1988 SOUTH AMERICAN HANDBOOK

SIXTY-FOURTH ANNUAL EDITION

Editor
John Brooks
Associate Editors
Joyce Candy & Ben Box

"Travel, in the younger sort, is a part of education; in the elder, a part of experience. He that travelleth into a country before he hath some entrance into the language, goeth to school, and not to travel."

Francis Bacon, Essays: Of Travel.

TRADE & TRAVEL PUBLICATIONS

TRADE & TRAVEL PUBLICATIONS LTD
5 PRINCE'S BUILDINGS
GEORGE STREET
BATH ENGLAND
TEL. 0225 69141
TELEX 265871 Ref DWL3004

© Trade & Travel Publications Ltd., 1987

64th annual edition, published September 1987

ISBN 0 900751 26 6

All rights reserved. No part of this publication may be reproduced, stored in a retrieval system, or transmitted, in any form or by any means, electronic, mechanical, photocopying, recording or otherwise, without the prior permission of Trade & Travel Publications Ltd.

Distributed in the United States of America by
Rand McNally & Company,
Chicago, New York, San Francisco

COVER

Hummingbirds are found only in North and South America. Although usually associated with humid, tropical conditions, they are found in most parts of the continent. There is a tremendous variety in no less than 320 species—some of which have the incredible ability to beat their wings up to 80 times per second and fly at speeds of 60 miles per hour, their energy coming from nectar-rich flowers. Whilst this mobility deters most predators, the bright iridescent colours of their plumage make them highly visible to would-be invaders of their home territories. Our cover illustration by Carl Melegari shows the migratory rufous hummingbird (*Selasphorus rufus*), which nests in south-eastern Alaska and winters in the Mexican Highlands.

Photoset by Nuffield Press Ltd, Oxford;
printed and bound in Great Britain by Richard Clay Ltd., Bungay, Suffolk.

CONTENTS

	Page		Page
Preface	5	Cuba	1193
Introduction and Hints	7	Hispaniola	1206
Health Information	21	Haiti	1207
Argentina	31	Dominican Republic	1214
Bolivia	152	Puerto Rico	1227
Brazil	205	West Indies	1235
Chile	372	Jamaica	1235
Colombia	450	Barbados	1243
Ecuador	533	Trinidad & Tobago	1247
Paraguay	606	Leeward and Windward Islands	1255
Peru	630	Bahamas	1270
Uruguay	766	Turks & Caicos Islands	1275
Venezuela	791	Cayman Islands	1277
The Guianas	836	Bermuda	1280
Guyana	837	Virgin Islands	1282
Suriname	849	Netherlands Antilles	1289
Guyane	859	French Antilles	1302
Falkland Islands (Malvinas)	864	Climatic Tables	1313
Mexico	867	Time Zones	1317
Central America	1006	Metric Equivalents	1319
Guatemala	1010	Exchange & Inflation Rates	1319
Belize	1057	Index to Maps	1323
El Salvador	1071	Index to Places	1325
Honduras	1088	Index to Advertisers	1341
Nicaragua	1116	Thomas Cook Assistance Points	1342
Costa Rica	1137	Sectional Coloured Map	Centre
Panama	1166		

THE LABEL
OF ACHIEVEMENT

JOHNNIE WALKER BLACK LABEL
· 12 YEAR OLD ·

JOHN WALKER & SONS LTD., SCOTCH WHISKY DISTILLERS, KILMARNOCK, SCOTLAND.

PREFACE

READERS OF THIS EDITION will notice a pronounced improvement in the economic sections, for which Sarah Cameron of Lloyds Bank Economics Department has assumed editorial responsibility, and which now include improved statistical information. Radical changes have also been made in parts of the Argentine and Guatemalan chapters; this is appropriate in view of the great increase in tourism to these two countries, the effect of which we have noticed from the growth in the number of letters we have received about them. Other countries that have received greatly improved coverage are Belize, Cuba, Ecuador and Honduras.

We have this year a new map of Quito, drawn by our friend Kevin Healey, and one of Belize from a traveller, Lisa Tenuta, for which we are most grateful. We must also express our thanks to John Lewis for again updating our hotel information, and to all the travellers—about 350 strong—who have written to offer new information and to point out our mistakes.

In October 1986 John and Sylvia Brooks visited North-East Brazil at the invitation of Quatro Rodas Hotéis do Nordeste, to see their hotels in Olinda (Recife), Salvador and São Luís. This most welcome invitation, for which we thank Quatro Rodas most warmly, also enabled us to visit other cities of the North-East—Aracaju, Maceió and Fortaleza—and revise the *Handbook's* coverage of all these places and their hinterlands.

We have much pleasure in amending our previous critical comment on Swiss Travel Service, of San José, Costa Rica, who have provided independent evidence that the comment was unjustified. We take this opportunity to advise people and organizations who receive unfavourable mention in this *Handbook* that we are always ready to re-examine our statements, if they can furnish us with independent testimonials giving more favourable opinions.

One fairly recent innovation in Latin American tourism has been the development in various countries of National Parks: Argentina, Brazil, Chile, Peru, Guatemala and Costa Rica are examples. We should be particularly interested in receiving further information on National Parks in these and other countries, and especially on details of access and accommodation.

Readers have asked us to support the suggestion that the provision of electric showers in hotels should be discouraged. These showers, in which the current is switched on by the flow of water through the shower rose, are inherently dangerous, and all the more so because of the poor state of maintenance and repair in which they are often found. Accidents are frequent and sometimes fatal, and we add our plea that the installation and use of these showers should be discontinued until the designs are modified to include improved safety features.

The Editor

ALL OUR EGGS ARE IN ONE BASKET*

*We specialise exclusively in travel to, from and within South and Central America.

We have a wide range of cut-price flight options — including oneways, returns, "Open Jaws", and student fares — and a host of permutations that can be tailor-made for the cost-conscious independent traveller. Ask for our Flights Bulletin, our invaluable guide to the cheapest ways of getting there.

We run our own fully escorted small-group holiday journeys in Latin America. For example:

Rio to Lima	3, 5 or 6 weeks
Peru, Bolivia	2, 3 or 4 weeks
Chilean Fjords	4 weeks
Guatemala, Mexico	3 or 4 weeks
Venezuela, Brazil	3 or 5 weeks
Ecuador, Galapagos	3 weeks

For full details, ask for a tour brochure.

In fact, amongst us all in the office here, we have a range of South American travel expertise which is almost certainly unequalled anywhere in the world. All this and maps, books and standard package tours too.

JOURNEY LATIN AMERICA

16 DEVONSHIRE RD.
CHISWICK, LONDON W4
Tel: 01-747 3108 (10 lines)

INTRODUCTION AND HINTS

THIS BOOK seeks to tell visitors, whether tourists or on business, what they most need to know. Each country chapter opens with a physical description of the country, its people, its history and its present form of government. There follows a survey of the cities, towns and other places of interest; under each town particulars are given of what is worth seeing, and of services of use to the visitor. There follows an account of the country's economy, and each chapter ends with "Information for Visitors", giving details about the best time for visiting a country, how to get there, what documents are necessary, what clothes should be worn, what the food is like, what health precautions should be taken, what the currency regulations are (at the time of going to press), and much else.

Travel to and in Latin America All the main airlines plying to each country are given in the "Information for Visitors" sections, together with any shipping lines that still carry passengers. Airlines will only allow a certain weight of luggage without a surcharge; this is normally 30 kg. for first class and 20 kg. for business and economy classes, but these limits are often not strictly enforced when it is known that the plane is not going to be full. On the other hand, weight limits for internal flights are often lower; best to enquire beforehand.

Chris Parrott, of Journey Latin America, has told us:

1. Generally it is cheaper to fly from London rather than a point in Europe to South American destinations.

2. There are no "charters" as such (but see para. 8 on next page), though most airlines offer discounted fares of one sort or another on scheduled flights. These are not offered by the airlines direct to the public, but through agencies who specialize in this type of fare*. The very busy seasons are as follows: all of Mexico and Central and South America; Dec.7—Jan. 15. Peru/Ecuador/Colombia/Venezuela/Central America/ Mexico July 10—Sept.10. If you intend travelling during those times, book as far ahead as possible.

3. Other fares fall into three groups, and are all on scheduled services:
   A. Student (or Under 26) fares. Some airlines are flexible on the age limit, others strict. One way and returns available, or "Open Jaws" where you fly into one destination and return from another. NB Some student tickets carry standby status only, and should be avoided in the busy seasons (see above).
   B. Excursion (return) fares with restricted validity e.g. 10-35 days, 14-90 days, 5-60 days. These are fixed date tickets where the dates of travel cannot be changed after issue of ticket.
   C. Yearly fares: these may be bought on a one-way or return basis, and usually the returns can be issued with the return date left open. You must, however, fix the route.

4. For people intending to travel a linear route and return from a different point from that which they entered, there are "Open Jaws" fares, which are available on student or yearly fares, or occasionally on excursion fares.

5. Many of these fares require a change of plane at an intermediate point, and a stopover may be permitted, or even obligatory, depending on schedules. Simply because a flight stops at a given

---

*In London, these include Trailfinders, 48 Earl's Court Road, London W.8. (Tel.: 01-937 9631); Melia Travel Ltd., 12 Dover Street, London W1X 4NS (Tel.: 01-491 3881), Steamond Ltd., 23 Eccleston Street, London SW1W 9LX (Tel.: 01-730 8646); Transatlantic Wings, 70 Pembroke Road, London W.8. (Tel.: 01-602 4021); and Journey Latin America, 16 Devonshire Road, Chiswick, London W4 2HD (Tel.: 01-747 3108). (Ed.)

8 INTRODUCTION

airport does not mean you can break your journey there—the airline must have traffic rights to pick up or set down passengers between points A and B before it will be permitted. This is where dealing with a specialized agency (like Journey Latin America!) will really pay dividends. There are dozens of agencies that offer the simple returns to Rio or Lima at roughly the same (discounted) fare. On multi-stop itineraries, the specialized agencies can often save clients hundreds of pounds.

6. Although it's a little more complicated, it's possible to sell tickets in London for travel originating in South America at substantially cheaper fares than those available locally. This is useful for the traveller who doesn't know where he will end up, or who plans to travel for more than a year. But a oneway ticket from South America is more expensive than a oneway in the other direction, so it's always best to buy a return. (I have heard of travellers buying an unused return seat on French charter flights—they're advertised in the small ads in some of the cheap hotels in Lima—and the charter company doesn't seem to mind who sits in the seat; very hit and miss though).

7. Certain South American countries impose local tax on flights originating there. Among these are Uruguay, Peru, Ecuador, Colombia and Mexico. This often applies if you happen to have bought a ticket, say, London—Rio—Santiago—Lima—Los Angeles and then on to Australia. Depending on the way it's issued the passenger could get charged tax on all the sectors from Lima onwards.

8. There are several cheap French charters to Mexico, Guatemala, Colombia, Ecuador, Peru, Bolivia and the southern countries, but no-one in the UK sells them. Try: Le Point, 4 rue des Orphelins, 68200 Mulhouse; 2 place Wagram, 75017 Paris (Tel.: 763-22-58) (with branches in various other European cities, such as Baden-Baden); or Uniclam-Voyages, 63 rue Monsieur-le Prince, 75006 Paris. A cheap Swiss charter firm is Sindbad, 3 Schoffelgasse, 8025 Zürich. It is reported that Aeroflot flies cheaply between Frankfurt and Luxembourg, and Lima. There are some special fares available on scheduled flights from Dublin. Líneas Aéreas Paraguayas flies weekly between Frankfurt, Brussels and Asunción and have one fare for all S. American destinations, including changes and "Open Jaws" journeys, of about US$900 from Brussels.

9. If you buy discounted air tickets *always* check the reservation with the airline concerned to make sure the flight still exists. Also remember the IATA airlines' schedules change in March and October each year, so if you're going to be away a long time it's best to leave return flight coupons open.

Beware buying tickets from the general sales agents in Europe of minor South American airlines. They are sometimes incorrectly made out and therefore impossible to transfer or cash in. If you buy internal airline tickets in South American countries you may find cash refunds difficult to get if you change your plans: better to change your ticket for a different one. On the other hand you can save money by buying tickets in a country with a black exchange market, for local currency, for flights on its national airline. Overbooking by Latin American airlines is very common, so always reconfirm the next stage of your flight within 72 hours of your intended departure. And it does no harm to reconfirm yet again in the last 24 hours, just to show them you mean it, and turn up for the flight in good time (at least 2 hours before departure).

We advise people who travel the cheap way in Latin America to pay for all transport as they go along, and not in advance. This advice does not apply to people on a tight schedule: paying as you go along may save money, but it is likely to waste your time somewhat. The one exception to this general principle is in transatlantic flights; here money is saved by booking as far as possible in one operation.

The national airlines of Argentina, Bolivia, Brazil, Chile, Colombia, Peru and Venezuela operate schemes for unlimited travel within those countries at a set price. See the respective country sections.

There is also an "Amerailpass", giving unlimited travel on the railways of Argentina, Bolivia, Brazil, Chile, Paraguay and Uruguay, which can be bought for 16 (US$120), 23 (US$140), 30 (US$175) or 60 (US$260) days. Payment must be in US dollars, so the savings may not be that great. Details in the paragraphs on rail travel under the principal cities, but remember that railway services are being progressively withdrawn. *Warning:* Not all railway staff know about the pass.

Warning Many countries in Latin America are reluctant to let travellers enter their territory if they do not already have outward tickets. (Look under "Information for Visitors" sections for the countries you intend to visit.) The purchase of a Miscellaneous Charges Order (open ticket) from an IATA airline for (say) US$100

INTRODUCTION

will satisfy this requirement in many but not all countries; it is valid for 12 months, can be exchanged for a ticket, or cashed at the airline offices in the country of issue. (The outward ticket requirement does not apply to travellers with their own vehicles.)

Money is best carried in US dollar travellers' cheques (denominations of US$50 and below are preferable) or cash. Sterling and other currencies are not recommended, outside the larger towns. Travellers' cheques are convenient but they attract thieves (though refunds can of course be arranged) and you will find that they are more difficult than dollar bills to change in small towns. Though the risk of loss is greater, many travellers take part of their funds in US dollar notes; better rates can usually be obtained for them. Low-value US dollar bills are very useful for shopping: shopkeepers and exchange shops (*casas de cambio*) tend to give better exchange rates than hotels or banks. The better hotels will normally change travellers' cheques for their guests (often at a rather poor rate), but if you're travelling on the cheap it is essential to keep in funds; watch weekends and public holidays carefully and never run out of local currency. Take plenty of local currency, in small denominations, when making trips into the interior. Spread your money around your person: less chance of thieves finding it all.

American Express (Amex), Carte Blanche and Diners Club credit cards are useful, and so are those of the Visa and Master Charge groups. Conceal them very carefully (*not* under the insole of a shoe, however: that may render them unusable!), and make sure you know the correct procedure if they are lost or stolen. Remember, though, that credit card transactions are at an officially recognized rate of exchange (sometimes, if there are several, the least favourable one); you may find it much cheaper to pay cash and get the parallel rate. Visa has been recommended as useful for getting cash advances in certain countries: Colombia, Chile and Venezuela have been mentioned.

We recommend in general the use of American Express or Thomas Cook US$ travellers' cheques, but should point out that less commission is often charged on Citibank or Bank of America cheques, if they are cashed at Latin American branches of those banks. These cheques are always accepted by banks, even though they may not be as well known outside banks as those of American Express or Thomas Cook. It is a good idea to take two kinds of cheque: if large numbers of one kind have recently been forged or stolen, making people suspicious, it is unlikely to have happened simultaneously with the other kind. Several banks charge a high fixed commission for changing travellers' cheques—sometimes as much as US$5-10 a cheque—because they don't really want to be bothered. Exchange houses (*casas de cambio*) are usually much better for this service.

In those countries where there is a black market, find out how much of their currency you are allowed to take in, and *buy before you enter*, preferably in a big city where banks are unlikely to make a charge on the transaction. (In small places the bank may charge up to 50 cents on a 10-dollar travellers' cheque.) There is always an active (but illegal) black market in local currency in all those countries that have no free exchange; it is, however, not illegal to buy currency outside the country you are about to enter, up to any limit that may be imposed. The City of London currency dealers are worth checking with: some find themselves overstretched from time to time with exotic currencies they can't get rid of and let them go at a large discount. Check in the publication *Banknotes of the World* that the notes you are being offered are still current, however.

N.B. If you are having additional sums of money sent out during a tour of Latin America, try to have it sent to one of the countries where you can exchange dollar travellers' cheques for dollars cash; at present these are Ecuador, Panama, and Uruguay. These countries, and Paraguay, are also good for getting US$ travellers cheques for a Eurocheque or Amex card, and for buying other Latin American currencies at favourable rates. In many countries, one can get at least US$500 in Amex travellers' cheques on the American Express card (US$1,000 on the gold card): quite the easiest way of adding to one's funds. Remember that a transfer of funds, even by telex, can take several days, and charges can be high; a recommended method is, before leaving, to find out which local bank is correspondent to your bank at home, then when you need funds, telex your own bank and ask them to telex the money to the local bank (confirming by air mail). It is possible to obtain money within hours by this method.

Whenever you leave a country, sell any local currency before leaving, because the further away you get, the less the value of a country's money.

10 INTRODUCTION

Americans (we are told) should know that if they run out of funds they can expect no help from the US Embassy or Consul other than a referral to some welfare organization.

Costs It seems, from travellers' accounts, that it is still possible to travel through Latin America (or at least Mexico, Central America and the Andean countries) spending no more for basic outgoings (travel, food and shelter) than US$50-60 p.p. per week. Argentina, Brazil, Chile and Venezuela are a little more expensive and the Caribbean islands much more expensive: say US$100 p.p. per week if camping and US$150-200 if staying in cheap hotels.

Passports Remember that Latin Americans, especially officials, are very document-minded. You should always carry your passport in a safe place about your person, or if not going far, leave it in the hotel safe. If staying in a country for several weeks, it is worth while registering at your Embassy or Consulate. Then, if your passport is stolen, the process of replacing it is somewhat simplified and speeded up. Keeping photocopies of essential documents is recommended.

Identity and Membership Cards Membership cards of British, European and US motoring organizations have been found useful for discounts off hotel charges, car rentals, maps, towing charges, etc. Student cards must carry a photograph if they are to be of any use in Latin America for discounts. (If you describe yourself as a student on your tourist card you may be able to get discounts, even if you haven't a student card.). Business people should carry a good supply of visiting cards, which are essential for good business relations in Latin America.

Law Enforcement Whereas in Europe and North America we are accustomed to law enforcement on a systematic basis, in general, enforcement in Latin America is achieved by periodic campaigns. The most typical is a round-up of criminals in the cities just before Christmas. In December, therefore, you may well be asked for identification at any time, and if you cannot produce it, you will be jailed. At first sight, on arrival, it may seem that you can flout the law with impunity, because everybody else is obviously doing so. If a visitor is jailed his friends should take him food every day. This is especially important for people on a diet, such as diabetics. It must also be borne in mind that in the event of a vehicle accident in which anyone is injured, all drivers involved are automatically detained until blame has been established, and this does not usually take less than two weeks. Sometimes these problems can be avoided by offering a bribe, but this, naturally, is illegal and may be extremely dangerous. Imported cigarettes from airport duty-free shops are very much appreciated by customs officials.

Never offer a bribe unless you are fully conversant with the customs of the country. (In Chile, for instance, it would land you in serious trouble if you tried to bribe a *carabinero*.) Wait until the official makes the suggestion, or offer money in some form which is apparently not bribery, e.g. "In our country we have a system of on-the-spot fines. Is there a similar system here?" Do not assume that an official who accepts a bribe is prepared to do anything else that is illegal. You bribe him to persuade him to do his job, or to persuade him not to do it, or to do it more quickly, or more slowly. You do not bribe him to do something which is against the law. The mere suggestion would make him very upset.

Security Try and look as little like a tourist as possible, especially in poor areas of cities; hide your main cash supply in different places or under your clothes; keep cameras in bags (preferably with a chain or wire in the strap to defeat the slasher) or briefcases; take spare spectacles (eyeglasses); don't wear wrist-watches (unless they're digital—too cheap and plentiful to attract thieves nowadays) or jewellery. If you wear a shoulder-bag in a market, carry it in front of you. If attacked, remember your assailants may well be armed, and try not to resist. It is best, if you can trust your hotel, to leave any valuables you don't need in safe-deposit there, when sightseeing locally. If you lose valuables, always report to police and note details of report—for insurance purposes. When you have all your luggage with you at a bus or railway station, be especially careful: don't get

INTRODUCTION 11

into arguments—or even conversations—with any locals if you can help it, and lock all the items together with a chain or cable if you are waiting for some time. Ignore strangers' remarks like "what's that on your shoulder?" or "have you seen that dirt on your shoe?" which are made to distract your attention and make you easy for an accomplice to steal from. Take a taxi between airport/bus station/ railway station and hotel, if you can possibly afford it. Finally, never accept food, drink, sweets or cigarettes from unknown fellow-travellers on buses or trains. They may be drugged, and you would wake up hours later without your belongings. In this connection, never accept a bar drink from an opened bottle (unless you can see that that bottle is in general use): always have it uncapped in front of you. A last point, from Canadian film-maker Russ Bentley: a courteous, friendly manner of speaking, including to beggars and market vendors, may avoid your being "set up" for robbery or assault.

Hotels A cheap but not bad hotel might run to US$5 a night in Argentina, Mexico or Brazil, but is less in the Andean countries (US$1-3) and more in the Caribbean islands (US$15-20). For the indigent, it is a good idea to ask for a boarding house—*casa de huéspedes, hospedaje, pensión, casa familial* or *residencial,* according to country; they are normally to be found in abundance near bus and railway stations and markets. There are often great seasonal variations in hotel prices in resorts. Remember, cheaper hotels don't always supply soap, towels and toilet paper. A useful tip: ask the Hertz employee at the airport for advice when you arrive—as long as he's not busy.

Our price ranges, for double rooms with taxes and service charges but without meals unless stated, are again unchanged from last year. The complete range remains as follows:

L—Over US$70   **A**—US$45-70   **B**—US$30-45
C—US$20-30   **D**—US$12-20   **E**—US$5-12
F—US$2-5   **G**—Up to US$2

Warning The electric showers used in many cheap hotels are extremely dangerous. If possible, hotels offering them should be avoided, and the reason given.

Youth Hostels Organizations affiliated to the Youth Hostels movement exist in Argentina, Brazil, Chile, Mexico, Peru and Uruguay. Further information in the country sections.

Meals In all countries except Brazil and Chile (where cold meats, cheese, eggs, fruit etc. generally figure) breakfast usually means coffee or tea with rolls and butter, and anything more is charged extra. There is a paragraph on each nation's food under "Information for Visitors". For reliable cheap meals, look in and near the markets and eat what the locals are eating, making sure that you can see it being cooked.

Travelling with Children We are grateful to Tim and Arlene Frost, of New Zealand, for the following notes:

People contemplating overland travel in South America with children should remember that a lot of time can be spent waiting for buses, trains, and especially for aeroplanes. On bus journeys, if the children are good at amusing themselves, or can readily sleep while travelling, the problems can be considerably lessened. Travel on trains, while not as fast or at times as comfortable as buses, allows more scope for moving about. Some trains provide tables between seats, so that games can be played.

Food can be a problem if the children are not adaptable. It is easier to take biscuits, drinks, bread etc. with you on longer trips than to rely on meal stops where the food may not be to taste. A small immersion heater and jug for making hot drinks is invaluable, but remember that electric current varies. A 220v heater can work on 110v (slowly), but not vice versa. (Good idea to take both: they're light and take little space—Ed.).

Fares: On all long-distance buses you pay for each seat, and there are no half-fares if the children occupy a seat each. For shorter trips it is cheaper, if less comfortable, to seat small children on

12 INTRODUCTION

your knee. Often there are spare seats which children can occupy after tickets have been collected. In city and local excursion buses, small children generally do not pay a fare, but are not entitled to a seat when paying customers are standing. On sightseeing tours you should *always* bargain for a family rate—often children can go free. (In trains, reductions for children are general, but not universal.)

All civil airlines charge half for children under 12, but some military services don't have half-fares, or have younger age limits. Children's fares on Lloyd Aéreo Boliviano are considerably more than half, and there is only a 7kg. baggage allowance. (LAB also checks children's ages on passports.)

Hotels: In all hotels, bargain for rates. If charges are per person, always insist that two children will occupy one bed only, therefore counting as one tariff. If rates are per bed, the same applies. In either case you can almost always get a reduced rate at cheaper hotels. (In restaurants, you can normally buy children's helpings, or divide one full-size helping between two children.)

Generally, travel with children presents no special problems—in fact the path is often smoother for family groups. Officials tend to be more amenable where children are concerned. Moreover, even thieves and pickpockets seem to have some of the traditional respect for families, and may leave you alone because of it!

Camping There is a growing network of organized campsites, to which reference is made in the text immediately below hotel lists, under each town. Géraldine des Cressonnières, of Linkebeek, Belgium, gives the following rules for "wild" camping: (1) arrive in daylight; (2) ask permission to camp from the parish priest, or the fire chief, or the police, or a farmer regarding his own property; (3) never ask a group of people— especially young people; (4) never camp on a beach. If you can't get information from anyone, camp in a spot where you can't be seen from the nearest inhabited place.

Gas cylinders and bottles are usually exchangeable, but if not can be recharged; specify whether you use butane or propane. (Liquid fuels are readily available.) The Camping Clube do Brasil gives 50% discounts to holders of international campers' cards. Many travellers have warned against camping on beaches, which are often infested, not only by sandflies but by thieves.

Souvenirs Remember that these can almost invariably be bought more cheaply away from the capital, though the choice may be less wide. Bargaining seems to be the general rule in most countries' street markets. Americans should remember that souvenirs made from, for example, sea-turtle shells may not be imported into the US, under the Endangered Species Act of 1973, and are advised to ask the US Fish and Wildlife Service, Department of the Interior, Washington D.C. 20240, for a complete list of the endangered species concerned.

If British travellers have no space in their luggage, they might like to remember Tumi, the Latin American Craft Centre, at 23 Chalk Farm Road, London NW1 (Tel.: 01-485 4152) and 2 New Bond Street Place, Bath (Tel.: 0225 62367), who specialize in Mexican and Andean products. There are similar shops in the USA; one good one is on the ground floor of Citicorp Center, Lexington Avenue and 53rd Street, New York.

Mail Postal services in most countries are not very efficient, and pilfering is frequent. All mail, especially packages, should be registered. Some travellers recommend that mail should be sent to one's Embassy (or, if a customer, American Express agent) rather than to the Poste Restante (*Lista de Correos*) department of a country's Post Office. Some Embassies and post offices, however, do not keep mail for more than a month. If there seems to be no mail at the Lista under the initial letter of your surname, ask them to look under the initial of your forename or your middle name.

Travellers' Appearance There is a natural prejudice in all countries against travellers who ignore personal hygiene and have a generally dirty and unkempt appearance. Most Latin Americans, if they can afford it, devote great care to their clothes and appearance; it is an appreciated compliment to do likewise. The general prejudice previously reported against backpacks has virtually disappeared, unless carried by those whom officials identify as "hippies". (Remember, however, that backpacks are much easier to pilfer from than conventional luggage; an electric motor-cycle alarm—or a flour sack—might stop this.) One tip we have received; young people of informal dress and life-style may find it advantageous to procure a letter from someone in an official position testifying to their good character, on official-looking notepaper. John Oliver, of Durban, tells us that a photograph of a pretty blonde young woman inside one's passport can have a similar salutary effect on Latin American officials!

Some countries have laws or prejudices against the wearing by civilians of army-surplus clothing. There is also a prejudice against shorts, which are only appropriate on the beach, or for jogging, or for sports and games. A medium weight shawl with some wool content is recommended for women: it can double as pillow, light blanket, bathrobe or sunscreen on occasion.

Drugs Users of drugs, even of soft ones, without medical prescription should be particularly careful, as some countries impose heavy penalties— up to ten years' *imprisonment—for even the simple possession of such substances.* In this connection, the planting of drugs on travellers—by traffickers or the police—is not unknown. Note that people who roll their own cigarettes are often suspected of carrying drugs and subjected to intensive searches. Advisable to stick to commercial brands of cigarettes—but better still not to smoke at all.

Toilets Many of the cheapest hotels in the poorer areas, also restaurants and bars, have inadequate water supplies. This may mean that used toilet paper should not be flushed down the pan, but placed in the receptacle provided. This is not very sanitary, of course, but a blocked pan or drain is infinitely more of a health risk.

Cockroaches These are ubiquitous and unpleasant, but not dangerous. Take some insecticide powder if staying in cheap hotels; Baygon (Bayer) has been recommended.

Language Without some knowledge of Spanish you can become very frustrated and feel helpless in many situations. English is absolutely useless off the beaten track. Some initial study, to get you up to a basic Spanish vocabulary of 500 words or so, and a pocket dictionary and phrase-book, are most strongly recommended: your pleasure will be doubled if you can talk to the locals. Not all the locals speak Spanish, of course; apart from Brazil's Portuguese, you will find that some Indians in the more remote highland parts of Bolivia, Guatemala and Peru, and lowland Indians in Amazonia, speak only their indigenous languages, though there will usually be at least one person in each village who can speak Spanish.

The basic Spanish of Hispanic America is that of south-western Spain, with soft "c's" and "z's" pronounced as "s", and not as "th" as in the other parts of Spain. Castilian Spanish is readily understood, but is not appreciated when spoken by non-Spaniards; try and learn the basic Latin American pronunciation. There are several regional variations in pronunciation, particularly in the River Plate countries, which are noted in the Argentine section "Information for Visitors". Differences in vocabulary also exist, both between peninsular Spanish and Latin American Spanish, and between forms of Latin American Spanish as spoken in the different countries.

It is permissible to speak Spanish in Brazil if you first apologize for not being able to speak Portuguese; you will be understood but you may not be able (because Portuguese uses on the whole fewer syllables than Spanish) to understand the answers.

Courtesy Remember that politeness—even a little ceremoniousness—is much appreciated. In this connection professional or business cards are useful (and have even been known to secure for their owners discount prices in hotels). Michael Davison makes the following suggestions: men should always remove their headgear and say "con permiso" ("com licença" in Brazil) when entering offices, and be prepared to shake hands (*this is much commoner in Latin America than in Europe or North America*); always say "Buenos días" or "Buenas tardes" ("Bom dia" or "Boa tarde" in Brazil) and wait for a reply before proceeding further; in a word, don't rush them! Always remember that the traveller from abroad has enjoyed greater advantages in life than most Latin American minor officials, and should be friendly and courteous in consequence. N. F. Hawkes adds: never be impatient or criticize situations in public: the officials may know more English than you think and they can certainly interpret gestures and facial expressions. Politeness can be a liability, however, in some situations; most Latin Americans are disorderly queuers. Russ Bentley stresses that politeness and friendliness, with small useful gifts for children such as pencils and scratchpads, not only increase the pleasure of one's trip, but may well improve one's personal security.

Moira Chubb, from New Zealand, suggests that if you are a guest and are offered food that arouses your suspicions, the only courteous way out is to feign an allergy or a stomach ailment.

Explorers The South American Explorers' Club is at Avenida Portugal 146 (Casilla 3714), Lima, Peru (Telephone: 31-44-80). For further details see under Lima, page 651). Large-scale topographical maps are usually obtainable from a country's Instituto Geográfico Militar or equivalent, on production of the price and your passport.

Wildlife Wildlife lovers might like to know about Kilverstone Wildlife Park, Thetford, Norfolk, IP24 2RL. This is a private zoo, open to the public, which specializes in Latin American fauna and is helping to preserve species threatened with extinction, by breeding and returning them to their native habitat.

Photography Take as much film in from home as you can; it is expensive everywhere. Some travellers have advised against mailing exposed films home; better to take them with you. The postal authorities may use less sensitive equipment for X-ray screening than the airports do.

Dan Buck and Anne Meadows write: A note on developing film in South America. Black and white is a problem. Often it is shoddily machine-processed and the negatives are ruined. Ask the store if you can see an example of their laboratory's work and if they hand-develop.

Jeremy Till and Sarah Wigglesworth suggest that exposed film can be protected in humid areas by putting it in a balloon and tying a knot.

A professional, John Burke, writes: "I used Agfa and Kodak for colour slides, all of which have come out true from Caracas to Arica. Suggest keep film on concrete floor. One canned reel was kept after use in refrigerator (for six weeks) before coming home from Lima and has been processed okay. At all costs avoid photographing shadows in the tropics, including shaded side of a person's face; they come out jet-black. Also avoid lens-hood, if possible; it tends to flatten colours. I used no lens other than ultra-violet. No special attention is needed when photographing high altitude areas like Bogotá, Cuzco or La Paz, when it is cloudy—if anything, the lens can be opened half a stop more than meter reads. (It may well be different in bright sunlight.) In Lima suggest photography between morning cloud clears and about 1100, and again after 1600. In April 0800-0930 is perfect. Officials tend to be officious and suspicious about photography of what they consider to be super-strategic areas (like a patch of desert near Tacna and the planning ministry in Caracas!). I was always in the fortunate position of being able to quell them with letters from higher authority, but the average tourist might come unstuck."

Surface Transport The continent has a growing road system for motor traffic, with frequent bus services. The buses are often comfortable; Brazil, Chile and Venezuela are the best; Ecuador is quite good; the other Andean countries are a long way behind, because of difficulties of terrain. Some services in Mexico and Central America are excellent. In mountainous country, however, do not expect buses to get to their destination, after long journeys, anywhere near on time. When the journey takes more than 3 or 4 hours, meal stops at country inns, good and bad, are the rule. See what the locals are eating—and buy likewise. For drinks, stick to bottled drinks or coffee (black). The food sold by vendors at bus stops may be all right: watch if locals are buying, though unpeeled fruit is of course reliable.

In most countries trains are slower than buses, and also less secure for luggage. They do tend, however, to provide finer scenery, and you can normally see much more wildlife than from the road—it is less disturbed by one or two trains a day than by the more frequent road traffic.

Keep a careful eye on your luggage at all stops, especially if it is on a luggage rack or piled on top of the bus. It's a good idea to chain and lock all items together, if possible.

INTRODUCTION

Warning Do not accept sweets—or indeed any food or drink or cigarettes—from unknown fellow-travellers. They may be drugged, and you would wake up hours later without your belongings.

Beware of Central American bus companies who claim to be in a position to sell tickets for travel in South American countries, which they don't themselves serve.

Hitch-hiking
This custom is increasing in Latin America, and travellers have reported considerable success in virtually all countries. Neatness of appearance certainly helps. Argentina, Brazil, Chile, Costa Rica, Ecuador, Panama and Venezuela are reported as good; Peru and Bolivia less so ("paying trucks" recommended here). If trying to hitchhike away from main roads and in sparsely-populated areas, however, allow plenty of time.

Joanna Codrington writes: Hitch-hiking in Latin America is reasonably safe and straightforward for males and couples, provided one speaks some Spanish/Portuguese. In Peru and Bolivia there is little private transport and trucks charge about ⅔ the equivalent fare. But elsewhere cars and trucks will carry you free of charge, and will generally treat you as their guests. It is a most enjoyable mode of transport—a good way to meet the local people, to improve one's languages and to learn about the country. Truck drivers in particular are often well versed in things of interest one is passing, e.g. crops and industries.

Here are a few general hints: in remoter parts, make enquiries first about the volume of traffic on the road. On long journeys, set out at crack of dawn, which is when trucks usually leave. They tend to go longer distances than cars.

And now, here are some guidelines for females hitching alone. You must remember the cultural differences, i.e. a local woman travelling in such a fashion would undoubtedly be of dubious moral status. Problems can arise through a genuine misunderstanding. Careful steering of the conversation to illustrate one's reasons for travelling alone is useful and can prevent the necessity of copious explanations later on. Also, probe your driver to find out as much as you can about him and his circumstances. Problems virtually never occur during daylight; so, if possible, plan your journey accordingly. If you should be in a vehicle after dark (it will probably be a truck) it is best not to talk, and perhaps to turn up the music so the driver can forget your presence. If the journey does entail a night, be a bit discriminating about your driver; the unshaven, barbaric sort should be avoided. Also, notice if the driver has a bed, so you can sleep on the seats. Discuss sleeping arrangements before night-time.

Overall, be friendly so that the driver enjoys having you with him, and let him feel that you trust him completely. Though, of course, be careful not to overdo it; you will soon work out the right balance. Should things go awry, the worst that is likely to happen is that you will be turfed out, and may suffer a consequent draughty night. The macho ego is fragile, but rape does nothing to boost it.

(Sylvia Brooks adds: Safe travel for lone women is assisted by dress and demeanour which is not sexually stimulating to men.)

Motoring
The normal saloon car reaches most destinations of interest to the tourist. High ground clearance is useful for badly surfaced or unsurfaced roads. In some places, service is not available for sophisticated items like automatic transmission, electronic ignition and fuel injection, so the simpler the car the better. It's an advantage if you can sleep comfortably in it; hence the liking for minibuses such as the VW (which can be "Africanized" by the makers, with protective grills and additional cranked exhaust pipe added and a converter for high altitudes). Four-wheel-drive utility vehicles are useful for the back country; on the other hand, luggage cannot be hidden, as in the boot of a car, so the contents are more susceptible to theft. Consider installing a large trunk for your bags.

Theft of all vehicles is common. Apply at least two anti-theft devices when parked, even in car parks, and remove easily detachable items such as hub-caps, mirrors and windscreen wipers. At least one locking wheel nut per wheel is useful. A policy of insurance may not satisfactorily solve the problem of a car stolen outside its country of origin. There will be a delay of at least a month in paying the claim, and the sum insured may be inadequate if the theft occurs in a country where cars are more expensive than in the country of origin. Import duty becomes payable on the stolen car, and again on any car bought for the return trip home. If, on the other hand, a cash settlement is made, there may be difficulties with exchange control. The same is largely true if a vehicle becomes a total loss in an accident.

Spare fuel should be in steel, not plastic, cans. You won't have travelled far before the plastic can will spring a leak, and there is danger of a spark from static electricity igniting the petrol when pouring. (In Venezuela, it is illegal to carry petrol from a garage in a can without a permit from the police, and this can only be obtained after paying a fine of Bs 500 for running out of fuel.) In remote areas, gas stations (few and far between, so keep well topped up) are unmarked. Look for a building with empty oil drums outside or ask. In this connection, it is wise to carry a funnel and/or hose to help fill the tank; often in rural areas there are no pumps and fuel must be taken from a drum. An in-line fuel filter is an advantage. (In Mexico, there are often few gas stations on main roads: you need to look in the villages off the road.—Ed.)

16 INTRODUCTION

If the motor is not to fail at high altitudes, the spark must be advanced and cold spark plugs changed for hot; alternatively, take sets of smaller carburettor jets for use at altitude, which is a more fuel-economic solution. You can reduce the risk of a broken windscreen on gravel roads by not following closely behind other vehicles, and reducing speed when other vehicles (especially trucks with double rear wheels) are passing. (Wire over-screens are available in some cities, such as Buenos Aires.) A reversing light is needed for driving on narrow mountain roads at night or in narrow unlit tunnels built on curves. Landslides are frequent in the mountains in the rainy season. Keep enough reserve of fuel to be able to turn back and take warm clothes and food in case you are delayed a day or so. The car is liable to be searched for arms and drugs with some frequency in certain areas.

In addition to the normal spares carried, fan belt, spark plugs etc., the more adventurous driver needs a spade, tow cable, planks for placing under the wheels when stuck in dust or sand, spare parts for the suspension and steering, jump leads in case of battery failure, and either an extra spare wheel or repair patches, air pump and valve screw. Help to repair a tyre is sometimes only available if you can provide these items yourself. An emergency fan belt which can be fitted without the use of tools is available from Flexicom Ltd, North Wing Mills, Bradford BD1 4EP, England.

If you are not a mechanic, or don't have one with you, try to get to know the general look of your engine so that at least you'll know after a repair if anything looks unfamiliar, and always get on chatty terms with the mechanics when you're having anything done to the car.

Make a check list to ensure you have everything before you start each journey. The list is also useful for establishing what it is essential to replace after the theft of a car's contents. If you carry a cooler for food and drink, any official on the highway who spots it is likely to ask for refreshments, so take plenty or you may end up with none for yourself.

The car freely crosses international frontiers without payment of customs duties provided it is eventually returned to its country of origin. In Central America, this is controlled by an entry made in your passport. In South America, it is controlled by a separate document, the *Carnet de Passages en Douanes* or *Libreta de Pasos por Aduana*, which must be stamped at both sides of each frontier. Failure to obtain a stamp will result in being turned back, perhaps after driving as much as 200 km., so it is important to find the Customs Office (*Aduana—Alfândega* in Brazil) in order to avoid this inconvenience; it may be at the border or in the town nearest the border. Most countries have special (and cheaper) arrangements for motorists visiting neighbouring countries only. Difficulties have been experienced in entering Peru: check with Peruvian Consulate before setting out.

A separate insurance policy has to be issued in each country if a claim is to be legally payable in the country where an accident occurs. Companies with the necessary international connections include American International Underwriters, Guardian Royal Exchange Assurance, AFIA and Saint Paul. Give them at least four months' notice of your requirements. Remember that in many countries third-party insurance for drivers may not be compulsory, or if compulsory, not enforced; you may have no claim on the other driver after an accident, except through the courts—a time-consuming exercise. If you are injured in an accident, people may refuse to take you to hospital; if you are found dead on arrival they could be jailed until it is proved that they were not responsible for the accident. An additional reason for always driving carefully.

Finally, overland motorists would be very well advised to read *Overland and Beyond*, by Theresa and Jonathan Hewat, who motored round the world over 3½ years in a VW minibus. The revised and expanded 5th edition, published by Roger Lascelles, 3 Holland Park Mansions, 16 Holland Park Gardens, London W14 8DY, contains a wealth of good sense on all aspects of overland motoring.

If driving and camping, the purchase of a 12-volt low-consumption neon light will add greatly to convenience.

If travelling from Europe with a car, do not sail to Panama if you are going south. You will still have the Darién Gap to negotiate. Much better to take the ship to Curaçao, where there is a car ferry to Venezuela. If shipping a car further south, Montevideo has much less bureaucracy and paperwork than any Argentine or Brazilian port. In any event you need a *Carnet de Passages* and an International Certificate of Registration.

Motorcycling Charles and Lucia Newall write: Motorcycling in South America is a great adventure, exhausting sometimes but not beyond the capacity of any experienced rider.

Machine: The bike should be tough and simple and capable of handling dirt roads (if you plan on going into the Andes). If riding solo a large 4-stroke trail bike, e.g. Honda or Yamaha 500, would be ideal; if carrying a passenger a larger machine might be needed. We used an 800cc BMW road bike which handled a variety of conditions with ease.

Preparations: Fit a handlebar windscreen rather than a large touring fairing, which will hamper low-speed handling and complicate shipping from Panama. Standard air filters should be replaced by cleanable types e.g. K and N. Carry a set of smaller carburettor jets to adapt the engine for high altitudes (we fitted jets two sizes smaller on the BMW, which gave good results from 8,000 to 12,000 ft).

The standard rear suspension on all motorcycles will only last a few thousand miles on unpaved roads; fit high-quality replacement units (Konis) with springs matched for the weight carried.

The luggage panniers and rack should be very robust; distribute the weight of luggage around the bike rather than just piling it on the back. A fuel range of about 250 (400 km.) miles is useful and also the ability to run on 80-octane petrol.

Spares: A modern well-maintained machine shouldn't need any major repairs on a 25,000-mile trip. Take the usual consumables with you, such as plugs, points, filters, bulbs, chains, tubes and a set of cables; add to this any other parts which might be weak points on your machine. Make arrangements to have parts sent out from home if you need anything unusual; a parts book and a good manual are invaluable. Find out how to service your machine and carry the correct tools. (Local mechanics are very good at making do without the proper parts.)

Clothes: Your clothing should keep you comfortable from 20° to 85°F and include a tough waterproof outer layer complete with overboots and overgloves.

Security: Security is not a problem; use a strong chain and lock. Hotel owners are very helpful and good about letting you bring your machine inside, but don't leave a loaded machine unattended. In general much safer than taking night buses or trains (cheaper too).

Documents: Passports, international driving licences, *carnet de passages*, motoring association membership card (for discounts etc.), registration certificate, Hoja de Ruta required in Bolivia. A letter from your Embassy, saying that you are a bona-fide tourist and have no intention of selling your bike, is very useful.

Shipping: Flying motorcycles from Panama is much easier than cars. SAM and Copa, space permitting, will take bikes in the baggage holds of their 737s. (It cost us US$130 for a 200-kilo machine.) For the adventurous, possibility of taking small boats down to Turbo, but at the high risk of losing the machine. If you want to ride the Darien Gap your bike had better be light enough to carry!

Warning: Do not try to ride the Andean roads in the rainy season as conditions are very dangerous, with muddy roads and deep river fords.

Hiking and Trekking Hilary Bradt, the well-known trekker, author and publisher, has very kindly written the following for us:

A network of paths and tracks covers much of Central and South America and is in constant use by the local people. In countries with a large Indian population—Guatemala, Ecuador, Peru and Bolivia, for instance—you can walk just about anywhere, but in the more European countries, such as Costa Rica, Venezuela, Chile, and Argentina, you must usually limit yourself to the many excellent national parks with hiking trails. Most Central and South American countries have an Instituto Geográfico Militar which sells topographical maps, scale 1:100,000 or 1:50,000. The physical features shown on these are usually accurate; the trails and place names less so. National Parks offices also sell maps.

Hiking and backpacking should not be approached casually. Even if you only plan to be out a couple of hours you should have comfortable, safe footwear and a daypack to carry your sweater and waterproof. At high altitudes the difference in temperature between sun and shade is remarkable. The longer trips mentioned in this book require basic backpacking equipment. Essential items are: backpack with frame, sleeping bag, closed cell foam mat for insulation, stove, tent or tarpaulin, dried food (not tins), water bottle, compass. Some but not all of these things are available in South America.

When planning treks in the Andes you should be aware of the effects and dangers of acute mountain sickness, and cerebral and pulmonary oedema (see pages 21). These can be avoided by spending a few days acclimatizing to the altitude before starting your walk, and by climbing slowly. Otherwise there are fewer dangers than in most cities. Hikers have little to fear from the animal kingdom apart from insects (although it's best to avoid actually stepping on a snake), and robbery and assault are very rare. You are much more of a threat to the environment than vice versa. Leave no evidence of your passing; don't litter and don't give gratuitous presents of sweets or money to rural villagers. Respect their system of reciprocity; if they give you hospitality or food, then is the time to reciprocate with presents.

Other Books We should mention the Bradts' "Backpacking Guide Series" published by Bradt Enterprises, 41 Nortoft Road, Chalfont St. Peter, Bucks, SL9 0LA, UK., and 95 Harvey Street, Cambridge, MA 02140, USA. They give detailed descriptions of hiking trails (mentioned in our country "Information for Visitors" sections) and much fascinating information, with many illustrations, in the following volumes: *Mexico and Central America; Venezuela, Colombia and Ecuador; Peru and Bolivia; Chile and Argentina, plus the Falkland Islands; Climbing and Hiking in Ecuador; South America, River Trips.* (2 volumes). (The Bradts also sell other trail guides, and import trekking and topographical maps from South America.) *South America on a Shoestring*, by Geoff Crowther (Lonely Planet Publications) has been recommended repeatedly for the quality of its maps.

Another very useful book, highly recommended, aimed specifically at the budget traveller is *The Tropical Traveller*, by John Hatt (Pan Books, 2nd edition, 1985).

River Transport Geoffrey Dempsey has sent us the following note, with particular reference to Amazonia:

Because expanding air services have captured the lucrative end of the passenger market, passenger services on the rivers are in decline. Worst hit have been the upper reaches; rivers like the Ucayali in Peru, but the trend is apparent throughout the region. The situation has been aggravated for the casual traveller by a new generation of purpose-built tugs (all engine-room and bridge) that can handle up to a dozen freight barges but have no passenger accommodation. In Peru passenger boats must now supplement incomes by carrying cargo, and this lengthens their journey cycle. In the face of long delays, travellers might consider shorter "legs" involving more frequent changes of boat; though the more local the service, the slower and more uncomfortable it will be. The Pucallpa to Iquitos run for example could be taken in three bites with changes of boat at Contamana and Requena.

From Iquitos downstream the situation improves and boats can be found to Leticia, Tabatinga or Benjamin Constant without too much delay. Another destination in the vicinity is Islandia, which consists of a nondescript Peruvian mudbank across a creek, the width of a village pond, from Benjamin Constant in Brazil. The last name is important to travellers as all boats sailing downstream to Manaus stop there. However, as neither Islandia nor Benjamin Constant has passport control facilities it is important if travelling from Peru to obtain an exit stamp from the immigration police in Iquitos before embarking. Brazil is more relaxed and formalities can await arrival in Manaus; otherwise take a ferry to Tabatinga (Brazil) where the immigration office is a short taxi ride from the port area. The most attractive (and expensive) of these river frontier towns is undoubtedly Leticia in Colombia, and visitors can both arrive and depart by river without passport formalities though these would need to be completed should the visitor decide to leave Colombia by air or wish to cash a travellers cheque at the bank or even stay at a hotel.

Once in Brazil, river services improve both in frequency and comfort. Delays of a week or more are not likely and become less so the further down-stream one goes. Unless sailing by an Enasa boat, the journey from Manaus to Belém is normally taken in two bites with a change of boat at Santarém. There are daily services to Santarém but there could be a day's delay between Santarém and Belém. The Enasa boats are more expensive and they offer no scheduled services upriver of Manaus.

Hammocks, mosquito nets (not always good quality), plastic containers for water storage, kettles and cooking utensils can be purchased in any sizeable riverside town, as well as tinned food such as sardines, meat loaf, frankfurters, ham and fruit. Fresh bread, cake, eggs, fruit—papaya, bananas, pineapple, oranges etc.—are available in most villages. Cabin bunks are provided with thin mattresses but these are often foul. Replacements can be bought locally but rolls of plastic foam that can be cut to size are also available and much cheaper. Eye-screws for securing washing lines and mosquito nets are useful, and tall passengers who are not taking a hammock and who may find insufficient headroom on some boats should consider a camp-chair. The writer yearned for a cushion.

Cycling Hallam Murray writes:

At first glance a bicycle may not appear to be the most obvious vehicle for a major journey, but given ample time and reasonable energy it most certainly is the best. It can be ridden, carried by almost every other form of transport from an aeroplane to a canoe, and can even be lifted across one's shoulders over short distances. We rode over 2,000 miles in the Andes, on unpaved roads which would have defeated even the most robust car or truck. Often we were envied by travellers using more orthodox transport, for we were able to explore the remoter regions and to meet people who were not normally in contact with tourists. To add to this we had virtually no transport costs.

Choosing a Bicycle: A thoroughly robust machine is a must. The Dawes Super Galaxy is ideal, with its indestructible frame of Reynolds 531 tubing and wide ratioed gears. It is essential that all parts conform to an accepted international specification to facilitate replacement (e.g. threads, wheels, spokes and gears). For approaching US$600 it is possible to buy such a machine.

Equipment for 2 Bicycles: A small, comprehensive tool kit (to include block and chain rivet removers and a spoke key), 2 spare tyres, 4 inner tubes, puncture repair kit with plenty of extra patches and glue, 4 brake blocks, set of brake and gear cables, 12 spokes, replacement set of nuts and bolts, selection of ball bearings, oil, grease, 2 pumps, a mileometer, a loud bell, a long case-hardened steel chain and cover lock.

Luggage: Strong back panniers, such as the Karrimor Iberian. Handlebar bags. Adhesive carpet tape is a must for protecting vulnerable parts of panniers which are easily frayed (e.g. where panniers rub against luggage rack). We carried a load of 23 kg. per bicycle and this was not excessive. Our most vital equipment included tent, sleeping bags, Optimus petrol stove (an absolute must—light and efficient), plastic survival bag for storing luggage at night when camping out (almost every night), 4 elastic "spiders", 4 one-litre water bottles, compass, altimeter, Swiss Army knife, torch, comprehensive medical kit, money belts, small presents such as postcards of home, balloons etc. Sunhats protect against hours of ferocious tropical sun.

Vital Tips: Always buy the highest quality equipment before you set out. In Europe and North America we are spoilt by quality. In the developing world, many indigenous manufactured goods are shoddy and rarely last.

Give the bicycle a thorough daily check for loose nuts and bolts and bearings. See that all parts run smoothly. Always camp out of sight of a road. Remember that thieves are attracted to towns and cities, so when sight-seeing, try to leave your bicycle with someone such as a café owner. Country people are invariably more honest than town folk and are usually friendly and very inquisitive. However, don't take unnecessary risks; always see that the bicycle is secure. In remoter regions the dogs are vicious; carry a stick to frighten them off. Keep to the small roads wherever possible. The traffic on some sections of the main roads can be a nightmare. Most towns have a

INTRODUCTION 19

bicycle shop of some description, but it is best to do your own repairs and adjustments. In an emergency it's amazing how one can improvise with wire, string, nuts and bolts! Richard's Bicycle Book makes essential reading for even the most mechanically minded.

Travel to the USA   Remember that all foreigners (except Canadians) need visas to enter the USA. If you are thinking of visiting the USA after Latin America, you are strongly advised to get your visa from a US Consulate in your own country, not while travelling. If you wish to visit a little-known part of the USA (and W Canada), David Stanley's *Alaska-Yukon Handbook* (Chico, CA 96927, Moon Publications), 230 pages, will be of the very greatest use. It costs only US$8 (book postage anywhere).

Final Hints   Everybody has his/her own list. Items most often mentioned include a small portable stove (liquid fuel is more readily available than gas—though the latter is becoming more common—and you need a combination canteen to go with it), air cushions for slatted seats, heavy shoes or boots for muddy and uneven streets and country walking (and remember that footwear over 9½ English size (or 42 European size) is difficult to obtain in Latin America except Argentina and Brazil), money-belt or neck pouch, obtainable from Journey Latin America (address on page 7); a small first-aid kit and handbook, rubber wedges for doors and windows, fully waterproof top clothing (cape, hat, leggings), rubber-thong Japanese-type sandals (flip-flops), a polyethylene sheet 2 x 1 metres to cover possibly infested beds and train floors and shelter your luggage, polyethylene bags of varying sizes, a toilet bag you can tie round your waist, a sheet sleeping-bag and pillow-case, a mosquito net (or a hammock with a fitted net), a clothes line, a nailbrush (useful for scrubbing dirt off clothes as well as off oneself), wax-type ear plugs, an airline-type eye mask, mosquito coils, a vacuum flask, a water bottle, a small immersion heater (you really need two: one 220v and one 110v, unless you can get a dual-voltage variety), tea bags, a light nylon waterproof shopping bag, a universal bath-and basin-plug of the flanged type that will fit any waste-pipe (or improvise one from a sheet of thick rubber), a ball of string, a roll of electrical insulating tape, large penknife preferably with tin and bottle openers, scissors and corkscrew—the famous Swiss Army range has been repeatedly recommended, collapsible drinking beaker, electric motor-cycle alarm for luggage protection, a flour sack for ditto, alarm clock or watch, candle, torch (flashlight)—especially one that will clip on to a pocket or belt, small transistor radio or battery cassette-player (Walkman type) with earphones, pocket calculator, an adaptor and flex to enable you to take power from an electric- light socket (the Edison screw type is the most commonly used), a padlock for the doors of the cheapest and most casual hotels, spare chain-lengths and padlock for securing luggage to bed or bus/train seat. Small coins, postage stamps, visiting cards and postcards of views from your own country to give away as souvenirs to friendly locals. Useful medicaments are given at the end of the "Health Information" section (page 27); to these might be added some lip salve ("Lypsil" has been recommended). Always carry toilet paper. Women travelling alone may find it useful to wear a wedding ring. A few extra passport photos may be useful, also photocopies of essential documents (passport, credit cards, air tickets).

Be careful when asking directions. Many Latin Americans will give you the wrong answer rather than admit they do not know; this may be partly because they fear losing face, but is also because they like to please. You are more likely to get reliable information if you carefully refrain from asking leading questions.

Lastly, a good principle is to take half the clothes (trousers with plenty of pockets are very useful), and twice the money, that you think you will need.

WARNING: Whilst every endeavour is made to ensure that the facts printed in this book are correct at the time of going to press, travellers are cautioned to obtain authoritative advice from consulates, airlines, etc. concerning current travel and visa requirements and conditions before embarkation. The publishers cannot accept legal responsibility for errors, however caused, which are printed in this book.

20 INTRODUCTION

For various hints, we are grateful to Dr Joseph L. Breault (Bronx, NY), Dr Sally Dealler (Leeds 8), W. Derksen (Driebergen, Neth.), Karel Devijver (Leuven, Belg.), Toñi García and Diego Caña (Barcelona), Ricardo Heyenn and Karin Kubitsch (Hamburg), Sara S. Hradecky (Ottawa), Warren L. Johns (CIIR c/o UK Embassy, Lima), Carmen Kuczma (Powell River, BC), Henry R. Laughlin (Norfolk, Ct.), Andrew Lawrence (Vancouver) and Jon Easterbrooke (Shaftesbury), Frans Mikkelsen and Karen Simonsen (Aarhus, Dmk.), Jens Plahte (Aas, Norway), and Sebastian Steib (Bottmingen, Switz.), and several other travellers.

Readers' Adventure Competition. The closing date for the next Readers' Adventure Competition is 31 May 1988. Further 250-word accounts of experiences will be welcome as we intend to run the competition each alternate year.

FOSTER-CHERRINGTON

We specialize in books about Latin America, Mexico and the West Indies. Catalogues sent on request.

39 Clarence Gate Gardens, Glentworth Street, London, NW1 6BA, England.
Telephones—: **01-262-7201 & 01-675-2624**

HEALTH INFORMATION

The following information has been very kindly compiled for us by Dr. David Snashall, who is presently Senior Lecturer in Occupational Health at St. Thomas's Hospital Medical School in London. He has travelled extensively in Central and South America, worked in Peru and in East Africa and keeps in close touch with developments in preventative and tropical medicine. We have included also some welcome observations on the text by Dr. C. J. Schofield, editor of Parasitology Today. The publishers have every confidence that the following information is correct, but cannot assume any direct responsibility in this connection.

THE TRAVELLER to Latin America is inevitably exposed to health risks not encountered in Britain or the USA, especially if he spends time in the tropical regions. Epidemic diseases have been largely brought under control by vaccination programmes and public sanitation but, in rural areas, the latter is rudimentary and the chances of contracting infections of various sorts are much higher than at home.

There are English-speaking doctors in most major cities. If you fall ill the best plan may be to attend the out-patient department of a local hospital or contact your Embassy representative for the name of a reputable doctor. (We give the names of hospitals and some recommended doctors in the main city sections.—Ed.) Medical practices vary from those at home but remember they have particular experience in dealing with locally-occurring diseases.

Self-medication is undesirable except for minor complaints but may be forced on you by circumstances. Whatever the circumstances, be wary of medicines prescribed for you by pharmacists; many are poorly trained and unscrupulous enough to sell you potentially dangerous drugs or old stock they want to get rid of. The large number of pharmacies throughout Latin America is a considerable surprise to most people, as is the range of medicines you can purchase over the counter. There is a tendency towards over-prescription of drug mixtures and in general this should be resisted. Many drugs are manufactured under licence from American or European companies so the trade names may be familiar to you. This means that you do not need to carry a whole chest of medicines, but remember that the shelf-life of some items, especially vaccines and antibiotics, is markedly reduced in tropical conditions. Buy your supplies at the better outlets where they have refrigerators, even though it is more expensive. Check the expiry date of all preparations you buy.

Immigration officials sometimes confiscate scheduled drugs (Lomotil is an example) if they are not accompanied by a doctor's prescription.

With the following precautions and advice, you should keep as healthy as usual. Make local enquiries about health risks if you are apprehensive and take the general advice of European or North American families who have lived or are living in the country.

Before you go take out medical insurance. You should have a dental check-up, obtain a spare glasses prescription and, if you suffer from a chronic illness (such as diabetes, high blood pressure, ear or sinus troubles, cardiopulmonary disease or a nervous disorder) arrange for a check-up with your doctor, who can at the same time provide you with a letter explaining the details of your disability, if possible in English and Spanish (or Portuguese for Brazil). Check current practice in malaria prophylaxis (prevention).

22 HEALTH INFORMATION

Inoculations Smallpox vaccination is no longer required anywhere in the world. Cholera vaccination is not required for Latin America. The following vaccinations are recommended:

Yellow fever: this is a live vaccine not to be given to children under nine months of age or persons allergic to eggs. Immunity lasts ten years. An international certificate of yellow fever vaccination will be given and should be kept because it is sometimes asked for.
Typhoid (monovalent): one dose followed by a booster in a month's time; Immunity from this course lasts two to three years.
Poliomyelitis: this is a live vaccine generally given orally and a full course consists of three doses with a booster in tropical regions every two to three years.
Tetanus: one dose should be given with a booster (vital) at six weeks and another at six months, and ten-yearly boosters thereafter are recommended.

Children should, in addition, be properly protected against diphtheria, and against pertussis (whooping cough) and measles, both of which tend to be more serious infections than at home. Teenage girls, if they have not had the disease, should be given rubella (German measles) vaccination. Consult your doctor for advice on tuberculosis inoculation: the disease is still widespread.

Infectious Hepatitis (jaundice) is endemic throughout Latin America and seems to be frequently caught by travellers. The main symptoms are pains in the stomach, lack of appetite, lassitude, and the typical yellow colour of the skin. Medically speaking there are two different types, the less serious but more common is hepatitis A, for which the best protection is the careful preparation of food, the avoidance of contaminated drinking water and scrupulous attention to toilet hygiene. Human normal immunoglobulin (gamma globulin) confers considerable protection against the disease and is particularly useful in epidemics; it should be obtained from a reputable source and is certainly useful for travellers who intend to live rough: they should have a shot before leaving and have it repeated every six months. The dose is 250 mg under 10 years of age and 750 mg above. It is fairly expensive and may be replaced soon by a specific vaccination.

The other, more serious, version is hepatitis B which is acquired usually by injections with unclean needles, blood transfusions, as a sexually transmitted disease and possibly by insect bites. This disease can be effectively prevented by a specific vaccination requiring three shots over six months before travelling but this is quite expensive. If you have had jaundice in the past it would be worthwhile having a blood test to see if you are immune to either of the two types because this might avoid the neccessity for vaccination or gamma globulin.
If at a particular occupational risk (e.g. zoologists or veterinarians), or in the case of epidemics, there are vaccines against other diseases such as rabies.

Common Problems, some of which will almost certainly be encountered, are:

Heat and Cold Full acclimatization to high temperatures takes about two weeks and during this period it is normal to feel relatively apathetic, especially if the relative humidity is high. Drink plenty of water (up to 15 litres a day are required when working physically hard in the tropics), use salt on your food and avoid extreme exertion. Tepid showers are more cooling than hot or cold ones. Large hats do not cool you down, but do prevent sunburn. Remember that, especially in the highlands, there can be a large and sudden drop in temperature between sun and shade and between night and day, so dress accordingly. Warm jackets and woollens are essential after dark at high altitude.

Altitude Acute mountain sickness or *soroche* can strike from about 3,000 metres upwards. It is more likely to affect those who ascend rapidly (e.g. by plane) and those who over-exert themselves. Teenagers are particularly prone. Past experience is not always a good guide: the author, having spent years in Peru travelling constantly between sea level and very high altitude, never suffered the slightest symptoms, then was severely affected climbing Kilimanjaro in

Tanzania. (Heavy smokers are reported to be particularly vulnerable to *soroche*.—Ed.)

On reaching heights above 3,000 metres, heart pounding and shortness of breath, especially on exertion, are almost universal and a normal response to the lack of oxygen in the air. *Soroche* takes a few hours or days to come on and presents with headache, lassitude, dizziness, loss of appetite, nausea and vomiting. Insomnia is common and often associated with a suffocating feeling when lying in bed. Keen observers may note their breathing tends to wax and wane at night and their face tends to be puffy in the mornings—this is all part of the syndrome. The treatment is rest, pain killers (preferably not aspirin-based) for the headache and anti-sickness pills for vomiting. Oxygen may help at very high altitudes. Various local panaceas ("Coramina glucosada", "Effortil", "Micoren") have their advocates and *mate de coca* (an infusion of coca leaves, widely available) certainly alleviates some of the symptoms.

On arrival at places over 3,000 metres, a few hours' rest in a chair and avoidance of alcohol, cigarettes and heavy food will go a long way towards preventing *soroche*. Should the symptoms be severe and prolonged it is best to descend to lower altitude and re-ascend slowly or in stages. If this is impossible because of shortage of time or if the likelihood of acute mountain sickness is high then the drug Acetazoleamide (Diamox) can be used as a preventative and continued during the ascent. There is good evidence of the value of this drug in the prevention of *soroche* but some people do experience funny side effects. The usual dose is 500 mg of the slow-release preparation each night, starting the night before ascending above 3,000 metres.

Other problems experienced at high altitude are sunburn, excessively dry air causing skin cracking, sore eyes (it may be wise to leave your contact lenses out) and stuffy noses. It is unwise to ascend to high altitude if you are pregnant, especially in the first 3 months (or if you have any history of heart disease—Ed.).

There is a further, albeit rare, hazard due to rapid ascent to high altitude called acute pulmonary oedema. The condition can affect mountaineers, but also occurs in Andean natives returning from a period at the coast. The condition comes on quite rapidly with breathlessness, noisy breathing, cough, blueness of the lips and frothing at the mouth. Anybody developing this must be brought down as soon as possible, given oxygen and taken to hospital.

Rapid descent from high places will aggravate sinus and middle ear infections, and make bad teeth ache painfully. (The same problems are sometimes experienced during descent at the end of a flight. One sinus sufferer has recommended continuous inhalation of McKenzie's anti-catarrh smelling salts at such a time— Ed.)

Despite these various hazards (mostly preventable) of high-altitude travel, many people find the environment healthier and more invigorating than at sea-level.

Intestinal Upsets Practically nobody escapes this one, so be prepared for it. Most of the time it is due to the insanitary preparation of food. Don't eat uncooked fish or vegetables, fruit with the skin on (always peel your fruit yourself), food that is exposed to flies, or salads. Tap water is rarely safe outside the major cities, especially in the rainy season, and stream water is often contaminated by communities living surprisingly high in the mountains. Filtered or bottled (make sure it is opened in your presence—Ed.) water is usually available and safe. If your hotel has a central hot-water supply, this is safe to drink after cooling. Ice for drinks should be made from boiled water but rarely is, so stand your glass on the ice cubes rather than putting them in the drink. Dirty water should first be strained through a filter bag (available from camping shops) and then boiled or treated. Water in general can be rendered safe in the following ways: boil for 5 minutes at sea level, longer at higher altitudes; or add three drops of household bleach to 1 pint of water and leave for 15 minutes; or add 1 drop of tincture of iodine to 1 pint of water and leave for 3 minutes. Commercial water-sterilizing tablets are available, for instance Sterotabs from Boots, England.

24 HEALTH INFORMATION

Milk, apart from canned varieties, is rarely pasteurized and, therefore, a source of tuberculosis, brucellosis and food-poisoning germs. This applies equally to ice-cream, yoghurt and cheese. Fresh milk can be rendered safe by heating it to 62°C for 30 minutes followed by rapid cooling, or by boiling it. Matured or processed cheeses are safer than fresh varieties.

The most effective treatment for simple diarrhoea is rest and plenty to drink (the Editor has benefited from a 24-hour fast, as well). Seek medical advice, however, if there is no improvement after three days. Much of the exhaustion of travellers' diarrhoea derives from the fact that water and salts are lost from the body and are not replaced. This can be done by proprietary preparations of salts which are dissolved in water, e.g. Electrosol (Macarthys) Dioralyte (Armour) Rehidrat (Searle) or simply by adding a tablespoonful of sugar and a teaspoonful of salt to a litre of water. If rest is not possible, or the lavatory is full of other people with the same trouble, or if the stomach cramps are particularly bad, then the following drugs may help:

Loperamide (Imodium, Janssen, or Arret) up to eight capsules a day. This is now available in the UK without prescription.
Diaphenoxylate with atropine (Lomotil, Searle) up to 16 tablets in any 24 hours, but do *not* use for simple diarrhoea, only to relieve cramps.
Codeine phosphate 30 mg. One tablet every 4 hours.
Kaolin and morphine or Paregoric, as directed by the pharmacist.

Severe vomiting may be calmed by metoclopramide (Maxolon, Beechams; Primperan, Berk) 10 mg. tablet or injection every 8 hours, but not more frequently.

The vast majority of cases of diarrhoea and/or vomiting are due to microbial infections of the bowel plus an effect from strange food and drink. They represent no more than a temporary inconvenience which you learn to live with and need no special treatment. Fortunately, as you get accustomed to Latin American germs, the attacks become less frequent and you can be more daring in your eating habits.

If, in addition to cramps and diarrhoea, you pass blood in the bowel motion, have severe abdominal pain, fever and feel really terrible, you may well have dysentery and a doctor should be consulted at once. If this is not possible, the recommended treatment for bacillary dysentery is Tetracycline or Ampicillin 500 mg. every 6 hours plus replacement of water and salts. If you catch amoebic dysentery, which has rather similar symptoms, do not try to cure yourself but put yourself in proper medical hands; the treatment can be complex and self-medication may just damp down the symptoms with the risk of serious liver involvement later on.

Dan Buck and Anne Meadows write: "Several days of chicken soup (especially *dieta de pollo*), mashed potatoes (*puré de papas*) and tea will do wonders for cramps, diarrhoea and other minor stomach ailments. (Some people swear by chewing raw garlic; we've never tried it.)"

John Streather writes: "If stuck in the bush literally hundreds of miles from the nearest doctor or reputable pharmacist, this unpleasant but foolproof remedy will cure you of intestinal parasites after seven whole days of rigorously keeping to it. Cut a medium-sized slice of papaya (mamão, pawpaw) and keep all the seeds from it. Eat the seeds—crunch them up! (really nauseating, I'm afraid!). Then eat the fruit. Then peel about a third of a (normal-sized) pineapple, cut into slices and eat that. If hungry after this, potato or rice boiled without salt can be eaten and as much fresh clean fruit as one likes. (The raw fruit replaces the mineral salts lost in the flux of dysentery and the papaya seeds (strongly alkaline) kill intestinal parasites; the papaya fruit itself is extremely calming for the digestion in general.)

"This awful meal should be eaten three times a day for seven entire days—the papaya seeds are essential. The cure is absolutely proven and foolproof: I have cured myself with it. Two or three mouthfuls of munched papaya seeds before meals on the Amazon may be better for one than endless preventative drugs, too.

"In very remote areas Indian herbal remedies are normally most efficacious. Resort to them *faute de mieux*!"

(The Editor stresses that these suggestions do not bear Dr. Snashall's authority.) John Streather emphasizes that after an apparent cure achieved by these means, one should still have one's stool analysed on return to civilization. Hans Walter Gerber, of W. Berlin, tells us that this remedy should not be persisted with if one begins to pass blood: indeed, it becomes actively dangerous at that point.

HEALTH INFORMATION 25

Enterovioform (Ciba), "Mexaform" in Latin America, gives some protection against amoebic dysentery but is useless in the general prevention of diarrhoea and can have serious side effects (nerve damage, especially to the eyes) if taken for long periods. The active agent, diodochlor-hydroxy-quinoline, is used in many antidiarrhoeals sold in Peru and Ecuador. If it is impossible to control the source of your food and you are likely to be far from medical attention (such as on Amazonian river trips) it is justifiable to take diloxanide furoate (Furamide) 500 mg. daily *plus* a sulphonamide drug e.g. Phthalylsulphathiazole (Thalazole, May & Baker) 500 mg. twice daily. Many businessmen and, for example, athletes who are on short visits of great importance take Streptotriad (May & Baker) one tablet twice daily to prevent diarrhoea and this has been proved to be effective.

Paradoxically, constipation is also common, probably induced by dietary change, inadequate fluid intake in hot places and long bus journeys. Simple laxatives are useful in the short term (the Editor recommends Sennacot) and bulky foods such as maize, beans and plenty of fruit are also useful.

Insects These can be a great nuisance, especially in the tropics, and some, of course, are carriers of serious diseases. The best way of keeping them away at night is to sleep off the ground with a mosquito net and to burn mosquito coils containing pyrethrum. Aerosol sprays have only a temporary effect. The best repellants contain di-ethyl-meta-toluamide (DET) or di-methyl phthalate—sold as "Deet", "Six-Twelve Plus", "Off", "Boots' Liquid Insect Repellant", "Autan", "Flypel". Liquid is best for arms and face (care around eyes) and aerosol spray for clothes and ankles to deter chiggers, mites and ticks. Liquid DET suspended in water can be used to impregnate cotton clothes and mosquito nets.

If you are bitten, itching may be relieved by baking-soda baths, anti-histamine tablets (care with alcohol or driving), corticosteroid creams (great care—never use if any hint of sepsis) or by judicious scratching. Calamine lotion and cream have limited effectiveness and antihistamine creams (e.g. Antihisan, May & Baker) have a tendency to cause skin allergies and are, therefore, not generally recommended. Caladryl ointment is also useful against bites.

Bites which become infected (commonly in the tropics) should be treated with a local antiseptic or antibiotic cream, such as Cetrimide BP (Savlon, ICI) as should infected scratches.

Skin infestations with body lice (crabs) and scabies are, unfortunately, easy to pick up. Use gamma benzene hexachloride for lice and benzene benzoate solution for scabies. Crotamiton cream (Eurax, Geigy) alleviates itching and also kills a number of skin parasites. Prioderm (5% malathion lotion) good for lice—but full-strength malathion can kill you.

(John Streather tells us that in remote grassland areas, insect larvae such as that of the bot-fly, which burrow into the flesh, are best removed by covering the breathing hole in your skin with aeroplane glue, then a circular piece of adhesive tape with more aeroplane glue round the edges. If this is allowed to dry well, with no lymph leaking out round the edges, you will be able to squeeze the maggot out next day.)

Malaria in South America is theoretically confined to coastal and jungle zones but is now on the increase again. Mosquitoes do not thrive above 2,500 metres so you are safe at altitude. There are different varieties of malaria, some resistant to the normal drugs. Make local enquiries if you intend to visit possibly infected zones and use one of the following prophylactic regimes. Start taking the tablets a few days before exposure and continue to take them for six weeks after leaving the malarial zone. Remember to give the drugs to babies and children also. Opinion varies on the precise drugs and dosage to be used for protection; all the drugs may have some side effects, and it is important to balance the risk of catching the disease against the albeit rare side effects. The increasing complexity of the subject as the malarial parasite becomes immune to the new generation of drugs has made concentration on the physical prevention of being bitten by mosquitoes more important, i.e. the use of long-sleeved shirts/blouses and long trousers, repellants and nets.

26 HEALTH INFORMATION

Prophylactic regimes:

Proguanil (Paludrine ICI) 100 mg, 2 tablets daily
or Chloroquine (Avlochlor, ICI; Nivaquine, May & Baker; Resochin, Bayer; Aralen 300 mg base (2 tablets) weekly (alternatively Amodiaquine can be substituted for Chloroquine).
Where there is a high risk of chloroquine-resistant falciparum malaria:
either take Chloroquine prophylaxis (as above) and carry Fansidar (Roche) for treatment.
or add Maloprin (Wellcome) 1 tablet per week to your routine Chloroquine prophylaxis.

(Dr Alex Williams, medical director of British Caledonian, has been quoted as saying that to get reasonable protection against all sorts of malaria one should take one tablet of Maloprin plus two tablets of Chloroquine a week—Ed.)

You can catch malaria even when sticking to the above rules, although it is unlikely. If you do develop symptoms (high fever, shivering, headache) seek medical advice immediately. If this is not possible, and there is a great likelihood of malaria, the *treatment* is:

Normal types: Chloroquine, a single dose of 4 tablets (600mg) followed by two tablets (300 mg) in 6 hours and 300 mg each day following.
Falciparum type or type in doubt: Fansidar, single dose of 3 tablets. (We have been told that this drug does not combine well with alcohol, so best to avoid drinking during treatment period.)

If Falciparum type malaria is definitely diagnosed, it is wise to get to a good hospital as the treatment can be complex and the illness very serious.

Pregnant women are particularly prone to malaria and should stick to Proguanil as a prophylactic. Chloroquine may cause eye damage if taken over a long period. The safety of Fansidar has been questioned and, at the time of writing, it is not recommended for prophylaxis.

Editorial Note The UK health authorities hold that malaria is on the increase throughout the world; prophylaxis should be used if travelling outside major cities in any humid tropical areas, particularly forest and coastal zones.

Chagas' Disease (South American Trypanosomiasis) is a chronic disease, very rarely caught by travellers, and impossible to treat, and transmitted by the nocturnal "kissing bug" (Triatoma or Rhodnius) known in the Spanish-speaking countries as the *vinchuca*, or in Brazil as the *barbeiro*, which lives in dirty adobe huts, identifiable by black and white excreta streaks on walls. Use a mosquito net and keep a candle burning (it dislikes light) if you cannot avoid sleeping in such conditions. If bitten do not scratch the bites; wash them at once in disinfected water. The disease is transmitted by excreta, not by bite.

Sunburn The burning power of the tropical sun, especially at high altitude, is phenomenal. Always wear a wide-brimmed hat and use some form of suncream lotion on untanned skin. Normal temperate-zone suntan lotions (protection factor up to 7) are not much good; you need to use the types designed specifically for the tropics, or for mountaineers or skiers, with a protection factor between 7 and 15. These are often not available in South America; a reasonable substitute is zinc oxide ointment. Glare from the sun can cause conjunctivitis, so wear sunglasses, especially on tropical beaches, where high protection-factor sunscreen cream should also be used.

Snakebite If you are unlucky enough to be bitten by a venomous snake, spider, scorpion or sea creature, try (within limits) to catch the animal for identification. The reactions to be expected are: fright, swelling, pain and bruising around the bite, soreness of the regional lymph glands, nausea, vomiting and fever. If any of the following symptoms supervene, get the victim to a doctor without delay: numbness and tingling of the face, muscular spasms, convulsion, shortness of breath and haemorrhage. The tiny coral snake, with red, black and white bands, is the most dangerous, but is very timid.

Commercial snakebite kits are available, but only useful for the specific type of snake for which they are designed. The serum has to be given intravenously so is not much good unless you have had some practice at making injections into veins. If the bite is on a limb, immobilize the limb and apply a tight bandage between the bite and the body, releasing it for 90 seconds every 15 minutes.

HEALTH INFORMATION

Reassurance of the bitten person is very important because death from snakebite is very rare. Do not slash the bite area and try to suck out the poison because this sort of heroism does more harm than good. Hospitals usually hold stocks of snake bite serum. Best precaution: don't walk in snake territory with bare feet or sandals—wear proper shoes or boots.

Spiders and Scorpions These may be found in the more basic hotels in the Andean countries. If bitten by *Latrodectus* or *Loxcosales* spiders, or stung by scorpions, rest and take plenty of fluids, and call a doctor. Precaution: keep beds away from the walls, and look inside shoes in morning.

Other Afflictions Remember that **rabies** is endemic throughout Latin America so avoid dogs that are behaving strangely, and cover your toes at night to foil the vampire bats, which also carry the disease. If you are bitten, try to have the animal captured for observation and see a doctor at once. Treatment with human diploid vaccine is now extremely effective and worth seeking out if the likelihood of having contracted rabies is high.

Dengue fever has made its appearance in southern Mexico and the lower-lying parts of Central America; also in Brazil. No treatment: you must just avoid mosquito bites.

Intestinal worms are common, and the more serious ones such as **hookworm** can be contracted from walking barefoot on infested earth or beaches. Various other tropical diseases can be caught in jungle areas, usually transmitted by biting insects; they are often related to African diseases and were probably introduced by the slave trade from Africa.

Onchocerciasis (river-blindness), carried by blackflies, is found in parts of Mexico and Venezuela. Cutaneous **leishmaniasis** (Espundia) is carried by sandflies and causes a sore that won't heal. Epidemics of meningitis occur from time to time. Finally, be careful about swimming in piranha- (or caribe-) infested rivers. It is a good idea not to swim naked: the candura fish can follow urine currents and become lodged in body orifices; swimwear offers some protection.

Prickly heat, a very common itchy rash, is avoided by frequent washing and by wearing loose clothing. Cured by allowing skin to dry off through use of powder, and spending 2 nights in an air-conditioned hotel! **Athlete's foot** and other fungal infections are best treated with Tinaderm.

When you return home, remember to take your anti-malarial tablets for 6 weeks. Thousands of people develop malaria after tropical holidays because they do not take this precaution and some of them die, because it is not realized at home that they are suffering from malaria. If you have had attacks of diarrhoea, it is worth having a stool specimen tested in case you may have picked up amoebic dysentery. If you have been living in the bush, a blood test may be worthwhile to detect worms and other parasites.

Basic supplies The following items you may find useful to take with you from home:

Sunglasses.
  Ear plugs ("Muffles") to be used when swimming to prevent outer ear infections, and when sleeping in noisy hotels.
  Suntan cream.
  Insect repellant, flea powder, mosquito net and coils.
  Tampons (they can be bought in the main cities), and contraceptives (very difficult to obtain).
  Water-sterilizing tablets, *e.g.* Sterotabs (Boots), Puritabs (Kirby & Co. Ltd.), Globaline.
  Antimalarials.
  Anti-infective ointment, *e.g.* Savlon (ICI).
  Dusting powder for feet, *e.g.* Tinaderm (Glaxo), Desenex.
  Travel-sickness pills, *e.g.* Dramamine (Searle), Gravol (Carter-Wallace).
  Antacids, *e.g.* Maalox.

28 HEALTH INFORMATION

Antidiarrheals, *e.g.* Lomotil (Searle) or Imodium (Janssen). (Charcoal tablets are useful for minor stomach ailments.)
First-aid kit.

The following organizations give information regarding well-trained, English-speaking physicians in Latin America:

International Association for Medical Assistance to Travellers, 745 Fifth Avenue, New York 10022.

Intermedic, 777 Third Avenue, New York 10017.

Information regarding country-by-country malaria risk can be obtained from the World Health Organization (WHO), or the Ross Institute, London School of Hygiene and Tropical Medicine, Keppel Street, London WC1E 7HT, which publishes a book strongly recommended, entitled *Preservation of Personal Health in Warm Climates*.

LEG POUCH
Money, Credit Cards, Passport
~ SUPER SAFE ~
FULL REFUND if not 100% convinced

Send $10 ($13 for airmail)
or equivalent in £, DM or Fr.

LEG-POUCH
17002 Cotter Pl
Encino CA 91436
USA

Request brochure

WANTED: MAPS

ARGENTINA – BRAZIL – MEXICO GUATEMALA – EL SALVADOR – THE CARIBBEAN ISLANDS

We would much appreciate receiving any surplus maps and diagrams, however rough, of towns and cities, walks, national parks and other interesting areas, to use as source material for the Handbook and other forthcoming titles.

The above regions are particularly needed but any maps of Latin America would be welcome.

**The Editor
Trade & Travel Publications Ltd
5 Prince's Buildings
George Street
Bath BA1 2ED
England**

THOSE WHO USE THIS BOOK SHOULD KNOW...

...that **TRAILFINDERS** provide a comprehensive information and booking service on behalf of all the best overland adventure and expedition operators in South America.

...that **TRAILFINDERS** can advise you on the cheapest ways to fly to South America, as well as offering unrivalled value air fares to all other parts of the world, including India, S.E. Asia, Australia and New Zealand.

...that **TRAILFINDERS** publish their own free colour magazine packed with worldwide information for the real traveller.

...that **TRAILFINDERS** offer the complete travel service, are licensed and bonded by the Civil Aviation Authority and are open 6 days a week from 9 am to 6 pm.

IT'S ALL AT:
Trailfinders, Travel Centre
42 - 48 Earls Court Road, London
W8 6EJ   01-938 3366

ARGENTINA

	Page		Page
Introductory	31	The Iguazú Falls	106
Buenos Aires and the		Up the Río Uruguay	112
Pampas	36	The Lake District	113
The Córdoba Region	59	Patagonia	125
Tucumán, Salta, Jujuy	66	Economy	144
Over the Andes to Chile	86	Information for Visitors	145
North of Mendoza	88	Maps	37, 60, 78, 96, 108
Mesopotamia	95		

ARGENTINA is the second largest country in area and third in population in South America. It covers an area of 2,807,560 square km., or 29% of the area of Europe; it is 3,460 km. long from N to S and is, in places, 1,580 km. wide. Apart from the estuary of the Río de la Plata its coast line is 2,575 km. long. Its western frontier runs along the crest of the high Andes, a formidable barrier between it and Chile. Its neighbours to the N are Bolivia and Paraguay and (in the NE) Brazil. To the E is Uruguay. Its far southern limit is the Beagle Channel.

Argentina is enormously varied both in its types of land and its climates. Geographers usually recognize four main physical areas: the Andes, the North and Mesopotamia, the Pampas, and Patagonia.

The first division, the Andes, includes the whole length of the Cordilleras, low and deeply glaciated in the Patagonian S, high and dry in the prolongation into NW Argentina of the Bolivian Altiplano, the high plateau. S of this is the very parched desert and mountain region S of Tucumán and W of Córdoba. The oases strung along the eastern foot of the Andes—Jujuy, Salta, Tucumán, Catamarca, La Rioja, San Juan, Mendoza and San Rafael—were the first places to be colonized by the Spaniards.

The second division, the North and Mesopotamia, contains the vast forested plains of the Chaco, and the floodplain and gently rolling land known as the Argentine Mesopotamia lying between the rivers Paraná and Uruguay. The Province of Misiones in the NE is actually on the great Paraná plateau. The plains cover 582,750 square km.

The third division, the flat rich pampa, takes up the heart of the land. These vast plains lie S of the Chaco, E of the Andes, W of the Atlantic and the Río Paraná and N of the Río Colorado. The eastern part, which receives more rain, is usually called the Humid Pampa, and the western part the Dry Pampa. The Pampas stretch for hundreds of km. in almost unrelieved flatness and cover some 650,000 square km.

The final division is Patagonia, the area S of the Río Colorado—a land of arid, wind-swept plateaux cut across by ravines. In the deep S the wind is wilder and more continuous. There is no real summer, but to compensate for this the winters are rarely severe. Patagonia has about 780,000 square km.

Three-quarters of Argentina's territory cannot be cultivated without irrigation but only 400,000 hectares are artificially watered.

History of Settlement and Economic Growth When, in the early 16th century, the first white men came to Argentina, the native Indians had already halted the Inca drive southwards from Peru through Bolivia into northern Argentina. The Spaniard Juan de Solís landed on the shores of the Plata estuary in

ARGENTINA

1516, but he was killed and the expedition failed. Magellan touched at the estuary four years later, but turned southwards to make his way into the Pacific. In 1527 both Sebastian Cabot and his rival Diego García sailed into the estuary and up the Paraná and the Paraguay. They formed a small settlement, Sancti Spiritus, at the junction of the Caraña and Coronda rivers near their confluence with the Paraná, but it was wiped out by the Indians about two years later and Cabot and García returned to Spain. Eight years later, in 1535, Pedro de Mendoza, with a large force well supplied with equipment and horses, founded a settlement at Buenos Aires. The natives soon made it too hot for him; the settlement was abandoned and Mendoza returned home, but not before sending Juan de Ayolas with a small force up the Paraná. Ayolas set off for Peru, already conquered by Pizarro, leaving Irala in charge. It is not known for certain what happened to Ayolas, but in 1537 Irala and his men settled at Asunción, in Paraguay, where the natives were friendly. There were no further expeditions from Spain to colonize what is now called Argentina, and it was not until 1573 that the settlement at Asunción sent forces S to establish Santa Fe and not until June 11, 1580 that Juan de Garay refounded the settlement at Buenos Aires. It was only under his successor, Hernando Arias de Saavedra (1592-1614), that the new colony became secure.

In the meantime there had been successful expeditions into Argentina both from Peru and Chile—the first, from Peru, as early as 1543. These expeditions led, in the latter half of the 16th century, to the foundation at the eastern foot of the Andes of the oldest towns in Argentina: Santiago del Estero, Tucumán, Córdoba, Salta, La Rioja and Jujuy by Spaniards from Peru following the old Inca road, and San Juan, Mendoza, and San Luis by those from Chile, across the Andes. Peru was given the viceroyalty over all the Spanish possessions in South America in 1543.

For 270 years after its foundation Buenos Aires was of little importance. Spanish stress was upon Lima, and Lima did not send its treasures home by way of Buenos Aires but through Panama and the Caribbean. Buenos Aires was not allowed by Spain to take part in any overseas trade until 1778; its population then was only 24,203. It was merely a military outpost for Spain to confront the Portuguese outpost at Colonia, across the estuary, and lived, in the main, by smuggling. Even when in 1776 the Viceroyalty of Río de la Plata was formed, it made little difference to Buenos Aires as a capital, for its control of the *cabildos* (town councils) in distant towns was very tenuous. When the British, following Spain's alliance with Napoleon, attacked Buenos Aires in 1806 and again in 1807 before being repulsed by local levies, there was no inkling of its future potential. But the attacks had one important result: a great increase in the confidence of the *porteños* (the name given to those born in Buenos Aires) to deal with all comers, including the mother-country, whose restrictions were increasingly unpopular. On May 25, 1810, the *cabildo* of Buenos Aires deposed the viceroy and announced that it was governing henceforth on behalf of King Ferdinand VII, then a captive of Napoleon. Six years later, when Buenos Aires was threatened by invasion from Peru and blockaded by a Spanish fleet in the River Plate, a national congress held at Tucumán declared independence on July 9, 1816. The declaration was given reality by the genius and devotion of José de San Martín, who boldly marched an Argentine army across the Andes to free Chile, and (with the help of Lord Cochrane, commander of the Chilean Navy), embarked his forces for Peru, where he captured Lima, the first step in the freedom of Peru.

When San Martín returned home, it was to find the country rent by conflict between the central government and the provinces. Disillusioned, he retired to France. The internal conflict was to last a long time. On the one hand stood the Unitarist party, bent on central control; on the other the Federalist party, insisting on local autonomy. The latter had for members the great *caudillos*, the large landowners backed by the *gauchos*, suspicious of the cities. One of their leaders, Juan Manuel de Rosas, took control of the country in 1829. During his second term as Governor of Buenos Aires he asked for and was given extraordinary powers. The result was a 17-year reign of terror. His rule was an international scandal, and when he began a blockade of Asunción in 1845, Britain and France

ARGENTINA

promptly countered with a three-year blockade of Buenos Aires. But in 1851 Justo José de Urquiza, Governor of Entre Ríos, one of his old henchmen, organized a triple *entente* of Brazil, Uruguay, and the Argentine opposition to overthrow him. He was defeated in 1852 at Caseros, a few km. from Buenos Aires, and fled to England, where he farmed quietly for 25 years, dying at Southampton.

Rosas had started his career as a Federalist; once in power he was a Unitarist. His downfall meant the triumph of federalism. In 1853 a federal system was finally incorporated in the constitution, but the old quarrel had not been solved. In 1859, when the constitution was ratified, the capital was moved to Paraná, the province of Buenos Aires seceded, and Buenos Aires, under Bartolomé Mitre, was defeated by the federal forces under Urquiza. Two years later Buenos Aires again fought the country, and this time it won. Once again it became the seat of the federal government, with Bartolomé Mitre as its first constitutional president. (It was during his term that the Triple Alliance of Argentina, Brazil, and Uruguay defeated Francisco Solano López of Paraguay.) There was another political flare-up of the old quarrel in 1880, ending in the humiliation of Buenos Aires, which then ceased to be the capital of its province; a new provincial capital was founded at La Plata, 56 km. to the SE. At that time a young colonel, Julio A. Roca, was finally subduing all the Indian tribes of the pampas and the S. This was an event which was to make possible the final supremacy of Buenos Aires over all rivals.

Politically Argentina was a constitutional republic with a very restricted suffrage up to the passage in 1912 of the Sáenz Peña law, which established universal manhood suffrage. From 1916 to 1930 the Unión Cívica Radical (founded in 1890) held power, under the leadership of Hipólito Yrigoyen and Marcelo T. de Alvear, but lost it to the military uprising of 1930. Though seriously affected by the world depression of the 1930s, Argentina's rich soil and educated population had made it one of the ten wealthiest countries in the world, but this wealth was most unevenly distributed, and the political methods followed by the conservatives and their military associates in the 1930s seemed to deny the middle and working classes any effective share in their own country's wealth and government. In 1943 came another military coup, which had a distinctly fascist tinge; in 1946 emerged, as President, Gen. Juan Domingo Perón (see also page 35), who based his power on an alliance between the army and labour; his contacts with labour were greatly assisted by his charismatic wife Eva (since commemorated in the rock-opera "Evita") and the living conditions of the workers were greatly improved—but at the expense of the economic state of the country. By the time a military coup unseated Perón in 1955 serious harm had been done; ever since, Argentina has been struggling to recover its lost economic health.

The Transformation of the Pampas The pampas, the economic heart of the country, extend fanwise from Buenos Aires for a distance of between 550 and 650 km. Apart from three groups of *sierras* or low hills near Córdoba, Tandil and Bahía Blanca, the surface seems an endless flat monotony, relieved occasionally, in the SW, by sand dunes. There are few rivers. Drinking water is pumped to the surface from a depth of from 30 to 150 metres by the windpumps which are such a prominent feature of the landscape. There are no trees other than those that have been planted, except in the *monte* of the W. But there is, in most years, ample rainfall. It is greatest at Rosario, where it is about 1,020 mm., and evenly distributed throughout the year. The further S from Rosario, the less the rain. At Buenos Aires it is about 940 mm.; it drops to 535 at Bahía Blanca, and is only 400 along the boundary of the Humid Pampa. The further from Rosario, too, the more the rainfall is concentrated during the summer. Over the whole of the pampa the summers are hot, the winters mild, but there is a large climatic difference between various regions: at Rosario the growing season between frosts is about 300 days; at Bahía Blanca it falls to 145 days.

When the Spanish arrived in Argentina the pampas were an area of tall coarse grasses. The cattle and horses they brought with them were soon to roam wild and in time transformed the Indian's way of life. The only part of the pampa occupied by the settlers was the so-called Rim, between the Río Salado, S of the capital, and the Paraná-Plata rivers. Here, in large *estancias,* cattle, horses and mules in great herds roamed the open range. There was a line of forts along the Río Salado: a not very effective protection against marauding Indians. The Spaniards had also brought European grasses with them; these soon supplanted the coarse native grasses, and formed a green carpet surface which stopped abruptly at the Río Salado.

The *estancia* owners and their dependent *gauchos* were in no sense an agricultural people, but towards the end of the 18th century, tenants—to the great contempt of both *estanciero* and *gaucho*—began to plant wheat in the valleys along the Paraná-Plata shore. The fall of Rosas in 1852, and the constitution of 1853, made it possible for Argentina to take a leap forward, but it must be remembered that its civilized population at that time was only 1,200,000.

The Modern Period The rapidly rising population of Europe during the latter half of the 19th century and the consequent demand for cheap food was the spur that impelled Argentina (as it did the United States and Canada) to occupy its grasslands and take to agriculture. This was made possible by the new techniques already developed: agricultural machinery, barbed wire, well-drilling machines and windpumps, roads and railways, and ocean-going steamships. Roads were, and are, a difficulty in the Argentine pampa; the soil lacks gravel or stones to surface the roads, and dirt roads become a quagmire in wet weather and a fume of dust in the dry. Railways, on the other hand, were simple and cheap to build. The system grew as need arose and capital (mostly from Britain) became available. The lines in the pampa radiate out fanwise (with intricate intercommunication) from the ports of Buenos Aires, Rosario, Santa Fe and Bahía Blanca. Argentina, unlike most other countries, had extensive railways before a road system was built.

The occupation of the pampa was made finally possible by a war against the Indians in 1878-83 which virtually exterminated them. Many of the officers in that campaign were given gifts of land of more than 40,000 hectares each. The pampa had passed into private hands on the old traditional pattern of large estates.

Cattle products—hides, tallow, and salt beef—had been the mainstay of Argentine overseas trade during the whole of the colonial period. In the early 19th century wool challenged the supremacy of cattle. The occupation of the grasslands did not, at first, alter the complexion of the foreign trade; it merely increased its volume. In 1877, however, the first ship with refrigeration chambers made it possible to send frozen beef to England, but the meat of the scrub cattle was too strong for English taste. As a result, pedigree bulls were imported from England and the upgrading of the herds began. The same process was applied to sheep. But the improved herds could only flourish where there were no ticks—prevalent in the N—and throve best where forage crops were available. Argentina adopted as its main forage crop alfalfa (lucerne), a plant like clover which proved extremely suitable on the pampa. It has since been supplemented with barley, oats, rye and particularly maize and sorghums.

The country given over to arable and pastoral farming is monotonously flat. It is astonishing to drive hour after hour and see no brook or river. Nor are there ponds or pools save in times of unusual rain. Tall windpumps stand in the fields, and from them radiate long lines of galvanized iron troughs for the cattle and sheep. Fields are fenced into very large *potreros,* or pastures, of from 40 to 2,000 hectares each. Cattle, sheep and horses usually graze in the same pasture. In the villages the roads are wide and commonly treeless, though now and then there are *estancias* where trees have been planted with care. The chinaberry tree is the favourite, for it is not devoured by locusts; next comes the eucalyptus.

A striking thing about the Pampas is the bird life. Flamingoes rise in a pink and white cloud as the trains passes, heron egrets gleam white against the blue sky, pink spoonbills dig in the mud and rheas stalk in the distance. Most fascinating are the oven birds, the *horneros,* which build oven-shaped nests six times as big as themselves on the top of telegraph and fence posts.

ARGENTINA

To sum up, the transformation of the pampa has had two profound effects. Because its newly-created riches flowed out and its needs flowed in mainly through Buenos Aires, that port grew from comparative insignificance into one of the great cities in the world. Also, the transformation of the Humid Pampa led, through immigration, to a vast predominance of the European strain. The first immigrants settled NW of Santa Fe in 1856. Between 1857 and 1930 total immigration was over six million, almost all from Europe. The process has continued; Italians have been by far the most numerous, followed by Spaniards, and then, far behind, groups of other Europeans and Latin Americans. British and North Americans normally came as stockbreeders, technicians and business executives.

The Argentine People In the Federal Capital and Province of Buenos Aires, where nearly half the population lives, the people are almost exclusively of European origin. In the far northern provinces, colonized from neighbouring countries, at least half the people are *mestizos* though they form less than 2% of the population of the whole country. In the highlands of the NW and in the Chaco, there are still a few pure-blooded Indians.

In 1985 the population was 30.6 million. Some 83.7% are urban and 40% live in cities of 100,000 or more. Population growth: 1.7%; urban growth, 2.1%. Death rate per thousand: 8.7; infantile mortality, 60; birth rate, 24.6. It is estimated that 12.8% are foreign born and generally of European origin. From 90 to 95% can read and write.

Communications Argentina has only four good seaports: Buenos Aires, La Plata, Rosario and Bahía Blanca. The two great rivers flowing southward into the Plate, the Paraná and the Uruguay, are not very reliable shipping routes. The Colorado and the Negro rivers in northern Patagonia are navigable by small vessels only. Internal air services are highly developed.

Most of Argentina is served by about 140,000 km. of road, but only 30% are paved and a further 25% improved. Even so, the network carries 80% of freight tonnage and 82% of medium and long-distance passengers. The 43,100 km. of railway line, owned mostly by British companies until they were taken over by the State in 1948, carry only 8% of freight and 15% of the passenger traffic, and are very heavily subsidized. Services have improved in recent years, but profitability is very low.

Political System The form of government has traditionally been a representative, republican federal system. By the 1853 Constitution (amended in 1880) the country is divided into a Federal Capital (the city of Buenos Aires), 22 Provinces and the National Territory of Tierra del Fuego, Antarctica and South Atlantic Islands. Each Province has its own Senate and Chamber of Deputies. The municipal government of the capital is exercised by a Mayor appointed by the President with the approval of the Senate.

Recent History After an uneasy alternation of three military and two constitutional regimes between 1955 and 1973, Gen. Juan Domingo Perón (see page 33) again became President in October 1973, but died on July 1, 1974, leaving the Presidency to his widow, Vice-President María Estela Martínez de Perón. A chaotic political situation, of which a high level of violence (including guerrilla warfare) was a regrettable feature, followed his death; by March 1976 conditions in the country, both of violence and of economic crisis, had deteriorated to the point when the military felt again obliged to intervene. Sra. de Perón was deposed from the Presidency by a military junta, led by Gen. Jorge Videla, and guerrilla warfare and the other features of dissidence were repressed with great brutality: about 9,000 people disappeared without trace during the so-called "dirty war". General Videla was appointed President in 1978 by the military leaders, for a three-year term. His nominated successor, General Roberto Viola, took over as President for three years in March, 1981 but was replaced by General Leopoldo Galtieri in December 1981. The latter was in turn replaced in June 1982 by General (ret.) Reynaldo Bignone. Confidence in the military began to ebb

36 ARGENTINA

when their economic policies began to go sour in 1980, and in 1982-83 pressure for a democratic restoration grew apace. General elections were held on October 30, 1983 and the Unión Cívica Radical was victorious, winning the Presidency and an absolute majority in the Chamber of Deputies, with 52% of the vote. Accordingly, Dr. Raúl Alfonsín, its candidate, assumed the Presidency on December 10, 1983. Mid-term elections in November 1985 strengthened the democratic process and confirmed the Unión Cívica Radical's majority in the Chamber of Deputies. During 1985 also, Generals Videla, Viola and Galtieri were sentenced to long terms of imprisonment for their parts in the "dirty war".

The Cities of the Pampas

The pampa is little more than a fifth of the total area of the country, but 35% of the people live in Greater Buenos Aires and 32% in the Pampas. The Pampa area has 70% of all the railways, 86% of the land used for cereals and linseed, 65% of the cattle, 40% of the sheep, 77% of the pigs, and nearly 90% of the industrial production.

The River Plate, or Río de la Plata, the main seaward entrance on which Buenos Aires lies, is not a river but an estuary or great basin, 160 km. long and from 37 to 90 km. wide, into which flow the Rivers Paraná and Uruguay and their tributaries. It is muddy and shallow and the passage of ocean vessels is only made possible by continuous dredging. The tides are of little importance, for there is only a 1.2 metre rise and fall at spring tides. The depth of water is influenced mainly by the direction of the wind and the flow of the Paraná and Uruguay rivers.

Buenos Aires, the capital, spreads over some 200 square km. Its municipal population is about 3,323,000, but the population of greater Buenos Aires is already estimated at 9.8 millions.

NB. In spite of its name (good air), extreme humidity and unusual pollen conditions can affect asthma sufferers if they stay over an extended period of time (i.e. after a month or so).

Buenos Aires has been virtually rebuilt since the beginning of this century and very few of the old buildings are left. In the centre, which has maintained the original lay-out since its foundation, the streets are often very narrow and are mostly one-way.

The heart of the city, now as in colonial days, is the Plaza de Mayo, with the historic Cabildo, the Town Hall, where the movement for independence from Spain was first planned; the pink Casa Rosada (Presidential Palace); the City Hall; and the Cathedral, where San Martín, the father of Argentine independence, is buried. Within a few blocks are the fashionable church of Nuestra Señora de la Merced, the National Library and the main banks and business houses.

Running W from the Plaza, the Avenida de Mayo leads 1½ km. to the Congress building in the Plaza del Congreso. Halfway it crosses the wide Avenida Nueve de Julio. A tall obelisk commemorating the 400th anniversary of the city's founding stands at its centre in the Plaza de la República, surrounded by sloping lawns. The Av. Nueve de Julio itself, one of the widest in the world, consists of three carriageways separated by wide grass borders.
In the N it meets the Avenida Libertador, the principal way out of the city to the N and W.

N of the Plaza de Mayo is the shopping, theatre and commercial area. The city's traditional shopping centre, Calle Florida, is in this district. This is the popular down-town meeting place, particularly in the late afternoon; it is reserved for pedestrians only, so taxis cannot drive up to hotels on Florida. Another shopping street is Avenida Santa Fe, which crosses Florida at the Plaza San Martín; it has become as touristy and as expensive as Florida. Avenida Corrientes is the entertainment centre, a street of theatres, restaurants, cafés and night life. Close by, in Calle Lavalle and in nearby streets, there are numerous cinemas and many good and relatively reasonable restaurants; Calle Lavalle is reserved to pedestrians.

A broad avenue, Paseo Colón, runs S to the waterfront and the picturesque

ARGENTINA 37

MAP OF BUENOS AIRES

old port district known as the Boca, where the Riachuelo flows into the Plata (reached by bus 152 from Av. L. N. Alem in the centre, US$0.95). It was here, near Parque Lezama, that Pedro de Mendoza founded the first Buenos Aires. For a tour of the Boca, start at Plaza Vuelta de Rocha, near Av. Pedro de Mendoza and Dr Del Valle Iberlucea, then walk up Caminito. Visit the Museo de Bellas Artes de la Boca, Av. Pedro de Mendoza 1835. The Boca, mostly Italian, has its own distinctive life, but the area, with the adjacent industrial and meat-packing suburb of Avellaneda across the high Avellaneda bridge, is now dirty and run down. Calle Brasil leads from this area to the far side of the docks and the spacious Avenida Costanera which runs along the river front. Here are bathing places (Balneario Municipal), gardens, many restaurants and public concerts: a pleasant place on a hot summer's day but overcrowded on Sundays and holidays. (The food at the outdoor restaurants is now said to be reliable, particularly

38 ARGENTINA

barbecues; reached by 33 bus from Retiro Station or Av. L.N. Alem.) Bathing in the River Plate is no longer allowed; the water is highly contaminated.

One of the few places which still have late colonial and Rosista buildings is the *barrio* of San Telmo, S of Plaza de Mayo, centred on Calle Independencia along the slope which marks the old beach of the River Plate. It is a recognized artistic centre and a charming area, with plenty of cafés, and a pleasant atmosphere; and there is a regular Sunday antiques market at the Plaza Dorrego (see page 45). The 29 bus connects the Boca with San Telmo, and passes the end of Calle Florida, the shopping street.

The theatre retains its hold on the people of Buenos Aires. About 20 commercial theatres play the year round. Recommended is the Teatro Liceo. There are many amateur theatres. You are advised to book as early as possible for a seat at a concert, ballet, or opera; the opera season at the Colón (April— early December) is certainly the finest in Latin America.

Principal Public Buildings

Casa de Gobierno on the E side of the Plaza Mayo, and called the Casa Rosada because it is pink, contains the offices of the President of the Republic. (The Foreign Minister's offices are at the Palacio de San Martín, Plaza San Martín). The Casa Rosada is notable for its statuary, the rich furnishing of its halls and for its libraries, but it is not at present possible to visit the interior. The Museo de los Presidentes is on the lower floors (see under **Museums**).

The **Cabildo** on the W side of the same Plaza, the old town hall, was put up in 1711 but has been rebuilt several times. Its original structure, fittings and furniture were replaced in 1940 and it was declared a national monument; it is guarded by soldiers in the red and blue uniform of San Martín's grenadiers. See under **Museums**.

Old Congress Hall on the S of the Square, built 1863, is a National Monument. It has been encircled and built over by a palatial bank building. Open Thursday.

Congress Hall (Palacio del Congreso) to the SW at the far end of Avenida de Mayo, of great size and in Greco-Roman architecture, is the seat of the legislature. It contains the Senate and the Chambor of Deputies. There is limited accommodation for the public at the sittings. It is open from 1700 onwards. Queue in front of desk assigned for minor parties, there they take your passport and give you a ticket for your seat and a pink slip to reclaim your passport. You may stay as long as you wish, but must remain seated.

Teatro Colón, one of the world's great opera houses, overlooks Avenida 9 de Julio, with its main entrance on Libertad, between Tucumán and Viamonte. The Colón's interior is resplendent with red plush and gilt; its vast stage is almost a block long. Salons, dressing rooms and banquet halls are equally sumptuous. Open daily to visitors, free guided tours every half hour, book in advance (closed Jan.-Feb., so check, Tel.: 35-5414/15/16). Male visitors must wear jacket and tie to gala performances, but dress smartly anyway. Tickets, sold three days before performance, from US$4 to US$8 on the Calle Tucumán side of the theatre.

The **Bolsa de Comercio**, built in 1916, a handsome building in Calle 25 de Mayo, corner Sarmiento, contains a stock exchange, a grain market and a general produce market.

Churches

All historic churches are open 1630-1900; some at 0900-1100 also. **Note** Very severe damage to some of the churches listed below was caused on the night of June 16, 1955, during *peronista* anti-Catholic riots. Restoration is now virtually complete.

The **Cathedral**, Rivadavia 437, on the N of Plaza de Mayo is flanked by the former residence of the Archbishop. On this site was built the first church in Buenos Aires, which after reconstruction in 1677 collapsed in 1753 and the rebuilding was not completed until 1823. The eighteenth century towers were never rebuilt, so that the architectural proportions have suffered. A frieze upon the Greek façade represents Joseph and his brethren. The tomb (1878) of the Liberator, General José de San Martín, is imposing.

The **Church of San Ignacio de Loyola,** at Calles Alsina and Bolívar 225, founded in 1710, is the oldest Colonial building in Buenos Aires. It has two lofty towers. The **San Francisco,** Calles Alsina and Defensa, controlled by the Franciscan Order, was inaugurated in 1754 and given a new façade in 1808.

La Merced, Calles Juan D. Perón (Cangallo) and Reconquista 207, was founded 1604 and rebuilt 1732. One of the altars has a wooden figure of Our Lord, carved during the 18th century by an

ARGENTINA 39

Indian in Misiones. It has one of the best organs in the country, and one of the few fine carillons of bells in Buenos Aires.

Santo Domingo, on Defensa and Av. Belgrano, was founded in 1756. During the British attack on Buenos Aires in 1806 some of Whitelocke's soldiers took refuge in the church. The local forces bombarded it (some of the hits can still be seen on one of the towers); the British capitulated and their regimental colours were preserved in the church. Adjoining is the Salón Belgraniano (with relics of General Belgrano and much colonial furniture). There are summer evening concerts in the church; check times.

El Pilar, Calle Junín 1904, is a jewel of Colonial architecture dating from 1717, in a delightful setting of public gardens. An exceptionally fine wooden image of San Pedro de Alcántara, attributed to the famous 17th century Spanish sculptor Alonso Cano, is preserved in a side chapel on the left. It has a huge, unusual graveyard.

Visitors may like to know about the following religious establishments: The **Holy Cross,** Calle Estados Unidos 3150, established by the Passionists. **St. John's Cathedral** (Anglican), 25 de Mayo 282 (service Sun. at 1000), was built half at the expense of the British Government and dedicated in 1831. **St. Paul's, St. Peter's, St. Michael and All Angels** and **St. Saviour's** are Anglican places of worship in the suburbs. **St. Andrew's,** Calle Belgrano 579, is one of the 8 Scottish Presbyterian churches. The **American Church,** Corrientes 718, is Methodist, and was built in 1863. Service at 1100. **First Methodist** (American) Church, Av. Santa Fe 839, Acassuso.

The **Armenian Cathedral** of St. Gregory the Illuminator at the Armenian Centre, and the **Russian Orthodox Cathedral** of The Holy Trinity (Parque Lezama) are interesting.

German Evangelical Church, Esmeralda 162.

Synagogues Anshe Galitzia at Uriburu 234; Temple at Alvear 1222.

The **Cemetery of Recoleta,** entrance at Junín 1822 near Museo de Bellas Artes (see below), is one of the sights of Buenos Aires (open 0700-1800). Evita Perón is now buried there; her tomb is now marked besides the inscription, Familia Duarte—guards will point out the grave. "A Doric portico gives on to the main, paved, cypress-lined avenue of a little city of the dead. At the end of the avenue there is a great bronze statue of the resurrected Saviour; on either side, hard up against each other, like houses in a street, there are the family vaults of the Argentine patricians. Every possible style of architecture is represented." G. S. Fraser, in News from Latin America. On Sundays there is a good craft market near the entrance. Another well known cemetery is that of La Chacarita, which has the much-visited, lovingly-tended tombs of Juan Perón and Carlos Gardel, the tango singer.

Museums, Libraries, Art Exhibitions, etc.

Note: Most museums close on Monday, and in January and most of February for summer holidays. State museums and parks are free on Wednesdays. Check opening hours with Tourist Office.

Museo de los Presidentes (basement of Casa Rosada), Hipólito Irigoyen 218. Historical memorabilia, particularly of former Presidents, closed to visitors in 1984.
Museo de Bellas Artes (National Gallery), Avenida Libertador Gral. San Martín 1473. In addition to modern Argentine, American and European works, there are paintings representing the conquest of Mexico, executed 300 or 400 years ago, and wooden carvings from the Argentine hinterland. Open Tues.-Sun., 0900-1245, 1500-1845.
The National Museum of the Decorative Arts is at Av. Libertador Gral. San Martín 1902. The building is shared with the **Museo Nacional de Arte Oriental;** both are open Wed.-Mon., 1500-1900.
Biblioteca Nacional (The National Library). Calle México 566, founded in 1810, moved here in 1902. About 500,000 volumes and 10,000 manuscripts.
Museo Histórico Nacional, Defensa 1600. It has 6 salons and a gallery. Trophies and mementoes of historical events. Here are San Martín's uniforms, a replica of his famous curved sabre, and the original furniture and door of the house in which he died at Boulogne. Open Thursday to Sunday, 1400-1800.
Museo de la Ciudad, Alsina 412, open Mon.-Fri., 1100-1900, Sat., 1600-2000. Permanent exhibition of architectural and urban development exhibits.
Museo y Biblioteca Mitre, San Martín 336, preserves intact the household of President Bartolomé Mitre. Open 1500-1700.
Museo de Ciencias Naturales at Avenida Angel Gallardo 490, facing Parque Centenario. It houses palaeontological, zoological, mineralogical, botanical, archaeological and marine sections. Open Tues., Thurs., Sun. 1400-1800. Library, Mon.-Fri., 1100-1700.
Museo Municipal de Arte Moderno (Tues.-Sun. 1600-2200) at Avenida Corrientes 1530, and **Museo Municipal de Artes Plásticas Eduardo Sivori** (Tues.-Sun. 1600-2000) at Junín 1930, where there are also a cinema, a theatre (Teatro Municipal San Martín, many free performances),

40 ARGENTINA

and the **Museo de Artes Visuales,** Tues.-Fri. 1600-2000. Free entry on Wed. 19th century and contemporary Argentine painting.

Museo de Motivos Populares Argentinos José Hernández, Av. Libertador 2373, Gaucho collection, open Tues.-Sun., 1400-1800.

Museo del Instituto Nacional Sanmartino, Sánchez de Bustamente and Av. A. M. de Aguado; Mon.-Fri. 0900-1200 and 1400-1700; Sat., Sun. 1400-1700.

Museo de Arte Español Enrique Larreta, Juramento 2291, in Belgrano. 1500-1945. Closed Thurs. The home of the writer Larreta. Also **Biblioteca Alfonso El Sabio,** Mon.-Fri., 1300-1930.

Museo de Cabildo y Revolución de Mayo, Bolívar 65, is the old Cabildo building, converted into a museum in 1940. It contains paintings, documents, furniture, etc., recording the May 1810 revolution, and memorabilia of the 1806 British attack. Entry US$0.33. Open Wed.-Sun., 1500-1900. Library, Mon.-Fri., 1100-1900.

Museo de Arte Hispanoamericano Isaac Fernández Blanco, Suipacha 1422. Contains a most interesting and valuable collection of colonial art, especially silver, in a beautiful colonial mansion. Open Tues.-Sun., 1400-1900, admission US$0.35. Thursdays free. Latin American art and history library at Suipacha 1444 nearby, 0900-1900, Mon.-Fri.

Museo y Biblioteca Ricardo Rojas, Charcas 2837, open Wednesdays and Fridays 1500-1800, US$0.10. The famous writer Rojas lived in this beautiful colonial house for several decades. It contains his library, souvenirs of his travels, and many intriguing literary and historical curios.

Numismatic Museum; fascinating, well kept, little known, at the Banco Central in San Martín, overlooks central foyer, ask guard for directions.

"Presidente Sarmiento", Dársena Norte, a sailing ship long used as a naval training ship; now a museum. Open on weekend afternoons. Small charge. Another sailing ship, the **"Uruguay",** tied up by the Boca bridge, is also due to become a museum.

Bank of London and South America, Bartolomé Mitre and Reconquista, has a miniature museum on its fifth floor. Open during banking hours; the building, designed by SEPRA (Santiago Sánchez Elia, Federico Peralta Ramos, and Alfredo Agostini) and completed in 1963 is worth seeing for itself. Next door is the **Banco de Córdoba,** designed by the brilliant Córdoba architect Miguel Angel Roca, completed in the early 1970s.

Museo Nacional de Aeronaútica, Av. Costanera Rafael Obligado, next to Jorge Newbery airport, Thurs., Sat. and Sun., 1600-1900. Many civil and military aircraft.

Museo Nacional Ferroviario, Av. Libertador 405, in Retiro station. Mon.-Fri., 0900-1800, free. Archives 1100-1800. For railway fans; no photographing.

Museo Botánico, Las Heras 4102 and Malabia 2690. Open 0800-1200 and 1400-1800, Mon.-Fri. Herbarium pleasant. Some 1,000 cats in residence.

Museo de la Dirección Nacional del Antártico, Angel Gallardo 470, Tues., Thurs. and Sun., 1400-1800. Dioramas.

Museo del Teatro Colón, Tucumán 1161. Mon.-Fri. 1200-1800. Documents and objects related to the theatre.

Museo Histórico Saavedra, Crisólogo Larralde (Republiquetas) 6309. Wed.-Fri., 1400-1800; Sat., 1800-2200; Sun., 1500-1800. City history from the eighteenth century. Free on Wed.

Yuchán Centro de Artesanía Aborigen, Defensa 788, has many interesting native artefacts on view, for sale.

Federal Police Museum San Martín 353, 7th floor, worth visiting, small entrance fee.

Museo International de Caricatura y Humorismo, Lima 1037, open Fri., 1700-2100 only, originals of cartoons and caricatures of 20th century, but small international section, admission US$0.05.

Museo de Armas, Maipú y Santa Fé. Open 1500-1900 daily, US$0.15. All kinds of weaponry.

Parks and Squares

Parque Lezama, Calles Defensa and Brasil, originally one of the most beautiful in the city, has been somewhat vandalized. Very lively on Sunday. It has an imposing statue of Pedro de Mendoza, the founder of the original city in 1535. The tradition is that the first founding took place on this spot. The Museo Histórico Nacional (see page 39) is in the park.

The **Palermo Parks** with their magnificent avenues are the city's Bois de Boulogne. They are famous for their rose garden, Andalusian Patio, Japanese garden with a lot of fish to feed (admission US$0.10) and the Hipódromo Argentino, the internationally-known Palermo race course, with seats for 45,000. Opposite the parks are the Botanical and Zoological Gardens (the Palermo Zoo and Japanese Garden are closed on Mondays). Nearby are the Municipal Golf Club, Buenos Aires Lawn Tennis Club, riding clubs and polo field, and the popular Club de Gimnasia y Esgrima (Athletic and Fencing Club). The **Planetarium** (just off Belisario Roldán, in the Park), is open Sat. and Sun. only (March-Nov., 1630, 1800, 1930, Dec.-Feb., 1800, 1930, 2100), entry US$0.22. The official name of the Palermo parks is the Parque Tres de Febrero. Reached by Subte line D. The **Show Grounds** of the Argentine Rural Society, on a site next to Palermo Park, stage the Annual Livestock Exhibition in July, the main agricultural show of the year.

ARGENTINA 41

There is another large and modern race course (one of the best of its kind) with grass track at San Isidro, 25 minutes from the city centre by train or road. The meetings alternate with those at Palermo. There are Saturday and Sunday races throughout the year, and upon all holidays other than May 25 and July 9. Betting is by totalizator only.

The **Municipal Botanical Gardens,** Santa Fe 2951, entrance from Plaza Italia (take Subte, line D), contain characteristic specimens of the world's vegetation. The trees proper to the several provinces of Argentina are brought together in one section. The Gardens are full of stray cats, fed regularly by benevolent local residents. The **Zoo** is next to the Botanical Gardens; it is attractive because several of the animals, such as the Patagonian *mara* (a local short-eared hare), are permitted to roam where they will. Latest reports indicate that it is getting run-down.

Plazas The most interesting are the Plaza de Mayo, containing so many public buildings; the Plaza San Martín, with a monument to San Martín in the centre; the former Plaza Británica, now known as the Plaza de la Fuerza Aérea, with the clock tower presented by British and Anglo-Argentine residents, "a florid Victorian sentinel, royal crest upon its bosom" (frequently vandalized); the Plaza Lavalle, which has secondhand bookstalls at the Calle Lavalle end; the Plaza del Congreso, the largest in the city, with a waterfall, floodlit at 2145. There is also the great Plaza de la República, with a 67-metre obelisk at the junction between the Diagonal Norte and the Avenida Corrientes.

Hotels The Dirección de Turismo fixes maximum and minimum rates for 1, 2 and 3-star hotels, guest houses and inns, but there have been complaints that at 3 stars and below the ratings do not provide very useful guidance. Four and five-star hotels are free to apply any rate they wish. The rates can be taken only as an indication. All hotels, guest houses, inns and camping sites are graded by the number of beds available, and the services supplied.

Most if not all of the hotels listed below include a continental breakfast in the price.

Name	Address	Single	Double	Star Grading
Panamericano	Carlos Pellegrini 525	85	96	5
Elevage	Maipú 960	75	85	5
Bauen	Callao 346	82	90	5
Libertador	Av. Córdoba y Maipú	77	95	5
Sheraton	San Martín 1225	129	160	5
Plaza	Florida 1005	77	88	5
Claridge	Tucumán 535	79	90	5
Regente Palace	Suipacha 964	60	70	4
Gran Colón	Pellegrini 507	84	96	4
Bizonte	Paraguay 1207	39	45	4
El Conquistador	Suipacha 948	57	66	4
De Las Américas	Libertad 1020	29	36	4
Principado	Paraguay 481	60	70	4
Gran Buenos Aires	M.T. de Alvear 767	45	50	4
Gran King	Lavalle 560	28	35	4
Continental	Av. Roque Sáenz Peña 725	34	58	4
Lancaster	Av. Córdoba 405	37	44	4
City	Bolívar 160	30	45	4
Crillón	Av. Santa Fe 796	39	48	4
Carsson	Viamonte 650	19	24	4
Salles	Cerrito 208	25	29	4
Rochester	Esmeralda 542	20	24	4
Sheltown	M.T. de Alvear 742	30	35	4
República	Cerrito 370	21	24	4
Los Dos Chinos	Brasil 780	17	27	4
Savoy	Av. Callao 181	24	34	3
Carlton	Libertad 1180	39	44	3
Gran Dora	Maipú 963	35	44	3
Colombia Palace	Av. Corrientes 1533	11	15	3
Wilton Palace	Av. Callao 1162	26	30	3
Italia Romanelli	Reconquista 647	13	17	3
Esmeralda Palace	Esmeralda 527	12	15	3
Embajador	Carlos Pellegrini 1181	25	32	3
Gran Argentino	Carlos Pellegrini 37	25	39	3

Other hotels: C price range, *Presidente*, Cerrito 850; *Promenade*, M.T. Alvear 444; *Regidor*, Tucumán 451; *Orly*, Paraguay 474, good position, helpful; *Bristol*, Cerrito 286; *King's*, Corrientes 623; *Napoleón*, Rivadavia 1364; *Phoenix*, San Martín 780, private bath, clean, traditional, warmly recommended but no a/c; *San Carlos*, Suipacha 39.

42 ARGENTINA

D range: *San Antonio*, Paraguay 372, with bath, nice atmosphere, clean; *Waldorf*, Paraguay 450, reasonable, clean, safe, pleasant; *Tucumán Palace*, Tucumán 384, moderate, front rooms noisy; *Plaza Roma*, Lavalle 110; *Acapulco*, Lavalle 472, hot-shower (cheaper without bathroom), convenient; *Regis*, Lavalle 813, nice atmosphere; *Liberty*, Corrientes 626; *Novus*, Sarmiento 631 (near Plaza de Mayo), recommended; *Sarmiento Palace*, Sarmiento 1953; *Diplomat*, San Martín 918, conveniently placed, private shower, good service; *Eibar*, Florida 328; *Cabilda*, Florida y Maipú, reasonable; *Florida House*, Florida 527, comfortable, hot shower, a little noisy, but quiet interior rooms available, recommended; *Camino Real*, Maipú 572, pleasant, clean, central, *Constitución Palace*, Lima 1697; *Nogaró*, J. A. Roca 562; *Don Juan*, Calle Dr Finochitto 842, recommended.

E range: *Tres Sargentos*, Tres Sargentos 345, clean, pleasant and helpful; *Frossard*, Tucumán 686, inexpensive, hot showers, but not quiet; *Apolo*, Tucumán 951, with or without shower, friendly, central; *O'Rei*, Lavalle 733, good, watch locks on doors; *N'Ontue*, Corrientes 3321; *Odéon*, Esmeralda 368 with Corrientes, clean, friendly; *11 de Setiembre*, J. D. Perón (Cangallo) y Castelli, English and French spoken, near Plaza Miserere; *Wilson*, Av. Sáenz Peña, between Pavón and Garay, 4 blocks West of Plaza Constitución, shared rooms; *De la Paix*, Rivadavia 1155; *Parada*, Rivadavia 1291, hot showers, central, very friendly; *Avenida Petit*, Av. de Mayo 1347; *Marbella*, Av. de Mayo 1261; *Gran Vedra*, Av. de Mayo 1350, good value, recommended; *De Mayo*, Av. de Mayo 776, central and friendly; *Novel*, Av. de Mayo 915, good; *Reyna*, Av. de Mayo 1120; *Chile*, Av. de Mayo 1297; *Concorde*, 25 de Mayo 630, more expensive with TV and fridge, helpful; *Central Córdoba*, San Martín 1021; *Petit Hotel Goya*, Suipacha 748, very central, dark rooms, with shower and toilet; *Victoria*, Chacabuco 726, clean and cheap, use of kitchens; *Brisas*, Tacuari 1621, bath, etc., clean; *Varela*, Estados Unidos 324 (San Telmo), pleasant; *Roxy*, Santiago del Estero 1677 (cheaper per week's stay), hot water, close to cheap restaurants.

F range: *Gran Sarmiento*, Sarmiento 1892; *Gran Vía*, Sarmiento 1450, Tel.: 40-5763, with bath, clean, friendly; *Aguila*, J. D. Perón (Cangallo) 1554, clean; *Mediterráneo*, Rodríguez Peña 152, basic, central, helpful, safe, clean; *Splendid*, Rivadavia 950; *Vila Seca*, Av. de Mayo 776, friendly; *Ocean*, Maipú 907, clean, comfortable, reasonable, with bath, cheaper in triple rooms; *Gran España*, Tacuari 80, Tel.: 30-5541, private bath, hot water, central heating; *La Giralda*, Tacuari 17, clean, cheap, unfriendly; *Central*, Alsina 1693, friendly and clean; *Patagones*, B. de Yrigoyen 1692, friendly, safe to leave luggage; *Cibelles*, Virrey Cevallos, 2 blocks from Congreso, with bath, safe (next to police HQ); *Bahía*, Santiago del Estero 3062; *Hispano Argentino*, Catamarca 167, some rooms with bath, clean, quiet, convenient. Women should be aware that they could attract unwelcome attention as prostitutes operate from Constitución station. Otherwise, this area is a short walk to centre and convenient for boats to Uruguay and trains to the N.

One can rent flats on a daily basis in *Edificios Esmeralda*, Marcelo T. de Alvear 842, Tel.: 31-3929, US$24-31 for one, US$25-33 for two a day, cleaning included. Facilities for up to 6 persons. Weekly renting at *Edificio Charcas*, M.T. de Alvear 776, US$128 d for one room per week, recommended (visiting singers at the Colón often stay there).

NB Additional charges at hotels: A service charge of about 24 % on which (including basic rate) VAT is charged (*IVA*) at 18 % but is included in the final price by most hotels and certainly the expensive ones. All the rates quoted are subject to alteration and it should be noted that for the most part they are the basic or minimum rates. Check when booking into a hotel whether breakfast is included or not. International telephone calls from hotels may incur a 40 %-50 % commission in addition to government tax of about the same amount. Tokens can be obtained and the call made from a public telephone box. International calls can be made from the central office on the corner of Maipú and Corrientes, about US$1 a minute.

Hotels with red-green lights or marked *Albergue Transitorio* are hotels for homeless lovers.

Laundry Laundry service in Buenos Aires hotels is very expensive. *Tintorería Constitución*, Av. Santiago del Estero 1572. Many dry cleaners, efficient and friendly. Several launderettes, e.g. Marcelo T. de Alvear 2018, in centre; Junín 15 with Rivadavia, Mon.-Sat. 0800-2100; Junín 529 with Lavalle, Paraguay 888; Super Lav, Juan D. Perón (Cangallo) 2009 with Ayacucho, owner speaks English.

Tips In spite of the high service charge it is customary to tip 10% of the total bill; porters at hotels expect a tip—about US$0.50 per day of stay or service rendered. Hairdressers expect 10% of the bill, cinema ushers about US$0.20.

Electric Current 220 volts, 50 cycles, A.C., European Continental-type plugs in old buildings, Australian 3-pin flat-type in the new. Adaptors can be purchased locally for either type (i.e. from new 3-pin to old 2-pin and vice-versa).

Camping Closest camp site to the city is about 12 km. out to the SW; information on all sites is available from the Automóvil Club Argentino. Those travelling by car might try at the German Sports Club, Sociedad Alemana de Gimnasia, 9 de Julio and Av. Márquez, Villa Ballester, 30 km. N of centre, cheap, or free. Easy to reach by Línea Suárez bus 90, get off at Chilavert.

Sleeping bags and tents direct from the factory at Acoyte 1622, Tel.: 855-0619, English, German spoken, reasonable prices, open 0800-1200, 1430-1900, Saturday 0900-1300.

ARGENTINA 43

Restaurants *The Buenos Aires Herald* publishes a handy *Guide to Good Eating in Buenos Aires* (with a guide to local wines) by Derek Foster. Eating out in Buenos Aires is very good, and cheap by international standards. David Mackintosh tells us that five of the best restaurants (US$15-25 per head) are: *Catalinas*, Reconquista 875; *Francis Malman*, Honduras 4963; *Blabs*, Florida 325; *Au Bec Fin*, Vicente López 1825; and *Montmartre*, Av. Libertador 3302, La Lucila. The *Sheraton* and *Claridge* hotel restaurants are also recommended. Other restaurants include *La Emiliana*, Av. Corrientes 1443, good; *London Grill*, Reconquista 435 (said to be declining), about US$12 p.p. *Lo Prete*, Luis S. Peña 749; *Hotel Español*, Av. de Mayo 1202 and *El Imparcial*, H. Irigoyen 1201, first-class service (Spanish); *Escorpión*, Av. Montes de Oca y Uspallata, good food and service; *El Mundo*, Maipú 550, is less good than it was, reasonably priced, as is the nearby *Maxim's* on Paraguay, between Florida and Esmeralda. Another good cheap restaurant is *Pippo's*, Paraná 356, near corner with Montevideo, and *Corrientes* near Montevideo (specializes in pasta and meat). For roast chicken try *Pepito*, on Uruguay, between Corrientes and Sarmiento. Many excellent middle-class restaurants on Maipú: *Maipú*, Maipú 480, excellent food, popular; *El Palacio de la Pizza*, Corrientes 751; popular and cheap is *Oriente*, Av. de Mayo and Av. 9 de Julio; *Las Vasijas*, Av. Tres Sargentos 496, corner with San Martín, food, service and atmosphere highly recommended, first class; *El Cuartito*, Talcahuano and Paraguay, good pizza; *El Ceibal*, food from the NE, at Pueyrredón and Las Heras, distinguished, expensive; *Irish Pub-Downton Matias*, San Martín 979, lunch only.

Alexandra (English, now expensive), Calle San Martín 780. Typical Argentine restaurants: *La Cabaña*, Entre Ríos 436, old tavern style not as good as it used to be, US$20-25; *Yapeyú*, Calle Maipú 389, recommended as good value and friendly; *El Fogón de Martín Fierro*, Palermo, highly recommended, huge barbecue; *Don Pipón*, Esmeralda 521, huge cheap grills; *Pizzería Iguazú*, Esmeralda 428, good pizza but not cheap; *Roma*, Lavalle, good pizzas, pleasant; *El Recodo*, Lavalle 130, recommended; *La Estancia*, Lavalle 941, barbecued meat and local dishes in typical surroundings, poor service: parrillada for 5, US$5, fillet steak US$2, very popular; *Otto's*, also on Lavalle (893), recommended. There are good restaurants all along Calles Lavalle 893 and Maipú e.g. *La Fonda* (Lavalle 542). Others serve à la carte dishes which are plentiful (US$ 5 each, upwards), and are open from 1500-2000 when most other restaurants are closed. In this category is *El Palacio de la Papa Frita*, which is more expensive than most. *Ligure*, Juncal 855, recommended; *Veracruz*, Uruguay 538, also recommended. There are also several economical restaurants along Florida, e.g. *Santa Generosa* (recommended), next to *Hotel Jockey Club*, *Cheburger* (hamburger about US$1, with french fries and soft drink US$2) and *Tía Vicenta* on Calle Carabelas. *Hunter's Place*, Lavalle 445, good. *La Blanca*, Tucumán and Florida, good and cheap; also *La Chacra* on Av. Córdoba, huge portions; *Corrientes 11*, Av. Corrientes 135; *Mesón Español*, Av. Caseros 1750, good food and very good show of folk music. The typical parrilla (mixed grill) is a speciality of *Tranquera*, in Palermo Park. *Chiquín*, Juan D. Perón (Cangallo) 920, is a well-known traditional restaurant. *Rocinante*, Carlos Pellegrini 715, diagonally opposite Teatro Colón, recommended as delicious and not expensive. Other restaurants near the Colón are *Hamburgo*, Carlos Pellegrini 581; *El Quijote*, at No. 663; *Don Luis*, Viamonte 1169; and *Zum Edelweiss*, Libertad 431. *Pichín No 1* or *No 2*, Paraná and Sarmiento, for gigantic asado de tira; *La Auténtica Banderita*, Moreno 1100, excellent meat dishes; *La Rural*, Suipacha 453, recommended, parrillada for US$13, bife de lomo US$4, potatoes US$1.50; *Los Troncos*, Suipacha 732, good grills; *El Pulpo*, Tucumán and Reconquista, Spanish sea-food, big portions, moderate prices, recommended. *El Pescadito*, P. de Mendoza 1483, recommended for pasta and sea-food. *Los Inmortales*, pizza-chain restaurants, very good. *Hispano*, Rivadavia 1200, reasonable, good sea-food. *El Repecho de San Telmo*, Carlos Calvo 242, excellent, reserve in advance. *La Veda*, Florida 1, is good and expensive. Well-known and sophisticated are *Hippopotamus*, Junín 1787, nouvelle cuisine, and *Clark's*, Sarmiento 646, and near the Recoleta cemetery. *Nazarenas*, L. N. Alem (North), good for beef. The Costanera along the river front is lined with little eating places: *El Rancho Inn* is best, try also *Los Años Locos*. Good snacks all day and night at Retiro and Constitución railway termini, also at *La Escalerita*, Lavalle 717. *La Cautiva*, Sucre 1546, typical local game dishes. *Sibaris*, Tucumán 933, good meal with wine, US$8; *ABC*, Lavalle 545, German cooking, good; *City Grill*, San Martín and Av. Córdoba, good steaks with salad and wine; *Smörgasbord*, Paraguay and Florida, Swedish food, also Swedish Club on Tacuarí, open to non-members. Hungarian, *Budapest*, 25 de Mayo 690, cheap. *Florida Grill*, at Florida 122, standing-only steak restaurant, excellent value; *Chez Moi*, Av. San Juan 1223 (Tel.: 270890), French, and Iranian food on Fri. and Sat. lunch, reservations necessary; *San Francisco*, Defensa 177, excellent, cheap lunches, dingy surroundings. *La Mosca Blanca*, right hand side of Retiro station, very good and busy; *El Tronio*, Reconquista 918, is very cheap and good. *El Jocoso*, reasonable, at Corrientes and Callao. *La Pipeta*, a little cheaper, very good, at San Martín and Lavalle. *Un Lugar*, on 1200 block of Av. Corrientes, is good for steaks and house wine. *China*, Paraná 342, recommended; *Kappo Benkei*, J.D.Perón 1228, Japanese, very good, on 3rd floor, no sign.

A vegetarian restaurant, *Grannix*, Florida 126 and 461, plenty of cheap food, open lunchtime Mon.-Fri. Another, *Ratatouille*, is at Sarmiento 1802 excellent value (nr. Calles). Natural food shop and restuarant, *Córdoba* 1599 with Montevideo, recommended. Other vegetarian restaurants: *Tamborá*, Pasaje del Carmen 768 (off Córdoba 1600 block); *La Onda Verde*, Corrientes 1580 (closed Sun.); *Hindú*, Mendoza 2175 (closed Sun., Mon.); *Sai Kai*, Suipacha 920 (lunch only, closed weekend); *Sr. Sol*, Billingshurst 1070 (p.m. except Sat., Sun., lunch also, closed Mon.); *Verde*,

ARGENTINA

Galería del Paseo, first floor, Santa Fe 1653 (closed Sun.); *Yin Yang*, Paraná 868 (lunch only, closed Sun.); *Manantial*, Montevideo 560 (closed Sun.). *La Esquina de las Flores*, Montevideo and Córdoba, excellent value. Other vegetarian restaurants: *Años Verdes*, Corrientes 1219, 1st floor; *Bon Manger*, Lavalle 835 (in arcade), 1st floor, recommended; *Verde Esmeralda*, Esmeralda (nr. Av. Corrientes); *El Jardín*, Suipacha 429; *La Huerta*, Paraguay 445, Tel.: 311-0470, macrobiotic, recommended; *Nueva Era*, Maipú 650, 2nd floor, good value.

Chung Kin, Calle Paraguay, near Maipú, Chinese, set lunch, US$2; *Pumper-nic* is a chain of fast food restaurants which are good but expensive compared to ordinary restaurants. *El Pasatiempo*, cheap and good, on Belgrano, near station, recommended. *Manolito's*, Piedras 566, *Barcito*, Piedras 554, and *Parrilla*, Piedras 442, provide cheap meals. *Lois*, across from *Hotel Orly* on Paraguay, is busy and good, as is *Juvenas* near the same hotel for stand-up lunches. *Kentucky Fried Chicken*, Roberto M. Ortiz 1815, Paseo de la Recoleta. For quick cheap snacks the markets are recommended, e.g. El Retiro market on the 900 block of Av. Libertador San Martín. Stalls of the Cooperadora de Acción Social offer cheap snacks, and can be found in several public areas, e.g. near the Recoleta. The snack bars in underground stations are also cheap; also *Hogar Obrero*, Rivadavia y Esmeraldas, US$0.65 for full meal (but not too good).

Typical Boca restaurant: *Spadavecchia*, Necochea 1180, set menu with wine US$8, seats some 500 people, loud band, dancing. There are several others in the same street. They all serve antipasto, pasta and chicken; no point in looking for beef here. All bands are loud; not attractive for those with sensitive ears. *Torna Sorrento*, Lamadrid 701/09 is Italian run, and has Chilean folk music. Nearby, is *Restaurant Napolitano*, which serves excellent set lunches of seafood (US$10 for 2), good atmosphere and young wine. *Cantina Nicoletta* is entertaining. *Cueva Zingarella*, lively at weekends (afternoon and evening), recommended, but costly. Try a family restaurant at corner of Necochea and Suárez known as *Cantina Los Tres Amigos*; live music from 2130, complete meal with wine under US$6 each, excellent, about 4 blocks from commercial centre.

Tea Rooms and Bars *Richmond*, Florida 468 between Lavalle and Corrientes (chess played between 1200-2400); *La Estrella* and *El Reloj*, Lavalle and Maipú; *Queen Bess*, Santa Fe 868; well-known are the *Confitería Suiza*, Tucumán 753, and the *Florida Garden* at Florida and Paraguay. *En El Patio*, Paraguay 886, very pleasant. *Exedra* at Carlos Pellegrini and Av. Córdoba and many on the Av. Libertador in the Palermo area, such as *Round Point*, *Café Tabac*, are fashionable. The more bohemian side of the city's intellectual life is centred on Avenida Corrientes, between Cerrito and Callao, where there are many bars and coffee shops, such as *La Paz* (opens very late) and *Politeama*. *Ideal*, Suipacha 834, nr. Corrientes, turn of the century atmosphere. *El Molino*, Rivadavia and Callas, popular with politicians, nr. Congress, Belle Epoque décor. Excellent ice-cream at *Freddo*, Callao 1400. On Lavalle there are *whiskerías* and *cervecerías* where one can have either coffee or exotic drinks (local whisky US$2, imported US$3.50, cocktail US$3.20, sandwich US$2.), *Bar-baro*, cosmopolitan, Tres Sargentos and San Martín. *Bar Rua* Nova, corner of Chacabuco and Av. de Mayo, cheap snacks. *Arrayanes*, Córdoba and San Martín, open Sunday. *Young Men's Bar*, Córdoba and Esmeralda. *Barila*, Santa Fe 2375, has excellent confectionery. *Café Tortoni*, Av. de Mayo 829-35, a haunt of artists, very elegant, over 100 years old, interesting *peña* evenings of poetry and music; *Handicap Bar*, on Paraguay, near *Hotel Orly*, has good, cheap breakfasts; *Cantón*, Córdoba 945, is overpriced and not recommended. *Bar Verona* in the Boca.

Night Clubs *Michelangelo*, impressive setting, restaurant and nightclub in an old converted monastery, US$20 each, including cover charges and first drink, good show, Balcarce 433; *Karina*, US$10 with cover charge and drink, good tango show at 0100, Corrientes 636; more locally coloured are *Mi Rincón*, Cerrito 1050; *La Querencia*, Av. de Mayo 870; *Achalay Huasi*, Esmeralda 1040; and many others (cover charge and first drink for US$10); tango music. *Caño 14*, Talcahuano 975, *El Viejo Almacén*, Independencia and Balcarce, tango shows at 2230 and 0115, (entrance US$15—no dancing for guests). *La Casa del Cantor*, P.Gollena 603. *El Rancho Ochoa*, Catamarca 999, has a good show and a reasonable meal. The best affordable tango bars are in the Boca, but it is apparently becoming increasingly difficult to find authentic tango for locals; most are tourist-oriented.

Bars and restaurants in San Telmo district, with live music (usually beginning 2330-2400, Fri., Sat., Sun., cover charge US$2): *Jazz y Pop*, Venezuela y Chacabuco; *Jazz Café*, Chile 400; *Players*, Humberto I° 528 (piano bar); *La Peluquería*, Bolívar, nr. Carlos Calvo (Samba).

The Luna Park stadium holds pop/jazz concerts. Teatro Alvear has free concerts Tuesday afternoons, usually Orquesta de Tango de Bs. As. Teatro Municipal General San Martín, Av. Corrientes 1530, organizes many cultural activities of which quite a few are free of charge. Many events are held in the large entrance hall. Centro Cultural General San Martín, Sarmiento 1551, has many free activities. Theatre ticket agency, La Cartelera, Lavalle 828.

Cinemas Many, centred on Lavalle and nearby blocks. The selection of films is as good as anywhere else in the world. Films are now shown uncensored, except for explicit sex. Cost per ticket, US$1.65, best booked early afternoon to ensure good seats. Reductions on Mon., Tues. and Wed. of 30% unless they are holidays. Tickets obtainable, from ticket agencies (*carteleras*). Most foreign films are shown with subtitles, but dubbing increasingly used for major box-office successes. Free films at Asociación Bancaria, Sarmiento 337/341, Tel.: 313-9306/312-5011/17; old films at

Ciné en el Teatro Hebraíca, Sarmiento 2255, Tel.: 48-2170, US$1. On Sat. nights many central cinemas have *transnoches*, late shows starting at 0100.

Markets Sunday markets for souvenirs, antiques, etc.: Plaza Dorrego (San Telmo), touristy, Sunday 1000-1700, on Humberto 1° and Defensa (only "antiques"). Also Feria de Las Artes (Fri., 1400-1700) on Defensa and Alsina. Saturday craft, jewellery, etc. market, 1000-1800, at Av. Santa Fe, Plaza Italia (underground line D). At Parque Rivadavia, Rivadavia 4900, around the *ombú* tree, stamps and coins, Sun. 0900-1300, Plazoleta Primera Junta, Rivadavia and Centenera, books and magazines, Sat. 1200-2000, Sun. 1000-2000. Plazoleta Santa Fe, Santa Fe and Uriarte (Palermo) old books and magazines, same times as Primera Junta, and again, plastic arts in the Caminito (Boca) section. Auction sales: some bargains at weekday auctions, Edificio de Ventas, Banco de la Ciudad de Buenos Aires, Esmeralda 660. Souvenirs can be found in area around San Martín and Paraguay (not markets). Once market is "cheap and cheerful, with many bargains."

Shopping Visit the branches of H. Stern, for fine jewellery at the Sheraton and Plaza Hotels, and at the International Airport. Kelly's, Paraguay 431, has a very large selection of Argentine handicrafts in wool, leather, wood, etc. Artesanías Argentinas, at Montevideo 1360 and Córdoba 770, a non-profitmaking organization selling handicrafts (clothing, weaving, basketware, wooden goods etc.) all with certificate of origin. Apart from shops on Florida and Santa Fe Av. Corrientes has many shops for men's clothes between 600 and 1000 blocks, on Cabildo in Belgrano district can be reached by 152 bus from Retiro for good shopping between 1600 and 2800 blocks. Many boutiques and places for casual clothes in Martínez suburb. The Mercado de Abasto, originally built in 1893, at Avs. Corrientes, Anchorena, Lavalle and Agüero, has been reopened as a commercial, cultural and entertainment centre.

Bookshops Acme Agency, Suipacha 245; ABC, Av. Córdoba 685 (quite a good selection of second-hand paperbacks and new English books) and Av. Libertador 13777 in Martínez suburb. French bookshop at Calle Rivadavia 743; Librería Goethe, Corrientes 365, English books, and a good selection of secondhand and German books. Italian books at Librería Leonardo, Av. Córdoba 335, also (with newspapers and magazines) La Viscontea, Libertad 1067. Secondhand/exchange inside shopping arcade in front of Once Station—good stock and prices. Good bookshop at Florida 340, El Ateneo, and Atlántida. (It is otherwise difficult to sell second-hand paperbacks in Buenos Aires.)

Libraries Biblioteca Lincoln, Florida 935, open 0900-1745 weekdays exc. Wed. US$10 per month; Harrods (2nd floor), on Florida, US$6 a month; Cultura Inglesa, Suipacha 1333 (for members only).

Laundry Tintorería Japonesa, in centre at 25 de Mayo 689, good.

Camera Repairs and Film Developing Casa del Flash, Av. de Mayo 839, with branch at Florida 37 (sales only): one-day service for small repairs; Esteban Psotka, Billinghurst 1565, 2nd Floor, H, Tel.: 84-4171. Also Attil, Viamonte 879 for service and developing. For film developing, Quick Lab, Av. Maipú 2786, for quality 2-hour service. Laboclick, Esmeralda 444, same day service for prints, 24 hrs for slides. Most others will take up to 3 days. Le Lab, Viamonte 612, near corner with Florida. Difficult to find colour film for slides under US$16 a roll—also check the "sell by" date.

Taxis are painted yellow and black, and carry Taxi flags. About US$1 per km. A charge is made for each piece of hand baggage. Tips not necessary. Beware of overcharging late at night. Check the notes you offer the driver; they have been known to switch a low-value note for your high one and demand the balance. Fares double for journey outside city limit (Av. General Paz).

Car Hire Cars for hire, expensive, can be got through hotel reception clerks. Use of Avis Car Credit card with central billing in one's home country is possible. Traffic drives on the right. Driving in Buenos Aires is no problem, provided you have eyes in the back of your head and good nerves. Avis agency in the *Sheraton Hotel* (vehicles reported not well serviced); A1 International, M.T. de Alvear 680, Tel.: 32-9475/76, 31-0247, Renault 12 US$160 a week + US$24 insurance, unlimited mileage, both have branches in all main cities. Hertz and Budget in Buenos Aires only. If you want to cross the border to another country you need a special written authorization from the car hire company.

Local Bus services (*colectivos*) cover a very wide radius, and are clean, frequent, efficient and very fast. The basic fare is **about** US$0.20 maximum. Give street destination and number to driver, who will charge accordingly. **NB.** The number of the bus is not sufficient indication of destination, as each number has a variety of routes. Look for the little plaques displayed in the driver's window. A guide to all routes is available at newsstands.

Tram A green and white old-fashioned street car operates on Sat. and Sun., free, from Emilio and Bonifacio. Operated by Asociación de los Amigos del Tranvía.

Underground Railways Five lines link the outer parts of the City to the centre. "A" line runs under Calle Rivadavia, from Plaza de Mayo up to Primera Junta. "B" line from central Post Office,

46 ARGENTINA

Avenida L. N. Alem, under Av. Corrientes to Federico Lacroze railway station. "C" line links Plaza Constitución with the Retiro railway station, and provides connections with all the other lines. "D" line runs from Plaza de Mayo, under the Diagonal Norte, Córdoba and Santa Fe to Palermo. "E" line runs from Plaza de Mayo through San Juan to Avs. Directorio and José María Moreno. The fare is about US$0.10, the same for any direct trip or combination between lines; tokens must be bought at booking offices (*boleterías*); buy a few in advance to save time. Stations closed between 0100 and 0500. The local name for the system is the *Subte*. Some stations on lines C and D have some very fine tile-work. Backpacks and luggage allowed. The tourist office gives out a map, which can also be bought on station platforms with a booklet giving bus schedules.

Sports Clubs Cricket is played by the British community and baseball by the American. Hurling is played by the Irish-Argentines. Polo of a very high standard is also played from Oct to Dec.; a visit to the national finals at Palermo in Nov. is recommended. The Tigre Boat Club, founded in 1888, is open to British or American visitors for a small fee and a limited period. The leading golf clubs are the Hurlingham, Ranelagh, Ituzaingó, Lomas, San Andrés, San Isidro, Sáenz Peña, Olivos, Jockey, Campos Argentinos and Hindú Country Club; visitors wishing to play should bring handicap certificate and make tele-phone booking. Weekend play possible only with a member. Good hotels may be able to make special arrangements. Tennis and squash are popular.

Gambling Weekly lotteries. Football pools, known as *Prode*.

Chess Club Argentino de Ajedrez, Paraguay 1858, open daily, arrive after 2000; special tournament every Sat., 1800. High standards.

Banks Bank of London & South America Ltd., corner of Reconquista and Bartolomé Mitre. It has 12 other branches in the city, and 10 othes in Greater Buenos Aires. Commission on travellers' cheques 5%. Probably best rate at Banco de la Nación, central branch just off Plaza de Mayo, although we're told it only exchanges Citicorp cheques.

Royal Bank of Canada, corner of Florida and J. D. Perón (Cangallo); branch at Av. Callao 291. Citibank, B. Mitre 502; branch at Florida 746. First National Bank of Boston, Florida 99, will exchange traveller's cheques for dollar bills with small commission. Bank of America, J. D. Perón (Cangallo) and San Martín (changes Bank of America traveller's cheques a.m. only, at 0.8% commission); branch at Paraguay 901, doesn't take American Express or Thomas Cook cheques. Banco Holandés Unido, Florida 359. Deutsche Bank (ex-Banco Alemán Transatlántico), Bmé. Mitre and Reconquista. Open 1000-1600 (exchange operations up to 1300 only), Mon.-Fri. Banco de la Provincia de Buenos Aires issues Visa Card, only place to obtain cash with this credit card in Argentina. Cheaper than exchanging US dollar bills.

There are many exchange shops, but few deal in travellers' cheques, most are concentrated around San Martín and Corrientes. Viatur, Reconquista 511; also Exprinter, Santa Fe; Aeromar, Corrientes 546; Teletour, Corrientes 571 (good rates); Forexcambio, M.T. de Alvear 566; various on San Martín, including Baires (215), Mercurio (229), Baupesa (363), Piano—for travellers' cheques (347) and Velox (298); open from 0900 to 1630, Mon.-Fri. and on Sats., 0900-1200, in rotation. City Service Travel, Florida 890, 4th floor, is the American Express Agency (for mail), but if you want emergency cash from a personal cheque backed by your card, go to Banco de Galicia, J.D. Perón 407, 4th floor; American Express main office: Alem 1110, 3rd floor, Tel.: 312-1661. Impossible to get money on American Express card on Sat. at the Amex office. Exchange shops offer the official rate but charge different commissions. **N.B.** Neither banks nor exchange shops are authorized to sell foreign currency. There is no service charge on notes, only on cheques. Many exchange shops ask for receipt of purchase of cheques, and practices vary all the time.

Clubs The American, English and German Clubs (addresses below) take temporary members and have reciprocal arrangements with many clubs in USA and UK. Both have excellent restaurants.

Useful Addresses

Argentine Association of English Culture, Suipacha 1333.
American Club, Viamonte 1133, facing Colón Theatre.
American Women's Club, Av. Córdoba 632, 11° piso.
Australian Embassy, Av. Santa Fe 846 (Swissair Building). Tel.: 312-6841.
Bolivian Consulate, 25 de Mayo 611, 2nd floor, open 0900-1400. Tel.: 311-7365
Brazilian Consulate, Pellegrini 1363, 5th floor, open Mon.-Fri., 1000-1800. (Easier to get a Brazilian visa from this consulate than in Montevideo; 2-day wait at latter.) Tel.: 394-5620.
British Chamber of Commerce, Av. Corrientes 457.
British Community Council, 25 de Mayo 444.
British Council, Marcelo T. de Alvear 590, 4° piso. Tel.: 31-4480 (Closed April 1982).
British Embassy and Consulate-General, Luis Agote 2412/52 (Near corner Pueyrredón & Guido), Casilla de Correos 2050. Tel.: 80-7071. (Closed April 1982 and British affairs looked after by Swiss embassy).
British Embassy Residence, Gelly y Obés 2301.
British Hospital, Calle Perdriel 74. Tel.: 23-1081. Cheap dental treatment at Av. Caseros y Perdriel 76.

ARGENTINA 47

British Tourist Authority, Av. Córdoba 645, 2nd floor, has recent newspapers. Open 1000-1300 and 1400-1630.
Canadian Embassy, Suipacha 1111 and Santa Fe, Tel.: 312-9081.
Centre of British Engineering & Transport Institute, Bmé. Mitre 441.
Comisión Nacional de Museos y Monumentos y Lugares Históricos, Av. de Mayo 556; professional archaeology institute.
Cultural Centre, General San Martín on Sarmiento 1551 has free concerts and plays almost every day. Monthly programme. Youth hostel connects with bus No. 7.
English Club, 25 de Mayo 581. Tel.: 311-9121. Temporary membership available to British business visitors.
West German Embassy, Villanueva 1055, Belgrano. Tel.: 771-5054/9.
German Hospital, Pueyrredón 1658, between C. Berruti and C. Juncal. Tel.: 821-4083.
Goethe Institut, Av. Corrientes 335 opp. Goethe bookshop, German library and newspapers, free German films shown. Next door is the German Club, Corrientes 327.
Irish Embassy, Av. Santa Fe 782, 7th floor, (1059) Buenos Aires. Tel.: 44-9987 No visa needed.
Italian Embassy, Billinghurst 2577, consulate at M.T. de Alvear 1149.
Paraguayan Consulate, Av. Maipú 464, 3rd floor, 0900-1300. Tel.: 392-6535.
Peruvian Consulate, Av. Corrientes 330, 2nd floor, open 0900-1300. Tel.:311-3374.
Uruguayan Consulate, Ayacucho 1616, open 1000-1800. Tel.:821-6031.
Salvation Army, Rivadavia 3255.
St. Andrew's Society, Perú 352.
South African Embassy, Marcelo T. de Alvear 590,8° piso. Tel.: 311-8991.
Spanish Embassy, Mariscal Ramón Castilla 2720, esq. Av. del Libertador 2075.
Swiss Embassy, Av. Santa Fe 846, 12° piso. Tel.: 311-6491.
USA Chamber of Commerce, Av. Roque Sáenz Peña 567.
US Embassy and Consulate General, Colombia 4300, Palermo. Tel.: 774-7611.
US Embassy Residence, Av. Libertador General San Martín 3502.
US Information Library (Biblioteca Lincoln), Florida 935. Reference library, free, take passport (closed Wed., Sat., Sun.).
Youth Hostel Association—information for all South America; Sarmiento 1262, 7° piso Tel.: 35-6690(take bus 23 to Uruguay 300 and walk 1½ blocks back towards centre). Buenos Aires hostel at Brasil 675 (Tel: 362-9133/8864) US$1.50 with YHA card (due to open Dec 1986).
N.B. A YHA card in Argentina costs US$12. Secretariat open Mon.-Fri. 1300-2000. (There are very few hostels going S from Buenos Aires on Route 3.)
YMCA (Central), Reconquista 439.
YWCA, Tucumán 844.
Municipality, Av. de Mayo 525, facing Plaza de Mayo.
Central Police Station, Moreno 1550. Tel.: 38-8041. (Emergency, Tel.: 101).
Migraciones (Immigration), Antártida Argentina 1365.

Urgent Medical Service (day and night) (Casualty ward: *Sala de guardia*). Tel.: 34-4001/4. The British and German hospitals (see above list) maintain first-aid centres (*centros asistenciales*) as do the other main hospitals. If affected by pollen, asthma sufferers can receive excellent free treatment at the University Hospital de Clínicas José San Martín, on Córdoba 2351.

Inoculations Centro Médico Rivadavia, S. de Bustamante 2531, Mon.-Fri., 0730-1900, or Sanidad de Puerto, Mon. and Thurs., 0800-1200, at Av. Ing. Huergo 1497, opp. Dique No.1, free, bus 20 from Retiro, no appointment required (typhus, cholera, Mon./Thurs. 0800-1200; yellow fever, Thurs. 1400-1600). Hospital Rivadavia, Calles Las Heras y Tagle, for polio inoculation. Free. Centro de Inmunización reported not to give vaccinations any more.

General Post Office (Correo Central), corner of Sarmiento and L.N. Alem. State Railways Building, Av. Maipú 4, in the Puerto Nuevo district; open 0800-2000 except on Sundays and national holidays. Small parcels only of up to 1 kg. Larger parcels from Centro Postal Internacional, Av. Antártida Argentina, near Retiro Station, about US$1 for 5 kg. Cheap packing service available (US$2). Open between 0900 and 1500. Poste Restante (US$0.30 per letter). KLM (Florida 989) has a special air mail service.

Cables and Telephones State CyT on Calle Corrientes, near corner of Calle Maipú, public telex in basement; alternatively in Central Post Office, Leandro N. Alem 300, also telex. Another office is in Calle San Martín 322. Entel, the state agency, has a monopoly. There are Entel offices for international calls and cables in Retiro and Once stations, open 7 days, 0700-2400. Entel also on 32-0849. Corrientes/Maipú and Agüero/Las Heras. *Fichas* (tokens) for calls in the city cost US$0.10, most easily obtained at Entel offices.

Language Schools which teach English to Argentines are: BBC, J. D. Perón (Cangallo) 961; Londonlab, Santa Fe 1424; Masters, Av. de Mayo 791; Berlitz, Av. de Mayo 847 (low rates of pay); Central Consultaret de Personal, Lavalle 1290 (office at 1103); Pullmen, Santiago de Estero 324. Before being allowed to teach, you must have a work permit; if unsure of your papers, ask at Migraciones (address above).

48 ARGENTINA

Tourist Information National office at Santa Fe 883 with masses of maps and literature. Open 1000-1700, Mon.-Fri.; Tel.: 312-5611, 312-5621. Has addresses of laundromats. There are also branches at either end of Calle Florida (Mon.-Fri., 0900-2000, Sat., 0900-1900). National Parks Information Service, Santa Fe 680, has a beautiful portfolio on all National Parks and the best film on the breaking of the Perito Moreno glacier in Calafate. There are also helpful *Casas de Turismo* for most provinces (open Mon.-Fri. usually, 1200-1900, depending on office, check); on Callao are Buenos Aires (no. 237), Córdoba (332), Chaco (322), La Rioja (755), Mendoza (445). Río Negro, Tucumán 1920; Chubut, Paraguay 876; Entre Ríos, J. D. Perón (Cangallo) 451; Formosa, H. Irigoyen 1429; Jujuy, Santa Fe 967; Misiones, Santa Fe 989; Neuquén, J. D. Perón (Cangallo) 687; Salta, Maipú 663; Santa Cruz, Córdoba 1345, 14th floor, Catamarca, Córdoba 2080; Corrientes, San Martín 333; La Pampa, Suipacha 346; San Juan, Maipú 331; Santa Fe, 25 de Mayo 358; Santiago del Estero, Florida 274; Tucumán, Mitre 836, Tierra del Fuego, Ushuaia and Lago Argentino, Esmeralda 351. Bariloche hotel, flat and bungalow service at Florida 520, enter *Galería* and walk up to room 116. Calafate bookings for *Motel La Loma* and *Refugio and Autocamping Lago Viedma*, excursions with Transporte Ruta 3 and lake excursions with Empresa Paraíso de Navegación booked from Turismo Argos, Maipú 812, 13th floor C, Tel.: 392-5460. Municipalidad de Buenos Aires, Sarmiento 1551, 4th floor, has an excellent free booklet about the city centre and maps. Further offices at Aeroparque (Aerolíneas Argentinas), Mon.-Fri., 0830-2000 and Sat. 0900-1900, and Ezeiza Airport, Mon.-Fri. 0830-2200; also Florida with Diagonal Norte and Florida with Córdoba, open at 0830-1930 Mon.-Fri. and 0900-1900 Sat. A useful local booklet is *Salimos*, printed in Spanish, with local information on festivals, etc. and free events (on Fri., the youth section of *Clarín—Sí*- lists free entertainments). *Where*, a tourist guide in English, published monthly, is available free in hotels, travel agencies, tourist kiosks on Florida, and in some newsstands at US$2.50. A good guide is *Guía Peuser*, US$1.30, available from magazine stands. Country-wide maps at Instituto Geográfico Militar, Cabildo 381, reached by 152 bus from Retiro station, open 0800-1300. Federico B. Kirbus has written *Guía de Turismo y Aventuras, de la Argentina desconocida, arqueológica y misteriosa*, obtainable at El Ateneo, or from the author at Casilla de Correo 5210, RA-1000. Bs. Aires. The Fundación Vida Silvestre (conservation organization and bookshop), L. N. Alem 968, has information and books on Argentine flora and fauna. Field guide to Argentine birds: *Las aves argentinas*, by Claes Chr. Olrog, US$35, bad drawings but good range maps.

Tourist Agents Exprinter, Santa Fe, and San Martín 176, Galería Güemes; Thos. Cook & Son, Av. Córdoba 746; Fairways, Viamonte 640, 3° piso (392-1716). City Service Travel Agency, Florida 890 (32-8416), which is the American Express agent, there are British staff to advise people travelling to the UK; Sol-Jet, Cerrito 1328, warmly recommended; EVES, Tucumán 702; Star Travel Service, Florida (392-2744); Astra Travel, Tucumán 358, 5th floor, English spoken by director, efficient; Furlong's; Agencia Marítima Mundial, S.A., Córdoba 653, helpful and efficient; Mitchell's, Av. Córdoba 657. Oficina Flyer, Reconquista 617, 8° piso, Tel.: 313-8165, Spanish, English, Dutch and German spoken, accepts credit cards, recommended. Schenker Argentina, Lavalle 530, German (Tel.: 394-2074). Gleizer Travel, on the ground floor of the *Sheraton Hotel*. Diners Travel, Avenida Sarmiento, takes Diners card, unlike most other travel agents. Germania, Lavalle 414, excellent service, (English not spoken) esp. for tours to the N, branch in Salta (Tel.: 393-1265/0035). English is widely spoken.

Tours A good way of seeing Buenos Aires and its surroundings is by using the day and night services of Autobuses Sudamericanos, Calle Neuquén, 1155, 1st floor, Apt. 8, Tel.: 431-16794 (with an information and booking office at Bernardo Irigoyen 1370, 1st floor, Offices 25 and 26, Tel.: 23-8073/23-2887/26-6061). For reservations in advance for sightseeing or other tours, with a 20% courtesy discount to *South American Handbook* readers, write to Casilla de Correo No. 29, Sucursal 34, 1434 Buenos Aires. A 3-hour tour of Buenos Aires in English and Spanish is run by City Tours, Lavalle 1444 (Tel.: 40-2304/90), US$9, recommended. Some tours (e.g. Buenos Aires Tur) include dinner and a tango show, or a gaucho *fiesta* at a ranch.

Motoring Associations Automóvil Club Argentino, Libertador General San Martín 1850, Tel.: 802-6061; Touring Club Argentino, Esmeralda 605 y Tucumán 781, 3rd floor, Tel.: 392-6742. See page 147 for details of service. Parking, safely, at El Balneario within the old port, but ask the military post for permission first.

Passenger Ships The *Buenos Aires Herald* (English-language daily) notes all shipping movements. The following services, among others, are by the Flota Fluvial del Estado (Corrientes 489, Tel.: 311-0728) with sailings from Buenos Aires, South Basin; Rosario (Paraná River), 2 weekly sailings; South Coast, down to Punta Arenas and intermediate Patagonian ports, served by the Imp. & Exp. de la Patagonia and Elma (state shipping line). Very irregular sailings. For connexions with Uruguay, see page 51.

ARGENTINA 49

To Antarctica with the Jefatura de Servicio de Transportes Navales in February, one sailing a year, for 30 days on Transporte ARA, *Bahía Buen Suceso*, stopping 2-5 days at each port of call, including Puerto Belgrano, Antarctica (6 days), Ushuaia, Puerto Madryn, including side trips. 2-4 berth cabins US$1,350-1,950, includes meals. Information from: Jefatura del Servicio de Transportes Navales, Reconquista 385, 7° piso, Tel.: 45-0034 and 45-1116, 0900-1200 and 1300-1700.

Airports Ezeiza, 35 km. from the centre by a good divided lane highway, which links with the General Paz circular highway round the city. The airport is up-to-date, has a duty free shop, and its hotel, the *Internacional*, is vey good (category B, all inclusive). Airport international, Tel.: 620-0217. Airport tax US$10. Ezeiza is used by international services but Jorge Newbery airport (normally known as Aeroparque), on the N side river front at the end of the New Port, 4 km. from the centre, is used for internal services and also flights to Punta del Este, most flights to Montevideo and a few to Asunción, Santiago and Santa Cruz (Bolivia). (Airport tax US$1.25.) If stuck for cash because banks are closed you can try the Newbery airport exchange facilities (bills only), run by Banco de la Nación.

Taxis called *remise* (from the Manuel Tienda León counter, in the airport, only, Tel.: 89-0661/6) to and from Ezeiza airport operate at a fixed price (US$12), to the centre (leave from *Hotel Colón*, on Carlos Pellegrini, more-or-less hourly, every day). There is now also a reliable standard taxi service operating from Ezeiza, US$20. Do not take an unmarked car, however attractive the fare may sound. Airport bus from Av. Carlos Pellegrini 509 (corner of Lavalle), US$6, approximately every 45 minutes from 0530. When landing at Ezeiza, buy tickets for city centre at the kiosk in the terminal building, before boarding the bus. (The company is often willing to deliver tourists by car to hotels in the city centre on arrival at the city terminal, at no extra cost, but if you haven't got a hotel booked or a friend's address they may try to deliver you to one of their own choosing or try to drop you off away from the centre). No. 86 bus can also be caught at corner of Perú and Av. de Mayo (500—starts at Irala 800 block in the Boca), cheap, but no good if you have much luggage. Make sure bus has sign "Aeropuerto" inside; many 86's stop short of the airport. Two or three stops in the Ezeiza airport area, journey about 1¾ hrs, *servicio diferencial* akin to shuttle bus comfort, every 20-30 mins. from Av. Colón y Estados Unidos, better than *común*, but US$1 against US$0.30. Other routes to the airport: train to Liniers, then bus 86, or train from Constitución to Ezeiza, then bus 138.

Journeys to and from Jorge Newbery (Aeroparque) by *remise* taxi, e.g. US$6.50 to Retiro, US$25 to Ezeiza. Taxis are charged according to meter (about US$2.75 from the centre, but up to US$5 to the centre), or you can catch the local No. 33 or 56 bus (US$0.25) from outside the airport to the Retiro railway station. You can also use your Pase Americano from De la Torre station (just past the race track) after having walked across the Palermo park or having taken a US$0.35 bus-ride to the station. Take train from there to Retiro.

Aerolíneas Argentinas and Austral offer daily flights to the main cities, for details see text below; see also page 146 for the Visit Argentina fare. If travelling in the south, book ahead if possible with LADE, whose flights are cheaper than buses in most cases.

Local Airline Offices Aerolíneas Argentinas, Calle Perú 2, with a branch office at Santa Fe and Esmeralda; reservations and enquiries, Tel.: 393-5122. Austral Líneas Aéreas, Flórida 429, Tel.: 49-9011. Líneas Aéreas del Estado (LADE), Calle Perú 710, Tel.: 361-7071. Aerolínea Federal Argentina (ex Aero Chaco), Perú 2, 30-8551.

Other Airlines Lufthansa, M.T. Alvear 636. Tel.: 312-81719. KLM, Florida 989, Tel.: 311-8921. Air France, Paraguay 610, Tel.: 312-7331. Eastern, Suipacha 1111, piso 23, Tel.: 34-0031. Iberia, Av. Pres. Roque Sáenz Peña 947, Tel.: 35-2057. Pan-Am, Av. Pres. Roque Sáenz Peña 832, 6th floor, Tel.: 45-0111. Varig, Florida 630, Tel.: 35-5431; CPAir, Av. Córdoba 656.

Air Fares AA to Córdoba, US$56; to Mar del Plata, US$42 return.

Railways Terminals (good snacks available at Retiro and Constitución at all hours).
Retiro: Ferrocarril Nacional Mitre (Central)—312-6596; Ferrocarril Nacional San Martín (Pacific)—311-8054; Ferrocarril Nacional Belgrano (North-Western)—311-5287/8/9.
Constitución: Ferrocarril Nacional Roca (Southern)—23-0021.
Once: Ferrocarril Nacional Sarmiento (Western)—87-0041/2/3.
F. Lacroze: Ferrocarril Nacional Urquiza (North-Eastern)—55-5214.

Principal Trains (The following table is designed merely as an indication; further enquiries will be needed, and details will be found under the provincial cities listed. Prices approximate only.

Destination	Departure Station	Trains per Week	Journey Time (hrs.)	Tourist	First	Fares (US$) Pullman	Sleeper
Bahía Blanca	Constitución	17	10-12	7.00	9.40	13.45	20.05
Bariloche	Constitución	3	32	19.00	26.00	37.00	45.00
Concordia*	F. Lacroze	15	8½	5.65	7.60	10.95	17.75
Córdoba*	Retiro	9	12	10.00	13.00	18.00	26.00
Mendoza*	Retiro	13	13-16	11.20	15.10	21.65	28.45

50 ARGENTINA

Paraná	F. Lacroze	6	10½	7.00	9.10	—	20.00
Paso de los Libres*	F. Lacroze	7	12	8.20	11.00	15.85	22.60
Posadas*	F. Lacroze	8	18	11.85	15.90	22.85	29.60
Rosario	Retiro	64	4	3.65	4.90	7.20	—
San Antonio Oeste	Constitución	4	19-22	11.85	15.90	22.85	29.60
Sante Fe	Retiro	32	7-10	5.40	7.20	—	—
Tucumán*	Retiro	11	18½-25	13.50	18.10	24.00	38.40
Zapala	Constitución	7	26	14.65	19.70	28.35	35.10

Some trains have car-transporters

NB The railways maintain an information centre and booking office beside the Galerías Pacífico, Florida 729 (311-6411/14), open 0700-2100 Mon.-Sat., Sun. 0700-1300. (If planning to travel in December, be at the booking office very early to avoid queues.) There is a good left-luggage facility at Retiro station. Book tickets well in advance wherever possible, also for connecting services, especially those going south of Buenos Aires. Outward journeys may be booked 45 days in advance, return journeys 60 days, but not later than 7 days in advance. Telephone reservations for named trains: 312-5680, 312-5686/9, 312-3686/9, 311-6325/9, 312-8610 and 312-8616/9. Pullman services are usually air conditioned. Tourist fares are about 30% cheaper than buses, but much slower and less reliable, and unlike the more expensive classes there is no guarantee of being able to stretch out to sleep. Buffet cars usually offer coffee and drinks; sandwiches and refreshments are usually touted down the train during journeys. Services have been speeded up in the last few years.

Buses The long-distance bus station, Estación Terminal de Omnibus, is behind Retiro, on Av. Ramos Mejía and Antártida Argentina (Subte C) Tel.: for information 311-6073/6088. Long distance buses now leave from here although some lines still make departures from their old terminals, including Plazas Constitución and Miserere. Some bus companies charge extra for luggage. Fares charged by the country-wide Chevallier company are: Bariloche, US$47; Córdoba, US$22.25; Mar del Plata, US$9.50; Mendoza, US$26; Rosario, US$8.10; San Martín de los Andes, US$48; and Tucumán, US$30. Fares may vary according to time of year and advance booking is advisable Dec.-March. In slack periods, the less popular companies may give discounts.

Hitch-hiking Heading S, take bus 96 to Ruta 3 for Comodoro Rivadavia, etc., US$0.35. Best to hitch from a service station.

Travel into Neighbouring Countries

By Road
Four branches of the Inter-American Highway run from Buenos Aires to the borders of Chile, Bolivia, Paraguay and Brazil. The roads are paved except when otherwise stated.

To Chile via Río Cuarto, Mercedes, San Luis, and Mendoza, Total: 1,310 km. Paved throughout (Three direct buses a week to Santiago, US$40, 23u hrs. e.g. TAC or Chevallier US$43, 1,459 km; same price to Valparaíso.) Car-transporter train to Mendoza on Fridays. There are also road connections between Bariloche and Osorno and Puerto Montt, and between Salta and Antofagasta.

To Bolivia via Rosario, Villa María, Córdoba, Santiago del Estero, Salta, Tucumán, and Jujuy. Total: 1,994 km. There is no direct bus service from Buenos Aires to La Paz but through connections can be booked, about US$80. Also a train/bus combination, train to Tucumán and then bus to Jujuy, but no sleepers. Try travel agent in Bernardo de Yrigoyen 957 shopping arcade. Car-transporter train to Tucumán, Mon., Tue., Wed. and Fri.

To Paraguay via Rosario (as for Bolivia), Santa Fe, Resistencia, Clorinda and Asunción (via new toll bridge—ferry service no longer operates). Total: 1,370 km (all paved). Buses take 20-22 hours, with N.S. de la Asunción, Juan D. Perón (ex-Cangallo) 2760; or Chevallier, Empresa Godoy, La Internacional or Expreso Brújula (all next to each other at the Retiro bus terminal). You have choice between *diferencial* (with food, drinks, about US$42) and *común* (without food, about US$32.50) services. Tickets can be bought up to 30 days in advance.

Those who wish to drive to Misiones to visit San Ignacio Miní or the Iguazú Falls should cross the river by the bridge between Santa Fe and Paraná, or the one between Resistencia and Corrientes. From there Route 12 leads NE through Posadas to the Iguazú Falls. The direct road from Buenos Aires to Posadas via the Zárate-Brazo Largo bridges is now reported fully paved. From Corrientes to Esperanza is paved, and from Posadas to Iguazú. (Singer and Tigre-Iguazú buses to Puerto Iguazú leave daily at 1130 and 1500 respectively, US$28.75, 22 hrs.) From Posadas you can cross the river to Encarnación by the ferry (bridge under construction) and take a good 370-km. road to Asunción (see Paraguayan chapter). Car-transporter train to Posadas, Tues. and Fri.

To Brazil To the Iguazú Falls, take the road given above to Asunción, Paraguay, and then a

ARGENTINA 51

paved 326-km. road to Ciudad Stroessner and cross by bridge to Brazil—or go by the ferry (which takes cars), from Puerto Iguazú, reached via Posadas. Another road to the border with Brazil, at Paso de los Libres, goes to Rosario, Santa Fe, cross by bridge and tunnel to Paraná; Villa Federal, Curuzú Cuatiá, Paso de los Libres, opposite Uruguaiana (Brazil), across the Río Uruguay. Total: 960 km. Direct buses to Brazil via Paso de los Libres by Pluma: São Paulo, 40 hrs. US$63.25, Curitiba, US$51.75, 38 hrs; Florianópolis, US$46, 32 hrs; daily at 1000 to Porto Alegre, US$40.25, 26 hrs. (The route across the River Plate and through Uruguay is a bit cheaper, not as long and offers a variety of transport and journey breaks; see also Uruguay under next section). Tickets from Onda, Florida 502 y Lavalle (392-5011), for any information also to combine travel via Uruguay. Buen Viaje, Av. Córdoba 415 (31-2953) or Pluma, Av. Córdoba 461 (311-4871 or 311-5986) or office branches in Rosario, Santa Fe and Paraná. Journey to Rio takes about 50 hrs, US$60; at least one bus per day. Car-transporter train to Paso de los Libres, Tues. and Fri.

To Uruguay Direct road connections by means of two bridges over the River Uruguay between Puerto Colón and Paysandú and between Puerto Unzué and Fray Bentos. "Bus de la carrera" links Montevideo and Buenos Aires (10 hrs). Departure from each city at 1000, 2200 and 2215 via Zárate-Gualeguaychú-Puerto Unzué-Fray Bentos-Mercedes-Montevideo, US$14.75. Book at Onda.

Air, River and Railway Services

Brazil Daily services to São Paulo, Rio de Janeiro and other Brazilian cities by air. Shipping service between Buenos Aires and Brazilian ports by various transatlantic lines. See *Buenos Aires Herald*, English-language daily.

Chile (Information about travel to Chile is available from Av. Córdoba 879.) The passenger-train service across the Andes between Mendoza and Santiago has been discontinued, but bus services are available. The train service to Antofagasta via Salta and Socompa has also been suspended, but there are buses between Salta and Antofagasta.

Foreign and national lines fly daily between Buenos Aires and Santiago, US$135. Time taken: 1½ to 2 hours. There are 2 flights weekly by Aerolíneas Argentinas to Punta Arenas on the S coast of Chile, via Comodoro Rivadavia, Río Gallegos and Río Grande. Aerolíneas Argentinas also flies to Antofagasta via Salta.

Bolivia There are now no international trains to Bolivia, via La Quiaca, and the connecting services from Salta and Jujuy to La Quiaca have been suspended. On arriving in La Quiaca by bus one must cross on foot to the Bolivian side and purchase a train ticket for the remainder of the journey, Villazón-La Paz. *El Norteño* train has no sleepers, leaves Retiro Tues. and Fri. at 1000, via Tucumán to Jujuy, US$20 1st cl. US$16 turista. Bus Panamericano Jujuy to La Quiaca. Villalonga Furlong, Balcarce 473, 2nd floor, open Mon.-Fri. 0900-1700, has information about trains (not Retiro); it is also a freighting company and sells the tickets. See under Tucumán (pages 68 for other train services. There are no sleepers beyond Tucumán. Sleeper tickets to Tucumán carry no seat entitlement elsewhere in the train. Sanitary facilities poor. Hot soup and local dishes brought round carriages. Bar and restaurant car with same food, adequate. Travel rug recommended on this part of the journey. Train Villazón-La Paz has sleepers, worthwhile but may need paying over the odds to secure. Carriages, old, noisy and crowded. Bad sanitary facilities but lavatory at Villazón comparatively clean. Local food available on train. Carriages soon become crowded. Cold night. Free baggage allowance 30 kg., and excess is charged. A weekly train (no sleepers) to Santa Cruz de la Sierra from Retiro Station via Salta, Güemes, Pocitos and Yacuiba takes 3 days; leaves Buenos Aires Tues at 1000, arrives Santa Cruz 2230 Thurs. From Santa Cruz, dep. 1000 Thurs., arrival 2100 Sat. at Retiro. See page 72.

There are also regular air services 5 or 6 times a week to La Paz by Eastern, Aerolíneas and Lloyd Aéreo Boliviano.

Paraguay The direct train to Asunción was withdrawn in 1984, but trains run daily to Posadas, and twice weekly from Encarnación to Asunción. From Encarnación you can get a connecting train (if it waits) or bus (saving up to 16 hrs.) to Asunción. There is a daily air service to Asunción by various companies. Time taken: 2 to 6 hours. See also Posadas, page 103

Uruguay Tickets heavily booked Dec.-March. **N.B:** No money changing facilities in Tigre, and poor elsewhere. For boat services, take the train to Tigre (Mitre suburban line), 50 mins. (US$0.25), leaves at 5 min. intervals from Retiro. (No good hotels in Tigre, but try *Astor*, reasonable-looking.) Two daily boats to Carmelo at 0800 and 0830, 3½ hrs., tickets at Cacciola, Lavalle 868, local 24, or Av. Cazón 1581, Tigre. It is advisable to book in advance; connecting bus to Montevideo (Onda, Florida y Lavalle, book in advance), arriving at 1530 and 1600; Tigre-Montevideo US$7.55. From Dársena Sud, the following services go to Colonia, where connecting Onda buses go to Montevideo (3 hrs., US$4.45). Night boat (*vapor carrera*) from Bs.As. to Montevideo from Dársena Sud Desembarcadero Fluvial (Pedro de Mendoza and Arzobispo Espinosa) with El Faro, Lavalle 388/92, 1047 Bs. Aires (Tel. 393-2306/33-3335/34-9881). Leaves at 2100, board between 1930 and 2030 only, single fare, shared cabin and breakfast, US$15.35; cars charged by

52 ARGENTINA

weight. Ferry services to Colonia, Ferrytur, Florida 780, 2nd floor, bus leaves from Florida and Córdoba to ferry, Uruguayan immigration on ferry.

Atlantic car ferry, daily, at 0800 arr. Colonia 1100, Montevideo 1430, US$32.65-53.35 p.p. w/o car, US$90 upwards per car; food on the ferry is not good, so take your own. Tickets from Flota Fluvial, Corrientes 375 or Onda.

Alimar S.A. (Tel.: 44-5959), hydrofoil at 0800, 1100, 1500, 1800 daily, 4 hrs. Belt SA, hydrofoils ten minutes earlier than those times, US$11.65 one way to Colonia; US$23 (incl. Onda bus) one way to Montevideo. All tickets from Onda, Florida 502, Tel.: 392-5011; reconfirm seat at Onda in Montevideo, Plaza Cagancha. Beware of overcharging by taxis from the harbour to the centre of Buenos Aires.

Air service from Jorge Newbery Airport (Aeroparque) to Colonia 15 mins., daily by Arco at 1000 (1400 Sun.) and 1900, Lapa at 0800 and 1750; US$14.40 one way. Tickets at Onda. Air service to Montevideo: shuttle 10 daily, 0730 to 2200, known as Puente Aéreo and run by AA and Pluna. Book at Jorge Newbery Airport or Tel.: 361-5008. Fare US$48; flight takes 35 mins. Punta del Este, daily with AA and Pluna US$66, 40 mins.

Suburbs of Buenos Aires

Avellaneda, a separate municipality of over 650,000 people, is one of the most important industrial centres in the country; the handling of hides, wool and animal produce is concentrated here. It is 5 km. from Plaza Constitución station, on the other side of the Riachuelo river from Boca. **Bank** of London and South America, Av. Gral. Mitre 553. First National Bank of Boston. 1000-1600.

Olivos, on the River Plate coast, 20 minutes by the Bartolomé Mitre Railway, is a favourite residential district. The presidential residence is there, many foreign residents. Population, about 160,000. Nearby, at La Lucila, there are many American families.

San Isidro, just beyond Olivos, a resort for golf, yachting, swimming, and athletics, is one of the most attractive suburbs on the coast. There is a magnificent turf racecourse, an attractive central plaza and fine colonial buildings. Pop.: 80,000. **Bank** of London and South America, Chacabuco 328. 1000-1600.

Martínez, nearby is an attractive residential area overloooking the River Plate, with an interesting shopping area. Sailing and windsurfing are well represented and river launches and other craft may be hired.

Quilmes has one of the world's largest breweries. It is an important industrial centre where textiles, ironware and glass are manufactured. Population about 150,000. St. George's College, an English boarding school, is here. Bathing is now both dangerous and prohibited; in one day 19 lives were lost. It is served by the Roca Railway and buses. **Bank** of London and South America, Hipólito Yrigoyen 616. 1000-1600.

The naturalist and writer W. H. Hudson (1841-1922) was born at Florencio Varela, near Quilmes, about 32 km. from Buenos Aires. His birthplace is now a national monument.

Tigre, on Tigre Railway from Retiro, US$0.70, amid rivers and streams, is about 29 km. (50 minutes) from Buenos Aires. It can also be reached by bus 60, which takes a little longer. Regattas are held in November and March on the River Luján. There are numerous "recreos" and restaurants on the river front, but sleeping accommodation is not good. Inland from Tigre is the Delta of the Paraná, with innumerable canals and rivulets, holiday homes, clubs, a profitable fruit growing centre and an attraction for holiday makers. The fishing is excellent and there is peace on the waterways, apart from motor-boats at week-ends. Regular launch services, each company with its own routes, for all parts of the Delta, including taxi launches— watch prices for these!—leave from wharf opposite railway station. The wharf where these are moored can be quite smelly. Two-hour excursion costs about US$5. Be warned that if you leave just before lunch the launch crew may stop along the way for a 1-1½ hr. lunch break! Catamarans make tours of canals and river channels, lunch included: a pleasant and inexpensive way of spending a lazy Sunday. Population: 40,000. Delta Youth Hostel at Colón y Río Luján, San Fernando (take bus 7 from train station, US$0.15) clean, hot showers; ask at Corrientes 1373, 1st floor, Buenos Aires. Good restaurant near Youth Hostel, around the corner. Direct ferry to Carmelo, Uruguay (see page 51) from opposite railway station. (If you miss the boat, Antonio J. Pissini has guest rooms for US$5 a night at Montes de Oca 142, Tigre, or try *Hotel Astor*.)

The Naval Museum is worth a visit. It contains models old and new, navigation instruments, flags and banners, and paintings of naval battles. There are also relics of the 1982 South Atlantic war on display outside. The Reconquista Museum celebrates the reconquest of Buenos Aires from the British.

Excursion to **Martín García** island (Juan Díaz de Solís' landfall in 1516), 45 km. from Buenos Aires, with La Valette Turismo, through channels in The Delta (approx. 12 hours there and back with day on the island (Tel.: 921-2050/2055).

Other Towns in the Pampas

There is one town which belongs to Argentina as a whole rather than to any province or area, though it is actually in the Province of Buenos Aires and only 71 km. W of the capital by Sarmiento railway from Once station (change at Moreno, 2 hours, US$2.30) or by bus from Once station, 1 hr. This is

Luján, a place of pilgrimage for all devout Catholics in Argentina. An image of the Virgin was being taken from church to church in the area in 1630 by ox cart. At a certain spot the cart got stuck, in spite of strenuous efforts by men and oxen to move it. This was taken as a sign that the Virgin willed she should stay there. A chapel was built for the image, and around it grew Luján. The chapel has long since been superseded by an impressive neo-Gothic basilica and the Virgin now stands on the High Altar. May 8 is her day. Each arch of the church is dedicated to an Argentine province, and two of the transepts to Uruguay and Paraguay. Population: 30,000. Very heavy traffic at weekends.

Museo Colonial e Histórico (The Colonial and Historical Museum) is in the old Cabildo building. Exhibits illustrate the historical and political development of the country. One of the most interesting museums. Open daily, except Monday and Tuesday, 1200-1800. No cameras allowed, and nowhere to store them, stroppy caretaker. General Beresford, the leader of an attempt to capture Buenos Aires, was a prisoner here, and so, in later days, were Generals Mitre, Paz, and Belgrano. There are also two transport and one art museums. The River Luján is picturesque at this point, and is a favourite spot for picnic parties.

Hotels *España, La Paz.* There are numerous **restaurants:** an excellent one is *L'Eau Vive* on the road to Buenos Aires at Constitución 2112; it is run by nuns, pleasant surroundings.

There are dozens of small, prosperous towns scattered throughout the vast area of the pampas. They serve as clearing centres for the cattle and grain and supply the rural population, which is much denser in the Humid Pampa than elsewhere in Argentina. Only the larger towns and resorts are dealt with here.

La Plata, capital of Buenos Aires Province, on the River Plate and only 56 km. SE of Buenos Aires, is reached by Roca railway and by many buses. This modern city, founded in 1882, has a population of about 406,000. Its port, accessible to ships of the largest tonnage, makes it a main outlet for the produce of the pampas. Its major industrial interest is the YPF petroleum refinery as all its refrigerated meat plants are now closed; a 72-km. pipeline runs to the South Dock at Buenos Aires. Its Museum of Natural History is one of the best in Argentina and has several unique exhibits (open 1300-1800). A motorway is being built to link La Plata with Buenos Aires, via Riachuelo, Avellaneda, Berazátegui, Gonnet and Tolosa.

Points of Interest The Museum at La Plata, famous for its collection of extinct animals, is open daily except in January and on public holidays (admission US$0.30, but free on Mon.). Its treasures are largely ethnological and include human skulls, mummies, and prehistoric implements. There are zoological, botanical, geological, mineralogical, palaeontological and archaeological sections. Well laid-out Zoological Gardens; fine racecourse and Observatory. The Museum, Zoological Gardens, and Observatory are all in the public park. The city has a Garden of Peace, each country in the world represented by one flower, with a plaque in front of it; on October 12 flags are put up there. The Town Hall and Cathedral are in the Plaza Moreno. Ten minutes in the train takes one to the Islas de Río Santiago and to the Yacht Club, Arsenal, and Naval Academy. Nearby is an interesting children's village with scaled-down public buildings, built under the first Perón administration.

Local Holiday Foundation of the City, November 19.

Hotels *Corregidor,* new, expensive, on plaza; *Roga,* Calle 54 No. 334, E, new, small. *Plaza,* Calle 44 y 3, E with bath; *Roca,* Calle 1 y 42, F with bath.

Restaurant *El Fogón,* recommended, main course about US$4.

Tourist Office In the old white theatre on the main plaza.

Buses To Buenos Aires, 1½ hrs. Fare US$0.85, about every quarter hour, Río de la Plata company (from Retiro in Buenos Aires).

On the coast 400 km. S of Buenos Aires, lies Mar del Plata, the most celebrated

54　ARGENTINA

Argentine seaside resort. The road and rail routes S to it are through Chascomús and Dolores.

Chascomús, 126 km. from Buenos Aires, is on a wide plain on the shores of Lake Chascomús, which covers 3,000 hectares and swells greatly in size during the rains. Its slightly brackish water is an important breeding place for *pejerrey* fish; up to 1,000 kg. have been caught in one day during the winter season, when amateur fishing competitions are held. There is a *gaucho* museum, and also a Regatta Club and bathing beaches and camping grounds at Monte Brown, on the far side of the lake. Chascomús is the birthplace of President Alfonsín.

Hotels *Del Lago; Riviera; Americano; Santa María.*

Camping Sites *Estancia El Carmen* (US$2.10 p.p) and *Casa Amarilla.*

Dolores, 204 km. from Buenos Aires, has a district population of 30,000; it was founded in 1818, destroyed by Indians three years later, and rebuilt. It is a grain and cattle farming centre which tends to suffer from flooding after prolonged rain.

Hotel *Argentina.*

About 130 km. N of Mar del Plata a new seaside resort, **Villa Gesell**, has sprung up, very popular with young people and families. The town offers dunes, pine forests and sandy beaches, over a dozen pleasant, intimate hotels (*Tejas Rojas, Aloha, Capri,* etc.), and villas to let. Direct bus service to Buenos Aires by Empresas Antón and Río de la Plata.

Camping Sites *Del Sol, El Faro, California.* The first is open all year round.

Air　Aerolíneas Argentinas flies to Villa Gesell several times daily in summer.

Pinamar, 22 km. N of Villa Gesell, is a rapidly growing resort, with a casino. It is now very much the "in" place, with good water-skiing. Fish, including conger eel (*congrio*) may be bought on the beach from local fishermen.

Hotels *Playa* and *Libertador.* All hotels fully booked throughout Jan.- March. **Youth Hostel** and *Moby Dick* campsite at Ostende. Many other campsites close to town.

Mar del Plata is 400 km. from the capital. The normal population is 350,000, but during the summer about two million visitors stay there; there are all classes of apartment blocks, boarding houses and lodgings. It is necessary to book in advance between late December and mid- March (when the night-life continues all night). For the rest of the year the town is fairly quiet. The city is famous for its casino: the upper floor is open to the public, for a small admission charge (men must wear jackets and ties).

There are fine squares, especially Plaza San Martín, and eight km. of beaches, including fashionable Playa Grande, with its private clubs and the summer estates of wealthy *porteños*; Bristol Beach, where the casino is; and Playa Perla, with moderately priced hotel accommodation. At Punta Iglesia there is a large rock carving of Florentino Ameghino, the palaeontologist who collected most of the fossils in the museum at La Plata. On other beaches are the municipal swimming pool, the pier of the Fishing Club, the Yacht Club, the Club Náutico, and the port, with the golf links behind it. (There is another golf club in the grounds of the Club Mar del Plata, 7 km. S of the Mogotes lighthouse, on the way to Miramar.) The wooded municipally owned Parque Camet is 8 km. to the N. It has polo grounds and playing fields. For those who do not care for surf bathing, there are salt-water pools. Fishing is good all along the coast and *pejerrey, corvina* and *merluza* (hake) abound; it is possible to charter a private launch for shark fishing. Football fans might enjoy seeing San Lorenzo play at their stadium—a very good atmosphere.

The port can be reached by bus, 15 mins. from bus terminal. There are a large fishing fleet, excursion boats, seafood restaurants.

Visits can be paid to the rocky promontory of Cabo Corrientes to watch the breakers; to Punta

ARGENTINA 55

Mogotes lighthouse (open Thursdays 1330-1700); to the Gruta de Lourdes, and the Bosque Peralta Ramos.

Local Holidays   Feb. 10 (Foundation of City); Nov. 10 (Day of Tradition); Nov. 22 (St. Cecilia). Mar del Plata is known for its hand-finished sweaters.

Hotels   Four-star (category A) are the *Provincial*, 500 rooms, Boulevard Marítimo 2500; the *Dos Reyes*, Av. Colón 2129; the *Hermitage*, Blvd. Peralta Ramos 2657, 150 rooms; and the *Sasso*, M. de Hoz 3545. The 3-star hotels (category B) are the *Astor*, Entre Ríos 1649; *Benedetti*, Av. Colón 2198, recommended; *Argentino*, Belgrano 2243; *Bizonte*, Belgrano 2601; *Gran Continental*, Córdoba 1929; *República*, Córdoba 1968; *Presidente*, Corrientes 1516; *Gran Opera*, Falucho 1938; *Corbel*, Córdoba 1870; and *Gran Dora*, Buenos Aires 1841. 2-star hotels (category C) include the *Flamingo*, Moreno 2155, has seen better days, but comfortable; *Roland*, Corrientes 1965; *Dover*, Santa Fe 1973; *Finisterre*, Garay 1786, without breakfast, clean, comfortable (near the bus station); and *Napoleón*, Santa Fe 1913. Two 1-star hotels (category D) the *Nuevo Dell'Acqua*, Sarmiento 2640; and the *Moli-Mar*, Alberti 1956. There are scores of good hotels at reasonable rates e.g. *Boedo*, Almirante Brown 1771 (Tel.: 24695), E, with bath, hot water, clean, good value, near beaches; *Residencial San Martin*, Arenales nr Alberdi, E with bath, friendly; *Hospedaje Paraná*, Lamadrid 2749, near bus terminal, E, with bath; *Hospedaje Misiones*, nr railway station, at Calle Misiones and Pedro Luro, F, clean; *Niza*, Santiago del Estero 1843, E (F out of season), bath, clean, safe, friendly, restaurant; *Little Hotel*, Lamadrid 2461, near bus station, nice and cheap; *Monterrey*, Lamadrid 2627, F, clean, good. During summer months it is essential to book in advance. In the off-season, bargain everywhere.

Camping   *Pinar de la Serena* and other sites, reasonable prices.

Restaurants   *Taverna Vaska*, 12 de Octubre 3301, very popular seafood. *Sorrento*, Av. H. Yrigoyen 1549, Italian family style, excellent and reasonable. *Hostería del Caballito Blanco*, Av. Rivadavia, excellent, German decor. *Cantina Capri*, Belgrano 2161 (near Casino), not cheap but excellent value; *Los Cercos*, Belgrano, between Entre Ríos and Corrientes, for meat; *La Paella*, Entre Ríos, between Bolívar and Moreno, good; *La Caracola*, Nuevo Complejo Comercial Puerto, seafood, good but dear; *Don Pepito*, opposite casino, big portions, reasonable prices, very popular, recommended; *Raviolandia*, Colón y Heras, good, cheap; *La Tablita*, Av. Rivadavia, excellent *asado*. *Montecatini*, Av. Colón, good and cheap; *Comedor Naturista*, vegetarian, Av. Salta 1571, cheap, *Los Inmortales*, Corrientes 1662, good, moderately priced. Tea, coffee and spirits in port area at *Cristóbal Colón*.

Casino   Open December to end-April, 1600-0330; 1600-0400 on Sats. Winter opening, May-December, Mon.-Fri. 1500-0230; weekends 1500-0300. Entrance US$2.

Bank of London & South America, Ltd., Av. Luro 3201. Open 1000-1600. Exchange houses on San Martín and surroundings.

British Council (Cultura Inglesa) on San Luís 2498.

Post Office   on Santiago del Estero, Pedro Luro.

Tourist Office   opp. Casino, near beach, free maps; also at bus terminal.

Trains (ten each day) leave Buenos Aires from Constitución, 10 minutes from the centre by any bus marked "Constitución". The best trains (a/c) take 5 hours (US$4.55 tourist, US$6.10 first, US$8.75 Pullman), 3 times a day (and others). Book very early for Dec.-March trips. 25% reduction for persons under 20 years of age. In Buenos Aires tickets from Galerías Pacífico, Florida 753.

Buses   Bus station at corner of Alberti y Las Heras, convenient. Companies from Retiro terminal in Buenos Aires: El Cóndor, Micromar, Costera Criolla. Chevallier US$9.50, 5½ hrs. Bus to Miramar from Mar del Plata, US$2.80. El Cóndor and Rápido Argentino to La Plata, day and night, US$9. La Estrella goes to San Martín de los Andes, US$26, and Bariloche, US$32.50 (none direct; change at Bahía Blanca or Tres Arroyos). To Bahía Blanca, only Pampa, daily at 0800 and 1300, US$12.25, 9 hrs. For hitch-hiking S, take a colectivo to the monument to El Gaucho.

Air Services   Camet airport, 10 km. from town. Many flights daily to and from Buenos Aires with Austral and Aerolíneas Argentinas. *Remise* taxi from airport to town, US$6.

Outside the city the country is undulating. To the N (34 km.) is a lagoon—the Mar Chiquita—joined to the sea by a narrow channel. There is good fishing, yachting, boating and bathing here. Picturesque spots reached from the road to Balcarce are (19 km.) Laguna de los Padres, and Sierra de los Padres and (32 km. beyond) the Laguna La Brava, at the foot of the Balcarce hills. In these hills, 68 km. by paved road from Mar del Plata, is the town of **Balcarce,** a centre for hill visits to La Brava, above Ruca-Lauquén, and the Cinco Cerros, five hills most strangely

56 ARGENTINA

shaped. Balcarce is the birthplace of the great racing driver Juan Fangio; it has a racing circuit.

Hotel *Balcarce*, good, D.

Beyond Balcarce a paved road runs 103 km. to Tandil, also reached from Mar del Plata (254 km.) by rail. Tandil is reached by road from Buenos Aires via Azul.

Tandil, at the northern end of the Sierra del Tandil, a ridge of hills which run W from the sea into the pampa for 250 km., is 390 km. by road from Buenos Aires. It is a resort with fine views of *sierra* scenery. The air is splendidly clear and refreshing, and the Holy Week festivities are outstanding. Excursions to the Sierra La Aurora. Population: 70,000.

A balancing stone, the Sentinel Stone, is on top of Cerro Américo Rossi nearby.

Hotels *Plaza*, General Pinto 438, E, very friendly, clean, comfortable and quiet. *Continental; Palace; Roma; Eden; California; Manantial*. Others near railway station.

By Air Lapa flight Buenos Aires-Tandil.

From Mar del Plata, along the rocky sea-front to the SW, there are a road (53 km.) and railway line to Miramar.

Miramar, like Mar del Plata, is a summer bathing resort, but the cliffs backing the beach are higher, the surrounding hills more picturesque, and it is a good deal cheaper to stay at. There is a fine golf course at *Hotel Golf Roca* and a casino. Fourteen km. by road or railway to the S, amongst dunes and black rocks, is Mar del Sur (*Atlantic Hotel*) with good fishing in a lagoon and bathing on the beach.

Hotels *Atlántico*, somewhat run down; *Normandie; Ideal; Putamar; Gran Rex; Royal; Palace; Villa Cruz*, friendly, clean, near the beach, D.

Camping *Escargot, El Fortín, Miramar*. Many sites, reasonably priced.

Restaurant *El Aguila*, good value.

Railway *Cruz del Sur* daily train, via Mar del Plata, leaves Buenos Aires (Constitución) daily at 2345, arrives Miramar 0550; leaves Miramar 2205, arrives Buenos Aires 0500. Fares are US$9.40 Pullman, US$5.85 first and US$4.70 tourist class. *El Atlántico* train, daily at 1520 from Buenos Aires to Mar del Plata arriving at 2000, connects with a railcar service (*automotor*) to Miramar (US$6.15 extra), arriving 2140.

Bus Buenos Aires-Miramar with Cóndor, five daily, US$8, and Costera Criolla, four a day.

About 110 km. further by road along the coast to the SW is another famous seaside resort:

Necochea, 500 km. from Buenos Aires, is reached by Roca Railway in 10½ hours. It stands next to Mar del Plata in repute. The surroundings are picturesque. Visits can be paid to the Paseo del Puente, Punta Negra, the Cascada (or waterfalls) 16 km. up the Río Quequén Grande, Los Manantiales, and the Laguna de los Padres. Grain is exported from the port. Urban population: 50,000. About 100,000 tourists visit during the season, for the 24-km. long beach is one of the best in the country. A new municipal recreation complex, boasting a large modern casino and various sports facilities has recently been opened; entry charge is nominal. The casino is open in summer. Airport.

Hotels *Royal; Atlántico; San Miguel; Trocadero; Marino; Moderno*, Av. 79, No. 311, D, close to beach, friendly, helpful, bath and breakfast.

Restaurants *Parrilla La Rueda*, excellent beef, cheap, recommended; *La Vieja Taberna*, Calle 85, reasonable, good chicken and beef dishes; *Caviar*, by fishing wharf, good steak, chicken, seafood.

Railway Train No 117 (Mon.-Wed.-Fri.) leaves Buenos Aires (Constitución) at 1930, arrives Necochea 0645; leaves Necochea at 0025 Sun.-Wed.-Fri. arriving at 1150 at Buenos Aires. Fares are US$11.30 Pullman, US$7.30 first, US$6.00 tourist class.

Bus El Cóndor from Buenos Aires six times a day, Costera Criolla 5 times a day.

About 3½ km. across the mouth of the river from Necochea is

ARGENTINA 57

Quequén, with an excellent beach, good bathing, and pleasant scenery. The channel to the port has to be dredged daily.

Hotels *Quequén; Faro; Costa Azul.*

Camping *Monte Pasuvio* and *Doble J* (recommended) sites.

Over 320 km. westwards from Necochea by paved road through the coastal area is the port of Bahía Blanca, which can be reached by rail (900 km.), by air, or by a 688-km. paved road (Route 3) through Las Flores, Azul, Juárez and Tres Arroyos.

Azul, 264 km. from Buenos Aires, is a cattle centre amid picturesque *sierras* with an attractive plaza. Population: about 45,000. A good stopping place if driving S from Buenos Aires. The Cathedral is worth a visit and the river has been dammed to provide a water-sports centre.

Hotels *Gran Hotel Azul,* C, excellent cafeteria; *Argentino; Roma; Torino.*

Restaurant *Mitre,* Av. Mitre, *Londres.*

Tres Arroyos, about 195 km. from Bahía Blanca, is a cattle and wheat growing centre of 40,000 people. The inhabitants are mostly of Dutch origin; there are a Dutch consulate and a primary school named Holanda, supported by funds of the Argentine Dutch. There is also an important Danish colony. A 68-km. paved road runs S to the sea at the pleasant little resort of **Claromecó,** with a beautiful beach of dark sand backed by high dunes.

Hotels at Tres Arroyos *Alfil, Parque,* recommended (restaurant) and *Andrea* are best. *City, París, Plaza* and *Tres Arroyos* (friendly), all modest. **Restaurant** *Di Troppo,* near *Hotel Parque,* good.

Hotels at Claromecó *Claromecó* (only open in summer; restaurant); *Residencial La Perla.*

Camping at Claromecó Good campsite *Dunamar,* hot showers, fire pits and laundering basins, US$1 a day; also ACA campsite.

Bus Buenos Aires-Claromecó with El Cóndor, US$20. Tres Arroyos-Claromecó twice daily off season, extra buses from mid-December in season. Pampa bus to Mar del Plata 0650, 4½ hrs., US$5.50. Modern, efficient bus terminal a few blocks from centre of Tres Arroyos.

Bahía Blanca, population 200,000, the most important centre S of Mar del Plata, stands at the head of a large bay where the river Naposta runs into it. The region has over a million people. Bahía Blanca consists of the city itself, built back from the river front, and five ports at various distances from the city strung along the N bank of the Naposta: Arroya Pareja and the naval base of Puerto Belgrano at the mouth of the estuary; Puerto Ingeniero White, 23 km. inland, Puerto Galván, 3½ km. beyond, and Cuatreros, 8 km. upstream. Bahía Blanca is also a rail, air and pipeline transport terminal for the rich Río Negro valley.

The city has some fine modern buildings and two parks. In the Parque de Mayo are lakes fed by the River Naposta and interesting statuary. There is a Zoological Garden in Parque Independencia, on the outskirts.

To the E of Bahía Blanca is an enormous stretch of almost unoccupied sandy beaches, scarcely developed for visitors (in the afternoon, however, it is usually windy). Pehuén-Có, 70 km. away, is an example of the beaches with camping places, well shaded by pine trees. Signs to it on the main road 24 km. from Bahía Blanca. Another fine beach, with hotels and camping places (*El Americano* and *Monte Mar*), is **Monte Hermoso,** 2 hours by bus at 0830 and 1830, US$2.50 (106 km.) from Bahía Blanca. Return daily at 0900 and 2100. Good cheap meals, several restaurants. (Its hotels are open only Jan.-March: *Isabel, Americano, Ameghino,* E, *América*).

Local Holidays Sept. 24 (Our Lady of Mercy); Nov. 10 (Day of Tradition).

Hotels *Austral,* C, and *Del Sur,* C, with restaurants (not good in the former); *City Hotel,* Chiclana 132, D. *Italia,* very noisy, C; *Central Muñiz,* O'Higgins 23. *Atlántico,* Chiclana 251, E; *Argentino* (restaurant), Chiclana 466, E. Opposite railway station: *Residencial Roma,* D with private bath, cheaper without; *Hotel Rivadavia, Hosp. El Sibarita, Sud América.* Cheap: *Hogar,* Rodríguez 64, F, clean, good, near Plaza; *Tizón,* Chiclana 422, E.

ARGENTINA

Camping Balneario Maldonado, 5 km. from centre, bus from Plaza every ½ hr. until 1930 (not very reliable in evening), US$1.60 per tent; salt water swimming pool, US$0.80.

Restaurants *La Cigala*, opp. railway station, very good; *Il Vesuvio*, Chiclana 231, cheap and good. *Gambrines*, Arribeños 174, central. *El Tren Mixto*, D, Cerri 765, opposite railway station for Zapala. Very good seafood and fish at the port of Ingeniero White, e.g. *Michos* and *El Greco*; buses go there.

Bank of London and South America, Calle Chiclana 102. Citibank. Open 0800-1400 on Nov. 15-March 31, 1000-1600 on April 1-Nov. 14. **Casa de Cambio** Pullman, O'Higgins (in a Galería), good rates.

Airport Comandante Espora, 15 km. from centre. Austral and Aerolíneas Argentinas flights to Buenos Aires daily. To Comodoro Rivadavia, Sun. at 0800 arrive 1005. To Neuquén daily at 1900, arrive at 1955. Flights to Río Gallegos and Trelew on Sun., at 0800 arrive at 1135 and 0905, respectively.

Trains Two trains daily from Buenos Aires, fairly comfortable, go via Olavarría from Constitución; *Estrella del Valle* daily at 1225, arrive at 2240 with dining car, return 1020 daily, arrive 2050; and at 2150 daily, arriving 0840, returning at same time, arriving Buenos Aires 0825. Five other trains on different days of the week. Sleeper US$20.25; Pullman US$13.45; 1st class US$9.40, tourist US$7. Daily train to Bariloche, 19 hrs., sleeper US$29, pullman US$24, first class US$17, tourist, US$12. To Zapala at 2220 (arrive 1000), same classes as Bariloche. Can be cold. There is no other link between the Bahía Blanca-Bariloche line and the more northerly Bahía Blanca-Zapala line.

Roads Well built asphalt highway (Route 3) S to Comodoro Rivadavia; major route W to Neuquén and the Lake District. Several routes go North.

Buses Terminal is 2½ km. from centre in old railway station; no hotels nearby. To Trelew, 3 per week, US$20, 734 km. Bahía Blanca-Río Gallegos with Don Otto US$60; Bahía Blanca-Mar del Plata bus, US$12.25 with Pampa, 7-8 hrs., 469 km. Bus Bahía Blanca-Río Colorado US$5.20. Bus Buenos Aires-Bahía Blanca frequent US$17. Bahía Blanca-Neuquén at 2130 and 2230, 9hrs, US$15.50, 580 km., one company only. To Zapala daily at 0630 and 1030.

Hitch-hiking S or W from Bahía Blanca is possible but not too easy. N to Buenos Aires, take bus 10 to outskirts, or bus 510 from centre to Ruta 51 (10 km).

Some 100 km. to the N is the Sierra de la Ventana, a favourite area for excursions from Bahía Blanca. The small town **Sierra de la Ventana,** with hotels (*Golf*, near station, is OK) and the excellent *Don Diego* campsite (hot water, open all year round) is a good centre for exploring the hills. Tres Picos, rising bare and barren from the rich farmlands of 1,070 metres, is only 6¼ km. away. There is a 9-hole golf course, and good trout fishing in the Río Sauce Grande.

193 km. N of Bahía Blanca by road/rail through Saavedra is

Carhué, served by three railways, one of which, via Bolívar, runs to Buenos Aires (603 km.). Five km. away is a sheet of water, Lake Epecuén, which covers over 40,000 hectares and is over twenty times saltier than the sea. No fish can live in it. These waters are recommended for chronic rheumatism and skin diseases, and thousands of visitors bathe in them. There are many hotels and *residenciales* at the lake side. A fort used in the wars against the Indians is now a museum of those wars. Pop.: 18,000.

Hotels at Lake Epecuén With restaurant: *Gran Parque Patera, Plage, Elkie, Victoria, Rambla, Cuatro Hermanos, Villa Marta, Italia, Española, Las Familias, Gran Rose*. Also: *El Lago, Castello*.

Hotels at Carhué With restaurant: *Buenos Aires, Marconi*. Without: *Volpe, Bristol*.

About 38 km. by road NE of Carhué, on the Roca Railway, which runs to the capital, is **Guaminí** (Hotels: *La Aragonesa, Roma*), a small but pleasant summer hill resort of 3,500 inhabitants on the shore of Laguna del Monte, not as salty as Lake Epecuén; *pejerrey* fishing is one of the attractions.

Santa Rosa (Hotel: *Calfacura*, 4-star, no restaurant, B without breakfast, but excellent steak restaurant around the corner), capital of the Province of La Pampa, is 332 km. NW of Bahía Blanca by road, and can be reached (619 km.) by Route 5, via Chivilcoy and Pehuajó, from Buenos Aires.

Córdoba and the North-West

The pattern of the land, from the crest of the Andes in the W to the river Paraguay in the E, consists of a high, dry Altiplano rising to a Puna cut into on its eastern face by rivers which flow into the Lowlands. This configuration of the land, similar to Bolivia, is carried southwards into all the north-western provinces of Argentina as far S as Tucumán, but the altitudes in Argentina are not so great as in Bolivia, and the whole area not so large. The E-running rivers born on the Puna flow into the Chaco; their broad valleys, or *quebradas*, make access to the heights comparatively easy. Between the base of the Puna and the Chaco lie a series of front range hogback hills running roughly from N to S; the lowlands between them are known in Argentina as the *valles*. Tucumán is the southern boundary of this kind of land. N of Tucumán crops can be grown without irrigation (though there is irrigation where the soil is absorbent) but S of Tucumán is droughty land, with long N-S ranges of low hills such as the Sierras de Córdoba, set in plains which have salt flats and swamps in the depressions.

Settlement and Economy The Puna is windswept, stony and treeless: the only growth is a low, blackish shrub (*tola*), and an occasional cactus. The first Spanish expedition from Bolivia came down the main Inca road (long since disappeared in Argentina) in 1542. A little later a better and lower route was discovered—the main route used today—descending from La Quiaca to Jujuy through the Quebrada de Humahuaca, with rugged and colourful mountain ranges closing in on both sides. Along this new route the Spaniards pressed S and founded a group of towns in the north-west: Santiago del Estero (the first) in 1551, Tucumán in 1565, Córdoba in 1573, Salta in 1582, La Rioja in 1591, and Jujuy in 1592. Mendoza (1561), San Juan (1562), and San Luis (1598) were all colonized by people who crossed the passes from Chile. All these colonies were hemmed in by the warlike tribes of the Pampas, and until the war of extermination in 1880 the route from Buenos Aires to Córdoba was often unsafe. The Indians raided frequently for cattle, which they drove S and over the Andes for sale in Chile.

During the whole of the colonial era the trade of the area, mostly in mules, was with Bolivia and Peru rather than with Buenos Aires, which was little more than a garrison and smuggling port. The mules were bred mainly in the plains between Rosario, Santa Fe, and Córdoba, and driven finally into Salta for the great fair in February and March.

Historically, Tucumán was always important, for the two river routes of the Salado and the Dulce across the dry belt forced the mule traffic to pass through Tucumán on the way to Salta. But Tucumán, unlike Salta, did not sink into insignificance with the ending of the mule trade: it was saved from that by the advent of sugar. Tucumán produced most of Argentina's sugar before the collapse of the industry in the 1960s. Tobacco is becoming important in the area, and an important factor in the North West is the growth of tourism.

In nearly all the provincial towns everything shuts between 1200 and 1600 except restaurants, hotels and post offices. There is nothing to do or see, and we suggest that this is a good time for travelling; buses are generally preferable to trains, being faster (except to Córdoba). (Panamericana buses have been recommended in the NW as new, clean and with a good service.)

From Buenos Aires to Córdoba

If hitch-hiking, take the train from Retiro (San Martín line) to Pilar to reach main Córdoba highway via Rosario. There are two main road routes: the shorter (713 km.) via Rosario and the longer (835 km.) via Río Cuarto. The latter goes through **San Antonio de Areco**—also on the Mitre Railway— 113 km. NW of Buenos Aires. Here is the Museo Gauchesco Ricardo Güiraldes, on Camino Güiraldes and Aureliano, a typical *estancia* of the late 19th century with manor house, mill, tavern, open Wed.-Sun., 1000-1200, 1500-1800 in summer; in winter 1000-1200 and 1400-1700. Check if it is open in Jan.-Feb. Güiraldes was a writer who described *gaucho* life; his best-known book is *Don Segundo Sombra*. Día de la

60 ARGENTINA

NORTH-WEST ARGENTINA

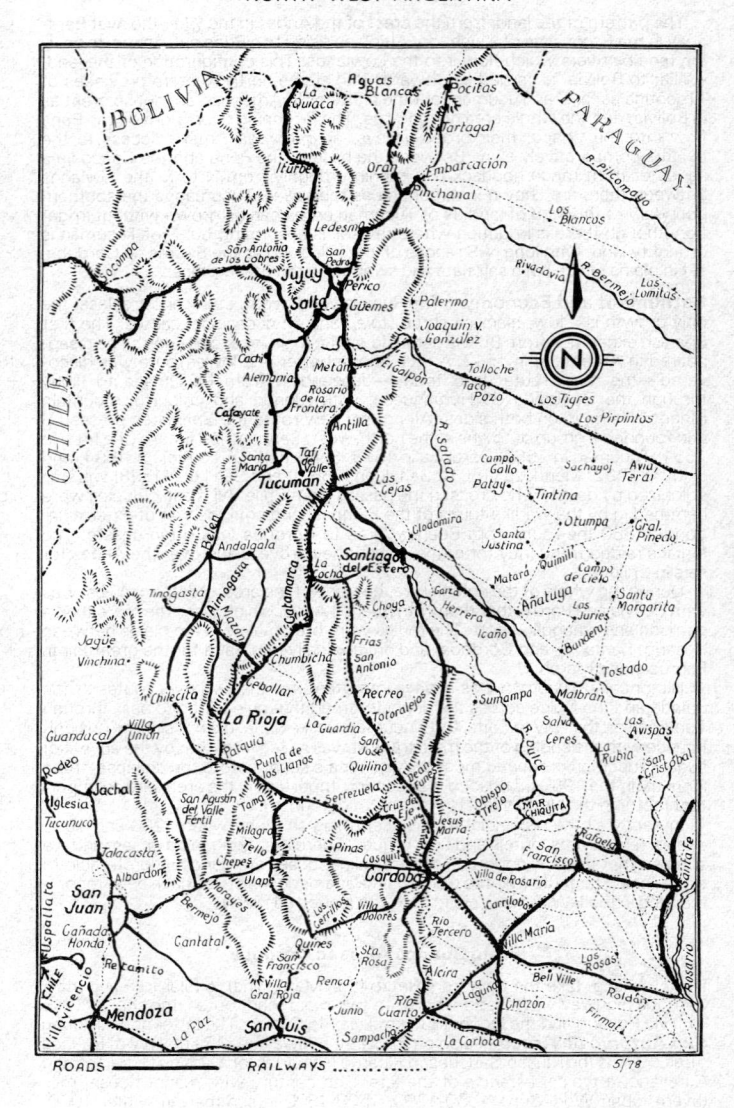

ROUGH SKETCH

ARGENTINA 61

Tradición is a *gaucho* festival with traditional parades, games, events on horseback, music and dance, celebrated on Nov. 10, 11 and 12 each year.

Camping near the centre of town; 12 km. from centre, auto-camping *La Porteña* on the Güiraldes *estancia*, good access roads. Six hotels. Many handicrafts, mainly *gaucho* objects, ceramics, silver, leather, colonial furniture. The Argentine artist Gasparini has a museum-school where he sells his drawings of *gauchos* to tourists; Calle de los Martínez, between Bolívar and Rivadavia. There is also a local natural history museum, Parque Metri, on Matheu and Hernández. For tourist information go to the Sub-Dirección de Turismo at Alsina and Lavalle. Tel.: 2101. Opposite Museo Gauchesco is *Hostería del Palomar*, typical barbecue; *Restaurant La Porteña* on the riverside, typical, very good.

Beyond Pergamino, 146 km., is **Venado Tuerto,** a pleasant town of 58,000 people with a fine Country Club at which race meetings and tournaments are held twice a year. At **Río Cuarto,** 70,000 people, there is a golf club and a fine old municipal building with an outlook tower worth seeing.

Hotels *Gran*, on Plaza, D, new, 1st class; *City Hotel*, good, D. *Opera*, 25 de Mayo, C; *Victoria*, Buenos Aires 183, E, small beds; *Gran Hotel Mendoza*, Constitución 483; *Alihué*, Sarsfield 69, E, good value, very friendly, big rooms. Near bus station on Calle Sobremonte 100-200 block are 3 cheap *residenciales*, *El Ciervo*, *Hospedaje El Bambi*, *Residencial Monge*, all F.

Restaurants *Cantina Italiana Sorrento*, fair. Best exchange rate at Banco de la Nación; post office on plaza. *Pizzería Costa Azul*, Belgrano 67, sit in or out, pleasant.

Buses Buenos Aires, US$22. Bus to Mendoza, US$24; to Córdoba US$7.75; frequent departures to Santiago US$35, daily.

Córdoba is 225 km. N of Río Cuarto across flatlands and rolling hills. About halfway along the road runs on the retaining wall of the great Río Tercero dam; the artificial lake here is used for recreation. Río Tercero has gained in importance with the development of groundnut plantations in the area and a local military factory. *Hotel Argentino*, adequate, D, with a/c.

Villa María, on the Mitre Railway and at a vital crossroads on the main Buenos Aires-Córdoba road, where it meets the most convenient highway route linking central Chile with Paraguay, Uruguay and Brazil, is a prosperous agricultural town. Hotel: *City*, D. Restaurant: *La Churrasquita*.

Córdoba, capital of Córdoba Province and Argentina's second city, has about a million inhabitants; it stands at an altitude of 440 metres. The district is well known for its countryside and the city for its buildings, for Córdoba was founded as early as 1573. Its university, founded in 1613, was the first in the country. The city faces eastward towards the pampas with ranges of *sierras* rising in three chains to the N, S, and W. The heart of the city is Plaza San Martín (the Liberator's statue is there). On the western side is the old Cabildo, now the police headquarters. Next to it stands the Cathedral, started in 1697 and finished 1787. The neo-gothic Church of the Sacred Heart (Sagrado Corazón), built in 1933, at Buenos Aires e Yrigoyen, is worth a visit. Córdoba was once a very picturesque place, but modernization is catching up fast. Pedestrianization schemes have recently improved the centre.

On Calle Independencia, leading S from the Plaza San Martín, is the Church and Convent of Santa Teresa (beautiful doorway, 1770). An old colonial building, the Viceroy's House (Casa del Virrey), is on Calle Rosario, E of the central plaza; it houses the Historical and Colonial Museum, open Tues.-Fri. 0830-1300, 1530-1930, Sat.-Sun. 0900-1200. N of Plaza San Martín, on Calle Rivadavia, is the Church of La Merced, whose old colonial pulpit is well worth seeing. The Church of La Compañía, on Calles Trejo y Sanabria, with a simple façade, dates from about 1650 and is a far better building than the Cathedral; its façade was rebuilt in the 20th century. The barrel vault and cupola, built entirely of Paraguayan cedar, are unique. There are some pleasant small 18th century churches with striking bell gables and undulating pediments. The Natural History Museum, previously in the Cabildo, has moved to Av. Yrigoyen 115 (open Mon.-Fri. 0830-1230 and 1430-1830, Sat.-Sun. 0900-1200). There is a very interesting and well

62 ARGENTINA

laid out Museum of Mineralogy; ask permission to visit from Dra. Hebe Gay at Universidad de Ciencias Exactas.

The Academy of Fine Arts, the theatre and the Olmos School are near the Plaza Vélez Sarsfield (there is a statue to this jurist, who gave Argentina its civil code). A diagonal, Avenida Yrigoyen, runs to the round Plaza España, where the Museum of Fine Arts (open Mon.-Fri., 0900-1300) is housed in a pillared building. E from this plaza is Parque Sarmiento, where there is a Zoological Garden with a serpentarium and a small waterfall. Argentina's main observatory is at the S end of Calle General Artigas. Córdoba is a good shopping city, but prices tend to be higher than in Buenos Aires. Pajas Blancas airport, 15 km. from the city, is modern and has a very good restaurant. Taxi to airport, US$10. **N.B.:** Churches are open mornings and after 1600.

The great San Roque dam defends the city from avalanches of water, regulates the flow of the Río Primero, provides drinking water and electric power, feeds two large systems of irrigation, and forms a blue lake ringed by hills which has become a tourist resort.

Local Holidays July 6 (Foundation of the City); September 30 (St. Jerome).

Industries Córdoba is the centre of Argentina's motor industry.

Hotels Best are: *Ritz*, San Jerónimo 495, B; *Mediterráneo*, Av. M.T. de Alvear 10, B; *Sussex*, Buenos Aires 59, B, comfortable, roomy, discounts for ACA members; *Palace*, Buenos Aires 101, C; *Royal*, Blvd. Reconquista 180, C; all these have garages. Also *Crillón*, Rivadavia 85, D, very friendly, comfortable. More economical: *Rivera*, Balcarce 74, near bus station, D, friendly, clean. *Grand Hotel Bristol*, Corrientes 64, F, bathroom, a/c, telephone. For economy: *Pensión Susy*, Entre Ríos, E; *Los Alpes*, near railway station; *Sportsman*, San Jerónimo 590, F, near bus and railway station; *Residencial Plaza*, Balcarce 336, 150 metres from bus station, dirty, friendly and quiet, E; *del Sol*, Balcarce 144, E with bath, clean, fan, close to stations, recommended; *Gran Terminal*, Pasaje Corrientes 64, a/c, next to bus station, E; *Central*, hot water, 100 metres from bus station, F, good; restaurant, cheap and good; *Mallorca*, on Balcarce, quite clean and near bus and railway station; *Hospedaje Apolo*, San Jerónimo 462, is nearby. Plenty of hotels of all classes on San Jerónimo. Cheap restaurants in the area. *Plaza* on Balcarce doesn't take singles, E, or F without bath, clean, friendly, quiet, one block behind bus terminal. *Hospedaje Suiza*, Corrientes 569, near bus terminal, very friendly; *Entre Ríos*, close to bus terminal on Entre Ríos, F, reasonably clean, hot water. Also on the same street, *Berlín*, F, clean and friendly. Small, clean and nice, family-run: *Residencial Mi Valle*, Corrientes 586, washing facilities, E; *Pasajeros*, Corrientes 564, F, pleasant. *Soledad* (not very clean), San Jerónimo, friendly, cheap. *Florida*, F, clean, Rosario de Santa Fe 459, recommended. Across the pedestrian bridge from the top of the bus station into a residential precinct are many low cost hotels and restaurants, around the precinct park or ½ block into bordering streets.

Camping Nearest site in Alta Gracia. Local bus takes 40 mins.

Restaurants Good but not cheap: *Crillón Hotel* (US$8 per head). Good food and moderate prices: *Florida Grill*, across from *Hotel Crillón*, good, informal meals. Next to *Crillón* is *Jerónimo*, simple, pleasant, US$7 per head. *Maxim's*, top floor of *Sussex Hotel*, good food, air conditioned, good view of plaza and cathedral. There are also numerous grills of all categories on the outskirts of the city, especially in the Cerro de las Rosas district, for meals out-of-doors when the weather is suitable. Restaurant in *Hotel Familiar*, S. Jerónimo, near railway station, cheap and good, recommended. *Pappagallo*, Av. San Jerónimo; *Café Gents*, Av. San Jerónimo. *La Cantina*, Rivadavia 30, central. *Restaurant Alborada*, nr bus station, good meals. Two reasonable restaurants: *Romagnolo*, opposite the Mitre railway station, recommended, and *Comedor Albéniz*, opposite Alto Córdoba station, a bit noisy. Try also at bus station. Not far from the *Romagnolo* are cheaper *Mayo*, *El Indio* and *Hotel Italia* restaurants (around the corner). *Rigoletto*, Entre Ríos 73, cheap meals, *La Cabaña*, Maipú 230, cheap and good. *La Casona*, Rivera Indarte 337, O.K.; *Don Pipo*, Santa Rosa 212, good, cheap *parrilladas*.

Rent-a-Car Avis and Al International at airport and in the centre. Entre Ríos 70. Tel.: 42-036/38 central depôt.

Casino Nearby, at Alta Gracia.

Bank of London and South America, Buenos Aires 23. Citibank. Oct.-March, 0730-1330; April-Sept., 0800-1400. Exchange at banks and following travel agencies: Exprinter, Rivadavia 39, opposite is Maguitur, Rivadavia 30, good rates, Viacor, Avincor, Epoca and Barujel, San Martín 37. If travelling N it is advisable to change money in Córdoba; not so easy further N.

Post Office Parcel Service on the ground floor of the Correo Central, Av. Colón 201, beside the customs office, up to 20 kg; wrapping service for small fee.

British Council Blvd. San Juan 137, has a good library.

ARGENTINA 63

Goethe Institut, Chacabuco 476, open Mon.-Fri., 1700-2100.
Laundry Laundromat (self-service) at Tucumán 135; also Chacabuco 32, and Av. Colón 300.
Tourist Office Dirección Provincial de Turismo, San Jerónimo 62, 1st floor. Information centres: Plaza San Martín on San Jerónimo and Obispo Mercadillo, Rosario de Santa Fe 39.
Club Andino, Duarte Quirós 1591.

Air Airport bus leaves terminal opposite railway station. Several flights to Buenos Aires daily, about 1 hr.; to Mendoza daily at 1400 (55 mins.); to Tucumán at 1235 daily exc. Sun. arr. 1335. Night flights: Buenos Aires to Córdoba Thurs. at 2230. Córdoba-Mar del Plata Thurs. and Sat. at 2350, returns Tues. and Fri. at 2330. Aerolíneas Argentinas, Av. Colón 520. Austral, Av. Colón 678.

Buses Excellent bus station with Tourist Office, many public telephones, shops, bank, post office, restaurants, and showers in bathrooms (about 6 blocks from centre), crowded at weekends when people travel to neighbouring resorts. Buenos Aires-Córdoba (US$17.50 with Costera Criolla or with Cacorba) by bus takes about 13 hours, and on from Córdoba to Salta and Jujuy with Panamericano, about 12 and 15 hours (US$24.50). Chevallier (Plaza Miserere) Buenos Aires to Córdoba via Route 8, four services, at 0600, 1600, 2015 and 2345; via Route 9 at 0745, 2100, 2200, and 2340, US$22.25. Many buses on both routes. Bus to Mendoza (10 hours), book early, US$13. Bus to Tucumán, US$10. Córdoba-Posadas (Expreso Singer) Tues., Thurs., Sat., 1730 arrive at Posadas at 1335; Thurs. and Sat. bus continues to Iguazú arriving 1930 next day, no air-conditioning. Onda operates a service from Paraná via Santa Fe and Rosario to and from Córdoba. Bus Córdoba-Asunción (Paraguay) direct with Brújula, four times a week, US$32.50. Also with Cacorba. Regular bus between Córdoba and Montevideo (Uruguay). In general, it is best to travel from Córdoba if you are going N, as at stations in between it may be hard to get a seat; a seat is only guaranteed if one pays US$1 extra. To La Rioja 3-4 a day with Cotil and Cotap; some go on to Catamarca. Córdoba-La Rioja-Aimogasta-Tinogasta-Fiambala with El Cóndor, Tues., Thurs., Fri.; leaves Tinogasta 1140 arr. Fiambala 1240, returns from Fiambala same day 1445, from Tinogasta at 1600 (see also p. 90). La Calera bus leaves Córdoba for Belén (Catamarca) on Mon., Wed., Fri., at 2100, arr. Belén 1030. Route: Córdoba, Dean Funes, Estación San Martín, Chumbicha, Saujil, Andalgalá, Belén. Return journey, via Andalgalá, Wed., Fri., Sun., dep. 1600 arr. Andalgalá 1735, dep. 1750, arr. Córdoba 0055. Cacorba, efficient a/c buses, serve Villa Carlos Paz, Cosquín and La Falda in the Sierras de Córdoba.

Railways The Mitre Railway *Rayo de Sol* night train takes 11 hours to and from Buenos Aires. Tourist class US$7.80, 1st class US$10.45, Pullman US$15.05, Sleeper US$21.85, car transporter daily. *Rayo de Sol* leaves Buenos Aires (Retiro) 2100 daily and Córdoba 2030 daily. The Belgrano Railway runs *El Norteño* train on Tues., and Fri., from Buenos Aires (Retiro) at 1000; from Córdoba, 0750, Wed., Sat. (12 hours), US$8 tourist, US$10.70 first class, no sleepers. The Alta Córdoba railway station for long-distance journeys is a good 2 km. from the city centre. The No. 6 bus will transport you from the Mitre railway station to the Belgrano station. Two trains per week to Salta via Tucumán, Tues., and Fri., 1000. It is advisable to check all trains as services are sometimes suspended without notice. The *Rayo de Sol* trains connect with bus services to various resorts in the Sierras de Córdoba, and the *Norteño* to La Rioja and Catamarca.

The **Sierras of Córdoba**, rising in undulating hills from the pampas, their lower slopes often wooded, particularly in the S, attract each year a large number of visitors. The highest peak, Champaquí (2,975 metres) has a small lake about 2,550 metres up. The hills run, roughly, for 500 km. from N to S; west of Córdoba they are 150 km. wide. There are three ranges of them: the Sierra Grande, the longest, in the middle, with Sierra Chica to the E and Sierra de Guisapampa and its continuation, the Sierra de Pocho, to the W. Swimming, riding, walking, climbing fishing, tennis and golf are the main recreations of a holiday in these hills. A network of good roads gives panoramic drives and dramatic contrasts of scenery: quiet valleys, deep gorges, mountain passes and plateaux. The region's climate is dry, sunny and exhilarating throughout the year.

At the foot of the Sierra Chica are three large dams to contain the waters of the Río Primero, One is at Río Molinos (29 km. from Córdoba, Route 5, good *pejerrey* and trout-fishing; bus to Villa Carlos Paz, US$2), and Río Tercero. There are two other large dams in the hills, at Cruz del Eje and La Viña. They provide power and irrigation, and the lakes are in themselves attractive. The Government keeps them stocked with fish. Sailing is popular.

Information can be obtained at travel agencies, at the Dirección Provincial de Turismo or at Casa de Córdoba at Callao 332, Buenos Aires.

Note There are innumerable good hotels and *pensiones* in the Córdoba mountain region; names are therefore not always given.

64 ARGENTINA

A road running NW from Córdoba through the Punilla valley leads to the following string of resorts shadowed by the Sierra Chica. Many of them have daily bus connection with trains between Buenos Aries and Córdoba:

Villa Carlos Paz (buses from Córdoba bus terminal every half hour, 36 km., US$ 1.00; Buenos Aires-Villa Carlos Paz with Costera Criolla—bus terminal on Calle Alvear), on lovely man-made Lake San Roque, a pleasant resort in the Punilla valley and the nearest to Córdoba. Tours possible on amphibian buses which go as far as the two dams on the lake. Launch trips, US$2.40 for 2½ hours. Much frequented by the British community in Argentina. At the Casa de Gaspar, Miguel Cané and El Redentor, roller-skating and optical illusions, Fri.-Sun. 1400-1900 out of season. A chair-lift (US$2.10) runs up the slopes to a tearoom and night club overlooking the valley, between 0900 and 1900. Bus tours to areas such as Sierra Chica, for those who like snack bars, fun slides and gravity-defying houses. Plenty of hotels, big and small, e.g. *Gran Lourdes*, Cassaffouth 63, C; *Hostal del Sol*, Av. San Martín y Lope de Vega, D; *Residencial Panambi*. Av. Uruguay y Liniers, D; *El Ciervo de Oro*, Hipólito Yrigoyen 995, on the lake, D. *Las Junturas*, Florida 181, excellent, clean and friendly, hot shower, use of barbecue and fridge. *Riviera*, E with bath, clean, recommended; *Hospedaje Don Edwards*, Calle Beethoven, 50 metres from Lake, F, run by a friendly Polish woman, clean, washing facilities, coffee, supply own food. Cheap *Recreo El Ancla* across the road. Cheapest and cleanest *Hostería Mil-Gui*, Irigoyen 615, with barbecue facilities. Camping at ACA campground, and associated sites at *Las Toldetías* and *El Mirador Lago San Roque*; there is a municipal campground with swimming at Bialet Massé, N of Carlos Paz. Best buys: leather mats, bags, pottery. Tourist office at bus station, very friendly. *Restaurant Carlos Paz* highly recommended for food and setting. *Restaurant Parrilla Mingo*, Av. Uruguay opp. *Hotel Uruguay*, not cheap but good, *Black and White*, reasonable, good food. Post Office and telephone on Av. Gral. San Martín.

Cosquín. Bus Córdoba-Cosquín US$1.40. with La Capillense; 1½ hrs., via Carlos Paz or with La Calera via the San Roque dam. 63 km. by Route 38 from Córdoba, on the banks of a river. Altitude, 720 metres. Beautiful surroundings, with a dry healing air. Camping on south bank of river. Friendly tourist office at San Martía 560, *Hotel La Serrana*, P. Ortiz 740, near bus station, F, friendly, good. Take a bus to the Pan de Azúcar (sugar loaf) from where there is a good view over the Punilla valley, at 0930 ret. 1630 or 2 hrs. walk. Chairlift to top (all year round). 19 km. on is **Valle Hermoso**, near La Falda (buses from Villa Carlos Paz). Altitude, 850 metres. Old restored chapel of San Antonio, a little gem. Riding, motoring. Youth hostel, address "Steinhaus", dirty, no heating, very cold, US$2 p.p., pay extra for gas. Camping near river, US$0.60 p.p., all facilities, but not too clean. A famous folklore festival is held in the last half of January at Cosquín, from 2200-0500, tickets from US$6 per night. (Recent reports suggest that the festival is becoming commercialized.)

La Falda, 82 km. from Córdoba. Bus 2 hrs., US$1.90. Altitude, 933 metres. Helpful tourist offices at bus station and in old railway station building. Pleasant at all seasons. Model railway museum at Las Murallas zoo at the end of Av. 25 de Mayo. *Hotel Fénix*, 25 de Mayo 218, good, F. *Restaurant El Bochín*, Av. España 117, good, cheap. Students of all nations welcome at Córdoba University holiday centre at Vaquerías, 2 km. from La Falda. Camping near small river. (Bus from Buenos Aires, US$19.50) Excursions to Quebrada Chica, Cascada del Molino. 3½ km. on by Route 38 is **Huerta Grande**, at 971 metres, a bathing resort with good fishing and medicinal waters.

Round trip excursion to **Cascadas de Olaén**. Take the road to Valle Hermoso back 10 km. towards Cosquín, then follow dirt road about 12½ km. to the crossing marked "Cascadas de Olaén"; from here walk 4½ km. to the falls: quite spectacular canyon—the water splashes into a small lake full of little fish. Return to the dirt road and 2½ km. to a monolith and another dirt road, which leads to La Falda. See the Pampa de Olaén, where there are many quartz mines.

Bus connections with Uruguay from La Falda on Mon., Fri., Sat. and Sun. at 1730, arriving at 1200 next day with CORA (of Uruguay). Connections to Rosario, Mendoza, Catamarca, Santiago del Estero, Tucumán, Salta and Jujuy. Route: La Falda-Córdoba-Santa Fe-Paraná-Colón-Paysandú-Montevideo. Expresso Encón operates a similar service with similar connections.

Candonga, altitude 810 metres, 11 km. from Huerta Grande, is in the Sierra Chica. The road from Córdoba city (55 km.) goes through Argüello, Villa Allende, Río Ceballos (campsites *Río Camping* and *La Quebrada*), and Salsipuedes (*AT Camping*) to El Manzano, where it branches off to the left leading to La Cumbre. The historic and beautiful Colonial church at Candonga, now a National Monument, was built in 1730 as an oratory of the Jesuit Estancia of Santa Gertrudis. The arch protrudes to form a porch which covers the entrance.

La Cumbre, 97 km. from Córdoba. Bus, US$7.50. Altitude, 1,141 metres. Trout streams with good fishing from November to April. Swimming, golf, tennis. Has an airport. Charming small inn, *Victoria*; *La Cumbre Inn*, large and commercial, grand view. Good restaurants, *La Perla* and *El Toboso*.

Cruz Chica, altitude, 1,067 metres, has very English houses and gardens in pine woods. Most attractive. Good English boys' school.

ARGENTINA 65

Los Cocos, just N of Cruz Chica, is a delightful, extremely popular mountain resort with 3 first rate hotels and many holiday houses. *Hostería Zanier*, E, full board C, recommended. Hang-gliding nearby at Cuchi Corral.

Capilla del Monte, 106 km. from Córdoba, (bus US$14, *Hospedaje Italiano*, C, good and clean, showers, opposite bus station; municipal campsite on the way to Cerro Uritorco and also some 9½ km. from Capilla del Monte) in the heart of the Sierras. Altitude, 914 metres. Medicinal waters, rocks and waterfalls and wide views; see particularly El Zapato rock, despite its graffiti. Excursions in the hills, particularly to Cerro Uritorco (1,950 metres). Good trout fishing at Los Alazanes dam; and good path on Uritorco, walk takes 2½ hrs. Permission to walk obtainable from a house beyond the river crossing (US$0.60). Grand views from the top if not misty. You can walk on to the direct dirt road to San Marcos Sierra (22 km.); many parakeets and small farmhouses. Along the way you will also see pretty views from a high spot to the *Cruz del Eje* dam and see one of the two villages with its own "micro-climate" (the other is Merlo in San Luis Province) and own honey production—try that made from carob (*algarrobo*) blossom (1 kg. about US$2). Excellent trout fishing at Tío Mayo, an hour from Capilla del Monte by car.

A road runs N from Córdoba to Asochinga and Jesús María.

Asochinga, 63 km. N of Córdoba by road via such pleasant little townships as Villa Allende, Unquillo, and La Granja. Altitude, 700 metres. Picturesque, dating from colonial days. Nearby is Santa Catalina, originally a Jesuit mission founded in 1622 and the most elaborate Jesuit establishment in the hills around Córdoba. (See the church begun in 1754, workshops and stone conduits.)

Jesús María, 51 km. N of Córdoba. Altitude, 533 metres. Good 18th century Jesuit church and the remains of its once famous winery; in the cloister is an excellent Museo Jesuítico, said to be one of the best on the continent (closed Mon.). Good trout, *dorado*, and carp fishing in winter. Road to Córdoba paved but rough. Some 4 km. N of Jesús María is Sinsacate, with an interesting church. There is also a fine colonial posting inn, with long, deep verandah and chapel attached. Beyond Jesús María the paved road runs another 132 km. to **Villa de María**, the birthplace of Leopoldo Lugones, a poet of country life. His house is a museum. *Hotel City*, good, at Villa de María, D.

From Jesús María you can take a bus to **Cerro Colorado**, 160 km. N. of Córdoba and 10 km. W of Route 9. There are more than 30,000 rock paintings by the Comechingones Indians. Cheap accommodation and camping in the Cerro Colorado archaeological park.

South-west of Córdoba a scenic road climbs through the Sierra Grande to another chain of resorts, Mina Clavero, Villa Dolores and Yacanto.

Mina Clavero, 140 km. from Córdoba by bus (US$9) through grand lake and hill scenery, and curious palm trees. A charming town, and good centre for exploring the high *sierra*. There is a nice church and a museum, dedicated by a French archaeologist, 5 km. from the main square, called "Rocsen" open 0900 till sunset. Furniture, minerals, instruments, animals, etc. Altitude, 915 metres. (Restaurant: *Rincón Suizo*, Calle Champaquí, good pastries.) Good new road from Mina Clavero over the Sierra Grande to *Hotel El Cóndor*, goes to Carlos Paz—not yet asphalted. Lovely views from El Cóndor over Lake San Roque. If hitching from Córdoba down this route to Mendoza, best starting point is Ycho Cruz, beyond Carlos Paz.

Villa Dolores, 187 km. from Córdoba (bus takes 5 hrs.), 48 km. from Mina Clavero. Altitude, 529 metres. Population: 10,000. The road from Córdoba crosses the two mountain ranges to reach finally the Pampa de Achala, a huge desert plateau of grey granite. (Camping: nearest site is Piedra Pintada, 15 min-bus-ride away, pleasant little village well situated for walks into mountains.) Bus to San Luis 5¼ hrs.

Rail Buenos Aires (Retiro)-Villa Dolores: *Sierras Grandes* train via Villa Mercedes, Mon., Wed., Fri. at 1615, arriving 0800; leaving V. Dolores 2240 Tues., Thurs., Sun, arriving Retiro 1350. Fares: Pullman US$23, first US$16.45, tourist US$12.75. Car transporter from Buenos Aires on Fri., from Villa Dolores on Sun.

From San Javier you can explore **Champaqui** (altitude 2,975 metres). For top, follow path to Capilla La Constancia, set in river valley with pine and nut trees, 2-3 hrs. Take water from here, then cross the river (path), keep left through a pinewood up to a mountain range and follow it up to the top of a huge plateau. Good path, about 4-5 hrs, and then you reach a square enclosure, whence you keep left. Follow stone mounds about 2 hrs. until you see the higher of two peaks, which is Champaqui. Lovely views, descent 4 hrs. to La Constancia. Not to be attempted in misty weather.

Yacanto, near Villa Dolores, at the foot of Champaquí, in a region of woods and waterfalls. Reached by road from Villa Dolores railway station. Curative waters.

A road S from Córdoba runs to Alta Gracia and to the Río Tercero dam.

Alta Gracia, altitude 580 metres, 48 km. SW of Córdoba. (Bus 40 mins, every 15 mins, US$0.75.) Interesting colonial church, finished c. 1762, and buildings housing a museum about the

66 ARGENTINA

Estancia de Alta Gracia, founded in 1588 and taken over by the Jesuits in 1643, beside Lake Trajamar. There is also the Museo Manuel de Falla on Pellegrini Final, open Tues.-Fri. 0900-1900, entry US$0.30, where the composer spent his last years. Also Museo del Virrey Liniers, open Tues.-Sun. 0900-1200 and 1500-1800. Take the local bus to La Paysanita or La Serranita for a quiet environment (but no cheap accommodation). *Hotel Sierras* (with 9-hole golf course and also croquet; not modern, but almost Edwardian comfort, attractive service, good, plentiful food but expensive, with 40% taxes *et al.*) *Hostería Reina*, Urquiza 129, good. Two camping sites, one scruffy, the other better and free in winter, which is by golf course. A few reasonably priced restaurants in town centre. Tourist office inside clock tower by Lake Trajamar. New casino. To the Bosque Alegre and Observatory it is 24 km., open Thurs. 1600-1800 Sun. 1000-1200 and 1600-1800. Good views over Córdoba, Alta Gracia and the Sierra Grande. To the Río Tercero dam is 79 km.; on the lake is a workers' holiday colony and an *Unidad Turística*.

Villa General Belgrano, 85 km. S of Córdoba on Route 36, is a completely German town founded by the surviving interned seamen from the *Graf Spee*, some of whom still live in the town. It is a pleasant resort and a good centre for excursions in the surrounding mountains. Fashionable expensive hotels and some cheaper guesthouses at *La Cumbrecita*, a Swiss-type hamlet, no regular bus-service.

Tucumán, Salta and Jujuy

The broad-gauge Mitre Railway and the metre-gauge Belgrano Railway both run N to Tucumán, 522 km. away. From Recreo on the Belgrano a branch runs W to Chumbicha, where it connects with a line N to Catamarca and S to La Rioja; they will be described later. The fastest route from Buenos Aires (1,149 km.) is by the Mitre line, via Córdoba and La Banda.

N.B. In Tucumán, Salta and Jujuy the only fuel one can get at the service station is *alconafta* (85% gasoline, 15% ethanol) which is a harmless substitute for gasoline.

Tucumán (properly San Miguel de Tucumán), capital of its province and with a population of 390,000, is the busiest and the most populous city in the N. Its natural beauties are great: it stands on a plain, at 450 metres, but to the W towers the Sierra de Aconquija. The city was founded by Spaniards coming S from Peru in 1565. There are still many colonial buildings left, and among rows of elaborately stuccoed, spacious, one-storey houses (many of them sadly dilapidated) rise three or four handsome churches with blue, yellow and white tiled domes. Summer weather can be very hot and sticky.

Tucumán's main square is Plaza Independencia. On its W side is the ornate Government Palace, next is the church of San Francisco, with a picturesque façade. On the S side is the Cathedral, with a rough rustic cross, kept near the baptismal font, used when founding the city.

To the S, on Calle Congreso, is the Casa Histórica where, in 1816, the Congress of the United Provinces of Río de la Plata met to draft and proclaim Argentina's Declaration of Independence. The simple room in which it was proclaimed survived the destruction of the original house in 1908 and has now been enclosed in a modern museum. A bas-relief on the museum walls shows the delegates proclaiming independence. Some distance to the W is Plaza Belgrano, with a statue to General Belgrano, who won a decisive battle against the royalists here in 1812. Two blocks E is the University, with a grand view from the *vivero*. Nightly, at 2030, *son et lumière* programme at Casa Histórica, US$1.50, no seats, in garden, disappointing.

There are two beautiful parks in the city: Nueve de Julio and Avellaneda. In the former there is an artificial lake as well as the house of Bishop Colombres, who introduced sugar cane to Tucumán in the early 19th century. In the house is his first milling machine, and in the back garden is a gigantic steam press imported from France in 1883.

Local Holiday Sept. 24 (Battle of Tucumán). Independence celebrations include music and speeches at the Casa de Independencia on July 8, followed by *gauchos* bringing in the National Flag at midnight. Next day there are many folklore markets and music.

Hotels *Grand Hotel del Tucumán*, Av. de los Próceres 380, B, large, new five-star hotel opposite the Parque Centenario 3 de Julio, efficient, outstanding food and service, swimming pool, tennis courts, discotheque; *Metropol*, 24 de Septiembre 524, expensive, B, but good service, worth it; *Versailles*, C. Alvarez 481, B, with bath and breakfast included, telex service very expensive, small

ARGENTINA 67

rooms; next door is *Francia*, C. Alvarez 465, same owner, but more comfortable and cheaper, D; *Premier*, with a/c, good, friendly, accepts Visa credit card, C. Alvarez 510, D; *Kings*, Chacabuco 18, D; *Claridge*, Maipú 545, C. Also good: *Viena*, Santiago del Estero 1054, E; *Corona*, on main square next to Tourist Office; *Plaza*, D, San Martín 435. In summer, best to stay at *Hotel St. James*, on top of Sierra de Aconquija, expensive, comfortable, good food, swimming pool, good views, and fine walking; *Los Arrieros*, on the Metán road, recommended; *Congreso*, Congreso 74, clean but old, recommended, friendly, E, with bath. There are other cheap hotels near the bus station, but some are very dirty. *El Bosque*, opp. bus station, F, clean, fan; *Palace*, 24 de Septiembre, F, with bath, overpriced; *Colonial*, San Martín 35, 5 mins. from bus station, fair, E; *Estrella*, just outside bus station, 24 de Septiembre, cheap and basic; next door is *Cristal*, similar. *Mendoza*, Mendoza 913, E; *Español*, Ayacucho 174, D; *Eros*, Mendoza 437, E, without bath, clean. *Alcázar*, Sáenz Peña 33 just in front of bus station, F; nameless hotel opp. bus terminal, F with bath, radio and heating; *Florida*, 24 de Septiembre and 9 de Julio, F, good value; *Italia*, Catamarca and Corrientes, F, by Mitre station, friendly, hot water, reasonably clean; *Congreso*, C. Alvarez 765, beautiful, very friendly, clean, F (shared bath), recommended. Many cheap hotels in streets around General Mitre station (Calles Catamarca and Marcos Paz). Marta Ruiz offers accommodation in her house at Rondeau 1824, F, not including food, very comfortable.

Camping Parque Nueve de Julio, good facilities, one site for locals, one for tourists (US$0.25 per tent, US$0.25 p.p.): hot showers, clothes-washing. Two roadside camp sites 3 km. E and NE of city centre.

Restaurants *Mi Abuela*, opposite casino, Maipú 942, on N side of town, self-service, US$6 meal (3-course), cheap and good; almost next to it an excellent, large corner restaurant open 1700-0500; *Palacio de las Empanadas*, also recommended, as is *El Duque*, San Lorenzo 440, excellent. Snacks at *El Buen Gusto*, 9 de Julio 29, good, but waiters can be hostile to foreigners; *La Leñita*, 25 de Mayo, inexpensive, good meat. *Los Dos Gordos*, 24 de Setiembre 450 on main plaza, average food and somewhat expensive; *Bar Risco*, B. Araoz and Avellaneda, nr. bus station, good cheap milanesas. *Rocca Bianca*, next to *Hotel Congreso* on Calle Congreso 32, good all round, very popular; *La Cantina*, San Martín 750, good; also good, cheap meals at *Champaquí*, Av. Sarmiento, corner with Catamarca, opp. Mitre station. *Sorrento*, C. Alvarez near 9 de Julio, cheap, all-you-can-eat, average food; *Comilandia*, cheap set meals, San Martín 181. *Café and Sandwichería*, corner of 24 de Septiembre and Buenos Aires, good. Set lunches near bus station good value. The local beer is very good (Cervecería del Norte).

Shopping An active centre, cheaper than Buenos Aires, but seedier. *Discoteque*, Galería at San Martín 675, good selection of records, English-speaking owner. In summer all shops close 1200-1600.

Casinos The Winter Casino is in an elegant 19th century building on the outskirts. It is open all year except January. The Summer Casino at the top of Aconquija is now closed.

Car Hire Al International and Avis; airport and in centre.

Museums Casa Histórica, open Tue.-Sun. 0830-1200 and 1730-2000, free, but you're encouraged to buy a guide, see previous page; Anthropological Museum, due to reopen at a new address in 1985; Folklore Museum, open Wed. and Sun. 0800-1230 and 1730-2030; the Instituto Miguel Lillo, associated with the natural history department of the University, has a large collection of animals, insects, and a herbarium, with the display greatly improved. One of the library's treasures is one of eight copies of the original edition of von Humboldt's travels in Spanish America; another is a sixteenth-century Pliny. Open Mon.-Fri. 1500-1800. All these four museums have been described as "quite exceptional". Casa de Padilla, next to government palace, houses a collection of international art and antiques in the home of a prominent Tucumán family. Next to *Hotel Colonia* on Av. Entre Ríos is Museo Iremaín, a very interesting memorial to the sculptor, open 0830-1200 and 1500-1800, Mon.-Fri. All museums are free.

Bank of London and South America, San Martín 622. Open 0700-1300; does not change traveller's cheques. **Casas de Cambio**, Noroeste Cambios S.A., 24 de Septiembre 549, good rates (2% commission on American Express and Thomas Cook). Also Maguitur, San Martín 677, near main square, cheques and cash.

Immigration Office Buenos Aires 2719, take bus No 6. Will only extend stay on the last day of the original permit.

Library North American Centre, Junín 567, open 1700-2100. Alliance Française, Mendoza 255, free events in French.

International Calls Entel, Muñecas 226.

Tourist Office In Plaza Independencia, 24 de Septiembre, 1st floor, open 0700-2300; sometimes helpful in finding accommodation in private houses (about US$3 with cooking facilities). Has details on Tafí (see page 68).

68 ARGENTINA

Rail and Road The daily *Estrella del Norte* train leaves Retiro station, Buenos Aires, at 1800, returns daily from the Mitre station in Tucumán at 1845, costs US$24 Pullman, US$ 18.10 first, US$13.50 tourist class; takes 18½ hours. The Belgrano train, the *Norteño*, leaves Buenos Aires 1000, Tues. and Fri.; and Tucumán (Belgrano station opp. bus station) 1845, Tues., Fri., taking 25 hours, no sleeper. *Independencia* train leaves Buenos Aires Tues. and Fri. at 1600, returns Sun. and Wed. at 1715 (Mitre station) sleeper, car transporter, can combine with bus La Veloz del Norte (5½ hrs.) to Salta, for about US$9 more, also to Jujuy (US$10, 5 hours) as can *Estrella del Norte* (to Salta only, daily at 1300).

Beyond Tucumán the Belgrano line runs N via Rosario de la Frontera to Jujuy. Trains no longer run to La Quiaca, on the Bolivian border, 644 km. from Tucumán. There are also buses to all these places and their use seems preferable; the trains N of Tucumán, though comfortable (with a dining car and crowded only when there are *fiestas*), are slow.

For travellers to Salta from Tucumán the road via Santa María (a very interesting journey through many microclimates, see page 69) and Cafayate is longer but more interesting than the direct road. Aconquija bus Tucumán to Cafayate via Tafí and Santa María leaves at 0600, Tues., Thurs. and Sat. (8 hrs.). Direct bus in summer from Tucumán to Cafayate 3 times a week, 6½ hrs., at 1000 (0600/0700 in winter), returning at 1100 from Cafayate. Direct Tucumán bus to Salta (but not via Cafayate), 4 hours, several daily, US$8. (slow bus 5½ hrs). Hitch-hiking from Tucumán to Salta is difficult beyond Tafí del Valle. Plenty of buses to Jujuy, e.g. Veloz del Norte, leaves at 0900, 6 hrs. (US$11.75).

For those who wish to travel direct from N Argentina to Central Chile, there are daily buses (US$20) from Tucumán to Mendoza, leaving 1230 and 2000 (16 hours), via Catamarca, La Rioja, Patquía, Chepes and San Juan, through interesting and little-visited arid country. Bus to Córdoba 480 km, US$10, 8 hours, many companies (incl. El Tucumano Panamericano). *La Veloz de Norte* serves free coffee, cake and soda. Train to Córdoba, US$5.65 tourist, US$7.30 1st class, no sleeper, at 2045, 13 hrs., Tues., Fri. (*El Norteño*). To La Paz, take a bus to the frontier since the line to La Quiaca no longer carries passengers, then, at frontier, Villazón, connect with train to Oruro at 1330, reach Oruro at 0450 and arrive at La Paz at 1045. Bus to La Rioja, 7 hours, US$10. To Catamarca, 7 a day with Bosio, about US$5. Buses also to Santiago del Estero, Paraná, Termas de Río Hondo, Orán (US$12), Resistencia and Tinogasta. Bus to Buenos Aires, Chevallier at 1250, arriving at 0805, US$30.

Air Airport: Benjamín Matienzo, 9 km. from town. Day and night flights to Buenos Aires with Aerolíneas Argentinas and Austral; discounts on night flights. Austral Tucumán-Mar del Plata at 0240 on Mon., Mar del Plata-Tucumán Tue. and Sat. at 0150; Tucumán-Córdoba with Austral daily exc. Sun. at 1355.

El Cadillal dam, in the gorge of the Río Salí, 26 km. N of Tucumán, supplies electricity and water for the city and permanent irrigation for 80,000 hectares of parched land. There are restaurants, a good ACA campsite, good swimming, and a small museum at the dam. Reached by frequent bus from the depot near the railway station, US$1.

Excursions 36 km. to Villa Nougués, an hour up the mountain side (one of the most interesting tours), the summer residence of the well-to-do Tucumanos; it has an excellent private hotel; Aconquija park, with glorious trees, is at the foot of the mountains. Bus at 1130 (the only one; returns immediately); tours from Terra, 9 de Julio 80, US$5.25. Another possible excursion is to San Javier (hotel), 20 km., beautiful views. To Salta via Cafayate, take the Ruta Nacional 38 SW, passing the Quebrada de Lules (20 km.), which is worth visiting. At Km. 46, Route 307 branches NW to **Tafí del Valle**, (97 km. from Tucumán, not to be confused with Tafí Viejo which is 10 km. N of the city) known to archaeologists as a holy valley of the precolumbian Indian tribes, where there is a dam (*Hostería ACA*, C; *Hotel Nuñorco*, D; *Colonial*, nr. bus station, friendly, clean, F. *Pensión La Cumbre*, F, hot water, basic). Camping, hotels, bungalows at El Pinar del Ciervo. Tafí del Valle, which is becoming touristy, is often shrouded in fog because of the dam. Try local cheese. Ten mins. from Tafí is Museo La Banda in an old chapel (San Lorenzo).

Bus, Tucumán-Tafí, with Aconquija, sit on left-hand side, travels through luxuriant gorge with subtropical vegetation, 0700 and 1600, 3½ hrs, US$3.25.

Just before Tafí del Valle are Dique El Mollar, formerly La Angostura dam, and nearby the menhir park of El Mollar, with 129 standing stones and good views. Small Ambrosetti museum nearby. Paved road between Tafí and El Mollar. Tours to El Mollar and Tafí from the agency next door to the tourist office, US$11.50 each for 4 people minimum. Apparently there are now local buses. Entrace to the park is 10 km. S of Tafí del Valle; you can drive around it by car, or walk.

NW of Tafí is **Amaichá del Valle** (bus US$5.25, leaves at 0930) with 360 sunny days a year, free municipal campsite, *Juan Bautista Alberdi*, 10 min. out of town (blue gate) (ACA hostel, recommended, *Pensión Albarracín*, F). La Pachamama festival at end of pre-Lent Carnival. Over the 3,040 metre Infiernillo pass 21 km. from Tafí and 15 km. from Amaichá the road is paved and again after Amaichá to the junction with the Ruta Nacional 40 (15 km.) which leads to Cafayate (55 km.-see page 73) and S, 24 km. to

Santa María, population 18,000.

Hotels *Plaza*, on plaza, clean, modern, recommended, D; *Provincial de Turismo*, San Martín, friendly, recommended, dining room, D, with bath; *Alemán*, E, Quintana 144, with restaurant, reasonable and friendly; *Windsor*, Mitre 200; *Residencial Palacios*, Mitre y Rivadavia; *Pensión Alvarez*, Belgrano; *Residencial Reinoso*, Av. 1° de Mayo, F, hot showers, clean, friendly. *Residencial Zanacchi*, Mitre 637, F, clean.

Restaurants: *Confitería Windsor*, off main plaza at Mitre and Sarmiento, no prices on menu, average food; *El Cardón*, Abel Acosta 158, cheap and good, regional dishes.

Buses Santa María-Tucumán 0220, 0800 (US$6). Santa María-Belén, 4 hrs., at 1330. Santa María-Cafayate daily at 0700 exc. Thurs. at 1030. Empresa Bosio goes from Santa María to Catamarca, Tues., Thurs., Sun. at 1330, 9 hrs., returns Mon., Wed., Sat. at 1130.

Excursions Several can be made from Santa María: to Fuerte Quemado (Indian ruins) 15 km. away, not as impressive as Quilmes (see below); Cerro Pintado, 8 km., coloured sandstone mountains; important ruins of Loma Rica, 18 km. away; Ampajango, 20 km. away, important indigenous finds; Quilmes, 37 km. away, with splendid views from the fortifications and interesting cacti, a small museum, camping facilities and a guide at the site from 0700 to 1730. It is 5 km. from the main road. There is also a provincial archaeological museum. Interesting winery in outskirts, "La Bodega Acialba", taxi US$2.50.

A railway and road run N from Tucumán to (145 km.) **Rosario de la Frontera,** a popular resort from June to September. Altitude: 769 metres. Eight km. away there are sulphur springs, famous for their curative properties. Casino. From Buenos Aires, by Belgrano Railway: 1,296 km.

Hotels *Termas*, rambling place, being remodelled, but beware of loose accounting, good food but many rooms without private bath (6 km. from bus station, taxi US$5), room with bath and 3 meals, C. Baths US$1.50. About 1 km from *Hotel Termas* is new ACA motel. Across the road is manmade lake owned by Caza y Pesca Club—ask in your hotel for permission to fish. *Real*, E, basic, clean, not all doors close.

Bus Rosario de la Frontera-Tucumán, Veloz del Norte, with stewardess, coffee and biscuits.

Excursions To *El Naranjo* (19 km.) a Jesuit colonial town; a church contains images and carvings made by Indians.
About 80 km. N of Rosario de la Frontera, at Lumbreras, a road branches off the Inter- American Highway and runs 80 km. NE to the Parque Nacional **Finca El Rey**, a 44,160- hectare tropical forest and wildlife preserve set among 900-1,500 metre hills with clear streams (good fishing). It can also be reached from Salta, 196 km., US$20 p.p. round-trip excursions of at least 6 with agencies. Public transport: take Benjamín Araoz bus at 0700 to Lumbreras, 2 hrs., US$2.50; there catch same line bus at 0915 to Paso de la Cruz, 45 min., US$1.30. From Paso de la Cruz it is 35 km. N to the park entrance and 10 km. from the entrance to the park hotel and administration. Only local farm and roadbuilding traffic, which may give a ride. A *National Tourist Hotel*, C, usually, but not always, closed at the height of the rainy season, Jan.-March (check at Terra Tours, Tucumán, Tel.: 214333, ask for Eduardo Cendoyo). It is clean and comfortable, has a large enclosed veranda overlooking the park. Also bungalows, and basic student accommodation. Mosquitoes, ticks and chiggers thrive; bring lotion. Camping allowed. Horseback riding. Landing strip for small planes. The access road is still poor and fords the river 9 times; passable for ordinary cars only in the driest of years.

From Güemes, 148 km. N of Rosario de la Frontera, a branch line and road run W through the mountains for 43 km. to

Salta, at 1,190 metres, 294,000 people, on the Río Arias, in the Lerma valley, in a mountainous and strikingly beautiful district. Salta, capital of its province, is a handsome city founded in 1582, with fine colonial buildings. Follow the ceramic pavement plaques for an interesting tour. The Cathedral (open mornings and evenings), on the N side of the central Plaza 9 de Julio, was built 1858-1878; it contains the much venerated images of the Cristo del Milagro and of the Virgin Mary, the first sent from Spain in 1592, and has a rich interior mainly in red and gold, as well as a huge late baroque altar. The miracle was the sudden cessation of a terrifying earthquake when the images were paraded through the streets on

ARGENTINA

September 13, 1692. They still are, each September, when 80,000 people visit the town. The Cabildo, on Calle Caseros, was built 1783. The Convent of San Bernardo, at Caseros and Santa Fe, was built in colonial style in the mid-19th century; it has a famous wooden portal of 1762. San Francisco church, at Caseros and Córdoba, built around 1880, is said to have the tallest church tower in South America. Take a cab to the Museo Arqueológico (US$1) on Av. Antártida Argentina, where there are many objects from Tastil (see page 75) reached by a 3-hr. bus ride. Salta, 1,600 km. from Buenos Aires by rail or paved road, is now a great tourist and handicraft centre (visit Mercado de Artesanía and shops—open 0800-2000 weekdays, 0800-1300 Sat. and the onyx factory) and the best starting place for tours of the NW.

In Salta, visit the Cerro San Bernardo (1,458 metres). Very beautifully set at the foot of the hill is an impressive statue by Víctor Cariño, 1931, to General Güemes, whose *gaucho* troops repelled seven powerful attacks by the Spaniards between 1814 and 1821. A steep path behind the Archaeological Museum with Stations of the Cross leads to the top of the hill, where there is an old wooden cross. The guards on the Plaza 9 de Julio (changing of the guard at 1200) wear red ponchos with black stripes to commemorate the death of General Güemes.

Festival Sept. 24, commemorating the battles of Tucumán and Salta. On June 16-17, folk music by youngsters in the evening and *gaucho* parade in the morning around the Güemes statue at the foot of the San Bernardo hill. Salta celebrates Carnival with processions on the four weekends before Ash Wednesday at 2200 in Av. Belgrano (seats optional at US$2-4); lots of shaving foam (*nieve*) in the early morning; also Mardi Gras (Shrove Tuesday) with a procession of decorated floats and of dancers with intricate masks of feathers and mirrors. It is the custom to squirt water at passers-by and *bombas de agua* (small balloons to be filled with water) are on sale for dropping from balconies on to unwary pedestrians below. Wear a light waterproof!

Hotels Salta is a favoured convention town. Many hotels are closed for a vacation during the Christmas season until January 10, so check. The last two weeks in July are often fully booked because of holidays. *Victoria Plaza* B, Zuviría 16, the foyer overlooking the plaza is one of the centres of *salteño* life, good porter has all information about travel, etc.; *Salta*, Buenos Aires 1, in main plaza, first class, refurbished, good restaurant, and *California*, Alvarado 646 (C), 1st class, one block from main plaza, singles are small, recommended. *Provincial*, Caseros 786, 4-star E; *Regidor*, Buenos Aires 9, opp. the *Salta*, English-speaking owner, avoid 1st floor, D, lunch US$5. *Continental*, 2 blocks from bus station, Hipólito Yrigoyen 295, C, with bath, expensive, poor. *Colonial*, D, with bath, Zuviría 6, a/ c. 24-hr. cafetería; *Colón*, J. B. Alberdi 165, old fashioned, central, opposite railway station, no hot shower, F.; *Plaza*, España 508, E, old, noisy, fair; *Portazuelo*, good hotel at foot of Cerro San Bernardo, D with breakfast, swimming pool, clean, helpful, better and cheaper than the ACA's *Motel Huaico*, Av. Bolivia, Campo Castanares; *Motel Flamingo*, at foot of road to San Bernardo; *Misoroj*, San Luis 190. *Crillón* (near main plaza, Ituzaingó 30), good; *Residencial Güemes*, on Necochea (600 block) near railway station F, basic, clean, private bath, laundry service. *Residencial Familiar*, Calle Santiago del Estero, E. *Savoy* (near railway station), E, or F without bath, basic, clean, with cheap restaurant; *Residencial Elena*, E, clean, friendly and quiet, Calle Buenos Aires 254; *Residencial San Jorge*, Ruiz de los Llanos 1164, corner of Esteco, F, with bath, parking, safe deposit, garden, washing facilities, horse- trekking expeditions organised by proprietor, Sr. Dejean; *Hospedaje Doll*, Pasaje Ruiz de los Llanos 1360 (7 blocks from centre), F with bath, friendly, safe; *Residencial Oriental*, on Ituzaingó, E. *Pensión Madrid*, B. Mitre, F; *Residenciales Viena*, Florida 184, F, *Florida*, D (no singles), hot showers, very friendly, clean, will store luggage, Calle Florida y Urquiza 722 and *Mendoza*, E, with shower, very clean; *Residencial Royal*, E, with bath, poor value, security suspect, basic but clean, 5 blocks from bus station, Lavalle and Alvarado; *Residencial Sandra*, Alvarado 630, E, private shower. *Residencial Italia*, Alberdi 210, modern, good value, E, with bath; *Residencial Cepmer*, Yrigoyen 1195, E, good. *Residencial Astur*, Rivadavia 508, F, no hot water. *Residencial Cayetano*, Balcarce 747, E, clean, hot water; *Residencial Balcarce*, Balcarce 460, friendly, clean, laundry, check price beforehand. *Residencial Centro*, Belgrano 657, friendly, F; *Residencial Rugantino*, Caseros 431, at San Francisco church, E; *Siria*, Ituzaingó 368. *Casa Familiar*, San Martín 540, 1st floor, Apt. 2, run by Sra Maria Florencia Zavalia de Márquez Valladares, E, hot showers, cooking facilities, very friendly but near bus station, so noisy. Very cheap fruit and veg. market in same street. *Motel Petit*, H. Yrigoyen 225, D, some rooms shared, two blocks from bus station, swimming pool, nice; *Candilejas*, Balcarce 980, E, without bath, erratic water supply, clean, comfortable, close to railway station. Many other cheap hotels near railway station.

Camping Casino Provincial municipal grounds, by river, swimming pool available, 3 km. from centre. Bus 13 to grounds. There is no signposting. In front of the Casino turn left, go to the *balneario* administration office, US$2.15 each, car US$3. Free hot showers available if there is gas, safe and excellent facilities. At *Motel Huaico*, Campo Castanares, and *Residencial Hispano*, San Juan 619.

ARGENTINA 71

Restaurants *El Rey de Bife*, recommended as best in town, with excellent cold buffet and *bife*; *Balcarce*, near railway on Balcarce 934, delicious and reasonable. *El Monumento*, Gurracharga 300 (opp. Güemes monument), recommended, owner Alberto Ax speaks English, good food, service and atmosphere, reasonably priced; *La Castiza*, Alberdi 134, huge, little atmosphere, reasonable; *Italiano*, Buenos Aires y Urquiza, 1st floor, highly recommended but not cheap. *Don José*, Urquiza 484, good, cheap, popular on Sun. *La Madrileña*, España 421, quite good; *La Posta*, España 476, good; *La Casona*, Caseros 511, good, reasonable; *Pepito*, Jujuy 1180 and *25 de Mayo*, 25 de Mayo 552, reasonable; *9 de Julio*, Urquiza 1020, recommended; *El Mesón de Pepe*, Rivadavia 714, fish specialities; *Chips*, corner of Caseros and Lerma, good and cheap. *Guisería Picantería Elite*, Belgrano 472, very friendly, local and some Arab dishes, small portions. Pleasant outdoor restaurants in Parque San Martín, at foot of Cerro San Bernardo. Good pizza at *La Selecta*, Belgrano 511. *El Quebracho*, near bus station, has *peña* show, at 2030. *El Antigal*, Balcarce, ½ block from railway station, cheap and good. *Mi Rancho*, cheap, on B. Mitre 301, good local food. Good set menu at *El Sorpaso* on Balcarce, cheap; *Miguel's Rotisería y Pizzería*, Balcarce nr. Belgrano, cheap, popular. Many good cheap restaurants on and near San Martín, by market. *Rotisería Pizzería Roque*, Alberdi y San Martín, cheap; *J.A.*, H.Yrigoyen y San Martín, cheap; also *Boliche Balderrama*, San Martín 1126, has folk music, US$5 entrance for the show, also US$1 for good 4-course lunch. *Restaurant Pinocho*, cheap, friendly. *Gauchos de Güemes*, for hearty food and music, Uruguay 750; *Ezeiza*, San Martín 1044, gives a cheap, good, 4-course lunch. *El Rincón del Artista*, in 1200 block of San Martín, also recommended. *Alvarez*, Buenos Aires y San Martín, cafeteria style, cheap and good. *La Casa de las Empanadas*, 12 de Octubre 720. *Café del Paseo* at Hotel Colonial, Zuviría 6, open 24 hrs. *Confitería Milk 1000*, 20 de Febrero y España, good ice cream. *Heladería Gianni*, España 486, ask for *copa del amor*. Cheap restaurants near the railway and bus stations, many lunch-only restaurants (closed Suns.) with meals at US$1-2. *Unión Sirio Libanesa*, San Martín 677, has a good restaurant open to the public.

Try local Cafayate wines, such as Michel Torino and Echart Privado, and typical Torrontés-grape wine. Also, the good local water makes excellent beer.

Markets Mercado Municipal, corner of San Martín and Florida, for meat, fish, vegetables and other produce and handicrafts, closed 1200-1700 and Sun. Mercado Artesanal is interesting; excellent quality goods, much better and cheaper are the tourist shops opposite, or in town. It is just out of town (San Martín 2555, Tel.: 219195), 0800-1930, take bus 2 or 3 from the centre. If going to Bolivia, however, remember that many handicrafts of similar description will be cheaper there. High quality, hand-made Botas Salteñas from Calle Vicente López 1046. Shoemakers on Calle Urquiza make boots to order in 48 hours.

Rent-a-Car Avis, airport and Alvarado 537; AI International in centre; several local companies.

Bathing Balneario Municipal on outskirts, reached by bus No. 13 from Calle Ituzaingó, entry US$1.00. Bus fare US$1.20.

Museums Cabildo Histórico, Caseros 549, fascinating colonial and historical museum, open Wed.-Sun., 1500-2100, US$0.20. Museo de Bellas Artes, Florida 18 open every day 1600-1900 and Wed.-Sun. 0900-1200. Casa Uriburu, Caseros 421, has relics of a distinguished *salteño* family. Museo Arqueológico behind the Güemes statue where the footpath to the San Bernardo mountain begins, good display but "closed until further notice". Museo de Ciencias Naturales, Mendoza 2, has a full display of stuffed birds. In the Casa del Alto Molino (Av. San Martín 2555), much rawhide work is on display. Centro Cultural, on Calle Caseros, has slide shows on Fridays about the local countryside, free.

Banks Banco de la Nación on Mitre and Belgrano, open 0730 until 1330, better overall rate (pays 5% more on cheques than on notes, but doesn't change money after 1000); Banco Provincial de Salta, España 526 on main square, closes at 1200 but changes travellers' cheques. Saltur on the main square will change US notes but at a very poor rate. Exchange house: Maguitur, España 678, cheques and cash, better rates than Denarium, España 613.

Post Office Deán Funes 140; also in shopping arcade at corner of Florida and Gral. San Martín.

Consulates Bolivia, Santiago del Estero 179; open Mon.-Fri., 0900-1300. Chile, Ejército del Norte 312; Spain, Las Heras 1229; Italy, Zuviría 380; France, Santa Fe 20; West Germany, España 671.

Tourist Office Buenos Aires 93 (one block from main square). Open every day, inc Sun., till 2100. Very helpful, gives free maps and offers slide shows some evenings, also a self-guiding tour, Circuito Peatonal, to see important landmarks on foot. This office will also arrange accommodation in a private house. Ask for the Tourist Market here, excellent leather goods.

Travel Agencies Saltur, Caseros 525, Tel.: 212012, very efficient. Continente Viajes, Zuviría 60 (on main plaza), has a wide variety of tours, recommended.

Bus Services Salta provides the most useful cheap land connection between Bolivia and Paraguay. Buses daily, US$22 (with La Veloz del Norte), 15 hrs. to Resistencia, 1700 for crossing into Paraguay (an arduous journey, hot, many stops in the night); for description of road, see page 101.

72 ARGENTINA

There is no direct bus from Salta to Asunción, but indirect links via Formosa, where there is a connection to Asunción. Bus Salta-Formosa, US$25, leaves 0830, arrives 0400 next morning. First bus from Formosa to Asunción 0430. Bus (Panamericano) Salta-Córdoba, 4 a day, 14 hrs, US$24. Bus to Cafayate, US$5, daily, also other services. To Mendoza via Tucumán, US$20, twice weekly. Daily bus to Tucumán, 4½ hrs, several firms, US$8. Bus to Embarcación daily at 0700. Bus to Jujuy, Atahualpa service 16 a day between 0600 and 2300, "directo", US$2, 2¾ hours. Bus to Calama and Antofagasta (Chile) leaves Wed. at 1600, US$30 (29-hour journey at least, very cold), run by Atahualpa; tickets from Balturis, Urquiza 272. Take own food. Güemes bus to Antofagasta on Sat. at 1600; reservations are hard to get on either service, have your name added to the list of reservations and try again on the evening before departure. Another company, Tramaca, is said to run the route, which is often suspended in winter. The bus station is eight blocks from the main square. Bus to Rosario de la Frontera, US$3.50, 2½ hrs, stewardess service, very pleasant trip. Taxi from bus station into Salta US$2.

Airport Bus connection from town on corner of the main Plaza to El Aybal airport. From London, cheapest to fly standby to Miami, connect with LAB flight via Santa Cruz once a week to Salta. Two AA flights a week to Santa Cruz (Bolivia), Wed. and Sun. at 1145, arr. 1215 Bolivian time, and also Lloyd Aéreo Boliviano (LAB office on Caseros 376). To Orán and Tartagal (Bolivia) with SEAL. One flight a week to Asunción. AA flies Antofagasta (Chile) on Tues. and Sat. AA flies to Bs. Aires (2 hrs.) Tucumán, Córdoba (US$70) and Rosario. There are flights across the N of Argentina; e.g. Salta to Resistencia by Alfa, US$60 via Formosa (tickets and reservations only in these towns, prop-jets). There is a flight to Iguazú on Tues., return Sun. Special bus service between airport and Plaza 9 de Julio, US$1.50. Taxi from airport to bus station US$9.

Railways Ticket office open weekdays 0900-1100, 1700-1900. (Salta is not on a direct line, it is connected with Güemes by local trains and by bus). Services to Buenos Aires also serve Tucumán (6 hrs.). Also bus/train combination with La Veloz del Norte (1) daily at 1230, arr. Tucumán 1700; see Tucumán section for details to Buenos Aires. *N.B.* If buying ticket from Buenos Aires to Salta via Tucumán, purchase train ticket to Tucumán and bus ticket to Salta at the same time so that you can transfer directly to the bus which meets the train, otherwise you must take local bus to bus terminal and wait (fare Buenos Aires-Salta US$28.20 and US$21) Ordinary train to Tucumán (continues to Córdoba), Tues., and Fri., 0835, 11½ hours (very slow). Train to Córdoba, leaves Tues. and Fri. at 1430, 20 hrs, no sleepers. From Salta to Mendoza, one takes a train to Villa María, near Córdoba, and after a 3-hr. wait gets another to Mendoza, takes about 40 hours. Slow but pleasant. Avoid during rainy periods as the track can get washed out; in summer can be hot and dusty. The Salta-Resistencia passenger service has been abolished, but for the hardy there is a regular freight service that leaves Metán (150 km. SE of Salta and a steam locomotive graveyard) after 1000 daily. The journey takes about 3 days, is very uncomfortable and involves frequent changes. It is best to buy all food before starting and to take plenty of drinking water with you. No direct train to Formosa. No direct trains between Salta and Jujuy, but connexions are possible; buses much quicker. Salta to Cafayate by train: buy tickets from any travel agency 2 days in advance, or 1700-1900 on day before departure at the station; a pretty run.

In October 1980 Chile suspended its rail service from Socompa to Antofagasta, so it is not now possible to travel from Salta to Antofagasta direct except air (see above) or by Atahualpa, Tramaca or Güemes bus. Argentine railways still maintain a train service from Salta to Socompa, where tourist cards are available (see page 75 for description of line, tourist train to San Antonio de los Cobres, and goods train, and also for road taking similar route.)

Routes to Bolivia To La Quiaca, on Bolivian frontier, 3 buses daily, Atahualpa (US$11.25), 8 hrs., at 0630, 1000 and 2130, can be very cold, dusty, with one-hour stop at Jujuy (except for 1000 bus, which stops there, so 2½ hr. wait); Atahualpa company stops in Humahuaca for lunch. Buses also NE to Orán, six hours, for connection with Tarija, Bolivia (can involve taking overnight bus to Aguas Blancas at 2200, arriving before dawn—cold—then crossing river in motor boats to Bermejo, Bolivia and the next bus out is often full. Spectacular 8 hr. mountain ride alternative to the latter in open-air pick-up: hair-raising!); and to Yacuiba, via Pocitos (Bolivian frontier), for Santa Cruz, Bolivia. US$6.50 with Atahualpa, 11½ hrs, very full, with passengers standing, can be uncomfortable and hazardous. Customs at Pocitos not to be trusted—beware of theft; and overcharging for "excess baggage" (on bus), for which there is no official limit written up anywhere. (Hotel at Pocitos, *Buen Gusto*, F, just tolerable.) No trains run to the border at La Quiaca since the line beyond Jujuy was washed away. The other route is served by train: Salta to Pocitos, Wed. 2000, arrive 0715 if you are lucky; go through Argentine exit formalities, cross the bridge into Bolivia then take a taxi to Yacuiba (US$0.25), whence the train leaves at 0815 to Santa Cruz (if you miss it, other trains to Santa Cruz on Wed. and Sat. at 1230—*rápido*, or Mon. and Fri. at 1900 - *mixto*) See also page 80 on the route via Orán.

Excursions Just S of Salta you pass Coronel Moldes: 26 km. from there is the dam of Cabra Corral, one of the largest artificial lakes in Argentina; water skiing, fishing, hotels. Paved road ends at the Presa General M. Belgrano, impressive views of the bridge across the lake. 11 km. NW of Salta is the picturesque village of San Lorenzo (new hotel with pool and meals, rather expensive; otherwise camping and picnicking beside rocky stream—meals at hillside lodge) and 2 km. further

ARGENTINA 73

the Lomas de San Lorenzo with a little river and subtropical vegetation (a popular Sunday picnic spot). Can be reached by regular transport daily from Salta. To Jujuy and Humahuaca, day trip through many agencies, about US$15 p.p. To Cuesta del Obispo and the Forgotten Valley, on return, with Saltur day trip, superb. In summer, guided tours are few and far between because of a lack of tourists. The El Rey National Park is about 80 km. E of Salta, at junction of Chaco and pre-Andean regions. Much wildlife and varied scenery.

A magnificent round trip of about 520 km. can be taken going SW from Salta to Cafayate, then N through the Valles Calchaquíes and Cachi, and back E to Salta. The first part of this trip, S from Salta, goes through El Carril (30 km.) where a road from Cachi intersects; continuing S for 25 km. Coronel Moldes is reached. Here, a side road to the left goes to Embalse Cobra Corral (see above). After Coronel Moldes, Route 68 goes through the Quebrada del Río de las Conchas with fascinating rock formations, all signposted: Anfieatro (a gorge), El Sapo, El Fraile, El Obelisco, Los Castillos. The road goes through wild and semi-arid landscapes with many wild birds, including ñandúes (rheas).

Cafayate (altitude 1,660 metres) A quiet, clean, little town, with low rainfall, lying between two ranges of Andean foothills and surrounded by vineyards. Its church is narrow but has 5 arches. About 18 km. S. is Tolombón, where there are reported Indian ruins among giant cacti and other scrub plants. (The ruins are vestigial; the cacti are far more interesting.) Cafayate is much frequented by Argentine tourists. A walk to La Cruz (3 hrs.) takes you to a view of the Aconquija chain in the S. to Nevado de Cachi in the N.

See Sr. Rodolfo Bravo's private museum of Calchaquí archaeology on Calle Colón, full of Indian artefacts dug up nearby, interesting slide show (US$0.50). Excursions to *bodegas* and vineyards possible, e.g. La Rosa owned by Michel Torino, open Mon.-Sat., 0800-1200 and 1600-1900, no need to book, 30 min. tours and tasting; also Etchart, 2 km. on road to Tucumán, no formal tours, but ask for the analyst, Jorge Riccitelli, who is knowledgeable and friendly—the Etchart Cabernet Privado, red, has been recommended. La Banda, a small vineyard near La Rosa, is interesting because it is more primitive. Near Bodega La Rosa a local kiln makes enormous pots. The Museo de Vitivinicultura is in an old cellar, on Av. Güemes, 2 blocks from main square, US$0.40, very well laid out. Locally woven tapestries are interesting, and very expensive; see them at workshops of Ricardo Miranda, Av. Güemes 330. Also Platería of Jorge Barraco, Colón 147, for metal craft work. Museo de Arte Popular y Artesanía Tradicional, Calle San Martín 157, recommended.

Hotels *Hostería Cafayate* (ACA), modern, quiet, colonial-style, D, good food; *Gran Real*, Güemes 128, *Asturias*, Güemes 158, *Melchor*, Güemes y Almagro, all C; *Pensión Arroyo*, Camila Q. de Niño 160, recommended, friendly, clean, F; *Colonial*, Almagro 134, basic, F; *Parador*, colonial style; *Güemes*, Salta 13, one block off main square, E; *Briones*, on main square, clean and comfortable, E with bath and hot water; *Savoy*, off main square, with nice restaurant, D; *Confort*, on main street, F with bath, good. Accommodation in private houses is available. Municipal campsite Lorohuasi at S access to town, hot water, best, not free, and autocamping with full facilities 1 km. on Tucumán road with camp site next to it, with taps only.

Restaurants *Miguelito*, simple, on plaza, good regional dishes and nice atmosphere, but lots of flies; *Bárbara*, also on plaza, good food and value; *La Carreta de Don Olegario*, also on plaza, good, pleasant, and spotless. *El Rancho*, for parrilla. Another parrillada is *La Tinaja* on the corner of the main square. Good cheap wine at café opposite El Indio bus station in street off plaza, provide own container. Try excellent *pan casero* (local bread).

At San Carlos 32, Pancho Silva and his family have a workshop selling and displaying their own and locals' handicrafts. A very informative and generous family; if it is convenient, Pancho will take you walking in the surrounding countryside (if you intend to visit them, it would be nice to take a small present).

Tourist Office Av. Güemes 101 (in art shop), 3 blocks from main square.

Bus Service from Cafayate to Tucumán (US$8) on Wed., Fri. and Sun at 0600. Alternatively go to Santa María with 1100 El Indio bus (2 hrs.) over good dirt road and take bus to Tucumán, Empresa Aconquija, leaving at 0200 and 0600, daily, taking 5-6 hrs. Colectivo leaves at 0400, taking 3½-4 hrs. (minimum 4 or 5 passengers). El Indio departs Salta 0700, 1100, 1800, 4 hrs. US$6; 0700 bus goes on to Angastaco, 2¼ hrs. Bus Cafayate-Salta 2-3 times a day, 4 hrs, US$5. Marcos Rueda bus leaves Salta daily at 0630, arriving Cachi 1130, leaves for Molinos at 1230, 2 hrs., US$2.30; leaves Molinos at 0645 daily. Same company from Molinos at 0900 to Cachi. The afternoon light on Cuesta del Obispo is the best. Marcos Rueda also has a service from Salta (Sat., 1300) to La Poma, arriving 1945 (via Cachi at 1750). The bus returns from La Poma next day at 1320. La Poma is reportedly a beautiful hamlet, and there is a *hostería*. Trout fishing is currently forbidden while stocks recover.

74 ARGENTINA

Taxi owner, Millán, can usually be found in *La Tinaja*, Cafayate, but he is expensive.

Reinhard Böhm-Raffay writes: "On entering Cafayate from Tucumán there is a municipal campsite (US$2). If you follow the Río Colorado on foot just before this campsite, you can cross and follow the road towards the mountains. (An alternative is to take Calle 25 de Mayo (a dirt road), 4 blocks from the main plaza; carry on along this road, including a sharp left turn, and you reach the start of the road to the ridge.) Adobe houses with orange trees and chickens, dogs and horses along the riverbank. The road becomes a path, leading past Indian village up 3,500 metres to a mountain ridge. Spectacular view down the river valley and towards Cafayate and its vast, flat valley. From the last hut in the valley is where the path leads up for about 3-5 hrs." Alternatively, hitch-hike, or take the El Indio bus to Salta as far as Km. 30, then walk the Quebrada de Cafayate; best done in the afternoon, take fruit and/or water.

Horses can be hired for US$1 for 1½ hrs. from La Florida, Bodega Etchart Privado (2 km. from Cafayate on road to Tucumán).

Continuing S from Cafayate, the road goes to Santa María (see page 69), and then SE to Tucumán.

About a day is needed for the 160 km. trip from Cafayate to Cachi (Route 40). The road is mainly gravel and can be very difficult after rain, but the views of the Andean-foothill desert country are fascinating for those to whom strange rock formations and unexpected colours have an appeal. The population is largely Indian, and regional costumes abound. Salta and the Valles Calchaquíes are the centre for U.S. archaeologist John Hyslo's study of Inca roads in the Andes.

About 24 km. N of Cafayate is **San Carlos** (altitude 1,660 m), a small settlement destroyed four times by Indians. It has a pleasant white church completed 1854, and another ACA *hostería*, as well as a municipal campsite. The Quebrada de Flechas, N of Cafayate on the road to Angastaco is beautiful and desolate.

Bus The El Indio bus on the Salta-Cafayate-Angastaco run arrives in San Carlos by noon and on the return journey at 0745. Cafayate to San Carlos daily at 1535 and 2205, 45 mins., US$0.60; returns at 0500 and 1655.

Entering the Calchaquí river valley, one comes N into a hillier region centred on **Angastaco,** 2 km. off the main road, another small town, expanding rapidly, surrounded again by vineyards. You can sample the local Vino Patero, red or sweet white, in a house close to the river bridge; apparently *bodegas* can be visited, *vino patero* is supposed to be made by treading the grapes in the traditional manner. (*Hostería* with pool, run by municipality, F, good; also a small *residencial* off the main plaza, G, clean, comfortable. Electricity is cut off at 2230 and remains off until at least 0630.). No buses run from Angastaco to Molinos. Ask in the main square for transport to Molinos, Cachi or Cafayate. Also ask for Sr. Gutiérrez in the shop by the bus stop, or for Yapura in the shop on the side of the same block; it's 1-1½ hrs. to Molinos, locals charge US$10-15. From the Angastaco turn-off it is 40 km. on a winding road through beautiful and desolate rock formations to **Molinos**. Its church (a national monument, built *c.* 1720, now covered in a yellowish paste to preserve it), contains the mummified body of the last governor appointed by Spain, Colonel Severo Siqueira de Isasmendi y Echalar, who died in 1837. This relic can be seen by arrangement with the priest. A pleasant walk is down from the church, crossing a creek and then climbing a gentle hill, from which there are good views of Molinos and surrounding country. Sra. de Guaymas, who runs a store, serves meals, and rents beds (3 to a room) in accommodation opposite the diesel electricity plant very noisy and basic. Ask at the municipality if there are rooms available at the sports centre, if stuck. On the left bank of the river, ask at the village of Seclantás for the hamlet of Solco, where the authentic *ponchos de Güemes* (red with black stripe) are woven.

From Molinos it is 46 km. to **Cachi** (Quechua for "salt"), a beautiful little town renowned for its weaving and other crafts; the natives claim people die only of old age, because the climate is very invigorating; height above sea level, 2,280 metres. The local archaeological museum is described by Federico Kirbus as the best such in Argentina. It is in the "Land of the Pimentón", the pepper-growing area. Hotel Nevado de Cachi, F, near bus station, good restaurant, also a good one opposite; good *ACA Hostería Cachi*, E. From Cachi, you follow Route 40 for 11 km. N, then turn right to Route 33. This road climbs continuously to the Cuesta del Obispo passing a dead-straight stretch of 14 km. known as Recta Tin-Tin

ARGENTINA 75

with magnificent views of the Los Cardones national park with the huge candelabra cacti, which grow up to 6 metres in height, reaching the summit (3,260 metres) after 43 km. Then it plunges down to through a luxuriously-wooded steep valley populated by Indians in local costumes. The road rejoins Route 68 at El Carril, from where it is 37 km. back to Salta.

If you wish to make a round trip just to Cachi, take a bus at 0630 from Salta (4 hrs.) stay the night and return the next morning at 0900. Take the bus from Marcos Rueda, Olavarría 658, *not* at bus station, where it arrives full (buy bus ticket the day before, from Islas Malvinas 339); sit on left-hand side, to see remarkable Quebrada de Escoipe. The bus goes on to Molinos. The church at Cachi has its floor, roof and confessional made of cactus wood. One-day excursions to Cachi from Salta (US$7) allow insufficient time.

Ask also at tour agencies about excursions to Quebrada del Toro, rugged and striking countryside (see below).

There is a metre-gauge railway from Salta through the little town of **San Antonio de los Cobres** to Antofagasta, in north Chile (trains only as far as Socompa, on the Chilean frontier). It is 900 km. long—571 km. lie in Argentina—and reaches an altitude of 4,453 metres as it passes over the Chorrillos pass. Do not eat, drink, smoke in excess on the way up; resident doctor on board for altitude problems. Take plenty of film. From Salta to San Antonio de los Cobres (a squat, ugly mining town on a bleak, high desert at 3,750 metres, pop.: 2,200 only of interest if you want to visit the copper, zinc, lead and silver mines with shuttle bus from La Concordia company office, about 20 km, from the mine you can walk to La Polvorilla viaduct, 20 mins., vicuñas and condors en route; *Hospedaje Belgrano,* painted blue, G, no heat, basic, use of kitchen and restaurant; *Pensión Los Andes,* G with restaurant; both on main street) it passes through the Quebrada del Toro, even more picturesque and impressive than the Humahuaca valley. Muñano, on a desert plateau after one goes over the mountains at Abra Muñano (4,165 metres), is the highest railway station in Argentina, 3,936 metres. The gorge is peculiar in that there is no pass over the mountains. The line is hewn out of the wall closing the end of the valley, zig-zags up and then across the top of the ridge at both El Alisal and Chorrillos. The Argentine side is a barren, rocky plateau 2,150-3,350 metres above sea level and inhabited by Coya Indians who bear a far closer resemblance to their cousins in Bolivia than to the Salteño lowlander. The train turns E at Puerto Tastil to climb to Muñano and misses the archaeological areas, which can however be reached by bus or car. The road from Salta to San Antonio de los Cobres (6 hours, bus four times a week, US$2.30; Empresa Quebradeño, unreliable timetable, serves Muñano 3 times a week, better to hire a car in San Antonio, US$10 return, to make the journey. Take your own water if hiking; there is none in mountains) follows much the same route as the railway but is at a much lower level, which makes it prone to flooding, and the view from the train is much more impressive. The vegetation is low scrub and cactus. Day trip from Salta by minibus US$6, stop at Santa Rosa de *Tastil* to see Indian ruins. The roofs of the houses are said to have been made of cactus. Try the *quesillo de cabra* (goat's cheese) from Estancia Las Cuevas. No through trains to Chile.

From Salta the main connexion with San Antonio is now the train to Socompa on the Chilean frontier. Train to Socompa leaves Salta Tues. 1500, Thurs. and Fri. 0800, Sat. 1500 and Sun. 1410, first class US$10.60, tourist US$7.90; returns 2 hrs. later. Wait in Socompa for the freight train which runs to and from Calama and ask officials if you can take this, a long, hard, cold ride, but cheap. In April 1982, the *Tren a las Nubes* (Train to the Clouds) was reinstated, running between Salta and La Polvorilla viaduct. The service operates on Sat. from May to November (1st and 3rd Sats. only in April, second half of July nearly every day), leaving at 0700 and arriving back at 2200, US$11, US$2 for lunch. Book well in advance at station; not possible through travel agents. Be warned, though, that its departure and arrival points are at 1,200 metres while it climbs to and descends from 3,960 metres in 15 hours—a recipe for *soroche,* despite what the tourist information claims. A goods train goes on Weds. from Salta at 1910 (arrive 0820) to Pocitos, beyond San Antonio. It serves the British-built borate plant at Campo Quijano. It is a single track line so you can change to come down at e.g. Diego de Almagro at dusk. Obtain authorization for travel by this train at the "Movimientos" bureau, 1st floor Office No. 110, change voucher for ticket at the downstairs counter. The train leaves from the goods depôt, a few metres from the Belgrano Railway station. Show up ½ hour early, on the platform where the big bell hangs and where the conductors (guards) meet; there is now one passenger coach (fares US$7.90, tourist US$5.90). Daily train at 1543 (except Weds.) to San Antonio but does not go to the La Polvorilla viaduct, take food; arrives 0205 (US$4.20 first class. US$3.15 tourist). Ask stationmaster in Salta for permission to travel.

There is a road from San Antonio de los Cobres over the pass of Huaytiquina (4,200 metres) to San Pedro de Atacama. At its highest, the road is 4,560 metres. It is a very beautiful trip: you cross salt lakes with flamingoes and impressive desert around. The road on the Argentine side is very good, but on the Chilean side there are very steep gradients. There are no service stations between San Antonio de los Cobres and Calama, or in San Pedro. Because of snow, this route is available only part of the year. A car must be in very good condition to cope with the heights. A bus service also runs from San Antonio to San Pedro on Saturdays; return journey on Wednesdays.

76 ARGENTINA

The direct road from Salta to Jujuy is picturesque with its winding 92-km. stretch through the mountains, now paved, known as *la cornisa*. The buses use the longer road, via Güemes, and this is the better road for hitch-hiking.

Jujuy (pronounced Hoo-hooey) properly San Salvador de Jujuy, the capital of Jujuy province, is 66 km. by rail N of the Güemes junction on the Belgrano railway. It was founded first in 1565 and then in 1575, when it was destroyed by the Indians, and finally established in 1593. The Government House is in a fine square lined with orange trees, Plaza Belgrano, in the eastern part of the city. On the western side of this plaza is a colonial Cathedral with very fine 18th century images, pulpits, walls and paintings finished about 1746. It has been heavily restored, but in the nave is a superb wooden pulpit, carved by Indians and gilded, a colonial treasure without its equal in Argentina. (The cathedral is often shut.) You can see the doorway on Calle Lavalle through which General Lavalle, the enemy of Rosas, was killed by a bullet in 1848, but the door is a copy; the original was taken to Buenos Aires. On Alvear, between Senador Pérez and Lamadrid, are the Teatro Mitre (worth a visit) and the Mercado Artesanal. In the western part of the city are the Parque San Martín and an open space, La Tablada, where horses, mules and donkeys used to be assembled in caravans to be driven to the mines in Bolivia and Peru. See the Palacio de Tribunales near the river, one of the best modern buildings in Argentina. Jujuy stands at 1,260 metres, completely surrounded by wooded mountains. Streets are lined with orange trees (the fruit is bitter). Pop.: 120,000. The scenery is as varied as it is splendid.

Public Holidays August 6, and 23-24.

Hotels Best is *Fenicia*, B, on riverside at 19 de Abril 427. Second best is *Internacional*, Belgrano 501 (main square), B. *Alto la Viña*, attractive, on hill 5 km. away, C, swimming pool. *Augustus*, Belgrano 715, D, modern, comfortable but noisy. *Sumay*, Otero 232, C, central, clean; *Avenida*, 19 de Abril 469, on riverside, with fair restaurant, D (F off season, cafeteria only); *Purmamarca*, El Exodo 825, E, 1½ blocks from bus station. *Residencial Los Andes*, Rep. de Siria 456, 3 blocks from bus station, clean, hot water, E. Across the street is *Residencial San Carlos*, Siria 459, E, friendly. *Santa Fe*, San Martín 134, E; *Motel Huaico* (good), just outside on road to Humahuaca. *Residencial Lavalle*, Lavalle 272, near station, recommended, E (dog bites if touched). *Del Norte*, Alvear 444, F, clean and friendly, near railway station, with cheap restaurant; *Savoy*, Alvear 441, opposite railway station, F, basic, clean. *Motel Posta de Lazano*, just N of Jujuy, F. *Chung King*, Alvear 627, friendly, very noisy, E; *Residencial Aramayo*, E, Salta 1058.

Camping *Autocamping Municipal*, US$2.40 per tent, ask for a cheaper rate for one person. 14 km. N of Jujuy on Humahuaca road, also *Autocamping*, 3 km. N outside city at Huaico Chico, US$1.50 per tent, motel opposite. Buses frequent. Hot showers, clothes washing facilities, very friendly.

Restaurants *Chung-King*, best, Alvear 627; *La Rueda*, Lavalle 320; *Conrad*, Belgrano 952, good; *La Royal*, on Belgrano, good food and atmosphere; *Internacional*, Av. Belgrano. *Bar-Restaurant Sociedad Obrera* for cheap food, General Balcarce 357, but not attractive, cheap bar opposite. Fair at *Hotel Avenida*. *Los Dos Gorditos* also called *Los Obreros*, on Alvear, near railway, cheap but not good. *Restaurant Sirio Libanesa*, Lamadrid 568 (don't be put off by the uninviting entrance). Very good ice cream around the corner of the Cathedral, made by Greek owner.

Museums Histórico Provincial, Lavalle 266; Museo de Paleontología y Mineralogía, Independencia and Lavalle; Galería de Arte, Balcarce 264.

Exchange at travel agencies on Calle Belgrano change cash and dollar travellers' cheques (e.g. next to *Helados Pingüino*). The latter can also be changed at Horus, about 50 metres from the Tourist office, on Güemes.

Consulates Migración is on Belgrano 499. Bolivia, Av. Mitre 32, Barrio V. San Martín; Spain, R. de Velasco 362; Italy, Av. Fascio 660.

Post Office Otero 262

Tourist Office on corner of Belgrano 690 and Lavalle, very helpful. Handicrafts here are higher-priced than in Bolivia.
   For information on bird watching, contact Mario Daniel Cheronoza, Pratonal 38, No. 848-830, Viviendos "El Arenal", Jujuy. The Estación Biológica de Fauna Silvestre, Av. Bolivia 2335, Jujuy, is open to the public on Sundays (for private tours on other days, contact Dr. Arturo A. Canedi, Tel.: 25617-25845), very interesting.

Train Direct services to Salta were cancelled in April 1981. Train to Buenos Aires only Tues. and

ARGENTINA 77

Fri. at 1240, very crowded and can be endlessly delayed. There is also a bus/train combination via Tucumán with La Veloz del Norte (US$9) Sun. and Wed. at 1100 arr. Tucumán 1600; Independencia train leaves at 1715, Bs. As. to Jujuy, Tues. and Fri. with *El Norteño* at 1000; Sun. and Thurs. at 1800. No sleepers. Since the line was washed away, no trains run to La Quiaca and Bolivia; there is no sign of the track being replaced.

Airport 40 km. out of town or 45 mins. by bus. Service to Buenos Aires by Aerolíneas Argentinas, at 1030, Mon., Tues., Thurs., and to La Paz. Check for weather conditions in connecting airports before you fly or you may find yourself stranded elsewhere.

Buses Jujuy via Tucumán to Córdoba, at 1400, 1845, 2130 (Panamericano), at 1100, with La Veloz, daily, Tucumán 5 hrs., US$11.75, and Córdoba, 14 hrs. US$20 with Atahualpa. Jujuy-Salta, from 0700 to 0930, 2¾ hours, US$2. To La Quiaca, leaves 0745, 1100, 1800, 2315, 8 hrs., Panamericano, US$10. Road paved only as far as Humahuaca, reasonably comfortable, but cold. To Orán daily at 1700; to Humahuaca, US$2.50, 3½ hrs., sit on left side. To Embarcación, US$5.25 with Agencia Balut, via San Pedro and Libertador San Martín. Jujuy-Purmamarca-Susques, leaves Purmamarca at 1330 on Wed. and Sat., returning Thurs. and Sun., crossing the Abra Potrerillos (4,164 m.) and the Salinas Grandes of Jujuy. Jujuy-Tilcara 1½ hrs., US$2.50.

Some 19 km. from Jujuy is **Termas de Reyes,** where there are hot springs. This resort, with the *Gran Hotel Termas de Reyes,* is set among magnificent mountains 45 mins. by bus from Jujuy (No. 14 from corner of plaza, 6 times a day). US$2 to swim in the thermal pool at the hotel; municipal baths free but closed Weds. It is possible to camp below the hotel free of charge.

Lovers of old churches will find Salta and Jujuy excellent centres. Franciscan and Dominican friars arrived in the area from Bolivia as early as 1550. The Jesuits followed about 1585. Along both the old Camino de los Incas and the new route through the Quebrada de Humahuaca the padres, in the course of two centuries, built simple but beautiful churches, of which about 20 still exist. They are marked by crosses on the map. All of them can be visited by car from Salta or Jujuy, though some of the roads are very rough. A spare fuel can should be carried because service stations are far apart. (There are ACA stations at Jujuy, Humahuaca and La Quiaca, and YPF stations at Tilcara and Abra Pampa.)

One group, in the Puna de Atacama, on the old Camino de los Incas (which has completely disappeared), can be reached by the road which runs W from Salta through the picturesque Quebrada del Toro to San Antonio de los Cobres (see page 75). The road S from San Antonio to Antofagasta de la Sierra is pretty severe going. The road N to Susques (105 km.), is comparatively comfortable, but runs through utter desert. There is lodging at Susques and an interesting 16th century chapel. The road on to Rosario de Coranzulí is a mule track. Close to the Bolivian and Chilean frontier is El Toro, lovely ride through *altiplano,* past Laguna Turilari, mining territory, bizarre rock formations. Lodgings may be available in first-aid room, ask male nurse, Don Juan Puca. From El Toro on to Coranzulí is very rough.

The second group can be reached from the road N from Jujuy to La Quiaca through the Quebrada de Humahuaca, which is itself extremely beautiful, with spectacular and dramatic rock colours and giant cacti in the higher, drier parts; the Inter-American Highway through it has been paved as far as Humahuaca. Beyond Tumbaya, where there is a church originally built in 1796 and rebuilt in 1873, a road runs 5 km. to Purmamarca, a very poor but picturesque village surrounded by hills of colourful rock strata; there is no hotel, but lodging can be obtained by asking at the ceramic shop opposite the church (mid-17th century) or at the police station. Not far N of the turn, on the main road, is Maimará (*Albergue Maimará,* also camping, 5 km. from Maimará, US$1.20 a day). Between Maimará and the turning to Purmamarca is a new folk museum called Posta de Hornillos, a recently restored old colonial posting house, of which there used to be a chain from Buenos Aires to the Bolivian border. The guide, Jorge Stande, speaks good English. Highly recommended. **Tilcara,** a short distance N in the *quebrada,* has a folk museum run by Buenos Aires University (closed in June), the Ernesto Soto Avendaño museum where a scaled-down model of the independence monument at Humahuaca can be seen, the regional museum José A. Terry with paintings, and the new *Hotel Tilcara* (Belgrano 599, D, swimming pool—usually dry); *Hotel Edén,* Av. Rivadavia, one block from plaza, clean, F; *El Antigal,* on same street, F. *Restaurante Pucará,* on main square, recommended. Within walking distance is a *pucará,* or Inca fort, incorrectly reconstructed but with good views of the valley, closed in June. Botanic garden at the foot of the *pucará* and museum at the main square with excellent display of Andean items.

78 **ARGENTINA**

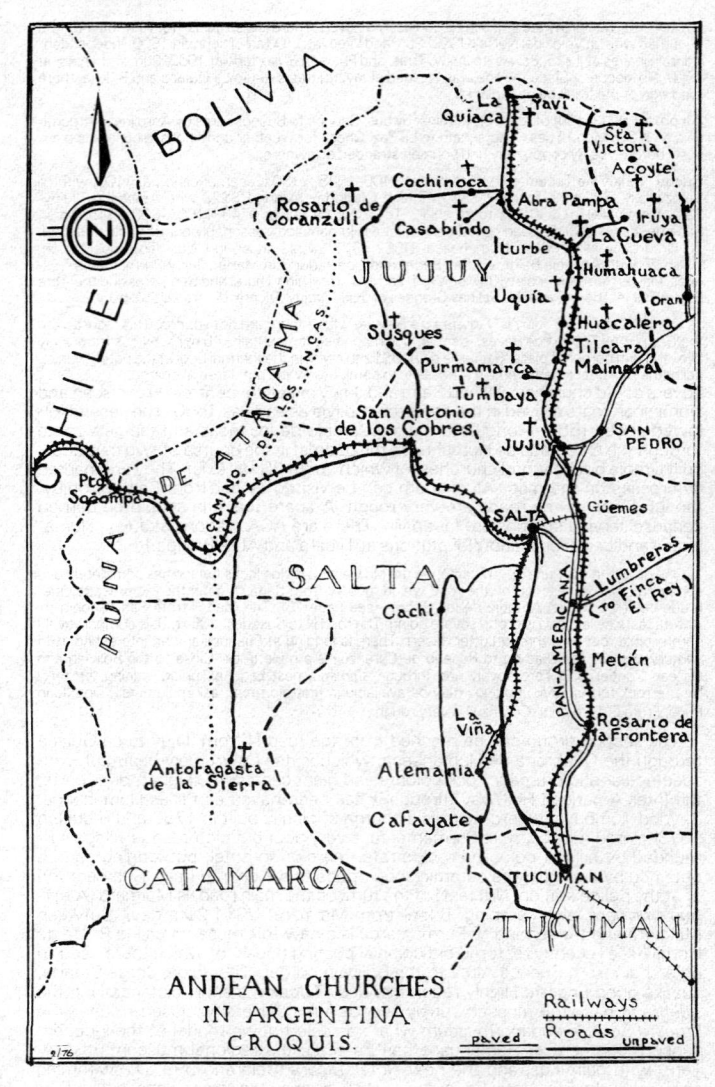

The churches of Huacalera, Uquía, and Humahuaca are on the main road. At Huacalera is the *Hotel Monterrey*, once comfortable. Two km. S of Huacalera, a small obelisk 20 metres W of the road gives the exact latitude of the Tropic of Capricorn. At Uquía (church built 1691) and Casabindo, the walls of the naves are hung with 17th century paintings of winged angels in military dress: the so-called *ángeles caballeros*. Cactus-wood decoration is found in many local churches.

Both in Tilcara and Humahuaca there are displays of pictures of the Passion made entirely of flowers, leaves, grasses and seeds at Easter and a traditional procession on Holy Thursday at night joined by thousands. No beef is sold during Holy Week in shops or restaurants. All along the Quebrada de Humahuaca the pre-Lent carnival celebrations are picturesque and colourful.

Humahuaca (alt. 2,940 metres), 126 km. from Jujuy, is a small traditional town with an attractive church (originally begun 1631, but totally reconstructed in 1873-80), a mechanical figure of San Francisco Solano which blesses the town from the town hall at 1200, and a large independence monument flanked by huge cacti. See the Estudio Museo Ramoneda, combined studio and museum, entrance US$0.50. Pleasant attraction: *Museo de Carnaval* (US$1). Market near Humahuaca railway station, where *colla* women sell everything from homeopathic herbs to fresh bread. On October 17 and 24 the Manca Fiesta, or the festival of the pots, is held here, and Indians from Jujuy and the Bolivian altiplano come, carrying all sorts of pots; local food is eaten. Folklore festival also around January 13-15, with local groups and dancing. Also Fiesta de la Señora de Candelaria, February 2, with a procession after 1400 with traditional dress and music. Near Humahuaca, 9 km. NE, is Coctaca, a large unexplained archaeological site; you can also see Indian artistic remains nearby at Hornaditas (18 km. on La Quiaca road) and Incacueva, and an Indian mine at Rinconada. Also near Humahuaca, at Estación Iturbe, a road leads right to La Cueva (6 km.) and on 70 km. over the 4,000-metre Abra del Cóndor to Iruya, a beautiful village with a fine 17th-century church and festival on October 6; daily bus from Humahuaca (highly recommended to make a visit). Roads to Cochinoca (25 km.) and Casabindo (62 km.) branch off left at a point 4 km. N of Abra Pampa, where mining is important. (*Residencial* nr. plaza in Abra Pampa on Senador Pérez, clean, hot water, F.) About 60 km away is Laguna Pozuelos, a natural monument and flamingo reserve. Truck transport daily exc. Sun. 15 km. from Abra Pampa is the vicuña farm at Miraflores, the largest in Argentina. Information offered, photography permitted.

The Instituto de Cultura Indígena offers guided tours of Indian communities, information, Quechua classes, exhibitions, concerts, lectures and a public library specializing in anthropology, folklore, history and archaeology, on Buenos Aires 740.

Hotels *Provincial de Turismo*, Buenos Aires 650,   D, swimming pool dry even in summer; *Hotel Humahuaca*, Córdoba y Corrientes, E, basic, run down, with hot water, food is not recommended; *Residencial Humahuaca*, F, traditional, clean, friendly. *Residencial Río Grande*, behind bus station, F, hot water, nice landlady, laundry. Several *residenciales* (F).

Camping   Across bridge by railway station, small charge includes use of facilities.

Restaurants *El Cardón*, at foot of large independence monument, good (try *cabrito al horno* with *queso de cabra*); *La Cacharpaya*, near church, good food and music, but avoid middle of the day when bus tours invade. Good place at bus station.

Yavi, with the fine church of San Francisco, which has magnificent gold decoration and windows of onyx, is reached by a good, paved road (16 km.) from La Quiaca; taxi available. (Find the caretaker at her house and she will show you round the church, open Tues.-Sun. 0900-1200 and Tues.-Fri. 1500-1800.) Opposite this church is the house of the Marqués Campero y Tojo. Three-room *hostería* at Yavi. Only a mule track leads on to the two churches of Santa Victoria (a forlorn Indian village in a rain forest valley) and Acoyte.

Beyond Humahuaca the *puna* is bleak and barren all the way, and the road unpaved, for the 167 km. to **La Quiaca**, on the Bolivian border and 292 km. from Jujuy. There is a market across the footbridge over the railway tracks, then one block on. La Quiaca is joined to its Bolivian neighbour, Villazón, by a concrete

80 ARGENTINA

bridge. Altitude, 3,442 metres. The climate calls for warm clothing the year round. If going on into Bolivia, buy your basic rations, medicaments etc. in La Quiaca. (Border on Argentine side closed 1200-1500.) When travelling by car between Jujuy to La Quiaca and it rains, wait, or you may find yourself on flooded roads.

Hotels *Turismo*, D, recommended, clean, modern, comfortable, two blocks S and one W of bus station; *Cristal*, best, four blocks from railway station, E, clean and comfortable, with café and bus office adjacent. The porter will exchange money, bargain for rates. Money exchange kiosk opposite this hotel will exchange US dollars and Bolivian pesos, but at a poorer rate than in Villazón. *Residencia Argentina*, clean; *Grand*, opp. railway station, clean, F; *Hotel Gran Victoria*, E; *Residencial El Turista*, very good, but expensive, has garages and swimming pool; *Club Social*; *Alojamiento Cruz del Sur*, cheap; cheap alojamiento, *Pequeño*, Av. Bolívar 236, friendly and clean. *Residencial Victoria*, near railway station and church, F, hot water.

Camping is possible near the control post on the outskirts of town.

Restaurant *Cristal*, opposite the Atahualpa bus office in small shopping arcade on the main shopping street, good, cheap; *Café Victoria* and *Panamericano* in same building as *Grand Hotel*.

Transport Difficult to obtain information in La Quiaca about buses leaving Villazón for points in Bolivia. 3 Atahualpa (next to *Hotel Cristal*) buses a day to Salta via Jujuy, 1115, 1600, 2130 (5-8 hrs. to Jujuy, 9-11 hrs. to Sa ta), also 1800 to Jujuy. La Quiaca-Salta, US$11.25. Panamericano (next to *Hotel Grand*) bus company has 5 buses a day to Jujuy, US$12. Some meal breaks, but take own food, as sometimes long delays. Buses may be stopped and searched for coca leaves. *Común* bus at 2130, 12 hours. The railway line between Jujuy and La Quiaca was washed away in many places during the heavy rains in February 1984. It is not known when services will be resumed. The railway goes up to 3,692 metres at Tres Cruces. Take warm sweaters, as temperature drops sharply after sunset. Go to Jujuy to take Tues. and Fri. train to Buenos Aires.

To Bolivia Take a taxi or hire a porter with a luggage barrow to take you through the immigration office opposite the Automóvil Club, and customs and final control on the frontier. There are few exchange facilities on the Argentine side (only until 1300 at Banco de la Nación in La Quiaca). Travellers' cheques can be cashed at the Turismo building; only dollar notes are accepted at the exchange shops. In La Quiaca some of the large supermarkets give good rates for the Argentine austral. You can also buy australes in Villazón for US notes', but not for travellers' cheques. *Cambios* are open on Sundays at Villazón but give a very poor rate. Food is good and cheap. Tip conductor at start and end of trip for service. Motorists should visit the Argentine Automóvil Club just off the international bridge for maps, gasoline, etc., and information; and in Villazón, the Servicio Nacional de Turismo to obtain the Hoja de Ruta, which all motorists must have. It is not restrictive in any practical sense; just a nuisance! If the Bolivian Immigration Officer at Villazón is not in his office, you can ask for him at *Hotel Panamericano*, just up from the Post Office. Taxis are available from the frontier to the Bolivian station.

Warning Those travellers who need a visa to enter Bolivia are advised to get it somewhere other than in La Quiaca because the consular staff try to charge US$15 per visa; pleading may reduce the charge.

Doctor There are a good hospital in La Quiaca and a doctor in Villazón.

Entering Argentina from Bolivia, Argentine immigration and customs are open 0730-1200, 1500-1800; Sats., Suns., and holicays 0900-1100. Buses arriving outside these hours will have to wait, so check before travelling. Porters US$1 from Villazón bus station to border; another US$1 from border to Argentine station. You can cross the border at night, without luggage, and your passport will not be stamped. Very thorough customs searches are made some 20 km. after the border (in Argentina).

N.B. Bolivian time is one hour earlier than Argentine. Lunch Bolivian side is 1200-1400 (Bol. time) and Argentine side 1200-1500 (Arg. time) so customs reopen at same time.

Make sure you book a seat when paying a railway fare; it is also essential to arrive well in advance of advertised time of departure to get your seat.

Bolivia can also be reached by road from **Orán**, an uninteresting place (*Hotel Centro*, E; dirty room at *Hotel Crillón*, E; *Residencial Crisol*, General San Martín, near bus stations, F, without bath, hot water, friendly, recommended; several hotels near bus station) where there are bus services to Agua Blanca (1½ hrs.) US$1.30, luggage checks on bus), on the frontier. There is nowhere to stay at Agua Blanca nor anywhere to change money, but there are restaurants (*El Rinconcito de los Amigos*) and shops; spend your remaining Bolivian money here, not accepted in Orán; buses to Orán every 2-3 hrs., e.g. 1615, 1830, 2100. The passport office at Agua Blanca is open from 0700 to 1200 and 1500 to 1900 hrs. There is no exit tax. There is a through bus service from Agua Blanca to Salta at 1100 caily. Buses run twice daily from Bermejo, across the river (ferry

ARGENTINA 81

US$0.10), to Tarija (6 hours, US$2). There is also a direct bus (Sat., US$15, 16 hrs journey) from Orán to Asunción, Paraguay.

Buses, five daily from Orán to Salta, last at 2100, 8½ hrs.; direct bus to Tucumán at 2130, connecting for Mendoza bus which leaves at 1300. Bus to Tartagal daily at 0630 and 1800; to Jujuy at 1200 daily; to Formosa, US$22, 14 hrs., leaving Tues., Thurs., Sat. at 0930; Orán to Embarcación, US$1.30.

Embarcación has several hotels (Sr. Sarmiento's Hotel; *Hotel Moderna*, E, *Universal*, hot water), of which the cheaper are near the railway station; just outside Embarcación you can walk to a Protestant mission for Mataes and Toba Indians, who sell unpainted pottery there. These Indians lead a fairly miserable existence. Buses go to Orán, 1 hour, US$1.30 on a paved road, from whence there are frequent buses to Agua Blanca (1 hour, US$1). Buses Embarcación-Pocitos. Bus Embarcación-Salta US$10. Embarcación-Formosa railway has *coche-motor* link run by Atahualpa bus company Mon., Wed., Fri. 1520, US$10, 19 hrs., but check details as this service is sometimes replaced by a bus when there is weather damage to the line. (Regular bus runs Tues. 1445.)

The Cuyo Region

In the Cuyo region, in the W, there is little rain and nothing can be grown except under irrigation. On the irrigated lands grapes and fruit are possible, and alfalfa takes the place of the maize grown in the N. Three of the more important oases in this area of slight rainfall are Mendoza itself, San Rafael, 160 km. to the S, and San Juan to the N.

Of the 15 million hectares in Mendoza Province, only 2% are cultivated. Of the cultivated area 40% is given over to vines, 25% is under alfalfa grown for cattle, and the rest under olive groves and fruit trees. Petroleum is produced in the Province, and there are important uranium deposits.

Generally speaking, the wine is less good than Chilean wines, but good types are produced when proper maturity is given.

The Transandine Route Travelling by rail or road from Buenos Aires westward across the pampa, one comes first to:

Mercedes, in Buenos Aires Province, an old but progressive city with a population of 40,000. It has many fine buildings, both public and private, and is a railway junction of some commercial importance. Travellers have been told here that it is against the law to take one's shoes off in the station! (Not to be confused with Villa Mercedes in San Luis Province—see below.) Tourist Office on plaza, very friendly.

Hotels *Aragón*, ½ block from Plaza, friendly, F, hot water. *Libertador*, E, opp. bus station, good.

The workshops of the San Martín railway are at **Junín,** 256 km. from Buenos Aires. (Eva Perón was born near here.) Also served by Mitre railway, the town is close to lagoons from which fish are taken to the capital. Population, about 60,000.

Hotels *Junín; Central. La Piemontesa*, E, reasonable.

Camping Chimihuin municipal campsite, US$1.50.

At La Boulaye, on Route 7, 517 km. from Buenos Aires, there are several good and cheap hotels, e.g. *Victoria*.

At **Villa Mercedes** (San Luis Province), 693 km. from Buenos Aires, a line runs NE to (122 km.) Río Cuarto. About 65 km. beyond Villa Mercedes we begin to run into the rolling hills of San Luis; beyond there are stretches of woodland. (ACA hotel, *San Martín*, Lavalle 435, restaurant, garages.)

Bus Villa Mercedes—Buenos Aires US$20.

Train Buenos Aires-Villa Mercedes, *El Aconcagua* daily at 2115, arrives 0730; returns 2206, arrives 0830; sleeper US$21.40, Pullman US$14.60; 1st Class US$10.25, tourist US$7.60.

Air Airport: Villa Reynolds, 10 km. from Villa Mercedes. Austral to Buenos Aires and to San Juan on Mon., Tues, Wed. at 1225, Fri., at 2000.

San Luis, 98 km. from Villa Mercedes, is the capital of the Province of San Luis. It stands at 765 metres at the southern end of the Punta de los Venados hills. It was founded by Martín de Loyola, the governor of Chile, in 1596, and is still

82 ARGENTINA

faintly colonial. The area is rich in minerals and an onyx quarry is worked. Visit the Centro Artesanal San Martín de Porras, run by the Dominican fathers, on 25 de Mayo, opp. Govt. Palace, where rugs are woven. Open 0700-1300 exc. Sat. and Sun. Population: 85,000. San Luis to Mendoza is 264 km.

A "Via Crucis" sculptured in white marble skirts the mountainside. Beyond Salto Grande, Salto Colorado and the Gruta de la Virgen de las Flores is El Volcán, in whose neighbourhood is Cruz de Piedra dam (drives, fishing), and Cañada Honda (placer gold mining, riding and fishing). Hotels and inns along the road.

Hotels *Dos Venados*, Junín and Sucre; *Gran Palace*, Rivadavia 657; *Aiello*, Av. Quintana 431, a/c, priv. bath, garages. *Gran San Luis*, Av. Quintana 470, pool, 50 metres from ACA; *Regidor*, San Martín 804; *Gran Hotel España*, Av. Quintana 300; and *Novel*, Junín 748, all category C. *Castelmonte*, Chacabuco 769; *Grisel*, Bolívar 321; and *Miramar*, Maipú 874, all category D. *Mitre*, Mitre 1043; *Rivadavia*, Rivadavia 1470; *Casino*, Uruguay 804; *Los Andes*, Los Andes 1582; *Royal*, Colón 878; and *Buenos Aires*, Buenos Aires 834; all category E. *Hotel Residencial 17*, hot water, friendly, opp. bus station, basic, F. *Hotel San Antonio*, with restaurant; many others opposite bus and railway station; these are category F.

Camping No site but plenty of waste ground between bus and railway stations.

Restaurants *Suany*, Bolívar 991, recommended; *Los Venados*, Colón and Bolívar. *La Cigüeña*, San Martín 723, good steaks, reasonable.

Exchange House *Alituris*, Pringles 983, opp. Plaza, no commission.

Tourist Office San Martín 741, excellent.

Train Buenos Aires-San Luis leaves at 2115, *El Aconcagua*, costs US$8.60 tourist, US$ 11.55 first, US$16.60 Pullman, and Sleeper US$23.40. Can continue with train to Mendoza, 4 hrs. Return daily at 2006, arrives 0830 next day.

29 km NE of San Luis is **La Toma** (*Hotel Gran Italia*, F, hot showers; *Residencial Days*, P. Graciarena 158, private bath) the cheapest place to buy green onyx—about 20 shops. From here you can make an excursion to Cerros Rosario, interesting hills and rock scenery, 10 km. NW; and San José del Morro, a group of mountains which were originally volcanoes (there is a model in the Museo de Ciencias in Buenos Aires). You will find a lot of rose-quartz.

Beyond San Luis (27 km.) the line climbs to a height of 460 metres and descends again along the valley of the Río Desaguadero. From the small junction of Las Catitas, 92 km. from Mendoza, a branch line runs S to (183 km.) San Rafael, through country typical of this region: sometimes arid, sometimes marshy, and sometimes cultivated. At **San Rafael** itself, at the foot of the Andes, irrigation makes it possible to grow fruit in large quantities. The town—there are some oil wells near—has a population of 46,000. There is a small but interesting natural history museum. A road runs W over El Pehuenche pass to Talca (Chile).

Above the town, up the Río Atuel valley, there is beautiful scenery (it is called Valle Hermoso, or Beautiful Valley) up to the dams of El Nihuil which provide irrigation water and hydroelectric power to Mendoza. There is fishing in the reservoir above the highest dam.

Hotels *Rex*; *España*, corner of San Martín and España, D with bath, clean but shabby, no restaurant. *Hospedaje Residencial Comercio*, F, opp. station on Rivadavia.

Campsite at Tunuyán, 77 km. before Mendoza from San Rafael; there are three more campsites on the road from Luján outside Mendoza to Potrerillos (52 km.).

Mendoza, at the foot of the Andes, 1,060 km. from Buenos Aires, is linked to it by air, the San Martín railway and a paved road. The road continues from Mendoza across the Andes to Chile. (No rail service now between Mendoza and Chile.)

Mendoza (756 metres) is an expanding and very pleasant city. Rainfall is slight, but irrigation has turned the area into a green oasis covered with fruit trees and vineyards. The city was colonized from Chile in 1561 and named in honour of the then governor of Chile. It was from here that the Liberator José de San Martín set out to cross the Andes, to help in the liberation of Chile. The city was completely destroyed by fire and earthquake in 1861, so Mendoza today is essentially a modern city of low dwellings (as a precaution against earthquakes), thickly planted with trees and gardens. There was a serious earthquake, which made

ARGENTINA 83

40,000 homeless, in January 1985. The main street is Calle San Martín, which runs S to N parallel to the San Martín railway line. Population of city and suburbs: 600,000.

See the Cerro de la Gloria, a hill above the great Parque San Martín on the W side of the city, crowned by an astonishing monument to San Martín. There is a great rectangular stone block with bas-reliefs depicting various episodes in the equipping of the Army of the Andes and the actual crossing. In front of the block, San Martín bestrides his charger. In the park at the foot of Cerro de la Gloria steep and twisting paths run to the Zoological Gardens, cageless, good and very well laid out. There are watercourses and an artificial 1 km-long lake in the park too, where regattas are held, and views of the Andes rising in a blue-black perpendicular wall, topped off in winter with dazzling snow, into a china-blue sky. The entrance to the Parque San Martín is ten blocks W of the Plaza Independencia and is reached by bus 3 from the centre; there is an open-topped bus ("Oro Negro") that will take you to the top of the Cerro de la Gloria, which regularly but infrequently runs from the eastern end of the park, on Av. Libertad, to the monument— it's a long walk (45 mins.). You can wait for the bus half-way up the hill, at the entrance to the zoo.

The San Martín Museum (US$0.15) is housed in a school building on Av. General San Martín, some 8 blocks N of the city centre (closed weekends). The Museum of Natural History is on Plaza Independencia, lodged underground; this, too, has some colonial exhibits but is best known for its collection of Argentine plants and animals. (Open Tues.-Fri. 0900-1300, 1500-2000 Sat.-Sun. 1600-2000.) The Palacio Municipal has a rooftop observation platform, no charge. The Municipal Aquarium is underground at Calle Buenos Aires and Ituzaingó, very interesting, admission US$0.50, open Mon.-Fri. 1000-1200 and 1530-2100, Sat. and Sun. same times a.m. but open an hour longer in the evening, until 2200. Worth seeing, also, are the ruins of the San Francisco church near Plaza Pedro de Castillo. The Historical Museum, on Calle Montevideo near Calle Chile, beautifully furnished, has a collection on San Martín and history of Mendoza. The best shopping centre is Avenida Las Heras, where there are good souvenir and handicraft shops; leather goods are cheaper here than in Buenos Aires. The vintage festival, Fiesta de la Vendimia, is held in the amphitheatre of the Parque San Martín in March. There is a wine museum (at the Gioll *bodega*), with good guides and wine tasting, just behind the Palacio de Gobierno, opening hours from the tourist office. Museums are open 0900-1230 and 1700-2000. Outside Mendoza, about 40 km. due E, there is a satellite town, very modern, called San Martín. N.B. Official tours of the city are a waste of time and money.

Wine Wine *bodegas* (wine-making season March/April) and fruit preserving; visiting times change with seasons, check: Gioll winery, take bus marked "Maipú" (every hour), visits possible weekdays, tours every hour, including a tasting, Spanish only, one of the world's biggest now. Bodega de Arizú, another of the biggest (in receivership, but being resold) 15 mins' walk from Correo or 10 minutes by bus from central bus station, direction Godoy Cruz, is open to inspection any time, bus No 7 from city centre; so are many of the others, and they are generous with wine after the visit. Visits at 0800 or 1500. Try Bodega Escorihuela (bus 15 from centre) if you are more interested in the information than the wine-tasting. The Toso bodega is close to the city centre and has excellent wines. Prices at the bodegas have roughly a 100% mark-up from supermarket prices. Recommended: Cruz del Sur from Bodega Arizú, Cuesta del Parsal, Valroy-Borgoña, Valroy-Cabernet Sauvignon, Viejo Toro, and Vino de Mesa Arizú Tinto Seco. Many tourist agencies include the bodegas in their half-day or day-long tours (but these visits are too short, with too few guides and little tasting).

Local Holidays January 18 (Crossing of the Andes); July 25 (St. James); September 8 (Virgin of Carmen de Cuyo). Annual wine festival at the beginning of March.

Hotels *Aconcagua*, B, comfortable, San Lorenzo 545, good restaurant, tourist advice and bookings available; *Plaza*, Chile 1124, B; *Gran Hotel Potrerillos*, Route 7, Luján de Cuyo, B; *Ariosto*, Infanta Mercedes San Martín 48, C; *Alcor*, Gral. Paz 86, E, central, good, accepts Amex; *Royal*, old part, Las Heras, 145, adequate value; *Palace*, Las Heras 70, C; *Nutibara*, Bartolomé Mitre 867, D, modern swimming pool, recommended; *Crillón*, Perú 1065, D, small, clean. Nearby is *Internacional*, good, Sarmiento 720. *Embajador*, C, Juan B. Justo 367, overpriced; *El Libertador*, Av. España 3-7, E without breakfast, D with, bath, clean, free taxi service to bus terminal; *City*, Gral Paz 95, D, clean, helpful; *Escorial*, San Luis 263, E, with bath, clean, central; *Cervantes*, Amigorena 63, restaurant; *Alem*, E, with bath, near bus station (opposite hospital), 5 mins. from centre; also near bus station; *Messidor*, Alberdi 690, D, reasonable, friendly, arranges tours; *Splendid*, San Martín 2215, E; *Santa Clara*, 9 de Julio, central, clean, hot water, own bath; *Terminal*, near bus station, F, basic, clean. Lower ratings: *Imperial*, Las Heras 88, F, good; *El Descanso*, Gral. Paz

84 ARGENTINA

463, F, without bath, clean, quiet, friendly, highly recommended; *Rincón Vasco*, Las Heras 590, D, with private bath; *República*, Necochea 541, E, pleasant, cheerful, English spoken; *Casius*, Gutiérrez 688, E; *Residencia Central*, 9 de Julio 658, F, immaculate, friendly, lashings of hot water; *Líbano*, Gral. Paz 227, excellent, clean, from E; *Petit*, Perú 1459, F with breakfast, 1½ blocks from railway station, clean, friendly, recommended; *España*, Perú 1525, good, clean, F, clothes-washing facilities. (There is another *Residencia España* at Vicente López, 420.) *Namuncua*, Chile 829, E, with bath; *El Rosario*, Chile 1579, between Las Heras and Paz, E, good, clean, hot water, heating, recommended; *Margal*, Juan B. Justo 75, clean, F; *Ideal*, Juan B. Justo 270, F, English spoken, transport to bus station; *Zamora*, Perú 1156, reasonable and friendly, converted house, E; *Vigo*, Necochea 749 (Tel.: 250208), D, good value, good *comedor*, E; *Galicia*, Av. San Juan 881, (near Av. L. M. Alem), F, very clean, hot water; *Quijote*, San Juan 1407, E, clean, friendly, restaurant; *Madrid*, Av. España, no hot water, E. Try *Pensión Janni*, junction 9 de Julio and Infanta Mercedes San Martín; *Motel Chacras de Coria*, S of town, Darragueina y Piedras, Luján, Tel.: 960309, for stays of over 4 days; *Residencial Unión*, Patricias Mendocinas, nr. Plaza España, E, without bath, breakfast, clean, hot water; *Santiago*, near railway station; many cheap *alojamientos* in this area; *Maxim*, Lavalle 32, F, hot shower, recommended; *Pensión Cuatro Ríos*, F, hot water; *Gran Marta*, Gen. Paz 460, clean, hot showers, recommended; *Residencial Ledesma*, Vicente López 511, F, nr. bus station. *Residencial Copihué*, between Rioja and Entre Ríos, E, hot water; *Residencial Miami*, Necochea 278, E, very clean; *Residencial Familiar*, Montevideo 145, E, with breakfast; *Savoy*, Belgrano 1377, F, good, clean, some rooms without window, tours offered at 20% discount. Several cheap *residenciales* in Calle Güemes, e.g. *Betty*, F, on 400 block, leading off Güemes; *Residencial Forli*, Coronel Plaza 315, F with short, hot showers; *Residencial Las Mellizas*, Federico Moreno 1819, F, with breakfast; *Residencial Sta. Paula* (behind bus station), F, with breakfast; *Center*, Alem 547, 150 metres from bus station, family atmosphere, comfortable, E; *Nevada*, Av. Perú, near railway station, F with bath, hot water, clean, cheap meals. Unnamed *pensión* at Montecaseros 1682, F, basic, hot water, cooking facilities. *El Piño Azul* apartments, San Martín 2872 (Tel.: 304593), D per day. Hotels also at Challao.

Camping In Parque General San Martín permitted, free, in cars, but not in tents. Three campsites at Challao, about 14 km. from the city centre, reached by colectivo No. 11 leaving every hour. *Camping Suizo* best value, has shop, US$1.50 p.p. and US$1.50 for tent, safest of all sites, friendly but loud music at night from nearby amusement arcade. About 13 km. from Mendoza, two sites near the turn-off for Barballón. *El Salto*, 50 km. W of Mendoza, near mountains, well situated.

Restaurants *Trevi*, Las Heras 68, de luxe. Good ones are the *Automobile Club*, Italian restaurants *Montecatini*, Gral. Paz 370, and *Marchigiana*, Patricias Mendocinas 1550; *San Marco*, on Las Heras, and the *Mendoza Regatta Club*, Av. de las Palmeras, Parque San Martín. Highly recommended is *Bárbaro*, San Martín 914, English spoken, US$6.25 for main course plus wine for 2. *Tristán Bajara*, Av. Sarmiento (parrilla), good. *Trattoria Aveni*, 25 de Mayo 1162, crowded, good, meal US$6.50. *Vecchia Roma*, Av. España 1619, recommended for good food, atmosphere and service. *El Rey de la Milanesa*, cheap and good; 1 block off Av. Las Heras, excellent value. *Don Angelo*, Lavalle 148, cheap; *Le Monde*, Mitre 1274; *Club Alemán*, Necochea 2261, Godoy Cruz, recommended. *Fritz y Franz*, Av. Gral. San Martín 1901. Good value is *Petit Progreso*, Córdoba with San Juan; *Boccadoro*, Mitre 1976; *San Agustín*, Av. L. M. Alem 477 opposite hospital, big meals at reasonable prices. *Chino*, 25 de Mayo 1553 (near Las Heras), very good; *La Tapita*, 25 de Mayo, 1½ blocks from *Hotel El Descanso*, serves 4 course set meal at low price. Good cheap menu at *Hotel Francia*, Las Heras. *Pizzería del Rincón de la Boca*, Las Heras 485, good, cheap pizzas; also at No. 475, *Pizzería Pic-Nic*. Many sidewalk cafés in Mendoza. *Bar San Marco*, on Espejo between 9 de Julio and España. *Confitería Bailable*, Av. Las Heras 449, good value. Ice cream at *Soppelso*, Las Heras 409, recommended. *São Paulo*, San Martín 1214, very popular standup coffee bar. *El Gran Lomo*, Rivadavia and San Martín, cheap filling sandwiches, open 24 hrs. Good snacks at *Cerrito Bar*, L.M. Alem 41. Cheap and good eating places near San Martín railway station. In bars 20% extra is charged if you sit at a table rather than at the counter.

Nightclubs in the suburb of Chacras de Coria. Discothèques: *Blow Up*, Mitre 1520; *Kangaroo*, Rivadavia 430; *La Cueva*, Chile 1285; *El Grillo*, Chile 1243; *Casino*, 25 de Mayo 1123; *Al Diablo*, Ruta Internacional Vistalba Luján.

Casino 25 de Mayo 1123, daily 02100-0300.

Car Hire Lis Car, San Lorenzo 110, Tel.: 291416; A.S. Rent-a-Car, Garibaldi 186, Tel.: 248317.

Mountain Climbing Information from Tourist Office. There is a three-day (Thurs.-Sat.) climbing and trekking expedition via Godoy Cruz and Cacheuta to Cerro Penitentes (4,351 metres), sleeping in mountain refuge, food included. See also page 87.

Bank of London and South America, Av. San Martín 1498. Good rates at Bank of America (not travellers' cheques though). Citibank (which does *not* give dollars for US travellers' cheques). Open 0715-1315. Currency changed between 0715 and 1030 only. **N.B.** No travellers' cheques changed at weekends, except at the *cambio* at Galería Tonsa, 1100 block of Av. San Martín, open till 2000 on Sat. Best rate for Chilean currency at the bus terminal (open from 0715). Good exchange house opposite LAN-Chile office in San Martín. Exprinter, San Martín 1198, and Santiago *cambio* opposite. Also recommended: Maguitur, Av. General San Martín 1203. Another at 9 de Julio, by Av. Las Heras. No exchange facilities Sun.

Consulates Bolivia, 9 de Julio 1357, 2nd floor; Peru, Av. España 533, Tel.: 241462.

Goethe Institut Morón 265, Mon.-Fri. 0800-1200, 1600-2230. German films.

English language magazines and *Buenos Aires Herald* usually available at kiosk at corner of San Martín and Alem.

Coin-operated **laundromat**, Colón 543.

There is a **gynaecological clinic** about three doors away from *El Descanso* hotel; helpful and relatively inexpensive.

Tourist Offices at airport, Tel.: 306484, helpful (frequently closed), one at the bus terminal, Tel.: 259709, at Av. San Martín 1143, Tel.: 242800, very helpful, which is also the Museum of Modern Art. They have a list of reasonable private lodgings, but not much other literature. Good town map available at most kiosks. Tourist cards are obtainable at the border, cost US$1.

Travel Agency Turismo Jocolí, Las Heras y 25 de Mayo, Tel.: 230-466, recommended for tours in and around the city, and to El Cristo Redentor statue.

Post Office Av. San Martín and Av. Zapata.

Airport Plumerillo, 8 km. from centre; *remise* taxis (US$2-3) and buses (infrequent) run. Bus No. 6 stops at corner of San Juan and Alem and takes you not to the terminal but to a stop some 2 mins. walk away. Flying time from Buenos Aires: 1¾ hours. Aerolíneas flies three times a day, and has one night flight; Austral twice a day. 40% discount on night flight from Buenos Aires (night flight to Buenos Aires, Sat. 2315). AA to Santiago, US$70, daily except Sun., fare must be paid in US$. AA to and from Bariloche, 3 times a week. Several flights to Córdoba with AA and Austral (1515).

Trains to Buenos Aires: *El Libertador*, leaves Mon. and Fri. at 2015, arrives at 0930; car transporters, luxurious bar, film show and airconditioning, steward service, good dining cars, meal US$4, good value; take drinks with you. *El Aconcagua* leaves Mendoza daily at 1545, arrives Bs. As. at 0830; *El Sanjuanino* at 2015, arrives at 0930 (Tues., Wed., Thurs.). Trains from Buenos Aires to Mendoza: *Libertador*, leaves at 2015, Sun. and Thurs., arrives 1000. *El Aconcagua* leaves at 2115, arrives at 1400 the next day, *El Sanjuanino* at 2015 Mon., Tues., Wed. Fares: Sleeper US$28.45, pullman US$21.65, first, US$15.10, tourist US$11.20. There are no trains to Chile. Train from Mendoza to San Luis 4 hrs., to San Juan 2½ hrs. daily. Bus from railway to bus terminal, No. 5, US$0.15.

Buses (all from smart new bus station) to Santiago, see page 86. To La Serena (Chile) via San Juan and the Agua Negra pass (US$10). Buses also run to Bariloche, leave 0900 Sun., Tues., Thurs., US$40, on a mostly paved road, about 27 hours; to Córdoba, daily at 2200 9 hrs., US$13; to San Juan every 2 hours US$3.75 (2 companies, TAC and Villa del Sur y Media Agua). To La Rioja US$14, 10 hrs., leaves 1430, 2030 or 2130. Catamarca overnight only, 12 hrs., daily, US$15. Daily at 1730 to Tucumán, US$17.25. Comodoro Rivadavia Tue., Thurs., Sat., 36 hrs., at 2000, US$80 incl. meal stops. Bus to Mar del Plata US$32; to Puerto Iguazú at 0700; Tues. and Sun. US$40, 38 hrs., Chevallier. To Buenos Aires via Route 8, 2nd class daily at 1315, arrives 0550, US$26, 1st class daily at 1750, arrives 0858, US$32; via Route 7 (Junín-Mercedes) at 2020, arrives 1205, US$26. Dull scenery, and very cold across the Pampas at night. Hitch-hiking between Mendoza and Buenos Aires is quite easy. If hitching to San Juan, take bus No. 6 to the airport near the highway. Hitching from Mendoza to Los Andes (Chile) is easy; go to the petrol station in Godoy Cruz suburb, from where all trucks to Chile, Peru and elsewhere leave.

Excursions If driving in mountains remember to advance the spark by adjusting the distributor, or weaken the mixture in the carburettor, to avoid the car seizing up in the rarified air. Buses run to the hot springs at **Cacheuta**, US$2.40 round trip, US$5 entry (thermal baths for those with doctors' certificates only, can be arranged at travel agents for US$4), 45 km. to the SW (hotels not recommended). The charming resort of **Potrerillos** is 13 km. from Cacheuta, with ski slopes not far away and excellent birdwatching in summer. *Gran Hotel*; *Hotel de Turismo*, B, with meals; ACA campsite (US$2 for members); the skiing at Vallecito (reached by tour bus or car only), however, is reported less good than at Portillo, on the Chilean side of the Andes. In summer, you can hike 20 km. from the resort of Potrerillos to Vallecito, taking two days. On the first you will see desert scenery, blooming cactus flowers, birds and an occasional goat or cow. The second you walk surrounded by peaks, a steep but not difficult climb to the San Antonio refuge, usually open with beds and meals. Two other popular resorts within a few km. of the city are Barballón, to the NE, and Challao, to the NW. An excursion is also available from the Mendoza bus station to the small ski resort of Los Penitentes, 170 km. away; equipment hire US$5 a day, lift ticket for a day US$9. The

86 ARGENTINA

best skiing is at (2,250 metres) **Valle de las Leñas**, S of Mendoza in the Valle Hermoso, about 70 km. from Malargüe. Excursions there on Sun. at 0300, return 2300. There are 15 ski-courses, three T-bars, three ski-lifts. Three stonebuilt hotels: *Escorpio, Acuario* and *Gemini* and a disco, shop renting equipment and expensive restaurant. It was built by an Argentine-French consortium in 1983. Malargüe is served by an airport; paved road Buenos Aires-Valle de las Leñas (1,180 km.). On the road to Luján de Cuyo (buses go every 15 mins. from near bus terminal) is a fine arts museum dedicated to Argentine artists, surrounded by sculpture in gardens, admission free (Museo Provincial de Bellas Artes Emiliano Guiñazu, *Casa de Fader*). The *El Oro Negro* buses take you to the top of Cerro de la Gloria. The Godoy Cruz bus takes you to adjacent vineyards. Day-trips can also be made to Puerte del Inca with Turismo Vitar for about US$10 (see page87). Turismo la Cumbre, Necochea 541, also includes in its price a 10-hr. 9 hour circular tour, as does Cata Turismo, Las Heras 426, 13 hours. Local bus for Puente del Inca at 1800, 6 hrs., last bus back at 1430.

Hotel *Termas* at Villavicencio is well worth visiting, B, offers breakfast and 2 enormous good meals. Unfortunately open only during short summer season. Many tourists come to visit the springs, which are all set in concrete. Pleasant walks round the area.

N.B. It is no longer possible to go from Mendoza to Santiago via the statue of Christ the Redeemer at 3,854 metres. To see it, you must go on an excursion from Mendoza (US$7 return, early a.m., all travel agencies) since the Chilean side of the frontier at the statue is closed. All buses and cars go through the tunnel to Chile, leaving the statue unseen above.

Over the Andes to Chile

N.B. No visas into Chile are available at the border, so if you need one and haven't got it, you will be turned back. There is a time change: travelling from Argentina into Chile remember to move your watch back 1 hr. between mid-March and mid-October.

There are 2 alternates of Route 7, which meet at the town of **Uspallata,** the only sizeable town between Mendoza and the Chilean frontier. Near Uspallata are the ruins of Las Bóvedas, built by the Huarpe Indians under the Jesuits, and an Inca *tambería*. They are just off the road which leads to Barreal and Calingasta (see page 89), unpaved for its first part and tricky when the snow melt-water crosses it after the summer. (Prices are usually much higher at frontier, temperatures much lower. Frontier closes early.) The fully-paved southern branch, via Cacheuta and Potrerillos, is wider and better than the northern branch, which goes via Villavicencio with a stretch of one-way traffic just beyond the resort, where the road leads up spectacularly to the 3,050 metres high Cruz del Paramillo. (The return loop, a little longer and less steep, is through the picturesque Quebrada del Toro.) This northern branch is still unpaved.

Uspallata Hotels *Hotel Uspallata*, C, dinner at 2100; payment for meals and drinks in cash, bowling alley. Quite good, but vast herds of people get driven through it. Also *Los Cóndores*.

Camping There is a pleasant municipal site at Uspallata, US$1 per head, full washing facilities hot water.

Beyond Las Cuevas, the road divides. The easier route goes through the new road tunnel (charge for car, US$10, for a VW bus, US$13); the other— negotiable on the Argentine side; in good condition on the Chilean side— goes over La Cumbre pass, and should be taken if at all possible. Pass open in winter except after heavy storms.

Transport to Santiago Turismo cars (Chi-Ar and Nevada) carrying 4 to 5 passengers (US$15, 5 hrs) and minibuses (6 hrs) do the trip to Santiago daily. If travelling by bus from Mendoza to Santiago take a direct bus as it is not possible to walk across the border. Buses Mendoza to Santiago daily at 0600-1200; several companies. Most of them are comfortable and fast (6½-8 hrs.), air-conditioned and hostess service (including breakfast), worth it when crossing the border as waiting time can be a matter of several hours. Criticisms have been received of O'Higgins and TAC companies. Passengers are normally collected from their hotels, fare US$13, those with hostess service US$17 (to Viña del Mar and Valparaíso US$15), children under 8 pay 60% of adult, but no seat; book two days ahead. Passport required. All buses go through the new tunnel, which is open 0800-1300 Chile to Argentina and 1300-1800 Argentina to Chile. The ride is rather rough and dusty, but spectacular. Information at main bus terminal. If you want to return, buy an undated return ticket Santiago-Mendoza; it is cheaper.

People travelling by car over the Andes in winter are advised to enquire about road conditions from ACA in Mendoza (San Martín y Amigorena).

All Argentine exit formalities are now dealt with at Punta de Vacas, 30 km. from Las Cuevas, where entry formalities are handled. One can hitch-hike, or possibly bargain with bus drivers for a

ARGENTINA 87

seat, from Punta de Vacas to Santiago, but if one is dropped at the entrance to the tunnel in winter, one cannot walk through. Travellers however report that customs men often help by asking passing motorists to take hitch-hikers through the tunnel to Chile. Chilean migration and customs check is just after the tunnel—searches for fruit, meat, etc., in a new building with the bus parked inside. Customs at the frontier are closed 1200-1400. Members of ACA need only the *Libreta de Pasos por Aduana*, otherwise you need the *Documento de Exportación* to enter Chile. Good food at frontier hotel, and there is an excellent motel on the Chilean side about an hour down.

The crossing of the Andes, taken by San Martín, is the old mountain trail the Spaniards named the Camino de los Andes. Beyond Uspallata is a vast, open, undulating plain, wild and bare. On all sides stand the grey, gaunt, barren mountains. On the far side of this plain the valley narrows till Río Blanco is reached, and there the mountain torrents rush and froth into the river. Soon we look up the Tupungato Valley at the majestic cone of Tupungato, one of the giants of the Andes, rising 6,797 metres. An equally majestic mass of pinnacled rocks, Los Penitentes, is passed. In the clear air it is difficult to realise that they are 65 km. away. The climber to their base (an easy task from Puente del Inca with a guide) sees a remarkable sight. The higher rocks look like a church and the smaller, sharper rocks below give the impression of a number of cowled monks climbing upwards. On the other side of the valley we get a good view of Aconcagua (6,960 metres), sharply silhouetted against the blue sky. In 1985, a complete Inca mummy was discovered at 5,300 metres on the mountain.

Best time for climbing Aconcagua is from mid-January to mid-February. Rob Rachowiecki writes: it is first necessary to obtain a permit from the Dirección de Deportes, Recreación y Turismo Social (offices at the Mendoza football stadium). The Club Andinista Mendoza will assist you with the paperwork; Sr. Parra is particularly helpful. Allow a couple of days for this. From Mendoza take a bus or colectivo to Puente del Inca. From here mules are available but cost US$20 per mule per day; you have to pay for 3 days there and back (1 day rest) and for the mule driver and his wages. This only takes you to the base camp at Plaza de Mulas (4,400 m) where there is a good hut about 2 km. beyond and behind the army barracks. Of the huts above this point only La Libertad (Berlín) hut at about 6,000 m is in serviceable condition. Both huts are small with no facilities. Bring a tent able to withstand 100 mph + winds, and clothing and sleeping gear for temperatures below -20°C. Allow at least one week for acclimatization at lower altitudes before attempting summit (4 days from Plaza de Mulas). Treks and climbs organized by Sr Fernando Grajales, J.F. Moreno 898, 5500 Mendoza, Telex 55-154.

In a short time we are at **Puente del Inca,** 2,718 metres above sea level, 160 km. from Mendoza, a sports resort set among mountains of great grandeur. The old hotel was destroyed by an earthquake; visitors now stay at the guest house on the army base. (*Hostería Puente del Inca*, C for room, about US$40 extra for full board, also bookable from *Plaza Hotel* in Mendoza, which manages it.) 5 km. from Puente del Inca on the road to Mendoza is a ski club, *Cruz de Caña*, with comfortable dormitories, E, and a good restaurant. The owner organizes trekking expeditions; prices: US$50 a day full board during expedition, and US$20 per mule.

The natural bridge after which Puente del Inca is named is one of the wonders of South America; it crosses the river Mendoza at a height of 19 metres, has a span of 21 metres, and is 27 metres wide, and seems to have been formed by sulphur-bearing hot springs. Puente del Inca is the best point for excursions into the higher Andean valleys or for a visit to the base of Aconcagua, which was first climbed by Vines and Zurbriggen of the Fitzgerald Expedition in 1897. Visits can be paid on horseback from Puente del Inca to Los Penitentes; or on foot to the green lake of Laguna de los Horcones; or by car (only with a well regulated engine) or on horseback to the statue of Christ the Redeemer set above La Cumbre (or Uspallata) pass on the frontier at an altitude of 4,200 metres. It was erected jointly by Chile and Argentina in 1904 to celebrate King Edward VII's decision in the boundary dispute of 1902. It is, unfortunately, somewhat disappointing from the road, for it is completely dwarfed by the landscape. (The road from the tunnel to the statue is closed for the season after the first snow fall in April.)

The frontier railway tunnel is no longer used by road traffic, which now takes the new 4-km. El Libertador-Las Cuevas toll road tunnel (US$10). The Chilean frontier is beyond **Las Cuevas,** a neat, modern settlement now being developed as a ski-ing resort (though there is no ski-lift as yet), but recently damaged by landslides and a fire. It has the Argentine customs station; customs formalities

88 ARGENTINA

take about 10 mins. It is wise to take snow chains from June to October. Officially, traffic without chains and a shovel is prohibited between Uspallata and the border, but this can be resolved in a friendly way with border policemen. Both ACA and Chilean Automobile Club sell, but do not rent, chains.

Hotel *Hostería Las Cuevas*, only one, poor food, no heating in annex.

North of Mendoza

There are three other oases standing between the plains and the mountains to the N of Mendoza, in much the same way as San Rafael to the S. San Juan is prosperous, La Rioja does fairly well with its wines and olive oil, but Catamarca has always lived on the brink of economic disaster. The first oasis, 177 km. from Mendoza by paved road or railway, is

San Juan, 400,000 people, the capital of the Province of San Juan, founded in 1562 by Don Juan Jufré de Loaysa y Montese, at 650 metres. An earthquake in 1944 practically destroyed the place but the centre, including the Cathedral, has been rebuilt. Sarmiento, the historian and educationist, and President from 1868 to 1874, was born here; his house contains the Sarmiento Museum, with a signed portrait of Lincoln. There is an Archaeological Museum 10 km. out of town, with a number of fascinating mummies. Also a Natural Sciences museum, open 0830-1230 and 1530-1930, US$0.15. The ruins of the Santo Domingo Convent are worth seeing. The Parque de Mayo has an artificial lake for boating, pretty gardens and a miniature railway. The surrounding country is picturesque. About 60 km. from San Juan is the famous religious site of Difunta Correa at Vallecito; the shrine in the desert commemorates a woman who died of thirst there, but whose milk kept her baby alive for 3 days until it was found. There is an interesting collection of items left for blessing.

Hotels Provincia (ex-*Estornell*), (no dining room), Mitre 31 Este, D, 10% discount for ACA members, parking; *Nogaró*, Ignacio de La Roza 132 Tel.: 227501/5, the best, pool, B (15% discount to ACA members); *Jardín Petit Hotel*, 25 de Mayo 345, B (10% discount to ACA members), bathwater sometimes cold, guarded car-park next door; *Selby*, Av. Rioja 183, C; *La Toja*, Rivadavia 494, C; *Argentino*, Estados Unidos 381, E; *Plaza*, Sarmiento 344, D, friendly; *Bristol*, Entre Ríos 368, C; *Brescia*, Av. España 336, opp. railway station, D; *Austria*, Sarmiento 246, E. Others are less good, including *Lido*, 9 de Julio 429; *Lara*, Rivadavia 213; *Hispano Argentino*, and *San Francisco*, on España, 410 and 284; *Oller*, Jujuy 45, pleasant, reasonable; *Rex*, Gral. Acha 187; *Central*, Mitre 131; *Roy*, Entre Ríos 180; *San Juan*, on Laprida, near tourist office, F, hot showers.

Camping "Camping permitted" signs along road from Mendoza to San Juan. Campsite in olive grove, 7 km. S of San José de Jáchal on the road to San Juan, and 23 km. after Jáchal, on Villa Unión road.

Restaurants *Nederland*, Salta y Circunvalación, on edge of town, international cooking and *parrillada*; many good grillrooms. *Club Español*, good, try Maravilla wine here, well-priced, on Rivadavia 32 Este. *Pizzería Cuyo*, Mitre 644 Oeste, near railway station, small, excellent food; *Un Rincón de Nápoli*, Rivadavia 175 Oeste, variable food but large glasses of fresh orange juice. *Club Sirio Libanés*.

Car Hire Parque Automotor, España y Libertador, Tel.: 226018, cash discount if you ask.

Tourist Office, opposite Sarmiento Museum, arranges tours, has good leaflets on the province. Large maps of the province available from bookshops, US$5.

By Air Airport: Chacritas, 14 km. from town. Daily flights to Buenos Aires stopping at Córdoba or Villa Mercedes.

Bus to Catamarca, 599 km., US$17.50 over secondary roads in arid country; no direct connexion with Santiago (Chile), only via Mendoza.

Rail The two named trains (see page 85) that ply between Mendoza and Buenos Aires (*El Sanjuanino* and *Aconcagua*) also serve San Juan. They reach San Juan 2½ hours after Mendoza, and leave for Buenos Aires 2½ hours before Mendoza departure times. Fares Buenos Aires-San Juan: sleeper (to and from Mendoza only on *Aconcagua*) US$31.55; pullman US$24.75, 1st class US$17.25; tourist US$12.90.

If hitchhiking to La Rioja, take route 141 to Chepes (ACA Hostería), then N to Patquía, because the road is paved and there is more traffic; to start with, take bus 39 to airport, out of town (this route is, however, less interesting than going via San Agustín or San José de Jachal, see below).

ARGENTINA 89

Along Route 20, heading West, one reaches Calingasta (135 km. from San Juan, *Hotel La Capilla*) in the valley of the same name. A spectacular drive: the road is open for traffic in one direction in the morning, in the other in the afternoon. South of Calingasta is Barreal (*Hotel Barreal*, also *Hotel Jorge*, F, clean, very simple. *Hostería San Eduardo*, small, quaint, few rooms with bath, open in summer only).

Route 40, the principal tourist route on the eastern slope of the Andes, heads northwards towards Cafayate and Salta, via San José de Jachal. After 55 km. is Talacasto, where the road to the Chilean frontier branches off to the left (Route 436). This road crosses the Puerta del Colorado pass (2,759 metres) with an extensive view to the north and reaches Las Flores after 125 km. Las Flores is on Route 150 from San José de Jachal to the Chilean frontier at the Agua Negra pass (4,765 metres), carrying on down the Elqui valley to La Serena. Turning left at Las Flores, you reach the customs post after about 45 km. in a river valley; if you do not want to go into Chile, leave your passport here and follow the road for another 30 km. (unpaved). The road may be closed from May onwards for the winter.

Turning right at Las Flores you reach the *Hotel Termas de Pismanta* (5 km.), an experience in itself: D p.p. for room, breakfast, dinner (good, but dining room not too clean), individual thermal bath and large swimming pool with thermal water under an orange tent. The hotel is in an isolated spot, with trees, in the desert. There is also a casino. Many people from Mendoza flock here in the summer. From Termas de Pismanta it is 61 km., partly on a very winding road high above the Río Jachal, to **San José de Jachal** (hotel, C; bus San Juan-San José, Expreso Argentino at 0730, arr. 0940).

From San José de Jachal, Route 40 continues to Villa Unión (see below). If you have your own car, you can take the old road (Route 491) for the first part, which offers good views from a pass and goes through a tunnel. Buses take the new road via Huaco. The road is paved to the border between San Juan and La Rioja provinces, but it is constantly up and down, passing dozens of dry watercourses.

Another interesting road from San Juan to Villa Unión goes via San Agustín del Valle Fértil, making it possible to do a round trip. Take Route 141 east towards Chepes; after 133 km. at Marayes, a paved road goes north for 114 km. to **San Agustín del Valle Fértil**. On a hill in town is the good ACA *Hostería*, with a wide view of the desert; at the foot of the hill is the ACA campsite, the municipal swimming pool, and on the other side of the hill a lake (fishing possible). Also *Pensión Andacollo*, E, and *Pensión Los Olivos*, similar prices. There are service stations. (Bus: Valle Fértil bus leaves San Juan at 2000, arr. 2300; a bus from San Juan to La Rioja passes San Agustín about midnight, if you wish to journey on; book in San Juan to get a seat).

From San Agustín the paved road runs north; after 56 km., a left turn at a police checkpoint goes 17 km. to the entrance of the interesting *Valle de la Luna (Ischigualasto)* park. Fossils found are exhibited in the Museo Bernardino Rivadavia in Buenos Aires. You may see around the park's coloured and strange rock formations only in a private car, and a guide will have to go with you. The circular tour, on a well-maintained, but unpaved road, lasts 2-3 hrs., entrance fee including guide US$1.25 p.p., children free.

4 km. beyond the police checkpoint, a junction to the right goes 51 km. over a lonely but paved road to Patquía and on to La Rioja or Chilecito. The left turn (Route 26) is the excellent road to Villa Unión. After 58 km. a paved road branches off to the right to the **Puerta de Talampaya** national park. The park entrance is at the turnoff, where guides wait with a pickup. Entrance fee including pickup for the tour and guide is US$10 for up to 8 people, US$1.25 for each additional person. After 14 km. the paved access road ends at the park centre (under construction). From here the actual visit starts, following the river bed of the Río Talampaya in a canyon. Herbert Levi writes: " There are 6,000 year old petroglyphs with pictures depicting animals. The whole area is said to have been covered with water long ago; now there are two visible strata, the *tarjado* and the *talampaya*. After that one enters a canyon with 'balconies', sheer overhanging walls. Across these is a small wood with many wild plants which are used for curative purposes. Coming out of the canyon there are rocks shaped like a cathedral, a bird, a castle, a chessboard, a monk and three kings on a camel." Finally, before returning the same way, you may go to the top of a little hill with a good view. The tour lasts about 2 hours. Buses from Chilecito to San Juan pass Talampaya.

From the park entrance it is 58 km. on the excellent Route 26 to **Villa Unión** (Hostería Provincial, simple, E, highly recommended; Sr. Werner Lorenz, the owner, who also owns vineyards, is very knowledgeable on the area and gives detailed plans for, and runs, excursions, including to Valle de la Luna and Talampaya). Excursions can also be made by jeep to Laguna Verde and Laguna Veladero. Bus station behind the plaza.

From Villa Unión to Chilecito, the road is only partly paved and goes over the Cuesta de Miranda, continuing down as a corniche through a deep, narrow canyon in a series of hairpin bends. After 92 km., it joins the paved Route 74 Patquía-Chilecito road, where you turn left for 18 km. to **Chilecito**, the second town in La Rioja province and a pleasant place, with good views of Sierra de Famatima. At Sra. Pizetti's souvenir shop, you can see her unique ceramic statues.

90 ARGENTINA

Hotels *ACA* on T. Gordillo and 9 de Julio, good, D; *Wamatinag*, 25 de Mayo 37; *Belsavac*, 9 de Julio y Dávila, good, paperthin walls; *Ferrito*, Pelagio Luna 661; *El Cordobés*, Dávila y Libertad; *Los Cerros*, Caminito 270; *Riviera*, Castro Barros 133, E-F, highly recommended, clean, hot showers; *Americano*, Libertad 68; *Bellia*, El Maestro and A. Marasso, and *Mis Montañas*, J. V. González 27.

Camping 15 km. from Chilecito on the road to Guauchía, near a Jesuit *estancia* established in 1652; also 6 km. along Calle de La Plata, at Santa Florentina, and 2 km. further at Los Tabas.

Restaurants at Chilecito: *Yayo y Silvia*, Independencia and 9 de Julio, good *chivito*; *Capri*, on main square, very good; *Comedor Club Atlético Newells Old Boys*, La Plata, opp. bus station, good.

Tourist Office at Chilecito, on 19 de Febrero and La Plata, very helpful; post office on J. V. González and Mitre. For treks, and trips to see gold washers at Famatima or to Talampaya, ask Carlos de Caro, at tourist office close to bus terminal.

Transport Líneas Aéreas Riojanas fly La Rioja-Chilecito, US$10 including transport to airport, 20-minute flight.

Bus to San Juan, Tues., Thurs., Sat. at 2200 (arrive 0705). Bus, Chilecito-Tinogasta (see page 90), Mon. and Fri., direct route at 0700, via Famatima, Angulas, Campanas, Santa Cruz, Costa de Reyes, returning from Tinogasta same day at 1600, same route. Tues. at 0700 and Sat. at 1330, same route to Campanas, then Pituile, San Blas, Cerro Negro junction, Salado, Carnival, Copacabana, Tinogasta. Return trip, Wed. at 0600, Sun. at 1400. Belén-Londres: No service Sun.; weekdays 0930 and 1215, Sat. 0900 and 1200. Reverse journey weekdays at 1630 and 1900, Sat. 1630 and 1930, about 20 mins. Connections with Catamarca and Córdoba (see relevant sections).

Excursions at Chilecito To La Mejicana mine at Santa Florentina (6 km.). Impressive cable car systems along which one could be conveyed to the railway station at Chilecito, built pre-World War I by a Leipzig firm, now disused. To Samay Huasi, the house of Joaquín V. González, founder of La Plata University, open 0800-1200 and 1500-1800, pretty garden (the view from the hill above the statue in the gardens is splendid, over Chilecito, the Famatima ridge and connecting valley; from the hill you can walk directly back to Chilecito; not far is the house of Sra. Inocente de Pizetti, who sculpts religious motifs. In Chilecito is a museum, at Jardín de Ocampo 63, corner of Famatima, open 0900-1300, 1800-2000. Half a block from the museum is the 17th-century flour mill of San Francisco. For the Valle de la Luna and Parque Nacional Talampaya, see above.

With the construction of an excellent new road, almost complete except in the area of Salicas, the numbering of the roads has been changed. Route 40 no longer goes north via Tinogasta but via Salicas (because the Cuesta de Zapata, N of Tinogasta, has been closed since the road was washed away in 1981). From Chilecito it is 21 km. to the junction of the old and new roads: to the left the old road goes via Famatima (ACA *Hostería*) to **Tinogasta**, a half-Indian copper-mining township, which lies cradled, by virtue of rare water, in a deep green valley lush with vineyards, olive groves and rows of poplar trees.

Hotels *Provincial de Turismo*; *Hostería Novel*, near airport.

Restaurants *Persegoni*, Tristán Villafane 375; *Rancho Huairipaca*, on Moreno; avoid *Virgen del Valle*.

Transport Bus Tinogasta-Tucumán, Empresa Gutiérrez, Tues., Fri., Sun. at 1700, Mon. at 0615, Fri. also at 0845. Return Tues., Fri. and Sun., arrives at Tinogasta at 0715, Thurs. at 1545. Tinogasta-Chubut, Empresa Ortiz; also Tinogasta-Comodoro Rivadavia, Caleta Olivia. For air services, see under Catamarca.

Fiambalá, on the road from the border, is reached from Tinogasta with El Cóndor on the Córdoba-Fiambalá route. Interesting mountain landscape. There is a *Hospedaje* at the end of the route (serves excellent *locro*). Drive from here (US$16 in a pick-up, asphalted road) to the *aguaditas*, hot water springs (bathing possible). Fiambalá-Tinogasta-Cerro Negro (junction)-Catamarca with Empresa Gutiérrez daily, depart Fiambalá 1345, depart Tinogasta 1500. Cerro Negro 1610, connects with Coop. Catamarca bus to Belén coming from Catamarca about 25 mins later; 85 km. trip Cerro Negro-Belén, bad road, about 2 hrs. Also departures from Fiambalá at 0530, dep. Tinogasta 0650, Cerro Negro 0810. 36 km. beyond Fiambalá is Palo Blanco, a township of the "*pre-puna*".

Turning right at the junction you follow the new Route 40 to Pituil, where the pavement ends at present, and on to Salicas (ACA *Hostería*), thence to the Cerro Negro intersection (59 km.) with Route 60, the Tinogasta (69 km. W of Cerro Negro)—Aimogasta road. Turning left at Cerro Negro for 2 km. you rejoin Route 40 heading north (right), well-paved, to **Londres**. This is the second oldest town in Argentina, founded in 1558 and named in honour of the marriage of Mary Tudor and Philip II in 1554. At the town hall one can see a glass coat of arms of the City of London and a copy of the marriage proposal. 15 km. further (paved) is **Belén** (*Hotel Provincial*, run down; *Hotel Doña Pilar*, forlorn-looking. Good breakfast at bus terminal; *Parrillada El Unico*, unexciting). Hot, but rewarding view after walking up a path where Calle General Roca (unnumbered) starts, about 20

ARGENTINA 91

mins. to a new but poorly decorated chapel. Belén is hemmed in by mountains, except towards the SE, lush vegetation along river; good *feria artesanal* near main square, ponchos, saddlebags, rugs. Then 177 km. to Santa María (only 16 km. paved), 22 km. (partly paved) beyond Santa María is Amaichá del Valle (see page 68); on 14 km. (paved) to Río Santa María and then 52 km. unpaved to Cafayate (see page 73).

Transport Belén-Villavil (springs), including side trip to Corral Quemado and end of line at Barranca Larga, 19 km. N of Villavil, Tues., Thurs. from Belén at 0800, returns from Villavil 1830. (Sit on right-hand side for best views of impressive *quebrada* and artificial lake.) Belén-Santa María, leaves Tues., 1330, Fri. and Sun. at 2020. Returns Belén Tues. and Thurs. at 0930, Sun., 1945. Belén-Salta, via Hualfín (curative waters), Santa María, Cafayate on Thurs. at 0600.

From Cerro Negro it is 38 km. east to Aimogasta and another 30 km. to the turn off to the Termas de Santa Teresita (7 km.), an ACA *Hostería*, with thermal bath in each room, and thermal swimming pool; excellent food at reasonable prices. From the turn off near Santa Teresita it is 15 km. east on Route 60 to where a good new road branches off north to Saujil (60 km.) and **Andalgalá** (130 km.); *Hostería Provincial*. This town, famous for strong alcoholic drinks, can also be reached by Bus 129 from Belén. The road passes, on the left, the long Salar de Pipanaco, and on the right, the Sierras de Ambato and Manchao.

Beyond Andalgalá, the road over the Cuesta de Capillatas in the direction of Santa María is very beautiful, but extremely difficult after the pass where you have to cross a river bed 15 km. wide. No public transport, only trucks to the mines at Capillatas, just beyond the pass, on weekdays.

(We are most grateful to Volker Filss of Oberhausen, W. Germany, for detailed information on the roads N of San Juan.)

For an alternative route to Salta, turn off the Ruta 40 52 km. after Belén on to Ruta 53 to Antofagasta de la Sierra and then on to 78 for Antonio de los Cobres (see page 75). This route is possible in ordinary cars, but you must carry enough fuel for 600 km. at high altitudes on unmade roads (fill up at Hualfín, 10 km. beyond turn off to Antofagasta de la Sierra). Also, the stretch beyond the right turn at Puerto de Corral Quemado is very difficult (37 km. of fords) and should not be attempted in the rainy season. At Km. 87 is Cerro Compo (3,125 metres), magnificent descent; at Km. 99 the road turns left to Laguna Blanca (don't go straight on at the junction). **Antofagasta de la Sierra** (260 km.) can be reached on the ground only by hiring a pick-up or by hitch-hiking, or by plane; enquire at Dirección de Aeronaútica, Aeródromo de Choya, Tel.: 24750. Bus L 22 goes from town centre to airfield. *Pensión Darín*; no petrol station, fuel may be obtained from the *intendencia* (fill up here). This is the main township of the NW of Catamarca, together with El Peñón and Laguna Blanca in the *puna*, and with Villavil and La Hoyada in the "pre-puna". La Hoyada can be reached from Sta. María in the NE via Provincial Route 118. There are lunar-like landscapes, with salt lakes, around Antofagasta, and several peaks of over 5,000 metres; Dos Conos, Bertrán, Sierra de Laguna Blanca. Deposits of marble, onyx, sulphur, mica, salts, borates and gold. There is a varied fauna including vicuña, guanaco, *suri*, chinchilla, pink flamingo and fox. The region is sparsely populated.

La Rioja, at 500 metres, 45,000 people, is the capital of La Rioja province. It has some colonial buildings and a folk museum, Instituto del Folklore Riojano at Pelagio B. Luna 811. (Tues.-Sat. 0900-1300 and 1600-2030, Sun. open 0900-1300 free); regional costumes are sometimes seen, and its peculiarly flavoured dry wine is interesting. Worth a visit is the solid adobe ruin of the Jesuit church (now encased in another building for protection) in which San Francisco Solano baptized the local Indians. A remarkable image of the Child Jesus can be seen in the Church of San Francisco. Ring the bell at 25 de Mayo 218 to see it. Inca Huasi museum (at Alberdi 650, Mon.-Fri. 0900-1300 and 1600-1900, Sun. open at 0900-1300) has Indian skulls, a fine collection of funerary urns, and "pregnant pots" or jars thought to belong to the Florescent Era around the time of Christ. Replicas sold in entrance hall. Casa de Joaquín V. González, a castle-like building, can be visited free at Rivadavia 952. There is a Museo Histórico, free, open Sat. at 1430-2000 and Sun., 0900-1230. Museo de Bellas Artes is at Copiapó 245, Mon.-Fri. 0700-1400 and 1430-2130, Sat.-Sun. 0900-1200. The Mercado Artesanal is interesting. There is a famous Casino at Avenida Sarmiento (now renamed Juan D. Perón) and Quiroga.

92 ARGENTINA

In the town are many examples of the strange *palo borracho* tree, with a bottle-shaped thorn-studded trunk at a drunken angle hung with pods like avocado pears which, when ripe, open to disclose large brown seeds in a kapok-like substance. The tree is also found in several parks and gardens in Buenos Aires.

Hotels *Internacional Sussex*, Ortiz de Ocampo 1551; *King's*, Av. Quiroga 1070; *Luxor*, Av. Quiroga 25; *Provincial Casino*, J.D.Perón 1235; *Libertador*, Buenos Aires 223; *Hotel de Turismo*, new. *Talampaya*, J.D.Perón 951; *Provincial de Turismo*, Santa Fe 950, well set up but poorly run; *Emperador*, San Martín 258; *Centro*, Rivadavia 499; *Plaza*, Bartolomé Mitre and 9 de Julio, recommended, but noisy street; all C. *Parlamento*, Rivadavia 549; *Savoy*, Roque A. Luna 14 and Bartolomé Mitre, excellent value, E, hot shower. *Ritz*, 25 de Mayo 195. *El Gringo*, Cnel. Lagos 427; *Aparicia*, Copiapó 119, all D, recommended. Good value from *La Rioja*, *Libertador* and *Central*. *Residenciales: Florida*, 8 de Diciembre 427, and *Margarita*, J.D.Perón 413, unfriendly and rundown; best is *Sumaj Kanki*, Castro Barros y Cnel. Lagos, but you can't leave before 0730. At Anillaco, on Highway 75, between La Rioja and Aimogasta, there is a *Hostería ACA*. The Tourist Office has a list of private lodgings; try Familia Lazzarotto, San Martín 156, friendly, hot showers, cooking facilities.

Restaurants *Café Corredor*, San Martín and Pelagio Luna, good, cheap menu; *La Cantina de Juan*, H. Yrigoyen 190, excellent *empanadas*, local white wine, local cheese with nuts; *La Posta* and *Don Facundo*, both on J.D.Perón.

Tourist Office One of the most helpful in Argentina, at Av. J.D.Perón y Urquiza, and near Plaza, maps, information, bus timetables for routes off the main road.

Transport From Córdoba or San Juan by San Martín railway or road. From Buenos Aires, 2,092 km., by train, 39 hours. *El Norteño* train goes via Córdoba Tues., and Fri. at 1000 and links with buses to La Rioja and Catamarca and tickets can be bought at Retiro. Return journeys (*automotor* returns from Córdoba Wed., and Sat. at 0751) can be booked from La Rioja and Catamarca bus offices. Tickets may be booked up to 90 days in advance. Villa Unión-La Rioja bus daily at 1440, reverse journey at 1330. Daily AA flights from Buenos Aires. Twice daily service, Mon.-Fri., at 0800 and 1330, La Rioja to Catamarca with Líneas Aéreas Riojanas, about 20 mins. Passengers have to go to Oficina Aeronáutica, Rivadavia 461 (Tel.: 28887); transport provided free. By road from Mendoza via San Juan. Bus to Mendoza and San Juan only by night, two companies: Bosio, 11 hrs, US$14, very comfortable, four per night. Bus terminal is about 5 blocks from the centre. Also bus to Tucumán, at least once a day, 7 hrs, at 0300 or 1200, US$10. The La Rioja-Catamarca bus linking the two capitals: Cotil, daily at 0615 and 1545, Bosio at 0515, 1645, 2200, about 2½ hrs, US$2.60. La Estrella and Libertador on the Mendoza-Tucumán run follow same routes, but arrival times are unreliable.

Excursions To Valle de la Luna and Talampaya (via Nonogasta, Cuesta de Miranda and Villa Unión), US$12 including transport and guide, and to Samay Huasi (see page 90). Good fishing at El Portezuelo dam (see below). Swimming and fishing at Los Sauces dam, 15 km. away; very good view of La Rioja from Cerro de la Cruz (1,680 metres). There is a bad 12 km. road from the dam to the top, which is now a centre for hang-gliding. Condors and falcons can be sighted.

A paved road runs NE to the third oasis, Catamarca.

Catamarca, capital of its province, lies on a river at 490 metres between two of the southern slopes of the Sierra de Aconquija, about 240 km. S of Tucumán. Cotton growing is added here to the cattle, fruit and grapes of the oasis. It is also famous for the hand-weaving of ponchos and for its preserves; an especially excellent one is from the fruit of a cactus (try Casa Valdés, Sarmiento 586). Pilgrimages to the church of the Virgen del Valle. The thermal springs of Catamarca are curative. A regional mountain wind, the Zonda, strong and dry, can at times cause depression. There is a *feria* in July, at which handicrafts are sold, the Festival del Poncho. Four nights of music, mostly folklore of the NW. Population about 79,000.

Hotels *Provincial de Turismo* (much as at La Rioja), República 108 y Caseros; *Ancasti*, Sarmiento 520, E, has first class expensive restaurant; *City*, San Martín 821; *Inti Huasi*, República 297; both D. *Pucará*, Av. Esquiú, 1 block from ACA station, D, clean, a/c, friendly; *Suma Huasi*, Sarmiento 547, E, ask for room *not* above TV lounge. Also *Carlos I*, Junín 1189, F. *Centro*, Juan M. de Rosas, esq. 9 de Julio, basic. *Sol*, Salta 1142, *Tempo*, Prado 367, *Colonial*, República 802, *Grand Hotel*, Camilo Meleb 41, all E. *Sussex*, Ruta Nacional 38, C. *Residenciales: Venecia*, Tucumán 115, *Plaza*, Rivadavia 278, *Sirio*, Salta 1184, *Familiar*, Güemes 811, *Esquiú*, Esquiú 365, *Avenida*, Av. Güemes 754, *Menen*, Av. Güemes 793, *Comodoro*, República 851, *Yunka Suma*, V. Segura 1255, *Valle Viejo*, Ruta Nac. 38, all F. The *Ancasti*, *Inti Huasi* and *Suma Huasi* grant a 10% discount to members of ACA (Argentine Automobile Club). Very cheap pensión, clean, unnamed, on Tucumán 1294, no shower or hot water, treble rooms, friendly.

ARGENTINA 93

Restaurants *Club Español; El Encuentro; La Cabaña*, on Esquiú; (and *Carlos I* at weekends) has folklore dancing. Roofgarden of *Hotel Ancasti* has restaurant. *La Abuela*, make sure what you eat is fresh. Avoid *Restaurante 25 de Agosto*. In this area soup is eaten after the meal, said to be a Chinese custom.

Shopping *Regionales Sevita*, next to Aerolíneas Argentinas office, Catamarca specialities. Artisan exhibition hall, *Casa del Poncho*, on General Urquiza, corner with Mota Botello, very worthwhile; handwoven articles. Open 0700-1330. The value of these depends on the number of knots used. Reached by infrequent colectivo 23 from centre.

Museum The Instituto Cultural Esquiú, Sarmiento 450 (archaeology, colonial history, iconography, mineralogy). Museo Arqueológico Adán Quiroga here opens daily at 0800-1300 and 1530-2130, Sat.-Sun. 0830-1230. Well worth a visit. There are traces of the Belén civilization elsewhere in the province, at Hualfín and Punta de Balasto.

Post Office San Martín 753, slow, closes at noon. Telephones at Rivadavia 758.

Tourist Office very helpful at Galería Virgen del Valle, Local 6, near cathedral. Also at Manzana del Turismo at Urquiza 951. Try Yokavil agency, on Güemes.

Buses Road to Tucumán is paved and in good condition except for the two *cuestas* (Cuesta del Tortoral) at the border between Catamarca and Tucumán provinces (steep gradients, hairpin bends, many potholes for 25 km.), bus US$6.50, 5½ hrs., 238 km., 7 a day with Bosio. To Buenos Aires, 2nd class at 2200, US$30; 1st class at 1900, US$37, daily. Catamarca-Belén, via Cerro Negro, with Coop. Catamarca, returns daily from Belén at 1300 (see page 90). Also Belén-Catamarca via Andalgalá; Coop. Catamarca via Saujil, Poman, Chumbicha, Tues. and Thurs. at 1000, Fri. and Sun., 1300, about 8 hrs. Catamarca-El Rodeo-Las Juntas, daily from platform 9 of the Catamarca bus terminal at 1300, arrive at Las Juntas 1500, returns at 1700. Buses to and from Córdoba, twice a week, connect there with *Norteño* train for Buenos Aires; about 5 buses a day to Córdoba in all.

Air Cooperativa de Transportes Catamarca, not as reliable as Aerolíneas Riojanas; service twice a week from Tinogasta to Belén, Tues. and Thurs. Officially departs Tinogasta at 0810, but one is told to show up at the municipal building at 0815 to be at the plane at 0830. Route is circular: Catamarca-Tinogasta-Belén-Andalgalá-Catamarca, in 6-seater Cessna or Piper. Aerolíneas Argentinas offices next to *Hotel Suma Huasi*.

Excursion to the Dique Las Pirquitas, 3 hrs with local bus 1A from bus station, with terminus at Isla Larga, pleasant hills and woods. Bus stops at *Hostería de Turismo* at Villa Pirquitas, about 45 min. walk. About 5 buses in the morning from 0700, last bus returns at 2200. Opening hours, Mon.-Fri., 1000-1900, Sat., Sun. and holidays, 0830-1900.

A road runs NE to Lavalle (on the way to Santiago del Estero). This 116-km. run over the **Cuesta del Portezuelo** pass (1,980 metres), with its 20 km. of steep gradients and numerous hairpin bends—small hairpins—is one of the toughest in the country (superb views of Catamarca). No bus service over Portezuelo to Lavalle, but a service to Frías, E and also in Santiago del Estero province—No. 9 and *not* No. 18 (which runs over the Tortoral) run by the Coop. de Transportes de Catamarca. Leaves at 0500, Tues., Thurs., Fri., Sat., arrives at Frías at 1000, returns from Frías on same days at 1400, arr. Catamarca at 1900. From Frías travel to Lavalle.

Catamarca to Lavalle or Frías via Tortoral: Bus 18, Mon., Wed., Fri., Sat., leaves at 0500, arrives at Frías 1030, returns 1330, back at Catamarca at 1900. Mon. and Fri., Bus 14 goes via El Alto, longer journey, at 0430, arrives at Frías at 1045. Catamarca-Lavalle via Tortoral, same Bus 18, leaves Tues., Thurs., Sun., at 1100, arrives Lavalle 1510.

The Chaco

Between the north-western highlands already described and the Río Paraná to the E lies the Argentine Chaco, containing the provinces of Formosa and Chaco, Santiago del Estero, and northern Santa Fe. Its southern limit is the Río Dulce valley. This great lowland is covered with thorn scrub and grassy savanna, the thorn bushes sometimes impenetrable and sometimes set widely apart on grassland. The highest summer temperatures in all South America have been recorded in the Argentine Chaco; the winters are mild with an occasional touch of frost in the S. Rain falls in the winter according to location: the further W, the less the rain.

Communications Before the recent building of highways, the only all-weather routes were provided by the Belgrano Railway. There are two main north/south lines from Buenos Aires: the international route to La Paz and the line through Rosario and Santa Fe to Resistencia. There are two east/west rail connections, Resistencia-Metán and Formosa-Embarcación; neither now carries passengers regularly. A third line runs SW from Roque Sáenz Peña to Anatuya in the province of Santiago del Estero. (It is advisable to check all rail services, since many were suspended years

94 ARGENTINA

ago without being formally abolished.) Roads are given in the text and air services link the major towns.

Tannin and cotton are the two great industries of the Chaco. The iron-hard *quebracho* (axe-breaker) tree grows only in the Chaco of northern Argentina and Paraguay; it is the purest known source of tannin. The industry is struggling against competition from synthetic tannin and the huge mimosa plantations in South Africa. The most accessible forest is worked out; most of the cutting is now in the N and W of the province.

Cotton growers, centred on Roque Sáenz Peña in Chaco Province, have had difficulty in maintaining production in the face of soil exhaustion. Sunflower is the chief crop replacing cotton, and there is also some maize and sorghum.

Roque Sáenz Peña can be reached by an excellent road from Puerto Pilcomayo. Hot springs have been found here and a modern hotel has been built to develop the city as a spa. Other hotels are: *Residencial Sáenz Peña*, near bus station, cheap, clean and friendly; *Residencia Asturias*, D, fair. Daily bus, La Internacional, to Buenos Aires, 2000, 19 hrs. From Buenos Aires, also 2000. Bus from Salta at 1700, 10 hrs., US$12.50; bus to Resistencia, US$3. North of Roque Sáenz Peña is the village of Castelli, which has a large Tobas Indian community and an *artesanía* shop. *Hotel Guc*, F, basic.

The rest of the Chaco is cattle country but there are few animals to the square km. Large *estancias* are the rule, some growing cotton, linseed and other crops by irrigation. The bird life of the area—flamingoes, black-necked swans, heron egrets, storks and various birds of prey—is most interesting.

Towns of the Chaco The most important ones—Resistencia and Formosa—are on the W bank of the Paraná and Paraguay and will be described, for convenience's sake, under "Up the Paraná River" when dealing with Argentine Mesopotamia. Apart from Roque Sáenz Peña, the only other town of any importance is Santiago del Estero, on the western boundary of the Chaco, 167 km. SE of Tucumán.

Santiago del Estero, the oldest Argentine town, was founded in 1553 by settlers pushing S from Peru. It is near the bank of the Río Dulce where that river, coming from Tucumán, flows into the plains of the Chaco; a 1½-km. steel bridge across the river carries the railway from La Banda (6½ km.) on the Buenos Aires-Rosario-Tucumán route. There is a branch line via Forres to Córdoba. Population, 92,000. The main square, Plaza Libertad, contains the Casa de Gobierno, and the Cathedral (the 5th on the site) stands next to it. Also on the plaza is the tourist office, open 0800 to 2000 daily, and very helpful. On Plaza Lugones is the pleasant old church of San Francisco, the city's first, which was founded in 1590 by San Francisco Solano, patron saint of Tucumán. His cell is in the near-by convent; his festival, celebrated with folk-music (he was himself a viol-player), is on July 24. Beyond the church is the pleasant Parque Aguirre, with a good zoo. Airport (Aerolíneas Argentinas flights daily, except Thurs.). Buses to Resistencia run by El Rey company.

In the convent of Santo Domingo is a "Holy Sheet", one of the three copies of the sheet that covered the body of Christ, given by Philip II to his "beloved colonies of America". The Provincial Museum of Archaeology (Calle Avellaneda) founded by Emil and Duncan Wagner, has over 10,000 samples of Indian pottery. There is also a provincial history museum, previously known as the Museo Gancedo.

Hotels *Palace, Savoy*, simple, well run, good and very ample food; *Bristol*, Moreno 67; *Gran Hotel*, Avellaneda and Independencia; *Residencial San Antonio*, Belgrano 485, E, very basic room but clean bathrooms. *Residencia Española*, 1 block from bus station, F; *Pensión Nueva España*, Pellegrini 59, E. *Premier*, E, pleasant with cheap, good restaurant.

Restaurant *La Rotonda*, at edge of town on road to Tucumán, reasonable *asado*. Easy to hitchhike N from here.

This arid area can be vividly experienced by a bus journey S from Santiago del Estero to Córdoba over paved roads, through continually varying semi-desert.

The **Termas de Río Hondo** are 65 km. from Santiago del Estero along the road to Tucumán, at 264 metres. Their water is recommended for blood pressure and

ARGENTINA 95

rheumatism; good to drink, too, and used for the local soda water. Swimming in public baths. A casino (roulette and card games) is open during the winter season. The huge Río Hondo dam on the Río Dulce is close by; it forms a lake of 33,000 hectares, used for sailing and fishing. Very popular in August, so book accommodation well in advance.

Hotels *Grand* (with casino); *Los Pinos*, the most pleasant; *Panamericano*; *Palace*; *Ambassador*.

Food In the main street is a corner shop where you can watch *alfajores*, the local sweet (see page 150) being made. Around the corner from there is a small restaurant with excellent homemade pasta. There are two restaurants on the plaza: *Sabot*, quite good, and *La Cabana*, rather poor. *Rancho de Doña María*, Alberdi 130, cheap but unfriendly and poor.

Some 320 km. SE of Santiago del Estero the Río Dulce, flowing in places through salt flats, runs into the shallow Mar Chiquita on the southern margin of the Chaco. People who live in the valley of the Río Dulce are so used to the taste of its water that they often add a pinch of salt to the water they drink when away from home. Mar Chiquita, 80 by 25 kms., is naturally salty, and the water is warm. No river drains it, though two other rivers flow into it from the Sierras de Córdoba in the flood season. There are several islands in the lake. On its southern shore is the small town of **Miramar.** Mar Chiquita is a very popular resort during the summer months; its salt waters are used in the treatment of rheumatic ailments and skin diseases. It is best reached by a railway W from Santa Fe to Deán Funes, which runs within a few km. of the southern shore. The lake is reached from Córdoba by road, 200 km.

Hotels *Gran Copacabana*, *Gran España*, *Miramar*, *Marchetti*.

Camping Autocamping Lilly.

(**Note** This Mar Chiquita and its town, Miramar, must not be confused with the other Mar Chiquita to the N of Mar del Plata and the seaside resort of Miramar, S of Mar del Plata.)

Mesopotamia

Between the rivers Paraná and Uruguay lies Argentine Mesopotamia: the provinces of Entre Ríos, Corrientes, and Misiones. The distance between the rivers is 390 km. in northern Corrientes, but narrows to about 210 km. in the latitude of Santa Fe. From the Alto Paraná, the northern boundary, to the River Plate in the S is about 1,130 km.

Mesopotamia was first colonized by Spaniards pushing S from Asunción to reoccupy Buenos Aires; both Corrientes and Paraná were founded as early as 1588. Misiones was first occupied by the Jesuit Fathers fleeing from the Brazilian Alto-Paraná region with their devoted Indian followers before the slave-hunting Bandeirantes. These missions and their history are described under Posadas (see page 103).

Misiones Province, in the far NE, is a hilly strip of land between the Alto Paraná and the Uruguay rivers, 80-100 km. wide and about 400 km. long; its capital is the river port of Posadas. Its boundary to the N is the river Iguazú, which here tumbles over the great Iguazú Falls. Misiones is on the Paraná Plateau; much of it is covered with forests of pine and cedar and broad-leaved trees, and the look of the land, with its red soil, reminds one strongly of Brazil. Here too the rainfall is heavy: twice as heavy as in Entre Ríos. The days are hot, and the nights cool.

The province of Corrientes, in the N, is marshy and deeply-wooded, with low grass-covered hills rising from the marshes. The normal rainfall is about 2,000 mm, but the rains are not spread uniformly and drain off quickly through the sandy soil. Entre Ríos, to the S, has plains of rich pasture land not unlike those of Uruguay. Winters in Mesopotamia are mild; the summers are hot and much rain falls in short, sharp storms, though both Entre Ríos and Corrientes often suffer from summer drought.

Much of Entre Ríos and Corrientes is still pastoral, a land of large *estancias* raising cattle and sheep. Maize (a gamble in the N) is largely grown in southern Entre Ríos, which is also the most important producer of linseed, citrus fruit and

96 **ARGENTINA**

NORTH-EASTERN ARGENTINA

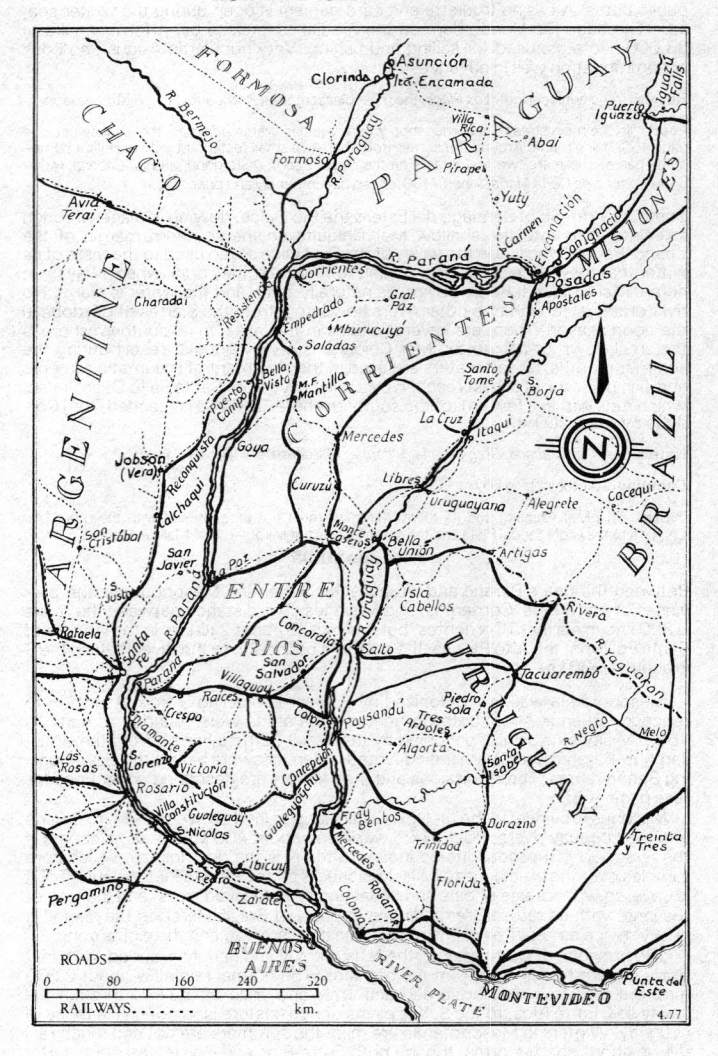

ARGENTINA

poultry in Argentina. In Corrientes, along the banks of the Paraná between the cities of Corrientes and Posadas, rice and oranges are grown.

It was the Jesuits who first grew *yerba mate* in plantations; Misiones has always been a large producer of this leaf, and also of citrus, tobacco, timber and tung oil. The province has of late years attracted immigrants from Eastern Europe, from Paraguay and from the rest of Mesopotamia. There is good fishing in many of the small river-towns. In NE Corrientes and in Misiones more Indian tea is now grown than can be absorbed by the internal market.

The Indian-tea industry was started by Sir Herbert Gibson, who sent for seed from Assam in 1929; it was sown in Playadito, Corrientes province. Six seeds developed into sturdy bushes. Year after year their seed was given to anyone interested. All Argentina's tea plantations today have their origin in Sir Herbert Gibson's enterprise.

Communications in the area are by road (now greatly improved), by railway, and by the two rivers the Paraná and the Uruguay, which bound it to E and W. Neither river is very good for navigation. Bridges between Fray Bentos (Uruguay) and Puerto Unzué, near Gualeguaychú, and between Paysandú (Uruguay) and Colón were opened in 1976, and there are a road and railway over the Salto Grande dam, near Concordia.

The area is served by the Urquiza railway, the only standard-gauge line in the country; the most important line runs from Buenos Aires to Posadas with connection over the river to Asunción, the capital of Paraguay, and a branch at Monte Caseros for Corrientes.

Most of the important towns of Mesopotamia lie on the E bank of the Paraná or the S bank of the Alto Paraná. A journey up these rivers is given here; the towns on both banks are described.

Up the Paraná River

River Shipping Line River boats carry passengers along various stretches of the river, though the Flota Fluvial del Estado (Av. Corrientes 389, Buenos Aires) is reported to have suspended its passenger services to Corrientes and Asunción, Paraguay. According to the tide, boats enter the Paraná river by either the Las Palmas reach of the delta, on which is Zárate, or the Paraná-Guazú reach, on which is Ibicuy.

Zárate, with 52,000 inhabitants, is industrially important, with large *frigorificos* and paper works. It is served from Buenos Aires (90 km.) by bus (US$2) and two railways: the Mitre and the Urquiza. Urquiza trains used to be ferried 84 km. across the river, but a link including two large and beautiful bridges has been built between Zárate and Brazo Largo, accelerating rail and road journeys alike (the bridge toll is US$6). The picturesque Ibicuy Islands can be visited by boat. Near Zárate is San Pedro, where fine riverfront camping can be had at either the *Centro Turístico, Club Pescadores* or *Camping Municipal*.

On the way upstream to Rosario, on the western bank, are two ports which export grain: San Nicolás (55,000 people), 80 km. below Rosario, and Villa Constitución, 37 km. below Rosario. Both are served by a railway from the capital. At San Nicolás is the General Savio steel plant. Pergamino, an important road/rail junction in the pampas, is 72 km. S by road or rail.

About 108 km. N of Ibicuy is **Gualeguay,** with a population of 26,000. It is the centre of one of the richest cattle and sheep ranching regions in Entre Ríos. The house in which Garibaldi was tortured by the local chief of police in 1837, in the time of Rosas, still exists. Eight km. S is its river port, Puerto Ruiz. The road from Gualeguay northwards along the E bank of the Paraná is paved most of the way to Posadas.

Hotels *Gran Hotel Gualeguay*, Monte Caseros 217, C; *Italia*, E. There is a municipal **campsite**. In the centre there are practically no **restaurants**, but the *Jockey Club* and the *Club Social*, both on the main square close to the *Gran Hotel Gualeguay*, cater also for non-members. The *Club Social* has a very nice atmosphere, good food, and you might be invited to see films on certain nights.

Rosario, chief city of the province of Santa Fe, 320 km. N of Buenos Aires, is the

98 ARGENTINA

third city of the republic, with a population of well over a million. It is a great industrial and export centre. The streets are wider than those of Buenos Aires, and there are fine boulevards and handsome open spaces. From October to early March it is warm, and from December to the end of February uncomfortably hot. Changes of temperature are sudden.

Points of Interest Monument of the Flag, a memorial on the river bank in honour of General Belgrano, designer of the Argentine flag, who raised it on this spot for the first time; Parque Independencia (Rose Garden): Boulevard Oroño; Cathedral in Calle 25 de Mayo; St. Bartholomew's Church (Anglican), Calle Paraguay; racecourse, the Alberdi and Arroyito boat clubs, and Saladillo Golf Club, with its own Links station on the Mitre line. The Aero Club is at the fashionable suburb of Fisherton, headquarters of the British community. The Juan B. Castagnino Municipal Museum and the provincial Historical Museum (open Thurs. and Sat. 1500-1800, and Sun. 1000-1200, 1500-1800) are in Parque Independencia. Swimming at sandy Florida beach, about 8 km. N of Rosario. The boat *Ciudad de Rosario* does a short trip round the nearby river islands at weekends and holidays, leaving from the Estación Fluvial near the Monument of the Flag.

Local holiday October 7 (Foundation of the City).

Hotels *Rivera*, San Lorenzo 1460, air conditioned, best, B; *Plaza*, Barón de Mauá, C; *Gran Hotel Italia*, Maipú 1065, C; *Presidente*, Av. Corrientes 919, C; *Micro*, Santa Fe 3650, D; *Onix*, Vera Mujica 757, D; *Río*, opp. railway station, F; *Moderno*, by Norte railway station, F with bath, OK; *Oviedo*, near railway station, F, with bath.

Restaurants *El Paco*, Plaza de Mayo, near Cathedral, specializes in *parrilladas*; *Doña María* in Calle Santa Fe does good Italian food; *Catay*, off Plaza Murillo, recommended for Chinese food; *Scaramouche*, just off Prado, on Loaysa, excellent US$4 *menú del oficinista*; *Maxim's*, Buenos Aires and San Luis, cheap, helpful.

Markets Mercado Central, Calle San Martín; also Mercados Norte, Sud, and Abasto. Best time, 0600-0800.

Bank of London and South America, Calle La Rioja 1205; Citibank, Santa Fe 1101; First National Bank of Boston, Córdoba esq. Mitre. Open 1000-1600.

Church German Evangelical Church, Boulevard Oroño 645.

Airport at Fisherton, 8 km. from centre. Taxi charges vary. Several flights daily to Buenos Aires. Austral to Corrientes once a week, to Posadas, three times and to Resistencia twice a week.

Rail Rosario is 4 hours from Buenos Aires (320 km.) on the Mitre Railway by express train, Pullman US$7.20, 1st class US$4.90, tourist US$3.65. It is served also by the Belgrano (metre gauge—5 hours). All trains heading N stop at Rosario.

Road Transport There are regular bus services to Arroyo Seco, Casilda, Cañada de Gómez, San Lorenzo and other important centres up to 80 km. from the city. Also from Buenos Aires, by paved roads via San Nicolás and General Pacheco on Route 9 (3¾-4 hrs) or via Pergamino, 309 km. less frequent on Route 8 (Chevallier bus, US$8.10), and from Rosario via Bell Ville NW to Córdoba (bus, US$8) and Tucumán. Local bus fare— US$0.50.

Rosario can be reached from Buenos Aires by Route 8 (marked Córdoba) to Pergamino, and then, following signs, by Route 188, and then 178 to Rosario. This is a better way than lorry-packed Route 9. Hitching to Salta along Route 34 is possible.

Ferries to Victoria, in Entre Ríos, which has a municipal **campsite**.

Above Rosario the river is very braided and islanded. Boat trips to river islands can be made at weekends. Canoes can be hired. Some 23 km. N of Rosario is **San Lorenzo,** where an associate company of ICI has one of the largest chemical works in Argentina. See the restored San Carlos monastery on the river bank, where in 1813 San Martín won his first battle in the War of Independence. Visitors are shown a pine tree grown from a cutting of the tree under which the Liberator rested after the battle. Some 180 km. above Rosario, on the E bank, is

Paraná, capital of Entre Ríos (pop., 200,000), founded in 1588. From 1853 to 1862 the city was the capital of the Republic; it is a handsome place, with a fine centre, the Plaza San Martín, where there are fountains and a statue of the Liberator. The Cathedral, E of the plaza, is notable for its portico and its interior; opposite it is the tourist information office. A modern building on Plaza Alvear houses the Bazán Museum of Fine Arts and the local history museum, open 0900-1200 and 1500-1800 except Mon. The Government Palace (Casa de Gobierno), in another plaza, has a grand façade. But the city's glory is the Parque

ARGENTINA 99

Urquiza, to the NW. It has an enormous statue to General Urquiza, and a bas-relief showing the battle of Caseros, at which he finally defeated Rosas; also an open-air theatre. There are excellent views of the country and of Santa Fe on the other side of the river. There is a paved road to Paso de los Libres, 483 km., on the Brazilian frontier (see page 113).

Hotels *Mayorazgo*, on Costanera Alta, with fine view of park and river, has casino and swimming pool, B; *Super Luxe*, Villaguay 162, C; *Gran Hotel Paraná*, Urquiza 976, D; *Almafuerte*, Av. Almafuerte 1295, D; *Las Colonias*, Cervantes 89, E. Cheap hotels near railway station, none by the bus terminal. The *Centro Autoturismo* motel on the road to the Hernandarias tunnel, C.

Restaurants *Molino Rojo*, down by river; *La Posta del Olivo*, just off Plaza San Martín; both good.

Santa Fe and Paraná do not face one another. It takes 20 mins. to get from one to the other by car, and 1 hour by bus, US$1, every half-hour. You cross a bridge close to Santa Fe, travel for some km. over an uninhabited island, cross another bridge, and run over another uninhabited island to dive into the 2-km. Hernandarias tunnel, which leads up to Paraná city (toll US$1.90).

Air Service Airport: General Urquiza, 12 km. from town; two flights to Buenos Aires daily with Austral. To Goya and Reconquista at 0820 thrice weekly.

Train *Río Paraná* train to Buenos Aires daily except Sat. at 2020, arrives 0710. From Buenos Aires (F. Lacroze) 2215, arrives 0857.

Santa Fe, a larger city of some 300,000 inhabitants, is the capital of its Province and the centre of a very fertile region. It was founded by settlers from Asunción in 1573, though its present site was not occupied until 1651. It was in its Cabildo (town hall) that the Constitution of 1853 was adopted. The oath of allegiance was taken before the crucifix in the sacristy of the church of San Francisco, built in 1680 from materials floated down the river from Paraguay; this old colonial church has been tampered with but is still fine, especially the carved wooden ceilings, which were fitted without nails.

Most of the best buildings are grouped round Plaza Mayo and Plaza San Martín in the eastern part of the city. Plaza Mayo, on Calle General López, has the small Jesuit church of La Merced (1660-1754), next to the majestic Casa de Gobierno, and (on the N side) a church begun in 1741 (see an old painting from Cuzco and the interesting archives). A block SE of the Plaza has the famous church of San Francisco (see above). Opposite it is the Museo Histórico Provincial. The buildings on Plaza San Martín are modern. In Calle General López is the Rosa Galisteo de Rodríguez Museum of Fine Arts, where local painters hold their exhibitions. The church of Nuestra Señora de Guadalupe has beautifully painted glass windows and may be reached by bus 8 or 14 from the centre. Twice weekly boats from Buenos Aires, 483 km. to the south; regular only in winter.

Local holidays Sept. 30 (St. Jerome); Nov. 15 (Foundation of City).

Hotels *Hostal de Santa Fe de la Vera Cruz*, best, genial management, well-kept and run, San Martín 2954, B; *Río Grande*, San Gerónimo 2586, B, modern, recommended; *El Conquistador*, 25 de Mayo 2676, C; *Corrientes*, Corrientes 2520, C; *Colón*, San Luis 2862, D; *Pacífico*, Obispo Gelabert 2950, D; *Hospedaje Nueva Tripolitania*, Vera 2230, F, friendly, good restaurant; *Royal*, clean, modern, private bath, opposite bus station, D; *Brigadier*, San Luis 3148, E, two blocks from bus station, good, clean, friendly, 50 rooms, a/c extra, but recommended if the river is in flood and there are lots of mosquitoes, some English spoken; *Bristol*, Belgrano 2859 by bus terminal, E; next door to it is *Gran Hotel Terminal*, Belgrano 2839, opposite bus terminal, E/F; basic, clean, water shortage; *Astur*, near the bus station, F (cheaper than most).

Camping Possible in municipal site near town centre, Parque Azul, bus No. 5. Site at Guadalupe beach by the lake.

Restaurants Many good ones, offering excellent meals with good wine for US$5. Excellent grills including *surubí* (local fish) at *Gran Parrillada Rivadavia*, Rivadavia 3299. *Apolo*, opposite bus terminal, good, cheap. Also good and cheap, *Comedor Tío Carlos*, Rivadavia y Suipacha, US$2 for unlimited *antipasto* and pasta or meat.

Bank of London & South America, Calle 25 de Mayo 2501, open 0715-1315.

Swimming On river at Guadalupe beach; local bus.

Tourist Office at the conveniently situated bus terminal: poor maps, not too friendly.

Railways The quickest link from Buenos Aires is by Mitre railway to Rosario, and connecting

100 ARGENTINA

bus (7 hours). Belgrano railway to Buenos Aires, 483 km., 8-10 hours (US$5.40 tourist, US$7.20 first class), also N to Resistencia.

Roads Fully paved to Rosario, 160 km. (3 hours by bus); to Formosa, 894 km.; to Roque Sáenz Peña, with spurs S to Villa Angela and General Pinedo and N to San Martín. Large and modern bus terminal. Bus for Asunción (Paraguay) leaves daily at 1640, US$28, arrives 0930. Bus to Córdoba takes 5 hrs. Many buses to Buenos Aires, Paraná and Rosario; daily to Mendoza (2100) and Santiago del Estero/Tucumán (2010).

Airport At Sauce Viejo, 17 km. from the city. Three daily flights (2 on Sun.) to and from Buenos Aires.

Upstream from Santa Fe the Paraná rapidly loses depth and is navigable only by river boats and small coastal vessels.

Between Paraná and Goya, on the left bank, is **La Paz (Entre Ríos)**, a small port with regional museum, riverside park and golf club. Buses to Buenos Aires, Rosario and Concordia. Small restaurants in port and near bus station.

Between Santa Fe and Corrientes the boat calls at several river ports, including La Paz, Goya and Empedrado. **Goya** (airport 7 km. from centre), on the E bank, the second town of the Province of Corrientes, is near the junction of the Paraná with the Santa Lucía river. It is a large tobacco centre on the Urquiza railway, with a population of 40,000. There is a vehicle-ferry service across the river to **Reconquista**. Both towns are served by air by Austral (which flies from the military base at Reconquista, between the airport and town, 10 km. from town). Austral to Reconquista, stopping at Paraná on Tues., Thurs. and Sat. at 0955. The road N from Goya to Empedrado and Corrientes is paved; many buses.

Empedrado, further up the river on the E bank, has a population of 21,000. It is on the railway line between Buenos Aires (1,014 km.) and Corrientes. Oranges and rice are grown in the neighbourhood.

Hotels at La Paz *Milton*, San Martín e Italia, modern; *Plaza*, main square; *Rivera*, San Martín 376; *San Martín*, San Martín 551, E, clean.

Hotels at Goya *Hotel de Turismo*, modern, recommended. *Cervantes*, J. E. Gómez 723; *Goya*, Colón 929; *España*, España 345, F, clean, hot water, friendly, near bus station. *Hoguimarsa*, B. Mitre 880/90 (the last-named also has establishments at Curuzú Cuatiá, Esquina, Empedrado and Mercedes in Corrientes province). *Restaurant El Colonial* said to be the best, US$4 for full meal, near bus station at Loza 415.

Hotels at Reconquista *Magui*, on main street, excellent restaurant. *Olessio*, opposite bus terminal, F. *Residencial San Martín*, F, with bath, on B. Mitre and Bolívar. *Motel Hostal del Rey*, located on the edge of town, clean, new, D, with bath. Many around bus station.

Hotel at Empedrado *Turismo*, with swimming pool and fine views. **Campsite.**

About 600 km. upstream from Santa Fe, on the W bank, is the little port of Barranqueras, served also from Santa Fe by railway (17 hours). It is on a steep bluff overlooking the Paraná. A paved road connects it with

Resistencia, the bustling, hot and energetic capital of the Province of Chaco, a galaxy of neon after dark, 6½ km. up the Barranqueras stream. Pop.: 94,000. The road N from Resistencia to Formosa (200 km.) and on to Puerto Pilcomayo (137 km.) is paved. There are many modern statues, mostly female nudes, promoted by the *Fogón de los Arrieros* (see below), along the streets and a museum, the Museo Histórico Ichoalay, at Donovan 425, in the Catholic girls' school, which follows the development of the city from its early days of conflict with the Indians to modern times. International airport.

Area Products Cotton, *quebracho*, cattle. Sculptured Chaco woods from Domingo Arenas, cubist-type wood-statues. Tradicional Pampeya, on Güemes 154, sells local handicrafts and has an Indian handicraft display. Handicrafts also sold by Toba Indians in the Toba district.

Hotels *Covadonga*, Güemes 200, C, a/c, *Tabaré* snack bar; *Lemirson*, Rawson 167, C; *Colón*, Sta. María de Oro 139, C, friendly, clean, recommended; *Sahara*, Güemes 169, D, Telex 71104. *Residencial*, Av. Alberdi 317, F; *Las Torres*, Güemes 757, D; *Residencia Monaco*, Tucumán 350, E, OK; *Aragón*, basic, F, near bus station. Several cheap ones near bus station, e.g. *Alfi*, E; *Residencia Santiago del Estero*, F, very basic; *Paraná*, clean and friendly, F, without bath; *Comedor El Oriente*, Av. 25 de Mayo 554, E, with bath. Avoid *Residencia Antártida*.

ARGENTINA

Camping *Parque Dos de Febrero*, very pretty, near artificial lake, tent US$2; adequate free site nearby. *Parque Mitre*, showers and toilets.

Restaurants *Círculo Residentes Santafecinos*, tasty meals at family style restaurant, US$6 for large meal, on Vedia 152. Try *chupín de surubí*, a sort of bouillabaisse, delightful. *Parrillada Clemente*, Santa María de Oro 399 near bus station, *Parrillada Las Brasas*, Brown 71, less good. Good pizzas at *San José* in main square. *Antiguo Farol* and *La Recova* both on Güemes and Don Bosco.

Fogón de los Arrieros, Brown 350, between López and French, a famous house-and-club full of local art and "objets" from abroad. No fee. Anyone can drink at the bar, open to the public from 2100 to 2300, but not every day and hours can vary, check. Good place to meet local people.

Car Hire Avis, French 701 and at airport.

Bank Banco del Chaco on Antártida Argentina 253. Espinosa travel agency, Santa María del Oro 125, changes travellers' cheques. Better rates for cheques than notes!

Tourist Office In main square, Vedia and Tucumán, maps, very helpful; open 0800-2000.

Air Airport 8 km. from town. Austral weekend night flights to and from Buenos Aires with 40% discount. Two flights a day to Buenos Aires, some stopping at Rosario. Aerolínea Federal Argentina (Alfa, ex-Aerochaco) flies to Salta Sat. 0800, US$60.

Rail S to Santa Fe, leaves on Tues. and Sat. at 1830, 12½ hrs, good food on train (Belgrano Railway). No regular passenger service to Formosa, Metán or Salta.

Buses Colectivo (Ataco Norte or Cotap) every 15 mins. to Corrientes over the Paraná River bridge, the Resistencia terminal is on Santiago del Estero, between Vedia and Sta. Maria del Oro. 3 *especiales* a day to Buenos Aires (US$23) 14 hrs., 3 *comunes* a day (US$19), 17 hrs.; bus to Santa Fe (US$11.50). 3 a day to Formosa and Puerto Pilcomayo, 6-7 hours, US$6.50. To Posadas, 6/7 hours, dull, hot journey. Daily Transchaco and Sáenz Peña buses direct to Salta (US$22) at 1700, 14-16 hours, bus may get bogged down on dirt roads; can be crowded. Few stops and no toilet on bus; one daily to Tucumán at about 1900. Bus to Rosario, daily, 2015, US$17.25. Bus to Paraguayan border US$5.20, 5 hours. Many searches, watch your belongings and make sure everything is there afterwards. Also to Formosa and Asunción with Godoy and Brújula, US$11.75, 6½ hrs.

Roads between Resistencia and Salta: Most of Route 16, through Roque Sáenz Peña, Avia Teray, Pampa del Infierno (good ACA Hostería), Río Muerto, Monte Quemado, El Quebrachal, Joaquín V. González, then on Route 30 to Las Lajitas and Lumbrera, is paved (there are two bad stretches of 30 km. each before Pampa del Infierno and J.V.González). No service stations along most of the route. It is 830 km. and can be done in one day by car, but it may be hot and there are several military check points—beware of cattle crossing the road. A south-western route (No. 94), from Avia Teray to Quimili, thence to Santiago del Estero, is very bad.

Across the river from Resistencia is Corrientes. The 2¾-km. General Belgrano bridge crosses the river (toll free); the best view of it is from the Corrientes side.

Corrientes, the site of Graham Greene's *The Honorary Consul*, is the capital of Corrientes Province. The river can make the air heavy, moist and oppressive, but in winter the climate is pleasant. Population, 200,000. The city was founded in 1588. The church of La Cruz (1808) houses a miraculous cross placed there by the founder of the city, Alonzo de Vera—Indians who tried to burn it were killed by lightning under a cloudless sky. The Cathedral is in the renaissance style. Plaza Sargento Cabral has a statue to the sergeant who saved San Martín's life at the battle of San Lorenzo. A beautiful walk along the Paraná river leads to Parque Mitre, from where there are good views of sunsets over the river. On the Costanera, above the bridge to Resistencia, is a small, pretty zoo with animals of the region. There is a Colonial, Historical and Fine Arts Museum. The pre-Lenten Carnival is said to be the most interesting in Argentina; reserve hotel in advance; otherwise stay in Resistencia, which is cheaper. Calle Junín is pedestrianized, with restaurants and shops, crowded at night. Road to Posadas, 320 km., now paved.

Hotels *Corrientes*, Junín 1559; and *Gran Hotel Guaraní*, Mendoza 970, B; *Turismo Provincial*, Entre Ríos 650; *Cadena de Oro*, Ruta Nacional 12; *Orly*, San Juan 861, C; *Waikiki*, Gobernador A. Ruiz 2260, D; *Colón*, Rioja 437, near river, 15 minutes' walk to centre, comfortable, D, with bath; *Buenos Aires*, C. Pellegrini 1058; *San Martín*, Santa Fe 955; *Sosa*, España 1050; *Pavón*, Av. Maipú, km 3. Residenciales *Aialay*, Córdoba 314; *Costanera*, Junín 565; *Avenida*, Av. 3 de Abril.

102 ARGENTINA

Camping Near bus terminal and railway station is *Camping-club Teléfono*, US$1 p.p., hot showers or bath, friendly.

Restaurants *Maximiliano*, H. Irigoyen 1331, open until 0300; *Yapeyú*, Av. Vera 1352; *Michelangelo*, C. Pellegrini y Catamarca; *Raviolandia*, Nueve de Julio 652; *Che Camba*, Av. Independencia 4175; *El Mangrullo*, Junín y Don Bosco. *Gran Hotel Turismo*, Entre Ríos 650; *La Rueda*, Av. 3 de Abril. *La Reforma*, Rioja and Julio. Ice creams at *Italia*, Nueve de Julio 1301 and *Verona*, Av. Ferré 1750. Tea rooms: *Confitería Viki*, San Juan 721 y Maipú 1198. *Café Mecca*, Junín 1264/66; *Gualeyan*, Junín 1426. Several on San Juan. Pizzerías: *Gaselli*, Av. Tres de Abril 686, *San Jorge*, Irigoyen 2265; *Los Pinos*, Catamarca and Bolivar; *Gandolfo*, Av. Tres de Abril 563.

Nightclubs Several on or near Mendoza, e.g. *Ka Ko Si, Teorema, Casa Blanca*; on or near Pellegrini, e.g. *Killer, Katyuska*.

Car Hire Avis at *Gran Hotel Guaraní* and airport; only credit cards accepted from foreigners.

Banks Banco de la Nación, Nueve de Julio 1298; Banco de Galicia y Buenos Aires, Córdoba 870; Provincia de Corrientes, Nueve de Julio 1098. Cambio Casa Ruiz, Junín 1243.

Tourist Office Junín and Córdoba.

Travel Agencies Quo Vadis, Pellegrini 1140; El Cabure, San Juan 671; Viamir, Junín 1459; Viajes Atlas, Mendoza 1073.

Shipping Buenos Aires and Asunción passenger services both reported suspended.

Airport Camba Punta, 10 km. from city. Aerolíneas Argentinas office Junín 1301, Tel.: 23850; Austral, Córdoba 935, Tel.: 25278. Daily AA and Austral flights to and from Buenos Aires. Austral to Rosario twice a week.

Rail Office on Córdoba 990, Tel.: 22009. *El Correntino* train leaves Lacroze station, Buenos Aires at 1500 daily, arriving at Corrientes (1,046 km.) at 1230 next day; it leaves Corrientes at 1825 daily, reaching Buenos Aires at 1545 next day. Fares: sleeper US$29, first US$15, tourist US$11.50.

Bus Terminal ½ block from *Hotel Colón* at Rioja and Plácido Martínez. Regular buses from terminal to town centre (US$0.15). Corrientes-Posadas US$7.50, 6½ hrs. Corrientes-Resistencia US$0.55, Cota, every 15 mins.; Buenos Aires-Corrientes, US$21.50.

At 20 km. along Route 12 from Corrientes is Santa Ana de los Guacaras, a 17th-century settlement with attractive colonial architecture. To the N of Corrientes is the small town of **Paso de la Patria** (38 km., Route 12), a paradise for *dorado* fishing, with plenty of bungalows to stay at. (Hotels: *Hostería Oficial*, C; *Cabaña Don Julián*, C, full board.)

A tiny port on the Alto Paraná—*Itatí* (pop. 5,700)—is reached by bus (73 km. on route 12). Here, on July 16, is held a gala festival which celebrates jointly the crowning of the Virgin of Itatí (housed in a sanctuary built 1638), and St. Louis of France. Thousands of pilgrims arrive on the 16th (when the religious ceremonies begin) from San Luis del Palmar (pop. 15,000) in picturesque procession. Also on Route 12 (250 km. from Corrientes) are the Saltos de Apipé, where one can fish or swim.

Corrientes is 40 km. below the confluence of the Paraguay and Alto Paraná rivers. Up the former is Asunción; up the latter are Posadas and Iguazú.

The only Argentine port of any note on the Paraguay river is **Formosa,** 240 km. above Corrientes. It is the capital of Formosa Province, and has a population of 40,000. There is an interesting colonial museum in the town centre. There are many Indians in the area. At the Casa de Artesanía ask about the ACA in Ingeniero Juárez, from where excursions to see Chaco Indian settlements may be made. The surroundings are flat and swampy, the climate and vegetation tropical. From the port a trip can be made to Isla Alberdi, a Paraguayan duty-free spot; no possibility of continuing into Paraguay, and can only be done if you have a multiple entry visa. Also from the port, try to go out with sport fishermen at weekends. By road from Buenos Aires; 1,365 km. Airport (at least one Aerolíneas Argentinas flight per day).

Hotels *Turismo*, best; *Residencial City*, near railway station, D; pleasant, but less friendly as *Residencial Colonial*, San Martín 879, F. Several others near this hotel at the same price. *Residencial Rivas*, ½ block from bus station, F, clean, friendly. *Hotel Royal*, E. *Residencial Italia*, on San Martín, nr. station, E, clean, hot showers.

Camping Possible on the river about 2 km. from the centre along a dirt road, upstream and over the railway lines.

Restaurant *Ser Bran*, near bus terminal, cheap and good.

ARGENTINA

Tourist Office España 318.

Banks close at about noon and there are no exchange shops; buy australes in Asunción or Clorinda if en route when they're closed. Banco de la Provincia de Formosa changes travellers' cheques.

Shipping Bolivian vessels (cargo and passenger) to Puerto Suárez (Bolivia), with call at Asunción. Irregular.

Roads S to Resistencia (200 km.); N to Clorinda and Asunción, paved, 150 km., via new toll bridge.

Bus Formosa-Puente Loyola US$4.25. Formosa-Asunción US$4, 0800 and 1630, Expreso Brújula and other companies on main street. Empresa Godoy to border. Six a day to Resistencia.

Railway across the Chaco to Embarcación, N of Jujuy and Salta. *Cochemotor* passenger service Mon. only, 1330, US$8, buy ticket 2 hrs. before departure, 19 hrs., noisy, uncomfortable but worth it for the birdlife. (This service may have been suspended: information, please.)

About 137 km. N of Formosa, almost opposite Asunción (Paraguay), are **Clorinda** and Puerto Pilcomayo, whence the new Loyola bridge crosses to Puerto Falcón, Paraguay. Border crossing is easy. Many buses from Argentine end of bridge: to Formosa (10 a day), Resistencia (4) and Santa Fe/Rosario/Buenos Aires (3). Clorinda has a well-known banana festival in early October. Street money changer at Clorinda bus station, gives good rates austral/guaraní.

At the confluence of the two rivers above Corrientes the Paraguay river comes in from the N, the Alto Paraná from the E. The Alto Paraná is difficult to navigate; it is, in parts, shallow; there are several rapids, and sometimes the stream is braided, its various channels embracing mid-stream islands. Much rice is grown on its banks. The main Argentine port, on the S bank, is **Posadas,** capital of the province of Misiones, 377 km. above Corrientes, and very hot in summer. A bridge is being built across the 2½ km. of river between Posadas and the Paraguayan town of Encarnación opposite, to link the rail and road systems of the two countries. A motor launch and car ferry link Posadas and Encarnación; the former runs 6 times a day Sat. and Sun., 7 daily in the week (US$1 plus US$0.10 for baggage), the car ferry runs 4 times a day. Thorough baggage and body searches when entering Argentina. Population, 130,000. *Yerba mate* (there is a *mate* museum in the Palacio del Mate), tea and tobacco are grown in the area. There is a Museo Regional near the amphitheatre on J. B. Alberdi, open daily 0800-1800, US$0.15. (not recommended, dilapidated). Better is the Museo Arqueológico e Histórico Andrés Guacurarí (on Gen. Paz, near municipal market), which has Jesuit remains and archaeological pieces from the areas to be flooded by the Yacyretá hydroelectric lake. There is a relatively expensive Mercado Artesanal (craft market). There is a head shrinker's museum in Dos de Mayo, near Posadas. A *mate* festival is held in San Miguel Apóstoles, near Posadas, at the beginning of November, otherwise a quiet town. Natural History Museum, with live birds and snakes, well-kept, extensive range. The roads to Corrientes and Iguazú are paved.

The route along the Río Uruguay from Zárate north (now fully paved) is the shortest and least crowded route to Posadas and avoids the major population centres.

Hotels Prices in the Province of Misiones are on the whole significantly higher than elsewhere, and double if you want a private bathroom. Best is *Libertador*, San Lorenzo 2208, C; *Continental*, Bolívar 314, D, comfortable, but noisy, reasonable breakfast; *Canciller*, Junín 258, D; *City*, Colón 280, D, dirty, but good restaurant, and *Posadas*, Bolívar 272, C; *Grand Hotel*, Ayacucho 272, swimming pool, central, reasonable, and *Río de Oro*, Colón 433 (ground floor, S side rooms coolest), both E; *Hotel de Turismo*, Bolívar 171, D, modern but poor maintenance; *Savoy*, Sarmiento 296, clean and pleasant, good restaurant next door, D; *Residencial Nagel*, Pedro de Mendoza 211, near bus station, noisy, basic, F; *Eldorado*, near bus station, Av. Mitre 84, basic, E, dirty, friendly; *Argentina*, corner of Colón and Sarmiento, basic, with fan; *Gran Hotel Misiones*, E, on Líbano, a/c, good restaurant, one block from bus terminal; *Tía Julia*, near bus terminal at Junín 880, F, hot shower. *Hospedaje Familiar*, Av. Mitre 58, E, friendly, convenient, next door to Expreso Singer bus terminal. Many adequate *residenciales* in the centre, F, but cheap hotels are hard to find.

Camping Municipal camping ground on the river, off the road to San Ignacio Miní, hot showers and shop, good.

104 ARGENTINA

Restaurants *El Tropezón*, San Martín 185, good, inexpensive, and *Jockey Club*, same street, 159. *Pescadería Bárbara*, corner of Junín and Entre Ríos, good, wide selection; excellent US$3 buffet on ground floor of *Hotel Savoy; Pizzería Los Pinos*, San Lorenzo 286; *El Litoral*, Av. Arrechea 35, opposite bus station. *Galaxia* on Mitre near bus station, open 24 hrs. but unfriendly. There is an excellent restaurant next door to the ACA service station called *La Querencia*, Córdoba 269; *Bar Itá* for good coffee and sandwiches, on San Martín. Breakfast at ACA.

Bank Only Banco de La Nación changes travellers' cheques. Opens very early, 0615-1215. Two **Casas de Cambio**, to change notes, one at Bolívar 443; neither accepts American Express. If stuck when banks and *cambios* are closed, cross the river to Encarnación and use the street changers.

Tourist Office Colón 393, Tel., 24360, helpful, maps and brochures in English of Posadas, Formosa and Iguazú Falls.

Paraguayan Consulate, San Lorenzo 179.

Bus from Buenos Aires, US$24.50, 16½ hrs; Expreso Singer, company leaves at 1030, 1500 and 1600. Tigre-Iguazú at 1500; some go via Resistencia, some via Concordia. Expreso Singer and Tigre bus terminal is 5 mins. walk from the main bus terminal. Tickets sold in both places. Express bus Posadas-Puerto Iguazú leaves at 0900 and 0500, 4½ hrs., US$11, daily; stops at San Ignacio Miní. Bus Posadas-Córdoba with Singer, Tues., Thurs., Sat. at 1730, arrive at 1335 next day. Bus to Corrientes US$7.50; to Formosa US$6.50; to Santa Fe US$11.50. Bus to Asunción (Expreso Singer), US$10. Bus to Montevideo, a roundabout journey because the main Asunción-Montevideo route passes through Corrientes. One can take Expreso Singer bus to Colón (US$15); two local buses over the bridge to Paysandú (US$1.50), then plenty of buses to Montevideo (US$8). Bus to Rosario US$14; to Paso de los Libres (7 hrs.) US$7.75, interesting, 60 km. not paved. For those continuing to Brazil (Uruguaiana) have the bus drop you off about 3 km. before Paso de los Libres at Puente Internacional—Argentine customs—the bus from here to the Brazilian border on the other side of the Río Uruguay costs US$0.25. Expreso Singer bus Posadas-Porto Alegre (via Oberá, Alba Posse and Porto Mauá) Mon., Wed., Fri. at 1500, arriving 0600 next day, US$18. If the bus is full it is possible to buy a ticket (without a seat) in Oberá. The bus usually empties before long and you can get a seat. Posadas-Resistencia, 5-6 hrs., dull trip, US$9. Bus Posadas-Concordia (Expreso Singer) US$14.50, 2100 daily, 8¾ hrs. Singertur, Av. Mitre 54 (Tel.: 4771, 4772) in Posadas. **N.B.** The bus station, at junction of Av. Uruguay and Av. Bartolomé Mitre, is at the upper level of the town, some distance from the ferry terminal.

Train from Buenos Aires (Lacroze Station). Information available in Galerías Pacífico, Florida 729, Tel.: 31-6411/5. *El Gran Capitán*, which leaves at 1500 daily, arrives at 0945. From Posadas *El Gran Capitán* leaves at 1950 daily, arrives in Buenos Aires about 1545 next day, sleeper US$29.60; pullman US$22.85; 1st class US$15.90; tourist US$11.85, not crowded. There is a car transporter on the Mon. and Fri. trains, returning to Buenos Aires on Thurs. and Sun. *Cataratas*, leaves Lacroze 1500 Sat., arrives 0750 Sun., returns 2300 Sun., arriving Buenos Aires 1545 Mon., was inaugurated in 1985; car transporter; same fares as *El Gran Capitán*. One advantage over the buses is that the wild life in woods and swamps may be seen more easily (because it is less often disturbed) from the railway than from the road. Meals on board, US$4.45. Train to Asunción leaves Encarnación 1100 Wed., arrives 0700 next day. Returns Tues. at 2000. There is a 4 hr. layover between Bs.As. and Asunción at Posadas. Tourist US$8, 1st US$12. *El Gran Capitán* from Posadas passes Paso de los Libres, for connection to Uruguaiana, arr. 0020. Trains from Posadas to Concordia, arrive at 0414. There is no rail connection between Posadas and Puerto Iguazú.

Airport General San Martín (12 km.), reached from Posadas by Bus No. 8 from opp. bus terminal in 20 mins., US$0.30. Daily flights to Buenos Aires with Austral (with one connection a week to Rosario), and Aerolíneas Argentinas; one night flight a week to Buenos Aires with each company; 40% discount.

From Posadas a visit should be paid to the impressive ruins of Jesuit settlements and to the magnificent Falls of Iguazú. It is possible, by leaving Posadas at 0700, to see the Jesuit ruins and continue on by bus or *colectivo* over the paved road to Iguazú the same day, arriving 2130: at Puerto Rico, on the road, there is a good hotel, *Suizo*, D; recommended restaurants are *Don Luís* and *Churrascaría Flach*, both on main street. The express bus takes 4½ hours (US$6.50), and leaves at 0200 and 0400, but will not stop at San Ignacio Miní (see 105); the ordinary buses, which will, take 11-12 hours for the journey and there are hourly departures from Posadas; these buses make 35 stops in all.

Not far from Posadas are thirty ruins of old Jesuit missions among the Guaraní Indians, from which the province of Misiones derives its name. Tourists should not fail to see those at San Ignacio Miní (very well maintained), reached by paved road in 1¼ hours (bus, US$1.45, every 1-1½ hours, from terminal, Nuestra

ARGENTINA 105

Señora, check return time with office). One and a half hours are sufficient for a leisurely look. There are heavy rains at San Ignacio in February.

At **San Ignacio Miní** the grass-covered plaza, a hundred metres square, is flanked north, east and west by 30 parallel blocks of stone buildings with ten small, one-room dwellings to the block. The roofs have gone, but the massive metre-thick walls are still standing except where they have been torn down by the *ibapoi* trees; it looks as if there was an arcade in front of each block. The public buildings, some of them still 10 metres high, are on the south side. In the centre are the ruins of a large church finished about 1724. To the right is the cemetery, to the left the school and the cloisters of the priests. Beyond are other buildings which were no doubt the workshops, refectory and storerooms. The masonry, a red or yellow sandstone from the Paraná River, was held together by a sandy mud. There is much bas-relief sculpture, mostly of floral designs. Now maintained as a National Monument (open 0800-1800, entry free, but tip appreciated if the guards look after your luggage).

The Jesuits set up their first missions among the Guaraní Indians about 1609. These were in the region of Guaíra, now in Brazil. One mission near the confluence of the Pirapo and Paranapanema rivers was named San Ignacio Miní. The missions flourished, and by 1614 there were 2,000 Indians living there. Cotton had been introduced, the Indians wove their own clothes, dressed like Europeans, raised cattle, and built and sculpted and painted their own churches. But in 1627 they were violently attacked by the slave-hunting Bandeirantes from São Paulo in Brazil. By 1632 the position of the mission had become impossible, and 12,000 converts, led by the priests, floated on 700 rafts down the Paranapanema into the Paraná, only to find their route made impassable by the Guaíra Falls. They pushed for eight days through dense virgin forests on both sides of the river, then built new boats and continued their journey; 725 km. from their old homes they founded new missions in what is now Paraguay, Argentine Misiones, and Brazilian Rio Grande do Sul. San Ignacio Miní was re-established on the banks of the small Yabebiri river, but moved 64 years later, in 1696, to the present site of its ruins. By the early 18th century there were, on both sides of the river, 30 mission villages with a combined population of over 100,000 souls. Only four of these show any signs of their former splendour: San Ignacio Miní, São Miguel (Brazil), and Jesús and Trinidad (Paraguay). At the height of its prosperity in 1731 San Ignacio contained 4,356 people. In 1767, Charles III of Spain expelled the Jesuits from Spanish territory; the Franciscans and Dominicans then took over. After the Jesuits had gone, there was a rapid decline in prosperity. By 1784 there were only 176 Indians at San Ignacio Miní; by 1810, there was none. By order of the Paraguayan dictator Francia, all the settlements were evacuated in 1817, and San Ignacio was set on fire. The village was lost in the jungle until it was discovered again in 1897. In 1943 an agency of the Argentine Government took control. Some of the craft work produced at the settlement can be seen at two museums in Buenos Aires: the Museo Colonial Isaac Fernández Blanco and the municipal Museo de Arte Colonial. Museo Jesuítico on site, close to ruins on main avenue. The caretaker, Sr Miguel Nadasdy, will show you a 350-mm. statue of Moses, said to be by Michelangelo, kept in the museum, and tell you of other worthwhile sites. Also Museo Provincial in main street. Interesting local crafts sold opposite ruins. Wooden carvings are especially worthwhile.

Accommodation There are ACA hostels (F; lunches at US$5 each) both at San Ignacio Miní and at Monte Carlo, half-way between San Ignacio and Iguazú. Also at San Ignacio is *Hotel San Ignacio*, friendly, good, clean, restaurant with nice food (closed in winter-August), E/F. There are 3 *comedores* (lunch only) opposite the entrance to the ruins. Festival July 30-31.

The caretaker at the Museo Jesuítico can give you the address of a young German, Michael Apel, who used to own a farm nearby but now owns one in neighbouring Paraguay. (Take the bus from *Ciudad Presidente Stroessner* on the international highway towards Asunción. Get off at Km. 88 near the radio transmission tower and ask villagers.) He will lodge respectable-looking travellers in exchange for a bit of housework or help in the fields. You only pay for things he has to pay for; fruit and farm produce free. **Camping** outside the ruins is permitted in the free municipal site; cold showers and toilets.

The most successful colonization in Argentina of late years has been at **Eldorado,** on this route. This prosperous small town is surrounded by flourishing *mate,* tung, citrus, eucalyptus and tobacco plantations. There are tung oil factories, sawmills, plywood factories, *mate* drying installations and a citrus packing plant. The ACA office is very helpful and has a large illuminated map of Eldorado and its surroundings.

Hotels at Eldorado *Alpa,* D; *Hostería ACA* and *Atlántida,* both E; *Castellar,* D with bath. *Ideal,* F, clean, opp. bus station. Restaurant: *Copetín al Paso,* excellent, reasonable for price, but doesn't cook every day.

Camping Camping site with showers and toilets; take the road toward the river from the main highway, for 2 km.

106 ARGENTINA

To see something of the Province of Misiones, the following way to return from Puerto Iguazú to Posadas is suggested by Reinhard Böhm-Raffay. If you are interested in flora and fauna, travel from Puerto Iguazú on Route 12 to Wanda; 2 km. away is an amethyst and quartz mine which sells gems, the only one in Misiones. Carry on to Eldorado, then follow Route 17 (buses 0800 and 1530), paved to Bernardo Yrigoyen, a nice village, lovely vegetation en route. Follow Route 14 to Tobuna, where you will see the Alegría falls. On to the small village of Paraíso, see Moconá falls 82 km. from there, then Dos de Mayo. There is a natural history museum, Juan B. Foerster, there, with quite a good collection of birds and animals, alive and stuffed. J. B. Foerster's family lives nearby. Pass through Oberá and follow Route 105 W to Santa Ana, with Jesuit ruins of Loreto, not restored. From here you can return via San Ignacio to Puerto Iguazú or turn 16 km. in opposite direction to Posadas.

The **Iguazú Falls** are the most overwhelming falls in South America. They lie about 350 km. upstream from Posadas where, 19 km. above the confluence of the Iguazú with the Alto Paraná, the waters fall thunderously in virgin forest bright with orchids and serpentine creepers festooning the branches. Above the impact of water on basalt rock hovers a perpetual 30-metre high cloud of mist in which the sun creates blazing rainbows. The Iguazú (Guaraní for great waters) rises in the Brazilian hills near Curitiba and receives some 30 streams on its course across the plateau. Above the main falls the river, sown with wooded islets, opens out to a width of 4 km. There are rapids for 3½ km. above the 60-metre precipice over which the water plunges in 275 falls over a frontage of 2,470 metres, at a rate of 1,750 cubic metres a second. Their height is greater than Niagara's by 20 metres or so and their width by one half, but most of the falls are broken midway by ledges of rock. The tumbling water in its setting of begonias, orchids, fern and palms with flocks of parrots and cacique birds, swifts dodging in and out of the very falls, and myriads of butterflies (at least 500 different species), is majestically beautiful, especially outside the cool season (when the water is much diminished, as are the birds and insects). One cannot cross the river at the Falls themselves; this can only be done by bridge or ferry between Porto Meira and Puerto Iguazú.

Visitors to the Falls should note that the Brazilian side (best visited in the morning because the light then is better for photography; half a day will suffice) shows the best panorama of the whole falls, but the Argentine side (which needs most of a day to explore it properly: the area is much greater) shows more close detail of the individual falls and is much more interesting from the point of view of seeing the forest with its wildlife and butterflies. There are a bird hide overlooking a marsh (Bañado), an interpreted (Spanish) nature trail (Macuco) in the jungle, a self-guided trail around the Lower Circuit, all of which are very lovely. Ideally, then, one should first visit the Brazilian side to get some idea of the size and magnificence of the whole, and then cross to the Argentine side to see the details; this can all be done in a day, starting at about 0700, but the brisk pace needed for a quick tour is very exhausting for the non-athletic in that heat. (An advantage in visiting the Argentine side first is that the information provided at the Visitors' Centre is far superior to anything offered in Brazil.) If one's time is limited, then the Brazilian side, with its marvellous distant views, is the one to visit, particularly since the Argentine side no longer has the spectacular catwalks at the top of the falls. To walk along the lower series of catwalks, at the level of the midway ledge, waterproof coats or swimming costumes are advisable but not absolutely necessary. Wear good shoes when walking around, e.g. tennis shoes, as the rocks are very slippery in places. Put your camera in a plastic bag. At the base of Dos Hermanas is a natural, idyllic swimming pool, so take bathing gear in summer to cool off.

The Devil's Throat the most spectacular fall, is best seen from Puerto Canoas, to which buses run (see below), or you can drive (parking US$1). There is also a short boat trip from Puerto Canoas to join the catwalk. Recommended in the evening when the light is best and the swifts are returning to roost on the walls, some behind the water. Below the falls the Iguazú runs swiftly for 19 km. through a deep canyon before it joins the Alto Paraná.

On the Argentine side the upper series of catwalks into the river, *Circuito Superior*, were largely destroyed by floods in 1983. The *Circuito Inferior* (lower

ARGENTINA 107

walk) is complete; of the upper walk, only from the Administration area to San Martín, and from Puerto Canoas to Devil's Throat has been replaced. It is unlikely that the middle section will be restored because debris from deforestation upstream poses too great a threat.

The Argentine Iguazú National Park embraces a large area. The fauna are rich and various but hunting is not allowed. Fishing is no longer permitted. The months to avoid are July (holidays) and December-March (hot). Information and permits can be got from the Visitors Centre Information Desk, open daily 0800-1800 in the old Cataratas Hotel, now converted. The Visitors' Centre organizes night-time walks between *Hotel Cataratas* and the falls when the moon is full. There is a museum of local fauna and an auditorium for periodic slide shows (on request for 8 or more people), no commentary, just music, though an educational show is planned. A good guide book on Argentine birds is for sale. Administration for the park's headquarters is in a colonial-style building at Puerto Iguazú.

On the Brazilian side, a 1½ km paved walk runs part of the way down the cliff near the rim of the Falls, giving a stupendous view of the whole Argentine side (the greater part) of the falls. It ends up almost under the powerful Floriano Falls, where a new catwalk was brought into use at the end of 1984. Waterproof clothing can be hired although it is not absolutely necessary. An elevator (from 0800) hoists the visitor to the top of the Floriano Falls and to a path leading to Porto Canoa. Helicopter flight over Falls—US$25 per head—lasts 5-6 minutes. There is a small but worthwhile museum 5 km. from the Falls on the Brazilian side (1 km. from park entrance is side road to museum, look for sign) and opposite it are some steps that lead down the steep slope to the river bank. Beautiful walk. It can be misty early in the morning at the Falls.

There is a US$1.50 charge which allows one-day entry to the Argentine Park, free information leaflet provided with ticket (guests at *Hotel Internacional* do not have to pay). Entry to the Brazilian side is about US$0.30, included in the bus fare out, or payable at the National Park entrance.

On the Argentine side Transportes Cataratas buses, about 6 a day, run from the bus station to the Falls, stopping in town outside the Aerolíneas Argentinas office, taking about 30 minutes for the 22½ km. These buses are sometimes erratic, even though the times are clearly indicated, especially when it is wet. They stop at the National Park entrance for the purchase of entrance tickets. Fare to the Falls, US$0.70; first bus at 0700, last at 1800; first back at 0815, last at 1900. The bus continues from the Park Adminstration to Puerto Canoas (for Devil's Throat). There are fixed rates for taxis, US$10, up to 5 people. A tour from the bus terminal, taking in both sides of the Falls, costs US$11. Hitch-hiking to the Falls is difficult, but you can hitch up to the Posadas intersection at Km. 11, then it is only 7 km. walk. From Foz do Iguaçu in Brazil, Transbalan buses (from local bus station—*Terminal Urbana*—on Av. Juscelino Kubitschek, opp. Infantry Barracks, 1½ blocks from *Rodoviária*— interstate bus station) marked Cataratas run the 32 km. to the falls every 2 hours from 0600-2200, but hourly on Sun. and holidays), past airport to *Hotel das Cataratas*, takes 40 mins. Buses return 0700-1900, about US$0.80 one way. (The taxi fare is US$4.50, plus US$2 for each hour of waiting.) The tours of the Falls organized by the various hotels have been recommended in preference to taxi rides.

Frontier crossing to see both sides is easy. If you are coming from one side and you just want to see the other, returning afterwards to the side you came from, tell the officials, and they won't stamp your passport. However, we have been advised that this may be difficult for British visitors (if you haven't a visa, you will not be allowed into Argentina unless very lucky). Similarly, U.S. citizens must have all necessary visas. Some say that, for fear of being stranded in no-man's-land, it is best to insist on having one's papers stamped at all posts.

Travel between Argentina and Brazil has been greatly improved by the opening of the 480 metre Puente de Fraternidad/Ponte Presidente Tancredo Neves, which joins Puerto Iguazú (Route 12) and Porto Meira (BR-469). Buses run from the Puerto Iguazú bus terminal to the Terminal Urbana in Foz, pausing at the border. Apparently the passenger and car ferries from Puerto Iguazú to Porto Meira still run: the passenger motor boats run frequently, the car ferry from 0800 to 2000,

108 ARGENTINA

but to 2200 in summertime. There are no exchange facilities on the ferries. From the local bus station (*Terminal Urbana*) in the centre of Foz the bus leaves every ¼ hr. to Porto Meira (12 km.). Bus ends at Brazilian customs, 1 km. away from the river; there will be another one, at busy times, from the customs down to the river. The boat crosses the river frequently; it costs about US$0.25 if you pay in the currency of the country you are leaving, but 3 times more if you pay in the currency of your destination. Minibuses over the new bridge leave the Terminal Urbana every ½ hr-1 hr., marked "Puerto Iguazú", US$0.85, 1 hr. journey to Puerto Iguazú, including stop at Argentine customs. If you have no australes, walk up the slope (10 mins.) and exchange money in Puerto Iguazú opp. the tourist office where the bus stops for the Falls.

Change some money into cruzados before going into Brazil: they try to charge you triple the true cost if you use Argentine money. The cruzado exchange rate is better in the town of Puerto Iguazú than in Brazil itself.

There is an immigration office on the road between Foz do Iguaçu and Porto Meira. Customs on Brazil-Argentina border do not now close until 0200; they can be very thorough with their luggage checks. Be sure to get a stamp on your passport if going on into Brazil. There is an entry tax on the Brazilian side for car passengers only, not for bus passengers. If driving into Brazil insist on visiting

ARGENTINA 109

customs. You *must* get entry papers for your car here or you'll have serious problems later. There is a Brazilian immigration office on the Brazilian side of the bridge into Paraguay; if you are just visiting Ciudad Stroessner and returning to Brazil, no need to have your passport stamped. There are Brazilian police control patrols looking for undeclared goods on the roads past the frontier.

It is not possible to go direct to Puerto Franco (Paraguay) from Puerto Iguazú; one must go through Brazil. If passing through Foz do Iguaçu en route from Puerto Iguazú to Paraguay, make sure that Brazilian officials stamp your passport.

On the Argentine side is **Puerto Iguazú**, a small town, above the river. There is a helpful tourist office (but no English) at Av. Victoria Aguirre and Brasil, open 0800-1200, 1500-2000 Mon.-Fri., 0800-1200, 1630-2000 Sat. and Sun.

Museum Imágenes de la Selva, housed in *Hotel Iguazú*, open daily, free, has wood sculptures by Rodolfo Allou who uses natural shapes of roots and branches.

Hotels *Internacional Iguazú*, L, five-star, pool, casino, good restaurant, business facilities, overlooking the falls, reportedly run down and unhelpful. Reservations at Av. Eduardo Madero 1020 (Tel.: 3114259, or 3136292), Buenos Aires, recommended. The *Iguazú Hotel*, on Paraguay, in the town (no swimming pool), is being used to offer last accommodation to the elderly, but transients are still welcome, D. A new hotel, the *Paraná*, is clean and friendly and same price, Brasil 367. *La Cabaña*, Av. Tres Fronteras 434 (D, with shower and breakfast, fan, good, clean and friendly) is nice, with an older part and a new annex, and has communal washing facilities and swimming pool. *Tierra Colorada*, Av. Córdoba and El Urú 265, very good, E with bath, nice restaurant. *Libertador*, next to bus station, Bonpland y Perito Moreno, C, looks good on the outside but quite run down inside, restaurant not up to standard either; *Esturión*, C, Av. Tres Fronteras 650, good, clean, friendly, comfortable, swimming pool, good restaurant, reservations at Belgrano 265, 10th floor, Buenos Aires. *Las Orquídeas*, Ruta 12, Km. 5 (Tel.: 2472), very comfortable, clean, set right in the jungle outside Puerto Iguazú, restaurant, C. At same location, *Tropical*, C. *King*, Victoria Aguirre 915, E; *El Pilincho de Don Antonio*, clean, hot shower. *El Descanso*, good, clean, basic, quiet hotel off the road going to the falls; *Alexander*, Córdoba 685, opp. bus station, C incl. meagre breakfast, swimming pool, like American hotel; *Residencial San Fernando*, close to bus station, E, with bath, clean, quiet; *Norte*, in centre, F. Bus to Falls passes *Residencial Paquita*, Av. Córdoba 731, F, very clean, just like a home, only 2 rooms, opposite bus station. *Turismo*, D with bath, hot water, charmingly old fashioned, spectacularly set above river. *Saint George*, Av. Córdoba 745, opp. bus station, C, with breakfast, comfortable, has good, expensive restaurant. Behind this hotel is *Residencial Los Helechos*, E, with bath, owner speaks German, clean, new, motel-style accommodation. Avoid *Rolón*, use only in emergency; *Residencial Los Naranjos*, E, clean, mosquito-free, private bath. *Residencial Arco Iris* (with private shower), basic, cooking facilities available, F.

Camping No camping allowed near the Falls in fee-paying area of National Park. The Ñandú camp ground has been destroyed by floods and a new camp ground will be opened near the Falls (Cataratas area). Camping sometimes permitted at the school just inside the Park entrance. Camping Pindó at the edge of town, charges US$0.60 p.p., US$6 per tent and US$0.60 for use of pool, now very run down, friendly, but for US$1.20 p.p., US$1.20 per tent, there are better ones at Camping América (Tel.: 2820/2788), incl. swimming pool.

Restaurants Restaurant (nameless), ½ block from *Hotel Sol de Iguazú*, Brazilian food, all you can eat for US$5. *La Rueda*, Av. Córdoba, good; *El Tío Querido*, Perito Moreno 345, friendly service, excellent cooking, guitarist at night; *Casa de Comercio*, on square opp. church, good food, moderate prices; *Barbas* and *Trébol* recommended. Good meals in the bus terminal.

Money Exchange three *casas de cambio* opposite the tourist office, change cash and travellers' cheques at good rates. Good rates for cruzados.

Car Hire Al International at airport and in town; *Hotel Internacional*, Avis plan to open an agency. Cars may be taken to the Brazilian side for an extra 10 australes.

Brazilian Consulate U.S. citizens continuing to Paraguay from Foz do Iguaçu must obtain visas here (2 passport photos required); takes a day.

Travel Agent Turismo Dick, Av. Victoria Aguirre 425, also in Foz do Iguaçu, good rates of exchange; does not close at lunchtime. Reports vary.

In Brazil, **Foz do Iguaçu** is a rapidly developing and improving town of 160,000 people.

On a height directly overlooking the Falls is the *Hotel das Cataratas*, an attractive colonial-style building with nice gardens and a swimming pool not without insects. Watch out for the tatty ostriches—they eat keys and watches. Rates: A, (but 30% discount for holders of the Brazil Air Pass). Non-residents can have lunch here (midday and evening buffets—good value, or else wait 45 minutes for *à-la-carte* dishes).

110 ARGENTINA

Hotels in Foz do Iguaçu Many out-of-town hotels state their address as km. from Foz, so you can work out the distance from the airport to the hotel. (Note that in Brazil breakfast is normally included in hotel price.) *Salvatti*, Rua Rio Branco 577, B, all a/c (with restaurant and cinema); *Internacional*, B, good; *Estoril*, Av. Rep. Argentina 892, *Rafahin Palace*, Br 277-Km. 727. *Rafahin*, Mal. Deodoro 909, B, good restaurant, pool, well spoken of; Recommended: *Foz Presidente*, near *Internacional*, superb value, E in winter, luxury room, shower, a/c, restaurant, swimming pool, English spoken; *Ambassador*, Rua Samways, E, breakfast and bath; *Ambassador Palace*, Av. Kubitschek 318, more expensive. On road to falls (Rodovia das Cataratas) are the *Bourbon* (Km. 2.5), *Carimã*, (Km. 16), *Dom Pedro I* (Km. 3), *Panorama*, (Km. 10), *Belvedere* (km. 6), *San Martín*, (Km. 17), no English spoken, unfriendly, 4-star (not deserved). On Av. Brasil: *Diplomata*, No. 678, some a/c, D with shower, value for money; *Astro*, No. 660, E. *City*, five blocks from centre, F, own bathroom, fan, hot water, clean; *Americano*, 3 blocks from bus station, run by Paraguayan couple, very noisy, hot showers, recommended; *Iris*, Brasil and Da Silva, F, left luggage possible, basic but adequate; in the vicinity of the Rodoviária: *Sol*, No. 90, D; *Foz do Iguaçu*, No. 97, B, good laundry and breakfast, will look after luggage, fair; *Bogari Palace*, No. 106, D, excellent restaurant, swimming pool; *Lord*, opp. Rodoviária, D, recommended, a bit like a youth hostel, with a/c, clean, good value, manager offers tours to both sides and to the Casino in Paraguay (with a room with about 30 poker machines—Paraguay is one hour behind); *Rio Mar*, No. 122, D, a/c with bath, good value, a bit run down; *Cisne*, N. 144A, D-E, good breakfast, shower, fridge; *Imperial*, No. 168, E with bath, clean; *Espanhol*, Kubitschek e Tiradentes, E; *Brasil*, opp. Rodoviária, F, no fan, hot water, clean, very basic; *Fortaleza*, ½ block from Rodoviária, F. *Itamaraty*, 1 block SW of bus station, Rua Xavier da Silva off Av. Brasil, F, basic, no breakfast; *15 de Julho*, E, German-owned, clean, friendly, hot water, recommended, Bartolomeu de Gusmão; 3-4 blocks from bus terminal; *Turis*, Rua Xavier da Silva 699, 2 blocks from bus station, D, a/c, bathroom, comfortable, good value, organizes tours; *Riviera*, Mal. Deodoro 559 with Bartolomeu de Gusmão, E, clean, friendly. On Rua Almirante Barroso, *Tropical*, E, basic but adequate; *Senhor do Bomfim*, E, newly refurbished and very clean, nr. bus station, next door is *Teresópolis*, F, near bus station, basic, fans, friendly. Recommended accommodation: house of Laura Coivo, Rua Naipi 629, 4 rooms with bath, D, friendly, helpful. Be sure to leave hotels punctually, or you will be charged an extra day. Many hotels have a minibus service to the airport for guests for a small fee and also offer excursions to Falls (Cheapest: Sun/Luz Hotel).

N.B. Sra Murro, at Estrada Velha das Cataratas, Tel.: 72-1808, rents rooms at her house, D, with fine breakfast, lovely atmosphere; it is in the country about 10 minutes' drive from Foz. Leave town on road to falls, drive 1 km. then on to road for Porto Meira for 1 km., then turn left for 3.4 km. at School of Agriculture; house is on left, painted red.

Camping (pretty cold and humid in winter) 8 km. from Foz, on road to Falls is the *Cataratas*, toilets not too clean, but 1 km. from *Churrascarias Boina Brasa* and (best) *Rafahin* at Km. 533 on Route 277 (Paraguayan music) next to *Rafahin Palace Hotel*. By National Park entrance Camping Club do Brasil, 17 km. from Foz, US$3 p.p. a night (half with International Camping Card), swimming pool, clean; park vehicle or put tent away from trees in winter in case of heavy rain storms, no restaurants, food there not very good, closes at 2300, there are cheaper sites nearer the town on the same road. Not permitted by hotel and Falls. Sleeping in car inside the park also prohibited.
N.B. There are increased reports of night-time thieving at Foz, with thieves carrying knives or guns. In particular avoid *Camping Internacional*, where several assaults have been reported, 5 km. from Foz centre.

Electric Current 110 volts a/c.

Restaurants Many open till midnight. *Rafahin* before the *policia rodoviária* post at Km. 533, with Paraguayan harp trio, good *alcatra* (meat), excellent buffet, next to *Rafahin Palace Hotel* on Route 277, km. 727. There are two other establishments called *Rafahin*: one at Av. Brasil 157 in Foz serves only *à la carte* meals, and a third at Av. das Cataratas Km. 7, between Foz and the airport, is a *churrascaria*. *Vienense*, Av. J. Kubitschek 527. *Hotel Astro*, Av. Brasil 660, cheap; *Arandela*, Brasil 1179, full meal, US$5.30, recommended. The pizzas at *Lanches Karlon*, Av. Brasil 1285, have been recommended; *Brasinha*, Av. Brasil, close to Rodoviária, reasonable; *Nosso Pão*, Av. Jorge Schimmelpfennig (3 blocks off Av. Brasil) cheap, honest menu with prices, masses of good food, sometimes unfriendly. *Bierhaus*, on J. Kubitschek, 4 blocks from the Rodoviária on the Porto Meira road. *Churrascaria Cabeça de Boi*, Av. Brasil 1325, wonderful smorgasbord, cheap, also for coffee and pastries. *Restaurant Malte 20*, corner of Rua Alm. Barroso, generous cheap meals. *Cataratas late Club* serves feijoada (bean stew) Sat. and Sun., fish and other specialities, Av. Gen. Meira, opp. agricultural college. *Casa do Frango*, chicken specialities, also take-away, on Alm. Barroso, opp. *Hotel Basso*. A fruit shop and restaurant are next to the Atlantic gasoline station, 2 blocks from the bus station, and one block behind the bus station is an excellent *churrascaria*, *Espetão*. *Italia*, behind bus station, cheap and popular; *Amigo John*, in the bus station, cheapest in town.

Beware of overcharging at *lanches* (small restaurants)—sometimes three times the posted price; have the right change available.

N.B. Travellers recommend not walking alone around Foz late at night.

ARGENTINA 111

Entertainment New discotheque *Whiskadão* with three different dance halls, Alm. Barroso 763, reasonable, lively at weekends. Fun fair, Centro de Diversões Imperial, on Av. Juscelino Kubitschek.

Consulates Argentina, Rua Eduardo Ramón Brandi 26 (in a residential district), open 0800-1300; Paraguay, Bartolomeu de Gusmão 777.

Post Office Praça Getúlio Vargas 72, next to Tourist Office.

Tourist Office Praça Getúlio Vargas 56. No English spoken at small office with list of accommodation; also kiosk on Av. Brasil and at airport, will book hotels.

Travel Agents and Currency Exchange Transatlântica Turismo, Av. Brasil 99, and others. Dicks Tours has been recommended for its all-day tour to the Brazilian side of the Falls, to Paraguay (Ciudad Stroessner) and to the Itaipú dam, US$12 with sumptuous lunch included. Small groups. Cambio Iguaçu, Av. Brasil 268; Casa Jerusalém, Av. Brasil 1055, for cruzados, australes, guaraníes, good rates.

Excursions You can make an excursion to the Itaipú dam, which is nearing completion, from Foz. The Sete Quedas Falls were flooded in 1982-83 under the project. Bus marked Canteira da Obra from Av. Brasil goes to the Public Relations office at the main entrance, visits free—film in Portuguese and then the dam. Tours start at 0830, 1000, 1430 and 1600. There are also an "executive' bus and agency tours but these are an unnecessary expense as the visit itself is free. If it's sunny, go in the morning as the sun is behind the dam in the afternoon and you will get poor photographs. You cannot go alone to the site as it is fenced in and guarded by its own security force. You can also visit the Paraguayan side, see page 620.

It is also possible to stay in Ciudad Stroessner (Paraguay) visiting both sides of the falls without immigration stamps (unless you are British); documents must be carried at all times, however. Take the Foz do Iguaçu bus or walk over the Ponte de Amizade (Friendship Bridge, Brazilian post open until 0200, pay US$2 in dollars, guaraníes or cruzados at the Paraguayan end) past Brazilian Customs and take Ponte-Cidade bus (US$0.05) to local bus station (10 mins. from *Rodoviária*) where buses go to the Falls or to Argentina.

How to get there There is an Argentine domestic airport near the Falls, and a Brazilian international airport about half-way between Foz do Iguaçu and the Falls. Taxi between the two airports over the new bridge costs US$20. It is recommended that when flying from Buenos Aires one should land on the Argentine side even if intending to stay on the Brazilian side. Travel by domestic flight avoids a long journey to the Buenos Aires international airport and is much cheaper than international flights. The air fare is cheaper from Buenos Aires than from Rio.

Also, if flying from Brazil to Buenos Aires from Iguaçu it is best to fly from the Argentine airport at Iguazú; it is not only cheaper but you arrive at the far more convenient Aeroparque airport in Buenos Aires. Aerolíneas Argentinas office in centre of Puerto Iguazú (bus from here to airport about 2 hours before plane's departure, 1445 and 2145); US$70 one way to Buenos Aires.

Taxis to town from the Brazilian airport are expensive (*comum*, US$5; *especial*, US$7); Transbalan town bus for US$0.35, first at 0515, does not permit large amounts of luggage. Varig/Cruzeiro office in Foz: Av. Brasil 821, Tel.: 74-3344; ground staff speak foreign languages.

By Air from Buenos Aires By Boeing 737 (Aerolíneas Argentinas and Austral) from Buenos Aires, via Rosario, Corrientes or Posadas, or direct to improved Iguazú airport (1 hr. 40 mins.) several daily. For best view on landing, sit on left side of aircraft. Flights back to Buenos Aires are very crowded. The Argentine side can be seen in one day from Buenos Aires: there is a flight between 0730 and 0830 with either Aerolíneas Argentinas or Austral on most days of the week from B.A. domestic airport, flight time 1 hr. 40 mins; bus to falls takes ½ hr., leaving according to plane arrivals. Bus from *Hotel Internacional* to airport leaves according to flight departure times.

By Rail and Road from Buenos Aires is comfortable, cheap, and picturesque. There are sleeping and restaurant cars, good meals and wines. Passengers take a train from Lacroze Station in Buenos Aires to Posadas (for details, see under Posadas, page 103). There is a road, now paved, from Posadas to Puerto Iguazú; express bus to Iguazú meets train, 4½ hrs.

Roads and Buses From Buenos Aires N to Clorinda, then by new toll bridge to Asunción. Or crossing the Paraná at Santa Fe or Resistencia, taking the paved road to Posadas, and on to the falls. The more direct run via Zárate and Concordia is now completely paved. Direct buses take some 22 hours, leaving at 1130 (returns at 1200), with Singer, no a/c, and Buenos Aires-Posadas-Iguazú (returns at 1700 to Buenos Aires) Expreso Tigre-Iguazú, daily at 1500, offices at Plaza Once, Buenos Aires leaving from Retiro terminal (US$28.75). Singer also goes to Córdoba Tues. and Sat. at 1130, via Posadas 26 hrs, US$34.50. Express Puerto Iguazú to Posadas, 6 hrs., US$11 (310 km.) with Transportes Iguazú at 0930 and 1530; ordinary bus takes 8 hrs., US$9.25, every 1½ hrs. All go by the Falls and stop at San Ignacio Miní. To Resistencia daily 0900 and 2000, 12 hrs., US$13.50. Alternative to direct bus to Buenos Aires (see page 111), take bus to Posadas

112 ARGENTINA

and take train from there; slower, but more comfortable. Puerto Iguazú to Eldorado, 2 hrs., US$3.50 with Cotal.

From Brazil Foz do Iguaçu can be reached by paved road from São Paulo or Curitiba (buses return to both at 2130). Rodoviária, Av. Brasil 99, Tel.: 73-1525; has trustworthy baggage store. Foz is reached by many buses from Curitiba (9 hours, US$5, *leito* US$10 Sul America), from Guaíra via Cascavel only (5 hrs., US$4.25), and from São Paulo (18 hours, about US$9 with Pluma, excellent service). Foz-Florianópolis, daily, 1900, US$7, 16 hrs., with Catarinense. Porto Alegre-Foz US$10, direct bus daily at 1900, 17 hrs. with Unisul; via Santa Catarina and Rio Grande do Sul, interesting but mainly completed by night. There are direct buses from Rio (US$18 one way pullman bus), 23 hours (return to Rio daily at 0900 with Pluma direct, or 1400 with Maringá, US$14; for a *leito* to Rio, you must change in Curitiba).

From Paraguay By daily plane from Asunción to Foz do Iguaçu, or by paved road from Asunción (book in advance to take the 0730 bus from Asunción, arriving at 1300 at the Brazilian border and at the bus terminal at 1500) about US$4. (If you wish to return to Asunción the same day, hire a small bus to the falls and return at 1730 to the bus station, to be back at 2400. Plenty of seats Foz-Asunción from 0715 to 1730.)

Up the Río Uruguay (1,510 km.)

The Río Uruguay is the eastern boundary of Mesopotamia and forms the western border of the Republic of Uruguay.

Boats leaving Buenos Aires go past Martín García island, and enter the wide estuary. At 193 km. from Buenos Aires, the Uruguayan town of Fray Bentos is to the right; a bridge has now been built to link Fray Bentos with the Argentine town of Puerto Unzué, near Gualeguaychú, but pedestrians and cyclists cannot cross it other than by vehicular means; officials will give lifts on either side. The river now becomes braided into channels and islands. Opposite Fray Bentos, on the left, is the mouth of the Río Gualeguay; 19 km. up is **Gualeguaychú,** which can be reached by rail and road from Buenos Aires (370 km.) and Concordia. It is a very pleasant town with a river promenade, a country club (free for tourists), street entertainment and a camping site. Lively Carnival at beginning of March. Population, 43,000, with quite a large German contingent, from up to 150 years ago. Airport. Customs formalities at Puerto Unzué take 10 minutes.

Hotels *Embajador*, C; *Posada del Charrúa*, D; *El Faro*, E; *París*, E; *Yapo*, E; *Entre Ríos*, F; *Mayo*, F; *Alemán*, F, friendly, German-speaking, recommended.

Exchange There are banks on either side of the bridge, but in Uruguay you can obtain only Uruguayan pesos and the Argentine-side bank is almost always closed. Next bank at Gualeguaychú has very good rates. There is also a service station a few km. beyond the border in Argentina, where you can sell Uruguayan pesos.

Concepción del Uruguay, the first Argentine port of any size on the river, was founded in 1778. There are train services to all parts of Mesopotamia. Population, 40,000. Paved roads to Paraná and Colón.

Hotels *Virrey*, Aceso Ruta 131, D; *Gran Hotel*, Colón 134, D; *General Ramírez*, Galarza y Blvd. Ramírez, E; *Residencial 3 de Febrero*, E; *Residencial La Posada*, E; *Centro Hotel*, E. Many hotels of all classes by the bus station, none near the railway station.

Local Boats Daily to Paysandú (Uruguay).

Some 37 km. above Concepción del Uruguay, past the Uruguayan port of Paysandú, is ***Colón.*** The river is more picturesque here with cliffs visible from a considerable distance; a road bridge now links Colón and Paysandú. (Toll for cars US$1.40. All border formalities, including stamping of vehicle carnets, are conducted at both ends of the bridge, easy crossing.) It is possible to get a bus from Colón to Paysandú, US$1.50, but there are none between 1145 and 1645, and none on Sundays. There are daily buses to Concordia (2½ hrs., US$2.65), Paraná and four a week to Córdoba.

Hotels *Nuevo Hotel Plaza*, D; *Palmar*, E; *Vieja Calera*, E; *Holimazu*, E; *Ver-Wei*, F; *Residencia 12 de Abril* and *Residencia Chacabuco*, both F.

About 105 km. above Colón, a little downriver from the Uruguayan city of Salto, is Concordia. Parque Nacional El Palmar lies between Colón and Concordia, has both free and paying camping facilities, a small hotel 8 km. N of the Park, with restaurant opposite, and a small shop. The Park contains varied scenery with a mature palm forest, Indian tombs and other remains, and many rheas and other birds.

Concordia is a prosperous city, with a population of 56,000, which has some fine public buildings, a racecourse, rowing clubs, and a 9-hole golf club. Five km. out is Parque Rivadavia, with a circular road used occasionally as a motor-racing track; there are pleasant views here of the river and a ruined French-style palace. Paved road to Buenos Aires, Paraná and Posadas.

The river is impassable for large vessels beyond the rapids of Salto Chico near the town, and Salto Grande 32 km. up-river, where there is a large international hydro-electric dam, providing a route for an international road and railway. Take No. 2 bus from bus terminal marked "Puerto", ferry crossing to Salto from Concordia US$1 (tickets obtainable at a small kiosk outside customs) departures 5 times a day on weekdays, 3 times Sat. but none Sun.; takes 15 mins. Few cars, but people willing to give rides. Above Salto Grande the river is generally known as the Alto Uruguay.

Hotels *San Carlos*, Parque Rivadavia, C; *Salto Grande*, Urquiza 575, C; *Palmar*, Urquiza 511, D; *Imperial Argentino*, E, very friendly; *Colonial*, Pellegrini 443, D, not recommended; *Gran Hotel Colón*, F, highly recommended, simple, clean and charming, longer stays only; *Embajador*, San Lorenzo 75, F, nr. bus station, good value, neat and clean. *Terminal* above bus station, surprisingly quiet, good value, F.

Camping *La Tortuga Alegre*.

Restaurants *Lion d'Or*; *Don Juan*, 1° de Mayo 21, near main plaza, excellent and cheap. *El Abrojito*, Pellegrini 1203, recommended.

Tourist Office, Plaza 25 de Mayo, helpful.

Rail *El Correntino* train has sleepers, pullman, 1st class and tourist class (US$17.75, US$10.95, US$7.60, US$5.65) and leaves Lacroze station at 1500, daily, arriving at 2314, returns daily at 0729, arr. 1545. *El Gran Capitán*, same prices, leaves at 1500 daily, arrives at 2314 daily. Returns daily at 0729, arrives 1545. This train also goes on to Paso de los Libres and Posadas from Buenos Aires, arrives at 0337 and 0945, respectively.

Buses To Buenos Aires, 6 daily; to Paraná 4, to Posadas 3, to Iguazú one. Bus to La Paz (Entre Ríos—see page 100, 1100, US$7.70, 8 hrs.

About 153 km. upstream from Concordia lies the small port of **Monte Caseros,** with the Uruguayan town of Bella Unión, on the Brazilian border, almost opposite. Above Bella Unión, the Alto Uruguay is the boundary between Argentina and Brazil. Ninety-six km. above Monte Caseros is **Paso de los Libres,** with the Brazilian cattle town of Uruguaiana opposite: a bridge joins the two. The railway from Buenos Aires to Posadas runs through the town. From Uruguaiana into Brazil the buses are much quicker than trains, though there is a comfortable railway service to Porto Alegre. Paso de los Libres was founded in 1843 by General Madariaga; it was here that he crossed the river from Brazil with his hundred men and annexed Corrientes province for Argentina. Road (paved) to Paraná.

Hotel in Paso de los Libres, *Alejandro I*, Coronel López y Pago Largo, best in town. For eating and dancing try the *Café Strauss*.

Rail See above under Concordia. Fares a/c sleeper US$22.60, Pullman US$15.85, first US$11, tourist US$8.20 Buenos Aires-Paso de los Libres.

The Lake District

Northern Patagonia has two railway lines. The more northerly runs westwards from Bahía Blanca to Neuquén and Zapala; the southern line runs from Bahía Blanca southwards across the Colorado to Viedma and then westwards through San Antonio Oeste to Bariloche and the Lake District. The roads along which buses ply, and airlines are mentioned in the text. (For map, see the Chilean section, page 421.)

The **Lake District** contains a series of great lakes strung along the foot of the

114 ARGENTINA

Andes from above 40° South to below 50° in the Los Glaciares National Park area. In the N the western ends of these lakes cut deeply into the mountains, their water lapping the forested skirts of some of the most spectacular snow-capped peaks in the world; their eastern ends are contained by the frontal moraines deposited there by the ancient glaciers which melted to form these huge fjord-like lakes. The water is a deep blue, sometimes lashed into white froth by the region's high winds.

On the far side of the Andes, in Chile, lies another system of lakes: these can be visited (unpaved roads) through various passes. The Puyehue route is given on page 121, with an alternative in the Chilean section.

National Park Lake Nahuel Huapí with its surroundings, an area of 7,850 square km., was set aside in 1903 as a National Park. It contains the most diverse and spectacular natural phenomena: lakes, rivers, glaciers, waterfalls, torrents, rapids, valleys, forest, bare mountains and snow-clad peaks. Most of the area is covered with abundant vegetation, though it is notably more abundant on the Chilean side, which gets more rain. Many kinds of wild animals live in the region, but they are extremely shy and seldom glimpsed by the explorer. Bird life, on the other hand—particularly swans, geese and ducks—is seen at any time and everywhere in large flocks. In the far N of this region, near Zapala, these species and many others can be seen in their hundreds in the nature reserve of Laguna Blanca.

The outstanding feature of this National Park is the splendour of the lakes. The largest is **Lake Nahuel Huapí**, 531 square km. and 460 metres deep in places. It is 767 metres above sea level, in full view of the snow-covered peaks of the Cordillera and of the forests covering the lower slopes. Towering over the scene is Cerro Tronador. Some 96 km. long, and not more than 12 km. wide, the lake is very irregular in shape; long arms of water, or *brazos*, which look like fjords, stretch far into the land. There are many islands: the largest is **Isla Victoria**, on which stands the forest research station where new species of vegetation are acclimatized. The Zoological Board is adding to the indigenous fauna; the trout and salmon of the lakes, for instance, have been introduced from abroad. Lake Nahuel Huapí is drained eastwards by the Río Limay; below its junction with the Río Neuquén it becomes the Río Negro. The Limay has good trout fishing but the rivers farther N—the Quilquihue, Malleu, Chimehuín, Collón-Curá, Hermoso, Meliquina and Caleufú—are much less fished. They are all in the neighbourhood of San Martín de los Andes (see page 124). The season is from early November to the end of March. Do not take fishing equipment out-of-season; it will only cause suspicion. Also remember that fishing in the National Park requires a permit.

A mere sand bar in one of the northern *brazos* separates Lake Nahuel Huapí from Lake Correntoso, which is quite close to Lake Espejo. Lake Traful, a short distance to the NE, can be reached by a road which follows the River Limay through the Valle Encantado, with its fantastic rock formations. S of Nahuel Huapí there are other lakes: the three main ones are Mascardi, Guillelmo, and Gutiérrez. On the shore of Lake Gutiérrez, in a grotto, is the Virgen de las Nieves (Virgin of the Snows). There is a road to these lakes from Bariloche.

Fishing The lakes are full of fish, and the best time for fishing is at the beginning of the season, that is, in November and December. Among the best are: Lakes Traful, Gutiérrez, Mascardi, Futalaufquen (in Los Alerces National Park), Meliquina, Falkner, Villarino, Nuevo, Lacar, Log-Log, Curruhué, Chico, Huechulafquen, Paimún, Epulafquen, Tromen (all in Lanín National Park), and, in the far N, Quillén. In the far S, the fishing in Lake Argentino is also good.

Bariloche (San Carlos de), on the southern shore of Lake Nahuel Huapí, founded 1898, is the best centre for exploring the National Park. It is a town of steep streets, its wooden chalets perched Swiss fashion upon a glacial moraine at the foot of Cerro Otto. To the S lie the heights of the Ventana and the Cerro Colorado (2,135 metres). The place is full of hotels and cheap *hosterías*. The main church, built in 1946, dominates the town; interior unfinished. There is a belvedere at the

ARGENTINA 115

top of Cerro Otto with wide views of lake and mountain. The main road into Bariloche from the E is paved and in good condition. Unhappily, because of its phenomenal growth, the town has become overcrowded, and the best time to visit it is out of season either in the spring or autumn. After March there are few tourists, the temperature is pleasant and there is no snow, wind or rain (however, in August and September the town is full of school parties). The 24 km. road to Llao-Llao is ribbon-developed, except near Cerro Catedral. Population, over 70,000. Lido swimming pool on the lake shore is beautifully sited but somewhat run down.

Hotels To check local hotel rates, the most complete listing with map is published by the Oficina Municipal de Turismo. Out of season, prices are quite reasonable, in all ranges, but in season everything is very expensive. Most hotels outside the town include half-board; all except *Tres Reyes* include breakfast. Hotels with lake views normally charge US$3-4 extra, per room per day, for the view; we give lake-view prices where applicable. The best are: *Huemul* (road to Llao-Llao, 1.5 km.); *El Casco* (Av. Bustillo, road to Llao-Llao 11 km.), German-run, excellent, luxurious; *Apart-hotel Casablanca* (same road, 23.5 km.), good, and *Tunquelén* (same road, 24 km.), are on a peninsula between Lakes Nahuel Huapí and Moreno, all A, some offering half-board. Also at Llao-Llao, 24 km. from Bariloche, is *Hostería Aunancay*, A, including 2 meals, friendly and delightful setting. Golf links, belonging to the *Gran Hotel*, on this peninsula. Other luxury class hotels (A): *Catedral Ski*, on Cerro Catedral, half-board; *El Monasterio* (5 km. out on Faldeo route); *Tres Reyes*, 12 de Octubre 135. *Residencial El Ciervo Rojo*, Quaglia and Elflein 115, very pleasant, C, with bath. *Austral*, San Martín 425, C, with bath, small rooms, has restaurant. First class: *Cristal*, Mitre 355, B; *Residencial Tirol*, Libertad 175, B, clean, friendly, good; *Casita Suiza*, Quaglia 342, very nice. *Edelweiss*, Av. San Martín 232; *Nevada*, Onelli y Moreno, C, with bath (E off-season); *Nahuel Huapí*, Perito Fco. Moreno 252; *Interlaken*, Vicealmirante O'Connor 383, A, all 3, 4-star. Just around the corner at Rolando 197 is *Val Gardena*, C with breakfast, excellent service, clean, no restaurant, 2-star; opp. is *Sunset*, C, 4-star. *Hostería Madinette*, Morales 534, very well run by charming couple, half-board; *Aguas del Sur*, P. Fco. Moreno 353; *Los Pinos*, 20 de Febrero 640, D, clean, spacious rooms, private bath, central heating. *King's Hotel*, P. F. Moreno 136, very nice, clean, warm, C, with bath (E off-season); *Colonial*, Quaglia 281, large tourist class hotel, C; *La Pastorella*, Belgrano 127, C, with bath and breakfast, German-run, recommended; *El Jabalí*, Av. San Martín 130, across the square from civic centre, A; *Residencial Portofino*, Morales 439, two blocks from plaza, D, small but spotless. Nameless guest house across the road. *Residencial Flamingo*, Mitre 24, C, with bath, and view of lake; *Los Andes*, Moreno 594, C, with shared bath; *Nevada*, Onelli y Moreno, D with shower, nice rooms; *Residencial Elisabeth*, J. J. Paso 117, E, cheaper rates for longer stays, German-run, clean, central, private bath, hot water, towels, good value; *Residencial Piuké*, Beschtedt 130, ½ block from Calle Mitre near Cathedral, D inc. breakfast (D p.p. in skiing season), clean, friendly, recommended; opposite is *Residencial Sur*, Beschtedt 101, opposite church, excellent value, D with bath and breakfast. *Residencial La Sureña*, San Martín 432, B; *Residencial Las Amapolas*, J. M. de Rosas 598; *Libertador*, Av. San Martín 441, C. *Residencial La Fontana*, Saavedra 689, Plaza Belgrano, clean, friendly, B; *Gracy Luz*, Villegas 146, E; *Residencial Matterhorn*, Swiss-run, Pasaje Gutiérrez 1122, E, recommended, good breakfast; *Residencial Andrea*, Goedecke 443, top of hill, D, with bath; *Ideal*, Libertad 121, behind police station, pleasant, clean, quiet, away from the commercial centre, D with private bath, cheaper without, restaurant, some doubles have lake view; *Hospedaje Nahuel*, Calle Gallardo 454, D, warm and clean, hot showers; *Residencial Panorámico*, P. F. Moreno 646, B, private shower, recommended; *Hostal de Los Alpes*, Diagonal Capraro 1034, D, very modern,

EL CASCO

The distinguished lake resort hotel in Bariloche

26 deluxe bed-sitting rooms
with private verandas
Conference room for 26 participants
Haute Cuisine   Very Personalized Service
P.O. Box 436-Ruta Llao-Llao KM. 11
8400-San Carlos de Bariloche, Argentina
Phone 0944-2.2532   0944-2.3083
Telex 80.705 CASCO

116 ARGENTINA

clean, friendly; *Victoria*, D-E, for a studio with bed, kitchen, bath with hot shower, Mitre 815, friendly but grubby. Others: *El Mirador*, Moreno 652-76, E, hot water p.m. only, owner speaks German, very pleasant, with lake views; *Residencial Premier*, Rolando 263, ½ block from main street, 1½ blocks from airport bus depot, E, clean, hot showers, breakfast, recommended; *Residencial Adquintue*, O'Connor 776, E, clean and comfortable; *Angelinas*, San Martín 66, E with bath and breakfast, good value, friendly, recommended; *Residencial El Nire* (Tel.: 2-3041), O'Connor 710, hot showers, clean, very pleasant, F; *Residencial Zagreb*, Quaglia 546, Tel.: 2-2022, E. *Huecho Ruca*, Moreno 816, D with bath, hot shower, recommended. Sra Milena de Arko, strongly recommended, Güemes 691, Tel.: 23109, speaks English and German, cooking facilities, four rooms, two showers. Also recommended, *pensión* of Sra Carlota Baumann, Av. de los Pioneros 860 (Tel.: 24502), close to main square, F p.p., kitchen, bath, hot water, laundry service, friendly, Sra Baumann speaks English and German. *Casa Tutzaner*, Av. Rosas 198, E. *Residencial Millaray*, Libertad 195, F, good and cheap, shower; *Hostería San Jorge*, 20 de Febrero 549, E, close to centre, clean, quiet, private bath; *Residencial Rosan*, Güemes 691, D, pricey; *Belgrano*, Güemes 648, E, friendly. Recommended family *pensión* at Salta 571, heated. Ask at tourist office, which has private homes listed. For longer stays try private house at Anasagasti 345, US$3. *Alojamiento Familiar Pire-Cuyen*, Anasagasti 840, E, clean, good, no single rooms. *Alojamiento Familial*, Frey 635, F, clean, hot shower, reasonable, recommended, has space for motorcycles. *Pájaro Azul*, at Puerto Moreno, Km. 10.8 on the Llao-Llao road, C. *Hostería Katy*, on Llao-Llao road Km. 24, warmly recommended, reasonable, C. *Refugio Challhuaco* is 16 km. outside town. Youth Hostel *El Yeti* on Llao-Llao road, 5.6 km. outside city, open all year, cabins with cooking facilities, campsites, bed and breakfast, half, or full board.

Camping Private campsite at Beschtedt 658, hot showers, US$0.50, pleasant. Other camping US$2.20 p.p.

Restaurants *Casita Suiza*, Quaglia 342, excellent and recommended, especially for fondue and trout; *Quintral*, Rolando 362, on a hill about 4 blocks above the centre, superb meat; *El Tronador*, Mitre 202; *Parrilla La Vizcacha*, Rolando 279, barbecues; *Viejo Munich*, good, Mitre 102; *Sobremonte*, Mitre 520, good meat and wine; *La Marmita*, Mitre, small, cosy, excellent; *El Rincón Patagonia* throws in folk singing entertainment with a good dinner for US$6. *La Andina* on Elflein and Quaglia specializes in inexpensive *empanadas* and pizzas, popular with travellers; *Caza Mayor*, Quaglia and Elflein, game and fish, good; *Nikola*, Elflein 49, very good value. *Dirty Dick's Pub* on Bustillo km. 5. Good pastries and hot chocolate at *Hola Nicolás*, Moreno 66 and Urquiza. *Jauja*, Moreno (near Villegas), good typical dishes; *Canguros*, Palacios 153, Australian run, try the hot wine. *La Andinita*, recommended, reasonable, trout a speciality, friendly; *Pizzería La Jirafa*, Palacios 288; *Pizza Vía Roma* on Mitre, big choice of good pizzas; *Villegas*, on Villegas 390, recommended for trout and friendly service; 4 km. towards Llao-Llao, *La Casona*, excellent; 5.2 km in same direction, *El Gato Andino*, dinner only; on same road, *La Posta del Río*, reasonable, and *La Glorieta*, good. Superb coffee and cakes at *Chocolate Casero del Turista* at Mitre 239. *La Mamadera*, on Mitre, recommended. *Saloom*, Mitre 208, restaurant with video films, open 24 hours, as are others on Mitre. Many good delicatessens in the area with take-away food, including chicken pizzas and cheeses, for picnics. *La Cosa Nostra*, B. Mitre 370, good cheap take-away pizzas. *América*, good *lasagne*, on Palacios 153 is a cheap restaurant. *Kaffe Status*, on Mitre, not cheap but very lively.

Best Buys Sweaters, beautiful but expensive; also alpaca and llama ponchos, stoles, jackets, scarves, woollen mittens and gloves. The products of the local chocolate industry are excellent: Fábrica de Chocolate Cerro León on Av. 12 de Octubre, near railway station. You can watch chocolates being made at La Turista on San Martín. Very good chocolate at Hugo on Morales and Gallardo (be sure to get the 10% discount). Try "Papas de Bariloche", the local chocolate speciality. Also chocolates at *Benroth*, Beschtedt 569, above Gallardo.

Museum The "Perito Francisco Moreno" Nahuel Huapí Museum in the Civic Centre, well worth seeing for collection of Indian artefacts, houses. The Museo de la Patagonia has a nice collection of stuffed animals, US$0.50, heated, not to be missed. Open 0900-1300. Closed public holidays. The clock in the Civic Centre has four figurines which rotate at noon; photos with St. Bernard dogs may be taken in the Civic Centre square.

Currency There are a couple of banks and official exchange shops, which buy virtually all European and South American currencies, besides US dollars. Exchange houses cash cheques for 5-10%. Casa Piano, B. Mitre 131, Tel.: 23733. Open 0900-1300 and 1600-2000 (charges US$3 on all cheques below US$100, 3% over US$100). Kiosko Suyoi, Elflein 87, for newspaper-quoted rate, cash only. If you get stuck on Sun. or at night change money at bus companies or Kiosko Anri, Mitre 339 (rear of Galería Arrayanes), US$ cheques and Chilean pesos accepted. Good exchange rates at *Kiwanis* (boot rental), Mitre 210. It is illegal to purchase Chilean pesos in Bariloche. The American Express Co. in Bariloche no longer issues travellers' cheques.

Laundry *Express*, Villegas 258, English manager, friendly, opp. cathedral. Laundromats on Palacios and on Villegas nr. Mitre.

ARGENTINA 117

Car Hire Avis, and A1 International, at airport and in town (latter at Bartolomé Mitre 26, Tel.: 24869, 22038); no flat rates. Permission to enter Chile may be obtained.

Tourist Office Oficina Municipal de Turismo en Centro Cívico, open Mon.-Sat., (ski season) 0800-2000, daily at those times in summer but check times out of season (March-April, October-November) when closed at weekends; very helpful. Has details of hikes in the area. Also has the address of a motorcycle hire company—a good way of getting around the National Park. National Park information (scanty) at San Martín 24, open 0800-2000.

Tourist Agencies Tour buses pick you up from your hotel. *Patagonia Travel*, Mitre 150 (Telex 80746 Patra), efficient, recommended, English spoken. *Catedral Turismo*, Mitre 399, mixed reports; *Alunco Turismo*, friendly. *Transport Mercedes*; *Turisur*, Quaglia 227, Tel.: 26109, organizes US$10 trips on lake. *Lake Travel Service*, Moreno 126, 3rd floor, efficient, English spoken. *Polvani Tours*, Quaglia 268 (Tel.: 23286), see Hans Schulz (speaks Spanish, German and English) to arrange horse trekking at the Estancia Nahuel Huapí, run by Carol Jones (from US$18 for ½ day to US$40 overnight); both the agency and the treks recommended. Arrange trekking with Sr Daniel José Gorgone, San Martín 127, DT 0706, Tel.: 26181. All tours are advertised at identical prices by the various agencies and tourist offices.

Chilean Consulate, Villegas, near Mitre, friendly, helpful.

Post Office Centro Cívico (same building as tourist office).

Clinic Cruz Azul, Capraro 1216.

Air Services Airport, 11 km. from town. Daily flights to Buenos Aires. Aerolíneas Argentinas US$93 by day or US$56 night flight. Also Austral and LADE. AA has a Mendoza-Bariloche flight via Neuquén and there is an Austral Neuquén flight daily, exc. Sun., from Bariloche at 1320, arrival 1405. LADE to Trelew, US$28, Mon. 1255, Fri. 1340. LADE flies to Comodoro Rivadavia Tues., Fri. and Sun., US$31; AA US$35. AA to Río Gallegos, US$62. LADE to Río Gallegos, 3 a week, US$36, usually booked 2 weeks in advance in season; continues to Calafate. Flights, 3-4 times a week, with Aerolíneas and LADE to Esquel. (It is reported that it is difficult to obtain LADE flights from Bariloche now, especially the cheaper night flights to Buenos Aires.) Small tax at airport on leaving. Taxi to or from airport, US$8-10; bus US$2 from Austral or Aerolíneas office. (Aerolíneas and LADE offices are, conveniently, in the same building.) Turismo Catedral, Mitre 399, give 10% discount on their tours with the ticket stub from their US$1.50 airport bus service into town.

Rail Services The railway station is 5 km. from centre, reached by local bus (US$0.20). *Expreso Lagos del Sur*, leaves Buenos Aires, Sun., (with car transporter), 30½ hrs (not much heat); *Lagos del Sur* Wed., Sat., 32½ hrs.; both at 0820; *Expreso* leaves Bariloche, 1150, Mon., *Lagos del Sur* Tues. and Fri. at 0855, all arrive at 1500 the following day, fares US$45 sleeper, US$36 Pullman, US$26 first, US$19 tourist class. Trip can be extremely dusty. Scenery not interesting till after Jacobacci (last 4½ hrs.); food on board reasonable (US$4 for 3 courses).

Road Services Paved road from Buenos Aires via Neuquén, 1,930 km. Chevallier, Buenos Aires to Bariloche, leaves at 1215, arrives at 1040 daily US$47. Also El Cóndor daily at 1315 and El Valle via Neuquén at 2030 (US$38.50). These three return daily at 1400, 1410 and 2230, respectively. For Mar del Plata, take Buenos Aires bus and change at Bahía Blanca or Tres Arroyos (e.g. La Estrella, 1500, arrive Tres Arroyos 0555, US$26). Bus to Mendoza, 27 hrs., mainly on an unpaved road via Zapala, Buta Ranquil and San Rafael, US$40, 3 times a week. Bus Córdoba-Bariloche, 25 hrs., US$46, Mon., Wed., Fri., and Sun. at 1200. Buses to El Bolsón (US$9.25) and Esquel (US$19.50 with Don Otto), bus stops at El Bolsón for lunch daily (we are told anti-British and US feeling exists at *Parrilla Achachay*, reflected in the bill!), exc. Sun., with a 4 times weekly extension to Comodoro Rivadavia. Fare Bariloche-Comodoro US$34 (Don Otto). To Esquel with Mercedes, US$11.50, daily except Sun., 0800. Buses also to Neuquén (550 km.) US$11.50 by Transportes Mercedes on Bartolomé Mitre or daily with La Estrella, Palacios 246 at 1415, 6½ hrs. (a dull journey). To Santiago (Chile), Tues., Fri. and Sun., 24 hours with tea and breakfast served en route. To Puerto Montt (Chile). (See the route to Chile from Bariloche, page 121.)

Activities Apart from sailing and boating, there are golf, mountaineering, walking, birdwatching, skiing, and fishing (for which you need a permit). The climbing may mean a ride on horseback or a skilled ascent of the slopes of Cerro Tronador (excursion by bus US$12, full day, including 1 hr. walk to black glacier, leaves at 0800, but too much time spent on the bus) which looms over the area. The Club Andino Bariloche, open 0900-1200, 1500-2000, arranges for guides; ask for Sr. Ricardo, the secretary, who organizes easy weekend climbs and walks with friendly visitors. It also provides maps and details of all campgrounds, hotels and mountain lodges. The Government has convenient rest lodges at from 1,000 to 2,000 metres on the mountains. Firing, light and food are provided at these points. Before going hiking you are recommended to buy moisturizing creams for exposed skin areas and lips; lemon juice is good for keeping away horse flies in summer. Excellent trout fishing Nov.-March; boat hire arranged with tackle shops. For horse riding, see above under Tourist Agencies.

Mountain Climbing In the area there is everything for every kind of mountaineer, from the

118 ARGENTINA

adventurous specialist to the enthusiastic amateur. National Park mountain guides are available but can be expensive. Book: *Excursiones, Andinismo y Refugios de Montaña en Bariloche*, by Tonek Arko, available in local shops or from the author at Güemes 691. In treks to *refugios* remember to add costs of ski lifts, buses, food at *refugio* and lodging (in Club Andino *refugios*: US$3 per night, plus US$1 for cooking, or US$1 for breakfast, US$2 for lunch, US$3 for dinner). Information from Club Andino Bariloche, 20 de Febrero 30, open 0900-1200 and 1500-2000 Mon.-Fri. and Sat. 0900-1200.

Swimming in the larger lakes such as Nahuel Huapí and Huechulafquen is not recommended, for the water is cold. But swimming in such lakes as Log-Log, Lacar, Curruhué Chico, Hermoso, Meliquina, Espejo, Hess and Fonck (all smaller lakes) is very pleasant and the water—especially where the bottom shelves to a shingly beach—can be positively warm.

Skiing There is grand skiing during the winter season (July to early October), supervised by the Club Andino at Bariloche. It is best organized with a tour company, through whom you can secure discounts as part of an inclusive deal. The favourite skiing slopes are on Cerro Catedral. (Regular bus service with seasonal timetable from Mercedes bus company on Mitre 161, US$3 return.) There are a cable car and a chair lift from the foot of Cerro Catedral to points high on the ridge. Red and yellow markers painted on the rock mark a trail from the top, which leads to Refugio Frey on the edge of a small mountain lake (allow 6 hours; one can return through the forest to the ski complex the next day and take a bus back to Bariloche). The seasonal cable car, with a chair lift from its upper terminus, takes one higher than the main (2-stage) chair lift (US$6 return). Bus tours from Bariloche to the foot of Cerro Catedral (US$6 including lift ticket which does not reach the top) give time for less than 2 hours on top of the mountain. Entrance to the Cerro Catedral ski slopes, below the snowline, is US$ 0.40. The only disadvantage at Bariloche is that the snow is unreliable except at the top. There are other skiing slopes 5 km. out of Bariloche, on Cerro Otto (cable car, US$7 p.p.), which can be reached in ½ day's walk from the town, stick to the paved road, ignore dirt track (splendid views), or in a minibus which goes every ½ hour from a car park near the National Park headquarters (closed public holidays), between 1400 and 1600, US$5 round trip (local bus US$1.50 return); also on López (try a car trip, rough road, US$10 for a tour, 1400-1830), Dormilón and La Ventana.

Excursions Whole-day trip to Lakes Gutiérrez, Mascardi, Hess, the Cascada Los Alerces and Cerro Tronador (3,554 metres) leaves at 0800, US$12.50. Turismo Llao-Llao organizes the following: 8-hour excursion to Río Limay, Valle Encantado, Lago Traful, Lago Correntoso, Villa La Angostura, returning via Paso Coihue. Catedral and Turisur have a 9-hour excursion, leaving at 1030 (afternoon dep. also Dec.-March), to Puerto Pañuelo, sailing down to Puerto Blest and continuing by bus to Puerto Alegre and again by launch to Puerto Frías (US$ 14). A visit to the Cascada de los Cántaros is made. Beautiful scenery at Llao-Llao for walking; one can walk the 17 km. "motor tour" route back to Bariloche (take the 3 de Mayo bus there from Moreno and Rolando, and the ferry for Isla Victoria; there is a chairlift at km 17.7 on Llao-Llao road (Campanario) one can walk to km. 18.3 and take the road to the left to Colonia Suiza and Punto Panorámico, which winds around Lago Moreno, unspoiled surroundings, all in 16 km. to Puerto Pañuelo). The chairlift at Campanario offers fine views of Isla Victoria and Puerto Pañuelo, 0900-1200, 1400-1800 daily, US$0.85. Another excursion involves going to Pampa Linda, which is 8 km. from the road ending at Tronador and has the *guardaparque* station. From there you can ask the ranger to show you a path for a two-day walk over Paso de las Nubes to Laguna Fría, which is not always well marked, especially one place early on where the track branches after crossing a river by a series of temporary footbridges. The right hand track should *not* be attempted by inexperienced walkers. The left hand track, once a road, leads one west up a spur to the edge of the glacier with a well appointed hut (3-4 hours journey). The road ends at Lake Frías and then there is a road across the frontier to Peulla, about 30 km. away. Journey Argentina-Chile downhill. Alun-Co Turismo, Mitre 22, 2nd floor, operates a rubber raft excursion mid-April to mid-Nov. until mid-April to Confluencia, leaves Bariloche at 1000 up River Limay, stopping for lunch at Valle Encantado, returns to Bariloche at 1900, US$16. A half-day excursion is possible taking a bus to Virgen de las Nieves, walking 2 km. to arrive at beautiful lake Gutiérrez; walk along lake shore to the road from El Bolsón and walk back to Bariloche (about 4 hrs.). A recommended one-day trip by car is Bariloche-Llao Llao-Bahía-Colonia Suiza-Cerro Catedral-Bariloche; the reverse direction misses the sunsets and afternoon views from the higher roads, which are negotiable in winter (even snow-covered). If one is staying only 1-2 days in the area the best excursions are to Cerro Tronador the 1st day, and on the 2nd to Cerro Catedral in the morning and Isla Victoria in the afternoon (possible only Dec.-March when there are afternoon departures for the island). Camping facilities for firing, food and water are good. Good walks to Lake Correntoso (4 km.) and Quetrihué Peninsula (15 km. to forest of Arrayanes). Also to the *refugio* at Laguna Negra (16 km. trail) and to Cerro López (3 hrs., with a *refugio* after 2); in both cases take Colonia Suiza bus and for the former alight at SAC, for the latter at Picada. Hitching to local sights is difficult.

A half-day excursion (1300-1830) may be taken from Bariloche to Puerto Pañuelo, then by boat to Isla Victoria. The full-day excursion (0900-1830, or 1300 till 2000 in season) at US$12 includes the Arrayán forest and 3 hours on Isla Victoria, picnic lunch advised. Half-day excursions to Isla

Victoria are available. Some boats going to Arrayanes call first at Isla Victoria, early enough to avoid boat-loads of tourists. These boats carry the names of Paraná river provinces—Corrientes, Misiones, Santa Fe—and they have no open deck. For open decks try the *Modesta Victoria* or the *Don Luis*. (Turisur have 3 fancy boats with a bar and cafeteria.) For a cheaper excursion take Transporte 3 de Mayo bus marked Estación Llao-Llao from Moreno and Rolando at 0900 or 0930 (Rte 609 1) for 1030 dep. from Puerto Pañuelo (1130 or 1200 for 1300 dep.) to go to Isla Victoria and Arrayanes by boat (US$7). From Puerto Pañuelo, opposite the *Hotel Llao-Llao*, boats also leave for Puerto Blest. All boats are very crowded in season, but operators have to provide seating for all passengers.

Roads There is good motoring on the 500 km. of highways (mostly unpaved) which run through the park. There are numerous excursions; prices vary very widely, and it is best to buy tours on the spot rather than in advance, although they get very booked up in season. The road to El Bolsón and Esquel (a new, faster, but less interesting road is being built between Bariloche and Esquel) is paved for the first 30 km. and goes past the beautiful lakes of Gutiérrez, Mascardi and Guillelmo and over fine mountain passes.

Río Villegas, about 80 km. S of Bariloche on the road to El Bolsón, is very beautiful. Cheap but pleasant *hostería* just outside the gates of the National Park, by the river.

Villa La Angostura on Lake Correntoso is picturesque, 80 km. W of Bariloche on the way to Chile, by excursion bus (day trip; try Turismo Llao-Llao, 8 hrs.) or local bus (at 1900 daily, returning 0730, Transporte Mercedes, US$5) which requires staying overnight; hotels a little dearer than Bariloche. The port, 3 km. from town, is spectacular in summer. It is best to return to Bariloche if going on to Osorno (Chile): otherwise you have to pay twice the fare to Osorno from Bariloche and arrange for the bus company to pick you up at La Angostura.

Hotels *Correntoso*, A. Cheaper are *La Cabañita* (Belvedere s/n) and *Don Pedro* (El Cruce), both E. Ask in the tourist office, opposite ACA, for lodgings in private houses, cheaper than hotels. *Hotel Ruca Malen*, warmly recommended, 24 km. away on lake shore.

Camping *El Cruce, ACA Osa Mayor* (2 km. along Bariloche road, pleasant, open late Dec. to mid-May), *Autocamping San Martín, Municipal Lago Correntoso*.

Restaurants *Guatraché*, grills; *Cuernavaca*; *Parrilla Gallegos, Confitería de los Amigos* (also lets rooms, E, no bath).

Excellent *Hostería Los Peraltoches* on Lake Gutiérrez, 116 km. from Bariloche, A with meals; magnificent views, English spoken, very homelike, open Nov.-March and June-Aug.

El Bolsón is 130 km. to the S, on the road to Esquel. It is a most attractive small town (pop. 8,000) in beautiful country, with many mountain walks and waterfalls nearby. Good fishing. Within half an hour's drive are Lakes Puelo and Epuyen (shops and petrol available). The valley, set between high mountains, is most attractive. The farms and the orchards sell their produce at Bariloche. Famous local fruit preserves can be bought at the factories in town. The Balneario Municipal is 300 metres from the town centre, pleasant river swimming. There is a full-day tour from Bariloche, about US$9, at 0800 (stops at Lake Puelo) Empresa Don Otto, very crowded and difficult to get on in high season, Mercedes or Turismo Llao-Llao, 11 hrs.

Accommodation *Hostería Steiner*, clean and pleasant, on the Lake Puelo route, F; *Hostería Amancay*, San Martín and Cervantes, E; *Alojamientos El Bolsón*, Angel del Agua, F; *Motel La Posta*, smart and new (Route 258). Up to 2 days' stay possible at the Franciscan school, but get recommendation from tourist agent. *Hotel Salinas*, in private house (everyone knows it), E, friendly, clean. *Arrayanes*, Av. San Martín, E. Several *residencias* and camping sites nearby. The campsite (US$1) at Lake Puelo has beautiful views across the lake to Tres Picos, but the walking is limited. Frequent public transport from El Bolsón. Very difficult to find accommodation in the high season.

Restaurants *Don Diego*, good; *Parilla Achachay*, where the buses stop; *Munich*, ½ block from tourist office; four or five others. Welsh tea room, *Casa del Té Galés*.

Tourist Office The agent, Sr. Sigfrido Janett, is most helpful, and a great authority on the area. Ask for sketch maps of the beautiful walks in the neighbourhood including up Cerro Piltriquitrón. Office open 0900-2000, on main plaza.

On the way from Epuyen to Esquel is Cholila, with superb views of Lake Cholila, crowned by the Matterhorn-like mountains of Cerros Dos and Tres Picos. There is a bus service between Bariloche, El Bolsón, and Esquel, and there is a direct

120 ARGENTINA

thrice-weekly bus service between Comodoro Rivadavia and Esquel. A recommended journey for motorists is to spend the night at El Bolsón, enter the Los Alerces park via Cholila and drive right through it to Esquel, travelling the whole length of Lakes Rivadavia and Futalaufquen.

Camping Parque Nacional camping ground at Lake Puelo, with hot showers (cold in winter) and small store on lake-shore, US$2; or free inside National Park.

Esquel, about 260 km. S of Bariloche, was originally an offshoot of the Welsh colony at Chubut, nearly 650 km. to the E. It is now a modern town with reasonable amenities (population 15,600). Major skiing location at La Hoya, ski-lift, 15 km. north of Esquel (more expensive skiing than at Bariloche). Restaurant. For skiing information ask at Club Andino Esquel. Esquel is known for its tulips, chocolate, jellies and jams (also for the mazard berry liquor made by the Braese family, interesting, but expensive). There is a museum on Belgrano and Ameghino, very varied exhibits, including stuffed local animals. Free, open Mon.-Fri., 0900-1200 and 1800-2100. Sat. at 1900-2100; 15 min. tour.

Hotels *Tehuelche*, 9 de Julio 961 y Belgrano, C, good but no restaurant; *Residencial Las Mutisias*, Av. Alvear 1021, D with breakfast, recommended, very helpful owner (Sr. Rubén Portscher); *Residencial Maika*, San Martín y 25 de Mayo, D; *Huenu*, San Martín 822, D; *Hostería Los Troncos*, San Martín 1380, D (without breakfast); *Residencial Sky*, San Martín 961, D, with bath, without breakfast. No youth hostel although it is still in the YHA handbook. *Hostería*, at Italian consulate, Ameghino 505, F, nice, friendly, clean, quiet, meals; *Residencial Esquel*, San Martín 1042, D; *Atalaya*, 9 de Julio 1086, D without breakfast; *Huemul*, Alvear 1009, D; *Europa*, very cold, F, on Calle 25 de Mayo; *Hostería Arrayán*, Antártida 767, E; *Al Sol*, Chacabuco 762. *Zacarias*, Roca 636, adequate, E. *Motel La Hoya*, Ameghino 2296, D, on road to airport, 1 km. Also *Hostería La Hoya* at the Centro Deportivo de Ski at La Hoya itself, E. *Residencial Maidana*, Chacabuco 666, E. *Residencial Alsol*, F. *Hospedaje Beirut*, 25 de Mayo 200, Ameghino, F, shared room, not very clean but friendly. Ask at tourist office for lodgings in private houses.

Camping Parque Nacional camping ground in the Park, by Lake Futalaufquen, 6 km.; hot showers and small store. Permit needed from Intendencia, who also provide fishing permits (US$51.35 for a whole season, with reductions for shorter periods). Camping facilities closed in winter; also on the way to El Bolsón. Camping at *Cabañas Tejas Negras*, (C), good facilities for US$3.50, by *Pucón Pai Motel*, which has its own campsite. Those with sleeping bags can go to the Salesian school and sleep in the school classrooms, Dec. to March; get recommendation from tourist office. On the road from Esquel to Trevelin, signposted on the righthand side, is *La Granja Trevelin*, owned by Domingo Giacci, macrobiotic meals, sells milk, cheese and onions; camping US$0.90, hot water and w.c.; bungalows US$15 a day.

Restaurants *Jockey Club*, Alvear 947, excellent, reasonably priced; *El Cóndor*, rotisería, near bus station, Alvear 1250, good for packed lunches; also for snacks. *Ahla Wasahla*, San Martín 1100, opposite Tour d'Argent, good cheap, friendly, TV, closed Sun.; *Red Fox*, Sarmiento 795 and Alvear, a British-style pub with light, but expensive meals, open from 2200, closed Tues. *Tehuelche*, 9 de Julio and Belgrano; *Esquel*, San Martín 1167, *El Fogón*, Av. Patagonia. *Bar San Jorge*, Av. Alvear, some of the best empanadas in Argentina. *Casa Suiza*, good confitería.

Bank and Post Office Banco de la Nación on Güemes and San Martín, very high commission on cheques, but none on cash; open Mon.-Fri., 1000-1300. Post Office at Roca 445. Opposite the bus terminal on Fontana and Alvear (open 0800-2000) is a new post and telecommunications office.

Tourist Office Operates from the bus terminal, very friendly, and good. Closed Sat. p.m. and Sun. off-season.

Tourist Agencies Mencué (for complete tours only), Lago Verde, Via Sur, all near Sarmiento. Esquel Tours, Fontana 754, Tel.: 2704, run a service to and from the airport (US$0.70) where they also have an office.

Airport 20 km. E of Esquel, by paved road, US$10 by taxi. US$4 by bus. One flight daily to Buenos Aires, 3 a week via Bariloche; 4 a week via Trelew. LADE flight to Ushuaia; also to Trelew and to Bariloche.

Rail (From Buenos Aires, *Lagos del Sur* train arrives in Jacobacci after 27½ hrs., returns at 1820 Wed.) A steam-operated, narrow-gauge branch has a train (described by Paul Theroux in *The Old Patagonian Express*) which leaves Jacobacci (E of Bariloche) Thurs. and Sun., at 1400, for Esquel (arrives 0415), which is the most southerly point in the connected South American railway system. It returns Mon., and Thurs., at 2200, arriving at Jacobacci at 1210. Fares from Bs.As. to Esquel: tourist US$19.35, 1st class US$26, pullman and sleeper, available only as far as Jacobacci, US$37 and US$44. Tourist train to Nahuel Pan leaves Mon. at 1500, returns same day,

ARGENTINA 121

US$5. Tickets from Tehuelche Viajes, Fontana 574, or Esquel Tours, Fontana 754. There are only two engines at Esquel, so go to El Maitén, where there are about 12, arriving at 0830. From El Maitén it is possible to hitch to Bariloche or take the Esquel-Bariloche bus.

Buses None direct from Buenos Aires to Esquel so travel via Bariloche. Transportes Patagónicos (Don Otto) leaves Comodoro Rivadavia on Tues., Thurs., Fri., and Sun., passing through Esquel at midnight. This bus runs slowly to El Bolsón, where it stays over one hour before leaving for Bariloche. Empresa Mercedes goes daily exc. Mon. to Bariloche at 0800 (also at 2200), US$11.50, but only three times a week in winter. Giobbi SA operates two routes to Comodoro Rivadavia; to Trelew, US$23 with Chubut; other bus companies on Av. Fontana and Alvear (bus terminal) are Empresa Don Otto, Chubut, Denis. Bus terminal Tel.: 2233, also for taxis.

Los Alerces National Park Sixty km. W of Esquel, which can also be reached by road from Rawson, is the Los Alerces National Park, with centuries-old larch trees. An interesting part of the park can be reached from a separate entrance through Trevelin (see below) following the Río Futaleufú. Because the Futaleufú hydroelectric dam has been built there, one can only go a short distance into the park this way, and entry to Lake Situación is forbidden. Entrance by car to see Futaleufú dam is only allowed at 1500, under police supervision; photography not permitted, except on top of the dam itself. There is no public transport, but Mencué in Esquel go there. (Hotels on Route 258, on E side of Lake Futalaufquen are, Quime Quipán and Cume-Hué, both closed in winter). The eastern side of Los Alerces has much the same natural attractions as the Nahuel Huapí and Lanín parks, but is much less developed for tourism. Esquel to Los Alerces, Mon. and Sat. at 0630, returns at 1800, US$4 round trip—check schedule as it varies. Its great Lake Futalaufquen has some of the best fishing in this huge area, begins Nov. 15. Bus to Lake Futalaufquen US$8.50, on Thurs., Sat. and Sun. at 0830 and 1730 (it passes 3 hotels and drives into 2 camp sites). Off-season, the bus only goes to the southern tip of the lake (the administration building, or Intendencia), US$5.15. Taxi, US$72. There are food shops in the area, near camping ground. The 0830 bus connects with the Trelew bus. The Hostería Los Tepúes, on the E side, is simple, rustic, and frequented by teenagers, A, open all year round, also has a family bungalow for rent. Recommended for fishermen are the Quime Quipán and Pucón Pai motels. (The Pucón Pai holds a fishing festival to open the season, A, friendly, open all year; reservations: Casilla 150, Esquel. It has a good restaurant.) On the W side, which is untouched by tourism (by law), is Hotel Futalaufquen just N of Puerto Limonao, recommended, especially rooms 2/3 and 4/5 which have balconies overlooking the lake, L, open all year (no heating in rooms); good walking around the hotel, e.g. to Cinco Saltos, and El Dedal. Regular full day launch trip from Puerto Limonao (reached by early morning minibus) on Lake Futalaufquen (a sheer delight) through Arrayanes river to windless Lake Verde (camping ground). From there one can walk out to Lakes Rivadavia and Cholila (Hostería El Trébol on Lake Mosquito), and to the end of Lake Menéndez, famous for its giant larch trees (US$15 incl. launch trip on Lake Menéndez, with Tehuelche Viajes y Turismo, Av. Fontana 574, from Esquel); the boat leaves at 1000 but book the day before, as it will not leave if there are not enough passengers. There are local guides with outboard motor boats for fishermen. From Lake Menéndez one can also take a launch to see the beautiful Cerro Torrecilla. Lovely view of Lago Cisne (Swan Lake) to the NW end of Lake Menéndez. One then walks a 3 km. nature trail looking across the Andes to Chile before returning. Tours arranged at Esquel. Other excursion tours offered are less interesting because they only involve short stops in front of points of interest. A road connects all the lakes.

From Esquel one can also drive to Perito Moreno (see page 133) via Teckia (95 km. paved), Gobernador Costa (84 km. unpaved), La Laurita (last 61 km. paved, ACA service station, breakdown truck and snack bar), 65 paved km. to join route 22 (60 km.) which is being paved, and on to Paso Río Mayo, with 121 km. unpaved road to Perito Moreno.

Trevelin (pop. 5,000), 23 km. SW of Esquel (local bus, US$0.60, every ½ hour, 0700-1900; Hostería Estafania, Pto. Moreno) is also an offshoot of the Welsh Chubut colony (see page 129). There is a modern Anglican church beside the Catholic one. It has a historical museum (entrance US$0.30) in the old mill. Grills at Che Ferrada, good mixed parrillada at El Quincho, and tea rooms offering té galés and torta negra. La Cabaña, 7 km. out on the road from Trevelin to Lake Futalaufquen, serves Welsh teas. There is a custom of giving a newly-married couple a "black cake" on their wedding day, to be eaten on their first anniversary.

The Route to Chile from Bariloche The preferred route is over Puyehue pass, being 4-5 times cheaper than via the lakes, on a good broad highway which is paved on the Chilean side up to Termas de Puyehue, but not yet on the Argentine ("120 km. of dirt road ... tough on the car and the nerves" - David Mackintosh). Road from Bariloche goes around east end of Lake Nahuel Huapí, then follows north side of lake through resort town of Villa La Angostura to junction with "Ruta de Siete Lagos" for San Martín at Km. 94, Argentine customs at Km. 109 and pass at Km. 125 at elevation of about 1,280 metres. (About 22 km. from the

122 ARGENTINA

Argentine customs is Camping Correntoso; 4 km. further is Camping El Cruce, ACA, and another 2 km. brings you to Camping Osa Mayor, ACA.) Chilean customs at Km. 146 in middle of a forest. The frontier is closed at night. *Hotel Termas de Puyehue* is at Km. 168. Possible to camp nearby, but bring own food as restaurant is expensive. Very pleasant *Motel Ñilque* on Lake Puyehue (Chile) is at Km. 174. A six-hour drive.

N.B.: You are strongly advised to get some Chilean pesos before you cross into Chile from Bariloche, as the austral is not easily exchanged in Chile. The Argentine and Chilean border posts are open every day; the launches (and hence the connecting buses) on the lakes servicing the direct route via Puerto Blest to Puerto Montt generally do not operate at weekends; check. There is an absolute ban in Chile on importing any fresh food—meat, cheese, fruit—from Argentina. Bariloche Tourist Office may not be up to date on lake crossings to Puerto Montt, check details at travel agencies, particularly if travelling to meet connections.

Four bus companies run services from Bariloche to Puerto Montt, Osorno and Valdivia, there is at least one bus every day from Argentine side. Two go the all-road crossing via Osorno: Visión Turismo and Bus Norte, Mitre 10, daily exc. Mon. and Wed. Perimel and T. Lanin (not recommended), Moreno 138, daily exc. Fri. and Sun.; all at 0800, 8 hrs., US$ 17.50 (although it is cheaper to go to Osorno and buy a separate ticket on to Puerto Montt). Sit on left side for best views. Turismo Catedral operates a one-day crossing to Puerto Montt, via the lake with lunch at Peulla. Alternatively you can buy a ticket to the Chilean border (US$10.50), then another to Puerto Montt (US$32), or pay in stages once in Chile. The route is Bariloche to Llao-Llao by road, Llao-Llao to Puerto Blest by boat (2½ hrs.), Puerto Blest to Puerto Frías (20 mins. by boat), then 1½ hrs. by road to Peulla. Leave for Petrohué in the afternoon by boat (2½ hrs.), cross Lake Todos Los Santos, passing the Osorno volcano, then by bus to Puerto Montt. All other agencies sell excursions to Puerto Frías using a Mercedes bus to Puerto Pañuelo, a Turisur boat to Puerto Blest and share a bus and boat to Puerto Frías with excursion groups going on to Chile. Request information at Turismo Catedral which owns the exclusive rights to the excursion via the lakes, using their own boats and bus from Puerto Pañuelo to Puerto Frías (Andina del Sud operates with them on the Chilean side). You can do the trip by paying as you go along but you need plenty of change. The most satisfactory way of doing the trip full-circle is by car from Bariloche, going first via Puyehue to Puerto Montt, returning via Tromen Pass (see the Villarrica volcano, good road), then Junín and San Martín de los Andes. It is reported that Peulla suffers from swarms of biting flies in summer and that the shorelines there are receding. No cars taken on ferry on Lake Todos Los Santos. There are daily boats from Puerto Pañuelo to Puerto Blest, with daily through connections by boat and bus to Puerto Montt.

Further information on border crossings in the Lake District, and details of accommodation in Peulla will be found in the Chilean section, page 429.

N.B. At the Futaleufú and Palena border crossings, Argentine border officials only give transit visas: legalize your stay within 10 days either by leaving the country or by renewing entry stamp at a migration office.

N.B.: Obtain maps and information about the district in Buenos Aires at the National Park Tourist Office at Santa Fe 690, or at the provincial offices (addresses given on page 48); it is hard to obtain these in the provinces themselves. Park wardens are also useful sources of information.

Neuquén, capital of Neuquén Province, is near the confluence of the Limay and Neuquén rivers. It is an industrial city of nearly 60,000 people, serving the rich oilfields to the W with heavy equipment and construction materials, and the irrigated fruit-producing valley to the E. There are also many wine *bodegas* nearby. Much farm machinery is sold to the orchards where apples, pears, grapes, hops and plums are grown. At the Parque Centenario is a *mirador* with good views of the city and the confluence of the Rivers Neuquén and Limay (be sure *not* to take the bus to Centenario industrial suburb). There is a jet airport (7 km. from centre) and Neuquén is the transport centre for Mendoza (N), Bahía Blanca and Buenos Aires (E), Zapala and Chile (W), and Bariloche (S).

Hotels *Apollo*, D-C, Av. Olascoaga 361, very good; *Cristal*, D-C, Av. Olascoaga 268, adequate; *Royal*, central, D without breakfast; *Comahue*, 4-star, new, very good; *ACA Cipolletti*, just outside Neuquén; *Residencial Imperio*, H. Irigoyen 65, E; other *Hospedajes* on F. San Martín, *Pani* (236), *Inglés* (534), *Monza* (552), all E; *Residencial Belgrano*, Rivadavia 283, F with bath. 13 km. S is *Hostería del Caminero* with pool and garden, popular. Some 50 km. W of Neuquén there is a motel at Arroyitos. Municipal camping site at Neuquén and various camping sites, mostly by the river.

Restaurant *Bariloche*, good food but poor service.

Bank *Casa de cambio* at Ministro Alcorta 144.

ARGENTINA 123

Museums Museo Histórico Provincial, Santa Fe 163; Museo de Ciencias Naturales, at entrance to airport (as is the Casino).

Tourist Office Félix San Martín y Río Negro.

Transport El Cóndor (La Estrella), El Valle and Chevallier bus Buenos Aires-Neuquén, daily US$24, 18½ hours; paved road throughout. Connections with Copahué and Córdoba. Bus to Zapala daily, 7 hours. To Bariloche, take La Estrella or Chevallier (not El Valle as it stops too often), and sit on left. Bus La Unión del Sud to Temuco (Chile) all year Mon., Tues., Thurs. and Sat. 0200, 16 hrs., US$23, returns on alternate days at 0430.

Daily train, *Estrella del Valle*, leaves Constitución station, Buenos Aires, at 1000, arriving Neuquén 0745; sleeper US$31, pullman US$24.40, first class US$17, tourist US$ 12.65; goes on to Zapala, 4 hours. Leaves Neuquén 2330, arrives Buenos Aires 2050. Takes car transporter Buenos Aires-Neuquén Thurs.; returns Fri.

If driving from Neuquén to Buenos Aires on Routes 151 and 21, via Catriel, fill up with fuel here because there is no other fuel for 323 km. of desert before General Achá.

Air Daily flights to and from Buenos Aires with AA and Austral (one night flight each). Connecting flights to San Martín de los Andes with TAN.

A road and railway go W from Neuquén to **Zapala** (247 km.) through the oil zone at Challacó and Plaza Huincul. There is an excellent geology museum in Zapala, visited by specialist groups from all over the world. Among the collections of minerals, fossils, shells and rocks, is a complete crocodile jaw, believed to be 80 million years old.

Hotels *Huincul*, Roca 313, F; *Coliqueo*, Etcheluz 159, E; *Odetto's Grill*, Ejército Argentino 455, moderate prices, 2 mins. from bus terminal. There is a municipal camping site.

Transport A Pullman bus, with hostess service, plies twice daily between Bahía Blanca and Zapala (15 hrs.). El Petróleo bus leaves Zapala 0230 and 1630 for San Martín de los Andes (5½ hrs.) via Junín de los Andes. In winter the direct route from San Martín de los Andes via the lakes may be impassable, so a bus must be taken back from San Martín to La Rinconada and then round to Bariloche (4 hrs.). There is also an overnight (at 2200) Neuquén-Zapala-San Martín bus that comes through Zapala at 0230; same service at 0915 (US$23). From Zapala to Bariloche by bus, one must change at La Rinconada. Zapala-Temuco (Chile) all year with La Unión del Sud at 0500, US$20, 13 hrs., as under Neuquén (see above). Also with Igi-Llaimi Wed. and Fri. at 0530, return 0330, twice weekly. Buy Chilean currency before leaving—if you can.

Train from Buenos Aires to Zapala, *Estrella del Valle*, 1,367 kms., 26 hrs.; daily via Bahía Blanca at 1000 from Constitución, arr. 1140. Zapala-Buenos Aires at 1925, arrives 2050 next day. On Sundays tickets go on sale at 1500, buffet car on train, scenery largely uninteresting. Fares: sleeper US$35, pullman US$28.35, first US$19.75, tourist US$ 14.65. The line follows the Río Colorado for some distance, then crosses it into the valley of the Río Negro where large fruit growing areas at (343 km.) **Choele-Choel** (ACA motel on edge of town, D, with bath, and fine modern *Hotel Choele-Choel*) and at (472 km.) Villa Regina are irrigated from the Río Negro dam. Two low-priced clean places: motel and *residencial* at edge of town near the main road. Cheap food at one of the service stations. There is an excellent free municipal campsite at Choele-Choel; shady, beside the Río Negro; no showers. Many local buses ply from Choele-Choel to El Chocón (large hydroelectric plant) and Zapala.

North of Zapala on the Chilean border is the Copahué National Reservation, best-known for its thermal baths and volcano of the same name. At 1,980 metres above sea-level in a volcanic region, **Copahué Termas** is enclosed in a gigantic amphitheatre formed by mountain walls, with an opening to the E. There are bus services from Neuquén and Zapala to Copahué, which may also be reached by road from Mendoza.

Hotels N of Zapala include those at Churriaca (131 km.), Chos Malal (202 km.) and Río Barrancas (at 340 km.). Road mostly unpaved.

The Laguna Blanca National Park to the W of Zapala is famous for its animal and bird life, but has not yet become a tourist centre.

Bariloche is 418 km. S of Zapala by a road through Junín de los Andes and San Martín de los Andes. A short detour from Junín leads to the very beautiful lake of Huechulafquen; from Junín, too, a road runs W over the Tromen Pass through glorious scenery to Pucón (135 km.) on Lake Villarrica, in Chile (easy to hitchhike to Villarrica from the Argentine border post); on the way there are splendid views of Lanín volcano, extinct and 3,975 metres high, one of the world's most beautiful mountains. At **Junín de los Andes**—a famous spot for salmon and rainbow

124 ARGENTINA

trout—is the *Chimehuín*, a very small fishing hostelry (C). Some 30 km. N of Junín are the *ACA Las Rinconadas* facilities; paved road. There is an airport between Junín and San Martín, but it is mainly used by the military.

The Tromen (Chileans call it Mamuil Malal) pass route between Argentina and Chile is much less developed than the Puyehue route, and definitely not usable during heavy rain or snow. Parts are narrow and steep. Argentine customs are at the pass. The Chilean *aduana* is at Puesco, 58 km. SE of Pucón and 16 km. from Tromen. Ferry at Lake Quilleihue, which is halfway between the posts, has been eliminated by road blasted across cliffs. It is possible to camp in the area, but take food as there are no shops at the pass. From the border, it is 24 km. to Currarrehue, from where several buses a day go (either at 0600 or at the latest at 1400) to Pucón. The international bus will officially only pick up people at Tromen but at the discretion of the driver can pick up passengers at Puesco (customs) at 0900 and Currarehue stops. Hitch-hiking over to the Tromen Pass is difficult.

San Martín de los Andes, 40 km. S. of Junín (paved road), and 196 km. from Zapala, is a lovely little town at the eastern end of Lake Lacar; it is the best centre for exploring Lanín National Park, with its sparkling lakes, wooded mountain valleys and the snow-capped Lanín Volcano. The numerous deer in the park are the red deer of temperate Europe and Asia. There is excellent ski-ing on Cerro Chapelco, to which there is a road. Tourist Office at Rosas 790, on main square, corner of San Martín, open 0800-2400, very helpful. Police station at Belgrano 611.

Hotels Motel, *El Sol de los Andes*, very expensive and nice, set above the town (Cerro Cnl. Díaz), A-L; *Berna*, Tcnl. Pérez 1127, B; *La Cheminée*, Roca y Moreno, B, very good, breakfast included, but no restaurant; in same range *Village* (Cap. Drury y G. Roca) and *Caupolicán*, San Martín 969; *Crismalu*, Roca 975, C; *Currahuinca*, Rivadavia (Cerro Cnl. Díaz), D; *Lacar*, San Martín 1015, old but central and good value, E-D, good meals; the *Hostería Arrayán*, one of 2 English-run guest lodges in the Lake District, is 3 km. from San Martín. (Self-contained cabins for 14 guests; superb view over Lake Lacar; US$25 a day, all in.) At San Martín is *Los Pinos*, D, Almte. Brown 420, German-run, reportedly run-down; *Turismo* is recommended; Mascardi and R. Roca, D-C, shared bathroom; *Hostería Anay*, Cap. Drury 841, F, central, good value, recommended. Also good, *Casa Alta*, Gabriel Obeid 659 E; *Residencial Peumayen*, Av. San Martín 851, very clean, C-B, with bath and breakfast. Private home, *Casa Ravelo*, Av. San Martín 413, E, excellent. Consult very good tourist office for other private addresses. *Residencial Villa Bibi*, E, with private bath, breakfast extra, clean, family-run, near lake, Cnl. Díaz 1186. At 24 km. from Villa La Angostura (see page 119) is *Hotel Ruca Malen* on Lake Correntoso, warmly recommended; at 53 km. *Hotel Pichi Traful*, and at 75 km. *Hostería Lago Hermoso*.

Camping ACA Camping and Autocamping San Martín de los Andes, both with hot water and laundering facilities US$2.20 p.p. Cabins on the camp site are US$5 p.p. Not open all year round. Hitchhiking to Bariloche and San Juan is slow.

Restaurants *Parrilla La Tranquera*, good value; *Los Ciervos* (opposite roundabout, with deer statues) and *Parrilla del Esquiador* on Belgrano 885, reasonable home-cooked food. *El Jockey* is also good. It is difficult to get dinner before 2200, but there are various good restaurants in the area. *Fan-Fani*, on San Martin, has good pasta.

Buses Station at Gral. Villegas 251, good toilet facilities. From Buenos Aires, US$48.

The most popular trips by car are to Lakes Log-Log, Alumine and Huechulafquen, to Villarrica Pass and Lanín Volcano. Shorter excursions can be made on horseback or by launch; recommended day excursion by El Valle at 0930, return 1700 on Lake Lacar for US$10. The road goes on via Lake Hermoso and Villa La Angostura to Bariloche, a beautiful drive of 220 km., 10 hours by bus, which stops for views and an hour for lunch at Angostura—an excellent, well organized bus route, but not in winter. Many buses, however, use a rather less scenic route following Río Traful, then Lake Lanín and joining the paved Bariloche highway at Confluencia (ACA station and a hotel, also motel *El Rancho* just before Confluencia).

Villa Traful, beside Lake Traful about half-way between San Martín and Bariloche on a side road, is described as a "camper's paradise'. Marvellous views, fishing (licence needed) excellent. All roads are dirt; drive carefully, avoiding wild cattle! *Hostería Traful* provides accommodation.

Camping along this "Seven Lake Drive" route is freely allowed to National Park permit-holders. No buses from Seven Lakes to San Martín de los Andes. If however you want to travel from Bariloche to San Martín via Junín and the Seven Lakes, you must buy a round trip excursion from one of the tour companies (e.g. Velox in Bariloche) for US$17.75, leaving at 0800, and not return with them. This is actually cheaper than a one-way ticket with the El Valle company who go there direct, via the less scenic route (US$20, at 1430). It is difficult to hitch-hike along this route as there is little traffic. When there is sufficient demand, there are two buses a day San Martín-Bariloche, 5 hours, making tourist day trips to San Martín, US$10.35. There are also daily buses San Martín-Bariloche via a paved road (least scenic) leaving San Martín at different times through four days in the morning and three days in early afternoon.

Excursion San Martín de los Andes-Panguipulli (Chile): boat leaves San Martín daily to Hua-Hum at the end of Lake Lacar, except Thurs., at 0900, US$4.25. Camping with shop at Hua-Hum. Hitching to the site is possible as a road now exists; start out from San Martín at 0700. Excursion buses run to Hua-Hum when the launch arrives across the border to Pirehueico, US$2.35. Boats also leave Puerto Fuy Mon., Tues. and Thurs. to Pirehueico for a day trip, US$3.45. Buses leave Puerto Fuy at 0600 to meet the boat from Choshuenco-Panguipulli on Mon., Tues., Thurs. and Sat. This route is open all year round and is an alternative service from Temuco to San Martín when the Tromen Pass is blocked by snow (usually June-mid-Nov.). When the pass is closed, the buses drive right on to the boat to cross between Puerto Fuy and Puerto Pirehueico. Check with customs at Hua-Hum about arrangements. Bus San Martín de los Andes to Pucón and to Temuco US$5.75; mid-Nov.-May Empresa San Martín Mon., Wed. and Fri., at 0700, returns from Temuco the following day at 0500, Igi-Llaimi Tues., Thurs. and Sat. at 0700, ret. next day at 0630, US$16 for Pucón, Villarica and Temuco. When the pass is closed Empresa San Martín switches its return and forward journey days but not the times. Igi-Llaimi goes Wed. and Fri. only at 0500, returning from Temuco Tues. and Thurs. at 0330. This route passes through Panguipulli, Villarica and Temuco only. For Pucón change to JAC bus in Villarica. The companies will not give information about each other, and do not run buses in winter when the pass is blocked. Bus Buenos Aires-San Martín, US$20, three a week, Chevallier goes Mon. and Fri. at 1430, arrives 1520 next day.

Skiing There is now a chair-lift on Cerro Chapelco and a ski-tow higher up. Very good slopes and snow conditions. As yet uncrowded and much cheaper than at Bariloche. Atmosphere friendly.

Patagonia

South of the Río Colorado is the vast plateau known generally as Patagonia. The area is sub-divided into the provinces of Neuquén, Río Negro, Chubut, Santa Cruz and the Territory of Tierra del Fuego. The area covers 780,000 square km.: 28% of the national territory, but has a population of only 600,000, little over 2.7% of the total population; and 57% of it is urban. Wide areas have less than one person to the square km., and there are virtually no trees except in the north and the Andean foothills.

Over the whole land there blows a boisterous, cloud-laden strong wind which raises a haze of dust in summer, but in winter the dust can turn into thick mud. Temperatures are moderated by the proximity of the sea and are singularly mild, neither rising high during the summer nor falling low during the winter. Even in Tierra del Fuego, where the warmest summer months average 10½°C, the winter days' average can reach a high of about 2°C. Make sure you have plenty of warm clothing, and anti-freeze in your car, available locally. Rain falls mostly in the winter, but not more than 200-250 mm. a year. The whole eastern part of the area suffers from a lack of rainfall and the land is more or less desert. Deep crevices or canyons intersect the land from E to W. Few of them contain permanent water, but ground water is easily pumped to the surface. The great sheep *estancias* are along these canyons, sheltered from the wind, and in the depression running N from the Strait of Magellan to Lakes Argentino and Buenos Aires and beyond. During a brief period in spring, after the melting of the snows, there is grass on the plateau. Most of the land is devoted to sheep raising. The wool, which is shipped N to Buenos Aires, is mostly the fine and finecrossbred wool used by the Argentine mills, and is often heavy with sand. Over-grazing leads to much erosion. Wild dogs and the red fox are the sole enemies of the sheep.

Because of the high winds and insufficient rainfall there is little agriculture except in the N, in the valleys of the Colorado and Negro rivers. Some cattle are raised in both valleys where irrigation permits the growing of alfalfa. A large area has been irrigated from the Río Negro dam near Neuquén and here, as a supplement to cattle raising, fruit growing has been highly successful: apples and pears are the chief crops, and many are exported.

Patagonia is rich in extractive resources: the oil of Comodoro Rivadavia and Tierra del Fuego, the little exploited iron ore of Sierra Grande, the coal of Río Turbio, the hydro-electric capacity of El Chocón, plentiful deposits of minerals (particularly bauxite) and marine resources, but their exploitation has been slow.

Tourism is opening up too. The wildlife is attractive. *Guanacos* and rheas are a common sight: there are also *maras*, Patagonian hares. On and off parts of the coast, particularly the Valdés peninsula, seals, sea-elephants, right whales and other aquatic mammals may be seen, as well as penguins. Further S, particularly in Tierra del Fuego, the antarctic wild goose (*quequén*) is the most commonly seen of the 152 species of birds.

N.B. We are informed that in summer hotel prices are grossly inflated (by as much as 100% in Ushuaia, 75% in Calafate); also that in some places there may not be enough hotel beds to meet the demand. Camping is increasingly popular, and *estancias* seem hospitable to travellers who are stuck for a bed.

Discovery and Colonization. The coast of Patagonia was first visited by a European late in 1519, when the Portuguese Ferdinand Magellan, then in the service of Spain, was on his voyage round the world. Early in 1520 he turned W into the strait which now bears his name and there struggled with fierce headwinds until he reached that Sea of Peace he named the Pacific. Later European expeditions that attempted to land on the coast were repelled by the dour and obdurate local Indians, but these were almost entirely wiped out in the wars of 1879-1883 against them, generally known as the "Campaign of the Desert". Before this there had been a long established colony at Carmen de Patagones; it shipped salt to Buenos Aires during the colonial period. There had also been a settlement of Welsh people in the Chubut Valley since 1865. After the Indian wars colonization was rapid, the Welsh, Scots and English taking a great part. Chilean sheep farmers from Punta Arenas moved northwards along the depression at the foot of the Andes, eastwards into Tierra del Fuego, and northwards to Santa Cruz.

Recommended Reading. *In Patagonia* by Bruce Chatwin, a good introduction to the area and its people.

In all Patagonia there is only one town—Comodoro Rivadavia—with a population over 100,000. Most of them are small ports, which used only to be alive during the wool-shipping season but have livened up since the local economy began to diversify. The high tidal range makes it impossible in most of them for ships to tie up at the docks (except at Madryn and Punta Arenas, Chile). The few railways inland form the ports have little traffic except during the sheep-shearing season.

N.B. Travellers are warned that during Argentine summer holidays (Jan., Feb., March) getting a hotel room in Ushuaia, Río Grande, Río Gallegos and Calafate is practically impossible. It is also difficult to change US dollars around the Lake Argentino area.

Communications Calls at the chief ports by passenger/cargo ships of the Flota Carbonera del Estado. Navy transport ships go as far as Ushuaia (Tierra del Fuego) once a month and carry 60 passengers for a nine-day trip.

Air Services Aerolíneas Argentinas from Buenos Aires either direct to Río Gallegos or calling at Bahía Blanca, Trelew and Comodoro Rivadavia on the way. Austral from Buenos Aires to Río Gallegos via Bahía Blanca, Trelew and Comodoro Rivadavia daily (night flight Mon. via Bahía Blanca). Cía. Argentina de Transportes Aéreos (CATA) from Buenos Aires to Bahía Blanca, Trelew, Comodoro Rivadavia and Río Gallegos. Beware delays for bad weather.

Many air force LADE flights in the region S of Bariloche—Río Gallegos to Bariloche, to Ushuaia, to Calafate—must be booked in advance from departure point of flight. The planes are small and fly low; passengers miss little of what there is to be seen. The baggage allowance is 15 kg. Travellers are warned that the flights are often heavily booked ahead, but always check again on the day of the flight if you are told beforehand that it is sold out. Sometimes, individual passengers are allowed to fly on air force carriers if planes are full or inopportune, through LADE. Also, LADE tickets are much cheaper for a long flight with stops than buying separate segments.

Roads The main road, Route 3, which runs near the coast, is paved from Buenos Aires to Fitz Roy, near Comodoro Rivadavia. From Comodoro Rivadavia to Piedra Buena the road has a very well maintained all-weather surface. The last 230 km. to Río Gallegos are paved. S of this town to Ushuaia is a combination of fair all-weather road and pavement in a bad state of repair. Sometimes passengers going South have to pay for baggage by weight.

The principal roads in Patagonia roughly form a triangle. Route 3 follows the Atlantic coast and has the advantage of being largely paved, with regular traffic and adequate services including accommodation. On the other hand, it has little to interest the tourist. At the southern end, this route enters Chile and crosses the Magellan Straits to Tierra del Fuego by the car ferry at Primera Angostura. The western route (Route 40) zigzags across the moors and is lonely and largely unpaved (advised speed 30 kph); there is hardly any traffic except in December, January and February, the tourist season. However, it is by far the more interesting road, with fine views of the Andes and plenty of wild life as well as the Alerces and Glaciares National Parks. Camping is no problem, and there are good hotels at Esquel, Perito Moreno, Piedra Buena, Calafate and (in Chile) Puerto

ARGENTINA 127

Natales. Third class accommodation also at Gobernador Gregores, Paso Río Mayo and Esperanza, and also in Coyhaique, Chile. The northern part of the triangle is formed by the paved highway running from Bariloche through Neuquén to San Antonio Oeste.

Many of the roads in Southern Argentina are gravelled; it is in your interest to buy a windscreen protector, costing US$50. This type is available in Buenos Aires, but more primitive versions can be bought for much less—e.g. US$5 in San Julián, and probably elsewhere. The best types to buy are the grid-type, or inflatable plastic ones which are made for some standard-type vehicles, the only disadvantage being some loss of visibility.

N.B.: Keep passport handy as examination is required when passing from one province to another. Also, be prepared for roadblocks at which one has to declare one's destination, nationality, vehicle particulars, etc.

The upper course of the Río Colorado is the northern limit of Patagonia. 160 km. S of where it reaches the sea (250 km. S of Bahía Blanca), about 27 km. from the mouth of the Río Negro, is

Carmen de Patagones, standing on high ground on the northern bank, with **Viedma** (20,000 people) the capital of Río Negro Province, across the river, which is spanned by a connecting rail and road bridge. There is also a frequent ferry service for pedestrians. On a hill behind Patagones a monument commemorates an attack on the twin towns by a Brazilian squadron in 1827. (Beware of pleasant-looking campsites near this monument; there is an artillery range nearby.) The Cuevas Maragatas, where colonists from Spain first lived on arrival here, can be seen at Patagones. There is a sign on Calle Rivadavia. There are air services to Viedma, 966 km. from Buenos Aires daily except Thursday (continuing either to Bariloche or General Roca). The swimming is recommended on the Viedma side of the river, where there is a nice shady shore.

Hotels at Carmen de Patagones: *Percaz*; *Gran Argentino*. At Viedma: *Roma*, F; *Viedma*; *Austral*, recommended, modern.

Tourist Office Belgrano 544, 9th floor, Viedma.

Camping Further camping sites on the Río Negro where the main route into Patagonia meets the river (some 170 km. from Viedma due NW) with all facilities including a small shop. Additional shops at General Conesa, 2 km. away. Mosquito repellant needed. There is another campsite N of General Conesa (about 140 km.) at Río Colorado again alongside the Patagonian road. All facilities.

Almost due W and 180 km. along the coast, on the Gulf of San Matías, is **San Antonio Oeste** (10,000 people). 17 km. S is a seaside resort, **Las Grutas**, developed in the 1960s with good safe beach; the caves are not really worth visiting, but there is a good seafood place, *Parrilla Bariloche*. ACA has a *Unidad Turística*, with 6-bed rooms, no restaurant. *Tour du Golfe*, friendly, 3-bed rooms, E, provide cooking facilities. There is also a camping ground. *Restaurant Rambla* recommended. The whole of Las Grutas closes down in mid-March and retires to Buenos Aires. Between San Antonio and Puerto Madryn is Sierra Grande, where iron-ore deposits are being rapidly developed. The ore is piped in solution to an ocean terminal 32 km. E.

Hotels at San Antonio *Iberia*, Sarmiento 241, E with bath; *Kandava*, 2 blocks from bus and railway station, E with bath, hot water, clean, good; *Vasquito*, just acceptable, F; *Albatros*, and *Americana*, F, not recommended. Good beach 7 km. away.

Railway via Viedma to Bahía Blanca and Buenos Aires and westwards to Bariloche and Zapala. Trains from Buenos Aires (Constitución) (19 hours) 0820 Wed. and Sat. (*Lagos del Sur*). Leaves San Antonio Oeste 2225 Tues., Wed., Fri. and Sat. Fares: sleeper US$ 29.60, pullman US$22.85, first US$15.90, tourist US$11.85.

Buses From San Antonio N to Bahía Blanca and S to Río Gallegos and Punta Arenas by Transportes Patagónicos. To Puerto Madryn, 2 a day, US$6.50. To Buenos Aires. US$23 via Bahía Blanca, frequent.

Route to Bariloche: paved. Continue 201 km. through bush country providing fodder for a few cattle, with a view to the S of the salt flats called Salina del Gualicho. The road then meets the Zapala-Buenos Aires highway at Choele Choel. Then 223 km. to Neuquén through an unbroken series of groves of tall trees sheltering vineyards and orchards. On (424 km.) to Bariloche along fast road, skirting the entire length of the reservoir formed by the Ezequiel Ramos Mejía dam. Then it drops

128 ARGENTINA

over an escarpment to cross the Collón Curá river. Continue through the valley of the river Limay to Confluencia and the Valle Encantado. The journey can be completed in 11 hours.

About 250 km. to the S, in Chubut, is

Puerto Madryn, a small port on the Golfo Nuevo. It was founded by the Welsh colonist, Parry Madryn, in 1865. Population, 22,000. A large aluminium plant is now operating (ask at tourist office for details of visits), and the town is becoming a popular tourist centre, with a casino, skin-diving and nature reserves. Museo de Ciencias Naturales y Oceanografía on J. García and J. Menéndez. Airport. No Youth Hostel. People staying more than two days should stay in Puerto Madryn or Puerto Pirámides (see page 129) to visit the area, otherwise Trelew is a better base.

Hotels (Very full in summer, make bookings early.) *Gran Madryn I,* L. Lugones 40, C, 2-star, friendly but rooms just acceptable; *Hostal del Rey,* Blvd. Brown, on beach, recommended, C, 2-star, with radio and television, breakfast included; *Motel ACA,* Ribera Marítima Norte, D; *Playa,* Av. Roca 181, B, 3-star; *Gran Palace,* 28 de Julio 390, C, some F rooms without bath, modern; *Yanco,* Av. Roca 627, on beach, C; *Hostería Carreras,* J.B. Justo 645; *Motel Hipocampo,* Vesta 33; *Península Valdés,* J.A. Roca 165, B, 4-star, sea view, suites available, comfortable, recommended; *Costanera,* Brown 759. *Motel Puma,* Roca 1140, closed temporarily; *Suyay,* 9 de Julio 57, E; *Anclamar,* 25 de Mayo 880, D; *Argentino,* 25 de Mayo 275, E, clean, quiet, hot water, cheaper with shared bath; *Atalaya,* Domec García 149, D, with bath, clean; *París,* Roque Sáenz Peña and 25 de Mayo, F, run down, beware of overcharging, basic; *Tolosa,* R. Sáenz Peña 253, B, 3-star, friendly; *Jo's,* Bolívar 25, E; *Vaskonia,* 25 de Mayo 43, F, hot water; *Motel El Cid,* 25 de Mayo 850, D; *Mora,* J.B. Justo 659, E; *Residencial Casa Blanca,* E; *España,* Calle San Martín, two blocks from bus station, E, good restaurant, cooking facilities available, friendly; *El Dorado,* San Martín, E, clean, shower, patio, but landlady not keen on backpackers; *Residencial La Posta,* J.A. Roca 33, F with bath (cheaper without), cooking facilities, clean, good; *El Antiguo,* 28 de Julio 147, near main square, possible to cook, F, clean; *Residencias Pérez,* two blocks from main square and also from Transportes Patagónicos bus terminal.

Camping At far end of bay, 6 km. S of town, is ACA site with hot showers and shady trees (Punta Cuevas) but many people camp on beach. There is a swimming pool in the rocks near the ACA camp site, which gets its water at high tide, very pleasant, and free. Also ACA and municipal at Ribera Sur, 2 km. S of town along beach. All facilities, very crowded. Camping out can be interesting as one can watch foxes, armadillos, skunks and ñandúes roaming around in the evening. Charges about US$2.50 a night p.p. and per car.

Restaurants *Aguila,* M.A. Zar and R.S. Peña, highly recommended, good for seafood; *Cantina El Náutico,* Julio Roca and Lugones, good value, good food, especially fish; *Comedor ACA,* Costanera Norte; *Cantina Club Náutico,* Costanera Norte; *Pizzería Cruz del Sur* and *Palace Hotel,* on 28 de Julio and San Martín; *París,* R.S. Peña, quite cheap; *Pizzería Quine,* J.A. Roca and R.S. Peña; *Pizzería Don Juan,* good; *Parrilla El Parquecito,* excellent steaks, but get there early; *La Cueva de Pepe,* San Martín 123; *El Mesón del Cazador,* Mitre 56; *El Rincón,* R.S. Peña 12; *La Tranquera,* D. García 479; *Hotel Vaskonia,* 25 de Mayo 43; *Parilla Las Brasas,* R.S. Peña 47. **Tea Rooms:** *Panadería La Proveedura,* good pastries; *Centenario,* on Belgrano and Paraguay. For Welsh afternoon teas, *La Goleta,* on Roca, 1700-1900.

Banks There are no *cambios,* and beware of poor rates from travel agents. *Receptivo Puerto Madryn,* Av. Julio A. Roca 141, does give good rates.

Tourist Agencies Tur-Mar, 25 de Mayo 157; Pu-Ma, 28 de Julio 40; Sur Turismo, J.A. Roca 39; Receptivo, J.A. Roca 141. The local tourist office, at Sarmiento 386, is open until after midnight in the tourist season. Recommended guide: Dr Pedro Fuentes Galliardo.

Sport Puerto Madryn is being promoted as a diving centre. Tours for those who have never dived before are organized by Safari Submarino, Mitre 80; Turismo Submarino, Av. Roca 743; Pimino in the harbour, about US$11 per excursion. Swim in the so-called *parque submarino* amid sunken cars and a few fish! Trained divers seriously interested in marine life who have at least a week's stay should contact the Centro Nacional Patagónico at Av. Roca.

Transport Sun., Mon., Thurs. and Fri., at 2030, with El Cóndor, daily with Costa Criolla at 2130, via San Antonio Oeste, change at Bahía Blanca, from Buenos Aires (US$29), 22-24 hrs. To Río Gallegos, also 24 hrs., four times a week. Bus to Bahía Blanca 0700 daily, 12 hrs. (US$17.50 with Don Otto); US$16.25 with La Puntual to Mar del Plata, changing at Bahía Blanca. Patagónicos to San Antonio Oeste at 0800 and 2230, US$6.50. Same times to Buenos Aires, US$29 (cheaper to go to San Antonio Oeste and change to the train, but 9 hr. wait). Bus to Trelew with 28 de Julio company (every 1½ hrs., 8 on Sun. US$1.80). Don Otto to Comodoro Rivadavia, Wed.,

Thurs., Fri., Sun. 0915 and 1830, US$11.50. No direct bus to Bariloche, change at Esquel (Aerolíneas Argentinas flight to Esquel Mon. and Tues. 1215). Taxi rank on the plaza. Bicycles rented at Roca and Yrigoyen.

Excursions There are nature reserves nearby at Punta Loma on Golfo Nuevo (sea-lions), only 15 km. from Puerto Madryn; Punta Pirámides (sea-lions) and Isla de los Pájaros (sea birds) Golfo San José and Punta Norte (killer whales), on the Valdés Peninsula (see below). (Check opening times of reserves in Puerto Madryn; they vary.) The natural history of the region is most interesting, with other seal and penguin colonies, breeding ground at Golfo Nuevo for right whales, fossils in the cliffs, and guanacos, rheas and armadillos in the countryside. Most animals (except the whale) can be seen in the warm seasons, until April. See whales at Puerto Madryn in Sept.-Oct. Past the lighthouse and Naval Zone at Punta Delgada on the other side of the Valdés peninsula is Salina Grande, Argentina's lowest point, 35 metres below sea level.

Excursion bus or hitch-hike (regular bus service now discontinued) to **Puerto Pirámides**, with a population of 70 (ACA motel, C, also ACA campsite, and small friendly hostería, the Posada del Mar, 10 km. from the sea, D: Also Cantina El Salmón, on the beach, good seafood. There is a shop that sells original Patagonian Indian work). Hydro Sports rents scuba equipment and boats, has a small restaurant, and organizes land and sea wildlife tours (ask for Mariano), boat trips US$10 for 1 hour. About 79 km. from Puerto Madryn is Isla de los Pájaros, on a good road. No one is now allowed to visit the island without special permission (only granted to recognised ornithologists), but free powerful telescopes are available on the opposite bank. At Punta Norte (176 km.) on the Valdés Peninsula, there are sea-elephants (breeding time in first fortnight in August, best seen at low tide), late spring and summer (Nov.-March), take own food, since the restaurant is expensive. At Caleta Valdés, you can see penguins and sea elephants at close quarters, but not at any specific point. Camping at hangar nearby, but bring fresh water with you as supplies are unreliable. At Punta Delgada (at the S of the Peninsula) most wildlife can be seen except the penguins, which have moved away. The peninsula is private property. One third belongs to one man, who grazes 40,000 sheep.

Tourist excursions are organized by Tur-Mar, Receptivo and Coyun-Co Turismo, Av. Roca 37. The usual tour takes in Puerto Pirámides, Caleta Valdés (or Punta Norte) and Isla de los Pájaros: the costs are US$22 p.p. on a bus tour, US$13 on a minibus (minimum 6 persons, e.g. Tur-Mar), US$90 for a car with guide, for 4-5 people, US$80 in a taxi for 4 (will stay as long as you like and may also go to Riacho San José to see flamingoes); tours including a boat trip to see whales charge US$12 extra. Trips last about 9 hours, starting at 0800. On all excursions take drink with you (binoculars are also a good idea). Most tour companies stay 50-60 minutes on location, not considered sufficient by some. The excursion buses run in Jan.-March, but the peninsula is easily reached if one has one's own car in fact, the best way to see the wildlife is by car). Peninsular roads are excellent and there is a permanently-stationed Conservation Officer at the entrance to the Peninsula (he is very helpful). Tour to Punta Tombo (see page 131) including a little sight-seeing tour of Rawson, Trelew and Gaiman, US$7.50. Turismo Receptivo runs full-day excursions to Punta Tombo, Gaiman, Rawson and Trelew (US$20). Taxis to Punta Loma for sealions charge official price, US$12; Tur-Mar does 12-hour US$20 p.p. trip to Punta Loma and the Ameghino dam (see below). The Punta Loma sealion reserve is open 0900-1200, 1430-1730 (easy hitch-hike from Madryn), Sept. and Oct. are best months. Tursur is the only agency that will arrange a minibus out of season, if you can gather eight people, to go to Punta Norte, Punta Pirámides and the shore opposite Isla de los Pájaros. You will not see whales between Dec. and June and there will only be young sealions as the older ones will have gone south.

N.B. If possible check all excursion dates in advance; it is very disappointing to arrive in Puerto Madryn only to find that one cannot reach the wildlife reserves.

The road from Puerto Madryn to Puerto Pirámides (94 km.) is now paved; Puerto Pirámides to San Antonio Oeste (328 km.) has 72 km. paved.

History On July 28, 1865, one hundred and fifty Welsh immigrants landed at Puerto Madryn, then a deserted beach deep in Indian country. After three weeks they pushed, on foot, across the parched pampa and into the Chubut river valley, where there is flat cultivable land along the riverside for a distance of 80 km. upstream. Here, maintained in part by the Argentine Government, they settled, but it was three years before they realized the land was barren unless watered. They drew water from the river, which is higher than the surrounding flats, and later built a fine system of irrigation canals. The colony, reinforced later by immigrants from Wales and from the United States, prospered, but in 1899 a great flood drowned the valley and some of the immigrants left for Canada. The last Welsh contingent arrived in 1911. The object of the colony had been to create a "Little Wales beyond Wales", and for four generations they kept the Welsh language alive. The language is, however, dying out in the fifth generation. There is an offshoot of the colony of Chubut at Trevelin, at the foot of the Andes nearly 650 km. to the west, settled in 1888 (see page 121). It is interesting that this distant land gave to the Welsh language one of its most endearing and best-written classics: Dringo'r Andes (Climbing the Andes), written by one of the early women settlers.

Gary Luton, of the Welsh Patagonia Expedition 1980, writes: "To me Chubut will always foster

130 ARGENTINA

memories of horses on an open wind-swept plain, or tethered, with brown sheepskin saddles, outside a *pueblo* inn. It is shuttered houses with poplar windbreaks. Chubut is relative prosperity surrounded by shanties of mud brick and tin; it is Coca-Cola and tea houses, sea lions and right whales sounding a short distance from shore; and *asados* washed down with red wine and *mate*. Chubut is a moonscape of neutral colours where sheep lose themselves in the grey-green saltpans of thornscrub, and dust and wind blow across scattered pockets of civilization. And it is the Eisteddfod at Gaiman, a Welsh festival of the arts in a chapel nestled among the poplars, on a cloudless night, where boys in white shirts recite poetry and choirs sing as a culture fights a subsiding battle to maintain itself."

The Florentino Ameghino dam, 110 km. inland on the River Chubut, covers 7,000 hectares with water and irrigates 28,000 hectares in the lower Chubut valley, as well as producing electric power.

Along the Río Chubut are several towns. **Rawson**, the capital of Chubut Province, 7 km. from the sea (*Hotel Provincial*, Mitre, C, good restaurant, hotel clean, but seems to be falling down), has law courts, a fishing port, and a riverside Tourist Office, 9 de Julio 64, Tel.: 213. (Puerto Rawson is about 5 km. down river.)

Some 20 km. up the Río Chubut is **Trelew** (90,000 people), a prosperous town which has lost its Welsh look. There is a pretty red-brick chapel in the centre. A paved road runs from Rawson through Trelew, Gaiman (see page 131) and Dolavon, all on the river, to Las Plumas (mind the bridge if driving) and the upper Chubut Valley, all the way to Esquel (see page 120) and Trevelin.

Local Holidays July 28 (Founding of Chubut); Dec. 13 (Petroleum Day).

Trelew Hotels *Centenario*, San Martín 150, C, good restaurant; *Argentino*, Gales y Moreno, clean, D, not a good location; *Libertador*, Rivadavia 73, D, without breakfast 4 blocks from Plaza, service good, quiet, *City*, Rivadavia 254, D; *Rayentray*, Belgrano and San Martín, A, overpriced; *Cheltum*, Av. Irigoyen 1485, modern, D; *Plaza*, F, on main square, clean, friendly, helpful; *Hostería Parque*, Irigoyen and Cangallo, D, good; *Grand Residencial*, Rawson and Pecoraro, D; *Residencial Rivadavia*, Rivadavia 55, F with bath, clean, recommended; *Touring Club*, Av. Fontana 240, excellent, E (with bath), the social hub of Trelew, chess is played here, colour TV, breakfast recommended, coffee the best in town; *Galicia*, 9 de Julio and Rivadavia, very warm, E; without bath, clean; *Riolo*, Don Bosco 461, D; *Amancay*, Paraguay 953, D. Cheapest are *Residencial San Carlos*, F, with private bath, Sarmiento 758, and *Provinciano*, Yrigoyen 525, F, poor and noisy. *Argentino*, Abraham Matthews and Moreno, F, clean, quiet, near bus station. *Hostal Residencial Plaza*, G in triple, clean, friendly, recommended. Camping possible south of the town on the road to Rawson and Comodoro Rivadavia, on right about 200 metres beyond the bridge over River Chubut; turn off at the sign Frasers Tea Room; one can camp by the river, but beware of mosquitoes.

Restaurants *Martín Fierro*, very good; *Luque*, H. Yrigoyen and Chile; *Parrilla Don Pedro*, intersection of Routes 3 and 25; *El Quijote*, 25 de Mayo 86, recommended; *El Mesón*, Rivadavia 540; *El Progreso*, San Martín 140; *Galicia*, Rivadavia and 9 de Julio; *Cantina Acapulco*, Belgrano and San Martín. *Taberna de Matías*, 25 de Mayo, good value, highly recommended.

Shopping *Roger's Shop*, Moreno 463, Tel.: 20696, serves Welsh afternoon teas, US$2, and sells traditional regional articles; also gives information on the Welsh of Patagonia, and is the local Aerolíneas Argentinas representative. Welsh and English spoken.

Car Hire Information at the airport; fixed rate plus charge per km. Also Alquilauto Fiorasi, España 344, Tel.: 31160.

Bank of London and South America, Av. 9 de Julio esq. Belgrano. Banco de Italia. Open 0700-1300 Oct.-March, 1200-1800 April-Sept. (1% commission).

Post Office and Entel 25 de Mayo and Mitre.

Tourist Office in the new Terminal Terrestre.

Tourist Agencies Sur Turismo (good rates for cash and travellers' cheques), Belgrano 320, *organize a few excursions. Recommended* tours by taxi to the Valdés Peninsula (see above) cost US$75 for 4 for a whole day.

By Air Airport 5 km. from centre. Airport bus to town, US$1, leaves after each arrival; taxis cost about US$4. Buses from Puerto Madryn do stop at the airport, however. LADE flies, Trelew-Río Gallegos, 1-3 flights daily US$40, US$50 with Aerolíneas. Daily flights to Buenos Aires (Aerolíneas and Austral, either coming from Bahía Blanca, or en route to Comodoro Rivadavia or Ushuaia). Buenos Aires-Trelew night flights once a week in each direction with each company. LADE Buenos Aires-Trelew US$33. Río Grande (via Río Gallegos), 2 flights a week with Aerolíneas, stopping at Comodoro Rivadavia, and Río Gallegos; to Comodoro Rivadavia/ Esquel/

ARGENTINA 131

Bariloche with LADE, Trelew-Bariloche US$28; crowded, book preferably in Buenos Aires in advance; 4 times a week, to Esquel with Aerolíneas.

Buses from Buenos Aires to Trelew daily at 2100, 25 hrs, US$28.75 (return 0700 and 2130 daily, 1705 Tues., Thurs., Fri. and Sat.). Bus, Trelew-Bahía Blanca, 734 km., US$20 daily with Don Otto, 0600, few a week with La Puntual, 0600; Trelew-Mar del Plata, changing at Bahía Blanca, US$17.25 with La Puntual; Trelew-Esquel, 14 hrs., bookable in Esquel only, US$23, Mon. (0700), Wed., Fri., Sun. (2130 express, 9¾ hrs.) with Empresa Chubut. Buses to Rawson every 20 min.; 6 a day to Gaiman; every 1½ hrs. to Puerto Madryn (last at 2200), US$1.80 with 28 de Julio, ask to be dropped off in the town centre on the way to the bus station to avoid backtracking; long-distance to Comodoro Rivadavia daily at 2000, and Sun., Wed., Thurs. and Fri. at 1035, US$9.20, 6 hrs; to Río Gallegos, Sun., Tues., Thurs. 2005, via Puerto Deseado. Rent-a-Car (Godfrey Davis) at Citrelew, 25 de Mayo and Entre Ríos. If hitching from Trelew, take the Rawson bus to the flyover 5 km. out of town.

Petrol at Garayalde, 193 km. from Trelew.

Gaiman, 18 km. from Trelew, a pretty place with well-built brick houses, is now the most Welsh of the Chubut valley towns, and has a museum of the colony (open in winter, Tues., Thurs. and Sat., 1500-1800). The only restaurant seems often to be closed, but tea rooms opposite the square, *Plas y Coed* and *Ti Gwynyn*, *Ty Nain*, and *Elma*, Tello 571, are open from 1500; interesting local agriculture. The Eisteddfodd, Welsh festival of arts, is held in early August each year.

Wildlife may be seen at **Punta Tombo** and Camarones. Punta Tombo is 120 km. S of Trelew, on a dirt road branching off 5 km. SE of Trelew on the road to Rawson, driving time 1¾ hours. There the wildlife is very varied: penguins, guanacos, etc. Season for penguins, Sept.-March (Dec.-Jan. is the time when the young are taking to the water). Check with the Tourist Office that it is all right to visit the penguins as from late March they are "off limits" as they prepare to migrate. You can share a taxi from Trelew; US$70 for one, US$90 for up to 4 passengers. Taxis available from J. A. Roca 200, Moreno 291, Av. Fontana y L. Jones, San Martín 470 and 751. Sur Turismo takes you there and back in a morning (0800-1300) for US$10. About mid-way between Rawson and Punta Tombo, a road leads off Ruta 1 to Isla Escondida (9 km., signed), no facilities, but lovely rock and sand beach with bird and wildlife; secluded camping.

Camarones, 275 km. from both Trelew and Comodoro Rivadavia, is less crowded. There is a large penguin colony 35 km. away at Cabo Dos Bahías along a dirt road (open in season only); free camping is possible there and in the town itself. In summer there is a sealion nursery nearby (binoculars are useful). Local buses very scarce; two a week from Trelew (Don Otto), book at Uruguay 590, Trelew; bus leaves 0800 from San Martín and Belgrano, arrives 1130, returns to Trelew same day 1600 (reports disagree on whether Don Otto bus continues from Camarones to Comodoro Rivadavia). In Camarones take a taxi to the penguin colony (US$15 return) and return to Trelew Tues. Hotels and restaurant at Camarones, *Kau-i-Keuken*, E, clean, friendly, good food. (We are grateful to Hans K. Wagner for helping us to reorganize this section.)

Comodoro Rivadavia, the largest city in the province of Chubut, is 396 km. S of Trelew. Petroleum was discovered here in 1907 and about 30% of all Argentina's oil production comes from wells to the S and W. A 1,770-km. pipeline carries the natural gas to Buenos Aires, and a petrochemical plant has been built. Renewed interest in the local oil industry is making the town boom. There is a regional Patagonian Museum at the ex-Hotel de Turismo, on the 2nd floor worth visiting. Population: 120,000. From here on, prices begin to rise very rapidly, so stock up before reaching Río Gallegos. Good beach at Rada Tilly, 5 km. south; walk along beach at low tide to see sealions (information from El Recreo campsite), beautiful walk.

Local Holidays July 28 (Founding of Chubut); Dec. 13 (Petroleum Day).

Hotels *Austral*, Rivadavia 190, D, noise from street traffic but otherwise comfortable; *Comodoro*, Rivadavia and 9 de Julio, 11 floors, large rooms, C (overpriced); *Colón*, on San Martín, E with private bath, cheaper without, seedy and noisy, poor value; *Residencial San Julián*, Belgrano 738; *Hospedaje Hamburgo*, E, with good restaurant on B. Mitre; *Hospedaje Praga*, España y Sarmiento, E, shower, clean; *Residencial Azul*, C, good service, Sarmiento 724; *Comercio*, Rivadavia 341, friendly, near bus station, hot showers, F (may be bargained lower), good meals, US$3.80; *Pensión Boedo*, Rivadavia 453, cheap restaurant, mediocre food; *Hospedaje Belgrano*, Belgrano 546, D, with bath, clean, hot water; *Cari-Hué*, Belgrano 500 block, clean, quiet, cheap; *Residencial Comodoro*, D, España 919; *Rada Tilly*, E, modern, clean, 5 km. S. see *Diana*, E. *Residencial del Sur*, Maipú 1083, *Su Estrella* and *El Patagón Motel*, access (S) of Route 3.

Camping ACA, 5 km. S at Rada Tilly, may be reached by hourly Expreso Rada Tilly bus from town and is at the far end of the beach, fresh water only; El Recreo, Rada Tilly, US$0.50 p.p., friendly, informative; and at 20 km. N signposted "Bar y Camping"; less inviting.

132 ARGENTINA

Restaurants No one eats at night until 2200. *Austral*, fair; *La Rastra*, Rivadavia 348, very good; *El Ancla de Oro*, Caleta Córdoba (18 km. from Comodoro); *Mar del Plata*, San Martín 371, good sea food, reasonable prices. *Mesón Español*, at No 674; *Il Vero Minicucci*, San Martín y B.Mitre, Italian; *La Tradición*, Bartolomé Mitre 683. *La Estancia*, Urquiza 863; *La Minuta*, Alem 35; *Los Troncos*, Av. Costanera and Rada Tilly; *El Náutico*, Playa Costanera. Several *rotiserías*, much cheaper, on 400 block of Rivadavia, in municipal market.

Bank of London and South America, Av. Rivadavia 264. Oct.-March 0700-1300; April-Sept. 1200-1800; no exchange transactions after 1000 in summer, 6% commission on travellers' cheques; the Banco de la Nación has the best rates on US$ but does not change travellers' cheques.

Post Office in central bus station (beware of overcharging).

Consulates Belgian Vice-Consul, Rivadavia 283; Chilean Consul, Sarmiento 936; Italian Vice-Consul, Belgrano 1053.

Tourist Office In the bus terminal. Travel agencies: Puelche EVT, Rivadavia 527; Richard Pentreath, Mitre 952; San Gabriel, Atlas, Monitur and Ceferino, at San Martín 488, 263, 811 and 372, respectively.

Buses Bus service to Buenos Aires daily at 1530 (Don Otto), 32 hrs., US$39 (also daily with La Puntual/Cóndor at 1300 and Sat. 2400). La Puntual buses to Coyhaique (Chile), US$45, 3 times a week in winter and 4 in summer (weather permitting). Four buses a week to Bariloche, US$34, (Don Otto leaves 1400, Sun., Tues., Thurs., Fri. stops at Esquel midnight, arrives 0600 at Bariloche), and daily to Río Gallegos (Patagónica, US$26.50). To Puerto Madryn US$11.50 (Don Otto). To Colonia Sarmiento, US$4, 2½ hrs. at 0700, 1300, 1900, returns at same times.

Air Services Airport, 9 km. Bus to airport from downtown terminal or opp. Aerolíneas Argentinas in main street hourly (45 mins), US$0.30; take bus No.6. 4-7 flights to Buenos Aires a day with Aerolíneas or Austral, stopping at Trelew, Bahía Blanca or both; offices on San Martín 421 and 291; Aerolíneas and Austral flight daily to Río Gallegos (US$41). Aerolíneas fly to Ushuaia; LADE flies twice a week Comodoro Rivadavia-Perito Moreno-Gobernador Gregores-Calafate-Río Gallegos-Río Grande-Ushuaia, with detour over Calafate glacier, weather permitting (fare to Calafate, US$16). Also to Río Gallegos via Puerto Deseado, San Julián, Santa Cruz, US$33. Taxi to airport, US$6.

Hitch-Hiking There is a truck stop outside Comodoro Rivadavia on the road to Bahía Blanca, where you can contact drivers if hitching. Take the bus leaving at 1200 from the bus station marked "Astra Km 20". Expensive truckdrivers' restaurants along the road; buy food in supermarkets.

A paved road (buses 0700, 1300 and 1700) runs inland from Comodoro Rivadavia to (156 km.) **Colonia Sarmiento** (commonly known just as Sarmiento), population: 12,000 (Archaeological museum next to cathedral, check opening times, may be closed at weekends), on Lake Musters, near the large Lake Colhué Huapí. 30 km. by dirt road S of Colonia Sarmiento there is a large petrified forest (Ormachea), well worth a visit. Taxis, US$15, leave from opposite *Hotel Lago Musters*, there are not many so book early. Sr. Gómez is reputed to do the cheapest tour, ask at bus station. The taxi allows only one hour to see the forest; bargain for longer. However, the warden, Juán José Valera, lives at Uruguay 43, Sarmiento, and is willing to give lifts to those in need when he makes his frequent journeys to the park. The bus to and from Comodoro Rivadavia stops at *Hotel Lago Musters*.

Hotels at Colonia Sarmiento *Lago Musters*, P. Moreno and Ing. Coronel, run down; *Hostería Los Lagos*, Roca and Alberdi, D, good, friendly, heating, has restaurant. Food at *Hotel Colón*, P. Moreno 645, F, clean and friendly, and *El Gaucho*, Route 20, access Sarmiento. In Dec.-March you may be permitted to sleep in the Agricultural School (bring sleeping bag) on the road opp. the petrol pump.

Travel Agency at Sarmiento: Julio Lew, Roca and Alberdi.

Bus Overnight buses to Esquel on Sun. Tues. and Thurs.

There is a road westwards from Colonia Sarmiento via **Paso Río Mayo** (which has three hotels, the *Covadonga*, E, very good, *La Ruta* and *San Martín*), to Puerto Aysén in Chile. A branch from this road goes 130 km. S to Perito Moreno, by Lake Buenos Aires. Another branch on the Paso Río Mayo-Perito Moreno road turns W at 31 km. to Lago Blanco, where there is a small *estancia* community, 30 km. from the border with Chile (about 150 km. from Paso Río Mayo). Population

130. No hotel, but police are friendly and may permit camping at the police post. No public transport to Chile; wild but beautiful place. From Colonia Sarmiento you can reach Esquel (448 km.), at the southern edge of the Lake District (see page 120). The first 210 km. from Sarmiento are paved, then it is mostly a dirt or all-weather road, though short stretches have been paved.

Perito Moreno (population 1,700), at 400 metres, with an airport, is close to Lake Buenos Aires, which extends into Chile as Lake General Carrera. Also nearby are Lakes Belgrano and Burmeister, and the source of the River Deseado. Daily buses (US$2) to Los Antiguos (service station) on Lake Buenos Aires (67 km. along Route 520) surrounded by orchards and where *pejerrey* can be caught. Halfway is Las Chilcas where Indian remains are found. The famous Cuevas de las Manos, a series of galleries with 10,000-years-old paintings of human hands and of animals, are interesting but do not warrant a detour unless you are particularly interested in rock art; they are beyond the "sprayed-on" version in the cave—red, orange, black, white and green colours. (The canyon on the way there is, however, very beautiful.) 118 km. S of Perito Moreno on Route 40, a marked road goes directly to the caves (68 km.) No buses, but the tourist office at Perito Moreno can supply names of drivers who can take you there, US$55, to be split among a party of visitors. Try hitching. On leaving Perito Moreno on the way to the caves you will pass Cerro de El Volcán, its crater is accessible; after pasing the Gendarmería on your right, take the first left (dirt road) at the 3-road junction with Route 40. It is 12 km. to the path to the crater—ask permission at the Estancia to continue. LADE flies from Perito Moreno to Comodoro Rivadavia (US$12.70), Calafate and Río Gallegos. Hitch-hikers to the S are warned that, outside the tourist season (Jan.-mid-Feb.), it is usually quicker to head for the coast at Caleta Olivia and go S from there than to take the road via Gobernador Gregores and Piedra Buena.

Hotels at Perito Moreno *Belgrano,* D with shower, clean, no heating, with good restaurant; *Austral,* same rates, open Dec. to Feb., both on San Martín; *Fénix,* F; *Argentina y Chile,* F, basic. Food is very expensive in Perito Moreno.

Camping Parque Laguna in town, good hot showers, well shielded, US$2.50 p.p., (slide shows at the tourist office there), free camping by the river at the Recreo Municipal 1½ km. from town. Municipal camping in town, with showers, toilets, shade, US$1 for tent, US$0.50 p.p., cars extra.

Exchange US dollars can be exchanged at *Hotel Austral* and *Hotel Belgrano,* former gives better rates. Difficult to exchange travellers cheques.

There are 3 routes from Perito Moreno to Coyhaique in Chile: Perito Moreno to Chile Chico, then by twice-weekly ferry boat across Lake Buenos Aires, and then on by road to Coyhaique (very little public transport); Perito Moreno to Río Gueuguel, Paso Huemules, Coyhaique; Perito Moreno to Río Mayo, Coyhaique Alto, Coyhaique. There is a bus connection from Caleta Olivia (see below) through Los Antiguos (border with Chile) every Mon. and Thurs., and back to Caleta Olivia every Tues. and Fri., with Empresa Comi.

The road to Fitz Roy, 110 km. S of Comodoro Rivadavia, is paved, and a major short-cut now bypasses Puerto Deseado. Fitz Roy to Piedra Buena (2,600 inhabitants, see page 135) is unpaved, but paving is complete (although in very bad condition) from Piedra Buena to Río Gallegos (231 km.). Fitz Roy (named for the captain of Darwin's *Beagle*) is a tiny town, only two small *hosterías,* very primitive, not recommended. Better stay 22 km. N at **Caleta Olivia** on Route 3 (13,400 inhabitants); hotels *Residencial Robert, Grand* and one other, all D; and camping at Yacht Club. Caleta Olivia is the urban centre for important oilfields, and is near Pico Truncado, the gas field which feeds the pipeline to Buenos Aires.

About halfway between Comodoro Rivadavia and Puerto Deseado, some 5 km. S of Fitz Roy, where the new short-cut starts, a road first goes S then SW 106 km. across bleak *estancia* country to a national park area called Bosque Petrificado, where there is a petrified forest, 70,000 years old, of fallen araucaria trees, nearly 3 metres round and 15-20 metres long: a remarkable sight. Taxi, Sarmiento to forests, US$7-15. It is best to do the trip by taxi or in groups, as tyre punctures are a menace.
    There are in fact three sites you can visit: the Bosque Petrificado José Ormachea, due W of Comodoro Rivadavia, about 140 km. by road (116 km. paved—the unpaved part is practically impassable in the wet season), 32 km. S of Sarmiento, in Chubut; the Víctor Szlapelis, some 40 km. further SW along the same road; and Monumento Natural Bosques Petrificados, W of Puerto Deseado in Santa Cruz, surrounding the Laguna Grande on a road SW from Fitz Roy, 113 km. away.
    South of Comodoro Rivadavia (254 km.), at Tres Cerros, is a new ACA hotel, C, quite attractive. At Piedra Negra, the previous turn-off for Puerto Deseado, there is a cheap hotel, *Florida Negra.* The only other building is a police post.

About 300 km. S of Comodoro Rivadavia is **Puerto Deseado,** with a population of 3,750 (airport), at the mouth of a river which drains Lake Buenos Aires, far to the W. (Hotels: *Los Acantilados*, C, and *Colón*, D.) The town was founded on July 15, 1884; its harbour takes large ships. A local tourist attraction is the Cañadón de las Bandurrias, sometimes known as the Grotto of Lourdes, 40 metres high. Nearby are islands with penguins and other birds, including the unique grey cormorant; local launches available. Lake Buenos Aires is reached by road in 7 hours; 280 km. to Las Heras, on to Perito Moreno, on the lake, 177 km., and a further 72 km. to the Chilean border at Chile Chico. This can only be crossed by walking across the river (you will wade waist-deep) or by going in a 4-wheel drive car.

It was at Puerto Deseado that a Welshman in Cavendish's expedition of 1586 gave the name of *pengwyn* (white head) to a certain strange-looking bird. It is only fair to relate the opposing theory that the name is derived from a Spanish word, *pingüe*, meaning fat.

Local holidays Jan 31 (St. John Bosco); Oct. 9 (Coat of Arms day).

From Puerto Deseado to Santa Cruz by the old road is about 470 km. Some 156 km. short of Santa Cruz and 4 km. off Route 3, it reaches **San Julián** (officially founded on December 17, 1901, population of 4,480), the best place for breaking the 925 km. run from Comodoro Rivadavia to Río Gallegos. There is much wildlife in the area: red and grey foxes, *guanacos*, wildcats in the mountains, rheas, etc. The main activities are sheep raising for export, fish canning, and production of kaolin and clay. Clay grinding can be seen at Molienda Santa Cruz and ceramics made at the Escuela Provincial No.4. There is a regional museum. The ruins of Florida Blanca, a colony founded in 1870 by Antonio Viedma, can be visited. The cascade of San Julián is formed by two different tides. Punta Caldera is a popular summer beach. The first Christian mass in Argentina was held here after Magellan had executed a member of his crew. Francis Drake also put in here to hang Thomas Doughty, after amiably taking breakfast with him. Near San Julián (15 km.) is Cabo Curioso beach, with an attractive natural cave.

Hotels *Municipal*, Av. Costanera and 25 de Mayo, very nice, well-run, good value, D, but no restaurant. *Residencial Sada*, on San Martín, E, nice, clean, hot water, own bathroom; *Piedrabuena*; *Argentino* on Urquiza and Saavedra; *Residencial 9 de Julio*, and *Hotel Colonial*, both F. Also older *Colón*, D, Av. San Martin 301 and *Águila*, F, friendly, clean. Good municipal campsite at town entrance, all facilities, but not suitable for tents, Av. Costanera between Rivadavia and Roca.

Restaurants *Sportsman*, Mitre and 25 de Mayo; *Dos Anclas*, Berutti 1080; *Mi Refugio*, Mitre and Vélez Sársfield, *Soc. Chilena de Socorros Mutuos*, Ameghino 961; *Astra* on Route 3. Restaurant at San Martín 1375. Bars and tearooms: *Nos Amis*, Ameghino 1091; *Sweet Helen*, San Martín 485, *Aero Bar*, J. B. Alberdi and Pellegrini. Dancing at *Franoi*, 25 de Mayo 1198.

Post Office At Belgrano and Av. San Martín; telephone exchange also.

Banks Banco de la Nación on Mitre and Belgrano, and Banco de la Provincia de Santa Cruz on San Martín and Moreno.

Pharmacy *Del Pueblo* on San Martín 570. Hospital on Av. Costanera between Roca and Magallanes. Good wire car-windscreen protectors for US$5.

Air Weekly services to Río Gallegos, other routes end in Buenos Aires; many connect with flights from Comodoro Rivadavia by Austral and Aerolíneas.

Bus Transportadora Patagónica comes from Río Gallegos en route to Buenos Aires; Transportes Staller goes weekly to Lago Posadas stopping in Gobernador Gregores, Hotel Riera, Las Horquetas, Caracoles and Río Blanco. Transportes El Cordillerano cover the previous route but also stop at Olivia.

Santa Cruz, one of the best of the coastal harbours (airport) is near the mouth of the Santa Cruz river which drains Lake Argentino. Founded on December 1, 1878 and capital of Santa Cruz province until 1904. A deep-water port is being built 22 km. outside Santa Cruz at Punta Quilla. Population 3,000 (ACA *Hostería*, D; *Hotel Anel Aike*, D). Isla Monte León, 66 km. away (Route 1601, then Route 3 and dirt track) has walruses, penguins, beaches, fishing and camping facilities.

An unpaved road (Route 521) runs NW from San Julián to Route 40 along the foothills of the Andes. About halfway is **Gobernador Gregores** (*Hotel San Francisco*, acceptable, similarly *Adelino*, C), with petrol pump.

ARGENTINA 135

At **Piedra Buena,** 35 km. W of Santa Cruz (10 km. N of Piedra Buena unpaved, but paved road to Río Gallegos and to Comodoro Rivadavia) is ACA motel, simple, functional but good, warm and nice food (E), also campsites N of town on Route 3. ACA breakdown station at Km. 247 on Route 3. Police tend to ask motorists for petrol or cigarettes on the road going S. Saves you from 2 hr.-long car search. The *Select* restaurant is very dear for what it offers. Route 1603 (unpaved, no petrol) from Piedra Buena to Calafate runs along the edge of a plateau with occasional panoramic views across the valley of the River Santa Cruz below. Then at about 170 km. it drops down into the valley itself to follow the river into the hills and to Lake Argentino. A pleasant run, without being spectacular.

Río Gallegos, at the mouth of the Río Gallegos, the capital of Santa Cruz Province, is 265 km. S of Santa Cruz; it has a deep-water port with a dry-dock. The tidal range here during spring tides may be as high as 16 metres. There is a large trade in wool and sheepskins. The town has recently improved greatly, and has a good shopping centre. (The cave paintings at Laguna Azul, 60 km. from Río Gallegos, are now reported not available for visiting.) Population: 42,000. Foundation Day: Dec. 9, 1885. Prices are high, and rise further in January each year. Museum at Perito Moreno 35. The Regional Provincial Museum has collections of local flora, fauna, rock samples. ACA service centre. 134 km. S of Río Gallegos there is a penguin colony at Cabo Vírgenes: follow Route 526. Cheap sheepskins (tanned) and very warm leather coats (*gamulanes*) at Puerto Aymond factory of Mr. Szasack (half-price compared with Buenos Aires). Handicraft market at Roca 658, open 1300-2000.

Hotels *Santa Cruz*, Roca and Rivadavia, C, without breakfast; *Comercio*, Roca 1302, C, good, with restaurant; *Gran París*, Roca 1030, D; *Oviedo*, Libertad 740, C; *Ampuero*, F Sphur 18, E; *Carrera*, España and Presidente Roca; *Nacha's Residencial*, Rivadavia 122, F, clean; *Río Turbio*, Zapiola 486 (opp. bus station for Punta Arenas), D, shared bath, English spoken, good. Strongly recommended: *Alonso*, Corrientes 33, C, simple, very clean and comfortable; *Covadonga*, Roca 1214, C, fairly good; *Maddalena*, Av. Roca 1127, E, central, quiet, cold showers; *Viejo Lafuente*, Vélez Sársfield 68/70, F p.p., reports vary; *Pensión Belgrano*, Calle Belgrano 119, very cheap, clean, has good restaurant; *Las Vegas*, Corrientes 257, D; *Puerto Santa Cruz*, Zapiola 238, F (more in season), with breakfast, tatty; *Residencial Fer War*, 25 de Mayo 196, E; *Cabo Vírgenes*, Rivadavia 252, and *Laguna Azul*, Estrada and Urquiza, both D; *Puerto Montt*, Roca 1614, E, cooking facilities available, also at a private house at Vélez Sársfield 505, same price range; *Residencial Internacional*, at Roca and Sphur 78, E, with heating, friendly; *Colonial*, Urquiza y Rivadavia, E, shower, friendly, clean, can be noisy; *El Trébol*, no sign, Rivadavia 122, F; *Residencial 9 de Julio*, cheapest, on Av. 9 de Julio; *Tehuelche*, 16 km. from ferry at Primera Angostura on junction of Punta Arenas-Río Gallegos route, F, old fashioned bar. *El Palenque*, inexpensive, good value.

N.B. Accommodation is hard to find in Río Gallegos because of the number of transient workers in town. Apparently no camping is allowed around Río Gallegos because it is a military zone. One is not allowed to take photographs either, for the same reason. "Car-camping" allowed, however, on waste ground opposite ACA garage, on seafront.

Restaurants Plenty and good, some specializing in sea food. *La Casa de Miguel*, Roca 1284, good. *Restaurant Díaz*, Roca 1157, good and cheap, recommended. *Montecarlo*, Zapiola 558, good seafood, not the cheapest; opp. is good *heladería*. *El Palenque*, Corrientes 73, good. *Hotel Carrera* has good but expensive breakfast, on España and Pres. Roca.

Car Hire Andrés Etura, Sarmiento 204..

Motorcycle Mechanic Juan Carlos Topcic, Costa Rica 25, friendly and helpful.

Bank of London and South America, Sarmiento 47. Open 1500-1600. Banco de Santa Cruz; *Sur Cambio*, Calle España (no travellers' cheques); *Casas de cambio*, best rates. Change travellers' cheques in Río Gallegos if going to Calafate, where it can be done even less easily; good rates at Cambio El Pingüino (Zapiola 443); may also change European and South American currencies.

Chilean Consulate Mariano Moreno 144, Mon.-Fri., 0900-1300 and 1500-1700.

Tourist Office at junction of Perito Moreno and Zapiola (police station on same block), friendly, helpful. (Also Libertad 156.) They will phone round hotels for you; they tend to get very booked up.

By Road Poor road to turn-off to Puerto Natales, then good road to Punta Arenas, 303 km. (one lane only); taxi US$50-70; Punta Arenas via Puerto Williams will cost some US$140, with boat trip, one night at the port and a flight to Punta Arenas; buses (US$10.35) Wed. and Sun. at 0900, Tues., Thurs. and Fri. at 1300 by Expreso Pingüino (booking office Zapiola 455, 0800-1250 and 1500-1930 Mon.-Fri. 0800-1230 and 1530-1900 on Sat.), take 6 hours including border-crossing process, now greatly simplified following the settlement of the Beagle Channel dispute.

Daily to Río Turbio: Expreso Pingüino goes at 1130 (1200 on Tues., Thurs., and Sat.), 6 hrs.,

136 **ARGENTINA**

US$15; San Caferino (Entre Ríos 371) Mon., Thurs. at 1130, US$12.30; one bus on Sat at 0830, US$11.50, to Puerto Natales. Make sure your car papers are in order if driving to Puerto Natales, Chile (go first to Tourist Office for necessary documents, then to the customs office at the port, at the end of San Martín, very uncomplicated); a weekly boat, but no air service. Bus to Puerto Madryn 28 hrs. Route 40, which goes to Calafate (312 km.) is paved for about 200 km., with an ACA motel at La Esperanza (146 km.). A provincial road that goes west from Route 3 to Calafate is rough. A better alternative is Route 1603, which branches off Route 3 some 43 km. from Piedra Buena. Occasional ships and buses (48 hrs.), to Buenos Aires, 2,575 km. Buses (Transportadora Patagónica, Gobernador Lista 330, Tel.: 2330) Tues., Thurs., Sat. at 1930, 14 hrs., also to Comodoro Rivadavia, 808 km., stops at Fitz Roy daily at 2200, arr. 1000 next day, US$26.50; Calafate (Patagónica, 4 times a week at midday in summer, 6 hrs., US$13, leaves Calafate on way back at 0600), Esquel and Bariloche. Hitchhiking to Buenos Aires is possible in about 3½ days; appearance important. Car parts and repairs at Repuestos Sarmiento, on Sarmiento, owner very friendly and helpful.

By Air Flights to Buenos Aires; Austral (office on Av. Roca), daily, stops at Comodoro Rivadavia, Trelew and Bahía Blanca; LADE, Tues. and Sat. at 0800, 11 hrs. with several stops, coffee and sandwiches, some discounts; Aerolíneas Argentinas cheap night flights are booked up several days in advance, US$75 (even in winter) also day (US$120) flights available. AA's Buenos Aires-Auckland, N.Z. flight (once a week) stops at Río Gallegos. Numerous flights to Ushuaia (Tierra del Fuego), direct or via Río Grande (LADE, US$22, cheaper than by bus, always booked). To Río Grande, 40 mins. LADE, or Aerolíneas Argentinas. Aerolíneas also has flights between Río Gallegos and Punta Arenas (Chile). LADE flights to Calafate US$14, 2 a day in summer (about 3 a week out of season); to Río Turbio (2 per week). LADE flights also to Bariloche via Santa Cruz, San Julián, Puerto Deseado, Comodoro Rivadavia (3 a week, US$33), Trelew (twice a week) and Esquel, twice a week, US$40. To Comodoro Rivadavia with Aerolíneas Argentinas, daily, 1 hr; LADE to Perito Moreno, Tues. and Fri. Personal controls and luggage search at Río Gallegos, delays of 30 min. to 2 hrs. Book seats in Buenos Aires to avoid difficulties with departures. Taxi to town, US$2.50, no bus, hitching from car park is easy. **N.B.** Flights may leave early, sometimes up to 40 mins.

From Río Gallegos a railway runs 260 km. to **Río Turbio** (6,000 people—no real tourist interest) where is found Argentina's largest coalfield; reserves are estimated at 450m tons and the state coal company YCF is building a deep-water port at Punta Loyola to service it. *Hostería Capipe*, Dufour, C; *Hotel Gato Negro*, expensive (D) and poor, *Victoria*, H.G. and *El Pionero* are cheaper, E. Ask at YCF office in Río Gallegos for possibility of taking the coal train to Río Turbio (steam locomotives, 10-12 hrs.); it usuallly leaves at 0900, passengers free, lots of wild life to be seen. Train stops 3 km. from town, hitch or walk. Río Turbio is reported to have better travel connections than Puerto Natales and once in Río Turbio it is easy to catch a local bus into Chile. (Río Turbio to Argentine border post: 3 km.,—bus, US$0.30, last at 2230, some reports suggest that there are no buses either side of the border, though—a further 4 km. to Chilean post and then 14 km. to paved section of road connecting Puerto Natales with Punta Arenas.) The bus from Río Turbio to Puerto Natales (31 km.) connects with the bus arriving from Río Gallegos. There is a LADE office and Expreso Pingüino runs daily at 0600 (5 hrs.) to Río Gallegos, but flights are cheaper and avoid the numerous passport checks as well as the essentially uninteresting ride. *Restaurant El Ringo*, near bus station, will shelter you from the wind. ACA station and motel between Río Gallegos and Calafate on unpaved but good Route 40, at La Esperanza; no direct bus connection Calafate-Río Turbio; you must change from the Calafate-Río Gallegos bus to the Río Gallegos-Río Turbio bus at La Esperanza, where there is a 10 hr. wait.

Calafate (population 1,500), on Lake Argentino, 320 km. NW of Río Gallegos, is an interesting, developing town. There is a chapel dedicated to Santa Teresa in the centre; behind it Calle Perito Moreno gently climbs the large hill S of the town, from which one can see the silhouette of the S end of the Andes, the Laguna Redonda and Isla de la Soledad on Lake Argentino. It is the southern gateway to the Parque Nacional de los Glaciares, which is 50 km. away (the northern end is at Lake Viedma). On the alluvial plain by the lake there are many interesting birds, and in the other direction there is scope for good hill-walking. At the far end of the lake (80 km.) the Ventisquero Moreno, one of the few glaciers in the world that is growing larger, descends to the surface of the water over a five-km. frontage and a height of about 60 metres. In a cycle of roughly three years it advances across the lake, cutting the Brazo Rico off from the Canal de los Témpanos; then the pressure of water in the Brazo Rico breaks up the ice and reopens the channel. Pieces break off and float away as icebergs. When visiting the glacier, do not go down too close to the lake as these icebergs can cause great waves when breaking off, and wash people off rocks. From Calafate there are daily minibus trips in the morning, Nov.-Feb. only, to the glacier's edge (return, US$11 from park administration area, Calle Dr. E. Bustillo and Av. del

Libertador), returning in the late afternoon; you have to pay return fare to go there and single to come back. Taxis, US$50 for 4 passengers round trip. There are four tourist agencies in Calafate running day trips. The ACA guest house gives information. The Parque Nacional truck leaves Calafate most mornings at 0800 and may give lifts (but arrive at 0500!); take food with you, as only expensive snacks and coffee are available at the glacier. Colourful cave paintings some 8 km. from Calafate, walking through the fields bordering the lake, or 12 km. by road. The Lake Argentino area is very popular; booking all transport in advance is a must. Out of season, trips to the glacier are difficult to arrange, but one can gather a party of up to 8 and hire a taxi, about 1 hr. 20 mins. one way; try asking at *Motel La Loma* (where they have 2 station wagons/kombis) or taxis at *Hotel Avenida* (for 4 people). The store *Las Plantas* in Calafate is helpful with travel arrangements and exchange. The tourist office has a list of taxis but undertakes no arrangements; it is helpful but some information may be incorrect, so check. There is a district hospital in Calafate.

Camping and fishing permits, limited to official sites, from the Parque Nacional rangers in Calafate. Although the mountains are snow capped, you can camp out in the pleasant woods around the lake in summer and even swim in it on warm days. (Campsite details below.) ACA bungalows at glacier's edge (10 blocks from it) charge US$30 without breakfast a day; sleep 4 (staple foods for sale); there are 10 bungalows, 4 beds each, bath and wood-burning stove, restaurant (good) and *confitería* (poor). In summer, they are very popular and difficult to book; there is often no food available (especially out of season), so, as cooking is not permitted in the cabins, take food to eat cold. There is utter stillness apart from squawking flocks of parakeets and an occasional roar as ice falls off the glacier and thunders into the lake. People flock to the February rural show and camp out with much revelry; dances and *asados* (barbecued sides of sheep). There are also barbecues and rodeo etc. on Día de la Tradición on November 10, and on February 15 (Lago Argentino Day).

Hotels *Los Alamos*, A, new comfortable, good food and service, has a mixed-media show, with dinner afterwards, recommended; *Kalken*, B, restaurant; *ACA Motel Calafate*, Av. Libertador 1153, C for non-members, much less for members (can be booked at ACA, Buenos Aires), extremely popular, capacity 27 rooms, washing facilities, bungalows with good restaurant; next to this is ACA *Hostería El Calafate*, on Manzana 36, D, modern, good view, 26 rooms; *El Quijote*, C, friendly, comfortable, good restaurant; *Carlitos*, Comandante Espora, C, modern, clean and very friendly, good restaurant; *Avenida*, Av. San Martín, D, with and without bath; *Tehuel Aike*, Av. Libertador 992, C, good meals, clean and modern; *Michelangelo*, Espora, C, modern, clean, excellent, reasonable, good restaurant, will accept travellers' cheques in payment (at a poor rate, though); *Hostería Kau-Yatún*, C, with bath, many facilities, 25 de Mayo (10 blocks from town centre), old *estancia* house, comfortable, barbecues, horses for hire; *Upsala*, Comandante Espora 139, C, with bath, good and clean; *La Loma Motel*, B in season (Jan., Feb., March)—C in low season, Roca and 15 de Febrero (can be booked in Buenos Aires at Av. Callao 433, 4° H,Tel.: 40-7476/40-9123), with bath, breakfast included, excellent view, modern, multilingual, restaurant, tea room, also has bungalows (14 rooms with bath) E p.p with special rate for International Youth Hostel members and owners of *South American Handbook*, also has two kombis for excursions for guests (run on most days); *Kapenke*, Gob. Gregores 1194, A; *Glanesa*, Av. Libertador 1108, C, central, bar; *Hostería Provincial*, C, with tea room; *Amado*, Av. San Martín. Several slightly cheaper hotels but none less than E, e.g. *Hospedaje Jorgito*, Gob. Moyano 934, F, clean, hot water, heating, breakfast extra, always full; *Hospedaje Echevarría*, Libertador 989, E, quiet, clean, recommended; *Casa 11 (casa familial)*, Los Inmigrantes 11, F, clean, hot shower, cooking facilities, crowded in season but recommended; recommended bed and breakfast at Espora 60, E p.p. Calafate has a tourist office from which caravans, tents (US$2 each, sleep 4) and 4-berth *cabañas* (US$3 p.p.) may be hired, showers extra. Note that all hotels except ACA are open only from October to April. Some private houses offer accommodation, two blocks away from main street. Ask at tourist office if in difficulty.

Camping The nearest camping sites with sanitary facilities (2) are 10 km. from the glacier. No tents for rent in Calafate. Sites include one near ACA service station in Calafate, US$1 p.p. A municipal camp site, US$2.50, and US$2.50 for warm showers, no tents for rent, but beds in trailers, US$3.75, near airport. Park *refugio* is free, with firing for cooking and heating supplied free, suitable for 3. Permission obtainable from the Intendencia in Calafate, some 77 km. away. There is no water at the *refugio*. Take enough food and drink with you. Key from warden at the site. Also two free camp sites by lake—the lower one sometimes floods (no facilities). Camp site with facilities at Lago Roca (S area of the Glaciares National Park), good restaurant, fishing, boating, horseriding, beautiful scenery, cave paintings nearby. Hostería and Autocamping on road to Lake Viedma (Route 40) at the base of Cerro Fitzroy (or Chaltén). Horses for hire.

Restaurants *ACA Grill*; *Pizzería Onelli* (good), stays open out of season; *Michelangelo*, Thomas

138 ARGENTINA

Espora, recommended; *La Posta*, restaurant and barbecues; *El Fogón del Lago*, opp. military HQ, covered, for barbecues; *Tehuel Aike*, tea rooms; *La Casita de la Loma*, one block from chapel, good cakes and chocolates, beautiful view; *Maktub*, tea room, excellent pastries, also at *Residencial Glanesa*, *Bar Don Diego de la Noche*, at end of main road in direction of the glacier, good atmosphere. At Moreno glacier, *ACA Unidad Turística* has a restaurant and a bar, expensive.

Bank Travellers' cheques and cash may be changed at the Banco de la Provincia de Santa Cruz (Av. del Libertador) which charges US$15 on top of the usual commission, but avoid changing US$ at the administration of the ACA motel, which charges 30% commission. YPF garage gives good rates for cash; also at reception of *La Loma Motel* for travellers' cheques.

Tourist Information At the Intendencia del Parque Nacional los Glaciares, opp. ACA Motel on Av. Libertador. Tourist office not Argentina's best but friendly (has no 'phone, so you must walk to the hotel of your choice to check on vacancies); the area's infrastructure still requires development, especially accommodation. Tour to Moreno glacier information available here, US$10. Good map available from National Park office. Hotel prices detailed on poster at the airport and on large chart at tourist office. Sr. Jorge Antolín Solache, Casilla de Correo 36, 9405 Calafate (Tel.: 16, Dec.-May), rest of the year Callao 433-4°H, 1022 Buenos Aires (Tel.: 40-7476), to whom we are very grateful for updating the Calafate section, has kindly offered to provide any information to travellers in the region. He speaks English, French, Italian and Portuguese.

Travel Agents Interlagos, Libertador 1175, do excursions and car-rentals. To Moreno glacier at 0900 return 1800, w/o lunch US$10. *Cir Tur* at *Hotel Glanesa*. Lake Tours (Libertador 932) runs tours to the Moreno and Upsala glaciers, also changes travellers' cheques, as well as accepting them, and bus once a week to Río Gallegos (more expensive than flight but not so heavily booked). Cost of car hire for trip to Cerro Fitzroy about US$200 (4-8 people). Also try at *Motel La Loma*, whose prices are US$11 to Moreno glacier, or to Lago Roca, US$7 to Gualichu caves, US$25 p.p. to Fitz Roy (one day).

Film and slide show (not very good) about Calafate, the Perito Moreno glacier and climbing the Cerro Torres at *Tío Cacho* discothèque, every night 2230, US$4, also good audiovisual at *La Posta* restaurant every day in summer, US$4.

How Reached By air from Río Gallegos (US$14, LADE, 2 a day in summer, out of season 3 per week) and Comodoro Rivadavia (often fully booked), US$33, Tues. only, also Río Grande (US$16, LADE), Ushuaia (US$20, LADE), 4 times a week and Perito Moreno, US$13 with LADE. To Esquel weekly on Tues., US$40. In winter there are often no flights for weeks if the weather is bad. The airport is about a ten-minute walk from the centre of town. Bus Calafate to Ushuaia requires four changes, and ferry; total cost of journey US$40. Transportadora Patagónica to Río Gallegos 4 times a week in summer at 0600, US$13, 6 hrs.; no buses in the winter to Río Gallegos. (Taxi van to Río Gallegos, 4 hrs., US$185, capacity 8). By a rough but interesting road from Santa Cruz, Route 1603 (Route 288 is 100 km. longer with two bridges replacing old ferry crossings), 5 or 6 hrs. by car, but not always possible after rain. From Esquel go via Perito Moreno, good accommodation; then via Gobernador Gregores (see page 134), or better via Piedra Buena and stay at ACA motel, making journey only 50 km. longer but avoids possible delay at ferry crossings near Lake Viedma. Very lonely road, occasional *guanacos*, flamingoes and armadillos, but mostly sheep. Few shrubs or trees. Sparse population. Taxi to Río Gallegos, 4 hours, US$30 irrespective of number of passengers, up to 5 people. There are no buses to Chile. The Río Gallegos-Calafate road trip is worth while (if going by car, but not the Río Gallegos-Calafate bus trip!), for the number of animals and birds one sees, takes about 6 hrs. (323 km.), reasonable road but very lonely, and no help in case of a breakdown: you need to be entirely self-supporting. It is reported the road trip from Calafate to Punta Arenas is very interesting: from Calafate take Route 507 (although Route 40 is shorter when passable), unpaved (209 km.) to La Esperanza, where there is a petrol pump and modest hotel; thence to Río Turbio, then paved road (14 km.) to Puerto Natales and 245 km. to Punta Arenas, 42 km. paved. The government is planning to open the stretch from La Esperanza to Cancha Carrera (126 km.), then to La Laurita (63 km.) and on 14 km. to Puerto Natales. The easiest way to Río Turbio for Puerto Natales is to fly to Río Gallegos then take the daily bus; this avoids a 10-hour wait to change buses at La Esperanza.

N.B. The road between Calafate and Torres del Paine National Park has been reopened, but requires 4-wheel drive as it is incomplete, and several large rivers have to be forded. It is nearly impossible to hitchhike from Calafate to Perito Moreno.

Excursions Travel by road to the most interesting spots is limited and may require expensive taxis; the best connections are to Perito Moreno. Tours can be arranged at travel agencies, *Motel La Loma*, *Hotel Avenida* or with taxi drivers at the airport who await arrivals. Two recommended walks: (1) From the Centro Cívico in Calafate, visit Capilla Santa Teresita in Plaza San Martín; behind it is Calle Perito Moreno; walk to the top of the hill for a view of Calafate. Then go S to the Río Calafate, then to the new section of the town, where the ACA grill is. (2) Leave from the Intendencia del Parque, go N to the hanging bridge on Río Calafate (5 blocks), follow the river along cultivated fields and orchards to Laguna de Los Cisnes, a bird reserve, with flamingoes, ducks, etc.

ARGENTINA 139

Walk down to Lake Argentino; 8 km. along the lakeside are the painted caves at Punta Gualichú. Unfortunately the paintings have greatly deteriorated but the caves are of geological interest. Excursion to La Gerónima, Lago Roca, 80 km. S from Calafate. Trout and salmon fishing, climbing, walking, camping and branding of cattle in summer. To Puerto Irma, fascinating geological formations caused by erosion, on the edge of Lake Argentino, 14 km. from Calafate on the road to Río Gallegos.

A worthwhile trip is by motor-boat (120-150 passengers) from Punta Bandera, 50 km. from Calafate, to the Upsala glacier at the end of Lake Argentino, Lake Onelli and glacier and Spegazzini glacier, leaves 0800 daily from Punta Bandera, returns 1600. Cia. Paraíso de Navegación (9 de Julio y Gregores) runs the lake excursions, tickets US$30 not including transport to the port (US$9). The boat passes by the 30-metre high glacier; it is reported however that the master often decides the weather is too rough and does not go to Upsala. Tourist Office is not always helpful about complaints. Put inshore and cross a little forest to reach the small Lake Onelli, quiet and very beautiful, beech trees on one side, and ice-covered mountains on the other. Small icebergs in the lake. Out of season it is extremely difficult to get to the glacier. Smaller boats (39 passengers) may run in winter; sometimes they don't run because of the danger of the glaciers "calving". Book tickets at Empresa Paraíso, and at least two days in advance; if you can't get tickets try to catch the boat in Punta Bandera with tickets from a travel agency, your own car (no car hire) or a taxi (US$10 p.p. round trip); bus Calafate-Punta Bandera US$9, at 0700. On the road from Calafate to Punta Bandera, at the foot of Cerro Comisión, is a rock formation that looks like a herd of elephants facing you.

Another worthwhile excursion is to the N end of the Glaciares National Park to Cerro Fitzroy and Cerro Torres, 230 km. from Calafate; organized trip US$24 p.p. return; a new highway has been built from Calafate to Lake Viedma, journey is about 4 hours. There is a very friendly hostel there, *Lago Viedma*, run by Juan and Mónica Vásquez, providing also a restaurant, shop, horse-hire and guide service. The Fitzroy massif can be seen from the hostel, and one can walk for 3 hours to see Cerro Torre, where there is a *refugio*. There is a base camp at Cerro Fitzroy. To reach the base camp here, and at Cerro Torres, one must ford the Río Fitzroy, which is not always easy. Ask at the *gendarmería* (border-police) in Calafate if you can join their truck which goes once or twice a week. On the way to Cerro Fitzroy (often bad weather) on Route 40, is the Southern Astronomical Observatory, managed by the Observatory of La Plata.

Transport in the Fitzroy area can be next to impossible. Arrange either through travel agencies in Calafate or contact Sr. and Sra. Vásquez (see above). There is a *hostería* at Fitzroy and a camping site nearby, US$2.50 no matter how many days (food very expensive). A certificate is required from the National Park Office in Calafate to camp elsewhere.

Organized trips to the Glaciares National Park are too short to appreciate it fully; either go on a tour bus, then camp (good gear essential) or hire a taxi/minibus. Lake Tours charge US$200 for up to 8 people, US$300 to take you and return later to collect you; private drivers (e.g. Martín Drake, Bo. Plan Alborada 390—speaks English) charge US$300 for up to 8 to take you and collect later (also does similar arrangements for the Moreno glacier).

Tierra del Fuego is the island at the extreme south of South America. It is bounded by the Magellan Strait to the north, the Atlantic Ocean to the east, the Beagle Channel to the south—which separates it from the southern islands—and by the Whiteside, Gabriel, Magdalena and Cockburn Channels etc, which divide it from the islands to the west. The western side belongs to Chile and the eastern to Argentina. The local Ona Indians are now extinct. Throughout Tierra del Fuego the main roads are narrow and gravelled. The exception is the road for about 50 km. out of Porvenir (Chile), which is being widened. The south has beautiful lakes, woods and mountain scenery. Part of this country is a new National Parks Reserve: trout and salmon in nearly all the lakes and rivers, and in summer wild geese, ducks, 152 other species of birds, and imported musk rats and beaver. Local tax exemptions apply throughout Tierra del Fuego.

N.B. Argentine time is normally one hour ahead of Chilean time.

Books: *Tierra del Fuego* (3rd edition), in English, by Rae Natalie Prosser de Goodall, US$10 (obtainable in Ushuaia and Buenos Aires), colourful maps by the same author. Also *Tierra del Fuego: The Fatal Lodestone*, by Eric Shipton, and *Uttermost Part of the Earth*, by E. Lucas Bridges. Available in U.S.A.: *Birds of Isla Grande (Tierra del Fuego)* by Philip S. Humphrey, and *A Guide to the Birds of South America*, by Rodolphe Meyer de Schauensee.

Feb.-March is a good time to visit because of the beautiful autumn colours.

Camping is very easy in Tierra del Fuego. You can, if so inclined, camp at most service stations. Many towns have municipal campsites which are either free or cost up to US$1. Private campsites can be very expensive.

There are two ways of crossing the Straits of Magellan to Tierra del Fuego. Coming S from Río Gallegos, an unpaved road turns left for Punta Delgada (1 hotel, 2 *hosterías*). (On the road Río Gallegos-Punta Delgada is Laguna Azul—3 km. off main road in an old crater; an ibis breeding ground, beautiful colours). A 30-minute crossing can be made by fast modern ferry from Punta Delgada to

Punta Espora (no hotel—if desperate, ask the lighthouse keeper). The boats, which take 4 lorries and 2 cars, run every hour, with schedule determined by tides and a 1200-1400 lunch hour rest. Under normal conditions they run from 0800 to 2100 daily, with tidal breaks lasting 4 hours (autumn and winter timetable). Ferry-operators accept US dollars or Argentine or Chilean currencies. If going by car, do not go before 1000, as first crossings are taken by buses, etc. However, there is no bus service from Punta Espora (or Punta Delgada); buses to and from the island only through Porvenir. From Punta Espora (Bahía Aril is ferry terminal) a road runs through Chilean territory to San Sebastián (Chile) and 14 km. further to San Sebastián (Argentina) (usually 15 min. delay in crossing borders), Río Grande and Ushuaia. There is an Esso petrol pump 38 km. from Punta Espora. Accommodation is scarce in the Chilean part (except for Porvenir—see page 443), and it is not always possible to cross it in one day because of the irregularity of the ferry. It is sometimes possible, coming and going, to spend the night at the guest house of ENAP at Cerro Sombrero (petrol there for employees only, but if you are running out, they may help), but do not count on it. Try Hostería Karu-Kinka.

The road from Río Gallegos goes on to Punta Arenas, from where (dock at Tres Puentes 5 km. E of town) there are two regular crossings a day to Porvenir (passenger US$4, motor car US$33, 2½-3 hours; there is a passenger saloon with small cafetería; get on first and you are invited on the bridge, get on last and you stand outside in the cold), at 0900 and 1400 (Sun. 0900), check from Porvenir at 1230 and 1630 (Sun. 1700); if you want to continue, Senkovic buses to Río Grande connect with 0900 ferries on Sat. and Wed. A 225-km. road runs from Porvenir E to Río Grande (6 hours) via San Sebastián; or by alternative route through Cerro Sombrero (see previous paragraph). On Chilean side of Tierra del Fuego, petrol available only at Porvenir. Reservations must be made at the hi-fi shop at Bulnes 637, Punta Arenas. The Argentine Consul in Punta Arenas is at Calle Valdivia 961 (Tel.: 22887). Border police at San Sebastián will sometimes arrange lifts to Ushuaia or Río Grande. Hitching after San Sebastián is easy. Distances are roughly as follows in this area: Border with Chile at Monte Aymont; to Río Gallegos 73 km.; road to Río Grande via Kimiri-Aike (114 km. from Río Gallegos)—no buses; from here to Punta Delgada 30 km.; Punta Delgada-Punta Espora (ferry, free for pedestrians) 20 km.; on to Punta Sombrero (60 km.) and San Sebastián (60 km.) reaching Río Grande 80 km. on. The best way to hitch from Río Gallegos to Punta Arenas is to take any lorry as far as the turn-off for Punta Delgada ferry. Then there is plenty of Chilean traffic from Punta Delgada to Punta Arenas. Hotel San Gregorio will put you up if you get stuck near the turn-off.

Entering Argentina from Chile, insist on getting an entry stamp for as long as you require—don't accept less.

The largest town in the Argentine part, with a population of 50,000 and growing, is

Ushuaia, the most southerly town in the world; its steep streets (there are mountains, the Cerro Martial, at the back of the town) overlook the green waters of the Beagle Channel, named after the ship in which Darwin sailed the Channel in 1832. It is reached from Buenos Aires by ship (monthly, US$32, 9 days) or plane (5 hours). There are impressive views of the snow-clad peaks, rivers, waterfalls and dense woods. There is a naval station at Isla de los Lobos. The people are engaged in sheep raising for the Río Grande *frigorífico*, timber cutting, fishing, and trapping, and Ushuaia's main street is lined with tax-free shops. There is a museum on the corner of Godoy and Maipú, on the sea front. A new road has been built between Ushuaia and Río Grande via Paso Garibaldi. Some skiing is done in the area. Ushuaia and its environs are worth a 2-3 day visit. Those arriving from Chile by road should report to Investigaciones on Kuanip 787. See Documents, page 148.

Hotels *Cabo de Hornos*, San Martín and Triunvirato, C, luxurious, TV, spotless, good value; *Las Lengas*, Goleta Florencia s/n, C, cold, no English spoken, breakfast only meal; *Maitén*, 12 de Octubre 138, D-C, good value, clean, English spoken by manager Herbert Locker, who is very helpful; *Canal Beagle*, Maipú 599, B (reductions for members of the ACA), good retaurant (catering usually for tour groups); *Albatros*, Maipú 505 and Lasserre, dark, clean, modern, B including breakfast; *Malvinas*, Deloqui 609, C, with bath, breakfast included, pleasant, helpful, central heating; *Antártida*, San Martín 1600, C, restaurant with fine views, recommended; *Capri*, San Martín 720, D, clean, friendly, permanent residents; *César*, San Martín 752, D, own bathroom, clean, no breakfast; *Mustapic*, Piedrabuena and Deloqui, friendly multi-lingual owner (Sr Miro, a Croat from Yugoslavia), C/D (may bargain lower), no singles, highly recommended, good breakfast, exceptionally clean, can leave luggage; *Ona*, 9 de Julio 27, on waterfront, all-night jazz club next door, E (without breakfast), heater in room, used by lorry drivers, difficult to get into. *Las Goletas* (no sign) Maipú 857 on waterfront, E, some rooms shared (3-6), in bunk beds, TV room (where they will allow sleepers if there is scarce accommodation), hot showers, heating. *Fernández*, Ochanaga 68, very friendly, hot water, good meals, D. *Ushuaia Apartment Hotel* for self-catering visitors, very friendly. Casa de Sra Hilda Sánchez, Deloqui 395 (corner Roca, Tel.: 92438), F, crowded, noisy,

ARGENTINA 141

clean, students and backpackers catered for; camping at the back, with use of facilities; cheap meals available. Rooms (reasonably priced) at home of Ismael Vargas, Kayen 394 (Tel.: 91125); Sra Vargas speaks English. Youth hostel in the Sports Complex. Lodging in Ushuaia has recently become rather a problem esp. Jan.-Feb., but even in winter hotels are very expensive. Enquire at Tourist Office for accommodation in private homes, and for campsites, some of which are free.

Camping At Almacén El Parque, Laserre y Magallanes, free, nice view, friendly, cold water, no bathrooms. At Lapataia, by forested shore of Lake Roca in Parque Nacional, with facilities for car and tent, US$1 p.p., caters for travellers without car, Dec.-March, including gas (18 km. from Ushuaia; weather can be bad). Can be reached by bus Jan.-Feb. Hot showers evenings, small shop, cafeteria. There is a free site by restaurant, with no facilities, on road to Parque Nacional about 4 km. from Ushuaia at Cascadas de Río Pipo. Camping at Monte Susana, 10 km. W, Ensenada, 14 km. W, and Río Olivia, 12 km. E of Ushuaia. Tents for hire at Parque Nacional Tierra del Fuego, US$3 per night.

Restaurants *Las Canelas*, on Av San Martín, good king crab; *Tío Rico* on San Martín is good. *Tante Elvira*, Av. San Martín 238 near Rumbo Sur—good food, expensive but probably best seafood in town. *Los Amigos*, San Martín, cheap; *Moustacchio*, San Martín, sea food, good value; *Los Inmortales*, on San Martín, good, cheap; *ACA Grill*, good value and food. *Restaurant-Hotel Canal Beagle*, Restaurant Hotel *Antártida*, San Martín 1600, limited choice, not very good. *Cafetería Acuario*, San Martín 124, pleasant. Cheap and good food at restaurant above the sports gymnasium at Maipú and 12 de Octubre. *Blanco y Negro Importaciones*, delicatessen; *Tío Carlos*, Colón 756, good *parrillada*; *Don Antonio*, Maipú y 9 de Julio, jazz bar, good atmosphere in wooden house; *Bar Ideal*, one of the few wooden houses left, good food and music. *Der Garten*, Swiss confitería, San Martín 620, in Galería shopping arcade, recommended. Excellent homemade chocolate sold at a shop at San Martín 785. *Panadería Primavera*, San Martín, good. The coffee bar at the airport is very expensive. Ask around for currently available *centolla* (king crab) and *cholga* (giant mussels). Food and drink (apart from the duty-free items) in Ushuaia are very expensive. Sados (with clean toilets) and Supercoop supermarkets on San Martín.

N.B. Restaurants here and elsewhere on Tierra del Fuego do not begin to serve until 2100-2130 in summer; it is advisable to book in advance in the high season.

N.B. also Cheap cigarettes, perfume, clothing, drink and chocolates available: local tax exemptions.

Car Hire Rentacar, San Martín 330, Tel.: 92185; Remisse, San Martín 987, Tel.: 92222.

Museum Museo Territorial, Maipú 173, open Mon.-Sat. 1600-2000, US$0.60, small but interesting display of early photos and artefacts of the local Indian tribes (4); relics from the missionaries and first settlers, etc. Also known as the "museum at the end of the world". Highly recommended.

Banks are open morning and afternoon in Ushuaia. Travellers' cheques can be changed at Banco de la Nación (San Martín and Rivadavia) at the official rate. No cash advance on Visa card available. In Southern Argentina it is easier to exchange cash than travellers' cheques outside banks. Change US dollars at Banco de Santa Cruz, Lasserre 140, no commission. Good rates at Monsieur Charles' shop, Av. San Martín; try also *El Globo Naranjo* (same street) or *Hotel Cabo de Hornos*.

Chilean Consulate on Maipú and Alapa.

Tourist Office Av. San Martín 524, office 3/4 (Tel.: 91423), friendly and helpful (will look after luggage while you trek). Large chart of hotels and prices. Tourist Office at airport has information on hotels. *Magnum Restaurant* on Av. San Martín has an audio-visual show (slides and music) most evenings at 2230, US$6 including first drink.

Buses run daily between Ushuaia and Río Grande at 0800 and 1200 and also at 1900 on Wed. and Sun., US$9.50, Transporte Los Carlos, Triunvirato 57. In winter the bus leaves before dawn so much of the beautiful scenery is missed. Taxi to Río Grande about US$60. There is a minibus (essential to book in advance during Jan.-March, ring Empresa Senkovic, stay the previous night in Río Grande) between Río Grande (see page 142) and Porvenir (in the Chilean part of the island (242 km., 6-8 hrs.) but no air connection.

Airport Aerolíneas Argentinas flights daily (twice, except Tues., and Sat.) from Buenos Aires all year round (change at Río Gallegos). (LADE and Aerolíneas offices on Av. San Martín open Mon.-Fri. 0900-1200, 1500-1800). To Río Grande US$10 (LADE and AA), daily at 0900 and several afternoons at 1300-1400; to Calafate via Río Grande and Río Gallegos (book early) US$20, 4 a week at 0900; to Trelew, US$125; to Comodoro Rivadavia, via Río Gallegos, US$84; to Río Gallegos, US$18, heavily booked (daily). To Bariloche, US$60, Tues. and Sun. at 0800, stops at Río Grande, Río Gallegos, Santa Cruz, San Julián, Puerto Deseado, C. Rivadavia, Trelew and Esquel. To Buenos Aires, day flight US$90, night flight US$50 (booked up at least 5 days ahead). LADE flies every Tues. and Fri. Ushuaia, Río Grande, Río Gallegos, Calafate, Gobernador Gregores,

142 ARGENTINA

Perito Moreno, Comodoro Rivadavia; with small detour over complete glacier, weather permitting. Get window seat on left side.

Weather often impedes flights in winter, and in the summer tourist season it is sometimes difficult to get a flight out. At the airport ask around for a pilot willing to take you on a ½ hr. flight around Ushuaia, US$16 for 2 people. Alternatively ask about flights at the tourist office. Taxi to airport, US$1, or 20 mins. walk.

Sport Ice skating rink at Ushuaia gymnasium. Diving: write to Club de Actividades Subacuáticas for information about scuba diving in the Beagle Channel. The Austral marine biology station has a display on Calle Roca of marine life. Director: Dr. C. Kuhnermann, Casilla 157, Buenos Aires. Beachcombing can produce whale bones. Fishing: trout, contact Asociación de Caza y Pesca at Maipú and 9 de Julio, with small museum. Fishermen may be interested in visiting the fish hatchery 7 km. E of Ushuaia, visiting hours 1000-1200 and 1400-1800 on Tues., and Thurs. There are brook, rainbow and brown trout and land-locked salmon. Take No. 1 bus E-bound on Maipú to the end of the line and continue 2½ km. on foot to the hatchery. Birdwatchers will also find this ride rewarding. Skiing, hiking, climbing: contact Club Andino, Solís 50. Skiing: A downhill ski area with chairlift, equipment rental and cafeteria is found on Cerro Martial. It is open June-July, has lights for night-skiing and is run by Club Andino. 20 km. E of Ushuaia is Valle Tierra Mayoria, a large flat valley with facilities for cross country skiing, snow shoeing and snowmobiling; rentals and a cafeteria.

Excursions Rumbo Sur, San Martín 342; Antartur, in *Hotel Las Lengas*. Onas Tours, 25 de Mayo 50, just off main street, very friendly. Tiempo Libre, San Martín 154, Tel.: 91296, recommended. Recommended guide: Domingo Galussio, Intervú 15, Casa 211, 9410 Ushuaia, bilingual but not cheap. Tour to Lapataia US$9 p.p.; Lake Escondido US$8, 50 km., 3-4 hrs, to *Petrel Inn*. Visit the Estancia Harberton, the oldest on the island, for tea, cakes and more, not cheap, but good. There are excursions to the Martial glacier (itself unspectacular but fine scenery) about 7 km. behind the town; take road behind *Hotel Antártida*, 2 km. to small dam, then 3-4 hour walk along trail. There is a chairlift to the glacier (operating schedule unclear). (In winter the glacier is inaccessible, even on foot.) Also to the so-called Indian Cemetery, 5 km. W of town (archaeologists on site pleased to tell of Indian history), to Lendegaia and Lapataia bays, the falls of the Olivia river. In winter the temperature drops to as low as -12°C, in summer it goes up to 25°C. In summer, 3 hr. boat trips may be taken to see sealions at the Isla de los Lobos (US$14), also Les Eclaireurs lighthouse (US$13, 4 hrs, in the *Angel B*), the Bridges islands and Isla Redonda, where the Government is breeding *guanacos*. Ask at Rumbo Sur, leaves at 1500 daily. Beaver inhabit the Parque Nacional near the Chilean border; one may see beaver dams and with much luck and patience the beavers themselves after dark, you need a torch; ask ranger. *Hosterías* at Lapataia (*Alakush*, D, 20 km. W of Ushuaia, on Route 3, in the Parque Nacional Tierra del Fuego, open for summer season from Dec. 1 to March); at Lake Fagnano (*Hostería El Kaiken*, also bungalows, nice site, well-run facilities, cheap drinks, on a promontory 93 km. from Ushuaia, C including real bath), and at Lake Escondido (*El Petrel Inn*, 54 km. from Ushuaia, D), after a spectacular climb through Garibaldi Pass, on the road to Río Grande; all three are good. Facilities at *Kaiken* are open all year round, but at *Petrel* only from Dec. to March. All are run by the ACA and offer reductions to its members; these inns are recommended for peace and quiet. Road-wise, the old Route 3 circles close to the lake while the newer Route 3 bypasses most of it. Even in the summer the climate can often be cold, damp and unpredictable. It is possible to hitch-hike, though with difficulty, as far as Lapataia; only tour buses go there. Rangers in the park are friendly and will sometimes put people up for a couple of days (as will police) and help with places to visit. A ranger truck leaves Ushuaia every weekday at 1300 and picks up hitch-hikers along the road. Park entrance US$1. Rumbo Sur runs good excursions: 3 hour trip to Tierra del Fuego Parque Nacional, US$5. Taxi to Park, US$9-12, shop around. Los Carlos bus to Lake Fagnano, 2½ hrs., US$4.70, then from Lake to Río Grande 2 hrs., US$5. Tours also arranged to Lake Fagnano and aerial excursions over the Beagle Channel (with local flying club, hangar at airport, 3-5 seater planes, 30 mins. US$19), Lake Fagnano, Lapataia and Ushuaia Bay. To Lake Escondido/Fagnano US$11.15; bus to Puerto Almanza (on Beagle Channel), 75 km., 4-5 hrs, US$9. Boat and bus 7 hr. tour to the Isla de los Lobos and Pájaros along the Beagle Channel, US$9.50. Take food, on board overpriced. There are 2-3 weekly tours to Antarctica by boat, 9 days, visit military base, in Jan. and Feb., US$1,250 and more. Boat trip Ushuaia—Puerto Williams (Isla Navarino, Chile), US$25, obtain Chilean pesos in Ushuaia because Argentine currency is not accepted anywhere in Puerto Williams. To Punta Arenas via Puerta Williams, ship *Vicente Padia*; ask for the captain at Don Bosco 56, Tel.: 92253, and check with the Chilean consul. The ship, *Ethel B*, captain Pedro Esteban Buchet (of Kilak Expeditions) does trips up the Beagle Channel to the Chilean border (he is also planning trips to Cape Horn, using the shelter of islands en route, weather permitting).

Interesting boat trips of 3 weeks' duration on the 2,346-ton *Lindblad Explorer* cost from US$4,600.

Río Grande (15,000 people) is a port in windy, monotonous sheep-grazing and oil-bearing plains; the oil is refined at San Sebastián, with ACA motel, D, (partly paved but bad road, most people seem to drive the tracks adjacent to the road,

ARGENTINA

which is narrow and winding over undulating country) in the smallest and most southerly refinery in the world (petrol station open 0700-2300). The *frigorífico* plant in Río Grande is one of the largest slaughterhouses in South America. A bridge is being built across the Río Grande so that the town may expand to the S. Accommodation is very difficult. ACA garage on sea-front has free hot showers for men, as has the gymnasium. Fill up with petrol here.

Local Festivals *Trout Festival*, 3rd Sunday in February; *Snow Festival*, 3rd Sunday in July; *Woodsman Festival*, 1st week of December.

Hotels Difficult (to say the least) to get hotel rooms because of number of oilmen and Chilean workers. *Federico Ibarra*, Rosales and Fagnano, recommended, good restaurant, B; *Villa*, San Martín 277, C, very warm; *Central*, behind it, E; *Arboleas*, E, Rivadavia 637, excellent value, recommended; *Atlántida*, Av. Belgrano and Rosales, under reconstruction; *Yaganes ACA*, Av. Belgrano 319, A, clean, comfortable, has a restaurant; *Argentino*, San Martín 86, D; *ACA Albergue*, on Luis Piedrabuena near Gymnasium, B, 4-bed rooms, very comfortable, central heating, hot showers, restaurant, US$10 a meal; *Miramar*, Belgrano and Mackinlay, E-D without bath, no breakfast, heated, hot water ("a plywood palace"); *Hospedaje Dany*, Moreno 781, D, heated, hot shower, clean; *Residencial Arboles*, Rivadavia 649, E, clean, heated, hot showers; *Anexo Villa*, Piedrabuena, E; *Albergue* at corner of Alberdi and Piedrabuena, F, very clean (obtain permit to stay from manager of Sports Centre next door). *Residencial Las Lenguitas*, Piedrabuena 436, E, bathroom shared between 2 rooms, good value; *Hospedaje Irmary*, Estrada 743, clean and pleasant, just off San Martín and 2 blocks from Senkovic bus office, F (being enlarged); *Residencial Rawson*, Estrada 750, E with bath, clean, recommended; *Pensión Río Bueno*, J. B. Alberdi 616, E, simple, clean and friendly, men only.

Youth Hostel, for boys only, but apparently always filled by local workers.

Restaurants *Las Malvinas*, reasonable; *Comedor Porteño; Cantina Restaurant; Fiori; Yaganes* (good for *centolla*); *Miramar; Villa; Rotisería El Trébol*, Calle Belgrano, counter snacks; very popular *Confitería Roca*, Roca 629, open all hours, reasonably priced food and bar. *Supermarket Sados* on San Martín, near 25 de Mayo. Smart place for a drink, *Paris*, Rosales 448.

Propane Gas from Gas del Estado, San Martín and Rivadavia.

Turkish Baths at San Martín 236.

Car Hire Rent-a-Car, Belgrano y Ameghino, Tel.: 22657.

Tourist Information at the Municipalidad, Mon.-Fri., on Calle Sebastián El Cano.

Airport 4 km. W of town. Río Grande-Buenos Aires flight (Aerolíneas Argentinas, several daily, 3 night flights weekly), 5 hours, stops at Río Gallegos and Comodoro Rivadavia (some also at Bahía Blanca). LADE flight Río Grande to Ushuaia, US$15.50 return, heavily booked (also Aerolíneas, US$10 one way). A bus Río Grande-Ushuaia also connects with the Aerolíneas night flight from Buenos Aires. To Río Gallegos, US$40 (book early in summer). To Calafate, stopping at Río Gallegos, US$16; to Comodoro Rivadavia, US$67. Telephone LADE office (behind *Hotel Yaganes*) open Mon.-Fri., 0900-1200 and 1530-1900, 0700-1200 on Sat., Tel.: 308. Conversely, travel with navy aircraft (if you're lucky), mostly Hercules transports, for half the price—enquire at airport. "Rent-a-plane" at airport, US$25 an hour.

Buses leave at 0600 Tues. and Fri. (Senkovic), US$15 each, for Porvenir, Chile (about 230 km.), no food or drink provided, no toilets, nor stops, for 6 hrs., passport and luggage control at San Sebastián (144 km. before Porvenir), then connect with ferry to Punta Arenas (2 hrs) which can be very rough and cold, US$4 p.p., US$33 per car. Senkovic offices at Av. San Martín 959. Bus from landing stage, Tres Puentes, into Punta Arenas (5 km.) necessary (US$0.85). Flight across Strait, US$20 each. Transportes Turicisne go to Porvenir, very crowded and filthy, avoid at all costs. Daily bus service at 1400 (and 2000 and 0200 Tues. and Thurs.) with Los Carlos, Estrada 568 to Ushuaia, 234 km., on an unpaved road, US$9.50, 5 hours, stopping at *Hostería El Kaikén*, Lake Fagnano, for a drink. Book tickets to Ushuaia at the *Hotel Antártida*. The bus leaves one block away from *Hotel Miramar*. In winter the bus leaves on Mon., Wed. and Fri. only (1830).

Excursion 11 km. N lies the Salesian mission and the regional museum housed in the original chapel and first parish church of Río Grande. Although the exhibits are not at all organized or classified, there is a great deal to see. There are Ona Indian materials, Salesian mission works, fossils, handicrafts and flora, fauna and mineral exhibits of the area. Just past the mission, on the right side of the road, is the old cemetery.

Isla de los Estados Robert T. Cook writes: "This long (75 km.) and guarded island lies east of Tierra del Fuego. Except for the caretakers of the lighthouse and an occasional scientist few people ever set foot on this cloud-shrouded reserve of Fuegian flora and fauna that no longer exist on the main island. During the 18th and 19th centuries hundreds of ships were wrecked or lost in the treacherous waters surrounding this island. Much gold, silver and relics await salvage." Information and tours from Rumbo Sur, San Martín 340, Ushuaia.

Argentina apparently has plans for tourist developments in **Antarctica** (accommodation at Marambio and Esperanza stations) and Argentina and Chile are planning a mountaineering camp about 600 km. from the South Pole.

The Economy

Argentina is one of the more highly developed countries of the region and is potentially one of the richest farming countries in the world. The importance of agriculture and livestock production is shown by the fact that this sector still provides about 70% of export earnings with sales of cereals, oilseeds, meat and processed foodstuffs. Although Argentina has lost its dominant position as an exporter of cereals and beef, it has great resources in relation to its population, which increases at a rate of only 1.7% a year. Agriculture, livestock, forestry and fishing account for about 16% of gdp. There has been a shift from livestock to crop production since the 1960s in line with changes in relative prices and the introduction of new technology which has sharply increased crop yields. Cereals account for a substantial proportion of crop production, with over 15m hectares under cultivation in the mid-1980s, of which nearly 6m were sown to wheat and produced about 12m tonnes a year. The area sown to oilseeds has risen steeply, now just exceeding that of wheat, and producing about 12m tonnes of soyabeans and sunflower seed a year. Livestock, faced with stiff competition abroad from other exporting countries, has declined in importance. The cattle stock fell from around 57m head in the late 1970s to less than 54m in the mid-1980s. Exports declined steadily while annual domestic consumption rose to about 82 kg per person.

The manufacturing sector has developed behind high import protection barriers; it accounts for a quarter of gdp and benefits from increased agricultural activity, so that natural resource-based and labour-intensive industries such as food processing, textiles and clothing are reasonably dynamic. Food processing and beverages account for a quarter of manufacturing output and a fifth of industrial employment, while they are the second largest foreign exchange earners after farming. Metal working, engineering and the steel industry were depressed in the first half of the 1980s as inflation surged, dampening domestic demand and creating investment uncertainties. In the construction industry, output plummeted by 53% in 1981-85.

Energy development has been a priority with emphasis on hydro and nuclear power sources to reduce dependence upon thermal power. In the mid-1980s, liquid fuels supplied 48% and natural gas 25% of energy consumption, while hydroelectricity was only 11%. By the end of the century it is planned to reduce liquid fuels' share to 37% and raise natural gas to 35%. Argentina is virtually self-sufficient in oil and there is exportable surplus of natural gas and petroleum derivatives. Hydroelectricity generating plants provided 50% of total electricity generation in the mid-1980s, thermal plants 36% and nuclear plants 14%. The country's hydroelectric potential lies on the rivers Paraná and Uruguay in the north and on the network of rivers in Río Negro and Neuquén provinces.

Extremely high rates of inflation were recorded in the 1980s through a combination of large fiscal deficits, monetary expansion and a high velocity of circulation. These were difficult to contain because of structural imbalances in the economy arising from supply shortages caused by inadequate levels of investment and inefficiencies in both the public and private sectors. As the economy reached hyperinflation at a rate of 1,129% in the twelve months to June 1985, the government introduced a stabilization programme known as the Austral Plan. This included a price and wage freeze, a new currency, the Austral, and as well as cutting the fiscal deficit it suspended financing of the deficit by the central bank. Results were mixed, but inflation was substantially cut.

The Government also tackled the problem of servicing the external debt, which had risen sharply by an annual average of 35% in 1978-82 to over US$50bn in the mid-1980s, making Argentina the third largest debtor in the

ARGENTINA

region. Several debt rescheduling agreements were negotiated with commercial bank creditors together with new loans and IMF financing facilities. Several World Bank loans were granted for restructuring a number of economic sectors, such as agriculture and foreign trade, and it is hoped that these arrangements would put Argentina on a stronger footing to face the 1990s.

	1961-70(av)	1971-80(av)	1981-85(av)	1986(est.)
Gdp growth (1980 prices)(%)	3.0	2.3	-2.1	4.7
Inflation %	21.3	119.4	322.6	90.1
Exports (fob) US$m	1,426	4,564	8,222	6,987
Meat	342	665	610	330
Maize	168	465	842	750
Wheat	178	361	1,003	500
Imports (fob) US$m	1,127	3,693	5,024	4,700
Current account balance US$m (cumulative)	-423	-2,729	-12,950	-2,641

Information for Visitors

In 1986 visa restrictions for British tourists were relaxed. For further details, see page 148.

How to reach Argentina

By Air Aerolíneas Argentinas flies to São Paulo, Rio de Janeiro, Caracas, Madrid, Lisbon, Rome, Lima, Mexico City, Los Angeles, Auckland, Paris, Amsterdam, Frankfurt, Miami, New York, Montreal, Quito, Guayaquil, Bogotá, Panama City, Zurich, Geneva, Tel-Aviv, Santiago de Chile, Antofagasta, Montevideo.

From New York there are services by Pan Am; by Eastern (stops at Miami, Santiago and Lima), 14 hours; by Aerolíneas Argentinas and by Varig. Lloyd Aéreo Boliviano (LAB) also flies between Buenos Aires and Miami, stopping at Santa Cruz, and Panama. Aeroperú flies Miami-Buenos Aires via Lima and Santiago and returns via Santiago, Lima and Panama. Two direct flights a week Jujuy-Miami. From Canada, Canadian Pacific Airlines fly to Buenos Aires via Peru and Chile. Other airlines include: Líneas Aéreas Paraguayas; Capetown via Rio by South African Airways; Viasa to Caracas; Bogotá, Lima, Santiago with Avianca; Aeroflot (via Dakar); Ecuatoriana, which flies to Santiago, Quito, Guayaquil, Mexico, Miami, Los Angeles. Also Cruzeiro, Iberia, KLM, LAN Chile, Lufthansa, Air France, Alitalia, Cathay Pacific, Swissair.

From the Continent of Europe the Italia Line sails from Mediterranean ports, Linea Costa "C" goes from Genoa-Barcelona-Lisbon-Rio-Santos to Buenos Aires, their luxury liner is Eugenio "C", followed by Enrico "C" and the smaller "Provence"; 9 days from Lisbon to Buenos Aires. Cars are cheaper to freight on the passenger ship than on the cargo boats which charge by the cubic metre bracket; the Johnson Line from Swedish and Baltic ports. Continental Shipping and Travel, 179 Piccadilly, London W1V 9DB, Tel.: 01-491 4968, offers a comprehensive service from France at reasonable prices. More expensive is Nedlloyd Lijnen, PO Box 240, 3000 DH Rotterdam, with limited passenger accommodation on cargo ships. A similar service is offered by Calmedia SpA di Navigazione, PO Box 349, 16123 Genoa.

From the USA There are sailings from New York to Buenos Aires by the American Republics Line, operated by Moore-McCormack Lines; sailings from San Francisco and Los Angeles by Pacific Republics Line, by the same operators; and from New Orleans by the Delta Line. Buenos Aires is 19 days by ship from New York or New Orleans.

Internal Air Services are run by Aerolíneas Argentinas, Austral, Lapa, and the army airline LADE (in Patagonia, highly recommended). There are frequent flights to all neighbouring republics. LADE flights are cheaper than the others, and there is a good extended schedule with new Fokker F-28 jets. **N.B.** LADE will not accept IATA MCOs. (Even though sometimes offices in various towns may tell you the flights are full, it is usually worth a try out at the airport.) The naval air passenger service, Aeronaval, carries paying civilian passengers, ⅓ cheaper than LADE. No firm schedule though; 2 flights a week between Ushuaia, Río Grande and Río Gallegos; once a week between Ushuaia and Buenos Aires. Aerolíneas and Austral have introduced a service of night flights, at fares 40-50= lower than the normal day tariff. **N.B.** All local flights are fully booked way in advance for travel in December. Don't lose your baggage ticket; you won't be able to collect your bags without it.

Visit Argentina Fare Those visiting Argentina should note the following excellent bargain. For US$299 one can buy from Aerolíneas Argentinas or Austral, in Buenos Aires, a voucher for this scheme, available to non-Argentines not resident in Argentina. The system permits travel anywhere on the domestic network of Aerolíneas or Austral for a period of 30 days, provided that no point is visited twice except to make an immediate or first available connection. The voucher is surrendered for a complete set of tickets which are not refundable (i.e. the whole tour must be planned before it is begun). There is also a US$199 ticket, for 14 days, permitting travel to 3 cities not including entry and departure points. Both tickets can be booked or bought in USA or Europe. Domestic timetables are given in *Guía Argentina de Tráfico Aéreo* and *Guía Internacional de Tráfico*. It is unwise to set up too tight a schedule because of delays which may be caused by bad weather; however, if your itinerary changes, it may be possible to trade off unused sections for others (there is a lot of confusion about this in local AA offices). Flights between Buenos Aires and Río Gallegos are often fully booked 2 to 3 weeks ahead, and there may be similar difficulties on the routes to Bariloche and Iguazú. Visit Argentina fare does not include Río Gallegos-Calafate (only LADE flies this route). It is advisable to have an "OK" status put on your flight coupons even if you are "wait-listed", to be sure of your seat. Reconfirmation at least 24 hours ahead of a flight is important and it is essential to make it at the point of departure. Extra charges are made for reconfirming LADE flights (useful in Santa Cruz and Tierra del Fuego) but they are not high.

Airport Tax US$10 for international flights, US$2.50 for flights to Chile, Brazil and Bolivia, and US$1.50 for internal flights. When in transit from one international flight to another, you may be obliged to pass through immigration and customs, have your passport stamped and be made to pay an airport tax on departure.

N.B. Do not send unaccompanied luggage to Argentina; it can take up to 3 days of form-filling to retrieve it from the airport. Paying overweight, though expensive, saves time.

Railways A permit (Argenpass) to travel anywhere by the Argentine railways costs US$95 a month, and US$150 for two months. There is no connected railway system south of Bariloche and Esquel. A "Pase Americano" (Amerailpass—check if still available) which enables you to travel on Pullman coaches through Uruguay, Argentina, Brazil, Chile, Bolivia, Paraguay, without mileage limit is US$120 for 16 days, US$140 for 23 days, US$175 for 30 days, US$260 for 60 days, also available for 90 days (payable in US$ only) free carriage, 30 kg. (children ½ price) and obtainable at the Centro de Información de Ferrocarriles Argentinos (CIFA) in Galerías Pacífico, Florida 729, Buenos Aires, open Mon.-Sat. 0700-2100, Sun. 0700-1300; also available in Mar del Plata, Bariloche, Mendoza, Córdoba, Tucumán and Posadas. There is no great difference between 1st and second tourist class in trains, but if uncrowded, you can sleep across 5 seats in the latter (3 + 2), and only 4 in 1st class. As a rule, tourist class is 20% cheaper than 1st class, Pullman 50% more than 1st.

N.B. Once out of Buenos Aires, train information is hard to come by, although we are informed that the CIFA has 328 agencies to book facilities for the named-train principal services from Buenos Aires. Stations have wall time-tables of complete schedules for their own line but no information for other systems. To avoid disappointments, make long-distance call to nearest station on the line you require—although this requires fluency in Spanish. The only general time-tables in circulation at present are those for named trains on the main lines to Mendoza, San Juan, Tucumán, Posadas, Córdoba, Mar del Plata, Bariloche, Zapala and Corrientes, which are available from the information centre at Galerías Pacífico; some of this information is summarized on page 49. The main services have been accelerated in recent years, but others remain slow and infrequent.

Motoring For entering Argentina by automobile the *Carnet de passages en douanes* (*Libreta de aduana*), issued by a recognized automobile club, is required. Tourists can now bring their cars into Argentina temporarily under international documentation. No specific papers are usually required to bring a Brazilian registered car into Argentina. A British international driving licence is valid only if it is endorsed by the Automóvil Club Argentino (ACA), and if the holder has a visa. Most main roads are paved, if rather narrow (road maps are a good indication of quality), and roadside services are good. Road surface conditions vary once one leaves main towns, though the dirt and gravel roads are well maintained: high speeds are quite possible on them, as long as you have the essential guard for the windscreen. You may not export fuel from Argentina, so empty spare jerry

ARGENTINA

cans while you are in the country. Do fill up when you can in less developed areas like Chaco and Formosa as filling stations are infrequent. Diesel fuel prices are about 60% of those for gasoline; it is known as *gas-oil*. Octane rating is as follows: regular gasoline 83 (US$0.90 per litre); super 93 (US$1.25); gasoline is called *nafta*.

To obtain documents for a resident to take a car out of Argentina, you can go to ACA in Buenos Aires, which may take up to 4 working days, or you can ask for a list of other ACA offices that can undertake the work; take forms with you from Buenos Aires, and papers may be ready in 24 hours. You will need at least 1 passport-size photo, which you can have taken at ACA at a fair cost. If the car is not your own, you require a special form signed by the owner and witnessed by a notary public.

Sometimes one may not be allowed to reach a border if one does not intend to cross it, stopping e.g. 20 km. from the border.

For those driving N to S through Argentina, Route 40 can be travelled most of the way from La Quiaca on the Bolivian border to Río Gallegos; all interesting places, with the exception of Iguazú, Buenos Aires and Trelew, can be reached from this route.

Automóvil Club Argentino (ACA), Av. Libertador General San Martín 1850, Tel.: 802-6061, has a travel document service, complete car service facilities, road information, road charts (*hojas de ruta*-about US$1 each to members, if available) and maps (dated with the code letters in the bottom corner—road map of whole country, with service stations and *hosterías* shown, US$3.20 to non-members), a hotel list, camping information, and a tourist guide book sold at a discount to its members and members of other recognized automobile clubs upon presentation of a membership card. (YPF, the state oil agency, also produces good maps for sale.) Members of other recognized automobile clubs can also, on presentation of membership cards, benefit from lower prices for their rooms and meals at ACA *hosterías*. The Club has service stations, some with parking garages, all over the country. The organization is efficient. Travellers do report, however, that if you are not a member of ACA you will not get any help when in trouble. ACA membership for 3 months costs US$40, which gives 20% discount on hotel rooms and maps, and discounts at associated hotels, and 10% discount on meals.

ACA accommodation comes in 4 basic types: *Motel, Hostería, Hotel,* and *Unidades Turísticas*. A *motel* may have as few as 3 rooms, and only one night's stay is permitted. *Hosterías* have very attractive buildings and are very friendly. *Hotels* are smarter and more impersonal. All have meal facilities of some kind. Anyone can get in touch by phone or radio with the organization to find out about accommodation or road conditions.

Hitch-hikers, as well as motorists, are recommended to contact the ACA for its wealth of information.

Touring Club Argentino, Esmeralda 605 and Tucumán 781 3rd floor, Tel.: 392-6742 has similar travel services but no service stations.

Car Hire Avis offers a good and efficient service with the possibility of complete insurance and unlimited mileage for rentals of 7 days or more. No one-way fee if returned to another Avis office, but the car may not be taken out of the country. Hire fees in early 1986 were US$305 for 7 days, US$530 for 15 days, US$955 for 30 days, for group B, i.e. Renault 12. Other companies are given in the text.

Camping is now very popular in Argentina (except in Buenos Aires) and sites with services are being installed, as well as good free municipal and paying private campsites in most tourist centres. Many are closed off-season. Camping is now allowed at the side of major highways and in all national parks (except at Iguazú Falls), at no cost. Many ACA gas stations have a site where one can camp, and in general gas-station owners are very friendly to campers. A list of camping sites is available from ACA (labelled for members, but should be easily available); see Autoclub magazine. References to sites will be found in the text. There are few Youth Hostels (many open only February to March), but some towns offer free accommodation to young travellers in the holiday season, on floors of schools or church halls; some fire stations will let you sleep on the floor for free (sometimes men only). Many garages have showers that you can use. No budget traveller should go to Argentina without a tent (no good, light-weight tents available), stove, etc. Regular (blue bottle) Camping Gaz International is available in Buenos Aires, at an electrical goods store on Av. 9 de Julio, near Teatro Colón.

Motorhomes US Motorhomes "Winnebago" is represented by Todotur, Av. de Mayo 1370-5th Floor, Room 92 (Tel.: 371552 or 380406) Buenos Aires. "Coachmen" Motorhome and "Pick-up" camper dealer at Av. Debenedetti 1285, (1871) Dock Sud, Avellaneda, Buenos Aires also represents Jensen, Wemac, Monogram, Peterson, Winegard, Monarch and Coleman (Tel.: 201-5289/6379). The best dealer for Motorhome equipment and repairs is Merello Hermanos S.R.L., Maipú 742, Vicente López, Prov. of Bs. As (Tel.: 795-3503/4335). Porta-Potti toilets are widely used in Argentina, sometimes under a different name.

Hitch-hiking Argentina used on the whole to be a good country for this (especially in Dec.-March), though recent problems with robberies have made hitch-hiking difficult. Carry little foreign cash on you, especially loose dollars (i.e. travellers' cheques better), because of frequent stoppages along the road. Don't rely on hitching absolutely, though; traffic can be sparse, especially in

148 ARGENTINA

Patagonia out of season (although oilmen and Chilean workers can be helpful). It may be useful to carry a letter from your Consulate. Backpack repairs in Buenos Aires at Mundo Náutico, Av. Santa Fe 4700.

Walking Information on trails in NW Argentina, the Lake District, Patagonia and Tierra del Fuego is given in *Backpacking in Chile and Argentina*, by Hilary Bradt and John Pilkington.

Buses In 1986 the price of bus journeys was approximately US$2.50 per 100 km. Most bus companies give a 25% student discount, but persistence is required to prevail with an international student card.

Documents Check visa requirements as they change frequently. In 1986 visa restrictions on British tourists were relaxed: they are now normally granted immediately on application. Passports are not required by citizens of neighbouring countries who hold identity cards issued by their own Governments. A passport visa from an Argentine consulate is necessary for US citizens (not available at borders), but not for nationals of other Western Hemisphere countries (excluding Cuba), Western European countries (excluding UK and Portugal), and Japan, who may stay for 3 months, a period which can be renewed for another 3 months at the National Directorate of Migration. For all others there are three forms of visa: a business "temporary" visa, a tourist visa, and a transit visa. Australians, New Zealanders and South Africans need visas. Tourist visas are usually valid for three months in Argentina and for any number of exits and entrances during that period. Visitors should carry passports at all times; backpackers are particular targets for thorough searches—just stay calm; it is illegal not to have identification handy. On arrival tourists are issued with tourist cards, the travellers' half of which must be surrendered on departure. US$1.20 is charged at borders on Sundays, holidays and after 1800.

Vaccinations Smallpox vaccination no longer required to enter Argentina. If intending to visit the low-lying tropical areas, it is advisable to take precautions against malaria, see page 47.

British Business Travellers are strongly advised to read "Hints to Exporters: Argentina", obtainable from Department of Trade, Export Services Division, Sanctuary Bldgs, 16-20 Great Smith Street, London SW1P 3DB. Similar information is provided for US citizens by the US Department of Commerce.

Customs No duties are charged on clothing, personal effects, toilet necessities, etc. Cameras, typewriters, binoculars, radios and other things which a tourist normally carries are duty-free if they have been used and only one of each article is carried. This is also true of scientific and professional instruments for the personal use of the traveller. Travellers may only bring in new personal goods up to a value of US$150 (up to US$50 for tourists from neighbouring countries); the amount of duty varies per item and according to exchange rates. However, the Argentine authorities allow goods to the value of US$500 to be introduced duty-free by travellers arriving in Tierra del Fuego. There are red and green divisions at airport customs, but officials make no difference between them. All incoming baggage is normally inspected.

Two litres of alcoholic drinks, 400 cigarettes, 50 cigars and 5 kg. of foodstuffs are also allowed in duty-free; for tourists originating from neighbouring countries the respective quantities allowed are 1 litre, 200, 20 and 2 kg. You can buy duty-free goods *on arrival* at Ezeiza airport.

If having packages sent to Argentina, do not use the green customs label unless the contents are of real value and you expect to pay duty. For such things as books or samples use the white label if available.

N.B. Never carry weapons, or drugs without prescriptions. The open season for fishing is between November and February or March. Enquire as to dates, so as to avoid carrying equipment unnecessarily, and remember that fishing in National Park requires a permit.

Climate ranges from sub-tropical in the N to cold temperate in Tierra del Fuego, but is temperate and quite healthy in the densely populated central zone. From mid-December to the end of February Buenos Aires can be oppressively hot and humid, with temperatures ranging from 27°C (80°F) to 35°C (95°F) and an average humidity of 70%. Beware of the high pollen count in the pollinating season if you have allergy problems. The winter months of June, July and August are best for a business visit, though spring weather in Buenos Aires is often very pleasant indeed. The skiing season in Bariloche ends by August 30. Corrientes and Misiones provinces are wet in August and especially September.

Clothing Shorts are not worn in city centres, though their use has become

ARGENTINA 149

more common in residential suburbs in spring, summer and autumn, and in Buenos Aires in the hottest months. In general, dress tends to be formal (unless casual wear is specified on an invitation) in Buenos Aires and for evening outings to shows, etc. The general standard of dress among Argentines is very high: collar and tie, with jacket, are very much the standard for men, and women "should always err on the side of elegance" - David Mackintosh.

Hours of Business Banks, government offices, insurance offices and business houses are not open on Saturdays. *Government Offices:* 1230-1930 (in the winter) and 0730-1300 in summer. *Banks:* generally 1000-1600 but time varies according to the city, and sometimes according to the season. (See under names of cities in text.) *Post Offices:* 0800 to midnight for telegrams. Stamps on sale during working days 0800-2000 but 0800-1400 on Saturdays. *Shops* are open from about 0900 to 1900, though many close at midday on Saturdays. Outside the main cities many close for the daily afternoon siesta, reopening at about 1700. 24-hour opening is allowed except on Mondays; this applies mainly to restaurants, foodshops, barbers, newspaper shops, art, book and record stores.

Language Spanish, with variant words and pronunciation. English comes second; French and Italian may be useful.

The chief variant pronunciations are the replacement of the "ll" and "y" sounds by a soft "j" sound, as in "azure" (though note that this is not done in Mendoza), the omission of the "d" sound in words ending in °-ado", the omission of final "s" sounds, the pronunciation of "s" before a consonant as a Scottish or German "ch", and the substitution in the north and west of the normal rolled "r" sound by a hybrid "rj". In grammar the Spanish "tú" is replaced by "vos" and the second person singular conjugation of verbs has the accent on the last syllable e.g. *vos tenés, podés,* etc.

For those who are staying some time, courses in Spanish at the Inlingua School, Corrientes y Callao, Buenos Aires, have been recommended. Also at Goethe Institut, Av. Corrientes 335, Buenos Aires, or free at Escuela Manuel Belgrano, La-Madrid 676, 1166 Buenos Aires (La Boca), 6 hrs. weekly, Tues., Thurs., and Fri., 1800-2000.

Cost of Living
Up to June 1985 the currency was allowed to depreciate against the US$ in line with inflation and Argentina became a much less expensive country for the tourist. However, it has since become dearer as depreciation of the austral is not strictly in line with inflation..

Standard Time is 3 hours behind GMT.

Holidays The main holiday period, generally to be avoided by business visitors, is January-March. No work may be done on the national holidays (May 1, May 25, June 20, July 9, August 17, October 12 and December 25) with the exceptions specifically established by the legislation in force. There are no bus services on May 1. On the non-working days (January 1, Holy Thursday and Good Friday, and December 8) employers are left free to decide whether their employees should work, but banks and public offices are closed. Banks are also closed on December 31. On New Year's Eve there is a ticker-tape tradition in downtown Buenos Aires: it snows paper and the crowds stuff passing cars and buses with long streamers.

Food National dishes are based in the main upon plentiful supplies of beef. There is a national tendency, however, to overcook it; "bien jugoso" will normally bring you a medium-rare steak. Many dishes are distinctive and excellent; the *asado*, a roast cooked on an open fire or grill; *puchero*, a pot- au-feu, very good indeed; *bife a caballo*, steak topped with a fried egg; the *carbonada* (onions, tomatoes, minced beef), particularly good in Buenos Aires; *churrasco*, a thick grilled steak; *parrillada*, a mixed grill, mainly roast meat, sausages (including *morcilla*, black pudding to the British, or blood sausage) and offal; and *humitas*, made with sweet corn, tasty but not strictly national. *Arroz con pollo* is a delicious combination of rice, chicken, eggs, vegetables and strong sauce. *Puchero de gallina* is chicken, sausage, maize, potatoes and squash cooked together. *Empanada* is a tasty meat pie, and *chorizo* a highly spiced sausage, though do not confuse this with *bife de chorizo*, which is a rump steak (*bife de lomo* is fillet steak). Try also local *milanesas* (Wiener Schnitzel), *mollejas* (sweetbreads) and *mayonesa de ave*, poultry mayonnaise. *Ñoquis* (gnocchi), potato dumplings normally served with meat and tomato sauce, are tasty and often the cheapest item on the menu. *Locro* is a thick stew made of maize, white beans, beef, sausages, pumpkin and herbs. Pizzas are excellent, and come in all sorts of exotic flavours, both savoury and sweet. Almost uniquely in Latin America, salads are quite safe. A popular dessert is *dulce de leche* (especially from Chascomús), milk and sugar evaporated to a pale, soft fudge; best eaten with cheese (*queso fresco*) to offset the sweetness. Other popular desserts are *dulce de batata* (sweet potato preserve), *almendrado* (ice-cream rolled in crushed almonds), *dulce de membrillo* (quince preserve), *dulce de zapallo* (pumpkin in syrup) with cream and *queso fresco*, and *postre Balcarce*, a cream and meringue cake. *Alfajores*, maize-flour biscuits filled with *dulce de leche* or apricot jam, are also very popular. Sweets: the Havana brands have been particularly recommended. Excellent Italian-style ice-cream with exotic flavours. For local recipes (in Spanish) *Las Comidas de Mi Pueblo*, by Margarita Palacios, recommended.

Rolls and coffee and perhaps fruit for breakfast. Offices close for 2 to 2½ hours for lunch between 1200 and 1400. Around 1700, many people go to a *confitería*—a cross between tea-room and cocktail lounge—for tea, sandwiches and cakes. The cocktail hour is 1900-2100. No one dines before 2100, and dinner often begins at 2200 or 2230; it is, in the main, a repetition of lunch.

Drink Argentine wines are sound throughout the price range, though probably the best are not as good as the best Chilean. The ordinary *vinos corrientes* are wholesome and extremely cheap (reds better than the whites). The local beers, mainly lager-type, are quite acceptable and cost about US$0.50 a litre in supermarkets. Hard liquor is relatively cheap, except for imported whisky, at about US$3 in shops for gin and vodka. Local liqueurs may be as cheap as US$0.70 a litre. *Clérico* is a white-wine *sangría* drunk in summer. Tap water in the main cities is safe, but often heavily chlorinated; it is usual to drink soda or mineral water at restaurants, and many Argentines mix it with their wine, as a refreshing drink in summer.

Best Buys Local leather goods in Buenos Aires, men's leather coats, US$200; suede, US$200-250 three-quarter-length coats are about US$130 and suede blousons about US$80; handbags and shoes (leather is much cheaper in Uruguay). *Ciudad del Cuero*, Florida 940, has clothing, footwear and luggage from 40 manufacturers. A gourd for drinking *yerba mate* and the silver *bombilla* which goes with it, perhaps a pair of *gaucho* trousers, the *bombachas*. Ponchos (red and black for men, all colours for women). *El Guasquero* in Calle Anasagasti specializes in old *gaucho* objects, saddlery, *bolas*, horn items, all genuine and reconditioned by Sr Flores, the owner. The shop is N of Av. Santa Fe, near Calle Bulnes, Buenos Aires (postcode 2028). Articles of onyx, especially in Salta. Silver handicrafts. In Buenos Aires, there is a good, reasonable and helpful souvenir shop on Av. de Mayo near Chacabuco. Knitted woollens, especially in Bariloche and Mar del Plata. If you like honey, the Casa de Miel has different honeys from every province. Try Mendoza or Tucumán varieties.

Value-Added Tax VAT is not levied on most medicines and foodstuffs but on all other products and services up to 20%.

Currency In mid-1985, a new currency was introduced, the *austral*, divided into 100 centavos (with an initial value of US$1.25), worth 1,000 of the existing pesos argentinos (themselves introduced as recently as mid-1983). Austral notes are being issued, but peso argentino notes are still being used, being gradually overprinted with austral denominations. Notes in circulation: A 10 (10,000 pesos argentinos), A 5 (5,000 pesos argentinos), A 1 (1,000 pesos argentinos), 50, 10, 5, 1 and ½ centavos (500, 100, 50, 10 and 5 pesos argentinos respectively). 5, 1 and ½-centavo coins have been introduced to co-exist with 50, 10 and 5-peso argentino coins, and coins for up to 50 centavos bearing the austral sign (A with an extra crossbar) are being struck. There is an acute shortage of small change, and the different series of coins in circulation are very confusing. It is usually difficult to change travellers' cheques in the smaller towns. Commissions can be as high as 6% and in general it takes a long time and many forms to transact these cheques. Other travellers have warned not to engage in unsolicited currency transactions in the streets, etc. as you may be tricked or land in prison—black market trading is an offence. Some of the major towns have exchange shops (*casas de cambio*) and these are given in the text. There is a 3% tax on cheques and an extra commission which can be avoided if you go to a branch of the issuing bank, especially if changing small amounts. Market rates, as opposed to official rates, are quoted in major newspapers daily, and available at some cambios; there is at the moment a premium of about 15% over the official rate. Money remitted to Argentina from abroad is normally paid out in australes. It is possible to obtain money from Europe through an express transfer, which takes 2-3 days, and the currency will be subject to tax. The sale of foreign exchange is prohibited; the only way to purchase dollars or other Latin American currencies, if not wanting to use the black market, is to try old coin shops.

When crossing a land frontier into Argentina, make sure you have some Argentine currency as there are normally no facilities at the border.

ARGENTINA 151

Credit Cards It is reported that American Express, Diners Club, Visa and Mastercard cards are all useful. At shops, hotels and places showing Argencard (head office, H.Yrigoyen, Buenos Aires) signs will accept Eurocard and Access, but you must state that these cards are affiliated to Mastercard. Argencard will not permit cash advances on these cards in outlying regions, and is itself very slow in advancing cash. The use of Mastercard/Access and Eurocard is very limited in the south and cash advances on credit cards are, in the main, impossible.

Weights and Measures The metric system is used.

Postage and Telephone Rates At end-1985 the minimum rate for airmail was about US$0.30. The local telephone system is hopelessly overloaded. On Sat., 1300-2200, and Sun., 0700-2200, Christmas to New Year and Easter Week international calls are half-price; there is a very well organised office in Calle Perú and Rivadavia for these in Buenos Aires. The normal rate for international calls is from US$1.50 to US$2.20 a minute, and for telex about US$1.00-1.75. Direct international telephone dialling is almost unknown in hotels and private homes. Letters from Argentina take up to a week to get to the UK, and about 5 days to the USA. No reverse-charge calls to Australia or South Africa.

Encomiendas Internacionales at the Centro Postal Internacional at Av. Antártida Argentina, NE of Retiro Station, Buenos Aires, has an efficient international parcel service, including obligatory customs inspection and wrapping for US$2. Open 1100 to 1700. Used clothes have to be fumigated before they will be accepted.

Press Buenos Aires dailies: *La Nación, La Prensa*. Tabloids: *Clarín, La Razón, Tiempo Argentino* Evening papers: *Crónica*. English language daily: *Buenos Aires Herald*. Magazines: *Siete Días, Gente, La Semana, Redacción, Mercado, El Gráfico* (sports). English language magazines: *The Review of the River Plate* (commercial, agricultural, political and economic comment), and *The Southern Cross* (Irish community).

Radio English language radio broadcasts can be heard daily on short wave: 0100-0130 on 6060 KHz 49m, 0230-0300 on 11710 KHz 25m, 0430-0500 and 2230-2300 on 15345 KHz 19m; Radiodifusión Argentina al Exterior, Casilla de Correo 555, Arg 1000, Beunos Aires. This is a government station and broadcasts also in Japanese, Arabic, German, French, Italian and Portuguese. Broadcasts by foreign radio stations (including the BBC) are receivable on short wave.

We wish to offer our profound thanks to Rosa M. de Bary de Ruiz Guinazú (Bs. As.),Philip Benson and Deirdre Ball (Quilmes), Romi and Olga Gandolfo (Bs. As.), Federico Kirbus (Bs. As.) for more most useful observations, Herbert S. Levi (Bs. As.) for yet more characteristically most useful contributions, G. Migoya (Bs. As.), Jorge Antolín Solache (El Calafate) for splendid information on that area, and Gustavo Steinbrun Bianco (Bs. As.). We also wish to thank the following travellers: Bill Addington (Warminster, Wilts), Richard and Sharon Alexander (Auckland 5), Stephen Appleby (Tynemouth), Mark Roy Battley (Toronto), Trond Bergquist and Ian Gjertz (Oslo), Barbera Bot and Bob Domberg (Maasland, Neth.), Mason Byles, Paulo Couto (São Paulo), Malcolm Craven (Weston-super-Mare), David Crowe (Sydney), Anke Cruse (San Francisco), Lynne and Hugh Davies (Mill Valley, Ca.), Diane De Mauro (Fort Lee, NJ), Karel Devijver (Leuven, Belg.), Kees Arthur van Dijk (Groningen), Grant Dixon (S.Hobart, Tasmania), Robert Edge and Renate Kronemann (London SW4), Julie Eisenberg and Andy Daitsman (Milwaukee), Roger Engetschwiler (Lucerne), Kurt Farner (Köniz, Switz.), Ferdinand Fellinger (Vienna), Volker Filss (Oberhausen, W Ger.) for a most valuable contribution, David Finn (Dallas) and Andrew Sherman (Los Angeles), Toni García and Diego Caña (Barcelona), Peter Gilmore (Guayaquil), William Gilmore-White (Watchet, Som.), Olivier Guize-Wiguiolle (Paris), Jürg Hangartner (Zürich), Brooke Hart (USPCV, Asunción), Suzanne Hartveld (Auckland), Hans Hendriks (Maasluis, Neth.), Ricardo Heyenn and Karin Kubitsch (Hamburg), John E.Hildeburn (San Marino, Ca.), Bastian Hiss and Daniela Fleischhauer (Krefeld, W. Ger.), Sara S.Hradecky (Ottawa), Marianne Hydara (Wels, Austria), Leo Joseph (Adelaide), Simón Keller (Montevideo), Peter W.Kenny (Minneapolis), Adelinde Klaus (Augsburg), Todd Knutson (Pittsburgh), Christian Küber (Hamburg), Carmen Kuczma (Powell River, BC), G.Lawson (Canberra), Peter Lonsdale (Taupo, NZ), Henry R. Loughlin (Norfolk, Ct.), Mark McHugh (Minneapolis) for useful information on Iguazú, Werner von Marinelli (Eindhoven), Sabine Marquardt and Mario Michalak (Leverkusen, W.Ger), Donna Mayer (Aarhus, Dmk.), Frans Mikkelsen and Karen Simonsen (Aarhus, Dmk.), Roland Moser (Ettingen, Switz.), Charles A.Muller, Paolo Nasuti (Venice), Hans and Ursula Niederndorfer (Lambach, Austria), Margherita Pedranzini (Milan), Vaclav Penkava (Seattle), David Phillips (London W11), Jens Plahte (Aas, Norway), H.L.Ravenswaaij (Curaçao), Beat Rebsamen (Buchs, Switz.), Eberhard Roth (Bühl, W.Ger), Stephen Saks and Andrea Keir (Melbourne), Erwin Sandvoss (Hannover), Dan Sarewitz (Cornell Univ., NY.), L.J.Schmit Jongbloed (Rotterdam), Barbara Simon and Peter Stobart (Cologne), Sebastian Steib (Bottmingen, Switz.), Carole Stroud (Tropical Tours, Belo Horizonte), R.Tucker (Natal, Braz.), Brian and Christina Turner (Caazapá, Par.), Dirk Vanmarcke (Brugge, Belg.), Doris Vaterlaus and David Froelicher (Thalwil, Switz.), Hans K.Wagner (Winterthur, Switz.), Jean de Wandelar (Brussels), Christopher W.Walker (Reston, Va.), Sabine Warko (Friedrichsdorf, W.Ger.), Haydn Washington (Sydney), Andrew Waterworth and Kerrie Oldfield (Neutral Bay, NSW), Susi and Alex Witteveen (Huizen, Neth.) and Roman Zukowski (Karlsruhe).

BOLIVIA

	Page		Page
Introductory	152	Santa Cruz	190
La Paz	157	The Beni	194
Lake Titicaca	171	The Economy	196
South from La Paz	175	Information for Visitors	197
Cochabamba	177	Maps	154, 158
Sucre	184		

BOLIVIA, straddling the Andes, is a land of gaunt mountains, cold desolate plateaux and developing semi-tropical and fertile lowlands. Its area of about 1,098,580 square kilometres makes it twice the size of Spain. It is land-locked, with Chile and Peru to the W, Brazil to N and E, and Argentina and Paraguay to the S. Of the population of some 6.4m people some 70% are Indians, 25% *mestizo* and 5% European; the population grew at a rate of 2.8% in 1981-85.

The Andean range is at its widest—some 650 km.—in Bolivia. The Western Cordillera, which separates Bolivia from Chile, has high peaks of between 5,800 and 6,500 metres and a number of active volcanoes along its crest. The passes across it are above 4,000 metres. To the E of this range lies the bleak, treeless, windswept Altiplano, much of it 4,000 metres above sea-level. It has an average width of 140 km., is 840 km. long, and covers an area (in Bolivia) of 102,300 square km., or nearly 10% of the country. Its surface is by no means flat, for the Western Cordillera sends spurs into it which tend to divide it into basins. The northern part is the more inhabited; the southern part is parched desert and almost unoccupied, save for a mining town here and there. Nearly 70% of the population lives on it, for it contains most of the major cities; almost half of the people are urban dwellers.

Lake Titicaca, at the northern end of the Altiplano, is an inland sea of 8,965 square km. at 3,810 metres: the highest navigable water in the world. Its maximum length and breadth are 171 and 64 km., and the greatest known depth is 280 metres. There are large annual variations between high and low water levels; 95% of the water flowing into it is lost by evaporation, making it more salty than most freshwater lakes. The immense depth of the water keeps the lake at an even all-the-year-around temperature of 10°C, and modifies the extremes of winter and night temperatures on the surrounding land. There is therefore a large farming population of Indians in this basin, tilling the fields and the hill terraces and tending their sheep and llamas.

The Altiplano is a harsh, strange land, a dreary grey solitude except for the bursts of green after rain. The air is unbelievably clear—the whole plateau is a bowl of luminous light. A cold wind blows frequently in the afternoons, causing dust storms. During the winter temperatures fall below freezingpoint; there is frost every night in July and August, but during the day the tropical sun raises temperatures over 20°C.

The animals of the Altiplano are fascinating. Llamas serve as pack animals—they carry up to 22 kg. loads up to 20 km. a day and yield about 2½ kg. of wool when sheared at intervals of from two to five years. The alpaca, bred not for work but for wool, belongs to the same group; the two may be distinguished by differences in the texture of their coats and shape of their tails. The vicuña, chinchilla and red fox are the main wild animals. The vicuña, an untamed member of

BOLIVIA 153

the family to which the llama and the alpaca belong, is found, though in diminishing numbers, on the bleak pampas. It may not be hunted, but its wool can be sold. It is smaller than the alpaca, and has a fine silky, tawny coloured wool.

Agriculture in the Altiplano is also interesting: the potato and the *oca* (another tuber), eaten in the dehydrated form of *chuño* and *tunta*, are the main crops. *Quinoa*, a kind of millet, and *cañava*, a smaller and darker grain, are the main cereals; both are extremely nutritious. *Chicha*, the national intoxicant, is brewed from maize (corn). Edible fish (small *boga*, large white-fleshed *pejerrey* and rainbow and salmon trout) are widely sold in the towns of the Altiplano.

Far more important to the economy of the Altiplano than agriculture is mining. 210 km. S of La Paz along the passageway at the base of the Eastern Cordillera is Oruro, where a low belt of hills supplies tin, copper, silver and tungsten. The Spaniards of Peru discovered the Cerro Rico in 1545. It is a mountain rising out of the Puna to a height of 4,780 metres, and was almost a solid mass of ore containing tin, silver, bismuth and tungsten. The Spaniards, interested only in silver, built Potosí at its base, 4,065 metres above sea level. The city grew till it had a population of 150,000, but rapidly dwindled after the richest deposits had been worked out. It remained a dead town till demand for tin rose early this century.

The presence of tin also accounts for the mining communities in the Cordillera to the SE of Oruro: the ex-Patiño mines at Catavi, to which there is a branch railway from Oruro, produce nearly half the tin of Bolivia. Bolivian tin production is high-cost; it can be maintained only by paying the miners extremely low wages. Silver is still mined or extracted from the tailings left by past generations, and variable amounts of lead, bismuth, antimony, tungsten and zinc from pockets in the Cordillera are exported. Large deposits of silver have been found south of the Altiplano, near Lípez, and mines are being reopened, and their tailings reprocessed, two centuries after the Spaniards abandoned them.

Recommended reading: *We Eat the Mines and the Mines Eat Us* by June Nash, New York, 1979, and *The Potosí Mita 1573-1700* by Jeffery Cole, Stanford University Press, 1985.

From the Altiplano rises, to the E, the sharp façade of the Eastern Cordillera. As luck would have it there is a gently graded passageway along the plateau at the foot of the Eastern Cordillera from Lake Titicaca, in the N, to the Argentine frontier, in the S. From Viacha, near La Paz, the main line of the Bolivian railways runs along this passageway to Villazón, with connections to Chile and Buenos Aires. The giant masses of the northern parts of the Eastern Cordillera rise to very great heights in the Cordillera Real to the east of Lake Titicaca: four peaks soar to above 6,000 metres. This magnificent sight can be seen on a clear day from the top of a ridge on the Titicaca-La Paz highway. Their far sides fall away to the NE, very sharply, towards the Amazon basin.

These heavily forested north-eastern slopes are deeply indented by the fertile valleys of the Nor Yungas and Sud Yungas, drained by the Río Beni and its tributaries, where cacao, coffee, sugar, coca and tropical fruits are grown. The problem of transport to the consuming centre of La Paz is formidable: the connecting all-weather road, hair-raising in places, climbs 3,430 metres in 80 km. to surmount La Cumbre pass, at 4,725 metres within 24 km. of La Paz.

From a point just N of Cochabamba to the S the Eastern Cordillera is tilted, not to the NE, but to the E. This part of the Eastern Cordillera rises abruptly in sharp escarpments from the Altiplano, and then flattens out to an easy slope eastwards to the plains: an area known as the Puna. The streams which flow across the Puna are tributaries of the Río Grande flowing NE to the basin of the Amazon, and of the Pilcomayo flowing SE through the Chaco to the River Plate system. They cut increasingly deep incisions as they gather volume until, to the E, the Puna is eroded to little more than a high remnant between the river valleys. These valleys deeply incising the surface of the eastern-sloping Puna are densely inhabited; a variety of grain crops and fruits is grown. All these semi-tropical mountain valleys are known as Yungas: the generic name is not confined to the valleys of the Provinces of Nor and Sud Yungas to the E of La Paz. Rainfall in the Yungas is from 700 to 800 mm. a year, as opposed to the 400 to 700 mm. of the northern Altiplano and much less further S. The heaviest rain is during

154 **BOLIVIA**

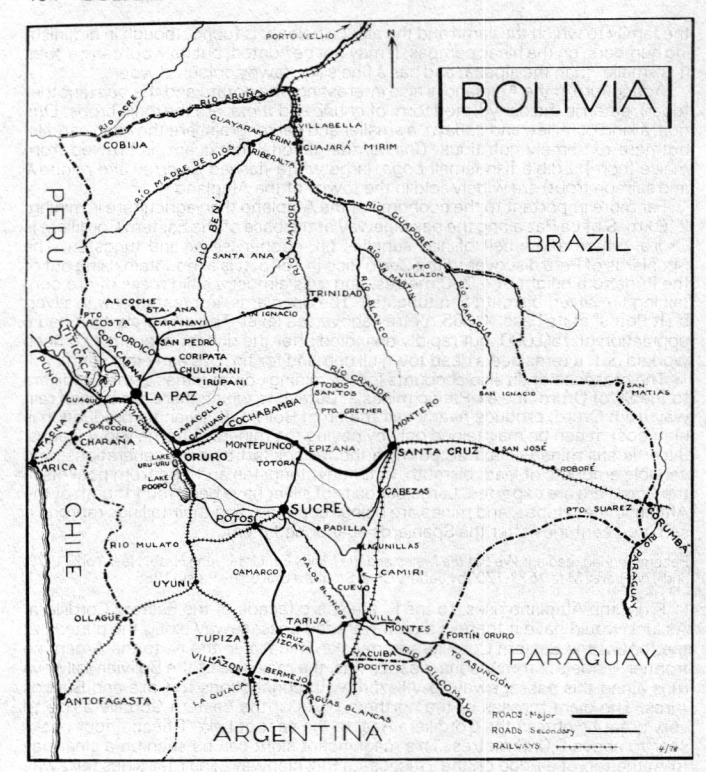

ROUGH SKETCH

December, January and February. The mean average temperature is between 16° and 18°C, but in spite of a high humidity the Yungas are not unhealthy. Chulumani in the Sud Yungas and Coroico in the Nor Yungas are popular resorts.

Typical valleys are the very fertile basins in which Cochabamba, Sucre, and Tarija lie. These send food and cattle to the towns of the Altiplano, but other valleys have no way of doing so. The basins and long ribbons of valley farmland are isolated, and transport to the areas where they might sell their produce is only now being developed.

The lowland tropics, stretching from the foothills of the Eastern Cordillera to the frontiers with Brazil to the NE and E and with Paraguay and Argentina to the SE and S, take up 70% of the total area of Bolivia, but contain only about 20% of its population. Rainfall is high but seasonal, and large stretches suffer from alternate flooding and drought. The climate is hot, ranging from 23° to 25°C in the S and to 27°C in the N. Occasional cold dust-laden winds from the S—the *surazos*—lower the temperature considerably. In the N and E the Oriente has dense tropical forest. Open plains covered with rough pasture, swamp and scrub occupy the centre. Towards the end of the 18th century this was a populous land of plenty; for 150 years Jesuit missionaries had controlled the area and guided it into a prosperous security. A symbol of their great effort is the cathedral at San José de Chiquitos: a gem of elegance and dignity. But the Jesuits were expelled in 1767; years of maladministration, spoliation and corruption reduced the area to lethargy.

This once rich land, drained by the Madre de Dios, Beni and Mamoré rivers into the Madeira, a tributary of the Amazon, has been isolated from the rest of the country. It is as difficult to get at from the E as from the W, for there are rapids and falls in the Madeira which limit navigation. In its heart lie the seasonally inundated tropical Llanos de Mojos, ringed in by rain forest or semi-deciduous tropical forest—230,000 square km. with only 120,000 people. Roads and river connections are still being improved; there are roads between Cochabamba and Todos Santos and between La Paz and Trinidad. Meat is already brought in from Trinidad, capital of Beni Department, and from airstrips in the area, to the urban centres of La Paz, Oruro, and Cochabamba.

The forests and plains beyond the Eastern Cordillera sweep S towards the Pilcomayo River, getting progressively less rain and merging into a comparatively dry southern land of scrub forest and arid savanna. The main city of this area is Santa Cruz de la Sierra, founded in the 16th century, now the second city of Bolivia and a large agricultural centre. Here conditions favour the growing of sugarcane, rice, oil plants and citrus fruit. The plains to the E are mainly used as grazing lands with small areas under cultivation, but in this area are extensive oil, gas, and iron-ore deposits, possibly Bolivia's greatest asset when developed. The Government hopes to develop the high-grade iron-ore deposits at Mutún, close to the Brazilian frontier.

Communications After centuries of isolation new roads are now integrating the food-producing eastern zones with the bulk of the population living in the towns of the Altiplano or the westward-facing slopes of the Eastern Cordillera. Under Spanish rule there were four great trails in use within the country: three of them led through passes in the Western Cordillera to the Pacific; the fourth led from La Paz southwards into Argentina. At the turn of the century, railways replaced the llamas and mules. By far the shortest line is the one from La Paz to Arica (Chile), completed in 1913. Arica ships a large part of the exports together with Antofagasta (Chile) and Matarani (Peru).

Bolivia has 3,774 km. of railway. There are two private railways: Machacamarca-Uncia, owned by the Corporación Minera de Bolivia (108 km.) and Uyuni-Pulacayo (52 km.) owned by the Empresa Minera Pulacayo. Plans to construct a railway to link Cochabamba and Santa Cruz, with Brazilian assistance, have often been studied. Bolivia has over 14,000 km. of navigable rivers, which connect most of the country with the Amazon basin. The national highway system at the end of 1983 totalled 40,969 km., of which only 3.75 % were paved and 20.1 % gravel-surfaced.

The People The racial composition varies from place to place: pure Indian around Lake Titicaca; more than half Indian in La Paz; three-quarters *mestizo* or European in the Yungas, Cochabamba, Santa Cruz and Tarija, the most European of all. Only 50 % of children of school age are attending school even though it is theoretically compulsory between 7 and 14.

About two-thirds of the population lives in adobe huts, and medical services are sketchy outside the towns and mining camps; birth rate, 43.2, general death rate, 15.4 per 1,000, but infantile mortality is 110 per 1,000 during the first year. Epidemics are comparatively rare on the Altiplano, but malaria and yellow fever are still problems in the Oriente and Santa Cruz, and hepatitis and Chagas disease (see page 26) are endemic in the warmer parts of the country. About 47.7 % is urban. Annual population growth: 2.8 %; urban growth: 5.1 %. Life expectancy at birth: 54 years; underemployment affects 37 % of the workforce, with 15 % without work (1984 estimate).

156 BOLIVIA

The Indians are mainly composed of two groups: those in the north of the Altiplano who speak the guttural Aymará, and those elsewhere, who speak Quechua, the Inca tongue. Outside the big cities many of them speak no Spanish, but knowledge of Spanish is increasing.

The most obdurate of Bolivian problems has always been that the main mass of population is, from a strictly economic viewpoint, in the wrong place, the poor Altiplano and not the potentially rich Oriente; and that the Indians lived largely outside the monetary system on a self-sufficient basis. Since the land reform of 1952 isolated communities continue the old life but in the agricultural area around Lake Titicaca, the valleys of Cochabamba, the Yungas and the irrigated areas of the south, most peasants now own their own land, however small the plot may be. There has also been appreciable migration to the warmer and more fertile lands of the eastern region, encouraged by the Government.

The Indian women retain their traditional costume, with bright petticoats, and in the highlands wear, apparently from birth, a flattish brown or grey bowler. In Cochabamba they wear a white top hat of ripolined straw. Indians traditionally chew the coca leaf, which deadens hunger pains and gives a measure of oblivion. On feast days they drink with considerable application, wear the most sensational masks and dance till they drop.

N.B. Remember to refer to rural Indians not as "indios" (an insult) but as "campesinos" (peasants).

History

At Tiahuanaco (Tiwanaku), near Lake Titicaca, stand a gateway and some restored terraces and roofless walls; the impressive remains of a pre-Inca civilization. The Aymará-speaking Indians in this area emerged around 1000 BC into a civilization characterized by massive stone buildings and monuments, exquisite textiles, pottery and metalwork. This phase seems to have been ended abruptly by some unexplained calamity, which greatly reduced the size of Lake Titicaca, around AD 900. When the Quechua-speaking Incas of Cuzco conquered the area around AD 1200, they found the Aymarás at Tiahuanaco living among ruins they could no longer explain. The Aymarás resisted obstinately and were not finally conquered until the latter part of the 15th century under the reign of Inca Túpac Yupangi (1471-93). Even so, they kept their traditional social structures and language, and fought for the Incas under their own leaders. Only religion was formally imposed by the Incas.

Francisco Pizarro landed in Peru in 1532. Six years later Spain conquered Bolivia, and the next year Sucre (then Charcas), still the official capital, was founded. By 1559 Bolivia had become the *audiencia* of Charcas, in the Viceroyalty of Peru, for it had become extremely important for the Spaniards after the discovery of the silver mountain at Potosí in 1545.

The excellent Inca communications and economic organization fell into ruin. Revolutionary movements against the colonial rule of the Spaniards began early; there were revolts at La Paz in 1661, at Cochabamba in 1730 and at Sucre, Cochabamba, Oruro and La Paz from 1776 to 1780. In 1809 the University of San Francisco Xavier, at Sucre, called for the independence of all Spain's American colonies. Finally, on December 9, 1824, Bolívar's general, Sucre, won the decisive battle of Ayacucho in Peru and invaded what is now Bolivia, defeating the Spaniards finally at the battle of Tumusla on April 2, 1825.

On February 9, 1825, when he first entered La Paz, Sucre had already promulgated the decree of independence, but his second in command, Santa Cruz, was for retaining links with Peru; Bolívar was in two minds. Sucre had his way and Bolivia was declared independent. On August 25, 1825, Bolívar named the new country after himself. In 1828, when Sucre left the country, Santa Cruz became President; pursuing his dream of amalgamation he proclaimed a Peruvian-Bolivian confederation in 1836, but Chile and Argentina intervened, and in 1839 Santa Cruz was overthrown and the confederation dissolved.

Since its independence, Bolivia has suffered a grievous contraction of its territory. It had never very actively worked its nitrate fields in the Atacama desert. In the War of the Pacific (1879-1883) Bolivia in alliance with Peru fought the Chileans for the right to retain this wealthy desert. After a year the Bolivians withdrew and Chile took over the desert and the port of Antofagasta, though it later compensated by building Bolivia the railway between Arica and La Paz. Railways traded for valuable territory has been Bolivia's fate. A railway to Yacuiba was Argentina's return for annexing some of the Chaco. When Brazil annexed the rich Acre Territory in 1903, Bolivia was compensated by yet another railway, but this Madeira-Mamoré line never reached its destination, Riberalta, and proved of little use; it was closed in 1972. A fourth railway, completed in the 1950s, connects Santa Cruz in East-Central Bolivia with Corumbá in Brazil.

There was not even an unbuilt railway to compensate Bolivia for its next loss. Constant disputes between Bolivia and Paraguay over the Chaco led to open warfare between 1928 and 1930, and again between 1933 and 1935. In 1938, by arbitration, Bolivia ceded to Paraguay three-quarters of the Chaco, but obtained a doubtfully valuable outlet to the Río Paraguay. Bolivia's failure to occupy its empty spaces is partly the explanation for these losses.

The moral results of this last defeat had revolutionary consequences. After over fifteen years of disorder, Víctor Paz Estenssoro was elected to the presidency in 1951 on a left-nationalist ticket. A military junta intervened, but in April 1952 a popular revolution overthrew it: Paz Estenssoro returned as president. His government committed itself to a profound social revolution, introducing the expropriation and the nationalization of the tin mines; universal suffrage without literacy or income qualifications; and a policy of land reform and redistribution of the large estates. Hernán Siles Zuazo, a revolutionary leader and vice president under Paz from 1952-56, was president from 1956-60. During his term the economy was stabilized. Paz Estenssoro was again elected president from 1960-64, but shortly after beginning a third term was overthrown in 1964 by General Barrientos, killed in an air crash in 1969. After three ephemeral governments, power was taken in August 1971 by a right-wing general, Hugo Banzer Suárez, who after seven years' rule called for elections in July 1978. Then came another sequence of short-lived military governments, despite disallowed elections which gave victories to ex-President Hernán Siles Zuazo. In August 1982 the military returned to barracks and Dr. Siles Zuazo assumed the Presidency in a leftist coalition government with support from the communists and trade unions. Under this regime inflation spiralled out of control. The elections of July 14, 1985 were won again by Víctor Paz Estenssoro, who imposed a most rigorous programme to stabilize the economy.

The Constitution of 1967 vests executive power in the President, elected by popular vote for a term of 4 years; he cannot be re-elected. There are nine departments; each is controlled by a Delegate appointed by the President.

Bolivia has, in effect, two capitals. Although Sucre is the legal capital, La Paz is in almost all respects the actual capital, being the seat of the Government and of Congress. On the other hand, the Supreme Court still holds its sessions in Sucre.

La Paz, the highest capital in the world, lies at 3,636 metres in a natural basin or canyon; it is sunk about 370 metres below the level of the Altiplano in its north-eastern corner. The Spaniards chose this odd place for a city on October 20, 1548, to avoid the chill winds of the plateau, and because they had found gold in the River Choqueyapu, which runs through the canyon. The mean average temperature is 10°C, but it varies greatly during each day, and the nights are cold. It rains almost every day from December to February, but the sun usually shines for several hours. The rest of the year the weather is mostly clear and sunny. Snow is rare. At first the visitor will probably feel some discomfort, known as *soroche* (altitude sickness), from the rarified air; a few hours resting when you arrive will put that right. Tea made from coca leaves (*mate de coca*) is recommended for *soroche*; if the discomfort persists many people take 'Micoren' tablets, a respiratory stimulant (though visitors with heart problems should consult a physician).

158 **BOLIVIA**

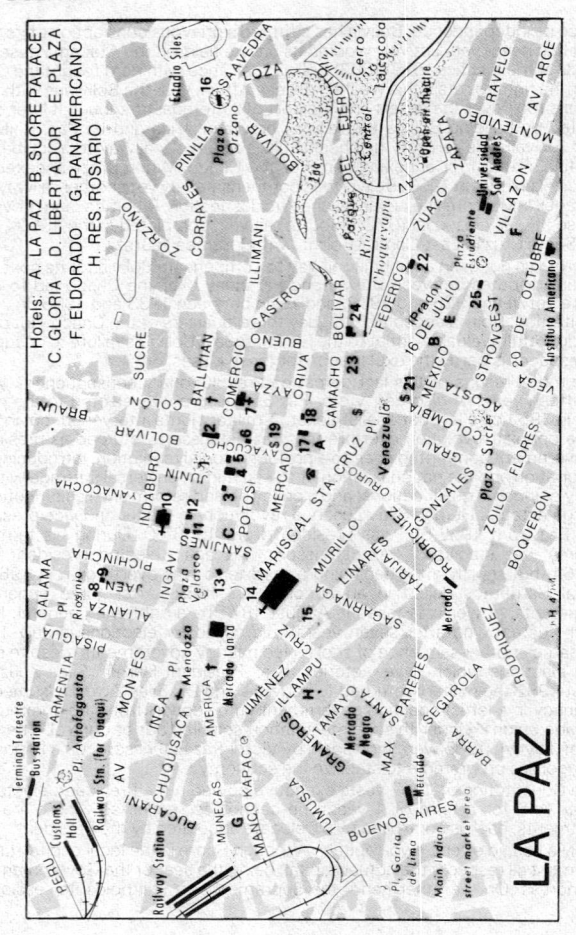

Hotels: A. LA PAZ B. SUCRE PALACE
C. GLORIA D. LIBERTADOR E. PLAZA
F. ELDORADO G. PANAMERICANO
H. RES. ROSARIO

LA PAZ

Key to Map
1. *Plaza* Murillo; 2. Congreso Nacional; 3. Museo Nacional de Arte; 4. Cathedral; 5. Government Palace (Palacio Quemado); 6. General Post Office; 7. Iglesia La Merced; 8. Museo de Costumbres; 9. Museo y Casa de Murillo; 10. Iglesia Santo Domingo; 11. Museo Nacional de Etnografía y Folklore; 12. Villaverde Palace; 13. Casa de la Cultura; 14. Basilica de San Francisco; 15. Witchcraft Market (Mercado de Hechicería); 16. Parque Prehistórico Tiahuanaco (Museo Semisubterráneo); 17. Alcadía; 18. U.S. Embassy and Citibank; 19. Banco Central; 21. Bank of Boston (Amex); 22. Museo Arqueológico de Tiahuanaco; 23. Lloyd Aéreo Boliviano; 24. Mercado Camacho; 25. Biblioteca Municipal.

Oxygen is available at the better hotels. In 1984, the population of La Paz was 953,000, half of it Indian.

Mount Illimani, with its snow-covered peaks (6,402 metres), towers over the city. Most of the Indians live in the higher terraces. Below are the business quarter, the government offices, the main hotels and restaurants and the university. The wealthier residential district is lower still: strung from Sopocachi to the bed of the valley at Obrajes, 5 km. from the centre and 500 metres lower than Plaza Murillo. Beyond Obrajes are the elegant districts of Calacoto and La Florida. The main sports and social clubs have moved to these districts.

There is some colonial building left; probably the best examples are in the Calle Jaén, but much of La Paz is modern. Plaza Murillo, on the north-eastern side of the river, is the traditional centre. Facing its formal gardens are the huge Cathedral (modern but very graceful); the Presidential Palace in Italian renaissance style, usually known as the Palacio Quemado (burnt palace) twice gutted by fire in its stormy 130-year history; and on the E side the National Congress. Across from the Cathedral on Calle Socabaya is the Palace of the Condes de Arana, now the Museo Nacional del Arte. Calle Comercio, running cross-wise past the Plaza, has most of the stores and shops. On Av. Bolívar (to which Mount Illimani provides a backdrop), continuing the Av. Camacho, is the Central Market (called "Mercado Camacho"), a picturesque medley of Indian victuals and vendors presiding raucously over stalls, their black braids topped by hard-brimmed bowler hats. Av. Camacho leads to the residential district of Miraflores.

From the Plaza Venezuela, Avenida Mariscal Santa Cruz leads to the Plaza San Francisco and to the church and monastery of San Francisco, well worth seeing; the church is colonial, richly decorated on native religious themes, and Indian weddings can be seen on Sats. 1000-1200. SW from Plaza San Francisco runs Calle Sagárnaga, with rows of handicraft shops (ponchos, alpaca rugs, wall hangings, devil masks, wood carvings, etc.) for visitors. Going higher still up Sagárnaga is a local market, and turning right on Max Paredes, heading west, one reaches Avenida Buenos Aires, one of the liveliest streets in the Indian quarter. A worthwhile walk is to Mirador Laicacota on Avenida del Ejército.

Other churches of more than passing interest are Santo Domingo (originally the cathedral) on Calles Ingavi and Yanacocha; La Merced, with its decorative 18th-century façade, on Calles Colón and Comercio; and San Sebastián, the first church to be built in La Paz, in Plaza Alonso de Mendoza (named after the church's builder).

Hotels Prices are inclusive of tax and service charge (20% in all).

Hotel	Address	Telephone	Single US$	Double US$
Sheraton	Av. Arce	356950	82-85	102-108
Plaza	Av. 16 de Julio	378300	68	76
Sucre	Av. 16 de Julio 1636	355080	60	63
Crillón	Plaza Isabel La Católica	352121	12	20
Copacabana	Av. 16 de Julio 1802	352242	15	19
Eldorado	Av. Villazón	363355	17	20
Gloria	Calle Potosí esq. Sanjinés	370010	33	40
Libertador	Calle Obispo Cárdenas 1421	343360	37	24
Emperador	Plaza del Stadium	340013	33	38
La Hostería	Calle Bueno 138	322925	11	15

The *Plaza* and *Sheraton* are excellent, and the latter's restaurant has possibly the best view in La Paz. This aside, the *Libertador* is very good value and nearest the business section and reported to be helpful (baggage stored). The *Eldorado* has been recommended. The *Sucre* gives good value, but hot water a problem, restaurant (car park at rear). A *Holiday Inn* is under construction. *Gloria* has a very good restaurant with excellent salads and pastries and gives a fair rate of exchange, but the hotel has been described as noisy and overpriced. For people staying several weeks, often looking for permanent residences, boarding houses (*pensiones*) are popular. Several can be recommended: *Pensión Colonial*, Av. Arce. For those wanting to stay in the suburbs at a lower altitude there is the *Hotel Calacoto*, Calle 13 on the corner of Bustamante, in Calacoto, D, with bath; *Panamericano*, Manco Kapac 454, clean, F with hot showers, recommended; *Residencial Rosario*, Illampu 704, travel agency downstairs, organizes trips to Puno and Tiahuanaco (recommended), D

160 BOLIVIA

with bath (electric showers), F without, popular with foreigners, laundry expensive, recently modernized and extended (Tel.:325348); *Residencial Copacabana*, Illampu 734, 3-star, E, hot water, safe, good restaurant, recommended. Hot water for baths and showers seems to be becoming even more of a problem than hitherto.

Try to arrive in La Paz as early in the day as possible, as accommodation, especially at the cheaper end of the market, can be hard to find. Economy: *City Hotel*, on the Prado, No. 1598, F, clean, basic, laundry facilities; *Neuman*, Loayza 442, E with bath. *Austria*, Yanacocha 531, E with bath, F without, double rooms only, can be unpleasant owing to drug dealing. *Florida*, C. Ingavi, F, newly decorated, good, warm water for shower; *Yanacocha*, Yanacocha 540, E expensive for what is offered (no breakfast) with bath, clean, but has seen better days; *Hostal República*, Comercio 1455, remodelled, clean, luke-warm water, E with bath (will store baggage); *Torino*, Socabaya 457, friendly, central, has seen better days, noisy, hot water on request, E with bath (F without), generally popular with young travellers, beware of drug-raids by police; *Búlgaro*, Colón 570, G, poor value, dirty. *Alojamiento Ideal*, Av. Mariscal Santa Cruz 1058, G without bath, E with. A few *residenciales* in the lowest price ranges include: *Plaza*, Plaza Pérez Velasco; *El Hostal*, Sucre 949; *Sucre*, Plaza Sucre 340; and *Miraflores*, Nanawa 1. A medium price hotel is *Sagárnaga*, Sagárnaga 326, D with bath, E without; next door and slightly cheaper, is *Alem*, No. 334, hot water but inadequate plumbing (both recommended). Hotels located in the Indian quarter include: *Grand*, Evaristo Valle 127, F without bath, E with, not satisfactory; *Andes*, Av. Manco Kapac 364, F with shared bath, clean, hot water, good value (one of the few that offers single rooms). Recommended is *Milton*, Illampu and Calderón, E with bath (with breakfast and hot water, friendly, helpful, will store luggage, has door-to-door bus service to Puno—US$12, local market outside Sat. and Sun.). *Oruro*, Plaza Alonso de Mendoza, E with bath; *Tumusla* Tumusla 580, near Indian market, E with bath, F without, basic, cold, unfriendly; *Alojamiento Metropoli*, Calle Tumusla, G, cheap, friendly; *España*, Av. 6 de Agosto 2064, E, with bath and breakfast; *Italia*, Av. Manco Kapac 303, E with bath, doubles only, hot shower (F without), can be very noisy (car park and peña); *Pullman*, Av. Montes, F, likely to be "full", spartan, good cheap restaurant. *Alojamiento Central*, Av. Manco Kapac 384, G, budget; *La Paz City*, N. Acosta 487, F; *Oriental*, Illampu 868, F without bath, E with, noisy; *Max Paredes*, on street of same name, modern, clean, F/G; *Residencial La Estancia*, Calle México, recommended, helpful; *Residencial Don Guillermo*, Colombia 222, F, good value, clean, hot water; *Alojamiento Los Angeles*, Calle Max Paredes, hot showers, recommended, F near market; *Urkupiñu*, nearby, F; *Residencial Imperial*, Av. General Pando 130, F without bath, E with, clean; *Residencial Illimani*, Av. Illimani 1817, F, highly recommended, often full. *Alojamiento Buenos Aires*, Pasaje Tumusla 651, F, hot showers; trucks to all parts of Bolivia leave from its yard, which tells you something about the level of noise to be expected. *Viena* in Calle Junín, F with bath, F without, beautiful old building, friendly staff; *Hostal Residencial*, Calle Sucre 949, F, is acceptable, as is *Plaza* on Plaza San Francisco, clean and hot water, F, without bath, E with. *Residencial Chuquisaca* is best avoided. Cheapest possibly is *La Carretera* (six to a room); hot shower extra.

Motel *Kori-Tambo*, Achocalla, outside the city, Tel.:327078. *San Bartolomé* recommended, own bus service to and from La Paz.

Camping No organized site, but the river gorge below the suburb of La Florida has been recommended; also Chinguihue, 10 km. from the city. Club Andino Boliviano (Tel.: 794016) rents equipment but stocks are tiny. Kerosene for pressure stoves is available from a pump in Plaza Alexander.

Restaurants in La Paz can be roughly divided into two categories: either they serve international cuisine and are expensive or they serve local dishes and are fairly cheap. The restaurants with international cuisine are to be found mainly on three streets, Av. 16 de Julio (the Prado), Av. 6 de Agosto and Av. 20 de Octubre. Service charges and tax of up to 23 % are usually included on the

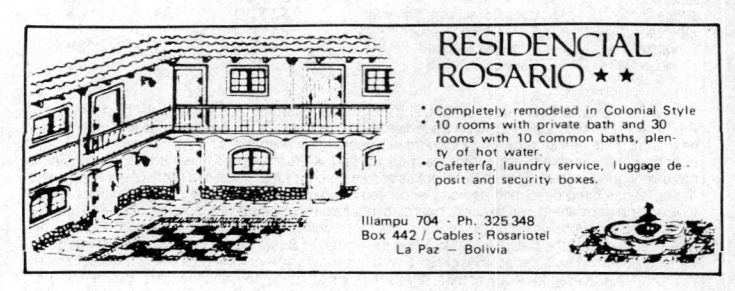

RESIDENCIAL ROSARIO ★★

* Completely remodeled in Colonial Style
* 10 rooms with private bath and 30 rooms with 10 common baths, plenty of hot water.
* Cafetería, laundry service, luggage deposit and security boxes.

Illampu 704 - Ph. 325 348
Box 442 / Cables : Rosariotel
La Paz — Bolivia

bill but it is customary to leave a few thousand pesos anyway as a tip. (Street numbers given in brackets.)

Av. 16 de Julio: there is the *Hotel Sucre* restaurant, which serves excellent food and has a pleasant view of the Prado, a favourite for lunch (fixed 4-course lunch for US$ 5.50 excluding taxes); there is also a good snack bar downstairs. The *Utana* restaurant at the *Plaza* has been recommended for food, service and view. All the other large hotels also have fairly good restaurants (e.g. *Crillón*). In the expensive range on the Prado: *El Bistrot*, French style, delicious food; *New China* (1577), good international cooking; the *City Hotel Restaurant* expensive, with shows Friday and Saturday nights. Slightly cheaper restaurants include the *China* (1549), good Chinese food; *Cuernavaca* (1490) has not very authentic Mexican food. *Picol*, corner of Prado and Bueno, good value.

There are many snack bars: there is the *Confitería Pick* on the 2nd floor of the Alameda Building, tallest building in La Paz; *La Gargantua*, in the same building serves fair "international food"; the *Tokio* (1832), good for *salteñas*; *La Llave* has good spicy Bolivian food (US$4 p.p.); *Confitería Elis* (1497), with good plate lunches, excellent soups, breakfasts and pastries. *Los Olivos* has good food at fair prices. The open air café next door to the *Hotel Copacabana* is popular with the Paceños at noon, to sip beer and watch people go by. *Club de la Paz*, Prado, near Camacho Bolívar, good tea room.

Off the Prado, on Calle Campero, one can recommend the *Club de la Prensa*, set in a pleasant garden, the food is typical Bolivian and moderately priced and the company is lively. The *Club Alemán*, off Calle Reyes Ortiz, is expensive but good; may need a member to introduce you. The *Carreta*, an Argentine-type restaurant at Batallón Colorados 32, serves a recommended mixed grill and very good steaks, a favourite of businessmen for lunch. Off the latter street at Capitán Ravelo 2070 (Edificio Venezuela, 2nd floor), is *El Tropero* which serves very good grills, expensive. A French restaurant, *Chez Pierre*, Calle Potosí 1320, is much frequented by visitors to La Paz; however standards appear to be falling here (won't accept American Express, despite sign).

On the continuation of the Prado going west, in Av. Mariscal Santa Cruz, is *Los Escudos*, Munich-type *bierkeller* with fixed 4-course lunch for US$2, food and shows (recommended) Friday and Saturday nights (2130, US$6 p.p.). *Lido Grill* (restaurant and confectionery), at No.815, popular meeting place, good food, reasonably-priced. *Parrillada Las Tablitas*, at Mariscal Santa Cruz 1283, excellent steaks, US$6; on the corner of Loayza with Santa Cruz is *Restaurant Verona* for economical *plato del día*, mixed reports. At Av. Ayacucho 206 is the *Internacional*, a lunch-time favourite of local businessmen and has good shows Friday and Saturday nights. At the other end of the Prado, at Av. Villazón 1936, is *Julio*, where lunch or supper costs only around US$1.

Av. 6 de Agosto: starting at the top end and heading southeast, there is the *Formosa* (2008), Chinese, tasty but slow; *Snack Shop* (2014), good hamburgers, doughnuts and milkshakes; *Oriental* (2179), good moderately-priced Chinese food; *Chifa Casa Lin* (2420), *Casa Argentina* (2535), good *parrilladas*; and *La Palizada*, excellent; also *Casa del Corregidor*, Calle Murillo 1040, a colonial mansion, attractive, recommended.

Av. 20 de Octubre: there is *Zlato's* (1824), regular international cooking; *Max Bieber's Restaurant and Tea-Room*, ice-cream, cakes and other dishes (2080); next door is *Stefano's*, art gallery by day, good Italian restaurant at night; *Chifa Gran Muralla* (2172); *Chifa Pletora* on corner of Rosendo Justiniano; *Churrasquería La Maison* (2344), good steaks.

In the shopping and business district: there are numerous snack bars and cheap restaurants. One can recommend: *Marilin*, corner of Potosí and Socabaya, *salteñas* and 3-course lunches, mixed reports (US$1), US$5 upwards for dinner; *Rayito de Luna*, Comercio 1072, is also good; *Haru*, Comercio 801; *Caravelle*, Mercado 1136, very clean, very good *salteñas*, ice cream and snacks; *Paulo*, on Potosí between Colón and Ayacucho for confectionery and coffee; *Galería Libertad*, on Socabaya, is a restaurant featuring an art gallery and good quality music; *Rojo y Negro*, Av. Manco Kapac (underneath the *Hotel Andes*), set meal for US$0.60, open for breakfast; on corner of Colón is the basement *Cafetería Verona*, fixed 3-course lunches US$3 (mixed reports). *Lasky*, on Plaza Venezuela, offers huge helpings and varied meals for less than US$4.

The best European and local food
Music bar open from 6.00pm to 1.00am.
The most typical corner of La Paz
Friday and Saturday Show and Folk music.

RESTAURANTE "EL HORNO" - BAR PEÑA "EL BODEGON"
Calle Murillo 1040 - Teléfono 363633 - Casilla 5889 - La Paz - Bolivia

162 BOLIVIA

Huari, corner of Manco Kapac and Tumusla, offers good value. Rather attractive, but out of the way, is the *Naira*, on Calle Sagárnaga 161, good *peña* every night from 2200, French-run *fondue* restaurant, expensive, do not be put off by dingy entrance. Vegetarian food can be had at *Ballivián*, Sagárnaga 123 (cheerless); *Los Buenos Amigos* (Chinese) is on the same street, good value. Cheap vegetarian restaurants to recommend are the *Restaurante Vegetariano Sra. Matilde*, Av. Armenia 545, second patio (lunch only), and *El Sol*, Calle N.A. Costa 222; also *Gran Fraternidad*, end of Calle México (1790) and *Aquarius* at 1844; *Man Jari*, Potosí 1315, Mon.-Sat. 0900-2100, Sun. 0900-1200, good value vegetarian food, bread, muesli. *Madre Tierra* has very slow bad service. Other recommendations include *Chingo's Hamburgers*, Av. Saavedra, clean; *Arabesque*, corner Loayza and Juan de la Riva, good coffee; *Gallo de Oro*, Lanza 567 (5) recommended, many cafés on Calle Comercio; restaurant beneath *Hotel Austria*, Yanacocha 531; *Don Francesco* Av. Arce 2312, good but expensive; *Pizzería* also on Av. Arce, moderate prices. Also on Av. Arce, opp. *Sheraton*, *Maison Suisse*, good attempt at Swiss food. *El Refugio*, Plaza Avaroa, not cheap, but best meat in La Paz; *Arte y Cocina*, Aspiazu 637, restaurant and bar at night, good, small selection. *La Italia*, Sanjinés 325, is poor with slow service.

Comedor Popular for the strictly limited budgets, cheap but filling local meals around US$1, available at Camacho and Loayza markets. The foodstalls at the top of Jiménez sell good T-bone steak cheaply. Bread from street vendors.

Books Foreign language books at Los Amigos del Libro, on Calle Mercado, at *Sheraton Hotel* and El Alto airport; they also sell tourist maps of the region from Puno to the Yungas, and walking-tour guides. Treat the details with caution. USIS has lending library and 2nd-hand paper-backs. Alliance Française, Calle Ingavi (open 1600-2000), has a library and recent papers in French. There are also 2nd-hand stalls on Av. Ismael Montes. Gisbert on Calle Illimani, and Juventud on Mercado and Yanacocha have good stocks.

Films For Kodak, Casa Kavlin, Calle Potosí 1130; Laboratorio Fuji Color, Potosí 1316; Foto Linares, Calle Loayza, will develop both Ansco and Agfa colour film 1-day service on black-and-white, but only repairs Minolta cameras. Repairs also at Av. Sánchez Lima 2178 by Rolando Calla C, just ring bell (1000-1200), there is no sign; also at Potosí 1316, between 1400—1900, Tel.: 373621, very helpful, professional, fair prices. Film is available at black market prices around Av. Buenos Aires, but otherwise it is expensive, as is developing. However in all cases check dates on film.

Souvenirs Shop around and bargain first. There is inexpensive silver and jewellery in the little cabinets outside Lanza market on Av. Santa Cruz. Up Sagárnaga, by the side of San Francisco church (Mercado Artesanal), are booths and small stores with interesting local items of all sorts. At Sagárnaga 177 is *Artesanía Nacional Tiwanaku*, for paintings, silver jewellery and woven goods. Although there have been complaints about quality and price, a visit is a must. Many Indian objects are sold near Av. Buenos Aires, and Indian musical instruments at *Colombiano*, Av. Mariscal Santa Cruz 1361, and on Calle Granier, near the General Cemetery. There are good jewellery stores throughout the city (La Joyería, Plaza Venezuela 1636, recommended), but visit the gold factories for lower prices and special orders. *Puma Punku*, Av. 16 de Julio, for weaving. *Artesanías Titicaca*, Av. Sánchez Lima 2320, retail and wholesale weaving. *Millma*, Sagárnaga 225, and in *Hotel Plaza*, for alpaca sweaters (made in their own factory) and antique and rare textiles. *Suri*, Av. Juan de la Riva 1431. *Curerex* has four shops in La Paz, recommended for leather goods. Best rings are from *Galería la Joyita* at the Edificio Alameda, in Colón. Good value is to be had at the *Sheraton Hotel* shops. *Artículos Regionales* in Plaza de los Estudiantes is recommended. Along Murillo and between Sagárnaga and Santa Cruz are various little shops selling old ponchos (better quality than in Peru) and rugs. The market between sells alpaca articles and other skins—but bargain hard. Generally, the higher up one goes along Calle Santa de la Sierra, the cheaper woollen goods seem to become. Also weavers' co-operative in central plaza. Alpaca goods are more varied than in Peru. Try *Inti Art* on the Prado (expensive modern designs), which is next to an antique store, in turn next to the *Restaurant China* and another on Calle Goitia. The Indian market is a good place for ponchos and local handicrafts. See also the "witchcraft market" on Melchor Jiménez, 3rd street on left walking up Calle Santa Cruz from Av. Mariscal Santa Cruz, fascinating items for sale. *Punchay Artesanías y Folklore*, Calle Santa Cruz 156 (Tel.: 362253), has been highly recommended—worth a visit; also *Rumillajta*, one of the Galería shops adjacent to the San Francisco church entrance. *Schohaus* at Calle Colón 260 has good pewter.

Taxis US$0.60 p.p., US$0.90 for two, for short trips within city limits. Between city and airport, up to US$10, can be shared, more at night including luggage. Current prices (incl. luggage) should be on display at the Airport exit. If not, enquire at the Airport Tourist Office(not too reliable, or their office in town). Moon Valley plus cactarium, US$17 for about two hours. Taxi drivers are not tipped; tip for porters—US$0.20 for each large piece of luggage. Sharing of taxis is common. Taxi to Tiahuanaco, US$30 return for 2; no time limit on stay at site.

Taxi-like vehicles flying variously coloured flags are *Trufis*, following fixed routes on a standard charge.

Car Hire Cars may be hired direct from Hertz Rent-a-Car, Tel.: 325592/332654 at Gen. Bernardo Trigo 429 or from their office at the *Sheraton Hotel*, or from Kolla Motors, Rosendo Gutiérrez 502, Tel.: 341660, or through a travel agent. Charges from US$26 a day, does not include

THE TRAVELLER'S HANDBOOK
EDITED BY MELISSA SHALES

New Edition - Completely Revised & Updated

New from Trade & Travel
The Completely Revised
5th Edition
864 pages
Paperback
ISBN 0 905802 04 7
£9.95

- designed to help plan any trip abroad
- everything the independent traveller needs to know
- 864 information packed pages
- 300 page Directory of useful names and addresses
- essential reference companion for foreign travel

"A gem of a guide. (Buy it to read in bed if you can't travel)."
OBSERVER

"Invaluable to the world-wide traveller."
VOGUE

"Justifiably billed as the indispensable guide to trouble-free travel".
GEOGRAPHICAL MAGAZINE

Available now from good bookshops, or from the publishers of The South American Handbook

Trade & Travel Publications Ltd.
5 Prince's Buildings, George Street,
Bath BA1 2ED. England.

164 BOLIVIA

gasoline or tax. Oscar Crespo, Av. Bolívar, rents Brazilian-made VWs, US$13/day plus US$0.18 per km.; Toyota jeeps, US$18/day plus US$0.25 per km.; for advance contact, telex via *Sheraton Hotel*. Rubén Hidalgo Nogales of Domicilio Graneros 304, Zona Rosario, hires out Dodge Darts for US$30 a day. One can also hire experienced drivers for US$12 a day plus accommodation and meals. You must have an international driving permit to drive in Bolivia, and outside the city you need an Hoja de Ruta (see page 198).

Local Buses Fares: US$0.10 in town; US$0.30 to Obrajes; US$0.40 to Calacoto. Minibuses (*Micros*) are dearer than buses, but much less crowded.

Festivals Particularly impressive is the Alacitas Fair held on Av. Montes in January. "It is dedicated to Ekeko, an Indian household god. You can buy plaster images of him at many of the booths. He is a red-nosed cheerfully-grinning little personage laden with an assortment of miniature cooking utensils, coins, balls of wool, tiny sacks of sugar, coffee, salt, rice and flour; a kind of Bolivian Santa Claus. Ekeko is said to bring prosperity and to grant wishes. If you buy a toy house, or a cow, or a sheep at the Alacitas, you will get a real one before the year is out. There are also model motor-cars and planes, for the extreme optimists." (Christopher Isherwood, "The Condor and the Cows.") See also page 200 for festivals outside La Paz.

Entertainment Best entertainment for visitors are the folk shows (*peñas*). Folk show at *Peña Naira* (US$5, includes drink), on Sagárnaga next door to restaurant, every night in August, and Fri. and Sat. evenings (very popular with tourists, repeatedly recommended). Various restaurants mentioned above have shows worth seeing. At these folk shows, visitors will be able to listen to the wide variety of local musical instruments, the different types of flutes, including the *queña*, and the *charango*, a small guitar with five strings, the back often made from the hide of an armadillo. Good peña at *Casa del Corregidor*, Calle Murillo, US$7, recommended, good food, Fri. and Sat. p.m. only; similarly *Marko Tambo*, US$7 (all incl.) repeatedly recommended. Indian dance halls, for example on Max Paredes, should only be visited in the company of Bolivians. There are a few discotheques of which the best are *Michelangelo's*, Av. 20 de Octubre 1832, and the *Viejoteca*, in Obrajes, which also has shows at week-ends, or the *Alamo*, or the *Baccara* in Calle 25 de Agosto. For drinks, there is *Giorgissimo* on Loayza, which is very popular (but not cheap by Bolivian standards) and also serves good meals, *Charlie's Bar* on Av. 6 de Agosto, and *St. George's Pub* at Av. 20 de Octubre 2019 (both expensive lounge bars). The *Sky Room* in the Hotel Gloria has been recommended. There are some good cinemas, films being mainly in English. La Paz has a resident ballet and symphony orchestra (*Teatro Municipal* on Sanjinés and Indabura) but no theatre company. The *Coloseo Cerrado* stages folk events on Sunday afternoons; so does the *Teatro al Avenida Libre*, near the university, at 1400. For film buffs there is the Cinemateca Boliviana, corner of Pichincha and Indabura, La Paz's art film centre with festivals, courses, etc. The Casa de Cultura (almost opposite Plaza San Francisco) sometimes has exhibitions, concerts or film festivals, most of which are free.

Sport There are two golf clubs (Malasilla, the world's highest, and Pinos), two tennis clubs (La Paz Tennis and Sucre Tennis), and two riding clubs. Football is popular and played on Thursday and Sunday at the Siles Stadium in Miraflores, two clubs (Micro A); there are reserved seats. Fishing and duck-shooting on Lake Titicaca and other lakes and rivers. There is a yacht club at Huatajata on Lake Titicaca (see page 172); sail and motor boats can be hired there and at Chu'a. (Non-members can play golf at Malasilla on weekdays subject to the usual payments, but it may be difficult to hire clubs.)

Mountain Sports Club Andino Boliviano, Calle México 1638, P.O. Box 1346, for mountain-climbing and skiing information (but does not hire ski equipment), Alfredo Martínez at the Club Andino is the country's foremost guide, or contact the well-regarded and friendly Bernardo Guarachi, Cañada Estrongest 1817, Casilla 20886, La Paz or Norbert Kloiber, Herrenstrasse 16, 8940 Memmingen, West Germany (Tel.: 08331-5258). Iván Blanco Alba, Asociación de Guías de Montaña y Trekking, Calle Chaco 1063, Casilla 1579, La Paz, Tel.: 350334, has been recommended (the association has about 10 guides in all and arranges climbing and hiking expeditions).

Museums Times: Mon.-Fri. 0930-1200, 1400-1800 (during winter months they close 30 minutes earlier), Sat. and Sun. 0900-1200. Some museums are closed on Monday.

Museo Nacional de Arte, across from the Cathedral on Calle Socabaya, housed in the 18th century baroque palace of the Condes de Arana, with beautiful exterior and patio. It has a fine collection of colonial paintings and also exhibits the works of contemporary local artists. Admission US$0.25. There are other exhibits at the Galería Municipal, on Colón, and at Galería Naira, on Sagárnaga.

Museo Tiahuanaco (Tiwanaku), or National Museum of Archaeology, easily reached by the flight of stairs by María Auxili church on the Prado. This modern building, simulating the Tiahuanaco style, contains splendid collections of the arts and crafts of ancient Tiahuanaco and items from the eastern jungles. Admission US$0.50.

Museo Semisubterráneo, in front of National Stadium, with restored statues and other artefacts from Tiahuanaco. It's in a sunken garden out of doors, and much can be seen from street level.

BOLIVIA 165

Museo Murillo, on Calle Jaén, was originally the home of Pedro Domingo Murillo, one of the martyrs of the abortive La Paz revolution for independence from Spain of July 16, 1809. This colonial house has been carefully restored and has a good collection of paintings, furniture and national costumes of the period; there is also a special room dedicated to herbal medicine and magic. Warmly recommended. Admission US$0.25, Sats. only, 1000-1200. Calle Jaén, a picturesque colonial street with many craft shops, is well worth seeing for itself.
Museo Nacional de Etnografía y Folklore, on Calle Ingavi 916, is housed in the palace of the Marqueses de Villaverde, worth seeing (especially the exhibit on the Chipaya Indians), small contribution requested.
Museo Costumbrista, Plaza Riosinio, at top of Calle Jaén. Miniature displays depict incidents in the history of La Paz and well-known Paceños 0900-1145, 1400-1745, Sundays 1000-1200.
Museo de Metales Preciosos, Calle Jaén 777, well set out, but no English labels, US$0.55.
Museo de Litoral, Jaén 789, with artefacts of the War of the Pacific and murals. 0900-1145.
Mineral Museum, Banco Minero, Comercio 1290, 3rd floor. Open Mon.-Fri. 0900-1300, 1400-1630. Slightly more expensive entrance fee than other museums but worth it for the gold and silver exhibits.
Nuñez del Prado, Ecuador 2034, Mon.-Fri., 0900-1200, 1400-1800, excellent sculpture.

Zoo at the upper end of Av. Bolivia, small, US$0.10.

Banks Citibank (will not cash its own travellers' cheques), Bank of Boston and other banks; American Express Agent: Magri Turismo, Av. 16 de Julio 1490, 5th Floor (American Express travellers' cheques are difficult to change elsewhere). Open 0900-1200, 1400-1630. Closed Saturday. Money is changed in hotels or *casas de cambio* rather than in banks.

Exchange Houses (*casas de cambio*): Best, Casa Nona Boutique, Ayacucho 413; América Ltda., Ayacucho 224; Sudamer, Colón 256; Titikaka Tours, Loayza 203; Tony Tours, Yanacocha y Asbún. Farmacia Hispani, Yanacocha, has been specially noted, also Visión Modas, Yanacocha 319. Many good rates obtainable in shops along Colón. Airport exchange booth will only change up to US$50 (commission) in travellers' cheques. Black market operates all over town, especially on Camacho, and is tolerated. It is very difficult to change money off the beaten track. You are advised to stock up in La Paz, or even before entering Bolivia, but watch out for unexpected devaluations. If you leave Bolivia with bolivianos you may not be able to change them in neighbouring countries. The best place for getting cheap bolivianos is still La Paz. However watch out for forged currency, especially Chilean pesos.

Addresses
Instituto Nacional de Arqueología de Bolivia, Calle Tiwanaku 93.
Immigration, Calle Gosálvez, between Av. Arce and Calle 6 de Agosto.
French Embassy, Av. 16 de Julio.
British Embassy and Consulate, Av. Arce 2732-2734. Tel.: 351400.
United States Embassy, Calle Colón (has a good reading room), Consulate on Av. Potosí.
West German Embassy, Av. Arce 2395. Telephone 35270 or 352389.
Goethe-Institut, Av. 6 de Agosto 2118.
Canadian Consulate, Edificio Alborada, Office 508, Calles Loayza y Mercado. Tel.: 375224.
Spanish Embassy, Av. 6 de Agosto 2827.
Swedish Consulate, Calle Mercado 1045, 5th floor, Tel.: 327535/377849.
Swiss Embassy, Av. 16 de Julio 1616, 2° piso. Tel.: 353091.
Brazilian Consulate, Fernando Guachalla 94, Tel.: 350718.
Peruvian Consulate and Embassy, 6 de Agosto y Calle F. Guachalla (a visa costs US$4 in US$ bills).
YMCA, 20 de Octubre 1839, Casilla 963.
Asociación Boliviana de Agencias de Viajes y Turismo, Edif. Litoral, Mariscal Santa Cruz 1351, Casilla 3967.

Doctor Dr René Coloma Rector, Edificio Cosmos, 11th floor, Office 1, Av. 16 de Julio (El Prado) Tel.: 377914/374893 (home). Recommended, speaks good English. Also Dr. César Moreno, Calle Pinilla 274, Tel.: 328805 (trained in Spain and Germany) Dr Mario Nava Guzmán, Buscamóvil 810-136/38 (home phone 784864) **Dentists** Dra Esperanza Aid, Rm 909, Edificio Libertad, Calle Potosí (Tel.: 320081); speaks English, or Dr Rigoberto Mena Morales, Rm. 705, Edif. Libertad (Tel.: 327636). Also Dr and Dra Osorio at *Hostal Austria*, Yanacocha 531.

Hospital Efficient and well run nursing homes such as Clínica Americana, Clínica Sta. Isabel opposite *Hotel Crillón*, Clínica Alemana, etc. Red Cross opposite Mercado Camacho will give inoculations if required. The Methodist Hospital (12th block of Obrajes, take "A" minibus from the Prado) runs clinic at US$5, telephone for appointment.

Church Protestant Community Church (inter-denominational), in English, American Co-operative School, Calle 10 Calacoto (Tel.: 795639 or 792052). The former pastor and his wife (The Rev. & Mrs. Charles F. King) have written an excellent duplicated guide to "Life in La Paz" which can be got on Sunday at the Community Church. Sunday service at 1045, but there are "lots of activities

166 BOLIVIA

during the week". Anglican-Episcopalian services are held at the Community Church on the third Sunday of each month.

Synagogues Calle Landaeta 330 (Sat. a.m. services only); Colegio Bolíviano Israëlito, Canada 1846 for Friday service—it looks like a private house.

N.B. In the San Pedro Prison (nr. Plaza Sucre) there are some Commonwealth, US., and European citizens held prisoner. Enquire at your consulate to see if one of your countrymen is "inside". A name of a prisoner helps to get a visitor in. Visiting hours, through the bars, are 0900-1730 each day and prison visits on Thursday and Sunday at the same time. These people would appreciate visits and old clothes (warm), books, food (milk, cheese), and company. *Beware:* You will be searched and have to leave all items of value with the guards. It may be better to leave these locked up somewhere securely. Passports also have to be shown, and these may sometimes be held by the guards during a visit.

Cables Public Telex booths at CWC offices.

Telephone service to the USA is now fairly good, though less so to the UK (now via satellite). Passports are kept to ensure prompt payment! Tolls are lower on Sundays. Calle Ayacucho near the Market (Entel).

Post Office on Ayacucho, just above Potosí (open Mon.-Sat. 0800-2000, and until 1800 on Sun. and holidays). Poste Restante keeps letters for 3 months. Procedure for sending parcels: customs (upstairs) must check contents first; then go to stamp counter to fill in customs declaration and purchase stamps; next have value of stamps checked and stamps franked, at a separate counter; finally, go to opposite window for *certificado* ticket. (Don't forget sack, needle and string for sewing up, and moth balls for textile items).

Electric Current 110 volts, 50 cycles A.C. in La Paz, 220 volts 50 cycles A.C. elsewhere. U.S.-type plugs can be used in most hotels.

Laundromat Wash and dry, US$2 per 4-kilo load, 6-hour service, at Lava-Sec, Ecuador y Guachalla, US$0.20/kilo, also at Arce 2660; laundry La Rápida, Calle Colón 445 (check your clothes afterwards).

Garage Volks Auto Motor, Jaime Freyre 2326, Tel.: 3-42279, friendly, Swiss.

Tourist Office Instituto Boliviano de Turismo (IBT) 4th floor Edif. Herrmann, Banco de Boston building, Plaza Venezuela, Tel.: 367463/367464. Very helpful. Maps and leaflets are available, but are not always up-to-date or accurate. A new kiosk is apparently being planned for the Plaza San Francisco.

Maps Servicio Nacional de Caminos, Av. México (next door there is a road conditions department). Instituto Geográfico Militar, Saavedra Rafael Subrieta (take Micro C or N), head office, but all enquiries are dealt with at the IGM's downtown office, on Av. 16 de Julio (near Plaza Venezuela). Passport is needed to get in, but worth it as they have the only railway map available in La Paz and a wide selection of others invaluable for the traveller. Topographic maps cost US$1.50 per sheet (scale 1:100 000 and 50,000) and about US$2 for standard tourist maps. For a clear but optimistic map, the Autómovil Club Boliviano at Av. 6 de Agosto 2993. Departmental road maps are meant to be available in the tourist offices in the capitals of each department but often they are out of stock. Maps are sold at Ichthus bookshop on the Prado; also at Librería La Paz and Amigos del Libro (page 162). Excellent range at Gisbert y Cía., Calle Comercio 1270.

Guides *La Paz Insólita* (7 maps) US$3 and *Guía de La Paz* by Jorge Siles Salinas (historical) US$5. *Guía Central de Bolivia,* US$2, information on transport, statistical and geographical data. In particular it contains the La Paz minibus schedules, which are unobtainable elsewhere.

Travel Agents Crillon Tours, Av. Camacho 1223 (Tel.: 320222), expensive, but increasingly good reports now being received; they are once again running a hydrofoil-bus service to Puno, US$129, via Copacabana and Sun Island, incl. lunch and breakfast. Transturin, Av. Camacho 1321 (Tel.: 363654/328560/320445; P.O. Box 5311, La Paz; Head Office Av. Mscal. Santa Cruz 1295, 3rd floor, Telex TRTURIN BV 2301; offices also in Cuzco and Puno), run an airport transfer service, city tour, and tours to Tiahuanaco, Lake Titicaca and Copacabana; they also have a new international service La Paz-Cuzco (see below). Tur-Bol, Mercado 1385 (Tel.: 324873); Turismo Balsa, Av. 16 de Julio 1650 (Tel.: 356566 and 355817, does inexpensive pathfinding tours round and near city); Pacific Tours; Turisbus (Illampu 704 Casilla 442, Tel.: 325348/326531), helpful, but mixed reports on its services (to Puno and Cuzco), and Marka Tambo, Calle Mercado 1328 (Ed. Mscal. Ballivián, Local 24) for local tours. Exprinter has tickets to Tumbes and Guayaquil (does not now operate exchange facilities). Taveline Tours, English-speaking, at Av. Camacho 1404, will cater for the unusual request. Taura Tours, Av. Arce, run jungle tours to their own camp as well as the Salt Lake areas, and the Amazon, friendly, good guides (also charter flights to Europe and U.S.A.); Profian Tours, Sra. Perales, Plaza Venezuela 1456, Tel.: 340729/342669, also organizes cheap flights—some payable in bolivianos, also recommended for local bus tours. Pan Tur, Edif.

BOLIVIA 167

Alamedo, Av. 16 de Julio, Tel.: 322454 is one of the largest. Atlas Tours organizes tourist guides and trips to Tiahuanaco, Isle of the Sun etc,; they use public transport and hence *seem* cheaper than the rest. However you should read what's offered carefully to avoid disappointments. Diplomatic Tours, managed by Rosario Zambrana, located at 2nd floor of Plaza Venezuela 1920, has been recommended (Tel.: 356372/310482); will provide airport transfer (US$8). Magri Turismo is the Amex agent, Av. 16 de Julio 1490, open Mon.-Fri., 0900-1200, 1400-1800, recommended. Leslie Iruzoque organizes "alternative" trips while her mother can provide accommodation near Moon Valley (Tel.: 360777 or 791767). Paititi S.R.L., Calle Juan de la Riva, Ed. Alborada (oficinas 106-107, P.O.Box 106, Tel.: 329625), organizes adventure tours, recommended, Javier Prudencio is helpful and speaks several languages. Shima Tours, Potosí 1310, recommended. Bolivian Adventure Tours in hall of *Hotel Sucre* has tents for hire. Also Carmoar Tours, which is headed by Günther Ruttger, Calle Campero 19; (Tel.: 370506), recommended as among the best and the cheapest. See also names and addresses under "Exchange Houses", page 165.

Airport El Alto, on plain above La Paz, the highest commercial airport in the world (4,018 metres), about ¼ hour by taxi (US$10, colectivo US$2) from centre. A motorway links city and airport. The ordinary road was damaged in January 1984 and now entails a detour of about 1 hour. International airport tax US$15 in bolivianos or dollars, internal US$1-3 (in bolivianos). There is a duty-free shop but it can sometimes forget to open. There are no exchange facilities. There is a small tourist office at the Airport which should know the price of a taxi to town, some maps available, English spoken, helpful. The coffee shop is slow but inexpensive.

Air Taxis US$250 per hour, contact Major Pericón of Taxi Aéreo Urkupiña, Tel.: 350580 or 812099.

Air Services Lloyd Aéreo Boliviano (LAB) and TAM (the air force and not recommended) fly to the main cities and towns, and also to Lima, Arica daily, and twice a week (Tues. and Sat. at 0900) to Cuzco (but not all the year round). Fares are comparatively low in bolivianos but foreigners tend to have to pay in dollars, especially for flights abroad. LAB, who are not IATA members, also have international flights which are cheaper than the IATA flights. However the only credit card LAB accept locally is American Express; they will not accept payment in bolivianos - nor will other international carriers. LAB have introduced a 28 day unlimited domestic flight ticket for US$99. However you must enter Bolivia using LAB or under the pooling arrangement LAB has with Lufthansa or Aeroperú at the moment. Also LAB is promoting limited stay tickets as well as the normal Apex type fares. Spouse fares (i.e. one goes free with one paying full fare) available on certain international flights. Insure your bags heavily as they tend to get left around.

Bus Services (for information, Tel.: 366783); to Copacabana (3½ hours, US$8, all companies) Oruro (3 hours, US$4.15), Potosí (14 hours, US$10.75), Sucre (24 hours, US$13), Cochabamba (12 hours, US$ 6.80, Nobleza), Santa Cruz (23 hours, US$24), Tarija (26 hours, US$15), Coroico (0900, Tues., Thurs., Fri., Sat. 5 hours, US$2.60), Villazón (US$16), Tiahuanaco (US$1). There are also services to towns in the Yungas from Av. de las Américas 344. Take Micro K, U or V to Villa Fátima, get off at the big service station—the booking office is 20 metres on. Buses to Sorata, Copacabana (except for Flota Copacabana, expensive, which does), Tiahuanaco do not leave from the bus station but from the Cementerio district (Micro M goes there). Companies located in the Cementerio district include Manco Kapac, 2 de Febrero, Ingavi, Morales. As so few roads are well paved, train is usually preferable to bus when there is a *ferrobus* service (see below). The services of Cóndor and Andino companies (they share a ticket window) are best avoided.

International Buses To Buenos Aires, 4 days a week at 1830, Expresos Panamericanos. Bus to Arica at 0630 Tues. and Fri, in each direction, US$20, Litoral (office at back of bus terminal), 18 hrs., a very hard trip on a dirt road in the Bolivian section to Tambo Quemado, subject to cancellation in the wet, no food but beautiful. Colectivos to Puno daily with different companies most easily booked through travel agencies, US$12-15, 10 hrs. Turisbus, who run to Copacabana, Puno and Cuzco daily in conjunction with Colectur, have had mainly favourable reports. A luxury service to Puno (US$50) and Cuzco (US$65) is operated by Transturin, Av. Camacho 1321 (Tel.: 363654-328560-320445), Mon. to Fri., 11½ hrs. to Puno via Huatajata and Catamaran to Copacabana, calling at Island of the Sun en route; stay overnight in Puno and continue next day to Cuzco, arriving 1850. Well worth the price for the extra comfort.

Trains There are acceptable *ferrobus* (railcar) services between La Paz and Cochabamba (8 hours, arriving Mon., Wed., Fri., US$5.80 *especial*, US$8.70 Pullman). Sundays and Wednesdays at 1720, to Potosí (11½ hours), and Sucre (16 hours, US$10.75 1st class, US$9.50 2nd). *Ferrobus* to Potosí, Mon., Thurs., Fri., Sat. 1900, US$10 Pullman, US$6.60 *especial*. You may only buy tickets the day before you travel; office opens 0700, but get there beforehand. To Argentina no through coach (via Uyuni and Villazón), Mondays, Thursdays and Fridays, departs 2010; no food or drink is served (very dusty journey). Book ahead at central station; queue for booking at 0600 on previous day, counter opens at 0800 (queuing numbers are given out), take passport. Phone to check times etc.: 352510 or 353510. It is always advisable to check times before travelling as there are often changes.

168 BOLIVIA

Railways from the Coast (1) By the Southern Railway of Peru from Arequipa to Puno, on Lake Titicaca. Getting to La Paz from Puno: by road (several lines, 10-hour journey); Crillon Tours run a daily hydrofoil service (0600 from Puno; 0830 bus departure from La Paz).

From Guaqui to El Alto, above La Paz, a railway follows the broad plateau on an almost level gradient, rising only about 300 metres to El Alto. The journey is done once a week in about 2 hours by modern diesel railcar. It stops for 20-40 minutes at Tiahuanaco to give passengers a quick look at the ruins. Not everyone can get onto the railcar; some have to go on by bus every hour on the hour, 3'T½ hours, or colectivo (2 hours), or by the ordinary train (4 hours). Travelling from Bolivia to Peru, the train leaves La Paz on Fridays at 1400.

Of the ordinary Guaqui-La Paz train, Nicholas Humphrey writes: "It drooled down to La Paz so slowly that the fireman on our train stepped off at one point, walked into a field, picked up a lamb from a flock, and trotted back to catch the train, which had not decelerated to help him in his larceny."

(2) Arica-La Paz International Railway, 447 km. with a change of trains at frontiers, taking 20 hours at least. Accommodation limited, tickets may be booked in advance of your journey, in La Paz (behind LAN-Chile on the Prado) and Arica only; it is common to tip seat reservers up to US$1, seats being safer than the floor from the danger of pickpockets.

The line from Arica skirts the coast for 10 km. and passes into the Lluta Valley, whose vegetation is in striking contrast with the barrenness of the surrounding hills. From Kilometre 70 there is a sharp rise of 2,241 metres, in 42 km. The line is racked for 48 kms., but the rack is no longer used. At Puquíos station, Kilometre 112, the plateau is reached. The altitude here is 4,168 metres. In the distance can be seen the snowcapped heights of Tacora, Putre, Sajama, and their fellows. The greatest altitude is reached at General Lagos (4,247 metres). The frontier station of Visviri is at Kilometre 205, with a custom house. Beyond, the train enters Bolivia and the station of Charaña where passengers swap trains, usually blacked-out after dark by smugglers.

In the Bolivian section the line runs via Corocoro, the copper mining town, to Viacha, the junction of the several railways running to Antofagasta, Guaqui, and Buenos Aires. The mountain peaks visible include Illimani, Sorata, Huayna-Potosí, Muruata, and many others. Fares: La Paz-Arica: 1st class slow train US$14; 2nd class (cattle trucks with no windows or toilets) US$11; train leaves La Paz every Tues. at 2300, arriving Charaña at 0700, connecting train to Arica every 2nd and 4th Wednesday morning.

(3) Antofagasta-La Paz, by Antofagasta and Bolivia Railway, 1,173 km., is now by train as far as Calama in Chile, then by bus (240 km.) to Antofagasta; the bus ticket (US$ 3) is given when entering Chile. This, the most southerly of the three railway routes connecting La Paz with the Pacific coast, passes through magnificent scenery. There is one train a week, leaves La Paz on Friday at 1200, arriving Calama Saturday 1700; arrive by bus in Antofagasta 2030 Sunday. Fare: US$19; bookable the day before. Be at La Paz station by 1200 Thursday (tickets are on sale to 1400) to be certain of a seat (all reserved). There are no sleeping cars and it can be very cold owing to broken windows and 1915 coaches. Money changers not allowed on the train, but still manage to operate. Watch out for forged Chilean notes especially if the light is bad. It is advisable to buy Chilean currency and sell bolivianos before journey. All passports are collected and returned about one hour later in the rear carriage, when your name is called (beware, as the train goes down to Chile, carriages are added; the reverse happens in the other direction). Someone should stay awake as unreclaimed passports are *not* returned.

Going from Chile to Bolivia, Calama, 2,255 metres above the sea, is a useful point at which to stay for a day or two to get used to the altitude before going higher. The summit is reached at Ascotán (3,960 metres), and the line descends to 3,735 metres at Cebollar, where it skirts a great borax lake, 39 km. long. The Bolivian frontier is crossed a short distance beyond (444 km.) Ollagüe station (a change of trains—be quick to get your seat), from which there is a 77 km. spur to the copper mines of Collahuasi. For the next 174 km. to Uyuni the line maintains an almost uniform level of 3,660 metres. The timetable is (approximately): leave Calama 1300, arrive at the border 2300 (1-2 hr. stop), arrive Uyuni 0500; the down train should leave Uyuni for Calama at 0400, fare US$10.40 (US$16 to Antofagasta from Uyuni). The train is full of smugglers who will throw others' bags out to get their gear on.

Uyuni, the junction with the branch line of 90 km. to Atocha, gives rail access, via Villazón on the Argentine border, to Buenos Aires, a route which is not interrupted by snowstorms. After crossing the Bolivian border there are no direct coaches for Potosí on the train. Change at Uyuni or Río Mulato for *tren mixto* from Villazón, or better at Oruro (which you can visit) and then *ferrobus* or express to Potosí or La Paz reserving your seats the day before. After crossing the Bolivian border you need bolivianos to buy food on the train; so if you have no bolivianos make sure you at least have some small dollar notes for changing into bolivianos at the first stop in Bolivia. Money can be changed at Ollagüe (Chilean Customs) and Oruro. **Watch baggage** at Oruro; the thieves are notorious.

From Río Mulato (716 km.) a branch line runs to Potosí and Sucre.

(4) Buenos Aires-La Paz: This railway journey of about 2,400 km. takes 71 hours. There is no through train service. Take Monday or Friday La Paz train (1600) to Villazón (arrives 1230 Tues. or Sat.), then cross frontier to La Quiaca to catch bus to Salta or Tucumán (for trains) to Buenos Aires

(Retiro) The railway line from La Quiaca to Jujuy in Northern Argentina has had a section washed away so it is not possible to travel by train into Argentina by this route.

Note that many travellers from La Paz on the Buenos Aires and Antofagasta lines take a bus to Oruro (more comfortable and quicker than the train) and board the train there. Again, you may have trouble getting a sleeper if you do this. Remember that in northern Argentina buses tend to be much quicker than trains.

Excursions from La Paz   There is trout fishing in the many glacier lakes and streams near La Paz.

The best near-by excursion is to Río Abajo and Malasilla golf course: through suburbs of Calacoto and La Florida follow the river road past lovely picnic spots and through some of the weirdest rock formations on earth, known as the "Moon Valley". About 3 km. from bridge at Calacoto the road forks; sharp right leads to the Caza y Pesca Club and Malasilla golf course. Small entrance fee at weekends and holidays. Moon Valley can also be reached by Micro 11, which seems the most reliable (the tourist office says there are no buses—this is not true), walking 1 km. to Ancillo Arce cactus gardens (free) and a further 1 km. uphill to road fork (always keep to the right). Most of the local travel agents organize tours to Moon Valley. You get puffed walking uphill though (so take something to drink!) but taxis are not dear (US$17), especially if shared, and you make sure the price is per car and not per person. Near the cactus gardens (wrecked by flooding in 1984) is the *Balneario Los Lobos*, popular for lunch at weekends and puts on a folklore show (*peña*) on Friday nights. To Zongo Valley: a steep but scenic ride down past several of La Paz's electric power plants. In 32 km. the altitude drops from 4,265 to 1,830 metres.

To Ashumani (past Valley of the Moon) take Micro 11. Good views of the valley and houses of the wealthy. Walk back along the valley and catch frequent buses into town.

To Los Organos del Diablo, take Micro "Ñ" (last stop Cotacota) or 21 from Calle México to the end of the route, then continue for 1 km. more and you will see the rocks on the left—"more impressive especially if the wind is blowing than Moon Valley". A further 4 km. on is the top of the mountain with a superb view of Illimani. The road continues to Ventilla, the start of the Inca trail.

For the Takesi (Inca) road hike, take a bus at 0830 from a street on the right below Plaza Belsiz (which is below the Mercado Rodríguez) to Ventilla on Palaca road (alternatively take a taxi to Ovejura vehicle checkpoint above Cota Cota, US$6.35, then truck to Ventilla), then follow 10 km. track to San Francisco mine. The "camino de Takesi" goes over the pass (4,650 metres) and then follows the valley which ends at Chojlla and on 5 km. to Yanacachi (*Hotel Panorámico*, F, very basic; some meals available in private homes)— colectivo to La Paz at 0800 (If you miss that, it's a 45-min. walk down to Santa Rosa, which is on the main La Paz-Chulumani road). The Bradts' book *Backpacking in Peru and Bolivia* (the tourist office in La Paz also publishes a leaflet with sketch map) describes this two-day walk, which shows exceptionally fine Inca paving in the first part. Please take care not to litter the route. The highest point is 4,650 metres and the lowest 2,100. The trail can also be used as a starting point for reaching Chulumani or Coroico. The scenery changes dramatically from the bitterly cold pass down to the humid Yungas. At Chojlla one can sleep at the school house for a fee.

Another trail is the Choro hike from La Cumbre pass to Coroico, descending from the snow-covered heights to tropical vegetation. (The tourist office's map of the trail is inaccurate and should not be trusted in bad weather.) Near the end of the trail, at Sandillani, a Japanese man welcomes hikers, allowing them to camp in his orchard (he is also keen to learn English and German); repay his hospitality with postcards, stamps or coins from your home country. From Chairo, trucks go to the main road, but there is a stiff climb remaining up to Coroico.

For the acclimatized only: A climb to Corazón de Jesús, the statue at the top of the hill reached via the steps at the north end of Calle Washington, then left and right and follow the stations of the cross. Worth the climb for the views over the city and the Altiplano, but watch out where you put your feet.

The route to **Huayna Potosí**, an attractive peak (2 days) starts from Zongo lake. Micro G to Alto Lima, then ordinary bus or truck at about 1300 to Milluni. Alternatively taxi to Zongo from about US$7 (buses return at about 1500). Huayna Potosí (about 6,000 metres) requires mountaineering experience with ice and crevasses on the way to the top; however bad weather, apart from mist, is rare. Alternatively Condoriri or Pequeño Alpamayo are reached in one or two days from Tuni at Km. 21 on the La Paz-Tiquina road.

Skiing Ninety minutes by car from La Paz (36 km.) is Chacaltaya, the highest ski run in the world. Season: December to March. Skiing equipment may be hired, and a rope-tow reaches 5,221 metres (out of order in 1986). Taxi US$25 (whole car) for a half-day trip, or similar to the top by rented car costs about US$60, and really only at weekends; no visitor should miss the experience and the views. Also on Sundays in season (very good in November). However the trip can be hair raising as the buses carry no chains and the drivers seem to have little experience on snow. The Club Andino runs its own Saturday and Sunday buses; the day trip, beginning at 0830 and returning at 1730, comes to about US$21 for bus ticket, ski pass and equipment hire for the day; your bus ticket (US$7) gives free access to the ski station restaurant. Equipment for hire is available from Club Andino (US$10 skis and boots, poor condition) or Ricardo Ramos, 6 de Agosto 2730, about US$ 10 per day (Tel.: 343441 or 372920). The lift pass costs US$4 (N.B. Club Andino's oxygen bottle at the Chacaltaya station is empty). Crillon also does a day trip, at US$15. Club Andino (Calle México 1638) also occasionally arrange trips to Mount Illimani. One can walk to the summit of Chacaltaya for a view of Titicaca on one side and La Paz on the other. Tiring, as it is over 5,000 metres, but one has most of the day to do the climb. Take plenty of mineral water when going to the mountains as it's thirsty work in the rarefied air. Laguna de Milluni, near Chacaltaya, is a beautiful lake to visit, but do not drink its water; it is dangerously contaminated by acid residues from mining.

Urmiri Take road S towards Oruro across the Altiplano, turn left at Urmiri sign at Km. 75. To get this far take Flota Bolívar or Flota Copacabana bus; lifts from the crossroads are few and far between. A steep scenic descent leads to pool filled by mineral springs and a pleasant primitive inn. Worth visiting. A 2½ hour trip one way. The La Paz Prefectura runs buses to Urmiri, where they have a hotel (D), price includes food.

Sorata is 105 km. from La Paz at 2,695 metres, giving appreciable relief, and is very beautiful. A 4-6 hour trip each way, bus every day with Transportes Flores, Calle Eyzaguirre (near Cemetery), 0645, or La Perla del Illampu, Calle Miguel Angel Bahía 1556 at 0700. It is in a valley at the foot of Illampu. Area has lovely views, mountain climbing, cave exploring (with lake inside, don't forget torch! Don't go swimming; people keep disappearing). Climbers of **Illampu** (experience and full equipment necessary) start here: hire horses at Candelaria mine and on to Coóco where llamas are hired to reach the base camp at 4,500 metres. Swimming pool 2 km. along road to river. Sunday market. Also Sunday market festival, including bull market, at village of **Achacachi** (Pensión, F, tiny) on the road. Not far from Sorata, along E shore of Lake Titicaca, is a tremendous marsh giving the best duck shooting in Bolivia. Typical *fiestas*, both at Sorata and Achacachi, on Sept. 14. Pleasant walks: splendid one to San Pedro village and cave with ice-cold swimming in underground lake, 75 metres below surface. Ulla Ulla vicuña reserve off the Achacachi-Puerto Acosta road around the northeast corner of Lake Titicaca, about 200 km. from La Paz.

Sorata Hotels *Prefectural*, recommended, good value, C, with meals, hot water. *Residencia Sorata* above Casa Gunther, C (recommended) with good meals. *Perlandina*, F, friendly and comfortable. *Alojamiento Central*, main plaza, No. 127, F, basic. *San Cristóbal*, near market, F, bargain. *Copacabana*, G, basic, clean and cheap.

Tiahuanaco (Tiwanaku) The ruins of Tiahuanaco (admission US$2—beware of overcharging) are near the southern end of Lake Titicaca, by partly paved road through the village of Laja (solid silver altar in church; entrance US$ 0.50), the first site of La Paz. Simple meals at US$0.80 available in village. There is a restaurant near the ruins, for those on booked tours (drinks are expensive). The village church is in striking contrast with the pre-Incaic statuary in front of it. The ruins, which are believed to date from AD 800 and are being reconstructed,

BOLIVIA 171

comprise four main structures: the Kalasasaya compound, the Acapana pyramid, the underground temple, and lastly the Gate of the Sun, with carved stone blocks weighing many tons; this is reported in a bad state as the locals used it for shooting practice. Ticket to Tiahuanaco also gives entrance to Puma Punku (down the road 1 km.), which contains a pair of andesite gates (among the finest examples of stone cutting in South America) while its sandstone platforms are made up of cut slabs weighing 13 tonnes each. There is a private museum near the ruins, but it is closed for repairs; in any event, most of the best statues are in the Museo Tiahuanaco or the Museo Semisubterráneo in La Paz. Indians trade arrowheads and bronze figures (almost all fakes). There is a very basic *alojamiento* on Calle Bolívar, cheap but good views.

Guidebook in English *Tiwanaku*, by Mariano Baptista, Plata Publishing Ltd., Chur, Switzerland, or *Discovering Tiwanaku* by Hugo Boero Rojo. They are obtainable from Los Amigos del Libro (or 2nd-hand from stalls in Av. Ismael Montes). *Guía Especial de Arqueología Tiwanaku*, by Edgar Hernández Leonardini, a guide on the site, recommended. Written guide material is very difficult to come by, so if you can hire a good guide take him with good grace (US$10).

Buses for Tiahuanaco (72 km.) can be caught outside the main La Paz railway station, but may be full already! Taxi for 2 costs about US$30 (can be shared), return, with unlimited time at site. Transportes Ingavi, Av. José María Asin y Eyzaguirre (take any Micro marked 'Cementerio') US$1 (2 hrs.), eight times a day, arrive at terminal by 0600. Some buses go on from Tiahuanaco to Desaguadero, US$0.50. Return can be slow because of frequent customs checks. Return buses can be caught at the crossroads in the village at the "Tránsito" sign; book return as soon as you arrive in the village (return on market day, Sunday, is very difficult). You can also go by train at 0700 from La Paz.

Lake Titicaca

The road and railway go to **Guaqui,** the port for the Titicaca passenger boats (service suspended in 1985/86; *Hotel Guaqui*, G, good value; tiny restaurant on the Plaza de Armas has been recommended). The road crosses the border at Desaguadero into Peru and runs along the western shore to the Peruvian port of Puno, at the northern end. Desaguadero is noted for its lack of accommodation. At Yunguyo a side road to the right re-enters Bolivian territory and leads to Copacabana. (Occasional buses, taking 45 minutes.)

Copacabana, 158 km. from La Paz, is an attractive little town on Lake Titicaca. It has a heavily restored church containing a famous 16th century miracle-working Dark Virgin of the Lake, also known as the Virgin of Candelaria, the patron saint of Bolivia. Candlelight procession on Good Friday. The church itself is notable for its spacious atrium with four small chapels; the main chapel has one of the finest altars in Bolivia. A *hospicio* (serving now as an almshouse) with its two arcaded patios is worth a visit; ask permission before entering. There are 17th and 18th century paintings and statues in the sanctuary and monastery. Good food and drink at the hotels and in the market. Bank only opens Wednesday-Sunday (does not change money); a few restaurants and shops give poor rates, so buy Bolivian money in Yunguyo (beware, much counterfeit money here) before

TURISMO BALSA LTDA.

Daily Tours

**TIWANACU   TITICACA LAKE
CITY TOUR AND MOON VALLEY
Balsa C
LA PAZ–COPACABANA–PUNO–CUZCO
or vice versa**

Visit our "Hostal Balsa" on Lake Titicaca

Operated by

Turismo Balsa Ltda, P.O. Box 5889, Telex BV2358, Phone 354049, La Paz, Bolivia.

172 BOLIVIA

crossing frontier, if coming from Peru. There is a *fiesta* every Saturday, followed by penance on following Sunday climbing up the hill to the Holy Sepulchre, past stations of the Cross. Other services include the blessing of cars and trucks. Major festival on August 5-8 makes town full, and dangerous. There are good walks beside the lake for those unwilling to do penance on the hill, or to an Inca site, Horca del Inca, on the hill behind the town overlooking the lake (recommended sunset walk). On the other side of the lake is El Baño del Inca, about 4 km. in direction of La Paz. Ask for directions on reaching the woods. Copacabana's water supply can be intermittent.

Hotels at Copacabana: *Playa Azul*, E, full board (rooms fair, meals and service good, half-board a possibility), hot showers, now generally recommended, bookable through Riveros bus company, Av. Montes, La Paz; new hotel being built on hill to replace the old one. *Ambassador*, F (bookings through the Copacabana bus company in Av. Montes, La Paz); *Patria*, in main square, E, dirty, cold water, good food; *Prefectural*, C, if with full board, no hot water, only hotel with view of lake; D, with no view of lake, risky for a single female, sloppy service; *Alojamiento Urinsuyo*, C, Destacamento 211, basic, G, water only in the morning. *Residencial La Porteñita*, off main plaza, E; *Alojamiento Santa Rosa*, E (C with full board); *Tunari*, F, clean and friendly, electricity only 1900-2200; *Alojamiento Copacabana*, corner of main plaza, F; *Alojamiento Imperio*, Calle V. Conde de Lemos, F, clean, new, some hot water, repeatedly recommended; *Residencial San Silvestre*, cheap and clean. Good value are *Pensión Titicaca*, ½ block from main Plaza, F; *Inca*, G, basic; recommended; *Residencial Copacabana*, G, noisy; *Alojamiento San José*, G, clean, laundry, with hot water during evening (take candles); *Santa Rosa*, by lake, G; and *Residencial Alojamiento Illimani*, F, with bath (food served). For the budget minded, *Emperador*, behind the Cathedral, G, friendly and clean, highly recommended, washing done, communal baths, hot showers; *Alojamiento Bolívar*, G, primitive. *Sucre* (noisy) E, with hot shower, Manco Kapac. *El Turista* at Calle 13 de Mayo and Jaure, recommended, cheap and clean. Just out of town is *Hotel El Peregrino*, a converted *hacienda*, French-run, check the price to be charged as they can be volatile, E with bath and dinner, excellent food.

Restaurant Aransay, Av. 6 de Agosto 130 friendly, acceptable food. Watch out for gringo pricing of food and in restaurants. *Puerta del Sol* on the plaza, unfriendly, expensive; *Peña Clima* has music on Saturdays, behind the market; *Restaurant Turistas* is recommended.

Transport By car from La Paz to Copacabana (direct), 4 hours. Bus (Ambassador, Manco-Kapac, Flota Copacabana, US$8, or book at office by *Hotel Tumusla*, at corner of Av. Buenos Aires and Calle Tumusla), 5 hrs., 0800, 1300 and 1500, last bus back to La Paz at 1400; book one day in advance. Bus, Copacabana-Yunguyo (for Peruvian frontier), hourly, (US$0.50) from plaza below *Hotel Playa Azul*. Minibus to Puno leaves 1200, US$3.75 from *Hotel Litoral* on Plaza. To reach Copacabana (or Tiquina) you cross the lovely straits of Tiquina (on the La Paz side of the Strait, there is a clean blue restaurant with excellent toilets). Vehicles are loaded on to a barge equipped with outboard motors. The official charge for a car is US$2, though they ask for more and there is a US$0.50 municipal car toll to enter Copacabana. Delays on the lake crossing during rough weather, when it can get very cold. Even when one has a bus ticket passengers pay US$0.20 each to cross. **N.B.** It is impossible to travel from Copacabana to Guaqui direct, because of border crossings.

Visiting the Lake (avoid Sundays). Sailing boats and motor-boats can be hired in Copacabana to visit the Island of the Sun. It contains a sacred rock at its NW end, worshipped as the site of the Inca's creation legend. In the middle of the E shore are Inca steps down to the water. A 2-km. walk from the landing stage to the SE takes one to the main ruins of Pilko Caima—a two- storey building with false domes and superb views. The Island of the Moon (or Coati) may be visited—the best ruins are an Inca temple and nunnery. A cheap way to visit the Island of the Sun is to catch the public ferry from the Bolivian naval station (passport required); it leaves 1300 on Weds., Sats., Sundays. Worth taking camping equipment and food as there is no boat back on the same day nor any accommodation. Ask permission at the *hacienda*, good spring water available opposite hydrofoil landing. Beware of thieves. Boats (not tackle) are hired at reasonable rates for fishing. Dawns and sunsets are spectacular. At **Chúa**, on the lake, there is duck shooting, fishing, sailing and at **Huatajata** a yacht club (*Hotel Chúa*, situated on lake between Huatajata and Tiquina, good). From Huatajata boats may be taken to Suriqui, where the reed boats are made (US$5 return). Thor Heyerdahl's *Ra II* and *Tigris* reed boats were constructed by craftsmen from Suriqui, and so was the balloon gondola for the Nazca (Peru) flight experiment (see page 692).

BOLIVIA 173

Boats on Lake   6 hours to Island of Sun and back, about US$25 for boat taking 12 (you can bargain) or US$10 for a 6 seater, best ruins on S, good scenery on N side, but difficult to persuade boatmen to go there. Similar rates for Island of the Moon. (Sailing boats, which take five and cost less, often suffer from lack of wind in the morning.) Rowing boat, US$5 an hour. Cheaper boats can be found by walking several km. along the lakeside outside Copacabana. Danger of sunburn on lake.

Crillon Tours, Avenida Camacho 1223, run a hydrofoil service on Lake Titicaca with a bilingual guide. Leaving La Paz at 0600 (except Saturday), you get to Huatajata on Lake Titicaca for breakfast by 0800. The hydrofoil sets off at 0830, moves past groups of reed fishing boats, and stops in the Straits of Tiquina for a few minutes to watch the wooden ferry boats crossing. Only the Island of the Sun is visited to see the ruins. You arrive at Copacabana for sightseeing and a trout lunch, with local folk music. The short tour returns to La Paz from Copacabana; the longer one continues to Juli (Peru) to see the fine colonial church. Charge: US$100 from La Paz to Copacabana; US$200 for the La Paz-Cuzco or Arequipa trip. Expensive but fascinating, not least for the magnificent views of the Cordillera on a clear day.

Tristan Jones, who crossed South America in his sailing cutter *Sea Dart* (see his book *The Incredible Voyage*, Futura Publications) wrote to us as follows: "During my crossing I spent over eight months cruising Lake Titicaca and probably know it better than anyone, including the Indians. On the Bolivian side, in Lake Huanamarca, i.e. from Straits of Tiquina south, the best way to visit the Lake from La Paz is to take a bus from Avenida Buenos Aires to Huatajata and there ask for Nicolás Catari. He is a great boatbuilder and knows the Lake well. Avoid Suriqui Island, which has become very commercialized. The best islands to visit are **Pariti,** where the weaving is very good indeed and, only a mile or so away, **Quebraya,** where there are pre-Inca *chulpas*, or tombs, stretching along the shore. This was the ancient port for Tiahuanaco, when the lake fell back from that city. No-one lives there, and it is best always to go with an Aymará guide, for the locals are very jealous of the place.

"The only hotel on Lake Huanamarca, at Chúa, is now expensive, but the trout is good. Nicolás Catari will also, if he likes you, arrange sleeping accommodation but it is very rough and you would have to take your own sleeping gear.

"Note   The Titicaca Indians' most interesting music, and quite rare, is at masses held for the dead."

Crossing the Peruvian Frontier

We give below the journey by road (see Peruvian section, page 710 for other routes). A visa to Peru will cost US$4 in US currency (if you need one). Also, the Bolivian navy (some assorted hovercraft and motor boats) may be seen at Tiquina. The road between La Paz and Tiquina is now paved.

No hotel at Tiquina, but ask for the Casa Verde, where you can stay for US$0.50 p.p. Two cheap eating places at Yunguyo.

Just as interesting as the water route is the bus journey from Puno along the western side of the lake via Juli, Pomata, Yunguyo (from there to Copacabana is 13 km. so take taxi or bus), then back almost to Pomata to take the main road on to Desaguadero at the border. Puno-Desaguadero takes 5 hours by taxi and 6 hours by bus. La Paz is reached any time between 1800 and 2100. This is a colourful trip, with wonderful views of the lake against the snow-capped Cordillera. The road on the Peruvian side is nearly all paved, and you really see the Indian life of the Altiplano.

A colectivo from Puno to La Paz costs US$12-15 p.p. (8 hours). A bus can be caught at Desaguadero for La Paz, 114 km., US$5, but this route is not really recommended because there is sometimes a shortage of buses. At the risk of another change it may be better to catch buses Puno-Yunguyo (get exit stamp) Yunguyo-Copacabana (frequent buses) and Copacabana-La Paz, via Tiquina. This is possible in one day in the reverse direction. Ferry at Tiquina, US$0.15.

If you are leaving Copacabana for Peru, get exit stamp at Bolivian immigration office (open 0800-1900) on Yunguyo road, or you can get exit/entrance stamp at Immigration Office on Copacabana near the edge of the town, if border post is closed. Generally, though, this is now a very straightforward border crossing, with customs and immigration posts at either side of the border; the buses stop at each one, 4 in all (or you can walk, but it is over 1 km.). Make sure, however, if arranging a through ticket La Paz-Puno, that you get all the necessary stamps en route, and ascertain whether or not your journey involves a change of bus.

It is also possible to enter/leave Bolivia via the east side of the lake. However, the Peruvians do not officially recognize the road as being a border crossing. (Officially, you must get your entry stamp in the Department of Puno, but as this is next to impossible on this route, you will run into difficulties later on.) The Bolivian frontier is at **Puerto Acosta** (there is an immigration office, but

174 BOLIVIA

it is advisable to get an exit stamp in La Paz first, especially if you have not been staying at a recognized hotel—see page 199). One *alojamiento* (G) and one restaurant (*pensión*) on the main plaza (2 smaller *pensiones*/kitchens on the smaller plaza). The road to La Paz (fine during the dry season only) passes through splendid scenery while the area around Puerto Acosta is good walking country and the locals are friendly. Ask for directions to the thermal water swimming pool. The Acosta road northwards to Peru rapidly deteriorates and is only recommended in the dry season (approximately May to October). The only transport beyond Acosta is early on Saturday mornings when a couple of trucks go to the markets, some 25 km. from Puerto Acosta on the border (no formalities); the Peruvian and Bolivian markets are completely different.

N.B. Remember that if you wish to enter Peru from Bolivia you must have an onward ticket (or return ticket) out of Peru. Bolivia sometimes (about one in ten) demands outward tickets, but the officials don't often check. A ticket outward from Peru to, say, Chile, Brazil or Colombia can be purchased at Exprinter in La Paz, but you will have to pay in foreign currency rather than bolivianos.

The Yungas

NE of La Paz an all-weather road runs to the Yungas. It circles cloudwards over La Cumbre pass at 4,725 metres; the highest point is reached in an hour; all around stand titanic snowcapped peaks and snowfields glinting in the sun. Then it drops over 3,400 metres to the luxuriant green Alto Beni in 80 km. The little town of **Coroico** is perched on a hill at 1,525 metres; the scenery is beautiful (a walk to the river for a swim is a must), but finding food can be a problem.

A two or three day walk is from La Cumbre to Coroico on the Coroico road, following the pointing hand of Christ along the Inca road to Coroico. Wonderful scenery from the snowy highlands to semi-tropical Coroico (full details in the Bradts' *Backpacking in Peru and Bolivia*). From Coroico one can go by road and boat to Puerto Linares and Santa Ana, starting points for trips on the Río Beni.

Hotels *Prefectural*, C, up the hill, biggest in town with full board (F without food) but run down and food poor. *Palmar* (near bus station) only three beds, a swimming pool and it is possible to camp there; the food, including home made ice cream, is delicious; *Lluvia de Oro* (good value, food recommended, cheap), swimming pool, F. *Alojamiento Pijoán* is very basic, filthy, and should be avoided, G. *Hostal Kori*, swimming pool (open to all), good value, F, top floors recommended, clean; *Alojamiento Coroico*, G. The hotel near the junction of the La Paz-Chulumani and Coripata-Chulumani roads has been recommended; C. A camping site will be found by the small church on the hill overlooking the town—a stiff climb though; at the church take the left-hand path for another stiff climb to a waterfall. Coroico is an attractive place to wander around, especially towards evening. Hotels can be difficult at holiday weekends.

Restaurants *La Tasca*, only one menu and under new ownership, not as good as before; *La Casa* is German-run. The convent has been recommended for its chocolate biscuits, peanut butter and coffee liqueurs, and interesting cheap wine.

Festivals There is a colourful four-day festival on October 19-22. On November 2, All Souls' Day, the local cemetery is festooned with black ribbons.

Buses from La Paz to Coroico (US$2.60) leave at 0900 on Tues., Thurs., Fri., and Sat., returning from Coroico on Wed., Fri., Sat., Sun. at 1400 and take 5 hours each way; sit left hand side (book return to La Paz well in advance). Flota Yungueña (Villa Fátima, La Paz—beyond petrol station). Trucks to and from La Paz are more frequent (daily) and cheaper, US$2.10. Take Micro B, 25 minutes from or to the suburb of Villa Fátima in La Paz, from where trucks leave, one block above the bus company. Transport can be a problem at holidays. Reconfirm onward bookings from and to Coroico as it is possible to get stuck for days at a time. From Coroico, trucks leave from the market.

The roads to Coroico and to Coripata and Chulumani divide at Unduavi at a height of about 3,000 metres on the E side of La Cumbre. There is no good place to eat at Unduavi, nor at Santa Rosa on the road to Coripata.

Chulumani, the capital of Sud Yungas, is the main regional centre. Citrus fruits are the main products from this area as well as some coffee. Along the road from Puente Villa to Coripata you enter the main coca growing area of northern Bolivia and the countryside is quite different from that near Coroico, where coffee, as well as coca and fruits, is the main crop.

Hotels *Hotel Prefectural*, D; *Motel San Bartolomé* (Tel.: 358386) and *Motel San Antonio*, both C, with pleasant cabins and swimming pools. *Hotel Bolívar*, cheap, clean and friendly.

Bus La Paz-Chulumani, Flota Yungueña, 120 km., 6 hours, US$3.30.

BOLIVIA 175

From below Coroico the road forks, the lower fork following the river NE to **Caranavi,** 164 km. from La Paz, at times along a picturesque gorge, towards the settled area of the Alto Beni, and Santa Ana. Truck from Coroico, US$1.65.

Hotels *Esplendido, Universo* and *Alojamiento Buen Amigo*, E; *Caranavi*, F, clean and friendly. *Prefectural* has a swimming pool. *Avenida*, G, very basic; *Residencial Rosedal*, clean, friendly, cheap.

Bus Yungueña buses leave La Paz for Caranavi at 0900 each day; the 164-km. journey (US$4.10) takes 6-7 hours and trucks 12½ hours. Direct bus Coroico-Caranavi on Sundays.

Some 70 km. from Caranavi lies the gold mining town of

Guanay, an expensive but interesting place. To stay, *Hotel Panamericano*, F, seems the best, though there are no locks on the doors. Permission to stay for only 48 hours is granted by the police. Other gold mining sites are Tipuani and Mapiri. Buses direct from La Paz (Yungueña).

South from La Paz

Oruro is built on the slopes of a hill at an altitude of 3,704 metres. The population, mostly Indian, is 162,213. It is about 190 km. from La Paz, and is important as a railway centre and for its tin, silver, and tungsten. A 20,000 tons-a-year tin smelter has been built nearby at Vinto; it can be visited in the morning, the vats are broached between 0930-1030. Take Micro D to terminus, and show passport at the gate. A pesticides plant is being built with Argentine assistance. There is good *pejerrey* fishing on a large nearby lake. Excellent daily market, near railway station. The zoo is not really worth a special visit. Airport. Rail travellers from Antofagasta can alight at Oruro and continue to La Paz by bus (quicker). Hotel prices at least double at Carnival time and a severe water shortage puts showers at a premium. In hotels hot water is only available in the mornings, owing to city ordinances.

Hotels *Repostero*, good by local standards but unfriendly, C with bath; *Prefectural-Oruro*, C, near station, improved, good restaurant; *Residencial Pagador*, Calle Ayacucho, G, *Residencial Ayacucho*, next door; *Los Arenales*, Calle Sucre, F; *Confort*, F, near bus terminal, poor value, dirty; *Hotel* and *Casa de Huéspedes La Plata*, Calle La Plata, E; *Alojamiento Porvenir*, near bus station, G; *Duchas Oruro*, showers, cheap, F; and *Lípton*, E, hot water, breakfast within two blocks; *Alojamiento Derby*, esq. Calles Pagador and Ayacucho; *Residencial Ideal*, Bolívar 392, F, reports vary. *Alojamiento Bolívar*, F, bad, but restaurant is good and cheap. *Terminal*, above bus depot, D, modern, good, hot water, night club, expensive restaurant. *Residencial Familiar* annex, F, 25 de Mayo, is clean. *Hispanoamericano*, opposite station, F, no hot water and no running water after 2200. *Alojamiento Ferrocarril*, G, basic, no hot water; better; *San Juan Apóstol*, Calles Sucre y Pagador, clean, friendly, communal bath, cold water, F, near train station. *Hospedaje Mutual*, Calle Sucre, has leaking roof and surly owner.

Restaurants *Fuente Suiza*, 6 de Octubre y Bolívar, very good but not cheap; *La Prensa*, Murguía (500 block, Press Club restaurant), quite good; *Pigalle*, Plaza 1 de Febrero, is well regarded but not cheap; *Confitería Chic*, Bolívar (500 block); *Comercio* and *Pagador*, both in Calle Sucre; cheap food at *Pensión 10 de Febrero*, at bottom end of Bolívar. *Pastelería La Polar*, C. Presidente Montes 5985, is good place to get warm; *Pastelería Suiza*, Bolívar, near 6 de Octubre, clean and excellent tea and pastries. *Donut Shop*, 6 de Octubre y Mier, for the obvious, and good hamburgers and beer; recommended nameless restaurant at 6 de Agosto 1166, huge portions.

Sauna Esq Ayacucho y Galvano, wet or dry, showers US$0.75. Duchas Oruro, 500 block of Av. 6 de Agosto (near bus terminal).

Shopping *Infol* on Ayacucho (near Potosí) for alpaca, high quality but not cheap nor a large selection and *Reguerín* on the junction with Mier; also sell devil masks. Items are generally cheaper in Cochabamba. Money changers operate near Entel offices. Also try LAB or *Casa de Huéspedes La Plata*.

Museums Casa de la Cultura, the former Patiño mansion, is well worth a visit as well as other Patiño legacies, e.g. the Sala de Conciertos (now a cinema). Museo Arqueológico Vivero Municipal, near the zoo on Calle Lizarraga (reached on foot, or Micro 'A Sud') has unique collections of stone llama heads and carnival masks. Guide available, US$0.75. Geology Museum at the university. Ask the tourist office whether they are open.

Exchange It is quite easy to change dollars (cash) on the street, specifically 1 block E of main plaza; travellers' cheques are hard to change and banks which accept them offer very poor rates.

176 BOLIVIA

They can be changed at a good rate at Ferretería Findel, Calle Pagador 1491, near the market (large hardware store; owner, Don Ernesto, speaks English and is helpful and friendly).

Post Office Presidente Montes 1456.

Tourist Office, Edificio Prefectural, Plaza 10 de Febrero (Tel.: 51764), open Mon.-Fri., 0900-1200, 1400-1800, has map of city, helpful. Also on Bolívar and Galvarro, Mon.-Fri., 0900-1200, 1400-1800, Sat. 0900-1200.

Cables Cables can be filed at the Empresa Nacional Office (Entel) with the routing via: Cable West Coast.

La Diablada At carnival on the Saturday before Ash Wednesday, Oruro stages the Diablada ceremony. Two figures, a bear and a condor, clear the way for a procession of masked dancers, led by two luxuriously costumed masqueraders representing Satan and Lucifer. Alternating with them in the lead are St. Michael the Archangel and China Supay, the Devil's wife, who plays the role of carnal temptress. Behind them come hundreds of dancers in ferocious diabolical costumes, leaping, shouting, and pirouetting. The parade ends in the crowded football stadium, where the masqueraders perform various mass and solo dances. These are followed by two masques: the first is a tragic re-enactment of the Conquest, in the second the golden-haired Archangel conquers the forces of evil in battle.

In the contest between good and evil, the result in favour of the good is pronounced by the Virgen del Socavón, the patroness of miners, and after the performance the dancers all enter her chapel, chant a hymn in Quechua and pray for pardon. The Diablada was traditionally performed by Indian miners, but three other guilds have taken up the custom.

The costume always features the heavy, gruesome mask modelled in plaster, with a toad or snake on top; huge glass eyes; triangular glass teeth; a horsehair wig; and pointed, vibrating ears. Tied around the neck is a large silk shawl embroidered with dragons or other figures, and the dancer also has a jewelled, fringed breastplate. Over his white shirt and tights he wears a sash trimmed with coins, and from it hang the four flaps of the native skirt, embroidered in gold and silver thread and loaded with precious stones. Special boots equipped with spurs complete the elaborate outfit. Satan and Lucifer wear scarlet cloaks, and carry a serpent twisted around one arm and a trident. The working-class Oruro district known as La Ranchería is particularly famous for the excellence of the costumes and masks made there. One of the most famous folklore groups is the stately Morenada. Carnival lasts 8 days with displays of dancing by day and night often superior to those given on the opening Saturday. It is compulsory to sit to watch the Diablada processions; benches line the streets and a seat costs from US$1 to US$4, although on the main square they are reserved for tourists and cost US$10. Seats can be booked at the town hall. Take raincoats as protection against water pistols and *bombas de agua* (water-filled balloons). Latest reports suggest that the processions on Saturday before Ash Wednesday are fine, but degenerate thereafter as all the participants are drunk; also participants now have to be wealthy to afford to take part, so *campesinos* have been forced to the periphery (selling food, etc.). Beware of sharp practices and prices for gringos during the period of carnival.

Guide *Carnival de Oruro*. Dance costumes and masks, Calle La Paz, 400 block.

Trains About 5 hours to La Paz (daily 0600, US$3 1st, US$2 2nd) and 7 to Cochabamba (daily 0820) Ferrobus US$3, Pullman US$1 *especial*; to Potosí, ferrobus Mon., Thurs., Sat., 2200, US$7, express Mon., Wed., 2020, US$5 1st, US$3 2nd; to Sucre, same timetable, ferrobus, US$9, express US$7 1st, US$5 2nd class. To Villazón, *mixto*, Sun., Wed. 1900, 18 hours, exhausting but exhilerating to hardy traveller, US$5.70 Express, Mon., Thurs., Fri. 0100 (ticket office opens 0700 Sun. for this train, be early), Uyuni Pullman US$ 3.60, *especial* US$2.40. Villazón US$8.40 Pullman, US$5.60 *especial*. Ticket office opens at 0800, best to be there early. Antofagasta (Chile), 29'7½ hours, US$17.50, train from La Paz calls here (Fri.), 1800), very crowded and dusty for first few stops.

Buses To La Paz, 3 hours, seven bus lines work the route, US$4.15; to Potosí, -10 cold and rough hours, US$6.85, two companies, both at 1900 daily; to Llallagua (6 a day), US$1.65; to Cochabamba, 4½ hours, US$5, six lines, most leave 0800-1500 (one night bus 2000). To Sucre, best to go via Cochabamba as the road to Potosí is so bad. Roads to Río Mulato and Uyuni are very bad, but some trucks work the route, train (8 hours) recommended, at 1900. Bus agencies all *near the railway station in the centre*. Bus terminal on outskirts. Take Micro E from main market. Trucks to Potosí and Sucre leave from Av. Cochabamba near the Mercado Bolívar.

Excursions From Machacamarca, 24 km. S of Oruro, a branch line runs to Uncia (108 km.) and the ex-Patiño tin mines.

A taxi to Lake Uru Uru costs US$6.50; or take Micro A to its terminus and then walk 1 hour along road, take Micro B for return trip, US$0.15 each way: flamingoes and other water-birds, highly recommended, but not at the height of the dry season (October) when wild life moves elsewhere. Boats may be hired only out of the rainy season.

There are hot springs at Obrajes, where there is the choice of private baths or swimming pool,

BOLIVIA 177

both hot. Wait at the bus stop at 6 de Octubre 1420 for the (intermittent) bus. Taxis sometimes make the run. Take picnic lunch.

Visitors with a Land Rover might explore the country W of Oruro towards the Chilean frontier. It's a day's drive to the western mountains following tracks rather than roads. There are no hotels in any of the towns, such as Escara or Sabaya, but lodging could be found by asking a schoolteacher or local mayor. From Escara it is only 25 km. S to **Chipaya,** the main settlement of the most interesting Indians of the Altiplano. They speak a language closely related to the almost extinct Uru; their dress is distinctive and their houses unique. This is a very difficult trip without your own transport. Sometimes trucks leave from Plaza Walter Khon for Chipaya; or the village may be reached by taking a bus to Sabaya or Turco, then a truck. At Chipaya you are welcomed by a US$5 tourist tax imposed by the Mayor! You should refuse to pay this— the tourist police will gladly supply free an exemption certificate. Bring your own food; shelter for US$0.25 per head in adobe *alojamiento*. Bicycles may be hired in Chipaya to visit lake 2 hours away with great variety of bird life.

A one-day drive to the west is the Parque Nacional Sajama, the world's highest forest. The road is reported to be very bad. To climb **Sajama**, Bolivia's highest mountain (6,530 metres) take the Litoral bus from La Paz to Arica and pay the full fare. Ask for the Sajama stop, 20 minutes past the village of that name, before Lagunas, and about 11 hrs. from La Paz. To return to La Paz, walk to Lagunas and take a truck or the Litoral bus (twice weekly). Crampons, ice axe and rope are needed for the climb, which is not technically difficult; the routes to base camp and beyond are fairly obvious. Water is available, but beware of sulphurous streams. It can be very windy.

About 100 km. S of Oruro is **Llallagua** (*Hotel Bustillo*, F; *Santa María*, *Hotel Llallagua*, F, the best). Nearby is the famous Siglo Veinte, the largest tin mine (ex-Patiño) in the country (trucks up from town). Tourist visits start at 0700. Prior permission to visit must be obtained from Comibol in La Paz. There is an acute water shortage. Llallagua can be reached by bus from Oruro, Mondays and Thursdays with connections to Sucre or Potosí; also buses 1900 from La Paz and 0730 from Sucre twice a week.

On the road to La Paz is Patacamaya which has a Sunday market (no tourist items); *Alojamiento 18 de Julio*, F (no w/c).

A recommended driver is Freddy Barron M., Casilla 23, Ouro, Tel.: 55270, for excursions.

From Oruro a railway runs eastwards to Cochabamba (204 km.). It reaches a height of 4,140 metres at Cuesta Colorada before it begins to descend to the fertile basin in which Cochabamba lies. Lake Uru Uru is seen fleetingly at the beginning of the journey. It is 394 km. from La Paz to Cochabamba by road, now paved to Oruro and from there paved except for 50 km. midway, where the going is very rough; about 8 hours by private car. A new highway is being built to Cochabamba, via Quillacollo. On the present road, a short cut from Caracollo to Colhuasi avoids Oruro and saves 65 km.

Cochabamba, Bolivia's third-largest city, founded in 1542, is set in a bowl of rolling hills and is an important agricultural centre. Population: 281,962; altitude 2,560 metres; excellent climate with average temperature of 18°C. It has fine buildings (though much of the modern building looks seedy), a University which has an excellent archaeological museum with a small but interesting collection of prehistoric pieces and Indian hieroglyphic scripts, and little-known collection of pre-Inca textiles (Mon.-Fri. only, 0830-1200, 1400-1800, passport required, Calle 25 de Mayo, same block as Palacio de la Cultura), many Spanish houses with overhanging eaves, and much for the tourist: a grand view from San Sebastián, a hill on the edge of the city; the Golf Club on Lake Alalay (you need a member to introduce you), and Los Portales, the Patiño mansion in the northern part of the city (take Micro G), set in beautiful grounds, completed after 10 years' effort in 1927 but never occupied (tours Mon.-Fri. at 1700, and Sat. at 1000 and Sun. at 1100, free, check times with tourist office). The Cathedral in the main plaza is pleasantly decorated; panels painted to look like marble. Just off the plaza is La Compañía, whose whitewashed interior is completely innocent of the usual riot of late Baroque decoration. The municipal market and the Cancha, a retail market (Wednesday and Saturday), are also full of local colour. *Fiestas* are frequent and fascinating; the merriest is Carnival, celebrated 15 days before Lent. Rival groups (*cumparsas*) compete in music, dancing, and fancy dress, culminating in El Corso on the last Saturday of the Carnival. Beware the rains around and after Carnival, and water-throwing the day after, when you are likely to get drenched. *Mascaritas* balls also take place in the carnival season, when the girls wear long hooded satin masks. To the N, in a high fault-block range of mountains, is Cerro Tunari, 5,180 metres. A road runs to within 300 metres of the top, usually sprinkled with a little snow. There are beautiful views of the Cochabamba valley from the mountain road which goes into the Parque Tunari from Cala Cala, ending at the lake which supplies drinking water; best in the afternoon, but no public transport.

An imposing monument overlooks the town from La Coronilla, part of the same hill as San Sebastián. It commemorates the heroic defence of Cochabamba by its womenfolk during the War of Independence. It has fine views and just below it is a charming little old bull ring, little used. There are thermal baths near the city. Small zoo, free (not recommended), on banks of river (bus 8 or 17). The Palacio de Cultura, Av. Heroínas y 25 de Mayo, has a group of local museums under one roof (entrance free, but exhibits usually locked). Churches worth a visit include Santo Domingo (Santiváñez and Ayacucho) and Santa Teresa (Baptista and Ecuador). Cochabamba is an expensive city, only surpassed by Santa Cruz.

Hotels *Gran Hotel Cochabamba*, Plaza Ubaldo Anze, Tel.: 43524, beautifully set in the northern part of the city (2 blocks from Los Portales at La Recoleta), with garden, swimming pool (guests only) and tennis courts, good food, the most expensive, A. In the city: motel-type *Berkeley* (French run, solarium with each room, swimming pool); *Ambassador*, Calle España 349 (Tel.: 48777), private bath, hot water, telephone, modern, central and reasonable, C, good restaurant. *Colón*, in Plaza Colón, E, hot water, breakfast included. *Boston*, 25 de Mayo 167, E. *Metropole*, 25 de Mayo, clean, E. *Residencial Copacabana*, Calle Esteban Arce, basic, clean, has water problems, and noisy, D. *Residencial Santa Cruz*, 25 de Mayo, F. *Residencial Familiar*, Calle Sucre 554, hot water, not very clean, D, with breakfast. *City Hotel*, Calle Jordán 341, near centre, F with shower but without breakfast, clean, noisy but modern. Both *Alojamiento Oruro*, F, and *Residencial Agustín López*, near bus station, E, clean, comfortable, hot water. *Residencial San Juan de Dios*, Calle

WANTED: MAPS
ARGENTINA – BRAZIL – MEXICO GUATEMALA – EL SALVADOR – THE CARIBBEAN ISLANDS

We would much appreciate receiving any surplus maps and diagrams, however rough, of towns and cities, walks, national parks and other interesting areas, to use as source material for the Handbook and other forthcoming titles.

The above regions are particularly needed but any maps of Latin America would be welcome.

The Editor   Trade & Travel Publications Limited
5 Prince's Buildings, George Street,
Bath BA1 2ED. England

BOLIVIA 179

Agustín López, F; *Residencial Anacris*, F, Calle Nataniel Aguirre 777, clean, recommended economy. *Resid. Brussillo*, Calle San Ravelo, clean, E, food. *Residencial Oriente*, Av. Aroma, G; *Residencial Kennedy*, E, Av. Aroma 152; *Resid. Bolivia*, E, Av. Aroma 158, hot water on request; *Residencial Pullman*, Av. Aroma 370, very clean, F, hot showers. *Las Palmas*, Av. Salamanca 5536, D, spotless. *Residencial*, Calle Uruguay 213, F, good; *Hotel Sucre*, Av. Aroma, G. *Gran Hotel Las Vegas*, E, bath, recommended, Esteban Arce 352. *Residencia Buenos Aires*, 25 de Mayo 329, E, courtyard; *El Dorado*, D, friendly, clean, hot water is also in 25 de Mayo; as is *Residencial Monterrey*, F, clean, safe to leave luggage, restaurant; *Alojamiento Cochabamba*, F, clean, recommended Calle Nataniel Aguirre; *Florida*, clean and friendly, E (hot showers); *Hostal Doria*, Junín 765, D with bath, good, clean; *La Coruña*, Junín 5961 (garden), recommended, D; as is, repeatedly, *Ideal*, Calle España, F, with breakfast, clean, Italian management; *Residencial El Salvador*, Av. 25 de Mayo 6995, good views from off-street rooms, but not recommended, F and *Residencial Ollantay*, corner of Calle Baptista 211 and Colombia, E (avoid front rooms); *Alojamiento Agustín López*, Calle Agustín López, F. *Residencial Urkupiña* at Calle Esteban Arce 750, F, clean, hot water, near bus station. Highly recommended is *Residencial Elisa*, C. Agustín López, F, cheaper without breakfast, modern, clean, friendly with garden, recommended; *Residencial Palace*, Av. San Martín 1023, F, recommended. Outside town (15 mins., bus 1) *Hostal Inca*, pool, tennis court, US$10 (E) per cottage, Tel.: 42732.

Restaurants *Guadalquivir* (N of town); good Spanish-type food out of doors (nice garden), and *Victor* (on Prado), same ownership and quality (recommended for duck, a local speciality). *Pasatiempo* on Plaza Colón serves very large steaks. *Don Gerardo*, 7 km. out of town, good and cheap, traditional Bolivian food. Good food at *Restaurant-Confitería Continental*, on main plaza; excellent pastries and ice cream at the *Zurich Tea Room*, Av. San Martín, 143, closes 2000, and *Café Berneck* on Colombia and San Martín, both expensive; medium-price *Shangai*, good food although like the *China* nearby, on Av. San Martín, overpriced, better at *Lai Lai* on España opposite *Hotel Ideal*; *Rosa Roja* is yet another Chinese establishment on the Plaza; *Paula*, 25 de Mayo y Bolívar, good cheap snacks, lunch US$3; also *Oki* and *Belgardo* on same street, cheap. *La Candela*, Av. San Martín, pleasant; *Moulin Rouge*, Santiváñez near Plaza 14 de Septiembre, US$3; meal; *Carlos V* (lunches only) good value; *6 de Agosto* on the street of the same name, but a long way out of town. *La Taquiña*, 500 metres below brewery 12 km. from city, roast duck lunches Friday, Saturday and Sunday (US$5), superb views, take bus No.3 to Cruce La Taquiña, then walk 30 mins. uphill, or take taxi from Cala Cala, reached by Micro A from plaza. *California Donuts*, 25 de Mayo (expensive), and *Café Boliche*, on 25 de Mayo or *Anexo Bar Comercio*, Calle Bolívar for lunches, good cheap food. *Hotel Boston*, Calle 25 de Mayo 167, expensive. *El Paruichi*, also on Calle 25 de Mayo, serves cheap snacks. *El Dragón de Oro* on main plaza, 4 courses for US$1.50, not clean, also *La Puerta del Dragón* on corner of Avenida Arce and Ravelo, 2nd floor. No vegetarian restaurant. International menu available at *Don Quixote*, Plaza Colón, and *La Costilla de Adán*, Aniceto Padilla 120, good value. *Karpels* on Calle Achá serves Black Forest cake. Recommended is *La Estancia*, next door to the *Hotel Cochabamba*, for steaks. Also out of town *El Virgil* serves typical food in a beautiful setting. *Pensión Oruro* on Av. Aroma, very good; *Al Spiedo Cafe Expresso* recommended for quick breakfast, as is *Restaurant España* at España 272; there are also many *confiterías* in the same street; *Heladería España* and *Heladería Imperial* (off Plaza de Armas) for good ice cream; also *H. Sabor* at Esq. Colón and Prado, nice surroundings; *El Sauce* on Quijarro 70 serves local specialities not too cheap but worth it; *Gallo de Oro*, Calle Lanza S 0567, recommended. Also worth trying are *Pollo a La Canasta*, Plaza Colón, delicious; *Pizzería El Golpe*, Colombia and 25 de Mayo—Argentine style. *Dallas*, 25 de Mayo, serves hamburgers, chips and ice cream. *Salón Berna*, Av. San Martín 209, Swiss pastry, ice creams inexpensive. *Quinta Miraflores*, Calle Tarija, good local food. Recommended *salteñas* at *Confitería Caravelle* on Calle Sucre, as well as *Confitería Maggy*, Sucre and 25 de Mayo, for breakfast and ice cream. The local place for cakes is *Dulce Ilusión* on Calle España.

Shopping Large market (La Cancha) near railway station (for tourist items). *Fotrama* for alpaca sweaters, stoles, rugs, etc. (expensive); there is also a branch at Av. de Heroínas, or Madame Eleska's *Adam* shop, now run by her son (expensive), or *Amerindia*, Calle San Martín, for good rugs and lengths of alpaca material, as well as ponchos and jumpers; or picturesque Indian market and nearby shops. Camera repairs recommended at shop on General Achá, next door to *Cromos*. A very good bookshop is *Los Amigos del Libro* on Av. de Heroínas. For leather try *Confecciones Gamucuer*, Destacamento 317. Market fruit and vegetables excellent and very cheap, but on more expensive articles do not expect prices to drop very much when bargaining. Try local hot drink, *api*, made from maize. Main markets Wed. and Sat.; beware pickpockets and thieves. The women's prison, near San Sebastián hill, is reported to be set up as a commercial laundry operation, and will take washing accordingly: "a good service".

Discotheques *Aladino*, recommended; also *Harliquinn*, *Monte Carlo* and *Sansiban*.

Exchange Houses Exprinter, Plaza 14 de Septiembre; American Ltda., Plaza 14 de Septiembre. Universo, on España, 1 block from plaza (poor rates). Money changers congregate in Plaza Colón.

Consulates British, Julio Méndez 1364, (Tel.: 41627); W. Germany, España 149; US, Av. de

180 BOLIVIA

Heroínas 464, office 115, Tel.: 25896; Brazil on Plaza 4 de Noviembre; Perú, Av. Pando 1143. At 25 de Mayo 25698, Telephone 21288; is the Centro Boliviano Norteamericano with a library of English-language books, open 0900-1200 and 1500-1900 Alliance Française, Santiuráñez 187.

Language School Spanish/Aymará/Quechua, at Instituto de Idioma, Casilla 550, run by Maryknoll Fathers, and Instituto Linguístico de Verano, Av. Beni or try Sra. Blanca de La Rosa Villareal, Av. Villazón 5218 (Tel.: 44298) who charges US$3 for a 45 minute lesson.

Festivals Fiesta de la Virgen de Urkupiña, Quillacollo, mid-August, see below; and September 14, dancing.

Swimming El Paraíso, halfway to Quillacollo, sauna and pool, US$0.50 entrance, accessible by bus or train. Pool at Club Social, Calle Méjico (US$1.20), is open to the public as well as La Rivera on Simón López (Micro A) or Los Chorrillos, both US$1, crowded on Sunday (Micro G), or outside town there is Posada de Los Cisnes at Quillacollo, at Km. 13 on Cochabamba road (entrance US$1.60). Also at Don Gerardo at Km. 7.

Fishing Excellent trout fishing in lake formed by the Corani dam, 48 km. N of Cochabamba.

Post Office Av. Heroínas, next to TAM office.

Cables can be filed at Empresa Nacional Office.

Tourist Office Calle General Achá, and Plaza 14 de Septiembre (helpful). Kiosks at Jorge Wilstermann airport and near Entel building. A useful photocopy map of the city can be obtained from Los Amigos del Libro, who also publish a guide book. Recommended travel agency, Gitano Tours.

Railway Tickets available on day before travel (office opens 0600-1000, be there early). There are ferrobuses leaving for La Paz Sun., Tues., Thurs. (0830) 8 hours; fares US$8.70 Pullman, US$5.80 Especial. Express train to Oruro 0830, Tues., Fri., Sun., US$2.10 1st class, US$1.50 2nd; ferrobus daily at 0725, US$3 1st, US$1 2nd. Train to Sucre on Mon. and Thurs. at 0700.

Air Service Jorge Wilstermann airport. Daily by LAB to and from La Paz (½ hour), US$20 one way (15 kg. baggage allowance), and to Santa Cruz, (½ hour, US$22.50) Sucre and Trinidad (connects with Riberalta flight), on Wed., Thurs., Sat. and Sun. Airport bus is Micro B from Plaza 14 de Septiembre. LAB in town at Ayacucho and Heroínas, open 0800; at airport LAB office opens 0500. TAM flights to Riberalta (Heroínas 235) US$100, but infrequent; best to fly from La Paz or Santa Cruz, via Trinidad.

Bus Services Buses (all overnight) and colectivos have day and night services to Santa Cruz, taking 12 to 16 hours (US$14), a beautiful trip; to La Paz via Oruro (0800, 1000 and 1300 with Nobleza), US$6.80, over a terrifying road (but good surface for all but 1½ hours), you have to change buses in Oruro and get a new ticket at the same time on a different floor, luggage is automatically transferred to the new bus; or via Caracollo, by night or by day, 10-12 hours (US$9.50). Bus to Oruro, US$5, 6½ hrs. Epizana (US$3.35). Daily to Sucre, by Flota Minera, Aroma 120, between 1800 and 1830, 12 hours, US$12, all but the first 2 hours are very bad. Villa Tunari, US$2.60 with Transportes Chapare and many others, very frequent. Also from Calle Lanza to Puerto Villaroel, US$6.50, but lorries run daily from Av. República, US$3.30. Most buses start from Av. Aroma, at foot of San Sebastián and Coronilla hills, about 1 km. S of main square. Most bus agencies are in the modern bus station near the centre. There is a decent hotel forming part of the bus station complex. Trucks to Oruro leave from Plaza San Sebastián. Trucks to Sucre leave from end of Av. San Martín (US$3.30). Bus to Quillacollo every 15 minutes, leaves from the corner of Av. Heroínas and Hamiaya or Plaza Guzmán Quibón.

The Cochabamba basin, dotted with several small townships, is the largest grain and fruit producing area in Bolivia. **Quillacollo** (20,000 people), a 20 minute bus ride from Av. Ayacucho, just beyond the markets in Cochabamba (good Sunday market but no tourist items; the campesinos do not like being photographed). Fiesta de la Virgen de Urkupiña in mid-August lasts 4 days with much dancing and religious ceremony (designed to make you rich); very interesting, plenty of transport from Cochabamba. 10 km. N of there is the Balneario Liriuni (thermal swimming pool and private baths, simple, not well-maintained, small restaurant, entry US$1 p.p.—to get there, take Calle Santa Cruz, the first on the right beyond the traffic circle coming from Cochabamba, no signpost, or bus on Sun. for 6 km. then take road to the right for 2 km. to the river—bridge washed away—then walk 2 km. Taxi, which may not get all the way there, costs US$25; it's not really worth the cost or the effort). Don't miss Tarata, a sleepy old village with beautiful Plaza, nearby, market day Thursday (bus also from Av. Ayacucho). A railway line runs from Cochabamba through the Punata Valley as far as Arani (60 km.). Another runs to Vila-Vila (132 km.). There is a large Sunday market at

BOLIVIA 181

Clisa, accessible by bus from Av. Ayacucho and another every Tuesday at Punata. Buses from Avenida Ayacucho. For those interested in *charangos* (of wood) a visit to Alquile (6 hrs) by train is recommended. To the north is the Parque Tunari, which is partly forested, and Laguna Wara Wara at 4,000 metres surrounded by 4,500 metre mountains.

Three seldom visited Inca ruins might be of interest: Inka-Rakay, a small outpost about 45 minutes' drive from Cochabamba and a 2-hour hike up a mountain; and Inkallakta and Samaipata (see below):

The Inka-Rakay ruins are near the village of Sipe-Sipe; the main attraction is the view from the site over the Cochabamba valley, as well as the mountains ringing the ruins. Take a bus to Quillacollo where the bus for Sipe-Sipe waits until there are enough passengers. From Sipe-Sipe to the ruins there is either a 4 km. footpath, or a 12 km. road with almost no traffic, which, to walk, takes three hours. Either hitch or hire guides and Land Rover in Cochabamba. Several letters indicate that it might be less terrifying to walk but all admit that this is a beautiful trip. Start early for it is a full day. Leave the Square at Sipe Sipe going up the street past the church, then left at the top and then right when you come to the wider road. Follow this road (easily graded) all the way to the top of the ridge ahead. Just below the ridge, the road loses a little height to take a bend. There is an outcrop of rock and here look for a track leading away downhill. The Inka-Rakay ruins are about 200 metres below and easily missed. (There is no clearly marked track). **N.B.** Carry plenty of water as there is none available.

The 500-km. road to Santa Cruz (page 190) is paved, but the surface has greatly deteriorated. Before the Siberia pass, 5 km. beyond Montepunco at Pocona (Km. 119), the 23-km. road to Inkallakta (unpaved and very bad) turns off. The ruins, on a flat spur of land at the mouth of a steep valley, are extensive and the temple is of special interest but nearly impossible to get to without your own transport. At Km. 386 are the ruins of Samaipata, worth a stop. At ***Epizana,*** 13 km. beyond Montepunco (Km. 128), with hotels and service stations, a branch road, right—dusty, stony, and narrow in parts, but very scenic—goes 233 km. to Sucre, 7-8 hours drive. Another road has been built to link Cochabamba with the Beni area (see page 194).

S of Oruro the railway from La Paz skirts Lake Poopó, over 90 km. long and 32 km. wide. From Río Mulato a branch line runs eastwards to Potosí (174 km.) and Sucre. The track reaches the height of 4,786 metres at Cóndor: one of the highest points on the world's railway lines.

Potosí, with a population of 103,183, stands at 4,070 metres, the highest city of its size in the world. The climate is often bitterly cold and fires are few; warm clothes essential. It was founded by the Spaniards on April 10, 1545, after they had discovered Indian mine workings at Cerro Rico, the hill at whose foot it stands.

Immense amounts of silver were once extracted from this hill. In Spain "éste es un Potosí" (it's a Potosí) is still used for anything superlatively rich. Early in the 17th century Potosí had a population of 150,000, but two centuries later, as its lodes began to deteriorate and silver had been found in Peru and Mexico, Potosí became little more than a ghost town. It is the demand for tin—a metal the Spaniards ignored—that has lifted the city to comparative prosperity again. Silver, copper and lead are also mined.

Large parts of Potosí are colonial, with twisting, narrow streets and an occasional great mansion with its coat of arms over the doorway. Some of the best buildings are grouped round the Plaza 10 de Noviembre, the main square. The Convent of Santa Teresa, which is under repair, has a collection of colonial and religious art. The old Cabildo and the Royal Treasury—Las Cajas Reales—are both here, converted to other uses. The Cathedral faces the square, and near-by is the Mint—the Casa Real de Moneda (founded 1572, rebuilt 1759)—one of the chief monuments of civil building in Hispanic America. The Moneda (entrance US$0.50) has a museum in many sections. The main art gallery is in a splendid salon on the first floor: the salon better than the paintings. Elsewhere are coin dies and huge wooden presses which made the silver strip from which coins were cut. You are advised to wear warm clothes, as it is cold inside; a

182 BOLIVIA

guided tour (essential) starts at 0900 and 1400 and takes two hours. The smelting houses have carved altar pieces from Potosí's ruined churches. Open Mon.-Sat. 0900-1200 and 1400-1700. Among Potosí's baroque churches, typical of the Andean or "mestizo" architecture of the 18th century, are the Compañía (Jesuit) church, with an impressive bell-gable (1700), San Francisco (museum of ecclesiastical art, open 1400-1600, Mon.-Fri.) with a fine organ, and San Lorenzo, with a rich portal (1728-1744—closed for repairs in 1985). San Martín, with an uninviting exterior, is beautiful inside, but normally closed for fear of theft. Ask the German Redemptorist Fathers to show you around; their office is just to the left of their church. Other churches to visit include Jerusalén, close to the *Hotel Centenario*, and San Agustín (only by prior arrangement with tourist office) on Bolívar, with crypts and catacombs. Tour starts at 1700, US$0.10 admission. From San Cristóbal, at Pacheco with Cañete, one gets a fine view over the whole city. The Franciscan School, Nogales 15, has a collection of stuffed animals. The University is also said to have a museum (Mon.-Fri., 1000-1200, 1500-1700, entrance US$1). In times of drought there may be rationing of water for showers etc. In that case the water is turned off at noon and restored at about 1800.

Hotels Best hotel is *Hostal Colonial*, Hoyos 8, C, a pretty colonial house with fires (Tel.: 24265) near the main plaza. *Turista*, Lanza 19, E, helpful, now remodelled, but no heating, intermittent hot shower, breakfast (US$1 only) highly recommended. *San Andrés*, Av. Camacho 283, F; *Residencial Sumaj*, F, Gumiel 10, friendly; *Casa de Huéspedes Hispano*, Matos 62, clean except for communal bath, F; *San Antonio*, Oruro 170 (communal showers and toilet), E with bath. *Central*, Bustillos 1230, E, cold, US$5 extra charge for hot shower, food available, clean; *Hotel IV Centenario*, E, hot water, but no heating, has seen better days but friendly, central; *La Paz*, F, Calle Oruro, hot water available; *Alojamiento Ferrocarril*, Av. Villazón 159, F, basic but clean (no hot water but hot showers available for US$0.55); best cheap lodgings (for which Potosí has a bad reputation) between Av. Oruro and Av. Serrudo, clean, but rarely with hot water; *Alojamiento Tumusla* (avoid ground floor—cold), near the bus station, F, which is reported to be good; *Residencial Copacabana*, Av. Serrudo, F, shared room, restaurant, safe car park; *Villa Imperial*, dirty, noisy, same prices, good motorcycle parking, US$0.20 for hot shower. *Residencial Rosario*, Oruro 526, F. *San José*, G, hot shower; *Alojamiento Barquito*, Oruro 7 (in 100 block), G, clean. *Alojamiento San Lorenzo*, Bustillos 967, G.

Restaurants *Sumac Orko*, Quijarro 46, reasonable, friendly; *As*, Matos 112, reasonable breakfast; *Confitería Royal*, on main plaza, small selection of good cakes and coffee; *Confitería Primavera* also very good; *Las Vegas*, three blocks above main plaza, three course meal, US$1.60 (very ordinary). *Pensión Florida*, US$0.50 each meal; *Scaramuch*, Bolívar 843 and *La Tranquita* at Bolívar 957, good and cheap. Reasonable priced restaurant (*salteñas*, soft drinks or beer) is *Imasumac*, Bustillos 987. *Café Aragón*, Linares 49, *salteñas*; also at Linares 20, both a.m. only. *Siete Vueltas*, Bolívar 816, serves a decent *almuerzo*. Cakes and ice creams along Linares and in Plaza 25 de Mayo. To get fresh bread you have to be up at 0630-0700 and go to Bustillos between Ingavi and Oniste and up a passage on the upper side of the street. *El Mesón* on corner of Tarija and Linares has been warmly recommended; *Don Lucho*, Oruro and Ingavi, has seen better days. *The Sky Room* at Bolívar 701 has interesting views of the town and the Cerro, unfriendly. Breakfast can be a difficult meal to find, but it is available in the Mercado Central, Calle Bolívar: worthwhile to see if the hotel serves it as most restaurants seem to be closed at this time. *El Alamena Confitería*, Hoyo y Sucre (opp. tourism kiosk), very good.

Shopping Silver (sometimes containing nickel) and native cloth; there are stalls in Calle Bustillos. Silver coins, jewellery and coca leaves in market between Av. Camacho and H. del Chaco. The best bookshop is at the University, open Mon.-Fri., 1000-1200, 1500-1700. Artesanías Pachamama, Hoyos 10, is recommended for textiles. There is also an interesting gift shop in the post office. Silver is sold in the main market near the Calle Oruro entrance. There is an informal swap market every Friday night at the Plaza, at Bolívar and Quijarro. There is a handicraft market at the junction of Calle Sucre and Plaza Saavedra. Some Fridays the merchants organize music, food and drink (*ponche*), not to be missed.

Taxi Within city limits US$1.20. Buses US$0.10.

Exchange at Tourist Office or *farmacías* nearby on Plaza. Also possible in other shops and hotels.

Tourist Agents Candería Tours, Bolívar 634, Tel.: 2458 and Tursul Ltda, Calle San Alberto, 24, Tel.: 1360.

Tourist Office On 2nd Floor, Cámara de Minería, Calle Quijarro (Tel.: 25288). ½ block from

BOLIVIA 183

main plaza, and booth on main plaza (both closed Sat. and Sun.); sells good town maps, information available, helpful.

Post Office, Lanza and Chuquisaca; unreliable for overseas mail.

Lloyd Aéreo Boliviano Lanza 19, at *Hotel El Turista*.

Sauna Bath and showers in Calle Nogales.

Transport To La Paz, *Ferrobus*: 4 a week—book previous day only; Express: twice weekly 2055—book Pullman class previous day. Flight to La Paz, US$30. To Sucre, express Mon., Thurs. at 0700, US$2.55 pullman, US$1.80 *especial*; *mixto* Sat. at 0800, US$2. To Uyuni/Atocha, *tren mixto* Thurs., Sun. at 1329 (1st and 2nd class only). To Oruro train (*ferrobus* US$7, express US$5 1st, US$3 2nd class), bus (US$6.85); connection to Cochabamba US$10.50, leaves 1800; to Villazón, daily, leaves 1700, US$4.50, 12-16 hrs., rough trip requiring warm clothing; or take *tren mixto* to Uyuni and change there. To Antofagasta, either take the *tren mixto* to Uyuni on Thurs. and connect with the La Paz-Antofagasta train/bus route on Fri. night, or take the Tues. *ferrobus* to Oruro and then book Pullman on Fri. train to Antofagasta; fares can be paid in Bolivian pesos. Mon. and Sat. bus to Tarija, except Weds, 0730; Tarija is reached by car or lorry leaving Plaza Minero (Bus 'A'), full range of scenery, to Uyuni, leaving Thursdays and Sundays at 1415 arrives 0145 the next day. Bus station out of town, below railway station and 20 minute walk from main Plaza; through buses from La Paz call here at the toll gate, as they are not allowed to enter city limits. Daily buses to Sucre (US$4.40, 2 a day, about 0830), *Micros* to Sucre wait until full, in p.m., Plaza Uyuni, 5½ hrs., US$4.40 also; Villazón, La Paz (12 hrs., US$10.75). Trucks for Tarabuco leave from Plaza San Francisco. Heavy overbooking reported on buses; the trucks from the plaza are an alternative if you are in a hurry.

Car Spares VW spares are obtainable at Hauwa Ltd, but it takes several days to get parts from La Paz.

A suggested tour round the town is to walk down Quijarro from San Agustín on Bolívar as far as Oniste then return by Junín, looking at "the passage of the seven turns" on the way. There is a fine stone doorway (house of the Marqués de Otavi) in Junín between Matos and Bolívar. Calle Lanza 8 was the house of José de Quiroz and of Antonio López de Quiroga. Along Millares between Chuquisaca and Nogales one sees on the right a sculpted stone doorway and on the left a doorway with two rampant lions in low relief on the lintel. Turning left up Nogales one comes to an old mansion in a little square. Turn left along La Paz and three blocks along there is another stone doorway with suns in relief. At the corner with Bolívar is the Casa del Balcón de la Horca. Turn left and one comes to the Casa de las Tres Portadas.

Visitors can see over the first level of the Pailaviri tin mine; visits can be arranged through hotels. Taxi up the hill to mine entrance before 0900, US$1.50, or go by bus, Línea A and B or up with miners in truck from Plaza 10 de Noviembre or 25 de Mayo, leaving at 0730. You can walk up in about an hour, but be there early as only 17 tourists allowed in the mine at any one time. Entrance fee about US$2 for up to 1½ hour tour, starting at 0900, special clothing provided, hot in mine though cold in access tunnels. Watch out for electric cable at head level. A (repeatedly) recommended guide to the private mines is Eduardo Garnica Fajardo, Hernández 1035, Casilla 33, Tel.: 2-3138; he speaks English, French and some Hebrew. (He charges about US$2 for a morning tour, which involves meeting miners and seeing them at work in conditions described as "horrific...like stepping back into the nineteenth century"; a contribution to the miners' cooperative is appreciated.) If visiting the private mines, wear old clothes. Another guide is Salustio Gallardo, Calle Betanzos 231, near Plaza Minero, price negotiable. Visitors can approach Padre Gustavo, a Belgian priest at the Concepción church who occasionally organizes visits to the cooperative mines. Rather more realistic and perhaps more interesting than a visit to the State mine.

A recommended Sunday trip is to Manquiri, a sanctuary in the mountains. Wait from 0730 at Garita de San Roque for a truck. Another trip is to Caiza on the fork off the Tarija road at Ingeniero Cucho; for this you will need a tent, etc., as there is no hotel. Only one bus a day from Potosí: it should leave from Plaza del Minero at 1330 but is often late. Caiza is where cooperatives produce handicrafts in tin. Their Caiza outlet is the Belgian Catholic Agricultural School in the main square. Cheap *mantas* and other hand woven goods can be purchased at villages betweeen Challatapa and Potosí, on the road from Oruro along Lake Poopó.

Thermal Baths at lake below city. Laguna de Tarapaya, Miraflores truck or van from Plaza Chuquimina to 25 Km. post, just before crossing the bridge. Above Tarapaya is the crater, which is reached by a track from 25 Km. point. When bathing after mid-day do *not* let go of the chain as the current is very strong; whirlpools can develop. There are buses back from Tarapaya at 1400 and 1600. A good place to spend a lazy day resting. Also Chaqui (by truck from police post at Garita San Roque), Tora and San Diego (on the main road to Sucre, it also has a restaurant). Alternatively

184 BOLIVIA

there is a thermal pool 1 km. before the village on the other side of the river. It is best to get off bus at the bridge 400 metres on the Potosí side of the river and pool.

Sucre, (pop. 79,941) the official capital of Bolivia, is reached from Potosí (175 km.) by daily train (a grand trip) or by road (the best *dirt* road in Bolivia). A branch road runs to it from the Cochabamba-Santa Cruz highway. The altitude is 2,790 metres, and the climate is mild (mean temperature 12°C, but sometimes 24°C in November-December and 7°C in June).

Sucre (originally Charcas) was founded in 1538. Long isolation has helped it to preserve its courtly charm; local law now requires all buildings to be painted original colonial white. Public buildings are impressive. Among these are the Legislative Palace (open 0900-1200 and 1400-1700, Sats., 0900-1200 US$0.25), where the country's Declaration of Independence was signed; the modern Santo Domingo (Palace of Justice), the seat of Bolivia's judiciary; the modern Government Palace; the beautiful 17th century Cathedral, open 0730-0915, and museum (US$0.25), open 1000-1200 and 1500-1700 (1000-1200, Sat.) (worth seeing are the Chapel of the famous jewel-encrusted Virgin of Guadalupe—1601, most easily seen just before or after mass (*fiesta* September 8), and the monstrance and other church jewels by appointment with the Padre Tesorero); the Consistorial building; the Teatro Gran Mariscal Sucre, and Junín College. Sucre University was founded in 1624. Early 17th century wooden ceilings (*alfarjes*) with intricate patterns of Moorish origin are found in San Miguel (see below) and San Francisco (0700-0930 and 1600-1930).

Behind the town a road flanked by Stations of the Cross ascends a gracious hill, Cerro Churuquella, with slim eucalyptus trees on its flank, to a statue of Christ at the top and views of Sucre and the countryside.

Churches San Miguel must be seen. Shut for 120 years, it is now restored and is very beautiful with carved and painted ceilings, pure-white walls and gold and silver altar. Don't be put off by the locked doors. In the Baptistery there is a painting by Viti, the first great painter of the New World, who studied under Raphael. In the Sacristy is another of his paintings and some early sculpture. It was from San Miguel that Jesuit missionaries went south to convert Argentina, Uruguay and Paraguay. (Open 1000-1200, 1500-1700, 1830-1945 daily, during masses.) The oldest church in Sucre, built in 1538, is San Lázaro, in Calle Calvo, with fine silverwork and alabaster on the baptistery. San Felipe Neri, church and monastery, attractive courtyard with cloisters. Roof gives view of city; open 1630-1730, US$0.50 entrance. Entrance requires a guide from tourist office. Other churches worth seeing are Santa Mónica (Arenales with Junín) perhaps one of the greatest gems of Spanish architecture in the Americas, note the main altar and pulpit in filigree (1000-1130 and 1500-1700, weekends during church services). San Francisco in Calle Ravelo has altars coated in gold leaf; the bell is the one that summoned the people of Sucre to struggle for independence. Capilla de la Rotonda (Av. L. Cabrera, near the station), Santa Rita, San Sebastián and Sta. Bárbara (Plaza Pizarro). Santo Domingo, corner of Calvo and Bolívar (1545), open only Fridays and Sunday night. Next door at Calvo 212 is the Santa Clara museum with art gallery and silver collection (see below), and Church of San Lázaro an Calvo, built in 1538 and regarded as the first cathedral of La Plata (Sucre). On the nave walls are six paintings attributed to Zurbarán, open 0700-0745 Sat. and Sun. after church service at 1900. La Merced has gilded altar pieces (Azurduy and Pérez) but was temporarily closed in 1984.

Hotels Best hotel is *Hostal Cruz de Popayán*, Calle Loa, C, a beautiful colonial house with interior courtyard, enthusiastically recommended, except for its restaurant; *Hostal Sucre*, 3 stars, Bustillos 113, D, good, clean, recommended; *Hostal Libertad*, esq. San Alberto y Aniceto Arce, B; also *Colonial*, Plaza 25 de Mayo, C, expensive (Tel.: 4709); *Tajibos Inn*, Av. Venezuela, new *Hostal los Pinos*, Colón 502, clean, comfortable, hot showers, C. *Londres*, Av. Hernando Siles, 3 blocks uphill from station, D, breakfast; *Residencial Bolivia*, near plaza in Calle San Alberto, E, with dangerous electric showers, good with hot water; *Grand*, Calle Arce 61, E; *La Plata* (noisy), Calle Ravelo, F; *Residencial Oriental*, Calle San Alberto, F, clean, friendly but basic, hot water; *Residencial El Turista*, Calle Arenales, F, good; *Alojamiento El Turista*, Calle Ravelo 118, G, clean, showers; even more basic *Alojamiento Urus*, Regimiento Charcas 85. *Alojamiento San Francisco*, esq. Av. Acre and Camargo, bath or shower, F has seen better days, but pleasant, meals available downstairs; *Residencial Copacabana*, 4 blocks up from station, G; also near station, *Municipal*, Av. Venezuela, E; *Residencial Bustillo*, Calle Ravelo, F, clean and modern but sometimes overcharges; *Residencial Oriental*, San Alberto, F (laundry); *Alojamiento Austria*, G, hot showers, good value, near bus station as well as *Alojamiento Central*, G, recommended (beware the buses which stop at 2000); *Alojamiento Avaroa*, good, F, Calle Loa, hot showers; *Posada San José*, F, cold showers but friendly.

BOLIVIA 185

Restaurants Best restaurant is *La Recoleta*, or *Aranjuez*, Calvo 16 (closed Tues.). *Hotel Municipal* restaurant; *Palet*, *Las Vegas* on east side of Plaza (icecream, no breakfast, at lunchtime no drink without food); *Pizzería Napoli* on main plaza, cheap with music; and *Piso Cero* (superb chateaubriand but cheap) Venezuela 241, together with *Restaurant China* (expensive). The *Alliance Française* on Calle Estudiante 49 serves crêpes, 1600-2000, soft music etc. For breakfast or quick food try cheap and friendly *Snack Paulista*; *Hawai* on Calvo for its chicken with pineapple. *Pizzería Love*, Aniceto Arce 369, Tel.: 22742, good, English manager, reasonably-priced (was seeking new premises in 1986); *Medeval*, Plaza San Francisco 105, international food. Good *almuerzo* at Hernando Siles 953. *Los Laureles*. Ortiz, is recommended for good cheap food. The *Plaza* restaurant, recommended *sopa de ajo* and steak tartare. *Los Bajos*, Loa 761, serves special sausages. *Doña Máxima*, Junín 411; *Austria*, good, attached to hotel, near bus station. Good value is given at *El Solar*, Bolívar 800 (Sun. closed); *La Casona*, Av. Ostria Gutiérrez 401, local food; *Municipal* in Parque Bolívar. Foodstores in the new *mercado*, highly recommended, serve clean cheap meals for US$1 until 1400. Most not open before 0930, then only for lunch (so breakfast is difficult to find) and reopen at 1600. *Bar El Tío*, Calle España, is pleasant as is *Pip* (breakfast especially), esq. Ravelo and Lourdes, Loa 581. The local brewery produces an interesting sweetish porter or stout.

Shopping Antique woven items must be sought. Small shops opposite Church of San Francisco for handicrafts or permanent market along Av. Jaime Mendoza, non-touristy, near railway line. There is also a wide selection in Calle Argentina, opposite Post Office and Coinca, Loa 622, and Candelaria at Bolívar 634 (expensive). Artesanías Calcha, Calle Hernando Siles 713. For sweaters try Packi at Ravelo 350, or Junín 403 (blankets). *Charangos* from Tarabuco are obtainable in the main plaza. Books in English available from Escuela Fox (if Mr Fox is there) just off the plaza. Postcards are 5 times as expensive as in La Paz.

Night Clubs Night Club Municipal, Av. Venezuela; *Peña Misky Huasi*, on San Alberto near Abarda, US$1 (with drink); *El Sótano* at the Parque Bolívar, acceptable; El Cuerno Colonial, España 162. Disco-Viva María, US$2.80, entrance includes a beer, San Alberto 6.

Folklore Centro Cultural Masir aims to promote traditional culture. It offers instruction in Quechua, traditional Bolivian music making and handicrafts. The director, Roberto Sahonero, who will give further details, is to be found at Colón 138 (Tel.: 23403). The Complejo Casa Capellánica—museum, theatre and handicraft workshop opened in 1984; esq. San Antonio and Potosí. Open 0900-1200 and 1500-2000. There are also tourist offices in the building (IBT and Desatur).

Museums These include the University's anthropological, folkloric, and colonial collections at the Charcas Museum (Bolívar 700), and its presidential and modern-art galleries. There are also the Museo de Santa Clara (Calle Calvo 212) sculptures, paintings, silver and ceramic collection; and the Museo de la Recoleta (Calle Pedro de Anzúrez), open 0930-1130 and 1500-1700 US$0.50 for entrance to all collections. The Recoleta monastery on a hill above the town is notable for the beauty of its cloisters and gardens; the carved wooden choirstalls in the chapel (upstairs) are especially fine (0930-1130 and 1400-1730). The Glorieta mansion, with the Princesa collection (leaflet available from tourist office), 5 km. outside the city (No. 5 bus) on the road to Potosí, has beautiful painted ceilings and Arabian gardens, and is being restored; worth a visit: "a delightful mixture of many styles", open Mon.-Fri. 0900-1200 and 1400-1800. At the back of the Grand Marshal's theatre, the faculty of medical sciences recently opened a museum of human anatomy and pathology—open 0830-1200 and 1400-1800 Mon.-Fri.

Post Office Argentina 50, between Estudiantes and Olañeta.

Banks Banco del Estado, no exchange facilities; Banco Nacional, cash only at a poor rate. Travel agencies' rates are not too good. Most shops and hotels will change money. Street changers on Hernando Siles below Arce.

Consulate West German, Arenales 215 (Tel.: 21862). The Goethe Institute shows films and has German newspapers and books to lend (1030-1230 and 1700-2000). Spain, Pasaje Argandoña (Tel.: 21435); Italy, Defensa 33 (Tel.: 22650). Alliance Française near Plaza de Armas.

Motor-cycle Mechanic Sr Jaime Medina, Motorservi Honda, Calle René Calvo Arana, Tel.: 5484. Will service all makes of machine.

Hospital Recommended, staffed by Japanese and locals. Doctor Roger Mortojo Panoso, Av. Hernando Siles 911, or Dr. Gastón Delgadillo Lona at Colón 33 (Tel.: 21692/ 21187), speaks English, French and German.

Tourist Office Calle Potosí 102 (esq. San Alberto), helpful map on request. Another office at Calle Ortiz 182. Check church and museum opening hours, also time of guided visit to San Felipe (see above). Tel.: 25983. Sub-office at airport, helpful. Tourist information office opp. San Felipe Neri is run by students studying tourism, who will show you around tourist sites for free.

Travel Agencies Candelaria Tours, Bolívar 634; Teresita's Tours, Bustillos 146; Solarsa Tours, Arenales 212; Itidalgo Tours, Bustillos 105; Sucre Tours, Bustillos 107.

186 BOLIVIA

Train Service to Potosí, Oruro and La Paz Mon. and Thurs. 1500 (book seats from 0800-1000 and then 1400-1700, Sats. 0800-1000, holidays 0800-0930), to Potosí, US$2.55 first, US$1.80 second (*tren mixto* to Potosí once a week, US$2); to Oruro, US$7 first, US$5 second class; to La Paz 20 hours (take food) US$10.75 1st, US$9.50 2nd, new coaches, Station Tel.: 1114-1115.

Air Service By LAB there is a Mon., Wed., Fri. La Paz-Sucre air service, to Cochabamba on Tuesdays, Thursdays and Saturdays and Santa Cruz daily Puerto Suárez, 0900 Mondays, TAM. There are also LAB flights to Tarija (Tues., Weds. and Fridays) and Yacuiba, and F27 flights to Camiri (Tues., Thurs., Sat.). LAB office at Calle Bustillos 121-127. TAM fly on Wed. to La Paz, Santa Cruz and Puerto Suárez, and on Sundays to Santa Cruz. All flights heavily booked but some "stand by" available. Your best chance is to lie in wait at the airport; they know nothing in town. Airport 5 km. from town. (Tel.: 24445). Airport bus service for passengers (LAB office next to *Hostal Sucre*). Taxi US$0.75. Beware of pickpockets at airport.

Bus daily to La Paz via Cochabamba (24 hrs., US$13), very rough and roads liable to flooding during the rainy season, but worthwhile; via Potosí, US$17 (18 hrs.); to Cochabamba daily, US$12; (also by truck for slightly less, night trip) 1800-1830, also daily buses and *micros* to Potosí (5 hrs., US$4.40). Bus to Santa Cruz, via Cochabamba, Flota Unificado, Mon. and Thurs., 1700, 18 hrs, US$16. Once a week to Tarija at 0500, Tuesdays, US$16, 18 hrs. (arrangements can be made to catch it in the main Plaza at 0700). To Monteagudo, Thurs. and Sun., 1500, US$5.30. Oruro, 14 hours, 0800, US$11. To Llallagua, Weds. and Sat., 0700, US$8.20, 10 hours. (Take Micro 2 to bus station 3 km. from centre, taxi US0.80, Tel.: 2029.)

On Sunday early (0600-0730) visit **Tarabuco**, *micro* looks around town for passengers until 0700, truck (US$1-1.50)—2½-3 hours— from open space at top of Calle Calvo (on Sun. many buses leave from here between 0700 and 0900, US$1.25 one way), or taxi, US$40, 2½ hours, (sit on right-hand side), for market starting 0930, good for ponchos and other typical garments. The road is good but dusty, take protection. There is a direct bus to Cochabamba, US$9.50, 11 hrs. There is a fairly basic hotel, *Prefectural*, and two *alojamientos* in plaza, G (*Bar California*, basic). Festival with fair: Virgen de Rosario, 1st Sunday in October and March 12. If you are hardy take a sleeping-bag and sleep in the only restaurant.

"Surely this is one of the most colourful Indian markets in S America. The costume of these Indians is unique and fantastic, and the men wander around playing the *charango*, a stringed instrument with an armadillo shell as a sound-box. Women do most of the work. The woven skirts and belts of the women are some of the finest to be found in Bolivia, and good weaving may be bought." - Hilary Bradt. Although the market is popular with tourists, it is still worth a visit. Best bargains are to be had on weekdays, or before the bulk of tourists arrive, or late in the day. Our latest reports indicate that prices at the market are high, but that the real appeal is the Indians in their authentic dress. On the other hand, to see the weaving in progress, visits to Candelaria (two hours truck from Tarabuco) or Macha (8 hours from Sucre), Pocata (one hour from Macha), or Ravelo will save you from hordes of other tourists (travel to Ravelo: by lorry or *micro*, mostly in the morning from departure point near airport, 3 hrs. one way; *micro*, US$1.30, check at shop at Hernando Siles 843 if it's running, it's supposed to leave at 0900, return 1600—lorries back to Sucre invariably full). Specially recommended is a trip to Potolo, where they weave red animals on a black or brown background. Trucks (Thurs. and Fri. in the dry season) go direct from near Sucre airport; in the wet, you can only get to Challanaca and then you walk for 3 hours to get there—the prices will probably be lower in the wet season. It has even been suggested that it is cheaper to buy in Peru or from street vendors in Sucre—so check and compare. Swimming in the rainy season only at Cachimayo, Yotala and Nujchu on the road to Potosí.

A main road runs SE from Sucre through Tarabuco and **Monteagudo** (*Hotel Salamanca*, G) for 216 km. to **Villa Serrano**, where the musician Mauro Núñez lived. A music festival is held on December 28-29. (The journey is beautiful through wild mountains.) 460 km. from Sucre is **Camiri** (20,000 people), growing rapidly because of nearby oilfields—the oil refinery may be visited. Flota El Chaqueño runs from Sucre to Camiri on Fri., theoretically at 0700, at least 20 hrs., US$16, returns, again in theory, on Tues. From Camiri there is a bus to Santa Cruz which should be booked up well in advance as it is always crowded (terrifying road), office on Av. Busch. Bus to *Gran Hotel Londres*, goes 4 times a week if enough passengers, 8 hrs., US$11; *camioneta* leaves from in front of the market when there are enough passengers, US$7.80, 7 hrs. (boring journey, dusty). As a garrison town it has some hotels (*Hotel Ortuño*, Calle Comercio, E; *Residencial Marieta*, Av. Petrolera 15, E; *Residencial Premier*, Av. Busch 60, E; *Residencial Familiar*, Calle Comercio, F; *Gran Hotel Londres*, Av. Busch 36, F), restaurants, bars (nothing is cheap) and also flights to La Paz and Santa Cruz, 180 km. If you arrive by car: at Tránsito checkpoint pick up a slip of paper with instructions on how to reach Guardia where you collect permits to stay overnight. Next visit army post on Plaza de Armas to be checked there. Before leaving town visit Guardia again to collect a permit to proceed—all permits cost about US$0.50 each. Hotels will *not* accept car passengers without permit. S along a very bad road is **Villa Montes**, more easily reached from Tarija (260 km., bus leaves Tues., Fri. and Sat. at 0700, US$11), famous for the highest temperatures in Bolivia; take mosquito repellant. Opposite the railway station 2 km. out of town is *Hotel El Rancho*, F, with bungalow-type accommodation; the food is expensive so eat in town. It is on the edge of the Gran Chaco and has a road and railway S to Yacuiba and Argentina and another dry-season road E to Paraguay which is O.K. for high clearance vehicles. *Hotel Pilcomayo*, G, dirty, communal

BOLIVIA 187

bath, and *Hotel Demia*, G, clean and friendly. The bus trip via Tarabuco and Camiri to Argentina is very rough; poor road and little comfort. Two buses a week (Wed. and Sat. 0730) to Llallagua (see page 176).

It is possible to drive from Camiri into Paraguay direct in a truck or 4-wheel-drive vehicle, carrying food and water for a week. No help can be relied on in case of a breakdown. At Camiri, obtain a US$1 permit from the Guardia to go 64 km. (1½ hours) over a rough road to **Boyuibe**, the last town in Bolivia (*Hotel Guadalquivir*, G, or *Hotel Chaqueño* next door, both serve meals); once there pay US$1 at the Tránsito office and US$2 at Customs for an exit stamp. (Neither is well sign-posted, so ask.) There are some rivers to ford and although they are dry in the dry season they could be impassable if there was any rain in the area. At Boyuibe gas and water are available, and it is on the Yacuiba railway. A new line is being built West out of Boyuibe, then North, to Tarabuco, to link up with Cochabamba (it has reached Monteagudo).

Tom Courtenay-Clack tells us: "¾ km. after the military checkpoint turn left past a large water tower. From then on just follow the most used road. The road is much better now than it used to be, owing to heavy black market fuel truck traffic. It's still quite difficult though and four wheel drive and high clearance is essential. A winch is also advisable especially if there's been rain. The insects are appalling.

"The road turns disconcertingly South for several km. at one point but it's O.K. We saw a tapir and a puma on this road. It is 134 km. from Boyuibe to the Bolivian border post at Villazón. It took us 6 hours. The officer at Villazón will give you your exit stamp. The nine soldiers at each of the fly-infested lonely posts on either side of the border will vie for your company if you arrive at nightfall. Enormously appreciated by these poor fellows are small gifts of soft drinks, beer, cigarettes or canned fruit. They do six month stints here.

"The Paraguayan post is 3 km. from the Bolivian post. Just a passport check here. Camping is better here than at the Bolivian post because they have a shower and will let you use their kitchen. 13 km. from the Paraguayan border post is Fortín Garay. Here the commanding officer will give you entry stamps. The road is somewhat better from here on, sandy and bumpy but straight.

"There is a police check point later at Mister Long, and still one more at an airforce base. All these take time. It took us nearly nine hours to get to Mariscal Estigarribia. Here there's a large military base and passports are cleared by the commandant. He is unavailable from 1300 to 1600, so be prepared for a wait. If you have to wait, there's a nice German-run pension 100 yards away where you can get excellent ice-cream, a meal and a room. They have a pet rhea (ostrich) if you want to see one close up.

"One and a half hours from Mariscal is Filadelfia (340 km. from Fortín Garay). About 20 km. South of Filadelfia the road is newly and beautifully asphalted all the way to Asunción. The birds along this road are incredible."

There are no buses beyond Camiri on this road. Petrol tankers and other trucks go through to Paraguay; they will sometimes take one passenger, as regulations forbid more, from Camiri to Filadelfia for US$5—possibly less.

The railway line S from Río Mulato goes through **Uyuni** (3,660 metres), the junction for the line to Antofagasta (train calls on Wednesday at 0500-*tren mixto*-$16). Warning: do not take photos between Uyuni and the border. Trains to Potosí, La Paz and Oruro (5 a week, 3 express, 2 *trenes mixtos*). (The road down from Oruro is sandy, and after rain very bad.) Uyuni lies bitterly cold and unprotected on the plain at the edge of a vast salt lake, the Salar de Uyuni.

"When it still has water in it (up to 4 or possibly 6 inches), being in the middle of the Salar de Uyuni is like being an ant on a gigantic mirror. The blue sky merges into the blue water, the islands are perfectly reflected and since there is no horizon they appear suspended in space. Some areas may be dry, in which case the salt crust is as blinding-white and featureless as the most perfect snowfield." - Stephen Saker, who endorses our warning on the Ollagüe-Uyuni track (see below).

Uyuni's 5,000 inhabitants are mostly Indian. Its market is the only point of interest (public showers). There is also supposed to be gasoline available. An interesting excursion by truck to Pampa Aullagas takes 3 hours, a picturesque village in the middle of a lake.

Hotel *Avenida*, basic, fairly clean, F, US$1, shower, food very basic. The *patrón*, Don Jesús Rosas, runs jeep excursions to the Salar (US$35). Banco del Estado will not change money. The pharmacy on the main street will change money, but it is very difficult to find out the current rate of exchange.

Motorists must be warned against a road from Río Mulato into Chile by way of Ollagüe. "Between Río Mulato and Uyuni it is deep soft sand and possible only for 4-wheel drive vehicles and trucks. Beyond there is the danger of getting lost on the many tracks leading over the deserted salt lakes, no petrol between Uyuni and San Pedro de Conchi (Chile), and little hope of help with a breakdown

188 BOLIVIA

on the Bolivian side unless you don't mind waiting for perhaps a week. After rain the route is impassable. Where the road has been built up, *never* forsake it for the appealing soft salt beside it. The salt takes a man's weight but a vehicle breaks through the crust into unfathomable depths of plasticine mud below." - Andrew Parkin.

Excursions Dan Buck and Anne Meadows write: "*Laguna Colorada,* about 350-400 km. SW of Uyuni, 12 hours' straight driving over unmarked, rugged truck tracks, is featured in Tony Morrison's two books, *Land Above the Clouds* and *The Andes.* It is one of Bolivia's most spectacular and most isolated marvels. The rare James flamingoes, along with the more common Chilean and Andean flamingoes, breed and live in its red algae-coloured waters. The shores and shallows of the lake are crusted with gypsum and salt, a bizarre arctic-white counterpoint to the flaming red waters. There is a *campamento* at the west end of the lake where visitors may be able to use one of the camp's *dormitorios,* space available, to spread their sleeping bags. The camp caretakers are Julio and Eustaquio Berna; gifts—oranges, candles, beer, etc.—are appreciated.

"The standard rate for hiring a truck or jeep, Uyuni-Laguna Colorada 3 day round trip, is US$300-400, negotiate. The Uyuni *Hotel Avenida* is a good contact for making arrangements. There are a welter of routes, and even locals easily get lost. Truck rides can be arranged at the Sindicato de Chóferes in town, behind the church. A map, compass, and a guide are all useful, plus asking directions of every person one meets along the way— which won't be many. In our round trip we met no vehicles, only 4 *campesinos* on bicycles and a handful on foot. Going out we went Uyuni-Corpina-Quetena Chica-east side Laguna Colorada; on the return we travelled west side Laguna Colorada-Alota-Uyuni. Beware: if approaching the lake from the east side, take the south shore of the lake to the *campamento,* it is longer but better than the north shore which is deep, treacherous volcanic ash and sand.

"There is no dependable transport linking any of the towns and mining camps in the Uyuni-Laguna Colorada area. No one should travel in the area without cold-weather camping gear, sufficient food, etc."

There is a truck on Saturdays which leaves Chiguana, a town on the Uyuni-Antofagasta railway, once the La Paz train arrives, going to Laguna Verde, 3 hrs., south of Laguna Colorada. There are also trucks which go to the Laguna Colorada and the Susana sulphur mine. The lorry back leaves on Friday afternoon, making this at least a one-week trip. At Chiguana and Laguna Verde the army will normally provide a place to sleep (no bedding). You may also be able to sleep on a floor at the sulphur mine at Laguna Verde, or at the workers' quarters for the Sol de Mañana geothermal project, 45 km. from Laguna Colorada. Hot food can also be purchased although there is none at Laguna Colorada. Travel in this region is possible anytime between May and October, but there is no petrol, mechanical assistance or supplies S of Salinas de Garci Mendoza (270 km. from Oruro) or Uyuni (petrol in Salinas de Garci Mendoza is twice as expensive as in Uyuni). The army can be helpful for transport in the area if you persist.

One can visit *Llica,* the capital of Daniel Campos Province, in 5 hours over the Salar by truck, or about 12 hours by boat, if there is enough water in the lake. There is a new, basic *Alojamiento Municipal* in town, F. Food is "difficult". There is a teachers' training college but not much special to see. Two fiestas: July 26 and August 15. Good though for llama and other wool handicrafts.

S of Uyuni, 200 km., is *Tupiza* (2,990 metres, 11,000 people), a centre of the silver, tin, lead, and bismuth mining industries (*Hotel Mitru,* F, private shower and bath; next to it is *Residencial Crillón,* F, with good motorcycle parking; also *Hotel Americano,* G, opposite railway station). Six trains to border every week. Bad road from Potosí which goes on S to Villazón; often closed in rainy season because there is no bridge over the Río Suipacha. Bus to Villazón US$1.25 (many daily).

From *Villazón* (13,000 people, good local market), on the border with Argentina, there is an improved road to Tarija, 965 km. by road from La Paz. The road linking Potosí with Villazón via Camargo is in poor condition and about 100 km. longer than the better road via Tupiza. For information on border crossing with Argentina see page 80; US$0.70 charged for crossings on Sunday. Little to see in Villazón (has two cinemas); border area must not be photographed.

Hotels at Villazón *Panamericano,* F, breakfast and lunch (showers extra); *Savoy,* just possible; *Grande,* F; *Residencial El Cortijo,* clean, E, good value, hot water, restaurant; *Residencial Avenida,* F, but try bargaining. *Grand Palace,* clean, E. Restaurants opposite bus station and on first floor of covered market.

Argentine Consulate in main plaza, open 1400-1700, Mon.-Fri.; officious, unhelpful.

Money-changing at Cambio Porvenir or other cambios on main street, rates said to be good; Banco del Estado changes travellers' cheques.

Buses from Villazón To Potosí at 1600 and 1700, 15 hrs., US$7.50 (terrible in the wet); to Tupiza, 0700 and 1500; to Tarija US$7.30, 6½ hours (see below). Bus passengers for La Paz must

BOLIVIA 189

cross from Argentina the previous day. Watch out for overcharging by Panamericano bus company— the "direct" La Paz bus sometimes goes only as far as Potosí. Bus station is near the main square. Taxi to border, US$0.20.

Trains from Villazón To La Paz (very dusty journey), Sunday at 1330, express arriving 1120 on Monday. Journey to La Paz is very crowded indeed, especially 2nd class. Train stops at Tupiza (no cutlery or napkins provided) for evening meal at 1900. To Oruro, express 3 times a week, US$8.40 pullman, US$5.60 *especial*; *tren mixto* twice a week (cold journey). The express from Oruro connects with a bus to Tarija, tickets from railway station, US$7.30 (one other bus a week). Station 500 metres from main square.

At *Camargo*, on road from Potosí to Tarija, is an excellent restaurant, *Media Luz*. Guest rooms have been built for overnight stop.

Tarija, at 1,956 metres (population, about 54,000) was founded July 4, 1574, in the rich valley of the Guadalquivir river. The road from Villazón, 183 km., is the shortest route from Argentina; there is also a road to Potosí via Camargo. The alternative route from Argentina via Bermejo (13,000 people), 269 km., is at a fairly low altitude and in a mild climate, but the views are rewarding; not recommended in the rainy season or a month or so after. There is no railway. Tarija had a tumultuous struggle against Spain, declaring itself independent in 1807, and has a strong cultural heritage. Its own university was founded in 1946. There is a large archaeological collection; the entrance is at the corner of the building. Maize, vegetables, wheat, potatoes and splendid grapes thrive in the basin. Bolivia's best wines are produced here. Its people are markedly religious and strongly individualistic, and the Indian strain is less marked here than elsewhere in Bolivia. The modern Avenida Costanera gracefully flanks the curves of the river. The Casa Dorada is being reconstructed with a view to becoming the Casa de Cultura (interested visitors may be shown round by the restorer), note the figures in the roof.

The city is famous for its *niño* (child) processions: colourful and charming. During processions of San Roque in a 3-day festival from the first Sunday in September the richly dressed saint's statue is paraded through the streets; wearing lively colours, cloth turbans and cloth veils, the people dance before it as it goes, and women throw flowers from the balconies. Dogs are decorated with ribbons for the day. On the second Sunday in October the flower festival commemorates the Virgen del Rosario, and another in Easter week.

Hotels *Prefectural*, D with bath and pool, shabby, poor service (2 km. from city centre, upstream on road); *Gran Hotel Max*, Calle Junín; *Internacional*, E with bath; *Club Social*, on main plaza; *Hostal Costanera*, Av. Las Américas, recommended, reasonably-priced, modern facilities; *América*, Bolívar 257, hot showers, good, F, restaurant attached (check bill carefully); opp. is *Residencial Bolívar*, F (E with bath), recommended, clean, comfortable, hot water, breakfast US$0.15; *Asturias*, clean and well furnished, F. *Sucre*, Sucre 771, D without bath, average. *Residencial Salta*, F, Cochabamba and Mcal. Sucre, basic; *Residencial Miraflores*, Calle Sucre, F, clean and recommended. *Residencial Londres*, F, shared room and bath, hot water; *Residencial Familiar*, F, friendly, good food; *Residencial Ocho Hermanos*, near main plaza, F, clean, collective rooms only.

Restaurants *Chapaco*, on main plaza, more expensive. *Guacho*, Av. Costanera, is recommended. *Siempre Primavera*, Chinese near Plaza. *La Cabaña de Don Pepe*, Campos 138, has excellent steaks at reasonable prices; *El Rinconcito Andaluz* on the Plaza is cheap and the food reasonable. Also on the Plaza, *Línea Carenajh*, for Italian food at night. On La Madrid, *La Princesa* (excellent *keperi*—meat that is first boiled, then fried); *Iscela* (same street), for pizza and ice-cream. Excellent food in market, but get there before 1300. After, go to Calle Carrero. Try the local wines, e.g. the white Aranjuez, Arce, Colonial or Kohlberg, also local beer.

N.B. Restaurants (and everything else in town) close in the middle of the day.

Shopping Craft goods in market and in co-operative shop in plaza; some cheap stuff, shoddy. Ceramics at Frial Susy, Sucre 776.

Tourist Office Calle Bolívar, near Sucre, unhelpful.

Zoo Out on Av. Costanera.

Bank Banco del Estado will not change money. Try Comercial Salinas at Mcal. Sucre 758.

Air Service TAM and LAB to Cochabamba, La Paz (twice a week), Santa Cruz, Trinidad, Yacuiba,

190 BOLIVIA

and Sucre (Tues). Flights are frequently cancelled and/or strike-bound. LAB office, Ingavi 244; TAM office between Sucre and Bolívar. Free bus to airport.

Buses Mon., Wed., Thurs. and Sat. on 935-km. route Potosí-Oruro-La Paz, leaving 1700 (26 hrs., US$15; check which company operates the best buses). To Potosí (386 km.), takes 13 hrs. (US$11.50), the last hour cold. To and from Villazón 3 days a week to connect with Villazón-La Paz train, and 1 other, taking 6 hrs., (US$7.30); otherwise you need to take a local truck. (Tip: expect to pay about half the bus fare for a truck.) Sucre, Weds., leaves 0730. Daily buses to Bermejo (7 hrs., US$5.75, truck US$3.50) not recommended in rainy season, leave in morning; at Bermejo cross river by ferry to Agua Blanca, Argentina. To Villa Montes (see page 186), 12 hrs., Wed., 0730 US$11. Also to Yacuiba, daily by Flota Tarija. The new bus station is in the outskirts on Avenida de Las Américas. Cía. El Chapaco uses poor quality vehicles. Trucks to Bermejo, Potosí and Villazón leave from the top of Calle Cochabamba.

Trains. There are three trains a week to La Paz and Sucre.

Swimming Municipal swimming bath down the hill from the Mercado Negro. Tomatitas, bus from San Juan at 0800, a trip of 5 km. For those with their own transport El Rincón de la Victoria, 18 km., or Tolomosita, 7 km., sandy beach on river bank, and Los Churros de Jurina with natural rock pools, 22 km., or the Ancón gorge. Sauna at Acuario, 15 de Abril 679. Also interesting walking tours.

Santa Cruz (437 metres) is the only other city of note, capital of the Department of Santa Cruz, Bolivia's largest and richest in natural resources, lying in the vast and now rapidly developing plains to the E of the Eastern Cordillera, 552 km. by air from La Paz. This hot, windswept (May-August) boom town, whose population is now 600,000, making it Bolivia's second city, was founded in 1561 by Spaniards who had come from Paraguay.

Santa Cruz is usually hot and dusty, although when the cold *surazo* blows from the Argentine pampas the temperature drops sharply (May-August); the rainy season is December-February. The Plaza 24 de Septiembre is the city's main square with the Cathedral (interesting hand-wrought colonial silver), the University and prefecture set around it. The Cathedral museum is open on Tuesdays and Thursdays (1000-1200, 1600-1800), and Sunday (1000-1200, 1800-2000). Worth seeing if only to wonder how such an isolated community maintained such high artistic standards (but entry is expensive). People stroll around the Plaza in the cool of the evening, and sloths live in the trees. Pleasant residential areas are being developed on the outskirts of town. The water supply is quite good, though typhoid and hepatitis are endemic in the area.

Cruceños are famous for their gaiety—their music, the *carnavalitos*, can be heard all over South America. Of the various festivals, the brightest is Carnival, celebrated for the 15 days before Lent: music in the streets, dancing, fancy dress and the coronation of a queen. Beware the following day when youths run wild with buckets and balloons filled with water—no one is exempt. The *mascaritas* balls also take place during the pre-Lent season at *Caballito Blanco*: girls wear satin masks covering their heads completely and thus ensuring anonymity!

Until recently Santa Cruz was fairly isolated, but new rail and road links in the 1950s ended this isolation and now there is an ever-increasing flow of immigrants from the highlands (*collas*) as well as Mennonites mostly from USA and Canada and Japanese settlers, such as the Okinawan colony 50 km. from Montero, to grow cotton, sugar, rice, coffee and other crops, which yield profusely. Cattle breeding and timber projects are also becoming important. A trip out of Santa Cruz to see these newly-settled areas is interesting, especially towards the Río Grande or Yapacaní (beautiful birds and butterflies; the fish are highly recommended). About 5 km. out of town are the Botanical Gardens, damaged in 1982 flooding.

The exploitation of oil and gas in the Department of Santa Cruz has greatly contributed to the city's rapid development. There are several oil fields: at Caranda, 50 km. to the NW, at Colpa, 32 km. to the N and a large gas field at Río Grande, 40 km. to the SE. YPFB has an oil refinery at Santa Cruz.

Warning The influence of drug-trafficking has made Santa Cruz into an expensive and, according to most travellers, unpleasant place. Always carry your passport with you as there are constant checks by Immigration. Failure to do so will result in extra hours at the police station. There seems to be no escape from plainclothes policemen "fining" foreigners for some misdemeanor or

BOLIVIA 191

other: "having an invalid visa"; at the airport "failing to pay the airport tax"; needing "safe conduct" to travel to Brazil. Bribes are charged arbitrarily at the bus station and, especially, at the railway station en route to Brazil. Watch out also for drug-plants. If possible never be without a witness, always ask for the policeman's identity card (green, embossed with a coat of arms), take his name and number, and say you will take the matter to his superior. Try also to enlist the help of the military police. There may be no alternative but to pay up: complaints, or requests for a receipt, have often led to jail.

Hotels Los Tajibos (Holiday Inn), the biggest and most expensive, A, Av. San Martín in Equipetrol Barrio out of town, swimming pool for residents only; Cortez, Av. Cristóbal de Mendoza 280, also out of town, on 2nd anillo near the Cristo, also has pool and good reputation, C, recommended for medium or long stays; Las Palmas, Av. Trompillo, near airport, new, friendly, recommended; in the centre of town is the Gran Hotel with pool and laundry service, English spoken; good value, C. Santa Cruz, central, Pari 59, good with pool, B, much used by British visitors (with English managers), not really recommended for families; Asturias, Moldes 154 with 2 pools, recommended for families C; Bolivia, Libertad 365, C; all those mentioned above are air-conditioned. La Paz, La Paz 65, C; Hotel Residencial Italia, René Moreno 167, no restaurant, C; Brasil, E, breakfast, bath and friendly; Pacífico, F, cheap, no bath, Denise, E, with bath and breakfast, —no air-conditioning; Roma, 24 de Septiembre 530, D, pleasant, no restaurant; Cataluña, 10 km. N on Montero road, pool, basketball, grounds, D, very popular at weekends with cruceños; Premier, René Moreno 258, small new hotel, C; Florida, Calle 27 de Mayo 209, centrally heated, noisy, D, with breakfast; Orion, E, shared room and bath; La Siesta, Vallegrande 17, D; Jenecheru, España 40, D; Chiquitania, Independencia, E with breakfast; Residencial Bolívar, Sucre 131, E, with breakfast (hot showers); Hotel Copacabana, Junín 129, D, with bath (E without); Residencial Copacabana, Junín 217, near centre, F, acceptable; Colonial, Buenos Aires 57, comfortable recommended, C; Alojamiento Ferrocarril, opp. station, E, washing facilities suspect; Residencial 27 de Mayo, Ayacucho, F, cheap; Santa Bárbara, Calle Santa Bárbara 151 (just off Junín), clean, F, Suárez, Ballivián 149; Alojamiento Tupiza, corner of Buenos Aires and Libertad, F, friendly. Posada Sucre, Vallegrande 93, fairly central and friendly, F. Residencial Santa Cruz, Junín, friendly, F; Posada El Turismo, Junín, F; Alojamiento Oriente, Junín, E, not recommended; Residencial Ballivián, Ballivián 71, F (hot showers); Alojamiento Boston, Florida 418, F; Hostalería Rojas, Cuéllar 257, F, central, cold showers, safe, adequate; Residencial Los Pozos, opp. Mercado Los Pozos, E, hot shower, clean, safe. The better hotels have some air-conditioned rooms but there is usually an extra charge. For those taking buses, Residencial Arze at the back of the terminal, F, or Querencia, F, is about half a block north of the bus terminal and Alojamiento San José, Canadá 136, cold water, clean, F, about 1½ blocks. La Quinta, Barrio Urbari, has individual chalets, good for families but out of town. For all hotels there is 3-tier pricing: locals, South Americans and others. All prices include taxes.

Restaurants The best restaurants are the Floresca, Av. Velarde 136, which has a good discotheque upstairs; the "85" at Bolívar 85 (very dear); La Fonda de Ariel (chicharrón on Sundays and pork), Av. Irala, and the Ambassador, Av. San Martín (all air-conditioned). On Calle 21 de Mayo, Oki and Belgrado are recommended for snacks or beer. La Empalizada, Barrio Cooper 3, has very good parrilladas (grills) in a very pleasant outdoor setting with discotheque. Don Miguel, on Av. Uruguay, has good parrilladas (repeatedly recommended). El Fogón, Av. Viedma 436 and La Buena Mesa, 2nd Anillo near Cristo, both excellent for parrillada and churrasquería; El Mauricio Rancho, Av. Ejército Nacional for excellent steaks. Portachuelo expensive but good. London Grill in Calle Beni is run by British ex-airman and his Bolivian wife. El Surubí, Av. Irala, serves only surubí (fish); El Boliche, Beni 222, serves good crêpes. Chinese restaurants include China, Sucre 209; China Law, Castedo Barba 127; China Town, Velasco 58; Patito, 24 de Septiembre 301; Shanghai, Av. 27 de Febrero 33; Nueva China on 24 de Septiembre or the expensive New Hong Kong on Ballivián 137. El Mandarín, Av. Irala 673, excellent. Japanese Kiku, near Loposo market. For good pizzas La Buena Napolí, Calle Independencia, to eat in, or take away. El Deportista a few doors down (Independencia 42) serves good cheap meals. Also good value is the Bonanza, Junín 177, across from the Post Office, hamburgers, clean; next door is Gandhis, opinions divided on the curries (ask if you want a hot one), English-speaking, Indian owner. The Costa Azul, and Monterrey, René Moreno, good value with cheap meals and snacks. New Orleans Bar, Av. Trompillo, hamburgers and pizza, English spoken; Yogi's Domino, Calle Campero, serves continental food, both English and German spoken. Two quite good duck restaurants are located on Km. 2 (Los Patos) and Km. 8 on the road to Cochabamba. La Pascana on the Plaza is a favourite of tourists and locals alike for ice-cream and snacks, though service is slow. Cheap, good parrilladas at Gauchito Moya, Av. Banzer. Cheap lunches at Chopp Alemana, Ayacucho 171. Many cheap restaurants near the bus terminal on the main avenida. Also on the extension of Calle 6 de Agosto behind the market Los Pozos (daytime). The bakeries on Junín, Los Manzanos and España look scruffy but sell the local specialities: empanadas de queso (cheese pies), cuñapés (yuca buns), rice bread and humitas (maize pies); try the Panadería Trieste, 21 de Mayo 369, not the cheapest, but good breakfasts as well. El Tropero, Av. Cañoto 310, is recommended for its churrasquería and parrillada, and Candilejas for quality parrilladas, next to Hotel Cortez. El Patio and the Palace on the main square sell good cakes. Ice-cream specialities at Ca-Ri-Na, Ingavi 213 and at Kivón. Ayacucho 267, highly recommended.

192 BOLIVIA

Clubs Tennis Club; Club Las Palmas, 2½ km. on road to Cochabamba, has 9-hole golf course and pool; Club Hípico, riding club, nearby.

Books Los Amigos del Libro, René Moreno 26, sells foreign language books (expensive) and *Newsweek*, and a useful guide *Con Usted La Señorial Santa Cruz de la Sierra* for US$0.25 (list of cheap boarding houses); Cruz del Sur, 21 de Mayo 62, sells *Time*.

Shopping Leather goods (Dorian, Florida 39, esq. Libertad, honest), baskets, hammocks. Carvings and other objects made from beautiful *guayacán* and *jacarandá* wood (though reported these crack in drier climates). The market Los Pozos is new, clean, good for mid-day meals and worth going to in summer for its exotic fruits: *ambaiba* (looks like a glove and the fruit is sucked out of the "fingers"), *guaypurú* (like a cherry), *ocoro* (like a prickly mandarin), *achachayrú* (mandarin-like with hard skin), *pitón* (like sour grapes) as well as better-known tropical fruits. There are plenty of smuggled Brazilian goods on sale, exchanged for Bolivian coca (made into cocaine). Beware of bag-snatching in the market. Another market (nothing for tourists, but also has a wide variety of fruit) is *Bazar Siete Calles*: walk down Vallegrande, past Ingavi.

Taxis US$0.40 anywhere within city limits. Luggage extra.

Entertainment Discotheques: El Mau-Mau, open only during Carnival (a vast auditorium), The Viva María is the largest night club. Another recommended night club is El Cuerno Colonial at España 162; on El Paso, Tramps Bar and The New Orleans Bar (both expensive). Also Caaly and Mermelade (Av. Uruguay 30). Tijuana Piano Bar Saloon has offered a courtesy drink to bearers of the SAHB at Av. Velarde 230. They also co-own Number One Disco, Calle Boquerón 83. There are numerous cinemas in town; see local press for details.

Museum Casa de la Cultura, on the plaza, with occasional exhibitions and also an archaeological display; has plays, recitals, concerts and folk dancing.

Banks Bank of America, Velasco 19; Banco do Brasil, Ayacucho 168; Banco Popular del Perú, 24 de Septiembre 156; Banco de la Nación Argentina, Sucre 31; also local banks. Open 0730 to 1300. Use Casas de Cambio for money exchange, on 24 de Septiembre, for example. Magri Turismo, Edificio Oriente, changes American Express travellers' cheques. Money changers on Av. Libertad, and Plaza de Armas.

Consulate Brazil, Florida 25, one block north of the main plaza. Argentina, Banco de la Nación Argentina building, Sucre 31. Uruguay, Ayacucho 296; Paraguay, Sucre 677; Peru, La Paz 726.

Post Office Calle Junín 150.

Cables can be sent from Entel just off the Plaza at Warner 83.

Tourist Agents Santa Cruz Tur and Orientur are on the Plaza; Exprinter is at Libertad 149; Chovy Tours, 21 de Mayo 309/317, Tel.: 24445, recommended; Camba Tur, Sucre 8; and Turismo Balas, Bolívar 16 recommended. Many agencies (there are over 100) are to be treated with caution since travel is not their primary "business".

Tourist Office Chuquisaca and Ñuflo de Chávez (Tel.: 48644). Open Monday-Friday, business hours only—no city maps. Also kiosk at bus station and airport.

Air Service LAB flies daily to La Paz and Cochabamba. LAB and Líneas Aéreas Paraguayas (LAP—recommended) fly twice a week Asunción-Santa Cruz. It is reported that up to US$40 can be saved by breaking your flight at Santa Cruz from Asunción and buying a La Paz ticket, than by flying direct. Cruzeiro do Sul has weekly flight to Campo Grande, S°o Paulo and Rio de Janeiro. LAB and Aerolíneas Argentinas also fly to Salta and Buenos Aires, four times a week. There are also three flights by LAB to S°o Paulo a week, and weekly ones to Manaus, Caracas and Miami. LAB flies to some of the outlying towns in the Dept. of Santa Cruz as also to Trinidad, Camiri, Sucre, San Ignacio de Velasco (daily, but check with LAB), Tarija (US$22.50) and Yacuiba. There is a weekly flight to Roboré and San Matías every Friday—one can then enter Brazil via Cáceres, taxi US$2.40.

A new international airport is open at Viru-Viru, about 16 km. from the city. Tel.: 44411 or 33473. The bus every 20 minutes to Viru-Viru leaves from the old Trompillo airport, or the bus terminal. Viru-Viru taxi, US$9. TAM, office on Independencia, flies to Puerto Suárez (US$16.50 Tues., Fri., Sun.) fills up quickly, book well in advance and Yacuiba (US$12, daily). On LAB internal services baggage allowance is 15 kg. (excess US$0.35 per kg.). Tax: internal US$1 (eq.) international US$15 (not payable in pesos). Often it is worth going out to the airport as neither LAB or TAM seems to be very aware of empty seats.

Buses Bus terminal on corner of Av. Cañuto and Av. Irala. Most buses seem to run at night. Two daily buses to Cochabamba (US$14, 15 hrs.) leave in the evening (Flota Boliviana, 1700, best) with connections to Sucre (US$16), Oruro and La Paz (US$22, 23 hrs.). For Sucre it is sometimes quicker and cheaper to fly, avoiding changing buses at Cochabamba, i.e. an extra 300 km. The only day time possibility for travel is by colectivo or truck to Cochabamba: either take Micro 17 to km. 12 were there is a police checkpoint at which all the trucks stop, or go to the office of Transportes Peco in Av. Landívar, half a block west from the Cañuto statue, on Calle Ayacucho. The fare after negotiation will only be marginally less than that for the bus, but at least you will get good views. To Camiri, bus US$11, 8 hrs., *camioneta*, 7 hrs., US$7.80. Minibus and colectivos now run to Trinidad; the office is below the *Alojamiento Cañuto* in Av. Cañuto, just south of the statue. Trinidad US$25, Samaipata buses leave at 0430; Yapacaní at 0725; and to Abapó and Puerto Banegas for river journey to Guayaramerín. Lorries also leave for Trinidad from the Plaza behind the statue.

Excursions The country surrounding the city is flat and scenically uninteresting—except for the agriculturist. The sand-dunes (Las Lomas de Arena) 20 km. to the south are worth a visit but impossible to get to without private transport. There is a fresh-water lake in the dunes, but a jeep with 4-wheel drive is required (not ideal on a windy day). Los Espejillos, where a mountain stream plunges over a waterfall and carves its way through limestone rocks down a beautiful green and forested valley is well worth the effort to get to—4-wheel drive, only in the dry season. Turn right at Km. 26 on Cochabamba road, cross the Piray river and drive some 12 km. up a forested valley. At a green field on the left (football goal posts) stop and walk a few hundred metres up to the stream. A favourite day trip is to the Yapacaní bridge where *surubí* from the river or *jochi* and *tatú* (armadillo) from the forest may be eaten in one of the riverside eating houses. The drive up to Samaipata, 120 km. along the Cochabamba road, takes a full day—visit the Inca site near the town, an exhausting walk, but the drive up the Piray gorge and "over the top" makes a splendid trip. Take daily bus to Vallegrande which passes the site (2"½-3 hrs.)

A recommended round trip taking about a week starts by arriving by train at San José de Chiquitos (with beautiful church that looks like a candle—see below). From there by truck to San Rafael (134 km.), San Miguel (169 km.) and then San Ignacio, and Concepción. From **Concepción** there are daily tours to San Javier or Santa Cruz, or there are LAB/TAM flights from Santa Cruz to Concepción and San Ignacio on Mon., Wed. and Friday. Accommodation is limited, but best at San Ignacio (*Hotel Santa Cruz*; also luxury bungalows, US$55d, or US$150 weekly for groups of over 6, contact Lucy Hartmann, Cochabamba, Tel.: 24258). Concepción is roughly 300 km. NE of Santa Cruz. Still reasonably wild though being opened up. Accommodation at *Grand Hotel Guarayas*, F; *Residencial 6 de Agosto*, shower, clean.

A good road has been driven into fertile lowland to the NW of Santa Cruz. It goes 37 km. N to **Montero** (30,000 people), where there are a sugar refinery and various cotton gins, and on to Puerto Grether, high on the River Ichilo, a tributary of the Mamoré. It will later connect at Todos Santos with the 200-km. road to Cochabamba. A non-stop shuttle minibus service leaves from Santa Cruz bus station for Montero when full. From Montero a minibus connects to Buena Vista (*pensión*); from there trucks run to El Terminal after which one can walk to the Surutú river, the eastern boundry of Amboró National Park (180,000 hectares)—walk to Cerro Amboró (guide required) recommended. The park is home to butterflies, humming birds, macaws, and other native animals (many of them endangered species). Beware of the insects—do not wear shorts or short-sleeved shirts; much wading is required to get around the park.

Travel to Brazil The Santa Cruz-Corumbá railway (take bus 4 from the centre to the station) is still rather primitive (and the time-table has been described as flexible, or pure fantasy) but has recently been improved; toilets are still dirty but there is an adequate dining car. Trains stop at Quijarro near the frontier. From there travellers must go by bus (US$0.60) or Land-Rover (US$10) to Corumbá in Brazil; these meet the trains as they arrive. The *ferrobus* train service is much faster and better, but also ends at Quijarro; it leaves Santa Cruz at 1700 Mon., Wed., Fri. 12-hr trip, returning from Quijarro the following day at 0800 (meals served at seats). (*Ferrobus* tickets are only available at the station, ticket office opens 0630-0700, but queuing starts at 0400; don't buy tickets for seats 2c and 2d, they don't exist.) There is also a fast train that leaves Santa Cruz Sun., Tues. and Thurs., but maybe daily, at 1210; returns following day at 1800. Stopping trains leave Thurs. and Sun. at 1404 and goods trains (mixed) Mon. and Fri. at 2115. Slow trains from Quijarro leave Mon. and Fri. at 1150 or goods (mixed) train at 1500 on Wed. or Sun. Fares: for ordinary trains "Pullman", US$12, first class US$10, second class US$6; *ferrobus*, "Pullman", US$14.50, "especial", US$13.50. Book in advance, early in the morning, at Brasileña station (phone 48488). Check *all* times before setting out. Take a torch, whichever class you are travelling. It is a monotonous journey through jungle except for the frequent stops at trackside towns, where the train's arrival is the chief event in life. A rail flat-car can be hired to transport cars, US$185; you may have to wait several days for a flat-car, however. Food is available on the train or at frequent stops. There is now an unpaved road between Santa Cruz and the Brazilian border, but not recommended, especially in the rainy season, take water, map food and compass. The ticket office at the station is not open before 0700 to Corumbá and Yacuiba; purchase only the day before. The customs and emigration post at Quijarro closes very soon after the arrival of the *ferrobus*. Taxi Quijarro-Corumbá (8 km.) about US$4 or colectivo, bus US$1.45. You are advised to book as early as possible on all services to Corumbá, which are reported to be getting very crowded. Failing that you can try to buy a ticket on the platform ½ hr. before train departure. Travel agent Orienturr sells tickets for the *rápido*. Foreign exchange generally little problem, but you are likely to be sold cruzados in largish denominations; also you will probably only be able to sell bolivianos in Bolivia, while a few dollars in cash have been known to make irritating border formalities less troublesome. However do beware of showing large quantities of money around. If there are heavy rains check that the line has not been washed out.

US citizens must visit Brazilian consulate (visa, one photo, yellow fever certificate and ticket out of Brazil) in Santa Cruz before travelling to Corumbá. They will be refused entry to Brazil unless they have a visa. Yellow-fever certificates are often asked for (failure to produce one is another "fineable" offence—see **warning** on page 190).

On the railway, half way between Santa Cruz and Corumbá, is **San José de Chiquitos**, with huge Jesuit church. (*Hotel San Sebastián Silvestre*, F, basic, clean, good food, near railway station.)

Puerto Suárez Beware thieves. *Hotel Sucre* on main plaza, G, barely adequate; *Hotel Banidi* (more comfortable and the most obvious), and *Residencial Puerto Suárez*, E, clean, fans and showers. *Hotel Bolivia*, D; *Hotel Domingo*, near railway station, dirty, unsafe. Beware the water, it is straight from the river. Most people prefer to go on to Corumbá where hotels are better.

The simplest way to Brazil is to fly La Paz-Puerto Suárez, US$85, then share a taxi to the border, US$7.30-US$10.90 (per car).

Travel to Argentina To Buenos Aires by train via **Yacuiba** (11,000 people; many cheap hotels in town centre) takes 3 days and is a long and tiring trip. First class and second class passengers must disembark at Yacuiba, taking taxi (US$0.25) to Pocitos on the border and walking across to Argentine side before boarding train for Buenos Aires. Tickets should be purchased from Incatur travel agents in Santa Cruz. A more comfortable alternative is to take the *ferrobus* from Santa Cruz to Yacuiba (9-10 hour journey) and then to take a bus from Pocitos on the Argentine side of the border to Güemes (2 buses daily with connections to Salta and Buenos Aires). Trains Yacuiba-Santa Cruz: Mon. and Fri., mixto, at 1900, 24 hrs., US$2; Wed. and Sat., rápido, at 1230, Pullman, US$8, 1st class US$4, 2nd class US$2.50, 10 hrs.; or Thursday at 0815. Trucks for Santa Cruz leave from Lourdes market, not advisable after rain. Be warned that the immigration police have been shaking tourists down for "smuggling dollars" and will offer you the option of jail or a fine. Contact a superior officer and/or Consulate to help stop this banditry. LAB flies to Santa Cruz and La Paz on Tues. and Sun., 1500; TAM also flies from here but has a much more flexible timetable.

Nearly every week there is a boat to Rurrenabaque (US$10, 11 hours) which has two hotels, F, all rooms with bath.

The Beni Lowlands

A road to open up the underinhabited Beni Department runs from Cochabamba NE for 200 km. to Todos Santos, on the Chaparé river, a tributary of the Mamoré (the previous narrow road has now been much improved and paved). To **Villa Tunari** by *micro* every 5-10 minutes (no standing allowed in the buses) from Calle Lanza, Cochabamba, US$2.60. *Hotel San Antonio*, E, water intermittent, *Hotel Las Vegas*, basic but clean, *Pilundui*, and others, F. Especially good is *Cabañas Sumuque*, D, pool and good view. Sr. Carlos at the *Hotel Rosas* does jungle trips to see birds and crocodiles.

A road goes through from Villa Tunari to **Puerto Villarroel** (*Hotels Rivera, Hannover*, best, E, and some cheap *alojamientos*) from where cargo boats ply irregularly to Trinidad in about 4-10 days (US$10, meals included). You can get information from the Port Captain's notice board. Take a hammock, mosquito net, plenty of reading matter, water-sterilizing tablets and any interesting food you can find beforehand (rain water available from pharmacy - on the boat one can only get river water tasting of mud). (There are very few stores in Villarroel. Sr. Arturo Linares at the Cede office organizes boat trips to the jungle—not cheap.) You get to Guayaramerín in 10-15 days (fare US$10), depending on the depth of the river (may be best in August/September when the water is lower but cleaner, and there are more animals around on the shore). The Cochabamba-Villa Tunari run is highly recommended for scenery, and fishing at San Fernando. However, the river boat people seldom fish although you might be offered turtle eggs, a local delicacy.

From Cochabamba you can get a bus to Puerto San Francisco, Todos Santos or Puerto Villarroel, and thence by boat down the Securé, Chaparé or Mamoré rivers to Guayaramerín, then by

BOLIVIA 195

road to Riberalta and back up river to Santa Ana on the River Santa Elena, or Puerto Linares, thence by road to Coroico and back to La Paz.

Ulricke Ramcke-Mensing writes:
Boat trip from Puerto Villarroel to Trinidad There are now daily except Sunday (US$6.50) buses from Cochabamba to Puerto Villarroel, taking about 6 hours. (Police checkpoints may ask for bribes from *all* bus passengers on the Cochabamba-Purto Villarroel route; similarly at the Capitanía del Puerto office in Puerto Villarroel where you are supposed to register. Either do not register, or demand a receipt and say you will check the facts with a superior—Ed.) Puerto Villarroel is the main port for the river transport to the north of Bolivia. As the road running from Santa Cruz to Trinidad can only be used in the dry season, river transport is still the most important means of communication. There are boats running between Puerto Villarroel, Trinidad and Guayaramerín on the Brazilian border, taking passengers. This trip is only for the hardy traveller. In the rainy season when the river is high it takes about 4 to 5 days to go from Puerto Villarroel to Trinidad, but in the dry season, i.e. between May or June and September or October, it may last 8 to 10 days. The launches do not provide berths; you just have to sleep on the cargo which, if you are lucky, may be sugar bags and the like. We paid US$15 for the trip including food. The food is native, that is to say all kinds of fish, dishes like *massaca* (stewed yuca with cooking bananas, *charque* or dried meat, oil and salt) and turtle eggs (rather delicious!). If you are fussy about food, don't make the trip because the kitchen is beyond description and the toilet facilities, too. Take your own drinking water, as the water served is taken from the river. The food served is very starchy and heavy because it is nearly always fried in oil. The trip is not as exciting as those in the real jungle; the countryside between Puerto Villarroel and Trinidad is more or less cultivated, with plantations of bananas and cattle ranches, some with 20-30,000 head. There is no jungle with orchids, crocodiles, etc., but one can see *petas*—small turtles basking in the sun, river dolphins, jumping fish, now and then monkeys playing on the beach, and many types of birds. At night, there are never-ending frog concerts. This trip could be described as quite relaxing if it was not for the poor food and the spartan accommodation.

Bathing in the river can be done without any harm. One night we caught quite a few *pirañas* but we were told that they do not usually attack men. (The Editor advises care, all the same!)

If one does not know how to enjoy the "green symphony" as it is passing by, one should take a good book, as the trip might otherwise get very long!

A mosquito net is a "must".

Trinidad, the capital of the lowland Beni Department (237 metres), founded 1686, population 36,200, is reached by air from La Paz, Cochabamba, Riberalta or Santa Cruz, or by river from Puerto Villarroel. Sleeping-bag and mosquito-net essential on boats; passengers sleep on the deck. The port is on a mud bank 8 km. out of town. Dry season, Oct.-Dec., boats do not reach Villarroel from the north. Food quite varied. A cheap restaurant is *El Dorado*, Santa Cruz 522, with set meals for US$0.60, or a Japanese restaurant near the market. The main mode of transport (even for taxis) is the motorbike. Excursions interesting for wildlife, as is the river trip. A road has been built to link La Paz with Trinidad (via San Ignacio, San Borja and Puerto Linares), and occasional colectivos, buses and trucks use it (but don't depend on it); the road is of typical "penetration" standard, not for use during the rainy season, and gasoline is very difficult to come by. Take water, and a compass. A railway from Santa Cruz to Trinidad, via Montero and Colonia San Juan, has reached the confluence of the Ichilo and Grande rivers, 105 km. from Trinidad. The flight to La Paz is cheaper by TAM than by LAB (book early in either case). Bus service to Cochabamba leaves 0700. A fleet of over 200 air taxis also provides local transport. LAB tend to cancel flights, especially during rainy season. Ask around at airport for private-hire air fare prices. Exchange cash dollars at Farmacia de Tarno, Santa Cruz 470.

Hotels *Ganadero*, C, recommended, roof top pool. *Cochabamba*, F, clean, three blocks from main Plaza; *Beni*, F; *Magdalena*, *Yaguma*, La Paz and Santa Cruz, F; *Trinidad*, F (poor value) or *Residencial Loreto*, Calle La Paz, F, clean. *Brasilia*, F, La Paz 662, communal bath, noisy, dirty, hard beds. Some cheaper alternatives on Calle 18 de Octubre: *Yacama*, (off Calle La Paz. *Al Brete*, F, not recommended; *Residencial Palermo*, F, Av. 6 de Agosto, clean with hot water. Slightly out of town (no transport) *Hostelería*, D, swimming pool, air-conditioned, friendly. *Restaurant Loreto*, recommended, between Plaza and Calle La Paz. Also *Churrasquería El Cachón de Mamita*, Av. Sucre 737, expensive, and, *Chifa Hong Kong* on the Plaza. *Snack Brasilia*, La Paz 662, serves a good dinner. *Carlitos*, on main square, recommended.

Guayaramerín A primitive small town (12,500 people) on the bank of the Mamoré river, N of Trinidad, opposite the Brazilian town of Guajará-Mirim. Passage between the two towns is unrestricted, but if going from Brazil into Bolivia

196 BOLIVIA

you need your passport stamped by the Bolivian consul in Guajará-Mirim before leaving Brazil, and by the Bolivian immigration office. Similarly, if you are travelling on into Brazil and not just visiting Guajará-Mirim, get your passport stamped when leaving Bolivia and entering Brazil (US citizens need visas to enter Brazil). Boat trip, US$0.20, speed boat US$ 0.50 during day, US$2.50 at night. If you don't want to stay, check the notice of boats leaving port on the Port Captain's board, prominently displayed near the immigration post on the river's bank. Boats up the Mamoré are fairly frequent—a three-day wait at the most.

Hotels *Santa Ana*, E, recommended. *Playa*, F. *Litoral*, F, cold water only, friendly. *Central*, F, just off the Plaza, and *Mexo Plaza*, E, on the main Plaza.

Restaurants *La Querencia*. Best is *La Puerta del Sol* for US$4-6 evening meals, or the old municipal market, two blocks west of the main square. *Snack Gino* at Av. 25 de Mayo 511 is also a possibility. At mid-day try the port area, where rapid short-order meals can be had for US$1-1.50.

Buses to Riberalta 3 hrs., US$4.75, 0930 and 1600 daily (first return bus at 0700). Also trucks available from the 1100 block of Gral. Federico Román.

Air Transport Daily flights to Trinidad and to La Paz (0930), and others to San Joaquín and Santa Ana. LAB and TAM offices at airport, 10 minute walk from town.

Riberalta Only 175 metres above sea level, another expanding town (20,000 people), which with the whole region attained temporary importance during the natural-rubber boom of the late 19th century; the cattle industry is providing a new boost for the town. It is at the confluence of the Madre de Dios and Beni rivers, which together flow into the Mamoré a few km. N of Guayaramerín. Electricity is turned off from 2300 to 0600.

Hotels *Noreste*, clean, friendly, *Cochabamba*, *Residencia*, *Santa Rita*, all F (without breakfast). *Comercial Lazo*, Calle N.G. Salvatierra (F, not too clean but comfortable), and *Colonial*, Plácido Méndez 1, are worth a try, E; *Residencial Los Reyes*, near airport, D, with fan.

Restaurants *Club Social Progresso*, US$1 a meal; *Club Social Riberalta*, better, on Maldonado; *Restaurant Popular Cochabamba*, US$0.50. Restaurants on main square are mediocre; good breakfast in market; food stalls outside *Comercial Lazo*, tasty meals.

Flight, Riberalta-Cochabamba (US$100 TAM, US$105 LAB). LAB to La Paz, via Santa Cruz and Tarija. Expect delays in the wet season. LAB office Linares 31, TAM office is opposite LAB. A motorcycle can be hired for US$2 an hour (no licence or deposit required) for visits to jungle; taxi drivers can give you the address.

Boat trip from Riberalta to Puerto Rico via River Aruña, from there to Conquista by road (US$4.10) and thence by River Madre de Dios to Riberalta (US$5.25). There are long gaps between boats from Riberalta.

Best rates of cash exchange at Swiss Consulate; the Swiss Consul also owns a few boats and knows all about what is going on on the river. Bazar La Paz on main Plaza buys dollars, cash and travellers' cheques.

N.B. Food in the Beni tends to be expensive, but the steaks are good. Electricity is turned off between 2300-0700: do not rely on the fan to keep the insects off.

Cobija, capital of the lowland Department of Pando, N of La Paz, population, 4,523 (252 metres), only connections by air (e.g. TAM to Puerto Rico and LAB to Guayaramerín and Riberalta) and river transport. It is close to the Brazilian and Peruvian frontiers and the area has many Brazilian residents.

The Economy

Bolivia is the poorest country on the South American mainland, with annual income per head estimated at about US$400. Its backwardness is partly attributable to its rugged terrain, which makes communications between the various parts of the country extremely difficult, and to its landlocked position.

The agricultural sector employs over 56% of the working population and contributes about 23% to gdp, but less than 2% of export earnings. Employment in agriculture has fallen since the mid-1960s because of increasing urbanisation. Production of crops for food takes place primarily in the Altiplano, mainly by subsistence farmers, while crops for industrial use (cotton, sugar and soya) are concentrated around Santa Cruz. Croplands cover about 5% of total land area.

Most commercial agriculture is in the east, where there are a number of food-processing plants: vegetable oils, a maize mill and sugar refineries. One of the major growth areas in agriculture is the cultivation of the coca leaf, used for chewing by the Indians and to make the drug cocaine. The extreme economic depression and rising unemployment has driven increasing numbers in search of the lucrative cocaine trade. Coca is easy to grow, up to four crops a year can be harvested, and Bolivia's production is believed to be worth about US$2bn a year, although less than a quarter of that actually returns to the country.

In contrast to agriculture, mining, including oil, employs only 2-5% of the labour force and contributes less than 7% of gdp, yet 95% of export earnings. Bolivia is a major producer of tin, antimony, wolfram and bismuth. Silver, lead and zinc are also produced and there are large unexploited reserves of lithium and potassium. Tin is the major mineral export, but because of the collapse of the world tin market, it has lost its first position in overall exports to natural gas. The mining sector is in decline and many mines are being closed.

Estimated reserves of natural gas are sufficient to meet domestic demand and export commitments for 30 years, but oil reserves, at 155m barrels in the mid-1980s, were being exploited faster than the rate of discovery. Production of around 20,000 b/d was just sufficient to meet domestic demand, but would be insufficient were there to be a general economic recovery.

The recession which afflicted most Latin American countries from 1980 hit Bolivia with six consecutive years of contraction of gdp, accompanied by accelerating inflation, massive and frequent devaluations of the currency and social unrest. Government spending to support key export sectors was hampered by widespread inefficiency, corruption and strikes in state enterprises, which led to massive public sector deficits and external indebtedness. Economic problems were compounded in 1983 by a severe drought in the Altiplano and floods in the eastern lowlands, which devasted farming. The resulting food shortages exacerbated existing inflationary pressures and led to hyperinflation with annual rates reaching over 20,000%.

In the mid-1980s the government of President Paz Estenssoro introduced severe austerity measures to stabilize the economy, in which price controls were lifted, subsidies removed, public sector wages frozen and the currency linked to the US dollar in a controlled float. Tax reform was passed, a new currency, the boliviano, was created, worth 1 million pesos, the IMF agreed to disburse a standby credit, bilateral and multilateral lending began to flow again and steps were taken to reschedule the external commercial bank debt. Inflation was volatile but was contained to less than 100% a year, although unemployment continued to rise and living standards to fall. Nevertheless, there were encouraging signs that growth could be renewed towards the end of the decade and structural adjustment would put Bolivia on a firmer footing for the 1990s.

	1961-70(av)	1971-80(av)	1981-85(av)	1986(est.)
Gdp growth (1980 prices)(%)	6.0	4.5	-0.04	-3.7
Inflation	6.1	18.7	610.6	67.0
Exports (fob) US$m	122	517	779	538
Natural gas	—	70	369	314
Tin	82	245	253	100
Zinc	5	33	36	30
Imports (fob) US$m	126	460	536	54
Current account balance US$m (cumulative)	-222	-965	-1,243	-450

Information for Visitors

To Bolivia by Air

(1) *From Europe*: Lufthansa, twice weekly from Frankfurt to La Paz, via San Juan and Lima. From other places, quickest to fly to Lima (more tiring) by Air France, etc., whence 12 flights a week to La Paz; or via Rio de Janeiro, São Paulo or Buenos Aires. Le Point have an office at Taura on Calle Sagárnaga, La Paz.

They can confirm or sell tickets on their Lima-Zürich flights. Cheapest route is with Líneas Aéreas Paraguayas: Frankfurt-Brussels-(Madrid)-Recife-Asunción-Santa Cruz; on the outward journey you will have to stay for 1,2 or 6 nights in Asunción (first night may be paid for by LAP), but the return connection is immediate.

(2) *From North America:* Eastern, 3 flights weekly from Miami to La Paz. Lloyd Aéreo Boliviano (LAB, non-IATA, cheaper, but timekeeping poor), daily from Miami via Manaus or Panama or Caracas to La Paz. From California, connections via Lima.

(3) *Within South America:* From Caracas twice weekly by LAB. From Lima, 10 a week by Lufthansa, Aero Perú (3 times weekly), LAB (cheaper) or Aerolíneas Argentinas. Twice weekly from Cuzco (Tues. and Sat. 0945). From Arica, twice weekly by LAB and LAN-Chile. From Santiago, 6 a week by LAN-Chile (via Arica and Iquique), Avianca, LAB or Lufthansa. From Buenos Aires, three flights by LAB or Aerolíneas Argentinas. From Asunción, two a week by LAB, or Líneas Aéreas Paraguayas. From Rio, two a week by Cruzeiro do Sul. From São Paulo, 7 a week by Cruzeiro or LAB. From Bogotá, once a week, Avianca. *Note:* LAB international flights to and from points E of La Paz tend also to call at Santa Cruz or Cochabamba, or both. TAM services are half as cheap again, but their record of timekeeping is even worse than LAB and your priority for a seat is low.

Tax on airline tickets 16%.

Airport tax of US$15 (only US$1-3 on internal flights, payable in bolivianos) is levied on leaving. No tax if leaving overland, or if you stay in Bolivia less than 24 hours.

By Sea   To Arica or Antofagasta, then by rail or road.

By Rail   From Argentina, Peru, and Chile (see page 168).

By Road   From Cuzco or Puno, several services. Peruvian and Bolivian roads mostly paved. Also links with Argentina and Chile (see below).

Motoring (1) From Puno (Peru) via border stations at Desaguadero (for Guaqui and La Paz) or Yunguyo (for Copacabana, the straits of Tiquina, and La Paz). Peruvian customs at Desaguadero do not work after 1730 unless you are prepared to seek out the officials and pay them "overtime" (US$3 at weekends). Bolivian customs now operate to 1900 but immigration formalities can be completed at Copacabana if the border post is closed. Peruvian time is an hour behind Bolivian time.

(2) From Salta-Jujuy-La Quiaca (Argentina) to Potosí or Tarija. Roads ford many rivers in Bolivia and are impassable in wet weather (Argentine section, despite much work, is reported still to be bad). Bolivian border controls work mornings and 1400-1800 only.

(3) Alternative routes lead from the Argentine province of Salta via Bermejo or Yacuiba into Tarija. Dry weather only.

(4) From Ollagüe (Chile) to Uyuni, very bad. A new dirt road has been built from Arica (Chile) via Tambo Quemado.

Internal Air Services are run by Lloyd Aéreo Boliviano (LAB) and TAM, the army airline, between the main towns. LAB offers a 28-day unlimited domestic flight ticket for US$99 for international travellers using LAB (one is not allowed to leave from the same airport twice, which may cause problems as so many flights radiate from La Paz or Cochabamba). There are also reductions for special excursion flights. LAB will be glad to supply current information on request.

Motorists (including motor-cyclists) must buy an Hoja de Ruta (driving permit) from local offices of the Servicio Nacional de Tránsito for every road journey, specifying final destination and date. These are checked and tolls charged outside each city (i.e. US$2 La Paz-Cochabamba). Cost of toll is about US$0.25 per 100 km. On arrival in La Paz one must report to Aduana to complete formalities. For hints on high-altitude motoring, see **Introduction and Hints** at front of book.

Petrol (gasoline) is bad; only one grade—less than 2-star. Gas oil is slightly cheaper. Costs are higher in Guayaramerín, Riberalta and Puerto Suárez.

Buses (interurban ones are called *flotas*, urban ones *micros*) ply on most of the roads. Reporting time for all Bolivia and Peru is half an hour before the bus leaves, but you should always try to reserve a seat as far as possible in advance. In the wet season, bus travel is subject to long delays and detours at extra cost. On all journeys, take food and toilet wipes.

Trucks congregate at all town markets, with destinations chalked on the sides, they are not much less comfortable than buses or ordinary trains and are normally about half the cost when there is

BOLIVIA 199

competition. Otherwise they charge what they judge the market will bear and can therefore seem expensive.

Internal Roads La Paz-Oruro, completely paved; Oruro-Challapata, paved first 30 km., then dirt (or mud in the wet season); La Paz-Tiquina, paved; Oruro-Cochabamba, all-weather; Cochabamba-Santa Cruz, paved, but in a very bad state; Cochabamba-Sucre, and on to Potosí, S of paved road, now all-weather road. Oruro-Potosí, all-weather. La Paz-Beni-Trinidad, mixed reports. Puerto Suárez-Arroyo Concepción open. Nearly all Bolivian road surfaces, even the paved sections, are bad, and after flooding or rough weather they are even worse.

Travel to Paraguay Apart from the adventurous journey described on page 187, a cheap way of getting to Paraguay is to travel by bus to Salta or Orán (Argentina), then on to Asunción via Resistencia (Argentina). Alternatively LAB have been tipped as a potentially cheap way to travel across South America.

Travel by Train The "Pullman" services are reported to be improving the general slow train service. The railways have recently renewed their rolling stock with Fiat railway coaches from Argentina. "Slow" trains have speeded up but they cannot take the curves and gradients at the same rate as the *ferrobuses*. Always check departure times in advance.

Documents A passport only is needed for citizens of the Western European countries, Canada and Israel; all others need visas unless they have tourist cards, which can be obtained free from the Consuls and travel agencies; they are good for 30 days and can be renewed twice, at the Ministry of Immigration in La Paz, Calle Gosálvez, between Av. Arce and Calle 6 de Agosto. Tourist cards are not available for nationals of communist countries. Extending tourist visas is time-consuming, and costs US$25. The exit-visa stamp, triangular in shape, which one used to have to get separately in La Paz, is now stamped in one's passport when entering and leaving Bolivia. Business visitors (unless passing through as tourists) are required to obtain a Determined Object Visa quoting reference Tasa-03.03. D from a Bolivian consulate. This costs US$60. Hotels automatically register their guests with the immigration authorities but visitors staying as private guests should present their passports at the nearest Ministry of Immigration office. We have repeatedly been asked to warn against people impersonating Interpol men who want to see all your money—ask (politely) to see identification first and then only in front of friendly witnesses. This warning applies especially to Santa Cruz and the rail link to Brazil, also the La Paz-Arica railway (point to the "Gratis" on the stamp, and stand your ground). One also needs an exit stamp at the airport or border town.

About one in ten travellers may be asked to produce an exit ticket, or the money to pay for it, and to show equivalent of US$10 a day for the amount of time they intend to stay in the country. No check, however, at the land frontiers. Visitors no longer need a valid smallpox vaccination certificate.

Duty-free Imports 200 cigarettes, 50 cigars and 1 lb. tobacco; one opened bottle of alcoholic drink.

Walking *Backpacking and Trekking in Peru and Bolivia*, by Hilary and George Bradt, describes 3-9 day hikes in the Cordillera Real within easy reach of La Paz. The local tourist office also produces a leaflet with sketch maps on walks available from La Paz. There are also some excellent guides available through local clubs.

Camping Chet and Jeri Wade, of Sacramento, California, tell us that one can camp almost anywhere in safety. Warm sleeping gear essential, even in the lowlands in the winter. Sleeping bags are also useful for getting some sleep on the buses or long distance trains, especially those crossing the Andes. Mosquito nets can be purchased in La Paz, but they are not cheap. Beware sandstorms S of Oruro. No camping gas is available in Bolivia.

British Visitors are strongly advised to consult "Hints to Exporters: Bolivia", which can be obtained from Dept. of Trade, Export Services Division, Sanctuary Blgs, 16-20 Great Smith Street, London SW1P 3DB. Similar publications for U.S. business visitors may be obtained from the Department of Commerce.

The best time for a visit is May to November, the dry season. May, June, and July are the coldest months.

200 BOLIVIA

Festivals January (last week), La Paz, "Alacitas", on Av. Montes. Feb. 2, Aug. 25: Virgin Copacabana. May 3: Fiesta de la Invención de la Santa Cruz, various parts, in La Paz at the "Calvario". June 23: San Juan, all Bolivia. June 29: San Pedro y San Pablo, at Tiquina. July 28: Fiesta de Santiago (St. James), Altiplano and lake region; Achocalla a convenient place to go to. Nov. 1 and 2: All Saints and All Souls, any local cemetery. For other festivals on the Altiplano enquire at hotels or tourist office in La Paz. Remember that the cities are very quiet on national holidays, but colourful celebrations will be going on in the villages.

Climate There are four distinct climatic zones: (1) The tropical departments of Santa Cruz and Beni, drained by the Amazon; altitude between 150 and 750 metres; average temperature, 29°C. (2) The Yungas, or low valleys, north of La Paz and Cochabamba, among the spurs of the Cordillera; altitude, 750-1,500 metres; average temperature, 24°C. (3) The Valles, or high valleys and basins gouged out by the rivers of the Puna; average temperature, 19°C. (4) The Puna and Altiplano; average temperature, 10°C, but above 4,000 metres may get down to -25°C in June-August (don't forget antifreeze). Little rain falls upon the western plateaux between May and November, but the rest of the year is wet. There is rain at all seasons in the eastern part of the country, and heavy rain from November to March.

Clothing suitable for Great Britain, with a raincoat or light overcoat, should be worn by visitors to the Altiplano and the Puna, where it is particularly cold at night. The climate in the Eastern Lowlands is tropical. Oruro and Potosí are colder than La Paz; Cochabamba can be very warm. There is a prejudice against the wearing of shorts in town centres.

Health Whatever their ages, travellers arriving in La Paz by air (too quickly, that is, for a progressive adaptation to the altitude) should rest for half a day, taking very little food and drink. They will be up and doing the next morning. In Bolivia, do as the Bolivians do: above 3,000 metres, walk slowly, very slowly uphill. Never go out for the whole day without taking an outer garment: the temperature drops sharply at sunset. Inoculate against typhoid and paratyphoid (also have yellow fever inoculation and anti-malaria tablets if visiting the lowlands) and stock up on necessary medicines; they are dear in Bolivia. Visitors are being asked for yellow-fever vaccination certificates when visiting Santa Cruz or the Oriente. We have also been asked to mention that hepatitis is very common. Chagas disease is endemic in the Yungas and other warmer parts of Bolivia. There is no known cure, so that adobe huts with thatched, or leaf-protected, roofs should be avoided as sleeping places because they play host to the *vinchuca* beetle which is the carrier; half Bolivia's population has the disease, which leads to heart failure but shows few other immediate symptoms (see **Health Hints**, page 26).

Hotels Throughout Bolivia the cheaper hotels impose their own curfews. In La Paz it tends to be midnight (check) but it can be as early as 2130 in Copacabana. These locking up times are strictly adhered to by hotel keepers.

Cost of Living Rents, appliances, and some clothing, and especially toilet goods and medicines, are high priced. Record inflation, which reached over 23,000% in the year ended August 1985, led to record devaluation against the dollar. This in turn lead to shortages of many personal items and other articles judged to be luxury goods. The U.S. dollar has become a convenient method of conserving value. Cash rather than travellers' cheques makes for easier and more rapid transactions.

Best Buys Llama-and alpaca-wool knitted and woven items are at least as good as those from Peru. La Cancha market in Cochabamba is highly recommended but you *must* bargain. Ponchos, *mantas*, bags, *chullos* (bonnets). Gold and silverware. Musical instruments such as the *charango* (mandolin with armadillo-shell sound-box) and the *queña* (Inca flute), and other assorted wooden items.

Food and Drink The normal international cuisine is found at most good hotels and restaurants. Some local dishes are interesting (see below). The 3 makes of

BOLIVIA 201

local beer (Pilsener), lager-type, are recommendable; the local hot maize drink, *api*, should be tried (usually US$0.12), as well as *singani*, distilled from grapes, good, cheap and bracing. Bottled water cannot always be found (rain water is sometimes offered as alternative); the local tap water should not be drunk without first being sterilised. We have been told that the prepared food found in Indian markets can not always be relied upon. We do not recommend Bolivian market food except to the desperate and, of course, to those accustomed to South American food but buy it only if it is cooked in front of you. Be very careful of salads; they may carry a multitude of amoebic life as well as vile green bacteria.

In the *pensiones* and cheaper restaurants a basic lunch (*almuerzo*—usually finished by 1300) and dinner (*cena*) are normally available at US$1-2. Lunch can also be obtained in many of the modern market buildings in the main towns.

Salteñas are meat stew baked in a wrapping of dough, eaten regularly by Bolivians, mostly in the morning. Some are extremely *picante* (hot) with red chili peppers. They come in lessening grades of heat as *muy picante*, *medio picante*, and *poco picante*. For milk, try sachets of Leche Pil (plain, chocolate or strawberry-flavoured), at US$0.10 each.

N.B. Bolivian highland cooking is usually very tasty and often *picante*, which means highly spiced with chili peppers. Local specialities, which visitors should try, include *empanadas* (cheese pies) and *humitas* (maize pies); *pukacapas* are *picante* cheese pies. Recommended main dishes include *sajta de pollo*, hot spicy chicken with onion, fresh potatoes and *chuño* (dehydrated potatoes), *parrillada* (a Bolivian kind of mixed grill), *fricase* (juicy pork dish served with *chuño*), *silpancho* (fried breaded meat with eggs, rice and bananas) and *ají de lengua*, ox-tongue with chilis, potatoes and *chuño* or *tunta* (another kind of dehydrated potato). The soups are also good, especially a *chairo* soup made of meat, vegetables, *chuño* and *ají* (hot pepper) to which the locals like to add *llajua* or *halpahuayca* (hot sauces always set on restaurant tables) to make it even more *picante*.

Currency The unit of currency is the boliviano, divided into 100 centavos. Change is often given in forms of other than money: e.g. cigarette, sweet, or razor blade. It is almost impossible to buy dollars at points of exit when leaving. Better unofficial rates can be obtained, especially for US dollar notes, in exchange shops, and outside Bolivia; many recommend Peru. The official rate of exchange in May 1987 was 1.95 bolivianos per US$. The black market is tolerated, and rates are no different on the street and in *casas de cambio*.

Creditcards are accepted hardly anywhere; it is impossible to get cash on them. Only American Express is of any use, and that is limited.

Post, telegraph, and telephone Post offices use the post box (*casilla*) system. Items sent by post should therefore bear, not the street address, but the *casilla* number and town.

Air-mail letters to and from Britain take between 5 and 10 days. Radio telephone services run by the Serval Company serve Cochabamba and other parts of the interior. There is now direct satellite communication with Bolivia. Direct calls possible from major cities to Europe, but no collect calls can be made.

Freight Lufthansa has been recommended.

Hours of Business are normally 0900-1200, and 1400-1800. Saturday is a half day. Opening and closing in the afternoon are several hours later in the provinces. Government offices are closed on Saturday. Banks 0900-1200, 1400-1630, but closed on Saturday. Local time is 4 hours behind GMT.

The Press In La Paz: morning papers—*Presencia*, daily (available in other main cities), about 75,000, the largest circulation, largely Catholic mouthpiece and good coverage of world events; *Hoy* and *El Diario*. *Meridiano* (midday): *Ultima Hora*, and *Jornada* (evenings). In Cochabamba—*Los Tiempos*, *Extra*. In Oruro—*La Patria*, mornings (except Mondays). *El Mundo* and *Crónica Deber* are the Santa Cruz daily papers; *Deber* also appears in Trinidad. La Paz papers are on sale in other cities. The *Miami Herald* is available in La Paz. Also, there are about 85 radio stations, a commercial government T.V. station as well as a university T.V. service.

Public Holidays

January 1—New Year's Day
Carnival Week—Monday, Shrove Tuesday, Ash Wednesday.

Corpus Christi (moveable)
July 16—La Paz Municipal Holiday.
August 5,7—Independence

202 BOLIVIA

Holy Week—Thursday, Friday and Saturday
May 1—Labour Day.
Oct. 12—Columbus Day.
November 2—Day of the Dead.
Christmas Day.

There are local holidays at Tarija, on April 15; at Sucre on May 25; at Cochabamba, Sept. 14; at Santa Cruz and Cobija Sept. 24; at Potosí, Nov. 10; at Beni, Nov. 18, and at Oruro, Feb. 22.

Our grateful thanks for help in revising this section go to the following travellers: Bill Addington (Warminster, Wilts), Richard and Sharon Alexander (Auckland 5), Susi Alexander and José Jacinto (Rosedo, Ca.), Stephen Appleby (Tynemouth), Nigel L.Baker, Christian Baudissin (Munich 40), Wolfgang Beck (Nuremburg), Åsa Bengtsson and Nils Johansson (Sweden), Trond Bergquist and Ian Gjertz (Oslo), Dr Michael Binzberger (Friedrichshafen), Barbera Bot and Bob Domburg (Maasland, Neth.), Christine Bräutigam (Basle), Joseph Breault (Bronx, NY), Stefan Brütt (Bonn), Jutta Christochowitz (Frankfurt) and Hanne Christensen (Hammel, W.Ger.), R.D.Copley (Cheshunt, Herts), Malcolm Craven (Weston-super-Mare), David Crowe (Sydney), Jonathan Curtis (Bury St.Edmonds), Carina Dahlstrom and Ulf Carlsson (Gothenburg), Lynne and Hugh Davies (Mill Valley, Ca.), Dianne De Mauro (Ft. Lee, NJ), W.Derkson (Driebergen, Neth.), Kees Arthur van Dijk (Groningen, Neth.),Dagmar Drescher (Bad Kreuznach, W.Ger.), Ivan Drouin (Club Aventure, Montréal), Brigitte Duttlinger (Berlin 61), Robert Edge and Renate Kronemann (London SW4), Julie Eisenberg and Andy Daitsman (Milwaukee), Christine Enkelaar and José Keldens ('s-Hertogenbosch, Neth.), Kurt Farner (Köniz, Switz.), Volker Filss (Oberhausen, W.Ger.) for a most valuable contribution, David Finn (Dallas), and Andrew Sherman (Los Angeles), Romi and Olga Gandolfo (Buenos Aires), Toni García and Diego Caña (Barcelona), Mark Gfeller (Richterswil, Switz.), Jürg Hangartner (Zürich), Hans Hendriks (Maassluis, Neth.), Ricardo Heyenn and Karin Kubitsch (Hamburg), Ronald Hijmans (Amsterdam), John E.Hildeburn (San Marino, Ca.), Richard Hoare (Calgary), Catherine Hooper (Aptos, Ca.), Allan Jarrett (London W10), John and Rosemary (Bolton), Walker Jones (USA), Deborah Karp (London N3) and Karin Schamroth (London NW8), R.Kavanagh and Judy Connor (Liverpool), Robyn Keen (Artarmon, NSW), Peter W.Kenny (Minneapolis), José Kiska (Pullman, Wash.), Todd Knutson (Pittsburgh), Christian Küber (Hamburg), Carmen Kuczma (Powell River, BC), Mme C.Lapostoue (Paris), Sarah Lauchlan, (Miami), Peter Lonsdale (Taupo, NZ), Jane Elizabeth Lunn (Killinghall, N.Yorks.), Cindy McNamara (Santiago) for a particularly valuable contribution, Margaret McOnie (London W12), Frank Mahoney (Portland, Or.), Anna Mia Marks (Utrecht), Hans and Ursula Niederndorfer (Lambach, Austria), Grace Osakoda (Hawaii), Martin J.Osbourne (Toronto), Vaclav Penkava (Seattle), Erick and Martine Perruche (Montargis, France), Jens Plahte (Ås, Norway), Harald Queseth, (Bnes, Norway), Annelies Roeleveld and Victor Kuijper (Amsterdam), Stephen Saks and Andrea Keir (Melbourne), Ulrich Sehalt (Eschborn, W.Ger.), Fredi Schmutz (Zürich), Gillian Scorfield and Alastair Mitchell (Spalding, Lincs.), Charlotte and Mike Sharp (Lima), Connie Sherrard (Portland, Or.), Frampton Simons and Libby Black (Atlanta), Gustavo Steinbrun Bianco (Buenos Aires), Nigel Talamo (London WC1), Tina Tecaru (Burton/Trent), Brian and Christina Turner (Caazapá, Par.), Rose Vandepitte (Bruges), Dirk Vanmarcke (Bruges), Mrs Z.Verlinden (Huizen, Neth.), Andrew Waterworth and Kerrie Oldfield (Neutral Bay, NSW), Paul Whitfield (Auckland), Steve Wingfield (Toronto), Alex and Susi Witteveen (Huizen, Neth.), and Arthur Yeandle (Southampton).

WILL YOU HELP US?

We do all we can to get our facts right in *The South American Handbook*. Each chapter is thoroughly revised each year, but Latin America and the Caribbean cover a vast area, and our eyes cannot be everywhere. A new highway or airport is built; a hotel, a restaurant, a cabaret dies; another, a good one is born; a building we describe is pulled down, a street renamed. Names and addresses of good hotels and restaurants for "budget-minded" travellers are always very welcome. We would especially like to receive maps and diagrams of towns and cities, walks, national parks and other interesting areas to use as source material for the Handbook and other forthcoming titles.

Your information may be far more up-to-date than ours. If your letter reaches us early enough in the year it will be used in the next edition, but write whenever you want to, for all your letters are used sooner or later.
Thank you very much indeed for your help.

**Trade & Travel Publications Limited
5 Prince's Buildings, George Street,
Bath BA1 2ED. England**

VARIG ARE NEVER FAR FROM BRAZIL.

Brazil is a country at the forefront of technological achievement. But it is also much more. There's a spirit about Brazil. A spirit of warmth and vitality. A spirit that's perfectly *reflected in the* friendly efficiency of its national airline.

VARIG is Brazil.

VARIG
Brazilian Airlines

BRAZIL

	Page		Page
Introductory	205	Northern Brazil	332
Brasília	212	The Centre-West	351
Rio de Janeiro	218	The Economy	359
Minas Gerais	248	Information for Visitors	360
São Paulo	261	Maps	207, 224
Southern Brazil	279		250, 265, 280
The North East	297		298, 319

BRAZIL, the fifth largest country in the world, has the eighth largest population. It is almost as large as the United States of America. Its 8,511,965 square km. is nearly half that of South America. For neighbours it has all the South American countries save Chile and Ecuador. Distances are enormous: 4,320 km. from north to south, 4,328 km. from east to west, a land frontier of 15,719 km. and an Atlantic coast line of 7,408 km. Its population of 133 million (1986) is half that of all South America, and one in every two is under 25 years of age.

Brazil's topography may be divided roughly into five main zones: the Amazon Basin; the River Plate Basin; the Guiana Highlands north of the Amazon; the Brazilian Highlands south of the Amazon; and the coastal strip. The two great river basins account for about three-fifths of Brazil's area.

The Amazon Basin, in northern and western Brazil, takes up more than a third of the whole country. This basin is plain, broadly based on the Andes and funnelling narrowly to the sea; most of the drained area has an elevation of less than 250 metres. The rainfall is heavy, for the winds from the north-east and south-east lose their moisture as they approach the Andes. Some few places receive from 3,750 to 5,000 mm. a year, though over most of the area it is no more than from 1,500 to 2,500 mm. Much of the basin suffers from annual floods. The region was covered by tropical forest, with little undergrowth except along the watercourses; it is now being rapidly cut down. The climate is hot and the humidity high throughout the year.

The River Plate Basin, in the southern part of Brazil, has a more varied surface and is less heavily forested than the Amazon Basin. The land is higher and the climate cooler.

Most of the remainder of Brazil's territory is highland. The Guiana Highlands, north of the Amazon, are partly forested, partly hot stony desert. Those that face the north-west winds get heavy rainfall, but the southern slopes are arid. The rainfall, which comes during the hot season, is about 1,250 mm. a year. The summers are hot and the winters cool.

The Brazilian Highlands lying SE of the Amazon and NE of the River Plate Basin form a tableland of from 300 to 900 metres high, but here and there, mostly in South-Eastern Brazil, mountain ranges rise from it. The highest peak in southern Brazil, the Pico da Bandeira, north-east of Rio de Janeiro, is 2,898 metres; the highest peak in all Brazil, the Pico da Neblina on the Venezuelan border, is 3,014 metres.

For the most part the Highlands cascade sharply to the sea. South of Salvador as far as Porto Alegre the coast rises steeply to a protective barrier, the Great Escarpment. In only two places is this Escarpment breached by deeply cut river beds—those of the Rio Doce and the Rio Paraíba; and only in a few places does the land rise in a single slope making for comparatively easy communication with the interior. Along most of its course, the Great Escarpment falls to the sea in parallel steps, each step separated by the trough of a valley.

The few rivers rising on the Escarpment which flow direct into the Atlantic do so precipitously and are not navigable. Most of the rivers flow deep into the interior. Those in southern Brazil rise almost within sight of the sea, but run westward through the vast interior to join the Paraná. In the central area the Escarpment rivers run away from the sea to join the São Francisco river, which flows northwards parallel to the coast for 2,900 km., to tumble over the Paulo Afonso Falls on its eastward course to the Atlantic.

The Great Escarpment denies to most of Brazil the natural valley outflows and lines of travel from the interior to the sea. Of its rivers the Amazon alone is directly navigable for a great distance inland.

The coastal strip, though on an average only 100 km. wide, is nevertheless extremely important. It contains only 7.7% of the total area of Brazil, but 30% of the population.

Climate The average annual temperature increases steadily from south to north, but even on the Equator, in the Amazon Basin, the average temperature is not more than 27°C, and the highest recorded has been only 36°C. Six degrees more have been recorded in the dry north-eastern states. From the latitude of Recife south to Rio de Janeiro, the mean temperature is from 23° to 27°C along the coast, and from 18° to 21°C in the Highlands. From a few degrees south of Rio de Janeiro to the boundary with Uruguay the mean temperature is from 17° to 19°C. Humidity is relatively high in Brazil, particularly along the coast.

It is only in rare cases that the rainfall can be described as either excessive or deficient: few places get more than 2,000 mm.—the coast north of Belém, some of the Amazon Basin, and a small area of the Serra do Mar between Santos and São Paulo, where the downpour has been harnessed to generate electricity. The north-eastern droughts are caused not by lack of rainfall, but by irregular rainfall; the area is also subject to floods.

The rainy season in the South is from December to March; as this is also the holiday season in Brazil when hotels and flights tend to be booked solid, it seems a good time for tourists to stay away—unless, of course, they want to see the famous Carnival seven weeks before Easter.

Distribution of the Population By 1986 the population of Brazil had reached 133 millions, but this population is heavily concentrated in a comparatively small area—chiefly along the coastal strip where the original Portuguese settlers exploited the agricultural wealth, and further inland in the states of Minas Gerais and São Paulo where more recent development has been centred. Much of the interior of Pará, Amazonas, Goiás and the Mato Grossos have densities of one person per sq. km. or less. Brazil's attention is officially focused on these relatively underpopulated regions as a means of syphoning off some of the population excess in the urban centres—the industrialized South-East contains more than 50% of the total urban population and its two largest cities, São Paulo and Rio de Janeiro, both have over ten million people in their metropolitan and surrounding areas.

The urban population of Brazil has been increasing at rates more than double the overall average rate, and much of this growth is concentrated in the larger cities—those over 100,000, which numbered 95 in 1980. Internal migration is the major cause of these phenomenal growth rates, bringing to the cities problems of unemployment, housing shortage, and pressure on services which are already stretched to breaking point; shanty towns—or favelas, mocambos, alagados, according to the region—are an integral part of the urban landscape and a constant reminder of the poverty of some of the rural areas from which these people come.

BRAZIL 207

208 BRAZIL

The deep interior (Sertão) has been relatively unaffected by European and Far Eastern immigration, which has gone to the big cities and the more intensely cultivated lands of the South-East and the South. Its inhabitants are people of mixed Portuguese and Indian origin (*mestiço*); most live off a primitive but ecologically effective method of cultivation known as "slash and burn", which involves cutting down and burning the forest for a small patch of ground which is cultivated for a few years and then allowed to return to forest.

The decision to found a new federal capital, Brasília, deep in the interior, was a symbolic act of faith in the future of the Sertão: a bold attempt to deflect population from the coastal regions to the under-developed central and western plateaux of the country.

Political and Social History The first system of government adopted by the Portuguese was a Capitânia, a kind of feudal principality—there were thirteen of them, but these were replaced in 1572 by a Viceroy. In the same year it was decided to divide the colony into two, north and south, with capitals at Salvador and Rio de Janeiro; it was not until 1763 that Rio became the sole capital.

The economic structure was, in the main, that of huge estates run by slave labour brought over from Africa, with an aristocratic white element that played the absentee landlord and did no manual (but much procreative) work. The Portuguese crown expected both a personal and a state revenue from its colony. This was raised partly by payment of a tenth of the produce from grants of land made to colonists, a fifth from mining production, and about forty other taxes.

The bulk of the colonists, right up to the early 19th century, lived along the coastal belt. The main exceptions were the settlers in the states of São Paulo and Minas Gerais, the Paulistas and Mineiros, who had thrust far into the interior in search of gold, precious stones, and slaves.

Three hundred years under the paternal eye of Portugal had ill-prepared the colonists for independent existence, except for the experience of Dutch invasion (1624 in Salvador, and 1630-1654 in Recife). The colonists ejected the Dutch from Brazil with little help from Portugal, and Brazilians date the birth of their national sentiment from these events. In 1789 infiltration of European thought led to the first unsuccessful revolution against Portuguese rule, the Inconfidência in Minas Gerais, led by Tiradentes. When the troops of Napoleon caused the Portuguese Royal Family to sail in British ships to Brazil in 1808, the fate of the colony was decided: Brazil became the senior partner, as it were, in the Portuguese empire. King João VI returned to the mother country in 1821, leaving his son, the handsome young Pedro, as Regent. The Portuguese Parliament (the Cortes) mistrusted this arrangement, and called on Pedro to return, but the Brazilians asked him to stay. On May 13, 1822, he agreed to stay, and assumed the title of "Perpetual Defender and Protector of Brazil". On September 7 he declared Brazil's independence with the cry "Independence or Death" by the Ipiranga River; on October 12 he was proclaimed constitutional emperor of Brazil, and on December 1 he was crowned in Rio de Janeiro.

Dom Pedro the First had the misfortune to be faced by a secession movement in the north, to lose the Banda Oriental (today Uruguay) and to get somewhat involved in his marital relations. In sum, he abdicated as the result of a military revolt in 1831, leaving his five-year-old son, Dom Pedro the Second, in the hands of a regent, as ruler. On July 23, 1840, the lad, though only 15, was proclaimed of age and the regency discontinued. Dom Pedro the Second, a strong liberal at heart, promoted education, increased communications, developed agriculture, stamped on corruption and encouraged immigration from Europe. Under his rule *the war with the dictator López of Paraguay ended in Brazilian victory.* Above all, it was he who declared that he would rather lose his crown than allow slavery to continue, and on May 13, 1888, it was finally abolished by his daughter, Princess Isabel, who was acting as Regent during his temporary absence.

There is little doubt that it was this measure that cost him his throne. Many plantation owners, who had been given no compensation, turned against the Emperor; they were supported by elements in the army and navy, who felt that the Emperor had not given due heed to their interests since the Paraguayan War.

BRAZIL 209

On November 15, 1889, the Republic was proclaimed and the Emperor sailed for Europe. Two years later he died in a second-rate hotel in Paris, after steadfastly refusing a pension from the conscience-stricken revolutionaries. At the time of the first centenary of independence in 1922 the imperial family was allowed to return to Brazil, and the body of Dom Pedro was brought back and buried in the cathedral at Petrópolis.

The history of the "Old Republic" (1889-1930), apart from the first ten years which saw several monarchist rebellions, was comparatively eventless, a time of expansion and increasing prosperity. Brazil declared war on Germany during both wars and Brazilian troops fought in the Italian campaign in 1944-45. In 1930 a revolution headed by Getúlio Vargas, Governor of Rio Grande do Sul, who was to become known as "the Father of the Poor" for the social measures he introduced, deposed President Wáshington Luís and Vargas assumed executive power first as provisional president and then as dictator. He was forced to resign in October 1945. In 1946 a liberal republic was restored and the following 18 years saw considerable economic development and social advance. There was, however, increasing government instability and corruption leading to growing military intervention in civil affairs; this culminated in the military movement of March 1964, which ruled until March 1985 with increasing liberalization and great economic success (up to 1980). In January 1985 a civilian, Tancredo Neves, representing a broad opposition to the military regime, was elected President by the electoral college introduced under the military's 1967 constitution. He was unable, because of illness, to take office: the vice-president elect, Sr. José Sarney, was sworn in as acting President in March 1985, and became President on Sr. Neves' death in April. A Constituent Assembly is to revise Brazil's constitution in 1987-88.

Settlement and Economic History Brazil was discovered for the Portuguese by Pedro Alvares Cabral in 1500. The first settlement was at Salvador da Bahia, and the settlers came mainly from southern Portugal, with its feudal tradition of great estates. For the first few years Portugal, then much concerned with the Orient, paid little attention to Brazil. But about 1507 a second colony was settled at São Vicente, near Santos, and in 1537 a third at Olinda, near Recife. The settlers at São Vicente, who founded the first settlement in the highlands at São Paulo in 1534, were unlike those at Salvador and Recife: they came from the poorer and more energetic north of Portugal. All of them were attracted less by the prospect of earning their living by self-supporting labour than by opportunities of speculative profit. To do the work they impressed the primitive Tupi-Guarani Indians, many of whom died from European diseases (see *Red Gold*, by John Hemming). They cohabited freely with the Indians and, later, with slaves imported from Africa.

Sugar cane had been introduced at São Vicente in 1532, but it was the wealthy settlers of the north-east who had the necessary capital to establish the crop and to buy African slaves to work it; the Indian, with his hunting-and-gathering culture, was a disappointment as a labourer. In the matter of sugar, Salvador and Recife had the advantages over São Vicente of being very much nearer home, and of having better ports and easier access to the interior. During the latter half of the 16th and the whole of the 17th centuries, the provinces of Bahia, Pernambuco, and Paraíba were the world's prime source of sugar.

The settlers at São Paulo, envious of the more fortunate north-east, sent out expeditions to explore the interior for gold, which had already been found in small quantities in their own streams. These hardy Bandeirantes pushed as far south as Colonia, opposite Buenos Aires, as far west as the River Paraguay, and north into the area west of the sugar plantations of the north-east. In 1698 they struck gold in central Minas Gerais. More was found soon after in central Mato Grosso, and in 1725 in Goiás. Diamonds were discovered in 1729 north of the goldfields of Minas Gerais.

There was a great gold and diamond rush in which the sugar planters took part. Sugar by that time was on the decline: there was competition from the Caribbean; profits had fallen, and the Brazilians had made no attempt to lower

BRAZIL

costs by ploughing back profits: that was not in their tradition. The gold boom started early in the 18th century, lasted a hundred years, and then petered out. Minas Gerais was transformed from a wilderness into a well populated agricultural, pastoral, and mining region. It was as an outlet for this area that Rio de Janeiro was developed. Some of the wealth went to create the extraordinarily beautiful city of Ouro Preto, to-day a national monument of superb building, painting and sculpture, and the similarly attractive cities of São João del Rei, Mariana, Congonhas do Campo, Diamantina and others.

Brazil was ready for the next speculation: coffee. Introduced about 1720 from French Guyane, coffee planting began near Rio de Janeiro and at many places round the coast as far as the Amazon, but by 1825 it had mainly been concentrated in the Paraíba valley, west of the capital. From there it spread into São Paulo, where its cultivation attracted a large number of immigrants after 1850. About a third of the total production normally still comes from São Paulo state.

There have been many other typical Brazilian booms and recessions. The best known is the famous rubber boom in the Amazon valley; competition from SE Asia wiped it out after 1912. Sugar, coffee, and cocoa were alike the subject of booms. In each case Brazil was challenged by other sources of supply, where more intensive methods of production were applied. The result in Brazil has been a lack of stability of settlement.

This boom tradition still holds, but it is shifting from agriculture to industry. Agricultural products accounted for the bulk of Brazil's exports until recently and some 40% of the people are still rural, but Brazilians today prefer to think of themselves as a rising industrial nation. Industrial production has increased greatly and now about half of total exports are defined as "of manufactures". Nevertheless, Brazil still remains a country where oases of prosperity are edged by deserts of poverty and wilderness.

One interesting aspect of the various booms is the large internal migration which has accompanied them: each product, as its popularity grows, has proved a magnet for people from the rest of Brazil. Because of its poverty, the North-East has lost many workers to the industries of the South-East; on the other hand many rural workers from southern Brazil have moved north, drawn by the rapid development of Amazonia.

The People At first the new colony grew slowly. From 1580 to 1640 the population was only about 50,000 apart from the million or so indigenous Indians. In 1700 there were some 750,000 civilized people in Brazil. Early in the 19th century Humboldt computed there were about 920,000 whites, 1,960,000 Africans, and 1,120,000 Indians and *mestiços*: after three centuries of occupation a total of only four millions, and over twice as many blacks as there were whites.

Modern immigration did not begin effectively until after 1850. Of the 4.6 million immigrants from Europe between 1884 and 1954, 32% were Italians, 30% Portuguese, 14% Spanish, 4% German, and the rest of various nationalities. Since 1954 immigrants have averaged 50,000 a year. There are some 500,000 Japanese in Brazil; they grow a fifth of the coffee, 30% of the cotton, all the tea, and are very active in market gardening.

Most of the German immigrants have settled in Santa Catarina, Rio Grande do Sul, and Paraná. The Germans (and the Italians and Poles and other Slavs who followed them) did not in the main go as wage earners on the big estates, but as cultivators of their own small farms. Here there is a settled agricultural population cultivating the soil intensively. It is only by such methods and by such an expansion that the wastes of the Sertão, given sufficient water, can be put to effective use.

Today the whites and near-whites are about 60% of the population, people of mixed race about 21%, and blacks 15%; the rest are either aboriginal Indians or Asians. There are large regional variations in the distribution of the races: the whites predominate greatly in the south, which received the largest flood of European immigrants, and decrease more or less progressively towards the north.

BRAZIL 211

The seven censuses of the present century show the growth of the population, from 17.3 million in 1900 to 119.0 million in 1980. The population in the cities is rising very rapidly: the two great metropolitan areas now hold 20% of the whole population, and in 1980 Brazil had 95 other towns with more than 100,000 inhabitants. In 1970, 56% of the population was urban; by 1980 this proportion had risen to 71%. Of the total labour force in 1980, 30% was occupied in agriculture and fishing, compared with 44% in 1970, 24% worked in industry (18% in 1970), 9% in commerce (8% in 1970) and 36% in government and services, compared with only 19% in 1970. The average life span has increased from 39 years in 1939 to 58 years today. The population grew by 2.9% between 1960 and 1970, and by 2.5% between 1970 and 1980. By region, population growth 1970-80 was: N, 5.0%; NE, 2.2%; S, 1.4%; and SE, 2.7%.

Though there is no legal discrimination against black people, the economic and educational disparity—by default rather than intent of the Government—is such that successful Afro Brazilians are active almost exclusively in the worlds of sport, entertainment and the arts. By the way, don't refer to black people as "pretos" or "negros": describe them as "oscuros" or "gente de cor"—more acceptable terms.

The following table gives the census returns by states for 1960 to 1980. The capital of each state is given in brackets.

	States	1960	1970	1980
North:	Acre (Rio Branco)	160	218	302
	Amazonas (Manaus)	721	961	1,406
	Pará (Belém)	1,551	2,197	3,411
North-east:	Maranhão (São Luís)	2,492	3,037	4,002
	Piauí (Teresina)	1,263	1,735	2,140
	Ceará (Fortaleza)	3,338	4,492	5,294
	Rio Grande do Norte (Natal)	1,157	1,612	1,900
	Paraíba (João Pessoa)	2,018	2,445	2,772
	Pernambuco (Recife)	4,137	5,253	6,145
	Alagoas (Maceió)	1,271	1,606	1,988
	Sergipe (Aracaju)	760	911	1,142
	Bahia (Salvador)	5,991	7,583	9,470
South-east:	Minas Gerais (Belo Horizonte)	9,799	11,645	13,382
	Espírito Santo (Vitória)	1,189	1,618	2,024
	*Rio de Janeiro (Niterói)	3,403	4,795	11,298
	*Guanabara (Rio de Janeiro)	3,307	4,316	—
	São Paulo (São Paulo)	12,975	17,959	25,023
South:	Paraná (Curitiba)	4,278	6,998	7,617
	Santa Catarina (Florianópolis)	2,147	2,930	3,628
	Rio Grande do Sul (Porto Alegre)	5,449	6,755	7,776
Centre-west:	†Mato Grosso (Cuiabá)	910	1,624	1,141
	†Mato Grosso do Sul (Campo Grande)	—	—	1,368
	Goiás (Goiânia)	1,955	2,998	3,864
	Federal District	142	546	1,176
Territories (4)	Amapá, Roraima, ‡Rondônia, Fernando de Noronha	177	275	753
	Total	70,976	93,244	119,024

*In 1975, the State of Guanabara was incorporated into the State of Rio de Janeiro, with the city of Rio de Janeiro as the capital.

†In 1977 Mato Grosso was divided in two, the southern portion forming the new state of Mato Grosso do Sul, with its capital at Campo Grande.

‡In 1981, the Territory of Rondônia became a State, with its capital at Porto Velho.

The most recent official surveys indicate that 25% of the population is illiterate. Of the 13 million children between 7 and 14, 2 million have no school to go to. Of those who go to school, not all stay long enough to learn how to read and write. Adult literacy campaigns have, however, recently improved the picture.

212 BRAZIL

Railways, of which there are about 30,500 km., were originally built to supply export markets and did not combine into a unified system. To join them effectively, however, would mean—besides 3,200 km. of new construction—the unifying of Brazil's five existing gauges. About 2,450 km. have now been electrified. Many lines have been closed in recent years.

Roads Though the best paved highways are still heavily concentrated in the South-East, those serving the interior are now being improved to all-weather status and many are paved. Brazil has over one million kilometres of highways, of which in 1980 over 90,000 km. were paved, and the recent road-building programmes have emphasized inter-regional connections and the opening up of the Centre, North and West of the country. Interurban bus services are frequent and good.

Air Services The first commercial flight in Brazil was in 1927. Because of the great distances and the comparative paucity of good highways and railways, aircraft have eased the traveller's lot more spectacularly in Brazil than in any other country. The larger cities are now linked with each other several times a day by air, and even the more remote points in the country can now be reached by light aircraft.

Government There is a federal form of government and legislative power is exercised by a Chamber of Deputies and a Federal Senate. The Federal Senate consists of two representatives from each of the States elected by direct suffrage for a term of eight years and a third elected by an electoral college. The Chamber of Deputies has 280 representatives elected for four years on the proportional system. The Federal District is not represented in either. The President and Vice-President are elected for a term of five years by an electoral college. By the constitutional reforms of 1967, the President has residual control over all aspects of federal government, authority to intervene in any of the 23 States without consulting Congress, and the right to declare a state of siege and rule by decree. There is universal suffrage for all citizens over 18 with the exception of beggars, illiterates, soldiers, prisoners and political exiles.

Local Administration Each State has a popularly-elected Governor who exercises the executive power, and a Legislative Assembly which legislates on all matters affecting provincial administration and provides for State expenses and needs by levying taxes. Each municipality has a similar structure, with a mayor (*prefeito*), also popularly elected, and a local council.

The New Capital

Brasília On April 21, 1960, Rio de Janeiro ceased to be the Federal Capital of Brazil; as required by the Constitution, it was replaced by Brasília, 960 km. away in the unpopulated uplands of Goiás, in the heart of the undeveloped Sertão. The population of the Plano Piloto (the official name for central Brasília) is 411,000 (1980 census—the Federal District as a whole, with an area of 5,814 square km., has nearly 1.2 million inhabitants).

The new capital lies 1,150 metres above sea-level on undulating ground. The climate, unlike that of the old capital, is mild and the humidity refreshingly low, but trying in dry weather. The noonday sun beats hard, but summer brings heavy rains and the air is usually cool by night.

The creation of an inland capital had been urged since the beginning of the last century, but it was finally brought into being after President Kubitschek came to power in 1956, when a competition for the best general plan was won by Professor Lúcio Costa, who laid out the city in the shape of a bent bow and arrow.

Along the curve of the bow are the residential areas made up of large six-storey apartment blocks, the "Super-Quadras". They lie on either side (E and W) of the "bow" (the Eixo Rodoviário) and are numbered according to their relation to *the Eixo and their distance from the centre*. Thus the 100s and 300s lie west of the Eixo and the 200s and 400s to the east; Quadras 302, 102, 202 and 402 are nearest the centre and 316, 116, 216 and 416 mark the end of the Plano Piloto. The numbering applies equally on either side of the centre, the two halves of the city being referred to as Asa Sul and Asa Norte (the north and south wings). Thus, for example, 116 Sul and 116 Norte are at the extreme opposite ends of the city. All Quadras are separated by feeder roads, along which are the local shops. There are also a number of schools, parks and cinemas in the spaces between the Quadras (especially in Asa Sul), though not as systematically as was originally envisaged. On the outer side of the 300s and extending the length of the city is the Avenida W3 and on the outer side of the 400s is the Avenida L2, both of these being similarly divided into north and south according to the part of the city they are in.

Asa Sul is almost complete and Asa Norte (which for years was looked down on) is growing very fast, with standards of architecture and urbanization that promise to make it more attractive than Asa Sul in the near future. The main shopping areas—with more cinemas, restaurants and so on, are situated on either side of the old bus station. Several parks—or at least green areas—are now in being. The private residential areas are W of the Super-Quadras, and on the other side of the lake.

At right angles to these residential areas is the "arrow", the 8-km. long, 250-metre wide Eixo Monumental. At the tip of the arrow, as it were, is the Praça dos Tres Poderes, with spacious grounds for the Congress buildings, the Palácio do Planalto (the President's office) and the Palácio da Justiça (Supreme Court). The Cathedral and the Ministry buildings line the Esplanada dos Ministérios, W of the Praça. Where the bow and arrow intersect is the old bus station (Rodoviária), with the cultural and recreational centres and commercial and financial areas on either side. There is a sequence of zones westward along the shaft of the arrow; a hotel centre, a radio city, an area for fairs and circuses, a centre for sports, the Praça Municipal (with the municipal offices in the Palácio do Buriti and a great cross marking the spot on which the first mass was said in Brasília, on May 3, 1957), and, lastly (where the nock of the arrow would be) the combined new bus and railway station (Rodoferroviária) with the industrial area nearby. The most impressive buildings are all by Oscar Niemeyer, Brazil's leading architect.

The main north-south road (Eixo Rodoviário), in which fast-moving traffic is segregated, follows the curve of the bow; the radial road is along the line of the arrow—intersections are avoided by means of underpasses and cloverleaves. Motor and pedestrian traffic is segregated in the residential areas.

The Palácio da Alvorada, the President's residence, which is not open to visitors, is close to the lake. The 80-km. drive along the road round the lake to the dam is attractive. There is a rustic but very pleasant restaurant, *Churrascaria do Paranoá*, at the dam, below which there are spectacular falls in the rainy season. Between the Praça dos Tres Poderes and the lake are sites for various recreations, including golf, fishing and yacht clubs, and an acoustic shell for shows in the open air. The airport is on the far side of the lake. Some 250 hectares between the lake and the northern residential area (Asa Norte) are reserved for the University of Brasília, founded in 1962. South of the university area, the Avenida das Nações runs from the Palácio da Alvorada along the lake to join the road from the airport to the centre. Along it are found all the principal embassies. Also in this area is the attractive vice-presidential residence, the Palácio do Jaburu, again not open to visitors. This area is almost completed and very scenic.

Sightseeing Apart from buildings open only during the week the main points of the city can be seen in a day by bus or taxi tour—don't try walking much unless fit and fairly impervious to heat (and even so not recommended for single females). The city can also be seen at night by taking the Alvorada circular bus from the old Rodoviária. Congress is open to visitors Mon.-Fri. 0800-1200 and 1400-1700, guides free of charge (in English 1400-1600), and visitors may attend debates when Congress is in session. The Planalto may be visited; admission restricted to men in lounge suits and women in dresses, Fri., 0900-1100 and 1500-1700. The marvellous building of the Ministry of Foreign Affairs, the Itamarati, has modern paintings and furniture, beautiful water gardens and offers one of the most rewarding visits (guided visits at 1000 and 1600, free). Opposite the Itamarati is the Palácio de Justiça, the Supreme Court building, with artificial cascades between its concrete columns. Visiting (lounge suits and dresses needed, Mon., Wed., Fri), 1400-1900; Tues. and Thurs. 0800-1030. A fine view of the city may be had from the television tower, which has a free observation platform at 75 metres up (lift will not ascend with less than 5 people; also bar and

214 BRAZIL

souvenir shop; open 0800-2000; the TV tower sways quite a bit), or from the old Rodoviária tower. The Cathedral, on the Esplanada dos Ministérios, a most spectacular circular building in the shape of the crown of thorns, is open 0900-1100, 1400-1700; see also the Ceschiatti statues of the evangelists and the baptistry in the shape of a large pebble. The outdoor carrillon was a gift from the King of Spain. W of the TV tower on Avenida W3 Sul, at Quadra 702, is the square Church of Dom Bosco, a most interesting building constructed largely of blue glass. Other religious buildings worth seeing are the Fátima church (the Igrejinha) in the Asa Sul at Quadras 307-308 and the chapel (Ermida) of Dom Bosco, on the other side of the lake opposite the Alvorada, though the site is not well maintained. Some 15 km. out along the Belo Horizonte road is the small wooden house, known as "O Catetinho", in which President Kubitschek stayed in the late 1950s during his visits to the city when it was under construction; it is open to visitors and most interesting. A permanent memorial to Juscelino Kubitschek, the "Memorial JK", containing his tomb together with a lecture hall and exhibits, is worth visiting (open Mon.-Fri. 0900-1200, 1300-1800, Sat.-Sun. 0900-1900, entry US$0.50).

Light industry alone is allowed in the city and its population is limited to 500,000; it is now about 411,000 and about 250,000 more live in a number of shanty towns, with minimal services, located well away from the main city.

Entertainment Social amenities are greatly improved, with more cinemas and night clubs opening. The three auditoria of the Teatro Nacional, the Sala Villa-Lobos (1,300 seats), the Sala Martins Pena (450), and the Sala Padre José Maurício (120) are now open; the building is in the shape of an Aztec pyramid.

The Federal District authorities have opened two theatres, the Galpão and Galpãozinho, between Quadra 308 Sul and Av. W3 Sul. Concerts are given at the Escola Parque (Quadras 507-508 Sul), the Ginásio Presidente Médici (Eixo Monumental, near TV tower), the Escola de Música (Av. L2 Sul, Quadra 602) and the outdoor Concha Acústica (edge of lake near Brasília Palace Hotel).

There are 15 cinemas in the Plano Piloto; programmes are available daily by dialling 139 on the telephone.

Information about entertainment etc. is available in two daily papers *Jornal de Brasília* and *Correio Brasiliense*. Any student card (provided it has a photograph) will get you into the cinema/theatre/concert hall for half price. Ask for "uma meia" at the box office.

Ceremonies The guard is changed ceremonially at the Palácio do Planalto on Tues., 0830 and 1730. The President attends if he is present.

Sculptures Brasília is famous for its wealth of modern sculpture. Examples are: "Culture" (on the University campus), "The Meteorite" (above the Itamarati water-mirror), and "The Warriors" (in front of the Planalto)—all by Bruno Giorgi; "Justice" (in front of Supreme Court building), the four evangelists in front of the Cathedral and "The Water-Nymphs" (above the Alvorada water-mirror)—all by Alfredo Ceschiatti; "The Rite of Rhythms" (Alvorada gardens), by Maria Martins; and the beautiful "Mermaid" in front of the Navy Ministry on the Esplanada dos Ministérios. A statue of Juscelino Kubitschek is adjacent to the "Memorial JK".

Hotels	Single US$	Double US$	Pool	Stars	Telex No. (061)
Nacional, Southern Hotel Sector	43	48	Yes	4	1062
Carlton, Southern Hotel Sector	44	50	Yes	4	1981*
Eron Brasília, Northern Hotel Sector	50	58	No	4	1422
Torre Palace, Northern Hotel Sector	35	39	Yes	4	1902
Américas, Southern Hotel Sector	29	36	No	3	1484*
Aracoara, Northern Hotel Sector	35	39	No	4	1589
Bristol, Southern Hotel Sector	36	44	Yes	3	1981*
Brasília Palace, Lake Sector	under renovation				
Alvorada, Southern Hotel Sector	23	25	No	3	1484*
Nações, Southern Hotel Sector	29	36	No	3	1484*

*Shared telex

Another good hotel is the *Casablanca*, Northern Hotel Sector, B. Other central hotels, all C, are the *Brasília Imperial*, *Itamaraty Parque*, *Planalto* (Sector Hoteleiro Sul, Quadra 3, Bloco A, Tel.: 225-6860, comfortable, reasonably-priced, city tours); *Riviera*, D, in the Southern Hotel Sector, and the *Aristos*, *Byblos* (D), *Diplomat* (C-good), *El Pilar* (D, friendly) and *Mirage* (D) in the Northern

Hotel Sector. Prices given include breakfast but 10% tax must be added to them. Moderately-priced hotels can be found in the Northern Hotel Sector only. The *Petrobrás Motel* at the Saída Sul is far from the centre but clean and cheaper (E) for motorists. Also at Saída Sul: Shell's *Motel Sabataia*, E, no breakfast; *Paranoá*, F, basic. Cheaper pensions available; enquire at airport information desk, e.g. Centro Cultural Padres Jesuítas Q601 L-2 Norte (Tel.: 23-0803). A cheap central place to stay is the headquarters of the Augusta Fraternidade Universalinha Solar (Centro de Cultura Integral Aquário), US$1.50 a night, meals US$4.20 (also, courses in yoga, dance, meditation, brown bread for sale).

However, the hotels outside the city in Taguatinga and Núcleo Bandeirante, though fairly basic, tend to be recommended for cheapness. Núcleo Bandeirante: *Olanda*, E; *St Moritz*, E; *Rio de Janeiro*, F; *Jurema*, at Av. Central 1390, E; *Valadares*, F with bath but no breakfast; *São Judas Tadeu*, F, noisy, clean but cockroaches, poor breakfast; *Ypacaraí*, round corner from *Hotel Rio de Janeiro*, F, O.K. for "young and hearty" but many mosquitoes; *Avenida*, F; *Buriti*, 2° Avenida 1415, F, with bath; has cheaper single rooms. Taguatinga is pleasanter than the Núcleo, which is full of shanties; there are many cheap hotels and restaurants of a reasonable standard, for example, *Olympus*, E, *São Paulo*, good, clean, friendly, F, close to Jumbo supermarket, good cheap eatery next door; *Aquarius*, E; *Rey*, F; *Pousada Brasília*, in the centre, F with bath and breakfast; *Globo*, CNB4, Lote 1, Tel.: 561-1716, F, with breakfast, clean, friendly, pleasant, basic. *Rodoviária*, F, without bath, E with, including breakfast, clean and friendly. *President* and *Central* much used by short-stay couples. Bus 702 from the old Rodoviária (0820-1750, every 10 minutes), passes Rodoferroviária (bus stops outside), continuing to Taguatinga Rodoviária where you change, without extra charge to 700 bus which passes, in order: *Rio Verde*, Bloco Norte QNE 26, F; *Camará*, QNE 16, F; *Palace*, CNB 11, F; *Taguatinga*, by roundabout near clocktower, about 10 mins. from Rodoviária, F with breakfast, hot showers, TV, clean, back rooms are quieter, clothes-washing facilities, used by prostitutes; *Solar*, near Jumbo Supermarket, F, basic and clean.

Camping The city's main site is 4 km. out, by the Centro Esportivo, Asa Norte, near the motor-racing track, with room for 3,100 campers. US$2 p.p., average charge, though apparently some travellers have stayed free. Take bus 109 (infrequent) from old Rodoviária. Agua Mineral Parque, 6 km. NW of city, direct buses only at weekend; US$1 p.p., mineral pool, showers. One site a few km. S on Belo Horizonte road, another out in the country about 70 km. E. Associação Brasileira de Camping (Edif. Márcia, 12th floor, Setor Comercial Sul, Tel.: 225-8768) has two sites: one at Km. 19 on the Belo Horizonte road and one 25 km. NE of Brasília at Sobradinho. Camping Clube do Brasil has site at Itiquira waterfall, 100 km. NE of the city, near Formosa; information from Edif. Maristela, room 1214, Setor Comercial Sul, Tel.: 223-6561. There is a Forestry Commission site 10 km. out of Brasília on the BR-041. There are signs to the sites. "Wild" camping is possible.

Restaurants There are new restaurants opening in Brasília every week. (The Southern Hotel Sector tends to have more; there are many cheap places on Av. W3 Sul, e.g. at Blocos 502 and 506.) At weekends few restaurants in central Brasília are open. The following are classified by their speciality:

International Cuisine: Aeroporto, terrace of international airport, very pleasant, food reported very good. Most of the big hotels' restaurants. *Restaurant Gaff*, Centro Gilberto Salomão, South Lake (reputedly the best restaurant in Brasília).

Churrascarias (barbecues): *Brasas*, first floor of Conjunto Nacional; *Boi na Brasa*, Km. 15 on Brasília-Belo Horizonte road; *Galetão*, Galeria dos Estados; *Júlio*, on road to Taguatinga; *Churrascaria do Lago*, beside *Brasília Palace Hotel*; *Pampa*, beside Carrefour hypermarket, *Tabu*, beside *Hotel Nacional*, overpriced; *Tordilho*, on edge of lake near *Brasília Palace Hotel*; *Muken*, in Taguatinga; *Toys*, a rancho among the trees below the Avenida das Nações; *Churrascaria do Paranoá*, beside the dam.

Brazilian food: Cantina Caipira, 104 Sul; *Fogão de Lenha*, 402 Sul; *Maloca Querida*, 107 Sul.

Northern Brazilian/Amazonian: Pororoca, 411 Sul; *Marajoara*, 113 Sul.

Seafood/Fish: Panela de Barro, Galeria Nova Ouvidor, Setor Comercial Sul; *Chorão*, 302 Norte; *Jangadeiro*, 213 Sul; *Sereia*, 212 Sul (open until the early hours); *Kastelinho*, 411 Sul.

Portuguese: Cachopa, Galeria Nova Ouvidor; *Ginga*, 104 Sul.

Spanish: O Espanhol, Avenida W3 Sul, quadra 506; *Salamanca*, 113 Sul.

French: Français, 404 Sul; *Bonapétit*, 203 Sul; *Le Coq*, Galeria Karim, 110/111 Sul; *La Chaumière*, 408 Sul.

Chinese: China, 203 Sul; *New China*, 209 Sul (the best according to Chinese diplomats); *Fon Min*, 405 Sul; *Fon Pin*, 403 Sul; *Fon Shian*, 201 Sul; *Pequim*, 212 Sul; *Ran Gon*, Praça dos Tres Poderes.

Japanese: Nipon, 314 Sul and 112 Sul.

Lebanese/Middle Eastern: Alef, 302 Sul; *Arabeske*, 109 Sul; *Beirute*, 109 Sul; *Beduino*, 102 Sul; *Almenara*, 204 Sul. *Chez Karam*, Centro Gilberto Salomão; *El Hadji*; Hotel Torre, N. Hotel Sector (self-service, very good).

German: Tirol and *Bierfass*, both in Centro Gilberto Salomão, South Lake.

Italian/Pizzerias: Kazebre 13, Avenida W3 Sul, quadra 504; *La Grotta Azzurra*, 208 Sul; *Roma*, Avenida W3 Sul, quadras 501 and 511; *La Romanina*, 303 Sul; *Tarantela*, 202 Sul; *Pizzaiola*, 310 Sul; *Prima*, 106 Sul; *Roma*, 311 Sul; *Romassas*, Avenida W3 Sul, quadra 505.

Macrobiotic/Vegetarian: Coisas da Terra, Avenida W3 Norte, quadra 706; *Vegetariano*, Avenida W3 Sul, quadra 505; *Portal*, 209 Sul, one at front of Setor Comercial Sul, close to Rodoviária, lunch only, set-price meal; *Ken's Kitchen*, Quadra 302 Norte (English spoken).

Pubs There are two "English style" bars: *Gates Pub*, 403 Sul and *London Tavern*, 409 Sul.

Snack Bars (*i.e.* those serving *prato feito* or *comercial*, cheap set meals) can be found all over the city, especially on Avenida W3 and in the Setor Comercial Sul. (e.g. *Max Burger*) Other good bets are the Conjunto Nacional and the Conjunto Venâncio, two shopping/office complexes on either side of the old bus station (Rodoviária), which itself provides the best coffee and *pásteis* in town (bottom departure level). For ice creams (especially tropical fruit flavours) try the two ice-cream parlours in 302 Norte or the *Marajoara* restaurant. Freshly made fruit juices in all bars; for Amazonian fruits try the bar at the eastern (*i.e.* Setor Bancário) end of the Galeria dos Estados.

Nightclubs *Aquarius* (gay), *Bataklan*, *Le Bateau*, all in Conjunto Venâncio; *Kako*, *Senzala*, in Centro Gilberto Salomão; *Eron Privé*, Eron Brasília Hotel; *Chateau Noir*, Hotel Diplomat; *Tendinha*, Hotel Nacional; *Odara*, 405 Sul; *Xadrezinha*, Avenida das Nações.

Local Holidays Ash Wednesday; Maundy Thursday, half-day; Dec. 8 (Immaculate Conception); Christmas Eve.

Shopping There are eight big shopping complexes, including the Conjunto Nacional on the north side of the Rodoviária (supposedly the biggest complex in South America), the Conjunto Venâncio on the south side, the Centro Venâncio 2000 at the beginning of Avenida W3 Sul and Park Shopping and the Carrefour hypermarket just off the exit to Guará, 12 km. from centre. For fine jewellery, H. Stern has branches in the *Nacional* and *Carlton* Hotels and at the Conjunto Nacional and Park Shopping. The embassy sector is good for low-priced, high quality men's wear. For handicrafts try *Galeria dos Estados* (which runs underneath the *eixo* from Setor Comercial Sul to Setor Bancário Sul, 10 mins. walk from old Rodoviária, south along Eixo Rodoviário Sul) with shops selling handicrafts from all the Brazilian states; *Lampião*, 208 Sul; *Di Barro*, 302 Norte; *Zé Artesanato*, 215 Sul. For Amerindian handicrafts, *Artindia* in the bus station and at the airport. Also at the bus station is a Funai shop. Dried flowers (typical of the region) outside the Cathedral. There is a *feira hippy* at the base of the TV tower every Saturday, Sunday and holiday: leather goods, wood carvings, jewellery, bronzes. English books (good selection) at Livraria Sodler in Conjunto Nacional and at the airport.

Historical Museum Praça dos Tres Poderes, really a hollow monument, with tablets inside; open Tues.-Fri. 0800-1200, 1300-1800.

Museum of Gold at the Banco Central exhibits old and new notes and coins and gold prospecting in Brazil; open Mon.-Fri. 1000-1600, Sat. 1400-1800.

Museo Postal y Telegráfico da ECT, Setor Comercial Sul, Ed. Apolo, Quadra 13, Block A. Very interesting, stamps, telegraphic equipment, etc. Entry, US$ 0.30. Closed Sun.-Mon.

Museo da Imprensa Nacional, Setor de Indústrias Gráficas, Quadra 6; bus 152 from old Rodoviária: admission free. Old printing and embossing equipment, etc.

Banks Lloyds Bank (ex. BOLSA), Avenida W3 Sul, quadra 506; First National Bank of Boston, Avenida W3 Sul, quadra 501; Citibank, Edifício Citibank, Setor Comercial Sul; Banco Francês e Brasileiro, Avenida W3 Sul, quadra 506; local banks. Open 0930-1630. Foreign currency can be exchanged at these banks and at the branches of: Caixa Econômica Federal at the airport; Banco Regional de Brasília and Banco do Brasil, Setor Bancário Sul. American Express, Kontik-Franstur, Setor Comercial Sul, Edifício Central, S/1007.

British Commonwealth Chamber of Commerce, at the British Embassy.

Addresses British Embassy: SES, Avenida das Nações 8, Caixa Postal 070586, Tel.: 225-2710. US Embassy: SES, Avenida das Nações 3, Tel.: 223-0120. Australian: Caixa Postal 11-1256, SHIS QL-09, Conj 16, Casa 1, Tel.: 248-5569 (in residential district, S of the lake). Canadian: SES, Avenida das Nações 16, Tel.: 223-7615. West German: SES, Avenida das Nações 25. Swiss: SHI-Sul QL 11, conj. 5, casa 13, Tel.: 248-3816. Austrian, Galeria do Hotel Nacional, Loja 74, Caixa Postal 07-1215, Tel.: 224-5397. Swedish: Av. das Nações 29, Tel.: 243-1444. British Council: CRN 708/709 Bloco 3 Lotes 1 e 3, Tel.: 272-3060. Cultura Inglesa, SEPS 709/908 Conj. B. American Library: Casa Thomas Jefferson, Avenida W4 Sul, quadra 706, Tel.: 243-6588 and 243-6625. Institut-Cultural Goethe, Edifício Dom Bosco, Setor Comercial Sul, Bloco A, 114-118, Mon.-Fri., 0800-1700, 1600-2000. Immigration Office, at end of W3 Norte.

Electric Current 220 volts, 60 cycles.

Tourist Offices at the Centro de Convenções (Detur); small stand at Rodoferroviária, not very helpful (open 24 hours, every day). Tourist office at the Air Terminal will book hotels, otherwise helpful; French and a little English spoken. Tours by bus (US$ 12-20), may be booked at the airport

BRAZIL 217

or *Hotel Nacional*: check that you will be taken back to the airport if you have a flight to catch. Touring Club do Brasil, on Eixo, has maps (members only).

Tours Presmic Tours, at old Rodoviária. A good and cheap way of seeing Brasília is by taking bus rides from the old Rodoviária at the centre: the destinations are clearly marked. The circular bus route 106 goes right round the city's perimeter. If you go around the lake by bus, you must change at the Paranoá dam. A one-day visit by air from Rio gives 4 hours in Brasília for a minibus tour, starting and ending at airport (US$ 25-30, but the city is worth much more of anyone's time than this). Cheaper tours, from 1300-1700, from US$7 up, start from the downtown hotel area and old Rodoviária. All tour operators have their offices in the shopping arcade of the *Hotel Nacional*; Toscana has been recommended as cheap and good. Tour guides meet arriving air passengers at the airport, offering city tours, ending at a destination of your choice (3-4 hrs., English commentary, inexpensive but bargain)—a convenient way of getting to your hotel if you have heavy baggage.

Roads From Saída Sul (the southern end of the Eixo) the BR-040/050 goes to Cristalina where it divides; the BR-040 continues to Belo Horizonte and Rio de Janeiro, the BR-050 to Uberlândia and São Paulo (both paved).

Also from Saída Sul, the BR-060 to Anápolis, Goiânia and Cuiabá; from Anápolis the BR-153 (Belém-Brasília) heads north to Belém (paved) and from Goiânia the BR-153 goes south through the interior of the states of São Paulo and Paraná (also paved).

From Saída Norte (the northern end of the Eixo) the BR-020 goes north to Formosa, Barreiras, and after Barreiras on the BR-242 (all paved) to Salvador and Fortaleza; in wet weather the Rio São Francisco is liable to flooding with consequent long delays on the ferry service (though smaller vehicles are used to complete the load after trucks and buses are loaded).

Road distances, in km.: Belém, 2,110; Campo Grande, 1,405; Corumbá, 1,834; Cuiabá, 1,127; Foz do Iguaçu, 1,415; Goiânia, 202; Manaus, 3,421; Porto Alegre, 2,021; Recife, 2,303; Rio, 1,204; Salvador, 1,520; São Paulo, 1,015.

Buses To Rio: 20 hours, 6 *comuns* (US$11) and 3 *leitos* (about US$22) daily. To São Paulo: 15 hours, 7 *comuns* (about US$12) and 2 *leitos* (about US$24) daily. To Belo Horizonte: 12 hours, 9 *comuns* (US$8) and 2 *leitos* (US$16) daily. To Belém: 36 hours, at 0715, 1200, 1915, 2400 (US$22, Trans Brasília), *leito* (US$45) Tues., Wed. and Sat. To Goiânia: 2½ hours, every hour from 0600 to 2000 and at 2200 and 2400 (US$2). To Cuiabá, twice daily 1200 and 1945 (São Luiz), US$17.50, 18-20 hours, book journey in advance. To Curitiba, US$14, Tues., Thurs. and Sat. To Porto Alegre: 35 hours, every evening at 2100 (US$19.50). To Natal: every evening at 2000. To Campo Grande, US$25, 23 hours. To Fortaleza: 40 hours, every day at 0800 (US$24). To Recife: 40 hours, daily at 1100 and Mon., Wed. and Fri. at 1830. To Salvador: 23 hours, daily at 1200 and 2000 (US$14). To Barreiras, 9 hrs. To Teresina: daily at 0900 and 2130. To São Luís: daily at 1400. To Anápolis, 2½ hours, US$1. Manaus via Porto Velho and Cuiabá involves several changes, taking up to 6 days. Bus tickets for major companies are sold in a subsidiary office in Taguatinga,Centro Oeste, C8, Lotes 1 and 2, Loja 1; and in centre of the city on a side street opposite the Pão de Açúcar store. Left luggage, post office, telephone and telegram facilities available at new bus terminal (Rodoferroviária) beside the railway station, from which long-distance buses leave; bus 131 between Rodoviária and Rodoferroviária, US$0.20. The waiting room at the Rodoferroviária is very comfortable, but one is not permitted to sleep stretched out. There are showers (US$0.50). Both bus stations have large luggage lockers.

Car Hire Critical reports on Hertz cars hired at airport.

Rail In 1981 a rail link from Brasília to Campinas was opened; at Campinas one changes train for São Paulo. The new train "O Bandeirante" leaves Brasília on weekdays only at 2050, arriving at São Paulo Terminal da Luz at 1920 next day; US$13.50 sleeper, US$8.50 first class. A cheap and interesting way to the South; very slow, but it passes through some interesting country. Cheap meals are served. The terminus is at the far end of the Eixo Monumental, past the TV tower.

Air Services Varig to Caracas and Miami on Tue.; to Rio and São Paulo regular shuttle service (2½ hours in both cases); daily flights to other main cities; regional services to the interior of Goiás, São Paulo, Pará, etc. Vasp to Corumbá via Goiânia and Cuiabá, US$112, daily. Transbrasil offers reduced-fare night flights to Manaus at 0145 twice weekly. Bus 102 to airport, regular, US$0.35, ½ hour. Taxi is US$4.50, worth it. Left luggage facilities at airport (tokens for lockers, US$0.50). Airport tax US$1.25.

Of the seven *cidades satélites* that contain between them over half the Federal District's population, five are new and two (Brazlândia and Planaltina) are based on pre-existing settlements.

218 BRAZIL

Planaltina, 40 km. N of the Plano Piloto via Saída Norte, was originally a settlement on the colonial pack route from the mines of Goiás and Cuiabá to the coast. The old part of the town (50,000 inhabitants) still contains many colonial buildings. There are two good *churrascarias* on the main street and it is a good place for a rural Sunday lunch. 5 km. outside Planaltina is the Pedra Fundamental, the foundation stone laid by President Epitácio Pessoa in 1922 to mark the site originally chosen for the new capital.

Just before Planaltina, at Km. 30 on the road from Brasília, lies the point known as Aguas Emendadas: from the same point spring two streams that flow in opposite directions to form part of the two great river systems—the Amazon and the Plate. Continuing along the same road (BR-020), at Km. 70 is the town of Formosa (*Hotel Mineiro*, F). Some 20 km. north of the town is the Itiquira waterfall (158 metres high). From the top are spectacular views and the pools at the bottom offer good bathing. It is crowded at weekends. There are four smaller falls in the area. Camping is possible. To get there take the road into the centre of Formosa and follow the signs or ask. It is not possible to get by bus to the Itiquira falls from Brasília in one day; the only bus from Formosa to Itiquira leaves at 1500 and returns the next morning.

In the other direction (S) is the Cristalina waterfall; take the BR-040 (Belo Horizonte road) and at Km. 104 take a left turn along a dirt road just after the highway police post. The waterfall is 11 km. along this road. The town of **Cristalina** is famous for its semi-precious stones, which can be bought cheaply in local shops.

Nearer Brasília, good bathing can be had at Água Mineral, two mineral pools 10 km. from the centre of the city. The newer pool is the better; turn right immediately after entering the main gate.

For information on the State of Goiás, which surrounds the Federal District, see page 351.

State of Rio de Janeiro

The State of Rio de Janeiro covers 43,305 sq. km. (the size of Denmark) and in 1980 had a population of 11.3 m., 88% of whom lived in metropolitan areas. The working population of 3.5 m. is about 15% of Brazil's total labour force, and the State is Brazil's second-largest industrial producer.

Rio de Janeiro, for 125 years the national capital, is on the south-western shore of Guanabara Bay, 24 km. long and from 3 to 16 km. wide. The setting is magnificent. The city sweeps twenty kilometres along a narrow alluvial strip between the mountains and the sea. The combination of a dark blue sea, studded with rocky islands, with the tumbling wooded mountains and expanses of bare grey rock which surround the city is very impressive. Brazilians say: God made the world in six days; the seventh he devoted to Rio. Man is now attempting to undo God's work, by putting up far too many high-rise concrete buildings.

The best known of these rocky masses are the Pão de Açúcar (Sugar Loaf, 396 metres), the highest peak of a low chain of mountains on the fringe of the harbour, and the Corcovado (Hunchback), a jagged peak rising 710 metres behind the city. There are other peaks, including Tijuca (1,012 metres), the tallest point in the foreground, and 50 km. away rise the strangely shaped Organ Mountains with the "Finger of God".

Rio has one of the healthiest climates in the tropics. Trade winds cool the air. June, July and August are the coolest months with temperatures ranging from 22°C (18° in a cold spell) to 32°C on a sunny day at noon. From December to March temperatures are high, from 32°C to 42°C. Sunstroke is uncommon, but humidity is high. It is important, especially for children, to guard against dehydration in summer by drinking as much liquid as possible. October to March is the rainy season, and the annual rainfall is about 1,120 mm. The population in 1980 was 5,093,000, while that of the Metropolitan Region was 9,019,000.

Points of Interest Two of the main streets are particularly impressive. The Avenida Rio Branco, nearly 2 km. long and 33 metres wide, is intersected by the city's main artery, the Avenida Presidente Vargas, 4½ km. long and over 90 metres wide, which starts at the waterfront, divides to embrace the famous Candelária Church, then crosses the Avenida Rio Branco in a magnificent straight stretch past the Central do Brasil railway terminal, with its imposing clock tower, until finally it incorporates the palm-lined canal-divided avenue formerly known as the Avenida Mangue. The Avenida Rio Branco is lined with ornate buildings, including the Brazilian Academy, National Art Museum, National Library, Municipal Council Chamber, and Municipal Theatre. The Rua

BRAZIL 219

Ouvidor, crossing the Avenida Rio Branco half way along its course, contains the centre's principal shops. Other shopping streets are the Ruas Gonçalves Dias, Sete de Setembro, Uruguaiana, Assembléia, and also the arcade running from Av. Rio Branco to the Rua Gonçalves Dias. The most stylish shops, however, are to be found in Copacabana and nearby in the huge Rio-Sul shopping centre. (The quality of souvenirs is higher in Copacabana than in the centre, and higher still in São Paulo.) The Av. Beira Mar, with its royal palms, bougainvilleas and handsome buildings, coasting the Botafogo and Flamengo beaches (too polluted for bathing), makes a splendid drive; its scenery is shared by the urban motorway along the beach over reclaimed land (the Aterro), which leads to Botafogo and through two tunnels to Copacabana, described on page 237. Some of the finest modern architecture is to be found along the Avenida Chile, such as the Petrobrás and National Housing Bank buildings, and the new Cathedral, dedicated in November 1976.

History The Portuguese navigator, Gonçalo Coelho, discovered Rio de Janeiro on January 1, 1502, but it was first settled by the French, who, under the Huguenot Admiral Villegaignon, occupied Lage Island on November 10, 1555, but later transferred to Sergipe Island (now Villegaignon), where they built the fort of Colligny. The fort has been demolished to make way for the Naval College (Escola Naval), and the island itself, since the narrow channel was filled up, has become a part of the mainland. In January 1567, Mem de Sá, third governor of Brazil, defeated the French in a sea battle and transferred the Portuguese settlement to the São Januário hill—the Esplanada do Castelo covers the site today.

WANTED: MAPS
ARGENTINA – BRAZIL – MEXICO
GUATEMALA – EL SALVADOR –
THE CARIBBEAN ISLANDS

We would much appreciate receiving any surplus maps and diagrams, however rough, of towns and cities, walks, national parks and other interesting areas, to use as source material for the Handbook and other forthcoming titles.

The above regions are particularly needed but any maps of Latin America would be welcome.

The Editor Trade & Travel Publications Limited
5 Prince's Buildings, George Street,
Bath BA1 2ED. England

220 BRAZIL

Though constantly attacked by Indians, the new city grew rapidly, and when King Sebastião divided Brazil into two provinces, Rio was chosen capital of the southern captaincies. Salvador became sole capital again in 1576, but Rio again became the southern capital in 1608 and the seat of a bishopric. There was a further French incursion in 1710-11.

Rio de Janeiro was by now becoming the leading city in Brazil. On January 27, 1763, it became the seat of the Viceroy. After independence, in 1834, it was declared capital of the Empire, and remained the capital for 125 years.

Hotels: All hotels in the following list are either partly or fully air-conditioned. A 10% service charge is usually added to the bill.

	Single US$	Double US$	Stars	Telex
Centre (Well placed for transport, 30 min. from the beaches. Most offices and commerce are located here)				
Ambassador, Senador Dantas, 25	36	40	3	21796*
Ambassador Santos Dumont, Sta. Luzia 651	42	48	3	32540
Center Hotel, Av. Rio Branco, 33	25	32	2	21817
Granada, Gomes Freire, 530	35	39	3	
Grande Hotel OK, Senador Dantas, 24	36	41	3	30366
Guanabara Palace, Presidente Vargas, 392	22	25	2	
Itajubá, Alvaro Alvim, 23	20	27	2	
Othon Aeroporto, Av. Beira Mar, 280	40	46	3	22655*
Presidente, Pedro I, 19	34	38	3	21244*
São Francisco, Visc. de Inhaúma, 95	34	37	3	21244*
Flamengo (Residential area midway between centre and Copacabana.)				
Argentina, Rua Cruz Lima, 30	34	37	3	
Flamengo Palace, Praia Flamengo, 6	37	39	3	
Glória, Rua do Russel, 632	60	70	4	21683
Imperial, Rua do Catete, 186	30	33	2	
Novo Mundo, Praia Flamengo, 20 (well rec.)	42	45	3	33282
Regina, Ferreira Viana, 29	31	34	2	
Copacabana (Seaside residential and commercial area.)				
Apa, República do Peru, 305	44	46	3	30394
†Astoria, República do Peru, 345	36	41	3	
Bandeirante Othon, Barata Ribeiro, 548	42	45	3	22655*
Castro Alves, Av. Copacabana, 552	42	45	3	
†Copacabana Palace, Av. Atlântica, 1702	125	140	5	22248
Califórnia Othon, Av. Atlântica, 2616	63	69	4	22655*
Debret, Av. Atlântica, 3564	32	37	3	
Excelsior, Av. Atlântica, 1800	36	39	3	21076
Lancaster, Av. Atlântica, 1470	50	60	4	23265*
Leme Palace, Av. Atlântica, 656	57	63	4	23265*
Luxor Continental, Gustavo Sampaio, 320	60	75	4	21469
Luxor Copacabana, Av. Atlântica, 2554	93	101	4	23971
Luxor Regente, Av. Atlântica, 3716	80	85	4	23887
†Meridien, Av. Atlântica, 1020	135	150	5	23183*
Miramir Palace, Sá Ferreira, 9	62	67	4	21508
Olinda, Av. Atlântica, 2230	36	39	3	23265*
Ouro Verde, Av. Atlântica, 1456	60	66	4	23848
Plaza, Av. Princesa Isabel, 263	58	63	4	
Rio Copa, Av. Princesa Isabel, 370	35	38	3	23988
†Rio Othon Palace, Av. Atlântica, 3264	104	114	5	23265*
†Rio Palace, Av. Atlântica, 4240	115	130	5	21803*
Savoy Othon, Av. Copacabana, 995	65	70	4	
Trocadero, Av. Atlântica, 2064	45	50	3	23265*
Ipanema/Leblon (Outer seaside residential and commercial area.)				
Arpoador Inn, Francisco Otaviano, 177	33	33	3	22833*
Carlton, João Lira, 62	31	36	2	
†Caesar Park, Av. Vieira Souto 640	140	160	5	21204
†Everest, Prudente de Morais, 1117	92	100	5	22254
Ipanema Inn, Maria Quitéria, 27	30	34	2	22833
Marina Rio, Av. Delfim Moreira, 696	65	70	4	30224*
Marina Palace, Av. Delfim Moreira 630	96	107	5	30224*

BRAZIL 221

†*Praia Ipanema*, Av. Vieira Souto, 706	65	70	4	31280*
San Marco, Visc. de Pirajá, 254	23	28	2	
Sol Ipanema, Av. Vieira Souto, 320	62	67	4	21979*
Vermont, Visc. de Pirajá, 254	30	35	2	

São Conrado and further out (Spectacular settings, but far from centre.)

†*Sheraton*, Av. Niemeyer, 121	115	130	5	21206
†*Nacional*, Av. Niemeyer, 769	100	108	5	21238
†*Intercontinental*, Av. Litorânea, 222	110	120	5	21790
Atlântico Sul, Recreio dos Bandeirantes	29	35	3	

Airport, Galeão

Luxor Hotel do Aeroporto	94	104	3	

*Shared telex.   †Swimming pool.

Other Hotels in Copacabana (all air-conditioned; number of stars in brackets) Our categories A-C: *Copacabana Sol*, Rua Santa Clara 141, Tel.: 257-1840 (3); *Acapulco*, Rua Gustavo Sampaio 854 (3), unfriendly service; *Praia Leme*, Av. Atlântica 866, pleasant, Austrian run, overlooking beach, English and German spoken (2); *Riviera*, Av. Atlântica 4122, very good, well placed, (3). *Atlantis Copacabana*, Av. Bulhões de Carvalho 61, a/c, TV, very good, close to Ipanema and Copacabana beaches (2); *Copacabana Praia*, Francisco Otaviano 30 (4); *Canadá* (2), Av. Copacabana 687, unfriendly, safe, reasonably priced.
Our category D, unless stated E: *Biarritz*, Rua Aires Saldanha 54 (2), good accepts American Express; *Angarense* (2), Trav. Angarense 25, clean, friendly, E; *Toledo* (2), Rua Domingos Ferreira 71, Tel.: 521-4443 or 257-1990, warmly recommended; *Santa Clara* (2), Rua Décio Vilares 316, Tel.: 256-2650, recommended, quiet; *Copa Linda*, Av. Copacabana 956, incl. breakfast, friendly and clean, suits Peace Corps, E (2); *Praia Lido*, Av. Copacabana 202 (2); *Copa Mar*, Rua Santa Clara 116.

Economy Hotels are found in three districts of Rio: Flamengo/Botafogo (best), Lapa/Fátima and Saúde/Mauá. Most hotel rates are for doubles, and include continental breakfast.
Flamengo/Botafogo (Residential area between centre and Copacabana, with good bus and metro connexions.) Walking from the centre, you will come across the hotels in this order: Rua Cândido Mendes, off Rua da Glória: *Alameda*, No. 112/118, E with bath, TV, radio, phone, good value, near Glória metro and Copacabana buses; *Cândido Mendes*, No. 117, F; *Monte Castelo*, No. 201, F (with bathroom), clean, central, safe, warmly recommended. *Benjamin Constant*, Rua Benjamin Constant 10, nr. Glória metro, F, men only, good; *Bahia*, Santo Amaro 42, F, clean; on same street, *Opera*, E, also good, near Glória metro. Across from here, on the hillside is Ladeira da Glória: *Turístico*, Ladeira da Glória 30, Tel.: 265-1698 (advance booking advisable), E, with bath, including breakfast, money and valuables can be left safely with owner, Sr Antônio, who speaks Spanish, tourist information provided, highly recommended. *Victória*, Rua do Catete 172, E, with breakfast, bath and hot water, a/c, clean and friendly, also on Rua do Catete: No. 233, *Rio Claro*, E, recently renovated, breakfast, shower, a/c, recommended; No. 160, *Monte Blanco*, F, breakfast, bath, a/c, radio, refurbished, clean, friendly, recommended; To the left is Rua Silveira Martins: No. 20, *Inglês*, D, reasonable breakfast; at No. 135, *Hispano Brasileiro*, E, a/c, with bath, clean, good, friendly owner speaks Spanish; *Pérola*, Silveira Martins 70, E, private bath, breakfast, very clean. Walking down Praia de Flamengo you will come across the next streets: Ferreira Viana: No. 58, *Ferreira Viana* (F, recommended, with bath and breakfast, always heavily booked, valuables may be left safely); No. 69-81, *Florida*, private shower and breakfast, good souvenir shop, recommended, safe-deposit, E; No. 20, *Antabi*, F. Correia Dutra: No. 19, *Cambuquirá*, E; *Mengo*, E (not very clean, friendly), No. 31 (Tel.: 225-5911); No. 141, *Leão*, E, clean, bath, a/c, unfriendly staff;

HOLIDAYS IN COPACABANA
LUXURY FURNISHED APARTMENTS
1 block from the beach
RENT: DAYS OR WEEKS
Fully equipped: air conditioning, telephone,
color TV, wall-safe, refrigerator,
linen & towels, maid service.
SWISS MANAGEMENT   English spoken
Call: Yvonne tels.: 227-0281 or 267-0054
RIO DE JANEIRO, Avenida Atlântica 4.066 apt. 605

222 BRAZIL

Caxambu, E with breakfast and radio, good; *Rondônia*, Buarque de Macedo, 58, E. *Monterrey*, Rua Artur Bernardes 39, E with bath, very good; at No. 29, *Rio Lisboa*, E with bath, a/c, cheaper rooms without bath, recommended—both hotels in this quiet street are family hotels. Rua Paissandu: No. 23, *Paissandu*, D, No. 34; *Venezuela*, E, with bathroom, very clean, but rooms small and breakfast poor. Beyond Largo de Machado: Rua Gago Coutinho: No. 22, *Serrano*, E, pleasant; *Hiedra*, Praia de Botafogo 296, F.

Lapa/Fátima (Area between Lapa and Praça Tiradentes, inner residential area, less desirable than Flamengo.) *Hospedaria Sul América*, Rua da Lapa, F, without breakfast, recommended. Near Cinelândia metro station are *Itajubá*, Rua Alvaro Alvim 15, E, good, and *Nelba*, Senador Dantas 46, E, with shower, friendly, also good. There are a lot of cheap hotels in this area, but many are hot-pillow establishments. In Lapa itself, near the Arches just beyond Passeio Público, is Rua Joaquim Silva: No. 69, *Americano*, F; No. 87, *Ipiranga*, F, old but clean; and No. 99, *Marajó*, D, with breakfast; also Joaquim Silva, F. Passing under the Arches you come to Av. Mem de Sá (bus 127 from bus terminal) No. 85, *Mundo Novo*, E, clean, air-conditioned; and No. 115, *Bragança*, F. In Rua Gomes Freire No. 430 is *Marialva*, D. In the same street is a hotel for men only (*para solteiros*), F. Turning towards Praça Tiradentes: Rua Riachuelo, *Nice*, D, a/c, shower, T.V., radio, very good; and Rua Resende, No. 31, *Estadual*, E, good; No. 35, *Pouso Real*, D, good, but the area is dubious. Praça Tiradentes, *Rio Hotel*, clean, noisy rooms on Praça, quieter overlooking São Sebastião Cathedral, E with breakfast (only served in rooms). Beyond Praça Tiradentes is Rua dos Andradas (towards centre): No. 19, *Globo*, E (without bath) and up (beware the sharp lift doors). No. 25, *Andradas*, E; and No. 129, *Planalto*, E.

Saúde/Mauá (Area between the railway station and the docks, a dubious part of town.) *Bandeirantes*, Rua Bento Ribeiro, 80, not very clean or cheap; *Rio Grande*, Rua Senador Pompeu 220, F, recommended; *Internacional*, Rua Senador Pompeu 82, F, clean and friendly; *Cruzeiro Tefé* and *Vital*, Rua Sacadura Cabral 167a and 107 respectively, F. The very cheapest hotels in town are in this area, but it is not too safe at night.

Near the Rodoviária: *Rio Preto*, Rua do Triúnfo 277; *Conceição*, Rua Garibaldi 165, good and cheap; *Rodoviária*, adequate, cheap, F without breakfast, fan, clean, hot water.

In the traditional Santa Teresa district, Rua Almirante Alexandrino 660, is the *Santa Teresa Hotel*, C, with swimming pool and full board. Take the "Dois Irmãos" tram from Largo da Carioca.

The Federal University puts up men during vacations. *Pousada Estácio*, Rua do Bispo 83, F in 4-bedded apartments with breakfast, recommended (in campus of Faculdades Integradas Estácio de Sá). There is a **Youth Hostel** on the tenth and eleventh floors of the *Casa do Estudante*, at Praça Ana Amélia 9 (Rua Sta. Luzia), near Santa Luzia church, open all year, F—student card required—international youth hostel card is best, you can check in at any time of day, and can come in at any time of night, but after 0100 you must pay the lift man US$0.10. (Adverse opinion from some travellers—uncomfortable, showers not working.) Cheap food at canteens for those with international student cards. Other Youth Hostels at Rua Almte. Gomes Pereira 86, Urca, F (girls only, Jan.-Feb. and July), and Rua Emílio Burla 41, Copacabana, cleaner than the one at Sta. Luzia. Youth hostels are fully booked between Christmas and Carnival; if intending to stay at this time reserve well in advance.

The city is extremely noisy. An inside room is cheaper and much quieter. (If you are desperate and it is late, some smaller hotels and hostelries may let you sleep on the floor.)

Apartments If they prefer, tourists can look after themselves in flatlets (small apartments) in Copacabana, Ipanema, Leblon, or more cheaply, in the centre or more northerly areas (for example, furnished apartments, accommodating up to 6, cost US$200 per month in Maracanã, about US$300 per month in Saúde, Cinelândia, Flamengo). Bookings for Copacabana by Rua Barata Ribeiro 90, room 205, Copacabana, Av. N.S. da Copacabana 583, room 1007, Tel.: 235-3748, and at Rua Barata Ribeiro 87/ 202, Tel.: 255-2016 or 237-1133. Also Rent Fiat Imobiliária Ltda, Rua Barata Ribeiro 207 s/101—CEP: 22011, Tel.: 256-9986. The *Praia Leme Hotel*, Av. Atlântica 866, has apartments, with maid and laundry service at Av. Princesa Isabel 7, close to the beach; US$12 a day. José Silva da Ferreira lets good apartment at Rua Pompeu Loureiro 56A, Apto. 401, Copacabana (Tel.: 256-9957), US$15 a day; Hans Peter Corr, Rua Belfort Roxo 158, Apto. 701, Copacabana (Tel.: 541-0615), several apartments, about US$40 d. *Rio Flat Service*, Almirante Guilhém 322, Leblon, reservations through SASS Ltda, Ataulfo de Paiva 566/305, Tel.: 274-9546, Telex: 30245. Estate agents dealing in more expensive apartments include Tower Real Estate, Rua Aníbal de Mendonça 157, Ipanema; Coroa Real, Rua Buenos Aires 4 and Av. Copacabana 647, Loja 205/206; Lowndes and Sons S.A., Av. Presidente Vargas 290, 2° andar, RJ20091, Tel.: 253-5622. For cheaper apartments, and rooms in private homes, try classified ads, e.g. *Jornal do Brasil*, under section 100, subsection 101—Temporada. The word "conjugado" abbreviated to "conj." means bedsitter, "vaga" a bed in a private home or a shared apartment and "quarto" room in a private house.

Camping Camping Clube do Brasil has beach site at Av. Sernambetiba 3200 (bus 233 from centre or 554 from Leblon, US$1.20—a long way from the centre), Barra da Tijuca, costing US$6 p.p. per night (half price for members). During January and February this site is often full and sometimes restricted to members of the Camping Clube do Brasil. Also at Recreio dos Bandeirantes, Estrada do Pontal 5900, and *Ostral*, Av. Sernambetiba 18790, US$2 p.p. and *Novo Rio*, at 17.5

BRAZIL 223

km. on Rio-Santos road, US$2.50 p.p. "Wild" camping possible on beaches further out; if trying it nearer centre, risk of thieves.

Electric Current 110-220 volts, 60 cycles, A.C.

Restaurants: Centre: *La Tour*, said to be the first revolving restaurant to be built in South America (it revolves hourly), Clube Aeronáutica building, Rua Santa Luzia 651, 45th floor. Marvellous views! (Reservations, Tel.: 224-2221 for French meals, 242-3221 for international and 252-8234 for fish). *Alba Mar* (fish, interesting location overlooking ferry station): *Academia*, Av. Pres. Wilson, not expensive; *A Cabaça Grande* (Casa das Peixadas, Rua do Ouvidor 12, best for fish, closed Sun./holidays); *Tokyo*, in Rua Teófilo Otôni (Japanese); *Miura*, Av. Rio Branco 156, 2nd mezzanine, No. 324/325 (Japanese); *Rio Minho*, Rua do Ouvidor 10, for seafood. Vegetarian: *Naranda*, Rua da Alfândega 112—1st floor, good value; *Health's*, Rua Benedito 18, Mon.-Fri. lunch only, *Zan*, Travessa do Ouvidor 25, *Lida* and *Saúde*, Rua Rosário 142, 2nd floor. There are several Arab restaurants on Av. Senhor dos Passos, also open Sat. and Sun. *Buksky* (*Paulista*), Rua do Rosário 133 (German), recommended for wholesome food and speedy service: on same street, *N.S. de Guia*, good, lunch only; *Monte Alegre*, corner Riachuelo and Monte Alegre, US$2.50; *Oxalá*, Rua Álvaro Alvim 36, good Bahian food, quick service, reasonable; *Churrascolandia*, Rua Senador Dantas, quick and simple, "but with character"; *Mesbla*, in store of same name (grand view of harbour and Sugar Loaf); *Museu de Arte Moderno* (excellent view of harbour and Sugar Loaf); *Pensão Guanabara*, Rua Buenos Aires by flower market, excellent meal for less than US$3. *Avis*, Av. Rio Branco 245; *Kit-Kat*, Primeiro de Março, near Post Office, Chinese, self-service, good selection. *Café Nice*, Av. Rio Branco 277, beside main Varig-Cruzeiro do Sul office, interesting, old-fashioned, not cheap. *Bar Americano Antártica*, Rua Evaristo da Veiga, near Opera House, cheap 2-course meals with drink; *Rei dos Galdos*, good for chicken, in Cinelândia. *Taverna do Galeto*, near Cinelândia metro station, good. *Navona*, Rua da Carioca, very good Italian food; *Lanchonette N.S. da Mo*, Rua São Bento 22, recommended; *Lanchonete Brasilândia*, Rua das Marrecas, and in same street, *Portuense*, recommended. Many *lanchonetes* for good, cheap meals in the business sector. Excellent cheap meals for US$1 at *Cantina São Roque*, Evaristo da Veiga 138, open in the evening. Also *Pensão Lord*, Av. Joaquim Silva, *Pensão Saramandaia*, Marechal Floriano. Cheap eating places on Praça Tiradentes. *Bar dos Estudantes*, opp. Casa dos Estudantes, *prato comercial* is cheap, filling and balanced, friendly staff. *Nova Carioca*, Rua Carioca 21, good snack bar. **Lapa:** *Mario*, Rua Joaquim Silva 130, and *Semente*, same street No. 138, both vegetarian. **Glória:** *Braseiro Galeto*, R. Cândido Mendes 116-C, good, cheap barbecued chicken, meats; *Vila Rica*, Rua Cândido Mendes, corner with Rua da Glória, good selection, inexpensive; *St. Moritz*, in same building as Swiss Consulate, Av. Cândido Mendes 157, bar/restaurant, good atmosphere; *Hobby Lanches*, R. da Glória, near Metro, good, cheap. **Flamengo and Catete:** *Planalto do Flamengo*, churrascaria, Rua Barão do Flamengo 35-S (Praça José de Alencar), recommended. *Bar KTT*, Rua do Catete, US$2 for 2-course meal, excellent; same road, No. 239, *Pastelaria Wong*, very cheap, good and, No. 234B, *Amazônia*, downstairs, one-price counter service, upstairs for good, reasonably-priced evening meals, recommended. *Rio Galicia*, Rua do Catete 265, near *Hotel Vitória*, very good pizza; *Big Bar Catete*, on R. do Catete next to metro station, recommended; *Rio's*, Parque de Flamengo, opp. Morro da Viúva, Tel.: 551-1131, French, expensive, good service, piano bar; *Oklahoma*, Rua Senador Vergueiro, US$2; *Restaurante Praia Bar*, Praia do Flamengo 144, elegant Italian, reasonable; *Galeto, Restaurante e Bar Cabanas*, Praia do Flamengo 122A, bar meals, reasonable; *Lamas*, Marquês de Abrantes 18-A, excellent value, good food; *Gaúcha*, Rua Senador Vergueiro 114, good and cheap. *Cozinha Arabe Brasileira*, Severo 176, US$2 for 1 dish or small Arab dishes; *Pensão*, Rua Arturo Bernardes 9, lunch or dinner US$1.50, good; *Rua Buarque de Macedo 60*, lunch all you can eat for US$2, very good. *Garoto Catete* (behind *Regina Hotel*), good value bar meals. **Largo do Machado:** *Churrascaria Minuano*, and near the Galeria Cóndor 2 small Arab bars, cheap and very popular. Plenty of pizza places, a *Macdonalds* and a *Big Bob's* at Largo do Machado. **Botafogo:** *Arataca*, Rua Voluntários da Pátria (Amazonian food); *Aurora*, Capitão Salomão 43 (Mon.-Sat. till 2330) good food, excellent value; *Do Arco da Velha*, R. Capitão Salomão 35. *Bismarque*, R. São Clemente 24A; *La Mole*, Praia de Botafogo 228, good, cheap Italian food (other locations in Rio); *Churrascaria Galeto na Brasa*, Praia de Botafogo 358-60, cheap and good; *Churrascaria Estrela do Sul*, Av. Repúbliver Néstor Moreira, s/n, excellent *rodízio* for US$5.30. *Chalé Restaurant*, Rua da Matriz 54 (N and NE Brazilian food) in a colonial-style house, good *feijoada*. *Café Pacífico*. Rua Visconde Silva 14, good, cheap, Mexican; *Sol e Mar*, beautiful terrace over bay, mediocre food, reasonable prices; *Restaurante Natural*, Rua 19 de Fevereiro 118. **Copacabana and Leme:** Hotels *Copacabana Palace*, *Excelsior*, *Leme Palace*, *Miramar Palace*, *Meridien* (restaurant called *St Honoré*), *Ouro Verde* (all international food, the last-named highly recommended); *Maxim de Paris*, at the top of the Rio Sul Shopping Centre, 44th floor, very elegant, good food and service, Tel.: 541-1900, tea 1400-1830, every Mon. concerts 1600-1700, dinner accompanied by live music and dancing, Belle Epoque decorations; huge grills at *Churrascaria Rio-Sul*, Rua Joaquim Nabuco, with *rodízio* for US$6, excellent; *Churrascaria Marius*, at Leme end of Av. Atlântica, good, cheap; also *Real*, Av. Atlântica 514 (Leme), seafood; *Príncipe Legítimo das Peixadas*, Av. Atlântica 974B, good but expensive; *Churrascaria do Jardim*, R. República do Peru, recommended; *Churrascaria Palace*, Rua Rodolfo Dantas 16-B, 22 different kinds of meat, very good value; *Baalbeck*, Rodolfo Dantas 225, Arab food and pastries, reasonable; also Arabic, *Novo Stambul*, Rua Domingos Ferreira 221-B, good;

224 **BRAZIL**

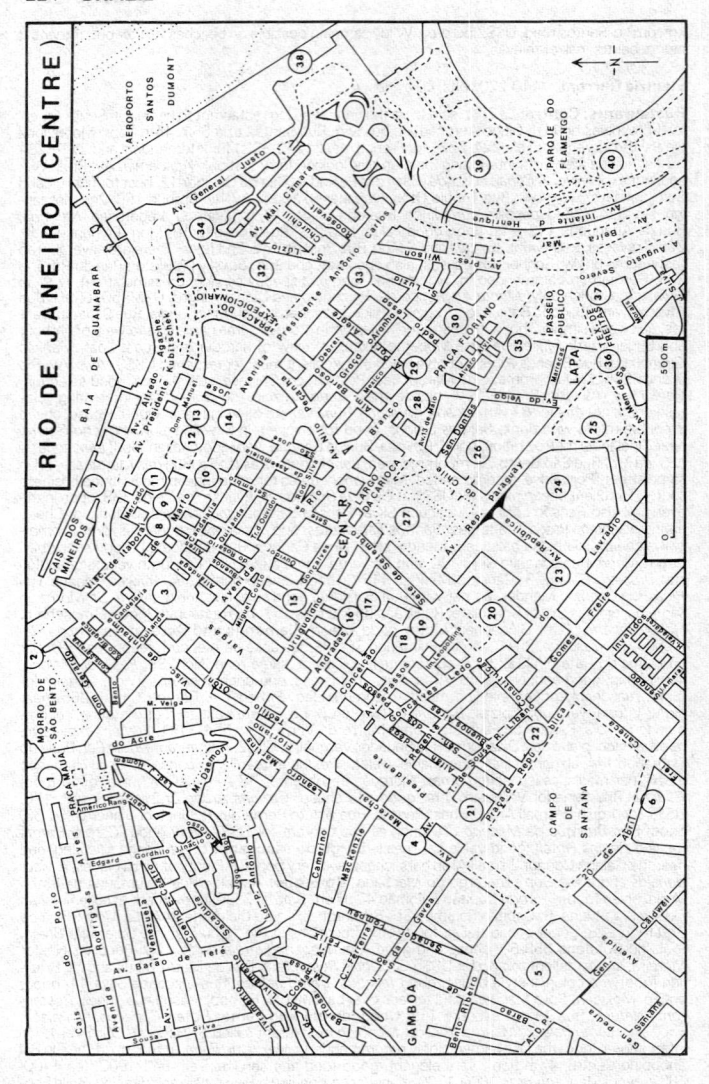

RIO DE JANEIRO (CENTRE)

ROUGH SKETCH

BRAZIL 225

same street, No. 242-A, *Nino*, good but not cheap; *Trattoria*, Bolívar near Av. Atlântica, Italian, reasonable; *El Pote Galetos*, Rua República do Peru 143B, good chicken; *Moenda*, Av. Atlântica 2064, live music but formal, good food; *La Mole*, Av. N.S. de Copacabana, good service; *Beliscão*, Rua Siqueira Campos 23A e B, good beef stroganoff; nearby is *Cantina Veneziana*, good and cheap. *Aux Tropiques* (French), corner of Rua Siqueira Campos and Rua Barata Ribeiro, 3rd floor, very good; *Akasaka* (Japanese) Av. Copacabana and Rua Joaquim Nabuco, recommended; *Oriento* (Chinese), Rua Bolívar 64; *Zingaro's* (Italian) Rua Figueiredo Magalhães, reasonable. *Bip-Bip*, R. Almirante Gonçalves 50 D, for *batidas*; *Ariston*, Santa Clara 18A and B, good; *Rian*, Santa Clara 8 (international), excellent and reasonable, especially seafood; *Galeto*, Rua Constante Ramos. *Le Streghe*, Rua Prudente Morais 129, *Baroni Fasoli*, Rua Jangadeiros 14-D, and *Enotria*, R. Constante Ramos 115, all Italian and 4 star. *La Polonesa*, Rua Hilário da Gouveia (Polish); same street Rio's first *Macdonalds*; cheap and good inclusive meal (US$4) at *Frango na Brasa*, Rua Constante Ramos 35; and also at *Cervantes* and *El Cid*. Cabral 1500, Rua Bolívar 8, and *Maxim*, Av. Atlântica 1850, both good. **Ipanema:** *Lagoa Charlies*, Rua Maria Quitéria 136, supposedly Mexican, not cheap (*margaritas* are prohibitively expensive). For a meal with a view, try the restaurant and nightclub at the *Panorama Palace Hotel*, Rua Alberto de Campos 12. *Hotel Caesar Park*, recommended for Saturday *feijoada*, all you can eat for less than US$9, also *Suiki* Japanese restaurant, excellent, expensive; *Lord Jim Pub*, Paul Redfern 63, does English food including tea, great atmosphere, not cheap, closed Mon. Ipanema is quieter than Copacabana, many nice places round main square, Praça General Osório, such as *Romanos*. *Porcão*, *churrascaria*, recommended; branches everywhere. Health food at *Restaurante Natural*, Rua Barão de Torre 171. **Jardim Botânico:** *O Philippe*, R.Jardim Botânico 617, very good and reasonable, close to the Garden. **Lagoa:** *Castelo da Lagoa*, on Av Epitacio Pessoa: on same road, No. 770, *Aleph*, Restaurant and bar; No. 987, *Carlitos*, 24 hrs.; No. 980, *Pizza Pino*, (Tel.: 259-4349). *Rive Gauche*, No. 1484 (Tel.: 247-9993), French, excellent; **Gávea:** *Schwarze Katz*, Estrada do Vidigal 471, German and international. **Leblon:** *Un*, *Deux*, *Trois*, Rua Bartolomé Mitre 123, very fashionable; restaurant and night club; *Le Relais*, Rua General Venâncio Flores 365 (French); *Les Templiers*, Borges de Medeiros 3207 (also French); *Pancake Bar*, Rainha Guilhermina 95C, German; *Antiquarius*, Rua Aristides Espínola 19, restaurant-cum-antique shop, seafood and international cuisine. *Sabor Saúde*, Av. Ataulfo de Paiva 624, very nice. *Mediterráneo*, Rua Prudente de Morais 1810, excellent fish, reasonable prices; *Vagos*, Cupertino Durão 78; *Bar Degrau*, Av. Ataulfo de Paiva 517b, good atmosphere.

Grill or barbecue houses (*churrascarias*) are relatively cheap, especially by European standards. There are many at São Conrado and Joá, on the road out to Barra da Tijuca (see page 239). Look for the "Churrascaria Rodízio", where you are served as much as you can eat. In São Conrado, *El Pescador*, Praça São Conrado 20, Spanish-style fish restaurant, excellent. There are plentiful hamburger stands (literally "stands" as you stand and eat the hamburger) and lunch counters all over the city. *Galetos* are lunch counters specializing in chicken and grilled meat, very reasonable. Most less-expensive restaurants in Rio have basically the same type of food (based on steak, fried potatoes and rice) and serve large portions; those with small appetites, and especially families with children, can ask for a spare plate, and split helpings. There are many juice bars in Rio with a wide selection. Most restaurants are closed on 24 and 25 December.

Tea Rooms For those who like their teas served English style, the sedate Belle Epoque 80-year-old *Confeiteria Colombo*, Rua Gonçalves Dias 32, is highly recommended for atmosphere, being the only one of its kind in Rio, with the original décor, open 0900-1800. It has also a most attractive branch at Av. Copacabana 890. More modern but similar establishments in *Rio Palace*, *Meridien* and *Trocadero* hotels, and at *Casarão*, Souza Lima 37A, Copacabana; *La Bonne Table*, Visc. de Pirajá 580 sala 407, Ipanema; *Chaika's*, also in Ipanema; and *Ponto de Encontro*, Barata Ribeiro

Key to Rio de Janeiro Map
1. Touring Clube do Brasil; 2. Monastery and Church of São Bento; 3. Church of Candelária; 4. Palácio do Itamarati (former Foreign Ministry); 5. Dom Pedro II Railway Station; 6. Hospital Sousa Aguiar; 7. Museu de Caça e Pesca; 8. Central Post Office; 9. Church of Santa Cruz dos Militares; 10. Old Cathedral and Church of Carmo; 11. Church of N.S. da Lapa dos Mercadores; 12. Palace of the Viceroys (now Post Office headquarters); 13. Church of São José; 14. Palácio do Tiradentes (former Chamber of Deputies); 15. Flower Market (Praça Olavo Bilac); 16. Church of Rosário; 17. Church of São Francisco de Paula; 18. Gabinete Português de Leitura; 19. Teatro João Caetano; 20. Teatro Carlos Gomes; 21. Library of the State of Rio de Janeiro; 22. National Archive; 23. Teatro Recreio; 24. New Cathedral; 25. Aqueduto da Carioca (Arches, or *arcos*); 26. Tram Terminus; 27. Monastery of Santo Antônio and Church of São Francisco da Penitência; 28. Teatro Municipal; 29. Museu Nacional de Belas Artes; 30. National Library; 31. Museu da Imagem e do Som; 32. Santa Casa de Misericórdia (convent) and Church of N.S. do Bonsucesso; 33. Church of Santa Luzia; 34. Museu Histórico Nacional; 35. Teatro Mesbla and Teatro Serrador; 36. Church of Carmo da Lapa; 37. Instituto Histórico e Geográfico; 38. Santos Dumont Airport—passenger terminal; 39. Museu do Arte Moderno; 40. Second World War Memorial.

226 BRAZIL

750B, Copacabana. *Café de la Paix*, Av. Atlântica, 1020; *Chá e Simpatia*, Av. Atlântica 4240; *Um Chorinho chamado Odeon*, Gávea Shopping Centre; *Bolo Inglês*, Cassino Atlântico Shopping Centre; *Concorde*, Av. Prudente de Morais 129. These establishments have become very fashionable.

Night Clubs Note that respectable night clubs permit entrance only to couples. Of most interest to the visitor will be shows featuring samba dancing. *Hotel Nacional* at São Conrado has the most lavish show in town, price for entrance and one drink is US$20. Other good samba shows at: *Sambahá*, Rua Constante Ramos 140; *Solaris*, Rua Humaitá 110; *Katakombe*, Av. Copacabana 1241; *Oba-Oba*, Visconde de Pirajá 499 e.g. US$32 for two dinners and show considered one of the best in Rio. *Olé-Iê*, Av. Copacabana 73. For the best Brazilian shows try *Canecão*, Rua Venceslau Bras 215, where the best-known Carnival ball is now held. *Plataforma I*, Rua Adalberto Ferreira 32, Leblon, receives mixed opinions. Rio has its share of lively discotheques; among the best are; *New Jirau*, Rua Siqueira Campos 12-A, Copacabana; *Ye Bateau*, Praça Serzedelo Correia 15-A, Copacabana; *Crocodilus*, Rua Xavier da Silveira 7, Copacabana; *Privé*, Praça General Osório, Rua Jangadeiros 28-A; *Papagaio Disco Club*, Av. Borges de Medeiros 1426, Lagoa (Fri. and Sat. only). For something quieter and more intimate, look in at any of the following piano bars: *Balaio* (Hotel Leme Palace), Av. Atlântica 656. *Franks Bar* and *Crazy Rabbit* next door to each other on Av. Princesa Isabel. *Open*, Maria Quitéria 83 (Ipanema). Two good (and expensive) restaurants with live shows are *Fossa*, Rua Ronaldo de Carvalho 55, Copacabana, and *Carinhoso*, Rua Visconde de Pirajá 22, Ipanema. On the beach, not far away, is *Albericos*, Av. Vieira Souto 240. *Scala*, Av. Afranio de Mello Franco, Leblon, large, 1¾ hr. show at 2300, lavish and loud, reasonably-priced drinks, entry US$11. *Assyrius*, Av. Rio Branco 277 and *Erótica*, Av. Prado Júnior 63-A, both have good erotic shows at midnight. Ladies, if you are looking for company, take a table at the pavement café and *churrascaria* of *Barril 1800*, Av. Vieira Souto 110, Ipanema, where the "younger set" congregate. *Jazzmaria*, on Ipanema beach, also recommended. Also in Ipanema on Rua Vinicius de Morais 49-A, *Garota de Ipanema*, where the song "Girl from Ipanema" was written, excellent atmosphere, food reasonable. *Help*, on Av. Atlântica, is also very popular with young people. On Fri., Sat. and Sun. nights, 2100-0200, there is dancing to live bands at *Circo Voador* beneath Arcos da Lapa, in a circus tent, popular. The beach at the end of Rua Vinicius de Morais, Ipanema, is considered the most elegant spot during the day.

One of the centres of gay life is Cinelândia, in the centre (another is Galeria Alaska); in this area extending up to the Viaduto is found the whole gamut of human life. The essentially local character of night life in this area seems to make it relatively safe.

Another good place to see Brazilians at play, and at the same time for the English to feel some *saudades* (homesickness), is *Lord Jim Pub*, Paul Redfern 63 (Ipanema). Authentic pub atmosphere, afternoon tea, English food upstairs—steak-and-kidney pie, fish and chips. Phone in advance to check opening hours.

All the rage now are *gafieras*, restaurants or night clubs with live Brazilian music for dancing. The best (and most expensive) is *Carinhoso*, Rua Visconde de Pirajá 22, Ipanema. Others, *Elite Club*, Rua Frei Caneca 4, 1st floor, in the centre. *Asa Branca*, Av. Mem de Sá 17, Lapa, high class, expensive, live music daily. *Roda Viva*, beside the Sugar Loaf cable car station, and *Cordão da Bola Preta* (pretty rough, but typical, only on Friday evening), Av. Treze de Maio 13, 3rd. floor, beside the Municipal Theatre, centre; *Gafiera Estudiantina*, Praça Tiradentes, and one, enthusiastically recommended, at Botafogo under the beach highway. Other bars which have music *shows* include: *Chucrute*, Largo de São Conrado; *Barbas*, Álvaro Ramos 408, Botafogo; *Equinox*, restaurant/bar, Av. Prudente de Morais 729 (piano music); *Jazzmania*, Av. Rainha Elisabeth 769, Tel.: 227-2447, show at 2200; *Western Club*, Rua Humaitá 380; *Gente da Noite*, Rua Voluntários da Pátria 466, both in Botafogo; *Klaus Bar*, Rua Dias Ferreira 410, Leblon (live music irregularly on Fri. and Sat.); *Existe um Lugar*, Estrada das Furnas 3001; *Four Seasons*, Paul Redfern 44, Ipanema, for jazz; *Vogue*, Rua Cupertino Durão 173, Leblon; *People*, Av. Bartolomeu Mitre 370, Leblon, where the beautiful people go. In Barra de Tijuca there are a multitude of small night clubs, discotheques and *gafieras*, as well as some very luxurious motels for very-short-stay couples.

Many people look for Macumba religious ceremonies. Those offered on the night tours sold at hotels are not genuine, and a disappointment. It is imperative you have a local contact to see the real ones, which are usually held in *favelas* and are none too safe for unaccompanied tourists.

Theatres The main theatres in Rio are: *Adolfo Bloch*, Rua do Russel 864, Glória; *Teatro da Bolsa*, Av. Ataulfo de Paiva 269, Leblon; *Carlos Gomes*, Praça Tiradentes; *Copacabana*, Av. Copacabana 327; *Dulcima*, R. Alcindo Guanabara 17; *Fonte de Saudade*, Av. Epitácio Pessoa 4866, Lagoa; *Teatro da Galeria*, Rua Senador Vergueiro 93, Flamengo; *Ginástico*, Av. Graça Aranha 187; *Gláucio Gil*, Praça Cardeal Arcoverde, Copacabana; *Glória*, Rua do Russel 632, Glória; *Ipanema*, R. Prudente de Morais 824; *João Caetano*, Praça Tiradentes; *Teatro da Lagoa*, Av. Borges de Medeiros, Lagoa; *Maison de France*, Av. Pres. Antônio Carlos 58; *Mesbla*, Av. do Passeio 48; *Miguel Lemos*, R. Miguel Lemos 51, Copacabana; *Teatro Municipal*, Av. Rio Branco, for concerts and opera; *Nacional de Comédia*, Av. Rio Branco 179; *Teatro Novo*, R. Gomes Freire 474; *Tereza Rachel*, R. Siqueira Campos 143, Copacabana (has samba shows, much cheaper than night clubs); *Teatro da Praia*, R. Francisco Sá 88, Copacabana; *Princesa Isabel*, Av. Princesa Isabel 186, Copacabana; *Sala Cecília Meireles*, Largo da Lapa (often free classical concerts); *Teatro Villa-Lobos*, Av. Princesa Isabel, Copacabana; *Senac*, Rua Pompeu Loureiro 45, Copacabana. Good value entertainment at "Seis e Meia" (1830) shows at various downtown theatres (e.g. João Caetano): 1½ hr. musical shows with top-name Brazilian artists—check local papers.

Cinemas Most give half-price tickets to students, and some reduce prices for first performance of the day. Listings in *O Globo* newspaper (best) and *Jornal do Brasil*.

Shopping A good jewellery shop is Badofsky Brothers, Av. Copacabana 680, Room 315, 3rd floor; English, German, French spoken. Maximino Jeweler, Av. Rio Branco 25, 11th floor, and other branches. H. Stern, jewellers, Rua Garcia D'Avila 113, Ipanema; they also offer a tour, with head-phone commentary, of their lapidary and designing workshops, arranged through representatives at better hotels. Gregory & Sheehan, jewellers, Rua da Alfândega 65, 1st & 2nd floors; Corcovado Jóias, Av. N.S. de Copacabana 209, Loja F; Roditi and Amsterdam Sauer offer free taxi rides to their workshops. For mineral specimens as against cut stones, try Mineraux, Av. Copacabana 195, Belgian owner. Good "hippy fair" at Ipanema (Praça General Osório on Suns.). Sunday market in Glória district (Rua da Glória), colourful, cheap fruit, vegetable and flowers. Excellent "shopping centre" Rio Sul, at city end of Túnel Novo, Copacabana, and two others, less classy, on Barra de Tijuca (see page 239). The Funai shop (Government Indian Agency) is very disappointing.

Camera Shop Dino's, Rua Buenos Aires 241; others in same street. Camera repair, Av. Rio Branco 151, 2nd floor, room 204. Kodachrome slide film difficult to get in Rio.

Bookshops For small international stock, Livraria Kosmos, Rua do Rosário 155, good shop (in the centre and Av. Atlântica 1702, loja 5) and there are many others, e.g. Livros Técnicos, Rua Miguel Couto 35, wide selection; Nova Livraria Da Vinci, Av. Rio Branco 185 loja 2/3, all types of foreign books; Livrarias Siciliano, Av. Rio Branco 156, loja 26, English, French and German books, also at N.S. de Copacabana 830 and other branches. Livraria Nova Galeria de Arte, Av. Copacabana 291D, international stock. El Dorado, Av. das Américas 4666, loja 207. **N.B.** Cultura Inglesa, Av. Graça Aranha 327 (subscription US$2 for 6 months, US$4 a year) takes main English papers and magazines: also has snack bar. Second-hand books also at Livraria São José, Rua Carmo 61 (only a few in English); under *Rio Hotel*, corner of Rua da Carioca and Praça Tiradentes; Livraria Antiquário, Sete de Setembro 207 and in Rua Pedro I, all in centre. Also on Av. Marechal Floriano, near Av. Rio Branco, especially at No. 63. On S side of Praça Tiradentes, Casa dos Artistas trades in second-hand paperbacks. Second-hand English books at the Anglican church, Rua Real Grandeza 99, Botafogo.

Buses Good services to all parts, very crowded, not for the aged and infirm during rush hours. Fare normally about US$0.10, watch your change! Bus stops are often not marked.

Trams Try the remaining tram service from Largo da Carioca (where there is a museum, open only Fri. 0830-1700) across the old aqueduct (Arcos) to Dois Irmãos or Santa Teresa— historical and most interesting, and now refurbished, US$0.05. **Warning:** do not walk from Dois Irmãos to Silvestre (for Corcovado)—robberies are very common. Also beware of theft in trams, particularly in rush hours; try to sit on the closed, wire-meshed side of the tram, not on the open side or at the back. There are police on trams.

Car Hire For self-drive, try Avis, Rio International airport, less helpful than office at Praia do Flamengo 224 (205-5796); Hertz, Av. Oswaldo Cruz 67 (245-0678) US$30 all-in for 24 hrs. in a VW Beetle. Hertz, US$40 for a VW Kombi, US$60 for a/c Ford Galaxie. Nobre, Gustavo Sampaio 826 (275-5297) and Av. Princesa Isabel 350 (Tel.: 541-4646) Copacabana, has special deal for 7 hrs. Telecar, Rua Figueiredo Magalhães 701 (257-2620). Many agencies on Av. Princesa Isabel, Copacabana. Remember service stations are closed in many places on Saturdays and Sundays; some agencies will supply gas to customers at the weekend.

Taxis start at US$0.60 and are quite reasonable. There is a 40% surcharge between 2300 and 0600 and on Suns. and holidays. Taxis have red number plates with white digits (yellow for private cars, with black digits) and have meters. Smaller ones (mostly Volkswagens) are marked TAXI on windscreen or roof. Meters are often out-of-date because of inflation and drivers will consult updating sheets (make sure the updating sheet is an original in black and red, and not a photocopy—this is a well-known fiddle!); all the same, beware of overcharging, which appears to be increasing (See also page 237 in Rodoviária section). Make sure meters are cleared. Radio Taxis (white with red and yellow stripe) are safer and not much more expensive, e.g. Cootramo, 270-1442, Coopertramo, 260-2022. Luxury cabs are allowed to charge higher rates.

Underground Railway Line 1 operates between Tijuca and Botafogo, via the railway station and Glória, with 30 of the 37 km. of basic metro and pre-metro network in operation. Substantial changes in bus operations are taking place because of the extended metro system; buses connecting with the metro have a blue-and-white symbol in the windscreen. Line 2, running past the Maracanã stadium northward to Irajá, is now complete. Line 1 operates 0600-2300, Line 2 0600-2000, but closed Sun and holidays. Fare US$0.10; integrated bus/metro tickets available (cheaper if bought in bulk). If you speak Portuguese, apply to the Municipality and allow 10 days for arranging a sightseeing tour.

Public Conveniences There are very few in Rio de Janeiro, but the many bars and restaurants

228 BRAZIL

(e.g. Macdonalds) offer facilities of a sort; just ask for the "banheiro" (banyairoo). Try the Castelo bus terminal in city centre.

Crime Rio has been getting worse, both for assaults and for pickpocketing, but the number of patrolling police has been steadily expanded in recent years. Precautions are advisable, especially on the famous beaches, where small boys work in gangs, some distracting your attention while others go through pockets and bags. So beware of groups of friendly small boys. It is suggested to women that they do not venture out alone at night or visit the cinema alone. Always carry some money: robbers may be incensed and very aggressive if their victims have nothing at all. Do not wear jewellery or carry openly tourist goods such as a camera, maps or guide books to make yourself an obvious target. Carry your belongings in a "day-pack", as the locals do (can be bought at any street corner—joggers' arm-bands have also been suggested). Pickpockets and purse-snatchers operate at bus stops, bus turnstiles and among passengers while the bus is passing through a tunnel. Among the more problematic areas are Dois Irmãos, Santa Teresa, on Copacabana's Av. Atlântica, Pão de Açúcar, Corcovado, Quinta da Boa Vista, Jardim Botânico/Jóquei Clube racecourse area, and around the *Hotel Intercontinental* at São Conrado. To avoid swindling in bars, especially if sitting outside, pay as soon as you receive your order (although contrary to custom) and always ask for an itemized bill and check your change; alternatively, pay at the cash desk. Be especially careful after changing money in a public place; thieves often wait outside *câmbios*. The Tourist Police (Poltur) office is at Rua Humberto de Campos 319, Leblon.

Sightseeing See, within the city, Candelária church, the monastery of São Bento, the convent of Santo Antônio, the Glória church (see under Churches), the Museum of National History, the National Museum of Fine Arts, the Museum of Modern Art, the Municipal Theatre, the National Library, the Ruy Barbosa Museum (see under Public Buildings). Outside the centre you should see Copacabana, Ipanema, Leblon and Barra da Tijuca beaches, the Sugar Loaf, Corcovado, Tijuca Forest, Botanical Gardens, Quinta da Boa Vista and Zoological Gardens, the Maracanã Stadium, Santa Teresa and, if there is time, Niterói and Icaraí, Paquetá Island, Petrópolis and Teresópolis.

A pleasant experience is to take bus number 206 from Praça Tiradentes as far as Silvestre. The route is partly up the side of the Corcovado mountain, and the road is narrow and twisty, lined with lovely trees and many picturesque houses, though some of them are coming down. The only remaining open trams (or *bondes*-pronounced "bon-jis") follow the same route, through the "traditional" suburb of Santa Teresa (see page 238); though they do not go as far as the buses, the ride is much more enjoyable. The cog railway to the top of the Corcovado (see page 238) does not stop at Silvestre, and it is not advisable to walk from Silvestre to the top: there are many muggers. Another scenic ride is that provided by the unnumbered Pegaso bus route between Santos Dumont airport and Santa Cruz, along the coast, but recent travellers suggest that it is no longer worth going beyond São Conrado because the coast beyond is being built up.

Carnival Carnival in Rio is still spectacular, though less so than formerly. On Shrove Tuesday and the three preceding days, the main avenues are colourfully lit, and many young people and children wear fancy dress. Special bandstands throughout the city are manned for public street-dancing (see *Daily Post/Brazil Herald* for where and when) and organized carnival groups, the *blocos carnavalescos*, are everywhere, dancing, drumming and singing. Visitors should be sure to get seats in stands in the Sambódromo (see below) for the main evenings of carnival (Sun. and Mon.) to see the great processions of the city's main samba clubs, or *escolas da samba*. Note that "tourist tickets", costing US$75, are not in the best places; tickets for main events, sold 3-4 weeks before Carnival (from branches of Banco do Estado do Rio de Janeiro (Banerj)—only 4 per person), range from US$3-$25. Tickets for other nights start selling after sales for the main event. Make sure you turn up about 6 hours before the event is due to begin: seats on stands are not numbered. Black market seat prices may go up to US$100 each, but tickets are often available at the official prices. The parades start at about 1900, and go on to 1000 next day. Each club represents a district, and chooses a theme to illustrate with its own samba; each has its own colourscheme for costumes and its own percussion band, or *bateria*. Some clubs are two to three thousand strong and take 1½ hours to pass the judges' stand—a film-spectacular in real life! There are three leagues of samba clubs using respectively the Sambódromo, the Avenida Rio Branco and Avenida 28 de Setembro, and promotion and relegation take place, as in football leagues. Competition is intense. Make sure you keep your ticket; gatecrashing is a problem on the stands. The main events on the other nights are the parade of clubs dancing *frevo* (a rather Cossack-like dance from the North-East) and *rancho* (the traditional Rio dance before the introduction of the samba in 1917) on Mon., and an amalgam of events on Tues., including a huge float parade by the *grandes clubes carnavalescos*, and exhibitions by the previous year's champion samba groups, *blocos carnavalescos* and *frevo* and *rancho* groups.

The **Sambódromo**, a permanent site at Rua Marquês de Sapucaí, Cidade Nova, not far from the centre, is used for the four main events. It has a length of 600 metres, with seats for 60,000 people. If you can't stand crowds, there is a less-frequented parade, of the winners and runners-up for each of the three leagues on the Saturday after the Carnival, at the Sambódromo. Tickets about US$2 from the São Cristóvão pavilion, available the Thursday after Carnival.

There are also innumerable fancy-dress balls (highly recommended); the main public one is at the Canecão (Sat. night) but there are scores more in hotels and clubs.

Carnival takes place at a time when Rio is packed with summer visitors enjoying the beaches. So visitors wishing to attend the Carnival are earnestly advised to make sure of their accommodation well in advance. Virtually all hotels raise their prices during Carnival.

Pickpockets and thieves are very active during Carnival. Don't wander into dark corners on your own, and take with you only as much money as you need for fares and refreshments. It gets hot! Wear as little as possible. Foreign males can often be identified by their long trousers.

If you can't be there at Carnival time, rehearsals are held at various places from November onwards; e.g. the Portela *escola* at Rua Arruda Câmara 81, Madureira, late Sat. nights. Samba shows are given at the Teatro Tereza Rachel, Rua Siqueira Campos 143, Copacabana, on Mon.

WANTED: MAPS
ARGENTINA – BRAZIL – MEXICO GUATEMALA – EL SALVADOR – THE CARIBBEAN ISLANDS

We would much appreciate receiving any surplus maps and diagrams, however rough, of towns and cities, walks, national parks and other interesting areas, to use as source material for the Handbook and other forthcoming titles.

The above regions are particularly needed but any maps of Latin America would be welcome.

The Editor   Trade & Travel Publications Limited
5 Prince's Buildings, George Street,
Bath BA1 2ED. England

230 BRAZIL

nights (not December), Tel.: 235-2119 (see also page 226); recommended. Also, Beija Flor, one of the best samba schools, performs on Mon. nights at Urca (half-way up to Sugar Loaf Mountain), dinner available at 2000, reservations required (on Fri. and Sat. at this venue is the "Noite Carioca" show, or a disco).

Other Festivals Less hectic than Carnival, but very beautiful, is the festival of Iemanjá on the night of December 31, when devotees of the spirit cults brought from Africa gather on Copacabana, Ipanema and Leblon beaches, singing and dancing around open fires and making offerings, and the elected Queen of the Sea is rowed along the seashore. There is a firework display on Copacabana beach. At midnight small boats are launched as sacrifices to Iemanjá. Again, if you go, beware thieves.

The festival of São Sebastião, patron saint of Rio, is celebrated by an evening procession on Jan. 20, leaving Capuchinhos Church, Tijuca, and arriving at the cathedral of São Sebastião. The same evening an *umbanda* festival is celebrated at the Caboclo Monument in Santa Teresa.

Museums and other Public Buildings
All museums and the Jardim Botânico are closed over Carnival.

The **National Library** (Biblioteca Nacional), at Avenida Rio Branco 219, was founded in 1810. Its first collection came from the Ajuda Palace in Lisbon, and to-day it houses over 2 million volumes and many rare manuscripts. The library is open Mon.-Fri. 1030-1830, and Sat. 1200-1800.

National Museum of Fine Art (Museu Nacional de Belas Artes), at Avenida Rio Branco 199. There are about 800 original paintings and sculptures and some thousand direct reproductions. Exhibitions of works by contemporary Brazilian artists are often held here. Open Tues.-Fri. 1230-1800; Sat., Sun. and holidays 1500-1800.

Those interested in contemporary art will also visit the former Ministry of Education, designed by Le Corbusier, to see the great murals of Cândido Portinári, whose canvas, "Café", is in the Museum of Fine Art.

Opposite the Art Museum is the **Municipal Theatre**. Opera and orchestral performances are given here; the small museum that used to be below the theatre is now at Rua São João Batista 103/105, Botafogo, open 1100-1700 Tues.-Sun.

The **Museum of Modern Art** (Museu de Arte Moderna), is a spectacular building at Avenida Infante D. Henrique 85, near the National War Memorial (see page 233). It is the work of A. E. Reidy, who has also built two neighbourhood units, one on the western slope of Pedregulho Hill, one in Gávea. It suffered a disastrous fire in 1978; the collection is now being rebuilt, and several countries have donated works of art. There is also a non-commercial cinema. Entrance US$0.85, Tues.-Sat. 1200-1900 (open till 2200 on Thurs.), Sun., 1400-1900. Closed periodically.

The **Brazilian Academy of Letters**, on Av. Presidente Wilson, is a replica of the Petit Trianon at Versailles; it was given to Brazil by the French Government after the Centenary Exhibition of 1922. The Academy was founded in 1897 by the writer Machado de Assis, and meets every Thurs. at 1700 hours. The new building next door includes some floors of the Academy's cultural centre.

The **National Historical Museum** on Praça Rui Barbosa (formerly Praça Marechal Âncora) contains a most interesting collection of historical treasures, colonial sculpture and furniture, maps, paintings, arms and armour, silver, and porcelain. The building was once the old War Arsenal of the Empire, part of which was built in 1762. Open Tues. to Fri., 1100-1700; Sat., Sun. and holidays 1400-1700. The building also houses the **Military Museum**.

Naval and Oceanographic Museum, Rua D. Manoel 15, daily 1200-1645. There is a particularly large collection of paintings and prints, besides the more usual display of weapons and figureheads.

The warship *Bauru* (*ex-USS McCann*) has been made into a floating museum, in the Glória Marina, opposite the war memorial on the Praia do Flamengo.

Museum of Image and Sound, also on Praça Rui Barbosa, has many photographs of Brazil and modern Brazilian paintings, open Mon.-Fri., 1200-1800; also collections and recordings of Brazilian classical and popular music and a non-commercial cinema open Fri.-Sun.

The **Museum of the Indian** (Museu do Índio) is at Rua das Palmeiras 55, Botafogo, Tel.: 286 0845, open Tues.-Fri. 1130-1700. Highly recommended. It contains 12,000 objects from many Brazilian Indian groups.

The **Museum of the City** (Museu da Cidade) at Estrada Santa Marinha, Gávea, in the delightful Parque da Cidade (see page 233), contains a collection of Rio's historical objects. Open Mon.-Fri., 1300-1700; Sat.-Sun., 1100-1700. Buses from centre, 176, 178; from Copacabana, 591 or better still 593 and 594.

BRAZIL 231

The **National Museum** in the Quinta da Boa Vista is one of the most important museums in South America. The building was the principal palace of the Emperors of Brazil, but only the unfurnished Throne Room and ambassadorial reception room on the 2nd floor reflect past glories (closed for repair in 1984). In the entrance hall is the famous Bêndego meteorite, found in the State of Bahia in 1888. It is possibly the largest metallic mass ever to fall on earth; its original weight, before some of it was chipped, was 5,360 kg. Besides several foreign collections of note, the Museum contains collections of Brazilian Indian weapons, dresses, utensils, etc., and of minerals and of historical documents. (Study of the ethnography section is recommended by Peter Worsley, of Manchester University.) There are also collections of birds, beasts, fishes, and butterflies. Open 1000-1645, closed Mon.; entrance US$0.10 (free Thursday). Buses: 472, 474, 475 from centre, Flamengo and Copacabana, 583 from Largo do Machado. Nearest metro São Cristóvão.

Museu de Fauna also at Quinta da Boa Vista, contains a most interesting collection of Brazilian fauna. Open Tues.-Sun. 1200-1700.

The **Fundação Raymundo Ottoni de Castro Maia,** generally known as **Chácara do Céu,** Rua Murtinho Nobre 93, has a wide range of art objects and particularly works of modern Brazilian painters. Take Santa Teresa tram to Rua Dias de Barros, then follow signposts. (Open Tues.-Sun. 1400-1700, Sun. 1300-1700, US$0.30.) Castro Maia's former residence on the Estrada do Açude in the Tijuca Forest bears the same name and is also a museum, currently under restoration.

Museo do Instituto Histórico e Geográfico, Av. Augusto Severo 8 (10th floor), just off Av. Beira Mar, has a very interesting collection of Brazil's products and the artefacts of its peoples. Open Mon.-Fri. 1300-1700.

The **São Cristóvão Pavilion,** a permanent exhibition hall designed by Sérgio Bernardes, has the world's largest open floor space without columns or transverse walls. Bus 472 or 474 from Copacabana or centre.

The **National Observatory** (founded 1827) is on São Januário hill, Rua Gen. Bruce 586, São Cristóvão. Visitors advised to call 248-1182 after 1700 to arrange a night viewing.

The **House of Rui Barbosa,** Rua São Clemente 134, Botafogo, former home of the Brazilian jurist and statesman, is open Tue.-Fri. 1400-2100. Buses 106, 176, 178 from centre; 571 from Flamengo; 591 from Copacabana. (Reported closed for renovation in mid-1986).

Itamarati Palace, the former Foreign Ministry, at Avenida Marechal Floriano 196, contains much interesting old furniture, tapestry and other objects of art. Now called Museu Histórico e Diplomático, open Tues.-Fri., 1200-1615 (doors close at 1700); admission free on Thurs.

Museum of the Republic, in Catete Palace (Rua do Catete 179), entrance in Rua Silveira Martins, was the official residence of the President for 63 years when Rio was the Federal Capital. Also contains Folklore Museum. Under renovation in 1985/86. Bus 571 from Copacabana, and close to Catete metro station.

Guanabara Palace, once the residence of the Princess Isabel, daughter of Dom Pedro II, is now the office of the Governor of the State of Rio de Janeiro.

Carmen Miranda Museum, Tues.-Sun. 1100-1700, Flamengo park area in front of Rui Barbosa 560 (small display of the famous singer's gowns etc). **Museum of Fringes of the Unconscious,** Ramiro Magalhães 521, Engenho de Dentro, Mon.-Fri. 0800-1600. **Villa-Lobos Museum,** Rua da Imprensa 16, Tues.-Sat. 1000-1600, with instruments, scores, books, recordings. **Capão do Bispo Estate,** Av. Suburbana 4616, Del Castilho, Mon.-Fri. 1400-1700 with archaeological exhibition.

Planetarium, Padre Leonel Franco 240, Gávea, Sat. and Sun. at 1600, 1700, 1830; inaugurated in 1970, sculpture of Earth and Moon by Mario Agostinelli. Free *choro* concert Fri. at 2100. Buses 176 and 178 from centre and Flamengo; 591 and 592 from Copacabana.

Aerospace Museum, Av. Marechal Fontenelle 2000, Campo dos Afonsos, Tues.-Fri. 0900-1600, early Brazilian civil and military aircraft.

Antônio Lago Museum, R. Andradas 96, centre, Mon.-Fri. 1400-1700. Reproduction of historical apothecary's shop.

Churches and Religious Foundations
Check opening hours before attempting to visit.

The oldest foundation is the **Convent of Carmo,** built early in the 17th century on Rua Primeiro de Março close to Praça 15 de Novembro, now used as a school. Its present church, the Carmo Church in Rua Primeiro de Março, next to the old cathedral, was built in the 1770s and rebuilt between 1797 and 1826. It has strikingly beautiful portals by Mestre Valentim, the son of a

Portuguese nobleman and a slave girl. He also created the main altar of fine moulded silver, the throne and its chair, and much else.

The second oldest convent is the seventeenth-century **Convent of Santo Antônio**, on a hill off the Largo da Carioca, built between 1608 and 1615. Its church has a marvellous sacristy adorned with blue tiles. St. Anthony is a particular object of devotion for women who want to find husbands, and many will be seen in the precincts.

The crypt contains the tomb of a Scottish soldier of fortune known as "Wild Jock of Skelater". He was in the service of the Portuguese Government during the Napoleonic War, and had the distinction of being appointed the first Commander-in-Chief of the Army in Brazil. The statue of St. Anthony was made a captain in the Portuguese army after his help had been sought to drive out the French in 1710, and his salary paid to the monastery. In 1810 he became a major, in 1814 a lieutenant-colonel, and he was granted the Grand Cross of the Order of Christ. He was retired without pay in 1914.

Separated from this church only by some iron railings is the charming church of **São Francisco da Penitência**, built in 1773. The carving and gilding of walls and altar are superb. In the ceiling over the nave is a fine panel painted by José de Oliveira. There is a museum attached to the church, open first and third Sun. of the month, 0700-1000.

The **Monastery of São Bento** (1641); entrance at Rua Dom Gerardo 68, contains much of what is best in the 17th and 18th century art of Brazil. "O Salvador", the masterpiece of Brazil's first painter, Frei Ricardo do Pilar, hangs in the sacristy. The carving in the church is particularly good. The Chapels of the Immaculate Conception and of the Most Holy Sacrament are masterpieces of Colonial art. The organ is very interesting. The monastery is a few minutes' walk from Praça Mauá, turning left off Av. Rio Branco just before the Rua São Bento. The intimate view of the harbour and its shipping from the grounds of the monastery (behind the church) is in itself worth climbing the hill on which it stands. (Male visitors must wear long trousers.)

The **Old Cathedral** of São Sebastião, in the Rua Primeiro de Março, was built between 1749 and 1770. In the crypt are the bones of many famous men, including those of Pedro Alvares Cabral, the discoverer of Brazil (though it is only fair to note that Santarém, Portugal, also claims to be his last resting-place).

The **New Cathedral**, on Avenida República de Chile not far from the Largo da Carioca, dedicated in 1976, is a very exciting cone-shaped building. Its internal height is 68 metres, diameter 104 metres, external height 83 metres; capacity 5,000 seated, 20,000 standing. The most striking feature is four enormous stained-glass windows (60 metres high). It is still incomplete.

The Church of **São Francisco de Paula**, at the upper end of the Rua do Ouvidor, was built in 1759. It contains some of Mestre Valentim's work—the carvings in the main chapel and the lovely Chapel of Our Lady of Victory. Some of the paintings, and probably the ceiling, are by Manuel da Cunha. The beautiful fountain at the back plays only at night.

The Church of **Nossa Senhora da Candelária** (1775-1810), on Praça Pio Dez, at the city end of Avenida Presidente Vargas, is well worth a visit to see its beautiful interior decorations and paintings. It is on the site of a chapel founded in 1610 by Antônio da Palma after he had survived a shipwreck, an event depicted by paintings inside the present dome.

In the Rua de Santa Luzia, overwhelmed by tall office buildings, is the attractive little church of **Santa Luzia**. When built in 1752 it had only one tower; the other was added late in the 19th century. Feast day: December 13, when devotees bathe their eyes with holy water, considered miraculous.

In the Rua Primeiro de Março, at the corner of Ouvidor (near the Old Cathedral), is the church of **Santa Cruz dos Militares**, built 1780-1811. It is large, stately and beautiful.

The beautiful little church on the Glória hill, overlooking the Parque do Flamengo, is **Nossa Senhora da Glória**. It was the favourite church of the imperial family; Dom Pedro II was baptized here. Built in 1791, it contains some excellent examples of blue-faced Brazilian tiling. Its main altar, of wood, was carved by Mestre Valentim. The church, open 0900-1200 (only Sat.-Sun.) and 1300-1700 weekdays, is reached by bus 119 from the centre and 571 from Copacabana. The adjacent museum of religious art is open on application to the priest.

The church of **Nossa Senhora da Penha**, in the N suburb of Penha (early 20th century), is on a bare rock in which 365 steps are cut. This staircase is ascended by pilgrims on their knees during the festival month of October; there is a funicular for those unable to do this. Bus 497 from Copacabana, 340 and 346 from centre.

When the Morro do Castelo was levelled to make the large new area known as the Esplanada do Castelo, the old church of São Sebastião had to be demolished. Its successor, the Capuchin church of São Sebastião in the Rua Haddock Lobo, Tijuca, built in 1936, contains the tomb of Estácio de Sá, founder and first Governor of Rio de Janeiro.

Churches where worship is conducted in English:

Christ Church, Rua Real Grandeza 99, Botafogo (Church of England/American Episcopalian). The British School, for children of 5-16, is nearby.
Chapel of Our Lady of Mercy, Rua Visconde de Caravelas 48, Botafogo. (Roman Catholic, with primary school.)
Union Church (Protestant undenominational) Services held at Rua Parque da Lagoa de Marapendi, C.P.37154-CEP 22609 Barra da Tijuca.

BRAZIL 233

International Baptist Church, Rua Desembargador Alfredo Russel 146, Leblon.
First Church of Christ Scientist, Av. Marechal Câmara 271, room 301.
Masonic Temple, in the British School at Rua da Matriz 76, Botafogo.
Synagogues, General Severiano 170, Botafogo; Rua Barata Ribeiro, Copacabana.
British Cemetery, Rua da Gamboa 181, granted to the British community by Dom João, Regent of Portugal, in 1810. It is the oldest cemetery in Rio.

Parks, Squares and Monuments

The city abounds in open spaces and squares, many of which have ornamental gardens and statuary.
On the Glória and Flamengo waterfront, with a view of the Sugar Loaf and Corcovado, is the **Parque do Flamengo,** designed by Burle Marx, opened in 1965 during the 400th anniversary of the city's founding, and landscaped on 100 hectares reclaimed from the Bay. Behind the War Memorial (see below) is the public yacht marina.

In the park are many sports fields and a botanical garden; for children, there are a sailboat basin, a marionette theatre, a miniature village and a staffed nursery. There are night amusements, such as bandstands and areas set apart for dancing.

The National War Memorial to Brazil's dead in World War II and the Modern Art Museum (see page 230) are at the city end of the park, opposite Praça Paris. The Memorial takes the form of two slender columns supporting a slightly curved slab, representing two palms uplifted to heaven. In the crypt are the remains of the Brazilian soldiers killed in Italy in 1944-45. It is well worth a visit, but beach clothes and rubber-thonged sandals will get you ejected—and don't sit on the wall. The crypt and museum are open Tues.-Sun. 1000-1700.

Those who want to see what Rio was like early in the 19th century should go by bus to the **Largo do Boticário,** Rua Cosme Velho 822, a charming small square in pure Colonial style. Buses to Cosme Velho from all parts of the city. The square is close to the terminus for the Corcovado rack railway (see page 238).

Botanical Gardens (Jardim Botânico) founded 1808, open daily, 0800-1800 in summer and 0830-1730 in winter (US$0.30); well worth a visit. The most striking features are the transverse avenues of 30-metre royal palms. There are over 7,000 varieties of plants, herbarium, aquarium, and library (some labels are unclear). The Gardens are 8 km. from the centre, 140 hectares in area; take any bus from the centre, e.g. 104, to Leblon, Gávea or São Conrado marked "via Jóquei" (the racecourse). From Copacabana any bus whose number begins with 5 and ends with an even number, except 592.

Bird-watchers who find themselves in Rio should visit the Botanical Gardens, preferably early in the morning. 140 species of birds have been recorded there. Flycatchers are very prominent (the social flycatcher, great and boat-billed kiskadees, cattle tyrant); also tanagers (the sayaca and palm tanagers, and the colourful green-headed tanager), and over 20 different kinds of hummingbird. Birds of prey include the roadside hawk, the laughing falcon and the American kestrel, and there are doves, cuckoos, parakeets, thrushes and woodpeckers, and occasional flocks of toucans. (John and George Newmark, Eastbourne.)

Parque Laje, near the Jardim Botânico at Rua Jardim Botânico 414, almost jungle-like, has small grottoes, an old tower and lakes. (The Institute of Fine Arts is housed in the mansion.) Open daily, 0730-1730, admittance free.

Quinta da Boa Vista, formerly the Emperor's private park, contains the zoo (see below) and many specimen trees. The Palace now houses the National Museum (see page 231).

Zoological Gardens, which contain Brazilian and imported wild animals, and a fine collection of birds (as well as many "visitors" - also good for bird-watchers), are in the Quinta de Boa Vista (admission US$0.05). Open 0800-1800 daily, except Mon. The gateway is a replica of Robert Adam's famous gateway to Syon House, near London. Near the Zoological Gardens is the Museum of Natural History which is small but excellent. Take bus 474 or 472 from Copacabana or Flamengo; bus 262 from Praça Mauá.

Parque da Cidade A pleasant park a short walk beyond the Gávea bus terminus. It was previously the grounds of the home of the Guinle family, by whom it was presented to the City; the house itself is now the Museu da Cidade (see page 230). Admission to the park is free; open Tues.-Fri. 0730-1730, Sat., Sun. and holidays 1100-1700.

Jockey Club Racecourse, at Praça Santos Dumont, Gávea, meetings on Mon. and Thurs. evenings and Sat. and Sun. 1400, entrance US$0.20. Take any bus marked "via Jóquei". Betting is by totalizator only.

Praça da República and **Campo de Santana** is an extensive and picturesque public garden close to the Central Railway station. At Praça da República 197 lived Marshal Deodoro da Fonseca, who proclaimed Brazil a republic in 1889 (plaque). The Parque Júlio Furtado in the middle of the square is populated by playful agoutis (or gophers), best seen at dusk; there is also a little artificial grotto, with swans.

Passeio Público (turn right at S end of Avenida Rio Branco) is a garden planted by the artist Mestre Valentim, whose bust is near the old former gateway. Coin and stamp market on Sun., a.m.

Praça Quinze de Novembro contains the original royal palace, the Paço, now used by the Department of Posts and Telegraphs; a beautiful Colonial building begun in 1743 and now under restoration. Every Sat. 0900-1900, handicraft fair and flea market; nearby on waterfront is Sun. antiques market, 1000-1800.

Praça Tiradentes, old and shady, has a statue to D. Pedro I, first Emperor of Brazil. Shops in nearby streets specialize in selling goods for *umbanda* and *macumba* - African-type religion and magic respectively. Several theatres nearby.

Praça Mahatma Gandhi, at the end of Avenida Rio Branco, is flanked on one side by the cinema and amusement centre of the city, known as Cinelândia. The fountain (1789) by Mestre Valentim in the ornamental garden was moved here from Praça Quinze de Novembro in 1979.

Praça Paris, built on reclaimed ground near the Largo da Glória, is much admired for the beauty of its formal gardens and illuminated fountains.

Fountains The oldest, the Fonte da Glória (1789), has eight bronze spouts. Possibly the finest is at the back of the church of S. Francisco de Paula, at the inland end of the Rua do Ouvidor. These, and nine other old fountains, are illuminated by night.

Sports Clubs Paissandu Athletic Club, Av. Afrânio de Melo Franco 330, Leblon (international)—Tennis, bowls, swimming. Leme Tennis Club (international), Rua Gustavo Sampaio 74—Tennis. Rio de Janeiro Country Club, Rua Prudente de Morais 1597, Ipanema (international)—Tennis and swimming. Gávea Golf and Country Club, Estrada da Barra da Tijuca 2005 (international)—Golf and polo. Itanhangá Golf Club, Jacarepaguá (international), visiting cards from Avenida Rio Branco 26, 16th floor. Clube Hípico Brasileiro, Av. Borges de Medeiros 2448, Jardim Botânico—Riding. Iate Clube do Rio de Janeiro, Av. Pasteur, Botafogo—Yachting. Jockey Club, Praça Santos Dumont, Jardim Botânico—Horse racing on Thurs., Sat. and Sun., pari-mutuel betting. Squash at Rua Cândido Mendes 581, Glória, Tel.: 242-0642. Ice skating at Barra Shopping, Av. das Américas 466, Barra da Tijuca. Roller-skating at *Roxy-Roller*, opp. Clube de Regatas Flamengo on Av. Borges de Medeiros, Lagoa.

Travel Agents Grand Tours, Av. Copacabana 166, Tel.: 237-0658; American Express Kontik Franstur, Av. Atlântica 2316A; Pioneer Turismo, Rua Santa Clara 33, sala 203; Wagon-Lits Cook; Ameuropa Turismo. Av. 7 de Setembro 55, Tel.: 222-2433; Roxy, Av. Winston Churchill 60, helpful, recommended (ask for Michael Weary who speaks English); Exprinter, Av. Rio Branco, 57a (said to be particularly good for money-changing); Casa Piano, Av. Rio Branco, 88; Itatiaia Turismo, Av. Rio Branco 120, helpful, will sometimes change money; Creditur, Av Almirante Barroso 63, suite 2508, for non IATA flights to N. America and Europe; for cheap flights to Europe, Líneas Aéreas Paraguayas, Rua Santa Luzia 827; Tourservice, Rua Alcindo Guanabara 24, sala 503; Casa Aliança, Av. Rio Branco 13a; Brazilian Holidays, Rua Visconde de Pirajá 414, Suite 819/820, Tel.: 267-5749, Ipanema, English and German spoken, helpful regarding tickets and information; Brazil Safari Tours, Visconde de Pirajá 156, s.217, Tel.: 521-3646; Soletur, Visconde de Pirajá 550, sala 1708, recommended. Victor Hummel, Av. Presidente Vargas 290/4, Tel.: 223-1262, Swiss-run, recommended. Tel.: 231-1800. Also Swiss-run and highly recommended, South American Turismo Ltda, Av. N. S. de Copacabana 788, 6th and 7th floors, Tel.: 255-2345. Americatur, Av. Rio Branco 156 (Tel.: 262-4293, 262-2659) runs tours on the Rio São Francisco, flying from Rio to Belo Horizonte (see page 258). Regular sightseeing tours operated by Gray Line (294-0393), American Sightseeing (236-3551), Sul América (257-4235), Canbitur (of Copacabana), Passamar Turismo, Av. Rio Branco 25 (233-8883, 233-4833, 253-1125; also at *Hotel Nacional*). Adrianotour, Tel.: 208-5103, for guided tours, reservations and commercial services (English, French, German and Spanish spoken). ENASA, for Amazon river travel, Rua Uruguaiana 39 (Sala 1402); they try to sell tickets on first-class boats only.

Tourist Information There are several excellent information centres. Embratur, Rua Mariz e Barros 13, near Praça da Bandeira, Tel.: 273-2177. Touring Club do Brasil, Pres. Antônio Carlos 130 and Av. Brasil 4294 (out of town) no English spoken. Riotur, Rua da Assembléia 10, 8th floor, good basic map available. Official Riotur information stands at Pão de Açúcar cablecar station (0800-2000); Marina da Glória, Flamengo; Rodoviária Novo Rio (the bus station—0600-2400; very friendly and helpful in finding accommodation). Riotur also has a multilingual telephone service operating 24 hours, Tel.: 580-8000. Flumitur at Rio International Airport, helpful with hotel information (where tourist packs are sold for US$15—these contain a map, restaurant list and a blank passport facsimile, which has no legal standing even though they may try to persuade you otherwise), and Rua da Assembléia 10-7th floor, Tel.: 221-8422. Best guide to Rio, with excellent map, *Guia Quatro Rodas do Rio* in Portuguese and English, US$3. *Guia Rex* street guide, US$8. *Guia Schaeffer Rio de Janeiro* (US$3) is an excellent sheet. Many hotels provide guests with the weekly *Itinerário* (*Rio This Month*).

Maps are available from Riotur information desks (US$0.50), Touring Clube do Brasil (US$0.40), touring agencies and hotels; Geomapas tourist map is clear, US$1.20. Also maps free from H. Stern, the jeweller, at Rua Visconde do Pirajá 490, Ipanema. Also from Paulini, Rua Lélio Gama 75 (outside the entrance of the downtown tram station): topographical and other maps of Brazil and of South America. **Note** Tourist agencies do not normally provide lists of cheap accommodation for travellers; some initiative is required.

Addresses

Australian Consulate, Rua Voluntários da Pátria 45, 5°, Botafogo, Tel.: 286-7922.
British Consulate, Praia do Flamengo 284, Tel.: 552-1422 (UK citizens can use telephone to phone UK at normal rates).
Irish Consulate, Rua Fonseca Teles 18, CEP 20940, Tel.: 254-0960.
Swiss Consulate, Rua Cândido Mendes 157, 11° andar, Cx. Postal 744-7c-00, Tel.: 222-1896 (open 0900-1200, Mon.-Fri.).
West German Consulate-General, Rua Presidente Carlos de Campos 417, Tel.: 285-2333.
French Consulate, Av. Pres. Antônio Carlos, 58, Tel.: 220-6022.
Austrian Consulate, Av. Atlântica 3804, CEP 22070, Tel.: 227-0040/048/049.
Swedish Consulate-General, Praia do Flamengo 344, 9° andar, Tel.: 205-8552.
U.S. Consulate General, Avenida Presidente Wilson, 147, Tel.: 252-8055.
USICA Reference Library, U.S. Consulate General, Av. Presidente Wilson 147.
U.S. Peace Corps, Rua Barão de Lucena 81, Botafogo.
Y.M.C.A., Rua da Lapa, 40.
The British Council, Rua Elmano Cardim 10 (formerly Rua Iguatu), Urca. Tel.: 295-7782.
The British School of Rio de Janeiro, Rua da Matriz 76.
The American School of Rio de Janeiro, Estrada da Gávea 132.
Sociedade Brasileira de Cultura Inglesa, Copacabana. Tel.: 227-0147.
American Chamber of Commerce for Brazil, Praça Pio Dez 15, 5th floor.
American Society and American Club, Avenida Rio Branco 123, 21st floor.
German Cultur-Institut (Goethe), Av. Graça Aranha 419, 9th floor; open Mon., Wed., Thurs., 1000-1400, 1500-1930, Fri., 1000-1300.
Republic of S. Africa, Consulate, Rua Voluntários da Pátria 45, 9th floor, Botafogo, Tel.: 266-6246.
Central Post Office, Rua Primeiro de Março, at corner of Rua do Rosário.
Policia Federal, Av. Venezuela 2 (near Praça Mauá), for renewal of 90-day visa, US$4.
Poltur, Tourist Police, Rua Humberto de Campos 319, Leblon (unmarked door beside main police station, helpful, English spoken, will type report for insurance).

Laundromats Lavandaria Automática, Rua Barão do Flamengo 42, and Rua Bambina 164 (Botafogo); Automática do Catete, Rua Andrade Pertence 42, Loja 6.

Doctor Rio Health Collective, Tel.: 511-0940 for medical referral service, Mon.-Fri., 0900-1700, which will direct you to doctors of all specializations, in languages other than Portuguese, belonging to a non-profit organization designed for travellers' use. Vaccinations at Climuno, Av. N.S. Copacabana 680, 5/604, Tel.: 255-3731. English-speaking. Everton Marques dos Santos, Rua Uruguaiana 10, S/708, Tel.: 232-6982/233-0836/222-0642. Policlínica, Av. Nilo Peçanha 38, recommended for diagnosis and investigation.

Dentist English-speaking, Amílcar Werneck de Carvalho Vianna, Av. Pres. Wilson 165, suite 811.

Banks Lloyds Bank (ex-BOLSA), Rua da Alfândega 33; Banco Internacional (Bank of America and Royal Bank of Canada), Rua do Ouvidor 90; Banco Holandês Unido, Rua do Ouvidor 101; Citibank, Rua Assembléia 100; The First National Bank of Boston, Av. Rio Branco 110; Banco de Crédito Real de Minas Gerais, S.A., Av. Rio Branco 116; Banco Lar Brasileiro, Rua do Ouvidor 98; Banco Econômico, Rua Miguel Couto 131, 2nd floor (accepts Master Charge); and many others. Banks are open 1000 to 1630. Closed on Sat. Banco do Brasil at the International Airport is open always. Official rate of exchange: black market is now illegal.

Exchange Houses Official rates only. American Express, Av. Atlântica 2316, Copacabana; at Exprinter, Av. Rio Branco 57A (good rates also at their Av. N.S. de Copacabana branch), Casa Piano, Rua Visconde de Pirajá 365, Ipanema (cash and cheques), also Praça da Paz, Ipanema, and Av. Rio Branco 88 (cash only); Turismo Portuguesa, Av. Rio Branco 45; Cualitour, Av. Rio Branco 25B; Kontik, Av. Presidente Vargas 309, Irmãos Capello, Av. Rio Branco 31A. In Copacabana: P. M. (no travellers' cheques), Av. Copacabana 391-B and Av. Rio Branco 124-A; Paladium Travel, 3rd floor of Shopping Casino Atlântico, Ipanema end of Av. Atlântica, Copacabana, Kraus, Praça

236 BRAZIL

Pio X 55, 2nd floor (German spoken), and Passamar, Rua Siqueira Campos 7. (Try Atlântica Joias, Rua Fernando Mendes 5. **N.B.** Exchange House rates are normally a little better than banks, but it is recommended to check first.

Cables Embratel, Av. President Vargas 1012. Telegrams may be sent through any post office. Larger offices have telex.

Telephones Buy *fichas* for calls from public phones (in acoustic shells) at chemists and news stands; they are hard to come by late at night. International calls at Av. Copacabana 462, 2nd floor, international airport, Praça Tiradentes 41 (centre), Rodoviária, or Rua Dias da Cruz 182-4, 24 hrs, 7 days a week, or at Santos Dumont airport, 1st floor (0530-2300). Collect calls, national and international, dial 107 (no charge).

Poste Restante American Express, Av Atlântica 2316, Copacabana, and all large post offices (letters held for a month, recommended).

Markets North-eastern market at Campo de São Cristovão, with music and magic, on Sun. mornings. Flower market at Praça Olavo Bilac, off Rua Buenos Aires, in centre. Saturday antiques market on waterfront, near Praça 15 de Novembro (1000-1800) and handicraft and flea market Sat. (0900-1900) in Praça 15. Sunday stamp and coin market in Passeio Público, a.m. Sunday open-air handicrafts market at Praça General Osório, Ipanema. Excellent food and household-goods markets at various places in the city and suburbs (see newspapers for times and places).

Portuguese Instituto Brasil-Estados Unidos, Av. Copacabana 690, 5° andar.

Rail Central do Brasil Railway to São Paulo and Belo Horizonte. To São Paulo there are only the "Santa Cruz" night trains with sleepers and lounge cars (from US$5 for a seat to US$20 for a double cabin, 9 hrs., leaving 2230— recommended, book cabins in advance: 2 weeks ahead for weekend journeys, 3-5 days for weekdays), provision of service is erratic, check! Thurs. and Sat. night service to Belo Horizonte (US$10 pullman, US$20 bunk, US$27 cabin for two, 11 hrs., leaves 2100). No service to Brasília. There are suburban trains to Nova Iguaçu, Nilópolis, Campo Grande and elsewhere. Buses marked "E. Ferro" go to the railway station. For guided excursions by rail, contact Platur.

Airports Rio has two airports. The Santos Dumont airport on Guanabara Bay, right in the city, is used exclusively for Rio-São Paulo shuttle flights (US$39), air taxis and private planes. The shuttle services operate every half hour throughout the day from 0630 to 2230. Sit on right-hand side for views to São Paulo, other side coming back. The main airport (Galeão), on Governador Island, some 16 km. from the centre of Rio, is in two sections, international and domestic. Duty-free shops are well-stocked, but not especially cheap. The Real company runs an air-conditioned bus (*frescão*) from Galeão to Santos Dumont Airport, via the city centre, every hour (US$1) and another goes to Copacabana, US$2, also every hour, with space for baggage (also stops at Rodoviária). Air-conditioned taxis (Cootramo and Transcopass) have fixed rates (US$15 downtown, US$17.50 Copacabana) and you buy a ticket at the counter near the arrivals gate before getting into the car. The hire is for taxi, irrespective of number of passengers, and therefore the possibility of sharing with other passengers arises. Ordinary taxis also operate with the normal meter reading (about US$8 downtown, US$10 Copacabana). A good policy is to check at the Riotur counter before leaving, for folders, maps and advice; watch out for pirate taxis, whose drivers will want to charge up to US$50! Town bus No. 322 goes to Rio International airport, first one with direction Bananal.

Buses Bus fares to the following cities, with approximate journey times (book ahead if you can), are as follows:

	distance km.	ordinary US$	executive US$	leito US$	hours
São Paulo	434	4.00	6.00	8.00	6
Brasília	1,134	11.00	17.50	22.00	20
Belo Horizonte	429	6.00	8.00	12.00	7
Curitiba	839	9.00	—	18.00	11
Florianópolis	1,154	10.00	—	20.00	20
Foz do Iguaçu	1,500	18.00	—	23.00	23
Porto Alegre	1,603	16.50	—	33.00	26
Juiz de Fora	177	1.65	2.25	—	4
Vitória	519	5.50	—	11.00	8
Salvador	1,690	15.00	—	30.50	28
Recife	2,309	20.00	—	40.00	38
Fortaleza	2,861	25.00	—	50.00	48
São Luís	3,093	31.25	—	—	50
Belém	3,187	35.00	—	—	70

To Campo Grande, 21 hrs. with Andorinha, US$24. To Santos, 6 a day with Normandy, US$4, 7½ hrs., but not along coast road—which can only be done by taking local buses (Atlântico to São

BRAZIL 237

Sebastião, US$4.50, 7 hrs., 1030 and 1800) and changing at Ubatuba, Caraguatatuba or São Sebastião. The trip to Santos along the coast road can be done in one day, in either direction, but it needs at least one change and a 0600 start. To Ouro Preto, direct bus 2330 daily US$5, 9 hrs.

International: Asunción, 1,511 km. via Foz do Iguaçu, 30 hrs., (Pluma) US$20, *leito* US$40; Buenos Aires (Pluma), via Porto Alegre and Santa Fe, 44 hrs., 1230, US$50, *leito* US$110 (book 2 days in advance); Montevideo, only from São Paulo; Santiago de Chile, US$70 with Pluma or Gral. Urquiza, about 70 hours. The Buenos Aires and Montevideo services are fully booked a week in advance.

You are allowed to sleep at the bus station, if you don't lie down. The main bus station (the Rodoviária, at Av. Rodrigues Alves, corner with Av. Francisco Bicalho, just past the docks, reached by buses 104 from the centre, 127 and 128 from Copacabana and 456, 171 and 172 from Flamengo, or taxi about US$2), has a Riotur information centre. From Rodoviária, take bus to Largo do Machado or to Catete for central location with buses and cheap hotels. The local bus terminal is just outside the Rodoviária: turn right as you leave and run the gauntlet of taxi drivers. If you do need a taxi collect a ticket, which ensures against overcharging, from the official at the head of the taxi queue. On no account give the ticket to the taxi driver.

Hitch Hiking To hitch to Belo Horizonte or Brasília, take a C-3 bus from Av. Presidente Antônio Carlos to the railway station, cross through the station to a bus station, and catch the Nova Iguaçu bus. Ask to be let off at the Belo Horizonte turn off. For the motorway entrance north and south take bus 392 or 393 from Praça São Francisco.

Ferry Service From the "barcas" at Praça 15 de Novembro, ferry boats and launches cross every 10 mins. to Niterói (20-30 mins., US$0.05); to Paquetá Island (70-90 mins., see page 239 for fares). There are also hydrofoils ("aerobarcas") to Niterói every 10 mins. (about 10 mins., US$0.70). The Niterói ferry service is still being maintained, despite the competition from the 14 km. bridge linking the two sides of Guanabara Bay. (The approach to the bridge is on the elevated motorway from the centre, or via Av. Rio de Janeiro, in the Caju district; take the Av. Rodrigues Alves past the docks.) Bus 999 from the Passeio Público crosses the bridge.

The Suburbs of Rio de Janeiro

Copacabana, built on a narrow strip of land—only a little over 4 square kilometres—between mountain and sea, has one of the highest population densities in the world: 62,000 per square kilometre, or 250,000 in all. Its celebrated curved beach backed by skyscraper apartments is an unforgettable "must" for visitors. On all Rio's beaches you should take a towel or mat to protect you against sandflies; in the water stay near groups of other swimmers; bathing is generally dangerous.

Copacabana began to develop when the Old Tunnel was built in 1891 and an electric tram service reached it. Week-end villas and bungalows sprang up; all have now gone. In the 1930s the Copacabana Palace Hotel was the only tall building; it is now one of the lowest on the beach. The opening of the New Tunnel in the 1940s led to an explosion of population which shows no sign of having spent its force. Buildings of less than 12 storeys are still being replaced by high flats and luxury hotels.

There is almost everything in this fabulous "city within a city". The shops, mostly in Avenida Copacabana and the Rua Barata Ribeiro, are excellent. A military fort at the far end of the beach commands the entrance to Rio Bay and prevents a seashore connection with the Ipanema and Leblon beaches. However, parts of the military area are now being handed over to civilian use, the first being the Parque Garota de Ipanema at Arpoador, the fashionable Copacabana end of the Ipanema beach. Buses to and from the city centre are plentiful and cheap, about US$0.10. If you are going to the centre from Copacabana, look for "Castelo", "Praça 15", "E. Ferro" or "Praça Mauá" on the sign by the front door. "Aterro" means the expressway between Botafogo and downtown Rio (not open Sundays). From the centre to Copacabana is easier as all buses in that direction are clearly marked. Aterro bus does journey in 15 minutes.

Beyond Copacabana are the beautiful seaside suburbs of Ipanema and Leblon; they are a little less built-up than Copacabana, and their beaches tend to be cleaner, though no less dangerous, than Copacabana's. (Posto 9 beach in Ipanema is a gay beach.) Backing Ipanema and Leblon is the Lagoa Rodrigo de Freitas, a salt-water lagoon on which Rio's rowing and small-boat sailing clubs are active; too polluted for bathing. Beyond Leblon the coast is rocky; the Avenida

238 BRAZIL

Niemeyer skirts the cliffs on the journey past Vidigal, a small beach where the *Sheraton* is situated, to the newest seaside suburbs of São Conrado and Barra da Tijuca (camp site). At the far end of Barra da Tijuca is the Recreio dos Bandeirantes, a safe bathing beach with good restaurants (700 bus from São Conrado). Buses from Botafogo Metro terminal to Ipanema: some take integrated Metro-Bus tickets, saving 25%; look for the blue signs on the windscreen.

On New Year's Eve the festival of Iemanjá is held by the *umbandistas* on the beaches of Copacabana, Ipanema and Leblon (see page 230).

Santa Teresa, a hilly inner suburb SW of the centre, well known as the coolest part of Rio, still has many colonial and 19th-century buildings, set in narrow, curving, tree-lined streets. See particularly the Convent (only the outside; the Carmelite nuns do not admit visitors), the Chácara do Céu Museum (see page 231), the Hotel Santa Teresa (the oldest house in the area), Vista Alegre, the Rua Aprazível, and Largo de Guimarães. Santa Teresa is best visited on the traditional open-sided trams, the only ones left in Rio, which leave from the Largo da Carioca in the centre of the city, for Dois Irmãos, crossing to Santa Teresa on top of the old 18th-century aqueduct known as the Arcos (fare US$0.05) Be careful: thieves sometimes run alongside the tram, jump on, and try to relieve you of watches, cameras etc.

Maracanã Stadium is one of the largest sports centres in the world. The football ground has seating capacity for 200,000 spectators and most matches are played on Sun. (entrance from US$0.25-standing-to US$6); matches are worth going to for the fireworks and samba bands of the spectators, even if you're not a football fan). A smaller covered gymnasium for basket-ball, boxing and other indoor sports, the Maracanãzinho, can accommodate 20,000 persons. There are an athletics stadium holding 8000 spectators and an aquatic sports centre with two Olympic pools and stands for 8000 more spectators. Open to visitors Mon.-Fri. 0830-1800 (non-match days) at Gate 18, at charge of US$0.50. Tours in Portuguese: admission to museum an additional US$0.30. Buses 433, 434 and 455 from Copacabana; 433 and 434 from Flamengo; from Leblon, 464 via Ipanema and Copacabana; 221 and 231 from Castelo; 249 and 269 from Praça Tiradentes; and 238 and 239 from Praça 15 de Novembro; from Praça Maua, 241 or 262; also Metro from Botafogo and Centre. Hotels can arrange visits to football matches: good idea Sundays when the metro is closed and buses very full.

Corcovado (710 metres) is the hunch-backed peak surmounted by a 40-metre high statue of Christ the Redeemer completed in 1931, weighing, with its base, 1,200 tons. There is a superb view from the top (sometimes obscured by mist), to which there is a road from the Laranjeiras district; both car and cog-train (30 mins. each way) put down their passengers behind the statue—there is a climb of 220 steps to the top, near which there is a café for light refreshments. Mass is held on Sun. in a small chapel in the statue pedestal. The floodlighting was designed in 1931 by Marconi himself.

Take a Cosme Velho bus (108, 422, 497, 498, 583) or taxi to the cog railway station at Rua Cosme Velho 513. Some buses from corner of Avs. Rio Branco and Getúlio Vargas in centre. Service every hour until 1900: about 1½ hrs. for the round trip, exclusive of waiting time (cost: US$2 return; single tickets available). Minibuses also operate from the station, return trip (1 hour stop) US$1.50, tickets obtained from office. Also, a 206 bus does the very attractive run from Praça Tiradentes (or a 407 from Largo do Machado) to Silvestre (the railway has no stop here now). An active walk of one hour will bring one to the top, and the road is shady. (Best done in company; robberies are very common in this neighbourhood.) Coach trips are not recommended because they are too brief.

Pão de Açúcar (Sugar Loaf, 396 metres) is a massive granite cone at the *entrance* to Guanabara Bay, ascended by thousands in the cable-car. The bird's eye view of the city and beaches is very beautiful. There is a restaurant (good, closes 1900) and a playground for children on the Morro da Urca, half way up, where there are also shows at night (weekends). You can get refreshments at the top. On the small path that leads down in the direction of Morro Cara de Cão there are toucans and macaws in cages. Buses 107 or 442 (from the centre or Flamengo) and 511 (from Copacabana) take you to the station, Av. Pasteur 520, at the foot.

The cable car timetable: Praia Vermelha to Urca: first car goes up at 0800, and the last comes down at 2215. From Urca to Sugar Loaf the first connecting cable car goes up at 0815 and the last leaves the summit at 2200; the return trip costs US$1.25 (US$0.65 to Morro da Urca, half-way up). The old cableway has been completely rebuilt. Termini are now ample and efficient and the present Italian cable cars carry 75 passengers. Even on the most crowded days there is little queuing. Beware of thieves at the cable car starting point.

Tijuca National Park, open 0600-2100, is for those interested in taking a forest walk through mountain scenery. An approximately 2-3 hr. walk will bring you to the summit of the Pico da Tijuca (1,012 metres), which gives a good idea of the tropical vegetation of the interior and a fine view of the bay and its shipping. On entering the park at Alto de Boa Vista, follow the sparse signposts to Bom Retiro, a good picnic place (1½ hrs walk), passing by the Cascatinha Taunay, Mayrink Chapel (built 1860) and the restaurant *A Floresta*. At Bom Retiro the road ends and there is another hour's walk up a fair footpath to the summit; take the path from the right of the Bom Retiro drinking fountain; not the more obvious steps from the left. The last part consists of steps carved out of the solid rock; take care of children at the summit as there are several sheer drops, invisible because of bushes. The route is shady for almost its entire length. All the facilities in the park were renovated in 1980. The panels painted in the Mayrink Chapel by Cândido Portinari have been replaced by copies and the originals will probably be installed in the Museu de Arte Moderna. Maps of the Park are available.

Take a 221 from Praça 15 de Novembro, 233 or 234 bus from the Rodoviária, or 454 from Copacabana or from Praça Sáenz Pena, Tijuca (reached by metro) to Alto da Boa Vista, for the park entrance. Other places of interest not passed on the walk to the peak are the Paul and Virginia Grotto, the Vista do Almirante and the Mesa do Imperador (viewpoints). A good restaurant in Parque Floresta is *Os Esquilos* (squirrels). Allow at least 5 to 6 hrs. for the excursion. Also, one of the Raymundo Castro Maia museums is nearby (see page 231).

Barra da Tijuca This new and very rapidly developing residential area can be reached from the Tijuca Forest by continuing on the 233 or 234 bus (from Praça Sáenz Pena, very good views of São Conrado and Barra), or from the city bus station at Rua São José, from Santos Dumont airport (Campo Grande or Santa Cruz bus, Pegaso) and from Copacabana via Leblon beach (bus 553). From Botafogo metro terminus, take bus 524.

Barra da Tijuca is also one of the principal recreation areas of Rio, the prime attraction being its 20-km. sandy beach. Bus 700 from Praça São Conrado (terminal of bus 553 from Copacabana) goes the full length of the beach to Recreio dos Bandeirantes. Apart from this, there are innumerable bars and restaurants, campsites (see page 223), motels and hotels. The facilities include Riocenter, a 600,000 sq.m. convention complex and the huge Barra Shopping and Carrefour shopping centres. Watch the hang-gliders jumping from the hilltops at weekends. Live concerts on São Conrado beach during summer (Nov.-Feb.).

The Autódromo (motor racing track) is beyond Barra in the Jacarepaguá district. The Brazilian Grand Prix is held here or at Interlagos, São Paulo, alternately in January.

Viewpoints Apart from the Pico da Tijuca, Corcovado and Pão de Açúcar, splendid views of different parts of Rio can be seen from the Vista Chinesa (420 metres), where from a Chinese-style pavilion one can see the inland lake (the Lagoa), Ipanema and Leblon; the Mesa do Imperador (Emperor's Table) and Vista do Almirante (Admiral's View) in the Tijuca Forest; and the Mirante de Dona Marta (340 metres) off the Corcovado road, with the same direction of view as the Corcovado, but as it is lower the details can be seen more clearly. There is as yet no public transport to any of these places. Above Botafogo is the Mirante do Pasmado viewing point, reached from Rua General Severiano.

Paquetá Island in Guanabara Bay can be visited by more or less two-hourly ferry services from Praça Quinze de Novembro (fare US$0.15 by boat, 1 hr.,

240　**BRAZIL**

US$1 by hydrofoil, every ½ hr., 20 mins. journey, which more than doubles its price Sats., Suns. and holidays). Horse-drawn carriages hire for US$6 per hr. (many have harnesses which cut into the horse's flesh). Tour by "trenzinho", a tractor pulling trailers, US$0.80. Bicycles for hire from US$1 per hr. (deposit US$2). Very crowded at weekends and public holidays, but usually very quiet during the week, though there can be aircraft noise. Reasonable food and drink prices.

Hotel Paquetá, E, *Flamboyant* and *Lido. Porto Fino Restaurant,* expensive and poor food.

Other boat trips, by *bateau mouche* (restaurant), around Guanabara Bay depart from Av. Néstor Moreira 11, Botafogo, first two trips at 0930, third at 1420, fares from US$25. Other companies: Aquatur (Tel.: 230-9273), Brazilian Marina Turismo, Camargo (Tel.: 275-0643), Passamar, Siqueira Campos 7 (Tel.: 236-4136), Greyline (Tel.: 274-7146), Soletur (Bay trips Sat. and Sun. only) and American Sightseeing, Av. N.S. Copacabana 605, Sala 1204 (Tel.: 236-3551). The last three offer a day cruise, including lunch, to Jaguanum Island (see page 245, under Itacuruçá) and a sundown cruise around Guanabara Bay, also deep-sea fishing expeditions and private charters.

Entering Rio from the W, an alternative to the BR-101 and Avenida Brasil, is to leave BR-101 on the road to Santa Cruz, continuing 6 km. to the fishing village of Sepetiba, quiet other than at weekends. Along the coast is Pedra de Guaratiba, from where you join Avenida das Américas, turning off right soon afterwards to Ponta do Picão and Guaratiba, a pretty seaside resort on a rocky, narrow, steep ledge between mountain and sea (good beaches and a playground for the rich). Another 2 km. along the main road is another (unmarked) right turn leading to a restaurant at the summit, with fantastic views, then down to Praia de Grumari, which is unspoilt except for 2 restaurants and a campsite (US$1 p.p.). It is then 30 km. to Copacabana, via Praia dos Bandeirantes (Dieter Reinmuth).

The State of Rio de Janeiro: East from Rio

Niterói, founded in 1573, the ex-capital of the State of Rio de Janeiro, across the bay by bridge or ferries, is a city with 386,000 population.

The Rio-Niterói bridge (Ponte Costa e Silva) has a length of 14 km. Toll for cars, US$0.30. Motorway connection to centre of Rio. Bus 999 from the corner of Senador Dantas and Av. Beira Mar, Rio, crosses the bridge to Niterói and Icaraí (US$0.30); also 996 and 998 from the Botanical Gardens (all three go to the Rodoviária in Rio).

Frequent ferry boat and hydrofoil service (see page 237) from Praça 15 de Novembro, Rio. There is a Flumitur tourist information booth to the right of the ferry-boat station. Nearby you can take the 33 bus (marked "via Froes") to the beaches of Icaraí, São Francisco and Jurujuba on the bay, a beautiful ride. Sit on the right-hand side. A few minutes' walk from where the bus route ends at Jurujuba are the attractive twin beaches of Adão and Eva, with lovely views of Rio across the bay. From Praça General Gomes Carneiro, near the ferry boats, take a 38 bus to Piratininga, Itaipu and Itacoatiara, fabulous ocean beaches and the best in the area, about 40 minutes' ride through picturesque countryside. The beaches inside the bay, though calm, are often overcrowded and polluted, but no more so than those opposite in Rio. The forts on this side of the bay include Santa Cruz (16th century, still a military establishment), Barão do Rio Branco (1633), Gragoatá and Nossa Senhora da Boa Viagem.

You should also visit the church of Boa Viagem (1633), built on an island connected to the mainland by a short causeway, a few minutes' walk from Icaraí beach. Nearby, on Rua Tiradentes, is the interesting Antônio Parreira Museum. The Museu de Arqueologia de Itaipu is in the ruins of the 18th century Santa Teresa Convent, and also covers the archaeological site of Duna Grande on Itaipu beach.

Hotels *Novotel Rio-Niterói,* Praia de Gragoatá, Telex 021-7252, B; *Samanguaia,* E; *Niterói Palace,* Rua Andrade Neves 134, D-C; *Imperial,* E.

Clubs Rio Cricket, bus 57 from ferry passes. Rio Sailing, bus 33 marked "via Froes".

Electric Current 110 volts, A.C., 60 cycles.

To the east of Niterói lie a series of salt-water lagoons, the Lagos Fluminenses. Two small lakes lie behind the beaches of Piratininga and Itaipu near Niterói, but they are polluted and ringed by mud. The next lakes are much larger, those of Maricá and Saquarema; though they are still muddy, the

BRAZIL 241

waters are relatively unpolluted, and wild life abounds in the scrub and bush around the lagoons. At the outlet to the lake of Saquarema (turn right off the main road at Bacaxá) is the holiday village of **Saquarema**. Of particular interest is the little white church of Nossa Senhora de Nazaré (1675) built atop a green promontory jutting into the ocean. Saquarema is the centre for surfing in Brazil, and the national championships are held here each year in May. Beware of strong currents, though.

The largest lake is that of **Araruama**, famous for its medicinal mud. It is so large that it seems more like a bay than a lagoon. The salinity is extremely high, the waters calm, and almost the entire lake is surrounded by sandy beaches, making it very popular with families looking for safe, unpolluted bathing. The major industry of the area is salt, and all around one can see the saltpans and the metal wind pumps used to carry the water into the pans. At the eastern end of the lake lies the village of **São Pedro de Aldeia,** which, in spite of intensive development, still retains much of its colonial charm, and has a lovely Jesuit church built in 1723.

Hotels in the lake district: Saquarema: *Sol e Mar*, C; *Katy Motel*, C; *Pousada do Holandés*, Av Vilamar 377, at Itaúna beach, E, highly recommended, many languages spoken by Dutch owner and his Brazilian wife (who runs the local day-care centre), good meals—follow the signs, or take a taxi (US$0.50), from Saquarema. Restaurant in Saquarema, *Term Uma Né Chama Teré*, very good, in main square. Araruama: *Senzala*, on Iguabinha beach, 10 km. from Araruama, B with meals; *La Gondola*, on the lake beach, D, overpriced; *Parque Hotel*, B; *Lakes Hotel*, over the bus station, B; *Chalés do Coqueiral*, chalets on lake beach, C. São Pedro de Aldeia: *Solar de Iguaba*, C; *Vilabranca Village*, over 100 chalets, B with meals, and *Costa do Sol*, B, on Iguaba Grande beach, 14 km. from São Pedro. At Ponta Negra is *Pousada Colonial*, suites and bungalows in B-C range, breakfast included, Tel.: Rio, 451-6254 for reservations.

The ocean beaches beside these lagoons, except for the sheltered coves of Ponta Negra and Saquarema, are rough and lonely. The whole area is perfect for camping; there are campsites (including Camping Clube do Brasil) at Araruama (close to the *Parque Hotel*) and São Pedro de Aldeia. A very steep road connects the beaches of Itaipu and Itacoatiara with BR-106 (and on to Araruama) via the village of Itaipu-Açu, with beach and good camping. Most maps do not show a road beyond Itaipu-Açu; it is certainly too steep for buses.

An alternative to the route from Niterói to Araruama through the lagoons is via Manilla, Itaboraí and Rio Bonito, on the BR-101 and RJ-124; this is a fruit-growing region.

Cabo Frio, 156 km. from Rio, about 2½ hrs. by bus (US$3), is a popular holiday and week-end haunt of Cariocas because of its cool weather, beaches, scenery, sailing and good under-water swimming (but mosquitoes are a problem). The ocean beach is much less frequented than the bay beach. The São Mateus fort nearby was built by the French; it is in a state of disrepair.

Hotels *Malibu Palace*, B, overpriced, unhelpful, not recommended; *Marliru Acapulco*, A; *Cabo Frio Sol* (motel), D. 20 other hotels with descending prices down to *Caravela* and *Colonial*, both E. *Nanaque*, 2 blocks from bus station (which is 2 km. from centre), 3 blocks from sea, F; two similar nearby. Youth Hostel, both sexes, open all year to IYHF members, G, very friendly.

Camping Camping Clube do Brasil sites at Estrada dos Passageiros, near town; at Km. 135 on the Rio road, 4 km. outside town, in Palmeiras; and at Arraial do Cabo on Praia dos Anjos, crowded beach. 10 km. to S. Cambrás has a site at Estrada dos Passageiros. Also site at Cabo Yacht club.

Tourists are also recommended to visit **Búzios**, NE of Cabo Frio, a resort built up in Portuguese colonial styles, with unmade roads so as to discourage fast drivers. It has 25 sandy coves, calm unpolluted waters (superb for windsurfing), beautiful scenery, plenty of good hotels and *pousadas* (mostly C upwards, e.g. *Casa D'elas Pousada*, and *Pousada do Sol*, Praia da Armaçaõ), but very expensive, as is everything else (except the vicious mosquitoes). Best route from Rio (2 hrs. by car) is the paved road towards Macaé, with a paved turnoff to Búzios. Direct road from Cabo Frio (bus 45 mins.) is unpaved. Camping is allowed. Tourist information office near bus station. Very crowded during Brazilian holiday season and extremely difficult to get hotel booking. Good restaurants: *Frank's* in Ossos and *Natural* in Armação. Popular bars are *Delikatessen* and *Tempero's*.

Continuing to the north, one comes to the seaside resorts of Barra de São João, **Rio das Ostras** (*Hotel Saint Tropez*, D; *Hotel Mirante do Poeta*, D) and **Macaé** (Hotels: *Colonial*, D, friendly, helpful, comfortable; *Turismo* and *Panorama*, D; *Central*, on main street, F, clean, nice, friendly, good breakfast, secure parking), all containing sheltered coves with good swimming and scuba diving. Macaé is also the supply centre for the offshore oil industry so there are usually several foreigners in town enjoying a beer.

From Rio and Niterói a first class highway, the BR-101, runs NE past Macaé to

242 BRAZIL

Campos (bus Rio-Macaé 2½-3 hrs., every ½ hr., Mil e Um or Rápido Macaense; to Campos, Mil e Um, hourly, 4½ hrs.). At Km. 222 is the Biological Reserve of Poço das Antas (2 hrs. drive from Rio). Many animals (including the *mico-leão*—this is its only natural habitat) roam in the forest.

Campos is a busy industrial city, some 276 km. from Rio de Janeiro (70 km. from Macaé). It stands 56 km. from the mouth of the Rio Paraíba, up which coffee planting originally spread to São Paulo state. Coffee is still grown near Campos, though the region is now one of the largest sugar-producing zones in Brazil. Important offshore oil discoveries have been made nearby. Town is not uninteresting. Population: 174,000.

Hotels *Terraza Tourist*, E, 2-star; *Planície*, Rua 13 de Maio 56, E; *Palace*, Av. 15 de Novembro 143, D. *Silva*, some way behind church on municipal *praça*, F, breakfast, clean, safe parking.

Travelling N, as an alternative to BR-101 to Vitória, one can take a detour inland, going through São Fidélis, Cambiasca, Itoacara and on to **Santo Antônio de Pádua**, 130 km. from Campos, a pleasant town on the Rio Pomba. (*Hotel das Aguas*, a short walk from the centre, E, a resort hotel in a park with pool, health centre and bottling plant for the local mineral water which is used for treating cardiovascular illness; *Braga*, in town, F, clean, friendly, good food.) Take road No. 393 to Itaperuna, Bom Jesus do Itabapoana and into Espírito Santo, then road No. 484 to **Guaçuí** (*Grande Hotel Minas*, F, friendly, clean; *Restaurant Kontiki*, very good), one of the starting points for the Parque Nacional do Caparaó (see page 248). Then take the road 482 to Cachoeira do Itapemirim and the BR-101 (see page 246).

Petrópolis (population: 149,000) is a summer hill resort and industrial city at 840 metres, 68 km. N of Rio. It is reached by bus along a steep, scenic mountain toll road (US$1 weekdays, US$1.50 weekends). Until 1962 Petrópolis was the "summer capital" of Brazil; it was founded in 1843 as a summer refuge by Dom Pedro II. Now it combines manufacturing industry (particularly textiles, which may be bought cheaply) with floral beauty and hill scenery. The Emperor's Palace (Museu Imperial), which seems to express very faithfully what we know of Dom Pedro II's character, is a modest but elegant building, fully furnished and equipped, containing the Crown Jewels and other imperial possessions. It is assiduously well-kept: one might think the imperial family had left the day before one's visit, rather than in 1889. Open Tues.-Sun., 1200-1730. Entry US$0.30 (Tues. free). Well worth a visit is the Gothic-style Cathedral, completed in 1925, which contains the tombs of the Emperor and Empress (guide in English, US$0.20).

Hotels *Casa do Sol*, 4-star hotel out on road to Rio, C; *Margaridas*, Monsenhor Bacelar 126, chalet-type hotel set in lovely gardens with swimming pool, charming proprieters, D; *Auto-Tour* (*Fazenda Inglesa*) at km. 51 on the Petrópolis by-pass, very chic, B, with meals; *Riverside Parque*, Rua Hermogéneo Silva 522, D; *Casablanca Center*, General Osório 28, C; *Casablanca*, Sete de Setembro beside Imperial Palace, D, good atmosphere in older part, pool, very clean; *Casablanca Palace*, Primeiro de Março 123, D; *Gran Solar* (*Pousado do Carmo*), Benjamin Constant 288, D; *Comércio*, opp. bus station, F, with breakfast; *Pensão Esther*, Rua do Imperador, F, incl. breakfast.

Camping Associação Brasileira de Camping and YMCA, Araras district. Can reserve space at Rio YMCA, Tel.: 231-9860

Restaurants *Churrascaria Majórica*, Av. do Imperador (ex 15 de Novembro) 754; *Mirthes Paranhos*, Irmãos d'Angelo 99; *Cantina Italiana*, Paulo Barbosa 48, clean, pleasant; *Maloca*, Wáshington Luís 466; *Bauernstube*, João Pessoa 297. *Vegetariano*, Rua do Imperador 288, sobreloja 1, good and cheap.

Attractions and Excursions Museu Ferreira da Cunha, Fernandes Vieira 390 (old road to Rio) shows large collection of arms, open Sat. and Sun. (only to groups, need to arrange in advance) 0900-1700. Summer home of air pioneer Santos Dumont, showing early inventions. Crystal Palace in Praça da Confluência, former imperial ballroom and now exhibition centre. Orquidário *Binot*, Rua Fernandes Vieira 390 (take bus to Vila Isabel; open Mon.-Sat., 0800-1100, 1300-1700), a huge collection of orchids from all over Brazil (plants may be purchased).

Buses leave from Rio every 10 mins. throughout the day (US$0.70). Return tickets are not available, so passengers must buy tickets for the return bus as soon as they arrive in Petrópolis. Journey 75 mins. each way. The ordinary buses leave from the Rodoviária in Rio; there is a new service of air-conditioned buses, every hour, from Av. Nilo Peçanha, US$0.90. There is a direct overnight bus from São Paulo.

Teresópolis (population: 80,000; 910 metres), near the Serra dos Órgãos, is

BRAZIL 243

124 km. NE of Rio. It was the favourite summer residence of the Empress Teresa Cristina. See the Colina dos Mirantes hill, the Sloper and Iaci lakes, the Imbui and Amores waterfalls, and the Fonte Judith. Tourist information office some way from bus station (not very helpful). São Pedro festival on June 29 is celebrated with fireworks.

About 30,000 hectares of the Serra dos Órgãos, so called because their strange shapes are said to recall organ-pipes, are now a National Park. The main attraction is the precipitous Dedo de Deus (God's Finger) Peak. There is also the rock formation Mulher de Pedra 12 km. out on the Nova Friburgo road, and the Von Martinó natural-history museum. The highest point is the Pedra Açu, 2,400 metres. A path leads up the 2,260-metre Pedra do Silo, 3-4 hours' climb. Entrance to park, US$0.25. IBDF (The National Forestry Institute) has some hostels, US$4.60 full board, or US$3.10 first night, US$1.50 thereafter, a bit rough. Camping, US$0.50. A good way to see the Park is to do the Rio-Teresópolis-Petrópolis-Rio circuit; a scenic day trip. The Rio-Teresópolis road is now a toll road (cars US$1, US$1.50 at weekends) from Km. 10.6.

Martin Crossland writes: Leave the Rodoviária bus station in Rio on the 0800 bus or before (Viação Teresópolis) for the 1¾-hour ride and up into the mountains to Teresópolis (sit on right side of bus). Upon arrival at the bus station, buy another ticket right away for Petrópolis (Viação Teresópolis) for the 1200 bus in order to get a good seat, as the bus fills rapidly. This gives you 2¾ hours to wander around. If you feel up to a steep 1½-hr. climb, try the Colina dos Mirantes for a sweeping view of the city and surroundings. For the less energetic, a taxi is not dear.

The drive from Teresópolis to Petrópolis is extremely beautiful (90 mins.), passing right through the Serra dos Órgãos. (Sit on left side.) The views on either side are spectacular. Again, upon arrival in Petrópolis at 1330, buy your ticket to Rio (Facil or Unica). Take the 1715 bus "via Quitandinha", and you might catch the sunset over the mountains (in May, June, July, take the 1615 bus). This gives you time to visit most of the attractions listed in the city description.

Hotels *São Moritz*, Swiss-style, outside on the Nova Friburgo road, km. 36, lowest rates, B, with meals; *Clube Caxangá*, resort-type, C; *Philips*, Rua Duval Fonseca, C; *Alpina*, Parque Imbui, on Petrópolis road, B; *Higino Palace*, Av. Oliveira Botelho 328, D, with meals; *Vila Nova do Paquequer*, Av. Alberto Torres 1149 (by the Guarani waterfall), E; *Várzea Palace*, Rua Sebastião Teixeira 41, F. *Florida*, Av. Lúcio Meira 467, F, with bargaining.

Camping National Park, entrance to Teresópolis from Rio, full facilities; Quinta de Barra, km. 3 on Petrópolis road; Vale das Choupanas, km. 30 on Rio road.

Restaurants *Taberna Alpina*, Duque de Caxias 131; *Cantina Riviera*, Praça Baltazar de Silveira 112; *La Cremaille*, Av. Feliciano Sodré 1012; *De Stéfano*, Av. Lúcio Meira 695. *Bar Gota d'Água*, Praça Baltasar da Silveira 16 for trout or feijoada.

Bus, Rio-Teresópolis Buses leave every half-hour from Rodoviária. As return tickets are not issued, passengers should book for the return journey as soon as they arrive at Teresópolis. Time, 1¾ hrs. each way; fare US$0.70. From Teresópolis to Petropólis, every 2 hrs. from 0900-2100, US$1.25.

Nova Friburgo (850 metres above sea-level), is a popular watering place (around 30 hotels) during summer months, in a beautiful valley with excellent walking and riding possibilities. Founded by Swiss settlers from Fribourg, it can be reached by bus (US$2.10) from Rio (every half hour) in 3 hrs. or by car in 1 hr. 45 min. Pop.: 80,000. Cable car from Praça dos Suspiros 650 metres up the Morro da Cruz, for view of rugged country. Road to Teresópolis paved.

Hotels *Bucsky*, 5 km. out on Niterói road, B, with meals; *Vale do Luar*, on outskirts, C; *São Paulo*, Rua Monsenhor Miranda 41, E; *Everest*, behind Chess Club, F, comfortable, good breakfasts; *Sans-Souci*, 1 km. out, B, with meals, D without; *Schumacher*, 2-star, E, Praça do Suspiro 114; *Garlipp*, German-run, in chalets, C, with meals, at Muri, km. 70.5 from Rio, 10 km. from Nova Friburgo, Tel.: 0245-421330. Under same ownership is *Fazenda São João*, D, Tel.: (0245) 42-1304, 11 km. from *Garlipp* up a side road (impassable in the wet), riding, swimming, sauna, tennis, hummingbirds and orchids. Also *Mury Garden*, with swimming pool, C, with meals, 10 km. away at Muri (km. 70 on Niterói road). 12 km. from Nova Friburgo at Amparo is *Jequitibá*, D, Tel.: 0245-221831, sports facilities, restaurant.

Camping Camping Clube do Brasil has sites on Niterói road, at Cônego (7 km. out) and Muri (10 km. out). Cambrás site also at Cônego, and private site at Fazenda Sanandu, 20 km. out on same road.

244 BRAZIL

Restaurants *Majórica,* traditional *churrascaria; Natural,* Rua Farinha Filho 2515, in centre, vegetarian, good and cheap.

The State of Rio de Janeiro: West from Rio

Volta Redonda, Brazil's chief steel centre, stands on a broad bend of the Rio Paraíba at an altitude of 565 metres, 113 km. W of Rio along the railway to São Paulo. In 1942 it was a little village; today it has one of the largest steel works in Latin America and a population of 178,000. The mills are on the river bank and the town spreads up the surrounding wooded and gardened slopes.

Hotels *Sider Palace,* Rua 33 No. 10, D; *Embaixador,* 1-star, F; *Bela Vista,* Alto de Boa Vista, on a hill overlooking town, C.

Visitors who have a permit from the Companhia Siderúrgica Nacional, Av. Treze de Maio 13, Rio de Janeiro (apply ten days in advance), or locally from the *Bela Vista* hotel, are allowed to inspect the mills. Visits start at 0900, and last 2½-3 hrs. The town can be reached from Rio by buses or minibuses in 2½ hrs., US$0.90.

North of Volta Redonda is Miguel Pereira, set in the mountain region with an excellent climate; nearby is the Javari lake, a popular recreational spot. Two *Hotel-Fazendas* (both C) near Miguel Pereira are *Quindins* and *Javari,* both with restaurant, swimming pool, sports grounds, etc. Further north, and still in the mountains are the university centres of Vassouras and Valença; both are historical monuments. 35 km. from Valença is Conservatória, another colonial town. Some 30 km. W of Volta Redonda, in the town of Resende, is the Military Academy of Agulhas Negras. Grounds, with captured German guns of World War II, are open to the public. Resende can be reached by bus from Aparecida do Norte (see page 279), several daily, US$1.25, or from Rio, 5 a day, 2½ hrs., US$1.50.

The **Itatiaia National Park** (founded 1937), on the Serra de Itatiaia in the Mantiqueira chain of mountains, is a few km. N of the Dutra Highway from a point 48 km. W of Volta Redonda: 174 km. from Rio. Road to it is paved. The town of Itatiaia is surrounded by picturesque mountain peaks and lovely waterfalls. It has good hotels, and plenty of camping sites: the Camping Clube do Brasil site is entered at Km. 148 on the Via Dutra. This is a good area for climbing (Pico das Agulhas Negras 2,787 metres, Pico da Prateleira 2,540 metres) and trekking; information and maps can be obtained at the park office. Worth seeing are the curious rock formations of Pedra de Taruga and Pedra de Maçã, and the waterfall Véu de Noiva (many birds). Basic accommodation in cabins and dormitories is available in the park; you will need to book in season, say 30 days in advance, by writing to Administração do Parque Nacional de Itatiaia, Itatiaia 27540, RJ. The Administração operates a refuge in the park which acts as a starting point for climbs and treks: information on these from Club Excursionista Brasileira, Av. Almirante Barroso 2, 8th floor, Tel.: 220-3695, Rio. Tres Picos wildlife trail near *Hotel Simon;* ask at hotel desk for info. There is a Museum of Flora and Fauna, closed Mondays. Entrance to Park, US$0.35.

Hotels *Simon,* Km. 13 park road, B, with meals, lovely views; *Repouso Itatiaia,* Km. 10 park road, B, with meals; *Hotel do Ypé,* Km. 13 park road, B, with meals; *Fazenda da Serra,* Via Dutra Km. 151, C, with meals; *Tyll,* Via Dutra Km. 155, C, with meals. *Motel Jahu,* Via Dutra Km. 156, E, very friendly, clean, comfortable.

In the same region, 175 km. from Rio, is the small town of **Penedo,** which in the 1930s attracted Finnish settlers who brought the first saunas to Brazil. This weekend resort, popular with the prosperous of São Paulo and Rio, hippies and naturalists, also provides horseback riding, and swimming in the Portinho river. Some 33 km. beyond Penedo (part of road unpaved) is the small village of **Visconde de Mauá,** which has cheap lodgings: enquire at *Vendinha da Serra,* natural food restaurant and store. Fine scenery and walks; roads to 3 other small hill towns, Maringá, Maromba and Mirantão, at about 1,700 metres. Buses to Visconde de Mauá from Resende, 1500 and 1630, 1½ hrs., US$1. Further along the Dutra Highway (186 km. from Rio) is the small town of **Engenheiro Passos,** from which a road (BR-354) leads to São Lourenço and Caxambu in Minas Gerais (see page 260), passing Agulhas Negras. One can climb Agulhas Negras from this side by taking the road from Registro pass (1,670 metres) to the Abrigo Rebouças refuge, which is manned all year round (take your own food, US$0.80 to stay), at 2,350 metres.

BRAZIL 245

Hotels Penedo: *Bertell*, C, with meals; also *da Cachoeira*, *Moradas do Penedo*, 2 campsites. Restaurants *Viking*, *Mariska* (Hungarian), and *Baianinha*. Engenheiro Passos: *Villa Forte*, C, with meals; *Pensão das Flores*, Visconde de Mauá, E, with meals. Nine campsites in the area.

The new Rio-Santos highway, and even more the parallel road along the coast, are making the beautiful coastal region SW of Rio more accessible. It is now complete right through to Bertioga (see page 273), which has good links both with Santos and (avoiding Santos) to São Paulo. There are direct Rio-Santos buses, and direct services from Rio to Angra dos Reis, Parati, Ubatuba, Caraguatatuba, and São Sebastião.

Itacuruçá, 91 km. from Rio, is a delightful place to visit if you like beautiful scenery and peace and quiet, with islands off the coast.

Hotels On Ilha de Itacuruçá, is *Hotel Pierre*, reached by boat from Coroa Grande, north of Itacuruçá on the mainland, 5 mins. (boats also go from Itacuruçá); hotel has 27 rooms in price range L, restaurant, bars, sporting facilities. For bookings Tel.: Rio 521-1546 or 289-7546, or Saveiros Tours, 267-2792. At S end of the island is *Pousada do Artur*, B; Tel.: Rio 256-6227. The *Hotel Jaguanum*, Ilha de Jaguanum, Itacuruçá, has apartments and chalets with private bathrooms. There are beautiful walks around the island. Reservations for the hotel, which include the boat trip to and from the island (at 1000 and 1700), cost US$120-130 per day for two with all meals. The only extra is the bus, US$3 return, which picks you up at your hotel. Book by calling 235-2893 or 237-5119, in Rio, or enquire at Sepetiba Turismo, Av. N.S. de Copacabana 605, s. 202.

Ilha de Itacuruçá can also be reached from Muriqui, a popular beach resort at Km. 27; bathing also in the Véu de Noiva waterfall. The next beach along the coast is Praia Grande.

Mangaratiba, half-way from Rio to Angra dos Reis, has muddy beaches, but pleasant surroundings and better beaches outside the town, for example Ibicuí, São Brás, Praia Brava, Saco, Guiti and Cação.

Hotels *Moreira*, F, cheapest; 2 others, more expensive. None is crowded because the town is not a tourist resort.

Daily ferry (Conerj) to Ilha Grande island (see below), at 0900 Tues., Sat. and Sun., 0830 all other days, and 1400, 1½ hrs., highly recommended; return ferry daily at 1600, fare US$0.20. Morning departures continue on to Angra dos Reis. Ferry departures and destinations can be checked at ferry station at Praça Quinze de Novembro, Rio. Buses from Rio Rodoviária every 15 mins, US$0.90.

Angra dos Reis, founded in 1502, is about 197 km. SW of Rio by bus; 50 km. S, near Cunhambebe, is the site of Brazil's first atomic-power stations. A small port with an important fishing and shipbuilding industry, it has several small bays with good bathing within easy reach and is situated on an enormous bay full of islands. Boat trips around the bay are available, some with a stop for lunch on the island of Jipóia. Of particular interest are the convent of Nossa Senhora do Carmo, built in 1593, the parish church (1626), the ruins of the Jacuecanga seminary (1797), and the Senhor do Bonfim church (1780).

Hotels *Frade* (A, the most expensive), *Da Praia* and *Pousada do Retiro*, small resort hotels, bookings Rio 267-7375, all C; *Palace*, D, and *Londres*, C; *Caribe*, central, and *Acrópolis* both D; *Angra Turismo*, E; *Cherry*, E. At Km. 115 on BR-101 is *Hotel Porto Bracuhy*, C, with lots of facilities for watersports, nightly shows and dancing, restaurant, etc. (23 km. from Angra dos Reis).

Restaurants *Costa Verde*, *Verde Mar*, both specializing in sea food. Also *Jaques*. For meat, *Adega dos Dragos*. *La Bambina* on Praça Lopes Trovão, expensive, poor service. *Chez Dominique*.

Bus Hourly from Rio's Rodoviária bus station, Viação Eval, take the "via litoral" bus and sit on the left, US$1.65, 2½ hrs.

The Hotéis do Frade group (*Frade*, *do Retiro*, *Pousada Dom João* in Parati and *Hotel Portogalo*, 1½ hrs. from Rio on a cliff top) in conjunction with Aquatur owns a schooner, the *Frade-Mar*, which runs cruises off Angra dos Reis, exploring islands, snorkelling, diving, etc. Trips are Mon.-Wed., or Fri.-Sun.; bookings for cruises,and for Frade hotels: Rua Joaquim Nabuco 161, Copacabana, 22080 Rio de Janeiro, Tel.: 267-7375, Telex: 31034, or Portuguese Tours Inc., 321 Rahway Av., Elizabeth, N.J. 07202, Tel.: 352-6112, Telex 138-203 or 178-051.

Two hours by ferry boat (Mon., Wed., Fri. at 1500) takes you on a most attractive trip through the bay to **Ilha Grande,** once an infamous pirate lair, and now occupied principally by fishermen and one of Brazil's larger prisons, with two

246 BRAZIL

good hotels, *Paraiso do Sol* (A, inclusive of meals, reservations, Rio, Tel.: 252-9158) and *Mar da Tranqüilidade* (C, reservations Rio, Tel.: 288-4162). Hotel reservations are necessary; alternatively you can camp on beaches; ask in the port at Angra dos Reis for a fishing boat going to Proveta, where you can stay in boat sheds or, if lucky, with a fisherman. It is a beautiful village, from which you can walk through tropical forest on a mountain to Praia do Aventureiro (a day's leisurely walk each way). Take mosquito precautions and register with police post in village of Abraão.

Beyond Angra dos Reis, the road continues 100 km. along the coast, past the new nuclear-power project at Itaorna, to **Parati,** a charming colonial town only accessible these last few years with the opening of the road. The centre has been declared a national historic monument in its entirety. It was one of the first planned towns in Brazil, being the chief port for the export of gold in the 17th century. The churches were built separately for each race, Indian, black and white. There is a great deal of distinguished Portuguese colonial architecture in delightful settings. There is a festival of sacred music in September. The town centre is out of bounds for motor vehicles.

In 1985 the road between Angra dos Reis and Parati was washed away near the site of the nuclear power station; passengers from Rio disembark from the bus and are taken in VW minibuses over the hill on a single track road—be prepared for delays until the main road is repaired.

Hotels *Pousada Pardieiro*, B, attractively housed in colonial building with lovely gardens, but always full at week-ends. Also *Pousada Dom João*, B, bookings Rio 267-7375; *Santa Rita*, Rua Santa Rita 2, E, good, with bath and breakfast; other central *pousadas*: *do Ouro*, A, *das Canoas* (recommended, clean, swimming pool, a/c) and *Aconchego*, both D; *Hotels Pescador* and *Sila Coupê*, central, D; *Hotel Solar dos Gerânios*, formerly *Johnny Gringo*, Praça da Matriz, F, clean, friendly, good breakfast. Good restaurant, *Vagalume*. The bus runs every 2 hrs. from 0600 (Colitur, US$0.90) from Angra and the run is 1½ hrs. There is a small Camping Club site on the fine Pontal beach, very crowded in January and February, and also a private camping site and a site next to the police station after the bridge, US$1.30 p.p. Apart from camping, very little cheap accommodation.

Bus From Rio, Eval, 0630, 0900, 1230 and 1400, 4 hours, (spectacular coastal views). From São Paulo 0900, and 2200 for Angra dos Reis (arriving 0730), stopping in Parati 0500. To São Paulo, 0900 and 2300 daily. To Ubatuba, several daily; change there for São Paulo.

The road continues from Parati into the State of São Paulo.

Espírito Santo

N of Campos (see page 242) is the State of Espírito Santo, with its capital at Vitória. The State has a mountainous interior and a hot, damp seaboard. It is an important grower of coffee. In the north there are large forests containing hardwoods. The people are known as Capixabas, after a former Indian tribe. Just across the frontier between the states is the resort town of **Marataizes,** with fair hotels and good beaches.

Hotels *Praia*, Av. Atlântica 99, on beach, E; *Saveiros Palace*, Av. Miramar 119, on beach, D; *Dona Judith*, Av. Lacerda de Aguiar 353, E; *Jona Balbina*, same street, No. 397, similar prices.

Camping Municipal site on Praia do Siri, 10 km. from centre; Xodó private site, Av. Atlântica, 2 km. from centre.

The main road N passes **Cachoeira do Itapemirim**, a busy city on both banks of the fast-flowing Rio Itapemirim; many hotels of all classes, a cheap one being *Planalto*, facing the river, F.

Further north, 58 km. south of Vitória, is **Guarapari,** whose beaches attract many people seeking cures for rheumatism, neuritis and other complaints, from the radioactive monazitic sands. Bus from Vitória, 1 hr., US$0.40. (Both Marataizes and Guarapari are very crowded mid-Dec. to end Feb., with visitors from Minas Gerais.)

Hotels *Porto do Sol*, Mediterranean style village on rocky point overlooking a calm beach, pool, sauna, etc., A, recommended, Tel.: 261-0011, Telex: 0272-488; *Coronado*, Av. Lourival de Almeida 312, C; *Hostess*, Rua Joaquim Silva Lima 701, B; *Thorium*, Praça Floriano Peixoto 17, D; *Atlântica*, Av. Edísio Cirne 332, on beach, recommended, D; *Guará*, Rua Getúlio Vargas 179, E.

Camping Camping Clube do Brasil, Setiba beach, 9 km. from centre. Cambrás site off Vitória highway close to beach, 4 km. from centre. Private site near Cambrás site.
Less crowded than Guarapari is Praia Iriri, 30 km. to the South, served by a regular bus; 2 beaches, beautiful setting, lodging in private houses is possible.

There are coastal and inland road routes to **Vitória**, 509 km. from Rio de Janeiro, reached irregularly by coastal vessels (24 hrs.), several times a day by plane (80 min.), and by bus (9 hrs.). Two bridges connect the island on which it stands with the mainland. The town is beautifully set, its entrance second only to Rio's, its beaches quite as attractive, but smaller, and the climate is less humid. On Avenida República is the huge Parque Moscoso, an oasis of quiet, with a lake, playground and tiny zoo. The upper, older part of town, reached by steep streets and steps, is much less hectic than the lower harbour area which is beset by dreadful traffic problems. Vitória is a growing centre for the sport of sea fishing. Population, one million.

Its growing importance is due to its connection westwards with Minas Gerais by the Vitória-Minas railway, which transports for export millions of tons of iron ore and a large tonnage of coffee and timber. Ships drawing 11 metres and 240 metres in length can enter the port. A supplementary iron-ore port has been built at Ponta do Tubarão, near Vitória, to load ships up to 250,000 tons. These installations have led to some beach and air pollution at places near Vitória, such as Camburi.

See the fortified monastery of Nossa Senhora da Penha, on a high hill above the small settlement of Vila Velha. Most of the (unremarkable) structure, now in ruins, is of the 17th and 18th centuries; the views are superb. The Dutch attacked it in 1625 and 1640. Vila Velha has an excellent beach, but it is built up and noisy: take bus from Vitória marked Vilha Velha or Praia da Costa. A bridge is being built across the bay, and when completed will bring even more crowds to Vila Velha.

Warning Robberies on the street are common. If you are robbed, yell "thief" or "*ladrão*" and give chase (if you think it safe to do so); most likely most of the street will join you and if the thief is caught he will receive a severe beating.

Hotels *Helal*, Jerônimo Monteiro 935, C; *Cannes Palace*, Jerônimo Monteiro 111, C; *Estoril*, Praça Pres. Roosevelt 532, D, some rooms overlook the port; *Tabajara*, Jerônimo Monteiro 60, E, dirty, noisy; *Vitória*, Cais de São Francisco 85, near Parque Moscoso, F, changes money; *Europa*, Sete de Setembro, corner of Praça Costa Pereira, F, clean, noisy but cheap, good value restaurant; *Imperial*, central, good although relatively simple; *Catedral*, opp. Cathedral in upper part of city, F, clean; *Avenida*, Av. Florentino Avidos 317 (Tel.: 223-4317/ 0770), F with breakfast, friendly, clean; *Moscoso*, Rua 23 de Maio 175, F; *Sagres*, Rua Gonçalves Lido 47, F; *São José*, Av. Princesa Isabel 300, C; *Pop*, C, dirty, on road to Vila Velha. *Senac Hotel* (Government-run hotel school), luxurious, swimming pool, restaurant, enthusiastic attention to guests by student staff, on the ocean at Rua 7, 417 Ilha do Boi, B, Tel.: 227-3222; *Novotel*, Av. Adalberto Simão Nader 133, B-A. Hotels located in beach areas, Camburi to the N, Vila Velha (*Hotel Alterosas*, F, dirty, run-down, unpleasant, *Hostess*, D) to the S, both about 15 mins. from city centre.

Camping Serra Verde and Dalla's, private sites with some facilities, about 30 km. N of the city on Manguinhos beach.

Restaurants *São Pedro* (fish a speciality). *Trattoria Toscana*, Av. República and Cleto Nunes, by Parque Moscoso, on first floor, good food and service.

Banks Local banks. *Casa de Câmbio* at Vitur, Av. Getúlio Vargas, next to *Bar Scandinave* (where moneychangers of a less trustworthy type can be found).

Cables Embratel, Palácio do Café, Praça Costa Pereira 52. Tel.:30914.

Tourist Information Emcatur, Rua Barão de Monjardim 30 (corner of Av. Jerônimo Monteiro), and at Rodoviária (bus. station, friendly, good free map). Plumatur, Av. Governador Bley (first floor), tourist information, coffee and parallel exchange rate.

Roads (distances in km.): Belém, 3,075; Brasília, 1,238; Belo Horizonte, 541; Foz do Iguaçu, 2,002; Manaus, 4,489; Porto Alegre, 2,038; Recife, 1,948; Rio, 509; Salvador, 1,175; São Paulo, 932.

Buses Rio, 8 hrs., US$5.50. To hitch to Rio, take Itapemirim bus to Aracatiba (26 km). Salvador, 18 hrs., US$11; Porto Seguro, overnight to Eunápolis, 9 hrs., US$5, then change buses which run

248 BRAZIL

every hour, US$1. To hitch to Salvador, take a bus to Sara, which is beyond Carapina; alight where the bus turns off to Sara. Diamantina, 5½ hrs., US$3. To Ouro Preto, 2215 only, Thurs., US$3.75; to Belo Horizonte, either by bus, 11 hrs., US$ 5.50, or take train at 0720 to Itabira, site of a large iron ore mine, where there is a connecting bus to Belo Horizonte at 2000, arrives 2200. Possible also to go by train to Ipatinga, site of the Usiminas steel mill (visits can be arranged); hourly buses Ipatinga-Belo Horizonte, 3 hrs. (no trains Vitória-Belo Horizonte).

Excursions Visit *Santa Leopoldina* or *Domingos Martins*, both around 45 km. from Vitória, less than an hour by bus (2 companies run to the former, approx. every 3 hrs.). Both villages preserve the architecture and customs of the first German and Swiss settlers who arrived in the 1840s. Domingos Martins (also known as Campinho) has a Casa de Cultura with some items of German settlement (Hotels *Campinho*, F, clean, breakfast, *Imperador*, 2 star, E). Santa Leopoldina has a most interesting museum (open Tues.-Sun., 0900-1100 and 1300-1800) covering the settlers' first years in the area, and a large number of fascinating constructions dating from the end of the last century showing Swiss and German influence.

To *Santa Teresa*, a charming hill town 2½ hours by bus from Vitória, US$0.50 (beautiful journey). There is a unique hummingbird sanctuary—difficult to visit because of illness of director, Dr Augusto Ruschi. Also the Nova Lombardia National Biological Reserve. Basic accommodation available. Previous permission must be obtained to visit from Instituto Brasileiro de Desenvolvimento Florestal in Vitória.

75 km. N of Vitória is the town of Aracruz. A whole new town is being built beside the impressive Scandinavian/Brazilian cellulose plant, surrounded by vast new eucalyptus forests.

136 km. N of Vitória is **Linhares**, on Rio Doce, with good hotels, for example *Linhares*, D, best in town; *Grande*, F, pleasant, and others; *Restaurant Mocambo*, good and cheap. Mid-way between Linhares and Vitória, 5 km. off BR-101 between Fundão and Ibiraçu, is a Zen Buddhist monastery. 84 km. N of Linhares is São Mateus, a pleasant town with no decent hotels (*Grande*, F, tiny, bad rooms), 13 km. from good beaches (buses).

The most attractive beaches in the State are around *Conceição da Barra,* 242 km. N of Vitória on the way to Salvador. Basic hotels *Cricaré; Nanuque;* and *Rio Mar*, F. Camping Clube do Brasil site with full facilities.

Minas Gerais

The inland State of Minas Gerais, somewhat larger than France, is mountainous in the S, rising to the 2,787-metre peak of Agulhas Negras in the Mantiqueira range, and in the E, where there is the Caparaó National Park containing the Pico da Bandeira (2,890 metres). From Belo Horizonte north are undulating grazing lands, the richest of which are in the extreme W: a broad wedge of country between Goiás in the N and São Paulo in the S, known as the Triângulo Mineiro. Most of the upland is also good grazing country. Being frost-free, Minas Gerais is again becoming one of the main producers of coffee.

Minas Gerais was once described as having a heart of gold and a breast of iron. Half the mineral production of Brazil comes from the State, including nearly all the iron ore. Diamonds are still found, and it has the only two gold mines working in Brazil.

Its exports move through Rio de Janeiro, Santos, Vitória and Angra dos Reis. The easy availability of power and the local agricultural and mineral production has created a large number of metal-working, textile, mineral water, food processing and timber industries.

There *is much to interest the tourist*: the old colonial cities built during the gold rush in the 18th century, some splendid caves, the Rio São Francisco in the N, and a number of splendid spas and hill resorts. You can easily visit the charming colonial cities from Rio or Belo Horizonte; many companies, including Tropical Tours of Belo Horizonte, provide tours.

The chief glory of the colonial cities is the architecture and, even more, the sculpture of one of the world's great creative artists, Antônio Francisco Lisboa (1738-1814), the son of a Portuguese architect and a black slave woman. He is known

BRAZIL 249

as "O Aleijadinho" (the little cripple) because in later life he developed a maiming disease (possibly leprosy) which compelled him to work in a kneeling (and ultimately a recumbent) position with his hammer and chisel strapped to his wrists. His finest work, which shows a grandeur and power not usually associated with the plastic arts in the 18th century, is probably the set of statues in the gardens and sanctuary of the great Bom Jesus church in Congonhas do Campo, but the main body of his work is in Ouro Preto, with some important pieces in Sabará, São João del Rei and Mariana (see following pages).

129 km. north of Rio by air and 155 km. by new highway is the pleasant city of **Juiz de Fora.** It lies on the Paraibuna river, in a deep valley between the Mar and Mantiqueira mountain chains, at 640 metres. Population: 299,000. The Museum of Mariano Procópio is well worth a visit.

Industries   Steel-making, textiles, brewing, timber sawing, sugar refining.

Hotels *Ritz* (best), *Barão do Rio Barras 2000*, D; *Imperial, Batista de Oliveira 605*, D (simple, but well run). Many hotels on Rua Getúlio Vargas. of (our) category F: declining street numbers for Hotels *Glória* (good), *Transmontana, Hilton* (no relation), *Brasília, Mauá* and *Big. Picache*, opp. Rodoviária. *Imperador,* Av. Rio Branco 25, F. Boarding houses (F and G) in side streets, e.g. Rua Marechal Deodoro, *Pensão Sulamericana* at No. 86, *Belo Horizonte* at No. 120.

Camping   Camping Clube do Brasil site at Represa Dr. João Penido.

Bus   Hourly from Rio 0600-2200, US$1.65, 3½ hrs. (spectacular trip), Belo Horizonte (many, US$3.50) and Petrópolis. Bus station outside town, Av. Brasil 3405.

From **Barbacena,** a rose-exporting town 103 km. on (rose festival in October), a paved road runs W to the colonial city of **São João del Rei,** with a fine bridge and three splendid 18th century churches: Pilar, the earliest, with rich altars and bright ceiling, and good *azulejos* in choir, and a sacristy with portraits of the Evangelists; São Francisco de Assis (1764), with exterior and interior sculptures by Aleijadinho (recent restoration has removed the plaster from the altars, revealing fine carving in sucupira wood) and the Carmo, on the other side of the river, designed by him and with interior sculptures by him, recently very well restored, all in white. Near São Francisco is the tourist office, in the same building as a small museum, whose chief treasure is the only known portrait of Aleijadinho. Museu da Arte Sacra, small but well recommended. Population, 50,000. There is also the Museu de Arte Regional do Patrimônio Histórico, in Praça Severiano (open Tues.-Sun., 1300-1600, US$0.25), the house of Bárbara Heliodora (1759-1819), one of the Inconfidentes (see page 255), and a pewter factory, exhibition and shop run by an Englishman, John Somers. A good view of the town and surroundings is from Alto Boa Vista, where there is a Cristo Redentor. See also **Tiradentes,** 13 km. away, now hardly more than a quiet village but attractive with silversmiths and other handicrafts, gardens, museum of Padre Rolim (another Inconfidente), and a beautiful church with a fine German organ (Santo Antônio, 1710, but with façade designed by Aleijadinho); the last two were restored in 1982-83. The simple pilgrimage church of Santíssima Trindade is also well worth seeing. Tourist Office in the Prefeitura, Rua Resende Costa 71.

Barbacena Hotel *Grogotó,* excellent, C; operated by Senac.

São João del Rei Hotels *Novotel Porto Real,* Av. Eduardo Magalhães, charming reconstructed colonial building, comfortable, C; *do Espanhol,* R. Marechal Deodoro, D; *Pousada Casarão,* opp. São Francisco church, D, converted mansion. *Glória; Colonial,* opp. *Porto Real,* E, clean and comfortable. *Pensão N.S. de Lourdes,* near bus station, F, meals US$1.10, good; *Brasil,* opposite railway station, clean, friendly, cheap, F, recommended, no breakfast (*Cafeteria Globo* in the same street, 2 blocks away, is good, though). *Hotel Porto Real* restaurant and *Restaurant Quinta do Ouro* recommended.

Rodoviária (bus station) 2 km. W of centre of São João, bus from Rio 0900, 6 hrs. For buses to Congonhas do Campo and on to Ouro Preto, see page 257.

Tiradentes Hotels *Pousada dos Inconfidentes; Pousada de Laurito; Solar da Ponte,* Praça das Mercês (prop. John Parsons), atmosphere of country house, B, including breakfast and tea, only ten rooms. Fresh flowers in rooms, a small bar, sauna, light meals for residents only, for larger

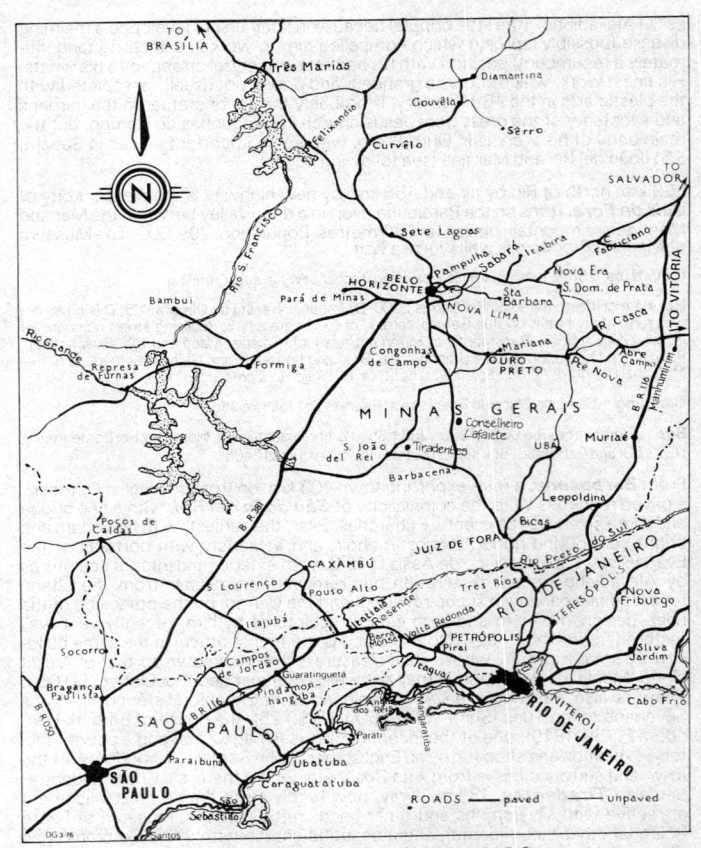

ROADS FROM RIO DE JANEIRO, SAO PAULO & BELO HORIZONTE

meals, the hotel recommends the three restaurants within 400 metres. *Quinta do Ouro* also recommended.

Martin Crossland and the Editor both recommend the train trip from São João del Rei to Tiradentes (13 km.). The train has been in continuous operation since 1881, using the same locomotives and rolling stock, running on 76 cm. gauge track, all now lovingly restored and cared for. Maximum speed is 20 km. per hour. Price: US$1, one class only. Fri., Sat., Sun. and holiday steam train service to Tiradentes, 1000 and 1400, returning 1300 and 1700. A railway museum was opened at the railway station in São João del Rei in 1981; opening hours: daily 0900-1200, 1330-1730; there are also an engine shed and a steam-operated machine shop, still working.

From Belo Horizonte, the shortest road to São João del Rei is via Lagoa Dourada. Just past Lagoa Dourada is the turning (12 km. on dirt road) for **Prados**, a small town 15 km. from Tiradentes known for its musical and handicrafts traditions. Near the turn is Entre Rios de Minas (*Hotel Camapuã*).

BRAZIL 251

Belo Horizonte, the capital of Minas Gerais, is the third largest city in Brazil. It is situated over 800 metres above sea-level, on a hilly site surrounded by mountains, and enjoys an excellent climate all the year round (except for the rainy season). It was Brazil's first modern planned city. Sights to be seen are the Praça da Assembléia, with three fine modern buildings: Legislative Assembly, church and Banco do Brasil; the Palácio da Liberdade, in Praça da Liberdade amid other fine *fin-de-siècle*-style public buildings (every Sun. morning an open-air craft market operates here); the Palácio das Artes, Afonso Pena 1567, which is in the Parque Municipal and contains the Centro de Artesanato Mineiro (craft shop open 0900-1700, Tues.-Sun.); the Museu Mineiro, Av. João Pinheiro, in old Senate building near centre; the City Museum; the Museum of Mineralogy, Rua da Bahia 1149, a Gothic building near the park, with interesting exhibits (open Mon.-Sat., 0800-1800, entrance free); the Museu Histórico, in an old *fazenda* house which is the last reminder of Belo Horizonte's predecessor, the village of Arraial do Curral d'el Rey, with most interesting historical exhibits (open 1100-1700 Tues.-Sun.); the Museu do Telefone, Av. Alfonso Pena 1180 (open Mon.-Fri., 0900-1800, Sun., 0900-1300); the railway station, with museum, and the railway headquarters in a mansion on the hill above the station, with locomotive and railway coach used by Dom Pedro II; the Municipal Park (an oasis of green, right in the centre of the city, small amusement park and playground, not too safe at night). Museo Histórico Natural, in the Instituto Agronómico, Rua Gustavo da Silveira 1035, Tel.: 461-7666, has a local geological and palaeontological display and good archaeological exhibits (take bus 3803A from Praça Rio Branco).

Eight km. from the centre is the picturesque suburb of Pampulha, famous for its modern buildings and the artificial lake (many infestations, do not swim in it), many buildings designed by the renowned Brazilian architect Oscar Niemeyer (who later designed much of Brasília); in Pampulha the glass and marble Museum of Modern Art may be visited (Av. Octacílio Negrão de Lima, open 0800-1800 daily), as well as the Chapel of São Francisco (the interior of which was decorated by the Brazilian painter Cândido Portinári). The bus from the city centre to the Jardim Zoológico (at the far end of the lake from the dam—not recommended) passes the chapel and also the Mineirão stadium (see below).

In the southern zone of the city, on the Serra do Curral, the Parque de Mangabeiras has forest trails, sports facilities and snack bars. The natural amphitheatre where the Pope spoke in 1982 is nearby; there is an iron monument marking the occasion (take bus 2001 from Afonso Pena). In 1984, the Minascentro, a convention centre for exhibitions and congresses, was opened in the city centre. The huge Mineirão stadium is the second largest in Brazil after the Maracanã stadium in Rio. The population of Belo Horizonte in 1980 was 1,442,000 and it is one of the fastest growing of Brazil's main cities.

The industrial area, about 10 km. from the centre, has now become the third largest industrial centre of Brazil, and apart from being the traditional centre of mining and agricultural industries (as well as diamond cutting and precious stones), it has steelworks and an automobile industry. The city has a good public transport system (red buses serve central and express routes, yellow are circular, and blue diagonal), and taxis are plentiful, although hard to obtain at peak hours.

Local Holidays Maundy Thursday; Corpus Christi; August 15 (Assumption); December 8 (Immaculate Conception).

Electric Current 120-220 A.C. 60 cycles.

Hotels *Othon Palace*, Av. Afonso Pena 1050, Tel.: 226-7844, A, deluxe, best; *Brasilton*, out of town at km. 3.5 on Rodovia Fernão Dias, Contagem, A; *Real Palace*, R. Espírito Santo 904, Tel.: 224-2111, A; *Internacional Plaza Palace*, R. Rio de Janeiro 109, Tel.: 201-2300, A, good but seedy part of town; *Boulevard Plaza*, Av. Getúlio Vargas 1640, Savassi district (chic), A, Tel.: 223-9000, very nice; *Del Rey*, Praça Afonso Arinos 60, B; *Normandie*, Rua Tamóios 212, B, excellent grill; *Excelsior*, Rua Caetés 753, B; *Serrana Palace*, Rua Goitacases 450, C, pleasant restaurant; *Amazonas*, Av. Amazonas 120, C; *Lorman*, Rua Guarani 165, C; *Brasil Palace*, Rua Carijós 269 (Praça Sete de Setembro), C; *Cecília*, Rua Carijós 454, D, pleasant; *Nacional*, Rua São Paulo 530, D; *Ambassy*, Rua Caetés 633, near bus station, D, good restaurant; *Itatiaia*, Praça Rui Barbosa 187, D; *Pampulha Palace*, Rua Tupis 646, D; *Esplanada*, Av. Santos Dumont 304, D, (E without bath), clean, good restaurant, own garage; *Financial*, Av. Afonso Pena 571, E, not too good; *Metrópole*, Rua Bahia 1023, D; *Sul America Palace*, Av. Amazonas 50, E, clean, friendly, warmly recommended; *Bragança*, Av. Paraná 109, E; *Paraná*, on same street, No. 437 (Tel.: 222-3472), F, with shower, clean, noisy at weekends from discothèque; *Gontijo*, Rua Tupinambás 731, E; *Presidente*, Av. Paraná 437, E; *Continental*, Av. Paraná 241, E, central, clean, friendly; *Minas*, Rua São Paulo 331, F, friendly, recommended; *Oeste Palace*, Av. Paraná 39, E; *Dom Pedro II*, R. Curitiba 248, F, clean, rather faded. Cheaper places are: *São Cristóvão*, Av. Oiapoque 284, F, near bus station; *Flamengo*, Av. Santos Dumont 624; *Magnata*, Rua Guarani 124, F, with breakfast, near bus station, cheap and clean, no hot shower; *Madrid*, F without breakfast, not very clean, near Rodoviária; on Rua Curitiba, *Vitória*, No. 224, good (near Rodoviária), F, and *Nova York*, No. 942, F with breakfast, fair; *São Bento*, Rua Guarani 438, E; *Pensão Nacional*, F, clean and very friendly. *Real*, Av. Santos Dumont 260, F, cheap (rooms cannot be locked from the outside). Near bus station many hotels are for very-short-stay couples; *Pensão Rodoviária* and away from traffic, *Pensão Nova Rodoviária*, Rua 21 de Abril 89, F, a bit dubious, basic, and many others; *Pensão N.S. Aparecida*, Av. de Fátima 1320 (near Rodoviária), F, basic, friendly but noisy. Within 10 mins. walk of Rodoviária: Rua Espírito Santo, No. 284, *Majestic*, F; No. 227, *São Salvador*, F; No. 237; *Magalhães*, Rua Espírito Santo 237, F, with good breakfast, clean, highly recommended; *Lux*, No. 220; Rua dos Caetés, *Solar*, No. 265, *Coimbra*, F, plus breakfast; *Luz Hotel*, Rua Guaicurus 344, F; *Guarani*, Rua Guarani 458, E. You may spend the night in the bus station only if you have an onward ticket (police check at midnight). *Dona Carolina*, Rua dos Timbiras 1969, unsigned, in centre, 20 mins ' walk from Rodoviária F p.p. per day with full board, most residents are students, good atmosphere and food. Two new hotels, the *Wembley Palace* and the *Grande*, are to be opened shortly.

Camping Wild camping near Alto do Palácio, near river and waterfalls.

Restaurants Grill at *Hotel Normandie* is good but expensive, few locals. *Tavares*, Rua Santa Catarina 64 (local dishes). Chinese: *Yun Ton*, R. Santa Catarina 946, recommended; *Dragon Palace*, Contorno and Getúlio Vargas, in Savassi. *Laçador*, in garden just up hill from Monjolo railway station. Churrascarias: *Carretão Guaiba*, Av. do Contorno 8412; *Rodeio*, Av. do Contorno 8222; *Minuano*, in the centre with cold-table; *La Greppia* next door; *Picanha na Tábua*, Rua Curitiba, unprepossessing but highly recommended; *Chico Mineiro*, Rua Alagoas, corner of Av. Brasil, local chicken specialities, good, closed Sun.; *Arroz com Feijão*, typical food, Av. Contorno 6510, Av. Contorno 7438 and R. Antônio de Albuquerque 440, all friendly, reasonably-priced; *Martini*, Rua Curitiba, and *Pizzaiolo*, Av. Contorno 8495, good for pizzas. *Hungaria*, Av. Pedro I, 2258; *Cosmo-Metropolitano*, Av. Cristóvão Colombo 544 and *Tokyo* (Japanese), R. Guajajaras 909; *Via Natural*, No. 1, Av. Afonso Pena 941, vegetarian, open till 2200 (except 2000 on Sun.), No. 2, Av. Andradas 367; *O Armazem*, Rua Alagoas 1468, also vegetarian, as is *Alquima Mercearia*, Rue Tomé de Souza 855, and *Folhas*, same street, No. 503; *Superbom* (vegetarian), R. São Paulo, 971, 1100-1500, Mon. to Fri. *Casa do Ouvidor*, near central praça, highly recommended but expensive. *Degrau*, Av. Afonso Pena 4221, excellent restaurant and bar, very pleasant; *Pinho's*, Rua Pouso Alto 740, set high above the city, tremendous views by day or night, can be very busy on Fri. and Sat.; *Mangueiras*, at Pampulha, next to Niemeyer chapel of São Francisco, very popular; *Dona Derna*, behind the Palácio de Liberdade, highly recommended; *Buona Távola*, R. Alagoas 777, Savassi, excellent Italian; *Cantina do Ângelo* (Italian), Rua Tupinambás 267, recommended, and in same street, No.253, *Torino* (Italian excellent, huge and varied menu; also at Guajajaras 460), and *Alpino* (German), same street, No. 173, both good value and popular, corned beef and fresh boiled vegetables available, open-air; *Monjolo*, Av. Assis Chateaubriand 525. *Contijo*, below *Hotel Magalhães* at Espírito Santo 237, cheap and good; *Quibelândia*, Rua dos Caetés 188, good. Good snack bar at corner of Av. Afonso Pena and Rua Bahia, *Doce D'ocê*, Av. Afonso Pena 2712. We are told that the splendid Minas typical dishes are more authentic— and more toothsome—outside Belo Horizonte.

Shopping Mercado Central, Av. Aug. de Lima 744, large and clean, open every day, Saturday social centre. Market for fruit, vegetables, meat and other items at corner of Rua Santa Catarina and Av. Amazonas (near Praça Raúl Soares). There are huge hypermarkets just outside the city on the highways to Rio and to São Paulo. Splendid delicatessen with foreign food and wines—and liquors—*Au Bon Gourmet*, Rua Tupinambás 187. For gemstones, try Manoel Bernardes, Rua Espírito Santo 835, very reasonable, ask for US saleswoman Manuela, who can arrange tours of workshops. "Hippie fair" Thurs. evenings and Sundays in Praça da Liberdade; other fairs on Fri. and Sat.

Bookshop Daniel Vaitsman, Rua Espírito Santo 466, 17th floor, for English language books. Foreign language books at Livraria Van Damme, Rua das Guajajaras 505, also good local and Portuguese selection.

Banks Lloyds Bank (ex-BOLSA), Av. Amazonas 303; Citibank, Rua Espírito Santo 871; Banco do Brasil, Av. Prudente de Morais 135; Banco Econômico, Rua Bahia 360, 9th floor, and other local banks, 1000-1630. American Express, Kontik-Franstur, Rua Carijós 244, Edifício Walmap, S/808/10. Exchange: Sr Abdul, Rua Caetés 323.

BRAZIL 253

Addresses British Vice-Consulate: Av. Afonso Pena 952, s. 500, Caixa Postal 2755. Sociedade Brasileira de Cultura Inglesa: as British Vice-Consulate. W. Germany: R. Carijós 244. Austrian consulate, Rua José Américo Cancado Bahia 199, Tel.: 33 33 622.

Tourist Information Turminas, Av. do Contorno 8471; Praça Sete de Setembro; at Rodoviária, railway station, airport. Touring Club do Brasil, Av. Afonso Pena 1915.

Travel Agent Tropical Tours, c/o Raptim, R.Grão Mogol 502, in Sion district, Tel.: 223-3811, telex 3823 RAPT, run by Douglas and Janice Trent, offer tours all over Brazil and have a special interest in ecology. Tours to Minas historic cities every day except Mon. Reliable information.

Roads (distances in km.): Belém, 2,827; Brasília, 747; Foz do Iguaçu, 1,663; Manaus, 3,948; Porto Alegre, 1,709; Recife, 2,137; Rio, 426; Salvador, 1,355; São Paulo, 588; Vitória, 541.

Buses Rodoviária is by Praça Rio Branco at end of Av. Afonso Pena (left-luggage lockers, no attended service). To Rio, 7 hrs., US$6 (ordinary), *leito*, US$12; to Brasília, 12 hrs., 9 a day incl. 2 *leitos*, only one leaves in daylight (0800), US$8, *leito* US$16; to Ouro Preto, 2 hrs., US$1.20, several daily (buy ticket well in advance); to Mariana (via Ouro Preto), 2¼ hrs., US$1.45; to Congonhas do Campo, 1½ hrs., US$1. To Sabará, US$0.30, ½ hr., from separate part of Rodoviária from main departure hall. To São Paulo, 9 hrs., US$7; route passes the great Furnas reservoir. To Salvador US$13, 22 hrs., at 1800 and 1900 daily. For Porto Seguro take Gontijo bus to Nanuque, then Rio Doce bus to Eunápolis, then Espresso São Jorge to Porto Seguro, total time 22 hrs., US$10. To Recife, US$21.50; to Belém, US$35. To Cuiabá, Expresso São Luiz, 0800 and 2000 daily, 26 hrs., US$15; to Vitória, 8 hrs., US$5.50.

Train Railway station is at Praça Rui Barbosa. Trains leave Friday and Sunday at night (the Vera Cruz) for Rio de Janeiro: cabin for two costs US$27 single fare. There are no trains to São Paulo or Brasília. No direct train to Vitória, but buses leave at 0530 for Itabira, where connecting train (dining cars) leaves 0800, arriving Vitória 1937.

Airport A new international airport near Lagoa Santa, at Confins, 39 km. from Belo Horizonte, has been opened. Taxi to centre, US$7; airport bus, either *executivo* from the exit, or comfortable normal bus from far end of car park every ½ hr., US$1. From centre, catch bus at Terminal Turístico JK, R. Olegário Maciel and R. Guajajaras.

Hitch-hiking to Rio or Ouro Preto, take a bus marked "Shopping", to the shopping centre above Belo Horizonte on the Rio road.

Excursions Within easy motoring distance from Belo Horizonte are several of the 400 caves and grottoes for which Minas Gerais is famous. The best and most famous is the Gruta de Maquiné with 7 chambers, well lit, with guides, but hot— 26°C, 126 km. NW of Belo (well signposted and with restaurants nearby, bus at 0915, return at 1500, 2¼ hrs., US$2; in the nearby town of Cordisburgo is a museum to the writer Guimarães Rosa), but the Gruta de Lapinha, almost as good, is only 51 km. N of the city (entrance to caves and small museum, US$0.50; bus at 0930, 1130 and others, via Pampulha, return 1210, 1600, 1hr., US$0.60 one way).

10 km. before Lapinha is the town of **Lagoa Santa,** a weekend resort for Belo Horizonte. The sandy beach on the lake (close to the town centre and bus station) is used for fishing, sun-bathing, swimming (not recommended) and boating. Along the beach are bars and restaurants, with more in the nearby main square which also has two small hotels and an interesting modernistic church. The road to Belo Horizonte (half-hourly bus service, US$0.60) passes Belo Horizonte's new international airport. Bus Lagoa Santa-Lapinha every half hour.

To the NE of the city, a few km. off the BR-262, is the Serra de Piedade, a high peak giving spectacular views over the surrounding countryside. A popular excursion point but only accessible by car or special bus service. There are a small chapel and a *churrascaria*. From the peak can be seen the small town of **Caeté,** which has one or two interesting churches and the remains of an old ironworks near the railway station. Take the Conceição do Mato Dentro bus to Alto do Palácio; near there are waterfalls and campsites.

From Belo Horizonte, excursions can be made to Nova Lima and the picturesque colonial cities of Sabará, Ouro Preto, Mariana and Congonhas do Campo. The road follows the Rio das Velhas in which, at points, one can see the *garimpeiros* waist-deep washing for gold.

Nova Lima, about 27 km. SE of Belo by a good road, is set in eucalyptus forests. Its houses are grouped round the gold mine of Morro Velho, opened by a British

254 **BRAZIL**

firm in 1834 but sold to Brazilians in 1959, the deepest mine in the Americas. The shaft has followed a rich vein of gold down to 2,591 metres. There are interesting carvings by Aleijadinho, recovered from elsewhere, in the (modern) parish church. Population: 34,000.

A paved road branching off the Belo Horizonte-Brasília highway leads (30 km., ½-hr.) to the colonial gold-mining (and steel-making) town of Sabará. Return by the old road over the mountain range of Serra do Curral for fine views. There is also a railway: 3 trains a day between Belo and Sabará, taking one hour.

Sabará is strung along the narrow steep valleys of the Rio das Velhas and Rio Sabará. Its old churches and fountains, its rambling cobbled streets, its simple houses with their carved doors, and its museum of 18th century gold mining in the Intendência de Ouro (built 1732, open 1200-1700 Tues.-Fri.) are of great interest. The churches are so spread out that a taxi is advisable if you wish to see them all. Population, 42,000.

Passeio a Sabará, by Lúcia Machado de Almeida, with splendid illustrations by Guignard, is an excellent guide to the place. The main sights are the Prefeitura, in Rua Pedro II, an old mansion, with oratory and main reception room (*salão nobre*) to be seen; the Imperial Theatre (1770, restored 1960) in the same street, for its fine interior; the Casa Azul, in the same street, for its portal; the Churches of Nossa Senhora do Carmo (1774), with doorway, pulpits and choirloft by Aleijadinho and paintings by Athayde; Nossa Senhora do Rosário dos Pretos (left unfinished at the time of the slaves' emancipation); São Francisco; Nossa Senhora da Conceição (1720) with much gilding, and paintings by 23 Chinese artists brought from Macau (under restoration in 1985); and, last of all, Nossa Senhora do O, built in 1698 and showing unmistakable Chinese influence (paintings much in need of restoration), 2 km. from the centre of the town (take local bus marked "Esplanada"). Also the fountains of Kaquende (1757), and Rosário. Hotel: *Pensão Bobagato*, above an art gallery, F; ask for Senhor Sérgio at the Sports Centre, he may have accommodation. Restaurant: *O Quinto do Ouro*, close to the bus station; *314*, Comendador Viana 314, near main praça; *Imperial Restaurant/Pizzaria*, in Rua Pedro II.

At 27 km. S along the Belo Horizonte-Rio de Janeiro highway a 68 km. road, the Rodovia dos Inconfidentes, branches off to Ouro Preto. On the way (48 km.) it passes Cachoeira do Campo, which was the centre of the regional mining administration in colonial times: now a sleepy, unspoilt village.

Ouro Preto, the famous former capital of the State, was founded in 1711. Population, 38,000. There is a famous School of Mining, founded in 1876, in the fortress-like Governor's Palace (1742), facing the main square (Praça Tiradentes); it has an interesting museum of mineralogy and precious stones (Museo de Mineralogia e das Pedras, a must, US$0.35, the only one open on Mondays). Opposite, next to Carmo Church, is the Museu da Inconfidência, a fine historical and art museum which has some drawings by Aleijadinho; the building, begun in the eighteenth century, has been a prison and also the local chamber of commerce (entry, US$0.45). See the Casa das Contas, now also a museum. Buy soapstone carvings at roadside stalls and bus stops rather than in the cities; they are much cheaper. (However, gems are not much cheaper from freelance sellers in the square in Ouro Preto than from the shops around the square—Brasil Gemas and De Bernardis recommended.)

The city, built on rocky ground 1,000 metres above sea-level, was declared a national monument in 1933. Its cobbled streets wind up and down steep hills crowned with 13 churches. Mansions, fountains, churches, vistas of terraced gardens, ruins, towers shining with coloured tiles, all blend together to maintain a delightful 18th century atmosphere.

Ouro Preto is famous for its Holy Week processions, which in fact begin on the Thursday before Palm Sunday and continue (but not every day) until Easter Sunday. The most famous is that commemorating Christ's removal from the Cross, late on Good Friday. This is very much a holiday period and many shops are shut—as indeed they are on winter weekends. Carnival is also memorable, with samba and happenings in the streets.

The topaz mine of Vermelho Topásios Mineração Saramenha can no longer be visited.

Ouro Preto displays many superb baroque carvings, in wood and in soapstone, of the sculptor Aleijadinho. The lovely church of São Francisco de Assis and the façade of the Carmo church are his work, and so are the two pulpits in the church of São Francisco, and much else.

BRAZIL 255

In the Praça de Independência there is a statue of José Joaquim da Silva Xavier, known as Tiradentes, leader of the Inconfidentes (unsuccessful revolutionaries of 1789), and thus regarded in Brazil as the precursor of independence. Another conspirator, the poet Tomás Antônio Gonzaga (whose house is close to São Francisco de Assis), was exiled to Africa. (Most Brazilians know his poem based on his forbidden love affair; visitors are shown the bridge and decorative fountain where the lovers held their trysts.) On June 24 of each year Ouro Preto again becomes, for that day only, the capital of the state of Minas Gerais.

Churches The following churches are all closed Mon., but are open at following times on other days: Santa Efigênia (1720, decorated with gold dust washed out of slaves' hair), Padre Faria, 0800-1200; Francisco de Assis, N.S. Conceição, 0800-1130, 1300-1700; Senhor Bom Jesus, N.S. Carmo, 1300-1700; N.S. Pilar (1733, heavily gilded work of Aleijadinho's father, Manuel Lisboa), Rosário, 1200-1700; das Mercês e Perdões, are open in afternoons only. The Antônio Dias parish church (1722), heavily gilded, contains Aleijadinho's tomb, and a museum devoted to him. Of the **museums** only Aleijadinho Paróquia is open a.m. and p.m.; Escola Minas, Inconfidência and Prata da Matriz do Pilar are open from 1200 onwards only; all except Escola Minas are closed Mon. At least two days are needed to see them all; the tourist office on Praça Tiradentes (opens 0800, Portuguese only spoken) and the hotels offer a leaflet showing the opening times; also sells good map for US$0.80. Most of the churches now charge for admission, usually about US$0.45. Shorts may not be worn in churches.

The mid-18th century paintings by Mestre Athayde (1732-1827), to be seen in S. F. de Assis, Sta. Ifigênia and elsewhere, are of particular interest: the pigments were obtained from local iron ore and from forest fruits. They are also very fine artistically; he was a worthy colleague of Aleijadinho.

N.B. In all churches and museums, all tourists' handbags and cameras are taken at the entrance and guarded none too securely (except at the Museum of Precious Stones).

Hotels *Grande*, Rua Sen. Rocha 164, largest hotel in town and the only modern structure, designed by Oscar Niemeyer, C, not well kept; *Pouso Chico Rei*, a fascinating old house with Portuguese colonial furnishings, very small and utterly delightful though extremely difficult to get a reservation, Rua Brig. Mosqueira 90, D (room No. 6 has been described as a "dream"); *Luxor Pousada*, Praça Antônio Dias 10, converted colonial mansion, no twin beds, friendly, clean, comfortable, Tel.: 551-2244, reservations in Rio, Tel.: 256-2680, C; *Hospedária Antiga*, Rua Xavier da Veiga 1, Tel.: 551-2203, a restored colonial house, reasonable rates, friendly, recommended; *Estrada Real*, 8 km. outside city, good but often fully-booked. *Quinta dos Barões*, Rua Pandiá Calógeras 474, C; *Pousada e Galeria Panorama Barroco*, Rua Conselheiro Quintiliano 722, fine views, Tel.: (031)551-3366, E, restored house with antique furniture, art gallery, music, videos, bulletin board for local events, run by John and Lucia Peterkin (US/Brazilian); *Solar das Lajes*, Rua Conselheiro Quintiliano 604 (Tel.: 551-2330), C with bath, a little way from centre, excellent view, being extended, friendly and well run; *Pilão*, Praça Tiradentes 57, on main square, E, noisy; *Colonial*, Rua Camilo Veloso 26, E; *Tófolo*, São José 76, near Contas fountain, D, cheaper rooms available, reasonable, sometimes overcharges, so pay in advance; *Pousada Tropical*, Rua Getúlio Vargas 10, E without breakfast, not recommended; *Pensão* at Rua Coronel Alves 2, Tel.: 551-2393, clean reasonable, friendly; *N. S. Aparecida*, Praça Cesário Alvim 21, E, well recommended, restaurant cheap. Hotels in Ouro Preto tend to be expensive, so there is some point in making a day trip, otherwise try *pensões* in Ruas Randolpho Bretas, Getúlio Vargas, Paraná, E. *Residencia of Doña Iva*, simple but nice, E. Also try *casas de família*, reasonably-priced, but more expensive if booked through tourist office. Difficult to get hotel rooms at weekends and holiday periods; a good idea to telegraph ahead. A number of travellers have recommended staying in Mariana where hotels are cheaper; three buses an hour to Ouro Preto.

Students may be able to stay, during holidays and weekends, at the self-governing student hostels, known as *repúblicas*, for about US$2 a night. (e.g. *República Vaticana*, Rua das Mercês 198, or *Pif-Paf*, in front of the Pilar church, *Tabu*, on road with main Post Office, or *Serigy*). Many are closed between Christmas and Carnival. Enquire at the city's tourist office on the main square (Praça Tiradentes 41), for this type, and other forms of accommodation. It shows filmstrips at 0900, 1200 and 1600 on weekdays, 0900, 1030, 1300, 1500, 1600 at weekends and holidays.

Camping Camping Clube do Brasil, 2 km. N of city, is quite expensive but very nice. Camping also possible at site of pleasant waterfall, Cachoeira dos Andorinhas, 1½ hrs. walk from city, or by car up a very steep hill at the top end of town: about 5 km. Also at picnic site 4 km. west of Ouro Preto, and at Rio Acima nearby.

Restaurants *Calabouço*, good (Conde de Bobadela 132, with an antique shop); *Pilão*, in main

256 BRAZIL

square (local painters), and good rooms above; *Quinta do Ouro*, Rua Camilo de Brito 21, good, a bit pricey, avoid window seats, recommended; also *Pelique*, US$2 *prato do dia* recommended, another branch at Rua São José 131, no sign; *Chafariz*, Rua São José 167, good local food; *Casa Grande* and *Forno de Barro*, both on Praça Tiradentes, good local dishes; *Casa do Ouvidor*, Conde de Bobadela 42, above De Bernardis jewellery shop (good), near main square, good, but expensive. On same street, *Chicken Inn*, No. 40, *Taberna La Luna* (very friendly), No. 138, good and cheap. *Bar Tropical*, near *Hotel N.S. Aparecida*, cheap. *Pousada Luxor*, cheap *lanchonetes* on opposite side of square to *Hotel Pilão*. Excellent sandwich bar, *Aupa*, Rua Cláudio Manuel 40, 1000-2200; good breakfast at *lanchonete* on corner of São José and Getúlio Vargas. Tea shop. *Doce a Doce*, fondue in basement, recommended. Students may be able to eat at the School of Mining on Praça Tiradentes.

Electric current 110 volts A.C.

Guide Book Bandeira's *Guia de Ouro Preto* in Portuguese and English (US$3.50 with coloured map, US$1 with black and white one), normally available at Tourist Office (helpful). Tourist Office's map costs US$0.80. A local guide for a day costs about US$3 (US$10 if obtained through Tourist Office).

Transport An early plane from Rio to Belo Horizonte and a bus (15 a day) gets to Ouro Preto by lunch (2 hrs.); bus fare, each way, US$1.20. Day trips are run; alternatively take an overnight bus from Rio, for example Util at 2330 (US$5, 9 hrs), return bus to Rio leaves at 2300. There is a new bus station (Rodoviária) at Ouro Preto, above the town near the São Francisco de Paula church. Book your return journey to Belo Horizonte early if returning in the evening; buses get crowded. There are also buses to Conselheiro Lafaiete for connections to Belo Horizonte and Congonhas, or to Rio via Barbacena and Juiz da Fora (direct bus to Rio is often fully booked 2-3 days in advance). Direct bus Ouro Preto to Vitória at 2130. Check that your bus ticket from Ouro Preto is in fact from Ouro Preto and not from Belo Horizonte. Three buses an hour to Mariana.

Mariana (population 20,000, 697 metres above sea level), another old mining city, founded 1696, much less hilly than Ouro Preto, is 12 km. E of Ouro Preto on a road which goes on to join the Rio-Salvador highway. See the beautiful old prison (Cadeia, 1768, now the Prefeitura Municipal), the Carmo church (1784, steatite carvings, Athayde paintings, chinoiserie panelling), next to it is the fine São Francisco church (1762, granite painted to look like marble, pulpits designed by Aleijadinho, Athayde paintings and tomb, fine sacristy, one side-altar by Aleijadinho, entry, US$0.15) and the old Palace of the Governors connected with it, the Museum (formerly the Bishop's Palace) for its church furniture, gold and silver collection, Aleijadinho statues and ivory cross (open 0900-1100 except Tues. and 1200-1700; entrance US$0.80), the city hall and the former post office, once a mansion. The Cathedral is at present closed for repairs. Between the old prison and São Francisco is a stone monument to Justice, at which slaves used to be beaten. Some people still pan for gold in the river running through the town. Between Ouro Preto and Mariana is the disused gold mine, the Minas de Passagem, dating from 1719.

Minas de Passagem A guided tour visits the mine workings and the processing plant, entrance US$3 each, visiting hours 0900-1800, Tel.: Ouro Preto 551-1068, Mariana 557-1340/1255. Bus between Ouro Preto and Mariana, every 20 mins., all stop, US$0.10 to Ouro Preto, US$0.20 to Mariana. Taxi from Ouro Preto, US$4.

Hotels *Itacolomi*, 6 km. out on Ponte Nova road, D; *Silva*, Rua Getúlio Vargas, E; *Faisca*, Rua Antônio Olinto 48, F in 3-bed room includes breakfast, spotless, excellent, cooking facilities, friendly; *Müller*, Av. G. Vargas 34, E; *Central*, Rua Frei Durão 8, F; *Avenida*, just off Praça Bandeirantes. The modern service station (*posto*) on the highway above the town offers good clean rooms at F, with hot showers.

Restaurant *Alvorada*, Praça Claudio Mansel 42, US$1-3; *Panetão*, Rua Dom Viçoso; *Taubaú*, Praça da Sé.

Tourist Office Praça Bandeirantes, helpful for a guide or pamphlet and map. Get off bus at first stop in Mariana rather than continuing to Rodoviária.

Congonhas do Campo (altitude 866 metres) is a small hill town with a good road through lovely farming country connecting with Ouro Preto, and a paved 3½-km. road link with the Rio-Belo Horizonte highway. It is also on the Central do Brasil railway between Rio and Belo Horizonte (but no through train to Rio). The town is dominated by the great pilgrimage church of Bom Jesus do Matozinho (1773); indeed there is little else of architectural interest. There is a wide view of the country from the church terrace, below which are six small chapels set in beautifully arranged sloping gardens, recalling (but excelling) the famous 18th century religious gardens of Braga in northern Portugal, showing scenes with life-size Passion figures carved by Aleijadinho and his pupils in cedar wood. The church is mainly famous for its group of prophets sculpted by Aleijadinho, standing on the parapets of the terrace. These twelve great dramatic statues (thought of as Aleijadinho's masterpieces), carved in soapstone with a superbly dramatic sense of movement, constitute one of the finest works of art of their period in the world—not just in Latin America. Inside the church, as well as the Room of Miracles, there are paintings by Athayde and the heads of four sainted popes (Gregory, Jerome, Ambrose and Augustine) sculpted by Aleijadinho for the reliquaries on the high altar. (Buses run from opposite the Rodoviária to Bom Jesus.)

Congonhas is also celebrated for its Holy Week processions, which centre on the Bom Jesus church. The most celebrated ceremonies are the meeting of Christ and the Virgin Mary on the Tuesday, and the dramatized Deposition from the Cross late on Good Friday. Pilgrimage season, first half of September, draws many thousands.

Hotels *Colonial*, good and comfortable, incl. breakfast, D; *Santuario*, Praça da Basílica 76, with fascinating restaurant downstairs full of colonial handicrafts and good local food, right next to Bom Jesus, E; *Freitas*, Rua Marechal Floriano 69, F, basic; *Globo*, F, without breakfast, rundown. There are handicraft shops selling soapstone artefacts

Bus From Belo Horizonte, US$1.20, 6 times a day, best to buy a return ticket. None direct from Rio; you have to change buses at Conselheiro Lafaiete (*Rhud's Hotel and Restaurant*, D; *Hotel Cupim*, on main Rio road, also D). To Congonhas from São João del Rei, take a São João-Belo Horizonte bus (5 a day) and alight at the crossing with the main Rio-Belo Horizonte highway; from there (it's an official bus stop) take a local bus (every ½ hr.) Bus to Ouro Preto: either go via Belo Horizonte (US$1 to Congonhas), or bus (every ½ hr.) to Conselheiro Lafaiete, US$0.30, then 0745, 1200, 1500 or 1845 bus to Ouro Preto, US$1.40, via Itabirito.

Diamantina, the most remote of these cities, is reached from Belo Horizonte by paved road (289 km., 6 daily buses via Pássaro Verde, US$3, 5½ hrs.) but there is no scheduled air service. Take the road to Brasília almost as far as the turnoff for Curvelo (a lively town, *Hotel Sagarana*—5-star, very good; *Restaurant Denise* with sleeping accommodation, on main highway, very clean), then through the impressive rocky country of the Serra do Espinhaço. The old railway service has been discontinued. 30 km. N of Belo Horizonte on the Brasília road, is the *Hotel Fazenda* at Ipê Amarelo—horses to ride, etc. Further on, between Paraopeba and Caetanópolis, is the *Flora Eunice* (Leite ao Pé da Vaca) snackbar (good toilets) with small private botanic garden and zoo with contented animals, recommended. About 120 km. N of Belo Horizonte, 33,400 square km. of the Serra do Espinaço has been named as the National Park of Serra do Cipó, in view of its scenic beauty and rich variety of plant and animal life.

Diamantina, centre of a once active diamond industry founded in 1729, has excellent colonial buildings. Its churches (difficult to get into, except for the modern Cathedral) are not so grand as those of Ouro Preto, but it is possibly the least spoilt of all the colonial mining cities, with carved overhanging roofs and brackets; try walking through the lower part of the town. This very friendly town is in the deep interior, 1,120 metres up amid barren mountains, with about 25,000 people; it is the birthplace of the late President Juscelino Kubitschek, the founder of Brasília. His house is a private residence, but the owner is very friendly and proud to show visitors round.

After repeated thefts, the diamonds of the Diamond Museum, in the house of Padre Rolim, one of the Inconfidentes (see under Ouro Preto) have been removed to the Banco do Brasil. Diamonds are still sought; see traditional methods at Guinda, 7 km. away. *Passeio a Diamantina*, an excellent guide, is written by the author of *Passeio a Sabará*. The town's latest industry is the making of Portuguese Arraiolos-style tapestry carpets by hand, at a cooperative in the centre; it was started by a diplomat, Sr Flecha da Silva, who was perturbed by the amount of local unemployment, and it has become very successful. Also etchings on leather are made locally.

The house of Chica da Silva, an 18th-century slave who married a rich diamond contractor, is at

258 BRAZIL

Praça Lobo Mesquita 266 (not worth a visit, entry US$0.30); Chica has become a folk-heroine among Brazilian blacks.

Hotels *Tijuco*, Macau do Melo 211, D, best, good food; *Grande*, Rua da Quitanda 70, E, *Carvalho*, same street No. 12, and *Dália*, Praça JK (Jota-Ka) 13, fairly good, E. *Pensão Avenida*, Av. Francisco Sá 243. Unnamed *pensão* at Rua Direita 131 (dona Tazinha), F; *Esplanada*, G; *Nosso*, opp. bus station, F without breakfast, good value; also opp. bus station, *J.K.* Other cheap hotels around the bus station. Wild camping near waterfall just outside town.

Restaurants *Bar-Restaurant Confiança*, Rua da Quitanda 39, good. *Capistrana*, R. Campos Carvalho 36, near Cathedral square, recommended. *Serestas* (serenades) Fri. and Sat. nights.

Voltage 110 A.C.

Tourist Information Dept. de Turismo in Casa de Cultura in Praça Antônio Eulalio 53 (no sign), 3rd floor, pamphlets and almost unreadable maps.

Excursion Along the river bank to (12 km.) Biribiri, a pretty village with an abandoned textile factory. About half-way, swimming pools in the river; opposite them, in cliff face, apparently prehistoric animal paintings in red, age and origin unknown. Interesting plant life along river, and beautiful mountain views.

Serro, 92 km. by paved road from Diamantina and reached by bus from there or from Belo Horizonte, is an unspoilt colonial town on the River Jequitinhonha (17,000 people) with six fine baroque churches, a museum and many beautiful squares. It makes *queijo serrano*, one of Brazil's best cheeses, being in the centre of a prosperous cattle region. The most conspicuous church is Santa Rita, on a hill in the centre of town, reached by steps. On the main square, at the bottom of the steps, is the Carmo, arcaded, with original paintings on ceiling and in choir. The town has two large mansions: those of the Barão de Diamantina, now in ruins, and of the Barão do Serro across the river, beautifully restored and used as the town hall and Casa de Cultura; there are old mine entrances in the hillside behind the courtyard.

Hotels *Itacolomi*, Praça João Pinheiro 20, E, fair restaurant; *Pousada Vila do Príncipe*, D, very clean, in old mansion on main street, contains own museum, the artist Mestre Valentim said to have been born in slave quarters; other cheap hotels. Restaurants: good one on main square, also *Churrascaria Vila do Príncipe* nearby on main street.

Just by the Serro turnoff is the town of Datas, with spacious church (1832) decorated in red and blue, which contains striking wooden image of Christ with the crown of thorns.

Tres Marias Some 240 km. NW of Belo Horizonte is a lake five times as large as Rio de Janeiro bay, formed by the Tres Marias dam on the upper reaches of the São Francisco river. There is a motel, and the power company, Cemig, runs a guest house (book in advance through its head office at Belo Horizonte). At Barreiro Grande is the *Clube Náutico Tres Marias*, E, simple. There are plans to develop the Tres Marias area for tourism.

(Almost the same distance SW of Belo is the even larger lake formed by the Furnas dam. It can be seen from the BR-381 road to São Paulo.)

Also north of Belo Horizonte is ***Pirapora***, terminus for boat journeys on the River São Francisco (see also page 315). The town itself is a tourist attraction because of the falls in the river which make for excellent fishing: catches weighing 73 kg. (160lb) have been reported.. The sandy river beaches are used for swimming. The grotesque figureheads of the riverboats, *carrancas*, are made in the workshops of Lourdes Barroso, Rua Abaeté 390. There are several hotels: *Pirapora Palace* and *Internacional*, both on Praça Melc Viana (7 blocks west and 1 block south of Rodoviária), and *Hotel Rex*, Rua Antônio Nascimento 357, F, good breakfast. Camping near the *Praça* on riverside. Restaurants: *Borretos* on the riverfront, and *Barrenko*, next door, better value. Watch the fishermen at work in their punt-like canoes.

The only passenger service in 1985/86 was that of the Companhia de Navegação do São Francisco (Franave), whose boat leaves Pirapora on the 5th of each month, taking 7-10 days to Juazeiro, departure 0900. The boat returns between the 13th and 17th of the month, taking 12 to 16 days for the journey upstream. Accommodation is in a *barranqueiro*, a cabin on a lighter, in tandem with cargo lighters: no private accommodation, take preferably, a hammock, or sleeping bag; no restaurant, but small canteen (take own plate and cutlery), male and female toilets (appalling).

BRAZIL 259

Cost is US$40 Pirapora-Juazeiro, US$30 Pirapora-Ibotirana (on the Salvador-Brasília highway), food included, but not beverages. Information from Franave: Av. São Francisco 1517, Pirapora (CEP: 39270, Tel.: 741 1744), or Rua José Petitinga s/n, Juazeiro (CEP: 48900, Tel.: 811-2465/2340). Information also from Mangabeira Turismo, Rua Goitacazes 71 (8° andar), Belo Horizonte, or Americatur, Av. Rio Branco 156, Rio de Janeiro (Tel.: 262-4293, 262-2659). Of the two remaining wood-burning stern-wheel boats, allegedly built for Mississippi services in the 1860s and imported from the USA in 1922 to work on the Amazon, one is being restored for tourist-agency use and was expected to be in service in 1987. The regular stops are at Januária (famous for Brazil's reputed best *cachaça*) and Bom Jesus da Lapa (a pilgrimage centre with a church built in a grotto inside a mountain, but a very poor town). Between Pirapora and Januária is the colonial town of São Francisco, with many attractive houses and a good handicraft market in the town hall; the boats do not always stop there. If you want to see the real Sertão, get off at Xique-Xique and take a bus to Utinga, Rui Barbosa and Itaberaba, then on to Salvador.

Eastern Minas

Eastern Minas Gerais is not of great cultural or historical interest, but is a centre of semi-precious stone processing and crystal carving, and also contains the Serra do Caparaó, where are found several of Brazil's highest mountains. The two principal towns, Governador Valadares and Teófilo Otôni, are both on the BR-116 inland Rio-Salvador road, and both have good connections with Belo Horizonte.

Douglas Trent writes:
Governador Valadares, 324 km. from Belo Horizonte, 5½ hours by bus (US$4 normal, US$8.50 *leito*) and also by regional air service, is a modern planned city of 250,000. The altitude is 170 metres. It is a centre of semi-precious stone mines and lapidation, as well as for the cut-crystal animals one finds in tourist shops all around Brazil.

Hotels *Governador Palace*, Av. Minas Gerais 550, C; *Real Minas*, Praça Serra Limaz 607, D; *Panorama*, D; *São Salvador*, Rua Prudente de Morais 915, E, new, clean.

Restaurants *Garfo de Ouro* in *Hotel Governador Palace*, international cuisine; *Panorâmico* in *Hotel Panorama*; *JB*, Rua Bárbara Heliodora 384, recommended, huge servings; *Joazeiro*, Rua Pessanha 639; *Tabu*, good fish dishes.

Airport is on the BR-381, 6 km. from the city centre with flights to Belo Horizonte and Ipatinga.

Excursion to the top of the Pico de Ibituruna, 960 metres.

Hospital São Lucas, Rua Barão do Rio Branco 662, Tel.: 70-0121.

Teófilo Otôni, 335 metres, population 129,000, 138 km. from Governador Valadares, is a popular buying spot for dealers of crystals and semi-precious stones. The best prices in the state are found here.

Hotels *Nobre Palace*, Av. Francisco Sá 43; *Teófilo Otôni*, BR-116 Norte km. 275, 5 km. from centre; *Lancaster*, Rua Frei Gonzaga 142, E; *Metropole*, Av. Francisco Sá 14, E; *Beira-Rio*, Av. Israel Pinheiro 671, E; *São Francisco*, Rua Dr. João Antônio 287; *Presidente*, Av. Getúlio Vargas 183.

Restaurants *Amigo do Rei*, Rua Benedito Valadares 161, Tel.: 521-4927; *Rio Grande*, next to *Teófilo Otôni Hotel*, *Intermezzo*, next to *Lancaster Hotel*.

Caparaó National Park, 49 km. of dirt road from **Manhuaçu** on the Belo Horizonte-Vitória road (BR-262), has the Pico da Bandeira (2,890m), Pico do Cruzeiro (2,861m) and the Pico do Cristal (2,798m). Arrive at the base of the waterfall by car (6 km. from park gate). From there it is a spectacular hike to the top of Pico da Bandeira (2-3 hours). The park features rare Atlantic rainforest in its lower altitudes and Brazilian alpine on top. It is best to visit during the dry season (April-October). Camping is permitted within the park at two spots and it can be quite crowded in July and during Carnaval.

Hotel *Caparaó Parque*, near park entrance in the town of Caparaó, nice, B, Tel.: (032) 741-2559.

Henri van Rooy writes that it is possible to reach the Pico da Bandeira from Ouro Preto, by using local bus services via Mariana and Ponte Nova to **Manhumirim** (*Hotel São Luiz*, F, meal $1.10, good value, but *Cids Bar*, next door, Travessa 16 do Março, has better food. 2 buses daily Ponte Nova-Manhumirim, or change at Manhuaçu. From Manhumirim, take a bus to Presidente Soares (several, 7 km.), then hitch 11 km. to Caparaó. Jeeps run from here to 1,900 metres, then it's a 3-4 hour walk to the summit. It is not possible to go to the Pico da Bandeira from Manhumirim and back in a day. This is good walking country. It may also be possible to visit local *fazendas*, for example Fazenda Modelo, 8 km. from Manhumirim. From Ponte Nova (bus 1½ hrs, $ 0.90, from Mariana) one can get the Belo Horizonte-Vitória bus to the coast. Also direct bus Manhumirim-Vitória 0900 and 1530, 5-6 hrs., passing Domingos Martins (see page 248).

Southern and Western Minas

The spas of southern Minas Gerais are easily reached by road and in some cases by air from Rio de Janeiro and São Paulo. They are also popular holiday places; the high season is from December through March.

São Lourenço, easily accessible from Rio de Janeiro or São Paulo, stands at 850 metres above sea-level. There is a splendid park, tennis, boating, swimming, a flying field, and fishing from the Ilha dos Amores in a lake ringed by gardens and picturesque forests. There is a grand ride through glorious scenery to the Pico de Buquerê (1,500 metres). Population: 15,000.

Its rich mineral waters are used in the treatment of stomach, liver, kidney and intestinal complaints. There is an up-to-date hydro establishment for douches and for the famous carbo-gaseous baths, unique in South America.

Bus service from Rio de Janeiro, 277 km., 5-6 hrs.; from São Paulo, 338 km., 6-7 hrs.

Hotels *Brasil,* nice; *Sul Americano Grande; Ponto Chic,* etc.

Caxambu, N of São Lourenço, at 900 metres, is one of the more sophisticated of these resorts. Its waters are used for treating stomach, kidney and bladder diseases, and are said to restore fertility. (They worked for Princess Isabel, daughter of Dom Pedro II, who produced three sons after a visit. The little church of Santa Isabel da Hungária stands on a hill as a thank-offering.) The mountains and forests around are very beautiful. View over the city from Morro Caxambu, 1,010 metres. Population: 12,000. Excellent hotels.

Hotels *Glória; Palace; Avenida; Caxambu; Bragança,* and 20 others.

Lambari, a lesser-known resort, is 56 km. W of Caxambu by road at 900 metres. It has a very luxurious casino, closed in 1945. Efforts are under way to reopen it. Hotels are not luxurious but fairly comfortable. The Parque das Águas has seven springs and a swimming pool. There are boat trips on the Lago Guanabara.

Hotels *Itaicy,* largest, on lake near Casino. Many others.

Cambuquirá, a little N of Lambari by road at 946 metres, very popular, with friendly atmosphere and picnic sites close by.

Hotels *Grande Hotel Empresa;* also *Santos Dumont,* and many others.

Poços de Caldas, in western Minas, is reached by road or plane from São Paulo (272 km.), Rio (507 km.) or Belo Horizonte (510 km.). The city is sited on the crater of an extinct volcano in a mountainous area. Venetians from Murano settled here and established a crystal-glass industry. It is the most luxurious and fashionable of the resorts, and is a traditional honeymoon centre. It has complete and up-to-date thermal establishments for the treatment of rheumatic, skin and intestinal diseases. Excursions include several lakes within a few km. of the city with boating and restaurants; the Véu das Noivas with its three waterfalls illuminated at night; the tall statue of Cristo Redentor at an altitude of 1,678 metres, which can be reached by cable car; nearby is an 80-metre granite rock, Pedra *Batão.* There are also the lovers' well, Fonte dos Amores, and the Japanese teahouse at the Recanto Japonês. Hippie fair every Sunday in Praça Pedro Sanches. Festivals include Carnival, São Benedito ending on May 13, and recently established Festival de Música Popular Brasileira. Excellent climate. There is now a small industrial estate. Altitude: 1,180 metres; pop.: 110,000.

Hotels Some 80 hotels and pensions. *Palace,* old fashioned but well run, with sulphur baths; *Continental,* Av. Francisco Salles 235; *Pousada Vale das Rosas,* Rodovia a Belo Horizonte Km. 5; *Minas Gerais,* Rua Pernambuco 615.

Restaurants *Castelões*, Praça Pedro Sanches 207; *Lareira*; *Sem-Sem*, Rua Assis Figueiredo 1080; *Cantina do Araújo*, Rua Assis Figueiredo 1705.

Buses Rio, 8 hrs., US$4; São Paulo, 4½ hrs., US$2; both by Viação Cometa.

Tres Corações, also in southern Minas but not a spa, is the birthplace of Pelé, the legendary football star (statue). Hotels: *Italian Palace*, E; *Capri*, F; good food at *Cantina Calabresa*. Reached by daily buses from Rio, São Paulo and Belo Horizonte. Daily bus to (32 km.) ***São Tomé das Letras***, beautiful hilltop village with frescoed 17th-century church and many caves in surrounding hills.

Uberaba, in the Minas Triangle, is on the Rio da Prata, 718 km. from São Paulo. It is an important rail and road junction, being on the direct highway between São Paulo and Brasília, and serves a large cattle raising district. At the beginning of May each year the Rural Society of the Minas Triangle holds a famous cattle and agricultural exhibition at Uberaba. There are local sugar mills and lime plants. Altitude, 700 metres. Population, 180,000. Hotels: *Palácio; Grande.*

Araxá, also in the Minas Triangle, about 193 km. from Uberaba at 970 metres, is a quiet little place with thorium and radio-active waters and sulphur and mud baths. It can be reached from Rio (848 km.) or São Paulo (549 km.) Belo Horizonte (374 km.), by bus. Pop.: 30,000. Airport.

Hotels *Grande de Araxá*, luxury, 8 km. away; *Grande Hotel Pinto; Colombo.*

Note that there are also mountain spa resorts (Serra Negra, Lindóia, Campos do Jordão) in São Paulo State (see page 278).

To the N of Uberaba is the city of ***Uberlândia***, founded in 1888; good communications by air and road (buses to Brasília, 6 hrs., US$3.60; to Belo Horizonte, 9 hrs., US$5, to São Paulo, US$5.40). Population, 230,000. *Hotel Nacional*, opposite Rodoviária, F, with view (cheaper without), shower and breakfast, clean.

The State of São Paulo

The State of São Paulo, with an area of 247,898 square km. and a population of 25 million, is larger than the states of New York and Pennsylvania together and about the same size as Great Britain and Northern Ireland. A narrow zone of wet tropical lowland along the coast rises in an unbroken slope to the ridge of the Great Escarpment—the Serra do Mar—at from 800 to 900 metres above sea level. The upland beyond the Great Escarpment is drained westwards by the tributaries of the Rio Paraná. The broad valleys of the uplands are surmounted by ranges of low mountains; one such range lies between the São Paulo basin and the hinterland of the state. West of the low mountains between the basin and the rest of the state lie the uplands of the Paraná Plateau, at about 600 metres above the sea. One of the soils in this area is the *terra roxa*, the red earth in which coffee flourishes. When dry it gives off a red dust which colours everything; when wet it is sticky and slippery. There is ample rainfall in São Paulo State; indeed, the highest rainfall in Brazil (3,810 mm.) is over a small area between Santos and São Paulo; at São Paulo itself it is no more than 1,194 mm. Temperatures on the plateau are about 5°C lower than on the coast, but it is only south of the latitude of Sorocaba that frosts occur and then not frequently. Temperatures are too low for coffee in the São Paulo basin itself, but the State produces, on average, about 7 million bags a year.

Between 1885 and the end of the century a boom in coffee and the arrival of large numbers of Europeans transformed the State out of all recognition. By the end of the 1930s there had arrived in São Paulo State a million Italians, half a million each of Portuguese and immigrants from the rest of Brazil, nearly 400,000 Spaniards and nearly 200,000 Japanese. The population is now almost equal to that of Argentina or Colombia. Today the State produces 50% of the country's cotton, 62% of its sugar, a third of its coffee and over 50% of its fruit exports. It turns out 90% of Brazil's motor vehicles, 65% of its paper and cellulose, and 60% of its machinery and tools, being also responsible for 60% of the country's industrial consumption of electric energy. All this comes, in sum, to some 20% of Brazil's agricultural output and 65% (40% in São Paulo city alone) of its industrial production. São Paulo provides 33% of the total exports of Brazil and takes 40% of the total imports: nearly all pass through the port of Santos.

São Paulo is 429 km. from Rio de Janeiro, and is connected with it by air, the Via Dutra highway, and the Central do Brasil railway. It was founded in 1554 by two Jesuit priests from São Vicente, Blessed José Anchieta and Padre Manuel Nóbrega, as a mission station. The original settlement, not yet effectively preserved, was at the Pátio do Colégio in the centre of the city, where a copy of Anchieta's original church has been built (it is open Tues. to Sun., 1300-1700).

São Paulo (altitude 730 metres) is one of the fastest growing cities in the world; people either love it or hate it. It is already the most populous city in South America, and the continent's leading industrial centre. Until the 1870s it was a sleepy, shabby little town, but it now covers more than 1,500 square km.—three times the size of Paris. The citizens are intensely proud of its skyscrapers, of its well-lit streets, of its efficient water supply, and especially of its underground line, the first in Brazil, which began operating in September 1975, linking Jabaquara in the south with Santana in the north. (A second line is now open.) The traffic pattern is extremely exasperating: you may have to drive around 10 blocks to reach a point half a block away. Also exasperating is the amount of air pollution: in dry weather eyes and nose are continually troubled. The city's population is now estimated at almost 8.5 million; in 1983 the metropolitan area population was estimated at 13 million, growing at about 150,000 a year, compared with 9.5 million for the metropolitan area population of Rio.

The two main reasons for the city's development lie in its position at the focus of so much agricultural wealth, and in its climate, which makes the Paulistanos the most hard working and energetic people in Brazil. Visitors, however, find the characteristic sharp changes of temperature troublesome and even Paulistanos seem to catch cold often. (Incidentally, one differentiates between Paulistas—inhabitants of the State—and Paulistanos— inhabitants of the city.) There is another and a most potent factor which explains its industrial growth: the availability of plentiful hydro-electric power.

The shopping, hotel and restaurant centre embraces the districts of Av. São Luís, the Praça da República, and Rua Barão de Itapetininga. The commercial quarter, containing banks, offices and shops, is contained within a central district known as the Triângulo, comprising Rua Direita, Quinze de Novembro, São Bento and Praça Antônio Prado, but it is already rapidly spreading towards the apartment and shopping district of Praça da República. Rua Augusta, near Avenida Paulista, once the home of the wealthier citizens, is now full of boutiques and fashion shops. Avenida Paulista houses most consulates in skyscrapers, many banking head offices, and the Assis Chateaubriand Art Museum (opened by Queen Elizabeth in 1968). It is becoming a new downtown area, more dynamic than the old centre, and so is Av. Faria Lima, 8 km. from Praça da República.

The park in Praça da República is worth going into between 0800 and 1400 on Sun.: birds, trees and Brazilians in all their variety, and a famous handicrafts fair. Near the Praça is the city's tallest building, the Edifício Itália on the corner of Av. Ipiranga and Av. São Luís. There is a restaurant on top (very reasonable), and a sightseeing balcony.

The Viaduto do Chá, which bridges the central avenue, Anhangabaú, leads to the opera house, one of the few distinguished 19th-century survivals that São Paulo can boast. The Av. Paulista and the "jardins" América, Paulista and Paulistano still contain some mansions of beauty and interest and are on one of the routes to the Butantã Institute or "snake farm". About 10 minutes' walk from the centre of the city is the old Municipal Market, covering an area of 27,000 square metres; a new Municipal Market has been built in the outskirts. The Municipal Library, surrounded by a pleasant shady garden, is well worth visiting.

The Cathedral's foundations were laid over 40 years before its inauguration during the 1954 festivities commemorating the 4th centenary of the city. This

BRAZIL 263

massive building in neo-Gothic style, with a capacity for 8,000 worshippers, is in the heart of the city. The sumptuous crypt chapel contains the tombs of São Paulo's ecclesiastical leaders.

The large Municipal Stadium in the Pacaembu valley, a flourishing residential district, is well worth seeing. Built on Olympic lines in an area of 75,500 square metres, it holds nearly 70,000 spectators. Besides the flood-lit football ground and athletics field and basketball court, there are also a covered gymnasium, open-air and covered tennis courts, an illuminated 50-metre long swimming pool, a youth hostel, and a great hall for receptions and rallies. There is a larger stadium holding 100,000 people in Morumbi, one of the more elegant residential districts.

Typical of modern development are the huge Iguatemi, Ibirapuera and Morumbi shopping centres. They include luxurious cinemas, snack bars and most of the best shops in São Paulo. Parking in each for over 1,000 vehicles. On a rather humbler level are the big supermarkets of El Dorado (Av. Pamplona 1704) and Pão de Açúcar (Praça Roosevelt, near the *Hilton*); the latter is open 24 hrs. a day (except Sun.).

The palatial Jockey Club racecourse is in the Cidade Jardim district with easy access by bus. Race meetings are held on Sat., Sun., Mon. and Thurs. nights. The new town premises of the Jockey Club (Rua Boa Vista) are well worth a visit.

Ibirapuera Take a Monções bus (675-C) from Ana Rosa metro station to Ibirapuera Park for the architecturally impressive new Legislative Assembly. There is also a planetarium equipped with the most up-to-date machinery (shows at 2000 Tues. and Thurs.; 1600, 1800 and 2000 weekends and holidays); a velodrome for cycle and motor-cycle racing; an all-aluminium covered stadium for indoor sports which seats 20,000 people. The Museum of Contemporary Art (of the Universidade de São Paulo), founded in 1963, has an important collection of Western and South American modern art. It includes works by artists such as Picasso, Braque, Matisse, Kandinsky, De Chirico, Klee, Ernst, Miró, Modigliani and many other European artists, and, from Brazil and South America, Malfatti, Tarsila do Amaral, Segall, Neri, Portinári, Di Cavalcânti, Ramos, Soto, Portocarrero, Toral and others. The collection is divided between the Bienal building in Parque Ibirapuera (entrance at back of building, open Tues.-Sun., 1300-1800, closed holidays, free) and a building at Rua da Reitoria, 109, Cidade Universitária, open Weds.-Sun. 1000-1700, closed holidays, students free (it is hoped to unite the collection at the Cidade Universitária). Buses to Ibirapuera, 5362 (Grajaú) from Praça da Bandeira; to Cidade Universitária 702U or 7181 from Praça de República.

In this park, too, are the Museums of Modern Art, Aeronautics (showing the Santos Dumont plane; US$0.40 entrance), Folklore (interesting) and Sciences. There is also a unique display of nativity scenes and scenes of the life of Christ. (Concerts held at Christmas-time). At the entrance is a majestic monument to the Bandeirantes, or pioneers. All the Ibirapuera museums are open Tues.-Sun., 1400-1800. (For other museums see page 267.)

Anhembi (Av. Assis Chateaubriand, Santana) is the largest exhibition hall in the world. It was inaugurated in 1970 and all São Paulo's industrial fairs are held there. It has a meeting hall seating 3,500 people, three *auditórios*, 24 conference rooms (*salas de reunião*) and two restaurants. Parking space is provided for 3,500 cars. It may be reached by underground (short walk from Tietê station).

Local Holidays Jan. 25 (Foundation of City).

Warning Beware of assaults and pickpocketing in São Paulo.

Hotels Among the most luxurious are the *Maksoud Plaza*, the *Caesar Park*, the *Grand Hotel Cà d'Oro* (superb restaurant), the *Brasilton*, the *Eldorado* (excellent) and the *Hilton*, all with swimming pools, nightclubs and convention halls. The *Grand Corona* has been recommended as best value. Here follows a selection in our categories L, A and B. Prices for the cheapest room in each category are as follows (incl. breakfast), in US dollars:

	Single	Double	Rooms	Class*
Maksoud Plaza, Alameda Campinas 150	163	179	420	L
Caesar Park, Rua Augusta 1508	120	140	200	L
Monfarrej Sheraton, Alameda Santos 1437	98	98		L
Eldorado Boulevard, Av. São Luís 234	95	105	154	L
Hilton, Av. Ipiranga 165	115	130	391	L
Grand Hotel Cà d'Oro, Rua Augusta 129 (recommended)	150	170	400	1+
Brasilton, Rua Martins Fontes 330	110	123	111	1+
Bristol, Rua Martins Fontes 277	63	73		
São Paulo Center, Largo Santa Ifigênia 40	34	42	253	1+
Othon Palace, Rua Líbero Badaró 190	39	43		
Samambaia, Rua Sete de Abril 422	33	37	65	1+
Vila Rica, Av. Vieira de Carvalho 167	32	37	215	1+
San Raphael, Av. São João 1173	40	47	197	1+
Jaraguá, Rua Major Quedinho 44	29	34	197	1+
Grand Corona (ex-Cà d'Oro), Basílio da Gama 101	33	55	82	

264 BRAZIL

Comodoro, Av. Duque de Caxias 525	44	55	132	
Excelsior, Av. Ipiranga 770	25	28	180	T
Planalto, Cásper Líbero 117 (Varig-Tropical chain)	25	29	268	1
Terminus, Av. Ipiranga 741	21	25	67	T
Normandie, Av. Ipiranga 1187	39	49	200	S
Cambridge, Av. Nove de Julho 216 (recommended)	18	21	120	S
Solar Paulista, Rua Francisca Miquelina 343	21	25	60	S

*Class: L—de luxe; 1+—first class plus; 1—first class; S—standard; T—tourist.

There are scores of cheaper hotels, of which we append a selection (asterisk * if breakfast included): *Hores Belgrano*, Rua Marquês de Paranaguá, 88, D, central, English spoken, special rates for long stays, rooms with kitchenette. Another residential hotel, recommended for longer stays, is *Metropolitan Plaza*, Alameda Campinas 474, A. *Triannon Residence*, Av. Casa Branca, C*; *Firenze*, Rua Frei Caneca 80, C* (Tel.: 255-6211); *San Marino*, Martinho Prado 173 (Tel.: 258-7833); C*; *Carillon Plaza*, Rua Bela Cintra 652, B*; *Las Vegas*, Rua Vitória 390 (corner Av. Rio Branco), F*, excellent; *Rio Branco*, Av. Rio Branco 234, near corner wih Ipiranga, E*, central, with bath, recommended; *Joamar*, Rua Dom José de Barros 187 (off São João), 50 rooms, E; *Marechal*, Av. Barão de Limeira 339, 67 rooms, E with bath and telephone, safe, excellent; *Planeta*, Al. Dino Bueno 54, E; *Danúbio*, Av. Brig. Luís Antônio 1099, D; *Senador*, Rua Senador Feijó 1066, E; *Kolins*, Alameda Gilete 1017 (off São João, nearest subway Praça República), F, clean, hot water, private toilet. *Banri*, Rua Galvão Bueno 209, D, good; *Isei*, Rua da Glória 288, F, good value, simple, nice, both near metro station Liberdade (Japanese quarter). *Adoro*, Matias Aires 425, near Rua Consolação, round beds, mirrors everywhere, appropriate TV, D.

Also suggested: *S. Sebastião*, 7 de Abril 364, E, recommended, cheap and clean, and now has rooms with bath; *Ideal*, R. Guaianazes 39, F*; *Cineasta*, Av. São João 613, 80 rooms, D*; *Plaza*, Av. São João 407, 42 rooms, E*; *Britânia*, Av. São João 300, F; *Central*, Av. São João 288 E with shower, F without, clean good, central; on Rua do Triúnfo: *Condeixa*, No. 145, F, showers; *Maringá*, F, friendly, basic; *Noroeste*, No. 285, F, basic, clean, hot showers; *Saturno*, F, hot water, soap and towel. *Carnate*, E; *Eiras*, E, showers. Very many of the cheap hotels are hot-pillow establishments.

Take the metro to Luz station and in the block behind the old Rodoviária, off Av. Rio Branco, there are scores of cheap hotels with prices ranging from category F to category C; try: Rua Santa Ifigênia: *Trinidade*, No. 737, F, recommended; *Lima*, F*, friendly, recommended; *San Remo*, No. 163 (corner of Av. Ipiranga), apartment 7000, F with breakfast, basic; *Diamantina*, No. 78. Rua General Osório, frequented by drug-addicts: *Aliança*, No. 235 (corner Santa Ifigênia), E, nice; *Ouro Fino Hotel Familiar*, No. 388, F, friendly; *øai*, No. 66, F, recommended; *Hotel Mauá*: *Pontal*, No. 248, E; *Comércio*, No. 512, E; *Queluz*, No. 438, F. Rua dos Gusmões: *Galeão*, No. 394, F, hot showers; *Hospedaria Apuliense Familiar*, No. 218, F, with shower; *Santa Ifigênia*, F, lunch available for US$1.70; *Londres* appears to be a brothel. Rua Timbiras, *Monaco*, No. 143, F; *Paulicea*, No. 216, F, cheap and clean, recommended; *Ofir*, No. 258, E. Rua dos Andradas; *Itaipu*, No. 467, E, good, clean. Rua Barão de Piracicaba; *São José*, F without breakfast, basic, good value; *Minister*, No. 105, 27 rooms, E. Also in this area are *Piratininga*, private shower, clean but no a/c, D*; *Osiris*, Cásper Líbero 591, F with bath and breakfast, clean, quite good, hot water, near Luz railway station; *Paraná*, next to old bus terminal, F without bath; *Rocha*, Av. Cásper Líbero, F; *Astória*, Rua Washington Luís, F; *Tatuí*, Praça Princeza Isabel 171 (on corner of Av. Duque de Caxias, 2 blocks from old bus station), F, clean with bath. **N.B.** the redlight district is in the blocks bounded by Ruas Santa Ifigênia, dos Andradas, dos Gusmões and Av. Ipiranga, and is definitely not recommended for women travelling alone. *Casa do Politécnico*, Rua Afonso Pena 272, cheap accommodation. A recommended "Apart-hotel" for longer stays is *Residencial Alameda Nothman* (Santa Cecília), Al. Nothman 682. Accommodation of the youth-hostel type is available at the Pacaembu Stadium at a fee in (our) category E. A letter addressed to the Secretário de Esportes is required. The Youth Hostel (*Albergue da Juventude*) is in the Ibirapuera gymnasium, Nóbrega e Estados Unidos, very cheap but you must first join the Brazilian YHA (15 de Novembro e Av. São João—office in centre) for about US$5 a year.

Electric Current 110-220 volts A.C., 60 cycles.

Camping Cemucam, at Cobia (Rodovia Raposo Tavares, km. 27). List of sites can be obtained from Camping Clube do Brasil, R. Minerva, 156—Perdizes (Tel.: 263-024).

Restaurants Apart from the international cuisine in the first-class hotels listed above, here are only a few out of many:

Portuguese *Abril em Portugal*, Rua Caio Prado 47; *Adega Lisboa Antiga*, Rua Brig. Tobias 280 (subsolo), and others.

Italian *Tibêrio*, Av. Paulista 392; *Famiglia Marcini*, Rua Avanhandava 81; *Trattoria do Piero*, Rua Caconde 323, popular and good; *Gigeto*, Avanhandava 63; *A Camorra*, R. de Consolação 3589; *Pastasciutta*, Rua Barão do Triúnfo 427 (Brooklin Paulista); *Cantina Roma*, Rua Maranhão 512 (Higienópolis); *Trastevere*, Al. Santos 1518; *Bongiovanni*, Av. 9 de Julho 5511; *Da Fierella*, R. Bernardino de Campos 294; *Don Ciccillo*, Praça Souza Aranha 185; *L'Osteria do Piero*, Alameda

BRAZIL 265

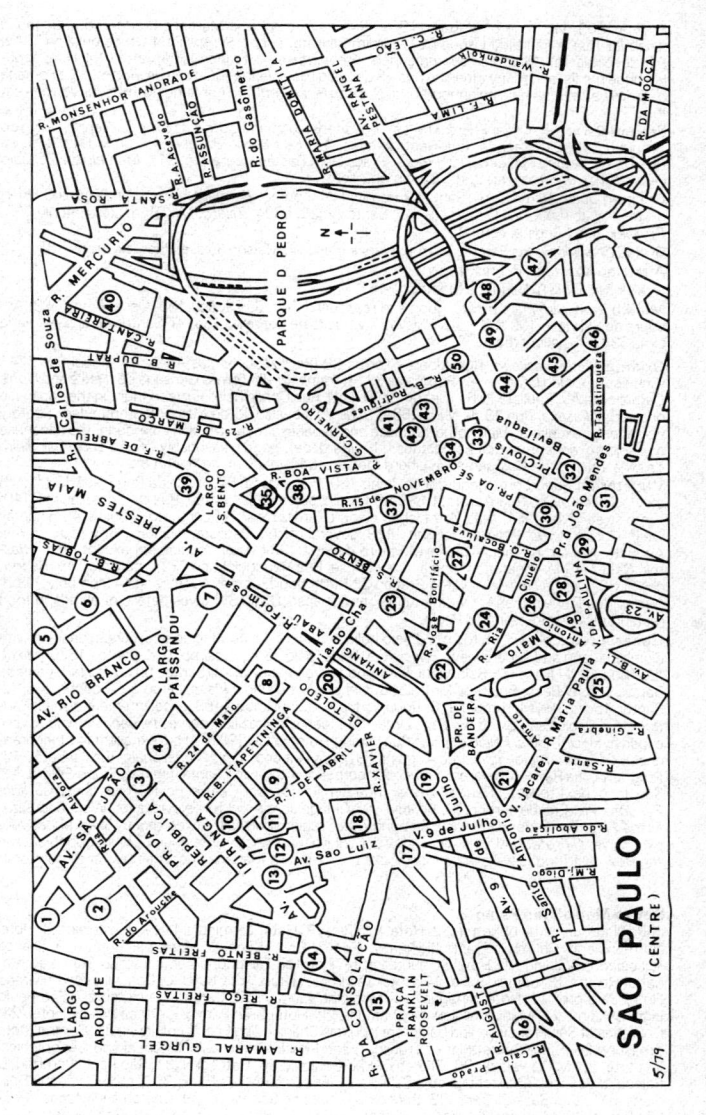

SÃO PAULO (CENTRE)

266 BRAZIL

França 1509; *Via Veneto*, Al. Barros 909; *Giovanni Bruno*, Rua Martinho Prado 165; *Il Sogno di Anarello*, Rua José Maria Lisboa 661, Jardim Paulista; *Grupo Sergei*, Post Office building in Av. São José near Rua Marconi (recommended); *Piemontese*, Al. França 1509, Jardim Paulista, popular, huge meals; and many others in Rua 13 de Maio (Bela Vista)— *Lazzarella*, *Roperto*, *La Fontana di Trevi*, *La Tavola*—and neighbourhood. *Casa de Pizza Rodízio*, Rua Augusta 1585, all you can eat for US$4.

French *David's*, R. Oscar Freire 913; *La Cocagne*, Rua Amaral Gurgel 378; *La Casserole*, Largo do Arouche 346; *La Gratinée*, Rua Bento Freitas, 42; *La Maison Basque*, Av. João Dias 239; *Le Bistrot*, Av. Adolfo Pinheiro 510; *Freddy*, Praça Dom Gastão Liberal Pinto 11; *Marcel*, Rua Epitácio Pessoa 98; *Coq Hardy*, nr. Borba Gato monument.

German *Juca Alemão*, Av. Santo Amaro and Al. Lorena; *Bierhalle*, Av. Lavandisca 263; *Biergarten*, Av. Ibirapuera 3174; *Kobes*, Av. Santo Amaro 5394; *Zillertal*, Av. Brig. Luís Antônio 909. *Bei Max*, Rua Augusta, central.

Swiss *Chamonix*, Rua Pamplona 1446, very expensive; *Maison Suisse*, Rua Caio Prado 183.

Austrian *Kitzbühel*, R. Frei Gaspar.

Greek *Mikonos*, R. Henrique Monteiro 218.

Middle East *Almanara* (Arab), good and reasonable, Av. São João 1155, Oscar Freire 523, Av. Vieira de Carvalho 109 and 124; *Rubayat*, Av. Vieira de Carvalho 134, Al. Santos 86 and Av. Faria Lima 5332, excellent meat.

Oriental *Sino-Brasileiro*, Rua Alberto Torres 39 (Perdizes); *Gengis Khan*, Av. Rebouças 3241 (Chinese); *Golden Dragon*, Av. Rebouças 2371; *Yamanga*, R. Tomás Gonzaga 66; *Heike* and *Notre Dame*, both Av. Paulista 2064 (Center 3); *Sukiaki*, Rua Conselheiro Furtado (right in the Japanese quarter); *Akasaka*, Rua 13 de Maio 1639; *Shushi-Kiyo*, also 13 de Maio, recommended. *Suntory* (Japanese), excellent. Many other Chinese and Japanese restaurants in Liberdade, the Japanese quarter. *Kokeche*, Rua dos Estudantes 41 (Liberdade), good, reasonably-priced *sushi* bar; *Hare Krishna*, Rua Pandiá Calógeras 54, Liberdade, near São Joaquim metro station.

Vegetarian *Superbom*, Viaduto 9 de Julho 180, Praça da Sé 62, Praça da República 128 (lunch only); *Salade e Chi*, Rua Aurora, US$2.50 for all you can eat; *Sattua*, Rua da Consolação 3140; same street, No. 2961, *Mãe Terra* (shop also); *O Arroz de Ouro*, Largo do Arouche 46 (shop as well); *Cheiro Verde*, Peixoto Gomide 1413; several off Av. Paulista, including *Boy Papi*, on Rua Augusta; *Nectar*, Alameda Gabriel Monteiro da Silva 1931 (open to midnight except Mon.); *Jasmin Casa de Chá*, vegetarian food and tea house, Rua Haddock Lobo 932; *Intergrão*, Av. Rebouças 2036; *Delícia Natural*, Av. Rio Branco 211 (4th floor), corner Av. Ipiranga, lunch only, good; *Herva*, Rua Pinheiros 541. "Vida Integral" newspaper (US$0.35) gives details of all health food restaurants and stores in São Paulo.

General *Terraço Itália*, on top of Edifício Itália, 41 floors up, good fixed price lunch, dancing with excellent band and superb view; *Bassi*, Rua 13 de Maio 334; *Massimo's*, Al. Santos 1826; *Mexilhão*, Rua 13 de Maio 62, Bela Vista, very good. *Don Fabrízio*, Al. Santos 65; *O Portal*, Alameda Barros 925; *O Beco*, Rua Bela Cintra 306, dinner only; *Dinho's Place*, Largo do Arouche 246, Al. Santos 45 and Av. Morumbi 7976; *Rodeio*, Rua Haddock Lobo 1468, excellent meat dishes; *Paddock*, Av. São Luís 228 and Av. Faria Lima 1541 (genuine Brazilian, serves *feijoada completa*, very expensive); *Um, Dois, Feijão e Arroz*, Rua Ipiranga, modest (US$3 or 4) but excellent (4 other branches); *Cantina Amigo Piolin*, Rua Augusta 89, excellent and cheap; *Amazonas*, Rua Guarará 212; *Programa*, Via Raposo Tavares; *Comercial*, corner of Vitória and Santa Ifigênia; *Grupo Sérgio*, Av. São João, next to *Hotel Central*; *Alvear*, Rua Seminario, near Central Post Office, cheap *surtido*; *Pandoro*, Av. Cidade Jardim 60; *Bolinha*, Av. Cidade Jardim 53 for *feijoadas* (on Wed. and Sat.); *Maria Fulô*, Av. 9 de Julho for Bahia and other regional dishes—fixed menu, fixed price, very expensive; *O Profeta*, Al. dos Aicós 40 (for Mineiro food); Airport Restaurant (very good); *Jack in the Box*, fast food, several locations. *Pizza d'Oro*, in Vila Mariana (local painters and sculptors);

Key to Map of São Paulo
1. Paulista Academy of Letters; 2. Hotel Vila Rica; 3. Hotel Terminus; 4. Hotel Excelsior; 5. Hotel Normandie; 6. Church of Santa Ifigénia; 7. Central Post Office; 8. Municipal Theatre; 9. Diários Associados Building; 10. Hotel Samambaia; 11. Brazilian Telephone Company; 12. State Secretariat of Health; 13. Edifício Itália; 14. Hotel São Paulo Hilton; 15. Church of Consolação; 16. Grand Hotel Cá d'óro; 17. Hotel Jaraguá; 18. Municipal Library; 19. Cambridge Hotel; 20. São Paulo Light Building; 21. Municipal Council Chamber; 22. Hotel Grão Pará; 23. Othon Palace Hotel; 24. Churches of São Francisco and São Francisco das Chagas, and Faculty of Laws; 25. Central State Treasury; 26. State Secretariat of Transport and Public Works; 27. Historical and Geographical Institute; 28. Mauá Palace; 29. Church of São Gonçalo; 30. Cathedral; 31. São Paulo Forum; 32. Palace of Justice; 33. Archbishop's Palace; 34. Federal Savings Bank; 35. Stock Exchange Buildings; 36. State Savings Bank; 37. State Savings Bank; 38. Banco do Estado de São Paulo; 39. Church and Monastery of São Bento; 40. Municipal Market; 41. Police Station; 42. Pátio do Colégio; 43. Gas Company; 44. Church of Nossa Senhora do Carmo; 45. State Cooperative Building; 46. Church of Boa Morte; 47. Policlínica Hospital; 48. Mauá Engineering School; 49. State Secretariat of Finance; 50. Accounts Tribunal.

BRAZIL 267

many snack-bars and pizzerias throughout the city. For fast food, there are now several McDonalds in São Paulo. There are plenty of atmospheric restaurants in the "artists' quarter" of Bexiga (Bela Vista), best Fri. and Sat. nights. Another atmospheric place is *Recanto Goiano*, just off Praça 14 bis (Av. 9 de Julho), typical dishes, *caipira* music.

Bars *Scotch Bar*, Rua 24 de Maio 35, conjunto 411; *Pepe's Bar*, Edifício Metrópole; several outdoor bars in Largo do Arouche and in Moema; all major hotels. Many gay and lesbian bars.

Tea Rooms Vienense, Jaraguá, Cha Mon (Edifício Metropole); Chelsea Art Gallery, *Hotel Eldorado. Jasmin*, Rua Haddock Lobo 932.

Night Clubs There are several first-class night-clubs serving excellent meals; they prefer couples to single people. Besides very good dance-bands, the majority have floor-shows in which internationally-famed artists perform. *A Baiúca*, Praça Roosevelt 256; *Silvio's* and *Plano's*, Oscar Freire 913 and 811 respectively; *Stardust*, Largo do Arouche 336. *Catedral da Samba* (Rua Rui Barbosa 333); *Igrejinha* (Rua Santo Antônio 973) and *O Beco* (Rua Bela Cintra 306), recommended for samba. Also recommended: *O Jogral*, Rua Maceió 66, Higienópolis (reasonable). Several small clubs with live music in the Bela Vista area of Av. Santo Antônio and Rua 13 de Maio.

Discotheques *Hippopotamus* (Av. Nove de Julho 5872); *London Tavern* (Hilton Hotel, subsolo); *Ton Ton* (Rua Néstor Pestana 115); *Moustache* (Rua Sergipe 160), among others. Jazz at *Opus 2004*, Rua Consolação 2004.

Shopping Rua Augusta for boutiques. All types of stores at Shopping Center Iguatemi, Av. Brig. Faria Lima, Shopping Centre Ibirapuera, Av. Ibirapuera (see page 263), and Shopping Centre Morumbi, also El Dorado Shopping Centre (corner of Av. Rebouças and Marginal Pinheiros). Souvenirs from Mimosa, Joaquim Nabuco 304, Brooklin Paulista; Indian handicraft, Artíndia, Rua Augusta 1371 (Galeria Ouro Velho), Tel.: 283-2102. Also good for souvenirs is the area between Rua 24 de Maio and bars and pizzerias Rua 7 de Abril (just off Praça da República); bargaining is recommended; plenty of jewellers here. H. Stern, jewellers, at Praça da República 242, Rua Augusta 2340 and at Iguatemi, Ibirapuera and Morumbi shopping centres and at main hotels. Below the Museu de Arte de São Paulo, a flea market takes place on Sun., 0800-1700. São Paulo is cheap for film and clothes.

Bookshops Livraria Cultura, Eva Herz e Cia., Av. Paulista 2073, loja 153. Livraria Triângulo, Alameda Tietê 46. Ilco, Barão do Triúnfo 371, Brooklin Paulista, books in English. Livraria Kosmos, Praça Dom José Caspar 134, loja 30, international stock. Librairie Française, R. Barão de Itapetininga 275, wide selection. Book Centre, R. Gabus Mendes 29 (near Praça de República), books in English.

Local Transport The metro is clean, cheap and efficient; book of ten tickets US$0.80. Combined bus and metro ticket are available, e.g. to Congonhas airport. The section Santa Cecília to Tatuapé is now open on line 2. The East-West line (2) is being extended 14 km. from Barra Funda (the interchange with Fepasa and RFFSA railways and site of a future, third Rodoviária) to Itaquera. (Apply to the Municipality, if you speak Portuguese and would like a sightseeing tour of the Metro system.) Local buses are normally crowded and rather slow, but clean. Maps of the bus and metro system are available at depots, e.g. Anhangabaú. Taxis display cards of actual tariffs in the window.

Golf Courses About half an hour's drive from the centre there are two 18-hole golf courses, one at Santo Amaro, and another, the São Fernando Golf Club, in beautiful surroundings. There is a sporting 9-hole course at São Francisco club, beyond the Butantã Institute.

Sport The most popular is association football. The most important matches are played at Morumbi and Pacaembu grounds. At Interlagos there is a first-class racing track (see page 271). There is yachting, sailing and rowing on the Santo Amaro reservoir.

Entertainment The Teatro Municipal, is used by visiting theatrical and operatic groups but has no resident company. There are several first-class theatres: Aliança Francesa, Teatro Arena, Itália, Maria Della Costa, Paiol, Ruth Escobar among others. There are also ballet companies and the usual multitude of luxurious cinemas.

Culture and Education There are three universities: the official university of São Paulo, the Pontifical Catholic University, and the Mackenzie University. The official University of São Paulo is now situated in the Cidade Universitária (buses from main bus station), outside the city beyond Pinheiros. There are a number of architecturally interesting buildings housing different faculties and the four museums of archaeology, ethnology, anthropology and mineralogy. (All keep different hours, but all are open Mon.-Thurs. 1400-1700.)

Galleries and Museums The Museu de Arte de São Paulo (at Av. Paulista 1578, immediately above the 9 de Julho tunnel, nearest metro is Paraíso, or circular bus 805A from Praça da República) has a large group of French Impressionists, Florentine and Umbrian painters (including

268 BRAZIL

Botticelli and Raphael), a magnificent Turner, several Hieronymus Bosch and Frans Post, sculptures by Degas, some interesting work by Brazilian artists, including Portinári. Particularly interesting are the pictures of the North-East done by Dutch artists during the Dutch occupation (1630-54); the exotic tropical landscapes— even the Paulo Afonso falls!—have been made to look incredibly temperate. (Exhibitions vary, not all the artists above may be on view.) Temporary exhibitions are held in the basement. Entrance US$0.25, 1400-1800 (main collection closes 1700), Tues.-Sun. **The Museum of Brazilian Art** is at Rua Alagoas 903, Higienópolis, entrance free, Tues.-Fri. 1000-2200, Sat.-Sun. 1400-1800. Here there are copies of Brazilian sculptures, including those of Aleijadinho. **The Museum of Anthropology and Ethnology** is on the fourth and fifth floors of Bloco D in the main Arts Complex just opposite the entrance to the Butantã Institute (see page 270). Every odd-numbered year the **São Paulo Bienal** at Ibirapuera has the most important show of modern art in Latin America, open from beginning of Sept. till Nov. For the other museums at Ibirapuera (including the Museum of Contemporary Art), see page 263, and for the Museu Paulista and Casa do Grito at Ipiranga, see page 271.

There are two museums on Av. Tiradentes, near the Luz Park; the **Museum of Sacred Art** in the Convento da Luz (open Tues.-Sun. 1300-1700, US$0.20) and the State Art Collection (**Pinacoteca do Estado**) at No. 141 (open Tues.-Sun. 1400-1800, free).

Not far from the Butantã Institute (see page 270) are the **Casa do Bandeirante** at Praça Monteiro Lobato, the reconstructed home of a pioneer of 400 years ago (Tues.-Sun. 1200-1730, free); and the **Casa do Sertanista**, a museum of Indian folklore and handicrafts mounted by the famous expert on the Indians, Orlando Villas Boas, at Av. Francisco Morato 2200, open Tues.-Sun., 1230-1730, entrance free.

The Casa Brasileira, Av. Faria Lima 774, has been established as a museum of Brazilian furniture. Open weekdays 0900-1200 and 1400-1700. Museo Padre Anchieta, Praça do Colégio, is a restored mission house; inside are examples and relics of the Jesuit era, entrance US$0.05. The Sound and Image Museum is at Av. Europa 158. The Museum of Lasar Segall, at Rua Alfonso Celso 362, Vila Mariana (near Santa Cruz metro station), shows the works of a German expressionist painter who emigrated to Brazil. Museo da Fundação Maria Luisa e Oscar Americano, Av. Morumbi 3700, Morumbi, a private collection of Brazilian and Portuguese art and furniture, well-displayed; hours Weds.-Sun., 1000-1700. There is a Museo da Discoteca e Biblioteca da Música at Rua Catão 611, 5th and 6th floors, open Mon.-Fri., 0900-1300 (take bus 819 P from Praça Princesa Isabel to Lapa district).

TREKS·SAFARIS
EXPEDITIONS

A unique selection of adventures in
ASIA·AFRICA·SOUTH AMERICA

from 3 weeks to 4 months at guaranteed prices you can afford. Phone (24 hours), write or come in.

ENCOUNTER OVERLAND

Involve yourself!

267 Old Brompton Road London SW5 Tel 01-370 6845

BRAZIL

Addresses

British Consulate General, Av. Paulista 1938, 17th floor; Caixa Postal 846. Tel.: 287-7722.
American Consulate General, Rua Padre João Manuel 933, Tel.: 853 2011.
Irish Consulate, Av. Paulista 2006, 5th floor, 01310 São Paulo, Tel.: 287-6362.
British Chamber of Commerce of São Paulo, Rua Barão de Itapetininga 275, 7th floor; Caixa Postal 1621. Tel.: 255-0519.
American Chamber of Commerce for Brazil, Rua Formosa 367, 29th floor, Tel.: 222-6377.
Canadian Consulate General, Av. Paulista 854-8th floor, Tel.: 287-2122.
West German Consulate, Av. Brig Faria Lima 1383, 12th floor, Tel.: 814-6644.
Swiss Consulate-General, Av. Paulista 1754, 4th floor, Caixa Postal 30588. Tel.: 289-1033.
Austrian Consulate-General, Al Lorena 1271, 01424 São Paulo, Tel.: 282-6223.
Swedish Consulate-General, Rua Oscar Freire 379, 3rd floor. Tel.: 883-3322.
Argentine Consul, Rua Araújo 216, 8th floor (open 0830-1430).
Bolivian Consul, Rua Cap. Salamão 80, 7th floor, S/11 (open 0900-1300).
Paraguayan Consul, Av. São Luiz 112, 10th floor, Tel.: 255-7818/259-3579.
Uruguayan Consul, Rua Gal. Jardim 770, 7th floor.
Samaritan Hospital, Rua Conselheiro Brotero 1486. Tel.: 51-2154.
Sociedade Brasileira de Cultura Inglesa, Avenida Higienópolis 449.
St. Paul's Anglican (Episcopal) Church, Rua Comendador Elias Zarzua 1231, Santo Amaro. Tel.: 246-0383.
American Library, União Cultural Brasil-Estados Unidos, Rua Coronel Oscar Porto 208, Tel.: 287-1022.
Goethe-Instituto, Rua Frei Caneca 1246 (open Mon.-Thurs. 1400-2030).
Instituto Hans Staden, Rua Cons. Crispiniano 53, 12th floor.
Lutheran church, Av. Rio Branco 34.
General Post Office, Praça do Correio, corner Av. São João.
Police, Tel.: 228-2276; Radio Patrol, Tel.: 190.

Emergency First Aid, Tel.: 71-8673, 71-0757.

Physicians (English-speaking) Edwin Castello, José Maria Lisboa 861, s/104, Tel.: 287-9071; Ruy Silva, Conselheiro Brotero 1505, No. 64, Tel.: 67-2470; Wilson Frey, Barão de Jacegua 1102, Tel.: 241-4474. Christel Schlünder, Rua Alvares de Azevedo 127, Sto. Amaro, Tel.: 247-5963, German speaking, and for children.

Banks Times when open vary from bank to bank. Lloyds Bank (ex-BOLSA), Rua Quinze de Novembro 143 165. (Open 1000-1630.) Banco Internacional, Rua Quinze de Novembro 240. Banco Holandês Unido, Rua Quinze de Novembro 150. Citibank, Av. Ipiranga 855. First National Bank of Boston, Rua Líbero Badaró 487. Banco Lar Brasileiro (Chase Manhattan owned), 131 Rua Alvares Penteado, and other national banks. Banco Mercantil de São Paulo, Av. Paulista 1450, for cash advances on Access/Master Charge, but most unhelpful and slow.

Exchange Many *câmbios* near Praça da República. Also PM Turismo/Cambio. Exprinter, Barão de Itapetininga 243, also deals in foreign currencies. Boreal Turismo, Rua Dom José de Barros 326, recommended.

Cables Embratel, Av. São Luís 50, and Av. Ipiranga 344.

Tourist Offices Praça da República, and Praça da Sé and Liberdade metro stations (small red kiosks). For information on São Paulo State, Praça Antônio Prado 9, 6th floor, Av. São Luís 115. On Sundays a free cultural tour of the city starts at Colégio do Passeio, near the cathedral (buses every 20 mins. from 0900 to 1600), to see Casa do Bandeirante, Casa do Sertanista, Capella do Morumbi, the old market, and Casa do Grito. For weekly information on cultural activities, addresses and recommended bars, see the supplement "Veja em São Paulo", of the magazine *Veja*. Tourist offices have free magazine, *Visão, Guia Turística Carto Plum* available from banks etc. around Praça da República.

Maps of São Paulo in train timetables at news-stands (US$1.50), and in the monthly tourist guide published by the Prefeitura. Also obtainable from the tourist offices, the Rodoviária (upstairs), the better hotels, American Express and H. Stern, the jeweller.

Travel Agents Wilson, Sons S.A., Av. São Luís 715; Exprinter, Rua Barão de Itapetininga 243; Receptur, same street, 221; Wagon-Lits Cook, Av. São Luís 285; Globe Trotter, Rua 24 de Maio 35; Tunibra, Praça da Liberdade 63, Tel.: 36-0101, helpful ; Itatiaia Publicidade e Turismo, Cons. Crispiniano 69 (for hotel reservations especially); Transatlântica Turismo, Rua Coronel Xavier de Toledo 98 (for local excursions); Kontik-Franstur (American Express representative), Rua Marconi 71. Panorama Turama, Av. São Luís 47, 257-7155/5348. Dicka Turística Ltda, Av. São Luís 50, Edif. Itália, 8th floor. Royal Turismo, Manoel da Nóbrega off Av. Paulista, helpful to budget travellers.

Railways The Estrada de Ferro Santos a Jundiaí (ex São Paulo Railway) to Santos "down the hill" (passenger service suspended in 1985), also to Jundiaí and the interior; Companhia Paulista

270 BRAZIL

de Estradas de Ferro, into the coffee, fruit and cattle districts; Central do Brasil Railway to Rio de Janeiro, 9 hrs. journey, night sleeper train (the Santa Cruz) leaving São Paulo Luz Station at 2230; warmly recommended, US$20 for a double cabin; Cia Mogiana to NE of state, from Campinas through Ribeirão Preto; Fepasa through Sorocaba to Bauru. No through tickets from São Paulo to Campo Grande or Corumbá are sold; you must go by bus or train (0830, 1925, 2225) to Bauru (risking a day's wait there for train connections) from where Estrada de Ferro Noroeste do Brasil goes at 1615 daily across Mato Grosso do Sul to Corumbá (34 hrs. from São Paulo), and on, after crossing frontier by road, from Quijarro (Bolivia) to Santa Cruz de la Sierra by the Estrada de Ferro Brasil-Bolívia. There is a railway from São Paulo to Brasília, changing at Campinas; US$24.50 sleeper, US$ 14.50 1st class, leaves Luz station on Sun. at 1000, reaching Campinas at 1125, and Brasília 0830 on Mon. (through tickets available). The track is bad, but the journey interesting. There are several railway stations in São Paulo; Júlio Prestes for former Sorocobana services into the State; Luz for Santos a Jundiaí commuters, night trains to Rio and former Paulista and Araquara Railways (metro links with Rodoviária at Tietê); Roosevelt for suburban trains.

RFFSA is planning to restore the uppermost stage of the São Paulo—Paranapiaçaba cog railway and the railway buildings; the line was the first to link São Paulo with the coast and Santos. Steam services are expected to recommence from São Paulo in 1988.

Roads Distances in km.: Belém, 2,917; Brasília, 1,100; Belo Horizonte, 586; Curitiba, 397; Florianópolis, 700; Fortaleza, 3,065; Foz do Iguaçu, 1,071; Manaus, 4,052 (last stretch not paved); Natal, 2,992; Porto Alegre, 1,143; Recife, 2,671; Rio, 429; Salvador, 1,944; Vitória, 932. Drivers to Rio can take the picturesque new coast road if they've time. Take the Via Anchieta to the Guarujá turn, before Guarujá take Bertioga turn and you're on the Santos-Rio highway.

Buses To get to the new Rodoviária, take the metro to Tietê, very convenient. Bus to centre, US$0.20. Bus to Rio, 6 hrs., frequent service, US$4 (*leito*, 8); to Curitiba, 6 hrs., US$4 (*leito*, 8); to Blumenau, 9½ hrs., US$6.50; to Porto Alegre, 18 hrs., US$10 (*leito*, 20); Rio Grande 25 hrs., US$16.25; to Belo Horizonte, 9 hrs., US$7 (*leito*, 14); to Salvador, 30 hrs., US$18.50 (*leito*, 37); to Recife, 40 hrs., US$20 (*leito*, 40); to Fortaleza, 48 hrs. US$28 (*leito* 56); to Cuiabá, 24 hrs., US$16 (Andorinha at 1700, connects with Cuiabá-Porto Velho bus); to Campo Grande (Mato Grosso do Sul), 16 hrs., US$15.75; to Porto Velho, 60 hrs. (or more), US$35; to Brasília, 15 hrs., US$12 (*leito*, 24); to Foz do Iguaçu, 18-20 hrs., US$9.50 (*leito*, 20). To Santos, US$1.15 (there is a bus station for Santos and São Vicente at the southern end of the Metro line, at Jabaquara, buses from here leave every 5 minutes, taking about 50 minutes); São Sebastião, 4 hrs. US$3.15 (say "via Bertioga" if you want to go by the coast road); to Parati, Angra dos Reis and also to Ilhabela, 2 daily, 8 hrs., US$3.50; to Montevideo, via Porto Alegre, with TTL, departs 2200, 31 hrs. US$40; to Buenos Aires 36 hrs., US$44 (*leito*, 90); to Santiago, Pluma or Gral. Urquiza (both start from Rio), 56 hrs., US$70; to Asunción (1,044 km.), 25 hours with Pluma or RYSA, US$16 (*leito* US$34.50).

Visits to coffee *fazendas* (May-June) and round trips into the surrounding country are organized by the travel agencies.

To hitch to Rio, take the metro to Ponte Pequeno, then a bus for Guarulhos, alighting where the bus turns off the Rio road for Guarulhos.

Air Services There are air services to all parts of Brazil, Europe, North and South America from the new international airport at Cumbica, near Guarulhos (about 40 km. from the city); the local airport of Congonhas, 14 km. from the city centre, is used for the Rio-São Paulo shuttle and private flights only (the taxis in the street outside are much cheaper than the airport taxis, at US$3.50) or take a bus (US$0.50) or metro/bus trip (US$2.50) to the Rodoviária do Tietê and Congonhas airport, every 20-40 mins., approx. 1 hr. Bus between Cumbica and Congonhas every 45 mins., ½ hr., US$1. There are about four hundred flights per week to Rio de Janeiro (about US$39). All airline offices in triangle formed by Av. São Luís, Av. Ipiranga and Rua da Consolação.

The Butantã Snake Farm and Museum (Instituto Seroterápico at the University), Av. Dr. Vital Brasil 1500, Pinheiros, is the most popular tourist attraction. The snakes are milked for their poison at 0930, 1030, 1130, 1400, 1500 and 1600, but you may not observe this; the antidotes made from the venom have greatly reduced deaths from snakebite in Brazil. Open daily from 0800-1700 (except 1300-1700 Mon.), entrance US$0.15. Informative museum. From Praça da República take bus 700, 701 or 702-U to beginning of Av. Dr Vital Brasil, then walk or take bus 715-F to Av. Corifeu de Azevedo Marqués, then walk. Also reached by bus 7181 and trolleybus 107-T.

Parque da Independência, in the suburb of Ipiranga, contains the famous Ipiranga Monument to commemorate the declaration of Brazilian independence; beneath the monument is the Imperial Chapel, with the tomb of the first emperor, Dom Pedro I, and Empress Leopoldina (open Tues.-Sun., 1300-1700). Take bus 4612 from Praça da República. The **Casa do Grito**, the little house in which Dom Pedro I spent the night before his famous cry of Ipiranga— "Independence or Death" - is preserved in the park (open Tues.-Sun. 1300-1730). The **Museu Paulista**, housed in a huge palace at the top of the park, has old maps, traditional furniture, collections of old coins and of religious art and rare documents, and a department of Indian ethnology. Behind the Museum is the Ipiranga Botanical Garden. Open Tues.-Sun. and holidays, 1300-1730. Take bus 478-P (Ipiranga-Pompéia for return) from Ana Rosa. There is a son et lumière show on Brazilian history in the park on Wed., Fri. and Sat. evenings at 2030.

Parque do Estado (Jardim Botânico), out at Água Funda (Av. Jabaquara), has a vast garden esplanade surrounded by magnificent stone porches, with lakes and trees and places for picnics, and a very fine orchid farm worth seeing during the flowering season, November-December. Over 32,000 different kinds of orchids are cultivated. Open Tue.-Sat., 0900-1700. The astronomical observatory nearby is open to the public Thurs. afternoons. Bus 475 from Brig. Luís Antônio or metro to Jaguaribe (2nd last stop), then a bus marked "Zoológico".

Zoological Gardens Near the Jardim Botânico, not more than half an hour's drive from the city centre. A very large variety of specimens can be seen in an almost natural setting of about 35 hectares of forest: a most interesting site. Open 0900-1800, admission US$0.45 (bus 4742, "Jardim Celeste", from São Judas Tadeu). There is a wild-life park, Simba Safari, nearby, admission US$0.75 per pedestrian, US$2 p.p. with a car, open Tues.-Sun. 0900-1800.

Aquarium, Av. Pacaembu 905, reportedly Brazil's best, is open Mon.-Fri., 1000-2000, Sat.-Sun., 0800-1800.

Parque Água Branca (Avenida Água Branca, 455) has beautiful gardens with specimens of tropical plants, Brazilian birds and wild life. Pavilions house a well stocked aquarium, a zoo, and exhibitions of food produce.

In Tremembé, a little beyond Cantareira, half an hour from the down-town area, is the **Horto Florestal**, containing examples of nearly every species of Brazilian woodland flora (admission daily, 0800-1800).

Santo Amaro Dam (Old Lake), is 3 km. from the centre of Santo Amaro suburb. This is a popular boating resort with several sailing clubs and many attractive cottages along the shore. There is a bus (30 min.) from São Paulo to Santo Amaro.

Interlagos, which has a motor-racing circuit with 18 km. of track, is São Paulo's lake resort on the Santo Amaro dam. It can be reached from Santo Amaro by bus. Close to the track, where the Brazilian Grand Prix takes place, usually in February, is the 32-km. long Guarapiranga artificial lake with good restaurants and several luxurious sailing and sports clubs. Camping Clube do Brasil site. Guarapiranga is less polluted than the other artificial lake, Billings, which also has restaurants.

Pico de Jaraguá (1,135 metres) the highest peak in the neighbourhood, gives good views of Greater São Paulo on a fine day. This peak is reached from km. 18 on the Campinas highway (Via Anhanguera) by a good road through Taipas and Pirituba.

Embu, 28 km. from São Paulo, is a colonial town which has become a centre for artists and craftsmen. On Sunday afternoons there is a large and popular arts and crafts fair; not to be missed. Buses from close to the Largo de Pinheiros, São Paulo, or Santo Amaro bus.

The Coast of the State of São Paulo

Santos, 63 km SE of São Paulo and 5 km. from the open sea, is the most important Brazilian port. (Over 40% by value of all Brazilian imports and about half the total exports pass through it.) It is reached from Rio by ship (320 km.) in 12-15 hrs., and a direct highway between the two cities has been completed (see pages 245 and 273). A railway and the Anchieta and Imigrantes highways run to São Paulo. A free-port zone for Paraguay, 1,930 km. by rail or road, has been established. A few km. outside the city there is an important industrial area round the steelworks, oil refinery and hydroelectric plant at Cubatão (known locally as the Valley of Death because of the pollution from chemical factories, among the worst in the world).

272 BRAZIL

The plain upon which Santos, a city of 411,000 people, stands is an island which can be circumnavigated by small boats. The city has impressive modern buildings, wide, tree-lined avenues, and wealthy suburbs. The streets around Praça Mauá are very busy in the daytime, with plenty of cheap shops. In the centre, an interesting building is the Bolsa Oficial de Café, in Rua 15 de Novembro. The night-life can best be seen in an area known as Gonzaga, which has the large hotels. Although best known for its commerce, Santos is also a holiday resort; visitors are attracted by the magnificent beaches and views.

The port is approached by the winding Santos Channel; at its mouth is a picturesque old fort (1709).

There are fine monuments, including one in Avenida Ana Costa to commemorate the brothers Andradas, who took a leading part in the movement for independence; one in the Praça Rui Barbosa to Bartolomeu de Gusmão, who has a claim to the world's first historically recorded airborne ascent in 1709; one in the Praça da República to Bras Cubas, who founded the city in 1534; and one in the Praça José Bonifácio to the soldiers of Santos who died in the Revolution of 1932. There are a disappointing municipal aquarium on Av. Bartolomeu de Gusmão (Ponta da Praia) and a Museu do Mar, Rua República do Equador 81.

Local Holidays (in addition to national): Jan. 26 (Foundation of Santos); Good Friday; Corpus Christi.

Hotels *Holiday Inn* complex at the centre of Gonzaga, Ana Costa 555, A, with shopping centre; *Atlântico*, Av. Pres. Wilson 1, D-B; *Gonzaga*, Av. Pres. Wilson 36 (Gonzaga), E with bath; *Pensão Curitiba* (Gonzaga), F without bath, basic but friendly; *Indaiá*, Av. Ana Costa 431, D; *Ritz*, Rua Marechal Deodoro 24, D; *Transmontana*, Rua Marechal Floriano Peixoto 202; recommended; *Maracanã Santos*, Pres. Wilson, beach front, D; *Avenida Palace*, Pres. Wilson 10, beach front, D; *Santos*, Bartolomeu de Gusmão 16, D with bath; *Estoril*, Rua Bitencourt 55, F, with bath, cheap (has round beds, red lights and mirrored ceilings); small, family-style hotels can be found in this area; *São Paulo*, Rua Macílio Dias 6, E without breakfast; many cheap hotels near the Orquidário Municipal, 1-2 blocks from the beach. *Potiguar*, Rua Amador Bueno 116, 300 m. from bus station, F, breakfast, showers, clean, good.

Restaurants *Cantina Dom Fabrízio*, Av. Ana Costa 482; *Jangadeiro*, Ponta da Praia; *Hong Kong Palace*, Av. Conselheiro Nébias 288 (Chinese food); *Rincón Argentino*, Av. Manuel da Nóbrega 666, at São Vicente (Gaucho food); *Ilha Porchat Grill*, on Ilha Porchat, off São Vicente, at edge of island, overlooking bays of São Vicente and Santos; first class *Pizzaria Zi Tereza*, Av. Ana Costa 451; also *Pizzaria Santa Izabel*, Av. Bartolomeu de Gusmão 165 (also serves seafood). *Chico's Bar*, Av. Floriano Peixoto (Boqueirão), good. *Fonte das Vitaminas*, Ana Costa 534, good for juices, lunches.

Electric Current 220 A.C. 60 cycles.

Tram Restored service along the Praia from 0800 to 2200 daily, US$0.10.

Taxis All taxis are supplied with meters. The fare is a fixed charge of US$0.25 plus US$0.10 per km. Taxi, Gonzaga to bus station, US$2.

Consulate (British) Largo Senador Vergueiro 2, first floor. Caixa Postal 204. Tel.: 25733, 29680.

All Saints Church, Praça Washington 92, José Menino. Services in English held every Sun.

Cables Embratel, Largo Senador Vergueiro 1 and 2.

Banks Banco Internacional, Rua General Câmara 24; Banco Holandês Unido, Citibank, Banco do Brasil, all in the Rua 15 de Novembro. The First National Bank of Boston, Praça Visc. de Mauá 14. Banks open: 1000-1630.

Exchange Houses Casa Faro, Rua 15 de Novembro, 80 & 260; Casa Bancaria Branco, Praça de República 29.

Tourist Information Praça dos Expedicionários 10, 10th floor; booths at Aquarium, Rodoviária, Casa do Café, Orquidário Municipal.

Coastal Shipping Irregular services by Companhia de Navegação Lóide Brasileiro, S to Porto Alegre, N to Belém (Pará) and intermediate ports, and Manaus. Consult their agents, Rua General Câmara 22, 2nd floor, conjunto 34.

Rail The British-built Santos a Jundiaí up the hill to São Paulo is one of the railway wonders of the world; it passes through Cubatão and then, running on toothed tracks up the escarpment, interesting hill scenery. Passenger services were suspended in 1985 although a daily freight train at 0600 from Ana Costa station includes a passenger car to Evangelista de Souza at the top of the hill, arriving 0757, return 1820 (arrive in Santos 2016); no connections at all to São Paulo from Evangelista de Souza, only for the hardy.

Air Services From São Paulo; Santos has no airport.

Bus Services Buses start for most suburbs from Praça Mauá, in the centre of the city. There are buses to São Paulo (50 mins., US$1.15) at intervals of approximately 15 mins., from the Rodoviária near city centre. Enquire about being picked up or put down outside usual terminal points. Express cars also run to São Paulo at regular intervals. Fare, US$2.75 each way, per passenger. (The two highways between São Paulo and Santos are sometimes seriously crowded, especially at rush hours and weekends.) Buses for Santos are caught in São Paulo in the Jabaquara bus station, not the new Rodoviária. There are direct buses to Rio but not along the coast road (Normandy company, 6 a day, *leito* at 2230, 7½ hrs., US$4); to get to Rio along the coast road, you must take an Atlântico bus to Ubatuba or Caraguatatuba, change there for Rio.

Excursions To the coasts E of Santos (Guarujá, Bertioga, Ilhabela) and SW (Praia Grande, Itanhaém). Short excursion along the Guarujá road to José Menino for the orchid gardens in the Praça Washington (flowering Oct.-Feb.). There is an open-air cage containing humming-birds of 20 different species and the park is also a sanctuary for other birds.

The *Ilha Porchat,* a small island reached by a bridge at the far end of Santos/São Vicente bay, has beautiful views over rocky precipices, of the high seas on one side and of the city and bay on the other. At the summit is a splendid night club, the *Top House Restaurante e Discoteca*. No entrance fee but there is a minimum charge of US$8.

To **Alto da Serra,** the summit of the forest-clad mountain range; magnificent panoramas and views. The return journey can be done in under 2 hrs. by road.

Monte Serrat A funicular railway to the summit (every ½ hr., US$1 return), where there is a semaphore station and look-out post which reports the arrival of all ships in Santos harbour. There is also a quaint old church, dedicated to Nossa Senhora da Monte Serrat, said to have performed many miracles. The top can be reached on foot. Seven shrines have been built on the way up; annual pilgrimages are made by the local people. Fine views.

Guarujá The route from Santos to the resort of Guarujá is along Av. Conselheiro Nébias, to the seafront, continuing along the beach to the Guarujá ferry (every 10 min., free for pedestrians) at Ponta da Praia. On the other side proceed as far as Turtle Bay. During the season and weekends there is a long delay at the Ponta da Praia vehicle ferry; to avoid this take the ferry on foot and get the bus on the Guarujá side. There is a strong undertow on nearly all the Guarujá beaches; the Jequiti-Mar beach (officially called Praia de Pernambuco) is the safest. Golf club at Guarujá; population, 94,000. (Trolleybus from Praça Mauá in Santos to the ferry, then buses.)

Turn left in centre of Guarujá and drive less than 1 km. to reach *Delfim Hotel* (B) and its restaurant *La Popote* at the beginning of the long beach of Praia da Enseada. Close by, at Av. Miguel Estefno 999, is *Casa Grande Hotel,* luxury, in Colonial style, with clean beach. Facing sea is the luxurious *Ferraretto Hotel,* B (night club, swimming pool). Camping Clube do Brasil site at Praia do Perequê (where the best fish restaurants are), near municipal nursery.

The Jequiti-Mar holiday complex, 8 km. beyond Guarujá on the road to Bertioga, is extremely attractive. There are private beaches (excellent swimming and boating) and very fine fishing grounds, and chalet accommodation, A or B, according to size and situation. There is an excellent restaurant and two night clubs; they are open each weekend and every night from December to March, in the holiday season. 2 km. further north is a beach where many fishing boats land their catch—a number of good seafood restaurants line the seafront.

There are good sea-food restaurants on the road to **Bertioga,** an attractive place, where the fort of São João houses the João Ramalho museum. (Hotels: *Marazul,* Av. Tomé de Souza 825; *Indaiá Praia,* same street, No. 1079, both D; restaurants *Zezé e Duarte* (2), *O Camarão de Bertioga*.) The coastal road beyond Bertioga is now paved, and the new Rio-Santos highway, 1-2 km. inland, is now completed, and provides a good link to São Sebastião. Going N, the beaches are Praia de Bertioga, Praia São Lourenço, Praia Guaratuba, Praia Boracéia (campsite, US$0.70 with meals), all are empty except for the light traffic. 30 km. beyond Boracéia is the beach resort of Maresia (hotels, campsite), from where it is 21 km. to **São Sebastião,** (two buses a day from Rio, 1030 and 1830, not along the coast, heavily booked in advance; 4 a day from Santos, 3½ hrs.; buses from

274 BRAZIL

São Paulo run inland, unless you ask for the service via Bertioga, only 2 a day), and (free ferry) to Ilhabela (4 hrs. by bus from Santos, 3 a day, US$2.55). There is a Museu de Arte Sacra in the Chapel of São Gonçalo in the town centre. Tourist Office; Av. Dr Altino Arantes 174, friendly and helpful except regarding Ilhabela. The São Sebastião beaches are polluted; foreigners can stay in the Camping Clube do Brasil grounds for US$3 a night. 6 km. S of São Sebastião is Camping do Barraquecaba Bar de Mar de Lucas, US$2 per night, recommended. (*Hotel Roma*, on the main square, excellent, E and upwards; *Recanto dos Pássaros*, *Porto Grande*, both C; *Arrastão*, C with most facilities; *São Paulo*, F with breakfast, clean, friendly.) Ilhabela tends to be expensive in season, when it is cheaper to stay in São Sebastião.

Half-way between Bertioga and São Sebastião, on the Praia de Juqueí beach, is *Hotel Timão*, D, German-owned, with excellent fish meals.

Ilha de São Sebastião (Ilhabela). The island of São Sebastião, known popularly as Ilhabela, is now easily accessible by car or bus from Santos. A bus runs along the coastal strip facing the mainland. Cavendish, the English pirate, had his secret anchorage in one of the sheltered caves there. Last century it was used as a landing place for illegal slave-traffic.

The island is of volcanic origin, roughly about 390 sq. km. in area. Its highest peak, Morro do Papagaio, rises 1,300 metres above sea-level, with its bare peak often obscured by mist; the slopes are densely wooded. There are many beautiful waterfalls, easily accessible to the enterprising walker. Most of the flatter ground is given over to sugar-cane for distilling *cachaça*; tourists may visit the distilleries.

The only settled district lies on the coastal strip facing the mainland, the Atlantic side being practically uninhabited except by a few fisherfolk. The place abounds in tropical plants and flowers of the most extraordinary variety, and many fruits grow wild, whose juice mixed with the local *cachaça* and sugar makes as delicious a cocktail as can be imagined.

No alterations are allowed to the frontage of the main township, **Ilhabela**: There are several hotels, ranging through the whole price-range. Visitors abound during summer week-ends; motorists are warned to avoid those days as the car-carrying capacity of the ferry is very limited.

The energetic can climb over the hump of the island down towards the Atlantic, sometimes through dense tropical forest following the old slave trail, but for this 50-km. return journey a local guide is required. A visit to the terraced Toca waterfalls amid dense jungle close to the foot of the 970-metre Baepi peak will give you cool freshwater bathing (entry, US$0.50). In all shady places, especially away from the sea, there abounds a species of midge known locally as *borrachudos*. A locally sold repellant (Autum) keeps them off for some time, however. Those allergic to insect bites should remain on the inhabited coastal strip.

Hotels in Ilhabela: *Mercedes*, C, Tel.: 7-0071; *Siriuba*, D, Tel.: 7-0265; *Ilhabela*, A, Tel.: 7-0083. Next door is *Itapemar*, windsurfing equipment rented at US$3 an hour, A. Also in the C price range are *Petit Village*, *Solar dos Bandeirantes*, *Ilhabela Praia*, *Colonial* and *Caiçara*. *Pousada dos Hibiscos*, D, good atmosphere, swimming pool, recommended. There are several other less expensive pensions, such as *Sul America*, E. *Camping Porto Seguro*, accessible by two-hourly bus from Ilhabela, US$1.40 p.p.

Restaurant *Les Boucaniers*, French-run, recommended, US$3.50 per head. *Telma*, Perequê, reasonable.

Sightseeing Visit the old Feiticeira plantation, where creepy underground dungeons will give you the shudders. The road is along the coast, sometimes high above the sea, towards the south of the island. You can go by bus, taxi, or horse and buggy.

Pedras do Sino (Bell Rocks) These curious seashore boulders, when struck with a piece of iron or stone, emit a loud bell-like note.

Bathing Bathing on the mainland side is not recommended because of oil, sandflies and jelly fish on the beaches and in the water. Praia dos Castelhanos, reached by a rough road over the island (no buses), is recommended.

Transport Ferry (free) every 15 mins. Modern passenger ferry to hotel district on island, every 2 hrs., US$1.60.

North of São Sebastião, on the Santos-Rio road, is São Francisco, a village with *Pontal Hotel* (not recommended, expensive, noisy), and *Restaurant Flipper* (excellent); good beaches. Further on is **Caraguatatuba**, with 17 good beaches to the NE and SW (several hotels, popular at weekends, good restaurants: *Brisa*, Av. Artur Costa Filho 1821, *Xamagu*, near main square). Good camping site US$1.60 per night on beach and other sites. Direct buses to Caraguatatuba from Rio de Janeiro, São Paulo and Santos; direct buses from São Paulo do not use the coast road. Further E is **Lagoinha**, 34 km. W of Ubatuba, with chalets and sailing boats for hire. Exotic birdlife and virgin forest. *Maier's Mar Virado* is owned by Hans Maier, who speaks English and arranges hirings. Then

BRAZIL 275

we come to **Ubatuba**, with two Camping Clube do Brasil sites at Maranduba and Perequê-Açu beaches. In all, there are 72 beautiful beaches, quite spread out, most with campsites (one 6 km. N of Ubatuba, US$1 p.p., is recommended). There is also a yacht haven. Ubatuba has numerous hotels; recommended are *Tropicana*, Praia da Enseada, D; *Restaurante Beija Flor* with apartments, E; *Solar das Aguas Cantantes*, Praia do Lázaro (11680 S.P., Tel.: 0124-42-0178), reached by local bus, swimming pool, restaurant, B; *Saveiros*, Praia do Lázaro (Tel.: 0124-42-0172), pool, restaurant, C, run by a Rumanian, Lucian Strass, English spoken, who welcomes users of *South American Handbook*. Furnished flats and cottages may be rented from Lúcio Martins Rodrigues, Rua Amaral Gurgel 158, Apto. 121—CEP.01221—Vila Buarque—São Paulo—SP; Tel.: 853-8101, 532-0496, 577-6482, 221-1357. The flats are in the town centre, 400 m from beach, the cottages 7½ km. from the centre in a green belt with a natural swimming pool, each can sleep a maximum of 5 (bedroom for 2-3, 2 extra in living room), and has kitchen with cooker and fridge, bathroom and laundry facilities. Cost is US$5 a day, payable in US or Canadian dollars, or any Western European currency. The road from São Sebastião is paved, so a journey from São Paulo along the coast is possible, 5 buses daily. Ubatuba is 70 km. from Parati (see page 246), several buses daily, on the hour, from *Lanchonete Nice*, near Rodoviária. If driving from Ubatuba along the coast to Rio, one can stop for lunch at Porto Aquarius, where there is a cave and hotel in a beautiful setting (not cheap). Direct buses from Rio, São Paulo and Santos.

In the opposite direction (SW) from Santos, it is 50 km. beside the Praia Grande to the town of **Itanhaém,** with its pretty colonial church and semi-ruined Convento da Conceição on a small hill. There are several good sea-food restaurants along the beach, and a Camping Clube do Brasil site nearby at Peruíbe beach, and many others which are cheaper. There are many attractive beaches here, and hot springs with medicinal mud (hotels *Maison Suisse*, *Príncipe*, *Glória*). The whole stretch of coast is completely built up with holiday developments. Frequent buses from Santos US$0.85, 1 hr.

Further south is the town of **Iguape**r, founded in 1538. Typical Portuguese architecture, the small municipal museum is housed in a 16th century building. (Buses from São Paulo, Santos, or Curitiba, changing at Registro.) It has a market, hotels and restaurants. Camping Clube do Brasil site on beach. Opposite Iguape is the northern end of the Ilha Comprida with beautiful beaches stretching SW for 86 km. A continuous ferry service runs from Iguape (passengers free; cars at a small charge); buses run until 1900 from the ferry stop to the beaches and campsite Britânia (clean, friendly, US$0.70 p.p., drinkable tap water, tastes bad). The island is being developed as a resort for Paulistas; good restaurants, hotels, supermarket—fresh fish is excellent. At the southern end **Cananéia** is more commercialized than Iguape; it has 3 or 4 hotels (mostly E).

From Iguape it is possible to take a boat trip down the coast to Cananéia and Ariri. Tickets and information from Dept. Hidroviário do Estado, Rua Major Moutinho 198, Iguape, Tel.: 41 1122. Boats leave Iguape on Mon. Thurs. (but check in advance). It is a beautiful trip, passing between the island and the mainland. The boat has a toilet, fresh water, and coffee. In wet weather, the cabin gets crowded and uncomfortable.

Caves Inland, W of the BR-116 are the caverns of the Vale do Ribeira; among the best known is the 8-km. Gruta da Tapagem, known as Caverna do Diabo (Devil's Cave), 45 km. from Eldorado Paulista. The caves are open 0800-1100 and 1200-1700; bar and toilets. *Hotel Eldorado*, friendly, clean, with breakfast, F. Bus to Eldorado Paulista from Santos or São Paulo, US$2.60, 4-5 hrs.; then hitch-hike on banana trucks or tourist buses (which run from both cities); most traffic on Sats. and Suns. From Curitiba, change buses at Jacupiranga for Eldorado Paulista. A suitable stopping place for visiting the caves area is **Registro** on BR-116, in the heart of the tea-growing region, populated mainly by Japanese Brazilians. (*Lito Palace Hotel*, D; *Hotel Continental*, F). 43 km. from Caverna do Diabo is Caverna de Santana, 10 km. from the town of Iporanga; it has 5.6 km. of subterranean passages and three levels of galleries. (Iporanga is the most convenient town for visiting both sets of caves; it is 42 km. from Apiaí, which is 257 km. SW of São Paulo.)

The Paraná River

For the Iguaçu Falls and neighbourhood, see Argentine section, page 106.

In the far W, on the great River Paraná, were the tremendous waterfalls known in Brazil as Sete

276 BRAZIL

Quedas (the Seven Falls), and in Spanish Latin America as the Guaíra Falls; they were drowned by the filling of the lake behind the giant Itaipu dam in 1982. (Some 130 km. S by air or road is Iguaçu, described on page 106.) A train for **Presidente Epitácio** on the Paraná leaves São Paulo (Júlio Prestes station) daily at 1600 (900 km.), reaching the port at 1020 the next morning. It has sleepers and a restaurant car. Price for a double sleeper, US$35. Normal 1st class fare US$8.50 (this service is under threat of closure-check). An alternative to the 17½ hour train ride is a ½hr. bus journey. Andorinha several daily, US$12. A luxury passenger vessel, the *Epitácio Pessoa*, sails twice monthly (weekly during holiday periods) on Wed. at 1700 downstream to **Guaíra**, 400 km. S; getting there at 1900 Thurs. evening. Return trips on Sat. at 1100, arrive at Pres. Epitácio at 2200 Sun., US$100. (Note: These schedules appear to be variable.) Guaíra will not be flooded, but much of its agricultural land and its clay beds will be. Prices per person using double cabin, including meals, US$170. Cheaper accommodation available on lower decks. Bookings should be made in advance with: Comércio e Navegação Alto Paraná Ltda., Praça da República 177, Loja 15, São Paulo, Tel.: 259-8255, Telex: 011-32400. Passages can also be purchased (subject to space available) at the office by the port in Presidente Epitácio, and in Guaíra from Ernst Mann, Americatur, Rua Alvorada 253. Alternatively it may be possible to obtain passage on a cargo boat.

Bus Guaíra-Campo Grande: buy a ticket (US$14) at the Guaíra bus terminal, take ferry to Ponta Porã, then bus to Mondo Novo, change bus there for Campo Grande; morning and night bus, 12 hrs. in all. (For journey from Campo Grande, see page 354.) There is a bus service between Curitiba and Guaíra, US$8, 10 hrs.; bus to São Paulo, US$8.25, 16 hrs.; Guaíra to Presidente Epitácio, US$1.20. The road is surfaced throughout. Also a bus from Londrina (US$5.25, 7½ hrs.) and Cascavel (connecting with bus from Iguaçu). The direct route Iguaçu-Guaíra is very bumpy, but interesting, takes 5 hrs. in the dry, but buses may be cancelled in the wet, US$3, or US$4 via Cascavel. There are also flights.

Railway No railway at Guaíra. Daily train Presidente Epitácio-São Paulo, 1535, 18 hours.

The 4 km. from Guaíra to the lake can be walked or done by car (US$1.50 one way, return taxi up to US$10). Entrance to park US$0.30; small museum three blocks from Guaíra bus terminal, 0800-1100 and 1400-1700.

Paraguay and Brazil are together building, nearby, the 12,600-megawatt Itaipu hydroelectric plant, which will be the largest in the world; it will enter into commercial production in 1988. The dam site can be visited (in groups; not alone), from visitors' centres on both the Paraguayan and Brazilian sides, in each case free. Visitors are first shown a film, and then taken on a tour of the project: on the Brazilian side, there is only one stop for taking photographs. Presentations on the Brazilian side are at 0830, 1000, 1430 and 1600, on the Paraguayan side at 0830 Mon.-Sat., 0830, 0930, 1030 Sun. and holidays. For how to get to the Paraguayan centre, see under Ciudad Presidente Stroessner, page 620; from Foz do Iguaçu, take a bus from the Terminal Urbana to Canteiro de Obras at 0740, 0925, 1405 or 1550 (US$0.10), 30 min. journey, then about 1 hr. at the site. (See also page 111.) Agency tours cost about US$3.50.

Presidente Epitácio Hotels *Primavera*, F, including breakfast, good value, near station.

Guaíra Hotels *Guarujá Motel*, Rua Alvorada 400, D. Near the bus station: *Palace Hotel*, E; *Majestic*, opposite bus station, F with or without bath, with breakfast, good; also *Hotel Itaipu*, F with bath, hot showers, good food (restaurant closed Sun.); *Sete Quedas*, Otávio Tosta 385, E, with breakfast and sandwich lunch, not too clean; *Ichapena*, F, not very clean but very friendly; and others.

Camping Municipal site at Bosque do Kartódromo, 2 km. out of town on the road from the bus station; ask at the Prefeitura for details. Basic facilities at each.

Restaurants *Recanto da Costela*, churrascaria, all you can eat for US$4. *O Chopão*, pleasant. Cheap snacks at *Bar São José*. *Restaurant Otto* for fish dishes.

Note If entering Brazil from Paraguay in the Guaíra region, make sure to get passport stamped at the nearest available location (probably Foz do Iguaçu)—there is no passport control when coming off the boat from Salto Guaíra, Paraguay. There is an hourly passenger ferry service from Porto de Lanchas and Porto Guaíra to Paraguayan side, US$0.50, and hourly car ferry from Porto Guaíra. There is a time change when you cross the Paraná.

Towns in the State of São Paulo

About 13% of Brazil's population lives within 200 km. of São Paulo city, a circle which includes 88 municipalities. Four of them—the big ABCD towns— sharing a population of over a million, are Santo André, São Bernardo, São Caetano and Diadema; they have many of the largest industrial plants. There are some 70 cities in the State with populations of over 50,000 and São Paulo is linked with all of them by road, and most of them by railway. One important line, the broad-gauge Santos a Jundiaí, runs from Santos to São Paulo (passenger services suspended on this stretch), and across the low mountains which separate São Paulo city from the interior to its terminus at

Jundiaí, 58 km. from São Paulo, which has textile factories and other industries. The district grows coffee and grain and there is an annual Grape Festival. Population, 210,000.

Hotel *Grande Hotel,* Rua do Rosário 605, with good restaurant.

The Paulista Railway, with the same broad gauge, continues from Jundiaí through Campinas, Limeira, and São Carlos do Pinhal—the richest part of the state. A metre-gauge line now links Campinas and Brasília.

Campinas, 88 km. from São Paulo by the fine Via Anhanguera highway (many buses, US$1.20), is important as a clearing point for coffee, for its Agricultural Institute, and its rapidly growing industries. The Viracopos international airport is 11 km. from Campinas, which also has its own airport. Population, 567,000 (1980), believed in 1987 to be over 1 million.

See fine cathedral, old market, colonial buildings, 8 museums, arts centre (noted symphony orchestra; the city is the birthplace of the noted 19th century Brazilian composer Carlos Gomes), and the modern university outside the city. Visits can be made to the Agricultural Institute to see all the aspects of coffee growing. Ten trains a day to and from São Paulo; trains also to Ribeirão Preto, Araguari and Brasília.

Hotels *Holiday Inn,* Praça Rotatória 88, A; *Vila Rica,* Rua Donato Paschoal 100, B; *Savoy,* Rua Regente Feijó 1064, C; *Terminus,* Av. Francisco Glicério 1075, C; *Opala Avenida,* Av. Campos Sales 161, central, D. *Solar das Andorinhas,* a health farm with pool, sauna, horses, sports, etc. 18 km. outside city on the Mogi-Mirim road, C, with meals. Many cheap hotels near Rodoviária.

Restaurants *Bar Restaurante Barão,* Barão de Jaguará 1381 and *Churrascaria Gaúcha,* Av. Dr Campos Sales 515, excellent for Brazilian food. *Kirinu's Place,* Av. Moraes Salles 1102, all you can eat for US$3.50. *Papai Salim,* Benjamin Constant 1293, Arab food, good. *Natureza* (vegetarian) at Rua José Paulino 1248, 2nd floor and Av. Francisco Glicério 984; lunch only, closed Sat. *Vegetariano,* Rua Barão de Jaguara 1260, 2nd floor, closed Sat. (and Fri. for dinner).

Shopping H. Stern jewellers at Shopping Centre Iguatemi.

Banks Lloyds Bank (ex-BOLSA), Rua General Osório 859. The First National Bank of Boston, Av. Francisco Glicério 1275, and local banks. Open 1000-1630.

Community Church Services in English at School of Language and Orientation, Rua Eduardo Lane 270.

Americana (pop. 122,000), an interesting town, is 42 km. from Campinas. This area was settled by Confederate refugees from the south of the U.S.A. after the Civil War. Most of the original settlers soon returned to the States, but some stayed, and there still exist reminders of their occupation here. A visit to the cemetery reveals an unusual number of English surnames. (*Hotel Bradesco,* 12 km. away at km. 118 on the Anhanguera Highway, D; *Cacique,* Rua Wáshington Luís 143, E.)

The metre-gauge Mogiana line, connecting with the broad-gauge Paulista at Campinas, serves the north-eastern part of the state. It goes through Ribeirão Preto and into the Triângulo of Minas Gerais, a great area for fattening beasts which are trucked to the *frigoríficos* of São Paulo. No São Paulo-Ribeirão Preto tickets are sold, so you may have to wait a day at Campinas for a connection (or go by bus). From Araguari there is a line into the state of Goiás (train Araguari-Goiânia once a week) and to Brasília (train from Campinas daily except Sunday). 25 km. from Campinas, at Jaguariúna, is a railway preservation group with steam engines and wagons; hourly bus from Campinas US$0.50. The group meets at weekends, just outside the town centre.

Ribeirão Preto, the centre of a rich coffee-growing district, also has a steel industry. The town is 422 km. from São Paulo city by rail via Campinas or paved road (5 hrs. by bus); airport has TAM flights to São Paulo, Rio, Poços de Caldas. Population 301,000. Altitude, 420 metres. It is a distribution centre for the interior of

278 BRAZIL

São Paulo State and certain districts in Minas Gerais and Goiás. Products: coffee, cotton, sugar, grain and rice.

Hotels *Black Stream*, Rua General Osório 830, C, with T.V.; *Umuarama Recreio*, Praça dos Cafeeiros 140, 6 km. from centre, very pleasant, pool, gardens, D; *Brasil*, Rua General Osório 20, F; *Holiday Inn*, Rua Alvares Cabral 1200.

All the southern part of the state and most of its western part are served by the metre-gauge Sorocabana railway. The main line runs from São Paulo through Sorocaba to Bauru, where it connects with the Noroeste, which crosses the Paraná river and the state of Mato Grosso do Sul to Corumbá, 1,223 km. (A continuation of this line into Bolivia goes on to Santa Cruz, 648 km. from Corumbá.) The line from a junction near Sorocaba extending (through connections with other lines) across the southern states to the border with Uruguay is for freight only.

Sorocaba, 110 km. west of São Paulo, is an important industrial centre. The altitude is 540 metres, and the climate temperate. The population is 255,000. It has textile mills; produces cement, fertilizers, footwear, hats, alcohol, wines; there are railway workshops, extensive orange groves and packing house installations. It is an important cotton centre. Other products are timber, sugar, cereals, coffee, and minerals. Communications with São Paulo are better by road than by rail; the Castello Branco highway passes nearby.

Hotels *Terminus*, Av. General Carneiro 474, D; *Nova Sorocaba*, Rua Mons. João Soares 158, E. Cheaper hotels: *Viajantes*, *Roma*, *Comércio*.

There is a picturesque paved road along the Tietê valley from São Paulo to Bauru, via the colonial towns of Pirapora and Itu.

Pirapora de Bom Jesus is a popular place of pilgrimage, in a most attractive setting on both sides of the river. **Itu** was founded by the Bandeirantes in the 17th century. The beautiful falls of Salto de Itu, 8 km. N, are flanked by a park and a textile mill.

Itu Hotels *International*, Rua Barão do Itaím 93, E; *Sabará*, Praça Padre Miguel 90, F.

Camping *Casarão de Itu*, km. 95 on the Jundiaí road; *Itu*, at km. 89 on the Cabreúva road.

Bauru (population: 179,000) was founded at the end of the last century. Its points of interest include the Horto Florestal, an experimental forestry station opened in 1928, the Vitória Regia amphitheatre in the Parque das Nações and the Tenrikyo temple, Rua Newton Prado. It is used by Paulistanos as a weekend resort. Currency exchange is difficult.

Hotels *Bekassin*, Av. Duque de Caxias 1717, swimming pool, D; *Colonial*, Praça Rui Barbosa 248, D; *Alvorada Palace*, Rua Primeiro de Agosto 619, D. Cheaper ones too, such as *Hotel Português* near bus station. Opp. railway station, *Lisboa*, F, clean, hot shower, restaurant, recommended, very friendly.

Restaurant *H 2 Churrascaria*; *Cantina Bello Nápoli*, cheap. Homemade ice-cream at *sorveteria* near *Hotel Lisboa*.

Rail to São Paulo, US$2 1st class, US$1.60 2nd class, three a day (6½ to 7½ hrs., compared to 4½ hrs., US$4, by bus); train from Corumbá arrives 1220, to Campo Grande 0530, US$4.50 2nd class. There are no reliable connections between São Paulo-Bauru and Bauru-Corumbá or Campo Grande trains in either direction. Daily train to Corumbá leaves 1615.

Presidente Prudente, in the West, is on the railway which runs to Presidente Epitácio on the Paraná river, and is a useful place to make bus connections for Campo Grande (US$6), Porto Alegre and São Paulo; also to Ribeirão Preto, US$5, 9 hrs. *Hotel Aruá*, B, single rooms poor but doubles said to be nice. *Hotel Alves* opp. bus station, F, clean, nice but noisy. Beware of assaults and pickpockets.

Serra Negra is a very pleasant spa town and summer holiday resort up in the mountains at 1,080 metres, 145 km. from São Paulo. Visitors tour the countryside in horse-drawn buggies. The population is about 5,000, and there are many first class hotels, a *balneário* and a small zoo.

Hotels *Rádio Hotel* (B, very nice indeed), and several others.

Near Serra Negra is the even better-known spa town of Águas de Lindóia, whose waters are bottled and sent all over Brazil.

BRAZIL 279

Another weekend resort, 70 km. north of São Paulo on the Dom Pedro I Highway, is **Atibaia**; nearby is the strangely-shaped Pedra Grande mountain summit. There are two campsites, Pedra Grande, and Taba, which is near the *Hotel Village Eldorado* (with sports facilities, American-plan accommodation).

Campos do Jordão, between Rio de Janeiro and São Paulo, is a mountain resort at 1,710 metres, in the Serra da Mantiqueira. It is prettily set in a long valley. The climate is cold and dry in winter and cool in summer, a great relief from the coastal heat and humidity. There are many hotels; but no airport, as yet. Population: 18,750.

The resort, about 190 km. from São Paulo, is reached by an 87 km. paved road from São José dos Campos, 100 km. from São Paulo, on the Presidente Dutra (BR-116) Highway. By car it takes about 3 hrs. from São Paulo, 6 to 7 from Rio de Janeiro.

Places of Interest Palace of Boa Vista, 4 km. from Abernessia Centre, Governor's residence and museum, open Wed., Sat., Sun., 1000-1200, 1400-1700; Pedra do Baú (1,950 metres), to get there take a bus to São Bento do Sapucaí at 0800 or 1500, then walk to Paiol Grande and then on an unmarked path to the Pedra. Return buses from São Bento at 0915 and 1615. Near Paiol Grande is the small waterfall of Cachoeira dos Amores. Pico do Itapeva (2,030 metres) and Imbiri (1,950 metres), command a beautiful view of the Paraíba valley; see also Morro do Elefante (chairlift available); Gruta dos Crioulos; nature reserve at Horto Florestal (20 km). Campos do Jordão is a popular place for hikers. The villages of Emílio Ribas and São Cristóvão are connected by a tram which runs frequently, US$0.10.

Hotels *Toriba; Vila Inglesa; Refúgio Alpino,* at Capivari; and others. *Casa de Juventude,* also called *Casa Azul* (Youth Hostel; membership card and permission from Dr Fernando at Tourist Office in the bus terminal required). Camping Clube do Brasil site in the Descansópolis district.

Transport Bus from São Paulo, US$2, 3 hrs.; from Rio, changing at São José dos Campos, US$2.75. No through rail service: railcars make three round trips weekly between Campos do Jordão and Santo Antônio do Pinhal, and there is a local tram service within the town. From Pindamonhangaba buses run to São Paulo, Taubaté and Aparecida do Norte, 1030, US$0.70. The short road down to "Pinda", starting from the paved road 24 km. SW of Campos do Jordão, is now paved. A new road branching off the BR-116 near Caçapava provides a quicker drive from Rio, or São Paulo, than the route via São José dos Campos.

Nearer to Rio than the Pindamonhangaba turn, just off the BR-116, is **Aparecida do Norte,** Brazil's chief place of pilgrimage and the seat of its patron saint, Nossa Senhora Aparecida. This small black image of the Virgin is said to have been taken by a fisherman from the nearby River Paraíba, and quickly acquired a miraculous reputation. It is now housed in a huge modern basilica in Romanesque style on top of a hill, with the pleasant clean white-walled, red-roofed town below.

Southern Brazil

This consists, from S to N, of the three states of Rio Grande do Sul, Santa Catarina and Paraná. The conformation of the land is not unlike what it is further north; the Great Escarpment runs down the coastal area as far as Porto Alegre, receding from the coast in a wide curve between Paranaguá and Florianópolis. South of Tubarão to the borders of Uruguay the hills of southern Rio Grande do Sul, which never rise higher than 900 to 1,000 metres, are fringed along the coast by sand bars and lagoons.

Rio Grande do Sul

North of the Rio Uruguai the land is deeply forested, but the area of prairie, small in São Paulo, Paraná and Santa Catarina, grows more extensive than the forest in Rio Grande do Sul, south of the Uruguai valley. In southern Rio Grande do Sul, south and west of the Rio Jacuí (draining into the Lagoa dos Patos) there are great grasslands stretching as far as Uruguay to the south and Argentina to the

280 BRAZIL

west. This is the distinctive land of the *gaúcho*, or cowboy (pronounced ga-*oo*-shoo in Brazil), of *bombachas* (the baggy trousers worn by the *gaúcho*), of the poncho and *ximarão* (or *mate* without sugar) the indispensable drink of southern cattlemen. There are many millions of cattle, sheep and pigs, and some 75 % of *all* Brazilian wine comes from the state. Its population (who all call themselves *gaúchos*) is now about 7.8 million. Rio Grande do Sul has the highest proportion of literate people in Brazil.

There are three sharply contrasted types of colonization and land owning in Rio Grande do Sul. During the colonial period, wars with the Spaniards of Uruguay were frequent, and the Portuguese government brought into the grasslands of the south a number of military settlers from the Azores; these soldiers inter-married with the Brazilian herdfolk in the area. In the colonial period,

BRAZIL 281

also, the Jesuits built several settlements to acculturate the local Indians; relics of this process include the impressive ruins of the Sete Povos das Missões Orientais (São Borja, São Nicolau, São Luiz, São Lourenço, São Miguel, São João, Santo Ängelo). West from Porto Alegre, in the floodlands of the Rio Jacuí and its tributary, the Rio Taquari, rice is cultivated in typical Brazilian fashion: large estates with tenant workers.

At São Leopoldo, north of Porto Alegre, a group of Germans were settled in 1824 on their own small farms, and during the next 25 years over 20,000 more were brought into the area by the Brazilian Government. The Germans concentrated on rye, maize, and pigs. Between 1870 and 1890, settlers from northern Italy arrived, bringing viticulture with them, and settled north of the Germans at Alfredo Chaves and Caxias do Sul.

Porto Alegre, capital of Rio Grande do Sul, lies at the confluence of five rivers which flow into the Rio Guaíba and thence into the great fresh-water lagoon, the Lagoa dos Patos, which runs into the sea. It is the most important commercial centre south of São Paulo. Population, 1,109,000 (1980).

Standing on a series of hills and valleys on the banks of the Guaíba, with its business centre jutting out into the water on a promontory, Porto Alegre has rapidly become one of the most up-to-date cities in Brazil. The older residential part of the town is on a promontory dominated previously by the Governor's Palace, the imposing modern stone cathedral, and the two high white towers of the old church of Nossa Senhora das Dores, but Governor and God have now been uttterly dwarfed by the skyscraper of the Legislative Assembly upon the promontory. The streets in the centre are famous for their steep gradients. The climate is temperate through most of the year, though the temperature at the height of summer can often exceed 40°C. The surrounding suburbs are very pleasant. For instance, Ipanema, on the banks of the Guaíba, has a selection of bars and small restaurants; a popular rendezvous, with spectacular sunsets over the river.

Do not miss that section of the Rua dos Andradas (Rua da Praia) that is now permanently closed to traffic. It is the city's principal outdoor meeting place, and by around 1600 it is full of people; at the peak hour of 1900 the street is jammed for about 6 blocks.

Points of Interest The Jockey Club at which races are held on Saturdays and Sundays; the Country Club (picturesque 18-hole golf course); the Parque Farroupilha, a fine park near the city centre; the interesting cathedral of the Anglican-Episcopal church of Brazil; the Zoological Gardens near São Leopoldo (bus US$0.50; Hotel: *Rima,* D, standard), the Botanic Gardens (Bairro Jardim Botânico, bus 40 from Praça 15 de Novembro) and the Cidade Universitária are well worth a visit. The Mercado Público (said to be a replica of Lisbon's Mercado da Figueira) is next to the Prefeitura, in the centre of town. In the Cidade Baixa quarter are the colonial Travessa dos Venezianos (between Ruas Lopo Gonçalves and Joaquim Nabuco) and the house of Lopo Gonçalves, Rua João Alfredo 582. The 5-km. wide River Guaíba lends itself to every form of boating and there are several sailing clubs. Tourist boat trips (2 hrs.) leave from the Doca Turística near the Guaíba bridge, for a journey among the river islands. The Museu Júlio de Castilhos, Duque de Caxias 1231, has an interesting historical collection, and there is the Museu do Trem in the old railway station of São Leopoldo. Museo de Arte do Rio Grande do Sul, Praça da Alfândega, Tues.-Sun. 1000-1700, entry free, is interesting. Varig airline museum, open Wed. and Fri. 0900-1200. Plays by local and visiting companies at São Pedro (opposite Government Palace) and Leopoldina (Av. Independência), theatres. Modern cinemas. Centro de Tradição Gaúcha has *gaúcho* shows every Sat., starting at 2200. A good view of the city may be had from the Morro de Santa Teresa, approached from Av. Padre Cacique (take bus 95 from Rua Salgado Filho).

Porto Alegre is a fresh-water port for ocean-going vessels of up to 7,000 tons and 4.87 metres draught. Vessels must come up through Rio Grande and the Lagoa dos Patos, some 275 km. from the open sea. Large areas of reclaimed land have been used for residential building and to extend the port facilities and quays, now among the most up-to-date in Brazil.

282 BRAZIL

Porto Alegre's most important industries are food and farm products, textiles, metal-processing, chemicals and leather products. Chief exports are pinewood, rice, wheat, soya, meat, hides, wool, animal hair, semi-precious stones, wine and tobacco. A visit to Varig's installations and workshops is well worth while.

Festivals February 2 (local holiday) is the festival of Nossa Senhora dos Navegantes, whose image is taken by boat from the central quay in the port to the industrial district of Navegantes. Semana Farroupilha, celebrating *gaúcho* traditions, main day September 20.

Warning The market area in Praça 15 de Novembro is dangerous at night.

Hotels *Plaza São Rafael*, Av. Alberto Bins 514, A; *Alfred Executivo*, Av. Otávio Rocha 270, C; *Plaza Porto Alegre*, Senhor dos Passos 154, C; *Embaixador*, Jerônimo Coelho 354, C; *Everest Palace*, Rua Duque de Caxias 1357, C; *Ritter*, Largo Vespasiano Júlio Veppo 146, in front of central bus station, C; *Umbu*, Av. Farrapos 292, C, noisy; *São Luiz*, Av. Farrapos 45, D, spotless, good service, but near the freeway and so a bit noisy; *Rishon*, Rua Dr. Flores 27, D; *Terminaltur*, opp. Rodoviária, E with bath, a/c, TV, breakfast, heating, but small rooms and tiny bathrooms; *Savoy*, Av. Borges de Medeiros 688, E; *Lido*, R. Andrade Neves 150, D; *Hermon*, Vigário José Inácio 541, D; *Motel Clube do Brasil*, Av. Farrapos 4655, E; *Santa Catarina*, General Vitorino 240, E; *Açores*, Rua dos Andradas 885, D; *Motel Charrua*, BR 116, km. 3, E; *Presidente*, Av. Salgado Filho 140, E; *Scala*, Av. Júlio de Castilhos 30/34, E; *Glória*, Travessa Eng. Acelino de Carvalho 67, E, with shower, central, quiet, clean; *Cedro*, Coelho and Vigário José Inácio, E; *Henrique*, General Vitorino 182, F; *Palácio*, Av. Vigário José Inácio 644, F, central, clean, friendly, hot water; *Ritz*, André da Rocha 225, E, friendly, central, helpful, German and Spanish spoken; next door is *Finks*, same price range; *Metrópole*, Rua Andrade Neves 59, F; *Marechal*, Rua Andrade Neves 123, F, basic, clean (not far from Mercado Municipal); *Laçador*, Rua Uruguai 330, E; *Garibáldi*, R. Garibáldi, F; *Vitória*, Voluntários da Pátria 459, F without breakfast, safe, comfortable, clean, highly recommended; *Minuano*, Farrapos 31, F without breakfast, good, and *Elevado*, Av. Farrapos 63, F with hot shower, clean, very friendly, both near bus station; *Lux*, Av. General João Mendel, just possible; two *Casas dos Estudantes* (for those with student cards), at Av. João Pessoa 41, and Rua Riachuelo 1355 (both not far from bus station), night free, breakfast and evening meal US$0.40, lunch US$0.60, if there's room. *Montevideo*, Rua Júlio de Castilhos, F, basic.

Camping Do Cocão, 10 km. out on Viamão road; Praia do Guarujá, 16 km. out on Av. Guaíba.

Restaurants (except on the *Everest Roof* and at the *Korote* and *Panarea* (US$8-16), the normal cost of dinner is US$6-8). General: *Everest Roof*, Duque de Caxias 1357; *Le Bon Gourmet*, Hotel Plaza São Rafael; *Mosqueteiro*, Estádio Olímpico; *Rodo Ferroviária*, Rua Voluntários da Pátria 1177, good; at No. 509 same street, *Panorama Lancheria*, always open, good large meals; *Adelaide's*, Rua Vigário José Inácio 685, good home cooking, cheap; *Martini*, Rua Leopoldo Froes 126; *Rancho Alegre*, Cristóvão Colombo 2168, good *gaúcho* music; also with folklore shows, *O Recanto de Seu Flor*, Getúlio Vargas 1700; *Moinho de Vento*, Protásio Alves 3284 and Dona Laura 424, and *Fogão de Chão*, Cavalhada 5200, for churrascos; *Tutty's*, Centro Comercial, Loja 15, Av. da Independência, recommended; *Churrascaria Quero-Quero*, Praça Otávio Rocha 47; also *Saci Estádio Beira Rio*, Av. Borges de Medeiros. Santa Teresa, Av. Assis Brasil 2750; *Ritter Hotel*; *Panorâmico*, Correia Lima 1949; *Grumete*, 24 de Outubro 905; *Umbu*, Av. Farrapos 292; *Ipanema*, Av. Coronel Marcos 1645; *Korote*, Silva Jardim 16; *Executivo*, Hotel Alfred; *Ratskeller*, Cristóvão Colombo 1654; *Panarea*, Eça de Queirós 819; *Scherazade*, Av. Protásio Alves 3284; *Barranco*, Av. Protásio Alves 1578; *Porto Velho*, Rua Andrade Neves, good steaks.

Vegetarian: *Aroma*, Rua Lima e Silva 292, 2nd floor; *Macrobiótico*, Rua Marechal Floriano Peixoto 72; *Ilha Natural*, Rua Andrade Neves, lunches only.

Chinese: *Palácio do Dragão*, Luciana de Abreu 471; *Chinatown*, Rua Andrade Neves (nr. Metrópole hotel), Chinese and other food, good value; *Gold Dragon*, Rua Dr. Valle 479; *Tai Seng Nhe*, Andradas 1097.

German: *Printz*, Protásio Alves 3208; *Steinhaus*, Paulino Teixeira 415; *Floresta Negra*, 24 de Outubro 905; *Germânia*, 24 de Outubro 945; *Franz*, Av. Protásio Alves 3250.

Portuguese: *Casa de Portugal*, João Pessoa 579; *Galo*, João Alfredo 904.

Italian: *Copacabana*, Praça Garibaldi; *Cantina del Peppe*, Getúlio Vargas 273; *Jardim Itália*, Av. Protásio Alves 3580; *Cantina Vila Romana*, Av. Carlos Gomes 1385.

Night Bars (beer and sandwiches, etc.) *Tivoli*, Av. Protásio Alves 766; *Hubertus*, Rua Professor Annes Dias 116; *Xuvisko*, Cristóvão Colombo 927; *Julius*, José de Alencar 480; *Bartok*, José de Alencar 173; *Barril*, Estádio Internacional; *Bar Occidentes*, Av. Osvaldo Aranha and Gral. João Telles, popular; *Bologna*, Av. Coronel Marcos 2359; *Dom Jayme*, Mostardeiro 112.

Discotheques Água na Boca, Discoate, Looking Glass, Maria Fumaça. Av. Farrapos has an assortment of less reputable establishments.

Electric Current 110-120 A.C. 50 cycles.

Bookshops Livraria Kosmos, Rua dos Andradas 1644 (international stock); Livraria Lima,

BRAZIL 283

Borges de Medeiros 539; Livraria Globo, Andradas 1416; airport bookshop. Livres e Artes bookstall in book market, Praia São Florencio, new English books with front covers missing!

Shopping H. Stern jewellers at Shopping Center Iguatemi and international airport. There is a street market (leather goods, basketware, etc.) in the streets around the central Post Office. Good leather goods sold on the streets.

Exchange on Av. Borges de Medeiros, good rate, cash only (e.g. Agência Platina, on corner with Andradas). Many câmbios in the centre will change travellers' cheques at parallel rates, for addresses consult tourist bureau brochure.

Addresses British Consulate, Caldas Júnior 20, sala 85, Tel.: 25-88-98. U.S. Consulate, Rua Uruguai 155, 11th floor. Austrian Consulate, Rua 7 de Setembro 1069, conj. 1714, Caixa Postal 1771, Tel.: 2460 77/85. British Club, Av. Carlos Gomes 534 (Montserrat). Lloyds Bank (ex-BOLSA), Rua General Câmara 249 (open 1000-1630). Citibank, Rua 7 de Setembro (open 1300-1700). Touring Clube do Brasil, Av. João Pessoa 623. Instituto Goethe, 24 de Outubro 122 (open Mon.-Fri., 0930-1230, 1430-2100). Instituto Cultural Americano Brasileiro, Mon.-Fri., 0800-2000 (Sats. 0800-1700).

Dentist Ursula Finkenwerder, R. Quintino Bocaiúva 655, Sala 301, Mon.-Fri. 0830-1130.

Cables Embratel, Rua Siqueira de Campos 1245. Tel.: 41233.

Post For sending parcels abroad: Rua Araújo Ribeiro 100.

Tourist Information Epatur, Travessa do Carmo 84 (head office), helpful as is branch in Praça 15 de Novembro; Branch offices: Salgado Filho airport; interstate bus station, very helpful; Rua General Câmara 368; Av. Salgado Filho 366. CRTur (Companhia Riograndense de Turismo), Rua dos Andradas 1137, 6th floor. Epatur maintains information booths at the frontier towns. A monthly booklet is available.

Swimming from the beaches near or in the city is forbidden because of pollution. See "Excursions", next page, for out-of-town beaches.

Rail The only long-distance passenger service from Porto Alegre is the line W to (386 km.) Santa Maria (pop. 151,000), and on to Cacequi, where the line branches for Uruguaiana (see page 286), where you cross the river to Paso de los Libres for buses or trains to Buenos Aires, and for Santana do Livramento, for connections to Uruguay. Every day except Sat. a diesel train leaves Porto Alegre 1900, arrives Uruguaiana 0720 next day, air-conditioned, buffet; also daily train at 2050 to Santa Maria, continuing to Cacequi, thence 3 a week to Uruguaiana and 3 a week to Santana do Livramento. None of these trains carry sleepers. There is also a suburban service from Mercado station (Rua da Praia) north to Sapucaia do Sul, serving Esteio and Canoas.

Buses Bus to Rio, US$16.50 (*leito* 33), 26 hrs.; São Paulo, US$10 (*leito* 20), 18 hrs.; Uruguaiana, US$6.75, 9 hrs.; Santa Maria, 4¾ hrs., frequent service with Planalto; Santana do Livramento, 1230 and 2300, 8½ hrs.; *leito* at 2330; to Pelotas, 8 daily, 4 hrs.; to Gramado, 8 daily, 2hrs.; to Canela, 5 daily, 2½ hrs.; to Caxias do Sul, almost hourly, 2 hrs., *executivo* service also. Florianópolis, US$3.75, 7 hrs. with Viação São Cristóvão (beware of overbooking on this route); Curitiba, US$8, 11 hrs.; Blumenau, US$4.60, 9 hrs.; Rio Grande, US$4, 8 per day, 0600 to 2000, 4½ hrs. Foz do Iguaçu, US$10, 18½ hrs.; Londrina, 22 hrs. To Cascavel (Paraná) for connections to Campo Grande, Cuiabá and Porto Velho: daily except Sat. with Aguia Branca, 21 hrs., or Unesul, 19 hrs. To Jaguarão on Uruguayan border at 2400, 6 hrs., US$ 5.50. Bus to Montevideo, with international buses TTL (daily 1730) or Onda (daily 2200), 12 hrs., US$19; alternatively take bus to border town of Chuí at 1200 or 2330 daily, 7½ hrs., US$6, then Onda or Rutas del Sol bus to Montevideo (US$7, cheaper bought in Porto Alegre or Chuí than in Uruguay). Ouro e Prata operates a 2-3 times weekly service to Salto and Paysandú (Uruguay), via Santana do Livramento/Rivera. To Asunción with Unesul at 1900 daily via Foz do Iguaçu. Expresso Singer bus Porto Alegre-Posadas (Argentina) via Oberá, Alba Posse, Porto Mauá, departs 2100 on Tues., Thurs., and Sun. arriving following day at 1135. There are bus services to Buenos Aires (US$35) 22 hrs. (depending on border) with Pluma, Mon., Fri., Sun., 2200, route is Uruguaiana, Paso de los Libres, Entre Ríos and Zárate, or US$40, with Onda, via Montevideo and Colonia. **N.B.** take your passport when purchasing international bus tickets. The new and excellent bus terminal on Av. Mauá with Garibáldi has good facilities, including a post office and long-distance telephone service until 2100. A regular bus runs from the Rodoviária to the airport, passing the central bus station.

Roads Good roads radiate from Porto Alegre, and Highway BR-116 has a paved surface to Curitiba (746 km.). To the S it is paved to Pelotas (though this stretch is in poor condition), and on from there to Chuí on the Uruguayan frontier. The new paved coastal road to Curitiba via Itajaí (BR-101), of which the first 100 km. is a four-lane highway, is much better than the BR-116 via Caxias and Lajes. The road to Uruguaiana is now entirely paved but bumpy.

Air Services There is a large modern international airport, Salgado Filho, 8 km. from the city. There are daily flights to Rio, São Paulo, Curitiba, Buenos Aires and Montevideo, and many other

284 BRAZIL

Brazilian cities. Vasp flies to Iguaçu and Brasília on Mon., Wed., Fri., and Sun. The airport is served by all Brazilian airlines, Pluna and Aerolíneas Argentinas.

Excursions from Porto Alegre The best beach resorts of the area are to the north of the city. The towns of **Tramandaí** (126 km.) and **Torres** (209 km.) are the most popular, with lots of luxury (and more reasonable) hotels and motels, bars, restaurants, and other standard requisites associated with seaside resorts. Between the two towns are the small resorts of Arróio Teixeira (Camping Clube do Brasil site), Capão da Canoa (*Hotel Kolman*, R. Sepé 1718, and others) and Atlântida. There is no lack of cheap accommodation, but hotels tend to be very full during the summer season. There are fully equipped campsites at both towns, and camping is also allowed on some beaches. Another popular beach area is around Cassino, near Rio Grande (see page 286). 40 km. to the south (towards Rio Grande) begins the Costa Doce of the Lagoa dos Patos; noted bathing points are Tapes, Barra do Ribeiro, Arambaré, São Lourenço do Sul (recommended camping site 3 km. out of town on lake shore) and Laranjal.

Torres Hotels *Torres Alfred*, R. Marechal Deodoro 48, C. *Farol*, Rua José A. Pirasol 240, D to B with full board; *Grande Hotel Torres*, Rua Júlio de Castilhos 124, D with bath, balcony and breakfast (off-season). *Camping* and *Mini-Torres*, both on Av. General Osório, F with breakfast and bath out of season; *Salth*, central, E with bath, friendly, clean. Other hotels, E, bath and breakfast are available.

Tramandaí Hotels *Samburá*, Av. Beira Mar. *Motel Junges*, on main street, E with bath and breakfast, friendly, German spoken. Many more.

Inland is the lovely Serra Gaúcha, the most beautiful scenery being around the towns of **Gramado** and **Canela,** about 130 km. from Porto Alegre (chocolate factory between the two towns). There is a distinctly Bavarian flavour to many of the buildings. In spring and summer the flowers are a delight, but on the other hand in the winter there are frequently snow showers. This is excellent walking and climbing country among hills, woods, lakes and waterfalls. There are many excellent hotels at all prices in both towns, but it is difficult to get rooms in the summer. Local crafts include knitted woollens, leather and wickerwork. Gramado has two fine parks, Parque Knorr and Lago Negro, and Minimundo, a collection of miniature models.

Gramado Hotels *Hortensias*, Rua Bela Vista 83, D; *Serrano*, Costa e Silva 1112, C; *Serra Azul*, Rua Garibáldi 152, C; *Pequeno Bosque*, Rua Piratina 486, E with bath, fridge, TV, good breakfast, located in wood close to Véu da Noiva waterfall; *Parque*, bungalows, good breakfast, friendly, maid will do laundry reasonably, D; *Ritta Höppner*, Rua Pedro Candiago 305, Tel.: 054-286-1334, D in cabins, very good value, friendly, good breakfasts, German owners, cabins have TV, fridge, some have own swimming pool, pool and miniature trains in grounds. *Letícia*, Rua Mons. Hipólito Constabili 707, D; *Planalto*, Rua Borges de Medeiros 505, E; *Tia Hulda*, Av Borges de Medeiros 1817, friendly, E; *Dinda*, Rua Augusto Zatti 160, cheapest, E; try in the private house opposite the tourist office (E).

Restaurant *Saint Hubertus*, Rua da Caixa d'Água. **Coffee shop**, *Tia Nilda*, Av. Pres. Costa e Silva. *Pyp* yoghurt factory, Av. S. Diniz 1030, has snack bar serving health food sandwiches and yoghurt. The local speciality is *café colonial*, a 5 o'clock meal of various dishes, including meats, recommended at *Café da Torre*. Visitors should also sample hot *pinhões* (pine nuts) and *quentão* (hot red wine, *cachaça*, ginger, cloves, sugar and cinnamon, often topped with *gemada*—beaten egg yolks and sugar).

Tourist Office Corner of Borges de Medeiros and Cnl. Diniz, (½ block from Rodoviária, helpful, English spoken).

Canela Hotels *Charrua*, Av. das Nações 351, D; *Bela Vista*, Rua Oswaldo Aranha 160, near Rodoviária, clean, good breakfasts, F (D with additional facilities). Cheap hotels: *Jubileu*, Oswaldo Aranha 223, F-G, and *Central*, Av. Júlio de Castilhos 146.

Camping Camping Clube do Brasil, 8 km. from Canela, near waterfall in Parque do Caracol; excellent honey and chocolate for sale here.

Electric current 220 volts A.C.

8 km. from Canela is the Parque Estadual do Caracol (bus marked "Caracol Circular" from corner R. Melvin Jones and Av. Oswaldo Aranha, adjacent to old steam engine, US$0.20, 20 mins. 4 a day, return about ½ hour after departure time); a slippery path leads to the foot of the falls, which

BRAZIL 285

are 130 metres high. Good paths lead to smaller falls above Caracol; from the high point at Ferradura there is a good view into the canyon of the River Cai. 80 km. from São Francisco de Paula is the Parque Nacional de Aparados da Serra, where the major attraction is the 7.8-km. canyon, known locally as the Itaimbezinho. Here, two waterfalls cascade 350 metres into a stone circle at the bottom. Tourist excursions, mostly at weekends, from São Francisco de Paula. At other times, take a bus to Cambara, get off at the *cruce*, from where it is 15 km. to the park—walk or hitch hike if you're lucky. There is a free campsite and a restaurant, which has a few rooms; in the park. From the restaurant one can walk to the canyon of Malacara. For experienced hikers (and with a guide) there is a difficult path to the bottom of Itaimbezinho. One can then hike 20 km. to Praia Grande in Santa Catarina (see page 287)—take a tent and food for two days.

24 km. W of Gramado (99 km. from Porto Alegre, 30 km. from Caxias do Sul) is **Nova Petrópolis** (bus US$0.40), another city with strong German roots; there is a Parque do Imigrante, an open-air museum of German settlement. (Hotels include *Veraneio dos Pinheiros, Recanto Suiço*, 3 star; *Petrópolis, Veraneio Schoeller*, one-star.) N of Nova Petrópolis is Jammerthal, a valley in the Serra Gaúcha with German farms, many of whose inhabitants still speak German (go to Joanette and walk from there).

Caxias do Sul, 122 km. from Porto Alegre, connected by regular buses, is the centre of the Brazilian wine industry. The population (199,000) is principally of Italian descent, and it is an expanding and modern town. One should not miss the opportunity to visit the many *adegas* (but do not always expect free wine-tasting), and the neighbouring towns of Farroupilha (Hotels *Don Francesco*, Rua Dr. J. Rossler 88, 2 star; *Grande*, Júlio de Castilhos 1064), Bento Gonçalves (hotels *Dall'Onder*, C; *Vinocap*, D) and Garibáldi (hotels *Pietá*, D; *Estação de Esqui*, D in cabins without breakfast; there is a "wine supermarket" on the road between Bento Gonçalves and Caxias; a selection of 40 wines at low prices). A good *adega*, with free tasting, is Cooperativa Viti Vinícola Emboaba Ltda, in Nova Milano (bus to Farroupilha, then change—day trip). Caxias do Sul's festival of grapes is held in February-March. The church of São Pelegrino has paintings by Aldo Locatelli and 5 metre-high bronze doors sculptured by Augusto Murer. Vines were first brought to the region in 1840 but not until the end of the century and Italian immigration did the industry develop. Good municipal museum at Rua Visconde de Pelotas 586 (open Tues.-Sat., 0800-1200, 1400-1800), with displays of artefacts of the Italian immigration. The best time to visit is Jan.-Feb. Garibáldi has the distinction of a dry ski slope (equipment hire, US$2 per hour).

Hotels *Volpiano*, Ernesto Alves, 1462, C; *Cosmos*, 20 de Setembro 1563, E-C; *Alfred Palace*, Rua Sinimbu 2302, C; *Itália*, Av. Júlio de Castilhos 3076, D; *Real*, Rua Marquês de Herval 606, E; *Alfred*, Rua Sinimbu 2266, C; *Bandeira*, same street, No. 2435, F with T.V. and bath; *Santa Rita*, Os 18 do Forte 2149, E without breakfast, cheap; *Pérola*, corner Ernesto Alves and Marquês de Herval (No. 237), E, good value; *Peccini*, Rua Pinheiro Machado 1939, E, shared bath, good breakfast. *Samuara*, 10 km. out on RS-25 road, D.

A good restaurant is *Angelo*; *Fogo de Chão*, Os 18 do Forte 16, reasonably priced, live music (not touristy), *gaúcho*-style; also *Cantina Pão e Vino*, Rua Ludovico Cavinato 1757, Bairro Santa Catarina, Caxias, good value.

Camping Municipal campsite, 4 km. out on Rua Cons. Dantas; *Palermo*, 5 km. out on BR-116 at km. 118; *Belvedere Nova Sonda*, 38 km. out in the district of Nova Pádua. At Garibáldi, near the dry ski slope.

Tourist Office Praça do Centro Administrativo; kiosk in Praça Rui Barbosa.

On the road north, 112 km. from Porto Alegre, is **Osório**, a pleasant town near sea and lakes, with a good cheap hotel, *Big Hotel*, E.

Rio Grande, at the entrance to the Lagoa dos Patos, 274 km. S of Porto Alegre, was founded in 1737. The city lies on a low, sandy peninsula 16 km. from the Atlantic Ocean. To-day it is the distribution centre for the southern part of Rio Grande do Sul. Its cattle and meat industries are important. Population, 125,000.

During the latter half of the 19th century Rio Grande was an important centre, but today it is a rather poor town, notable for the charm of its old buildings. (Museu Oceanográfico, US$0.30, interesting, 2 km. out of centre.) At Praça Tamandaré is a small zoo.

Hotels *Charrua*, Rua Duque de Caxias 55 (recommended for good value), D; *Paris*, Rua Marechal Floriano 112, E; *Europa*, Rua Gen. Neto 165, main square, E. *Noivo do Mar*, R. Marechal Floriano 481, F, basic, no breakfast. Cheap hotels on Luis Loréa and Silva Paes; on former *City, Iria*, both F; on latter *Ritter Anexo*.

BRAZIL

Restaurants *Haiti* (Italian); Chinese restaurant on Rua Luís Lorea, good but not cheap; *Pescal*, for fish, fairly expensive and a long taxi ride from the centre.

Exchange *Hotel Charrua* for US$ notes.

Cables Embratel, Rua Andrade Neves 94.

British Vice-Consul.

Tourist Office Rua Gral. Bacelar, near Cathedral; good map.

Transport Frequent daily buses to and from Pelotas (56 km.), Bagé (280 km.), Santa Vitória (220 km.), and Porto Alegre (US$4, 4½ hrs.). To Itajaí, 14 hrs., US$7.75. Road to Uruguayan border at Chuí is paved, but the surface is poor (4 hrs. by bus, at 0700 and 1430, US$2.10).

Boat Trip By boat across mouth of Lagoa dos Patos, to pleasant village of São José do Norte, US$0.25.

Excursions To ***Cassino***, a popular seaside resort on the Atlantic Ocean, 24 km., over a good road. The breakwater (the Barra), 5 km. north of town, through which all vessels entering and leaving Rio Grande must pass, is a major tourist attraction. Barra-Rio Grande buses pass the Superporto, very impressive. Very good fishing. The coastline is low and straight, lacking the bays to the N of Porto Alegre; unfortunately the beach is used as a roadway. The Cassino beaches are always populous (note the statue of Yemanjá); those further N are mainly used in summer. One attraction is railway flat-cars powered by sail; the railway was built for the construction of the breakwater.

Hotels *Atlântico*, Av. Rio Grande, E; *Cassino*, Av. Rio Grande, D, poor. Private campsite on Avenida 33, on the way out to Rio Grande. Camping Clube do Brasil site near town.

Pelotas, on the BR-116, 56 km. N of Rio Grande, is the second largest city in the State of Rio Grande do Sul, on the left bank of the River São Gonçalo which connects the Lagoa dos Patos with the Lagoa Mirim. Its proximity to Rio Grande has hindered the development of its own port. Pelotas is prosperous, with an array of shops and pleasant parks. Like Rio Grande, it is rather damp, but Rio Grande is a better place to stay. Population: 197,000.

Within a radius of 60 km., say an hour's drive, there are numerous excursions into the hilly countryside. Simple and clean accommodation and cheap, good and plentiful food can be found on the farms of settlers of German descent.

Hotels *Curi Palace*, Gen. Neto 1279, D; *Curi*, Gen. Osório 719, E; *Estoril*, Rua Gen. Osório 718, a/c, reasonable, D; *Tourist Parque*, motel-type, 7 km. south on the BR-116, D; *Rex*, Praça Pedro Osório 205, F, friendly, dowdy; *Grande*, Praça Pedro Osório 51, old, some rooms with electric shower, F; *Germano*, next bus station, owner speaks some German, F.

Camping 60 km. out at the Arco Iris waterfall, no facilities; *Cascata*, 25 km. out on the Cangussu road. Between Pelotas and Chuí, 1 km. S of junction with Rio Grande road, 1,200 metres from road at a working ranch, recommended, clean, meals included.

Restaurant Tyrolean restaurant, opposite *Hotel Rex*, excellent, cheap.

Communications Plane a day to Porto Alegre. Rodoviária is far out of town, with bus every 15 mins. to centre. Frequent daily buses to Porto Alegre, 244 km. (US$4, 3-4 hrs., paved road); Rio Grande, 75 min. (paved but in poor condition); Jaguarão, on frontier with Río Branco, Uruguay (dirt); and inland to Bagé (*Hotel Medronha*, near bus station, F, without breakfast, clean) and other towns. The road to the Uruguayan frontier at Chuí (paved), has international bus service. Onda and TTL bus services (Montevideo-Porto Alegre) stop at the bus station for Montevideo (Ruas Chile and Venezuela); tickets must be purchased from agency during day. If travelling by car, buy as much gasoline as possible in Uruguay. Bus to Buenos Aires (via Uruguaiana), US$28.75. From Bagé, the Uruguayan company Núñez runs buses 3 times a week to Melo, via Aceguá.

The southern interior of the state is the region of the real gaúcho. Principal towns of this area include ***Santana do Livramento*** (population: 64,000, bus and train—3 a week—services to Porto Alegre) with its twin Uruguayan city of Rivera (see page 785)—a great attraction of the latter being its casino. Rivera is generally considered to have the better hotels and better exchange facilities. (Livramento hotels: *Piranga*, cheap and clean, F; *Uruguaiana*, E, close to bus station).

In the extreme west are ***Uruguaiana***, population 75,000, a cattle centre 772 km. from Porto Alegre (*Hotel Glória*, Rua Domingos de Almeida 1951, E, good; *Califórnia* and *Pampa*, near the bus station, both E; *Moderno*, Rua Santana, F; *Palace*, Praça Rio Branco, F, without breakfast) and its twin Argentine town of Paso de los Libres, also with a casino (see page 113). A 1,400-metre bridge over the River Uruguai links the two cities; taxi or bus across about US$2. Buses connect the railway and bus stations, and centres of each city every half-hour; if you have to disembark for visa formalities, a following bus will pick you up without extra charge. There are train and bus services to Porto Alegre. The west of Rio Grande do Sul also contains the Sete Povos das Missões Orientais (see page 281). The only considerable Jesuit remains in Brazilian territory are at **São Miguel** (church, 1735-45, and small museum) some 50 km. from **Santo Ângelo,** (*Hotel Nova Esperança*, behind bus station, F, without breakfast; other cheap central hotels near old railway station). At São Miguel there is a son et lumière show, weekdays at 2000, weekends at 1930, but ends too late to return to Santo Ângelo; in São Miguel village is *Hotel-Churrascaria Brillante*, F. East of Santo Ângelo is Passo Fundo, "the most *gaúcho* city in Rio Grande do Sul", so much so that the town's square boasts a statue of a maté gourd and bombilla—otherwise not much of interest; *Hotel dos Viajantes* opposite bus station, F. Planalto buses run from Uruguaiana via Barra do Quaraí/Bella Unión to Salto and Paysandú in Uruguay.

Entering Uruguay Those requiring a visa face problems: a medical exam is required before a visa can be issued, cost approximately US$20 and US$10 respectively. All buses, except those originating in Pelotas, stop at customs on both sides of the border; if coming from Pelotas, you must ask the bus to stop for exit formalities. (The Brazilian border town, Chuí, is much cheaper than its Uruguayan neighbour, so stock up with food and drink before crossing.) At Santana do Livramento all one need do is cross the main street, but the Uruguayan immigration is hard to find, in a side street. No customs formalities, but luggage is inspected on boarding bus for Montevideo, and there are checkpoints on the roads out of town. Bus to Montevideo, US$7; trains to Montevideo (night only) start 8 km. from border. For motorists there are 3 customs offices in Santana do Livramento, about ½ hr. needed for formalities.

Entering Brazil from Uruguay, on the Uruguayan side, the bus will stop if asked, and wait while you get your exit stamp (with bus conductor's help); on the Brazilian side, the appropriate form is completed by the Rodoviária staff when you purchase your ticket into Brazil. The bus stops at Polícia Federal and the conductor completes formalities while you sit on the bus. Buses run from Chuí to Pelotas (6-7 daily, US$4, 4 hours), Rio Grande (0700, 1400, 4 hrs., US$2.10) and Porto Alegre (1200, 2300, 7½ hrs., US$6); also from Chuí to Santa Vitória nearby, where there are a few hotels and rather quicker bus services to the main cities.

Santa Catarina

Further up the coast, in Santa Catarina, a group of Germans was settled at Lajes in 1822. In 1848 a new German-speaking settlement was founded at Blumenau. The Germans spread inland over the mountains to Joinville, inland from the port of São Francisco. The Italians came later. Over northern Rio Grande do Sul and Santa Catarina the vast majority of people to-day can trace their origin to these immigrants.

In Santa Catarina, a state of small holdings, the farmer owns his land and cattle: the familiar European pattern of mixed farming worked by the family. Sixty per cent of the population is rural. There is coal in the S, and flourishing food processing and textile industries. Itajaí and São Francisco do Sul are the main ports, handling 90 % of the trade. Except for the summer months of January and February, the coast of Santa Catarina is pleasant and uncrowded.

386 km. NE of Porto Alegre is the small fishing port of **Laguna** (pop.: 50,000; *Hotel Laguna Tourist*, first class; *Hotel Itapirubá*, 4-star with beach and pool; several others, medium-priced, *Grande*, opp. post office, clean, F, without breakfast), in southern Santa Catarina. At Laguna is the Anita Garibaldi Museum, containing documents, furniture, and the personal effects of the Brazilian wife of the hero who fought in the 1840s for the independence of Rio Grande do Sul and later helped to unify Italy (US$0.05). Laguna's beach, 2 km. from the centre, is pricey and unspectacular, but 16 km. from Laguna (by ferry and road) are beaches and dunes at Cavo de Santa Marta. South of Laguna is Praia Grande, on

288 BRAZIL

the Ilha de São Francisco (cheap hotel at bus station, F). Buses from Praia Grande to Ararangúa and Laguna. Also from Laguna, take a Lagunatur or Auto Viação São José bus to Farol (infrequent, US$0.70). You have to cross the mouth of the Lagoa Santo Antônio by ferry to get to Farol, but it runs all day taking vehicles and pedestrians; look out for fishermen aided by dolphins (botos). Here is a fishing village with the third oldest lighthouse in the world (Farol Santa Marta) — guided tours available (taxi, US$8.25, not including ferry toll). No hotels, but it is possible to bargain with fishermen for a bed. (Bus Laguna-Florianópolis, 2 hrs., US$2.10, several daily.) Another 32 km. to the north of Laguna is the port of **Imbituba,** where there is a carbo-chemical plant, from which air pollution is very bad. Imbituba sends the coal mined in the area between Ararangúa and Tubarão in coastal vessels to Rio de Janeiro, where it is railed to the steel mills at Volta Redonda for coking. The rail link between Imbituba and Tubarão is one of the busiest steam services in South America (freight only). There are good beaches (those near Garopaba and Araçatuba have been particularly recommended), and bus services to Porto Alegre and Rio de Janeiro.

The coalfield towns of **Tubarão** (Hotel Mossi, in centre, E, excellent), Criciúma and Içara are interesting, and the nearby beaches are good.

From Tubarão one can visit the Termas do Gravatal. (There is one first class hotel, and two others, good value, quiet, good food.) Also, buses go inland to Lauro Müller, then over the Serra do Rio do Rastro (beautiful views of the coast in clear weather). At Bom Jardim da Serra there is an apple festival every April. A dirt road continues to São Joaquim (see page 290), and over Pericó to Urubici (Pensão Anderman, F, clean, friendly, big meals). A new paved road is being built, as far as Santo Amaro da Imperatriz. There are direct buses from São Joaquim to Florianópolis.

J. P. Monnickendam, of Elstree, writes: About 60 km. inland from Tubarão is Orleães. It has one of the most interesting and least known museums in the area, which has an original water-powered workshop and sawmill, complete with waterwheel. It dates from the original settlers (late 19th century), and is still in working order. To get there one must get off the bus at the junction about 3 km. from the town.

The festival of São João in June can be seen best in Santa Catarina at Campo Alegre, the first town on the road inland to Mafra. There are bonfires, a lot of (German) folk dancing, and large quantities of quentão (a hot drink made of red wine, cinnamon, ginger and cachaça) and pinhões (the nuts of the Paraná pine tree). It is a beautiful climb on the road from the BR-101 to Campo Alegre. The road continues through São Bento and Rio Negrinho to Mafra, from where a good road (the BR-116) goes to Curitiba.

124 km. N of Laguna is **Florianópolis** (founded in 1726), capital of the State, on the Ilha de Santa Catarina joined to the mainland by two bridges, one of which is Ponte Hercílio Luz, the longest steel suspension bridge in Brazil (closed to all traffic in 1983, the newer Colombo Machado Salles bridge has a pedestrian and cycle way beneath the roadway). It is a port of call for coastal shipping, 725 km. from Rio de Janeiro and 420 from Santos. The natural beauty of the island and bays are making Florianópolis a popular tourist centre (only January and February are very crowded); it seems a pity that the waterfront, scene of a traditional market, has been filled in and reclaimed. Many of the older houses are typically Portuguese: pastel colours with white ornamentation like sugar icing. The metropolitan cathedral on Praça 15 de Novembro has a life-size sculpture in wood of the flight into Egypt, originally from the Austrian Tyrol. Forts include the Santana (which houses a Museum of Military Arms), São José da Ponta Grossa and Nossa Senhora da Conceição. There are three other museums, the Museum of Historical and Modern Art near the municipal market, the Anthropological Museum at the Federal University and the Sambaqui Museum at the Colégio Catarinense, Rua Esteves Júnior (all museums open 0800-1200, 1400-1800, Mon.-Sat.). There is a look-out point at Morro da Cruz (take Empresa Trindadense bus). Urban population 170,000 (municipality, 220,000).

Hotels Florianópolis Palace, Rua Artista Bittencourt and Rua dos Ilhéus 26, new, best, C; Royal, Trav. João Pinto, E, good; Oscar Palace, Av. Hercílio Luz 90, C, watch the bill carefully; City Hotel, Rua Emílio Blum 31, F, very basic, friendly. Within 10 minutes' walk of the Rodoviária: Rua Felipe Schmidt, Faial Palace, No. 87, C, good restaurant; Valerim, No. 74, central, D with bath, E without (cheaper off season), fridge, radio, T.V., stove; Sumaré, No. 53, F, acceptable; Querência Palace, Rua Jerônimo Coelho 1, D, clean, good; Levi, opp. bus station, F, basic; on Conselheiro Mafra: Colonial, No. 45, very basic, clean, F; Regencia, No. 20; Cruzeiro, No. 68; Center Plaza, D, No. 70;

BRAZIL 289

Majestic, Trajano 4, F; *Felippe*, F, friendly, clean, 10% off to Youth Hostel members. On the mainland: *Oasis*, Rua Gral. L. Bittencourt 201, F, with breakfast, clean, good (take bus 201 from here to bus terminal); *Bruggeman*, Rua Santos Saraiva 300 (bus 236 or 226 from Terminal Urbano do Aterro), E for motel-type rooms and 2-star accommodations.

Camping Camping Clube do Brasil, São João do Rio Vermelho, near the lagoon, 21 km. out of town; also at Lagoa da Conceição, Praia da Armação, Praia dos Ingleses, Praia Canavieiras. "Wild" camping allowed at Ponta de Sambaqui. Beaches of Brava, das Aranhas, da Galheta, Mole, Campeche, das Campanhas and dos Naufragados. 4 km. S of Florianópolis, camping site with bar at Praia do Sonho on the mainland, beautiful, deserted beach with an island fort nearby. Take bus to Laguna and walk or hitch to beach (5 km. from highway). "Camping Gaz" cartridges from Riachuelo Supermercado, on Rua Alvim with Rua São Jorge.

Restaurants *Braseiro*, R. Trajano 27 (behind Governor's Palace), crowded at lunch-time. *Dalton's*, Rua Trajano 29, first floor meals better than ground floor pizzas, etc.; *Manolo's*, Rua Felipe Schmidt 71, near centre, good, but not cheap. *Lindacap*, Rua Felipe Schmidt 178 on outskirts (closed Mon.), good views. *Hotel Faial*, Rua Felipe Schmidt, roof-top restaurant. All the above give a good meal and beer for around US$7. *Dom Dom*, Praça Pereira Oliveira 6, cheap, good; *Rotisserie Acapulco*, Rua dos Ilhéus 20, central, cafeteria-style, popular. Shrimp dishes are good everywhere. *Polly's*, Praça 15 de Novembro, good food and service, reasonable prices; *Macarronada Italiana*, Av. Beira Mar Norte 196, good. *Churrascaria Ataliba*, Rua Jau Guedes da Fonseca s/n, 2 km. from centre at Coqueiros, excellent *rodízio*, US$3.75. Vegetarian: *Sol da Terra*, Rua N. Ramos 13, popular, *Vida*, Rua Visconde Ouro Preto 62, *Neu Sol*, Rua Vida Ramos 36 (all closed Sun.). *Padaria União*, R. Tenente Silveira, very good.

Electric Current 220 volts A.C.

Car Hire Auto Locadora Coelho, Felipe Schmidt 81, vehicles in good condition.

Banks for exchange: Banco do Brasil, Praça 15 de Novembro 20; Banco do Estado de São Paulo, Tenente Silveira 55; Banco Estado de Santa Catarina, Trajano 33.

Post Office Praça 15 de Novembro 5, Tel.: 22-3188.

Cables Telesc, Praça Pereira Oliveira 20, Tel.: 23-3700 (interstate and international telephones).

Tourist Office Head office: Portal Turístico de Florianópolis (Setur), at the mainland end of the bridge, 0800-2000 (Sat., Sun. 0800-1800); Praça 15 de Novembro, 0800-1800 (2200 in high season); at bus terminal (0700-2200, 0800-1800 Sat., Sun.), and airport, 0700-1800, (0800 Sat., Sun.); maps available, free.

Communications Daily flights to Porto Alegre and São Paulo. There is a new bus terminal with helpful tourist information at the east (island) end of the newer Ponte Colombo Machado Salles; the Terminal Urbano do Aterro for the island nearby, between the Rodoviária and the Mercado Municipal, which serves the northern beach towns, the east coast and most of the Southern ones, and a further terminal at the junction of Rua José da Moelmann and Av. Mauro Ramos which serves the other towns. All local bus destinations and schedules are clearly posted. Regular daily buses to Porto Alegre (US$ 3.75, 7 hrs.), São Paulo, US$6, Rio, US$8 ordinary, Brasília, 3 a week at 0300, US$14; Curitiba (US$3.50, 5 hrs.), Blumenau (US$1.50, 4 a day, 3 hrs.), Joinville (2½ hrs. direct, 3½ with stops) US$2.25 and other towns in the State. Also regular daily buses to Foz do Iguaçu (with Catarinense, US$7.20, continuing to Asunción); daily to Buenos Aires, US$ 32 via Uruguaiana, 3 a week to Santiago, Chile, US$53. The coastal highway (BR-101) is preferred as an alternative to the congested inland BR-116; it runs close to Florianópolis but it is bad in places and has many lorries.

Excursions To Lagoa da Conceição (Emflotur bus 403) for beaches, sand dunes, fishing, church of N.S. da Conceição (1730), boat rides on the lake (restaurants: *Oliveira*, excellent seafood dishes; *Miguelão*, Praça Pio XII 5, excellent *seqüência de frutas do mar*; *Leca*, try *rodízio de camarão*, prawns cooked in a dozen ways) Across the island at Barra da Lagoa is a pleasant fishing village and beach which can be reached by Emflotur bus 401 or 402. The latter goes to beach at Joaquina (surfing championships in January). Hotel near Barra da Lagoa: *Gaivota* (Família Coelho), Praia do Moçambique. Also visit the "city of honey bees" with a Museo da Apicultura, and the Church of Sto. Antônio Lisboa on the way to Sambaqui beach and fishing village. There is a pleasant fishing village at Ponta das Canas, and the beach at Canavieiras is good. There are 42 beaches around the island almost all easily reached by public buses from the centre (buses of the Empresa Canavieras go to the northern towns and beaches, Empresa Ribeironense to the southeastern ones, schedules from Tourist Office). Excursions can be made on the mainland to the hot springs at Caldas da Imperatriz (41° C) and Aguas Mornas (39° C); at the former are 2 spa hotels (*Caldas da Imperatriz*, D, meals and baths included, built in 1850 under the auspices of Empress Teresa Cristina, houses public baths; *Plaza Caldas da Imperatriz*, from B, with baths, swimming pools, very well appointed), at Aguas Mornas, the *Palace Hotel* is on the site of the springs, A,

290 BRAZIL

baths open to public Mon.-Fri. a.m. only. Boat trips can be made from Florianópolis in the bay, Tel.: 22-1806, from US$4.50-6.80.

From Florianópolis a poor road runs SW inland via São Joaquim (see below) to **Lajes,** a convenient stopping place on BR-116 between Caxias do Sul and Curitiba. Despite the poor road, however, this journey is perhaps the most interesting in the State (2 buses a day do this journey, via Alfredo Wagner, otherwise go via Blumenau). (New *Grande Hotel*, good, but no heat; cheaper is *Presidente*, F; *Natal*, cheap, adequate; *Rodalar*, *Centauro*, both G, near bus station; *Pensão Nelson*, to be avoided. Bus station is ½-hr. walk S.E. of centre. Voltage 220 A.C.) Population, 109,000. On the coast N of Florianópolis there are many resorts. They include Porto Belo, a fishing village with a calm beach (and wilder beaches reached by rough roads nearby—bus Florianópolis—Porto Belo with Praiana or Biguaçu, 8 daily, 4 on Sat., 3 on Sun.); Itapema (66 km., many hotels); **Camboriú** (86 km., beautiful beach, hotels *Dinamarca*, *Paraná*, *Motel San Carlos*, all near bus station, E, *Balneario de Camboriú*, central, on beach, E, friendly, clean; camping *Mag-Mar* is good; buses from Florianópolis, Joinville and Blumenau); and Meia Praia, which is quieter and cleaner than Camboriú. Between Itajaí and Camboriú is the beautiful, deserted (and rough) beach of Praia Brava.

São Joaquim, at 1360 metres, the highest town in Southern Brazil, regularly has snowfalls in winter; very pleasant town with an excellent climate (Camping Clube do Brasil site). Hotels: *Nevada* (expensive meals) and *Maristela*, F (good breakfast) both on Rua Manoel Joaquim Pinto, 213 and 220 respectively (5 mins'. walk from Rodoviária). Bus to Florianópolis 0830 and 2230, 7½ hrs., US$5. To Caxias do Sul, 4½ hrs., US$3.

One hundred km. up the coast N of Florianópolis by the BR-101 paved road or by sea is the most important port in Santa Catarina:

Itajaí, at the mouth of the Itajaí river. It is well served by vessels up to 5½ metres draught, and is the centre of a district largely colonized by Germans and Italians. Main exports: timber, starch, tapioca, sassafras oil, and tobacco. Population, 64,000. Airport. You can walk to Cabeçudas beach, which is quiet and small.

Hotels *Balneário Cabeçudas*, at Cabeçudas beach, best, 6 km. out of town, D; *Grande*, Rua Felipe Schmidt 44, good value, E; *Maringá*, N of town, friendly, cheap and clean, with Shell service station next door, providing good food, open all night. *Castro*, Almirante Barroso 229, F, recommended; *Rex*, *Cacique*, both on R. Asseburg, cheap, near market. Recommended **Bar**, *Trud's*, on riverfront at end of main street.

Resorts north of Itajaí include Piçarras, with sandy beaches interspersed with rocky headlands (ideal for fishing), and Barra Velha (*Hotel Mirante*, F, good, cheap restaurant, and 2 dearer hotels).

There is a 61 km. paved road to **Blumenau** (population, 145,000), 47 km. up the Itajaí river. It is in a prosperous district settled mostly by Germans; see Museo da Família Colonial, German immigrant museum, Av. Duque de Caxias 78, open Mon.-Sat., 0830-1130, 1330-1730, US$0.05. German Evangelical Church. Places of interest include the houses, now museums (open 0800-1800) of Dr Bruno Otto Blumenau and of Fritz Müller (a collaborator of Darwin), who bought the Blumenau estate in 1897 and founded the town. The town was devastated by floods in 1983 but most of the damage has been repaired. A "traditional" Oktoberfest beer-festival was started in 1984 here, and in other cities of German settlement (Blumenau's is repeated, but called a "summer festival", in the 3 weeks preceding Carnival). The Rodoviária for interurban travel is in the village of Fortaleza, US$0.10 by Rodoviária-7 de Setembro bus from the old bus station at Av. 7 de Setembro and Padre Jacobs (US$2.50 by taxi).

Hotels *Himmelbleu Palace*, Rua 7 de Setembro 1415, D; *Garden Terrace*, Rua Padre Jacobs 45, D; *Grande Hotel*, Alameda Rio Branco 21, D; *Glória*, Rua 7 de Setembro 954, D, German-run, excellent coffee shop (all aforementioned hotels have heating in rooms); *Plaza Hering*, 5-star, 7 de Setembro 818, C, heating and a/c; *Paraíso dos Poneis*, motel 9 km. out of town on the Itajaí road, D; *Rex*, Rua 7 de Setembro 640, D; *Geranium*, Rua Uruguai 266, E; *Central*, Rua 7 de Setembro 1036, basic, E with bath, F without, both without breakfast, clean, but not safe for luggage; *Beira-Rio*, R. 15 de Novembro 1330, F, for very short-stay couples; *Oliveira*, Alameda Duque de Caxias 109, F, without breakfast, basic; *Herrmann* (formerly *Durma Bem*), central, F. Peixoto 213, recommended, F. *City*, Rua A½ngelo Dias 263, F; *Junior*, Duque de Caxias 21, F. Many cheap hotels do not include breakfast. Most hotels and restaurants very clean.

Camping Municipal campsite, 2 km. out on Rua Pastor Osvaldo Hesse; Paraíso dos Poneis, 9 km. out on the Itajaí road; Refúgio Alpino, 11 km. out on Rua da Glória.

Restaurants Good German food at *Frohsinn* (panoramic view) and *Cavalinho Branco*, Av. Rio Branco 165, huge meals, international eating at *Moinho do Vale*. *A Cantina de Mai*, Rua R.C. Deeke 165, large helpings, good; *Blumental*, 15 de Novembro 962 and Av. Castelo Branco 671, good value; *Caféhaus Glória*, in Hotel Glória, excellent coffee shop; *Rancho Alegre*, 7 de Setembro 1335, good value; *Das Cafehaus*, serves huge, delicious cakes (*tortas*); *Gruta Azul*, Rodolfo Freygang, good, popular, not cheap.

Voltage 220 A.C.

International Telephones Corner of Av. Brasil and República Argentina.

Tourist Office in town hall, Rua 15 de Novembro 420, corner of Rua Nereu Ramos; also at bus station; helpful, but prices out of date. Only Portuguese spoken.

Amenities Teatro Carlos Gomes is also exhibition centre; public library open 0800-1800; German bookshops, Librerias Alemãs, at bus station and Ruas 7 de Setembro and 15 de Novembro. Craft shop, Casa Meyer, 15 de Novembro 401.

Excursions By bus to Timbo and Pomerode past rice fields and wooden houses set in beautiful gardens. At **Pomerode**, 32 km. (*Hotel Central*, F, big lunches) there is an interesting zoo (US$0.40). The North German dialect of *Plattdeutsch* is still spoken here. Rex Bus goes to Iraguã from Pomerode; change for connection to Joinville, US$1.50. Boat trips down the River Itajaí, daily in season, Sat. and Sun. out of season, unspectacular. ½-day excursion to Gaspar to visit the cathedral set high above the river (Verdi Veli bus company from stop outside the huge supermarket on Rua 7 de Setembro in the centre).

To Iguaçu We have received from Gerry Monahan and Gary Rubkin an interesting account of a bus journey from Blumenau to Iguaçu by mostly unpaved roads, through rich and interesting farming country (as an alternative to direct Catarinense bus, daily from Florianópolis and Itajaí to Iguaçu via Blumenau). They stopped at **Joaçaba**, a town of German immigrants (8 hrs. by bus; *Hotel Colonial*, at bus station, *Lotus*, across bridge, both F), Erechim (6 hrs. by bus, *Hotel Rex*, F, strong *gaúcho* influence), **Iraí** (6 hrs. by bus, Italian immigrant area, town with thermal springs, *Hotel São Luís*, E, with full board, town good for semi-precious stones), and Pato Branco (8 hrs. by bus, immediate connection to Cascavel for Foz do Iguaçu). The Tourist Office has details of combined ticket to Iguaçu—bus to Curitiba, then flight to Iguaçu—for US$ 62.

São Francisco do Sul, 80 km. up the coast (population 15,000), is the port for the town of Joinville, 45 km. inland at the head of the Cachoeira river. Most of the colonial architecture has been replaced by modern buildings. There are some excellent beaches nearby such as Ubatuba, Enseada (3 camp sites, Pascerella recommended) and Cápri. (At weekend trips to Ilha do Farol in port's supply boat.) Petrobrás oil refinery. *Hotel Avenida*, F with breakfast, clean, friendly; *Kon-Tiki*, E, near waterfront, opp. market; *Central*, R. Rafael Pedrinho, F; *Zibamba*, R. Fernandes Dias 27, central, C. The *Restaurante Franciscano*, on the Praia dos Coqueiros, is recommended, so are the *Metralhas* and *Flutuante* (good seafood.) Bus terminal is 1½ km. from centre. Direct bus (Penha) daily to Curitiba at 0730, US$1.80, 3½ hrs. Train from Joinville leaves daily at 0810 and frequent buses. Men are not allowed to wear shorts here.

Joinville, the state's second largest city (population, 217,000), lies 2 km. from the main coastal highway, BR-101, by which Curitiba and Florianópolis are less than two hours away. To Guaratuba (see page 296) by bus, 1¼ hrs., US$0.75 (connexions to Paranaguá). To Blumenau, US$ 1.25, 2¼ hrs. The bus terminal is 2½ km. outside the town (regular bus service).

See the Museum of History in the Prince of Joinville's mansion, which has a collection of objects from the original German settlement. The interesting Museo de Arte is in the old residence of Ottokar Doerfeu, Rua 15 de Novembro 1400 (open Tues.-Sun., 0900-1800). The Archaeological Museum has a collection of the Sambaquis period dating back to 5000 BC (open Tues.-Fri., 0900-1800, Sat., Sun., and holidays, 0900-1200, 1400-1800; US$0.20). Other museums are Museum of Immigration and Colonization, R. Rio Branco 229 (closed Mon.) and the Museum of the sculptor Fritz Act, Rua Aubé (closed Mon.).

292　BRAZIL

At Expoville, 4 km. from centre on BR-101 (continuation of 15 de Novembro) is an exhibition of Joinville's industry and an industrial museum. The industry does not, however, spoil the considerable charm of the city. There is an annual flower festival in the first fortnight of September.

Hotels *Tannehof*, Visconde de Taunay 340, 4 stars, restaurant on 14th floor; *Colón Palace*, São Joaquim 80; *Joinville Palace*, Príncipe 142, D; *Anthurium Parque*, São José 226, D, colonial style, good value, English spoken, friendly; *Ideal*, Jerônimo Coelho 98, E, with excellent breakfast, friendly, clean; *Fiedler*, Jerônimo Coelho 188, F; same street, No. 27, *Principe*, F. *King*, F, clean, friendly. *Novo Horizonte*, at bus station, basic, clean; *Konig*, 15 de Novembro 937, F; same street No. 811, *Matles*, F.

Camping Camping Clube do Brasil, Rua Saguaçu, Horto Florestal. Municipal site, same road, 1 km. from centre.

Restaurants *Petisqueira Pinheiro*, 7 de Setembro, is well worth a visit for excellent fish and shrimp dishes for about US$5. For meat or German specialities, *Churrascaria Rex*, *Churrascaria Ataliba*, near Expoville, *Familiar*, *Bierkeller*, 15 de Novembro 497, or the more expensive *Tannehof*, Visconde de Taunay 340; *Dietrichs*, Rua Princesa Isabel, excellent beer and German food (especially cakes). Similar are *A Cerejão* and *O Gato Preto*, on Dr João Colin. *Pasteleria Japoneza*, R. Princesa Isabel, excellent *pásteis*; *Jerke*, a bar on Dr João Colin, has good *empadas*; *Padaria Brunkow*, 9 de Maio, good snacks. The cheapest place to eat is the *Sociedade Ginástica*, Rua Ginásticos—you don't have to be a member.

Banks Banco do Brasil. Open 1000-1630.

Tourist Office corner Praça Nereu Ramos with Rua Príncipe; no information on cheap hotels. Good exchange rates

Air Service Airport 5 km. from city. Daily flights to major cities.

Excursions Four daily buses go to Ubatuba beach, a week-end resort (see above under São Francisco do Sul). The Sambaqui site of Rio Comprido can be reached by Gideon Bus, but there is not much to see.

The State of Paraná

The Italians were first in Paraná, but apart from a few Germans most of the later settlers were of Slavonic origin—Poles, Russians, Ruthenians and Ukrainians. Paraná made astonishing progress until the past few years. It is now the leading producer of wheat, rye, potatoes and black beans, but its population, 7,630,200 at end-1982, no longer expands as quickly as it did, partly as a result of internal migration following the uprooting of coffee plants in the more frost-prone areas and the turning of the land over to cattle; this has led to much displacement of rural workers. The latest boom crop, soya, also employs fewer workers throughout the year than coffee.

Curitiba, capital of Paraná state (pop. 1.5 million), is a modern city at 900 metres on the plateau of the Serra do Mar. The commercial centre is busy Rua 15 de Novembro (old name: Rua das Flores), which has a pedestrian area where there are Sat. morning painting sessions for children. Another pedestrian area is behind the cathedral, near Largo da Ordem, with sacred art museum, flower clock and old buildings. Art market Sat. morning in Praça Rui Barbosa, and on Sun. morning in Praça Garibáldi (recommended), beside attractive Rosário church. The Civic Centre is at the end of Avenida Dr. Cândido de Abreu, 2 km. from the city centre: a monumental group of five buildings dominated by the Palácio Iguaçu, headquarters of the state and municipal governments. In a patio behind it is a relief map to scale of Paraná. In contrast is the old municipal government building in French Art Nouveau style, now housing the Museu Paranaense (free, open Mon.-Fri. 0900-1800, Sat., Sun. 1200-1700, recommended), in Praça Generoso Marques. Nearby, on Praça Tiradentes, is the Cathedral (1894). The most popular public park is the Passeio Público, in the heart of the city (closed Mondays); it has a good little zoo, a network of canals with boats, and a small aquarium. On the north east edge of the city is Parque do Barigui, take bus 450 "São Braz" from Praça Tiradentes. Near the shores of Lake Bacacheri on the northern edge of the city (R. Nicarágua 2453) is an unexpected Egyptian temple (the Brazilian centre of the Ancient and mystical order of Rosicrucians—visits can be arranged—take Santa Cândida bus to Estação Boa Vista, then walk). There are three modern theatres, the Guaíra for plays and revues (also has free events—get tickets early in the day), one for concerts and ballet, and the Teatro Paiol in the old arsenal. Nearby is the Santa Felicidade district, which is mainly Italian, with good eating places. Many of the main streets have been widened and the city is being rapidly transformed.

Local Holidays Ash Wednesday (half-day); Maundy Thursday (half-day); September 8 (Our Lady of Light).

Hotels Those in the following list are in our category A or B:

Name	Address	Double (US$)	Rooms	A/c	Category*
Caravelle Palace	Rua Cruz Machado 282	57	100	yes	1+
Iguaçu	R. Cândido Lopes 102	41	200	yes	1
Mabu	Praça Santos Andrade 830	44	109	yes	S
Deville Colonial	R. Com. Araújo 99	41	95	yes	S
Lancaster	R. Voluntários da Pátria 91	40	106	yes	T
Del Rey	Ermelino de Leão 18	37	154	yes	S
Ouro Verde	R. Dr. Murici 419	37	90	yes	S+
Guaíra Palace	Praça Rui Barbosa 537	38	108	yes	T
Eduardo VII	Praça Tiradentes	39	163	yes	T

*1—first clas; S—standard; T—tourist

Charrua Motel, BR-116, Km. 389, exit for São Paulo, pool, heated rooms, D; *Tourist Universo*, Praça Gen. Osório 63, C, recommended; *Climax*, Rua Dr. Murici 411, good value, popular, C; *Los Angeles*, D with shower, a/c, T.V. and breakfast; *Braz*, Av. Luís Xavier 65, E; *Palace*, Rua Barão do Rio Branco 62, E with bath, F without, central, European atmosphere; *Regência*, Rua Alfredo Buffern 40, E; *Cacique*, Rua Tobias Macedo 26, E. *San Rafael*, Av. 7 de Setembro 1948, near bus and railway station, E with breakfast, bargain for cheaper rates without breakfast. Lots of cheap hotels around new railway/bus station; *Itamarati*, Tibagi 950, 500 m. from Rodoferroviária, E, clean, with bath, fan, friendly; *Joçoaba*, Rua João Negrão 340, on site of old bus station, F; *Marajó*, R. João Negrão 294, F; *Rheno*, Praça Carlos Gomes, F. *Vitória*, Rua São Francisco, F, central, pleasant, clean, friendly. Hotels near railway/bus station are also close to wholesale market, which operates noisily through the night. They include the *Império*, Av. Pres. Afonso Camargo 367, E, good breakfast, quiet, recommended (take insect repellant); next door, *Maia*, F without bath, E with, incl. breakfast, clean and quiet, owner speaks German and Dutch; *California*, opposite station, very clean, noisy, fair breakfast, recommended (but not the buffet supper), D; *Doral*, TV, frigobar in room, good breakfast, D; *Filadélfia*, E, clean, good breakfast, private bath, 4 blocks from station through market; *Espanha*, 3 blocks from terminal towards centre, F with bath; *Damasco*, Rua da Paz 660, G, not too clean, reasonable. *Blumenau*, Inaco Lustosa 161 (near Passeio Público), F; *Casa dos Estudantes*, Parque Passeio Público, F, with student card.

Camping Official site 7 km. N of city, on São Paulo road, US$1 a night. Camping Clube do Brasil, 14 km. out on same road.

Restaurants at the *Tourist Universo* and *Iguaçu* hotels. Foreign food at the *Emir* (Arab); *Pinheirão* (meat dishes); *Mouraria* (Portuguese); *Ile de France* (French), Praça 19 de Dezembro 538; *Bavaria* and *Frau Leo* (German); *Schwartze Katz* (German and international), Rua Francisco Torres 18; *Schwarzwald*, Claudino dos Santos 63, beerhaus/ restaurant, in centre (German); *Matterhorn* (Mateus Leme 575, centre) and *Locanda Suiça* (Swiss); *Lido* (Chinese), near Praça Osório. Lunch at *Nino's*, on 20th floor of a building near Praça Carlos Gomes, for grand views. *Golden Chopp*, Rua André de Barros (near corner with Rua Barão do Rio Branco), good value, recommended; *A Sacristia*, Rua João Manuel 197, restaurant, pizzeria, bar, very good; *Commercial Club*, Rua 15 de Novembro; *Tempo*, Rua Marechal Deodoro, good; good *feijoada* at *Hotel Del Rey* on Sats. *Oriente*, Rua Ebano Pereira 26 (1st floor), excellent, huge Arab lunch. Good Arab food also at *Casa de Efina*, Cruz Machado 247, and *Cantina Árabe*, Al. Augusto Stellfeld 143. Local and Italian food and local red wine in nearby Santa Felicidade (10 km. out of town on road to Ponta Grossa). Sukiyaki at *Restaurant Vemura*, near Cine Arlequin, on the Rua Vicente Machado, and also at *Yuasa*, Av. Sete de Setembro, cheap and good, recommended. *The Silver Dragon* (Chinese; good). *Dragão de Ouro*, Presidente Camargo 451 (opp. Rodoferroviária), good value. Vegetarian: *Transformação* (macrobiotic, shop also), Al. Augusto Stellfeld 781; *Vegetariano*, Carlos de Carvalho 127, 13 de Maio 222; *Ao Natural*, Rua São Francisco 332 (lunch only, shop also); *Super Vegetariano*, Rua Pres. Faria 121, Cruz Machado 217, Rua Dr. Murici 315, lunch and dinner Mon.-Fri., very good and cheap. At the corner of R. 15 de Novembro and General Carneiro is a nameless restaurant, good value for lunches. *Paláchio*, Barão Rio Branco, is all-night restaurant, good food and cheap; cheap

294 BRAZIL

food also near old railway station. *Restaurant e Pizzaria Mama Aurora,* Tibagi 1000, near Rodoviária and hotels in the area, OK. Close to the new bus and railway station is the market, where there are a couple of *lanchonetes*. Students can eat at University canteen (student cards required). Hot sweet wine sold on the streets in winter helps keep out the cold.

Electric Current   110 v. 60 cycles.

Bookshop   Livrarias Ghignone, Rua 15 de Novembro 409, has good selection of English books.

Shopping   Curitiba is a good place to buy clothes and shoes. H. Stern jewellers at Mueller Shopping Centre.

Local Transport   The city has a very efficient bus system; all bus stops have maps. Tickets must be purchased at booths before entering bus. Express buses on city routes are orange: for example, from centre (Praça Rui Barbosa) take Leste bus marked "Villa Oficinas" or "Centenário" for Rodoferroviária (combined bus and railway station).

Museums   The Museu Paranaense, Praça Generoso Marques (opening hours given above). Museu David Carneiro, on Rua Comendador Araújo 531, Sat., 1400-1600. Museo Guido Viário, R. São Francisco 319, painter's house; Museum of Contemporary Arts, Rua D. Westphalen 16 (closed Sats., and Sun. morning). Casa Andersen, R. Mateus Leme 336, house of painter, open Mon.-Fri. Railway Museum, Av. 7 de Setembro, in the old railway station, open Tues.-Fri., 1300-1900, Sat.-Sun., 0800-1300, Sunday steam-hauled excursions, book at Rodoferroviária; Second World War Museum, Casa Expedicionária, Rua da Paz 187; Museo do Automóvel, Av Cândido Hartmann 2300, all worth a visit.

Addresses   Centro Cultural Brasil-Estados Unidos (Mon.-Fri., 0800-1200, 1400-2100); Sociedade Brasileira de Cultura Inglesa (British Council), Rua General Carneiro 679 (Caixa Postal 505). Instituto Goethe, Duque de Caxias 4, open Mon., Wed., Thurs., Fri., 1500-1900. Austrian Consulate, Rua Marechal Floriano Peixoto 228, Edif. Banrisul, 17 andar, Caixa Postal 2473, Tel.: 22 46 795.

Banks   Lloyds Bank (ex-BOLSA), Rua Quinze de Novembro 317, and national banks. Open 1000-1600. **Money Exchange**; Best exchange rates at Jade travel agency, Rua Quinze de Novembro 477 (cash only); Triangle Turismo Travel, Praça General Osório 213, cash and travellers' cheques; Diplomata, Rua Presidente Faria 145 in the arcade, cash and travellers' cheques.

Tourist Office   Rua da Paz 54, maps and information in English. *Guía Turística de Curitiba e Paraná,* annual, US$4, on sale at all kiosks, has been recommended. Paranatur has booths at Rodoferroviária, in the old rail car at Rua 15 de Novembro 141, and at airport, helpful, English spoken, but no maps. Free weekly leaflet, *Bom Programa,* available shops, cinemas, paper stands etc.

Church services held in German at the Evangelical Church.

Cables   Post Office, Rua 15 de Novembro and Rua Pres. Faria. Main post office is at Marechal Deodoro 298. Embratel, Galeria Minerva, Rua 15 de Novembro.

Transport   Passenger trains to Paranaguá (book ahead). Frequent buses to São Paulo, including night bus at 2320 (6 hrs., US$4; *leito* 8) and Rio de Janeiro (11 hours, US$9, *leito* 18). To Santos, 3 a day (*leito* at 2300), 6½ hrs., US$3.35. Buses to Buenos Aires, US$37 (*leito* US$81) with Pluma; to Foz do Iguaçu, 10 buses a day, 10 hrs., US$7 (3 *leito* buses at night, US$14); to Porto Alegre, US$8, 10 hrs (*leito* US$16); to Londrina via Ponta Grossa, 8 hrs.; to Guaíra, 0700, 1915 and *leito* 1930 (12 hrs). Itajaí, 4 hrs., US$2.20; Blumenau, 4½ hrs., US$2.50. Florianópolis, US$3.50 (*leito* US$7); Santiago de Chile, US$60. New combined bus and railway station (Rodoferroviária) at end of Av. 7 de Setembro, very efficient (bus to centre US$0.10); short-distance bus services (up to 40 km.) begin at old bus station at Rua João Negrão 340. If travelling by car to Porto Alegre or Montevideo, the coastal highway (BR-101) is preferable to the inland road (BR-116).

Excursions   One Sun. a month the beautiful Ouro Fino estate (34 km.) is open to the public. 20 km. from Curitiba (at Km. 119) on the road to Ponta Grossa on the Museu Histórico do Mate, an old water-driven mill where *mate* was prepared (free admission). On the same road is **Vila Velha,** now a state park, 97 km. from Curitiba: *the sandstone rocks have been weathered into most fantastic shapes.* There is a Camping Clube do Brasil site near Vila Velha, 85 km. from Curitiba. Alternatively, stay in Ponta Grossa, from which buses leave for Vila Velha at 0900. The park office is 300 metres from the highway and the park a further 1½ km. (entrance US$0.20). Transport from the Park to a (free) swimming pool, 2 km. away. Princesa dos Campos bus from Curitiba at 0730 and 0930, 1½ hrs., US$1 (return buses pass park entrance at 1500 and 1800). The Lagoa Dourada, surrounded by forests, is close by. Nearby are the Furnas, three water holes, the deepest of which has a lift (US$0.30) which descends almost to water level (the same level as Lagoa Dourada); entrance US$0.05. Bus from Vila Velha at 1310, US$0.30, 4½ km. to turn-off to Furnas (another ¼-hr. walk) and Lagoa Dourada (it's not worth walking from Vila Velha to Furnas because it's mostly uphill along the main road). From the turn-off buses to Curitiba pass 10 minutes before they pass Vila Velha.

Popular expeditions during the summer are by paved road or rail (4½ hrs.) to Paranaguá. Two trains a day do the journey, the most spectacular railway trip in Brazil. Book well ahead. The normal train leaves Curitiba at 0700, arriving in Paranaguá at 1030 (US$1.60 1st class, US$1.30 2nd class, tickets on sale at 0600, except for Sun. train where on sale on Fri., no seat reservations—ticket office is closed on Sun.). Avoid the front coach. A modern air-conditioned railcar (the Litorina, called the *automotriz*) leaves at 0830, arriving at 1100 (US$4.25 round trip, US$3 one way, reserved seats bookable 2 days in advance—on Sat., Sun., and holidays tickets cannot be bought on day of departure; must be bought in advance), with recorded commentary (in Portuguese, French, Spanish and English) and stops at the viewpoint at the Santuário da N.S. do Cadeado and at Morretes (only a few minutes). There is an extra train on Sats. only at 1330. Sit on the left-hand side on journey from Curitiba (in the *automotriz*, the seats, not the car, are turned round, so you sit the same side in each direction). If Litorina is full, take bus to Paranaguá, US$1.65, then take Litorina back: return journeys start at 1630 and 1530 respectively so remember that in winter part of the journey is covered in the dark. The train is usually crowded on Saturdays and Sundays. Many travellers recommend returning by bus (1½ hrs.), buy ticket immediately on arrival), if you do not want to stay 4½ hrs. A tour bus meets the train and offers a tour of town and return to Curitiba for US$3. There are numerous tunnels, with sudden views of deep gorges and high peaks and waterfalls as the train rumbles over dizzy bridges and viaducts. Near Banhado station (Km. 66) is the waterfall of Véu da Noiva; from the station at Km. 59, the mountain range of Marumbi National Park can be reached: good hiking.

You can also visit **Antonina** (not on main route) and **Morretes** (on main route), two sleepy colonial towns which can be reached by rail and also by bus on the old Graciosa road, which is almost as scenic as the railway. Bus Paranaguá to Morretes at 1830, US$0.80, to Antonina, stopping en route at Morretes, 6 a day, (US$1.15). 3 buses daily Morretes-Curitiba. An *automotriz* train runs to Antonina on Sun. only (US$3).

Morretes hotel: *Nhundiaquara*, in town centre, beautifully located, F and up; good restaurants in town and a river beach. Antonina hotels: *de Lazer*, B, 3-star; *Christine*, F and up, clean. Antonina is a port, but there are no beaches. 14 km. N of Morretes is the beautiful village of São João de Graciosa, 2 km. beyond which is the flower reserve of the Marumbi Park. The Graciosa road traverses the park for 12 km., with 6 rest stops with fire grills, shelters and camping. The park is very beautiful; you can also hike the original trail which follows the road and passes the rest-stops. Take food, water and plenty of insect repellant. The Marumbi Park can be entered at a gate 3-4 km. from the BR-116 Curitiba-São Paulo highway.

The chief port of the state of Paraná is

Paranaguá, one of the main coffee-exporting ports, founded in 1585, 268 km. south of Santos. The port is on a lagoon 29 km. from the open sea and is approached via the Bay of Paranaguá, dotted with picturesque islands. The fort of Nossa Senhora dos Prazeres was built in 1767 on a nearby island; one hour's boat trip. The former Colégio dos Jesuitas, a fine Baroque building, has been converted into a Museum of Archaeology and Popular Art (Tues.-Fri., 1000-1700, Sat.-Mon., 1200-1700; entrance US$0.10). Other attractions are a 17th century fountain, the Church of São Benedito, and the shrine of Nossa Senhora do Rocio, 2 km. from town. There is an interesting market near the waterfront. Population, 68,366. Paranaguá is a free port for Paraguay.

The paved 116-km. road to Curitiba is picturesque, but less so than the railway (see page 295), which offers one of the most beautiful trips in Brazil.

Hotels *Santa Mônica*, Praia de Leste, 30 km. from town, on fine beach, D; *Líder*, Rua Júlia da Costa 169, D; *Auana*, Rua Correia de Freitas 110, E, good value, recommended. *Ribamar*, F, with

296 BRAZIL

breakfast; *Litoral*, Rua Correia de Freitas 66, F without breakfast, clean and comfortable; *Rio Mar* and *Mar de Rosas*, both on waterfront, F.

Camping Camping Clube do Brasil site at Praia de Leste, on the beach, 27 km. from Paranaguá.

Restaurants *Bobby's*, Faria Sobrinho 750. Fish, shrimps and oysters are recommended. *Danúbio Azul* 15 de Novembro 91, good, not cheap, view of river. A very good T-bone steak (with good salads) at *Churrascaria Cacique*, Dr. Leocádio 290. *Bar Bela Vista*, Rua General Carneiro; *Aquarius*, Av. Gabriel de Lara 40, near bus station, good but not cheap seafood.

Tourist Information kiosk outside railway station.

Air Services Curitiba airport.

Bus Station Praça João Gualberto, nr railway station; all buses operated by Graciosa. To Curitiba, US$1.65, many, 1½ hrs. (only the 0745 in either direction takes the old Graciosa road).

Excursions *Matinhos* is a Mediterranean-type resort, invaded by surfers in October for the Paraná surf competition; several cheap hotels, including *Bolamar*, (F, basic, cheapest) and *Beira Mar*. 3 camp sites, but the municipal site is closed until November. Cruises on Paranaguá Bay by launch, daily from Cais do Mercado. Bus from Paranaguá at 1000, 1400 and 1615, US$0.60. 6 buses a day to Guaratuba, US$0.60. **Guaratuba** (which is less built up than Caiobá) has *Pensão Antoinet*, F, clean, dangerous showers, and other hotels; campsite. All Guaratuba buses pass **Caiobá** (*Hotel Caiobá*, D, cheapest). Caiobá to Guaratuba by ferry, free for pedestrians, US$0.80 for cars, 10 minutes, frequent departures.

To **Ilha do Mel**, take bus to Pontal do Sul (many daily, 1 hr., US$0.50); turn left out of the bus station and walk 25 metres to main road, turn right for 1½ km. and bear left along a sandy road for 2 km. to fishermen's houses from where a ferry runs (US$0.75). On the island, at Praia dos Encantados, one can camp or rent a fisherman's house—ask for *Valentim's Bar*, or for Luchiano. Dona Ana and Dona Maria sell bread and cakes, and meals if you ask in advance. There are two bars, fresh water, but no electricity. The beaches, caves, bays and hill walks are beautiful. 4 hrs.' walk from the village is an old Portuguese fort, possible to hitch a ride in a fishing boat back. If camping, watch out for the tide, watch possessions and beware of the *bicho de pé* which burrows into feet (remove with a needle and alcohol) and of the *borrachudos* (discourage with Autum repellent). In summer and at holiday times the island is very crowded.

A launch leaves Paranaguá each Wed. and Fri. at 0600 from the quay behind the Yacht Club for Cananéia and Iguape in São Paulo State (see page 271). (This service was reported withdrawn in December 1986).

About 117 km. from Curitiba the road inland (which passes Vila Velha—see page 294) reaches **Ponta Grossa**, a town of 186,618, at 895 metres. It now calls itself the "World Capital of Soya" (as does Palmeira las Missões, in Rio Grande do Sul). Roads run north through Apucarana (Camping Clube site) and Londrina to São Paulo, and south to Rio Grande do Sul and the Uruguayan border.

Hotels *Vila Velha Palace*, Rua Balduino Taques 123, D; *Planalto Palace*, Rua 7 de Setembro 652, plain and clean, F-E; *Gravina*, Rua Cnel. Bittencourt 92, F. *Scha Fransky*, Rua Francisco Ribas, 104, E, very good breakfast; almost next door, same street No. 162, is *Central*, F, with fan and basin, good breakfast; *Luz*, bargain, near railway station. *Esplanada*, in bus station (quiet, however), F with bath and breakfast. Try area around Praça Barão de Garaúna.

Camping Camping Clube do Brasil, 26 km. out at the entrance to Vila Velha.

Restaurants *Chopin*, for excellent *churrascos*. *Shanadu*, on main square, good value.

In Alto Paraná in the extreme NW of the State, connections have traditionally been with São Paulo rather than with Curitiba. Large new centres of populations have risen in a short time. In 1930 four Japanese and two Germans arrived in **Londrina** (developed by a British company). Today it is a city with skyscrapers, modern steel and glass cathedral, wide streets and 309,420 people. (*Hotel Coroados*, Sen. Souza Naves 814, E, standard; *Hotel Aliança*, nr. bus station, E, very clean, good breakfast; *Granada*, Av. São Paulo, near bus station, F with breakfast.) **Maringá**, 80 km. W of Londrina, founded in 1947, has 168,619 people, half of them Japanese. There is a conical cathedral here; Parque Ingá is shady, with a Japanese garden. (*Hotel Santos*, nr bus station, F, basic, clean; others in this area. *São Carlos*, Joules de Carvalho 422, F, recommended.) Londrina and Maringá are good points for connections between the south (Porto Alegre), Foz do Iguaçu and Mato Grosso do Sul (Campo Grande). Bus from Londrina to Porto Alegre takes 22 hours; to Campo Grande 11 hours, via Presidente Prudente (see page 278). A number of bus services from Paraná state to Porto Alegre (Aguia Branca, Unesul) and to Campo Grande, Cuiabá and Porto Velho (Eucatur) commence at Cascavel, further S on the Curitiba-Iguaçu road.

The North-East

The nine states of the north-eastern bulge of Brazil are best considered as one entity. They cover 2.6 million square km. and contain a third of Brazil's people. The birthrate is the highest in Brazil, but so is the infant mortality rate. The average annual income from subsistence farming is deplorably low. Despite the misery, both regional and state loyalty remain ineradicable.

There was a brief period of colonization from northern Europe in the NE, when the Dutch West India Company, based at Recife, controlled some seven captaincies along the coast. They gained control in 1630, when Portugal was subject to Spain. After 1640, when Portugal freed itself, the Portuguese colonists fought the Dutch and finally expelled them in 1654.

The nine states are Bahia, Sergipe, Alagoas, Pernambuco, Paraíba, Rio Grande do Norte, Ceará, Piauí, and Maranhão. They by no means form a homogeneous unity, but may be roughly divided into three contrasting parts. One is the sugar lands of the Zona da Mata along the coast between Salvador (Bahia) and Natal, where the rainfall can be depended upon. This was the first part of Brazil to be intensively colonized; hence the number of 16th century buildings and the density of old settlements are way above the national average. Inland from the Zona da Mata is the Zona do Agreste, with less rainfall, but generally enough for cattle raising. Inland again is the true interior, the Sertão, where rainfall cannot be depended upon; there is a little agriculture where water allows it but the herding of goats, and occasionally cattle is more important. There are few blacks in the interior; the inhabitants are mostly of Portuguese-Indian stock, one of the most distinctive in Brazil. They are known as the *flagelados,* the scourged ones.

When there is rain, food in the zone is plentiful and varied. Manioc is a basic food; in addition, there are goat's milk and cheese, beef, beans, and sweet potatoes. But in the years of drought, when the hot dry winds from Africa scorch the earth, the effects can be tragic. Migration towards the coast and the southern towns begins, and the people are exposed to castigation of yet another sort: exploitation by grasping labour contractors. But at the first news that there is rain, the *flagelado* heads for home.

The main export crops of the north-east are sugar, cotton and cacao. Sugar and cotton have long been in decline, and now the southern states grow more than half of the Brazilian total. But cacao is grown almost entirely in southern Bahia, inland from the port of Ilhéus.

Brazil's main oilfields are in the State of Bahia; there are also offshore wells in the coastal waters of Alagoas, Sergipe and Rio Grande do Norte.

South of Cape São Roque there is abundant rainfall, but in Pernambuco the zone of ample rain stretches only 80 km. inland, though it deepens southwards. São Luís in Maranhão also gets plenty of rain, but between eastern Maranhão and Pernambuco lies a triangle, with its apex deep inland, where the rainfall is sporadic, and occasionally non-existent for a year. Here the tropical forest gives way to the *caatinga,* or scrub forest bushes which shed their leaves during drought. In this area grow the carnauba palm, the babaçu palm and the tree that produces oiticica oil.

Cities of the North-East

Salvador is the capital of Bahia state and the fifth city of Brazil; Brasillia is 2,099 km. away. São Paulo 1,972 km. and Rio 1,702 km. The BR-116 inland road to Rio and the shorter coastal road, the BR-101, are both paved through-out. Salvador is a good city to slow down in and relax on the beaches. It rains somewhat all the year, but the main rainy season is between April or May and September. In

298 **BRAZIL**

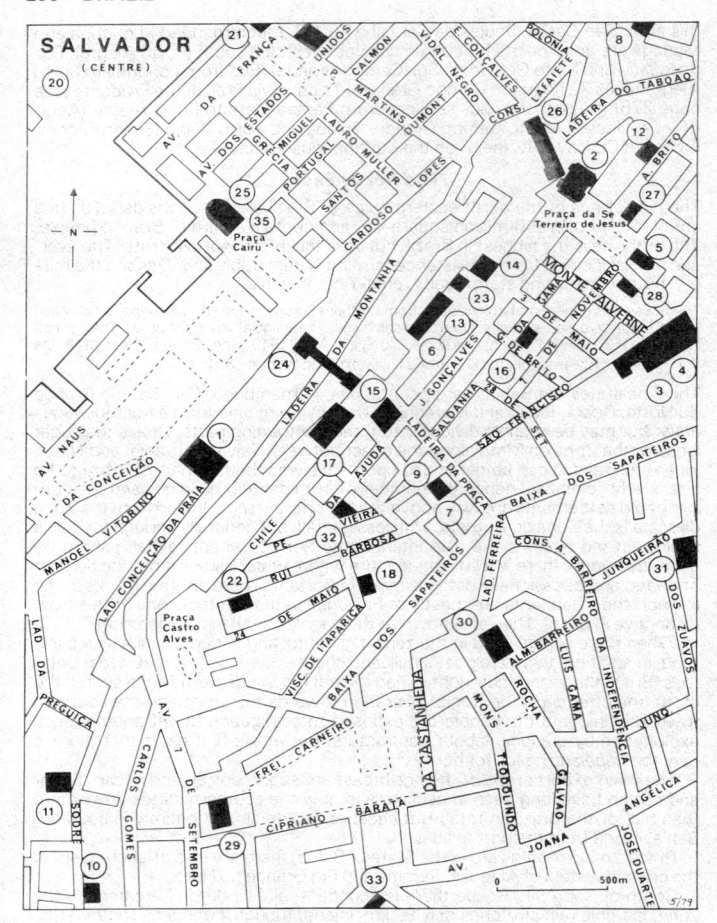

Key to Map of Salvador

1. Church of Conceição da Praia; 2. Cathedral; 3. Church and Convent of São Francisco; 4. Church of the 3rd Order of São Francisco; 5. Church of the 3rd Order of São Domingos; 6. Church of Santa Casa de Misericórdia; 7. House of Rui Barbosa; 8. House of the Seven Dead Men (Sete Mortes); 9. House of the Seven Lamps (Sete Candeeiros); 10. Colégio Ipiranga (Castro Alves Museum); 11. Museum of Religious Art; 12. Museum of the Nina Rodrigues Institute; 13. Museum of the Santa Casa; 14. Archbishop's Palace; 15. Town Hall (Palácio Municipal); 16. Palace of Saldanha; 17. Palace of Rio Branco; 18. Berquó Mansion (Solar); 20. Fort of São Marcelo; 21. Customs House (Alfândega); 22. Post and Telegraph Office; 23. Municipal Tourist Office; 24. Lacerda Lift; 25. Market (Mercado Modelo); 26. Gonçalves Funicular (Plano Inclinado); 27. Church of São Pedro dos Clérigos; 28. São Dâmaso Seminary; 29. Church and Convent of São Bento; 30. Church of Palma; 31. Church of Sant' Ana; 32. Church of Nossa Senhora da Ajuda; 33. Convent of Lapa; 35. State Tourist Office.

general the climate is pleasant, and the sun never far away. Temperatures range from 25°C to 32°C, never falling below 19°C.

Salvador's population is 1,496,000. It was founded in 1549, and was till 1763 the capital of Brazil. Most of its 135 churches, the fortifications, and some other buildings date from the 17th and 18th centuries. The centre of the city is divided into two, the Baixa (or lower part, known as Comércio), and the Alta (or higher part, known as Centro) on a small plateau some 70-odd metres above the lower city and overlooking the sparkling bay. The commercial quarter, the picturesque market near Praça Cairu, and the old port are in the lower city. The older parts of the upper city, from the Praça Terreiro de Jesus to beyond the Carmo church, are now a National Monument and extensive restoration work is being undertaken. A new administrative centre has been built near the airport.

Salvador is the main centre of the cigar-tobacco trade, and is famous for its excellent mild cigars. There is a small oil refinery at Mataripe, across the bay, serving the nearby oilfields of the Recôncavo area. The new industrial centre is at Aratu, and at Camaçari nearby there is a petrochemical centre.

The upper city is reached from the lower by steep slanting streets (*ladeiras*), and various public lifts and funiculars. The Lacerda lift raises passengers 71 metres from Praça Cairu in the lower city to Praça Municipal in the upper, where are the old Government Palace and the Biblioteca Municipal (1811); a steep road runs from the Customs House to Largo dos Aflitos, just behind the Governor's Palace; it has been continued under a viaduct at Campo Grande and on to the Canela valley, where the University is. The Gonçalves funicular railway runs from near the Praça da Sé down to the lower city. From Praça Municipal runs Rua Chile, with the best shops; several hotels are in its further extension, Rua 7 de Setembro, which continues along the Atlantic coast as Av. Presidente Vargas. New roads have been built inland: the Periférico Vale dos Barris, a divided-lane highway, runs from close to the centre, behind the Atlantic coast suburbs, to the administrative centre and the airport.

In the upper city interesting walks and drives can be taken across Praça Castro Alves, past the São Bento church (rebuilt after 1624 but with fine 17th century furniture), the Instituto Geográfico e Histórico, São Pedro fort (1646-1877), and the fine Praça 2 de Julio (also known as Campo Grande), with its column. At Campo Grande (magnificently lit at night) is the Castro Alves theatre. The route can be continued past the British Club (the sea side of Campo Grande, at Rua Banco dos Ingleses 20), the old Legislative Assembly, the Vitória and the Graça church (rebuilt 1770), down the Barra hill, past forts and the lighthouse at the bar, to Avenida Oceânica and along the sea front to Rio Vermelho and beyond. On Av. Oceânica, half-way to Rio Vermelho, there is a Zoo (daily 0800-1700, entrance free) in the Botanical Gardens at Ondina, and a restaurant at the top of Ondina hill, overlooking the sea. A road between Rio Vermelho and the airport, 32 km. from the city, runs picturesquely beside the sea for 13 km. before turning inland to the airport. Some of the best hotels are on the sea front at Ondina and Rio Vermelho, and beyond at Pituba, Placafor and Itapoan. Piatã beach is less polluted than most.

Near the turning to the airport is the palm-fringed beach of Itapoan (primitive eating stands, with good sea food), where the traditional fishing rafts (*jangadas*) may occasionally be seen. There are two campsites on the beach, past the lighthouse. Quite near is the dark-green freshwater lake of Abaeté, circled by brilliant white sand dunes, now becoming built-up (bus direct from Praça da Sé and Campo Grande, marked "Aeroporto" or "Itapoan", 1 hr. US$0.10).

Many of the old forts are worth looking at, though most are closed to the public. The oldest, Santo Antônio da Barra (1598), is by the beach at Barra, where you can choose between bay and ocean bathing. One of the forts normally open to the public is that of São Marcelo in front of the Mercado Modelo (closed for repairs in 1985). The best bathing inside the bay that can be easily reached from the city is at Itapagipe, near the Bomfim church (Ribeira bus, from Elevador, lower station) but bathing inside the bay is not recommended because of pollution. A clean and uncrowded beach is at Boca do Rio.

Near the old churches in the upper city are untouched colonial mansions and

300 **BRAZIL**

dwellings (especially in the Rua Gregório Mattos), some with heavily carved doors. See particularly the church of the monastery of São Francisco de Assis for its sculptures in wood, and the cloisters of the monastery itself for its excellent tiles and paintings (Sr. Salvador is the guide here, extremely helpful, worth asking for even when the monastery is closed, a guide is compulsory, US$1.50); the church (1701) of the Ordem Terceira (the Franciscan Third Order), next door to São Francisco, for its rich façade and, within, a quite remarkable Chapter House (0830-1130 and 1400-1700) with striking images of the Order's most celebrated saints; the Cathedral (Terreiro de Jesus, upper city), formerly the Jesuit church, for its general design, the tomb of Mem de Sá, coloured marble and inlaid furniture (0730-1130 and 1500-1730); Santa Casa de Misericórdia (late 17th century), for its high altar and painted tiles; the Convent of Santa Teresa, for the gate and the tiles in the floor of the kitchen; the 18th century church and monastery of Nossa Senhora do Carmo, for its altar and stalls, and statues in the sacristy; the church of Rosário dos Pretos, next to the Senac restaurant, Largo do Pelourinho, for its *azulejos* and its fine painted ceiling.

See also the famous church of Nosso Senhor do Bomfim on the Itapagipe peninsula in the suburbs, whose construction began in 1745; it draws endless supplicants (particularly on Fri. and Sun.) offering favours to the image of the Crucified Lord set over the high altar; the number and variety of ex-voto offerings—often of parts of the body deemed to have been cured by divine intervention—is extraordinary. The processions over the water to the church on the third Sun. in January are particularly interesting.

Also on the Itapagipe peninsula is a colonial fort on Mont Serrat point, and at Ribeira the church of Nossa Senhora da Penha (1743). The beach here has many restaurants (bus from Praça da Sé or Av. França).

Local Holidays Jan. 6 (Epiphany); Ash Wed. and Maundy Thurs., half-days; July 2 (Independence of Bahia); Oct. 30; Christmas Eve, half-day. An important local holiday is the Festa do Nosso Senhor do Bomfim, on the first Sun. in Feb., but the colourful washing or *lavagem* of the Bomfim church takes place on the preceding Thurs. The Festa da Ribeira is on the following Mon. The most colourful feast of all is that of the fishermen of the Rio Vermelho district on Feb. 2; gifts for Yemanjá, Goddess of the Sea, are taken out to sea in a procession of sailing boats to an accompaniment of *candomblé* instruments. The Holy Week processions among the old churches of the upper city are very colourful.

The pre-Carnival festive season begins towards the end of Nov. with São Nicodemo de Cachimbo (penultimate Sun. of Nov.), then comes Santa Bárbara (Dec. 4), then the Festa da Conceição da Praia, centred on the church of that name at the base of the Lacerda lift. (Dec. 8 is the last night—not for those who don't like crowds!) The last week of Dec. is the Festa da Boa Viagem in the lower city; the beach will be packed all night on the 31st. On January 1 is the beautiful boat procession of Nosso Senhor dos Navegantes from Conceição da Praia to the church of Boa Viagem, on the beach of that name in the lower city. The leading boat, which carries the image of Christ and the archbishop, was built in 1892. You can follow in a sailing boat for about US$1; go early (0900) to dock by Mercado Modelo. A later festival is São Lázaro on the last Sun. in January.

Folklore Carnival in Salvador is particularly lively, with nearly everyone in fancy dress and dancing in the streets; parades are centred on Campo Grande (grandstand seats cost about US$4.20). Visitors find it exciting and entertaining, but look out for the more violent elements and don't carry any valuables. The pre-Carnival festive season is very long—the first *festas* start at the end of November (see page 300). The *blocos* (samba groups) can be seen practising at this time; ask locals, Bene at *Zanzi-bar* or Bahiatursa for details. Many clubs have pre-carnival and Carnival dances; Baile das Atrizes has been recommended (always book tickets early).

The *Bahianas*—black women who dress in traditional 18th century costumes—are street vendors who sit behind their trays of delicacies, savoury and seasoned, made from the great variety of local fish, vegetables and fruits.

See *capoeira*, a sport developed from the traditional foot-fighting technique introduced from Angola by African slaves. The music is by drum, tambourine and *berimbau*; there are several different kinds of the sport. If you want to attempt *capoeira*, the best schools are Mestre Bimba in Terreiro de Jesus, at Rua Francisco Muniz Barreto 1, and Os Inocentes in Pelourinho, at Rua Alfredo Brito 33.

BRAZIL 301

Classes are held in evenings. There are two more schools in Forte de Santo Antônio behind Pelourinho, but check addresses at tourist office. Exhibitions take place in the Largo do Pelourinho, very picturesque, in the upper city (cost: US$2). You can also see the experts practising outside the Mercado Modelo on most days and at Campo Grande and Forte de Santo Antônio on Sunday afternoons; they often expect a contribution.

Candomblé, the local Africa-derived magico-religious ceremonies (counterpart of Rio's *macumba*) may be seen by tourists—but not photographed—on Sundays and religious holidays. Contact the tourist office, Bahiatursa, or see their twice monthly calendar of events.

One of the best ways to get the "feel" of Salvador before visiting it is to read the works of the great Brazilian regional novelist Jorge Amado, most of which are set in and around the city. Several are in English translation. The Casa da Cultura Jorge Amado is being installed in a colonial building at the top of the Largo do Pelourinho.

Warning Salvador is not free of crime, ranging from armed robbery to pickpocketing and bagsnatching, though the picture is improving, thanks to an increased police presence. Be very careful of your money and valuables at all times and in all districts. Avoid the more distant beaches out of season, when they are empty (e.g. Itapoan, Piatã, Placafor); on Sundays they are more crowded and safer. Leave valuables securely in your hotel (inc. cameras if possible), particularly at night. Be careful if you stay in hotels around the Praça da Sé; parts of the centre of the upper city nearby are run down and rather dubious, and one is warned not to walk down the Ladeira de Misericôrdia, which links the Belvedere, near the Lacerda lifts, with the lower city.

Hotels There are over 120 in the city and suburbs. Most of those away from the centre have swimming pools. Prices are lowest available. Those listed below are in our categories L, A, B and C.

Name	Address	Single (US$)	Double (US$)
Quatro Rodas	Rua da Passárgada, Farol de Itapoan (*recommended*)	75	82
Meridien	Rua Fonte do Boi 216, Rio Vermelho	67	79
Bahia Othon Palace	Av. Oceânica 2456, Ondina	78	86
Salvador Praia	Av. Oceânica 2032, Ondina	65	72
Farol	Av. Presidente Vargas 68	48	54
Grande da Barra	Av. Sete de Setembro 3564	45	54
Marazul	Av. Sete de Setembro 3937	54	62
Paulus	Av. Otávio Mangabeira, Pituba	30	36
Pituba Plaza	Av. Manoel Dias da Silva 2495, Pituba (*recommended*)		
Ondina Praia	Av. Oceânica 2275, Ondina (*recommended*)	40	48
Luxor Convento do Carmo	Largo do Carmo 1	48	60
Praiamar	Av. Sete de Setembro 3577, Vitória	50	56
Vilha Velha	Av. Sete de Setembro 1791	35	39
Pelourinho	Rua Alfredo Brito 20	20	24
Vela Branca	Av. Antônio Carlos Magalhães, Pituba	36	40
Itapuã Praia	Jardim Itapuã, Placafor	35	48
Armação	Av. Otávio Mangabeira, Armação	28	35
Ondimar	Av. Presidente Vargas (*recommended*)	36	42
Palace	Rue Chile 20 (*recommended*)	33	38
Bahia Praia	Av.Presidente Vargas 2483, Ondina	37	44
Bahia de Todos os Santos	Av. Sete de Setembro 106 (Ladeira de São Bento)	30	35
Villa Romana	Rua Lemos Brito 14	24	29
Bahia do Sol	Av. Sete de Setembro 2009, Ondina	40	45
Praia do Sol	Praia de Piatã	28	36

For people who like something out of the ordinary the *Luxor Convento do Carmo*, in a converted monastery dating from 1580 with colonial-type furniture and decoration, swimming pool, is recommended, sometimes cheaper in mid-year. *Quatro Rodas* is a complete vacation hotel, extensive grounds, peaceful but plenty of activities available. *Chalê Enseada das Lajes*, Av. Presidente Vargas 511 (Morro da Paciência), A-L, 9 rooms in what used to be a private house, good service, good but expensive meals, ocean-views, 2 mins. from beach. *Da Bahia*, Praça 2 de Julho 2 (Campo Grande), new, deluxe, very expensive, recommended.

Paraíso, Rua Demócrata 45, F, centre, good views, not too clean. *Ilhéus*, Ladeira da Praça 4 (200 metres from Elevador Lacerda), F, clean, unsafe, friendly but a little noisy; *Chile*, Rua Chile 7,

302 BRAZIL

also with good views across bay, F, with bath and breakfast, friendly, secure, clean (very strange night-life in this area); *Solara*, Rua José Alencar 25, Largo do Pelourinho, central, F with shower, toilet, breakfast, clean, facilities for laundry, recommended; *Vigo*, Rua 13 de Mayo 8, 2 blocks from Praça da Sé, F with bath and breakfast, not too clean, safe, owner is Spanish (also owns *Hotel Center*); *Joana Angélica*, in street of same name, cheap, friendly, no breakfast; *Santiago*, Rua Visconde de São Lourenço 52 (near Praça Campo Grande), F with shower, breakfast, friendly, good; *Mater Café Teatro Hotel*, Rua M. Floriano 5 (also near Campo Grande), E, clean (but poor locks on doors), breakfast, with good café, *dos Artistas*, next door (Spanish spoken); *Caramuru*, Av. 7 de Setembro 2726, no baths, very clean, friendly, safe parking, E. *Benfica*, Rua Monte Alverne 6, near Praça da Sé, F; *Center*, also R. Monte Alverne, F. *São José*, Travessa do Rosário 1, E; *Estrela Dalva*, 7 de Setembro 1013, cheap and clean; opposite is *Mercês*, recommended, not recommended. Nearby, on Largo São Bento, is *São Bento*, E, friendly, good cheap restaurant. *Imperial*, Av. 7 de Setembro, E, bath and breakfast, good bar-restaurant next door; *Anglo Americano*, Av. 7 de Setembro 1838 (near Campo Grande) Tel.: 247-7681, F with breakfast, fan, laundry facilities, safe, pay in advance, good gringo hotel, pleasant district, clean. *Granada*, Rua 7 de Setembro 512, F, good value, good breakfast. *Pousada Cosme e Damião*, Av. 7 de Setembro 76, 2nd floor, F, clean; also *Carata*. *Amaralina*, Av. Amaralina 790, F, clean but a bit out of the way; *Barra Praia*, Av. Almirante Marques de Leão 172, Barra (one street from beach) F, clean, recommended; *Casa Grande*, in Barra, E; *Enseada Praia de Barra*, Barão de Sergy 49, D, clean, safe; *Acácia*, Rua Carlos Gomes 21, E; *Residencial* (formerly *Pensão Amides*), Rua do Paraíso, F; *Jequié*, Rua Saldanha de Gama 14, F with breakfast; *Miramar*, Rua Artur Catrambi 5 (1st and 2nd floors), near railway station, F; *Bella Vista*, Rua Ruy Barbosa 51, F, with bath, fan, clean, not very friendly, used by short-stay couples; same street, *Paris*, E, plus breakfast, recommended; also *Pousada da Praça*, at No. 5, F, without bath, clean, friendly, recommended, bar and sandwiches, safe. *Nova Esperança*, Ladeira das Hortas, friendly, F; *Guadalajara*, Ladeira de Santa Rita 2, F. *Pensão* at Rua Independência 63, F; *Internacional*, Rua Senador Costa Pinto 88, being renovated; *Oxalá Lanches*, R. da Mangueira, F, with all meals; *Meridional*, Rua do Paraíso 330, friendly and clean, F. Cheap hotels near Terreiro de Jesus, upper city, e.g. *Império*, F, incl. breakfast. *Solar São Francisco*, Praça Anchieta 16A, F, noisy but recommended, friendly, good breakfast; next door (No. 20) is *Colón*, F with breakfast and washbasin in room, clean, safe, recommended. *Pensão Moderno*, Rua Monte Alverne, F, laundry service, friendly; next door is *Glória*, F; *Real*, Rua Direita da Piedade, F with breakfast. Three places further out are: *Atlântico*, Av. Otávio Mangabeira, Itapoan, C; *Pousada do Itapoan* (1 hr. from centre), F, without breakfast; *Pituba*, Av. Manoel P. da Silva, Pituba, one star (no sign), F. *Pensionatos* are cheap places to stay in shared rooms (up to four persons per room); e.g. *Pensionato No. 20*, Av. Cerqueiro Lima; part or full board available. A huge Hilton hotel complex is being built 16 km. from the city, along the road to the airport. Youth Hostel, Rua da Graça 99, in centre, Tel.: 241-0591, no singles, groups of 4 or more only, unhelpful.

Camping Near the lighthouse at Itapoan, take bus from Praça da Sé to Campo Grande or Barra, change there for Itapoan, about 1 hr., then ½ hr. walk; two campsites, one Camping Clube do Brasil, at US$6 p.p. per night (members half price), and a cheaper one opposite. Camping de Pituaçu, Av. Prof. Pinto de Aguiar, Jardim Pituaçu. Sea bathing is dangerous off shore near campsites.

Restaurants Upper City: *Palace Hotel*, Rua Chile, serves a different traditional Portuguese *entrée* each lunchtime, except Sunday; *Mini Cacique*, Rua Rui Barbosa 29, behind *Palace Hotel* but lower down hill, good Bahian cooking, lunch only, very popular; *O Tempo*, Largo do Pelourinho, through antique shop of the same name, run down, not very clean; *Hotel Pelourinho*, indoor and outdoor, good views, good food, US$5; *Quindins de Iaiá*, Rua Direita de Santo Antônio 376, good, cheap (north of Pelourinho); *Pérez*, behind Governor's Palace, international food, view over bay; *La Portuguesa*, Av. 7 de Setembro 600 block, good, cheap; *Xangai*, Av. 7 de Setembro 1755 (near Campo Grande), Chinese, very good and cheaper than Chinese restaurants in Barra. *Casa d'Italia*, corner of 7 de Setembro and Visconde de São Lourenço, good, reasonable prices, good service; opposite *Bela Nápoli*, Av. Joana Angélica, Italian and fairly good. *Frutas do Mar*, Rua Marquês de Leão, good seafood. *Tong-Fong*, Av. Joana Angélica 101, Chinese, highly recommended. *D. Velázquez*, Rua Direita da Piedade, good; opposite is *Baita-Kão* which serves good, cheap sandwiches. *Kowloon*, off Politeama do Baisco, next to Cinema Bristol, all you can eat for US$2.50; *Teng Teng*, snackbar, Rua Carlos Gomes; same street, *Lanchoneta O Camarade*, good and cheap. *Lotus*, Rua do Paraíso 34, macrobiotic, good, excellent value. *Fruta de Terra*, Rua Carlos Gomes 21, vegetarian, good food, fine views of city and the bay; *Tao Chi*, Rua General Labatut 23 and *Nectar*, Rua A. França 16, also vegetarian; *Nutre Ben*, Av. Joana Angélica 148 and *Trigal*, Rua Prof. Américo Simas 48, vegetarian, both open Mon.-Fri. for lunch only. Reported best vegetarian restaurant is *Grão de Arroz*, Coqueiros da Piedade 83, Barra. *Solar do Unhão*, in modernized sugar-estate house off Av. do Contorno, right on the side of the bay, is beautiful and expensive (US$20); folkloric dancing and *son et lumière*; closed Sundays. *Don Quichoppe*, Av. Carlos Gomes, US$1.50-3, good variety. *Casa de Gamboa*, Rua Newton Prado 51, old colonial home, reported best place for Bahia's regional food; *Cantina*, opposite cathedral, wholesome meal for under US$2; *Lanches Apolo*, R. Portugal and Miguel Calmon 3, clean, daily specials under US$2. There is a good hamburger stand near Igreja N.S. da Piedade, good value, real orange juice; *Kentefrio*, Av. 7 de Setembro 379, excellent clean snack bar, counter service only, closed Sunday; in same street, Chinese restaurant opp. *Hotel Anglo Americano*, good but not cheap; *Perini Sorveteria*, R. Miguel Bournier 22, superb ice cream, cakes, savouries, chocolates, branches also at Iguatemi shopping centre, Pituba and Rua Portugal (Comercial district). *Salada de Frutas*, on A. Brito, is a good fruit salad bar. Opposite the fire station, a Chinese *lanchonete* serves good fruit juices. *Baby Beef*, Hipermercado Paes Mendonça, Pituba (Av. Antônio Carlos Magalhães s/n), very good food and service; *Juarez*, Mercado de Ouro, Av. Federico Pontes s/n, Cidade Baixa, good, cheap food; *Mão de Vaca*, Rua Mont' Alverne 10, downtown. Opposite the Mercado Modelo, you can eat cheaply at the self-service counter of Paes Mendonça supermarket. *Cantina Lua*, Praça 15 de Novembro, cheap, good atmosphere, live samba shows outside on Sats. 1900-2100; nearby is *Bar Ibiza*, recommended.

Senac runs a restaurant school at Largo do Pelourinho 19, serving 40 dishes including regional ones, US$2.50 for Bahian supper, US$4.25 for all you can eat, open Mon.-Sat., 1130-1530, 1830-2230; at 2000 there is a folklore show, US$1.50 entrance fee (recommended for an introduction to Bahian culture).

Famous atmosphere and local food at *Maria de São Pedro* and *Camafeu de Oxóssi*, on the second floor of the Mercado Modelo, overlooking the port. The *Chez Bernard* (French food and grand view), small, on street below the Praça, is one of the city's best. Excellent French cuisine, though more expensive than average, at *Le Privé*, Av. 7 de Setembro 554, and *Le Bistroquet*, Rua Santos Dumont 9. Another recommended French restaurant is *La Grille*, near Teatro Castro Alves, very popular, especially with artists and actors. Good churrascaria: *Las Palmas*, Rua Manuel Dias da Silva.

Restaurants and bars in the Atlantic coast suburbs: *Ondina Restaurant*, Ondina hill, local dishes and shows; *Churrascaria Alex*, Boca do Rio (half-way to the airport) on the road by the sea, *Yemanjá*, Av. Otávio Mangabeira, Armação. *Agda*, *Yemanjá* (both serving local dishes), *Panelinha* and *Alfacinha* at Boca do Rio; *Churrascaria Moenda* and *Bargaço* (Rua P, Quadra 43, Jardim Armação, Tel.: 231-5141), Bahian seafood dishes, reasonable) at Praia da Armação; *Popular* (bar), *Rodaviva Churrascaria*, Av. Octávio Mangabeira (on the beach, good value), and *Gererê* (typical food) at Largo de Amaralina; *Oxalá*, *Clave do Sol*, *Chez Bernard* (not recommended) and *O Marisco* (for good seafood, very popular, recommended) at Rio Vermelho; also *Cheiro de Mar*, Rua Borges dos Reis 14, typical food, live music, Tel.: 247-1106, English spoken; *Vagão*, Rua Almirante Barroso 315, Rio Vermelho, bar with drinks (but little food) and live music, open air among trees and flowers, worth visiting. Another good restaurant serving Bahian food is *O Jangadeiro*, Av. Otávio Mangabeira (at Pituba beach). *Chez Bouillon*, Barra hill, next to Yacht Club; *Taverna Romana*, Italian dishes, at Barra; also at Barra, *Restaurante Van Gogh*; *Manga Rosa*, Rua César Zama 1, Porto da Barra, health food and fish, good; several good pizzerias on Rua Afonso Celso in Barra; *Fino Real*, Rua Barão de Sergy, Barra, good steaks, good sandwich bar; *Fugitivo*, Barravento, *Habeas-Copus* in Farol and Porto da Barra. *Restaurant-bar Berro d'Agua*, Rua Barão de Sergy, Barra, good steaks, pleasant.

Bahian food is spiced and peppery. Typical dishes are those which feature oysters, shrimps and crabs, as well as *vatapá*, made from fish, rice, cashew-nuts, ginger, mint and parsley cooked in an earthenware dish and garnished with *dendê* (palm) oil. *Muqueca* is fish or shrimp in spicy stews, and *xin-xin* is chicken stewed with fish or shrimp, onion and squash. Good food on the streets from the Bahianas. Delicious *acarajés* (deep-fried bean cake stuffed with *vatapá*, green salad and usually shrimp, with optional hot sauce) are sold in the streets.

Nightlife Most of the modern night clubs are between Barra and Itapoan: *Lingua de Prata* at Praça Dorival Caymmi (small); *Close-up Drinks*, Rua Fernando Luz 12, Barri; *Casa Verde*, Av. Otávio Mangabeira 1230, Boca do Rio; and *Zum Zum* next door at No. 1240; *Bual Amour*, same street, further out in Corsário; *Pá de Baleia*, even further out on same street, in Piatã; and *Charles Night* at Itapuã Praia Hotel, Placafor. *Hippopotamus*, Othon Palace Hotel (both latter require membership or invitation). Typical show after dinner (at 2300) at *Tenda dos Milagres*, Amaralina.
Bars *Banzo Bar*, Praça José de Alencar 6, Pelourinho, pleasant, cheap food, popular with travellers. *Ibiza* and *Bauru*, both on Rua Alfredo Brito, and *Cantina da Lua*, Terreiro de Jesus, all friendly; *O Bilhostre*, Rio Vermelho, a bar with modern jazz on Sat. night. Also in Rio Vermelho, *Bleff* at the Maria Bethania theatre, and *Graffiti*, Rua Odoricio Odilon, highly recommended, open night only, dancing, good food, owners speak several European languages.

Cinema Maria Bethania film theatre, Rio Vermelho, art and foreign films.

Markets The Mercado Modelo, at Praça Cairu, lower city, offers many tourist items such as wood carvings, silver-plated fruit, leather goods, local musical instruments. Lace items for sale are often not handmade (despite labels), are heavily marked up, and are much better bought at their place of origin (e.g. Ilha de Maré, Pontal da Barra and Marechal Deodoro, see page 314). Bands and dancing, especially Sat. (but very much for money from tourists taking photographs), closed at 1200 Sun.; two restaurants on top floor, large balcony provides good view over harbour; restaurants on ground floor are cheaper. (Many items are often cheaper in the Praça da Sé in the nearby Cidade Alta.) Largest

304 BRAZIL

and most authentic market is the Feira de São Joaquim, 5 km. from Mercado Modelo along sea front: barkers, trucks, *burros*, horses, boats, people, mud, all very smelly, every day except Sun., busiest on Sat. morning; interesting African-style pottery and basketwork; very cheap. (Car ferry terminal for Itaparica is nearby.) Instituto Mauá, Av. 7 de Setembro 261, and at Barra, sells good handicraft items, but prices are fixed. There is also a good gift shop at the Convento do Carmo museum, and at the Instituto Mauá shop in the Iguatemi Shopping Centre near the bus station (Rodoviária). Centro Artesanal do Maciel, Largo do Pelourinho 12, good for handicrafts. Mosquito nets can only be bought in O Mosquiteiro, in Calçados, or sometimes in the market area. Beware money-changers in street outside market, and at foot of Lacerda lift: many are thieves.

Bookshops Livraria Selso, Rua Barbosa 4-B, Tel.: 243-5383, secondhand and English books. Currupio, Dra. Dragner Froes, Barra, is bookshop selling posters of old Salvador, and high quality books.

Shopping H. Stern, jewellers, at Hotels Meridien and Othon, Iguatemi Shopping Centre, and at the airport. Another jeweller is João Teobaldo Silva, Praça Anchieta 19, 1st floor. Also Frank Ribeiro da Silva, Praça do Alencar, precious stones and handicrafts. Jewellers along Rua do Carmo (e.g. Gérson Joalheiros, Largo do Carmo 26), and in the Convento do Carmo.

Hairdresser Edmea Penteados, Praça da Sé, Edificio Themis, 3rd floor, recommended.

Local Transport Taxi meters start at US$0.25 for the "flagdown" and US$0.10 per 100 metres. They charge US$5 per hour within city limits, and "agreed" rates outside. Taxi-drivers tend to overcharge, especially at night; the night-time charge should be 30% higher than daytime charges. Teletaxi (24-hr. service), 243-4333. Local buses US$0.20, air-conditioned *frescões* US$0.50. On buses and at the ticket-sellers' booths, watch your change and beware pickpockets. Hitching out of Salvador, take a "Cidade Industrial" bus from the bus station at the port; it goes on to the highway.

Theatres Castro Alves, at Campo Grande (Largo Dois de Julho), daily concerts; Teatro da Gamboa; Teatro Vila Velha; Senac; Instituto Cultural Brasil-Alemanha (ICBA); Teatro Santo Antônio, part of the Escola de Teatro da Universidade Federal da Bahia; Teatro de Arena, Alto de Ondina, Ondina; and the Tenda dos Milagres in Amaralina.

Museums The city has 27 museums. The **Museum of Contemporary Art**, converted from an old estate house and outbuildings off Av. Contorno, is only open for special exhibitions. The good restaurant (*Solar do Unhão*) is still there, and the buildings are worth seeing for themselves (*son et lumière* most evenings).

There is a remarkable **Museum of Sacred Art** in the 17th century monastery and church of Santa Teresa, at the bottom of the steep Ladeira de Santa Teresa, at Rua do Sodré 276. Many of the 400 carvings are from the Old World, but a number are local. Among the reliquaries of silver and gold is one of gilded wood by the great Brazilian sculptor Aleijadinho. Open Tues.-Sat. 1300-1800, US$0.40. Many of the treasures which used to be in an old mansion, the Casa de Calmon, Av. Joana Angélica 198, are here now. This important collection is well worth a visit.

The **Carmo Church** has a collection of icons and colonial furniture, including carvings by Francisco Manuel das Chagas, known as "O Cabra"; see particularly his statue of Christ bound to the pillar (open daily, 0800-1200, 1400-1800, US$0.35). Next door is a State museum which is architecturally notable and has period furnishings. **Museu Abelardo Rodrigues**, in the Solar Ferrão, Pelourinho (Rua Gregório de Mattos 45, open Mon.-Fri. 1000-1200, 1400-1700, closed Tues., Sat.-Sun. 1100-1700), is another religious art museum, with objects from the 17th, 18th, and 19th centuries, mainly from Bahia, Pernambuco and Maranhão.

Museu Costa Pinto, Av. 7 de Setembro 2490, US$0.35 (1500-1900 except Tues.) is a modern house with collections of crystal, porcelain, silver, furniture etc.

Museu de Arte da Bahia, Av. 7 de Setembro 2340, Vitória, Tues.-Sun. 1400-1800, poor.

Afro-Brazilian Museum, in former Faculty of Medicine building, Terreiro de Jesus, open Tues.-Sat., 0930-1130, 1400-1730, (free on Tuesdays) comparing African and Bahian Orixás (deities) celebrations, beautiful murals and carvings, highly recommended.

City Museum, Largo do Pelourinho (centre of old quarter), arts and crafts, old photographs, entrance free, Mon.-Sat. 0800-1200, 1330-1800. **Hydrographical Museum**, Forte de Santo Antônio, free (Tues.-Sun. 1100-1700).

Thirty-six km. from the city is the **Museu do Recôncavo** (Museu do Wanderley Pinho, 0900-1200, 1400-1700) in the old Freguesia mill (1552), (closed for refurbishing in 1985) in which one can find artefacts and pictures of three centuries of the economic and social life of this region. The Casa Grande e Senzala (the home of the landowner and the combined dwelling and working area of the slaves) is still intact. It is a peaceful way to spend an afternoon, but difficult to get to by public transport, the museum is 7 km. from main highway. The **State Geological Museum** is at Av. 7 de Setembro 2195, Vitória, open Mon.-Fri. 1000-1200, 1400-1800 and Sat. and Sun. 1400-1800. Opposite the Museum of Sacred Art is Tempostal, a private museum of postcards, open

Tues.-Sat., 1000-1130, 1400-1730, at Rua do Sodré 276 (proprietor, Antônio Marcelino do Nascimento). Convention Centre at Praia Armação in operation.

Tourist Office (with lists of hotels and pension stays in private homes) Bahiatursa, Palácio Rio Branco (former government palace, which may be viewed), Rua Chile on Praça Municipal, open 0800-1830. Visitors can obtain weekly list of events and itineraries (on foot or by car) planned by the city, well worth doing, but be warned that the itinerary goes through some very run down areas of the city. Map, US$0.90, good; offices have noticeboard for messages. Also at corner of Mercado Modelo, Praça Cairu, lower city, and at bus station (good, English spoken) and airport (not helpful regarding cheap hotels); other offices at Porto da Barra, and church of São Francisco, Praça Anchieta. Also details of travel throughout State of Bahia, including boats on River São Francisco (see page 315). Maps from Departmento de Geografia e Estatística, Av. Estados Unidos (opp. Banco do Brasil, lower city); free Bahia maps; maps of Brazil US$ 1.50.

A multilingual tour guide is Manfred von Büttner (Manfredo), to be found at *Hotel Colón*, Praça Anchieta, Tel.: 241-1531. Tours in English, French, German, Italian and Spanish. Helpful with exchange.

Electric Current 110-220 A.C., 60 cycles.

Banks Lloyds Bank (ex-BOLSA), Rua Miguel Calmon 22; Citibank, Av. Estados Unidos; Banco Holandês Unido, Praça da Inglaterra; and national banks. Banco Econômico, Av. 7 de Setembro 302, 5th floor. Banco Mercantil de São Paulo, Rua M. Calmon, near Mercado Modelo, and Banco Nordeste, close by, accept Master Charge cards, Banco Real, Rua Ourivés (Visa). Banco Mercantil do Brasil, Rua Portugal, good rates for exchange; Open 1000-1630. Also exchange shops, e.g. Watt Representações, Rua Miguel Calmon 63, room 601; also Casa de Câmbio Salomão, Rua Estados Unidos 379 (Edifício INAMPS), first floor, Tel.: 242-0837 for rates); travel agency at Estados Unidos 4 (in the arcade of Edifício Visconde de Cayru) changes travellers' cheques; López e López, Rua Conselheiro Dantas 57, Edifício Paraguassu, Room 101. Also Catedral Corretora de Câmbio, Rua Miguel Calmon 382-5°, in the Banco Francês e Brasileiro building.

American Consulate Av. Presidente Vargas 1892, Tel.: 247-8540.
British Vice-Consulate, Av. Estados Unidos 4, Edifício Visconde de Cayru, Salas 1109/1133, CEP 40000, Caixa Postal 38, Tel.: 241-3120/241-3222.
Austrian Consulate Av. Almirante Marqués Leão 46, apt.33, Caixa Postal 4032, 40000 Salvador, Tel.: (071)24 76 013.

Post Office Main post office and poste restante is in Praça Inglaterra, in the Lower City.

Immigration on Rua da Bélgica (for extensions of entry permits), behind Mercado Modelo.

Communications Embratel, Av. Estados Unidos, near Mercado Modelo. Cia. Rádio Internacional do Brasil, Rua Miguel Calmon 41. Tebehahia has offices at Campo da Pólvora, on Rua Hugo Baltazar Silveira (open always), airport, Rodoviária and Mercado Modelo.

British Club Campo Grande. **Associação Cultural Brasil-Estados Unidos**, Av. 7 de Setembro, opp. *Hotel Anglo Americano*, has a library and reading room with recent U.S. magazines, open to anyone, and nearby on the same avenue is the German **Goethe Institut**, also with library and reading room with recent papers.

Clinic Barão de Loretto 21, Graça. Dr Argemiro Júnior speaks English and Spanish. First consultation US$24, second free. Dr Manoel Nogueira, (from 1000-1200), Av. Joana Angélica 6, Tel.: 241-2377, English-speaking. Yellow fever vaccinations free at Delegação Federal de Saude, Rua Padre Feijó, Canela.

Buses Bus station 5 km. from city but regular services to centre; bus to Campo Grande, then Circular Campe Grande-Praça da Sé or "Barroquinha", is best way to get to the hotel section; journey can take up to 1 hr. especially in peak periods. Transur bus between Praça da Sé and Campo Grande, US$0.05 then bus Campo Grande to Rodoviária. Executive bus from Praça da Sé runs to Iguatemi Shopping Centre from where there is a walkway to the bus station. To Recife, US$6.50 (*leito*, 13), 12 hrs.; plenty to Rio (28 hrs., US$15, *leito* 30), São Paulo (30 hrs.), US$18.50, *leito* US$37, Belo Horizonte 22 hrs, 2 normal (US$13), 2 *leito* (29) buses; to Fortaleza, 19 hrs., US$12.50 at 0900 and 2100 with Viação Brasilia; Ilhéus, 7 hrs., US$4, several (e.g. Sulba at 2210 daily); Valença, 5 a day, 5 hrs., US$2.50; Porto Seguro, 2000, 2100, 12 hrs., US$5.50; Maceió, US$6, 4 a day, 11 hrs, advised to book (best service, Empresa Bomfim at 2000); Belém US$24, 37 hrs. There are daily bus services to Brasília along the new (fully paved) road, BR-242, via Barreiras; buses leave at 1200 and 2000, 23 hrs. (US$14); the journey can be broken at Lençóis (see page 308, an inn on the River São Francisco; at Barreiras on the River Negro, where the bus stops for 2-3 hrs. (*Hotel Vandelena*, E, full board); or at Posse (Goiás). To Paulo Afonso, US$4, 10 hrs., leaving 0430, 2000, and 1910 on Sun., Wed. and Fri, partly paved road. (Travel agency Remundi, Rua da Grécia 8, 1° andar, Cidade Baixa, Tel.: 242-5286, sells bus tickets.)

306 BRAZIL

Motorists to Rio can do the trip on the BR-116 highway in 3 days, stopping at *Vitória da Conquista* (524 km. from Salvador), *Hotel Bahia*, E, with huge meals; *Hotel Aliança*, D and *Hotel Livramento*, E, with restaurant; also Camping Clube do Brasil site at Km. 1,076; Teôfilo Otôni see page 259(946 km.); or Governador Valadares (1,055 km.) see page 259, and Leopoldina (1,402 km.). There are also various motels; two in the State of Bahia are at km. 1,076, at Vitória da Conquista; and km. 1,470, at Feira de Santana; also between Feira and Salvador. Fairly good hotels are also available in Jequié (*Itajubá, Rex,* and motels), and basic ones in Milagres. Stopovers on the BR-101 coastal road can be made at Vitória and Itabuna (or Ilhéus), and there are many other towns on or near the coast.

Rail From Salvador there are only local train services, though the tracks are continuous to Rio; the nearest inter-city service leaves from Iaçu, 260 km. from Salvador (Belo Horizonte train Fri.), but no passenger service Salvador-Iaçu.

Air To Brasília, daily, 2 hrs; to Rio, about 2 hrs., Brazilian Air Force (FAB) fly Rio-Salvador-Recife and return Mon. Wed. Fri; it is possible to get a free flight—telephone or ask at FAB desk at airport. Dois de Julho airport is 32 km. from the city. Buses go between airport and city centre, bus "Aeroporto-Politeama" goes to Av. 7 de Setembro, US$0.10, 1 hr., or special taxi (buy ticket at airport desk) US$7.50. Air-conditioned bus service from Praça da Sé to Pituba and airport US$0.50.

Shipping The Spanish Ybarra from Europe is the only regular transatlantic line to call. National coastal vessels.

Excursions From the lower city the train (Trem do Leste) leaves Calçada for a 40 min. journey through the bayside suburbs of Salvador—Lobato, Plataforma (canoes and motor boats for Ribeira on the Itapagipe peninsula), Escada (17th century church), Praia Grande, Periperi and Paripe (take bus for 17th century church at São Tomé de Paripe). The same trip can be made by bus, less picturesquely. From Ribeira a small boat goes 25 km. to *Ilha da Maré* between 0900 and 1100, connecting the island's villages of Itamoaba, Praia Grande and Santana (US$0.70); boat returns next day from Santana at 0400-0500. Santana is a centre for lace making, Praia Grande for basket-weaving. None of the villages has a hotel, but there are restaurants and bars and camping is possible.

The Bahia de Todos os Santos has 34 islands.

There are ferries every hour (40-min. journey) from next to the Mercado Modelo (US$0.75, more on Sundays, good juices at the landing stage) to the island of *Itaparica,* on the other side of the bay from the city; the car ferry leaves from São Joaquim (bus from in front of Lacerda lift to São Joaquim), check sailings. Ferry from Mercado Modelo goes to Vera Cruz (US$0.20 each way, ½ hr., last boat back from island is 1630) where there are good beaches, swimming, horses and bikes for hire, but to other parts of the island one has to take a taxi. Car ferries go to Bom Despacho (from where buses go to other parts of the island) between Porto Santo and Gameleira. The island has beaches (most of which are dirty, but good ones at Barra Grande in the south, at Ponta de Areia (1 hr. walk from Itaparica town), and at Club Méditerranée), adequate hotels (*Grande Hotel de Itaparica*, near sea, *Icaraí*, Itaparica, E, fair food, now run by Fernando Mesquita, very friendly and obliging, and one at Gameleira) *Club Méditerranée*, of which some very poor members; restaurants are expensive, but there are food shops and a self-service restaurant at the Paes Mendonça shopping centre in Gameleira. Camping is worthwhile. The church and fortress of São Lourenço are in Itaparica town. *Mar Grande,* which can be reached direct by ferry from Mercado Modelo (first one at 0630, last back at 1700, every half-hour, but hourly after 1600), US$0.50, or by launch from Itaparica (0630, 0900, 1400, 1700—may not leave until full), is very unspoilt, but beach rather dirty. To rent houses costs up to US$55 for one month. (*Hotel Galeão Sacramento*, suites in four separate buildings, swimming pool and other sports facilities; *Arco Iris Pousada*, D, magnificent building and setting in mango orchard, overpriced hotel, good restaurant; next door is a campsite, same owners, filthy but shady, 1 block from beach and town centre. Another *pousada*, C, 4-star.) Eat at *Philippe's Bar and Restaurant*, Largo de São Bento, good French and local food, local information in French and English. There is a minibus service between Mar Grande and Itaparica. From Bom Despacho on the island, trips can be made to the picturesque small Colonial port of *Jaguaribe* and to Nazaré (see below), with its market (both on the mainland). Jaguaribe can be reached by boat from the Mercado Modelo, leaving Thursday and Saturday and returning Friday and Monday.

BRAZIL 307

The Companhia de Navegação Bahiana provides excursions in the ship *Bahia de Todos os Santos*, from near the Mercado Modelo. An excursion along the city front (Tues., Thurs., Sat.), taking 3 hours, costs US$4.90; an all-day trip around the bay's islands, including a 3-hour stay at Itaparica, costs US$8 (Wed., Fri., Sun.). Small boats for trips round the bay may be hired privately at the fishing port (Porto dos Saveiros) at the W side of the Mercado Modelo. There is also an excursion to all parts of the city accessible by boat. For other excursions by boat contact agencies such as L. R. Turismo, Av. Sete de Setembro 3959; Grey Line, Av. Presidente Vargas 2456; Remundi, Rua da Grécia, 8 (1st floor); Kontik, Praça da Inglaterra, 2. For cheaper excursions to the bay's islands, watch for notices in lunch bars and in bank windows in the lower city bank district, put up by employees looking for people to go on trips (US$2.50-3.75, including a beer and sandwich).

Nazaré das Farinhas, 60 km. inland from Itaparica, and reached over a bridge by bus from Bom Despacho, is an 18th-century town celebrated for its market, which specializes in the local ceramic figures, or *caxixis*. There is an especially large market in Holy Week, particularly on the Thursday and Good Friday. 12 km. from Nazaré (taxi US$3, also buses) is the village of Maragojipinha, which specializes in making the ceramic figures. Bus from Salvador, 1530, takes 5 hours.

Northwest from Salvador is **Feira de Santana** (225,000 people), 112 km. away on both the coastal BR-101 and the inland BR-116 roads to Rio, the centre of a great cattle breeding and trading area; its Monday market, known as Feira do Couro (leather fair), said to be the largest in Brazil, attracts great crowds to its colourful display of local products. James Maas tells us that the permanent Artesanato market in the centre has a bigger selection, including leather, than the Monday market. Bus every half hour from Salvador, 2 hrs., US$1. (Bus station has a wall of painted tiles made by Udo-Ceramista, whose workshop is Brotas, Av. Dom João VI 411, Salvador.)

Hotels Half-way to Feira from Salvador is the turn off to the *Hotel Fazenda*, Alto da Ipê. At Feira: *Luxor Pousada da Feira*, Km. 1,470 on BR-116, C; *Vips Hotel Restaurante*, Rua Visconde do Rio Branco 367; *Flecha Motel Feira*, F, about 20 km. away at Km. 1,067 BR-101; *Hotel da Bahia*, Rua Visconde do Rio Branco 562; *Vitória*, Rua Marechal Deodoro, F, with breakfast; several cheap ones in Praça da Matriz and near the bus station, which is quite near the centre.

Bar Restaurant *A Kaskata*, Rua Presidente Dutra, good food, open terrace.

The Recôncavo The area around Salvador, known as the Recôncavo Baiano, was one of the chief centres of early sugar-and tobacco-based settlement in the 16th century.

Leaving Salvador on the Feira road, at km. 33 one forks left on the BR-324 to the Museu de Recôncavo Wanderley de Pinho (see page 304). Further W, round the bay, is São Francisco do Conde, 54 km. from Salvador, with a church and convent of 1636 and the ruins of Don Pedro II's agricultural school, said to be the first in Latin America.

At 60 km. from Salvador the BA-026 road branches off the BR-324 to Santo Amaro, Cachoeira and São Félix.

Seventy-three km. from Salvador is **Santo Amaro da Purificação,** an old sugar centre now with a population of 20,000 noted for its churches (often closed because of robberies), municipal palace (1769), fine main square, house of the poet Caetano Velloso, and ruined mansions including Araújo Pinto, former residence of the Barão de Cotegipe. Other attractions include the splendid beaches of the bay, the falls of Vitória and the grotto of Bom Jesus dos Pobres. Festivals in January and February (Santo Amaro and N.S. da Purificação) are interesting. Craftwork is sold on the town's main bridge. No good hotels or restaurants.

At 54 km. from Santo Amaro, and only 4 km. from the BR-101 coastal road, are the twin towns of **Cachoeira** (Bahia's "Ouro Preto"), and **São Félix,** on either side of the Rio Paraguassu below the Cachoeira dam. Cachoeira, recently declared a national monument, was twice capital of Bahia: once in 1624-5 during the Dutch invasion, and once in 1822-3 while Salvador was still held by the Portuguese. It was the birthplace of Ana Néri, known as "Mother of the Brazilians", who organized nursing services during the Paraguayan War (1865-70). There are beautiful views from above São Félix. Cachoeira's main buildings are the Casa da Câmara e Cadeia (1698-1712), the Santa Casa de Misericórdia

(1734), the 16th-century Ajuda chapel (now containing a fine collection of vestments), and the Monastery of the Carmelites' Third Order, whose church has a heavily gilded interior. Other churches: Carmo (1548) and its Third Order (fine *azulejos* and gilding), the Matriz with 5-metres-high *azulejos*, and Nossa Senhora da Conceição da Monte. Beautiful lace cloths on church altars. All churches either restored or in the process of restoration. Ruined Jesuit seminary. Tourist office in the Casa de Ana Néri. In the same building is the Hansen-Bahia collection of wood-engravings (see also the Hansen house on the hill above São Félix, where the engravers Karl and Ilse Hansen lived; it is to be opened as a museum). Festivals: São João (June 24) "Carnival of the Interior" celebrations, well-attended by tourists, Boa Morte (early August), and a famous *candomblé* ceremony at the Fonte de Santa Bárbara on December 4. Try the local dish, *maniçoba* (meat, manioc and peppers). Craftwork in ceramics and wood readily available. Buses from Salvador (Carnurujipe) every hour or so.

Hotels Cachoeira: *Pousada Cachoeira* (run by Bahiatursa), in newly restored 16th-century convent, D, good restaurant; *Pousada do Guerreiro*, 13 de Maio 40, no restaurant; *Pousada do Convento*, recommended, swimming pool, reasonable. Restaurants: *Cabana do Pai Thomaz*, excellent Bahian food; *Recanto de Oxum*, nearby, *Gruta Azul*, lunch only. São Félix: *Xang-hai*, F.

Excursion 6 km. from Cachoeira, on the higher ground of the Planalto Baiano, is the small town of Belém (turning 2½ km. on road to Santo Amaro). Church and seminary of Carmo. Healthy spot: people from Salvador have summer homes. We are told there is an 8 km. secret passage between the Carmo churches here and in Cachoeira, but have not seen it—reports welcome.

The tobacco centre of **Cruz das Almas** can also be visited, although transport is poor. The São João celebrations here (June 24) are not recommended: very dangerous games with fireworks are involved.

Maragogipe, a tobacco exporting port 22 km. SE of Cachoeira along a dirt road (BA-123), can also be reached by boat from Salvador. See the old houses and the church of São Bartolomeu, with its museum. The main festival is São Bartolomeu, in August. Good ceramic craftwork.

Inland from Salvador 400 km. W of Salvador on the BR-242 to Brasília is **Lençóis**, a town which is a historical monument, founded in 1844 because of diamonds in the region (there are still some *garimpeiros*), pop. 2,000. *Pousada de Lençóis*, C, with breakfast, swimming pool; *Hospedaria São José*, central square, E with good regional breakfast, friendly, hot showers, good restaurant; 2 campsites, one 2 km. before Lençóis, one in the town centre (friendly, recommended). Restaurant: *Dom Ratão*, armadillo, snake, toad, piranha and alligator included on the menu. Near the town are waterfalls (including the Cachoeira de Glass, 400 metres, the highest in Brazil), large caves, rivers with natural swimming pools and good walking tours (guides essential). Ask for Álvaro or Luís near the central campsite (US$5 a day), or in the Pousada for Ray Funck, an American resident guide, who also runs a craft shop, Funkart. There is also a Casa do Artesão, where children learn to fill bottles with patterns of coloured sand, a local speciality. There is a local liquor factory. Paraíso bus from Salvador, Feira de Santana, Ibotirama, Barreiras or Brasília stops here.

South from Salvador John Holmes, of São Paulo, writes: 271 km. from Salvador, on an asphalted road, is **Valença** (5 buses a day to Salvador, 5 hrs., US$2.50, and to Itabuna, 4½ hrs., US$1.70) and Ilhéus, a small, attractive and bustling town at the mouth of the River Una. Two old churches stand on rising ground above the town; the views from Nossa Senhora do Amparo are recommended. The town is in the middle of an area producing black pepper, cloves and *piaçava* (used in making brushes and mats). Other industries include the building and repair of fishing boats (*saveiros*). Tourist office opposite Rodoviária on other side of river, friendly. The River Una enters an enormous region of mangrove swamps.

The main attraction of Valença is the beaches on the mainland (Guabim, 14 km. N) and on the island of Tinharé. Main hotels are *Tourist Hotel*, Marechal Floriano 167, E, good; *Rio Una* (fairly chic, expensive, swimming pool); *Guabim* (Praça da Independência, modest, E); good *Akuarius* restaurant; *Universal*, F, Marquês de Herval 98, clean, helpful, good breakfast, restaurant.

Tinharé is a large island (with good walking, beaches and camping, but no banks or exchange) separated from the mainland by the estuary of the River Una and mangrove swamps, so that it is hard to tell which is land and which is water.

BRAZIL 309

Boats (US$0.75) leave every day from Valença for Galeão (1½ hrs.) and also for Gamboa (1½ hrs.) and Morro de São Paulo (2 hrs.). The boat for the two last named leaves at 1200 on weekdays and 0700 on Sun., returning from Morro de São Paulo at 0600. There is an extra boat Dec.-Feb. at 0600, returning at 1200. Other small boats make the trip. *Morro de São Paulo* is very popular in summer, situated on the headland at the northernmost tip of the island, dominated by the lighthouse and the ruins of a colonial fort (1630). The village has a landing place on the sheltered landward side, dominated by the old gateway of the fortress. *Pousada*, D, *Pousada Rola*, E, plenty of restaurants (*Gaúcho* recommended) and bars, and rooms to rent in almost every house, F-G (just ask by the fountain). Camping is possible, but not too safe on the long deserted beach to the S of the village; fresh water from springs in the village, washing at the public fountain. Fish can be bought from the fishermen in summer, but you must bring most necessities, apart from bread, from the mainland. The place is expensive December-March, cheaper during the rest of the year.

Galeão is another village in the island, but there is no beach, only mangrove swamps. The church of São Francisco Xavier looks imposing on its hill. (Another island worth visiting is Boipeba.) It is sometimes possible to get a direct boat from Salvador, 2-3 times a week in summer, 6-7 hrs, ask for Sr. Cacu and the *Natureza* at the fishing port next to the Mercado Modelo.

On the coast, south toward Ilhéus, is the picturesque fishing village of **Itacaré**. Hotels: *Bom Jesus*, at bus station; *Sta. Bárbara*, Praça Izaac Soares 4, clean, good food. Camping site.

Ilhéus, near the mouth of the Rio Cachoeira, 380 km. south of Salvador, serves a district which produces 65% of all Brazilian cocoa. Shipping lines call regularly. A bridge links the Pontal district (where the airport is) to the mainland. Population, 108,000. The town is the scene of the famous novel by Jorge Amado, "Gabriela, Clove and Cinnamon". The local beaches are splendid (except those in the bay and close to town—polluted) and the place is highly recommended for a short stay. Among the churches to visit: Nossa Senhora da Vitória, in Alto da Vitória, built in 17th century to celebrate a victory over the Dutch; São Jorge, in city centre; and the cathedral of São Sebastião on sea shore. Tourist office on Av. Soares Lopes, near cathedral.

Hotels *Hotel Barravento* on Malhado beach, Rua N.S. das Graças, ask for the penthouse—usually no extra charge, D, including bath, breakfast and refrigerator; next door is *Motel Barravento*, E. In same street at 574 is *Panorama*. *Britânia*, Rua 28 de Junho 16, and at 29 the *San Marino*, F, friendly, clean. *Lucas*, Rua 7 de Setembro 17, E-D, central, O.K.; *Central*, Araújo Pinho 115, E with bath and breakfast, adequate; *Vitória*, Rua Bento Berilo 95, Tel.: 231-4105; *Pontal Praia*, Praia do Pontal, C, swimming pool; *Florida*, Rua General Câmara, F without bath; *Ilhéus Praia*, Praça D. Eduardo, C, pool, recommended; *Litorânea*, Rua Antônio Lavigne de Lemos 42; *Tio San*, F with breakfast, near beach, friendly; *Motel Cana Brava*, Km. 6 on Ilhéus-Olivença road; *Real*, Rua General Câmara 102. *Rio Cachoeira*, road to Itabuna, Km. 7, pool, also good churrascaria. In Rua Carneiro da Rocha are *Tropical*, No. 129 and *Bahiano*, No. 94, each F, and two *dormitórios*. Plenty of cheap hotels near municipal bus station in centre.

Restaurants *Pontal Praia Hotel, Motel Barravento, Luande Beira Bahia, Av. Soares Lopes* s/n, *Moqueca de Ouro. Cabana do Mirante*, Alto do Ceará, with good views. *Vesúvio*, Praça D. Eduardo, next to Cathedral, made famous by Amado's novel (see above). Local drink, *coquinho*, coconut filled with *cachaça*, only for the strongest heads! Also try *suco de cacau* at juice stands.

Local Festivals include Festa de São Sebastião (January 17-20), Carnival, Festa de São Jorge (April 23), Foundation day, June 28, and Festa do Cacau (October).

Buses Station is some way from centre, but Itabuna-Olivença bus goes through centre of Ilhéus. Several daily to Salvador; 0620 bus goes via Itaparica, leaving passengers at Bom Despacho ferry station on the island—thence 50-minute ferry to Salvador.

Buses run every 30 mins. to **Itabuna** (32 km.; 130,000 people), the trading centre of the rich cocoa zone. (Ceplac runs tours to its model cocoa plantation between Itabuna and Ilhéus; it is possible to visit *fazendas*.) Of the hotels, the *Príncipe, Lord* and *Itabuna Palace* (Av. Cinquentenário 1061, C, restaurant) are probably the best (*Rincão Gaúcho*, F, small, friendly, overlooking river; opposite Rodoviária is *Dormitório Rodoviária*, F, basic; several motels on the outskirts).

310 BRAZIL

The paved BA-415 links Itabuna to Vitória da Conquista (275 km.) on the BR-116. Ceplac installations at Km. 8 on the Itabuna-Ilhéus road show the whole processing of cocoa. Tours of cocoa plantations can be arranged through the *Ilhéus Praia* hotel; Jorge Amado's novel "The Violent Lands" deals with life on the cocoa plantations.

The beaches between Ilhéus and Olivença are good, e.g. Cururupe, and frequent buses run to Olivença.

About 400 km. south of Ilhéus on the coast is the old town of **Porto Seguro**, now developed for tourism (the airport has been enlarged to take jets). Direct buses from Rio, São Paulo and Salvador. For the routes from Vitória see page 247 and from Belo Horizonte page 253. At Brazilian holiday times, all transport north or south should be booked in advance. Across the Rio Buranhém (10 minutes, US$0.10, ferries between 0600 and 1900), and a further 5 km. (US$0.20 in bus), is Arraial da **Ajuda**; the village is about 15 mins. walk from the beach (better for camping than Porto Seguro). Pilgrimage in August to the shrine of Nossa Senhora da Ajuda (interesting room in church, full of ex-voto offerings). Ajuda has become very popular with tourists and there are a number of cheap *pousadas*, a Japanese restaurant, bars and small shops. Many rooms for rent (for days, weeks or months); best accommodation in private houses behind the church (F). Beach protected by coral reef. At Brazilian holiday times it is very crowded, and with the coastline up for sale, it may become overdeveloped in a few years. The beaches in this neighbourhood are splendid, for instance Pitinga, also protected by coral reef; camping at Da Gringa, BR-367 (beach), and Mucugê, Ajuda.

25 km. to the S of Porto Seguro is **Trancoso**, reached by rickety bus from the other side of the Rio Buranhém, 4 a day, (US$0.80, 1½ hours), (more buses and colectivos in summer), by colectivo, hitch-hiking or by walking along the beach; the village is simple but also popular with tourists and many Europeans have built or bought houses there. Stay at the French-owned *Pousada do Gilberto*, F, *Pousada Miramar*, next to church (good view, hammock space), several other *pousadas*, mostly in E/F range (of which Henry Giese's *Pousada do Bosque*, Rua de Cuba, is recommended), in private houses, also houses for rent. Trancoso has a historic church. Colectivos run from Trancoso 15 km. to Ajuda (1 hr., US$1.20). Between Ajuda and Trancoso is the village of Rio da Barra.

It was N of the site of Porto Seguro that Cabral first landed in 1500; a cross marks the supposed site of the first mass in Brazil on road between Porto Seguro and Santa Cruz Cabrália. 23 km. to the N of Porto Seguro is Santa Cruz Cabrália (simple accommodation, good restaurant *Coqueiro Verde*—try *pitu*, a kind of crayfish); dugout ferry crosses the river, then a short walk to the beach at Santo André. Trips on the river can be made. Bicycles for hire at hardware shop, Dois de Julho 242, US$2 a day. In this area there are *borrachudos*, little flies that bite feet and ankles in the heat of the day; coconut oil keeps them off; at night mosquitoes can be a problem.

Porto Seguro Hotels *Porto Seguro Praia*, 3 km. N of city on coast road, B; *Vela Branca*, Cidade Histórica, C, top of cliff, good; *Pousada Coroa Vermelha*, Getúlio Vargas 12, F, with bath, clean and good, run by Dutchman; a number of cheap *pousadas* on Av. Getúlio Vargas, most without breakfast; *Pousada Tapuia* at No. 40 is over-priced and not recommended; *Mar Azul* at No. 109, F with bath, clean, friendly; *Real*, same street, No. 70. *Pousada Inaiá, Pousada Colonial* (both traditional houses, E, on Av. Portugal, Nos. 526 and 344), *Pousada São Luiz*, E, recommended. *Estrela d'Alva*, Rua da Misericórdia 10, Cidade Histórica, E; *Pousada Casa Azul*, E, Rua 15 de Novembro 11, Pacatá; *Pousada do Cais*, Portugal 382, Tel.: 2121, E with bath, colonial house on sea-front; on same street *Turismo* (No. 344), *Pousada Rio do Prado* (No. 236), recommended, F with big breakfast; *Rio Mar*, Praça Inaiá 12, F, with bathroom; *Porto Brasília*, Praça Antonio Carlos Magalhães 234, E with breakfast, F without, clean, friendly; *Pousada Vera Cruz*, Av. 22 de Abril 100, F with bath, good breakfast, clean. *Repousada*, Marechal Deodoro 100; *Pousada Navegante*, near port, recommended, but *Pousada Comba* is unsafe and to be avoided. *Pensões* and *dormitorios* near the port are cheap; those near the bus station are dearer.

Ajuda Hotel *São João*, good set lunch. *Pousada dos Guaiamuns*, on the road to Ajuda, E, very good, no electricity in the cabins, French owner is very knowledgeable.

Porto Seguro Restaurants *Cruz de Malta*, Av. Getúlio Vargas 358, good seafood; *Arrastão*;

Preto Velho, Praça da Bandeira, 30; *Marisqueira* at *Rio Mar Hotel; Arrecife*, good and cheap, near harbour. *Calda de Pau*, Av. Getúlio Vargas, recommended; *Santa Luzia*, Av. 22 de Abril on the seafront; *Casa da Esquina*, very good, moderately priced. *O Circo*, good sandwiches.

Tourist Office: Rua Dois de Julho 172, open daily 0800-2200. Public telephone, same street, No.71.

Buses from Porto Seguro: Salvador, daily, 12 hrs., US$5.80; Vitória, daily, 11 hrs.; Ilhéus daily, US$4.60; Eunápolis, many, 1 hr., US$0.60. For Rio direct buses, leaving at 1745, US$10, 18 hrs. To São Paulo direct, 1045, 25 hrs. US$16; other services via Eunápolis or Itabuna. All now leave from terminal by boat dock.

Air Varig from Rio via Macaé and Campos, Sat., return Sun.

North from Salvador

The paved BA-099 coast road from near the airport is known as the Estrada do Coco (coconut road) and for 50 km. passes some beautiful beaches. The best known from south to north are Ipitanga (with its reefs), Buraquinho, Jauá, Arembepe, Guarajuba, Itacimirim, Castelo Garcia D'Avila (with its 16th century fort) and Forte. Buses serve most of these destinations.

Some 50 km. to the north of Salvador is the former fishing village of **Arembepe,** an "in-place" of hippies and others in the late 1960s. It is now a quiet, enchanting place. *Pousada da Fazenda* on the beach, thatched huts, good seafood, not cheap. *Privé* seafood restaurant, very good. Best beaches 2 km N of town. Bus from Terminal Francés, Salvador, every 2 hours, 1½ hrs., US$0.45, last one back at 1700; or from Itapoan.

247 km. N of Salvador, on BR-101, is Estância, with pleasant hotels: *Turista*, F, and *Dom Bosco*, opposite, F, slightly cheaper, bath and breakfast, both pleasant.

Monte Santo About 270 km. N of Feira da Santana, via the direct BR-116 road to Fortaleza (partly paved but bad between Petrolina and Juazeiro del Norte), is the famous hill shrine of Monte Santo in the Sertão, reached by 3½ km. of steps cut into the rocks of the Serra do Picaraça. This is the scene of pilgrimages and great religious devotion during Holy Week. Not far away is Canudos, where religious rebels led by the visionary Antônio Conselheiro defeated three expeditions sent against them in 1897 before being overwhelmed. These events are the theme of two great books: *Os Sertões* (Revolt in the Backlands) by Euclides da Cunha, and *La Guerra del Fin del Mondo* by the Peruvian writer Mario Vargas Llosa.

Hotel At Euclides da Cunha, on the BR-116 and 39 km. from Monte Santo, is *Hotel Lua*, simple.

Buses From Salvador via Euclides da Cunha, about 8 hours.

Aracaju, capital of Sergipe, 327 km. N of Salvador, founded 1855, clean and lively, and the largest port between that city and Maceió, has a population of 288,000. It stands on the right bank of the Rio Sergipe, about 10 km. from its mouth, and can be reached from Maceió or Salvador by road. The city—unusually for Brazil—is laid out in the grid pattern. It has a beautiful park, clean streets (some in centre reserved to pedestrians); there is a handicraft centre, the Centro do Turismo, open 0900-1300, 1500-1900, in a restored colonial building on Praça Olímpio Campos, the cathedral square. A 16-km. road leads to the fine Ataláia beach: oil-drilling rigs offshore. There is another better beach, Nova Ataláia, on Ilha de Santa Luzia across the river, reached by boat from the ferry station. On December 8 there are both Catholic (Nossa Senhora da Conceição) and Umbanda religious festivals.

Hotels *Parque dos Coqueiros*, A, Ataláia beach, large pool, luxurious and attractive; *Praia Avenida*, very clean and friendly, C; *Palace*, in tall building on Praça Gen. Valadão, C, cockroaches, dangerous electric showers, no a/c; *Brasília*, Rua Laranjeiras 580, Tel.: 222-5112, E, good value, good breakfasts; *Serigy*, Rua Santo Amaro 269 (Tel.: 222-1210), D, comfortable, no hot water in rooms; *Turista*, opp. Rodoviária in centre, F, friendly; *Guanabara*, noisy, cold water in rooms, Rua Florentino Menezes 161 (near market), F, good meals. Many cheap hotels in Rua Gen. Caru and Rua Santa Rosa.

312 BRAZIL

Camping Camping Clube do Brasil site at Atalaia beach.

Restaurant *Tropeiro*, on boulevard, seafood and live music, highly recommended.

Tourist Information Emsetur, Av. Barão de Maroim 593, near Praça Fausto Cardoso, maps of Aracaju, Laranjeiras, São Cristovão. *Artesanato* interesting: pottery figures and lace particularly. Fair in Praça Tobias Barreto every Sun.

15 km. from Aracaju is **Laranjeiras**, reached by São Pedro bus, from old Rodoviária in centre, 30 mins-1 hr. A small pleasant town, with a ruined church on a hill overlooking it, it has two museums (Museu Afro-Brasileiro and Centro de Cultura João Ribeiro), and the Capela de Sant'Aninha with a wooden altar inlaid with gold.

São Cristóvão, SW of Aracaju on the road to Salvador, an unspoiled colonial town, was the old state capital of Sergipe, founded in 1590 by Cristóvão de Barros. Worth visiting are the Museu de Arte Sacra e Histórico de Sergipe, the Assembly building, the Provincial Palace and five churches including Misericórdia and Nossa Senhora da Vitória (all closed Mon.). Outdoor arts festival in 2nd half of October. Buses (São Pedro) from Aracaju, from old Rodoviária in centre, 30 mins.-1 hr. (No hotels, but families rent rooms near the bus station.)

Between Aracaju and the next port to the north—Maceió—is the mouth of the São Francisco river, whose great Paulo Afonso falls upstream (see page 314) can be visited from Maceió or (if travelling from Aracaju to Maceió by bus) from Penedo by river and bus. The BR-101 between Aracaju and Maceió is now paved, crossing the São Francisco by bridge between Propriá and Porto Real do Colégio.

Penedo, in Alagoas down the River São Francisco, 451 km. from Salvador (US$9, 10 hrs., by daily bus at 0830; 115 km. from Maceió), is a surprisingly charming town. It has a nice waterfront park with stone walkways and walls. Long two-masted sailing vessels cruise on the river (they can be rented for US$2.40 per hour, regardless of the number of people, possibly stopping to swim or visit beaches on islands in the river). Frequent launches across the river to Neópolis, 25 mins., US$0.45. Also free car ferry (take care when driving on and off). Daily street market. Good hammocks. Buses from Maceió, US$2, 4 hrs. One bus to Aracaju daily, 0600.

Hotels *São Francisco*, Av. Floriano Peixoto, E, recommended except for poor restaurant; *Pousada Colonial*, Praça 12 de Abril 21, E with bath, clean (reconstructed boys' school), most rooms with view of Rio São Francisco; *Turista*, Rua Siqueira Campos 148, E with bath, recommended, close to bus station; in same street *Majestic* and *Victoria*, both F; *Imperio*, Av. Floriano Peixoto, F. Good **restaurant**, *Forte da Rocheira*, Rua da Rocheira, good food, especially *ensopado de jacaré* (alligator stew).

Tourist Office in Casa da Aposentadoria, Praça Barão de Penedo, helpful.

Maceió, capital of Alagoas state, is about 287 km. NE of Aracaju by road, and 244 km. S of Recife. It is mainly a sugar port, although there are tobacco exports handled also, with a lighthouse on an eminence built in a residential area of town (Farol), about one km. from the sea. Population of Maceió is 376,000.

Maceió still has a colonial flavour. Two of its old buildings, the Government Palace and the church of Bom Jesus dos Mártires (covered in tiles), are particularly interesting, as is the recently restored Cathedral. The Associação Comercial has a museum, near the beach, in a beautiful, though deteriorating building. There is an enjoyable lagoon (Lagoa do Mundaú), 2 km. S at Pontal da Barra: excellent shrimp and fish at its small restaurants and handicraft stalls. Bus to Marechal Deodoro passes Praia do Francês, clear water, coconut palms and small restaurants, beautiful (but crowded on Sundays; last bus back to Maceió, 1800). Beyond is the equally fine beach of Barra de São Miguel. It is a ten-minute taxi ride from the town centre (or take "Porta da Terra" bus) to Pajuçara beach, where there are a nightly craft market and several good restaurants. The beaches, some of the finest and most popular in Brazil (such as Jatiúca, Jacarecica, Guaxuma, Mirante, Garça Torta, Riacho Doce, all within 30 mins. taxi ride from town; buses to the last two from terminal, US$0.65, or local "Fátima" bus, US$0.10), have in most cases a protecting coral reef a kilometre or so out.

BRAZIL 313

Beaches fronting the old city and between Salgema terminal and the modern port area (Trapiche, Subra) are not recommended for swimming.

Jangadas take passengers to a natural pool 2 km. off Pajuçara beach, at low tide you can stand on the sand and rock reef. Jangadas cost US$2.50 per person per day—negotiable (there is a jangada anchored at the reef selling food and drink). From Maceió, a ferry crosses the lagoon to Coqueira Seca (30 mins., US$0.20), a small pretty fishing village.

Local Holidays   August 27 (Nossa Senhora dos Prazeres); Sept. 16 (Freedom of Alagoas); December 8 (Nossa Senhora da Conceição); Christmas Eve; New Year's Eve, half-day.

Hotels   *Othon*, Av Antônio Gouveia 1113, Pajuçara, good cinema downstairs; *Luxor*, Av. Duque de Caxias 2076, first class, 4 star, A; behind is *Praia Avenida*, Artur Jucá 1250, 2 star, D, clean, comfortable; *Ponta Verde*, B/C; *Jatiúca*, Lagoa da Anta 220, A, a/c, on the beach, swimming pool, heavily booked, good breakfasts, but small rooms with thin walls; *Beira Mar*, Av. Duque de Caxias 1994, B; *Beiriz*, Rua João Pessoa 290, comfortable, E-C, dear; *Califórnia*, Rua Barão de Penedo 33, E; *Parque*, Praça Dom Pedro II 73, D, a/c, good, central, comfortable; *Golf*, Rua Prof. Domingos Moeda 38A (near Praça D. Pedro II), clean, F; *Pousada Sol e Mar*, Av. Rosa da Fonseca s/n, E without bath, good breakfast, helpful owners, recommended; *Florida*, Rua Senador Luiz Torres 126, central, F with bath but without breakfast, noisy on street side, does not charge by the hour (unlike most other cheap hotels); *Castelinho*, reasonable. Cheap hotels (mostly without windows) in Rua Barão de Atalaia, e.g. *Real*, at No. 778, F without breakfast. Pajuçara, F, clean friendly; *Bomfim*, *Rodoviária* (friendly), *Atalaia*, all F; also *Riviera*, small rooms, noisy, F. Near Rodoviária: *Oasis*, F; *Sany*, next to bus station, F with shower and fan, clean; *Reencontro*, next door, F. Avoid both hotels *Maceió*. Good *pousadas* can be found in the Pajuçara beach district, not too expensive; e.g. *Pousada Rex*, Antônio Pedro de Mendonça 311, E, clean, friendly, honest, helpful.

Camping   There is a Camping Clube do Brasil site on Jacarecica beach, a 15-min. taxi drive from the town centre. Camping also possible on the Avenida beach, near the *Hotel Atlântico*.

Electric current   220 volts A.C.

Restaurants   *Gstaad*, Av. Roberto Kennedy 2167, Ponta Verde; *Bem*, Praia de Cruz das Almas, good seafood and service; *Ao Lagostão*, Av. Duque de Caxias 1348, seafood, fixed price menu; *O Gaúcho*, Av. Duque de Caxias 1466, good Brazilian food from all regions; *Recanto*, Rua Artur Jacá 10, Centro; *Alagoas late Clube*, Av. Roberto Kennedy; *Adega do Trapiche*, Av. Siqueira Campos, Prado; *Calabar*, Antônio Gouveia 293, Japanese; *Passaporte Santa Lucia*, Praia da Avenida, good cheap sandwiches, juices on beach. Vegetarian: *O Natural*, Rua Libertadora Alagoana (Rua da Praia) 112; *Nativa*, Osvaldo Sarmento 56; *Chegança*, Rua do Imperador 342A; *Paraíso*, Av. Antônio Gouveia 631, Pajuçara. Italian and Arab cooking at *Comes e Bebes*, Antônio Gouveia 943. Good eating places on the road to Marechal Deodoro and at Praia do Francês. Local specialities include oysters, *pitu*, a crayfish (now becoming scarce), and *sururu*, a kind of cockle. Local ice-cream, Shups, has been recommended.

Entertainment   Teatro Deodoro, Praça Marechal Deodoro, in centre; Cinema São Luiz, Rua do Comércio, in centre; the other cinemas tend to be fleapits. *Bar Chapéu de Couro*, Jos̀ée Carneiro 338, Ponto da Barra, is a popular music bar for young people. Many bars at end of Av. Roberto Kennedy by Parque de Sete Coqueiros, e.g. *Bar Lampião* (or *Tropical*), R. Kennedy 2585, food and *forró* every night.

Museums   Instituto Histórico, Rua João Pessoa 382, good small collection of Indian artefacts and Lampião relics. Museu de Arte Sacra, same street (closed indefinitely). Museu Folclórico Theo Brandão, in the old University building, Mon.-Fri., 0800-1200, 1400-1700, Sat., 1400-1700, free, Av. Duque de Caxias 1490, interesting local artefacts.

Bank   Banco do Brasil, etc. Open 1000 to 1630. Aeroturismo, Rua Barão de Penedo 61 or Pajuçara Turismo on same road, which begins opposite Ferroviária at Praça Valente de Lima (but not named on all maps).

Cables   Embratel, Rua João Pessoa 57, Praça Dom Pedro II 84. Telegráfico Nacional.

Tourist Information   Ematur, Praça do Centenário 1135 (Tel.: 243-6868), Farol; at Largo do Livramento, on Av. Senador Mendonça, and on ground floor of *Hotel Othon*. Also at airport and at Rodoviária. Helpful, has good maps.

Tourist Agencies   Alatur, Duque de Caxias 1416; Dreamar Turismo, Av. Cons. Lourenço Albuquerque 261; Lysturismo, Duque de Caxias 1338.

314 BRAZIL

Buses Rodoviária is 5 km. from centre; take bus marked "Ouro Preto p/centro" or "Serraria Mercado" which has a circular route from centre to suburbs and bus terminal (taxi quicker—all local buses are very crowded). Bus to Recife, 20 a day, 4 hrs., US$3; to Salvador, 11 hrs., 4 a day (3 at night), US$6. **N.B.** If travelling to Salvador, or if booking through Bom Fim, check all details on your ticket; they are not reliable. To Penedo, several, 4 hrs, US$2. Train to Recife on Sun. only.

Airport 20 km. from centre, taxi about US$8.50. Buses to airport from near *Hotel Beiriz*, Rua João Pessoa 290, signed "Rio Largo"; alight at Tabuleiro dos Matrices, then 7-8 min. walk to airport, bus fare US$0.25. Tourist flights over the city.

Excursion By launch or bus (22 km. South) past Praia do Francês to the attractive colonial town and former capital of Alagoas, **Marechal Deodoro,** with the fine old churches of São Francisco, Terceira Ordem (being restored) and Rosário. There is also the State Museum of Sacred Art, open Tues.-Sun., 0900-1300. The town is the birthplace of Marshal Deodoro da Fonseca, founder of the Republic; the modest house where he was born is on the Rua Marechal Deodoro, close to the waterfront, open Tues.-Sun. The cleanliness of this little town is exemplary: on Mondays everyone is required by local law to sweep the streets. The trip by launch, leaving from Trapiche on the lagoon, is very pleasant indeed. Good local lacework. *Restaurant São Roque*, simple but good. A recommended excursion is to take Real Alagoas bus from Rodoviária to Marechal Deodoro (every 30 mins., US$ 0.45, 1 hr.) then after visiting the town spend some time (beware the *borrachudos* behind the beach) at beautiful **Praia do Francês** (recommended restaurants *O Pescador* and *Chez Patrick*; try *agulhas fritas* on the beach), where Quatro Rodas are to build a new hotel; existing ones are *O Pescador* and *Pousada das Águas*, both D. Return to Maceió by bus (last one leaves 1800) or *kombi* van, 20 mins.

There are many interesting stopping points along the coast between Maceió and Recife, such as Barra de Santo Antônio, 45 km. N, a busy fishing village, with beach on a narrow peninsula, a canoe-ride away; *Hotel Peixada da Rita*, F, good food in the restaurant. Also Japaratinga (*Hotel Solmar*, F, 2 rooms, basic, good restaurant—bus from Maceió at 0515) and São José da Coroa Grande (*Hotel Lar Ana Luiza*, E (cheaper without breakfast); *Hotel do Francês*, D, further from beach; a few families rent rooms); at low tide watch colourful fish in the rock pools on the reef. Along this coast, the protecting reef offshore prevents garbage and silt from being taken out to sea at high tide, so water is muddy and polluted.

The Falls of **Paulo Afonso**, once one of the great falls of the world but now exploited for hydroelectric power, are 270 km. up the São Francisco river, which drains a valley 3 times the size of Great Britain. There are 2,575 km. of river above the Falls to its source in Minas Gerais. Below the Falls is a deep gorge clothed with dense tropical vegetation. The lands around are a national park. The best time to visit the Falls is Jan.-Feb.; only in the rainy season does much water pass over them, as almost all the flow now goes through the power plant. The best view is from the northern (Alagoas) bank. The Falls are in a security area; no admission for pedestrians, so need to visit by car or taxi (US$4.50 an hour). Admission is from 0800 onwards, but it depends on the availability of guides, without whom one cannot enter.

There are the new *Hotel Casande* (B), *Grand Hotel de Paulo Afonso* (expensive) and a guest house (apply for room in advance) at the Falls. The town of Paulo Afonso (35,000 people; Hotels *Guadalajara* and *Paulo Afonso*, friendly, cheap; *Belvedere*, D, a/c, swimming pool and *Palace*, F, a/c, swimming pool, both on Rua André Falcão; *Hospedagem Lima*, very basic, F, near *Hotel Guadalajara*; *Hotel Dormitório*, F—all hotels within walking distance of bus terminal), is some distance from the Falls, reached by paved road from Recife, bus, 7 hrs., US$4, from Salvador, bus (475 km., 160 paved, the rest bad), or from Maceió (306 km.) via Palmeira dos Índios, partially paved. For information about Paulo Afonso and the *sertão*, ask the Italian fathers (Mario, Antonio and Riccardo) who are most helpful. Handicrafts (embroidery, fabrics) from Núcleo de Produção Artesanal, Av. Contorno s/n. It is possible, with plenty of time, to go upstream from Penedo (see page 312) to about Pão de Açúcar or Piranhas, but on to the Falls is complicated and involves nonconnecting buses. Piranhas, 80 km. from Paulo Afonso (road almost completely paved, buses difficult), is a charming town with good beaches on the Rio São Francisco; it has picturesque houses and an old station which is now a *Pousada* (3-4 rooms, F, restaurant) with a small museum (photographs of the severed head of Lampião, the Brazilian "Robin Hood").

BRAZIL 315

Travel on the River São Francisco (see also page 258). The river is navigable above the Falls from above the twin towns of **Juazeiro**, in Bahia, and **Petrolina**, in Pernambuco (buses from Salvador, 6 hrs., also from Recife, Fortaleza, Teresina) to Pirapora in Minas Gerais, linked by road to the Belo Horizonte-Brasília highway. River transport has changed rapidly in the past few years; for information telephone Juazeiro (075) 811-2465: the Companhia de Navegação do São Francisco boat to Pirapora sails once a month, between the 13th and 17th.

John Hale writes: Juazeiro and Petrolina are thriving towns compared with many others on the upper São Francisco. Petrolina has its own airport and close to this is the small Museu do Sertão—relics of rural life in the North-East and the age of the "coronéis" and the bandit Lampião. *Hotel Grande Rio* and *Restaurante Rancho Grande*. Juazeiro is the poorer of the two cities. Hotels: *Grande Hotel*, Rua Pititinga, *Vitória*, and *União* (recommended) and *Oliveira*, the last two in Rua Conselheiro Saraiva. Unique restaurant known as the *Vaporzinho* is high and dry on the river front, a side-wheel paddle steamer, the *Saldanha Marinho*, built at Sabará in 1852. Market on Fri. and Sat.

About 244 km. to the north of Maceió is

Recife (Pernambuco), founded on reclaimed land by the Dutch prince Maurice of Nassau in 1627 after his forces had burnt Olinda, the original capital, is the capital of Pernambuco state and the fourth largest city in Brazil. It is 835 km. N of Salvador by road. It consists of three portions, all on islands: Recife proper, Santo Antônio, and Boa Vista. The three districts are connected by bridges across the rivers Capibaribe and Beberibe. The town centre is is in poor condition. The population is 1,500,000 and the proportion of blacks is large, though less than in Salvador. Olinda, the old capital, is only 6 km. to the North (see page 321).

Churches The best of them are the churches of São Francisco de Assis (1612), on Rua do Imperador; São Pedro dos Clérigos in São José district (1782, for its façade, its fine wood sculpture and a splendid *trompe l'oeil* ceiling); Santo Antônio (1753), in Praça da Independência, rebuilt in 1864; Conceição dos Militares, in Rua Nova (1708), grand ceiling and a large 18th century primitive mural of the battle of Guararapes; Nossa Senhora do Carmo, Praça do Carmo, (1675); Madre de Deus (1706), in the district of Recife, with a splendid high altar, and sacristy; the Pilar church (1680), Rua do Pilar; the Espírito Santo (1642), the original church of the Jesuits, in Santo Antônio district; Santo Antônio do Convento de São Francisco (1606, beautiful Portuguese tiles), in the Rua do Imperador; the Capela Dourada (Golden Chapel, 1697), in Rua do Imperador (the finest sight of all, 0900-1100 and 1500-1700, Sat. 0900-1100: no flash photography); S. José do Ribamar (19th century), in São José. There are many others. The best way of seeing them is to buy a local booklet: *Templos Católicos do Recife*, which has excellent photographs, or join an agency tour. Many of them are closed for most of Sunday, because of services.

A few km. S of the city, a little beyond Boa Viagem and the airport, on Guararapes hill, is the historic church of Nossa Senhora das Prazeres. It was here, in 1654, that a Brazilian victory finally ended the 30-year Dutch occupation of the North-East. The church was built by the Brazilian commander to fulfil a vow. Boa Viagem's own fine church dates from 1707.

Other Attractions You may be able to visit Fort Brum (1629), built by the Dutch (does not appear to be open to the public, but soldiers may let you wander around), and the star-shaped fort of Cinco Pontas (with Museu da Cidade do Recife—cartographic history of the settlement of Recife, and Museu de Imagem e Som, Mon.-Fri. 0800-1800, Sat.-Sun., 1400-1800) built by the Portuguese in 1677. Visit the city markets in the São José and Santa Rita sections. Go fishing on log rafts—*jangadas*—at Boa Viagem with a fisherman who charges US$2. Visit sugar plantations in interior (though few tour agencies offer such trips), try Sevagtur, Tel. 341-3956, in Casa da Cultura.

Boa Viagem, now a southern suburb, is the finest residential quarter. The 8 km. promenade commands a striking view of the Atlantic, but the beach is

316 BRAZIL

crowded at weekends. The main square has a good market Sats., with *forró* being danced. Good restaurants along sea shore. 901 or 902 bus from centre.

Excursions About 30 km. S of Recife, beyond Cabo, is the beautiful Gaibú beach, reached by bus from Cabo.

The artists' and intellectuals' quarter is based on the Pátio de São Pedro, the square round São Pedro dos Clérigos (see under **Churches**). Folk music and poetry shows in the square on Fri., Sat. and Sun. evenings and there are pleasant little restaurants, with good atmosphere, at Nos. 44, 46 and 47, and No. 20 *Caldeira de Cana e Petisqueira Banguê*. The square is an excellent shopping centre for typical North-East craftware. Not far away is the Praça de Sebo, where the city's second-hand booksellers concentrate; this Mercado de Livros Usados is bounded by Av. Guararapes, Rua Dantas Barreto and Rua Siqueira Campos.

The former municipal prison has now been converted into a cultural centre, the Casa da Cultura, with many cells converted into art or souvenir shops and with areas for exhibitions and shows (also public conveniences). Most weeks, local dances such as the *ciranda* and *bumba-meu-boi* are held as tourist attractions.

The State Museum (closed Mon.), has excellent paintings by the 19th-century landscape painter, Teles Júnior. The Popular Art Museum, containing ceramic figurines (including some by Mestre Vitalino and Zé Caboclo), the Museu do Açúcar, Av. 17 de Agosto 2187 (sugar museum, 1100-1700, Sun. 1300-1700, closed Mon.), are most interesting; the latter contains models of colonial mills, devices for torturing slaves, collections of antique sugar bowls and much else; at the same address are the Museum of Anthropology, the Nabuco Museum and the modern museum of popular remedies, Farmacopéia Popular; the complex is known as O Museu do Homem do Nordeste, and is excellent. Take the "Dois Irmãos" bus (check that it's the correct one as there are two) from in front of the Banorte building near the Post Office on Guararapes, half-hour ride 10 km. outside the city to the zoo (US$0.20, not very good) and Botanical Gardens; it passes the museum complex, and together with the zoo they make a pleasant day's outing. See also the beautiful houses at Av. Rui Barbosa 960, the former home of Joaquim Nabuco at Av. 17 de Agosto 2223 (afternoons). Also the Museu do Trem, Central Station, Rua Floriano Peixoto, small but interesting, especially the Garrett steam locomotive (open Tues.-Fri., 1000-1200, 1300-1700, Sat.-Sun., 1400-1800). The first Brazilian printing press was installed in 1706 and Recife claims to publish the oldest daily newspaper in South America, *Diário de Pernambuco*, founded 1825. Museu da Abolição (of Slavery), corner of Av. Caxangá and Rua João Ivo da Silva, is worth a visit, in an early 19th-century tiled house. You may like to visit Cerâmica Brennand, a factory in the western suburbs on the Camaragibe road (take a taxi, or walk the 3 km. along Rua Gastão Vidigal—past hotels *Costa Azul* and *Tropical*—from the end of the bus line along Av. Caxangá). They make ceramic tiles, and one of the brothers is a sculptor of idiosyncratic works on display, for those interested in the wilder shores of artistic endeavour. Entry is free, and it is very friendly.

Local Holidays January 1 (Universal Brotherhood). June 24 (São João). July 16 (Nossa Senhora do Carmo, patron saint of the city). São João, though cancelled by the Pope, is still celebrated with bonfires and fireworks on June 24 all over the State of Pernambuco—and, indeed, throughout Brazil. December 8 (Nossa Senhora da Conceição).

Carnival The carnival groups dance at the doors of all the churches they pass; they usually go to the Church of Nossa Senhora do Rosário dos Pretos, patron saint of the slaves, before proceeding in procession into the down-town areas. A small car at the head bears the figure of some animal; it is followed by the king and queen under a large, showy umbrella. The *bahianas*, who wear snowy-white embroidered skirts, dance in single file on either side of the king and queen. Next comes the *dama do passo* carrying a small doll, or *calunga*. After the *dama* comes the *tirador de loas*: he chants to the group which replies in chorus, and last comes a band of local percussion instruments.

Still flourishing is the dance performance of the *caboclinhos*. The groups wear

BRAZIL 317

traditional Indian garb: bright feathers round their waists and ankles, colourful cockades, bead and animal-teeth necklaces, a dazzle of medals on their red tunics. The dancers beat out the rhythm with bows and arrows; others of the group play primitive musical instruments, but the dance is the thing: spinning, leaping, and stooping with almost mathematical precision.

There is a *pre-carnavalesca* week, followed by the main days Sunday to Tuesday; on the Saturday the *bloco* "Galo da Madrugada" officially opens Carnival (wild and lively), see local press for routes and times. The groups taking part are *maracatu*, *caboclinhos*, *trocas*, *blocos*, *ursos*, *caboclos de lança*, *escolas de samba* and *frevo* (the costumes are better than the music). Usually they start from Av. Conde da Boa Vista and progress along Rua do Hospício, Rua da Imperatriz, Ponte da Boa Vista, Praça da Independência, Rua 1° de Março and Rua do Imperador. During Carnival (and on a smaller scale throughout the year) the Casa de Cultura has *frevo* demonstrations where visitors can learn some steps of this unique dance of Pernambuco (check local press for details of "Frevioca" truck and *frevo* orchestras during Carnival in the Pátio de São Pedro). The best place to see the groups is from the balconies of *Hotel do Parque*.

In the "Festivais Juninos", the June *festas* of São João and São Pedro, the *forró* is danced. This dance, now popular throughout the North-East, is believed to have originated when the British builders of the local railways held parties that were "for all".

Hotels (for Olinda hotels see page 321)

Name	Address	Price (US$) Single	Double
Miramar‡	Rua dos Navegantes 363 (Boa Viagem)	55	66
Internacional Othon Palace*	Av. Boa Viagem 3722	48	52
Quatro de Outubro	Rua Floriano Peixoto 141	28	34
Mar‡	Rua Barão de Souza Leão 451 (Boa Viagem)	48	53
Vila Rica*	Av. Boa Viagem 4308	50	54
Jangadeiro*	Av. Boa Viagem 3114	44	50
Savaroni*	Av. Boa Viagem 3772	50	54
Pousada Casa Forte	Av. 17 de Agosto	28	32
Do Sol*	Av. Boa Viagem 978	37	43
Casa Grande e Senzala‡	Av. Conselheiro Aguiar 5000 (Boa Viagem)	28	35
Boa Viagem‡	Av. Boa Viagem 5000	42	50
Grande	Av. Martins de Barros 593	32	36
Praiamar*	Av. Boa Viagem 1660	30	35
São Domingos	Praça Maciel Pinheiro 54/66	20	25
Duzentas Milhas Praia*	Av. Boa Viagem 864	20	24
Sea View‡	Rua dos Navegantes 101 (Boa Viagem)	25	32

*On beach   ‡Near beach

There are several other hotels and pensions. A new 5-star *Recife Palace* has just been opened in Boa Viagem. *Recife*, Rua do Imperador 310, Tel.: 2240799, E, central, pleasant; *Gálica*, Rua Jequitinhonha 301, D; *Treze de Maio*, Rua do Hospício 659, F with breakfast; next door (and better) is *Suíça*, at No. 687, F, and up, safe parking, clean, but a bit run-down, friendly; *Lido*, Rua do Riachuelo 547, F, good breakfast, hot water, friendly, recommended. *Palácio*, Rua Henriques Dias 181, Boa Vista, E, Tel.: 221-0222, shower and breakfast, quiet, friendly, a/c, mangoes in the patio. *Nassau*, Largo do Rosário 253, E, clean, hot showers, but a bit noisy (breakfast only, served on 7th floor, with a balcony overlooking the city). *Praia*, corner of Praia and Arsenal da Guerra, 5 minutes from bus station, F; *Sete de Setembro*, Matias de Albuquerque 318, F including plus breakfast, recommended, but not very clean or quiet; *Parque*, Rua do Hospício 51, good value, F, friendly, noisy, clean, safe, highly recommended, good bars and restaurants nearby; *Avenida*, Av. Martins de Barros 292, F with breakfast; *Central*, Av. Manoel Barba 209, E without bath, clean; *Hospedaria Rigor*, Praça 17, central, F, including breakfast, fan, mosquito net. *Santini*, Rua Barão de Vitória 295, near railway station, E, with shower, clean, friendly, helpful, reasonably quiet. There are several hotels in Boa Viagem, e.g. *Marazul*, José Brandão 135, D, comfortable, clean, friendly, pleasant, care with electric shower; *Veraneio*, Rua Conselheiro Sérgio Henrique Cardin 150, Boa Viagem, E, close to beach; *Saveiro*, R. Conselheiro Aguiar 4670 (Tel.: 326-6073), no pool, mosquitoes, but new and clean, a/c, D; *Pousada Aconchego*, Rua Félix de Brito 2382 (Tel.: 326-2989) D, swimming pool, good meals, English-speaking owner; *Beira Mar*, Av. Boa Viagem 5426, D, with breakfast, no bath, hot water, clean, friendly; *Gaivota*, Rua Barbosa, F. For longer stays rooms may be rented in the centre for about US$20 a month, make inquiries on the streets. For example, contact Dr. Bezerra dos Santos, Rua Floriano Peixoto 85, Edif. Vieira da Cunha

318 BRAZIL

S/511, Tel.: 224-1098 (English-speaking dentist). Hotels near the bus station are not recommended; this area, especially Santa Rita, is dangerous at night.

During Carnival, private individuals rent rooms and houses in Recife and Olinda; Lins Turismo has listings as does the *Diário de Pernambuco*, or ask around the streets of Olinda. This accommodation is generally cheaper, safer and quieter than hotels, which inflate prices at Carnival

Electric Current 220 volts A.C.

Restaurants There are many good restaurants, at all prices, in the city, and along beach at Boa Viagem.

City: *Adega da Mouraria*, R. Ulhoa Cintra 40; *Casa d'Itália*, R. Fernandes Vieira 73, not recommended; *Panorâmico AIP*, Av. Dantas Barreto 576 (12°); *Varanda*, Av. Eng. Abdias de Carvalho (Sport Clube); *Laçador*, R. Fernandes Vieira 171; *Pierre* (French), R. Ulhoa Cintra 102; *Faia*, R. Ulhoa Cintra 122; *Bella Trieste*, R. Fernandes Vieira 741; *Clube de Engenharia*, Av. N.S. do Carmo 110 (4°); *Buraco da Otília*, Rua da Aurora 1231 (lunch only). *Toca do Guiamum*, Av. Herculano Bandeira 865; *Bar Restaurante Pia Você*, Herculano Bandeira 115, good fish; *Bar Restaurante OK*, Av. Marquês de Olinda 174; *Rex*, Rua do Hospício, and next door, *Viena*, better value; *Le Buffet*, Rua do Hospício, Japanese food and vegetables, helpful, friendly, English-speaking owner; *Fuji* (Japanese), R. do Hospício 354, good *tofu* dishes; *Restaurante Leite* (lunches only), Praça Joaquim Nabuco 147/53 ; *Popy*, for snacks, on Rua Matias de Albuquerque. *Torres de Londres*, Praça 13 de Maio; *Galo de Ouro*, Gamboa do Carmo 83, recommended, US$3 for main course; *Dom Pedro*, Rua do Imperador 376, specializes in fish dishes. *Bar Esquina 17*, Grande Hotel, recommended. *Grande Vida*, Rua Riachuelo 581, *O Pirata*, on Av. 17 de Agosto (Casa Forte) near Museu do Homem do Nordeste. *O Vegetal*, Rua Cleto Campelo (2nd floor) behind Central Post Office, lunch only, less than US$2, good. *Rosa de Ouro*, Rua das Flores 59, delicious food and cheap. Good baker *Nabuco* opposite park at Rua do Sol and Rua Concórdia.

Boa Viagem: Main hotels. *Canton* (Chinese), Rua Desembargador João Paes 123; *Golden Dragon* (Chinese), Rua Barão de Souza Leão 691; *Le Mazot* (French), Av. Boa Viagem 618; *La Pinha*, Praça de Boa Viagem; *Maurício de Nassau*, Av. Boa Viagem 908; *Costa Brava*, Rua Barão de Souza Leão 698; *Mustang Praia*, Av. Boa Viagem 5566; *Lobster*, Av. Boa Viagem 2612 and *Churrasco*, Av. Boa Viagem 1700, both recommended; *Coqueiro Verde*, Av. Boa Viagem 5388; *Moenda*, Rua dos Navegantes 1417; *Tio Pepe*, Av. Boa Viagem 5444; *Baiúca*, Praça Boa Viagem 16; *Shangai* (Chinese), Av. Cons. Aguiar 4700, excellent, plenty of food; *Pajuçara*, Rua Tomé Gibson (no number); *O Chocalho*, Av. Barão de Souza Leão 297, for local dishes. *Bar Branco e Azul*, near bus station, good.

(For Olinda restaurants see under Olinda, page 321). Be careful of eating the local small crabs, known as *guaiamum*; they live in the mangrove swamps which take the drainage from Recife's shantytowns (*mocambos*).

Bars From Gerard Moxon's extensive personal research the following are suggested: *Lapinha*, Praça Boa Viagem; *O Veleiro*, Primeira Jardim. Also try *Café Passacole*, Av. Visconde de Suassuna 871, Boa Vista and the cafe/ice cream parlours *Fri-Sabor* and *Eskimo*, both close to Praça Boa Viagem.

Discotheques tend to be expensive and sophisticated: Esquina 90 Disco Club, corner Av. Conselheiro Aguiar and Wilfred Shorto (Boa Viagem); Misty, Riachuelo 309, Boa Vista; Caktos, Av Conselheiro Aguiar 2328, Boa Viagem; Disco 34, Av. Boa Viagem 3114 (*Hotel Jangadeiro*); Gaslight, Rua dos Navegantes 363 (*Hotel Miramar*), Boa Viagem; Skorpios, Rua Barão de Souza Leão (*Mar Hotel*), Boa Viagem; Aritana, Rua José de Alencar 44, Loja 4, Boa Vista; Leandro's, Av. Conselheiro Aguiar 5025, Sobreloja, Sala 116, Boa Viagem.

Also visit a typical North-Eastern *forró* where local couples dance to typical music, very lively especially on Fridays and Saturdays. Among the best are: Belo Mar, Av. Bernardo Vieira de Melo, Candeias; Casa de Festejo, Praça do Derby; Torre.

Key to Map of Recife

1. Church of Rosário de Boa Vista; 2. Presbyterian Church of Boa Vista; 3. Matriz (Principal Church) de Boa Vista; 4. Presbyterian Church of Recife; 5. Faculty of Law; 6. Municipal Council Chamber; 7. State Institute of Education; 8. State Legislative Assembly; 9. State College of Pernambuco; 10. Church of Piedade; 11-13. TV stations (channels 2 and 6); 14. Central Technical School; 15. University of Pernambuco TV Station; 16. New Municipality Building; 17. Church of Pilar; 18. Moinho Recife SA (Flour Mill); 19. Port Captain's Office; 20. Banco do Brasil; 21. Governor's Palace; 22. State Secretariat of Finance; 23. Santa Isabel Theatre; 24. Palace of Justice; 25. Monastery of Santo Antônio and Church of São Francisco; 26. Central Post Office; 27. Geographical and Statistical Institute (IBGE); 28. *Diário de Pernambuco* (newspaper); 29. Church of Rosário dos Pretos; 30. Church of Espírito Santo; 31. Church of Nossa Senhora do Livramento; 32. Church of São Pedro dos Clérigos; 33. Basilica of Nossa Senhora do Carmo; 34. (none); 35. Casa de Cultura; 36. "Metrô" Railway Station; 37. Fort of Cinco Pontas; 38. Church of São José de Ribamar; 39. Central Bus Station; 40. Church of Nossa Senhora da Penha.

BRAZIL 319

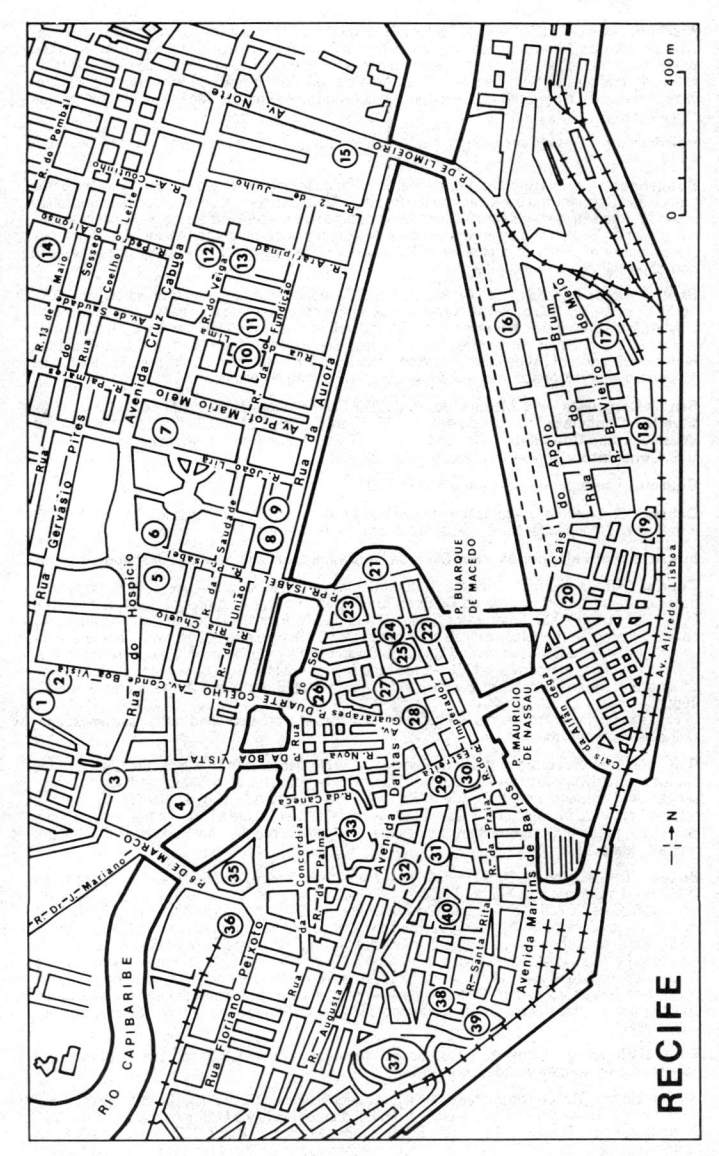

ROUGH SKETCH

320 BRAZIL

Markets Mercado São José (1875) for local products and handicrafts. Casa Amarela for a truly typical market on Sats. Sun. evenings: "hippy fair" at Praça Boa Viagem, on the sea front, life-sized wooden statues of saints (a good meeting place is the *Bar Lapinha* in the middle of the square). New Sat. craft fair at Sítio Trindade, Casa Amarela: during the feast days of June 12-29, fireworks, music, dancing, local food. On April 23, here and in the Pátio de São Pedro, one can see the *xangô* dance.

Hairdresser Dellos Cabeleireiros, Av. Visconde de Jequitinhonha 106, Boa Viagem, Tel.: 326-4414.

Bookshops Livraria Brandão, Rua da Matriz 22 (good selection of used English books and some French and German) and bookstalls on the Rua do Infante Dom Henrique. Perhaps best bookshop is Livro 7, Rua Sete de Setembro 329 and Guararapes airport. Ao Livro Técnico, R. Princesa Isabel, has thrillers in English and beginners' readers. Also a great local character, Melquísidec Pastor de Nascimento, second-hand bookseller, at R. Bispo Cardoso Aires, 215; he also has a second-hand bookshop at Praça de Sebo.

Banks Lloyds Bank (ex-BOLSA), Rua do Fogo 22; Banco Internacional; Citibank. Open 1000-1600. Lins Câmbio, Rua da Palma corner with Guararapes, better rate than banks, but dollars cash only. Agência Luck (Edifício Bancomérica, 3* andar, Rua Matias de Alberquerque 223) takes cash and travellers' cheques. Good rates from Sr Jesus Cal Malleiro, Hospedaria Senhor do Bomfim, Rua dos Pescadores (just behind bus station). Jacinto at 7th floor, Banco Comércio, Rua Matias de Albuquerque, and Monaco men's clothing store, Praça Joaquim Nabuco.

British Consulate Av. Marquês de Olinda 200. Caixa Postal 184. Tel.: 224-0650.
Swedish Consulate Travessa do Amorim 66, 1° andar, Tel.: 224-1622.
West German Consulate Dantas Barreto 191, Edif. Santo Antônio, 4th floor.
U.S. Consulate Gonçalves Maia 163. Tel.: 221-1412.

Church Episcopalian, Rua Carneiro Vilela 569.

Cables Embratel, Av. Agamenon Magalhães, 1114, Parque Amorim district, Tel.: 221-4149; also Praça da Independência. Telex, public booth, Av. Guararapes 250.

International Telephones Rua Diário de Pernambuco, 38; also at airport (first floor).

Tourist Offices Empetur (for the State of Pernambuco). Main office, Av. Cruz Cabugá 553, near corner of Coutinho; Casa da Cultura, Rua Floriano Peixoto (old prison), Mon.-Sat., 0900-2000, Sun. 1400-2000. Emetur (for Recife), Pátio de São Pedro, loja 10. At Carnival-time they have a full programme. Maps available: Empetur, US$0.33, who also publish walking tour schedules for Recife and Olinda in several languages; also central map in monthly guide *Itinerário Pernambuco*. Offices at Rodoviária (0700-2100) and airport—24 hrs. (will book hotels, helpful, English spoken). Information trailer parked corner Av. Dantas Barreto and Av. Guararapes, 0800-1900.

Hours of opening of museums, art galleries, churches etc. are published in the daily newspaper *Diário de Pernambuco*.

Rail Recife is the centre of the Rede Ferroviária do Nordeste, with lines from the Cinco Pontas station south to Maceió (train Sun. 0840, 10 hrs, no dining car), north to Paraíba and Natal (no passenger services), and a central route to Salgueiro (train Sat. 0700, with de luxe car to Caruaru, returns from Caruaru Sun. 1700). Commuter services, known as the Metrô but not underground, leave from the Central station; they are being extended to serve the new Rodoviária at São Lourenço da Mata.

Buses To Salvador, US$6.50 (*leito*, 13), 12 hrs. to Fortaleza, US$6.50, and 5 hrs. to Natal US$2.50. To Goiana, every ½ hr., US$0.90. To Rio, 38 hrs., US$20 (*leito* 40); to São Paulo, 40 hrs., US$20 (*leito*, 40). To Teresina (Piauí), 19 hrs. (US$10), and further to São Luís, 26 hrs., US$11.25; to Belém, 34 hrs., US$22 (Boa Esperança bus recommended). To Paulo Afonso, US$4, 7 hrs. on completely paved road; to Brasília via Belo Horizonte 52 hrs. US$27. Good roads N to João Pessoa, Natal and Fortaleza, W to Arcoverde and Caruaru (and ultimately Belém), SW to Garanhuns and S to Maceió, US$3, 4 hrs. (Maceió can be reached either by the main road or by the coast road "via Litoral"); in all 20 buses daily. A new bus station for interstate services is under construction outside the city at São Lourenço da Mata. Old Rodoviária is at Av. Sul and Rua das Calçados.

Coastal Shipping Lóide Brasileiro ships run frequently between Brazilian coastal ports. They have several up-to-date vessels, some de luxe.

Air Services The principal international and national airlines fly to Guararapes airport, 12 km. from the city. Three direct flights a week from London to Recife via Lisbon by Varig and by TAP. Direct flights from Paris with Air France. Bus to airport, No. 52, US$0.33, 30 minutes from N.S. do Carmo. Tourist taxis at the airport are twice as expensive as ordinary red taxis picked up on the main road.

BRAZIL 321

Olinda, the old capital, founded in 1537 and named a "Patrimônio de Humandade" by Unesco in 1982, 6 km. to the north, is served by buses (from Recife any bus marked "Rio Doce", e.g. No. 902 which runs from Boa Viagem, No. 981 which has a circular route around the city and beaches, No. 33 from Av. N.S. do Carmo, US$ 0.25) and taxis (US$3). This city contains many fine old colonial churches, monasteries and convents; tourist handout gives schedule of opening times. Particularly interesting are the Prefeitura, once the palace of the viceroys; the monastery of São Bento, founded 1582, restored 1761, the site of Brazil's first law school and the first abolition of slavery, by the Benedictine monks (paintings, sculpture, furniture) and the beautifully restored Rua São Bento; the monastery of São Francisco (splendid woodcarving and paintings, superb gilded stucco, and azulejos, in Capela de Sant'Ana); the Igreja da Misericórdia and Academia Santa Gertrudes; the Cathedral, the first church to be built in the city, of simple and severe construction; São João Batista dos Militares, the only church not burnt by the Dutch; and the colonial public fountain, the Bica de São Pedro. There are some houses of the 17th century with latticed balconies, heavy doors and pink stucco walls. There is a large colony of artists (as the superb grafitti at election times testify), and excellent examples of regional art, mainly woodcarving and terra-cotta figurines, may be bought very cheaply in the Alto da Sé, the beautiful square on top of the hill by the Cathedral, or in the handicraft shops at the Mercado da Ribeira, Rua Bernardo Vieira de Melo (Vieira de Melo gave the first recorded call for independence from Portugal, in Olinda in 1710.) There is a Museum of Sacred Art in the beautiful 17th century Bishop's Palace at Alto da Sé 7. At Rua 13 de Maio, in the old jail of the Inquisition, is the Museum of Contemporary Art; also the old slave market. A programme of restoration, partly financed by the Netherlands Government, has been undertaken in order to comply with the recently-conferred title of National Monument. The Regional Museum, Rua do Amparo 128, is excellent. Apparently, churches can only be visited in the company of a guide, and even then entry is not guaranteed. The Tourist Office, helpful and friendly (Rua de São Bento 225), has a map with a recommended walking tour of the sights, opening times, as well as churches, museums and other places of interest, and houses to stay during Carnival. Taxis between Olinda and Recife put their meters on to higher rates at the new Convention Centre (between the two cities), best to start a journey either way here. Population: 360,000.

Hotels At Casa Caiada, Av. José Augusto Moreira 2200 (Tel.: 431-2955), is *Quatro Rodas* (L), with swimming pool, excellent restaurant, tennis courts, gardens, very good. *Quatorze Bis,* Av. Getúlio Vargas 1414, D, friendly, helpful, clean, run by Dutchman. *Pousada dos Quatro Cantos,* Rua Prudente de Morais 441, D-C (E without bath), in a converted mansion, very good, highly recommended, Tel.: 429-0220/1845; *Albergue da Olinda,* Rua do Sol 237, E, new, reasonable, popular with gringos; *Pousada Barlovento,* Av. José Augusto Moreira 1745, E, average; *Pousadas do Mar* and *da Praia,* E-F, Av. Beira Mar 497 and 633, Bairro Novo, Tel.: 429-2883 for either, each has 16 rooms with bath, some a/c, cheaper for stay longer than 3 days. Also on Av. Beira Mar, *Hospedaria do Turista* (No. 989), run down and noisy, D; *Marolinda* (No. 1615, 2 star, D, recommended), *Pensionato Beira Mar* (No. 1103, E) and *Hospedaria Olinda Beira Mar* (No. 1473, E). At Carnival, houses or rooms may be rented for 5-10 days (up to US$800 for a house, US$230 for a room, often without bed); try Maria da Silva, Rua Epitácio Pessoa Sobrinho, Bairro Umuaramê, Tel.: 429-0320, 2 rooms to let (US$50 a week each).

Restaurants *Mourisco,* Rua João Alfredo 7, calm and pleasant, discotheque attached; *Las Vegas,* Av. Beira Mar 1571, food good (watch the bill) but sanitary facilities not reliable; *Zé Pequeno* and *Samburá,* Av. Beira Mar (no number—both with terrace) recommended to try *caldeirada, agulhas fritas* (at former) and *pitu* (crayfish), also lobster in coconut sauce or daily fish dishes at latter, very good; *La Mer,* Av. Beira Mar 1259; *Rei da Lagosta,* Av. Beira Mar 1255; *Agulha Frita, Itapoã* and *Rainha do Mar,* Av. Beira Mar (no numbers); *Las Vegas,* Av. Beira Mar 2619; same street, *Ouriço,* local food good; *Taizan,* Chinese, same street; *Cantinho da Sé 305,* lively, good view of Recife; *Ancora Mar,* Av. Getúlio Vargas 1336; *Chin Lee,* Av. Getúlio Vargas, excellent Chinese food; *Saúde,* Av. Prudente de Morais 411, serves vegetarian meals; *Quebra Mar,* Av. Getúlio Vargas (no number). *L'Atelier,* Rua Bernardo Vieira de Melo 91, Ribeira, small converted workshop with beautiful view, run by Swiss tapestry artists, excellent international food, local dishes with reservation (necessary), open Wed.-Sun. *O Cachorrão* (lunch stand), Praia do Quartel, good cheap sandwiches. The traditional drinks, Pau do Índio (which contains 32 herbs) and Retetel, are both manufactured on the Rua do Amparo.

322 BRAZIL

Discotheques *Menphis*, Av Beira Mar 1051, Bairro Novo; *Restaurant Mourisco*.

Entertainment At Janga beach on Fri. and Sat., you can join in a *ciranda* at the bar-restaurant *Ciranda de Dona Duda*. For the less active, there is the *Casa da Seresta*, also in Janga on the beach side of the main road. On Praça do Carmo is *Cheiro do Povo*, a *forró* dance hall.

Beginning at dusk, but best after 2100, the Alto da Sé becomes the scene of a lively street fair, with arts, crafts, makeshift bars and barbeque stands, and impromptu traditional music. Street urchins try to tell you the history of Olinda (for a price). The fair becomes even more animated at Carnival.

At Olinda's carnival thousands of people dance through the narrow streets of the old city to the sound of the *frevo*, the brash energetic music which normally accompanies a lively dance performed with umbrellas. The local people decorate them with streamers and straw dolls, and form themselves into costumed groups to parade down the Rua do Amparo; Pitombeira and Elefantes are the best known of these groups.

Beaches North from Olinda, there are beautiful, usually deserted, palm-fringed beaches beyond Casa Caiada, at Rio Doce, Janga, and Pau Amarelo (though they are said to be dirtier than Boa Viagem, S of Recife). At many simple cafés you can eat *sururu* (clam stew in coconut sauce), *agulha frita* (fried needle-fish), *miúdo de galinha* (chicken giblets in gravy) and *casquinha de caranguejo* (seasoned crabmeat and *farinha de dendê* served in crabshells). Visit the fort on Pau Amarelo beach; small craft fair here on Sat. nights. A beautiful beach, reached by direct bus from Recife at weekends, US$0.75, otherwise via the town of Nossa Senhora do Ó, 2 hrs., is Porto de Galinhas. It has cool, clean water, and waves. No hotels, but *pensão* of Dona Benedita in the street where the bus stops, very basic, clean; food at *Rang Bem* in same street.

Igaraçu, 32 km. N of Recife on the road to João Pessoa, has the first church built in Brazil (SS Cosme e Damião), the Livramento church nearby, and the convent of Santo Antônio (being restored) with a small museum upstairs. The church of Sagrada Coração is said to have housed Brazil's first orphanage. Much of the town (founded in 1535) has been declared a National Monument; it is an attractive place, with a number of colonial houses and Brazil's first Masonic hall. (Pop.: 55,000.) Camping Clube do Brasil has site nearby at Engenho Monjope, an old sugar estate, now a historical monument and interesting (it is 3 km. before Igaraçu coming from Recife—bus US$0.30—; alight at the "Camping" sign and walk 5-10 mins.).

N of Igaraçu you pass through coconut plantations to Itapissuma, where there is a bridge to ***Itamaracá*** island, where, the locals say, Adam and Eve spent their holidays. It has the old Dutch Forte Orange, an interesting penal settlement with gift shops, built round the 1747 sugar estate buildings of Engenho São João, which still have much of the old machinery; charming villages and colonial churches, and fine, wide, clean beaches. Buses from Recife (Av. Martins de Barros opp. *Grand Hotel*) and Igaraçu. (*Hotel Caravela*, C with shower, good restaurant, on beach; *Hotel Pousada*, pool etc., some minutes from beach.)

Goiana, on the Recife-João Pessoa road, is one of the most important towns for ceramics. Carmelite church and monastery, founded 1673, impressive but poorly restored; San Benedito, needs restoring; Matriz do Rosário, only open for 1800 mass. The uniformity of many of the dwellings is due to their construction, for his workforce, by the owner of a now-defunct textile factory. Hospedaria Durma Bem, open weekends only; ask at Prefeitura at other times. Beach is not good for swimming. Visit the workshop of Zé do Carmo, opposite the *Buraco da Giá* restaurant (excellent seafood; owner has tame crab which will offer you a drink), R. Padre Batalha 100. Just north of Goiana is a sugar-mill, Usina Nossa Senhora das Maravilhas, which can be visited during the week; ask for Dr Jairo.

At the Pernambuco-Paraíba border, a 27 km. dirt road to the fishing village of Pitimbu— *jangadas*, lobster fishing, surf fishing, lobster-pot making. No tourist facilities but camping is possible; food from *Bar do Jangadeiro*. Bus from Goiana, US$0.50.

Another possible excursion is by a slow railway or a good road to the city of ***Garanhuns***, 200 km. SW of Recife. It claims to be the best holiday resort in the North-East, partly because of its cool climate—it stands at 890 metres, and has an average temperature of 19°C—and partly because of its mineral waters. Population: normally 74,000, swells to about 100,000 during the summer.

Hotels *Familiar*, Av. Santo Antônio 12; Tel.: 1173. *Grande Hotel Petrópolis*, Praça da Bandeira 129; Tel.: 1097. *Sanatório Hotel*, Av. Rui Barbosa 296; Tel.: 1280-1386.

BRAZIL 323

Tracunhaém, 30 km. from Recife, is a peaceful town where ceramics are made and can be bought. To get there, turn off the Limoeiro road at Carpina, on to the road to Nazaré da Mata. Even the children are adept in working in clay.

Caruaru (pop. 138,000), 130 km. W of Recife by paved road (many buses, 2 hrs., US$3), has a big Fri. to Sun. market with a separate site across the river for leather goods, pottery and articles of straw, although it is disappointingly tourist-oriented now (smaller market on other days of the week). See the hand-painted textiles of Sr Valério Cristóvão, Rua 13 de Maio 94, 1st floor; he is very helpful and his work depicts local history. The little clay figures (*figurinhas de barro*) originated by Mestre Vitalino and very typical of the North-East, are a local speciality; many local potters live at Alto da Moura 6 km. away, where a house once owned by Vitalino is open, but has no examples of his work. Bus, ½ hour, bumpy, US$0.30. Rodoviária is 4 km. from town, take bus marked "Rodoviária". Bus to Maceió, 0700, 5 hrs., US$ 2.10. Bus to Fazenda Nova 1030, 1 hr., returns for Caruaru 1330. Train to Recife, de luxe car, 1700 Sunday.

Hotels *Do Sol*, B (4-star) on hill outside town, good restaurant, pool; *Frevo*; *Grande São Vicente de Paula*, Av. Rio Branco 365, run down, not clean or friendly, swimming pool; D. *Centenário*, 7 de Setembro 84, D, clean, friendly, restaurant; also *Expedicionário*, C. Cheap *hospedarias* around central square, Praça Getúlio Vargas: *Capri* (very dirty), *Bella Vista*, *7 de Setembro*, *Continental Familiar*, F, cheap but unsafe.

Restaurants *Mãe Amara*, R. São Paulo, for regional food. *Guanabara*, clean, cool, not too expensive. *Churrascaria São Luís*, Rua dos Guararapes 15, near Praça Getúlio Vargas, good and cheap; *Churrascaria Trêvi*, said to be good.

On the way to Caruaru is Gravatá (*Hotel Fazenda*), known as the Switzerland of Pernambuco for its scenery and good hill climate.

During Easter Week each year various agencies run package tours to the little country town of **Fazenda Nova**, a few km. from Caruaru. Just outside the town is **Nova Jerusalém**, where from the Tuesday before to Easter Sunday, an annual passion play, suggested by Oberammergau's, is enacted. The site is one-third the size of the historic quarter of Jerusalem, with 12 permanent stages on which scenes of the Passion are presented; the audience moves from one to another as the story unfolds.

Hotels in Fazenda Nova *Grande*, best; *Mansão Verde*; *Fazenda Nova*.

Camping Close to site.

Arcoverde, about 126 km. W of Caruaru, is a market town in the Sertão, market every Saturday, cool at night. Hotel: *Grande Palace Majestic* (fair), F, with breakfast.

Triúnfo, about 200 km. W of Arcoverde via Serra Talhada, delightful small town in Serra de Borborema, good climate, with great variety of crops and fruits. Stay at *Hotel-Orphanage Lar St. Elizabeth*, run by German religious sisters, D, with private apartment and 3 excellent meals. Two buses daily to and from Recife (6½ hrs.); trains run from Recife to Serra Talhada, *Hotel Municipal* on main square, F with breakfast.

Fernando de Noronha is a small archipelago 345 km. off the NE coast, under military control; only one island is inhabited. Total population about 1,340, of whom many are fishermen or civilians working for military. Only hotel, *Pousada Esmeralda*, C, runs a tour boat for guests. Most food is brought from mainland but prices are reasonable. The islands were discovered 1503, and were for a time a pirate lair. In 1738 the Portuguese built the Forte dos Remédios, of which remains exist as well as a deserted town nearby, and a prison. Sea landing is difficult, but an airstrip has been built; there are flights to Recife with VASP, weekly (all flights and hotel bookings operated by Toulemonde, Av. Ipiranga 313, 4th floor, São Paulo, Tel.: 231-1329, bookable through any travel agency). The island, which is dominated by a 321-metre peak, has interesting wildlife; fishing is very good, and so is scuba-diving. Take sufficient cruzados: travellers' cheques and dollars are heavily discounted. **NB** The time is one hour later than Brazilian Standard Time.

It is a bus ride of 2 hours through sugar plantations over a good road from Recife (126 km.) to

324 BRAZIL

João Pessoa, capital of the State of Paraíba, on the Paraíba River, with 290,000 inhabitants, port for coasting traffic. Ocean-going ships load and unload at Cabedelo (6,872 population), 18 km. by road or rail. The old monasteries are worth seeing, and the 18th century church of São Francisco is a beauty (currently under restoration). Other tourist points include the Casa da Pólvora, an old gunpowder store which has become the city museum, the Cabo Branco lighthouse at Ponta do Seixas, the most easterly point of continental Brazil, with palm-lined but oil-polluted beaches (½-hr. trip); the city parks; and trips on the River Paraíba. Airport for internal services.

Hotels *Tambaú*, A, comfortable, good service (Tropical chain), recommended, and *Tropicana*, Praia de Tambaú; *Aurora*, Praça João Pessoa 51; *Globo*, Praça São Pedro Gonçalves 36; *Pedro Américo*, Praça Pedro Américo, F (no breakfast on Sun.); *Motel Veraneio* on BR-230; *Motel Fogeama* Rua das Trincheiras (with restaurant); *Pousada do Conde*, BR-101 Sul (with churrascaria); cheap hotels near the old bus station, e.g. *São Pedro*, Rua Irineu Pinto 231, clean, basic, friendly, E; *São Domingos*, R. Gabriel Malagrida, F.

Electric Current   220 volts A.C.

Restaurants *O Circo*, Av. Ruy Carnerio. *Casino da Lagoa*. Parque Solon de Lucena. *Cabo Branco Clube* has two restaurants, one in Rua Peregrino de Cavalho and the other in the Miramar district. *Olivio*, Rua Monsenhor Walfredo 714, *Paraibambu*, Parque Arruda Camara. *O Elite*, Av. João Mauricio Tambaú; two good restaurants on Tambaú beach are *Adega do Alfredo* (Portuguese) and *Wan Li* (Chinese); *A Caravela*, Quadra 3, Jardim Beiramar; *Badinaldo*, Praia do Poço (20 km. from centre) and also *Bardilucena*. Marambaia, Av. 24 de Maio, Jaguaribe; *Marisco*, Av. Cabo Branco; *Itacoatiara*, near *Hotel Tambaú*; *Pescador*, near Cabo Branco lighthouse; *O Luzeirinho*, Av. Vasco da Gama, Jaguaribe; *O Boiadeiro*, Av. Coração de Jesus; *A Gameleira*, Av. João Maurício, Tambaú.

Tourist Information   PB Tur, Av. Getúlio Vargas 301, Centro João Pessoa; also bus terminal (helpful). Crafts at Casa do Artesão, R. Maciel Pinheiro near city bus station.

Tourist Agencies   Planetur, Av. Miguel Couto 5, Loja 12, and *Hotel Tambaú*. Agência de Viagens e Turismo Arnaldo von Sohsten, Rua Gama e Melo 100.

Cables   Embratel, Rua das Trincheiras 398.

Bus   Station is 10 mins. from centre. To Recife, every 60 mins., US$1.10, 2 hrs. To Natal, every 2 hrs., US$1.80, 3 hrs.; to Fortaleza, 2000 only, 10 hrs., US$6. Warning: you will be refused permission to travel from João Pessoa Rodoviária wearing shorts, whether or not you arrived in shorts (Bermuda shorts are acceptable).

Excursions   Twenty minutes by car or taxi, or 30 by bus, to Tambaú, fishing village and seaside resort with lovely beach and excellent bathing. Halfway along is Cabo Branco club, open to visitors: good food, beautiful views; hotels (none less than US$10, fully-booked in season) and restaurants also at Tambaú. At Cabedelo are the impressive walls of the 17th-century fortress of Santa Catarina.

Campina Grande, the "Porta do Sertão", is 120 km. from João Pessoa (bus 2 hours), a rapidly growing centre for light industry and an outlet for goods from most of the North-East. There is a museum of modern art, and another of the cotton industry. Most genial climate. Population: 222,000. Near Campina Grande is Lagoa Seca, where the local craft is the making of figures in wood and sacking.

Hotels *Rique Palace Hotel* (excellent) is on the top floors of the tallest building in town: the restaurant is on the 11th floor. Other hotels: *Ouro Branco*, F; *Honor Hotel*, cheaper; *Barborema*, near old bus station, F, friendly. *Dormitório São Paulo*, also near bus station, F, cheap, clean. Many others near old bus station. **Restaurant** *Miura*, Rua Major Juvino 262, good steaks, and in old bus station.

W of Campina Grande the main highway, still paved, leads on through **Patos** (*Hotel JK*, F) to Ipaumirim (Ceará). Here a left turn leads to the twin towns of **Crato** (*Hotel Crato*, E) and **Juazeiro do Norte** (Ceará), oases of green in the dry Sertão. Mosquitoes can be a problem at night.

Juazeiro do Norte is a small pilgrimage town; it was the home of Padre Cícero, one of the unofficial saints of the North-East. A statue to him stands in the Logradouro do Horto, a park overlooking the town; either take the pilgrim trail up the hill or go by bus. Hotels: *Panorama*, D, good value; *Vieira*, corner of Rua São Pedro and Rua Santo Antônio, F, private bathroom and breakfast; and *Municipal*, F, recommended.

BRAZIL 325

Many beautiful fishing villages along the coast, often difficult to reach; one of the most popular is Baía Formosa in Rio Grande do Norte (daily bus from Natal, 2½ hrs.). No hotel; ask in town for accommodation in fishermen's houses, infinitely preferable to the overpriced accommodation at the *Miramar* bar.

Natal, 377,000 people, capital of Rio Grande do Norte, a friendly town on the estuary of the Rio Potengi, is about 180 km. to the north of João Pessoa. It is served by weekly coastal vessels and there is a railway S through the State of Paraíba to Recife and Maceió (only suburban passenger services). There is a large airport 13 km. from the city (taxi US$6.50). Natal has excellent beaches (for example Ponta Negra, with two *pousadas*, 20 mins. by bus from centre), some on the far side of the Potengi river (for example Redinha and Genipabu reached by direct bus from old Rodoviária, or by bus to Redinha then walking 8 km. along deserted beach). The main square, the Praça João Maria, oblong in shape, has a traditional cathedral at one end and a fine modern bank building at the other. The city is centred on the Av. Rio Branco. The Forte dos Reis Magos is a 16th-century fort on the coast, it is open 0800-1100, 1400-1700. The Casa da Música Popular Brasileira has dancing on Sunday afternoon, very popular. The Marine Research Institute at the Praia da Areia Preta can be visited; bus marked "Areia Preta" from Av. Rio Branco. Good local craftware Sats. at Mercado do Alecrim, along Rua Quaresma near Rua Gonçalves. At Mãe Luiza is a lighthouse with beautiful views of Natal and surrounding beaches (take city bus marked Mãe Luiza and bargain entrance fee). Some 20 km. from Natal is the rocket base of Barreira do Inferno, near Eduardo Gomes, which can be visited (first Wed. of each month only, make prior appointment).

Hotels *Reis Magos,* Av. Café Filho, Praia do Meio, facing sea, overpriced, obligatory full board in high season, food not recommended, B; *Ducal Palace* on Av. Rio Branco in centre, C, restaurant not recommended; *Marsol Natal,* Via Costeira 1567, km. 7, Parque das Dunas, 3-star, new; *Marabá,* Av. Rio Branco 371, F; *Bom Jesus,* Av. Rio Branco 374, clean, friendly, good breakfast, F with bath; *Fenícia,* Av. Rio Branco 586, F (more with a/c), with breakfast and shower, friendly; *Casa Grande,* Rua Princesa Isabel 529, F without bath, good breakfast, pleasant, excellent value; *Casa da Maçã,* near *Casa Grande,* good value, friendly; *Pousada Meu Canto,* Manoel Dantas 424, Petrópolis, F incl. good breakfast, clean, friendly, nice garden; *Pousada Esperança,* F without breakfast, basic, clean; *Samburá,* Rua Prof. Zuza 263, C, recommended; *Majestic,* Rua Dom Pedro I 20, clean, friendly, F; *Beira Mar,* Praia dos Artistas, on the beach front, F, with breakfast, small, good value, popular; *Tirol,* Av. Alexandrino de Alencar 1330 D, good but noisy; *Pousada do Sul,* BR-101, Km. 18; *Motel Tahiti,* Estrada da Ponta Negra, Km. 2; *Santo Antônio,* R. Santo Antônio 724, F; *Nordeste,* Voluntários da Pátria, F; *Natal,* Av. Rio Branco 727, F with breakfast and bath, but said to be less good than *Fenícia* nearby; *Caicó,* Av. Princesa Isabel 735, basic, noisy, F, central; *Central,* next door, basic. Cheap accommodation at *Casa de Estudantes,* near the Tourist Centre (separate facilities for men and women), "Via Tirol" bus from Rodoviária to centre passes here.

Camping on the Praia do Forte beach, near the Forte dos Reis Magos, not recommended because of rubbish and courting couples, also unsafe. Camping Clube do Brasil site at Sítio do Jiqui.

Electric Current 220 volts A.C.

Restaurants *Mirante,* Av. Getúlio Vargas; *Casa de Mãe,* near *Hotel Reis Magos,* regional food; luxury restaurants *Nemésio* and *Xique-Xique; Casa Grande,* Rua Princesa Isabel 529; same street, No. 717-C, *O Amarelinho* good; *Casa da Maçã,* Av. Marechal Deodoro, central, beer and good, cheap dishes; *Bosque dos Namorados,* Av. Alexandrino de Alencar; *América,* Av. Rodrigues Alves 950; *Assen,* Av. Prudente de Morais 760; *Marinho,* Rua do Areial 265, 15 mins. walk from centre, clean, friendly, inexpensive; *Raizes,* Av. Campos Sales, with C. Mossoró, good regional dishes; *Tirraguso,* Av. Café Filho 27, good; *Lira,* Rua Pereira Simões 71; *Rampa,* Rio Potengi, good for grilled fish but not service; *Pescada da Comadre,* Rua São João 101. Vegetarian (with shops): *Amai,* General Varela 624, and *A Microbiótica,* Princesa Isabel 524. For snacks try the stalls outside the *Hotel Reis Magos;* there are also various restaurants along the beach road nearby, where itinerant musicians play.

Cables Embratel, Av. Duque de Caxias 99. Tel.: 1230.

Tourist Information Centro de Turismo (a converted prison with handicraft shops) Rua Aderbal de Figueiredo s/n, off Rua General Cordeiro, Petrópolis; Rodoviária (helpful) and Aeroporto Augusto Severo. Natal is a very poor place to change money.

Tourist Agencies Aertur, Rua João Pessoa 219; Bradesco, Av. Rio Branco 692, 1°andar; Aparecida Turismo, Av. Rio Branco, Ed. Barão do Rio Branco.

326 BRAZIL

Airport Augusto Severo, 15 km. from centre; flights to Belém, Belo Horizonte, Fortaleza, Manaus, Rio, Salvador, São Paulo.

Bus (terminal is about 6 km. out of town, bus "Cidade de Esperança Av. 9", "Areia Preta via Petrópolis" or "Via Tirol" to centre); to Recife, 5 hrs., US$2.50; to Fortaleza, 9 hrs., US$5; to João Pessoa, US$1.80, 3 hrs.

At Pirangi, 30 mins. by bus from new Rodoviária, is the world's largest cashew-nut tree (*cajueiro*); branches springing from a single trunk cover an area of some 5,000 square metres. Opposite is a good beach. The snack bar at the tree has schedules of buses back to Natal.

The state of Rio Grande do Norte (whose people are called "Potiguares" after a former Indian tribe) has three main paved roads radiating from Natal: S to João Pessoa and Recife, SW to **Caicó** and W to **Mossoró** (pop. 118,000) and Fortaleza. Between Caicó (*Hotel Guanabara*, recommended, F) and Mossoró (*Hotel Termas*, C, with pool; *Hotel Grand*, F, *Hotel Pax* next to market; *Hotel Zenilândia*, F, highly recommended) there are earth roads leading to some interesting small towns (including **Patu** with its huge basilica on a hillside), with passable "hotels", rather primitive. Trains run twice a week S from Mossoró to Sousa, via Patu.

Fortaleza, capital of the State of Ceará, with a population of 1,308,000, is about 520 km. from Natal, NW along the coast. Fortaleza is 1,600 km. by road from Belém and 885 km. from Recife. There are fair dirt roads throughout the State, and paved roads W to São Luís and SE to Recife; the federal highway S to Salvador (BR-116) is now largely paved but much is in poor condition. A beautiful tourist centre in the old prison on the waterfront (Av. Senador Pompeu 350) includes the Museu de Arte e Cultura Popular (open daily, 0800-1200, 1400-1800, most interesting), shops and restaurants. Other museums: Museu Histórico e Antropológico do Ceará, Av. Barão de Studart 410 (open Tues.-Fri., 0730-1230, 1430-1730, Sat.-Sun., 0800-1200, 1400-1800; take bus marked "Dom Luís"); in the next street, the Museum of Ceará's Minerals, Rua José Vilar 196 (open Mon.-Fri., 0700-1300), bus to centre, "Praia do Futuro" or "Serviluz". Museu das Secas, Pedro Pereira 683, 0800-1100, 1400-1700, collections of photographs and anti-drought equipment. A festival takes place on the last Sunday in July, during which the traditional *jangada* (raft) races take place. Also visit Forte Nossa Senhora da Assunção, originally built by the Dutch. The mausoleum of President Castello Branco (1964-67), next to the state government building, may be visited. The new cathedral, in gothic style but built in concrete, stands opposite the Mercado Central; it has beautiful stained glass windows.

Beaches are fine (take bus marked "P. Futuro" from Praça Castro Carreira, or bus marked "Caça e Pesca", which passes all SE beaches on its route), and you can watch the boats coming in before sundown with their catch. The majority of high class hotels are at Praia de Iracema, which is the most popular beach, though rather polluted. Another near town is Barra do Ceará, where the Rio Ceará flows into the sea. Praia do Futuro is 8 km. to the SE, Praia de Icaraí 22 km. to the NW (it is under development); also Cumbuco where one can swim safely and there are palm trees (bus from Av. Tristão Gonçalves to Caucaia, then another bus). Iguape beach is recommended, but is at end of 40 min. bus ride— São Benedito bus from Praça Escola Normal (trips on *jangadas* for US$7). The Serra de Maranguape with thick tropical growth and distant views back to the city is 30 km. inland. The local dance, *forró*, can be experienced at the *Clube dos Vaqueiros* out on the BR-116 road South, Wed. 2230; or at *Viva Maria*, Vieira e Estados Unidos, Sat. at 2200 (check by phone first).

Local Holidays Jan. 6 (Epiphany); Ash Wed.; March 19 (São José); Christmas Eve; New Year's Eve, half-day.

On August 15, the local Umbanda *terreiros* (churches) celebrate the Festival of Iemanjá on Praia do Futuro, taking over the entire beach from noon till dusk, when offerings are cast into the surf. Well worth attending (members of the public may "pegar um passo" - enter into an inspired religious trance—at the hands of a *pai-de-santo*). Beware of pick-pockets and purse-snatchers.

Hotels *Beira Mar*, on beach, swimming pool, B; *Novotel*, Av. Pres. Kennedy 2380, A; *Othon Palace*, 5-star, beach front location; *Esplanada Praia*, Av. Presidente Kennedy 2000, A; *Colonial*,

BRAZIL 327

4-star, said to be pleasantest, with best grounds and biggest pool. *Savanah*, central, noisy, C, Trav. Pará 20 (Praça do Ferreira); *Samburá Praia*, Av. Beira Mar 4530, C, new, cheaper than most beach hotels; *Cabana Praia*, at Rua João Lourenço 441 (224-2557) and at Av. Rui Barbosa 555, both D, small, friendly; *Internacional*, Rua Barão do Rio Branco, D, with shower, try to get a room with a fan; *Excelsior*, Guilherme Rocha 172, D, with good breakfast, no bath; *Premier*, Rua Barão do Rio Branco 829, D, good. *San Campio*, Guilherme Rocha 1156, a/c, D, quiet, friendly. *Chevalier*, Av. Duque de Caxias 465, E with bath and fan, pleasant; *Blumenau*, Rua 25 de Março 705, E, noisy, a/c, TV, friendly, helpful; *Minas Gerais*, Av. Duque de Caxias, E, friendly; *Lord*, Praça José de Alencar, E and up, private bath, hot water, fan, large and clean (restaurant not recommended). *Pousada da Praia*, Av. Mons. Tabosa 1315, Iracema, 2 blocks from beach, E, fan, valuables may be left in safe of English-speaking owner, mixed reports, buses to centre stop at door; *Pousada do Mar*, behind *Esplanada*, near Av. Mons. Tabosa, F, clean and friendly; *Pousada Ideal*, Av. Kennedy beside Iracema beach, E, fan, fair; *Apart-hotel*, at beginning of Praia Iracema, 20 mins.' walk from centre, F and up, with bath, pool and bar, clean, quiet; *Nossa Pousada*, Rua Ana Bilhar 123, Meireles, E without bath, near beach, friendly, helpful; *Praia Fortaleza*, Caça do Peixe, C; *Praia Sol*, Praia do Futuro, C; *Temporada Atlantica*, Praia do Futuro, F, clean, friendly, good. Inexpensive hotels along Rua Senador Pompeu (e.g. No. 706, *Fortaleza*; No. 492, *Savoy*, F (cheaper rooms without bath), basic; No. 1012, *Primavera* (ex-*Sobral*), E, friendly, good value; *Joia*, F with bath; *Maranhense* at No. 716, F with fan, without bath, breakfast included friendly; *Universo*, at No. 1152, F with breakfast, clean, friendly, some rooms have mosquito nets); No.725, *Tio Patinho 2*, F, less good than *Tio Patinho 3*. *Druaux*, 24 de Maio 214, F, with bath, central; *Jacanã*, Rua 24 de Maio 845, F with breakfast, safe; across street are *Tio Patinho 3* and *Dormitório Belo Horizonte*, both F. *Passeio*, Rua Dr. João Moreira 221, F with bath, fan, good breakfast, good value. *Caxambu*, General Bezerril 22, a/c, D with breakfast, central (opposite Cathedral, in market area). Note that the cheaper, central area, is deserted at night. *Nossa Senhora de Fátima*, by bus terminal (6 km. from centre), F, cheap, basic. Try student houses on Av. Universitários, cheap or even free.

Camping Official site about 5 km south of city.

Electric Current 220 volts A.C.

Restaurants Several good fish restaurants at far end of Av. Presidente Kennedy, where the boats come ashore between 1300 and 1500, for example, *Trapiche*, No. 3950 (a little expensive, but excellent), and *L'Osteria*, No.4320, good, reasonably-priced, Italian. At Praia de Mucuripe are *Alfredo* and, next door, *Peixada do Meio* (better). *Kebramar*, on beach, good pizzas. Lobster meals are famous, but expensive. Another local speciality is crab: *Sandras*, Av. Perimetral, Praia do Futuro, lobster from US$7 upwards, has been specially recommended. *Rancho Gaúcho*, Praia Náutica (between *Novotel* and *Othon Palace*), good. Good restaurant in Clube Náutico. A short taxi ride from Clube Náutico is *O Ozias*, Rua Canuto de Aguiar 1449 (Tel.: 224-9067), good for seafood, but hard to find. Good Chinese: *HongKong*, Av. Pres. Kennedy 4544, Mucuripe, and *Tung Hua*, Av. Visconde de Mauá 81, Meireles. Vegetarian: *Caminho á Saúde*, lunch only, very good value, Barão do Rio Branco 1468; next door is *Alivita*, Barão do Rio Branco 1486, good, lunch only Mon.-Fri.; *Céu da Boca*, Rua Franklin Távora 114, lunch and 1800-2000 Mon.-Fri., good and inexpensive. *Caminho á Saúde* also has *lanchonete* and store at Mons. Tabosa 1326. *Hollyday Lanches*, ask at *Hotel Maranhense*. *Kury*, Rua Senador Pompeu 959, good food at reasonable prices. Another good place in centre is *Belas Artes*, Major Facundo 82, just up from Passeio Público. Cheap meals at railway station. Emcetur restaurant, in old prison, good atmosphere.

Shopping Fortaleza has an excellent selection of textiles at reasonable prices (among the cheapest in Brazil) and some handicrafts. Also good for clothes. The local specialities are lace (some hand-made) and embroidered textile goods; also hammocks, fine alto-relievo wood carvings of North-East scenes, basket ware and clay figures (*bonecas de barro*). Bargaining is O.K. at the Mercado Central in the Praça da Sé, and the Emcetur tourist market in the old prison (more expensive). Every night (1800-2300), there are stalls along Av. Pres. Kennedy, lively but more expensive than the Mercado Central, where some stallholders will accept a better price if you're paying in dollars. The Centro de Artesanato Lucila Távora is decaying. Boutiques along Monsenhor Tabosa between Senador Almino and João Cordeiro.

Theatre Teatro José de Alencar, near railway station in centre, built 1810, building contains also newer theatre built 1910.

Banks Lloyds Bank (ex-BOLSA), Rua Barão do Rio Branco 862; and national banks. Open 0900-1630. Exchange at travel agent for cash and cheques.

Cables Embratel, Rua Castro e Silva 286/290.

Tourist Information Emcetur, in ex-municipal prison, helpful, has maps. Open 0700-1800, Sun. 0700-1200. Also at Rodoviária, free town map.

Tourist Agencies Mundiatur (helpful, English spoken), Turismo Viagens, Itala Viagens Turismo and Intertur.

Rail South to Baturité (tourist train round trip Sun.), Iguatu and Crato (twice weekly), Sun. and

Fri. 1640. Fortaleza-Teresina, 738 km., 17½ hrs. (once a week Mon. 1900, 1st class US$5.60, 2nd, US$4.30).

Air Service Direct flights to Belém, Recife, Rio and other cities in Brazil. Bus from airport to Praça José de Alencar.

Bus Service New bus station 6 km. from centre, bus to Praça José de Alencar marked Aguanambi 1 or 2 (and others). The Expresso de Luxo runs daily to Recife (12 hrs., US$ 6.50), also Rio de Janeiro, 48 hrs., US$25 (*leito* 50), São Paulo, 48 hrs., US$28 (*leito* 56), Crato, Parnaíba, and many other cities. To Brasília, Expresso Ipu-Brasília, same company to Belo Horizonte, 42 hrs. Salvador, 19 hrs., US$ 12.50, several bad stretches; Natal, US$5.50, 9 hrs.; Teresina, US$5.50, 9 hrs. (at least); São Luís, US$7.75, 18 hrs.; Belém US$ 12, 5 buses a day, 24 hrs., bad road. To Piripiri, for Parque Nacional de Sete Cidades, US$3.50, 9 hrs.

Excursions Caponga Beach, to the SE, is reached by direct bus from Fortaleza (2 a day) or by taking a local bus to Cascavel, thence a taxi or bus to Caponga; accommodation at *Caponga Praia*, on the beach front, simple cheap rooms and good meals, and at *Hotel-Restaurant Sereia*, E. A ½-hour walk S along the deserted white-sand beach leads to a river outlet, offering a combination of fresh-and salt-water bathing. *Jangadas* set sail in the early morning (arrangements can be made to accompany fishermen on overnight trips); there is a fish market on the beach. 174 km. SE of Fortaleza is Aracati (bus every 2 hrs., US$1.50; bus to Natal, via Mossoró, 6 hrs., US$3.50). From this town take a VW Combi-Bus (US$0.50, ask locals for bus stop) to **Canoa Quebrada** (US$0.50, ask locals for bus stop), a fishing village on a sand dune, 10 km. from Aracati. There are no hotels, no electricity, no running water, but villagers will let you sling your hammock or put you up for about US$1.50 (Brendan is recommended, but his food is expensive, European books exchanged; Sr Miguel rents good clean houses for US$7.50 a day); bars and restaurants for food, vegetarian food in *Espácio Cultural*, cheap seafood (don't drink the water). The village is famous for its *labirinto* lacework and coloured sand sculpture, for sand-skiing on the dunes, for the sunsets, and for the beaches, though beware of jiggers (*bicho de pé*) there, best to wear shoes. Canoa Quebrada has been "discovered" and is becoming a major tourist attraction.

40 km. from Fortaleza, along the coast, is **Prainha**, a fishing village and weekend resort. It is possible to see *jangadas* coming in daily in the late afternoon. The beaches are clean and largely empty. There are several small, cheap and good restaurants, where it is possible to see displays of the *carimbó*, the main local dance of Ceará. 87 km. from Fortaleza (too far for a day trip) is **Morro Branco** (4 km. from Beberibe, bus), with spectacular beach, craggy cliffs and beautiful views. *Jangadas* leave the beach at 0500, returning at 1400-1500; hotel-restaurants, E; *Cabana do Morro, Pousada do Morro*, F, clean, but mosquitoes, fan and shower, *Novo*, F, clean, noisy at weekends and *Recanto Praia*, F, clean, good breakfast, recommended (first two have swimming pool); or you can rent fishermen's houses; meals can also be arranged at beach-front bars (try *O Jangadeiro*). Double room for rent at *Bar São Francisco*, F, or 7-room house for rent. São Benedito bus from Fortaleza, US$1; 2½ hrs., 4 a day. To get to Natal, take 0600 bus to Beberibe, then 0800 bus (only one) to Aracati, US$0.50, then on to Natal. Town is very crowded at holiday time.

Alex Bradbury and Jayne Overmeyer of Joyce, Washington State, write: 2 hours NW of Fortaleza is **Paracuru**, which is being developed as Ceará's carnival city (hotel *Cantinho do Mar*, F with bath, run by a young Paulista; restaurant *Ronco do Mar*, good fish dishes). It has some lovely deserted white sand beaches with good bathing. Some 7 hours from Fortaleza is the sleepy fishing village of Almofala, served by many buses. There is electricity, but no hotels or restaurants, although locals rent hammock space and cook meals (usually US$2 p.p., food and lodging). Bathing is better elsewhere, but the area is surrounded by dunes and is excellent for hiking along the beach to nearby lobster-fishing communities. In Almofala, the church and much of the town was covered by shifting sands and remained covered for 50 years, reappearing in the 1940s.

Nestled in the dunes near the border with the state of Piauí is the tiny fishing community of Jericuacuara (known as Serrote by locals). Described as one of Brazil's most secluded primitive beaches, it is becoming increasingly popular with adventurous travellers, despite the difficulty of getting there. There is no real road, so the trip is part of the adventure; the least difficult route is to take the bus from Fortaleza to Gijoca at 0800 (8 hrs.), then a jeep meets the bus: Jericuacuara from Gijoca costs about US$2 per person for the hour's journey. Once there, the visitor is rewarded with towering sand dunes, deserted palm-fringed beaches, cactus-covered cliffs rising from the sea, and a chance to savour life in a sleepy, primitive fishing community. Pigs, chickens and donkeys roam the streets at will; there is no electricity and no running water (take your showers at the town pump). Fortunately, ice-cold beer is available in several tiny lantern-lit bars and there is *forró* on Fri. and Sat. nights. No hotels, but many locals rent hammock space, hammocks, and cook food (about US$2 per day, room and board). Returning, the bus leaves Gijoca for Fortaleza at 0630.

The pilgrimage centre of Canindé may be visited, 3-hour bus ride from Box 21 of the Rodoviária (Viação Nova Esperança). Large modern church on hill with carved bapistry doors, many ex-votos, interesting dry-land vegetation along route. (Hotels: *Plaza*, by basilica, food OK; *Santo Antônio*). Another inland town, Baturité, can be seen, 3 hrs. from Rodoviária (Box 45) by Redenção bus, mornings only, also a tourist train round trip Sundays.

The Ubajará cave in the Ubajará National Park is regarded as one of the State's premier tourist attractions; it is 18 km. off the road to Teresina, on a good paved road, near the Piauí border. A cablecar descends the cliff to the cave entrance (guided tour plus cablecar ride, US$0.50 return); the views of the *sertão* from the upper cablecar platform are superb. Here is the state-run *Pousada Neblina*, D, near caves, with swimming pool, new (moved from town centre), with breakfast and private shower, meals not recommended. In **Ubajará** town are *Hotel Gruta*, Rua 31 de Dezembro 74, F, basic, good breakfast, helpful owner, and *Hotel Churrascaría Ubajará*, Rua Juvencio Pereira 370, F, clean and friendly, hot water, good breakfast, restaurant. Interesting Sunday morning market. Several buses a day to Fortaleza.

The road to Sobral and Teresina is paved, but in poor condition. To hitch-hike to Teresina, take a bus W to the BR-222, the Teresina road.

Sobral, the principal town in western Ceará and well-known for straw hats, has *Hotel Municipal*, F, meals available. South of Sobral is the remote town of **Crateús** (rail link, but no paved roads there), with the *Crateús Palace Hotel*, very reasonable and clean, F, with breakfast. Good restaurant, *Churrascaria Pequena Cabana*, at back of hotel. Bus service from Crateús over very bad road to Teresina, every two days.

Between the states of Maranhão and Piauí, which has a coastline of only 27 km., runs the river Parnaíba. Near its mouth is the anchorage of Luís Correia, where ships unload for final delivery by tugs and lighters at **Parnaíba**, 15 km. up river, the collecting and distributing centre for the trade of Piauí: tropical products and cattle. Population, 79,000.

Hotels *Parnaíba Palace; Rio Parnaíba. Cívico*, F with bath and a/c, good breakfast, friendly, recommended; *Rodoviária*, F and other basic hotels in the centre.

Beaches at Luís Correia, which with Parnaíba has radioactive sands (good hotel at Luís Correia, F). Some 15 km. from Parnaíba is Pedra do Sal: dark blue lagoons and palm trees.

Teresina, about 435 km. up the Parnaíba river, is the capital of the State of Piauí, reputed to be the poorest in Brazil. There are paved road and rail connections with the neighbouring state capitals. The town has high temperatures but the heat is dry. The Palácio de Karnak (the old governor's palace), just South of Praça Frei Serafim, can be visited, Mon.-Fri., 1530-1730; it contains lithographs of the Middle East in 1839 by David Roberts R.A. There is an interesting open market by the Praça Marechal Deodoro and the river is picturesque, with washing laid out to dry along its banks. The market is a good place to buy hammocks, but bargain hard. Every morning along the river bank there is the *troca-troca* where people buy, sell and swap, but it is no longer spontaneous; an under-cover complex has been built at Rua Paissandu 1276 (Praça Dom Pedro II), open daily 0800-2200. Most of the year the river is low, leaving sandbanks known as *coroas* (crowns).

Hotels *Luxor Hotel do Piauí* and *Teresina Palace*, luxury class; *Grande*, Firmino Pires 73, F, very friendly and clean; *Fortaleza*, Praça Saraiva, F, basic but expensive; *Sambaíba*, Rua Gabriel Ferreira 230-N, 2-star, D, central, good; *Victoria*, Senador T. Pacheco 1199, F, friendly, basic, clean; *São João e São Pedro*, G p.p., recommended; *Central*, N, average, with fan, 13 de Maio 85 N; *São José*, João Cabral 340, E, reasonable restaurant; many cheap hotels and *dormitórios* around Praça Saraiva. *Rex*, Rua Barbosa 36, E, central, clean, good breakfast; *Viana*, R. Senador T. Pacheco 899, F, cheap. Many cheap ones in Rua São Pedro: *Bom Clima*, No. 890, E; *São Pedro*, No. 905, F; *Globo*, No. 861, F.

Restaurants *Churrascaria Gaúcha*, ½ km. W of newer river bridge, with all the meat you can eat for US$2.50. For fish dishes, *Pesqueirinho*, near the confluence of the rivers in Poti Velho district. Many eating places for all pockets in Praça Dom Pedro II.

Exchange Only possible to change dollars cash on parallel market: try Banorte Turismo, Av. Pacheco and Barbosa.

Tourist Information Piemtur, Rua Alvaro Mendes 2003, Caixa Postal 36, information office at Rua Magalhães Filho s/n (next to 55 N -English spoken); kiosks at Rodoviária and airport.

Buses The bus trip from Fortaleza is wonderfully scenic and takes 9 hrs. (US$5.50). Another road, very bad, leads inland to Porto Franco and Imperatriz (Restaurant: *Bar Central*, OK) on the Belém-Brasília highway; daily bus takes 26-40 hrs. for the trip to Imperatriz (US$6.50), depending on the state of the road; these buses are very crowded. The road to São Luís is reckoned just about OK. Another main road, also very bad, runs SE via Picos to Petrolina, on the River São Francisco opposite the Bahian town of Juazeiro. Bus, one or two a day, 15 hrs., US$5.50. Buses from Petrolina/Juazeiro (see page 315) SE to Salvador. Bus to Belém, about 16 hrs., US$7.25. To São Luís, bus takes 7 hrs., US$2.

330 BRAZIL

Rail Trains to Fortaleza, Mon. 1050, 17½ hrs, and São Luís, 453 km., Thurs. 0400, 16½ hrs (for the stout-hearted only). Teresina-Parnaíba, mixed train, once a week but often cancelled

Excursion Some 190 km. NE of Teresina and 12 km. from Piracuruca is the beautiful 20-sq. km. Parque Nacional de *Sete Cidades* with its strange eroded rock formations, just off the Parnaíba-Teresina road. From above, the formations appear to make up seven small towns with streets and squares; from the ground it is more a medley of weird monuments. The inscriptions on some of the rocks have never been deciphered; one Austrian researcher in the 1920s suggested links with the Phoenicians. If hiking in the park, beware of rattlesnakes. Small booklet with sketch map (not really good enough for walking), US$0.20; entrance US$0.30. There are camping facilities (US$0.60) and two natural swimming pools.

At park entrance is the hotel *Fazenda Sete Cidades*, D, with private bathroom, swimming pool, restaurant and free bicycle or horse transport; also has a free pick-up to the park. In the park is a IBDF (Forestry Institute) hostel, G p.p., rooms with bath, pleasant, good restaurant, natural pool nearby. Ask the park administration (Sr Joaquim Menor) if there is room to sleep in the workers' house.

A free bus service leaves the Praça in *Piripiri* (in front of Telpisa office), 26 km. away, at 0700; return at 1700, or hitch-hike. Taxi from Piripiri, US$4.50, or from Piracuruca, US$ 10. Bus Teresina-Piripiri 0600, 0730, 0800, 0900, 3 hrs.; return buses to Teresina 1100, 1530:, 1800, 2000, US$1.10. Bus São Luis-Piripiri, 1200, 1630, 2130, 10 hrs., US$5.50. Several daily buses Piripiri-Fortaleza, 9 hrs. US$3.50. From Piripiri, a bus goes to Tianguá, and on to Ubajará (see previous page). Hotels in Piripiri: *Dos Viajantes*, G, basic and clean; *Resende*, both near bus offices and behind the church.

In the south of the state is **Oeiras**, old capital of Piauí, where the state government is restoring some of the old buildings, such as the bishop's palace and the church of Nossa Senhora da Vitória.

Warning We have been asked to tell readers that the adjoining parts of northern Goiás, southern Maranhão and southern Piauí were "bandit country" in 1986 in view of resistance to land reforms.

Maranhão state is about the size of Italy; its land is flat and low-lying, with highlands to the S. The Atlantic coastline—a mass of sandbanks and creeks and sandy islands on one of which stands São Luís—is 480 km. long. A quarter of Maranhão is covered with *babaçu* palms, and by far the most important products are *babaçu* nuts and oil. Rice often takes second place, but well behind *babaçu*. There are salt pans along the coast. The huge Boa Esperança hydroelectric plant on the Parnaíba river now floods the State with energy, and some petroleum has been discovered.

São Luís, the capital and port of Maranhão state, founded in 1612 by the French and named for St. Louis of France, is about 560 km. west of Fortaleza (1,080km. by road) and 400 km. SE of Belém (830 km. by road) in a region of heavy tropical rains and deep forest. The city stands upon São Luis island between the bays of São Marcos and São José. The urban area extends to São Francisco island, connected with São Luís by three bridges. The old part, on very hilly ground with many steep streets, is still almost pure colonial: the damp climate stimulated the use of ceramic tiles for exterior walls, and São Luís shows a greater variety of such tiles than anywhere else in Brazil, in Portuguese, French and Dutch styles. See the Governor's Palace (state rooms open Mon., Wed., Fri. 1500-1800, take passport, beautiful floors of dark wood (*jacarandá*) and light (*cerejeira*), marvellous views from terrace) and the old slave market. The best colonial churches to see—some of them rebuilt and not improved by it—are the Cathedral and the churches of Carmo, São João, Rosário, and Santana. On Largo do Desterro is the church of São José do Desterro, finished in 1863, but with some much older parts. The Forte do Ribeirão, Largo do Ribeirão, was begun in 1796. The Museu do Estado, in a fine early 19th century mansion (complete with slave quarters) at Rua do Sol 302, US$0.35, is open Tues.-Fri., 1400-1800, Sat.-Sun., and holidays, 1500-1800. The commercial quarter is still much as it was in the 17th century; best shopping area is Rua de Santana near Praça João Lisboa. Population: 182,000.

São Luís is reached by air and road and by ships of Lóide Brasileiro and Cia. Navegação Costeira.

Festivals On June 24 (São João), the "Bumba-Meu-Boi", a fantastic bull

BRAZIL 331

dance and masque with traditional words. For several days before the festival street bands parade, particularly in front of the São João and São Benedito churches. The São Benedito, at the Rosário church in August. Festival in October, with dancing, at Vila Palmeira suburb (take bus of same name).

Hotels Good accommodation is in short supply, and the situation will worsen when Texaco begins oil exploration off-shore. *Quatro Rodas*, 8 km. from centre on Calhau beach, L, excellent, with all facilities; *Vila Rica*, 5-star, Praça D. Pedro II, A, central, many amenities; *Lord*, D, Rua Joaquim Távora 258 (Tel.: 222-5544), facing Praça Benedito Leite, friendly, comfortable, clean, recommended, good breakfast; nearby is *Central*, Av. D. Pedro II 258, more expensive, D. *São Marcos*, restored colonial house, family-run, recommended. More basic, but with excellent food, *Pousada Solar do Carmo*, Praça João Lisboa 400, D-E, pleasant; *Guarani*, Rua da Palma, E with full board, F without, friendly; *Aliança*, Rua das Palmas, E, without bath, basic poor, rat-infested, but reasonable restaurant; *Colonial*, Rua dos Afogados 84, basic, F without breakfast. *Atenas*, facing municipal market, D, dirty. Many cheap hotels in Rua das Palmas, very central; *Lusitano*, Rua das Palmas, F, cheap, noisy, hot; *Klauss*, in side street off Rua Formosa, F, friendly, dirty; *Nazaré*, Rua de Nazaré (extension of Rua do Sol), F, central, fair facilities and breakfast; *Grande*, Rua das Palmas, near market, F, rats; *Globo*, F, with bath and breakfast, friendly, quite clean; *Rio de Janeiro*, Rua Afonso Pena; full board, very dirty. *Casa do Estudante*, Rua do Passeio, 2 km. from centre.

Restaurants *Solar do Riberão*, Rua Isaac Martins 141, Tel.: 222-3068, good buffet lunch and seafood, not cheap, regional cuisine, closed Sat. p.m. and Sun.; *Hibiscus* and *Tia Maria*, recommended; *Base do Germano*, Av. Wenceslau Bras in Canto da Fabril district, excellent *caldeirada de camarão* (shrimp stew), about US$4 per head. *Atenas*, Humberto de Campos 175, good stew for US$2; *Aliança*, Praça Benedito Leite, good regional food. *Egito*, friendly, good food and atmosphere. *Naturaleza*, Rua da Formosa, vegetarian, good, lunch only, Mon.-Fri. *Grande*, *Marjuce* in Rua das Palmas, good value; *Lusitano* on same street, overcharges.

Exchange Travellers' cheques only at Banco do Brasil; Agetur, Rua do Sol 33.

Cables Embratel, Avenida Dom Pedro II 190. Tel.: 2500.

Tourist Offices, Av. dos Franceses and Av. Pedro II; good information on walks in city. Recent travellers report Maratur offices of little use. Taguatur, in *Hotel Central* building, good. Town maps from agencies. Funai shop at Rua do Sol 371. Centro do Artesanato in main street of São Francisco suburb, over a bridge from the city.

Airport Internal flights only. 15 km. from centre; buses to city until midnight, US$0.20. Flight to Belém, US$46 (US$32 at night).

Railway 453 km. S to Teresina, through the Maranhense towns of Caxias and Senador Furtado, both on the left bank of the Parnaíba. Train leaves 0400, Mon., 20 hrs. US$2 1st class, US$1.90, 2nd class. A delightful if hard and dusty trip (no lights on train); frequent stops at country halts to buy coffee, cakes, fruit (but take food and water). Two trains a week on Carajás railway to Paraupebas, 17 hrs., 890 km., leave São Luís Mon., Thurs. 0930, return Tues., and Sat. 0530.

Road Bus station 5 km. from centre, "Alemanha" bus to centre. The Teresina-São Luís road is paved ("just about OK"), bus service, US$2, 7 hrs. Bus to Piripiri, US$5.50, 10 hrs.; Expresso de Luxo continues to Fortaleza, buses in poor condition. Bus to Fortaleza, US$ 7.75, 18 hrs. (road also paved). Also to Recife, US$11.25, 25 hrs.

To Belém Direct road via Santa Inês and Alto Bonito paved but in poor condition. There is a bus service 14 hrs., US$5.50, once daily (no *leito*). There are occasional coastal ships of the Costeira line, but best to go by air.

Excursions Calhau is a huge beach, 10 km. away; Ponta D'Areia is nearer to São Luís but more crowded. An hour's bus ride from São Luís is Raposa, a fishing village built on stilts; another fishing village is Ribamar, a half hour's bus ride from São Luís, from in front of the market.

Some 22 km. away by boat is **Alcântara**, the former state capital, on the mainland bay of São Marcos. Construction of the city began at the beginning of the seventeenth century and it is now a historical monument. There are many old churches (e.g. the ruined Matriz de São Matias) and colonial mansions (see the Casa, and Segunda Casa, do Imperador), the traditional pillory, the Pelourinho, in the Praça Gomes de Castro, also a small museum in the square (US$0.20) and the Forte de São Sebastião (1653) now in ruins. See also the Fonte de Mirititiva. The city has a population of 2,000. Good beaches, good walking around the coast, but mosquitoes after dark. A rocket-launching site is being built nearby. Principal festival: Festa do Divino, at Pentecost (Whitsun).

332 BRAZIL

Transport A boat service leaves São Luís daily at 0800, 80 minutes, from close to the Governor's palace, for Alcântara, returning between 1200 and 1300, but check return time, US$1.50 plus US$0.25 each to get on to a boat, sea can be rough.

Hotels *Picandinho*, Praça Gomes de Castro, E, converted 17th-century house; *Pousada do Pelourinho*, Praça Gomes de Castro, D, clean, friendly, good restaurant, communal bathroom; one can also stay cheaply in houses (e.g. Dona Maria, 3rd house on left on Rua Neto Guterres, near harbour, US$1.50 for hammock space and 2 meals), or in restaurants, *Dois Amigos*, Rua da Miritítiva, US$3 for hammock space and a meal. Try bargaining for hammock space in private houses. Children who offer themselves as guides can help arrange accommodation in private houses, friendly but no great comfort; provide your own mineral water.

Northern Brazil

Northern Brazil consists of the states of Pará, Amazonas, Rondônia and Acre, and the territories of Amapá and Roraima.

The area is drained by the Amazon, which in size, volume of water—12 times that of the Mississippi—and number of tributaries has no equal in the world. At the base of the Andes, far to the west, the Amazonian plain is 1,300 km. in width, but east of the confluences of the Madeira and Negro rivers with the Amazon, the highlands close in upon it until there is no more than 80 km. of floodplain between them. Towards the river's mouth—about 320 km. wide—the plain widens once more and extends along the coast south-eastwards into the state of Maranhão and northwards into the Guianas.

Amazonia, much of it still covered with tropical forest, is 56% of the national area, equivalent to two-thirds of Canada. Its jungle is the world's largest and densest rain forest, with more diverse plants and animals than any other jungle in the world. But it has only 8% of Brazil's population, and most of this is concentrated around Belém (in Pará), and in Manaus, 1,600 km. up the river. The scarcity of population is owing to these reasons: other areas are easier to develop; the rainfall is heavy, the humidity high and the climate hot; and the soil, as in all tropical forest, is poor.

The Government is now making strenuous efforts to develop Amazonia. Roads have been built parallel to the Amazon to the south (the Trans-amazônica), from Cuiabá (Mato Grosso) northwards to Santarém (Pará), and NE from Porto Velho through Humaitá to the river bank opposite Manaus. Agricultural settlements are being established along these roads, and great concern has been expressed at the wholesale destruction of the forest over the past 12 years. The area is changing rapidly, especially under the impetus of major energy and mining projects for bauxite and iron ore now in progress. This is reflected in the burgeoning cities. Manaus now suffers from air pollution.

Anyone interested in the Amazonian development programme and its ecological, social, economic and political effects should read Richard Bourne's masterly "Assault on the Amazon" (London, Gollancz, 1978).

Along the Transamazônica

The Transamazônica, about 5,000 km. in length, represents the greater part of a direct road connection between Brazil's furthest E and furthest W points. It skirts the southern edge of the Amazonian plain, linking the following places: Estreito (junction with the Belêm-Brasília highway, N of Araguaína, see below), Marabá (on the Tocantins river), Altamira (on the Xingu), São Luís do Tapajós, near Itaituba (on the Tapajós), Jacarèacanga, Humaitá (on the Madeira), Rio Branco, and Japim, in the far W of the State of Acre. The road was officially *opened in December* 1973; parts are paved and buses will shortly be running along the whole length; they are operating between Marabá and Humaitá and there are also services from Santarém to the Belém-Brasília road and to Cuiabá (very bad road, can take a week in the rainy season-October onwards-and it is dangerous to stay in small villages en route).

From **Marabá**, pop. 14,776 (*Hotel São Félix, Hotel Hilda Palace*, E; *Norte-Sur*, F; *Pensão Nossa Senhora do Nazaré*, F, clean, near bus terminal; *Avenida*, F) buses leave daily at 0430, 1200 and 1500 for Belém, for Santarém at 1730 and many daily for Imperatriz; buses can be caught going south at Toncantinópolis, opposite Porto Franco on the Belém-Brasília road. Also a bus can be taken to Araguaína, 12½ hrs., US$8; bus Marabá-Goiânia (change at Araguaína), US$25. Bus to Santa Inês (Maranhão), 1700, 19 hrs., US$8. On these bus trips take plenty of food and drink—local supplies are expensive. With the filling of the Tucuruí dam the town has been moved; even so it suffers from flooding. A new city of 200,000 is planned. Marabá is the jumping-off point for the gold mines of Serra Pelada; 15 days needed for authorization from Dr. Sérgio at Rua 7 de Junho next to Posto São Francisco (filling station). Banco do Brasil will not cash travellers' cheques; parallel market in larger stores.

From Marabá, or from Belém, one can reach the Carajás iron mine (the largest mineral development in Brazil) by road—quite an adventure. Between Marabá and Belém, on the Tocantins river, is the Tucuruí hydroelectric scheme (which is causing much ecological damage), reached either by bus or by day and night riverboat from Belém. **Hotel Transamérica** best in Tucuruí.

Araguaína is a small settlement of some 3,000 on the Brasília-Belém road (Brasília, 1102 km.; Belém 842 km.; Imperatriz, 174 km.). Several hotels near Rodoviária including *Esplanada*, F p.p., may have to share a room, friendly, clean, fan, no breakfast, good; *Líder*, *São Jorge*, *do Norte* and *Goiás* (all F). Bus leaves Araguaína for Marabá 0700 and 1400. Ordinary bus to Goiânia takes 24 hours: try to get an express. If travelling to Belém or Brasília by bus, reservations are not usually accepted: be at the terminal 2 hrs. before scheduled departure as buses tend to leave early; as soon as bus pulls in, follow the driver to the ticket counter and ask if there are seats. Buses also to Santarém.

Rurópolis lies at the junction of the Transamazônica and the Santarém highway. **Hotel** run by Incra.

In **Humaitá** there are several basic hotels on the eastern edge of town; *Hotel Humaitá*, F, basic but friendly; *Aquarius Palace*, E with breakfast, is also the Expresos Humaitá bus stop; a similar hotel is the Andorinha bus stop. The Soltur bus station is in the centre.

There is very little traffic on the Transamazônica between Humaitá and Itaituba; local drivers may give lifts. The road is very good for about 350 km. from Humaitá, then it deteriorates badly. It is hilly, narrow, and the jungle usually grows over the side of the road. Expresos Humaitá depart at 1500 daily. It takes 24 hours to Jacarèacanga (which is 8 km. off the highway). One must stay overnight and catch the Transbrasiliana bus to Itaituba (24 hours, schedule erratic; the bus is replaced occasionally by a truck). There are two insanitary and expensive hotels in Jacarèacanga (try the gas station on the Transamazônica near the Jacarèacanga turn-off, they may have hammock space). Bus fare Humaitá-Jacarèacanga, US$15.60; Jacarèacanga-Itaituba, US$8; travel time depends on the weather conditions, the condition of the bus, and whether the driver decides to stop somewhere for a sleep at night.

At Itaituba, the Transbrasiliana company has a bus station on the river Tapajós, near the ferry docks. Bus fare Itaituba-Marabá, US$17. At Marabá, a new bridge is being built over the river Itacaiunas. The ferry service no longer runs at night. Buses arriving at night from Santarém or Itaituba stop near the river, opposite the town; passengers must take a ferry across (US$0.10), and then walk or take a taxi to the Transbrasiliana bus station in the old market area.

Up the Amazon River

The Amazon system is 6,577 km., long, of which 3,165 km. are in Brazilian territory. Ships of up to 4/5,000 tons regularly negotiate the Amazon for a distance of about 3,200 km. up to Iquitos, Peru. Distances upstream from the river mouth to Manaus in nautical miles are:

Belém	80	Santarém	538
Narrows (entrance)	225	Óbidos	605
Narrows (exit)	330	Parintins	694
Garupa	334	Itacoatiara	824
Prainha	452	Manaus	930

What to wear Remember that some Enasa boats' restaurants do not permit shorts. At night put on a sweater or coat, for it gets quite cold. From April to October, when the river is high, the mosquitoes at night can be repelled by Super Repelex spray or K13; protective clothing is advisable. Leather sandals fall apart in the wet, rubber ones are better, but proper shoes or boots are best for going ashore: there are many foot-attacking parasites in the jungle. A hammock is essential on all but the most expensive boats; often too hot to lie down in cabin during day.

Health There is a danger of malaria in Amazonia. On the smaller boats sanitary standards are low and one is very likely to contract intestinal infections; take plenty of tablets (Colestase are the locally available brand), toilet paper, soap, water sterilization tablets (none available in Belém) and some plain biscuits. A good idea also to take oranges, mineral water, tea bags, seasonings, sauces and jam. A yellow-fever inoculation is strongly advised, too.

334 BRAZIL

N.B. If going in the smaller boats, be prepared for mechanical breakdowns that prolong the journey. Also remember that coming downstream from Manaus boats often keep to the middle of the river, leaving little to see but water. If you have the choice, remember that the journey upstream in small boats often keeps close to the banks; the patient watcher can see plenty of wildlife.

Exchange facilities are sparse in Amazonia, outside Belém and Manaus. Bargaining with the masters of small boats may be greatly helped if one has some low-value dollar bills.

Food in Amazonia Inevitably fish dishes are very common, including many fish with Indian names, e.g. *pirarucu*, *tucunaré*, and *tambaqui*, which are worth trying. Also shrimp and crab dishes (more expensive). Specialities of Pará include duck, often served in a yellow soup made from the juice of the root of the manioc with a green vegetable (*jambo*); this dish is the famous *pato no tucupi*, highly recommended. Also *tacaca* (shrimps served in *tucupi*), *vatapá* (shrimps served in a thick sauce, highly filling, simpler than the variety found in Salvador), *maniçoba* (a green vegetable mixed with cheaper cuts of meat). Avoid food from street vendors.

Belém (or Pará), founded in 1616, 145 km. from the open sea and slightly S of the equator, is the great port of the Amazon. It is hot (mean temperature, 26°C), but frequent showers freshen the streets. There are some good squares and fine buildings. The largest square is the Praça da República; the main business and shopping area is along the wide Avenida Presidente Vargas leading to the river and the narrow streets which parallel it. The Teatro da Paz is one of the largest theatres in the country and is of baroque splendour, worth visiting. Population 934,330.

Places to visit are the Bosque (0900-1200, 1500-1630), a public garden (which is really a preserved area of original flora, renovated to include a good collection of archaeological items of Amazonian Indians) with a small animal collection (admission free, yellow bus marked "Souza" or "Cidade Nova" - any number—30 mins. from "Ver-o-Peso" market), and the Goeldi Museum. Both can be reached by bus from the Cathedral. The Goeldi Museum, Av. Magalhães Barata, takes up a city block and consists of the Museum proper (with a fine collection of Marajó Indian pottery), a zoological garden (including anacondas, gold hares and manatees), and botanical exhibits; open Tues. to Sun, 0900-1730 (Sat. afternoon, garden and zoo only). Entry US$0.15 (partly under renovation in 1985).

In the Belém market, known as "Ver-o-Peso" (see the weight) after the large scales on which the fish landed nearby were weighed, there is now little for tourists to buy, apart from the charms on sale for the local African-derived religion, *umbanda*. In the old town, too, is the fort, which you can enter on request; the site also contains the *Círculo Militar* restaurant. Visit the Cathedral (1748) with several remarkable paintings, and directly opposite the 18th-century Santo Aleixandre church (now Museum of Religious Art) noted for its wood carving. The 17th-century Mercês church, near the market, is the oldest church in Belém; it formed part of an architectural group known as the Mercedário, the rest of which was almost entirely destroyed by fire in 1978. The Basilica of Nossa Senhora de Nazaré (1909), built from rubber wealth, is an absolute must for its beautiful marble work and stained glass windows.

Local Holidays Maundy Thurs., half-day; June 9, Corpus Christi; August 15, accession of Pará to independent Brazil; Our Lady of Nazaré, second Sun. and fourth Mon. in October, known as Cirio. Oct. 30, half-day; Nov. 2, All Souls Day; December 8, Immaculate Conception; Christmas Eve, half-day.

Cirio, the Festival of Candles in October, is a remarkable festival based on the legend of the Virgin of Nazaré, whose image is kept in her Basilica; it apparently was found on that site around 1700. To celebrate, on the second Sun. in October, a procession carries a copy of the Virgin's image from the cathedral to the Basilica. On the Mon., two weeks later, a further procession takes place, to return the image to its usual resting-place.

Hotels Expensive: *Hilton*, Av. Pres. Vargas 882, A-L, swimming pool, sauna, restaurants; *Selton*, 2 km. from airport, B, swimming pool; *Novotel*, Av. Bernardo Sayão 4808, B-A, unprepossessing neighbourhood, far from centre; *Excelsior Grão Pará*, Av. Presidente Vargas 718, C, fair breakfast, noisy a/c and internal rooms, reports vary, but good food; *Equatorial Palace*, Av. Braz de Aguiar 612, B, *Vitória Régia* restaurant, bars, swimming pool, sauna, Lusotur travel agency. Less expensive: *Sagres*, Av. Gov. José Malcher 2927, opp. bus station, air conditioning, good meals, swimming pool, recommended, C; *Regente*, Av. Gov. José Malcher 485, C; *Vanja*, Travessa Benjamin Constant 1164, C, one very adverse report; *Executivo*, Av. Alcindo Cacela 866,

BRAZIL 335

20 mins. walk or US$1 taxi ride from centre, D, good. Medium priced: *Solar Belém*, Marquês de Pombal 48, E, overlooking market and port, restaurant set meal US$1.50, clean and friendly; *Diplomata*, Trav. 1 de Queluz 29, near bus station, E. *Terminal*, Av. Gov. José Malcher 2953, near bus station, hot, F, not good value; also *Triângulo*, Av. Ceará 81, F, directly behind bus station; also *Panorama*, F, including breakfast, not very good; *Central*, Av. Presidente Vargas 290, F, without bath, no restaurant, noisy, but friendly, clean, comfortable, good breakfast; *Vidonho*, same ownership, good, E-C with abundant breakfast, Rua O. de Almeida, 476, Tel.: 225-1444, in a side street opp. *Avenida*, Av. Presidente Vargas 404, F; central, recommended but some rooms better than others, ask to view several, good breakfast; *Transbrasil*, Av. Cipriano Santos 243, behind bus station, D with a/c; *São Geraldo*, R. Padre Prudêncio 54, F with breakfast, also rooms with a/c, E. Cheaper: *Lis*, Rua João Diogo 504 (old city), 1 star, F, with bath, a/c, fridge, has good cheap restaurant; *Hilea*, Av. Gov. José Malcher 312; *Vitória Régia*, Frutuoso Guimarães 260, F, with breakfast, good, clean, friendly, convenient for Enasa boats, owner changes money and cheques at good rates; *Transamazônico*, Travessa Indústria 17, waterfront by docks, F, with breakfast, clean, will store luggage for short periods; *Manaus*, Rua 13 de Maio, F; *Sete Sete*, Rua 1° de Março 77, behind Praça da República, F, good; *King*, R. 28 de Setembro 269, F, not too clean. Cheap, very shabby: *Palácio das Musas*, Frutuoso Guimarães 275, G p.p., without breakfast, very basic; *Fortaleza*, Frutuoso Guimarães 276, G, with fan, breakfast extra, good and cheap restaurant; *Belém Palace*, Rua Gaspar Viana, F. Many cheap hotels close to waterfront, in old part of town, for example dormitory bed in *Pensão Canto do Rio* opposite the dock, a "classic and unspoilt waterfront dive", F; try bargaining for cheaper rate if you have hammock; next door is *Grajaú*, F with or without breakfast, reasonable.

Camping at Benfica, 16 km. from Belém, US$2.

Restaurants All the major hotels have good but expensive restaurants. *Hotel Internacional*, Av. Lobo nr. Presidente Vargas, *prato do dia* US$2, recommended. *Círculo Militar* recommended for its food and situation in the grounds of the fort with view over river (good choice and good value). *Churrascaria Sanambaia*, Quai Kennedy. Also recommended; *Augustus*, Av. Almirante Barroso; *Lá em Casa*, Av. Gov. José Malcher 982; *Nazaré*, good but rather expensive local dishes; *Regatão*, Av. Senador Lemos 3273; *Internacional*, near *Hotel Excelsior Grão Pará*; *Marisqueira do Luiz*, Av. Senador Lemos 1063; *Capitol*, Av. Presidente Vargas near docks; *Casa Portuguesa*, Rua Manoel Barata 897, good, inexpensive; *Miako*, Rua Caetano Rufino 82 (menu includes very good medium-priced oriental food); *Hakata*, 13 de Maio and Pres. Vargas, excellent, cheap Japanese food; *Avenida*, Praça Justo Chermont 1294 (opp. Basilica), very friendly; *La Romana*, Av. Gentil Bittencourt 574 and *Pizzaria Napolitano*, Praça Justo Chermont 12 (in particular pizzas and Italian dishes); *Pato de Ouro*, Rua Diogo Môia 633 (next to *Sorveteria Santa Martha* ice-cream parlour) and *Renasci*, Travessa José Pio 322 (in particular for regional dishes); *Paraense*, US$2, recommended; *Churrascarias Linda Cap* and *Tucuravi*, both on the highway leading out of Belém.

Specially recommended for tourists are also some very good snack-bars (mostly outdoors in Belém) where you can buy anything up to a full meal, much cheaper than restaurants: *Onda*, Av. Gentil Bittencourt 663; *Pappus*, Av. Conselheiro Furtado 637 (nr. Padre Eutíquio); *Garrafão*, Av. Serzedelo Correa (below Ed. Manuel Pinto); *Café do Parque*, Praça da República, popular with young people, a good meeting place; *Bug*, near airport; *Bos's*, Av. Gentil Bittencourt/Travessa Quintino Bocaiúva (snacks, standing only); *Milano*, Av. Presidente Vargas, next to *Hotel Grão Pará* (especially for espresso, desserts, cakes; pizzas not recommended); also a good bar next to *Hotel Central* on same street. *Só Delicias*, Nazaré 251, recommended for pastries, sweets, soft drinks. *Casa dos Sucos*, Av. Presidente Vargas, Praça da República, serves 41 types of juice (including Amazonian fruits) and delicious chocolate cake (disappointing vegetarian restaurant upstairs). *Bar do Parque*, next to Municipal theatre, excellent place for meeting local people. There are also many street vendors, who, although they should be viewed with care, often sell delicious local food.

Curio Shops in Av. Presidente Vargas; also try the Indian handicrafts shop at Praça Kennedy, set in a garden with Amazonian plants and animals. Funai (Indian agency) shop, Av. Presidente Vargas 762, loja 2, near Casa dos Sucos, is highly recommended.

Camera Repairs Henri van Ligten, Conjunto Parklandia, Quadra B, Casa 9, Tel.: 231-5839 (take Nova Marambaia-Telégrafo bus from Praça Dom Pedro, ½ hr.). Recommended: a Dutchman who speaks English and German.

Local Buses Buses marked Arsenal or Canudos go from the Rodoviária to the centre and to the docks.

Banks Lloyds Bank (ex-BOLSA), Rua Quinze de Novembro 275, and Brazilian banks (open 0900-1630, but foreign exchange only until 1300). Travel agent at Rua Sen. Manoel Barata 704, or Dias Lopes e Cia, 5th floor Rua Santo Antônio 316, also photo shop, 15 de Agosto on Av. Presidente Vargas, Orion Perfume Factory, Trav. Frutuoso Guimarães, Sr. Milo, Travessa Campos Sales 28, and Casa Santo Antônio on Av. Presidente Vargas 698. *Central* and *Victória Régia* Hotels; *O Canto do Uirapuru*, Av. Presidente Vargas 594, souvenir shop, also exchange.

336 BRAZIL

Electric Current 110 A.C., 60 cycles.

Post Office Av. Presidente Vargas.

Cables Embratel, Travessa Quintino Bocaiúva 1186 (Tel.: 22-9099) or at the Post Office, Av. Presidente Vargas. For phone calls: Telepará, Av. Presidente Vargas.

Consuls British, Av. Presidente Vargas 119. Caixa Postal 98. Tel.: 23-5319. U.S. Av. Oswaldo Cruz 165. Tel.: 23-0800. Colombian and Venezuelan: both at Trav. Benjamín Constant 1303.

Health Clinic Clínica de Medicina Preventativa, Av. Bras de Aguiar 410 (Tel.: 222-1434), will give injections, English spoken, open 0730-1200, 1430-1900 (Sat. 0800-1100).

Tourist Office Municipal office, Av. Nazaré 231, near Edifício Manuel Pinto, friendly but not very helpful, good free map. Paratur, Praça Kennedy on the waterfront, inside the handicraft shop; has a good map of Belém in many languages. Office at Rodoviária, free, but useless map of city. Town guidebook, US$2.75. Street map from news stands US$ 0.60.

Roads A good asphalted road leads E out of the city to the coast town of Salinópolis, some 228 km. away, at the extreme end of the eastern part of the Amazon Delta. Various paved roads branch off: 118 km. out of Belém one turns right on to the paved highway S to Brasília (2,100 km.). Straight on, the road leads to Bragança, which was the centre of an early, unsuccessful, attempt in the 1900s to transfer population to Amazonia. At Capanema (*Hotel São Luís*, F, good), on the road to Bragança, the road for São Luís, Teresina, Fortaleza and Recife branches right.

Bus Services The Rodoviária is located at Av. Presidente Vargas, 5 km. from centre, take Aeroclube, No. 20 bus. It has a good snack bar and showers (US$0.10). There are four buses a day to Brasília (US$22), modern and comfortable, and also a *leito* bus— US$45, 36 hours. Belém-Imperatriz bus takes 10-12 hrs. (US$7). There are also direct buses from Belém to Marabá (16 hrs.), on the Transamazônica, via Porto Franco and Toncantinópolis, and then change to Santarém (Marabá-Santarém 34 hrs.). One direct bus Belém-Santarém once a week (US$36, more expensive than by boat and can take longer). To Salvador and also to Recife, 1 daily, to each, 2000, US$22, 34 hrs. The trip to Recife can be broken at Teresina, Picos (*Picos Hotel*, F, with meals) and Ouricuri (*Hotel Independência*, F, with bath). To São Luís, once a day, 14 hrs., US$5.50 (*leito*, US$10, Trans Brasília); to Fortaleza, 1,595 km. 24 hrs., US$12; to Rio, US$35; to Belo Horizonte, US$35.

Hitch-hiking Going south, take bus to Capanema, 3½ hrs., US$2, walk ½ km. from Rodoviária to BR-316 where trucks stop at the gas station.

Shipping Services Regular coastal services to Southern Brazil. Agency for international services, Agências Mundiais Ltda, Av. Pres. Vargas 121, Tel.: 224 4078.

Infrequent services to Manaus and Porto Velho by the Government's Enasa boats (office: Av. Presidente Vargas 41, Tel.: 223-3011 or 223-3572, Telex 2064, or Rua Uruguaiana 39, sala 1402, Tel.: 222-9149 or 224-7267, Rio de Janeiro) whose schedules are published the 20th for the next month: they leave for Manaus at 2200 on the same day of the week in each month, normally Wed., but the day may change monthly, taking 5 days; they take cars and motorcycles (Sanave are reportedly cheaper than Enasa). You must show your passport when buying an Enasa ticket, at boat dock on Av. Castillo França. Fare to Manaus, US$40, hammock space only, terribly crowded (least crowded are the couples' and single women's sections). Sanitary conditions are appalling, but the 3 meals a day now not too bad (take your own cutlery to speed up the queuing). A hammock and rope are essential (easily bought for between US$5 and US$25, buy cotton ones); also useful is a light blanket. Arrive early (some say 8 hrs.) to ensure a good hammock space, chain belongings to a post in the hammock area (thieves abound) and don't drink from the drinking fountains on board: the small canteen sells mineral water, beer and soft drinks. For an inducement of say US$100, the captain may let you have a cabin. Enasa has a 12-day tourist service Belém-Santarém-Manaus-Santarém-Belém in new boats (*Pará, Amazonas*), leaving Belém every other Wed., Manaus every other Thurs., at 2000 with air-conditioned cabins, restaurant, swimming pool, bar, night club, with fares from US$370 per person in a 4-berth cabin, to US$430 internal double, US$520 external double cabin, US$1,300 special cabin. Also bookable through Soletur, International Service Division, Rua Visconde de Pirajá 500, Suite 1708, 22410 Rio de Janeiro (Tel.: 239-7145, Telex 212 3858, 213 0237 SOLE BR); can include at extra cost a night in Manaus or Belém, or a week in Rio. Belém-Manaus (about US$70 less to Santarém in 4-berth and double cabins); foreigners allowed only to travel 1st class. Service to Santarém by *Franz Rossy*, every second Thursday at 1800, 3 days, US$23 hammock space, US$26 cabin, from Armazem 09, Portão 15, Cais do Porto.

Non-Enasa fare to Manaus US$50 in covered hammock space (cabins US$100)—take food and water; look afer your equipment, especially at night and in port. Ask guards at the dock gate for permission to look for a boat. Two companies that are recommended are Rodomar for destinations close to Belém (office near cathedral) and Fe em Deus, Av. Bernardo Sayão 3590 (take bus to Cremação), recommended to Santarém (US$20 in *Fe em Deus IV*, 1st class hammock space, basic, crowded, take fruit, mineral water, books, 3 days, 4 nights). Also recommended to Santarém, *Terra Santa I*, also from Doca 15, Av. Bernardo Sayão, US$22.25 hammock space,

US$26.70 cabin space, 3 meals included. Take a bus 514 from the city centre to the intersection 10 mins. beyond the Cata textile factory, and ask directions from there to the *posto comercial* area.

There is an Enasa ferry to Macapá; check at docks; the Sanave vessel, *Idalino Oliveira*, sails approximately once a month, departs Belém 0300 Weds., arrives Macapá 1000 Thurs., crowded, US$16 1st class, US$8 2nd, free chilled drinking water, good food and bar on board, passengers may embark at 2000 on night prior to sailing (tickets from Av. Castilhos 234), boat goes through the channels of Marajó Island; Representação do Governo do Território de Macapá ferry Belém-Macapá every 4 days or so, tickets from Av. Castillo França 234 (opp. Ver-o-peso), US$8 for hammock space, US$12 for cabin, 28 hrs. Other non-regular sailings, *Príncipe do Mar* and *Príncipe do Mar II*, US$16 upper deck, US$14 lower, with food, 2 days. Also *Barco Souza*, every Friday, return Tuesday, US$12 for hammock space, US$13.50 for cabin (only 2), wait on board while cargo is loaded at Porto Santana; *São Francisco de Paula*, US$15, friendly, clean, food not too good, best to take some of your own. Weekly Enasa boat to Tucuruí on the Tocantins River at 1730 (with 6 stops).

Joanna Burrill and Henry Perks (of Hornsea, E. Yorkshire) have sent us the following information on river travel: Most boats have two decks and are divided into three classes: 1st class cabins (upper deck), which can be very hot and cramped; 1st class hammock space on upper deck, seems best as this is pleasanter during daytime; 2nd class hammock space on the lower deck, can be cramped because of cargo, and hot and noisy from the engine. Food is ample but monotonous. Fresh fruit is a welcome addition. Fresh coffee available; most boats have a bar of sorts. Plates and cutlery may not be provided. A strong fishing line and variety of hooks can be an asset to supplementing one's diet; with some meat for bait, *piranhas* are the easiest fish to catch. Negotiate with the cook over cooking your fish. "The sight of you fishing will bring a small crowd of new friends, assistants, and lots of advice—some of it useful."

Light cotton hammocks seem to be the best solution. Buy a wide one which you can lie across: lying straight along it leaves you hump-backed. Mosquito nets are not required when in motion as boats travel away from the banks and too fast for mosquitoes to settle, though repellant is a boon for night stops. Most boats begin their journeys in the evening, but stops en route come at any hour. If making en route connections it is easy to miss a boat in the night. On arrival at the final destination it is usually possible to negotiate with the captain to stay an extra night on the boat (perhaps more) for no extra charge. This can be useful if arriving in a town late.

Warning Boat passengers arriving from Manaus (a free trade zone) may experience long delays at customs. Note that dress in Amazonia is often more conservative than further south.

Air Services Regular flights N to Miami and New York and S to Brazilian cities, Montevideo and Buenos Aires; to Brasília and to Santarém and Manaus, the latter with connection for Leticia, Colombia, with Saturday flight giving connection for Bogotá. Nightly flight to Manaus costs only US$58; to Fortaleza US$64. To Iquitos; weekly to Paramaribo and Cayenne; Barbados (with stopovers). Bus "Perpétuo Socorro-Telégrafo" or "Icoaraci", every 15 mins. from Prefeitura to airport, US$0.10. Taxi to airport, US$6. Airport has a hotel booking service but operated by, and exclusive to, 5 of the more expensive hotels, discounts offered. There are now no flights between Belém and Trinidad and Guyana. To Oiapoque on French Guyane frontier by Taba (Rua O. de Almeida 408, Tel.: 223-8811). Travellers entering Brazil from Guyane may find it necessary to obtain a 60-day visa (takes two days) before airlines will confirm their tickets. Check, as there is only one flight a week (Sunday). Daily service (except Sun.) to Macapá at 0400 (40 mins.).

Tour Volker Filss, a German traveller, has sent us the following suggestion for a one-day sightseeing tour, subsequently revised by Philip A. Smith, recently of BOLSA, Belém: "Go to the Ver-o-Peso market early in the morning when the boats are coming in and watch the unloading of the fish and the vendors in the market. Take a bus marked Souza at the market and ask the driver to drop you at the Bosque (open 0800-1100 and 1400-1700). Take the same bus back and get off at the Museu Paraense (Goeldi) in Av. Magalhães Barata (formerly Independência). After visiting museum and gardens, walk down avenue to the Basilica (Nossa Senhora de Nazaré) and then on to the Praça da República (on the way the Tourist Office will be passed on the right). From the Edifício Manuel Pinto de Silva at this end of the Praça, you walk to the Teatro da Paz and along Av. Presidente Vargas. Before reaching the docks, turn left along, say, Av. Santo Antônio and Av. João Alfredo, through the shopping and commercial area (interesting narrow streets and open-fronted shops) to reach the harbour with its fishing boats and to the left the Prefeitura Municipal and Palácio do Governo. Beyond stand the Cathedral and the old fort (entry US$0.10) and *Círculo Militar* restaurant. Depending on your progress, lunch can be taken by the Basilica (e.g. *Avenida* restaurant directly opposite), or on the terrace of Edifício Manuel Pinto, or, say, at *Hotel Central* on Av. Presidente Vargas".

Excursions Travel agents offer short and longer visits to the rivers and jungle, e.g. Ciatur, or Turismo Bradesco, both Av. Presidente Vargas, 3½ hrs., US$13, or Marajó tour, 32 hrs., US$200. The nearest beach is at **Outeiro** (35 km.) on an island near Icoaraci, about an hour by bus and ferry (the bus may be caught near the Maloca, an Indian-style hut near the docks which serves as a night-club). Further north is the island of **Mosqueiro** (86 km.) now accessible by toll bridge (US$0.20) and an excellent highway, with many beautiful sandy beaches and jungle inland.

Many hotels and weekend villas at the villages of Mosqueiro and Vila; recommended *Hotel Farol*, on beach, D, traditional building; and *Hotel Chapéu Virado*, E, basic, poor value, friendly but haphazard service. Restaurants at Mosqueiro: *Ilha Bela*, Av. 16 de Novembro 460; *Sorveteria Delícia*, Av. 16 de Novembro, good local fruit ice creams, owner buys dollars. At Praia do Farol (Mosqueiro) is *Bar-restaurant O'Stop* which has a shower and will let you leave luggage and hang your hammock. The traffic is heavy in July and at weekends, and hotels are full. Food at hotels US$3.50, but same quality costs US$2 at stalls along beach. Camping is easy. Buses Belém-Mosqueiro every hour from Rodoviária, US$0.75, 80 minutes.

Marajó Island is worth visiting for a weekend's buffalo hunting (use a camera, not a gun, or the buffalo won't last long). Enasa boats to Marajó leave every 5-7 days at 2000 or 1400. Trips to the island are arranged by the *Grão Pará Hotel* and travel agents. Alternatively, a light aircraft may be hired to see Marajó from the air (with pilot, about US$80 for 2 hours) e.g. from Kovacs, Av. Dr. Freitas, opposite the airfield of the Aero Clube do Pará. (Cheap weekend flights are easier to find than boats.) The island was the site of the precolumbian Marajoaras culture.

At Soure, on the island, are *Pousada Marajoara*, and *Pousada Parque Floresta*, nearby, E, friendly and clean, good meals. There are fine beaches, Pesqueira and Araruna.

Salinópolis (228 km.) about 4 hrs. by bus (US$3) on excellent highway, also worth a visit. Seaside resort with many small places where you can eat and drink at night by the waterfront, and fine sandy beach nearby (buses and cars actually drive on to the beach). Best during holiday month of July. Atalaya, opposite Salinópolis, is nice, reached by taxi (US$5) or with a fisherman.

Hotels *Solar*, Av. Beira Mar s/n, D with bath, best in town, good restaurant; *Salinas*, on beach, E; *Jeanne d'Arc*, F with breakfast.

There are ferries (check departures at Porto São Benedito, Av. Bernardo Sayão 868, Tel.: 222-6025, see page 337) two 45-minute flights daily (Cruzeiro do Sul, Varig, at 2200 and 0500), US$20.50, from Belém to **Macapá**, a town on the northern channel of the Amazon Delta, which used to be decrepit but is now improving, particularly along the riverfront. (The ferries often go to Porto Santana, 30 km. from Macapá, to which there are frequent buses, US$ 0.30, and shared taxis US$2 pp., boats readily hired to visit river communities). Macapá is the capital of the Territory of Amapá (agriculture, gold, manganese, coal, timber), one-quarter the size of France but with only 180,000 inhabitants, of whom 95,000 live in Macapá. There are interesting old Portuguese fortifications (the Fortaleza de São José do Macapá, built 1764), with each brick brought from Portugal as ballast. Interesting market behind the Fortaleza. A handicraft complex has been built next to the *Novotel*. The riverfront has been pleasantly developed. There is a monument marking the equator halfway between Porto Santana and Macapá, known as Marco Zero, with nightclub underneath and more nearby. Gold is sought by washing sand in the river, using a gallon kerosene can: if you find less than 5 grams of gold in a canful of sand you move on.

The popular local beach is at Fazendinha (take bus of same name), extremely lively on Sundays.

Hotels *Novotel* (formerly *Macapá*), French-owned, on waterfront, small, 4-star, A/B, all rooms a/c, swimming pool, service and cleanliness strongly criticized as being far below acceptable standard; *Excelso*, F, has been recommended. *Sylvestre*, F, acceptable, fan, shower, breakfast; *Santo Antônio*, near main square, F, very clean, fan, shower, good breakfast; *São Luís*, as you enter town from Pto. Santana, E. The following are 10-mins.' walk from port and from Praça São José (where bus from Porto Santana stops): *Amapaense Palace*, Rua Tiradentes, F and up, 2 star, clean (*lanchonete* in same building, poor); *Palace*, Rua Cora de Carvalho 144, F with breakfast; *Silvestre*, Rua São José 2390, F with fan; *Mercúrio*, Rua Cândido Mendes, 1200 block, F.

Restaurants *Lá em Casa*, opp. *Amapaense Palace*, quite good; *Lennon*, also good; *Lanchonete Zero Grau*, in city centre, recommended for food. Excellent ice cream sold in Macapá.

Exchange Banco do Brasil, near *Novotel*, or in *Novotel* itself.

Rubber was almost the only other product of the Territory until the 1950s, when manganese was discovered 150 km. NW of Macapá. A standard-gauge railway, 196 km. long, the only one in Brazil, has been built from the mining camp to Porto Santana, from which there is an excellent road. Malaria is rampant in Amapá; the illiteracy rate is 85%; smuggling goes on in a big way. But the mining area—Icomiland; pop. 4,000—is a startling exception: swimming pools, football fields, bowling alleys, supermarkets, dance halls, movies, a healthy oasis in the wilderness.

Sr João Batista de Oliveira Costa in Macapá is a good pilot who flies around the delta, particularly to the mouth of the Araquari river to see the *pororoca*, a tidal wave that travels upriver in the high tides of spring and autumn.

An unpaved road has been built from Macapá northward to the small town of **Oiapoque** (one hotel), on the coast near the French Guyane border; road completed halfway to Calçoene (government-owned hotel by bus stop F, expensive food in adjoining canteen; sleeping space advertised in a café on Macapá road, very cheap), via Amapá (*Tourist Hotel* and one other, F, clean, comfortable—one block from square towards docks, turn right, 2nd house on left). Amapá is better than Calçoene for travelling on. Macapá-Amapá bus, US$6.50, 6 hrs.; daily Estrela de Ouro bus Macapá-Calçoene from Praça Vega Cabral (timetable varies), US$8, 7 hrs. (minimum), many delays, book at least 2 days in advance. 80 km. from Calçoene is Lourenço, the centre of the local gold rush. For the 216 km. from Calçoene to Oiapoque there is a bus scheduled for 0700, Mon., Wed., Fri. (US$5), but it often does not run (also an unscheduled government lorry, which does not run in the rainy season, Jan.-Apr.); you can hitch from Macapá, take a private lorry (little traffic), costing US$7 to 15, or hire a vehicle—for all means you will be overcharged. From Oiapoque a ferry goes to St. Georges (Fr. Guyane), US$2—a bridge is being built; be sure to get exit and entry stamps on either side of the border: in Oiapoque the Federal Police station is past the church on the road to Calçoene, and in St. Georges visit the Gendarmerie Nationale (no customs). Accommodation in Oiapoque for US$2 p.p. near ferries, basic. It is very difficult to get francs anywhere (the Gendarmerie may change dollars if you are stuck).

A government boat makes the trip from Macapá to Oiapoque once or twice a month, US$10. The boat service on its journey south stops at Calçoene (24 hrs., US$8.50, including food) and from there a trip can be made by lorry (US$5) to Macapá. There are Taba flights from Macapá to Oiapoque on Tues., Fri., Sat. (return Tues., Wed., Sat., continuing to Belém), US$52 (US$107 to Belém); Taba office in Oiapoque on the quay by the ferry, rarely open (flights usually booked up). It is possible, but hard, to fly Amapá-Oiapoque. (Taxi into Oiapoque US$4, bus US$1.25.) If using Paris-Cayenne route as a cheap way to/from South America, it is recommended to fly Cayenne-Belém, US$135, compared with five days of discomfort and delays overland from Cayenne to Macapá (you have to fly Cayenne-St. Georges anyway, or else go by heavily booked boat, *São Pedro*, from S.T.M.G., 136 Monnerville (opp. Market), Cayenne, Tel.: 311388).

Belém to Manaus

A few hours up the broad river the region of the thousand islands is entered. The passage between this maze of islets is known as "The Narrows". The ship winds through lanes of yellow flood with equatorial forest within 20 or 30 metres on both sides. In the Furo Grande the vessel rounds a hairpin bend almost touching the trees, bow and stern. For over 150 km. these lanes of water lead through the jungle.

After the Narrows, the first point of special interest is formed by the curious flat-topped hills, on one of which stands the little stucco town of Monte Alegre (airport), an oasis in mid-forest.

Santarém, 2-3 days upstream on the southern bank, stands at the confluence of the Tapajós River with the Amazon, just half-way between Belém and Manaus. It was founded in 1661, and is the third largest town on the Brazilian Amazon, with 52,665 people. The yellow Amazon water is mottled with greenish patches from the Tapajós; the meeting of the waters is said by some to be nearly as impressive as that of the Negro and Solimões near Manaus. There is now a road southwards towards Cuiabá (Mato Grosso), meeting the Transamazônica at Rurópolis (see page 333.) (The southward leg from the Transamazônica to Cuiabá begins about 90 km. W of this point, or 20 km. from Itaituba.) Timber, bauxite and gold discoveries have promoted very rapid growth of the city. It is the jumping off point for gold prospectors in the Mato Grosso territories to the

340 BRAZIL

South. It is reported that prospectors are exploited by high prices, and that lawlessness abounds in the goldfields. The unloading of the fish catch between 0500 and 0700 on the waterfront is an interesting scene. There are good beaches nearby on the river Tapajós.

N.B.   Santarém is one hour behind Brazilian Standard time.

Hotels *Santarém Palace*, close to city centre, Rui Barbosa 726, good, D with bath and TV; *Tropical*, Av. Mendonça Furtado 4120, D, de luxe, swimming pool seems to be unrestricted, friendly staff, good chef (but not "de luxe" cooking), meals for around US$ 5; *City*, Trav. Francisco Correia 200, E with bath, a/c, TV, radio, frigobar; *Uirapura*, Av. Adriano Pimentel 140, E, for a/c with breakfast and bath, single room with fan, F, good breakfast, view of "meeting of the waters" from front porch and some rooms, but filthy. *Camino*, Praça Rodrigues dos Santos 877, F, with bath and fan, run-down, friendly; *São Luís*, near market, E, good value, meals; *Hospedaria Rai-Fra*, Travessa Senador Lemos, F; *Alvorada*, E, reasonable; *Brasil*, F, including breakfast, clean; *Mocorongo* on waterfront, breakfast US$0.60, dilapidated but clean.

Restaurants *Mascote* bar and restaurant, haunt of young people, but expensive; *Pirâmides*, good local fish dishes; good value restaurant beneath *Equatorial Hotel*. Good ice-cream at *Sorveteria Go-Go*, Siqueira Campos 431. *Luci's* snack bar in the main square, good.

Banks   Banco do Brasil changes foreign currency and travellers' cheques.

Airport   15 km. from town. Internal flights only (US$70 to Manaus). No buses to centre or waterfront, only taxis (US$5 to waterfront); *Hotel Tropical* has a free bus for residents, you may be able to take this.

River Services   Small launches leave for Manaus 2-5 days, most days, e.g. Luciatur, US$20 including food, 3rd class. Other examples of fares to Manaus: US$37.50 1st class (upper deck cabin), US$20, 2nd class (upper deck hammock), US$18.50, 3rd class (lower deck). You may sleep on board (in hammock) days before departure. Enquire at the waterfront. Enasa, Trav. Agripina Matos 1089; Tel.: 522-1138. For Belém, *Franz Rossy*, every second Thursday at 1200, 2-3 days, US$23 hammock space, US$26 cabin. For Macapá (Porto Santana), 36-48 hrs., US$18, e.g. *São Francisco de Paula*, clean, efficient, friendly, good food. All boats, to Manaus or Belém, including Enasa, leave from the "Cais do Porto" dock, about 4 km. from the centre; take bus marked "Circular" or "Circular Externo", both of which go to Cais do Porto, and pass Rodoviária. Guards will allow you to enter the dock and look for boats, but you may have to wait several days for a cargo/passenger boat going in either direction. Along the river, closer to the centre, are numerous boats, usually leaving daily, for Itaituba, Óbidos, Oriximiná, Alenquer or Monte Alegre.

Buses   Rodoviária is on the outskirts, take "Rodagem" bus from the waterfront near the market, US$0.12. Santarém to Itaituba, 8 hrs. US$5.40; there connecting service east to Marabá on the River Tocantins, 28 hrs. (if lucky, can be 60 hours, or even 6 days), US$ 21.60, 1830 with Trans Brasiliana. Also to Imperatriz, 46 hrs., US$24.50, office on Av. Getúlio Vargas and at Rodoviária. (Beware of vehicles that offer a lift, which frequently turn out to be taxis.)

Excursion to Altar do Chão, a village of mud houses, set amid Amazonian vegetation; nice restaurant next to the church, good swimming in the Tapajós from the beautiful, clean beach; bus leaves 0400, returns 1800 (rugged, but fun). Also by 1000 bus to Porto Novo, 3 hrs. into jungle by a lake, bus returns 0330 next morning (you can sleep in it). Interesting wildlife on lake; canoe can be hired.

About 40 km. S from Santarém on a dirt road is **Belterra**, where Henry Ford established rubber plantations in the late 1920s, in the highlands overlooking the Tapajós River. Ford built a well laid-out new town; the houses resemble the cottages of Michigan summer resorts. Many of the newer houses follow the white paint with green trim style. The town centre has a large central plaza that includes a band stand, the church of Santo Antônio (circa 1951), a Baptist church and a large educational and sports complex. There is a major hospital which at one time was staffed by physicians from North America and attracted people from Manaus and Belém.

The whole project was turned over to the Ministry of Agriculture in the late 1940s. Little replacement of old trees has been done; extraction has been the only activity. As a result, the rubber forest is in bad condition, and the government is attempting to dispose of Belterra. (*Hotel Seringueira*, F, with about 8 rooms and pleasant restaurant). Bus from Santarém, 1000, 1230, 1630, Mon.-Sat., Sun. at 1630, return 0530, 0700, 1300, US$1 (office in Santarém at Getúlio Vargas and Travessa Moraes Sarmento—note: one hour time difference between Santarém and Belterra). There is an older and similar rubber enterprise established by Henry Ford, known as Fordlândia, further up the Tapajós River.

110 km. up-river from Santarém is Óbidos, with a population of 27,000. There the river is comparatively narrow, and for many kilometres little is seen except the wall of the great Amazonian forest. Small airport.

BRAZIL 341

Manaus, the next great city upstream, was until recently an isolated urban island in the jungle. This remote "free port" is, in fact, the collecting-point for the produce of a vast area which includes parts of Peru, Bolivia, and Colombia. There is superb swimming in the natural pools and under falls of clear water in the little streams which rush through the woods, but take locals' advice on swimming in the river; electric eels and various other kinds of unpleasant fish, apart from the notorious *piranhas*, abound.

Until recently Manaus' only communications were by river and air, but now a road SW to Porto Velho, which is already connected with the main Brazilian road system, has been completed and partly paved. Another, as yet unpaved, has been built due N to Boa Vista, from where other roads already reach the Venezuelan and Guyanese frontiers.

Manaus (613,000 people) is the capital of the State of Amazonas, the largest in Brazil, with a population of almost 1.2m. Though 1,600 km. from the sea, it is only 32 metres above sea-level. The average temperature is 27°C. The city sprawls over a series of eroded and gently sloping hills divided by numerous creeks (*igarapés*). Dominating the centre is a Cathedral built in simple Jesuit style on a hillock; nothing distinguished inside or out. Nearby is the main shopping and business area, the tree-lined Avenida Eduardo Ribeiro; crossing it is the wide, attractive Av. Sete de Setembro, bordered by ficus trees. The main shopping area between Av. Sete de Setembro and the rear of *Hotel Amazonas* is now reserved to pedestrians. There is a modern air-conditioned theatre. Manaus is building fast; 20-storey modern buildings are rising above the traditional flat, red-tiled roofs. It was the first city in South America to instal trams, but they have now been replaced by buses.

Other attractions are the Botanic Gardens (to enter you must have the mayor's permission), the military zoo (not to be confused with small town centre zoo), the well stocked public library, and the legendary Opera House, the Teatro Amazonas, completed in 1896 during the great rubber boom and rebuilt in 1929. It seats over a thousand people and was restored in 1974. It is used about once a month for plays; entry to view, US$0.50, open Tues.-Sun., mornings only. See the two markets near the docks; best early in morning. There is a curious little church, the Igreja do Pobre Diabo, in the suburb of Cachoeirinha; it is only 4 metres wide by 5 metres long, and was built by a worker (the "poor devil" of the name); take Circular 7 Cachoeirinha bus from cathedral to Hospital Militar.

The Rio Negro has an average annual rise and fall of 14 metres. The remarkable harbour installations have a floating ramp about 150 metres in length leading from street level to the passenger-ship floating dock. When the water is high, the roadway floats on a series of large iron tanks measuring 2½ metres in diameter. The material to build the large yellow Customs building near the harbour was brought block by block from Scotland as ballast. Tourists can visit the docks on Sun., 0600-1000.

Manaus is a free trade zone, established in 1967. All travellers are required to fill out a customs declaration on all articles bought there, which you are requested to pack in your hold luggage; in fact it is a good idea to declare goods of non-Brazilian origin such as cameras, radios, tape-recorders etc. on arrival in order to avoid any problems. It is only necessary to give information to Customs on goods already possessed if one is travelling into Brazil. You have to go through customs when leaving the Rodoviária. If flying from Manaus outside Brazil, no such documentation is required.

Duty-Free Imports Travellers entering Brazil through Manaus may import from the zone, duty-free, foreign electrical or electronic goods and food products, up to maximum values that are often changed.

Local Holidays Jan. 6 (Epiphany); Ash Wed., half-day; Maundy Thurs.; June 24 (St. John); July 14; Sept. 5; Oct. 30; Nov. 1, All Saints Day, half-day; Christmas Eve; New Year's Eve, half-day.

The annual Folklore Festival (dates vary, but about end of June) is well worth seeing for its colour, noise, and pleasure. On Sept. 5 there is a celebration march-past between 0800 and 1100, with bands of marchers from all the local schools, clubs, associations, etc.

N.B. Manaus time is one hour behind Brazilian standard time.

Museums The Museu do Índio (formerly the Museu Indígena Salesiano), in

342 BRAZIL

Catholic school at end of Av. Sete de Setembro, corner of Rua Duque de Caxias, has most interesting exhibits of Indian culture in Amazonas (entry 0800-1100 and 1400-1700, Mon.-Sat., US$0.30). In the next block, on Rua Duque de Caxias, is a rubber factory that may be visited free. The coin museum, Museu Numismático, is at Rua Henrique Martins 458, free. Indian artefacts and documents can also be seen at the Instituto Geográfico Histórico, Rua Bernardo Ramos 117 (Tues.-Sat., 0900-1700; entry US$ 0.20). Museu do Porto de Manaus, a small museum of memorabilia, Vivaldo Lima 61, near port (Mon.-Fri., 0800-1100, 1400-1700, Sat., 0800-1100); Museu do Homem do Norte, showing the way of life of the local population and their products.

Zoo Run by the military; known as CLOS. Bus 205 or 217 (marked "Ponta Negra"), US$0.40, every ½ hr from Banco do Brasil in centre, alight 400 metres past the 1st Jungle Infantry Barracks (a big white building). The zoo is in the Headquarters of the Jungle Training Centre (CIGS); entrance free. There is also a small zoo in town, less interesting, but has two souvenir shops; entrance free. Instituto Nacional de Pesquisas Amazonas (INPA), Estrada de Aleixo, at km. 3 (any bus to Aleixo), has named trees and supposedly manatees and dolphins; good for birdwatchers.

Hotels *Tropical*, Praia de Ponta Negra, Tel.: (92)234-1165, a lavish, 5 star Varig hotel 20 km. outside the city, in a superb setting by the river, L, good food. Reserve as far ahead as possible through Varig; non-residents may use pool on weekdays, the park and small zoo with healthy animals, river boats, tennis; *Novotel*, Av. Mandu 4 in the Industrial Area, A, 4 star, luxurious, pool, US$1.75 taxi ride from centre, reported markedly less good than *Tropical*; *Imperial*, Av. Getúlio Vargas 227, 3 star, B a bit rundown, huge new hotel alongside blocks windows on that side; *Amazonas*, Praça Adalberto Vale, 4 star, A, good; opp. *Amazonas*, *Ana Cassia Palace*, expensive, Rua dos Andradas 14, B; *Lord*, Marcílio Dias 217/225, C, some rooms a/c, expensive for what they offer, with breakfast, restaurant has been recommended; has a cheaper annex. *Da Vinci*, Rua Belo Horizonte, about 2 km. from centre (convenient bus route), C, swimming pool, all facilities; *Manaus*, Rua Lobo D'Almada 48, D, a/c, clean, friendly, reported overpriced; *Rio Mar*, R. Guilherme Moreira 325, incl. breakfast and bath E, good, clean, central; *Flamboyant*, Av. Eduardo Ribeiro 926, E, quite good. In Av. 7 de Setembro; *Palace* (593), old building, now refurbished with a/c but poor, D; *Topaz* (711), D, incl. breakfast, central, rooms have fans, new but scruffy, still recommended; *Líder* (827), C, expensive; *Martins* (1429), F, with breakfast; *Modelo*, near Av. 7 de Setembro, F, clean, friendly, recommended. *Monaco*, Rua Silva Ramos 20, 3 star, C; *Regente*, Coronel Sérgio Pessoa 189, D with a/c and bath, said to be run down; *Fortaleza*, Rua dos Bares, F with fan, reasonable. In Rua Dr Moreira: *Kyoto Plaza* (232), D with a/c, some rooms E, good breakfasts; *Central* (202), Tel.: 234-7374, E, some a/c, quiet; *Internacional* (168), D, a/c, clean, friendly, central, coffee most of the day, good exchange rates; *Nova Olinda*, next door, F with bath, a/c, TV; *Hospedagem Familiar Garrido* (148), F, as much as you can eat for US$2, dirty, friendly, showers; *Solimões* (119), D with breakfast, pricey, poor standards of hygiene; *Nacional* (59), F with bath, fridge, a/c, good value. In Av. Joaquim Nabuco: *Hospedaria Manaus* (703), F, clean, spacious, washing facilities; *Doral* (687), E/C, Tel.: 232-4102, a/c, friendly, excellent breakfast, recommended; *Hostal Rondônia* (565), F, dirty, noisy, coffee most of the day, cold water, fan, friendly; also *Pensão Rondônia*, clean, F, no breakfast, pleasant; *Vidal* (681), F, no breakfast, pleasant rooms at rear, cheap; *Pensão Sulista* (347), Tel.: 234-4185, F with fan, no breakfast, laundry facilities, very clean, friendly; *Bons Amigos* (307), F, no breakfast; *Alugam* (154), rented apartments, E full board; *Aurora* (130), F with bath, a/c, friendly, clean, noisy TV; *Artêrio*, near corner with R. Lima Bacuri, D with a/c, E with fan, without breakfast, clean, large rooms with bath; *Karam*, waterfront end, F with bath, a/c, fridge, coffee all day, friendly, has sauna and TV; *Hospedaria Paulista*, F with breakfast, fan, popular; next door is *Astoria*, F with breakfast, a bit run down. *São Francisco*, just off Av. Joaquim Nabuco, F; *Rio Branco*, Rua dos Andradas 485, F, highly recommended, friendly, clean, cheap, clothes-washing facilities; *Rio Branco* also at Miranda Leão 485; cheap *pensão* at Miranda Leão 432, F with fan, good rooms, *agua mineral* on tap. *Pensão Buenos Aires*, near Cathedral, E, full board; *Pensão Bolívia*, 24 de Maio 542, F, without, and E with bath, full board; Spanish spoken, all shared rooms. **N.B.** Lori Kornblum suggests keeping your room key, in view of reports of staff allowing bogus police officers into guests' rooms. **N.B.** also, when taking a taxi from the airport, insist on being taken to the hotel of your choice, and to not one which pays the driver commission.

Camping It is possible to camp "wild" on the bank of the Rio Negro near the *Hotel Tropical*; through outskirts of city via Taruma bathing waterfalls to Ponta Negra bathing beaches, 20 km. Good swimming. Bus daily (US$0.15). Campsite under construction at Praia Dourada (1983).

Electric Current 110 volts A.C.; some hotels 220 volts A.C.

Restaurants *Tarumã*, Hotel Tropical, over US$15 disappointing (*churrascaria* every night for US$6); *Canto da Alvorada*, Comendador Clementino 183, fair; *Florentina*, Rua José Paranaguá, Italian, reasonably priced, good salad, pizza (government rating A); *Kavako*, Av. 7 de Setembro;

BRAZIL 343

Suan Lung, Rua 24 de Maio; *São Francisco*, Rua Vista Alegre, ½ hr. walk from centre, in Educandos suburb, good fish, huge portion, US$ 5.50, highly recommended; new *Panorama* next door (also good for fish). Good cheap Chinese at *Mandarim*, Av. Eduardo Ribeiro 650, has buffet lunch, US$2 all you can eat; also *China*, Av. Getúlio Vargas 1127, warmly recommended; Japanese at *Mikado*, Rua São Luís 230, and at *Tokyo*, Rua Silva Ramos 456, good; *O Gauchão*, Av. Castelo Branco 2009, fixed price of about US$5 for as much as you can eat, recommended. Another *churrascaria* is *Rodaviva*, Av. Ajuricaba 1005, open air, all you can eat for US$4, also *Churrascão*, Av. Castello Branco, Cachoeirinha. *O Vegetariano*, Av. 7 de Setembro 874 (6th floor), good, also takeaway, open 1100-1430 Mon.-Fri.; *La Fiorentina*, pizzeria and Italian food at Praça da Policia, Av. 7 de Setembro, also at Rua J. Paranaguá 44, moderate prices, good food. Cheap: *Hotel Assis*, R. Mauá, US$1.25-2.00; *Sorveteria Pingüim*, Av. Eduardo Ribeiro, good, medium-priced; *Cantinha Carioca*, Rua Dr. Moreira, 2nd floor of Edifício Moreira, excellent food, good value; *Sirva-Se*, Rua Dr. Moreira 124, plenty of choice, recommended, good value; *175*, Rua Dr Moreira 175, menu in Portuguese and English; *Forasteiro*, same street, No. 178; *Central*, Rua José Clemente, US$1.50; *Jangada Bar*, opp. *Hotel Amazonas*, good for snacks; *O Bem Amado*, Joaquim Nabuco 497, excellent value, especially *prato feito*; *Alemã*, cafeteria, Rua José Paranaguá, good for juices, sandwiches, cakes; good *pratos* at Brasileiros department store, Av. 7 de Setembro; *Lanchonete Bali*, Rua Marechal Deodoro 172, US$1.50 for *prato comercial*. Snack-bar top of 13-storey building next to *Lider Hotel; Arigato*, R. Guilherme Moreira and Av. 7 de Setembro, for American food. On river front at end of Av. Joaquim Nabuco are several floating restaurants serving fish very cheaply, less than US$1. Reasonable, but probably not completely hygienic. The floating retaurant in the harbour below the market building is recommended for best *tucunaré* fish. Many restaurants close on Sunday nights and Mondays. City authorities grade restaurants for cleanliness: look for A and B.

The fishing catch is brought to the waterfront between 2300-0100, including the giant *pirarucu*.

Cinema on R. J. Clemente, opp. Teatro Amazonas.

Bookshop Livraria Nacional, Rua 10 de Julho 613 opp. Teatro Amazonas, stocks some English and French books. 2nd-hand English books at corner of 24 de Maio and Rui Barbosa.

Souvenirs Indian handicrafts in the Museu do Índio, Sete de Setembro 217. Funai shop on main market street, near *Hotel Amazonas*. H.Stern, jewellers, at *Hotel Tropical* and International Airport. The Humming Bird, Rua Quintino Bocaiuva, 224, good.

Clubs Ideal; Athletic Club of Rio Negro; Bosque (bathing pool, tennis courts). For evening entertainment (including gambling): Vogue Club (jacket and tie obligatory), Boite Inglês, The In Crowd, Danielo´s.

Tourist Information Emantur, Praça 24 de Outubro, Rua Taruma 329 (not very good), airport (where Margaret is very informative, speaks English) and floating harbour. Town map from *Hotel Amazonas* or from Amazon Explorers, *Hotel Lord*. Guide Book of Manaus, US$3, available from *Hotel Amazonas* and other places, in English, useful.

Banks Lloyds Bank (ex-BOLSA), Rua Guilherme Moreira 147; Banco do Brasil, Av. Rui Barbosa; many local banks. Open 0900-1600. Most offices shut afternoons. Foreign exchange operations 0900-1200 only, or close even as early as 1100. Reported that only Banco do Brasil and Lloyds will change US$ notes. It is possible to change US$ at the airport; open 24 hrs. per day (official rates only). Exchange at the main hotels (poor rates at *Tropical*, through), at Souvenirs de Manaus shop and at Luciatur, Av. Eduardo Ribeiro 365, Minitur and Selvatur; try also bakery opp. *Hotel Rio Branco* for cheques, and Sr. Ayoub, Av. 7 de Setembro 711. Exchange rates in Manaus are better than elsewhere in Northern Brazil, but less good than in the South.

Post Office Praça Congresso, 1 block N of Opera House; poste restante at post office in Marechal Deodoro. For airfreight and shipping, Alfândega, Av. Marones Santa Cruz (corner of M. Deodoro), Sala 106.

British Consul, Eduardo Ribeiro 520, 12th floor.
United States Consular Agency, Rua Maceió 62, Adrianópolis, Tel.: 234 4546 (office hours) and 232 1611 (outside office hours), Mr. James R. Fish. Will supply letters of introduction for US citizens.
Peruvian Consul, Rua Tapajós 536 Tel.: 234-7900.
Colombian Consul Please note that apparently the Colombian consul (Rua Dona Libânia 62, near opera house) has been advising travellers from Manaus to Leticia that if they are only visiting Leticia they do not require a tourist card. Either get your Colombian tourist card before reaching Manaus or tell the consul you are travelling further into Colombia, which will probably then require proof of money and return ticket.

Tours Amazon Explorers Tour Service, run by Manoel (Bebê) Barros from office in *Hotel Lord*; his day's tour including "meeting of the waters", Parque Januário and rubber collecting, US$20 including lunch, has been highly recommended by most users; 32-hour trips, require a minimum of

344 BRAZIL

4 people; other tours available. Boat *Amazon Explorer* available for hire at about US$230 per day. Kurt Glück, Quintino Bocaiúva 224, Caixa Postal 361, offers a more personal service at US$100 day excl. food and fuel; his shortest boat trips, which need to be booked as far in advance as possible, last five days in an open 5.5 metre canoe, and he explores many of the tributary rivers of the Amazon; maximum two persons. Transamazonas Turismo, Leonardo Malcher 734, Tel.: 232-1454/232-4326 (reservations in Rio through South American Turismo, Av. N.S. de Copacabana 788, Tel.: 255-2345, 22050 Rio de Janeiro), for parties of 10 or less offers a 3-days-plus stay on a floating lodge on Lake Periquitão, 80 km. from Manaus (US$260 p.p. with extras for 3 days). The better hotels also arrange tours (ask for Joe Sears in *Hotel Tropical*), and so do Selvatur (office in *Hotel Amazonas*, unfriendly staff), Rio Negro trip per person, US$10, 0800-1300, with lunch at Janaurylândia floating hotel, returning at 1500, US$30 or 2-day trip for US$200 p.p. Luciatur, Av. Eduardo Ribeiro 355, 0800-1500, US$35; Amazon Explorer 0730-1500 with lunch US$27; Jungle Trips, R Guilherme Moreira 281, 3-day jungle trip, all included, irrespective of numbers, for US$130; and Mundial (Av. Pres. Vargas) agencies.

Also recommended for trips by canoe on the Amazon and Rio Negro is Moacir Forbes, R. Miguel Ribas 1339, Santo Antônio, Manaus, Tel.: 232-7492 (4 passengers maximum), he speaks English and German (US$100 per day, plus fuel and food). Also Arlendo da Vicente Silva (Rua Vista Alegre, Educandos, Tel.: 233-3531, or seek him out at the waterfront), for 3 day tours on tributaries of the Solimões and into the jungle—very little English spoken, but recommended, maximum 8 people, about US$65 p.p. inclusive. Other guides: Elmo de Morais López and Cássio Serra Vieira, Rua Henrique Martins 369, Centro, for 2-5 day tours, 2-4 people, sleeping in hammocks, US$100 a day per couple, recommended; Gustavo, a Peruvian, 3-day tours for US$110 p.p. for 2 (less for more people), he speaks several languages, Tel.: 233-0958; Cristóvão, Rua Barão São Domingos 169, Apt. 9, Centro, (Tel.: 233-3231), experienced jungle guide, reasonably-priced tours for 1, 2 or more days, speaks German, English. Rubens Silva, Eduardo Ribeiro 420, has been recommended for his 3-day trip up the Rio Branco for 2-5 people, US$110 p.p. However, avoid the Janauaca jungle tour sold by Concya-Tours: overpriced, overcrowded, incomplete. Motorized canoes can be hired from behind Mercado Municipal, US$50 for 6-hr. trip, takes 8, with navigator/guide, goes to inaccessible places.

R. D. Ranft writes: "It should be realized that all these river tours are limited to areas close to Manaus, which have been visited often. Few animals, though some exotic vegetation, are seen—disappointing anyone who wants a taste of real jungle life. For those prepared to spend around 10 days in the interior, contact Carlos Colares (Tel.: 234-6260, Rua Marechal Deodoro 89, 17° andar sala 1701/1702, 69.000 Manaus, or P.O.Box 360) who conducts private excursions, with fishing, hunting and exploring in the more remote regions of the Rio Negro (6-10 people)." Carlos Colares has been highly recommended by other readers as an excellent, well-informed guide and biologist (British-educated). He and his Indian guide provide well-planned, informative trips which do not follow the usual tourist routes.

Generally, between April and September excursions are only by boat; in the period October-March the Victoria Regia lilies virtually disappear. Fishing is best between September and March (no flooding).

Many people have expressed disappointment with the shorter tours. The problem is that authentic jungle life, whether human or animal, does not easily co-exist with a large city. However, bird-watchers can see many kinds of birds in and around the grounds of the *Hotel Tropical* (for instance: fly catchers—kingbirds and kiskadees—, swallows, yellow-browed sparrows, aracaris—member of the toucan family—, woodpeckers, woodcreepers, thrushes, anis, three species of tanager, two of parrots—the dusky and blue-headed). Sloths and monkeys may also be seen. Bird-lovers anxious to pursue their hobby on the Amazon River and its backwaters should contact Sr. Moacir Forbes, see above for address and further details (we are grateful to John and George Newmark of Eastbourne for this information).

The enterprising go to the Capitânia do Porto and find out what boats are making short trips; e.g., Manaus-Itacoatiara, US$6 first-class. For swimming, it is possible to travel to Ponta Negra beach (no shade) by Soltur buses for US$0.25, though beach virtually disappears beneath the water in April-August and is now reported to be polluted. Good swimming at Bolívar Falls: take Taruma bus (very few on weekdays), getting off at the police checkpoint on the road to Itacoatiara.

About 15 km. from Manaus is the confluence of the Solimões (Amazon) and the Rio Negro, which is itself some 8 km. wide. Here you can see the meeting of the blue-black water of the Rio Negro with the yellow-brown Solimões flood; the two rivers run side by side for about 6 km. without their waters mingling. Tourist agencies run boat trips to this spot, or if travelling on a tight budget you can get up about 0330 in Manaus, take a "milk boat" such as the *Capitão Braga* (try to arrange the day before) at about 0400. It returns about 1300, passing through the confluence. Also the *Joanne d'Arc* leaves the dock area around 0730 and returns late afternoon, and the *Castelo*, 0800 to 1500 to the confluence, US$2. Alternatively hire a motorized canoe from near the market for about US$10 per

BRAZIL 345

hr. (you'll need 3 or 4 hrs. to take in the experience properly). The simplest way is to take a taxi or bus to the Careiro ferry dock, and take the ferry across (take airport bus to the old military airport, marked Aeroporto (US$0.15), it's a short walk from the end of the bus line, or bus 407 or 601 from near cathedral, US$0.15, to ferry, or "Ceasa" bus from Cathedral which terminates at Ceasa, 2 km. from the ferry). The ferry goes at 0700, returning 0900, 1100, returning 1400, and 1500, returning 2000 (approx.). You can also take small private launches across. A 2-km. walk along the Porto Velho road from the Careiro ferry terminal will lead to a point from which Victoria Regia water lilies can be seen in April-September in ponds, some way from the road. If you continue over the Capitari bridge, you reach unspoilt jungle. There are several small restaurants on the S bank in Careiro, where the road SW to Porto Velho and the South begins.

Urs Bucher, of Zug, Switzerland, recommends a trip to Manacapuru, by bus 304 (30 mins.) at 0800, ferry from São Raimundo (30 mins.)and 2-hr. bus ride (bus every hour), to see a typical Amazon town (buy bus ticket before you get on the ferry: don't wait till you arrive at the other side). A small market town on the Solimões W of Manaus, with three basic hotels and *Il Maccarone* pizzeria, Av. Eduardo Ribeiro 1000, with its friendly Italian owner Mário. Another village one can visit is Araça, a 3-hr bus ride from Rodoviária in the direction of Castanho; the journey includes a ferry crossing at the confluence of the Negro and Solimões (fare to Araça US$0.70). The village is on the banks of the River Mamori; canoes can be hired for US$3-5 for a day (night trips also possible) and you may be able to sling your hammock in a private house. Plenty of wildlife close at hand. 3 buses a day return to Manaus.

Roads To *Itacoatiara,* 285 km. E on the Amazon, with Brazil-nut and jute processing plants (bus service); now paved. An unpaved road runs N (759 km.) from Manaus to Boa Vista (daily by Andorinha at 1800 and 2100, 20 hrs., US$10, book at least 4 days in advance, 2 daily, often extra buses put on; also Eucatur bus to Boa Vista, continuing to Santa Elena on Venezuelan border, insect repellant advisable for ferry crossings, also a good idea to take food and water). The Catire Highway from Manaus to Porto Velho, which is partly paved with work continuing, and sometimes closed during the rainy season (877 km.), starts at Careiro on the southern bank of the Amazon opposite Manaus. Bus, Manaus-Porto Velho, 3 a day (sometimes extra ones), US$10, 24-6 hrs., best to book in advance. Bus to Humaitá; 670 km., where the Catire Highway crosses the Transamazônica, more than one a day, 17 hrs., (including 4 ferry crossings), US$6; three buses a day from Humaitá to Porto Velho (3 hrs. with one ferry crossing, paved stretch), 257 km., US$2. Bus tickets can be bought from a booth at Eduardo Ribeiro with 7 de Setembro. Bus station is 5 km. out of town at the intersection of Av. Constantino Nery and Rua Recife; take local bus from centre, US$0.30, marked "Aeroporto Internacional" or "Cidade Nova". Local buses to Praça 14 or airport leave from opposite *Hotel Amazonas* (take airport bus and alight just after Antártica factory) or take local bus to Ajuricaba. Hitch-hiking from Manaus can be very difficult. For Boa Vista, take a Taruma bus to the customs building and hitch from there.

Air Services direct from Miami, Bogotá, La Paz, Lima, Santa Cruz, Caracas and from most Brazilian cities. Two Air France 747s a week, Paris-Cayenne-Manaus-Lima. On Thurs. Avianca goes on to Bogotá, Varig on Fri. (Avianca is represented by Luciatur, Av. Eduardo Ribeiro 365; tickets can only be bought if you have an onward ticket out of Colombia). Three times a week, Cruzeiro do Sul (accepts Access/Mastercharge) flies to Cayenne, US$198 (make sure you have onward ticket). To Paramaribo, Sun. Cruzeiro, Fri. Suriname Airways. Manaus-Iquitos, Cruzeiro do Sul, Sat. and Wed. at 1015, US$270 one way, stopping at Tefé and Tabatinga for Leticia (separate Manaus-Tabatinga—US$85, Tabatinga-Iquitos—US$79 available and cheaper). Flights to Benjamin Constant, opposite Leticia, 3 times a week. There are also flights to Boa Vista, Cruzeiro do Sul, Tues., Thur., Fri. 1000, Sun. 1715, 55 mins., return flights 1 hr. after arrival, Porto Velho, Corumbá, Santarém, Teresina. About 17 flights a week to Belém. The taxi fare to or from the airport is US$5, but settle price before journey or obtain a ticket that fixes flat-rate fares, or take bus 608 or hourly bus 201 marked Aeroporto Internacional from Rua Tamandaré near cathedral, US$0.20. Last bus at night to airport from R. Tamandaré at 2345. (Taxi drivers often tell arrivals that no bus to town is available, be warned!) Check all connections on arrival. N.B. Allow plenty of time at Manaus airport, formalities are very slow, and there are queues for everything.

Shipping Taxi from centre to docks, US$1.20. Occasional German vessels. Fairly frequent (irregular) river boats to Tefé (3 days, US$20, including food), and Benjamin Constant (see below). Boa Vista (not good), and Porto Velho (US$70 in 2-berth cabin, US$30 2nd class, 7 days, 3 days downstream at high water, recommended boat, *Clívia*). Buy a hammock (*rede*—pronounced "hedgie") if travelling 2nd or 3rd class, and plenty of books to read; often the boats only stop at night. Boats to Santarém every evening, from E end of dock, prices vary, roughly US$14 lower deck, US$15 upper deck, US$37.50 cabin (Navio Motor Emerson); *Dejard Viera*, leaves Wed., 1800 37 hrs., US$16 lower deck, US$20 upper, US$28 cabin, US$12 by *Cidade de Natal*, well recommended; *Ayapua*, US$28 d, a/c cabin (cold at night) including meals, leaves Manaus every Fri. 1830 (no guaranteed connexion to Belém). Also recommended to Santarém, M.V. *11 de Maio*, leaving each Tues. evening, its sister ship doing return at same time, good meals, top deck with chairs, tables. Enasa to Belém once a week at 2000, the day is normally Wed., but may change every month, but in any one month it's the same day of the week (buy ticket in advance, Enasa office closes 1130 on Sat. very crowded, board early); 4 days, one class, hammock space only, US$40 inc. meals; bar on board (foreigners 1st class only fare comparable with night flight). The address of the Enasa line is Rua Marechal Deodoro 61. Shipping a car: either with Enasa, or Sanave Cia, Entrada de Bombeamento 20, Compensa, Manaus, Tel.: 234-4803/4302, telex 092-2463 SOCN, recommended, driver free, one passenger and car US$250 to Belém, inc. meals (no variety), sleep in car or hammock; cheaper if you load the car on to an empty truck. The Capitânia do Porto, Av. Santa Cruz 265, Manaus, has a list of all shipping. All boats, when berthed, display destination and time of sailing so you can check facilities and costs. Boats for Belém and international shipping leave from west end of the docks (entrance at Capitânia do Porto), all others from east end.

N.B. Be careful of food on the boats; may be cooked in river-water. You may need a visa to travel to Peru; consulate at Rua Tapajós 536. Those arriving from Leticia should go to the police for their immigration entrance stamp, but you should get this in Tabatinga. Departures to the less important destinations are not always known at the Capitânia do Porto, Av. Oswaldo Santa Cruz 264.

Passports For those arriving by boat who have not already had their passports stamped, the immigration office is on the first of the floating docks next to the tourist office. Take the dock entrance opposite the cathedral, bear right, after 50 metres left, pass through a warehouse to a group of buildings on a T section.

Tefé lies approximately halfway between Manaus and the Colombian border. A small town of some 22,000; the waterfront consists of a light sand beach; waterfront market Mon. a.m.; the nuns at the Franciscan convent sell handicrafts and embroidery; there are three small hotels and five pensions (Anilce, Praça Santa Teresa 294, E, clean, a/c, recommended), and an airport with connection to Manaus. Recommended boat, Captain Noonan (safe food, plenty of space, drinks on sale). Also Jean Filho, leaves Manaus 1800 Sat. (arrives Mon. p.m.), leaves Tefé Tues. 1900 (arrives Wed. p.m. or Thurs. a.m.). US$10.50 first class with food bottled water, 2nd class and small cabins available.

For jungle tours, contact Joaquim de Jesus López, Rua Hermes Tupina No. 740, Barro Holaria, Tefé not a professional guide, but he has been recommended for self-organized trips (cost for 4 for 1 week, US$200). No English spoken.

Benjamin Constant A small river-town on the frontier with Peru, with Colombian territory on the opposite bank of the river. Several hotels, including, Benjamin Constant, beside ferry, D, all a/c, some with hot water and TV, good restaurant, arranges tours, postal address Apartado Aéreo 219, Leticia, Colombia. Hotel São Jorge, F, meal US$2, try bargaining; Araponga, C, run down; Hotel Lanchonete Peruana, F, good food. Eat at Pensão Cecília, meals US$ 1.80 each; Bar-21 de Abril for less than US$1. Boat services from Manaus, 7 days, or more, US$40, to Manaus, 4 days, or more, cabin (Wed. and Sat. evenings) US$25. Boats go to Benjamin Constant only. Prices do vary, try bargaining. Recommended vessels are Almirante Monteiro, US$24 with hammock space, US$28 in cabin; Dominique and Cidade de Teresina, cabin US$60; Clívia, from Manaus every 2nd Sat., 6½ days, returns Wed., 3 days, cabins US$100 for 2 with fan, hammock space US$25 each. The frigorífico Conte Maciel returns empty to Manaus every 10 days, comfortable, clean, good food, 3 days, US$22.50. It is wise to bring food to supplement the rice, beans, chicken and salt fish, and sterilized water (some boats sell chilled beer or Coca Cola); mosquito spray is a must when you are in port, all year round. Ferry (Recreio) to Leticia (Colombia) twice daily, US$0.50, 1½ hrs., ferry calls at **Tabatinga** (Hotel Miraflores, expensive; São Jorge, F, reasonably priced, clean; Residencial Aluguel Paji, F with bath, fan, clean, unfriendly; Solimões, run by the military—in army camp—E with breakfast, excellent value, clean—some taxi drivers are unaware that this hotel accepts non-military guests), only 4 km. from Leticia, hitch or get a ride for US$0.20, or a taxi. Cruzeiro flies Wed. and Sat. Manaus-Tabatinga-Iquitos (US$270 inc. tax) and return. (Flights may be booked up 10 days in advance from Manaus.) The regional company, Taba, operates 3 flights a week Manaus-Tabatinga-Manaus (US$52—be prepared for delays at takeoff), via Eirunepé on the Juruá river. Hammock (good) will cost US$12 in Tabatinga or Benjamin Constant, much more in Leticia. It is difficult to change travellers' cheques in Tabatinga, and far harder to purchase Peruvian intis than in Leticia. Airport to Tabatinga by car (VW) is expensive (US$4 by taxi). The Port Captain in Tabatinga is reported as very helpful and speaking good English. N.B. The port area of Tabatinga is called Marco.

Entering Brazil from Colombia Cross frontier between Leticia and Tabatinga; Boats to Manaus depart from Benjamin Constant (see preceding paragraph). Brazilian exit/entry formalities at Marco (Tabatinga): walk through docks and follow road to its end, turn right at this T-junction for one block, white immigration building is opp. Café dos Navegantes (ten minutes' walk) from docks, Mon.-Fri., 0800-1200, 1400-1800 (airport immigration only works Wed. and Sat.), proof of US$500 or exit ticket may be required. This is a frontier area: carry your passport at all times, but travel between Leticia and Tabatinga is very informal. Taxi to Leticia, US$4. Brazilian

Consulate in Leticia, Calle 8, No. 8-71, Mon.-Fri., 1000-1600, requires two black-and-white passport photos and 36 hrs. for visa (best to get your visa beforehand); go there if you have entry problems coming from Peru into Brazil.

Entering Brazil from Peru Boats from Iquitos to the Brazilian border stop at Ramón Castilla, or at an anchorage off this town, or at Islandia, a mud-bank anchorage off Benjamin Constant (passengers are ferried by canoe between the two-Peruvian boats are not allowed to stop at Benjamin Constant); catch boats from Benjamin Constant to Manaus. You must have a Peruvian exit stamp (obtained on the boat, or at Peruvian consulate in Leticia, or at Puerto Alegria or Ramón Castilla, practice seems to vary so check first in Iquitos), and you must get an entry stamp in Tabatinga; without either you will be sent back to Peru. Leave boat at Ramón Castilla for Tabatinga. Alternatively, take one of the ferries from Benjamin Constant to Tabatinga (1½-2 hrs., US$0.80, or hire a canoe, US$3), get off at first stop, walk 1 km. to the main road, police offices are on the right. Tans flies Islandia to Iquitos (US$12.75), but there are no guarantees of flights.

To Peru and Colombia Tabatinga-Iquitos flights available on Wed. and Sun; get your Brazilian exit stamp at the airport. Entering Colombia from Brazil, you must have a tourist card to obtain a stamp to go beyond Leticia, but there appears to be no problem in staying in Leticia without a stamp; check these details on arrival. The best places for boats to Manaus or Iquitos are Benjamin Constant and Islandia (or Ramón Castilla) respectively. Frequent sailings from Peruvian border jetties (Islandia) to Iquitos, US$10, 3 days. Peruvian tourist cards obtained from Puerto Alegría, 2 hours up river where boats stop for police checks (these formalities may change).

Boa Vista

(population 45,000), capital of the extreme northern Territory of Roraima, is 759 km. N of Manaus, to which there are air and bus services. The connecting road is a rough dirt road (except for the last 50 km. to Boa Vista which are paved) with a ferry crossing at the Rio Branco. On some sections of the road S of the Equator, traffic is not allowed at night. It is difficult to buy gasoline or supplies between Caracaraí and Manaus. Boa Vista has road connections (buses) with the Venezuelan frontier at Santa Elena de Uairen (237 km.) and Bomfim for the Guyanese border at Lethem. Mount Roraima, after which the Territory is named, is possibly the original of Sir Conan Doyle's "Lost World". There is swimming in the Rio Branco, 15 mins., from the town centre (too polluted in Boa Vista). This town has a modern functional plan, which often necessitates long hot treks by the traveller from one function to another. Industrial estate S of town. New government district is being built on the NW edge of town. Taxi from airport should cost no more than US$3.50 (45 min. walk) and will assume you want *Hotel Tropical* unless you indicate otherwise.

Hotels *Tropical* (Varig), D, security recently improved, good pool, friendly, manager speaks English, good food; *Eusébio's*, E, always full, book ahead, demand single if on your own, very good restaurant, swimming pool, free transport to bus station or airport, recommended; *Paraíso*, above Varig office, E with bath, popular with Guyanese shoppers (reportedly a centre for narcotics trading); *Roraima*, Av. Cecília Brasil, F, fair; *Universo*, sleazy, very basic, F; *Central*, E, noisy and seedy, good restaurant; *Brasil* in Rua Benjamin Constant, G (do not confuse with sleazy *Hotel Brasília* in same street); also *Lua Nova*, No. 591, G without, E with a/c, recommended, English spoken. *Rodoviária*, at bus station about 1½ km. from town centre, F, communal rooms, clean, shower; *Tres Nações*, also close to bus station. There are also two missions who offer hospitality to those in need.

Camping Rio Caviné, 3 km. N of town.

Restaurants *Hotel Tropical* and *Eusebio's Hotel*, both very good; *Senzala*, Av. Castelo Branco 1115, where the town's high society eats; *Churrascaria Venezuela*, bus station; *Bigode*, on waterfront, fish, music at weekends; *Góndola*, Praça do Centro Cívico; restaurant and bar in Parque Anana, near airport. Snacks at *Top Set*, Av. Jaime Brasil, *Hotel Lua Nova*, *Central*. Catequeiro, Araújo Filho with Benjamín Contant, recommended *prato feito*.

Exchange US$ and Guyanese notes can be changed in Boa Vista; try Ramiro Silva, Rimpex, Av. Jaime Brasil. Travellers' cheques in Banco do Brasil; rates reported rather poor. There is no official exchange agency and the local rates for bolívares are low: the Banco do Brasil will not change bolívares. Try *Hotel Tropical* where manager is helpful, speaks English, some German and French; try the chemist/drugstore opp. *Hotel Tropical* for dollar exchange.

Bus To Manaus, 2 daily by Eucatur, 2300 and 2400, and two by Andorinha, 1000 and 1300, US$10, 24 hrs., may need to book because sometimes buses are fully booked days in advance, check times. To Bomfim (for Guyana) 1300 and 1500; to Santa Elena (Venezuela) 0800. Buses often run late, and have to wait up to 4 hrs. for the Rio Branco ferry. Boa Vista-Caracaraí US$4. To border, see below. Rodoviária is on town outskirts, 3 km.; taxi to centre, US$2.30, bus US$0.10.

348 BRAZIL

Hitch-hiking from Boa Vista to Manaus is fairly easy on the many trucks travelling to Manaus; try from the police checkpoint S of Boa Vista. You may have to change trucks at Caracaraí. At the ferry crossing over the Rio Branco there is usually a long queue of waiting hikers; try to arrange a lift on the ferry. Hitching to Santa Elena, Venezuela, is not easy; either wait at the bridge and police checkpoint on the road to the border—be there early in the morning or about 1800-2200, or try to find a Venezuelan driver passing the *Hotel Tropical*. Drivers often charge for hitches—maybe as much as a bus fare.

Air Travel To Manaus; to Georgetown, Guyana, with Guyana Airlines; tickets sold at Cruzeiro office in town. Aircraft maintenance, baggage checking and handling are unreliable; Guyanese come to Boa Vista to buy goods unavailable in Guyana—make sure your luggage is not among the excess that has to be taken off the plane. Also to Lethem.

Border Crossing, Guyana Get exit stamp at police station in Lethem, Guyana, then take rowing-boat over border river Tacutu. No car ferry, but river can be forded in dry season. Once in Brazil, register at military camp at Bomfim (no hotels) and get entry stamp (closed for lunch). Phone Boa Vista 2290 (for one G$) for car to take you to Boa Vista (US$45), or if lucky, take a colectivo (US$15, 3 hrs.) or daily bus at 1500. The bus leaves Boa Vista for Bomfim at 1300 and 1500, US$6, 3 hrs.; luggage is checked at the Ministério da Fazenda checkpoint, before Bomfim, from where a jeep takes travellers to the Brazilian immigration post and then to the river, US$0.35, 5 km. in all. It is very difficult to hitch between Boa Vista and Bomfim. From Bomfim to Boa Vista the road is acceptable (2 buses daily), but subject to washouts; bridge over Rio Branco and car ferry operates every two hrs. Peter McAlpine (Totnes, Devon) tells us that there is another border crossing at Arimatung from where it is a hard, but rewarding walk to the Guyanese town of Orinduik. A weekly jeep connects Arimatung with Boa Vista (US$25), also twice-monthly flights. A good rate for cruzados is reported in the Guyana border area. Cruzados can only be changed into G$ in Guyana at Lethem; Bomfim is a much better place for exchange, but Boa Vista is best.

Border Crossing, Venezuela Everyone who crosses the border from Boa Vista, regardless of nationality, requires a visa. These can be obtained (allow at least 24 hrs.) from the Venezuelan Consulate in Boa Vista, Av. Benjamín Constant 525E, next to *Hotel Lua Nova* (open Mon.-Fri. 0800-1300); requirements are a yellow-fever vaccination certificate (obtainable at the airport—at Km. 350, Department of Health officials inoculate anyone arriving in Boa Vista who cannot produce a yellow fever vaccination certificate), an onward ticket (an MCO will suffice, but not a copy) and a passport photograph. (Venezuelan consulates in Rio and Manaus are *not* authorized to issue visas for overland travel into Venezuela. Border officials may also insist on a ticket out of Venezuela and US$20 a day—however, regulations state that a visa is sufficient. Trucks leave for Venezuela from Rua Benjamin Constant, drivers are not officially supposed to take passengers. Jeep service, Expresos la Reina, to Ciudad Bolívar in Venezuela. Eucatur runs a daily bus from Santa Elena to Manaus, via Boa Vista, US$4; the Eucatur bus leaves Boa Vista 0800, dep. Santa Elena 0730 from *Café Las 4 Esquinas*, journey 8 hrs. Border search may be thorough and you may be asked to show US$300. Entry stamp can now be obtained at border, which closes at 1700. There are a bank and a basic hotel, *Pacaraima Palace*, on Venezuelan side and you can camp. The road from the frontier is rough and hilly for the first 100 km., then flattens out and improves; many travellers find the journey worthwhile.

Caracaraí Hotels: *Márcia*, F; *Roraima*, F, cold shower, basic. A busy river port with modern installations; boats will take passengers to Manaus. N.B. The Perimetral Norte road marked on some maps from Caracaraí E to Macapá and W to the Colombian frontier does not yet exist; it runs only about 240 km. W and 125 km. E from Caracaraí, acting at present as a penetration road.

It is possible to get a launch up the Rio Negro to São Gabriel da Cachoeira, and continue from there to Venezuela (see Venezuela section). São Gabriel is near the Pico de Neblina National Park (Pico de Neblina is the highest mountain in Brazil, 3,014 metres); in São Gabriel, Tom Hanly, an Irish Salesian brother, is helpful, friendly and informative. The town has one hotel, cheap, clean, good food (ask for it), shops and, in the river, rapids for 1½ km.

Southern Amazonia

Porto Velho (300,000), capital of the State of Rondônia with a population of 700,000, stands on a high bluff overlooking a curve of the River Madeira; at the *top of the hill* is the cathedral, built in 1950. The principal commercial street is Av. Sete de Setembro, which runs from the railway station and market hall to the upper level of the city, past the Rodoviária. Parks are under construction. Rondônia is the focus of experimental development in agriculture, with concomitant colonization of the area. At the same time, much of the state is being reserved for Indians and national forests. Porto Velho is expensive because of the local gold rush. About 20 km. from Porto Velho, the Samuel hydroelectric scheme is under construction, with a new town to house the workers. The first phase was

BRAZIL 349

due to enter in operation in 1987, and eventually will provide power for the states of Rondônia and Acre. Malaria is common.

The Madeira is one of the major tributaries of the Amazon. The four main rivers which form it are the Madre de Dios, rising a short distance from Cuzco (Peru); the Beni, coming from the southern Cordillera bordering Lake Titicaca; the Mamoré, rising near Sucre, Bolivia; and the Guaporé, coming out of Mato Grosso, in Brazil.

Hotels *Rondón Palace,* C, opp. bus station, recommended; *Samaúma Palace,* Rua Dom Pedro II, 1038, C, nice rooms but said not too friendly (221-3159); *Seltom,* a/c, C, (nice swimming pool), and *Floresta,* D, a/c, swimming pool, which non-residents may use for the price of a drink or two; *Vitória,* E, plus private bath, quiet, good food. Hotels within sight of the Rodoviária: *Libra, Avenida Palace,* 2-star, *Porto Velho Palace,* 2-star, *Príncipe da Beira,* Rua Getúlio Vargas 2287, D (221-6135). From Rodoviária, take bus No. 301 "Presidente Roosevelt" (outside *Hotel Pontes*), which goes to railway station at riverside, then along Av. 7 de Setembro, passing: *Yara,* Gral. Osório 255, F; *Guaporé Palace,* 7 de Setembro 927, E, a/c, restaurant; *Nunes,* 7 de Setembro 1087, F; *Sonora,* 7 de Setembro 1103, F, clean, fan, clothes washing facilities; *Leyzer,* Av. Joaquim Nabuco 2110, F, basic, clean, good breakfast, friendly, fairly good cheap meals; *Laira,* Joaquim Nabuco 2005, F with fan; *Tres Irmãos,* Av. Nações Unidas 30. Hotels often full.

Electric Current 110 volts A.C., elsewhere in Rondônia 220 volts.

Restaurants At hotels: *Tarantella,* Av. Joaquim Nabuco with 7 de Setembro, fairly good pizza; *Juazeiro, Carreteiro, Dejoca, Tóquio* (cheap).

Shopping Bookshop off Av. 7 de Setembro, near the port, a few English paperbacks; manageress speaks English. Indian handicrafts at Casa do Índio, Rua Rui Barbosa 1407.

Travel Agent Rotur, near *Hotel Floresta.* Guaportetur, Av 7 de Setembro 925, Helga speaks English and German.

Exchange Banks, official rates; try *Hotel Seltom, Hotel Leyzer,* Varig or Cruzeiro do Sul office. Difficult elsewhere in Rondônia.

Air Services Airport 8 km. W of town. Daily flights to Manaus (US$120), Brasília, Cuiabá, Rio Branco, Corumbá (US$105.50), Cruzeiro do Sul, via Rio Branco, Mon., US$83.

River Services Manaus, 1st class, with passable food; 2nd class very crowded US$30. Journey takes 3-4 days when river high; as much as 7 days when low. The boat leaves on Sat. at 1800. 1st class means upper deck, with more hammock-hanging room, or, if lucky, one of two 2-person cabins (US$70). Advantages to 1st class: more room, better view, coffee with milk, meals served first. Food is safe to eat, though monotonous; water-purifying tablets or bottles of sterilized water strongly recommended. Wait at the Capitânia do Porto in the centre of town for a possible passage on a cargo boat; these boats leave from Porto Bras, down river from Porto Velho. Six days a week a boat leaves at 1800 for Manaus from Manicoré, at the confluence of the Rivers Madeira and Manicoré, US$32 for two nights, and one day's journey, including food. Porto Velho-Humaitá US$6.66 (boat *Dois de Junho*).

Roads to Cuiabá (BR-364, 1,450 km., fully paved; see page 357); Rio Branco, 490 km., following Madeira-Mamoré railway, due to be fully paved by 1987; to Humaitá (205 km.) on the Madeira river (fully paved), connecting with the Transamazônica Highway, and on to Manaus (877 km.), not completely paved. Road journeys are best done in the dry season, the second half of the year; the Manaus road (Catire Highway) is sometimes closed in the rainy season.

A result of the paving of BR-364 is the development of towns along it: Aviquemes (159 km. from Porto Velho, buses hourly from 0600, 3-4 hrs., Banco do Brasil, some hotels); Nova Vida (200 km.), Jaru (257 km.), Ouro Preto d'Oeste (297 km.), Ji Paraná (337 km.—bus to Porto Velho, US$7, 12 hrs.; hotels *Horizonte,* E, recommended with reasonable restaurants, *Sol Nascente,* F with *churrascaria, Hotel Transcontinental,* C, recommended; trips to frontier towns possible, e.g. Nova Colina), Presidente Médici (373 km.), Cacoal (404 km.), Pimenta Bueno (440 km.) and Vilhena (658 km. from Porto Velho, 710 km. from Cuiabá; *Diplomata Hotel,* D, near bus station; *Rodoviária,* F, recommended; *Gastão,* F). At Vilhena proof of yellow-fever inoculation required; if no proof, new shot.

Buses New Rodoviária on outskirts of town, Av. Pres. Kennedy (15 min. walk from *Seltom Hotel* on same street). Bus to Manaus, 1600, and 2000 normal (US$10), 1700 and 1800 (*leito* US$18), 24-26 hrs.; to Humaitá, US$2; to São Paulo, sixty-plus hrs., US$ 35; to Cuiabá, 24 hrs. US$27, take plenty of food and drink. To Guajará-Mirim, see below. To Rio Branco, twice daily, 18 hrs. (but can take 3-5 days), US$12. Daily bus with Eucatur from Cascavel (Paraná) via Maringá, Presidente Prudente, Campo Grande and Cuiabá to Porto Velho. To Cáceres for the Pantanal, Colibri, 18 hrs., US$12. Hitching difficult, try at the *posto* 2 km. out of town. For Manaus try at the ferry crossing just outside town.

Porto Velho was the terminus of the Madeira-Mamoré railway of 367 km. (closed 1971), Brazil's

350 BRAZIL

price to Bolivia for annexing the Acre territory during the rubber boom. It cost a life for every hundred sleepers, 6,208 in all, during construction. The line, built 1907-12, by-passed the 19 rapids of the Madeira and Mamoré rivers, and gave Bolivia an outlet of sorts to the Atlantic. It was supposed to go as far as Riberalta, on the Rio Beni, above that river's rapids, but stopped short at **Guajará Mirim** (12,000 people). The railway expert will enjoy the ancient steam locomotives in the railway station and on a siding 2 km. away. There are still two engines in working order, which run Sunday excursion trains as far as Santo Antônio, 25 km. away (US$0.10). Small railway museum at station has been moved so that the station can accommodate passengers on the newly restored line. (The conductor on the Saturday train, Silas Shockness, who also runs the shop where the locomotives are being repaired, is from Grenada and so speaks English; his brother Denis runs the museum and speaks English too.) The railway is now replaced by a fair road, which uses its bridges (in poor condition); the 370-km. bus ride (3 buses a day, US$7, takes 14 hrs. or more depending on season—road often closed March-May) is far faster than the train was. The Bolivian town of Guayaramerín is across the Mamoré river (expensive speedboat service or ferry, which is free for foot passengers); it is connected by road to Riberalta, and there are air services to other Bolivian cities. An ancient stern wheeler plies on the Guaporé; 26-day, 1,250 km. trips (return) can be made on the Guaporé from Guajará Mirim to Vila Bela in Mato Grosso, fare including food, is US$5. 170 km. from Guajará Mirim, on the Guaporé river, is the Forte Príncipe da Beira, begun in 1777 as a defence of the border with Bolivia. The fort, which is being restored, can be reached from Costa Marques (20 km. by road), which can only be reached by air or by river.

If travelling by road between Porto Velho and Guajará Mirim, two possible stops are at Maluca dos Índios, from where you can visit villages of gold prospectors by the Madeira river; the other is from the railway bridge just before Vila Murtinho where you can see gold panners, and, walking a few hundred metres, the rapids on the Mamoré river.

Guajará Mirim Hotels *Comercial*, F; *Mini-Estrela*, Av. 15 de Novembro 460, E; *Fénix Palace*, Av. 15 de Novembro 459, E; *Hudson*, Av. Marechal Deodoro s/n, F, recommended. *Camponês*, F.

Restaurant Best is *Oasis*, at Posto Nogueira service station, Av. 15 de Novembro 837, US$5 with drinks.

Museum Museu Municipal at the old railway station beside the ferry landing—small, with railway memorabilia and a few stuffed birds.

Exchange Banco do Brasil (foreign exchange a.m. only). Loja Nogueira, Av. Pres. Dutra, esq. Leopold de Matos (cash only).

Note If you need a visa to enter Brazil, apply to the Brazilian Consul at Guayaramerín (Bolivia), open 1100-1300, before crossing the Rio Mamoré into Brazil. If the Policia Federal are not on duty at the waterfront, you must get passport stamped at their office in town, address below. Similarly, before crossing into Bolivia you may need a visa (free) from the Bolivian consul in Guajará Mirim (2 photos needed) in 600's block of Av. 15 de Novembro. Western Europeans can cross river and visit the Immigration Office; which closes at 1100 on Sat. You will need a Brazilian exit stamp from Policia Federal, Av. Antônio Correia da Costa 482.

From Abunã, 220 km. from Porto Velho (*Hotel Ferroviário*, E, including meals, however town is best avoided if at all possible) the road from Porto Velho continues W to **Rio Branco**, the capital of the State of Acre, 90,000 people (*Hotel Chui*, most expensive but not clean, dirty swimming pool, a bit peculiar; *Inacio's*, rated locally as the best, good restaurant, on same street as *Chui*; opposite *Chui*, Rio Branco; *Amazonas*, *Fontes* (best of a bad bunch of budget hotels, F, not clean), *Fortaleza*, all on left bank; on right bank, *Sucessor*, F, showers, fan, clean, comfortable, friendly. Cheap meals at *Dos Colonos* near market. *Marayina*, next to *Chui*, for pizzas, sandwiches, cakes, ice cream, popular at night; *Churrascaria Triângulo*, near airport, as much charcoal-grilled meat as you can eat, recommended; *Churrascaria Modelo*, Rua Marechal Deodoro 360, less good). In front of the *Hotel Chui* is a park with a military garrison on one side; beyond is the Governor's palace and another park leading to the market on the bank of the Acre river. There is a bridge across the river, which is only navigable to Manaus in the wet season. The city has a Cathedral, an airport and an agricultural research centre.

Warning The road from Porto Velho to Rio Branco should be travelled with much caution; not only does the journey take as much as 3 to 5 days, but the area is seriously affected by malaria.

At Rio Branco the Transamazônica Highway meets the road from Brasília and goes on to Cruzeiro do Sul and Japim; it is expected to reach the Peruvian frontier further N when completed; it is hoped that it will be continued by the Peruvians to the river port of Iquitos. It is very difficult to get from Rio Branco to Cruzeiro do Sul by road because there is no bus service, and the occasional lorry goes mainly in the dry season. There is a plane (Varig) every Monday at 1130 to Cruzeiro do Sul (originating in Porto Velho).

Cruzeiro do Sul, an isolated Amazonian town of 10,000 people, is situated on the river Juruá; cheap excursions can be made on the river, for example to the village of Rodrigues Alves (2-3 hrs., return by boat or by road, 15 km.). In the jungle one can see rubber-tapping, and collecting the latex into "borrachas" which weigh up to 45 kg. Hotels: *Sandra's*, D; *Novo do Acre*, F, recommended, a/c, clean; *Hospedaria Janecir*, F; *dos Viajantes*; *Flor de Maio*, F, facing river, clean, showers, full board available. Restaurant *O Laçador*, good food. Money changing is very difficult; none of the banks will change dollars. Try the airline staff (poor rates). From Cruzeiro do Sul to Pucallpa one can go either by air: Sasa, US$37.50, 50 mins.,—details from Blvd. Taumaturgo 25 (no phone), flies only when plane is full, it seats 5; undertake all formalities at Policia Federal before leaving. Alternatively one can go by boat when river is high (Nov.-Feb.): only for the hardy and well-equipped; journey takes about 10 days: 4 by boat to Tamburiaco, on rivers Juruá and Juruá-Mirim, then 2 days' walk through the jungle to the Peruvian border at Canta Gallo, then 3-4 more days by boat on the rivers Amonia and Abojao to Pucallpa. The regional airline Taba have a permit to fly to Eirunepé on the Juruá river from Manaus and Tabatinga; Eirunepé is a small town near Carauari, where Dutch missionaries live.

A road from Rio Branco (the BR-317), paved as far as Xapuri, goes to Brasiléia (bus daily, 6 hrs., US$4, basic hotel, Federal Police give exit stamps), opposite the Bolivian town of Cobija on the Acre River, and finally to Assis Brasil at the intersection of the Peruvian, Bolivian and Brazilian frontiers; across the Acre River are Iñapari (Peru) and Bolpebra (Bolivia). There is no public transport, and little else, beyond Brasiléia to Iñapari. In Assis Brasil, there is one small hotel (a dormitory, basic but clean, friendly), one snack bar, a bank which does not change US dollars (the hotel owner may be persuaded to oblige) and river transport only, which is dependent on the seasons.

N.B. Rio Branco time is one hour behind Manaus time; this means two hours behind Brazilian Standard Time.

The Centre-West

The so-called centre-west of Brazil is occupied by the states of Goiás, Mato Grosso and Mato Grosso do Sul. Goiás is one of Brazil's most rapidly developing agricultural areas, producing cattle, coffee, soya and rice. The Federal District of Brasília (see page 212) was subtracted in 1960 from the territory of Goiás.

Goiânia, 202 km. SW of Brasília, the second (after Belo Horizonte) of Brazil's planned state capitals, was founded in 1933 and succeeded Goiás Velho as capital of the State of Goiás in 1937. It now has a population of 703,000. Goiânia is an exceptionally spacious city, with its main avenues excellently lit and ornamented with plants; tourists can enjoy the Parque Mutirama with its planetarium on the city's eastern side and the Horto Florestal, with good zoo and anthropological museum in the west; there are a racecourse and a motor racetrack. The Jaó Club on the edge of a reservoir provides for sun bathing and water skiing. Every Sunday morning there is a handicrafts fair in the city's central square, the Praça Cívica, where there is a small museum of local handicrafts, animals and Indian artefacts.

Hotels *Samambaia*, Av. Anhanguera 1157; *Bandeirantes*, same street, No. 3278; *Umuarama*, Rua 4, No. 492; *São Conrado*, Rua 3, No. 652; *Augustus*, Praça Antônio Lizita 702 (all good D-C). Many cheap hotels e.g. *Olímpia*, F, shower, near bus station, unfriendly; *J. Alves*, also opp. Rodoviária, better; *Santo Antônio*, Av. Anhanguera 6296, F.

Restaurants *Jaó Club*; *Long Feung*. Goiânia is much cheaper for eating and sleeping than Brasília. Restaurant at the Rodoviária for good food at very low prices, and plenty more eating places nearby.

Banks National banks.

Tourist Office Goiastur, in the football stadium (Estádio Serra Dourada), very friendly; it's rather remote!

Travel Agents Cardealtur, Av. Goiás 382; Incatur, Av. Goiás 151; Transworld, Rua 3, 560, in Galeria Central. All good for exchange.

Airport Nearby, with daily flights to main cities.

Roads and Buses To Cuiabá (Mato Grosso) paved, 4 buses a day, US$9, 13 hrs.; continues to Porto Velho (Rondônia) and Rio Branco (Acre); this stretch is now being paved, but will take years to complete. To Brasília (about 17 a day, 2½ hrs.) and São Paulo (bus services, US$8.25, 14 hrs. to São Paulo); Campo Grande 18 hrs. US$11. To Goiás Velho, 136 km. Distances by road (km.): Belém, 2,017; Brasília, 202; Campo Grande, 1,212; Corumbá, 1,641; Cuiabá, 934; Foz do Iguaçu, 1,232; Manaus, 3,222; Porto Alegre, 2,025; Recife, 2,505; Rio, 1,354; Salvador, 2,301; São Paulo, 918.

Anápolis, 61 km. nearer Brasília, with a population of 161,000, is an important trading centre.

352 BRAZIL

Hotels *Itamarati; Príncipe; Central Palace; Anápolis.* Many cheap ones around bus station.

Goiás Velho (25,000 population), a picturesque old gold-mining town founded in 1727, was capital of the State of Goiás until 1937. There is a regular bus service between Goiânia and Goiás Velho. The city has seven baroque churches, the oldest being São Francisco de Paula (1761).

Museums The Museu da Boa Morte in the colonial church of the same name has a small but interesting collection of old images, paintings, etc. The Museu das Bandeiras is in the old town hall and prison (Casa da Câmara e Cadeia), by the colonial fountain. The old Government Palace, with fine rooms, is now open to the public, next to the red-brick Cathedral in the main square. A local tradition is the Fogaréu procession in Holy Week.

José Joaquim da Veiga Valle, who was born in Pirenópolis in 1806, was the "Aleijadinho" of Goiás. Many of his works are in the Boa Morte museum. British artist Robin Macgregor, whose paintings are widely collected throughout Brazil, is a resident of Goiás Velho.

Hotels *Vila Boa*, large, C, pool, views; *Municipal*, simple, F; *Minas Goiás*, F incl. small breakfast, clean, in Rua Dr Americano do Brasil.

Restaurants *Pito Aceso*, grills; *Hotel Vila Boa*; *Pedro's Bar*, good cold beef. Try the local meat pie, *empadão goiano*.

Shopping Centro de Tradições Goianas, in *Hotel Vila Boa*.

Excursion Cachoeira Grande, 7 km. from Goiás Velho on the Juçara road, has bathing place and snack bar.

Pirenópolis, another colonial town, is 128 km. from Goiânia, 220 km. from Brasília. There is a regular bus service between Anápolis and Pirenópolis (66 km.). **Hotels**: *Rex*, F, *Central*, G (for the desperate).

Caldas Novas 187 km. SE of Goiânia (many buses; best reached via Morrinhos on the BR-153 Goiânia-São Paulo highway, population 10,000) is a newly-developed thermal resort with good hotels and camp sites with hot swimming pools. Daily bus from Morrinhos, US$0.50, 1½ hrs. There are three groups of springs within this area: Caldas Novas, Fontes de Pirapetinga (7 km. from the town) and Rio Quente (25 km. from the town); water temperatures are 37-51°C.

Hotels 48 in all. *Tamburi*, R. Eça de Queirós. Very fashionable is *Hotel Turismo* (5-star, L, full board, a/c) at Rio Quente, and, sharing some of its facilities, *Pousada do Rio Quente*, 3-star, B, full board, but not a/c. (The *Turismo* has a private airstrip; flights from Rio and São Paulo with agencies.) *Parque das Primaveras*, R. do Balneário, A/B, recommended by locals, cheaper than the Rio Quente places. Also *Motel Aguas Calientes* and *Cabanas do Rio Quente*. *Goiás*, F with breakfast, recommended. Camping at Esplanada, and Camping Clube do Brasil site on the Ipameri road, 1 km. from the centre. Many other "Clubes e Campings": *Tropical*, US$1 p.p., 2 sites in town, can use both in 1 day, others mostly US$1.30 a day, all have snack bars; *Berro d'Água* in Bairro do Turista recommended.

Two other natural attractions in Goiás are the Cachoeira do Salto (160 km. from Brasília) and the thermal waters of the Lagoa de Aporé on the border with Mato Grosso. At Cristalina (120 km. from Brasília) there is a waterfall; also semi-precious stones for sale (see page 218). The River Araguaia, forming the border between Goiás and the two Mato Grosso states, provides many sandy beaches and good fishing: 1,600 km. of the river are navigable by boat.

A dirt road connects Goiás Velho with Aragarças (on the Goiás side) and **Barra do Garças** (on the Mato Grosso side) on the River Araguaia (Barra can also be reached by a more southerly route from Goiânia). A road to the north of Barra extends as far as São João do Araguaia; where this road crosses the Rio dos Mortes is the town of **Xavantina** (*Hotel Xavantina*, F, basic; *Churrascaria Arca de Noé*, highly recommended). Anti-malaria precautions are recommended for the Rio Araguaia region. May is said to be the best time to visit the region; low water allows camping on beaches and islands, but others say Oct.-Feb., avoiding the rainy season. Avoid July, when the *fishermen and their families all come*. Boats and guides can be hired in Aruanã, Britânia or Barra do Garças. The river also contains the island of **Bananal** (20,000 sq. km.) the largest river island in the world, with a 460,000-hectare national park of virgin forest. *Hotel Chapéu de Palha* (20 km. from island, 80 km. from São Miguel do Araguaia) A, full board; fishing equipment and boats can be hired. Alternatively "botels" i.e. floating hotels.

To the west of Goiás are the states of Mato Grosso and Mato Grosso do Sul, with a combined area of 1,231,549 sq. km. and a population of only about 2.5 million, or just over two persons to the square km. The two states are half covered with forest, with a large swampy area (220,000 sq. km) called the Pantanal (roughly west of a line between Campo Grande and Cuiabá, between which there is a direct road), partly flooded in the rainy season. East of this line the pasture plains begin to appear. The Noroeste Railway and a road run across Mato Grosso do Sul through Campo Grande to Porto Esperança and Corumbá, both on the River Paraguay; much of the journey is across swamps, offering many sights of birds and other wildlife.

Campo Grande, the capital of the State of Mato Grosso do Sul (pop. 283,000), is a pleasant modern town. In the centre is a shady park and nearby the Casa do Artesanato (Av. Calógeras) has a good collection of Indian jewellery and arrows on sale. Mato Grosso do Sul is a good region for buying cheap, good leather shoes.

Regional Indian Museum (Museu Regional Dom Bosco), Rua Barão do Rio Branco 1843 (open daily 0700-1100, 1300-1700), has interesting exhibits and handicrafts of the Pantanal and Mato Grosso Indians. There is also a collection of animals and birds (particularly good and well-preserved) from the Pantanal, and a fossil collection.

Hotels *Jandaia,* Rua Barão de Rio Branco 1271, well located, best, B. *Campo Grande,* Rua 13 de Maio 2825, a/c, luxury, C. *Concord,* Av. Calógeras 1624, very good, swimming pool, a/c, C. *Fenícia,* Av. Calógeras 2262, a/c, D. *Anache,* Rua Marechal Rondón 1396, D. *Condor,* D, central, swimming pool; *Iguaçu,* opposite bus station but quiet, modern, clean, pleasant, D; *Gaspar,* Av. Mato Grosso 2, opp. railway station, F with bath, ask for quiet room, good breakfast, clean. *Rio,* Marechal Rondón 1499, in city centre, E, with bath, breakfast, a/c, good value, friendly, good restaurant; *Hospedaria Califórnia,* good, F. *Esperança,* near railway station, F, basic, hot water; many cheap and shabby *pensões* on Avs. Calógeras and Mato Grosso within a few blocks of railway station. *União,* E, Calógeras 2828, near the station, good breakfast, clean, but noisy, friendly; *Continental,* Rua Maracaju 229, 2 blocks from railway, 5 from bus terminal, F, clean, comfortable; *Plaza,* same street, F, clean, unfriendly; *Tupi,* between bus and railway stations, cheap, basic; *Cosmos,* at bus station, E, reasonable; *Nacional,* Rua Dom Aquino 610, near bus station, F, fair; *Campos,* Av. Calógeras 2668, F; basic; *Caçula,* Av. Calógeras, F, cheap, near railway station; *Tropical,* E, at bus station. Some hotels near bus station relatively cheap, best go into town. *Dormitório,* opposite bus station, F, basic.

Restaurants at Campo Grande: *Cabana Gaúcha,* Av. Afonso Pena, 1919, recommended, live music evenings; *Vitório,* next door, slightly cheaper, also live music evenings; *Churrascaria do Papai,* at bus station, huge meal; *Carinca,* SE corner of main *praça,* modern, clean, good plain food. *Hong Kong,* Rua Maracaju 131, centre, good Chinese food; *Lanchonete Arabe* recommended. *Cafeteria Lojas Americanas,* Marechal Rondón 1336, in a supermarket; *El Café,* R. Dom Aquino 1248, both good. Plenty of good, cheap places in Rua Barão de Rio Branco, e.g. *Sabor e Artes,* No. 1016.

Bank Banco do Brasil changes travellers' cheques.

Post Office on corner of R. Dom Aquino and Calógeras.

Tourist Information, maps, etc. at MSTur at Av. Afonso Pena 3149. Also maintains a counter at the airport.

Tourist Agencies Tainá Viagens e Turismo, R. Ruy Barbosa 2646, English spoken. Time Tour Turismo not recommended.

Roads Distances in km. from Campo Grande: Belém, 3,299; Brasília, 1,405; Corumbá, 429; Cuiabá, 712; Foz do Iguaçu, 1,141; Goiânia, 1,212; Manaus, 3,006; Porto Alegre, 1,786; Recife, 3,708; Rio, 1,475; Salvador, 2,935; São Paulo, 1,046.

Buses (Taxi to Rodoviária, US$1.75.) São Paulo, paved road, US$15.75, 16 hrs. 6 buses daily, 1st at 0800, last at 2100, *leito* buses at 1600 and 2000. Cuiabá, US$7, 10 hrs., 12 buses daily, *leito* at 2100 and 2200. To Brasília, US$25 (Motta recommended), 23 hrs. at 0900. Rio de Janeiro, US$24, 21 hrs., 4 buses daily, *leito* at 1745. Corumbá, 1 daily bus at 0930 (be at ticket office at 0700), US$7, 7½-11 hrs., on surfaced road (often flooded). Campo Grande-Corumbá buses connect with those from Rio and São Paulo, similarly those from Corumbá through to Rio and São Paulo. Ponta Porã, 5½ hrs., Expresso Queiroz, US$5, 5 ordinary buses a day, 2 executive buses, US$7.50, 8 buses daily, 1st at 0630, last at 2130. Dourados, same schedule as Ponta Porã, 4 hrs., US$3. Beyond Dourados is Mundo Novo, from where buses go to Punta Porã (0530) and to Porto Frajelli (many between 0420 and 1900,½ hr.); from Mundo Novo ferries for cars and passengers go to Guaíra for US$0.20. Buses Campo Grande-Mundo Novo, 0900, 10 hrs. in dry weather, US$4.20, return 0730 and 1800; buses Dourados-Mundo Novo, unpaved road, four a day. No direct service to Foz do Iguaçu; journey takes 21 hrs. via Londrina, with good connections, or 24 hrs. via Maringá, with less good ones.

354 BRAZIL

Air Daily flights to São Paulo, Rio, Corumbá, Cuiabá, Brasília, Manaus, Porto Velho. To Foz do Iguaçu, 4 a week, 1 hr. flight with VASP. Reduction of 30% on VASP night flights to Rio and São Paulo. City bus stops outside airport. Taxi to airport, US$3.

Trains The railway station is 5 blocks from the bus terminal. Ponta Porã, slow train (6 hrs.) daily at 1200 (not Sun.). Ponta Porã to Campo Grande at 0845, US$4 1st class, US$2.25 2nd class on the train (this service is under threat—check). To Corumbá: twice daily. Fast night train at 2010, arriving 0640, US$20 double sleeper (recommended), US$5.50 pullman, no 2nd class. Day train leaves at 0815, arriving 1915, meals served at seats, US$3. Fares US$3 1st class, US$2 2nd class (no advance ticket sales, office open 0640-0815), a very tiring journey. Thefts and drugged food reported on this journey. To São Paulo: twice daily, with change at Bauru, where connections to/from São Paulo are not guaranteed and you may have to wait a day. Fast train at 1830, arriving 2000 the next day. Slower train at 0930, arriving Bauru 0505 next day, should catch São Paulo train at 0800. 1st class US$13.75, 2nd class US$8.75 (sleeping cars only from Bauru to São Paulo). Restaurant on train. 2nd class to Bauru, US$4.50.

The Campo Grande—São Paulo journey can be broken at **Tres Lagoas** near the Paraná river and on the railway, and 10 hours by road to São Paulo (bus Campo Grande—Tres Lagoas, 8 hrs., US$8, dep. 1100, a bumpy, interesting journey). *Novo Hotel* near bus station, F. friendly.

A road (being paved) and railway run SW from Campo Grande to **Ponta Porã** (14,500 people), on the Paraguayan border opposite the town of Pedro Juan Caballero.

Hotels *Pousada do Bosque*, very nice motel type with a/c, restaurant and swimming pool, Av. Pres. Vargas, out of town, D. *Barcelona*, Rua Guia Lopes, maze-like building, pool, restaurant, a/c, D-E. *Internacional*, Rua Internacional 1267, E with a/c, F with bath or without, hot showers, clean, good breakfasts, recommended; *Francia*, F, opposite *Barcelona*, bath, clean, friendly, restaurant, US$3 for big meal. *Grande*, Av. Brasil 1181, E. *Cacique*, F; *Palace*, F; *Alvorada*, F, clean and pleasant; *Amambaí*, F. *Dos Viajantes*, opp. railway station, G, very basic, clean.

Restaurants *Top Lanches*, beside *Hotel Barcelona*, cheap and friendly. *Chapão*, good food at reasonable prices. *Pepe's Lunch e Pizzeria*, good, fairly cheap; *Karina Lanches*, near federal Police office, good, cheap; *Santa Antônia*, recommended.

Electric Current 220 volts A.C.

Exchange Banco do Brasil changes travellers' cheques. Several *cambios* on the Paraguayan side, but none deal in cheques.

The border post at Ponta Porã normally closes at 1700 (it is also closed on national holidays). The Federal Police office is in a new white building shared with an engineering supply company in the same block as the Expresso Queiroz Rodoviária; open 0800. To reach Paraguayan control, follow the Rua Guia Lopes 4 blocks into Paraguay. If crossing into Paraguay some nationalities require visa from Paraguayan consulate next door to *Hotel Internacional*, Rua Internacional.

A new area of tourist interest in Mato Grosso do Sul is being established in the municipalities of Bonito (hotels: *Bonanza*, *Alvorado*, *Florestal*, all F; campsite at Ilha do Padre, 10 km. N of Bonito, very pleasant, no regular transport; restaurant, *Tapera*) and Aquidauana (several hotels around railway station, including *Fluminense*, F with fan and breakfast, a/c more expensive), where cave formations comparable to those found in the Lagoa Santa region of Minas Gerais are encountered. Two of the first to be opened are the Lago Azul and N.S. Aparecida (Sérgio Gonzales in Prefeitura of Bonito controls entry), both 26 km. from Bonito (no buses) and 320 km. from Campo Grande. Lago Azul has a lake 150 metres long and 70 metres wide. It is best visited in Jan.-Feb., 0700-0900 for the light, but there are no organized visits as yet, so Brazilian holiday times are best. Bus Bonito-Campo Grande, US$4, 3 hrs, 0545 and 1600. Also possible by changing at Jardim. Daily bus between Bonito and Aquidauana, about 3 hrs. on dirt road.

Corumbá, on the River Paraguay, with Bolivia on the opposite bank, has a population of 180,000 people and millions of mosquitoes. River boats ply occasionally between it and Buenos Aires. The Forte de Coimbra, the city's most historic building, which may be visited, was built in 1775. In the hills to the south is the world's greatest reserve of manganese, now beginning to be worked. From the Bolivian border town of Quijarro a 650-km. railway is open westwards to Santa Cruz de la Sierra, and there is a road of sorts. The Campo Grande-Corumbá road, via Aquidauana, crosses the Paraguay by ferry (very rough, often flooded, no gasoline between Miranda and Corumbá). The scenery between Campo Grande and Corumbá is most interesting, the road and railway follow different routes, but the train is more reliable, cheaper and less tiring than the bus (though slower).

BRAZIL 355

Warning Police have very strict controls on drug-trafficking in Corumbá; there are many drug-runners, searches are very thorough and none too polite. We have received reports of drug-planting by customs officials.

Hotels *Santa Mônica*, R. Antônio Maria Coelho, 369, a/c, D, good restaurant; *Alphahotel*, next door, E, clean and new (opened 1984); *Nacional*, R. América 934, C, good pool, river trips arranged; *Grande Hotel*, R. Frei Mariano 468, F without bath; *Santa Rita*, Dom Aquino 860 (unsigned), E, with bath, F without, bathrooms dirty otherwise clean but basic, noisy, good lunch in restaurant; *Paris*, R. Antônio Maria Coelho, E, with fan, quiet, many very short-stay couples. *Loja*, Delamaré 903, F; *Salette*, same street, No. 893, F, recommended; *Santa Cruz*, No. 909, E, restaurant, improved; *Camba*, R. Portocarreiro 1064, F, near railway; next door is *Crucenho*, No. 1056, F. *Schabib*, Rua Frei Mariano 1153, E, basic but clean, owner friendly, multilingual and helpful, recommended. *Residencila*, opposite railway station, F, basic adequate, friendly, meals available; *Internacional*, opposite station, which has day and night prices—one night and day F, friendly, basic, cockroaches; *Mini Corumbá*, Frei Mariano 1354, F, with breakfast; *Esplanada*, across from railway station, F, cold shower; *Central*, G, basic but clean. *Espanha*, Rua 13 de Junho 776, F, meals for US$2. *Nelly*, pretty good value, excellent breakfast. There are cheap hotels within sight of railway station; most are reported dirty.

Restaurants *Churrascaria Gaúcha*, R. Frei Mariano; *Tarantella* (Italian), R. Frei Mariano and América, good, large helpings; *Peixaria de Lulu*, nr. centre, good; *Churrascaria Rodeio*, very good; another good, cheap *churrascaria* in Rua Antônio Maria Coelho. *São Paulo*, Rua Delamaré, in centre, good juices and sandwiches, cheap. Good beer at *Bar Zico*, Rua Frei Mariano. *El Pacu*, on the waterfront, run by a German, Hermann, and his Brazilian wife, good source of information on river travel and Pantanal excursions.

Museum Museu Regional do Pantanal, Rua Delamaré 939, 0800-1100, 1400-1800; Sat. 0800-1200; closed Sun. Arts and Crafts Centre, Rua Dom Aquino Correa, in a converted prison.

Exchange Banco do Brasil changes travellers' cheques (open a.m. only). Try *A Favorita* shop, Rua Antônio Maria Coelho, or at the border—cash only (it is impossible to change pesos into cruzados in town). Street traders in shopping street between Rua Delamaré and Post Office.

Travel Agents Turismo Pantanal, R.Manoel Cavassa 219, good one-day river tour with *Lancha Pérola*.

Shipping Paraguayan FME to Asunción, beautiful trip. When you enter Corumbá by boat, officials board vessel to stamp passports. No regular passenger service. Seek information at *El Pacu* restaurant, or from small cargo boats at the waterfront. (See page 357, under Cáceres.)

Air To Cuiabá, Manaus, Porto Velho. VASP daily to Campo Grande at 1110, and on to São Paulo. VASP daily to Rio, US$120. Daily private flights to Santa Cruz, Bolivia, especially in rainy season, US$100 per person—cheaper to travel overland to Asunción and fly from there.

Trains and Buses The day train from Corumbá to Bauru, via Campo Grande and with very poor connections to São Paulo, leaves at 0715, arriving in Campo Grande at 1827 (US$4 in 2nd), and Bauru at midday the next day US$17.25, (very crowded and tiring). Tickets can only be booked as far as Bauru (tickets can be bought from 1300 on previous day), US$6, 1st class. Buses from Campo Grande to São Paulo are quicker, but dearer. Fare Corumbá to Campo Grande US$3 1st., US$2 2nd; ordinary train takes 11 hours. A second train (express) leaves Corumbá for Campo Grande at 2055, arriving 0700 (US$15.50 double sleeper—good, US$5.50 pullman, no 2nd class). Trains pretty comfortable, but dusty; good food on board. Thefts and drugged food reported. The Corumbá-São Paulo bus journey takes 24-30 hrs. (US$10). Bus, Corumbá-Brasília, 24 hrs., US$13.75; bus, Corumbá-Campo Grande, 11 hrs., US$7, leaves at 2100. Four buses (Andorinha) to Rio daily, US$14. Bus station is on R. Antônio Maria Coelho, half way between railway station (where passport control is done) and town centre (also for Andorinha buses; Viação Motta bus terminal is nearby). Taxis from railway station to centre are extortionate. Don't rely on getting a supply of cruzados in Bauru; exchange is difficult there. Stock up in Corumbá.

There are four train services to Santa Cruz in Bolivia, the *ferrobus*, *rápido*, *omnibus* and *mixto*; all leave from Quijarro, the Bolivian frontier station, not from Corumbá. The schedule of each appears to change frequently so check on arrival in Corumbá; also check when the ticket office is open for the train you wish to take, to purchase tickets as early as possible. Quijarro-Santa Cruz *ferrobus*, Tues., Thurs., Sat., 0800 (Santa Cruz-Quijarro, Mon., Weds., Fri., 1700) Pullman US$14.50, special US$13.50; *rápido* Quijarro-Santa Cruz, Mon., Weds., Fri. (perhaps daily), 1500 (Santa Cruz-Quijarro Tues., Thurs., Sun., 1210); *omnibus* (stopping train), Quijarro-Santa Cruz, Mon., Fri., 1150 (Santa Cruz-Quijarro, Thurs., Sun., 1404); *mixto* Quijarro-Santa Cruz Weds., Sun., 1500 (Santa Cruz-Quijarro, Mon., Fri., 2115), fares on last 3, pullman US$12, first US$10, second US$6 (all converted from pesos). If immigration is closed, buy your train ticket before going there. It is worth buying a 1st class seat, which is much more comfortable on night trips than the 2nd class, but these are often mysteriously "sold out". 2nd class is on the baggage van floor, is crowded and there are no toilet or water facilities. Stops at stations are brief; take your own water; journey time 19½'Y hrs (not recommended). Colectivo Corumbá-Quijarro, US$0.15, from in front

356 BRAZIL

of Dona Aparecida's store, *A Favorita*, R. A. Maria Coelho (Dona Aparecida changes money outside banking hours; bargaining recommended). Also taxis, US$4.30; colectivo border—Quijarro US$1. The railway to Santa Cruz is liable to flood damage.

Going to Bolivia Immigration and emigration formalities are constantly changing so check procedure in advance. Have passport stamped by Brazilian Policia Federal at Corumbá train station (published opening hours, 0600-1130, 1300-1600, 1915-2100, Sat. and Sun. 0600-0730, 1030-1130, 1900-2100). Take taxi, or walk, to Rodoviária, then bus to Bolivian border post (15 mins.), go through formalities, then take colectivo to Quijarro for train. Best to get some Bolivian pesos in Corumbá. Bolivian Consulate in Corumbá: Rua Antônio Maria Coelho 825 (colectivos may be caught nearby for frontier), Mon.-Fri., 0700-1100, 1500-1730, Sat. and Sun. closed. Alternative to train: Bolivian TAM flight, from border to Santa Cruz, daily between 1100 and 1300, US$27.

Coming from Bolivia If you arrive at the border when the Bolivian offices are closed (e.g. at night) and you therefore have no exit stamp, be prepared to be sent back for an exit stamp by Brazilian officials in Corumbá (the Bolivian border post opens at 0700). If you arrive in Brazil without a yellow fever vaccination certificate, you must go to Rua 7 de Setembro, Corumbá, for an inoculation. When travelling from Quijarro, take a colectivo (bargain fare) to the Bolivian border, go through formalities (US$0.15), outside office take bus to Corumbá Rodoviária (US$0.10). Taxi or walk to railway station for Brazilian formalities (some buses go direct to the station): be quick to catch the office open.

Pantanal This vast swampy area, located between Cuiabá, Campo Grande and the Bolivian frontier, is one of the world's great wildlife preserves, slowly being opened up to tourism. The flora and fauna are similar in many ways to those of the Amazon basin, though because of the more veldt-like open land, the wildlife can be viewed more easily than in the dense jungle growth. Principal life seen in this area are over 600 species of birds, in the main, waders and water fowl, storks (the *tuiuíu* is almost two metres tall), herons, coots, ducks, as well as pheasants, quails and parrots. There are some 350 varieties of fish, from the giant *pintado*, weighing up to 80 kilos, to the voracious *piranha*. Fishing here is exceptionally good, especially during the season, December through March. Animal life is represented by deer, ocelot, puma, boar, anteaters, *pacu*, tapir, rhea and the ubiquitous *capivara*, a species of giant aquatic guinea-pig. Probably the most impressive sight is the *jacaré* (Brazilian alligator). The extraordinary thing is that man and his domesticated cattle thrive together with the wildlife with seemingly little friction. Local farmers and the National Parks Authority protect the area jealously. (Only one area is officially national park, the Biological Reserve of Cará-Cará in the municipality of Cáceres, 80,000 hectares of land and water, only accessible by air or river. Permission to visit at Delegacia Estadual do IBDF, Av. Jaime Figueiredo 550, Cuiabá.) Hunting in any form is strictly forbidden. Fishing is allowed throughout the year, but not encouraged in the breeding season (August to beginning of the rains). The International Union for the Conservation of Nature is concerned at the amount of poaching, particularly of *jacaré* skins and *capivaras*, so further restrictions on visiting may be introduced.

There are two distinct seasons. In the rainy season, most of the area floods, and animals crowd on to the few islands remaining above water. It is extraordinary to see ocelots and pumas living side by side with deer and *capivara*. During the dry season (July to beginning of October), is the nesting and breeding season. At this time the birds form vast nesting areas, with hundreds and thousands crowding the trees creating an almost unsupportable cacophony of sounds. At this time the white sand river beaches are exposed, where *jacarés* bask in the sun.

The Pantanal is not easy to visit. One finds public transport all around the perimeter, but none at all within. Litter is becoming a problem; don't contribute to it.

There are several lodges with fair to good accommodation, some only approachable by air or river; most are relatively expensive. Following is a list of those presently operating:

From Cuiabá: *Santa Rosa Pantanal Hotel*, reservations at the Santa Rosa Hotels or Selva Turismo in Cuiabá, 250 km. from Cuiabá near Porto Jofre. A, with full board, an old *fazenda*, a good starting point for trips into the rivers. Buses run from Cuiabá to Poconé (100 km., US$1.50) from where one can hire a car from hotel in the main square or hitch (very difficult) to Porto Jofre, or hire a vehicle to get there, around US$150 (see under Cuiabá). *Hotel Pixaim*, D, 170 km. from Cuiaba, halfway between Poconé and Porto Jofre. *Hotel-Fazenda Cabanas do Pantanal*, A, 142 km. from Cuiabá, 50 km. from Poconé by the rivers Piraim and Cuibá, on the northern edge of the Pantanal, 10 chalet bedrooms with bath, restaurant, boat trips (few in dry season), horse-riding, fishing, helpful proprietor and staff, everything except boat trips and bar drinks included in price (booking: Praça da República 108, Cuiabá, Tel.: 065-322-1353). *Pousada do Barão*, near Barão de Melgaço, reservations through Onlytur, R. Siqueira Campos 43, conj. 901, Copacabana, Rio 20031 (Tel. 257-7773), 150 km. from Cuiabá, access by bus to Barão de Melgaço and boat from there on, A, with full board, transport from Barão de Melgaço to the lodge, US$20 p.p. *Jauru-Taiamã* camp, 140 km. south of Cáceres, bus to Cáceres (see 357) then by boat, or air taxi from Cuiabá, reservations at Tel.: 321-6808, or Toulemonde Turismo, Av. Ipiranga 313, office 42, São Paulo, no rates available. Fishermen will not give lifts on the Pantanal since none have been murdered. Boats ply between Porto Cercado (near *Cabanas do Pantanal*) via Porto Jofre to Corumbá (48 hrs.) about once a week, e.g. *San Antônio* and *Elza*.

BRAZIL 357

From Corumbá: *Pousada do Pantanal*, 125 km. from Corumbá near the Campo Grande road, easy access by bus, reservations from Pantanal Empreendimento Turísticas Ltda, Rua Frei Mariano 295A, Corumbá, Tel.: 231-5797/5894, or from an agency in Rua 13 de Julho, Corumbá, or São Paulo Tel.: 258-8086, A with full board (try bargaining in the off-season for reduced rates), recommended; horses, canoes, simple fishing gear, guides included, motor boats for rent. *Fazenda Santa Blanca*, S of Porto Esperança, C, full board, very clean and friendly, good kayak excursions, information from *Hotel Schabib*, Corumbá. *Fazenda Morrinhos (Motel do Severino)*, 67 km. from Corumbá on the Campo Grande road, easy access by bus, reservations in Corumbá, Tel.: 231-4460, A with full board. *Fazenda Santa Clara*, also on Campo Grande road, comfortable, relaxing, B, good excursions but many mosquitoes. *Rancho Kué*, 120 km. by air from Corumbá, or 210 km. by river, on the junction of the São Lourenço and Paraguai rivers; located in the centre of the Pantanal, probably the best location of all, and the most difficult to reach; at present in refurbishment; reservations in Aquidauana, Tel.: 2-1875, or São Paulo, Tel.: 228-8015, Rua Beneficência Portuguesa 24, 3rd floor, room 317, Ms. Cristina Schmitt. or Sr. Macedo, Rua 13 de Junho 1044, Suite 44, Tel.: 231-1460. An American, Bill Seffusatti, takes day trips by boat into the Pantanal, September-February, 0800-1800, for US$32 for 4, recommended; contact him on the quay, at *Hotel Schabib*, or at Travessa Mercúrio, Corumbá, Tel.: 231-4834. Contact also Hermann, at *El Pacu* bar (see above). In the wet season, access to the Pantanal from Corumbá is only by boat. Boats can be hired for US$25 a day through the Varig/VASP tourist agency. Cattle boats will take passengers on their round trips to farms in the Pantanal, 3 days, US$6.50 but take your own food—it is not possible to disembark. Ask at Bacia da Prata, 10 mins. out of Corumbá on the Ladário bus (the gatekeeper is unhelpful). Road trips from Corumbá into the Pantanal US$35 for 6 hours per vehicle.

From Campo Grande: *Hotel dos Camalotes*, Porto Murtinho, 440 km. from Campo Grande; access by bus long, tedious, bumpy and dusty; best access by air taxi. 4-star luxury hotel on the shores of the Paraguai river, favoured by wealthy Paulistas, A, with full board. *Cabana do Pescador*, 50 km. from Aquidauana on the Miranda river, access by bus to Aquidauana, and local bus to Bonito, possible to visit the impressive Bonito Caves, A, includes breakfast. *Pesqueiro do Lontra*, 180 km. from Aquidauana on the Corumbá road, access by bus, same rates as *Cabana do Pescador*. Both the latter lodges can be reserved at the same place as *Rancho Kué*.

A suggestion from Stephen L. Meredith, London SW19, is to take the 0715 train from Corumbá to Agente Inocêncio, where you change for the local train to Porto Esperança, a 10-minute journey. There you may be able to hire a boat for a 2-3 hr. trip on the River Paraguai (about US$15, but bargain). The return train connects with the main line train at 1718. You can walk back along the track, but this is dangerous on the bridges, which have gaps between the sleepers.

It seems that wildlife has already disappeared from the River Paraguai, so it is now necessary to make trips on the smaller rivers to see it.

Tours to N or S Pantanal arranged in Rio de Janeiro by Pelajo Turismo, Av. Rio Branco 52, 16th floor, Tel.: 296-4466 or 233-5085: from 4 to 8 days.

River trips from Cuiabá to Corumbá are very difficult since boats on the Cuiabá river are few and irregular. It may be possible from **Cáceres**, a riverside town (pop. 60,000), 250 km. west of Cuiabá, very hot and not much to do if you get stuck there. *Hotel Fénix*, C-D, fridge, a/c, TV; *Santa Terezinha*, Rua Tiradentes 485, F with fan, breakfast, not clean, friendly. Many other cheap hotels, e.g. *Hispano*, F, clean. Good restaurant: *Paraná*, on 7 de Setembro. Change money elsewhere: travellers' cheques take 10 days to change at the banks, Soteco by the main square changes cash at the official rate. From Cáceres the *28 de Setembro* sails to Corumbá; it is a cattle boat in the service of Serviço de Navegação da Bacia da Prata, leaving Cáceres at most twice a month. The 2-3 day journey covers 482 km., US$16 with meals (excellent food—recommended) or US$4 with no food. The Serviço de Navegação has no office in Cáceres: you must wait until the boat arrives to see if you can get on. For information on boat sailings, ask at the Capitânia dos Portos, on the corner of the main square at the waterfront. If possible phone in advance to Cáceres, Posto Arrunda, 221-17-07 to find out which boats are going. Also Portobrás on the outskirts at the waterfront (Tel.: 221-1728), helpful, but ultimately it is up to the boat's captain. If you ask at Portobrás you may (with a lot of luck) be able to get passage on a cement boat; they run about twice a month, US$4, food extra, 3 days to Corumbá (8 the other way). These boats are officially not allowed to take passengers. You may have a better chance of getting a boat in Corumbá since there are more head offices and river traffic. Bus Cuiabá-Cáceres, US$5, 10 a day (book in advance, very crowded), 3½ hrs. now that the road is paved, one stop in the jungle at a restaurant.

From Cáceres to the Bolivian border: Get passport stamped by the Federal Police then take the 1600 bus to San Matías, Bolivia, where you must have your passport stamped. Spend your last cruzados in San Matías, a small town, which is cheaper than Cáceres but more expensive than the rest of Bolivia (*Residencial Génova*, F, recommended; military flights on Fri. and Sun. to Santa Cruz via Roboré—book in advance).

Cuiabá, the capital of Mato Grosso state, on the Rio Cuiabá, an upper tributary of the River Paraguai, has an imposing government palace and other fine buildings round a green main square. Alt.: 165 metres; pop.: 168,000. There is a

358 BRAZIL

paved road to Campo Grande (712 km.), on the Noroeste railway to São Paulo, and the 2,400 km. BR-364 road from Brasília to Porto Velho and Rio Branco passes through Cuiabá; it is paved all the way between Brasília, Cuiabá and Porto Velho. The more direct road to Brasília through Barra do Garças and Goiás Velho is not yet paved. A road to connect Cuiabá with Corumbá (which can be reached by water in the rainy season), across the Pantanal, has reached Porto Jofre on the Cuiabá River. Work has been suspended indefinitely because of difficulties, costs and ecological considerations. A mark in the Praça Moreira Cabral shows the geographical centre of South America. It is very hot; coolest months for a visit are June, July, and August, in the dry season. Good fishing in the Cuiabá and smaller Coxipo rivers (fish and vegetable market, picturesque, at the riverside); wildlife for photography, and the Aguas Quentes hot springs, 90 km. (*Hotel Aguas Quentes*) can be visited. The University of Mato Grosso has an attractive museum of Indian objects (closed Sat. and Sun.), and the military post near the University has a small zoo.

Hotels *Santa Rosa Palace*, Av. Getúlio Vargas 600, A, overpriced, not recommended except for its swimming pool, and *Santa Rosa Excelsior*, Av. Getúlio Vargas 246, not recommended either, C, a/c, restaurants. *Aurea Palace*, Gen. Melo 63, B, pleasant rooms, restaurant, swimming pool, good; *Fenícia*, Av. Getúlio Vargas 296, D, with a/c, no restaurant, good. *Bandeirantes*, Av. Coronel Escolástico 425, D, a/c, out of centre; *Almanara*, Av. Coronel Escolástico 510, D, new, opposite *Bandeirantes* and better. *Mato Grosso*, Rua Comandante Costa 2522, almost opposite the *Fenícia* and down a side street, small, clean, restaurant, E. *Capri*, F, good food. *Santiago*, Av. General Mello 115 (centro), F, very friendly, clean, laundry, meals. *Samara*, Rua Joaquim Murtinho 150, central, E, breakfast, hot shower, fan, good, clean, friendly; *Presidente*, Av. Getúlio Vargas 119, central, fans in rooms, F. Cheap clean hotel near old bus station, *Cidade Verde*, F. *Dormitório Cézar*, near bus terminal, F; others in same area. incl. *Danúbio*, F with bath, breakfast, friendly, excellent restaurant.

Restaurants average except for the excellent restaurant at the Casa do Artesão (see below under souvenirs); try *Novo Mato Grosso*, next *Sayonara Club* on Coxipo river (club is a good place for children). Try also *Tip-Top*; or at Várzea Grande, nearby, there is a floating fish-restaurant on the river. *Churrascaria Majestic*, Av. Coronel Escolástico 585, very good; *Bierhaus*, Rua Bolívar; *Cristóvão*, Av. Isaac Póvosa 1200, good *churrascaria*. *Beija Flor*, Rua Galdino Pimentel, good and cheap.

Electric Current 110 volts A.C.

Entertainment Cuiabá is quite lively at night; *Disco Keda d'Agua* and nearby *Pino's Ball* bowling alley, both on Av. C.P.A.

Souvenirs Handicrafts in wood, straw, netting, leather, skins, Pequi liquor, crystallized *caju* fruit, compressed *guaraná* fruit (for making the drink), Indian objects on sale at airport, bus station, and craft shops in centre, such as the Casa do Artesão, Av. Mário Correa 310, interesting; Funai (Indian Foundation) shop, poor stock, Rua Barão de Melgaço 3900, opposite Shopping Cuiabá.

Money Exchange at *Santa Rosa Palace* and *Fenícia* hotels.

Car Hire Locadora de Veículos Frescino, Rua Comandante Castro with Av. Dom Bosco; a VW Beetle costs about US$30 a day. (Beyond Poconé on the Transpantaneira, only diesel and gasoline available in Porto Jofre, no alcohol.)

Tourist Information Turimat, state tourist authority, Praça República, next to Post Office building. Good maps, friendly, helpful regarding boats to Corumbá, but double-check information. Maintains a counter at the airport, frequently unstaffed. Santa Rosa Hotels also has a counter there. Ramis Bucair, Rua Pedro Celestino 280, is good for detailed maps of the region. Confiança, Praça da República 108, very helpful travel agency. Also recommended is Cuiabá Tour, Rua Barão de Melgaço 3508 (Edif. Irene), Sala 4, only Portuguese and Spanish spoken. Selva Turismo (Tel.: 32-2007) can take bookings for Pantanal hotels.

Excursions To **Chapada dos Guimarães**, 68 km. from Cuiabá, a pleasant ride into the mountains (bus from Cuiabá US$0.80). See the Véu de Noiva (Bridal Veil) waterfall (70 metre drop), strange rock formations, canyons, and the beauty spots of Mutuca, Salgadeira, Rio Claro, Portão do Inferno, and the falls of Cachoeirinhas—all unspoilt but none easy to reach. Chapada itself is a small village with the oldest church in the Mato Grosso, Our Lady of Santana (1779), a huge spring-water public swimming pool, and a good *churrascaria*; it is still inhabited mainly by *garimpeiros* (diamond-seekers), but a craft community is being established, complete with health food shops.

To the Pantanal by the Transpantaneira Highway to Porto Jofre. Excursions (very expensive) can be arranged by Santa Rosa hotels to the *Santa Rosa Pantanal Hotel*, or by bus to Poconé, and hitch-hike to Porto Jofre (see section on Pantanal). Very little traffic on this road. Watch out for park rangers, who can be very helpful and friendly, after you have persuaded them you are not poachers or hunters. The research station 40 km. from the end of the Transpantaneira is for Brazilian scientists only.

Transport By air to Corumbá, São Paulo, Manaus, Campo Grande, Goiânia, Brasília, Rio de Janeiro and Porto Velho. One may be lucky enough to get an air force flight to Porto Velho—a letter of introduction may help. Comfortable buses (toilets) to Campo Grande, 719 km., 10 hrs., US$7, 12 buses daily, *leito* at 2000 and 2100. To São Paulo, 24 hours, US$16, Rio de Janeiro, 32 hrs., US$22.15, Goiânia, 14 hrs., US$9; direct to Brasília, São Luiz company, 18-20 hours, US$17.50. Direct São Luiz bus to Belo Horizonte, 2000, 26 hrs., US$15; from Belo Horizonte bus passes through Ituiutaba (*Hotel São Luiz*, F, recommended), Nova São Simão (a new dam nearby), and Jataí. Now 4 buses daily (including one *leito*) to Manaus, via Porto Velho, around 80 hrs. Spectacular scenery between Cuiabá and Porto Velho, road newly paved, 1,450 km., bus journey takes 24 hrs., leaving Cuiabá 2030, arriving Porto Velho next day at 2030 (can take 30 hrs.), US$27 (Andorinha; their 1700 bus São Paulo-Cuiabá connects with Porto Velho service). (Eventually a paved road from Brasília to Caracas is envisaged). Hitch-hiking from Cuiabá to Manaus is possible—ask truck drivers for lifts at the roadside eating places. The road due N to Santarém has been completed and is being paved to Alta Floresta; daily bus at 2000. Yellow fever inoculations sometimes insisted on when travelling this route. Rodoviária at Cuiabá is now on outskirts: bus link (No. 117) with centre costs US$0.15.

Road Distances (km.): Belém, 2,955; Brasília, 1,127; Campo Grande, 712; Corumbá, 1,141; Foz do Iguaçu, 1,849; Goiânia, 934; Manaus, 2,294; Santarém, 1,777 km.; Porto Alegre, 2,356; Recife, 3,430; Rio, 2,118; Salvador, 3,226; São Paulo, 1,758.

From **Rondonópolis,** population 60,000 (many cheap hotels, such as *Dormitório Beija Flor*, near bus station, or *Sumaré*, clean, extremely good value, friendly, helpful owner regarding changing money and local attractions, both F) about 215 km. SE of Cuiabá on the road to Goiânia, a paved road branches southwards to Campo Grande and thence to the western parts of the State of São Paulo.

Buses from Rondonópolis Brasília, US$12, 14½ hrs.; Goiânia, US$10, 11 hrs.; Campo Grande, US$5, 6½ hrs.; Presidente Epitácio, US$4; Presidente Prudente, US$6.

Airport, for internal flights.

Indians The Bororo tribe, on a reservation three hours by truck from Rondonópolis, have long been "civilized". It may be possible to visit the Xavantes at Poxoreu, or at one of the Reservas Indígenas along the BR-158, N of Barra do Garças (see page 352). Funai is reluctant to permit travellers to visit Indian reservations on their own.

A journey along the Porto Velho road from Cuiabá demonstrates the amount of development along Brazil's "Far West" frontier, see page 349.

N.B. When travelling N of Cuiabá, yellow fever vaccination is obligatory; if you do not have a certificate, you will be (re)vaccinated.

The Economy

Brazil is the world's tenth largest economy and eighth largest market economy. It has abundant and varied natural resources and a long-standing development record, obtaining a positive growth rate every year since 1931 apart from 1963 and 1981-83. The most striking features of economic development since 1945 have been state intervention and control, and industrialization, particularly in the areas of energy, heavy industry, transport equipment and capital goods. The vast majority of consumer goods are now manufactured locally, as well as a wide range of capital goods. Since the 1970s there has been a rapid expansion of technology-based industries. Manufactures now account for well over one half of total exports. In 1985, industry accounted for 35% of gdp and 25% of total employment.

Brazil remains a large farming country and is generally self-sufficient in food production apart from wheat. It is the world's largest producer and exporter of coffee and sugar cane. Since the mid-1970s soya and orange juice production have been developed, so that dominant positions in international markets in these products have been secured. Agriculture customarily produces about two-fifths of foreign exchange earnings, and in the mid-1980s accounted for 9% of gdp and 30% of total employment. However, the sector is backward in its use of techniques and yields are comparatively low. Mechanization is largely

BRAZIL

limited to southern areas. A concentrated land holding structure and a preference for export cash crops have generated structural problems which have prevented satisfaction of domestic demand for food.

The country is richly endowed with metals and other minerals. Their exploitation has only recently begun, since low demand and high transport costs have previously rendered them uneconomic. Brazil has up to a third of the world's total iron ore reserves, found mainly in Minas Gerais and certain parts of the Amazon basin, especially the Serra dos Carajás region (Pará). Brazil is also a significant exporter of manganese and gold and produces increasing amounts of tin and copper.

Energy sector development has aimed at substituting local for imported energy. Oil reserves are estimated at 2.1 bn barrels with substantial additions in recent years from the Campos basin off the coast of Rio de Janeiro state. Oil production has risen steadily to a current 0.6 m barrels a day, and this satisfies two-thirds of local requirements. Large investments have been made in hydroelectricity, alcohol and nuclear power. Hydroelectric plants produce 90% of electricity and several major schemes are in preparation, including Itaipú on the River Paraná, a joint project with Paraguay and reportedly the world's largest. The Pro-álcool programme begun in 1974 aims to substitute alcohol derived mainly from sugar cane for oil products, and in 1986 90% of the country's vehicles were powered by alcohol. A 620-Mw nuclear reactor at Angra dos Reis (Rio de Janeiro) came on stream in 1985, but financial restrictions have slowed nuclear power development.

High rates of inflation have been recorded particularly in the 1980s because of domestic and external factors. These included urbanization and food supply bottlenecks, energy consumption patterns heavily dependent on oil imports, public accounts disequilibrium, and generalized indexation covering wages, prices and financial instruments. A stabilization programme, known as the Cruzado plan, was introduced in February 1986, including a price freeze, introduction of a new currency, the cruzado, and partial dismantling of indexation. Inflation was sharply cut but the generation of excess demand caused the plan to collapse by the end of the year.

During the 1970s large-scale, high cost projects and current account deficits were financed by foreign borrowing, and Brazil accumulated the region's largest external debt, at US$111 bn at end-1986. From 1982 annual rescheduling agreements were concluded with creditors, with new money and, in 1983-85, IMF standby facilities. The World Bank and Inter-American Development Bank granted large loans for sectoral development. These arrangements were hoped to maintain the economic external balance into the 1990s.

	1961-70 (av)	1971-80 (av)	1981-85 (av)	1986
Gdp growth (1970 prices)	6.0%	6.7%	1.7%	8.2%
Inflation	48.0%	36.8%	148.9%	65.0%
Exports (fob) US$m	1,829	9,994	23,600	22,393
Coffee	779	1,552	2,087	2,360
Soya	38	1,291	2,595	1,562
Iron ore	104	654	1,674	1,720
Imports (fob) US$m	1,462	13,007	18,301	12,866
Current account balance US$m (cum)	-2,515	-62,142	-34,100	-2,849

Information for Visitors

How to Get to Brazil

By Air Brazil is connected with the principal cities of Europe by Air France, KLM, Scandinavian Airways, Lufthansa, Alitalia, Iberia, Swissair, Aerolíneas Argentinas, Varig and TAP. Varig flights from London to Rio (twice a week) take only 11½ hrs. British Airways flies twice weekly, non-stop London to Rio and on to São Paulo. Cheap carriers to Europe are Pluna and LAP (non-IATA) from Rio to Madrid (latter also from Recife).

Brazil is connected to the USA direct by Varig, Pan American, Aerolíneas Argentinas and Japan Airlines (Varig and Japan Airlines fly twice a week, Tokyo-Los Angeles-Rio, and Pan Am, LA-Rio). The cheapest route is probably from Miami. Non-stop New York-Rio by Pan-Am or Varig is 9 hrs. 20 min. Lloyd Aéreo Boliviano flies twice weekly from Miami to Manaus.

All South American capitals are connected by air services to Rio. Caracas, 7 weekly (Varig, Viasa, Pan-Am); Bogotá, 5 weekly (Varig, Avianca); Lima, 7 weekly (AeroPerú, Varig); La Paz, 3 weekly (Cruzeiro; also LAB to São Paulo); Quito/Guayaquil, once a week with Varig; Asunción, 11 weekly (Varig, LAP, Iberia); Santiago, 19 weekly (LAN-Chile—also daily from São Paulo, Ladeco, Varig and others); Montevideo, 22 weekly (inc. Varig, Cruzeiro, Pluna); Buenos Aires, several daily; Paramaribo, twice a week by Cruzeiro do Sul and Suriname Airways to Belém; Cayenne-Manaus twice weekly by Air France; Cayenne-Belém by Cruzeiro do Sul (once a week), Suriname Airways, SLM (once a week) both heavily booked. Iquitos, Peru, via Tabatinga (on the Brazilian border with Colombia, a few km. from Leticia) to Manaus by Cruzeiro on Wed. and Sun. La Paz and Santa Cruz twice weekly to São Paulo.

For many travellers flying to Rio de Janeiro from Europe via South Africa, there is little difference in air fares compared to the direct route. Varig and SAA have two flights each per week between Rio and Johannesburg, and SAA has a weekly flight Rio-Capetown. Varig has a weekly flight from Rio to Luanda and Maputo, and to Lagos. Iraqi Airways fly from Rio to Baghdad via Lisbon and Amman. Varig and Japan Airlines each fly twice a week Tokyo-Los Angeles-Rio. Airline tickets (international and internal) are expensive in Brazil, so buy them with cruzados.

N.B. Regulations state that you cannot buy an air ticket in Brazil for use abroad unless you first have a ticket out of Brazil.

Airport Tax   US$9 is charged for international flights and US$3 (or US$0.50 for 2nd-class airports) for local ones. Tax is waived if you stay in Brazil less than 24 hrs.

By Sea   Cargo ships carrying up to 12 passengers are run by several European shipping lines. The voyage takes about 14 days. The Booth Line serves North Brazil, from Liverpool and New York. Continental Shipping and Travel of London have sailings to Santos, and Nedlloyd of Rotterdam to Rio. Cargo ships, taking a few passengers, ply between Recife and African ports. Cars can be shipped from Genoa, Barcelona and Lisbon to Rio, Santos and Buenos Aires by Linea C.C. Costa, now the only regular passenger line from Europe. It charges on a 1,000 kg basis and is cheaper than other cargo lines which transport cars, and charge on a cubic metre basis usually quoted in Deutsche marks.

Regular services from the United States are: from New York by Moore-McCormack Lines, Booth Line, and Lamport & Holt Line; from New Orleans by Delta Line; from San Francisco and Los Angeles (via Panama Canal) by Moore-McCormack Line, returning by the Straits of Magellan; from Los Angeles to Rio de Janeiro and Santos and vice-versa by Mitsui O. S. K. Lines; from California via Chilean ports, and Straits of Magellan by Grace Line fortnightly. **N.B.** There is an 8% tax on international shipping-line tickets bought in Brazil.

By Car   The *Carnet* issued by the automobile clubs of other countries is not valid in Brazil (except that issued by the Touring y Automóvil Club de Venezuela), though the Touring Clube do Brasil does issue *carnets* for travel in other countries. There are agreements between Brazil and border countries (Uruguay, Paraguay, Argentina and Bolivia) whereby a car can be taken into Brazil (or a Brazilian car out of Brazil) for a period of 60 days; an extension of up to 60 days is granted by the customs authorities on presentation of the paper received at the border; some reports suggest this may be done at most customs posts.

For Expert Help Planning Travel for SOUTH AMERICA

Contact the travel planning professionals at LADATCO TOURS — North America's largest travel company specializing in South America.

20 YEARS EXPERIENCE

With over 20 years experience planning travel for both individuals and groups LADATCO TOURS is the recognized leader in creating outstanding travel itineraries throughout South America.

INDEPENDENT OR GROUP TRAVEL

LADATCO TOURS welcomes your individual or multi-country requests for travel. We prepare computerized itineraries for all types of special interest travel.

CRUISE DEPARTMENT

We also maintain the largest cruise department in North America specializing in South American cruises — Amazon, Galapagos, Panama Canal, Chilean Fjords and Antarctica.

1-800-327-6162

Contact LADATCO TOURS for our comprehensive catalogue of cruises and tours to all South America. Call tollfree in the USA 1-800-327-6162 (Florida 800-432-3881) or write:

LADATCO TOURS
The Ladatco Building
2220 Coral Way • Miami FL 33145

BRAZIL 363

This now applies to cars registered in other countries; the requirements are proof of ownership and/or registration in the home country and valid driving licence (international or from home country). It is better to cross the border into Brazil when it is officially open (from 1300 to 1800 Mon. to Fri.) because an official who knows all about the entry of cars is then present. The motorist should in any case insist on getting the correct paper "in accordance with Decree No. 53.313/63", or he might find it impossible to get the 60-day extension. You must specify which border station you intend to leave by, but application can be made to the Customs to change this. If you want to leave by ship the Touring Club in Rio (possibly also elsewhere, but this is less definite) will arrange it for about US$60; you can also arrange the paper yourself by taking your car away by ship, but it takes about two days and costs about US$15 in port and police charges; the Touring Club provides information on how to go about it. (Klaus Elgner, of Hannover, reports this can be done with a letter in Portuguese saying you wish to leave by ship plus passport number, vehicle number, entry forms data plus an *ordem de embarque* supplied and stamped by the shipping agent. These should be presented to the Customs.) Crossing by a land border is, in any case, easier and probably cheaper. The law allowing for free entry of tourist vehicles applies only to vehicles entering from Argentina, Uruguay, Paraguay and Bolivia; a large deposit is still required if shipped from other countries.

Any foreigner with a passport can purchase a Brazilian car and travel outside Brazil if it is fully paid for or if permission is obtained from the financing body in Brazil. These cars will not necessarily meet safety regulations in N. America and Europe, but they can be easily resold in Brazil.

Most main roads between principal cities are now paved. Some are narrow and therefore dangerous. Service stations are rare on some roads, e.g. Belo Horizonte-Brasília. There is a 80 km. per hr. speed limit, to save gasoline, and there are frequent radar checks. Penalties for speeding (which can be negotiated with difficulty) vary from US$40 to US$160.

Warnings Motorists are warned that it is virtually impossible to buy premium grades of gasoline anywhere. Gasoline in Brazil is expensive; about US$2 a US gallon. It is only 65 octane (owing to high methanol content), so be prepared for bad consumption and poor performance. However, diesel fuel is cheaper and a diesel engine may provide fewer maintenance problems for the motoring tourist. Service stations on main roads within 20 km. of cities close for the sale of gasoline (but not diesel or methanol) from 2000 to 0600, and Fri. 2000-Mon. 0600; there are some exceptions in designated tourist areas (see below). In these areas the stations close for gasoline at 1200 Fridays, but are open 1200-2000 Sundays. For alcohol and diesel they are open Sats. also. All stations everywhere are closed from 2000 to 0600 (except Sun.) and from 2000 Sat. to 1200 Sun. The special tourist areas include (see index) Penedo (Alagoas); Cachoeira and Valença (Bahia); Aracati and Juazeiro do Norte (Ceará); Guarapari and Marataizes (Espírito Santo); Araxá, Cambuquirá, Caxambu, Diamantina, Lambari, Ouro Preto, Poços de Caldas, São João del Rei, São Lourenço and Serro (Minas Gerais); Salinópolis (Pará); Foz do Iguaçu and Guaíra (Paraná); Caruaru, Fazenda Nova and Garanhuns (Pernambuco); Parnaíba and Piracuruca (Piauí); Angra dos Reis, Búzios, Cabo Frio, Nova Friburgo, Parati, Resende and Teresópolis (Rio de Janeiro); Mossoró (R. G. do Norte); Canela, Gramado, Iraí, Torres and Tramandaí (R. G. do Sul); Camboriú, Gravatal, Laguna and São Francisco do Sul (Santa Catarina); Aparecida, Campos de Jordão, Cananéa, Caraguatatuba, Lindóia, São Sebastião, Serra Negra and Ubatuba (São Paulo). There is no black market for gasoline.

Motor Spares Volkswagen spares in Brazil are not always interchangeable with German VW spares, but in the main there should be no problems with large components (e.g. gears).

Young tourists crossing the frontier may get "shaken down" by police on both sides for alleged infringements; one way of overcoming this is to refuse to pay and wait to be released—generally an hour or so. (Advisable only for the strong-minded with plenty of time!)

Passports Consular visas are not required for stays of up to 90 days by tourists from Western European (except for French nationals) or Latin American countries, Morocco and the Philippines. For them, only the following documents are required at the port of disembarkation: valid passport (or *cédula de identidad* for nationals of Argentina, Chile, Paraguay and Uruguay); and adequate proof that you can pay your way and your return fare, subject to no remuneration being received in Brazil and no legally binding or contractual documents being signed. (Some consulates, e.g. Santiago, ask to see an onward ticket). 90-day renewals are easily obtainable, but only within 15 days of the expiry of your 90-day permit (e.g. from Policia Federal, Praça Mauá, Rio, open till 1600, US$10); for longer stays you must leave the country and return (immediately if you wish) to get a new 90-day permit. US and French citizens and people of other nationalities, and those who cannot meet the requirements above, *must* get a visa before arrival, which may, if you ask, be granted for multiple entry. Do not lose the emigration permit they give you when you enter Brazil. Leaving the country without it, you may have to pay up to US$100 per person.

Officially, if you leave Brazil within the 90-day permission to stay and then re-enter the country, you should only be allowed to stay until the 90-day expires. Usual practice, though, is to give another 90-day permit, which may lead to charges of overstaying if you apply for an extension.

Clothing and personal articles are free of import duty. Such articles as cameras, movie cameras, portable radios, tape-recorders, typewriters and binoculars are also admitted free if there is not more than one of each. Tourists may also bring in, duty-free, 2 litres of spirits, 2 litres of champagne, 3 litres of wine, 600 cigarettes, 25 cigars, 280 grams of perfume, and 700 grams of toilet water.

British Visitors are referred to "Hints to Exporters: Brazil", obtainable from Dept. of Trade, Export Services Division, Sanctuary Bldgs, 16-20 Great Smith Street, London SW1P 3DB.

Internal Transport There is no lack of transport between the principal cities of Brazil; few are connected by railway, but almost all are by road. Ask for window seats (*janela*), or odd numbers if you want the view. Brazilian bus services have a top speed limit of 80 kph (buses are supposed to have governors fitted). They are extremely comfortable, stopping fairly frequently (every 4-5 hrs.) for snacks; the cleanliness of these *postos* has greatly improved, though generally less good in the poorer regions. Buses only stop at official stops. Take something to drink on buses in the North. The bus terminals are usually outside the city centres and offer fair facilities in the way of snack bars, lavatories, left-luggage stores, local bus services and information centres. *Leito* buses ply at night between the main centres, offering reclining seats with foot and leg rests, toilets, and sometimes in-board refreshments, at double the normal fare. For journeys over 100 km., most buses have chemical toilets. Air conditioning can make *leito* buses cold at night, so take a blanket or sweater (and plenty of toilet paper); on some services blankets are supplied; others have hostess service. Bus stations for interstate services and other long-distance routes are usually called *rodoviárias*. It is not easy to sell back unused bus tickets. Some bus companies have introduced a telex system enabling passengers to purchase return tickets at point of departure, rather than individual tickets for each leg. Buses usually arrive and depart in very good time; you cannot assume departure will be delayed. In the South East and South a *Horário de nibus* is available at *rodoviárias* (not available for North or North East). Many town buses have turnstiles which can be inconvenient if you are carrying a large pack. Urban buses normally serve local airports.

Hitch-hiking Information on hitch-hiking (*carona* in Portuguese) suggests that it is difficult everywhere. Try at the highway-police check points on the main roads (but make sure your documents are in order) or at the service stations, or *postos*. Large increases in the price of gasoline and restrictions on its sale have diminished the amount of road traffic, especially pleasure traffic at weekends.

Rail Trains tend to be appreciably slower than buses. The sleeper services between Rio and São Paulo, and Rio and Belo Horizonte, can be recommended. There are services in the state of São Paulo and between Campinas and Brasília. There is a service between Porto Alegre and the Argentine and Uruguayan frontiers at Uruguaiana and Santana do Livramento. More and more services are being withdrawn; travellers are normally advised to go by air or road. Timekeeping is good on the whole. To obtain the Amerailpass (see Introduction) you are *theoretically* required to purchase the ticket in cruzados equivalent to US$120 (16 days), US$140 (23 days), US$175 (30 days), US$260 (60 days), exchanged at the official rate. The Ministry of Transport, Esplanada dos Ministerios, Bloco 9, DF 70 062 Brasília, or Praça Mauá 10, Rio, insist on seeing the exchange receipt; Fepasa, Praça Júlio Prestes 148, São Paulo (Tel.: 011-233-7211) do not insist on the receipt. However, a number of travellers have suggested that, as rail travel in Brazil is so cheap, the Amerailpass is not good value for money.

Air Internal air services are highly developed. A monthly magazine, *Guia*

Aeronáutico, gives all the timetables and fares. All four national airlines—Varig, Vasp, Cruzeiro and Transbrasil—offer excellent service on their internal flights. Between 2400 and 0600, internal flights cost 30% less than daytime flights. On some flights couples can fly for the price of one-and-a-half. Varig, Vasp and Transbrasil each offer a 21-day, unlimited travel, round-trip ticket, which costs US$330. The ticket must be purchased outside Brazil, no journey may be repeated, it is not transferable between airlines and may not be used on the Rio-São Paulo shuttle, but unlimited stop-overs are allowed, and certain hotels give discounts to ticket-holders. Excellent value. Varig also has a Brazil Airpass II, valid for 14 days, and four sectors, for US$250, purchasable outside Brazil. Make sure you have two copies of the Airpass invoice when you arrive in Brazil; otherwise you will have to select all your flights when you book the first one. Hotels in the Tropical and Othon chains, and others, offer discounts between 10-40% to Airpass travellers; check with Varig. The small feeder airlines have been formed into scheduled domestic airlines, and now operate Brazilian-built *Bandeirante* 16-seater prop-jets into virtually every city and town with any semblance of an airstrip. **N.B.** Beware of Cruzeiro do Sul and Varig combining their flights, with consequent last minute changes in flight time and/or number. Foreigners are not allowed to travel on Brazilian air force flights. Most airports have left-luggage lockers (US$0.30 for 24 hours).

Information All Brazil's States, and most cities and towns have their own tourist information bureaux. They are not usually too helpful regarding information on very cheap hotels, tending to imagine that no foreign tourist should consider staying in anything of that kind. It is also difficult to get information on neighbouring states. *Quatro Rodas*, a motoring magazine, publishes an excellent series of guides in Portuguese and English at about US$5 each. Its *Guia do Brasil* is a type of Michelin Guide to hotels, restaurants, sights, facilities and general information on hundreds of cities and towns in the country. The same company also publishes a camping guide and more specialized guides to Rio, São Paulo, Salvador and the South, with other cities and areas in preparation. These guides can be purchased at street newspaper vendors throughout the country. Quatro Rodas Guides may be bought in Europe from Distribuidora Jarim, Quinta Tau Varais, Azinhaga de Fetais, Camarate 2685, Lisbon, Portugal, Tel.: Lisbon 257-2542. There is also the "Transbrasil Guide to Attractions and Services" with maps, in Portuguese, English and French.

Many of the more expensive hotels provide locally-produced tourist information magazines for their guests. Travel information can be very unreliable and it is wise to recheck details thoroughly.

Climate and Clothing Conditions during the winter (May to September) are like those of a north European summer in Rio de Janeiro, but more like a north European autumn in São Paulo and the southern states. Summer-weight woollens can be worn without discomfort in winter in Rio de Janeiro, but further south something heavier is often required. In São Paulo, which is in the Highlands, lightweight clothing is only required in the summer; the climate can be treacherous, however, with large temperature changes in a brief space of time. It can get surprisingly cold S and W of Rio, and on high ground anywhere in Brazil, at night; warm clothes are needed. The season of heavy rains is from November to March in Rio and São Paulo, January to April in the north, and from April to August around Recife.

Summer conditions all over the country are tropical, but temperatures of 40°C are comparatively rare. On the coast there is a high degree of humidity. The luminosity is also very high; sunglasses are advisable.

Casual clothing is quite cheap to buy; indeed we are advised that even fashionable clothing is cheap by London and Paris standards. In general, clothing requirements in Brazil are less formal than in the Hispanic countries. It is, however, advisable for men visiting restaurants to wear long trousers in Rio and Manaus (women in shorts are also likely to be refused entry), trousers and jackets or pullovers in São Paulo (also for cinemas). As a general rule, it is better not

366 BRAZIL

to wear shorts in official buildings, cinemas and inter-state buses. Trousers and long-sleeved shirts are advisable for visits to government offices.

Security As pointed out in the chapters on Rio de Janeiro and Salvador, personal safety in Brazil has deteriorated of recent years, largely because of the economic recession of the early 1980s. The situation is now improving, with a larger police presence in tourist areas.

Apart from the obvious precautions of not wearing jewellery, do not travel alone (this applies especially to women), do not camp or sleep out in isolated places and if you are hitch-hiking, never accept a lift in a car with two people in it. Money belts are safer than bags for your valuables.

Warning Most houses and hotels outside the large cities have electric showers operated by water pressure, delivering a supply of tepid to warm water. Despite electrical earthing, these showers are potentially dangerous. Care must be exercised in their use.

Best Time for a visit is from April to June, and August to October, inclusive. Businessmen should avoid from mid-December to the end of February, when it is hot and people are on holiday. January and February are not good months for seaside tourism either, because hotels, beaches and means of transport tend to be crowded. July should also be avoided: it is a school holiday month.

Health Vaccination against smallpox is no longer required for visitors, but vaccination is necessary against yellow fever for those visiting or coming from countries with Amazonian territories, e.g. Bolivia, Colombia, Ecuador and poliomyelitis for children from 3 months to 6 years. If you are going to Amazonia, or to other low-lying forested areas, malaria prophylaxis is advised (pills are not difficult to find in Brazil) and water purification tablets are essential (not always easy to buy locally). Also, in the Amazon basin, sandflies abound; take a good repellant. South of the Amazon beware of *borrachudos*, small flies with a sharp bite that attack ankles and calves; coconut oil deters them. Water should not be drunk from taps unless there is a porcelain filter attached or unless you have water sterilizing tablets ("Hydrosteril" is a popular local brand); there is mineral water in plenty and excellent light beer, known as "chopp" (pronounced "shoppi"), and soft drinks. For those who have been in Brazil for a while, *água gelada* (chilled water) is usually safe to drink, being filtered water kept in a refrigerator in most hotels, restaurants and stores. Avoid ice in cheap hotels and restaurants; it is likely to be made from unfiltered water.

Yellow fever (see page 359) and some other vaccinations can be obtained from the Ministério da Saúde, Rua Cais de Pharoux, Rio de Janeiro. Less common vaccinations can be obtained at Climuno, address in Rio 'phone book (it is behind the beach front, not far from the American Express office).

An excellent hospital, supported by the American and British colonies in São Paulo, is Hospital Samaritano, Rua Conselheiro Brotero 1486, São Paulo (Tel.: 51-2154). Good Brazilian medical service is dear.

If staying in Brazil for any length of time, it is recommended to take out Brazilian health insurance; Banco Econômico and Citibank are reported to provide good advice on this matter.

Hotels The best guide to hotels and prices in Brazil is the *Guia do Brasil Quatro Rodas* (although it does not list the cheapest places), with good maps of regions and towns. Motels on the outskirts of cities are primarily used by very short-stay couples. The type known as *hotel familiar*, to be found in the interior—large meals, communal washing, hammocks for children—is much cheaper, but only for the enterprising. Usually hotel prices include breakfast; there is no reduction if you don't eat it. In the better hotels (our category D and upwards) the breakfast is well worth eating: rolls, ham, eggs, cheese, cakes, fruit. Normally the *apartamento* is a room with a bath; a *quarto* is a room without bath. The service stations (*postos*) and hostels (*dormitórios*) along the main roads provide excellent value in room and food, akin to truck-driver type accommodation in Europe, for those on a tight budget. The star rating system for hotels (five-star hotels are not price controlled) is not the standard used in North America or Europe. Low-budget travellers with student cards (photograph needed) can use the Casa dos Estudantes network. **Warning** Hotel safe-deposits are not always secure: take a substantial part of your funds in travellers' cheques.

Business visitors are strongly recommended to book accommodation in advance, and this can be easily done for Rio or São Paulo hotels with representation abroad.

N.B. Taxi drivers will try to take you to the expensive hotels, who pay them commission for bringing in custom. Beware!

Camping Members of the Camping Clube do Brasil or those with an international campers' card pay only half the cost of a non-member, which is US$8 p.p. (US$6 for meals). The Club has 43 sites in 13 states and 80,000 members. For enquiries, Camping Clube do Brasil, Divisão de Campings, Rua Senador Dantas 75—29° andar (Tel.: 262-7172), Rio de Janeiro. For those on a very low budget, service stations can be used as camping sites; they have shower facilities and food. There are also various municipal sites; both types are mentioned in the text. Campsites often tend to be some distance from public transport routes and are better suited to those with their own transport.

Good camping equipment may be purchased in Brazil and there are several rental companies: Rentalcenter, Av. Brig. Luís Antônio 5088, São Paulo (Tel.: 852 0081 and 853 5147) and Av. Bernardino de Campos 661, Santos (Tel.: (0132) 41489); Camping Service, Rua Tibiriçá 115, Brooklyn, São Paulo. For special jungle equipment, Selva SA, Rua do Carmo 65-3° andar, Rio de Janeiro (Tel.: 242 9695); for equipping camping vans, Camp Car, Rua Piauí 375, Todos os Santos, Rio de Janeiro. It may be difficult to get into some Camping Clube campsites during the high season (Jan.-Feb.). *Guia de Camping* is produced by Artpress, Rua Araçatuba 487, São Paulo 05058; it lists most sites and is available in bookshops in most cities. Quatro Rodas publishes a *Guia de Áreas de Camping* annually.

Tipping is usual, but less costly than in most other countries, except for porters. Hotels and restaurants, 10% of bill if no service charge but small tip if there is; taxi drivers, none; cloakroom attendants, small tip; cinema usherettes, none; hairdressers, 10-15%; porters, fixed charges but tips as well; airport porters, about US$0.50 per item.

Cost of Living There has been heavy inflation in Brazil for some years; an attempt to halt it was made under the Cruzado plan of February 1986. Good rates of exchange on the parallel market, especially in Rio, have made Brazil inexpensive for travellers, except for high-class hotels and restaurants, but the parallel market is now definitely "black" and illegal. Taxi meters are out of date. Drivers have a list of price alterations which should be consulted: make sure it's not a photocopy as that is a well-known minor swindle! Taxis have a 40% surcharge on Sundays.

Currency The currency unit is the cruzado (Cz$), which in February 1986 replaced the cruzeiro at a rate of 1:1,000. Existing 100, 200, 500, 1,000, 5,000, 10,000, 50,000 and 100,000 cruzeiro notes are still circulating; new cruzado notes, of identical design to the equivalent cruzeiro notes they are replacing, are entering circulation, and a 500-cruzado note has been introduced. Any amount of foreign currency and "a reasonable sum" in cruzados can be taken in; residents may only take out the equivalent of US$1,000. Money sent to Brazil is normally paid out only in Brazilian currency, so do not have more money sent to Brazil than you need for your stay in the country itself. Tourists cannot change US$ travellers' cheques into US$ notes, nor can they obtain US$ travellers cheques on an American Express card. The Banco do Brasil in most major cities will *change cash and travellers' cheques at the official rate;* also Lloyds Bank (ex-BOLSA) branches. For the latest rate, see "Inflation and Exchange Rates" near end of book. If you keep the exchange slips, you may convert back into foreign currency one-third of what you changed into cruzados. This applies to the official rate only; there is no right of reconversion unless you have an official exchange slip. There is an illegal black market, offering up to 100% over the official rate, to be found on the street and among hotel staff (ask for "mercado paralelo"). Loiterers outside hotels will often direct travellers to money changers—they will expect a tip. It is generally possible to exchange US dollars (cash) virtually anywhere in Brazil at black market rates, but only in larger cities can the black market for travellers' cheques be found, and this sometimes involves a search. Remember that the black market is now illegal; if you want to use it take plenty of US$ cash for exchange. Black market and official rates are quoted in the papers and on TV news programmes. Cruzados can also be bought more cheaply outside Brazil, for instance in Asunción, Lima, La Paz, Montevideo, or Puerto Iguazú (Argentina). Credit cards are widely used; Diners Club and American Express are useful. Visa-Elo is the Brazilian Visa but many places will not take overseas Visa. Master Charge/Access is accepted by Banco Econômico and Banco Real and some airline offices, but hardly at all outside Rio. Credit card transactions are charged at the official rate, so are expensive. Cash advances on credit cards will only be paid in cruzados.

368 BRAZIL

Working in Brazil   Work-permit restrictions are making it harder to find work as an English language teacher than it used to be. One's best bet would be in a small language school. Charges: private, US$5 per hr.; school, US$2 per hr. Or advertise in the Press.

Weights and Measures   The metric system is used by all.

Cables   Cables are listed under cities. Cable facilities are available at all post offices, and the main ones have public telex booths. Post offices are recognizable by the ECT (Empresa de Correios e Telégrafos) signs outside. There is a 40% tax added to the cost of all telegraphic and telephonic communications, which makes international service extremely dear. Local phone calls and telegrams, though, are quite cheap. Make sure that hotels equipped with telex facilities can send outgoing telexes; some are unable to do so, or only at certain times of day.

Telephone   The system has been greatly improved. There is a trunk-dialling system linking all parts; for the codes look up DDD in the telephone directory. There are telephone boxes at airports, post offices, railway stations, hotels, most bars, restaurants and cafés, and in the main cities there are telephone kiosks *for local calls only* in the shape of large orange shells, for which *fichas* can be bought from bars, cafés and newsvendors; in Rio they are known as *orelhões* (big ears). Phone calls are half-price after 2000. Phone calls abroad are US$4 for first 3 mins. to Europe. Note that Brazil is now linked to North America, Japan and most of Europe by trunk dialling (DDI). Codes are listed in the telephone directories. For collect calls from phone boxes (in Portuguese: "a cobrar"), dial 107 and ask for someone who speaks English or French. No collect calls available to New Zealand, though to Australia is OK. It is useless trying to dial long-distance from hotels or orange *orelhões*, as a blocking device is installed on those lines. There are special blue *orelhões* for long-distance DDD calls; for these you need to buy *fichas interurbanas* from telephone company offices. Making phone calls abroad from hotels is subject to a surcharge and is therefore very expensive.

Postal charges are high. Air mail takes 4 to 6 days to or from Britain or the U.S.; surface mail takes some 4 weeks. "Caixa Postal" addresses should be used when possible. Leaflets on postal rates are not issued; ask at the post office. Some post offices will not accept picture postcards unless enclosed in an envelope. Postes restantes usually only hold letters for 30 days. Letters from abroad may be subject to random checks by Brazilian officials. The Post Office sells cardboard boxes for sending packages internally and abroad (they must be submitted open); pay by the kilo; you must fill in a list of contents; string, but not tape, provided. In general, postal services have greatly improved in recent years.

National Holidays
are January 1 (New Year); 3 days up to and including Ash Wed. (Carnival); April 21 (Tiradentes); May 1 (Labour Day); Corpus Christi (June); September 7 (Independence Day); October 12, Nossa Senhora Aparecida; November 2 (All Souls' Day); November 15 (Day of the Republic); and December 25 (Christmas). The local holidays in the main cities are given in the text. Four religious or traditional holidays (Good Fri. must be one; other usual days: November 1, All Saints Day; December 24, Christmas Eve) may be fixed by the municipalities.

Working hrs. are 0900-1800 Mon. to Fri. for most businesses, which close for lunch some time between 1130 and 1400. Shops are open on Sat. till 1230 or 1300. Government departments are open from 1100-1800 Mon. to Fri. Banks are closed on Sat. The British and American embassies' hrs. are 0830-1245 and 1415-1700 Mon. to Fri. The consular section's hrs. are 0830-1230; 1330-1630 Mon. to Fri.

Language   The language is Portuguese. Efforts to speak it are greatly appreciated and for the low-budget traveller, Portuguese is essential. If you cannot lay your tongue to "the language of the angels", apologize for not being able to speak Portuguese and try Spanish, but note that in remoter parts you may well not be understood and you will certainly have difficulty in understanding the answers.

One important point of spelling is that words ending in "i" and "u" are accented on the last syllable, though (unlike Spanish) no accent is used there. This is especially important in place names: Paratí, Iguaçu. Pronunciation peculiarities worth mentioning are: final "o" is often dropped; final "de" and "te" are often produced "jee" and "chee", but in some words, the final "e" is dropped as in "tarde", pronounced "tarj", "quente" pronounced "kench". On the other hand, words ending in a consonant often have a final "ee" added, as in Varig, pronounced "Várig-ee". Final "l" is pronounced like a "w", so that Pantanal rhymes with "cow". Note also "dia°: "jee-a"; initial "r" and double "rr" can sound like "h", as in "rede" (hammock): "hedgie". Audioforum, 31 Kensington Church Street, London W8 4LL, Tel.: 937-1647 does cassette course on Brazilian Portuguese.

Time   Brazilian Standard Time is 3 hrs. behind GMT; of the major cities, only Manaus, Cuiabá, Campo Grande and Corumbá are different, with time 4 hrs. behind GMT. Clocks move forward one hour on the second Sunday in November for summer time, and return to normal time on the second Sunday in March.

BRAZIL 369

Press: Rio *Daily Post/Brasil Herald*, the only English-language daily in Brazil, Rua do Resende 65, Rio de Janeiro 20231, Tel.: 221 2772. Not published Mons. The main papers are *Jornal do Brasil*, *O Globo*, and *Jornal do Commércio*. **São Paulo** Morning: *O Estado de São Paulo*, *Folha de São Paulo*, *Gazeta Mercantil* and *Diário de São Paulo*. *Daily Post/Brasil Herald* (except Mons.) Evening: *A Gazeta*, *Diário do Noite*, *Ultima Hora*. A monthly publication, *Jornal de Turismo* (Largo do Machado 29, Rio), gives notes on tourism, hotel prices, timetables, etc. There is a similar monthly magazine in English, *Rio Visitor* (Rua Marquês de São Vicente 52, Loja 318, Gávea, Rio).

English-language radio broadcasts daily at 15290 kHz, 19m Short Wave (Rádio Bras, Caixa Postal 04/0340, DF-70 323 Brasília).

Food The food can be very good indeed. The most common dish is *bife* (*ou frango*) *com arroz e feijão*, steak (or chicken) with rice and the excellent Brazilian black beans. The most famous dish with beans is the *feijoada completa*: several meat ingredients (jerked beef, smoked sausage, smoked tongue, salt pork, along with spices, herbs and vegetables) are cooked with the beans. Manioc flour is sprinkled over it, and it is eaten with kale (*couve*) and slices of orange, and accompanied by glasses of *aguardente* (unmatured rum), usually known as *cachaça* (booze), though *pinga* (drop) is a politer term. Almost all restaurants serve the *feijoada completa* for Saturday lunch (that means up to about 1630). Bahia has some excellent fish dishes (see note on page 303); some restaurants in most of the big cities specialize in them. *Vatapá* is a good dish in the north; it contains shrimp or fish sauced with palm oil, or coconut milk. *Empadinhas de camarão* are worth trying; they are shrimp patties, with olives and heart of palm. A mixed grill, including excellent steak, served with roasted manioc flour (*farofa*; raw manioc flour is known as *farinha*) goes under the name of *churrasco* (it came originally from the cattlemen of Rio Grande do Sul), normally served in specialized restaurants known as *churrascarias* or *rodízios*; good places for large appetites. Minas Gerais has two splendid special dishes involving pork, black beans, *farofa* and kale; they are *tutu a mineira* and *feijão tropeiro*. A white hard cheese (*queijo prata*) or a slightly softer one (*queijo Minas*) is often served for dessert with bananas, or guava or quince paste. Meals are extremely large by European standards; if your appetites are small, you can order, say, one portion and one empty plate, and divide the portion. Unless you specify to the contrary many restaurants will lay a *coberto opcional*, olives, carrots, etc., costing US$0.50-0.75. **NB** The main meal is usually taken in the middle of the day; cheap restaurants tend not to be open in the evening.

For vegetarians, there is a growing network of restaurants in the main cities, where a main meal is unlikely to cost more than US$2. We list several. Most also serve fish. Alternatives in smaller towns are the Arab and Chinese restaurants.

There is fruit all the year round, ranging from banana and orange to strawberries (*morango*), pineapple (*abacaxi*) and avocado pear (*abacate*). More specialized fruits include mango (*manga*), pawpaw (*mamão*), custard-apple (*fruta do conde*) and guava (*goiaba*). One is especially recommended to try the *manga de Uba*, a non-fibrous small mango. Also good are *mora* (a raspberry that looks like a strawberry), *jaboticaba*, a small black damson-like fruit, and *jaca* (jackfruit), a large yellow/green fruit.

The exotic flavours of Brazilian ice-creams should be experienced. Martin Crossland recommends readers to try *açaí*, *bacuri*, *biribá*, *buruti*, *cupuaça*, *marimari*, *mucajá*, *murici*, *pajurá*, *pariri*, *patuá*, *piquiá*, *pupunha*, *sorva*, *tucumá*, *uxi* and others mentioned below under "drinks".

If travelling on a tight budget, remember to ask in restaurants for the *prato feito* or *sortido*, a money-saving, excellent value *table-d'hôte* meal for US$2 or less. The *prato comercial* is similar but rather better, costing up to US$2.50. *Lanchonetes* are cheap eating places where you must pay before eating. *Salgados* (savoury pastries), *coxinha* (a pyramid of manioc filled with meat or fish and deep fried), *esfiha* (spicey hamburger inside an onion-bread envelope), *empadão* (a filling—e.g. *ckicken*—in sauce in a pastry case), *empadas* and *empadinhas* (smaller fritters of the same type), are the usual fare. Hamburgers are referred to as "X" (pronounced "shees" - often spelt on menu-boards "cheese"), e.g. *X-Salada*. In Minas Gerais, *pão de queijo* is a hot roll made with cheese. A *bauru* is a

370 BRAZIL

toasted sandwich which, in Porto Alegre, is filled with steak, while further north has tomato, ham and cheese filling. *Cocada* is a coconut and sugar biscuit.

Drinks Imported drinks are expensive, but there are some quite good local wines. The beers are good and there are plenty of local soft drinks. *Guaraná* is a very popular carbonated fruit drink. There is an excellent range of non-alcoholic fruit juices, known as *sucos: caju* (cashew), *pitanga, goiaba* (guava), *genipapo, graviola* (= *chirimoya*), *maracujá* (passion-fruit), *sapoti* and *tamarindo* are recommended by the Editor personally. *Vitaminas* are thick, mixed fruit or vegetable drinks, often with milk. *Caldo de cana* is sugar-cane juice, sometimes mixed with ice. Remember that *água mineral*, available in many varieties at bars and restaurants is a cheap, safe thirst-quencher (cheaper still in supermarkets). Apart from the ubiquitous coffee, good tea is grown and sold.

Recommended wines are Conde de Foucauld, Château d'Argent, Château Duvalier, Forestier, Dreher, Preciosa and Bernard Taillan. Acqua Santiera Rosé Suave, Baron de Lantier and the cheaper Mosteiro have been recommended, so have the excellent red Marjolet from Cabernet grapes, and the Moselle-type white Zahringer. A white-wine *Sangria*, containing tropical fruits such as pineapple and papaya, is worth looking out for. The Brahma and Antárctica beers are really excellent, of the strong lager type, and are cheaper by the bottle than on draught (buying bottled drinks in supermarkets, you may be asked for empties in return).

Scotch whisky essence, imported, then diluted and bottled in Brazil, is very popular because of the high price of Scotch imported in bottle; Teacher's is the most highly regarded brand. Locally made gin, vermouth and campari are very good. The local firewater, *aguardente* (known as *cachaça* or *pinga*), made from sugar-cane, is cheap and wholesome, but visitors should seek local advice on the best brands; Martin Crossland recommends São Francisco and the Editor Praianinha; Maria Fulô, "51" and Pitu are other recommended makes. Mixed with fruit juices of various sorts, sugar and crushed ice, *cachaça* becomes the principal element in a *batida*, a delicious and powerful drink; the commonest is a lime batida or *batida de limão*; a variant of this is the *caipirinha*, a *cachaça* with several slices of lime in it. *Cachaça* with Coca-Cola is a *cuba*, while rum with Coca-Cola is a *cuba libre*.

Best Buys Jewellery (especially in Minas Gerais), costume jewellery, and articles made of gemstones, such as lamps; ornamented articles of jacaranda and other tropical hardwoods; clay figurines from the North-East; lace from Ceará; leatherwork; strange pottery from Amazonia; carvings in soapstone and in bone; tiles and other ceramic work, African-type pottery and basketwork from Bahia. Good general shops for those with little time to search are "Folclore" shops in Copacabana next to *Rio Othon Palace* and also in Ipanema. Brazilian cigars are excellent for those who like the mild flavours popular in Germany, the Netherlands and Switzerland; in the Editor's opinion, those manufactured by Suerdieck of Bahia are the best of the easily available brands, but C. Loughnane recommends trying the unbranded ones when you go to Salvador.

Indian artefacts are perhaps best obtained from the Funai shops: *Brasília*, bus station and airport; *Rio de Janeiro*, airport and Museu do Indio; *São Paulo*, Galeria Ouro Velho, Rua Augusta 1371; *Cuiabá*, Rua Pedro Celestino 305; *Manaus*, Praça da Matriz; *Belém*, Galeria do Edifício Assembléia Paraense, Avenida Presidente Vargas.

We wish to offer our grateful thanks for help in revising the Brazilian chapter to Robin Chapman, of Lloyds Bank Economics Department, who revised the Economy section; and to Rita Davy (Rio), Theodor A. Gevert (São Paulo), John Hale (Lloyds Bank (now in London)), Senta Verena Mikesch Germano de Matos (Olinda), Kathryn Sikkink (Rio), Janice and Douglas Trent (Tropical Tours, Belo Horizonte) for some splendid updating material, Dimitrije Wenter (Olinda). Finally to the following travellers: Bill Addington (Warminster, Wilts), Richard and Sharon Alexander (Auckland 5), Stephen Appleby (Tynemouth), Sven Arnemann-Krieg (Hamburg), Pierre-Yves Atlan (Paris 18), Kees van der Avort (Nijmegen) for valuable information on the North-East, Åsa Bengtsson and Nils Johansson (Sweden), Trond Bergquist and Ian Gjertz (Oslo), Michael Biró (Vienna 1090), Erik Bloom (Davis, Ca.), Barbera Bot and Bob Domburg (Maasland, Neth.), Christine Bräutigam (Basle), Gerd Hans Bremer (Bielefeld, W.Ger.), Celia and Tom Bruneau (Westmount, Que.), Catherine Burry (London W4) and Joan Gitelman (Maine, USA), Tal Carmi (NY), Cristina Conti (Fribourg, Switz.), David Crowe (Sydney), Anke Cruse (San Francisco), Jonathan C.Curtis (Bury St.Edmunds), Michael Dachler (Vienna 1190), Lynne and Hugh Davies (Mill Valley, Ca.), Michael Davison (Caracas) for a most valuable contribution, R.E.Deighton (London E17) for excellent information on Rio, Robert Edge and Renate Kronemann (London SW4), Julie Eisenberg and Andy

Daitsman (Milwaukee), Christine Enkelaar and José Keldens ('s-Hertogenbosch), Jonathan Fleischer and Susan Leopold (Toronto), Toñi García and Diego Caña (Barcelona), Mark Gfeller (Richterswil, Switz.), Peter Gilmore (Guayaquil), Timothy Gluch (Welland, Ont.), Noah Goodman (NY), Odete R.Gregus (West Milford, NJ), Suzanne Hartveld (Auckland), Hans Hendriks (Maassluis, Neth.), Ricardo Heyenn and Karin Kubitsch (Hamburg), Ronald Hijmans (Amsterdam), Bastian Hiss and Daniela Fleischhauer (Krefeld), B.van Houten (Amsterdam) for some excellent information, Esther Hunziker (Liestal, Switz.), Marianne Hydara (Wels, Austria), Ralph Jacobson (Fairfax, Ca.), John and Rosemary (Bolton), Leo Joseph (Adelaide), Mary Kanasch (USA), R.Kavanagh and Judy Connor (Liverpool), Peter W.Kenny (Minneapolis), José Kiska (Pullman, Wash.), Sabine Koch, Christian Küber (Hamburg), G.Lawson (Canberra), Peter Lonsdale (Taupo, NZ), James Maas (London W3) for a fine contribution, Mark McHugh (Minneapolis), Frank Mahoney (Portland, Or.), Louis Maine, Robert E.Manley (Cincinnati) for some excellent Amazonian updatings, Werner von Marinelli (Eindhoven), Anna-Mia Marks (Utrecht), Sabine Marquardt and Mario Michalak (Leverkusen, W.Ger.), Heinz Maul (Erlangen, W.Ger.), Donna Mayer (Aarhus, Dmk.), Jim Moore (Issaquah, Wash.), Gwynne Murray (Palo Alto, Ca.) for most useful North-East updatings, Jill Nord (Glendale, Ca.), A.Okle and M.Dürig (S.Pasadena, Ca.), Vaclav Penkava (Seattle), Chuck Phillips (St Petersburg, Fl.), Jens Plahte (Ås, Norway), H.L.Ravenswaaij (Curaçao), Stephen Saks and Andrea Keir (Melbourne), L.J.Schmit Jongbloed (Rotterdam), Dr Sidney A.Schwartz (Canajoharie, NY), Sebastian Steib (Bottmingen, Switz.) Gustavo Steinbrun Bianco (Buenos Aires), Jon Taylor (Middlestown, W.Yorks), Brian and Christina Turner (Caazapá, Par.), Dirk Vanmarcke (Bruges), Doris Vaterlaus and David Froelicher (Thalwil, Switz.), Geuko Vos (Oudorp, Neth.), Paul W.Wallig (Washington, DC), Jean de Wandelar (Brussels), Sabine Warko (Friederichsdorf, W.Ger.), Haydn Washington (Sydney 2068), Andrew Waterworth and Kerrie Oldfield (Neutral Bay, NSW), and Jeff White (La Habra, Ca.).

John and Sylvia Brooks, who travelled in the North-East in October-November 1986, would like to acknowledge their debt to Quatro Rodas Hotéis do Nordeste and their staff, particularly Laudeman Cavalcanti (Olinda), Ivo Sousa (Salvador) and Francisco Esteves (São Luis); also to Empetur in Recife, Bahiatursa in Salvador, and their staff.

WILL YOU HELP US?

We do all we can to get our facts right in *The South American Handbook*. Each chapter is thoroughly revised each year, but Latin America and the Caribbean cover a vast area, and our eyes cannot be everywhere. A new highway or airport is built; a hotel, a restaurant, a cabaret dies; another, a good one is born; a building we describe is pulled down, a street renamed. Names and addresses of good hotels and restaurants for "budget-minded" travellers are always very welcome. We would especially like to receive maps and diagrams of towns and cities, walks, national parks and other interesting areas to use as source material for the Handbook and other forthcoming titles.

Your information may be far more up-to-date than ours. If your letter reaches us early enough in the year it will be used in the next edition, but write whenever you want to, for all your letters are used sooner or later.

Thank you very much indeed for your help.

**Trade & Travel Publications Limited
5 Prince's Buildings, George Street,
Bath BA1 2ED. England**

CHILE

	Page		Page
Introductory	372	**Forest Chile**	418
Desert North	376	**Patagonia**	438
Heartland	390	**Economy**	444
Santiago	392	**Information for Visitors**	445
Pacific Islands	407	Maps 374, 391, 395, 410, 415, 421	
Central Valley	412		

CHILE, with an area of 756,946 square km., is smaller than all other South American republics save Ecuador, Paraguay and Uruguay, but is nonetheless larger than France. Its territory is a ribbon of land lying between the Andes and the Pacific, 4,200 km. long and, on average, no more than 180 km. wide. Of this width the Andes and a coastal range of highland take up from a third to a half. Chile contains within itself wide variations of soil and vast differences of climate; these are reflected, from area to area, in the density of population and the occupations of its 12,081,000 people.

In the extreme north Chile has a frontier with Peru running ten km. north of the railway from the port of Arica to the Bolivian capital of La Paz. Its eastern frontier—with Bolivia in the north and with Argentina southwards—is along the crest of the Andes, gradually diminishing in height from Santiago southwards to the southern seas, where the Strait of Magellan lies, giving access to the Atlantic. Chile's western and southern coastline is 4,500 km. long.

Down the whole length, between the Andes and the coastal range, there runs a valley depression, though it is less well defined in the north. North of Santiago transverse ranges join the two massifs and impede transport, but for 885 km. south of the capital the great longitudinal valley stretches as far as Puerto Montt. South of Puerto Montt the sea has broken through the coastal range and drowned the valley, and there is a bewildering assortment of archipelagos and channels.

From north to south the country falls into five sharply contrasted zones:
1. The first 1,250 km. from the Peruvian frontier to Copiapó is a rainless hot desert of brown hills and plains devoid of vegetation, with a few oases. Here lie the nitrate deposits and several copper mines.
2. From Copiapó to Illapel (600 km.) is semi-desert; there is a slight winter rainfall, but great tracts of land are without vegetation most of the year. Valley bottoms are here cultivated under irrigation.
3. From Illapel to Concepción is Chile's heartland, where the vast majority of its people live. Here there is abundant rainfall in the winter, but the summers are perfectly dry. Great farms and vineyards cover the country, which is exceptionally beautiful.
4. The fourth zone—Forest Chile—between Concepción and Puerto Montt, is a country of lakes and rivers, with heavy rainfall through much of the year. Cleared and cultivated land alternates with mountains and primeval forests.
5. The fifth zone, from Puerto Montt to Cape Horn, stretches for 1,600 km. This is archipelagic Chile, a sparsely populated region of wild forests and mountains, glaciers, fjords, islands and channels. Rainfall is torrential, and the climate cold and stormy. There are no rail and few road links S of Puerto Montt. Chilean Patagonia is in the extreme south of this zone. To make the most of this trip, read Darwin's *Voyage of the Beagle* beforehand.

A subdivision of the fifth zone is Atlantic Chile—that part which lies along the Magellan Strait to the east of the Andes, including the Chilean part of Tierra del Fuego island. There is a cluster of population here raising sheep and mining coal. Large offshore oilfields have now been discovered in the far South, and the area is developing rapidly.

History A century before the Spanish conquest the Incas moved south into Chile from Peru, moving across the desert from oasis to oasis at the foot of the Andes. They reached the heartland and conquered it, but were unable to take the forest south of the Río Maule; there the fierce Mapuches (Araucanians) held them. In 1537 Diego de Almagro, at the head of a hundred Spaniards and some thousands of Indians, took the Inca road from Peru south to Salta and across the Andes. Many of the Indians perished, but the heartland was reached; bitterly disappointed at not finding gold they returned to Peru. The next *conquistador*, who took the desert road, was Pedro de Valdivia; he reached the heartland in 1541 and founded Santiago on February 12. Reinforced by fresh colonists from Peru and Spain, Valdivia widened his conquest and pushed S into Mapuche land, but was able to hold only the settlement to which he had given his name. The Mapuches fought desperately—they soon mastered the use of the horse—and in 1554 they captured Valdivia himself and killed him. Fighting continued for three centuries, and it was not until the late 19th century that immigrants were able to settle in the Mapuche lands.

The colonial period was greatly troubled by constant wars against the Mapuches and by internal dissensions, particularly between the landowners and the priests, who strongly objected to a system of Indian serfdom—the Indians were constantly in revolt. There have been, too, natural disasters in the form of earthquakes and tidal waves which have wiped out the cities again and again. From the end of the 16th century British and French pirates frequented the coasts. From the first, Chile formed part of the Viceroyalty of Peru; it was controlled from Lima, and trade was allowed only with Peru. This led to uncontrolled smuggling and by 1715 there were 40 French vessels trading illegally along the coast. It was not till 1778 that trading was allowed between Chile and Spain.

In 1810 a group of Chilean patriots, including Bernardo O'Higgins— the illegitimate son of a Sligo-born Viceroy of Peru, Ambrosio O'Higgins, and a Chilean mother—revolted against Spain. This revolt led to seven years of war against the occupying troops of Spain—Lord Cochrane was in charge of the insurrectionist navy—and in 1817 General José de San Martín crossed the Andes with an army from Argentina and helped to gain a decisive victory. O'Higgins became the first head of state: under him the first constitution of 1818 was drafted. But there was one thing which was dangerous to touch in Chile: the interests of the dominant landed aristocracy, and O'Higgins's liberal policies offended them, leading to his downfall in 1823. A period of anarchy followed, but in 1830 conservative forces led by Diego Portales restored order and introduced the authoritarian constitution of 1833. Under this charter, for almost a century, the country was ruled by a small oligarchy of landowners. It was during this period, from 1879 to 1883, that the War of the Pacific was fought against Peru and Bolivia; all three contestants were claiming the new nitrate wealth of the desert in the north. Chile emerged victorious—even Lima was occupied—and for 40 years thereafter it drew great wealth from the nitrate fields. One unexpected result of the war was that the Chilean land workers or *inquilinos,* after a taste of liberty, were unwilling to return to the bondage of the big estates; the demobilized soldiers migrated to the cities, or pushed south into the new lands beyond the Bío-Bío recently opened by pressure on the Mapuches. The free labourer had made his appearance.

The rule of the Right was challenged by the liberal regime of President Alessandri in 1920. Acute economic distress in 1924, linked to the replacement of Chile's natural nitrates with artificial fertilizers more cheaply produced in Europe, led to army intervention and some reforms were achieved. In 1932, when elections were again held, Alessandri was again elected president, but he was prevented from carrying out his programme. The next president, Aguirre Cerda (1938-1941) was the first to come from the ranks of the poor; with his passion

374 **CHILE**

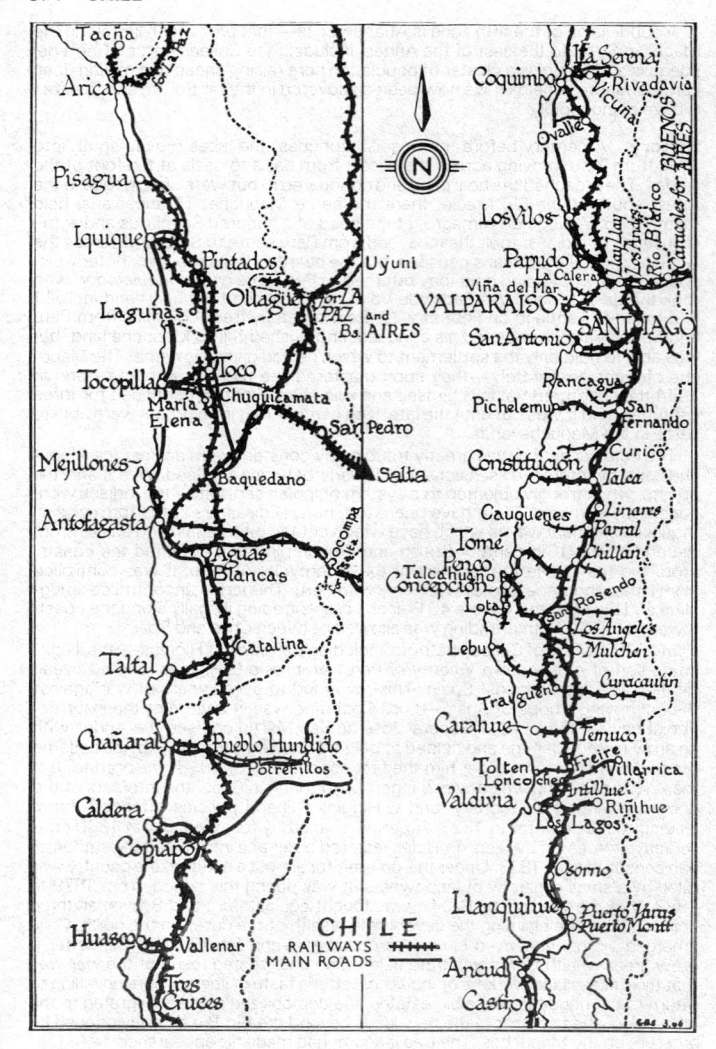

CHILE 375

for education, health and industrial development he was able to achieve something, but the inequalities in Chilean society grew ever sharper, despite the maintenance of political democracy, and gave rise to powerful socialist and communist parties. President Eduardo Frei's policy of "revolution in freedom" (1964-70) was the first concerted attempt at overall radical reform, but it raised hopes it could not satisfy. In 1970 a marxist coalition assumed office under Dr. Salvador Allende; the frantic pace of change under his regime polarized the country into Left-and Right-wing camps. Gradually increasing social and economic chaos formed the background for Allende's deposition by the army and his death in September 1973. A military regime now rules the country. Under the new Constitution put into effect on March 11, 1981, President Pinochet is expected to remain in office until March 1989, when the military junta will nominate a single presidential candidate for election (see page 376).

The People There is less racial diversity in Chile than in most Latin American countries. There are about 150,000 pure blooded Mapuche Indians; 95% of them live in the forest land around Temuco, between the Bío-Bío and Toltén rivers. A fifth is European; the rest is *mestizo*, a compound of bloods. The stock has been much less modified by immigration than in Argentina and Brazil. The German, French, Italian and Swiss immigrants came mostly between 1846 and 1864 as small farmers in the forest zone S of the Bío-Bío. Between 1880 and 1900 gold-seeking Serbs and Croats settled in the far S, and the British took up sheep farming and commerce in the same region. The influence throughout Chile of the immigrants is out of proportion to their numbers: their signature on the land is marked in German colonization of Valdivia, Puerto Montt, Puerto Varas and Osorno.

The population is far from evenly distributed: Middle Chile (from Copiapó to Concepción), 18% of the country's area, contains 77% of the total population. The Metropolitan Region of Santiago contains, on its own, about 39% of the whole population. The rate of population growth per annum—1.7%—is slightly under the average for Latin America.

The death rate has fallen recently; the birth rate is highest in the cities, particularly of the forest zone. Illegitimacy fell from 39% in 1917 to 27.6% in 1980. The death rate, 6.3%, is highest in the cities. Infant mortality is 19.6 per thousand live births; it is highest in the rural areas. There are 300 hospital beds per 100,000 population and 1,038 inhabitants per doctor. Life expectancy is 67. Of the total population, 8.9% are illiterate.

Today, there is in process an intense urbanization of the populace. The cities are expanding, partly because so many people have left the land, and some 84% now live in the towns. Housing in the cities has not kept pace with the increased population; about 200,000 Chileans live in slum areas called *callampas* (mushrooms) in the outskirts of Santiago and around the factories.

Chile grows only a third of the food it needs; about 25% by value of the total imports are food. An inheritance from colonial days of huge estates (1.1% of the owners held 63.7% of the land) coupled with wretched farming methods was largely reponsible for this. Agricultural production is still growing very slowly because of the institutional chaos on the land that followed the acceleration of agrarian reform under Allende, and the free-market policies of his successors, but there has been a great expansion of exportable crops.

Communications Chile's difficult topography—archipelagos, forests, mountains, deserts—makes communications a formidable problem. It would be much more serious if 90% of the Chilean population did not live in the compact central rectangle, with good roads and adequate railways, between La Serena and Puerto Montt. The three southern provinces are best reached by sea or air, or circuitously by road through Argentina. Only a short distance along one river—the estuary of the Bío-Bío—is navigable.

Railways There are 10,100 km. of line, of which most are state owned. Most of the privately owned 2,130 km. of line are in the desert north, where the northern terminal is Iquique. From the longitudinal Iquique-Puerto Montt trunk line

376 CHILE

branches run westwards to the ports and seaside resorts, and eastwards to mines and mountain resorts. The main gauge on the Valparaíso-Santiago and southern lines is 5 ft. 6 in. (1.676 metres). Passenger services on the metre-gauge lines N of La Calera have virtually ceased.

Five international railways link Chile with its neighbours. There is a local line between Arica and Tacna, linking Chile with Peru. There are two railways to Bolivia: between Arica and La Paz (448 km.), and from Antofagasta via Calama to La Paz. Between Chile and Argentina there are two lines: one between Antofagasta and Salta, in the Argentine north-west, and the Transandine Railway linking Santiago with Buenos Aires. International passenger services on both these lines have now ended. The Ferrocarriles del Estado publish an annual *Guía Turística*, available in various languages from the larger stations.

Roads About one-half of the 88,000 km. of roads can be used the year round, though a large proportion of them are unimproved and only about 9,700 km. are first class. The region round the capital and the Central Valley is the best served.

The Pan-American (Longitudinal) Highway runs from Arica through Santiago to Puerto Montt; from Llay-Llay a branch goes to Los Andes and over La Cumbre (Uspallata) pass to Argentina. Another main international road in the Lake District goes from Osorno across the Puyehue pass to Argentina. The Longitudinal Highway, vital to the Chilean economy, is paved throughout, but many sections are in a bad state.

Constitution and Government Since the deposition and death of President Salvador Allende on September 11, 1973, Chile has been ruled by a military president, Gen. Augusto Pinochet Ugarte, and a 4-man-junta with absolute powers. The pre-1973 constitution has been replaced by a new one, which was approved in a plebiscite held on September 11, 1980. This authorizes President Pinochet's stay in office until March 1989. The Junta, of which President Pinochet is not a member, is also remaining in office with legislative powers and in March 1989 will nominate a single presidential candidate for election. Despite growing demands for reform, no concessions have been made to bring forward the proposed timetable for elections. The Constitution provides for an eight-year non-renewable term for the President of the Republic, a bicameral Congress (to function from 1989), and an independent judiciary and central bank.

N.B. In 1974 Chile initiated an administrative reform establishing twelve regions and a metropolitan area, to replace the old system of 25 provinces. The twelve regions are subdivided into 44 new provinces. **The Desert North**

Regions	Old Provinces	Population ('000) 1975	1982
I	Tarapacá	210	273
II	Antofagasta	287	341
III	Atacama	179	183

The 1,250 km. between Arica and Copiapó are desert without vegetation, with little or no rain. The inhospitable shore is a pink cliff face rising to a height of from 600 to 900 metres. At the bottom of the cliff are built the towns, some of considerable size. The far from pacific Pacific often makes it difficult to load and unload ships. The nitrate fields exploited in this area lie in the depression between Pisagua and Taltal. Copper, too is mined in the Cordillera; there are two large mines, at Chuquicamata, near Calama, and at El Salvador, inland from Chañaral.

Life in the area is artificial. Water has to be piped for hundreds of km. to the cities and the nitrate fields from the Cordillera; all food and even all building materials have to be brought in from elsewhere. Only the small populations of the oases, such as Calama, are self-supporting.

There is some difference of climate between the coast and the interior. The coast is humid and cloudy; in the interior the skies are clear. The temperatures on the coast are fairly uniform; in the interior there is often a great difference in the

CHILE 377

temperature between day and night; the winter nights are often as cold as -10°C, with a cruel wind.

The map on page 374 shows the Longitudinal Highway running S from Arica to Santiago and Puerto Montt. Drivers must beware of high winds and blowing sand, and a paucity of service stations N of Copiapó.

Chile's most northerly city, 19 km. S of the Peruvian border, is

Arica, with a population of 150,000, built at the foot of the Morro headland and fringed by sand dunes. The Andes can be clearly seen from the anchorage. The Morro, with a good view from the look-out park on top (an hour's walk along the road from town, ½ hr. by footpath from the south end of Colón, or 10 mins. by taxi), was the scene of a great victory by Chile over Peru on June 7, 1880. There is a Pacific War museum here.

There is no rain, winter or summer. The average winter temperature is 15°C, and the average summer temperature 22°C. It is frequented for sea-bathing by Bolivians as well as the locals. The attractive cathedral church, San Marcos, built in iron by Eiffel and fitted with bright coloured windows, is in the Plaza de Armas. It was brought to Arica from Ilo (Peru) in the early 1900s, as an emergency measure after a tidal wave swept over Arica and destroyed all its churches. Eiffel also designed the customs house (under repair in 1985/86). A 63-km. railway connects the town with Tacna, in Peru, and another (448 km.) with La Paz, the capital of Bolivia; the old steam locomotive (made in Germany in 1924) once used on this line can be seen outside Arica station. In the station is a memorial to John Roberts Jones, builder of the Arica portion of the railway. It is this railway, over which today flow about half the imports and exports of Bolivia, that makes Arica important; it will become more important now that the international highway to Tambo Quemado, Bolivia, is completed for normal traffic. An oil pipeline runs from Bolivia. There are large fishmeal plants.

The Free Zone in the First Region now imposes customs duties on many articles, but vessels, aircraft and other transport still enter the Zone without payment of customs dues and other charges. Articles such as calculators are cheaper here for Peruvians and Chileans, but not for Europeans. Spirits are slightly more expensive than in Santiago, cigarettes marginally cheaper.

Hotels *Hostería Arica* best, B, about 2 km. along shore, reached by frequent bus service along front (Nos. 7, 8), outstanding beaches with clean water and sand; *El Paso*, bungalow style, pleasant gardens, Av. Gral. Velásquez, 1109, Tel.: 31965-32288, C; *King*, Colón 376, D, with bath, overpriced; *Motel Azapa*, attractive grounds but several km. from beaches and centre: G. Sánchez, Azapa, Tel.: 42612-42613; *Savona*, Yungay 380; *Lynch*, Lynch 589, E, with bath, clean, quiet and pleasant; *Español*, Pasaje Bolognesi 340, D; *Ostería*, B, with bath, right on the sea (reportedly those who reserve through Hotelería Nacional, J. Miguel de la Barra 433 (Casilla 4190), Tel.: 391133, or cable Honsa in Santiago, are entitled to a discount); *Diego de Almagro*, Sotomayor 490, Tel.: 32927, immaculately clean, E; *Latino*, Junín 857, F; *Residencial Blanquita*, Maipú 472, clean, no hot water, F; *Residencial Chang*, 21 de Mayo 186, F; *Residencial Ibáñez*, Sotomayor 580, F; *San Marcos*, same street No. 367, D; *Res. Balkys*, Sotomayor 380, F; *Alojamientos Chillán*, Velásquez 611, F; *Residencial Madrid*, Calle Baquedano 685, poor beds but good value, F (including shared hot showers); *Residencial El Cobre*, General Lagos, basic, clean, F. *Residencial Patricia*, Maipú 269, F, recommended, but tiny rooms; *Residencial Núñez*, No. 516, F, basic but friendly. *Residencial Leiva*, Colón 347, F, incl. breakfast, shared bath, hot water a.m. only; *Residencial Maipú*, Maipú 479, F. On Calle Colón, *Residencial Atenas*, F, with bath, noisy; *Residencial Universo*, (No. 682) F, inexpensive and clean; *Res. Leira*, Pasaje Colón, F, good. Private house, Don Manuel, Población Juan Noé, Pasaje 15, No. 921, in alley behind main road opposite bus station. Also at Av. D.Portales 885 (Barbino Guajardo C.), room for rent in F range (opp. bus station, friendly). Youth Hostel, Av. 18 de Septiembre 2221.

Camping On beach at S end of town, past fishmeal factories. Interesting shoreline; caves, waves, blow-holes and birdlife.

Restaurants *Aduana*, Baquedano 373, excellent fish; *Aquarius*, Máximo Lira, Terminal Pesquero; *890*, pizzeria, 21 de Mayo; *Centro Español*, Bolognesi 311, good and cheap; *Restaurant Santiago*, Colón 359, good hamburgers; *Schop 18*, Calle 18 de Septiembre 240, serves excellent *pastel de choclo*. Restaurant at foot of El Morro on sea, recommended. Also, *El Rey de Mariscos*, corner Colón and Maipú, 2nd floor. Good eating at fire station, *Casino de Bomberos*, on Colón; also at *El Conquistador*, Baquedano 365; *El Corral*, 18 de Septiembre 482, 3 courses for US$2; *El Fascinador*, Av. Cdte. San Martín 1010. *Las Rocas*, on beach near *Hostería Arica*. **N.B.** In this area, *pensión* means restaurant, not hostel.

378 CHILE

Cafés *La Tranquera*, 21 de Mayo 431; *Chez Cristián*, P. Lynch 587; *Yovicar*, 18 de Septiembre 675; *Petit Pingüino*, Colón 423; *Ice Stop*, 21 de Mayo 248. Good cheap lunches at *The Snack*, 18 de Septiembre 431. Good *jugos* from central market and bread from Maipú 510.

Night-Clubs Casino, Gral. Velásquez 955, open all year. High Club and Vejescotec, 18 de Septiembre 482, 795; Disco Beach, Playa Arenillas Negras; Orbita 757, 21 de Mayo 757; Africa 2000, Rotonda Libertador Bernardo O'Higgins; Crazy Duck, Bajos del Chinchorro; Manhattan, Maipú 543; El Dorado, Sotomayor 367.

Cinemas Colón, 7 de Junio 190; Rex, 21 de Mayo 570.

Shopping Handicrafts: Pueblo Artesanal Arica, Rotonda Libertador Bernardo O'Higgins; Cema-Chile, Baquedano 311; Hugali, Pasaje 10, No. 932; Casa Martínez, 21 de Mayo 423; Feria Sangra, Sangra 350; Feria Dominical, Av. Costanera, Sun. a.m. only; Mercado Central, Sotomayor, 0800-1500 daily.

Car Hire Alen Rent a Car, Gral. Velásquez 750, Tel.: 42477.

Automóvil Club de Chile, Chacabuco 460, Tel.: 32780.

Car Service Shell, Panamericana Norte 3456; Esso, Av. Diego Portales 2462; Shell Cánepa, Chacabuco, San Martín. Volkswagen/Michelin, very helpful for repairs and assistance.

Museum at San Miguel, 12 km. along road towards Azapa Valley, small but good for pathological analysis of mummies, including one dating from 5000 BC if you are feeling strong. Open Tues.-Fri., 1100-1800; much of the information is in English. Colectivo with "Azapa" sign, from Calle Lynch, passes museum (US$0.70 one way).

Currency Many banks and money changers on 21 de Mayo and junction of Colón and 18 de Septiembre. Also at tourist office on main square. When banks closed money can be changed at *Hotel International*, *Hotel King*, or at the exchange houses (Yanulaque, Colón 380 or 21 de Mayo 175; Marta Daguer, 18 de Septiembre 330), which stay open until 2000.

British Vice-Consul (the only one in Chile outside of Valparaíso) and Instituto Británico reading room, opposite *Restaurant Aduana*, both on Baquedano, between 21 de Mayo and Sotomayor.

Consulates Argentina, Av. Prat and Chacabuco; Belgium, Sotomayor 504; Bolivia, Bolognesi 344; Costa Rica, Sotomayor 802; Denmark, 21 de Mayo 399; Peru, Yungay and Colón; Holland, 18 de Septiembre, with San Martín; Italy, Chacabuco with San Martín; France, Santa María 2860; Spain, Santa María 2660.

Telephones 21 de Mayo and Baquedano.

Tourist Office National office: Calle Arturo Prat 375, 2nd floor; post-office complex. Tel.: 32101. Very helpful, but not all information is accurate.

Travel Agencies Arica City Tour, Baquedano 769; Galantur, 7 de Junio 291; Tacora, 21 de Mayo 171; Turismo Payachatas, Bolognesi 332, Tel.: 51514; Jurasi, Bolognesi 360 A., Tel.: 32635; Parina Tours, Av. Prat 430. Huasquitur, P. Lynch, between Maipú and O'Higgins; Aricamundi, A. Prat 358; Mar y Tour, Colón 301.

Bathing Nice sandy beach 5 mins. from town by Balneario bus from Plaza de Armas. La Lisera and El Laucho, good for swimming; Playa Brava (surf beach) to south with fine, white sands; Playa Arenillas Negras, 3 km. to south; Playa Corazones, 15 km. to south, recommended not for swimming but picnics and fishing; Playa Chinchorro, north, swimmimg in Olympic pool.

Airport Chaculluta, to town costs US$5 for taxi. Airport tax US$5. Lan-Chile run a free bus service to their office in Plaza de Armas. Flights to La Paz (US$70, also with LAB and Aeronor, San Marcos 261, cheaper), Iquique, and Santiago (also with Aeronor). Ladeco, 18 de Septiembre 370, fly to Santiago direct once a week, or via Iquique and Antofagasta or El Salvador.

Road Services Terminal at corner of Av. Portales and Santa María, Tel.: 41390; station at 21 de Mayo 53, Tel.: 31105 (No. 8 taxi from centre). The Longitudinal (Pan-American) Highway S is mostly good, fast, 2-lane, concrete with hard shoulders and well signposted and served. All buses are modern, clean and air-conditioned, but ask carefully what meals are included. You must buy a platform ticket (US$0.15) in terminal to get to your bus. To Antofagasta, Flecha Norte, US$8.50, 10-11 hrs., via Tocopilla, not a comfortable trip. To Calama and Chuquicamata, 5 a day, 10 hrs., US$9. To Iquique, Agencia Norte Sur (Maipú 100, Esquina Prat) daily at 1600 or 1700, US$5, 4½ hrs. To Viña del Mar, US$30. To Santiago, 28 hrs., Chile Bus (1030 and 1530, 28-30 hrs.), with meals, good, US$30; several other companies, some more luxurious, student discounts available. To La Serena, Andes Mar Bus is the cheapest, daily at 1400, 18 hrs. There is now a road via Tambo Quemado into Bolivia; Litoral bus, tickets from A. Pedro Montt, journey to La Paz via Chungará takes 12 to 20 hrs., leaves on Tues. and Fri. at 0630, US$20. US$ cash only can be exchanged with the Bolivian Immigration Officer at Tambo Quemado.

Several checkpoints on the Longitudinal south from Arica. There is a checkpoint for fruit at Cuya

CHILE 379

(Km. 105), 20 km. further on are petroglyphs to the right (signposted), a checkpoint for buses and lorries at Huara (Km. 234, also petrol station), and customs and fruit control at Quillagua on Río Loa (Km. 430, where there is a museum of local Indian artefacts—key held by lady in telephone exchange). Also customs check at Arica bus terminal before departure south (painfully slow). **N.B.** If driving S, en route to Quillagua there are some steep ascents and descents best tackled in daylight (at night, sea mist, *camanchaca*, can reduce visibility).

Rail To La Paz by Arica-La Paz Railway (see page 168 for description of the line). No sleeping cars, 20 hrs. 2nd and 4th Tues. in month, 2300 (US$14 1st; US$11 2nd); latest reports indicate that the Fri. train no longer runs. Food, soft drinks and tea available. **Warning.** You have to change train at the Bolivian side of the border; be quick, as it is likely to be crowded. If you buy a 1st class ticket in Arica, you get reserved seat on the second train; if you travel 2nd class, don't bother to go to the ticket office at the border, just find space where you can (in, or on, the train). There are frequently long delays at the border.

Excursions To the fruitful Azapa valley by colectivo (US$1), from Patricio Lynch and Maipú; book through tourist agency. To the Lluta valley, 10 km. to north, figures built with stones on sandy hills, and to the wild desert and mountain scenery at the foot of the Andes.

Colectivo taxis run to and from Tacna for about US$2.80 p.p. (telephone Arica 31376 or Tacna 2288) one way and take about an hour for the trip. If there are not enough travellers to fill a taxi, the bus costs only US$1.30 between Tacna and Arica and leaves from Baquedano and Chacabuco. Money-changing at frontier, but reported better rates for pesos in Tacna; certainly best to buy Peruvian intis in Chile. By rail costs US$1.20, daily at 1130, 1630 and 1800, 1 hr. (exit stamp obtainable at station, but allow ½ hour for this—it is preferable to relying on the Town Hall); it is best to avoid Sats. because of crowds and delays at the border. The railway journey is sometimes suspended owing to problems with the one and only diesel engine.

Drivers are required at the Chile-Peru frontier to file a form, *Relaciones de Pasajeros* (6 copies), giving details of passengers, obtained from a stationery store in Tacna, or at the border. The first checkpoints outside Arica on the road to Santiago also require the *Relaciones de Pasajeros* from drivers. If you can't buy the form details on a piece of paper will suffice or you can get them at service stations. The form is *not* required when travelling south of Antofagasta.

Lauca National Park A visit to the Parque Nacional Lauca, some 120 km. E of Arica, is highly recommended. It is in the Altiplano (so beware of *soroche*, if you are not coming from Bolivia); the scenery shows snowy volcanoes reaching to 6,300 metres, blue cold lakes swarming with waterfowl, and much mammalian life including vicuñas, pumas and vizcachas. The Park is maintained by the Corporación Nacional Forestal (Conaf), Sotomayor 216, 3rd and 4th floors, Arica (Tel.: 31559), and it is advisable to obtain their advice before making the visit and essential to obtain a letter of introduction if you wish to stay in the *refugios*; they may also give you a lift. There are 4 refuges in the Park, but only those at Parinacota and Lake Chungará allow sleeping: at Putre (a scenic village at the Park entrance); at Las Cuevas (good for seeing wildlife, 20 km., inside the Park), at **Parinacota** (need sleeping bags, plenty of space, only 4 beds though, US$0.80, fully equipped kitchen) 4,392 metres up, at the foot of the Payachatas volcano (interesting 17th-cent. church with wall paintings and churchyard statuary; local resident Lorenza de Calle will knit alpaca sweaters for US$18-20; weavings of wildlife scenes also available), and at Lake Chungará (2 beds and floor space, cooking facilities) one of the highest lakes, a must (4,600 metres above sea-level). Limited possibilities of purchasing food at Chucuyo, a village just beyond the police control 30 km. from Putre, better to take your own (enough for yourself and the Park guards). Trips can be arranged with Turismo Payachatas, Jurasi (addresses above, US$15 p.p.) or Huasquitur, reported unreliable (contact Sr. Eric Vásquez Berutt, 7 de Junio 174, Casilla 566, if interested). Public transport to Lauca: The Arica-Bolivia road passes through the Park. Lorries leaving port of Arica early in the morning will often give lifts to the Park on their way to La Paz. Best place to wait is at the Pocón Chile control point, about an hour out of Arica on the Putre road. Hitching is best on Sunday when there is some tourist traffic. Buses leave from Germán Riesco 2071, Arica, for Putre on Tues., Thurs., Sat. at 0630 (returning Tues., Thurs., Sun. at 1200), US$2.50, then take daily "Vialidad" truck at 0700 into the Park. On Tues. and Fri. buses from Arica to Visviri on the Bolivian border (to connect with the La Paz train, but see above) pass Parinacota (6-7 hrs.), US$7: e.g. Martínez and Bus Sector Chile Norte on Av. P.Montt, Palomas Blancas, Velázquez 705 y Maipú, unreliable departure times in p.m. From Parinocota you can hitch to Visviri on Tues. or Fri. with lorries going to meet the train; catch the train to La Paz at Charaña. Lake Chungará is on the road route to La Paz, it is a 1 hr. walk to the border (Tambo Quemado), which opens at 0800; trucks pass infrequently, or you may be lucky and get on the Litoral bus which will charge full Arica-La Paz fare. The road into Bolivia is terrible, especially in the wet.

Dr. Klaus Busch, of Osnabrück, describes driving in the Park (he used a Toyota Landcruiser): "The road can be managed with a city car. Leave Arica via Panamericano North/Aeropuerto. After 9 km. turn off right; at 39 km. you will reach Pocón Chile, the control point for cars, and at 62 km. Molinos. Zapahuira, at 3,270 metres, marks the end of the paved road, with a marvellous view over the mountains. Later, at 152 km., at the turn off to Putre, you can see the Nevado de Putre

(5,825m.) The track to Chucuyo and back to Zapahuira is not even suitable for 4-wheel cars, or at least must be taken very slowly."

Humberstone, at the junction of the Pan-American Highway and the road to Iquique, is a large nitrate ghost town; ancient Indian drawings are to be seen and there is an interesting British cemetery 10 km. to the north. 2 km. beyond the junction to Humberstone is the Oficina Santa Laura, an impressive early nitrate plant, through which you can walk.

Iquique, the capital of the First Region and one of the main northern ports, is 304 km. by road south of Arica. The name of the town is derived from the Aymará word *ique-ique*, meaning place of "rest and tranquillity". It was founded in the 16th century on a rocky peninsula sheltered by the headlands of Punta Gruesa and Cavancha. The city was partly destroyed by earthquake in 1877. It has some old wooden houses, gaily painted, in a Victorian style, an outstanding square, Plaza Prat, with a clock tower and bell, and wide avenues bordered by trees. One, Av. Balmaceda, runs along the coast. The Archaeological Museum of the University of Chile, Calle Serrano 579, open Tues.-Fri. 0900-1300, 1500-1900 and Sat., Sun. 1000-1200, 1600-1800, small but well displayed, includes a section on minerals and a shop selling goods made by Chilean Aymarás. At the back of the Customs House is a Naval Museum. The Palacio Astoreca on Calle O'Higgins, built in 1903, formerly the Intendencia and now a cultural centre, is also of interest, not least because of its fine pinewood architecture and its exhibitions of shells and on the history of the nitrate industry. Population: 150,000. There are checkpoints on the road N to Arica, on the road S at Quillagua, and on the road inland (to Mamiña). One traveller reports being required to have an exit visa to travel internally from Iquique.

The harbour is well protected and ships tie up to load at modern docks. Many sealions and pelicans can be seen from the harbour. It was at Iquique that the *Esmeralda* and another wooden ship, under Captain Arturo Prat, resisted the attack of the Peruvian ironclad ship *Huáscar* on May 21, 1879, during the War of the Pacific (see page 416). The main exports are fishmeal, fish oil, tinned fish and salt.

Iquique has a Free Zone, at the north of town: it is worth a visit, goods from Hong Kong and Taiwan, reasonably priced cameras, electronics and cheap Ektachrome films are sold.

Local holiday During the ten days before July 16 there is a religious festival, "La fiesta de Tirana", at a village 70 km. E of Iquique (near Pica, see next page). Over 100 groups dance night and day, before making their pilgrimage to the church of the Virgen del Carmen.

Hotels *Hostería Cavancha*, A, south of city, on water's edge; *Arturo Prat*, in Av. Aníbal Pinto, facing Plaza Prat; *España*, Tarapacá 465, near Plaza Prat, recommended, F; *Tamarugal*, Tarapacá 369, central, clean and modern, E. Plenty of basic but cheaper hotels on Av. Amunátegui (700s); *Victoria*, F; *Vienna*, F; *Res. El Cobre* on Legaos F; *Turística*, F, clean, basic, the hotel shop sells extremely cheap film. Reasonably priced *pensiones* include *Residencial Catedral*, España 590 D, E; *Res. Bolívar*, Bolívar 478, F; *Residencial Marclaud*, Juan Martínez 753, F, recommended, quiet, clean, motor-cycle parking (good cheap restaurant at the corner); *Alvimar*, San Martín, F, cheap, pleasant; *Motel Primeras Piedras*. Youth Hostel, Av. Pedro Gamboni 2828.

Restaurants *Quinta José Luis*, near old airport, primitive, but food good; *Las Urracas*, Avenida Balmaceda 551, on seafront regarded as best place for fish; *Tamarugal Hotel* for seafood; *Chifa Tung Fong*, Tarapacá 835; *Parrilladas Misiacarmela*, Barros Arana 794, and *Yugoslavenki Dom*, Plaza Prat, for barbecues; *El Oasis* on Baquedano Norte; *Jorge Pedrero*, Thompson 882, cheap, English spoken; *Club de la Unión*, reasonable lunch. Also, the *Sociedad Protectora de los Empleados de Tarapacá* (Plaza Prat) is open to tourists and has reasonable prices. Several good, inexpensive seafood restaurants can be found on the second floor of the central market, Calle Barros Arana with Latorre. *Portofino*, Thompson 650, 3 courses for US$2. Yacht Club serves inexpensive lunch.

Cafés *Salón de Té Chantilly*, Tarapacá 520 and Barros Arana 716; *Café Diana*, Vivar 836, speciality mango ice cream; *El Mastique*, Thompson 728.

Clubs Casino Español, excellent meals well served in cool, Moorish decorated 100-year-old rooms; attractive. Club de la Unión; Club Yugoslavo, Plaza Prat; Círculo Italiano on Calle Tarapacá.

Discotheque Domino's, Sotomayor 657.

CHILE 381

Theatre Teatro del Norte at Sotomayor 728.

Cables Post and Telegraph Office, Calle Bolívar y P.Lynch; telex available.

Banks National banks.

Tourist Information Aníbal Pinto 436. Tel.: 21499.

Fishing Broadbill swordfish, striped marlin, yellowfin tuna, oceanic bonito, March till end of August.

Beaches Balneario Cavancha and Huaiquique, reasonable, November-March. Restaurants at Cavancha.

Buses To Arica, daily at 0830, 1400 and 2000, US$5, 4½ hrs., comfortable in spite of various checkpoints. To Antofagasta, daily 2000, US$10, a dusty, hot 8-hr. drive through the desert, relieved by the occasional oasis. To Calama and Chuquicamata, four times a week at 2230, 8 hrs. to Calama (US$12.50). To Santiago at 0830, arriving about 1330 the following day; Ramos Cholele and Tarapacá are the cheapest, about US$25 incl. meals. All buses leave from terminal at N end of Obispo Labbe.

Airlines Diego Aracena international airport, 35 km. S at Chucumata. Free airport bus to city centre. Lan-Chile, Av. Aníbal Pinto, next to *Hotel Prat*; Ladeco, San Martín 191 (Santiago-Iquique daily). To Antofagasta, Arica and Santiago daily by Lan-Chile.

Excursions Good roads run to the nitrate fields, which are 900 metres above sea level. A road runs NE to the hot mineral springs in the mountains at Termas de **Mamiña** (2,700 metres), where there is good accommodation for tourists (*Hotel Termas de Salitre*, D, full board, thermal pool in each room, electricity till midnight; *Residencial Ipla*, D, cheapest). The rainy season in Mamiña is mainly in January and is called *Invierno Boliviano* (Bolivian winter). Near Mamiña, 5 km. SW, is an Inca village with lots of pottery lying around.

The Iquique-Mamiña bus trip (130 km.) takes about 3 hrs. (The police control point just outside Iquique requires registration by foreigners, but the bus waits.) Bus, run by *Hotel Salitre*, leaves from market in Iquique every day except Sun. at 1600 (US$ 10). The road is well paved for the first 50 km., but from Pozo Almonte (a small town with a petrol station, hotel) onwards is unpaved and very bad. There is a large ravine, Quebrada Duplisa, where no vehicle can pass another, but as it is located slightly on a bend it is easy to avoid trouble.

The Pan-American Highway continues South: 13 km. after the turn-off to Iquique is a detour to Tirana (10 km.—see above) and the fertile oasis of **Pica** (2,750 metres), famous for its citrus groves and two natural springs. Hotels: *O'Higgins*, D; *San Andrés*, E. Campsite US$0.80 p.p. Yellow bus leaves Iquique from near market at 0900, returns from Pica at 2000; US$3.75. Beyond Pica is the oasis of Matilla, whence a road in poor condition returns to the Pan-American Highway.

Tocopilla, 195 km. S of Iquique, exports nitrate and iodine from two famous nitrate fields—María Elena (68 km.), and Pedro de Valdivia (85 km.). Population: about 42,000.

In the centre is the copper concentrate plant of Cía. Minera de Tocopilla. There is a sporting 18-hole golf course and fine deep sea fishing if you can find a boat and a guide. There are two paved roads out: a 193-km. coast road S to Antofagasta, and the other E up the narrow valley 72 km. to the Pan-American Highway (with a short spur to María Elena and Pedro de Valdivia, both working nitrate mines, the former with petrol station) and on to Chuquicamata. From Tocopilla to Chuquicamata is poor, particularly the eastern half which is eroded by the heavy lorries which use it (requires careful driving). A new coastal road runs N to Iquique and continues S to Antofagasta, via Mejillones (see page 383).

There are two sports stadiums and two good beaches: Punta Blanca and Caleta.

Hotel *América* (middling). *Hostal Bolívar*, Bolívar 1332, F, clean, friendly.

Restaurants *Kongton*, very poor; *Leo's*.

Cables All America Cables & Radio, Inc., Calle Serrano 1180.

Bus To Santiago, Tues. and Sat. To Antofagasta daily, 0730 and 1730, US$6.

Airport At Barriles, 12 km. from Tocopilla.

Antofagasta is 1,373 km. N of Santiago and 700 km. S of Arica. It is the capital of the Second Region, and its population of 190,000 makes it the largest city in northern Chile. It exports the nitrates of the area and the copper of Chuquicamata. A huge anchor stands high in the mountains, and was used as a navigational aid by ships. The main historical interest lies in some ruins at the edge of town, and a Bolivian silver refinery dating from 1868 (Huanchaca, now a military zone—you may visit, but not take photos), but it is lively and attractive, with a university of high standing, quite good parks and public gardens, an interesting waterfront, a clock tower on the main plaza donated by the British community, and very expensive shops. There is a small museum near the university, which has an interesting handicraft shop; museum opens Tues.-Fri., 0900-1200; 1500-1900; Sat. 0900-1200; Sun. 1100-1300. There is also a Geographical Museum on Balmaceda 2786, and an Archaeological Museum on Pasaje López (Prat y Latorre), Tues.-Fri. 1030-1300, 1530-1900, Sun. 1000-1300; Museo Regional (formerly University of the North museum in Iquique) on Balmaceda y Bolívar is also interesting. The modern sports stadium is close to the most popular beach (S end of city) where there is also a restaurant-pool-discotheque complex. Pavements are bad outside the shopping centre. The delightful climate (apart from the lack of rain) never varies more than a few degrees (18-20°C), but the best time for a visit is from May to September. The tap water is not potable.

Local Holiday June 29, San Pedro, patron saint of the fishermen; the saint's image is taken out by launch to the breakwater to bless the first catch of the day.

Festivals On the last weekend of October, the foreign communities put on a joint festival on the seafront, with national foods, dancing and music.

Hotels *Turismo Antofagasta*, Calle Prat, run-down, garage, swimming pool, lovely view of port and city, A with breakfast, beach; *Diego de Almagro*, very good; *San Marcos*, Latorre 2946, B; *San Martín*, Calle San Martín 2781, ½ block from main plaza, F; *Prinz*, Matta 2321, D; *Residencial El Paso*, very near bus station, F, basic but friendly; *Imperio*, Condell 2736, F; *San Antonio*, Condell 2235, E, clean, good but noisy from bus station; *Residencial La Riojanita*, Baquedano 464, F, and full of young people, use of kitchen permitted; *Comercial*, San Martín, friendly, clean; *Residencial Calama*, San Martín 2772, F; *Residencial Paola*, Prat 766, good value, friendly, clean, F; *Res. Cobre*, Prat 749, F, dirty; *Plaza*, Baquedano 461, D, modern, clean; *Res. Colón*, Baquedano 329; *Res. O'Higgins*, Sucre 665, F (no hot water); *Res. Venecia*, F, near station on Serrano; *Tatio*, Av. Grecia 1000, D, out of old town on the beach, has buses converted into caravans, friendly, beautiful views. Youth hostels: men: Matias Rojas 522; women: Díaz Gana y Eduardo Lefort.

Camping Las Garumas, 16 km. on route to Coloso, US$10 for tent, US$15 for cabins; hot water, showers and beach. Official campsite at S end of beach beyond university.

Restaurants *Helénico*, Sucre 456; *Don Lucho*, Latorre 2356; *Londres*, Sucre y Matta; *Protectora de Empleados*, San Martín 2544; *Apoquindo*, Prat 616, self-service, reasonable, good, as is *Club Náutico*, Pinto 3051; *Italiano*, Prat 732, excellent lunch; *Tío Jacinto*, Calle Uribe, by Tramaca terminal, friendly, good seafood; *Air Port Station Restaurant*; *Rancho Coloso* near the Auto Club at the southern end of city; *El Galeón*, old fishing boat converted into an imitation galleon, recommended for quick lunches and romantic late dinners. The al fresco luncheons at the Auto Club are fashionable both in summer and winter. *Club de la Unión*, Calle Prat 470 (quite good). *Societá Italiana*, next to *Residencial Paola* on Prat, recommended. *Tatio*, Av. Costanera; *El Arriero*, good grills, Spanish-style, Condell 2632; *Chico Jaime* above the market, seafood, US$3 p.p. incl. wine. Many eating places in the market.

Clubs Club de Tenis Antofagasta, Av. Angamos 906, connected with Av. Brasil, and the Automobile Club, 6½ km. from Antofagasta; Yachting Club, Calle Balmaceda.

Market Municipal market, corner of Matta and Uribe.

Car Rental Rent-a-Car, Prat 810, Tel.: 225200; Hertz, Balmaceda 2646, offer city cars and jeeps (group D, Toyota Landcruiser) and do a special flat rate, with unlimited mileage, if you hire the car for over a week.

Discotheques *Eden* is popular.

Theatres In centre: Nacional, Latorre, Imperio, Gran Vía to the S. El Universitario.

Cinema There are two cinemas showing triple features.

Banks in main square will not buy or sell Argentine or Bolivian money, but will change dollars. N.B. There is practically no official opportunity to change currency S of Antofagasta until you reach La Serena.

CHILE 383

Post Office Washington 2623; Telephones, Uribe 746.

Tourist Office Helpful, Edif. Centenario, piso 12, Washington 2675, Tel.: 223004; also Prat y Matta, Tel.: 224834, and Airport.

Roads To Tocopilla, 185 km.; to Mejillones, 64 km.; to Pedro de Valdivia, 168 km.; to María Elena, 199 km.; to Taltal, 309 km.; to Calama, 214 km.; to Chuquicamata, 230 km. **N.B.** the Pan-American Highway between the N and S exits to Antofagasta is not paved (20 km.).

Buses To Santiago, 20 hrs., US$19.75 (luxury double decker bus, Flota Barrios, US$26 including drinks and meals; 30% reduction on Inca and Gemini buses for students; Flecha Norte cheapest, US$18, book 2 days in advance). Bus station at S end of town (Av. Argentina, Díaz Gana) often has seats left when buses from N terminal (at Uribe) are booked. Alternatively, catch a bus to La Serena (US$14 or 25 with lunch and supper) or Ovalle and travel to Santiago from there. To Arica, US$8.50 (Flecha Norte), 13½ hrs. (It is forbidden to take fresh fruit south from Antofagasta because of fruit-fly control.) To Chuquicamata, Flecha del Norte leaves at 0700, returns at 1900, as well as many others. To Calama, Wed. at 0900, US$3, gets to Calama (3 hrs.), in time to catch the train (see page 384). Bus leaves from railway station. Tickets to La Paz can be bought at railway office, corner Bolívar and Pinto (US$19). Direct to Copiapó on Thurs. and Sat. at 2230, US$10.50. Frequent buses to Iquique; US$10 by colectivo, 8 hrs., checkpoints near Iquique for foreigners. To Mejillones, twice a day from Latorre 2700. To San Pedro de Atacama, US$2, bus; US$1 truck. Bus station has a left luggage office.

If hitching to Arica or Iquique try at the beer factory a few blocks N of the fish market on Av. Pinto, or the lorry park a few blocks further N.

N.B. There are no more railway passenger services from Antofagasta. The famous journey to Bolivia now starts from Calama (see page 384), and the line into Argentina has been closed to passengers for some years. However, Empresa de Transportes Atahualpa runs a weekly bus service to Argentina; via Calama, immigration check at San Pedro de Atacama, then on to high Cordillera (very cold) and to San Antonio de los Cobres; change bus at Salta. There is nowhere to change Chilean pesos en route.

Air To Santiago, Ladeco flies daily and Aeronor on Tues., Wed., Fri. and Sat. To Iquique, Aeronor daily. To Salta, Aerolíneas Argentinas Sat., US$62. Taxi to airport US$7, but cheaper if ordered from hotel.

Excursions to derelict nitrate *oficinas*, over good roads (140 km.). (Some of the old nitrate towns are being repopulated as a result of renewed demand for natural nitrates following the oil price rises.) The most interesting are Rica Adventura, Buenaventura, Puelma and Ibérica. There are two favourite spots for picnics: near the town of La Chimba, and the fantastic rock scenery at La Portada (16 km.) taxi fare, US$1.50. Alternatively, ask the driver of the airport bus, which leaves every 2 hrs. from *Hotel Turismo*, to drop you at the junction for La Portada—only 1 km. walk to beach. Last bus back leaves at 1830. A number of bathing beaches are within easy reach, including La Portada. Oficina Chacabuco is a military camp and "off limits"; in 1938 it was a town with 7,000 inhabitants (at junction of Antofagasta-Calama and María Elena roads). 50 km. from Antofagasta at Juan López is a windsurfers' paradise. Buses leave from Latorre 2700.

Mejillones, 64 km. N (130 km. S of Tocopilla), has a good natural harbour protected from westerly gales by high hills. Since the export of tin and other metals from Bolivia ceased, Mejillones lives solely by fishing. The town comes alive after 1700 when the fishermen prepare to set sail. There is a Museo del Mar in the old customs building (1866) on Aníbal Pinto. The sea is very cold because of the Humboldt current. Population: 6,000.

Hotels *Posada San Juan*, A.Goñigg, with restaurant; *Residencial Elisabeth*, Alto Latorre 440, F, friendly, restaurant. *Juanito Restaurant*, Las Heras 24.

215 km. NE of Antofagasta is the oasis town of **Calama,** population 88,000, at an altitude of 2,265 metres. The Cía. Sud Americana de Explosivos manufactures high explosives. The town is modern and has a developed commercial centre. There is a Jugoslav Club. Travellers by car coming from the N can drive via Chuquicamata, although the road is quite poor on either side of that town, or, from the S, by a paved road (94 km.) leaving the Pan-American Highway 98 km. N of Antofagasta. 2 km. from the centre on Av. B.O'Higgins is Parque Loa, with

an exhibition of pre-cordillera life, 2 museums, a zoo and a copy of Chiu Chiu church; open Tues.-Sun. 0930-1230, 1430-1700, US$0.20.

Hotels *Hostería Calama*, Latorre 1521, A, good food; *Lican Antai*, Ramírez 1937, A; *Motel Pukará*; *Rolando* (clean and small); *Prat*, Vivar 1970, F, friendly; *Residencial Internacional*, hot water, F, friendly but noisy; *Residencial Casa de Huéspedes*, Sotomayor 2073, clean, quiet, shared hot shower, E; *Res. Tacora*, Sotomayor 1992, friendly, clean, F; *Res. Toño*, Vivar 1970, next to Kenny bus, F, shower (extra); *Capri*, Vivar, F, clean and friendly, hot water; cheap hotel at Flecha del Norte bus terminal; *Universo*, near railway station, good value, F. *Los Andes*, F, basic, cheapest.

Restaurants *El Arriero*, on Calle Vivar, *La Nueva Florida*, Calle Vargas 1975, excellent and cheap, *Ollantay*, on Vivar, set lunch for US$1.75, good. *Lascar*, on Calle Ramírez, cheap, as is *Santa Teresa* on Vargas. *Osorno*, not cheap, but live music from 2200. *El Hotelero*, Av. Tocopilla 2546; good eating at fire station (*Casino de Bomberos*). Yugoslav club serves good, cheap lunches.

Car Hire Comercial Maipo S.A., Barrio Industrial, sitio 14, Tel.: 211965, take taxi—½ hr. out of town, cheapest, US$28/day for car, US$37/day for pickup. Hertz, Latorre 1510.

Exchange Farmacia Frankfurt will change travellers' cheques and cash at a good rate, also Casatel (electricity shop), Ramírez between Latorre and Vivar, and *Hotel Los Andes*; Banco de Crédito e Inversiones will only change cash. Money changers selling Bolivian money for Chilean can be found outside the railway station (last chance before Oruro or La Paz).

Consul The Bolivian Consulate (Vicuña Mackenna 1976) is open 0900-1230 and 1530-1830, Mon.-Fri., friendly, helpful.

Laundry Ramírez, corner Vivar, cheap, US$1 for 2½ kg.

Tourist Office, José La Torre and Mackenna; Parque Ramírez and La Torre. Good map of town, arranges car hire. Open Mon.-Fri. 0900-2000, Sat.-Sun. 0900-1400.

Transport Daily bus services to Santiago (22 hrs., US$20), Arica (Tramaca, at 2130 daily, except 2230 on Sunday, US$9), and Iquique and Ovalle. Student reduction on Tramaca Bus. Also to San Pedro daily (US$3) with Tramaca on Félix Hoyos and Morales Moralitos, Av. Balmaceda y Ramírez (see below for schedules), Morales bus continues to Toconao Tues., Thurs., Sat.; to Chuquicamata (see 384). Antofagasta, 3 hrs., US$3. Bus to Salta, Argentina, Wed., a.m. and Sat. p.m. (2), 17 hrs., US$27. 3 companies: Geminis (Av. Granaderos), Tramaca and Atahualpa.

Air Ladeco flights to Antofagasta and Santiago leave daily—except Sat.

Rail Antofagasta (Chile) and Bolivia Railway to Oruro and La Paz: train departs from Calama now. Bus leaves Antofagasta Wed. 0900 to connect with train leaving Calama at 1255, Ollagüe 2000, Uyuni at about 0500 on Thurs. and La Paz at 1500 (all times are "pure fantasy"). No sleeping cars available from Calama to La Paz so take blankets or sleeping bag. The frontier is reached about 2300 to the accompaniment of considerable palaver. There is a change of trains at the border (just after Ollagüe); your ticket is supposedly valid for both, but ensure that it is stamped with a reservation for the second, and be quick at the changeover. One class only to La Paz is US$17; to Oruro US$13; scenery beautiful but journey crowded (especially with smugglers), very slow and uncomfortable. Many passengers leave train at Oruro, and go on by bus to La Paz (3¾ hrs.). For Potosí and Cochabamba change trains at Río Mulato and Oruro respectively; note that the connection is not always assured. There is a freight-train to Potosí (free) some hours later, a bus one day later and a train on Sat. Note that before leaving you must visit (a) the Bolivian consulate for visa if needed, and (b) the railway station. It is advisable, but not necessary, to visit the railway office at Bolívar 255, Antofagasta (open Tues. 0900-1300 and 1500-1630, and Wed. 0900-1230) to make sure if there is a seat, but they can be purchased (with luck) at Calama (office opens Tues. p.m. and Wed. a.m.). You must have your passport with you when buying ticket. It can be very cold at night (-15°C) and into the day. Meals available at Ollagüe and Río Mulato (only for the conditioned).

Excursion Just E of Calama is the village of Chiu Chiu, with a very interesting old church and nearby a unique, perfectly circular, very deep lake. An ancient fortress and rock carvings are to be found in the Río Loa valley. This excursion is only possible by private or hired car.

At **Chuquicamata**, 16 km. from Calama at 2,800 metres, is the world's largest open-cast mine, a state-owned copper mine that used to belong to a U.S. firm. It is an astoundingly large hole. All the processes can be seen; there are daily guided tours with a film show three times a week on Mon., Wed. and Fri. at 1330 from the Public Relations Office, near Puerta Una, taking 2 hrs. (very interesting but only given in Spanish); fee of US$1 goes to workers' social fund. Register at 1300; passport essential; photography with permission only. You must wear a

CHILE 385

long-sleeved garment (shorts not allowed) and strong footwear if you wish to see the industrial plants.

Travellers can eat inexpensively beforehand at the works canteen, "club social", next to the tourist-reception office. The clean, modern and pleasing town has about 30,000 people. (Guest house at east end of Plaza, nice, but book at Santiago or Antofagasta; overnight accommodation may be difficult.) There is a country club with a golf course at Río Loa. Within 30 km. of Chuquicamata there are several small towns and villages nestling in remote oases in the Andean massif. Due E of Chuquicamata, 37 km. on the way to Ayquina (see page 386), are the pre-Incaic ruins of Lasana, a national monument, with explanatory tablets. They are arguably the most impressive in Chile; the road from Calama through the *quebrada* is more scenic than that via Ollagüe.

Bus marked "Chuqui" from main plaza in Calama to Chuquicamata, US$0.40, ½ hr., frequent, then colectivo (marked "Local Chuqui") to mine, US$0.25. To Arica at 2200 (weekends at 2300), US$9, 9 hrs. To Antofagasta, ten a day, US$6 single. To Iquique at 2300. To Santiago at 1400, US$25, 24 hrs.

419 km. from Antofagasta, at 3,690 metres, on the dry floor of the Salar de Ollagüe near the Bolivian border, is **Ollagüe,** surrounded by a dozen volcanic peaks of over 5,000 metres. Population: 500; one service station (with unusual opening hrs.). A 77-km. spur railroad of metre gauge runs to the copper mines of Collahuasi, and from there a 13-km. aerial tram to the highest mine in the world: the Aucanquilcha, at 6,100 metres. Its sulphur is taken to Aruncha, a town at the foot of the volcano, to be refined. The highest passenger station in this spur is Yuma, at 4,400 metres. A train can be taken from Calama on Wed. at 1255, US$3.30 to Ollagüe, but if you stop off, you will have to hitch back, the daily freight trains are not allowed to take passengers. Bad unmade road from Ollagüe into Bolivia (see page 187).

At this altitude nights are cold, the days warm and sunny. Minimum temperature at Ollagüe is -20°C, and at the mine, -37°C. There are only 50 mm. of rain a year, and water is very scarce.

The main stock animals are llamas and alpacas, whose principal forage is the *ichu* bunch-grass covering the lower slopes. There is no timber. *Taqui*—dried llama dung— and *tola* heath are used for cooking fires, but the main fuel is *yaretal*, a resinous moss growing in pillow-like masses in rocky outcrops from 3,500 to 5,000 metres high. Its calorific value is 6,300 British Thermal Units per pound—half that of bituminous coal. It apparently is an Ice Age relic, growing very slowly but now worked out in this area. Across the border in Bolivia there is plenty, which is used as fuel for the Laguna Verde sulphur mine. It is claimed, like mineral land, and broken up with dynamite into chunks for transport.

103 km. SE of Calama—road now completely paved—is **San Pedro de Atacama,** (2,436 metres, pop. 2,500), a small town more Spanish- Indian looking than is usual in Chile, well worth a visit. Both Diego de Almagro and Pedro de Valdivia stopped in this oasis (Valdivia's house on the main square may be visited by knocking at the green door next to it and asking for the key). A most impressive archaeological museum now under the care of the Universidad del Norte (Mon.-Fri., 0900-1300, 1500-1900; Sat., and Sun., 1000-1200, 1500-1900) is stocked with Indian skulls and artefacts, as well as the contents of the study of the late Father Le Paige, who used to run the museum. The Director's Brazilian wife gives an excellent guided tour in Spanish. Labels on displays are good (English pamphlet soon to be available). Graham Greene tells us that "the striking feature of the museum is . . . the mummies of Indian women with their hair and dresses intact dating from before the Conquest, and a collection of paleolithic tools which puts the British Museum in the shade". Along the road are mounds of lava ash and dried-up geysers, making the landscape look rather lunar (see also below) as well as various archaeological remains. There are Tramaca buses daily at 0900, 1000 on Sun. and Morales Moralitos Mon.-Sat. 1700 (1600 in winter), 1¾ hrs., US$3 from Calama to San Pedro de Atacama, returning from the plaza at 1800 (Tramaca) and 0800 (Morales Moralitos, Tues.-Sat.). Extraordinary sunsets.

The Valle de la Luna, with fantastic landscapes caused by the erosion of salt mountains, is traversed by a road 13 km. before reaching San Pedro; the bus does not pass through the valley but the San Pedro-Calama bus passes the old road which crossed the valley (most bus drivers know where it is and will let you out—the sign is not visible if coming from Calama). From here it is a 3-hr. walk back to San Pedro (best done at sunset, take torch and food). Alternatively, a trip can be arranged through *Residencial Chiloé*. A recommended guide is Robert Sánchez (he speaks German). Driving through the Valle de la Luna at sunset, with the Licancábur volcano, 5,916 metres, in the background, is incredible. If you are in your own car, make the detour on your way south (i.e. from Calama), as from N drifting sand makes uphill driving difficult. There are also some pre-Inca

386 CHILE

ruins about 3 km. from San Pedro at Pucará, and a fine sandstone cave nearby. Pucará can be reached on foot by following the river bed, or US$1.20 for pick-up truck, seats 6.

Hotels *Hostería San Pedro*, recently refurbished, D, recommended, Australian joint proprietors Luis Hernández and Mrs. Bobbee Andrews have prepared a short guide to the area in English, German, French, Spanish and Japanese; the *hostería* has a swimming pool, shop and a Copec petrol station, tents for hire, US$3 for 2 people, camping in grounds, US$0.75 p.p., 2 cabins with 6 and 3 beds, hot water, electricity 1800-2300, restaurant and bar, Tel.: 21-1511. *Residencial Chiloé*, F; *Pukará*, F, clean, pleasant; *Pensión Florida*, good, F, no hot water, but has a friendly parrot.

Restaurants *Juanita's*, reasonably priced; *Cobreloa*.

Swimming Pool Pozo Tres, 3 km. outside village, 40 mins. walk from centre, was drilled in the late 1950s by Unesco as part of a mineral exploration project, US$0.50 to swim. Camping.

An interesting route from San Pedro de Atacama to Calama is to go north on a maintained road which passes the Baños de Puritama (27 km., truck drivers leaving from behind the police station for the sulphur mine at 0500 may give you a lift and collect you on return), then to the geysers at El Tatio. The geysers, at an altitude of 4,500 metres, are at their best 0630-0830. There is no public transport, so if going in a hired car, make sure the engine is suitable for very high altitudes and is protected with antifreeze; 4-wheel drive is preferable. It is easy to get lost if driving in the dark. Taxi drivers Héctor Ochoa and Segundo Ugalde (contact through *Hostería San Pedro*) are recommended for this trip. From Calama, trips for El Tatio leave at 0400, continuing to San Pedro and the Valle de la Luna, arriving back at 2000 (US$120-140 for six). Villages between El Tatio and Calama include Caspana, beautifully set among hills, with an interesting museum, and **Ayquina**, in whose ancient church is enshrined the statue of the Virgin of Guadalupe. Her feast-day is September 8, when pilgrims come from far and wide. There is day-long group dancing to Indian rhythms on flute and drum. Towards sunset the Virgin is carried up a steep trail to a small thatched shrine, where the image and the people are blessed before the dancing is renewed at the shrine and all the way back to the village. The poor people of the hills gather stones and make toy houses all along the route: miniatures of the homes they hope to have some day. With a detour, the thermal waters and ruins of Baños de Turi may be visited and, 35 km. north, Copo, on a scenic road with herds of llama and alpaca, giant cacti and flamingos on the mudflats. The route to Calama continues via Lasana, Chiu Chiu or Chuquicamata.

SE of San Pedro, 39 km. on a reasonable unpaved road, is the lush oasis of **Toconao**, with some 500 inhabitants on the eastern shore of the lithium-salt lake Salar de Atacama. All houses are built of bricks of volcanic stone, which gives to the village a very characteristic appearance totally different from San Pedro. Its colonial clock tower is modelled in the same volcanic stone by the local craftsman and it has an attractive oasis called Quebrada de Jérez. (Worth visiting are the intricate irrigation systems on both sides of the canyon.) Morales Moralitos buses to Toconao from San Pedro Tues., Thurs., Sat. 1800, returning Wed., Fri., Sun. 0630, US$1. An alternative is to hitch from San Pedro (most traffic at weekends). Camping possible along river bank of Quebrada de Jérez.

Ask the *jefe de carabineros* in San Pedro or Toconao for a chance to go with police patrols to the Bolivian or Argentine border areas (paying your share of fuel).

From San Pedro de Atacama one can cross into Argentina over the pass of Huaytiquina to San Antonio de los Cobres. Travellers by car should make careful enquiries into road conditions (often impassible in rainy season, Jan.1 to mid-March, and blocked by snow in winter); gasoline may be bought in Calama or at *Hostería San Pedro*. Passport control and customs clearance must be undertaken in San Pedro.

The first village reached is Toconao (see above; cars registered at the entrance to the village); the Atacama desert can be seen in the distance. A detour can be made to the scenic villages of Camar (where handicrafts from cactus may be bought), Socaire (which has domesticated llamas, knitwear for sale) and Peine (woollen goods and knitwear); good views of the Quebrada de Jérez and Lascar Volcano. After a steep climb, you reach the Laguna Lejía (4,190 metres), where flamingos abound. You then pass through the high plains of Huaytiquina (4,275 metres), where only a few herdsmen are found. Before reaching Catua, the first Argentine settlement, you cross the *salares* (salt lakes) and the road winds its way through the Socompa pass (3,880-4,200 metres). The highest altitude reached during the trip is at Chorrillos (4,560 metres). The road crosses the railway, descends into the ghost-like town of Agua Castilla, and after 8 km. reaches San Antonio de los Cobres. It is a further 3½ hours by car to Salta. Buses from San Pedro to San Antonio de los Cobres, US$15; to Salta, Geminis, Wed. 2030, Tramaca, Sat. 2200, from Interpol office (take passport), US$20.

The next important port to the south is

CHILE 387

Taltal, 309 km. S of Antofagasta, connected with it by the Pan-American Highway and a poor but scenic road along the coast. It is a nitrate and copper ore centre with 12,200 people. There is an airport, but few flights.

Hotels *Plaza; Hostería de la Corfo* (modern; 12 bedrooms, D). *Hostería Norhoteles,* Esmeralda 641, C. Several boarding houses; one, *La Goyesca,* Martínez 279, has a pleasant cheap restaurant. "The water supply is random, and the Salón de Te has no tea" (J. D. H. Smith).

Buses Three a week to Santiago; several to Antofagasta.

Chañaral, a neglected looking port and town with wooden houses perched on the hillside and beset by water shortages. It is 100 km. S of Taltal and 400 km. S of Antofagasta by sea or Pan-American Highway. Population, including Potrerillos and Caleta Barquito: 50,000. Anchorage is very near jagged rocks which rear out of the sea all round.

Hotels *Hostería El Sarao; Jiménez; La Marina; Hostería Chañaral,* D, with evening meal.

Buses Three leave for Antofagasta between 1100 and 1230; these departures are subject to alteration at short notice.

Copiapó, 240 km. S of Chañaral, capital of the Third Region, is an inland town in a ribbon of farms and orchards about 150 km. long on the river Copiapó, the river generally regarded as the southern limit of the Atacama desert. It is an attractive mining centre with an important mining school, and a population of 65,000. There is a monument to Juan Godoy, a pioneer of the mining industry. The best mineralogical museum in Chile is in a new building, 1 block from Plaza de Armas (east), no fee; Mon.-Fri. 1000-1300, 1830-2200. Many ores shown are found only in the Atacama desert. Also Museo Regional Atacama Copiapó; entrance US$0.35, interesting. Open Tues.-Sat. 0930-1300, 1600-1900, Sun. 1000-1300. Airport.

Hotels *Inglés,* D, recommended; *Turismo* (good); *Carrera* (small rooms round courtyard, good food, D); *Derby,* Yerba Buena 39, E, clean; *Res. Norte, Res. Party, Res. Kennedy,* all F, recommended. *Willy Beer* restaurant, Maipú 386, has fancy hot-dogs, hamburgers and entertainment. *Bavaria Restaurant,* on main square, excellent but not cheap.

Tourist Office Los Carrera 691, Tel.: 2838.

About 70 km. W of Copiapó is the port of **Caldera,** which has a pier of 230 metres; 1½ km. to the S there is a terminal for the loading of iron ore.

Camping Bahía Inglesa, 6 km. W of Highway, 3 km. S of Caldera. Swimming in the Pacific.

A road runs NE through the pass of San Francisco in the Andes to Tinogasta, in Argentina (suitable only for 4 wheel-drive vehicles, often closed by landslides). South of the pass rises the Ojos del Salado mountain, believed to be the second highest peak in the Americas; its height is now thought to be in the range of 6,875-6,887 metres. There is fumarolic activity 300 metres below the summit of Ojos del Salado, which makes it a contender with Cotopaxi in Ecuador for the title of the world's highest active volcano.

From Copiapó to Illapel

The second geographic zone, lying between the valleys of the Copiapó and the Aconcagua, contains the southern half of the Third Region and the whole of the Fourth (population at 1982 census, 419,956). The zone is about 600 km. long.

This is a transitional zone between the northern desert and the fruitful heartland. S of Copiapó the central valley is cut across by transverse spurs of mountain which link the Andes and the coastal *cordillera.* Between these spurs several rivers flow westwards. Southwards the desert gives way slowly to dry scrub and bush interspersed with sand dunes. Winter rainfall (there is no rain in summer) is still light and lasts only a short time: it is about 115 mm. at Copiapó and 500 mm. at Illapel. In the river valleys under irrigation, fruit, vines, and barley are grown, and some alfalfa for cattle. There are many goats.

Vallenar (airport), inland up the Huasco valley, is 144 km. S of Copiapó; it is the second city of the Third Region, with a population of 42,000. Good wines are produced in the Huasco valley, in particular a sweet wine known as Pajarete. A road runs down the valley to **Huasco** (Hotel Miramar), an interesting port: 1½ km. S of Huasco is a terminal for loading iron ore from the deposits at Algarrobal, inland 35 km. N of Vallenar. Population: 6,347.

Vallenar Hotels Real Hotel Turismo; Hostería Vallenar (good); Hotel Atacama.

La Serena, on the coast 187 km. S of Vallenar, 480 km. N of Santiago (93,000 people), is the capital of the Fourth Region, an attractive old-world town built on a hillside, which has become a tourist resort. It was remodelled in the 1950s and is now one of the pleasantest towns in Chile, with many colonial-style buildings, pretty gardens and a lot of azulejos, or coloured tiles. It has a Cathedral, 29 churches and several old convents. Many rodeos are held, and Chilean independence is celebrated on September 20 with a huge open-air picnic on the sands at nearby Coquimbo. The most popular nearby beaches are Peñuelas, half way to Coquimbo, and La Herradura. A road (about one-third paved) runs 500 km. E over the pass of Agua Negra (4,775 metres) to San Juan in northern Argentina (closed in winter). The climate is often damp and rarely hot. Market on Sun. New market on Cienfuegos, cheap food and souvenirs.

History La Serena was founded by Juan de Bohón, aide to Pedro de Valdivia, in 1544, destroyed by Diaguita Indians in 1546, rebuilt by Francisco de Aguirre in 1552, and sacked by the English pirate Sharpe in 1680. Legends of buried treasure at Guayacán Bay, frequented by Drake, persist.

The Archaeological Museum, in a colonial-style building, has an interesting collection of Diaguita and Molle Indian exhibits, especially of most attractively decorated pottery, at corner of Calles Córdovez and Cienfuegos. It is closed all day Mon., Sun. afternoon, and from 1300 to 1600 daily, entrance, US$0.35. There is a mineralogical museum near the Technical University.

Hotels Turismo, B; Francisco de Aguirre, Córdovez 210, good, but poor sound insulation; Londres, Córdovez 566, D, fair restaurant; Baños los Socos, C, good; Pucará (on Balmaceda), D; Alameda, E, clean and comfortable, towels supplied; Residencial Brasilia, Brasil 555, F, good, friendly; Res. La Florida, E, friendly; Hostería Chile, Matta 561, basic, fairly clean, F. Residencial El Loa, Bernardo O'Higgins 362, E with shower, good inexpensive home cooking (US$2.50-3 per main meal), friendly; Residencial Petit, F, basic; Residencial Americanas, Calle Andrés Bello, F; Residencial Carreras, Los Carreras 682, Tel.: 51-213646, F. Family pensión of Isabel Ahumada, Eduardo de la Barra 315, good, cheap. Lodging at Calle Vicuña, F, good. Youth hostel, Colegio Santa Inés, Pedro Pablo Muñoz y Cirujano Videla.

Motel on Pan-American Highway.

Campsite Maki Payi, 153 Vegas Norte, about 5 km. N of La Serena, near sea, friendly, recommended, self-contained cabins available; US$3.10 per tent and US$9.50 p.p. for chalet. Also on the beach near the Drive-In Donde ya Sabemos (expensive snacks).

Restaurants Club Social, Córdovez 516, unpretentious but excellent. Also, restaurant and bar at Hotel Berlin (popular with the locals) and Parrillada El Pino, recommended; also Restaurante O'Higgins. Restaurant Galeón, Brasilia, good seafood; El Candil, Balmaceda 545; Mi Casa, Av. Aguirre 596, 2nd floor, cheap almuerzos; Café Milan, Balmaceda 655, good pastries. Pizzería on Calle O'Higgins. Fish meals on 1st floor of market hall. Copec gas station an S-bound side of Pan-American Highway, excellent food. N.B. All restaurants are closed on Sundays.

Discotheques Oriente, Balmaceda 677.

Tourist Office Room 108, Edificio de Servicios Públicos, Plaza de Armas, next to Post office (open Mon.-Fri. 0830-1300, 1430-1800); kiosk in market area (Cienfuegos y Prat).

Transport Buses daily to La Calera and Santiago at 0800 and evening, 8 hrs, US$7.50; to Arica, US$20; to Calama, US$17, 16 hrs. Only freight trains to Santiago. By bus to Antofagasta takes 13 hrs., US$14 and to Iquique 20 hrs, US$21. Bus to Vicuña and Pisco Elqui, 3 hrs., US$2.35. Bus to Coquimbo, from Av. Aguirre, US$0.25.

Air From Vallenar and La Serena, Aeronor flies 6 times a week (Mon.-Sat.) to Santiago.

Excursion La Serena is at the mouth of the Elqui river valley, where the Nobel Prize-winning poet Gabriela Mistral was born. She described the valley as "confined yet lofty, many-sided yet simple, rustic yet a mining area". The road up the valley has been rebuilt and paved as far as Vicuña; "its branches all lead to fertile nooks, to shady vegetation, to dense groves, to gardens fed by the very sap of the hills". Except for Vicuña, most of the tiny towns have but a single street. Of the elquinos, the people of the valley, she says that "even the most taciturn of them come out with

CHILE 389

witty and charming remarks". There are still a few descendants of the Diaguitas, the tribe that inhabited the valley at one time.

Vicuña (66 km.; *Hostería*, swimming pool; *Hotel Plaza*, F, with breakfast; camping at airstrip a few km. from town—ask police), capital of the valley, is on the way to Rivadavia at an altitude of 600 metres and has a population of 16,000. Beautiful hand-woven rugs may be purchased at the village of Chapilca (25 km. from Vicuña). There are mines, vineyards and orchards in the district, which produces pisco and dried fruits. Vicuña is picturesque, fairly clean and friendly; it is within reach by car (120 km.) of Termas del Toro in the mountains. A small Gabriela Mistral Museum has been opened. Her grave is at Monte Grande, 20 km. S of Rivadavia. Tourist Office at Plaza de Armas will also arrange a visit to the Pisco distillery, Capel, between 0800-1200 and 1400-1800.

The road to Rivadavia continues up the valley, in which there are orchards and orange groves. Beyond Rivadavia the road runs to the small towns of Paihuano and Pisco Elqui (*Hotel Plaza*, F) (34 km.), where you can visit old-fashioned pisco distilleries. Table wine is made at Pisco Elqui.

The La Serena district is one of the astronomical centres of the world. On a peak about 35 km. S of Vicuña is the new Cerro Tololo Inter-American Observatory, which has a 400-cm. (the largest in the Southern Hemisphere), a 150-cm., a 100-cm., a 60-cm. and two 40-cm. reflecting telescopes. Visits only on Saturdays at 0900 and 1300 and permission must first be obtained from the AURA office in La Serena or write to Observatorio, Cerro Tololo, Casilla 603; La Serena in English or Spanish. In peak season booked two months in advance. Between 0900-1300 there is a free guided excursion to the mountain for 5-45 people. No transport provided, takes 1½ hrs. by car from La Serena. On Cerro La Silla, 100 km. NE, is the European Southern Observatory, with 13 more large telescopes, the largest of which is 360 cm. Visiting with permission from ESO, Av. Alonso de Córdoba 3107, Las Condes, Santiago, or AURA in La Serena; free excursion every Sun.

Only open on first Saturday of the month. 54 km. from La Silla, are three large telescopes, a 250 cm., and a 100 cm. run by the Carnegie Institution of Washington, and a 61-cm. telescope owned by University of Toronto. Permission to visit must be obtained from office at Colina El Pino, La Serena.

From La Serena, 51 km. SE by road, is the little town of **Andacollo**. Here, on December 25 and 26, is held one of the most picturesque religious ceremonies in South America. The pilgrimage to the shrine of the miraculous Virgen del Rosario de Andacollo is the occasion for ritual dances dating from a pre-Spanish past. The church is huge. Alluvial gold washing and manganese and copper mining in the area. No hotel, but some *pensiones*.

Coquimbo, 11 km. S of La Serena and on the same bay, is a port of considerable importance and with several industries. The city has one of the best harbours on the coast. A pleasant walk is along Aldunate, past the port and fishmeal factory to view a guano covered rock, 50 metres offshore, with many seabirds, penguins and an occasional sealion (binoculars a help). Population: 78,000.

Hotels *El Bucanero* at La Herradura, on Guayacán Bay, 1½ km. from Coquimbo port, listed "de luxe" but is not; *La Valle*, F, in front of bus station. Cheap hotels near bus terminal at south end of Aldunate, e.g. *Castex*, No. 459, a rambling barn with large rooms, F.

Campsites Guanaqueros, at km. 430 on the Pan-American Highway, 30 km. S of Coquimbo. Camping also available at Morrillos (several sites), km. 442 on the Pan-American Highway. Both are beside clean beaches. There are also several campsites between Coquimbo and Los Vilos.

Restaurants *La Barca; Mai Lan Fan* (excellent Chinese cuisine), *Don Pepe* (seafood).

Museum In 1981 heavy rain uncovered 39 ancient burials of humans and llamas which had been sacrificed. A small museum has been built behind the Post Office to exhibit these.

Excursions Good beaches to the S at Totoralillo (good swimming), Guanaqueros (30 km.) and Tongoy (56 km.). If motoring, watch the fuel gauge; the nearest service station is at Coquimbo. In the suburb of Guayacán there is one of Eiffel's steel churches.

From here to Santiago, the Pan-American Highway mainly follows the coastline, passing many beautiful coves, alternatively rocky and sandy, with good surf, but the water is very cold, as is the air. The last stretch before Santiago is through green valleys with rich blue clover and wild artichokes. Beware, the green caterpillars crossing the road in November sting! Buses Bejean, US$10-12.

Ovalle is in the valley of the Limarí river, inland from the sea. There is a bus service 3 times a day from Coquimbo. It is the centre of a fruit, sheep-rearing, and mining district. Population: 65,000. 115 km. S by gravel road is the town of Combarbala, where there is a sanatorium for tuberculous patients. Campsite. A 30

390 CHILE

km. road runs NW to the small port of Tongoy. The Paloma dam, at the confluence of the Grande and Huatulame rivers, SE of Ovalle, is one of the largest in Chile.

Hotels *Hotel de Turismo; Roxy; Residencial Lolita*, F, friendly, clean; *Residencial Londres*, F. *Residencial Atenas*, Socos, F. Youth Hostel, Vicuña Mackenna 783. **Restaurant** *El Bosco*, Benavente 88, good, cheap.

Museum Museo Regional, Calle Vicuña Mackenna 521, open Tues.-Sat. 0900-1300, 1500-1900, Sun. 1000-1300, has 3 rooms, information on petroglyphs.

Excursions The Parque Nacional Valle del Encanto, about 22 km. from Ovalle, has Indian petroglyphs as well as dramatic boulders, its own microclimate, cacti and lizards. No local bus service; you must take long distance bus and ask to be dropped off; may be necessary to hitch back. Camping facilities are being upgraded. The Parque Nacional Fray Jorge (40 km.) has interesting forest land, which contrasts with the otherwise barren surroundings. Round trip in taxi, US$30. 2 km. N of Ovalle along Monte Patria road is Balnearia Los Peñones, on a clean shallow river.

Termas de Socos, 35 km. S of Ovalle, has fine thermal springs (entrance US$1.30), a good hotel and a campsite (about US$1.50 p.p.) nearby. Bus US$2.

About 165 km. S of Ovalle by road, and 59 km. by new paved road from Los Vilos, is *Illapel*, in the basin of the river Choapa. Population: 14,000. Fruit, grains and cattle are raised in the valley.

Hotel *Illapel*.

Los Vilos, 280 km. S of Coquimbo, is a small seaside resort with frequent launches to the off-shore Isla de La Reina and a beautiful nearby beach (26 km. S) at **Pichidangui** (*Hotel Kon-Tiki*, owned by the army—sometimes not open to the public). The *Panamerican Motel* is right on the highway, and is a convenient stopping place between La Serena and Viña del Mar or Santiago; it claims to be American style, which will surprise Americans, but is quite good. Also *Hostería Arrayán*, clean, E. Campsite on Av. El Bosque.

The Heartland
(From the River Aconcagua to the River Bío-Bío.)

Nearly 70% of the people of Chile live in the comparatively small heartland. The capital, Santiago, is here, and so is the largest port: Valparaíso. The rural density of population in the area is exceptional for Latin America: it is as high as 48 to the square km. in the Central Valley running S from Santiago to Concepción.

Region	Old Provinces	Population ('000) 1975	1982
V	Aconcagua, Valparaíso	1,124	1,205
Metropolitan	Santiago	3,806	4,295
VI	O'Higgins, Colchagua	529	585
VII	Curicó, Talca, Linares, Maule	685	723
VIII	Ñuble, Concepción, Arauco, Bío-Bío	1,406	1,517

From a third to half of the width of the area is taken up by the Andes, which are formidably high in the northern sector; at the head of the river Aconcagua, the peak of Aconcagua, the highest in the Americas, rises to 6,964 metres. S of Talca, and to the W of the main range, there is a series of active volcanoes; the region suffers from earthquakes. There is a mantle of snow on the mountains: at Aconcagua it begins at 4,300 metres; at Curicó at 3,350; at Bío-Bío at 1,980. The lower slopes are covered with dense forests. Between the forest and the snowline there are alpine pastures which narrow towards the S; during the summer cattle are driven up to these pastures to graze.

The coastal range takes up another third of the width. It is lower here than in the northern desert, but the shoreline is still unbroken; it is only at Valparaíso, San Antonio and Talcahuano (the port for Concepción) that good harbourage is to be found. The coastal range is over 2,130 metres high in the N, but it falls gradually to about 600 metres near Concepción.

Between the coastal range and the Andes lies the Central Valley; most rivers

CHILE 391

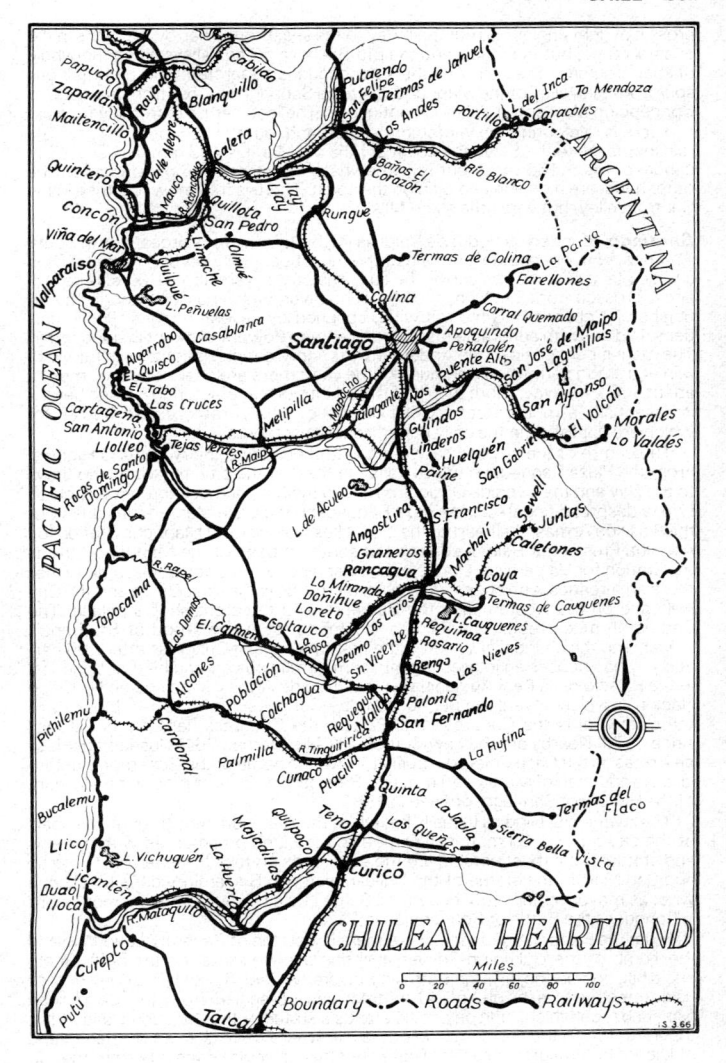

ROUGH SKETCH

cross it at right angles and cut their way to the sea through narrow canyons in the coastal range, but the Maule and the Bío-Bío have broad valleys along the whole of their courses. The valley of the Aconcagua is separated by a mountainous spur from the valley of the Mapocho, in which Santiago lies, but from Santiago to Concepción the Central Valley is continuous. The land here is extremely fruitful.

There is rain during the winter in the heartland, but the summers are dry. The rain increases to the S. On the coast at Viña del Mar it is 483 mm. a year; at Talcahuano it is 1,168 mm., but is somewhat less inland. Temperatures, on the other hand, are higher inland than on the coast. There is frost now and then in the Central Valley, but very little snow falls.

Santiago, founded by Pedro de Valdivia in 1541, is the fifth largest city in South America, with 4m people, and one of the most beautifully set of any. It stands in a wide plain, 600 metres above the sea. The city covers about 100 square km. and is crossed from E to W by the Mapocho River, which passes through an artificial stone channel, 40 metres wide, spanned by several bridges. Public gardens, laid out with admirable taste, are filled with flowers and kept in good order. The magnificent chain of the Andes, with its snow-capped heights, is in full view, rain and smog permitting, for much of the year: there are peaks of 6,000 metres about 100 km. away. More than half the country's manufacturing is done here; it is essentially a modern capital, full of bustle, noise, traffic, smog (tables for which are published in the daily papers) and skyscrapers.

The centre of the city lies between the Mapocho and the Avenida O'Higgins. From the Plaza Baquedano (Plaza Italia), in the E of the city, the Mapocho flows to the NW and the Avenida O'Higgins runs to the SW, at much the same angle as two widespread fingers. From Plaza Baquedano the Calle Merced runs due W of the Plaza de Armas, the heart of the city; it lies 4 blocks S of Mapocho Station (on Avenida Presidente Balmaceda, on the southern bank of the Mapocho); this is the station for Valparaíso. On the eastern and southern sides of Plaza de Armas there are arcades with shops; on the northern side is the Post Office and the City Hall; and on the western side the Cathedral and the archbishop's palace. The Cathedral, much rebuilt, contains a recumbent statue in wood of St. Francis Xavier, and the chandelier which lit the first meetings of Congress after the liberation; it also houses an interesting museum of religious art and historical pieces. In the Palacio de la Real Audiencia on the Plaza de Armas is the Museo Histórico Nacional, which covers the period from the Conquest until 1925. A block W of the Cathedral is the Congressional Palace; the Congress has held no sittings since 1973. Nearby are the Law Courts. At Calle Merced 864, close to the Plaza de Armas, is the Casa Colorada, built in 1769, the home of the Governor in colonial days and then of Mateo de Toro, first President of Chile. It is now the Museum of the History of Santiago, opened in 1981.

The Avenida O'Higgins (usually known as the Alameda) runs through the heart of the city for over 3 km. It is 100 metres wide, and ornamented with gardens and statuary: the most notable are the equestrian statues of Generals O'Higgins and San Martín; the statue of the Chilean historian Benjamín Vicuña Mackenna who, as mayor of Santiago, beautified Santa Lucía hill; and the great monument in honour of the Battle of Concepción in 1879.

From the Plaza Baquedano, where there is a statue of General Baquedano and the Tomb of the Unknown Soldier, this fine avenue skirts, on the right, Santa Lucía hill, and on the left, the Catholic University. Santa Lucía hill, a cone of rock rising steeply to a height of 70 metres, can be scaled from the Caupolicán esplanade, on which, high on a rock, stands a statue of that Mapuche leader, but the ascent from the northern side of the hill, where there is an equestrian statue of Diego de Almagro, is easier. There are striking views of the city from the top (reached by a series of stairs), where there is a fortress, the Hidalgo Castle (the platform of which is its only colonial survival): each day the report from its midday gun reverberates down the city streets. In the basement is an Indian historical museum, often closed. It is best to descend the eastern side, to see the small Plaza Pedro Valdivia with its waterfalls and statue of Valdivia. The area is famous, at night, for its gay community.

CHILE 393

Beyond the Hill the Avenida goes past the neo-classical National Library on the right, which also contains the national archives. Beyond, on the left, between Calle San Francisco and Calle Londres, is the oldest church in Santiago: the red-walled church and monastery of San Francisco. Inside is a small statue of the Virgin which Valdivia carried on his saddlebow when he rode from Peru to Chile. Beside the church is the Museum of Colonial Art, well worth seeing (Av. Bernardo O'Higgins 834). On the left, a little further along, is the University of Chile; the Club de la Unión is almost opposite. N of Plaza de la Libertad, hemmed in by the skyscrapers of the Civic Centre, is the principal government building, the Palacio de la Moneda (1805), containing historic relics, paintings and sculpture, and the elaborate "Salón Rojo" used for official receptions. With some persistence, you can see some of the rooms by applying at about 1400 to the building's secretariat. The Moneda was damaged by air attacks during the military coup of September 11, 1973; repairs are now completed and the presidential offices have been restored.

In front of the Palace is the statue of Arturo Alessandri Palma, who was President of the Republic for two terms. The Municipal Theatre is on Calle Agustinas with Calle San Antonio 149, and nearby on Calle Nueva York is the Bolsa de Comercio. Further along, any of the streets on the left leads to the great Parque O'Higgins, with a small lake, playing fields, tennis courts, swimming pool, an open-air stage for local songs and dances, a discothèque, the racecourse of the Club Hípico, an amusement park, Fantasilandia, admission US$1.50, and a group of about twenty good "typical" restaurants, some craft shops and a small insect and shellfish museum at El Pueblito (local 12). Cars are not allowed in the Parque. The Avenida runs westwards to Plaza Argentina, on the southern side of which is the Alameda (Central) railway station for the S. On Avenida Matucana, running N from Plaza Argentina, are the National Museum (entrance US$0.50) and the Quinta Normal de Agricultura, the latter a large area of ground containing a very popular park. Pieces of armour worn by Valdivia's men are to be found in the National Museum, which was renovated for its centenary in September 1980. The Natural History Museum, in the Parque Quinta Normal has an excellent exhibition of Chilean landscapes. A railway museum has recently opened in the Quinta Normal; it has 13 steam engines built between 1884 and 1953 (open Tues.-Sun. 1100-1300, 1500-1900, on Thurs. till 2000). The Museo de Aviación by the Parque Quinta Normal (Av. Portales 3530) is also worth a visit; open on Sun. and holidays 1000-1300, 1500-1800; other days by appointment only, Tel.: 90 888. There is a Museo de la Escuela Militar, Los Militares 4800, Las Condes, with displays on O'Higgins, the Conquest and the Pacific War. Also interesting are the Museo del Huaso; the Museo Chileno de Arte Precolombino, Bandera 361, open Tues.-Sat. 1000-1800, Sun. 1000-1400 and the Museo de la Merced, MacIver 341 (colonial art). The Centro Cultural Mapoche, J. V. Lasterria, near Alameda, has art galleries and a good café. The Alhambra Palace, Compañía 1340 (with Amunátegui) is a national monument sponsored by the Society of Arts; it stages exhibitions of paintings (open Mon.-Fri., Tel.: 80875).

On Calle Dieciocho, some 5 blocks S of the Alameda, is the Palacio Cousiño, a large elaborate mansion amongst crumbling buildings and shanties; it contains some good oriental rugs and second-rate European furniture. It is run by the Municipality as a museum and official guest house. Can be seen by written permission from the Municipalidad. Open Mon., Wed., Fri., 1000-1300.

There are several other parks in Santiago, but perhaps the most notable is the Parque Forestal, due N of Santa Lucía hill and immediately S of the Mapocho. The National Museum of Fine Arts is in the wooded grounds and is an extraordinary example of neo-Moorish architecture; it has a large display of Chilean and foreign painting and sculpture, and art exhibitions are held several times a year (open Tues.-Sat. 1000-1315, 1400-1800, Sun. 1000-1330), the Art School is in the building. Also in the Parque Forestal is the Museo de Arte Contemporáneo, containing Chilean art. The Parque Balmaceda, E of Plaza Baquedano, is perhaps the most beautiful in Santiago (the Museo de los Tajamares is here), but the sharp, conical hill of San Cristóbal, to the NE of the city, is the largest and most interesting. A funicular railway goes up the 300-metre-high hill every few

394 CHILE

minutes for US$2 return. There is also a chairlift (same price) from Av. Pedro de Valdivia Norte (only taxis go there). The hill has several summits: on one stands a colossal statue of the Virgin, which is floodlit at night; on another is the astronomical observatory of the Catholic University; and on a third a solar observatory (Victoria Castle). The hill is very well laid out with terraces, gardens, and paths; there are good restaurants with splendid views from the terrace, especially at night, and an Enacoteca, or exhibition of Chilean wines (with restaurant and tastery) has been opened. (You can taste one of the three "wines of the day" - US$0.30, and buy if you like.) If you alight at the intermediate stop on the funicular railway, there is a cultural centre in a small castle, where free concerts are held on Sundays. There is also a beautiful swimming pool (US$1.50, US$3 on weekends). The Zoological Gardens (not very good) are near the foot of the hill (entrance US$0.75). The interesting Central Market is at Puente 21 de Mayo.

Ballet is popular. During the summer, free performances are given in the city parks, but seats are usually hard to get. The theatre (there are 12 houses) is more active than in most Latin American capitals. The Lastarria neighbourhood (Santa Lucía metro) is worth a visit for those interested in antique shops (for instance Mulato Gil de Castro, on Alameda and Av. José V. Lastarria, an old estate with crafts, antiques, etc.), art studios and theatres.

N.B. The earthquake in March 1985 destroyed and damaged many buildings, including the main post office, Mapocho station and those on Santa Lucía hill. Reconstruction is still under way.

Things to do Daily list of events in *El Mercurio* should be consulted. During November there is a free Art Fair on the banks of the Mapocho River flowing through Parque Forestal, lasting a fortnight.

In October or November there are a sumptuous flower show and an annual agricultural and industrial show (known as Fisa) in Parque Cerrillos. Religious festivals and ceremonies continue throughout Holy Week, when a priest ritually washes the feet of 12 men. The image of the Virgen del Carmen (patron of the Armed Forces) is carried through the streets by cadets on July 16.

Climate In the central region (including Santiago and Valparaíso) the climate is Mediterranean: temperatures average 29°C (84°F) in January, 10°C (50°F) in July. Days are usually hot, the nights cool.

Shopping There is a fairly good shopping area on Paseo Ahumada and Paseo Huérfanos, two intersecting streets now reserved to pedestrians, in the centre of the city. About 3 km. from the centre there is a very contemporary shopping centre full of boutiques in Providencia (Metro stop, Los Leones, *dirección* Las Condes). Gucci has three shops; authentic Gucci footwear at about ½ NY prices. Best bargains are handicraft articles, black pottery (best bought in Pomaire, 50 km. away, see page 402) and beautiful wrought copper and bronze. Cocema is a good store for Chilean handicrafts, near the centre, with two branches on Av. Providencia. The best place for handmade tapestries is Talleres Artesanales, Lyon 100, in a subway near Los Leones metro, Providencia. Good shops for local copper work are Bozzo, at Ahumada 12 in the centre, and at Av. Providencia 2125. The gemstone lapis lazuli (only found in Chile and Afghanistan) is best bought in the numerous workshops on Bellavista. H. Stern jewellery shops are located at the San Cristóbal Sheraton and Carrera hotels, the Crowne Plaza (Holiday Inn), and at the International Airport. Cema-Chile (Centro de Madres, the women's organization presided over by Sra. Pinochet), Portugal 351 and at Universidad de Chile metro stop, Artesanía Popular Chilena, Av. Providencia 2322 (near Los Leones metro), and Artesanía Chilena, Estado 337, have a good selection of handicrafts, and so do Cema-Chile branches in the provinces. There is a good outside fruit market at Puente 815, by Frutería Martínez. There is an antique fair on Sun. (1000-1400) in the summer and a Fiesta de Quasimodo on the first Sunday after Easter at Lo Barnechea, 30 min. by bus from Santiago, other antique stores near Merced and Lastarria (Santiago).

CHILE 395

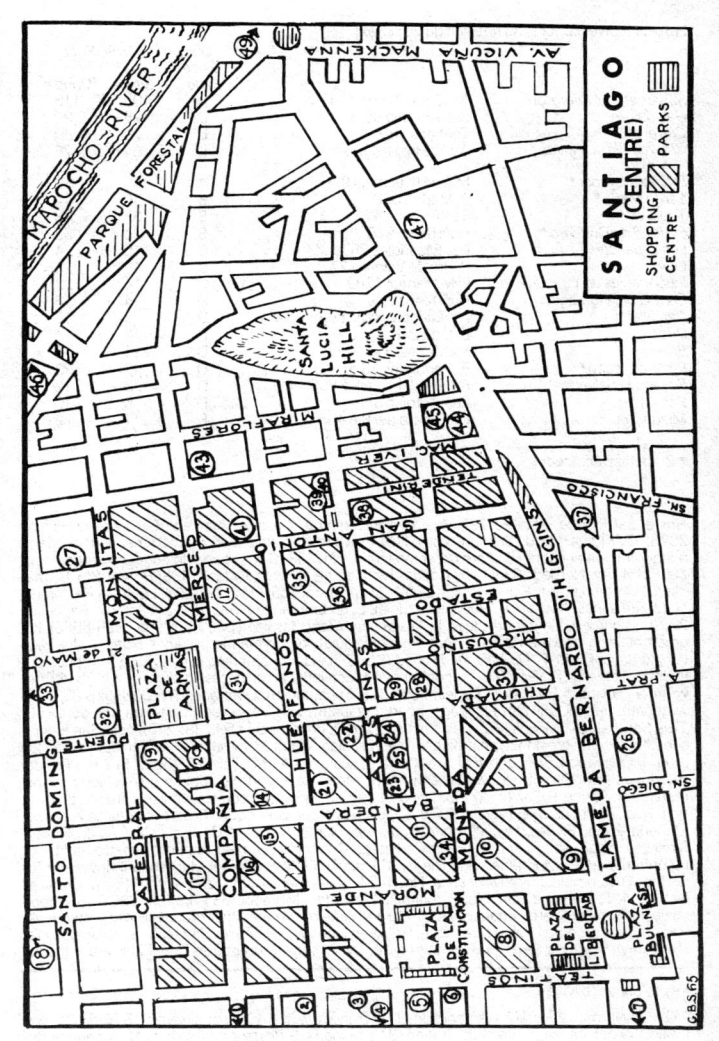

ROUGH SKETCH

396 CHILE

Hotels (Lowest prices, do not include 20% tax)

		Our Price Range	1986 Price Single	Double
San Cristóbal Sheraton	Av. Santa María 1742	L	105	115
Galerías	San Antonio 65	L	78	90
Carrera*	Teatinos 180	L	70	80
Crowne Plaza (Holiday Inn)	Av. O'Higgins 136	L	64	76
El Conquistador*	Miguel Cruchaga 920	A	45	50
Santa María*	S. María 2050	B	36	44
Tupahue*	San Antonio 477	B	35	43
El Hotel de Don Tito*	Huérfanos 578	B	20	33
Los Españoles	Los Españoles 2539	C	15	24
Orly	Pedro de Valdivia 27	C	18	23
Las Acacias de Vitacura	El Manantial 1782	C	14	22
Santa Lucía (garage)	Huérfanos 779	D	14	18
Canciller*	Av. Eliodoro Yáñez 867	D	9	16
Ritz*	Estado 248	D	12	15
Riviera	Miraflores 106	D	11	14
Panamericano*	R. Rodrígues 1314	D	11	13
Posada El Salvador*	Av. Eliodoro Yáñez 896	D	8	12
São Paulo	San Antonio 359	E	6	10
Miami	Dr. Sótero del Río 465	E	7	9

* Breakfast included.

Hostal del Parque, Merced 294, A, excellent, central; *Delicias*, Alameda Bernardo O'Higgins 2828, C; *Monte Carlo*, Subercaseaux 209, bottom of Santa Lucía, recommended, modern, restaurant, with heating, D; *Foresta*, same street, No. 353, C, less good. In our price range D are: *Del Pasos*, Av. Noruega 6340, Las Condes (with bath); *Larssen*, Nataniel 139; *Bristol*, Pte. Balmaceda 114, restaurant; *France*, Puente 530; *Mauri*, Tarapacá 1112; *Mundial*, La Bolsa 87. *Apart-Hotel Agustinas*, Agustinas 1990, clean, quiet, E, recommended. *Residencia Alemania*, República 220 (no sign), excellent food, clean, F; *Residencial Mery*, Pasaje República 10 (Tel.: 696-8883), big green building down an alley, F, hot-showers, quiet, recommended; *Lucy's Hotel*, Calle París behind Santa Lucía, F. *Du Maurier*, Moneda 1512, handy for catching early (0630) Aerobus Tour Express; *Indiana*, Rosas 1334, recommended, convenient for buses to centre, with bath, hot water, F; *Hostería Tramanual*, D, near Plaza de la Constitución; *Libertador*, Av. O'Higgins 853, E-D with bath, helpful, will store luggage, good restaurant, bar; *Versailles*, nr. station, Bandera 860; *Tres Coronas*, Av. Molina 152; *Residencial Londres*, Londres 54 (Tel.: 382215), near San Francisco Church, with breakfast, charming former mansion, Victorian furniture, F, E with bath (often full after 1000). Good *Residencial* of Sra Marta at Alameda 4134 (Tel.: 79-7592), E. *Gran Palace*, Huérfanos 478, D, with shower, clean, noisy rooms facing street (others quiet), good simple restaurant; *Caribe*, F, San Martín 851, clean, basic, hot showers, convenient to centre and bus station; *Real*, Alameda B. O'Higgins 2876 (airport bus stops near door); *Residencial Alicia Adasme*, Moneda 2055, F; *Residencial Tabita Gutiérrez*, Marco A. Reyes 81, Tel.: 71-5700, pleasant family, E, clean, safe, central; *Colonial*, Ricardo Cumming 88, near República metro, cold, not recommended, E; *Montemar*, San Diego 369, clean. On Av. General Mackenna (convenient for northern bus terminal) are *Mackenna*, No. 1471, clean; *Retiro*, No. 1264, without bath; *Colonial*, No. 1414, F; *Annex d'Elite*, clean, friendly; *Cervantes*, Morandé 631, E, Tel.: 696-7966, good value; on San Pablo are *Pudahuel*, No. 1419 and *Nuevo*, corner with Morandé, F, hot water, quiet (except rooms on San Pablo side), safe, will keep luggage, recommended (although also used for short stay), nearby is *Cairo*. **N.B.** Hotels on Gen. Mackenna, Morandé and San Pablo are in the red

---

Key to Santiago Map

1 Quinta Normal, 2 *Hotel Panamericano*, 3 US Consulate, 4 SAS (Scandinavian), 5 *Hotel Carrera*, 6 Ministry of Finance, 7 Alameda Station, 8 La Moneda, 9 *Restaurant Escorial*, 10 Argentine Airlines, 11 Transradio, 12 City Museum, Casa Colorada, 14 Pre-Colombian Museum, 15 *Restaurant Santiago*, 16 Palace of Justice, 17 Congress, 18 Mapocho Station, 19 The Cathedral, 20 *Hotel City*, 21 Air France, 22 Lastarria neighbourhood, 23 Exprinter SA, 24 PSNC (B. Cal.), 25 Lufthansa, 26 University of Chile, 27 *Taberna Capri*, 30 *Restaurant Ahumada 79*, 31 *Chez Henry*, 32 Post and Telegraph Office, 33 Santo Domingo (burnt out), 34 Entel, telephone company for long distance calls, 35 *Hotel Kent*, 36 *El Pollo Dorado*, 37 San Francisco Church, 38 Teatro Municipal, 39 KLM, 40 *Restaurant Nuria*, 41 *Hotel Santa Lucia*, 43 Merced Church, 44 National Library, 46 Museum of Fine Arts, 47 Catholic University, 49 *El Parrón*.

CHILE 397

light district and are therefore cheap in both senses of the word. *Residencial O'Higgins,* San Ignacio 882, friendly, cold water only, no kitchen, US$46 s, US$62 d, per month. Sra. Marianne Corvely's *pensión*, Los Jardines 462 B, recommended; the owner is a professional translator and works as a tourist guide. Sra. Maria Aguilera, Av. Eliadoro Yáñez 809, apt. 93, (metro, Salvador) also rents rooms, very friendly. Family *pensión* at Pasaje de Gales 81 (at Moneda 1452), opp. YHA, 1 block W of Plaza Constitución, convenient for airport bus and metro, F with small breakfast, hot water, clean, safe; *hospedaje* at Amunátegui 712, F, hot shower, friendly, incl. breakfast. Private house/*residencia* at Los Algarrobos 2135, E incl. 3 large meals, friendly, helpful landlady. Casa del Estudiante Americano, Huérfanos 1891, F (7 blocks from centre over motorway). YMCA rooms, at Marco Antonio Reyes 84, Moneda, San Martín, with card only, D, hot water and heating. Youth hostel, Pasaje de Gales 84 (Metro Moneda, behind Entel tower), open only Jan. and Feb. YH information available from Villavicencio 352 (worth getting list of YH addresses around country as these change year by year).

Camping A campsite has been opened on the top of the San Cristóbal hill. If full, the Farellones road near the river. Or S of Santiago near Puente Alto. Take Av. J. Pedro Alessandri S to Las Vizcachas to Puente Alto and La Obra where there is a small park on left side of road. At Km. 25 S of city on Panamericana, Esso garage with free hot showers and free and clean camping. Club Camping Maki, and Casino Camping, both 70 km. from Santiago, see page 401. Standard camping gas cartridges can be bought at Unisport, Providencia 2503, or Santo Domingo 1079., Other equipment for camper-vans from Bertonati Hnos, Manuel Montt 2385. Caravans (US model Tioga) can be rented from Castanera Turismo, Av. Providencia 1072, local 14 D. Sleeping bags, tents etc. can be bought at Lomas Spfá, branches at Apoquindo 3363 and A. Vespucio Sur 1650. Tent repairs: Juan Soto, Silva Vildosola 890, Paradero 1, Gran Avenida, San Miguel, Santiago, Tel.: 555-8329.

Electric Current 220 volts A.C., 50 cycles.

Restaurants In addition to those at the main hotels and those in Parque O'Higgins there are, in the centre of the city; *Portada Colonial,* Merced 88 (1st class); *El Pollo Dorado,* Agustinas 881 (closed Sun.); *Le Due Torri,* San Antonio 258 (closed Sun.); *Pinpilinpausha,* Matías Cousiño 62; *Restaurant Auerbach* (German), MacIver 165, US$8 for four course lunch (closed Sun.); *Da Carla,* MacIver, Italian food, very good; *La Peña,* Alameda and San Isidro, folk music, reasonable prices; *Bar Central,* San Pablo 1063, good chicken and sea food, typical, recommended; *Savoy,* Morandé 526, good and cheap; *El Rey del Pescado,* Banderas, good seafood; *Atelier,* Tenderini 171, recommended, good expensive seafood. *Danubio Azul* (Chinese), Reyes Lavalle 3240 (near Metro El Golf); *Lung Fung* (Chinese), Agustinas, good, but beware of the high cost of tea; *Los Rubíes,* Lira 75, Chinese, 3 courses for US$2.30; *Chez Henri,* on Plaza de Armas, excellent *empanadas, parrillada de mariscos* a speciality, reckoned best in Santiago, dining room at back has live music and dancing; *Picorocio* on San Pedro, recommended for sea food and wine; also at 21 de Mayo and Rosas, good seafood; *Moulin Rouge,* Estado between Huérfanos and Agustinas, recommended for complete meal (US$10); *Los Adobes de Argomedo,* Argomedo 411, Chilean food and spectacular floor show including *cueca* and Easter Island dancing; *Marco Polo* in Plaza de Armas, good local dishes, immaculately clean surroundings; *Catalán,* Av. Suecia, near Av. Lota, very good, reasonable prices; *Da Vinci,* Suecia 113, Italian; *San Marcos* (Italian), Huérfanos 612; *Mermoz,* Huérfanos 1048, good; *Restaurant Fuente de Soda,* San Ignacio 802, fried fish with rice US$1.15; *Las Alemanes,* Huérfanos 837, good value; *Restaurant Full,* Alameda B. O'Higgins, reasonable; *Café Dante,* Merced 801, for *pastel de choclo*; *La Danze,* San Antonio, cheap, open till 0100. *Savory Tres,* Ahumada 327, good and reasonable, particularly seafood; *Hotel Aport,* Américo Vespucio, has good restaurant; *Internacional,* Victoria Subercaseaux 15 (near Sta. Lucía), good, cheap *almuerzos*; *München,* good, out of town on road to Farellones and La Parva; *El Parrón,* Providencia 1188. Vegetarian restaurants: *El Huerto,* Orrego Luco 54 (Providencia), metro Pedro de Valdivia, recommended, open daily, live music Fri. and Sat. evenings; *Alternativa Macrobiótica,* Santa Beatriz 84, *El Naturista,* Moneda 846, recommended, and *El Vegetariano,* Huérfanos 827, Galería Victoria. *La Pirámide,* Av. Américo Vespucio; *La Pizza Nostra,* Providencia and Pedro de Valdivia sells good Italian food; typical Chilean dishes at *El Pollo Al Coñac,* Lo Barnechea 127, expensive (local delicacy of sea-urchins, *erizos*, may not always please the visitor). *Pollo Montserrat* on main plaza, alleged to have the cheapest chicken in Chile. For snacks and excellent ice cream, try *Coppellia*. Excellent ice cream and good hamburgers can be found in many places on Ahumada. Airport meals and snacks are good. If really travelling "economy", do not sit at tables in bars, etc.; the extra service charge for tables is 20%. There are many cheap restaurants around the Municipal Market and fish stalls serving lunch (e.g. *La Playa Chonchi*). Good, cheap snacks can be had from stalls in the arcade of the Plaza de Armas. For fast food try *El Rápido* on Bandera.

First-class restaurants out of the centre are *Bric-a-Brac* (French), Av. Las Condes 9100; *Banco de Turismo la Rueda,* Av. Las Condes 9739, Tel: 2208054, also offers typical food. Drive-in *Lo Curro,* Las Condes; *Linfá,* Av. Apoquindo 6230, Las Condes, serves good Chinese food. *Rodizio,* Av. El Bosque 0380, Las Condes, assorted grills and seafood salad bar, US$10; *Baltazar,* Av. Las Condes, Estoril, open all night at weekends, dancing, lively, excellent food, particularly salads; *El Alero de Los de Ramón,* Av. Las Condes 9889 (Chilean cuisine and music, expensive but really excellent in both departments); *Canta Gallo,* Av. Las Condes 12345 (ditto); *Buenos Aires de Paine,* popular and excellent grill restaurant, ½ hr. south by car of San Bernardo (Panamericana); *La*

398 CHILE

Cascade, Av. Bilbao 1947 (French, good and dear); *La Querencia*, Av. Las Condes 14980, not dear for the quality; *Los Gordos*, Av. San Enrique 14880 (perhaps the best food of all); and *La Estancia*, around 9000 on Av. Las Condes; *La Paz*, excellent German-run restaurant on road to El Volcán, famous for its apple cake.

Cafés and Bars Many bars (some serve snacks) on Pedro Valdivia, very popular. *Cross Keys* (Los Leones Metro). *Claerie Drugstore*, Av. Providencia; *Full Bar Ltda.*, Alameda 833, good and cheap; *Café di Trevi*, Av. El Bosque; *El Lugar de Don Quijote*, good, corner Morandé and Catedral; *Café Paula*, Estado and Pasaje España, excellent coffee and cake. *Café del Cerro*, Ernesto Pinto Lagarigue 192 (at foot of San Cristóbal) has different concert or cabaret each evening, highly recommended. *Bar-Restaurant Nacional No. 1*, Huérfanos 1087, good; *Cosnes Bar* on Moneda, good soups. Try *Café Haití*, *Café Caribe* and *Café Santos*, Paseo Ahumada (last named at No. 312) for delicious coffee. *Dunkin Donuts*, Paseo Ahumada, and *Tiptop Cookies* recommended for freshly baked biscuits. Note that almost all hotel bars are closed Sun.

Tea Rooms *Carrera*, Teatinos 180; *Villa Real*, Compañía 1068; *Nuria*, Agustinas 715; *Oriente*, Plaza Italia; *Paula*, San Antonio 218.

Clubs Nuñoa (Tel.: 223 7846), with swimming pool, tennis courts and school; Polo y Equitación San Cristóbal; Chess Club, Alameda O'Higgins 898, Mon.-Sat. 1800, lively, reasonable competition.

Bookshops Librería Kuatro, Vitacura 2726; Librería Albers, Merced 820, local 7 and Av. Tobalaba 032 (English and German); Librería Altamira, Huérfanos 669; Librería Ivens, Moneda 730; Andrés de Fuenzalida 36 and Tenderini, for books in English. Pedro de Valdivia 47, classical and pre-C19 books. Second-hand English books from arcade at San Diego 121, 1½ blocks south of Alameda and *Librería El Patio*, Providencia 1652; exchange for best deal. Also, from Henry at Metro station, Los Leones. Reading rooms at British and U.S. cultural associations (see **Addresses**). German books at Humboldt, 645, 2216 Providencia.

Camera Repairs, Harry Müller, Ahumada 312, oficina 402, recommended; speaks German and English. For Minolta and Canon repairs, Nueva York 52, Of.1004, recommended. Developing (Fuji), Reifschneider Laboratory, Carmen 1313, 1 day service.

Buses and Taxis There are three kinds of buses: the small fast kind called *liebres* (hares) which cost US$0.25-0.35 a ride; the regular buses at US$0.25, and the large buses marked Expreso. At present charges are slightly higher at night and on Sun. Taxis are now abundant (black with yellow roofs), and not expensive, about US$1 per km., with a minimum charge of US$1.05. At bus terminals, drivers will try to charge more (illegally)—best to walk a block and flag one. Large blue taxis do not have meters. There are also colectivo taxis to the suburbs. Visitors going outside the city should arrange the charge beforehand. **N.B.** from 0200 to 0600 there is a vehicle curfew; no buses or taxis, but you can walk.

Underground Railway The first line of the underground railway system (Metro) runs between San Pablo and Escuela Militar, under the Alameda, and the second line runs from Los Héroes to Callejón Ovalle. Line 3 is to be constructed between Buen Pastor and Vivaceta. The ticket for Line 1 costs US$0.15; save queuing by buying a ten-ticket booklet (US$1.30). Fares on Line 2 are half this price. The trains are fast, quiet, and full. The first train is at 0700, the last about 2245.

Car Hire Hertz, Avis and Budget available from airport. Hertz (Av. Costanera 1469, Tel.: 225-9328, and airport) appears to have the best network in Chile and cars are in good condition.

Theatres Plays in Spanish at Petit Rex, L'Atelier, Antonio Varas, Camilo Henríquez; Maru, Moneda, Talia, La Comedia and Municipal, where the Chilean ballet company performs and concerts are given. Lunchtime concerts on Tues. at 1315, for US$1.25. Three others, the Opera (Huérfanos), Humoresque, and Picaresque, show mostly Folies Bergères-type revues. Outdoor rock concerts from March onwards at the National Stadium Velodrome.

Cinemas Films of famous operas shown on Mon. at Salón Fildamério, Teatro Municipal building, free. Most other cinemas cost about US$1.25 p.p., films start at 1100. Poor accoustics in many but good in Lido, Cervantes, Gran Palace. Several cinemas along Huérfanos.

Night Clubs *El Pollo Doro* and *La Casa de San Isidro* (near Estación República), both folklore; *Dancing Brazil* on Plaza Brasil, cheap; *Gato Viudo*, on Vitacura, very popular, live music, cheap, fun; *Gato Hydráulico*, in big shopping centre E of Santiago, also popular, but slightly older clientèle than *Gato Viudo*; *Red Pub*, Av. Suecia, very international, American-style.

Discotheques *Gente*, Av. Apoquindo; *Las Brutas*, Av. Príncipe de Gales, Parcela 158, Las Condes; *Caledonia*, Av. Larraín Parcela; *Eve*, Av. Vitacura 3418.

Swimming Pool Antilen, at Cerro San Cristóbal, beautiful (US$1.25 weekdays, US$2 weekends); in Parque O'Higgins, same prices. Take colectivo "Plaza Caupolicán", Calle Pío Nono.

CHILE 399

Tennis Santiago Tennis Club; Tenis Centrum Alemán, Parcela 68, Santa Ana de Chena, Camino Lonquén, run by Dieter and Myriam Mittelstaedt, recommended; 5 good courts, hot showers, small restaurant, US$1.50 p.p. per day. Also, Club de Tenis Jaime Fillol, Rancho Melnichi. Par.4.

Bowling at Bowling Center, Av. Apoquindo 5012.

Racecourses Club Hípico, racing every Sun. morning and every other Wed. afternoon (at Viña del Mar, January-March); Hipódromo Chile every Sat. afternoon; pari-mutuel betting.

Banks Banco Central de Chile, one block from Plaza Constitución, demands the minimum of formalities, although there is usually a commission charge for most transactions. Financiera Ciga, Agustinas 1287, and Exprinter are recommended for good rates, low commission. Most exchange houses are on Agustinas (American Express is at No. 1360 for Exchange and No. 1173 for travel information and collection of mail) and Huérfanos and some, such as Huso, Providencia 1990 (Metro Pedro de Valdivia), are open on Sat. mornings. Banco O'Higgins will cash personal cheques. Citicorp will give U.S.US$ cash for U.S.US$ travellers' cheques, useful for black market and travel S of Santiago. Banco do Brasil, national banks, open from 0900 to 1400, but closed on Sat. Official daily exchange rates are published in *El Mercurio*. Black market rate can be obtained at corner of Agustinas and Ahumada and around the Moneda; agents on the street take you to exchange offices. American Express and Afex, Moneda 1162, will change travellers' cheques into US dollars for 2% commission. Cash cannot be obtained with a Master Card or Eurocard in Chile.

British Community maintains the British Commonwealth Society (old people's home etc.), the interdenominational Santiago Community Church, at Av. Holanda 151 (Metro Tobalada), Providencia, Tel.: 44970, which holds services every Sunday at 1045. Schools (The Grange and Redlands—coeducational, and Craighouse and Braemar—girls).

Addresses *British Embassy and Consulate*, La Concepción 177, 4th floor, Providencia 1800, Casilla 72-D; *British Chamber of Commerce*, Bandera 227, Casilla 536, Tel.: 698-5266; *British Council*, Av. Eliodoro Yáñez 832, nr. Providencia, Tel.: 694-6005; *Chilean-British Institute*, San Martín 949 (has English papers in library, open 1000-1200, 1600-1900 except Mon.). *U.S. Embassy*, Agustinas 1343; *U.S. Consulate*, Merced 230 (visa obtainable here); *Chilean-North American Cultural Institute*, Moneda 1467, good for US periodicals, cheap films on Fri.; *Canadian Embassy*, Ahumada 11. *Australian Embassy*, Gertrudis Echeñique 420, Las Condes. *New Zealand Embassy*, Av. Isadora Goyenechea 3516, Las Condes (Tel.: 487071). *West German Embassy*, Agustinas 785 (Tel.: 693-5031/ 693-5035); *German Chamber of Commerce*, Ahumada 131. *Goethe Institut*, Esmeralda 650. *Austrian Embassy*, Av. Pedro de Valdivia 300, Barros Errázuriz, 3rd floor. *Spanish Consulate*, Av. Providencia 329, 4th floor; *Swiss Embassy*, Av. Providencia 2653, 16th floor (metro Tobalada); *Belgian and Japanese embassies* in same building. *Argentine Embassy*, Vicuña Mackenna 41 (Tel.: 226947), Australians need letter from their embassy to get visa here, open 0900-1400; *Brazilian Embassy*, Av. Varas 647 (Tel.: 749159); *Bolivian Embassy*, Av. Santa María 2796 (Tel.: 2256950, Metro Los Leones); *Panamanian Embassy*, Bustos 2199 (open 1000-1330); *Paraguayan Consulate*, Burbos 245, Las Condes (metro Alcántara); *Peruvian Embassy*, Andrés Bello 1751 (Tel.: 490045). *Emergency Pharmacy*, Portugal 155 (Tel.: 382439). Academia Chilena de la Historia, Clasificador 1349, Correo Central, for information and help on archaeology.

Laundry Dry cleaning, Merced 494. **Laundromat** Dr. Luis Middleton 1738, nr. Providencia 1777. US$3 for 5 kg., US$4 for 8 kg. Also at Providencia 1033, and Merced y MacIver.

Vaccinations Almost the only place in Chile to obtain a yellow fever vaccination is the Hospital San Salvador, Salvador 420, Tel.: 2256441. Arrive at correct time, Tues. 0900-1000, or you have to pay for a whole capsule (enough for 20!).

Post Office Agustinas 1137, Plaza de Armas, poste restante well organized (though only kept for 30 days), list of letters received in the hall of central Post Office; also has philatelic section, for stamp collectors. Go to Moneda 1155, fourth corner, for mailing postcards and letters. If sending a parcel, the contents must be checked at Post Office; parcel is then sealed for US$0.75. If receiving a parcel, you must collect it from international branch at Marsella, near Parque O'Higgins.

Cables and Telephones Compañía de Teléfonos de Chile, Moneda 1145. International phone calls: Entel, Huérfanos 1132, Mon.-Fri. 0830-2200, Sat. 0900-2030, Sun. 0900-1400, 20% discount after 2000. International telex service, Bandera 168.

The National Tourist Bureau Sernatur, Servicio Nacional de Turismo, is at Catedral 1165 (Casilla 3927, Correo Plaza de Armas), Tel.: 698-2151/696-0474, opposite the Congreso Nacional, open Mon.-Fri. 0900-1700, Sats. 0900-1300. Closed all week-end in winter. English is spoken and maps (which distinguish between paved and dirt roads), brochures and posters are available. Off-season discount booklets available. They also sell *Qué Hacemos*, which is a monthly magazine about events in Chile. Information Office at Antofagasta-La Paz railway, Agustinas 972, oficina 904. Excellent road maps may also be obtained from the **Automóvil Club de Chile**,

400 CHILE

Pedro de Valdivia 195. Shell also produce a good map, as do Guía Banco Osorno and Rutas Camineras. Geophysical and topographical maps are available from **Instituto Geográfico Militar,** at their sales office, Alameda 240 (Universidad Católica Metro) or main office Dieciocho 407 (opposite Palacio Cousiño, Toesca metro) (closed in holiday season) and from **Conaf** (Corporación Nacional Forestal), General Bulnes, 285 (Tel.: 696-0783/3801). Walkers' maps are not available outside Santiago. The Chilean Telephone Company also publishes a tourist guide of most of the country.

Tourist Agencies Wagons-Lits Cook (Calle Agustinas 1058, Casilla 1534), La Universal, Exprinter, Turismo Cocha (American Express representatives), Gondrand Brothers (Chile), (all in Calle Agustinas). Agency Pudahuel, Paseo Ahumada 312, oficina 1024, highly recommended. Sportstours, German-run, at Hotel Panamericano, are helpful. Viajes Litvak, Cía. Chilena de Viajes y Turismo, Civit, Turavion Shipping Express (all in Calle Bandera), Turismo Magallanes, Providencia 1357. Latour, Hotel Carrera; Atitur (Agencia de Viajes Automóvil Club), Moneda 1162. Ugarte International, Huérfanos 1178, Loc. A, very helpful. Most of these offer routes in the Lake District. Blanco, Pedro Valdivia near Providencia, good for flight information and exchange. Rapa-Nui, Huérfanos 1160, specializes in trips to Easter Island. Turismo Grace, Victoria Subercaseaux 381, Tel.: 693-3740, good service.

Airport Arturo Merino Benítez (at Pudahuel), 26 km. from Santiago with a speed limit. Airport taxi, US$10, US$0.10 per suitcase. Fixed taxi fares on board by cab rank. Pullman service by Aerobuses Tour Express from Moneda 1523, Tel.: 717380 (US$0.85) though internal Lan-Chile customers travel half-price (slip issued), buses every ½ hr., 0630-2100, ½-¾ hr. journey; plenty of luggage space; Flota LAC from Metro Los Héroes, and others, also run a bus service, US$0.80. Los Cerrillos airport (20 min.) is used for Aeronor flights; other internal flights such as Lan-Chile and Ladeco operate from the International Airport. For schedules, see under individual towns. Airport tax US$8 if leaving country, not included in ticket price. Bank and cambio (better rates) outside customs hall; tourist office in same area will book accommodation. No duty free shop, so buy your wine etc. in town.

For information on flights with the Air Force, Relaciones Públicas Fuerza Aérea, Alameda O'Higgins 1170, first floor.

Rail International service to Buenos Aires suspended. No passenger trains to northern Chile. Trains to Viña del Mar, Valparaíso and Llay-Llay leave from Mapocho station at Independencia; others leave from Estación Central at O'Higgins 3300. To Viña del Mar and Valparaíso ("Puerto") 3 daily from 0800, 3 hrs., US$2. To Concepción, 5 daily, Temuco, 2 daily; Valdivia ("Rápido del Calle Calle" 2030 daily) and Puerto Montt, one Rápido a day at 1830 with sleepers, about 18 hrs., reservations necessary (at O'Higgins 853, or at station). Recommended, train built in Germany in 1926, bunks lie parallel to rails so comfortable despite poor track; an attendant for each car; bar car shows 3 films—no cost but you must purchase a drink ticket in advance. Expreso, 2100, about 23 hrs., no reservations (get your ticket the morning of the day the train leaves and sit on the train as soon as you can get on; otherwise you'll stand for the whole journey). Free hot water supplied, so take own mug and coffee. To Osorno Rápido at 2000, 14½ hrs. Also a car-transporter service to Temuco, Osorno and Puerto Montt. Also trains to Rancagua, Curicó, Talca, Chillán and Pichilemu (direct Fri.-Sun., otherwise via Chillán). Trains are still fairly cheap, meals are good though expensive. For a family it may be cheaper to buy one ticket for an apartamento, rather than separate seats. Booking offices: for State Railways, Alameda O'Higgins 853 in Galeria; Tel.: 301818/ 330746, 331814 for "autotrén"; or Metro Esc. Militar, Galería Sur L-3, Tel.: 228-2983; central station, Tel.: 699-2157/699-1682; Mapocho, Tel.: 696-0923; for Antofagasta-La Paz, Agustinas 972, oficina 904. Left luggage office at Estación Central.

Buses There are frequent, and good, interurban buses to all parts of Chile. The longest journey within the country, N to Arica (2,113 km.), costs about US$30, and takes 27 hrs., check if student rates available (even for non-students), or reductions for travelling same day as purchase of ticket. Worth bargaining over prices. Fichtur and Chile-Bus recommended for Arica, fully reclining seats with footrests on each bus. Antofagasta, 20 hrs., US$18 (Flecha Norte), US$19.75 ordinary, US$26 (Flota Barrios, with sleeper, meals, hostess, 1500), an interesting trip to see the changes in landscape, but cold at night. To Viña del Mar, daily, 2 hrs., US$2.10 (Pullman, Tur-Bus, others cheaper); Los Andes, US$2; to La Serena, US$7.50, 8 hrs. (sit on left); San Felipe, US$2; Valparaíso, US$2-4, 2 hrs. Bus to Valdivia, US$13.75-US$8. To Puerto Montt (1,060 km.), US$15, first class, US$10, second, 16 hrs.; to Concepción, 8½ hrs. US$9.50; to Chillán, US$7.50, to Temuco, 10 hrs., US$8.50. Varmontt buses (own terminal) to Puerto Montt, 17 hrs., are US$25, including reclining seats, meals and wine, colour TV, stereo headphones, highly recommended. In winter most fares on this route are reduced. Igi-Llaima (near La Moneda bus station) runs a comfortable service to Temuco and points south, at 1700, arrives 0600. Bus offices all along Morandé. You can bargain for lower fares. Buses to Valparaíso, Viña del Mar, Osorno, S and coast leave from Terminal de Buses Santiago, Al. B. O'Higgins 3878, Tel.: 791385, 796452 for Valparaíso and Viña del Mar (Metro, Universidad Técnica). In general, buses N leave from Terminal del Norte, Gral. Mackenna and Amunátegui (metro Mercado, Tel.: 712141). Beware: Buses very punctual: Do not be late for departure!

International Buses Long distance: to Buenos Aires, leaves from Santiago terminal, Av. O'Higgins 3878, take Metro to Universidad de Santiago, US$40, 22 hrs.; also to Montevideo; Caracas (Tues. and Fri. 0900); Lima 51 hrs., it is cheaper to take a bus to Arica (US$30), Colectivo to Tacna (US$2.80), thence bus to Lima. Bogotá (7 days); Rio de Janeiro; Guayaquil; and Quito. Short distance: there are frequent minibus services from the North Station over the Andes to Mendoza, about US$13 (Cata bus), 10 hrs., other companies, 7 hrs., book as far ahead as possible; they do not run in winter. Transportes Caracoles sell a combination ticket but there are many changes. All buses now go through the completed Cristo Redentor tunnel, and it is no longer possible to go to the Cristo Redentor statue from the Chilean side. Chi-Ar taxi company, Morandé 890, recommended, leaves at 0800 and charges US$15 for Santiago-Mendoza.

Bus companies: Tepsa, Amunátegui 324 (not recommended, no food on bus in Peru); Pul-Bus-Norte (not recommended); Flota Barrios, Morandé 766; Igi-Llaima. Fenix Pullman Norte, good. Try to change money before entering Chile, as Santiago bus station lies far outside the city (beware taxi drivers overcharging).

Shipping M/n *Evangelistas*: Puerto Montt to Puerto Natales and return, Navimag, Av. Suiza 248, Cerrillos, Santiago, Tel.: 572-650, Telex 240069 MAGSA CL. M/n *Skorpios*: Luxury cruise out of Puerto Montt to Laguna San Rafael, Constantino Kochifas C., MacIver 484, 2° piso, Oficina 5, Santiago Tel.: 336-187, Telex 240764 NATUK CL. M/n *Quellón*: cruise out of Puerto Montt to Laguna San Rafael, early December to late March, Transcontainer S.A., Estado 360, Oficina 502-c, Santiago, Tel.: 337-118, Telex 340002 TCSA CK VTR. P.S.N.C., Agustinas 1066-70, Casilla 4087; Empresa Marítima del Estado, Estado 359, 5th floor.

Hitch-hiking to Valparaíso, take Metro to Pajaritos and walk 5 minutes to W—no difficulty. Or, take bus "Renca Panamericana" from MacIver and Monjitas. To hitch south, take "Panamericana Sur" bus from Teatinos and Plaza Libertad.

Excursions from Santiago

Several small resort towns are easily reached by car from the capital: Peñalolén, 16 km., with a lovely park and a beautiful view of the city (bus in front of Mapocho station at Av. Independencia and Balmaceda, take your bathing gear); Colina (915 metres), an attractive, popular spa in the mountains 32 km. to the N (bus from Calle Independencia 225, or Av. La Paz and Juárez, US$0.50 one way), thermal baths, US$3.70, swimming pool, US$2.70, last return bus at 1900; San José de Maipo, some 80 km. to the SE (return journey by car: 3 hrs., buses every 15 mins. from N end of Parque O'Higgins, return fare US$1.75), particularly beautiful in spring; just beyond is the mountain town of Melocotón (*Millahue Hotel*). Just past Melocotón between San José de Maipo and El Volcán is San Alfonso, in the Callejón del Maipo (*Hostería Café Cordillera*, D, full board, warmly recommended, ring 72-4082 in Santiago, also others). Buses at hourly or 2-hour intervals from Parque O'Higgins, Santiago. Beautiful mountain-river area, with vineyards. Three buses a day (US$2) run from Parque O'Higgins (same metro) to El Volcán in the Andes, 77 km. to the SE (1,400 metres), a small poor mining village, uninteresting except for the astounding view. (Bus, 0800 Sat. and Sun., to Puente Alto.) From El Volcán the road runs 12 km. E and then N to the skiing slopes of *Hotel Lo Valdés*, C. A splendid region which deserves the walk, drive or hitch-hike required to get there. *Refugio Alemán*, D, with full board, recommended. 12 km. away are hot natural baths, Baños Morales (bus leaves daily from Parque O'Higgins at 0800, arriving at Baños Morales 1130, US$2 each way; returns at 1800). Several *residenciales* incl. *Hostería Inesita*, F. Drinks can be obtained from Negro José nearby. The Lo Valdés area is popular at weekends and holiday times, but is otherwise deserted. The small towns in the Aconcagua Valley to the N—San Felipe, Jahuel and Los Andes—are described in the section "To Buenos Aires across the Andes", page 411. The road over the Andes to Mendoza is excellent except when snowed up in winter; the last 900 metres of the climb can be avoided by passing through the new road tunnel, 3¼ km. long. There are few service stations in the area so come prepared.

The National Votive Temple of Maipú, of fine modern architecture and stained glass, 30 min. by car (or about 45 mins. by bus from corner of Calle Teatinos and Av. Bernardo O'Higgins) from Santiago, which commemorates O'Higgins' battle, is interesting, and so is the attached museum of carriages, furniture, clothing and other colonial and later items, Sun. only, 1000-1200, 1600-2000.

Campsites Excellent facilities about 70 km. from Santiago at Laguna de Aculeo, called Club Camping Maki. Facilities include electricity, cold water, swimming pool, boat mooring, restaurant,

US$2 p.p. daily, but only available to members of certain organizations. An alternative site is Casino Camping, 1 km. away, on edge of lake, US$2 per family per night. Very friendly, café sells fruit, eggs, milk, bread and kerosene. Good fishing. No showers, water from handpump.

Pottery is best bought in **Pomaire**, a little town about 50 km. from Santiago towards the coast, where the artists can be observed at work. The area is rich in clay and the town is famous for its cider (*chicha de manzana*, 3 strengths: *dulce, medio* and *fuerte*) and Chilean dishes. Pomaire may be reached by Mellipilla bus from San Borja 60 (behind supermarket on O'Higgins 3390) leaving daily at 1130, Sat.-Sun. at 0800 also, about US$1, 2 hrs.; en route, delicious *pastel de choclo* can be obtained at Restaurant *Mi Ranchito*.

Vineyards Another agreeable excursion is to the vineyard of Concha y Toro at Puente Alto, 40 km. south of Santiago. Tours of the *bodega*, and wine can be bought direct from vineyard. Pirque vineyard of Concha y Toro, entry free, bus from Alameda and Santa Rosa, ¾ hour, US$0.50. The Undurraga vineyard at Santa Ana, north-west of Santiago, also permits visits on weekdays (tours given by the owner-manager, Pedro Undurraga).

Horse-Breeding A specially recommended excursion is to Los Lingues, a private *hacienda* 120 km. S of Santiago, where it is said the best horses in Chile are bred. Rosie Swale was lent two of them for her epic ride from Antofagasta to Cape Horn, described in *Back to Cape Horn* (Collins, London, 1986). Visits are arranged by the main hotels to the C.17 house, a gift of the King of Spain.

Skiing There is an excellent ski centre at **Farellones,** 51 km. E of Santiago at 2,470 metres, and reached by car, bus, or truck in under 90 min.:two hotels, one third-class *pensión* and annex. Most skiers stay in the two *refugios* belonging to Santiago's universities (full board US$10 p.p.). High season: June to September/October, weather depending. An excellent network of five ski-lifts. There are excursions for a day from Santiago at US$15, including ski-lifts ticket; enquire Ski Club Chile, Ahumada 312. If you cannot find Sr. Grez there, go direct to corner of Plaza Italia where bus leaves at 0800, returns at 1700. Alternatively, go by ordinary bus which leaves at 0800 from front of Apumanque shopping centre, Av. Apoquindo, US$4 return. Beautiful views for 30 km. across ten Andean peaks. Incredible sunsets. Large restaurants. No telephone, only communication is by radio. Five min. away by car (6 km.) is the village of La Parva with eight lifts (good hotel and restaurant), where the runs are a little easier. In summer, this is a good walking area. Lift ticket and equipment rental, US$40 each. Another skiing area close by is El Colorado. Sunglasses are a must for skiers.

Other skiing and mountaineering clubs: Club Andino de Chile, Enrique Foster, 29, ski club (open 1900-2100 on Mon. and Fri.). Federación de Andinismo de Chile, Almirante Simpson 77, open daily, sells guides. Club Alemán Andino, Arrayán 2735, open Tues. and Fri., 1800-2000.

Portillo, 139 km. from Santiago and 62 from Los Andes, is the greatest centre for skiing and winter sports in Chile. The weather is ideal, the snow conditions excellent, the runs many and varied; seven lifts carry skiers up the slopes. The season is from June to September/October, weather depending. Cheap package can be arranged at the beginning and out of the season. On three sides the mountains soften into snow-clad fields and finally slope gently into the Laguna de Inca, 5½ km. long and 1½ km. wide; this lake, at an altitude of 2,835 metres, has no outlet, is frozen over in winter, and its depth is not known. Out of season this is another good area for walking, but get detailed maps before setting out.

Portillo is easily reached from Santiago by daily bus services (except in bad weather). In summer, ask the bus driver to stop, as it is not a routine call and on the way down you may have to hitch to the customs station with your baggage. In summer take a bus to Los Andes (US$2.25), then to Río Blanco (US$0.70), then hitch (see page 411). Alternatively, the skier can catch the 1108 train from Los Andes and get to Portillo in the afternoon after one of the most beautiful train journeys on *the continent*. (The train does not run daily from Portillo to Los Andes, but for a small extra fee, one can ride on the freight train.)

Hotels Hotel Portillo (L), including a cinema, night club, swimming pool, sauna baths and medical service, on the shore of Laguna de Inca. Rates, meals, tax and service included, in US dollars: 180 to 200 a day for lake front suites; single room and bath, 60 to 75; double room and bath, 100 to 110; family apts. for 4, 75; bunk room, community bath, 15 up; bunk room and private bath, 30. A fabulous view, and parking charges even if you go for a meal; jacket and tie must be worn in the dining room. Self-service lunch, US$12 p.p. Lift charges are US$12 per day. Check to make sure the hotel is open in the summer. Reservations, Don Carlos 3227, Santiago, Tel.: 28-6501. Cheaper food available at *Restaurant Yuly* across the road, and *Restaurant Los Libertadores* at the customs station 1 km. away. *Hostería Alborada*, A, including all meals, tax and service. During Ski Week (last in Sept.), about double normal rate, all included. Reservations; Agencia Tour Avión, Agustinas 1062, Santiago, Tel.: 72-6184, or Calle Navarro 264, San Felipe, Tel.: 101-R.

There are boats for fishing in the lake; but beware the afternoon winds, which often make the homeward pull 3 or 4 times as long as the outward pull. There are some gentle ski slopes for beginners near the hotel. The major skiing events are in August and September. Mules for stupendous expeditions: to the Cristo; to the glacier at the head of the valley or of the Cerro Juncal; to the pass in the west side of the valley.

Lagunillas is a favourite ski-resort only 50 km. from Santiago, 2 hours by gravel road along the beautiful Maipo valley road to the Ojo de Agua area. Accommodation in the lodges of the Club Andino de Chile (bookings may be made at Ahumada 47, Santiago). Tow fee US$12; long T-bar and poma lifts; easy field.

Valparaíso, the principal port of Chile, is built on the shores of a sweeping bay and on a crescent of hills around it. Seen from the ocean, the city presents a majestic panorama: a great circle of hills is backed by the snow-capped peaks of the distant Cordillera. Population, 270,000.

There are two completely different cities. The lower part is the business centre, with fine office buildings on narrow, clean, winding streets. Above, in the hills, is a fantastic agglomeration of tattered houses and shacks, scrambled in Oriental confusion along the littered back streets. *Ascensores*, or funicular railways, and winding roads connect the lower and the upper cities.

The climate is good, for the summer heat is tempered by fresh breezes and sunshine mitigates the unkindness of a short winter. (The mean annual temperature is 15°C, with -1°C and 31°C as the extremes.) The city was founded in 1536, but not many antiquities have survived the sequence of pirates, tempests, fires and earthquakes. A remnant of the old colonial city remains in the hollow known as El Puerto, grouped round the low-built stucco church of La Matriz. The last devastating earthquake was in 1906, and most of the principal buildings date from that time. Until recently, all buildings were low, as a precaution against earthquakes, but during the last few years modern multi-storey blocks have appeared. There was another serious earthquake in July 1971 and, most recently, in March 1985.

The main business quarter stands on land reclaimed from the sea. A further large tract has been regained for the port works, which are partially protected by a sheltering mole; but there is always a high swell, particularly when a north wind blows. Mail and passenger vessels moor alongside.

The Plaza Sotomayor is opposite the passenger landing pier. It has a fine statue to the "Heroes of Iquique"; the Palacio del Intendencia (Government House) is across the way. Near the landing pier is the railway station (for Santiago), with the information services of the State Railways and the Empresa Marítima del Estado. Long distance buses start from a bus station near the end of Calle Chacabuco, 2 blocks from Av. Argentina, about 1½ km. from Plaza Sotomayor; the local buses from Plaza Aduana. The streets of El Puerto run N and S from Plaza Sotomayor. To the N Calle Cochrane runs for 7 blocks to the Plaza Echaurren, on which stands the old church of La Matriz. A block beyond rises the bold hill of *Cerro Artillería*, crowned by the huge Naval Academy and a park. To the W of the Cerro the Avenida Playa Ancha runs to a stadium, seating 20,000 people, and to Playa Ancha park. From the western base of the hill the Avenida Altamirano runs by the sea to Las Torpederas, a picturesque bathing beach.

The narrow Calle Prat, the financial centre, runs S from Plaza Sotomayor. After three blocks it becomes Calle Esmeralda; this is the main shopping street, twisting along the foot of the Cerro Alegre; further along, across Plaza Aníbal Pinto, are Calle Condell, the Plaza Victoria, and the spacious Avenida Pedro Montt with its cafés and theatres and its little Parque Italia leading on to the large Plaza O'Higgins. The Avenidas Brasil and Errázuriz, with trees and many monuments, run parallel until near the Barón district from which Avenida España skirts the shore as far as Viña del Mar.

Leaving Plaza Sotomayor by the Calle Serrano and Plaza Echaurren, the Plaza Aduana is reached, where there is a public lift for the Paseo Veintiuno de Mayo,

404 CHILE

a terrace on Cerro Artillería giving views of the bay and the hills. The New Year is celebrated by a firework display on the bay, which can be seen from the many terraces on the surrounding hills.

Hotels *Prat*, Calle Condell 1443, Tel.: 7634, 220 beds; *Reina Victoria*, Plaza Sotomayor, F, with small breakfast, hot shower, clean and central, recommended; *Residencial Dinamarca*, E, excellent value; *España*, Plaza Victoria, E, without meals (monthly rent only). *Copihues*, Chacabuco 2883, behind bus terminal, clean, F; *Pensión Sra. Isabel*, Calle Fernando Lessops, Los Placeres. Many cheap hotels on Cochrane and Blanco Encalda, S of Plaza Sotomayor; for example, *Embassy*; *Zurich*, Blanco Encalda 328, F. *Mackenna*, Av. Mackenna, near north bus terminal, clean, good, F; *Nuevo*, Morandé 791, F. *Residencial* at Calle Valparaíso 618, F, good. Many of the "cheap" hotels in the Chacabuco area (*Restaurant-Pensión*, F) are for short-term occupation only.

Restaurants *Prat Hotel*, *El Castillo* (Av. Altamirano, on the sea front), *Marisquería La Sureña*, Valdivia 169, near market, lunch only, very good. Others are *Monico*, Calle Prat; *La Nave*, Calle Serrano, next door to Intendencia; *Café Express Delmónico*, Av. Prat (near Plaza Sotomayor), good, cheap lunches, popular; *El Faro*, same street, good; *Krill Restaurant*, Errázuriz 210, across street from docks, excellent service and sea food—many main dishes under US$3; *Port Station Restaurant*; *Buque Salvavida*, tourist menu at US$4; *Natur-in*, Francia 549, 2nd floor, vegetarian; fresh juices at *Salud*, Condell 1678; *Bernal Fuente de Soda*, Esmeralda 1140. *Menzel*, Las Heras 563; *Trattoria Italiana*, Esmeralda; *Rotonda* on same street good for lunch; *El Rey del Pescado*, Avenida Ecuador; the "casino" of the Asociación de Clubs de Regata, on the waterfront, is recommended for good seafood. *Café Apollo*, Av. Argentina 179, cheap and sustaining. Chocolate from the factory and retail store, Hucke on Gral. Cruz 824, recommended.

Discotheques: *Topsi-Topsi* and *La Nouvelle Epoque*. *Bar Roland* and *Yako Bar* on Cochrane are "classic sailors' dives".

Transport Cars for hire by the hr. or day. Taxis; more expensive than Santiago: a short run under 1 km. costs US$0.50. Public transport good. Fares within city limits US$0.20.

Museums Museum of Fine Arts, Museo Baburiza, in fine old house overlooking harbour (recommended; free), take *Ascensor El Peral* from Plaza Sotomayor opposite Law Courts. Severin Library; Museo del Mar Almirante Cochrane, in Lord Cochrane's house overlooking city, take *ascensor* from Plaza Sotomayor to Cordillera (closed temporarily for restoration).

Banks Centrobanco will change travellers cheques. National banks. Open 0900 to 1400, but closed on Sat. Rate of exchange at Banco de Chile and Banco de Crédito e Inversiones good. Parallel market outside Exprinter, corner Cochrane and Esmeralda.

Addresses The British Consulate, Blanco 737, Tel.: 56117; YMCA, Blanco 1113; YWCA, Calle Melgarejo 45; Chilean-British Cultural Institute, Calle Blanco 725, Tel.: 2828; Valparaíso Seamen's Institute, Blanco 394, Tel.: 2717; The Pacific Steam Navigation Co., Calle Almirante Señoret 48; Instituto Chileno-Norteamericano, Esmeralda 1061.

Cables Transradio Chilena, Esmeralda 932.

Tourist Agents Exprinter, Calle Prat 895 (corner of Cochrane); Gondrand Bros., Calle Prat 725; Turismo Forestier, Bellavista 409; Turismo Oroco, Esmeralda 960; Servitur, Esmeralda 1028. Agentur, Esmeralda 940.

Rail The main services, subject to changes, are: to Santiago by State Railway (3 hrs.), 3 daily *automotores*, and 7 on certain days, US$2. (No student concessions.) Trains southward, to Concepción, Temuco, Valdivia and Puerto Montt, are caught at Santiago. 2 trains daily to Los Andes. No trains going North.

Buses Excellent and frequent bus service runs between Valparaíso/Viña del Mar (25 min.) US$2 and Chorrillos; fare US$0.30. No. 9 company "Central Placeres" bus gives fine scenic drive over hills to fishing port. To Santiago, 2 hrs., US$2; to Concepción, 11 hrs., US$10. La Serena, 7 hrs., 1000. Terminal Rodoviario is on Pedro Montt, corner of Rawson, 1 block from Av. Argentina.

If driving from Santiago there are two tunnels, toll of US$2.25 paid at the first.

Hitch-hiking to Santiago is easy from service station on Calle Argentina.

Lighthouse The Faro de Punta Angeles, on a promontory just beyond the Playa Ancha, was the first on the West Coast; you can get a permit and go up it. On another high point on the other side of the city is the Mirador de O'Higgins, the spot where the Supreme Dictator exclaimed, on seeing Cochrane's liberating squadron: "On those four craft depends the destiny of America".

CHILE 405

Pleasure Resorts near Valparaíso

Laguna Verde, a couple of hours' dusty walk over the hills (or a short road journey, buses from Calle Buenos Aires) to the W of Valparaíso, is a picturesque bay for picnics. Wayside restaurant.

Viña del Mar, one of the foremost South American seaside resorts, is 9 km. from Valparaíso by electric train or one of the innumerable express buses, which run along a narrow belt between the shore and precipitous cliffs. Halfway, on the hill of Los Placeres, is the Universidad Técnica. The popular bathing resort of El Recreo is passed, then Caleta Abarca with its crowded beaches, floral clock and big Hotel Miramar. Beaches are often closed because of pollution.

At the entrance to Viña del Mar a steep bluff rises above the Miramar station, worth climbing for the views over Viña from its *paseos*. Here also is Cerro Castillo, the summer palace of the Presidents of the Republic. Below, to the left, is the lagoon of the Marga Marga, crossed by a bridge which leads direct to the Casino, built in the 1930s and set in beautiful gardens. Population: 284,000 (1982).

From September 15 to March 15, and on Sat. and Sun. throughout the year, roulette and *chemin de fer* are played at the Casino, which has a poor restaurant, an excellent cabaret and jazz orchestra.

One of the sights is the municipally owned Quinta Vergara, set in superb gardens with a double avenue of palms; it houses a collection of pictures and an art school. Take bus or train to El Salto. Part of the grounds is a children's playground, and there is an outdoor auditorium where concerts and ballet are performed in the summer months, and an international song contest is held every February.

"The Song Festival is recommended as a fascinating experience not to be missed, but make sure you have a place to stay before going to Viña! It may be better to watch for the first 3 nights on the television (to familiarize yourself with the songs and performances), and then to attend in person the last two nights. Pay the extra money and sit down near the Quinta Vergara stage (reserved seats and much better views). Otherwise, for the economy seats, you will have to arrive several hours in advance. Doors open at 1700 (except for the last night, when they open at 1500)—show doesn't start until 2130, so bring a hat for sun protection, snacks and something to read!" (Richard Crowe, Univ. of Toronto).

The Teatro Municipal is on Plaza Vergara. Near the Valparaíso Sporting Club with its racecourse and playing fields are the Granadilla Golf Club and a large stadium. In the hills behind a large artificial lake, the Tranque Sausalito, is frequented by picnic parties, and popular with waterskiers; not far away is the Salinas golf course.

Festival El Roto, Jan. 20, in homage to the working men and peasants of Chile.

Hotels *San Martín*, 8 Norte, 186 rooms each with bath, radio, and telephone; *O'Higgins*, A, Plaza Vergara, 350 rooms each with bath and telephone (very good); *Miramar*, Caleta Abarca, private beach and swimming pool (not always clean), 101 rooms, A; *Hotel Residencial 555*, A; *Alcázar*, Alvarez 646, 48 rooms, and 19 modern motel units with parking area, C, pricey, restaurant; *Residencial Sauce*, D, near railway station. Other *residenciales*: *Victoria*, Valparaíso 40, E; *Veronica*, Calle Dr. von Schroeders at end of Calle Arlegui, E, b. and b.; *Von Schroeders*, same street 392, 70 rooms, radio, telephone and TV, recommended; also, *José Francisco Vergara*, on same street, which has garden houses for up to 5. *Blanchait*, Valparaíso 82A, clean, D; *Larramendy*, Ecuador 17, D; *Cousiño*, Pasaje Cousiño, C (with meals); *Oxamas*, Villanello 136; *Arica*, Alvarez 102; *Maggie*, Montana 743, C; *La Frontera*, Libertad 342, Montaña 853, D; *Magallanes*, Villanello, D; *Park Hotel*, 3 Norte 817, D; *Española*, on plaza, D, incl. breakfast; *Residencial Sandy*, Quillote near Valparaíso, near bus and railway stations, E.

Motels at Reñaca (5 km. from Viña del Mar): *Holiday*, Angamos 367, A; *Presidente*, Sotomayor, B; *Nilahue*, Borgoño 14920, B; *Castalera*, recommended; and many others.

N.B. It is cheaper to stay in Valparaíso and commute to the Viña beaches.

Youth Hostel at Sausalito stadium, US$0.80 p.p. a night for YHA card holders, or join in Santiago. Open all year round, basic.

Camping At the *Aku-Aku* at Reñaca, US$3 p.p.; *Doña Panchita* and *Internacional*, also at Reñaca; *Marbella* and *Quintay* on Playa Grande, Quintay, 42 km. from Viña del Mar. At Sausalito.

406 CHILE

Unofficial site in woods behind Quinta Vergara park. Camping gas and similar articles for sale at Valparaíso 464.

Restaurants The *Miramar* and *O'Higgins* hotels, the *Chez Gerald*, *Los Lilenes*, and *San Marco* are all good as is *Chez Jaques*, on beach. *Cap Ducal*, also on beach near Naval Museum, expensive, highly recommended. *El Rincón de Carlos*, in family house, 1 Poniente 714, good cheap menu. *Mapuche*, San Martín 529, excellent. *Airport*, Valparaíso 503, reasonable. Many restaurants on Av. Valparaíso, try in the Galerías (arcades, e.g. *Café Big Ben*). Many smaller ones along the sea front. *Terminal Pesquero*, 1st floor, interesting. Discotheque *Topsy Topsy*, with fantastic views.

Market At intersection of Av. Sporting and river, open Wed. and Sat.

Museums The Museum of Naval History, in the Castle, good, next door is a small Aquarium. Institute of Oceanography, in Montemar, worth seeing; Palacio Rioja, built at turn of century by a prominent local family and now used for official municipal receptions, main floor open to visitors during season, Archaeological Museum on a lower floor. On the coast road between the Naval Museum and the *Hotel Miramar* there is an Easter Island statue (easy to miss as it is on a small traffic island, opposite side of street from beach).

Cultural Associations North American Institute, in fort off Avenida Alvarez; British, Calle 3 Norte. Goethe Institut, in plaza opposite station.

British Community The community here maintains two schools: St. Margaret's and Mackay. There is also an Anglican church, with a resident English chaplain, postal address Casilla 561.

Exchange Agencia de Viajes Star, Valparaíso 328, Exitour, Ecuador 140, La Araucana, Valparaíso 322.

Tourist Office Av. Valparaíso 507, 3rd floor, Tel.: 684117. Arrangements may be made at the Tourist Office for renting private homes in the summer season.

Bus to Santiago, US$2.10; to La Serena, 6 daily, 7 hrs., US$7; to Antofagasta, 20 hrs., US$20. Terminal at Av. Valparaíso and Quillota.

Rail 3 daily to Santiago, 3 hrs., US$2, via Los Andes (US$1).

Excursions Beyond Reñaca beach is Cochoa with its large sealion colony, 100 metres offshore.

Resorts N of Valparaíso There is a very fine drive N of Viña del Mar along the coast (many motels being built) through Las Salinas to Concón, then inland to Quintero. Las Salinas, beach between two towering crags, is very popular. **Concón**, on the NE point of Valparaíso Bay, is 16 km. further. Main attractions: tennis, bathing, fishing, and riding. Main eyesore: an oil refinery (not visible from beach). Near the Concón beach there is a very interesting pelican colony. There is also a new inland road, much faster than the coast road, between Viña del Mar and Concón.

Concón Hotels *Playa Amarilla*, *Inter Motel*, *Motel Bosquemar*, *Motel Embassy*, B. Good seafood *empanadas* at bars.

Campsite Las Gaviotas.

Another 16 km. to the N of Concón over the new bridge is the resort of **Quintero**, the naval aviation centre. **Hotels** *Isla de Capri*; *Hotel Yachting Club*.

Horcón, set back in a cove surrounded by cliffs, is a pleasant small village, mainly of wooden houses. Vegetation is tropical with many cacti on the cliff tops. Seafood lunches with the catch of the day recommended. **Hotels** *Horcón*, *Aranciba* and *El Faro*, all E and on beach. Restaurant *El Ancla* recommended.

From Las Ventanas the road continues N to the fashionable resort of **Zapallar** and the once fashionable **Papudo**. Excellent bathing, but water is cold. Hotels are 3rd class. **Hotels** at Zapallar: *Motel Aguas Claras*; *César*. At Papudo: *Moderno*; *Di Peppino*.

Excursions There is a fascinating drive to Cachagua, where a colony of penguins may be viewed from the northern end of the public beach.

Several excellent sea beaches are frequented by people from Santiago: some lie N of Valparaíso (already described), and some at the mouth of the Río Maipo. The railway runs to the port of **San Antonio**, 113 km. from Santiago and 112 km. south of Valparaíso. Its shipping shows a considerable growth, mostly at the expense of Valparaíso. The port exports copper brought by railway from the large mine at El Teniente, near Rancagua. Population: 60,826. Itself a popular resort, it is also the centre for other resorts to the N and S: **Cartagena**, the terminus of the railway 8 km. to the N, an old town, is a great playground for Santiago residents (there are several small resorts— El Tabo, El Quisco with a beautiful white sand beach, and particularly Algarrobo with its yacht club, marina and penguin colony—to the N of Cartagena); **Llolleo** (a famous resort for those who suffer from heart diseases, 4 km. to the S), and **Maipo**, at the mouth of the Río Maipo, are other

CHILE   407

resorts. Near Llolleo are many beautiful places, including La Boca. **Santo Domingo,** with a good hotel, is about 10 mins. by road S of San Antonio. It has a golf course, and is by far the most attractive place on this coast.

Hotels   At San Antonio: *Jockey Club*. At Cartagena: *Biarritz; La Bahía; Prince*. At Llolleo: *Oriente; Allhambra*. At Santo Domingo: *Rocas de Santo Domingo*. At El Tabo: *Hotel El Tabo*, quite nice, and *Motel El Tabo*, next door. At Algarrobo: *Pacífico; Aguirrebeña; Internacional; Cantábrico*. At El Quisco, *Hotel El Quisco*, F p.p. with breakfast, clean; *Motel Barlovento* and *Motel Los Acantilados*.

N.B. This entire coastal area, and especially San Antonio, was damaged in the severe earthquake of March 3, 1985.

The Chilean Pacific Islands

Juan Fernández Islands, some 650 km. W of Valparaíso, were discovered by Fernández in 1574. One of them was the home (1704-09) of Alexander Selkirk (the original of Defoe's *Robinson Crusoe*), whose cave on the beach of Robinson Crusoe island is shown to visitors. The main island has 550 people housed in log huts, who fish for lobsters which they send to the mainland. The village of San Juan Bautista has a church, schools, post office, and wireless station.

The climate is mild, the vegetation rich, and there are plenty of wild goats—and some tourists, for the islands are now easily reached by air and there is a boat service about every three weeks from Valparaíso (US$35 return). Tickets available from Empremar, Almirante Gómez Carreño 49, Valparaíso (Tel.: 258061) or Estado 359 (4th floor), Santiago. There is an air taxi daily in summer from Santiago (Los Cerrillos airport, US$370 round trip), by Taxpa, Nueva York 53; also from Valparaíso. The plane lands on an airstrip in the W of the island; passengers are taken by boat to San Juan Bautista (1½ hrs., US$8 one way).

The anvil-shaped peak, El Yunque, is a landmark, and it was upon this hill that Selkirk lit his signal fires. A tablet was set in the rock at the look-out point by British naval officers in 1858, to commemorate Selkirk's solitary stay on the island for 4 years and 4 months. The official names of the three islands are: Robinson Crusoe (previously Más a Tierra), Alejandro Selkirk (previously Más Afuera) and Santa Clara (the smallest island).

Hotels *Hostería Robinson Crusoe*, L (US$170-190 d, full board, plus 20% tax), about 40 minutes' walk from the village. Another motel in village, charges similar prices. No other cheaper places to stay, and lodging with villagers is difficult. Tel.: Valparaíso 81573. *Renaldo Green Pensión*, good.

Easter Island (Isla de Pascua) is just S of the Tropic of Capricorn and 3,790 km. W of Chile; its nearest neighbour is Pitcairn Island. It is triangular in shape, 24 km. across, with an extinct volcano at each corner. The population was stable at 4,000 until the 1850s, when Peruvian slavers, smallpox and emigration (encouraged by plantation-owners) to Tahiti reduced the numbers. Now it is about 2,000, of whom about a quarter are from the mainland, mostly living in the village of Hanga Roa. Just north of Hanga Roa, there is a reconstructed site with a temple, houses and a ramp leading into the sea. Further along, there is a mediocre museum. (Mon. to Sat., 0900-1700, Sun. 0900-1500, admission US$0.30). About half the island, of low round hills with groves of eucalyptus, is used for sheep and cattle, and nearly one-third constitutes a National Park. The islanders, of Polynesian origin, have preserved their indigenous songs and dances, and are extremely hospitable. Tourism has grown rapidly since the air service began in 1967. Paid work is now more common, but much carving is still done; the better items are no longer cheap (about US$30), but are readily bartered for clothing. Airport shop is expensive; there are cheaper stalls in the *mercado municipal*, east of Tahai, and Cema store. You may find cheaper carvings still in Santiago. The islanders have profited much from the visits of North Americans: a Canadian medical expedition left a mobile hospital on the island in 1966, and when a US missile-tracking station was abandoned in 1971, vehicles, mobile housing and an electricity generator were left behind. Unique features of the island are the 600 (or so) *moai*, huge stone figures up to 9 metres in height and broad in proportion.

One of them, on Anakena beach, was restored to its (probably) original state with a plaque commemorating Thor Heyerdahl's visit in 1955. Heyerdahl's theories, as expressed in *Aku-Aku, The Art of Easter Island* (New York: Doubleday, 1975), are not as widely accepted as they used to be, and South American influence is now largely discounted (see below). Other *moai*, at Ahu Tepeu and Ahu Tahai, have since been re-erected. The rainy season is from February to the end of August. Useful information is contained in David Stanley's *South Pacific Handbook*, and there is a very thorough illustrated book by J. Douglas Porteous (a frequent, and valued, correspondent of ours), *The Modernization of Easter Island* (1981), available from Department of Geography, University of Victoria, BC, Canada, US$6.

David Bulbeck, an anthropologist from Adelaide, writes: Far from being the passive recipient of external influences, Easter Island shows the extent of unique development possible for a people left wholly in isolation. It is believed to have been colonized from Polynesia about AD 800: its older altars (*ahu*) are similar to those of (French) Polynesia, and its older statues (*moai*) similar to those of the Marquesas Islands. The very precise stone fitting of some of the *ahu*, and the tall gaunt *moai* with elongated faces and ears for which Easter Island is best known were later developments whose local evolution can be traced through a comparison of the remains. Indigenous Polynesian society, for all its romantic idylls, was competitive, and it seems that the five clans which originally had their own lands demonstrated their strength by erecting these complex monuments. The *moai* were sculpted at the Rano Raraku quarry and transported on wooden rollers over more or less flat paths to their final locations; their red topknots were sculpted at and brought from the inland quarry of Puna Pau; and the rounded pebbles laid out checkerboard fashion at the *ahu* all came from the same beach at Vinapu. The sculptors and engineers were paid out of the surplus food produced by the sponsoring family: Rano Raraku's unfinished *moai* mark the end of the family's ability to pay. Over several centuries from about AD 1400 this stone work slowed down and stopped, owing to the deforestation of the island caused by roller production, and damage to the soils through deforestation and heavy cropping. The birdman cult represented at Orongo is a later development after the islanders had lost their clan territoriality and were concentrated at Hanga Roa, but still needed a non-territorial way to simulate inter-clan rivalry.

Things to See The visitor should see the crater of the volcano Rano Kau with its reed-covered lakes; best for photographs in the afternoon. The adjacent ceremonial city of Orongo with its petroglyphs (entrance US$1, pamphlet in English or Spanish extra) is famous for the birdman cult and gives good views of Motu Nui, Motu Iti and Motu Kaokao, the so-called bird islets. The volcano Rano Raraku; the statues at Ahu Tahai; the beaches of Ovahe and Anakena (Thor Heyerdahl's landing place, also restored *moai*); and the *ahu* and *moai* at Vinapu, Akivi/Siete Moai, Pitikura, Vaihu and Tahai. Ahu Tongariki, once the largest platform, was badly damaged by a tidal wave in 1960. Cave paintings at Ana Kai Targata. Music at the 0800 Sun. mass is "enchanting". Museum near Tahai. If you are hiring a car, you should do the sites from south to north since travel agencies tend to start their tours in the north (also a high-wheelbase vehicle is better-suited to the roads than a Suzuki minivan).

Accommodation and Food A comprehensive list of all accommodation available is displayed at the airport information desk. *Hotel Hanga Roa* (L) including all meals (120 beds), helpful manager; *Hostal Nanatura*, A, excellent food; *Iorana Hotel*, new, on Ana Magara promontory (5 mins. from airport), 12 rooms, friendly, excellent food, Tel.: 345; convenient for visiting Ana Kai Targata caves; *Residencial Evert House*, Arapiku-Nui-on-Hill, comfortable and homely; *Residencial Apina Nui* (B), US$30 s, 45 d, full board, not recommended, complaints of overcharging, poor food and inadequately-guided tours; *Residencial Taheta One One*, A; *Residencia Oronco* and *Toro Nui* on main street of Hanga Roa, B, full board with private bathroom, will provide packed lunch. *Hostería Robinson Crusoe* at Pangal, B, but far from village; *Hostería Green* opposite landing stage, B, full board; *Aldea Daniel Defoe*, B; *Residencial Vaiarepa*, B, including two meals; *Residencial El Tauke*, B, with meals; *Residencial Rano Raraku* (near airport), A, including all meals; *Ote Rangui* (motel), C; *Hotel Hotu Matu'a*, no a/c, cockroaches, very expensive; a new hotel is being built at Ahu Tahai (a part of the latter is like a *casa bote*, the oldest form of house on the island) A or *Rapa Nui Inn*, A, full board; Sr. Martín Rapu provides excellent tours around the island. Islanders' rates vary from US$20-30, again including meals. Some such recommended homes are Yolanda Ika's (*Residencial Tiare Naoho*), Rosita Cardinale's, A, recommended, modern, will arrange Land Rover at US$100 per day; Krenia Tucki's *Residencial Kai Poo* (US$30 p.p.), small, clean, friendly with hot water; Maná Reina Paoa and Juan Edmunds (US$40 p.p.); Gonzalo and Elsa Nahoe (US$30 p.p.); *Residencial Pedro Atán* (US$25 p.p., full board); Sophia Gomero and María Luisa Pakarati. Some families (such as Anakena and Raraku) and *Residencial Pedro Atán* will rent their garden to travellers with a tent, US$7, with meal; the lack of natural water makes this uncomfortable. Tour guides and guest-house keepers meet arriving air passengers. *María Hey*, B, incl. breakfast and dinner; half pension is convenient and cheap; you can buy good fresh fruit and vegetables at Hanga Roa market. There is a restaurant opposite the airport as well as several others on the island. Wine and

CHILE 409

beer expensive because of freight charges. There are two discotheques in Hanga Roa. Both are popular, but drinks are expensive: a bottle of wine costs US$4, canned beer US$1.50. Little in the way of shops—be prepared; bring with you what you can from the mainland. Beware of extras such as US$3 charge for hot water.

Camping   Free in eucalyptus groves near the Ranger's house at Rano Raraku, and at Anakena.

Warning   "The water is relatively safe to drink on the island but its high magnesium content may make you sick. Also, although the islanders are very nice about getting you a horse—they will get you *any* horse, so beware," writes Lani Yoshimura of Los Gatos, CA.

Bank at Tahai, open 0900-1400 daily. Bank charges US$5 commission per cheque. Credit cards are not accepted on the island, but most places accept travellers' cheques. **Post Office** (in winter) 0900-1200 and 1500-1800. Opens at 1200 on Wed. for one hour when plane arrives.

Tourist Office   Tuu Maheke, Hanga Roa, Tel.: 55.

Travel Agency   Mahinatur Ltda, will make your car reservations in advance.

Medical   There is a 20-bed hospital. 2 resident doctors and 2 dentists on the island.

How to Get There   Since September 1985, following the replacement of Boeing 707s with DC 10s, Lan-Chile fly only once a week, 5 hrs. Normally Wed. at 1130 from Santiago. Return to Santiago is on Fri. at 0700, arriving 1300. This means that visitors from Chile may have to choose between a 1½ day and 8½ day visit to the island. Lan-Chile's *insular* air-ticket, which includes length of Chile and Easter Island for US$449, is cheaper than the normal Lan-Chile return, but must be purchased outside Chile. Cheaper flights with Aeronor; islanders also hoped to start charter flights in 1986, with Latour, Agustinas 1472, Santiago. Students studying in Chile eligible for 30% discount. The flight to Tahiti stops at Easter Island for ¾ hr. going east, but 1½ hrs. in the other direction; a taxi may be hired during the stopover. Leaves Tahiti for Easter Island once a week, on Fri., from April to November and twice a week, Fri. and Sun., between December-March. Coming from Tahiti, you can stay for 2 days on Easter Island, Lan-Chile flight arriving Sat. 0600, leaving Mon. 0630 for Santiago (enough time to see all the important sites, but not to take it all in properly). (From Tahiti, connections can be made *direct* to Santiago, Lima, USA, Japan, Australia/New Zealand, S. Pacific in general.) The airport runway has been improved. There is strict plant quarantine on the island and luggage is searched at arrival and departure. There is an airport (departure) tax of US$1. Construction has started on a US project to extend the airfield, ostensibly to provide an emergency landing for space shuttles. It is advisable to book in advance for all flights to Easter Island, and to reconfirm your return booking.

Transport on Easter Island   Lan-Chile office in *Hotel Hanga Roa* provides tours of the island. Hitch-hiking up main road is possible. Jeep tours of archaeological sights cost US$40 per day (lunch included). It is possible to split the cost between up to 6 people. A horse can be hired for US$8 a day or less, and is the best way to see the island. Motorbikes can be rented for about US$20-30 a day (Suzuki 125 recommended because of rough roads), or truck US$15 p.p./day. Aku-Aku Tours arrange accommodation with islanders and excursions around the island, US$25 per person for full day, US$13-14 for half-day. Krenia Tucki of *Residencial Kai Poo* will also organize jeep tours, US$25 per day, as will Michel Fage. Some islanders, including Martín Rapu and Edmundo Edwards, a trained archaeologist, also provide tours. Charles Wilkins, Agencia de Viajes Mahinatur Ltda, Tel.: 20, English-born guide, recommended, as is Victoriano Giralde, Kia-Koe Tours: provides transport for groups, arranges various activities and owns a local supermarket. Others may provide internal transport at a discount but be discreet, as an islander so doing is subjecting himself to social disapproval. The English of other tour guides is often poor.

Dr. R. H. Webber, to whom we are most grateful for the sketch map writes:

"It is possible to walk around the main part of the island in two days, either camping at Anakena or returning to Hanga Roa and setting out again the next day. From Hanga Roa, take the road going past the airport and continue northeast until you come to a right turn at a wireless station. Continue along the south coast, past many *ahus* to Rano Raraku (20 km.). The statues have been pushed over in some places, exposing the hollow chambers where human bones are still to be found.

"There are also many temple sites in the Hanga Nui area nearby; the road goes past "the trench of the long-ears" and an excursion can be made to Poike to see the open-mouthed statue that is particularly popular with local carvers. The jeep-track continues to Ovahe, passing many temple sites and conical houses. At Ovahe, there is a very attractive beach with pink sand and some rather recently carved faces and a cave.

"From Ovahe, one can return direct to Hanga Roa or continue to Anakena, site of King Hotu Matua's village. From Anakena the coastal path is variable in quality, but there are interesting remains and beautiful cliff scenery. At Hanga o Teo, there appears to be a large village complex, with several round houses, and further on there is a burial place, built like a long ramp with several ditches containing bones.

"From Hanga o Teo, one can venture inland to Aku Akivi, where there are several other sites and

410 **CHILE**

WILL YOU HELP US?

We do all we can to get our facts right in *The South American Handbook*. Each chapter is thoroughly revised each year, but Latin America and the Caribbean cover a vast area, and our eyes cannot be everywhere.

Your information may be far more up-to-date than ours. If your letter reaches us early enough in the year it will be used in the next edition, but write whenever you want to, for all your letters are used sooner or later.

Thank you very much indeed for your help.

**Trade & Travel Publications Limited
5 Prince's Buildings, George Street,
Bath BA1 2ED, England**

CHILE 411

a cave at Tepahu. Near here there is a trail to Puna Pau; a track near the church leads to the top of the volcano.

"Rano Kau, south of Hanga Roa, is another important site to visit; one finds the curious Orongo ruins here. One final place not to be missed is Vinapu, where the *ahu* masonry work rivals that of the Incas.°

A shorter walk is from Hanga Roa to Ahu Akivi, down to the South West coast, and back to Hanga Roa (8 km. one way).

To Buenos Aires across the Andes Most of the Chilean section of the Transandine Railway (no international passenger service) and the Pan-American Highway run through the rich Aconcagua Valley, the so-called Vale of Chile. The line from Valparaíso runs through Viña del Mar, climbs out of the bay and goes through (16 km.) **Quilpue,** 1½ km. from El Retiro, a popular inland resort with medicinal springs. It crosses a range of hills and reaches the Aconcagua Valley at **Limache** (40 km. from Valparaíso); population 22,511 (*Hotel Colegio Alemán*). Between Quilpue and Limache is Peñablanca, the town of the white windmills. San Pedro, the next station, is the junction for a branch line to Quintero, on the coast. The line runs NE to **Quillota,** an orchard centre (hotel near station; Balneario El Edén, 5 km out of town, good swimming), and La Calera (88 km. from Valparaíso), the junction with the N-S line. Beyond La Calera the line swings SE and E for Las Vegas, San Felipe, Los Andes and the pass over the mountains to Mendoza. Llay-Llay is the junction for the railway S to Santiago.

San Felipe, the capital of Aconcagua Province, is 96 km. from Santiago and 128 km. from Valparaíso; it is an agricultural and mining centre with 42,000 inhabitants, 635 metres above sea level, with an agreeable climate. Part of the Inca highway has recently been discovered in the city; previously, no traces had been found further south than La Serena. A paved highway (13 km.) runs N from San Felipe to the old town of Putaendo. By rail via Llay-Llay to Santiago is 125 km.

Hotel *Hostería Pedro Aguirre Cerda*, Merced 204, D.

Termas de Jahuel (hotel), is high in the Cordillera (1,190 metres) 18 km. by road from San Felipe. The hill scenery includes a distant view of Aconcagua. Good roads in the neighbourhood.

Cuimón, between San Felipe and Los Andes, has a historic church, with a small museum attached.

Sixteen km. SE of San Felipe is **Los Andes,** in a wealthy agricultural, fruit-farming and wine-producing area. There are monuments to José de San Martín and Bernardo O'Higgins in the Plaza de Armas, and a monument to the Clark brothers, who built the Transandine Railway. It is 77 km. to Santiago by road. Population: 30,500. Altitude: 730 metres.

Hotels *Continental*, D; *Balneario El Corazón*, *Hostería La Ribera*, E; *Plaza*, E, good. *Baños El Corazón*, take colectivo from Los Andes, E, lovely pool.

Beyond Los Andes the Pan-American Highway passes into the Cordillera and winds along the Río Aconcagua for 34 km. until it reaches the village of **Río Blanco** (1,370 metres), set at the confluence of two rivers which go to form the Río Aconcagua: the Blanco and the Juncal. There is a fish hatchery with small botanical garden at the entrance of the Andina copper mine. *Hostería Luna*, 8 km before Río Blanco on road from Los Andes, good value, clean, helpful, but poor food. *Hostería Guardia Vieja*, expensive but untidy. Possible to camp. Trains and buses run daily from Los Andes; from Santiago, Bus Ahumada, at 1930 daily, direct, 2 hrs., US$2.

(Do not wait around at Los Andes for bus transport to Argentina as the local buses only go as far as Río Blanco; much better from Santiago. Hitch-hiking over Andes possible on trucks from Aduana building in Los Andes).

Beyond Caracoles (Customs post; long delays; no fruit can be taken across) the highway over La Cumbre (Uspallata) pass rises by steep grades to the Redentor tunnel: the road over the pass is more scenic, but is often closed. The top, at an altitude of 3,856 metres, is 8 km. beyond the tunnel and can be reached only on foot. The frontier is crossed at the foot of the statue of Christ the Redeemer, dwarfed by the scenery. The mountain views (including Aconcagua) are stupendous; as are the wild flowers in late January and early February. On the far side of the Andes both road and railway descend 203 km. to Mendoza, where there are rail connections for Buenos Aires. The road from the tunnel to Mendoza is in fair condition, most of it paved.

South through the Central Valley

Road and railway run S through the Central Valley, one of the world's most fruitful and beautiful countrysides, with the snowclad peaks of the Andes delimiting it to the E. It is in this valley that most of Chile's population lives.

The railway has been electrified from Santiago to S of Chillán. Along the road from Santiago to Temuco there are several modern motels.

Rancagua, the capital of the Sixth Region, 82 km. S of Santiago (1½ hrs. by train, less by bus), is an agricultural centre with a population of 140,000, where a battle was fought in 1814 by O'Higgins against the Royalists. Its Merced church is a national monument; it also has a historical museum. El Teniente, the largest underground copper mine in the world, is 67 km. to the E, at 2,750 metres; a permit to visit may be obtained at the office in Millán 1040, Rancagua. On this line, 37 km. from Rancagua by rail or road, are the thermal springs of Cauquenes, and nearby is the hydroelectric plant of Rapel, with large lake.

Festivals at Rancagua The national rodeo championship is held there at the end of March. Festival del Poroto (Bean Festival), Feb. 1-5.

Hotels *Central; Turismo; Santiago; Ducal*, all D. *Termas de Cauquenes*, D, quiet, clean, expensive but excellent food (colectivo from Rancagua market, US$1.10). Many hotels do not accept guests before 2000 hrs., or may charge you double if you arrive in the afternoon. Some 50 km. south is a beautiful colonial residence, *Hacienda Los Lingues*, L, and horse-breeding centre, set in 1,000 acres of fertile land; riding, swimming, windsurfing, shooting all available.

Tourist Office Germán Riesco 277, Tel.: 25777.

San Fernando, founded in 1742, capital of Colchagua Province, with 44,500 inhabitants, is 51 km. S of Rancagua. It stands in a broad and fertile valley at a height of 340 metres. A branch railway and road (buses) run W to the seaside resort of Pichelemu (train daily at 1815, 3¼ hrs., returns 0730, US$1.75). A road runs E towards the Cordillera and bifurcates: the northern branch runs to the Termas del Flaco, near the Argentine frontier; the southern branch goes to the resort of Sierra Bella Vista, a private *fundo* where many Santiago businessmen have holiday houses, but there is also a *hostería* which caters for about 20 to 25 guests. Cowboy rodeos in October and November.

Hotel *Imperio*.

Curicó, 60 km. S of San Fernando and 192 km. from Santiago, is in the heart of the wine country; population: 74,000. The surroundings are picturesque and the town's main Plaza de Armas is one of the finest in the country. A branch railway runs W to Licantén, 26 km. from the popular sea beaches of Iloca and Retén Llico (*Pensión Chile*, F, no hot water, basic). There is a toll (US$2.10) on the Longitudinal Highway south of Curicó.

Hotels *Luis Cruz Marines; Comercio* (recommended); *Curicó; Prat*, near Plaza de Armas, cheap and good value.

Camping Elfenwald, on Lake Vichuquén, near Llico.

Buses To Santiago, US$3.

Talca, 56 km. S of Curicó (258 km. from Santiago) is the most important city between Santiago and Concepción and an important maufacturing centre; it is the capital of the Seventh Region, with a population of 300,000. It was founded in 1692, and destroyed by earthquake in 1742 and 1928; it has been completely rebuilt since 1928. Chilean independence was declared in Talca on January 1, 1818. A 175 km. road runs E through the pass of Pehuenche (2,490 metres) to San Rafael (Argentina). Near the border is Lake Maule (2,130 metres), reached by bus from terminal; it has been stocked with salmon and rainbow trout; the road passes through some of the finest mountain scenery in Chile. A visit to an old estate at Villa Cultural Huilquelleru is recommended, 10 km. away.

Hotels *Plaza*, good commercial standard, and *Claridge*, both D; *Alcázar*, recommended as

CHILE 413

reasonable and clean. Also, *Los Angeles,* 2 Sur 1728, E; *Favorit,* 2 Sur 1716; *Cordillera Residencial,* 2 Sur 1360, near new bus terminal; *Paris,* F (red light area). Youth Hostel: 1 Norte 998 (near plaza).

Museum Museo O'Higgins, 1 Norte 875, entrance US$0.35, open Tues.-Fri. 0930-1300, 1500-1900, Sat. till 1830, Sun. 1000-1300; interesting on history, especially the Pacific War, excavations, Vilches.

Tourist Office Edificio Intendencia (at the town hall), Tel.: 33669.

Bus Terminal, corner 12 Oriente and 2 Sur. To Chillán, frequent service, US$2; also frequent to Constitución.
 To Vilches, the starting point for the climb to the volcanoes Quizapu and Descabezado (3,850 metres) 3 a day there, 4 on Sun., US$12.

Constitución, 90 km. from Talca by rail, and also reached by paved road from San Javier, is the centre of a wealthy district producing grain and timber, but its main attraction is as a seaside resort. The beach, an easy walk from the town, is surrounded by very picturesque rocks, The nearby scenery is attractive, though rather blighted by nearby factory. There are plenty of hotels and *pensiones,* but accommodation is difficult from January to March, and bookings must be made well in advance.

Hotels *Hostería Constitución,* best; *Gran Hotel; De la Playa; Negri; Plaza. Residencial Mistral,* D, very friendly.

About half-way between Talca and Chillán is the road and rail junction of Parral, 342 km. S of Santiago, celebrated as the birthplace of the Nobel Prize-winning poet Pablo Neruda.

Chillán, 105 km. S of the road junction of Linares (youth hostel, Av. Valentín Letelier 1162), was the birthplace of Bernardo O'Higgins. (Chile's naval hero, Captain Arturo Prat, was born 50 km. from the town, at Ninhue.) It is an important agricultural centre with a population of 121,000. When the city was destroyed by earthquake in 1833, the new city was built slightly to the N; that, too, was destroyed by earthquake in 1939 and there was a further earthquake in 1960. It is a pleasant city with a modern cathedral (containing a famous mural). Visit the outdoor Municipal Market for handicrafts and good restaurant; open daily, Sun. until 1300. Leather work can be bought at Av. Libertad 281. Murals by David Alfaro Siqueiros, the great Mexican artist, in library of Escuela México.

Hotels *Gran Hotel Isabel Riquelme,* Arauca 600, A; *Quinchamalí, Rucamanqui* (off Plaza de Armas, D, clean, spartan); *Las Encinas, Martin Ruiz de Gamboa; Chillán,* D, good service though dirty, full board only; *Real,* Libertad 219, E; *Hostería Sur,* O'Higgins 770, E; *Victoria,* nr. railway station, F.

Restaurants *Café Paris, Las Tinajas, La Tranquera, Quick Lunch.* 3 course meal in *Hotel Chillán* for US$2. *O'Higgins,* Constitución 199, good *almuerzo; Español* for snacks.

Exchange Both Banco de Concepción and Banco Sudamericano give poor rates.

Tourist Office Av. O'Higgins 198, Chillán Viejo, Tel.: 23338.

Train To Concepción daily at 0700, Sun. at 1550, 5 hrs., US$1.75 (can only buy ticket to Dichato—see page 416, then onwards). To Santiago, 4 daily, 6 hrs., saloon US$6.60, *económico* (one train only) US$4.50, 1st US$3.70, 2nd US$3.15.

Bus Terminal at Maipú and Sgto. Aldea for local buses. For Santiago, 7 hrs, US$7.50, buses leave from the interprovincial terminal at Constitución 10 (near railway station).

Excursions 20 km. SW of Chillán is **Quinchamalí,** a village famous for the originality of its craftsmen in textiles, basketwork, black ceramics, guitars and primitive paintings. Its ferry, powered by the flowing river and manned during daylight hours, except 1200 to 1400, is a must for enthusiasts of alternative technology. To the thermal baths, Termas de Chillán, 88 km. E, 1,850 metres up in the Cordillera, reached by a good road all the way. Season: middle December to the end of March. Here the Ski Club de Chile has a tourist centre with hotel (L, full board) and skilifts. There is excellent ski-ing on the slopes and views of the

414 CHILE

Chillán volcano, E of the Termas. Cheaper than centres nearer Santiago; packages available.

From Chillán there are various road routes to Concepción: (1) SW to Penco and S along the coast—there is a scenic railway; (2) along the Longitudinal Highway to Bulnes, where a branch road goes SW to Concepción; or (3) along the Highway past the Salto del Laja to Los Angeles, from which a main road and a railway run NW to Concepción. The **Salto del Laja** is a spectacular waterfall in which the Laja plunges 47 metres over the rocks. There is a good motel (the *Motel Salto del Laja,* C) with fine restaurant, 2 swimming pools and chalet-type rooms on an island overlooking the falls. Campsite, Los Coyuches (US$3.50 per tent). It is 6 hrs. drive from Santiago (by bus, US$7.25). To see the falls, buy bus ticket (Bus Sur or Bio Tal) from Los Angeles (US$0.60, ½ hr.) or Chillán (US$2).

Concepción, the capital of the Eighth Region, 15 km. up the Bío-Bío river and 580 km. from Santiago, is the most important city in southern Chile and the third city of the Republic. Its port, Talcahuano, is 15 km. away. Population: 240,000 (with Talcahuano: 468,000).

The climate is very agreeable in summer, but from April to September the rains are heavy; the annual average rainfall, nearly all of which falls in those six months, is from 1,250 to 1,500 mm. Concepción has been outstandingly unfortunate in the matter of earthquakes; it was founded in 1550, but its site has had to be moved more than once during its history.

In the attractive Plaza de Armas at the centre are the Intendencia, the city hall and court house and the Cathedral. The old arcades have given way to a new shopping area. In the Parque Ecuador, there is a craft fair every February.

Cerro Caracol can easily be reached on foot starting from the statue of Don Juan Martínez de Rozas in the Parque Ecuador, arriving at the Mirador Chileno after 15 minutes (necessary to obtain permission first from Entel office). Chile's largest river, the Bío-Bío, and its valley running down to the sea lie below. On the far side of the river you see lagoons, the largest of which, San Pedro, is a watersport playground. On the city side, among cypress trees, is the modern Barrio Universitario. A stroll through the grounds, which are beautifully kept with geese, ducks, swans, hummingbirds and a small enclosure with *pudu-pudu* (miniature deer) is recommended; the Casa del Arte here contains a fine allegorical mural, 35 by 6 metres, the *Presencia de América Latina,* by Jorge González Camerena. There is a golf club on the road to Coronel, La Posada, by the side of a picturesque lake.

There are striking massive rock formations along the banks of the Bío-Bío estuary. Concepción is linked with Talcahuano, on the bay, by railway and 2 good roads, half-way along one of which is the Club Hípico's racetrack. Races are held on Sun. and holidays. A branch road leads to good beaches, including Penco with two good seafood restaurants. It passes through the Parque de Hualpén, which can be reached by bus in summer (US$1) and taxi all the year (US$10). In it, on a farm, is a small museum containing curious local and Mapuche Indian items. Nearby is the strikingly set beach of Desembocadura del Río. Two other beaches are Las Escaleras (a private club)—a flight of natural stairs down sheer 53-metre sea cliff leads to it—and Ramuntcho, named after a novel by a visitor in 1875: Pierre Loti.

Concepción is one of Chile's industrial centres. It has plenty of the most important industrial raw material, water, and good port facilities at Talcahuano and other places in the bay. It is near the coalfields, has ample sources of hydroelectric power, good rail and road communications with the consuming centres of the N, and plenty of room to expand.

Hotels *El Araucano,* Caupolicán 521, *City, Castellón* 510; *Cruz del Sur,* Freire 889, all three C; *Bío Bío,* better, but smaller, near main square, B, with private bath; *Concepción,* luxury, C; *Ritz,* Barros Arana 721, D, good; *Central,* 1½ blocks from main square, D, without bath; *El Dorado,* D, Barros Arana 348; *King,* Av. Prat, opp. railway station; *Res. Turismo,* Calle Caupolicán 67, reasonable; *Alonso de Ercilla,* Colo-Colo, between O'Higgins and Caupolicán, small rooms, cold; *Romani,* Barros Arana 790, C, clean; *Santiago,* Av. Prat 438, F, across from railway station; *Res. Oriente,* Freire 552, across from the market; *Res. O'Higgins,* Av. O'Higgins 457, F, good value; *Youth Hostel,* Colo Colo 354, dirty, not recommended.

CHILE 415

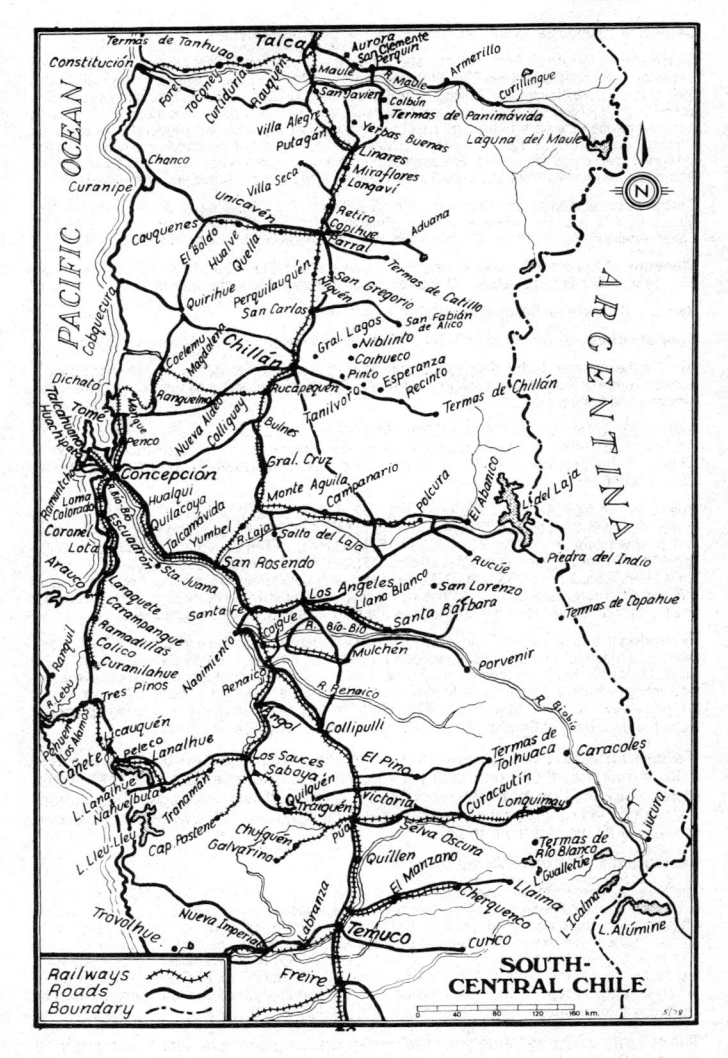

SOUTH-CENTRAL CHILE

ROUGH SKETCH

416 CHILE

Campsite Fundo Santa Sara, at Yumbel (1½ hrs. drive from city).

Restaurants Rincón de Pancho (international), Pasaje Cervantes 469; specializes in Italian food; Le Château (French), Colo Colo 334; Chung Hwa, Barros Arana 270; Los Copihues (typical), Rozas 899; Da Salvatore (Italian), Av. O'Higgins 448; Carnoteca, Bulnes; Fortín Bulnes, same street; Colacho (Arab), Ejército 452; Rincón Campesino, outside city in Nonguén, folk music Fri. and Sat.; Molino, on road to airport, famous for roast sucking-pig. "Acceptable with moderate prices" is the Concepción grill room at Barros Arana 101. Many fuentes de soda in centre; Fuente Alemana, Av. O'Higgins, recommended. Also, El Estribo, one block from main plaza. Nuria Café Bar, Barros Arana, serves excellent "lomo a lo pobre", steak with 2 eggs, chips, bread and brown ale.

Clubs Concepción at Los Copihues; Alemán; Círculo Francés; Chilean-British Institute, San Martín 573 (British newspapers, library); Chilean-North American Institute, Caupolicán 301; Chileno-Italiano, Barros Arana. Country Club, Pedro de Valdivia, outside swimming pool, tennis.

Museum Museo de Concepción, near Barrio Universitario, Tues.-Sat. 1000-1300, 1400-1700, Sun. 1430-1730. Entrance US$0.30. Interesting on history of Mapuche Indians.

Banks Best rates at Banco Concepción.

Tourist Office Aníbal Pinto 460, Tel.: 29201. Will advise on the more expensive hotels.

Air In the summer, flights daily to and from Santiago (in winter, only four a week) and connections to Temuco, Puerto Montt and Punta Arenas. The new jet airport is by the fast road from Talcahuano and Concepción.

Rail Daily to Temuco at 0800 and 1220, US$3, 7½ hrs.; to Puerto Montt three times weekly, 18 hrs., change at Temuco; to Santiago daily and in the summer special fast diesel trains three times weekly, 10 hrs., saloon US$7.35, económico (one train daily) US$4.75, 1st US$4.50, sleeper US$11.60/16.85.

Buses to and from Santiago, 8½ hrs., US$9.50; to Loncoche, 7 hrs., US$7; to Puerto Montt US$8.50, leaves Concepción 0745, arrives Puerto Montt 2000, only one ½ hour stop to take food and drink with you; to Pucón, 8 hrs., US$7.35. Igi-Llaima, to Temuco, 5 hrs., US$3.75, at 0800 and 1130. To Los Angeles, buses leave from 700 block of Aníbal Pinto. Best direct bus line to Chillán is Línea Azul, 2 hrs., US$2, at 0700, connects with 0900 train to Santiago. For a longer and more scenic route, take Costa Azul bus which follows old railway line, through Torné, Coelemu and Nipas on to Chillán (part dirt-track, takes 5½ hrs.). Frequent service to Coronel.

Excursion to Lirquén, a small, old, pretty town of wooden houses with a good beach (walk along railway to reach it). Plentiful cheap seafood for sale. Local buses from Av. Prat 484 take 20-30 mins., US$0.40. 16 km. further along is Torné, 1½ hrs., US$0.70, another picturesque village. An interesting cemetery, Miguel Gulán Muñoz, is set on a cliff overlooking the ocean. **Dichato**, a 1-hr. bus ride away, is also worth visiting: it is a beautiful fishing village and has the oceanographic centre of the Univeriosity of Concepción. Take a local bus to the tiny village of Cocholgüe.

Talcahuano, on a peninsula jutting out to sea, has the best harbour in Chile. It is Chile's main naval station; its dry docks accommodate vessels of 30,000 tons. PSNC ships call on both their northward and southward voyages. Population: 228,000. 1½ km. away the steel plant at Huachipato has its own wharf to unload the iron ore shipped from the N.

Restaurant El Alero de los Salvo, Colón 3396.

The Huáscar, a relic of the War of the Pacific, is in the naval base. On May 21, 1879, at the beginning of the war, the Peruvian Navy's huge ironclad, the Huáscar, and a small one arrived at Iquique. Chile sent two small wooden ships under Captain Arturo Prat to challenge them. Prat fought with ferocity. When his broken vessel, the Esmeralda, was rammed by the Huáscar Prat called upon his men to follow him, boarded the enemy and continued fighting until he was killed. Chile later captured the Huáscar at the battle of Angamos, Mejillones, on October 8, 1879. The ship is open 1000-1200 every day except Fri., but it seems admittance is sometimes not granted. Cameras must be handed in at main gate.

The railway to Curanilahue links the coal-producing districts near Concepción. It crosses the Bío-Bío by a 1,885-metre bridge, the longest of its kind in Chile. A new road bridge has been built. The town of **Coronel**, in the heart of the coal area, is 27 km. on. Coronel was the scene of the British naval defeat in 1914, which was later avenged at the Falklands with the destruction of the German squadron. The coast is very picturesque, the country wooded.

Buses Buses to Concepción every hour.

CHILE 417

Lota, 8 km. S of Coronel, is a coal-mining centre with 52,000 inhabitants. In the neighbourhood is the famous Parque Cousiño Isidora, laid out with views of the sea by an English landscape architect about a century ago. It contains many flower gardens, romantic paths, and peafowl and pheasants roaming freely. (Admission US$0.60, no picnicking; open 1000-1800 daily, till 2000 in summer.) The Cousiño mining company runs an excellent ceramic factory. The road is paved beyond Lota as far as the seaside resort of Laraquete (an hour's run by car from Concepción), where there are mile upon mile of golden sands, and on to Arauco (*Hotel Plaza*; *Hostería Celulosa Arauco*), past the Celulosa Arauco woodpulp plant.

Hotel Third house (blue, no numbers) in Calle Condell recommended, F. Bus drivers from Agencia Miramar stay there. *Residencial Central*, Cousiño 656, F. Campsite at Playa Blanca, free.

Buses to Coronel (20 min.), and Concepción (1½ hrs.). No rail services.

From Curanilahue, 96 km. from Concepción, a 32 km. road runs to Los Alamos, where a bus (26 km.) can be taken W to **Lebu**, a coal port with a population of 17,000. It lies at the mouth of the Río Lebu, and is the capital of Arauco province. The lower river reach and the beach are popular with tourists in summer, and one can go via Los Alamos to Puerto Peleco on the highly picturesque Lake Lanalhue, 63 km. S of Lebu. From Lanalhue a launch service connects with the *Hostería Lanalhue* (adequate, nice location) on the opposite shore of the lake. There is a 16-km. direct road to the *hostería* from Peleco. (Take the left branch about 3½ km. S of Peleco.) By taking the right branch of this road for about 25 km. and then asking the way to Contulmo, you can reach the south-eastern end of the lake after crossing a high ridge from which you can see both the ocean in the W and the snow-capped Andes to the E. From Contulmo (*Hotel Contulmo*, E) the road goes along the N shore of the lake.

Between Puerto Peleco and Los Alamos, 15 km. N, is **Cañete**, a small town on the site of Fort Tucapel where Pedro de Valdivia and 52 of his men were killed by Mapuche warriors in 1554. Museo Mapuche de Cañete, half-hour walk from town in direction of Contulmo. Open, Tues.-Sun. 1000-1230, 1400-1800. Entrance US$ 0.60. Interesting for its architecture, landscape, gardens with flowers cultivated by the Mapuches. Ask for Sr. Mauricio Rivera Osorio.

Accommodation Some shops rent rooms, F. Mormons in Calle Condell offer accommodation, free and friendly.

Buses Buses to Purén, US$1.50; sit on right-hand side to get good views of Lake Lanalhue. To Concepción, 3 hrs., US$2.75.

Travelling on the Longitudinal Railway S from San Rosendo, the junction for Concepción, we come (24 km.) to Santa Fe, from which there is a branch line E to (21 km.) **Los Angeles,** a town of 106,000 inhabitants in a wine, fruit and timber district. It is a pleasant city, with a large Plaza de Armas; Colón is the main shopping street. There is a good daily market. A road runs to the Parque Nacional Laguna de Laja past the impressive waterfalls and rapids of the Laja river. A car can take about 3 hours to get to the lake, where there is stark volcanic scenery of scrub and lava, dominated by the Antuco volcano and the glacier-covered Sierra Vulluda. Take a bus to Abanico, 20 km. past Antuco (US$1.35), then 4 km. to park entrance (details from Conaf in Los Angeles). 7 km. further on from the lake there is the Hotel Los Canelos F, while 14 km. on is the *Refugio Chacay* offering food, drink and bed (B). Following the road one reaches the Club de Esquí de los Andes with two ski-lifts, giving a combined run of 4 km. on the Antuco volcano (season, May-August). There is swimming in the Río Dugueco, ten minutes away by bus, US$0.80.

Hotels *Salto del Laja*, B, Casilla 562, Los Angeles. *Mariscal Alcázar*, Lautaro 385 (Plaza de Armas), D; *London Bar*, Lautaro 281, E; *Motel Mallorca*, D; *Central*, Almagro 377, E. On Caupolicán, *El Fogón Criollo*, No. 639, F; *Los Angeles*, No. 638, E; *Residencial Capri*, No. 659, F. *Familia González*, Camilo Enríquez 156, E inc. breakfast, highly recommended. Campsite: *Los Cabañas*, US$0.25 per tent.

Restaurants *Centro Español*, *Fogón Gaucho*. *Rincón Alemán*, Colo Colo 423; *Julio's Pizzas*, Colón 452; *Brasilia*, Colón 431.

418 CHILE

British Cultural Institute on Vicuña 648.

Tourist Office Av. Caupolicán and Villagrán.

Bus to Santiago, 9 hrs., US$7.50. To Viña del Mar and Valparaíso 10 hrs., US$8.25, 4 daily to Concepción, US$1.50, 2¼ hrs. To Curacautín, daily at 0600, 3 hrs., US$2.25. All buses leave from Plaza de Armas or nearby.

Road continues from Los Angeles to Santa Bárbara on the Bío-Bío river, and then via Collipulli, Victoria, Púa and Lautaro to Temuco.

From Collipulli and Los Angeles paved roads run W to **Angol** (25,000 people), capital of the Province of Malleco (Ninth Region), founded by Valdivia in 1552, seven times destroyed by the Indians and rebuilt. Bus from Los Angeles, US$1.20. Worth seeing are the Vergel experimental fruit-growing station, the Dillman S. Bullock regional museum with stone-age Indian artefacts (open Mon.-Sat. 1000-1230, 1500-1800, Sun. 1500-1800; free, a 5 km. bus-ride from town) and the San Francisco church. 35 km. W is the Parque Nacional Nahuelbuta, in the coastal mountain range, reached by bus to Vegas Blancas, 0700 and 1600 Mon., Wed., Fri., 1½ hrs., US$1, 27 km. from Ayol, then walk (or possibly hitch) 7 km. to park gate, and a further 7 km. to the campsite (US$0.70 to enter park, US$0.70 to camp). The park has many araucaria trees (monkey-puzzles) and viewpoints over both the sea and the Andean volcanoes. Roads run W to Los Sauces and Purén. Bus to Temuco, US$2.15.

Hotels *Residencia Angol*, F; cheaper, unmarked *residenciales* on Prat.

Restaurant *Angol*, Lautaro 194.

Mulchén, a small, old-fashioned town, 32 km. to the south, has few cars, no concrete and is a glimpse of a world gone-by.

A small town which has hot springs nearby, **Curacautín**, is some 25 km. E of Púa, 111 km. S of San Rosendo and can be reached by paved road from Victoria; bus from Los Angeles. The beautiful pine-surrounded Termas de Tolhuaca, with hot springs, are 37 km. to the NE of Curacautín by road (under repair in 1986). (Good hotel, D with full board; camping near the river, good.) SE of Curacautín (32 km. by road) are the hot springs and mud baths of Río Blanco (hotel), at 1,046 metres on the slopes of the Sierra Nevada and near Lake Conguillo (bus to Conguillo National Park only at 1800). 18 km. from Curacautín (direction Lonquimay) are the Termas de Manzanar, reached by bus from Temuco and Victoria (*Hotel Termas*, luxury, but also has cheaper rooms which are poor value; *Hostería Abarzua*, simple, friendly). The nearby Lonquimay volcano has the Puelche ski-run, open June-Oct.

Curacautín Hotels *Turismo; Internacional; Plaza.*

Forest Chile: Temuco to Puerto Montt and Chiloé

Region	Old Provinces	Population ('000) 1975	1982
IX	Malleco, Cautín	649	698
X	Valdivia, Osorno, Llanquihue, Chiloé	693	848

South from the Bío-Bío river to the Gulf of Reloncaví the same land formation holds as for the rest of Chile to the N: the Andes to the E, the coastal range to the W, and in between the central valley. The Andes and the passes over them are less high here, and the snowline lower; the coastal range also loses altitude, and the central valley is not as continuous as from Santiago to Concepción. The climate is cooler; the summer is no longer dry, for rain falls during all the seasons, and more heavily than further N. The rain decreases as you go inland: some 2,500 mm. on the coast and 1,350 mm. inland. This is enough to maintain heavy forests, mostly beech, but there are large clearings and an active agriculture; irrigation is not necessary. The farms are mostly medium sized, and no longer the huge *haciendas* of the N. The characteristic thatched or red tiled houses of the rural N disappear; they are replaced by the shingle-roofed frame houses typical of a frontier land rich in timber. The farms raise livestock and food crops, and the timber industry is being encouraged.

CHILE 419

About 20,000 pure blooded Mapuche Indians live in the area, more particularly around Temuco. There are possibly 150,000 more of mixed blood who speak the Indian tongue, though most of them are bi-lingual.

A Mapuche music festival is normally held mid-February in one of the Region's main towns. Enquire at the Santiago or Temuco tourist office.

Between parallels 39° and 42° S is found one of the most picturesque lake regions in the world. There are some 12 great lakes of varying sizes, some set high on the Cordillera slopes, others in the central valley southwards from Temuco to Puerto Montt. Here, too, are imposing waterfalls and snowcapped volcanoes. Anglers revel in the abundance of fish, the equable climate, and the absence of troublesome insects (except for enormous horseflies between mid-December and mid-January). The season in the lake district is from mid-December to mid-March, when prices are higher and it is best to book well in advance. It is a peaceful area, with fewer tourists than across the border in the Argentine lake district.

The Lake District proper does not begin until we reach Chile's newest city, Temuco, founded 1881 after the final treaty with the Mapuches.

Temuco, 676 km. S of Santiago, has 220,000 inhabitants. It is the capital of the Ninth Region, and one of the most active centres in the S. Wheat, barley, oats, timber and apples are the principal products of the area. The cattle auctions in the stockyards behind the railway on A. Malvoa, Mon. and Thurs. are interesting; you can see the *huasos*, or Chilean cowboys, at work. Also, cattle sales at Nuevo Imperial, 35 km. away, on Mon. and Tues. Poultry and geese are sold in the market near the railway station, where Mapuches may be seen; Temuco is their market town and you see many of them, particularly women, in their typical costumes. The best places to look for Indian textiles, pottery, woodcarving, jewellery etc. are the indoor market in centre of town (corner of Aldunate and Diego Portales); or, for textiles, early in the morning, near the bus station. There is a grand view of Temuco from Cerro Ñielol, where there is a fine array of native plants in the natural state, including the national flower, the *copihue rojo*. There are also a casino and a bathing pool (US$0.40). On Cerro Ñielol is also La Patagua, the tree under which the final peace was signed with the Mapuches in 1881.

Hotels *Turismo,* slightly run-down restaurant, B, near main square; *Nuevo Hotel de la Frontera,* A, opposite, excellent; *Nicolás,* Mackenna 420, D with shower and heating, restaurant; *Espelette,* Claro Solar 492, E, clean, friendly; *Continental,* good, old fashioned, E with bath; *Terraz,* Av. Prat 520, F, not always hot water, restaurant, fair; *Lautaro,* Calle Lautaro 1444, E, no hot water; *Pensión Limache,* nearby, D, better, Lautaro 1359; *Central,* E, near main square; *Hostería Rodríguez,* main street, E; *Residencial Prat,* Calle A. Prat, F; *Hogar Emaus,* Las Quilas 1435, F. Many cheap *residenciales* and *pensiones* near railway station such as *Rupangue,* in market area. Also *Omega,* opp. bus terminal, overlooking market, F p.p., hot shower, friendly. Sra. Veronica Kiekebusch, Av. Alemania 0649 (Tel.: 32079), F with breakfast, good transport connections. Youth Hostel, Av. Prieto Norte, basic.

Restaurants *Hostería Allen Cley,* Bulnes 902 at bus station, excellent; *El Fogón,* Aldunate 288; *Pehuén,* Bulnes 315; *Centro Español,* Bulnes 483. Outside town: *Hostería La Estancia* (dancing), highly recommended; *Hostería Yacará, Frontera Country Club* (dancing), all on Longitudinal Norte; *Casino Ñielol* (dancing), on top of Cerro Ñielol. Several in indoor market in centre, quite good; also *Restaurante Capri,* cheap, clean.

Museum Museo Araucano de Temuco, Alemania 084, a well-arranged Indian collection. Open Tues.-Sat. 0900-1230, 1500-1830; Sun. 1500-1800, US$0.50.

Car Hire Hertz, Bulnes 726-733, Tel.: 36190/31226.

Exchange Frontera Tours, Bulnes 750 and Turismo Narquimalmal, Av. Prat 540, for parallel market.

Tourist Office on main square, at Calle Bulnes 586, esquina Clara Solar, Tel.: 34293. Open Mon.-Sat. 0830-2030. Has full list of places to stay. Also at Balmaceda and Av. Prat. Automóvil Club de Chile, Bulnes 763, has good maps.

Rail Station at B. Arana and Lautaro. Twice daily to Talcahuano; daily to Puerto Montt, US$3.75, at 0630 and 0920 and to Concepción at 1300 and 1315. To Valdivia: once a day in winter, twice a day in summer. To Carahue: daily. To Santiago: twice a day (2230 for sleeper) saloon US$10, *económico* US$5.75, 1st US$5.50, 2nd US$4.75, sleeper US$14.75/21.05. Ticket office at Bulnes 582, open Mon.-Fri. 0900-1300, 1430-1800, Sun. 0900-1300 as well as at station.

Air Ladeco has several flights a week to Valdivia, Osorno and Santiago; also one to Concepción.

Bus to neighbouring towns from Terminal Rural at Pinto and Balmaceda, near Mercado Municipal. To Curacautín, 0745, 1315 and 1645, US$2.50. Frequent buses to Villarrica (US$2, 1½ hrs.) and Púcon (US$2.50, 2 hrs.); Buses JAC from Terminal Rural and V.Mackenna 798 y Bello, every hour. Long-distance buses leave from individual company terminals. To Valdivia, Osorno, Puerto Montt, Ancud and Castro, Buses Cruz del Sur from V.Mackenna 653, 3 a day to Castro, 5 a day to Puerto Montt. To Junín de los Andes (Argentina) Mon.-Sat. To Valdivia US$2; to Osorno US$3. Day and night buses to Santiago (Igi-Llaima), 11 hrs., US$8.50. Bus to Concepción (US$3.75), six daily.

Excursions A road and railway run W through picturesque scenery to (55 km.) Carahue (*Hotel El Sol*), through Indian country. About 30 km. further, at the mouth of the navigable River Imperial, is Puerto Saavedra (hotel), where there is a stretch of beach with black volcanic sand. It is reached from Carahue by car (1 hr.), or by bus.

From Puerto Saavedra there are interesting excursions to Nehuentue, on the other side of the river, or to Lakes Budi and Trovolhue, both well worth seeing. Trovolhue is reached by a specially chartered launch which takes 4 hrs. to go up the Moncul River. Puerto Domínguez, on Lake Budi, a picturesque little place famous for its good fishing, is reached by dirt road from Carahue (40 km.).

"Another pleasant trip through Mapuche country is to take a "micro" from the Central Market to the country town of Chol-Chol, 30 km. to the west. There are several buses per day, laden with corn, vegetables, charcoal, animals, as well as the locals. The trip traverses rolling countryside with panoramic views. On a clear day it is possible to see five volcanoes. Nearer Chol-Chol, the traditional round houses of thatch (*rucas*) can be seen. There is not much to see in Chol-Chol itself, but it does have a delicious wild west flavour somehow." (Ian H. Dally, Iglesia Anglicana de Chile). You can continue from Chol-Chol to Imperial and Puerto Saavedra, but bus connections few and slow (stay overnight in Puerto Saavedra).

The smoking 3,050-metre Llaima volcano has at its foot one of the prettiest skiing resorts in Chile: **Llaima**, at 1,500 metres, 80 km. E of Temuco. It stands in the middle of two large national parks, Los Paraguas (named for the umbrella-like araucaria pine trees) and Conguillo (open 20 Nov.-13 March). The latter, too, is full of araucaria forests and contains the Laguna Conguillo and the snow-covered Sierra Nevada. It is one of Chile's most popular parks, but is deserted outside the Jan./Feb. season. Take a bus from Temuco to Curacautín (see page 418) then a bus at 1830, Mon., Thurs., and Fri. towards the park, 1 hr., US$1, or hitch, to Conaf hut (you can camp nearby). It is then 10 km. to Laguna Captren situated in araucaria forest, where you pay a park entrance fee of US$0.50; campsite (US$4 including firewood), good hiking. 6 km. further on is Laguna Conguillo (take the Sendero de los Carpinteros), with a visitor's centre, campsites and café/shop, from where you can hike into the Sierra Nevada. At Laguna Verde in the Park is a free campsite without facilities. 15 km. beyond Laguna Conguillo, mostly across deserted lava fields, is the other entrance to the park, and then it is 13 km. though farmland to the village of Melipeuco (*Hotel Central*, F, good; *Hosteria Hue-Telén*, E, good; buses to Temuco, US$1.75, several daily, last at 1630).

For details of these excursions visit the Corporación Nacional Forestal, IX Región, Caupolicán y Bulnes, Temuco. Tours are arranged to lakes, sea beaches, Indian settlements, and salmon and trout streams. For best touring, hire a 4-wheel drive vehicle in Temuco.

The way from Temuco to Villarrica follows the paved Longitudinal Highway as far as Freire (24 km.), then (also paved) runs 63 km. SE. A road to Villarrica from the S runs substantially parallel with the old railway line from Loncoche. Wooded Lake Villarrica, 21 km. long and about 7 km. wide, is the most beautiful in the region, with snow-capped Villarrica volcano (2,840 metres) in the background.

Villarrica, pleasantly set at the extreme SW corner of the lake, was founded in 1552 but destroyed by the Indians; the present town (24,000 population) dates from the 1890s.

CHILE 421

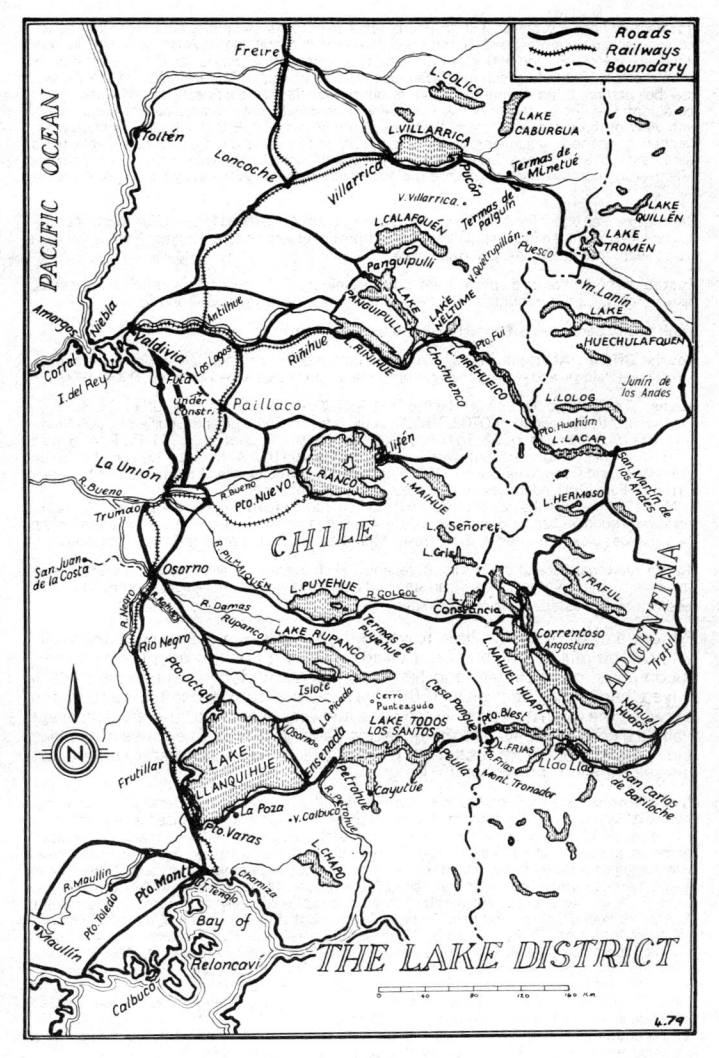

THE LAKE DISTRICT

ROUGH SKETCH

422 CHILE

Hotels *Yachting Club*, pleasant atmosphere, terraced gardens, swimming pool, restaurant, boating and fishing, recommended, B, but cheaper rooms in motel annex; *Hostería Riñimapu*, outstanding, B; *Hotel El Ciervo*, German-run, also recommended, C; *Parque Unión*, E; all one block from lakefront. *Central*, French-run, clean, good meals, E; *Alcázar*, F, clean; *Residencial Royale*, near bus station, E, no private bathroom or hot water; *Residencial Puechi*, E, hot water, good restaurant; *Fuentes*, by JAC terminal, F; *Aravena*, E, cold water only, clean, pleasant, some rooms with view of the volcano; *Hostería Rayhuen*, Pedro Montt 668, E/D, full board, highly recommended, good food; *Alojamiento La Cabaña*, F, very cold; *Termas de Liquiñe* is reasonable, has a restaurant; *Casa San Jorge*, Calle Catedral, F, is a Scouts' hostel, good value dormitory accommodation. Also, rooms in private homes, e.g. Calle Francisco Bilbao 969, run by Tom Funk, F; also at No. 827.

Camping See under Pucón (below). Also 25 km. south of Villarrica (1 hour, US$1 bus), at Lican-Ray on Lake Calafquén (see below). Bus leaves from near tourist office. Summer houses available in Dec.-Feb. Also nearby *Acapulco* campsite.

Restaurant *Club Social*, on main street, good, Henríquez 379, for snacks and ice-cream dishes. Also *Yandally*, Camilo Henríquez 401. *Panaderías*, at Gral de Aldunate 632 and 635.

Bank Only Banco de Osorno will change travellers' cheques.

Tourist Office At Vicente Reyes and Pedro Montt, near Esso station. When closed the municipal office at Valdivia and Acuerdo will give information and maps. Open Mon.-Fri. 0900-1800.

Buses To Santiago, US$13.50. To Pucón, US$0.60; 4 a day to Valdivia, US$1.85, 3-5 hrs.; daily service to Panguipulli at 0700, US$2, scenic ride. To Coñaripe and Liquiñe at 1600 Mon.-Sat., 1000 Sun. Temuco, US$2. To Loncoche (road and railway junction), US$1.15. To Argentina at 0615 on Tues., Thurs. and Sat. with Empresa San Martín (Av. A. Muñoz 417) and at 0730 on Mon., Wed. and Fri. with Igi-Llaima, US$12, but passes can be blocked for four months by snow. If Tromen Pass is closed, buses go via Panguipulli instead of Pucón.

About 25 km. S of Villarrica and 125 km SE of Temuco is **Lican-Ray**, on Lake Calafquén, full of islands and good for fishing. Buses twice daily. 4 km. away to the E is the river of lava formed when the Villarrica volcano erupted in 1971. Buses Mon.-Sat. at 0730 from Lican-Ray to Panguipulli.

Hotels *Anakena*, *Bellavista*; *Refugio*, B, recently taken over by Mr and Mrs Jack Douglas Feka, Canadian couple, with North American standards, on Playa Grande; *Rio Negro*, Gerónimo 776, F; several motels, *hosterías*, and camping sites.

Pucón, a most attractive little town on the south-eastern shore of Lake Villarrica, can be reached by bus from Villarrica (26 km.) or Temuco, not by water. Pucón has a good climate and first-class accommodation. Queen Elizabeth II stayed there during her visit in 1968. The season is from December 15 to March 15, when the town is extremely crowded and very expensive. There is a pleasant walk to a convent above the town, also to La Peninsula for fine views of the lake and volcano, pony rides, golf, etc. There is a large handicraft centre where you can see spinning and weaving in progress.

Pucón Hotels State owned *Grand Pucón* (9-hole golf course), open mid December to end-February, L (US$100 full board), C room only, accessible in off season for entrance fee; *Interlaken*, A-B, on lakeside 10 minutes from town, Swiss run, chalets, recommended; *Antumalal*, luxury class, 30 metres above the shore, 3½ km. from Pucón, very small (18 rooms), picturesque chalet-type, with magnificent views of the lake (take lunch on terrace), expensive and excellent (the Queen stayed there), L, with meals (open year round). Poor beach, but good fishing up the river. *Hostería Suiza*, F, clean, has a small café which is cheap and serves excellent *empanadas*; *Indian Hotel*; *Residencial Pucón*, Palguin and *Res. Caburga*, Arauco, both F; *Vista Hermosa*, a modest *residencial*; *Gudenschwager*, Pedro de Valdivia 12, classic Bavarian type, D, views over lake, specializes in natural food. *Los Castaños*, in centre, recommended; *Residencial Araucarias*; *Residencial Lincoyán*, Av. Lincoyán, clean and comfortable; *Residencial Frontera*, Av. Gral. Urrutia and Arauco, F; *Hostería Viena*, clean and pleasant, E, being extended; *Hostería El Principito*, Av. Gral. Urrutia and Fresia, E, with bath, very friendly; *Hostería Rodríguez*, E, clean. *Salzburg*, F, recommended; German spoken. Jorge Arancibia, Gerónimo de Alderete 403, has 10 beds, hot water, cooking facilities, recommended, simple but welcoming, also acts as guide on walking tours, has crampons for hire. Also ask in bars/restaurants, e.g. next to garage opp. *Gran Hotel Pucón*.

Camping Next to lake, 20 mins. walk from town, US$1.50 for two. There are several campsites between Villarrica and Pucón: *Huimpalay*, 12 km. from Villarrica; *Lorena*, 10 km. from Villarrica; *El Gaigue* in the Villarrica National Park; *Acapulco*, *Playa Linda* (Villarrica), *Suyay*, *Honsa*, *Millaray*, 7 km. S of Pucón; *Trancura* and *Saltos del Molco*; *Albergue Juvenil*, US$1 p.p./night, tent provided, sleeping bags required, 2 km. out of town. Other sites between US$12-20, regardless of number of people. Cheaper sites en route to Caburga.

CHILE 423

Pucón and Villarrica are celebrated fishing centres, for the lake and the very beautiful Lincura, Trancura and Toltén rivers. The fishing is now reported to be even better further S, in Lake Ranco (see page 426) for example. Local tourist office will supply details on licences and open seasons etc. Windsurfers and laser dinghies can be hired by lakeside (US$3.50).

Restaurant *Munich 2000*, Fresia 291, recommended, owner speaks German and English and has excellent colour slides.

Tourist Office   Av. Caupolicán and Av. Brasil, arranges tours. If closed, Municipal at O'Higgins and Palguin will provide information.

Telephone   International service at O'Higgins 170.

Excursions from Pucón may be made to Rinconada; to the active Villarrica volcano in a National Park 8 km. S of the town for the grand view (bus leaves Pucón, summer only, at 0900, returns 1300; taxi to volcano, US$16.50). There is a refuge without beds 4 km. inside the Park, in need of renovation (which is due to start soon). The volcano can be climbed up and down in 7 hrs., iceaxe and crampons needed—beware of sulphur fumes at the top; it is not an easy hike, ask Jorge Arancibia, Gerónimo de Alderete 408, for details of how to reach the crater. To Lake Colico to the N and Lake Caburga, very pretty, to the NE, both in wild settings (row boats may be hired, US$1.50 per hour). Two buses a day. Lake Caburga is unusual for its beautiful white sand beach whereas other beaches are black sand of volcanic origin (campsite expensive in season, US$2.50 car, US$6.50 tent, but cheap out of season, US$2.50 for tent). Bus departs 1215, returns 1400, 2nd bus leaves in the afternoon and returns next morning (US$1 single). No shops, so take own food. Two more beautiful lakes are Verde and Toro in the Huerquehue National Park, W of Lake Caburga; there is a well-signed track to them from the car park at Lake Tinquilco (it is more-or-less straight uphill, 5 km., but worth it). To the thermal baths of Menetue, N of the road to Argentina, Palguin, S of the same road and Liquiñe, 52 km. E of Lican-Ray. To Panguipulli (see page 425), on the lake of the same name.

There is a road from Pucón to the Argentine town of Junín de los Andes. The route is past the volcanoes of Villarrica and Quetropillán and round Lake Quilleihue, a gem set between mountains at 1,196 metres above sea level. On the border, to the S, is the graceful cone of Lanín volcano (3,421 metres), and beyond the border is Lake Tromen, much visited by Argentine tourists. The Argentine road from the border to Junín de los Andes goes on to San Martín de los Andes, and via Lago Hermoso and Villa Angostura (a beautiful drive) to Bariloche. There is a more direct road from San Martín de los Andes to Bariloche but it is not so interesting (see under Argentina, page 124).

The Longitudinal Highway runs from Loncoche through Lanco to Valdivia, then cuts SE to Paillaco and S to Osorno. It by-passes all towns except Chillán and Valdivia.

From Antilhue, 148 km. S of Temuco, a road runs 40 km. W to Valdivia.

Valdivia, a city standing where two rivers join to form the Río Valdivia, is 18 km. from the port of Corral and the Pacific Ocean. It is the capital of Valdivia Province and has a population of 140,000. It is 820 km. by rail or road (about 16 hrs.) from Santiago.

The city is set in a rich agricultural area receiving some 2,300 mm. of rain a year; it was founded by Pedro de Valdivia in 1552. From 1850 to 1860 a comparatively small number of German colonists settled in the area; their imprint in terms of architecture and agricultural methods, order, education, social life and custom is still strong. In particular they created numerous industries, most of them on Teja Island (5 by 2 km.) facing the city. The Universidad Austral de Chile was founded in Valdivia in 1954. Valdivia was badly damaged in the earthquake and tidal wave of May 22, 1960. The riverside market is fascinating.

Hotels *Pedro de Valdivia*, Carampangue 190, B with bath; *Naguilán*, Gen. Lagos 1927, Tel.: 2851/52/53, B, clean, quiet; *España*, Calle Independencia, E with bath; *Melillanca*, recommended but pricey, C; *Isla Teja*, Las Encinas, D with bath; *Pumantú*, General Lagos 1946, E with bath; *Nuria*, Calle Independencia, *Unión*, Av. Prat, E. On Calle Chacabuco are *Henriques, Buxton*, D, *Plez*, E, *Palace* (No. 308), D. *Regional, Hostal Montserrat* (No. 849), E with breakfast, clean, comfortable, both on Av. Picarte, as is the Salvation Army (US$1.50). *Raitúe*, Gral. Lagos 1382, E with bath; *Villa del Río*, D with bath, Av. España 1025, restaurant recommended (try salmon in almond sauce), rents apartments with kitchen for US$20 a day; *Las Encinas*, same street No. 181 (E) and *Tejas* (C), same street; *Central*, Av. Caupolicán, F; *Schuster*, Calle Maipú, is an old Victorian-type

424 CHILE

German hotel, a godsend to those who dislike modern ones, deteriorating, noisy, D with bath—F without, hot water; *Residencial Anilebu*, Av. Picarte 875, (nr. bus station) and *Residencial Germania*, F, No. 871, clean but no heat in rooms, both F; *Residencial Varas*, E; *Palace*, E, with bath, hot water, clean, central; *Hospedaje* at Arauco 905, F, clean, friendly; also, Anwanter 880 and *hospedaje* (no name) at Picarte 953, F, good. Student *pensiones* include *Juan XXIII*, Lagos, and Arauco 852. The house at Aníbal Pinto 1335 (Tel.: 3880) is friendly and cheap; also, Farias family at Cochrane 375 Tel.: 3089; *pensión* of Sra. Armida Navarrete Uribe, Calle A.R. Phillippi 878, E/F, full board if desired, hot water, good value; and Sra. Paredes, García Reyes 244, F. Several inexpensive hotels opposite or near bus terminal (best one is white *hospedaje* without a name). Youth Hostel at Houachocopihues.

Campsite Quillín, between Ranco and Valdivia. Also in Parque Saval, Valdivia and at Av. Picarte 1160, US$1.80 per tent.

Restaurants *Centro Español*, Calle Henríquez, good; *Café La Cabaña*, Plaza, popular, good, US$1.75 for 4-course meal; *Café Palace*, Av. Pérez Rosales and Arauco, central but overpriced; *Club de la Unión*, on Plaza, serves a large lunch US$2 p.p.; *Selecta*, Av. Ramón Picarte 1093, reasonable, clean, good fish; *Café Haussmann*, O'Higgins 394 (good tea and cakes); *Bomba Bar*, Saval on Teja Island; *El Conquistador*, good food, reasonable prices; *El Rey de Mariscos*, seafood; *Hostería Costanera*, beside town's boat dock, has good food and good atmosphere. *Restaurante Roma* for *empanadas*. *Pizza Trattoria la Nonna*, Chacabuco 325, good. *Restaurant y Bar La Posada del Turista*, Puerto 13, does cheap, seafood lunches. Bakery: *La Baguette*, Libertad 110, French-style cakes, brown bread.

Clubs Chilean-North American Institute, Calle Beauchef; Santa Elvira Golf Club (9 holes); tennis, sailing, motor, and rowing clubs like Phoenix on Teja Island; also Club Español.

Museum run by University on Teja Island, free and worthwhile, closed Sun. afternoons, cartography, archaeology, history of German settlement (including cemetery), local Indian crafts, etc. Open Mon.-Fri. 0900-1200, 1400-1800, Sat.-Sun. 0900-1200. Also on the island, a botanic garden and arboretum with trees from all over the world. "Lago de Lotos" on the island—slightly neglected but has beautiful November blooms.

Festival Semana Valdiviana, Feb. 12-18.

Exchange Polla Gol Lotería, O'Higgins 444. Turismo Cochrane, Percy Rosales 624, recommended for changing Chilean pesos to Argentine australes.

Tourist Office Calle Arturo Prat 555, by dock. Good map of region and local rivers. Regional office, 2 km. from market.

Rail Station at Ecuador 2000, off Av. Picarte; information and booking office at Arauco 220. Daily to Santiago; 3 times a week the Pullman Express to Santiago leaves 1830, Saloon US$11.60, *económico* US$6.85, 1st 6.30, 2nd US$5.50, sleeper US$16.85/23.70. Daily at 0700 and 1135 to Osorno and on to Puerto Montt, US$2. To Trumao (for launch to La Barra) daily at 1115, 40 mins., US$0.50 (see page 427). No train services to Pucón.

Bus Terminal is at Muñoz and Arturo Prat, by the river. To Santiago: Pullman daily, leaving 2100, arriving next morning at 0830, about US$8-13.75. Pullman daily to and from central and southern towns. ½ hourly buses to Osorno, 1½ hrs., US$1.50 (cheapest). To Lanco, US$2. Thrice daily to Llifén, US$2.50. 15 buses daily to Panguipulli, US$2. Many daily to Puerto Montt, US$2.50, 3 hrs. To Puerto Varas, ETC bus, 3 hrs., US$2.35. To Villarrica, by Bus JAC, 3-5 hrs., US$1.85, daily at 0700, 1100 and 1600. For Pucón change at Villarrica, to Bus JAC, Vicente Reyes 621. The road is unpaved from Loncoche. To Bariloche via Osorno (10 hrs.) with Bus Norte and Tas Choapa, 5 a week. Twice daily to Riñihue, Mon.-Sat., 1630 and 1830, Sun. 1945 and 2015.

Air Ladeco operates jet flights to Santiago via Temuco 3 times a week.

Excursions The district has a lovely countryside of woods, beaches, lakes and rivers. The various rivers are navigable and there are pleasant journeys to Futa, Putabla, and San Antonio, behind Teja Island and through the Tornagaleanes, the Isla del Rey. Among the waterways are countless little islands, cool and green. Ferryboats (almost every hour in summer) leave from dock, Muelle Fluvial, behind tourist office on Av. Prat 555, making the beautiful trip down the river to Corral in about 1¼ hours (US$1.50 one way; occasional buses are cheaper) where there is *Residencial Maviel*, F, on Calle Arica, and *Santa Clara*, E. The boats call at the seaside resorts of Niebla, 10 mins. away, US$0.80 extra (less hectic than Corral, with good Youth Hostel on top of the hill; can also be reached by bus, every 1½ hrs. from Valdivia bus terminal to Los Molinos), and Mancera. 4 km. along the coast from Corral is San Carlos, with its *Hostería los Alamos* (F), a delightful hideout for those seeking a quiet life. The tourist boats (*Neptuno* or *Calle-Calle*) to Isla Mancera and Corral, including a guided half-day tour (US$8.45 with meals) leave at 1330 and return at 1630. A service boat, *Panguipulli*, which is cheaper, also goes to Corral; leaves at 0800 and 1230 from Valdivia and returns at 1000 and 1600 from Corral (1230, returning 1530 on Sun.). In Corral is the Castillo, a national monument with a battery of 24 guns, and opposite it, on a promontory W of Niebla is the Fuerte San Luis de Alba; a substantial earthwork fort. The coastal walks are splendid. A cruise boat, *Capri*, run by *Hotel Pedro de Valdivia*, can be hired to take you to Fuerte San Luis de Alba.

A road runs from Valdivia along the River Calle Calle to Los Lagos (61 km.), and on to the beautiful Lake Riñihue (39 km.). The road from Riñihue to Enco around the southern edge of the Lake is now closed, so Choshuenco can only be reached by road from Panguipulli or Puerto Fuy. To avoid an overnight stay in Los Lagos, catch the bus from Riñihue to Los Lagos, departing 1530 Sun., US$0.50, train north from Los Lagos at 1620 to Lanco, US$1.30, and bus in evening (1920) on to Panguipulli. Riñihue, a beautiful but very small and isolated village, is worth a visit. Campsite by the lake; *Restaurant del Lago* has rooms, E (no meals). The road to Coñaripe, a small village on the east side of Lake Calafquén, offers superb views of the lake, and of Villarrica volcano. Afternoon bus goes on to Lican-Ray (see page 422), a particularly beautiful spot and a good start for hiking expeditions. Bus north, five times a day to Villarrica, US$1.

Panguipulli, on the W bank of the lake of the same name, is in a beautiful setting, with roses planted in all the streets. Excursions can be made to Lakes Panguipulli, Calafquén, Neltume and Pirehueico, and south to the northern tip of Lake Riñihue at El Desagüe (*Hostería Riñimapu*, B, excellent). There is a new 30-km. road around the lake to Choshuenco, a beautiful coastline, wooded, with cliffs and sandy beaches. Buses leave daily at 1530 and 1600 along the North bank of the lake, but it is not possible to return from Choshuenco on same day. (Bus returns from Choshuenco at 0630 and 0645.). Launch service across lake now discontinued. Choshuenco volcano is at the SE end. For fishermen, daily excursions on Lake Panguipulli are recommended (see Donald Nash, a Canadian living in Panguipulli, Martínez de Rozas 646). The waterfalls of Huilo-Huilo are most impressive and reached by the Choshuenco bus, get off beyond Choshuenco at *Alojamiento Huilo Huilo*, where the road crosses the Huilo Huilo river. From here it is a 1½ hr. walk the following day to the falls. Alternatively, walk from Choshuenco along Puerto Fuy road for 3½ hrs. and turn right at sign to the falls. A scenic road, through rainforest, runs around the Chosuenco volcano from Puerto Fuy to the river Pillanleufú, Los Llolles and Puerto Llifén on Lake Ranco (see below); only possible by car or on foot, and permission must be obtained from the lumber factory at Neltume (Sr. Thomas Morefield), 5 km. from Neltume, 3 km. from Puerto Fuy.

Since there are no longer any ferries across Lake Pirehueico, to reach San Martín de los Andes (Argentina), on the eastern shore of Lake Lacar, you must go via Choshuenco and Liquiñe to the pass of Carirriñe.

Hotels At **Niebla**: *Hostería Rucantu*, E; *Hostería Santa Clara*, F. At **Panguipulli**: *Hotel-Bar El Ciervo* (nr. supermarket), F, clean, hot water, friendly; *Central*, clean, hot water, E; *Hostería Panguipulli*, F; *Hostería Quetropillán*, Etchegaray 381, E, comfortable, food; also, private house opposite; Sra. Pozas, Pedro de Valdivia 251 (F); *Residencial Riquelme*, good value. Youth Hostel, F (open all year round). *Las Brisas* restaurant, has rooms to let, F; *Waldorf*, F; *Restaurante Valparaíso*, recommended. At **Liquiñe**: *Hostería Termas de Liquiñe*, D; private houses, F. At **Choshuenco**: *Hotel Choshuenco*, F; various hosterías, including *Los Notros*, F, *Hostería Pulmachue*, E, and *Club Andino*, on Independencia 625; free camping. At **Pirehueico**: *Hostería Pirehueico* occupied by military, but beds available for US$1 or so in private houses. At the edge of Lake Ranco: *Puerto Nuevo* (very good), A. At **Río Bueno**: *Plaza*, *Río Bueno*, Casilla 157, A. At **Carboneros**: *Villa Lucía*. At **La Unión**: Hotels *Turismo* and *La Unión*.

Campsite Imahuito, on Lake Ranco, 8 km. from Futrono. Free camping on lakeside at Panguipulli possible. Also, at Los Molinos.

Tourist Office in plaza next to police station.

NB No foreign exchange facilities.

426　**CHILE**

Bus to Santiago daily at 1845, US$9; frequent buses to Valdivia, 2 hrs., US$1.50 and Temuco, 3 hrs., US$2.25. To Calafquen, 3 daily at 1200, 1545 and 1600. To Lican Ray and on to Villarrica at 1530, 2 hrs., US$2. Bus to Villarrica leaves from depot in Calle Etchegaray, 100 yards uphill from *Hostería Quetropillán*.

Rail　To Puerto Montt at 0730, change at Antilhue, arrive 8 hrs. later; a long, slow trip but worthwhile for the scenery around the lake.

Sports　The Club Andino Valdivia has ski-slopes on the Mocho and Choshuenco volcanoes. The southern shore of Lake Ranco offers excellent fishing.

Mehuin, 2 hrs'. bus ride from Valdivia; post office, good sea bathing and several hotels: *Hostería Pichicuyín* (E), 1 km. away, highly recommended. Don Kurt who lives in Ing. Haverbeck may be able to put up guests. He is also planning to build a youth hostel on the peninsula of Chanchán, 13 km. S. Quelle, 6 km. from Mehuin, has two simple *residenciales*. Good beach but bathing dangerous at high tide because of undercurrents; safer to bathe in the river near ferry.

The 76-km. road from Valdivia to La Unión and Río Bueno on the Longitudinal Highway goes on to Puerto Nuevo on lovely, island-starred Lake Ranco and to Lake Maihue. A branch of this road curves round the north of Lake Ranco to **Llifén,** a picturesque place on the eastern shore. From Llifén, visits can be paid to Lakes Maihue and Verde.

Llifén Hotels *Llifén*, B and *Hostería Cholinco*, 3 km. out of town on the road towards Lake Maihue, B, poor food, limited electricity, and also the *Calcarrupe Lodge*, run by *La Cascada*, on Correo Llifén, A; *Huequecura*, Casa 4, *Cumilahue Fishing Lodge*, A, including meals and fishing services.

On the south side of Lake Ranco is Lago Ranco, an ugly town (one *residencial*) and Riñinahue; the road is terrible (lots of mud and animals, including oxcarts), but is worth taking to see an older lifestyle, the beautiful lake, waterfalls and sunsets on the distant volcanoes (if walking, beware the numerous guard dogs in the area).

Some 42 km. S of Río Bueno is Osorno, another centre for exploring the Lakes.

Osorno, 900 km. from Santiago and 105 km. N of Puerto Montt (103,000 people) was founded in 1558. It was destroyed shortly after its foundation, and was later settled by German immigrants, whose descendants are still of great importance in the area. The Argentine town of Bariloche is reached by a road E through Puyehue pass (bus 2-3 times a week, daily in summer, US$17.50) or via the lakes of Todos los Santos and Laguna Verde, both crossed by ferries. The trip via the lakes takes at least a whole day; maybe 2-3 in winter (April-Nov.). The road via Puyehue (120 km.) is more reliable, and still a very beautiful trip.

Hotels *Waeger*, Cochrane and Bilbao, A; *Gran* (good restaurant), main square, A, with bath; *Osorno*, D; *Tirol*, O'Higgins 810, E, with bath; *Ferrari*, Cochrane 515, D, with bath; *Madrid*, Av. Bulnes, D, a bit overpriced; *Residencia Maara*, P. Lynch and Colón, E; *Residencia Hein*, Cochrane 843, D; *San Martín*, Cochrane and J. MacKenna, E; *Residencia Astoria*, Julio Buschmann 2277, E without bath, clean; *San Fernando*, Bulnes 836, F, good supper for US$2; *Germania*, Rodríguez 741, F; *Residencial Riga*, Amunátegui 1058, E, highly recommended but heavily booked in season. *Roma*, near centre, E with breakfast; *Hospedaje Eliana del Río Cortés*, Bulnes 876, F and *Alcázar*, F, next door; *Residencial Macera*, E; *Residencial* at Amunátegui 520, run by Sra. Gallardo, near Provincial bus terminal, good, D; *Turismo*, E, rather basic; *Residencial Ortega* (strongly recommended) and *Royal*, both near bus terminal, F. For youth hostels, contact Secretaria Provincial de la Juventud, Bilbao 850. Private houses at Freire 530, Martínez de Rozas 544 (near railway station) and Los Carrera 1174 recommended.

Restaurants *German Club*, O'Higgins 563; *La Playa* (excellent but expensive seafood); *Cautín*, Lynch 1591. *Bahía*, Ramírez 1076, recommended for quality and economy; *Lincanyon*, Freire 526, friendly and good food; good ice cream at Ramírez 939. The *Club de Campo* is open to non-members for meals. *Parrillada Argentina*, Calle Lynch; *Café Dino*, a new and expensive restaurant on the plaza. Good restaurant in the bus station. *Café Central*, good choice of German küchen; *Hostería Socavi*, 25 km. S on the Longitudinal Highway, excellent roast chicken. Try chicha (cider) or local pisco sour.

Shop　Reinares and Thone, Ramírez 1100, for good fishing gear.

Museum　Museo Histórico Municipal, Matta and Bilbao.

Garage　Good Volkswagen garage in Calle Los Carrera—owner speaks German. **Car Hire,** Hertz, Bilbao 857, Tel.: 5401/2.

CHILE 427

Laundry Av. Arturo Prat 678.

Exchange Banco Osorno y La Unión, on Plaza is the only official place; poor rate and minimum commission of US$5. For parallel rates try Globus Viaje, Cochrane 646; Café Waldis, O'Higgins 611.

Tourist Office Provincial government office, 1st floor, Tel.: 4104. Has details of accommodation. Closed at weekends. Instituto Chileno-Norteamericano, Bilbao 934, offers advice to tourists (open 0830-1300, 1400-1730). Also, office in upstairs of 1st class bus terminal, Errázuriz 1400.

Buses Most leave from next to municipal market at Errazúriz 1400. Varmontt buses every ½ hr. (from 0700 to 2200) to Puerto Varas and Puerto Montt (to former, 1½ hrs., US$2). To Puerto Octay, from market on Mon., Wed. and Fri. at 1545 or from station on Bulnes at 0600, daily, US$1.25, return 1200 or 1800. Frequent buses to Santiago, US$11, 16 hrs. Buses to Valdivia, every half hour, 1½-hr. journey, US$1.50 and up, Entre Lagos, US$2. Local bus to Anticura (Chilean customs post) leaves at 1620, 3 hrs., 22 km. from border. Left luggage at terminal, open 0730-2030. Local bus fare, US$0.30.

Rail Station at Juan Mackenna 600. To Santiago one Rápido daily, 14 hrs., Saloon US$12.10, *económico* US$7.90, sleeper US$18.40/25.25.

Air Ladeco operates flights 3 times a week to Santiago, via Temuco.

Excursions Drive 48 km. SE to **Puerto Octay**, on northern shore of Lake Llanquihue, a small town in a lovely setting (buses daily). Follow the road along the lakeside, with the Osorno volcano on your left, to Ensenada for lunch, a short distance up the road (20 mins.) is Petrohué with its beautiful falls, and the Osorno volcano again in the background, and Lake Todos los Santos; continue to Puerto Varas for tea, then along the W side of the lake to Octay and back. *Café Kali* on main square at Octay, Amunátegui, recommended. Playa Maitén, 5 km. from Puerto Octay; "highly recommended, nice beach, marvellous view to the Volcán Osorno, no tourists"; campsite.

Hotels There are hotels at **Puerto Octay**, *Haase*, very pleasant, C (rooms with and without bath), US$70 for rooms, breakfast and supper for family of 6; *Posada Gubernatis*, Calle Santiago, lakeside, motorboat, excellent food, clean, comfortable, D; *Hostería La Baja*, Casa 116. **Centinela;** *Hotel Centinela*, Casa 114, C (rooms with or without bath).

E to the Pilmaiquen waterfall, and on to Lake Puyehue and the thermal waters at **Termas de Puyehue** (US$4 p.p. for bathing); 2 hrs. by car; Empresa Buses Puyehue depart 0930 from Osorno bus station (return 1600); tickets can be bought from booth 10 in shop parade, return US$3. Bus does not stop at Lake (unless you want to get off at Gran Hotel Termas de Puyehue and clamber down), but goes to Aguas Calientes, which has National Park headquarters, an open air swimming pool with hot thermal water, US$0.57 p.p. (free after 1900), a Conaf campsite, at entrance to park (US$4.50), private sites (US$6.85) and a café. Return bus at 1630. In the Puyehue National Park is surviving temperate rain-forest. Continue 18 km. to Volcán Antillanca (good *hostería*, C, developed as a ski resort with two ski lifts) through a lovely region of small lakes and fairytale forests. The views from Antillanca are breathtaking, with the snow-clad cones of Osorno, Puntiagudo, and Puyehue forming a semicircle. The tree-line on Antillanca is one of the few in the world made up of deciduous trees (southern beech). *Bus continues from Aguas Calientes to Antillanca in winter only.*

Hotels Puyehue, *Gran Hotel Termas de Puyehue* has a hot-springs swimming pool, large and well kept, A, main meals US$8 each, breakfast US$3, in beautiful scenery, heavily booked Jan.-Feb. (Telex 273146, SOTERCL); also near Lake Puyehue, about 4 km. from Termas is *Aguas Calientes*, cheaper and less commercial (take food if you want to cook) than the *Termas*, cabin-type accommodation C per cabin, or good camping, meals available. *Hostel Ensenada* and *Centro Juvenil Verbo Divino*, San Ignacio 979 (acts as a boarding school in term time), F, at **La Ensenada**, a string of farmhouses and hotels along the lakefront; 7 km. E. of Entre Lagos is the *Hostería Tramahuel* (six rooms and two family cabins), C; *Hostería Irma*, 1 km. between Puerto Octay and Ensenada, D, good food; *Motel Nilque*, cabins, B, half-price April to November, by Osorno-Bariloche road on S shore of Lake Puyehue; *Hostería Isla Fresia*, located on own island, transport provided.

Drive or take bus N to Río Bueno, celebrated for its scenery, to La Unión, and to Trumao, a river port on the Río Bueno, whence a launch may be taken to La Barra on the coast. Leaves Wed. and Sat. only at 0900, 5 hrs., US$6; returns Sun. at 0900.

Bus to Las Cascadas (Mon.-Fri. at 1700, Sat. 1400, Sun. 1900), next day to La Picada (24 km.),

428 CHILE

stay at *Refugio La Picada*, then on to Lake Todos los Santos and Petrohué (14 km.). From Petrohué (see page 429) go to Saltos de Petrohué or by bus to Ensenada and Puerto Varas.

A further excursion can be made to the S shore of Lake Rupanco (65 km.) taking the road to Puerto Octay and turning E after 33 km.

The sea beaches at Maicolpue (60 km. from Osorno—*Hostería Müller*, on the beach) and Pucatrihue (*Hostería Incalcar*, summer only) are worth a visit in the summer (daily bus service).

Two hours' walk to top of Volcán Casabla, though no path; excellent views over Osorno, Puntiagudo, Puyehue, Cerro Tronador.

The Club Andino Osorno has three shelters (US$3 p.p.) at La Picada (84 km. from Osorno), on the ski slopes on the Osorno volcano at 950 metres and on a road off the main road between Octay and Ensenada; *Las Pumas* on the Volcán Osorno at 900 m., with plenty of beds at about US$1.75 p.p. and cooking facilities. Apply at the Oficina de Turismo de Osorno, *Gran Hotel*. At 1200 metres is Refugio Teski Club; both open in summer. If you wish to climb Volcán Osorno, ask first at Las Pumas or Refugio Teski for advice. To reach Volcán Osorno, take bus to Ensenada from Puerto Varas (US$1) then walk 12 km. to Las Pumas. A ski resort is under construction on Volcán Osorno.

Campsites Lake Puyehue, Camping Municipal. Entre Lagos, Camping Muelle de Piedra (7 km. E of Entre Lagos); Camping Los Copihues (9 km. E of Entre Lagos); campsite at Centinela. Wild camping allowed at Aguas Calientes; ask the rangers.

From Osorno it is 117 km. S to Puerto Montt, including 25 km. along the shore of Lake Llanquihue which, together with Lake Todos los Santos to the E of it, is the best known of all the lakes (there is a boat service across Lake Todos los Santos, US$4.50). Across the great blue sheet of water can be seen two snowcapped volcanoes: the perfect cone of Osorno (2,680 metres) and the shattered cone of Calbuco, and, when the air is clear, the distant Tronador (3,554 metres). Lake Llanquihue covers over 540 square km. and is the third largest natural lake in South America. There is a road, 187 km. long, round it.

Puerto Varas, a beauty spot of about 23,300 inhabitants, is on the shore of Lake Llanquihue, with standard roses grown along the streets. Parque Philippi, on top of hill, recommended for good views and an interesting craft centre. It is 1,046 km. from Santiago and only 26 by rail or 24 by paved road from Puerto Montt. Casino charges US$2.65 entry, including first drink.

Hotels *Puerto Varas*, Klenner 349 (*Gran Hotel Turismo*), B, luxury class with casino; *Cabañas del Lago*, Klenner, cabins, B; *Residencial Central*, E; *Residencial Alemania*, E; *Hospedaje Loreley*, Maipo 911, D, recommended, homely, quiet, good restaurant; *Bella Vista*, E, run by friendly old German ladies; *Playa*, lakeside position, Salvador 24, clean, but spartan, C, restaurant is good, though comparatively expensive; *Licarayén*, small, B with bath, highly recommended, book in season; *Residencial Hellwig*, F, San Pedro 210, very good, reasonable; *Grand Hotel Heim*, San Pedro and San José, basic, but good food, E; Student hostel, *Centro Juvenil*, Colón 251, US$1.50 p.p., including bathing and cooking facilities, TV, games room; *Hotel Atalaya*, Santa Rosa 710, D, incl. breakfast, comfortable, English spoken. Also cheap *residenciales* opposite bus station and in Plaza de Armas. *Motel Altué*, Av. V. Pérez Rosales, C, incl. breakfast; *Motel El Trauca*, Imperial 433, E; *Motel Sacho*, San José 581, E. *Residencial Unión*, Calle San Francisco 669, (opp. bus station), clean, basic, hot water, F. Residencial at Salvador 423, D, run by a German lady, recommended, as is María Schilling Rosas' *hospedaje* at La Quebrada 752. *Hospedaje Bellavista*, 33 km. outside Puerto Varas en route to Ensenada, recommended, a model farm, D.

Campsite Playa Venado, apply to Playa Venado Municipal Office. Camping Municipal Puerto Varas (4 km. E), good beach; Camping Playa Niklitschek (8 km. E), full facilities, US$5 per night.

Restaurants *Club Alemán*, best, dinner, expensive; *Mercado*, next to market, good and reasonable, about US$4 for lunch; *Café Asturias*, San Francisco 316, good *empanadas*; restaurant on shore road to Puerto Chico. *El Molino*, an excellent coffee house in an old mill, on road to Ensenada.

Banks Better rate of exchange for travellers' cheques obtained in Puerto Montt.

Tourist Agent Graytur; Andina del Sur (beside Igi-Llaima bus office) offer trips for US$42 to Lake Todos los Santos, Peulla, Cerro Tronador and return.

Buses To Santiago: Igi-Llaima leaves from Salvador at 1830, arrives 1130 (US$11.50). To Puerto Montt every ½ hr. from Varmontt station, 30 mins., US$0.65.

Excursions Buses run on the southern side of the lake between Puerto Varas and (50 km.) Ensenada (see below), in the south-eastern corner of the lake, and on to Petrohué (for lunch), both served by Transporte Esmeralda, Del Salvador 57 (see below). In summer, Varmontt excursion on Sat. and Sun. to Ensenada,

Petrohué, Laguna Verde and Osorno Volcano, US$3.50, good value. The drive around the lake is very picturesque. On the northern road are Puerto Octay and Centinela (see page 427).

It is not possible to go by private car from Puerto Varas direct to Bariloche, Argentina, as the ferry on the Argentine side does not take cars; one must go via Osorno.

Puerto Varas is within easy reach of many famous beauty spots—Desagüe, Totoral, Frutillar, Los Bajos, Puerto Octay (direct bus only from Osorno), Puerto Chico, Puerto Fonck, Ensenada, La Poza, the Loreley island, the Calbuco volcano, La Fábrica, Puerto Rosales, Playa Venado, Ralún and Río Pescado. The Falls (Salto) of Petrohué should not be missed. The whole countryside with its prirneval forest, deep blue rivers and snowcapped volcanoes is very beautiful; interest is added by the timber-frame buildings with shingle roofs—even the churches.

Bus every half hr. from Varas to Alto **Frutillar** (where windsurf boards can be hired), US$0.75 from Varmontt terminal on San Francisco, then another half-hourly colectivo to Bajo Frutillar, 4 km. away and possibly the most attractive town on the lake. Frutillar, a beautifully kept town, offers a classical music festival in late January to early February. Museo Colonial Alemán, including watermill, and a German colonial house are open to the public. *Hostería Alemán* by lakeside, very clean, excellent food, C, including breakfast. Also, *Casona del 32*, C with bath and breakfast, comfortable old house, central heating, English and German spoken, Tel.: 323, P.O.Box 101; and *Posada Campesino Frutillar*, German-run, good food. *El Retiro*, run by Betty Heim, friendly, E; *Frutillar Alto*, Calle Principal 168, F, clean. Many German-style cafés and *Salons de Té* on Calle Philippi (the front).

La Poza is a little lake to the S of the main lake and reached through narrow channels overhung with vegetation; a concealed channel leads to yet another lake, the Laguna Encantada. The motorboats that tour Lake Llanquihue stop at Loreley Island, very beautiful and well worth a visit.

East of Lake Llanquihue is the most beautiful of all the lakes in southern Chile: Lake Todos los Santos, a long irregularly shaped sheet of water with the ports of **Petrohué** at its western and **Peulla** at its eastern ends; a boat trip costing US$4.50 can be taken between the two, leaves Petrohué at 1100, Peulla at 1900 (2½ hrs.). If you prefer to go walking, ask for the park guard, Hernán, who organizes expeditions from Petrohué in the summer months. Peulla is a good starting point for hikes in the mountains. Trout and salmon fishing at Petrohué are excellent. The waters are emerald green. It is only 18 km. by a scenic gravel road from **Ensenada**, a lovely spot on Lake Llanquihue (3 buses a day from Varas, 1½ hrs., 50 km., US$1.50); to Petrohué, Tues. and Thurs. (US$1.75; schedules vary). (**N.B.** Do not confuse this Ensenada with La Ensenada on S shore of Lake Puyehue, page 427). There are shops in Petrohué, but bread is sometimes short. There is also a post office. The Salto de Petrohué (entrance, US$0.75) is 6 km. from Petrohué on the Ensenada road.

Petrohué is infested by *tavanos* (local horseflies) in Jan. and Feb. Cover up as much as possible.

Hotels At **Ensenada:** *Hotel Ensenada*, B with bath, olde-worlde, (closed in winter) good view of lake and Osorno Volcano; *Millantu*, reminiscent of cheap hotels in the Alps, used by climbers, E; *Hostería Los Pumas*, 3 hrs. up the hill also highly recommended, in season only, D; *Ruedas Viejas*, E; in next door house, you can lodge or camp in back garden. *Pucara*, D; opp. is *Hospedaje Opazo*, F with breakfast, no hot water, friendly; *Refugio Teski*, 4 hrs. walk up the volcano from *Hotel Ensenada* (where you should call to check if *refugio* has food), bleak site above tree line (see page 428). Youth Hostel, *Centro Juvenil*, US$2, rather noisy as shared with an orphanage. *Bellavista*, E, a few km. N, serves excellent meals. At **Petrohué;** *Hostería Petrohué*, C, with bath, built for Queen Elizabeth; *Familia Küscher* on other side of river, F, recommended; *Refugio* above being repaired. At **Peulla**, on the opposite shore: *Hotel Peulla*, C without meals, B with full board, big, simple, service sketchy, but cold in winter (tiny shop at back of hotel); 3 private houses, F (including *casa de familia*, yellow house, of one of the Andino Sur bus drivers). Homemade marmalade, *dulce de leche* available from Mrs. Gisela Schwitzgaeble, Ruiz Moreno 938. Otherwise food hard to find in Peulla, so take your own. Reported that other lodgings may be found through asking locals (F); the customs official puts people up for US$4.50 p.p., including two meals.

Bus To Puerto Montt via Puerto Varas on Tues., Thurs. and Sat. (2 hrs.) leaves 1820 (US$1.50); stops at Salto de Petrohué for 15 minutes. To Lake Frías (1½ hrs.).

Market On Tues. and Thurs. mornings; a number of lorries sell food, wine and clothes.

Campsites on Llanquihue: Alcalde Manuel Droquett, Chinquahue, Playa Maki, and at Petrohué, a

National Parks Environment Centre with display and slide show (camping US$4.50), near *Hotel Petrohué*; an unofficial one by lake shore 1 km. beyond *Hotel Ensenada* at Playa Larga, basic.

A dirt road runs 31 km. SE from Ensenada along the wooded lower Petrohué valley to **Ralún**, on the salt-water Estuario de Reloncaví. Here is the *Hotel Ralún*, a magnificent timber building to a fine modern design by Cristián de Groote, with a choice of rooms or cabins, warmly recommended, A (25 % more in summer than rest of year) plus US$35 p.p. full board. Telex 40048 Santiago or 70071 Puerto Montt; address Casilla 1044, Puerto Montt. Bus from Ensenada, US$0.70, daily 1015; also from Puerto Varas, 3 times a week.

Lake Todos los Santos has no roads round it, but from Petrohué a rather poor road (recommended only for jeeps) runs N through mountain land to the ski-ing hut on La Picada; the hut is more usually reached from Ensenada or Osorno.

As for the lake itself, its shores are deeply wooded and several small islands rise from its surface; in its waters are reflected the slopes of Osorno volcano. (Only experienced climbers should attempt to climb right to the top, ice climbing equipment required; there is a shelter for hikers.) Beyond the hilly shores to the E are several graceful snow-capped mountains, with the mighty Tronador in the distance. To the N is the sharp point of Cerro Puntiagudo (2,278 metres), and at the north-eastern end Cerro Techado (1,720 metres) rises cliff-like out of the water. Visitors stay at the *Hotel Peulla* for the night when going into or coming out of Argentina. (Tours have priority at hotel.) For those who stay longer there are motor launches for excursions on the lake; two good day trips are to Cayutué and Río Blanco. The only way to reach Petrohué from Cayutué is by boat, US$28, and you may have to wait several days. The *Esmeralda* (or *Don Ricardo*) crosses Lake Todos los Santos in 2 hrs.

Puerto Montt, capital of the Tenth Region, 1,064 km. from Santiago, is the terminus of the railway; the Longitudinal Highway is being extended south towards Aysén. The first German colonists arrived in 1852; they have remained to this day a small but influential percentage of the 106,000 inhabitants. The houses are mostly faced with unpainted shingles; here and there stand structures in the Alpine manner, all high pitched roofs and quaint balconies. The handicrafts market by the port merits a visit. See the little fishing port of Angelmó and sample its shellfish or fresh cooked crab; Angelmó is 2 km. from the centre of town and is also noted for its handicrafts. It has become a tourist centre.

The port is much used by fishing boats and coasting vessels, and it is here that passengers embark for the island of Chiloé, for Puerto Aysén, and for the long haul S to Punta Arenas. A paved road runs 55 km. SW to Pargua, where there is a ferry service to Chiloé, and to Chaitén, where it connects with the new highway to Coyhaique in the south.

Hotels Check Tourist Office. *Vicente Pérez Rosales*, Antonio Varas 447, Tel.: 2571-3, A, with bath, recommended, excellent restaurant, seafood and tourist information; *Colina*, Talca 81, D, with bath, new; *Montt*, Av. Varas and Quillota, C, with bath, D without, poor water supply but clean, friendly, good value (good restaurant); *Royal*, E, reasonably-priced, good meals; *Hostal Panorama*, San Felipe 192, E, crowded meeting place for Europeans and Americans (good restaurant), great view; *Benavente*, on Benavente, E; *Millahue*, D, Copiapó 64, good food; *Ramwiller*, Quillota 108, near railway station, E; *Burg*, Pedro Montt and Portales, modern, central heating, centrally located, C; *Bahía*, opposite dock gates, E; *Royas*, Quillota 136, E, near railway station, very nice. *Los Abedules*, Agr. Esc. 55 Pelluco, C, with bath; *Miramar*, A. Bello 972, E, opposite bus terminal; *Melipulli*, Libertad 10, D, poor, dirty; *Bologna*, Ibáñez; *Petorca*, San Martín 233 good, residential, E, with breakfast; *El Nave*, on hill by bus station, F with breakfast, spotless. Many private homes give you a bed for US$4, look for signs in windows, particularly recommended is *Casa Haraldo Steffen*, Serrano 286 (Tel.: 3823), F, with breakfast, excellent, homemade bread and jam, free transport to/from bus station; Sr. Altmann, Guillermo Gallardo 552; *Uncle Renato*, Guillermo Gallardo 621, US$1 with own sleeping bag; Balmaceda 300, F, incl. breakfast, good dinners, US$1.50, warmly recommended; *Residencial El Sol*, Chorrillo 1592, shabby, run down, F; *Residencial Embassy*, Calle Valdivia, E, clean; *Residencial Talquino*, Pérez Rosales 114-116, near bus terminal, F, hot water, clean; at Gmo. Gallardo 415, Sra Luciana Lazo, E. *Hospedaje Alemán*, F. Student hostel at Guillermo Gallardo 190, F; there are also several inexpensive hostels in Calle Huasco, e.g. at Nos. 2, 16 and 126, F, with breakfast, and private house at No. 131, with large garden, E, as well as in Calle V. Pérez Rosales, near bus station. Also J. J. Mira 1002, F, excellent, breakfast included; Aníbal Pinto 328, F, friendly, recommended; Sr. Raúl Arroyo at Concepción 136, F (recommended); Illapel 129, D; and Calle Vial 750, Ida Soto de Arras, F, very friendly.

Youth Hostels Information is available from Albergues Juveniles de la X Región, Urmeneta 183, Puerto Montt, Tel.: 2384, open only in summer.

Camping At Chinquihue, 10 km. W of Puerto Montt (bus service), about US$1.50 p.p. open October-April US$8 per site, for any size of tent. Each site has table, two benches, barbecue and plenty of shade. Toilets and showers. Small shop, no kerosene. Good camping shop, "Winkles", on Calle Varas. "Wild" camping possible along the front. 4 km. E of Puerto Montt, Copec have a network of 18 "Rutacentas" between Quillagua and Puerto Montt, which, apart from selling petrol and oil, have good shower (US$0.25) and toilet facilities and restaurants.

Restaurants *Embassy*, Ancud 104 and Pelluco, is recommended for reasonably priced seafood; *Club de Yates*, good, Av. J.S. Manfredini, on waterfront beyond railway station; *Super Yoco*, Urmeneta 478, very reasonable and good; *Patache* in Angelmó, try *picoroco al vapor*, a giant barnacle whose flesh looks and tastes like crab; *Café Real*, Rancagua 137, near main plaza, good for coffee and cakes; *Nettuno*, Illapel 129, cheap Italian food, good atmosphere; *Al Passo*, A.Varas 626; *Savoy*, Rancagua 256; *German Club*, Varas 264, reasonable set meal, good beer; *El Bodegón*, popular, Mexican as well as local music; *Café Thomas*, Copiapó, pub with local music; *Café-Restaurant Kiel*, Capilla 298, Chinquihue, 9 km. from centre, owner Helga Birker de Bauer speaks excellent German, Danish and English, lovely view over bay. *La Rinconada*, Antonio Varas 1101, highly recommended, friendly, large portions and live music; *Café Central*, Rancagua 117 and A. Varas, good atmosphere and pastries. *La Llave*, by the sea, in railway station. On road to Chinquihue, *Restaurant Stop* recommended. *Café Amsel*, Pedro Montt y Portales, good variety and quality; fish restaurants in market and along wharves, recommended. Restaurants in market at Angelmó highly recommended for fish (not so good for hygiene), as is the "restaurant-ship" at the ro/ro terminal with its *congrio frito* and *erizos* (ask prices first as there is no menu). *Curanto*, a national dish (seafood, chicken, sausages and potatoes), at the "restaurant-ship" *Catepumontt*, highly recommended. Bakery: *La Estrella*, Gallardo 174, self-service, good.

Shopping Woollen goods and Mapuche-designed rugs. Cheaper at roadside stalls between port and market than at tourist shops in town. Angelmó, west along the waterfront, sells reasonably priced wool articles.

Museum at Quillota 124, interesting. Open Mon.-Fri. 0915-1245, 1415-1740; Sat., Sun. 1000-1300, 1500-1900. See also private collection at Museo Chiloye, Calle M. Rodríguez.

Car Hire Hertz, Urmeneta 1036; Automóvil Club de Chile, Cauquenes 75 and airport.

Banks You are advised to change money here if visiting Chiloé as reports indicate that few banks offer that service on the island. Only Banco del Estado, Banco Chile and Lan-Chile office offer good rates. *Hotel Pérez Rosales*, Andino Sur travel agency and Patagonia Tours will change money at parallel market rate. Viajes Alerce, A.Varas 445, will change travellers' cheques as well as cash. Try also *Café Real*, Calle Rancagua 137.

Consulates Argentine (US citizens need visas), Cauquenes 94, 2nd floor; Dutch, Talca 119; German, O'Higgins 114, and Spanish, Rancagua 113.

Laundry Opposite Banco O'Higgins on Pedro Montt.

Books Useful pamphlet, in English, published monthly "Bienvenidos a Puerto Montt" - NSD Publications, Calle Quillota, or free from certain hotels.

Tourist Office Edif. Intendencia Regional, Av. Xa. Región 480, Tel.: 4580. Open 0900-1400 Mon.-Fri., 0900-1300 Sat., Sun. Also at bus terminal and annex in railway station. Town maps available. Best map for the region is the blue "Atlas Caminero de Chile".

Rail Station at San Felipe 50. Daily to Santiago, via Osorno (US$1.50), and Temuco. Daily *expreso* to Santiago leaves at 0900, 23 hrs. Rápido at 1715, 16-19 hrs., US$18.45-25.25 for beds in compartment; *salón* US$12.65, *económico* US$9.20. Ticket office opens at 0830 for Expreso and 0900 for Rápido.

Bus Service Bus station on sea front, at Av. Diego Portales and Av. Lota. To Puerto Varas (US$0.65) and Osorno every 30 min., US$1.70, 1½ hrs.; to Santiago, express 15 hrs., US$15 first class, 10 second; Varmontt are the most expensive, double-decker bus (US$25 including cocktails, cold dinner, breakfast). Bus service to Punta Arenas, Bus Norte, Fri. 1300, 38 hrs. US$55, also Turibus US$60. Many buses daily to Valdivia, US$2.50, to Bariloche, US$17.50 with Bus Norte (daily 0830), Tas-Choapa (thrice weekly) and Rápido Argentino Lanín (4 times), or with Andina del Sud, Mon.-Sat. 0900, US$42 inclusive (see also routes to Argentina given on page 435 and 437). Quellón, US$4. Ferry-buses to Chiloé (several), to Ancud, US$1.75, Castro US$2.50. Empresa Andina del Sud, very close to central tourist office, Varas 437 (Casilla 15-D, Tel.: 3253) sells tour to Puerto Varas, Parque Nacional V.P. Rosales, Petrohué, Lago Todos los Santos, Peulla and back.

Hitch-hiking is difficult and may take as long as four days between Puerto Montt and Bariloche.

432 CHILE

Air Service Ladeco run 3-5 flights a week to Coyhaique/Balmaceda, and daily flights to Santiago, US$65, and Punta Arenas, US$88. In January, February and March you may well be told that the plane to Punta Arenas is booked up; however, cancellations may be available from the airport. There are air force flights to Punta Arenas about once every two weeks (ask at Tourist Office for telephone number); seat availability is only known when plane arrives from Santiago, price about US$27 compared with US$70 Lan-Chile which has daily flights to Santiago. TAC, Fokker 27, run twice daily flights to Chaitén and Coyhaique (will stop at Puerto Aysén if 6 or more passengers want to get off there). El Tepual airport is 16 km. from town, bus from ETC Terminal, Pedro Montt. Bus to centre of town, US$1. Lan-Chile and Ladeco offices at Benevente 305 and 350, TAC, Gmo. Gallardo 167.

Shipping Service The roll-on/roll-off vehicle ferry m/n *Evangelistas* of Nisa-Navimag (Naviera Magallanes S.A.) run about every ten days to Puerto Natales, taking 3-4 days. Fares range from US$170 to US$300 depending on cabin (all double with bath, 4 meals included per day). Book as far ahead as possible (at least 6 weeks). First-class reservations handled in Santiago (see page 401). The dramatic 1,460 km. journey first goes through Seno Reloncaví and Canal Moraleda. From Bahía Anna Pink along the coast and then across the Golfo de Peñas to Bahía Tarn it is a 12-17 hrs. sea crossing, usually rough. The journey continues through Canal Messier, Angostura Inglesa, Paso del Indio and Canal Kirke (one of the narrowest routes for large shipping). The only regular stop is made off Puerto Edén (1 hr. south of the Angostura Inglesa), where the local Alacalufe Indians come out to sell their shellfish.

The m/n *Calbuco* of Empremar (Empresa Marítima del Estado) leaves Puerto Montt every Tuesday at 2000. One week she serves the "Línea Cordillera" with stops at Ayacará, Buill, Chaitén, R. Marín Balmaceda, Melimoyu, Puyuhuapi, Puerto Cisnes, Puerto Aguirre, Puerto Chacabuco; the next week she serves the "Línea Combinada" with stops at Ayacará, Chaitén, Quellón, Melinka, Seno Gala, Puyuhuapi, Puerto Cisnes, Puerto Aguirre, Puerto Chacabuco. Arr. Puerto Chacabuco on Fridays at 0800, sails at 2200 and returns to Puerto Montt on Mondays at 0800. From late December through early March she sails from Puerto Chacabuco on Fridays at 2100, stays Saturdays 0900 to 1900 at Laguna San Rafael, calls again at Puerto Chacabuco on Sundays at 0800 and returns to Puerto Montt on Tuesdays at 0800. She is a simple ship with only 4 berths in 2 cabins plus 36 seats in tourist class and 53 seats in 3rd class. Sailing dates are published in "El Mercurio" newspaper.

Between early December and late March, the m/n *Quellón* of Empremar leaves Puerto Montt on Saturdays at 1400, calling at Melinka, Pto. Aguirre, Pto. Chacabuco, Laguna San Rafael, Puerto Cisnes, Puyuhuapi, Castro and returns to Puerto Montt on Fridays at 0800. This journey is sold on a round-trip basis only by Transcontainer S.A. in Santiago and Puerto Montt. Fares range from US$396 to 510.

The m/n *Skorpios* of Constantino Kochifas C. leaves Pto. Montt on Saturdays at 1100 for a luxury cruise with stops at Puerto Aguirre, Quitralco, Laguna San Rafael, Melinka, Castro and returns to Puerto Montt on Fridays at 0800.

Transmarchilay Ltda. run the ferry *Pincoya* from Pargua or Conchi to Chaitén and back and the ferry *El Colono* between Quellón and Puerto Chacabuco. For sailing dates, their timetable should be consulted.

Shipping Offices in Puerto Montt: Navimag, Terminal Transbordadores Angelmó, Tel.: 3754, Telex 270055. Empremar/Transcontainer, Av. Diego Portales 1450, Tel. 2548, Telex 370001 EMAR CK. Constantino Kochifas C., Angelmó 1660 (Castilla 588), Tel.: 2952, Telex 270028 NATUK CL. Transmarchilay Ltda., Angelmó 1668, Tel.: 4654, telex 270031. Fares: Pto. Chacabuco-Laguna San Rafael rt. US$60-85; Pto. Montt.-Pto. Chacabuco. o.w. US$20-30. We are deeply grateful to Hans K. Wagner (Winterthur, Switzerland) for this revised information.

Excursions The wooded island of Tenglo, close to Puerto Montt and reached by launch, is a favourite place for picnics. Magnificent view from the summit. The island is famous for its *curantos*, a local dish. (*Hostería Miramar*, F, with breakfast, basic, but a nice view overlooking the port of Angelmó; *Hoffmann*.) Chamiza, up the River Coihuin, has fine fishing. There is a bathing beach at Pelluco (*Gran Papa*, opposite ETC bus terminal, good chicken; *Restaurant Juan Pazos*, recommended), a fair walk from Puerto Montt. The (cargo) launch trip up the Reloncaví estuary (8 hrs.) is very beautiful, fjords, sealions, local colour, and recommended. At **Cochamó**, at the end of the estuary, there is a small hotel, *Hotel Cochamó*, basic but clean, F, good meals; *Hostería Bayer*, Pocoyhúen (one can stay at the village hall at Cochamó for US$1.05). Sra. Flora Sauvientes also offers rooms above her bar/restaurant/drugstore, F; cheapest accommodation in a house by the pier (floor space only). Cochamó itself is pretty but limited; a side trip is to the Termas de Sotomó, but this requires an affinity for mud. Boats to Cochamó from Puerto Montt leave Tues. to Sun. at 0830, US$4, taking up to nine hours (tip the locals who row you to the launch), returning to Puerto Montt next day. Once road to Puelo is complete, it will be possible to go by bus to Puelo then walk to Cochamó. Advisable to take warm clothes and plenty of food, check at Angelmó port for details. An alternative by land is by bus to the head of the estuary, near Ralún (see page 430) then cross the Petrohué river by small boat, 3 times daily, US$0.80, then by bus to Cochamó. There is a beautiful hike from Cochamó through forests to Cayutúe (see the Bradts' book, *Backpacking in Chile and Argentina*, for route); the settlement is on Lake Todos los Santos and occasional boats go to Petrohué (see page 429); you can camp by the lake. The Maullin River, which rises in Lake Llanquihue, has some interesting waterfalls and good fishing (salmon). The little old town of **Maullin** (Motel El Pangal, A), at the mouth of the Maullin River, is worth a visit. **Calbuco** (Hostería Huito), centre of the fishing industry, with good scenery, can be visited direct boat or by road. Puerto Montt is a good centre for excursions to the lakes via Puerto Varas. From Puerto Montt to Puerto Varas by the old (dirt) road is a short but beautiful journey.

Isla Huar may be visited by boat from Angelmó harbour (1600, 2 hrs.); boat returns from other end of island at 0730. The north shore is rocky. Accommodation, if lucky, at the church; best to camp.

Chiloé island is 250 km. long, 50 km. wide, 9,613 sq. km., and has a population of 116,000. There are two main towns, Ancud and Castro (airport), and many fishing villages. Seaweed is harvested by Celpers for export to Japan. Typical of the island are substantial wooden houses ("*palafitos*") built on stilts over the water. The hillsides in summer are a patchwork quilt of wheat fields and dark green plots of potatoes. Inland are impenetrable forests. There has recently been appreciable development, and power and water shortages and poor sanitation are now things of the past. Though the weather is often cold and foggy, the island is extremely beautiful when the sun is out. Sweaters and woollen caps are good purchases. Music is popular, with many players in the waterfront cafés in Castro. The local sailing sloops, *lanchas*, are fast being replaced by diesels, in fact more can be seen in Puerto Montt now.

From Puerto Montt buses run 15 times a day to Pargua (55 km.) on the Straits of Chacao. (At Chacao, *Pensión Chiloé*, F; *Hospedaje Angelino*, F.) The harbour water is beautifully clear. Buses drive onto ferry across the Chacao Strait to Chiloé, then to Ancud and Castro. The trip passes through beautiful scenery with a great variety of wildlife: pelicans, seals, penguins and albatross. There are 12 trips a day to Chiloé by the ferryboat (US$0.50); cars US$3.50. The Tourist Office brochure, *Conozca a Chiloé*, free, is recommended.

Ancud Beautiful views, Spanish fort (Fuerte San Antonio) and powder magazine restored in 1975-76, a regional museum on the Plaza de Armas (entry, US$0.25), the tourist office, Libertad 370, and craft shops (speciality is basketwork). Oyster beds interesting. Buses everyday to Mar Brava and Playa de Pumillahue, 20 km. east of Ancud.

Hotels *Hostería A. de Ercilla*, San Antonio 30, a most interesting building, C, recommended; *General Quintanilla*, Libertad 751, recommended, C, with bathroom and breakfast, good but expensive restaurant; *Lidia*, D with bath, E without, breakfast extra; *Convento de la Concepción Imaculada*, Calle Chacabuco 841, offers youth-hostel type accommodation, F, somewhat unfriendly, no showers; *Residencial Montenegro*, Río Blanco and Dieciocho, F, fair, hot water; *Residencial* on Aníbal Pinto 515, good, F. *Talleres Artes*, F; *Hospedaje de T. Germania*, E, clean; Sra. María Aguilar de Pávez, Cochrane 407, F, hot water, use of kitchen, family meals; *Residencial Wescheler*, D, clean, unfriendly. In summer, the school on Calle Chacabuco is open for lodging, US$1.30 p.p.

Campsite 5 km. W of town.

Restaurants Excellent. Seafoods, especially king crabs (very cheap), *almejos* and cheese in market area. *Polo Sur*, on seafront, good but not cheap; *Coral*, Pudeto 346, good, cheap; *Jardín*, same street No. 263; *Macaval*, Chacabuco 691; *Pica del Loco*, A.Prat; *El Tirol*, Maipú 746.

Bus Ancud-Castro, US$1; frequent buses daily on both routes, 1½ hrs. No direct Sunday bus from Ancud to Dalcahue, need to stay in Castro. To Puerto Montt, US$1.75.

Shipping Transmarchilay has offices in Ancud, Libertad 669 (Tel.: 317-279, Telex 270071).

Castro Capital of the Province and a very friendly town, 88 km. from Ancud. Tremendous variety of styles in housing. Waterfront market (Thurs.). Large cathedral (1906) with excellent

434 CHILE

wooden interior on the Plaza de Armas, built by Italian architect, Eduardo Provosoli; the outside of the cathedral is an unusual shade of orange. One-room museum (Blanco Encalada 261) contains history, folklore, handicrafts and mythology of Chiloé. Very good views of the city from Millantuy hill above the cemetery, which is legendary. Helpful tourist office in main square.

Hotels Several cheap hotels near main plaza, F; *Residencial Mirasol*, San Martín 815, good, F; *Splendid*, Blanco Encalada 266, F with breakfast, and a modern, attractive *hostería*, A. *La Bomba*, Esmeralda, E, without bath, decent, hot water (showers may be rented for US$1), 3 course menu (US$4). *Residencial Lidia*, Blanco Encalada 278, F, clean, cold shower; *Hostería Castro*, Chacabuco 202, Tel.: 301, A (restaurant) but 20% surcharge, interesting building; *Costa Azul*, F, Lillo 67; *Pensión Victoria*, San Martín 745, F; *Estrella*, O'Higgins 657; *Plaza*, Blanco 366, D, recommended on 3rd floor, breakfast included, good restaurant; *Motel Anquilda*, on way to Aeropuerto Gamboa, D. Rooms above *Restaurant Roto Chileno*, Calle Blanco Encalada, basic, F.

Restaurants *Café Plaza*, excellent; *Krill Café* and *La Amistad* (seafood); *Sampayes*, Calle Thompson 243, good food; *El Cangrejo*, good; *El Sacho*, Balmaceda 286, just off main plaza towards post office, good food, not too dear, clean; and others, like *Palafito*, on the waterfront and *Vista Hermosa*, south end of Calle Esmeralda, clean, wonderful views. *Confitería Haití*, Blanco Encalada 60, good pies.

Camping with permission from controllers at airfield; some water available. Motel opposite will change money. Banco del Estado de Chile on main square accepts travellers' cheques (at a poor rate). The Punta Arenas-Puerto Montt cargo boats call at Castro occasionally; US$2.50 to Puerto Montt (3¼ hrs.), last bus to ferry each day at 1715. Bus to Quellón (2 hrs.), US$1.50; to Ancud (1½ hrs.) US$1.

Doctor Muñoz de Las Carreras, near police station, surgery 1700-2000 on weekdays, recommended.

Tours Trans Chiloé, San Martín 359, Tel.: 497, day trips around the island, US$3 without food.

Dalcahue 21 km. N of Castro, the wooden church dates from 1858, on older foundations. Market on Sundays, excellent for woollens, from 0700 to 1300 at this picturesque village. Good choice early on, but better bargains in late morning. Tourist kiosk in season. Bus service from Castro. Colectivos also available. (*Pensión Montaña*, F, basic; *Pensión San Martín*, F).

From Castro, buses every day in summer, 3 a day (but none Tues. and Thurs.) otherwise, 2 hrs. US$1.40 (via Dalcahue and Curaca de Vélez de Achao; Dalcahue-Achao, US$0.75) and a ferry takes one to **Achao**, 39 km. away (*Hotel Splendid*, F, hot water; *Hotel Sao Paulo*, recommended, hot water, F; *Restaurant Octavio*, at waterfront, cheap and good; *Restaurant El Porvenir*, humble appearance but first class food and service; *Cocinería Insular*, F, friendly, recommended excellent breakfast; *Restaurante Cristina*, excellent seafood), a quiet, pretty fishing village with a lovely old wooden church, built in 1730, which inspired most other churches in the area (2-roomed museum close to church). It is possible to return to Castro same day. Many excursions S and W are available (best to take sleeping bags if visiting remote islands). Tourist office on the Plaza de Armas, highly recommended, provides excellent literature and good advice on accommodation. Good place to buy woollen goods. Camping possible on the shore—ask. Tenaún, 56 km. NE of Castro, is an interesting fishing village with a good 18th-century church, as has Vilpulli, 20 km. S of Castro. Quilquico, between Castro and Rilan, has a wooden church from 1767.

Chonchi, 25 km. S of Castro, is a picturesque fishing village with rambling shingled houses painted in many colours and a lively wharf for fishing (neo-classical wooden church, 1850). *Hotel El Sacho*, Centenario 102 (main street), F with breakfast and bath, recommended, and *Pensión Turismo*, also F. Rooms available at *Almacén la Patagonia* with Sra. Gamín Chacón, Calle Itudrade, corner Alvarez and Manuel Gómez, baker at P.J: Andrade 184, G with breakfast. Transmarchilay company runs a ferry service to Chaitén Tues., Thurs./Fri. 0800 (foot passengers must board much earlier) US$3.50 p.p., 5-6 hrs., return same day; office on Av. Costanera, Tel.: 66.

Visits to Queilen beach, the island of Lemuy and the village of Cucao are recommended. Lemuy Island, 90 sq. km., is quiet, with good walking through undulating pastures and woodland. Daily ferry service from Chonchi. The main town is Puqueldén which offers basic accommodation, clean, F, in Calle J. M. Carrera. *Restaurant Lemuy* is next to the municipal offices and *Café Amancay* opposite. Good walks to Lincay, 5 kms., or Lincura, one-day expedition.

Cucao, a village 40 km. west of Chonchi and the only settlement on the West coast of Chiloé, can now be reached by road. There is an immense 15 km. beach with thundering Pacific surf. Nearby is the Chiloé National Park (opened in 1984), with reception centre, small museum, helpful staff, guest bungalow available for visiting scientists (apply to Conaf, through your Embassy, stating environmental interests). The forests in the park are vast and impenetrable; ask at Conaf for directions or guides. Camping US$4.50 (beware of theft in Jan./Feb. season). Accommodation, F, with full board or *demi-pension* at Provisiones Pacífico, Sra. Boreuel or with Sra Luz Vera, next to school. Buses from Castro at 1100 on Tues., Thurs., and Sat., returning at 1430, and Sun. 0900, returning 1500; hitching is very difficult.

Quellón Southernmost port on Chiloé; 92 km. from Castro, fishing boats built at wharf, pleasant beaches (*Hotel Playa*, P. Montt 255, F; restaurant; same street, *Hostería Quellón*, E, basic; new hotel, *Yungay*; *Pensión Vera*, F, good, clean; *Hostería La Pincoya*, La Paz 64, F). Daily service from Castro to Quellón, US$1.50, 2 hrs. Transmarchilay ferries leave 1500 for Puerto Chacabuco, Aysén, Tues., Thurs. and Sun., returning from Chacabuco Mon., Wed. and Fri. (more sailings in summer), 18-hr. trip, US$18 for Pullman seat, US$9.50 ordinary seat (IYHF card holders can buy spare tickets for US$5.75) all luggage has to be stowed (tickets must be bought the day before travelling; can be purchased in Coyhaique at 0900 the day before or in Transmarchilay office in Quellón-Pedro Montt 265, Tel.: 290, Ancud, or Puerto Montt) takes vehicles. A cargo boat, *Marítimo*, also does this route, but takes longer. Timetable should be obtained from tourist office and foot passengers should note that priority is given to those travelling in vehicles. Lovely trip (forested islands, snow-capped peaks in background) dolphins and small penguins may be seen en route.

The islanders of Chiloé were the last supporters of the Spanish Crown. When Chile rebelled the last of the Spanish Governors fled to the island and, in despair, offered it to Britain. Canning turned the offer down. The island finally surrendered to the patriots in 1826, the last remaining Spanish possession in South America.

Currency If going on south, stock up well with Chilean pesos. It is difficult to change money at the weekend.

Part of Chiloé Province is on the mainland. The port of **Chaitén** (a drab, expensive place), has grown in importance because of the military camp and surveying for the new road (*Restaurant/Hotel Mi Casa*—on a hill—recommended, E with bath, negotiable; large youth hostel, F, sleep on floor; also, *Hostería Schilling*, C, on waterfront; shopping and most facilities); ferry to Chonchi, 1500, Tues., Thurs. and Fri., US$3.50, 5-6 hrs each way; m/n *Calbuco* from Quellón every second week, and weekly from Puerto Montt (but check schedules in Puerto Montt in advance); flights to Puerto Montt, US$37.50. A road runs to Puerto Cárdenas (good *hostal*) on Lake Yelcho (public bus service), 46 km. (26 km. from Chaitén on this road are thermal springs, free bathing in mud bath or covered pools, camping, refreshments available); at the other end of the lake, around which a road now runs, is Puerto Ramírez (*Hostería Río Malito*—Sr. Soto—nearby, rooms, camping, fishing), whence there are two roads to the Argentine border at Futaleufú (*Hotel Carahue*, F, and others) and Palena. It is possible to travel from Chaitén, via border towns of Futaleufú and Palena, to Esquel in Argentina, the starting point for several Argentine national parks. **N.B.** Only transit visas are issued at border points, so you must either leave within 10 days or renew your entry stamp at an immigration office.

In February 1982 a road was opened from Puerto Chaitén to Coyhaique, known as Carretera Austral Presidente Pinochet. Useful information about the state of the road can be obtained at Chaitén. Once complete (in 1988) the road will link Puerto Montt to Coyhaique. It goes through tall forests and wild mountain scenery; on fine days many peaks, icefields and glaciers may be seen. Few buses: Coyhaique—La Junta weekly and minibus Coyhaique—Puerto Cisnes twice a week. Private *micros* charge US$18.50 from Puerto Chaitén to Coyhaique, with an overnight stop in La Junta. To appreciate the route fully, you can hitch and walk (because little traffic) the unpaved, but well-maintained 420 km. from Chaitén to Coyhaique (can be done in 2 days with a lot of luck, but allow up to 10 days if stopping en route). There is superb salmon fishing in the rivers, and the local people are very friendly. 25 km. from Chaitén is Amarillo; 5 km. from the village are thermal baths (2 wooden sheds with very hot pool inside), camping possible. From the thermal baths it is possible to hike along the old trail to Futaleufú, 4-7 days, not for the inexperienced, be prepared for wet feet all the way. The trail follows the River Michinmawida (passing the volcano of the same name) to Lake Espolón. Ferry across early Mon. and Thurs., US$1, then 8 km. to Futaleufú. Campsite at this end of the lake also has bungalows. At Puerto Cárdenas there are 2 places to stay (out of 3 houses and a police post), full board available; beautiful setting. At Costa Brava (a few km. S of Santa Lucía—one shop, bread from a private house) there is a military camp with no accommodation or shops. It is necessary to continue to La Junta, at the confluence of Río Rosselof and Río Palena, Km. 270 from Coyhaique, a drab village, but the fishing is good; *pensión* available and walks to Lake Rosselof beautiful. Puerto Puyuguapi, about half way, at the end of the Puyuguapi Canal, is an intriguing town built by Germans fifty years ago. There are several springs with 50° C water filling two pools near the beach. Accommodation is available in a large wooden house on the right-hand side of the road which leads from the quayside through the village, 150 metres before the police post, owned by Sra. Ursula Flack Kronscheky, very good board and lodging; alternatively, 300 metres south at Sur Rolando, stay at Sra. Sophía's house. There is a general store behind the petrol station. Transport out of Puyuguapi is very scare. At Puerto Cisnes along the Seno Ventisquero (33 km. from the main road), you can buy food and find accommodation (*Posada del Graal*, E, recommended, as is *Posada Gaucho*, F with breakfast, dinner available, also a youth hostel). Parque Nacional Queulat (Km. 160 on Carretera Austral) near-by, is, according to legend, the place where the rich town of Césares once was. The Colgado glacier can be seen from the park. The Río Cisnes is recommended for rafting or canoeing; 160 km. of grand scenery, with modest rapids except for the horrendous drop at Piedra del Gato; there is a 150 metre cliff at Torre Bright Bank. Good camping in the forest. At Cisne Medio, there is a road to La Tapera and to the Argentine border. Villa

436 CHILE

Mañihuales, 20 km. S of El Tocqui copper mine, is connected by bus with Coyhaique and Puerto Aysén; there is a hotel (F) or you may be able to sleep in the school during the holidays.

Archipelagic Chile   From Puerto Montt and Chiloé to Cape Horn.

		Population ('000)	
Region	Old Provinces	1975	1982
XI	Aysén	57	67
XII	Magallanes and Antarctic Territory	101	131

South of Puerto Montt lies a third of Chile, but its land and its climate are such that it has been put to little human use: less than 3 % of the country's population lives here. It is one of the wettest regions on earth: over 5,000 mm of rain fall on some of it and the sun only shines through a blanket of mist and cloud on 51 days of the year. Storms occur most often in spring, though the heaviest rain falls in the winter. Impenetrable forest covers most of the land. It is only the northern part, as far south as Coyhaique—and the far S that are inhabited. S of Chiloé, for 1,100 km., there is a maze of islands—the tops of submerged mountains—separated by tortuous fjord-like channels, a veritable topographical hysteria. It is fortunate for shipping that this maze has a more or less connected route through it: down the channel between Chiloé and the mainland, about 290 km. of open sea beyond the southern tip of Chiloé and then down the Moraleda, Mesier, Inocentes and Smyth channels into the Straits of Magellan. In some places along this route the tide levels change by 12 metres. In one particular place two sharp-cut walls, 900 metres high, enclose the constricted channel which leads to Puerto Natales; here the waters are deeper than the cliffs are high and slack water lasts for 30 mins. only. The Smyth Channel enters the Straits of Magellan at Cape Thamar. January and February are probably the best months for a trip to this region.

Lan-Chile has excellent air services to Balmaceda (for Puerto Aysén), Coyhaique and Magallanes from Puerto Montt. Air force flights half-price.

The rainy Eleventh Region (Aysén) lies between Chiloé and Magallanes. The main port of Aysén, **Puerto Chacabuco** (with *Parque Turístico Loberías de Aysén*, B, *Hotel Moraleda*, *Res. Chacabuco* and *Res. El Puerto*, all F), is 15 km. from Puerto Aysén. There is a bus service (daily except Sun.), US$0.20, but make sure to reserve seats.

Puerto Aysén, no longer a port, population 20,000, has good connections with Argentina and daily bus service at 1000 to Coyhaique, 67 km. away. The road from Puerto Aysén to Coyhaique passes through the Parque Nacional Río Simpson, with beautiful waterfalls. Folklore festival in 2nd week of November. Walk to Laguna los Palos, 2 hrs., recommended.

Hotels *Gran Hotel Aysén*, Chacabuco 130, E; *Central*; *Plaza*, O'Higgins 217, F; *La Bomba*, Merino 791, F; *Roxy*, Aldea 796, F. *Residencial Marina*, Sgto. Aldea 382, E, clean, only cold water. *Rosey*, F; *Gastromonía y Residencial Carrera*, Carrera 1031, off main plaza offers excellent lunch for under US$2. No campsite but free camping easy.

Bank on Plaza de Armas will only change cash, not travellers' cheques.

Post Office on other side of bridge from Plaza de Armas.

Bus to Puerto Chacabuco, US$0.20, colectivo US$6.

Shipping Empremar office at Teniente Marinero 778; luxurious cruise line, Constantino Kochifas Carclamo, Teniente Marinero 868; Tel.: 342; the owner of a 65 ft. sailing yacht, who organizes 4 day cruises to Laguna San Rafael (US$500), lives on the plaza opposite Ladeco office.

A ferry service runs from Puerto Chacabuco (Aysén) via the Canal Moraleda to Quellón on Chiloé on Mon. and Fri. and takes 19 hours (US$9.50 seat, US$18 Pullman seat); meals are available. Beware of fleas. Information from Transportes Marítimos Chiloé-Aysén (Transmarchilay), Ancud, Puerto Montt (addresses under towns), or Av. O'Higgins s/n, Pto. Chacabuco (144).

Coyhaique (population, 30,000) is the administrative and commercial centre of the region, located in a large green valley surrounded by mountains. The town provides a good base for hiking and skiing excursions in the area and has a good museum on the corner of Condell and Coyhaique. Excellent views of the Río Simpson valley from the hill, 4 hrs. walk north of town, at Reserva Forestal.

Hotels at Coyhaique (rooms in short supply): *Chible*, José de Moraleda 440, C; *Residencial Puerto Varas*, Serrano 168, F hot water, recommended; *Hostería Coyhaique*, on La Onza, B, poor beds, unreliable hot water, good restaurant *Los Nires*, Baquedano 315, Tel.: 21329, C; *Pensión América*, 21 de Mayo, F, basic and cheap. *Motel Hostal del Rey*, near buses, D with kitchen, bath and heater; *Residencial Tejas Verdes*, Baquedano 198, E; Sub-Teniente Cruz 57, F, off Plaza de Armas, basic. *Residencial* at Cochrane 532 (no sign), F, quite nice. Camping at Laguna Verde in Reserva Forestal is free.

Restaurants *Parador Munich*, Prat y Dussen, pizzas and sandwiches; *Café Oriente*, Calle 21 de Mayo y Condell, good bakery, tea; *El Colonial*, Barroso 713, Tel.: 22452, good food and folk music; *Café Kalu*, A. Prat 402, serves good hamburgers. *Café Ricer*, Calle Horn, cheap.

Shopping Three large well stocked supermarkets; dehydrated camping food available. Food, especially fruit and vegetables, is much more expensive than in Santiago.

Car Hire Automóvil Club de Chile, Prat 348, rents Suzuki jeeps if reserved in advance in Santiago (see page 399).

Bank will change travellers' cheques.

Tourist Office Av. Baquedano and Lillo, ground floor, good, Tel.: 21752. Conaf office on Parra and Moraleda.

Empremar/Transcontainer office, 21 de Mayo 758, Tel.: 22586, Telex 281060 EMAR CL. Transmarchilay, 21 de Mayo 417, Tel.: 21971, Telex 281057.

Buses Comodoro Rivadavia (Argentina), twice weekly, US$45, 12 hrs.; Puerto Aysén-Coyhaique, 3 times daily, US$1.75, Puerto Chacabuco, US$2. Puerto Cisnes on Tues. and Sat. at 1400; La Junta, Mon. at 0900. There are now daily buses to Mañihuales and Balmaceda and to Chile Chico; to Chaitén on Mon. (overnight at La Junta;) Wed., Fri., Sat. to Puerto Ibáñez on Lake Carrera, the Chilean section of Lake Buenos Aires (US$4.50); ask at *Residencial Tejas Verdes*, Baquedano 198.

Travel to Argentina Unless hiking, better to go via Coyhaique Alto rather than by Balmaceda, where crossing only allowed to Chileans and Argentines. Transport to Los Antiguos in Argentina by van (US$4). Beware, many border posts closed at weekends.

Air Ladeco (office at Gral. Parra 210, Tel.: 21188) to Puerto Montt (US$31), Punta Arenas, March-Dec. only and Santiago. To Comodoro Rivadavia (Arg.), departs Tues. 0700. Air taxi to visit glaciers, US$400 (five passengers), also to southern archipelagic region. Charter flights: Taxi Aéreo Hein, Bilbao 968, Tel.: 21028, 21172. TAC, Lillo 315, Tel.: 21889, to Puerto Montt. Transporte Aéreo "Don Carlos", Subteniente Cruz 65, Tel.: 21981 to Chile Chico and Cochrane.

Excursions Several reserves: Reserva Forestal Mañihuales, 76 km. from Coyhaique, has largely been destroyed by forest fires, but Reserva Forestal Lago Las Torres, 126 km., is worth a visit. There is a free camping place and the lake is full of fish. To reach **Chile Chico** (population of town 800, of region 2,400), a flourishing town on Lake Carrera, one can either go by boat from Puerto Ibáñez or go through Argentina. The town feels much like Argentina, and will remain isolated from the rest of Chile until the Carretera Gen. Pinochet is completed in 1988. The region prides itself in having the best climate in Southern Chile with some 300 days of sunshine; much fruit is grown as a result. Rainfall is very low but strong winds are common. The lake itself covers 2,240 sq. km.; the Chilean end is predominantly Alpine and the Argentine end (Lake Buenos Aires, 881 sq. km.) dry pampa. **Hotels** at Chile Chico: *Aguas Azules*, E, recommended; *Refugio*, on Plaza. *Residenciales Frontera*, E and *Nacional*, F. Youth hostel in school from Jan. to end Feb. **Restaurants** *Almacén Elizabeth* on Plaza serves coffee and delicious homemade cakes; will prepare meals if asked. Ask at the Municipalidad for help in arranging tours.

Regular services by Transmarchilay car ferry, *El Pilchero*, along the lake, leave Chile Chico for Puerto Ibáñez twice a week (3 times in January) each way (1½ hrs, each way: US$2 p.p. US$26 for car; offices in Ancud or Coyhaique). At **Puerto Ibáñez** there are three *residenciales*: *Ibáñez*, *Mónica* (both F), and *Hostería Batada Río Ibañez*, E. Chile Chico is connected by road S only as far as Fachinal (50 km.); from where there is a trail to Mallín Grande and Puerto Guadal. A road from Guadal leads to Puerto Bertrán and on to Cochrane on Lake Cochrane. Trails through the valley of Río Baker to Puerto Yungay are recommended for serious walkers and horses can be hired to go up into the mountains. There are bus services to Coyhaique (Particular thanks are due to Dieter Reinmuth of Kiel, W. Germany, for help with this section.)

Some 150 nautical miles south of Puerto Aysén is the Laguna San Rafael glacier, 30 metres above sea level, and 45 km. in length. It calves small icebergs, carried out to sea by wind and tide. The thick vegetation on the shores, with snowy peaks above, is typical of Aysén. The glacier is one of a group of four that flow in all directions from Monte San Valentín. This icefield is part of the Parque Nacional Laguna San Rafael (1.35m. hectares), one of Aysén's 12 national parks, all set up in

438 CHILE

1967 and now regulated by the National Forestry Council (Conaf). The only way there is by plane or by boat: Air Taxi from Coyhaique (C. Fischer, Bilbao 563, Tel.: 21712), US$160, or US$100 each if party of 12; some pilots in Puerto Aysén will fly to the glacier for about US$85, but many are unwilling to land on the rough airstrip. The glacier is best seen from the sea: there are expensive cruises (for instance those of Empremar, or Kochifas—offices in Santiago and Puerto Aysén); local fishing boats from Chacabuco/Puerto Aysén take about 18-20 hrs. each way, charging about US$120; the *Calbuco* of Empremar, a government supply ship, leaves Chacabuco on Fri. at 2100, returning from the Laguna on Sat. at 1800, arriving Chacabuco on Sun. at 0800, two lifeboats make the trip to the glacier (bring food as you may be left at the glacier for 3 hours). Operates to San Rafael only between December and March, book in advance in Aysén in Jan./Feb. season (all year round the *Calbuco* runs from Puerto Montt to Puerto Chacabuco). Cost Chacabuco-San Rafael and back is US$75 in cabin, US$18 1st class seat, US$9.50 bench seat; food is available at extra cost (on the return journey you can continue to any of stops back to, and including Puerto Montt, 48 hrs.). A hotel opened in 1984; also rooms can be hired for US$2 p.p. (bring a week's supply of food if planning to return on the *Calbuco*; also bring anti-mosquito cream). At the glacier there is a small ranger station. The rangers are willing to row you out to the glacier, a 3-hr. trip. Robert af Sandeberg (Lidingö, Sweden) describes this journey as follows:

"The trip in the rowboat is an awesome venture. At first it is fairly warm and easy to row. Gradually it gets colder when the wind sweeps over the icy glacier (be sure to bring warm clothes). It gets harder to row as small icebergs hinder the boat. Frequently somebody has to jump onto an icefloe and push the boat through. The glacier itself has a deep blue colour, shimmering and reflecting the light; the same goes for the icebergs, which are an unreal, translucent blue. The glacier is very noisy; there are frequent cracking and banging sounds, resembling a mixture of gun shots and thunder. When a hunk of ice breaks loose, a huge swell is created and the icebergs start rocking in the water. Then great care and effort has to be taken to avoid the boat being crushed by the shifting icebergs; this is a very real danger."

N.B. If you plan to go to Laguna San Rafael by boat, check first with the Gobernación Marítima in Puerto Aysén that the boat is licensed for the trip.

Chilean Patagonia

The Province of Magallanes, which includes the Chilean part of Tierra del Fuego, has 17.5% of Chile's total area, but it is inhabited by under 1% of Chile's population. In summer rains are frequent. In winter snow covers the country, except those parts near the sea. The country is then more or less impassable, except on horseback. Strong, cold, piercing winds blow, particularly during the spring, when they reach a velocity of 70 to 80 km. an hour. During the winter they do not blow all that hard, and from May to August a strong wind is almost exceptional. The dry winds parch the ground and prevent the growth of crops, which can only be cultivated in sheltered spots.

Until the discovery of oil—Tierra del Fuego and N of Magellan Strait produce all Chilean oil—the most important industry was the breeding of sheep. At one time there was a large British colony there; it has been diminishing steadily of late. Coal has been discovered on the Chilean side of the frontier, at Pecket, but the mine is considered uneconomic; miners still cross into Argentina to work at Río Turbio.

Punta Arenas, the most southerly city in Chile, and capital of the Twelfth Region, 2,140 km. S of Santiago, is on the Straits of Magellan at almost equal distance from the Pacific and Atlantic oceans, 1,432 nautical miles from Valparaíso, and 1,394 from Buenos Aires. The population is about 80,000. Most of the smaller and older buildings are of wood, but the city has expanded rapidly, and practically all new building is of brick or concrete. All the main roads are paved and the country roads are of gravel; when driving in Patagonia, some form of windscreen protection is absolutely essential. Punta Arenas is a busy little city somewhat neater looking than the average Chilean town. The cemetery, at Bulnes 900, is even more fantastic than the one at Castro (Chiloé), with a statue of Indiocito, the little Indian, and many memorials to pioneer families and crews of shipping disasters (open 0800-1800 daily).

Punta Arenas is the centre of the sheep farming industry in that part of the world and exports wool, skins, and frozen meat. Besides the export of oil and gas, there is the regular carriage of crude between the Strait oil terminals and the refineries in central Chile. Good roads connect the city with (255 km.) Puerto

CHILE 439

Natales in Ultima Esperanza and Río Gallegos in Argentina. There are no railways. Punta Arenas has certain free-port facilities; the Zona Franca is 3½ km. N of the centre (open 1000-2000).

There is a modern museum in the Colegio Salesiano, "Mayorino Borgatello" dealing with the Indians, animal and bird life of the region, and other interesting aspects of life in Patagonia and Tierra del Fuego, at Av. Bulnes 374, entrance next to church. Open Tues., Thurs., Sat. 1500-1800, and Sun. 1000-1300 and 1500-1800. There is a municipal museum in Hernando Magallanes (open 1100-1300), with good dioramas (entry: US$0.50). Museo Histórico Regional de Magallanes, on Navarro, just off Plaza de Armas, located in a mansion built by one of the early millionaires, is well worth visiting; it contains a painting of two geese by Picasso's father as well as many marble sculptures. Tours in English, 1100 and 1300 only. Closed Mon. (entry US$0.35). The best sight is the Patagonian Institute at the N end of Av. Bulnes, which contains a collection of work tools from the colonial period. It has a small zoo with puma and condors, and a collection of old local vehicles and machinery. The Institute also has a botanical garden, and locally-spun woollen goods are sold nearby. The Cervantes theatre is so ornate it is worth buying a cinema ticket just to see it. The British School on Waldo Seguel, and St. James' Church next door, are wooden, in colonial style.

Festivals Festival Folclórica de la Patagonia, July 26-30.

Hotels *Cabo de Hornos*, telegraphic address Capotel, Plaza Muñoz Gamero 1025, Tel.: 22134, A, excellent, recommended; *Los Navegantes*, José Menéndez 647 (Casilla 230, Tel.: 23968), A, excellent restaurant, slightly cheaper than *Cabo de Hornos*; *Savoy*, same street, No. 1073, C; *Turismo Plaza*, José Nogueira 1126, D (cheaper without bath); *Posada del Tehuelche*, D, restaurant, bus to/from Río Gallegos makes lunch stops there; *Cervantes*, Calle Pedro Montt; *Colón*, Avenida Colón, E; *Lucerna*, Bories 624; *Monte Carlo*, Av. Colón 605, F, with breakfast, clean; *Residencial Ritz*, 3 blocks from main square toward ocean, D; *Residencial Villegas*, Boliviana 238, friendly, F with meals; *Residencial La Selecta*, O'Higgins, F; *Residencial París*, J. Nogueira 1116, at Plaza de Armas, 4th floor, D, recommended, though some rooms are without windows. *Residencial* at Armando Sanhuesa 965, F, hot shower, recommended, pleasant atmosphere, meals available; *Residencial Roca*, Calle Roca 973, clean and pleasant, 3 blocks seaward from main square, F, incl. breakfast; *Residencial* above *Restaurant Sobota* on Independencia, F, also good; *Casa Deportista*, O'Higgins, E, cheaper without breakfast, pleasant, quiet; *Albergue Juvenil*, Ramírez 845, F, 50 rooms; another in Jan. and Feb. on Escuela Portugal and Mejicana. *Pensión* at Boliviana 366, F, quiet, friendly, warm and comfortable. Also, private houses at Boliviana 340 (Nena's), 3 rooms, friendly, F, and Boliviana 288, highly recommended, central heating, use of lounge, F (but *Casa de familia* at Boliviana 238 is not recommended). Cheap floor space for the hardy at the Salvation Army building, Calle Bella Vista 577, US$0.50 per head, or ask for private house accommodation at tourist office. Camping is possible near the warden's house in Parque María Behety, 2 km. south of centre.

Restaurants Main hotels. *Asturias*, Lautaro Navarro 967. Good inexpensive food served at restaurant without visible name, Calle Chiloé 968, with Waldo Seguel. *La Taverna Silver*, on Av. Colón, good; *Union Club*, Plaza Muñoz Gamero 714, accepts non-members for meals, and is reported to be very good. *Español* is excellent; *Iberia*, Av. O'Higgins, highly recommended, try steak au poivre. Seafood at *Sotitos*, O'Higgins 1116, good service and cuisine; Italian food at *Pepino*, O'Higgins 1134, expensive, good pizzas. *Mi Cosa*, Balmaceda, pleasant bar. American Service restaurant good. Local specialities at *Moreau*, Chiloé 1132. *Café Garogha*, Bories 817, open Sun. p.m., pleasant but busy at night. *Café Monaco*, Bories y Menéndez, cheap snacks and drinks. Restaurant above fish market offers *centolla* and oysters, but slow service and expensive. Cheap fish meals available at stalls near the fishing cooperative near the docks. The bakeries on Calle O'Higgins are well worth a visit, with excellent rye bread sold on Mons. and Thurs. Also, try Polar beer. Lobster has become more expensive because of a law banning the use of fishing with nets, allowing only lobster pots.

Night Club *Pollón de Oro*, excellent traditional floor show; expensive.

Car Hire Hertz, Lautaro Navarro 1064, Tel.: 22013.

Banks National banks. Open 0900 to 1400 but closed on Sat.; but the Casa de Cambio Andino is open until 1900 on Fri. Banco O'Higgins good for exchange. If buying Argentine australes with dollars it is advantageous to do so at a bank, if with Chilean pesos at Casa de Cambio. Good rates at Cambio Gasic, Lautaro Navarro 549, La Hermandad, same street No. 1099 and at Bus Sur office on Menéndez (accepts travellers' cheques). If banks and *cambios* are closed, exchange is available at Hotel *Los Navegantes*, José Menéndez 647, or Hotel *Cabo de Hornos*.

440 CHILE

British Vice-Consul Mr Bill Matheson at Rocaca 858 above Chamber of Commerce. Pedro Montt 841, Casilla 327, Tel.: 23008. Helpful and friendly.

Argentine Consulate Av. 21 de Mayo 1878, open 1000-1400.

Cables Calle Pedro Montt 841.

Tourist Office Sernatur, Waldo Seguel 689, Casilla 106-D, Tel.: 24435, at the corner with Plaza Muñoz Gamero, may be closed in the afternoon. English spoken.

Touring Club Main square, Casilla 127. Correspondence in any European language.

Travel Agents Skartour and Cabo de Hornos Tur, Plaza Muñoz Gamero 1013 and 1039. Ventistur in lobby of *Hotel Las Navegantes*, Tel.: 24677, competent, run by Sr. Ernesto Fernández de Cabo.

Baths Steam and Turkish, Valdivia 999 O'Higgins, US$0.70. Open in winter only.

Shipping Cruise vessels visit this port or Castro. Navimag, office at Independencia 830, Tel.: 26600 and 22593, have the only service north to Puerto Natales (tickets N of Puerto Natales can only be bought in Punta Arenas). Also try truck companies, or truck drivers at the dock (male passengers only should try this). Government supply ships are recommended for the young and hardy, but take sleeping bag and extra food, and travel pills. *Río Cisnes* of Empremar runs once a month from Punta Arenas to Puerto Williams and Beagle Channel islands; fare US$63 return, 3½ day journey. Carries only ten passengers in bunks in a converted container on deck. Take warm sleeping bag and be prepared to share toilets with crew. Ask at Tourist Office for details or enquire at Empresa Marítima del Estado (Empremar), Punta Arenas (Lautaro Navarro 1338, Tel.: 21608). To Ushuaia, through the Beagle Channel, the *Argonauta* runs irregularly, US$75-120 for 2-day trip with food, drink and hot water (but not luxurious); fascinating journey, but can be rough and cold. Also calls at Puerto Williams, where the vessel appears to be based.

Ferries Regular services between Punta Arenas and Puerto Porvenir (Tierra del Fuego) in *Melinka*, leaving Tres Puentes (5 km. from Punta Arenas) at 0900 daily (1000 on Sun.), depending on tides, US$2 p.p., US$2 per bike, US$25 per vehicle. Buy tickets on board. It returns from Porvenir (Sampaio 302) at 1400 (1500 Sat.), 2¾ hrs. each way. Bus to ferry at either end is US$0.25, but stops 1 km. before ferry at Punta Arenas, leave time to walk or take taxi-colectivo (US$1.50) all the way. Alternative transport on navy supply ships—enquire at Tercera Zona Naval, Calle Lautaro Navarro.

Air Services Lan-Chile and Ladeco run daily flights to Puerto Montt and Santiago. From March to early December Ladeco also stops at Balmaceda on Tues., Thurs. and Sat. (US$65). In summer no direct flights to Balmaceda, transfer at Puerto Montt. With Lan-Chile flights there is a free bus service to Ancud and Castro on Chiloé. Aeorolíneas Argentinas flights to Río Grande, Río Gallegos, Bahía Blanca and Buenos Aires on Tues. and Fri. in summer. Aerovías DAP, Carrero Pinto 1022, Tel.: 23958, fly to Porvenir, to Puerto Williams and to Río Gallegos (on Mon. and Fri.), with a Twin-Otter aircraft. (Heavily booked so make sure you have your return reservation confirmed.) Flights to Tierra del Fuego, see page 443. Also, military (FACh) flights US$27, approx. twice a month to Puerto Montt. Information and tickets from airforce base at Bahía Catalina, 4 km. out of town, along airport road (or take bus E to Zona Franca and 5 mins. walk); need to book well in advance. Reserve passages in advance in January and February. Bus from airport, US$0.75. DAP and Ladeco have their own services from town. The airport restaurant is good.

Bus Service To Río Gallegos, daily, 4 companies (at least 2 a day except 1 on Sun. and Mon.—El Pingüino and Luis Lopetegui most frequent; all leave before 1200), US$10.35, 7 hrs., including ½ hr. lunch at km. 160. Time should be allowed for visit to customs prior to departure from inside dock gates. Puerto Natales, 4 a day, 4 hrs. (US$6.50) with El Pingüino, Lautaro Navarro 971. Also Fernández, Chiloé 930 and Buses Sur, José Menéndez 565 (cheapest). To Puerto Montt (via Argentina) and Santiago once a week in summer. Private cars can be hired.

Excursions

Within easy reach are Puerto Hambre and Fuerte Bulnes (reconstructed, old fort, a 56-km. trip). At Río Penitente is Morro Negro, a large rock outcrop. The trip can be done in a day. The most interesting excursions are to the Ultima Esperanza region (see below under Puerto Natales) and so to the Torres del Paine National Park. Ventistur offer excursions from Fri. night to Sat. night, US$110 p.p. if they have at least 15 passengers. Cabo de Hornos Tur organize tours with station wagons. Sr. Mateo Quesada, Chiloé 1375, Tel.: 22662, offers local tours in his car, up to 5 passengers.

The fjords and glaciers of Tierra del Fuego (70 km. by schooner) are exceptionally beautiful. Once a fortnight there is a 22-hr. 320-km. round trip to the fjord d'Agostino, 30 km. long, where many glaciers come down to the sea. A three-day tour to Puerto Natales, the glacier, Balmaceda and Torres del Paine can be arranged from Punta Arenas for US$120, inclusive of meals. Empresa

CHILE 441

Buses Fernández, Calle Chiloé 930, run afternoon excursions to (1) Club Andino and the Fuerte Bulnes (US$6), (2) penguin hatchery on Otway Sound (US$6), (3) 3-day trip to Torres del Paine, which includes Milodon Cave. Buses Sur also run (3) for US$50 Mon.-Wed., US$60 Fri-Sun.; on Mon. and Fri. their bus to Torres del Paine at 1500 costs US$22 return.

Antarctica Punta Arenas has become the number one starting point for touristic visits to Antarctica. The following possibilities exist: Turismo Cabo de Hornos, Plaza Muñoz Gamero (Casilla 62-D), Punta Arenas, Tel.: 22599, Telex 280342 HORNO CL, now offers in March and November six-day packages, which include three nights accommodation at the *Hotel Estrella Polar* at the Teniente Rodolfo Marsh base on King George Island in the South Shetlands. Air transport is by Chilean Air Force (FACh) C-130 Hercules aircraft. Cost US$1,600. Lindblad Travel, P.O. Box 912, Westport CT 06881, USA, Tel.: (203) 226-8531, made five cruises to Antarctica with the luxury chartered Chinese ship m/v *Yao Hua* of 10,151 grt during the 1985/86 season. Fare range US$2,490-15,325 for land/cruise arrangement. Telex 643443 LIND UR.

Society Expeditions Cruises, 723 Broadway East, Seattle WA 98102, Tel.: (206) 324-9400, (800) 426-7794, Telex (910) 444-1381, are now operators of the luxury small cruise ships *World Discoverer* of 3,153 grt and *Society Explorer* of 2,367 grt (formerly *Lindblad Explorer*) During the 1985/86 season, they made 8 cruises to Antarctica, fare range US$4,750-17,775. In addition, the *World Discoverer* made an Antarctica Circumnavigation from Ushuaia, Argentina to Wellington, New Zealand in Jan./Feb. 1986. Fare range US$8,900-23,900. (Again, thanks to Hans K. Wagner, Winterthur.)

Joe and Cristina Kessler of New York write: "From Punta Arenas we went with the Chilean Navy to Antarctica. To say it was an exceptional trip is a vast understatement. We went from Punta Arenas through the southern canals to Puerto Williams, then S past Cape Horn, across the Drake Passage to the Antarctic Peninsula. We traversed back and forth between 5 Chilean bases including Deception Is. The furthest south we went was the American Palmer station at 65° S. The trip was for three weeks and the cost US$33 per day. Information, in person only, from Tercera Zona Naval, Calle Lautaro Navarro, Punta Arenas. There are two trips a year with limited space for tourists. It is possible to get passage with the Navy to Puerto Williams, or almost anyplace they go to in the area; information from the same office."

Skiing Cerro Mirador, only 12 km. from Punta Arenas, one of the few places in the world where one can ski with a sea view. Transtur buses 0900 and 1400 from in front of *Hotel Cabo de Hornos*, US$3, return. Daily lift-ticket, US$4.50; equipment rental, US$6 per adult. Mid-way lodge with food, drink and equipment. Season June to September/ November, weather depending. Contact the Club Andino at the *Hotel Cabo de Hornos* about crosscountry skiing facilities. Also skiing at Tres Morros.

Puerto Natales (17,000 people) is 254 km. N of Punta Arenas and close to the Argentine border at Río Turbio. It stands on the Ultima Esperanza gulf amid spectacular scenery, and is the jumping-off place for the magnificent Balmaceda and Paine national parks.

Puerto Natales Hotels *Eberhard*, Pedro Montt and Señoret, A, excellent views, good; *La Ultima Esperanza* nearby, recommended, C; *Natalino*, Eberhard 371, Tel.: 168, clean and very friendly, E, breakfast included, recommended (tours to Milodon Cave arranged); *Palace*, D, has new extension, good food, on Eberhard, as is *Plaza*, also D; *Austral*, Valdivia 955, Tel.: 193, clean, friendly, good food, run by Eduardo Scott, E, without bath. *Valdivia*, Kouger, B, old-fashioned but friendly. *Residencial Temuco*, friendly, reasonable, good food, F; *Hostería Kiki*, simple, clean; *Hostería Paine*, expensive. *Florida*, O'Higgins 431, F or E, with full board; *Pensión La Busca*, Calle Valdivia 845 (no sign outside), F, recommended, good and cheap food available; and *Pensión Magallanes* on Calle Magallanes (no sign), F, hot water, recommended, clean and friendly; many mountaineering parties stay here, the owner's son runs day excursions to Lake Grey. Accommodation with family above *zapatería* at Bulnes 80, F, friendly, comfortable. *Pensión Bahía*, Teniente Serrano 346, excellent food, especially king crabs. *Residencial Bulnes*, Calle Bulnes (no sign), beside police station, good, F. *Pensión* at Baquedano 745, F; also at O'Higgins 413 and Perito 443. *Restaurant Socorro* is also recommended as is *Don Alvarito*, Blanco Encalada 915; *Restaurante La Ultima Esperanza*, Pedro Montt and *Midas*, Rogers 169, both good, clean. *Café Tranquera*, Bulnes 579, good coffee, snacks. *Centro Español*, Magallanes 247, reasonable restaurant.

Hotels in the countryside and around include: *Hostería Llanura de Diana*, 30 km. away, on road to Punta Arenas (hidden from the road), highly recommended; *Posada de Cisne de Cuello Negro*, a former guest house for meat buyers at the *frigorífico*, D, friendly, clean, reasonable, all rooms with bath, excellent cooking, new owners, 5 km. from Puerto Natales at Puerto Bories; *Patagonia Inn*, D, at Dos Lagunas, 23 km. from Puerto Natales, open only in summer, from November to March; *Tres Pasos*, E, 40 km. from Puerto Natales, highly recommended (Gabriela Mistral wrote one of her books there); and *El Pionero*, 62 km. from Puerto Natales, D. The youth hostel at Sec. Nac. de la Juventud, Ramírez 856, accepts IYHF cards, US$2.50 (open summer only). If locked contact

442 CHILE

Srta. Nancy Segura at Domeyco 621 or secretary of YH at Ramírez 857. No other cheap accommodation in Puerto Natales except *Pensión Ritz*, F, near hospital, at Carrera 443. At Cerro Castillo, the mayor may let you sleep in the school during holidays for US$1.

Shipping The m/n *Evangelistas* of Navimag runs the 1,460 km. between Puerto Natales and Puerto Montt and carries passengers (see page 432). Navimag offices: Independencia 830, Punta Arenas, Tel.: 22593, 26600, Telex 280009 COMAP CL, and Pedro Montt s/n, Terminal Marítimo, Tel.: 287, Puerto Natales (unhelpful, direct telex with Punta Arenas office, which is much better). The cutter *21 de Mayo* (if enough tourists and weather permitting), goes up to Balmaceda and Serrano glaciers, US$14 (take lunch). An interesting trip, viewing glaciers and the rugged mountains at the S end of the Patagonian ice cap. On the trip one usually sees dolphins, sea-lions, black-neck swans, penguins and the quaint steamer ducks.

Buses to Punta Arenas, 4 times daily, 4 hrs. US$6.50. Once a week to Río Gallegos (Argentina), hourly to Río Turbio (Argentina), 2 hrs. (depending on customs—change bus at border). Bus Fernández, Eberhard 555 and Bus Sur, Baquedano 553.

Tourist Office in kiosk on main street, Av. Pedro Montt.

Exchange *Casas de Cambio* on Blanco Encalada 226 and 266 where Argentine australes (and sometimes US$) can be changed. Another two at Bulnes 683 and 1087. Australes are accepted everywhere.

Travel Agent   Turismo Paine, Calle Eberhard.

Museum   Museo De Agostini, Tierra del Fuego fauna.

Laundry at *Tienda Milodón*, on Bulnes.

Excursions A recommended walk is up to Cerro Dorotea which dominates the town, with superb views of the whole Ultima Esperanza Sound. Take Río Turbio bus and alight at jeep track for summit. 25 km. NW of Puerto Natales the Cueva Milodón can be visited. It now contains a plastic model of the prehistoric ground-sloth whose bones were found there in 1895. Fernández bus is cheapest, going on Fri. and returning Sun., mid-Nov. to mid-March only; at other times, take a taxi.

"Some 150 km. NW of Puerto Natales is the **Torres del Paine** National Park, covering 1,630 sq. km., a "must" for its wildlife and spectacular scenery. Along the (gravel) road it is common to spot the Andean condor and herds of *guanaco*. The Torres and Cuernos del Paine are oddly shaped peaks, surrounded by glaciers, which fall straight down to the valleys, now covered with beautiful lakes at 50 to 200 metres above sea level. The glaciers Grey, Dickson and Zapata are three of the big glaciers branching off the huge mass forming the Patagonian icecap.

"There are about 250 km. of well marked hiking trails and nine National Park shelters, bring food, sleeping bag and cooking gear. A popular hike is from the Pehoé guardhouse, N of Lake Pehoé, past Lakes Nordenskjold and Grey up to the Grey glacier, 8 hrs. with a shelter half-way. The area is very popular in summer and the shelters often crowded, extensions are being built.

"The park is administered by the forestry department (Conaf) with a centre at the southern tip of Lake Pehoé and seven guardhouses located throughout the park. There the friendly wardens (*guardaparques*) give advice and one should register with them before setting out for a hike." They estimate about 15 hrs. between Glacier Grey and Lake Paine, so you would need a tent for this trip. (Hans K.Wagner)

Refugios cost US$0.15, and an entrance fee to the Park (US$1.20) is charged. Most of the *refugios* have good areas, so take your own food (beware of mice!) as it is expensive to buy and limited in the Park. Maps (free with Park entrance fee, or obtainable at Conaf offices in Punta Arenas or Puerto Natales, but beware, some of the trails marked peter out and bridges get washed away) and protective clothing are essential. Recommended guide: Eduardo Scott can be contacted at his hotel, *Austral*, Valdivia 955, Puerto Natales (Tel.: 193), he runs tours of the Park in a 12-seater bus. Also José Torres of Sastrería Arbiter in Calle Bulnes. The Visitor Information Centre, an old *estancia*, has a good slide show on Wed. and Sat. at 2030; guards will store luggage and arrange transport back to Puerto Natales.

Accommodation *Posada Río Serrano*, E, shared facilities, 2 km. from park administration, with restaurant and a shop. (Reservations: Serco Ltda., Casilla 19-D, Punta Arenas, Tel.: 23395).

Hostería Pehoé, B, 60 rooms, private facilities, 5 km. S of Pehoé guardhouse, 11 km. N of park administration, on an island with spectacular view across the Lake to Paine Grande and Cuernos del Paine (Reservations: Turismo Pehoé, 21 de Mayo 1460, Punta Arenas, Tel.: 23610).

Camping Pehoé (32 lots, hot shower US$2.15 p.p.) and Camping Río Paine (25 lots) are operated by Serco Ltda., Camping Laguna Azul (10 lots) and Laguna Amarga (15 lots) by Conaf.

Buses Fernádez and Sur (addresses above) run a twice-weekly service to Paine National Park if there are 5 or more passengers (US$11); Sur buses leave Puerto Natales on Mon. and Fri., returning from the Park headquarters Wed. and Sun. For these 2 companies' 3-day, all-in trip from Punta Arenas, twice a week in summer, see page 441. Enap weekend tours in summer cost US$45 including accommodation and meals. Taxi costs US$80 per day, run by Sergio Zaley (Arturo Prat 260). A minibus can be hired for about US$20 at Puerto Natales, to take a party of up to 8 to a *refugio* in the Paine National Park. Off season there is no public transport and trucks are irregular. It may be possible to arrange a lift at Conaf in Puerto Natales (opposite the hospital on Av. Carrera) with one of their buses going to the Park Administration twice a month (US$5).

The most popular hike starts from the administration building at the south end of Lake Pehoé, and takes seven days going from *refugio* to *refugio* past the spectacular Grey Glacier and round the back of the Cuernos and Torres del Paine. It is tough, the longest lap being 30 km., but not too steep. (Note that the main footbridge to Glacier Grey was washed away by floods in 1983.)

The scenery in the Park is spectacular. Walking along the trails one is constantly rewarded by changing views of fantastic peaks, ice-fields, vividly coloured lakes of turquoise, ultramarine and grey and quiet green valleys. Many describe it as the best walking they have done. Wild life abounds: one can expect to see *guanaco*, hares, foxes, condors, black-neck swans and many other birds. Apparently the park has a micro-climate especially favourable to plants and wild life. The Park is open all year round, although snow may prevent access in the winter: best time is January-April.

Another recommended walk is to Valle Francés, 2 hrs. from Pehoé to the Río Francés, 5 hrs. on to Campamento Británico.

Descriptions of several walks in the Torres del Paine area are found in *Backpacking in Chile and Argentina*, by Hilary Bradt and John Pilkington.

Tierra del Fuego is the island off the extreme south of South America. It is surrounded by the Magellan Strait to the north, the Atlantic Ocean to the east, the Beagle Channel to the south—which separates it from the southern islands—and by the Whiteside, Gabriel, Magdalena and Cockburn channels etc. which divide it from the islands situated to the west. The western side belongs to Chile and the eastern to Argentina. It produces most of Chile's oil.

In Chilean Tierra del Fuego the only town is **Porvenir,** with a population of 4,500, several hundred from Yugoslavia. There is a small museum with stuffed animals and an Indian mummy.

Porvenir Hotels *Los Flamencos*, Teniente Merino, best, B; *Tierra del Fuego*, Carlos Wood 489, D, good food; *Turismo*, Soto Salas 698, E, good value; *Residencial Cameron* (ask at bar called *Somos o no Somos*), F, for shared room, "friendly folk", good meals, sleep on dining-room floor for US$1; *Central*, Phillips 298, D, hot water; *Bella Vista*, D, with restaurant, clean and friendly; *España* is central and reasonable, good lunch; *Colón*, F. Many good *pensiones*, E, with full board, such as *Posada Los Cisnes*.

Yugoslav Club does wholesome and reasonable lunch (about US$5), also *Restaurante Puerto Montt* for seafood. Many lobster fishing camps where fishermen will prepare lobster on the spot.

Exchange at *Estrella del Sur* shop, Calle Santos Mardones.

Buses on Tierra del Fuego Two a week between Porvenir and Río Grande (Argentina), US$15; Senkovic in Porvenir at *Hotel Tierra del Fuego*. Bus from Río Grande arrives 1300, ferry to Punta Arenas leaves 1400; from terminal to ferry, taxi US$2.75, bus (if running) US$1, ferry US$2; trip takes 7-8 hrs. depending on border crossing. Beware: taxis are not allowed to cross the border. If you go to the police station and ask for a ride to the border on a truck, you can save the fare to Río Grande. Hitch-hiking elsewhere is difficult as there is so little traffic. Argentine time one hour ahead of Chilean time.

Puerto Williams is a Chilean naval base on Isla Navarino, S of the Beagle Channel, the most southerly place in the world with a permanent population (about 1,000). The ferry service between Puerto Williams and Ushuaia (Argentina), has been resumed following the peace treaty between Chile and Argentina over the Beagle Channel. The island is totally unspoilt and beautiful, with a chain of rugged snowy peaks, magnificent woods and many animals, including beaver. There is one hotel, the *Hostería Wala*, with attractive locally-made furniture and

444 CHILE

soft furnishings, roaring log fire in lounge, it is now owned by the Navy (but run by civilian management), C in summer, D in winter (monthly rates available); splendid walks nearby. Hotel can arrange car trips to the beaver dams, cascades, and other sights. There is a supermarket. Only one other hotel; you can also stay at private houses. You can camp near the *Hostería*: collect drinking water from the kitchen, bring food from Punta Arenas as it is expensive on the island, but you can buy gasoline for stoves at the *Hostería*. Aeropetrel will charter a plane, if a sufficiently numerous party is raised, to Cape Horn. Near Puerto Williams there is a *centolla* crab canning factory which is well worth a visit.

Museum Excellent museum in Puerto Williams, full of information about vanished Indian tribes, local wildlife, and voyages including Charles Darwin and Fitzroy of the *Beagle*. Open Mon.-Fri. 0800-1200, 1400-1600, so if you catch the ferry across from Punta Arenas for the day, you will find it closed.

Transport to Tierra del Fuego For ferry services from Punta Arenas, see page 440. There are two ferries running across the Primera Angostura (First Narrows) between Delgada and Espora points, 170 km. NE from Punta Arenas, schedule varying with the tides. Reservations at the ferry. Price US$1 p.p. and US$12 per car, one way. By air from Punta Arenas—weather and bookings permitting, Tama (Mexicana 782, Tel.: 22965) flies to Porvenir (15 mins., US$ 10) and Puerto Williams (US$40 one way) on Mon., Wed. and Fri.; Aerovías DAP (Ignacio Carrera Pinto 1022, Tel.: 23959 Punta Arenas and Oficina Foretic, Tel.: 80089, Porvenir) cover the same routes on Tues., Thurs. and Sat. (same prices). Heavily booked so make sure you have your return reservation confirmed. The flight to Puerto Williams is beautiful, with superb views of Tierra del Fuego, the Cordillera Darwin, the Beagle Channel, and the islands stretching S to Cape Horn.

The Economy

Chile is endowed with a diversified environment, allowing the production of all temperate and Mediterranean products. Agriculture, however, supplies only about 10% of gdp, employs 20% of the labour force and contributes about 12% of merchandise exports. Given the country's topography, only 7% of the land is devoted to crop production, while 14% is used for pasture. Traditional crops, such as cereals, pulse, potatoes and industrial crops (sugarbeet, sunflowerseed and rapeseed) account for about 37% of the value added of agriculture, and vegetables for about 25%. The area showing fastest growth is fresh fruit. Another area of expansion is forestry. Chile has over 9 m hectares of natural forest of which planted forests cover 1 m hectares, with more than 90% planted with insignis radiata pine, a species which in Chile grows faster than in other countries. Chile is the most important fishing nation in Latin America and the largest producer of fishmeal in the world. Industrial consumption absorbs about 93% of the fish catch; fresh fish and fish products contribute about 11% of merchandise exports.

The dominant sector of the economy is mining. Chile has been the world's largest producer of copper since 1982 and also produces molybdenum, iron ore, manganese, lead, gold, silver, zinc, sulphur and nitrates. Chile has a quarter of the world's known molybdenum ore reserves (3m tonnes), and is believed to have around 40% of the world's lithium reserves. The fall in world prices for metals in the 1980s put pressure on the country's external accounts. In real terms, the copper average price contracted by 23% in 1982-85. Mineral ores account for 56% of total export revenue, most of which is copper.

Chile is fortunate in possessing reserves of oil, natural gas and coal, and abundant hydroelectricity potential. About 60% of its energy requirements are met by oil and gas, 15% by coal, 24% by hydroelectricity and the balance by biomass. Almost all the country's hydrocarbon reserves are in the extreme south, on Tierra del Fuego, in the Strait of Magellan and the province of Magallanes. Oil reserves are estimated at 736 m barrels, 188 m of which are offshore.

Manufacturing has been particularly vulnerable to changes in economic policy: nationalization during the Allende administration in the early 1970s; recession brought about by anti-inflationary policies in the mid-1970s; increased foreign competition resulting from trade liberalization in the early 1980s, and greater exports together with import substitution in the mid-1980s. The contribution of manufacturing to total gdp has fallen from 25% in 1970 to 20% in 1985 although its share of exports has risen. Activity is mostly food processing, metal-working, textiles and fish processing.

High rates of inflation were recorded in the first half of the 1970s, but were brought down from over 500% at the end of 1973 to less than 10% by end-1981, largely because of fiscal balance and an overvalued currency. Following the freeing of the exchange rate in 1982 inflation accelerated somewhat, but was successfully moderated by tight monetary control and a lower public sector borrowing requirement. Monetary policy was formulated to cope with high domestic indebtedness in the light of restrictive IMF programmes. IMF involvement was sought following a sharp fall in international commercial lending in 1982 and a decline in Chile's terms of trade. The average annual rate of growth of exteral debt fell from 32% in 1978-81 to 6% in 1982-84. Chile has successfully negotiated several debt refinancing packages with commercial banks and with the Paris Club of creditor governments. In the second half of the 1980s, Chile's foreign debt actually began to fall as the government introduced schemes whereby debt could be converted into equity in Chilean companies.

	1961-70 (av)	1971-80 (av)	1981-85 (av)	1986 (e)
Gdp growth (1980 prices)	4.2%	2.5%	-0.4%	5.0%
Inflation	21.2%	120.4%	20.4%	19.0%
Exports (fob) US$m	674	2,120	3,753	4,050
Copper	581	1,266	1,726	1,761
Imports (fob) US$m	628	2,286	3,862	3,074
Current account balance US$m (cum)	-1,162	-6,381	-11,521	-1,091

Information for Visitors

How to get there: by Air

From Europe: Air France (3 per week), Iberia (4), KLM (2), Lufthansa (2), Sabena, SAS, Swissair (1) and Alitalia (1) fly to Santiago. Some flights go via Rio/São Paulo, Montevideo and Buenos Aires; others via New York, Lima and/or other points in northern S. America. Also, Varig, Aerolíneas Argentinas, Viasa and Avianca offer services between Europe and Santiago, with connections via Rio, Buenos Aires, Caracas and Bogotá respectively. Sobelair has regular charters from Brussels and Spantax from Madrid.

From North America: Eastern has flights from Miami, New York and/or Washington, and Los Angeles; one service is non-stop from Miami, taking 8 hrs.—others stop at Panama City, Lima or Quito. Lan-Chile has 5 flights per week from New York and Miami. Also from Miami, Ladeco flies either via Bogotá and Guayaquil or Bogotá and Arica; Aeroperú has 7 flights and Aerolíneas Argentinas 2 per week; Pan Am 3 per week. Also to Miami fly Avianca, Ecuatoriana, LAB and Líneas Aéreas Paraguayas (LAP); change at Asunción for Miami. There are good connections to Bogotá (by Avianca) or Lima (by several other carriers). CP Air have one flight per week from Montreal and Toronto, and 2 from Vancouver—all via Lima. Lan-Chile flies once or twice a week, depending on season, between Tahiti (making connections from Japan, Australia and New Zealand) and Santiago; they stop over at Easter Island. For excursion fares between Australia/New Zealand and Chile, the stopovers at Easter Island now carry a surcharge of about US$125.

Within South America: from Buenos Aires (over 30 per week) by Lan-Chile, Aerolíneas Argentinas, Varig, Aeroperú, Avianca, CP Air, Air France, Iberia, KLM or Lufthansa; from Rosario, Córdoba or Mendoza (5 per week) by Aerolíneas Argentinas; Ladeco flies twice a week to Mendoza. From Montevideo (5 per week) by Lan-Chile, Iberia, KLM, SAS or Sabena; from Asunción (three times a week) by Ladeco or LAP; from Rio/São Paulo, non-stop by Lan-Chile, Ladeco, Varig, Swissair or by several other airlines via Buenos Aires; from La Paz (6 per week) by Lufthansa, Lloyd Aéreo Boliviano (LAB), Lan-Chile, Avianca; from Caracas via Lima 2 a week; from Lima (up to 30 per week) by Aeroperú, Lan-Chile, Lufthansa and others; from Bogotá (6 per week) by Avianca.

446 CHILE

To Arica, from Cochabamba and La Paz (4 per week) by LAB and Lan-Chile.

Airport Taxes US$8 for international flights; US$1 for domestic flights. There is a tourist tax on single air fares of 2%, and 1% on return fares beginning or ending in Chile (these taxes are just about the lowest in South America). There is a sales tax of 5% on all transport within Chile.

From the U.S.A. by Sea: By Lykes Line from New Orleans via Panama Canal, Time taken: 20 days, 2 departures monthly.

From Europe by Sea: By Compagnie Générale Maritime from La Pallice, France, via Panama Canal. Time taken: 28 days. Every 6 weeks.

From Neighbouring Countries by land. There are railways from La Paz (Bolivia) to Calama for Antofagasta, and to Arica (see Bolivia section). All passenger services have been suspended on the lines between Chile and Argentina. Roads connect Santiago with Mendoza, and Osorno and Puerto Montt with Bariloche, in Argentina. Less good road connections N of Santiago are described in the main text.

Internal Air Services Lan-Chile serves Santiago, Antofagasta, Iquique, Arica, Puerto Montt and Punta Arenas. The private airline Ladeco flies between Santiago and El Salvador, Antofagasta, Calama, Iquique, Arica to the north and between Santiago and Balmaceda, Puerto Montt, Punta Arenas in the south. Both Lan-Chile and Ladeco now offer a 21-day "Visit Chile" ticket (five prices: US$269 takes you to Santiago, Antofagasta, Iquique, Arica, Pto. Montt and Pta. Arenas; US$310 takes you to Coyhaique also; there are three island prices, of which the highest, US$510, takes you to Easter Island) which enables you to visit the length of country both ways. It must be purchased abroad and reservations made well ahead since many flights are fully booked in advance.

N.B. The ticket cannot be changed, though reservations can, so it is worth including as many destinations as possible. It is also possible for the route Santiago-Antofagasta-Arica-Santiago to take a coupon ticket which allows greater flexibility.

Surface Transport Reservations are sometimes problematic. Buses are frequent and on the whole good. As a general rule long-distance buses cost US$1-2 per 100 km., depending on services. Prices are highest between Dec.-March. Trains in Chile are moderately priced, and not as slow as in other Andean countries, though dining car food is expensive. There is a railway information office at O'Higgins 853 (at end of arcade), Santiago, for all lines except the Antofagasta-Bolivia (Agustinas 972, room 904). English spoken. Shipping information at Empresa Marítima del Estado (Empremar), Estado 359, 5th floor, and Kochifas, Av. Maciver 484, 2nd floor, Room 5. Transcontainer, Estado 360, Of. 502-C and Navimag, Avda. Suiza 248, Cerrillos, Tel.: 572650. Local newspapers are useful for all transport schedules.

Motoring in Chile Car drivers require the usual *Carnet de Passages en Douanes* issued by a recognized automobile club, as do motor cyclists. The Carta Caminera from the Dirección de Vialidad is the most detailed road map (series of twenty-six) but is only available at Vialidad, Marsende and Alameda, Santiago. Reasonable road maps may also be obtained from the Automóvil Club de Chile, Pedro de Valdivia 195, Santiago; or other regional offices. Town maps from the Automóvil Club and Copec service stations. Hydrographic maps from Instituto Hidrográfico, Malgarejo 59, Valparaíso.

Walking Serious walkers are advised to get *Backpacking in Chile and Argentina*, by Hilary Bradt and John Pilkington, published in 1980.

Travel Documents Passport and tourist card only are required for entry by all foreigners except citizens of France, Guyana, Haiti, Suriname, Kuwait, African countries and the Communist countries, who require visas. National identity cards are sufficient for entry by citizens of Argentina, Bolivia, Brazil, Ecuador and Uruguay. The tourist card is valid for 90 days and is renewable for 90 more; it is available from Chilean consulates, immigration office at the Ollagüe land frontier, as well as at Arica, airline offices and most aircraft bound for Chile; it will be surrendered on departure. If you wish to stay longer than 180 days (as a tourist), it is easier to make a day-trip to Argentina and return with a new tourist card, rather than to apply for a visa, which involves a great deal of paperwork. Visa is required for French passport holders, US$5.25; valid for no more than 90 days, strictly one entry only.

All foreigners who wish to work in Chile must obtain visas. Smallpox vaccination and health certificates no longer required.

Customs Allowed in free of duty: 500 cigarettes, 100 cigars, 500 grams of tobacco, 3 bottles of liquor, camera, and all articles of personal use. Fruit, vegetables, flowers and milk products may not be imported.

Time GMT minus 4 hrs.; minus 3 hrs. in summer. Clocks change on second Sat. in March and October.

CHILE 447

Seasons The best time for a visit to Santiago is between October and April when fine weather is almost assured, but business visits can be made any time during the year. During the holiday season, between January and March, it is sometimes difficult to make appointments.

Clothing Warm sunny days and cool nights are usual during most of the year except in the far S where the climate is like that of Scotland. Ordinary European medium-weight clothing can be worn during the winter (June to mid-September). Light clothing is best for summer (December to March), but men do not wear white tropical suits.

Health Tap water is fairly safe to drink in the main cities but bottled water is safer on trains and away from the larger centres. Hotels and restaurants are usually clean. Inoculation against typhoid is a wise precaution. Travellers should not eat salads, strawberries or ground-growing food; hepatitis and typhoid are all too common as the result of the use of untreated sewage for fertilizer.

Hours of Business Banks: 0900-1400, but closed on Sat. Government offices: 1000-1230 (the public is admitted for a few hrs. only). Business houses: 0830-1230, 1400-1800 (Mon. to Fri.). Shops (Santiago): 1030-1930, but 0930-1330 Sat. British business visitors are advised to obtain "Hints for Exporters: Chile" from the Department of Trade, Sanctuary Bldgs, 16-20 Great Smith Street, London SW1P 3DB.

Taxis have meters, but agree beforehand on fare for long journey out of centre or special excursions. A 50% surcharge is applied after 2100 and Sun. Taxi drivers rarely know the location of any streets away from the centre. There is no need to tip unless some extra service, like the carrying of luggage, is given.

Language The local pronunciation of Spanish, very quick and lilting, with final syllables cut off, can present difficulties to the foreigner.

Telephones Local telephones use four 1 peso coins.

Advice It is reported that the police are less exigent about travellers' dress than they were a few years ago.

Living Conditions and Cost Shops throughout Chile are well stocked and there is a seasonal supply of all the usual fruits and vegetables. Milk in pasteurized, evaporated, or dried form is obtainable. Chilean tinned food is dear. Food is reasonable, but food prices vary tremendously. Santiago tends to be more expensive for food and accommodation than other parts of Chile. Southern Chile can be expensive between December 15 and March 15.

Shopping There is an excellent variety of handicrafts: woodwork, pottery, copperware, leatherwork, Indian woven goods including rugs and ponchos in the South. Good quality at the Cema-Chile shops (Av. Portugal 351, Santiago, and main provincial cities).

Hotels On hotel bills service charges are usually 10%, and taxes on bills are 20%. Whether or not the 20% is added to bills in hotel restaurants that are signed and charged to the hotel bill depends on the policy of the establishment. When booking in make certain whether meals are included in the price or only breakfast or nothing at all, and don't rely on the posted sheet in the bedroom for any prices. Small *residenciales* are often good value.

Youth Hostels There are youth hostels throughout Chile; average cost about US$0.50 p.p. The youth hostel at Viña del Mar is open to IYHF card holders all the year round. The others are open only from Jan. to the end of February and a Chilean membership card is necessary (US$5). An additional stamp costing US$2.50 enables one to use the card in Argentina, Uruguay and Brazil. This can be obtained from the Secretaría Nacional de la Juventud, Programa Albergues Juveniles, Calle Estados Unidos 359, Santiago; together with a useful guidebook of all Youth Hostels in Chile, *Guía Turística de los Albergues Juveniles*. If you carry an IYHF card you can stay in summer in makeshift hostels in many Chilean towns, usually in the main schools.

Camping is easy but no longer cheap at official sites. A common practice is to charge US$10 for up to 5 people, with no reductions for less than 5. "Camping Gaz International" stoves are recommended, since green replaceable cylinders are available in Santiago.

Motoring Spare car parts available from many shops on Calle Diez de Julio, Santiago. Diesel fuel is only available along Longitudinal Highway. **Skiing** Season from June to September/October, weather depending. For information write to: La Federación de Ski de Chile, Casilla 9902, Santiago

Tipping Standard is 10% in hotels and restaurants and 20% in bars and soda fountains. Railway and airport porters: US$0.10 a piece of luggage. Make a deal with dock porters. Cloakroom attendants and cinema usherettes: US$0.05. Hairdressers: 10% of bill. Taxi-drivers are not tipped.

448 CHILE

Currency and Exchange The unit is the peso, its sign is US$. Notes are for 100, 500, 1,000 and 5,000 pesos and coins for 1, 5, 10, 50 and 100 pesos.

Travellers' cheques must be changed before 1200 except in exchange shops (*cambios*) and hotels, which give better rates than banks. Changing travellers' cheques can be time-consuming and has become difficult in most towns apart from Arica, Antofagasta, Santiago and Puerto Montt. Foreigners may no longer exchange pesos for dollars when leaving the country. Visa and Mastercharge are common in Chile, but American Express is less useful. Try and change as much as you can in Santiago.

N.B. Prices in dollars in this chapter are converted at the official exchange rate. Travellers can buy pesos on the parallel (black) market, which is tolerated, at slightly better rates. *El Economista* quotes black market, *mercado paralelo*, rates, and you can get fairly close to the *paralelo* nowadays in *cambios* and hotels.

The **metric** system is obligatory but the quintal of 46 kilos (101.4 lb) is used.

Posts and Telegraphs Airmail takes 3-4 days from the UK. Seamail takes 8-12 weeks. There is a daily airmail service to Europe with connections to the UK. Poste restante only holds mail for 30 days; then returns to sender. Lista de Correo in Santiago, Central Post Office, is good and efficiently organized. Telegrams to Britain: ordinary rate, US$3.40 (minimum 7 words); L.T. rate: US$5.60 (minimum 21 words). A 3-min. telex call to Britain costs US$5.65.

International telephone and telegraph communications are operated by the Entel; by Transradio Chilena (2 offices); and by the Cía. Internacional de Radio (2 offices). Calls may be made collect. International calls cost US$11 for first 3 mins. to North America and Europe (US$9 between 2000 and 2200); US$2.25 for each subsequent min.

Astonishing how throughout Chile one post office official will charge rates different from the next, and they are all "right". Public telex booths are available at the offices of Transradio Chilena in Santiago and Valparaíso. Amex Card holders can often use telex facilities at Amex offices free of charge.

Public Holidays

Jan. 1—New Year's Day.
Holy Week (2 days).
May 1—Labour Day.
May 21—Navy Day.
Aug. 15—Assumption

Sept. 18, 19—Independence Days.
Oct. 12—Discovery of America.
Nov. 1—All Saints Day.
Dec. 8—Immaculate Conception.
Dec. 25—Christmas Day

Santiago daily papers *El Mercurio*, *La Nación*, *La Segunda* and *La Tercera*. *Las Ultimas Noticias*, *El Cóndor*, weekly in German.

Weekly magazines; *Hoy*, *Qué Pasa*; *Ercilla* and *Panorama Económico* are best economic journals. Monthly: *Rutas* (official organ, Automobile Association).

Local Dishes A very typical Chilean dish is *cazuela de ave*, a nutritious stew containing large pieces of chicken, potatoes, rice, and maybe onions, and green peppers; best if served on the second day. Another popular Chilean dish is *empanadas de horno*, which are turnovers filled with a mixture of raisins, olives, meat, onions and peppers chopped up together. *Pastel de choclo* is a casserole of meat and onions with olives, topped with a maize-meal mash, baked in an earthenware bowl. The popular *empanada frita*, a fried meat pasty, is delicious. A normal *parrillada* is a giant mixed grill served from a charcoal brazier. The *pichanga* is similar but smaller and without the brazier. Goat cheese is a delicacy of the Fourth Region, but can be a source of food poisoning.

What gives Chilean food its personality is the seafood. The delicious conger eel is a national dish, and *caldillo de congrio* (a soup served with a massive piece of conger, onions and potato balls) is excellent. *Paila Chonchi* is a kind of bouillabaisse, but has more flavour, more body, more ingredients. *Parrillada de mariscos* is a dish of grilled mixed seafood, brought to the table piping hot on a charcoal brazier. Other excellent local fish are the *cojinoa*, the *albacora* (swordfish) and the *corvina*. An appetizing starter is the shellfish *loco* (known to Australians as abalone), and in the S one should try the *centolla* (king crab). Avocado pears, or *paltas*, are excellent, and play an important role in recipes. The *erizo*, or sea-urchin, is also commonly eaten. Make sure whether vegetables are included in

CHILE 449

the price for the main dish; menus often don't make this clear. Always best, if being economical, to stick to fixed-price *table d'hôte* meals or try the local markets. Ice cream is very good; *lúcuma* and *chirimoya* are highly recommended flavours.

Lunch is about 1300 and dinner not before 2030. *Onces* (Elevenses) is tea taken at 1700 often accompanied by a couple of fried eggs. The cocktail hour starts at 1900. Waiters are known as *garzón*—never as *mozo*.

It seems impossible to get real coffee unless you go to expresso bars and specify *café-café, expresso*. If you ask just for *café*, you get soluble coffee. The soluble tea should be avoided. After a meal, instead of coffee, try an *agüita*—hot water in which herbs such as mint, or aromatics such as lemon peel, have been steeped. Very refreshing.

Drinks Imported whisky and other spirits are still cheap, but are increasing relatively in price. The local wines are very good; the best are from the central areas. Among the good *bodegas* are Cousiño Macul, Santa Carolina, Undurraga, Concha y Toro, Tocornal, San Pedro and Santa Helena. Santa Elena (no H) is less good. The bottled wines are graded, in increasing excellence, as *gran vino, vino especial* and *vino reservado*. A small deposit, US$0.30, is charged on most wine bottles. Beer is quite good and cheap; the draught lager known as Schop is good; also try Cristal Pilsener or Royal Guard. Malta, a brown ale, is recommended for those wanting a British-type beer.

Good gin is made in Chile. Champagne-type wines are cheap and good. Reasonably good brandy, *anís* and crème de menthe are all bottled in Chile. *Vaina* is worth trying, and so is the traditional Christmas drink, *cola de mono*, a mixture of *aguardiente*, coffee, milk and vanilla served very cold. *Pisco* is worth sampling, especially as a "Pisco Sour" or with grapefruit or lemon juice. *Chicha* is any form of alcoholic drink made from fruit; *chicha cocida* is 3-day-old fermented grape juice boiled to reduce its volume and then bottled, when cool, with a tablespoonful of honey. Cider (*chicha de manzana*) is popular in the South.

Sports The Chilean State Railways and the tourist agencies will give all the necessary information about sport. Skiing is popular. Horse racing is also popular and meetings are held every Sunday and on certain feast days at Viña del Mar, Santiago and Concepción throughout the year; horseback riding is also popular. Santiago and Valparaíso residents fish at the mountain resort of Río Blanco, and some of the world's best fishing is in the Lake District. The licence required can be got from the local police or such angling associations as the Asociación de Pesca y Caza, which gives information on local conditions. Other popular sports are football and basket ball. Viña del Mar has a cricket ground; on Saturdays there are polo matches at Santiago.

We are deeply grateful to the following travellers for help with this section: Bill Addington (Warminster, Wilts), Richard and Sharon Alexander (Auckland), Stephen Appleby (Tynemouth), Dr Paul G.Bahn (Hull), Nigel L.Baker, Mark Roy Battley (Toronto), Wolfgang Beck (Nürnberg), Trond Bergquist and Ian Gjertz (Oslo), Paulo Couto (São Paulo), Malcolm Craven (Weston-super-Mare), David Crowe (Sydney), Lynne and Hugh Davies (Mill Valley, Ca.), Diane De Mauro (Ft. Lee, NJ), James Derry (Courtenay, BC), Grant Dixon (S.Hobart, Tasmania), Kurt Farner (Köniz, Switz.), Harry Floyd (London W8), Thomas Frisch (Ottawa), Romi and Olga Gandolfo (Buenos Aires), Toni García and Diego Caña (Barcelona), Peter Gilmore (Guayaquil), Jürg Hangartner (Zürich), Hans Hendriks (Masshuis, Neth.), Ricardo Heyenn and Karim Kubitsch (Hamburg), Catherine Hooper (Aptos, Ca.), Marianne Hydara (Wels, Austria), Simón Keller (Montevideo), David Kellie-Smith (London SW6), Todd Knutson (Pittsburgh), Christian Küber (Hamburg), Peter Lonsdale (Taupo, NZ), Henry R.Loughlin (Norfolk, Ct.), Dr Richard Luckett (Cambridge), Shelly Lurie (Ramat Gan, Israel), Gary MacLake (Sheboygan, Mich.), Frans Mikkelsen and Karen Simonsen (Aarhus, Dmk.), R.B.Ll.Morgan (Repton, Derbys.), Roland Moser (Ettingen, Switz.), Paulo Nasuti (Venice), Hans and Ursula Niederndorfer (Lambach, Austria), C.H.Palmer (São Paulo), Sue Penn, Beat Rebsamen (Buchs, Switz.), Antoine Hilaire Rucker (Schlangenbad, W.Ger.), Stephen Saks and Andrea Keir (Melbourne), Thomas Schmidt (Rindögt, Stockholm), L.J.Schmit Jongbloed (Rotterdam), Charlotte and Mike Sharp (Lima), Kathryn Sikkink (Rio), Barbara Simon and Peter Stobart (Cologne), Gustavo Steinbrun Bianco (Buenos Aires), Tim Sutton (Silver Spring, Md.), R.Tucker and James Fraser Darling, Chris and Kathy Van Straaten (Asunción), Dirk Vanmarcke (Bruges), Doris Vaterlaus and Daniel Froelicher (Thalwil, Switz.), Hans K.Wagner (Winterthur, Switz.), Christopher W.Walker (Reston, Va.), Haydn Washington (Sydney 2068) Steve Wingfield (Toronto) and Susi and Alex Witteveen (Huizen, Neth.).

COLOMBIA

	Page		Page
Introductory	450	Cauca Valley	508
Bogotá	454	The Economy	524
North Coast and Islands	465	Information for Visitors	525
Magdalena River	478	Maps	451, 456, 465,
Central Cordillera	502		468, 479, 518

COLOMBIA, with 1,138,618 square km., is the fourth largest country in South America and has the second largest population (28.6 millions), being now more populous than Argentina. It has coast lines upon both the Caribbean (1,600 km.) and the Pacific (1,306 km.). Nearly 55% of the area is almost uninhabited lowland with only 4% of the population; the other 96% are concentrated in the remaining 45%, living for the most part in narrow valleys or isolated intermont basins, or in the broad Caribbean lowlands. The population is infinitely varied, ranging from white, Indian, and black to mixtures of all three.

The 620,000 square km. of almost uninhabited land in Colombia lie E of the Eastern Cordillera. Near the foot of the Cordillera the plains are used for cattle ranching, but beyond is jungle. Islands of settlement in it are connected with the rest of the country by air and river, for there are no railways and very few roads: communication is by launch and canoe on the rivers.

In the populous western 45% of the country four ranges of the Andes run from S to N. Between the ranges run deep longitudinal valleys. Of the 14 main groups of population in the country, no less than 11 are in the mountain basins or in the longitudinal valleys; the other three are in the lowlands of the Caribbean.

The first 320 km. along the Pacific coast N from the frontier with Ecuador to the port of Buenaventura is a wide, marshy, and sparsely inhabited coastal lowland. Along the coast N of Buenaventura runs the Serranía de Baudó. E of this range the forested lowlands narrow into a low trough of land; E of the trough again rise the slopes of the Western Cordillera. The trough—the Department of the Chocó—is drained southwards into the Pacific by the Río San Juan, navigable for 200 km., and northwards into the Caribbean by the Río Atrato, navigable for 550 km; there are vague plans to link the two rivers by canal. The climate is hot and torrential rain falls daily. The inhabitants are mostly black.

From the borders of Ecuador two ranges of mountain, the Western Cordillera and the Central Cordillera, run N for 800 km. to the Caribbean lowlands. Five peaks in the Western Cordillera are over 4,000 metres but none reaches the snowline. The Central Cordillera, 50-65 km. wide, is much higher; six of its peaks, snow clad, rise above 5,000 metres and its highest, the volcano cone of Huila, is 5,439 metres. There is hardly any level land, but there are narrow ribbons of soil along some of the rivers.

Between the two ranges, as they emerge from Ecuador, lies a valley filled in the S to a height of 2,500 metres by ash from the volcanoes. Not far from the frontier there is a cluster of self-subsisting Indians around Pasto. Further N between these two ranges lies the Cauca valley; in its northern 190 km., roughly from Popayán N past Cali to Cartago, there is an important agricultural region based on a deep bed of black alluvial soil which yields as many as five crops a year. This valley, which is at a height of about 1,000 metres and up to 50 km. wide, is drained northwards by the Cauca river. Cali is the business centre of the valley, and a road and railway run from Cali over a low pass of less than 1,500 metres in the Western Cordillera to Buenaventura. Sugar cane was the great crop of this valley in colonial times, but has now been varied with tobacco, soya, cotton, pineapple, and every other kind of tropical fruit. There is still some cattle raising. Coffee is grown on the Cordillera slopes above 600 metres. A "Tennessee Valley" scheme of development to drain the swamps, control floods, irrigate parched areas, improve farming, and produce electric power has been applied in the Cauca Valley since 1956.

At Cartago the two Cordilleras close in and the Cauca valley becomes a deep gorge which runs all the way to the Caribbean flatlands. In the Cordillera Central, at an altitude of 1,540 metres, is

COLOMBIA 451

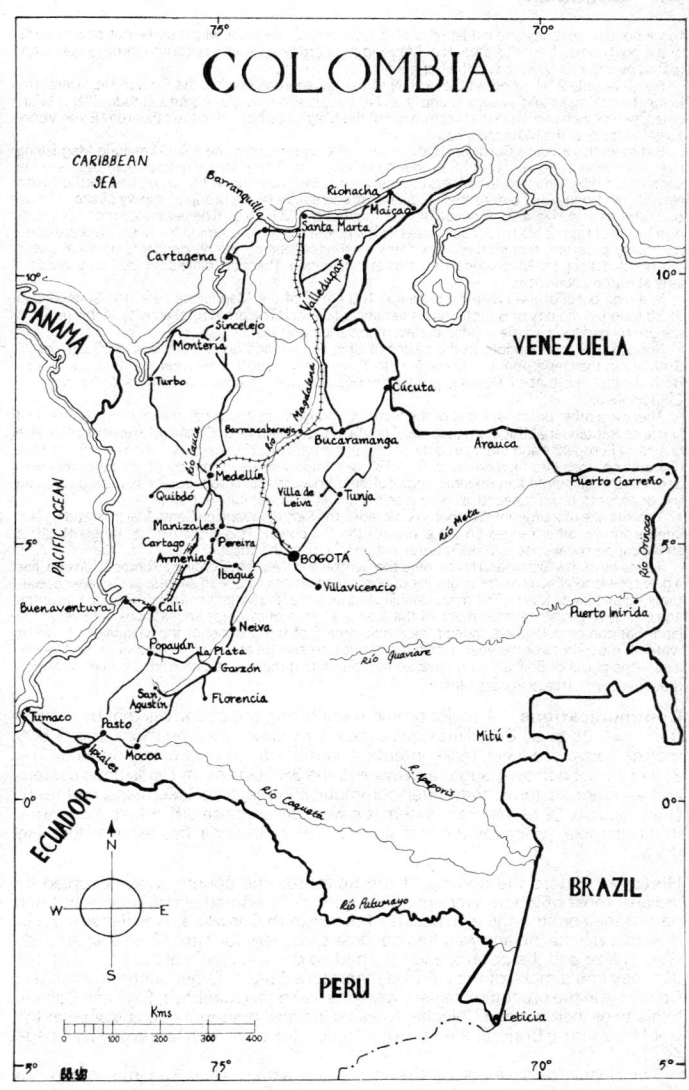

452 COLOMBIA

the second largest city and industrial centre in Colombia: Medellín. Much of the coffee and 75% of the gold comes from this area. N of Medellín the Cordillera Central splits into three ranges, separated by streams flowing into the Caribbean.

Near Latitude 2°N, or about 320 km. N of the Ecuadorean border, the Eastern Cordillera, the longest of all, rises and swings N and then NE towards Venezuela. About Latitude 7°N it bifurcates; one branch becomes the western rim of the Maracaibo basin and the other runs E into Venezuela, to the S of the Maracaibo basin.

Between this Eastern Cordillera and the Central Cordillera runs the 1,600 km. long Magdalena river, with the Caribbean port of Barranquilla at its mouth. There are more intermont basins in the Eastern Cordillera than in the others. Some of its peaks rise above the snow line. In the Sierra Nevada del Cocuy (just before the Cordillera bifurcates) there is a group of snowy peaks, all over 5,200 metres; the highest, Ritacuba Blanca, reaches 5,493 metres. The basins are mostly high, at an altitude of from 2,500 to 2,750 metres. In the Lower Magdalena region the river banks are comparatively deserted, though there are a few clearings made by the descendants of black slaves who settled along the Magdalena after their emancipation. There are oilfields in the valley, particularly at Barrancabermeja.

In a high basin of the Eastern Cordillera, 160 km. E of the Magdalena river, the Spaniards in 1538 founded the city of Bogotá, now the national capital. The great rural activity of this group is the growing of food: cattle, wheat, barley, maize and potatoes.

Roads run N from Bogotá to the basins of Chiquinquirá and Sogamoso, over 160 km. away. Both are in the Department of Boyacá, with Tunja, on a mountain between the two, as capital. Both basins, like that of Bogotá, produce food, and there are emerald mines at Muzo, near Chiquinquirá.

There are other basins in the N of the Eastern Cordillera: in the Departments of Santander and Norte de Santander at Bucaramanga and Cúcuta, and a small one at Ocaña. Movement into these basins by Europeans and *mestizos* did not take place until the 19th century, when chinchona bark (for quinine) rose into high demand. By 1885 this trade was dead, but by that time coffee was beginning to be planted. In Bucaramanga coffee is now the main crop, but it has been diversified by cacao, cotton and tobacco, all grown below the altitude suitable for coffee.

There is one more mountain group in Colombia, the Sierra Nevada de Santa Marta, standing isolated from the other ranges on the shores of the Caribbean. This is the highest range of all: its snow-capped peaks rise to 5,800 metres within 50 km. of the coast.

To the W of this Sierra, and N of where the Central and Western Cordilleras come to an end, lies a great lowland which has three groups of population on its Caribbean shores; at Cartagena, Barranquilla and Santa Marta. The rivers draining this lowland (the Magdalena, Sinú, Cauca, San Jorge and César) run so slowly that much of the area is a tissue of swamps and lagoons with very little land that can be cultivated. Indeed the whole area E of the channel of the Magdalena is under water at most times of the year. When the floods come, large areas of the land W of the Magdalena—the plains of Bolívar—are covered too, but during the dry season from October to March great herds of cattle are grazed there.

Communications A major problem still facing the country is that of surface transport. Its three Cordilleras, separated by valleys often no more than 1,500 metres above sea-level, make internal communications extremely difficult. The 3,700 km. of narrow-gauge railways and the 38,200 km. of roads have eastern and western systems, with inter-communicating laterals (see maps and text). Only about 10% of the road system is paved. Given these difficulties it is natural that Colombia, which ran the first airline in South America, has taken ardently to the air.

History Before the coming of the Spaniards the country was occupied by Indians, most of whom were primitive hunters or nomad agriculturists, but one part of the country, the high basins of the Eastern Cordillera, was densely occupied by Chibcha Indians who had become sedentary farmers. Their staple foods were maize and the potato, and they had no domestic animal save the dog; the use they could make of the land was therefore limited. Other cultures present in Colombia in the precolumbian era were the Tairona, Quimbaya, Sinú and Calima. Exhibits of their and the Chibcha (Muisca) Indians' gold-work can be seen at the Gold Museum in Bogotá, the one total "must" for all visitors to the city (see page 462).

The Spaniards sailed along the northern coast as far as Panama as early as 1500. The first permanent settlement was by Rodrigo de Bastidas at Santa Marta in 1525. Cartagena was founded in 1533. In 1536, Gonzalo Jiménez de Quesada (who wrote a full account of his adventures) pushed up the Magdalena river to discover its source; mounting the Eastern Cordillera in 1536, he discovered the Chibchas, conquered them, and founded Santa Fe de Bogotá in 1538.

COLOMBIA

In the meantime other Spanish forces were approaching the same region: Pizarro's lieutenant, Sebastián de Benalcázar, had pushed down the Cauca valley from Ecuador and founded Pasto, Popayán and Cali in 1536. Nicolás de Federmann, acting on behalf of the Welser financiers of Germany, who had been granted a colonial concession by Charles V, approached from Venezuela. Benalcázar reached Bogotá in 1538 and Federmann got there in 1539. As in Peru, the initial period of settlement was one of strife between contending *conquistadores*. The royal Audiencia de Santa Fe set up in 1550 gave the area a legislative, judicial and administrative entity. In 1564 this was followed by a presidency of the kingdom of Nueva Granada controlling the whole country and Panama, except Benalcázar's province of Popayán. The Presidency was replaced in 1718 by a viceroyalty at Bogotá which controlled the provinces now known as Venezuela as well; it was independent of the Viceroyalty of Peru, to which this vast area had previously been subject.

The movement towards independence from Spain was set going in 1794 by a translation into Spanish by the *criollo* Antonio Nariño of the French Declaration of the Rights of Man. The movement was given point and force when, in 1808, Napoleon replaced Ferdinand VII of Spain with his own brother Joseph. The New World refused to recognize this: there were several revolts in Nueva Granada, culminating in a revolt at Bogotá and the setting up of a *junta* on July 20, 1810. Other local juntas were established: Cartagena bound itself to a *junta* set up at Tunja. Late in 1812 the young Bolívar, driven out of Venezuela, landed at Cartagena. In a brilliant campaign in 1813 he pushed up the Magdalena to Ocaña, and from there to Cúcuta, and obtained permission from the *junta* at Tunja to advance into Venezuela. In 90 days he marched the 1,200 km. to Caracas over mountain country, fighting six battles, but he was unable to hold Caracas and withdrew to Cartagena in 1814.

Napoleon fell in 1815, and the Spanish Government immediately set about reconquering, with some success, Venezuela and New Granada. General Pablo Morillo took Cartagena after a bitter siege of 106 days—Bolívar had withdrawn to Jamaica—and was later "pacifying" Bogotá with a "Reign of Terror" by May 1816.

Bolívar had by now assembled an army of Llaneros, fortified by a British legion recruited from ex-servicemen of the Peninsular wars, in Venezuela at Angostura, or Ciudad Bolívar as it is called today. In the face of incredible difficulties he made a forced march across the Andes in 1819. After joining up with Santander's Nueva Granada army, he defeated the royalists at the battle of the Swamps of Vargas in July and again at Boyacá on August 7. He entered Bogotá three days later.

Bolívar reported his success to the revolutionary congress sitting at Angostura, and that body, on December 17, 1819, proclaimed the Republic of Gran Colombia, embracing in one the present republics of Venezuela, Colombia, and Ecuador. A general congress was held at Cúcuta on January 1, 1821, and here it was that two opposing views which were to sow such dissension in Colombia first became apparent. Bolívar and Nariño were for centralization; Santander, a realist, for a federation of sovereign states. Bolívar succeeded in enforcing his view for the time being, but Gran Colombia was not to last long; Venezuela broke away in 1829 and Ecuador in 1830. The remaining provinces were named Nueva Granada; it was not till 1863 that the name Colombia was restored.

Almost from its inception the new country became the scene of strife between the centralizing pro-clerical Conservatives and the federalizing anti-clerical Liberals. The Conservative president Tomás Cipriano de Mosquera (1845) encouraged education, began building roads, adopted the metric system, and put steamers on the Magdalena. The Liberals were dominant from 1849 for the next 30 years of insurrections and civil wars. In 1885 the Conservatives imposed a highly centralized constitution which has not been modified in this respect to this day. A Liberal revolt in 1899 turned into a civil war, "the War of the Thousand Days". The Liberals were finally defeated in 1902 after 100,000 people had died. It was in 1903 that Panama declared its independence from Colombia, following U.S. pressure.

454 COLOMBIA

After 40 years of comparative peace, the strife between Conservatives and Liberals was re-ignited in a little-publicized but dreadfully bloody civil war known as *La Violencia* from 1948 to 1957 (some 300,000 people were killed); but this was ended by a unique political truce. It was decided by plebiscite in 1957 that the two political parties would support a single presidential candidate, divide all political offices equally between them, and thus maintain political stability for sixteen years. In 1978 the agreement was ended, though some elements of the coalition— representation of the main opposition party in the Cabinet, for instance— were allowed to continue. The presidential election of May 1982 was won by Sr. Belisario Betancur, the Conservative candidate, who offered a general amnesty to guerrilla movements in an attempt to end violence in the country. Following an initial general acceptance of the offer, only one of the four main guerrilla groups, the FARC, upheld the truce in 1985-7. The Liberal candidate, Sr. Virgilio Barco, won the presidential elections of May 1986. FARC set up a political party, the Unión Patriótica, which won 10 seats in the 1986 congressional elections; the Liberal party took the majority.

The People of Colombia The regions vary greatly in their racial make-up: Antioquia and Caldas are largely of European blood, Pasto is Indian, the Cauca Valley and the rural area near the Caribbean are African or *mulatto*. No colour bar is legally recognized but it does exist in certain centres. Colombia has 19 cities with over 100,000 people.

About 50% live in the cities, and 50% are engaged in agriculture, pastoral and forest pursuits, hunting and fishing. The birth and death rates vary greatly from one area to the other, but in general infant mortality is very high. Hospitals and clinics are few in relation to the population. About 66% of the doctors are in the departmental capitals, which contain 12% of the population, though all doctors now have to spend a year in the country before they can get their final diploma. Deplorable *barrios clandestinos* (shanty-towns) have sprung up around Cali, Barranquilla, Cartagena and Buenaventura.

Education The literacy rate is 56%. Education is free, and since 1927 theoretically compulsory, but many children, especially in rural areas, do not attend. There are high standards of secondary and university education, when it is available.

Constitution and Government Senators and Representatives are elected by popular vote. The Senate has 112 members, and the Chamber of Representatives has 199. The President, who appoints his 13 ministers, is elected by direct vote for a term of four years, but cannot succeed himself in the next term. Every citizen over 18 can vote.

Administratively the country is divided into 22 Departments, 5 Intendencias, 5 Comisarias, and the Special District of Bogotá.

Liberty of speech and the freedom of the press are in theory absolute but in practice more limited. The language of the country is Spanish. Its religion is Roman Catholicism. There is complete freedom for all other creeds which do not contravene Christian morals or the law.

President, 1986-90: Sr. Virgilio Barco Vargas (Liberal).

Bogotá

Bogotá, capital of the Republic and a city of 4.4 million people, is on a plateau at 2,650 metres. The average temperature is 14°C (58°F). It is built on sloping land, and covers 210 square km. The central part of the city is full of character and contrasts: colonial buildings stand side-by-side with the most modern architecture. For the most part the houses are low, with eaves projecting over the streets; they are rarely brightly painted. The traffic is very heavy.

Visitors should take it easy for the first 24 hrs. Some people get dizzy at Bogotá's altitude. Be careful with food and alcoholic drinks for the first day also.

There is a very good view of the city from the top of Monserrate, the lower of the two peaks rising sharply to the E. It is reached by a funicular railway and a cable car. The new convent at the top is a popular shrine. At the summit, near the

COLOMBIA 455

church, a chairlift (US$0.20) and a platform give a bird's-eye view of the red-roofed city and of the plains beyond stretching to the rim of the Sabana. Also at the top are a Wild West-style train for children, a single restaurant (good *tamales*, US$1), and the Calle del Candelero, a reconstruction of a Bogotá street of 1887. Behind the church are popular picnic grounds. The fare up to Monserrate is US$1.30 return (US$ 0.70 children); four trips per hour. The funicular works only on Sun. and holidays; the cable car operates 1000-1800 weekdays, 0600-1800 on Sun. The neighbourhood can be dangerous, however; muggings are frequent even in daylight. Take a bus or taxi to the foot of the hill, and never be tempted to walk down from the top. (This warning cannot be overemphasized.) Taxi to foot, allowing 1 hour at the top, US$5.30.

At the foot of the hill is the Quinta de Bolívar, a fine colonial mansion, with splendid gardens and lawns. There are several cannons captured at the battle of Boyacá. The house, once Bolívar's home, is now a museum showing some of his personal possessions and paintings of events in his career. (Open 1000-1630, except Mon., mornings only on holidays; its address is Calle 20, No. 3-23 Este; charge US$0.50.)

The Plaza Bolívar, with a statue of the Liberator at its centre, is at the heart of the city; around the Plaza are the narrow streets and massive mansions of the old quarter (known as the Barrio La Candelaria), with their barred windows, carved doorways, brown-tiled roofs and sheltering eaves. The district is becoming popular as a residential area and has a growing artists' community. Most of the mansions and best colonial buildings are in this district: the Palace of San Carlos, the house of the Marqués de San Jorge (housing an archaeological museum), the Municipal Palace, the Capitol, and the churches of San Ignacio, Santa Clara, San Agustín, and the Cathedral.

The Calles (abbreviated "Cll.", or "C") run at right angles across the Carreras ("Cra." or "K"). It is easy enough to find a place once the address system, which is used throughout Colombia, is understood. The address Calle 13, No. 12-45 would be the building on Calle 13 between Carreras 12 and 13 at 45 paces from Carrera 12; however transversals and diagonals (numbers with letters appended) can complicate the system. The Avenidas, broad and important streets, may be either Calles (like 19) or Carreras (like 14). Av. Jiménez de Quesada, one of Bogotá's most important streets, owes its lack of straightness to having been built over a river-bed.

The street map of Bogotá on page 456 is marked with numerals showing the places of most interest for visitors. Each place will be described under the numeral which stands for it in the map.

1. The Plaza Bolívar, heart of the city, coeval with the city's foundation. On the eastern side rises the Archbishop's Palace, with splendid bronze doors. To one side of it is the colonial Plazuela de Rufino Cuervo. Here is the house of Manuela Sáenz, the mistress of Bolívar. On the other side is the house in which Antonio Nariño printed in 1794 his translation of "The Rights of Man" which triggered off the movement for independence.

See the Casa del Florero or 20 de Julio museum in a colonial house on the corner of Plaza Bolívar with Calle 11. It houses the famous flower vase that featured in the 1810 revolution and shows collections of the Independence War period, including documents and engravings. Entry fee US$0.40, open 1000-1830. On the northern side of the Plaza is the spectacular Palace of Justice, spectacularly wrecked in a guerrilla attack in 1985.

2. The Cathedral, rebuilt in 1807 in classical style. Notable choir loft of carved walnut and wrought silver on altar of Chapel of El Topo. Several treasures and relics; small paintings attributed to Ribera; banner brought by Jiménez de Quesada to Bogotá, in sacristy, which has also portraits of past Archbishops. There is a monument to Jiménez inside the Cathedral. In one of the chapels is buried Gregorio Vásquez Arce y Ceballos (1638-1711), by far the best painter in colonial Colombia. Many of his paintings are in the Cathedral.

3. The beautiful Chapel of El Sagrario, built end of the 17th century. Several paintings by Gregorio Vásquez Arce.

4. The Municipal Palace.

5. The Capitol, an imposing building with fine colonnades (1847-1925). Congress sits here.

9. The church of Santa Clara, another colonial church, is now a religious museum and concert hall.

10. San Ignacio, Jesuit church built in 1605. Emeralds from the Muzo mines in Boyacá were used in the monstrance. Paintings by Gregorio Vásquez Arce.

11. The Palace of San Carlos, where Bolívar lived. He is said to have planted the huge walnut tree

456 **COLOMBIA**

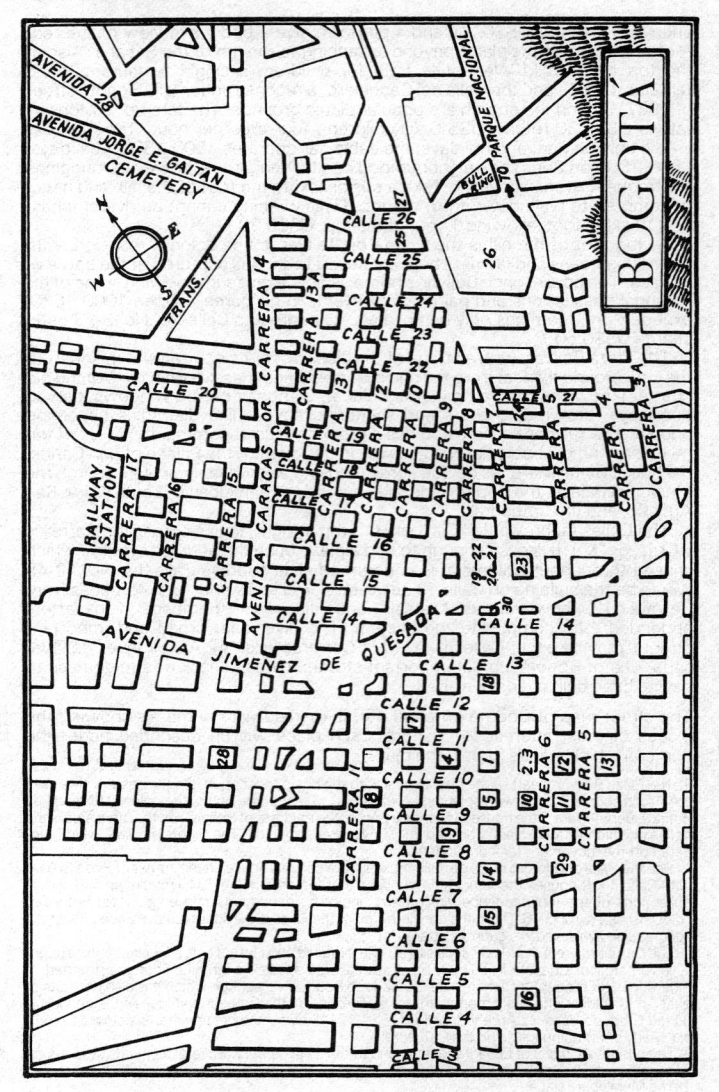

ROUGH SKETCH

in the courtyard. On September 25, 1828, there was an attempt on his life. His mistress, Manuela, thrust him out of the window and he was able to hide for two hours under the stone arches of the bridge across the Río San Agustín. Santander, suspected of complicity, was arrested and banished. Now the Presidential Palace, with a huge banquet hall used for state affairs. The guard is changed—full-dress uniform—every day at 1700.

The Museum of Colonial Art, across from the Palace of San Carlos (Carrera 6, No. 9-77) is one of the finest colonial buildings in Colombia. It belonged originally to the Society of Jesus, and was once the seat of the oldest University in Colombia and of the National Library. It has a splendid collection of colonial art and paintings by Gregorio Vásquez Arce, all kinds of utensils, and 2 charming patios. Open Tues. to Sat. 0930-1830; Sun. and holidays, 1000-1700. Entry fee US$0.40 for adults; students US$0.20.

12. Colón Theatre, Calle 10, No. 5-32 (operas, lectures, ballets, plays, concerts, etc.), late 19th century with lavish decorations. Seating for 1,200, and very ornate.

13. The Mint (Casa de la Moneda), built in 1720, is at Calle 11, No. 4-93; contains a museum of religious paintings and numismatics. Open Mon.-Sat. 0900-2100, Sun. and holidays, 0900-1800. In the same street, No. 4-16, is the Banco de la República's Luis Angel Arango library, one of the best endowed and arranged in South America, with 3 reading rooms, research rooms, an art gallery and a splendid concert hall. There are free concerts and exhibitions. The architecture is impressive and the lavatories are recommended.

14. Palacio de Nariño (1906), the presidential palace. Spectacular interior, fine collection of modern Colombian paintings. Free tours every Sun. morning with guide, leave whenever 15 people gather at main entrance gate.

15. Church of San Agustín, strongly ornamented (1637). Fine paintings by Gregorio Vásquez Arce and the Image of Jesus which was proclaimed Generalísimo of the army in 1812 (closed for restoration—1984).

16. Santa Bárbara church (mid-16th century), one of the most interesting colonial churches. Paintings by Gregorio Vásquez Arce (closed for restoration—1984).

17. Church of San Juan de Dios, well worth a visit.

18. Palace of Communications (postal and telegraph), built on the site of the old colonial church of Santo Domingo.

19. Government Palace of Cundinamarca Department, almost as imposing as the Capitol. Corinthian style.

20. San Francisco church (mid-16th century), with notable paintings of famous Franciscans, choir stalls, and a famous high altar (1622). Remarkable ceiling is in Spanish-Moorish (*mudéjar*) style.

21. Church of La Veracruz, first built five years after the founding of Bogotá, rebuilt in 1731, and again in 1904. In 1910 it became the National Pantheon and Church of the Republic. José de Caldas, the famous scientist, was buried along with many other victims of the "Reign of Terror" under the church. Fashionable weddings.

22. La Tercera Orden, an old colonial church famous for its carved woodwork, altars, and confessionals.

23. The Banco de la República, next to Parque Santander. Next to the Bank is the wonderful Gold Museum (see page 462). In Parque Santander there is a bronze statue of Santander, who helped Bolívar to free Colombia and was later its President.

24. Las Nieves, old colonial church, has been demolished and replaced by an ugly modern church.

26. Planetarium, Natural History Museum and Museum of Modern Art (Calle 26, Carrera 7), in Parque de la Independencia. Two daily showings of best foreign modern painters, US$0.30. (see also page 462)

27. *Tequendama Hotel*. Nearby (on Carrera 7 and Calle 26) are the church and monastery of San Diego, a picturesque old building recently restored. The Franciscan monastery with fine Mudéjar ceiling was built in 1560 and the church in 1607 as its chapel. It is now used as a crafts shop by Artesanías de Colombia (municipal tourist office opposite). SE of the *Tequendama Hotel* is the National Library, with entrance on Calle 24.

28. Parque Mártires (Park of the Martyrs) with monument, on the site of the Plaza in which the Spanish shot many patriots during the struggle for independence.

29. Church of María del Carmen, with excellent stained glass and walls in bands of red and white.

Warning In addition to the advice on personal safety given on page 527, be especially careful of people who describe themselves as plain-clothes police: ask for identification or offer to go to the police station—as long as it isn't dark! The old part around Plaza Bolívar and from Calle 28, extending to the centre and South (i.e. declining Calle numbers) are reported as dangerous. Mugging, however, may still occur in other parts of the city, and some Bogotanos carry "mugging money" to hand over in such a situation. There are now special police patrolling the centre in pairs; the situation is reported to have improved.

Under state-of-siege legislation police may shoot and kill a suspect during any narcotics operation and it will be automatically classified as self-defence. A large number of would-be drug traffickers have been killed in this way.

The Judicial Unit for Tourism offers 24-hour service for tourists at Carrera 7, No. 27-50, Tel.: 283-49-30 or 284-50-47.

458 COLOMBIA

Hotels

Name	Address	Single (US$)	Double (US$)	No. of Stars	Category
Hilton	Cra. 7, No. 32-16	60	72	5	A
Tequendama	Cra. 10, No. 26-21	55	67	5	A
La Fontana*	Diagonal 127A, No. 21-10	50	67	5	A
Bacatá	Calle 19, No. 5-20	42	52	4	A
Continental	Av. Jiménez, No. 4-16	19	25	4	C
Dann	Calle 19, No. 5-72	30	41	3	B
Nueva Granada*	Av. Jiménez 4-77	19	30		B
Maria Isabel	Calle 33, No. 15-05	28	38		B
El Presidente	Calle 23, No. 9-45	21	28	3	C
Las Terrazas	Calle 54a, No. 13-12	17	22	2	C
Del Duc	Calle 23, No. 9-38	18	24	2	C
San Diego*	Cra. 13, No. 24-82	11	15	1	D

(The prices above are minimum rates in February 1987)
* = recommended. Whenever possible, book hotel reservations in advance.

For comfort, El Belvedere, on Calle 100 with Transversal 18, A, has been recommended. Aparta-Hotel América, Carrera 8, No. 65-89 (Aptdo Aéreo 59859, Tel.: 212-81-10, 212-44-90, 212-42-09), A for apartment for one to four persons, clean, comfortable, quiet; Cosmos 100, Av. 100, No. 21A-41, B. There are many others, rather cheaper, some recommended, as follows: Bogotá Plaza, C. 100, 18A-30, A; Magdalena, Carrera 13A, No. 38-91, Tel.: 232-6314, C; Monserrat, Av. Caracas, 18-08, D, recommended, clean, impeccable service; Cristal, Calle 17, No. 7-92, C, similar quality; Menéndez, Calle 20, No. 5-85, E, meals extra, hot water, very clean, good view of Monserrate, unsafe, in a dangerous area; Regina, Carrera 5, No. 15-16, D, with private bath, TV, phone, friendly, good; La Hostería de la Candelaria, Calle 9, No. 3-11, Tel.: 283-5258/242-1727, Aptdo. Aéreo 15978, D, highly recommended for comfort, atmosphere and service (good for longer stays); Residencias Steves, Carrera 10, No. 16-67, D; Comendador, Carrera 8, No. 38-41, high class, D, reasonable, but poor service and poor plumbing, in central residential section. On Calle 14 with Carrera 4 are: Turístico Trianon, No. 4-13, D in restored colonial house, nice; Dann Colonial, No. 4-21, C; opposite is Santa Fe, No. 4-48, bath and hot shower with good service, E, recommended; Residencias San Sebastián, Carrera 4, No. 4-80, E; Residencias Florián, Calle 14, No. 4-67, F; also recommended, Hospedaje Zaratoga, Av. Jiménez, No. 4-56, D (F without bath), safe, pleasant, hot water—all are near the centre; Del Dorado, Calle 18, No. 3-98, F; Residencia Aragón, Carrera 3, No. 14-13, clean and safe, F, run down, but friendly and honest, no hot water, special rates for long stay (cheap taxi to airport can be arranged); Residencias Las Vegas, Calle 13, No. 3-81, F, clean, central. Residencias Panamericano, Calle 15, No. 12-70, 3-star but not in a safe area, E; similarly, De Lujo, Carrera 13, No. 22-46, Tel.: 242-8849, D, with bath, clean, safe, friendly, recommended; Centro International, Carrera 13, No. 38-97, friendly, small rooms, D; Avenida 19, Avenida (Calle) 19, No. 5-92, D, with shower, good price considering its central location, clean, very helpful service; Pensión Alemana, Carrera 14, No. 25-15, E, recommended; Pensión Halifax, Calle 93, No. 15-93, English spoken, friendly, B with all meals included in daily rate; Regis, Calle 18, No. 6-09 (also known as Residencias María), E (C with shower), sometimes hot water, old-fashioned, run down but safe, clean, poor value; Del Parque, Calle 24, No. 4-93, C; La Virgen del Camino, Calle 18A, No. 14-33, D, without bath, but not clean, no hot water, breakfast US$1, not recommended; Residencia Claudia, Carrera 8, No. 17-66; Kayser, Carrera 4, No. 13-18, E, safe; Ile de France, Calle 18, No. 14-56, C, hot water, good food, either breakfast or dinner; Hostal Alexander, Calle 23, No. 5-23, D, safe, clean, friendly, hot water; Residencias Alemanas, Carrera 16, No. 16-48, E (about US$1 more for room with bath), some shared rooms, recommended, noisy front rooms, laundry service (except when raining), hot water, very friendly, breakfasts are expensive (US$1.30) and not recommended; El Buen Amigo, Carrera 16, No. 14-45, E, friendly, cheap, noisy at night; opposite is Manizales, E; Teuscaá, Av. 33, No. 14-64, D; Hostal Residencias Moreno, Transversal 33 No. 95-28, Tel.: 257-9127, D inc three meals, two house taxi drivers, nearby frequent bus service to town centre, very friendly, safe for left luggage, quiet, comfortable, hot water, highly recommended; Los Cerros, Avenida 19, No. 9-18, D, clean, friendly, restaurant, recommended, TV in rooms; under same management, Quiratama, Calle 17, No. 12-44, bar, restaurant, TV, phone, C, safe; Motel Tropicana, Avenida Caracas (Carrera 14), cheap, friendly and good food; Residencial Capri, Carrera 13, No. 15-89, E; Residencial Casablanca, Carrera 15, between Calles 16 and 17, F, with bath, not very good; Vas, Calle 12-30, E, with bath, safe, clean and friendly; Residencias Schlief, Calle 33A, No. 14-38, E, with breakfast, hot water, pleasant; Residencias La Casona, Calle 14, No. 4-13, old-fashioned, English spoken, E, with bath, good meals for US$1; María Luisa, Carrera 14, between Calles 15 and 16, very reasonable and food is good; Residencias Picasso, Calle 17, No. 15-47, F, dirty, shared bath, unsafe area, often full, not very secure, breakfast US$0.60 (poor food); next to Picasso is Pensión Armenia, F, after bargaining, clean; Residencia Cacique, Carrera 17, Calle 15, F, hot water, safe; Geber, Carrera 10, No. 22-45, D, good, but water supply can be faulty; under same management, Quindio, Calle 17, No. 16-94, F; Serranía, Calle 17, No. 14-55, F; Residencia Dorantes, Calle 13, No. 5-07, very clean, E (F without bath), hot water, reasonable; *Ferlen*, Calle 8a, No. 16-52, basic, F; *Zaddi*, Carrera 13, No. 12-32, D; *Residencias R-B*, Av. Jiménez with Carrera 4, central, clean, E; *Residencia Candelaria*, Carrera 4, No. 18-87, F, clean, hot water, safe, recommended for motorcyclists; *Residencias Real No. 1*, Carrera 15, No. 17-71, E, safe, dubious water supply, good value, as is *Residencias La Villa*, E, which is opposite; *Niagara*, Carrera 3a, No. 20-35, D, with turkish bath; *Residencias Liliana*, D, Carrera 5, No. 12-55; *Residencias Elis*, Calle 14, between Carreras 14 and 15, good and cheap; *Italia*, Carrera 7 y Calle 20, E, run down, poor value, not recommended; *Alcron*, Calle 20 y Carrera 5, F, restaurant; *Residencias Ambala*, Carrera 5A, No. 13-46, D, cheap, clean, friendly and central. *Alexia*, Carrera 9, No. 16-33, fair; *Calli Valle*, Carrera 15, Calle 16, E, basic; *España*, Carrera 7, Calle 23, D, clean, safe; *Regio*, next to Gold Museum, E, clean, noisy. We are informed that from Calle 12 southwards, Carrera 13 westwards is not salubrious: visitors are therefore advised to pick hotels in streets NE of Calle 12, with higher numbers. There are certainly many hotels between Calles 13 and 17 and Carreras 15 and 17, many of which are cheap, some of which are clean. *Residencias Españolas*, Calle 13 and Carrera 16, is one such, clean, E; *Residencias El Hogar*, Calle 16, No. 15-87, is another, clean, small rooms, warm water, G (gringos pay a US$1 surcharge). *Camelia*, Calle 16, No. 15-20, G, clean, safe, hot water, Tel.: 243-4131; *Asturias*, next door (No. 15-36), Tel.: 242-0931, also G, same standard but no hot water; many other cheap hotels in this area, which is dangerous especially for women alone; *Residencias Panamá No. 2*, Carrera 16, No. 16-88, Tel.: 241-04-05, F, friendly, clean, safe, hot shower. Private vehicles should be parked in lockable, guarded *parqueaderos*.

Restaurants Hotel food has become very expensive and 10% value-added tax is now charged. The restaurant of *Hotel Nueva Granada* has been highly recommended. The *Refugio Alpino*, Calle 23, No. 7-49, is an excellent Swiss restaurant: meals cost about US$9 and service is superb. *Gran Vatel*, Carrera 7, Calle 70, French and Belgian food, meals cost US$5-10, highly recommended food, but gloomy atmosphere; *Montserrate*, Tel.: 243-65-30, Ext. 05 (Colombian food, overpriced); *Casa San Isidro*, on Monserrate, good, not cheap; *El Pollo Dorado*, Carrera 9, No. 17-38; *Eduardo*, Carrera 11, No. 90-43, international and expensive; *Las Acacias*, Carrera 11, No. 65-46, for typical Colombian food, US$5-6; *Verners*, Calle 25, No. 12-23, near *Hotel Tequendama* (very good German food); *Casa Vieja del Claustro*, Carrera 3, No. 18-60, offers typical food; *El Café de Rosita*, Carrera 3, No. 8-65, connected with *Hostería de la Candelaria*, breakfast, lunch, bar and *tapas*, concerts Thurs. and Fri., recommended; *Casa Viejo de San Diego*, Carrera 10, No. 26-50; *Casa Vieja*, Av. Jiménez 3-73 (traditional Bogotá food in traditional atmosphere, live music), close by on Av. Jiménez is *La Guayacana*, Colombian food, reasonably priced lunches; *El Zaguán de Las Aguas*, Calle 19, No. 5-62, local dishes, atmosphere and national dancing in evening, but expensive and poor cooking and drinks (beer and soft drinks not available) very expensive; *Los Sauces*, Carrera 11, Calle 69, also has traditional music and dancing, expensive with cover charge; *Chalet Suizo*, Carrera 7, No. 21-51, Swiss and international food; *Donde Canta la Rana*, Carrera 24-C, No. 20-10 Sur, a few km. from centre, is refreshingly local and unspoilt, open 1400-1900. Also try *La Polla*, Calle 19, No. 1-85. *Doña Bárbara*, Calle 82, corner of Carrera 11, dinner costs US$ 4-7, excellent latino jazz played; *La Barba*, Calle 22, between Carreras 9 and 10, Spanish atmosphere; *La Piragua*, corner of Av. Jiménez and Carrera 5, cheap and good; *Temel*, Carrera 19 at Calle 118, good steaks, expensive; *Giuseppe Verdi*, Calle 58, No. 5-85, excellent pasta; *Petit Paris*, Carrera 4 and Calle 74, expensive French food; *Jeno's*, Carrera 15, near Calle 85, serves good, though not cheap, pizzas, another outlet at Calle 19, near Cra. 6; *Berlín*, Carrera 15 and Calle 74, German food; *Chalet Europa*, Carrera 9, No. 16-91, 4-course meals for US$5; *Balalaika*, Calle 15, No. 32-83; *Cafetería Romano*, Av. Jiménez, between Carrera 6 and 7, all meals, very clean and reasonable, well recommended, as is its sister restaurant *Salerno*, Carrera 7, No. 19-43; *Brisas del Valle*, Carrera 7, Calle 22, good, reasonably priced; *Barra Llanera*, Carrera 9, No. 21-45, open weekends and recommended for cheap fish. *Robin Hood*, near *Hotel Nueva Granada*, very good, three-course weekday lunch for US$4, there are also other branches. Also on Avenida Jiménez, *Avenida*, good local food, meals starting from US2, recommended; *Balmoral*, No. 4-92, good food, reasonable prices, open Sun. and holidays, and *Restaurante Briceño*, Av. Jiménez, 5-19, large portions, cheap. For local food, *Teusacán*, Carrera 15, No. 39-16; *Tierra Colombiana*, Carrera 10, No. 27-27, good, expensive food, evening floor show. There are two restaurants called *Sandricks*, one on Carrera 16, No. 91-25, the other on Carrera 15, No. 79-92; they are run by two brothers and are highly recommended, though not cheap (US$6-9 for a main dish). There is a small chain of restaurants called *La Sultana*: the best is at Carrera 7, No. 21-14; *El Parrillón*, 1½ blocks from *Hotel Kayser*, serves good steaks and other dishes for less than US$4; *Doña Hertha*, Calle 19, No. 8-61, 3-course meal US$3, specialty is goulash; *Ranch Burger*, Centro El Lago, on Carrera 15, serves hamburgers; *Burger King*, Cra. 7 with Calle 34 next to Hilton, also *Centro Granahorrar*, Av. Chile with Cra. 9, in Chapinero at Carrera 13 with Calle 64, and more; *Dominó*, a chain of good, fairly cheap, typical food restaurants, at Calle 19 with Cra. 3, Cra. 11 with Calle 71; *La Gran Barilla*, Carrera 4, with Calle 13, cheap, rich meals; *Parrilla de Oro*, Carrera 4, No. 17-94, excellent inexpensive typical food; *Delphi*, opposite Teatro Gaitán, on Carrera 7, recommended for cheap meals; *Trattoria Bistro*, Calle 59, No. 8-50, with branch at Unicentro (Local 2-45), not cheap, but good food, must book at weekends; *Taverna Alemana*, Avenida Caracas (Carrera 14) with Calle 64; for US$1.20 a two-course meal can be had in the cafeteria of the Ley and Tía supermarkets; also Cafam, Calle 17 y Carrera 9 (Centro Colseguros). Snackbar *La Puerta Falsa*, on Calle 11, No.

460 COLOMBIA

6-50, *El Vegetariano*, Calle 22, No. 8-89, set meals for US$1, recommended (the restaurant on 3rd floor with only a small sign); there is another branch at Calle 8, No. 5-74; *El Trópico*, Carrera 8, No. 17-72, vegetarian restaurant, good food (especially the fruit cake) and whole wheat loaves for US$1.20 (4-course meal, US$3); also vegetarian: *El Vegetariano Fleber*, Carrera 17, No. 10-49, good, *Vegetariano de Sol*, Calle 63, No. 10-62 with Yoga Institute in Plaza de Lordes. *Jugos Cali*, Carrera 11, No. 64-60, mostly juices, with pastries. 4 recommended vegetarian restaurants, all with the same owner, are: *El Champiñón*, Transversal 20, No. 122-05 (Tel.: 213-2278), near Unicentro, *Samovares*, Carrera 11, No. 69-99 (Tel.: 249-4549), Carrera 11, No. 67-63 (Tel.: 249-6515) and Av. Caracas No. 32-64 (Tel.: 285-6095). *Los Vegetarianos*, Calle 41, No. 8-65 (good) and another location with courtyard, very nice; *Acuarius*, Carrera 16, No. 43-30 and also at Calle 18, good vegetarian food, recommended; *Gran Fraternidad*, Carrera 8, No. 21-39, also recommended. Vegetarian food, excellent, at Calle 74, No. 12-30. *El Dorado*, Carrera 15, No. 16-39, good meal for US$2.60. *Monte Blanco*, Carrera 7a, No. 17-31, and other branches, very good. *Diana*, Calle 8 with Carrera 6. Good pizzas are served at branches of *Little John's*; *Tío Tim's*, Carrera 13, Calle 67, for pizza, beer and mechanical bull (owned by a Welshman); *Pizzería*, Calle 33, No. 15 (opp. *Hotel María Isabel*), excellent food, atmosphere and music; opposite the US embassy; *La Candelaria*, Calle 11, No. 3-89, 3-course meal meal for US$2; *Residencias Lido*, Calle 11, No. 8-79 (just off Plaza Bolívar) serves good, cheap, complete meals; *La Fregata*, Calle 15, No. 9-30 and Calle 77, No. 15-36, expensive but excellent for sea food. Spanish food at *El Mesón de la Paella*, Calle 69, No. 12-14. Typical Colombian food at *Mesón las Indias*. French food at *La Reserva*, Calle 39 and Carrera 15, expensive (dinner for 2, US$30), good food and service in an old house with open fire. For Italian food, *Il Piccolo Café*, Carrera 15, No. 96-55, very good. *Longaniza*, Carrera 15, No. 92-73, very good for meat, with salad bar. For Chinese food, the *Hong Kong* (overpriced); *Nanking*, Calle 23, between Carreras 6 and 7; and *Pagoda China* on Calle 69, Cra. 6. Japanese and Korean dishes at *Restaurant Arirang*. For excellent inexpensive Arab food, *Ramses*, Carrera 7, No. 18-64. For the traveller on a budget, *bandeja* (the local *plato del día*) can cost US$1.50- 2 for a 2-course meal at the right places. *Mi Ranchito*, Calle 21, No. 5-77, good cheap bar, drinks only. Good ice cream at *Yeti Helados*, Carrera 11 with Av. Chile. On Sunday nights it is difficult to find anywhere open; try Calle 22 (the entertainment district).

All along Carrera 15 in El Chicó are shops, bars and restaurants, many of which have tables out on the pavement. *Pimm's*, Carrera 15, Calle 83; *Tony Roma's*, Carrera 15 esq. Calle 77, good quality food and excellent service. Also on Carrera 15, 85-42, interior 7, is *Academia de Golf* which has a good beef/fish and salad restaurant, as well as golf and driving and putting ranges, and equipment for sale. *Arte y Cerveza Taberna*, 2 locations, at Calle 43 near Av. Caracas, and one in North of city, bar with some food, live music (Colombian and Andean); *Quiebracanto*, 2 locations, Carrera 5 near Calle 16, and next to University of Los Andes, Calle 18 and Carrera 2, student places with recorded music, occasional films, talks, etc.; *Café Libre*, Carrera 5, near Universidad Católica, bar with live music, also serves lunches; *Café Omo Lago*, Carrera 15, No. 82-60. For those visiting the Centro Administrativo Nacional (CAN, on Av. El Dorado near airport), a good restaurant nearby is *La Casa de Fernando*, Transversal 42, Diag. 40, No. 43-22; others nearby.

Tea Rooms *Benalcázar*, near Plaza de las Nieves on Carrera 8, No. 20-25, excellent pastries and quite all right for women alone; *La Suiza*, Calle 25, No. 9-41, excellent pastries; as good, but cheaper, is *Pastelería Castilla*, Calle 19 and Carrera 10 and 12; *William Tell*, Carrera 13, Calle 23. *Fábrica del Pan*, Av. Jiménez at Carrera 8, good for breakfasts, teas, snacks, reasonably priced. A chain of *Cyranos* throughout the city offers good pastries.

Clubs Anglo-American Club, Country Club (golf, polo, swimming), Magdalena Sports Club (tennis), San Andrés Golf Club, Club de Los Lagartos (social; with a pool heated by hot springs, water-skiing, a golf course and tennis courts), Club Campestre Fontanar (tennis), America Tennis Club, Lions' Club, Bogotá Sports Club (cricket, football, tennis, squash, rugby and hockey). Both the Lagartos and the Country Club have beautiful gardens designed by Enrique Acosta.

Shopping 10% value-added tax on all purchases. *Artesanías de Colombia* (state-owned), Almacén San Diego, in the old San Diego church, Cra. 10, No. 26-50, Almacén Las Aguas, next to the Iglesia de las Aguas, Carrera 3A, No. 18-60, Almacén del Norte, Cra. 15, No. 95-74, has best selection of folk art and crafts, at fair prices. A good place for handicrafts is *El Lago*, Carrera 15, No. 73-64; some way from centre; also a branch at the Avianca building. Another good place is *El Balay* on Carrera 15, No. 74-38, and, of course, there is the shop in the Museo de Artes y Tradiciones Populares, which is recommended. *Artesanía* shop at Carrera 15, No. 83-30 often has cheap objects. See H. Stern's jewellery stores at the International Airport, *Hilton Hotel* and *Tequendana Hotel*. A street market on Avenida Jiménez and Carrera 14 (Avenida Caracas) sells cheaper *ruanas*, blankets, leatherware, etc. Good *ruanas* can be bought at *Tipicentro*, Calle 17, No. 5-46 and No. 5-37, with better prices at the smaller shop although bargaining can bring them down a bit further. The lot at Carrera 7, corner of Calle 24, often has *artesanía* or book fairs. Shopping centre at Chapinero, Carrera 13, Calles 55-60, specializes in men's shoes and leather. Women's shoes are found on Calle 18 between Carrera 7 and 9. Boutiques are to be found in El Chicó on Carrera 15, Calles 76-100. There is another market, which is good for handicrafts, at Carrera 10, Calle 10. A handicrafts market is held around Carrera 14 and Calle 28 at the beginning of July and before Christmas. High-quality leather goods on Calle 19, between Carreras 4 and 7,

COLOMBIA 461

especially at *Todo en Cuero*, Calle 19, No. 6-56; also Carrera 10, between Calles 13 and 19. Also the *Boots and Bags* and *Pecarí* chains for high-quality leather. *Galería Cano*, Edificio Bavaria, Carrera 7, Bogotá Hilton, Unicentro, Loc. 218, Airport, sells gold and gold-plated replicas of some of the jewellery on display in the Gold Museum. *Mitus* (in *Hotel Tequendama*) also sells reproduction jewellery from its own workshop, and Indian pottery. *Galería 70*, Avenida 13, No. 70-14, exhibition of and shop selling hand-woven textiles and rugs. Primitive paintings are often on show in the *Galería El Callejón*, Calle 16, No. 6-34, as well as old maps and prints. Banco de Fotografías Movifoto, Calle 15, No. 4-66, has a very large selection of postcards from all over Colombia. There are several antique shops around Calle 66 and Carrera 11; check yellow pages for precise addresses. Antiques also at *Hijos de Antonio Cancino* on Plaza Bolívar.

The pavements and cafés along Av. Jiménez, below Carrera 7, Parque de los Periodistas, and Calle 16 and Carrera 3, are used on weekdays by emerald dealers. Great care is needed in buying: bargains are to be had, but synthetics and forgeries abound. (Beware of stones that seem too perfect or have a bluish colouring.) Three shops selling good emeralds at reasonable prices are: *Joyería Frida*, Carrera 7, No. 18-31; *Willis F. Bronkie*, Carrera 9, No. 74-08, oficina 801; *Jewelry Prado*, Carrera 7, No. 16-50. Also *El Palacio de la Esmeralda*, Carrera 10, No. 26-7, int. 126, reasonable prices, certificates given. Also jewellery shops in the basement of *Hotel Tequendama*. Modern textiles and knitwear (many Rodier products are made in Colombia) can be bought at low prices at *Unicentro*, a large shopping centre on Carrera 15 at Calle 127A, with restaurants, night clubs, cinemas, post office, and a bowling centre as well as shops (take "Unicentro" bus from centre, going N on Cra. 10—takes about 1 hr.). Centro Granahorrar, Av. Chile (Calle 72) between Carreras 10 and 11 is a good shopping centre, comparable in size with the Unicentro. *Only*, supermarket, Carrera 13, Calle 60. *Pomona* supermarket on Calle 100, esq. Av. Suba, has many imported items, more impressive than *Carrulla*. *Ley* and *Tía* supermarkets are inexpensive for necessity items; they can be found throughout the country. *Técnica*, Carrera 7A, No. 16-13 (first floor) will put gold lettering on leather goods quickly and cheaply. *Oma*, Carrera 15, Calle 79/80, is good for coffee.

Bookshops *Librería Buchholz*, Carrera 7, No. 27-68, also at Calle 59, No. 13-13 (Chapinero); useful advice in a number of languages, low prices. *Librería Aldina*, Carrera 7, Calle 70-80, most helpful on books and Bogotá alike, excellent stock of English-language books, open 0930-1930, Sat. 0930-1700. *Librería Nacional*, Carrera 7, No. 17-51. *Librería Francesa*, Calle 65, No. 9-07. *Librería Lerner*, Av. Jiménez, No. 4-35. Books in Colombia are generally expensive. Book Exchange Stalls, Calle 19, between Carreras 7 and 10.

Taxis have meters (although newer ones are reported not to have them); insist that they are used. Starting charge, US$0.35, plus US$0.07 for every 90 metres, minimum charge US$0.85. Additional charge of US$0.35 after 2000 and on public holidays and Sun. (a list of legal charges should be posted in the taxi).

Tan and green tourist taxis can be rented by the hour or the day through the *Tequendama Hotel*, most of the drivers speak English and are very helpful. Taxis are relatively cheap, so it is worthwhile taking one if you are carrying valuables, or at night. Taxi tours with Jaime Carvajal (Spanish spoken only), Tel.: 203-1063.

Travel in Bogotá Flag buses down; no stops to speak of. Bus fares are US$0.10, *busetas* charge US$0.05. Green buses with letters TSS (i.e. unsubsidized) are more expensive. Urban buses are not good for sightseeing because you will be standing as likely as not. Most scenic route is 149 "Capilla—via La Calera", which starts on Carrera 14 (Av. Caracas) with Calle 71 and goes up into the mountains to the east of the city, ending at Calle 64. A metro is under consideration.

Car Rental Rentacarro, at the airport, and Carrera 7, No. 29-34; Hertz, at the airport, and at Carrera 10, No. 26-35; National, Carrera 7, No. 32-33; Hernando Zuluaga & Cía, Carrera 7, No. 20-80; Aquilautos Ltda., Carrera 7, No. 34-81. Avis also have an office. Large cars can be hired at US$25 a day plus US$0.20 per kilometre. Volkswagens cost US$15 daily plus US$0.12 per kilometre.

Night Clubs The most fashionable is the Monserrate Room at the *Tequendama*. Others are Casbach, Candilejas, La Casina delle Rose, Kyreos, As de Copas, Balalaika, La Pampa, Sahara, and La Zambra (Spanish). Unicorn, Calle 94, No. 7-75, now expensive and spectacular; El Padrino, very good. The red light area is near the corner of the Calle 20 and Carrera 13.

Theatre Many of the theatres are in the Candelaria area. Colón Theatre details on page 457. The following are the equivalent of the British fringe theatre: La Candelaria, Calle 12, No. 2-59; Sala Seki Sano, Calle 12, No. 2-65; Teatro Libre de Bogotá, Calle 13, No. 2-44.

Cinema Cinemateca Distrital, Carrera 7 No. 22-79. Good films, US$0.85. Also on Carrera 7: Teatro Municipal, No. 22-53, Metro, No. 21-78, Tisquesa, No. 27-29. Consult *El Tiempo* for what is on; frequent programme changes. Admission, US$0.70.

Sports Bull fighting on Sats. and Suns. during the season at the municipally owned Plaza de Santamaría, near Parque Independencia. (Local bullfight museum at bullring, door No. 6.) Boxing matches are held here too. Horse races at Hipódromo los Andes, on Autopista Norte, races at

462 COLOMBIA

1400 (entrance US$1 and US$0.35), and at the Hipódromo del Techo, in the SW, on Sats., Suns. and public holidays. Near-by is the Municipal Stadium, which can hold 50,000 spectators. Football matches are played here. The Country Club has two 18-hole golf courses, several tennis courts, indoor swimming pool and many other facilities. There are two polo clubs. Some streets, for instance parts of Carrera 7, are closed on Sundays for cycling and roller-skating; the former is particularly popular.

Football Tickets for matches at El Camplin stadium can be bought in advance at *Cigarrería Bucana*, Calle 18, No. 5-92. But not normally necessary to book in advance, except for local Santa Fe-Millionarios derby. Take a cushion; matches Sun. at 1545, Weds. at 2000.

Museums (all closed on Mondays) The National Museum, on Carrera 7, No. 28-66, the Panóptico, an old prison converted into a Museum (to the NE of the map), founded by Santander in 1823. Its top floor houses a fine art section, comprising national paintings and sculptures. Open Tues.-Sat. 0930-1830, Sun. 1000-1700, US$0.25. Many of its pre-conquest exhibits have been transferred to the Archaeological Museum at Carrera 6, No. 7-43, open Tues.-Sat. 1000-1700, Sun. 1000-1300, US$0.15. See 11 for Museum of Colonial Art, under 1 for Museo 20 de Julio, under 26 for Planetarium and under 13 for the Banco de la República's Luis Angel Arango library.

The Museum of Modern Art, Calle 26, No. 6-05, entry US$0.15 (open Tues.-Sun. 0900-1900). It has a programme of films. The Planetarium and Natural History Museum, Calle 26 with Carrera 7, open Tues.-Fri. 0900-1800, Sat., Sun., and holidays, 1000-1800. The Museo de Arte Colonial, Calle 6, No. 9-77, in an old convent with a garden.

The Museo Mercedes de Pérez, formerly the Hacienda de El Chicó, a fine example of colonial architecture, is at Carrera 7, No. 94-17. It contains a world-wide collection of mostly 18th century porcelain, furniture, paintings, etc. Open Tues-Sun., 0930-1230, 1430-1700.

The Museum of Popular Art and Tradition is at Carrera 8, No. 7-21. This museum is in an old monastery and exhibits local arts and crafts. It has a shop, selling handicrafts more cheaply than at Artesanías de Colombia, and a reasonably-priced bar and restaurant (dishes typical of different regions of Colombia served in colonial setting, usually with regional traditional music). Open 0900-1730, Tues.-Sat., Sun. and holidays 1000-1400. The shop is not open on Sun. and holidays. Entry fee US$0.25.

Museo Siglo XIX, Carrera 8, No. 7-91, founded by the Banco Cafetero, has a collection of 19th-century painting, clothes and furniture. Open Mon.-Fri., 0900-1800, Sat., 1300-1700.

The Museo Arqueológico (belonging to the Banco Popular) is a fine and extensive collection of precolumbian pottery, assembled in the restored mansion of the Marqués de San Jorge, Carrera 6, No. 7-43. The house itself is a beautiful example of 17th century Spanish colonial architecture. US$0.30 entry. Open: 1000-1700, Tues. to Fri.; 1000-1300, Sat.-Sun. There is a restaurant.

Museum of Urban Development, Calle 10 No. 4-21 (open Tues.-Sat., 0900-1800, Sun. and holidays, 1000-1800), interesting maps and photos of the development of Bogotá in an attractive colonial house near the Palacio San Carlos.

Museo del Oro (the Gold Museum), is in splendid premises at the Parque de Santander (corner of Calle 16 and Carrera 6-A). This collection is a "must", for it is unique. No less than 30,000 pieces of precolumbian gold work are shown. Open: Tues. to Sat., 0900-1600; Sun. and holidays, 0900-1200. (People in shorts not allowed). Charge, US$0.18, a bargain (US$0.10 for children). Do not miss seeing the collections kept in a huge strong-room on the top floor. Several film shows a day; at 1000 and 1430 they are in English.

The ancient gold objects discovered in Colombia were not made by the primitive technique of simple hammering alone, but show the use of virtually every technique known to modern goldsmiths.

The **Universidad Nacional** (about 13,000 students) is off our map, to the NW. The fine buildings are coated with political graffiti, and foreigners are not usually welcome on the campus. The most ancient centres of learning in Bogotá are not, however, grouped here. Oldest of all is the Colegio Nacional de San Bartolomé (C 10, No. 6-57), in the same block as the Chapel of El Sagrario (3), founded 1573. The second oldest, founded on December 18, 1653, is the Colegio Mayor de Nuestra Señora del Rosario (C 14, No. 6-25); its beautiful colonial building is well worth a look.

Banks Banco de la República, the only bank permitted to exchange travellers' cheques in denominations of US$50 or less (up to 1530 Mon.-Thurs., to 1630 Fri., no commission charged), will give cash on American Express card, but not Visa, which is accepted at most other banks; Banco Anglo Colombiano, Carrera 8, No. 15-60, and eleven local agencies. Banco Royal de Colombia, Av. Jiménez with Carrera 8; Banco Internacional de Colombia; Banco Francés e Italiano de Colombia; Banco Franco Colombiano, and other Colombian banks. Open 0900-1500 Mon. to Thurs. and 0900-1530 on Fri. Closed on Sat.; also closed at 1200 on last working day of month.

Currency American Express, Tierra Mar Aire Ltda, edif. Bavaria Torre B, Local 126, Carrera 10, No. 27-91, Tel.: 283-2955, Telex 41424 BOGCL. International Money Exchange, Carrera 7, No. 32-29, open till 1600 on Sats., check all transactions carefully; exchange at Av. 19, No. 15-35. Exprinter on Av. Jiménez and Carrera 6. Inside you can only get pesos and no travellers'

COLOMBIA 463

cheques are exchanged, but the black market operates on the pavement outside including for Peruvian and Ecuadorean currencies (rates generally little different from official rates). Check the rate first, though, and if using it, be extremely careful.

Addresses

British Embassy Calle 98, No. 9-03. Tel.: 218-2899/1867. Postal Address: Apartado Aéreo 4508.
U.S. Embassy Calle 37, No. 8-40. Tel.: 285-1300.
W. German Embassy Carrera 4, No. 72-36, 6th floor, Tel.: 259-2501.
Canadian Embassy Calle 76, No. 11-52; Tel.: 235-5066, open 0900-1700.
Norwegian Consulate, Carrera 13, No. 50-78, Oficina 506, Tel.: 235-5419.
Venezuelan Consulate Avenida 13, No. 103-16, Tel.: 256-3015, hrs. of business 0900-1230, 1300-1500, visa free, but allow 3 days.
Panamanian Consulate Calle 87, No. 11A-64, Tel.: 236-7531; Mon.-Fri., 0900-1300 (take "Usaquén" bus going north from centre, US$0.15).
Mexican Consulate, Calle 99, No. 12-08, Mon.-Fri., 0900-1300.
Costa Rican Consulate, Carrera 15, No. 80-87, Mon.-Fri. 0900-1300.
Guatemalan Consulate Carrera 15, No. 83-43, Ap. 301, Mon.-Fri., 0900-1200, visa takes 24 hrs., US$5.
British Council Calle 87, No. 12-79, Tel.: 236-25-42/257-96-32. Has a good library and British newspapers.
Anglo-Colombian School Transversal 30, No. 152-38. Postal address: Apartado Aéreo 52969, Bogotá 2.
English School Calle 170, No. 31-98 (Tel.: 254-1318 or 254-8874), Apartado Aéreo 51284, Bogotá.

Postal Services Main airmail office and foreign *poste restante* in basement of Edificio Avianca, Carrera 7, No. 16-36, open 0700-2200 Mon. to Sat. closed Sun., and holidays (0830-1200, 1530-1700, Mon. to Fri. for *poste restante*, letters kept for only a month). At weekend the Post Office only franks letters; stamps for postcards are not sold. Pharmacies and newsagents in Bogotá have an airmail collection. Surface mail, Calle 13 and Carrera 8, US$1.50 per kilo (3 months.)
International telephone calls made from Empresa Nacional de Telecomunicaciones, Calle 17, No. 7-15.

Laundry La Solución No. 2, Carrera 5, 21-84, 0800-1200, 1400-1900, US$0.75 for 1 kg. Piccadilly, Calle 63, No. 7-10; Auto Servicio Burbujas, Edificio Procoil, Avenida 19, No. 3A-37, open Mon.-Sat. 0730-1930. Panorama, Carrera 7, Calle 67. Drycleaners: *Lavaseco*, Av. Jiménez, No. 4-30.

Health Cruz Roja Nacional, Avenida 68, No. 66-31, open 0830-1800. Centro Médico La Salud, Carrera 10, No. 21-36, 2nd floor, Tel.: 243-13-81/282-40-21. For hepatitis (gamma globulin), Clínica Bogotá, Carrera 17, No. 12-65, US$10 a shot. Walter Röthlisberger y Cía Ltda. imports medicines, including Vivotif for typhoid and gamma globulin, and stores them correctly; trade prices. The US Embassy will advise on doctors, dentists, etc. Profamilia, Calle 34, No. 14-46, for contraceptives.

Tourist Office Calle 28, No. 13A-15, ground floor, Edificio Centro de Comercio Internacional (the name at the top of the building is Banco Cafetero), Tel.: 283-9466 (Mon.-Fri., 0900-1300, 1400-1700); they will tell you which parts of the country are unsafe; at Eldorado Airport and new bus terminal (both helpful, will book hotel rooms). Municipal tourist office just opposite San Diego church (27). Inderena, the National Parks Office, is on Calle 34, No. 5-84. Good hiking maps from Instituto Geográfico, US$0.75 each. Esso road maps from service stations, US$0.40.

Travel Agent recommended: Lands of Colombia, Carrera 16, No. 72A-16, friendly, (helpful, English-spoken). Tierra Mar Aire, Cra. 10, No. 27-91, is Amex agent.

Thefts Most hotels charge US$0.10 a night for insurance against theft. If you have something stolen go to the Corporación Nacional del Turismo for help and collect the insurance; this will probably take a few days of strenuous effort, but it has been known to work.

Immigration (DAS, División de Extranjería) Carrera 27, No. 17-85.

Airport The airport at El Dorado has the world's second largest landing field. "Tourist Guide" policemen have white armbands. The taxi fare from airport to city is usually about US$2.75. There are colectivos (US$0.30 plus luggage p.p.) from airport to centre; also buses, US$0.10. In the city centre buses and colectivos leave from Calle 19, going W between Carreras 10 and 14, to airport; buses marked "Aeropuerto" or "Universitaria Dorado"; colectivos marked "Aeropuerto". Alternative routes: Z8-Aeropuerto *buseta* along Autopista Norte and Avenida Caracas, thence along Calle 57 West, take bus marked "El Dorado" from Calle 34, US$0.10; ask driver to let you out at stop nearest airport, walk 15 mins. to first terminal then take free airport *buseta* to international airport. Airport shops are beautiful, and there is a restaurant. Free Colombian coffee inside the customs area, between gates 2 and 3. There are luggage lockers at the airport. Hotel reservations can be

464 COLOMBIA

made at the airport but their hotel rates are often out of date. The cheapest is in our Category D. Exchange rates are marginally lower than in the city, but pesos cannot be changed back into dollars at the airport without receipts.

For internal flights, which serve all parts of the country, see page 526. For domestic shuttle flights to Medellín/Montería, Cali/Pasto, and Barranquilla, go to Puente Aéreo terminal, 1 km. before main terminal on Av. El Dorado. Avianca international flights also use this terminal. It is more comfortable but there is not as much duty-free shopping. You have to cross eight busy lanes of traffic to get a bus into town, and negotiate two drainage ditches. As a rule, all flights are overbooked, so book well in advance. The Avianca office is at Carrera 7, No. 16-36, Tel.: 266-97-00. Satena, Avenida 19, 13A-18, Tel.: 283-55-57/282-55-57. SAM office is on Av. Jiménez, 5-14 (closed 1200-1400, then open till 1830). Many international airline offices are closed on Sat. and Sun. See page 525 for procedure to obtain refunds on unused tickets.

Rail Although there are 3,700 km. of railways (metre gauge) in Colombia, the only long-distance route carrying passengers from Bogotá is to Santa Marta, via La Dorada, 0800 Tues., and Fri., 30 hours, US$20. Tourist trains (with sleeper) run Dec.-March, with connections to/from Medellín. Station is at Calle 13 and Carrera 20. "Germania" bus goes from railway station to the city centre. Special excursions on steam trains go to Zipaquirá and Nemocón, Sat. and Sun., 0900, returning 1800, US$6 return; to Facatativá each Sun. and holiday, US$2.50 return; to Parque Duque, a pleasure park on the road to Tunja, Sun. and holidays, US$3 return, leave 1000, return 1830.

Buses There is a long-distance bus terminal on Av. Boyacá between El Dorado (Av. 26) and Av. Centenario (Calle 13). There is also access from Carrera 68. To get to the terminal take bus marked Terminal Terrestre; to get into town take Route No. 1 or No. 3 at the terminal and get off at Carrera 13 esq. Calle 13, closest to the centre (from this junction "Germania" bus goes to the centre). A *buseta* (US$0.05) runs from Carrera 68 to the terminal and back. Taxi US$1.60 (plus US$0.15 at night—police give price slip. The terminal is well-organized, comfortable and safe; free self-service luggage trolleys are provided. There are shops and restaurants. Companies are grouped according to routes, so you choose a company, time, seat and price that suits you. Buses to: Cali, 12 hrs., about US$10; Medellín, 12 hrs., on new autopista US$11; Manizales, 9 hrs., US$7-8.50; Honda, 4 hrs., US$3; Tunja, 2½ hrs., US$3; Villa de Leiva, US$3.50; La Dorada, 5 hrs., US$4; Popayán, 16 hrs., US$15; Florencia, US$19.50; Neiva, 6½ hrs., US$5; Girardot, US$2.70; to Sogamoso, US$4, 4 hrs. (US$5 by executive minibus, 3 hrs.); Bucaramanga, 10-11 hrs., US$9; Cúcuta, 18 hrs., US$12 (the daily service by Berlinas del Fonce, 1600, recommended); Cartagena, 23 hrs., US$19; Santa Marta US$20, 4 a day, 22 hrs., check if bus is going to Santa Marta, those continuing to Barranquilla may drop you short of town; Pereira, 9-10 hrs., US$6.50, via Girardot, Espinal, Ibagué, Cajamarca, Armenia (fly if you wish to avoid the Quindío pass, 25 mins.); San Agustín, 12 hrs., US$10; Villavicencio, 3 hrs., US$2.75; Ipiales, 24 hrs., US$20, only gets crowded at Cali (the bus stops for an hour in Cali; it leaves from a different level of the terminal from that on which it arrived—don't lose your bus!). Pasto, 23 hrs., US$19.50. Velotax busetas are slightly quicker and more expensive, as are colectivos, which go to several long-distance destinations. For an early morning start to Neiva (approx. hourly), Pitalito (0730 and 1030) and San Agustín take Taxis Verdes or Taxi-Exito, the latter will pick you up at your hotel. Buses can be caught along Av. Caracas, north of Calle 10, and can be stopped at street corners for: Zipaquirá, 1¼ hrs., US$0.45; Guatavita, 2-3 hrs., US$1.25; Chía, US$0.30.

Bus to Venezuela It is better not to buy a through ticket to Caracas with Exp. Berlinas as this does not guarantee a seat and is only valid for 2 Venezuelan companies; moreover no refunds are given in Cúcuta. Sometimes the border with Venezuela is closed because of illegal immigration; in this case, tickets can be refunded in Bogotá, but the best way to Caracas is by plane.

Excursions from Bogotá

The salt mines of Zipaquirá are described on page 492. Other excursions are to the beautiful artificial lake of Muña, formed by a dam; to **Sopó**, in the Sabana (63 km.), where they venerate an image of the Saviour which has appeared in an eroded stone; the paintings of angels in the church are very strange and worth seeing (ask at the Casa Cural for entry to church—give a tip); in Sopó a restaurant (previously *Nicolás*) serves good local dishes. Nearby are the Alpina yoghurt factory (no free samples), Parque Puerto de Sopó (with artificial lake) at km. 32.5 on Autopista Norte, and an amusement park a few km. N. For the Falls of Tequendama, see page 489. For Tunja (2 hrs. over first-class road), and Guatavita Nueva, see page 494. To the east of Bogotá is **Choachí**, an attractive village set in a valley, where there are hot springs (good food at *El Colonial*, 1½ blocks from main square). Flota Macarena bus, Av. 17, No. 23-96, Tel.: 277-39-00, several a day.

Hiking "Salsipuedes" is a hiking group based in Bogotá, hiking 15-25 km. every Saturday on trails in Cundinamarca; a very friendly group which welcomes visitors. Contact Alfonso Gamboa, Diagonal 123, No. 50-30, Bogotá.

COLOMBIA 465

The North Coast and the Islands

The climate is much the same for the whole area: the heat is great—ranging from 26° to 36°C, and there is a difference of only 2° between the hottest and coolest month. From November to March the heat is moderated by trade winds.

Character, like climate, seems to change in Colombia with the altitude. The *costeños* (the people of the coast) are gayer and more light-hearted than the more sober people of the highlands, particularly the Antioqueños of the Cordillera Central. (The contrast is sharply drawn in the great modern Colombian novel, *Cien Años de Soledad*, by Gabriel García Márquez.) The coastal people talk very fast, slurring their words and dropping the final s's.

N.B. In this region hotel prices are subject to high and low season variations: high season is December 15-April 30, and June 15-August 31.

Barranquilla, with 1.1 million, is Colombia's fourth city. It lies on the western bank of the Magdalena river, about 18 km. from its mouth, which has been deepened and the silted sandbars cleared so that it is now a seaport (though less busy than Cartagena or Santa Marta) as well as a river port.

Barranquilla is a modern industrial city with a dirty central area near the river, and a good residential area in the north-west, beyond Calle 53. The principal boulevard is Paseo Bolívar; there is a handsome Cathedral in Plaza San Nicolás, the central square, and before it stands a small statue of Columbus. The commercial and shopping districts are round the Plaza Bolívar, a few blocks N of the Cathedral, and in Calle Murillo. The colourful and vivid market is between Paseo Bolívar and the river, the so-called Zona Negra on a side channel of the Magdalena. Good parks in the northern areas, the favourite one is Parque Tomás Suri Salcedo on Calle 72. Stretching back into the north-western heights overlooking the city are the modern suburbs of El Prado, Altos del Prado, Golf and Ciudad Jardín, with the German-run *El Prado Hotel*. Not far away is the Country Club. There are three stadiums in the city, a big covered coliseum for sports, a bull ring and the Amira de la Rosa theatre. There is also the best zoo in Colombia, well maintained, with many animals (anteaters, tree porcupines) not often seen in zoos. Calle 77, 0830-1200, 1400-1800. All the trees have name-signs.

Festivals Carnival, lasting four days, parades, floats, street dancing and beauty contests.

Hotels *El Prado,* the social centre, swimming pool and tennis courts, B, good restaurant, some distance from the centre (Carrera 54, No. 70-10); in same category and district, *Royal,* Carrera 54, No. 68-124, Tel.: 35-78-00, E, good service, with swimming pool, modern; *Génova,* swimming pool, Calle 44, No. 44-66, 10 blocks from centre, C; *Caribana,* Carrera 41, No. 40-02, C; *Arenosa,* Carrera 48, No. 70-136, C, with bath, TV, pleasant staff and surroundings; *Majestic,* Carrera 53, No. 54-41, out of city centre, C, very good; *Riviera,* Calle 34, No. 41-81, D, very noisy if you have a room on the street; *Central,* Calle 38, No. 41-121, D, clean, safe, hot water, friendly, good restaurant; *Spanish-American,* Paseo Bolívar, D, with bath, clean, meals available at about US$2; *Victoria,* Calle 35, No. 43-140, D; *Las Villas,* Calle 35-84, E, with bath; *Zhivago,* Plaza Bolívar, very good, E, without bath; *Santa Sofía,* Calle 38 and Carrera 38B, E, with bath, friendly; *Residencia,* on Carrera 53 with Calle 55, E, breakfast included, no air conditioning and not very attractive; *San Blas,* Calle 33, No. 4-46, E; *Colón,* NW of Cathedral, F, very simple, but described as dangerous; *Real,* Paseo Bolívar, next to Plaza, D, clean, friendly, English and German spoken; *Roxy,* Plaza Bolívar (Calle 34 and Carrera 45), F, with bath, clean and safe. At Puerto Colombia (20 mins.), *Esperia,* and just outside, *Pradomar.* **Note:** hotel prices are much higher during Carnival. Watch for thieves in downtown hotels.

Restaurants In El Prado and Alto Prado, between Calles 72 and 84 and Carreras 40 and 60: *Metropole, Sorrento* (Italian and South American food), *Masia Catalana,* Spanish, Calle 76; *Petit Chalet* and *Chez Catherine,* French and expensive; *El Calderito,* also local, tropical garden atmosphere; *Gambrinus* and *Taverna Gunter,* German; *Los Techos Rojos,* steak-house; various Lebanese (*Baalbek, Biblios, Tripoli*) with belly-dancers; several Chinese and *pizzerias. El Mesón de Morgan,* excellent sea-food, good service, but very expensive; *El Famoso Chino,* Paseo Bolívar, good and cheap self-service, clean; *El Pez que Fuma,* in front of football stadium, sea-food; *Chop Suey Steak House. Brandes, Don Brisi,* recommended. Local dishes at *José Pazos,* Calle 69F, La Colonia.

Clubs Country (golf, tennis, swimming pool); Barranquilla; Anglo-American; German; Italian; Centro Israelita. La Cabaña at *Hotel El Prado.*

Market San Andrecito, or "Tourist Market", Vía 40, is where smuggled goods are sold at very

466 COLOMBIA

competitive prices; a good place to buy film. Picturesque and reasonably safe. Any taxi driver will take you there.

Bookshop Librería Nacional, Carrera 53, English, French and German books and a café which serves excellent fruit juices. Maps from Instituto Agustín Codazzi, Calle 36, No. 45-101.

Banks Banco Royal de Colombia; Banco Anglo Colombiano, Calle 34, No. 44-43, with agency on Calle 72; Banco Internacional de Colombia. Open: Mon.-Thurs, 0800-1130, 1400-1600; Fri. 0900-1130, 1400-1630; last working day of month 0800-1130.

Addresses US Consulate, Calle 77, opposite zoo. Tel.: 41-40-99 or 41-49-92. W. German Consulate, Calle 80, near Vía 40 (ask for Herr Schnabel). American Express agency at Tierra Mar Aire, downtown.

Tourist information at main hotels and at Carrera 72, No. 57-43, of. 401, Tel.: 45-44-58 or 33-66-58. A recommended taxi-driver/guide to the city is Henry Robinson, Tel.: 35-37-14; he speaks English.

Museum Small archaeological collection, Calle 68 No. 53-45 (Mon.-Fri. 0900-1200, 1400-1700).

Airport The new Ernesto Cortissoz airport is 10 km. from the city; there is plenty of transport of all types. City bus from airport to town, US$0.20. Taxi to town, US$4.50. Special bus from outside the airport, US$2.50; the bus to the airport (marked Malambo) leaves from Carrera 44 up Calle 32 to Carrera 38, then up Calle 30 to Airport. ALM to Aruba and Curaçao; Lacsa to Maracaibo and Caracas, and Mexico City. It is advisable to pay airport taxes in dollars, since poor exchange rates are given for pesos.

Roads Regular buses from Plaza Bolívar and the church at Calle 33 and Carrera 41 to the attractive bathing resort of *Puerto Colombia*, 19 km. (US$0.50, ½ hr.). Beach clean and sandy, water a bit muddy. S along the Magdalena to the little town of Palmar de Varela. On this road, 5 km. from the city, is the old colonial town of *Soledad*, with 16,000 inhabitants. The Cathedral and the old narrow streets round it are worth seeing.

Barranquilla-Cartagena, a good paved road but driving is violent. From Baranoa a branch road runs to Usicurí (72 km. from Barranquilla), known for its medicinal waters and for the grave of the popular Colombian poet, Julio Flores. The main road goes on via Sabanalarga (50 km. from Barranquilla) to Cartagena. From Sabanalarga an all-weather road continues to Puerto Giraldo, a port on the Magdalena River linked by ferry with the small town of Salmina (ferry 0500 to 1800). A spectacular new bridge over the River Magdalena gives a fine view of Barranquilla and the river, a highlight on the Cartagena-Santa Marta road. An all-weather road leads to Fundación, on the Atlántico Railway, and a junction point with the road from Santa Marta to Bucaramanga and Bogotá, which is now paved throughout, though surface somewhat uneven.

Buses Most bus companies operate from Calle 34 and Carrera 45. To Santa Marta, US$1.50, Pullman, about 2 hrs., also direct to Santa Marta's famous Rodadero beach; to Montería, US$9.25, 8 hrs.; to Medellín by Pullman, US$16, 16hrs.; to Bucaramanga, US$13.50 with Copetran, air-conditioned, first class, departures at 1130 most days, arriving 2030; to Bogotá, 20 hrs. with a change of bus in Bucaramanga (there is only a 1-hour stop to purchase ticket on to Bogotá); to Caucasia, US$9, 11 hrs. To Maicao, US$6.50, 6 hrs. (with Rápidos Ochoa); to Cartagena, 3 grades of bus, 3 hrs. (US$2.15 with Transportes Cartagena, US$2.50 with Expreso Brasilia, by Brasilia Van Tours mini-bus, US$2, from their downtown offices as well as the bus terminals), 2 hrs. by colectivo, US$2.50.

Warnings When leaving by air for the USA, you may be searched by drug squad police; they are very civil, but acquisitive—check your belongings afterwards. Tourist Police can be very rough when searching foreigners. Beware also of people claiming to be ships' officers who say they can arrange a passage if you pay in advance; buy a passage only in a recognized shipping office or agency. If shipping a car into Barranquilla allow 2 days to complete all paperwork to retrieve your car from the port.

Cartagena, old and steeped in history, is one of the most interesting towns in South America. Its population is 437,000. An arm of the river, 145 km. long, canalized in 1650 by Spain—the Canal del Dique—from Calamar to Cartagena allows free access for ships from the up-river ports.

What interests the visitor is a comparatively small part of Cartagena, the old walled city almost completely surrounded by the Caribbean sea on the W, the waters of the Bay of Cartagena on the S, and lakes and lagoons to the N and E. Cartagena was one of the storage points for merchandise sent out from Spain and for treasure collected from the Americas to be sent back to Spain. A series of forts protecting the approaches from the sea, and the formidable walls built around the city, made it almost impregnable.

COLOMBIA

Cartagena was founded by Pedro de Heredia on January 13, 1533. There were then two approaches to it, Bocagrande, at the northern end of Tierra Bomba Island—this was a direct entry from the Caribbean—and Boca Chica. Bocagrande was blocked after Admiral Vernon's attack in 1741, and thereafter the only approach was by the narrow channel of Boca Chica from the S. Boca Chica leads into the great bay of Cartagena, 15 km. long and 5 km. wide. The old walled city lies at the head of it.

On our left, as we enter Boca Chica, is the curiously shaped island of Tierra Bomba. At the tip of a spit of land is the fortress of San Fernando (entrance fee, US$1; guide, US$1.50 for one to five people); boat trips to it (1 hr.) are worth while. Opposite it, right on the tip of Barú Island, is the fortress of San José. The two forts were once linked by heavy chains to prevent surprise attacks by pirates. North of Barú Island stretches Manga Island, much larger and now an important suburb. At its northern end a bridge, Puente Román, connects it with the old city. This approach was defended by three forts: San Sebastián del Pastelillo built between 1558 and 1567 (the Club de Pesca has it now) at the north-western tip of Manga Island; the fortress of San Lorenzo near the city itself; and the very powerful fortress of San Felipe inland on a height to the E of the city. Yet another fort, La Tenaza, protected the walled city from a direct attack from the open sea. The huge encircling walls were started in 1634 and finished by 1735. They were on average 12 metres high and 17 metres thick, with 6 gates. They contained, besides barracks, the old city water reservoir.

In spite of its daunting outer forts and encircling walls Cartagena was challenged again and again by enemies. Sir Francis Drake, with 1,300 men, broke in successfully in 1586. The Frenchmen Baron de Pointis and Ducasse, with 10,000 men, beat down the defences and sacked the city in 1697. But the strongest attack of all, by Sir Edward Vernon with 27,000 men and 3,000 pieces of artillery, failed in 1741 after besieging the city for 56 days; it was defended by the one-eyed, one-armed and one-legged hero Blas de Lezo, whose statue is at the entrance to the San Felipe fortress.

Cartagena declared its independence from Spain in 1811. A year later Bolívar came to the city and used it as a jumping-off place for his Magdalena campaign. After a heroic resistance, Cartagena was retaken by the royalists under Pablo Morillo in 1815. The patriots finally freed it in 1821.

The old walled city was in two sections, inner and outer. Much of the wall between the two was razed a few years ago. Nearly all the houses are of one or two storeys. The houses in El Centro were occupied by the high officials and nobility. San Diego (the northern end of the inner town) was where the middle classes lived: the clerks, merchants, priests and military. The artisan classes lived in the one-storey houses of Getsemaní in the outer city.

The streets are narrow—in the Getsemaní neighbourhood both walls can be touched as you walk along—and rarely straight. Each block has a different name, a source of confusion, but don't worry: the thing to do is to wander aimlessly, savouring the rich street scenes, and allow the great sights, the "musts", to catch you by surprise. Our map is marked with numerals for the places of outstanding interest. The most attractive streets have been given a star (*). All the "great houses" can be visited.

The numbers stand for the following places:

1. The Puente Román, the bridge which leads from the island of Manga into the Getsemaní district. Visitors should on no account miss the *casas bajas* or low houses of Getsemaní, but be careful; it is not a very safe neighbourhood.
2. The Chapel of San Roque (early 17th century), near the Hospital of Espíritu Santo.
3. The Church of Santísima Trinidad, built 1643 but not consecrated till 1839. The plaza in which it stands is most interesting. North of the church, at number 10, lived Pedro Romero, the man who set the revolution of 1811 going by coming out into the street shouting "Long Live Liberty".
4. The Monastery and Church of San Francisco. The church was built in 1590 after the pirate Martin Côte had destroyed an earlier church built in 1559. The first Inquisitors lodged at the monastery. From its courtyard a crowd surged into the streets claiming independence from Spain on the morning of November 11, 1811. The Church of the Third Order is now the Colón Theatre.

Immediately to the N is Plaza de la Independencia, with the landscaped Parque del Centenario just off it. At right angles to the Plaza runs the Paseo de los Mártires, flanked by the busts of nine patriots executed in the square on February 24, 1816 by the royalist Morillo when he retook the city. At its western end is a tall clock tower. Passing through the tower's arches (the main entrance to the inner walled city) we get to

5. The Plaza de los Coches. Around almost all the plazas of Cartagena arcades offer refuge from

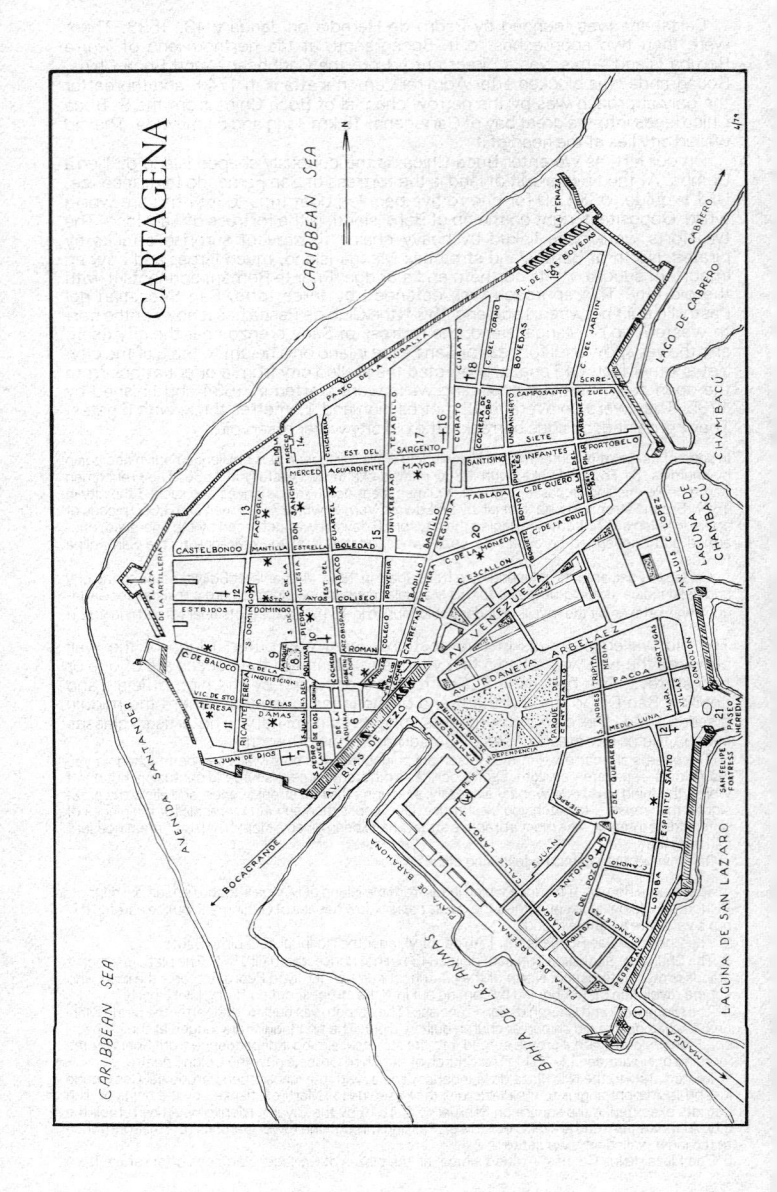

COLOMBIA

the tropical sun. On the W side of this plaza is the famous Portal de los Dulces, a favourite meeting place.

6. Plaza de la Aduana, with a statue of Columbus and the City Hall.

7. Church of San Pedro Claver and Monastery, built by Jesuits in 1603 and later dedicated to San Pedro Claver who was a monk in the monastery and was canonized 235 years after his death in 1654. He was called the Slave of the Slaves: he used to beg from door to door for money to give to the black slaves brought to the city. His body is in a glass coffin on the high altar, and cell in the monastery and the balcony from which he sighted slave ships are shown to visitors. Entry, US$0.50. Guides charge US$1.

8. Plaza de Bolívar (the old Plaza Inquisición), very pleasant, and with a statue of Bolívar. On its W side is

9. The Palace of the Inquisition, established in 1610, but the building dates from 1706. The stone entrance with its coats of arms and well preserved and ornate wooden door is very notable. Indeed the whole building, with its overhanging balconies, cloisters and patios, is a fine example of colonial baroque. There is a very pleasant historical museum at the Palace, and a library. Entry charge US$0.40; good historical books on sale. Open Mon.-Sat., 1000-1700, Sun., 0900-1300.

On the opposite side of the Plaza to the Palace of the Inquisition, the Museo del Oro y Arqueológico has been installed in an old building. Gold and pottery, very well displayed. Entrance free.

In the NE corner of Plaza de Bolívar is

10. The Cathedral, begun in 1575 and partially destroyed by Francis Drake. Reconstruction was finished by 1612. Great alterations were made between 1912 and 1923. A severe exterior, with a fine doorway, and a simply decorated interior. See the guilded 18th century altar, the Carrara marble pulpit, and the elegant arcades which sustain the central nave.

11. Church and Convent of Santa Teresa, founded 1609, now occupied by the police.

12. The Church and Monastery of Santo Domingo, built 1570 to 1579 and now a seminary. The old monastery was replaced by the present one in the 17th century. Inside, a miracle-making image of Christ, carved towards the end of the 16th century, is set on a baroque 19th century altar. Most interesting neighbourhood, very little changed since the 16th century. In Calle Santo Domingo, No. 33-29, is one of the great patrician houses of Cartagena, the Casa de los Condes de Pestagua, now the Colegio del Sagrado Corazón de Jesús. North of Santo Domingo, at

13. Calle de la Factoria 36-57 is the magnificent Casa del Marqués de Valdehoyos, now owned by the tourist authority and containing a Tourist Office; open to visitors.

14. The Church and Convent of La Merced, founded 1618. The Convent—a prison during Morillo's reign of terror—is now occupied by the Law Courts and its church is the Municipal Theatre.

15. The Monastery of San Agustín (1580), now the University. From its chapel, now occupied by a printing press, the pirate Baron de Pointis stole a 500-pound silver sepulchre. It was returned by the King of France but the citizens melted it down to pay their troops during the siege by Morillo in 1815. Adjoining the University is the Edificio Ganem, which offers a good, free view of the city from the 9th floor.

16. The Church of Santo Toribio de Mongrovejo. Building began in 1729. In 1741, during Admiral Vernon's siege, a cannon ball fell into the church during Mass and lodged in one of the central columns; the ball is now in a recess in the W wall. The font of Carrara marble in the Sacristy is a masterpiece. There is a beautiful carved ceiling (*mudéjar* style) above the main altar. Opens for Mass at 0600 and 1800, closed at other times.

17. Casa del Consulado (Calle Sargento Mayor) was one of the great houses but has now become a teachers' college.

18. Church and Monastery of Santa Clara of Assisi, built 1617-21, now the Hospital of Santa Clara.

19. Plaza de las Bóvedas. The walls of Las Bóvedas, built 1799, are some 12 metres high and from 15 to 18 metres thick. Cars can drive along the rampart, from which there is a grand view of the harbour. At the base of the wall are 23 dungeons, now containing tourist shops. Both a lighted underground passage and a drawbridge lead from Las Bóvedas to the fortress of La Tenaza on the sea shore.

Also worth visiting is the Casa de Núñez, just outside the walls of La Tenaza in El Cabrero district opposite the Ermita de El Cabrero and 5 minutes from the bullring. Here lived Rafael Núñez, president (four times) and poet (he wrote Colombia's national anthem). His grandiose marble tomb is in the adjoining church.

Three of the sights of Cartagena are off our map. One of them is the Fortress of San Fernando, already mentioned.

The Fortress of San Felipe, across the Puente Heredia (21) from the outer walled city, stands on the hill of San Lázaro, 41 metres above sea-level. Building began in 1639 and it was finished by 1657. Under the huge structure are tunnels lined with living rooms and offices. Some are open and lighted; visitors pass through these and on to the top of the fortress. Baron de Pointis, the French pirate, stormed and took it in 1697, but Admiral Vernon failed to reach it in the abortive attack of 1741. Entrance fee US$1. Guide US$ 1.50 for one to five people.

A lovely road leads to the summit of La Popa hill, nearly 150 metres high, from which there is a fine view of the harbour and the city. Here are the church and monastery of Santa Cruz and restored ruins of convent dating from 1608. In the church is the beautiful little image of the Virgin of La Candelaria, reputed a deliverer from plague and a protector against pirates. Her day is February 2.

470 COLOMBIA

For nine days before the feast thousands of people go up the hill by car, on foot, or on horseback. On the day itself people carry lighted candles as they go up the hill. The name was bestowed on the hill because of an imagined likeness to a ship's poop. It is dangerous to walk up on your own; either take a guided tour, or take a public bus to Teatro Miramar at the foot of the hill, then bargain for a taxi up, about US$2. The Tourist Office recommends a guided tour from an agency opposite the *Hotel Playa* in Bocagrande, for US$5.50, which also takes in San Felipe and San Pedro Claver.

Feasts The other great feast, apart from Candlemas and Carnival, is on November 11-14 to celebrate the independence of Cartagena. Men and women in masks and fancy dress roam the streets, dancing to the sound of *maracas* and drums. There are beauty contests and battles of flowers and general gaiety. This festival tends to be wild and can be dangerous.

Warnings Carry your passport with you at all times. Failure to present it on police request can result in imprisonment and fines. Regarding sea passages, see warning under Barranquilla (page 466). In addition, if offered a job on a ship to the Galápagos or to New York, insist on full documentation at the Seamen's Union office and do not make any arrangements on the street.

The north of Colombia is generally reported to be more dangerous than the centre and south, partly because of the drugs trade. Beware also of self-appointed tourist guides who charge very highly for their services, and can turn nasty if thwarted.

Hotels On Bocagrande beach, 10 mins by bus from city: *Cartagena-Hilton*, El Laguito, L, Tel.: 50666 (Apto. Aéreo 1774); *Capilla del Mar*, B, Calle 8, Carrera 1, excellent French restaurant, swimming pool on 4th floor, be careful of their travel desk and check any reservations they make for you, no connection with restaurant of same name ½ km. away; *Las Velas*, Calle Las Velas, No. 1-60, C, opposite *Caribe Casino*, warm water all day, showers, good restaurant; *Hotel del Caribe*, B, all rooms a/c, administration could be better, swimming pool in the (expensive) restaurant, pancakes recommended; *India Catalina*, Carrera 2, No. 7-115, C, very good, with a/c, safe, clean; *Bahía*, Calle 4, Carrera 4, C, not very well kept, swimming pool; *Residencias Internacional*, Av. San Martín 4110, Tel.: 50-675, C, with bath and a/c, clean, safe, friendly; opposite at No. 5-86 is *Flamingo*, C, with bath and a/c, not so good; *Del Lago*, Calle 34, No. 11-15, B, not recommended; *El Dorado*, Av. San Martín, No. 4-41, B, clean, a/c, swimming pool, restaurant; *Playa*, on Av. San Martín, C, all rooms with private bathroom, open air bar, restaurant (breakfast, US$1), swimming pool, noisy disco next door, Av. 2a, No. 4-87; *Residencias Bocagrande*, D, with shower, no hot water, clean and friendly, but noisy, try to get a room with a balcony and a view over the sea, good restaurant; *Leonela*, Carrera 3a, 7-142, D, quiet, comfortable; *Residencial Olga Luz*, D, on the sea, O.K.; *New Royal*, D, not on beach, air conditioning, clean; *Residencias Astoria*, D, bath, fan (air conditioning 25% extra), friendly, breakfast US$1.50, good, not actually on beach, but nearby; *Residencia Mansiomar*, Carrera 3, No. 4-64, E. On Carrera 3, there are plenty of small *residencias*, for instance Carrera 3, No. 5-29, D in season, clean and friendly.

In town: *Bucarica*, Calle San Agustín 6-08, near University, F, good value, rooms of varying standard, take sleeping bag. English and French spoken, acts as brothel; *Veracruz*, Calle San Agustín, opp. San Agustín church, E, clean, safe, with or without a/c; *Residencial Pacoa*, Calle Pacoa, E, noisy; friendly; *Real*, Calle Espíritu Santo 29-70, F with shower, basic, clean, friendly; *Candy*, same street, E; *Residencias Valle*, E, on San Andrés; *Colombia*, F, basic; *Hernando*, F, smelly; *Roma*, F, without bath, on San Andrés; *Residencias Stella*, F, near the University, basic but clean; *Plaza Bolívar*, Plaza Bolívar No. 3-98, D, good, nice restaurant, accepts dollars cash and credit cards; *Residencias Venezia*, Calle del Guerrero No. 29-108, F, may require bargaining, some rooms with fan, clean and secure, and many others; *Berlín*, F, friendly but no hot water, dirty, not recommended; *Pensión la Presentación* in old city, D, breakfast US$1; *Doral*, Media Luna, friendly, nice, fan, recommended, F; *Residencia Nelsy*, Media Luna 10-20, poor value, F; *Medellín*, Calle Ayos, F, negotiable, simple but clean, small, friendly, central, fan, communal bathroom, safe. On the road to the airport are several hotels and *pensiones*, particularly at Marbella beach (e.g. *Bellavista*, Av. Santander, D, clean, nice patio, English-speaking owner, secure; *Playa Blanca*, Av. Santander, E, very nice; *Residencia Nicol's* 80, Malecón, *Hotel del Mar*, Miramar, D, with toilet and shower, clean, secure; *Kalaman*, *España*). Except for *Cafetaría San Felipe*, No. 943, with rooms in F range, and good cheap meals, many cheap hotels on Calle Media Luna are brothels.

N.B. Hotel prices tend to go up by as much as 25 per cent from December 20 to January 20, and hotels tend to be heavily booked. Either book well in advance yourself, or avoid the city at this time. For hotel insurance, add 5%, plus US$0.05 p.p. per day.

Camping In a secure walled garden at *Hotel Bellavista*, Av. Santander, on the beach, US$2.50 p.p. People camp on the beach, but may be troubled by thieves—and the police.

Restaurants *Nautilus*, in the old wall of the city, facing the statue of La India Catalina, seafood; another *Nautilus* (same menu and service) on road to airport in Marbella; and yet another *Nautilus*, Carrera 3, Bocagrande. *Capilla del Mar*, recommended, sea food dinner for 2, US$20-30; *Hansa*, in Bocagrande, good for seafood; *El Toboso*, opp. Centro Comercio Bocagrande; also in Bocagrande, Av. San Martín, *Da Marisa*, pizzas; *Alexander*, Bocagrande, German food; *El Arca de Noé*,

COLOMBIA 471

in Bocagrande, very good steaks; *El Patio de la Atarraya*, Bocagrande, good fish restaurant overlooking the sea; *Rincón Argentino* for good steaks (US$4); *La Olla Cartagenera* and *La Petite Sensation*, both on Carrera 2, Bocagrande, very good, but not cheap; *La Heladería Arabe*, Carrera 3, Bocagrande, good ice cream; *Little Chicken*, Americanized Colombian food, clean, good food and juices (US$4 for steaks), English spoken by Ivan, helpful manager; *La Hormiga*, Calle Bocagrande, good, cheap; *Kokoriko* is a chain of barbecued chicken restaurants, US$6 for a whole chicken; *Club de Pesca*, at the Fuerte del Pastelillo: you can dine in the open air in a lovely setting, expensive (taxi, US$3.50-4.50); *Marcel Hostería Sevillana*, Malecón 70, near *Residencias Ligia*, *Barú* and *El Arabe* (Arab dishes), all in Bocagrande; *El Candilejo*, more expensive than it looks, but good food (in Candilejo); *El Candil*, behind the Plaza Aduana. *Loon Foon*, Chinese, good, on first street into city from the statue of La India Catalina; *Kon-Nam*, Calle San Pedro Claver, good Chinese cuisine; *Nuevo Oriente*, near Santo Domingo, Chinese, good; *El Ganadero*, Calle Media Luna, good food, friendly; *Paco's Restaurant* on Plaza Santo Domingo, pleasant atmosphere, excellent food, not cheap; *Bodegón de la Candelaria*, Calle de las Damas (Tel.: 47251), excellent food and service, but expensive; *El Rinconcito*, near Plaza Fernando de Madrid, good cheap meals; also *El Pollo Dorado* on Calle Ricuarte, opposite Banco de Bogotá. *Maria's*, on Guerro, half-a-block from *Hotel Romar*, meals for US$2. *Restaurant Americano*, near central post office, good meals for US$1.50; *Bar La Vitrola*, on Calle de la Chinchería by the city wall, recommended for its atmosphere; *La Fragata*, in old town, two blocks behind *Hotel Bolívar*, French *maître d'hôtel*, German cook; many restaurants around Plaza Independencia have good meals for about US$2. Restaurants in Calle San Andrés cost about US$1.30, with plenty to eat; cheap meals at *San Martín*, Calle de las Damas, and in a restaurant on the corner of Plaza de los Coches; *Madrid*, near *Residencias Venezia*, is very good value; *Panificadora la Española*, Calle 8, No. 7-61, fresh bread and pastries; *Heladería Almirante Vernón*, a block from San Pedro Claver church towards Plaza Bolívar, has hearty, reasonable meals and good fruit juices; *Heladería Cecilia* for good ice-creams. *Juguería Dino* (near the clocktower at entrance on landward side to the city walls) for fruit juices, good. *Lucho Delicatessen* in the Centro Comercial in Bocagrande has local and imported food, cheeses, meats, wines and beers. Many restaurants around the Plaza Independencia have good meals for about US$2. At cafés try the *patacón*, a biscuit made of green banana, mashed and baked; also in Parque del Centenario in early morning. *Stella Maris*, near the harbour in Barrio Manga, used mainly by seamen, is a bar and shop, selling stamps (0900-2300) and souvenirs, administered by the Salvation Army.

Market There is a new market out of town, which is disappointing; bus from Av. Urdaneta Arbeláez. The fish market is in the SE suburbs of the old city.

Shopping A good selection of *artesanías* on Plaza Bolívar, but in general (except for leather goods) shopping is much better in Bogotá. Woollen *blusas* are good value, US$8-12; try the *Tropicano* in Pierino Gallo building in Bocagrande. Also in this building are reputable jewellery shops. H. Stern has a jewellery shop in the Pierino Gallo shopping centre and at the Hilton Hotel. Suntan oils and lotions can vary in price as much as 100% —shop around.

Gambling at Casino Turístico, Av. San Martín and Casino de Caribe at Pierino Gallo shopping centre, Bocagrande.

Taxis From Bocagrande to the centre, US$1.25; to the airport US$4; centre to airport, US$3 (more at night). Try to fix price for journey before committing yourself. A horse-drawn carriage can be hired for US$9, opposite *Hotel El Dorado*, Av. San Martín, in Bocagrande, to ride into town at night (romantic but rather short ride).

Buses Within the city large buses (with no glass in windows) cost US$0.05, short-wheelbase type (with glass windows), US$0.10.

Sport Fishing; yachting; also bullfights and cockfights. The former take place mainly in January and February, the latter throughout the year on Sat., Sun. and holidays. On Sat. cockfighting takes place at the Teatro Granada and on other days at Ternera, a village 16 km. away.

Swimming Take bus from Plaza de la Independencia to Bocagrande, which has good beaches. The Boca Chica beach is now reported to be dirty, and the boat service there unreliable. Boats leave from Plaza de la Independencia; the round trip can take up to 2 hrs. each way. *Ferry dancing*, about half the price of luxury boats, and carries drunk, dancing passengers. For about US$1.50 you can take a tour round the fort of San Fernando in a dugout canoe. There are boats from the city; the last return trip is at 1230. Swimming is good. Boats taking in Boca Chica and San Fernando are US$5 return without lunch or US$10.50 with lunch (children under 12, half price); Alcatraz run a daily trip from the Muelle Turístico leaving at about 1000, returning at 1530. There is a daily cruise to Islas del Rosario, US$14.50 including lunch (possible to bargain in low season), with Alcatraz, leaving 0630, returning 1630. The boat stops first at Playa Blanca on the mainland for 1 hr. (bargain with boatman to leave you for a day, camp on the beach, and continue the cruise next day—Playa Blanca is crowded a.m., but peaceful after the tour boats have left). At the Islas del Rosario is an aquarium in the sea, worth visiting, US$0.60. There are cheaper boats to the islands. Marbella beach, just North of Las Bóvedas, is good for swimming.

Art Gallery Contemporary Latin American paintings, Banco Ganadero, Plaza de la Aduana.

472 COLOMBIA

Nearby is the Museo de Arte Moderno (open Mon.-Fri., 0900-1200, 1500-1800, Sat., 1000-1200), opposite the San Pedro Claver church.

Banks Banco Anglo Colombiano. Banco Royal changes American Express travellers' cheques up to a maximum of US$300, with US$10 commission. Banco de la República, on Plaza Bolívar does not charge American Express cheques. There are many *cambios*; none change travellers' cheques. Be sure to count the pesos yourself before handing over your dollars. Never change money on the street, they are nearly all crooks and will short-change you. American Express (Tierra Mar Aire Office), Bocagrande, Carrera 4, Calle 8, is only a travel agency and does not change travellers' cheques.

Venezuelan Consulate.
French Consulate very helpful.

Anglican Church Calle Ricuarte, services in English can be arranged.

Post Office beside Avianca office between Avs. Venezuela and Urdaneta Arbeláez.

Tourist Office Carrera 3, No. 36-57 (Plaza Bolívar); also at Casa del Marqués de Valdehoyos, Calle de la Factoría (Tel.: 47017 and 46515).

Shipping There are modern wharves. It is possible to ship a car from Cartagena to Panama (see Panama section, page 1187). Interoceánica, Centro Carrera 4a, No. 31-14, Tel.: 45976/44047; cargo ships.

Airport Crespo, 1½ km. from the city, reached by local buses from Blas de Lezo, SW corner of inner wall. Bus from airport to Plaza San Francisco US$0.10. Flights to Maracaibo. Commuter flights to Barranquilla. Tourist information desk gives list of taxi prices. Good self-service restaurant. No exchange facilities. There is a Copa office in Cartagena.

Buses All long-distance buses leave from Calle 32, with Av. Pedro Herrera, near foot of San Felipe fortress (any bus marked "E-Villa" goes to the old city and Parque Centenario). Pullman bus from Cartagena to Medellín 665 km., US$12. Several buses a day, but book early, takes 13-16 hrs. The road is now paved throughout, but in poor condition. From Cartagena by bus to Santa Marta, US$4.75 (with Brasilia, Calle 32, No. 20D-55), 4 hrs., also cheaper lines, US$3.50. To Barranquilla US$2.15 with Transportes Cartagena, 2½ hrs., or US$2.50 with Expreso Brasilia pullman. To Bogotá via Barranquilla and Bucaramanga with Expreso Brasilia pullman, US$19, at 1445, may take 23 hrs., depending on number of check-points. To Valledupar with Expreso Brasilia, pullman US$8.50 (with a ½ hour stop in Barranquilla), for Sierra Nevada and Pueblo Bello. To Riohacha, US$7.50. Bus to Maicao on Venezuelan frontier US$4.75 (with Expreso Auto Pullman, Expreso Brasilia at 2000, or Unitrasco, Av. Pedro Heredia), 12 hrs.; the road is in good condition, except for 30 km.

Travel from Cartagena To the little fishing village of **La Boquilla**, E of Cartagena, about 20 mins. past the airport. One small hotel (E, clean, good food). On Sat. and Sun. nights people dance the local dances. Go there by taxi, US$3 (there is a reasonable bus service, and Carlos drives a green Dodge regularly to the bus terminal, US$0.50); can be dangerous for pedestrians. Visit the mangrove swamps nearby to see the birds. To **San Jacinto**, 1½ hrs. by road S of Cartagena, good place for local craft work. To **Turbaco,** 24 km. SE by road (Botanical Garden, 1½ km. before village on the left, student guides) and on S through Sincelejo (193 km., see below), **Planeta Rica** (320 km.) and Yarumal (*Restaurante La Nena*) to Medellín. 60 km. beyond Planeta Rica there is a camping site in the grounds of the *Parador Chaubacú* (US$4 per tent); next door is the *Mesón del Gitano*. Five km. further on is **Caucasia**, which makes a good stopping point if you want to break the journey from Cartagena to Medellín. *Auto Hotel*, new, best, quiet, heavily booked; *Hotel Playa Mar*, F, good food available, friendly, but noisy; *Residencias San Francisco*, Carrera 49 esq. Calle 45, E, with bath, good value. Chinese restaurant, 3 doors up, good cheap food. A nice place to visit, Jardín Botánico, entrance fee US$0.25.

Ninety-six km. S of Cartagena along the coast is **Coveñas**, the terminal of the 420-km. crude oil pipeline from the Barco oilfields to the N of Cúcuta, on the Venezuelan frontier (*Hotel y Motel Fragata*, on the beach, recommended). 20 mins away, E, is Tolú village (*Residencias Manuelito* and *Residencias El Turista*, both F; *Residencias La Cabaña*, at western end of beach road, F, no running water, friendly; many fish stalls along the beach) whose beaches are not as nice as those at Coveñas, which are unsigned—ask to be let off the bus. W. of Coveñas are beautiful beaches at Porvenir, no food available, afternoon buses infrequent. Coveñas is 40 minutes from

Sincelejo, capital of Sucre Department (*Hotel Majestic*, Carrera 20, No. 21-25, E; same range are *Palace*, Calle 19, No. 21-39, and *Marcella*, Calle 21, 23-59; *Finzenu*, Carrera 20 and Calle 22, D, with a/c. and some good basic eating; *Sincelejo*, Plaza Santander, F with shower, clean, friendly, fair restaurant; *Gran Hotel*, F, to be avoided), is a cattle centre 193 km. S of Cartagena on the main road to Medellín (population, 109,000). It is well known for the dangerous bull-ring game, likened to the San Fermín festivities in Pamplona, Spain, in which bulls and men chase each other. The town is hot and dusty and power cuts are a factor of life.

Montería, capital of Córdoba Department, on the E bank of the river Sinú, can be reached from Cartagena by air, by river boat, or from the main highway to Medellín. (Bus from Cartagena, US$8.40, with Brasilia, 2nd class.) It is the centre of a cattle and agricultural area turning out tobacco, cacao, cotton and sugar. Present population is 144,000. Compared with other Caribbean cities there is little to attract the tourist except for the one fine church, picturesque street life and the extremely friendly people. Average temperature: 28°C. Road to Planeta Rica (airport). Hotels: *Sinú*, Carrera 3, Calle 32, C, a/c and swimming pool, watch out for short changing in the restaurant; *Tocarema*, Carrera 2, No. 34-32, F; *Alcázar*, Carrera 2, No. 32-17, F, comfortable and friendly, restaurant not always open; *Pensión Rincón*, F, reasonable, clean, meals, US$1; *Santa Rosa*, F, with water, good.

Warning There is a high risk of kidnapping in rural areas of Sucre and Córdoba departments; tourists are advised not to stray from the beaten track.

On the Gulf of Urabá is the port of **Turbo,** now a centre of banana cultivation, which is booming. It is a rough frontier community; not too law-abiding, tourists are advised to be very careful. Turbo may be reached from Cartagena and from Medellín (6 buses a day, a gruelling 13-16 hrs., US$7.50). Hotels: *Playa Mar*, D, the best; *Sausa*, D, running water in early morning only, helpful owners, pleasant dining room; *Residencia Sandra*, F, good; *Residencia Turbo*, *Residencia Marcela*, both F; most hotels are brothels; in Playa district: *Miramar*, *Rotitom*, both D. No banks are open for exchange of travellers' cheques on Monday or Tuesday, either don't arrive then, or have dollars in cash with you. A description of an overland journey from Panama to Colombia via Turbo will be found in the Panama section; note that if going from Colombia to Panama via Turbo you should get an exit stamp from the military post in the centre of town before leaving. We have also been informed that the immigration office at the Panamanian port of Puerto Obaldía can be extremely obstructive. Think twice about taking a small boat between Panama and Colombia: the majority are contraband, even arms runners and if stopped, you will be in trouble. (Even if not stopped you will have difficulty obtaining a DAS entry stamp because the captain of the boat must state officially that he is carrying passengers into Colombia.) If taking a reputable cargo boat from Panama to Colombia, be sure to arrange with the captain the price and destination before departure.

186 km. S of Turbo, on the road to Antioquia (see page 505), is Dabeiba (*Residencia Diana*, on main street, F, simple, clean; very helpful, free morning coffee).

San Andrés and **Providencia,** two small and attractive islands in the Caribbean Sea, have belonged to Colombia since 1822. They are 400 km. SW of Jamaica, 180 km. E of Nicaragua, and 480 km. N of the Colombian coast— ferry or plane from Cartagena. Henry Morgan had his headquarters at San Andrés. A beautiful road circles the island, of coral, some 11 km. long rising to 104 metres. The 8,000 mostly black people speak English. San Andrés is a regular stop for Avianca and SAM, also Lacsa and Sahsa airlines fly in from Barranquilla. (SAM, not Avianca, flies from Cartagena, but you can use an Avianca "Conozca a Colombia" ticket for this flight.) Main products: coconuts and vegetable oil. Places to see: the beautiful Keys, like Johnny Key with a white beach (US$3.80 return, you can go in one boat and return in another,) and the so-called Aquarium (US$3 return), off a Key where, using a mask and wearing sandals as protection against sea-urchins, you can see myriads of colourful fish. Snorkelling equipment can be hired on San Andrés for US$4-5, but it is better and cheaper on the shore than on the island. The Hoyo Soplador is a geyser-like hole through which the sea spouts into the air most surprisingly when the wind is in the right direction. Less spoilt parts of the island are San Luis, Sound Bay and the west side. Buses US$0.25. Bicycles are a popular way of getting around on the island and are easy to hire— usually in poor condition (US$1.10 per hour, US$6 per day); motorbikes also easy to hire, US$3.60 per hour. Cars can be hired for US$15 for 2 hours, with US$6 for every extra hour. Pedalos can be hired at US$4 per hour.

The islands are a customs-free zone; they are often very crowded with Colombian shoppers looking for foreign-made bargains, but San Andrés, on the whole, is an expensive island. Although alcoholic drinks are cheap, essential goods are extremely costly, and electronic goods are more expensive than in the UK. There is an airport tax of US$15 when leaving on international flights and of US$2.25 for domestic flights. In July and August, it is very difficult to get on flights out of San Andrés, especially to Cartagena; book in advance if possible. Checking in for flights can be difficult because of queues of shoppers with their goods. There is a customs-tax of about US$2 (rarely enforced) on merchandise exported from the islands. Banco de la República (Mon.-Fri., 0800-1300) will exchange dollars and travellers' cheques. Also Casa Colombina de Cambio at the

474 COLOMBIA

airport drug store, 0800-1800, 7 days a week, or try the Photo Shop on Av. Costa Rica. (Rates are lower than in Bogotá.) Many shops will change US$ cash; it is impossible to change travellers' cheques at weekends. (Airport employees will exchange US$ cash at a poor rate.)

Only cruise ships and tours go to San Andrés; there are no other passenger services by sea. To ship a vehicle costs US$900 with bargaining (officially US$1,300). To ship a vehicle to Panama costs US$400-450. Interoceánica cargo ships, Tel.: 6624-6625.

There are Panamanian and Costa Rican consulates on San Andrés.

Airport Flights to most major Colombian cities: to Bogotá with SAM (you can arrange a 72-hr. stop-over in Cartagena), with Aerotal (one flight every three days) to Bogotá; to Cartagena, with SAM, US$50; to Barranquilla (SAM, Aerotal and Eastern Airlines, from Miami). SAM also flies to Cali and Pereira. Also to Belize, Guatemala City (twice a week), San José, Tegucigalpa, Panama. If flying to Guatemala, ask at *Residencia Restrepo* for unwanted return tickets, good value. Note that Panama, Costa Rica and Honduras all require onward tickets which cannot be bought on San Andrés, can be in Cartagena. 15 mins. walk to town (taxi US$2.50 p.p.). All airline offices in town, except Satena at airport.

Hotels on **San Andrés** *Gran Internacional*, Av. Colón, No. 2-77, B, a/c, swimming pool, decrepit; *Aurora*, Av. de las Américas, B, fan and private bath; *Bahía Marina*, expensive but has swimming pool, the largest on San Andrés, and good restaurant; *El Dorado*, Av. Colombia, No. 1A-25 (casino, swimming pool), D; *Abacoa*, Av. Colombia; also *Royal Abacoa* on same avenue at No. 2-41; *Bahía Sardina*, across the street from the beach, a/c, comfortable, clean, no swimming pool; *Europa*, Av. 20 de Julio, No. 1-101, D, with bath, clean; *Isleño*, Av. La Playa, No. 5-117, D; *Calypso*, C; *Palace*, Av. Colón and Costa Rica, C; *Capri*, Av. Costa Rica, No. 1A-110, C, with bath and a/c, good value; *Victoria Princess*, Av. 20 de Julio, C; *Cacique Toné*, Av. Colombia, Cra. 5, A, deluxe, a/c, pool, on sea-front; *Mediterráneo*, Av. Colón, D, dirty, no running water on upper floors; *Tiuna*, Av. Colombia, No. 3-59, B, a/c, swimming pool; *Turista Natania*, in front of Coliseo, C; *Residencias San Martín*, E, with meals, basic; *Residencia Restrepo*, near airport, noisy, mosquitoes, run down, F, clean, some rooms with bath, meals US$ 1.50, only lunch worth it; *Kingston*, Av. Las Américas, D, with fan and bath (some rooms less), with breakfast; *Astor*, D inc. 3 meals; *Residencias Mary*, opposite *Astor*, E, clean; *Residencias Hernando Henry*, F, restaurant, fan, clean, good value, on road from airport; *Residencial Barú*, E, with fan; *Playa*, E, cheap, pleasant; *Residencia y Cabinas South End*, recommended, if you write to Luis Alberto Avila at this address in advance, he will collect you at the airport.

Restaurants on **San Andrés** *Oasis* (good); *Lyons* (with bar); *La Parrillada* (Argentine) and *Aldo's* (Italian), good meals US$4; *Popular*, on Av. Bogotá, good square meal for US$4; *comida corriente* at *Don Joaco's* for US$2, good fish. *Mercapollo*, good value; *San Andrés* and *High Seas* are also recommended for cheap, typical meals; *La Fonda* on Av. Colombia near the main beach, and Av. Colombia at Av. Nicaragua, both good; *Miami*, special for US$3; excellent fruit juices at *Jugolandia*, Calle 20 de Julio; *Jugosito*, Av. Colombia, 1½ blocks from tourist office towards centre, cheap meals; *Mundo Acuático*, snacks of fresh fish and *papaya* for US$1, cheaper beer, soft drinks and mangoes. *Fisherman's Place*, in the fishing cooperative at N end of main beach, very good, simple. Good ice cream next to Hotel *Gran Internacional*. *The Barboat*, a floating bar, off the beach between the Centro Comercial Dann and Club Naútico, English and German spoken, waterskiing and windsurfing rental, also instruction available, water taxi to the Keys.

Taxis are expensive. Round the island, US$8; to airport, US$2.50; in town, US$0.60; *colectivo* to airport, US$0.50.

Tourist Information, Avenida Colombia, friendly, helpful.

Providencia, commonly called Old Providence, 80 km. back to the NNE from San Andrés, is 7 km. long and is more mountainous than San Andrés, rising to 610 metres. There are waterfalls, and the land drops steeply into the sea in places. It is also an expensive island. The 3 main beaches are Manchineal Bay, the largest, most attractive and least developed, South West Bay and Freshwater Bay, all in the South West. Most of the accommodation is at Freshwater: *Cabañas El Recreo* (Captain Brian's), E, p.p.; *Cabañas El Paraíso, Cabañas Aguadulce* and *Hotel Royal Queen*; *Ma Elma's* recommended for cheap food; at Santa Isabela on the N end of the island, *Flaming Trees Hotel*, E, clean, restaurant, good value, but a long way from the beach; at Smooth Water Bay, *Dutch Inn* (C full board) and several houses take in guests. Camping is possible at Freshwater Bay. Truck drivers who provide transport on the island may be able to advise on accommodation. The sea food is good, water and fresh milk are generally a problem. Horse riding is available, and boat trips can be made to neighbouring islands such as Santa Catalina (an old pirate lair), and to the NE, Crab Key (beautiful swimming). Superb views can be had by climbing from Bottom House or Smooth Water to the peak. Day tours are arranged by the Providencia office in San Andrés, costing US$30 inclusive. Satena fly from San Andrés, US$30, 30 mins., once a day, sometimes twice, never on Sun., bookable only in San Andrés. (Return flight has to be confirmed at airport. Tourist office at airport.) Boat trips from San Andrés take 8 hours, and are regular.

Santa Marta, capital of Magdalena Department (pop.: 131,000), the third Caribbean port, is 96 km. E of Barranquilla, at the mouth of the Manzanares river. It is best reached from Barranquilla by the paved road along the coast, which skirts an extensive and most interesting lagoon, the Ciénaga de Santa Marta, in which all types of swamp birds, plants and animals may be seen.

Santa Marta lies on a deep bay with high shelving cliffs. The climate ranges seasonally from hot and trying to hot but pleasant in February and March; occasionally one can see snow-clad peaks to the E, less than 50 km. away and 5,800 metres high.

Its sandy beaches stretch from the Simón Bolívar airport to Punta Aguja across the Rodadero de Gaira, the little fishing villages of Villa Concha, surrounded by meadows and shady trees and Taganga (nice for swimming, has a pleasant and inexpensive hotel; a 25 minute walk around the bay leads to the beautiful, popular and thief-ridden Playa Grande: do not go alone). A jutting rock—the Punta de Betín—rises from the sea in front of the city and is topped by a lighthouse. Rugged Moro Island, 3 km. off Santa Marta, completes the panorama. Altogether, Santa Marta is the most popular Colombian seaside resort, and Rodadero Bay is the most fashionable and tourist-oriented part of Santa Marta, though it lies some distance W of the city (local bus service, taxi, US$4.50). It is extremely dangerous to wander off the beaten track at Rodadero: correspondents have been robbed at gunpoint. Many of the buses coming from Barranquilla and Cartagena stop at Rodadero on the way to Santa Marta. There is also a dirty, unsafe beach with a seaside promenade close to the centre of town.

Santa Marta was the first town founded (1525) by the *conquistadores* in Colombia. Founder: Rodrigo de Bastidas. Most of the famous sea-dogs—the brothers Côte, Drake and Hawkins—sacked the city in spite of the two forts built on a small island at the entrance to the bay. It was here that Simón Bolívar, his dream of a Great Colombia shattered, came to die. Almost penniless he was given hospitality at the *hacienda* of San Pedro Alejandrino, 5 km. to the SE. He died on December 17, 1830, at the age of 47, and was buried in the Cathedral, but his body was taken to the Pantheon at Caracas 12 years later. The simple room in which he died and his few belongings can be seen today (admission, US$0.10, open Tues.-Sat. 1330-2000); take the "Mamatoca" bus from the waterfront (Carrera 1C) to the *hacienda*, US$0.20.

Hotels In town: *Residencia Park Hotel,* Carrera 1C, No. 18-63, on sea front, D with shower, reasonable; *Tairona,* Carrera 1, No. 11-41, Tel.: 32408, D, with fan, bath, clean and safe; *Dos Virreyes,* Calle 12, No. 1-34, near waterfront, can be bargained to E, only 5 rooms, with fan and shower, friendly, recommended; *Residencias Miramar,* Calle 10C, No. 1C-59, F with fan (cheaper rooms without), friendly, safe, 2 blocks from railway station and beach (not to be confused with *Hotel Residencias Miramar,* Carrera 1C, No. 18-23); several others nearby; *Bucanero,* Calle 22, E; *Hotel Residencias Yarimar,* Carrera 1A, No. 26-37, E; *Español,* Calle 17, No. 1 C—48, E; *Zulia,* Carrera 1C, No. 20-23; *Residencias Medellín,* Calle 23 and Carrera 1, E, with bath, rooms overlook the sea and there is a cool patio, but very run down; *Residencias Aurora,* Carrera 9A, No. 14-08, E, very dirty; *Yuldama,* Cra. 1, No. 12-19, C, clean a/c, reasonable food; *Residencias Adelita,* Calle 24 and Carrera 8, D; many on Calle 22. *Andrea Doria,* 300 m. from seashore, E, friendly, clean.

At Rodadero Bay: *Tamacá* (best, Carrera 2, No. 11A-98, B); *Irotama,* L (km. 14, between airport and Rodadero Bay; has bungalows); *Titimar,* Calle 29 and Carrera 1A; *Residencias Edma,* Carrera 3, No. 5-188, Rodadero, D, a/c, new, clean, cafeteria, run by two ladies, welcoming; *La Sierra,* Carrera 1, No. 9-47, C, good and relatively inexpensively restaurant; *La Riviera,* Carrera 2, No. 5-42, D, (food US$3-5); *Valladolid,* E, Calle 2, good value; *Puerto Galleón,* L, at km. 18 (difficult to reach by taxi at night); *Santa Mar,* at km. 8, D; *Residencias Costa Azul,* E, with bath and shower, recommended as impeccably clean with good mattresses, fan and window on to courtyard, in town, very friendly. In season, it is difficult to find a single room for less than US$4.

Motels *Rodadero; Taboga* (new); and *Lilium,* secure parking.

Restaurants *Grill Venecia,* in roof garden of Posiheuica building, facing the bay; the *Pan American,* on the beach walk, is pleasant; good food and service; *Yarimar,* Carrera 1A, No. 26-37, next to hotel of same name, good seafood; opp. is *La Terraza Marina,* also recommended for seafood. *La Gran Muralla,* Carrera 5, No. 23-77 and *Oriental,* Calle 22, No. 3-43, both good Chinese. A good breakfast in *Colonial,* on corner of *Hotel Zulia. Bermuz,* Calle 14, No. 4-08, good, cheap. *Ley* department store on Carrera 5, No. 9-01, in town, has cheap cafeteria. At Rodadero: *La Bella Napolés,* first class; *Pacabuy,* on seafront, highly recommended; *Cumbeiros,* one block from *Motel Lilium; Porto Fino,* three blocks from *Tamacá,* good food, not too expensive; *Restaurante Karey,* highly recommended. *Restaurante Pekin,* Calle 22, between Carreras 4 and 5, good value.

476 COLOMBIA

Museum Casa de la Aduana, Calle 14 y Carera 2, displays an excellent archaeological collection, including a large number of pre-Columbian gold artefacts. Open Tues.-Sat., 0800-1200, 1400-1800, Sun. 0800-1200, during the tourist season, Mon.-Fri., 0800-1200, 1400-1800, the rest of the year; entry US$0.15.

Bank Change money at the Banco de la República, on Carrera 5, No. 17-04; open 0800-1100 and 1400-1530. *Casas de cambio* in 3rd block of Calle 14.

Tourist Office in the former Convent of Santo Domingo, Carrera 2, No. 16-44. There is also an office at Rodadero, Calle 10, No. 3-10. Inderena office, Carrera 1C, No. 22-77.

Train Expreso del Sol leaves on Mondays and Thursdays at 0700 for Bogotá, stopping at La Dorada; 24 hrs. to La Dorada (US$10), 30-50 hrs. to Bogotá (US$20), long delays possible. One class only; meals at US$1.50 each, quite good. From La Dorada, one can also take a bus to Bogotá (see page 480). Extra trains with sleeper to Bogotá and to Medellín run in the Dec.-March tourist season. The *autoferro* from Santa Marta to Barrancabermeja at 1500 costs US$8.50, it gets crowded early and is a slow 16 hr. journey.

Buses Terminal is at Calle 24 and Carrera 8 (take a taxi or walk to Calle 22, then take "Playa" bus to centre, passing waterfront—Carrera 1C). The Copetran bus to Bucaramanga takes about 13 hrs. (US$15). Journey time will also be affected by the number of police checks (may be as many as 40). There is a good meal stop at Los Límites. From Bucaramanga the buses take 8 hrs. to Bogotá (11 minimum by 2nd class). Buses to Barranquilla, 2 hrs. (US$1.50); to Cartagena, 4 hrs. (US$3.50, or US$4.75, Brasilia). To Riohacha US$1.75; Pullman to Maicao, US$5.75. The buses stop at the Venezuelan border on the way to Maracaibo for exit and entry stamps, usually better organized than at Cúcuta. There are three buses a day (Brasilia) direct to Rodadero Beach from Barranquilla, taking 2 hrs. and costing US$1.50. They return to Barranquilla at 1300, 1530 and 1730.

Airport Simón Bolívar, 20 km. from city; bus, US$0.20, taxi from Santa Marta, US$7, from Rodadero, US$6. During the tourist season, get to the airport early.

Port It can take up to 4 working days to get a car out of the port, but it is usually well guarded and it is unlikely that anything will be stolen.

Sightseeing Tours in air-conditioned jeeps run by Airline travel agency at centre. Launches leave Rodadero beach every hour for the Aquarium and the closest safe view you can get of hammerhead sharks, US$3 return (includes admission). From the Aquarium, one can walk over slippery rocks (1½-2 hrs.) to the Playa Blanca (White Beach) where one can swim in less crowded conditions than elsewhere—food available at the beach.

Excursions On the E shore of the Ciénaga de Santa Marta, is **Ciénaga,** a town of 75,000 people. Passengers from Barranquilla transfer here to the Atlántico Railway from Santa Marta to Bogotá (the station is a busy journey from the town). Cotton, bananas, tobacco and cacao are grown in the area. Hotels in Ciénaga: *Tobiexe; Naval.* (Granturismo tours to Ciénaga are not recommended; much too fast). South of Ciénaga, just before Fundación, is **Aracataca,** birthplace of Gabriel García Márquez, fictionalised as Macondo in some of his stories (notably *One Hundred Years of Solitude*). His home, called a museum, may be seen in the backyard of La Familia Iriarte Ahumada— just ask for directions. There are *residencias* (G), but it is better to stay in Fundación. Best hotel is *Caroli,* Carrera 8, No. 5-30, Fundación, F (E with a/c); others all in this price range. Do not walk between Aracataca and Fundación at night, otherwise it is safe. Bus Fundación-Aracataca, US$0.15; Fundación-Ciénaga, US$0.75; Fundación-Barranquilla, US$3.50. Banana growing in the area has now been replaced almost entirely by African Palm plantations.

The Sierra Nevada, covering a triangular area of 16,000 sq. km., rises abruptly from the sea, or from lowlands where nowhere reach over 300 metres above sea-level. "Indeed, the north slope is one of the most striking anywhere, lifting from the Caribbean to 5,800-metre snow peaks in about 45 km., a gradient comparable with the south face of the Himalaya, and unequalled along the world's coasts. The interior is made up of some eight E-W ranges with their intervening valleys. . . . The lower parts of these interior valleys are flanked by forests—the homes of primitive Indians as well as pumas, jaguars, and a variety of snakes and birds—but for the most part the Sierra is almost lunar in its sterile grandeur, bleak *páramos* leading to naked crag and scree and glacier, where only an occasional questing condor moves. In the rocky heart of the area are a large number of small, beautiful lakes, many in cirques." - Frank F. Cunningham, in an excellent illustrated article on exploring the Sierra in *The Geographical Magazine*.

It is difficult to visit the Sierra Nevada and it is necessary to obtain a safe-conduct pass from the Casa Indígena and the police in Valledupar (see next page) before doing so. From Valledupar the best route is along the Guatepuri valley; also there are jeeps to Pueblo Bello (US$1), running hourly from 0700 to 1400 from near the bus stations. In Pueblo Bello enquire for transport (irregular and infrequent), to San Sebastián de Rábago, the central village of one of the four tribes of Indians living in the Sierra, the Arhuacos. It is set in beautiful surroundings and is the epitome of an Indian village, as yet unspoilt by tourism. The Indians of the Sierra distrust strangers and do not take kindly to being photographed, especially without permission. However they like to be given sea-shells which can be ground into powder and mixed with coca leaves and such a gift may improve their reaction to strangers and cameras. Those interested in the Arhuaco culture should seek out Celso Domingo, a dentist in Pueblo Bello, himself an Arhuaco. At Pueblo Bello there is *El Hogar de Mami*, E, full board, very clean. Also *El Hogar de Mercedes*, where room and board is reasonably priced.

To go to the recently uncovered Ciudad Perdida, take a truck at 0720 from Santa Marta market to El Campano and La Tague, then hike for 2 days. Permission required from Inderena and the police.

N.B. The Sierra Nevada is a marijuana-growing area—take care.

The **Tairona** national park, 35 km. E of Santa Marta in the Riohacha direction, wild woodland on the coast, is beautiful and unspoilt. Take a Maicao or Riohacha bus to the park entrance (US$0.70), then walk or hitch 5 km. to beach at Cañaveral. Alternatively, there is a tour bus at 1000 from *Hotel Zulia* in Santa Marta, direct to Cañaveral, return at 1500, US$3 (not long enough). Bathing not recommended as there is heavy pounding surf and the tides are treacherous. The place is not without thieves, but a most attractive spot for camping; the beach is less crowded and cleaner than Rodadero. (There are splendid and deserted sandy beaches, to which you have to walk, about 5 km. E of Cañaveral.) Relics of ancient Tairona culture abound. A taxi to Cañaveral and back from Santa Marta costs US$14. A guided tour round the Pueblito archaeological site costs US$7 for the 6 hrs. involved (a full tour from *Hotel Irotama*, including transport and guide, costs US$55). Camping in the Park at Cañaveral costs US$5.70 per tent. Many camping and hammock places on the path from the Park to Pueblito (also refreshment bars). The camping at Cañaveral has facilities but there is only one restaurant with a tiny store, so take all supplies. There are plenty of mosquitoes. Good camping at Arrecifes (US$1.75 for tent, US$1.10 for hammock space, US$2.85 for hut), no facilities but meals and soft drinks available, beautiful beach nearby (sea dangerous). Avoid, if possible, camping at Finca Martínez—dirty, narcotics centre; there is another, much better Finca at which one may camp (on the road to Pueblito). Walking in the park, it is 1 hour from the entrance to Cañaveral, then another hour to Arrecifes; follow the beach for ¼ hour to Rancho Viejo from where a clear path leads S to Pueblito (1½ hrs.). At the site there are Indians; do not photograph them. From Pueblito you can either return to Cañaveral, or continue for 2 hours to Calabazo on the Santa Marta-Riohacha road. It is advisable to inform park guards when walking in the park as it is a marijuana-growing area; also wear hiking boots and beware of bloodsucking insects. In the wet, the paths are very slippery.

Riohacha, capital of Guajira Department, 160 km. E of Santa Marta, is a port of 44,000 people at the mouth of the Río César: low white houses, sandy streets, no trees or hills. It was founded in 1545 by Nicolás Federmann, and in early years its pearling industry was large enough to tempt Drake to sack it (1596). Pearling almost ceased during the 18th century and the town was all but abandoned. (The contraband element can make it dangerous for visitors.)

Hotels *Campestre* (state-owned); *Gimaura*, (also state-owned), on beach, D, including breakfast, they allow camping (free) in their grounds, with outside shower; *Almirante Padilla* and *Líbano* (neither very good). *Hostal* opposite the bus station, E, fan, clean, friendly, expensive food; *Nelly*, F, basic but convenient for bus stations on the edge of town.

Many small restaurants along sea-front including *Europa*, German run. *Tizoles*, recommended for *chiva* (goat); *Golosinas*, café near the beach, good food, friendly service. All accommodation and food is expensive (no hotel or *pensión* costs less than US$5). You can sling your hammock for free at the police station. There are an airport, a cinema, a tourist office on the beach front and a bank, which changes dollars cash, but not if you're in your beachwear. At the weekend, Riohacha fills up, and bars and music spring up all over the place. The sea is clean, despite the red silt stirred up by the waves.

Venezuelan Consulate Calle 7, No. 3-75. With two passport photographs and an exit ticket UK citizens can get a visa on the same day.

There is a road from Riohacha to Bucaramanga. At La Paz (Hotel: *Turismo*; Restaurant: *La Fogata*) you join the road that leads through **Valledupar,** capital of César Department-population 202,000 (Hotels: *Sicarare,* two-star, Carrera 9,

No. 16-04, C; cheaper 2-star hotel is *Kurakata*, Calle 19C, No. 7-96; bus from Santa Marta, 8½ hrs., US$1.75; from Cartagena, US$8.50 with Expreso Brasilia) to Barranquilla and Santa Marta via Fundación (see above). On to Codazzi is asphalted, but not beyond until the paved Bucaramanga-Santa Marta highway. There is a possible overnight stay at Curumaní (*Hotel Himalaya*), or at Aguachica, just off the road.

Beyond Riohacha to the E is the arid and sparsely inhabited Guajira Peninsula. The Indians here live primitively, collecting dividivi, tending goats, and fishing. To visit a small part of the Peninsula you can take a pick-up truck from Riohacha (they leave twice a day from the Indian market) to Manaure for US$1.50, or a daily bus, 0830 from bus station, which may be safer. It is an uncomfortable 3-hr. drive through fields of cactus but offers glimpses of the Indians. Manaure, which is known for its salt flats, has a *residencia*—restaurant (G). From Manaure there are trucks to Uribia (one basic *residencia*, no running water, but fresh water is a problem throughout the Guajira) and thence to Maicao. In Uribia you can buy handicrafts intended for local, not tourist, use by asking around. Sometimes it is possible to get a lift to Cabo de la Vela, further round the coast, where the lagoons shelter vast flocks of flamingoes, herons and sandpipers. Sunsets in the Guajira are magnificent. There is a paved road from Riohacha to Maicao near the frontier. Travellers will need a visa to enter Venezuela; essential to get it elsewhere because the delays in Riohacha or at the frontier posts can be unconscionable and many are turned back. Reports suggest that only 3-day tourist cards are given at Maicao. For those entering Colombia at this border, immigration is at Riohacha. The Caribbean coastal highway, now paved, runs direct from Santa Marta along the coast to Riohacha, and the Riohacha-Maicao road (also paved) has been greatly improved. A large coal-mining industry is being set up at El Cerrejón, in the Guajira.

Maicao Following the decline in border contraband, it has lost much of its attraction as the centre for smuggled goods entering Colombia from Venezuela. It is still at the centre of the narcotics trade. Its streets are unmade and it has a considerable reputation for lawlessness; most commercial premises close before 1600 and after 1700 the streets are highly unsafe. If at all possible travellers should avoid Maicao and the road services that go there, which are liable to ambush. Also, all isolated areas of César and Guajira Departments are unsafe for tourists.

Entering Venezuela at this border, everyone needs a visa; a transit visa will only suffice if you have a confirmed ticket to a third country within 3 days.

Hotels in Maicao: *Maicao Juan Hotel*, C, the only safe one; *Residencia Gallo*, E, private bath and pool; *Hotel Hilda*, C, reasonable; *El Parador*.

Buses (basic): Maicao-Riohacha, US$2; Maicao-Santa Marta, US$5.75; Maicao-Maracaibo, US$3.15 (last bus 1530); Maicao-Barranquilla, US$6.50. Maicao-Cartagena, US$4.75-7.50. There are bus services along the Caribbean coastal highway, and also flights Barranquilla-Maicao. Colectivo, Maicao-Maracaibo, US$15.

Air Services with Avianca, Satena.

Up the Magdalena River

Passenger travel by the lofty and top-heavy paddle boats on the river has now come to an end, though the adventurous traveller may still find an occasional passage by cargo paddle boat. But in general the only way of getting from one place to the other along the river is by motor boat, and this is more expensive. Insect repellants should be taken, for mosquitoes are a nuisance.

The Magdalena is wide but shallow and difficult to navigate because of surface eddies, and there are little whirlpools over submerged rocks. Away to the NE, in the morning, one can see the high snow-capped peaks of the Sierra Nevada de Santa Marta.

At Tenerife Bolívar had his first victory in the Magdalena campaign. At Zambrano, a cattle centre 96 km. beyond Calamar, there are tobacco plantations. Population, 4,000. There is a road W to the N-S Cartagena-Medellín road, and a trail E to the oil fields at El Difícil. Near Pinto the river divides: the eastern branch, silted and difficult, leads to **Mompós**, an old town of 20,000 people: cattle farming and tobacco, and the scene of another victory for Bolívar: "At Mompós", he said, "my glory was born." Mompós was founded in 1537 and, thanks to its comparative isolation, preserves its colonial character more completely than any other town in Colombia. Old buildings are the Casa de Gobierno, once a home of the Jesuits, and the Colegio de Pinillos. There are 7 churches and the Easter celebrations are said to be among the best in Colombia. The town is well known in Colombia for handworked gold jewellery. Airport. Malaria is endemic in the surrounding countryside.

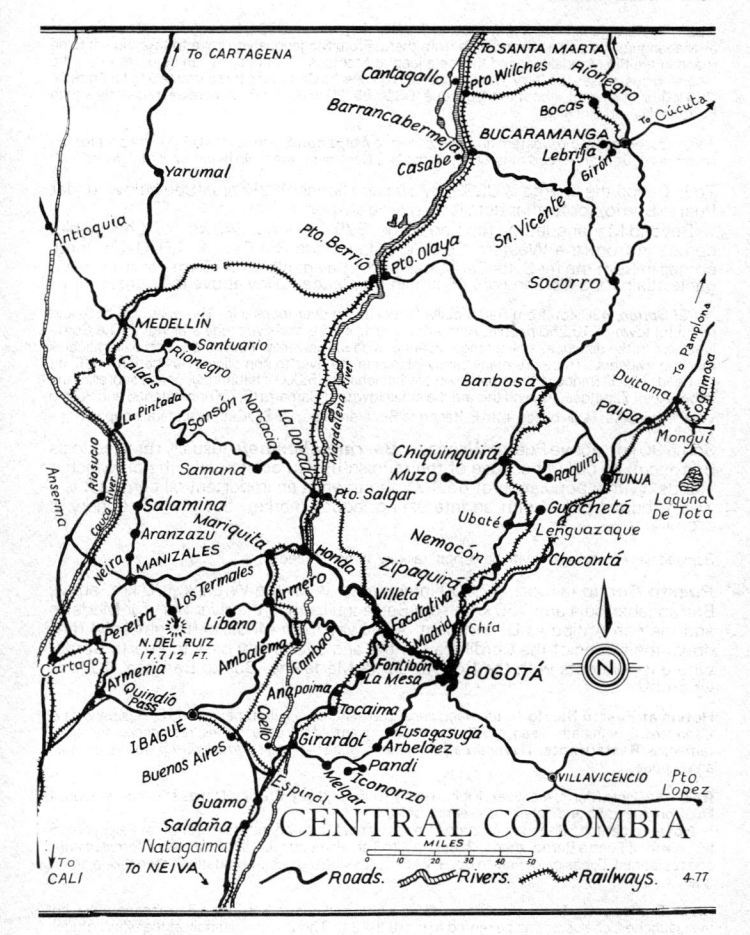

Mompós Hotels *Residencias Unión*, Calle 18, No. 3-43, F, with bath and fan; *Hostal Doña Manuela*, Calle Real del Medio, 17-41, D, a converted colonial house, quiet and peaceful but run down; with cockroaches; also *Tropicana*, *Núñez*.

Restaurant *La Brasa*, facing river.

480 COLOMBIA

Bus To Cartagena with Unitransco and Brasilia daily, 4 hrs., US$4, but you can only book as far as Magangué; you pay a second time from there. From Magangué you have to take launch to an island in the Río Magdalena, and thence a jeep to Mompós. Connections can be unreliable if the incoming bus misses the ferry. It is cheaper and quicker to Cartagena by shared taxi to La Bodega, US$1, 1 hr., then motor boat to Magangué, US$0.85, 20 mins. From Magangué, buses also go to Barranquilla and Sincelejo.

Most vessels go by the western arm of the loop to **Magangué,** a town of 40,800, the port for the savannas of Bolívar. A road runs W to join the N-S Cartagena-Medellín highway. Hotel: *Mardena*.

To El Banco the charge is US$3, by *chalupa* (launch), 2¼ hrs. (See below, under Puerto Berrío, for further details on river transport.)

Beyond Magangué, the Río San Jorge, 379 km. long, 240 km. of it navigable, comes in from the Western Cordillera. Later the Río Cauca, 1,020 km. long, comes in from the far S. Its Caribbean end is navigable for 370 km., and it is navigable again for a distance of 245 km. in the Cauca Valley above the gorge.

At **El Banco,** 420 km. from Barranquilla (airport), the river loops join. This is an old, dirty and beautiful town of 10,250 people. Along the river front are massive stone stairways. The Cordilleras are in the distance, a blue range on either side of the valley. Pink herons and blue macaws much in evidence. There are many sandy islands in the river to complicate navigationA difficult trail leads N of El Banco to the small town of Chimichagua (5,000 inhabitants), on the shores of the large lake of Zapatosa. Beyond this are the small towns of Gamarra (3,700 inhabitants) and Puerto Wilches (5,600). Daily buses from El Banco to Bucaramanga, US$7, Cúcuta and Valledupar.

Some 30 km. above Puerto Wilches is **Barrancabermeja** (usually referred to as Barranca), so called because of the reddish-brown oil-stained cliffs on which it stands. With a population of 66,400, the town is an important oil centre; it is a warm, humid place with an interesting indoor market, but the oil refinery is prominent.

Residencias Ferroviario, F with bath, opp. railway station, friendly.

Puerto Berrío (airport; 12,750 inhabitants) is on the W bank 100 km. above Barrancabermeja and 756 km. from Barranquilla. It is the river port for Medellín and the rich Antioquia Department. A railway from Medellín (freight only) runs down the slopes of the Cordillera Central and over a low pass to Puerto Berrío, where it connects with the Bogotá-Santa Marta line. Bus to Barbosa, 10 hrs., US$4.50.

Hotels at Puerto Berrío *Hotel Magdalena*, pleasant, on a hilltop near river, E; *Residencias El Ganadero*, F, with bath, clean, modern, with ceiling fans. Many other hotels, *residencias* and *apartamentos*. **Restaurants:** *Tabrona*, *La Buena Mesa*, good big meals; *Heladería Joi*, good ice cream and sundaes.

Rail To Santa Marta: 4 a week, Mon., Tues., Thurs. and Sat. Check all times at Grecia station, 4 km. from the town and hotels, taxi service only.
Note: to get to El Banco or Mompós from a Santa Marta-bound train, get off at Palestinos, 8 hrs. north of Puerto Berrío, then a shared taxi to Tamalameque (US$1; *Residencia Tamalameque* and restaurant, F, basic), or Puerto Boca, 2 km. further on (no accommodation), then take a motor boat.

River Transport There is no regular service between Puerto Berrío and Barrancabermeja, but river launches, *chalupas*, can be rented to make the 2 to 3 hour journey (apply at the wharf office). From Puerto Boca, *chalupas* run from 0500 till dusk; Cootrafluvial has a service to Barrancabermeja, Gamarra, San Pablo, La Gloria, El Banco (US$2.25, 45 mins.), Mompós (changing at El Banco, US$4, 2 hrs.). Don't be bullied into taking an *expreso* service, or you'll pay for all the empty seats.

5 hours by road from Puerto Berrío is **Puerto Boyacá**. The road is mostly unpaved, passing zebu *fincas*, swamps and oil fields. There are army checkpoints on the road, owing to guerrilla activity in the area. (Hotels: *Residencias Lusitania*; *Santa Fe*; *Hotel* and *Heladería Embajador*.) Rápido Tolima has a daily 1100 bus to Puerto Berrío, US$3.50.

It is 151 km. up river from Puerto Berrío to **La Dorada** (6,000 people) on the W bank, but only 134 km. by rail (7½ hrs.) along the W bank. (Hotels: *Rosita*, Calle 17, No. 3-28, Tel.: 72301, F, with bath, friendly, pleasant, recommended; *Departamental*; on highway to Honda, *Magdalena Motel*; *Hospedaje La Floresta*,

COLOMBIA 481

in centre, F, with bath and toilet, good, clean). This railway crosses the Magdalena by a bridge from La Dorada to **Puerto Salgar,** on the E bank, from which the Cundinamarca Railway (198 km.) goes up the slopes of the Eastern Cordillera to Bogotá. (This journey, which takes 10 hours, is described on page 488.) Bus La Dorada-Bogotá, US$4, La Dorada-Medellín, US$4.25. Train La Dorada-Bogotá twice a week; to Santa Marta, Tues. and Sat. at 1500, 24 hrs. US$10. Hotels: *Salgar; Residencia Antioquia,* G, with fan. The Lower Magdalena river navigation stops at La Dorada as there are rapids above, as far as Honda. Cargo is taken by railway to Honda, where it is re-embarked. The Upper Magdalena is navigable as far as Girardot.

Honda (airport) on the W bank of the river, is 32 km. upstream from La Dorada (149 km. from Bogotá). It is a pleasant old town with many colonial houses. The streets are narrow and picturesque, and the town is surrounded by hills. El Salto de Honda (the rapids which separate the Lower from the Upper Magdalena) are just below the town. Population: 31,600. Average temperature: 29°C. Altitude 230 metres. Several bridges span the Magdalena and the Guali rivers, at whose junction the town lies. In February the Magdalena rises and fishing is unusually good. People come from all over the region for the fishing and the festival of the Subienda, as the season is called.

Hotels *Ondama* (swimming pool), recommended; *América,* with pool, similar standard; *Río Ritz,* good restaurant; *Residencias Las Mercedes,* E, with bath, clean and friendly; *La Piscina,* E, fan, swinmming pool, clean, friendly, arranges safe parking at reasonable rates with neighbours, recommended; *Moderno,* G; *Residencias Virrey,* F with or without fan; *Las Villas,* F, clean, pleasant; *Los Puentes,* next to cinema, a bit run down, across river from *La Cascada,* F; *La Riviera,* E, friendly, good value, swimming pool, reported destroyed by flooding in 1985.

Restaurants *La Cascada,* overlooking river, a good meal for US$3. There is a good *panadería* at the entrance. *Hotel Río Ritz* has a good meal for US$1.50. Good ice cream (La Campiña brand) at *heladería* next to Teatro Unión; *Fuente Mar* for yoghurt and ice cream. There is a row of good cheap restaurants across the Magdalena River bridge in Puerto Bogotá.

Buses from Bogotá by Velotax US$4, and Rápido Tolima, US$3. Manizales, US$3. Rápido Tolima run half-hourly buses to La Dorada (1 hour), and beyond, to Puerto Boyacá (3 hrs.), US$2.25. To Puerto Berrío, 8 hrs., departures at 0300 and 0800 with San Vicente.

West from Honda a paved road goes 21 km. to **Mariquita** (13,000 people; *Hotel Bocaneme* and others, campsites), the centre of a fruit-growing country. Buses depart from Honda every half hour, US$0.30, ½ hr. with Rápido Tolima. On the way is the clean and pleasant bathing pool of El Diamante. On again is the Club Deportivo: private, but visitors are welcome to its swimming pool, a blessing in this climate. There is another, El Virrey, in Mariquita. The town has several old houses and buildings: a mint, the viceroy's house, the parish church. Here José Celestino Mutis lived for 8 years during his famous Botanic Expedition towards the end of the 18th century (when he and his helpers accumulated a herbarium of 20,000 plants, a vast library, and a rich collection of botanical plates and paintings of native fauna). The collection was sent to Madrid, where it remains. Mariquita was founded in 1551, and it was here that the founder of Bogotá, Jiménez de Quesada, died in 1579. From Mariquita a road runs W up the slopes of the Central Cordillera to Manizales.

Motel *Las Acacias,* outside Mariquita, on the Armero road.

Fresno, in the heart of a big coffee growing area, is 30 km. from Mariquita. The road to Honda is appalling. Bus to Manizales (83 km.) US$2.80 (Rápido Tolima).

From Mariquita the road turns S to (32 km.) Armero (7,500 inhabitants), which used to be a cotton growing centre. This town and surrounding villages were devastated by the eruption of the Nevado del Ruiz volcano (see page 508) in November 1985. (Armero can be reached by colectivo from Honda; no lodging in Armero, nearest at Mariquita or possibly Guayabal; no drinks available in Armero, either, only icecream and flowers; there are lots of mosquitoes, though). A branch road runs 35 km. W to **Líbano,** 29,700 inhabitants. (Hotels: *Cumanday; Rex.*) Coffee is the great crop here, with potatoes in the uplands. Away to the W looms the peak of Nevado del Ruiz, which before its eruption was the second highest in the Cordillera Central. Bus from Líbano to Ibagué, US$2.25, 4 hrs..

From Armero a branch road runs down to the Magdalena past Gambao to

482 COLOMBIA

Ambalema (Hotels: *Barcelona; Nariño*). (At Gambao the river is crossed for the road to Bogotá.) The main road from Armero goes direct for 88 km. to Ibagué.

Ibagué, capital of Tolima Department, is a large city (304,000 inhabitants), lying at the foot of the Quindío mountains at 1,250 metres. It is cooler here (22°C) than in the valley. Parts of the town are old: the Colegio de San Simón is worth seeing, and so is the market. The Parque Centenario is very pleasant. The city specializes in two things; hand-made leather goods (there are many good, cheap shoe shops) and a local drink called *mistela*. There is an excellent Conservatory of Music.

The National Folklore Festival is held during the last week of June. The Departments of Tolima and Huila commemorate St. John (June 24) and Sts. Peter and Paul (June 29) with bullfights, fireworks, and music.

Hotels There are many hotels of reasonable quality which are quite comfortable. *Ambala*, Calle 11, No. 2-60, C, not good value, slow service, no hot water; *Italia*, cheap, reasonable; *Athabasca*, D, with restaurant; *Bram*, E, Calle 17 and Carrera 4, convenient and insect-free; *Acapulco*, near bus station, E, hot water, shower, clean and pleasant; *Ambeima*, Carrera 3 No. 13-32, E; *Raad*, E, next door; both good. *San Luis*, near Expreso Bolivariano bus station, G, good but noisy. *Residencia Puracé* (opposite Tolima bus station), E.

Restaurants *Parador Los Cristales*, S side of town, reasonable; *Casino Chamaco*, with excellent, typical *tamales* at weekend. For Chinese food, *Toy Wan*, Carrera 4. 24 hr. restaurants include *Punto Rojo*, in the shopping precinct on Carrera 3, and *Punto Fácil*, Calle 15 with Carrera 3.

Tourist Office Carrera 3, between Calles 10 and 11; helpful.

Just outside, on the Armenia road, a dirt road leads to the slopes of the Nevado del Tolima. Gerhard Drekonja of Vienna writes: For climbing the Nevado del Tolima (5,200 metres) take in Ibagué at 0600 the *mixto* train to Juntas and El Silencio (2 hrs.). From there half-an-hour walk to the primitive but fabulous thermal waters (90°C) of El Rancho (simple sleeping accommodation and food available). The climb starts from El Rancho. It takes 8 to 10 hours to the top. The equipment (crampons and pica) indispensable. The final climb has to be done at sunrise because clouds and mist invariably rise around 0800. From the top a breathtaking view across the other snowcapped mountains of the Cordillera Central.

There is a road to Girardot, 79 km. E on the Magdalena, going on to Bogotá on the far side: Bogotá is 224 km. by road from Ibagué. On this road is the village of **Gualanday**, with *Hotel Rozal*, F, clean, friendly, safe for motorcyclists and 4 good roadside restaurants (*Dona Eva's* also has accommodation). **Espinal**, pop. 80,000, is an important agroindustrial town at a road junction, but of little interest to the tourist. A 2-star hotel is being built outside the town. Restaurant *Parador Rokoko*, on the main street is costly but has decent meals. Bus to Ibagué, 1 hr., US$0.75, just flag one down. Toll between Ibagué and Espinal, US$0.50; between Espinal and Girardot, US$0.40. W of Ibagué the road runs over the 3,350-metre high Quindío Pass to Armenia, 105 km. from Ibagué across the Cordillera Central. The bus trip to Pereira takes 4 hrs. and costs US$2.55. To Cali, on Flota Magdalena pullman, 7 hrs., US$5.75; ordinary buses US$4; Velotax US$5. To Bogotá, 4½ hrs., US$3.75 with Velotax, US$3.50 by bus. Bus to Popayán, US$6.75.

Between Ibagué and Armenia, on the E side of the Quindío Pass, is **Cajamarca**, a friendly town in a beautiful setting; *Residencia Central*, E; *Residencia Balmoral*, E; both on same street, friendly and clean.

Girardot (airport) is on the Upper Magdalena. Altitude, 326 metres; population, 70,000. The climate is hot and there are heavy rains. Here the navigation of the Upper Magdalena ends, although in dry weather boats cannot get this far; walk across the fine steel bridge to see merchandise being loaded and unloaded—coffee and hides are the main items, although shipments of the former have declined considerably. Launch rides on the river can be taken, starting from underneath the bridge. Large cattle fairs are held on June 5-10 and December 5-10. There is a two-storey market, at its best in early morning but nevertheless good all day, and another good market on Sun. mornings. Bogotanos come down here at weekends to warm up.

Hotels *El Peñón*, on site of former *hacienda* just outside town, fashionable bungalow complex, casino, huge pool, lake, B per bungalow. *Bachue*, Carrera 8, No. 18-04, C, large pool, excellent;

Los Angeles, on main plaza, D, clean, friendly, recommended; *Canala*, comfortable and reasonable; *Residencias La Paz*, Carrera 1 E, No. 11-33; *Flamingo*, near market, E. Opp. new bus terminal, *Maroti*, F, and *El Cid*, F with fan.

Restaurants *Laresa*, Carrera 8a, US$2-3 for a meal; *Cali*, not very good, but cheap; *Club 60*, across the bridge, US$3-8. There is a good food market.

Banks Only the Banco de la República will change travellers' cheques in Girardot.

Roads To Bogotá, 132 km.; bus costs US$3, about 3½ hrs.; bus to Neiva, US$2.55, 3½ hrs.; to Ibagué, 78 km. To Fusagasugá, US$1.65.

Train daily *autoferro*, except Sunday and public holidays, to Neiva at 1400.

Another centre of population—though a small one—in the Magdalena Valley lies upstream from Girardot with Neiva as its capital. Coffee and tobacco are grown on the slopes here, and cattle are raised in the valley.

The road, and its short branches E and W, runs through a number of small towns of under 25,000 people. One of these, 35 km. from Girardot, is **Guamo,** with 21,000 inhabitants. Eight km. beyond Guamo is **Saldaña,** where there are irrigation works that have made 15,000 hectares available for rice, sesame and cotton.

Hotel at Guamo: *Lemayá* (modern; swimming pool), best in region. At **Saldaña,** *Hotel Saldaña,* not too good.

A pretty spot is the reservoir located near **Prado,** Tolima. Turn off the Ibagué-Neiva road at Saldaña for 25 km.; it is well signposted. There is a dirt road for the last 12 km. past Purificación. Buses can be caught in Bogotá, Ibagué and all intermediate towns. A pleasant government hotel is at the lake (D, B for cabin for 6-10, free camping on the shoreline, water-skiing US$2.50, short trip with a boat). The pretty part of the lake is hidden from the end of the road and must be seen from a boat. Official boat trips to the islands are about 3 times cheaper than those of "sharks" operating here; the official mooring-point is down the slope at the end of the road. Swimming is good and the water is warm, but wading is not advisable because of the presence of the fresh-water stingray. Cheap hotels are available in Prado, 4 km. from the lake. There are restaurants of questionable quality in town. Excellent food can be obtained at the end of the road in the boat-dock area, but sanitation leaves something to be desired.

A little beyond the 50 kilometre stone from Neiva you can turn to the left, cross a fence, and see the Piedra Pintada de Aipe, a stone not in fact painted but carved by precolumbian Indians with designs akin to the shapes of some of the gold pieces in the Museo del Oro at Bogotá.

Neiva, capital of Huila Department, has a population of 139,000. It was first founded in 1539, when Benalcázar came across the Cordillera Central from Popayán in quest of El Dorado. It was soon after destroyed by the Indians and refounded in 1612. It is now a pleasant, modern city. There are rich coffee plantations around Neiva, for here the valley bottom is high enough to be in the coffee zone. The cathedral was destroyed by earthquake in 1967. There is a large and colourful market every day. Tourist information is given at the cultural centre with museum and gallery on the main square. Altitude: 470 metres.

Hotels *Hostería Matamundo*, in old *hacienda* 6 km. out of town on road to Garzón and San Agustín, C, a/c, swimming pool, good meals, US$2.50-7, disco (does not accept Visa card; will not put extra beds in room for children); *Tumbaragua*, C, no swimming pool or hot water but nevertheless recommended; *Americano*, Carrera 5, No. 8-65, D, clean, swimming pool; *Avirama*, Calle 7, No. 2-40, E; *Plaza*, Calle 7, No. 4-62, D, a/c, swimming pool; *Central*, Cra. 3, No. 7-82, E, meals US$1 each, near market, good value. *Residencias Pacandé*, near Taxis Verdes office, D, overpriced, clean. *Cali*, F, basic, reasonable, next door is *San Jorge*, F, cheaper, clean, adequate. Several cheap hotels are to be found off the square where the bus companies are centred. Many small boys meet the buses and suggest accommodation.

Restaurants *Hostería Los Cerros*, Calle 11, No. 32-39; *El Caimo*, Calle 8, No. 7A-22; *Los Gauchos*, Carrera 15, No. 5-12; *Neiva Viejo*, Calle 9, No. 6-49.

Fiesta from June 18 to 28, when the Bambuco Queen is elected, with folklore, dances and feasting.

Airport La Marguita, 1½ km. from city. Aires and Satena fly from Bogotá (Aires to Bogota daily, US$27; to Cali, US$33; to Medellín, either direct or via Ibagué, US$34). Satena flies to Leguizamo, via Florencia daily.

Train *Autoferro* daily except Sun. and public holidays to Girardot.

484 COLOMBIA

Bus from Bogotá (331 km., paved road), 6 hrs., US$5. Regular bus service with Autobuses Unidos del Sur (Carrera 2, No. 5-32, Tel.: 24800) and Coomotor to San Agustín, US$4 (US$4.50 by colectivo). To Garzón, US$3; to Pitalito, US$4.35. To Espinal, 3 hrs., US$2.25, good road except for stretch between Nataguima and Aipe. To Pasto, US$9; to Popayán, US$7.75, ordinary bus at 0330, 1000, 1930, to Florencia, US$6.50. Long-distance buses leave from Carrera 2, Calles 5 and 6.

Warning At the bus stations in Neiva, Garzón and especially Pitalito, theft is rife—take extra care of your belongings.

Beyond Neiva lie the plains of Huila Department, arid, but still capable of supporting cattle, and dominated by the snow-capped Nevado del Huila to the NW. The road runs S from Neiva, past (92 km.) **Garzón**, a pleasant cathedral town set in mountains with roads W across the Cordillera to Popayán and SE to Florencia, capital of the Intendencia of Caquetá (see page 487), and is paved past Pitalito to San Agustín. **Pitalito** (12,000 people), has little to offer the tourist. If you hitch you'll find it fairly easy to Garzón; slower on to San Agustín, but plenty of buses and colectivos (US$1). Buses in Pitalito go from Calle 3a; Taxis Verdes from the main square (US$9 to Bogotá). See map of area, page 518.

Hotels at Garzón: *Damasco*, D, good meals for US$3; *Cecil*, near bus station, E, with private bath; *Arizona*, E; *Miami*, E, good. The *Abeyma*, a state hotel, is recommended, D; it is possible to camp in the grounds, US$1. *San Luis*, F, not recommended, dirty, basic. At **Pitalito** there is a *Hotel de Turismo*. There are 2 hotels with swimming pools: the *Calamó*, C, hot water, and *Timanco*, a 3-star hotel; *Pigoanza*, on main square, E; *Residencia Pitalito*, F, without shower, reasonable, Calle 5 round corner from police station; *La Laroyano*, on main street, cheap, adequate; *Residencial El Globo*, main street, F, clean, basic. Other hotels: *Grand Hotel*, F, bath, good food; *Nacional*; *Pachito*; *Residencias Londres*; *Residencias California*. Restaurant *Cando* recommended; also *Napolitano*, good, cheap.

South of Pitalito is the **Cueva de los Guácharos** National Park; take a bus to Palestrina, US$1, 1 hour, and then walk for 6 hours along an eroded, muddy path. Between December and June swarms of oilbirds (*guácharos*) may be seen; they are nocturnal, with a unique radar-location system. The reserve also contains many of the unusual and spectacular cocks-of-the-rock. The rangers are particularly friendly, providing tours and basic accommodation; permission to visit the park must be obtained from the Inderena offices in Pitalito, Neiva or Bogotá.

The way to the remarkable Tierradentro underground burials in man-made caves painted with geometrical patterns is given on page 517; they can be reached by Popayán bus from San Agustín, Pitalito or Garzón, with a change at La Plata, or at the Cruce San Andrés. The bus from La Plata leaves at 0500, and on Fri. only, at 1200.

San Agustín (altitude 1,700 m.) is 27 km. from Pitalito (all paved). Here, in the Valley of the Statues, are some hundreds of large rough-hewn stone figures of men, animals and gods, dating from roughly 3300 B.C. to just before the Spanish conquest. Nothing is known of the culture which produced them, though traces of small circular bamboo straw-thatched houses have been found. Various sculptures found here are exhibited in the National Museum at Bogotá, and there are some life-sized copies of San Agustín originals along the highway from Bogotá to the superseded Techo airport, near Fontibón. There are about 20 sites; information can be obtained from the tourist office, Calle 5a, No. 14-45, Tel.: 73019 (open 0830-1230, 1330-1730, Mon.-Fri., 0900-1200, 1300-1700, Sat. and Sun., Sr Joaquín Emilio García is most helpful in all matters). Free maps to the area can only be obtained here or in Bogotá. It is recommended that visitors arriving in San Agustín should go initially to the tourist office which has a list of all hotels, their prices and quality, and a price list for taxi rides and horse hire.

The nearest sites are the Parque Arqueológico and the Bosque Arqueológico (open 0800-1800 daily, entrance to both costs US$0.15), both about 2½ km. from San Agustín town, 1½ km. from the *Hotel Yalconia*, and less than 1 km. from the *Motel Osoguaico*. It is a steady uphill walk. The statues in the Parque are *in situ*, though some have been set up on end and fenced in with wire; those in the Bosque (a little wood) have been moved and rearranged, and linked by gravel footpaths. Of particular interest are the carved rocks in and around the stream at the Fuente de Lavapatas in the Parque, where the water runs through the carved channels (visitors should not miss the Cerro de Lavapatas which has an extensive view, closes at 1600); refreshment stands at "Fuente" and on the way up to

Lavapatas. There is a museum in the Parque which contains pottery and Indian artefacts (entry included on Parque ticket, closes at 1700 and on Mondays). The whole site leaves an unforgettable impression, from the strength and strangeness of the statues, and the great beauty of the rolling green landscape.

Hotels *Yalconia*, outside town, government financed, being remodelled, B, swimming pool, bookable by phone from *Hotel Monasterio*, Popayán (camping allowed next door, sheltered tents available); *Central*, Calle 3, No. 10-32, near bus offices, E, with bath (F, in the 3 rooms without bath), good meals at US$1.50, it is possible to do laundry here (but keep an eye on your clothes), clean and friendly, secure motorcycle parking, will hire horses, English and French spoken; *Residencias Dorada*, Calle 3, 10-41, also Autobuses Unidos office. There is accommodation in private houses for about US$2 p.p., which is often preferable. *Colonial*, Calle 3, No. 10-54, F, shower, clean, pleasant, restaurant, recommended; *Residencias Náñez*, Calle 5a with Carrera 16, F, singles may have to share room, hot water, friendly and clean; guests may use kitchen; also the owners have horses for rent (US$5 for 5 hrs., check them first) and will act as guides to the archaeological sites (price of guide included in price of horse, but US$1.15 each hour over 5 hours). *Mi Terruño*, Calle 4, No. 15-69, 5 rooms, F, colonial house, some rooms with bath, hot water, friendly, morning coffee, recommended, owner Carlos Arturo Muñoz also has 3 cabins, *Los Andaqui*, for rent. *Residencias Luis Tello*, Calle 4a, No. 15-33, run by a teacher, clean, hot water, very pleasant and friendly, F, good meals, US$1.50; also *Residencias Cosmopólita*, E, recommended. *Residencias Eduardo Motta*, Calle 4, No. 15-71, has five rooms, friendly, clean, hot water, F, hard beds, but with morning coffee; similar establishment run by Luis who runs the post office, F; *Residencia Familiar*, on main street one block down from Coomotor-Autobuses Unidos del Sur office, 7 rooms, hot water extra, laundry, friendly, G p.p., book meals in advance, horses for hire; *Residencias La Gaitana*, Calle 6A, No. 14-47, F, clean, friendly management; *Residencia y Restaurante La Floresta*, see below (has hot water). Sr. Noé Ortiz López can arrange accommodation at a farm for F category price, with breakfast and dinner, recommended, contact him at Carrera 14, No. 5-69. Small boys (and thieves **beware**) will meet you off the bus with offers of such accommodation; they are also remarkably competent guides in many languages. Between San Agustín and the Parque Arqueológico is the *Motel Osoguaico*, recently rebuilt after fire, good food, F p.p.; swimming pool, camping site, US$1 p.p. Accommodation at the farm of Constantino Ortiz is recommended, 6 km. from town, bordering on the Parque Arqueológico, 4 rooms, meals and horses available, peaceful, inexpensive; reservations at Calle 5, 1113 in town. *El Camping* and *Camping Ullumbe* both provide tents or charge per site, both good.

Restaurants *Los Idolos* restaurant recommended. *Restaurante Brahama*, Calle 5A, No. 11-15, vegetarian meals and *comida* including soup and drink (also meat dishes), good fruit salads (has horses for rent); *Superpollo*, Diagonal a la Iglesia, US$2 for half chicken, good; *Cambi*, near bus station, Calle 3, No. 10-60, cheap and pleasant; *Pandi's* does European-style food at reasonable prices. *Esmeralda*, Calle 12, Carreras 11 y 12; *La Negra*, Calle 5, good *tamales*; *Palacio de Jugos*, Carrera 13, No.3-32, excellent fruit juices; *El Ullumbe*, opp. *Hotel Yalconia* and 200 metres past *Floresta*, pleasant, nice salads, friendly owner, not cheap, has rooms to let. Also opp. *Yalconia*, *Villadolly*, local and international food, recommended. Further on, *Casa Blanca*, opp. *Motel Osoguaico*, good cheap breakfast.

Transport San Agustín may be reached directly from Bogotá by taxi (Taxis Verdes have one service a day, leaving at 0300, US$12, 10-12 hrs. or Taxi-Exito will pick you up at your hotel in Bogotá, leaves at 0300) or by bus (Coomotor, Carrera 27, No. 13-58, 3 times a day, US$10, 12 hours). Alternatively there are frequent services from Bogotá to Neiva (US$7, 6 hrs.) as well as some to Pitalito (Taxi Verde costs US$9, leaving Bogotá at 0730). From Neiva there are 6 buses a day to San Agustín, taking 6 hrs. and costing US$4. The return journey to Bogotá with Coomotor (3 a day) takes 12 hrs. US$10 (US$5 to Neiva), and with Autobusco. To Neiva with Autobusco, US$4, 6 a day. The journey from Pitalito takes 1½ hrs., costs US$1 by jeep. To Popayán, La Gaitana daily at 1600, 11 hrs., US$7; Coomotor daily at 0600, 13 hrs., US$9. The bus stops at La Plata (for Tierradentro), US$3.50, 5 hrs. See also page 517. San Agustín-Cali daily at 0600, US$9, with Coomotor. A new direct route has been opened between Popayán and San Agustín (via Isnos); it is unpaved, with one stretch of 20 km. single track, suitable only for jeeps and lorries. Jeeps leave daily for Popayán along the new road from Pitalito at 0600, 6 hrs., wait until full (book a day in advance and be there at 0500). The company, Cootranslaboyana, was to start direct service from San Agustín in 1987. (For information ask in the tourist office.)

There is good riding in the neighbourhood. The rate for hiring horses works out at around US$3.80 per ½ day. (Check the horses carefully before you hire them—they do not all, for instance, have shoes.) You must pay for the guide's horse, plus usual tip of US$3. There are 3 types of guide: *Baquianos* (white identity cards), permitted only to accompany visitors to sites reached on horseback; *Alquiladores*, who own horses, but may not explain the statues or enter the Archaeological Park; and qualified, *Guiatur* guides (orange cards) who are fully trained, may explain all the sites, and charge US$6 to explain the Archaeological Park, US$12 for full day's guidance. Recommended guide: Sra. Luz Omayra González, employee of the Corporación Nacional de Turismo. Rafael Gómez (next to *Hotel Yalconia*) hires good horses, and will act as a guide for a little extra.

486 COLOMBIA

Lucas Peña at *Hotel Central* will act as guide on treks in the area; he also provides information on money exchange, etc.

Alternatively, jeeps may be hired and about 8 people can fit in one! Prices vary according to the number of sites to be visited, for example: to Alto de los Idolos, Alto de las Piedras, and the waterfalls de Mortiño and de los Bordones, costs about US$6 p.p. Be clear about what you are to be shown before setting out, don't be rushed, don't let the driver pick up people *en route*, and don't let the driver charge more than the tourist-office-approved rate. The tourist office itself runs tours by jeep (max. 7 people) to Alto de los Idolos, Alto de las Piedras, and Mortiño, US$6 p.p.; trip lasts 5 hrs., departure at 0900, book the day before. The *Hotel Central* offers a one-day excursion by jeep to Alto de los Idolos, Alto de las Piedras, and the 2 waterfalls, Salto de Mortiño and Salto de los Bordones. Jeeps, however, have difficulties on the road to Alto de los Idolos in the rainy season and ordinary vehicles should not even attempt it. The area offers excellent opportunities for hiking, although some trails to remote sites are not well marked. Two sites easily reached on foot are El Tablón and La Chaquira. At the site of El Purutal (previously called La Pelota), two painted statues were found in 1984. The leaflets given out by the Tourist Office disagree about distances to the sites; check before starting out to walk.

The best books on the subject are *Exploraciones Arqueológicas en San Agustín*, by Luis Duque Gómez (Bogotá, 1966, 500 pages) or *San Agustín, Reseña Arqueológica*, by the same author (1963, 112 pages); a leaflet in English is obtainable from tourist offices. The Colombian Institute of Archaeology has published a booklet (English/ Spanish), at US$1.80, on San Agustín and Tierradentro (see page 517), available at museums in San Agustín and San Andrés (also available at the Tourist Office, free).

The visitor with time to spare should visit Alto de los Idolos, 5 km. as the crow flies, or about 10 km. by horse or on foot, a lovely (if strenuous) walk via Puente de la Chaquira, but 27 km. by road via San José de Isnos village (which is 5 km. from Alto de los Idolos), and to which a bus can be taken, US$1, 0500 on Sat. return bus at 1100, 1300, or catch a bus from the *cruce* on the Pitalito road or hitch, well signposted (the site is open until 1600, entry US$0.20). Here on a hill overlooking San Agustín are more and different statues known as *vigilantes*, each guarding a burial mound (one is an unusual rat totem). The few excavated have disclosed large stone sarcophagi, some covered by stone slabs bearing a sculpted likeness of the inmate. It is a 6 hr. walk from San José de Isnos to Alto de los Idolos and back to San Agustín. It needs 1½ days by vehicle and on horseback to see the most important sites in and around San Agustín, though much can be seen in the Parque and Bosque in three hours. Alto de las Piedras, 5 km. from San José, has a few interesting tombs and monoliths, including the famous "Doble Yo" (admission US$0.40). The Director of the Parque (Don Hernán Cuéllar Muñoz) will arrange transport and guide to outlying sites. Only less remarkable than the statues are the orchids growing nearby. A new government-financed hotel has been built at Alto de los Idolos. From San Agustín the Bordones waterfalls can be visited; best with a car; there is a 3-room government guest house at Los Bordones, D in season, otherwise E.

Market day is Mon. in San Agustín and Sat. in San José—bus at 0500 from San Agustín for Sat. market (Hotel in San José: *Hospedaje Nueva*, F). The *fiesta* of Santa María del Carmen is held in mid-July (not on a fixed date) in San Agustín. There are cockfights in San Agustín on Sundays at 2030.

Bring lots of film. Rainy season April-June/July, but it rains somewhat during most of the year, hence the beautiful green landscape; the driest months are Nov.-March. The days are warm but sweaters are needed in the evenings; average temperature 18°C. Travellers are warned to change travellers' cheques before arriving in San Agustín; the Caja de Crédito Agrario will exchange cash only, at a poor rate; the Banco de Colombia will not change money but does give cash on Visa cards; 0800-1300 Mon. to Fri., 0800-1000 Sat. Leather goods are beautiful and priced reasonably. Many local shops make boots to your own design for about US$27.50 (double-check the price beforehand); *Calzado Líder* is highly recommended.

Caquetá

Lying to the E of the Cordillera Oriental is the Intendencia of Caquetá, reached by air, or by road from Neiva or Garzón. This region, although still sparsely populated (total pop. about 300,000) is an area of intensive settlement. The population has trebled since about 1965; people have been moving down from the highlands to turn the area into a productive livestock region. The natural forest cover around Florencia, the capital of the Intendencia, has been cleared and for a radius of 10-15 km. lie well-established, undulating pasturelands, dotted with tall palms—the fruits of which are a delicacy for grazing cattle. To the SE, beyond the cleared lands, lie little-touched expanses of tropical forest inhabited by indigenous tribes and wide varieties of Amazonian flora and fauna.

The road Neiva-Florencia is 260 km.: possible in one day, but it is recommended that travellers should try to complete the last 100 km. over the mountains into Florencia by daylight. From the Garzón-San Agustín road, the only route for vehicles into Caquetá branches off at Altamira. Here the surfaced road ends and becomes a single-track dirt road, originally engineered in 1932 during the Leticia dispute between Colombia and Peru. The climb up over the mountains passes through a region of small farms (some of their cultivated fields appear to be on almost vertical valley sides),

COLOMBIA 487

through sugar-cane cultivation and up into cloud at the higher points of the route. Here there is rain-forest, sporadically cleared for farms. Soon after the summit, and on a clear day, there are extensive views out over Caquetá and then the road winds down through substantial forests—ablaze with the colours of tropical flowers in the dry season (Jan.-March) and into the lowlands. The lower section of the road into the lowlands is prone to frequent landslides (or *derrumbes*) because of weak geological structures.

The roads in Caquetá run from Florencia along the foothills of the Cordillera; eventually a road is planned to run from Puerto Asís through Florencia to Villavicencio, skirting the foothills of the eastern Andes. Other routes are difficult and seasonal (although tracks, or *trochas*, are being laid out as part of the settlement scheme, financed by the World Bank) and the main lines of communication into the lowlands are by boat along the rivers Caquetá and Guayas and their tributaries.

Florencia (pop. 78,000) is the capital of the region and the centre for settlement in Caquetá, originally established in 1908. The square contains sculptures, fountains, a large forest tree (*saba*) and flower beds. When the road to Garzón is obstructed by landslides, petrol supplies are limited.

Hotels *Plaza*, Carrera 1, No. 30-70, C; *Apartamentos Capri*, E, with bath, clean and safe; those located around the central square are reputed to be more salubrious, and charge about US$3-4 per night. *Residencia Cordillera*, E.

Cafés, Restaurants Plenty, but prices tend to be high because much food is trucked in. For good value try *Tocarema*, 4-course meal US$2, large portions. Vegetarian restaurant on main street for good *patacones*.

Fiesta The local Saint's day is on July 16, when there is a candlelight procession in the evening around the town.

Bank Cash cheques at the Banco de la República.

Car parking Overnight, cars are best left in the care of the fire-station (US$0.20 a night).

Buses There are regular services from Neiva (US$6.50, 7 hrs.), Garzón and Altamira to Florencia (bus Altamira to Florencia, US$3.15) and frequent services as far as Puerto Rico and Belén. Bus to Bogotá costs US$19.50.

Air Services To Puerto Asís, with Satena, on Mon., Wed., Fri., daily to Neiva and to Leguizamo, with Satena.

Excursions From Florencia down the Orteguaza river: take a morning bus to Puerto Lara or a bus to San Antonio (US$3.25) where there is a cheap hotel; you can visit Indian villages.

From Florencia the road runs as far as Puerto Rico: it is paved for 34 km. to La Montañita and then unsurfaced, passing through El Paujil (2,750 pop.), where the *residencias* are unnamed and are situated alongside the road into the town. A dry-weather road runs from here for 21 km. towards Cartagena before giving way to a mule track. Then comes El Doncello (5,500) a very pleasant town, overlooked by the church which has a brightly painted steeple. The *Residencias Americanas* is highly recommended, F. Popular Sun. market. Next comes Esmeralda, a small settlement located on a ford that is too deep for cars, although trucks and buses may cross, and there is a wooden suspension bridge over the river for which the toll is US$0.20. The hotel there provides a very plain but excellently cooked breakfast.

Puerto Rico (4,950) is at the end of the road—which is interrupted by the River Guayas. It is possible to cross the river by ferry (US$0.08) and travel by bus as far as San Vicente where a muletrack goes over the Cordillera to Algeciras in Huila Department. Puerto Rico is a river port; ferries travel downstream to Río Negro (1½ hrs.) and Cartagena (4½ hrs.). Houses built down by the river are raised on stilts above possible flood levels. River boats are made and repaired by the riverside. **Hotels** and *residencias* are full on Sat. nights—book a room early in the day. *El Gran Hotel*, despite its name, provides basic amenities. *Hotel Almacén* is the only place in Puerto Rico serving fresh fruit juices.

The road from Florencia to San José is unsurfaced. At Morelia there is a poor branch road S to the River Pescado, where a ferry will take you across the river to the town of Valparaíso (1,175). *Hotel Ceilán* is cheap and friendly; there is also the *Hotel Turista*. From Valparaíso mule tracks go further into the lowlands. If travelling to Valparaíso by car, make sure it is left well away from the river when catching the ferry as, during times of flood, the river may rise rapidly overnight. Morelia to Belén de los Andes is an unsurfaced road, passing through some very interesting scenery, and crossing very clean, fast-flowing rivers by metal bridges. For some reason prices are higher in ***Belén*** (2,235) than in other towns in Caquetá. Hotels fill up very quickly, and mosquito nets are not always provided, although they are needed. In the area are a group of co-operative farms, and an oil palm plantation. From Belén an unsurfaced road runs to Albania (1,075) which is a small frontier settlement with only one hotel. A semi-surfaced road runs from here for 11 km. further towards the new areas of settlement.

Anyone wanting to look at wildlife in Caquetá must travel beyond the settlement area. Toucans, monkeys, macaws etc. are kept as pets, but there is little wild-life. Boats and canoes are easily

488 COLOMBIA

hired, but horses and mules are more difficult, especially in the dry season when they are needed to transport the harvest.

From the Magdalena to Bogotá

From Puerto Salgar, by railway, 198 km.; the line is a narrow-gauge and often sharply-curved single track. From the river it passes through wooded ravines, with palm trees growing to the summits, the black Río Negro plunging amongst the rocks below. The climb goes on, through tall woods with glimpses of precipice and gorge, until **Villeta** (84 km.; 9,700 inhabitants), which has become a popular weekend resort for the Bogotanos, is reached. Not far away are the waterfalls of Quebrada Cune. The road from Honda joins the railway route at Villeta. Hotels: *Pacífico* and *Mediterráneo* (both have swimming pools and are expensive); less expensive is the *Colonial Plaza*, Carrera 4, No. 6-07 (corner of main square), good restaurant, with swimmimg pool, pleasant. Nearby is *Llamarade* restaurant, good value; many good ice cream parlours around the square.

Midway between Honda and Villeta is **Guaduas;** in the main square is a statue of the female liberator Policarpa Sala Varrieta. Also in the main square is a delightful colonial hotel. Public swimming pool in town. There is a Sunday market. Best local dish is *quesillos*. Bus to Honda, US$1.20, 1 hr. The surrounding countryside is beautiful, including waterfalls at Versalles (10 km.). Hotel: *Tacuara*, swimming pool, riding, *cabañas*, B.

Beyond, the climb continues, and suddenly the train is over the top and making a short descent to the flat land of the Sabana of Bogotá. Over the top, 71 km. beyond Villeta, is **Facatativá,** a town of 22,460 people, 40 km. from Bogotá. The road from Gambao joins the railway route just before Facatativá, and a road from Girardot at Facatativá. Some 3 km. from Facatativá, on the road to the W, is the Piedras de Tunja, a natural rock amphitheatre of enormous stones; it has numerous Indian pictographs and has now been established as a park with an artificial lake.

From Facatativá to Bogotá the flat green plain is dotted with white farms and groves of eucalyptus. The line and the accompanying Gambao road pass through two small towns, Madrid and Fontibón, as they approach Bogotá, built at the far end of the plateau, under encircling mountains, and for that reason, wetter than the rest of the Sabana. **Fontibón,** 10 km. from Bogotá, has a good colonial church, and about 3 km. outside the town are more stones with Indian pictographs; nearby, on the road from the old Techo airport to Bogotá, there are replicas of San Agustín statues.

The Simón Bolívar Highway runs from Girardot to Bogotá; this 132-km. stretch is extremely picturesque, running up the mountains through **Melgar,** a popular weekending place for Bogotanos who like a little warmth (there are lots of hotels in the area most of which have swimming pools; it is best to try whichever you like the look of and move on to another if it is full; the *Esmeralda* and *Nuevo Guadaira* have been recommended; there are also camping sites and the state-subsidized Cafam vacation centre, best visited in mid-week), Boquerón, the charming town of Fusagasugá, and within 5 km. of the Salto de Tequendama. Toll at 14 km. S of Fusagasugá, US$0.50, and 20 km. S of Bogotá, US$0.40. From Boquerón, a side road goes about 10 km. to **Pandi** where there is a park with ancient stones. Nearby, on the road to Inconzu, is a famous natural bridge in a spectacular and very deep gorge through which runs the Sumapaz river.

Fusagasugá lies in a rich wooded valley famous for its fruits. A few kilometres before we reach it is the *Hotel Catama*. Fusagasugá is noted for its good climate and Sunday market. Population: 22,460, with an admixture of the wealthiest families from Bogotá during the summer. A visit should be paid to the Jardín Luxemburgo for its splendid orchids, best flowering Nov.-Feb. but it is a long walk out of town; the Jardín Clarisa for orchids, and that at the Casa de la Cultura are pleasant. There are bathing spots on the Sumapaz river. Altitude: 1,740 metres.

From Bogotá, Autos Fusa (Carrera 22, No. 14-27) and Cootransfusa (Carrera 14, Calle 10), US$1.

Hotels *La Scala*, F, recommended; *Europa*, overpriced and poor; *Sabaneta*; *Manila*; *Castillo*, E, recommended. There are many luxury hotels on the road to Melgar.

Forty km. further on, by the Embalse de Muna, is a 5-km. branch road runs to the **Salto de Tequendama,** where the water of the Río Bogotá or Funza falls 132 metres over the lip of the Sabana; the water is dirty with sewage but the falls are still a spectacular sight though the smell can be most unpleasant. The site is 31 km. from Bogotá in an amphitheatre of forest-clad hill sloping to the edge of a rock-walled gorge. There is a good bus service from Bogotá.

From **Tocaima**, a small, attractive holiday town (several hotels; *Bella Vista*, D, clean, friendly, good simple food, swimming pool, no hot water), a road runs through beautiful mountain country, via La Mesa, to Mosquera on the road between Madrid and Fontibón. This is a good alternative to the Simón Bolívar highway from Girardot to Bogotá.

The Llanos

A spectacular 110-km. road (due for improvement) runs from Bogotá to **Villavicencio,** capital of Meta Department in the Llanos at the foot of the eastern slopes of the Eastern Cordillera. Population: 175,000. Rice is now grown near Villavicencio and milled there for transport to Bogotá. Altitude: 498 metres. The town fills up at weekends. It is also full of Military Police owing to guerrilla activity to the SE.

Hotels *Del Llano*, Carrera 30, No. 49-77, B, out of town, swimming pool, overpriced, not recommended; *Villavicencio*, in town, D, suites available, a/c, hot water, very comfortable, good restaurant; *Centauros*, in centre, E, reasonably clean and quiet, small rooms; *Inambú*, E plus extras, Calle 37A, No. 29-49, central; *Savoy*, Carrera 31, No. 41-01, E, with shower and air conditioning, clean and friendly; *Carimagua*, F, shower, recommended; *El Gran Hotel*, F, with bath; *Residencias Nuevas*, F, adequate. *Residencias Don Juan*, Carrera 28, No. 37-21 (Mercado de San Isidro), attractive family house, E, with bath and fan, sauna, safe, recommended. *El Nogal*, F, clean, comfortable, good value. *Residencias Myriam* (off main square), F, fairly clean, check roof for leaks.

Restaurants On main square: *Palace*, recommended; *La Brasa*. One Chinese; others, some with swimming pools, on the road to Puerto López.

Tourist Office on main square, helpful.

Airport Flights to Miraflores and Mitú for those who want to see "uncommercialized" jungle. To Puerto Carreño: Urraca, a freight service with some seats, 0630, Mon., Wed., Fri., arrive early to get a seat, 1½ hrs. Taxi to town, US$2; bus US$0.30.

Buses La Macarena and Bolivariano run from Bogotá about every half-hour, US$2.75, 3 hrs.; alternatively there are colectivos (e.g. Velotax, US$3.50, or Autollanos who run every hour, US$5.25).

Villavicencio is a good centre for visiting the Llanos and jungles stretching 800 km. E as far as Puerto Carreño, on the Orinoco, with Venezuela across the river. Cattle raising is the great industry on the plains, sparsely inhabited by *mestizos*, not Indians. The cattle town of San Martín may be visited by bus from Villavicencio, 1½ hrs., US$1.20 each way.

A good asphalt road has been built E from Villavicencio to **Puerto López** on the Meta river, a port of call for large river boats. Hotels: *Tío Pepe*, D, with swimming pool; *Marichal*, E, fans but no a/c, swimming pool; two good *residencias: Doña Empera*, F, and *Popular*, F, cheaper, friendly, every bed with mosquito net, good meals. Good food also at *Restaurante Yamiba*. Armando Mildenberg, at *Res. Popular*, speaks German, some English and French, is helpful; he may be able to arrange tours in the *llanos*, or trip to Puerto Carreño. The road E (unpaved and poor, but reported to be about to be improved) continues for another 150 km. through Puerto Gaitán, where there are hotels and restaurants, and San Pedro to Arimena. Here the road branches: one road goes N to the Río Meta at El Porvenir, where a ferry (dry season only) takes you across the river to the Orocue tourist centre, E, swimming pool, excursions. The main road, now degenerated to a rough track impassable in the wet season, continues E through Vichada to Puerto Carreño.

Puerto Carreño (population about 5,000) has two banks (one of which changes travellers' cheques); shopkeepers will exchange Venezuelan bolívares.

490 COLOMBIA

The DAS office and Venezuelan Consulate are on the Plaza Bolívar. Passports are checked at the waterfront, then you must go to the DAS office and insist on having your passport stamped on entry. You may encounter problems over documents; the military are active in the area and frequently demand permits and proof of how much money you have, and carry out spot checks. There is a Satena office; next to it is *Residencias Mami*, F; *Hotel Samanave*, F (more expensive) with fan, clean, but breakfast is poor value; *Residencias La Vorágine*, F, friendly, clean, safe, good; the *residencia* on the waterfront doubles as a brothel.

For boats to Puerto López, be prepared to wait 4-5 days; check with Ulises, a bar owner on the river front by the moorings (he gives free coffee to those prepared to help with his son's English lessons). Between December and May, a bus runs on Thursday between Puerto López and Puerto Carreño at 0500, taking 2 days, night spent at La Primavera, US$25 (Flota La Macarena).

Air Services To Villavicencio and Bogotá with Satena on Tues., Thurs., and Sat., about US$50 to Bogotá; to Villavicencio, 4 hrs., following the Orinoco south as far as San Fernando de Atabapo, stopping at Inírida, not far from the confluence of the river of the same name with the Orinoco (*Hotel Orinoco* and *Refugio Safari*).

To Venezuela Launches take about 25 minutes to cross to Burro, stopping at Puerto Páez, from which Caracas can be reached by road. *Por puesto* service is available to Puerto Ayacucho.

The road S from Villavicencio is surfaced as far as San Martín. It runs on to **Granada** (*Hotel Yali*; *Tío Pepe Motel*, very clean) and from there deteriorates rapidly. **Vistahermosa**, situated near the break-point between the Llanos and the jungle, lies further S along this road (*Residencias Royal* is cheap and comfortable; *Lilian's* restaurant). It is a good place from which to visit the Sierra de la Macarena, a Tertiary outcrop 150 km. long by 35 km. broad. Its vegetation is so remarkable that the Sierra has been designated a national park exclusively for scientific study, although latest reports suggest that the flora is rapidly being destroyed by colonization. The Inderena office in Vistahermosa will advise you on trips to the Sierra. The road from Vistahermosa to the Sierra de la Macarena is very muddy in June (ankle-deep or more). For the energetic, a worthwhile trip is to the Sardinata or Cañones falls. Both can be reached from Maracaibo, which is a day's walk from Vistahermosa.

To the SE of Villavicencio, along the river Vaupés, and near the border with Brazil, is **Mitú**, which can be reached by air from Villavicencio and Bogotá. On arrival in the town you must fill in an entry card at the police station. Several anthropological studies are being carried out in the Mitú area and trips can be made from the town to Indian villages. The cost of a trip down river to visit an Indian village where you stay overnight is approximately US$10, plus the cost of the fuel used by the boat. Take your own food. The proprietor of Señor León's hotel (E) in Mitú will help you arrange such a trip. The hotel has the only restaurant in town, meals about US$2 each. Good local buys are baskets and bark paintings.

You can get a good away-from-it-all holiday in the Llanos. Plenty of reserve gasoline should be carried when travelling by car, as there are few service stations. Take food with you, unless you can live by gun and rod. Everybody lets you hang up your hammock or pitch your tent, but mosquito nets are a must. "Roads" are only tracks left by previous vehicles but easy from late December till early April and the very devil during the rest of the year. More information on the Llanos and particularly the Macarena national park can be obtained from the office of the Gobernación del Departamento de Meta, Calle 34 and Carrera 14, Bogotá.

Leticia, 3,200 km. up the Amazon on the frontiers with Peru and Brazil, a fast-growing community of 7,000, is now becoming a clean modern town. It is rapidly merging into one town with neighbouring Marco in Brazil. There is a modern, well equipped hospital. Prices have soared, and accommodation can be scarce. The best time to visit the area is in July or August, the early months of the dry season. A police drive against drug trafficking, which has displaced tourism as the major industry, has led to an economic depression in the town. Tourist services, although deteriorated, are still better than in Tabatinga or Benjamin Constant (Brazil).

Hotels and Restaurants The *Parador Ticuna*, B, has 13 apartments (all with bathrooms which have hot and cold running water, but no lights or water between 2300 and 0600) which can each sleep up to 6; six more apartments are being built. The hotel has a swimming pool (uncleaned), bar and restaurant, but is a little run down. The owners of the *Ticuna* also operate the *Parador Yaguas* in Leticia and the *Jungle Lodge*, on Monkey Island, an hour's boat ride from Leticia. *Hotel Colonial*, 16 double rooms and one triple, all with airconditioning or fans, hot and cold water, there are a swimming pool, cafeteria and ATA flights service, friendly staff, B, US$6 per additional person, not including tax and insurance. Cheaper accommodation: *Residencias Monserrate*, E without bath or food, water rare, rather dirty; *Residencias La Manigua*, comfortable rooms, E, with bath, clean satisfactory. *Hotel Anaconda*, C, overpriced, no hot water; there is a restaurant (beware overcharging) which serves meals for about US$6, swimming pool; *Hotel Alemanas*, D, with bath, Romanian-run, clean; *Residencias Amazonas*, F, without meals; *Hotel Americano*, near *Colonial*, D, noisy, not safe; *Residencial Quina*, E, clean, not very good; *Tacana*, D, possible to sling your hammock for US$1, not recommended; *Residencia Leticia*, Calle 8, No. 11-93, F, very friendly (not possible to sling hammock), good value, laundry facilities, clean, good cheap meals, use of kitchen; *Residencia Familiar*, Carrera 8, cheap, F, friendly, laundry facilities; *Residencias Copacabana*, E, with bath, friendly, English spoken. (*Parador Ticuna* and *Hotel Colonial* boil water.) *Café La Barra* serves beer, wine, and excellent fruit juices, serves sandwiches occasionally. Restaurant opposite *Residencia Leticia* serves good lunches and dinners, and *Señora Mercedes*, 3 doors from *Residencia Leticia*, serves good, cheap meals until 1930. *Restaurante Río Grande* serves excellent steaks. No meal with chicken or meat costs less than US$3-4. Cheap food (fried banana and meat) is sold at the market near the harbour. Also cheap fruit for sale. The campsite also has a good restaurant.

Tourist Office   Calle 10, No. 9-86. DAS office, Calle 9 (between Carreras 9 and 10).

Brazilian Consulate very efficient and helpful; 2 black and white photos needed for visa (photographer nearby).

Leticia is a good place to buy typical products of Amazon Indians, but the growth of Leticia, Tabatinga, Marco and Benjamin Constant has imposed an artificiality on the surrounding Amazon territory. There are good telephone and telegraph communications with Bogotá and the rest of the world. The *cambio* next to the *Anaconda Hotel* has good exchange rates for dollars, cruzados or intis. The money changers and *cambios*, of which there are plenty, give a better rate of exchange than the banks, which charge a 15% levy on travellers' cheques, except Banco de la República on American Express. Travellers' cheques cannot be changed at weekends, and are hard to change at other times.

Excursions   If you choose to go on an organized tour, do not accept the first price and check that the supplies and equipment are sufficient for the time you will be away. It is cheaper and better to find yourself a local guide. You can hire a dug-out for about US$3 a day. Motorboats cost much more, of course (e.g. US$54, 8 hrs, for 10 people). Turamazonas, *Parador Ticuna*, Tel.: 7184, offers a wide range of tours; provisions and bedding for overnight safaris are supplied by the agency, whose staff are all expert, especially Rolf Heumann, at Monkey Island. Not cheap but worth the extra money. Other reputable tour services are those of Amatours, right off *Hotel Anaconda's* lobby, and Amazonia (whose boatman, Hans, is recommended). The following tours are available: to Benjamin Constant to see a rubber plantation, 8 hrs., US$38 for 1, US$30 each for 2; to Monkey Island to see Ticuna and Yagua Indians, overnight trip, US$55 including full board. Turamazonas offers tours up the river to visit Indian communities, US$130 p.p. for 3 days (price depends on number of people in group), recommended. A cheaper guide is Guillermo Bueno, Tel.: 72-91. Many independent guides can be found on the river front; for example Bautista offers one day excursions to Yagua Indians (gifts of food and provisions much appreciated), Victoria Regia waterlilies, Monkey Island and more, for about US$15 p.p. Make sure the guides bring rubber boots as it can be quite muddy. Cheap guides do not have the experience or first aid equipment of the main tour companies. A small airline, ATA, offers flights in a Cessna plane at reasonable rates. An interesting walk is along the river bank to Marco and Tabatinga, in Brazil. (The bars in Marco, sometimes spelt Marcos, are friendlier and serve better (local) beer, than in Leticia.)

When going upstream remember that the slower and dirtier the boat, the more mosquitoes you will meet. (You can swim in the Amazon and its tributaries, but do not dive; this disturbs the fish. Also do not swim at sunrise or sunset when the fish are more active, nor when the water is shallow in the dry season, nor if you have a wound, however slight, which might open up and bleed.)

Transport   Avianca flies to Leticia (Tabatinga airport if Leticia's is closed) from Bogotá, daily except Fri. and Sun. for US$120 (US$58 if bought in pesos); Leticia to Bogotá, departs 1420, arrives 1605; to Cali (via Bogotá), US$62; Satena has flights on Thurs. and Sun. afternoon, US$50; it is possible to return to Bogotá by freight plane, but you have to sit with the cargo, often fish. Check with Satena crew, who stay in the *Hotel Colonial*, if there is a seat available, or at the airport. (From Bogotá by freight plane, you have to be at the halls of the cargo companies—all at the same place—at 0400, and ask which company is flying.) Líneas Aero Caribe cargo flights twice a week; flight time 3½-4 hrs. Cruzeiro do Sul flies Manaus-Tabatinga (for Leticia)-Iquitos and back on Wed. and Sat. (there is a connection on Wed. for Pucallpa from Iquitos); fare from Tabatinga (for Leticia) to Iquitos US$49 + US$3 tax; Taba operates three flights weekly Manaus-Tabatinga-Manaus. TANS, the Peruvian military jungle airline, usually offers flights between Iquitos and Ramón Castilla nearby, in Peru, for about US$20, but you must book well in advance and make sure of getting to the airport well ahead of the flight time. These flights are on Fridays and Sundays. It is also possible to get a seat on a Petrobrás plane to Manaus. This leaves every Friday, and can be arranged with the crew, who stay at the *Anaconda Hotel*. A letter of recommendation helps. Taxi to airport, US$1.50.

The cheapest way to get to Leticia is by bus to Puerto Asís, and then by boat (see page 522).

492 COLOMBIA

There are ferries from Leticia to Benjamin Constant, Brazil (US$0.50, 1½-2 hrs., US$15 in private launch); if leaving Brazil by this route, disembark at Tabatinga and obtain exit stamp from office which is 1 km. from boats: turn right one block at main street, office is on the left. There is a Colombian Consular Office near the border on the road from Tabatinga, where Colombian tourist visas are issued on presentation of 2 passport photographs. Most boats down to Manaus take passengers—all leave from Benjamin Constant, Islandia (a mud bank off Benjamin Constant), perhaps Tabatinga—none from Leticia. The *Ayapua* has a comfortable passenger capacity of about 70, takes 5 days and costs US$40 for a basic cabin or US$50 for first class passage on the top deck. Second class is below decks with the cargo and not recommended. Most passengers sling a hammock on deck, which is much cooler. Departure times are uncertain, and the boats tend to be overcrowded. Recommended is the *Marcia Maria*, about US$37 for hammock space, US$45 p.p. in 2-person cabin. The *Cidade de Teresina*, a cargo vessel, has four cabins with four berths in each, and a top deck for slinging hammocks; passage in a cabin is US$62.50, to be arranged with the captain. The trip takes at least 4½ days; there is a better selection of provisions in Leticia, but purchases are much cheaper in Benjamin Constant. Boats to Peru from Tabatinga wharf La Ronda sail daily at 1800 and take passengers and cargo. Boats to Ramón Castilla cost US$6 each way. There are irregular sailings for Iquitos on the *Huallacha*, cost US$40 (at least 10 days between sailings, on this and other vessels). Food is provided but is not recommended. Remember to get your passport stamped by the DAS office near the church, just off main square in Leticia before you leave the area; (there are no customs formalities for everyday travel between Leticia and Tabatinga in Brazil, taxis cost US$5 from a rank, or US$0.70 as colectivos (N.B. colectivos increase their charges after 1800); bus, US$0.20; 24-hour transit stamps can be obtained at the DAS office for one-night stays in Leticia, although it appears that these are not necessary if you are not going beyond Leticia—best to check, though; also see below). From Ramón Castilla to Iquitos or Pucallpa the *Oro Negro* is highly recommended. The captain and owner is a characterful elderly lady and her crew a family affair. Passage for the 5-day journey costs only US$20-25, food included but take your own water, unless you want to drink river water, and your own eating utensils. Passengers' aid is sometimes solicited to gather firewood or yuca on the river bank.

N.B. Robert Smith and Geoffrey Dempsey tell us that if entering Colombia at Leticia, from Brazil en route to Peru, you should try to get your tourist card before Manaus because the Colombian consul there will tell you that a card is not needed just for passing through Leticia. This is not true: you must have a card. If you do have to see the consul in Manaus tell him you are going further into Colombia—you may have to show an onward ticket, or money—this may get you a card.

It is reported that for travellers interested in Amazonian wild life the Putumayo is more accessible than Leticia; it is best reached from Pasto (see page 522).

Chía-Zipaquirá-Chiquinquirá

An interesting trip from Bogotá can be made to the salt mine of Zipaquirá and to the large centre of population around Chiquinquirá to the N of Bogotá. Bogotá is left by an *autopista*, a northern extension of Avenida Caracas and Carrera 13. The *autopista* ends after 24 km. at an intersection where a road leads off left at a right-angle for Chía and Zipaquirá. Taking this road you soon come to a fork which takes you left to Chía and right to Zipaquirá. At the beginning of the road to Zipaquirá is the *Restaurant Arrieros*, where *antioqueño* food is served by waiters in the appropriate dress and *antioqueño* music is sometimes played.

Chía has a graceful colonial bridge and a typical Sunday market. Near Chía is Terijo, whose metalworks is famous. On the way there you pass through Fonqueta where simple tapestries are made. Walk, or take a bus to La Barbanera church on a hill overlooking the *sabana* of Bogotá. Good restaurant just outside Chía, *Andrés Carne de Res*.

From Chía (via Cájica, 22,000 pop., pleasant town with good shopping) to **Zipaquirá** (40,850 people), centre of a rich cattle farming district, and famous for its rock salt mine, which has enough salt to last the world 100 years, though it has been exploited for centuries. The church in the central Plaza is also worth a visit for its stonework (despite its external appearance, it has a modern interior).

The immense black galleries of salt gleaming under electric lights are most impressive and a little eerie. A road has been opened into the galleries but because of damage cars are no longer allowed to drive in. You can walk its whole length in 15 mins. An underground cathedral dedicated in 1954 to Our Lady of the Rosary (patron saint of miners) is about 4 mins. on foot from the entrance and very impressive. The roof is 23 metres above the floor and the main altar table is a block of salt weighing 18 tons. It took ten years to complete. Entry (adults US$0.65, children US$0.30, open Mon.-Sat. 0930-1200, 1300-1630, Sun. 1030-1630) is on a hill, which is a 20 mins. walk from the Plaza. Many buses from Avenida Caracas, Bogotá, US$0.45 each way, 1¼ hours. The Zipaquirá bus station is 15 minutes' walk from the mines and cathedral. Tours are also arranged by some of the Bogotá hotels and cost about US$20. Zipaquirá can also be reached from Tunja (see page 494), by taking a Bogotá-bound bus and getting off at Alcaro for connection to Zipaquirá, US$2. Leave plenty of time for the return journey as it can be difficult to stop Bogotá-Tunja buses at Alcaro. Minibus Zipaquirá- Chiquinquirá, US$2.75, 2 hrs.

The *Hostería del Libertador*, near the mines, good food, but no longer a hotel. *Hotel Colonial*, E, without bath, clean and friendly. Restaurants on main square, *El Mesón del Zipa*, good, cheap food, US$1.50-2.00; *Los Pijaos*, pleasant; *Begoña*, Calle 1, No. 1-00.

Not far from Zipaquirá, at **Nemocón**, there are salt mines and a church. You can walk through the salt-mine galleries, which offer a good view of the process.

Ubaté is 48 km. by road to the N. On Sunday, the market in the big plaza has nothing of interest for the tourist. It is the cheese-making centre of the Sabana; the church is being refurbished. Here a branch road runs E to Lenguazaque (6,125 people). Close by, at Chirbaneque, is a worked-out emerald mine in lovely scenery. A spur from this road branches left to Guachetá, 21 km. from Ubaté, and slightly larger than Lenguazaque. Nearby is the Laguna de Fúquene (Devil's Lake, hotel), about 4,850 hectares of water with four cultivated islands.

Chiquinquirá, 50,000 people, 134 km. by road from Bogotá, is on the W bank of the Suárez river at 2,550 metres. It is a busy commercial centre and the focus of a large coffee and cattle region. In December thousands of pilgrims honour a painting of the Virgin whose fading colours were restored by the prayers of a woman. In 1816, when the town had enjoyed six years of independence and was besieged by the Royalists, this painting was carried through the streets by Dominican priests from the famous monastery, to rally the people. The town fell, all the same.

Hotels *Sarabita*; F; *El Dorado*, F, with bath; *Moyba*, Carrera 9, No. 17-53, facing square, F, with bath (cheaper without); *Residencias San Martín*, Carrera 9, No. 19-84, F, basic; *Residencias Viajero*, G, opposite Banco de Colombia, good, cheap meals.

Restaurant *El Escorial*, good but expensive.

In the shops of Chiquinquirá are displayed the toys made by Indians: some ceramics painted in gay colours and others white and porous as they come from the kiln; tops and teetotums and other little things carved from tagua nuts; orange-wood balls to catch on a stick; the most durable tambourines in the world; shining, brightly coloured gourds; diminutive nine-stringed guitars on which children try the first measures of the *bambucu*; many scapularies; but better than anything else, the little pottery horses from Ráquira, or, by the same Indian craftsmen, little birds that whistle, hens with their chicks, and enchanting little couples dancing to an orchestra of guitars and mandolins.

Chiquinquirá has a new bus station. Bus from Chiquinquirá to Villa de Leiva takes 1¾ hr.; US$1.70; we describe it under excursions from Tunja (see page 495). Bus to Tunja, 3 hrs., US$3.25; to Zipaquirá, US$2.75; to Bogotá, 2½ hrs., US$3 (last returns at 1730).

A steam-hauled *tren turístico* runs on Saturday and Sunday at 0900 from the main station in Bogotá, calling at a halt at Calle 100 and Carrera 15 at 0927, going to Zipaquirá and Nemocón: 2 hrs. 20 mins. to Zipaquirá, 2 hrs. 45 mins. to Nemocón, when the train is met by the town band. At Nemocón there is time to visit the mines and have lunch before train returns at 1800. Tickets in Bogotá from Tierra Mar Aire travel agency.

Excursion A road runs 105 km. SW to **Muzo,** on the banks of the Rio Carare, 600 metres above sea-level. Population: 5,000. Sixteen km. away a famous open-cast emerald mine has been worked since 1567, and long before that by the Muzo tribe of Indians.

There are roads from Chiquinquirá to Tunja, the capital of the Department, and to Barbosa. Both are on the Bogotá-Cúcuta highway and are described below. On the Tunja road a short branch right at Tinjacá leads to **Ráquira,** where Indians make the pottery described above (sold in about 10 shops on the main street, including branch of Artesanías de Colombia). There's nowhere to stay, not much to eat. Market day Sunday. 30 minutes' walk along a very rough road is a beautiful 16th-century monastery, the Convento de la Candelaria, with anonymous 17th-century paintings of the life of St. Francis; they sell honey to finance the monastery. Also nearby are some waterfalls. The old colonial town of Villa de Leiva is also on this road. Ráquira is best reached from Tunja although there are direct buses from Bogotá (Rápido El Carmen, 0545, 0715, US$2.50, 6 hrs., returning 1300) on an appalling road. Last bus to Tunja 1330. If stuck after 1330, walk 5 km. to Tres Esquinas on Villa de Leiva-Chiquinquirá road, where buses pass between 1530-1630, mostly going E.

494 COLOMBIA

Bogotá to Cúcuta

There is a 618-km. road running NE from Bogotá to Cúcuta, near the Venezuelan border, through Tunja, Barbosa, Monquirá, Socorro, San Gil, Bucaramanga and Pamplona. It runs through some beautiful scenery, and is good most of the way. Toll points 10 km. N of Bogotá, US$0.40, and at La Cara, S of Tunja, US$0.40. The railway via Tunja to Duitama and Sogamoso is now for freight only. The road out of Bogotá is the *autopista* to near Chía (see page 492), then follow Tunja signs.

At Sesquilé you can take a minor road to the right, to Guatavita Nueva.

Guatavita Nueva This modern town, 75 km. from Bogotá, was built in colonial style when the old town of Guatavita was submerged by a new hydroelectric reservoir. Although the blend of old and new is fascinating, Guatavita Nueva has failed as a social experiment. All the country folk have left and it is now a weekend haunt for Bogotanos and tourists. (During the week the town is empty.) Cathedral, artisan workshops, museum, and small bull-ring for apprentices to practise Sun. afternoons. Sun. market best in morning, before Bogotanos get there. Bus from Bogotá (Flota Valle de Tenza, Carrera 25, No. 15-72, recommended; Flota Aguila, Carrera 15 No. 14-59), US$1.25, 2-3 hrs.; departures 0730, 0800 and 0930; last return bus at 1730. You can walk (or ride, US$7 per horse) from the town to the Laguna de Guatavita (also called Lago de Amor by locals), where the legend of El Dorado originated, but it is a long (2-3 hr.) walk. It is easier to approach the lake from a point on the Sesquilé-Guatavita Nueva road (the bus driver will let you off at the right place) where there is a sign offering "Alpina Yoghurt" and a kiosk. It is a 2 hr. walk along a dirt track from the main road to the lake. This track can be driven to the lake (in the dry season, in a good car); turn right near the barn with the red door, and right again opposite small lake; car can be left at the farm 1-2 km. beyond this turning (pay farmer US$1). Beside the lake are houses of rich Bogotanos.

There are no hotels in Guatavita Nueva, although rooms are sometimes to be found.

The basis of the El Dorado (Gilded Man) story is established fact. It was the custom of the Chibcha king to be coated annually with resin, on which gold dust was stuck, and then to be taken out on the lake on a ceremonial raft. He then plunged into the lake and emerged with the resin and gold dust washed off. The lake was also the repository (as with the *cenotes* in Yucatán, Mexico) of precious objects thrown in as offerings; there have been several attempts to drain it (the first, by the Spaniards in colonial times, was the origin of the sharp cut in the surrounding hills) and many items have been recovered over the years. The factual basis of the El Dorado story was confirmed by the discovery a few years ago of a miniature raft with ceremonial figures on it, made from gold wire, which is now one of the most prized treasures of the Museo de Oro in Bogotá. Part of the raft is missing; the story is that the gold from it is now reposing in one of the finder's teeth! (Read John Hemming's *The Search for El Dorado* on the subject.)

Beyond Chocontá (15,300 inhabitants), 88 km. from Bogotá, the route is across the western slopes of the Eastern Cordillera to Tunja, 137 km. from Bogotá.

Tunja, 150,000 inhabitants, capital of Boyacá Department, stands at 2,820 metres in an arid mountainous area. The climate is cold; mean temperature, 12°C. One of the oldest cities in Colombia, it was refounded as a Spanish city by Gonzalo Suárez Rendón in 1539. It was then the seat of the Zipa, one of the two Chibcha kings. The old city has been compared with Toledo, but the modern city is far less attractive. Of the many colonial buildings the most remarkable is the church of Santo Domingo, a masterpiece begun in 1594; the interior is covered with wood most richly carved. Another is the Santa Clara Chapel (1580), now the hospital of San Rafael, with some fine wood carving. In Parque Bosque de la República is the adobe wall against which three martyrs of the Independence were shot in 1816. The Tourist Office in the Casa del Fundador (see below), on Plaza Bolívar, is helpful. Market open every day (good for *ruanas* and blankets). Bus from Bogotá, 2½-4½ hrs., US$3 (Duitama, Cotrans, and others). The bus station is a steep 500 metres from the city centre. Friday is market day.

The house of Don Juan de Vargas has been restored as a museum of colonial Tunja. The Casa del

Fundador Suárez Rendón on the main square dates from 1540-43 and is one of the few extant mansions of a Spanish *conquistador* in Colombia; open as a museum (except Mon. and Tues.); see the unique series of plateresque paintings on the ceilings. The church of Santa Bárbara is full of colonial woodwork, and in the nearby parish house are some notable religious objects, including silk embroidery from the 18th century. Some houses still have colonial portals. There are some fine colonial buildings on the main plaza (Plaza Mayor) opposite the Cathedral, which is of little interest.

The city formed an independent Junta in 1811, and Bolívar fought under its aegis during the campaign of the Magdalena in 1812. Six years later he fought the decisive battle of Boyacá, nearby (see below). For the Piedras de Tunja see under Facatativá (page 488).

Hotels *Hunza,* Calle 21, No. 10-66, B, good service; *Pensión Suárez Rendón,* main plaza (good food, D, friendly but basic); *Centenario,* hot water, good restaurant, D; *Residencias El Cid* (Carrera 10, No. 28-78) and *Tunja* (Carrera 9, No. 18-64), both E, basic; *Residencias Saboy,* near main plaza, to be avoided, F, unfriendly, no water, doors shut at 2100; *San Francisco,* Carrera 9, No. 18-90, on main plaza, near cathedral, E, clean but figuring not accurate, not recommended; also *Residencias Continental,* opposite cathedral, F, clean, meals US$1.25, but of poor quality; *Boyacá,* F (without bath); *Suiza, Bolívar, Boyacense* (not recommended), all E, near bus stations, 5 mins. from main plaza. Fairly cheap is *Dux,* off the main square, F, quaint, basic; *Residencias Fundador* on the corner of Plaza Bolívar, F, has hot water, is safe and clean.

Restaurants Good cheap meal at *Bolo Club* and at a restaurant through an archway leading off the main plaza opposite the cathedral; *La Fonda,* US$1.50 for a big meal; *Bodegón de los Frayles,* beside the church of San Ignacio, one block from the Plaza Bolívar, recommended as friendly with good food. On Carrera 10, there is a restaurant in a converted Jesuit church.

Bank Banco de la República, Carrera 11, No. 18-12.

Excursions from Tunja The battle of Boyacá was fought about 16 km. south of Tunja, on the road to Bogotá. On the bridge at Boyacá is a large monument to Bolívar. Bolívar took Tunja on August 6, 1819, and next day his troops, fortified by a British Legion, the only professional soldiers among them, fought the Spaniards on the banks of the swollen Río Boyacá. With the loss of only 13 killed and 53 wounded they captured 1,600 men and 39 officers. Only 50 men escaped, and when these told their tale in Bogotá the Viceroy Samao fled in such haste that he left behind him half a million pesos of the royal funds. There is now a huge modern restaurant overlooking the site.

On a hillside outside Tunja is the carved rock throne of the Chibcha king, the Zipa; ask for directions from the Tourist Office.

At **Paipa** there are municipal thermal baths, US$0.75, 30 mins. bus ride from Tunja, US$1. *Hotel Sochagota,* overlooking the lake, has a swimming pool fed by hot springs, C, cabins for hire, with 2 bedrooms, bathroom, log fires and private hot spring pools. Other places to stay include *Casona El Salitre* and *Panorama* (D), *Cabañas El Portón, Hotels Victoria* and *La Posada, Posadero La Casona, Las Palmeras, Residencias Daza,* and *Minihotel Familiar* (all F p.p.). There are 7 restaurants: it's a popular centre for Colombians.

Villa de Leiva,

an extremely pretty place, is reached by a branch road, left, at Arcabuco. (Toll at Arcabuco, US$0.40.) The drive affords some beautiful views and passes the Iguaque National Park which is the site of interesting oak woods. (Camping is allowed and safe.) The town dates back, like Tunja, to the early days of Spanish rule, but unlike Tunja, it has been declared a national monument so will not be modernised. There are two colonial houses which are worth a visit: the house in which Antonio Nariño lived (Carrera 9, No. 10-39, open Tues.-Sun. 0900-1230, 1400-1800)—he translated the *Rights of Man* into Spanish—and the building in which the first Convention of the United Provinces of New Granada was held. Also worth a visit is the restored birthplace of the independence hero Antonio Ricuarte. A palaeontological museum has been opened 15 mins. walk N of the town on Carrera 9. The shops in the plaza have an excellent selection of Colombian handicrafts, while the Sat. market, not yet geared to the tourist trade, still offers many good bargains. On the Plaza Mayor is the Casa-Museo Luis Alberto Acuña, housing fascinating examples of Acuña's work (recommended, entry US$0.40, US$0.35 extra to take photographs). The Monasterio de las Carmelitas has one of the best museums of religious art in Colombia, open Sat. and Sun. 1400-1700. The mountains around Villa de Leiva abound in fossils. 7 km. along the road to Chiquinquirá can be seen the complete fossil of a dinosaur; there are road signs to it, ask for *El Fosil* (open 0800-1200, 1300-1500); the children sell fossils and rough emeralds. 20 mins. walk along this road is the archaeological site known as El Infiernito, where there are several huge carved stones believed to be giant phalli and a solar calendar. 8 km. further on, and one

496 COLOMBIA

hour by bus (one per day) from Villa de Leiva is the Monastery of Ecce-Homo (founded 1620), which is worth a visit. The road goes through the desert of La Candelaria, a beautiful, highly-eroded countryside. Note the rectangular cromlech with 24 menhirs. Tourist Office just N of main square (Carrera 9, No. 13-01) most helpful.

Hotels *El Molino la Mesopotamia*, Calle del Silencio, which used to be a colonial mill, very good, A, including all meals (US$12.50), 10% rebate for booking 10 days ahead (closed during the first weeks of January), a meal costs about US$2.50, home cooking, excellent food, beautiful gardens; next door is *La Candelaria*. *Mesón de la Plaza Mayor*, Calle 79, No. 10-11, C (B full board), beautifully restored *hospedería*, owner, Mauricio Ordóñez, speaks English, helpful; *Convento*, *La Rosita* and *Posada Don Juan de Castellanos* all D; *El Marqués de San Jorge* is D, pleasant, on Calle 14, No. 9-20; *Hospedaje El Mesón de Los Virreyes*, Carrera 9, No. 14-51, D, with bath, good restaurant; *Cabaña Jequeneque*, opposite *la Mesopotamia*, D, with breakfast, open only at week-ends but recommended. Unnamed *residencia* on Plaza Bolívar (the only one), F, hot water, pretty. *Hospedería Convento de San Francisco*, E, one of the cheaper hotels, quiet, spartan rooms, helpful staff, swimming pool not always filled; *Hospedería La Villa*, Carrera 10, No. 11-87, just off main square, F, basic, noisy; *Los Olivos*, F; *Hospedería Duruelo*, C, above the town, magnificent view, good cooking, horse riding, recommended for its high standards. Accommodation with Señora Carmen Castaneda, Calle 14, No. 7-51, 4 rooms, all giving onto a flower-filled patio, E, clean, friendly; also Familia Fitortá, Calle 12, No. 7-55, E (F in week), breakfast extra, friendly, clean, safe. The telephone connection from Bogotá is poor and most hotels have reservation numbers in Bogotá. Information from the Tourist Office. Booking essential during holidays, and advisable at weekends (try bargaining Mon.-Thurs.). Accommodation also in *Hostería La Roca*, Calle 13, No. 9-54, F, hot water, very clean and pleasant, with rooms overlooking main square and reasonable breakfast, noisy at night because of bar music; cheap rooms available in bar-cum-bus-agency at entrance to town, also at restaurant/ *hospedaje* on the corner of the plaza near the Caja Agraria on the road out to Chiquinquirá, but some beds only have blankets, not mattresses over the springs. **Camping** at Los Olivares near village of Sáchica, 4 km. from Villa de Leiva (no services).

There are reasonable **restaurants** on the main square (try *Pueblito Viejo*), and in and opposite the bus station. *La Parrilla*, Carrera 9, No. 9-17 and *Los Kioskos*, Carrera 9, No. 11-52; *Nueva Granada*, Carrera 9, No. 13-69, good value; *Los Balcones*, just off plaza, cheap, early breakfasts; *El Parrilón de los Caciques*, W side of town on Carrera 9, No. 9-05, warmly recommended, good value. Visit the shop of Marcos A Buitrago set in tropical gardens on El Paraíso de los Sachos, near the main square—he likes to talk to visitors.

Post Office in Telecom building, Calle 13, No. 8-26.

Another way of getting to Villa de Leiva is via Sáchica, either directly from Tunja or, coming from Bogotá, turning left (W) at the Boyacá monument, via Samacá. The houses are closed Monday-Friday out of season, but the trip is worth while just for the views. In any event, the town and surrounding hills are excellent for long, peaceful walks. Buses to Leiva from Tunja, 1 hr. 5 mins., US$1 with Flota Reina or Valle de Tenza company. (From Bogotá to Villa de Leiva, via Tunja, takes 4 hrs.) Colectivo taxis leave the bus station in Tunja for Villa de Leiva every hour and return from the main square. Leiva bus station in 8th block of Carrera 9. It is recommended to book the return journey on arrival. If driving from Tunja, watch out for rockfalls.

N.B. It is better not to visit Villa de Leiva on Mondays as almost everything is closed.

From Tunja there are two possible routes to Cúcuta: the main road, almost entirely paved, goes via Bucaramanga, but the other via Duitama and Málaga, rejoining the main road at Pamplona, is also interesting. In **Duitama** there is the interesting tourist complex Punta Larga, close to a furniture manufacturer. (*Hospedería D'la 18*, Carrera 18, No. 18-60, clean, quiet, F; many others nearby). About 3 km. from Duitama, on the road to Belencito, there is another hotel, also in an old *hacienda*, the *Hostería San Luis de Ucuenga*. In Málaga, *Hotel Príncipe* near main square, F, shared bathroom, clean, friendly, good meals. Bus Málaga-Duitama at 0400, or truck at 1000 with lots of stops, 6 hrs. Bus Duitama to Bucaramanga at 0900, 9 hrs., US$9. At Duitama turn right for **Sogamoso**, where a good museum of archaeology has been opened on the site of the centre of the precolumbian city. It is possible to camp in the museum grounds if you ask permission. A museum of religious art is open on the road from Duitama to Sogamoso (its most valuable exhibits were stolen in 1981). *Hotel Hacienda Suescún*, E, nearby in old *hacienda*, excellent service (but food not too good); *Hotel Santa Marta*, near bus station, F, clean, friendly (many others near Sogamoso bus terminal). E of Sogamoso the churches of Monguí (a pleasant colonial town) and Topaga are worth a visit, and so is the mountain-ringed **Lago de Tota** (3,015 metres above sea level). The *Refugio el Pozo Azul*, on the lakeside, is a private club run by Gary Clements and his Colombian wife, who will extend membership to readers of *The South American Handbook*; an excellent place to stay, in D price range, also has cabins for up to 7 people, US$60. Good food, fresh trout caught in the lake, suitable for children, very friendly atmosphere. Boats and fishing tackle for hire; good walking, and bird-watching country; recommended to book in advance, postal address: Apartado Aéreo 032, Sogamoso, Boyacá (or through Gladys García, Representative, Calle 80, No. 12-37, Bogotá, Tel.: 255-8682). Also on the lake is *Las Rocas Lindas*, D with bath and hot water, US$2.50 for each extra person, 2 cabins for 7 (US$30) one for 8 at Playa Blanca across the lake (US$40), boats for hire, dining room, bar, fireplaces, recommended. The owner, Sr. Mauricio Moreno Arenas, is very friendly. Aquitania is a cold, expensive town on the lake, reached by bus from Sogamoso, US$0.75, 1 hr.; bus from Bogotá (Rápido Duitama), via Tunja and Sogamosa, goes round the lake to Aquitania, passing Cuitiva, Tota and the *Rocas Lindas* and *Pozo Azul* hotels (3 hr. wait in Aquitania). In Aquitania, *Residencia Venecia*, Calle 8, No. 144, F, with restaurant *Lucho* below, reasonable.

Just before the descent to the Lago de Tota, a road branches left, leading in 4 hours to **Yopal,** capital of the Intendencia of Casanare in the Llanos. (Pop. 10,000.) The road passes through *páramo* and virgin cloud forest. A fine waterfall can be reached in one hour's walk from the DAS checkpoint just above Pajarito. The best *residencias* in Yopal are usually full; direct buses from Sogamoso. **N.B.** Casanare and Arauca beyond are centres of guerrilla activity.

NE of Duitama, on the road to Málaga, is the turning at Belén for Paz de Río, where Colombia's national steelworks is sited; visitors can see over it. The road goes N to Soatá (*Residencias Colonial,* excellent, good restaurant; *Hotel Turístico,* E, swimming pool) and then descends to the very dry, spectacular valley of the Río Chicomocha.

By the bridge over the river at Capitanejo is the turning to the very attractive **Sierra Nevada del Cocuy** in the Eastern Cordillera. The Sierra extends in a half circle for 30 km., offering peaks of rare beauty, lakes and waterfalls. The area is good for trekking and probably the best range in Colombia for rock climbers. The most beautiful peaks are Cocuy (5,100 m.), Ritacuba Negra (5,200 m.), Ritacuba Blanca (5,200 m.) and El Castillo (5,400 m.). The area is good for trekking—details can be found in *Backpacking in Venezuela and Colombia* by George and Hilary Bradt. The main towns are **Cocuy,** on one side of the sierra, reached by Paz de Río bus from Bogotá, Av. 6, Carrera 15 (13 hrs., US$10), tourist office on Carrera 3, No. 8-06, *Residencia Cocuy,* F, cold water, laundry; and **Guicán,** on the other side, one hotel, F, good meals (extra), cold water. Both towns are 1-1½ hrs. drive by jeep from the mountains, so it is recommended to stay higher up. Above Guicán, you can stay at some farms or, at 3,600 metres, 3 tourist cabins have been built, from which it is 3 strenuous hours' walk to the snowline on Ritacuba Blanca. This would also be the best base for the 2-3 day walk (described in the Bradts' book) round the N end of the Sierra and into Ratoncito valley, which is surrounded by snow-capped mountains. Above Cocuy, accommodation is available at Estadero Don Pastor and, probably, Hacienda La Esperanza. Horses can be hired at both places. La Esperanza is the base for climbing to the Laguna Grande de la Sierra (3-4 hours), a large sheet of glacier-fed water surrounded by 5 snow-capped peaks, and also for the 2-day walk to the Laguna de la Plaza on the E side of the Sierra, reached through awesome, rugged secnery. Permission to camp can easily be obtained from the friendly people. It takes 1 to 2 days to walk between the two towns; maps available in Cocuy and at La Esperanza. It takes 8-10 days to trek from one end to the other through a central rift, but equipment (crampons, ice pick, rope etc.) is necessary. The perpendicular rock mountains overlooking the Llanos are for professionals only. The area can also be reached by bus from Pamplona and Bucaramanga. The best weather is from December to April.

The main road goes on to **Barbosa** (*Hotel Príncipe,* clean rooms with private bath; *El Palacio del Pollo,* good, simple roadside restaurant), 64 km. NW in the Department of Santander. Eleven km. from Barbosa, at Puente Nacional, is *Agua Blanca,* a splendid hotel with a swimming pool.

A road runs NW to the Magdalena at Puerto Olaya, opposite Puerto Berrío. Eighteen km. from Barbosa is **Vélez,** a charming little town where horses and mules are raised. (*Hotel Galés,* G.)

The road (toll at Santana, US$0.40) goes NE for 84 km. to

Socorro (23,500 people), with steep streets and single storey houses set among graceful palms. It has a singularly large and odd stone church. The local museum, La Casa de la Cultura, is worth seeing, as is the market which is open every day.

At Socorro, in 1781, began the revolt of the peasant *comuneros*: not a movement for independence but a protest against poverty. It was led at first by a woman, Manuela Beltrán, and then, when other towns joined, by Juan Francisco Berbeo. They marched as far as the salt town of Zipaquirá, N of Bogotá, rebel terms were accepted by the Spaniards, and sworn to by the Bishop of Bogotá, but when they had returned home troops were sent from Cartagena and there were savage reprisals. Another woman from Socorro, Antonia Santos, led guerrillas fighting for independence and was captured and executed by the Spaniards in 1816; her statue is in the main square.

Hotels *Tamacara,* swimming pool, new, B-C; *Saravita; Venezia,* F, with shower, has dining room, nice old rooms; *Sucre.* **Restaurant** *Chanchón.*

About 21 km. beyond Socorro is **San Gil,** an unspoilt colonial town which has the tourist attraction of El Gallineral, a riverside spot whose beautiful trees are

498 COLOMBIA

covered with moss-like tillandsia. Bus to Bogotá, US$6; to Bucaramanga, US$1.90.

Hotels *Bella Isla* (swimming pool), C, a good stopover on the Bogotá-Cúcuta run (locked parking); *San Gil*, F, showers, clean, friendly; *Alcantuz*, Carrera 11, No. 10-15, E, clean, good location, pleasant but noisy facing street; *Residencias Guananta*, Calle 11 (same block as *Hotel Bogotá* and *Colombia*), F, small, clean, hard beds, noisy in daytime; *Galés*, G; *Pensión Elba*, F.

Restaurants Just outside Pinchote on the road from Socorro to San Gil is the *Mesón del Cuchicote*, which specializes in dishes from the Santander region. A good, cheap restaurant in San Gil is the *Santandereano*; *El Turista* is adequate.

A road runs E from San Gil to Onzaga (bus), through Mogotes and San Joaquín, dropping from high mountain ridges to tropical valleys. From Onzaga it is 20 km. to Soatá (see previous page); no public transport, if walking make sure you take the right road.

21 km. from San Gil is **Barichara,** a beautiful colonial town at 1,830 metres, founded in 1714 and designated as a national monument to preserve its character. There are many places of historical interest, the most important being the house of the former president Aquiles Parra (the woman next door has the key).

No hotels, but 3 rooms for visitors available in the restaurant (not museum) *Casa de la Cultura* (F, and excellent meals for US$2); *La Notoria*, F, clean, comfortable, showers in rooms, no meals, you can make your own coffee, "elegant, friendly, talkative" landlady. Buses from San Gil, from main plaza, 1 hr. An interesting excursion is to Guane, a town 9 km. away by road, or 1½ hrs. walk by trail, where there is an interesting archaeological museum in the priest's house, large collection of coins and a mummified woman (admission, US$0.25).

About 24 km. beyond San Gil, a little off the road, is the picturesque village of Aratoca, with a colonial church. Ten km. further on, the descent from the heights along the side of a steep cliff into the dry canyon, with spectacular rock colours, of the Río Chicamocha is one of the most dramatic experiences of the trip to Cúcuta, but, if driving, this is a demanding and dangerous stretch.

Bucaramanga, 420 km. from Bogotá, is the capital of Santander Department. It stands at 1,018 metres on an uneven plateau sharply delimited by eroded slopes to the N and W, hills to the east and a ravine to the S. The city was founded in 1622 but was little more than a village until the latter half of the 19th century. The metropolitan area has a population of 700,000, which has expanded rapidly because of the success of coffee, tobacco and staple crops. The Parque Santander is the heart of the modern city, while the Parque García Romero is the centre of the colonial area. Just off Parque García Romero is the Casa de Bolívar, Calle 37, No. 12-15, an interesting museum (0900-1200, 1400-1700, free, closed Sat. and Sun.). Opposite is the Casa de Cultura. Casa Perú de la Croix, Calle 37, No. 11-18, is a beautiful colonial mansion, housing the Corporación Cultural (excellent information on the region), and a small photography museum. There is a large, colourful market next to the bus station. The city's great problem is space for expansion. Erosion in the lower, western side topples buildings over the edge after heavy rain. The fingers of erosion, deeply ravined between, are spectacular. The Club Campestre is one of the most beautifully set in Latin America. There is an amusement park, Parque El Lago, in the suburb of Lagos I, SW of the city on the way to Floridablanca.

Average maximum temperature is 30°C; average minimum, 19.4°C. Rainfall is about 760 mm., and humidity is high (68% to 90%).

Hotels *Chicamocha*, luxury, Calle 34, No. 31-24, B, a/c, clean; *Bucarica*, spacious, on main plaza, C, private bathroom, telephone, not always hot water, good restaurant and snack bar; *Andino*, Calle 34, No. 18-44, D, private bathroom; *Carolina*, next best, near bus terminals, E, private bathroom, no hot water, some air-conditioned rooms; *Zulima*, Calle 36, Carrera 22, E, with bath, no hot water, also has an annex on Calle 31; *Balmoral*, uphill from centre, Calle 35, Carrera 21, E, with bath; *El Pilar*, Calle 34, Carrera 25, E, clean; *El Príncipe*, Carrera 17, No. 37-69, E (very good value with superb food—but book ahead); *Embajador*, Calle 37, No. 17-18, E; *El Edén*, Calle 31, No. 19-25, one block from bus station, F, clean, safe; *Tamana*, Carrera 18, No. 30-31, F, clean, friendly. A few blocks uphill from the bus terminal are several *residencias*; one is *Residencias Colonial*, recommended, D, with hot shower and w.c., T.V., bar, expensive; another is *San Pablo*, G, clean and good; *El Pilos*, E, strongly recommended, friendly service, good food, view from roof; *Hospedaje y Lanchería La 55*, one block uphill from the Copetran terminal, F, good lodgings and restaurant. *Residencias Magdalena*, Calle 31, No. 20-17, F, with private bath, noisy, dirty; *Amparo*, Calle 31, Carrera 20, E, with bathroom, good; *Residencias Tayrona*, F, clean, good, no hot water;

COLOMBIA 499

Hospedaje Díaz, Carrera 18, 28-69, near bus station, F, basic; *Pasajeros*, F, clean, comfortable, near bus station. *Morgan*, Calle 35 y Carrera 19, E-F, 2 blocks from bus station, central, old and new wings, O.K. Wide variety of hotels on Calle 31, between Carreras 18-21. Accommodation at the *Club Campestre*, E, is good, but you must have an introduction; try the mayor's office or Chamber of Commerce. **Note:** Since Bucaramanga is the site for numerous national conventions, it is sometimes hard to find a room. You may find it more pleasant to stay at San Gil (see above).

Restaurants *La Carreta*, Calle 27, No. 42-27, excellent, not cheap, delightful surroundings, music at times; *Mi Bodequín*, Carrera 17, No. 31-77, also good; good food at *Club del Comercio* (by invitation or introduction). *Di Marco*, Calle 48, No. 28, excellent meat; *La Brasa*, Carrera 33, No. 34, good typical meals; *Corcobado*, on hill overlooking town Km. 4 road to Pamplona (another branch in Cabecera), slow service, but good, expensive; *La Puerta del Sol*, Carrera 30, No. 62-304 and *La Fonda*, Vía Girón Km. 4, serve typical dishes; *El Maizal*, Calle 31, No. 20-74, and *Consulado Antioqueño*, Carrera 19, No. 33-81, both serve *platos antioqueños*; *Portofino*, Calle 37, No. 13-13, good; *Fujiyama*, Calle 38, No. 33-34, good value Chinese food; also oriental, *Oriental* and *Tokio*, both on Carrera 18, between Calles 35 and 34; in same area, *Aldana*, good *asadero*; *Pesquera*, Carrera 33, for seafood; pizzas at: *Piz Pon Pum* (next to Cinema Rivera), *Oskar's* and *Alero del Castillo* in Centro Comercial Cabecera; *Lonchería La 36*, Calle 36, No. 13-02, very good savoury pasties and snacks; *Desayunadero La 18*, opposite the Copetran terminal, cheap, friendly, English spoken, open every day till late; good snack bars including *Más Pin...chos* (Carrera 31 y Calle 30), *Mar Villa* (in the centre and at Centro Comercial Cabecera); *Almuerzo Colonial*, Carrera 33, No. 38-33, good fixed price lunch only; *Los Arrayanes*, Calle 32, No. 29, good value, especially lunchtime; *El Tony*, Carrera 33, No. 33, very popular, live music late at night; *Gran Gastby* (correct spelling! Carrera 33, No. 30-30). *El Toronjil*, vegetarian at Carrera 33, No. 52-123, a bit dear; *Berna*, Calle 35, No. 18-30, best pastries in town. Try the *hormigas* (large black ants), a local delicacy. Service in Bucaramanga's many restaurants is slow, so be warned.

Discotheques On road to Girón are *El Pulpo* and *Capricornio*; *Ulisses 2000*, Av. Quebrada Seca y Carrera 28, gay.

Shopping Camping equipment, *Acampemos*, Calle 48, No. 26-30, last place in Colombia to get camping gas cartridges before Venezuela. Handicrafts in Girón (expensive—see below) and typical clothing upstairs in the food market, Calle 34 y Carreras 15-16. Similar articles (*ruanas*, hats) in San Andresito. *Fería de artesanías* in first 2 weeks of September, usually near the Puerta del Sol.

Banks Banco Anglo Colombiano, Calle 36, No. 20-04, and agency on Carrera 15. Banco de la República, on central plaza, is the only bank authorized to cash travellers' cheques; also 2 agencies (one on Carrera 15). Many other banks. Open Mon.-Fri. 0800-1130, 1400-1600, and last working day of month, 0800-1030. Closed Sats.

Tourist Office Carrera 19, Calle 35.

Transport Taxis do not have meters but the fare within the city is US$0.70 (US$0.75 at night). Buses charge US$0.10.

Airport Palonegro, on three flattened hilltops on other side of ravine S of city. Spectacular views on take-off and landing. 3 Avianca flights to Bogotá, US$35, regularly overbooked; US$16 to Cúcuta. Taxi, US$3-4; colectivo, US$1. Buses are scarce despite the fact that some bus boards say "Aeropuerto" (direction "Girón/Lebrija" from Diagonal 15).

Roads To the Magdalena at Barrancabermeja, 174 km.; to Cúcuta, 198 km.; to Bogotá, 420 km.; to Medellín, 1,010 km.; to Santa Marta, 550 km., all paved.

Buses Bus terminals around a plaza at Calle 31 and Carrera 18. To Bogotá, 8-11 hrs., US$9 (Pullman) with Berlinas del Fonce, Carrera 18, No. 31-06 (this journey is uncomfortable, there are no relief stops, and it starts off hot and ends cold in the mountains, come prepared), Copetran, Calle 55, No. 178-57, has 3 classes of bus to Bogotá including Pullman, 10 hrs., US$10; Tunja, 9 hrs., US$5.10; Barranquilla, 9 hrs. (US$13.50 first class with Copetran); Cúcuta, 6 hrs., US$4.25 (Pullman). Berlinas buses often arrive full from Bogotá, Cotran also to Cúcuta; colectivo to Cúcuta, US$6; Santa Marta, 13-20 hrs., according to season, US$15 with Copetran; Barrancabermeja, 3 hrs., US$1.90, a scenic ride with one rest stop permitted; this road is now paved. Hourly buses to San Gil, US$1.90. To Berlín, US$1.

Excursions In the neighbourhood are several small towns: **Floridablanca,** 8 km. SW, with famous El Paragüitas gardens, belonging to the national tobacco agency, reputed locally as "a replica of the Garden of Eden" - and known particularly for its pineapples; you can get a free pass to the gardens from the agency's office in town. The gardens are not open at weekends. Take the Cotandra bus (US$0.25) from Carrera 22, Bucaramanga, either Florida Villabel which goes by El Paragüitas, or Florida Autopista which goes direct to the square in Florida and you have to walk about a km. Toll on road to Floridablanca, US$0.20.

Lebrija (20,400 people), 17 km. to the W, is in an attractive plain. Rionegro (36,750 people) is a coffee town 20 km. to the N with, close by, the Laguna de Gálago and waterfalls. **Girón** (27,500 people) a tobacco centre 9 km. SW of Bucaramanga on the Río de Oro, is a quiet and attractive

500 **COLOMBIA**

colonial town, filled with Bumangueses at weekends, with a beautiful church. The buildings are well preserved and the town unspoilt by modernization. By the river are *tejo* courts and popular open air restaurants with *cumbia* and *salsa* bands; in the square at weekends, sweets and *raspados* (crushed ice delights) are sold. (Hotels: *San Juan de Girón*, B, outside town on road from Bucaramanga, swimming pool; *Río de Oro*, in centre. Restaurant: *Mansión del Fraile* on the square, in a beautiful colonial house, good food—Bolívar slept here on one occasion, ask to see the bed.) Take the bus from Carrera 15 or 22 in Bucaramanga, US$1.45, or walk, jog or cycle as the Sunday trippers do. In **Piedecuesta,** 18 km. SE of Bucaramanga (bus from Carrera 22, US$0.35, 45 mins.), you can see cigars being hand-made, furniture carving and jute weaving—cheap, hand-decorated *fique* rugs can be bought. There are frequent buses to all these places; a taxi costs US$5. Corpus Christi processions in these towns in June are interesting.

Another excursion is to **California**, about 30 km. NE of Bucaramanga, where there are gold mines that tourists can visit.

Our road runs E to Berlín, and then NE (a very scenic run over the Eastern Cordillera) to Pamplona, about 130 km. from Bucaramanga. The road is very bad and narrow.

Berlín has been recommended to the hardy camper as challenging and rewarding. The village lies in a valley at 3,100 metres, the peaks surrounding it rise to 4,350 metres and the temperature is constantly around 10°C, although on the infrequent sunny days it may seem much warmer. The scenery is awesome. The inhabitants are tolerant of visitors; ask a farmer for permission to camp in his field. There are no hotels or restaurants, although food is made available. It has been recommended as an ideal place to appreciate the grandeur of the Eastern Cordillera and the hardiness of the people who live on the *páramo*.

Pamplona, Department of Santander del Norte, lies amid mountains at 2,200 metres. Population, 23,200. The climate is cold and uninviting, but the town is definitely worth seeing. Founded in 1548, it became important as a mining town but is now better known as a university city. Few modern buildings have as yet broken its colonial harmony. Cathedral in the spacious central plaza. The earthquake of 1875 played havoc with the monasteries and some of the churches: there is now a hotel on the site of the former San Agustín monastery, but it may still be possible to visit the ex-monasteries of San Francisco and Santo Domingo. The Iglesia del Humilladero, adjoining the cemetery, is very picturesque and allows a fine view of the city. See the Casa Colonial archaeological museum, Calle 6, No. 2-56, open Tues-Sat., 0900-1200, 1400-1800; Sun., 0900-1200.

Hotels *Cariongo*, Carrera 5, Calle 9, C, very good, excellent restaurant (locked parking available); *Montaña*, Carrera 6, No. 8-02, E; *Sandoval* and *Santander* hotels poor. *Lincoln*, C, on main square. *Residencias Doran*, E with bath (F without), large rooms, good meals, US$1.50; *Anzoátegui*, F with bargaining, for dinner, bed and breakfast. *Orsua* on main square, F, clean, friendly, hot water usually, cheap, good food also available; *Pensión Victoria*, 1½ blocks from main square, G, basic, dirty, also used for prostitution, not recommended by locals, large meals for US$1.25 in restaurant. Hotel accommodation may be hard to find at weekends, when Venezuelans visit the town.

Restaurant *El Doran*, meals for US$1.60. *El Gran Duque*, on main square, student-run, good music. *Los Bucaros*, close to main square, good value *menú fijo*, US$2.

Shopping Pamplona is a good place to buy *ruanas*. Good indoor market.

Banks do not change dollars or travellers' cheques in Pamplona.

Buses To Bogotá, US$10; to Cúcuta, US$1.35; to Bucaramanga, US$2.75, 4 hrs.; to Málaga, 0930 8 hrs. in dry weather, beautiful but very hard journey; to Tunja, US$9, 12 hours (leaving at 0600). To Berlín, US$1.75.

Warning DAS can be difficult with "hippies" as the Venezuelan border is close.

It is a run of 72 km. from Pamplona through sparsely populated country, descending to an altitude of only 215 metres, to Cúcuta.

Cúcuta, capital of the Department of Santander del Norte, and only 16 km. from the Venezuelan frontier, was founded 1734, destroyed by earthquake 1875, and then rebuilt, elegantly, with the streets shaded by trees, and they are needed for it is hot: the mean temperature is 29°C. Population: 500,000. Coffee is the great crop in the area, followed by tobacco. There are also large herds of cattle.

Cúcuta, because it is the gateway of entry from Venezuela, was a focal point in the history of Colombia during the wars for independence. Bolívar captured it after his lightning Magdalena campaign in 1813. The Bolívar Column stands where he addressed his troops on February 28, 1813. At El Rosario de Cúcuta, a small town of 8,000 inhabitants 14½ km. from Cúcuta on the road to the frontier, the First Congress of Gran Colombia opened on May 6, 1821. It was at this Congress that the plan to unite Venezuela, Ecuador, and Colombia was ratified; Bolívar was made President, and Santander (who was against the plan) Vice-President. (Santander was born at a *hacienda* near El Rosario which is now being developed as a tourist centre.) The international bridge between Colombia and Venezuela is a few km. from El Rosario; just beyond it is San Antonio del Táchira, the first Venezuelan town, and 55 km. on is San Cristóbal.

Hotels *Tonchalá*, Calle 10, Av. 0, B, good restaurant, swimming pool, air conditioning, airline booking office in hall; *Tundaya*, Calle 10, No. 6-21, E, comfortable; *Victoria Plaza*, Calle 8, No. 2-98, D; also D are *Frontera*, Calle 12, No. 7-36 and *Sol*, Calle 10, No. 7-51; *Casa Blanca* (swimming pool), D, good, reasonable meals, recommended; *Nohra*, on main square, E, friendly; *Residencias Los Rosales*, near bus station, Calle 2, 8-39, fan and private bath, good, F; *Hospedaje Danubio*, Calle 2, 8-88, cheaper but not as good; *Residencia Mary* at bus station, E, with bath (cheaper per person in triple room), good. Also near the bus station are *Zulia*, F, with bath, clean; and *Residencias Catacumba*, F, good value. *Residencias Los Dos Santanderes*, Calle 1 between Av. 9 and 10, F; *Amaruc*, Av. 5, No. 9-37, E, with fan, private bath, no hot water.

Restaurants *"M"*, also called *Chez Esteban*, on road to Venezuela, very good; *El Aire y Sol*; *Bahía*, just off main square, pleasant; other good restaurants at reasonable prices are *El Pollo Especial*, *El Jarrón de Baviera*, *Cantón* (Chinese), *Auto Lunch El Palacio* (run down). *Jarrón Reviejo*, informal restaurant/bar, live music nightly.

Shopping A good range of leather goods at possibly the best prices anywhere in Colombia.

Currency A good rate of exchange for pesos is to be had in Cúcuta, or on the border. There are money changers on the street all round the main square and many shops advertise the purchase and sale of bolívares. The price is usually better than at the Banco de la República (Calle 11 and Avenida 5). Change pesos into bolívares in Cúcuta or San Antonio—difficult to change them further into Venezuela. AmEx and Citicorp travellers' cheques can be exchanged only in Banco de la República.

Tourist Office Calle 10, No. 0-30, helpful, has maps, etc. At airport. Other maps obtainable from Instituto Geográfico, Banco de la República building, in the main plaza.

Airports At Cúcuta for Colombian services (to Bogotá US$40 if paid in pesos, with Avianca; less with Satena, and with Aerotal), and at San Antonio, Venezuela (30 minutes) for Venezuelan domestic lines. At latter, be sure all baggage is sealed after customs inspection and the paper seals signed and stamped.

Note Cúcuta is a great centre for smuggling. Be careful.

Transport To San Cristóbal colectivo, US$2; bus, US$1 (Bolivariano); to San Antonio taxi US$6; bus US$0.30. Bus to Bogotá, hourly, 17-24 hrs., US$12, Berlinas del Fonce 1400, several stops, including 15 mins. in Bucaramanga, or Bolivariano, 20 hrs., often delayed at check points. There are frequent buses, even during the night. To Bucaramanga, US$4.25, 6 hrs, with Berlinas del Fonce Pullman, several departures daily; from there a connection to Barranquilla can be made. To Tunja, US$9. The road is bad for the first part of the journey. Bus station: Avenida 7 and Calle O (a really rough area). Taxi from bus station to town centre, US$2.

There are good roads to Caracas (933 km. direct or 1,046 km. via Mérida), and to Maracaibo (571 km.). Bus to Caracas, 14 hrs., Expreso Occidente, two daily, US$13; taxi colectivo US$15.75.

If travelling from Venezuela to Colombia, it is cheaper to fly Caracas-San Antonio (US$30 approx.), take a taxi to Cúcuta (US$6), then take an internal Colombian flight, than to fly direct from Caracas to Colombia. It will, of course, take longer. The airport transfer at San Antonio is well organized, with taxi drivers calling at necessary immigration offices, and at exchange places, the trip taking 25 mins. You must buy your Colombian ticket in Cúcuta, but you can make a reservation in a travel agency in Venezuela some days in advance. With a computer (*localizador*) reference number, you can avoid queues.

N.B. All visitors need a visa and tourist card to enter Venezuela. There is a Venezuelan Consulate at Cúcuta (Av. 0, Calle 8—open 0800-1300, Mon.-Fri.) which supplies tourist cards—same applies at Venezuelan Embassy in Bogotá. You must also provide one photograph for a visa; evidence of onward transportation out of Venezuela, often with a date, is officially required, and proof of funds is sometimes requested. You are strongly advised to obtain visa and card from the Venezuelan embassy in your own country, if you know in advance when you will be arriving at the frontier. It is necessary to obtain a DAS exit stamp from the offices in Cúcuta (open every day, 0800-1730, except Sun.; Calle 17, No. 2-60) before leaving the country as there are no Colombian exit/entrance formalities at the international border bridge. If you do not, you will be turned back

502 COLOMBIA

by Venezuelan customs officials, and the next time you enter Colombia, you will be subject to a fine of US$7.50. Similarly, if arriving from Caracas, make sure bus stops at border for Venezuelan exit formalities. Obtain Colombian entrance stamp from the DAS in Cúcuta because your passport will not be checked again until Pamplona. Border checks in Cúcuta are very strict. Entering or leaving Colombia by car, you must have car papers and passport stamped at the DAS in the centre of town *and* at the airport. On the road to the airport stop at the Customs Office—watch hard for the small sign—for a Customs stamp. At the Customs Office is a restaurant serving excellent, large meals for US$2. Venezuelan car documentation is checked at the border post in San Antonio.

7 km. from Cúcuta is Zulia (Petróleo *buseta*), worth a visit if waiting for a Venezuelan tourist card.

The Andes chain N of Cúcuta is the branch which sweeps north to the Guajira Peninsula after the bifurcation of the Eastern Cordillera near Cúcuta: the other branch crosses into Venezuela. This western branch is the Sierra de Perijá y Motilones, in which live the Motilones Indians, the only Indians in Colombia who have refused to accept absorption into the larger nation. Little is known of them, for so far they have persisted in killing many of the missionaries sent to convert them, and the anthropologists sent to study them.

The Central Cordillera: Medellín and Manizales

The Central Cordillera lies W of the Magdalena River. In it are two of the most important cities in Colombia: Medellín, the second largest city in the country, and Manizales. Manizales can be reached by a road (309 km.) passing through Facatativá and Honda; or through Girardot to Ibagué, then over the high crest of the Quindío pass via Armenia. (For the road from Manizales to Medellín, see, page 508.) Medellín can be reached from Bogotá by road three ways: the highway opened in 1982 (see page 505); the old direct road (478 km.) with a 207-km. unpaved stretch from La Dorada to La Unión; and the third via Manizales. The journey from Bogotá to La Dorada can still be done by train.

The town of Antioquia was founded in 1541, but the Spaniards, eager for gold, were not interested in the hinterland, which was then very sparsely inhabited by nomadic Indians who made very poor agricultural labourers. But during the 17th century a new wave of settlers came to Colombia from Spain; many of them were Jewish refugees who were deliberately seeking isolation, and found it in the little valley of the Río Aburrá, where they founded the city of Medellín in 1616. They were farmers with their families rather than *conquistadores*: they had an extraordinarily high birth rate; they intermarried very little with either Indian or black; and they divided the land into small farms which they worked themselves. Their exports were small: a little gold and silver from their streams. They lived on the food they themselves produced: maize, beans, sugar-cane, bananas, fruit.

In the early 19th century the settlement began to expand and to push out in all directions, particularly to the S. The settlers followed the forested slopes on the western side of the Central Cordillera and occupied all the cultivable land. Manizales, 120 km. S, was founded in 1848. In the second half of the century new lands were occupied further S.

It was coffee that brought stability to this expansion, but they were slow to adopt it. Coffee appeared in the Magdalena Valley about 1865, but none was being exported from Antioquia before the end of the century. It was the 1914-18 war that suddenly gave a fillip to the industry: within 20 years the Departments of Antioquia and Caldas were producing half the coffee of Colombia, and they are by far the most important producers today. The industrialization of Medellín followed the coffee boom. There has been little immigration since the original settlement, but the natural growth in population has been extraordinary.

Medellín capital of Antioquia Department, is a fast growing city of 2.2 million people, at an altitude of 1,487 metres. It could hardly be less advantageously placed, for it faces forbidding mountain barriers in nearly all directions. Its climate alone, that of an English summer day (21°C), is in its favour, despite a certain amount of smog. Yet Medellín is one of the main industrial cities of Colombia, and seethes with energy. The first looms arrived in 1902. Today the city produces more than 80% of the textile output of the country, and textiles

COLOMBIA 503

account for only half its industrial activity. A metro is planned for the city. Excellent views from Cerro Salvador (statue on top), SE of city, and from Cerro Nutibara, S of city, where there is an outdoor stage for open air concerts, souvenir shops and restaurants.

Medellín is a well-laid-out industrial city. There are four universities, together with other higher educational institutions. The old colonial buildings have nearly all disappeared, but there are still some 17th century churches left: the old Cathedral on Parque Berrío and the churches of San Benito, La Veracruz, and San José. The new Cathedral of Villanueva, one of the largest brick buildings in the world, is on Parque Bolívar, an attractive place. Three churches of the 18th century survive: San Ignacio, in Plaza San Ignacio, San Juan de Dios, and San Antonio. The city's commercial centre, Villanueva, is interesting for its blend of old and modern architecture, including many skyscrapers. There is a fine sculpture, Monumento a la Vida, next to the Edificio Seguros Suramericana on Calle 50, where exhibitions of work by leading South American artists are held on the ground floor. The cattle auctions on Tues. and Thurs., held in specially built cattle yards on the outskirts, are interesting. There is a zoo, Zoológico Santa Fe, in the southern section of the city, mainly of South American animals and birds; reached by the Guayabal bus (US$0.07; admission US$0.80). In the zoo grounds is a Historical Museum (closed Mon. and Tues.), costing an extra US$0.20 to enter.

Warning Medellín is not a safe city at night; be particularly wary of the prostitutes, of both sexes.

Hotels *Intercontinental*, the best, but some distance from the centre, A, excellent; *Amaru*, Carrera 50A, No. 53-45, A, central, quiet, but overpriced, good, expensive restaurant with excellent service, poor rate for travellers' cheques; *Ambassador*, Carrera 50, No. 54-50, B, in connection with *Veracruz*, Carrera 50, No. 54-18, B, with bath, swimming pool, very good, restaurant on 11th floor gives fine view over city; *El Balcón*, near *Intercontinental*, in Transversal Superior, A, beautiful view of the city, good meals, US$6 p.p.; *Nutibara* (casino and swimming pool), Calle 52A, No. 50-46, A; *Residencias Nutibara*, an annex facing hotel of same name, slightly cheaper with all the same facilities; *Gran Hotel*, Calle 54, No. 45-92, C, fair, unremarkable food (do not use its telephone, telex or cable services); *Europa Normandie*, Calle 53, No. 49-100 (Tel.: 41-99-20), C, restaurant, cafeteria, sauna, disco, central, fair; *Casa Blanca*, Calle 50 and Carrera 47, C, central but rather a run-down area; *Casa Blanca 70*, Carrera 45 and Calle 70, D; *Residencias Las Mercedes*, Calle 47, No. 43-84, near centre, D, with bath; *Horizonte*, Carrera 47 No. 49A-24, C, good and popular restaurant; *La Montaña*, Calle 48, No. 53-69, E, with shower, good meals available, in the dangerous market area; *Residencias Los Llanos*, Carrera 51, No. 44-41, E, clean, comfortable, cold showers, inside rooms quieter; *Lido*, Carrera 49 and Calle 47, E, with bath; *Residencia Hotel Centro*, Carrera 45, No. 50-25, E, with bath; *Residencias Plaza*, Calle 54, D; *Viajes*, E, good cheap meals, friendly; *Eupacla*, Carrera 50, No. 53-16, C, central, recommended; *Bristol*, Calle 46, No. 49-27, F with shower, water supply erratic; *Pensión Mon Amour*, E, Calle 47 and Carrera 51; *Comercial*, Calle 48, No. 53-94, E, friendly, clean, hot water available in some rooms, the best of which are on the top floor, doors barred to all but residents after 1800, meals US$2; *Residencial Cordillera*, Calle 46, No. 49-26, F, for room with bath, not recommended; *Residencias Hotel Gladys*, Carrera 48 and Calle 45, E, modern, clean, friendly and helpful, but rather noisy; all rooms face street. Nearby, *Residencias Kennedy*, E, Carrera 49; *Príncipe*, Bolívar and Carrera 51, E, clean and friendly; *Nuevo*, Calle 48 and Carrera 53, E, with bathroom, noisy but clean, good meals for US$1; *San Francisco No. 2*, Carrera 54, No. 48-44, F, good and clean, friendly but noisy; *Mora*, Carrera 53, good meals, pleasant atmosphere. *Pensión Estrella*, Carrera 48, F, clean, secure; *Doris*, Carrera 45, No. 46-25, F, clean and friendly; *Gómez Córdoba*, Carrera 46, No. 50-41, F, basic, safe; *París*, Carrera 45, No. 49-57, F with cold shower, noisy, watch figuring. Many *residencias* on Carreras 54 and 55, but this is not a safe area; a safer area for accommodation is around Carrera 43. An excellent private house to stay in is on Carrera 58, No. 53A-36, 3rd floor, US$3 a night, very safe. Calle 45 is said to be an unsafe street.

If you are due to arrive in Medellín late at night and do not wish to risk looking for accommodation at such an hour, alight at Barbosa, which is safe (hotels *Imperial* and *Familiar*, both on main square, E). Frequent buses Barbosa-Medellín, US$0.75.

Restaurants *Salvatore*, Calle 53, with Carrera 49, opp. *Hotel Europa Normandie*, *Lombardo* and *Tonino* (Italian); *Cacique Nutibara*, on Cerro Nutibara, offers excellent views of the city and good, reasonably-priced food; *Aquarius*, on road past *Intercontinental Hotel*, first class; on same road, and good also, *Las Sombrillas*, *La Yerra*, *Los Cristales*. Local dishes are served at branches of *La Fonda Antioqueña*, about US$3 for a meal, but something of a tourist trap and not recommended. Roast chicken is provided at the four branches of *Kokoriko*, for US$3; good steaks at *Texas Steak*

House, Calle 44 and Carrera 80; good *arroz con pollo* from *Los Alejos* in Centro Comercial Boyacá. *Finale*, Av. El Poblado with Calle 8, bar serving excellent food, art gallery upstairs, manager speaks English, very friendly; also in El Poblado, *Bar-Pizzería Julio's* (Tel.: 46-04-37) open till 0300. Other restaurants in El Poblado, all near Parque Poblado: *Arepizza* on Calle 10 (local food, juices, cheap); *Che's*, Calle 9, good steaks; on Av. 43B, one block from Parque, *Frutos del Mar*, good seafood; *La Crêperie*, opposite, French; *La Torre de Pizza*, good. On Av. Poblado (Av. 43A), *Presto* hamburgers and 2 good chicken restaurants. *Piemonte* and *La Bella Epoca*, very good and expensive, both on road to Envigado, as are *La Mesa* and *Isla Verde* (good, but expensive); *Hostería* (very good); *Sebastiano* (fair); *El Boquerón*, on the mountain top; good German restaurant close to University Centre. *Doña María*; *Aguacatala* and *La Posada de la Montaña*, both outside off road to Envigado, good, Colombian food, but expensive; *Posada de la Montaña* in centre, too; *Noche y Día*, Carrera Junín, between Maturín and Amador, good meals for US$0.80; in fact there are several of these round-the-clock cafés in the vicinity which serve cheap meals. *La Vida*, round corner from *Hotel San Francisco No. 2*, US$1.60 for *comida*, excellent fruit juices, friendly, also, 2 doors from this hotel, *Popular*, is good. Two good self-service restaurants are *La Estancia*, Carrera A49, No. 54-15, on Plaza Bolívar, and *Contenalco*, Calle la Playa, between Av. Oriental and El Palo, clean, cheap, very busy in rush hours. *Cirus*, Calle 53, meals for US$1, good value. *Restaurant Palma Sola*, Carrera 51 and Calle 48, *comidas* for US$1.50. Many good, cheap restaurants on Carrera 49, e.g. *Versalles*, on pedestrian precinct between Av. La Playa and Plaza Bolívar. For hamburgers and sandwiches, *Mr Ham, Hardy's*, four of each in the city. Excellent pastries at *Salón de Té Astor*, Carrera 49, No. 53-39. Many cheap cafés near bus station.

Clubs Campestre (good food, rooms, golf, tennis, swimming pool); Ejecutivos (lunch club in centre).

Shopping Silver seems cheaper than in Bogotá; there is also a good branch of *Artesanías de Colombia* (Carrera 50, No. 52-21). Cercado San Alejo, Parque Bolívar, open on the first Saturday of every month (handicrafts on sale). Plaza de Flores is worth a visit. Carrera 47 has 3 antique shops. Many of the textile mills have discount clothing departments attached where good bargains can be had; ask at your hotel. *La Piel*, at Calle 53, No. 49-131, has an excellent selection of leather goods at very reasonable prices (the selection and price of leather goods in Medellín is better than Bogotá). *Supermarket Exito* is good for cheap leather bags. There are 2 new shopping centres, San Diego and Oviedo, with many shops, restaurants, etc.

Bookshop Librería Continental, Junín No. 52-11, sells foreign-language books.

Taxis Pay what is on the meter plus US$0.90. From airport, about US$2.70.

Discotheque Delfos (in *Hotel Europa Normandie*); others in central hotels, and in El Poblado district.

Music Monthly concerts by the Antioquia Symphony Orchestra. Band concerts in the Parque Bolívar every Sun. at 1130. Open air concerts, on Sundays, of Colombian music on Cerro Nutibara.

Museums Museo Etnográfico Miguel Angel Builes, Carrera 81, No. 52B-120, has an extensive collection of artefacts housed in beautiful new building. The Museum of the Missionary Sisters of Mother Laura has a good collection of indigenous costumes and crafts from Colombia, Ecuador and Guatemala. Museo El Castillo, Calle 9 Sur, No. 32-269, formerly a landowner's home, has interesting objects and beautiful grounds; entry US$1.20; take bus to Loma de los Balsos, El Poblado (US$0.07), then walk 1 km. up the hill until you see the road lined with pine trees to the right. Open 1300-1700, closed Sun. The Museo Zea, now called "de Antioquia" (Carrera Cundinamarca and Diagonal Carabobo) shows Colombian pictures and sculptures, including works by Fernando Botero, Colombia's leading contemporary artist (now living in U.S.A.). Museum of Modern Art, Carrera 64B, No. 51-64, small collection, open Tues.-Fri., 0900-1300, 1500-1800. The Chamber of the Chamber of Commerce, Carrera 46, No. 52-82, (exhibitions of modern art). Casa Museo Maestro Pedro Nel Gómez, Carrera 51B, No. 85-24, Tel.: 332633/440725, house of the contemporary painter and sculptor. Museo Antropológico at University of Antioquia (new campus). (In the old University of Antioquia building, beside San Ignacio church, is a Museo Histórico.) Philatelic Museum in Banco de la República building. Most museums are closed on Mondays.

Botanical Gardens Joaquín Antonio Uribe gardens, near the new campus of the University of Antioquia, which include an aviary, are open daily, 0900-1730, US$0.40 entrance, well worth a visit (but the plants are not named); there is a restaurant, pleasant but not cheap. There is also a zoo (see page 503). Also visit El Ranchito, an orchid farm between the towns of Itagüí and La Estrella (entry US$0.50; April to June is the best time to visit).

Bullfights at the bull-ring of La Macarena in February.

Banks Banco de la República, Calle 50 (opp. Parque Berrío), changes travellers' cheques, but your photo will be taken; has other branches; Banco Anglo Colombiano, Calle 50 (Bolívar), No. 51-06; agency on Calle 45, No. 55-65 and two others; Banco Internacional, Banco Royal, Banco Francés e Italiano de Colombia, and various other Colombian banks. Open: Mon.-Thurs. 0800-1130, 1400-1600; Fri. 0900-1130, 1400-1630; last working day of month 0830-1100. Main

COLOMBIA 505

hotels will cash travellers' cheques for residents when banks are closed. (The owner of *Café Arturo* is reported to cash cheques.)

Post Office Main airmail office in Avianca building, Carrera 52, Calle 51A, Mon.-Sat., 0700-2200.

Telecommunications Pasaje Junín and on corner of Calle 49 and Carrera 50.

Travel Agents Empresas Diversificadas, Carrera 81A, 51-79 (Tel.: 34-91-42: day, 34-36-65: night), Apartado Aéreo 13053; full information on Antioquia, many tours arranged. Tierra Mar Aire (American Express agents), Calle 52, No. 43-124, helpful. Viajes Marco Polo, Calle 48, No. 65-94, Tel.: 230-5145, recommended; also Terra Nova, Calle 5A, No. 39-114, Tel.: 266-5000, who run an excursion by train to Cisneros, 3 hrs. journey, with 3-4 hours for a picnic and swim (US$5.20). Viajes Turandina, Calle 53, No. 49-80, Tel.: 455815.

Tourist Office Calle 57 No. 45-129, in bus station, and Turantioquia, Carrera 48, No. 58-11, Tel.: 254-3864, has good maps, good information on Antioquia and owns 5 good hotels in the Department. For a cheap tour of the city take any "Circular" bus, for US$0.06.

Airport A new airport, José María Córdova, 38 km. from Medellín and 13 km. from Rionegro, has been opened; *buseta* to centre, via bus terminal, US$1, frequent service, about 1 hr. journey, sit on right going to town (catch bus in town by *Hotel Nutibara*). To Rionegro, bus US$0.15, taxi US$8.50. By air to Bogotá, 45 mins. with Avianca, on shuttle flight, every ½ hour between 0730 and 1630. Copa office, Carrera 45B, No. 33-24. Daily flight to Panama with SAM or Copa, US$101 (excluding taxes), but you will have to buy a return unless you have another exit ticket out of Panama. See page 526 regarding transport of motorcycles by air to Medellín.

Roads A paved road, 665 km. long, goes N to Cartagena, and another S to Manizales. There are two other important roads: one, 383 km. NW through Antioquia to Turbo, on the Gulf of Urabá; and another, 478 km. SE from Medellín through Sonsón and La Dorada and on to Bogotá. The latter is paved as far as Rionegro, but from Rionegro to Sonsón is in a bad state of repair. The scenery compensates for this to some extent. The new Medellín-Bogotá highway has been completed, but beware of landslides in wet weather (near the Magdalena Valley is the California wildlife park, well-signposted). The road is totally paved but there are potholes, waterfalls and detours between Medellín and Honda. There are many campgrounds along the route, for example 130 km. and 150 km. from Medellín.

Buses The new bus terminal for all long-distance buses, Carrera 48m No. 42-88, is about 3 km. south west of the town centre, with shops, cafeterias, left luggage (US$0.30 per day) and other facilities. Quite safe. Bus service to city centre, US$0.15, buses to station marked: "Terminal de Transporte". To Bogotá, 9-12 hrs. US$11, every 40 minutes or so, with 5 companies, or to La Dorada, US$4.25. Frequent buses for Cali, Flota Magdalena US$11, 10-13 hrs. Frequent buses to Manizales, 7 hrs. (US$6.50 1st class, 5.25 2nd, by Empresa Arauca). To Cartagena, Brasilia, 17-20 hrs., or 14 hrs., by Pullman bus, US$12; road paved throughout but poor. To Barranquilla, US$16 by Pullman, 16 hrs. To Cartago, 8 hrs., Flota Magdalena, US$5. To Pereira, 8 hrs., US$6.25 by Flota Occidental Pullman. To Sincelejo, 9½ hrs. To La Dorada, 9 hrs. To Popayán, US$13.25, 16 hrs. To Turbo, US$7.50.

Rail There are no regular passenger services from or to Medellín, except the tourist train from and to Cisneros. See above under Travel Agents.

Excursions A run N along the Cartagena road to (132 km.) **Yarumal,** with 61,250 people, or NW to (80 km.) **Antioquia** (13,275 people) will give a good idea of the very beautiful countryside. Antioquia lies just W of the Cauca river; it was founded as a gold mining town by the Spaniards in 1541, the first in the area, and still retains its colonial atmosphere. Until 1826 it was the capital of the Department. The fine old Cathedral is worth seeing, as is the church of Santa Bárbara. There is an interesting wooden bridge, 300 metres long, 3 km. downstream from the first bridge which the buses use—ask for directions or take a taxi. Hotels: *Mariscal Robledo* (D, 37 rooms, swimming pool); *Hostería Real*, 2 km. from town, C full board, good food, pool; *Turismo*. Bus from Medellín US$1.50 (Flota Urbara or Transporte Sierra), 2½ hrs. The road goes on to Turbo, on the Gulf of Urabá (see page 473).

Another interesting excursion from Medellín is along the Sonsón road SE to (39 km.) the town of **Rionegro**, in a delightful valley of gardens and orchards. Here was born one of Bolívar's generals, José María Córdova, the hero of the battle of Ayacucho. Medellín's new airport has been built nearby. The Casa de Convención (where the 1863 Convention took place) is now an archive museum, entry US$0.20. The cathedral, with its gold and silver altar, deserves a visit. A museum of religious artefacts beside the altar (entry US$ 0.20) and you can climb up behind the Virgin donated by Philip II to look down into the cathedral. There are processions in Easter Week. Many interesting pottery and ceramics factories in Rionegro area, hardly mechanized, as well as metal working; they welcome visitors and explain the processes. A day trip can cost US$15, but the Medellín-Rionegro *rápido* taxi service is very cheap. Bus to Rionegro, from Calle 44, No. 44-43, US$1, one hr. Rionegro has become something of a tourist trap, and those thinking of buying

506 COLOMBIA

leather goods should be warned that prices are high. 10 km. from Rionegro (15 minutes by colectivo, US$0.60) is *Carmen de Viboral,* well-known for its pottery; there are several factories just N of the market place.

Rionegro Hotels Aymará, E, hot showers, meals available; Rionegro, F, friendly, dark rooms, cold water; *residencia* on main square; Oasis, Carrera 50, No. 46-23, with restaurant, bar, laundry, TV in rooms. **Restaurants** Pizza at *La Mansarola* and *Capuccino; Kokorico* on main square for chicken.

Beyond Rionegro is El Peñol, a precipitous, bullet-shaped rock which towers above the surrounding hills and lakes. It has been eroded smooth, but a spiral staircase has been built into a crack which extends from the base to the summit. A snack bar has been built at the summit, and the views are breathtaking. Cabins can be rented at the foot of the rock for about US$28 per day (sleep six, everything except food provided), Tel.: Medellín 234-6966, Santamaría y Cía; architects, Calle 81A, No.51-79. Bus to the rock and to the pretty town of Guatapé with Cía. Fco. López, US$1.20.

On the road to El Retiro is Fizebad, an old estate house, restored with original furniture and artefacts, and a display of flowering orchids; entry, US$1.75. In El Retiro itself is a small colonial church and an even older chapel which is seldom open: ask for the caretaker. On the road to La Ceja, have lunch in *Parador Tequendamita*, in a beautiful setting by a waterfall. The route is through splendid scenery, and one can see typical Antioquian costume and life. (To Fizebad by bus, catch a La Ceja or El Retiro bus).

La Ceja, also on the Sonsón road, is well worth a visit. Transportes La Ceja cover the route; the journey takes 1¾ hrs. For the energetic, any one of the surrounding hills affords an excellent view of the area. *Hotel Primavera* and one other, both delightful, have rooms (F). At *Sonsón*, there are the *Tahami* (F, very good value) and *Imperio* (F) hotels.

At *Bello,* 6½ km N of Medellín (pop. 153,000), is the hut in which Marcos Fidel Suárez, President 1918-1922, was born. It is completely covered in with glass for its better preservation.

A good trip is by car to *Hatillo,* 32 km. along a road which parallels the railway to Puerto Berrío, and then another 80 km. along a new road to Caldas. There are many restaurants along this road.

To the SW of Medellín, the towns in the coffee-growing district (Fredonia, Jericó, Jardín, Venecia) are worth visiting; all have basic inns which are cheap to stay in. The scenery is beautiful.

At *Envigado,* 10 km. S of Medellín, craftsmen have for generations turned out the traditional *antioqueño* pouch called *carriel*, carried by the men. Now used for money, its original use was for coffee samples. Further S (half an hour from Medellín) is Caldas Department, which has some of the finest scenery in Colombia. 55 km. S of Medellín is **Santa Bárbara**, at 1,857 metres on a green hill top, with stunning views in every direction of coffee, banana and sugar plantations, orange-tiled roofs and folds of hills. *Hotel Palomares* on main square, F, clean, well-maintained; restaurants and cafés also on square, as is the large church. Bus to Medellín, US$1.

Quibdó, the capital of Chocó Department, is a small jungle town (41,000; *Hotel Citará*, D; *Dora Ley*, E with bath, F without, rooms vary greatly in quality, meals available; *Pacífico*, E, good, with bath, its restaurant, *Club Náutico*, on 2nd floor has good food and views; several *residencias* including *Del Río* and *Darién*; Restaurant *El Paisa* recommended; *Chopán* bakery, good pastries and coffee.). There is a good museum at the Normal School. The huge concrete church looks very out of place. Sunday market is attended by many Indians, some painted, who arrive by canoe. Most of the platinum of the Chocó Department is shipped from Cartagena. Boats can be hired for river trips; try Ruffo at the sawmill, US$20 an hour. Quibdó can be reached (1) by bus from Medellín; (2) from Buenaventura by boat up the Río San Juan to Istmina and on by road (see page 513; (3) by the Río Atrato: small speedboats go to and from Riosucio, US$40 p.p., from where there are boats to Turbo, and an overland trail to the Darién Gap (hotels, restaurants, bars and shops in profusion at Riosucio); large cargo boats go from Quibdó to Riosucio, Turbo and Cartagena (one week, US$28 p.p. inc. meals, warm clothes and blankets necessary at night, wash in river water, stops allow enough time to disembark and look around); (4) by plane from both Medellín and Cali. Chocó Department, thickly wooded and mountainous, is impressive; travel is rough but the rewards are high. A road is planned from Quibdó to the Pacific Coast at Bahía Solano (good for skin-diving; *Cabañas El Almendral*, 40 mins. by decrepit taxi from Bahía Solano, recommended for its setting on the Pacific, for river trips and accommodation, E p.p., book through ACES which runs the airlink; see page 1187 for boats from Panama).

Manizales, built on a mountain saddle, is dominated by its enormous (still unfinished) concrete Cathedral and the Nevado El Ruiz volcano, which erupted so catastrophically in November 1985. The city was founded in 1848 by settlers from the Department of Antioquia; it has a population of 350,000 and is the capital of the small Department of Caldas, which originally (until 1965) contained what are now the new Departments of Quindío and Risaralda. The old Department, now known as Viejo Caldas, produces about 30% of all Colombian coffee and picturesque coffee farms abound.

Manizales, at 2,153 metres above sea level, rides its mountain saddle uncompromisingly, the houses falling away sharply from the centre of the city into the adjacent valleys. The climate is extremely humid—average temperature is 17°C, and the annual rainfall is 3,560 mm.—and frequently the city is covered in cloud. The best months of the year are from mid-December through to early March, and early in January the Fair and Coffee Festival is held, with bullfights, beauty parades and folk dancing. The city looks down on the small town of Villa María, "the village of flowers", although with the rapid expansion of Manizales, Villa María is now almost a suburb.

The architecture is predominantly modern with high-rise office and apartment blocks, although traditional architectural styles are still seen in the suburbs and the older sections of the city. The departmental government building, the Gobernación, opposite the Cathedral in the Parque Bolívar, is an imposing example of neo-colonial architecture; the bull-ring built 25 years ago is an impressive copy of the traditional Moorish style. The suburbs stretch away North (with poshest shopping around Calle 59) and South of the city centre and are reached by the main *avenida*, a four-lane highway lined with flowers—marguerites—which grow to enormous proportions (as also the geraniums) because of the damp and the altitude. Chipre, a recreational park, provides a good view of the city (well-visited on Sundays); El Tanque, near Chipre, is another vantage point.

Hotels N.B. in January, during the *fiesta*, hotel prices are grossly inflated. *Carretero*, B, good (Tel.: 33206); *Fundadores*, C, good (Tel.: 22333); *Las Colinas*, Carrera 22, Calle 20 (Tel.: 29400), three-star, two bars, good restaurant, very comfortable, C; *Bonaire*, above Ley supermarket, not too noisy, spacious, very clean, hot water, D, shared rooms cheaper, recommended; *Europa*, Av. Centenario, No. 25-98 (Tel.: 22253), near the bull-ring, restaurant for breakfast only, comfortable and clean, D; *Rokasol*, Calle 21, No. 19-16, near bus station so noisy, not water, clean, all rooms have bathrooms, E, good restaurant, set meal US$2; *Pensión Margarita*, Calle 23, 22-45 (Parque Bolívar), fairly noisy, E, with bath, breakfast, lunch and supper, US$1.00 per meal; *Villa Kempis*, on road to Pereira, about 2 km. past bull-ring, old religious retreat house, beautiful view over the valley, very quiet, hot water a.m. only, restaurant and bar, good food at moderate prices, but slow service, Tel.: 32961/ 30187, D; *Tama Internacional*, Calle 23, No. 22-43, next to Cathedral, E, with bath, meals US$1, warmly recommended, but noisy in daytime. Cheaper: *Residencias Nueva York*, Calle 18 between Cras. 22 and 23, extremely clean, hot water, shared washing facilities, some bar noise in front, F; *Casablanca*, above Bolivariano bus station, F, a bit noisy, rooms of varying quality; *San Francisco*, Calle 23, No. 18-50, no hot water, clean but noisy, F; *Residencias Avenida*, Carrera 18, No. 21-21, dirty, not recommended; *Residencias Avenida 2*, Calle 21, No. 20-07, figuring needs watching, F, hot water; *Residencias Colonial*, Calle 20, No. 17-32, no hot water, F; *Residencias Monaco*, near bus station, F, adequate, English spoken; *Residencias Caldas*, Carrera 19, No. 22-45, near bus station, F, US$1 surcharge on holidays, hot water, quiet, good; *Escorial*, Calle 20 and Carrera 22; *Residencias El Cónsul*, one block from plaza where buses stop, towards Cathedral, F (US$1 more for bathroom).

La Rochela hotel in the "hot country" about 30 km. (1 hr.) W from Manizales on the road to Arauca, large swimming pool for adults and smaller one for children, E, for a room for six; no smaller accommodation, family holiday atmosphere, good food at moderate prices; in process of building separate cabins. *Hotel Termales Arbeláez*, 45 km., or 55 mins., from Manizales on the road to the Nevado El Ruiz, D, hot swimming pool, private bathrooms, restaurant.

Restaurants *Los Arrayanes* and *Las Torres*, both beautifully set in the Chipre area of town overlooking valleys: *Los Arrayanes* has plain food at moderate prices; *Las Torres*, local specialities, more expensive. *El Cable*, so-called because it stands beside the remaining tower of a disused cable-way for coffee, good food, two-course meal US$5.50 *Las Redes*, Carrera 23, No. 75-97, predominantly sea food, good but about US$8-10 per head; *Cuezzo*, Carrera 23, No. 63-112, Argentine restaurant with very good meat—try the *parrillada*, moderate prices but wine expensive; *Vitiani*, Carrera 23, No. 25-32, Italian and European food, quite smart, food and wine fairly expensive, has good trout (*trucha*) and excellent crab-claws (*muellas de cangrejo*); *El Dorado Español*, moderate prices, good food, *carne a la parrilla* highly recommended, on road to Chinchiná; *Holandesa*, Carrera 19, good, plentiful meals, about US$3; *El Pilón*, moderate prices, *plato montañero* and *sopa de mondongo* recommended; *Epsilon*, one block from plaza, average price US$3 per meal; *Hong Kong*, opp. Carretero Hotel, good Chinese; *Chung-Mi*, Chinese, does takeaway meals; *La Suiza*, Carrera 23, No. 26-57, good fruit juices and cakes; *Caballo Loco*, Calle 21, No. 23-40, expensive pizzas; *Domo*, modern-type hamburger joint and pizzeria, moderate prices;

508 **COLOMBIA**

Picaflor, very good food at moderate prices; *El Ruiz,* Carrera 19, No. 22-25, US$2 for filling 3-course meal.

Teatro de los Fundadores Supposedly has the largest stage in Latin America, a modern cinema-theatre auditorium. Interesting wood-carved mural by local artist, Fernando Botero, who also has murals in the entrance hall of the Club Manizales and *Hotel Las Colinas.*

Museums Bellas Artes, anthropology museum with interesting selection of findings from Indian tombs (and a marvellous view of the Nevado El Ruiz), open in the afternoon (erratically) after 1400. Banco de la República, Carrera 23, No. 23-06, gold and anthropology museum open during banking hours, classical music every afternoon in the Bank. Universidad de Caldas, natural history museum open every day from 0800 to 1200 and 1400 to 1800 (take a "Fátima" bus to the University). La Galería del Arte, Av. Santander at Calle 55, exhibitions of work by local artists, pictures can be bought.

Bank Banco Anglo Colombiano, Carrera 22, No. 17-10, and other banks. Open 0800-1130, 1400-1600, Mon. to Thurs., 0900-1130, 1400-1630 Fri. only. Last working day of the month 0830-1130.

Tourist Office Parque Bolívar, opposite Cathedral, well-organized.

Manizales has an airport, La Nubia, and the regional airline ACES provides an efficient and punctual service to Bogotá, Medellín, and other cities.

For excursions to see the full process of coffee growing, apply to the Comité Departmental de Cafeteros de Caldas, Carrera 22, No. 18-21, Tel.: 41706.

Parque de los Nevados national park includes El Ruiz, Santa Isabel, El Cisne, El Nevado del Tolima—all snow-capped peaks. Contact Inderena (National Conservation Institute) for details. Also La Laguna del Otún, where there is trout fishing by permission of Inderena.

Roads To Medellín direct, 265 km. via the winding mountain road through the picturesque towns of Salamina (*Residencia Puerto Nuevo,* F, opp. bus office, clean, good meals), Pácora and Aguadas, all perched on mountain ridges, to La Pintada (*Hostería Los Farallones,* C, nice pool, meals fair), but further if we go West across the Cauca river via Arauca, Anserma, *Riosucio* (a delightful old town with fine mountain views all round and a large colonial church next to the Arauca bus terminal) and then on to La Pintada. Buses Autolegal via Neira and Aguadas, 9 hrs., US$5.25; Empresa Arauca via Anserma, 10 hrs., 1st class, US$6.50 ordinary, US$5.25; colectivo to Medellín, US$8.55. Both routes offer impressive scenery, but the shorter route is largely unpaved between Aranzazu and La Pintada. Bus to Bogotá, 8-10 hrs. by Expreso Bolivariano Pullman, US$7, 9 hrs.; 7½ hrs. by Flota El Ruiz *buseta,* US$8.50—beautiful scenery. To Honda, US$3 (Expreso Bolivariano). Cali by bus Expreso Palmira, 5½ hrs., US$4.50 ordinary; Pullman 6 hrs., US$6. Pereira, Expreso Palmira, Expreso Trejos, hourly, 1¼ hrs., excellent road, beautiful scenery, US$1 ordinary. Armenia, Expreso Palmira, 3 hrs., US$2. **N.B.** Unlike other places, town buses stop only at bus stops.

The Cauca Valley

From Manizales a road runs S to Pereira (fine scenery) and then to Cartago, at the northern end of the rich Cauca Valley, which stretches S for about 240 km. but is little more than 30 km. wide. The road goes S up this valley to Cali and Popayán, at the southern limit of the valley proper. There it mounts the high plateau between the Western and Central Cordilleras and goes all the way to Ecuador. From Cali a railway (no passengers) and a road run W to the Pacific port of Buenaventura. The Valley, which has been described in the introduction to this chapter, is one of the richest in Colombia. From Cartago S the river Cauca is navigable by barges as far as Cali.

Pereira, capital of Risaralda Department, 56 km. SW of Manizales, stands overshadowed by green mountains, at an altitude of 1,476 metres, above the Cauca Valley. Population, 343,000; a considerable centre for coffee and cattle. It is a modern city, founded in 1863, with an undistinguished cathedral and four parks: the best is the Parque del Lago, with an artificial lake; a fountain is illuminated several times a week. There is a lively market. Matecaña airport is 5 km. to the S (bus, US$0.05). Outside it is a good zoo (bus from town centre to zoo, US$0.06.)

Hotels *Soratama,* main plaza, C; *Gran,* Calle 19, No. 9-19, C, restaurant, bar, travel agency, etc.; *Residencia San Francisco,* near buses, E, with bath; *Residencia Colón,* F, no hot water, dubious plumbing, O.K.; *Residencias Bolívar,* opp. Cathedral, F, friendlier but plumbing also suspect, meals available; *Cataluña,* E, clean and friendly, good set meal in dining room; *Residencia Edén No. 1,*

COLOMBIA 509

Calle 15, Carrera 10, near market, F, clean, friendly. Plenty of *residencias* in Calle 19, e.g. *Savoy*, F with bath.

Restaurants *El Pollo Campestre* (near airport), *La Ricura*, Carrera 8, No. 22-21, very good meal, US$1.50; *Bonanza* and *El Manolo*, Calle 20, No. 8-22, which has excellent meals for less than US$2 near the market; good self-service restaurant on main square; *El Norteño* is recommended.

Clubs *Club Rialto; Club Campestre*, 5 km. from town.

Banks Banco Anglo Colombiano, Carrera 9, No. 17-48. Banco Internacional. Open 0800-1130, 1400-1600, Mon.-Thurs., 0900-1130, 1400-1630, Fri. Last working day of month, 0800-1030.

Transport New bus terminal, clean, with shops, outside city centre. Bus to Armenia, 1 hr., US$1, a beautiful trip. SAM flights to and from Bogotá, Cartagena, Cúcuta, Medellín and San Andrés. Bus to Cali, US$3.50, 4½-5 hrs.; Manizales, US$1, 1½ hrs.; to Bogotá, US$6.50, 7 hrs., rough journey, not recommended for motorbikes.

Excursion 15 km. away, at Santa Rosa de Cabal, a poor 11-km. road branches off to Los Termales, where waters from a hot spring cascade down a mountain into a swimming pool. There are also cold showers fed from a natural spring. Restaurant so-so. Bus Pereira-Santa Rosa, US$0.20; package tours from Santa Rosa to Los Termales cost US$11.50 including meals and one night's lodging.

Armenia, capital of Quindío Department, is in the heart of the Quindío coffee district; population 200,000; altitude 1,838 metres; mean temperature 19°C. This modern city, founded in 1889, is the seat of Quindío University. The Bogotá-Armenia-Cali road is fully paved, but slow through the mountains; fog, reckless drivers and stray animals make the Quindío Pass (3,350 metres) a hazard at night. A new, more direct road from Armenia to Cali, joining the Panamericana S of Zarzal, has lighter traffic than the main road.

Hotels *Zuldemaya*, Calle 20, No. 15-38, C, poor service and water shortages reported; *Palatino*, Calle 21 at Cra. 14, E-D, central, comfortable; *Izcay*, Calle 22 with Cra. 14, D, restaurant not recommended; *Atlántico*, F; *Embajada*, E; *Pensión Nueva York*, basic but clean and cheap, G; *Moderno Aristi*, Calle 18, Carrera 20, a block from Palmira bus station, E, with bath, hot water, clean; opposite is *Superstar*, F.

Restaurants *La Fogotá*, near university; *La Chalet*; *Frisby*, Carrera 16, No. 20-22, good pizza or fried chicken; *El Pollo Campestre*, near Country Club.

Archaeological Museum Calle 21, No. 16-37.

Airport El Edén, 13 km. from city. Fog often makes air services unreliable.

Bus to Neiva, Flota Magdalena, 0100, 0400, 2230, US$4.75. To Bogotá: Velotax bus, US$6, hourly, 9 hrs.; Velotax colectivo, US$8, 7 hrs.

Before the road drops into the Cauca Valley, between Armenia and Buga is Sevilla; *Hotel Araucarias*, in square next to Plaza Bolívar, E, with or without bath, clean, pleasant, parking. Restaurant: *Chicken Loco*. 30 minutes' bus-ride from Armenia is Montenegro, a coffee centre (ask at FNC office on Plaza Bolívar about visits to *fincas* in the district); Plaza Bolívar is heavily wooded.

Cartago, 64,830 people, about 17 km. SW of Pereira, is on a small tributary of the Cauca river before it takes to the gorge separating the two *cordilleras*. Coffee, tobacco and cattle are the main products. Founded in 1540, it still has some colonial buildings, particularly the very fine House of the Viceroys (Casa de los Virreyes). Visit the cathedral, with the cross set aside from the main building. Local train service to Cali, but the one carriage is always crowded, US$3, 4 hrs. Bus to Cali, US$3, 3½ hrs.

Hotels *Mariscal Robledo; Alhambra*, Carrera 5a, No. 9-59, F; *Villa del Río*, F, recommended. *Residencial Paraíso*, Carrera 9, No. 8-99, F, cold showers only, clean, Sat. noisy at night. Many others in same area, i.e. around bus terminals and railway stations; those in the same block as Flota Magdalena are better value than the others.

About 27 km. S of Cartago is **La Victoria** (the Pan-American Highway bypasses it to the east), a pleasant, small colonial town with a shady plaza. There is a *Hotel Turista* (F, family atmosphere, clean and friendly, will change US$ cash), one block from the plaza, and several restaurants. La Victoria is in the centre of a beautiful area where cattle are raised, and cotton, sorghum, maize and soya are grown. You can cross the Cauca River by turning right off the road going to the south (good fishing Jan., Feb. and July) and 10 km. (paved road) further on is **La Unión** at the foot of the

510 COLOMBIA

mountains on the west side of the valley. Stop at the 4th house on the right before the public swimming pool for excellent *pan de yuca* straight out of a brick oven. La Unión is a small agricultural town, a centre for grape production. *Residencia Los Arrizos*, and *Residencia El Cacique*. The countryside around offers lovely walks. Just south of La Unión is Rondanillo, a small town in the hot Cauca Valley, with a museum of paintings by the Colombian artist, Omar Rayo. A road runs E to the main highway at Zarzal.

About 50 km. S of Cartago is Zarzal, and 71 km. S again is **Buga,** an old colonial city of 75,220 people and a centre for cattle, rice, cotton, tobacco and sugar cane. Founded in 1650, and its modern Cathedral contains a famous image of the Miraculous Christ of Buga to which pilgrimages are made. N of Buga, at Uribe (50 km.), is the junction of the road S from Medellín with the one from Bogotá and Venezuela. Bus to Cali, US$1.50.

Hotels *Guadalajara* (swimming pool), D, recommended, cabins for family groups, excellent restaurant and self-service cafeteria; *España*, F; *Real* (not recommended); *Capacari*, E, with bath, clean (swimming pool), overpriced, poor restaurant; *residencias* around Cathedral better value.

At La Manuelita, 40 km. S of Buga, is a famous sugar estate. Before reaching La Manuelita any of 3 roads running E will reach, in 12 km., the fine colonial *hacienda* of El Paraíso, where the poet Jorge Isaacs (author of *La María*, a Colombian classic) lived and wrote. To visit the *hacienda*, take a bus from either Buga or Palmira to El Cerrito, and bargain for taxi to take you on, wait and return. This should be about US$4. On Sundays there are tourist buses from Palmira. The trip is recommended. Toll between Buga and La Manuelita, 25 km. N of Palmira, US$0.40.

If you take the road from Buga to Buenaventura you come to the man-made Lake Calima. Taking the southern route round the lake, 42 km. from Buga is the *Hotel del Lago Calima* (D) set in very pleasant surroundings on the edge. There is no swimming pool, but some brave people swim in the lake, which is cold at about 16°C, and a kilometre deep.

Five km. S of La Manuelita and 47 km. S of Buga is **Palmira,** in the Department of Valle; population, 163,000. Good tobacco, coffee, sugar, rice and grain are grown, and there is a College of Tropical Agriculture. The paved Pan-American Highway runs direct to Popayán via Pradera, but the road through Cali is preferable. (Taxi connection with Cali, 29 km. south, US$5.55; bus US$0.45).

Hotels *El Dorado*, D without bath, clean; *Residencias Benalcázar*, F, with bath, clean, friendly, good value. *Escorial*, F, and many other cheap places.

Restaurants *La Fonda*, good; *Grill Caña de Oro*, nice; *Paradero los Parrales*, good breakfast, good service, clean loos.

Cali, capital of Valle Department (1.4 million people), is the third largest city in Colombia, set in an exceptionally rich agricultural area producing sugar, cotton, rice, coffee and cattle. Altitude: 1,030 metres; average temperature: 25°C, hot and humid at mid-day but a strong breeze which blows up about 1600 hrs. makes the evenings cool and pleasant. It was founded in 1536, and until 1900 was a leisurely colonial town. Then the railway came, and Cali is now a rapidly expanding industrial complex serving the whole of southern Colombia. South of Carrera 10 are many one-and a few two-storey houses, tiled and wide-eaved. Through it runs the Cali river, a tributary of the Cauca; it is beautiful, with grass and exotic trees on its banks. On one overlooking mountain, from which the best views are obtained, there is a statue of Christ visible for 50 km. and there are three large crosses on another mountain. The statue of Benalcázar, the city's founder, is worth a look, beautiful views of the city. Two nearby *haciendas*, the very attractive and renovated El Paraíso (see above under Buga) and Cañas Gordas, have important historical associations. There is a sugar cane museum in the Hacienda Piedechinche (open 0930-1600; admission, US$0.50; 42 km. from Cali, take a bus to Palmira, then taxi); tours of this and Hacienda El Paraíso arranged by Comercializadora Turística Ltda, Carrera 4, No. 8-39, local 101 (US$10, including transport, entrance fee, guided tour and lunch).

The church and monastery of San Francisco are Cali's best buildings. Inside, the church has been renovated, but the 18th century monastery has a splendidly proportioned domed belltower. The 18th century church of San Antonio on the Colina de San Antonio is worth seeing and there are fine views. Cali's oldest church, La Merced (Calle 7, between Carreras 3 and 4), has been beautifully restored by the Banco Popular. The adjoining convent houses two museums:

COLOMBIA 511

Museo de Arte Colonial (which includes the church) and the Museo Arqueológico with precolumbian pottery. More Indian pottery can be seen in the Sociedad de Mejoras Públicas, across the street from La Merced; this collection belongs to the Universidad del Valle. Another church worth seeing is La Ermita, on the river between Calles 12 and 13. The orchid garden along the Río Aguacatal, near the centre, is well worth seeing.

The city's centre is the Plaza de Caicedo, with a statue of one of the independence leaders, Joaquín Caicedo y Cuero. Facing the square are the Cathedral, the Palacio Nacional and large office buildings. Across the river from the Plaza de Caicedo is the splendid new Centro Administrativo Municipal (CAM) and the main post office. Lovely walks and parklands stretch along both sides of the river here, with the Intercontinental Hotel, Museum of Modern Art, and zoo (entrance fee US$0.50) on its South bank. See also the Museum of Natural History, Carrera 2 Oeste, No. 7-18, which has some precolumbian exhibits as well as biological specimens from the area (entrance fee US$0.13).

The Museo de Arte Moderno La Tertulia, Av. Colombia, No. 5-105 Oeste (10 mins. from centre) has an exciting exhibition of South American art (good films shown nightly, except Mon., at 1900 in the *cinemateca*, admission US$1). Within its Villa Olímpica in San Fernando, Cali has three stadiums: the Pascual Guerrero Stadium, holding 50,000 people; the Olympic Gymnasium, holding 7,000 people; and the Piscinas Olímpicas, holding 3,000 people. Another stadium holding 18,000 spectators, the Monumental de Cali, is 10 mins. from the city on the road to Meléndez. Outside the city also is the new first-class bull-ring.

Warning Cali has recently become a centre of guerrilla and counter-insurgency activity. Nowhere is safe after midnight. Carry your passport at all times and be prepared for frequent police checks.

Hotels A Hilton is under construction, on Av. Colombia, Carrera 10 Oeste. Intercontinental, Av. Colombia, No. 2-72, recently extended, tennis and pool, recommended despite mediocre service, A (weekend discounts); Americana, for businessmen, B, a/c, Carrera 4, No. 8-73; Dann, opposite Intercontinental, new, A, (with weekend discounts), service could be improved, but good; Don Jaime, Av. 6, No. 15N-25, B, good, restaurant recommended; Menéndez, Av. Colombia, No. 9-80, D, all rooms have own bath, good, reasonably priced meals available, nice old colonial building, popular with Colombians; Petecuy, Cra. 9, No. 15-33, modern, rooftop pool, not-so-good area, B; del Puente, Calle 5, No. 4-36, D, with bath, clean, will store luggage, recommended; Aristi, Carrera 9, No. 10-04, 3-star, C, but weekend discounts, recommended, large and old by Cali standards, turkish baths, rooftop pool, restaurant; New York, Calle 12, No. 3-62, D, clean, hot water, basic, near bus station and market; Plaza, Carrera 6, No. 10-29, D; Residencial María Eugenia, near bus station, Calle 11, No. 6-9, E, beware of overcharging, not recommended; Tikal, Carrera 10 esq Calle 9, D, modern, quiet, but on edge of dubious neighbourhood; Los Angeles, Carrera 6, No. 13-109, E, good; Calima, Calle 15, No. 3-66, E, noisy, not recommended; La Merced, Calle 7, No. 1-65, 4 blocks from Intercontinental, D, swimming pool, pleasant young staff are very helpful, English spoken, recommended; Hotel Residencias Stein, Av. 4N, No. 3-33, B, full board, C, bed only, friendly, very good, quiet, excellent food, dinner for non-residents US$5, French, German and English spoken, Swiss-run, swimming pool; Miami, Carrera 7, 13-55, E, with bath (no hot water), central, clean, safe; María Victoria, Calle 10, No. 3-38, E with bath, F without; Franco, Calle 11, No. 6-9, E, beware of overcharging, not recommended; Bremen, Carrera 6, No. 12-61, Tel.: 761998, without bath, F; Residencias las Américas, near new bus terminal, Calle 25, 2N-31, F, dirty; Amoblador Bolívar, Calle 25, No. 2N-47, near bus terminal, E, basic, good meals, safe, highly recommended for friendly atmosphere; Casa del Viajero, several, found in converted homes, e.g. Calle 15 Norte, No. 4-44 (Tel.: 621477), F or E, many on other side of river round Av. 6. Arca de Noé, on road leading up to the Cristo Rey, D, fabulous views, marvellous gardens, good food in restaurant, poor service but worth the effort.

Restaurants Cali is a good place for eating, as the attached list attests (but restaurants close early, and many close on Sun.): Don Carlos, Carrera 1, No. 7-53, excellent seafood, elegant and expensive; Hostería Madrid, Calle 9, No. 4-50, European specialities, good service, above-average price; Canarias, Calle 8, between Carreras 3 and 4, recommended for cheap meals; Torremolinos, Carrera 7a, No. 13-31; Restaurante Suizo, Calle 5, No. 24A-11, Swiss, excellent fondue bourguignonne, pleasant atmosphere, reasonably priced; Los Farallones, at Hotel Intercontinental on 9th floor, is Cali's most atmospheric restaurant, with shows starting at about 2230-2300; try their Chateaubriand for two with drinks and desserts, less than US$25 including tips, a real buy; also their weekday noontime buffet at about US$6.50 a head is very reasonable, eat all you want; El Quijote, Carrera 4, No. 1-64, atmospheric, European dishes, expensive; Simonetta, Diagonal 27, No. 27-117, pleasant, reasonable, Italian dishes; La Terraza, Calle 16, No. 6N-14, elegant, music and dance, nice atmosphere; El Cortijo Andaluz, Carrera 38 and Calle 53, atmospheric (converted residence), Spanish and European foods; Los Girasoles, Av. 6N, Calle 35, steaks, other

512 COLOMBIA

meat grills, good atmosphere; *Los Gauchos del Sur*, Calle 5 about Carrera 60, Argentine-style grilled meat, dancing, excellent food, very reasonable; *China*, Av. 6N, No. 24-52, excellent food and service, pleasant atmosphere, large servings for reasonable price; *Shanghai*, Av. 8N, No. 17-33, Chinese, excellent food in utilitarian setting, takeaway, very reasonable; *Embajada Antioqueña*, Av. Roosevelt, Antioquian regional food, relatively cheap; *Cali Viejo*, in the Bosque Municipal, about US$10 p.p. for very good local food in pleasant surroundings; also good is *La Cazuela*, Avenida Roosevelt, 26-30; *Las Valles*, Av. 6N, No. 47-197; *International Tourist Centre*, a complex of nightclubs and restaurants, so-so food; *Los Panchos*, Carretera a Meléndez with Autopista Sur, very good Colombian food, a favourite of Caleños; *Gloria*, Carrera 6, Calle 14, good and cheap; *La Amistad*, beside main Post Office, meals US$1.60; *Eduardo VIII*, piano bar, attempt at English pub atmosphere, good food, well-stocked bar; *Mauna Loa*, Centro Comercial del Norte, seafood a speciality, reasonably priced, Lebanese food too; *Taberna Olafo*, Calle 15, No. 6-37; *Mac Club*, Centro Comercial Imbanaco (Calle 5a and Carrera 39), American-style food, world's biggest hamburgers and hotdogs, excellent, cheap; *Sears Cafetería*, open 0930-1930, excellent food, rather expensive but large servings. *Kokorico*, places all around town, spit-roasted chicken; *La Calima*, Carrera 3, No. 12-06, good meal US$1.30, always open; *El Galeón*, Calle 8a, No. 1-27, very good seafood and atmosphere, expensive; *Jino's Pizza*, held to be Cali's best pizzas, reasonably priced; *La Veda*, near bus station, good *gaucho* food. At least 10 eating places in the bus station, *Doble Vía* is the best, the *Autoservicio* is overpriced.

You can find lots of European-style side-walk places along the Av. 6 at good prices. Try Mexican food at *Mexitaco*. Cheaper are the *fuentes de soda* you'll find all around, mostly with Colombian-style cooking, which is generally plentiful and tasty; a decent meal for US$3-4. There are also *Masserna* on Carrera 7 between Calles 10 and 11 and *La Sultana*, Calle 10, on the corner with *Hotel Aristi*. Try their *buñuelos* (cheesy fritters) and the *pandebono* (cheesy buns) next door at *Montecarlo*. Cafés and ice-cream parlours abound in the vicinity of the university, across the river from the main part of town.

Clubs Club Colombia; Club de Tennis de Cali; Club San Fernando, modern and luxurious; Club Campestre, as good as any club anywhere, with a magnificent golf course, tennis courts and swimming pool; Club La Ribera y Náutico.

Shopping *Platería Ramírez*, Carrera 11b, No. 18-64, for gold, silver, brass, jewellery, table settings, etc. *Artesanías de Colombia*, Calle 12, No. 1-20 and for larger purchases Av. 6 N, No. 23-45. For leather goods and shoes, try *Boots and Bags*, *Carlo's* and *Clogs*, all in the same precinct. For boots and shoes *Chaparro* (*Botas Texanas*), Av. 6, No. 14N-14, Tel.: 651007, good, owner Edgar speaks a little English. Posh shopping district: Av. 6N, from Río Cali to Calle 30 Norte.

Bookshop Librería Nacional, on main square, has English books and a café.

Taxis Black taxis are the most reliable; ensure that meters are used. Prices, posted in the window, start at US$0.11. On holidays an extra charge is made.

Nightclubs Locally known as "Grills". The ones along the Av. Roosevelt and along Calle 5a are safest and best known. *Arca de Noé*, *Farallones* at the *Intercontinental* and *El Peñol* on the Buenaventura road are probably Cali's best (and most expensive).

Fair Held during December; bullfights, masquerade balls, sporting contests. National Art Festival in June (painting, sculpture, theatre, music, etc.). Also in June Feria Artesanal at Parque Panamericano, Calle 5, handicrafts and excellent leather goods.

Banks Banco Anglo Colombiano, Calle 11, No. 4-48 (Plaza de Caicedo), and agencies on Avenida Roosevelt and Av. 6; Banco Internacional; Banco Royal de Colombia, Calle 3; Banco Francés e Italiano; Banco Colombo Americano and other national banks. Open: Mon.-Thurs., 0800-1130, 1400-1600; Fri., 0900-1130, 1400-1630. Last working day of month, 0800-1130. Closed Sats. Money can be changed at Almacén Estella, Calle 10, Carrera 8 (by *Hotel Aristi*) out of banking hours, or at travel agents.

British Consul Edificio Garcés, oficina No. 410, Calle 11, No. 1-07. Tel.: 721752-3. Postal address: Apartado Aéreo 1326.

Swiss Consul Carrera 5, No. 12-16, 6th floor; Tel.: 87-1771

Tourist Office Corporación Nacional de Turismo, Carrera 3, No. 8-39. Maps, posters and general information. DAS office, Av. 3N, No. 50N-20. Also co-operative for shopping. There is a Thomas Cook office just off the Plaza de Caicedo.

Rail No passenger service, except to Cartago.

Buses New bus terminal (connected by tunnel to railway station) is at Calle 30N, No. 2A-29, 25 mins. walk from the centre. Hotel information available. *Casa de cambio*, cash only. There are plenty of local buses between the bus station and the centre, which charge US$0.06. Taxi from centre to bus station, US$2. Buses to Popayán, US$3, 2½-hrs. (Colectivo to Popayán, US$3.50); to Pasto, US$9.50, 9 hrs.; to Ipiales (direct), US$9, 11 hrs. or by Bolivariano Pullman, US$8, departures at 0400 and 0615 and 0800; Coomotor have a direct service to San Agustín; to

COLOMBIA 513

Cartago, 3½ hrs., US$3; to Ibagué, US$6, 7 hrs.; to Buenaventura, US$3.15, 4 hrs.; to Manizales, US$4.50, 5 hrs.; to Medellín, US$11, 11-15 hrs.; to Bogotá, 10-15 hrs., by Magdalena (recommended) and Palmira, US$10. *Busetas* (Velotax and others) charge about 50% over bus prices but save time; taxi-colectivos about 2½ times bus prices and save even more.

Airport Palmaseca, 20 km. from city, has *casa de cambio*. International standard. Services to Bogotá, Medellín, Pereira, Cartagena, Barranquilla, San Andrés, Leticia. Microbus from airport to bus terminal (2nd floor), every 10 minutes, approx. 30 mins., US$0.75. Colectivo to city about US$1; taxi, US$6. Two flights a week to Quito (Weds. and Sat.); direct flights (Eastern Airlines, Avianca) to Panama; also to Miami.

145 km. by road (4 hrs.) over a pass in the Western Cordillera is **Buenaventura,** Colombia's only important port on the Pacific, and one of the busiest on the West Coast. It was founded in 1540, but not on its present site. It stands on the island of Cascajal, 16 km. inside the Bay of Buenaventura. Port works are in progress. Beaches such as La Bocana, Juanchaco and Ladrilleras may be reached by motor launch, but they are not very safe. Trips to beaches cost between US$10-40 for 10-person launch (rate per launch, not per person).

Buenaventura is 560 km. by sea from Panamá, 708 km. by road from Bogotá. Population, 122,500, mostly black. Mean temperature, 27° C. It rains nearly every day, particularly at night; the average annual rainfall is 7,400 mm. (relative humidity 88%). There are still problems with malaria. The port handles 80% of Colombia's coffee exports, and 60% of the nation's total exports, including sugar and frozen shrimp.

The toll road to Cali is 80% paved; the toll is about US$0.40 for cars and US$0.10 for motorcycles. The ordinary road is not paved. (Both give beautiful views of mountains and jungle.) There are plenty of buses to Cali, US$3.15 each way, 3 hrs. Colectivos run at half-hourly intervals to Cali, US$4.75 p.p.

The commercial centre is now entirely paved and has some impressive buildings, but the rest of the town is poor, with steep unpaved streets lined with wooden shacks. It is more expensive than Cali and it is difficult to eat cheaply or well. Festive atmosphere every night. S of the town a swampy coast stretches as far as Tumaco (see page 521); to the N lies the deeply jungled Chocó Department, where the most important gold and platinum mines are found.

Hotels On Carrera 3 with Calle 3, *Del Mar*, C, restaurant, TV, phone in rooms, *Balmoral*, E with bath, and *Felipe II*, D with bath, restaurant. *Comfort*, E, a/c; *Bahía*, Calle 3, F, clean, friendly. *Gran*, E with bath; *Continental*, Carrera 5, No. 4-05, E with bath; opposite is *Europa*, F without bath. *Estación*, being remodelled.

Camping With the permission of the commandant, it is safe to camp in the police compound at the docks while awaiting your ship.

Restaurants Self-service restaurant on main plaza, clean, modern, open 24 hrs. *La Sombrita de Miguel*, on road to El Piñal, good seafood, reasonable prices. Good seafood at Pueblo Nuevo market, but not very cheap.

Exchange Do not change money in Buenaventura, but in Cali.

American Consular Agency Grace Building.

Tourist Office Calle 1, No. 1-26, Mon.-Fri., 0800-1200, 1400-1800. Cámara de Comercio nearby is also helpful; has plan of city.

Air Services Local airport only; flights to Cali.

Shipping Passenger service from France: arrange with Continental Shipping and Travel, 179 Piccadilly, London W1V 9DB, Tel.: 01-491 4968.

Grace Osakoda from Hawaii tells us that you can get from Buenaventura to Quibdó on the Río San Juan, but that boats are scarce out of Buenaventura (lumber boats from El Piñal only go about a day and a half upstream, and port authorities are strict about allowing passengers on cargo boats). One way is to take a bus from Pueblo Nuevo, Buenaventura, to San Isidro on the Río Calima (28 km., 6 hrs., terrible road), then a motorized dugout (*panga*) to Palestina on the Río San Juan. From there take a dugout going upstream; they rarely go as far as Istmina, which is connected by road and bus to Quibdó (see page 506). Try to get as far as Dipurdú (no hotels, but friendly locals who offer sleeping space, shops with tinned goods), from where daily boats go to Istmina.

The paved Pan-American Highway (142 km.) runs S through the Cauca Valley

514 COLOMBIA

from Cali to Popayán. (Toll, US$0.40.) It takes 2½-3 hrs. by bus through splendid scenery. At first we pass through a land of rich pastures interspersed with sugar-cane plantations. To left and right are the mountain walls of the two Cordilleras. The valley narrows and we begin to climb, with occasional glimpses E of the towering Nevado del Huila (5,750 metres).

Warning All of rural Valle Department off the main roads is unsafe because of guerrilla activity. Similarly, Cauca Department E of the Highway, is not recommended for tourists.

Popayán is in the garden valley of the Pubenza, at 1,760 metres, in a peaceful landscape of palm, bamboo, and the sharp-leaved agave. (Pop. 103,000.) The early Spaniards, after setting up their sugar estates in the hot, damp Cauca valley, retreated to Popayán to live, for the city is high enough to give it a delightful climate. To N, S, and E the broken green plain is bounded by mountains. To the SE rises the snowcapped cone of the volcano Puracé (3,960 metres).

Popayán was founded by Benalcázar, Francisco Pizarro's lieutenant, in 1536. After the conquest of the Pijao Indians, Popayán became the regional seat of government, subject until 1717 to the Audiencia of Quito, and later to the Audiencia of Bogotá. It is now the capital of the Department of Cauca. The equestrian statue of Benalcázar on the Morro de Tulcán overlooks the city; it is worth climbing up for the views. The streets of two-storey buildings are in rococo Andalusian style, with beautiful old monasteries and cloisters of pure Spanish classic architecture.

In March 1983, an earthquake devastated the city. Following restoration work, Popayán is gradually coming back to life and has managed to retain its colonial character. The churches of San Agustín and Santo Domingo are again open to the public. The latter is used by the University of Caldas. All other churches remain closed. Walk to Belén chapel, seeing the statues en route, and then continue to El Cerro de las Tres Cruces if you have the energy, but do not go alone (there are plenty of guides offering their services). Security has deteriorated since the earthquake. Popayán was the home of the poet Guillermo Valencia; it has given no less than seven presidents to the Republic.

The versatile Francisco José de Caldas was born here in 1771; it was he who discovered how to determine altitude by variation in the boiling point of water, and it was to him that Mutis (of the famous *Expedición Botánica*) entrusted the directorship of the newly founded Observatory at Bogotá. He was a passionate partisan of independence, and was executed in 1815 during Morillo's "Reign of Terror".

Festivals Easter processions are spectacular; the city is very crowded. The childrens' processions in the following week are easier to see. As at Pasto (but less violent), there are the Día de los Negros on Jan. 5 and Día de los Blancos on Jan. 6; as at Carnival, the tourist and his belongings are likely to be drenched in water.

Hotels The following hotels survived the earthquake: *Monasterio*, Calle 4, No. 10-50, in what was the Monastery of San Francisco, lovely grounds, swimming pool, B, very good; *Los Balcones*, Calle 3, No. 6-80, C, hot water, Spanish-style restaurant for breakfast and lunch, good, will change traveller's cheques; *Chayaní*, Panamericana Calle 17 Norte, D, travellers' cheques accepted, and change given in US dollars; *Camino Real*, Calle 5, No. 5-59, Tel.: 21546/21254, P.O.Box 248, new; *Viajero*, Calle 8, No. 4-45, F, with bath, hot water, friendly; *El Príncipe*, Calle 8, No. 4-35; *Hostal Santo Domingo*, Calle 4, No. 5-14 (Tel.: 21676), E, with bath, in colonial building; *Residencia Comercio*, Calle 6, just off Carrera 17, clean, friendly; *El Viti*, F, clean, with bath, no hot water, near old bus station; *Casa Familiar Sra Haydée*, Carrera 5, No. 2-41, F, hot shower, clean, very friendly (ask for Sra. Haydee Gasca de Varela at the tourist office; she also has details of a *residencia* outside Popayán); *Casa Don Sebastián*, Calle 4, No. 7-79; *Residencias El Castillo*, Carrera 4 esq. Calle 1, D, bath and hot water, clean, very friendly, cafeteria and bar; *Residencias Bolívar*, Carrera 5, No. 7-11, F, clean, pleasant, good restaurant, parking across street; nearby *Residencia Panamá*, G, hot water, doors close at 2200; there are many others on Carrera 5 e.g. *Venicia*, No. 7-45, *Manizales*, No. 7-55 (F), *Viena*, No. 7-56, *Cecilia*, No. 7-60. *Residencias San Agustín*, F, behind the old bridge, clean, good beds, washing facilities.

Restaurants *Ricuras del Mar*, Carrera 4, No. 6-21, good fish restaurant; *La Castellana*, Carrera 6, No. 5-47 (meal and soft drinks for two, US$4.50); *El Mesón del Arriero*, Carrera 6, No. 7-37; good value but limited menu; *Taberna La Tolda*, next to Hotel Los Balcones, friendly student-type place; *Vitapán*, Carrera 6, No. 6-09 and Calle 4, No. 7-81; *El Danubio*, Carrera 8, No. 5-33; *Mei Chow*, Carrera 10A, No. 10-81; *Pizzería Los Alamos*, Calle 3, No. 2-54, very good pizzas, recommended; *Pizzería El Recuerdo*, Carrera 6 Vía Cauca, cheaper. For good lunches (US$1) *Los Olivares*, Carrera

4, No. 7-37; and *Punto Aparte*, Carrera 9, No. 6-09. *Astoria*, Calle 7, No. 4-33, good for breakfasts; lunches at *Bogotá*, Carrera 5, No. 6-57; *La Oficina*, Calle 4, No. 8-01, good *criollo* cooking, friendly, good value; *Pollo Pío Pío*, carrera 6, No. 8-11 open, till 0300, good. *El Bambo*, restaurant with swimming pool, on outskirts on road from Cali, friendly, camping permitted (US$0.50 for 2). Wholemeal bread, information and occasional accommodation from Heinz Rose, Calle 5, No. 2-28 (Aptdo. Aéreo 1851).

Museums Museo Negret, with works, photographs and furniture of Negret. All others damaged and closed.

Banks Banco de la República, Calle 3, No. 2-78, is the only one that changes foreign currency. (Open 0800-1130; 1400-1600, Mon.-Thur., until 1630 on Fri.) However, the *Hotel Monasterio* will accept travellers' cheques when you pay your bill and will give you change in pesos.

Tourist Office Carrera 6, No. 3-69, between Puente del Humilladero and Plaza Mayor (Tel.: 22251), has good maps of the city, prices of all hotels and pensions, and bus schedules and prices. They are very friendly and helpful, giving information on places of interest, will tell you where horses may be hired for exploring, and will store your luggage. Ask at the Tourist Office about which areas of the city are unsafe. They also offer coffee, and sell local crafts; telephone and mail service. The Tourist Office and the Colegio Mayor de Cauca have details on art exhibitions and concerts.

Travel Agent Avialoi Ltda, Calle 4, No. 7-59, good prices for air tickets bought with cash dollars.

Buses Popayán has a new bus terminal, next to the airport, 15 mins. walk from the centre (Ruta 2-Centro bus, terminal to centre, US$0.10). Luggage can be stored safely (receipt given); there is a charge to use the toilets, and a US$0.07 departure tax. To Bogotá, US$15. To Cali, US$3, 2½-3 hrs., or Velotax microbus, US$4.25, colectivos leaves from the main plaza (US$3.50); to Pasto, with Coop de Nariño, Carrera 6, No. 2-16, 1130, Cootranar, Flota Magdalena, Exp. Bolivariano and Supertaxis del Sur, US$5, 5-8 hrs.; spectacular scenery (sit on right); to Medellín, US$13.25, 16 hrs.; to Ipiales, Supertaxis at 1230, US$10, or bus, US$7.50, every two hours (Transportes Ipiales, Bolivariano, the best), 7½-10 hrs. To San Agustín, La Gaitana, 11 hrs., US$7, Coomotor, 13 hrs., US$9, each once a day, a jeep runs over the new road via Isnos to Pitalito for San Agustín (direct to San Agustín due in 1987) from bus terminal at 1000 (or when full), 6 hrs., US$6. To Tierradentro (Cruce de San Andrés), with Sotracauca (Tel.: 26-46), US$3, 4 hrs.; and goes to La Plata. Flota Magdalena to La Plata, US$3.75, 5 hrs, also Unidos del Sur (not via Tierradentro). To Puracé, US$1, 2 hrs. (Pullman is slightly more). To Silvia (see below), daily Coomotorista *buseta* at 0800 (US$1.30) or: take Expreso Palmira bus to Piendamó on Cali road, every ½ hour, US$0.60; from there, colectivo to Silvia, US$0.70. On market day (Tuesdays) buses leave directly to Silvia at 0600.

Air Services Service to Bogotá with Aires, every day except Weds., 1650, Mon.-Sat. at 0825. Avianca office for airmail, Carrera 7, No. 5-77.

Excursions A favourite is the drive to Silvia, at 2,521 metres, one way through Totoró (unpaved) and the other through Piendamó (paved) two beautiful routes. In Piendamó there is one, unnamed hotel, behind the former railway station (E, clean, quiet, but has seen better days).

Silvia lies in a high valley. (Hotels: *Hotel de Turismo*, C, expensive and not recommended. Next door is *Hotel Cali*, an old house, with good craft shop, E, including food, a little primitive, but very pleasant. *Pili*, F, on plaza, very clean, friendly, English spoken, helpful, recommended; *Silvia*, F, simple; *Ambeina*, F (3 beds per room), clean, friendly, efficient, recommended, good meals; *Residencias La Villa*, about 200 metres up main road past *Cali*, F, good meals. *La Parrilla*, F, water supply erratic, basic, restaurant is good. *Taberna El Buho*, friendly, with live music Sats. p.m.). Silvia is no longer an Indian town, but there is an interesting Indian market on Tues. mornings until 1300. Guambiano Indian farms can be reached by local bus: ask for the "paradero de los Guambianos". A typical Indian settlement, La Campana, is ½ hour on the bus; 1½ hours' walk downhill back to Silvia. The Indians wear their typical blue and fuchsia costumes, and are very friendly and communicative (Ettore Grugni and Martha Quintero). It is not safe to park cars in the street at night in Silvia, and guerrilla activity has been reported in the area. Horse hire from Sr. Marco A. Mosquiro, under US$1 per hour. On market days you can take a bus to Totoró (on the Popayán-Tierradentro road), departs 1200, US$0.50, and then a bus from Totoró to Tierradentro, US$1.25.

For those who like to go off the beaten track, Sr. Camilo Arroyo (address: Carrera 3, No. 4-65, Popayán) arranges trips towards the coast, W of Popayán, for birdwatching or gold-panning (his family has a *finca* on the coast). He charges about US$50 a day p.p., depending on the length of the trip, size of the party, etc. His trips into the mountains are reported as less interesting—obtain full details before embarking on one.

Road to Neiva (page 483) across the Central Cordillera, which is paved from Puerto Seco to Neiva, has interesting sights off it (best seen from left-hand side of the bus). Drive 37 km. along it (or take 0400 bus) to the small town of **Puracé**, which has several old buildings. *Residencias Cubito*, F, clean, cold showers, secure parking, no restaurant in the town but two stores will prepare meals on request. Drive to the Escuela and walk 5 mins. to see Chorrera de las Monjas waterfalls. About 11 km. E of Puracé towards Neiva a road branches S from the main road; 1 km. along this road is another fork at El Cruce de la Mina, the right branch leads to the Puracé sulphur mines (3,000 metres) 5 km. away; 1 km. along this road is a left fork to Pilimbalá, signed "Piscinas" (1½ km.) where are the Puracé National Park office, 5 warm sulphur baths in stone pools (which can be smelt a km. away), and a path leading to Puracé volcano. The Park is open all the week, but reduced service on Mondays. The volcano is steep; loose ash makes footholds difficult. It takes up to 5 hours to get to the top. Close to the main road (which continues to La Plata), and more easily reached from El Cruce de la Mina are Laguna San Rafael (10 km. from Pilimbilá), the Cascada de Bedón (15 km.), the Cueva de los Guácharos (26 km.), and the Termales de San Juan (17 km., but only 700 metres from the main road; cafeteria; entry US$0.10). 112 hot sulphur springs combine with icy mountain creeks to produce spectacular arrays of multi-coloured mosses, algae and lichens—a must if you are in the area. Buses on the Popayán-La Plata route go near Pilimbalá and will drop you near any of these places (fare from Popayán about US$1). The Tourist Office in Popayán will supply full information. The Park's fauna include the spectacled bear and mountain tapir. The only accommodation in the Park is at the thermal baths of Pilimbalá—cabins with up to six beds, D per cabin (warm blankets and wood for the fire provided—rooms for 2 in the cellar can be hired at F rates); power goes off at 2200, but candles are provided. Camping costs US$3 p.p. and there are an expensive, but good restaurant/bar and a picnic area.

Take warm clothes (and a sleeping bag) if climbing the volcano or visiting the baths; the nights are cold and blankets in the mountain cabins are thin. The weather is best, especially for climbing the volcano, in July and August. The highest point on the road is Quebrada Honda, at 3,340 metres above sea level.

Ute Lindner (of Freiburg) tells us that one may stay at a *finca* called Merenberg, 5 km. from Santa Leticia, on the road between Popayán and La Plata; the owners speak English and German. Take your own food (Santa Leticia is the only town in the mountains with shops); a good centre for walking.

Coconuco, at 2,734 metres, has beautiful landscapes. Turn to the right off the Popayán-Neiva road after 21 km. (16 km. short of Puracé); then 7 km. along is Coconuco (*Hotel de Turismo*; *Casa Familiar*, G, basic). There are good thermal baths near the village (camping US$1.50). Drive on 12 km. to the impressive scenery of the Paletará highland, where you can traverse vast areas of primeval forest; a bus to the village of Paletará takes 1 hour and costs US$0.40. Bus to Popayán, US$ 1, 1 hr. The direct road from Popayán to San Agustín (see page 484) through Coconuco was opened in March 1985.

The Tierradentro Archaeological Park can be reached from Popayán, or San Agustín via **La Plata** (20,000 people), 147 km. from Popayán, 210 km. from San Agustín. Direct bus service with Coomotor from La Plata to Bogotá, 10 hrs., at 0900 and 2100.

Hotels at La Plata *Berlin*, by church on square, near the bus office, F with bath, clean, friendly; *Residencias Tunubalá*, F, dirty, unfriendly, meals served, *Brooklyn*, clean, F, and *Norteño*, in the same price range; *Pensión Murucuju*, basic place to sleep and eat; *Residencias Nariño*, F; *Continental*, F (but prices rise at weekends), dinner good value. There is a café in the house where Bolívar stayed in 1829. *Patolandia*, good, cheap fruit juices. There is a cinema (2030).

From La Plata drive 35 km. NW to Guadualejo where one road goes N to Belalcázar (12 km.—a dusty drive). Another road continues NW to

Inzá (17 km.); hotels *Inzá* and *Ambalá*. Nine km. before Inzá is the Cruce de San Andrés, where a road turns off to **San Andrés de Pisimbalá** (4 km.), the village at the far end of the Tierradentro Park.

At San Andrés there is a unique and beautiful colonial church with a thatched roof; for the key ask behind the church. Some few km. before reaching San Andrés you pass the Tierradentro Museum, hours: 0700-1100 and 1200-1700, entrance US$0.40, camping is not allowed.

At San Andrés hire horses (US$2 an hr.)—or you can walk—for visiting the **Tierradentro** man-made burial caves painted with geometric patterns. There are four cave sites—Segovia, El Duende, Alto de San Andrés and El Aguacate. Guards at these sites no longer carry torches; essential to take your own. The surrounding scenery is splendid. It is very crowded at Easter-time.

For people on a one-day visit: go to Segovia, which has over 20 tombs, 5 of which are lit (these 5 are not opened until 0800-0900). Nos. 9, 10 and 12 are best decorated; Nos 8 and 28 are also impressive. The site is a 20 min. walk uphill from the administration building. El Duende (two of the four tombs are very good), is 15 mins. beyond Segovia. El Aguacate is a good, though hard, 2 hrs. hike one way and worth it, and one can return via El Alto de San Andrés (Nos. 1 and 5 tombs the best—the guard at El Alto is very helpful).

At El Tablón in the Parque there are 8 stone statues. There are several more in the new plaza at Inzá. A beautiful area for walking. From behind El Tablón, you can walk back to the museum via El Duende and Segovia in 2½ hrs. The surroundings have spectacular natural beauty; see small Indian villages in the mountains, e.g. Santa Rosa, 2 hours' hard walk beyond El Duende (get exact directions before setting out).

The Páez Indians in the Tierradentro region can be seen on market days at Inzá (Sat.), San Andrés (Wed.), and Belalcázar (Sat.); all start at 0600. The second floor of the museum at San Andrés is dedicated to their work: not to be missed. Take bus (US$0.50) from Tierradentro to Inzá market, on Sat. (buses leave from 0200); best to go into San Andrés and out again to be sure of getting a seat. On Saturdays there is plenty of transport going to and from Inzá on the Tierradentro road.

Hotels at Tierradentro A short way up from the museum, *Albergue de San Andrés*, E, good, but not cheap, meals (swimming pool also available to non-residents, US$0.80). Houses on either side of the Albergue offer accommodation, F, meals for US$1.50; 2 houses up from the museum, 2 rooms available, G; *Residencia Turista*, in the village, basic, clean, F p.p., insufficient bedding; house of Sra. Marta de Angel, F, friendly, meals US$1.20 excellent; between San Andrés and museum, *hospedaje* of Sra Poli Angel de Velasco, Carmelita's house (*Hospedaje Lucerna*) next to museum, clean and friendly, F, showers. Other cheap accommodation in village: *Residencias Murujuy*, F (breakfast, US$0.65, lunch and dinner, US$1); *Dormidero La Gaitana*, F, with shower, clean, owner also has a restaurant where all meals cost US$0.70. *Residencias Las Veraneras*, F p.p. 2 houses, 300 metres from Archaeological Park, rent rooms for US$2 p.p., clean, no hot water, food available if requested in advance. *El Gauchito* in San Andrés village, F, family atmosphere, recommended; camping.

Restaurants There is a restaurant, meals about US$1; good fruit juices at the *Fuente de Soda y Artesanía* store. Villagers provide meals—at a price. The house of Nelli Parra de Jovar, opposite the museum with the long antenna, is recommended for abundance but not cheapness; you must book meals in advance. She can also give up to date information on accommodation.

Transport The road from Popayán to Tierradentro is difficult and narrow, but this is compensated by the beautiful scenery. Sotracauca buses from Popayán cost US$3. Take 4 hr. bus to Cruce San Andrés. Walk (about 2 km.) from there to the museum. The village is another 20 mins. walk from the museum. Bus Cruce San Andrés-Popayán, 0800, 1000 and 1300. If you want to go to Silvia, take this bus and change to a colectivo (US$1) at Totoró. There are buses on market day, or trucks (US$1). Buses from Tierradentro to La Plata leave at 0900 and 1500 (unreliable) from the Cruce, US$1.50, 3 hrs.; if you cannot get a direct Cruce-La Plata bus, take one going to Belalcázar (US$1), alight at Guadualejo from where there is a more frequent service to La Plata; or one can hitch. On Fri. only, a bus leaves from San Andrés village for La Plata at 0400. Similarly, on Fri. only, a bus from La Plata to San Andrés goes at 1200, otherwise the only La Plata-Tierradentro bus leaves daily at 0500 for Inzá; alight at Cruce. Private jeep hire La Plata-Tierradentro, US$15 after bargaining. The road follows the spectacularly beautiful Páez valley.

From San Agustín, take Coomotor at 0600 to La Plata, 5 hrs., US$3.50. Many others a day with change at Pitalito. Next morning, take the 0430 bus from La Plata to Cruce de San Andrés, arrives

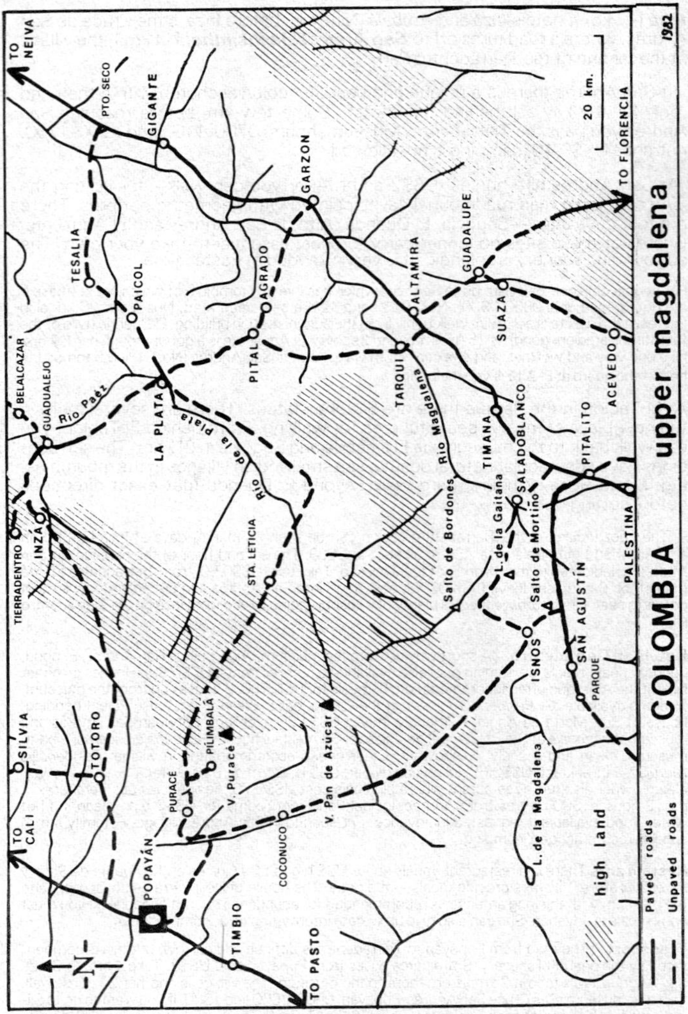
COLOMBIA upper magdalena
1982
20 km.
high land
Paved roads
Unpaved roads
N
TO NEIVA
TO CALI
TO PASTO
TO FLORENCIA
PTO. SECO
GIGANTE
GARZON
TESALIA
PAICOL
AGRADO
PITAL
ALTAMIRA
GUADALUPE
SUAZA
ACEVEDO
TARQUI
BELALCAZAR
GUADUALEJO
Rio Paéz
LA PLATA
Rio de la Plata
Rio Magdalena
TIMANA
SALADOBLANCO
PITALITO
PALESTINA
TIERRADENTRO
INZÁ
STA. LETICIA
Salto de Bordones
L. de la Gaitana
Salto de Mortiño
SAN AGUSTÍN
PARQUE
ISNOS
L. de la Magdalena
SILVIA
TOTORO
PILIMBALÁ
V. Puracé
PURACÉ
V. Pan de Azúcar
COCONUCO
POPAYÁN
TIMBIO

0800 (continues to Inzá and Popayán). Alternatively, on arrival in La Plata, take a pick-up to Guadualejo (US$1), then hitch, or try to get a bus going past Tierradentro (about 3 per day). Buses from La Plata to San Agustín at 0700, 0900 and 1500.

The Pan-American Highway continues S from Popayán to Pasto. The entire road is now paved. After El Bordo (*Residencias Confort*, on main road, F, simple but recommended) the road takes a new route and the 294-km. drive takes 4-5 hrs. The express bus takes 7 hrs. in ordinary conditions, though landslides often block the road. 93 km. S of Popayán is a tourist complex including hotel, swimming pool and campsite.

If one has time, the old route via La Unión and Mercaderes can be done by bus; enquire at Popayán or Pasto bus terminals. There are three basic hotels at La Unión (beware of overcharging at the *Hotel Nevada*). In El Bordo, the *Aquí Jaramillo* restaurant serves good Colombian dishes (US$3 per head).

163 km. S of Popayán is **Mercaderes**, a small town with a pleasant climate. Hotels (F) are good and the *Restaurante Tropical* is recommended. 30 km. before Pasto is Chachagui, where the *Hotel Imperio de los Incas* is recommended, E with bath, friendly, swimming pool, 2 km. from Pasto airport. Toll N of Pasto US$0.30.

Pasto, capital of the Department of Nariño, stands upon a high plateau (2,534 metres) in the SW, 88 km. from Ecuador, with a population of 300,000. The city, which has lost its colonial character, was founded in the early days of the conquest. Today it is a centre for the agricultural and cattle industries of the region, which exports little. Pasto varnish (*barniz*) is mixed locally, to embellish the strikingly colourful local wooden bowls. A visit to the church of Cristo Rey near the centre is recommended. Also La Merced, Calle 18, is worth seeing for its rich decoration and gold ornaments.

There are some gold mines in the area. The volcano, Galeras (4,069 metres), is to the W. The last eruption took place in 1934. A highway traversing all kinds of altitudes and climates has been built round it; the trip along it takes half a day. A rough road goes to the summit where there is an army post guarding a TV relay station; you can scramble down into the crater. A taxi will take you to about 200 metres from the top; there is a fine view and the soldiers are glad to see people. On it lies the village of **Sandoná** where Panama hats are made; they can be seen lying in the streets in the process of being finished. Sandoná market day is Saturday. (It is a worthwhile trip to Sandoná, 4 buses daily, the last back to Pasto is at 1700).

During the new year's *fiesta* there is a Día de los Negros on Jan. 5 and a Día de los Blancos next day. On "black day" people dump their hands in black grease and smear each other's faces. On "white day" they throw talc or flour at each other. Local people wear their oldest clothes. Things can get quite violent. On December 28 and Feb. 5, there is also a Fiesta de las Aguas when anything that moves—only tourists because locals know better—gets drenched with water from balconies and even from fire engines' hoses. In Pasto and Ipiales (see page 523), on December 31, is the Concurso de Años Viejos, when huge dolls are burnt; they represent the old year and sometimes lampoon local people. On Suns. a game of paddle ball is played on the edge of the town (bus marked San Lorenzo) similar to that played in Ibarra, Ecuador.

During the wars of independence, Pasto was a stronghold of the Royalists and the last town to fall into the hands of the patriots after a long and bitter struggle. Then the people of Nariño Department wanted to join Ecuador when that country split off from Gran Colombia in 1830, but were prevented by Colombian troops.

Hotels *Morasurco*, Avenida de los Estudiantes, B, recommended, reasonable res-taurant; *Agualongo*, Carrera 25, Calle 17, B; *Zorocán*, Calle 18, No. 22-33, C, bath, TV, a/c, indifferent restaurant; *San Diego*, Calle 16A, No. 23-27, E, with bath, reasonably priced but uncomfortable; *Sindagua*, Calle 20, No. 21B-16, D, recommended; *Cuellar's*, Carrera 23, No. 15-50, D, roomy, well-furnished, new, some noise from bowling centre underneath, but recommended; *Real*, Calle 18A, 20-20, F; *Winnipeg*, Carrera 19, 16-40, F; *Res. Santa Ana*, Carrera 25, 16-45, E with bath, F without, top floor rooms are quiet; *Residencias El Carmen*, near bus station, clean and comfortable, E; *Mayasquer*, Av. de las Américas, 16-66, E, with bath, clean, friendly, restaurant. *Res. El Dorado*, Calle 19, 19B-08, F, shared bath; *Residencias Texalia*, Calle 19, 21-50, F, both old and basic; *Residencias Colón*, Carrera 22, No. 19-61, F, clean, friendly, hot water; *Varcono*, on pedestrian mall linking Carreras 23 and 24, between Calles 16 and 17, E; *Mallorca*, Calle 18, 21a-45, F, pleasant, hot water a.m.; *Hotel Nueva York*, Carrera 19 bis, 18-20, F, clean rooms, dirty toilets, hot shower, friendly, near Magdalena bus company, the only place in the town where you can put

520 COLOMBIA

a motorcycle inside; *Londres*, Calle 19, No. 19-28, above a bakery, F, hot water; near bus station are *Líbano* (O.K., hot water), *Las Pensas* (quiet, no hot water), *Cartagena* (cheap, adequate), *Jordán*, and others, in F price range; *Manhattan*, Calle 18, 21B-14, F, clean, pleasant, hot water old-fashioned, big rooms; *Residencia Indi Chaya*, Calle 16, No. 18-23, Tel.: 4476, F, good value, clean, good beds, carpets, hot water, safe; *Residencias Isa*, clean, F, Calle 18, No. 23-49, good; *Residencias Monserrate*, Calle 19, 20-21, near bus station and market (hence extremely noisy), hot showers, F, not very safe, but does provide towels and soap; *Residencia Santa Isabel*, Calle 19, No. 20-39, F, clean, close to bus station. *Roma*, Calle 18A, No. 20-37; *Real*, Calle 18A, No. 20-20; *Magdalena*, Calle 19, No. 19B-09; *Viena*, calle, Carrera 19B, No. 18-36, all cheap and near bus station. *Pensión Pasto*, Calle 18, 20-22, G, ghastly, cheapest.

Restaurants *El Chalet Suizo*, Calle 20, 41-80 (Tel.: 4419), high class food; *Barú*, Calle 18 between Carreras 19 and 20, good and cheap; *Viena*, opposite *Hotel Nueva York*, good, cheap; *Parma*, on same street as *Residencia Santa Ana*, good, large meals; *Metropolitano*, Carrera 23, 16-76, good, cheap food; *La Cabaña*, next to *Hotel San Francisco*, pleasant, good meat dishes for US$3. *Pollorrico*, Carrera 25, 17-50, good. *Pollo Listo*, opp. *Agualonga Hotel*, cheap, good chicken dishes. *La Picantería*, Calle 19, cheap, good food; *Alberto's*, Calle 17, No. 27-26, friendly; *Bar Concorde*, Calle 17, Carreras 26 and 27, French and English music, pleasant. *El Encinar*, Calle 16, No. 13-48, US$0.80, good value, recommended. *El Superior*, Calle 18, next to bus station. A cheap but good place to eat is the self-service cafeteria at the Amorel shopping centre. Most restaurants on main street are OK. In the nearby village of Catambuco (15 mins. drive), the restaurant *Catambuey* is recommended if you like guinea pig.

Shopping Artesanías de Colombia have a branch on Carrera 25. Casa del Barniz de Pasto, Calle 13, No. 24-9, Artesanías Nariño, Calle 26, No. 18-91; Artesanías Mopa-Mopa, Carrera 25, No. 13-14, for *barniz*. See Colegio Artesanías, run by a government institute (Sena), 5 km. N on road to Popayán. Visitors welcome. Leather goods are cheaper here than in Bogotá, Ecuador or Peru. Most of the shops are on Calles 17 and 18. Also try the municipal market for handicrafts. Supermercado Confamiliar de Nariño, Calle 16b, No. 30-53, recommended, and, more convenient, Ley on Calle 18, next to Avianca postal office.

Cinema Carrera 25 and Calles 17 and 18, good.

Banks For changing travellers' cheques, Banco de la República on the main square. Banco Anglo Colombiano, Calle 17, No. 21-32, and at Amorel, and other national banks. Open Mon.-Thur., 0800-1130, 1400-1600; Fri., 0900-1130, 1400-1630; closed Sat. Last working day of month, 0800-1100. This is the last place before crossing to Ecuador, or going to Tumaco, where travellers' cheques can be cashed. A *cambio* off the main square will change sucres into pesos, but the Banco de la República will not, though it does change Amex cheques without charging commission. An optician on the main square changes sucres into pesos.

Airmail Carrera 23, 18-42 and Calle 18, 25-86.

Ecuadorean Consulate Calle 17, No. 26-55, 2nd floor. Four photos needed if you require a visa.

Tourist Office Just off the main square, Calle 18, No. 25-25, friendly and helpful. It will advise on money changing. Maps of Colombia and cities from Instituto Geográfico Agustín Codazzi, Calle 18, No. 23-36, 1st floor (Banco del Occidente building).

Buses Most buses leave from Calle 18. To Bogotá, 23 hrs., US$19.50 (Bolivariano Pullman). To Ipiales, 2 hrs., US$2.45, Cooperative Supertaxis del Sur. To Popayán, ordinary buses take 10-12 hrs.; expresses take 5-8 hrs., cost US$5. To Cali, US$9, expresses, 8½-10 hrs. To Tumaco, 11 hrs. by bus, 10 hrs. by minibus, US$6.50. To Puerto Asis, 11 hrs., US$4.75 with Trans Ipiales or Bolivariano (both Calle 18), 0500 and 1100.

Air Services Daily to Popayán, 20 mins., and Bogotá; to Cali with Avianca at 0800, and to Ipiales by Avianca on Fri. Aerotal, Pasto to Cali, daily at 0800; to Medellín. The airport is at Cano, 40 km. from Pasto; by colectivo (beautiful drive), 45 mins. US$1.75 or US$8.35 by taxi. There are no currency exchange facilities, but the shop will change US$ bills at a poor rate.

Tumaco Region

The 250-km. road W from Pasto to Tumaco is paved for 20 km. beyond Túquerres, but is then unsurfaced. The region is very different from highland Colombia, with two-storey Caribbean-style wooden houses and a predominantly black population. Small farms are mixed with cattle ranches, rice farms and oil-palm plantations. Cocoa is grown. The coastal area around Tumaco is mangrove swamp, with many rivers and inlets on which lie hundreds of villages and settlements; negotiate with boatmen for a visit to the swamps or the beautiful, newly-developed island tourist resort of **Boca Grande** (US$7.50 minimum, the trip takes 30 mins.; ask for Señor Felipe Bustamante, Calle Comercio, Apto. 224, Tel.: 465, who rents canoes and cabins, has a good seafood restaurant and owns *Hotel Los Manglares* on the island; water and electricity supplies are irregular on the island).

Tumaco has a population of about 100,000; the unemployment rate is very high, the living conditions are poor, and the services and roads in the town are not good. It is in one of the world's rainiest areas; the yearly average temperature is in the 25°-35°C range. The movement of the tides governs most of the activities in the area, especially transport. A natural arch on the main beach, N of the town and port, is reputed to be the hiding place of Henry Morgan's treasure. Swimming is not recommended from the town's beaches, which are polluted; stalls provide refreshment on the beach. Swimming is safe, however, at El Morro beach, north of the town, only on the incoming tide (the outgoing tide uncovers poisonous rays). Hotels are well subscribed and of varying quality - it is advisable to get a bed early in the day. The northern part of the town is built on stilts out over the sea. Visit it during the daylight as it is reported to be dangerous at night, and not just because you could fall through the holes in the wooden pavements into the sea. There is an airport, and the area is also noted archaeologically for the finds associated with the Tumaco culture. The town has problems with water and electricity supplies. There is one cinema. There are no money exchange facilities (except in some shops that will buy dollars and sucres at a poor rate; change money in Cali or Pasto). (We are most grateful to Monique van't Hek, of Amsterdam, for updating information on Tumaco.)

Hotels *Villa del Mar*, D, Calle Sucre, modern, clean, with shower, toilet and fan, no hot water, good café below; *Claudia*, Calle Mosquera, E, with restaurant; *Calamares*, E, not good; *Ipiales*, fair; *Residencias Don Pepe*, near water-front and *canoa* dock, friendly but basic. Children meet arriving buses to offer accommodation; most cheap places are in Calle Comercial, many houses and restaurants without signs take guests—nearly all have mosquito nets. Try opp. Trans Ipiales, under Cootranor sign, or 2 doors from Trans Ipiales (Barbería Nueva), both F. **Food:** The main culinary attractions of the town are the fish dishes, in the market and restaurants, fresh from the Pacific. A number of good restaurants on the main streets (Calles Mosquera and Comercial): *La Tropicana*, *La Tortula*, *La Brasa*. **N.B.** Be very careful of food and water because there are many parasites.

Transport Tumaco to Pasto, 11 hrs. (10 hrs. by minibus), US$6.50, with Supertaxis del Sur or Trans Ipiales (better), 4 a day, very rough but interesting ride. An alternative is to catch a bus from Ipiales to Espino (US$0.60, colectivo, US$0.90) and there change buses for Tumaco (US$4, 7½ hrs., rough ride). There are no hotels in Espino. There are daily flights to and from Cali with Aces (US$40 one way) and on Wed., Fri. and Sun. with Satena (US$35), 1 hr. Flights also to Pasto.

To Ecuador It is possible to travel to Ecuador by water, but only by motorized canoe. Part of the trip is by river, which is very beautiful, and part on the open sea, which can be very rough; a plastic sheet to cover your belongings is essential. Daily service at 0800 to San Lorenzo, 7 hrs. US$6.50, Coop. de Transportes, tickets from Calle Comercial (protective plastic sheeting provided). Señor Pepello, who lives in the centre of Tumaco, owns two canoes: he leaves on Wed. and Sat. at 0700 for San Lorenzo and Limones in Ecuador—book in advance. Also enquire for Señor Lucho, or ask around the water-front at 0600. DAS stamp for leaving Colombia and visa for Ecuador (if required) should be obtained in Cali or Pasto (although there is a DAS office in Tumaco, Calle Sucre, No. 6-13); offices are open on weekdays only. Entry stamps for Ecuador must be obtained in the coastal towns.

Barbacoas, 57 km. from Junín, is interesting—a former Spanish gold-producing centre which still retains the remains of an extensive water-front, a promenade and steps coming down through the town to the river. Gold is still panned from the rivers by part-time prospector-farmers. *Hotel Telembi*, F, basic, friendly; *Residencial*, F, poor, unfriendly. Restaurant *Telembi* on the river front, good food. Problems with water and electricity supplies. River trips on the supply boats are possible, about US$6.75 for 8 hrs. Bus to Pasto, US$6, rough trip. The road to Barbacoas is limited to one-way traffic in places—enquire at the chain barring the road at Junín and the operator will telephone down the line to see if the route is clear for you to pass.

The *Putumayo*

One hour E of Pasto, on the road to Mocoa (capital of the Intendencia of Putumayo) is **Laguna La Cocha,** the largest lake in S Colombia (sometimes called

COLOMBIA

Lago Guámez). By the lake is the Swiss-run *Chalet Guámez*, D, well recommended, particularly for the cuisine, cabins sleeping up to five can be hired, US$21 for two. Rafael Narváez has cheap, basic rooms to let. The chalet will arrange a US$22 jeep trip to Sibundoy, further along the road. Boats may be hired for US$2.20 per hour. La Cocha may be reached by taking a bus to El Encano and walking the remaining 5 km. Or walk 20 mins. from the bus stop to the fishing village of El Encano, where you can enjoy trout at very low prices at one of the many small restaurants, and from here take a *lancha* to the chalet for US$2-3. There is also a new government hotel nearby called *Sindamanoy*, but we have no information yet about it. Taxi from Pasto, US$11.

The road from Pasto to the Putumayo deteriorates rapidly after El Encano. It is dangerous between Sibundoy and El Pepino and care should be taken, but there is a magnificent view out over the Putumayo by a large statue of the Virgin, just before the final descent.

Sibundoy There is a beautiful church on the main plaza, completed in 1968. About a quarter of the valley is now reserved for Sibundoy Indian occupation. Craft goods and fashionable striped *manas* are for sale; market Sunday. Marcelino Chindoy, Carrera 18, 18-66, should be visited for woven and carved goods. He travels a lot around Colombia and you can normally find him at handicrafts fairs in Bogota. He has newspaper clippings supporting his claim to be the "original" and the best. Also for woven goods, Don Manuel, Carrera 18, 16-44. Roasted guinea-pig (*cuy*) may be eaten in the restaurant here. Bus from Pasto (3 hrs., US$2.25), passing through Colón (*residencias*) and Santiago. *Hotel Turista*, F, clean; *Oriente*, F, pleasant, with restaurant, best value in town; better meals at *Hotel Sibundoy*, also F; *Residencias San Francisco* and *Colón*. Restaurant *Viajero*, just off main street. You can camp in the hills, where there are lovely walks and you can see all kinds of flora and fauna.

Mocoa, the administrative capital of the Intendencia of Putumayo, is small (21,000 people), with a number of hotels (*Viajero*, D) and *residencias*. The town has a very modern square, new offices and modern developments. Sugar-cane is grown in the area. The road (buses) to Puerto Asís is good, passing through an area cleared mainly in the last 15 years and supporting cattle ranching. 12 hrs. by bus to Pasto. Bus from Sibundoy, US$2, 5 a day, continuing to Puerto Asís; very uncomfortable, police checks.

Puerto Asís is the main town and port of the Putumayo. River traffic is busy. All boats that leave for Leticia (with connections to Manaus) are cargo boats, and only sail when they have cargo. Those carrying gasoline (and most do) are forbidden to take passengers. Only one company, Navenal, normally take passengers, and it can be weeks between their sailings. One can also try the army for a passage. Fares are about US$100; at least 8-10 days; it is best to see the Jefe de la Marina, or the Oficina de Transporte Fluvial, about a passage. Another possibility is to take a *canoa* to Leguizamo (see below), and try for a passage there. By boat to Leguizamo takes 2-3 days, US$4.50, food US$2.50 per day. For those interested in flora and fauna it is necessary to travel down river, beyond new areas of settlement. Boats will not go unless the rivers are high; sometimes, they get stuck halfway.

There are regular flights to and from Puerto Asís three times a week by Satena to Bogotá, via Florencia. Flights to Florencia are on Mon., Wed. and Fri. at 1000 with Sarpa, who also fly to Leguizamo. Occasional flights to Leticia.

Hotels *Residencias Nevado*, Carrera 20, close to the airport, well kept and comfortable, air-conditioning optional, F, without board. *Residencias Liz*, Calle 11, F, with bath, very friendly; *Res. San Martín*, Carrera 20, F, beds clean, rooms not so, poor value; *Residencias Patiño*, G, recommended; *Meri*, F, with fan; *Residencias Gigante*, Calle 10, 24-25, F, clean. There are plenty of cheap hotels in the port, but it is hard to find a room late in the day.

Buses may be taken to Pasto (a 10 hr. journey, at 0500, 0600 and 0900 daily, mostly on mountainous roads, US$4.50, be prepared for military checks). Bus Sibundoy-Puerto Asís, US$3.25. Local bus to San Miguel near the Ecuadorean border where the Sun. market provides a meeting place, and where *canoas* may be hired to visit villages 2-4 hrs. away on the river.

San Miguel Accommodation is very limited: *Residencias Olga* is the only place available and has only 6 single rooms. Accommodation beyond San Miguel is non-existent, except in Orita, W of Puerto Asís, a small town on the oilfield.

Leguizamo, upstream from Puerto Asís, can also be reached by air from Florencia, with Satena, daily, flight originates in Neiva. There are boats to Leticia and to Peru, but transport on all boats carrying gasoline is forbidden. For information go to Naval at the port, Transporte Fluvial Estrella del Sur (Carrera 27, off Calle 10) or Transporte Fluvial Amazonas (Carrera 20, 14-59—English spoken). Hotels: *Leguizamo* and *Putumayo*, both G, basic. Further upstream are El Encanto and the nearby village of **San Rafael,** which is a good place to see the Huitoto Indians, the most important of the many tribes which live along the Putumayo river. At San Rafael there is a mission at which it is possible to stay.

We are informed that travellers interested in Amazonian plants, birds and animals will find Putumayo more accessible, with more abundant wild life, than Leticia. Restaurant food in the Putumayo region is often uninspiring; take some canned goods for variety. There is a road of a sort from Mocoa to Puerto Limón, on the Río Caquetá (see Caquetá section, page 486).

South to Ecuador

Passing through deep valleys and a spectacular gorge, buses on the paved Pan-American Highway cover the 84 km. from Pasto to Ipiales in 1½ -2 hours. (Toll US$0.40). The road crosses the spectacular gorge of the Guaitara River near El Pedregal, 40 km. from Pasto. A detour via Túquerres (later unpaved) and its plain takes over an hour more; it reaches 3,050 metres at Túquerres, dropping to 2,440 at Guachucal, and rising again to 2,740 metres at **Ipiales,** "the city of the three volcanoes", with about 30,000 people; not a very attractive town but famous for its colourful Sat. morning Indian market.

The Catedral Bodas de Plata is worth visiting, and so is the near-by Sanctuary of the Virgin of Las Lajas. San Luis airport is 6½ km. out of town.

On days set apart for religion, dazzlingly clean Indians come down from the hills in their traditional bright colours. Seen from afar the Sanctuary is a magnificent architectural conception, set on a bridge over the canyon: close to, it is very heavily ornamented. There are great pilgrimages to it from Colombia and Ecuador and the Sanctuary must be second only to Lourdes in the number of miracles claimed for it. The Church recognizes one only. Colectivo from Carrera 6 y Calle 4, Ipiales, US$0.25 p.p., taxi, US$5 return (it's about a 1½-hour walk, 7 km.); 3 basic hotels and a small number of restaurants at Las Lajas.

Hotels *Mayasquer*, 3 km. on road to frontier, D, very good, swings for children, discothèque; *Pasviveros*, bright and clean, E, with bath and hot water; *Alcalá*, D, TV, radio, private bath; *Central*, Carrera 6a, 14-48, E, pleasant, clean; *Las Lajas*, E, hot water in the morning, good restaurant; *Zaracay* (opposite *Internacional*), E, quiet; *Buchue*, F, clean, comfortable, very good; *New York*, near main square, G, run down, friendly; *Bahamas*, F, just off main square, hot water; *Colombia*, Calle 13, No. 7-50, F, hot water, quite clean; opp. at No. 7-59 is *Valparaíso*, F, hot water; *Residencia Italiana* (F, hot water); *Kurawasy*, F, not bad; *Residencias El Dorado*, F; *Residencias Horizonte*, F, friendly, no hot water; *Oasis*, G, hot shower, clean; *Rumichaca Internacional*, E, clean and comfortable with good basic restaurant; *Pensión Bolívar*, G; *Residencias La Cabaña*, F, basic; *Residencias Victoria*, good; *Residencial Belmonte (Hotel B)*, Carrera 4, No. 12-111 (near Expreso Bolivariano), F, very clean, hot water, highly recommended; *Residencia Miramar*, Calle de Atrás 12A-89, G; *Residencia Miami*, on main plaza, F; *Residencia Tequendama*, Carrera 5, No. 14-08, F, family atmosphere, very basic; *San Andrés*, Carrera 5, No. 14-75, F, clean, hot water; same street, No. 14-25, *Residencias Santa Fe*, F; *Hotel Los Andes* refuses to take backpackers. Young travellers can expect to be questioned and searched by police soon after checking in to a hotel.

Camping Possible above the bus parking lot, or free behind last Esso station outside town on road north.

Restaurants *Himalaya*, on the main square, for a three-course meal for US$2.50 average; *Valparaíso*, very good value; *Vitapán*, comparatively clean; *Don Lucho*, Carrera 5, No. 14-13 (*antioqueño*); *Munich*, Calle 10, good; *Bar D'Albert*, small, quiet, on main road from Bolivariano bus station into centre; *Greenhouse*, Carrera 6, No. 16-73, good, reasonable prices. Plenty of cheap restaurants. Meals in Almacenes Ley cost US$1. Many good bakeries on Carrera 6.

Cinemas 2 on Calle Principal on road to Las Lajas.

Currency It is possible to cash travellers' cheques only at the Banco de la República, a few blocks from the main square (closed 1100-1400); you will have to show two different pieces of identification and may have to recite passport number from memory. Casa de Cambio at Carrera 6, No. 14-09. There are money changers in the street, but better rates are to be had in Quito. There is an agency of Banco Anglo Colombiano, Carrera 6, 3 blocks from main square.

Frontier Ipiales is 2 km. from the Rumichaca bridge across the Carchi river into Ecuador. The frontier post stands beside a natural bridge, on a new, concrete bridge, where the customs and passport examination takes place from

0800 to 1800 (closed at lunchtime). (It is possible to bathe in the hot springs under the bridge, US$0.10.)

You obtain your Colombian exit stamp from the DAS at the frontier post. You have to get your entry stamp and tourist card for Ecuador at the frontier; if the border office is closed, you must go to the police station just before Tulcán. This applies at weekends, closed 1200-1400; taxis on the fast road to the border do not pass the police station. Ecuadorean officials do not usually give more than 30 days for visiting the country, but extensions are easy to obtain, from Amazonas 2639, Quito and the Migración offices in provincial capitals. Motorists have their *carnets* stamped at the border (very efficient). You may be required by Ecuadorean customs to show that you have enough money for your stay in the country. Colombian customs have the same requirement; US$20 a day is necessary (US$10 for students), though you are not always required to show that you have this amount. Entering Colombia, tourist cards are issued at the frontier. If entering Colombia by car, the vehicle must be fumigated against diseases that affect coffee trees. This is done at the ICA office at the border; the certificate must be presented in El Pedregal, a village 40 km. beyond Ipiales on the road to Pasto. There is a duty-free shop about ½ km. from the border. There are frequent police checks on the buses going to Popayán and neighbouring areas.

Transport From Ipiales to Tulcán: seat in car (waits till all seats are full), US$0.30, to the frontier, and same again from there to Tulcán; bus US$0.30 to Tulcán, US$0.20 to the frontier. Colectivo from frontier to Tulcán will charge extra (US$0.60) to go to the bus terminal. Taxi to border, US$1.50 after bargaining; from border to Tulcán, US$1.75. From Tulcán's modern bus terminal buses go to Quito throughout the day; a beautiful five-hour Andean trip.

Bus to Popayán, Expreso Bolivariano, US$7.50, 7½ hrs., 2-hourly departures, 0430-2030; Transportes de Ipiales, US$7, Super Taxis and Cootranar *busetas*, US$6, beautiful trip. Bus to Cali, US$9, 11-12 hrs. To Pasto with minibus from main square, US$2.45 (frequent police checks); Flota Bolivariano buses every hr., US$1.50. Buses to Bogotá leave every other hour between 0500 and 0830.

TAME (of Ecuador) has flights to Quito from Tulcán.

The Economy

Agriculture is the most important sector of the economy, contributing about 22% of gdp and employing 34% of the labour force. It is also the largest earner of foreign exchange, with over 57% of total legal exports. The traditional crops are coffee, sugar cane, bananas, rice, maize and cotton. Colombia is the leading producer of mild Arabica coffee and second to Brazil in world production. Output has declined since 1984 as the Government has tried to diversify into other crops, but coffee remains the dominant export item with 50% of total revenues.

Manufacturing contributes almost as much to gdp as agriculture, with agricultural-related activities such as food processing, drink and tobacco accounting for 35% of the sector's value added. Textiles and clothing are also important, and provide an outlet for home-grown cotton. Heavy corporate indebtedness in the first half of the 1980s affected the growth of manufacturing and led to a decline in employment to only 15% of the total labour force. This was expected to improve in the second half of the decade, however, with strong growth being shown by chemicals, textiles and clothing, transport equipment, cement, metalworking and paper.

Although contributing only 2% of gdp, mining, mainly oil and coal, was the most dynamic sector of the economy in the mid-1980s, with growth rates of over 20% a year. With the exception of a few major projects, mining is concentrated in the hands of small scale producers with little technology or organization. Much of their output remains outside the formal economy. Colombia is, however, the largest producer of gold and platinum in Latin America, and these two metals, together with emeralds, have traditionally dominated the mining sector. Mining of precious metals, including silver, is primarily in the Departments of Antioquia and El Chocó; huge gold deposits have also been discovered on the borders of the Departments of Cauca and Valle, while others have been found in the Guainía, Vaupés and Guaviare regions near the Brazilian border. In 1984, Colombia became self-sufficient in energy. Rising production of hydrocarbons moved the oil trade into surplus for the first time in ten years. Development of energy sources has been given high priority to satisfy domestic requirements and to diversify exports. Most of the oil production comes from the Magdalena basin, but these are older fields which are running down. The discovery of the Caño Limón field near Arauca has raised output to around 365,000 barrels a day. As well as oil and gas, Colombia has the largest coal reserves in Latin America, which partial surveys have put at 16.5 bn tonnes. The largest deposits are in the Cerrejón region, where a huge project has been set up to mine and export steam coal from a new port at Bahía de Portete. Hydroelectricity now accounts for 70% of installed generating capacity. It has an advantage over thermal power because 75% of the nation's hydroelectric potential is in the central zone, where 80% of the population live. Total potential is said to be 100,000 MW, of which only about 5% is harnessed.

Current account surpluses in the late 1970s during the coffee price boom were turned into large deficits in the first half of the 1980s, reaching over US$3bn in 1982 and 1983, because of lower export receipts and rapidly rising imports. However, Colombia was able to avoid having to reschedule its foreign debts, and took steps to adjust its external accounts. The devaluation of the peso was speeded up, reinforced by import restrictions and export incentives, until in 1986 a current account surplus was recorded. The fiscal accounts were also turned around and the public sector deficit was reduced from 7.5% of gdp in 1984 to 2.0% in 1986. The World Bank and the IMF endorsed the Colombian economic strategy and commercial banks continued to lend to the country with a US$1bn jumbo loan agreed in 1985.

	1961-70 (av)	1971-80 (av)	1981-85 (av)	1986 (e)
Gdp growth (1980 prices)	5.5%	5.5%	2.1%	5.0%
Inflation	11.2%	21.1%	22.3%	20.9%
Exports (fob) US$m	575	2,162	3,446	5,638
Coffee	350	1,162	1,631	3,107
Fuel oil	9	94	307	530
Imports (fob) US$m	575	1,910	4,443	3,800
Current account balance US$m (cum)	1,619	-195	-10,809	529

Information for Visitors

Travel by Air British Airways has a weekly service from London to Bogotá, via Caracas. Airlines with services from continental Europe are Air France, Viasa, Iberia, and Lufthansa. Avianca, the Colombian national airline, flies from Frankfurt via Paris and Madrid.

Frequent services to and from the U.S. by Avianca and Eastern. Varig and Avianca fly from Bogotá to the U.S. West Coast. The cheapest flight from Miami to Bogotá is via Panama with a couple of hours' stopover with Air Panama. Another cheap route is Miami-San Andrés, then take a domestic flight to your Colombian destination. Other flights from Miami: to Bogotá, Cali and Barranquilla with Eastern; to Barranquilla with Aeroperú; Avianca to Medellín, Cali, and San Andrés. Aerotal also fly to Miami. Lacsa flies to Barranquilla from Mexico City, and from San José to San Andrés and Cartagena. To Mexico City with Aeroméxico from Bogotá, from Barranquilla with Lacsa. Sahsa flies to San Andrés from Honduras, 4 times a week, and from Guatemala, Costa Rica and Belize. SAM flies to San José, 3 times a week; to San Salvador, Thurs. and Sun.; to Guatemala (calling at Cartagena and San Andrés), Thurs. and Sun.; also Barranquilla and San Andrés to San José, San Salvador and Guatemala. Fares to Central America may be cheaper with a change in San Andrés, rather than direct.

From Neighbouring Republics Avianca, Pan-American Airways, SAM and Eastern connect Colombia with republics to N and S. Turismo Aero flies from Panama to Colombia. Bogotá-Panamá, via Medellín—do not be persuaded by SAM desk at Panama airport to buy an onward ticket out of Colombia—this may not be needed—if you fail, SAM in Bogotá will give refunds: first you must go to the DAS, Extranjería section, show your passport and ticket and obtain a permit for a refund; then go to the SAM office. Panama-Cali; Panama-Cartagena. Medellín-Panama with Copa: one may not enter, or obtain a visa for, Panama without a return or onward ticket, so you must buy a return ticket and then sell half in Panama once you have purchased a flight ticket out of Panama. Panama to Cali with Eastern. Motorcycles may be taken as luggage with Aerolíneas Medellín or Copa; remove oil, petrol, battery and anything breakable. Insist on supervising loading and unloading. Medellín customs take more than a day and you have to go from the airport to the *aduana interior*, in town; six copies of relevant papers have to be completed and delays can be experienced in getting hold of your property at Medellín. Officials, however, are helpful and friendly, despite the bureaucratic nightmare. The cheapest way to fly to Quito is to fly to Ipiales (Aeropesca from Bogotá), cross the border by road and take another 'plane at Tulcán. Avianca, Lufthansa, Air France and Ecuatoriana go S from Colombia.

For a cheap means of flying from Venezuela to Colombia, see page 501.

For travel overland from Panama, see note at end of Panama section.

N.B. There is an airport exit tax of US$15, from which only travellers staying less than 24 hours are exempt. When you arrive, ensure that the entry stamp is put in both your passport and the tourist card; if your card is not stamped you will have to pay US$30 on leaving. Visitors staying more than 30 days have to pay an extra US$15 tax, which can only be avoided by bona-fide tourists who can produce the card given them on entry. There is a 15% tax on all international air tickets bought in Colombia for flights out of the country (3% on international return flights). Unfortunately it is no longer possible to avoid the purchase tax by buying tickets outside the country, as the charge is included automatically. Do not buy tickets for domestic flights to or from San Andrés island outside Colombia; they are much more expensive. When getting an onward ticket from Avianca for entry into Colombia, reserve a seat only and ask for confirmation in writing, otherwise you will pay twice as much than if purchasing the ticket inside Colombia.

Internal Air Services are flown by Avianca, SAM and 15 smaller companies. Avianca offers a round ticket (*Conozca a Colombia*) giving unlimited domestic travel for 30 days; conditions are that it allows up to ten stops, it must be bought outside Colombia, one may not pass through each city more than once, and a proposed itinerary (not firm) must be submitted when buying the ticket. There are two prices: US$325 if your 10 stops include San Andrés and Leticia; US$224 if they don't. For single flights, however, the army airline Satena, tends to be cheaper than Avianca. Avianca's domestic shuttle flights (Puente Aéreo) go from Bogotá to Medellín/Montería, Cali/Pasto and Barranquilla; for example to Medellín every ½ hour between 0730-1630. But it is best to book a ticket as for an ordinary flight: just turning up will involve a long wait. Stand-by tickets are available to Barranquilla, Cali, Medellín; known as PET, *pasajero en turno*. Domestic airports are good, but in-flight service and airline services on the ground tend to be poor. There is an airport tax of US$2.25.

Travel (in General) If driving yourself, avoid night journeys; the roads are often in poor condition, lorry-and bus-drivers tend to be reckless, and stray animals are often encountered. Hitch-hiking (*autostop*) seems to be quite easy in Colombia, especially if you can enlist the co-operation of the highway police checkpoints outside each town. Truck-drivers are often very friendly, but be careful of private cars with more than one person inside, especially if you are travelling on your own; they may be unmarked taxis.

Buses Travel in Colombia is far from dull. The buses are generally fairly comfortable. The luggage compartment is normally locked, but it is wise to keep an eye on your bags. Breakdowns are many. In all parts, police checks on buses are frequent. Note that meal stops can be few and far between, and short; bring your own food. Be prepared for climatic changes on longer routes. A full colectivo, such as a "Taxi Verde", costs only twice as much per person as a bus seat. The excellent minibus (*buseta*) services of Velotax have been recommended. If you entrust your luggage to the bus companies' luggage rooms, remember to load it on to the bus yourself; it will not be done automatically. There are few interdepartmental bus services on holidays.

Taxis Whenever possible, take a taxi with a meter, and ensure that it is switched on, otherwise you will be overcharged. All taxis are obliged to display the additional legal tariffs that may be charged after 2000, on Sundays and fiestas. If a taxi has a meter, do not haggle the price; if it does not

COLOMBIA 527

(and most taxis on the N coast do not), fix a price beforehand. Don't take a taxi which is old; look for "Servicio Público" on the side. Women do not travel alone in taxis at night. If the taxi "breaks down", take your luggage out if you are asked to push, or let the driver push; it may be a trick to separate you from your luggage.

Motoring Roads are given in the text. Motor fuel: "premium" 95 octane (only in large cities), US$1.10 per US gallon; "corriente" 84 octane, US$1 per US gallon. Roads are not always signposted. If you are planning to sleep in your car, it is better to stop in a parking lot (*parqueadero*); you will be charged a little extra, but the lots are guarded. In many guarded carparks, only the driver is allowed in; passengers must get out at the entrance.

National driving licences may be used by foreigners in Colombia, but must be accompanied by an official translation if in a language other than Spanish. Carry driving documents with you at all times.

Walkers are advised to get *Backpacking in Venezuela, Colombia and Ecuador*, by Hilary and George Bradt, who consider that Colombia offers some of the best hiking in South America. They describe 3-8 day treks in the Sierra Nevada de Santa Marta, Sierra Nevada del Cocuy, Sierra Nevada de Huila, and the hike from San Agustín to Popayán.

Documents A passport and (according to the Colombian Consulate in London) an onward ticket is always necessary. According to Decree 3106 of November 9, 1983, nationals of the following countries do not need visas: Argentina, Austria, Barbados, Belgium, Chile, Costa Rica, Denmark, El Salvador, West Germany, Finland, Holland, Ireland, Israel, Italy, Japan, Liechtenstein, Luxemburg, Norway, South Korea, Spain, Sweden, Switzerland, Trinidad and Tobago, UK, Uruguay. All other countries need visas for which taxes are payable as follows: US$5, France, Paraguay, Haiti, Jamaica, Dominican Republic, Kenya, Guyana; US$10, East Germany, Bulgaria, China, Ivory Coast, Egypt, Hungary, Iran, Nicaragua, Portugal, USSR; US$15, Poland; US$20, all other countries. Normal validity is 90 days; extensions for a further month can be obtained in Bogotá. A visa (US$20) is required by U.S. citizens, who must show 2 photographs, an onward or return ticket, as well as a passport (allow 24 hours). Alternatively, in the USA only, Avianca issues tourist cards (transit visas), valid for 15 days, costing US$10—these cards are renewable only by leaving the country. In Miami insist at the Consulate, as they will assume that you can work it all out through the airline. If you do not receive an entry card when flying in, the information desk will issue one, and restamp your passport for free. Visitors are sometimes asked to prove that they have US$20 for each day of their stay (US$10 for students). Note that to leave Colombia you must normally get an exit stamp from the DAS (security police). They often do not have offices at the small frontier towns, so try to get your stamp in a main city, and save time. However, you may find that your onward ticket, which you must show before you can obtain a visa, is stamped "non-refundable". The DAS does not give any "certificado" for cancelling onward tickets; insist on cancelling them without it.

N.B. It is highly recommended that you have your passport photocopied, and witnessed by a notary (about US$0.20). This is a valid substitute, and your passport can then be put into safekeeping. Also, photocopy your travellers' cheques and any other essential documents. For more information, check with DAS or your consulate.

Duty-free admission is granted for portable typewriters, radios, binoculars, personal and cine cameras, but all must show use; 200 cigarettes or 50 cigars or 250 grams of tobacco or up to 250 grams of manufactured tobacco in any form, 3 litres of alcoholic beverages per person.

Tourist Information The Corporación Nacional de Turismo (CNT), with its headquarters at Bogotá, has branches in every departmental capital and other places of interest. They should be visited as early as possible not only for information on accommodation and transport, but also for details on areas which are dangerous to visit. The Coordinadora de Turismo de Bogotá (Carrera 13, No. 27-95) has daily tours of the city with interpreters. The Automobile Club in Bogotá has offices on Avenida Caracas, No. 46-64 (Tel.: 2451534 and 2452684). Branches are at Manizales, Medellín, Cali, Barranquilla and Cartagena. It supplies Esso, Texaco and Mobil maps: good, but not quite up-to-date; a full set of Hojas de Ruta costs US$2.50. The Texaco map has plans of the major cities. Even the Shell series lacks detail. Maps of Colombia are obtainable at the Instituto Geográfico Militar, next to the University in Bogotá. A good road map is obtainable from Instituto Geográfico Agustín Codazzi, Carrera 30, No. 48-51, open 0800-1530, Bogotá, or from their office in Pasto. Drivers' route maps are available from the CNT. Buchholz and Central bookshops have a few country and Bogotá maps.

Warnings Though the majority of Colombians are honest and friendly, visitors should be warned that Colombia is very well known for pickpockets and thieves. However, this reputation has been exaggerated to the point where Colombia is regarded as far worse than other Latin American countries. This is not so: it used to be, but other countries, particularly Brazil and Peru, are getting worse and Colombia, with the help of better policing, is tending to improve. In large cities, especially, watch your pockets, handbag, camera, watch and luggage

528 COLOMBIA

closely and it is better not to wear a watch, eyeglasses or jewellery. Bags should be worn across the shoulder if possible. Documents and high-value notes should be pinned to inside pocket, or carried in special pouch tied under shirt, or round waist under skirt, or kept in trouser pocket inside waistband. It is socially acceptable for women to keep banknotes in their bras. Observe how locals carry their belongings and follow suit. When travelling by bus keep your luggage close to you, or else get out at each stop to check that no one else takes it from the luggage compartment. In town buses, do not open windows so wide that belongings may be snatched; beware of pickpockets by the doors. Small *busetas* are marginally safer than buses because there is only one door for escape. Travelling by car, always keep an eye on your petrol cap at filling stations. Thieves tend to be particularly active in and around bus and railway stations.

The following warning cannot be emphasized too strongly: on buses, do not accept cigarettes, chewing gum, sweets or any other type of food from fellow-passengers because it may be poisoned with sleeping drugs, allowing you to be robbed with ease. This crime is particularly common between Popayán and San Agustín, and Bogotá and Ipiales. We have received a number of reports confirming this practice of drugging tourists, not only in the Popayán area, but in other parts of Colombia, and, sadly, in other Andean countries.

Avoid money changers on the street who offer over-favourable rates of exchange. They often short-change you or run off with your money, pretending that the police are coming. Beware of counterfeit dollars.

Colombia is also part of a major drug-smuggling route. Police and customs activities have greatly intensified and smugglers increasingly try to use innocent carriers. Travellers are warned against carrying packages for other people without checking the contents. Penalties run up to 12 years in none too comfortable jails, and the police sometimes behave very roughly towards those they choose for a spot check at airports; complaints have been made in this connection to the Colombian authorities. All young travellers are suspect, so be very polite if approached by policemen. If your hotel room is raided by police looking for drugs, try, if possible, to get a witness to prevent drugs being planted on you. Colombians who offer you drugs may well be setting you up for the police, who are very active on the north coast and San Andrés island, and other tourist resorts. Again, this warning cannot be stressed too emphatically.

The best advice at all times is to take care, and above all use your common sense.

Also be prepared for frequent bus stopping and searches which are conducted in a rather haphazard and capricious manner. Travellers in private cars are also stopped often, but not necessarily searched. Some roads are more heavily policed than others, and you can expect to be stopped several times when travelling to or from the Caribbean coast and when coming from Ecuador into Colombia. It is strongly advisable to get a window seat on the side of the bus where your luggage is stowed; this will be pulled out and rummaged through by heavy-handed police. All luggage is searched leaving Leticia airport and most tourists are checked arriving in Cartagena from the airport. It has been reported that the police charge 10% of the value of stolen articles for making out a declaration for insurance claims.

Working hours Mon. to Fri., commercial firms work from 0800 to mid-day and from 1400 to 1730 or 1800. Certain firms in the warmer towns such as Cali start at 0700 and finish earlier. Government offices follow the same hours on the whole as the commercial firms, but generally prefer to do business with the public in the afternoon only. Embassy hours for the public are from 0900 to noon and from 1400 to 1700 (Mon. to Fri.). Bank hours in Bogotá are 0900 to 1500 Mon. to Thurs., 0900 to 1530 on Fri. except the last Fri. in the month when they close at 1200; banks in Medellín, Cali, Barranquilla, Bucaramanga, Cartagena, Pasto, Pereira and Manizales open from 0800 to 1130 and 1400 to 1600 on Mon. to Thur.; on Fri. they are open until 1630 but shut at 1130 on the last Fri. in the month; banks in Popayán, Cúcuta, Neiva, Tunja, Ibagué and Santa Marta open from 0800 to 1130 and 1400 to 1530 on Mon. to Fri. and 0800 to 1100 on Sat. and the last day of the month. Shopping hours are 0900 to 1230 and 1430 to 1830, including Sat.

British Business Travellers should consult "Hints to Exporters: Colombia", from Room CO7, Export Services Branch, Department of Trade, Sanctuary Bldgs, 16-20 Great Smith Street, London SW1P 3DB. Similar U.S. publications may be obtained from the Department of Commerce, Washington, D.C.

Climate and Clothing Climate is entirely a matter of altitude: there are no seasons to speak of, though some periods are wetter than others. Tropical clothing is necessary in the hot and humid climate of the coastal fringe and the eastern *llanos*. In Bogotá medium-weight clothing is needed for the cool evening and night. Medellín requires light clothing; Cali lighter still; Manizales very similar to Bogotá. A dual-purpose raincoat and overcoat is useful in the uplands.

The **best time for a visit** is December, January and February: the driest months. But pleasure— it happens sometimes—is in conflict with duty, because most business people are then on holiday. There is heavy rain in many places from June to September.

Health The larger cities have well-organized sanitary services, and the water may be safely drunk. Take sterilizer with you, or boil the water, or use the excellent mineral waters, in the smaller towns of the tropical coast and the interior. Choose your food and eating places with care everywhere. Fruit juices made with milk should be avoided. Hepatitis is common; have a gamma-globulin injection before arriving. Mosquito nets are useful in the coastal swampy regions. There is some risk of malaria and yellow fever in the coastal areas and the eastern *llanos*/jungle regions; prophylaxis is advised.

Hotels There is a tourist tax of 5% on rooms and an insurance charge, but no service charge, and tipping is at discretion: 10% is generous. The more expensive hotels and restaurants also add on 10% VAT (IVA). Food is not expensive. A good lunch costs about US$5-6. A restaurant meal that business people might give to prospective customers would cost from US$6 to US$12 p.p. In many hotels outside the main cities you can only stay (very cheaply) at *en pension* rates and no allowance is made for missing a meal. The Colombian tourist office has lists of authorized prices for all hotels which are usually at least a year out of date. If you are overcharged the tourist office will arrange a refund. Most hotels in Colombia charge US$1 to US$6 for extra beds for children, up to a maximum (usually) of 4 beds per room. On the Caribbean coast and San Andrés and Providencia, high season is 15 December-30 April, 15 June-31 August. Although most hotels, except the very cheapest, offer private WC and shower as a matter of course, hot water often comes only in the more expensive hotels or in colder zones. Wash basin plugs are universally in short supply.

Camping Sites are given in the text. Colombian Tourist Office has a list of official sites. Permission to camp is readily granted by landowners in less populated areas.

Tipping Hotels and restaurants 10%. Porters, cloakroom attendants, hairdressers and barbers, US$0.05-0.25. Taxi-drivers are not tipped.

Electric Current 120 volts AC., as is general for the rest of Colombia. Transformer must be 110-150 volt A.C., with flat-prong plugs. Be careful with electrically heated showers.

Weights and Measures are metric, and weights should always be quoted in kilograms. Litres are used for liquid measures but US gallons are standard for the petroleum industry. Linear measures are usually metric, but the inch is quite commonly used by engineers and the yard on golf courses. For land measurement the hectare and cubic metre are officially employed but the traditional measures *vara* (80 centimetres) and *fanegada* (1,000 square *varas*) are still in common use. As in many other countries food etc. is often sold in *libras* (pounds), which are equivalent to ½ kilo.

Postage There are separate post offices for surface mail and airmail. Send both internal and external letters by airmail, for surface mail is very unreliable. Avianca controls all airmail services and has offices in provincial cities. Correspondence with U.K. is reported to be good. It costs US$0.25 to send a letter or postcard to the U.S., and US$0.27 to Europe; a 1 kg. package to Europe costs US$13 by air (Avianca).

Telecommunications Empresa Nacional de Telecomunicaciones has offices in all main cities.

Telephone systems have been automated; the larger towns are interconnected. Inter-city calls must be made from Telecom offices unless you have access to a private phone. Long-distance pay 'phones are located outside main Telecom offices, also at bus stations and airports. They take 20 peso coins. 1 peso coins for ordinary 'phones may be bought in 20 peso packets from Banco de la República. From the larger towns it is possible to telephone to Canada, the U.S.A., the U.K., and to several of the Latin American republics. International phone charges: for 3 mins., to USA or Canada, US$8 (20% discount on Sun.), to UK, US$9; a deposit is required before the call is made which can vary between US$18 and US$36, US$1 is charged if no reply, for person-to-person add an extra minute's charge to Canada, 2 minutes' to UK; all extra minutes' conversation costs ⅓ more. Collect, or reversed-charge, telephone calls are only possible from private telephones; make sure the operator understands what is involved or you may be billed in any case.

530 COLOMBIA

Difference in Time GMT minus 5 hours.

Currency The monetary unit is the peso, divided into 100 centavos. There are coins of 5, 10, 20, 25 and 50 centavos and of 1, 2, 5, 10 and 20 pesos; there are notes of 1, 2, 5 (all 3 very rare), 10, 20, 50, 100, 200, 500, 1,000, 2,000 and 5,000 pesos. Large notes of over 1,000 pesos are often impossible to spend on small purchases as change is in short supply, especially in small cities, and in the morning. There is now a limit of 500 on both the import and export of pesos. It is difficult to change pesos back into dollars on departure. Travellers' cheques are not easy to change in Colombia; only Banco de la República is permitted to exchange travellers' cheques. Owing to the quantity of counterfeit American Express travellers' cheques in circulation, travellers experience great difficulty in cashing these cheques except in main cities, where the procedure is often slow, involving finger printing and photographs. The best advice we can give is for the traveller to ascertain on arrival what conditions obtain because there appears to be no rule concerning where and when one may be able to change travellers' cheques. Sterling travellers' cheques are practically impossible to change in Colombia. As it is unwise to carry large quantities of cash, credit cards are widely used, especially the Diners' Club and Visa; Master Charge is less common, while American Express is only accepted in high-priced establishments in Bogotá. Many banks advance pesos against Visa. It is generally dangerous to change money on the streets; the safest way to obtain black market rates is at the border in a neighbouring country.

Public Holidays are on the following days:

January 1: Circumcision of our Lord.	June 29: SS. Peter and Paul.*
January 6: Epiphany*.	July 20: Independence Day.
March 19: St Joseph.*	August 7: Battle of Boyacá.
Maundy Thursday.	August 15: Assumption.*
Good Friday.	October 12: Discovery of America.*
May 1: Labour Day.	November 1: All Saints' day.*
Ascension Day.*	November 11: Independence of Cartagena.*
Corpus Christi.*	December 8: Immaculate Conception.
Sacred Heart.*	December 25: Christmas Day.

When those marked with an asterisk do not fall on a Monday, or when they fall on a Sunday, they will be moved to the following Monday.

Best Buys Emeralds in Bogotá; handworked silver (excellent); Indian pottery and textiles. The state-run Artesanías de Colombia for craft work (see under Bogotá). In Antioquia buy the handbag—*carriel antioqueño*—traditionally made from otter skin, but nowadays from calf skin and plastic trimmed at that. At Cartagena crude rubber is moulded into little dyed figurines: odd but attractive. Clothing and shoes are cheap. The Colombian *ruana* (poncho) is cheap, chic and warm in any cool climate, and comes in an incredible variety of colours. Silver and gold work is cheaper than in Peru. Good duty-free shop at Bogotá airport. Leatherwork is generally good and not expensive.

Other shopping tips Colombia is one of the few countries which sell "white gas" for camping stoves etc., so stock up here.

Food Colombia's food is very regional; it is quite difficult to buy in Medellín, say, a dish you particularly liked in Bogotá.

Locro de choclos is a potato and maize soup so rich and nourishing that, with salad and coffee, it would make a meal in itself. Colombia has its own variant of the inevitable *arroz con pollo* (chicken and rice) which is excellent. For a change *pollo en salsa de mostaza* (chicken in mustard sauce) is recommended. *Ajiaco de pollo* is a delicious chicken, maize, manioc, cabbage and potato stew served with cream and capers, and lumps of avocado; it is a Bogotá speciality; another

Bogotá speciality is *sobrebarriga* (belly of beef). *Bandeja antioqueña* costs US$3 in most places and consists of meat grilled and served with rice, beans, potato, manioc and a green salad; the simpler *carne asada* may be had for as little as US$2. *Mazamorra*, boiled maize in milk, is a typical *antioqueño* sweet. *Lechona* (sucking pig and herbs) is a speciality of Ibagué. Cartagena's rice with coconut can be compared with rice *a la valenciana*. In Nariño, guinea pig (*cuy, curí* or *conejillo de Indias*) is typical. *Tamales* are meat pies made by folding a maize dough round chopped pork mixed with potato, peas, onions, eggs and olives seasoned with garlic, cloves and paprika, and steaming the whole in banana leaves (which you don't eat); the best are from Tolima. A baked dish of squash, beaten eggs and seafood covered with sauce is known as the *souffle de calabaza*. *Magras* is a typical Colombian dish of eggs and chicken baked together and served with a tomato sauce. *Sancocho* is a filling combination of all the tuberous vegetables, including the tropical cassava and yam, with chopped fresh fish or any kind of meat, possibly chicken. From stalls in the capital and the countryside, try *mazorcas* (roast maize cobs) or *arepas* (fried maize cakes). On the Caribbean coast, eat an egg *empanada*, which consists of two layers of corn (maize) dough that open like an oyster-shell, fried with eggs in the middle, and try the *patacón*, a cake of mashed and baked plantain (green banana). *Huevos pericos*, eggs scrambled with onions and tomatoes, are a popular, cheap and nourishing snack for the impecunious—available almost anywhere. A good local sweet is the *canastas de coco*: pastry containing coconut custard flavoured with wine and surmounted by meringue. *Arequipe* is very similar to fudge, and popular (it is called *manjarblanco* in other parts of South America). *Almojábanas*, a kind of sour-milk bread roll, are delicious if fresh: "one day old and they are a disaster". There is, indeed, quite an assortment of little fruit pasties and preserves. Then there are the usual fruits: bananas, oranges, mangoes, avocado pears, and (at least in the tropical zones) *chirimoyas, papayas*, and the delicious *pitahaya*, taken either as an appetizer or dessert and, for the wise, in moderation, because even a little of it has a laxative effect. Other fruits such as the *guayaba* (guava), *guanábana* (soursop), *maracuyá* (passion fruit), *lulo* (*naranjilla*), *mora* (blackberry) and *curuba* make delicious juices, sometimes with milk added to make a *sorbete*—but be careful of milk in Colombia. Fruit yoghurts are nourishing and cheap (try Alpina brand). *Tinto*, the national small cup of black coffee, is taken ritually at all hours. Colombian coffee is always mild. (Coffee with milk is called *café perico*; *café con leche* is a mug of milk with coffee added.) *Agua de panela* is a common beverage (hot water with unrefined sugar), also made with limes, milk, or cheese.

Drink Many acceptable brands of beer are produced. The local rum is good and cheap; ask for *ron*, not *aguardiente*, because in Colombia the latter word refers to a popular drink containing aniseed (*aguardiente anisado*). Try *canelazo*—cold or hot rum with water, sugar, lime and cinnamon. Local table wines include Santo Tomás; none are very good. General food and wine tips: wine is normally about US$3.50-4.50 in restaurants for an acceptable bottle of Chilean or Argentine; don't buy European wines as they don't travel well to South America and are very expensive.

Warning Great care should be exercised when buying imported spirits in shops. It has been reported that bottles bearing well-known labels have often been "recycled" and contain a cheap and poor imitation of the original contents. This can be dangerous to the health, and travellers are warned to stick to beer and rum. Also note that ice is usually not made from potable water.

Press Bogotá: *El Tiempo, El Espectador* (both Liberal); *La República* (Conservative), *El Siglo* (extreme Conservative). Medellín: *El Mundo*; Cali: *El País, Occidente, El Pueblo*, all major cities have daily papers. Magazines are partisan, best is probably *La Semana*. U.S. and European papers can be bought at a stall in Bogotá on Av. 19 between Carreras 3 and 4.

Sport The game of *tejo* is still played in Cundinamarca, Boyacá and Tolima. In Pasto it is played under the name of *sapo* (toad). This is the Spanish *juego de la rana*, in which a small quoit has to be thrown from an improbable distance into a metal frog's mouth. There are bullrings at Bogotá, Cali, Manizales, Medellín, Sincelejo and Cerete. Polo is played at Medellín and Bogotá. Most of the larger towns have stadiums. Association football is the most popular game. American baseball is played at Cartagena and Barranquilla. Cockfights, cycling, and basketball are also popular.

Fishing is particularly good at Girardot, Santa Marta, and Barranquilla; marlin is fished off Barranquilla. There is good trout fishing, in season, in the lakes in the Bogotá area, particularly at Lake Tota, in the mountains.

COLOMBIA

This section has been revised with the very welcome help of John S. Benson (Medellín), John E Eyberg (Medellín), Frank Farrell (Colegio Anglo-Colombiano, Bogotá), Joaquín Emilio García (CNT, San Agustín) for a most valuable contribution, Mark Paramo (CEVCA, Bogotá), Lesley Willcoxson (former resident of Bucaramanga), Veronika Winkler (Bogotá), and the following travellers: Richard and Sharon Alexander (Auckland 5), Susan Basnett (Warwick Univ.), Erik Bloom (Davis, Ca.), Joyce M. Bogner (Boise, Idaho), Klaus Bryn (Oslo), Malcolm Craven (Weston-super-Mare), Lynne and Hugh Davies (Mill Valley, Ca.), Morgan Davis (Monteville, Ont.), Dagmar Drescher (Bad Kreuznach, W.Ger.), Peter Ehrat and Rolf Ramsperger (Switz.), Julie Eisenberg and Andy Daitsman (Milwaukee), Christine Enkelaar and José Keldens ('s-Hertogenbosch, Neth.), Andrew Frigaard and K. Gould (Maids Moreton, Bucks.), Pierre-Marie Gagneux (Taulignan, Fr.) and Nathalie Baudouin (Bar-le-Duc, Fr.), Theodor A. Gevert (São Paulo), Gerhard Glattli (Bonstetten, Switz.), Jean M Guest (Banbury), Leo Joseph (Adelaide), William Kelty (Northridge, Ca.), Dan and Sue Koenigshofer (Chapel Hill, NC), Michael Kreder and Heinz Rose (Fellbach-Schmiden, W.Ger.), Jean Laberge (Montreal), Andrew Lawrence (Vancover), and John Easterbrooke (Shaftesbury), Roger Lemercier (Nice), Gary MacLake (Sheboygan, Mich.), Louis Maine, Claus Mayer (Stuttgart), Robert S. Millar (Tela, Hond.), Robert Monk (Los Gatos, Ca.), Hans and Ursula Niederdorfer (Lambach, Austria), Grace Osakoda (Hawaii) for a most useful contribution, Vaclav Penkava (Seattle), Jens Plahte (Aas, Norway), Steven Powell (London N4), Annamarie Reichmuth and Roger Müller (Schwyz, Switz.), Felz Reinhard (Hoechst, Austria) and Thomas Stevenson, Elliott Roseman (Arlington, Mass.) for a very valuable contribution, Josyane Sechaud (San Salvador), Barbara Simon and Peter Stobart (Cologne), Ellen D. Steinberg (River Forest, Ill.), Sophie Stirling (Buchlyvie, Stirling) and others, Richard Stolter (Durham, NC) for a very fine contribution, Catherine Strauss and Gregory Groth, Asle Strmsvaag (Steinkjer, Norway), A.C. Tanswell (Walsall), Stefan Thommen (Liestal, Switz.) and Thomas Meier (Schaffhausen, Switz.), Dirk Vanmarcke (Bruges), Paul Whitfield (Auckland), John Wood (Liss, Hants), and Rolf Würtz (Heidelberg).

WANTED: MAPS
ARGENTINA – BRAZIL – MEXICO GUATEMALA – EL SALVADOR – THE CARIBBEAN ISLANDS

We would much appreciate receiving any surplus maps and diagrams, however rough, of towns and cities, walks, national parks and other interesting areas, to use as source material for the Handbook and other forthcoming titles.

The above regions are particularly needed but any maps of Latin America would be welcome.

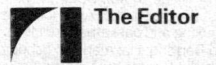

The Editor Trade & Travel Publications Limited
5 Prince's Buildings, George Street,
Bath BA1 2ED. England

ECUADOR

	Page		Page
Introductory	533	**Guayaquil & Lowlands**	580
Quito	537	**Oriente**	588
North of Quito	550	**The Galápagos**	594
N & W Lowlands	556	**Economy**	601
Guayaquil to Quito	564	**Information for Visitors**	602
Southern Sierra	574	**Maps**	536, 538, 540, 582

ECUADOR is bounded by Colombia to the north, Peru to the east and south and the Pacific Ocean to the west. Its area is about 283,520 square km., which makes it the second smallest republic in South America. About 40% of its 8,073,000 (1983 census) people are Indians, 40% *mestizo*, 10% European; the remainder are black or Asian.

The Andes, running from the Colombian border in the north to the borders of Peru in the south, form a mountainous backbone to the country. There are two main ranges, the Eastern Cordillera and the Western Cordillera, separated by a 400-km. long trough, the Central Valley, whose rims are from 40 to 65 km. apart. The rims are joined together, like the two sides of a ladder, by hilly rungs, and between each pair of rungs lies an intermont basin with a dense cluster of population. These basins, which vary in altitude between 1,800 and 3,000 metres, are drained by rivers which cut through the rims to run either west to the Pacific or east to join the Amazon. The whole mountain area is known as the Sierra.

Both rims of the Central Valley are lined with the cones of more than thirty volcanoes. Several of them have long been extinct, for example, Chimborazo, the highest (6,310 metres), Cayambe (5,790 metres), standing directly on the equator, Iliniza (5,263 metres) and Altar (5,319 metres). At least eight, however, are still active; Cotopaxi (5,897 metres), which had several violent eruptions in the nineteenth century; Tungurahua (5,016 metres), which had a major eruption early this century; Antisana (5,704 metres), which showed signs of activity in the 1960s; Pichincha (4,794 metres), which erupted in 1981, and Sangay (5,230 metres) one of the world's most active volcanoes, continuously emitting fumes and ash. Nowadays all the main peaks except for Altar and Sangay, which are less accessible, are climbed fairly regularly.

East of the Eastern Cordillera the forest-clad mountains fall sharply to the plains—the Oriente—through which meander the tributaries of the Amazon. This eastern lowland region makes up 36% of Ecuador's total territory, but is only sparsely populated by native Indians and agricultural colonists from the highlands. In total, the region has only 3% of the national population, but colonization is now proceeding rapidly in the wake of an oil boom. There are substantial oil reserves in the northern Oriente near the Colombian border, and exports began in 1972.

Between the Western Cordillera and the Pacific lies the Costa, 685 km. from north to south and some 100 km. wide. It is from this area that Ecuador draws the majority of its agricultural products for export. Guayaquil, the main city of this region, is 464 km. from the capital, Quito, which lies high in a northern intermont basin.

The Sierra There are altogether ten intermont basins strung along the Sierra from north to south. There is little variation by day or by season in the temperature in any particular basin: temperature depends on altitude. The basins lie at an

534 ECUADOR

elevation of between 2,100 and 2,750 metres, and the range of shade temperature is from 6°C to 10°C in the morning to 19°C to 23°C in the afternoon. Temperatures can get considerably higher in the lower basins. There is one rainy season, from November to May, when the average fall in Quito is 1,270 mm; the skies are mostly cloudy or overcast at this time and there are frequent rainfalls during the afternoons and nights. Over half the area is now grassy *páramo* on which cattle and sheep are raised and subsistence crops grown. What crops are grown is determined by altitude, but the hardiest of them, the potato, cannot thrive above 3,800 metres or so. The intermont basins produce livestock, poultry, wheat, barley, oats, maize, quinoa, fruit and vegetables, some of which find their way down to the coastal plain.

The headwaters of the rivers which drain the basins have cut deep, sharp valleys in the limestone and soft volcanic ash which lies thick upon the basin floors. The general level of the Ibarra basin floor is 2,300 metres, but just to the N is the Chota valley bottom in which cotton and sugar are grown at only 1,500 metres above sea-level.

Some 48% of the people of Ecuador live in the central trough of the Andes, and the majority of the valley people, again, are pure Indians. Most of the land is held in large private estates worked by the Indians, but some of it is held by Indian communities. With the limited application of an agrarian-reform programme, the *huasipungo* system whereby Indians were virtual slaves on the big highland *haciendas* is now disappearing, and co-operatives are proliferating. Though many Indian communities live at subsistence level and remain isolated from national centres, others have developed good markets for products using traditional skills in embroidery, pottery, jewellery, knitting, weaving, and carving.

The Costa Most of the Costa region is lowland at an altitude of less than 300 metres, apart from a belt of hilly land which runs west from Guayaquil to the coast and trends northwards. In the extreme north there are two rainy seasons, as in Colombia, and a typical tropical rain forest. But the two rainy seasons soon merge into one, running from December to June. The further south we go, the later the rains begin and the sooner they end: at Guayaquil the rains normally fall between January and April. The forests thin out too as we move south, and give way to thorn and savanna. The Santa Elena Peninsula and the south-western coast near Peru have little or no rainfall.

Along the northern coast, the main areas of population are at Esmeraldas, along the highways inland, in the irrigated lands of northern Manabí, and near Manta, Montecristi, and Jipijapa. It is from this area that tagua nuts, the fruits of a palm fern, come to Guayaquil for export, but appreciable quantities of castor seed, tagua nuts and coffee are exported through the port of Manta.

The main agricultural exports come from a small area of lowland to the SE and N of Guayaquil. It lies between the coastal hills and the Andes; rains are heavy, the temperature and the humidity high: ideal conditions for the growth of tropical crops. One part of this Guayas lowland is subject to floods from the four rivers which traverse it: bananas, normally accounting for half the exports of the lowland, are grown here, as well as rice. Cacao too is farmed on the natural levees of this flood plain, but the main crop comes from the alluvial fans at the foot of the mountains rising out of the plain. High on these same alluvial fans excellent coffee is also grown; cacao, bananas, coffee and sugar, whether processed or unprocessed, are about 30% of the exports by value. Cotton is developing. Add to this that the Guayas lowland is a great cattle-fattening area in the dry season, and its importance in the national economy becomes obvious. A good network of paved roads now links Guayaquil with the major zones of agricultural production, and the once thriving river-ports have now declined.

Two areas of the coastlands have experienced spectacular rises in population and agricultural production: El Oro Province in the extreme south, centred on the town of Machala, and the Quevedo-Santo Domingo zone along the Andean fringe to the north of Guayaquil. In both areas, highland settlers have mixed with coastal entrepreneurs to produce a particularly progressive agriculture. Irrigation in El Oro has produced a thriving zone of very intensive banana plantations.

In the Quevedo-Santo Domingo area, large areas of forest have been cleared; bananas used to be the main crop, but are now being replaced by African palm. Further north, in Esmeraldas Province, there still remain large areas of land which could be cleared and developed for farming, although the fertility of this zone is reputedly much lower than that of the Quevedo, Guayaquil and Machala areas.

Population About 49% of Ecuador's inhabitants live in the Costa region west of the Andes, and 48% in the Andean Sierra. Migration is occurring from the rural zones of both the coast and the highlands to the towns and cities, particularly Guayaquil and Quito, and agricultural colonization by highlanders is occurring in parts of the coastal lowlands and the Oriente. About 18% of the inhabitants over 15 years of age are illiterate. 52% of the population is urban (living in a cantonal or provincial capital), and 48% is rural. National average population density is 30 per square kilometre, the highest in South America. Average income per head has risen fast in recent years like that of other oil-exporting countries, but the distribution has not improved and a few citizens are spectacularly wealthy.

History The Incas of Peru, with their capital at Cuzco, began to conquer the Sierra of Ecuador, already densely populated, towards the middle of the 15th century. A road was built between Cuzco and Quito, and the empire was ruled after the death of the Inca Huayna Capac by his two sons, Huáscar at Cuzco and Atahualpa at Quito. Pizarro's main Peruvian expedition took place in 1532, when there was civil war between the two brothers. Atahualpa, who had won the war, was put to death by Pizarro in 1533, and the Inca empire was over.

Pizarro claimed the northern kingdom of Quito, and his lieutenants Sebastián de Benalcázar and Diego de Almagro took the city in 1534. Pizarro founded Lima in 1535 as capital of the whole region, and four years later replaced Benalcázar at Quito by Gonzalo, his brother. Gonzalo, lusting for gold, set out on the exploration of the Oriente. He moved down the Napo river, and sent Francisco de Orellana to prospect. Orellana did not return: he drifted down the river finally to reach the mouth of the Amazon: the first white man to cross the continent in this way.

Quito became an *audiencia* under the Viceroy of Peru. For 280 years Ecuador more or less peacefully absorbed the new ways brought by the conqueror. Gonzalo had already introduced pigs and cattle; wheat was now added. The Indians were Christianized, colonial laws and customs and ideas introduced. The marriage of the arts of Spain to those of the Incas led to a remarkable efflorescence of painting, sculpting and building at Quito. In the 18th century black slave labour was brought in to work the plantations near the coast.

There was an abortive attempt at independence in the strongly garrisoned capital in 1809, but it was not until 1822 that Sucre, moving north from Guayaquil, defeated the Spanish at Pichincha and occupied Quito. Soon afterwards Bolívar arrived, and Ecuador was induced to join the Venezuelan and Colombian confederation, the Gran Colombia of Bolívar's dream. On July 26 and 27, 1822, Bolívar met San Martín, fresh from liberating Lima, at Guayaquil. What happened at that mysterious encounter is not known, but San Martín left it silently for a self-imposed exile in France. Venezuela separated itself from Gran Colombia in 1829, and Ecuador decided on complete independence in August, 1830, under the presidency of Juan Flores.

Ecuador's 19th century history was a continuous struggle between pro-Church conservatives and anti-Church (but none the less devotedly Catholic) liberals. There were also long periods of military rule from 1895, when the liberal General Eloy Alfaro took power. During the late 1940s and the 1950s there was a prolonged period of prosperity (through bananas, largely) and constitutional rule, but the more typical pattern of alternating civilian and military governments was resumed in the 1960s and 1970s. Apart from the liberal-conservative struggles, there has been long-lasting rivalry between Quito and the Sierra on one hand and Guayaquil and the Costa on the other.

The country's eastern jungle territory has been reduced from that of the old Audiencia of Quito by gradual Peruvian infiltration, which means that the country's official claim to be a "país amazónico" has little relation to present reality.

536 **ECUADOR**

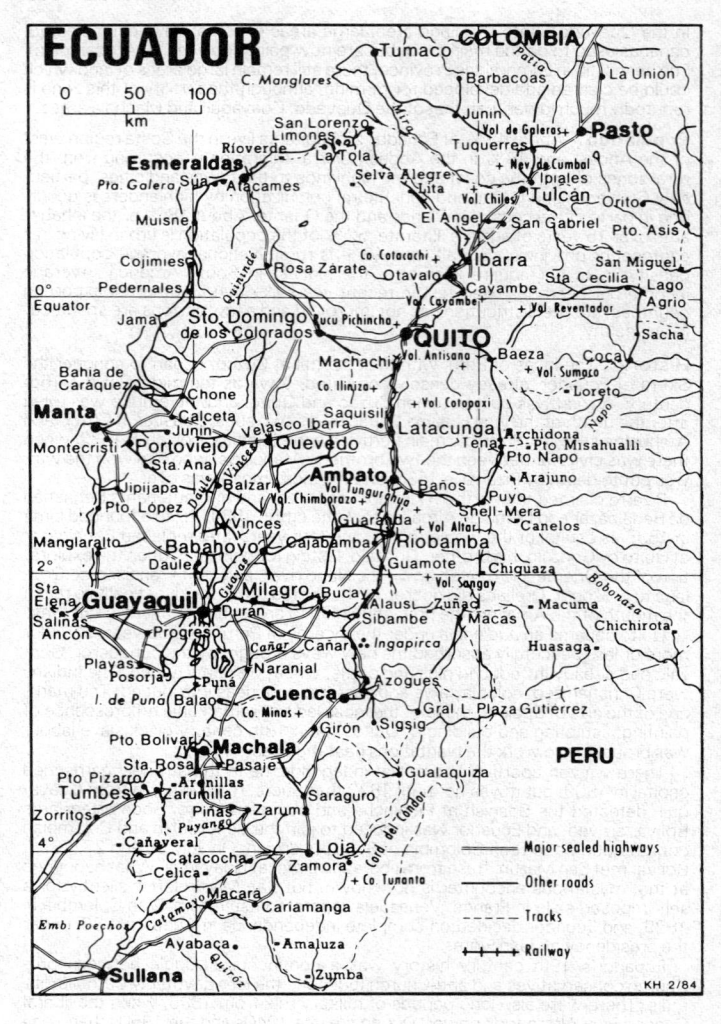

ECUADOR 537

This process reached an acute phase in 1941 when war broke out with Peru; the war was ended with the Rio de Janeiro Protocol of 1942 which allotted most of the disputed territory to Peru. Ecuador has denounced the Protocol, and the country's official policy remains the recovery of all the territories of the Audiencia of Quito. Border skirmishes occur at times although there has been no serious incident since 1981.

Government

There are 20 provinces, including the Galápagos Islands. Provinces are divided into cantons and parishes for administration.

Under the 1978 constitution, the vote was extended to include all literate citizens over the age of 18. The president and vice-president are elected for a five-year term. The president may not stand for re-election. The legislative branch consists of a single Chamber of Representatives of 69 members, which meets for two months of the year. The first presidential and congressional election under the new charter took place on April 29, 1979. Prior to then there had been military rule for seven years, attended by growing oil-based prosperity, until August 10, 1979 when President Jaime Roldós Aguilera was inaugurated for a five-year term. His policy was to follow a programme of gradual reform. In May 1981, President Roldós was killed in an air crash and was succeeded by the vice-president, Osvaldo Hurtado Larrea. In 1984 he completed his term of office and handed power over to his elected successor and political opponent, the conservative Sr. León Febres Cordero, the first time in 23 years that such a transfer of power had occurred.

Quito

Quito (2,850 metres), with a population of 881,000, is within 25 km. of the equator, but it stands high enough to make its climate much like that of spring in England, the days warm or hot and the nights cool. Because of the height, visitors may initially feel some discomfort and should slow their pace for the first 24 hours. Mean temperature, 13°C, rainfall, 1,473 mm.; rainy season: Sept. to May with the heaviest rainfall in April, though heavy storms in July are not unknown. The day length (sunrise to sunset) is constant throughout the year.

Few cities have a setting to match that of Quito, the second highest capital in Latin America. The city is set in a hollow at the foot of the volcano Pichincha (4,794 metres). It was an Inca city, refounded by Sebastián de Benalcázar, Pizarro's lieutenant, in 1534. The city's charm lies in its colonial centre, where cobbled streets are steep and narrow, dipping to deep ravines. Through this section hurries the Machángara river, nowadays too polluted to wash clothes in. Westwards the valley is closed by Cerro Panecillo; from its top, 183 metres above the city level, there is a good restaurant and a fine view of the city below and the encircling cones of volcanoes and other mountains. Don't walk up the series of steps and paths which begin on García Moreno (where it meets Ambato) as assaults are becoming common: take a taxi up. There is a new statue on the hill to the Virgen de las Américas; Mass is held in the base on Sundays. There is a good view from the observation platform up the statue.

The heart of the city is Plaza Independencia, dominated by a somewhat grim Cathedral (open 0600-1000, 1400-1600) with grey stone porticos and green tile cupolas. On its outer walls are plaques listing the names of the founding fathers of Quito, and inside are the tomb of Sucre (tucked away in a corner) and a famous Descent from the Cross by the Indian painter Caspicara. Beside the Cathedral, round the corner, is El Sagrario, being restored. Facing the Cathedral is the old Archbishop's Palace, which has been renovated and now houses shops. On the northeast corner is the old Municipal Palace whose street floor, built in a series of graceful arcades, has more shops. The new concrete Municipal Palace is now complete, and fits in quite well, despite its material. The low colonial Palacio de Gobierno, on the northwest side of the Plaza, is silhouetted against the great flank of Pichincha; on the first floor is a gigantic mosaic mural of Orellana discovering the Amazon, and the President's offices are on the second floor.

538 **ECUADOR**

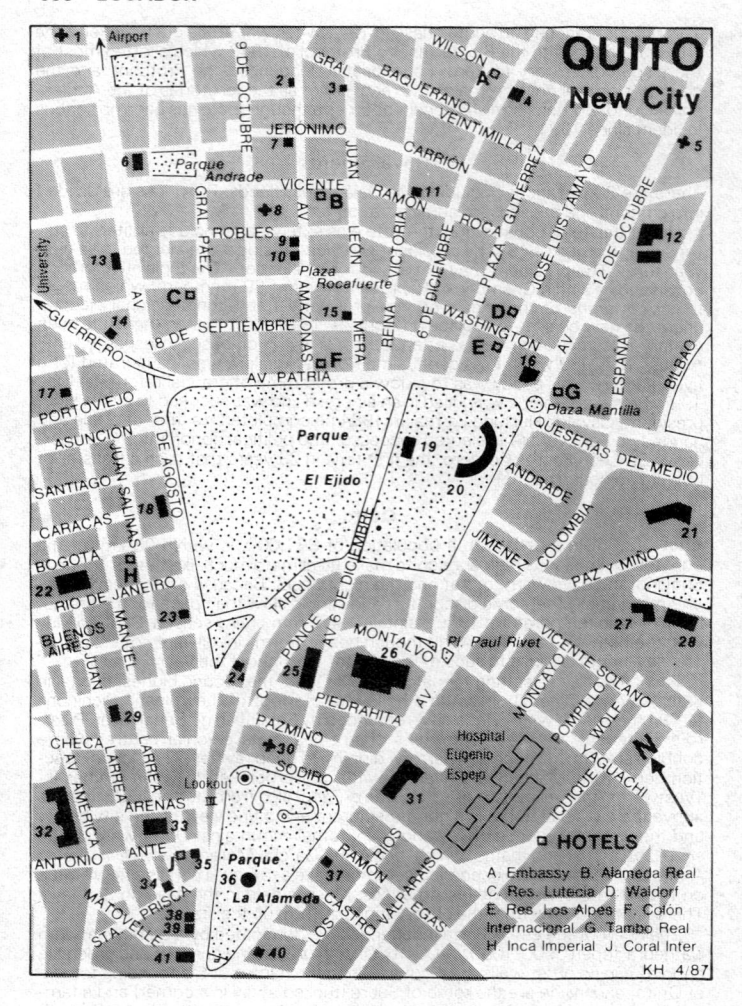

QUITO New City

HOTELS

A. Embassy B. Alameda Real
C. Res. Lutecia D. Waldorf
E. Res. Los Alpes F. Colon
Internacional G. Tambo Real
H. Inca Imperial J. Coral Inter

KH 4/87

ECUADOR 539

The best way to see old Quito is to walk its narrow streets. Wander down the Calle Morales, main street of La Ronda district (traditionally called Calle Ronda), one of the oldest streets in the city, past Plaza Santo Domingo to Carrera Guayaquil, the main shopping district, and on to shady Parque Alameda, which has the oldest astronomical observatory in South America (open Sat. 0900-1200). There are also a splendid monument to Simón Bolívar, various lakes, and in the NW corner a spiral lookout tower with a good view. The traditional colonial area is being preserved, with the buildings painted white and blue, but other parts of the city are being radically altered as a result of road improvements.

From Plaza Independencia two main streets, Carrera Venezuela and Calle García Moreno, lead straight towards the Panecillo to the wide Av. 24 de Mayo, at the top of which is a new concrete building where the Indians are supposed to do their trading since the street markets were officially abolished in 1981. Street trading still takes place, however, and there are daily street markets from Sucre down to 24 de Mayo and from San Francisco church west up past Cuenca.

Plaza San Francisco (or Bolívar) is west of Plaza Independencia; on the northwestern side of this plaza is the great church and monastery of the patron saint of Quito, San Francisco, the earliest religious foundation in South America (1535); a modest statue of the founder, Fray Jodoco Ricke, a Flemish Franciscan who sowed the first wheat in Ecuador, stands at the foot of the stairs to the church portal. The fine Jesuit church of La Compañía is in Calle García Moreno, one block from Plaza Independencia, and not far away to the north-east is the church of La Merced. In the monastery of La Merced is Quito's oldest clock, built in 1817 in London. Fine cloisters entered through door to left of altar. La Merced church contains many splendidly elaborate styles; note the statue of Neptune on the main patio fountain.

Plaza Santo Domingo (or Sucre), to the south-east of Plaza San Francisco, has to the SE the church and monastery of Santo Domingo, with its rich wood-carvings and a remarkable Chapel of the Rosary to the right of the main altar. In the centre of the square is a statue to Sucre, pointing to the slopes of Pichincha where he won his battle against the Royalists. The modern University City is on the NW side of the city, on the lower slopes of Pichincha by the Avenida de las Américas. Notice also the curious new "French Gothic" basilica under construction (since 1926) on a hill in the centre of the town. (You go up Carrera Venezuela to see it, puffing all the way, but it's worth while to see the local sculptors and stonecutters at work, if you can get friendly with the administrator.)

There are altogether 86 churches in Quito. La Compañía (open 1000-1100, 1300-1800) has the most ornate and richly sculptured façade and interior. See its coloured columns, its ten side altars and high altar plated with gold, and the gilded balconies. Several of its most precious treasures, including a painting of the Virgen Dolorosa framed in emeralds and gold, are kept in the vaults of the Banco Central del Ecuador and appear only at special festivals.

The church of San Francisco, 1535 (open 0600-1200, 1430-1930), Quito's largest, is rich in art treasures. The two towers were felled by an earthquake in 1868 and rebuilt. See the fine woodcarvings in the choir, a magnificent high altar of gold and an exquisite carved ceiling. There are some paintings in the aisles by Miguel de Santiago, the colonial *mestizo* painter. His paintings of *the life of Saint Francis* decorate the monastery of San Francisco close by. Adjoining San Francisco is the Cantuña Chapel with sculptures.

The house of Sucre is at Venezuela 573, a beautiful restored house, open daily, entry free. The

1. Iglesia Sta. Clara de San Millán; 2. Turismundial; 3. Libri Mundi; 4. Ministry of Public Works; 5. Iglesia El Girón; 6. Ministry of External Relations; 7. Bank of London & South America; 8. Iglesia Santa Teresa; 9. Casa de cambio 'Rodrigo Paz'; 10. Ecuadorian Tours (Amex); 11. DITURIS (Tourist Office); 12. Universidad Católica (museums); 13. Ministry of Finance; 14. Expresso Turismo (bus); 15. Casa de cambio 'Unicambios'; 16. United States Embassy; 17. Flota Imbabura (bus); 18. Immigration; Dept. of Social Security; 19.Cultural Library; 20. Casa de la Cultura; 21. Nuevo Hospital Militar; 22. Colegio Militar; 23. Banco Holandés Unido; 24. Alitalia; 25. Palacio de Justicia; 26. Palacio Legislativo; 27. Instituto Panamericano de Geografía y Historia; 28. Instituto Geográfico Militar (IGM); 29. Ministry of Public Health; 30. Iglesia El Belén; 31. Maternity Hospital; 32. Colegio Mejía (museum); 33. Consejo Provincial de Pichincha; 34. Banco Internacional; 35. First National City Bank; 36. Astronomical Observatory; 37. Ciné Capitol; 38. TAME; 39. Banco de los Andes; 40. SAETA and Red Cross; 41. Banco Central (museums).

540 **ECUADOR**

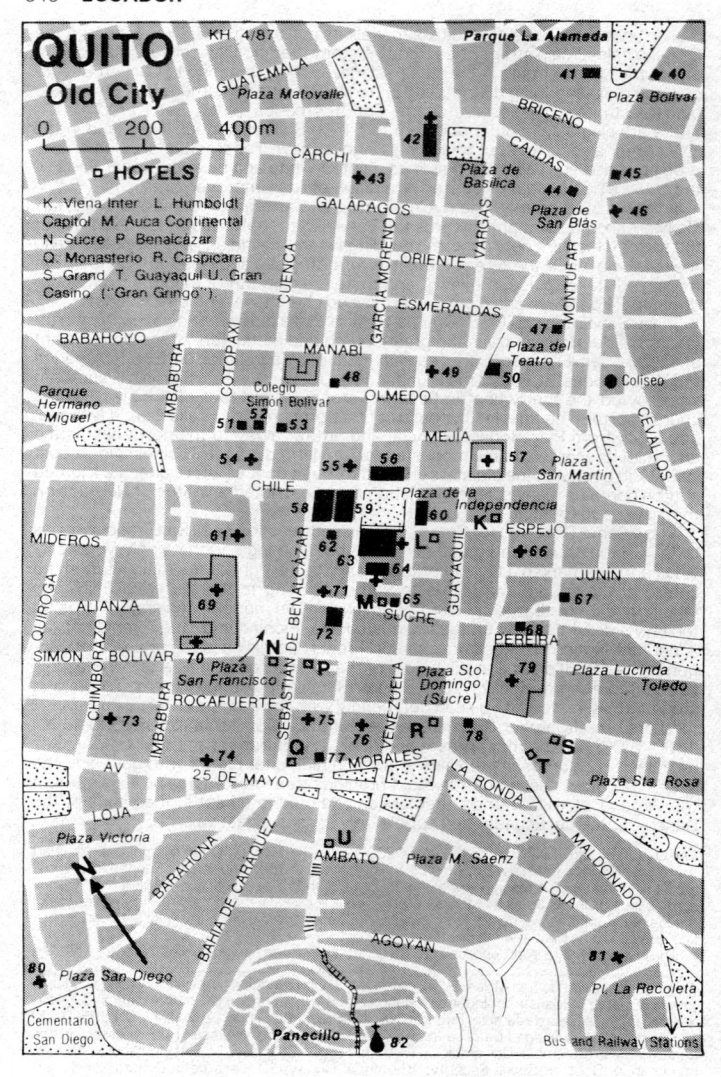

QUITO
Old City

KH 4/87

0 — 200 — 400m

□ **HOTELS**

K. Viena Inter L. Humboldt
Capitol M. Auca Continental
N. Sucre P. Benalcazar
Q. Monasterio R. Caspicara
S. Grand T. Guayaquil U. Gran
Casino ("Gran Gringo").

ECUADOR 541

house of Benalcázar is on Olmeda with Benalcázar, a fully-restored colonial house. The house of Camilo Egas, a recent Ecuadorean artist, on Venezuela, has been restored by the Banco Central; it has different exhibitions during the year; entrance US$0.75.

Many of the heroes of Ecuador's struggle for independence are buried in the monastery of San Agustín (Flores and Mejía), where the treaty of independence from Spain was signed. The church of El Carmen Moderno has a fine collection of Quito ceramics. In the recently restored monastery of San Diego are some unique paintings with figures dressed in fabrics sewn to the canvas -a curious instance of our present-day "collage". Ring the bell to the right of the church door to get in; entrance US$0.75, 0900-1200, 1500-1700, all visitors are shown around by a guide. Also La Concepción, Mejía and García Moreno; San Blas, Guayaquil and 10 de Agosto. The Basílica de Guápulo (1693), perched on the edge of a ravine SE of the city, is well worth seeing for its many paintings, gilded altars and the marvellously carved pulpit. Take bus 21 (Guápulo-Dos Puentes) from Plaza de Santo Domingo.

Modern Quito extends northwards into a wide plain; it has broad avenues, fine private residences, parks, embassies and villas. Av. Amazonas, from Av. Patria to about Av. Colón, and the adjoining streets comprise Quito's modern tourist and business area: travel agencies, airlines, hotels and *residenciales*, exchange houses, moderate to expensive restaurants—several with sidewalk cafés, arts and crafts stores and stalls, jewellery stores, book stores, car rental agencies, and pastry shops are all clustered in this neighbourhood. Av. Amazonas is closed to most commercial wheeled traffic, but has British double-decker buses running its length and on to the airport. On Sun. La Alameda and El Ejido parks are filled with local families.

Museums Quito prides itself on its art. The **Casa de la Cultura Ecuatoriana,** a large circular building at the east side of Parque El Ejido, has good murals, a picture gallery, the Natural History Museum previously in the Eloy Alfaro military college, an exhibition of Ecuadorean books, and a unique museum of musical instruments. An open-air amphitheatre is under construction (open 0900-1230, 1500-1815, Tues.-Fri., 0930-1600 Sat.). There is a good collection of Ecuadorean sculptures and painting at the **Museum of Colonial Art,** on the corner of Cuenca and Mejía, but this was closed for renovation in 1982. The **Museo de San Francisco** has a fine collection of religious art, open 0900-1130, 1500-1730, entrance US$0.35 (closed 1986 for renovation), while the **Museo de Santo Domingo** has a further collection open Mon.-Fri., 0800-1100, 1500-1700, but not of quite the same quality. Similar collection in **Museo de San Agustín,** Chile y Guayaquil, open Mon.-Sat. 0830-1230, 1430-1800, interesting exhibition of restoration work (closed for reconstruction). The **Museo Jijón y Caamaño,** now housed in the Catholic University library building, has a private collection of archaeological objects, historical documents, portraits, uniforms, etc., very well displayed. Open 0900-1200, 1500-1800. Admission: US$0.30. There is also a Shuar ethnographic museum at the university. There are two first class museums in the Banco Central (Av. 10 de Agosto), the **Archaeological Museum** on the fifth floor with beautiful precolumbian ceramics and gold and the **Museo Colonial y de Arte Religioso** on the 6th. Open 0900-1500, Sat. 1000-1430; closed Sun.-Mon. There are guided tours in English, French and German—Entrance fee is US$0.75 for foreigners, US$0.35 for Ecuadoreans, US$0.20 for students, but free on Sunday and every day between 1800-2000. At the Banco Central library on Av. 10 de Agosto, between the Alameda and El Ejido parks, you can see video film of Ecuadorean culture and the different Indian tribes, and listen to cassettes of music. Admission free. Leave your passport at the entrance. Open Tues.-Sat., 1300-2000. In Eloy Alfaro military college, Av. Francisco Orellana y Amazonas, is a zoo of Ecuadorean animals, open daily, with several condors and a large group of Galápagos tortoises. Passports must be shown for entry. There is a fine museum in Bella Vista north east of Quito, **Museo Guayasamín:** as well as the eponymous artist's works there is a precolumbian and colonial collection; open Mon.-Sat. 0900-1230 and 1500-1830, free admission. Works of art may be purchased. The museum is near the Channel 8 TV station, take Batán-Colmena bus no. 3 marked Bella Vista. Other museums: **Municipal Museum of Art and History,** Espejo 1147, near main plaza, Tues. to Fri., 0830-1830, Sat. and Sun. 1000-1700, was the old municipal offices; underneath is the cell where the revolutionaries of 1809 were executed

---

42. The Basílica; 43. Iglesia San Juan; 44. Ciné Alhambra; 45. Ministry of Agriculture; 46. Iglesia de San Blás; 47. Ciné Central; 48. Instituto Ecuatoriano de Cultura Hispánica (Casa de Benalcázar); 49. Iglesia de Carmen Bajo; 50. Teatro Sucre; 51. Academy of History; 52. Museum of Colonial Art; 53. National Art Museum; 54. Basílica de la Merced; 55. Iglesia de la Concepción; 56. Archbishop's Palace; 57. Iglesia de San Agustín (and museum); 58. General Post Office; 59. Government Palace; 60.Municipal Palace (inc. Tourist Office); 61. Templo Evangélico; 62. Municipal Museum of Art and History; 63. Cathedral; 64. El Sagrario chapel; 65. Casa de Sucre (museum); 66. Iglesia de Santa Catalina; 67. Ciné Rumiñahui; 68. Flota Imbabura (bus); 69. San Francisco: Church, monastry and museum; 70. Catuña chapel; 71. Iglesia de la Compañia; 72. National Library; 73. Iglesia San Roque; 74. El Robo chapel; 75. Convent of Carmen Alto; 76. Hospital Chapel of San Juan de Dios; 77. Transportes Esmeraldas (bus); 78. Ministry of Public Education; 79. Iglesia de Santo Domingo (museum); 80. Iglesia San Diego (Convent and museum); 81. Iglesia San Sebastián; 82. Panecillo lookout and restaurant.

542   **ECUADOR**

(waxwork); **Museum of Ethnology,** Departamento de Letras, Ciudad Universitaria, Tues. to Fri. 0900-1230, Wed. and Fri. 1500-1700, Tues. and Thurs. 1500-1830; **Museo Histórico Casa de Sucre,** the beautiful house of Sucre on the corner of Venezuela and Sucre, open 0900-1200, 1300-1600, Tues.-Sat.; closes 1500 Fri. **The Museo-Biblioteca Aureliano Polit** at the former Jesuit seminary beyond the airport has a unique collection of antique maps of Ecuador. Open Mon. to Fri. 0900-1200 and 1500-1800. Take the Condado minibus from the Plaza San Martín in Av. Pichincha. **Cima de los Libertadores,** museum at the site of the 1822 Battle of Pichincha, splendid view. The Tourist Office recommends taking a taxi there as the suburbs are dangerous, but you can take a bus to the south of the city and walk up.

Hotels *Intercontinental Quito,* with casino and pool, A, meals dear, often empty on weekdays as business travellers prefer the more central and convenient *Colón Internacional,* Amazonas y Patria, A, impersonal, excellent food, good discotheque, shopping arcade, casino. *Alameda Real,* A, can be booked through KLM airline, on Amazonas y Roca, all rooms are suites and many have kitchenettes, recommended. *Tambo Real,* 12 de Octubre y Patria opp. US Embassy, A, warmly recommended as best value for money; *Chalet Suisse,* Calama 312 y Reina Victoria, C; *Residencia Los Alpes,* D, Tamayo 233 with Washington, behind the US Embassy and popular with Americans, clean, friendly, comfortable, water pressure poor on third floor, recommended; *Savoy Inn,* Yasuni 304 y El Inca, C, between new town and airport; *Apartotels Amaranta 1,* Veintimilla 187, C, and *Amaranta 2,* L.Plaza 196 y Washington, B; *Apartotel Mariscal,* Robles 958, D; *República,* Av. República y Azuay, D, clean and reasonable; *Príncipe,* E, Av. América 660, recommended, good breakfasts; *Dan,* Av. 10 de Agosto 2482, E, a/c, private bathrooms, rooms over Av. 10 de Agosto are noisy, food and services improved, laundry facilities good, recommended; *Residencial Florida,* Versalles 1075, E, with full board, excellent. Near the *Quito,* at Caamaño 213 y Colón, is *Posada Real,* E; *Auca Continental,* corner of Venezuela and Sucre in centre, E, bath, be careful of your belongings, little service; *Coral Internacional,* Manuel Larrea 164, E, spacious rooms, equidistant from new and old city, cafeteria open 0730-2200, popular with families, clean, friendly; *Rapa-Nui,* Av. 6 de Diciembre 4454, F; *Zumag,* Av. 10 de Agosto y Mariana de Jesús, E, parking; *Residencial Santa Clara,* F, Gustavo Darquea Terán 1578, just off 10 de Agosto, friendly, clean, no meals, laundry service, some English spoken; *Residencial Carrión,* Carrión 1250 y Versalles, E, 20 rooms with private bath, 'phone, restaurant, bar, "clean, quiet, attractive, reasonable"; *Embajador,* 9 de Octubre 1046 y Colón, E, full board available, run down, good service; *Residencial Cumbres,* E, Baquedano 148 y Av. 6 de Diciembre, clean, very helpful, large breakfast; *Inca Imperial,* D, Calle Bogotá 219, built in Inca style with lavish Inca-style decor, large, lock-up car park, very good restaurant, highly recommended; *Real Audiencia,* Bolívar 220, C, spacious, lavishly furnished rooms, highly recommended, front rooms a bit noisy, restaurant O.K., central, parking, in general good value; *Majestic,* E, Mercadillo 366 y Versalles, little hot water but clean and friendly; *Hostal Imperio,* good for modern area, Portoviejo 188 y 10 de Agosto, C; *Residencial Bethania,* Pres. Wilson y Juan León Mera, F, hot water, hard beds, rather run down, cold house; *Residencial Los Geranios,* F, Cotopaxi 240, only one shower, dirty but friendly; *Quitumbe,* Espejo 815 y Flores, E, centre of old town in pedestrian area, recommended, friendly, clean, not enough bathrooms, secure for left luggage. Students can try *La Buena Esperanza,* Calle Morales 755 and Guayaquil, F, basic, if all else fails there are other places, same price range, same street; *Residencia Dali,* Calle Caldas 718 y Vargas, near Basílica (D full board, F without, hot water, recommended); *Royal Inn,* 6 de Diciembre 2751, E, comfortable, helpful owner; *Residencial Lutecia,* Av. Jorge Washington 909 y Páez, in a restored colonial house (C with bath and full board), popular with overlanders; *Embassy,* D, Presidente Wilson 441 y 6 de Diciembre, highly recommended, friendly, clean, well-furnished, showers, parking, good restaurant (French); *6 de Diciembre,* Av. 6 de Diciembre 1230, D, private bath, quiet, but a bit grubby; *Colonial,* Maldonado 3035 in centre, F, G if without shower, helpful, clean, quiet room, cheaper rooms in annex, laundry service, television, but robberies have been reported; *Santa María,* Inglaterra 933, D, good breakfasts, safe to store luggage, en route to airport; *Europa,* Guayaquil 1373 y Olmedo, E, basic, close to Plaza Teatro, *Residencial Italia,* E, Av. 9 de Octubre 237, clean, rather cold at night, friendly, family-run, recommended; *Viena Internacional,* Flores y Chile, E, English spoken, hot water, telephones, laundry service, friendly, good meals, secure; *Viena,* F, opposite, disorganized, dirty bathrooms; *San Agustín,* Flores 626 y Chile, E, clean, friendly, hot water, private bath, cheap restaurant; *Amazonas,* Maldonado 915, F, restaurant, friendly, highly recommended, convenient for buses to the south; *Residencial New York,* on Guayaquil, F, friendly, basic, failing water supply; *Residencial Bolívar,* Calle Espejo 832, F, cold water, clean. *Residencial Pichincha,* Elizalde and Colombia, F, rates vary according to length of stay, will store luggage, parking, convenient to old and new city, only one very dirty bathroom and constantly failing water supply, public baths opposite, US$0.30, lots of hot water; *Rocafuerte,* G, Rocafuerte 1066 y Paredes, dirty bathrooms, thefts, fleas; *Grand Hotel,* E, Rocafuerte 1001, bathroom, safe, friendly; *Hostal El Ejido,* E, Juan Larrea 535 y Riofrío, clean and friendly, meals overpriced; *Residencial Marsella,* Los Ríos 2035, F, clean, modern, friendly, washing facilities, no hot water, recommended, overlooks Parque La Alameda; *Residencial Andaluz,* Calle Morales, F, grimy; *Hogar,* Montúfar 208, F, with parking, overpriced, luggage can be stored; *Pensión Minerva,* Loja 654, G, hot shower, clean and cheap, and *Astoria,* Loja 630, G, both in noisy red-light area; *Juana de Arco,* Rocafuerte 1311 y Maldonado, E, friendly, only back rooms with shower, recommended, front rooms cheaper but noisy, good restaurant next door; *9*

ECUADOR 543

de Octubre, 9 de Octubre 1047 y Colón, E, shower, warm water, quick laundry service, friendly, safe deposit; *Montúfar*, Sucre 162 near Plaza Santo Domingo, F, safe, clean, hot water, recommended; *Residencial Dorado*, 18 de Septiembre 805, F, intermittent water, toilet paper supplied, basic, another wing of same hotel across the street, more expensive, higher standard; *Monasterio*, 24 de Mayo 1250, F, dirty, not recommended; *Sucre*, Bolívar 613 e Imbabura, G, basic, by the market, friendly, spacious rooms, hot water on demand; *Los Andes*, F, on Maldonado; *Huasi Continental*, Calle Flores and Sucre, F, clean, friendly, rooms on street noisy, convenient for the old city. *Guayaquil No. 1*, F, Maldonado 3248, near Plaza San Domingo, hot water, basic, will store luggage for small charge, safe; *Gran Casino*, García Moreno and Ambato, G and F (preferable rooms), hot water 0600-1500, good meals, popular with gringos and a good meeting place, will store luggage, US$0.25 per bag per week, laundry available, book exchange, dirty. Washing and toilet facilities limited, but Turkish bath, sauna and shower next door. There is also the new *Gran Casino Internacional*, E, at 24 de Mayo y Bahía, round the corner, both GCs are owned by the same family. *Pensión Americana*, Av. 6 de Diciembre 2751, D with breakfast; *Pensión Ramírez*, Morales 781, La Ronda, owned by Freddy Ramírez who also runs very reasonable trips to jungle and mountains; *Zulia*, Maldonado y Morales, G; *Hilton* (no relation!), Cordero near 10 de Agosto, F; *Ingatur*, Maldonado 3226, F, hot water, clean, washing facilities, safe to store luggage, open nearly all night; *Capitalino*, opposite Ingatur on Maldonado, F, pleasant, hot water; *Indoamérica*, F, hot water, well-furnished, clean, recommended, Maldonado 3022; *Canarias*, F, Flores 856, recommended.

If you prefer not to stay in a hotel, 'phone Rosa Jácome, José Bustamante 153 y Zaldumbide, Tel.: 451-590, who has several rooms for guests, near airport with direct bus to centre, you may cook for yourself if you want, about US$5 p.p. She is a taxi driver and can make arrangements for visits to the city for tourists. For longer stays with room, kitchen, TV, laundry service etc., the following have been recommended: *Suites Ejecutivos*, 10 de Agosto 4032 y Rumibamba, F, US$150 a month; *Apartamentos Colón*, Leonidas Plaza 326, Casilla Postal 2103, Tel.: 230360, US$320 a month for two people; *Apartamentos Calima*, Luis Cordero y 10 de Agosto, US$140 a month for two people. Rates depend on length of stay and number of people. *Aparthotel El Sol* has suites for two people, Av. Orellana 1757, between 10 de Agosto y 9 de Octubre, Tel.: 524150, also suites for between 1 and 5 people. Also *Casa Paxi*, F, Pasaje Navarro 364 y Av. La Gasca, Tel.: 542-663, complete with cooking facilities, telephone and roof terrace, owned by Dutch guide Pieter van Bunningen.

Note Those travelling by car may have difficulty parking in the centre of Quito and are therefore advised to choose the less central hotels.

Restaurants Excellent food at *Hotel Colón Internacional* for non-residents; cheaper in snack bar. Also a "limitless" buffet, where Sunday lunch, US$5, is worth fasting for. In old city, *Hotel Auca* restaurant, Venezuela 625 y Sucre, has been mentioned. *Moby Dick*, Amazonas 272, for oysters and lobster, excellent; *El Cholito*, Av. Guayaquil 1255; *Le Toucan*, Camino El Inca 1934, expensive; *Los Faroles*, Av. de la Prensa, Spanish food; Italian food at *Rincón de Sicilia*, Av. 10 de Agosto 9-71, and at *Vieja Europa*, Reina Victoria 1226. *Excalibur*, Calama 380, international cuisine. At lunchtimes *Chifa Epicur*, Av. 10 de Agosto 13-23, sometimes serves local specialities, though the normal fare is Chinese. *La Jaiba*, Reina Victoria y Av. Colón, has good seafood. *El Cebiche*, Juan León Mera 1232 y Calama, delicious seafood, open 1000-2100. Also for seafood, *Los Redes de Mariscos*, Amazonas 845 y Veintimilla, American-run, excellent; *Ron Coffey's Hyatt*, Juan León Mera and Bruna, also American (Southern menu), very select, recommended; *Chalet Suisse*, Calama 312 with Reina Victoria, dear but excellent steaks. *Rancho Suizo*, Juan León Mera y Sta. María, about US$10 p.p. for 3-course meal, food good but service slow, closed Sat.; *Tokio*, Asunción 1388; *La Choza*, 12 de Octubre y Cordero, good typical Ecuadorean food. *Emperador*, García Moreno 8-66, is reasonable. Simple food at *Chifa Chang* (not only Chinese), at Chile y Flores, it also has good pastries, self-service, dear for what's offered; good Chinese food at *Pekin*, Bello Horizonte 197; *Chifa Mayflower*, 6 de Diciembre 1149; *Casa China*, Mariana de Jesús with Amazonas, good, reasonable; *Salón Fénix*, also Chinese, Amazonas y Carrión, serves vegetarian; *Mandarín*, Suárez 162, in front of *Hotel Quito*, very good Chinese food about US$3.50 p.p.; *El Oriente del Sur*, Calle Olmedo y Venezuela, cheap, good; *Fondue Bar*, Juan Rodríguez 175, good bar, fondues, French dishes, fairly priced, closed Sun.; *Manolo's Churrería*, Amazonas 4-20, very reasonable hot snacks. Excellent meats and vegetables at Mrs Groner's *Casa de mi Abuela*, Luis Cordero 1922 y Páez, home cooking, warmly recommended; *Columbus* steak house, Av. Colón 1262 y Amazonas, good and popular; *El Hobo*, Av. Amazonas 3837, steaks and *paella*, English spoken. *Churrasquería al Rodizio*, Av. Amazonas, look for stuffed bull on first floor terrace, Brazilian style, US$4, inc. tax, for meat, salad, as much as you can eat. Seafood at *El Tartaro Internacional*, Calama 163 y 6 de Diciembre, is recommended and reasonably priced. *Restaurant do Brasil*, Venezuela y Chile, cheap speciality of the day, fair. *La Ronda*, on Bello Horizonte, good food, nice atmosphere, quite expensive; *Terrazón de El Tanturo*, Amazonas y Veintimilla, no signs, at top of building, beautiful views, good food, good value. Good place to eat cheaply is *Salón Italia*, Olmedo 651 y Guayaquil; *Una Terraza Increíble*, on corner of 6 de Diciembre y Veintimilla, upstairs, through the art gallery to a plant-filled terrace, good food, moderate prices, open Mon. to Fri., 1000-1800; *Marisquería El Delfín*, Av. Coruña e Isabel la Católica. *Café Madrillón*, Chile 12-70

544 ECUADOR

y Benalcázar, recommended. *Asia*, Guayaquil y Mejía 236, for lunch. Excellent food at *Restaurante Viena* on Chile with Flores. *La Cosecha*, Mariscal Foch 881 y Amazonas, good, cheap, friendly, vegetarian; *Salud y Vida*, Reina Victoria 11-38, is a good and reasonably priced vegetarian restaurant; *La Cabaña*, new vegetarian, Cordero 1489 y Amazonas, expensive and good; also *Tierra Buena*, close to *Chalet Suisse*. *Rincón de Francia*, Roca 779 y 9 de Octubre, posh and expensive but food excellent, especially seafood; *La Bella Epoca*, Whimper 925, reasonably priced, excellent food; *Oasis*, Espejo 812, cheap, excellent *jugos*; *Mamá Clorinda*, Reina Victoria y Calama, cheap and good for Ecuadorean food; next door to *Salud y Vida*; *Rues del Mundo*, Robles y Amazonas, good for lunch, tea and dinners; *El Ciervo* or *Hirsch*, Dávalos 250 y Páez, German-run, German cuisine, highly recommended; *Taberna Quiteña*, Amazonas 12-59 y Cordero and Patria y Gral. Páez, live music from 2030, also Manabí with Luis Vargas, in centre, better, with good folk music nightly and great atmosphere, good Ecuadorean food but on the dear side; *Las Cuevas de Luis Candela*, not cheap, in old town opposite Post Office, Benalcázar y Chile and Orellana y Coruña, usually open until midnight, but closed Sun; *Pizza*, Colón y 10 de Agosto. In the old town, *El Criollo*, Flores 825, cheap and clean, creole specialities, big helpings; *El Amigo*, on Calle Guayaquil, good food, moderate prices, set lunch for US$0.60; *Inti*, Mariana de Jesús y Hungría, good "typical" food, clean, good service; *Casa Española*, Calama entre J. L. Mera y Reina Victoria, reasonably-priced Spanish restaurant, good fish, owners perform flamenco when in the mood; Similar is *Costa Vasca*, 18 de Septiembre 585, good food and excellent atmosphere, see eccentric owner's bathroom décor; *Rincón Cubano*, Amazonas 993 y Veintimilla, recommended for Cuban food, English-speaking owner; *Toto Restaurante Lotto*, Av. 10 de Agosto y Orellana, run by Colombians, good, cheap, recommended; *Taverna Bavaria*, Calle Cordero y Juan León Mera, also German-run but French and English spoken, very good value, proprietors will arrange small group tours to the Galápagos and Oriente, also trekking in the mountains; *Fortunato Steak House*, Diego de Almagro 534, good salad bar, good steaks; *La Trattoria de Renato*, San Javier y Orellana, good meals, nice atmosphere, expensive; *Cafetería Dominó*, Calle Venezuela y Mejía near Plaza Independencia, snacks, juices, cheap *almuerzo*, clean and friendly, good coffee. *Vecchia Roma*, Roca 618, run by Venetian lady, good food and atmosphere; *Sorrento*, Calama 339, Italian food, Chilean wine, run by Italians, recommended but not cheap; *Pizza Nostra*, Amazonas 252 y Washington, good Italian food, but not cheap; *Pizza Hut*, on Espejo down hill from Plaza Independencia, and at Juán León Mera y Carrión; *Nuevo Shanhay*, J. Carrión 742 y Amazonas, cheap and recommended; *Pollo Chino*, Av. Américas y Portoviejo, specializes in chicken, good value. *Porky's*, Mejía 285 y Guayaquil, good, clean. There is a *Kentucky Fried Chicken* opposite the Post Office on Plaza Santo Domingo and on Benalcázar; better value is *Pollos Gus*, 24 de Mayo 1246 y Moreno, US-style self-service chicken and meat cooked on open fire, waitress service downstairs, good helpings, recommended for fussy eaters; also recommended is *Pollo Broster*, Sucre 258 y Venezuela, ice cream, bread and pastries especially good; *King Chicken*, Guayaquil y Manabí, wide menu, modern and clean; *Self-Service El Americano*, 10 de Agosto 666 y Cheta, large selection of dishes, clean and pleasant setting. Open late is *Sucre* (not bad), on Plaza Sto. Domingo (Rocafuerte y Maldonado); *El Pub*, opposite *Hotel Quito*, with an English menu including Cornish pasties and fish and chips. For hamburgers, *McDonalds* (an imitation of the real thing), Av. Amazonas y Cordero; *Dimpy*, Av. Amazonas and in most shopping centres, quick service, hot dogs, sandwiches etc, clean, reasonable. Inexpensive spit-roasted chicken can be had at cafés in the old city, e.g. *Piko Riko*, Chile y Cuenca. Markets are also a good source of food. An excellent bakery for cakes and pastries is *El Túnel*, Amazonas 1036 y Pinto; *Panadería Sevilla*, Edificio Torre Reina, Luis Cordero, try the sweets, excellent cakes; *Baguette*, Amazonas y Mariana de Jesús, sells good bread, pastries and pasteurized cheeses; *Pastelería Frederica*, 10 de Agosto 679, recommended for very fresh *cachos*; *El Torreón*, on Plaza del Teatro, good for cakes, juices, ice creams and sandwiches, though a little more expensive than usual. **N.B.** Many of the restaurants in the old city close at about 2200 every evening. Also, prices listed on menus may not be true prices; it is worth checking.

Bookshops Libri Mundi, Juan León Mera 851 y Veintimilla and at the *Hotel Colón Internacional*, Spanish, English (some second-hand available), French, some German and Italian books, international magazines, records, Ecuadorean maps in stock, has a notice-board of what's on in Quito; very highly recommended. Librería Universitaria, García Moreno 739; Su Librería, books in English and German, García Moreno 1172 y Mejía; Librería Científica, Av. Colón y Juan León Mera; Librería Cima, Av. 10 de Agosto y Sta. Prisca; Pomaire, Av. Amazonas 863 (Spanish mainly). The United States Information Service has an excellent library. Biblioteca Luz, Manabí 568, runs a book exchange: Foreign newspapers at newsstand in *Hotel Colón*.

Shopping Articles typical of Ecuador can be bought in the main shopping districts centred on Avenidas Amazonas and Guayaquil or at the two main markets. One of these, Mercado Ipiales, on Chile from Imbabura uphill, is where you are most likely to find your stolen camera for sale. The other is on 24 de Mayo and Loja from Benalcázar onwards. There are carved figures, plates and other items of local woods, balsa wood boxes, silver of all types, Indian textiles, buttons, toys and other things fashioned from tagua nuts, hand-painted tiles, hand-woven rugs and a variety of antiques dating back to colonial days. Panama hats are a good buy; Eljuri, Chile 1062. Indian garments (for Indians rather than tourists) can be seen and bought on the north end of the Plaza Sucre and along the nearest stretch of the nearby Calle General Flores. Ocepa, at Carrión 1336 y Versalles,

ECUADOR 545

good selection, government-run, also Jorge Washington 252 y Amazonas, near *Hotel Colón*, Amazonas 2222 and La Granja, and in town centre on Espejo y Venezuela; branches also in Guayaquil and Cuenca. Shops under Palacio de Gobierno. Near *Hotel Quito* at Av. Colón 260 is Folklore, the store of Olga Fisch, a most attractive array of handicrafts and rugs, but distinctly expensive, as accords with the designer's international reputation; also at *Hotel Colón* and *Hotel Quito*. Productos Andinos, an artisans' co-operative, Urbina 111 y Cordero, good quality, reasonably priced, recommended; there is a smaller branch store at Robles 900 y 9 de Octubre. After it in quality is Artes, Av. 6 de Diciembre 1118 y Veintimilla. La Bodega Exportadora, Juan León Mera 614 y Carrión, is recommended for antiques and handicrafts, and so is Renacimiento, Carrión y Mera. Coosas, Juan León Mera 838, the factory outlet for Peter Mussfeldt's attractive animal designs (bags, clothes etc.). Goldwork from Antigüedades el Chordeleg, 6 de Diciembre y Cordero. Artesanías El Jaguar, Juan León Mera 234 and 18 de Septiembre, behind *Hotel Colón*, souvenirs especially from the Oriente, the owner, Gladis Escobar, paints balsawood birds in colours of your choosing (not cheap). Handicrafts Otavalo, Calle Sucre 255 and García Moreno, good selection, but expensive. Galeria Latina, next to Libri Mundi at J.L.Mera 823 y Veintimilla, has fine selection of handicrafts from Ecuador, Peru and Bolivia. On Av. Amazonas, NE of *Hotel Colón*, are a number of street stalls run by Otavalo Indians, who are tough but friendly bargainers; recommended shops include Hamiltons, for jewellery, and Bonita Fashions where you can have a leather jacket made to order in 48 hours. La Guaragua, Washington 614, sells *artesanías* and antiques, excellent selection, reasonable prices; Joe Brenner sells folk art and handicrafts at reasonable prices at Galería Sul, Pontevedra 698 y Salazar near *Hotel Quito*, recommended for quality and price and better value than more tourist-oriented shops, particularly where ceramics and balsa-wood carvings are concerned. El Scarabejo Azul, Portugal 948 y Shyris, near southern end of La Carolina, Indian handicrafts and works by modern craftsmen using prehispanic materials. Rainproof ponchos at shops along Flores between Espejo and Bolívar. You need to bargain. Casa de los Regalos, Calle Mañosca 456, for souvenirs and antiquities. Bargaining is customary in small shops and at street stalls. "Typical" articles tend to be cheaper outside Quito. Recommended watchmaker, Sr. Torres, Relojería Patek Phillippe, Mejía 329. Food is cheap at Centro Comercial Iñaquito (CCI) supermarket if you have their credit card, but you pay 10% extra without. There is one in the Multicentro shopping complex on Av. 6 de Diciembre y La Niña, about two blocks N of Colón, open 0830-1230, 1530-1900. See H. Stern's jewellery stores at the airport, *Hotel Colón* and *Hotel Intercontinental*. Cheap food at Frigorífico Los Andes, Calle Guayaquil. Casa Americana, on Venezuela, inexpensive department store. Camping gaz cartridges hard to find, buy in Peru if convenient; otherwise Importadora Vega, opp. Banco Central, or Deportes Cotopaxi, 6 de Diciembre y Baquedano, or Globo, 10 de Agosto, sometimes have it in stock but it's expensive. For hiking boots, Calzado Beltrán, Cuenca 562. For mosquito nets, hunting and climbing gear: Capitán Peña, Flores 200 y Bolívar.

Camera Repairs and Equipment Foto Gómez, Olmedo 827; Fujicolor, Roca y Gutiérrez.

Warning Pickpocketing is becoming more common in Quito, especially round Plaza S. Francisco, in market areas and on public transport. Quito is not, however, a dangerous city, apart from some of the poorer suburbs.

Night Clubs Licorne, at *Hotel Colón Internacional*; discos at JK, Amazonas 541, Mamma Rosa, Amazonas 553, Tobujas, Amazonas y María, La Diligencia, 9 de Octubre 158, Luis XVI, Cordero 994 y Foch, recommended. Casinos at *Chalet Suisse*, *Intercontinental* and *Rapa Nui* hotels. Tulsa, República 471 next to Ciné República, is a dance hall frequented by US expatriates.

Local folk music is popular and the entertainment is known as a *peña*. Places include Lira Quiteña, Amazonas y Orellana; Rincón Sentimental and Pan y Canto, both at Veintimilla y 6 de Diciembre; Peña del Castillo, Calama 270 y Reina Victoria; Billy Cutter, Cordero 1952; Peña del Chino, and Ñucanchi Llacta, both at Rodríguez y Almagro; Las Jarras and Inti Illimani, both at Baquedano y Reina Victoria. *Taberna Quiteña* restaurants (best at Luis Vargas and Manabí in the centre), also recommended. Most places do not come alive until 2230.

Theatre Teatro Sucre, Calle Flores with Guayaquil, the most elegant. Weekly concerts during the rainy season, but buy tickets in advance. Symphony concerts are free. Teatro Prometeo adjoining the Casa de la Cultura Ecuatoriana, 6 de Diciembre y Tarqui. Also, plays at the Patio de Comedia, 18 de Septiembre, between Amazonas and 9 de Octubre.

Cinema The Colón (10 de Agosto y Colón), República (Av. República) and Universitario (Av. América, Plaza Indoamérica, Universidad Central) usually have the best films, the former often has documentaries with Latin American themes. The *Hotel Colón* shows films on video in the bar at weekends (free).

Festivals A New Year *fiesta*, the Inocentes, from Dec. 28 to Jan. 6, fills the streets with people; much bitter satire on the politicians. Another festival, for week ending Dec. 5, celebrates foundation of city. Hotels allowed to charge extra. Bullfights, and music in streets.

Carnival at Shrovetide is celebrated, as elsewhere in the Andes, by throwing plastic bags of

546 ECUADOR

water at passers-by, so you need a raincoat and umbrella at that season. The Good Friday processions are most impressive. Fancy-dress parades for Hallowe'en, celebrated last Sat. in October, along Av. Amazonas.

Sport Horse racing on Sun. at La Carolina track; pari mutuel betting. A local game, *pelota de guante* (stone ball), is played, Saturday afternoon and Sunday, at Estadio Mejía. Football is played Sat. afternoons and Sun. mornings at Estadio Atahualpa, and basket-ball in the Coliseo. The first week of December is the main bullfighting season. Tickets are on sale at 1500 the day before the bullfight; an above-average ticket costs US$2.70 but you may have to buy from touts. There is a cold spring-water swimming pool on Maldonado beyond the Ministry of Defence building (US$0.10), hot shower (US$0.10). Rugby is played at Colegio Militar on Sun. 1000. Inquire at *El Pub*.

Climbing Nuevos Horizontes Club, Venezuela 659, on Pasaje Amador near Plaza Independencia, in a room which is also used by the Academía Americana, meets evenings (1900 or 2000 hrs.), will advise on climbing Chimborazo and Cotopaxi, including purchase or hire of crampons, ice axes etc., but does not hire them (best to have with you). Non-members may go on the club's trips if these are not fully-booked. Cóndores, Padre José Ribas of Colegio San Gabriel is helpful. Sr. Enrique Veloz of Riobamba arranges trips to Chimborazo (see page 569). Useful climbing equipment stores (and sources of information) are Equipo Cotopaxi, 6 de Diciembre 1557, and Campo Abierto, on same street. Other clubs for climbers: Sadday, Manabí 621, near Plaza Independencia; the International Andean Mountaineers' Club is open to visitors and residents of Ecuador; equipment rented, call G. Rae on 230070. Those needing a professional climbing guide can try Alan Cathey (Tel.: 230847) who is fluent in English, Spanish and German and can also arrange ice climbing trips. Marco Cruz, guide for Sierra and Selva, can be contacted through Metropolitan Touring. Freddy Ramírez G., Juan de Dios, Morales 781, La Ronda, Quito, Tel. 613-579, runs a *pensión*, is a member of the Inti-Nan Club, works at the Dituris office in the Palacio Municipal and can act as a mountain guide, not expensive, highly recommended. Freddy and his brother Milton speak English and French and also do jungle tours. He has a 4-wheel drive Toyota jeep for rent, and will also rent climbing equipment. A Dutch guide, Pieter van Bunningen, Andrés de Artieda 444 y Av. La Gasca, Quito, takes small parties on mountain and jungle treks at reasonable rates, he is an experienced walker and climber and speaks Spanish, English and German. Nelson de la Torre, La Cumbre 189, Sector 32, Quito, Tel.: 242704, is a climbing guide and can organize climbing and trekking tours; he is fluent in English. The agencies offer climbs up the Illinizas (2 days, US$125), Cotopaxi (3 days, US$230), Tungurahua (4 days, US$260).

Academia de Español Quito

★ Specially designed programs for foreign students.

★ Up to 7 hours daily of individual instruction (one to one with teacher), Monday through Friday.

★ Essentially practical courses, based on vocabulary, grammar and conversation, at all levels.

★ The system is self-paced and you can start at any time.

★ You can live at the home of an Ecuadorian family where you get 3 meals, have your own bedroom and laundry.

★ It is also possible to contract for classes only, at a reduced fee and with flexible schedules.

**130 Marchena St. and
10 de Agosto - 3rd Floor,
P.O. Box 39-C, Quito-Ecuador**

ECUADOR 547

Bank of London and South America, Av. Carrión y Amazonas, with Torres de Colón, Jipijapa and San Agustín agencies, quick service, recommended; Citibank (own cheques only); Banco Holandés Unido, 10 de Agosto 911; Bank of America, Patria y Amazonas; Banco Internacional, opposite B. of A., notes only; Banco Popular, Amazonas 648. Open 0900-1330. Closed Sat. Bank open all day Sat. and Sun. a.m. in departure lounge at airport. The American Express representative is at Ecuadorian Tours, Amazonas 339, Tel.: 528-177.

Exchange Houses Rodrigo Paz, Venezuela 659, and Av. Amazonas 370, will change travellers' cheques into US$ cash up to US$200 without question. We have been told that more can easily be changed, if you give a good reason. Jaramillo Arteaga, Mejía 401 y Venezuela, and Colón y Amazonas, will change up to a maximum of US$100, passport copy required. The airport *cambio* and the *Hotel Colón* are the only places you can change money on Saturdays and Sundays. If you have trouble cashing American Express or Thomas Cook's travellers' cheques, try the *Hotel Colón* or the Banco Popular. You are advised not to buy Peruvian intis in Ecuador; you will get a much better rate in Peru. If you have sucres left over, change them into US dollars, not intis.

Post Office Toledo y Madrid (for *poste restante*), letel, the telephone company is at Benalcázar 769 y Chile, where there is also a post office that accepts parcels over 1 kg. There is also an Ietel office at Av. Colón y Av. Amazonas, open until 2200. Parcels take three months by sea (US$12.30) to Europe, US$25 by airfreight. Ecuadorian Tours accepts air mail packages with a minimum charge. Transpak (also called STAIR), Av. Amazonas y Veintimilla, will ship out packages for a minimum charge of US$50.

Embassies U.K., Av. González Suárez 111 (opposite *Hotel Quito*), letters to Casilla 314, Tel.: 521-755. U.S.A., Av. Patria y 12 de Octubre, Tel.: 548-000. (The US embassy does not hold mail for US citizens.) West Germany, Av. Patria y 9 de Octubre, Edificio Eteco, 6th floor, Tel.: 232-660. Austria, Av. Patria y Amazonas, Edificio Cofiec, 11th floor, Tel.: 545-336. Swiss, Av. Amazonas y Catalina Herrera, Tel.: 241-504. Canadian, Edificio Belmonte, 6° piso, Avenida Corea 126 y Amazonas, Tel.: 458-102. Dutch, Naciones Unidas 1204, Tel.: 456-800. Colombian Consulate, Av. Amazonas 353, insists on a ticket to leave Colombia before issuing a visa. Peruvian and Brazilian Consulates both in Edificio España, Av. Colón y Av. Amazonas.

British Council, Amazonas 1615 y Orellana, Tel.: 236-144, postal address: Casilla 1197. There is a library, open Mon.-Fri., 0800-1245, 1500-1915, which stocks back copies of British newspapers.

Language Courses at the Universidad Católica, Av. 12 de Octubre 1076 y Carrión, Instituto de Lenguas y Lingüística, Tel.: 529-240: 6-week Spanish courses, US$100; courses in Quechua. They will provide student cards, valid for reductions in Peru. The Academia de Español Quito, Marchena 130 y 10 de Agosto, 3rd floor, offers individual teaching, 7 hours a day, with full board and lodging with an Ecuadorian family for US$578 a month, recommended. Special reduced rates of about US$52 a month (or US$3 a day) can be negotiated for classes only.

Anglican Church St Nicholas, Gustavo Darquea y Carrión, service in English, Sun. at 0930. Joint Anglican/Lutheran service is held (in English) at the Advent Lutheran Church, Isabel la Católica 1419, Sun., 0900.

Charity The Centro del Muchacho Trabajador, or Working Boys' Centre, run by the Christ of the Andes Mission, is a charitable organization which welcomes visitors who wish to see the progress it is making in improving the conditions of the shoe-shine boys. It is located on one side of the Plaza San Martín coming down the Calle Chile from the Plaza de la Independencia. Handicrafts made by the boys are on sale at Caperucita Roja in the Palacio Arzobispal, Calle Venezuela with Chile, shop 12 and at some *artesanías*.

Medical Hospital Voz Andes, next to Voz Andes radio station, Villalengua 263 (Tel.: 241-540), emergency room, fee US$4, some English spoken (American-run), has out-patient dept., reached by No. 1 bus to Iñaquito; Centro Médico Alemania (Dr Klier speaks German), Eloy Alfaro y Alemania. Clínica Pichincha, Veintimilla 1259; Clínica Americana Adventista (some English spoken) 10 de Agosto 3366, 24 hrs., US$5. Dentist: Dra. Rosa Oleas, Amazonas 258 y Washington (Tel.: 524-859); Dr Roberto Mena, Tamayo 1255 y Colón, speaks English and German. All-night chemist, Farmacia Alaska, Venezuela 407 y Rocafuerte (Tel.: 210-973).

Immigration Office Independencia y Amazonas 877. For visa extensions, Av. Amazonas 2639, open 0800-1200 and 1500-1800; take bus 15, go early and be prepared to wait; service more reliable a.m. in Extranjería, Reina Victoria y Colón, Mon.-Thurs., 0830-1230, for visas other than tourist.

Laundromat Lavanderías Modernas, can take 2 days, Av. 6 de Diciembre 24-00 y Orellana (US$0.37 per 450 grams). Lavanderías Populares on Riofrio y Venezuela, central. Ropa Limpia, J. L. Mera y Lizardo García, good service. For dry-cleaning try Martinizing, Av. Colón y Mera (same day service).

Casa de Cultura Many cultural events, usually free of charge; see daily press for details. *Café*

548 ECUADOR

Artes, 6 de Diciembre y Veintimilla, near Libri Mundi, houses a modern art gallery and a lively restaurant which is a popular meeting place for local "intelligentsia".

Tourist Office Dirección Nacional de Turismo (Dituris) at Reina Victoria 514 y Roca (Tel.: 239-044), at airport, and the new Palacio Municipal, Plaza Independencia (Tel.: 514-044; Freddy Ramírez, the climbing expert, works here) provide maps and other information although help is often in short supply and few staff speak English. Their information on bus departure times is reported as being extremely inaccurate, so check at bus stations.

Maps may be obtained from the helpful and efficient Instituto Geográfico Militar on top of the hill at the eastern end of El Ejido park, on corner of Patria. Their maps are also sold by Libri Mundi, and by the shop at Venezuela 573. Opposite the entrance to the Casa de Cultura on 12 de Octubre, running SE up the hill is a small street, Jiménez, which becomes Paz y Miño, follow this up and round to the IGM on the right. You have to exchange your passport for a visitor's pass. Map and air photo indexes are all laid out for inspection. The map sales room is open 0800-1500, Mon.-Fri.

Tourist Agencies Ecuadorian Tours (American Express agent), Av. Amazonas 339, Tel.: 528-177 (Poste Restante can be sent for clients, Aptdo. 2605, Quito); Metropolitan Touring, helpful for information for non-customers, Amazonas 235, Tel.: 524-400; also downtown and at *Hotel Quito*; general agents for Galapagos Cruises and Transturi; runs tours to the Galápagos, also arranges climbing, trekking expeditions led by world-known climbers. Interturis, Av. Colón y 6 de Diciembre; Turismundia, friendly, Av. Amazonas 657 (reservations to Galápagos). Seitur, for the Galápagos and elsewhere, Pinto 525 y Amazonas, helpful, fluent English. Transturi, part of Metropolitan Touring, operate a cruise ship, the *Flotel Francisco de Orellana*, in 4-5 day trips from Coca along the jungle rivers, from US$285 p.p. Freddy Ramírez, Morales 781, La Ronda, does 8-day jungle trips by bus to the Cuyabeno National Park, US$150 all inclusive. Yanasacha, Av. República 189 with Diego del Almagro, Tel.: 528-964, arranges trips to the Galápagos and Oriente as well as mountaineering expeditions. National Tours, Foch 831, Tel.: 547-614; Macchiavello Tours, Juan León Mera 1414, Tel.: 525-320. Alpa Tours, Amazonas 631 y Carrión, recommended, very helpful. Samoa Turismo, Victoria 907 y Wilson, Tel.: 551-597, P.O. Box 9107, Suc. 7, Quito. Reliable tours to the Galápagos (8-day cruise for US$300, plus airfare); Coltur, Robles y Páez, also have office in Puerto Ayora, Galápagos, reported to be very good and helpful. For other agencies organizing tours to the Galápagos, see page 595.

Galasam Cía. Ltda., Pinto 523 y Av. Amazonas, operates Economic Galapagos Tours as well as Condor Tours, Uniclán, Yanasacha, Sol Mar Tours and their tours can be purchased in Switzerland: Artou, 8 rue de Rive 1204, Geneva; France: Delta Voyages, 11 Rue Edouard Jacques, Paris 75014; Italy: Nouvelles Frontières, Vicolo del Divino Amore, 180, 00186 Rome; Peru: Top Tours, A. Miró Quesada 247, Of. 704, Lima and El Punto, Av. Gonzalez de Piérola 742, Lima 1; USA: Latin American Student Travel, 43 Millstone Road, Randallstown, MD 21121, Tel.: (301) 922 2409; Canada, Galapagos Tour, 161 Dupont St., Toronto M5R 1VF (Tel.: (416) 968-3664, Telex 06-217682), exclusive representatives, prices are the same as in Ecuador. The Icaro flying school will organize trips in a light plane along "Avenue of the Volcanoes", 4-5 people, US$25 each. (US$30 an hour for lessons.)

Airport Mariscal Sucre Airport. Taxi to centre US$2-2.50. From airport catch bus 16 to go to Plaza Santo Domingo. The No. 1 Iñaquito and Aeropuerto buses go to the airport, look for a sign "*Aeropuerto*" on the windscreen; also No. 43, Marím-Carcelén. British Leyland double decker buses run all the way along Av. Amazonas to the airport. There is a US$5 airport and police departure tax on international flights, payable in sucres or US$. Beware of self-styled porters: men or boys who will grab your luggage in the hope of receiving a tip. There are no facilities for long-term left luggage at the airport, but there are at *Hotel Aeropuerto*, just outside the terminal, US$2 per day. Watch out for thefts by security officials when searching your bags; it has been reported that while you walk through the metal detector they remove money from your hand baggage. There are three duty-free shops in the international departure lounge, they sell few appliances and no film.

Internal Flights There are about 10 flights a day to and from Guayaquil US$12 (Tame, Saeta, SAN) and 3 to Cuenca (US$12). There are daily flights to Esmeraldas, Manta, Tulcán, Lago Agrio and the Galápagos; 2-3 flights a week to Loja, Portoviejo, Coca and Macas. Tame, Reina Victoria y Colón (Tel.: 549-100, another Tame office is at Av. 10 de Agosto 239); Saeta, Av. Colombia y Elizalde (Tel.: 217-681).

Local Transport Standard fare on local buses is US$0.06. The British double-decker bus running along Av. Amazonas to the airport costs US$0.08 (buy ticket in kiosk, not on the bus) and passengers may not stand, even when it's raining. Other buses are allowed along Av. Amazonas only before 0830. For trips outside Quito taxi tariffs should be agreed beforehand: usually US$30-32 a day. Outside main hotels drivers have a list of agreed excursion prices. Standard tariff in the city is US$0.60 to US$2 and not more than double by night; no increase for extra passengers; by the hour, US$4 up. Although the taxis now have meters, drivers sometimes say they are out of order. Insist on the meter being used, it is always cheaper! If they have no meter, it is imperative to fix fare beforehand.

ECUADOR 549

Car Rentals All the main car rental companies (Hertz, International Avis, Ecuacar, Budget, Dollar and Carros Inteligentes) are at the airport, with some having small offices in the city. It is best to ignore these and catch bus directly to the airport. Cars are available at US$33 per day, unlimited mileage, but there is a minimum three-day rental period. Insurance is US$5, and tax is 6 per cent on the total transaction. Some car hire firms do not have adequate insurance policies and you will have to pay heavily in the event of an accident. Also be sure to check the car's condition, not forgetting things like wheelnuts. We have received bad reports of Budget and Inteligentes, whilst Ecuacar is recommended. Land Rover specialists at Calle Inglaterra 533, Talleres Atlas. Also Luis Alfredo Palacios, Iturralde and Av. de la Prensa, Tel.: 234341 and Expo, Av.América 1116 y Bolivia.

Buses The Terminal Terrestre in the southern Villa Flora district, at Maldonado and Cumandá, enlarged in 1986, handles all long-distance bus services. From Terminal Terrestre to Av.Amazonas area take bus "Colón-2-Camal". Take No. 10 bus marked "*terminal terrestre*" from city, No. 1 Bartolo-Miraflores from Plaza Santo Domingo, or a taxi. Most buses marked "*terminal terrestre*" do not go right to the bus station but stop 300-500 metres away, which is awkward if you have luggage. There are company booking offices but staff shout destinations of buses leaving; you can pay them and get on board. Buses to Esmeraldas, US$2.50, 6 hrs., good buses, 19 daily, or by Aerotaxi minibus, 5½ hrs., 8 a day (for which you need a reservation), US$2.10, 12 passengers. Buses to Otavalo, 2 hrs., US$0.80, 9 a day. To Ibarra, 2½ hrs., US$1; to Tulcán, 4 hrs., US$2, about 30 a day; buses to Guayaquil, 8½ hrs., about US$3 on an ordinary bus or US$4.50 on a pullman coach; Ambato, US$1, 3½ hrs.; Cuenca, 10 hrs. US$4 (minibus, 8 hrs., US$4.50). To Santo Domingo de los Colorados, 2½ hrs., US$1; to Quevedo via Santo Domingo, US$2, 4 hrs.; to Latacunga, 2 hrs., US$0.75; to Riobamba, 4½ hrs., US$1.50. To Baños 3 hrs., US$1.50. To Huaquillas, 12 hrs., US$4; to Machala, US$3.50 first class, 10½ hrs. (Also minibuses.) Panamericana, Maldonado 3077, runs an "international" bus to Bogotá, but this involves many changes and greater expense; it is better to take a bus to the border and change. To Oriente: Lago Agrio, US$4, 9½ hrs.; Coca, US$5, 12½ hrs; Puyo, US$2, 7 hrs. (US$2.50, 9 hrs. via Baeza); Tena, US$2.50, 6½ hrs. (US$3, 8 hrs. via Ambato). There are now no direct through buses to Peru so take a bus to Huaquillas via Machala, cross the border and catch one of the Peruvian long-distance buses from Tumbes on to Piura, Trujillo and Lima. The alternative route for crossing the Peruvian border via Loja and Macará takes much longer than the Machala route. For buses out of Quito it is often advisable to reserve the day before as they may leave early if they are full. Tepsa has an office at Pinto 539 y Amazonas but avoid buying Peruvian bus tickets here as they will be half the price in Peru.

Drivers should note that there is now a ring road around Quito, and a by-pass to the S, the Carretera de Amaguaña.

Railway station is two km. from centre, along continuation of Calle Maldonado, reached by buses along that street (e.g. Colón-Camal, No. 2). The ticket office at the station is frequently closed. Severe rains and flooding destroyed much of the track in 1983. Daily train leaves for Riobamba 0830, US$1, 5 hrs.; *autoferro*, 1500, US$1, 4½ hrs. Metropolitan Touring does 2-day tour: down to Riobamba by train, overnight Riobamba, back by bus, US$120.

Cruz Loma and Rucu Pichincha Cruz Loma is one of the two antenna-topped peaks overlooking Quito from the west (it has two antennae, its neighbour one). On a clear day you can see about 50 km. down the central valley and to the east. Hiking up from Calle 24 de Mayo in central Quito takes 3-4 hrs. and the descent about 2. (To save time and energy one can take a cab or bus, e.g., Toctiuco, No. 14, to the upper reaches of Quito and start from there.) There are roads up to both peaks, but traffic is sparse. Try hitching early in the morning, but remember that it is difficult to hitch back after about 1730 and you will have to walk in the dark: some streets go through dangerous districts which should be avoided in the late afternoon and evening. The road to the northern hill is better for hitching; it leads to the radio station at the top of the hill; take bus no. 5 from Calle Gabriel García Moreno. Take a stick to ward off dogs. **Rucu Pichincha** (4,700 metres) cannot be seen from Quito, but can be climbed either via Cruz Loma or via its neighbour. The path to its foot runs due west over and around hummocks on the rolling, grass-covered *páramo*. The climb up to the peak is not technical, but it is rocky and requires a bit of endurance. About half an hour beyond Rucu Pichincha, is a second peak, Paso de Muerte. From Cruz Loma to Rucu Pichincha peak takes about 3 hrs. and the return about 1½. Take rainproof and cold-weather gear just in case. (*Note:* please pick up your flotsam; the area is rubbish-strewn enough as it is.)

Excursions 23 km. N of Quito (½ hour by taxi or 1 by bus, US$0.12), is the Equatorial Line Monument. On overcast days it is chilly, for the Monument stands at an altitude of 2,374 metres. The exact equatorial line here was determined by Charles de la Condamine and his French expedition in 1735. The monument forms the focal point of a park and leisure area with restaurants, gift shops, etc., and has a museum inside (open Tues.-Fri., 0900-1500, Sat.-Sun., 1000-1300). Admission to the monument and museum, US$0.75. Various Indian cultures are well explained by a pleasant, helpful guide who speaks good English. The T-shaped Solar Museum 2 km. SE, in village of San Antonio, is closed for

550 ECUADOR

repairs. The two entrances to the building are marked Northern Hemisphere and Southern Hemisphere. A paved road runs from Quito to the Monument, which you can reach by a "Mitad del Mundo" bus from University, Av. América y Pedro Guerrero. Two minutes' walk before the Monument is the restaurant *Equinoccio*, good food, good service, live music. Available at the restaurant are "certificates" recording the traveller's visit to the Equator. Other restaurants are now being opened.

A few km. beyond the Monument is the Pululagua crater, well worth visiting, and there is now a paved road. Continue on the road past the Monument towards Calacalí. After a few km. (1 hr. walk) the road bears left and begins to climb steeply; the paved road to the right leads to the rim of the volcano and a view of the farms on the crater floor. Buses to Calacalí (infrequent) will drop you at the fork, from where it is a ½ hr. walk. There is a rough track down from the rim to the crater, to give an impression of the rich vegetation and warm micro-climate inside the crater. Also in the vicinity of the Monument, 3 km. from San Antonio beyond the Solar Museum, is the ruined Inca fortress of Rumicucho. Restoration poor, but situation magnificent. Start early if you want to visit all these in one day.

The Equator line also crosses the Inter-American Highway 8 km. south of Cayambe, where there are a concrete globe beside the road and a mark on the road itself. Midday by the sun, incidentally, is between 1200 and 1230. Take Cayambe bus (2 hrs., US$0.80) and ask for Mitad del Mundo.

According to the vulcanologists, the best hot springs in Ecuador are the Baños de **Papallacta**, 80 km. E from Quito on the road to Lago Agrio. The natural pools are pleasanter than the commercial baths, and there are plenty of them so it is never very crowded; the water is wonderfully hot and there is a freezing river alongside. As you enter the village of Papallacta from the baths the first shop on the right, *Salón La Quiteñita*, has rooms to let upstairs and a small restaurant, no signs, basic but very cheap; you can also camp in the pastures up towards the baths, or sleep in the shelter at the hot springs themselves (no extra charge after the US$0.25 admission fee). There are showers, toilets and changing rooms. The restaurant is poor and open at weekends only. The farm next door sells milk and cheese. Bus Quito-Papallacta US$1, 2½ hrs. In the valley of Chillos (SE, 1 hr. by car) are the thermal pools of Alangasí and El Tingo. A few km. from El Tingo is La Merced, which has thermal baths. Camping is allowed in the vicinity. Further on from La Merced is Ilaló, a semi-private swimming club, admission US$2 but clean, fewer mosquitoes and people.

Another interesting trip is to **Sangolquí** about 20 minutes away by bus. There is a colourful Sun. market (and a lesser one on Thurs.), with Indians in traditional costumes and few tourists, and there are thermal baths nearby (pop. 18,000).

Day tours via Cotopaxi to Indian fairs at Pujilí and at Saquisilí (see page 573), about 93 km. each way, or to Cotopaxi itself.

North of Quito

A railway and the Pan-American Highway run north-east from Quito to Otavalo (121 km.) and Ibarra (145 km.). At Ibarra, the railway and Highway separate. The railway goes north-west to the Pacific port of San Lorenzo, a very spectacular trip: the highway runs north for another 108 km. to Tulcán and on to Ipiales in Colombia. The Pan-American Highway is now paved for the whole stretch Quito-Tulcán.

Calderón, 30 km. N of Quito, is the place where miniature figurines are made of bread; you can see them being made, and prices are much lower than in Quito. Especially attractive is the Nativity collection. Prices start from about US$0.15. See the Indian cemetery on November 1-2, when the graves are decorated with flowers, drinks and food for the dead. Corpus Christi processions are very colourful. Many buses from Quito (W end of Av. Colón).

The road for the north traverses the Indian area around Calderón, descends the spectacular Guayllabamba gorge and climbs out again to the fertile oasis of Guayllabamba village, noted for huge avocados and chirimoyas. Further north the road runs through dry, dusty land before irrigated land is reached again at **Cayambe** (pop. 14,168), dominated by the snow-capped volcano of the same name. This area of rich dairy farms produces a fine range of European-style cheeses. Cayambe is the Agrarian Reform Institute's showplace; its only major project. The monastery of the Salesian fathers in Cayambe has a superb library on indigenous cultures.

ECUADOR 551

Between Guayllabamba and Cayambe, before entering Tabacundo, a narrow dirt road to the left leads to Tocachi and further on to the Estancia **Cochasqui** national archaeological site; the whole area is covered with hills of pyramid shapes and ramps built between 900 and 1500 AD by Indians of the Caras or Caranquis tribe. Festivals with dancing at the equinoxes and solstices. Note the spectacular wind-eroded rocks. Students offer free, 20-min. guided tours which are recommended.

Rob Rachowiecki writes that about 1 km. before Cayambe is an unmarked cobbled road heading right for 26 km. to the Ruales-Oleas-Berge refuge at 4,400 metres. Opened in 1981 it costs US$2.50 p.p. a night and provides beds (bring sleeping bag), food, water and a kitchen. It is named after three Ecuadorean climbers killed by an avalanche in 1974 while pioneering a new route up the Cayambe volcano from the west. This has now become the standard route, using the refuge as a base. The climb is heavily crevassed, especially near the summit, and is more difficult and dangerous than either Chimborazo or Cotopaxi. Cayambe (5,790 metres) is Ecuador's third highest peak and the highest point in the world which lies directly on the Equator.

The road forks north of Cayambe: to the right a cobbled road, the very scenic *carretera vieja*, runs through Olmedo (just outside Olmedo, *El Coche Rojo* restaurant is reasonable and serves excellent seafood), Zuleta and Esperanza, to Ibarra; to the left, the main paved road crosses a *páramo* and suddenly we descend into the land of the Otavalo Indians, a singularly lively and prosperous group who have been making commercial woollens for over fifty years. The men are recognizable by their white, bell-bottomed, mid-calf-length trousers, long braided hair and blue ponchos. Although some work on *haciendas* between San Pablo and Ibarra, most of the scattered homes in the fields belong to Indians.

An alternative route from Quito to Otavalo is via San Antonio (Inca ruins of Rumicucho) and San José de Minas. The road curves through the dry but impressive landscape down to the Río Pita, then climbs again, passing some picturesque oasis villages. After Minas the road is in a very bad condition and a jeep is necessary for the next climb (beautiful views) and then descent to join the Otavalo-Selva Alegre road about 15 km. from Otavalo. The journey takes about 3 hours altogether and is rough but magnificent.

Otavalo (2,530 metres, population 18,000) is notable for its colourful Indian fair on Sat. (see below). Near the market, a ball game is played in the afternoons. It is similar to the game in Ibarra described below except that the ball is about the size of a table-tennis ball, made of leather, and hit with the hands, not a bat. From June 24 to 29, at the Fiesta de San Juan, there are bullfights in the plaza and regattas on the beautiful Lago de San Pablo, 4 km. away (bus to Espejo, US$0.20) and there is the *Fiesta del Yamor* in early September. At the Lago de San Pablo is the Club de Tiro, Caza y Pesca where one can rent canoes. It is worth walking either to or back from Lago de San Pablo for the views, the walk back via the outlet stream from the lake (staying on the right hand side of the gorge), taking 2-3 hrs., is particularly recommended. The new 13-roomed *Hotel Chicapán*, C, on the lakeshore is recommended; from the restaurant there is a fine view of the lake and Imbabura mountain. *Cabaña del Lago*, on the lakeside, D, has cabins with bunk beds, clean, good food. Boats and pedalos for hire, pony rides etc. Also in San Pablo del Lago (half-hourly buses from Otavalo) is *Hostería Cusín* in a converted *hacienda*, D, both often open only Fri.-Sun. Pleasant setting but awful food. There are also other restaurants. There are several lakes in the mountains around, such as Lake Cuicocha (see page 553), and the four very picturesque Lagunas Mojanda, with a simple hostel (take food).

There is a network of old roads and trails between Otavalo and the Lago San Pablo area, none of which takes more than an hour or two to explore. It is only half an hour's walk to the Cascadas de Peguche through woods. Four km. from Otavalo are lukewarm ferrous baths at the Fuente de Salud, said to be very curative (John Streather). It is also possible to hike much further south to Lagunas Mojanda and on to Tocachi (turn left after second lake); on the way you can visit the pyramids of Cochasqui (see above), a new and important excavation. Free guides. For maps and information contact García Mora in Ateneo Móvil, Bolívar y Roca, or his brother Rodrigo Mora in Zulaytour, Sucre y Colón, who arrange good guided tours (8 hours, US$5.50) for information on local history and Indian handicrafts (including visits to several homes).

We have received many reports of stealing from Otavalo hotel rooms; you are advised to ensure that your door is always locked, even if your absence is very brief.

Hotels May be full on Fri. nights, before fair, when prices go up. *Yamor Continental*, at northeast end of town, E, very comfortable, sometimes water shortages, lovely building, saunas,

552 ECUADOR

swimming pool, indoor and outdoor restaurants; *Otavalo*, E, hot water, cheaper rooms without bath, clean, fine old building with attractive patio, slightly run down but recommended, the new part across the street is clean but noisy, Indian music in nice restaurant, set menu; *Mariscal*, G, not safe; *Riviera y Sucre*, F, Moreno y Sucre, hot water, clean, safe, recommended, table-tennis table downstairs, the owner, Sr. Antonio Andrade, is an expert on the area; *Residencias Sami Huasi*, F, near market, friendly, clean, recommended; *Pensión Los Andes*, G, very grimy; the old dueña seems to be almost blind. (The landlady's brother will show you his small museum of archaeological and anthropological artefacts, entrance US$0.30, or free if you stay at the *pensión*.) *Isabelita*, Roca 1107 y Quiroga, F, quiet, spacious rooms, hot water, washing facilities, very clean, helpful, recommended. *Pensión Los Angeles*, G, clean, basic, hot water on request; *Pensión Otavalo*, G, quiet, clean, showers, laundry facilities, friendly; *El Mesón del Arrayán*, good, reasonable prices; *Pensión Vaca No. 2*, G, hot water, clean, friendly; *La Herradura*, G, very friendly, clean, restaurant; *Residencia Santa Ana*, F, on Calle Colón, pretty courtyard, large rooms, often only cold water, clean, cheap breakfast.

Restaurants *La Parenthesis*, Morales 813 y Miguel Egas, bar/restaurant once run by French people but has changed hands; *Sumak Mikuy*, Jaramillo y Pasaje Saona, criollo food; *El Triunfo*, Moreno y Jaramillo, good breakfast early, English spoken. *Camba Huasi* (with enclosed parking), self-service, good coffee, mixed reports; *El Mesón del Arrayán*, good, reasonable prices (check bill); *Ajadero Crystal*, Bolívar, clean, noisy jukebox. *Ali Micuy*, Jaramillo y Quiroga, vegetarian food, *jugos*, and cheeseburgers, also on Plaza de los Ponchos, cheap and good value, good map of town. *El Indio*, good value for money. For good "gringo" food, try the *Prime Burger* in the *Hotel Otavalo*. *Casa de Corea*, opposite *Hotel Otavalo*, Ecuadorean food, ordinary; *Chifa Tien An Men*, near Moreno and Bolívar, very good, generous portions, inexpensive; try *pollo pilipina*, chicken roasted in a thick, black hot sauce; *Copacabana*, Montalvo y Bolívar, basic, clean, reasonable, *merienda* about US$1, good for breakfast; *Cafetería Shanandoa*, Salinas y Jaramillo, good pies, milk shakes and ice cream, recommended for breakfast; *Centro Latino*, Sucre y Calderón, good fried chicken; *Royal*, on main plaza, clean (even the toilets), meal with cola about US$1.40.

Entertainment Local music at *Peña de los Chaskís*, Plaza de los Ponchos, *Peña de los Chozas*, Rescuate y Morales, and *Peña Folklórica*, Quiroga y Jaramillo; all on Fri. and Sat. nights, from 2200. There is also a cockpit (*gallera*), near the market, fights Sat. and Sun. 1500.

Swimming Pool Neptuno, open air (5 sucres) at end of Calle Morales, near the railway track, 3 blocks from station.

Museums Instituto Otavaleño de Antropología, exhibition, on Panamericana Norte; Museo Arqueológico César Vásquez Fuller, at *Pensión Los Andes*, Roca y Montalvo; Museo Jaramillo, Bolívar, off Parque Central.

Tourist Information Municipal Tourist Office at city hall, Moreno y Sucre; Zulaytour, English spoken, Sucre y Colón 1014.

The fair is a "must" for tourists. There are 4 markets in different places: (a) woollen fabrics and shawls, 0500-1330, in Plaza de Ponchos; (b) animal auction, 0530-1400 (Barrio San Juan at Cotocachi turnoff); (c) produce, 0800-1300, in Plaza 23 de Mayo; (d) *artesanías* at Plaza Centenario, Salinas y Sucre, Sats. only. The market is rated highly for woollen goods, though it is now rather highly organized and touristy and prices are not especially low; very little of the traditional weaving is now to be seen and many of the ponchos are made of orlon (these are easily recognizable). The earlier you get there the better. Bargaining is essential. All the same, Otavalo is the best place in Ecuador to buy a man's woollen poncho. Watch out for pickpockets and bag slashers in the market. (Goods sold in the market can also be bought in local shops, sometimes cheaper and with less bargaining.)

The Otavalo Indian weavers come from the villages of Peguche, Iluman and Quinchuqui, close to Otavalo. They are very friendly and will indicate where you can buy their products more cheaply from the loom. For a tour contact Rafael Perugachi, Calle Sucre 12-16; or Rodrigo Mora of Zulaytour, Sucre y Colón. Otavalo textile shops include *Tejidos y Artesanías Atahualpa*, Bolívar 1015, and *Coop. Indígena de Tejidos Peguche*, Bolívar 910. **Note:** If planning a spending spree, bring plenty of cash; Otavalo can be as expensive as Quito, and the exchange rate is very unfavourable, even in the bank.

Transport Bus to Ibarra, every 15 mins., US$0.15, ½ hr. From Quito by taxi takes 1½ hrs. (US$15); by minibus (Transportes Andinas) from 18 de Septiembre and Av. Guerrero, 1½ hrs., US$1; by bus (Cooperativa Otavalo, Coop Las Lagos) 1 hr., US$0.80, every ½ hr. The Tourist Office in Quito will help with reservations; the organized tour sold by hotels is expensive. Travelling on Friday is recommended as the best prices and best goods are found early on Saturday morning before the tourist bus arrives.

ECUADOR 553

Off the road between Otavalo and Ibarra is **Cotacachi**, where beautiful but expensive leather goods are made and sold. (Hotels: *El Mesón de las Flores*, D, converted ex-hacienda off main plaza, excellent meals; *El Mirage*, D, very good rooms and food.) A few km. before Cotacachi (turn off at Quiroga), at an altitude of 3,070 metres lies Lake **Cuicocha**, which has been developed for tourism. This is a crater lake with two islands, although these are closed to the public for biological studies. There is a well-defined path around the lake, which takes about 5 hrs., and provides spectacular views of Cotacachi, Imbabura and glacier-covered Cayambe peaks. The Ministry of Agriculture also maintains a research station/visitors centre on the lake edge, open 0800-1600 every day. The restaurant on the lake edge, *Muelle*, is rather run down and dirty, food moderate, 2 terrible rooms for rent, no view. Nearby is *El Mirador* with food, excellent view. Motor boats can be hired for groups of five or more. The slopes of Cerro Cotacachi, N from the lake, are a nature reserve. From Otavalo or Ibarra take Cotacachi bus, get off at Quiroga and take the *camioneta* (or hire a taxi) for 12 km., US$0.50. It is also possible to get a truck or colectivo from Cotacachi to Lake Cuicocha, US$1.60, one way; they await the buses from Otavalo.

Warning Many people have been badly poisoned by eating the blue berries which grow near the lake; they are *not* blueberries; they render the eater helpless within 2 hrs., requiring at least a stomach pump.

Also off the main road between Otavalo and Ibarra is **San Antonio de Ibarra,** famous for its wood carvings. The part near the main road is rather touristy but if you walk uphill, away from the main square, you will find cheaper carvings and a better selection. Visit the workshop of Moreo Santacruz, and the exhibition of Osvaldo Garrido in the Palacio de Arte. The Galería Luís Potosí on the main square has some beautiful carvings: he is a famous artist. (Buses from Ibarra, 13 km., ten mins.)

John Streather recommends a visit to **Apuela**, in the lush tropical valley of the Zona del Inca (*Pensión Apuela*, G, grim; small restaurant) for the thermal baths of Nungulví nearby (1 hr. walk). Apuela buses from Otavalo on a good new road (6 a day) pass Nungulví, where the swimming pool is emptied for cleaning on Tues. and Fri. About 2 hrs. drive (bumpy track) from Ibarra are the clean, hot mineral swimming pools of Cachimbiro in the parish of Tumbariro. Buses there reportedly run only at weekends; enquire in Ibarra.

Ibarra, founded 1606, at 2,225 metres, population 80,000, is a pleasant colonial town with some good hotels. A unique form of paddle ball is played on Sat. and Sun. near the railway station. The players have huge spiked paddles for striking the 2 lb. ball. On weekdays they play a similar game with a lighter ball. Local festival, Fiesta de los Lagos, last weekend of September, Thurs.-Sun.; also July 16, Virgen del Carmen. Some interesting paintings are to be seen in the church of Santo Domingo and its museum. Office for visa extensions is at Villamar y Oviedo.

Hotels The better class hotels tend to be fully booked during Holy Week. S on Quito road; *Hostería San Agustín*, C; *Hostería Chorlavi*, off highway 2 km. S of Ibarra, D, US$2.10 per extra bed, recommended, swimming pool open to non-residents, US$0.30, elegant surroundings of converted *hacienda*, Sun. excellent buffet, folk music and crafts, discotheque at weekends; nearer town, *Ajavi*, D, very good restaurant; *Ibarra*, Mosquera 6158 y Bolívar, E; *Residencial Madrid*, F, Olmedo 857 near main plaza, clean, comfortable; *Imbabura*, Oviedo 9-33, G, pretty and pleasant; *Residencial Vaca*, F, Bolívar 753; *Residencial Familiar*, Moncayo 726 y Olmedo, E, clean and good; *Residencial Imperial*, F, Bolívar 622 on Parque Pedro Moncayo; *Los Alpes*, E, Velasco 732 y Bolívar, clean with private bath; *Pensión Olmedo*, Velasco 855, G, basic, no hot water; *Pensión San Lorenzo*, Olmedo 1056, F, no hot water, clean; *Residencial Astoria*, G, Velasco 809, hot water, safe, can store luggage, friendly, basic, not very clean, upper rooms have beautiful view, large terrace, laundry facilities; *Pensión Descanso*, F, Grijalva 712, basic; *Parador de Yaguarcocha*, Diturisrun, 8 double rooms, restaurant seating 240; *Residencial Colón*, G, Narváez 5257 y Velasco, pleasant, clean, friendly, laundry facilities, will change money. *Residencial El Príncipe*, Sánchez y Cifuentes 882, G, basic but clean, restaurant. Several others, F and G, along Moncayo and Olmedo.

Restaurants *Hostería Chorlavi* restaurant recommended, likewise Hotel *Ajavi*. *El Chagra*, Olmedo 7-48, recommended, reasonable prices; *Marisquería Las Redes*, Oviedo 572 y Sucre, seafood, clean, good, breakfast for US$1, accept US$ at top rate. Good breakfast and excellent bread at *Café Pushkin*, Olmedo 7-75 and at *Mejor Pan*, Olmedo 7-52. *El Caribe*, Flores 757,

554 ECUADOR

chicken and local food, excellent three-course *merienda* for US$0.60. *Nueva China*, Olmedo 732, and *Rojo Oriental*, Calle Olmedo 748, Chinese; *Chifa Muy Buena*, Olmedo 723, does a good *Chaulafan*; *Pollos Gus*, Olmedo 888; *Don Quijote*, Rocafuerte 836; *El Dorado*, Oviedo y Sucre, seafood, snacks; *Portón de Sevilla*, Oviedo 764, seafood; *Caldera del Diablo*, G. Moreno 443, cafeteria, snackbar, good; *Koco Rico*, Olmedo 724, and *Asadero a las Doradas*, Oviedo 720, both chicken; *La Estancia*, García Moreno 7-66, very good grill but not cheap. *Los Helados*, Calle 27, near main plaza, for good ice cream; also *Heladería La Nevada*, Velasco 837. Local specialities are sweets made from walnuts, blackberries (*arrope de mora*) and other fruits, and nougat (*nogada*). Many good pastry shops.

Exchange It is reportedly difficult to change travellers' cheques in banks. Intipungo, a travel agency on Rocafuerte y García Moreno and Bolívar 4-43, will change them at a poor rate. *Las Redes* restaurant and *Residencial Colón* will change US$ notes.

Tourist Office Dituris, Sucre y García Moreno, very helpful.

Things to Do Museo Fray Pedro (open 0900-1200, 1500-1800, US$0.15, closed Sun.), Santo Domingo church, religious art. Balneario Primavera, Sánchez y Cifuentes 323, pool, sauna, turkish bath. Peña Folklórica at Poncho Libre, Olmedo 935. Piano bar, *El Encuentro*, Olmedo 953.

Bus to Quito 3 hrs., US$1, about 50 departures a day. Colectivo taxis for about double. To Yaguarcocha, US$1. To Tulcán, US$1, 2½ hrs. To Otavalo, ½ hr. Bus station is 1 km. S of town, reached by bus No. 2 from centre.

Excursions Alexander Tkany, of Karlsruhe, recommends a visit to Guachara, NW of Ibarra, reached by bus from Ibarra railway station, or by train from Ibarra to Carchi and then bus. Tourists unknown, people friendly, mountains beautiful and hitch-hiking very possible. A pretty village to visit close to Ibarra, 10 km. directly south on the road to Olmedo is **La Esperanza**, in beautiful surroundings with an Inca road which goes to Cayambe. Accommodation: *Casa Aída*, F, nice, friendly, Aída speaks some English and cooks vegetarian food; *Café María*, cheaper if you sleep on the floor than in a room, excellent fruit yoghurt and cheese. Eugenio makes leather clothes cheaply to measure; e.g. US$60 for trousers. One particular lady does extremely fine embroidery; ask in village for her house.

At edge of **Yaguarcocha Lake** are *Parador El Conquistador*, 8 rooms, D, large restaurant, run by Dituris, and *Hotel del Lago*, no accommodation, only refreshments.

It is possible to walk to Lake Yaguarcocha (4 km.) in about 1½ hrs. Follow Calle 27 to the end of town, cross the river and walk to the right at the first junction. At the end of this road there is a small path going steeply uphill. There are beautiful views of Ibarra and then from the top of the hill over the Lake surrounded by mountains and the village of the same name. Yaguarcocha, "bloody lake" in Quechua, named because legend says that the water turned red when the Incas threw in the bodies of the defeated Otavalo Indians. There are frequent buses back to Ibarra from the village. The beauty of the lake has been disfigured by the building of a motor-racing circuit round its shores.

Laguna Puruanta, 45 km. SE of Ibarra on Río Pisque, can be visited by bus to Pinampiro (US$0.40, 1 hr.), then walk to San Francisco de Sigsipamba (15 km.) and on trails from there to the Laguna. Return to Ibarra via Mariano de Acosta to complete 2-day excursion.

A 193 km. railway runs from Ibarra to the port of San Lorenzo (see page 563), N of Esmeraldas. An *autoferro* runs once a day at 0700, taking from 9 to 12 hrs. (US$1.75). The train is very crowded and reservations two days in advance are necessary. You can get a reservation in Quito at the railway office on Av. Bolívar, but you still need to queue up at 0600 in Ibarra for the tickets. Sit on the right side of the train; the track is on the left side of the valley down to San Lorenzo. The track is in poor condition and derailments are common.

Leaving Ibarra, the train descends past Salinas into the narrow gorge of the Río Mira (called Chota upstream) inhabited by blacks growing fruit and sugar cane, who sell fruit at the station. After three hours the valley widens near Collapi (730 metres) and the land becomes better watered and has been more recently colonized. Lita (460 metres) is reached after seven hours and a stop is made for refreshment. Through the lowlands cultivated land becomes commoner until we reach San Lorenzo.

North of Ibarra the Pan-American Highway goes past Lake Yaguarcocha, and descends to cross the Chota valley. The Highway divides in the valley, and you can go to Tulcán either via El Angel over a long stretch of *páramo* or, like most of the heavy vehicles, further east over eroded hill sides via San Gabriel (see below). On the El Angel road at the village of Chota and on the San Gabriel road at El Juncal, the highway descends to a mere 1,520 metres; in the tropical Chota valley

ECUADOR 555

you can buy excellent fruit from the local blacks, descendants of slaves brought from Africa in the 17th century by Jesuits to farm their estates. The El Angel route is still heavy going; the San Gabriel route is a good paved road but is subject to landslides, when the traveller is taken over poorly marked or unmarked dirt roads.

About 20 mins. to the west, off the El Angel road, is the town of **Mira** (pop. 5,000). Some of the finest quality woollens come from this part of the country; there are two women in Mira who produce them for export and a cooperative which sells in the town. There are two carnivals held each year, on February 2, and August 18, with fireworks and free flowing Tardón, the local *aguardiente*. There is a clean *residencia*, and numerous restaurants; the best is the *Bar Latino*. Stretches of virgin rain and cloud forest along the River Mira are accessible to the adventurous. (We are grateful to Bruce C. Tettemer Jr., of the U.S. Peace Corps, for this information.)

John Streather writes: **San Gabriel** (pop. 13,000) is a good place from which to visit the **Gruta de la Paz,** about 10 km. to the south, on the way to Bolívar. (Buses from Ibarra and Tulcán; *Hotel Inti Huasi* and *Restaurant Oasis* on opposite sides of main plaza). (If you are driving, the road branches off the Panamericana at the village of La Paz. The sign says 7 km. to "Grutas", but it is more like 4 km., on a cobblestone road which leads down into mosquito country, but with beautiful views and at least two thundering waterfalls.) There is a huge hotel, but it only opens sporadically and unpredictably—mainly for religious conferences. Buy tickets (US$0.20) for the hot showers and hot swimming pool from the convent before going down to the grotto, near which are the showers and the pool, which is only open from Thur. to Sun. inclusive. There is a restaurant of sorts on the bridge above the grotto. To get back to the main road, cadge a lift!—very long walk. There is a weekly excursion to the Gruta de la Paz from Tulcán.

Tulcán is a chilly town of 33,000 people at an altitude of 2,960 metres, the centre of a rich farming area. It is not particularly interesting for the tourist except for the famous cemetery, where the topiarist's art reaches its apogee; bushes are trimmed into fantastic figures of animals, plants, geometrical shapes etc. Camera essential. Ecuador's unique form of paddleball is played every afternoon by the south side of the cemetery. The migration office is situated at the border at Rumichaca, so all exit formalities are carried out there. The office and the border are open 0900-1800 with skeleton staff at lunch-time. U.S. citizens, Australians and New Zealanders need a visa and most nationalities a tourist card to enter Colombia, which can be obtained at the Colombian Consulate, Bolívar y Junín (closed 1230-1430). Two photos and an onward ticket or MCO are needed. Colombian entry stamp is given at the border. Because of the high volume of local traffic, border crossing is fairly relaxed. Coming from Colombia into Ecuador, entrance stamp is given at the border. If entering Ecuador by car, fumigation costs US$1.50 and *carnet* must be stamped at Edificio Portuario, 2nd floor, corner of main square with Bolívar. A new 4-km. highway leads from Tulcán to the border. The old road descends tortuously for 6½ km. through the mountains to the River Carchi, on the border, which is crossed by the natural bridge of Rumichaca (*Parador de Rumichaca*, D, pool, restaurant, casino, discotheque) and a new concrete bridge. Ipiales is 1½ km. beyond the bridge. Airport between Tulcán and border, Mon.-Fri. TAME flight to Quito at 1400, US$6.

Hotels *Quito*, Ayacucho 450, G, clean, central; *San Francisco*, F, Bolívar y Atahualpa, hot water, clean; *La Frontera*, G, Bolivia y Calderón, basic, noisy; *Residencial Ecuador*, G, Bolívar y Arellano, opp. bus station; *Pensión Minerva*, G, 10 de Agosto y Bolívar, clean but cold; *Residencial Carchi*, G, Sucre 576 y Pichincha, friendly, no hot water; *Residencial Oasis*, F, 10 de Agosto 395 y Sucre, private showers; *Granada*, G, Bolívar y Pichincha, communal shower sometimes has hot water; *El Paso*, F, Sucre y Pichincha, communal shower sometimes has hot water. *Mallorca*, F, two blocks north of main plaza, friendly, hot water, but thin walls. If all are full, try police station.

Restaurants *Avenida*, Bolívar y Ecuador, opp. bus station; *Terminal*, in bus station, reasonable. Many along Sucre: *Restaurant El Paso*, Chinese, good; *Chifa Tulcán*, *Chifa China*, *Chifa Pusán*, *El Sabor Latino*, *El Paraíso*, *Max Pan* for good breakfasts. Good cheeseburgers at *Café de la Rueda* just off main square.

Camping Possible at the sports field next to the cemetery.

Transport Taxi to border, US$1.60; to Ipiales, US$3, however many people share it. Bus, if you can get one, is cheaper, US$0.15. Bus to Quito 4 hrs., US$2, about 100 a day; to Ibarra, 2½ hrs., US$1. Otavalo, US$1.40, 3 hrs. To Guayaquil, 20 a day, 11 hrs., US$5. Plenty of colectivos also. Bus terminal is long uphill walk from centre; best to take taxi or little blue bus.

556 ECUADOR

Exchange Those travelling from Ecuador into Colombia should change all their sucres into dollars before they reach the frontier, making sure they bargain for a good rate; this is better at Tulcán than at Ipiales, where you can get only Colombian pesos. Bad rates at bus station. There are many money changers who will exchange cash on both sides of the border. Travellers' cheques are reportedly difficult to exchange, but try Rodríguez Paz Casa de Cambio, on Ayacucho in front of *Hotel Quito*, or Carlos Burbano, Bolívar y Junín. For those arriving in Ecuador, change only what you need to get to Quito. Banco de los Andes, Sucre y Junín, is the only bank which will undertake foreign currency transactions (cash only).

Excursions Weekly minibus trips with Cooperativa 11 de Abril, US$2 return, from opp. *Hotel Carchi*, to Gruta de la Paz (see above) at 0800 on Sats., and to Aguas Hediondas at 0800 on Suns. There are two daily buses from Boyacá y Arellano, Tulcán, 0600 and 1200, to Tufiño, 1 hr. From Tufiño walk 2 km. to turnoff for Aguas Hediondas, then 6 km. to springs themselves. You can probably hitch back to Tufiño. John Streather tells us that Aguas Hediondas (stinking waters) is a pool of boiling sulphurous mineral waters in a wild, impressive, lonely valley. An ice-cold stream of melted snow water passes nearby—one needs to direct it into the pool to make it cool enough to enter! These waters are said to cure spots, rheumatism, etc. If one takes one's passport one can walk from Tufiño over the border to the various hot, warm and cold mineral baths, with a restaurant (friendly and cheap) about 2 km. away in Colombia. One can spend the day at these baths and return to Ecuador in the evening without any fuss, so long as the passport is shown at the border (a rope over the village street). There are five pools at Tufiño—the top, hot, one is good for liver and kidneys, the one below the restaurant for the nerves and rheumatism. The cold pool is some distance from the four others which are all close together. The landscape and the plants on the way up to Aguas Hediondas are really marvellous.

Another, longer but rewarding, trip from Tulcán is to go down to the hot jungle riverside town of Maldonado—buses Mon. and Wed. at 0600 from Boyacá y Arellano, Tulcán—small *pensiones*, good swimming. The road to Maldonado passes the foot of the trail to the Chiles volcano. On the way up you see many Frailejón plants (related to the Puya Raimondii of Peru and found also in Venezuela).

The Northern and Western Lowlands

From Quito, a scenic bus trip can be taken to (129 km. US$1.05, 2½ hrs.) **Santo Domingo de los Colorados**, in the W lowlands (pop. 66,661). There is a small daily market and a large Sun. market, but very few Indians now come to the town so both it and the market itself are unexciting and scruffy. You would do better to hire a taxi and go to their villages to see the Colorados. Very few of them now wear the traditional hair dress. Santo Domingo, now the hub of roads radiating to Quito, Guayaquil (by bus 5 hrs.), Esmeraldas (bus, 4 hrs.—the road is very bad N of Rosa Zárate) and Manta, once had the boom town air of the American west a century ago, but is now dusty, noisy, and decaying. Shops in the town are open Tues.-Sun., and banks Tues.-Sat. There is a cinema.

Carnival water throwing is particularly vigorous in Santo Domingo.

Hotels *Zaracay*, C, 2 km. out of town on the road to Quito, with a very good restaurant, casino, gardens and a swimming pool, refurbished, best available, advisable to book, especially at weekend. At 1 km. on same road is *Hotel del Toachi*, D. On the same road, 20 km. from Santo Domingo, is *Tinalandia*, pleasant and small, C, with its own golf course, and excellent food. Many species of birds, flowers and butterflies in the woods behind the *hostal*. Poorly signposted, take small road between Km. 16 and 17 from Santo Domingo on the right. Nearer the town centre, still on the Quito road, is *La Siesta*, German-run, D, and opposite, *Victoria*, F, basic, restaurant, recommended; *Caleta*, Ibarra 137, E, good restaurant, private bath, good; *Colorado*, 29 de Mayo y Quininde, F, good; two *Hostales Turistas*, No. 1 at 3 de Julio y Latacunga and No. 2 at Ambato y 29 de Mayo, both F with bath (hot water); *Residencial Jessica*, 29 de Mayo y Latacunga, G, English spoken; *Residencial Ontañeda* and *Ambato*, both on Esmeraldas y Iturralde, both G. *Hostal San José*, G, clean, Latacunga y 3 de Julio; *Pensión Don Pepe*, Calle Quito, F, clean, friendly, quiet. *Residencial Madrid*, G, Av. 3 de Julio 438, good and clean but used as a brothel and many rooms without windows.

Restaurants *Parrilladas Chilenas*, on Quevedo road, for good barbecues. *Mocambo*, Tulcán y Machala, good; *La Fuente*, Ibarra y 3 de Julio, good; *Rico Pollo*, Quito y Río Pove, for chicken; two *chifas*, *Nuevo Hongkong* and *Nueva China*, on the Parque Zaracay; *Corea*, 3 de Julio y San Miguel. Several snackbars and pizzerias.

Exchange Banco Internacional, Esmeraldas y Quito.

A busy paved highway connects Santo Domingo de los Colorados with Esmeraldas to the North (see page 561), and **Quevedo** (78,000 people) to the South

ECUADOR 557

(1½ hrs. by bus). Set in fertile banana lands and often flooded in the rainy season, Quevedo is known as the Chinatown of Ecuador, with a fair-sized Chinese colony. It is a dusty, noisy, crowded town which has grown exceptionally rapidly over the last 25 years.

Hotels None of Quevedo's hotels offers a quiet night. *Olímpico*, Bolívar y 19a, D, good restaurant, near stadium; *Continental*, 7 de Octubre y 8a, F with bath, good; *Mirador*, 7 de Octubre y 10a, G; *Guayaquil*, Calle Cuarta 205 y 7 de Octubre, G *Ejecutivo Internacional*, F, 7 de Octubre y Calle Cuarta, modern, large rooms, a/c, private bath, good value, clean, the least noisy; *Pensión Azuay*, F, very basic, on main road.)

Restaurants *Hotel Olímpico*, best; *Royal Chick*, 7 de Octubre y 13a. Most others along 7 de Octubre: *Rincón Caleño* (Colombian), 1103; *Chifa 51* (best Chinese), 928; other *chifas* at 806, 809 and 707; *Tungurahua* (local food), 711. Snackbar, *Quevedo City*, Bolívar y 4a.

Roads and Buses Quevedo is an important route centre; the old paved highway from Latacunga in the highlands to Portoviejo and Manta in the lowlands carries very little traffic, but for a leisurely traveller it is the most beautiful of the routes connecting the highlands with the coast. (Bus, Quevedo-Latacunga, Cotopaxi line, 6 hrs., US$1.50. Bus, Quevedo-Portoviejo, 5 hrs., US$1.40, watch your possessions.) On this road is the *Selva Negra* hotel, basic accommodation, but excellent food.

Quevedo is connected with Guayaquil by two paved highways (bus, 3 hrs., US$1.25), one through Balzar and Daule, one through Babahoyo (41,000 people). The roads give a good idea of tropical Ecuador, with its exotic birdlife and jungle and plantations of cacao, sugar, bananas, oranges, tropical fruits and rice. To Quito, 4 hrs., US$1.80.

Popular beach resorts of the Western lowlands can be reached along a paved highway (toll) from Guayaquil. The road divides at Progreso (63 km.). One branch leads to Villamil, normally known as **Playas,** the nearest seaside resort to Guayaquil (1½ hrs. by frequent bus—US$1). Its old charm as a fishing village has almost gone, although every day single-sailed balsa rafts can still be seen among the motor launches returning laden with fish. These rafts are unique, highly ingenious and very simple. The beaches are sandy and shelve gently; excellent

---

ECUADOR TRAVEL LTD
37-39 GT. MARLBOROUGH ST. LONDON W1V 1HA

"INTERNATIONAL TOURIST ORGANIZATION"
(112 OFFICES WORLDWIDE)

LOOKING FOR ASSURANCE WITH PROFESSIONAL SERVICE AND COMPETITIVE RATES TO **LATINAMERICA?**

YOU NEED TO LOOK NO FURTHER!

WE OFFER YOU A WIDE RANGE OF SERVICES FROM ECONOMIC AIR FARES TO HOTEL BOOKINGS, TOURS, ETC AND A PERSONAL SERVICE WITH THE HELP OF OUR 12 OFFICES IN SOUTH AND CENTRAL AMERICA.

FOR ANY ENQUIRIES, CALL US ON: **01-437 7534**

GALAPAGOS IS. TOURS & INFORMATION

558 ECUADOR

for shell collectors. As an alternative to the main beach take the unsurfaced road going north which leads to a long sandy beach backed by salt flats and giant cactus. Ecuadoreans flock to the sea from January to April and traffic is very heavy along the coastal roads. Anyone who goes to the beach in May-December will have it largely to himself, except on Sundays.

Hotels *Residencial Cattan* (D, good food); *Miraglia*, F, run down but clean, sea view; *Playas*, E, beach hotel with seawater showers and plain rooms without fans or a/c, good restaurant; *El Galeón*, E, beside the church, friendly, clean, good beds, mosquito nets, water all day, cheap restaurant attached; *Hostería La Gaviota*, 500 metres out on Posorja road, D, colour TV, a/c, but rooms shabby with cockroaches, friendly, good clean restaurant. *Residencial California*, and *Restaurant Jalisco* nearby, good cheap food. *Hostería Costa Verde*, cheap, clean, F. Camping at S end of beach. Casino.

There is a water shortage all along the coast; drinking water has to be brought by tanker from Guayaquil and no hotel can guarantee water in the rooms at all times. There are showers on the beach.

An interesting place to visit, a walk or short drive from Playas, is the little village of El Morro. There is a picturesque wooden church and a large rock formation known as El Muerto. Beyond Playas lies **Posorja**, at the mouth of the Guayas estuary, home to a large commercial fishing fleet and fish processing plants. The ocean front is rubbish-strewn and muddy. Posorja and other coastal towns are receiving a population influx because of the economic boom caused by shrimp farming. Local people catch young shrimp in the sea and estuaries and sell them to large commercial ponds where they are grown to market size. Up and down the coast, from Esmeraldas to Machala, the ocean front is being transformed, as every available piece of land is developed for shrimp farming. Native mangrove swamps are being destroyed rapidly; heavy construction equipment can be seen everywhere.

West of Progreso the road to Salinas runs through a vast area of arid thorn-scrub land whose inhabitants look very Indian and produce little besides charcoal. At Santa Elena the road forks. To the left, south, we pass a petroleum refinery and enter the busy port and regional market centre of **La Libertad** (Hotel Villa María, D, friendly; *Hostería Samarina*, E, Dituris-run, some bungalows, swimming pool, restaurant, coffee shop, bar; *Hotel Viña del Mar*, E; *Hotel Turis Palm*, on main street (noisy in front), F, fan, bath, older place and a bit run down). Buses every hour to Manglaralto, Puerto López and Jipijapa from near market.

A few km. further on is **Salinas**, the self-styled best resort in Ecuador (population, 21,000, buses from Guayaquil, US$1.25, at the corner of Montúfar and Alcedo, about 3½ hrs.; return journey via La Libertad). The beaches are sandy and clean, but the town is becoming increasingly more developed; it is very quiet outside the holiday season. The flat-topped hill at Punta Santa Elena dominates the landscape. Good deep-sea fishing and water-skiing. Pesca Tours, on the seafront, rents boats for US$180; four lines from the boat, you may keep any dorado you catch but Pesca Tours keeps the marlin. Car racing at the Autódromo.

Hotels *Salinas*, D, modern, off Malecón, restaurant reported good; *Miramar*, with casino, B, with bath and telephone. *Samarina*, C, or US$32 bungalow with 6 beds, acceptable; *Cantábrico*, D, lines of hammocks outside, 4-course *merienda*; *Samarina Tivoli*, E, meals; *Yulee*, D, with own bath (but try bargaining), clean, excellent food, friendly, well placed for beaches; *Residencial Rachel*, 2 blocks from beach, F; *Herminia*, very basic, G, close to beaches but no running water.

Restaurants *Saavedra* recommended for large portions of well cooked fish for about US$1.50. Discothèque, *El Caracol*. Night club, *Che Papusa* (near town hall), normally known after its owner as *Donde el Roy*.

Cables Ietel public telex booth at Radio Internacional.

At Baños San Vicente, about 7 km. E. of La Libertad, just off the main road to Guayaquil, Dituris has opened a large tourist complex, where for US$0.30 admission you have use of the whole facility, including swimming pools, thermal baths and a mud hole to cure assorted ailments. There is still more construction work to be done; a hotel is planned when finance is available.

Punta Carnero is on the S shore of the Santa Elena peninsula. Magnificent 15-km. beach with wild surf and heavy undertow, virtually empty during the week. To the E of Punta Carnero, along the coast, lies Anconcito, a picturesque fishing port at the foot of steep cliffs, but nowhere at all to stay; further on is Ancón, centre of the declining local oilfield.

The northward fork of the road at Santa Elena leads us along the coast (past

ECUADOR 559

Ballenita, pleasant beach, surfing with two good *ceviche* restaurants, cottages can be rented) as far north as La Entrada. Manta can be reached by going inland from La Entrada via Jipijapa. Part of the road is along the beach and therefore fast, but care should be taken as the tide rises fast and suddenly. La Entrada can be reached in less than 5 hrs. from Guayaquil, and because of this a number of attractive fishing villages along this stretch of coast contain the modern bungalows of Guayaquileños. Almost all the villages have good beaches, and there is particularly good swimming near the attractive fishing villages of Palmar and Ayangue (latter crowded at week-ends). Many kinds of cactus are found in this area because of the dry climate (fewer than five days of rain a year). A typical dish from this region is *sopa de bola de verde*, made from several kinds of vegetable: green *plátano* is crushed, kneaded and formed into balls filled with green peas and diced carrots.

At Valdivia, a small port, is the site of the supposed Japanese-Jomón culture contact, via fishermen, about 3000 B.C. Little for the visitor to see except the little museum (reported closed); most artefacts discovered at the site are in museums in Quito and Guayaquil.

Manglaralto, the main centre of the region north of Santa Elena, is reached by bus from Guayaquil (change at La Libertad) as well as by numerous trucks. 3 km. N, at Montañita beach, reported best surfing in Ecuador, cottages to let, 2 hrs., US$0.70, by bus or truck from La Libertad or Santa Elena.

Hotels: *Alegre Calamar*, N end of town, F, good seafood restaurant; *Corona del Mar* restaurant has basic and dusty rooms, F, shared bath. Sra. de Arcos' house next to post office. The first row of houses nearest to the sea was washed away in the 1983 floods. It is still a nice place to stay and bathe, however; there is a good, quiet, clean beach, but little shelter. The *Comedor Familiar* is a place to eat; also *Comedor Florencia*, cheap and friendly.

North of Manglaralto the rainfall increases and at La Entrada the road peters out in the wet season (Dec.-Feb.; July-Sept.). One of the bumpier rides in Ecuador takes one from Manglaralto through lush tropical scenery to **Puerto López**, set in an impressive bay with hills on either side. Buses often can not make it all the way (2 hrs., US$1, Manglaralto-Puerto López; 2½ hrs., US$1.75, Manglaralto-Jipijapa), be prepared for a muddy walk to complete your journey. The main attraction is the busy scene on the beach when the fishermen come in at 0800 and again at 1630. The whole town seems to assemble on the beach to greet the hordes of small boats and buy the fish. It seems to be easy to go out with the fishermen in their boats (*Residencial El Pacífico*, F, on sea front, clean, basic; *Carmita*, recommended restaurant on sea front, friendly and clean.) From Puerto López it is a 2 hr., US$1, ride by fairly regular bus to Jipijapa. To La Libertad, 2½ hrs., US$1.

A new dirt road has been made from Manglaralto to the main Guayaquil-Manta road. This road climbs into the humid hills of S Manabí, then descends to the dry savanna scrub around **Jipijapa** (27,500 inhabitants), an important centre for the region's farmers, trading cotton, fruit and kapok (from the fat-trunked ceiba tree). It appears that the Panama hats for which Jipijapa was famous are no longer produced there. (*Pensión Mejía*, F, 2 blocks from plaza, clean, basic, noisy.) Thirty-two km. across dusty hills is **Montecristi** (8,190 people), below an imposing hill, high enough to be watered by low cloud which gives the region its only source of drinking water. The town is also famous for its Panama hats which, along with cane-work products, are found here, much cheaper than in Quito.

Soon after, we reach **Manta** (100,000 people), the main commercial centre of western Ecuador, a noisy and dirty town—steep streets and a fine wooden church—and economically very active. With its twin town, Tarqui, it has the largest population W of Guayaquil. The Tarqui beaches are reported to be good for sunbathing and swimming, but watch your belongings. Fishing boats are built on the beach. The beach at the Manta end is smelly, but fairly quiet, with moderate surf. The Banco Central museum, Calle 9 y Av. 4, has interesting specimens of the Huancavilca-Manteña culture (AD 800-1550); open during banking hours, curator speaks English and French. Sites can be visited from Bahía de Caráquez. All streets have been given numbers; those above 100 are in Tarqui. Dituris is in the Edificio Emapa. Ecuadorian Tours is at Av. 2 y Calle 13, and Metropolitan Touring at Av. 3 y Calle 12.

Hotels *Las Gaviotas*, Malecón y Calle 106, E, on beach, a/c, restaurant, tennis; *Manta Imperial*, D, Calles Playa y Murciélago, on beach, a/c, disco and dancing; *Haddad Manabí*, Av. 105 y Calle 103, E, on the beach in Tarqui; *Panorama Inn*, Calle 103 y Av. 105, E, a/c, bath, TV, recommended, swimming pool and restaurant; *La Cascada*, opposite, *Rivera*, Av. 4, Calle 7, E, a/c, noisy, run down, near bus station; *Residencial Las Mantas*, G, Calle 12 y Av. 8, good, clean. Also on Tarqui beach, *Residencial Eugenia*, Malecón y Calle 105, F, safe, comfortable, hot water, clean; *Las Rocas*, Calle 101 y Av. 105, restaurant, E; *Residencial Boulevard*, Av. 105 y Calle 104, E; *El Inca*, Calle 105 y Malecón, F, restaurant, private bath; *Miami*, Malecón y Calle 107, F, private bath, good; *Residencial Astoria*, Av. 105 y Calle 105, F with bath. *Residencial Niza*, Malecón y Calle 103, G, restaurant, shared bath, clean. There are two hotels with the same name: *Lun Fun*, one is near the bus station, Alfaro y Calle 2, E, with restaurant, while the *residencial*, G, is at Av. 4 y Calle 8 in the centre.

Restaurants Hotels. Cheap restaurants by Tarqui market, Av. 108 y Calle 102; and on the nearby beach. *El Ceibo*, in the centre, is recommended. *El Boulevard* on Tarqui beach near the Plaza Tarqui, good fish and seafood, reasonably priced; *La Cascada*, Av. 105 y Calle 103, cafeteria with swimming pool; *Georgie* on Calle 16 with Av. 7, good fish, cheap. *Pelicán*, Malecón y Calle 105; *El Shirley*, *Playero* and *Costa Mar* seafood places nearby. In centre, *Andes Cafeteria*, Av. 1 y Calle 12, and *La Choza*, Calle 13 y Av. 7.

Post Office above Banco de Pichincha; **Telephone** Ietel on road to the beach.

Exchange *Casa de Cambio* Zanchi, Banco de Pichincha and Banco del Pacífico change travellers' cheques.

Air Service Eloy Alfaro airport nearby. Every day by Tame to Quito, US$10, every day except Sun. to Guayaquil, US$6.50.

Buses To Quito, 8 hrs., US$3; Guayaquil, 3½ hrs., US$2; Esmeraldas, 8 hrs., US$3; Santo Domingo, 6 hrs., US$2.10; Portoviejo, ½ hr., US$0.30; Jipijapa, 45 mins., US$0.45; Bahía de Caráquez, 3 hrs., US$1. All from bus station.

•24 km. inland from Montecristi is **Portoviejo** (101,771 inhabitants), a major commercial centre with connections by road with Quito and Guayaquil.

Hotels *París*, off main plaza, E; *Residencial Maroles*, 2 Av./Calle 1, F, friendly, noisy. Also *Internacional*, Olmedo 503; *Cristal*, Calle Ricaurte 106, F; *Bahía*, Olmedo y P. Gual; *Cabrera Internacional*, P. Gual y García Moreno; *San Marcos*, Olmedo y 9 de Octubre; *Residencial Pacheco*, 9 de Octubre, near San Marcos, F, shower, basic, no windows but lots of cockroaches. The restaurant *Chifa China* on the plaza has a clean, cheap hotel upstairs.

From Portoviejo a road goes E to Quevedo (147 km). At Calderón, branch NE for Calceta, Chone (36,000 people) and on to Santo Domingo de los Colorados. From Calceta and Chone paved roads run 50 km. to **Bahía de Caráquez** (13,000 people), a tranquil town in a pleasant setting on the seaward southern end of an inlet; the river front is attractively laid out, but there are water shortages except in the better hotels. Smart new homes fringe the seaward side. The town is a centre of banana and other agricultural exports. On Isla de los Pájaros in the bay are many seabirds; launches can be hired to visit mangrove islands. There is a friendly tourist office; the local coordinator, Sr. Darío Proaño Leroux, very helpful and friendly, is at Centro Vocacional "Life", Tel.: 690-496.

Hotels *Herradura*, Bolívar y Malecón (beach), D; *Centro Vocacional "Life°*, Dávila y García Moreno, D, full board; *Apart Hotel Bahía*, Malecón y G. Moreno, E; *Mantas*, clean, good, F; *Americano*, Ascazubi y Morales, E; *Manabí*, nearby, G, clean and friendly; *Residencial Vera*, Ante y Bolívar, F, with bath and mosquito net; *Residencial Los Tamarindos*, opp. *Vera*, clean but less good, F; *Palma*, Bolívar y Arenas, G, clean and friendly.

Restaurants *Moby Dick*, Bolívar y Ante; *Miramir*, Malecón Santos near Ante, seafood and local dishes; *Los Helecheros*, cafeteria, good and clean, Bolívar y Malecón; *Chifa China*, cheap, at Bolívar y Ascazubi.

Bus from Bahía de Caráquez to Quito, 8 hrs., US$3, Esmeraldas, 8 hrs., and Portoviejo, 2 hrs., with Reina del Camino. To Guayaquil, 5½ hrs., US$2.80; to Manta, 3 hrs., US$1.

Airport at San Vicente (see below): Air Transportes Bahía flies twice a day to Guayaquil, US$12.

Those interested in exploring the coast further north can take the ferry (every 15 mins., US$0.10) from Bahía de Caráquez to **San Vicente**, on the far side of the Río Chone, a thriving market (*Hotel*

ECUADOR 561

Vacaciones, E, restaurant, TV in rooms; about 3 km. from San Vicente are *Cabañas La Playa*, US$20 for beach chalet sleeping 5, good food in restaurant; other *cabañas* on beach), and on by bus, truck or car north along the beach to Canoa, thence inland, cutting across Cape Pasado through the more humid pasture-lands to the small market centre of *Jama* (small *pensión*). From there the road runs parallel to the beach past coconut groves, inland across some low hills and across the Equator to **Pedernales**, another small market town on the coast, bus from San Vicente, 6 hrs., US$3.50; several houses where you can stay, a friendly spot (*Hotel Turismo*, F, clean, helpful; *Cabañas Cañaverales*, F; *Residencial-Restaurant La Buena Esperanza*, G, no electricity in rooms, not recommended; *Residencial Comedor El Gitano*, F, meals, friendly) and 2 or 3 eating places. A new road is being finished between Pedernales and El Carmen (thence to Sto. Domingo and Quito) and the two towns are expected to become booming tourist resorts. Northwards there is now a very poor dry-season road (buses—one or two a day—use the beach at low tide, one hour's journey; also trucks, 45 mins.) between Pedernales and **Cojimíes** (*Hotel España*, G, shabby, no water; *Cabañas Coco Solo*, F. Flower-decorated house on same street will serve meals at any hour; *Restaurant Lord Byron; Comedor Costa Norte*). Cojimíes was a major pre-conquest centre; little of this is noticeable now, although many artefacts are still dug up; it is being continually eroded by the sea and has been moved about three times in as many decades. It is reached by daily bus from San Vicente at 0700 (Costa Norte, 12 to 14 hrs.) or truck from Pedernales and San Vicente (make enquiries between 0700 and 0900). After heavy rain there may be a 2 or 3 day delay before road transport is resumed. A boat leaves at high tide every Sat. for Esmeraldas, stopping at Chamanga (US$4, 7 hrs.) and one from Esmeraldas on Sat. as well. There is a boat to Manta on Wed. (sometimes calling at Muisné). The entry into Cojimíes and Muisné is treacherous and many boats have been thrown into the shallows by swell.

North of Cojimíes is a rich banana-growing region, and **Muisné**, an island reached by road from Esmeraldas (bus US$1, 3 hrs., and a canoe over to the island). Muisné is the centre and main outlet of this area; through it some 50,000 stems of bananas a month are exported via Esmeraldas. On the Río Sucio, inland from Muisné and Cojimíes, is an isolated group of Cayapa Indians, some of whom visit the towns on Sun. Muisné is a pleasant place (only 4 vehicles!) All hotels F, but women should avoid *Residencial Narcisita*; we have been warned of sexual attacks by the owner; *Sarita*, F, has been recommended, clean, fan, mosquito nets, private bathroom; you can also rent small huts on the beach, F, electric light, some with water, beautiful setting, beaches nearby and simple seafood *comedores*. The beaches are large at low tide but practically disappear at high tide. There is a lot of wood lying around and hordes of mosquitoes. In the wet season there are boats between Muisné and Cojimíes, mostly early a.m., US$2.25, 2 hrs. Cargo boats ply between Muisné and Manta. A new road has been built between Muisné and Bolívar inland, behind the beaches; easier but less scenic. Be careful on the beaches; we have received further reports of rape and other violent attacks.

Esmeraldas, Ecuador's fifth city (117,000 people) is improving, although some travellers have reported it dirty and over-priced. The electricity and water supplies are still inadequate. The main street is closed to traffic from 1930 to 2130 nightly. Gold mines nearby, tobacco and cacao grown inland, cattle ranching along the coast, timber exported, and an oil pipeline from the Oriente to an ocean terminal at nearby Balao; an oil refinery has been built nearby. A new road bridge over the river at San Mateo upstream from Esmeraldas gives a direct road link to the General Rivadeneira airport. Daily TAME flight to Quito at 1000, US$6.50. (Taxi to centre, about US$3). Las Palmas, just N of Esmeraldas, is being developed as a resort and several hotels have been built and a number of restaurants opened. There is a broad sandy beach but it received severe damage in the 1983 floods and is reported as unsafe (theft) and dirty. White people have been advised to avoid the shanty-town on the Malecón. Even the water is muddy as it is close to a naval harbour and people use the beach as a speedway. Buses to Las Palmas (US$0.05) leave regularly from the main square in Esmeraldas.

Mosquitoes and malaria are a problem throughout the province of Esmeraldas. All the beaches have mosquitoes that come out in hordes at night and bite through clothing. Take plenty of insect repellant because the Detán sold locally does not work well. Most *residencias* provide mosquito nets (*toldos* or *mosquiteros*); don't stay anywhere that does not. Carry your passport at all times, failure to do so may result in a few days in police custody. Best to visit in dry season, June-December.

Hotels Best in Esmeraldas are *Apart Hotel*, Av. Libertad 407 y Ramón Tello, D, good restaurant, and *Roma*, E, Olmeda y Piedrahita, with its *Restaurant Tres Carabelas*; *Galeón*, opposite *Roma*, F, private showers; *El Barracón*, Olmedo 1100, F, *Royal*, Libertad y Rocafuerte, F; *La Pradera*, 7½ km. S on Atacamés road, D, a/c, swimming pool, tennis courts, restaurant, and *Europeo*, D, between Esmeraldas and Las Palmas, no a/c, but the restaurant is very good, German-owned

562 ECUADOR

but under Chilean management. *Corea*, Mañizares y Bolívar, F, recommended, private shower, fan; *Chaber Inn International*, Libertad 200 y Montalvo, F with a/c. *Americano*, Sucre y Piedrahita, F with fan, good value; *Diana*, Mañizares y Sucre, good, private showers, F. *Hostal Domínguez*, G, on Sucre near Plaza Central, noisy, hot water, open all night; *Valparaíso I*, Libertad y Pichincha, G, very basic but good value, cheap restaurant, *Oro Negro*, next door. Other cheaper hotels include *Bolívar*, F and cheaper still, *Central*, F, and *Asia*, F, both are basic but clean. *Rito* is a brothel. Generally, hotels in the town centre are not up to much and you are recommended to stay in the outskirts. Some hotels are not keen to take single travellers.

Las Palmas offers the best hotels along Av. Kennedy: *Cayapas*, D, a/c, showers and hot water in all rooms, good restaurant; *Hotel del Mar*, D, on sea front, modern. *Atahualpa*, E, 14 rooms, private bath, hot water, garage, garden, Swiss-run, recommended; *Hippocampo*, D, new; *Colonial*, Platat y L. Tello, D; *Hostal Familiar*, G, dirty, little water; *Chimborazo*, G, cheap and noisy.

Restaurants In Esmeraldas: *Chifa Restaurante Asiático*, Mañizares y Bolívar, Chinese, rather expensive; *Tía Carmen*, Sucre y 9 de Octubre, recommended for good, cheap, fish soup and stew. *La Marimba Internacional*, Libertad y Lavallén, has been recommended; *La Pampa* grill is on Colón y Rocafuerte; *Daruma*, Olmedo y Mejía, is Japanese and local. *Café Congenita*, near *Hotel Americano*, for iced tea, milk shakes; other soda fountains at Olmedo y Piedrahita. In Las Palmas, *Atenas Tiffani*, Kennedy 707, good food but expensive; *Bayardo*, on main seafront road, the Malecón, good food, lively host, cheaper than *Tiffani*. There are numerous typical restaurants and bars by the beach selling *ceviches*, fried fish and *patacones*, etc. Throughout Esmeraldas province a cheap meal is the *comida típica*, fish, rice, boiled *plátano*, sometimes beans (*minestre*), called *tapao*. There is also *cocado*, fish, crabs or shrimp cooked in coconut cream served with rice and plátano. There is a soup made of shellfish and coconut milk which is very good. *Cocada* is a sweet made of brown sugar and grated coconut, *conserva* is a paste of *guayaba*, banana and brown sugar, wrapped in banana leaves.

Shopping There is a Cayapa basket market across from the Post Office, behind the vegetables. Also three doors down, Tolita artefacts and basketry. Exchange at Botica Koch, Sucre y 9 de Octubre, good rates.

Entertainment In Esmeraldas, *El Portón peña* and discotheque, Colón y Piedrahita; *El Guadal de Ña Mencha*, 6 de Diciembre y Quito, *peña* upstairs, marimba school at weekends; good *Bar Asia* on Bolívar by main Parque. *Los Cuervos*, discotheque. In Las Palmas, *El Náutico* and *Déjà Vue* on the Malecón, a/c, discotheques. Cockfights, Eloy Alfaro y 9 de Octubre, weekends.

Music Esmeraldas is called "the capital of rhythm" with good reason. The people prefer the livelier sound of Caribbean *salsa* to the *cumbia* heard in the sierra, and have retained the African-influenced *marimba*, usually accompanied by a *bomero*, who plays a deep-pitched bass drum suspended from the ceiling, and a long conga drum. Where there is a *marimba* school you will also find dancers, and the women who are too old to dance play percussion and chant songs handed down the generations, many with Colombian references. In Esmeraldas the *marimba* school practises Sat. p.m. in the school in front of the Parque Central. The best *marimba* can be seen in the backwoods of the province on Sundays and holidays. (Nancy Alexander, Chicago.)

Cinema *Ciné Bolívar*, Bolívar y 9 de Octubre, is the best, with a/c and upholstered seating. Three other cinemas offer more basic accommodation with bats and rats.

Tourist Information The tourist office (Dituris) is in the Edificio de la Alcaldía, Bolívar 517 y 9 de Octubre, 2nd floor, half a block from the main square, singularly unhelpful.

Transport No central terminal. Buses to Quito, US$2.50, 6 hrs., 30 a day, good paved road, Trans-Esmeraldas, Av. Piedrahita 200, recommended, or by Occidental; by Aerotaxi, 5 hrs., 12 passengers, reserved seats, office on main square. To Santo Domingo, US$1.40, 4 hrs.; to Ambato, 5 times a day with Coop. Sudamericana, 8 hrs., US$2.50; to Guayaquil, 20 a day, US$3, 8-9½ hrs.; to Portoviejo and Manta, US$2, to Quevedo, 6 hrs. To La Tola (road good to Río Verde), 3 daily, US$1.60, 5 hrs.; to Muisné, 28 daily with La Costeñita, US$1, 3½ hrs. To Súa (road reasonable) and Atacames every half hour from 0630 to 2030, US$0.20, 1-1½ hrs. Boats to Limones and San Lorenzo: service irregular; ask at Port Captain's office at Las Palmas. Combined boat/bus service leaves for San Lorenzo at 1330.

Atacamés, a beach resort 25 km. S of Esmeraldas, is still attractive, but much of it was destroyed in the 1983 floods when palm trees on the beach were washed away and houses, terraces and streets leading on to the beach were damaged. Atacamés is famous for its black coral and the local people make handicrafts from it. Most accommodation has salt water in the bathrooms; fresh water is not always available and not very good. *Hotel Tahiti*, with shower, F, serves breakfasts, full meals in holiday periods, good restaurant, try the prawns, but check your bill carefully, also has new bungalows, F; *Las Vegas*, F, with shower; *Hostería Los Bohíos*, C, prices cheaper (F) in low season (June, July, August), for a bungalow, safe, clean; *Hostería Cayapas*, beach huts, F, cooking and barbecue; *San Sebastián* and *Marbella*, beach huts for 5, both F; *Chachis*, F, beach, shares bathrooms; *Residencial Sol de Oriente*, F, clean, near beach. *Residencial Bachita*, F, clean, near beach. Tents or beach bungalows can be hired at under US$1 a night; no facilities but can

ECUADOR 563

arrange with hotels. *Lumbaye* bungalows are recommended, cheaper off-season. Beach bungalows with showers at *Cabañas Costa del Sol*, D, good breakfast and seafood; *Cabañas South Pacific*, F, clean, American owner, fresh water showers; *Cabañas Casas Rogers*, E, cheap huts, running water, space for camping with private beach and beach chairs, English spoken, restaurant. Rats are common in all these beach huts, and insect repellant is essential. Restaurants on beach, mostly seafood, are reasonable; try *Comedor Pelícanos*, fresh fish, chicken, ceviche, occasionally music, recommended; also *Cafetería Pelícanos*, best, includes vegetarian dishes and salads. *Comedor Maribar*. *Copacabana* discotheque on beach. *Cocada*, a sweet made from different nuts, brown sugar, cocoa, etc., is sold in the main plaza. **Warning:** It is reported that there have been many assaults on campers and late-night beach strollers. The sea can be very dangerous, there is a powerful undertow and many people have been drowned.

Súa, another beach resort a little S of Atacamés (20 min. walk at low tide), is quiet, friendly, with a beautiful bay with pelicans and frigate birds, but the sandy beach is very dirty. *Pensión Palmar*, G, cabins; *Residencial España*, F; *Residencial Quito*, G, *Mar y Sol*, G, washing facilities poor. The hotels along the seafront vary little in standard but quite significantly in price. *Motel Chagra Ramos*, on beach, F, with good restaurant. Insect repellant is essential along this coast. **Tonchigüe**, 1 hr. S from Esmeraldas beyond Súa, is also lovely during the rainy season (Dec.-May). Muisné is a better place for swimming than either Atacamés or Súa.

There are no good beaches for swimming north of Esmeraldas. Río Verde, where the paved road ends, has a lovely beach but nothing else. It was the setting for Morriz Thompson's book on Peace Corps Life, *Living Poor*. Beyond Río Verde is **Rocafuerte**, recommended as having the best seafood in the province, including oysters and lobsters. Beyond here there is nothing interesting, except the scenery, until you get to San Lorenzo. At **La Tola**, where one catches the boat for Limones and San Lorenzo, the shoreline changes from sandy beaches to mangrove swamp. The wildlife is varied and spectacular, especially the birds. La Tola is 3½ hrs. (US$1.50) from Esmeraldas, by bus, four daily a.m., dusty, uncomfortable, buses often get stuck. Four boats go daily from La Tola to San Lorenzo via Limones, 2 hrs., US$1.50; seem to connect with boats from Esmeraldas. Try to avoid staying overnight in La Tola; take a raincoat.

Mangrove coastlands stretch north into Colombia, and have only two towns of note, Limones and San Lorenzo.

Limones, the main commercial centre, largely a saw-mill town, is the focus of traffic down-river from much of northern Esmeraldas Province where bananas from the Río Santiago are sent to Esmeraldas for export. The Cayapa Indians live up the Río Cayapas and can sometimes be seen in Limones, especially during the crowded weekend market (uninteresting), but they are more frequently seen at Borbón.

Limones has two good shops selling the very attractive Cayapa basketry; one is run by an Indian woman and is the cheaper, the other, run by a Colombian, has a very good selection with some items from Colombia. The first is opposite *Restaurant El Bongó* and the second by the dock opposite Banco de Fomento.
　　Two hotels, both execrable. Limones is "the mosquito and rat capital of Ecuador". A hired launch (6 pers. US$ 1.40 p.p., 1½ hrs.) provides a fascinating trip through mangrove islands and passing hundreds of hunting pelicans. Information on boat journeys from the Capitanía del Puerto, Las Palmas, reached by bus No. 1 from the main square in Esmeraldas. From Limones you can also get a canoe or boat to Borbón and another one from there up the River Cayapas to Zapallo Grande, a friendly village with many gardens. Better to stay at San Lorenzo.

Borbón (*Residencial Capri*, F, with marimba dance hall next door), with population almost entirely black, is on the Río Cayapas past mangrove swamps. Buses to Esmeraldas, US$1.40, 4 hrs. Upstream are Cayapa Indian villages. From Borbón hire a dugout to Boca de Onzole one hour upstream, which is the confluence of the Cayapas and Onzole rivers. There is a fine lodge built by a Hungarian (for advance bookings write to Stephan Tarjany, Casilla 187, Esmeraldas), E with full board, good value, clean, warm showers. Water skiing available on request. You can hire a dugout with him for US$50 to Santa María (board and lodging with Sra. Pastora at missionary station, F, mosquito nets) and on upstream to San Miguel passing Zapallo Grande where the American missionary Dr Meisenheimer has established a hospital, pharmacy, church and school. You will see the Cayapa Indians passing in their canoes and in their open long houses on the shore. San Miguel is the last outpost of civilization with a church and a few houses, beautifully situated on a hill at the confluence of two rivers. From there you go back 5 hrs. downstream to La Tola where you can pick up the bus from Esmeraldas or go on to Limones and San Lorenzo.

San Lorenzo is relatively more attractive than Limones. There is a beach nearby at San Pedro, reached by boat; make enquiries in the village for transport. The

564 ECUADOR

best places to see *marimba* are two schools, one Esmeraldeña and one Colombiana. The latter practice between the *Residencial Pailón* and the *Residencial Ibarra*, you can't miss the sound. The former practice Wed. and Sat. nights, are more disciplined, better musicians and dance more. They have toured the continent and are led by a woman called Lydia who can make marimbas to order. *Marimba* can be seen during the local fiesta on Sept. 30.

Hotels *Wilma*, F, basic, ask for rooms 15 or 16, they are newer and bigger; *Residencial Margaritas*, F, friendly, clean, good showers, Imbabura y Ortiz; *Pailón*, Ayora y 24 de Mayo, satisfactory, G; *Restaurant Jhonny* upstairs; *Ecuador*, Alfaro y 10 de Agosto, F, restaurant OK, basic, laundry facilities, mosquito net provided; *Colón*, Imbabura y 24 de Mayo, water irregular, G, basic; *Residencial Vilmar*, Imbabura y Mariano, G, near the station, is better. *San Lorenzo*, Alfaro y 10 de Agosto, G, recommended for meals, but not so good to stay; *Residencial Turista*, next to post office, G, multilingual staff, recommended; *Residencial Ibarra*, Coronel y 24 de Mayo, possibly the best, G, clean, friendly. *Residencial Flora*, Alfaro y Ortiz, G, noisy, next to dance hall. **Restaurants**: *Cabaña del Sol*, recommended for good, cheap fish, Ayora y Alfaro. *Jhonny* (sic), Ayora y 24 de Mayo, upstairs, best in town, large helpings for US$1. *Rumory's marimba* and discotheque at Imbabura y 10 de Agosto. Insect repellant is a "must" in San Lorenzo. Be sure to check your bedding for scorpions.

Train The *Autocarro* (motor rail-coach) leaves daily from the station 10 mins. from town centre (usually overcrowded; reserve day before travelling). The train journey gives an excellent transect of Ecuador (see page 554). To Ibarra, US$1.75, up to 12 hrs., departing at 0700. Because of heavy rains, roadworks and landslides, delays are inevitable.

Boats Dugouts, with motors, to La Tola (2 hrs., US$1.50) and Borbón (2½ hrs, US$2), via Limones, US$1. Boats leave daily at 0730 and 1400 (stops at Tambilla and Limones en route), bus from there to Esmeraldas, through ticket US$2.75. Beautiful journey but dusty bus trip. Boat to Esmeraldas, infrequent.

From San Lorenzo there are occasional boats to Tumaco in Colombia, but gringos are not normally welcome as passengers because contraband is being carried. When arriving in San Lorenzo from Tumaco, the customs office run by navy personnel is in the harbour, but you have to get your passport stamped at the immigration office in Ibarra, because the immigration police in the *Hotel Imperial* office do not handle passports.

Nancy Alexander, of Chicago, writes that about 75% of the population of Limones, Borbón and San Lorenzo has come from Colombia in the last fifty years. The people are mostly black and many are illegal immigrants. Smuggling between Limones and Tumaco in Colombia is big business (hammocks, manufactured goods, drugs) and there are occasional drug searches along the N coastal road.

From Guayaquil to Quito

Note to Motorists There is a 3¼-km. bridge from Guayaquil across the river to Durán. A good paved road from there (summit at 4,120 metres) connects with the Andean Highway at Cajabamba, near Riobamba (see page 565).

The floods in 1983 closed the Guayaquil-Quito railway for through traffic and the only services were by *autoferro* or ordinary train between Guayaquil and Bucay (87 km.) and between Riobamba and Quito (223 km.). Contracts for repair work were awarded in 1985 but it will be several years until normal service can be resumed, though some sections have reopened: for example, service on the Alausí-Huigra section was resumed in 1985. Departures are at 1130 daily from Alausí, and 1300 daily from Huigra. The ride takes 1 hour. The sections km. 87-116 and km. 143-166 have to be entirely rebuilt. We have retained the description of the full journey in the hope that finance will soon be made available for the work to start.

The 464-km. railway line (1.067 metre gauge) passes through 87 km. of delta lands and then, in 80 km., climbs to 3,238 metres. At the summit, at Urbina, 3,609 metres is reached; it then rises and falls before debouching on to the Quito plateau at 2,857 metres. The line is a most interesting piece of railway engineering, with a maximum gradient of 5.5 per cent. Its greatest triumphs, the Alausí loop and the Devil's Nose double zigzag (including a V switchback), are between Sibambe and Alausí, on the reopened section.

Leaving the river the train strikes out across the broad, fertile Guayas valley. It rolls through fields of sugar cane, or rice, past split cane houses built on high stilts, past sugar mills with their owners' fine homes. Everywhere there are waterways, with thousands of water-birds, and down them ply the big dugouts piled high with produce bound for Guayaquil.

The first station is **Yaguachi.** On August 15 and 16 more than 15,000 visitors pour into this little town to attend the feast day celebrations at the church of San Jacinto, who is honoured in the region for having put an end to many epidemics.

The first stop of importance is **Milagro**, a large but uninteresting town of 77,000 people (*Hotel Viker*, F, no food, communal washing facilities; *Hotel Marta*, F; *Restaurant Topo-Gigio*, nearby, good, cheap food). Women swarm about the train selling pineapples which are particularly sweet and juicy. About 87 km. from Durán the train stops at **Bucay,** at the base of the Andes (market Sunday). Buses run parallel to the train between Bucay and Guayaquil, but take only 2 as opposed to 4 hrs.

The landscape spreads before you in every shade of green; row on row of coffee and cacao trees, with occasional groves of mango and breadfruit trees, banana plantations, fields of sugar cane, tobacco, and pineapple. The train follows the gorge of the River Chanchán until it reaches **Huigra.** By road Bucay to Huigra is still rough going. After leaving Huigra the train crosses and recrosses the River Chanchán, and then creeps along a narrow ledge between the mountain and the canyon. Here begins the most exciting part of the trip. The first mountain town reached is Chanchán, where the gorge is so narrow that the train has to pass through a series of tunnels and bridges in its zigzag course. Next is **Sibambe,** the junction for trains to Cuenca. A train leaves Sibambe at 0500 for Cuenca (service resumed), arrives at 1100. There are buses to Cuenca, but they miss some of the stunning scenery. The train to Cuenca is worthwhile, with spectacular views. Shortly after leaving Sibambe the Quito train starts climbing the famous Nariz del Diablo (Devil's Nose), a perpendicular ridge rising in the gorge of the Chanchán to a height of 305 metres. This almost insurmountable engineering obstacle was finally conquered when a series of switchbacks was built on a 5½ per cent grade. The air is chilly and stimulating.

Next comes **Alausí,** an old and colourful village (Sunday market), in the mountains on the Pan-American Highway, popular with Guayaquileños. It is best reached from Riobamba by road: the Cuenca and Guayaquil links are less good. (*Residencia Tequendama*, G, clean, friendly, hot water; *Hotel Panamericano*, G, clean, but poor food; *Hotel Gampala*, G, basic but adequate, breakfast not available; *Hotel Europa*, G, safe parking in courtyard.) Restaurants: *Hotel Panamericano*, *Paradero Chumpisti*, *Salón Oriental*. All buses stop in front of *Hotel Panamericano*. You can walk on the railway track to Chunchi, a friendly village with a Sunday market, 15 km. An Inca trail to Ingapirca (see page 578) can be followed: it starts at Achupallas, 25 km. from Alausí.

After crossing the 120 metre long Shucos bridge, the train pulls into Palmira, on the crest of the first range of the Andes crossed by the railway. The train has climbed nearly 3,350 metres in less than 160 km. Precipitous mountain slopes covered with temperate-climate crops such as wheat and alfalfa gradually change to a bleak, desolate *páramo* (moor) where nothing grows except stiff clumps of grass. Now and then the drab, depressing landscape is brightened by the red poncho of an Indian shepherd watching his sheep. One by one the great snow-capped volcanoes appear: Chimborazo, Carihuairazo, Altar, Tungurahua, and the burning head of Sangay. They all seem very close because of the clear air.

Guamote is another point on the Pan-American Highway, five hours by car from the capital. There is an interesting market on Thursdays and some good ½ day walks in the area. There is a *pensión*, F, near the railway station and also some places to eat nearby. There have been reports of finds of Inca pottery and gold in the area. The train skirts the shores of Lake La Colta, before reaching the fertile Cajabamba valley. A road is being built to Macas (see page 594).

Cajabamba is a small, rather poor town. In 1534 the original Riobamba was founded on this site, but in 1797, a disastrous earthquake caused a large section of the hill on the north side of the town to collapse in a great landslide, which can still be seen. It killed several thousand of the original inhabitants of Riobamba and the town was moved almost twenty kilometres north-east to its present site. The new Riobamba has prospered, but Cajabamba, where some of the inhabitants of the original Riobamba remained after the earthquake, has stagnated. Indian market on Sun., small but uncommercialized and interesting. There are no hotels and few restaurants.

Cajabamba is connected to Riobamba and Quito by a good paved highway and there is another paved highway from Cajabamba to Bucay and Guayaquil. A fairly good dirt road leaves the Pan-American Highway soon after Cajabamba, to the west; it is one of the oldest of the coast-Sierra routes and links Cajabamba with Guaranda and Babahoyo.

Riobamba (2,750 metres) is the capital of Chimborazo Province. It has 75,000 inhabitants, is built on a large, almost wide plain and has broad streets and many ageing but impressive buildings. Altogether, it seems a quiet, dignified place, with the nickname "Sultan of the Andes". Riobamba has many good churches

566 ECUADOR

and public buildings, and magnificent views of three of the great volcanic peaks, Chimborazo, Altar and Tungurahua. Four blocks NE of the railway station, along Calle Juan de la Valle, the Parque 21 de Abril affords an unobstructed view of Riobamba and environs; the park also has a colourful tile tableau of the history of Ecuador and is especially fine at sunset.

Riobamba has a new market building, but only a small part of the activity at the Saturday market takes place there. Buying and selling go on all over town. The "tourist" market in the small plaza south of the Convento de la Concepción museum is particularly fascinating and a good place to buy local handicraft—*ikat* shawls (*macanas*), embroidered and finely woven belts (*fajas*), blankets, embroidered dresses and shirts, Otavalan weavings and sweaters, *shigras*. Indian women come to the plaza each week with sacks full of bead and coin necklaces, old belts and dresses, blanket pins (*tupus*), and much more. Since Indian-style clothing is also sold here, the plaza is full of colourful Indians from different parts of Chimborazo province, each group wearing its distinctive costume. Two blocks east, there is a huge produce market in another plaza, also pottery, baskets, hats. All the streets in this area are filled with traders. (Karen J. Elwell, Urbana, Illinois, USA.) There are also 2 markets on Weds.: Mercado La Condamine and Mercado San Alfonso. A variety of *pelota* games can be seen on Sunday afternoons. On Saturdays at 1800 there are cockfights on the corner of Tarquí with Guayaquil, entrance US$0.25. Open-air restaurants do a flourishing business in that Andean delicacy, roast *cuy* (guinea-pig). Hotel prices rise during independence *fiestas* around April 20, and rooms are difficult to obtain during the November basketball tournament. There are three cinemas.

The Convento de la Concepción, Orozco y España, has been carefully restored by the Banco Central and now functions as a religious art museum, open Tues.-Sat. 0900-1230 and 1500-1830, Sun. 0900-1230. Admission: US$0.60 for Ecuadoreans, US$0.90 for others. The guides are friendly and knowledgeable (tip expected). The priceless Custodia de Riobamba Antigua is the museum's greatest treasure, one of the richest of its kind in South America. Well worth a visit.

Hotels A good but somewhat run down hotel with a recommended restaurant is *El Galpón*, D, Argentinos y Zambrano, pool, sauna, and very quiet (some way from centre); next to it is *Chimborazo Internacional*, D, spacious rooms, fully carpeted, neat, clean, highly recommended, restaurant with fair food at reasonable prices; *Hostería El Troje*, Km. 4½ on road to Chambo, D, tourist centre, restaurant; *Liribamba*, Pichincha y Primera Constituyente, E, only serves breakfast, recommended; *Humboldt*, Av. Daniel León Borja 3548, F, inc. breakfast, clean, with bath; *Segovia*, F, Primera Constituyente 2228, modern, friendly, hot water, ask for front room, food recommended; *Los Shiris*, 10 de Agosto y Rocafuerte, E, with private bathroom, clean, nicely furnished, friendly, restaurant good; *Imperio*, Rocafuerte 22-15 y 10 de Agosto, F, a good quality hotel, hot water, private or shared bathroom, laundry facilities, can store luggage, friendly and comfortable, but loud music from bar on Sat. nights; *Whymper*, P.Constituyente 3230, F, private bath, cafeteria; *Zeus*, Borja 4139, E with bath, clean, friendly, good restaurant, English spoken; *Las Retamas*, La Prensa y Calle D, F with bath, near bus station; *El Altar*, Km. 2 on Ambato road, F, good; *Americano*, G, pleasant, above restaurant of same name on Borja near station; *Colonial*, G, clean, usually hot water, uncomfortable beds; *Venecia*, Dávalos 2221 y 10 de Agosto, G, hot water; *Metro*, Borja y Lavalle, F with or without bath, a pleasant, central, traditional hotel; *Residencial Rocío*, F, Brasil 2168, clean, quiet, friendly, with bath; *Residencial Camba Huasi*, 10 de Agosto 2824, G, laundry facilities, clean, dormitory beds, pots by the beds, hot water, spacious, friendly, owner is a mountaineer and organizes trips to Chimborazo, safe parking in courtyard; *Metropolitano*, Borja y Lavalle, F, pleasant, with bath; *Residencias Villa Ester*, Unidad Nacional y Lavalle, F, hot shower, basic; *Puruha*, F, opposite bus station at Eplicachima 2076 y Borja, friendly, fairly clean, but noisy; nearby is *Monterrey*, Rey Cacha y Eplicachima, G.

Restaurants *Chuquiragua*, 2 km. out on Quito road, best typical restaurant; *Candilejas*, reasonable food, cheap prices, but unfriendly, 10 de Agosto y Pichincha; *El Mesón*, Veloz 4199 y Los Sauces, some way out, good, high-class; *Léon Rojo*, P.Constituyente y Pichincha, German and international cuisine; *El Rodeo*, 10 de Agosto y García Moreno, a bistro, not cheap but good; *Chifa Chang*, 10 de Agosto near railway station (does not serve Chinese food); *Alexander*, Falconi y Brasil, bistro style, reasonable; *Chifa Internacional*, Veloz y Dávalos, Chinese food, good; *Chifa Chung Wah*, 10 de Agosto 2558, good food; *Amazonas*, Borja y Lavalle; *La Biblia*, Primera Constituyente and Miguel León, piano bar, reports vary; *El Botecito*, Veloz y G. Moreno, cheap; *El Pailón*, Pichincha y 10 de Agosto, clean, good *merienda*; *El Molino*, 10 de Agosto, clean, friendly, cheap, good food; *Su Casa*, Primera Constituyente, between Pichincha and García Moreno, good food, nice serving; *Cabaña Montecarlo*, García Moreno 2140, beautiful, clean, good food, not expensive; *Pato Juan*, España y 10 de Agosto, snack bar, pleasant. Many other snackbars along 10 de Agosto.

Entertainment *Peña*-restaurants *Media Estocada*, Borja y Duchicela, and *Parrillada Gaucha*, Unidad Nacional. Peñas at *Taquí Huasi*, Orozco y 4a Transversal, and *La Casa Vieja*, Orozco y Tarqui. Disco, Thurs.-Sun, at *Zero*, Km. 1½ on road to Cajabamba.,

Exchange Banco Internacional, 10 de Agosto y García Moreno.

Tourist Office Dituris, Calle Tarqui 2248 y Primera Constituyente. Open Tues.-Sat. 0800-1200, 1430-1700. Addresses for renters of climbing equipment. Souvenir shops on 10 de Agosto between Carabobo and Rocafuerte.

Transport All trains to Guayaquil were suspended in 1983 after heavy rains destroyed much of the track. A daily *autoferro* runs to Quito, 0630, 5 hrs., US$1, buy tickets in advance. Bus to Quito, US$2, 4 hrs., about every 15 mins. Bus to Guaranda, US$0.80, 2 hrs., beautiful views. Bus to Cuenca, 5 a day via Alausí, 6½ hrs., US$3. A more popular route to Cuenca, entirely on paved roads, is via El Triunfo, on the Guayaquil bus US$2 to El Triunfo, where you change buses, then US$2.50 to Cuenca; good roads and scenery. Bus to Santo Domingo, US$2, 5 hrs. Bus to Baños, US$0.50, 1 hr. Bus to Puyo, US$1.10, 3½ hrs. direct. There are 2 buses (US$3.50, 10 hrs.) to Huaquillas every evening, which avoid Guayaquil. Bus to Guayaquil, about 35 a day, US$2, 4½ hrs., the trip is really spectacular for the first two hours. There are pirate buses which charge more than the regular lines and do not sell tickets in the bus station, first come first served, they can be useful when all the others are full up. There is a well-run *terminal terrestre* on Eplicachima y Av. D. L. Borja for buses to Quito, Ambato, etc., but buses to Baños and the Oriente leave from the Terminal Oriental, 10 de Agosto y Puruhua. This can be confusing.

Excursions Two are of great interest: the first, to **Guano**, an attractive hemp-working and carpet-making town of 6,000 inhabitants 10 km. to the north, with prehistoric monoliths nearby; there are frequent buses but nowhere to eat. After Guano you can take the bus on to Santa Teresita from where it is a 1 km. walk downhill to Balneario Las Elenas: 3 pools, 1 tepid, 2 cool. The second is to Baños, scenic route along Chambo River (see page 569).

Climbing To climb Chimborazo contact Enrique Veloz Coronado, mountain guide and technical adviser of the Asociación de Andinismo de Chimborazo, Chile 33-21 y Francia, Riobamba (Tel.: 960916). He will provide all the necessary equipment; you must agree on a fee with him for the trip you want to make (see page 569). He is best reached after 1500 and is very helpful even if you don't need his services as a guide. For Sangay, take a taxi to Alao and hire guides or carriers of food, tents, etc. there; remember you have to pay for and organize the food for your porters separately, otherwise you have to pay them a lot more. Make sure the fee covers the return journey as well. Also Expediciones Andinas (Marco Cruz), Argentinos 3860 y Zambrano, Tel.: 964-915.

To the crater of **Altar**: Travel to Penipe by bus (bargain for the price) from Baños or Riobamba/Ambato, then to Candelaria by truck, or bus which passes between 1200 and 1400. Walk out of the village, cross the bridge and go up to Hacienda Releche on your left (about 2 km.). There is a *refugio* (US$1.10) about 1 km. from Candelaria, a white building at the turning for the Hacienda, marked by a Sangay National Park sign. It is not always open, ask in Riobamba beforehand at the Ministry of Tourism or the Sangay National Park office, Primera Constituyente y Pichincha, Ministry of Agriculture. The track to the Altares leads on past the Hacienda, but it is best to ask someone to point out the faint track which branches to the left about 30-40 minutes after the Hacienda and leads up a hill to a ridge where it joins a clear track. This goes south first and then turns east up the valley of the River Collanes. It is about 6 hrs. to the crater which is surrounded by magnificent snow-capped peaks. It is possible to camp in the crater, but better still, about 20 mins. before you turn into the broad U-shaped valley leading up to the crater there is a good-sized cave, the floor of which is lined with dry rushes; there is a fire ring at the entrance. Guides to Altar can be hired for about US$3.50 a day, and horses are US$3.50 each a day. Because of damage done to the track by mudslides the route is hazardous and you would be unwise to do it alone. Consult the National Park Office about conditions, they are in radio contact with the Guardería at Candelaria.

From Riobamba to Quito the road is paved. Between Riobamba and Cevallos the railway reaches its highest point at Urbina Pass (3,609 metres). At the pass, there are fine views in the dry season (June is probably the first safe month) of Chimborazo and its smaller sister mountain, Carihuairazo. Then the railway and the Pan-American Highway wind down towards the Ambato basin. Between Riobamba and Ambato is Mocha, where guinea-pigs (*cuy*) are raised for the table; you can sample *cuy* at stalls by the roadside. Fine views of the valley and its patchwork of fields give an impression of greater fertility and prosperity than the Riobamba zone. The houses seem larger and better built, and almost universally, a small crucifix crowns the roof, where figurines of domestic animals

568 ECUADOR

are also found. Large areas of apple orchards and onion fields are passed before Ambato is finally reached.

Ambato (population 110,000) is the sixth largest city in Ecuador. It was almost completely destroyed in the great 1949 earthquake. The modern cathedral faces the attractive Parque Montalvo, where there is a statue of the writer Juan Montalvo (1833-1889) who is buried in a memorial in a neighbouring street. His house (Bolívar y Montalvo) is open to the public; entrance free (ring 821-024). In the Colegio Nacional Bolívar, at Sucre y Lalama, there is a museum of stuffed birds and other animals and items of local historical interest (US$0.05, closed Sat. and Sun.). The Quinta de Mera, an old mansion in gardens in Atocha suburb, open 0900-1200, 1400-1800, can be reached by bus from Espejo y 12 de Noviembre. Out along the River Ambato (a pleasant walk) is the prosperous suburb of Miraflores. Ambato has a famous festival in February, the *Fiesta de frutas y flores*, during which it is impossible to get a hotel room unless you book ahead; similarly in Riobamba, Baños and Latacunga. It is an important centre for the manufacture of rugs and has some excellent tourist shops in the centre, e.g. Artesanías Montalvo, Eguez y Cevallos: look for colourful and good-quality cloth shoulder bags. Leather clothes can be specially made quite cheaply. On a clear day Tungurahua and Chimborazo can be seen from the city.

The main market is held on Mon., and smaller markets on Wed. and Fri., but they are rather disappointing for the tourist.

Hotels *Ambato*, Guayaquil y Rocafuerte, C, best, restaurant, casino, squash; *Miraflores*, Av. Miraflores 227, E, English spoken; *Florida*, Av. Miraflores 1131, D, set meal good at US$3; *Villa Hilda*, E, in Av. Miraflores, German spoken, recommended, laundry, restaurant good, limited menu but lots to eat. Buses from the centre stop outside the *Florida*. *Tungurahua*, Lalama y Vela, E, restaurant; *La Lira*, Montalvo y Cevallos, E, good, cheaper for long stay; *Cumandá*, F with bath, 12 de Noviembre 2494; *Carillo*, F, Av. de las Américas; *Residencial Americano*, Plaza 12 de Noviembre, G, basic, hot water; *Asia*, Espejo y 12 de Noviembre, F, hot water, central; *Residencial La Unión No. 1*, Espejo 323, G; *La Unión No. 2*, Cotachi 118 (far from centre), G, reasonable; *Vivero*, Mera 504 y Cevallos, E, good. There are a lot of cheap *pensiones* and hotels; close to each other on Calle Mera are *Residencial Europa*, *Residencial Laurita* and *Hotel Guayaquil*, all G with hot water, shared bathrooms.

Restaurants Good but expensive meals at the *Villa Hilda*; *Cabaña del Negro*, Av. Miraflores 263, good seafood; *El Alamo*, Swiss-owned, excellent meals, now three restaurants, one at Sucre 660, *El Alamo Júnior*, self-service, for snacks, and the *Gran Alamo*, round the corner at Montalvo 520. *Florida*, uninteresting food but inexpensive. *La Borgoña*, 13 de Abril y Mera, French; *Chambord*, Quito y Rocafuerte, international; *El Pollo Loco*, Lalama y Sucre, chicken, likewise *Pollo Rico*, Alfaro 521; local cooking at *Rincón Criollo*, Eguez y Bolívar. Seafood at *Monarca*, Bolívar y Eguez (best), *Los Sauces*, Mera y Bolívar, and *El Tiburón No. 2*, Primera Imprenta y 5 de Junio. Oriental at *Chifa Nueva Hongkong*, Bolívar y Martínez, and *Chifa Internacional*, 12 de Noviembre y Aillón; also along Cevallos. Grills: *La Brasa*, Montalvo y Olmedo, *El Gaucho*, Bolívar y Castillo, and *El Faraón*, Bolívar y Lalama. Many good cafeterias and snackbars. *Chifa Jao Fua* at Cevallos 540, good food and friendly service but arrive early to avoid the rush. *Mama Miche*, Centro Comercial, open 24 hrs. For rockbottom prices with rather dubious hygiene, try the markets. *Happy Chicken*, next to *Hotel Vivero* for clean, cheap, fast food.

Exchange Only Citibank travellers' cheques can be changed at Citibank, Calle Sucre; Banco del Pacífico changes notes only. Cambiaria Pichincha, Darquea y Sevilla, accepts travellers' cheques; money exchange at *Café Español*, Montalvo 607, Mon.-Sat., 0900-1800.

Tourist Office Dituris is next to the *Hotel Ambato* on the 900 block of Calle Guayaquil. Open 0830-1230, 1430-1830, Mon.-Fri.

Travel Agents Metropolitan Touring, Bolívar 471; Coltur, Cevallos 536; Ecuadorian Tours (American Express) Bolívar 678. There is a *peña* on Fri. and Sat., *Peña del Tungurahua*, in block 2 of the Centro Comercial.

Buses To Quito, 3 hrs., US$1. To Guayaquil, 6½ hrs., US$2.50. To Cuenca, US$3, 9 hrs., to get to Cuenca in daylight take a morning Guayaquil bus to El Triunfo and pick up a Guayaquil—Cuenca bus, or take a bus to Biblián and change there. (There can be some discomfort from descent to under 200 metres and subsequent climb up to 2,600.) To Baños, paved road, lovely scenery, 45 mins., US$0.40. To Latacunga, 30 mins. US$0.50. To Santo Domingo de los Colorados, 4 hrs., US$1.60; to Tena, US$2.20, 6 hrs. To Puyo, US$1.10, 3 hrs. To Esmeraldas, US$2.50, 8 hours. Main bus station is 2 km. N from centre, near the railway station; town buses go there from Plaza Cevallos in the city centre.

ECUADOR 569

Ambato is connected by the excellent paved Pan-American Highway south to Riobamba and north to Latacunga and Quito. To the west, a narrow, winding road (now paved) leads up the valley of the Ambato river, over a high area of desert called the Grande Arenal, past Carihuairazo and Chimborazo, and down into the Chimbo valley to Guaranda. This spectacular journey takes about three hours.

Excursions To Salasaca (see below); to Picaihua by frequent bus to see the local work from *cabuya* fibre, and to Pinllo to see the leather work.

Chimborazo, 6,310 metres: there are two routes up the mountain:

1) The South West face: there are no direct buses so take a taxi (US$30, return, next day or later, US$13 one way) from Riobamba to the Edward Whymper refuge, which takes 1 hr., 47 km., or a bus to San Juan village and hitch from there. The road ends at 4,800 metres, where there is a new refuge, or you can walk up to the Edward Whymper refuge at 5,000 metres which is at the foot of the Thielman glacier. There should be two keepers at this refuge, which provides water and a bed (US$1 p.p. a night, plus US$0.50 charge for gas in gas stove). Beware of thieves if you leave anything in the refuge or even in your car at 4,800 metres. From the refuge to the summit the climb is 8-9 hrs and the descent about 4 hrs. There are three routes depending on your experience and ability. Recommended to start at 2400 or 0100. There is a road from San Juan to Pogyos round Carihuairazo, making a round trip by jeep, Riobamba-Chimborazo-Ambato, possible.

2) The North West face, or Pogyos route: Take the Guaranda bus from Ambato along the new paved road or a truck along the spectacular old road (50 km.) to the valley of Pogyos. At Pogyos (4,000 metres) there is a house with a metal roof where you can hire mules for US$4 each to carry your luggage. (Beware of pilfering from your bags on ascent.) Walk about 3 hrs. to the Fabián Zurita refuge (4,900 metres); there are no facilities or furniture here, only the stone-floored building, which shelters about 20 people. Some climbers prefer to take their own tent. Take water up (obtainable at Pogyos, containers in Ambato). From the refuge to the summit is about an 8-hr. climb and 3-4 hr. descent. Advisable to start at 0100. (We are grateful to Enrique Veloz Coronado—see page 567—for much of this information.)

Dr Sverre Aarseth writes that in order to climb this mountain it is essential to have at least one week's acclimatization above 3,000 metres. The best season is December and June-September. Sr. Héctor Vásquez at Colegio National Bolívar, Ambato, has helped many expeditions with travel arrangements and information; he is a top-grade mountaineer. The original Whymper route is an attractive one, but is harder than the Pogyos route; especially the scree where rolling stones present a hazard during the afternoon descent (the upper part is quite straightforward with two or three on a rope). Previous parties will most likely have left marker flags; these are often needed for descent in a cloud. Very soft snow between first and second summit but usually there will be a good path from previous parties (otherwise snow shoes might be needed). The ascent to the summit is very steep and partly exposed (falling could be fatal). No one without mountaineering experience should attempt the climb, and the use of rope, ice-axe and crampons is a must. Carihuairazo (5,020 metres) is a spur of Chimborazo.

Guaranda (14,000 inhabitants) is the capital of Bolívar Province. It is a quiet, rather poor town which, because it is built on seven hills, proudly calls itself "the Rome of Ecuador". Market day is Sat. Guaranda is connected by a new paved road to Ambato (several buses) and Babahoyo, and a poor, narrow road to Riobamba. It is the main centre for the wheat and maize-growing Chimbo valley, but has long stagnated since newer, faster routes replaced the old Guayaquil-Quito road through Babahoyo and Guaranda.

Hotels: *La Colina*, high up on Av. Guayaquil, D, well kept, good value; *Cochabamba*, García Moreno y 7 de Mayo, F with bath, best in town; *Pensión Ecuador*, opposite, F; *Residencial Bolívar*, Sucre y Rocafuerte, F; *Matiaví*, Av. Eliza Mariño, F, clean, next to bus station; *Residencial Acapulco*, 10 de Agosto y 9 de Abril, G, basic.

Restaurants Hotel *Cochabamba*, best; *Santa Fe*, opp. *Resid. Acapulco*, reasonable; *Guaranda* soda bar on G. Moreno y Pichincha.

Buses Bus station on road to Ambato. To Ambato, US$1.20, 3¼ hrs.; Riobamba, US$0.70, 2½ hrs.; Guayaquil, US$1.75, 3½ hrs. None direct to Quito.

To the east of Ambato, an important road leads to Salasaca, Pelileo, and Baños and then on along the Pastaza valley to Mera, Shell Mera, Puyo and Tena in the Oriente (see page 590). It is paved to Puyo.

Salasaca is a small modernized village 14 km. (½ hr.) from Ambato, at the centre of the Salasaca Indian zone. The Salasacas wear distinctive black ponchos with white shirts, trousers and broad white hats. Most of them are farmers, but they are best known for weaving *tapices*, strips of cloth with remarkable bird and animal shapes in the centre. A co-operative has fixed the prices on the *tapices* it sells in its store near the church. Throughout the village the prices are the same, and no cheaper than in Quito. If you have the time you can order one to be specially made; this takes four to six weeks, but is well worth the wait. You can watch the Indians weaving in the main workshop opposite the church, and there is a small, but very interesting *feria artesanal* on Sundays at which the fine local work can be bought.

Pelileo, 5 km. beyond Salasaca, is a lively little market town which has been almost completely rebuilt on a new site since the 1949 earthquake. In all Pelileo has been destroyed by four earthquakes during its 400-year history. The new town springs to life on Saturday, the main market day. The ruins of Pelileo Viejo can be seen about 2 km. east of the present site on the north side of the road to Baños. *Fiesta* on August 15.

From Pelileo, the road gradually descends to Las Juntas, the meeting point of the Patate and Chambo rivers to form the Pastaza river, and where the road from Riobamba comes in. It then continues along the lower slopes of the volcano Tungurahua to Baños (25 km. from Pelileo). The road gives good views of the Pastaza gorge and the volcano.

Baños (1,800 metres) is a holiday resort with a supposedly miraculous Virgin and hot springs; very busy at weekends. The central Basilica attracts many pilgrims; the paintings of miracles performed by Nuestra Señora de Santa Agua are worth seeing. There is a *fiesta* in her honour in October with processions, bands, fireworks, sporting events and a lot of general gaiety. The Basilica de Baños has a museum (stuffed birds, Nuestra Señora's clothing). There is another *fiesta* on December 15 to celebrate the town's anniversary when each *barrio* hires a *saka* band and there is much dancing in the streets. The following day there is a parade in which spectators are outnumbered by participants. There is a zoo off the road to Puyo on the left, about 1 km. from town, run by the Church authorities, US$0.20 entrance, cages far too small and excessive loudspeaker noise. The Pastaza river rushes past Baños to the Agoyán falls 10 km. further down the valley, marred by engineering works connected with the construction of a hydroelectric scheme. The whole area between Pelileo and Baños has a relaxing subtropical climate (the rainy season is from May to October, especially July and August). It is from here that Ecuador's best *aguardiente* comes. Street vendors sell *canelazo*, a sweet drink of *aguardiente*, lime, water and cinnamon, also jaw-sticking toffee made in ropes in shop doorways, and painted balsa-wood birds (see *El Chaguamango* shop by Basílica). Two sets of thermal baths are in the town: the main set is by the waterfall close to the *Hotel Sangay*; the Santa Clara baths are about ½ km. further W, up against the mountain, and the third, the Salado, which is pleasanter (entrance to each is US$0.20), is 1½ km. out of town on the Ambato road. There are regular buses every 30 mins. between the Salado baths and the Agoyán Falls, passing by the centre of town. All the baths can be very crowded and the water not very hot. Interesting side trips are possible from the main Pelileo-Baños highway across the main valley, north to Patate, or up the Chambo valley to Penipe and Riobamba, or take taxi to Puente Vendas, 2 hrs., US$2.20, beautiful ride.

Hotels *Sangay*, D, with bath, beautifully situated close to waterfall, tennis court, swimming pool, squash courts, accommodation good, but chalets dearer and better than rooms; meals are recommended. Information and some equipment for expeditions to the jungle and volcanoes can be provided by the hotel. *Villa Gertrudis*, Montalvo 2975, good situation on edge of town, with lovely garden, D, full *pensión*, also good; *Paraíso (Humboldt)*, Ambato y Haflans, D with board or F without food, bath, clean, beautiful view from front rooms; *Palace*, opposite *Sangay* (even closer to waterfall) good facilities, clean, D, restaurant, breakfast US$1, dinner US$3. *Residencial Magdalena*, Oriente y Alfaro, E with bath, clean, warm water, recommended; *Hostal Los Helechos*, E, run by former owners of *Acapulco*, on Parque Central, close to Post Office and Ietel, restaurant, warmly recommended; *Hostal La Basílica*, new, Plaza de la Basílica, F with bath, *Restaurant El Marqués 2* in building, parking, safe; *Pensión Patty*, Eloy Alfaro 556, near market, G for stays of over one night, highly recommended, clean, good facilities, use of kitchen, laundry, comfortable and quiet, family-run, the helpful owner is a mountaineer and can offer good, free advice, sell maps and hire

ECUADOR 571

equipment; *Residencial Los Pinos*, Rocafuerte y Maldonado, F, clean, friendly, ask for front room with view, preferably on second floor; *Residencial Baños*, F, Ambato y Alfaro, good, washing facilities; *Residencial Teresita*, on the Parque de la Basílica, G, cooking facilities, hot water, clean, prices vary, recommended; *Americano*, G, 12 de Noviembre y Martínez, basic but friendly, cooking facilities available, thin walls. There are two *Residenciales Las Delicias*, *1*, on the Parque Central, front rooms have lovely view, but are noisy, good, clean, friendly; *Las Delicias 2*, Ambato y Haflans, is newer; *Agoyán*, F, opposite Basilica, clean, good, ask for front room overlooking square; *Anita*, Rocafuerte y 16 de Diciembre, F, behind the market, clean, friendly, quiet, use of kitchen; *Residencial Olguita*, G, Rocafuerte y Haflans, front rooms best (lovely view), clean rooms but not the communal bathroom, no hot water; *Chile*, in nearest square to bus station, clean, comfortable, private bath; *Santa Clara*, 12 de Noviembre y Montalvo, G, use of kitchen possible, nice garden, recommended; *Pensión Guayaquil*, on Parque de la Basílica, F, old and picturesque, good food, but no private baths. Several near corner Ambato with Alfaro: *Residencial Guayas*, G, no hot water, communal bath; *Residencial Guadeloupe*, G, ditto, *Residencial Puerto del Dorado*, clean and *Residencial Santa Fe*, G, opposite the market, no hot water, fairly clean; next door, *Residencial Bolívar*, G, clean. Many more *residenciales* on Parque and cathedral square. Also, houses for rent on a weekly basis: the owners of *El Paisano* restaurant have three houses, US$24 for the most expensive. Camping is not recommended on the mountainsides as several people have frozen to death.

Restaurants *El Marqués No. 1*, on Montalvo, just beyond Hotels *Sangay* and *Palace*, in old house, closes early, good steaks for US$2, quiet and friendly. *El Marqués No. 2*, 16 de Diciembre y Rocafuerte, international food; *Monica's*, down the road from *Pensión Patty*, well-prepared and interesting menus, popular gringo meeting place, book exchange, good, but be careful with overcharging, slow service; *Cumandá*, ex-*Puerto del Dorado*, not terribly clean but reasonably priced; *El Gaucho*, opposite the church, serves excellent mixed grills and salads; *Chifa Cantón*, on Maldonado, warmly recommended; *Chifa Oriental*, Ambato y Alfaro, fair food, low prices, friendly; *El Paisano*, recommended; *Martínez* y *Santa Clara*, vegetarian, but meat also served, also good for breakfast, with yoghurt, houses rented, on road to *Sangay* hotel; *Restaurant Acapulco*, Rocafuerte y 16 de Diciembre, no longer recommended, yoghurt and wholemeal bread. *Suecia*, opposite *Acapulco*, pizzas, evenings only, Swedish and English spoken; *La Fuente*, on main street, good *merienda*; *Lucerno*, also on main street, clean, friendly, good value *merienda*; good vegetarian restaurant next to *Pensión Guayaquil* on main square. The bakery, *Pan de Casa*, next to the market, is recommended for breakfast; hot bread at 0600, also good butter and jam; *Hotel Humboldt* recommended for breakfast, in main street.

Entertainment Cockfighting, Coliseo, Sun. 1400-1800. Horses to hire on the square in front of the Post Office, US$0.75 per hour, without guide, for trekking in the mountains. Peñas *La Burbuja* and *Agoyán* (near main baths), Fri. and Sat.

Bank Banco del Pacífico, Martínez y 12 de Noviembre, one block up from the Basílica, changes all travellers' cheques and foreign currency, but only from 1100-1330.

Laundry Clothes can be washed at the municipal washhouse next to the main baths for US$1.20 a bundle.

Warning Many people have been bitten by dogs in Baños. If you are bitten, report to the hospital where you will be treated, free of charge, and passed on to the public health inspector who will find out whether the dog concerned is rabid.

Tourist Office on Parque Central (Haflans y Ambato) open Tues.-Sat., 0800-1200, 1400-1800.

Buses To Quito, via Ambato, US$1.50, 4½ hrs.; to Ambato, ¾ hr., US$0.40; to Riobamba, 1 hr., US$0.50; to Latacunga, 2 hrs., US$0.60; to Puyo, 2 hrs., US$0.80 (paved road); to Tena, 5½ hrs., US$1.80 by bus (more leg room) with Coop. Riobamba, or US$2 by *buseta*, only three direct buses Baños-Tena, but frequent passing buses from Riobamba and Ambato; seat reservations recommended; to Misahuallí, change at Tena, buses leave every 20 mins., US$0.30, 1 hr. The bus station is on the Ambato-Puyo road a short way from the centre, and is the scene of vigorous volleyball games most afternoons.

From Baños it is possible to climb **Tungurahua** (5,016 metres); follow road opposite police control on Ambato side of town, then first mule track to right of store and follow the path to Pondoa; do not follow the road up to the baths. If you are driving to Pondoa, take the main Ambato road and turn off to the left about 1 km. from the town centre. The road runs parallel to the main road for several km. before turning east into the mountains. Park the car at the shop in Pondoa. The walk from the shop to the beginning of the trail takes 30 mins. *Pensión Patty* in Baños arranges equipment, guides (min. US$32 a day for two climbers and US$16 for each extra one), and jeeps to Pondoa Tues., Wed., Thurs., Sat. 0830, US$0.60 p.p.; there is also an occasional bus from Baños to Pondoa. It takes 5-10 hrs. to reach the Santos Ocaña *refugio* (3,800 metres) situated 4 hrs. below the snowline, then about 4 hours from the *refugio* to the summit early next morning. Leave summit about 0930 as clouds come down later in the day; allow 2 hours for descent to *refugio*. Those

572 ECUADOR

wishing to use the mountain hut should purchase a ticket (US$0.70 p.p. a night) at the shop in Pondoa, where sketch-map of route can be obtained. Allow a second day for exploring higher and return on the third day. Take a sleeping bag and food; there are cooking facilities at the *refugio*, but no heating and it can be cold. For a guide and pack animals enquire at Baños tourist office or Pondoa shop; guide and mule for 1 pack US$5, for 2 packs, US$7. Horses can be hired for US$0.90 an hour (see Julio Albán, Segundo Sánchez or Víctor Barriga near the Plaza Central or through tourist office). A tiring but rewarding climb; requires experience.

There are many interesting walks in the Baños area. You can cross the Pastaza by a suspension bridge across the main road from the bus station. Short hikes include San Martín shrine, 3 hrs., which overlooks deep rocky canyon with the Pastaza River thundering below; along the old road to Ambato to Lligua, a flowery little village straddling the Lligua River at its junction with the Pastaza; to Runtún, a village of a dozen mud dwellings, each sporting a billiard table, from which there is a splendid view of Tungurahua (2½ hrs.). Cold drinks sold at the billiard hall, no food. There are two paths from Baños to Runtún, one from south end of Calle 9, the other from Calle 6.

20 km. from Baños on the Puyo road are the Río Verde falls. Cross river and take path to right of last house on right; take immediate left fork, trail down to suspension bridge with view of falls.

North from Ambato the railway and Pan-American Highway (many buses) pass through **Salcedo,** good Thurs. and Sun. markets (*Hostería Rumipamba de las Rosas*, D, restaurant, swimming pool, exchanges US$ notes; *Hostal Las Piedras*, G, on Parque; *Residencial Las Vegas*, Bolívar y Paredes, F, hot water, private showers; *Restaurant Ritz*, Bolívar y Sucre, chicken.) to Latacunga, the capital of Cotopaxi Province.

Latacunga, with 30,000 inhabitants, is a place where the abundance of light grey lava rock has been artfully employed. Cotopaxi is much in evidence, though it is 29 km. away. Provided they are not hidden in the clouds, which unfortunately is all too often (try the early morning), as many as nine volcanic cones can be seen from Latacunga. The central plaza, Parque Vicente León, is a colourful and beautifully maintained botanical garden, where the shrubs are sculpted into various shapes (e.g., fans, globes, wedding cakes). There are several other gardens in the town including Parque San Francisco and Lago Flores. The colonial character of the town has been well preserved.

Just off the Parque Vicente León is the Pasaje Catedral, a colonial building renovated into an arcade of shops, offices, and a small art gallery that features a 17th-century aerial view painting of Latacunga (open Tues.-Sat. 0830 to 1800). Casa Cultural, the Museo Etnográfico (closed Sun. and Mon.). There is a Sat. (also, but smaller, on Tues.) market on the Plaza de San Sebastián; goods for sale include *chigras* (cactus-fibre bags), llama wool (in the fleece but poor quality) and homespun wool and cotton yarn. Tourist Office in Centro Comercial, Pasaje Quito.

Festival The Fiesta de Nuestra Señora de la Merced (Sept. 22-24) is celebrated with dancing in the streets. Some of the masks and costumes used are on display in the Casa Cultural. Mama Negra festival, colourful costumes, headdresses and masks, in November.

Hotels *Cotopaxi*, on main square, F, with bathroom, good, safe for luggage, clean, parking, hot water, highly recommended, ask for view over plaza; *Estambul*, F, Belisario Quevedo 7340 y Salcedo, soap, toilet paper, recommended, friendly. *Turismo*, nice, noisy, good restaurant; *Hostal Jacqueline*, G, near market, clean, no showers, no water except from 1900-2300, unfriendly. Also *Costa Azul*, G, unfriendly, good meals; this, the *Residencial Los Andes* (F) and the *Hotel Residencial Turismo* (G) are along the Ambato road. Accommodation is not abundant.

Restaurants *Los Copihues*, on main square, best in town; *El Fogón*, south on the Ambato road, overpriced, (closed Sun.); *La Carreta*, Quito 150, good 4-course lunch; *Cyrano*, 2 de Mayo 7674, chicken; *Chifa Gran Pekin*, 2 de Mayo 7660; *Chifa Tokio*, Quito 7396, moderate prices, good value; *Salón Coseñita*, Echeverría 1143, good cheap meals; El Estudiante, Antonio Vela 78, almuerzo US$0.50. *Pollo Dorado*, 5 de Junio y Vela, good value, US$ 1.30; milkshakes and real coffee recommended at *Pingüino*, Quito y Salcedo; inside *Hotel Cotopaxi* is a good Chilean restaurant; *Los Alpes*, opposite the *Cotopaxi*, good. *Pollos Gus*, cheap roast chicken, on Ambato road. Ice cream store off main square, Salcedo y Quito. Bakery at Amazonas 25-76 has superb bread, and so does Hector's, opposite *Pingüino*. Difficult to eat after 2000.

Exchange Banco de Pichincha on Plaza, cash only.

Buses to Quevedo, 6 hrs., US$1.60; to Quito, 2 hrs., US$0.75; to Ambato, 1 hr., US$0.40; to Guayaquil, US$2.50, 6 hrs.

Day trips to Cotopaxi (see page 574) can be arranged with a taxi for about US$16.

A fine paved road leads west to **Pujilí** (good Sun. market; also, but smaller, on Wed.; beware

ECUADOR 573

local illicit liquor and pickpockets), 15 km. away (bus, US$0.18) and then on over the Western Cordillera to Zumbahua, Macuchi and Quevedo. **Zumbahua**, a cluster of 40 houses by an old *hacienda*, 65 km. from Pujilí, has a fine Sat. morning market (a local market for produce and animals, not tourist items, but rated as one of the most interesting and colourful in Ecuador and not to be missed) with llamas on view (bus US$0.60 from Latacunga at 0500, 0630, 0700 leaves from corner of *Hotel Turismo*, 2 hrs., beautiful ride. Bus drivers on the Latacunga-Quevedo line often do not want to take tourists to Zumbahua as they want to fill up the bus with people going to Quevedo. Car hire has been recommended. A taxi can cost the same as the bus). Many interesting crafts are practised by the Indians in the neighbouring valley of Tigua: skin paintings, hand-carved wooden masks, baskets. Zumbahua is the point to turn off for a visit to **Quilotoa**, a volcanic crater filled by a beautiful emerald lake, to which there is a steep path from rim. From the rim of the crater several snowcapped volcanoes can be seen in the distance. It is reached by a dusty road which runs north from Zumbahua (turn right and over the bridge at the fork in the road, there are no road signs and the crater can only be recognized when you are on top of it) to Quilotoa and on to Chugchilán (this last stretch is the worst). Chugchilán is a very poor village in one of the most scenic areas of Ecuador. At the crater, itself, expect to be besieged by persistent beggars. It's wise to carry some food or small bills to buy them off, and take a stick against dogs on the road. Also be prepared for sudden changes in the weather. There is now a very basic refuge, just inside the crater's rim. The walk to Quilotoa is 9-10 km., or about 2-3 hrs. hike from Zumbahua; take water as that from the lake is quite sulphurous and water is generally hard to find. Alternatively, you can get a bus on Saturdays, US$0.15, but it will only go part of the way, leaving you with a ¾-hr. walk to the crater. Trucks go up after the Saquisilí market on Thurs. p.m. During the wet season, the best views are in the early morning so those with a tent may wish to camp. Alternatively, hitch a truck (which is easy on market day); you will be dropped close to the volcano; the last truck from Zumbahua leaves at 1100 on market day, so get to the market very early if you want to do both in one day. Vehicles bound for Chugchilán drop the traveller 5 mins. from the lagoon, those for Ponce on the Ponce turnoff, still about a 40-min. walk north. Hitching a return trip should not be left till late in the afternoon. The Sat. trip to Zumbahua market and the Quilotoa crater is one of the best excursions in Ecuador, but there are only two very small *pensiones* in Zumbahua, without plumbing; one has no beds and they do not like to rent rooms to foreigners, often claiming to be full. In Zumbahua, two houses sell cooked food. Hugo Rengifo (contact through *Hotel Interandino*) has a 4-wheel drive vehicle and for the trip to Pujilí, Zumbahua, Quilotoa and Chugchilán, charges US$40. Macuchi, on the main road to Quevedo some way beyond Zumbahua, is a mining centre for gold and various non-ferrous metals. The mines were developed in the 1930s by an American company, and now they are almost abandoned.

The Zumbahua-Quilotoa road follows the Zumbahua River about half the distance to the lagoon; The scenery is vast, barren, and spectacular. The houses range from straw shepherd huts the size of dog-kennels to thatched adobe, usually windowless, cottages.

About 30 min. by bus north-west of Latacunga is the small but very important market town of **Saquisilí**. Its Thurs. (0700-1100) market is famous throughout Ecuador for the way in which all eight of its plazas and most of its streets become jam-packed with people, the great majority of them local Indians with red ponchos and narrow-brimmed felt hats. The best time to visit the market is between 0900 and 1000; be sure to bargain, prices may be inflated. Rated the best market in Ecuador by a traveller who has visited them all, but less good for textiles than Otavalo. Saquisilí has colourful Corpus Christi processions.

Dan Buck and Anne Meadows write: Tightly woven decorated baskets plentiful but expensive, though somewhat cheaper than in Quito. Bargain hard, there is a lot of competition for your custom. Livestock market hectic and worth a visit. Some animal buyers set up small corrals in which they collect their purchases. Trucks brimming with oranges and yellow and red bananas; reed mats, fans, and baskets; cow, pig, and sheep parts piled on tables; Indian women hunkered down beside bundles of onions, radishes, and herbs, and little pyramids of tomatoes, mandarin oranges, potatoes, okra, and avocados; *cabuya* and *maguey* ropes and cords laid out like dead snakes; and a food kiosk every five feet offering everything from full *almuerzos* to *tortillas de papa*.

Accommodation *Pensión Chavela*, main plaza, G, billiards and gambling hall downstairs, noisy; *Salón Pichincha*, Bolívar y Pichincha, G, good restaurant-bar below, friendly, not very clean, secure motor cycle parking. Some basic restaurants can be found in the same district (at the entrance to the village).

Transport The Saquisilí and Cotopaxi bus companies have frequent services between Latacunga and Saquisilí (US$0.10, ½ hr.) and several buses a day run between Saquisilí and Quito (catch them in Quito on the Avenida 24 de Mayo in the old centre, US$0.65, 1½-2 hrs.). Alternatively you can catch an Ambato bus from Latacunga, ask the driver to let you off at the junction for Saquisilí and get a passing pick-up truck (US$0.25) from there. The *Hotel Intercontinental Quito* and the *Hotel Colón Internacional* in Quito both organize efficient but expensive taxis for a 2-hr.

574 ECUADOR

visit to Saquisilí market on Thurs. Bus tours cost about US$17.50 p.p., taxis can be found for US$25, with 2 hr. wait at market.

North of Latacunga, the railway and the Pan-American Highway cross one another at Lasso, a small village with a milk bottling plant and two recommended cafés serving dairy products. Just north of Lasso, east of the highway, is the San Agustín hill, thought to be a prehistoric pyramid.

The area around San Agustín is owned by the Plaza family, which has two large *haciendas* and breeds bulls for the bull-fights in Quito in December. One of the two *haciendas* is actually at the base of the San Agustín hill and includes some converted Inca buildings.

About 2 km. off the road from Latacunga to Quito, near Lasso, is the Hostería La Ciénega, a good restaurant also operating as a small hotel in an old *hacienda* with outstanding gardens and a small private chapel. It used to belong to the Lasso family when their land spread from Quito to Ambato (Tel.: Quito 541-337).

A little beyond San Agustín, a poor road leads off towards the Cotopaxi volcano, at Parque Nacional de Cotopaxi sign. National Park authorities are breeding a fine llama herd on the lower slopes. Just north of Cotopaxi are the peaks of Sincholahua (4,893 metres), Rumiñahui (4,712 metres) and Pasochoa (4,225 metres).

Cotopaxi (6,005 metres) Rob Rachowiecki writes: There are two entrances to the Cotopaxi National Park: the first is near a sign for the NASA satellite tracking station, from where one can walk (or hitch hike on weekends and holidays) the 3 km. to the NASA station (can be visited with preauthorization from Instituto Geográfico Militar in Quito) and then continue for over 30 km. more along a signposted dirt road, past two campsites, through the National Park gates, past Lake Limpio Pungo (a popular camping site), past the old Armada Nacional refuge and on to the parking lot (4,600 metres) where the road ends. From here it is 30 mins. to 1 hr. to the José Ribas refuge (4,800 metres). The second entrance, about 6 km. further south, is marked by a small Parque Nacional de Cotopaxi sign. It is about 28 km. from here to the refuge. Nearly 1 km. from the highway, turn right at a T junction and a few hundred metres later turn sharp left. Beyond this the road is either signed or you take the main fork; it is shorter and easier to follow than the first route which you join just before the Park gates.

The ascent from the refuge takes 6-11 hrs. Equipment and experience are required. Climb the sandy slope above the hut and head up leftwards on to the glacier. Getting on to the glacier is the steepest and technically hardest part of the climb. The route then goes roughly to the right of Yanasacha and on to the summit. Allow 2-4 hrs. for the descent.

Dr. Sverre Aarseth writes that the best season is December-April; strong winds and clouds in August-December but still possible for experienced mountaineers. The route is more difficult to find on Cotopaxi than on Chimborazo (see page 569); it is advisable to seek information from Quito climbing clubs (Nuevos Horizontes is the best). The snow and ice section is more heavily crevassed than Chimborazo and is also steeper; however it is less climbing time.

Visitors to the Parque Nacional de Cotopaxi must register when entering and leaving the park. The park gates are open 0700-1800 with lunch 1200-1400. The refuge (US$0.85 p.p. a night) has a kitchen (you may use the stove for a small charge), water, many beds (bring sleeping bag) and lock-up facilities for your excess luggage when you climb. There are many campsites in the Park. If you have no car, the best bus to take from Quito is the Latacunga bus. Do not take an express bus as you have to get off before Latacunga.

Thirty-seven km. beyond, at Cotopaxi, the line begins to dip into the Quito basin. In a valley below the bleak *páramo* lies the town of **Machachi,** famous for its mineral water springs and very cold swimming pool (US$0.35). The water, "Agua Güitig", is bottled and sold throughout the country. There are no buses but it is a nice walk to the plant about 4 km. from the town, or take a taxi, US$1. On the way back you may be able to get a lift in a Güitig truck. Machachi produces a very good cheese. Cockfights on Sun. *Pensión El Tiempo*, F, clean. Bus to Quito US$0.35. Taxi to Cotopaxi, US$16 per car.

The Southern Sierra

The Pan-American Highway and railway S of Sibambe to Cuenca run through mountainous country and high above the valleys of the west-bound rivers. The countryside is poor, dry, chilly and wind-swept, and the Indians small, withdrawn and wrapped-up. Near Gun and Cañar, more Indians, dressed in black, are seen. At Gun an all-weather road runs to Cochancay in the coastal lowlands, from where there are paved roads to Guayaquil and Machala. Towards Cuenca the road loses height and the land is more intensively farmed. There are excellent

ECUADOR 575

roads linking Quito-Guayaquil and Guayaquil-Cuenca, which meet at El Triunfo on the coastal plain. Some transport goes this way rather than using the direct road, although there the scenery is magnificent; there are often detours which lead to deep ravines and precipitous peaks. The main road south divides at Cajabamba into two equally respectable-looking paved roads to Cuenca and Guayaquil, but the paving of the Cuenca road is complete only as far as Alausí (see page 565). Beyond here to the junction with the Guayaquil-Cuenca road at Zhud, roadworks can make the road almost impassable, or even close it. On this route, near Alausí, is Chunchi, a small, welcoming village with a Sunday market.

Azogues (14,452) is 31 km. before Cuenca and a centre of the panama hat industry, though good quality hats for sale only at the large Sat. market (*Reskdencial Tropical*, G, no competition, showers sometimes electrocute guests). Both Azogues and Biblián have attractive churches overlooking the towns from neighbouring hillsides.

Cuenca (2,595 metres), with 151,000 people, is the third largest city in Ecuador. It was founded by the Spaniards in 1557 on the site of the indigenous settlement of Tomebamba. A 146 km. railway runs from Sibambe on the Guayaquil-Quito line to Cuenca. The climate is spring-like, but the nights are chilly. The city has preserved its colonial air, with its cobblestone streets and old buildings, many of them built of the marble quarried nearby. A fine new cathedral, which contains a famous crowned image of the Virgin, has now been built in the central square, Parque Calderón, where the old cathedral still stands. The University is now on the other side of the Tomebamba river. Part of the Padre Crespi collection can be seen at the Banco Central "Pumapungo" museum (open Tue.-Fri. 0930-1630 and Sat. 0900-1230, free), Calle Larga y Huayna Capac, on the edge of town at the Tomebamba site (excavation continuing). (It is often shut if the exhibition is being changed.) Padre Crespi (died June 1982) used these artefacts to support his theory that the Phoenicians reached Cuenca via the Amazon. The Instituto Azuayo de Folklore, Sucre 176, San Blas district (open Mon. to Fri., 0800-1200, 1400-1800) has an excellent exhibition of popular art, with a few items on sale. The old Casa de Gobierno (now demolished) where Humboldt was a guest in 1802 formerly stood on this site and there is a plaque over the doorway. There is a municipal museum at Calles Sucre y Talbot (modern art and Indian artefacts, open Mon.-Fri. 0800-1300, 1500-1800). A pleasant walk is upstream along the river.

The churches which deserve a visit are the old Cathedral, which has a fine organ; La Concepción (convent founded 1599, religious art museum, obtain permission to view from the Bishop), San Blas, San Francisco, Santo Cenáculo, and Santo Domingo. Inca ruins have been found on the banks of the river: about 300 metres from the Pumapungo site, at Larga 287, there are excavations at the Todos Los Santos site (open Mon.-Fri., 0800-1600).

Festivals On Christmas Eve there is a parade; children and adults from all the *barrios* and surrounding villages decorate donkeys, horses, cars and trucks with symbols of abundance: strings of dollar bills, bottles of Cinzano, strings of lemons and peppers, bunches of bananas, whole roasted chickens with banknotes in their beaks, toys etc. Little children in colourful Indian costumes or dressed up as Biblical figures ride through the streets accompanied by Indian musicians. The parade ends in the Plaza de Armas, which is a good place to watch it. Travellers in Cuenca over New Year's Eve report that the festivities include the parading and burning of effigies (some political, some fictional) which symbolize the old year; there is also much water throwing and tourists are a prime target. The festivities seem to go on all through January. The burning of straw puppets (*el hombre viejo*) takes place at the moment of the New Year throughout Ecuador. There are also festivals on April 10-13 (Foundation of Cuenca) and November 3 (Independence). There are also festivities involving the throwing of water balloons at Carnival time before Lent and around Easter, and tourists in Cuenca and throughout southern Ecuador can expect to be soaked. Don't be afraid of the water: Cuenca has the best drinking water in Ecuador and visitors are welcome at the water plant, with its gardens.

The main market is on Thursday when pottery, clothes, guinea pigs and local produce, especially baskets, are sold in the 9 de Octubre and San Francisco areas. There is also a colourful daily market. Be careful of pickpockets in the market. If you are robbed, however, contact the police, their efficiency has been

ECUADOR

praised by one traveller who had most of his money returned to him after paying them a small fee.

Cuenca has been criticized as not well organized for tourism; many places of interest are closed at weekends. Police searches of tourists' luggage at their hotels are not unknown.

Warning There is a short, dark, pudgy man who asks lone female travellers to write letters for him to non-existent friends, and then invites them out. He is a known rapist and dangerous, but seems to have close relations with the police. Avoid him.

Hotels *El Dorado*, Gran Colombia y Luis Cordero, B, night club, the best in town, good restaurant, small portions, but good view; *La Laguna*, Swiss-run, on lake in outskirts of town, A, the best available, lovely rooms, restaurant reasonable; *Hostería El Molino*, D, Km. 8.5 on road Azogues-Cuenca, pleasant position between road and river, Spanish run, typical Ecuadorean dishes, pool, rustic style, recommended, advisable to book; *Crespo*, Calle Larga 793, C, good service and food with restaurant overlooking river, very clean, a lovely building, recommended; *Crespo Annex*, comfortable, nice, Cordero 422 y Larga, E; *Presidente*, Gran Colombia 651, D; *París Internacional*, Sucre 694, D, restaurant; *Atahualpa*, Sucre 350, E; *Tomebamba*, Bolívar y Torres, E; *Alli-Tiana*, Córdova y Aguirre , E; *Resid. El Puente*, 12 de Abril 4189, E, parking; *Hurtado de Mendoza*, Sangurima y Huayna Capac, E, good, restaurant; *Las Américas*, Mariano Cueva 13-59 y Vega Muñoz, E, good value, carpets, hot water, telephone, friendly, helpful, good cheap restaurant next door; *El Conquistador*, Gran Colombia 665, E, without breakfast, sauna, good, friendly; *Tours Cuenca*, Borrero 1069, large rooms, TV, central, E, reasonable; *Catedral*, Padre Aguirre 8-17 y Sucre, E, cheaper rates for Peace Corps and other service organizations, spacious, modern, English-speaking manager, safe, laundry service, good food; *Gran Hotel*, Torres 970, F; *Resid. Samay*, Ordóñez 1186, F, cafetería; *La Alborada*, Olmedo 1382, F; *Internacional*, Benigno Malo 1015, F, cheerful, good value for set meal; *Majestic*, Luis Cordero 1129, F, no longer majestic; *Pichincha*, Gral. Torres y Bolívar, F, clean; *Milán*, Pres. Córdova 989 y Aguirre, F, friendly, helpful, reliable for storing luggage, good breakfast, warmly recommended; *Paris*, Gral. Torres 1048, E; *Londres*, Huayna Capac y Núñez, F; *Residencial Niza*, Mariscal Lamar 4/51, F, clean, water not too hot; *Residencial Atenas*, Cordero 1189, F, clean, comfortable, but not safe for left-luggage; *Pensión Azuay*, Padre Aguirre 775, G, market area, basic; *Pensión Granada*, Sucre 1074, G, basic; *El Galeón*, Sangurima 240, F, large, modern rooms, own bathroom, hot water, parking; *Pensión El Oro*, Gabriel Ullauri 509, F, market area, hard to find; *Pensión El Inca*, Gral. Torres 842, G, hot showers, clean, friendly; *Hostal Norte*, Mariano Cueva 1163, G; *Residencial Colombia*, Mariano Cueva 1161, G, clean but noisy, overlooking market, hot showers, thieving staff; *Residencial Tito*, Sangurima 149, F, clean, good restaurant, recommended; *Pensión Andaluz*, Mariano Cueva 1221, G; *Residencial España*, Sangurima 117, G, recently refurbished, friendly, laundry facilities, hot water, clean; safe parking for motor cycles; *Residencial Santo Domingo*, Calle Padre Aguirre y Gran Colombia, opposite Sto. Domingo church, F, clean, central, rather unfriendly; *La Ramada*, Sangurima 551, F, friendly, clean and pleasant but noisy; *Residencial Sánchez*, G, Muñoz 428 y Mariano Cueva, *merienda* recommended; *Emperador*, G, Gran Colombia 1077, clean, front rooms noisy; *Siberia*, G, Gran Colombia 531, hot water, bargain for room rates, laundry facilities, central and convenient; *Los Alamos*, F, modern, communal hot shower, clean, recommended, Av. España, opposite main bus terminal.

Furnished two-bedroom apartments are available; *El Jardín*, Av. Pumapungo y Viracochabamba, US$5 per day p.p., cooking facilities and parking. Tel.: 830 330, or write to address above, Casilla 298.

Restaurants *El Jardín*, Presidente Córdova 7-23, lovely restaurant, good food, French (nouvelle) cuisine, US$8 p.p. (shut on Sundays); *El Fogón*, España 2472, Argentine, live music, superb steaks. The dining room at the *Crespo Hotel* has lovely views and excellent food; *Hotel La Laguna* restaurant warmly recommended; *La Reforrna*, Coronel Talbot 10-27, vegetarian, cheap; *Chifa Manila*, Sangurima 2-20 and *Chifa Hong Kong*, Huayna Capac 1137, both reasonably priced, good food; *Govinda*, Honorato Vásquez 7-56 y Cordero, vegetarian, excellent fruit juices, very clean; *El Paraíso*, Ordóñez 1023, 3rd floor, vegetarian also. *El Escorpión*, Malo y Larga, criollo, good food, recommended; *Rancho Chileno*, España y Elia Liut, good steak and seafood; *Cafetería Roma*, Luis Cordero y Sucre, try the *lasagna*, European, not cheap. Also Italian is *Pizza de Colores*, Torres 1079 y Lamar, Italian (not only pizzas) and international, English spoken, recommended; *Balcón Quiteño* (Nos. 1 and 2) Sangurima 649 near market, frequented by the locals, good value, rapid service; *Nutibara*, also on Sangurima at Luis Cordero, inexpensive, but limited menu; *Los Copihues*, Simón Bolívar 6-31, for *empanadas chilenas*, juices and coffee; *Yogur*, Benigno Malo 635, yoghurt with fruit; *El Cangrejo*, seafood bar for lunch on Av. 12 de Abril, near the hospital and medical school, just beyond El Vergel church, a pleasant walk down the river. Seafood also at *El Acuario*, Huayna Capac 138, and *El Calamar*, Pizarro 148 y España. Chilean food at *Tupahue*, 12 de Abril 1107 (also near El Vergel church); *La Cantina*, Borrero y Córdova, criollo food in refurbished mansion, good. Snackbars at *Los Pibes*, Gran Colombia y Cordero, good, and *Trattoría Césare*, Cordero y Larga, fair food, clean. *Heladería Holanda*, Benigno Malo 9-45 with Bolívar, half a block from main plaza, Dutch recipes for good ice-cream with fresh whipped cream; *Helados Honey*, Mariscal Lamar, clean, cheap, milkshakes recommended; *Raymipampa*, on main plaza, cheap but slow; *Mi Pan*, Presidente Córdova 842, excellent cakes, tarts, doughnuts, good breakfast; *El Bucanero*, Sangurima 617, good breakfast and à la carte menu, cheap, clean but small helpings; *El Trigal*, Cordero 9-38, a bakery for good fresh bread. *Primavera*, Borrero 5-29, whole food shop; *Panificadora El Molino*, Simón Bolívar 12-33, good whole wheat rolls; *Pío-Pío*, on main square for roast chicken and real coffee; also in bus station, good for breakfast. Cuenca's best sandwich bar at *Los Chorizos*, Cordero 1067 y Gran Colombia; hamburgers at *Pity's*, Gran Colombia 2087, recommended.

Shopping Many craftware shops along Gran Colombia, near *El Dorado* hotel, and on Benigno Malo. These include Ocepa, Productos Andinos, Artesanías Atahualpa, Arte Artesanías, Arte del Pacífico and Artesanías Paucartambo. Good souvenirs are carvings, leather, basketwork, painted wood, onyx, woven stuffs (cheapest in Ecuador), embroidered shirts, etc. Joyería Turismo, owned by Leonardo Crespo, at Gran Colombia 9-31, has been recommended; he will let wholesale buyers tour his factory. Jewellery prices are reported as high: shop around. High quality Panama hats are made by Homero Ortega, Vega Muñoz 9-33, Tel.: 823-429, who exports all over the world. Interesting market behind new cathedral.

Entertainment Discos at Hotels *Conquistador* and *Alli-Tiana*, and *Las Galaxias*, Núñez de Bonilla 239. Peñas at *Hotel la Laguna*, outside town, and *La Pantera Rosa*, España 1080.

Taxis US$0.32 for short journey; US$0.75 to airport; US$1 per hr.. Local buses US$0.05.

Exchange Citibank, Gran Colombia 749 (charges commission, even on its own cheques), and local banks. Cambistral in City Hall on Sucre y Malo. Generally, the rates are quite good.

Post Office and letel on corner of Calles Gran Colombia and Borrero.

Tourist Office Dituris, Benigno Malo 735, just off main Plaza. Very helpful. Maps of Cuenca. They have little information on Ingapirca but a little booklet: *Ingapirca, guía para visitantes* can be bought for about US$0.40 in bookshops (out of print in 1985). Yroo Tours, Larga y Malo, English spoken, recommended. Also Metropolitan Touring and Ecudorean Tours, both at Sucre y Malo. A recommended guide for the Cuenca area is Vicente López Cárdenas, Tel.: 823-790, well-informed on local flora and culture, Spanish speaking only.

Buses The *Terminal Terrestre* is on Av. España, a 20-min. walk northwest of the city centre, or take a minibus, US$0.05. To Loja, 8 hrs., US$2.30, major construction work on this road, long delays; Ambato, US$3.25, 9 hrs. (travel during day because scenery is magnificent, the road, not all paved, goes from 2,600 metres to under 200 and up again); Quito, 10½ hrs., US$4.10; Machala, 5 hrs., US$2.70; to Guayaquil, 5 hrs., US$2.65 (road now entirely paved). To Huaquillas, 6 hrs., US$3.10, at 2100 (the bus sometimes stops for 2 hrs. in Machala, it is often better to get a local bus from there to Huaquillas). The evening bus arrives in Huaquillas at 0300, but passengers sleep on the bus till daylight. Be prepared for frequent police checks on the way. To Riobamba 5½ hrs., US$3; scenic. To Saraguro, US$2, 6 hrs. To Macas, 11 hrs., US$2.80.

Trains In 1985 the train to Sibambe, leaving daily at 1500, was restored. A pleasant round trip by train and bus can be made to El Tambo and back, to see Ingapirca (see next page).

Air Service Daily connections with Quito (US$12) and Guayaquil (US$7.50) with TAME and SAN.

Excursions There are sulphur baths at Baños, with a beautiful church in a delightful landscape, 5 km. S of Cuenca. Two separate warm baths, of which the lower one is better (US$0.80 for private bathroom, US$0.40 for swimming pool, the upper one is rather dirty (US$0.40). There are *Residenciales Baños* and *Rincón de Baños*, both F with bath, on the main road, and the *Hostelería Durán*, C, with restaurant, pool and amenities, at the baths. Buses from Cuenca (Calle Larga), US$0.05, taxis US$1.80.

Cañar, 65 km. N of Cuenca (36 km. N of Azogues), is famous for its double weaving and is a good area for walking (*Residencia Patricia*, F, overpriced, insist on hot shower; *Pensión Guayaquil*, G, Calle Guayaquil 76, OK; unmarked *pensión*, Av. 24 de Mayo 235, green house, on a corner on left side going towards Cuenca; restaurants close early in the evening about 1830, one good one on corner of same street as *Resid. Patricia*). About 40 km. NE of Cuenca in the beautiful Paute Valley is the *Hostería Uzhupud*, C, deluxe, swimming pool, very good food, excellent value, highly recommended, Casilla 1268, Uzhupud, Paute, Tel.: Cuenca 821-853; also *Residencial Cutilcay*, G.

E to **Gualaceo** (Sun. market), 25 mins. by bus every ½ hr., on a recently-paved road, US$0.25 (leave from corner of *terminal terrestre*) pretty town in beautiful landscape, with charming plaza and fine new church with splendid modern glass; embroidered goods sold from private home above general store on main square; hotels: *Hostería Rivera*, E; *Gran Hotel Gualaceo*, F; *Residencial Gualaceo*, F; and *Español*, G; restaurant *Manabí* on main road to Cuenca. Good shoes made locally; splendid bargains. To **Chordeleg** by colectivo (plenty), or by local bus, US$0.10 from Gualaceo market square (every ½ hr.—from Cuenca), a village famous for its crafts in wood, silver and gold filigree and pottery, also panama hats, although reported to be

578 ECUADOR

very touristy nowadays. Watch out for fake jewellery. Joyería El Brillante has been found to sell gold-plated silver for solid gold. Joyería Puerto del Sol, on Juan B. Cobos y Eloy Alfaro, has been recommended. The church is interesting. Gualaceo is a very pleasant hour's walk downhill from Chordeleg. Chordeleg has a small Museo de Comunidad of fascinating local textiles, ceramics and straw work.

Ingemar Tholin of Västerås, Sweden, recommends taking a bus (US$0.50, 1½ hrs.) from Cuenca to Sígsig (S of Gualaceo, 83 km. from Cuenca, *residencial*, G), and from there another to Chiguinda (stay overnight with Sr. Fausto, the teacher). A trail from Chiguinda goes to Aguacate (4-5 hrs. walking), a village of 70 people. Sr. Jorge Guillermo Vásquez has a *hospedaje*, horses can be hired for trekking to caves. There are shops, electricity at night only, and good *fiestas* at Christmas and New Year, and carnival in February (very popular). From Aguacate either walk or hire a horse to continue SE to Río Negro, a friendly village, from where daily buses at 1300 and 1600 go to Gualaquiza (1 hr., US$0.35—see page 594). A road is being built between Sígsig and Gualaquiza, along a beautiful and unspoilt route; the trail can be hiked by the intrepid but is not yet passable by wheeled vehicles.

NW of Cuenca, **El Cajas**, 2 hr. bus trip (daily except Thurs. at 0600 and 0630, buses back at 1400, hitchhiking impossible, no traffic) is a national park with about 60 lakes. Ideal but strenuous walking, 4,200 metres altitude. Obtain a permit for entry to the park from the Ministry of Agriculture above the Banco Azuay, Bolívar 6-22. They are supposed to provide maps but these are often unavailable. There is a refuge with four bunks in the park which you can book at the Ministry. The park is easy to miss; avoid being carried 8 km. further to the village itself. Warm clothing and waterproofs therefore recommended. To the **Laguna de Surucucho** catch the bus at the Plaza Santo Domingo to Sayausi (US$0.05) and walk from there; about 1¼ hrs. from Sayausi take a dirt road to the left and walk a further 45 minutes. There is good trout fishing in the lake and the river.

A beautiful hour-long bus trip on the Machala road from Cuenca takes one to the town of Girón, whose beauty is spoiled only by a modern concrete church. From there trucks take passengers up a winding road to the hamlets of San Gregorio and Chumblín. Friendly inhabitants will act as guides to three lakes high in the *páramo* where excellent trout-fishing is to be had. Take camping gear.

Ecuador's most important Inca ruin, **Ingapirca,** can be visited from Cuenca by bus. Alternatively you can take a taxi for the 5-hr. round trip, recommended on Sundays particularly, when it is impossible to complete a round trip by bus. There are also buses and occasional trucks along the Panamericana to Cañar; the traveller is dropped 2 km. before Cañar at a side road to the right, 14 km. from Ingapirca, but there are colectivos from Cañar to Ingapirca, or a bus from Cañar leaves at 0600, and the ride is quite beautiful despite the bad road, or try to get a lift, which is quite easy. Another recommended method is to take a bus (US$0.75 from Calles Sangurima y Machuca), to the village of El Tambo, beyond Cañar (and 7 km. from the site) from where a train goes to Ingapirca at 0800, returning 1700. Alternatively, wait on the other side of the railway tracks for a *colectivo* or pick-up truck to pass, usually about every 30 minutes. There is an *hospedaje* at El Tambo. A third possibility is to go to San Pedro, where there is a municipal *hospedería* where travellers can stay free of charge (although difficulties have been reported in obtaining the key); a 3 km. dirt road leads to the ruins. On Fri. there is an Indian market at Ingapirca. There is a good co-operative craft shop next to the church. Camping at the site is possible. There is no hotel at Ingapirca: the (free) *refugio* has benches, table and fireplace but no beds. It is not available at night, cannot be locked during the day, and to use it at all you must surrender your passport.

Ingapirca is commonly known as a fortress complex although this is contradicted by archaeologists. The central structure is an *usnu* platform probably used as a solar observatory. It is faced in fine Inca masonry, and it is interesting to note that the length is exactly three times the diameter of the semicircular ends. This may have been connected with worship of the sun in its morning, midday and afternoon positions. (John Hemming)

Warning Be careful of overcharging by truck drivers. The guardian at the entrance is very helpful.

From Cuenca, the Pan-American Highway runs S to La Y, about 20 km. away near the village of Cumbe. Here the road divides into two all-weather gravel roads: one continuing the Pan-American to Loja (beautiful views on both sides) and the other, which is faster (or less slow), running to Pasaje and Machala. (One traveller reports that on a night trip on this route, the bus driver stopped before beginning the descent, made a collection from the passengers and having made the sign of the Cross, apparently tossed the money over the edge of the cliff.) Santa Isabella and Pasaje (pop. 27,000), the main towns along the route, have little to recommend them. Most buses travel NW to

ECUADOR 579

El Troncal and then S down the coast road to reach Machala and Huaquillas for the Peruvian border (see page 587).

The Pan-American Highway climbs S from La Y and rises eventually to the 3,500 metres high Tinajillas pass. The road descends sharply into the warm upper Jubones valley past cane fields and rises again near the small town of Oña. From there it weaves through highland *páramo* pastures and then descends towards Saraguro. Here we meet Indians once more, the most southerly Andean group in Ecuador, dressed all in black. They wear very broad flat-brimmed hard felt hats: the men are notable for their black shorts (sometimes covered by a whitish kind of divided apron) and a particular kind of double bag, the *alforja*, and the women for their pleated black skirts, necklaces of coloured beads and silver *topos*, ornate pins fastening their shawls. They have entered the money economy with vigour: many now take cattle across the mountains east to the tropical pastures above the Amazonian jungle.

The road runs through **Saraguro** (picturesque Sun. Indian market), over the mountain and then makes a long, very tortuous, descent towards Loja. The direct Cuenca-Loja road is under reconstruction and when the widening is completed it will be one of the most beautiful and breathtaking in Ecuador without the discomfort offered by the longer, alternative route via Arenillas.

In Saraguro, two pensions, one over the *farmacía*, F, friendly, family-run, freezing shower. Restaurant: *Salón Cristal*, behind the church The restaurants are poor and the shops sell little. It is a very cold town.

Loja (2,225 metres, 71,130 inhabitants), lies near the Oriente. There are crude but original paintings on the patio walls of many of the old houses. There are two universities, with a well-known law school. The cathedral and San Martín church have painted interiors. The town, encircled by hills, can be reached by air from Quito or Guayaquil to La Toma and then 35 km. by paved road. There is a market on Sat. and Sun. Travellers' cheques cannot be changed in the banks; good rate for US$ in gift shop in front of *Hotel Acapulco*, but there are no *casas de cambio*. Souvenir and craft shops on 10 de Agosto between Kennedy and 18 de Noviembre. Dituris on 10 de Agosto near 18 de Noviembre.

Hotels *Imperial*, with restaurant, Sucre 945, E; *Residencial La Rivera*, Universitaria y 10 de Agosto, E, good; *Hostal Quinara*, opp. *La Rivera*, E, also good; *Inca*, F, hot water; *Saraguro Internacional*, Universitaria 724, E, hot water, TV, restaurant open Mon.-Fri.; *Ejecutivo Sudamérica*, Universitaria 1076, F, good, also "video club"; *Metropolitano*, 18 de Noviembre y Colón, F with bath and TV, hot water, clean; *París*, 10 de Agosto 1637,clean with electric hot showers, F, bargain for good rate, near food market, recommended; *Residencial Santa Marianita*, Colón 1638, G, cheap, clean, safe; *Miraflores*, 10 de Agosto 1656, G, can bargain, clean; *México*, Eguiguren 1571, G, basic; *Londres*, Sucre y 10 de Agosto, F, constant hot water, clean; *Acapulco*, Sucre 743, F, clean, pleasant, private bathroom with copious hot water, safe for leaving luggage, recommended. Basic *residenciales* in G range: *Caribe*, Rocafuerte 1557; *Cristal*, Rocafuerte 1539; *Alborada*, Sucre 1279; *Internacional*, 10 de Agosto 1528; *Loja*, Rocafuerte y Sucre; *Don Juan*, Colón 1644.

Restaurants *Mesón Andaluz*, Bolívar y Eguiguren, best in town; *Suizo Lojano*, Guerrero y Eguiguren, international; *Palace*, Eguiguren y Sucre, local food; *Trece*, Universitaria y Colón, also Eguiguren 1468, good; *Beirut*, Rocafuerte y Primera Paralella; *Restaurant Popular*, Rocafuerte 1516, serves freshly brewed coffee. Other *criollo* places are *Ocaso*, 10 de Agosto 1639; *Cordillera*, 10 de Agosto 1419; *La Choza*, Sucre y Riofrío. Chicken at *Rico Pico*, 18 de Noviembre y Colón. Seafood at *Pescadería Pacífica*, Bolívar 931; and *Doscientas Millas*, Bolívar y Eguiguren (evenings only). *Chifa 85* on main plaza, new, clean, good quality food, including Chinese dishes. Chinese also at *Chifa Feliz*, Eguiguren y 18 de Noviembre. Good *Unicornio* piano bar on main square; good snacks at *Pastelería Persa* (2 locations).

Excursions A 1½-hr. bus ride, Sur Oriente, Calle Azuay and Av. Kennedy, 4 a day (US$ 0.50) from Loja is **Vilcabamba**, where people were reputed to live to over 100 as often as not; recent research has eroded this belief, but it's still a very pleasant and healthy valley, with an agreeable climate, 17°C min., 26°C max. There is the attractive *Parador Turístico*, E, with restaurant and bar; *Hotel Valle Sagrado*, G, on main plaza, clean, friendly, hot showers rarely work; there are 4 restaurants on the plaza, including *Cabañita*. *Cabañas Amala*, cabins, E, reductions for a long stay, health food (home made, home grown), horses to rent, steam baths, mud treatment, private sun bathing, beautiful setting, English and French spoken; the Mendoza family make travellers very welcome. A small and peaceful farmhouse, owned by Sra. Leticia Jiménez de Macanchi, may be rented; very pleasant for a long stay.

580 ECUADOR

The scenic road to Zamora (40 km.) is narrow but in good condition. You can carry on from there into the Oriente.

Buses To Cuenca, 7 hrs., 7 a day, US$2.60 with Viajeros (18 de Noviembre e Imbabura), the only company which leaves at 0500; Machala, 10 a day, 7 hrs., US$2.75. Cooperativa Loja (10 de Agosto y Cuarto Centenario) runs many buses in all directions, including Quito, 4 a day, 18 hrs., US$5, and Guayaquil, 5 a day, 11 hrs., US$4.40, and two nightly buses to Huaquillas at 2030 and 2230; Macará, 4 a day, US$2, 7 hrs. **Warning** You are advised to avoid late-night buses on the Loja-Macará road; recently several have been robbed by armed gangs.

Most road travellers enter and leave Loja via Machala (see page 586). There are two routes from Loja to Machala, one of which goes through Piñas and is rather bumpy with hairpin bends but has the better views, the other is paved and generally quicker (depending on the driver). Machala can be avoided, however, if you take a Machala bus to the Huaquillas crossroads, called La Avanzada, and there catch another one straight to Huaquillas, the border town. There is also a road into the Oriente, at Zaruma (on this road), where there are interesting carved wooden houses. The old Portovelo gold mines at Zaruma are worth a visit.

An alternative, more scenic route to Peru is, however, available from Loja via **Macará**, a small dusty town on the border, in a rice-growing area, with road connections to Sullana near the Peruvian coast (Hotels: *Paradero Turístico*, F, pool, restaurant may not be open, 1½ km. outside the town on the road to the frontier; *Residencial Paraíso*, G, Veintimilla 553, new and clean; *Guayaquil*, G, with shower, clean, large cell-like rooms; *Internacional*, G, filthy, dubious, rats, by Loja bus office and *Amazonas*, G, friendly, clean, basic, on same street; restaurants *Colonial Macará*, Rengel y Bolívar, and *Macará*, opposite, a cafeteria). Leaving Loja on the main paved highway going westward, the airport at La Toma is reached after 35 km. At La Toma, the Pan-American Highway divides into two branches, one, the faster, via Catacocha, and the other going to Macará via Cariamanga. The road is mainly paved and offers lovely views. The bank at Macará does not change money, so change sucres through the *ambulantes* to give you enough intis to last you until you can find an open Peruvian bank, but no more. A Peruvian tourist card can be obtained at the border if not already obtained in Quito or Guayaquil. There is a 2½ km. walk or taxi ride (US$0.50) to the international bridge over the Río Macará. Border crossing formalities (0800-1800) can last about 1 hr. Peruvian officials may ask to see an onward ticket out of Peru. A lorry (US$2, 1100, uncomfortable) is then taken from La Tina on the Peruvian side to Sullana, or buses leave La Tina at 1400 for Sullana, and at the same time for Piura. Coming from Peru into Ecuador, buses to the *puente internacional* run from Sullana at between 0700 and 0800, be there at 0630 for a seat. There are many military checkpoints along the route but these are not usually a problem. Coop Loja runs four buses a day from Macará to Loja (6 to 8 hrs., US$2), at 0600, 1300, and 1800 (but see warning on page 580), so the whole journey can be done in a day if you arrive at the border at noon. There is less likelihood of bureaucratic hassle or of drug-pushing at Macará than at Huaquillas, but officials are not above asking for a bribe if you do something unusual, such as crossing the border after 1800 hrs and returning the next day to get your passport stamped.

Guayaquil

Guayaquil, the chief seaport and commercial city, founded in 1537 by Francisco de Orellana, stands on the west bank of the Guayas river, some 56 km. from its outflow into the Gulf of Guayaquil. Its population of 1,600,000 makes it the largest city in the Republic. The climate is at its best from May to December with little or no rain and cool nights, though the sky is overcast more often than not. The heat and humidity during the rainy season, January to April, are oppressive. The Puerto Marítimo, opened in 1959, handles about 90% of the country's imports and 50% of its exports.

The city is dotted with small parks and pleasant gardens. (Don't miss the tame iguanas in the Parque Seminario or Bolívar.) A waterfront drive, known as the Malecón, runs along the shore of the Guayas river. Here are the splendid Palacio

ECUADOR 581

Municipal and the severe Government Palace. From the landing pier of the Yacht Club the drive is known as the Paseo de las Colonias. The main street, Avenida 9 de Octubre, runs due west from a central pier; there are 11 piers in all, 6 to the north of 9 de Octubre, 4 to the south. About half-way along it is the Plaza Centenario, the main square of the city, where stands the large liberation monument set up in 1920. On Calle Pedro Carbo, between Vélez and 9 de Octubre, the restored interior of the colonial church of San Francisco is truly beautiful. At La Rotonda, on the waterfront near the beginning of Av. 9 de Octubre, is a statue depicting the famous and very mysterious meeting of Bolívar and José de San Martín in 1822. The dazzling white cemetery, north of the city at the foot of a hill, is worth seeing, but best to go on Sundays when there are plenty of people about. The snow-capped peak of Chimborazo can sometimes be glimpsed from Guayaquil.

The city is bustling and prosperous, and much cleaner than it used to be. The locals are much livelier and more open than the people of Quito. There are clubs for golf, tennis, yachting, and a race track set in delightful surroundings some 5 km. outside the city: there is a football stadium and an enclosed coliseum for boxing, basketball, etc. The pleasant suburb of Urdesa, NW of the city, contains some of the best restaurants and places of entertainment.

One of the oldest and most interesting districts is Las Peñas, at the foot of Cerro Santa Ana, by the river. Here is the city's first church, Santo Domingo (1548). Nearby is an open-air theatre, the Bogotá. Then, up the hill, there is a flat space where two cannon point riverward, a memento of the days when pirates sailed up the Guayas to sack the city. Here begins a curving, narrow colonial street, Numa Pompilio Llona. Paved with huge stone slabs, and lined with many fine houses which used to be an artist's colony, it is picturesque but somewhat neglected. To reach Las Peñas, turn left at end of Av. 9 de Octubre and carry on along the Malecón, to its end. It is a picturesque but still poor area, though improving; even the locals say it is unsafe and you are not advised to walk up the adjacent streets on Cerro Santa Ana.

The pride of Guayaquil is the enormous River Guayas bridge linking the city with Durán, the rail terminal on the east bank of the Guayas River. About half an hour is saved in comparison with the ferry journey, which costs US$0.06 (and leaves every 15 min. from Muelle 5). From Durán, paved highways fan out to Babahoyo, Milagro, Riobamba (pass 4,120 metres high on the way), Cuenca and Machala.

Warning Guayaquil has many thieves and pickpockets, especially outside the hotel entrances and on the waterfront, often working in pairs, and the area south of Calle Ayacucho is generally unsafe. Guayaquil is, however, a safer place on the whole than many cities in Colombia or Peru. Except in the best hotels, there is a chronic water shortage.

Local Holidays October 9 and 12. July 24 and 25, Bolívar's birthday, and Foundation of the City; Carnival is in the days before Lent: watch out for malicious throwing of water balloons, mud, ink, paint etc.; women are prime targets. In contrast New Year's Eve is lots of fun, there is a large exhibition of tableaux, featuring *Años Viejos*, along the Malecón, children begging for alms for their life-size *viejos*, families with cars taking their *viejos* for rides through the centre of town, and a vast conflagration at midnight when all these figures are set on fire and explode.

Museums The Museo Municipal is housed in the Biblioteca Municipal, at Sucre with Pedro Carbo (near the *Hotel Continental*) where there are paintings, gold and archaeological collections and also a good newspaper library. The museum (which contains Shuar heads) is open Wed.-Fri. 0900-1200 and 1500-1800; Sat. 1000-1500, Sun. 1000-1300. Entrance US$0.15 for Ecuadoreans and US$0.40 for foreigners (free on Sat., but passport must be left at desk). The Central Bank's anthropological museum is at José de Anteparra 900 and 9 de Octubre, open Mon.-Fri. 1000-1800, Sat. and Sun. 1000-1300. There is an impressive collection of prehistoric gold items at the museum of the Casa de la Cultura, together with an archaeological museum, Av. 9 de Octubre 1200 and Moncayo, open Mon.-Fri. 0900-1200 and 1500-1830, Sat. 0900-1600. The archaeological museum of the Banco del Pacífico, Icaza 200 and Pichincha, is open Mon.-Fri., 0900-1300. There is a small zoo, open Sun., at the Colegio Nacional.

Hotels Hotel prices in Guayaquil are set by the Tourist Board and should be posted inside hotel. Rooms are much in demand in better hotels, the cheap ones being pretty basic, and singles seem very hard to find. All tend to be heavily booked, particularly in the week before July 24, the *fiesta*.

582 **ECUADOR**

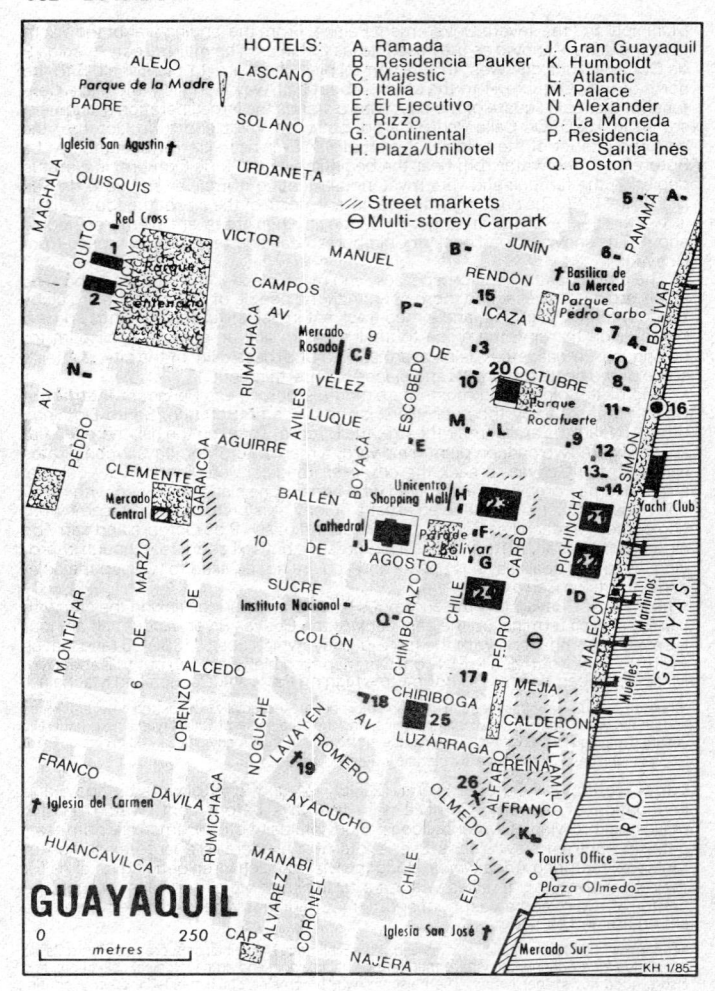

ROUGH SKETCH

Key to Map of Guayaquil
1. Casa de la Cultura; 2. Supreme Court; 3. TAME; 4. Banco del Pacífico/archaeological museum; 5. Clínica Panamericana; 6. Banco Central; 7. Bank of London & South America; 8. Iberia Airlines; 9. Librería Científica; 10. Avianca; 11. Ecuatoriana de Aviación; 12. Bank of America; 13. Lufthansa; 14. Air France; 15. Servitours; 16. La Rotunda & Bolívar/San Martín monument; 17. Banco Continental; 18. Chamber of Commerce; 19. Medalla Milagrosa church; 20. San Francisco church; 21. Palacio de Gobernación, Immigration & Extranjería; 22. Palacio Municipal; 23. Main Post office; 24. Biblioteca Municipal/Museum; 25. University; 26. San Alejo church; 27. Clock tower.

ECUADOR 583

The best hotel is probably *Oro Verde*, 9 de Octubre y García Moreno, A; followed closely by *Unihotel*, Clemente Ballén 406 y Chile, A, good restaurant, and *La Moneda*, P. Icaza y Pichincha, A; *Gran Hotel Guayaquil*, Boyacá 1600 y Clemente Ballén, A; *Continental*, Chile y 10 de Agosto, A, recommended; *Ramada*, Malecón y Orellana, B; *Atlantic*, Chile 303 y Luque, B, good restaurant; *Palace*, Chile 214 y Luque, C, restaurant not clean; *Sol de Oriente*, Aguirre 603 y Escobedo, C, good Chinese restaurant; *Majestic*, 9 de Octubre 709, D; *Plaza*, Chile 414 y Clemente Ballén, D, friendly, some cheaper rooms, excellent restaurant; *Doral*, Aguirre y Chile, D; *Humboldt*, Malecón 2309, D; *Italia*, 10 de Agosto 115 y Pichincha, E, reasonable, convenient, quiet, a/c, rooftop restaurant; *Alexanders*, Luque 1107 y Pedro Moncayo, D, very comfortable but restaurant poor; *Rizzo*, Clemente Ballén 319 y Chile, D, one key opens several doors, so watch your belongings; *Sanders*, Pedro Moncayo y Luque, F, moderately clean and safe, but deteriorating, a/c, no bath; *Residencial Cervera*, E, Gral. Córdoba 1036, a/c, clean, some rooms with bath; *Residencial Metropolitana*, V.M. Rendón 120 y Panamá, F, hot water, a/c, clean, friendly, safe for luggage; *Los Andes*, Garaycoa y Aguirre, E, clean, friendly, recommended; *Londres*, 9 de Octubre 903, F, basic, clean, dark rooms, quieter off street, will store luggage, safe; *Residencial Embajador*, Chimborazo 1106, F, clean but shower rarely works; *Imperial*, Urdaneta 707, F, private shower but water supply only in mornings and evenings, safe, clean, good; *Pensión Pauker*, Baquerizo Moreno 902, F, friendly, clean, rooms on street side noisy, safe for luggage; *Francisco de Orellana*, Villamil 106, F; *San Francisco*, 9 de Octubre y Boyacá, D, check your bill carefully, not recommended; *San Juan*, Vélez y Boyacá, E, own bathroom, no a/c, acceptable but most rooms without windows; *Colón*, Moncayo y Colón, F, shower, clean but noisy; *Santa María*, E, Villamil 102, central, adequate, restaurant; *Orchidea Internacional*, Centro Comercial at Villamil 210, E, good, clean, TV, a/c, hot water; *Residencial Comercio*, Escobedo y 9 de Octubre, F, cheap, basic; *Luz de América*, F, also on Villamil, basic, noisy; *Libertador*, Malecón, F with bath; *Danubio*, also Malecón, F with shared bath; *Residencial Ayacucho*, Chimborazo 1026, F, shared bath; *Residencial Centenario*, Vélez y Garaycoa, F; *Residencial Medellín*, Rumichaca 1502 y Sucre, G, not recommended for women travelling alone; opposite, *Ecuatoriana*, Sucre y Rumichaca, F, dirty, cockroaches, some rooms with no window; *Delicia*, Clemente Ballén 1105, G, clean, fair, try to get room away from street; *Astoria*, E, Av. Quito y C.Ballén; *Marco Polo*, 6 de Marzo 948, F, basic, not safe for women; *Residencial Viena*, Montúfar 534, E. Sra Greta Portugal at Imbabura 214 y Rocafuerte, Aptdo 4-2, lets rooms at price category D, recommended. Total tax of 15 % on all hotel rates.

Restaurants (Centre) *El Fortín* restaurant in the *Hotel Continental* won the Gran Collar Gastronómico Internacional competition worldwide and has excellent food; the cheaper *La Canoa* has local food. Good dining at *Le Gourmet* and *La Fondue* in Hotel Oro Verde, its coffee shop, *El Patio*, has nice and reasonably priced *platos típicos*. Good food at other hotels. *El Parque*, top floor of Unicentro, highly recommended, buffet lunch, overlooks Parque Bolívar; *1822* restaurant at the *Grand Hotel Guayaquil*, expensive, but pleasant surroundings, high quality cuisine with good daily outdoor barbecue at pool-side. Next to the well-known and expensive *Caracol Azul* on 9 de Octubre, is *Grillo Amarillo*, same management but cheaper, wonderful seafood and meats; *Tertulia de Hilda*, Hurtado y Tungurahua, exotic *encocados* Esmeraldeño style, lobster, crab, fish etc., prepared with vegetables and coconut milk, expensive, recommended; *Melba*, General Córdoba 1036, cafeteria; *Bagatelle*, excellent but expensive. *Anderson*, Tulcán 810 y Hurtado, good, French, closed Sun.; *Clérico*, Junín 213 y Panamá, local cooking, reasonable; *Don Vito*, Carchi 803 y 9 de Octubre, disco and bar, closed Sun.; *Muelle 5*, Malecón opp. Roca, local food; *La Piñata*, in Unicentro, Aguirre y Chile, also local food, closed Sats. *La Rotonda*, 9 de Octubre 432, first floor of casino, good, large portions, not cheap; *The Steak House*, García Moreno 811, opposite *Hotel Oro Verde*, pleasant atmosphere, good food and service; *Los Checitos*, Rumichaca 916, good, cheap, take-away available; *Olmos*, Av. P. Ycaza 705 (steaks); *Mamma Rosina*, on road to Urdesa (Italian); *La Cruz de Lorena*, French, small, clean, Junín 413 y Córdova; *Candilejas*, Chile y Carbo, good, quick and cheap; *Res Chan*, ½ block S of post office on Pedro Carbo, very fast and cheap, good Chinese as well as typical meals, packed at lunch time; *Gran Chifa*, Pedro Carbo 1018, ornate, good food at reasonable prices. Typical food at *Pique y Pase*, Alejo Lascano 16-17 y Carchi, not dear, and also at the art gallery, *Galería El Taller*, Calle de las Peñas 183. *Joun Yep*, Los Ceibos; *Central*, 10 de Agosto with Rumichaca; *Mayflower*, Colón 524, Chinese, good food and service, try the Wantan *fritos*; *Chifa Mandarin*, 9 de Octubre 828, for shrimp and fish dishes, passable but a bit dirty; *Chifa China*, on road to airport, run down; *Palacio Dorado*, Chile 712, Chinese also; *Chifa Chan* (not Chinese), Pedro Carbo 816, cheap, generous servings; *Fontana de Soda Germánica*, Ballén y Chimborazo, good. *Pizzalandia*, Carchi and 1º de Mayo, for best pizza in town; *Pizzería Italia*, 9 de Octubre 706, expensive for what you get; *Bavaria*, same street 1313, German run, good for meat. *El Super Cangrejo*, V.M. Rendón 729 y Ximena, cheap seafood. There are a lot of American-style snack bars on 9 de Octubre, but they are fairly expensive. *Burger King*, two branches, one in Urdesa and the other at 9 de Octubre 610. *Kentucky Fried Chicken*, 9 de Octubre 514, recommended. *El Camino* on the corner of Pedro Ycaza and Córdova, owned by English-speaking Jaime Mendoza, has local dishes at economical prices, chicken and seafood also served, best for lunch as they tend to run out of things in the evening. *Baguette*, Aguirre 322, provides good, clean and cheap food; also bakes French bread twice daily. Best ice cream at *Il Gelato Italiano*, 9 de Octubre y Carchi, also in Urdesa.

584 ECUADOR

Restaurants outside the Centre are mostly in Urdesa and Kennedy suburbs. Urdesa: *Juan Salvador Gaviota*, Boloña 603 y Décima, good seafood, closed Sun.; *Il Fiorentino*, Datiles y V.E. Estrada, international, closed Mon. *Trattoria Da Migliorini*, La Primera 604 y Las Monjas, opposite Ietel, very good Italian food, service excellent; *Colombus Steak House* in Urdesa for good steaks and *parrilladas*; *Parrillada del Ñato*, V.E. Estrada 1219 y Laureles, steak and salad; *Costa Brava*, Catalan food, Las Monjas 303 y Cuarta; many others of all kinds along V.E.Estrada. Kennedy: several on Francisco Boloña and Av. Kennedy.

Shopping   Guayaquil has four shopping centres, the Policentro, the Unicentro, the Centro Comercial Urdesa and the Albán Borja shopping centre. The Policentro, on Av. San Jorge, Kennedy, contains a large supermarket and anything else that you might be looking for; catch the minibus labelled "Policentro" from the Malecón. The Unicentro at Aguirre 411 between Chile and Chimborazo is mainly small boutiques and restaurants. The Albán Borja centre, Av. C.J.Arosemena, Km. 2.7, has the most modern branch of the Super Maxi chain of supermarkets. To buy handicrafts, the best places are Madaleine Hollander's shop in the *Oro Verde*, (expensive), and *Manos* (offshoot of *La Bodega* in Quito) at the *Gran Hotel Guayaquil* and also in Urdesa. *Lo Nuestro* (Olga Fisch) and *Galería Guayasamín* are at Policentro. Every day except Sun., Otavalan Indians sell their handicrafts under the *portales* along Calle Chile between 9 de Octubre and Vélez. Beware of newly manufactured "Inca relics" and "Jívaro shrunken heads" sold in souvenir shops. *Artesanías del Ecuador*, 9 de Octubre 104 y Malecón, are good and reliable, and so are *Ocepa*, V.M.Rendón 405 y Córdova. The prices here differ little from those in the towns where the goods are made. Good shops include *Inca Folklore* in the Edificio Gran Pasaje, Av. 9 de Octubre 424, *Arte Folklore Otavalo*, 9 de Octubre 102 y Malecón; *Artesanías Cuenca*, Vélez 110; and *Artesanías Mariel*, Vélez y Chile. There is an H. Stern jewellers shop at the airport. There are souvenir shops in front of, or next to, the hotels *Gran Guayaquil* and *Continental*. Stands in street near Post Office, and a small market in Calle Chile, between 9 de Octubre and Vélez, next to San Francisco church, open daily. Everyone in Guayaquil, rich, poor and in-between, does their shopping at the Bahía, or black market, located along Pichincha, S of Colón and along Olmedo. A wide selection of shoes, appliances, T.V.s, radios and houseware can be found along Pichincha. Clothing is along Pedro Carbo and Olmedo. There is a food market ("bahía") in a covered area on Huancavelica near Pichincha, behind the Cepe gasoline station. Watch your valuables; however the area is generally safe, lots of police. Most name-brand goods will probably be counterfeit. Camping gas at Casa Maspons, corner of Ballén 517 y Boyacá.

Entertainment   Discos and bars in the good hotels. Also *El Corsario*, Los Ríos y Piedrahita; *Cuartito Azul*, Luque y Garaycoa; *Zebras*, Los Ríos y 9 de Octubre. There is a *peña* (folklore show) at *Rincón Folklórico*, Malecón 208 y J.Montalvo. Casinos at *Oro Verde*, *Unihotel* and *Boulevard* hotels.

Books   Librería Científica, for English and US books, Luque 223 and Chile, also good for field guides to the flora and fauna of South America and the Galápagos. Librería Selecta, Aguirre 717. Librería Cervantes, Aguirre 606A and also at Pedro Carbo 827 with 10 de Agosto. Su Librería at Chimborazo 416, Librerías ABC, Policentro Urdesa. Book Exchange at Nuevos Horizontes, 6 de Marzo 924.

Conveyances   Buses and colectivos about US$0.06 (most visitors dare not try them, but they are not lethal although once on it is difficult to get off). The *busetas*, or mini-buses, are cheap and safe to ride. Ruta 15 will take you from the centre to Urdesa, 13 to Policentro, 14 to Albán Borja. *Buseta* passengers and drivers have been occasionally robbed by armed thieves, but generally in the poorer areas of the city. For more roomy travel the *Servicio Especial* buses marked with blue and white diagonal stripes are clean and convenient. Both *busetas* and *Especial* buses in theory, allow no standing passengers. To get off at your stop, yell *pare*. Taxis: short runs, US$0.50; to Policentro or Urdesa, US$0.08; to the airport US$2; by the hr. US$1.50. To Durán, across bridge, US$4.50; also ferry. Taxis are notorious for overcharging; check on fare before entering.

Car Hire   Hertz, Avis, Budget, Dollar at airport, town centre offices and main hotels, prices around US$30 a day, inc. insurance and tax, for a small car. Dollar offers competitive prices but the cars are often reported in poor condition.

Horse-Racing   Hipódromos Buijo and Río Verde in Salinas. Parimutuel betting. Amazingly low standard.

Bank of London and South America, Calle Pichincha 108-110 and Mercado Central and Urdesa agencies; Banco Holandés Unido, P. Ycaza 454 y Baquerizo Moreno, Tel.: 312900; Citibank, Av. 9 de Octubre, Citicorp cheques only; Bank of America, Elizalde 100. Open 0900-1330. Closed Sat. Banco del Pacífico recommended.

Exchange Houses   There are several on Av. 9 de Octubre, also many on Av. Pichincha, between Aguirre and 9 de Octubre. All the *cambios* in the centre will exchange Amex travellers' cheques, though the banks may offer rates as good, or better. Cambiosa, 9 de Octubre 113 y Malecón, recommended. Most open 0900-1900, shut on Saturday. Wander Cambios at airport open 7 days a week.

ECUADOR 585

Consulates UK, c/o Agripac Cía Ltda, Córdova 623; Tel.: 300-400. Telex 3379. Switzerland, Illingworth 108, 4th floor; Tel.: 307-570. Austria, Av. 9 de Octubre 1310, Tel.: 392307. Peru, Av. 9 de Octubre 411, 6th floor, Tel.: 512-738. 0900-1330. Bolivia, P. Ycaza 302 of. 601, Tel.: 304260. Uruguay, V. M. Rendón 1006, Tel.: 513-461. Brazil, L García 103, Tel.: 362-772. Argentina, Aguirre 104. USA, 9 de Octubre y García Moreno, Tel.: 511570. Netherlands, Av. 9 de Octubre 2309, 5th floor. Tel.: 366410. Italy, 9 de Octubre y Baquerizo Moreno. W.Germany, 9 de Octubre 109; Canada, Córdova y Rendón; France, Boyacá 1215. Visa extensions at the Gobernación office, Malecón y Aguirre, 0800-1200.

Telecommunication Instituto Ecuatoriano de Telecomunicaciones (letel). Telephone company and post offfice share same block, Pedro Carbo y Aguirre. Public telex booth. Many kiosks in arcades all round it, each with the flag and name of a different country, plenty of stationery, airletters and postcards.

Medical Dr. Angel Serrano Sáenz, Av. Boyacá 821, Tel.: 301-373, English speaking. The main hospital used by the foreign community is the Clínica Kennedy, Tel.: 396-963. It also contains the consulting rooms of almost every kind of doctor.

Churches Episcopalian Church of U.S.A.; Lutheran Church; Anglican Church, Luis Urdaneta y Malecón del Salado, Urdesa.

Schools US and German. School year, May -mid-January. The Inter-American Academy (US system), August-May.

Tourist Bureau Dituris, Malecón 2321 y Av. Olmedo, first floor; Tel.: 518926, 526241. Helpful, English spoken by some staff, open 0900-1600, Mon.-Fri. Map of Ecuador. A Policía de Turismo man can be hired for a guided tour of Guayaquil. Cost will be about US$4 per hr. for taxi (2 hrs. will do) and US$3 to the Policía de Turismo.

Travel Agents Reportedly, none is open at weekends. Galasam Cía Ltda., Edificio Gran Pasaje, sala 1107, Av. 9 de Octubre 424, Tel.: 306289, their Galápagos programme is called Economic Galápagos Tours. See Galápagos section (page 594) for details. Metropolitan Touring, Pichincha 415 y Aguirre; Orbitours, Aguirre 100 y Malecón. Machiavello Tours, 9 de Octubre y Anteparra (recommended). Galápagos Cruises, Los Ríos 0-80, Tel.: 390-893. Ecuadorian Tours, 9 de Octubre 1900 at corner of Esmeraldas, is agent for American Express, Tel.: 397-111.

Rail Service to Quito suspended in 1983. Travellers arriving in Durán and ferrying to Guayaquil land about 8 blocks still from the main city area, Av. 9 de Octubre. The last ferry is 2130 but buses run later. *Autoferro* and ordinary train run 87 km. from Durán to Bucay.

Bus Services The new bus station (Terminal Terrestre) is near the airport, just off the road to the Guayas bridge. To Cuenca, US$3, 5 hrs.; Riobamba 4 hrs., US$2. Santo Domingo de los Colorados, 4¾ hrs., US$2. Manta 3 hrs., US$2; Esmeraldas 9½ hrs., US$3; to Portoviejo, 3½ hrs., US$2, and to Bahía de Caráquez, 5½ hrs., US$2.80. Machala (for Peru) 3½ hrs., US$2, frequent, or by minibus 2½ hrs., leave at 20 minute intervals between 0600 and 1900, 10 kg. baggage limit. For the Peruvian border, to Huaquillas, avoiding Machala, US$2.50, 5 hrs.; via Machala, 6 hrs. To Ambato, US$2.50, 6½ hrs. To Alausí, 4 hrs., US$2. Several bus companies to Quito, US$3, 8½ hrs. **Trucks** carry freight and passengers, slower, bumpy, cheaper than buses, and you see better. Inquire at Sucre 1104. Regular and frequent buses to Playas (2¼ hrs., US$0.90) and to Salinas (2½ hrs., US$1). Colectivos are not recommended for journeys to the Sierra, they drive too fast and are dangerous. Town buses 2 and 3 from new bus station to centre, US$0.06.

Simón Bolívar Airport, near the centre. US$0.12 for bus, No. 2 from Malecón, No. 3 from Centro Cívico, US$1.50 for taxi from centre, but if you are arriving in Guayaquil and need a taxi from the airport, walk ½ block from the terminal out to Av. Las Américas, where taxis and camionetas wait for passengers. The fare will be at least half of what you will be charged for the same trip by one of the drivers who belong to the airport taxi cooperative. Dituris advises that visitors should not pay more than US$2.50 for taxis from the airport to town. There are several car hire firms at the airport; an information desk; Dituris office; a *cambio*.

Air Services About 12 flights daily to and from Quito, US$12 (TAME, Saeta, SAN). Sit on the right side for the best views. Flights to Machala daily (except Sundays) with TAME or in light 5 or 7 seater planes with Cedta and Lansa about six times a day from the Avioneta terminal on the city side of the international airport. There are flights to Cuenca (2 a day, US$7.50), Manta (1-2 a day, US$7.40), and Loja (1 a day, US$7.50). Daily to Galápagos, US$156 one way (see page 594). TAME, 9 de Octubre, Edif. Gran Pasaje (Tel.: 305-800); Saeta, Escobedo 1114 y 9 de Octubre (Tel.: 303-024). Flights to Lima: Aero Perú (9 de Octubre), US$169 one way. Andes Airlines will ship vehicles to Panama.

Excursions To Playas, Salinas and the Santa Elena peninsula (see page 558).

586 ECUADOR

The Southern Lowlands

On the southern shore of the Gulf of Guayaquil is **Puerto Bolívar** (Hotels: *Pacífico* (restaurant) and *Jambelí*, both basic, G), built above a mangrove swamp and backed by jungle. Approximately one million tonnes a year of banana exports pass through this port. It serves (6½ km.) **Machala,** Ecuador's fourth city, a growing agricultural town of 122,000 with an annual banana fair in September. The area is an unattractive (mosquitoes) but prosperous irrigated banana zone. From Machala paved roads run inland to Pasaje (26 km.), and Arenillas (76 km.), and NE from Puerto Bolívar via Pasaje and Girón to Cuenca. An all-weather road runs SE through Arenillas to Loja (161 km.). In 1983 heavy rainfall destroyed bridges and washed out roads in the area and now there are major construction and improvement works which can cause frequent delays.

Buses run every 10 min. from Puerto Bolívar to Machala (20 mins. journey), and taxis are available. There are daily (except Sunday) Tame flights from Guayaquil and Quito; alternatively, Cedta and Lansa have about 3 flights a day to Guayaquil by *avioneta*. The airport is about 1 km. from town centre, beside local prison.

Machala Hotels *Encalada*, Tarqui y 9 de Octubre, D, Tel.: 920681, restaurant, bar, cafetería, disco; *Rizzo*, Guayas y Bolívar, D, Tel.: 921511, a/c, T.V., suites available, slightly worn luxury, pool, casino, cafetería, restaurant, recommended for breakfast as well as dinner; *El Oro*, Sucre y Juan Montalvo, D, Tel.: 922408, refurbished, good, excellent restaurant; *Perla del Pacífico*, Sucre 603 y Páez, D, Tel.: 920915, T.V., a/c, no hot water; *Gran Hotel Machala*, Juan Montalvo y Rocafuerte, C, Tel.: 920530; *Suites Guayaquil*, Carrera 2a, F, no hot water; *Inés*, Montalvo y Pasaje, E, Tel.: 922301, good restaurant; *Residencial Machala*, Boyacá y Guayas, G (rooms with and without windows, but neither recommended), basic, unfriendly; *Residencial La Delicia*, Montalvo y Rocafuerte, clean, safe, electric fans, F; *Residencial El Oro*, 9 de Mayo y Bolívar, G, basic but OK; *Residencial Almacha*, Sucre 542, G, rough, basic, near Azuay bus station; *Residencial Pichincha*, Sucre y 9 de Mayo, G, basic, dirty, central; *Las Cuevas de los Tayos*, F, clean, parking, recommended; *Residencial Paula*, 9 de Octubre 912, F, with bath, a/c; *Hotel Ecuatoriano*, 9 de Octubre y Colón, F, bath, a/c; *Residencial Patty*, Av. 4a Norte, G, basic, shared bathrooms. *Residencial Hilton*, 9 de Octubre 1656, G, very basic. A mosquito net may be needed for sleeping.

Restaurants *Cafetería San Francisco*; Sucre block 6, good filling breakfast; *Pepe's Parrillada*, Av. 9 de Octubre y 9 de Mayo, food and service recommended, but not cheap, specializes in kebabs and steaks, *bife* better than *lomo*; *Parrillada Sabor Latina*, Sucre y Guayas, steaks and grills; *Pío Pío Rico Pollo*, Av. Guayas, chicken; *Fortaleza*, Sucre y Guayas, open 0600-2100; *Chifa China* and *La Peña*, both 9 de Octubre y Guayas, restaurant of *Hotel Inés*, good seafood; two branches of *Kingburger* offer good hamburgers, clean; *La Fogata*, near telephone office, for good chicken. In Puerto Bolívar *El Acuario* offers excellent value in seafood dishes (on main street which runs back from the pier). A good spot for a beer and toasted sandwich or *ceviche* is the *Miramar* bar at the pierhead.

Tourist Office Dituris is at the junction of Tarqui and Primera Constituyente. Maps are in the basement.

Peruvian Consulate At the corner of Av. 3a Sur, on Píchincha y Guayas.

Post Office Bolívar y Montalvo; telephone and cable office, Ietel, 9 de Octubre near stadium.

Travel Agent Ecuadorian Tours, Bolívar y Guayas.

Exchange Banco del Pacífico, Rocafuerte y Tarqui, changes travellers' cheques and notes; the *casas de cambio* prefer notes.

Cinema There are several, of which *El Tauro* is the best, a/c, cushioned seats, good sound. The *Teatro Municipal* has wooden benches and rats, US$0.32 a seat.

Sport A development just outside Machala on the Pasaje road has two large outdoor swimming pools. The Machala tennis club has three clay and two concrete courts, a swimming pool and a club house. It is situated on the left-hand side of the Santa Rosa road just after the roundabout where the Pasaje road branches off, about 5 km. from Machala. Cockfighting takes place every Saturday afternoon at the cockpit on Calle 9 de Octubre.

Buses The bus companies Occidental, Panamericana, Ecuatoriano Pullman and Rutas Orenses (the best safety record) have depots in the town with direct services to Quito (10½ hrs., US$3.50), Guayaquil (3½ hrs., US$2), Esmeraldas, (11 hrs., US$3.70). Loja (7 hrs., US$2.75). Hourly (a.m.) service to Cuenca by Empresas Pullman Sucre, Sucre block 7, US$2.70, 5 hrs., "exciting ride guaranteed" along a winding road!

ECUADOR 587

Excursions From the old pier on the Puerto Bolívar waterfront motorized canoes go to the tourist beach at Jambelí, on the far side of the mangrove islands which shelter Puerto Bolívar from the Pacific. The beach is long and safe but there is no shade. Canoes cost US$12 return (arrange return time with boatman) or there is a regular boat service (US$1 p.p.), 1000 and 1300 returning 1500 and 1700 on weekdays, more frequent at weekends. A trip to the quieter beach at La Bravita can be arranged, but there are no facilities and again no shade, so take drinks, etc. If arranging a trip to the beach at Costa Rica (2 hrs.) be sure to carry passport as a military post has to be passed. This beach is pleasant but the waves and currents can be dangerous. The trip through mangrove channels is interesting, especially for bird watchers. All the above locations suffer from ferocious mosquitoes after about 1630 and it is better not to stray off the sand at any time as the driftwood is infested with biting insects. The gold mines at Zaruma can be visited. Frequent buses to Zaruma, Transportes TAC, Colón y Rocafuerte.

Crossing the Border into Peru The normal route overland to Peru is via Machala. Buses run 8 times a day (US$0.50, 1¾ hrs.) to **Huaquillas,** the Ecuadorean border town, something of a shopping arcade for Peruvians (all shops close about 1730), described by one traveller as a "seedy one-horse banana town full of touts with black briefcases". Travellers who haven't obtained their Peruvian tourist cards in Guayaquil or Quito can get them at the border.

Hotels at Huaquillas *Parador Turístico Huaquillas,* E, at N of town, Dituris-operated, swimming pool, restaurant and bar; *Continental,* Av. de la República 440, G, basic, noisy, clean, mosquito nets; *Residencial Huaquillas,* Córdovez y 9 de Octubre, G, basic, clean; *Guayaquil,* Gómez y Portovelo, F, mosquito nets provided, expensive, dirty; *Residencial San Martín,* opp. Customs on main street, G, clean, noisy, mosquito nets, convenient; *Pensión Internacional,* G, Av. República, basic; *Mini,* Av. República, G, mosquito net, adequate, reasonable restaurant downstairs; *Resid. Fabiolita* and *Atahualpa,* both G.

Restaurants: Best at *Parador Turístico;* also *Rapa Nui,* on ground floor of *Residencial Mini.* Expect bananas with everything here. There appear to be no *meriendas.*

Complete Ecuadorean formalities at a building in the main street of Huaquillas, then walk along the main street and across the bridge. At the bridge, the police check passports. Then take a colectivo or bus to the new Peruvian customs and immigration (US$0.30, about 3km.); from here colectivos and buses run to Tumbes, US$0.35. The border is officially open 0800-1800, but long lunches are common. It is often best to cross just after lunch when the officers are still sleepy and do not pay you much attention. Peruvian time is one hour earlier than Ecuadorean. Take a colectivo or bus to the Peruvian border town of Zarumilla, or to Tumbes, the first large Peruvian town further south; from there, fast long-distance buses run to Lima. Coming from Peru into Ecuador the reverse applies; take a bus to Tumbes or Santa Rosa and a colectivo from there. Some travellers crossing border from Peru to Ecuador at Huaquillas report being required by the Ecuadorean authorities to show an exit ticket (a bus ticket will do) but this is now less common. Border practices tend to vary, so check to make sure what the authorities require. For example, Australians need a consular visa (US$2, available in Machala) from Peru's consular office near the main plaza. There are a few direct buses from Huaquillas to Quito each day, 14 hrs., US$4; most go via Quevedo but if you get one via Riobamba and Ambato you may see all the great volcanoes. To Guayaquil about 5 hrs., including several stops at military checkpoints, US$2.50. If in a hurry to reach Quito or Guayaquil, it may be advisable to change buses in Machala. Ecuatoriano and Panamericana have a reciprocal arrangement regarding tickets across borders and onwards, but there are no through bus services between Ecuador and Peru. To Cuenca several daily, 7 hrs., US$3.10. The road is completely paved, going up the coast towards Guayaquil and then turning inland at El Triunfo; a circuitous route but quicker than taking the more direct road (10 hrs.) via Girón which is still under reconstruction.

An alternative point for crossing the Peruvian border is Macará in Loja Province (see page 579).

Warning Officially, a ticket out of Peru is necessary for entry into the country. Although rarely asked for, some agencies reportedly still sell cheap tickets for non-existent runs out of Peru. (Tepsa sells tickets in Quito at twice the price they are in Peru). If you are required to show a ticket, you can buy a Miscellaneous Charges Order, valid one year, minimum US$150, but remember there is a 10%

588 ECUADOR

tax on all tickets bought in Ecuador. (We have been told that one traveller's MCO was not accepted by Peruvian officials as an exit ticket.) Peruvian customs and police have asked for bribes at this crossing.

The Peruvian inti has been greatly devalued recently, so verify the rate with travellers leaving Peru. Exchange only what is needed immediately; a better rate is normally obtained in Peru and the Banco de la Nación in Tumbes will give you the official rate. At the border, the best rate is for cash dollars. Be sure to count your change carefully; the money changers (recognizable by their black brief cases) are positively dishonest, and clever. Travellers leaving Peru should get rid of their intis inside Peru, and buy sucres on the Ecuadorean side. At Huaquillas, better rates are obtained in the town than in the vicinity of the border post when buying sucres, though it is difficult to change travellers' cheques.

The Oriente

Ecuador's eastern tropical lowlands can now be reached by four different road routes, from Quito, Ambato, Cuenca or Loja, all described below. These roads are narrow and tortuous, but all have regular bus services and all can be attempted in a jeep or in an ordinary car with good ground clearance. Their construction has led to considerable colonization by highlanders in the lowland areas. Several of the towns and villages on the roads can be reached by air services from Quito, Cuenca and Guayaquil, and places further into the immense Amazonian forests are generally accessible by river canoe or small aircraft. The country is particularly beautiful, and some of the disadvantages of other parts of Amazonia, such as the inadvisability of swimming in the rivers, are here absent. Anti-malaria tablets are recommended, however, and be sure to take a mosquito net. A yellow fever vaccination is recommended for travel into the Oriente.

Most visitors to the Oriente make a circular route Quito-Baeza-Tena-Puyo-Baños-Ambato-Quito. Another popular route is Quito-Baños-Puyo-Tena-Misahuallí-Coca-Lago Agrio-Baeza-Quito, using both bus and boat. Allow at least a week. Metropolitan Tours of Quito do trips to the Oriente for about US$600; and a Napo River tour, US$250, meals, flights, lectures included. Transturi of Quito (Orellana 1810 y 10 de Agosto, Tel.: 544963) do trips from Coca into the jungle on a floating hotel, *Flotel Oreliana*, US$200 (3 days) per person in double cabin, US$375 (4 days) or US$465 (5 days) including Quito-Coca air fare and all meals, guides, etc. and visits to Lake Taracoa, Limón Cocha, Monkey Island, Hacienda Primavera, and Pompeya Catholic mission. Going by bus etc. you can do a round trip much cheaper. The Oriente also has an unpredictable air service provided by army planes; passengers pay insurance, US$1-2; apart from that, fares are low. Frequent military checks; always have your passport handy. You may be required to register at Shell-Mera, Coca, Misahualli, Puerto Napo and Lago Agrio.

From Quito to Coca or Misahuallí From Quito as far as Pifo the road is paved and in excellent condition, but then it gradually worsens until it becomes a narrow, muddy, gravel-covered track, often impassable in the rainy season. It crosses the Eastern Cordillera at an altitude of 4,064 metres at a pass just north of the extinct volcano **Antisana** (5,704 metres, which, according to Cliff Cordy, gets vast quantities of snow, has huge glaciers and is the hardest peak in Ecuador to climb), and then descends via the small villages of Papallacta (see page 550), and Cuyuja to the old mission settlements of Baeza and Borja. The trip between the pass and Baeza has beautiful views of Antisana, high waterfalls, tropical mountain jungle, *páramo* and a lake contained by a glacial moraine almost on the equator.

Baeza is a small town in the beautiful setting of the Quijos pass, recommended for long scenic walks (beware trucks passing) with many waterfalls (the village is about 2 km. off the main road—get off Lago Agrio bus at the police checkpoint and walk up the hill; Tena bus goes through the town). The old Spanish cobblestone trail can be seen down the hill from Baeza, winding along the banks of the Quijos river. Because of the climate, *ceja de montaña*, orchids and bromeliads abound. Trout in the rivers. The pass also has numerous megalithic ruins and petroglyphs (see the books of Padre Porras Garcés, Centro de Investigaciones Arqueológicas, Pontífica Universidad Católica del Ecuador, Quito).

ECUADOR 589

Hotels *Samay*, G, clean, cold shower, and *Nogal de Jumandy*, G, food, bar, parking, friendly, both on main Tena road.

Restaurants *Gina*, good, friendly and clean, and *Lupita*, good, both on Calle Chimborazo. Everything closed by 2030.

At Baeza the road divides, one branch heading S to Tena, the other NE, following the Quijos river past the villages of Borja, a few km. from Baeza (small hotel on roadside; *residencial* on corner of plaza, clean, cold shower, meals provided; basic restaurant *Costa Azul*) and El Chaco (hotel and eating places all reported as dirty) to the slopes of the still active volcano Reventador, 3,485 metres. (At the village of Reventador there is a *pensión*, *Las Orquídeas*, F, and a restaurant.) The road winds along the north side of the river, past the impressive San Rafael falls (145 metres high and discharging an average of 325 cubic metres of water per second; to see them, get off bus at Inecel sign, walk down side road, and then down a steep path, about 1 hr.), until it crosses the watershed between the Coca and Aguarico rivers. A ferry operates 0600-1800 across the Aguarico river until the bridge is rebuilt. The road runs along the north bank of the river to the oil camps and developing towns of Santa Cecilia and Lago Agrio.

Lago Agrio is growing rapidly: it is still a rough place but the infrastructure is improving; excursions into the jungle can be made. Virtually everything in the town is along the main road, Av. Quito.

Hotels *El Gofán*, E, a/c, best, good restaurant; *La Mexicana*, F, reasonable, mosquito nets; *Willigram*, F with own bath, clean, recommended; *Putumayo*, F, shared bathroom; *Hilton*, *Oro Negro*, *Chifa China* (restaurant) and *Chimborazo*, all G with shared bathrooms.

Exchange Several *casas de cambio* on Av. Quito, good rates for notes.

Transport Daily TAME flights to Quito at 1200, US$8. Buses to Quito (US$4, 9½ hrs.), Baeza (US$2.10, 6 hrs.), Coca (US$1.10, 3 hrs.) and Tena (US$3.20, 9 hrs.). Transportes Baños should be avoided.

From Lago Agrio it is possible to take a bus to Chiritza and then a 2 hour boat ride to San Pablo de Kantesiya, a small village on stilts which has one hut where visitors can stay. There are buses north to La Punta (US$0.40, 1¼ hrs., visit Migración in Lago Agrio), where you get a boat across the Río San Miguel to Puerto Colón, in Colombia. There are canoes along the river to the village of San Miguel in Colombia and from there you can catch a bus (5 hrs.) to Puerto Asís (border formalities).

At Lago Agrio, a temporary ferry crosses the Aguarico River (bridge washed away), then the road heads south to **Coca** (officially named Puerto Francisco de Orellana), a river port at the junction of the Coca and Napo rivers; described as a typical oil town, dirty, noisy, with heavy drinking. All foreigners have to register with the police.

Coca Hotels: *Auca*, F, clean, big garden with monkeys roaming free, reasonable food but crowded, manager speaks English; *Florida*, F; *Ecuador*, G, not recommended, noisy; *Residencial Rosita*, G, noisy, hot, showers don't always work; *Tungurahua*, F, favourite with oil workers; and 3 basic *residenciales*, G: *Turingia*, *Lojanita* and *Camba Huasi*.

Restaurant *Doña Erma*'s set meal is cheap and filling; *Venecia*, good food, away from main market area; *Cubayne*, delicious barbecues; *Mama Carmen*, good for early breakfast.

Canoes (irregular service, best to hire your own) pass Coca carrying passengers and cargo down-river to Limón Cocha (where *Flotel Orellana* has a lodge, closed to guests other than their own tour parties), the Capuchin mission at Pompeya with a school and museum of Napo culture, and Nueva Rocafuerte. Local tours can be hired from Limón Cocha and also canoes to return to Coca. In Nueva Rocafuerte, the missionaries and Sra. Jesús let rooms; there are no restaurants. There is a Monday boat from Coca to Nueva Rocafuerte but you must get a military permit to enter the area. The officer has to write exactly the area you wish to visit (e.g. Yasumi river, 2 Auca villages). The boat takes 24 hrs. at least (hammocks provided) US$5.50. You can stay overnight at the mission in N. Rocafuerte. There you can hire boat and guide for US$15 a week. Take plenty of food, tinned meat, ammunition, salt and lighters as present for the Aucas. There is a boat back on Mon. but it doesn't always run and you may have to wait until Fri. To Coca it is a 2-day ferry ride (US$9) with an overnight stop at Sinchichieta and

590 ECUADOR

a meal stop at Pañacocha. From Coca there are also boats (daily) going upstream to Misahuallí (see page 591), from which a bus can be caught to Puerto Napo (officially known as Puerto Nuevo), and then another to Puyo (Coca to Misahuallí via motorized canoe, US$5 for gringos leaving at 0830, 9 hours in average conditions. Take a cushion and waterproofs for self and luggage). The canoe trip upstream to Misahuallí takes about 14 hrs.; if it is not reached before nightfall, the party will camp beside the river. For the less hardy the return trip downstream is advised, 6 hrs. For a price, of course, the willing traveller can hire his own canoe with owner and outboard motor to take him anywhere along the Napo. (To Misahuallí the charge is about US$120.)

Canoes and guides for jungle trips can be hired from Fernando Silva, who lives at the end of the riverside lane next to the bridge. Large canoe for 6 people, 6 days, about US$250, exclusive of food and equipment. Kevin Johnsrude warns "Insist that there be no hunting or dynamite fishing or the only animals you will see will be in your soup!" This price is about half that charged by Misahuallí guides, but since few other trips originate from Coca, you may have to arrange boat trips along the River Napo from Misahuallí.

Two hours downstream from Coca is the Hacienda Primavera owned by Transturi of Quito, who own the *Flotel Orellana*. There are clean and pleasant rooms available, or you can camp. There is a generator now but candles are used for after-generator hours. It is highly recommended for relaxing and enjoying the wildlife; 1 hr. walk to the beautiful Lake Taracoa where there are canoes. You can hire canoes from the *hacienda* to visit other places along the Napo. The *Flotel Orellana* also stops here for a visit.

Transport Bus to Quito, 12½ hrs., US$5; to Lago Agrio, 3 hrs., US$1.10; to Tena, 12 hrs., US$4.20; to Baeza, 9 hrs., US$3.25. There are TAME flights from Coca to Quito Mon., Wed., Fri. at 1100. Ticket office on the riverside, by the bridge, and you have to move your own luggage to the airstrip (20 mins. walk). (Quito-Lago Agrio is the usual alternative; we are also told that the Cepe and Texaco oil companies fly Quito-Coca and sometimes take travellers on board their small planes). Flight Quito-Coca US$12 (Coca-Quito, book 3-4 days in advance), Quito-Lago Agrio (with TAME) US$8, daily except Sun.

From Ambato Beyond Baños (see page 570), the road eastward winds along the north side of the Pastaza river until eventually, after a long descent, the broad extent of the Amazonian plains becomes visible. The road between Ambato and Baños is paved, and from Baños to Puyo it has been reconstructed. It is a dramatic and beautiful journey with superb views and a plethora of waterfalls. **Shell-Mera** (50 km. from Baños, 1½ hrs, *Hotel Esmeraldita, Residencial Azuay*) is the first major stop. Here there are an army checkpoint where foreigners must register, and an airfield. Shell-Mera can also be reached by military flight from Quito, ½ hr.; also flights to Macas. Military flights from Shell-Mera to Montalvo and Tiputini. A few km. on is the larger and busier town of **Puyo,** the most important centre in the whole Oriente. The pioneer fringe has now left Puyo far behind, and its wooden buildings are giving way to concrete and cement. The electricity supply is turned off promptly at midnight. There is a cinema, Coliseo, the Nucaloma discotheque, and a cock-pit (cockfights Sun. 1400).

Hotels in Puyo: *Hostería Turingia*, Orellana y Villamil, E, small huts with bath, in tropical garden, comfortable but noisy, restaurant quite expensive but good; *Europa*, F, with bath, good value and good restaurant, also newer *Europa Internacional*, E, and *California*, F, slightly cheaper, noisy, all on Calle 9 de Octubre; *Grenada*, Calle 27 de Febrero y Orellana, G, clean, recommended; *Pensión Susanita*, 9 de Octubre y Orellana, E, cafetería, recommended; *Pensión Tungurahua*, 27 de Febrero y 24 de mayo, G, basic; *Pensión Paris*, F, Marín 651. Some other *pensiones*.

Restaurants *Hostería Turingia*, best; *California*, 9 de Octubre y Marín, good; *Rincón Ambateño*, Atahualpa y 24 de Mayo, local food, *Delicia* (local), *Viña del Mar* and *El Delfín* (both seafood), all on Marín; *Chifa China*, 9 de Octubre y 24 de Mayo, clean.

Buses to Baños, US$0.80, 2 hrs.; Ambato, US$1.10, 3 hrs.; Quito, US$2, 7 hrs.; Tena, US$1, 3 hrs. Riobamba, US$1.10, 3½ hrs.

From Puyo, a short road goes east to Vera Cruz, but the main highway (unpaved) runs northward to Puerto Napo and Tena. The whole area is a large-scale producer of sugar cane, yuca and *naranjillas* (an orange fruit related to the tomato, used for making a delightfully refreshing fruit drink), and tea has been introduced around Shell-Mera by two foreign companies. Puerto Napo, 72 km. north of Puyo (bus US$1), has a bridge across the Napo river.

On the north bank, a road leads eastwards to **Misahuallí**, about 17 km. downstream, a small port at the junction of the Napo and Misahuallí rivers. From the bridge you can get a ride in a truck, US$0.50, or colectivos, thus avoiding going into Tena. There are downriver canoe services with anything from 10 to 25 people in the vessel. Misahuallí provides one of the best opportunities to visit the jungle and is one of the easiest places to get to, as it is only a day from Quito and 5 hrs. from Baños; it is also one of the cheapest, since other jungle centres such as Iquitos, Manaus, and Leticia are more remote and more developed. However, there is not a great deal of wildlife around Misahuallí, although butterflies are plentiful, and for animals and birds you are advised to go further into the jungle to Coca or to take an excursion lasting several days; the 1-and 2-day trips have been described as disappointing. There is a fine, sandy beach on the Río Misahuallí, but don't camp on it; the river can rise suddenly and unexpectedly.

There are many guides available to take parties into the jungle for trips of 1 to 10 days, seeing river and jungle flora and fauna, visiting Indian villages, the Cuyabeno National Park and other jungle locations, all involving canoeing and varying amounts of hiking. The going rate is between US$12 and US$30 p.p. per day, depending on season and length of trip. This should include food and rubber boots, which are absolutely essential. Overnight tours are recommended only for the hardy.

Hotels *Anaconda*, B, on Anaconda Island in the Río Napo, about 1 hr. by canoe downstream from Puerto Misahuallí; consists of three bungalows of bamboo and thatch, with space for about 32 guests, no electric lights, but flush toilets and cold showers, with water available most of the time. Watch out for thieving monkeys. The meals are good. Canoe and hiking trips to see Indians arranged. Expensive. *Hotel Jaguar*, 1½ hrs. downstream from Misahuallí, congenial atmosphere, B, with full *pension* although the food is rather poor, reservations from Quito, Ramírez Dávalos 653, Tel.: 239400, a full tour (minimum 3 days) including transport from Quito, all meals and excursions into the jungle costs US$170 p.p. with an extra charge of US$32 for each additional day. Avoid paying in US$ as they give you a very bad rate. In the village all the hotels are in the F price range (or G where stated): *El Paisano*, clean, washing facilities, hammocks, nice garden, recommended, four rooms behind excellent vegetarian restaurant (the owner's son, Pablo, arranges trips); *Negrito*, near beach, friendly, restaurant, run by Héctor Fiallos; *Sacha* owned by Héctor, basic, bamboo walls, can be noisy, very good restaurant, at point where rivers meet, dirty but friendly, apes in the garden, path to hotel floods when rains heavy, buy souvenirs of the Oriente here, cheaper than in Baños or Quito; *Balcón del Napo*, basic, central, meals available, clean, friendly; *Residencial Bolívar*, you need to bargain. *La Posada*, G, basic, reports of cheating; *Etsa*, F with or without bath, owner is guide Carlos Cordero. Douglas Clarke now provides cheap, basic accommodation in bamboo huts with bunk beds behind the restaurant, showers available. Beware of thieves poking hooks through the floor.

Restaurants Douglas Clarke's *Restaurant Dayuna* is reasonably good and cheap, as is *El Paisano*, mostly good vegetarian food (but meat should be treated with caution), and popular meeting place for gringos, hence its nickname *Restaurant Paleface*.

Héctor Fiallos, of Fluvial River Tours, (information in Quito Tel.: 239044) arranges one-day outings, recommended, and it is possible to make 3- and 4-day tours. A 6-day tour takes in the Cuyabeno National Park (special permit needed and may be difficult to get), the Shushufindi tribe and the Aguarico River. A 10-day tour goes down the Napo to Nuevo Rocafuerte, up the Aguarico to the Cuyabeno National Park and various Indian tribes. Reports have reached us, however, that Héctor does not accompany his parties, leaving them in the care of less experienced guides: Domingo, Enrique and Bolívar have been recommended but not others. The longer tours cost between US$14 and US$25 p.p. a day and are recommended only for the hardy. Julio Los Angeles is very knowledgeable on the flora and fauna. His two-day trip includes one day of fairly rigorous hiking and one day of light hiking and canoeing down river, but he will arrange anything you wish to do; his 4-day tour on Río Tiputini to see animals is the minimum time, US$14 a day (you can see very little in a shorter time); his cooking is good; a 6-day tour includes floating downriver on balsa rafts made by Julio, highly recommended by those who like peace and quiet and offering the opportunity of sighting wildlife undisturbed by motor launches. Adonis Muñoz of Caiman Tours has also been warmly recommended as good English-speaking guide (and cook). He was born in Limón Cocha and studied biology in the U.S.A. Douglas Clarke (speaks English), who runs the *Restaurant Dayuna*, and his sister, Billy, arrange trips. Their one-and two-day walks are recommended, but expensive. Also trips to Coca, to smaller rivers and lagoons, Limón Cocha, and longer ones into the jungle of up to ten days, similar to those organized by Héctor Fiallos but reportedly slightly more expensive. A short canoe trip to El Ahuano gives a good idea of the jungle river life.

592 ECUADOR

Carlos Lastra has worked with other guides and is now independent. He offers much the same programmes of short or long trips, to various Indian villages and has been recommended for his style and good cooking. At *Hotel Balcón del Napo* contact Galo, who does 7-day jungle tours, or Carlos Sevilla, whose tours are 1-2 days; both charge US$11 p.p. per day, both are well recommended. Another tour operator is Walter Vasco, of Experiencia en Selva y Río, who has 2 or 3 canoes for fairly inexpensive trips. Carlos Cordero, at the Etsa Tours office in main square, is recommended for walks between 1 and 10 days to see plants and butterflies, and trips to the Jumandí caves, also to see a friendly local witchdoctor (*brujo*). You need to be fit for the longer walks. Good food is provided (US$12 p.p. per day). Some tours have been criticized for too much walking for too few rewards, so make sure your guide knows enough to make your effort worthwhile; an inexperienced guide can mean a boring, or even distressing, walk. Travellers into the Oriente must have their passports stamped at the naval office, which is clearly marked as the canoe embarkation point. Fees for chartering a canoe are open to bargaining; fares on excursions are fixed. Every canoe pilot is supposed to have his passenger list checked before going downstream but this is not always done. For your own safety ensure that the authorities have a record. Essential items for a trip of any length are rubber boots, sleeping bags, rain jackets, binoculars, insect repellant, sun tan lotions, mosquito net, water-purifying tablets, sticking plasters.

No buses run directly Misahuallí-Quito or Misahuallí-Baños. Buses to Puerto Napo and Tena. From Misahuallí, canoe services to the downriver ports of Coca, Limón Cocha and Nueva Rocafuerte. By motorized canoe to Coca, 1130, foreigners are charged US$5 p.p. for the six-hour trip (boats often crowded, best to be early, tickets sold early in the morning from the hut next to the police station; take waterproofs); there is also a mail boat in both directions twice a month. During and after heavy rainfall there are obviously no services, nor are there any services during a long dry period.

The main road from Puerto Napo runs 10 km. north to **Tena,** the capital of Napo Province, and then on to Archidona, a small mission settlement about 10 km. further on. Tena is a quiet, rather dignified town, and Archidona is a village (*Residencial Carolina*, F) centred around its mission and an extraordinary church. Both settlements have good views of Sumaco, an extinct volcano to the north (3,807 metres), and both have a large lowland Quechua Indian population living in the vicinity, many of whom are panning for gold in the rivers. These Indians are unlike the Indian groups further into the Oriente forests. "They are Quijos, of Chibcha stock, and their old territory extended in pre-conquest times from Puerto Napo up the Quijos pass to Papallacta and from there down to Coca. Their forthright character, bravery and their inherent honesty have not changed since the days when they held the Spaniards back from their efforts to find "El Dorado'." (Jay Louthian, Florida). From Tena or Archidona (bus from Archidona, ½ hr.), a visit can be made to the famous Jumandí caves by the Río Latas, 10 km. N. of Archidona (bus from Archidona, ½ hr.). The front entrance is normally flooded and you have to enter through a rear entrance. Take good boots and a strong torch. It is very muddy so it can be useful to take spare clothes. The side ducts of the caves are extremely narrow and claustrophobic. There are several colonies of the vampire bat (*Desmodus rotundus*) in the caves.

Hotels *Tena*, G, noisy at night, due to restaurant below; *Amazonas*, G, clean, near main square; *Jumandy*, G, clean, friendly, breakfast from 0600; *Enmita*, G, near bus station, reasonable restaurant; *Residencial Cumandá*, G; *Hostería Amazónica*, F, near airport; *Resid. Hilton*, G, good and clean; *Resid. Alemania*, F, good and clean, own bath. *Residencial Alexander*, F, 2 rooms with bathroom, near bus station, clean. A modern resort-style hotel is *Auca*, E, on the river out of town, 1½ km. on road to Archidona, Dituris-run, restaurant and bar, nice grounds, discotheque, casino, swimming in river, electricity and water unreliable.

Restaurants In Tena, *Don Quiño*, good, reasonable; *Niagara*, *Oriental*, *Tena*. Throughout the Oriente there are small, set-menu restaurants, about US$1. It is difficult to find a meal if you arrive on a late bus and you may prefer to go hungry rather than eat what is on offer.

Buses Quito (via Baeza), 5 daily, US$2.50, 6½ hrs.; Baeza, US$1, 3 hrs.; Ambato (via Baños), 11 a day, US$2.20, 6¼ hrs., Archidona every 20 mins., US$0.08, 15 mins.; Misahualli every 20 mins., US$0.30, 1 hr. (via Puerto Napo, US$0.08, 15 mins.), Puyo, US$1, 3 hrs.

From Cuenca The journey into the Oriente via El Descanso, Gualaceo, Limón (*Res. Limón*, clean, modern), Méndez, Sucúa and Macas is longer than and as spectacular as from Quito or Ambato; there are several beautiful stretches. **Sucúa** (9-hr. bus trip from Cuenca US$2.05, *Hotel Oriente*, clean, friendly, restaurant; *Hotel Cuhanda*, *Colón*, *Rincón Oriental*, *Cuenca*, all F), is of particular interest as the centre of the now-civilized branch of the ex-head-hunting Shuar

ECUADOR 593

Avenue of the volcanoes

Explore it...

in a different way:
by train with the unique
EXPRESO METROPOLITAN
Leaves Tuesdays and Saturdays

Galapagos Islands

Explore them...

with the excellent
SANTA CRUZ or charter
one of our private yachts.

Amazon Jungle

Explore it...

with the comfortable
FLOTEL ORELLANA
Departures every Friday
and Monday.

Bookings and information.

METROPOLITAN TOURING

Amazonas 239 P.O.Box 2542
Quito - Ecuador
Telex 22482 METOUR-ED

SOUTH AMERICAN TOURS
Adalbertstrasse 44-48
D-6000 Frankfurt/Main 90
West Germany

ADVENTURE ASSOCIATES
13150 Coit Road, Suite 110
Dallas - Texas 75240
United States of America

594 ECUADOR

(Jívaro) Indians; their crafts can be seen and bought but it is tactless to ask them about head-hunting and shrinking! You can visit the Shuar Federation and enquire about visits to Indian villages. There is an interesting bookshop and ten minutes walk from the town centre there is a small museum in the Centro de Formación.

Macas (10 hrs., US$2.25 bus trip from Cuenca, hourly buses from Sucúa), the capital of Santiago-Morona province, is developing rapidly thanks to nearby oil deposits. Its environs are very beautiful and the surrounding hills give excellent views of the volcano **Sangay**, 5,230 metres, within the Sangay National Park, entrance US$10, reached by bus to village of 9 de Octubre, Wed. and Sun. 1600, then walk. You can cross the River Upano (footbridge) and take bus (½ hr.) to the Salesian Sevilla-Don Bosco mission (most welcoming, with Jívaro artefacts to show), and various Indian villages. Good swimming. The whole settlement area has been developed for beef production. Malaria precautions essential. Flight to Quito, TAME, Mon. and Fri. 1500, US$10.

Macas Hotels *Orquídea*, best, roof restaurant, 9 de Octubre y Sucre, F; *Hostería del Valle*, 5 km. out on Sucúa road, self-contained cabins, F. Others are all G: *Residencial Macas*, clean and friendly; *Hotels Encalada, Amazonas, Residenciales Emperatriz* and *Elvira* (over liquid gas store); *Pensión Turismo*, basic.

Restaurants Hotels *Orquídea* and *Encalada, Fredy*, below Resid. Macas. *Chifa Perla Oriental*, *Mesón Dorado* and bus station restaurant, all on 10 de Agosto.

A round trip Cuenca—Gualaceo—Limón—Sucúa—Macas—Mera and onwards to Quito will be possible on completion of the road between Macas and Mera and construction of the bridge on the Pastaza river. This road is now completed from Macas to the Pastaza river (hourly bus Macas-La Punta, US$1, 2 hrs., then 4-hr hike to Pitirico) and from Mera S to Pitirico. A road is virtually completed between Macas and Guamote, S of Riobamba (see page 565), which will give quicker access to Quito.

From Loja The road to the Oriente (see page 579) crosses a low pass and descends rapidly to **Zamora**, an old mission settlement about 2 hours' drive away. From Zamora, the road follows the Zamora river to **Gualaquiza** (also bus from Cuenca, 2 a day, 8 hrs., US$2.80). The valley produces large quantities of *naranjillas* and some sugar cane, maize, bananas and yuca. Regular bus services from Loja to Zamora and beyond on Cenepa-Pacífico and other companies. Cheap, basic hotels are available in Zamora and Gualaquiza.

Galápagos Islands

Lying on the Equator, 970 km. west of the Ecuadorean coast, the Galápagos consist of 6 main islands (San Cristóbal, Santa Cruz, Isabela, Floreana, Santiago and Fernandina—the last two uninhabited); 12 smaller islands (Baltra, with an airport, and the uninhabited islands of Santa Fe, Pinzón, Española, Rábida, Daphne, Seymour, Genovesa, Marchena, Pinta, Darwin and Wolf) and over 40 small islets. The islands have a total population of just over 6,000. The largest island, Isabela (formerly Albemarle), is 120 km. long and forms half the total land area of the archipelago. Its notorious convict colony was closed in 1958; some 650 people live there now, mostly in and around Puerto Villamil, on the S coast. San Cristóbal (Chatham) has a population of 2,321 with the administrative centre of the archipelago, Puerto Baquerizo Moreno. Santa Cruz (Indefatigable) has 3,154, with Puerto Ayora, the main tourist centre; and Floreana (Charles) fewer than 50. The group is quite widely scattered; by boat, *Puerto Baquerizo Moreno and Puerto Ayora are 6 hours apart*.

The islands are the peaks of gigantic volcanoes, composed almost exclusively of basalt. Most of them rise from 2,000 to 3,000 metres above the seabed. Eruptions have taken place in historical times on Fernandina, Isabela, Pinta, Marchena, Santiago and Floreana. The most active today are Fernandina, Isabela, Pinta and Marchena, and fumarolic activity may be seen intermittently on each of these islands. There have been recent eruptions on Volcán, Sierra Negra, Isabela and Fernandina.

The Galápagos have almost certainly never been connected with the continent. Gradually, over many hundreds of thousands of years, animals and plants from over the sea developed there and as time went by they adapted themselves to Galápagos conditions and came to differ more and more from their continental ancestors. Thus many of them are unique: a quarter of the species of shore fish, half of the plants and almost all the reptiles are found nowhere else. In many cases different forms have evolved on the different islands. Charles Darwin recognized this speciation within the archipelago when he visited the Galápagos on the *Beagle* in 1835 and his observations played a substantial part in his formulation of the theory of evolution. Since no large land mammals reached the islands, reptiles were dominant just as they had been all over the world in the very distant past. Another of the extraordinary features of the islands is the tameness of the animals. The islands were uninhabited when they were discovered in 1535 and the animals still have little instinctive fear of man.

The most spectacular species to be seen by the visitor are the giant tortoise (species still survive in 6 or 7 of the islands, but mostly on Isabela); marine iguana (the only seagoing lizard in the world and found throughout most of the archipelago; it eats seaweed); land iguana (on Fernandina, Santa Cruz, Santa Fe, Isabela, Seymour and Plaza); Galápagos albatross (which nests only on the island of Española); Galápagos hawk, red-footed, blue-footed and masked boobies, red-billed tropic-bird, frigate birds, dusky lava gulls, mockingbirds, 13 species of Darwin's finches (all endemic and the classic examples of speciation quoted by Darwin); Galápagos sea-lion (common in many areas) and the Galápagos fur-seal (on the more remote and rocky coasts). Santiago and Plaza islands are particularly interesting for students of these species.

In 1959, the centenary of the publication of Darwin's *Origin of Species*, the Government of Ecuador and the International Charles Darwin Foundation established, with the support of Unesco, the Charles Darwin Research Station at Academy Bay 1½ km. from Puerto Ayora, Santa Cruz, the most central of the Galápagos islands, open daily 0700-1300, 1400-1800. Collections of several of the rare races of giant tortoise are maintained on the station as breeding nuclei, together with a tortoise-rearing house incorporating incubators and pens for the young. The Darwin Foundation staff will help bona fide students of the fauna to plan an itinerary, if they stay some time and hire a boat. Avoid visiting in July and especially August (high season).

Travel to the Islands There are daily flights with SAN to the new airport at Puerto Baquerizo Moreno (San Cristóbal) from Guayaquil and connecting flights from Quito (except Sun.). The round trip in July 1986 cost US$324 from Guayaquil, and US$365 from Quito. One-way tickets are available and it is now possible to buy an open-ended ticket (valid one year—e.g. from Manatours, Av. Amazonas, Quito). SAN will change dates for return to mainland. Tour operators still buy up blocks of seats in advance and they always try to sell you one of their excursions. For this reason, if time is limited, it is probably advisable to go for a package tour. If you cannot get a flight within a week, try going to the airport to get a seat on stand-by. It has been reported that the airport at Baltra, close to Puerto Ayora, Santa Cruz, is now used exclusively by the military, but it seems the TAME daily flight is still being maintained.

The Air Force flights, known as *logísticos*, are now available only for the Ecuadoreans who live on the islands, and in the rare cases when foreigners are allowed on to make up numbers they are usually charged the same fare as with TAME or SAN. It is reported to be easier to get a *logístico* back to the mainland but much depends on the pilot. Official documents, determination, and the Spanish language help. *Logísticos* are unpredictable; the military frequently suspend the service to use the aircraft for other purposes. Beware of agencies offering bogus military flights for US$170, they cannot deliver and are probably doing something illegal. The student organization, Oetej, 6 de Diciembre 159 y Paz Miño, Quito, can get 30% discounts for students: ask for Martha Jiménez. Don't confuse Oetej with Ceptej, another student organization, which can't help in this way. Apparently a letter of introduction in relation to scientific study will secure a *logístico* flight for students: take it to the Ministerio de Defensa, Av. Maldonado y la Exposición, Quito, and you may be lucky. César, in the *Hotel Gran Casino Internacional*, Quito, is reputed to be able to get people on *logístico* flights if they enquire 2-3 weeks in advance, but getting a flight back may not be easy.

There are now many travel agencies operating tours of the Galápagos Islands. Their quality and price varies considerably so shop around. Prices in the low season (Feb.-May, Sept.-Nov.) are considerably cheaper, sometimes making a difference of several hundred dollars. Alternatively ask if an agency has 1-3 spaces to fill on a cruise and you can sometimes get them at 20% discount.

In Guayaquil, Galasam (Economic Galapagos Tours), Av. 9 de Octubre 424, Edificio Gran

WANTED: MAPS

ARGENTINA – BRAZIL – MEXICO GUATEMALA – EL SALVADOR – THE CARIBBEAN ISLANDS

We would much appreciate receiving any surplus maps and diagrams, however rough, of towns and cities, walks, national parks and other interesting areas, to use as source material for the Handbook and other forthcoming titles.

The above regions are particularly needed but any maps of Latin America would be welcome.

The Editor
Trade & Travel Publications Ltd
5 Prince's Buildings
George Street
Bath BA1 2ED
England

Pasaje, 11° piso (Tel.: 306 289) sell flights as well as their own tours and can sell air tickets for their tours at a discount by using the free market. If you buy your air ticket from their office they throw in one night and lunch at a hotel in Puerto Ayora even if you do not purchase their tour. In Quito, Galasam is at Pinto 523 y Av. Amazonas. The Galasam 8-day tours, Wed. or Sat. departure, normally cost about US$400, but can vary between low (US$250) to high (US$700) season (negotiation essential), on 4 small boats taking 8 people, on which conditions are fairly spartan; however their two new 12 passenger boats, the M/Y *Yolita* and *San Pedro*, are more comfortable, and have specially trained bilingual guides; their newest boat, *Dorado*, is more luxurious still. Galasam say the guides on the smaller boats are English-speaking, but their knowledge of English may be very limited. It has also been alleged that their boats sometimes travel in convoy. Metropolitan Touring, Av. Amazonas 239, Casilla 2542, Quito (represented in the USA by Adventure Associates, 5925 Maple, Suite 116, Dallas, Texas 75235), Tel.: 524-400 offers 7-night cruises on the M.V. *Santa Cruz* (90 passengers), about US$120 a day, said to be the best boat, very professional service, with multilingual guides. They also have five yachts for private charters. Galapagos Cruises, Los Ríos 0-80, Guayaquil, Tel.: 390-893, Telex 3610 ETICAG. Galapagos Inc., 150 S.E. Second Ave. Suite 1109, Miami, Florida 33131, organizes tours on the *Bucanero* (90 passengers) operated by Gordon Tours, Baquerizo Moreno 1120 and 9 de Octubre, Casilla 5284, Guayaquil, Tel.: 309-201, Telex MIGOR. A very professional service, some guides are fluent in French and German as well as English and Spanish. If you take the boat from Guayaquil, the two-day cruise to the islands is used for lectures on natural history by specialists. The price for foreigners is about US$1,000 but if there are places to fill you can sometimes get included as an honorary Ecuadorean for about half-price. Macchiavello Tours of Guayaquil (Anteparra 809 y 9 de Octubre, Tel.: 392-892) is ordering two new boats from Italy.

A tourist agency in Quito, Samoa, Victoria 907 y Wilson, Tel.: 551597, has relatively cheap and reliable 8-day tours (US$300, plus air fare) from Puerto Ayora. Other agencies with tours to/in the Galápagos are: Coltur, Robles y Páez 370, Quito, Tel.: 545-777, Telex 2302, with an office in Puerto Ayora; Nuevo Mundo, Av. Amazonas 2468, Quito Tel.: 552-617, Telex 2484; Castro Turismo, Vélez 205, Guayaquil, Tel.: 512-174; Viajes Wang, 10 de Agosto y Bolivia, Quito, Tel.: 551-946, is reported to arrange an all-in 7-day trip for about US$520—the cheapest we have heard of. Kayaking trips in the Islands are organized by Northern Lights Expeditions, 5220 NE 180th, Seattle, WA 98155, USA.

There are usually cargo ships making the trip, but dates are irregular and some interesting but

GALAPAGOS CRUISES

We offer weekly expeditions at reasonable rates on the sailboats BRONZEWING and PIRATA as well as on the motorvessels TIP TOP, EL DORADO, BARTOLOME. We also arrange scuba and special interest tours for groups. Contact us for all your vacation needs in Ecuador: flight tickets, hotels, train excursions, Amazon adventures. Extensions to Cuzco and the Sacred Valley of the Incas.

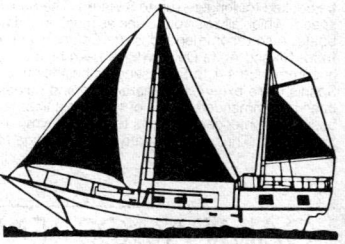

Brochures, information,
GALAPAGOS HOLIDAYS
745 GERRARD STREET EAST
TORONTO, ONT. M4M 1Y5
CANADA.
Tel: 416/469 8211
Tlx: 217682

598 ECUADOR

remote ports are missed; check with the naval port authorities on the Malecón in Guayaquil. One such is the *Iguana*, which visits San Cristóbal and Santa Cruz monthly, 16 passengers in doubles (dirty) with WCs, US$100 p.p. incl. 3 meals a day, owned by Gerardo Aguilera, La Quinta 401 y Las Lomas, Urdesa, Guayaquil (Casilla 3552, Tel.: 385-996). It takes 5 days to reach the islands and allows a reasonable amount of time to explore near the ports and to make day excursions from Puerto Ayora and Puerto Baquerizo Moreno. The more basic *Piquero* also does the trip once a month, leaving Guayaquil on the 27th for Puerto Ayora, making the return journey after about 8 days; one 2-berth cabin, others sleep wherever there is space, US$90 p.p. including 3 meals a day (US$165 return); it is owned by **Rafael Castro**, Tramfsa, Oficina 602, Baquerizo Moreno 1119 (at 9 de Octubre) Guayaquil; If buying a return on either boat, ensure that you can get a refund if you are not able to use it: return dates are not very reliable.

From Britain, inclusive tours can be booked through Twickers World, 22 Church Street, Twickenham, TW1 3NW, or through the Coltur representative in London, Cecilia Irivalo, Tel.: 01-221 0968. David Howell, ex-naturalist and author of a forthcoming book on the Galápagos, arranges tailor-made tours to Ecuador and the Galápagos islands. For further details write to him at 29 Palace View, Bromley, Kent, BR1 3EJ, England.

From the airport on Baltra, one takes a combination of bus (US$1), ferry (US$0.20) and bus (US$1.50) to Puerto Ayora, Santa Cruz. The whole process takes at least 3 hours. Airport buses leave Puerto Ayora (Pyky supermarket) at 0800 and 0830 for Baltra. Tame office in P. Ayora closes Sat p.m. and Sun. Hotel may make prior arrangements. There is a National Park Tax which every visitor has to pay; in 1986 it was US$40, payable only in US$ cash.

Travel between the Islands There are official (Ingala) boats travelling Tues. and Thurs. between Santa Cruz and San Cristóbal (US$4), visiting Isabela from Santa Cruz fortnightly; local inhabitants and tour passengers booked in advance get preferential treatment. The best centre from which to visit the Islands is **Puerto Ayora,** Santa Cruz. Here you can hire boats (lists available from National Park Service) and a two-week sojourn will allow you to see most of the Islands. If you only have a short time, the northern islands are the more scenic with the more interesting wildlife. Reservations are strongly recommended for June-August and December-April. The Capitanía del Puerto will give information on fishing boats' movements. For cheaper tours it is generally recommended that you form a group of six to ten people once you reach the Islands, talk to people about the boats they may have used and then talk to the boat owners (known as *dueño*), not the captains, about what you wish to do. Bargain over the route and the price, and get a firm commitment from the owner on dates and itinerary, leave a deposit "to buy food" and get a receipt; the rate for a small boat taking about six to eight people will start at approximately US$25-$30 p.p. per day in the low season for a full load rising to US$30-$40 p.p. in the high season. Larger, more comfortable boats can cost twice as much, especially if they have bilingual guides. Each boat has to be accompanied by a Park-trained guide, either a naturalist (who will be English-speaking, more knowledgeable and therefore more expensive), or an auxiliary; this is arranged by the boat owner. Most boats operate 4-8 day cruises, it appears that only the 50-berth *Isabela*, owned by Etica, can be booked for longer—up to 3 weeks. The *San Juan* is recommended for its friendly crew and its speed, which allows you to see as much in 7 days as some do in 10; it is also one of the cheaper boats. Also recommended is the *Golondrina*; friendly crew, knowledgeable guide and excellent food. Gil and Anita De Roy have been highly recommended for tours on their yacht *Inti*, which accommodates 4 to 5 passengers besides two crew; they speak French, German, English and Spanish, are experienced naturalists and guides and serve excellent food. Eduardo García has been recommended as one of the best guides. Coltur, an agency in Quito and Puerto Ayora, has been recommended for visits to North Seymour and Caleta Tortuga Negra on the north coast of Santa Cruz. Their representatives can arrange tours on the *Pirata* (Augusto and Georgina Cruz),

GALAPAGOS EMPIEZA EN COLTUR

BRITISH AGENT
For information telephone
CECILIA IRIVALO
01-221-0968

Coltur
Robles 370 y Páez
Telfs: 545 777 - 545 264
P.O. Box 2771 Télex 2302

ECUADOR 599

which has been recommended for its friendly and helpful staff and good cooking; Georgina Cruz is English. The *Angelito* has been highly recommended, partly because the captain navigates by night so that you have more time on the islands by day; this makes it slightly more expensive. Others recommended in this category are *Española* (10 passengers, good crew and cooking, fast, US$25 p.p.—high season), *Cachalote* and *Sulidae*, also 10 passengers, *Daphne* and *San Antonio* (one of the cheapest, US$170 a day for a party of 8). It must be stressed, however, that a boat is only as good as its crew and when the staff change, so will these recommendations. Check that the small boats can carry enough food and supplies for the length of journey so you do not waste a day restocking. We have received persistent reports that tour operators are unreliable in sticking to their agreed programme, and that some of the guides deviate from the scheduled route, wasting time in port and leaving out some islands. Many travellers recommend that you insist on a written itinerary or contract prior to departure as any effort not to provide this probably indicates problems later; not spending more than a half-day on either Santa Cruz or San Cristóbal for restocking of provisions; counting your money regularly and not leaving your beach gear unattended if other boats are in the vicinity when you are ashore. If you have problems afterwards, take your contract to the Capitanía (port captain). Warning: it can take several days to arrange a tour, so allow yourself plenty of time (up to a week in high season). If you do get stuck, the Tourist Office in Puerto Ayora offers one-day tours (US$36 p.p. with lunch) to either South Plazas or Santa Fe. These smaller islands have a good sample of animal species (although fewer in numbers) and, together with sightseeing on Santa Cruz, can be a worthwhile experience for the tourist with only limited time. Never miss the chance to do a bit of snorkelling, but enquire carefully about the likelihood of sharks (*tiburones*).

Byron Rueda offers day trips for 10 in his dinghy *Santa Fe* to Santa Fe and to the Plaza islands (US$18). His office is on the Ninfa dock and he also represents other boats (open 0800-1800).

The Cost of Living in the Galápagos is not cheap. Most food has to be imported although certain meats, fish, vegetables and fruit are available locally in the Puerto Ayora market.

Hotels at Puerto Ayora Hotel space is limited (more are being built) and reservations are strongly recommended in high season. *Galápagos*, B (local class 1), bungalows with private bathroom, hot water, ocean-view, laundry service, generator, restaurant with fixed menu, price and time, fruit and meat from hotel farm, near Darwin Research centre, reservations can be made through Ecuadorean travel agencies, day excursions can be made from hotel in Pedro and Sally García's own dinghy for 10, the *Fernandina*. *Delfín*, on far side of Academy Bay, with lovely beach, D (1), well recommended, accessible only by boat, write to Rolf Sievers. *Residencial Angermeyer*: about 20 beds, F; small restaurant just opened, banana pancakes unbeatable! You can also buy your own food and cook it over wood fire in the garden. Mrs Angermeyer and her daughter keep the place spotlessly clean. They have information, for guests, on good and bad boats. There is a *peña* next door. *Sol y Mar*: 20 beds (double, triples and quadruples) in cabins; E (1), without meals; B, with 3 meals; 10% discount for stays of 2 weeks or more. Recommended, comfortable, friendly, well-informed, good food; reservations can be made by writing to the owner (Sr. Jimmy Pérez), or Macchiavello Tours, Casilla 318, Guayaquil. *Castro*, F, (2), with private bath, owned by Sr. Miguel Castro, he arranges 7-day inclusive tours, including Friday TAME flight. He is an authority on wildlife and his tour includes one or two nights away visiting the islands of Plazas and Santiago, and a day-trip to Santa Fe, with visits to the tortoise reserve and the Darwin Institute. *Colón*: 22 beds (doubles) in third class rooms; F (3), without food; D, including 3 meals. Write to Sra. Piedad Moya. *Elizabeth*, E (3), now remodelled, has running water; *Ninfa*, E (2), has its own boat at reasonable price for day trips and Fernando Jiménez is helpful with arrangements; *Lobo de Mar* E (2), 30 beds; *Gloria*, G (3), 12 beds, simple, Sr. Bolívar very friendly, clean, you can cook your own food over a wood fire, mosquito repellant needed; *Darwin*, F, with bath, clean, friendly, recommended, as is *Las Palmeras*, F (2), private bath, cafeteria, laundry facilities, pleasant, clean; *Salinas*, opposite, also F, 20 beds. *Santa Cruz*, F (3).

Restaurants at Puerto Ayora Good food served at *El Túnel* (US$0.80 for breakfast) on main road; *Don Enriques*, same road, local dishes; *Los Gemelos*, near the school; *La Garrapata*, open air, on road to research station, pizzas, hamburgers, cakes, morning and evening but not Sun.; *Fausto's*, between Gloria and Angermeyer hotels, good pizzas, friendly owner speaks English; *Four Lanterns*, good, reasonable (dinner US$1.50); *Pastry Shop* (in front of hospital) for snacks and drinks; *Ninfa Dock Bar/Restaurant*, on dock, excellent grilled lobster, changes money, meeting place; nearby is *Pasty Pan* for bread and cakes (not open Sun.). *Bambú*, good light food, Spanish specialities, pleasant atmosphere; *Bibu*, yoghurt and good breakfasts; *Fragata Bar*, good, on road to research station, as is *Galaps Pizzería*. *Pelikano* and *Pastik-Shock* cafeterias. Restaurants serve lobster dinners at US$5; *merienda* costs between US$1.50-2.

Entertainment Two discos (*La Terraza* and *Disco Light*) and one *peña-disco* (*Peter Cheese*) in P.Ayora.

Hints For boat charters and camping trips most basic foodstuffs generally can be purchased in the islands (e.g. Pyky supermarket in Puerto Ayora), although occasionally there are shortages.

600 ECUADOR

However, no special items (dehydrated or freezedried foods) are available other than a few common ones such as oatmeal and dried soups. Fresh milk available in Puerto Ayora from Christine Aldaze, 0930, next to *Túnel* restaurant (24 hrs. notice appreciated).

Medicines, sun lotions (only up to factor 4 available in Ecuador), mosquito coils, film, pipe tobacco, and other useful items are either not available or cost a lot more than on the mainland. Take plenty of film with you; the birds are so tame that you will use far more than you expected; a telephoto lens is not essential. A good supply of sun block and skin cream to prevent windburn and chapped lips is essential. There is a souvenir shop next to Angermeyer's hotel, Galápagos Souvenirs, and a camera repair place next to the cemetery near the Darwin Station.

Warning: Valuables should be watched.

Some of the prices charged are exorbitant. There is a cinema at Puerto Ayora—each evening at 2015. Information and retrieval of lost property from Radio Santa Cruz, next to Catholic Church. Short-stay camping permitted at the Caseta in the highlands and at Tortuga Bay.

There is a hospital in Puerto Ayora; consultations are free, medicines reasonably-priced.

Currency It is advisable to take plenty of cash; there are few facilities for cashing cheques in P.Ayora, and rates for them are about 5% less than for cash. The *Hotel Sol y Mar* and *Ninfa* restaurant will change notes and cheques, but at a poor rate. There is a bank at Puerto Ayora but it gives a poor rate of exchange and will not accept credit cards. Several shops change US$ notes.

Immigration The police will extend visas with a little persuasion for those who overstay their visa or tourist card; but such extensions are reportedly not valid.

Tourist Office Dituris, near the pier, open Mon.-Fri. 0800-1200, 1500-1800. Information also available at the boat owners' cooperative office nearby.

Excursions on Santa Cruz Walk to Tortuga Bay. A new, shorter track, 2 km. long (1½ hours) has been opened: turn at *Hotel Elizabeth* off main road, then left at *Hotel Santa Cruz*.

Hike to the higher parts of the island called Media Luna, Puntudo and Mt. Crocker. Trail starts at Bellavista (which can be reached on foot, or by car, or 3 buses a day US$0.20, or hitch), 7 km. from Puerto Ayora. Round trip from Bellavista is 4 to 8 hrs., depending upon distance hiked, 10-18 km. (permit and guide not required).

There are two natural tunnels (lava tubes) 1 km. from Bellavista (on private land, US$0.70 to enter, torch provided—it takes about ½ hr. to walk through the tunnels). There is a barbecue each Sun. at La Choza, Bellavista; information in *El Túnel* restaurant, Puerto Ayora.

Hike to the Chato Tortoise Reserve; trail starts at Santa Rosa, 22 km. from Puerto Ayora; 3 buses a day, or hitch. Horses can be hired at Santa Rosa, US$5 each, guide optional US$6.50 extra. Round trip takes one day. Again, the Puerto Ayora-Bellavista bus stops at the turnoff for the track for the reserve (US$0.50). It's a hot walk; take food and drink. From Santa Rosa, distance to different sites within the reserve is 6-8 km. (permit and guide not required).

Two sinkholes, Los Gemelos, straddle the road to Baltra, beyond Santa Rosa; if you are lucky, take a *camioneta* all the way, otherwise to Santa Rosa, then walk. A good place to see the Galápagos hawk and barn owl.

Visit the giant Galápagos tortoises in pens at the Darwin Station, a short distance from Puerto Ayora. Small tortoises in rearing pens may be observed. The Station has a museum (explaining the geology and natural history of the islands) and a library. There are also public lectures (details from Dituris office near the pier).

Puerto Baquerizo Moreno, on San Cristóbal island to the E, is the capital of the archipelago, with a new airport with flights Wed. and Sat. by the SAN airline. Two boats a week to Puerto Ayora; fishing boats also take passengers.

Hotels *Residencial Northia*, E with bath; *Resid. San Cristóbal*, F, shared bath, not clean; *Resid. Miramar*, F; *Resid. Flamingo*, F, basic.

Restaurants *Rosita*, best in town; *Chatham*, good; *Laurita*, fair; *La Terraza*, on beach; *Fragata*, on road to airport.

Excursions Bus (shuttle) to El Progreso, then short walk to El Junco lake, tortoises may be seen on the way. From El Progreso (eating places), a trail crosses the high lands to Cerro Brujo and Hobbs Bay; also to Stephens Bay, past lakes.

The climate can be divided into a hot season (January to April), when there is a possibility of heavy showers, and the cool or *garúa* season (May to December), when the days generally are more cloudy. Daytime clothing should be lightweight. (Clothing generally, even on "luxury cruises" should be casual and comfortable.) At night, however, particularly at sea and at higher altitudes, temperatures fall below 15°C and warm clothing is required. Boots and shoes soon wear out on the lava terrain and there is need for protection against rain and sun. Apart from Tortuga Bay, there are no beaches on Santa Cruz, but several on San Cristóbal.

Information The *Galápagos Guide* by Alan White and Bruce White Epler, with photographs by Charles Gilbert, is published in several languages; it can be bought in Guayaquil in Librería Científica and the airport, Libri Mundi (US$5) in Quito, or at the Charles Darwin station. Also available and a must for birdwatchers, is *Field Guide to the Birds of the Galápagos* (US$20). A map of the Galápagos, drawn by Kevin Healey and illustrated by Hilary Bradt, has been published by Bradt Enterprises. The National Park now publishes a good guide in English and Spanish, with plans of all the places where visitors are allowed to land: *Guide to the Visitor Sites of Parque Nacional Galápagos*, by Alan and Tui Moore, US$3.30. National Park Office, Puerto Ayora, Santa Cruz, Mon.-Fri. 0800-1200, 1400-1800, Sat. 0800-1000. For more information write to the Director of the Charles Darwin Research Station or the Superintendent of the Galápagos National Park Service, Isla Santa Cruz, Galápagos (correspondence in English.)

(With acknowledgements to the Charles Darwin Foundation and the Galápagos National Park Service.)

The Economy

In the early 1970s, Ecuador underwent a transformation from an essentially agricultural economy to a predominantly petroleum economy. From 1972 when substantial domestic oil output began, economic growth has largely followed the fortunes of the oil market, except in 1983, when freak weather conditions resulted in large crop losses. Agriculture's contribution (including fishing) to gdp has dwindled from over 22% in 1972 to less than 14% by the mid-1980s and although it still employs a third of the labour force, it provides less than 25% of export revenues, compared with 64% in 1972. The major export crops of bananas, coffee and cocoa are grown on the coast. Ecuador is the world's largest exporter of bananas, although it is not a member of the Union of Banana Exporting Countries (Upeb). Production is being promoted with increased plantings of high-yielding varieties and provision of technical assistance and quality control. Coffee is the most extensive of Ecuador's cash crops, accounting for over 20% of total agricultural land, but it is also the lowest yielding crop. Cocoa production has been increased by a rehabilitation programme after the 1983 floods, but although yields have trebled, output of 498 kg per hectare is still well below Brazil's 914 kg/ha.

Fishing is a growing industry, offering lucrative export potential. As well as tuna, sardines and white fish, shrimp is being caught in increasing amounts and is the most valuable catch. Shrimp farming is booming along the coast and has provided much-needed jobs for agricultural workers. Mining has been relatively unimportant historically, but the discovery of about 700 tonnes of gold reserves around Nambija (Zamora) in the southeast created intense interest in precious metals and over 12,000 independent miners rushed to prospect there.

Although Ecuador's share of total world oil production is small (0.65% in 1985), foreign exchange earnings from oil exports are crucial to the economy. The main producing area is in the northern Oriente, and a 495-km. trans-Andean pipeline carries the oil to Esmeraldas on the coast, where it is refined and/or exported. There are also reserves of natural gas, mainly in the Gulf of Guayaquil, but these have not yet been fully developed. Hydroelectric potential is estimated at 90,000 MW, but generating capacity in the mid-1980s was only 2,000 MW. New projects on the Paute, Pastaza and Coca rivers could raise capacity to 12,000 MW by the end of the century.

Ecuador's foreign debt rose sharply in the 1970s when oil exports began and in the 1980s it joined other debtor nations in refinancing its external obligations. Adherence to free market economic policies in IMF programmes brought international approval and by 1985 Ecuador was widely acclaimed as a model debtor with sufficient creditworthiness to return to the voluntary market for loans. However, in 1986 oil prices crashed, cutting Ecuador's oil receipts by half, followed in 1987 by an earthquake which destroyed part of the trans-Andean pipeline and damaged other oil installations, causing a cessation of oil exports. It was clear that huge amounts of finance would be necessary for reconstruction of economic infrastructure and villages which had been destroyed. The international financial community rallied to support Ecuador under the aegis of the World Bank, but it was expected to be some time before the economy could be restored to its former health.

602 ECUADOR

	1961-70 (av)	1971-80 (av)	1981-85 (av)	1986 (e)
Gdp growth (1980 prices)	5.2%	8.9%	2.0%	1.7%
Inflation	4.5%	12.6%	27.5%	27.3%
Exports (fob) US$m	195	1,232	2,545	2,186
Crude oil	1	555	1,618	984
Bananas	93	158	186	271
Coffee	30	132	152	227
Imports (fob) US$m	169	1,132	1,826	1,631
Current account balance US$m (cum)	-440	-2,725	-2,445	-642

Information for Visitors

By Air Air France and Avianca between them fly 3 times a week from Paris to Quito. Some Aero Perú flights stop in Guayaquil en route to Miami. Iberia flies from Madrid to Quito and Guayaquil and KLM weekly from Amsterdam to Guayaquil (Tues.). KLM also fly to Caracas, Aruba and on to Quito (Thurs.). Lufthansa has connections with Frankfurt. Loftleidir (cheaper) flies from Luxembourg to Nassau where you can make a connection with Ecuatoriana. There are flights from New York via Miami by Eastern Airlines, which also flies to Panama, as does Air Panamá. Ecuatoriana, the national company, has international runs to Mexico City (three weekly), Lima, Nassau, Miami and Barbados. Avianca also flies to Mexico City via Bogotá. Remember cheap French charters to Lima; bus to Ecuador. Direct flights from other South American countries to Ecuador: from Chile (Ecuatoriana, 2 a week), Argentina (Ecuatoriana, 2 a week, Aerolíneas Argentinas weekly to Guayaquil), Brazil (weekly Varig flights); Paraguay and Bolivia (twice a week by Eastern); there are none from Uruguay. There is a 10 per cent tax on international air tickets for flights originating in Ecuador, regardless of where bought, and 8 per cent on domestic tickets, and a tax of US$20, payable in sucres, on all passengers departing on international flights.

By Sea The cargo (no passengers) route from England to Ecuador is by the Pacific Steam Navigation Company via the Panama Canal to La Libertad or Guayaquil. Gran Colombiana ships sail from New York, Baltimore and New Orleans. New York to Guayaquil takes 10 days with 20 days from a U.K. port to Guayaquil by a cargo-passenger vessel. Serving the Continent of Europe are the Hamburg American Line and the North German Line jointly; Knutsen Line (from Copenhagen, Oslo, Stockholm, Göteborg, Hamburg, Bremen, Antwerp and Lisbon), and occasional Cie. Générale Maritime boats from La Pallice, Marseille. The only passenger service to Guayaquil is offered by Continental Shipping and Travel, 179 Piccadilly, London W1V 9DB, Tel.: 01-491 4968, with departures from France.

Documents Passport (valid for at least six months required on arrival at Quito airport), and a tourist card valid for 90 days (tourists are now allowed only 90 days in any one calendar year) obtainable on arrival. You are required to say how many days you intend to stay and the card will be stamped accordingly; most travellers are given 15 or 30-day stamps irrespective of their requests (at Huaquillas, Macará and Tulcán), and travellers arriving by air may be given a stamp valid for only 10 days (transit pass) unless they request otherwise. It is therefore better to overestimate as you can be fined on leaving the country for staying too long. An extension can be routinely obtained at the Department of Immigration in Quito or Guayaquil, or at the government offices of several provincial capitals; evidence of sufficient funds (see below) is sometimes required. A visa is required only for business people who stay longer than 90 days, application to be made in home country, and they must get an exit permit with both tax and police clearance. Tourists crossing from Colombia or Peru may be asked for evidence that they possess US$20 p.p. for each day they propose to spend in Ecuador. Theoretically you must have an onward ticket out of Ecuador, but this is almost never enforced if you are travelling overland. However, travellers arriving from Miami with Ecuatoriana have been refused entry without a ticket and an MCO may not be sufficient. For a car a *carnet de passage* is required; failing that a bond equal to the value of the car will be demanded. **Warning** Always carry your passport with you; if it is not in your possession you may be taken to prison.

Personal effects, a litre of spirits and a reasonable amount of perfume are admitted free of duty. No foreign cigarettes are allowed to be brought into Ecuador.

ECUADOR 603

The **best time for a visit** is from June to October, during the dry season, though September can sometimes be wet. The coastal area is extremely hot and wet from December to May.

Clothing Spring clothing for Quito (mornings and evenings are cold). In Guayaquil tropical or light-weight clothes. Laundering is excellent, but dry-cleaning is expensive.

Local Time is 5 hrs. behind GMT (Galápagos, 6 hrs. behind.)

Health Amoebic dysentery is a danger. Visitors should drink mineral water (Güitig or Manantial), avoid uncooked vegetables or salads, and be inoculated against typhoid. Hepatitis (jaundice) is a very real risk and should be inoculated against with gamma globulin; see "Health Information" in front of book. Travellers in the Oriente and the Costa are advised to take anti-malaria tablets; mosquito netting is also useful. Yellow-fever vaccination is recommended for travel into the Oriente. There are excellent hospitals both in Quito and Guayaquil. Climbers are warned to undergo a period of acclimatization before attempting to scale the volcanoes.

Food Well worth trying are *humitas* (*tamales* made of sweet maize), *llapingachos* (fried mashed potatoes with cheese), and *locro* (a soup of stewed potatoes and cheese topped with an avocado), served, with a beer, at bars. Local food is highly spiced only when *ají* (red pepper) sauce is added, and then it is very hot, but the food is often unspiced. *Tamales de moracho* (not unlike Venezuelan *hallaca*) and *empanadas de moracho* are delicious (same insides, breadcrust outside). A typical food (but a matter of taste) is roast *cuy* (guinea pig). *Cacho*, a croissant-like pastry, is cheap and filling. If economizing in restaurants ask for the standard meal, *merienda*—very cheap; it costs between US$1 and US$2. There are interesting *encocada* (coconut) dishes on the coast. The fruits are magnificent: try *mamei colorado*, a fruit of the avocado family. A good sweet is *quimbolito*, a sweet sponge pudding made with maize flour.

Drink The local wines, often made from bananas, are safe but sickly, and cannot be recommended. Argentine and Chilean wines are cheaper than European or US ones. The best fruit drinks are *naranjilla*, *taxo* and *mora* (blackberries). Beers available are Pilsener, Club, Malta (dark) and Löwenbräu. International drinks, when they can be had, are costly. Good *pisco*, *aguardiente* (Cristal is recommended), *paico* and *trago de caña*. The usual soft drinks, known as *colas*, are available. Instant coffee or liquid concentrate is common, so ask for *café puro* if you want real coffee.

Accommodation outside the main towns; almost standard prices are charged of US$1 p.p. (without bath) in a *pensión*, *residencial*, or hotel (where this is the minimum charge). One can bargain at cheaper *pensiones* and *residenciales*. Outside the provincial capitals and the resorts of Salinas and Playas, there are few of what the well-to-do tourist would call good hotels. Service of 10% and tax of 5% are added to 1st and 2nd class hotel and restaurant bills. The cheaper hotels charge at most 5%, generally. Hotel owners tend to try and sell their less attractive rooms first, but they are not insulted if you ask for a bigger room, better beds or a quieter area. The difference is often marked.

Tipping Hotels and restaurants, 10% usually in the bill. Taxi, nil. Airport and railway porters, US$0.08-0.20, according to number of suitcases; cloakroom attendants, US$0.04; hairdressers, 20%.

Electric Current 110 volts, 60 cycles, A.C. throughout Ecuador.

Internal Air Travel The local airlines Saeta, SAN and TAME operate internal flights between the main cities. TAME and SAN fly to the Galápagos. Also local airlines Lansa and Cedta operating Machala-Guayaquil. Ecuavia operates charter flights. There are air taxis (Cessnas or Bonanzas) to anywhere you want to go to, also helicopters. On internal flights passengers may have to disembark at intermediate stops and check in, even though they have booked all the way to the final destination of the plane. Seats are not assigned on internal flights.

Railway Travel The railways are not too comfortable or reliable. The total track length is 1,043 km., but floods in 1983 damaged much of the system. The Quito-Riobamba, Guayaquil-Bucay, Alausí-Huigra, Sibambe-Cuenca and Ibarra-San Lorenzo stretches are now in operation.

Road Travel Bus travel has improved greatly and is generally more convenient than in other Andean countries: more roads are paved, and since most buses are small they fill up and leave at frequent intervals. We have received a number of reports recently that late night buses have been subject to attack by armed gangs. Half the 17,700 km. of road are open the year round. The length of paved highway is developing rapidly, including Quito-Guayaquil, Quito-Riobamba, Quito-Tulcán, Guayaquil-Cuenca, Guayaquil-Riobamba, Riobamba-Baños, Ambato-Puyo and the lowland (Costa) road Huaquillas-Machala-Guayaquil-Babahoyo-Santo Domingo-Esmeraldas. When touring by car, beware the bus drivers, who often drive very fast and rather recklessly. The lack of road signs can be a nuisance. Hitch-hiking on the main roads is reported to be easy in the north, but nearly impossible south of Riobamba, and it can be very cold in the mountains in the back of a truck. In the arid S the unpaved roads are dusty; use a wet cotton handkerchief to filter the air you breathe. In 1983 the country suffered a disastrous rainy season in which many coastal roads were washed out. Many are still in a bad state and will take time to repair, so if you are hiring a car make sure it has good ground clearance. Always carry your passport and driving licence; there are police checks on all the roads leading out of main towns and you can be in serious trouble if you are unable to present your documents. Car hire charges are about US$33 a day, unlimited mileage. Gasoline costs US$1.00 per US gallon for 80 octane and US$1.30 for 92 octane (only in the main cities). Gasoline shortages are common, so fill up where you can.

The Instituto Geográfico Militar, on top of the hill at the E end of El Ejido Park, Quito (see page 548), produces a large detailed map of Ecuador on four pages which is among the best available for any South American country. A comprehensive road map is also available as well as various other maps, US$0.50-$0.80 apiece. Maps of the Oriente take a day to be photocopied. If you don't have time to go to the IGM, Libri Mundi bookshop has some maps. There are also road maps issued as a small booklet (US$2) with 26 partial maps published by Nelson Gómez, Editorial Camino.

Walking Walkers are advised to get *Backpacking in Venezuela, Colombia and Ecuador*, by Hilary and George Bradt, and Rob Rachowiecki's book (see next para.).

Sport The Sierra country is excellent for riding, and good horses can be hired. Quito, Guayaquil and Riobamba have polo clubs. There are golf clubs at Guayaquil and Quito and on the Santa Elena Peninsula. There is excellent big-game fishing for bonito and marlin off Playas, Salinas and Manta. Bull fighting is rarely seen at Guayaquil, but there is a well-known bullfight festival on Dec. 6 at Quito. A favourite sport is cock fighting; every town has its pits, but association football is fast taking over as the national sport. Baseball, volleyball and basket-ball are also popular. There is Sunday horse-racing at Quito and Guayaquil. Climbing can be arranged through climbing clubs in Quito and other cities, or those associated with universities. Recommended guides to climbing, *Climbing and Hiking in Ecuador*, by Rob Rachowiecki (published by Bradt Enterprises) and *The Fool's Mountaineering for Ecuador and Peru* (from the South American Explorers' Club in Lima, US$3.50, which may only be available in Peru). The quality of hired equipment needs scrutiny.

Wild Life includes the jaguar, puma, tapir, several kinds of monkey, the armadillo, ant-bear, squirrel, porcupine, peccary, various kinds of deer, and many rodents, including the guinea pig. There are also tortoises, lizards and iguanas. Among the birds are condors, falcons, kites, macaws, owls, flamingoes, parrots, ibises, cranes, and storks. Unhappily, every type of insect is found in the coastal towns and the Oriente. The Galápagos Islands have their own selection of nearly tame wildlife.

National Parks All foreigners are charged US$10 for entry into each national park, except for the Galápagos which now costs US$40.

Public Holidays New Year's Day; January 6; Monday and Tuesday before Lent (Carnival); Holy Thursday; Good Friday; Holy Saturday; May 1-Labour Day; May 24-Battle of Pichincha; July 24-Birthday of Bolívar; August 10-Independence of Quito, Opening of Congress, October 9-Independence of Guayaquil, October 12-Discovery of America; November 1-All Saints' Day; November 2-All Souls' Day; November 3-Independence of Cuenca; December 6-Foundation of Quito; Christmas Day.

Telecommunications All the principal towns have long-distance telephone facilities. Ietel, the state telecommunications agency, has offices at Guayaquil, Quito and Salinas.

Telephone call to Europe is US$7.50 for first 3 min. and US$2.50 per min. thereafter; cheaper on Sunday. For international operator dial 116, normally only 5-20 minute wait for call to UK. You can call collect to the USA and to Canada but not to Australasia. A charge is made for person-to-person calls even when the person is not there. Telegrams, ordinary US$4.30 first 7 words and US$0.57 per word thereafter, nightletter US$0.20 per word. There are public telex booths in the best hotels in Quito and Guayaquil (US$10.50 for 3 mins.), and at Cuenca.

Posts Many post offices away from Quito may not know the foreign rates (10g air-mail to Europe about US$0.20) and give incorrect ones. Postal service is extremely unreliable, with frequent thefts and losses. For a small extra charge you can certify your letters and parcels; ask for "*con certificado*" when you buy stamps, so that they are stamped separately. Packages sent from Encomiendas Internacionales are opened for inspection by customs (20 kg. costs US$12).

For shipping out packages contact Transpak, Av. Amazonas y Veintimilla, Quito.

Currency The sucre, divided into 100 centavos, is the unit of currency. Bank

ECUADOR 605

notes of the Banco Central de Ecuador are for 5, 10, 20, 50, 100, 500, and 1,000 sucres; there are nickel coins of one sucre, 50, 20 and 10 centavos. The one sucre coin is also sometimes called an *ayora*.

There is no restriction on the amount of foreign money or sucres you can take into or out of Ecuador. It is said to be easier to cash Bank Americard cheques than American Express cheques. It is very easy to change US$ cheques into US$ notes at the *cambios*; the commission varies so it is worth shopping around and *cambios* sometimes run out of US$ notes. Rodrigo Paz *cambios* are recommended as reliable, with only 0.5% commission, but may offer a slightly lower rate than banks. M. M. Jaramillo is also recommended and you can try to bargain for a better rate than shown on the blackboard. Ecuador, together with Panama, is the best place in South America to have money sent to. Note that Diners Club and Visa credit cards are widely accepted. It is quite difficult to change US$, whether cheques or bills, outside the main towns, especially in the Oriente.

Weights and Measures The metric system is generally used in foreign trade and must be used in legal documents. English measures are understood in the hardware and textile trades. Spanish measures are often used in the retail trade.

Newspapers The main newspapers are *El Comercio, Hoy, Tiempo,* and *Ultimas Noticias,* in Quito; *Expreso, El Telégrafo, El Universo, La Prensa, La Razón* and *Extra* (an afternoon paper), in Guayaquil; *El Mercurio,* in Cuenca; *La Opinión del Sur,* in Loja; and *El Espectador,* in Riobamba. Newspapers cost more outside their town of publication, up to double the price in the Oriente.

Information for business travellers is given (1) in "Hints to Exporters: Ecuador", available from Department of Trade, Sanctuary Buildings, 16-20 Gt. Smith Street, London SW1P 3DB; (2) the Ecuadorean-American Association, Inc. (55 Liberty St., New York, NY 10005) issues monthly bulletins and a free sample copy may be requested. Telephone directories in Ecuador have "green pages" giving useful tourist information, sometimes in English.

For extensive improvements to this chapter we are most grateful to Glenn Germaine (Guayaquil), Peter Gilmore (Guayaquil), Gerhard R.Leitner (c/o South American Explorers' Club, Lima) for a systematic updating that has transformed this chapter, Laura M.Miller (Cuenca), and Gene Rainone (Cuenca); and to the following travellers: Susi Alexander and José Jacinto (Resedo, Ca.), David and Kathy Anderson (Chico, Ca.), Claude Arnaud-McVay (Bainsdale, Vict.), Dr J.R.J.Asperen de Boer (Amsterdam), Paul Bader (Sulzberg, W.Ger.), Nigel L.Baker, Nicoline Beck (Doorn, Neth.), Trond Bergquist and Ian Gjertz (Oslo), Dr Michael Binzberger (Friedrichshafen, W.Ger.), Joyce M.Bogner (Boise, Idaho), Christine Bräutigam (Basle), Klaus Bryn (Oslo), G.D.Claridge (E.Grinstead), Malcolm Craven (Weston-super-Mare), Anke Cruse, Carina Dahlstrom and Ulf Carlsson (Gothenburg), Lynne and Hugh Davies (Mill Valley, Ca.), Dr. Sally Dealler (Leeds 8), Dagmar Drescher (Bad Kreuznach, W.Ger.), Peter Ehrat and Rolf Ramsperger (Switz.), Christine Enkelaar and José Keldens ('s Hertogenbosch, Neth.), Kurt Farner (Köniz, Switz.), David Finn (Dallas), and Andrew Sherman (Los Angeles), Axel Flörke (Darmstadt), Pierre-Marie Gagneux (Taulignan) and Nathalie Baudouin (Bar-le-Duc), Romi and Olga Gandolfo (Buenos Aires), Mark Gfeller (Richterswil, Switz.), Harold Goldstein and Janet Young (Washington DC), Richard Guichard (Montreal), John E.Hilderburn (San Marino, Ca.), Bastian Hiss and Daniela Fleischhauer (Krefeld), Catherine Hooper (Aptos, Ca.), Nils Kaltenborn (Lillestrm, Norway), Deborah Karp (London N3) and Karin Schamroth (London NW8), Marion Klaus (Ranchester, Wyo.), Dr J.Kleinwächter (Hamburg), Todd Knutson (Pittsburgh), Dan and Sue Koenigshofer (Chapel Hill, NC), Mrs C.Lapostolle (Paris), Roger Lemercier (Nice), Trevor Long (London NW6), Suzanne Maillet (Montreal), Jason Malinowski (San Bruno, Ca.), Rosemary Marcus and Ian Fleming (Bolton) for a most useful contribution, Anna-Mia Marks (Utrecht), Heinz Maul (Erlangen, W.Ger.), Claus Mayer (Stuttgart), Steve Michmerhuizen (Michigan), William and Joellyn Milligan (Philadelphia), Josef Moser (Mels, Switz.), Gilberto Mundaca (Deerfield Beach, Fla.), Hans and Ursula Niederndorfer (Lambach, Austria), Grace Osakoda (Hawaii), Vaclav Penkava (Seattle), Erick and Martine Perruche (Montargis, France), Jens Plahte (Aas, Norway), Sally Purbrick (Berlin 21), Miss J.Randall (London E7), L.Rathfelder (Mannheim), Annamarie Reichmuth and Roger Müller (Schwyz, Switz.), Beat Rebsamen (Buchs, Switz.), Bengt Roos (Helsingborg, Swe.), Mari-Ann Roos and Charlotte Gottfries (Swedish Emb., Lima), Elliot Roseman (Arlington. Mass.) for a particularly good contribution, Hugh and Emilie Salvesen (Bad Honnef, W.Ger.) for another fine contribution, Gillian Scourfield and Alastair Mitchell (Spalding, Lincs.), Connie Sherrard (Portland, Ore.), Prof. Alfred Siemens (Vancouver), Martin Silva-Moeller, Barbara Simon and Peter Stobart (Cologne), Frampton Simons and Libby Black (Atlanta), Gustavo Steinbrun Bianco (Buenos Aires), Sophie Stirling and friends (Buchlyvie, Stirling), Catherine Strauss and Gregory Groth, Asle Strmsvaag (Steinkjer, Norway), Melissa A.Swan (Pullman, Wash.), A.C.Tanswell (Walsall), Roy Thomas (King's Lynn), Brian and Christina Turner (Caazapá, Paraguay), Kristien Veckert (Belgium), Sabine Warko (Friedrichsdorf, W.Ger.), Andrew Waterworth and Kerrie Oldfield (Neutral Bay, NSW), Paul Whitfield (Auckland), Edward Willis (Worthing), and Rolf Würtz (Heidelberg).

PARAGUAY

	Page		Page
Introductory	606	Economy	624
Asunción	609	Information for Visitors	626
The Interior	617	Maps	607, 611

PARAGUAY is entirely landlocked, encircled by Argentina, Bolivia and Brazil. Its total land area is put at 406,752 square km., cleft into two quite distinct parts by the great river Paraguay. It has over 3.5 million people (roughly 40% living in towns). It has not as yet fully developed its potential, partly because it was deeply involved in two out of the three major wars staged in Latin America since independence.

To the W of the Paraguay river is the Chaco (246,950 square km., nearly 61% of the country's area), a sparsely inhabited tract of flat and infertile country. E of the river is Paraguay proper (159,800 square km.), a rich land in which almost all the population is concentrated. Paraguay proper is itself divided into two contrasting areas by a high cliffed formation which runs almost due N from the Alto Paraná river, W of Encarnación, to the Brazilian border. E of this cliff lies the Paraná plateau; W of it, as far as the Paraguay river, lie gently rolling hills and flat plains.

Paraguay's southern boundary with Argentina from the confluence of the Río Paraguay to that of the Río Iguazú is the Alto Paraná river. From the Iguazú Falls, the Itaipú Lake and the Alto Paraná form the eastern border with Brazil; from Guaíra Falls the northern boundary with Brazil runs north-westwards across the land mass to the confluence of the Apa and Paraguay rivers. From Corrientes as far N as Asunción the Río Paraguay is the western boundary with Argentina. From Asunción as far N as the confluence with the Apa, the river divides Paraguay into two. For some distance N of the entry of the Apa, the Paraguay river is the Chaco's eastern boundary with Brazil. The S border of the Chaco with Argentina is along the Río Pilcomayo; its W and N borders are with Bolivia.

The Paraná Plateau, ranging from 300 to 600 metres in height, has comparatively heavy falls of rain and was originally forest. Across the plateau, much of which is in Argentina and Brazil, runs the Paraná river. West of the high cliff which forms the western edge of the plateau lies a fertile plain stretching to the Paraguay river. This plain is diversified by rolling, wooded hills. Most of Paraguay's population is concentrated in these hilly lands, stretching SE from Asunción to Encarnación.

Much of the flat plain is flooded once a year; it is wet savanna, treeless, but covered with coarse grasses. On this plain, rice, sugar, tobacco, grains, soya and cotton are grown. Several heavily forested rivers drain the plain and hill lands into the Paraguay.

The Chaco, lying W of the Paraguay river, is mostly cattle country or scrub forest. Along the river there are grassy plains and clumps of palms, but westwards the land grows drier and more bleak. Much of the north-western area is almost desert. The marshy, unnavigable Pilcomayo river forms the boundary with Argentina. Apart from Mennonite colonies, small settlements on the river banks, and a number of *estancias* in the SW, only a few nomadic Indian tribes live in the vast region. (The average density is less than 1 person to the square km.) The *quebracho* (axe-breaker) tree, the world's principal source (with mimosa) of tannin, comes from the scrub forests of the Chaco and of the Paraná river.

PARAGUAY

ROUGH SKETCH

Some 54% of the country is covered with forest, 40% is pastoral, 4% is agricultural but only 1% is intensively cultivated. In eastern Paraguay, the land supports only 11 people to the square km.

Communications The only practicable water route is by the Paraná to the Plate estuary, and Buenos Aires is 1,450 km. from Asunción. So difficult is the river that communication with Buenos Aires was mainly by road before the railway to Asunción was opened in 1913. Most freight is now moved to Buenos Aires, or to Santos or Paranaguá in Brazil, by good paved roads, though river barges still ply along the Paraná.

History The original inhabitants of Paraguay were the Guaraní Indians; they had spread by the 16th century to the foothills of the Andes, along the coast of Brazil, and even into the basin of the Amazon. They did not contest the coming of the Spaniards, the first of whom, under the navigator Diego de Solís, arrived at the River Paraguay in 1524. A member of Solís's expedition, Alejo García, the discoverer of the Iguazú falls, was the first European actually to enter Paraguay; his career included an attack on the Incas of Peru with a Guaraní army from Paraguay in 1525: he was thus also the first European to fight against the Incas. The main expedition, led by Juan de Ayolas, came from Buenos Aires, where the earliest Spanish settlement was planted in 1536. Finding no gold, and harassed by the hostile Indians of the Pampa, they pushed north along the river, seeking a short route to the gold and silver of Peru. They reached the friendly Guaraníes in 1537 and a member of the party, Juan de Salazar de Espinosa, is generally credited with founding Asunción on August 15. The shifting sands and treacherous channel of the Paraná river made it almost impossible for further forces to be brought that way: what little reinforcement there was came overland across Brazil.

Asunción became the nucleus of Spanish settlement in southeastern South America. Spaniards pushed NW across the Chaco to found Santa Cruz, in Bolivia, eastwards to occupy the rest of Paraguay, and southwards down the river to re-found Buenos Aires in 1580, 43 years after they had abandoned it.

During the colonial era one of the world's most interesting experiments in dealing with a native population was carried out, not by the conquerors, but by their missionaries, over whom the civil power had at first little control. In 1609 the Society of Jesus sent missionaries to Paraguay to civilize the Indians. During the 158 years until they were expelled in 1767, the Jesuits formed 30 "reductions", or settlements, run along theocratic-socialist lines. They induced the Indians to leave the forests and settle in townships, where they helped build magnificent churches, employing unsuspected native skills in masonry, sculpture, and painting. Selected natives were even given a sound classical education. The first reductions were further north, but they were forced to abandon these because of attacks by the Bandeirantes of São Paulo, Brazil. They settled finally in Misiones; parts of the area of settlement are now in Argentina and southern Brazil. After the expulsion of the Jesuits, the reductions fell to pieces: the Indians left, and were reduced to peonage under other masters. Most of the great churches have fallen into ruin, or been destroyed; the few that remain are dealt with in the text.

Paraguay got its independence from Spain, without bloodshed, on May 14, 1811. Gaspar Rodríguez de Francia, known as "El Supremo", took power in 1814 and held it until 1840. His policy of complete isolation was brought about by the landlocking of Paraguay by the *porteños* of Buenos Aires who wished to annex it: no one might leave the country, no one might enter it, and external trade was not permitted, but Paraguay achieved a high level of self-sufficiency. Francia was followed as president by Carlos Antonio López, who ruled until his death in 1862. He reversed Francia's policy of isolation and in 1854 began the building of the Central Paraguayan Railway from Asunción to Encarnación. He was followed by his son, Marshal Francisco Solano López, who is today the most venerated of Paraguay's heroes. His Irish mistress Madame Eliza Lynch, who encouraged him in his ambitions, is also held in high esteem. In 1865 he became involved in a war against Brazil, Argentina and Uruguay—the war of the Triple

Alliance. His motive was that Uruguay, with whom Paraguay had a treaty of reciprocal help, had been occupied by Brazil and Argentina and forced to oppose Paraguay. The war was disastrous for the Paraguayans, who held out against overwhelming odds until Marshal López was killed at Cerro Corá in 1870, when the war ended. Out of a population of 800,000, only 194,000 were left alive after the war, and of these only 14,000 were male (only 2,100 of whom were over 20); out of 400,000 women at the beginning of the war, 180,000 survived. Paraguay was occupied for eight years during which time it was deprived of all its gold reserves, many national treasures and 156,415 square km. of territory. (Brazil took 62,325 square km., Argentina 94,090 square km.; previously Paraguayan were the Iguazú Falls and the town of Posadas, once called San José del Paraguay.) (For further reading on the origin and aftermath of the War of the Triple Alliance, see *Paraguay: un destino geopolítico*, by Dra. Julia Velilla Laconich de Aréllaga; *Genocídio Americano: A Guerra do Paraguai*, by Júlio José Chiavenalto; *Women on Horseback*, by William E. Barrett.) After 1870 a certain number of European immigrants arrived; their descendants are still powerful in the social life of Paraguay. Various religious and ideological communities were among them; the Mennonites, mostly of German descent, who are largely responsible for the development of the Chaco, are the most notable.

The country's history since 1870 has been the story of a recovery from disaster, but this process received a severe setback in the wars with Bolivia which broke out intermittently between 1929 and 1935 over the Chaco. The Paraguayans, fighting with their customary courage and tenacity, triumphed, and were given a large area of the Chaco in the final settlement. Bolivia was given an outlet, of little use, to the Paraguay river. Paraguay is still in the process of opening up and settling the Chaco.

After the Chaco War, Paraguay endured several years of political dictatorship, followed by disorder. This period was ended by the seizure of power in 1954 by General Alfredo Stroessner, soon appointed President. Thereafter he gained the support of the Colorado Party (founded in the 1890s), which has been an integral part of his regime ever since. He is still in power as the result of repeated reelection, and in 1981 he surpassed El Supremo's 26-year tenure.

The People of Paraguay Because the proportion of Spanish blood is smaller than elsewhere, the people of Paraguay today are bilingual, speaking both Spanish and Guaraní. Outside Asunción, most people speak Guaraní by preference. There is a Guaraní theatre, and books and periodicals are published in that tongue, which has official status as the second national language. There are about 40,000 pure-bred Indians left; most of them are in the Chaco.

Population: 3.70 m. (1985 estimate). Urban growth: 4.0%; annual growth: 3.1%. Life expectancy at birth: 62.8 years. Infant mortality: 51.2 per thousand. Some 40% live in towns. Over 44% work on the land, nearly 15% in industry (185,500 jobs). Per capita income US$1,777 (1985). 25% of all Paraguayans live abroad.

Government There was a new Constitution in 1967. Executive power rests with the President, elected for five years. There is a two-chamber Congress. Voting is secret and obligatory for all citizens over 18. Uniquely in Latin America, the Constitution permits the immediate reelection of the President.

Asunción, the capital and only large city in Paraguay, is built on the shores of a bay cutting into the eastern bank of the Paraguay river, almost opposite its confluence with the Pilcomayo. Its population is 600,000 (excluding suburbs). The city, built on a low hill crowned by the large modern church of La Encarnación, is laid out in the colonial Spanish rectangular manner; many avenues are lined with beautiful trees, including orange, rubber and jacaranda. The central plazas of the city are drenched in colour during July-August with the prolific pink bloom of the *lapacho* trees, which grow everywhere. The oldest part is down by the water's edge, but none of the public buildings is earlier than the last half of the 19th century. Dwelling houses are in a variety of styles; new villas in every kind of taste have replaced the traditional one-storey Spanish-Moorish type of house, except in the poorer quarters.

You see most public buildings by following Calle El Paraguayo Independiente from the Customs House. The first is the Government Palace, built during the Triple Alliance War in the style of the Louvre. In Plaza Constitución stands the Congressional Palace (debates can be attended during the session from April to December, on Thursdays and Fridays), with the Cathedral at the corner of the square. (When walking in this area, keep your passport handy as the police conduct frequent checks; ask to see plain-clothes agents' identity documents, and be careful about showing too much money.) Two blocks SW, along Calle Chile, is Plaza de los Héroes, with the Pantheon of Heroes, based on the Invalides in Paris, begun during the Triple Alliance War and finished in 1937. It now contains the tombs of Carlos Antonio López, Francisco Solano López, two unknown Paraguayan soldiers, and Marshal Estigarribia, the victor of the Chaco War in the 1930s.

The best of several parks are Parque Carlos Antonio López, set high and with a grand view; Parque Caballero, laid out along a stream, with waterfalls and plantations (both these parks have in attendance a doctor and sports supervisors); and Parque Gaspar Rodríguez de Francia. The Botanical Gardens are 6½ km. out, on Av. Artigas with Primer Presidente at Trinidad, quickly reached by rail or bus (Nos. 5, 6, 2, 7, 23, 40 and 172, US$0.15, about 45 mins.; outward they can be caught on Luis A. Herrera, or Nos. 35 or 44 on Cerro Corá). They lie along the Paraguay river, on the former estate of the López family, and have an enormous range of plants, an eighteen-hole golf course, and a little zoo (animals kept in appalling conditions). Entrance fee US$0.10, or US$0.60 for 2 persons and a car. The Gardens temporarily housed the Maca Indians when they were moved from their reservation across the river; they were moved again in 1985 to very poor conditions (if you wish to photograph the Indians, bargain with them first). Near the entrance to the Botanical Gardens is a restaurant (recommended), which serves excellent steak with good service. The López residence is in the Gardens; a typical Paraguayan country house with verandahs, which has become a natural history museum and library. The beautiful yellow church of Santísima Trinidad (on Santísimo Sacramento, parallel to Av. Artigas), where Carlos Antonio López was originally buried, dating from 1856 with paintings inside, is well worth a visit. N.B. Av. España may also be referred to as General Genes or Generalísimo Franco (not to be confused with Presidente Franco).

Hotels Hotel prices are given at the parallel exchange rate at the time of going to press. *Excelsior*, A, Chile 980 between Manduvirá and Piribebuy, reported best, telex 5192, Tel.: 95632/5; *Chaco*, Caballero y Mariscal Estigarribia, B, highly recommended, parking (but no garden), rooftop swimming pool, good restaurant; *Cecilia*, recommended, Estados Unidos 341, Tel.: 91.271/3, C, very smart, good restaurant; *Guaraní* on Plaza Independencia reported closed indefinitely; *Husa* (a Brazilian chain hotel), 15 de Agosto 420 y Estrella, C, 1st class, all rooms a/c, TV, swimming pool, restaurant, recommended *Bistro* cafeteria, bars, laundry service; *Gran del Paraguay*, C, Residente y Padre Pucheu, out of town, in a park, with swimming pool and a night club on Fridays, was the palace in which López lived; the dining-room, with floral murals, was the private theatre of Eliza Lynch; an air-conditioned annex has been built in the gardens; with breakfast. The *Hotel y Casino Itá Enramada*, 7 km. S of Asunción, C, with breakfast (recommended), free bus link with town, 7-hectare park, swimming pools, sauna, tennis, mini-golf, water-skiing on river, open to non-residents, reservations through KLM, or Hugen Int., Fort Lauderdale, Fla. (Tel.: 1-800-327-8571) or London (01-629-6611), fishing nearby, "Honeymooners get 20% off", Tel.: 33041/9; *Touring 25*, 25 de Mayo 1091, D, small, modern, includes breakfast. *Paraná*, 25 de Mayo y Caballero, D, with breakfast; *Amalfi*, D, Caballero 877, recommended, modern; *Córdoba*, Oliva 1275, D with bath, friendly, clean, 1 km. from centre (take taxi); *Atlántico*, México y Azara, F (beware dangerous *electrical* equipment) with bath, unfriendly; *Premier*, Curupayty y 25 de Mayo, C, with breakfast, restaurant not recommended; *Terraza*, Caballero y Comuneros, central, lovely view overlooking the "bay", F, with shower and a/c, an old house, converted and recently redecorated; *La Paz*, Colón 350, D, with breakfast; *Gran Renacimiento*, Chile 388 y Estrella, central, D, a/c, with poor breakfast in room, good service; *Sahara*, Oliva 920 near Montevideo, good, clean, air conditioning, small pool, E; *Residencial Chaco*, Yegros y Ayala (don't confuse with *Hotel Chaco*), E, after bargaining, *Imperial*, Oliva y Colón, F, clean and friendly; *Presidente*, Azara 128, D, with breakfast and a/c, has seen better days; *Grand Hotel Armele*, Palma y Colón, a/c, D, with breakfast; *Montserrat*, E, 14 de Mayo 474 y Oliva; *La Estancia*, Caballero y Abay, F, clean and friendly; *Señorial*, colonial

PARAGUAY 611

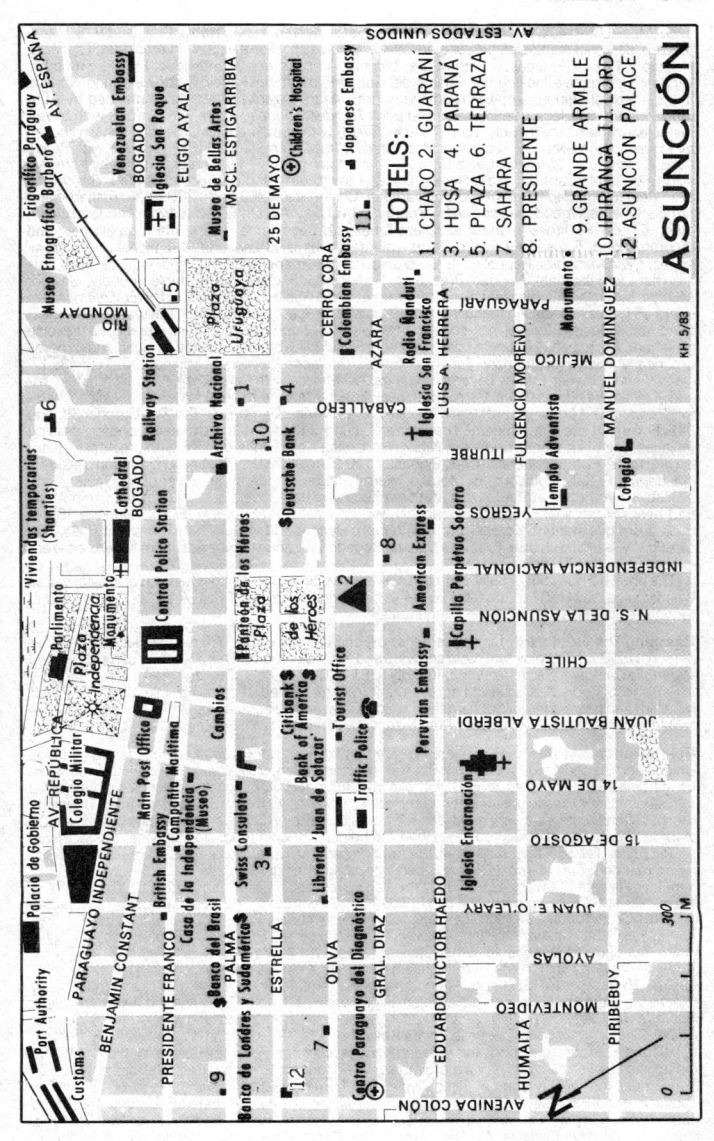

612 PARAGUAY

style (Mcal. López 475 y Perú), D, with breakfast, a/c, swimming pool; *India*, Gral. Díaz 918 y Montevideo, dark, quiet and clean; *Asunción Palace*, Colón 475 y Estrella, E, with breakfast; *Española*, Herrera y Yegros, F, laundry, with meals, friendly; *Ambassador*, Montevideo 111, F, with bath, very old (rooms overlooking the Palacio del Gobierno must close their windows during working hours—fear of snipers—makes rooms very hot); *Azara*, Azara 860, F, recommended by Auto Club, most rooms face a shady patio and pool; *Residencial Ideal*, Azara with Perú, F with breakfast, clean, quiet, very friendly; *Lord*, Tacuary 576, F with bath, breakfast, friendly, English spoken by Korean owner, Mr Lee, recommended; *Stella d'Italia*, Cerro Corá 945, F (popular with Peace Corps volunteers); *Hispania*, Cerro Corá 277, near main plaza, F, with breakfast, run by Koreans, said to be unpleasant but the cheapest place in town, dirty and not recommended; *Residencia* (also Restaurant) *Japón de Kikoyo Uchiyamada*, Constitución 763 (Tel.: 22038), E, management prefers Orientals, good meals; *Cardel*, Ygurey (1145) esq. Av. Dr. Eusebio Ayala, modern, clean, quiet, E, near Pettirossi market, excellent breakfast; *Lago Ypoa*, Azara 1161, small, new and recommended, F, used by Peace Corps volunteers, as is *El Lapacho*, Kubitschek, near Mcal. López; *Casa Menonita*, República de Colombia 1050, E, friendly, German spoken, plain food (bus stop here for Filadelfia); *Nandutí*, Presidente Franco 551, F, clean, comfortable, friendly; *Gasthof Munich*, E, Ayala 163, pleasant; rooms for rent at Eligio Ayala 376, D; *Hospedaje El Viajero*, Antequera 451, noisy, clean and friendly, F *América*, Montevideo 160, not much hot water, fans, mosquito nets; specially for German-speaking travellers: *Ayuda Social Germano-Paraguaya* (hospice attached), Av. España 202, near railway station, F, including breakfast, central, clean, most rooms a/c, nearly always full, friendly, Tel.: 49485; also *Deutsche Pensión*, E, Milano 222, Tel.: 43217, clean friendly, owner's name Federau. *Ipiranga*, Av. México with Cerro Corá, F, with breakfast, friendly, clean; *Residencial Rufi*, Cerro Corá, near Antequera, F, with breakfast, friendly, clean, helpful; *Residencial Mirava*, just off Plaza Uruguay, E, very friendly; *Pensión Fru-Fru*, Coronel Bogado 848, F with hot showers. Unnamed *pensión* at Tacuary 348, near Plaza Uruguaya, cheap, washing facilities, use of kitchen. *Residencial Nuevo Horizonte*, Calle Eligio Ayala, F with breakfast, clean, comfortable; *Hotel Residencial Cadi*, Piribebuy 150 (Tel.: 96901), also F, recommended; *Residencial Itapúa*, F, Calle Fulgencio R. Moreno, warmly recommended with decent breakfasts, lunch available; two hotels at the railway station, cheap and bad, E. *Residencial Familiar*, Eligio Ayala 843 near rail terminal F, breakfast, friendly, will do washing. *Hospedaje El Sol*, Lapacho 185 (2 mins. from bus station), Korean-run, F with bath, clean, good value. There are two motels, *San Martín*, Av. San Martín 889, F, and *La Cuesta*, Bogado y Cacique Lambaré, E. Family *pensiones* are expensive, in the D range.

The hotel bill does not usually contain a service charge. It pays to tip when you arrive as well as when you go, say US$1 to the table waiter at both ends of a week's visit. A tip of 10% is enough for non-residents, at hotels and in restaurants.

Camping The site at the Botanical Gardens now charges a fee, US$1.20 per car plus US$0.30 per person, US$0.60 p.p. plus tent, cold showers and 220v electricity. There is a new campsite called *Westfalia Camping*, German owned, friendly (US$1.20 a car, cold showers), at Av. Gral. Santos y J. F. Bogado, good steaks served at restaurant, recommended. If camping, take plenty of insect repellant and beware large (but harmless) toads. Caravan and camper repairs at *Rodantes Ypacaraí Metalint*, Av. Benjamín Aceval y Ruta Mariscal Estigarribia km. 36, Ruta 2, Tel.: (0513) 290.

Restaurants At the hotels *Chaco*, *Presidente* and *Gran del Paraguay*; *La Preferida*, Estados Unidos and 25 de Mayo (1005) Tel.: 91.126, recommended; *Talleyrand*, French and expensive, Estigarribia 932; *La Pergola del Bolsi*, Estrella 389, full meal US$6, good, wide choice of wines; *Da Vinci*, Estrella 695, disco upstairs, recommended; *Asunción*, Estrella y 14 de Mayo (opp. Deutsche Bank), bar and restaurant very good, service a bit slow; also on Estrella, *Tirol*, *Pizzería Cábala* (602 y 15 de Agosto, good cakes too); *Peppone*, big helpings of cold food, slow service; *Castel Blanc*, on Pacheco, Tel.: 66079, very good; *Bistro*, cafeteria of *Hotel Husa*, 15 de Agosto y Estrella, recommended; *San Marcos*, Oliva y Alberti, good; best cheap Chinese are *Gran Oriente*, Brasil near Luis Herrera, *Taiwan*, Azara 535 (they also have sleeping accommodation US$6 p.p. incl. 3 big meals—US$1 accommodation only). *Suki Yaki*, Constitución 763 y Pettirossi, for reasonably-priced authentic Japanese food; *La Majestad*, Chinese, cheap, Perú 332; *Noodle House Pynong-Ynong*, Perú y Francia, excellent; *Taiwan*, Av. Herrera 919, Tel.: 90524, English spoken, highly recommended and reasonable. Other Chinese: *Sinorama*, Azara near Brasil; *Taipei*, Brasil y Teniente Fariña; *Kung Fu*, L.A. de Herrera 1031, also vegetarian. *La Carreta* serves local dishes; *Hermitage*, 15 de Agosto 1360, food is good, mostly international, as is the music, and moderately expensive, there is a cover charge; *Munich*, Eligio Ayala 163, good German food, excellent value; *Hostería del Caballito Blanco*, Alberti 631, Austrian-run, good food and service (US$10 p.p.); *Chalet Carina*, Av. España 252 1 esq. Santa Rosa, Tel.: 662739, German, Paraguayan and international food, German-run, good, and *Restaurant Deutscher Ecte*, near the university, good value for those who like German food. For a more mixed type of cuisine (traditional and German) try the *San Roque* near the railway station, Eligio Ayala esq. Tacuary; *Santa Rosita*, next to *Hotel Lord* on Tacuary, good Paraguayan food, friendly; *El Jardín de la Amistad*, Estados Unidos 442, good home cooking, open Sun. and all week; *Lucho*, Estados Unidos y Cerro Corá, good local food, cheap. *Jardín de la Cerveza*, Av. Rep. Argentina y Castillo, good food and good entertainment. Good place is the *Lido*, a lunch counter in Plaza de los Héroes, corner Palma and Chile, open until midnight, recommended; also on Palma, *El Mundo*, good. *Chucks*, close to Plaza Uruguaya on

PARAGUAY 613

Ayala is quick and clean. *Imagen*, Pte. Franco 586; *Tío Toms*, quiche and pizza, Av. Perú y Estigarribia; *El Molino*, Calle España near Brasil, good service and food; nearby is *Casa Nostra*, good pizza. *Kentucky Fried Chicken* on Plaza de los Héroes. The *Restaurant Rum-Rum*, Caballero y Estigarribia, excellent *empanadas*, cheap. *Subito*, 500 block of Palma, a/c, also recommended for *empanadas*. *Germania* in Cerro Corá has been warmly recommended, not cheap. For good roast chicken for about US$1.50 try *rotisería*, known as *Nick's Restaurant*, on Azara near Iturbe. The Paraguayan harp can be heard at *Restaurant El Rosedal*, Estados Unidos y Figueroa; also at the beer-garden opposite the Hospital Bautista in Av. República Argentina, Villa Mora; there is a cover charge of US$2 and meals are expensive, the show starts at 2000 hrs. Music, folk show and good food and service at *Yguazú*, at Chóferes del Chaco 1334 (San Lorenzo) US$30 for two, but some distance from centre. About 20 mins. out of town on bus route 26 or 27 is the *Ñandutí Parrillada* (Tel.: 24643), an open-air restaurant with good atmosphere, highly recommended, on Av. Eusebio Ayala y Bartolomé de las Casas. Good ice cream at *Confitería Vertua*. Good Paraguayan harp/guitar *conjunto* at *Churrasquería Sajón*, Av. Carlos A. López, bus 26 from centre. Various ice cream parlours and fast food outlets are to be found in Av. Brasilia, near Av. España e.g. *La Paraguayita*, Brasilia y Siria, opp. is *Heladería París*, very popular. Several restaurants serving good *parrilladas* can be found on Av. Brasilia and Av. Quinta, and around bus station. *Bar Estrella*, 25 de Mayo e Yegros, cheap; *El Trigal*, 25 de Mayo y Tacuary (2 blocks from Plaza Uruguaya), popular with Peace Corps for good, cheap lunches; *Bar de la Estación* (railway station), Eligio Ayala 587, cheap, but that's all that can be said for it; *Futuro*, Quinta y Yegros, regional specialities, quite cheap. You can get a fantastic view of the city from the *Zodiac*, 14 de Mayo 150, 13th floor, expensive, but good; *La Valencia* serves excellent *parrilladas*, always full but far from the centre; *Don Vitos* is well known for *empanadas*, San José 585. Plenty of good, cheap places on Colón (e.g. *Restaurant Vienna*) south of Estrella. A huge pot of tea at *Don Otto Restaurant* costs US$0.35 (but US$1.15 with milk). The *Liverpool Bar*, Pte. Franco 590, and the *Taurina*, at No. 583 are reasonable bars; *Bar Victoria*, corner of Chile and main Plaza, has good food; English breakfast and bed from *Dispensia Chaco Boreal*, Loma Pyta (phone 290-797, take bus 44 or 23).

Other recommendations include: *Kalis*, Antequera 120, excellent service, cheap lunches; *Chino Embajador*, Ed. V. Haedo 668; also *Hoy*, Chinese, good value at Azara 830; *Peña Folklorica*, Refugio del Cantor, San Martin y Sucre; *La Taberna*, Franco, excellent, Spanish; *La Pérgola*, Perú casi España; *Zürich*, Calles Ultima y Ayala. *Chalet Suizo*, Av. Kubitschek 975 (Ethiopian Goulash recommended). *Mastropiero* has 130 types of pizza at Av. España 1372 (Tel.: 60160); another Italian restaurant is *La Bettola*, recommended at C. del Maestro 1698, off the Av. San Martín; *La Piccola Góndola* is very good for Italian (and other) food, so is *Buon Apetito*, 25 de Mayo near Hotel Premier, Av. Mariscal López y Juan Motta. *Natural Mente*, Juan O'Leary 689, good health food restaurant. *Superpán*, 25 de Mayo 845, "pan integral" and good sweets. *Wagner*, Presidente Franco 828 y Ayolas, excellent bread and sweet shop; good icecreams next door.

Clubs Centenario; Unión; Yacht y Golf Club at Itá Enramada; Club Mbiguá; Club Deportivo de Puerto Sajonia; Asunción Tennis Club; Asunción Garden Club, Club Hípico Paraguayo; Jockey Club del Paraguay; Paraguay Kennel Club; Asunción Golf Club; Deutscher Turn und Sport Verein. Instituto Anglo-Paraguayo.

Shopping Calle Colón, starting at the port, is lined with good tourist shops, and so are Calles Pettirossi, Palma and Estrella. Casa Arnoldo, Calle Palma 640, is worth a try for hand-embroidered blouse lengths. Catedral, at Eligio Ayala y Yegros, manufactures shirts or dresses in 3 days. La Asunceña, Palma 766, leatherware; Galería Colón, good for leather, near port. Calle Franco for handmade furniture. For wooden articles and carvings go to Artes de Madera at Ayolas (222), Palma y Pte. Franco. Also Artesanía Raity at Pai Pérez 778, woodcraft, prints and paintings, recommended; Arte Popular, 25 de Mayo 1138 and Casa Vera at Estigarribia 470 for Paraguayan leatherwork, cheap and very good. Other recommended shops, Artesanía Kuarajhy, Juan O'Leary y Pte Franco, Artesanía Hilda (same location), for *aho poi* embroidery and *encaje jhy* lacework. *Casa Overall*, Mcal. Estigarribia, nr. Plaza Uruguaya, good selection. On Rioja near the main park for all local handicrafts and imported items (4 floors). Pistilli has a fine selection of canework and furniture, Estados Unidos esq. Azara. Check the quality of all handicrafts carefully, lower prices usually mean lower quality. A small but excellent fruit and vegetable market is to be found at San José behind the España supermarket. The markets are worth a visit, especially the Pettirossi (food and ordinary clothes). There is a daily market on Av. Dr. G.R. de Francia. Outside Asunción, visit Luque (musical instruments and jewellery—see below) and Itauguá (lace)—see page 618.

Bookshops Librería Universal, English stock, Mcal. Estigarribia 430 (casi Caballero); Librería Internacional, Oliva and main square, Estrella y Juan O'Leary and Palma y 15 de Agosto; also "Books" at Mcal. López 3971, at the shopping centre, also carries English stock (at 3-4 times UK prices); the Cultural Centre (ex-Librería Francesa) at Alberdi 439 and magazine/newspaper kiosk El Lector on Plaza Uruguaya and 25 de Mayo have a full selection of foreign material. There is a small German bookshop at Av. Luis A. de Herrera 292. The best historical bookshop is Librería Juan de Salazar at O'Leary 482 y Oliva (Tel: 49329).

614 PARAGUAY

Taxis Minimum fare in Asunción is US$0.40 plus US$0.10 for every 100 metres. The average journey costs about US$2. Hire by the hour; about US$4. Tip 10%.

Trams No longer in operation.

Buses The system is extensive, running from 0600-2400; buses stop at signs before every street corner. Journeys within city, US$0.15, including from the centre to the new bus terminal.

Night Clubs and Discotheques Kaktus, Teniente Vera y San Martín; Musak, Bertoni y José Ocampos, J y C; Boggiani y O'Higgins; Fantasio, Av. Bogado and Felicidad, in front of Radio Primero de Marzo; *Piper's*, in the centre, good disco, drinks not expensive, popular; Torremolinos, Costa Azul Urbanización, 2001; and one in the *Hotel Casino Itá Enramada* (open every day in summer, Saturdays in winter).

Municipal Theatre, Pte. Franco, nr. Alberdi, has an extensive winter programme of concerts and ballets (entry US$4). Cinema programmes are given in the press; some offer 3 films at one price (US$1). Art gallery and dance studio (Taller de Movimiento Creativo), 15 de Agosto 530, English-speaking owner.

Banks Lloyds Bank (ex-BOLSA), Palma y O'Leary (and six agencies in Greater Asunción - will give US dollars); Bank of America, Oliva esq. Chile; Citibank, Estrella y Chile (will change Citibank travellers' cheques into dollars for a small commission); Chase Manhattan Bank, V.E. Haedo e Independencia Nacional; Banco de Boston, Pte. Franco y O'Leary (will give US dollars); Bank of Commerce and Industry, Caballero esq. Eligio Ayala, also gives dollars; Interbank, 14 de Mayo 339; Deutsche Bank, Estrella y 14 de Mayo; Banco Sudameris (ex-Francés e Italiano), Oliva e Independencia Nacional. Banco Holandés Unido, Independencia Nacional y V.E. Haedo. Also Argentine, Brazilian and local banks. Unionbank branch at Alberdi will give quick cash advances on Visa or Mastercard in about 15 minutes, English spoken, friendly. Open Mon.-Fri. 0730-1100. Several *casas de cambio* on Palma (open Mon.-Fri. 0730-1200, 1500-1830, Sat., 0730-1200; rates for neighbouring countries' currencies usually good, except bolivianos), Deutsche Marks can be changed at good rates, and all rates are better than at the various frontiers. Be careful to count money received from street exchange-sellers (Palma and surrounding area—they give a poor rate when banks and *cambios* closed). *Casas de cambio* do not like changing sterling travellers' cheques, the only one that will do it is Cambio Paraná on Palma. Some only change one type of dollar travellers' cheque. *Cambios* give 3% less on travellers' cheques than on cash. Cambio Guaraní, Palma 449, between 14 de Mayo and Alberdi, is good, will change dollar cheques into dollars cash, but charges 1% commission for this. German spoken at Cambios Menno Tour, Azara 532. Cambios Yguazú (Palma) is O.K., Luís will negotiate for the best U.S. dollar rates.

General Post Office Alberdi, Benjamín Constant y El Paraguayo Independiente. Tel.: 48891, 0700-2000, but closed for lunch. Also philatelic museum, open 0700-1800, Mon.-Fri.; 0700-1200, Sat. Post boxes throughout the city carry address of the nearest place one can purchase stamps. Register all important mail; you must go to main P.O. for this. Poste Restante charges about US$0.25 per item collected. There are sub-offices at the railway station and at the docks.

Museums National Museum of Fine Arts (closed in November 1986), and the Asunción Seminary Museum, both showing some "mission" art. At the Museum of Fine Arts (in Calle Mariscal Estigarribia, off Plaza Uruguaya), the paintings are very badly displayed; it has a Murillo and a Tintoretto and collections of Acevedo (about 1910) caricatures. In the Botanical Gardens are the Museo de Historia Natural and the Museo Etnográfico, both open Mon.-Sat. 0730-1130, 1300-1700, Sun. 0600-1200, 1300-1700, both well worth seeing. In the Casa de la Independencia (14 de Mayo y Presidente Franco) is an interesting historical collection; entry free. Panteón Nacional de los Héroes, esq. Palma y Chile, open every day. Historical and military museum at Ministry of Defence at Mariscal López esq. Gen. Santos. Most museums are small and basic.

Laundry Lavamático, Yegros 808 y Fulgencio Moreno. Lava Pronto, Azara 850, Tel.: 45147, good, quick service.

Addresses British Embassy and Consulate: Presidente Franco 706, esquina O'Leary, 4th floor (Casilla 404), Tel.: 49146; U.S. Embassy and Consulate: Av. Mcal. López esq. Kubitschek, Tel.: 201041; Swiss Embassy: O'Leary 409 esq. Estrella, Tel.: 48-022; Spanish Embassy: Calle 25 de Mayo 175, esq. Yegros; Dutch Consulate, Presidente Franco y 15 de Agosto; W. German Embassy: José Bergés 1003-1007. Brazilian Consulate, in Banco do Brasil building on main square (open 0800-1200, Mon.-Fri.), Nuestra Señora de la Asunción y Oliva; Argentine Consulate, in Banco de la Nación building, also on main square, open 0700-1100, visas processed in 1-2 hours, photograph needed. South African Embassy, Banco Sudameris, piso 4°, esq. Cerro Corá e Independencia Nacional; Chilean Embassy, Guido Spano 1740, Tel.: 660344; Bolivian Consulate, Eligio Ayala 2002, Tel.: 22662; Peruvian Consulate, Estrella 451, piso 3°, Tel.: 41741; France, Av. España 676, Tel.: 23111; Israel, Ed. Líder, piso 3°, O'Leary y Gen. Díaz; Uruguay, Av. Brasil y Siria, Tel.: 44242; Mexico Ed. Ytá Ybate, esq. Cerro Corá y Juan O'Leary. The US-Paraguay cultural centre has a good library at España 352; Instituto Anglo-Paraguayo, España 457, where you can acquire much useful information and read English newspapers (take Tram No. 5). Compañía Marítima

PARAGUAY 615

Paraguaya S.A., Presidente Franco 199 esq. 15 de Agosto, for all shipping enquiries. Anglican Church: St. Andrew, on España with Uruguay; Synagogue at Gen. Díaz 657. Peace Corps, Chaco Boreal 162, Tel.: 65622/662871. Police, Tel.: 46105.

Electricity Domestic and industrial: 220 volts A.C., 50 cycles.

Camera Repair Panatronic, Benjamín Constant 516; Olympus agency at Libería Universal, Mcal. Estigarribia 430, no repairs undertaken. Rodolfo Loewen, Camera Service, Blas Garay y Morelo, Tel.: 23807.

Tourist Office Alberdi y Oliva. Open 0700-1200, 1500-1800. Tel.: 45306, 49521, 47865. Free map, also one available for sale in bookshops. Helpful, but information usually incorrect. There is a display of lace and handicrafts.

Tourist Agencies (all very helpful) Inter-Express (Am-Ex), Yegros 690, Maral on 25 de Julio and Caballero are helpful; Continental, Benjamín Constant 777. American Tours, Independencia Nacional, under *Hotel Guaraní*, both German and English spoken. Grupo Cataldi, Estrella 876, Tel.: 90458, can occasionally pick up at airport; real estate agents (German run) with good contact in hotels and apartment accommodation. Menno is also staffed by Germans and will book buses to Foz etc.

Airport Presidente Gral. Stroessner, 15 km. NE of centre. Taxi to centre, US$15; Bus 30A to the centre (US$1.10) stops every 15 minutes just outside the airport perimeter at the road fork, 300 metres from the main entrance. Ask to be set down at road fork. (Do not walk on the grass outside the airport or the police will fine you). Buses 30 and 18 to the bus terminal. Buses only recommended outside rush-hours, with light luggage. The *Asunción Palace Hotel* runs a colectivo service from the airport to hotels, and in the other direction, US$2 p.p. (don't pay more than the fixed tariff). Líneas Aéreas Paraguayas (LAP) has its own colectivo which collects from hotels, US$3.10 p.p., as does TAM. Enquire at airline offices. LAP office at Oliva 467; Eastern at Independencia Nacional y Azara.

A new airport terminal has been built (duty free facilities, small *casa de cambio*—turn left as you leave customs and immigration, handicraft shop and restaurant), 1 km. from the old building. There is a helpful tourist office on the ground floor at the airport; they will book for the Varig flights to Foz do Iguaçu, as well as arranging transport into town (minibus arrives and leaves from Iberia Office), finding accommodation and changing money at poor rates.

Rail Presidente Carlos Antonio López Railway to Encarnación and Buenos Aires (1,510 km.) journey of 44 hours, Tues. only (better to take bus to Encarnación and catch train in Posadas). To Encarnación: with wood-burning steam locomotive, Tues. and Fri. 1800, at least 18 hrs. (first 12 hrs. in the dark), US$3, 1st class (recommended), US$1.90 2nd class; tickets on sale 2 hrs. before departure. Good hot food can be ordered for US$1.50, drinks US$0.30. In dry weather dust, and in wet weather rain, gets into 2nd-class carriages. Track liable to flooding. (Trains may be cancelled on public holidays, such as Christmas.) See under Excursions for a trip to see the wood-burning locomotives.

River Boats To Concepción (24 hrs.) with Flota Mercantil del Estado, Estrella 672-682 (tickets from here only). Weekly (every Tues., 0800 hrs.—returns on Wed., 1400), US$7.50 1st class, US$5.50 2nd class (4 beds to a cabin, men and women segregated, comfortable, but 2nd class food is bad and service worse—take food with you), US$4.50 3rd class (wooden benches on upper deck, bring hammock and mosquito repellant). Restaurant on board. Boats are modern, elegant and comfortable. Other boat lines work this route, but they are less comfortable, although cheaper, with no regular sailings; enquire at the small boat dock to the right of the main dock; you will have to take your own food. Ferries sail thrice weekly to Balletín one day's journey N of Concepción, 2 day's journey in all (seats and cabins). On the 2nd and 4th Tuesday of each month FME sails to Corumbá, Brazil, leaving at 0700, arriving Friday a.m., leaving Corumbá Monday 0800; 1st class US$26, 2nd class US$18 (1st class to Bahía Negra en route US$20, 2nd class US$13). All 1st class cabins on the upper deck to Corumbá are taken in advance by an Argentine tour company for the whole 12 day round trip, including, excursions into the Pantanal, bookable in Asunción from Chacotur, Montevideo 1447, Tel.: 80318, US$210 in all (exit stamps not needed for the round trip, official on board takes charge of passports). Ferry to Puerto Pilcomayo about every two hours.

Roads There is a 10 km. road N from Asunción (passing the Botanical Gardens on Primer Presidente) to a concrete arch span bridge (Puente Remanso—US$1 toll) which leads to the border at Puerto Falcón and then to Clorinda in Argentina. The border is open 24 hours a day; last bus from Falcón to the centre of Asunción at 1830. The bus fare from Asunción to the border (at Falcón) is US$0.60; from Falcón to Clorinda costs US$0.25. Taxi from border to centre, US$15, shared. There is a good bus service to Resistencia and Buenos Aires from the Argentine side, by Empresa Godoy. There is a 32 km. road NW to Villa

616 PARAGUAY

Hayes (bridge) and on through the Chaco (Route 9) to Filadelfia (paved to here) and Bolivia, 805 km. (an account of a direct journey from Bolivia by this road will be found on page 187). Route 8 is now paved N from Coronel Oviedo, 100 km. to San Estanislao (see also under Coronel Oviedo, page 619), where it becomes successively Routes 3 and 5 (being paved for about 100 km.) and runs 305 km. N and then NE, to Pedro Juan Caballero on the Brazilian frontier. Also paved are the long-distance Route 1 to Encarnación (372 km.), and Route 2 to Coronel Oviedo, which leads to Route 7 to Ciudad Presidente Stroessner and the Iguazú falls (362 km.). A round trip Asunción—Ciudad Stroessner—Encarnación—Asunción is easily done. The roads are described in the text.

Buses To Ciudad Stroessner, about 20 buses a day, most with toilet, with the following companies: Sirena del Paraná, Rápido Caaguazú, Nuestra Señora de la Asunción and RYSA (Rápido Yguazú),US$4. Nuestra Señora and Pluma (serves coffee on board) continue to Foz do Iguaçu; all luxury bus fares to Foz are US$5, 5-7 hrs., at 0100, 0400, 0700/0730 and 1330. Seat reservations recommended; take the 0100 bus (easy to sleep), which arrives at Foz at 0700 if you want to visit the Brazilian side of the Iguaçu Falls in one day; take 1200 bus from Falls to bus station, then 1320 bus back to Asunción—remember to buy cruzados in Asunción. Pluma continues from Foz to Florianópolis, Brazil.
   Bus to Encarnación (for Posadas in Argentina), 8 daily, Alborada SRL, 6 hrs. Rápido Iguazú, at 0800, 6 hrs. US$3.50, Flecha del Oro (7 a day); Nuestra Señora de la Asunción, and La Encarnaceña, recommended, US$3. To Villarrica, La Guaireña, US$1.50, La Yuteña, US$0.85. To Concepción, US$4.50, 10 hrs., La Encarnaceña (0100), San Jorge (1950, 2400),US$5; San Jorge runs to Guaíra for US$3.70, and to Pedro Juan Caballero for US$4 (Amambaya also to P.J. Caballero). Bus to Filadelfia 0730, 8-10 hrs., US$4, and 2200, 7 hrs., US$5. San Bernardino, US$ 0.65; Itauguá, US$0.50; Yaguarón US$0.60; Caapucú (on Encarnación road), US$0.70.
   COIT runs to Montevideo, 0800, Sat. and Wed., 24 hrs. (the route is Clorinda, Resistencia—for connection to Cochabamba at 1700—Reconquista, Santa Fe, Paraná, Colón, Paysandú). To Curitiba, US$16 with Pluma, buses daily, 17 hrs.; to São Paulo, Rápido Yguazú, Pluma and Brújula, US$16 (*leito*, US$34.50). Pluma to Rio de Janeiro, US$27.50. Unesul run to Porto Alegre on Thurs. and Sun., Nacional Expresso to Brasília 3 times a week.
   Asunción-Buenos Aires (*diferencial*, US$42, *común*, US$32.50), via Rosario, and Santa Fe (US$28), with Godoy, Brújula and La Internacional, each 6 times a week. To Resistencia (US$11.75) and Formosa (US$4), daily, with Compañía Brújula and Godoy; Brújula and Cacorba to Córdoba (US$32.50), each twice weekly.
   All buses now leave from the new bus terminal, out of town at República Argentina esq. Fernando de la Mora; entry to terminal US$0.10. Take local bus numbers 8, 10, 31, 38, anywhere on Haedo in the centre for Terminal Nuevo; from the terminal to the city, get off the bus at the corner of General Díaz and Chile. The terminal has tourist information desk, restaurant (quite good), café, shops, and lots of noisy televisions. No sleeping accommodation nearby. Taxi from down town, recommended if you have luggage, US$2 p.p. Many bus companies still maintain ticket offices around Plaza Uruguaya.

Excursions At Barrio San José de Olera (follow the river bank north) is the local brick works with about 20 kilns. Everything is still done by man and horse power. To **Villeta** (27 km., 5,232 people), a cotton and tobacco town on the E bank; it has an industrial park and has undergone a rapid economic expansion. A little North is a park at Ytororó where trenches used in the war of the Triple Alliance can still be seen. By road to see the Chaco and its wild life. The town of **Luque** (population, 24,917), close to Asunción, is famous for the making of Paraguayan harps, difficult to find though (Guitares Sanabria is one of the best-known firms), and for fine filigree work in silver and gold. There are also many fine musical instrument shops on the road to Luque; get off the bus—No. 30—from Asunción just before the major roundabout. Marshal López' house may be visited, and there is a good restaurant, *El Aljibe*. 8 km. from Luque is Balneario Yukyry, with an artesian well, springs, swimming pools, football pitches and a snackbar; for details and reservations, Tel.: 23731 (closed in winter, but pleasant trip anyway).
   Parque Nacional **Ybicuy** is reached by bus two to three times daily US$1.85, 4 hours. Good walks, a beautiful camp site (hardly used in the week, no lighting, some facilities may not be available) and lots of waterfalls; it is one of the few areas of protected forest in the country. At the entrance is a well-set out park and museum as well as the reconstructed remains of the country's first iron foundry (La Rosada). The only shops are at Ybicuy, 30 km. away (*Hotel Pytuúrenda*, E/F, cooking facilities, friendly; *Pensión Santa Rosa* and *San Juan*, both F).

Bus from Ybicuy at 0430 and 1120, returning 0700 and 1345, goes as far as camp site, 2 km. beyond the museum. Crowded on Sundays but deserted the rest of the week.

The most popular trip is east to Itauguá, and San Bernardino and Aregua on Lake Ypacaraí (see page 619).

A short steam train trip to Aregua leaving Asunción station at 1215 daily, takes 1½ hrs., US$0.20, to the shores of Lake Ypacaraí. Bus for return trip via Itauguá: a good outing. For a longer look at the countryside, hire a car with driver for US$12 from any travel agent (pick-up at your hotel) to drive the "Circuito Central" also called "Circuito de Oro": Asunción-San Lorenzo-Itá-Yaguarón-Paraguarí-Chololó-Piraretá-Piribebuy-Caacupé -San Bernardino-Ypacaraí-Itauguá-Aregua-Capiatá-Asunción. Some 200 km. on paved roads, 7 hrs. Lions, at Alberdi 454, 1°, Tel.: 90.278, run a full service of trips. Beware of the Argentine Hugo, otherwise O.K. Alternatively, from San Lorenzo, take Route 1 towards Encarnación and at Km 28 (Shell Petrol station) turn right to Guarambaré, a sleepy town in the sugar area with many Peace Corps trainees. From May to November bullock carts and trucks take the cane to the factory, 1 km. past the electricity sub-station. For the steam enthusiast a visit is a 'must'. There are 20 different working steam engines. After your visit continue to Guarambaré. Take the second dirt road on the right after the Plaza and for about 10 km. continue through typical farmlands and citrus orchards. The road then continues through Ypané, Nemby and back to Asunción via Lambaré. In Lambaré, near the *Itá Enramada Hotel*, is Lambaré hill with very good views.

A 3-hour colectivo ride from Asunción is Sapucay, 88 km. away, where the main workshops for the wood-burning steam locomotives are located. There are cheap *hospedajes* in Sapucay; either stay there, or take the Asunción-Encarnación train which passes through Tues. and Fri. at 2130.

North from Asunción

A boat trip up the Paraguay to Concepción, about 312 km. N of Asunción, is one of the easiest ways of seeing more of the country. The winding river is 400 metres wide, with shoals of vicious *caribe* fish. There is a lot of traffic, for in the absence of a direct road between Concepción and Asunción (though there are roads via the Chaco and by Coronel Oviedo) this is the main trade route for the products of northern Paraguay: cattle, hides, *yerba mate*, tobacco, timber and *quebracho*. Nevertheless, for passengers there is only one weekly boat. Every second Tuesday in the month there is a boat as far as Corumbá.

Concepción (22,866 inhabitants), a free port for Brazil, lies on the E bank. This pleasant, friendly, quiet and picturesque town is the trade centre of the N, doing a considerable business with Brazil. There is an interesting market. Buses run every two hours to Asunción. A bridge is being built across the river; the regular ferry operates in the dry season; motor boats cross in the rainy season.

Hotels *Francés*, Presidente Franco 1016, E with bath and a/c, F bath and fan, cheaper without bath, inc. breakfast, excellent restaurant, has character. There is a hotel above *Bar Victoria*, Franco y Caballero, F without breakfast, cheap and clean, hot water, recommended, being extended; on same street, *Center*, F with breakfast, and *Concepción*, F with bath and breakfast. *Paraguay*, F, restaurant excellent, good food at low prices. Also F, *Boquerón*, basic. *Cosmos* (clean, fan, breakfast included) and *Bar Estrella del Norte* (near port), both F, basic but possible. Other restaurants include *Copetín Chino*, A. F. de Pinedo 1188, fair. Bread shop at Mcal. Estigarribia 229. Prices may rise rapidly during Brazilian tourist seasons.

Exchange Banks give a poor rate for travellers' cheques; *casa de cambio* in the store beside the ticket office for weekly boat to Asunción.

Communications The bus station is on the outskirts: from Pte. Franco, with your back to the port, it's 8 blocks up Gral. E. A. Garay (to the left). Arriving in town by bus, get out in town centre, don't wait for bus station. There is a bus from Concepción to Horqueta, 56 km. to the E (1½ hrs., US$0.55), a cattle and lumbering town of 10,000 people. There is now a dry-season road from Concepción-Pozo Colorado (ferry) W across the Chaco, to Pozo Colorado on the Trans-Chaco highway. The Concepción-Pozo Colorado bus takes 2 hours, US$2.75, but it is difficult to get onward connections. Once a week the "Camioneta Cristo Rey", a jeep belonging to the Anglican Church, goes across to the Trans-Chaco highway. Concepción-Asunción via Chaco takes 7 hours (departure 0830), road impassable with heavy rains; via Coronel Oviedo, bus departs at 0700, 1800 (US$4, 12 hrs.) and 1900 (direct service US$5, 9 hrs.—boring), bad road as far as Coronel Oviedo, rains often delay departures. Bus to Pedro Juan Caballero at 0830, 1030 and 1400, US$2.50.

Air Service Asunción-Concepción flights are operated by LATN, Aeronorte and TAM (which tends to be cheapest). TAM to Asunción daily at 0800, US$10, book as early as possible (only 25

618 PARAGUAY

seats), free colectivo from TAM office on main street to airport. TAM flies from Concepción to Bella Vista on Brazilian border (from there a poor road goes to Aquidauana on the Corumbá-Campo Grande railway); to Vallemí, Puerto Casado and Bahía Negra, all three villages to N of Concepción on the Río Paraguay. From Puerto Casado, 210 km. N of Concepción, a 200 km. railway runs W into the heart of the Chaco (used mainly by Mennonite settlers, and soldiers). There is no direct air connection between Concepción and Pedro Juan Caballero.

Shipping To Asunción, Weds. 1400, US$7.50 1st class, US$5.50 2nd class, US$4.50 3rd class, 19 hrs., also Sun. 0900 and 1900. To Balletín, once a week, 24 hrs. To Fuerte Olimpo, Mon. only; contact Agencia Marítima Ramón Velázquez, Presidente Franco 2, near dock.

There is a 260 km. road (Route 5—almost all paved) to the border town of **Pedro Juan Caballero** (pop.: 37,331), opposite Ponta Porã, Brazil, which has a road and railway to São Paulo and the Atlantic coast. The two towns are divided only by a road and the locals come and go as they please. To cross into Brazil officially, (i.e. if you don't need a Brazilian visa) first obtain a Paraguayan exit stamp then go to the Brazilian consul (closed 1200-1400) in P. J. Caballero, and then report to Brazilian federal police in Ponta Porã. From P. J. Caballero there are daily flights to Asunción (they may be suspended after heavy rain). Much cheaper here than Asunción for most purchases.

Hotels *Peralta* (F) and *Holiday* (E) are on the same street as the TAM offices. Recommended *Eiruzú*, D, with breakfast, modern, swimming pool; *La Siesta*, modern, luxury, good restaurant, close to border with Ponta Porã; *Paraguay*, D, with breakfast, good, friendly. *Corina*, very clean with breakfast, F, recommended. Try to pay in cruzados as you may find it cheaper than in guaraníes. For a good meal, cross the border to *Viviani's*.

Buses The bus terminal is situated opposite the Brazilian Consulate, one block on the left. P.J. Caballero-Concepción at 0200, 0430, 0800, 1030, 1200 (direct) and 1400, US$2.50, 6 hrs. To Asunción at 0900, 1700 and 1900 (direct), US$4, 11-12 hrs.

Exchange There are two *casas de cambio* on the corner of Dr. Francia and Mcal. Estigarribia, 3 blocks on the left opposite the Brazilian Consulate. For travellers' cheques you can go to the *casas de cambio*, or to *Hotel Eiruzú*, one block behind the *casas de cambio* (also deal in the European currencies). Reports vary as to which gives the better rates; some say neither changes travellers' cheques. There are illegal exchanges.

South from Asunción

Another trip, this time down the river, can be made to **Pilar** (13,135 inhabitants), 306 km. S of Asunción, opposite the confluence of the Paraguay and the Bermejo, coming in from the Argentine Chaco. A road (Route 4) is open E to San Ignacio Guazú, on the Asunción-Encarnación highway; in the other direction, it continues to the extreme SW tip of Paraguay, near Humaitá, the site of a heroic siege during the War of the Triple Alliance. Flights from Pilar to Asunción and Resistencia, Argentina, on Mon. and Thurs. by LAP.

Hotels *Gardel*; *Prinquelli*.

East from Asunción

Route Two The Mariscal Estigarribia Highway leaves Asunción past typical markets, reached by 26 bus from Asunción. At km. 12 is **San Lorenzo** (pop.: 74,359), an industrial town with the National School of Agriculture (Universidad de Agronomía—it has an extensive insect collection; also excellent Museo de las Indígenas, by the Cathedral, handicrafts for sale at reasonable prices, non-profit-making organization run by Catholic Relief Services). Here is the Balneario El Tigre, with swimming pool and shady trees. At km. 20 is **Capiatá**, founded in 1640, where there is a fine cathedral with remarkable 17th century sculpture made by Indians under the tutelage of the Jesuit Fathers. Here there is a left turn sign-posted to Lake Ypacaraí via an inexpensive toll road, 7 km. to the lake, worth a visit.

Km. 30, **Itauguá** (5,369 inhabitants), founded in 1728, is where the famous ñandutí, or spiderweb lace, is made. The blocks of uniform dwellings in the broad plaza, with their reddish tile roofs projecting over the sidewalk and their lines of pillars, are very close to the descriptions we have of Guaraní Jesuit settlements.

PARAGUAY 619

The church and the market are worth seeing, and the town looks most attractive with the ñandutí work spread or hanging outside the houses; you can buy the most beautiful hammocks, tablecloths, shirts, hats and dresses locally made. There is a 3-day festival in mid-July, including processions and the crowning of Señorita Ñandutí. Accommodation poor (there is only one *pensión*, F), but Itauguá is only one hour by bus from Asunción, US$0.50. At km. 36 the garage Metalint Rodantes Ypacaraí has been recommended for camper vehicles and caravan repairs; ask for Sr. Gauto.

At km. 40 a branch road, 5 km. long, leads off to **San Bernardino**, on Lake Ypacaraí, by bus from Asunción (Route 2, 56 km. 1½ hrs., US$0.65) or partly by rail. The lake is 24 km. by 5. Crowded from December through February. Facilities for swimming and water sports, with sandy beach, but water is a bit dirty (*Restaurant La Retonda* on the lake is not recommended). **Aregua**, a pretty town on the far shore (church), is also a resort. The lake area is still unspoilt from commercial tourism, is peaceful and with an idyllic countryside. Riding is possible. (It is possible to camp right on the lake but you will be charged as much as in the camp site and on top of that you would have more mosquitoes, inadequate sanitary facilities and less safety for your personal belongings.)

Hotels *del Lago*; *Acuario*, new; IPS (the Medical Social Service of Paraguay) has a first class hotel, open for tourists. *Santa Rita*, E, bed and breakfast, friendly (good German food, and Paraguayan folk music at weekends). It is possible to find rooms in private houses.

Camping Camping Alt. Heidelberg, Avenida Presidente Stroessner, 200 metres from Lake Ypacaraí; full services including home-cooking.

At km. 54 is **Caacupé**, a popular resort and religious centre with 9,105 inhabitants. Its sights include the beautiful Basilica of Our Lady of the Miracles. Her day is December 8, when pilgrims come to the town from far and wide. The old church is being demolished, but the new basilica is very beautiful. There is an interesting market next to it, where one can buy pottery, etc., and swimming pools in the streams nearby. Parque Anka has a swimming pool, tennis courts, ponies, a Disneyland, camp site and good restaurants.

Thousands of people from Paraguay, Brazil and Argentina flock to the shrine. Besides fireworks and candle-lit processions, pilgrims watch the agile gyrations of Paraguayan bottle-dancers; they weave in intricate measures whilst balancing bottles pyramided on their heads. The top bottle carries a spray of flowers and the more expert dancers never let drop a single petal.

Hotels *Gran Hotel Victoria*; *El Uruguayo*, F, with good restaurant, friendly service.

Excursions Poor roads lead to several interesting churches. One is at Tobati, a tobacco centre 16 km. to the N. At km. 64 beyond Caacupé a paved road runs 13 km. SE to **Piribebuy** (pop.: 5,902, *Pensión Santa Rosa*, F, basic; *Restaurant Rincón Viejo*, reasonable), founded in 1640 and noted for its strong local drink, *caña*. In the central plaza is the church (1640), with fine sculptures, high altar and pulpit. Near the town are the attractive small falls of Piraretá. The road goes on to Chololó, with good views from a hill, and you can visit the Chololó falls (motel); it reaches Route 1 at Paraguarí, 22 km. from Piribebuy.

At km. 132, but off the main road (buses drop passengers at La Cruz) is **Coronel Oviedo**, an important road junction (21,782 people; *Pensión Ñanda Roga*, F, without breakfast, basic but friendly; on main road to the West, *Hotel Alemán*, recommended, or in centre, *El Sueño Feliz*, F, clean and friendly). Here the road branches: one branch, Route 8, is paved for 42 km. S to Villarrica and continues S (unpaved) through Caazapá to Boquerón. The road N is paved as far as San Estanislao.

Villarrica, 173 km. by road or rail from Asunción and 219 from Encarnación, with 21,203 people, is delightfully set on a hill rich with orange trees. It has a fine Cathedral. A public, open-air swimming pool has recently been opened. Products of the region are tobacco, cotton, sugar, *yerba mate*, hides, meat and wine produced by German settlers.

Hotel *El Mesón III*, F, and *Guaíra*, F, near bus terminal, both very pleasant. Also various F places: *Hospedaje Restaurant San Miguel*, Natalicio Talavera and *Pensión el Toro*. *Hospedaje Leticia*, overpriced. *Internacional*. Bus to Coronel Oviedo US$1.50; also direct service to Ciudad Presidente Stroessner, US$2.75.

620 PARAGUAY

There are three German colonies near Villarrica. At Colonia Independencia, a hotel, and Señora Bürg has two rooms for about US$6, full board; very good food, fresh milk, lemon juice. Makes a good stop, especially for German-speaking travellers, who can also visit the German cooperative farms. Direct bus to Asunción, twice daily, as well as to Villarrica.

The other branch, the paved Route 7, runs 195 km. from Coronel Oviedo through cultivated areas and woods and across the Caaguazú mountain to the spectacular 500-metre single span "Friendship Bridge" across the Paraná at **Ciudad Presidente Stroessner,** where there is a grass-strip airport. This was the fastest growing city in the country (83,000 inhabitants) until the completion of the civil works of the Itaipú hydroelectric project, for which it is the centre of operations. Ciudad Presidente Stroessner has been described as the biggest late-night shopping centre in Latin America, with little to excite the tourist (except the prices for electrical goods, watches, perfumes, etc.)—but watch the exchange rates if you're a short-term visitor from Argentina or Brazil. The nearby towns of Hernandarias (pop.: 32,000) and Puerto Presidente Franco (pop.: about 24,000) have also had a tremendous increase in population and activity. The **Monday** falls, 10 km. from Ciudad Stroessner, are worth visiting by taxi. There is good fishing below the falls.

Hotels (incl. breakfast) *Acaraí Casino*, B, a/c, with swimming pool and casino, quiet; *Catedral*, C, a/c, with swimming pool, restaurant; *Munich*, D; *Hanga Roa* chalet, D; *Itaipú*, D; *Motel Mi Abuela*, highly recommended, F, including breakfast; *Tres Monedas*, D, on the main street, decent breakfast. *Mi Abuelo*, E, with breakfast, Av. Gen. Adrián Jara, recommended; other cheap ones near market: *Ocampo*, G, to be avoided. *Executive*, Av. Adrián Jara y Curupayty, Tel.: 8981/8982, B (incl. breakfast—restaurant recommended), and *San Juan*. Also in this class are *Floresta*, Av. Teniente Cabello y C.A. López, Tel.: 8255/8197, and *Santo Domingo*, Emiliano R. Fernández y Alejo García, Tel.: 2505, superb.

Restaurants *Mburucuyá*, with music, at Alejo García y A. Jara; *Hostería del Lago* at the same address; *Rosa de Lago* at B. Caballero (opposite the park); *Cary-Bar* at Nanawa y Monseñor Rodríguez; *Tripolis* for good moderately-priced meal. *Tai Fu*, Chinese, very good value, on 8th floor above *Casa Mona Lisa*, good views. *Dolíbar*, clean and fair value. Cheaper ones in market.

Banks Banco Holandés Unido; Lloyds Bank (ex-BOLSA) agency; local banks (open Mon.-Fri. 0730-1100). Good rates for changing dollars into cruzados available in town.

The leather market at Ciudad Presidente Stroessner is well worth a visit, be sure to bargain.

Communications The road links with the Brazilian road system at Foz do Iguaçu across the bridge (no money changers reported to be available on Brazilian side), from where another 32-km. road leads to the Iguazú Falls. The International bus calls at the town office in Ciudad Stroessner to let people off, then does a circuit to the bus station, airport and then tourist cards are handed out just before crossing into Brazil. Passengers disembark on each side of the bridge. The international bus then goes to the inter-city depot, behind Av. Brasil, at the edge of Foz do Iguaçu. Crossing from Paraguay to Brazil other than on the international bus, you just pay US$2 (in dollars, guaraníes or cruzados) on the Paraguayan side of the bridge, walk across, visit Brazilian immigration, then take a bus to the city terminal (*terminal urbana*), US$0.05, just outside Foz, opposite a military training camp. Remember to put your watch forward 1 hr. From the *terminal urbana*, buses run to the Falls; if only visiting the Brazilian side of the Falls, immigration procedure on the Paraguayan and Brazilian sides of the Friendship Bridge is minimal, even for those normally requiring a visa to visit Brazil.

Many buses (US$4) and colectivos (up to US$5) run to Asunción, 5½-7 hrs. Nuestra Señora and Rysa reported to run the best buses. Bus to Encarnación, along fully paved road, US$3.50.

The **Itaipú** hydroelectric project is close to Ciudad Presidente Stroessner, and well worth a visit. Take a bus to the visitors' centre, about half-way (17 km.) in the direction of Hernandarias. The Visitors' Centre is open 0730-1200, 1330-1700, Sun. and holidays 0800-1200, 1330-1630. Free conducted tours of the project, including film and bus tour, start from here at 0830 Mon.-Sat.; on Sundays and holidays they are at 0830, 0930, 1030 (check times in advance). Take passport. If you don't like guided trips but still wish to visit the largest "hydro" project in the world, apply to head office in Asunción.

Another road from Coronel Oviedo, now paved, runs N to San Estanislao (5,538 people, small historical museum), then (Route 10) NE for 323 km. to the Itaipú dam area, past numerous "colonies" where the jungle is being cleared. There are daily buses from Asunción (14 hrs.).

South-East from Asunción

Route One runs through some of the old mission towns to Encarnación, 370 km. away, on the Alto Paraná.

Km. 37, **Itá** (9,308 inhabitants), an old town turning out rustic pottery. At Carapeguá there is a turn off Route 1 to Ybycuy; 18 km. away is one of the more accessible National Parks (see page 616). Km. 48, **Yaguarón,** founded in 1539, was the centre of the Franciscan missions in colonial times. It is set on a river at the foot of a hill in an orange-growing district, and has a famous church, begun by the Franciscans in 1640 and finished in 1720, and reconstructed in 1885. (Open 0700-1100, 1400-1900.) The tints, made by the Indians from local plants, are still bright on the woodcarvings. Most of Paraguay's petit-grain comes from the area. (For the by-road to Caacupé see page 619.) Buses every 15 mins. or so from Asunción (US$0.60). (*Hotel Silva, Bar Elsi,* both F.)

"The corridor, or outside walk under a projecting roof supported by pillars, is a typical feature of Paraguayan churches. Generally it runs all the way round the church, forming an entrance portico in front. An excellent example is the church at Yaguarón. It is the prototype of the mission sanctuaries of the early 18th century, when the structure was built with a sturdy wooden skeleton and the walls—simple screens of adobe or brick—had no function of support. The belfry is a modest little wooden tower somewhat apart from the church; in the missions it also served as a *mangrullo*, or watch tower." - Paul Dony.

Museum Museo Doctor Francia, 700 metres from church, with relics of Paraguay's first dictator, "El Supremo". Open Tues., Thurs., Sat. 1500-1700; Sun. and holidays 0930-1130; 1500-1700.

Km. 63, **Paraguarí,** founded 1775, the N entrance to the mission area, is on the railway (5,724 people), set among hills with many streams. Its church, though cruder, is reminiscent of the famous church at Yaguarón. It has a curious bell tower.

Hotels *Paraguarí; Domínguez. Pensión San Luis,* F, cheapest, on edge of town.

24 km. north of Route 1 from Eusebio Ayala (pop.: 5,316) is the Vapor Cué National Park, with peaceful swimming and fishing in the river in the middle of fertile cattle country. It contains the remains of seven steamships sunk during the War of the Triple Alliance. Several boilers and one ship have been reconstructed. Camping is permitted, public transport runs to within 4 km. of the site. Transport can be hired in the village.

Just before Km. 141 where the Tebicuary river is crossed by bridge (toll) is Caapucú (*Hotel Misiones,* F). At Km. 161 is **Villa Florida,** an ideal holiday resort for sailing, fishing and relaxing, with first-class hotel, 2 *paradores*, camping near the river (good fishing); also at **Centú Cué,** 5 km. away, on the shores of a lake, there are hotels and camping facilities, for reservations at either, Tel.: Asunción 206570 or directly to Centú Cué 083219. The delightful Jesuit town of **San Juan Bautista,** about half-way between Asunción and Encarnación, is worth stopping at (population 6,872, *Waldorf Hotel*).

Km. 226, San Ignacio Guazú; there is a museum of Guaraní carvings in the old Jesuits' home. About 16 km. to the NE is the new church of Santa María de Fe, with some 60 to 70 Guaraní sculptures in the chapel. From San Ignacio Guazú a road, 156 km., runs W to Pilar (see page 618). Coronel Bogado (5,180 people), km. 319, is the southern limit of the mission area. Turn off Route 1 just before Coronel Bogado to reach the Jesuit ruins of **San Cosme y Damián** (343 km. from Asunción)—church, refectory, etc. The road reaches the Alto Paraná at Carmen del Paraná, km. 331, 40 km. W of Encarnación, the terminus of the railway from Asunción.

Encarnación (pop. 27,632), a busy port on the Alto Paraná, is connected by ferry to the Argentine town of Posadas, from which there is a road and air service to the Iguazú Falls (a bridge is under construction). The town is the centre for the

622 PARAGUAY

construction of the Yacyretá-Apipé dam to be shared by Paraguay and Argentina. Encarnación exports the products of a rich area: timber, soya, *mate*, tobacco, cotton, and hides; it is fast losing its traditional and very rural appearance. A monument to a soldier from the Chaco War, to be found near the harbour, is worth a visit; it is guarded day and night by the military and it is forbidden to take photographs. (Travellers should be prepared for cold weather, despite the latitude). The upper part of the town is not especially interesting, although prices here are lower than downtown near the river. The lower, older part of the colonial town will be flooded when the Yacyretá dam is completed. The cost of living is higher in Encarnación than in other parts of Paraguay, and souvenir prices are much the same as in Posadas. The road along the Alto Paraná to Puerto Presidente Stroessner is now paved.

Hotels *Novohotel Encarnación*, A, first class, Route 1, km. 2, Tel.: 071-5120/24; *Repka*, Arquitecto Pereira 43, a small grey house in pretty garden, private baths, very good home cooking, E, bed and breakfast; *Viena*, Caballero 568 (Tel.: 071-3486), F with bath and breakfast, German-run, friendly, good food, garage; *Paraná*, E without breakfast, new, satisfactory; *Central*, Mcal. López 542, includes private bath and meals, *Viera*, a/c, good location, F, Estigarribia and 25 de Mayo, breakfast, gambling, private bath; *Hospedaje San Cayetano*, F, near station, clean, fan, hot shower, good restaurant downstairs; *Rueda*, F, near bus station, hot water, clean, fan, mosquito repellant required. *Suizo*, Mcal. Estigarribia 562, just below bus terminal, F with breakfast, clean; *Latino*, next door clean, hot water, fan, F; *Colón*; others near railway station such as *Hospedaje Comercio* and *Hospedaje El Torbellino*, *Pensión la Yuteña*, all F (basic). *Pensión Vila Alegre*, Antequera 951, F, very primitive but the people are pleasant and the food excellent.

Restaurant *Ara-Mi*, centrally located in the upper town, good food, pleasant. *Rubi*, Chinese, Mcal. Estigarribia 519, near railway, excellent but pricey; and *Restaurant Paraná*, international cuisine, on Mcal. Estigarribia (main street) and Memmel. *Bar-Restaurant Imperial*, Iturbe, corner Estigarribia, good and cheap; *Rosita*, Mcal. Estigarribia 1109, good meal, US$3.50; *Karanday*, Gral. Caballero, good grill but poor wines; *Confitería Tokio*, Estigarribia 484, good.

Taxis Horsedrawn (about US$0.25), but prices tend to be high if drivers suspect you don't know the distance you want to travel. Some motor driven ones for those in a hurry. Horse-drawn taxi from railway station US$1.25 (compared to US$3.75 by car).

Bank Lloyds Bank (ex-BOLSA), agency at Villarrica y Mariscal Estigarribia, open Mon.-Fri. 0730-1100. Many money-changers at the Paraguayan side but will only change notes—better rates for australes here than in Argentina. For travellers' cheques you need a *casa de cambio*, to be found in Mariscal Estagarribia (Thomas Cook cheques preferred), it is difficult to change money at weekends.

Tourist Office Kiosk on the ferry pier.

Consulate Argentine, at Cabañas y Mallorquín.

Transport Bus to Asunción, about 6 hours, US$3.50 with Rysa, colectivo with Halcones. (Bus terminal is above the town, up the main street; good cheap snacks at the terminal.) Train to Asunción, 18 (can take 24) hours, US$3, 1st class, US$1.90, 2nd class, Sun. at 0500, Wed. at 1130. Bus to Trinidad, US$0.40, 30 mins., every hour. Bus to Puerto Stroessner US$3.50, several daily, 3 hrs. Buses also to Villarrica. Boats to Asunción leave Wed. 1600.

Passenger ferry to Posadas, 6 a day (last at 1720), 3 on Sat. and 2 on Sun., less than US$1, baggage extra; car ferry 4 times a day. Taxi from dock to bus terminal, US$0.75. The bridge linking Encarnación with Posadas will be open for cars and trains.

Warning On arrival, foreign travellers are searched at the ferry terminal (principally for "communist" literature), and then you have to purchase an entry card for US$3, payable in dollars.

Nearby is the village where *anillas de coca*—wooden rings inlaid with mother-of-pearl designs—are made.

Beyond Encarnación, the road goes on 28 km. to Trinidad, and beyond to the thriving German settlements of Obligado and Bella Vista (another, Colonia Hohenau, is due E of Trinidad on the Alto Paraná); this road continues N, fully paved, as Route 6, paralleling the Alto Paraná, to meet Route 7 near Ciudad Presidente Stroessner. Beyond again, 71 km. from Encarnación, is the Japanese Colonia Pirapó.

At **Trinidad** there is a great Jesuit church, once utterly in ruins but restoration should be finished soon and a museum set up. The church was founded in 1706 by Padre Juan de Anaya; the architect was Juan Batista Primol. For information, or tours of the ruins, contact Sr. Augusto Servián Goana, Ruinas Trinidad, Itapúa, Encarnación. A visit is recommended, also for the surrounding countryside. Ten km. N of Trinidad, at Jesús, there is another ruined church, which is also being restored (frequent but irregular minibuses between Trinidad and Jesús). Bus service to Encarnación hourly from 0630 (US$0.25, ¾-hr. journey).

Next to the ruined church at Trinidad is a small modern church; it contains a large carved wooden statue of the Deity, so hollowed at the back that a priest in hiding could simulate the resounding voice of the Eternal Father to impress the Indians of the mission.

Twenty km. before Encarnación on the highway from Trinidad is *Hotel Tirol del Paraguay* (Capitán Miranda, Ruta 6, km. 20), a stunning hotel with 3 swimming pools, chalets with private terrace, bath, TV, a/c for 40 people and a landing strip; Belgian-run, with good food.

The Paraguayan Chaco

Michael Wigan writes:

The Paraguayan Chaco covers 24 million hectares, but under 100,000 people live there. A single road, the Transchaco Highway, runs in a straight line northwest to the Bolivian border 20 km. beyond Nueva Asunción. It begins as an excellent asphalt top turning into a levelled earthen road of average quality. It seldom rains but if it does all vehicles slither about hopelessly: you cannot move till it dries. The elevation rises very gradually from 50 metres opposite Asunción to 450 metres on the Bolivian border.

The Chaco is divisible into 3 terrains. The first, the Low Chaco, leaving Asunción, is open palm forest and marshes, much of which is permanently beneath shallow water. The lack of slope and the impermeable clay hardpan mean the water hardly moves. The palm forest is used for cattle ranching of the most extensive type, some *estancias* lying several hundred km. down tracks off the highway. The cattle are very mixed—English Herefords, Indian Brahmins, and Brazilian. Most *estancias* are chronically overstocked and overgrazed; calving rates are very low. Remote *estancias* have their own airfields, and all are equipped with 2-way radios.

The Middle Chaco, around the capital, Filadelfia, has been settled by Mennonites, latterday Baptists chiefly of German extraction who arrived in Paraguay from 1930 onwards. They set up three distinct colonies: Menno (from Canada and Mexico, but originally from Russia); Fernheim (the first group directly from Russia) and Neuland (the last group to arrive, also from Russia, after 1945). The Mennonites speak "plattdeutsch" - a cross between Dutch and German, and normal "hochdeutsch"; very few speak Spanish. Altogether there are 118 villages with a population of about 10,000 Mennonites, 10,000 Indians and a very small number of other immigrants. The natural cover is scrubland with a mixture of hardwoods, and more cactus further north. The bottle-tree with a pear-shaped, water-conserving, trunk, and the *quebracho* (axe-breaker), used for tannin, are native. The Mennonites, who run their own banks, schools, hospitals and a cooperative agricultural system, are the only organized community in the Chaco. They are mainly crop-farmers (though they also run dairy cattle and make cheese and butter) and grow grapefruit, lemons, groundnuts, sorghum and cotton.

From Filadelfia an alternative route goes north and into the north-west Chaco where most of the remaining jaguars are found. This road is very rough, but the main highway remains negotiable by car although it narrows. In the western sector scattered military outposts are the only human presence. The whole area is under military jurisdiction; the visitor may find a letter of authorization or military introduction useful.

The north-western part, the High Chaco, is a low thorn forest, an impenetrable barricade of hard spikes and spiny branches resistant to fire, heat and drought. Occasional tracks lead off the highway for a short distance. Towards Bolivia cactus becomes more concentrated. In this remote and extremely inhospitable region the Government has deliberately discouraged mining and oil companies, and is restricting land sales. However, there are a few *estancias* further

624 PARAGUAY

south, where the brush is bulldozed into hedges and the trees left for shade. In summer it is very hot. The animal life—wild hog, puma, jaguar, tapir—congregates around the water-holes at night. The whole area is a national park.

The primeval character of the Chaco is reflected in the 1975 discovery of a kind of wild hog, formerly thought extinct since the Pleistocene era, now listed as Wagner's peccary. When camping out fires should be kept up to deter the local fauna; the greatest danger is from several species of poisonous snakes. Grass round the tent should be cut. The highway is a smuggling route from Bolivia, so it is unwise to stop for anyone in the night. In the High Chaco there is almost no traffic.

The Chaco's Indian population is nomadic and Guaraní-speaking, and sets up little brushwood and mud villages wherever there is a plentiful food-supply. The Indians eat everything, bird and mammal, and even the poisonous snakes. The great delicacy is armadillo. Anthropologists have found the Indians' social structures, marriage and death rites as inscrutable as the surrounding countryside. They are friendly and peaceful, and periodically work on the *estancias*.

No expedition should be without supplies of water, food and fuel. Although there are service stations in the Middle and Low Chaco self-sufficiency is advised. Ill-equipped expeditions have had to be rescued by the army or have come to grief. In winter temperatures are warm and comfortable by day, cooler by night. In summer heat and mosquitoes make it very unpleasant. The Low Chaco is one of the foremost bird habitats in the world, and although bird-life may be enjoyed from the road it is still comparatively unknown and rarely visited. Tourists are unheard-of. Until recently entry into the Chaco was by plane only. The rapid development of the Highway will surely open it up before long.

Martin Crossland writes: A bus ride to **Filadelfia** (472 km.), in the Chaco, from Asunción, costs US$5 with the Nueva Asunción bus company, daily at 2200 (direct, 7 hrs.) and a slow bus, 8-10 hours (US$4). After about 350 km., one starts seeing the Mennonites' neat little homes with painted wooden shutters, surrounded by flowering plants and orchards. The paved section ends at km. 386, so avoid the trip on rainy days as the buses often get stuck. The centres are Filadelfia and Loma Plata, clean modern agricultural communities with wide dusty streets. The Unger Museum at Filadelfia gives a good idea what this industrious people had to go through to make this rich area what it is today (open Tues. and Fri. 1100-1730; at other times ask at the Information Office, two doors left of *Hotel Florida*). Some Indian tribes live nearby, but have been "civilized", seemingly to their disadvantage.

The Mennonite bus company, Chaco Boreal, leaves from the colonies for Asunción on Mon., Wed., and Fri., US$5; leaves Asunción at 1600 from the Comité Central Menonita, Colombia with Estados Unidos, make reservations early; the bus passes all 3 communities and ends at Neuland.

Hotel *Florida*, in Filadelfia, new wing with a/c and private bath, D, old section, fans and shared bath, F. **Restaurants:** *Girasol*; *La Estrella* recommended for good ice cream and *asados*; another good restaurant opposite. Plenty of good ice cream parlours (you need them in the heat), but no bars. Nearby is **Loma Plata** (*Hotel Loma Plata*, E, with restaurant). There is also the Unger museum (see above) and an Indian handicraft shop. 2 km south-east is the Parque Trébol, a charming public park, with facilities where one can camp. Lots of frog noise at night, however. Good hotel in the village of Neu Hallestadt, Neuland, is *Boquerón*, E with breakfast. Ask around in Filadelfia for people to drive you round the Mennonite communities (US$0.15 per km.). A useful tip, if space permits is to buy a ticket for the 2100 Filadelfia-Asunción bus, but take the 1430 bus, get out at Loma Plata to see the town, then catch the 2100 bus when it passes through at 2130. See also notes on travel into the Chaco under Concepción, page 617.

To Bolivia From Filadelfia to the Bolivian border at General Eugenio A Garay is 304 km. Work on paving the road is progressing seven days a week. There are facilities every 50 km. (cafés, petrol). Oil trucks travel all the way to Bolivia. You can try to hitch. Frequent Army identity checks are inevitable. It is important to have photographs on documents which are a good likeness to the bearer. Backpackers need expect no special difficulties. Take plenty of food and water since even the smallest amount of rain can cause delays. If entering Bolivia by this route it is important to visit the Bolivian Consul in Asunción first, as the papers and instructions he will supply can help reduce the problems of crossing considerably.

The Economy

Paraguay is essentially an agricultural country; farming employs 50% of the labour force, and accounts for 27% of gdp. Agricultural exports earn over 93% of Paraguay's foreign exchange with normally about 80% coming from cotton and soya. Cattle raising and meat exports used to be the principal agricultural activities, but their importance has declined as a result of uncompetitive pricing policies and import restrictions in potential markets. Fluctuations in the value of

PARAGUAY

exports characterize the performance of Paraguay's main commodities, since they are so subject to the weather and world prices. For example, in 1986 there was a dramatic turn-around as meat exports increased from US$1.5m in 1985 to US$44.3m to satisfy Brazilian demand. Other major products are timber, tobacco, tung and other industrial oilseeds, essential oils (mainly petit grain) and *quebracho*. Self-sufficiency in wheat has been achieved since 1985, and the country now grows most of its basic food requirements.

Industry has traditionally been dependent upon agriculture: for instance, cotton ginning, sugar milling, textiles, meat packing, timber processing and extraction of *quebracho*, industrial and essential oils. The country industrialized fast in the 1970s and early 1980s, and manufacturing now accounts for 17% of gdp. As a result of economic recession since 1983, between 40% and 50% of industrial capacity is unused. On the back of hydroelectric development, Paraguay has its own cement industry and a steel plant opened in 1986. Both these, shipbuilding and the distillation of alcohol for fuel and other purposes, are state-owned. 14% of the workforce are employed in manufacturing, 8% in onstruction.

The massive hydroelectric scheme undertaken by Brazil and Paraguay at Itaipú on the river Paraná is reported to be the largest of its kind in the world. Both the total cost, of about US$15.3bn, and the final capacity, of 12.6m kilowatts, are to be shared equally between the two countries. Paraguay's share already exceeds domestic requirements and the surplus energy is being sold to Brazil now that a high-tension line to São Paulo is in place. Paraguay is cooperating with Argentina on the construction of the Yacyretá-Apipé plant, also on the river Paraná, to produce 2.7m kilowatts. Civil works have begun, but the project has been frequently delayed, not least by financing difficulties in Argentina. A third Argentine-Paraguayan hydroelectric project, Corpus, has been postponed until the turn of the century at the earliest. Paraguay has its own hydroelectric facility at Acaray. Ample electricity reserves are not matched by hydrocarbons. Exploration is being undertaken in the East and in the Chaco, so far without success.

Until 1983, Paraguay managed to offset its current account and trade deficits with capital inflows for Itaipú. Since the completion of civil works, the overall balance of payments has fallen into deficit, with a consequent drain on international reserves. In 1986, the situation was exacerbated by the World Bank and the Inter-American Development Bank refusing to disburse loans until a more realistic exchange rate was adopted. This was eventually done at the year's end, but too late to eliminate the effects of a long-overvalued guaraní on trade and industry. It is estimated that unrealistic exchange rates encourage about half of Paraguay's exports to leave the country illegally, while contraband imports have adversely affected industry's sales on the home market.

Paraguay has not yet needed to reschedule its external debt, but a combination of grace periods ending, a poor export performance and dwindling reserves, led the authorities to hold talks with the IMF. In 1986, total external debt was US$1.9bn; amortization and interest payments in that year were estimated at 82% of exports, compared with 43% in 1984.

	1961-70 (av)	1971-80 (av)	1981-85 (av)	1986 (e)
Gdp growth (1980 prices)	4.3%	8.6%	2.3%	-4.0%
Inflation	3.3%	13.1%	15.8%	30.0%
Exports (fob) US$m	50	231	361	233
Cotton	3	46	151	78
Soyabeans	—	29	101	44
Imports (fob) US$m	59	300	640	509
Current account balance US$m (cum)	-158	-897	-1,539	-258

Information for Visitors

By Air from Europe Iberia has a twice weekly service to Asunción from Madrid, via Rio and São Paulo. Air France via Rio. Líneas Aéreas Paraguayas (LAP—now a member of IATA) has a twice-weekly service from Frankfurt, via Brussels, Madrid (once a week) and Recife (cheaper than most). From other points in Europe, slow connections can be made via Rio or São Paulo (Varig).

From North America Eastern operates twice a week to Asunción from Washington and/or New York, via La Paz (only once a week) and one or two other points. LAP also operates flights (four weekly) from Miami to Asunción. Alternatively from New York, connections every day via Rio, but Varig's connecting flights are slow. From California, connections most days via Lima; cheapest, Lloyd Aéreo Boliviano (LAB), Fridays.

Within South America From Montevideo (5 flights a week) by Líneas Aéreas Paraguayas (LAP) or Pluna; from Buenos Aires (15 a week) by Aerolíneas Argentinas (via Resistencia or Corrientes), LAP or Iberia; from Santiago (3 a week) by Ladeco (Chile) and LAP; from Lima (4 a week) by LAP or Eastern; from Guayaquil (twice a week) by Eastern; from La Paz (twice a week) by Eastern, or via Santa Cruz (2 a week) by LAP or LAB (probably now payable in U.S. dollars or credit card only); from Rio, São Paulo and Iguazú Falls (daily) by Varig; also from São Paulo (daily) and thrice weekly to Rio de Janeiro by LAP.

Airport Tax is US$2 (exit), US$3 (arrival) payable in US$ or guaraníes.

From Europe Lamport & Holt Line (sailings from Glasgow), Paraguay Linie (from Grangemouth and continental ports), Flumar and Rotterdam-Zuid Amerika Lijn (ex-continent only)—The Paraguay Linie occasionally goes on from Asunción to Concepción. UK agent: Scottish Express, Argyll Av., Renfrew PA4 9ET (Tel.: 041-886 5931) or Belgian agent: Westcott Shipping, NV Brouwersvliet 21, B-2000 Antwerpen (Tel.: 03-231 29 20).

From the U.S.A. The Holland Pan-American Line, New York office: 233 Broadway, New York 10004. Tel.: 791-8450 (bookings also through van Nievelt, Goudriaan & Co. B.V., Veerhaven 2, 3016 CJ Rotterdam), has a direct service between New York and Asunción.

From Argentina The international rail route from Buenos Aires to Posadas is given on page 104. At Posadas the train passengers cross the Alto Paraná to Encarnación, from which there is a line to Asunción; 44 hrs. total journey, distance, 1,510 km. (trains will use the new bridge when it is open). There is a paved road from Buenos Aires via Santa Fe to Clorinda and then on new paved roads via the border at Puerto Pilcomayo (Falcón) and the new Remanso Castillo suspension bridge to Asunción: 1,370 km., about 23 hrs. Good bus service on this route. After the border at Puerto Pilcomayo (Falcón), before the Remanso Castillo bridge, a road forks to the Paraguayan Chaco (paved as far as Filadelfia) and on to Bolivia.

From Brazil The headwaters of both the Paraguay and the Alto Paraná are in Brazil. There are unscheduled boat services from Asunción northward along the Paraguay river to Porto Esperança, Brazil (from which there is a railway to São Paulo), and scheduled services to Corumbá (1,220 km.—see page 615), which is connected by road, rail and air with Bolivian and Brazilian cities. Frontier with Brazil is officially closed at weekends but it is worth checking as sometimes passports will be stamped on Sunday.

International Bus Services. See under Asunción, page 616.

Travel in Paraguay: By Rail There are more than 600 km. of public railways, and 732 km. of private industrial lines, mostly forest lines of metre gauge or narrower. The standard-gauge railways are the 370 km. from Asunción to Encarnación, the 200 km. from Puerto La Victoria into the Chaco, and 64 km. from Borja (on Asunción-Encarnación line) to Abaí.

By Air There are scheduled services to most parts of the country by the Paraguayan Transportes Aéreos Militares (TAM) and Líneas Aéreas de Transporte Nacional (LATN). Planes can be chartered.

By Road Buses ply on the main roads. For motorists, there are sufficient service stations in Paraguay, except in the Chaco area. Motorists should beware stray cattle on the road at night. Diesel fuel is US$0.25 per litre in Paraguay but car users should only use *super*, US$0.45 per litre (which is 93 octane; regular petrol (*alconafta*) contains 10-15% alcohol at US$0.40 per litre). It is

PARAGUAY

highly recommended that drivers in Paraguay (and neighbouring countries) use diesel-powered vehicles: not only is diesel usually cheaper than gasoline, but a diesel engine will not stop in water, has no ignition/carburettor problems, and will not encounter the corrosive effects of alcohol in the fuel. Gasoline in Paraguay is the most expensive on the South American continent: motor fuel and oil is sold in Paraguay by the litre. The documents needed in Paraguay for private cars are *carnet de passages en douanes*, international car registration and driver's licence. For entry into Brazil the only document necessary is the title to the car (or other proof of ownership). There are Esso and Shell road maps of Paraguay. It is essential to drive at walking pace through military areas and stop completely if a flag ceremony is in progress.

Motor Repairs A recommended mechanic is Lauro C. Noldin, Dr. Moleón Andreu y 4ta (at Felix Bogado y General Santos, on the way to Itá Enramada), Tel.: Asunción 26788; he repairs Land Rover, Range Rover, Jaguar and all makes of British, European, American and Japanese cars, diesel and petrol engines. Motorcycles, power generators for motor homes. Bosch Garage Office, Chispa S.A., Carios y José Rivera, Asunción, Tel.: 27290/1. For diesel service (all British makes, inc. Lucas-CAV), M.B.T. service garage at Av. Eusebio Ayala y Lapacho km. 4, Tel.: Asunción 27350. Land Rover body repairs at Taller San José of José Escobar at Battilana, casi Santo Domingo; Tel.: 203311. A recommended Land Rover parts source is Repuestos Agromotor at Herrera 604, Asunción. Good mechanics at Premetal Alemán, near crossing Eusebio Ayala with Rep. Argentina (Tel.: 64131). Spares are available in Paraguay for all makes of car (European, North American, Asian); also available are most makes of tyre.

Tourist Information The Dirección Nacional de Turismo has an office at the corner of Alberdi and Oliva, Asunción. More fruitful sources of information, particularly about weather and roads, are the Touring & Automobile Club of Paraguay at 25 de Mayo y Brasil, and the office of the traffic police in Asunción. The best map is available from Instituto Geográfico Militar, Av. Artigas (on the way to the zoo), price US$4.50, take passport. The USAID office has a good booklet on Paraguay. Other books: *Así es el Paraguay* (with maps and very useful information) and *Paraguay, Land of Lace and Legend* (reprinted 1983, available from bookshops and Anglo-Paraguayan and US-Paraguay cultural institutes in Asunción); also *Green Hill, Far Away*, by Peter Upton.

Passport The entry requirement is a passport. Visitors are registered on arrival by the immigration authorities and get their documents back immediately. Visas are normally not required for a stay of up to 90 days, by visitors who hold tourist cards, which are issued to non-visa holders on arrival by air or land; they cost US$3. If you do not complete formalities you can be turned back at the border, or have trouble when leaving Paraguay. This concession does not apply to citizens of France and the communist countries, who need visas (US$8—we have received a report that Canadians also need visas, but this is not so according to the Embassy in London). Visitors with U.S.S.R., Cuban and various Central American entry stamps in their passports may be refused entry, others may have to surrender their passports and undergo interrogation by the police; there appears to be no hard and fast rule so a lot depends on the official's mood or even your appearance. (Restrictions on Asians are being applied for immigration purposes.)

Customs "Reasonable quantities" of tobacco products, alcoholic drinks and perfume are admitted free of duty.

Warnings The prejudice against "hippie-looking" people carrying rucksacks seems to have diminished. The proverbial "official-looking" letter is, however, still useful. Searches for "communist" literature are made at land borders. Any public criticism of the Government is unwise and can result in a stay in prison; as can taking pictures of "military" installations, for instance, Itaipú. Backpackers entering via Clorinda may have problems crossing the International Bridge; it is therefore recommended that they enter Paraguay via Puerto Pilcomayo or Ciudad Presidente Stroessner. Apparently, hitch-hiking is still illegal, although possible in rural areas.

Currency The Guaraní (plural Guaraníes) is the unit of currency, symbolized by the letter G (crossed). There are bank notes for 100, 500, 1,000, 5,000 and 10,000 guaraníes and coins for 1, 5, 10 and 50 guaraníes. It is possible to buy US dollar bills in Asunción (see page 614), and rates for all foreign currencies, except Bolivian bolivianos, are reasonable. Get rid of all your guaraníes before leaving Paraguay; there is no market for them elsewhere (except in some *cambios* in Buenos Aires or Montevideo). *Casas de cambio* will cash travellers' cheques for U.S. dollars in Asunción for a 1% commission. Visa and Mastercharge cash advances are a possibility in Asunción. Street dealers operate from early in the morning until late at night, even at weekends or public holidays. In Asunción their rates are marginally better than the *casas de cambio*, but they are not recommended at Ciudad Presidente Stroessner. Many cheap hotels will neither accept nor change travellers' cheques although they may accept credit cards.

Visa and Mastercharge credit cards are widely accepted even for small purchases. Foreign-issued Visa cards may not always be accepted though a phone call will often resolve the problem; Visa is displayed as Unioncard. Credit card transactions are subject to a 10% tax.

628 PARAGUAY

Sports Football is very popular. Tennis and horse-racing are popular. There are two rowing and swimming clubs of some 2,000 members, and a motor-boat club with 150 members, in Asunción. Golf is played in the Botanical Garden, and there is a Paraguayan Aviation Club. There are two boxing rings. Fishing, basketball and rugby football are popular.

Business Visitors Nearly all foreign business is transacted in Asunción; business visitors do not generally find it worth while to visit other parts of the country. From May to October is the best time for a visit. British business travellers are advised to get a copy of "Hints to Exporters: Paraguay", obtainable from the Department of Trade, Sanctuary Buildings, 16-20 Gt. Smith Street, London SW1P 3DB.

Business Hours Paraguayans are up early and many shops, offices and businesses open between 0630 and 0700. *Siesta* (generally observed during the hot season) is from 1200 to 1500. Commercial office hours are from 0730 to 1100 or 1130, and 1430 or 1500 to 1730 or 1900. Banks: from 0700 to 1030 in summer and 0700 to 1130 in winter, closed on Sat. Government offices are open 0630 to 1130 in summer, 0730 to noon, in winter, open on Sat.

Weights and Measures The metric system is used except by carpenters, who use inches.

Electricity 220 volts and 50 cycles.

Postal and Telegraph Services The telephone service links the main towns, and there is a telephone service with most countries. Time is 3-4 hrs. behind GMT (clocks go on one hour in the local summer).

A phone call to Europe, Australia, and South Africa costs US$2.50 a minute; U.S.A. Canada, US$2 a minute; Spain, US$1.50 a minute. A telex message to Britain is US$5 (1 minute). A normal airmail letter to Europe costs US$0.50 and a registered air letter US$2. Register important mail if you want it delivered. Parcels may be sent from main post office on El Paraguayo Independiente, Asunción. Rates: up to 5 kg., US$3 by surface, US$10 by air; 15-20 kg., US$10 by surface, US$35 by air. Customs inspection of open parcel required.

Climate and What to Wear The climate is sub-tropical, with a marked difference between summer and winter and often between one day and the next throughout the year. Summer (Jan.-March), is hot. Temperatures range from 25 to 43°C: tropical clothing; sunglasses and an umbrella are needed. The autumn (April-June) is mild, but nights are cold. During winter (July-Sept.) the temperature can be as low as 5°C, though it can equally well be much higher. Temperatures below freezing are rare, and it never snows. The best time for a visit is from May to September; at other times the heat is often oppressive. The heaviest rains are from October to April, but some rain falls each month.

Cost of Living is generally cheap. Hotels in our G range are hard to find although there are many good ones in our F-E ranges, with breakfast, private shower and toilet. Hotels near the hydroelectric construction sites are often more expensive and require booking.

Tipping Hotels, restaurants, 10%. Railway and airport porters US$0.15 a suitcase. Porters at docks US$0.40 a suitcase. Cinema usherettes are not tipped.

Car Hire Hertz offers unlimited mileage for reasonable rates, free delivery to airport, minimum rental 3 days, but no insurance whatsoever. You will be responsible for any accident, damage or theft.

What to Buy The famous *ñandutí* lace, made exclusively by the women of Itauguá (see page 618). The local jewellery is also attractive. Handmade *ahopoí* (fine cloth) is suitable for shirts and blouses, and there are cotton thread belts in all colours. The best place to buy these items is Villarrica. Tourists are often attracted by the leather articles, the pottery and small wooden articles made from Paraguayan woods. Some of these are exhibited, and sold, at the Inter-Express Travel Agency's shop, Galería del Turista. See also "Shopping", under Asunción (see page 613). Imported goods, especially cameras and film, are cheaper in Paraguay than in most other Latin American countries, particularly in Ciudad Presidente Stroessner, which is a free port (although prices in the U.K., for instance, are cheaper).

Health Tuberculosis, typhoid, dysentery, and hepatitis are endemic. Hookworm is the most common disease in the country, and there is much venereal disease, goitre and leprosy. Visitors should be inoculated against tetanus, typhoid, and paratyphoid. Be very careful over such things as salad and tap water. Medical fees and medicine costs are high. The Centro Paraguayo del Diagnóstico, Gral. Díaz 986 y Colón, Asunción, is recommended as inexpensive,

PARAGUAY 629

foreign languages spoken. Dentists can be found either at the centre, or at Odontologia 3, Mcal. Estigarribia 1414 y Pai Pérez, Tel.: 200175, Asunción.

Newspapers *La Tribuna; Hoy, Ultima Hora. Sendero*, Catholic.

Official Holidays Jan. 1, Feb. 3, March 1, Maundy Thursday, Good Friday, May 1, 14, 15, Corpus Christi, June 12, Aug. 15, 25, Sep. 29, Oct. 12, Nov. 1, Dec. 8, 25.

Food and Drink Typical local foods include *chipas* (maize bread flavoured with egg and cheese) and *sopa paraguaya* (a kind of dumpling of ground maize and onion). *Soyo* is a soup of different meats and vegetables, or sometimes just soya, delicious; *albóndiga* a soup of meat balls; *bori bori* another type of soup with diced meat, vegetables, and small balls of maize mixed with cheese. *Palmitos* (palm hearts) should not be missed; the beef is excellent in better class restaurants (best cuts are *lomo* and *lomito*). *Parrillada completa* is recommended. *Surubí*, a Paraná river fish, is delicious. Sugar-cane juice, greatly beloved, is known as *mosto*. Fruit is magnificent. Very typical of Paraguay is *tereré* (cold *mate* with digestive herbs) for warm days and hot *mate* to warm you up on cold days. The national wine is not recommended.

We would like to thank Brooke Hart (Peace Corps, Asunción), Brian and Christina Turner (Caazapá), and Chris and Kathy Van Straaten (Asunción). We are also grateful to the following travellers: Richard and Sharon Alexander (Auckland 5), Barbera Bot and Bob Domburg (Maasland, Neth.), Lynne and Hugh Davies (Mill Valley, Ca.), Karel Devijver (Leuwen, Belg.), "F" (London NW1), Volker Filss (Oberhausen, W.Ger.) for some extremely useful notes; Harry Floyd (London W8), Toni García and Diego Caña (Barcelona), Theodor H.Gevert (São Paulo), Timothy Gluch (Welland, Ont.), Bill Hammond (Madrid), Ricardo Heyenn and Karin Kubitsch (Hamburg), Marianne Hydara (Wels, Austria), Doeke de Jong and Wigle Sinnema (Friesland, Neth.), Carmen Kuczma (Powell River, BC), G.Lawson (Canberra), Frank Mahoney (Portland, Ore.), Werner von Marinelli (Eindhoven), Sabine Marquardt and Mario Michalak (Leverkusen, W.Ger.), Paolo Nasuti (Venice), Jens Plahte (Aas, Norway), Eberhard Ruth (Bühl, W.Ger.), Stephen Saks and Andrea Keir (Melbourne), Charlotte and Mike Sharp (Lima), Tina Tecaru (Burton-on-Trent), Doris Vaterlaus and David Froelicher (Thalwil, Switz.), and Andrew Waterworth and Kerrie Oldfield (Neutral Bay, NSW).

WILL YOU HELP US?

We do all we can to get our facts right in *The South American Handbook*. Each chapter is thoroughly revised each year, but Latin America and the Caribbean cover a vast area, and our eyes cannot be everywhere. A new highway or airport is built; a hotel, a restaurant, a cabaret dies; another, a good one is born; a building we describe is pulled down, a street renamed. Names and addresses of good hotels and restaurants for "budget-minded" travellers are always very welcome. We would especially like to receive maps and diagrams of towns and cities, walks, national parks and other interesting areas to use as source material for the Handbook and other forthcoming titles.

Your information may be far more up-to-date than ours. If your letter reaches us early enough in the year it will be used in the next edition, but write whenever you want to, for all your letters are used sooner or later.

Thank you very much indeed for your help.

**Trade & Travel Publications Limited
5 Prince's Buildings, George Street,
Bath BA1 2ED. England**

PERU

	Page		Page
Introductory	630	The Inca Road	754
Lima	634	The Economy	755
North-West from Lima	657	Information for visitors	756
South-East from Lima	689	Maps	635, 661, 676, 693,
Cuzco	710		713, 720, 747
Inland from Lima	734		

PERU, the third largest South American country, over twice the size of France, presents formidable difficulties to human habitation. The whole of its western seaboard with the Pacific is desert on which rain seldom falls. From this coastal shelf the Andes rise steeply to a high Sierra which is studded with massive groups of soaring mountains and gouged with deep canyons. The highland slopes more gradually eastwards; the mountains in its eastern zone are deeply forested and ravined. Eastward from these mountains lie the vast jungle lands of the Amazon basin.

The coastal region, a narrow ribbon of desert 2,250 km. long, takes up 11% of the country and holds 44% of the population. When irrigated, the river valleys are extremely fertile. Almost 600,000 hectares are watered today, creating 40 oases which grow cotton throughout the country, sugar-cane and rice in the N, and grapes, fruit and olives in the S. Petroleum comes from the N and Amazonia. The coastal zone is the economic heart of Peru; it consumes most of the imports and supplies half of the exports. Climate is determined by cold sea-water adjoining deserts: prevailing inshore winds pick up so little moisture over the cold Peruvian current that only for five months, from June to October, does it condense. The resultant blanket of cloud and sea-mist extends from the S to about 200 km. N of Lima. This *garúa* dampens isolated coastal zones of vegetation (called *lomas*) and they are grazed by livestock driven down from the mountains. The Peruvian coastal current teems with fish, and Peru has had the largest catch in the world; however, in recent years, the *anchoveta* shoals have moved southward into Chilean waters. At intervals during December-April a current of warm water, known as "El Niño", is blown S from the equator over the cold offshore waters and the surface temperature rises, the fish migrate, and evaporation is so great that the desert is deluged with rain which creates havoc (most recently in 1983).

In the Sierra, at an average altitude of 3,000 metres, which covers 26% of the country, live about 50% of the people, an excessive density on such poor land. This high-level land of gentle slopes is surrounded by towering groups and ranges of high peaks. Ten are over 6,000 metres; the highest, Huascarán, is 6,768 metres. There are many volcanoes in the S. The continental divide is the western rim of mountains looking down on the Pacific. Rivers which rise in these *mountains and flow towards the* Amazon cut through the cold surface of the plateau in canyons, sometimes 1,500 metres deep, in which the climate is tropical. Pastoral farming is possible on about 13 million hectares of the plateau; the deep valley basins contain the best land for arable farming.

The plateau, mountains and canyons are inhabited mostly by Indians. There are 5,000 Indian communities but few densely populated settlements. Their literacy rate is the lowest of any comparable group in S. America and their diet is 40% below acceptable levels. Nearly 99% of the rural population and 60% of the town dwellers have no running water or drainage. About two million Indians speak no Spanish, their main tongue being Quechua, the language of the Incas; they are largely outside the money economy.

A mostly Indian labour force of over 80,000 is engaged in mining, and mineral exports from the Sierra represent half of total exports. Minerals are extracted as far up as 5,200 metres. Some of the sheep-farming areas are at altitudes ranging up to 4,250 metres.

The wide areas of high and wind-swept Altiplano in S Peru are near the limit of agriculture—though some potatoes and cereals (quinoa and cañihua) are grown—but the Indians use it for grazing llamas, alpacas and sheep; it cannot support cattle. The pastoral Indians of the area live off their flocks; they weave their clothes from the wools, eat the meat, use the dried dung for fuel and the llamas for transport. They are, in short, almost entirely self-supporting.

The **Montaña,** or **Selva,** the forested eastern half of the Andes and the land beyond covered with tropical forest and jungle, is 62% of the country's area but holds only about 5% of the population. Its inhabitants are crowded on the river banks in the cultivable land—a tiny part of the area. The few roads (given in the text) have to cope with dense forest, deep valleys, and sharp eastern slopes ranging from 2,150 metres in the N to 5,800 metres E of Lake Titicaca. Rivers are the main highways, though navigation is hazardous and the draught of the vessels shallow. The area's potential is enormous: immense reserves of timber, excellent land for the production of rubber, jute, rice, tropical fruits and coffee and the breeding of cattle. Few of these products come out by road to the W; most of them converge by river on Iquitos, which is 11,250 km. from Callao via the Panama Canal and the Amazon but only 1,010 km. as the condor flies.

Oilfields have been discovered southwards from the Ecuadorean border E of Iquitos down as far as Pucallpa. An intensive oil search is going on; estimates indicate that about 83% of Peru's oil reserves are in the jungle area. The Nor Peruano oil pipeline linking the Amazon area with the coast is in operation and Occidental Oil has discovered a large oil deposit; Peru is now a net exporter.

Climate The climate of the highlands is varied: the W side is dry, but the northern and eastern parts get very heavy rains from October to April, and are heavily forested up to a limit of 3,350 metres: the grasslands are between the forest line and the snowline, which rises from 5,000 metres in the latitude of Lima to 5,800 metres in the S. Most of the Sierra is covered with grasses and shrubs, with Puna vegetation (bunch grass mixed with low, hairy-leaved plants) from N of Huarás to the S.

Communications Several roads and two railways run up the slopes of the Andes to reach the Sierra. These railways, once British owned, run from Lima in the centre and the ports of Matarani and Mollendo in the S. There are in all 2,740 km. of railway. There are three main paved roads: the Inter-American Highway runs N-S through the coastal desert and sends a spur NE into the Sierra to Arequipa, with a partially paved continuation to Puno on Lake Titicaca which then skirts the lake to Desaguadero, on the Bolivian frontier, a total of 3,418 km.; the Central Highway from Lima to Huancayo, which continues (mostly paved) to Pucallpa in the Amazon basin; and the direct road from Lima N to Huarás. Both roads and railways are given in the text and shown on sketch maps.

Pre-History Two Harvard archaeologists, Michael Moseley and Robert Feldman, concluded, following excavations at coastal sites at Ancón, Supe, etc., that an early civilization sprang up on the coast on the basis of a fishing economy and was well developed by 2100 BC. (This is in complete contradiction of one of archaeology's basic tenets that development of agriculture must invariably precede civilization.) The key site is Aspero near Supe, where low mounds facing the shore revealed stone walls, plaster clap-board shaped friezes, wall niches, a trapezoidal doorway (predating the Incas by 3,500 years) and unbaked clay figurines. One of the mounds is bisected by a gigantic looters' pit which gives an interesting cross-section across the mound, showing at least fifteen different occupation levels defined by floors and bands of ash and burnt rocks (heated and dropped into gourds or tightly-woven baskets to cook fish before the days of cooking pots). The hypothesis of Moseley and Feldman has, however, been seriously questioned by further study such as that of David J. Wilson of the University of Michigan. He argues that a mixed agricultural-maritime economy based primarily on plant cultivation is evident at coastal sites such as El Paraíso and

632 PERU

Aspero, and that El Niño conditions must be taken into account as a recurring and biologically devastating phenomenon creating critical lean periods in the diet of maritime-oriented coastal populations at all levels in the food chain.

This early start on the coast developed into a *huaca* (mound)-building culture of whose works the easiest to visit is Garagay, within sight of Lima airport and identified easily by an electricity pylon built on top. It is a U-shaped complex of three mounds with magnificent adobe friezes (not open to the public as there is no way of preserving them) half way up the main mound, dated by Dr. Roger Ravines to 1000 BC. In the huge plaza enclosed by the mounds a circular subterranean plaza has been found with symmetrical staircases. This is an important find, as a similar circular plaza was found recently at Chavín. The Chavín culture flourished mainly in the highlands near the coast from Piura S to Pisco, from about 800 to 200 BC. Whether it had origins on the coast or in the highlands is a matter for debate because it is unknown where the fusion of styles which characterized the Chavín cult took place. Its centre was Chavín de Huantar, which was a cross-roads of trade between coast, Sierra and jungle; the University of San Marcos has an interesting museum including a collection of Chavín pottery. It influenced heavily the Paracas culture of the S at about 200 BC to AD 200 (see under Nazca), the high Nazca culture (AD 400-800) the more primitive culture around Lima in the centre, and the Mochica culture in the N which had its beginnings just before the Christian era—some say as early as 300 BC—and lasted until the sixth century AD, characterized by realistic moulded pottery, sculptured wood and worked metals and by the huge adobe pyramids of the Moche valley (see under Trujillo). About AD 600, the Huari empire, based at Huari near Ayacucho, came to prominence; at its greatest its influence spread from Cajamarca and the Chicama valley in the North to almost the Titicaca basin and the Ocaña valley on the South coast. It overlapped with the Tiahuanaco culture, which was possibly an indigenous development, even if complementary to Huari and the Nazca culture. The classical Tiahuanaco culture, whose great monument is the ruins of Tiahuanaco, E of Lake Titicaca in Bolivia, dominated the coast until the 9th century. Possibly towards the end of the 11th century, the Incas had begun to rise in the Cuzco basin; their conquest of Peru and Ecuador was only completed around 1450. (Their civilization is briefly described under Cuzco.)

History A short time before the Spaniards arrived Peru was being ruled from Cuzco by the Inca Huáscar and from Quito by his half-brother Atahualpa, who was victorious in the civil war between the two. When Francisco Pizarro and Diego de Almagro landed a tiny force in Peru in 1532, Atahualpa, no doubt anxious for allies, allowed them to reach the Sierra. Pizarro's only chance against the formidable imperial army he encountered at Cajamarca was a bold stroke. He drew Atahualpa into an ambush, slaughtered his guards, promised him liberty if a certain room were filled with treasure, and finally killed him after receiving news that another Inca army was on its way to free him. Pushing on to Cuzco, he was at first hailed as the executioner of a traitor: Atahualpa had killed Huáscar after the battle of Huancavelica two years previously. Panic followed when the *conquistadores* set about sacking the city, and they fought off with difficulty an attempt by Manco Inca to recapture Cuzco in 1538. (For the whole period of the Conquest John Hemming's *The Conquest of the Incas* is invaluable; he himself refers us to Ann Kendall's *Everyday Life of the Incas*, Batsford, London, 1978.)

In 1535, wishing to secure his communications with Spain, Pizarro founded Lima, near the ocean, as his capital. The same year Almagro set out to conquer Chile. Unsuccessful, he returned to Peru, quarrelled with Pizarro, and in 1538 fought a pitched battle with Pizarro's men at the Salt Pits, near Cuzco. He was defeated and put to death. Pizarro, who had not been at the battle, was assassinated in his palace in Lima by Almagro's son three years later. For the next 27 years each succeeding representative of the Kingdom of Spain sought to subdue the Inca successor state of Vilcabamba, N of Cuzco, and to unify the fierce Spanish factions. Francisco de Toledo (appointed 1568) solved both problems during his 14 years in office: Vilcabamba was crushed in 1572 and the last reigning Inca, Túpac Amaru, put to death. For the next 200 years the Viceroys closely followed

PERU 633

Toledo's system, if not his methods. The Major Government—the Viceroy, the High Court (*Audiencia*), and *corregidores* (administrators)—ruled through the Minor Government— Indian chiefs put in charge of large groups of natives: a rough approximation to the original Inca system.

The Indians rose in 1780, under the leadership of an Inca noble who called himself Túpac Amaru II. He and many of his lieutenants were captured and put to death under torture at Cuzco. Another Indian leader in revolt suffered the same fate in 1814, but this last flare-up had the sympathy of many of the locally-born Spanish, who resented their status, inferior to the Spaniards born in Spain, the refusal to give them any but the lowest offices, the high taxation imposed by the home government, and the severe restrictions upon trade with any country but Spain. Help came to them from the outside world: José de San Martín's Argentine troops, convoyed from Chile under the protection of Lord Cochrane's squadron, landed in southern Peru on September 7, 1820. San Martín proclaimed Peruvian independence at Lima on July 28, 1821, though most of the country was still in the hands of the Viceroy, La Serna. Bolívar, who had already freed Venezuela and Colombia, sent Sucre to Ecuador where, on May 24, 1822, he gained a victory over La Serna at Pichincha. San Martín, after a meeting with Bolívar at Guayaquil, left for Argentina and a self-imposed exile in France, while Bolívar and Sucre completed the conquest of Peru by defeating La Serna at the battle of Junín (August 6, 1824) and the decisive battle of Ayacucho (December 9, 1824). For over a year there was a last stand in the Real Felipe fortress at Callao by the Spanish troops under General Rodil before they capitulated on January 22, 1826. Bolívar was invited to stay in Peru, but left for Colombia in 1826.

Important events were a temporary confederation between Peru and Bolivia in the 1830s; the Peruvian-Spanish War (1866); and the War of the Pacific (1879-1883), in which Peru and Bolivia were defeated by Chile and Peru lost its southernmost territory. A long-standing legacy of this was the Tacna-Arica dispute, which was not settled until 1929 (see under Tacna).

Population 19.7m. (1985 estimate), growing at an annual rate of 2.6%. Birth rate, 36.4 per 1,000 (1984); death rate 10.3 per 1,000 (1984).

Constitution Legislation is vested in a Congress composed of a Senate and a Chamber of Deputies. Men and women over 18 are eligible to vote; registration and voting is compulsory until the age of 60. The President, to whom is entrusted the Executive Power, is elected for five years and may not be re-elected until after one presidential term has passed. He exercises his functions through a Cabinet of 12 members. A new Constitution was approved in July 1979. Peru's 25 Departments are divided into 150 Provinces, and the Provinces into 1,321 districts.

Government A reformist military Junta took over control of the country in October 1968. Under its first leader, Gen. Juan Velasco Alvarado, the Junta instituted a series of measures to raise the personal status and standard of living of the workers and the rural Indians, by land reform, worker participation in industrial management and ownership, and nationalization of basic industries, exhibiting an ideology perhaps best described as "military socialism". In view of his failing health Gen. Velasco was replaced in 1975 by Gen. Francisco Morales Bermúdez and policy (because of a mounting economic crisis and the consequent need to seek financial aid from abroad) swung to the Right. Presidential and congressional (60 senators, 180 deputies) elections were held on May 18, 1980, and Sr. Fernando Belaúnde Terry was elected President for the second time. His term was marked by growing economic problems and the growth of the Maoist guerrilla movement Sendero Luminoso (Shining Path). The April 1985 elections were won by the APRA party leader Alán García Pérez, who took office as President on July 28, 1985.

Education is free and compulsory for both sexes between 6 and 14. There are public and private secondary schools and private elementary schools. There are 32 State and private universities, and two Catholic universities. A new educational system is being implemented as too many children cannot complete secondary school.

Language Spanish. Quechua, the language of the Inca empire, has been given some official status; it is spoken by millions of Sierra Indians who have little or no

Lima

Lima, capital of Peru, was the chief city of Spanish South America from its founding in 1535 until the independence of the South American republics in the early 19th century. It is built on both sides of the Río Rímac, lying at the foot of the Cerro San Cristóbal. From among the traditional buildings which still survive soar many tall skyscrapers which have changed the old skyline out of recognition. The city, which is now very dirty and seriously affected by smog for much of the year, is surrounded by "Pueblos Jóvenes," or shanty settlements of squatters who have migrated from the Sierra; much self-help building is in progress. There are still signs of earthquake damage after the disastrous 1970 earthquakes nearby, especially in the Rímac section of the city. Many of the hotels and larger business houses have moved to the plush seaside suburbs of Miraflores and San Isidro. In early 1987 there was a curfew between 0100 and 0500. If you arrive at the airport between these hours you are given a pass.

Half of the town-dwellers of Peru now live in Lima and Callao. The metropolitan area contains five million people, nearly 30% of the country's total population, and two-thirds of its industries.

In the older part the way the streets are named may confuse the visitor. Several blocks, with their own names, make up a long street, a *jirón* (often abbreviated to Jr.). The visitor is greatly helped by the corner signs which bear both the name of the *jirón* and the name of the block. The new and old names of streets are used interchangeably: remember that Colmena is also Nicolás de Piérola, and Carabaya is also Augusto N. Wiese. The city's urban motorway is often called "El Zanjón" (the ditch).

Only 12° S of the equator, one would expect a tropical climate, but from June to at least October the skies are grey; it feels almost chilly, clothes take ages to dry, and a damp *garúa*, or Scotch mist, is common. The rest of the year is mild and pleasant with temperatures ranging from 10° to 27°C.

History The University of San Marcos was founded in 1551, and a printing press in 1595: among the earliest of their kind in S. America. Lima's first theatre opened in 1563. The Inquisition was introduced in 1569 and was not abolished until 1820. For some time the Viceroyalty of Peru embraced Colombia, Ecuador, Bolivia, Chile and Argentina. The city's wealth attracted many freebooters and in 1670 a protecting wall 11 km. long, which was demolished in 1869, was built round it.

Lima's power was at its height during the 17th century and the early 18th, until the earthquake of 1746 destroyed all but 20 houses and killed 4,000 inhabitants. There were few cities in the Old World that could rival its wealth and luxury. It was only comparatively recently, with the coming of industry, that Lima began to change into what it is today.

Sightseeing The heart of the city, at least in plan, is still what it was in colonial days. A single block S of the Río Rímac lies the Plaza de Armas; the Desamparados Station of the Central Railway is quite near. Most of what the tourist wants to see is in this area. The newer parts of the city are based on Plaza San Martín, S of Jirón de la Unión, with a statue of San Martín in the centre. One and a quarter km. W is the Plaza Dos de Mayo. About 1 km. due S of this again is the circular Plaza Bolognesi, from which many great *avenidas* radiate.

The Jirón de La Unión, the main shopping street, runs to the Plaza de Armas, usually the first objective of visitors to Lima; it has now been converted into a *pedestrian* precinct (street theatre, street vendors, etc., in the evening). Later the pedestrian area will be extended to cover the southern half of Jirón de la Unión, from Plaza San Martín to Plaza Grau. In the two northernmost blocks of Jr. Unión, known as Calle Belén, several shops sell souvenirs and curios: the nearer the shops are to the best hotels the dearer the souvenirs are. Around the great Plaza de Armas stand the Government Palace, the Cathedral (see page 636), the Archbishop's Palace, the City Hall and the Unión Club. The Central Post Office is opposite the visitors' entrance to Government Palace. Running along

PERU 635

Key to Map.
1. Plaza de Armas. 2. Palacio de Gobierno. 3. Cathedral. 4. Union Club. 5. Plaza San Martín. 6. Torre Tagle Palace. 7. Plaza 2 de Mayo. 8. Plaza Bolognesi. 9. Plaza Grau. 10. Palacio de Justicia. 11. National Museum of Art. 12. Museum of Italian Art. 13. Panteón de los Próceres. 14. Museum of Peruvian Culture. 15. Las Nazarenas Church. 16. National Library. 17. *Hotel Bolívar.* 18. *Hotel Crillón.* 19. *Hotel Riviera.* 20. *Hotel Savoy.* 21. *Hotel Maury.* 22. Municipal Theatre. 23. Teatro Segura. 24. *Hotel Continental.* 25. *Hotel Sheraton.* 26. Civic Centre. 27. City Hall. 28. Parque Universitario.

N.B. A good map of Greater Lima may be bought at the Jorge Chávez airport and in the main shopping streets; it has street references and the main bus routes on the back (US$2).

two sides are arcades with shops: Portal de Escribanos and Portal de Botoneros. In the centre is a bronze fountain dating from 1650.

The **Palacio de Gobierno** (Government Palace) was built from 1921 to 1938, on the site of and with some of the characteristics of Pizarro's palace. Visitors' entrance is on Jirón de la Unión. Guided tours at 1230, but you must present your documentation on previous day (Mon.-Thur. only). The ceremonial changing of the guard is worth watching, most days 0800 and 1245-1300 (check with the Tourist Office).

The **Municipalidad de Lima,** built 1945, has a picture gallery (open 0800-1500 Mon.,-Fri., free).

Near San Pedro, at Jirón Ucayali 363, is **Torre Tagle Palace,** the city's best

636 PERU

surviving specimen of secular colonial architecture: a Sevillian mansion built in 1735. Now occupied by the Foreign Ministry, but visitors are allowed to enter courtyards to inspect fine wood-carving in balconies, wrought iron work, and a 16th-century coach complete with commode. During working hours Mon.-Fri,. visitors may enter the patio only.

A short taxi ride across the Río Rímac takes you to the Convent of Los Descalzos (see page 637) and the Quinta de Presa (incorrectly reputed to be the house of La Perricholi), now the Viceregal Museum (Museo Virreynal— see page 639), closed at present for repairs.

La Perricholi—real name Micaela Villegas—was a beauty, wit, actress, and mistress of Viceroy Amat (1761-1776). Legend says he installed her in this mansion, but the house the Viceroy built for her was torn down last century. She has inspired plays, an opera (by Offenbach) and many books, the best known of which is Thornton Wilder's *The Bridge of San Luis Rey*.

The Puente de Piedra, behind the Presidential Palace, is a Roman-style stone bridge built 1610. Hundreds of thousands of egg whites were used to strengthen its mortar.

Other important mansions worth visiting are the **Casa Pilatos**, opposite the San Francisco church at Jirón Ancash 390, now the Casa de Cultura, open 0830-1645, Mon.-Fri.; **Casa de la Riva** at Jirón Ica 426, now the German Institute; **Casa de Oquendo** at Conde de Superunda 298, in a state of dilapidation and closed for renovation; **Casa Negreiros** (a restaurant), at Jirón Azángaro 532; and **Casa de las Trece Monedas** (also a restaurant), at Jirón Ancash 536. The **Casa Aliaga**, at Unión 224, is still occupied by the Aliaga family and has recently been opened to the public; Vista Tours has exclusive rights to include the house in its tours (Tel.: 27-6624, or any travel agent). The house contains what is said to be the oldest ceiling in Lima and is furnished entirely in the colonial style. Don Jerónimo de Aliaga was one of the 13 commanders to arrive with Francisco Pizarro, and all 13 were given land around the main square to build their own houses when Lima was founded in 1535. The house of the author Ricardo Palma is open to the public, Mon.Fri. 1000-1230, 1600-1900 (a.m. only Sat.), small entrance fee, Gral. Suárez 189, Miraflores—a 19th-century middle-class residence.

"Other old mansions worth seeing: **Museo Berckemeyer**, Jr. Lima 341, a typical 17th-century *limeño* house—one of the few left; phone for an appointment to visit. **Casa Barbieri**, Jr. Callao, near Jr. Rufino Torrico—a fine old 18th-century town house in the Sevillian style; ring bell in entrance hall for permission to look at the patios. **Casa Museo Prado**, Jr. Cuzco 448, visitable when Sr. Prado is in residence, a beautifully maintained house with early 19th-century front and, apparently, a 17th-century patio. **AAA Theatre**, Jr. Ica 323, is in a lovely 18th-century house. **Casa de la Rada**, Jr. Ucayali, opposite Palacio Torre Tagle—an extremely fine mid-18th-century town house in the French manner; patio and first reception room open occasionally to the public (now belongs to a bank)." (John Streather)

Churches

The Cathedral (open to visitors 0930-1200, 1400-1700 every day) is on the Plaza de Armas. See the splendidly carved stalls (mid-17th century); the silver-covered altars; mosaic-covered walls bearing the coats of arms of Lima and Pizarro and an allegory of Pizarro's commanders, the "Thirteen Men of Isla del Gallo"; in a small chapel, the first on the right of the entrance, are remains in a glass coffin originally said to be those of Pizarro, but later research indicates that his remains lay in the crypt. Museum of Religious Art in the cathedral (temporarily closed in 1984), all-inclusive entrance ticket, US$0.20. The Archbishop's Palace was rebuilt in 1924, with a superb wooden balcony.

Four notable churches are quite near the Plaza de Armas: La Merced, Santo Domingo, San Francisco, and San Pedro. **La Merced** (open 0700-1230, 1600-2000 every day) and its monastery (open 0800-1200 and 1500-1730 daily) are in *Plazuela de la Merced, Jirón de la Unión,* two blocks from the Plaza de Armas. The first mass in Lima was said on this site. Very fine restored colonial façade, and attractive cloister. See the choir stalls and the vestry's panelled ceiling. At independence the Virgin of La Merced was made a Marshal of the Peruvian army. **Santo Domingo**, built 1549, is in Jirón Camaná (first block). In an urn in one of the altars are the remains of Santa Rosa de Lima (1586-1617), the first saint of the New World: August 30 is her day. Pope Clement presented, 1669, the alabaster statue of the Saint in front of the altar (entrance, US$0.30, open

0700-1300, 1600-2000 daily; monastery and tombs open 0930-1230, 1530-1730 Mon.-Sat.—Sun. and holidays a.m. only). The University of San Marcos was at the monastery for the first 20 years of its existence, from 1551 to 1571. The main hall has some interesting relics. **San Francisco,** open 1000-300 and 1500-1730, in first block of Jirón Lampa, corner of Ancash, is a baroque church with Arabic influences, finished 1674, under reconstruction. See carved "Sillería Coral" (1622), gold monstrance set with jewels made in Cuzco (1671), and Zurbarán's paintings (1672). The monastery is famous for Sevillian tilework and panelled ceilings in the cloisters (1620). Catacombs under church and part of monastery, well worth seeing; entry charge is US$0.70, by guided tour only, last groups start at 1245 and 1745 daily. The baroque Church of **San Pedro** (open 0700-1300, 1740-2030 every day), 3rd block of Jirón Ucayali, finished by Jesuits in 1638, has marvellous altars with Moorish-style balconies, rich gilded wood carvings in choir and vestry, and tiled throughout. Several Viceroys buried here; the bell called La Abuelita, first rung in 1590, sounded the Declaration of Independence in 1821.

Santuario de Santa Rosa (Av. Tacna, 1st block), small but graceful church. A pilgrimage centre; here are preserved the hermitage built by Santa Rosa herself, the house in which she was born, a section of the house in which she attended to the sick, her well, and other relics. Open 0930-1245 and 1530-1830 daily; entrance US$0.05.

Las Nazarenas Church (Av. Tacna, 4th block, open 0700-1130 and 1630-2000 daily), built around an image of Christ Crucified painted by a liberated slave in 1655. This, the most venerated image in Lima, and an oil copy of El Señor de los Milagros (Lord of Miracles), encased in a gold frame, are carried on a silver litter—the whole weighing nearly a ton—through the streets on October 18, 19, and 28 and again on November 1 (All Saints' Day).

San Agustín (Jirón Ica, 251), W of the Plaza de Armas, is a much changed old church, but its façade (1720) is a splendid example of churrigueresque architecture. There are carved choir stalls and effigies, and a sculpture of Death, said to have frightened its maker into an early grave. Open 0830-1200, 1530-1730 daily; since being damaged in the last earthquake the church has been sensitively restored, but the sculpture of Death is in storage.

Fine 18th century carving also in gilt altars of **Jesús María** (Jirón Moquegua, 1st block), and in **Magdalena Vieja** (1557, but reconstructed in 1931), with altar pieces, of gilded and carved wood, particularly fine; it should be seen during visit to the Museum of Archaeology, Plaza Bolívar (in Pueblo Libre). Another church worth seeing for its two beautiful colonial doors is **San Marcelo**, at Av. de la Emancipación, 4th block.

The **Convent of Los Descalzos** on the Alameda de Los Descalzos in Rímac contains over 300 paintings of the Cuzco, Quito and Lima schools which line the four main cloisters and two ornate chapels. The chapel of El Carmen was constructed in 1730 and is notable for its baroque gold leaf altar. The museum shows the life of the Franciscan friars during colonial and early republican periods; the cellar, infirmary, pharmacy and a typical cell have all been restored. The library has not yet been incorporated into the tour. The convent is open Mon.-Sat. 0930-1300, 1400-1730, entrance US$1. Guided tour only, 45 mins. in Spanish, but worth it.

The church of **Santo Tomás** is now a school (Gran Unidad Escolar "Mercedes Cabello de Carbonera", on corner of Junín and Andahuaylas); it is said to have the only circular cloister in the world apart from St. Peter's in Rome, and a fine 17th-century Italian-designed baroque library. The headmistress is glad to show people round.

Note: Churches are open between 1830 and 2100 unless otherwise stated.

Museums

Museum of National History, Plaza Bolívar, Pueblo Libre, in a mansion built by Viceroy Pezuela and occupied by San Martín (1821-1822) and Bolívar (1823-1826). Exhibits: colonial and early republican paintings, manuscripts, portraits, uniforms, etc. Paintings mainly of historical episodes. 0900-1730, except Sat. Admission US$0.20. Bus 12 from corner of Tacna and Emancipación, minibus 2 from Rufino Torrico, bus 21, 42, 48 from Parque Universitario.

The Gold Museum (Museo Miguel Mujica Gallo), is in 7th block of Prolongación Av. Primavera (Av. de Molina 1110), Monterrico, several km. from centre (Tel.: 352919); bus 76 from Av. Alfonso Ugarte, or bus 2 from Plaza San Martín to Miraflores (corner of Avenida Arequipa and Angamos), then change to microbus 72 to Monterrico, alternatively, take any of the buses going up Angamos, they go past the side road to the museum—bus 59b goes from Parque Unversitario to Angamos (get out before the bridge under Panamericana Sur); by taxi, with 2½ hrs. at the museum, US$10 (US$3 without wait). It is still privately owned. An underground museum contains items which have been exhibited in the world's leading museums including precolumbian metals (99% pre-Inca), weavings, mummies and a remarkably complete arms collection. Well worth seeing. Open daily (incl. Sun. and holidays) 1200-1900. Admission: US$4, students half price. No photography allowed. Good copies of ancient pottery are on sale.

National Museum of Art, Paseo Colón 125, in the Palacio de la Exposición, built in 1868 in Parque de la Exposición. More than 7,000 exhibits, giving a chronological history of Peruvian cultures and art from the 2,000-year-old Paracas civilization up to today. Excellent examples of 17th and 18th century Cuzco paintings, a beautiful display of carved furniture, heavy silver and jewelled stirrups. During the autumn and winter seasons, starting in April, there are guided tours, lectures and films every Friday evening. Several good, English-speaking guides. Several times a day there is a multi-screen slide show called "Afirmación del Perú", covering all aspects of Peruvian life. 0900-1900 Tues.-Sun. Admission US$1. Recommended guide: José Luis Vilches, who speaks English and French, and is most helpful and informative.

Museum of the Inquisition, Plaza Bolívar, Calle Junín 548, near corner of Av. Abancay the main hall, with splendidly carved mahogany ceiling, remains untouched. Court of Inquisition held here 1569-1820; until 1930 used by the Senate. In the basement there is an accurate re-creation *in situ* of the tortures. A description in English is available at the desk. Students offer to show you round for a tip; good explanations in English. Open 0900-1930 Mon.-Fri., 0900-1630, Sat.; entrance free.

Museum of Anthropology and Archaeology, Plaza Bolívar (San Martín with Antonio Pola), Pueblo Libre (Tel.: 623282—not Av. José de la Riva as shown on Cartografía Nacional map), a museum for exhibition and study of art and history of aboriginal races of Peru. Most interesting textiles from Paracas and ceramics of Chimú, Nazca, Mochica and Pachacámac cultures, and various Inca curiosities and works of art. See the Raimondi stella and the Tello obelisk from Chavín, and the marvellous Mochica pottery, and a subterranean reconstruction of one of the galleries at Chavín. An impressive model of Machu-Picchu in the Sala Inca, and mummies upstairs. Easily the most interesting museum in Peru. Open Mon.-Sat., 1000-1830, Sun., 1000-1800. Admission US$1.20, plus US$ 0.40 to take photographs with flash. Bus 12 from corner of Tacna and Emancipación, Bus 41M from Cuzco and Emancipacíon, Minibus 2 from Rufino Torrico, also bus 21, 24, 41 or 42 from Parque Universitario. Direction "Avenida Brasil", alight at General Vivanco.

In San Isidro, on the corner of Av. Rosario and Nicolás de Rivera, are the pre-Inca ruins of Huallamarca, consisting of a mound of small adobe bricks. Specimens found in the tombs are in a museum. Open daily 0900-1700. Admission US$0.30. Bus No. 1 from Av. Tacna, or microbus 13 or 73 to Choquecharca, then walk. "Another excavated precolumbian mound, with a small museum, is that of Santa Catalina in the Parque Fernando Carozi in La Victoria (an insalubrious district). Minibus 1 or 46 from Plaza Dos de Mayo." (John Streather). A third, Huaca Juliana, is currently being excavated on Av. Arequipa in Miraflores.

There is also an archaeological museum at Puruchuco (see page 656).

Museo Banco Central de Reserva, Av. Ucayali and Lampa (one block from San Pedro Church, on same side as Torre Tagle Palace). Large collection of pottery from Vicus or Piura culture (AD 500-600) and gold objects from Lambayeque, as well as 19th and 20th century paintings. Both modern and ancient exhibitions highly recommended. (Don't be put off by the sombre bank exterior!) Admission US$0.05, Tues.-Fri. 1000-1700. Photography prohibited.

Museo Etnográfico de la Selva, Av. Tacna 120 (4 blocks NW of Plaza de Armas), houses cultural and household objects from Madre de Dios; run by Dominicans, open every day (except Mon.) until 1900, US$0.10.

Museum of Peruvian Culture, Av. Alfonso Ugarte 650, showing pots and popular art, and costumes worn by Indians in various parts of Peru, includes exhibition of *mate burilado* (carved gourds); open 1000-1700, Mon.-Fri., 0900-1700, Sat. Admission US$0.10; US$0.70 to take photographs.

Rafael Larco Herrera Museum, Av. Bolívar 1515, Pueblo Libre, is the Chiclín pottery museum brought from Trujillo. The greatest number of exhibits stem from the Mochica period (AD 400-800). The Cupisnique period, dating back to 1000 BC, and the Nazca, Chimú, and Inca periods are also well represented. There is an erotica section in a separate building. This is a museum for the pottery specialist; it is more like a warehouse than a museum, but the general visitor will enjoy the excellent collection of precolumbian weaving, including a sample of two-ply yarns with 398 threads to the inch. Also several mummified weavers buried with their looms and a small display of gold pieces. Admission US$4 (US$2 student-card holders), open Mon.-Sat., 0900-1300, 1500-1800, Sun. and holidays, 0900-1300. Photography not permitted. Bus 23 from Avenida Abancay, or minibus 37 from Av. Nicolás de Piérola (Colmena) or taxi (US$2).

Museum of the Viceroyalty (Quinta de Presa), is a fine 18th century mansion. Exhibits: colonial portraits, furniture, dresses, candelabra, and so on; one of the Viceroy's carriages is shown. Closed 1986-87 for repairs.

Museo Histórico Militar (Real Felipe Fortress, Callao), has interesting military relics: a cannon brought by Pizarro, a cannon used in the War of Independence, the flag that flew during the last Spanish stand in the fortress, portraits of General Rodil and of Lord Cochrane, and the remains of the small Bleriot plane in which the Peruvian pilot, Jorge Chávez, made the first crossing of the Alps from Switzerland to Italy: he was killed when the plane crashed at Domodossola on Sept. 23, 1910. Open 0900-1200 and 1500-1700, Tues., Wed., Thurs.; 1400-1730, Sat., Sun. Entrance free. Closed April-August. Bus No. 63 from Post Office in Jirón Lima. The **Museo Miguel Grau**, Calle Lezcano 170 (near Basílica La Merced, just off Jr. Unión), is the house of Admiral Grau and has mementoes of the War of the Pacific. **Museo Morro de Arica,** Cailloma 125, Tues.-Fri., 1130-1900, gives the Peruvian view of the famous battle. **Museo Naval** (Av. Jorge Chávez, off Plaza Grau, Callao), open 0900-1230, 1500-1730 on Mon., Wed., Fri. and Sat. Admission free. Bus 63 from Post Office in Jirón Lima.

Museo Hospital Dos de Mayo open 0900-1800 daily, admission US$1.25.

Museo Peruano de Ciencias de la Salud, Jr. Junín 270 (just off Plaza de Armas), houses a collection of ceramics and mummies, showing precolumbian lifestyle; divided into five sections: *micuy* (Quechua for food), *hampi* (medicine), *onccoy* (disease), *hampini* (healing) and *causay* (life). Minibus Nos. 35 or 42 from Miró Quesada. Open: Mon.-Sat., 0900-1700, very interesting indeed. Admission, US$1. A guide is available in Spanish.

Pinacoteca Municipal (Municipal Building, Plaza de Armas), contains a large collection of paintings by Peruvian artists. The best of the painters is Ignacio Merino (1817-1876). Open: Mon.-Fri., 0900-1300.

Museum of Italian Art (Paseo de la República, 2nd block), is in a building, Italian renaissance style, given by the Italian colony to Peru on the centenary of its independence. Open Tues.-Sun., 0900-1900, but 0900-2000 on Fri., US$0.50. Large collection of Italian works of art, but most of the paintings are reproductions. Now also houses Institute of Contemporary Art, which has many exhibitions.

Museum of Natural History (Av. Arenales 1250) belongs to University of San Marcos. Exhibits: Peruvian flora, birds, mammals, butterflies, insects, minerals and shells. Prize exhibit is a sun fish (more plaster than fish)—only two other examples known, one in Japan and another in New Zealand. Open Mon.-Fri. 0830-1530, Sat. 0830-1200, 0900-1300; admission US$0.12. Bus No. 54A or minibuses 13 and 73 from Av. Tacna.

Philatelic Museum (Central Post Office, off Plaza de Armas). Open 0800-1330, 1400-1600, Mon.-Fri., 0800-1330, Sat., 0900-1200, Sun. Incomplete collection of Peruvian stamps. You can buy stamps here as well (shop hours: Mon.-Fri., 0800-1200, 1400-1500), and the museum has information on the Inca postal system.

Bullfight Museum (Hualgayoc 332, Plaza de Acho, Rímac). Apart from matadors' relics, contains good collections of paintings and engravings— some of the latter by Goya. Open 0900-1300, 1500-1800. Closed Sat., Sun. and holidays in the afternoons. Admission US$0.20.

Contemporary Folk Art Museum, Seco Olivero 163, between Arenales and 3rd block of Arequipa. Shop in museum grounds. Open Tues.-Fri., 1430-1900; Sat. 0830-1200.

WILL YOU HELP US?

We do all we can to get our facts right in *The South American Handbook*. Each chapter is thoroughly revised each year, but Latin America and the Caribbean cover a vast area, and our eyes cannot be everywhere. A new highway or airport is built; a hotel, a restaurant, a cabaret dies; another, a good one is born; a building we describe is pulled down, a street renamed. Names and addresses of good hotels and restaurants for "budget-minded" travellers are always very welcome. We would especially like to receive maps and diagrams of towns and cities, walks, national parks and other interesting areas to use as source material for the Handbook and other forthcoming titles.

Your information may be far more up-to-date than ours. If your letter reaches us early enough in the year it will be used in the next edition, but write whenever you want to, for all your letters are used sooner or later.

Thank you very much indeed for your help.

**Trade & Travel Publications Limited
5 Prince's Buildings, George Street,
Bath BA1 2ED. England**

PERU 641

Amano Museum (Calle Retiro 160, Miraflores). A very fine private collection of artefacts from the Chancay, Chimú and Nazca periods owned by Mr. Yoshitaro Amano—one of the most complete exhibits of Chancay weaving. Particularly interesting for pottery and precolumbian textiles, all superbly displayed and lit. Open Mon.-Fri. Guided tours 1400, 1500, 1600, 1700. Phone 412909, at least one day in advance, for an appointment; try to get a small group (under 10) first. Admission free (photography prohibited). Bus No. 1 or Santa Cruz minibus (no. 13) from Av. Tacna, get out at Av. Angamos. Calle Retiro is unmarked: it is the street on your right as you stand with your back to the Pacific on the 11th block of Angamos.

Pedro de Osma Museum (Av. Pedro de Osma 421, Barranco). A private collection of colonial art of the Cuzco, Ayacucho and Arequipa schools. Phone 670019 for an appointment. No. 54A bus from Av. Tacna. (Apparently this museum is now closed.)

Numismatic Museum, Banco Wiese, 2nd floor, Cuezo 245, Tel.: 275060 ext. 553, open Mon.-Fri., 0900-1300, free admission. Peruvian coins from the colonial era to the present day.

Museum of Mineral Specimens at Krystal S.A., León Velarde 537, Lince, Lima 14 (Tel.: 710713, 711379).

"**Museo Miniatura de la Plaza de Armas del Siglo XIX** in the house of Dr. César Revoredo, Salaverry 3052, is a private small scale reproduction of the Plaza de Armas in the last century. Dr. Revoredo also has a fine collection of prints by Rancho Fierro, the 19th century *costumbrista* watercolour artist.

"**Casa Galería de Esculturas de Sra. Marina Núñez del Prado**, Antero Aspillaga 300, Olivar de San Isidro, another private collection, of fine sculpture; phone for an appointment on Weds., or Sats. Two more private collections that are occasionally open to visitors on application by telephone are: the collection of precolumbian artefacts belonging to Sra. Elsa Cohen, Esquina Larraburre Unánue 392 (Bus 54A, or minibus 13 from Tacna), and, at Parque Hernán Velarde 199, the collection of rural handicrafts (pottery, engraved gourds, etc.) belonging to Sra. E. Luza (bus 13, Tacna with Emancipación, or bus 2 from corner of Plaza San Martín)." (John Streather)

Galería Wari 69, Cailloma 630, exhibits the tapestries of the Sulca family of Ayacucho; traditional designs and techniques are used in their beautiful work.

For those interested in modern Peruvian art, a new gallery has been opened at Independencia 812, Miraflores, Tel.: 451058, by Gaston Garreaud, who speaks English and French and will kindly guide you if you make an appointment. Admission free.

Note Some museums are only open between 0900 and 1300 from Jan. to March, and some close altogether in January. Many are closed at weekends and on Monday.

Parks and Gardens

Lima has many fine parks and gardens, with a profusion of flowers and trees in leaf the year round, the results of well concealed artificial irrigation. Alameda de los Descalzos, at the foot of the Cerro San Cristóbal, was laid out as early as 1610; it is a walk shaded by ancient trees and fenced by a wrought-iron grille. It was once a haunt of Lima's aristocracy, though today it is very run-down. The marble statues, each representing a month of the year, and the marble seats date from 1856. Nearby is another walk, the **Paseo de Aguas**, created by the Viceroy Amat in the 18th century to please his mistress, La Perricholi. The great arch with cascades was rebuilt in 1938. This walk, too, is in extremely poor condition.

Campo de Marte (Plaza Jorge Chávez and Av. Salaverry), a large open park. In the centre is a huge monument to the Peruvian soldier. The National Symphony Orchestra plays in the auditorium on the W side during the summer.

Parque Universitario, where the old San Carlos Jesuit church was turned into a **Pantheon of the Heroes** (Panteón de los Próceres) on the 100th anniversary of the Battle of Ayacucho. A graceful 18th century church with a circle of famous tombs under the rotunda. General Miller, the Englishman who fought in the wars of independence, and whose memoirs contain an excellent picture of the time, is buried here, and so is Admiral Guise, of Gloucestershire, who was killed at Guayaquil. Also the poet and composer who wrote the Peruvian national anthem. Next to the church is the former building of San Marcos University, which has now been restored and is used for meetings and conferences. Worthy of a visit are the beautiful patio and the small archaeological museum. In the centre is the clock tower presented by the German colony on the centenary of Peruvian independence. On the far corner of the park is the tall Ministry of Education building.

Between Paseo Colón and Av. 28 de Julio is **Parque de La Exposición**, a quiet place shaded by trees; several of the main avenues border it. It was opened for the 1868 International Exhibition. The great Palace of the Exhibition, facing Paseo Colón, is now the Museum of Art. South of the Parque de La Exposición is the **Parque Japonés**, which has a small admission fee.

Parque de la Reserva (Av. Arequipa, 6th block). In the middle is a statue of Sucre; of the other

642 PERU

two statues, one is of Tangüis, who selected the famous cotton. By the park is the Edificio El Pacífico-Washington (British and Israeli embassies).

Parque las Leyendas, between Lima and Callao, is an interesting park, beautifully arranged to represent the three regions of Peru: the coast, the mountainous Sierra, and the tropical jungles of the Montaña, with appropriate houses, animals and plants, recommended, children's playground. It has been refurbished, with new zoo facilities. Elephants and lions have been introduced so it is no longer purely Peruvian. The Park is open 0900-1700 (closed Mon.), entrance US$0.35. There is a handicrafts fair (Feria Artesanal) at the entrance to the park; particularly good insect specimens can be bought here. Buses 23 and 57 leave from Plaza Dos de Mayo; also minibus 75 from Jirón Azángaro goes direct to the park.

Warning Thieves and pickpockets have been on the increase, especially around the Plaza San Martín, Plaza Dos de Mayo, and the city centre generally at night, but latest reports suggest that an increase in the number of police and soldiers on the streets at night has made Lima safer. There have been reports of theft from hotel rooms left briefly unattended; also, small, sparsely-populated hotel lobbies are popular targets. Be especially careful in or near bus stations; never carry unnecessary money or valuables, and don't wear jewellery. Backpack slashing is very common; it may be wise to take a taxi if carrying one.

Festivals January 18, Founding of Lima; last week of August, Cañete; October, month of Our Lord of the Miracles with imressive processions (see *El Comercio* for dates and routes); November (every other year), Pacific International Fair.

Hotels Prices very negotiable outside peak July-August holiday season.

Name	Address	Beds	Single (US$)	Double (US$)	Tax & Service	Price Range
Miraflores César	La Paz y Diez Canseco Miraflores		80	95	21%	L
Lima Sheraton	Paseo de la República 170	650	80-90	80-90	18%	L
Gran Bolívar	Plaza San Martín (Tel.: 276400 Telex: 25201 PECP)	440	55	72	18%	L
Crillón*	Nicolás de Piérola 589 (Tel.: 283290, Telex: 25274PE)	700	56	75	18%	L
Country Club	Los Eucaliptos, San Isidro	150	45	55	18%	A
Plaza*	Nicholás de Piérola 850	56	36	43	13%	B
Continental	Puno 196	150	20	28	17%	C
Gran Maury	Ucayali 201	140	30	40	17%	B
Savoy	Cailloma 224	400	23	33	18%	B
Ariosto†	Av. La Paz, Miraflores(Tel.: 441414, Telex: 21195)	230	31	41	15%	B
Riviera	Inca Garcilaso de la Vega 981	300	36	46	18%	A
Columbus*	Av. Arequipa 1421	150	14	23	17%	C
La Granja Azul Country Inn	16 km. out, off Central Highway		30	43	18%	B
El Pardo	Av. Pardo 420, Miraflores (Tel.: 470283)		52	67	18%	A
María Angela	Calle La Paz, Miraflores		60	70	18%	A

* Recommended. †Rates include service and tax.

Accommodation in Miraflores: *El Condado* (close to *César*), L, deluxe. *Residencial 28 de Julio*, 28 de Julio 531, Tel.: 470636/473891, C, with breakfast, parking, café and bar, phone and bathroom with each room, lax security; *Gran Hotel Miraflores*, Av. 28 de Julio, A, overpriced; *Hostal El Ejecutivo*, Av. 28 de Julio 245, Tel.: 476310, D, including bath and breakfast, clean, tariff negotiable for long stay, safe, luggage can be left; *Hostal La Alameda*, Av. José Pardo 931, D with limited breakfast, pleasant, quiet, safe; *Hostal Residencial Torreblanca*, Av. José Pardo 1453, C, including breakfast and tax, quiet, friendly, clean, helpful; *Hostal La Castellana*, Grimaldo del Solar 222 (3 blocks E of Larco, between Schell and Benavides), Tel.: 443530, 444662, C (D off season), with bath, pleasant, good value, nice garden, safe, cafeteria, laundry. English spoken; *Ovalo*, Av. José Pardo, Plaza Morales Barros, C, quiet, good, breakfast served; *Hostal Señorial*, José Gonzales 567, (Tel.: 459724/457306), C, 60 rooms all with bath, including tax and breakfast, recommended, clean, friendly, well-appointed, garden; *Hostal Palace*, Av. Miraflores 1088, C, friendly; *Pensión San Antonio*, Paseo de la República 5783, Tel.: 477830, E, shared bathroom, clean, comfortable, ask for hot water; *Hostal Huaychulo*, Av. Dos de Mayo 494, excellent (German owner-manager); *Hotel Benavides*, Av. Benavides, block 22 (out of centre of Miraflores), D, good for longer stays; *Hostal Residencial Kimari*, Pasaje Los Pinos 156, piso C, Edificio El Comodoro, Tel.: 422266/422177, D for stays of more than week, clean, modern, safe, friendly; *Pensión Lucerna*, Calle Las Dalias 276 (corner Av. Largo), C with breakfast, friendly, clean, Tel.: 457321, recommended; *Hostal Catalina*, Toribio Polo 248 (½ block W of Av. Ejercito blocks 7/8), D negotiable, friendly, English spoken, bath, good transport connexions, Tel.: 410192/424037; *Pensión Antoinette*, D with breakfast; *Hostal Miraflores*, Av. Petit Thouars 5444, D, leave valuables at desk, English and German spoken; *Bailiwick's Lodge*, Colón 577-79, Tel.: 471749 (no sign), E, English spoken, clean; Sra Grety Jordan, Porta 274, Tel.: 459840, E, friendly, German lady, who speaks English. *Residencial Inn*, General Borgoño 280, Tel.: 471704, D, plus tax, access to kitchen and laundry, friendly, English spoken. *Winnie's Bed and Breakfast*, La Calera de Monterrico, M-13, Lima 34 (close to Miraflores), Tel.: 455864, C, run by Winnie Reyes de Espinosa of VIP Travel Service, warmly recommended. Those with vehicles are recommended to stay in Miraflores, since parking is difficult in the centre.

Accommodation at San Isidro, *Hostal San Isidro Inn*, Av. Pezet 1761, just off Salaverry; *Hostal Limatambo*, Av. Aramburú 1025, B, Tel.: 419615, 24-hour snack bar, won the "América-86" award for good service and quality; *Residencial Beech*, Los Libertadores 165, Tel.: 40-5595, C, with bath, including breakfast; *Garden*, new, recommended; *Hostal Callacocha*, Coronel Andrés Reyes 100, C, very good; *Hostal El Olivar*, Raymundo Morales de la Torre 385, Tel.: 417745, C with bath, friendly, garden, nice restaurant; *Hostal Firenze*, Chinchón (2 blocks from Las Camelias), Tel.: 227382, D, clean, family-run, hot water, English and Italian spoken, highly recommended; *Pensión Doratina*, Los Cedros 285, D, excluding food (which is pricey), very good; *Sans Souci*, Av. Arequipa 2760, towards Miraflores, B with bath, comfortable, recommended; *Residencial Javier Prado*, Av. Javier Prado Este 461, C with bath, toilet and breakfast (front rooms noisy), good, 4 blocks from colectivo to centre, transport to airport US$8; *Residencial Ritz*, Av. Salaverry 2599, Tel.: 401595/406091. In Barranco, *Barranco*, D, Malecón Osma 104, converted mansion above the cliffs, swimming pool, access to beach, good views of sunset from the garden. In Magdalena del Mar, *Hostal Magdalena del Mar*, Jirón Miraflores (off Av. Brasil), Tel.: 611336, E (triples available), all rooms with bath and hot water, good restaurant (also hourly rates). In Lince is *Hostal Ambassador*, Julio C. Tello 650, clean, safe, hot water, E, highly recommended.

In central Lima: *Pensión Astoria*, Camino Real 155, C, with bath and breakfast; also has small apartments with kitchenette and maid service, US$22 per night. *Hostal Los Virreyes*, Jirón Cañete 826, C, comfortable, clean, hot water, central position, recommended; *Hostal Renacimiento*, Parque Hernán Velarde 52, D, in a quiet cul-de-sac 2 blocks from central bus station, 10 mins walk from centre, not all rooms with bath but clean, helpful, recommended, Tel.: 318461/324821; *Pensión* at Hernán Velarde 72, run by Pablo W.See, C, very good, 5 mins. by bus from centre. *Damasco*, Jirón Ucayali 199, a block from Plaza de Armas, F, shower, hot water, drab, friendly,

---

Hostal **Barranco** Lima 4 Peru
Tel. 671753 Fax 671719

Only ten minutes (10 km) from the noisy and congested center of Lima (23 km from the airport) located above the cliffs, overlooking the ocean. A converted mansion with a quiet, relaxing and homely atmosphere. At your feet Lima's most popular beaches (private access – beach Las Sombrillas). Swimming pool, sauna, dining room (also vegetarian food) piano bar, fitness room, billiards, ping-pong, front and inner gardens. Spacious double rooms, some with private bath, balcony, fireplace, bar-refrigerator, television and telephone. English, German, French spoken. Great security against robberies, etc. Double $ US 8 to $ 30 (depending on room).

MALECON OSMA 104, Barranco. Tel. 671753 (Prix. 671738 Fax. 671719)

644 PERU

luggage can be stored. Good middle income hotels are *Hostal del Sol*, Rufino Torrico 773, C, with shower, helpful, fairly quiet, clean, safe, and *Oriental*, Jirón Cuzco 696, D, with bath, recommended, but noisy disco at weekends; *Universo*, Azángaro 754A, central, 1 block from Parque Universitario, F, with bath, poor service, dirty, safe, P.C. Volunteers US$2; *Claridge*, Cailloma 437, D, with bath, friendly, good, hot water. *Hostal San Martín*, Av. Nicolás de Piérola 882, 2nd floor, Plaza San Martín, recommended, good value, C inc. taxes, a/c, with bath, breakfast served in room, helpful, money changing facilities, Japanese run, good restaurant, good service; *Granada*, on Huancavelica, D without breakfast, English spoken, friendly; *Grand Castle*, Av. Carlos Zavala Loayza 219, opp. Ormeño bus station, D, including breakfast (poor), hot water, comfortable, good service, Japanese restaurant, recommended; *Residencial Santa Rosa*, Camaná 218, D, with bath, quiet, some hot water, laundry service. *Wilson*, D, with bath, good service, friendly, safe to deposit valuables, a bit noisy, disappointing restaurant; *El Dorado*, N. de Piérola, E with bath, clean and friendly, some rooms rented by the hour; *Hostal Niza*, N. de Piérola 206, G (triples available), breakfast, friendly, central, clean but not so the toilets, basic, noisy; *Wiracocha*, F, Junín 270, same block as Cathedral, clean, TV, central, hard beds; *Hostal La Bayamesa*, Angamos 8100, corner of Colmena, D, including continental breakfast, good, clean, English spoken. *Casa Vasca*, Carabaya 1033, good full board, D; *Hostal Belén*, Belén 1066, just off San Martín, Italian spoken, F, very popular, basic breakfast extra, hot water, friendly, music groups practising; *Asociación de Amistad Peruano Europea*, Jirón Camaná 280, 7th floor, F, two dormitories (8 and 16 beds), three showers, clean, friendly, laundry facilities, will store luggage; *Pensión Machu-Picchu*, Jirón Cailloma 231, central, D, dirty, hot shower. *Richmond*, Jirón de la Unión, 706, F, with bath (occasional hot water), not recommended, but cheap and central. Cheaper accommodation includes *Corona*, Calle Montevideo, off Av. Abancay near Parque Universitario, F, with bath, dingy but cheap; *Europa*, Jirón Ancash 376, near Plaza San Francisco, "gringo" hotel and popular with budget travellers in Lima, G (s, d, or shared rooms), no hot water, safe, will store luggage, some rooms without windows, beware rucksack-eating mice, fleas, three cafés in same block; *Pacífico*, Augusto N. Wiese 113, near presidential palace and station, F, only front rooms have windows, basic, hippy, convenient; next door is *Comercio*, F, similar, but less friendly, communal bathrooms are basic, US$0.30 extra for hot shower; *Residencial La Casa*, Jirón Huancavelica 572-574, E, reasonably clean, noisy at weekends because of parties; *Hostal San Sebastián*, Ica 712, Tel.: 23-2740, run by Nellie de Viana, E, clean, friendly, English spoken, popular, safe to leave luggage, bit noisy on street corner, restaurant and laundry facilities (runs taxi service to airport); *Residencial Roma*, Ica 326, Tel.: 277576, E, hot water, safe to leave luggage, quiet, basic but clean, recommended, often full (good pastry shop below); *Gran*, Av. Abancay 546, F, spacious rooms, old, eccentric, safe, private bath; *Alojamiento Hamburgo*, Av. N. de Piérola 459, F, dirty, hot water, friendly, special arrangements can be made for longer stays; *Pensión Ibarra*, Av. Tacna 359, Apt. 162, no sign, E, including breakfast (less if staying several days), clean, friendly, very helpful owner, full board available; *Colmena*, N. de Piérola 1177 (near Plaza San Martín, opp. Parque Universitario) F, with or without bath; *Hostal El Paraíso* (Jirón Unión 428, down a passageway, past bookshop), F, hot water all day, but erratic water supply, safe, dormitory and communal bathroom; *Pensión Lima*, Jirón Unión, recommended. *Hostal San Francisco*, Jirón Ancash 340 (Tel.: 283643), C, with bath, D, without shower, you can bargain the price down, some rooms without window, central, restaurant not recommended; *Hostal El Tambo*, Av. Bolognesi 373, D, including breakfast, laundry, dry cleaners and supermarket all nearby. Also try *La Casona*, Moquegua 299, clean, E (negotiable) including breakfast, good 4-course lunch, friendly, old fashioned, recommended; and *Pensión Alemana*, Av. Arequipa 4704 Tel.: 456999, C, comfortable, clean, excellent breakfast (triple-rooms available) book in advance, laundry service extra; *Hostal Colombia*, Av. Colombia 137 (with Av. Brasil), D, beware overcharging, with breakfast, clean, friendly, good; *Residencial María Fernanda*, Av. Brasil 351, F, good, clean, friendly, safe, continental breakfast available, *Hostal Samaniego*, Av. Emancipación 184, Apto. 801, near Plaza San Martín, G, recommended, 15 spaces available, hot water, friendly, safe; *Callao*, Av. Callao, F; *Moderno*, Av. Manco Capac, F; *Latino*, Jr. Paruro 1127, in Chinese quarter, F, cold water, basic, convenient for Roggero bus terminal; *Montevideo*, on Montevideo, F, reasonable; *Leticia*, F, Jirón Leticia 618; *Casa de Hospedaje*, Pasaje Acisclo Villarán 365, no sign, central, E, not including breakfast, clean, homely, good; *Pensión Sra. Bertha Bonilla de Barboza*, Montero Rosas 1379, E, including 3 meals; *Familia Rodríguez*, Av. N. de Piérola 730, 2nd floor, Tel.: 236465, F, clean, friendly, will store luggage, dormitory accommodation with only one bathroom; *Pensión Olga*, Av. Arequipa 292, E, including 2 meals. Family accommodation with Familia Konja, Garcilaso de la Vega 302, Salamanca, Lima 3 (bus No. 50 "Salamanca" from Parque Universitario), Tel.: 355619, double room (F), clean, cold shower. *Residencial Francia*, Samuel Velarde 185, Av. Ejército, Tel.: 617054, C not including taxes and breakfast, bath, hot water, laundry facilities, swimming pool, gardens, very friendly and helpful, 20 min. bus ride from centre; *Pensión Flory*, E, Urb. Sta. Florencia, Calle Guido 182, San Miguel, clean, hot water, popular with Germans; *Los Condores*, Domingo Ponte 874, Magdalena Mar, C with bath, cheaper rooms available, safe, warm water, clean, free transport from airport, tour guide (Alfredo) operates from here. Sra. López, Jr. Carlos Baca Flor 443 in Urb. Ingenería, near Avenida Eduardo Habich, also good (family also runs a good *hostal* in Huarás), F. Spanish-speaking travellers who prefer family accommodation can contact Yolanda Cueva, Tel.: 363277. If arriving by air, especially at night, a visit to the tourist office at the airport (beyond passport control) is helpful if you want to arrange a hotel room. **Hotel reservations** for Lima and elsewhere in

PERU 645

Peru can be made through Centro de Reservaciones, Garcilaso de la Vega 732, oficina 401, Lima 1.

Warning The tap water in Lima should not be drunk untreated by the health conscious, particularly between June to October when risk of contamination is greatest. This warning also applies to ice in drinks.

Youth Hostel *Albergue Juvenil Internacional*, Av. Casimiro Ulloa 328, Miraflores, Tel.: 465-488, E, basic cafeteria, travel information, laundry facilities, private and public rooms, swimming pool, "spacious, clean and safe, but run by a dragon". Open to non-members of the Youth Hostel Association, ten minutes walk from the beach. (Bus No. 2 from Av. Tacna to Miraflores passes in front, 30 mins. to centre.)

Camping Under no circumstances camp on or near beach at Miraflores, theft and worse is rife in these areas. Propane gas in heavy iron gas bottles available from Delta-Gas, Av. Benavides (former Colonial) 5425, Lima. Camping gas (in small blue bottles) available from Técnica Import S.A., Calle Palca 201, Tel.: 32-30-88, 0900-1300 and 1400-1700. Oechsle sell butane gas cartridges. N.B. Airlines do not allow the carriage of gas bottles.

Baths Baños Pizarro, Unión 284, steam rooms, US$3, cold showers only, café and swimming pool.

Restaurants In central Lima we can recommend the restaurants at the *Crillón* and *Bolívar* hotels. *Gran Bolívar* offers a quick lunch for US$3 and a 3-course executive lunch for US$6. *L'Eau Vive*, Ucayali 370, across from the Torre Tagle Palace, run by nuns, open Mon.-Sat., 1245-1430, 2030-2230, fixed-price US$4 lunch menu, Peruvian-style in interior dining room, or à la carte in either of dining rooms that open on to patio, excellent, profits go to the poor; *Roof Garden 91*, Avenida Inca Garcilaso de la Vega 911; *Tambo de Oro*, Belén 1066, lavish, colonial decor, international and *criollo* cooking, music and a select handicraft market, expect to pay at least US$20 a head with a beer but no aperitifs. *Domino*, in an arcade off Unión, near San Martín, good, Swiss-owned, expensive, recommended. *Vista Alegre* (the view is better than the food), Av. Atocongo 1401, Surco (Peruvian and Chinese); *Casa Vasca*, good food and atmosphere; *Goyescas*, Plaza S. Martín, good food (full meal including drinks, US$6.20 p.p.); *Parrilladas San Martín*, Plaza San Martín (opposite *Bolívar*), recommended (especially the *anticuchos* and sauces), US$4; *Café Bolívar*, Plaza San Martín, good, overlooking N. de Piérola; *Versailles*, Plaza San Martín, not recommended. *1900*, Belén 1030, very good, US$15 for dinner, drinks and salads in patio, live music from 1930. *La Reserva*, Emilio Fernández 330 (near Parque de la Reserva), very good, expensive. *Balcón Colonial*, intersection of Jr. Cuzco and Camaná, open 1130-1530, good lunches. *Akropolis*, Jirón Huancavelica 116, Chinese and Peruvian, set lunch for US$1. *Chifa*, Jr. Callao 189; *Chifa Santos*, N. de Piérola, opp. *Hotel Colmena*, recommended. *Giannino*, Rufino Torrico 899 (good Italian food), *La Granja Azul* (also hotel—see list above), Carretera Central (turn off between Km. 13 and 14 of Carretera Central, buses from Parque Universitario every 15 minutes; last bus back leaves 2000 but a minibus leaves the hotel for Lima at 2200), specializing in exotic cocktails and chicken dishes, dancing every night, recommended; *Rincón del Pescador*, opposite *Hotel Crillón*, excellent but expensive, US$20 per head; *Atlantic*, Jr. Huallaga 146, overlooking Plaza de Armas (on 2nd floor), excellent, changing of the guard can be seen from here; *Darri's Restaurant* on Av. Abancay, recommended; *Las Trece Monedas*, in an old colonial mansion off Av. Abancay (Ancash 536), excellent, dear, but insist on an itemized bill; *Rico's Pizzeria Americana*, Nicolás de Piérola 514, good, friendly service; *Chalet Suisse*, Av. Nicolás de Piérola 560, recommended, international and Peruvian cuisine. *Rosita Ríos*, Av. El Altillo 100, Rímac section, for highly seasoned Peruvian food at reasonable prices, to and from centre by bus No. 10; *Mesón La Ronda*, in the bullring, has an excellent bullfight museum. *Raimondi*, Miró Quesada 110, excellent, not too expensive. Cheaper restaurants include: *Alberto*, Carabaya 322, good food, plenty of it, reasonably priced,

★★★ **Hostal Torreblanca** ★★★

INTERNATIONAL CATEGORY IN MIRAFLORES, THE DISTRICT OF THE PEACE AND FLOWERS

Av. José Pardo 1453 - Miraflores
Telf.: 452874, Lima 18, PERU
Telex N° 21002 - 25002 CP CESAR

24 rooms. Exclusive bar, Cocktail Lounge, Room Service, Colour T.V., Interior garden, Sun terrace plus a Health and Beauty Club with beautiful Ocean view.

Tourist Information and free Baggage keeping.

Rates: SWB US$ 15. DWB US$ 20. TR US$ 24. Breakfast Included.

friendly; *Jerry's Restaurant and Coffee Bar*, Carabaya 336, simple, clean, cheap, open Sun. p.m.; *Rincón Toni*, Nicolás de Piérola, friendly service, recommended, main dishes US$3 (German and Swiss food, good); *El Torreón* (Jirón Camaná 571), good, US$1.50 p.p.; *Ciervo de Oro*, Jr. Ica 322, next to *Res. Roma*, good *empanadas* and cakes; *Centro*, Belén; *Don Juan* (off Plaza de Armas), good and cheap, open from about 1000, but not open late or on Sundays. *Don César*, Moquegua 113. Recommended is *Casa Camaná* on Camaná, south of N. de Piérola. Also try Rímac section of city, over Puente de Piedra, for cheaper food, e.g. the chicken restaurants on Av. Trujillo. There are several inexpensive restaurants on Av. Venezuela, and good snack-bars on Unión, particularly *Las Vegas*, western-style, good, cheap. On Jirón Ancash and Av. Abancay (near Buena Muerte church) there are restaurants serving good lunches. *Machu Picchu*, Azángaro 142, good, cheap, popular, also Jr. Ancash, next to *Hostal San Francisco*. There is a reasonable vegetarian restaurant at Carabaya 744, where a meal costs US$1.05; also *Asociación Naturista Peruana*, Jirón Ucayali 133; *Natur*, Moquegua 132, some English spoken; *Cooperativa de la Naturaleza*, good, Moquegua 305 and Camaná 489; *Gran Fraternidad Universal*, Garcilaso de la Vega 911, 11th floor, lunch only US$1, another branch in Lince, César Vallejo y Arequipa; other vegetarian restaurants on 200 block of Moquegua, 300 block of Ucayali, 800 block of Camaná, names and exact addresses, please! For students, *Comedor Universitario Congallo*, filling meal for US$0.20. *Soda Bar La Esquina del Sabor*, Junín 500 and Moreno, recommended; decor basic but typical food good. A good coffee bar for snacks and sandwiches is *Googies* in Plaza San Martín; also *Bar Zata* nearby and *Tivola* bar, Nicolás de Piérola 820; *Sandwich Tacna*, Tacna 327, popular and crowded at lunchtime. *Balkan*, Av. Tacna 555, good (German spoken). *Restaurantes Populares* near Hotel Crillón on Jirón Ocoña (full course meal US$0.50), these are principally for poor Peruvians and foreigners are unlikely to be welcome; *Cordano*, Ancash with Carabaya, near Desamparados station, 1920s décor, a good meeting place, but poor food and overpriced; at corner of Ancash and Lampa is *Sayumi*, good food, low prices; the *Lukyi* at Jirón Callao 300 Chinese food at reasonable prices; as does the stand behind Banco de la Nación, Av. Abancay. There are good cheap fish restaurants near Parque Universitario. *El Rinascate*, NW corner of Parque Universitario, good and cheap. Budget meals (called the *menú*) cost about US$0.75; try *Colonial* on Emancipación by Cailloma); *El Criollo*, Cailloma 225, cheap and clean. Also recommended, *Luigi* near Panteón de los Próceres, US$1.20 meal; *Huérfanos*, corner of Huérfanos and Gallinazos, a bar that serves food, and also has a shop. *La Buena Muerte*, Jr. Paruro 394, corner Ancash, seafood, popular, open Mon.-Sat. 1200-1400. *El Abuelo*, Jr. Camaná, spit-roast chicken, moderately clean; *Snack-bar Koala*, Camaná, Italian and Peruvian food, good, friendly, clean. Lima is good for natural fruit juices. *Alemania* pastry shop (near *Pensión Ibarra*, Swiss-run) is good, as is *Munich Cakehouse*, Cailloma 329 and Ica. Good bread rolls at corner of Moquegua and Unión. *Helados Alpha*, Jr. Unión 514, delicious icecream; *Pastelería Lobatón*, Jr. Unión 672, good *churros*; *El Pan Nuestro*, Jr. Ica 265.

In San Isidro these restaurants are recommended: *Aquarium* (at the Country Club Hotel); *La Calesa*, good steaks, good value; the restaurant formerly called *La Barca*, Av. del Ejército 2195, excellent but expensive sea food; *Los Condes de San Isidro* (Av. Paz Soldán 290—an 18th-century mansion—Tel.: 222557) excellent as is its companion, *El Otro Sitio* (also *peña*), Calle Sucre 317, in Barranco. *Valentino's*, Calle M. Bañón (near Camino Real and Av. Javier Prado), excellent food and service; *Saint Tropez*, good European cuisine, expensive; *The Key Club*; *Beverley Inn*; *Todo Fresco*, more reasonable than *La Barca* while still very good sea food; *Chifa Mandarín*, recommended, cheap and excellent; *Lung Fung* (Chinese); *Ebony 56*; *Micasa* (Japanese); *Todos* (American style); *Blue Room* at Las Begonias 379; *La Caleta*, Dionisio Derteano 126, recommended in the local guide books, has been found to be below standard despite the high prices charged for its fish; *Kentucky Fried Chicken*, Av. Arequipa, salads unsafe. *Steak House*, Las Camelias 870, open 1200-2400, serves Argentine steak (about US$20 for 3 courses).

In Miraflores we recommend the following: the *Miraflores César Hotel* has five restaurants at varying prices, the rotisserie has excellent meat; *Roxy* (quite good, Italian); *Dom Beta*, José Gálvez 667, excellent seafood, moderate prices; *Rosa Náutica*, built on old British-type pier (Espignon No 4) in Lima bay, near Miraflores, not to be missed, delightful opulence, finest cuisine, sunset recommended (discotheque upstairs, good); *Pizza Hut*, Av. Comandante Espinar; *La Pizzería* (Avenida Mariscal Benavides Diagonal) very good, wide selection, but expensive; *Indianapolis*, good food and service, rather expensive; Italian restaurant at Benavides 346, also good; *Café Restaurant Strauss*, Benavides 500, recommended for Peruvian and seafood dishes in German style at moderate prices; *El Faisán*, Canseco 10, for traditional food; *Las Tejas*, Diez Canseco 340, good *anticuchos* and seafood at reasonable prices; *Parrillada en la Parque*, Av. Petit Thouars (N end), good steaks, expensive; *Bavaria*, Av. Benavides (German style); *Casiopeia Bar* at Centro Comercial Aurora, Swiss and Peruvian dishes, Swiss-owned; *Pío Pío*, specializes in chicken, and so does *Wolfie's*, opp. Hostal Torreblanca; *El Dorado* (Chinese), Av. Arequipa, good food, expensive; *Kuo Wha*, Paseo de la República 5046; *Ajinomen*, Calle Los Pinos (between Benavides and Schell), Chinese, good; *Lau's Chifa*, Ricardo Palma 322, good and cheap Chinese food; *La Costa Verde* (on the beach, excellent food and wine, but expensive).

Rincón Gaucho on Malecón at Av. Larco end and *El Gaucho*, not far away on Av. Larco, two of the best steak-houses in Peru, both serve superb steaks imported from Argentina; *Café Lusitania*, Av. Larco, good international cooking; *Restaurante Daworís* and *El Tieber* recommended, to meet local people. *Haiti*, Av. Benavides, good food, cheap, recommended. *Super Gordo*, Av. Larco 201, family-type, not very good; *La Colina*, Schell 727, cheap and good; *Kentucky Fried Chicken*, also

PERU 647

Av. Schell. *Whatta Burga*, Av. Bolognesi, just off José Pardo, good burgers etc., and salads; *Govinda*, Schell 630, vegetarian; European cuisine is served at *Steffan*, Juan Fanning 331. *Salad House*, Av. Grau 164, 42 different salads, very good, open (except Mon.), 1230-1530, 1930-2300. Typical Peruvian restaurants can be found at the end of Avenida Brasil, including *Gran Chifa Brasil*, opposite Av. Javier Prado. Vegetarian restaurants are the *Bircher Berner*, Av. Schell 598, good value, and *Koricancha*, Petit Thouars 2686, 3rd floor. Try also *Carlín*, Av. de la Paz 644 (excellent, expensive, seafood specialities); *La Belle Epoque*, La Paz 646, Miraflores, Local 7, in El Suche shopping arcade, US$10 p.p. inc. wine, well prepared, delicious seafood, recommended; *Le Bistro*, in El Suche pedestrian mall, small, French restaurant, expensive; also in El Suche, *El Condado*, recommended, and other restaurants (and good shopping) in same area is *La Crêperie*, delicious filled pancakes; *The Brenchley Arms*, Atahualpa 174, Tel.: 459680, English pub serving English food, English speaking, informal and relaxed, tourist information. *Café Suisse*, main square, for cakes, coffee, European-style food and delicatessen; *Manolo's*, good desserts; *El Cortijo*, excellent steaks. *La Tiendecita Blanca*, opp. *El Pacífico*, tea rooms/delicatessen, good cakes, sandwiches, coffee. Good ice cream at *Lamborghini*, Av. Larco. *Helados Sabores*, Av. Larco, good ice creams; *Pastelería Sueca*, Av. Larco 759, good hamburgers, pastries and salads. Good pisco sours at *El Estribo*, Av. Larco; just off Av. Larco are *Vivaldi's*, expensive but good and *Liverpool*, good food, Beatles music and décor. In Magdalena, *José Antonio* (Peruvian food, music after 2200), Monteagudo 210 B, strongly recommended. In Monterrico, near the Gold Museum, *Pabellón de la Caza*, expensive, but very good food and service, "sumptuous gastronomic treat". Also *Puerto Fiel*, Av. Primavera 1666, 3 blocks from Gold Museum, recommended, seafood.

N.B. Most restaurants now have 13%-16% added to the bill: 10% for tip and 3%-6% for taxes (although this can vary according to the restaurant; some show no extra charges at all).

Electric Current 220 volts A.C., 60 cycles throughout the country, except Arequipa (50 cycles).

Clubs Phoenix Club, Av. Nicolás de Piérola 1014, 3rd floor (Plaza San Martín). Club Callao, Lima Cricket and Football Club, Justo Vigil 200, Magdalena del Mar, Tel.: 610080/ 614030; anyone with a Commonwealth passport can become a temporary member (for a small fee)—ask the staff to phone a committee member. The club has extensive sports facilities, as well as football, rugby and cricket, squash, swimming, snooker, etc. (Rugby players and cricketers are always welcome!). Also cheap restaurant, pub and friendly place to meet people.

Chinatown Lima's Chinese district is centred on Jirón Paruro and Calle Ucayali, south of Av. Abancay. Chinese clothing, food and souvenirs. Watch out for pickpockets and thieves.

Shopping Silver and gold handicrafts of all kinds; Indian hand-spun and hand-woven textiles; manufactured textiles in Indian designs; llama and alpaca wool products such as ponchos, rugs, hats, blankets, slippers, coats, sweaters, etc.; fine leather products mostly hand made. *Silvania Prints*, Nicolás de Piérola 714, Conquistadores 905 (San Isidro) and in lobby of *Miraflores César Hotel*, sell modern silk-screen prints on Pima cotton with precolumbian designs. *Plaza México*, jewellery in preColumbian designs. On Av. Nicolás de Piérola vendors sell oil paintings of Andean scenes, bargains abound. The *mate burilado*, or carved gourd found in every tourist shop, is cheap and a genuine expression of folk art (cheaper in villages near Huancayo). One of the best selections of folk art, but not the cheapest, will be found at the *Artesanías del Perú* shops in Lima. *Cerámica Los Reyes*, Av. Nicolás de Piérola. Ground floor of *Hotel Bolívar* for all metal, pottery, woollen and handicraft items, reasonably priced, credit cards accepted. *Artesanía Huamanqaqa*, Belén 1041 between Hotels *Sheraton* and *Bolívar*, the best store for high-quality weaving (but very expensive), specializes in Indian weaving from San Pedro de Cajas. Next door is a permanent exhibition with a century-old loom. Also try the stores in *Tambo de Oro*, Belén 1066 and the 24 stores in *Restaurant*

Silvania Prints

Pima cotton handprinted with Peruvian designs
Sold by the meter or made up into pillows,
placemats, dresses, scarves, ties etc.

* Colmena 714, Between Crillón and Bolívar, Tel 243926
* Conquistadores 905, San Isidro, Tel 226440
* Miraflores Cesar's Hotel, Lobby, Av. La Paz 463, Tel 441212

1900, Belén 1030. *EPPA (Empresa Peruana de Promoción Artesana)* government store for Peruvian handicrafts in San Isidro (Av. Orrantia 610). *Antisuyo*, Jr. Tacna 460, an Indian cooperative run by an Englishwoman, sells high-quality handicrafts from all regions, reasonable prices, Tel.: 472557. *Art-Andina*, Belén 1045, good selection of Indian weaving and rugs at very reasonable prices. Precolumbian textiles can be bought from the *Casa de Antigüedades*, Av. de Emancipación 253. On Unión is *Casa Mas*, with a wonderful display of gold and silver handicrafts. In Miraflores, lovely shopping arcade called *El Suche* at La Paz 646, but high prices in the woollen goods, ceramics and leather shops. Antiques available at *Casa Mas* and in Miraflores on Calle La Paz. *Mon Repos*, Urbanización El Club, sells excellent quality blankets, sweaters and ponchos. (Take Chosica bus, get off at Km. 12.5.) Vicuña is unobtainable for the time being in Peru and Bolivia alike. See H. Stern's jewellery stores at *Hotels Miraflores César, Bolívar* and *Sheraton*, and at the International Airport. (Note: It is better to buy pullovers in the Sierra. However, although Lima is more expensive, it is often impossible to find the same quality of goods elsewhere.) Alpaca cloth for suits, coats, etc. (mixed with 40% sheep's wool) can be bought cheaply from factories: Cirsa, Av. Argentina 2400, microbus 93, 70 or 84 from Plaza Castilla; Lanificio, Alberto del Campo 285, bus 59 from Av. Abancay (gives 10% discount to foreigners attached to their embassies). Beware of thieves on your return journey. Made-to-measure cotton shirts in 24 hrs. from Sr. Hurtado, "Sir", Jr. Carabaya 1108. A good tailor is Navarro Hermanos, in Belén, below the Tourist Office. Good Indian market on Avenida de la Marina, San Miguel, bus No. 10 from Miraflores. Records: Discos del Mundo, Unión 779, allows you to listen, in sound-proof booth, before you buy.

Markets Kevin Johnsrude of Fargo, ND, has sent us the following details: Parque Diagonal, Miraflores (by *Restaurant Haiti*): paintings and other handicrafts, Sat. and Sun. nights; Feria Artesanal, Av. de la Marina 790 and Av. Sucre westwards, in Pueblo Libre (take bus 2, 7, 10, or 48 on Av. Abancay, but watch your possessions, as thieves are numerous): extensive market selling woollen goods, leatherwork, bric-a-brac and Peruvian goods and souvenirs; sidestreets off Lampa: hardware; sidestreets off Av. Colmena: books; Parque Universitario: bargains; Plaza San Martín, behind *Hotel Bolívar*: ambulantes (money-changers, see **Banks**, page 649. There is an interesting flower market with enormous arrangements near Plaza George Washington, on the way to the Gold Museum.

Bookshops *ABC Bookstores S.A.*, N. de Piérola 689, Todos shopping area, Galax commercial centre (Todos and Galax are the largest stores), Miraflores and Jorge Chávez airport. Books and magazines in English, French and German. *Librería Studium*, Plaza Francia 1164 (also on N. de Piérola), sells history/travel books in English; has an excellent selection. *Studium* and *Librería de la Universidad de San Marcos* give student discounts. Tourist books in English, French and German also available from *Librería Ayra*, Jirón Unión 560, recommended, will supply works in Quechua. *Librería Internacional*, Jirón Unión (corner of Plaza San Martín) has a wide selection of books on South America in all languages. The *Book Exchange* at Ocoña 211a (near Plaza San Martín), will exchange foreign-language books (mainly science-fiction, detective and porn) another shop is on Benavides 286 in Miraflores. *Librería El Pacífico* in Miraflores has a good selection of English paperbacks. *Librería Alemania*, Av. Larco 1150, Miraflores, secondhand English, French and German books. Rare books, many shops on Av. Azángaro. Sr. Schwaub, Iturriaga, Jirón Ica 441a (mornings only), exports books, has huge secondhand stock, ideal for browsing (Spanish only). French bookshop, *Plaisir de France*, Colmena 958.

Film The Agfa distributor, at Av. Tomás Marsano 390, sells film at reduced prices. Foto Mare, Belén 1047. Many developers using Kodak equipment offer same-day service; all at similar prices. Many on Jr. Unión and Plaza San Martín; also Av. Larco, Miraflores. Fujicolor offer a free film with developing. Quality tends to be poor. **Camera Repairs** Casa Hindú, Jr. Unión, repairs Olympus cameras.

Pharmacy Botica Inglés, Jirón Cailloma 336, sells Dr. Scholl foot supplies for those contemplating or recovering from the Inca Trail.

Buses Standard fares in Lima: buses and minibuses, US$0.10, sometimes half price with student card, not very reliable. The main routes, such as from Plaza San Martín down Av. Arequipa to Miraflores and on to San Isidro, are also served by colectivos, US$0.25, which continue late at night after many buses stop.

Taxis No taxis use meters, you must bargain the price beforehand and don't give in to demands for payment in dollars, unless you get a bargain! Also, insist on being taken to the destination of your choice, not the drivers': about US$0.50 for short journeys and US$1.50 from the centre to the suburbs. After 2400 and on holidays, 35%-50% surcharge. Be careful of black "pirate" taxis; they usually charge 50% more. Pako, Tel.: 616394, is dependable for phone hiring.

Drivers don't expect tips; give them small change from the fare. If hiring a taxi for over 1 hour agree on price per hour beforehand. To Callao, La Punta, San Miguel, Magdalena, Miraflores, Barranco, Chorrillos, by agreement, basis US$5 per hour. Colectivos are fine, with legally fixed prices, e.g. US$0.25 from Miraflores to Lima centre. Taxi to or from airport (US$3-8, depending on size of vehicle).

PERU 649

Car Hire Self-drive from US$17 a day plus US$0.17 per km. depending on size, plus US$2 a day for insurance. Cars can be hired from Hertz Rent-a-Car, Ocoña 262 (beside *Hotel Bolívar*), Tel.: 289477; Budget Rent A Car, Airport, Tel.: 528706 and Miraflores; Graf Automóviles Seleccionados, S.A. (Avis), Av. Petit Thouars 915, Miraflores, Tel.: 233486; Turamérica, Ocoña 164 (beside *Hotel Bolívar*), Tel.: 276413, or Nicolás de Piérola 590 (opp. *Hotel Crillón*), Tel.: 278970. The condition of vehicles is usually very poor. Beware of deep street potholes. The standard of driving in Lima is very low. Make sure that your car is in a locked garage at night. Russian-made Fiat four-wheel drive Niva vehicles are often rented; they are up to the conditions of Andean driving, but the ordinary Lada saloon cars of the same make are not.

Motor Parts International Motors S.A. in Lima is the only Land Rover agent in Peru. Some BMW parts seem to arrive in Lima. BMW motor cycle service: Las Américas 386, Tel.: 724493, service manager Sergio Boza, very helpful.

Night Clubs International cabaret—*Sky Room* at the *Crillón Hotel* (folk shows— disappointing, US$7), *Embassy* in the Plaza San Martín and *Yorkas* on Av. Nicolás de Piérola. *Charlie's Night Club*. Many *peñas* have opened in recent years; these are generally cheap, tavern-like places with Peruvian music, much dancing and audience participation, *Hatuchay Peña*, Trujillo 228 (across the bridge past the Post Office), Fri., Sat., 2100, inexpensive, crowded, good, but best to phone for taxi late at night; *La Peña de Pocho Ugarte* in Miraflores; *Peña El Ayllu*, Jr. Moquegua 24, open Fri., Sat.; *La Palizada*, Av. del Ejército 800, Miraflores; *Las Guitarras*, Miraflores, recommended.

Folklore Every Sunday at the Coliseo Cerrado, Av. Alfonso Ugarte. AAA Theatre, Ica 323, has folklore evening every Tues., 2015, admission US$3. Also at the Teatro Municipal, Jirón Ica (tickets US$0.60-3.60), Tues. 2000 and at the Teatro La Cabaña. Cooperativa Santa Elisa, Cailloma 824 (3rd floor) has a folk group every Wed., 2000. *Hatuchay* (see under night clubs) is considered the best *peña* by most travellers. The Museo de Arte has seasons of Peruvian folklore on Weds., at 2000, US$1.20 entrance.

Bars (with music) *Charlie's Peppermint Bar*, Av. Corpac, *Percy's Candlelight Room*, at Todos shopping centre, all in San Isidro. *Satchmo Jazz Bar*, Av. La Paz 538, Miraflores, good quality music.

Discotheques Ebony 56 in San Isidro. Las Rocas in San Isidro is good and not expensive. Recommended in Miraflores, La Miel, min. consumption US$5.50 (pay as you go, don't wait for a big bill!), and Arizona, US$4. Unicorn del Mar at Herradura beach in summer.

Theatre Most professional plays are put on at the Teatro Segura, Teatro Municipal (Jirón Ica, 300 block—also orchestral and ballet performances); Teatro Arequipa and Sala Alzedo; Teatro Marsano, Av. Petit Thouars, Miraflores. Others are produced by amateur and university groups. See the newspapers for announcements. Teatro Cabaña in the Parque de la Exposición puts on a strong programme of progressive theatre. Theatre Workshop, Jirón Ica 323.

Cinema Tickets cost about US$0.65 in Lima. Good films can be seen cheaply at the Cooperativa Santa Elisa, Cailloma 824, Thurs., Fri., Sat., and Sun. each week, Tel: 322641. Museo de Arte, Alianza Francesa (every Tues.), Av. Garcilaso 1550, as well as at the British and North American-Peruvian Culture Associations (usually Thurs.). Ciné Pacífico Miraflores, in central Miraflores, most films in English with Spanish subtitles.

Sports There are two bullfight seasons, one in October-November and a short one in March. They are held in the afternoons on Sun. and holidays. Tickets at 2nd block of Calle Huancavelica, or at the Plaza de Acho bullring early on the day of the *corrida*. Famous *toreros* practise in the Lima ring, the oldest in the Americas, and fighting bulls are of Spanish stock. Cockfights are frequently organized and advertised: the Plaza de Gallos at Calle Sandía 150, near Parque Universitario, is recommended, US$6 for best seats. Horse racing on Tues. and Thurs. evenings and Sat. and Sun. afternoons in summer, and in winter on Tues. evening and Sat. and Sun. afternoons. Colectivos on race days leave from the Plaza San Martín, fare US$0.10. The popular stand is not recommended. Pelouse and Primera stands US$0.60. Tourists may enter the members' stand on production of their passports. For Paso horses, which move in four-step amble, extravagantly paddling their forelegs, National Paso Association, Miraflores, Tel.: 476331. The Lima, Inca, Granja Azul and La Planicie golf clubs and the Country Club de Villa all have 18-hole courses. The Santa Rosa, Cruz de Hueso and Huampani golf clubs have 9-hole courses. (Contact Gerard Astruck of Sudex S.A., telephone 28-6054, for particulars.) Polo and tennis are also played. Boxing or all-in wrestling (Sat. night) at the Coliseo Nacional.

Association football matches and various athletic events take place at the National Stadium, seating 45,000, in the centre of the city on ground given by the British community on the 100th anniversary of Peru's Declaration of Independence.

Banks Banco de la Nación (e.g. Av. Abancay 491). Bank of London & South America, Carabaya 442, and agencies at Avenida Arenales, San Isidro, Callao and Miraflores will give you US$ cash for American Express travellers' cheques, minimum US$200, maximum US$300; Citibank, Av. N. de Piérola 1062, charges 1% or US$3 min. on travellers cheques (will change its own travellers' cheques into cash without commission), open 0830-1245 in summer. Bank of America, Augusto Tamayo 120, San Isidro; will change Bank of America travellers' cheques into dollars or intis, no commission. Banco de Crédito, Lampa, block 4, will change travellers' cheques into dollars with 1% commission, and a daily limit of US$300; also good with telex transfers. Citibank and Banco de Lima will not change American Express travellers' cheques into intis. Interbanc on Unión changes cash and travellers' cheques. Peruvian banks. Open: Jan. 1 to March 31—0830 to 1130; April 1 to Dec.31—0915 to 1200. Closed Sat. except Banco de la Nación at Rufino Torrico 830 (opposite *Hotel Crillón*), which is open Sat. 0900-1200 (for changing dollar bills only—poor rate) and also open in the afternoons 1600-1830; small and crowded, it can be quicker elsewhere. Visa (Banco de Crédito), Jr. Lampa 499. Many *casas de cambio* near San Martín, on Ocoña and Av. Nicolás de Piérola; also on Av. Larco in Miraflores. Compare the rates, travellers cheques are mostly changed without commission but at a lower rate (though not all change travellers' cheques). Always check your money in the presence of the cashier, particularly bundles of pre-counted notes. Official *casa de cambio* on Jirón Unión, corner of Moquegua. Casa de Cambio Casanova, Ocoña 144, gives good rates for Bolivian pesos as well as US$. Brazilian cruzados can be changed at good rates. Best rates for US dollars cash at Av. Larco 321, Miraflores (Tel.: 440830), Av. Benavides 218, Miraflores (Tel.: 473620), Miguel Dasso 111, San Isidro (Tel.: 220265). The *cambio* in *El Pacífico*, Miraflores, changes travellers' cheques. Many money changers at corner of Plaza San Martín and Jirón Unión, and in the streets behind *Hotel Bolívar*, identified by their calculator and hiss of "dollars", change money at the very profitable (for you) parallel rate; some change other south American currencies (beware, many forgeries in circulation). Don't change money at your hotel: rates are invariably better at *casas de cambio* or on the street.

British Schools Markham College, for boys of all ages, is one of only four Headmasters' Conference Schools outside the Commonwealth. Colegio San Andrés, for boys, run by the Free Church of Scotland. Colegio San Silvestre, a school for girls at Miraflores, is represented in the Association of Headmistresses. Colegio Peruano-Británico, San Isidro, co-educational.

American Schools Colegio Franklin Roosevelt, the American School of Lima, Monterrico, co-educational: Villa María, La Planicie (for girls); María Alvarado, Lima (girls).

Addresses

British Embassy and Consulate: Edificio Pacífico-Washington, Plaza Washington, corner of Av. Arequipa (5th block) and Natalio Sánchez 125 (Casilla de Correo 854). Tel.: 283830. (Yellow bus No. 2 passes the Embassy.)
U.S. Embassy and Consulate: Grimaldo del Solar 346, Miraflores, Tel.: 443621/443921.
Canadian Embassy: F. Gerdes 130, Miraflores, Tel.: 46-3890.
Irish Consulate, Carlos Povias Osores 410, San Isidro, Tel.: 230808.
Australian Embassy: Natalio Sánchez, 220. Tel.: 288315.
New Zealand Embassy: Av. Salaverry 3006, San Isidro. (Casilla 5587.) Tel.: 621890.
South African Embassy and Consulate: Natalio Sánchez 125. Tel.: 247948.
West German Embassy: Av. Arequipa 4202, Miraflores. Tel.: 459997.
Bolivian Consulate: Los Castaños 235, San Isidro, Tel.: 228231 (0830-1330).
Chilean Consulate, Javier Prado Oeste 790, San Isidro, Tel.: 407965.
Ecuadorean Consulate, Las Palmeras 356, San Isidro, Tel.: 228138.
Colombian Consulate, Arequipa 2685, Lince, Tel.: 40-7835, Mon.-Fri. 0900-1230.
Venezuelan Consulate, Arequipa 298, Tel.: 23-3540.
French Consulate, Plaza Francia 232. Tel.: 238618.
Belgian Consulate, Angamos 380, Miraflores, Tel.: 463335.
Brazilian Consulate, Cmdte. Espinar 181, Miraflores, Tel.: 462635.
Swiss Consulate, Av. Salaverry 3240, San Isidro, Lima 27, Tel.: 227706.
Swedish Embassy, Las Camelias 780, San Isidro, Tel.: 406700.
Norwegian Consulate, Canaval Moreyra 595, Tel.: 404048.
Netherlands Embassy, Avenida Arequipa 1155, Lince, 8th floor, Tel.: 721925.
Italian Embassy, Av. G. Escobedo 298, Jesús María.
PSNC: Nicolás de Piérola 1002-06, Plaza San Martín. Tel.: 283250.
YMCA: Carabaya 664. New building with more facilities on Avenida Bolívar in suburb of Pueblo Libre.
Biblioteca Nacional, Av. Abancay (cuadra 4) y Miró Quesada.
Peruvian-British Cultural Association, Av. Arequipa 3495, San Isidro, with reading room and British newspapers (bus 1, 2, 54A). For other offices, library and film shows, Jirón Camaná 787, Tel.: 277927, classes only; theatre, Av. Benavides 620, Miraflores, Tel.: 454326.
British Council, Alberto Lynch 110, San Isidro, Tel.: 704-350.
Teatro Británico (amateur productions of plays in English), Calle Bella Vista, Miraflores.
Peruvian North American Cultural Institute, Cuzco 446, in centre, with library; branch at Av. Arequipa 4798, Miraflores. Language tuition, US$30 for 4 weeks.
Anglo-American Hospital, Av. Salazar, 3rd block, San Isidro. Tel.: 403570 (recommended for injections; stock gamma globulin).
American Chamber of Commerce, Juan de Arona, San Isidro.

PERU 651

The Union Church of Lima (Interdenominational), Av. Angamos 1155, Miraflores.
Trinity Lutheran Church of Peru, Las Magnolias 495, Urb. Jardín, San Isidro.
Church of the Good Shepherd, Av. Santa Cruz 491, Miraflores (Anglican).
First Baptist Church of Lima, Av. Garcilaso de la Vega 1734.
Christian Science Society, 1285 Mayta Capac (near Av. Salaverry), Jesús María.
English Benedictine Monastery, Jirón Olivares de la Paz, Las Flores (57M minibus from Plaza de Acho); Sunday Mass 0900, weekdays 1900.
Goethe-Institut, Ica 426. Mon.-Fri., 1100-2000, library, theatre, German papers, tea and cakes.
Alliance Française, Avenida Garcilaso de la Vega 1550, also in Miraflores.
The American Society of Peru, Av. Angamos 1155, Miraflores. Tel: 414545.
Hospital de Niñas, Av. Brasil, vaccination centre at the side.
Anti-rabies centre, Chacra Ríos.

N.B. During the summer, most embassies only open in the morning.

Doctor Dr. Manfred Zapff-Dammert (German), Monte Grande 109, Of. 406, Centro Comercial Chacarilla, Lima 33—Monterrico, Tel.: 361532 (private), 350292 (home), recommended.

Post Offices Jirón Junín, west of the Plaza de Armas, hours: Mon.-Sat., 0800-1915, Sun., 0800-1200. On Av. Nicolás de Piérola, opp. *Hotel Crillón. Poste restante*, Camaná 195. The Central Post Office near Desamparados Station is open 0800-1200 on Sundays (stamp collectors meet in yard to exchange stamps). Also at the intersection of Av. Larco and Av. Miraflores (Av. 28 de Julio), in Miraflores, open 6 days a week. Express letters can only be sent from the Post Office at the airport. Be careful with the rates charged at this Post Office, they sometimes try to charge more than in the city. Parcels for abroad to Aduana Exterior, Juan del Mar with Bernedo, Chacra Ríos (see page 762, **Mail**).

Cables Hotels *Bolívar, Crillón, Miraflores César*, and *Country Club*, also Jirón Lampa 667 and San Isidro. Public telex booths.

Air Freight Emery, in Callao, Tel.: 52-3643; to USA US$50 plus US$3 per kg.

Laundry Rápido, Carabaya 1027-1029, off Plaza San Martín, modern machines, charges per item of clothing. Continental, Cailloma 430, same-day and next-day laundry and dry-cleaning, good. Miraflores, Tarapacá 199 and Inclán, Miraflores. Insist on an itemized receipt. Autoservicio, Porta 198, Miraflores, fast, US$1.20 per machine. Av. Petit Thouars 3139, Miraflores, US$2 wash and dry. Lava Velox, Atahualpa 175, Miraflores, US$2 a load, good. Businessman, A. N. Wiese, fast. Good dry cleaning at Jirón Lámpa 1180 in centre.

Spanish Classes offered by group of teachers, including background to Peru. Information available from Centro de Idiomas de Lima, P.O. Box 772, Lima 100 (Av. Manuel Olguín 215, Monterrico, Tel.: 350601), 1, 2 and 4-week courses (US$300, 450, 720), accommodation with families can be arranged (room with bath, about US$150 a month).

Tourist Offices Enturperú, which administers the State Tourist Hotel chain, is at Av. Javier Prado-Oeste 1358, San Isidro (a 15-min. taxi ride from the centre), open Mon.-Fri., 1000-1900, Sat., 0900-1300 (telex. 20394; P.O. Box 4475), very helpful; rooms in the *hoteles de turistas* may be booked in advance. There is a tourist office at the airport, not too good, which only has a list of hotels and will ring to reserve a room for travellers, or will book taxis. The Dirección General de Turismo, Unión (Belén) 1066 (open Mon.-Fri., 1000-1900, Sat., 0900-1300), highly recommended, many languages spoken, knowledgeable and helpful to budget-minded travellers, sells maps and has free brochures, Cuzco, Puno, Iquitos, etc.

The Ministerio de Industria y Turismo, Calle 1 Oeste, Corpac, Lima 27, is very helpful regarding complaints and problems connected with travel agencies and touring.

Maps For Lima bus routes you can get a "transit map" from news stands for US$0.50. A good map of the whole country is available from street sellers in N. de Piérola and Plaza San Martín (published by Lima 2000, US$3.50). The Instituto Geográfico Militar (Av. Aramburu 1190, Surquillo, Lima 34), also sells a standard map of Peru (1:2,200,000), US$1.15, department maps, US$0.85 and a 4-sheet map of Peru, 1: 1,000,000, US$8.70, good value, but only available as seperate sheets at Av. Aramburu, black-and-white aerial photos available; passport may be required; they are open 0900-1600, Mon.-Fri.; Av. Aramburu open for map sales Mon.-Fri., 0800-1230, 1400-1530. Maps of N and S border areas are not sold. If you submit a letter to the IGM, giving your credentials and adequate reasons, plus a photocopy of your passport, you may be able to obtain maps of the border regions. No accurate maps of the jungle regions have yet been prepared. The Instituto Nacional de Planificación, Avenida República de Chile, also sell a large atlas of Peru, US$25. Petroperú maps for town centres recommended.

South American Explorers' Club Av. Portugal 146, Casilla 3714, Lima 100 (telephone 31-44-80), has been formed to bring together all in Peru (and by extension, all in Latin America or visiting it) who are interested in the activities off the beaten track. It is producing a magazine, *The South American Explorer*. Don Montague, editor of the magazine, 1510 York Street, Denver, CO 80206 (Tel.: (303) 320-0388), will provide further information, including trip reports for journeys you want to make. Open 0930-1730 Mon. to Fri.; non-members are asked to limit their visits to 30 mins., staff very helpful. They will buy and sell used equipment. Some maps available. Their map of the Inca Trail is good (US$4), but has been criticized for being too big. They have also recently published an excellent guide to hiking in the Cordillera Blanca and the Cordillera Huayhuash. They also publish a map of the Cordillera Vilcanota (Ausangate)—1:100,000 (dyeline). (Also see the Bradts' *Backpacking* book, listed in "Information for Visitors".)

Trekking and Backpacking Percy Tapiá, Casilla 3074, Lima 100, leads treks for groups on the Inca Trail, Cordillera Vilcabamba and Cordillera Blanca. Club Andino Peruano, Las Begonias 630, also helpful. Instituto Nacional de Recreación, Educación Física y Deportes (Inred), have an Andean specialist, César Morales Arnao, at the Estudio Nacional, Tribuna Sur, 3rd floor, Tel.: 329177. Trekking and Backpacking Club Peruano, Jr. Huáscar 1152, Jesus María, Lima 11 (Tel.: 232515), also at Huarás; free information on Peru and South America, storage and gas cylinders available. Issues a magazine, *El Trekkero*, write for information. Open Mon.-Fri., 1730-1900, phone first at weekends. For hiking and rafting, Expediciones Mayoc, Conquistadores 199, San Isidro, Lima 27 (Casilla 270137), Tel.: 225-988.

The Peruvian Touring and Automobile Club, at Av. César Vallejo 699 (Casilla 2219), Lince, Lima (Tel.: 403270), offers help to tourists and particularly to members of the leading motoring associations. Good maps available of whole country; regional routes and the S. American sections of the Pan-American Highway available (US$2.10).

Tourist Information Best guide to archaeological sites is *Manual de Arqueología Peruana*, by Kaufmann Doig, on sale from stalls and most bookshops, published in Spanish, US$8; an abridged version, *El Perú Arqueológico*, US$2, covering pre-Inca remains, is also available. Booklet *Lima, City of Treasures and Traditions* by Frances E. Parodi (published by the American Woman's Literary Club, Lima). *Guía "Inca" de Lima Metropolitana* is invaluable for finding less well known, but interesting, parts of Lima, as is the *Guía de Transportes de Lima Metropolitana* (US$1.75) for getting to them. For those interested in architecture, *Itinerarios de Lima*, by Héctor Velarde (in Spanish and English), and *Guía Reparaz del Perú*, by Gonzalo Reparaz Ruiz (Spanish, English and French) are very useful. Also useful is *Guide to Lima* by J. E. Maguiña. Spanish and English news in the lobby of the *Sheraton Hotel*. *Lima Times* publishes a monthly "Where, When, How . . ." booklet.

Professional archaeologists should contact the Instituto Nacional de Cultura, Casilla 5247, Lima, or Centro de Investigación y Restauración de Bienes Monumentales del Instituto Nacional de Cultura, Jirón Ancash 769, Lima.

Travel Agents Sudex S. A. (Gerard Astruck), Sudamérica building, Carabaya 933, Of. 310-317; Lima Tours, Belén 1040, just off Plaza San Martín, slow for money changing, publishes a tourist guide. America Tours, Av. Nicolás de Piérola 672 (Víctor Melgar); Exprinter, N. de Piérola 805; Coltur S.A., Jr. Camaná 868, recommended; Melitur, Av. Emancipación 328; Wagons Lits/Cook, Jr. Ocoña 170; Universal Travels, Rufino Torrico 965; Dasatour, Jr. Augusto N. Wiese 671; Turamérica S.A., Jirón Ocoña 164; Receptur, Rufino Torrico 889; Laser Tours, Av. Nicolás de Piérola 757; Casapia Express Tours, Tel.: 289-551, Av. N. de Piérola 661; Puno-Cusco Tours, Av. N. de Piérola, 742, oficina 302, Casilla Postal 10356, Tel.: 239502, 230132, 235854; Atlas Tours, Ocoña 234, nr. Plaza San Martín, recommended (has connections with agent, Sabina de Valle, very helpful, in Cuzco); Lambayeque Tours, Jr. Ocoña 234, Tel.: 275324, 280420. Creditio S. A., Schell 319, Oficina 706, Miraflores (Tel.: 444200/444727), efficient, helpful, English spoken; Viajes Universal, Av. Arequipa 2885, San Isidro (Tel.: 421111/421112), helpful, contact María del Rosario Berio; Explorandes, Av. Bolognesi 159, Miraflores, recommended; Aries Tours, Camaná 851, Tel.: 247207, satisfactory; Olga García Li, Jr. Unión 1033-2, for cheap flights out of Peru, English and other languages spoken; Key Tours (Jorge Gonti Angeles), Av. Nicolás de Piérola 677, Of. 9, Tel.: 284311 recommended for swift and efficient service arranging tours throughout Peru

Peruvian Amazon Adventure Vacation

Enjoy moonlit excursions up the Amazon River. Guided biological, zoological & pictorial tours through Amazon virgin forest. Choice of lodges with full amenities or primitive camp on private 50,000 acre reserve.

Special rates for 1988 . . . $60/day. Available year round for groups or individuals. Free color brochure. Call now.

Wilderness Expeditions
310 Washington Ave., S.W. • Roanoke, Va. 24016
1 (800) 323-3241, (703) 342-5630 in Va. Telex - 901238

Amazon Selva Tours
Putumayo 133 • Iquitos, Peru
Telephone - 236918 Telex 91002

PERU 653

and to La Paz. Turismo Inkaiko, Av. Garcilaso de la Vega 911 (also in Cuzco) has been strongly criticized.

Chávez Tours will arrange drivers to take small groups (or individuals) on trips for US$22 per day. Cecilia Toso Stagi, Turispa, Av. La Paz 1101, Miraflores (Tel.: 474903), recommended. Julio E. Figueroa Cubas, Fco. Sarmiento de Gamboa 289, Urb. La Colonial, Callao, Tel.: 514748, private guide, recommended particularly for non-Spanish speakers, Lima tours, US$5 per hour. A good archaeological tour guide is Rolando Peceros, Tel.: 276720.

Airport The Jorge Chávez airport is 16 km. from the centre of Lima. Taxi, about US$3-8 to centre, US$13 to Miraflores (hang on to your bag if surrounded by taxi touts—if you walk 100 metres outside the airport gate you can probably bargain a much cheaper price from taxis not working the airport route—but not recommended at night). Airport bus to centre leaves from right-hand end of building as you step out of the door. Municipal blue bus 35 (US$0.10) and colectivo (outside the Air France office), and to and from Plaza Dos de Mayo in the day-time, US$0.50 p.p. and per item of luggage. Minibus every 20 mins., US$0.75, from Calle Serrano, opposite Iberia office. Also, 15 and 35 from the Plaza Dos de Mayo leave for the airport; service about every 30 mins. There is a cheap colectivo service from in front of Café de París or Galería Internacional, Colmena (N. de Piérola) 733, from 0400 to 2000, colectivos wait until they have 5 passengers, US$0.50 p.p., and US$0.25 for luggage. Buses go from Trans Hotel, Camaná 828 (Tel.: 275697, 289812), every 30 mins. from 0430, except Sun. will also collect passengers from hotels (fares range from US$1.75 p.p. with one bag leaving from Camaná office or a hotel nearby, to US$5 if they pick you up from a hotel away from the centre). Also from Miraflores (Avenida Ricardo Palma 280), every 20 min., US$2 p.p. (buses will collect travellers from private houses, US3.20), Tel.: 469872. If using this service, book well in advance at Trans Hotel. Hoteltours operate a bus service from the airport to hotels in town for US$4; they have desks near both the domestic and international arrival gates. The big hotels also have their own buses at the airport, and charge about the same. There is a duty-free shop but no duty-free cigarettes. Only official Corpac porters are allowed in the customs area. Airport tax of US$10, payable in intis or dollars, for international flights. Avoid getting left with intis at the airport when leaving, there is no way of changing them back into dollars. Left luggage costs US$1.90 per day, US$0.40 per hour per item. The Prohotel agent at the airport is very helpful with hotel bookings of all classes; there is a second hotel booking agency. Taxi drivers also tout for hotel business, offering discounts—don't be bullied. Safe to stay all night in 24-hour expresso-snack bar.

Internal Air Services To Andahuaylas, Anta, Arequipa, Ayacucho, Bellavista, Cajamarca, Chiclayo, Chimbote, Cuzco, Huánuco, Iquitos, Juanjui, Juliaca, Moyobamba, Piura, Pucallpa, Puerto Maldonado, Rioja, Tacna, Talara, Tarapoto, Tingo María, Trujillo, Tumbes and Yurimaguas. Prices are relatively low in comparison with other countries.

Air Lines Most international airlines have moved out to San Isidro and Miraflores because of bomb threats. Faucett (Plaza San Martín, Tel.: 282930), Aeroperú (Plaza San Martín Tel.: 317626, domestic, 287825 international). Office hours are usually 0900-1700, Mon.-Fri., 0800-1930, Sat. For Aeroperú, internal flights, Cailloma 818.

Rail Central Railway of Peru maintains passenger and freight service to La Oroya (with an extension N to Cerro de Pasco, with Centromín) and S to Huancayo (with an extension to Huancavelica). Desamparados station, behind Presidential Palace. Train to La Oroya, US$1.50, 2nd class, departs 0740 (Tues., Thurs., Sat.), 6½ hrs. (from La Oroya to Cerro de Pasco, US$1.35; but one cannot buy a through ticket from Lima because the Cerro de Pasco train leaves La Oroya at 1430 regardless of whether the train from Lima has arrived). If not wishing to go beyond La Oroya, colectivo back to Lima costs US$5.50, 5 hrs., you can make a day trip of it, being back by 2000. You can also return by bus, 7½ hrs., for railway enthusiasts especially. The train to Huancayo (reported suspended in Oct. 1986 after damage to a bridge) leaves Desamparados station Tues., Thurs., Sat. at 0740, arriving 9-14 hrs. later (simple breakfasts and lunches served on the train). The return Mon., Wed., Fri., leaves 0700, arriving Lima 1700. Single, 1st class, US$4.20, 2nd class, US$3.50; good cheap breakfast and lunch served. (1st class and buffet seats can be reserved for US$0.25—take a torch for the long, dark tunnels; ticket office opens 0700-1200, 1330-1600 Mon.-Fri., 0700-1100 Sat.); tickets can only be bought one day in advance in Lima; in the high season, tickets are often sold out for 1st class by 1200. Sit on the left; remember that the train changes direction at San Bartolomé, so you will be on the right to begin with). Guard your possessions very carefully against pickpockets at the station. Only ticket holders are allowed on the platform. The station is closed on Sundays.

Roads The Pan-American Highway is open from Lima N along the coast N to Ecuador (but was heavily damaged in the floods of 1983 N of Chiclayo), and S to Arequipa and Chile. It is mostly through desert, with occasional valley oases. The Central Highway from Lima goes through La Oroya NE to Cerro de Pasco, Huánuco, Tingo María and terminates at Pucallpa on the Ucayali River (paved most of the way, but interrupted by mud-slides in the Huallaga valley). From La Oroya a

654 PERU

good road goes SE to Huancayo, and on (not good) to Ayacucho, Cuzco, Puno on Lake Titicaca, and on into Bolivia. The Puno-Bolivia stretch is now almost entirely paved. The two roads to Cuzco, one by the Central Andes and the other by Arequipa and Puno, make a most spectacular circuit of 2,400 km. possible. Preferably it should be done clockwise: there would be less driving on the outsides of precipices; it would be downhill on the poor stretch between Puno and Arequipa, and the return to Lima would be by a good road. Another road from Lima to the Sierra deviates from the Lima-Oroya highway at Chosica; it goes along the Río Santa Eulalia and joins the road from La Oroya to Cerro de Pasco just beyond Marcapomacocha. (This road is spectacular, but is mainly used for local access; it is not recommended for long-distance driving.) The Puno-Cuzco section has paved stretches at each end. Most of the high Sierra roads are narrow, unsurfaced and liable to landslides; many accidents. Be sure to check with the Peruvian Touring and Automobile Club regarding road conditions before driving in the Sierra.

Bus Companies   Coastal buses are usually good although liable to delays. Buses of companies which operate in the Sierra, in view of the road surfaces, often break down. The services of the Ormeño group, who operate modern Scania buses, are generally recommended throughout Peru; Cruz del Sur are also generally well thought of. Tepsa, Paseo de la República 129 (Tel.: 321233) run N and S on the coast and to Pucallpa and Arequipa; their services have been improved, but we are told they still tend to drive too fast for safety. Expreso Continental (Ormeño) to Trujillo, Piura and Tumbes, recommended; Chinchay-Suyo (northwards), Apurímac 391 and Av. Grau 525; also going north, Perú Express, Pacífico El Norte (to Chimbote), Atahualpa, Jr. Sandía 266, Tel.: 275838/287255 (to Cajamarca, Celendín, etc.), good; Sudamericano buses (Av. Nicolás de Piérola 1117) to Tumbes are unreliable and slow. Along the South coast route, Ormeño, Av. Carlos Zavala 145, reliable, also to Arequipa and Cuzco; Cruz del Sur, Paseo de la República corner with Almirante Grau (also go to Santiago). To Cuzco: via Arequipa, Cruz del Sur; via Nazca and Puquío, Ormeño, El Cóndor. To Huancayo, Compresa Cáceres, Av. 28 de Julio 2195, and Comité 22 colectivo, Av. Ayacucho 997, Tel.: 289082. To Huánuco: León de Huánuco, Av. José Gálvez 1734 (also to Pucallpa not recommended, buses in bad condition); Nor Oriente, Luna Pizarro 365. Expreso Intersa, Av. Nicolás de Piérola, 1631; El Trome, Montevideo 949. Colectivos leave for all parts of Peru from Parque Universitario. For prices of routes and more details, see under individual cities in pages following.

International Buses   Turismo Expreso Pullman (Tepsa) runs a twice weekly service to Santiago, Chile (3,500 km.) leaving Lima on Thurs. and Sun. at 1645, fare US$125 not including meals or hotel room for overnight stop (take some food with you). Arrives on the third day at 1800. Pul Bus Norte to Santiago, US$135. Also connecting twice weekly services to Guayaquil and Quito (although there are no through buses; you can buy through tickets but they are very expensive and give no priority), leaving Lima on Wed. and Sun. at 0845. The trip takes 2½ days; often long frontier delays.

The international trips are much cheaper if one is prepared to take buses to frontier posts only, walk across frontiers, and buy tickets as one goes along; on the other hand the extra paperwork involved, as compared with the through bus, is irritating. To enter Peru, a ticket out of the country may be required. If you have to buy a bus ticket, be warned: they are not transferable or refundable.

Warning   Luggage is often snatched at terminals. Make sure your luggage is well guarded and put on the right bus. It is also important not to assume that buses leave from the place where you bought the tickets.

In the weeks either side of July 28/29 (Independence), it is practically impossible to get train or bus tickets out of Lima.

Short Excursions   Two short excursions in the neighbourhood of Lima, one to Pachacámac and one to Chosica, are well worthwhile. The road to Pachacámac, the Avenida Arequipa expressway from the centre of Lima, is a 4-lane highway, 10 km. long, with gardens and a double row of trees in the centre. Parallel to this, a few blocks away, is the Paseo de la República expressway where the large Sears-Todos shopping complex is located. At **San Isidro** is El Olivar, an old olive grove turned into a delightful park. Beyond this is the Lima Golf Club where the Country Club is found, primarily a hotel, which incorporates the Real Club with swimming pools, tennis courts, etc. This is an 8 km. taxi ride from the centre of Lima. Between San Isidro and Miraflores is the Pan de Azúcar, an adobe pyramid of the Maranga culture, of about AD 100-500 (Calle Nicolás de Rivera 201, small museum). One km. from Puruchuco (see page 656) are Huaquerones and

PERU 655

Catalina Huaca (in Parque Fernando Carozi—also called Santa Catalina), sites now being restored. Nearby, at Chivateros, is a quarry said to date from 10,000 BC.

The road reaches the sea at **Miraflores,** the largest, most important suburb of Lima, with well stocked shops and many first class restaurants. There is a handsome park in the middle of the shopping centre and at the end of Avenida Mariscal Benavides, which is commonly called Av. Diagonal, you can get the best view of the whole Lima coastline from Chorrillos to La Punta. The Mariscal Necochea clifftop park overlooks the Waikiki Club, a favourite with Lima surfers. On no account camp on Miraflores beach; it is extremely dangerous as well as pebbled and dust-blown because of cliff erosion. (In fact, any of the beaches near Miraflores are unsafe regarding theft, especially during school holidays.) You can see thousands of sea birds fishing off-shore.

Buses to Miraflores No. 2 from Plaza de Armas, Nos. 2 and 53 from Emancipación and Tacna; No. 2 from Plaza San Martín (US$0.12). Taxi-colectivos recommended, from Plaza San Martín in front of Ciné Colón, US$0.15.

The road passes through **Barranco,** with an attractive plaza and nearby the interesting *bajada*, a steep path down to the beach, where many of Lima's artists live and exhibit their work; many old houses are under restoration. (Take bus No. 2 to Miraflores and Barranco beaches from Plaza San Martín, for US$0.15.) The next development on the coast is at **Chorrillos,** a fashionable resort (*Café Suizo* overlooking beach) with a cliff promenade, and boating. At Hacienda La Villa, an old Spanish *hacienda* worth visiting, there is occasionally open air dancing to *salsa* music. Near Chorrillos is the Playa de los Pescadores with seafood stalls, Playa Agua Dulce (a clean beach), and the Club Regatas de Lima. Beyond Chorrillos is **La Herradura,** another bathing resort with several restaurants. The private Club Unicornio is open to tourists. Some of the beaches round Lima are none too clean; La Herradura, however, is a welcome exception. A new beach road runs round the entire bay; the main access to it is either at the end of the Paseo de la República in Barranco or by the Bajada de Balta, which is at the end of Av. Diagonal in Miraflores. Bathing at all points, but be careful of the currents. Pucusana, 50 km. from Lima, Silencio, Santa María and Cerro Azul, 90 km., are fishing villages with beaches that are much cleaner than those near Lima. Robbery is common on the beaches and you are advised to sit on your clothes and other possessions. Do not leave anything unattended when swimming.

Pachacámac is some distance further along the coast, in the Lurín valley, 31 km. from Lima. When the Spaniards arrived, Pachacámac was the largest city on the coast. The ruins encircle the top of a low hill, the crest of which was crowned with a Temple of the Sun, a large pyramid built in 1350 of sun-baked bricks. (There are also a reconstructed Temple of the Virgins and the ancient temple of the Creator God.) Hernando Pizarro, brother of Francisco, was the first European to come to Pachacámac; in 1533 he destroyed images, killed the priests and looted the temples. The setting is marvellous, but the restoration has been criticized and vandals have been at work. Bus or colectivo from Lima, caught at the Plaza Santa Catalina, near the Parque Universitario at the crossing of Puno with Andahuaylas. The buses (US$0.25, 1 hr.) and colectivos (US$0.50) go by way of Miraflores and Chorrillos, but tell the driver you are going to the *ruinas* or he will land you in Pachacámac town further on. Taxi, 3 hr. trip, US$40. Closed Mon. and May 1, open 0900 to 1700. Entrance US$0.40.

Return by Avenida Costanera along the top of the cliffs and with beautiful views over the bay. Beyond Miraflores it passes through a seaside resort, **Magdalena del Mar,** served by a separate road and bus route from Lima. A little inland, along this route, is **Pueblo Libre,** where the Museum of Anthropology and Archaeology, the Museum of the Republic and the Rafael Larco Herrera Museum are found (see under Museums), as well as the old church of Magdalena Vieja (1557), which was unfortunately heavily damaged in the 1974 earthquake. A good restaurant here is the *Pejerrey De Oro*, near the Museum of Anthropology.

656 PERU

The second drive is to **Chosica**, 40 km. up the Rímac valley (see also page 734). In the residential district of Chaclacayo, just before Chosica, are the *Huampani Hotel*, C, modern, attractive, good meals, swimming pool (US$0.40), run by the Government's hotel chain, and *Residencial La Casa de los Olivos*, at Los Ficus 373 y Los Olivos, with restaurant and ten rooms. An excellent lunch or light refreshments can be had at *San Jorge* in Chosica; or chicken meals at the *Granja Azul* (take bus 88M or 204 from Parque Universitario) and several other places on the road from Lima to Chosica. The *Hotel El Pueblo* has swimming pool, horse riding, tennis, a beautiful garden, entrance, US$3, used heavily for conventions. Try restaurant and campground of *Puerto del Sol*, owned by Sr. Italo de Neqzi Herreros. A delightful place for dinner and dancing is the restaurant *Fiesta*, at km. 6 on the Central Highway. At km. 33 is *El Bosque* Country Club (anyone may enter on payment of US$85), private lake, 4 swimming pools, tennis and ball courts, riding stables, bull ring, etc. Colectivos for Chosica leave from just W of Parque Universitario, near the Ministry of Education building. Buses, 204, 1M.

On the way to Chosica a diversion may be made at Km. 4½ to **Puruchuco**, to see the reconstructed palace of a pre-Inca Huacho noble; with small museum (ceramics, textiles, etc., from the lower Rímac or Lima valley) and a selection of indigenous plants and animals, including hairless dogs and guinea pigs, open 0900-1700, Tues.-Sun. (closed May 1 and July 28). Entrance US$1; Chosica bus or colectivo from Parque Universitario. The large adobe pre-Inca city of **Cajamarquilla** may also be visited, for which the turnoff (left, at Huachipa) is about 6 km. on from the Puruchuco turn. The site is difficult to find—you can't see it from the road—but look for a sign "Zona Arqueológica" in the middle of a brick yard. Keep on driving through the yard, and you will find Cajamarquilla at the end of an ill-kept dirt road. Open every day, 0900-1700. Beyond the Huachipa turn-off for Cajamarquilla, along the main road, there are precolumbian ruins at San Juan de Pariache and Huaicán-Tambo, 13½ and 16½ km. respectively from Lima.

Beyond Chosica, near the Santa Eulalia river (80 km. from Lima), is **Marchuasi**, a table mountain about 3 km. by 3 km. at 4,200 metres, near the village of San Pedro de Casta (accommodation in a cold shelter only, less than US$1). The *meseta* has been investigated by Daniel Ruzo: there are 3 lakes, a "monumento a la humanidad" (40 metres high), and other mysterious lines, gigantic figures, sculptures, astrological signs and megaliths which display non-American symbolism. Ruzo describes this pre-Incaic culture in his book, *La Culture Masma*, Extrait de l'Ethnographie, Paris, 1956. Others say that the formations are not man-made, but the result of wind erosion. Truck to San Pedro de Casta from Chosica, 3 hrs., colectivo 2 hrs (US$1.70). Trail starts behind the village of San Pedro bending to the left—about 2 hours to the *meseta* (guides about US$3 a day, advisable in misty weather). Buses available for US$1.85 from San Pedro de Casta to Lima. Take food as no-one lives on the *meseta*, although there is a hut which provides good basic shelter; nights are cold. Srta. Paquita Castillo, Tel.: Lima 275251, arranges group tours.

The Central Highway to La Oroya opens up possibilities of excursions by car with attractive stopping places like Matucana (1 hr.), San Mateo and Río Blanco (2 hrs.). The trip to La Oroya takes over 5 hrs., and crosses the Andean divide at 4,843 metres. An excursion may be made to Infiernillo ("Little Hell") Canyon, beyond Matucana, which is well worth seeing.

There are bathing, tennis, and a yacht club at **Ancón**, 30 km. NW of Lima, reached by a double-lane asphalted highway. It is the only real seaside resort in Peru, but no hotels apart from *Restaurant Cinco Luches*, which has rooms, E. Beaches are very small. Crowded Jan.-March holidays, good for fish. There are the ancient (from 1500 BC) ruins of a small town on the hill of San Pedro de Casta, a fortress on the hills of Loma de los Papas (daily bus from Chosica at 0800), the ruins of Tambo Inca, and an ancient cemetery to the S. Beyond Ancón is a Chancay cemetery, from which has come much Chancay weaving and pottery (as seen in the Amano Museum). There are also Inca ruins at Maranga and Chuquitanta, near Lima; unfortunately the latter cannot be visited at present.

Other Excursions from Lima To the South, up the Omas valley beyond Coalla to the Inca adobe structures at Los Gentiles (on the right, well before Omas) and, nearer Omas, Pueblo Viejo, Yampa and Viracocha. Take a colectivo from Plaza Santa Catalina, Jr. Puno (2 blocks from Av. Abancay), Lima to Mala, then hitch, or taxi, via Asia to the sites. To the North, up the Chillón valley is Cantamarca. "Beyond Cantamarca one comes (writes John Streather) to the beautiful Abra de la Viuda pass, where one passes through the Bosque de Piedras (rocks in extraordinary shapes and sizes) and the Junín pampa to Cerro de Pasco." In the Chancay valley are Chiprac, Rupac and Añay. John Streather writes: "These extraordinary ruins are very little visited, especially the last two which are more or less perfectly preserved. They have roofs on them and are extraordinarily well built. For Chiprac and Rupac, go with food, tent and sleeping bag to Huaral on the coast (bus from Lima from the Plaza de Acho, by the bullring, over the Puente de Piedra—beware of thieves). From Huaral, get a lift or a bus (one a week) to San Juan up beyond Acos. Best go first to Acos where there is a restaurant and accommodation and wait at the road junction a few km. out of the village for a lift up to San Juan. Chiprac is high above the village and can be reached on one's own;

PERU 657

it is a good day's walk there and back with time to take photographs and eat. In San Juan, a man called Chavelo will act as a guide to Rupac, which can be reached via the pretty and deserted town of Pampas—also a day there and back. For Añay, go to Huaral as for the other ruins, then get transport to Huayoapampa (basic accommodation) or La Perla whence the visit to the ruins can easily be made; get a guide to show you up from either village." Further on are Sayán, Oyón and Churín (near here, at Chinchín, is *Albergue San Camilo*, C, excellent; bus from Lima, US$5 with Espadín y Hnos at Ormeño terminal to Churín, Oyón and Huamahuanca); at Churín, there are hot, sulphurous baths. From Chinchín, there are buses to nearby villages, such as Huancahuasi, where one can buy woven goods, see interesting churches, and spot *vicuña* in lovely surroundings.

Callao Passengers coming to Peru by sea usually land at Callao (now contiguous with Lima). It handles 75% of the nation's imports and some 25% of its exports.

Callao's maritime terminal or inner harbour covers 100 hectares, and the largest vessels go alongside. Population, 411,200. San Lorenzo island, a naval station, protects the roadstead from the S; inland stretches the green Rímac valley. It is a commercial place with no architectural beauty. Lima is reached by road (20 mins. by car or bus, US$0.12). Passengers are expected to be on board half-anhour before the vessel's departure. (Some have been attacked and robbed just outside the dock gates.) There are some interesting shops in the area between Calle Constitución and Av. Sáenz Peña, and a market between Sáenz Peña and Buenos Aires. "The Club", the oldest English club on the W coast, is at Pasaje Ronald, Calle Constitución, Callao.

History Drake and others raided Callao in the 16th century. An earthquake wiped it out in 1746. On November 5, 1820, Lord Cochrane boarded and captured, after a bloody fight in which he was wounded, the Spanish frigate *Esmeralda*. The Real Felipe fortress (1774), last stronghold of the Royalists in S. America, withstood a siege of a year and finally gave in after terrible sufferings in 1826. It is still a military post, and tourists are allowed to visit it. The Military Museum (see page 639) is in the old barracks. The railway to Lima, opened May 17, 1851, was one of the first in S. America.

Leading Restaurant *El Chalaquito*, Calle Constitución. A number of good fish restaurants can be found on Av. Sáenz Peña. There are a number of reliable bars in the Pasaje Ríos and Calle Constitucíon.

Taxis In Callao use taxis recommended by U.S. Embassy or port authorities—for safety's sake. About US$15 for 3 hrs.

Addresses British Vice-Consulate, Sáenz Peña 154. P.S.N.C., Calle Independencia 150 (Casilla 368), Tel.: 299040.

Bank of London & South America, Av. Sáenz Peña 352. Open 0830-1130 January-March, 0915-1245 April-December.

Cables Pasaje Ronald y Constitución 258. Sáenz Peña 160; Tel.: 29-0117 (Public Telex booth).

The Naval College is at ***La Punta***, just beyond Callao, served by municipal buses and colectivos through Callao from Lima. La Punta is on a spit of land stretching out to sea; once a fashionable beach, but water is cool. A new yacht club has been built on the N side. The walk along the seafront between Callao and La Punta has its charms.

The road from Callao to Lima is lined by factories. Shipyards, far from sea, load the fishing vessels they build on huge lorries and launch them into the ocean at Callao. San Marcos University (founded May 12, 1551) has now been transferred to a new University City, near the Naval Hospital.

On Avenida Marina between Lima and Callao, a turn-off opposite the entrance to the Feria del Pacífico grounds leads to the Parque Las Leyendas (see page 642):

North-West from Lima

From Lima to Chimbote Between Lima and Pativilca there is a narrow belt of coastal land deposited at the mouths of the rivers, but from Pativilca to the mouth of the Río Santa, N of Chimbote, the Andes come down to the sea. Between Lima and Pativilca cotton and sugar-cane are grown, though the yield

658 PERU

of sugar is less than it is further N where the sunshine is not interrupted by cloud. Cotton is harvested from April to September by Indian migrants from the basins of Jauja and Huancayo. Much irrigated land grows vegetables and crops to supply Lima and Callao. Cattle are driven down from the Highlands to graze the *lomas* on the mountain sides when the mists come between June and October.

The Pan-American Highway parallels the coast all the way to the far N, and feeder roads branch from it up the various valleys. Just N of Ancón, the next port N of Callao (see page 656), the Pasamayo sand dune, stretching for 20 km., comes right down to the seashore. The old road which snakes along the base beside the sea is spectacular, but is now closed except to commercial traffic. The new toll road (US$0.85), which goes right over the top, is much safer and you get spectacular views over the nearby coast and valleys. Chancay on the coast, suffers from severe water shortages, but there is a fresh water source on the beach; *Pensión Chancay*, F, safe, friendly, can wash clothes.

Turn right 5 km. along road to Sayán where there is a national reserve, Loma de Lachay, which has thousands of snail shells, locust-trees and much bird life. Or continue north to the small port of **Huacho**, 132 km. from Lima. It is the outlet for cotton and sugar grown in the rich Huaura valley; a branch road runs up to Sayán and beyond to Churín and Raura. There is a cemetery near Huacho where mummies may be found. There are cotton-seed oil and other factories. Port and sea are sometimes alive with monstrous jellyfish. Pop.: 35,900.

Hotels *El Pacífico*, F, safe, dirty, water problems, inadequate clothes-washing facilities; *Italia*; *Grace*; *Hostal Maury*, E, basic but friendly. Camping is possible at El Paraíso beach.

The journey inland from Huacho is splendid (Lima to Huacho by bus: Transportes América S.A., Av. Colonial 129, Lima). Beyond Sayán are terrific rock formations, then road passes through subtropical vegetation around Churín (see page 657), which is visited for its mineral springs. There are coal mines. Above 4,000 metres is a chain of lakes which reflect the Cordillera Raura (up to 5,800 metres). Road ends at Raura mine.

Just across the river is **Huaura**, where the balcony is still preserved from which San Martín declared the country's independence from Spain. Try *guinda*, the local cherry brandy. We pass from the wide valley of Mazo through the irrigated valley of San Felipe. There is more desert and then the cotton-fields of San Nicolás lead to **Supe,** a small busy port shipping fishmeal, cotton, sugar and minerals (*Hostal Supe*, G; better is *Hostal Grau* (basic, G, clean, safe, comfortable, laundry, good value), next to which is a poor restaurant: *El Norteño*). At Aspero, near Supe, is one of the earliest prehistoric sites in Peru (see History section, page 632). We pass through the town of **Barranca** (*Hotel Chavín*, F, nice, with bath, clean, good value, front rooms are noisy, also restaurant on first floor for lunch and dinner (try *arroz con conchas*), breakfast bar and café opens onto street by main entrance; *Pacífico*, F with bath, clean, good value; *Jefferson*, Lima 946, F, reasonably clean, friendly; *Hostería Central*, F, basic; many others on main street, and plenty of bars and restaurants, e.g. *Chifa*). The beach is long, not too dirty, though windy. Next is the straggling town of **Pativilca**, which has a small museum (bus from Lima US$4, 2½ hrs.—*Restaurant Cornejo*, good and cheap) from which a well-paved road turns off for the Callejón de Huaylas and Huarás (see page 664). 4 km. beyond the turn-off, beside the Highway, are the well preserved ruins of the Chimú temple of **Paramonga**. Set on high ground (view of the ocean), the fortress-like mound is reinforced by 8 quadrangular walls rising in tiers to the top of the hill (admission US$0.25, well worth visiting, taxi from Paramonga and return after waiting, US$4.50, otherwise hitch from Barranca). Not far from the fortress, the Great Wall (La Muralla) stretches across the Andes. Paramonga is a small port, 3 km. off the Pan-American Highway, 4 km. from the ruins and 200 km. from Lima, shipping sugar.

Hotel There is no hotel at Paramonga. There are several in Barranca; as bus companies have their offices there, buses will stop there rather than at Pativilca or Paramonga. No buses run to the ruins, only to the port.

Bus from Lima to Paramonga, Compañía Fortaleza or Empresa América recommended. From Lima to Barranca, 3 hrs. US$2, Empresa América, very comfortable. 1st class from terminal on

PERU 659

outskirts; Compañía Fortaleza and Comité Cinco (2nd class) go to Barranca from Parque Universitario in Lima. Buses cover the 7-8 km. from Barranca to Paramonga. Bus from Barranca to Casma US$1; Ancash bus to Huarás, 4 hrs., US$3. Truck, Pativilca-Huarás, 5-6 hrs., US$1.70; many buses, first at 1030.

Between Paramonga and Chimbote (225 km.) the mountains come down to the sea. The road passes by a few very small protected harbours in tiny rock-encircled bays—Puerto **Huarmey** (small *Hotel de Turistas*, D, clean and good service, but noisy, being on Pan-American Highway, rebuilt and reopened after earthquake, at Huarmey town, not port), Puerto Casma, and Vesique. Tepsa bus Lima-Huarmey, US$5.10, US$8.50 by colectivo, from Parque Universitario. From Casma a road runs through the Callán pass (4,224 metres) to Huarás. A difficult but beautiful trip. Not all buses take this route, so check before leaving. From Casma to the pass (apart from the paved first 30 km.), the road is appalling (many land-slides), but once the Cordillera Negra has been crossed, the road is better (gravel, wide) with spectacular views.

Casma The town was largely destroyed by the 1970 earthquake, but has since been rebuilt. A good new food market.

Hotels *Central*, G, on Plaza de Armas, dirty, basic; *Hostal El Farol*, E, ask for cheaper rate in low season, good, with bathroom (no hot water), breakfast and dinner available (and sandwiches and coffee), pleasant garden setting despite crickets and cockroaches in rooms; *Hostal Madeleine*, Plaza de Armas, F, very basic *Restaurant Tumi*, recommended; *Chifa Tío Sam*, good, and *Chifa San Chan*, all on Plaza de Armas. Also *Restaurant Libertad*, fair.

Bus From Parque Universitario, Lima, colectivo to Casma, US$8.80. Bus to Lima leaves 1100 daily (Tepsa) US$4.25 also Chinchay-Suyo, on main street, and Turismo Chimbote (main road opp. road on which *Hostal El Farol* is located), 4 a day, US$3.40. Bus to Huarás, Chinchay-Suyo, 2300, daily and Moreno, 0700, 10 hrs., US$3.40. It is well worth making this trip in daylight to get the view of the Cordillera Blanca. Bus to Trujillo, Tepsa and Chinchay-Suyo, US$2.40, 3 hrs.

Excursions From Casma, take a truck going to San Rafael and ask for Castillo (departs 0900 from the garage opposite Huarás bus stop). After alighting, walk 2 km. uphill to a cemetery with pottery on the ground, and a Chimú castle of 4 concentric rings, with 3 towers in the middle, the Castillo de Chanquillo. Further on is a large wall with 13 towers on a ridge. Take water with you. There are several other sites around Casma: Sechín Alto, Pallka, Tokán, Mojeque, La Cantina, Tokachi and Huanchay.

Sechín At km. 370 on Pan-American Highway, shortly before reaching Casma from Lima, watch for a large concrete sign to Sechín on the right. Follow the road indicated for about 2 km. until you reach the ruins (about one hour's walk). Three sides of the large stone temple have been excavated and restored. You cannot see the adobe buildings inside the stone walls, which belong to an earlier period. They were later covered up and used as a base for a second storey which unfortunately has been completely destroyed. Some experts think the temple and surroundings were buried on purpose. Others believe it was engulfed by natural disaster. The latter theory is supported by finds of human skeletons. Tombs have been found in front and at the same level as the temple. A wall of a large adobe building under excavation can be seen and runs round the sides and back of the temple. The site is open to tourists, 0800-1700 (US$0.75, children half price); ticket also valid for Pañamarca (see page 660), and there is an attractive, shady picnic garden. The Max Uhle Museum opened in 1984 (interesting display of Sechín artefacts). It is quite easy to walk to the ruins from Casma. One must walk about 3 km. S to a well posted sign showing a left turn, then simply follow the road for 2 km. to the ruins. (Frequent colectivos from Casma, easy to hitchhike from Casma to Sechín, but leave early in the morning; no buses.) 2 km. further along there are two pyramids of the late Chavín period, but these have not yet been excavated.

Sechín is one of the most important ruins on the Peruvian coast. It consists of a large square temple completely faced with carved stone monoliths—probably over 500 of them—which depict gruesome battle scenes: men being eviscerated, heads with blood gushing from eyes or mouths, dismembered legs, arms, torsos, ears, eyes and vertebrae. The style is unique in Peru for its naturalistic vigour. Within the stone temple is an earlier, pre-ceramic mud temple with painted walls. The temples are pre-Chavín, about 1500 BC. (John Hemming)

Chimbote, 420 km. from Lima, is one of the few natural harbours on the W coast, ample in area and depth of water. Rapidly growing population of 185,000; a new port has been built to serve the national steel industry: iron ore from Marcona field is shipped from the port of San Juan, 547 km. S of Lima; anthracite comes by railway from the hinterland, and power comes from the hydroelectric station at the Cañón del Pato, 129 km. inland. Chimbote is Peru's largest fishing

660 PERU

port; fishmeal is exported and the smell of fish can be overpowering. Bathing is forbidden on the beach near the hotel. Flocks of brown pelicans and masked boobies may be seen from the beach. Shanty towns have burgeoned around. Small airport.

Hotels *Chimú*, now a State Tourist Hotel (D, with bath, meals US$3.50, uninspiring), Chimbote's cleanest snack bar, there are some cheaper rooms at the back, must ask, safe parking; *Presidente* (3 star), E, with bath, clean, friendly, hot showers, safe parking, poor snack bar, recommended; *Rivera*, E, clean, hot water, restaurant on top floor with good view but poor food; *San Felipe*, E, unfriendly, dingy, warm showers; *María Isabel*, F, dingy, helpful; *El Santa*, E, with bath, clean and good; *Venus*, F, near Roggero bus station, useful if you arrive at 0200; *Augusto*, Aguirre 265, F, with shower and toilet, overpriced, clean, front rooms noisy, water intermittent as everywhere in town; opp. is *Huáscar*, G, clean and friendly; *Oriental*, G, in market; *Felic*, Av. José Pardo, 552, F, noisy.

Restaurants *Pollo Gordo*, Prado y Aguirre, good chicken and cold beer; *San Remo*, Pardo y Villavicencio, seafood, good and cheap, good pisco sours; *Buenos Aires*, Aguirre near beach, popular lunch place; *Marisquito*, Bolognesi near Palacios, good local food, disco at night; *Franco* and *Venecia*, same block, good seafood.

Tourist Office Av. Bolognesi 421.

Buses To Lima, best is Turismo Chimbote on Pardo, US$4.50, 6-7 hrs. The Santa valley road via Huallanca to the Callejón de Huaylas and beyond has been rebuilt, but is still hair-raising (scenery is superb). Bus leaves Chimbote for Huarás daily at 0700 via Casma, US$4.75, and 0800, via Carás and Cañón del Pato, US$4.90 (Transportes Moreno, Av. Pardo 758), 8 hrs. (12 hrs. in rainy season). Road is unsurfaced to Carás (bus to Carás, US$3.65, 6 hrs., daily); bus to Huallanca, US$3.25. Colectivo to Casma, US$1.25. Buses run Chimbote to Trujillo, US$1.10 (Empresa El Aguila, José Gálvez 317, hourly from 0600-2000); Tepsa at 1600; Colectivo to Trujillo, US$1.90, 2 hrs.

Warning Thefts are common around the Moreno Hermanos bus station.

John Streather tells us that about 25 km. S of Chimbote a paved road leads E to the Nepeña valley, where a sculpted precolumbian tomb and the temple of Cerro Blanco may be found; also ruins at **Pañamarca** (pre-Mochica temple), 10 km. from the crossroads. Pañamarca is a town from the Mochica culture, where buildings and animal sculpture remains can be seen. 20 km. from Pañamarca is the site of Paredores with the "Puerta del Sol", and a stone carving, the "monolito de siete huacas".

From Chimbote a road branches off to the NE and, joining another road from Santa, goes up the Santa valley following the route, including tunnels, of the old Santa Corporation Railway. (This used to run as far as Huallanca, 140 km. up the valley, but was largely destroyed by the 1970 earthquake.) At the top of the valley the road goes through the very narrow and spectacular Cañón del Pato before reaching the Callejón de Huaylas and going on S to Carás and Huarás.

Just before the Cañón del Pato is **Huallanca**, an unfriendly village (where everything closes early) with an impressive hydroelectric plant built into a mountain. This can no longer be visited because of terrorism (similarly, the Cañón del Pato is closed to tourist excursions). *Hotel Huascarán*, F, good value (the only saving grace).

Carás, also badly damaged by the 1970 earthquake, is now almost totally restored, and is reported a pleasant place and a good centre for walking; splendid views of Huandoy and Huascarán. Information on mountaineering obtainable from the director of the Huascarán National Park in Huarás, or the Tourist Office in Yungay. Excellent views of the northern *cordilleras* in July and August; in other months, mountains often shrouded in cloud. One has to cross a river by cable (20 mins.) and go to Pueblo Libre to climb Tunaspampa. Carás has a milder climate than Huarás and is more suited to day excursions.

Hotels *La Suiza Peruana*, in main square, F, without or with bath, quiet, not clean, not secure for left luggage (restaurant); *El Cafetal*, friendly, clean, hot water; *Hostal Carás*, Calle Sucre, F, dirty, hot showers; *Chavín*, just off Plaza, F with bath, new, clean, good value (but no views); *Morovi*, just outside town on Yungay road, F, clean, friendly, helpful, with bath and hot water; *Herrera*, F.

Restaurants *Le París* on main square, dirty; *Jeny*, on plaza, good food and prices; *La Copilliana*, excellent local dishes; *Juventud*, recommended; *La Punta Grande*, on corner of turn-off to Lake

PERU 661

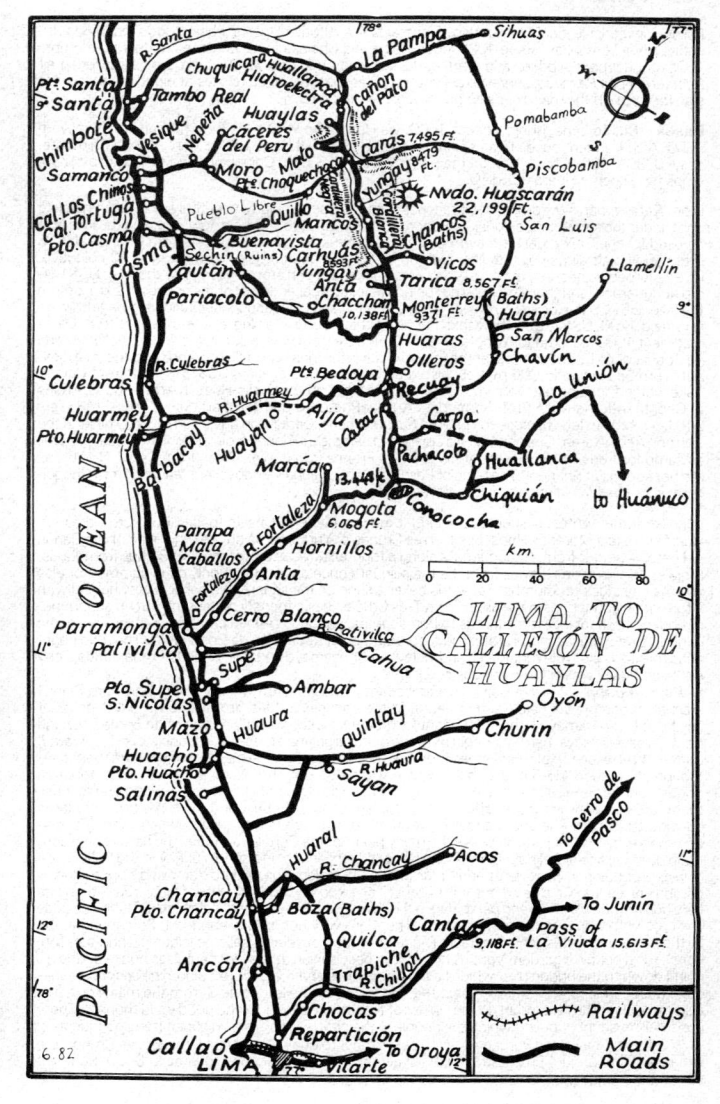

662 PERU

Parón, inexpensive local meals. Also, *Esmeralda* Av. Alfonso Ugarte, cheap, good local food, friendly; *Chifa Lorena*, Jr. Sucre 1021, cheap local and Chinese food; unnamed restaurant at Sucre 1003, good, English spoken and *Centenario*, not recommended. About 1 km. S of Carás, open-air *Restaurant Las Palmiras*, serves excellent trout, reasonably priced (closes at nightfall); follow the sign for trout off the main road and go through carnation farm.

Buses Bus to Lima 14 hrs., direct 1500, via Huarás (to which the 67-km. road is now paved) 0600. Also frequent buses to and from Huarás, US$1.20 (last at 1900), 2 hrs. Bus to Chimbote, daily, 0630, 1230, 6 hrs., through the Santa Valley, US$3.65. Chinchay-Suyo to Trujillo at 1730, stops for dinner at Huarás, US$10.

From Carás a narrow, rough road branches E to the spectacularly beautiful Lake Parón nestling right under the snow-capped peak of Huandoy (the water level has been lowered, and the lake is to be used for the Cañon del Pato hydroelectric scheme—taxi from Carás, or from Huarás, US$15 return, will wait all day at the lake, pick-up US$3 approx., bargain hard), Comité 20 colectivo, US$3; 10 people needed, max. 15—1-2 hrs. at lake, one can stay at a lodge by the lake, US$1.60 p.p. (unguarded, and therefore may not be possible, at weekends), or at the houses 1-2 km. before the lake, US$1 p.p. Comité 20 colectivos also go to Lake Llanganuco (see following page), 0730, returning 1200, US$2, US$15 by taxi. For hikes in the Cordillera Negra, a truck leaves from Carás market at 1000 to Huata (dirty hotel, F; 2,700 metres) from where one can climb to the Quebrada de Cochacocha (3,500 metres) at the top of which is the Inca ruin of Cantu, and on to the Inca lookout, Torreón Andino (5,006 metres); also reached from Rocracallán, US$1 by truck from Carás). Take water, food and tent with you. 6 km. down a track off the Carás-Huata road are the Inca ruins of Chonta. Alternatively, Prof. Bernardino Aguilar Prieto (former teacher), San Martín 1143 (Tel.: 2161—rooms to let, G), close to *Hotel La Suiza Peruana*, Carás, can advise on 2-3-day hikes in the Torreón Andino area. One can visit his apiary and sample the honey (sold at his town house) as well as camp for free and hire horses at his farm, La Fronda (run down), 7 km. from Carás. N of Carás are hot springs at Shangol. The ruins of Pashash Cabana and Huandoval are reached from Chuquicara, about halfway along the Santa Valley road.

John Streather writes: A spectacular circuit may be made to Chavín (page 666) from Carás (or Huarás). Take a Morenos Hnos. bus to Tres Cruces or Yuracmarca on the other side of the Cañon del Pato. A detour from Yuracmarca is along a frightening road to Corongo (0530 bus from Carás, Empresa Callejón de Huaylas from the main square once a week), but only go in summer, or else you may be stuck for months. Eat at the baker's shop on the square, the baker is very helpful with information about ruins in the area. From Tres Cruces (basic friendly restaurant, but no accommodation) one can take daytime lorries to Pomabamba, passing pre-Inca *chullpas*, Yanac, Tarica, the mining town of Pasacancha (hotel and restaurant) and the Callejón de Conchucos. The road continues through cold, wild mountains and valleys to Andaymayo and Palo Seco to Pomabamba, "city of the cedars" - where I saw not one cedar tree.

Pomabamba is worth a visit on several counts. Several good walks into the Cordillera Blanca start from nearby: via Palo Seco or Laurel to the Lagunas Safuna, from which one can go on, if hardy, to Mt. Alpamayo ("the most beautiful mountain in the world") and down to Santa Cruz and Carás—several days' hard walking. Up to the quite large and extensive, though sadly dilapidated, ruins of **Yaino**, on top of a very steep mountain and visible from the main square of Pomabamba—though still a good 4½-5 hours walk away. Ask directions in the village and on the way too. If in doubt, veer left after about two hours of going fairly straight uphill. The ruins, when one reaches them, are certainly worth the effort. The walls are beautifully built and there are two very large buildings, a square one and a circular one, the like of which I have seen nowhere else. The site commands far and majestic views of the many peaks of the Cordillera. Again, the hardy could continue their walk (several days) to the two lakes of Llanganuco and so to Yungay in the Callejón de Huaylas, or down to Santa Cruz and Carás on the other side. The walk to Yaino and back to Pomabamba can be done in a day if one starts early. Take a good lunch, and lots of juicy fruit—one gets very dehydrated climbing and perspiring in the thin dry air. It's also very cold high up if the sun goes in, so go with warm, waterproof clothes. There are very hot natural springs in Pomabamba, the furthest are the hottest and the best. The lady of the house also sells delicious orange-blossom honey from her own garden. Various hotels; the best is in an at present nameless house on the hill going down to the bridge over which lie the hot springs and the path to Yaino. The second best—quite adequate and very cheap—is up the first street on the left going S from the main square—also nameless. The restaurant on the corner of that street is friendly and good (cold though). There is a small museum opposite which the *people in the courtyard offices* will open free on request.

Cóndor de Chavín and Peruano Andino buses run S to Chavín and on to Lima. Buses to and from Lima via Chimbote are Empresa Marino (Ayacucho 1140, Lima), leaving Lima at 0800, Sun. and Wed., and Pomabamba at 0600 on the same days, 20 hrs.

The main road goes on to **Yungay**, which was completely buried by the 1970 earthquake—a hideous tragedy in which 20,000 people lost their lives. The survivors are housed just north of the old town, which is now recovering, with houses and a concrete market. A new church is being built. The site now has a few monuments and a field of rose bushes. A tourist complex is being built near the buried town.

Bed and Board A hotel without a signboard is on the left of the Carhuás road (F); *El Señor Blanco's Hotel* (past maternity hospital), G, breakfast and dinner US$1.40, recommended, luggage can be left safely; *Hostal Gledel*, Av. Arias Graziani (owned by Sra. Gamboa, who is hospitable and a good cook), F, clean, secure, good; *Hostal Yungay*, on plaza, F, clean; *Alojamiento Acuña*, F, clean, meals available. There is also private accommodation. Good food and drink can be found in the new market, and there is a good restaurant run by the local co-operative; also *Comedor Yungay* (good) and *El Portal*.

Tourist Office on the plaza (rarely open); opposite is *Café El Palmero*, which offers simple accommodation, F. There are several trucks which leave from the café for Lake Llanganuco (provided there are at least 10 passengers, US$2 single or return). A return allows only about an hour at the lake. Times of departure always change, so check at the Tourist Office. A tourist minibus to the lake leaves at 0800 on Sat., 2 hrs.

For trekkers, one of the finest walks (trees, flowers, birds, midges) is over the path by Huascarán and Lake Llanganuco (2 lakes: Orkoncocha and Chinancocha) from Yungay to Piscobamba (Yungay to Lake Llanganuco, trucks on Mon., Wed., Fri., at 0400, US$3, and Sun. from Huarás, no trucks will go unless there are enough passengers, and departure is often delayed; trucks to Llanganuco continue on the new road to the Portachuelo Pass at 4,750 metres, beautiful views of Huascarán; return to Yungay at 1000). It is a 5-6 day hike over a well-travelled route, but don't try it unless you are properly equipped. After 3-4 days you reach Llumpa on the Chavín-Piscobamba road (basic accommodation, unfriendly people), from here there are 2 buses per week to Piscobamba, and 2 per week to Chavín. After Llumpa, the trek to Piscobamba becomes rather boring and tiring. There are 2 buses per week between Piscobamba, Pomabamba (see page 662) and Huarás. (Advice and registration for mountain hut at Llanganuco from National Park office, Av. Centenario 912, Huarás and from local Club Andino at Electropo.) N.B. If making an excursion to photograph Huascarán and Huandoy, note that they are usually hidden by cloud after midday.

Deservedly the most popular walk in the Cordillera Blanca is from Llanganuco through the Portachuelo Pass to Colcabamba, and then through the Punta Unión (4,750 metres) to Cashapampa, Santa Cruz and Carás. This hike takes 5-6 days with guide and donkey (for baggage) from National Park office, who charge US$9 p.p. per day for all necessary equipment. Entrance to the National Park costs US$3 and is vaild for 3 days. Some of the route is on Inca roads (see pages 754-755). The mountain flowers and humming birds at these altitudes are magnificent. The road to the lake (full of trout) continues up to the tongue of the glacier of Cerro Chopicalqui (not suitable for cars, 4,830 metres)—insect repallant needed; take food, warm clothes, tent, sleeping bag and a stove. The early morning trucks from Yungay on a new road running from Llanganuco over the Portachuelo Pass go to Vaquería, the first settlement after the pass; get off the truck at the tin shacks on the left after Vaquería; from there the trail descends on S side of stream to Colcabamba, or crosses stream below thatched farmhouse to join Colcabamba-Punta Unión trail above Colcabamba. At Yanamá, on the eastern side of the Cordillera Blanca, there is lodging and food; a day's hike to the ruins above the town affords superb views (truck Yungay-Yanamá, US$2.50—ask at plaza in Yungay). At Colcabamba, the Calonge family welcome travellers with good meals and basic accommodation (G), and small shop—no sign but a white flag and red geraniums. Cashapampa, the first village at the bottom of the Santa Cruz valley has basic accommodation; meals at the house of Sra. Zenaida Pajuelo. Bus to Carás leaves at 0500 (US$1), there are also trucks; or follow footpath from Santa Cruz village a few km. further uphill. Above Santa Cruz (very basic accommodation—dirty and for midgets!) are hot springs at Huancarhuás. Lorries for Santa Cruz and Cashapampa leave Carás market at 1230, US$0.50, 3 hrs.

After Yungay, the main road goes to Mancos at the foot of Huascarán (*Hotel Mancos*, F, lovely setting, but bathroom dirty, water rationing) and on to **Carhuás** (daily bus service to Huarás, and to Huallanca via the Cañón del Pato), with fair hotels (*Perú*, F, good restaurant; and *Gran Hotel*, E, pleasant, no hot water *Hospedaje La Merced*, F, excellent, clean, friendly, recommended; *Restaurant Palma*, good value) and very good walking in the neighbourhood; precolumbian baths at Vicus and La Merced, ruins at Cuntuyoc, Hualcan, Huacoy, Torojirca, Tuyo and Huamanvilca. Carhuás has a *mestizo* festival on October 24, followed eight days later by an Indian festival. Before Huarás the road goes to Marcará (bus to Huarás, US$ 0.50), where there is a branch road 3 km. to **Chancos**, another thermal resort (*Hotel Chancos* closed but you can camp in the neighbourhood, 2 restaurants, minibus from Huarás). Further up the Huandoy valley is Vicos, set in superb surroundings with views of Nevados Tocllaraju and Ranrapalca. From Vicos, one can walk through the Quebrada Honda to Chacas (*Hostal Pilar*); a road has been built to Chacas (a tunnel through the pass was due for

664 PERU

completion in 1985). From Chacas you can get transport to San Luis (see page 755). The main road goes on to Tarica where there is cheap accommodation.

The valley's focus is **Huarás** (population 50,000), capital of the Department of Ancash, at 3,028 metres, 398 km. from Lima. One-third of Huarás was swept away and 6,000 people killed when the Laguna Palacocha above the city ruptured in December 1941. The city had been totally reconstructed when it was half destroyed in the earthquake of May 1970. Reconstruction of the city is again well advanced; the Plaza de Armas has been mainly rebuilt, except for the Cathedral, which is being resited elsewhere. The setting, with the peaks of Huascarán, Huandoy, and San Cristóbal in the background, is tremendous. Good panoramic views are to be had from the *mirador* at the cross (visible from Huarás) one hour's walk from the town (turn left past the cemetery and head uphill through a small forest). Huarás is now becoming a very lively place, popular with young gringos and Peruvians alike.

Festival Patron saints' days, September 27-30, parades, dancing, music and fireworks; much drinking and overcharging.

Hotels *Termas de Monterrey*, 7 km. N, run by State Tourist Hotel chain, recommended for walking, swimming in warm springs, D (accepts American Express), with bath, good, meals US$4.50; bus (marked "Monterrey" 1) Huarás-Monterrey, US$0.25, leaves every few minutes, takes ½ hr.; US$0.20 swim in tepid pool or US$0.20 for private bath tub (closed Mon.) Don't be too vigorous at the start; it's over 2,750 metres up. In town, *Hotel de Turistas*, Av. Centenario (Tel.: 2696), large rooms, clean, C; *Los Portales*, Raymondi (9th block), E, clean, helpful, quiet, hot water, reasonable restaurant; *El Pacífico*, Luzuriaga 630, F with bath, comfortable, locked parking facilities; *Los Pinos del Puente*, E, good value; *Tumi*, San Martín 1122, E, with bath, good restaurant, recommended; *Hostal Huandoy-Cusco*, F (triple rooms available), communal bathrooms, good; *Saxofón*, E, run down and poorly maintained; *Hostal Andino* (*Chalet Suisse*), C, Jr. Pedro Cochachín 357 (some way from centre), good, clean, meals served, safe parking, Swiss run, recommended, beautiful view of Huascarán, climbing and hiking gear for hire; *Hostal Colomba*, Calle Francisco de Zela 210, bungalow, rooms D, plus 21%, family-run (German), garden, friendly, safe car parking, English spoken; *Barcelona*, Av. Raymondi 612, F, with bath, no hot water; next door is *Cataluña*, Av. Raymondi 622, E or F in dormitory, restaurant, somewhat expensive, clean, safe, noisy, hot water; *Hostal Tabariz*, Av. Raymondi 827, F, clean, cold water; *Raymondi*, Av. Raymondi 820, F, central, bath, hot water (a.m. only in ground floor shower), comfortable, unfriendly, charges for left luggage, with café; *Janett*, Av. Centenario 106, E, friendly, hot water, clean, large rooms, recommended; opposite is *Su Casa*, E, with bath (F, without); *Alojamiento Amalia*, F, English spoken; *Edward's Inn*, Av. Bolognesi 121, F, clean, hot shower, laundry, friendly, food available, recommended, popular, Edward speaks English and knows a lot about trekking; under same ownership, *Alojamiento de Quintera*, Juan de la Cruz Romero 593, F, hot shower, laundry facilities, clean, popular with trekkers. *Hostal Premier*, Av. Luzuriaga 651-53, Tel.: 721954, F with bath (cheaper without), hot showers, clean, modern, English spoken by owners' son, helpful, informative, recommended; *Landauro*, on Plaza de Armas, E, cheap, clean, basic, friendly; *Hostal Los Andes*, Av. Tarapacá 316, G, hot water, clean, friendly, with laundry, but prices shoot up in the peak season; *Albergue El Tambo*, Confraternidad Internacional—Interior—122 B, F, clean, clothes washing, 3 rooms with 12 beds, and cooking facilities, nice people. Accommodation in private houses also available: 3 rooms for 2-4 people with Señora Andrea behind *La Casa de los Pantalones*, which is opposite the entrance to the market, clean, friendly, F; *Pensión Maguiña*, Av. Tarapacá 643, opposite Rodríguez bus terminal, G, hot water, rooms single to 4-bed, garden, clothes-washing facilities, breakfast available, rucksack store, recommended; *Alojamiento Galaxia* (de Inés Herrera) Jr. Romero 638, hot water F, friendly, recommended; *Familia Estella*, Jirón Nueva Granada 519, F, hot water, friendly, safe, recommended; *Casa de Señora López* (ask near Estadio just off Avenida Bolognesi at Santa river end), F, luke-warm showers, safe, washing facilities for clothes, a patio, very friendly, recommended. *Albergue Juvenil Los Capulíes*, Jr. Los Capulíes 160, Centenario—Huarás (15 mins., walk from the centre—information from the owner's *bodega* at San Martín 618), F, clean, friendly, showers, cooking and washing facilities, recommended. There are usually people waiting at the bus terminals offering cheap accommodation in their own homes.

Hot Public Showers on Av. Raymondi, 9th block, US$0.25.

Restaurants *Chifa Familiar*, cheap and good, serves local food as well; several other Chinese restaurants. Restaurant and bar at *Ebony 76*, Plaza de Armas, friendly, clean and *menú* not expensive; *Ebony 84*, behind plaza. *Tabariz*, corner of Av. Centenario and Av. Raymondi, good food. At Raymondi 809 is *Oja-Yo*, Chinese, good. *El Cosmos*, Fitzcarrald; *Recreo Unión*, Manco Capac, and *Los Pilatos*, both serve local food. *Eboli* is good; *Freddie's Tavern*, Av. Centenario 307, pop music. *Tik-Tok*, Raymondi 639, is indifferent and dear. *Rincón Trujillano*, next to *Hotel Raymondi*, good value, recommended, daily *pensión* (3 meals), US$1. *Restaurante D'Orropio* is

PERU 665

recommended, also good is *La Fontana* on Av. Mariscal Luzuriaga; *La Familia* at No. 431 (popular with gringos, impersonal) and *Gerard's* on same street. Behind La Fontana is *El Anzuelo*, good fish. Good breakfast at *San Miguel*, next to Hotel San Isidro. *La Cabañita* is also good and cheap, as is *Rivioli*, Av. Guzmán Barrón 244. *Francos Parrilladas*, Luzuriaga 410, good grills; *Pepe's Place*, Raymondi 622 (upstairs from Hostal Cataluña), expensive but good; *Ticino*, Luzuriaga 651, good pizzas and pastas; *Creperie Patrick*, across from *Ticino*, good crêpes; *Pizzería Trattoría*, good, popular, expensive; *Las Puyas*, Morales 535, good cheap meals and breakfasts, popular with gringos; *Pío Pío*, Av. Centenario 329, recommended; *El Gondolero*, or *Chifa Ton Fon*. *Pacccha'k Pub*, Centenario 290, folklore shows, local and international food, travel information.

Entertainment There are discotheques at *Tabariz*, *Bodega* (recommended). *Peña El Rizzo*, Luzuriaga 455, shows Thurs., Fri., Sat.; *Imantata*, Luzuriaga 424, disco and folk music; *Amadeus*, snack bar and music, on Plaza behind Banco Internacional, good; *Tambo*, José de la Mar, folk music daily.

Museum Museo Regional de Ancash, Instituto Nacional de Cultura, containing stone monoliths and *huacos* from the Recuay culture has been set up in the *Casa de Cultura*. Open 1000-1700, Tues.-Sun., US$0.25, students cheaper, pay to take photographs.

Camping Several shops of the trekking agencies sell camping gaz cartridges. Bodega Santillana, Centenario 417, good for all supplies. Andean Sport Tours, Av. Luzuriaga 571, Tel.: 721612, German-owned, rents or sells camping equipment, incl. camping gaz cartridges; treks, climbing, donkeys for hire, US$2 a day, guides, US$5, tents, US$1.50 a day. Tent hire for five days about US$13. All prices standard, but not cheap, throughout town.

Car Hire Empresa de Transporte Turismo Huascarán, Av. Raymondi 870, Tel.: 310099; VW Beetles for US$18 a day, plus US$0.18 per km., vehicles not up to much.

Exchange behind Banco de la Nación on Plaza de Armas, open till 1800.

Travel Agencies Cordillera Negra Tours, Av. Luzuriaga, organize trips to Chavín, Lake Llanganuco etc., guide speaks Spanish rapidly, very autocratic, take care that driver has a licence and that the same driver is with you after the police checkpoint. Explorandes, 28 de Julio y Luzuriaga, adventure travel, good. Foptur, main Plaza beside post office, for Chavín tour and treks; ask there for Miguel Chiri Valle, English speaking. Pablo Tours, Luzuriaga 501 (have information on horses for rent from Sr Quinta Paloma) and Chavín Tours, Av. Luzuriaga 502, organize trips to Chavín (US$9, all day), Llanganuco and the Puya Raimondii park, the latter is more expensive. Azul Tours, Av. Luzuriaga 658, helpful, friendly staff, hires good quality trekking equipment, recommended. Montrek, Luzuriaga 640, good for rafting on Santa river. Peruvian Exciting Tours, next to *Hotel Raymondi*, also offers a tour to Lake Llanganuco, US$11 p.p., but is not recommended; its vehicles are not sturdy and the management is elusive if you want to complain. In the main, tours to sites other than Chavín are too short; private arrangements with taxis are preferable.

Tourist Office Ministerio de Turismo, Luzuriaga 459; maps available, good for backpacking in the Cordillera Blanca. Pomabamba 415, 1st floor, and ground floor of Palacio Municipal, Plaza de Armas. Information on trekking, and equipment hire, at corner of Av. Fitzcarrald 458 and Calle Raymondi, maps and information but no English spoken (Tel.: 2394). Trekking & Backpacking Club Pernano, San Martín 995 (Casilla 112), issues magazine *El Trekkero*, maps and library at office. Asociación de Guías de Montaña, at Casa del Guía, behind Banco Internacional. Better maps of the area are available in Lima. However, the Instituto de Geología y Minería (Av. Guzmán Barrón 582, open a.m. only) sells useful maps for hikers.

Buses from Lima Transportes Rodríguez, 3 a day, leaves from office at Roosevelt 354, Lima (Tel.: 280-506)— recommended—and Tarapacá 622, Huarás; Expreso Ancash, 4 a day (recommended), Av. Carlos Zavala 177, Lima, and Raymondi 881, Huarás; Arellano-Intersa, Colmena 1635, Lima, and Raymondi 408, Huarás; El Trome, Montevideo 1049, Lima, and Raymondi 422, Huarás (not recommended); Empresa Huarás, Leticia 655 (Tel.: 275260), Lima, and Fitzcarrald 241, Huarás; Empresa Callejón de Huaylas, Leticia 626 (leaves at 0730); Co-op. de Transportes Huarás Ltda, Prolongación Leticia 1059, Lima, and Fitzcarrald 303, Huarás (neither too good). Transportes Tadeo, Arenillas 139, Act. Cda. 4, Av. Zarumilla, San Martín de Porras, Lima (an extremely dangerous area of Lima) and Raymondi 450, Huarás. All leave daily in both directions at approx. 0900 and 1400 to 2100, 8 hrs., average price US$5 (we are grateful to John Streather for much of this information). Colectivos to Lima, Comités 11 (Leticia 587) and 14 (Leticia 604, Tel.: 286621), Fitzcarrald 216, Huarás, recommended, leaves at 0200 but will collect passengers from hotels for US$1.50 extra), 6 hrs., US$11. Taxi to Lima, US$70 for 5.

Other Buses To Casma (150 km.) 6¼ hrs. US$3.40. Bus to Chimbote (Moreno, Av. Fitzcarrald 309) at 0930, 2000, US$4.90, 9½ hrs. via Cañón del Pato, overcrowded, often delayed; 0800 via Casma, US$4.75; colectivo to Chimbote, daily, leave early, 6 hrs. Bus to Marcará, US$0.50. Colectivos take visitors to see the Cordillera, and there is also a trip to the Chavín site, Huari and Huascarán. To Trujillo, US$6, only with Chinchay Suyo (Juan Bautista 845) departs 2030, 10 hrs. via Pativilca. Truck to Pativilca on coast, 5 hrs., US$2.75, or buses Intersa (old, poor service) and El

666 PERU

Trome. To Barranca, Ancash, US$3, 4 hrs. Bus to Carás, US$1.20, 2 hrs., (Ormeño) colectivo frequent; to Yungay US$1 hourly. Buses Huarás-Carhuás-Yungay-Carás run every ½ hr.

Huarás, which is the climbing centre of Peru, particularly between May and October, is the headquarters of the Huascarán National Park (entrance US$ 3—Unesco wants to make the park a worldwide natural heritage). The office is on Av. Centenario 912 (Prolongación Av. Raymondi—5th block), behind the Ministry of Agriculture building, helpful staff. For organised treks, contact Percy Tapiá, Casilla 3074, Lima 100: prices range from US$26 (16-20 people), to US$40 (under 8 people) daily. One should also contact Andes Adventures, Jr. Simón Bolívar 925, Casilla Postal 925, Tel.: 721646, Telex 46502 PE CP, Huarás, run by a Belgian, efficient, Spanish, English, French, German and Dutch spoken, reasonably-priced; also Pablo Morales Flores at Pyramid Adventures, Casilla 25, office: Av. Las Américas 330, Huarás. On the second floor of the *Hotel Residencial Cataluña*, Av. Raymondi, Tel.: 72117, José Valle Espinosa, "Pepe", hires out equipment (pricey), organizes treks and pack animals, sells dried food, and is generally helpful and informative. Treks organized by Ranra Tours, Casilla Postal 110, Huarás, offer guidance in English, French, German and Dutch.

Excursions About 8 km. into mountains is **Willcawain** archaeological site (entrance, US$0.60, students US$0.30), the ruins of a Tiahuanaco-style temple, dating from about AD 1000. The site is now signposted: walk down Av. Centenario and take the signed right turn 1 km. out of town. Alternatively, take a colectivo towards Yungay or Monterrey, get out 2 stops past the *Hotel de Turistas*, turn right and then left at a house for "pirotécnicas" (fireworks). Bring torch. Snacks are usually available at the ruins. Don't miss the extra ruins at the end of the track, which goes on 27 km. to Laguna Llaca (beautiful surroundings; taxis go there, bargain for fare, about US$3 one way). Excursion by taxi to the Parque Nacional de **Puya Raimondii** costs about US$15; in the park, puya plants, with the largest flowers (April-May) in the world, reach heights of 10 metres; they grow in the Quebrada Pachacoto valley, some 57 km. S of Huarás and 26 km. E of the road; there is a sign (entrance to Park, US$3). Carpa, in Puya Raimondii Park, can be reached on foot, by truck, or by San Cristóbal bus from Catac (continuing to La Unión). You can see the Park cheaply by getting the early Huarás-Lima bus to Pachacoto crossing, then hitch a ride on the road through the Park. Chavín Tours to the Puya Raimondii Park includes a visit to the glacier on the Quebrada Pachacota and to ice caves; take gloves and food, recommended, 7 hrs., US$5 p.p. Punta Callán, on the Cordillera Negra between Huarás and Casma, may be reached (20 mins.) by Empresa Soledad bus; spectacular views of the Cordillera Blanca. Hitch, or walk virtually straight down, 2-3 hrs. Inca ruins in the Huarás vicinity include Honcopampa, Canray Grande, Llasha, Pallasca, and Quequepampa. To the hot springs and sauna at Chancos (see page 663); minibuses and trucks go there.

S of Huarás is **Recuay**, a provincial capital (*Hotel Santa*, F, basic) where unusual pottery is sold. There are a museum and the Pueblo Viejo de Catac ruins here. Truck from Recuay to Chavín, US$1.50; many buses run from Recuay to Huarás.

Chavín The Chavín de Huantar ruins, of a fortress temple built about 600 BC, are about 3½-7 hrs. drive (depending on the bus, 109 km., avoid back seats) from Huarás, reached by a rather rocky spectacular road branching E from the main Huarás-Catac road. Unesco has proposed that the site be designated a worldwide cultural heritage. (Transport is difficult from Catac except in early morning and late evening.) Entry US$0.60, students US$0.40. The 1970 earthquake destroyed many of the underground structures and now only the first few levels can be toured, but work is now in progress to excavate and light the tunnels closed by the earthquake as well as other temple mounds so far unexplored. Open 0800-1200, 1400-1600. The main attraction is the marvellous carved stone heads and designs in relief of symbolic "gourd" figures. The carvings are in excellent condition, though many of the best sculptures are in Huarás and Lima. The famous Lanzón dagger-shaped stone monolith of 800 BC is found inside the

PERU 667

temple tunnel. **N.B.** Entrances to the temple buildings are locked: you must either hire a guide at the gate or get a child from the caretaker's house to open them for you. You cannot rely on the chambers being lit, so take a torch.

John Streather writes: There is only one carved head *in situ* on the walls of Chavín now. The best things are the finely drawn stone reliefs of condors, pumas and priest warriors— by far the finest work in stone of any Peruvian, or indeed any Andean, culture of any period. The lines are outstanding for their fluidity, sinuousness, complexity and precision. Nothing like them seems to have existed either before or after them: the earlier Sechín art is clearly a fount of inspiration, but is very clumsy when compared with the delicate exactitude of the Chavín... In many ways it resembles early Chinese art more than anything Andean—in its spirit and manner, though not in its symbolism, which is entirely Andean and American.

There are hot sulphur baths about 3 km. S of Chavín (US$0.08 for a bath; camping possible here). Beware of thieves in Chavín village; children try to sell fossils and stonework, or swap them for ballpens. Electricity 1800-0600.

Hotels *Gantu*, F (not recommended) and *Inca*, F, bathrooms filthy, basic but friendly; also *Monte Carlo*, F, fairly clean; *Monterrey*, F; *Casa de Alojamiento Geminis*, Jr. Túpac Yupanqui, F, fork left after bridge just past ruins, basic (no bath or shower, toilet in outhouse), but clean and friendly, all meals extra; *Albergue de Turistas*, D, with bath, modern, clean breakfast expensive, beautiful setting, 7 km. from the town on road to Huari. **Restaurants** *Montecarlo*, very slow, indifferent food; *Comedor de Cooperativa de Chavín*, behind church, good but difficult to get in, closed between mealtimes. All eating places appear to close after 1830. (Better hotels in Huari, 44 km. further on.) Nowhere to change money in or near Chavín.

Bus to Chavín Huascarán from Huarás, 1000 daily, returns 1000, US$2 (tickets available from the *Comedor El Sol*) and Cóndor de Chavín at 1000, returns at 0930 (slow, run-down, careless with luggage). Wait in the main plaza between 0900-1000 and take the best-looking bus, rather than buying ticket in advance for a bus that may not show up. A magnificent 6-hr. scenic journey, passing through the mountains and along the River Mosna gorge; spectacular views of the Yanamarey peaks and of many snow-fed waterfalls (sit on top of the bus if you can). Trucks US$1.25, 7 hrs., but very cold. Chavín Tours and Pablo Tours (tours about US$6) make daytime excursions to Chavín and other places of interest; collection from hotels at 0700, Comité 11 also does the return trip in a day with 1-2 hours at ruins, US$35 per car, taking up to 5. Andino Tours also organizes trips to Chavín, US$5 p.p. Taxi, Huarás-Chavín, US$15, 3-4 hrs. return. Direct bus Chavín to Lima, 13 hrs., Ancash Tours, also US$8.80 by Cóndor de Chavín, main office in Lima, Montevideo 1039. Tel.: 288122. Also Peru-Andino, Ayacucho 1152, Lima, Tues. at 1400, Sat. at 1300 to Huarás, returning Mon. and Thurs. The Lima-Chavín bus goes on to Pomabamba or Huari. From Barranca, every second day by truck, US$1.50, 17 hrs., trip is very bumpy and cold.

Hiking For the active, there is the possibility of a 4-day walk from Olleros, reached by bus or truck from the *frigorífico* in Huarás (US$0.25). The Olleros village carpenter, on the square, has a room where one can stay. Enquire at National Park Office about necessary equipment for walk. A good map of the route is available from the Instituto Geográfico Militar in Lima, line maps from Don Pepe at *Hotel Cataluña*, Huarás, (ask directions from anyone you meet along the way). The first day you go half-way along the meadows to the first, nameless Quebrada; on the second, you climb the first pass and sleep in the next valley; on the third, you pass Punta Yanashallash and camp in the valley somewhere after it, but before Jato; on the last day you reach Chavín. The area is isolated, so be sure to take good camping equipment, extra food and plenty of warm clothing. A longer walk may also be made to the Laguna Verdecocha, a glacier lake; this is recommended for experienced climbers only. On the first day of the walk, one reaches the Quebrada Quilloc: the second day, the Quebrada Otuto and the Punta Yanashallash (altitude: 4,680 metres); several Inca remains may be seen en route. On the third day, the trail dips and rises like a roller coaster, passing through the River Shongo valley (spectacular views of the Huachecsa gorge), finally reaching Chavín. A two-day walk from Huarás to the Laguna de Chulup (4,250 metres) a beautiful blue lake in a crater beneath a mountain peak beyond the small village of Pitec is possible; a guide is necessary for the inexperienced, or a very good map to find the Laguna. A pick-up is supposed to go half-way there, but it is hard to find. It is 18 km. from Huarás, of which the first 15 km. are easy, in the valleys (locals will advise on the route)—follow Av. Raymondi E out of Huarás. Just before Pitec, turn right at a fork, and in Pitec, turn left, just before a mountain stream. From here it is very hard going, initially with no path, then occasional trail markers—the general direction is NE towards the snow-covered peak. The hike can be done in a day, with an early start; take sun cream and food.

Warning Recent reports suggest that tourists in the Callejón de Huaylas have been attacked, not so much by local people, but particularly by dogs (a stick is most useful— otherwise, throw stones).

Probably the best way to see the Santa Valley and the Callejón de Huaylas, which contain some of the most spectacular scenery in Peru, is to take the paved

668 PERU

road which branches off the coast road into the mountains just N of Pativilca (see page 658), 187 km. from Lima. This route also gives a more spectacular view of the Cordillera Blanca. In 120 km. it climbs to Lake Conococha (delicious trout available in Conococha village), at 4,100 metres, where the Santa River rises. After crossing the high level surface it descends gradually for 87 km. to Huarás, and goes on to the Callejón de Huaylas, where it runs between the towering Cordillera Negra, snowless and rising to 4,600 metres, and the snow-covered Cordillera Blanca, whose highest point is the 6,768 metres high Huascarán. Farms appear at about 4,000 metres, but most of the farming is around Huarás. The inhabitants grow potatoes and barley at the higher and maize and alfalfa at the lower altitudes. The valley has many picturesque villages and small towns, with narrow cobblestone streets and odd-angled house roofs. (At weekends and holidays beware of reckless Lima drivers on the roads.)

The alternative routes to the Callejón de Huaylas are via the Callán pass from Casma to Huarás (see page 659), and via the Cañón del Pato (page 662).

Advice to Climbers: The height of the Cordillera Blanca and the Callejón de Huaylas ranges and their location in the tropics create conditions different from the Alps or even the Himalayas. Fierce sun makes the mountain snow porous and the glaciers move more rapidly. The British Embassy advises climbers to take at least six days for acclimatization, to move in groups of four or more, reporting to Club Andino or the office of the guide before departing, giving date at which search should begin, and leaving telephone number of Embassy with money. Rescue operations are very limited and there are at present only eight guides with training (by the Swiss). Insurance is essential, since a guide costs US$40-50 a day and a search US$2,000-2,500 (by helicopter, US$10,000).

Robert and Ana Cook (formerly of Lima) write of the **Callejón de Huaylas**. The heavy rainy season lasts from Jan. to Mar., while the dry season is from May to Sept. The mean daily temperature is determined by the altitude and hardly varies throughout the year. For instance, at 3,000 metres (the altitude of Huarás) the mean temperature is 14°C.

Apart from the range of Andes running along the Chile-Argentina border, the highest mountains in South America are along the Callejón and perfectly visible from many spots. From the city of Huarás alone, one can see over 23 snow-crested peaks of over 5,000 metres, of which the most notable is Huascarán (6,768 metres), the highest mountain in Peru. Although the snowline now stands at the 5,000 metres level, it was not long ago (geologically speaking) that snow and ice covered the Callejón at 3,000 metres. Despite its receding snowline, the Cordillera Blanca still contains the largest concentration of glaciers found in the world's tropical zone. From the retreating glaciers come the beauty and the plague of the Callejón. The turquoise-coloured lakes which form in the terminal moraines are the jewels of the Andes and visitors should hike up to at least one during their stay. At the same time these *cochas* (glacial lakes) have caused much death and destruction. Rarely a decade passes in which at least one major tragedy does not occur, due to the breaking of a dyke, sending tons of water hurtling down the canyons wiping out everything in their path. Now government engineers combat this problem by monitoring water flows and dyke stability.

Hilary Bradt writes: The Cordillera Blanca offers the most popular backpacking and trekking in Peru, with a network of trails used by the local people and some less well defined mountaineers' routes. Most circuits can be hiked in five days. Although the trails are easily followed, they are rugged and the passes very high—between 4,000 and nearly 5,000 metres—so backpackers wishing to go it alone should be fit and properly acclimatized to the altitude, and carry all necessary equipment. Essential items are a tent, warm sleeping bag, stove, and protection against wind and rain (climatic conditions are quite unreliable here and you cannot rule out rain and hail storms even in the dry season). Trekking demands less stamina since equipment is carried by donkeys. There are various trekking companies in Huarás.

Backpackers should buy a copy of *Trails of the Cordilleras Blanca and Huayhuash* by Jim Bartle, an excellent book detailing every important trail in the Cordillera, plus much useful background information. The book includes a large map which is the best available on the area. The book may be purchased in Huarás or from Bradt Enterprises (or from the South American Explorers' Club in Lima).

Only photocopied maps of inferior quality can be bought in Huarás so it's best to do your map shopping in Lima. The South American Explorers' Club publishes a good one with additional notes on the popular Llanganuco to Santa Cruz loop, and the Instituto Geográfico Militar has mapped the area with its 1:100,000 topographical series. These are more useful to the mountaineer than hiker, however, since the trails marked are confusing and inaccurate. Recommended guides through the Cordillera Huayhuash are Catalino Rojas and Cerillio Zambrano, both from the village of Llamac. "Jefe", who sells maps and key chains in Chiquián, is to be avoided.

PERU 669

Apart from the books by the Bradts and Jim Bartle (see "Information for Visitors"), recommended reading includes *Guide to the Peruvian Andes* by John Ricker, and *Randonées dans la Cordillère Blanche*, published by Uniclam (Paris). Librería Studium in Lima have a good selection of books on the Cordillera Blanca.

There are two spectacular transandine routes from Huarás to La Unión (and on to Huánuco for Cerro de Pasco, La Oroya, etc.; see page 743). The first is by twice weekly direct bus or bus leaving Huarás at 1100 (Señor Huascarán) to Conococha and from there another bus, via Chiquián to La Unión. At **Chiquián** (*Hostal San Miguel*, clean, simple) one can walk into the Callejón de Huayhuash. There are two poor bus services Lima-Chiquián: Landano, Ayacucho 1040, Lima, Mon., Wed., Sat. at 1100, returning to Lima Mon., Wed., Fri., 1100; Tubsa, Leticia 633, Lima, Mon., Wed., Fri., 1900 to Chiquián, and in both directions Tues., Thurs., Sat., 1400 (bus Huarás-Chiquián from Av. Tarapaca 133, at 1130; then Chiquián-La Unión with Tubsa, Mon., Wed., Fri. at midnight). Or one can take a truck from the crossroads at Lake Conococha (a very cold place). The second is to take a Comité 5 bus to Catac (US$0.85, 1 hr., frequent service from 0630); ask to be set down at Griffo's garage on the edge of Catac. Take a taxi or walk the 5 km. to Pachocoto (2 cafés with accommodation if stranded). If you cannot get a truck Pachocoto-La Unión (9 hrs., US$2.30), wait for a truck from Lima going to the mines at Huansalla (take warm clothes). The road passes through the Puya Raimondii National Park and ascends to a high section with most rewarding views of gigantic geological features. From Huansalla, bus, truck or walk to Huallanca (8 km.) and take transport on to La Unión "through an entertaining gorge by a demanding gravel road" (Friedrich Dürsch). There are occasional trucks Huarás-La Unión. Bus Huarás-Huallanca, 3½ hrs., US$2.80.

Warning If driving this route, beware of armed robbery; at road blocks it is best not to get out of your car.

The Northern Oases N of the mouth of the River Santa the Andes recede, leaving a coastal desert belt of from 8 to 16 km. wide containing the three great oases of Northern Peru—the areas of Trujillo, Chiclayo and Piura.

N of Chimbote we cross the valleys of Chao and Virú, arriving after 137 km. at the first great oasis of northern Peru, Trujillo. Coming down from the desert

GUIDES TO SOUTH AMERICA
BACKPACKING SERIES:
In addition to detailed trail descriptions of all the popular as well as the lesser known hiking areas of South America, this series includes background information on Indians, archaeology, wildlife, mountain and jungle ecology, health, security, transport and accommodation.

Backpacking in Mexico & Central America
Backpacking in Venezuela, Colombia & Ecuador
Backpacking & Trekking in Peru & Bolivia (New edition)
Backpacking in Chile & Argentina, plus the Falkland Islands
OTHER GUIDES:
Exploring Cuzco
Climbing and Hiking in Ecuador
Maps of South America (2 sheets)
Northwest South America, and the Galapagos Islands
Also, Up the Creek: An Amazon Adventure (travel narrative)
We also stock a wide selection of South American road, topographical and trekking maps and imported books pertaining to Latin America.
Send for a catalogue.

BRADT PUBLICATIONS	OVERSEAS DISTRIBUTORS HUNTER PUBLISHING	REX PUBLICATIONS
41 Nortoft Road,	300 Rariton Center Parkway	413 Pacific Highway
Chalfont St. Peter	CN94 Edison.	Artarmon, NSW 2064
Bucks. SL9 0LA, England.	New Jersey, 08810 USA	Australia

there is an abrupt line between desert and greenery; cultivation can only be carried out with irrigation ditches which take their water from far up in the mountains. The area's port is **Salaverry,** exporting sugar and minerals, importing consumer goods and machinery. There is an 8 km. road to Trujillo.

The Quiruvilca copper mines are 120 km. inland by road from Salaverry. The concentrating plant at Shorey is connected with the mines by a 3 km. aerial cableway, and with its coal mine by a further 8 km. The ore is then taken by a 40 km. cableway to Samne, whence it is sent by road to Salaverry.

Trujillo, capital of the Department of La Libertad, disputes the title of second city of Peru with Arequipa. Population 750,000. The traveller entering Trujillo is delighted with its surrounding greenness against a backcloth of brown Andean foothills and peaks. Founded by Pizarro, 1536 (and named after his native town in Spain), it has moved with the times, but still retains many old churches, graceful colonial balconies and windows overhanging its modern pavements, of homes built during the reigns of the viceroys. Besides the Cathedral it has 10 colonial churches as well as convents and monasteries. Its University of La Libertad, second only to that of San Marcos at Lima, was founded in 1824.

Near the Plaza de Armas is the spacious 18th century house in which General Iturregui lived when he proclaimed the city's freedom from Spain in 1820. It is now the exclusive Club Central and Chamber of Commerce, at Pizarro 688 (may be visited in mornings). Two other beautiful colonial mansions on the Plaza have been taken over by the Banco Central and Banco Hipotecario, which maintain as museums the parts they do not need as offices (they may be visited a.m.). Certain other mansions, still in private hands, may occasionally be visited with the help of Trujillo Tours; they include the magnificent Orbegoso house at Pizarro 316 and the one at Junín 682; also the Casa de los Condes de Aranda, Bolívar y Gamarra; the Casa del Mariscal de Orbegoso in the 5th block of Calle Orbegoso; Casa del Mayorazgo; Casa Ganoza Chopitea, 4th block of Independencia (which has a private museum that can be seen when Sr. Ganoza is in residence); Casa Madalengo, Pizarro y Gamarra; Casa Baanante, in Grau near Almagro.

The focal point is the spacious Plaza de Armas, with a sculptured group to the heroes of the Liberation. Fronting it is the Cathedral, with the old palace of the Archbishop next door; the *Hotel Trujillo*; the building in colonial style of the Sociedad de Beneficencia Pública de Trujillo housing the Peruvian North American Cultural Institute; and the Municipality building. Many churches damaged in the 1970 earthquake. One of the best, La Merced at Pizarro 550, with picturesque moulded figures below the dome, is being restored, but part of the dome has collapsed because of building work next door. El Carmen church and monastery, described as the "most valuable jewel of colonial art in Trujillo", is still closed after the earthquake. Other old churches include La Compañía, near Plaza de Armas; San Francisco on 3rd block of Gamarra; Belén on 6th block of Almagro; Santa Clara on 4th block of Junín; San Agustín on 6th block of Mariscal Orbegoso; Santa Ana on 2nd block of same street; Santo Domingo on 4th block

---

Adventure in South America

If you want to explore the mountains and jungles of Peru, Bolivia and Ecuador, visit the Galapagos Islands or take a five-month journey right round the continent, there's no better place to start than our brochures. We organize holidays throughout Latin America to suit *all* tastes and capabilities, including walking and adventure trips from 19 days, and overland journeys from 6 to 22 weeks long.
Full details from:

Exodus Expeditions (Dept SH)

100 Wandsworth High Street, London SW18 4LE, UK. Tel. 01-870 0151; Telex 8951700 EXODUS G.

PERU 671

of Bolognesi. There are also two markets, one on Gamarra and the Mercado Mayorista on Calle Roca.

Warnings As with all Peruvian cities, Trujillo is troubled with theft—beware of robbers working in pairs, especially beyond the inner ring road, Av. España, towards the hill. Its water supply has a bad reputation.

Hotels *Turistas*, Plaza de Armas, E with bath (cheaper without), accepts American Express, full of character, rooms on street are noisy, meals US$4, excellent buffet lunch on Sun.; *El Golf* (near California district), C, swimming pool, burglars at night; *Los Jardines*, 4 km. from centre, bungalows in garden, buses to town, D; *Turismo*, 7th block of Gamarra, E, occasional hot water, laundry service, restaurant, good; *San José*, E, in 5th block of Grau, private bath, no hot water, unsafe, noisy, dirty but cheap; *San Antonio*, E, also in 8th block of Gamarra; *San Martín*, in 7th block of San Martín, F, with bath (scant hot water), clean but some rooms damp, has more than 100 rooms, good restaurant. *Opt Gar* (5th block Grau), C, with bath, good, friendly, recommended, excellent restaurant (try sea food) and snack bar; *Los Escudos*, Orbegoso 676, Tel.: 243523, E, with bath and hot water, breakfast, small garden, recommended; *Continental*, Gamarra, opp. market, F, clean, good, safe, restaurant; *Palermo*, E, hot water, by market; *Premier*, Gamarra 631, opposite market, dirty, water intermittent, central, E, with shower (front rooms are noisy), parking one block away; *Los Incas*, Av. César Vallejo, G, not very clean; *Acapulco*, Gamarra 681, E, with bath, F without, noisy, dirty, worth bargaining here; *Hostal España*, Jirón Unión 546, F, clean and friendly (near Antisuyo/Quiroz bus station); *Hostal Monterrey*, Av. Los Incas 256, Tel.: 241673, open 24 hrs., F, friendly, comfortable (close to Tepsa, good for late arrivals); *Primavera*, Nicolás de Piérola 872, E, noisy on the street side; *Internacional* (6th block Bolívar—F, without bathroom) much better in a new section at rear, F, with bath, very good; *Lima*, Ayacucho 718, F, poor, cheap, dirty, many gringos; *Hostal Central*, Ayacucho 728, G, dirty, but not as noisy. *La Giralda*, Gamarra 830, F; *Americano*, Pizarro 758-768, is a vast, old building, damp, with cockroaches, F, with bath, rooms without bath are worse (back on to cinema), most rooms without window, occasional warm water, parking; *Latino* (5th block Grau), not recommended, F; *Hostal Colón*, Jirón Colón 5th block, F, to be avoided, cheap; *París* and *Perú*, opposite each other on Ayacucho, both G; *Vogi*, also on Ayacucho, E, highly recommended. *Hostería El Sol*, D, opened by the late Dr. Kaufmann of Coina (see page 674) and now run by his family, 55 beds, 10 mins. from centre by bus to Santa Inés or Huanchaco (US$0.50 by taxi), at Calle Los Brillantes 224, in front of the Parque Ramón Castilla, in Urbanización Santa Inés. For a private *pensión* contact the family Bravo Díaz, Huayna Capac 542, Urb. Sta. María, Tel.: 243347, very friendly, cheap.

Restaurants *Hotel Opt Gar*, lunch only except for guests, recommended; Chinese food at *Gallo Rojo*, Grau 579, and *Kuon Wha* (8th block Gamarra); *Chifa Oriental* on Gamarra recommended; *El Pesquero*, Jurín 118, good fish; *El Portal*, Plaza de Armas; *Morroco*, Av. Bolívar, smart and cheap; *Chifa Oriental*, Gamarra 735; *Santa Inés*, Calle Los Robles, good fish, try the *corvina*; *Oriental*, (on Grau), lunch only, good Criollo food; Vegetarian restaurants: *Salud y Vigor*, Bolívar 787; *Alfa y Omega*, Bolívar 767; *Viva Sano*, Colón 578, cheaper; *Gran Fraternidad Universal*,Bolívar y Colón. *Pollos Bolívar*, Bolívar 577, chicken and salad. Excellent local dishes at *Pedro Moriallas* in nearby seaside resort of Buenos Aires. Good Argentine-style food at *Parrillada El Gaucho*. *24 Horas*, Jr. Gamarra, reasonably priced meals for about US$1, always open, as the name implies; *Oasis* (next to *Hotel Turismo*), good *fritos*. *ABL*, San Martín 427, large, good portions of chicken; *De Marco*, Pizarro 725, good, especially the ice creams, desserts and cakes. *La Calesa*, Pizarro 716, good snack bar; *Romano*, opp. *Hotel Americano*, at Pizarro 747, good cheap menu; *El Mesón de Cervantes*, Pizarro, bar-restaurant, polite, good cheap food; avoid *Bar-Restaurant El Rosado* on Pizarro; *Pizzería* on Pizarro, near *Hotel Americano*, very good. *Subterráneo*, Plaza Murillo, set lunch US$1. More reasonably priced restaurants include *La Pileta* (next to Tepsa bus office, Astete 472, strongly recommended for good local food) and *El Recreo*, Pizarro 879. *La Miel*, Jirón Bolívar 600, good breakfasts, poor coffee, friendly; at 522 on same street, *Juguería San Antonio*, no seating, window onto street; at 610, same street, *Cafetería La Rueda*. Wholewheat bread at *Panadería Chalet Suizo*, Av. España e Independencia.

Note Tourists may be approached by vendors selling *huacos* and necklaces from the Chimú period; the export of these items is strictly illegal if they are genuine, but they almost certainly aren't.

Taxis Town trip, US$0.45; out of town US$0.60. Chan Chan, Huanchaco, US$ 1.20. Taxi driver Jorge Enrique Guevara Castillo, Av. del Ejército 1259, Altos 1, recommended. By the hour, in town, US$3, outside US$4.

Night Club Granja Azul—country club. Billy Bob's for drinking. Discotheques: Las Rocas, The Drive Inn, Nancy's.

Fiestas Second half of September or first half of October transport and hotels booked. Other busy periods are around Mothers' Day (in March/April) and the last week of January, when the Nacional Marinera contest is held (dancing by all ages, public participation and viewing welcomed).

672 **PERU**

Archaeological Museum, normally open 0800-1300 in Jan.-March and 0800-1200, 1500-1800 the rest of the year, Pizarro 349 (entrance, US$0.60). The museum has an interesting collection of pottery and a mummified parrot in a sewing box. Another place to visit in Trujillo is the basement of the **Cassinelli** garage on the fork of the Pan-American and Huanchaco roads; it contains a superb private collection of Mochica and Chimú pottery. Be sure to ask for a demonstration of the whistling *huacos;* entry, US$0.60, open 0830-1130, 1530-1630. Sr. Cassinelli has plans to construct a larger museum. The University has a Zoological Museum, San Martín, corner with Bolognesi (0745-1300, 1500-1900).

Pedro Puerta, an English speaking expert on Chan Chan and former college librarian, who has an office at Km. 560 on the Panamericana Norte, 2½ km. from the Plaza de Armas offers interesting tours to Chan Chan, Huaca El Dragón, and Huaca La Esmeralda. He charges US$3 per hour for a 6-7 hr. tour, not including taxi hire and lunch for him and the taxi driver. He also sells prints of Chan Chan reliefs and Mochica pottery motifs, beautiful but expensive. He gives a slideshow at 2000 nightly at the *Hotel Turistas.*

Laundry Opposite *Hotel Americano.*

Post Office corner of Independencia and Bolognesi. Entel for international phone calls: Calle de la Puerta Aranda 680.

Hospital Anglo-American Hospital, good, reasonable fees.

Bank Banco NorPerú on Pizarro, recommended for changing cheques (but US$2 commission) and cash with no delay, good rates. Banco Popular del Perú, Gamarra, for cheques (a protracted operation). There are *casas de cambio* for cash only, in main square and around courthouse. Ghia Tours, near Plaza, changes travellers' cheques outside banking hours.

Tourist Office Pizarro 402, very helpful, and at airport. Information also from Sra. Carmen Melly, Trujillo Tours, Gamarra 440 (Tel.: 233-069), recommended for knowledgeable guides and efficient service. Maps and information also from Touring and Automobile Club, Almagro 707, and from Gira Tours on Calle Independencia; maps from Librería Ayacucho, Ayacucho 570. Tourist Police have an office on the Plaza de Armas; they wear white uniforms and are extremely helpful; will even help lone travellers to visit Chan Chan safely.

Immigration Edificio Demarco, 3rd floor, Diego de Almagro 225. Gives 60-day visa extensions (for 90 days proof of funds and onward ticket required). Involves taking forms to Banco de la Nación, and waiting for papers to be stamped—time-consuming.

Air Transport Faucett, Pizarro 532, and AeroPerú, Junín 537, daily flights from Lima, 1 hr., Faucett from Tumbes. AeroPerú fly to Cajamarca (Mon., Fri., low season), 25 mins. Tarapoto and Juanjui (Tues. and Sat.). Faucett and AeroPerú to Iquitos, change at Tarapoto, US$28. Flights by Faucett to Cajamarca, Chiclayo and points N and to a multitude of small jungle towns. Taxi to airport, US$2.50; or take bus to Chan Chan and get out at airport turn-off.

Buses To Lima, 551 km., colectivo, 7-9 hrs., US$11, or by bus, 8-9 hrs. US$8.50 with Tepsa (3 a day—station in Trujillo, Av. Almagro, between Avs. España and Grau, tickets Astete 482), Peru Express, Chinchay-Suyo (office at Bolívar 720 for tickets, González Prada 337 for bus, insist on ticket before you board or you may get charged extra for luggage), Expreso Continental (part of Ormeño), US$6, or Roggero; mostly at night. Try to book your bus to Lima a day in advance: they fill up quickly. Buses to Lima quite frequent but difficult to go north as buses booked for days; try Emtrafesa (Av. Miraflores with España) N to Pacasmayo (US$1, 2½ hrs.), Chiclayo, Piura, Tumbes. To Lima, Roggero departs at 0930, Chinchay-Suyo at 1000 and Panamericana at 1100, 2200 and 2330. To Huarás (via Pativilca) with Chinchay-Suyo, US$6, 10 hrs., depart 2030, daily (Jirón Bolívar 720, book ahead). To get to Huarás by day you have to spend the night in malodorous Chimbote and change there (El Aguila at 0545 no longer connects with 0800 Moreno bus to Huarás). Chinchay-Suyo and Tepsa have buses to Casma, 3 hrs., US$2.40 and to Tarapoto, departing at 1200 daily. Bus to Chimbote US$1.10, Empresa Cajamarca, Av. España 2023-27, Empresa El Aguila, Av. Nicaragua y Moche, Empresa Chinchay-Suyo leaves 1300; Empresa San Pedro, Av. España 2011, every 2 hrs.; colectivo to Chimbote, 2 hrs., US$2. Colectivo to Cajamarca US$6.50, daily at 2200, 0500, 8 hrs., with Empresa Cajamarca (comfortable), 2100, 2300 with Díaz bus (Jirón Colón 537), US$3, El Cóndor buses (Pizarro 789) at night, 6-9 hrs.; US$4.50 (also Etucsa); to Cajamarca in daylight, take Chiclayo bus to la Cruz, turn-off for Cajamarca, and wait there for a collectivo to Cajamarca, US$3, 8 hrs. Colectivo to Piura, 1000 daily, US$10; bus to Piura (Tepsa, 2000, Chinchay-Suyo 1300 and at night), US$5, 8-9 hrs.; to Chiclayo, US$3, 3-4 hrs. Tepsa to Tumbes, several daily US$6.50 and up, Expreso Moderno and Sudamericano (Jr. Montevideo 618), US$7.30, 15 hrs. Bus to Sullana, Sudamericano, also Chinchay-Suyo at 2300, arrive about 0800, sleep impossible, potholes.

From Antarctica to the Galapagos, from Rio Carnival to the Wilds of Costa Rica, South America is Our Oyster

We have spent the last 22 years perfecting wildlife, cultural and wilderness journeys to the continent. No matter where in Latin America you want to go we have the tours, the excitement, the adventure you are seeking.

We can show you what gave Cortez the wanderlust, what inspired Pizzaro to lust for gold that destroyed two nations. From Darwin's "Enchanted Isles" The Galapagos, to the Amazon Jungle and bird watching in Ecuador. From climbing to skin diving, from Aztec and Inca ruins to photography and trekking, we make South America come alive with all the colour, fiesta and excitement of this great continent. Yet we also concentrate on the amazing flora and fauna that make this region so rare.

For all enquiries and a full colour brochure call TWICKERS WORLD today. South America really is your oyster when you go with us.

TWICKERS WORLD

22 CHURCH STREET, TWICKENHAM TW1 3NW, ENGLAND   TEL 01-892 7606   TELEX 25780

ABTA/IATA/PATA
Agents for Metropolitan Touring Galapagos Cruises of Ecuador and Society Expeditions of Seattle.

Books on South & Central America, Mexico & the Caribbean

A Burton-Garbett

35 The Green
Morden, Surrey
SM4 4HJ England

Telephone: 01-540 2367
Cables:
Garbo, Morden, Surrey

© John Bartholomew & Son Ltd., 1983

These maps are for interest only
and are not of political significance

KEY TO
MAP SECTIONS

ON THE SAME SCALE

Map: Gulf of Mexico and Central America

United States

States/Regions: ARKANSAS, MISSISSIPPI, ALABAMA, GEORGIA, LOUISIANA, CAROLINA

Cities:
- McAlester, Ft Smith, Little Rock, Memphis, Tennessee, Gainsville, Athens, Savannah
- Hot Springs, Arkansas, Tupelo, Gadsden, Atlanta, Augusta, Orangeburg
- Durant, Red, Pine Bluff, Columbus, Birmingham, Macon, Charleston
- Texarkana, Greenwood, Tuscaloosa
- Dallas, Greenville, Columbus, GEORGIA
- Longview, Monroe, Jackson, Meridian, Montgomery, Phenix City, Albany, Savannah
- Tyler, Vicksburg, Flint, Waycross
- Lufkin, Natchez, Hattiesburg, Laurel, Alabama, Valdosta, Brunswick
- Alexandria, Dothan, Tallahassee, Jacksonville
- Baton Rouge, Mobile, Pensacola, Panama City, Gainesville, St. Augustine
- Beaumont, Lake Charles, Lafayette, Biloxi, Ocala, Daytona Beach
- Houston, Orange, Pt Arthur, Orlando
- Galveston, NEW ORLEANS, Clearwater, St. Petersburg, Tampa Bay, Tampa, Lake Okeechobee
- Matagorda B., Ft. Myers, The Everglades
- Corpus Christi
- C. Sable, Key West, Marquesas Keys
- Brownsville, Matamoros
- Madre

Gulf of Mexico

CUBA: Habana (Havana), Matanzas, Pinar del Rio, Guane, G. de Batabano, I. de la Juventud

- C. San Antonio
- C. Catoche
- Yucatan Channel
- Pto Juárez

Mexico / Yucatan

- Tamiahua, Rojo, Tizimin, Valladolid, I. de Cozumel
- Progreso, Mérida, Ticul, Peto
- Bahía de Campeche, Halachó
- Campeche, Felipe C. Puerto, B. de la Ascensión
- Jalapa Enriquez, Veracruz
- Córdoba, Escárcega, Chetumal
- S. Andrés Tuxtla, Cd del Carmen, Frontera, Bco Chinchorro
- Tierra Blanca, L. de Términos, Ambergris Cay
- Cuicatlan, Coatzacoalcos, Villahermosa, Turneffe I.
- Oaxaca, Minatitlán, Tenosique, BELIZE, Swan (Hond)
- Tlacolula, Istmo de Tehuantepec, Tuxtla Gutiérrez, Flores, Belmopan
- Cd Ixtepec, Hondo, Dangriga
- Tehuantepec, San Cristóbal, Usumacinta, G. of Honduras
- Salina Cruz, Comitán, Pta Gorda, Is. de la Bahía, Trujillo, L. de Caratasca
- Golfo de Tehuantepec, Tonalá, GUATEMALA, G. of Cortés
- Pijijiapan, Cobán, S. Pedro Sula, HONDURAS, Coco (Segovia), Patuca
- Huixtla, Tapachula, Barrios, Tela, La Ceiba, Juticalpa, Bonanza
- Quezaltenango, Sta Rosa, Comayagua, Tegucigalpa, Cordillera, rio grande, P. Cabezas
- Escuintla, Sta Ana, Guatemala, San Salvador, Matagalpa, Prinzapolca
- San José, Sonsonate, S. Miguel, La Unión, Chinandega, León, L. de Managua, NICARAGUA, Bluefields
- EL SALVADOR, Managua, Masaya, Granada, L. de Nicaragua
- San Juan del Sur, San Juan
- G. de Papagayo, COSTA RICA, Puntarenas, Alajuela
- Pen. de Nicoya, San José, Pto Cortés
- G. de Nicoya, Pen. de Osa

Scale

0 100 200 300 400 miles
0 200 400 600 km.

16M

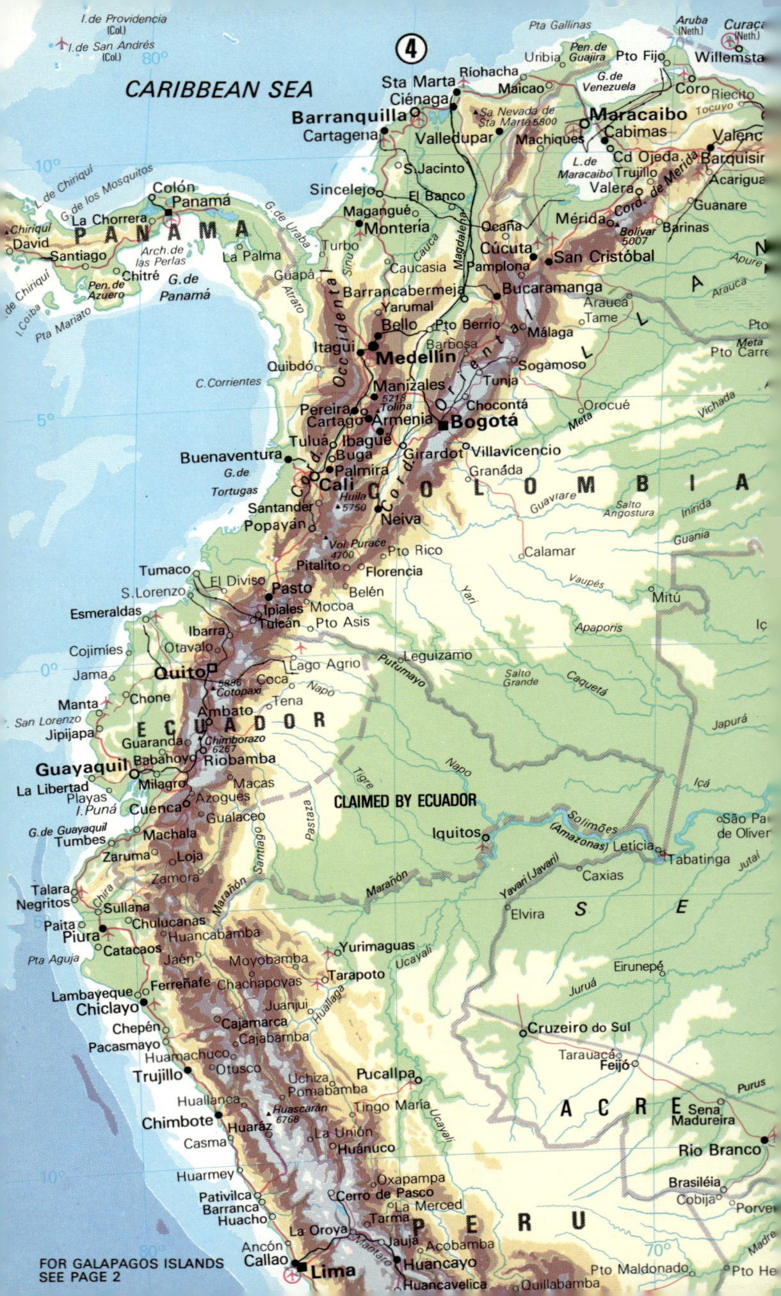

FOR GALAPAGOS ISLANDS SEE PAGE 2

The Grenadines
GRENADA
I. de Margarita
St George's
5
Tortuga
La Asunción
Pen. de Paria
Tobago
Carúpano
Güiria
Port of Spain
Cumana
TRINIDAD AND TOBAGO
la Cruz
Caripito
G. de Paria
Trinidad
San Fernando
arcelona
Anaco
Maturín
El Tigre
Tigre
Tucupita
Barrancas
Boca Grande
Cd Bolívar
Orinoco
Cd Guayana
Upata
Mabaruma
Cd Piar
Emb. de Guri
EZUELA
La Paragua
El Dorado
Charity
Suddie
Leguan I.
Georgetown
V. en Hoop
Bartica
New Amsterdam
Nieuw Amsterdam
Paramaribo
Marienburg
Salto del Angel
La Gran Sabana
Roraima 1280
Kaieteur Fall
Linden
Nieuw Nickerie
Totness
Albina
Sinnamary
Kourou
I. du Diable (Devil's I.)
Cayenne
San Maigualida
Paragua
Sta Elena
Apoera
Witagron
Blommesteinmeer
GUYANA
SURINAME
FRENCH GUIANA
Julianatop 1280
Sa Pacaraima
Sa Parima
Bonfim
Lethem
Boa Vista
Ireng
Corantijn
Maroni
Oiapoque
Orinoco
RORAIMA
Essequibo
Litani
Caracaraí
Serra Tumucumaque
Calçoene
Amapá
AMAPÁ
Branco
Sa do Navio
Jari
Equator
Macapá
Pto Santana
Paru
Barcelos
Negro
Carvoeiro
Oriximiná
Obidos
Amazonas
Gurupá
Monte Alegre
Manaus
Parintins
Santarém
Xingu
Manacapuru
Careiro
Itacoatiara
Tefé
Codajás
Altamira
AZONAS
Coari
Purus
Borba
Tapajós
Aveiro
Itaituba
Pimenta
Madeira
Novo Aripuanã
Coari
Manicoré
Aripuanã
anutama
Jacareacanga
Iriri
S. Félix
Lábrea
Humaitá
Prainha
Serra do Cachimbo
Madeira
Porto Velho
Xingu
Jiparana
Aripuanã
Teles Pires
Cachimbo
Abunã
T. Roosevelt
BRAZIL
Juruena
Sa dos Caiabis
Arinos
Guajará-Mirim
Rondônia
RONDÔNIA
Mamoré
Serra dos Parecis
Sa Formosa
São Félix
Guaporé
Vilhena
Rogaguado
65°
60°
55°
10°
0°
5°
0 100 200 300 400 miles
0 200 400 600 km.
1:16M

6
SURINAME
FRENCH GUIANA
Apoera
Witagron
Albina
Sinnamary
Kourou
Cayenne
I. du Diable (Devil's I.)
Cabo Orange
Oiapoque
Julianatop
1280
Blommesteinmeer
Corantijn
Maroni
Essequibo
Litani
Calçoene
Ilha de Maracá
Amapá
Serra Tumucumaque
AMAPÁ
Sa do Navio
Jari
Macapá
Pto Santana
Paru
I. Caviana
C. Maguarinho
B. de Marajó
I. de Marajó
Salinópolis
Bragança
Capanema
Belém
Abaetetuba
Pará
Curralinho
Gurupá
Amazonas
Oriximiná
Obidos
Monte Alegre
Santarém
Parintins
Xingu
Cametá
Altamira
Aveiro
Tapajós
Itaituba
Pimenta
P A R Á
Tucuruí
Tocantins
Jatobá
Capim
Gurupi
Pindaré
Alcântara
Pinheiro
B. de São Marcos
São Luís
Rosário
Parnaíba
Camocim
Acaraú
Equator
50°
45°
0°
5°
Monção
Chapadinha
Brejo
Bacabal
Coroatá
Codó
Caxias
MARANHÃO
Teresina
Campo Maior
Castelo
Crateús
Sobral
Itapipoca
Caucaia
Fortaleza (Ceará)
Sta Quitéria
Piripiri
Ipu
Nova Russas
Canindé
Aracati
Quixadá
Morada-N
CEARÁ
Mombaça
Tauá
Iguatu
Acopiara
Areia Branca
Macaú
Pta do Calcanhar
Mossoró
RIO GRANDE DO NORTE
Natal
Patu
Caicó
Sousa
Cajàzeiras
J. do Norte
Crato
Patos
Borborema
PARAÍBA
Cabedelo
Picos
Oeiras
Floriano
PIAUÍ
Parnaíba
Marabá
Imperatriz
Barra do Corda
Grajaú
Tocantinópolis
Pto Franco
Carolina
Balsas
Araguaína
Araguaia
C. do Araguaia
S. Félix
Xingu
Iriri
Jacareacanga
Serra do Cachimbo
Cachimbo
Teles Pires

7
MATO GROSSO
GOIÁS
BAHIA
SERGIPE
MINAS GERAIS
ESPÍRITO SANTO
SÃO PAULO
PARANÁ
MATO GROSSO DO SUL
Rio de Janeiro
São Paulo
Belo Horizonte
Salvador (Bahia)
Brasília
Goiânia
Anápolis
Cuiabá
Campo Grande
Curitiba
Vitória
Vila Velha
Niterói
Santos
São Vicente
Maceió
Aracaju
Arapiraca
Penedo
Propriá
Estância
Lagarto
Serrinha
Alagoinhas
Feira de S.
Cachoeira
Nazaré
Jequié
Ilhéus
Itabuna
Vitoria da Conquista
Montes Claros
Uberlândia
Uberaba
Ribeirão Prêto
Campinas
Sorocaba
Londrina
Maringá
Cascavel
Ponta Grossa
Guarapuava
Juiz de Fora
Volta Redonda
Petrópolis
Nova Friburgo
Campos
Governador Valadares
Teófilo Otôni
Caratinga
Colatina
Linhares
São Mateus
Planalto de Mato Grosso
Chapada Diamantina
Serra do Espinhaço
Sa de Mantiqueira
B. de T. os Santos
Tropic of Capricorn
1:16M
0 100 200 300 400 miles
0 200 400 600 km.

Huascarán 6768
Tingo María
Ucayali
ACRE
8
Sena Madureira
Abunã
Huaraz
La Unión
Huánuco
Casma
Rio Branco
Brasiléia
Cobija
Riberalta
Guajará-Mir
Porvenir
Madre de Dios
Mamoré
Huarmey
Oxapampa
Cerro de Pasco
La Merced
Huacho
Tarma
PERU
La Oroya
Jauja
Acobamba
Mantaro
Ancón
Callao
Lima
Huancayo
Pto Maldonado
Pto Heath
L. Rogaguado
Beni
Quillabamba
MACHU PICCHU
Huancavelica
Ayacucho
Cuzco
Quince Mil
Santa Ana
Apurimac
Abancay
Chincha Alta
Pisco
Andahuaylas
Ica
Pen. de Paracas
Sicuani
Ayavari
Rurrenabaque
Trinidad
CORDILLERA DE LOS ANDES
Nazca
Huanay
Sta Ana
Juliaca
L. Titicaca
Ancohuma 7014
Coroico
Chulumani
Coropuna 6425
Majes
Puno
Chala
Arequipa
Misti 5822
Juli
Guaqui
La Paz
BOLIVIA
Camaná
Matarani
Mollendo
Moquegua
Quillacollo
Cochabamba
Santa C
Ilo
Pta Coles
Desaguadero
Sajama 6520
Oruro
Cliza
Aiquile
Tacna
Arica
L. Poopó
Huanuni
Sabaya
Sucre
S. de Coipasa
Rio Mulatos
Potosí
Salar de Uyuni
Uyuni
Camarg
Cotagaita
Iquique
Ujina
Vol. Ollagüe 5870
Ollagüe
Tarija
Tupiza
Loa
Tocopilla
Chuquicamata
La Quiaca
Tocorpuri 5833
Abra Pampa
Bermejo
Pedro de Valdivia
Calama
Jujuy
Orán
Iturbe
Mejillones
Salar de Atacama
Tilcara
S. Salvador de Jujuy
Antofagasta
Tropic of Capricorn
Desierto de Atacama
Llullaillaco 6723
S. de Arizaro
Salta
PACIFIC OCEAN
Puna de Atacama
Cachi
Taltal
Catalina
Metán
Cafayate
Chañaral
Potrerillos
S. Miguel
Tucumán
Felix
San Ambrosio
(Chile)
Caldera
Ojos del Salado 7104
Catamarca
Copiapó
Pissis 6858
Londres
Tinogasta
Santiago del Estero
1:16M
0
100
200
300
400 miles
0
200
400
600 km.
Huasco
Vallenar
Grl Manuel Belgrano 6250
Catamarca
Chilecito
Cabo Bascuñán
Co. del Toro 6380
Guandacol
La Rioja
Salinas Grandes
La Serena
Coquimbo
Rivadavia
6282 Olivares
Jáchal
Cruz del Eje
S. Agustín
Ovalle
San Juan
Córdoba
80°
Punitaqui
V. Dolores
Illapel
S. Juan
Pampa de la Salinas
Los Vilos
Mercedario 6770
Aconcagua 6960
Islas Juan Fernández
(Chile)
Quillota
S. Felipe
Mendoza
San Luis
Robinson Crusoe
Sta Clara
Viña del Mar
6800 Tupungato
Valparaíso
S. Antonio
Santiago
Mercedes
ON THE SAME SCALE
S. Bernardo
Vol. Maipó 5290
Rançagua
S. Rafael
V. Huidobro
Pichilemu
S. Fernando

9
BRAZIL
MATO GROSSO
GOIÁS
MATO GROSSO DO SUL
SÃO PAULO
PARANÁ
SANTA CATARINA
RIO GRANDE DO SUL
PARAGUAY
URUGUAY
Chaco
Santa Fe
Entre Rios
Corrientes
Misiones
SOUTH ATLANTIC OCEAN
Cristalândia
Porto Nacional
São Félix
Ilha do Bananal
Gurupi
Vilhena
Utiariti
Pto Artur
Diamantino
Mato Grosso
Uruacu
Aruanã
Planalto de Mato Grosso
Cuiabá
Fatima do Sul
Aragarças
Goiás
Ceres
Formosa
Jaraguá
Brasília
Pirenópolis
Anápolis
Goiânia
San Ignacio
San Matías
Cáceres
Rondonópolis
Iporá
San José de Chiquitos
Roboré
Mineiros
Rio Verde
Jataí
Caldas Novas
Paracat
Ipameri
Goiandira
Catalão
Itumbiara
Araguari
Coxim
Taquari
Corumbá
Pto Suarez
Uberlândia
Patrocínio
Mayor P. Lagerenza
Paranaiba
Iturama
Uberaba
Pres. Vargas
Fernandópolis
Grl E.A. Garay
Aquidauana
Campo Grande
Três Lagoas
S. José do R. Prêto
Barretos
Franca
Passos
Ribeirão Prêto
Fte Olimpo
Jardim
Araçatuba
Panorama
Catanduva
Pres. Epitácio
Tupã
Pto Murtinho
Dourados
Pres. Prudente
Araraquara
São Carlos
Filadelfia
Pedro J. Caballero
Ponta Porã
Pto E. Cunha
Marília
Bauru
Jaú
Limeira
Assis
Ourinhos
Piracicaba
Campinas
Paranavaí
Londrina
Maringá
Botucatu
Jundiaí
Concepción
Pozo Colorado
Horqueta
Umuarama
Jacarezinho
Apucarana
Itapeva
Sorocaba
São Paulo
Esteros
San Pedro
Ygatimi
Guairá
S. del Guairá
C. Mourão
Goio-Erê
Pitangao
Assis Ch.
Toledo
Itararé
Juquiá
Castro
Iguape
Luque
Caacupé
Asunción
Cascavel
Ponta Grossa
Paraguarí
Cnl Oviedo
Foz do Iguaçu
Ciudad Pres. Stroessner
Guarapuava
Curitiba
Paranaguá
Villarrica
Quedas do Iguacu
Formosa
Caazapá
Mafra
S.J. Bautista
Palmas
União de Vitória
São Francisco do Sul
Joinville
Pres. R.S. Peña
S. Miguel d'Oeste
Blumenau
Pilar
S. Ignacio
Itajaí
Resistencia
Encarnación
Chapecó
Barranqueras
Corrientes
Posadas
Erechim
Florianópolis
I. de Sta Catarina
Lajes
Empedrado
Sto Angelo
Passo Fundo
Sto Tomé
Imbituba
S. Borja
Cruz Alta
Vacaria
Tubarão
Itaqui
Criciuma
Reconquista
Tostado
Mercedes
Araranguá
Goya
Vera
Caxias do Sul
Paso de los Libres
Sta Maria
N. Hamburgo
Canoas
Uruguaiana
Alegrete
Cachoeira do Sul
Rio Pardo
Osório
Porto Alegre
Artigas
La Paz
Rivera
Santana do Livramento
Rafaela
Concordia
Salto
Tacuarembó
Bagé
Santa Fe
Pelotas
Paraná
Colón
Paysandú
Rio Grande
Bell Ville
Concepción
P. de Los Toros
Melo
Rosario
Jaguarão
Cda de Gómez
San Nicolás
Gualeguaychú
Mercedes
Durazno
Treinta y Tres
Pergamino
Trinidad
Ibicuy
Zárate
San José de Mayo
Florida
Chuí
Santa Vitória do Palmar
Canelones
Colonia
Minas
Buenos Aires
Avellaneda
Las Piedras
Rocha
Lincoln
Junín
Mercedes
La Plata
Montevideo

10
SOUTH
ARGENTINA
URUGUAY
PARANÁ
SANTA CATARINA
RIO GRANDE DO SUL
GRAN CHACO
ANDES
CORDILLERA DE LOS ANDES
PAMPAS
Puna de Atacama
Salta
Catamarca
La Rioja
San Juan
Mendoza
San Luis
Córdoba
Santiago del Estero
Tucumán
Santa Fe
Entre Rios
Corrientes
Misiones
Chaco
Formosa
Buenos Aires
La Pampa
Neuquén
Asunción
Santiago
Montevideo
Porto Alegre
São Paulo
Curitiba
Florianópolis
Rosario
Mar del Plata
Bahía Blanca
La Plata
Avellaneda
Valparaíso
Viña del Mar
Concepción
Talcahuano
Coquimbo
La Serena
Copiapó
Mendoza
Paraná
Corrientes
Resistencia
Posadas
Encarnación
Rio Grande
Pelotas
Santa Maria
Passo Fundo
Lajes
Blumenau
Joinville
Paranaguá
Ponta Grossa
Cascavel
Foz do Iguaçu
Ciudad Pres. Stroessner
Río de la Plata
L. dos Patos
L. Mirim
Aconcagua 6960
Tupungato 6800
Ojos del Salado 6880
Llullaillaco 6723
Cabo San Antonio
Cabo Bascuñán

⑪

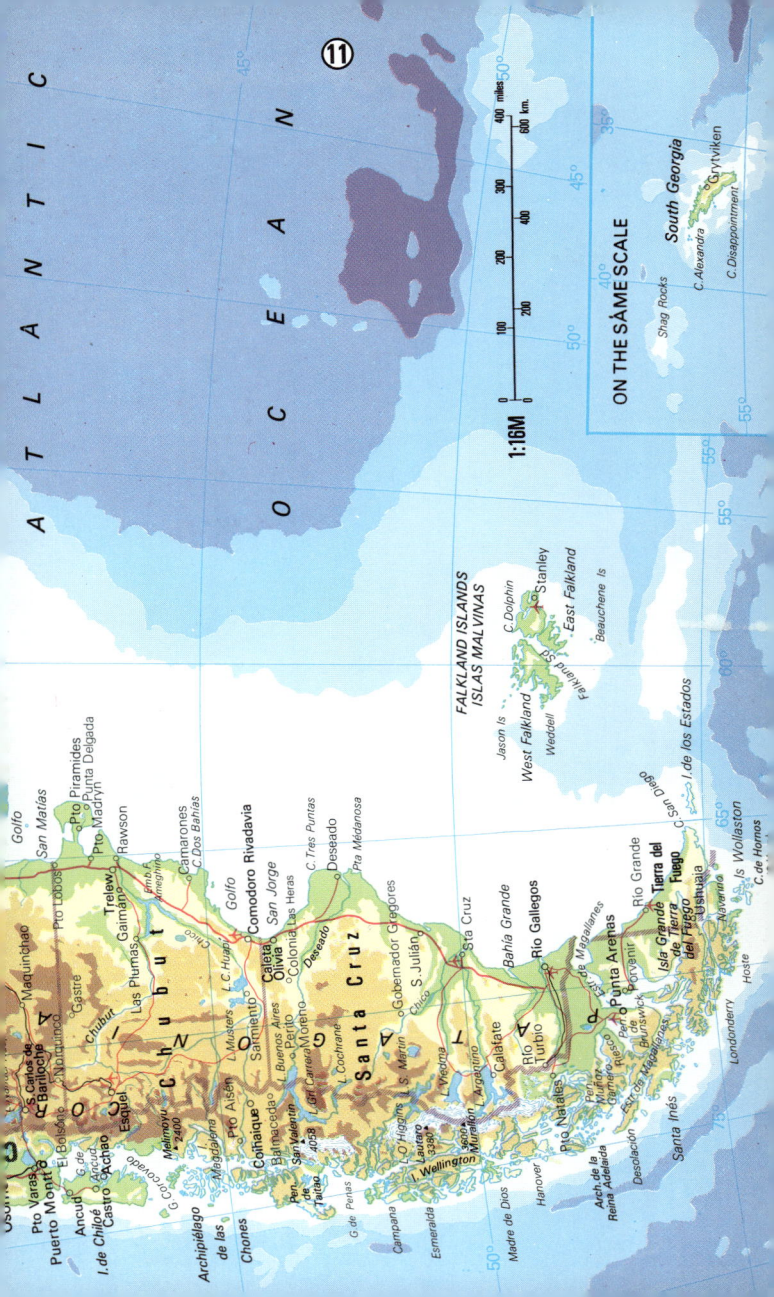

ATLANTIC OCEAN

1:16M

ON THE SAME SCALE

0 100 200 300 400 miles
0 200 400 600 km.

South Georgia
Shag Rocks
C. Alexandra — Grytviken
C. Disappointment

Pto Varas
Puerto Montt
Ancud
I. de Chiloé Castro
Archipiélago
de los
Chones
G. Corcovado
S. C. de Bariloche
Nahuel
El Bolsón
Esquel
Maquinchao
Pto Pirámides
Pto Madryn
Punta Delgada
Rawson
Trelew
Gaimán
Chubut
Castre
Las Plumas
CHUBUT
Pto Lobos
Golfo
San Matías
Camarones
C. Dos Bahías
Comodoro Rivadavia
Golfo
San Jorge
C. Tres Puntas
Deseado
Pta Médanosa
Emb. F. Ameghino
L. C. Huapi
Musters
Sarmiento
Colonia Las Heras
Caleta Olivia
Balmaceda
Coihaique
Pto Aisén
Magdalena
Pen. de Taitao
Melmoyu 2400
L. Buenos Aires
L. Pueyrredón
Perito Moreno
G. de Penas
Campana
Esmeralda
Madre de Dios
Hanover
Ach. de la Reina Adelaida
Wellington
Lautaro 3380
San Valentín 4058
L. Gt. Carrera
L. Cochrane
L. O'Higgins L. S. Martín
Viedma
Argentino
Río Turbio
SANTA CRUZ
Gobernador Gregores
S. Julián
Sta Cruz
Bahía Grande
Río Gallegos
Pto Natales
Calafate
E. de Magallanes
Punta Arenas
Porvenir
Río Grande
Pen. de Brunswick
Santa Inés
Desolación
Londonderry
Hoste
Tierra del Fuego
Isla Grande de Tierra del Fuego
Ushuaia
Navarino
Is. Wollaston
C. de Hornos
C. San Diego
I. de los Estados

FALKLAND ISLANDS
ISLAS MALVINAS
Jason Is.
West Falkland
Weddell
Falkland Sd.
C. Dolphin
Stanley
East Falkland
Beauchene Is

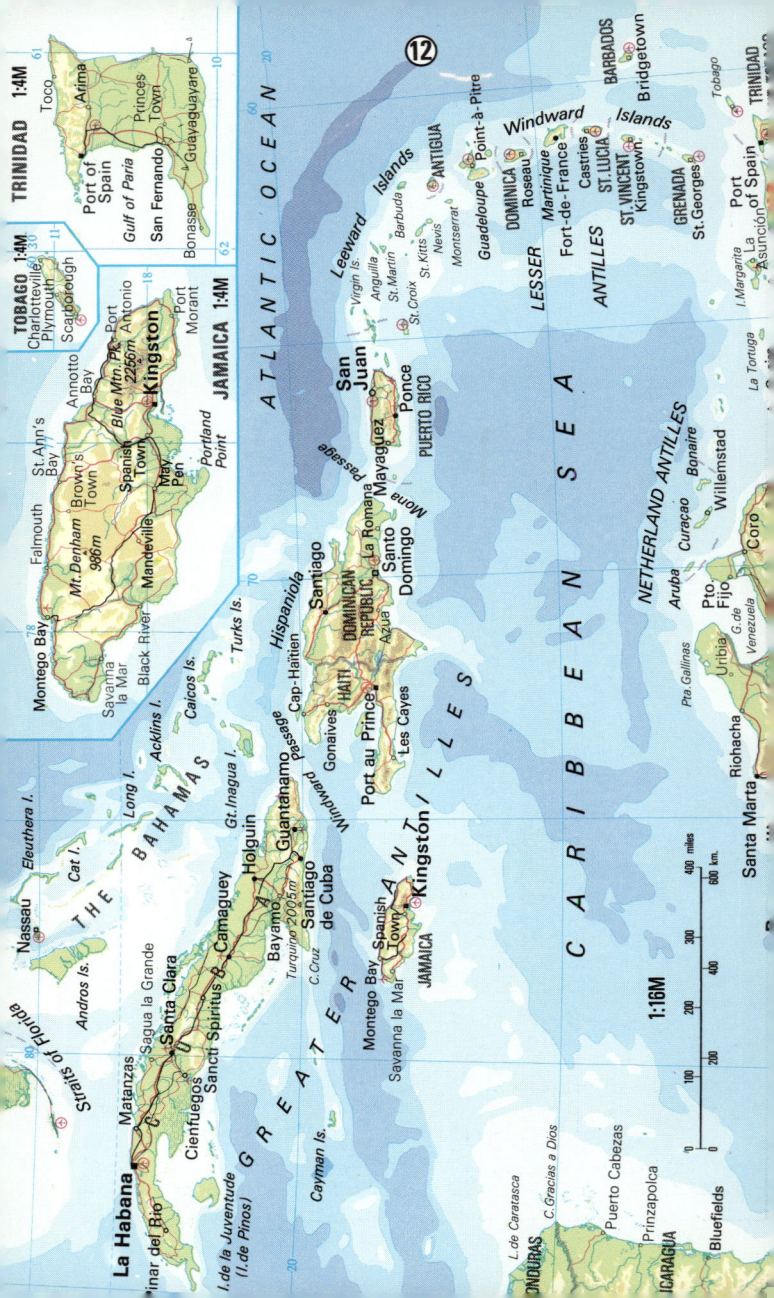

Caribbean Region Map

TRINIDAD 1:4M
- Toco
- Arima
- Princes Town
- Port of Spain
- Gulf of Paria
- San Fernando
- Bonasse
- Guayaguayare

TOBAGO 1:4M
- Charlotteville
- Plymouth
- Scarborough

JAMAICA 1:4M
- Montego Bay
- Falmouth
- St Ann's Bay
- Annotto Bay
- Port Antonio
- Port Morant
- Mt Denham
- Brown's Town
- Blue Mtn. Pk. 2256m
- Kingston
- Savanna la Mar
- Black River
- Mandeville
- Spanish Town
- May Pen
- Portland Point

Main Map 1:16M

Greater Antilles
- La Habana
- Pinar del Rio
- Matanzas
- I. de la Juventud (I. de Pinos)
- Cienfuegos
- Sagua la Grande
- Santa Clara
- Sancti Spiritus
- Camaguey
- C. Cruz
- Bayamo
- Turquino 2005m
- Santiago de Cuba
- Holguín
- Guantánamo
- Cayman Is.
- Montego Bay
- Spanish Town
- Kingston
- JAMAICA
- Savanna la Mar

Bahamas
- Nassau
- Eleuthera I.
- Cat I.
- Andros Is.
- Long I.
- Acklins I.
- Caicos Is.
- Gt. Inagua I.
- Turks Is.

Hispaniola
- Cap-Haïtien
- Gonaïves
- Port au Prince
- Les Cayes
- HAITI
- Santiago
- Azua
- DOMINICAN REPUBLIC
- La Romana
- Santo Domingo

Puerto Rico
- Mayagüez
- Ponce
- San Juan
- PUERTO RICO
- Mona Passage
- Windward Passage

Lesser Antilles
- Virgin Is.
- Anguilla
- St. Martin
- St. Kitts
- Nevis
- St. Croix
- Barbuda
- ANTIGUA
- Montserrat
- Guadeloupe
- Point-à-Pitre
- DOMINICA
- Roseau
- Martinique
- Fort-de-France
- ST. LUCIA
- Castries
- ST. VINCENT
- Kingstown
- BARBADOS
- Bridgetown
- GRENADA
- St. Georges
- Windward Islands
- Leeward Islands
- Tobago
- TRINIDAD
- Port of Spain
- I. Margarita
- La Asunción
- La Tortuga

Netherland Antilles
- Aruba
- Curaçao
- Bonaire
- Pto. Fijo
- Willemstad
- Coro
- G. de Venezuela

South/Central America coast
- Uribia
- Pta. Gallinas
- Riohacha
- Santa Marta
- L. de Caratasca
- C. Gracias a Dios
- Puerto Cabezas
- Prinzapolca
- Bluefields
- HONDURAS
- NICARAGUA

Seas & Oceans
- ATLANTIC OCEAN
- CARIBBEAN SEA
- Straits of Florida
- Gulf of Paria

Scale: 0 100 200 300 400 miles / 200 400 600 km

1:16M

At the doorstep of the Nazca Lines

Flights over the Lines every hour

Hotel Las Dunas

Perú — Ica Nazca

The newest and most complete resort hotel, with swimming pools, discotheque, tennis courts, golf, horseback riding. Wine tasting tours to the Ica valley, close to the National Reserve of Paracas, ideal for swimming, snorkeling, fishing and wild life observation of the Pacific Ocean. Located 168 miles south of Lima on the Panamerican Highway, 5 minutes from downtown Ica. Group rates available, upon request.

80 standard rooms presently available, 50 additional rooms in 1986.

SINGLE US$36 **DOUBLE US$40**

AV. LA ANGOSTURA — ICA — PERU

Sales and Reservations; P.O. Box 4410 Lima, Peru

Telex 21162   PE INVERTUR Phone 424180   Ica's Phone 231031

READERS' ADVENTURE COMPETITION!

Readers are invited to send to the publishers an account in English, in not more than 250 words, of the most interesting, adventurous, exciting or bizarre experience that has befallen them when visiting Latin America or the Caribbean, being careful to mention any role that the **South American Handbook** may have played in the experience.

Entries will be judged by the editors, and the winning entry, which will be rewarded with a £25 prize, will be published in the 1989 **South American Handbook**. A selected number of entries will be named as runners-up, and their authors will receive free copies of our 1989 edition.

Entries to be received by the publishers at the address below by 31 May 1988, please.

The winning entry for our last competition, reprinted here, is from David Ridges of Caldy, Merseyside, England.

'Mexico Mix-Up'

I was travelling northwards through Nicaragua during June 1986 with my Japanese friend, Toshiro, and we had been told of a one-off boat sailing from Bluefields to the Yucatan Peninsula, Mexico. Our plane to Bluefields was delayed in leaving Managua, so we barely had time to get an exit stamp before arriving at the dock just as a boat was preparing to leave. Toshiro asked an old sea-dog engrossed in cutting heads off fishes, "¿Es para Mexico?", and being answered with a positive-sounding grunt, we jumped aboard. As the boat set sail, we wondered why there were so many soldiers around, and upon making enquiries from an obviously inebriated captain, we made the horrifying discovery that we had mistakenly boarded a Sandinista army patrol boat, not returning to Bluefields for three days. We decided, despite the tremendous setback to make the most of this "cruise", but on the morning of the third day shots rang out from the riverbank, and everyone dived for cover. We were sitting on deck reading and ran for our cabin, but we were very exposed, and suddenly I felt that I had been hit and fell onto the deck. However, upon inspection, I was both amazed and relieved to discover that the bullet had penetrated and got lodged in my South American Handbook which I had been reading. So now I would never criticise the Handbook's thickness – after all, I owe it my life!

Trade & Travel Publications Limited
5 Prince's Buildings, George Street, Bath BA1 2ED, England.

Excursions from Trujillo About five km. to the crumbling ruins of **Chan Chan,** imperial city of the Chimú domains and largest adobe city in the world. The ruins consist of nine great compounds built by Chimú kings. The nine-metre high perimeter walls surrounded sacred enclosures with usually only one narrow entrance. Inside, serried rows of storerooms contained the agricultural wealth of the kingdom, which stretched 1,000 km. along the coast from near Guayaquil to Paramonga. Most of the compounds contain a huge walk-in well which tapped the ground water, raised to a high level by irrigation higher up the valley. Each compound also included a platform mound which was the burial place of the king, with his women and his treasure, presumably maintained as a memorial. The Incas almost certainly copied this system and transported it to Cuzco where the last Incas continued building huge enclosures. Chan Chan was taken by the Incas about AD 1450 but not looted; the Spaniards, however, despoiled its burial mounds of all the gold and silver statuettes and ornaments buried with the Chimú nobles. The dilapidated city walls enclose an area of 28 square km. containing the remains of palaces, temples, workshops, streets, houses, gardens and a canal. What is left of the adobe walls bears well-preserved moulded decorations and painted designs have been found on pottery unearthed from the debris of a city ravaged by floods, earthquakes, and treasure seekers. Heavy rain and flooding in 1983 damaged much of the ruins and although they are still standing, many of the interesting mouldings are closed to visitors. The Ciudadela of Tschudi has been reconstructed (15 min. walk from the road), open 0830 to 1600 (but it may be covered up if rain is expected). A ticket which covers the entrance fees for Chan Chan, the Huaca El Dragón and the Huaca La Esmeralda (for one day only) costs US$0.60 (students, US$0.30), it is recommended (some say, compulsory—US$1.50) to take a guide (Oscar, who is normally to be found at Chan Chan when not working, has been recommended). Minibuses leave from José Gálvez 394, corner of Los Incas, near market, or corner of España and Orbegoso/Mansiche, or from Salaverry, US$0.15, last one returns about 1200; Trujillo-Huanchaco bus, US$0.10 to Chan Chan entrance; Colectivo, US$0.15; taxi, US$1.20.

Warning If you walk to the ruins from the main road, keep to the path. Do not go to Chan Chan alone or in couples; it is preferable to go with a guide. Do not walk on Buenos Aires beach near Chan Chan as there is serious danger of robbery, and being attacked by dogs.

The restored temple, Huaca El Dragón, dating from the Mochica empire of between 800 and 100 BC, is also known as Huaca Arco Iris (rainbow), after shape of friezes which decorate it. It is on the W side of the Pan-American Highway in the district of La Esperanza; Taxi costs US$1; open 0800-1700.

The Caballo Muerto ruins, about 11 km. inland up the Moche valley, are now forbidden to visitors, and the sculptures have been re-buried to protect them from robbers.

The poorly restored Huaca La Esmeralda is at Mansiche, between Trujillo and Chan Chan, behind the church. Buses from Pasaje Agustín, between Orbegoso and Gamarra, 2 blocks from Plaza (not a friendly district).

A few km. south of Trujillo are the huge Moche pyramids, the Huaca de Sol and the Huaca de la Luna (open all the time, entry free, taxi, US$6 return, colectivo from the Mercado Mayorista US$0.25, marked Moche El Alto or La Compiña, stops right in front of the ruins, alternatively bus marked Salaverry US$0.15, get out at Bodega El Sol on the right hand side of the road; opposite is a huge Sprite sign. Here starts a path to Moche, about an hour's walk; it is inadvisable to walk unless in a large group). The pyramids consist of millions of adobe bricks and are the largest precolumbian structures in South America (they are being restored, and the interior passageways of the Huaca de la Luna can now be seen; the site is under the control of the tourist police). An interesting feature of the site is the innumerable number of ancient pottery shards lying around on the ground.

The small fishing village of **Huanchaco** is worth visiting to see the narrow pointed fishing rafts, known as *caballitos*, made of tortora reeds and used in

674 PERU

many places along the Peruvian coast. Unlike those used on Lake Titicaca, they are flat, not hollow, and ride the breakers rather like surfboards. These craft are depicted on ancient Mochica and Chimú pottery. The village is overlooked by a huge church from the belfry of which are superb views. Children sell precolumbian *objets d'art* and beads; beware of eating fish in the hut-like restaurants as they aren't very hygienic. Bus to Huanchaco from corner of Av. España and Av. Mansiche (regular, ringroad bus), or, after 1830, Pasaje Agustín, Trujillo, 2 blocks from Plaza.

Hotels and Restaurants *Hostal Sol y Mar*, Jirón Ficus 570, F (more expensive with hot water) some rooms with bath and balcony, kitchen facilities, friendly owner, garden, swimming pool, recommended; *Bracamonte*, F, friendly, comfortable, good, chalets with private bath, pool, secure, bar nearby, good pies and cakes; *Hostal Huanchaco*, on Plaza, also F, clean and friendly, swimmimg pool; *Hostal Las Palmeras*, Calle Las Palmeras, G-F, 6 rooms, hot water in bathrooms, cooking facilities, clean, American owner has extensive folk-art collection; *Barraca*, F, private showers; *Caballitos de Totora*, E, swimming pool, the owners are to open a vegetarian restaurant and hold cultural events at the hotel; cheap accommodation at the house of Señora Consuelo, about US$0.50 p.p. Ask around for rooms in private houses for long stays. Good fish restaurants on the sea front (*Viña del Mar*, *El Peón*, *El Erizo* recommended; *Violleta*, a private house (good meals provided) and *Familia Flores*, popular; *El Tramboyo*, near the pier; *Lucho del Mar*, excellent sea food, *Piccolo*, 5 blocks from plaza, cheap, friendly, sometimes live folk music). Bus from Trujillo, hourly, US$1 (taxi US$2 for 4).

A visit may be made to one of the sugar estates, say the Hacienda Cartavio, in the Chicama valley (43 km.). At Laredo (bus from Trujillo, near central market, 7 km.), a sugar refinery can be visited—the tour is free; apply to public relations office in administration building; there are also interesting ruins at Galindo, near Laredo. One of the biggest sugar estates in the world, also in the Chicama valley, is the Casa Grande cooperative. It covers over 6,000 hectares and employs 4,000 members. Visits (guided) are only possible before 1200; US$0.70 by bus. The Chiclín museum, once famous for items from Chan Chan, now contains interesting collection of colonial religious paintings and statuary. Ruins in the Chicama valley: Huaca Prieta and Chiquitoy; colectivos from Av. España, change at Cartavio.

132 km. E from Trujillo is the village of **Coina**, at 1,500 metres in the Sierra Alto Chicama, where the late Dr. Kaufmann, from Germany, opened a hospital for Indians and built the *Hostería El Sol*, with glorious views, E, for full board, F, bed only. Walking. English, French and German spoken. Information from the *Hostería El Sol*, at Calle Los Brillantes 224, Santa Inés, Trujillo (Tel.: 231933). Mail can be forwarded to Apartado 775, Trujillo.

To the NE of Trujillo is Cajamarca, which can be reached either from Trujillo or from Pacasmayo (paved throughout). The old road from Trujillo is poor, taking 12-15 hours (as opposed to 8 hrs. via Pacasmayo), but it is more interesting, passing over the bare puna before dropping to the Huamachuco valley. Off it lies **Otusco**, an attractive Andean town with an imposing but unfinished church and narrow cobbled streets. Further on, at the mining town of Shorey, a road branches off to **Santiago de Chuco**, birthplace of the poet César Vallejo, where there is the annual festival of Santiago El Mayor in the second half of July. The main procession is on July 25, when the image is carried through the streets. The road runs on to the colonial town of **Huamachuco**, 181 km. from Trujillo, which has a huge main plaza and a modern cathedral which is not universally popular. There is a colourful Sunday market. A 2-hr. walk (take the track which goes off to the right just after crossing the bridge on the road to Trujillo) takes you to the extensive ruin of a hilltop pre-Inca fortress, Marcahuamachuco (car US$5 p.p.).

Hotels Best is *La Libertad*, G, rooms fairly clean, bathrooms filthy; also *Sucre*, G. Recommended restaurants: *Caribe*, quite good, probably best in town, and *El Sol* (both on main square) and *Danubio*. Good snacks at *Salón Venecia*, Carrión near main plaza.

Buses Transportes Quiroz from Trujillo, US$5, 12 hrs., at 1530, 1700, 1800, take warm clothing; Antisuyo to Trujillo three daily, US$4, 10 hrs. There are also colectivos from Trujillo. Buses to Cajamarca, US$1.50; to Casa Grande, US$0.85. Direct bus to Lima, 24 hrs.

From Huamachuco buses (Empresa Huancapata which start in Trujillo) run to Tayabamba (important ruins nearby), on the far bank of the Marañón, passing through the old gold-mining centres of Pataz province, such as Parcoy and Buldibuyo. This journey takes a good 18 hours in "normal" conditions. Not far, but a time-consuming journey on mule-back, from Pataz itself (a friendly gold-mining town, about 100 km. from Huamachuco) are the unique circular ruins of El Gran **Pajatén** (pre-Inca); ask at Tourist Office in Cajamarca for details. (A national park, Río Abisco, incorporating Gran Pajatén, four other sites—La Playa, Las Papayas, Los Pinchudos and Cerro Central—and

PERU 675

the surrounding cloud forest, is scheduled to open for visitors in 1990; until then you need a permit (hard to get) from the Instituto Nacional de Cultura in Lima.) Also worth seeing in the Huamachuco area are Laguna Sausacocha (with Inca ruins, similar to those of Vilcashuamán, near Ayacucho, nearby) and *haciendas* Yanasera and Cochabamba, deep down in the valley of the river Chusgón, about 2-3 hrs. by truck east of the town. Yanasara, noted for its fighting bulls, is still in the hands of its long-term owner, Francisco Pinillos Montoya, a well-known local character. There is a guest house at Cochabamba, which used to be the Andean retreat of the owners of the Laredo sugar plantation, near Trujillo. The climate, at about 2,300 metres, is mild.

There is a 2-day walk from Bolívar in the NE to Huamachuco, parts of which follow an Inca trail used by Túpac Yupanqui (see also page 754). One walks from Bolívar to Bambamarca, then down the stone steps leading to the Calemar trail, which crosses the River Marañón. At Pallar, there are trucks to Huamachuco. Be sure to take food, water, a small kerosene cooker and a compass; this is an arduous trip and not recommended for beginners.

From Huamachuco the road runs on 48 km. through impressive eucalyptus groves to **Cajabamba,** which lies in the high part of the sugar-producing and once malaria-infested Condebamba valley. It has an attractive Plaza de Armas. Several buses daily to Huamachuco; Quiroz, Antisuyo, about 3 hrs., US$1.75, also trucks and lorries. Two direct buses a day from Trujillo, 12 hrs.

The best hotel is the *Flores* (F, with toilet, friendly, clean) on the Plaza de Armas; *Hostal Bolívar*, F, including fleas but without bath; also *Ramal*, F, friendly; *Hostal Comercio*, G, basic, not recommended; *Restaurant Gloriabamba* good.

Cajabamba can also be reached in a strenuous but marvellous 3-4 day hike from Coina (see above). The first day's walk brings you to Hacienda Santa Rosa where you stay overnight. Then you cross the mountains at about 4,000 metres, coming through Arequeda to Cajabamba. The ruins at Huacamochal may be seen en route; the scenery is spectacular. It is advisable to hire a guide, and a donkey to carry the luggage. The cost for both is about US$4 a day. A map of the route is available from the Post Office in Coina.

The road continues from Cajabamba through San Marcos (basic hotel), important for its Sunday cattle market, to Cajamarca. Bus to Cajamarca (124 km.), Atahualpa and Empresa Díaz leaving early in the morning, takes 6 hrs., US$3.

Pacasmayo, port for the next oasis northward, is 100 km. N. of Trujillo on the Pan-American Highway running N to Chiclayo (bus, 2 hrs., US$0.75). Population: 12,300.

Hotel *Ferrocarril*, F, on seafront, quiet and clean, no hot water (ask for water anyway); *Panamericano*, Leoncio Prado 18, F, with private cold shower, good value, friendly, clean, safe, reasonable restaurant downstairs. Several cheap restaurants on the main street.

Pacasmayo is the best starting point for visiting Cajamarca (2,750 metres). The new paved 180 km. road to it branches off the Pan-American Highway soon after it crosses the Jequetepeque River. The river valley has terraced rice fields and mimosas may often be seen in bloom, brightening the otherwise dusty landscape. A few km. to N on other side of River Jequetepeque are the ruins of Pacatnamú—pyramids, cemetery and living quarters of nobles and fishermen, seem to have been built in Chavín period (Kaufmann Doig maintains that they are later). Evidence also of Moche tribes. At the mining town of **Chilete**, a worthwhile diversion is to take the road N to San Pablo; 21 km. from Chilete are the stone monoliths of the Kuntur Huasi culture, which resemble those of San Agustín in Colombia. There are occasional buses from Chilete to the site, 1½ hrs., then 20 mins.' walk (no signs; you must ask locals), then a long wait for transport back, best to hitch. In Chilete, hotels *Amazonas* and *San Pedro*; restaurant *Montecarlo* serves cheap *cuy* and other dishes. Truck to Chilete from the police control 1 km. from main plaza in Cajamarca, US$0.85. On the road to Cajamarca is Yonán, where there are petroglyphs.

An alternative route from Trujillo to Cajamarca, via Contumazá, passes through the cane fields and rice plantations of the Chicama valley before branching off to climb over the watershed of the Jequetepeque. From Contumazá, an attractive little town, trucks can be taken to Cajamarca, via Chilete.

Cajamarca (pop. 70,000), the chief town of the northern mountain area, has kept its colonial air. Here Pizarro ambushed and captured Atahualpa, the Inca emperor. The Cuarto de Rescate (not the actual ransom chamber but in fact the room where Atahualpa was held prisoner—closed on Tues. and after 1200 on Sat. and Sun.) can be seen (US$0.50, ticket also valid for nearby Belén

676 **PERU**

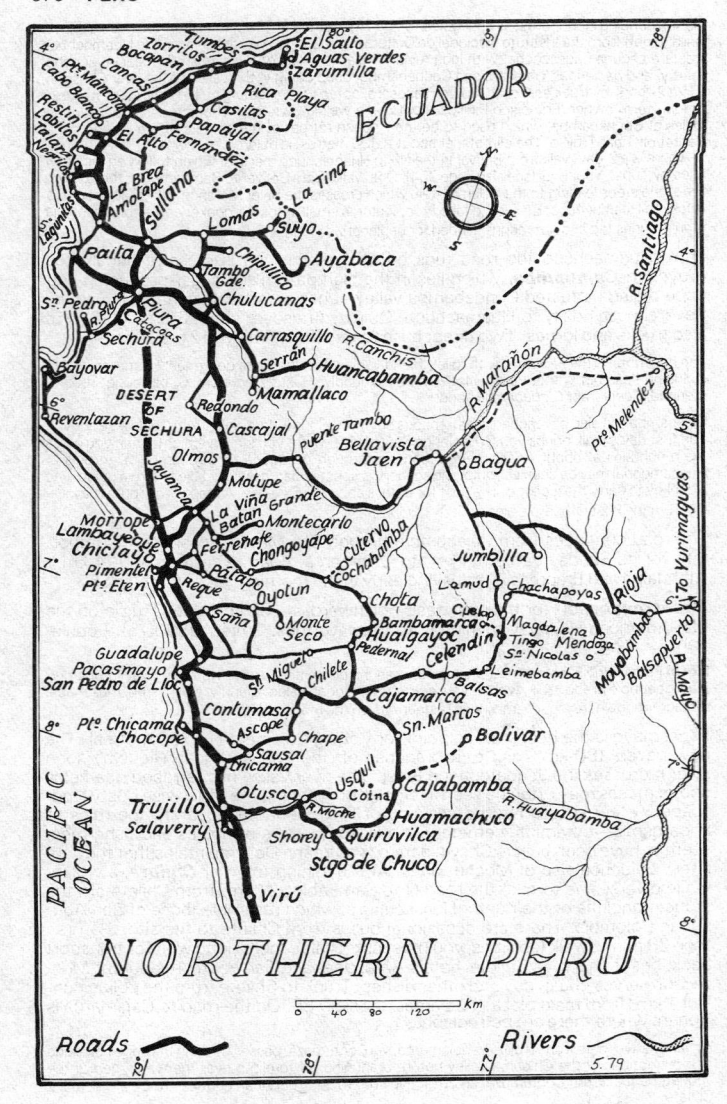

church); a red line purporting to be the height of Atahualpa's hand was only recently painted in. (The room was closed to the public for centuries, and used by the nuns of Belén hospital). The chamber also has two interesting murals and unusual trapezoidal doors (Spanish). The Plaza where Atahualpa was ambushed and the stone seat set high on a hill where he reviewed his subjects are also shown. The Cathedral, San Francisco (with catacombs) and Belén churches are well worth seeing; so are San Pedro (Gálvez and Junín), San José (C. M. Iglesias and Angamos), La Recoleta (Maestro and Casanova) and Capilla de La Dolorosa, close to San Francisco. Many belfries were left half-finished in protest against a Spanish tax levied on the completion of a church. The Cathedral, which took 350 years to build, was completed in 1960; it still has no belfry. Next to the Belén church (closed on Tues.) is an ancient hospital; the two, known as the Conjunto de Belén, are being restored as a centre for the handicraft trade.

Points of interest include the Bishop's Palace, next to the Cathedral, and many old colonial houses with garden patios, and elaborate carved doorways: see palace of the Condes de Uceda, now occupied by the Banco de Crédito on Jr. Apurímac 719; the house of Toribio Casanova, Jr. José Gálvez 938; the house of the Silva Santiesteban family, Jr. Junín 1123; and the houses of the Guerrero and Castañeda families. The Education Faculty of the University has a museum on Jirón Arequipa with objects of the pre-Inca Cajamarca culture, not seen in Lima; the attendant knows much about Cajamarca and the surrounding area. Open 0800-1200, 1500-1700, in winter, and 0800-1200 in summer, US$0.20 (guided tour). The Museo de Arte Colonial, at the Convento de San Francisco, is also worth a visit. Nearby are the warm sulphurous thermal springs known as Los Baños del Inca, where there are a public pool and private rooms (US$0.30, excellent). Atahualpa tried the effect of these waters on a festering war wound. Here can also be seen a lake and gardens, and a farm of the Ministry of Agriculture with bulls for breeding (open 0830-1200, 1400-1600). There is a minibus service from the main square, US$0.10.

The surrounding countryside is splendid. Other excursions include Ventanillas de Otusco, part of an old Inca sanctuary (airport road, 14 km., minibus from town, US$0.10), gallery of niches. A good walk, 10 km., is from Baños del Inca on Celendín road to Ventanillas de Otusco (start from the bridge and take the path along the brook), through beautiful countryside. A new road continues to Ventanillas de Combayo, some 20 km. past those of Otusco; these are more numerous and more spectacular, being located in a rather isolated, mountainous area, and are distributed over the face of a steep 200-metre-high hillside. Cumbemayo, mountain village (23 km. SW of Cajamarca but no bus service; it is dangerous to go alone, take a guided tour, US$4; taxi US$12), sanctuary and canal which can be followed for several km., very remarkable; also, be sure to take a strong torch; guides are available, but alternatively you can walk and ask local passers-by the way. The trail starts from the hill of Santa Apollonia (Silla del Inca), and goes to Cumbemayo straight through the village and up the hill; at the top of the mountain, leave the trail and take the road to the right to the canal. The walk takes 2-3 hours, but is not difficult and you do not need hiking boots. The Indians use the trail to bring their goods to market. Other Inca ruins in the area include Tantarica, Torrecitas, and San Pedro de Pacopampa. The hill of Santa Apollonia is in fact a sacrificial altar dating to Chavín times. The town is a favourite among Peruvians for holidays, and has an interesting market with some crafts, especially noted for cotton and wool saddlebags (*alforjas*). Bargains of hand-tooled leather goods can be bought from the prisoners at the jail beyond the white arch on Calle Lima (7 blocks from Plaza de Armas). All museums are closed on Tuesdays (shops take a long lunch) but open at weekends.

Festivals Plenty. Corpus Christi is a favourite. The pre-Lent Carnival has been revived; it is spectacular but includes much throwing of water, oil and paint, which can develop into fights between local youths and gringos. July 28/29, Independence: *fiesta*, with bullfight and agricultural fair.

Warning Beware of pickpockets in the Plaza de Armas and in cinemas.

Hotels *Turistas* (60 rooms) in the Plaza de Armas, with its 350-year-old fountain (very good, E, with private bath, meals US$3.20). *Laguna Seca*, at Baños del Inca, a converted *hacienda* in pleasant surroundings, private hot baths in rooms. *Sucre*, Amalia Puga 815, near Plaza de Armas, F, with toilet and wash basin in each room, sometimes noisy and no water, poor restaurant upstairs; *Amazonas*, Jiron Amazonas 528, modern, medium-priced. *Gran Hostal Plaza*, Plaza de Armas

631, F, old building with handmade wood furnishings, private bath and balcony, poor water supply, with new annex (dirty but is open at 0200 when bus arrives); *San Francisco*, Jr. Belén 570, F, good, no hot water; *Bolívar*, Jr. Apurímac 670; *Jusovi*, Amazonas 637, F, comfortable, all rooms with private baths, recommended; *Becerra*, Jr. Arequipa 195 (unsigned), F, intermittent tepid water, recommended; *Casablanca* on Plaza de Armas, F, basic, hot water, clean, Dos de Mayo 446, noisy, not friendly; *Hostal Cajamarca*, E, in colonial-style house at Dos de Mayo 311, clean, hot water, noisy but recommended; *Hostal Dos de Mayo*, Dos de Mayo 585, F; *Prado*, Plaza de Armas, F, cold water; *Hostal José Galves*, E, thermal water; *Hostal Atahualpa*, E, private bath, clean, good value, but hard beds, recommended. *Hostal* (without name) in Calle Lamar recommended; *La Mar*, F, cheap, beds only in dormitories. Try to get a room in the sun, no heating for the cold nights.

Restaurants *Arlequín*, corner of Plaza de Armas, good; *Salsas*, very good, popular with locals; *El Zarco*, Plaza de Armas at Arequipa 170, very highly recommended, much frequented by local residents, inexpensive, try the *sopa fuchifú*, *humitas de maíz*; *La Namorina*, on edge of town on road to Baños del Inca, opposite Ché service station, renowned for its speciality, *cuy frito* (fried guinea pig); *Hotel Casablanca* has good dining room. *La Taverna*, Plaza de Armas, recommended, clean, good variety, but food cold as in most places, reasonable prices, *tamales* are a speciality, best in town; *Super Pollo* on Plaza, recommended for its *jugo especial* (made from *algarrobina*); *Buen Amigo*, Jirón Apurímac, recommended; *Playa Azul*, good food, clean, in Magdalena (about 1 hr. from Cajamarca by car); *Central*, cheap, good; *Charlie's*, Jr. Lima, just W of *Hotel Turismo*, friendly, good apple tart; *Capri*, Jirón Lima, good ice cream; *Rescate* has been recommended for its *cuy*. Also try *El Cumbe* and *Taverna Johnny*.

Tea Rooms *Café Florida* and *Casa Blanca*, both on Plaza de Armas.

Food Specialities *Queso mantecoso* (full-cream cheese); *manjar blanco* (sweet); *humitas* (ground maize with cheese); *cuy frito*; eucalyptus honey (sold in the market on Calle Amazonas; said to be a cure for rheumatism). Try the delicious flaky pastries filled with apple or *manjar blanco* from the street sellers.

Addresses Banco Nor Perú, corner of Lima and Tarapacá, exchanges dollars for 1% commission. Banco de Crédito will not even change cash. Post Office, Jr. Lima 406; Entel Perú, Jr. San Martín 363; Hospital, Av. Mario Urteaga; Guardia Civil, Plaza Amalia Puga.

Tourist Information Dirección de Turismo, Conjunto de Belén, opp. Jr. Belén 628, 1 block from Plaza de Armas, helpful (has city maps, not much use). Ask here for car hire. Also Cajamarca Tours, Dos de Mayo 323, guides do not speak English, despite what they claim. A group of local guides has formed Cumbemayo Tours, and do good economical trips, e.g. to Cumbemayo itself (US$3 p.p.), the pottery workshop at Ayllambo, 3½ km. out, and the Palm Sunday celebrations at Porcón, 1 hr. out on the Bambamarca road.

Air Service AeroPerú flights to Lima via Trujillo on Tues., Sat. mornings (US$75). Cheaper to pay for each stage separately. **Warning:** Delays at Cajamarca are all too frequent.

Buses Daily buses and colectivos to Lima (bus, US$13), Trujillo (7-8 hrs., US$3-4.50 by bus) and Chiclayo (US$3.25, 4 hrs. by Empresa Díaz, 1230 and 2100, with El Cumbe, Amazonas 860, US$3, at 1100 and 1500, with Atahualpa at 1430, US$2.50, Comité de Autos 2, and Chinchay-Suyo). Tepsa leaves for Trujillo and Lima at 1800; Empresa Díaz for Trujillo at 0630 and 2000, for Lima at 1800 (1730 from Tourist Hotel, "Presidential service" non-stop) and for Celendín at 1530. Atahualpa to Lima, 15 hrs., US$9, overnight, recommended; to Celendín daily at 1300 (also to Cajabamba, Chota, Cutervo). Expreso Cajamarca, Amazonas 807, Comité de Autos 12 and 40 also go to Trujillo. Also daily to and from Cajabamba (Empresa Díaz, Calle Ayacucho 717 or Atahualpa at 1000), US$3, 6 hrs. (milk trucks will also take passengers to Cajabamba).

North of Cajamarca is Hualgayoc (see page 684). Trip with fantastic scenery. There is excellent trout served in restaurant on the way there; easy to find as it is the only place for a long way. Order on your way there to eat on the way back.

South of Cajamarca, through Santa Catalina and Trinidad, are the Inca and pre-Inca ruins of Tantarica, near Cholol.

Cajamarca is the starting point for the northern route to Iquitos. From Cajamarca there are several buses daily to **Celendín** (5 hrs., US$2.50), where there are several hotels off the main plaza (*Hotel Jorge Girón*, F; *Amazonas* and *José Galves*, both F and recommended; *Hostal Celedín*, F, with bath; *Maxmar*, Jr. Dos de Mayo 349, G, dirty, unfriendly; *Bolívar*, F; *Restaurant Jalisco* on Plaza de Armas, simple, not cheap) and cock fighting weekends in the local arena for the *aficionados*. Festival July 24 (Virgen del Carmen). There is also an interesting local market on Sunday. The town has electricity only between 1800 and 2200. The road follows a winding course through the northern Andes, crossing the wide and deep canyon of the River Marañón at Balsas. Balsas is reached after 2½ hrs. and then the road climbs steeply with superb views of the mountains and the valleys below. The fauna and flora are spectacular as the journey alternates between high in the mountains and low in the rain forest. After rain; landslides can be quite a problem. There are some interesting Inca ruins on the road between Celendín and Leimebamba.

Leimebamba is a pleasant town with 2 hotels, the better of which is *Escobedo*, G, friendly owner has lots of local information, toilets, cold shower; 3 restaurants, including *Oasis*, just off Plaza de Armas, and *El Caribe* on the Plaza; one truck a week Leimebamba-Celendín; Mon. only to Chachapoyas. Of the ruins in the area **La Congona**, a Sachupoyan site, is 2½ hrs.' walk away, take the trail at the end of the street with the hotels and climb up (next to police station). The trail levels out and follows round the mountain, then down into a little valley. La Conga, a system of 3 hills can be seen: aim for the right-hand (easterly) conical hill with a visible small cliff. The trail does not go all the way up the hill; you must cross a field and climb through moss forest. This is the best preserved of 3 sites, with 30 decorated round stone houses (some with evidence of 3 storeys) and a watch tower. The other hills have been levelled. It is worth following the trail along the crest beyond these hills, and then to the left, down through rain forest (muddy), eventually to join the main trail. (A good day's walk—Haydn Washington, Australia.)

The road on to Chachapoyas (10 hrs. from Celendín by car, probably 14 by truck) is poor (dry weather only), but the scenery is magnificent. Food and warm clothing are necessary; usually only chicken and rice is available in the villages where the trucks stop. If you want to go through to Iquitos, better to fly.

Chachapoyas, population 18,000, is the capital of the Department of Amazonas and has been called, by the American explorer Gene Savoy, "the friendliest town in Peru". Chachapoyas is a military zone, so foreigners must present their documents at P.I.P. on arrival. If you have any problems contact the Guardia Civil (green uniforms), very friendly and more helpful than P.I.P., in the town and countryside. Archaeological and anthropological information can be sought from the local anthropologist, Carlos Torres Mas, who is the head of the Instituto Nacional de Cultura, in the municipal building on the main plaza (will store luggage). For most thorough information, contact Padre Pedro Rodríguez Arista, Sto Domingo 643 (see also below under Kuelap). Those interested in the abundant archaeological sites in the area should read Gene Savoy's *Antisuyo* (British edition: *Vilcabamba*). There is also a Tourist Office on the Plaza de Armas, the director, Don Segundo Pastor, is helpful, luggage can be stored here (there is a small but good museum in the same building).

Hotels *Marañón*, F, with bath, filthy, cold, not recommended; *Johumaji*, Jr. Ayacucho 711 (Tel.: 138), F, with bath, cheaper without, clean and safe for luggage; *Casa Blanca*, F; *Amazonas* in Plaza de Armas, F, good. A new tourist hotel is planned at Laguna Pomacocha, 3 hrs. by bus from Chachapoyas.

Restaurants *Chacha*, on Plaza de Armas, good for *bistec apanado*, not friendly; *Oh Qué Bueno*, limited menu; good pastries also at *Patisserie*, Jr. 2 de Mayo 558; *Kuelap*, same street as *Johumaji*, good; good pizzas on the Plaza de Armas below the Acción Popular sign; *Café Bar Mary*, Plaza de Armas, clean, good, cheap; *Monte Carlo*, opp. market entrance, cheap, friendly; *Mio Mio*, near Post Office, good value chicken restaurant; good fruit juices at stall 67 in the market, also *Juguería Montes Chávez*, Ayacucho 824-32, friendly, also restaurant.

For leatherwork, Zapatería "El Cairo": a pair of boots costs US$27.

Buses Daily to Chiclayo (Olano, US$10, 1000, 1100, on Sat., none on Sun.) via Bagua and Jaén (18-25 hrs.). There is a truck and *camioneta* on Wed. only, at 0200, 14 hrs., US$4.50, to Celendín (not for those without a head for heights), other *camionetas* run, but to no fixed schedule and only occasionally. Empresa Díaz leaves Cajamarca Wed. and Sun. at 1200 for Chachapoyas, arriving 1600 next day after an 8-hr. stop in Celendín to sleep, US$9.25. You can alight in Tingo (for Kuelap). Some trucks will take passengers to Moyobamba and to Tingo in afternoon.

Air Service A new airport has been built; AeroPerú fly Lima (US$50)-Chiclayo (US$25)-Chachapoyas on Weds., arriving 1100, departing 1200. Also Wed. flights to Rioja.

The road is now open via Chachapoyas to Mendoza, a five-hour journey from Chachapoyas by lorry and occasional minibuses. Mendoza is ethnologically interesting because of a high incidence of very fair people.

"Two hours by truck on the road to Mendoza is Molinopampa, which marks the starting point of an an adventurous five-day hike to Rioja. Only experienced hikers should attempt this journey, which is very difficult. Food supplies for the whole journey should be purchased at Chachapoyas and a guide, absolutely essential, hired at Molinopampa for about US$5. The steep trail leads through waist-high unbridged rivers, over the cold, high Sierra and then for three days one follows the muddy trail down to the dense and humid jungle. We were accompanied by exotic butterflies, and never a quiet moment with the chattering of birds and monkeys. The whole magic of the jungle—trees, birds, animals and insects—can be seen untouched in their natural surroundings." (Katrina Farrar and Andy Thornton).

Kuelap By driving S up the Utcubamba valley from Chachapoyas (several trucks or *micros*, 0800-0900), US$1, 2 hrs.; trucks infrequent from Celendín US$3.85—leave at 0300, 12 hrs., driver collects you from hotel) to Tingo (1,800 metres; there are two cheap *pensiones*, at the entrance to the village, a blue house with dark basement, F, mouldy, good restaurant and white building opposite, called *Bar Restaurant Kuelap*, F; no water or electricity in Tingo), and a 4-5 hr. steep walk uphill (take waterproof, food and drink, and start early a.m.), one can reach Kuelap (3,100 metres), a spectacular pre-Inca walled city. Its massive stone walls are as formidable as those of any preColumbian city. A road and hotel are being built—slowly (there is crude lodging for US$0.50, 2 beds, and food sometimes available at the summit to save you the walk down to Tingo—take candles). Entrance fee is US$0.05 (the ruins are locked; the proprietor of the lodging has the keys and accompanies visitors). It was proposed that Kuelap would be fully excavated and the road completed in 1987; a minibus sevice from Chachapoyas is planned. These developments will lessen the remoteness, and perhaps the charm, of Kuelap. Recommended guide in Tingo: Domingo, who works for the Director of the Institute of Culture. The whole area is full of largely unexplored remains; some of them have been studied by the Swiss archaeologists Henri and Paula Reichlen (who surveyed 39 sites in 1948—see *Récherches archaeologiques dans les Andes du haut Utcubamba*, in *Journal des Américanistes*, which includes an accurate map), and the American archaeologist Gene Savoy (who went further than the Reichlens-see his book *Antisuyo*); Kaufmann Doig refers to them as the "12 Cities of the Condors"; his map showing their location is in his *Arqueología Peruana*. See also the booklet on Kuelap, available at the Tourist Office in Chachapoyas, very informative. Some scientists have tried to prove that the fair-skinned, blonde people of this area, described by the Spanish chronicles, were Celtic. Mark Babington and Morgan Davis write:

"Kuelap, discovered in 1843, was the last outpost of a lost white race, known variously as the Sachupoyans or the Chachas, who were in retreat from the advancing Inca around the years 1450-1470. Up till now Kuelap and La Congona were the only Sachupoyan ruins to have been explored in any detail whatsoever. The fact is that Kuelap was the final refuge of the Sachupoyans in a region which must have supported at least one million people before the arrival of the Inca. The known area inhabited by the Sachupoyans extends north from Leimebamba to Chachapoyas, and west as far as the Marañón.

"In 1977 a team of three Americans explored the area between the Marañón and Utcubamba Rivers; they were the first to do so. They left an account of their journey in the American magazine *Outside*. Inspired by their account the two of us decided to retrace their steps. This is surely a region which overwhelms even Machu-Picchu in grandeur and mystery. It contains no less than five lost, and uncharted cities; the most impressive of which is Pueblo Alto, near the village of Pueblo Nuevo (25 km. from Kuelap). It was discovered some 60 years ago by the father of a local farmer, Juan Tuesta, with whom we stayed. By far the majority of these cities, fortresses and villages were never discovered by the Spaniard; in fact many had already returned to the jungle by the time the Spaniard arrived in 1532. The sites are situated in the tropical rain forest, and on the upper slopes of the *puna*. Furthermore many of them are to be found on or near the trails which today still provide the only medium of transport in this heavily populated and agricultural region. On a recent map of the area, with which we were provided in Chachapoyas, no less than 38 sites can be counted; but Ojilcho and Pueblo Alto, for example, are not charted on this new 1977 map in spite of their enormous dimensions. If all this sounds a bit exaggerated and inaccessible, we must add that the local farmers are conversant with the ruins, whether charted or not. It is among these people that one must look for information, provision and hospitality and, most important of all, guides and mules. The area, though well populated, provides virtually no facilities for the traveller. One should be cognizant of the difficulties ahead before attempting this journey, though this is not to say the trip is beyond the ability of most. Hiking gear is essential: sleeping bags, tents and canned goods (and a machete—ed.). Small gifts are also much appreciated by the local people in return for their hospitality. (Take money in small notes as villagers do not have change for larger.) Water is no problem, *unless it is the rainy season* (Feb.-May). Travelling at this time is not advised as the mountain passes are shin-deep in mud.

"Padre Pedro Rodríguez Arista, Sto. Domingo 643, whom everyone in Chachapoyas knows well, will be only too willing to help the prospective explorer. It was he who provided us with maps and letters of introduction. We can also recommend others who will be of help to the traveller, such as Oscar Arce Cáceres based at "El Chillo" 4½ km. outside Tingo, who owns a farm and knows the area very well. The trek into this area, like the walk up to Kuelap, starts from Tingo; easily accessible from Chachapoyas by daily *camionetas* for about $1 per person. From Tingo the way is all mule track. In Magdalena (a 15-minute walk from Tingo), Abram Torres will be happy to provide one with his services as guide, and his mule, for the first leg of the journey as far as Choctamal, about 4 hours away.

Levanto is 2 hrs by new road (*camioneta* at 0600-0700, no scheduled return) or 6 hrs. walk from Chachapoyas. Levanto was the first Spanish capital of the area and the Spaniards built directly on top of the previous Sachupoyan structures. Although, not many years later, the capital was moved to Chachapoyas, Levanto still retained its importance, at least for a while, as it had been one of the seven great cities of the Sachupoyans as described by Cieza de León and Garcilaso de la Vega. Nowadays Levanto is a small, unspoilt, and very beautiful colonial village set on flat ground overlooking the massive canyon of the Utcubamba river. Kuelap can, on a clear day, be seen on the other side of the rift. Levanto is a good centre for exploring the many ruins around, being the centre of a network of ancient ruins, fortified redoubts, residential areas and many others. Very close to Levanto are the ruins of **Yalape**, recently cleared under the supervision of Sr César Torres Rojas, a resident of Levanto. Yalape seems to have been a massive residential complex extending over many hectares and including many well-preserved examples of typical Sachupoyan architecture and masonry with quite elaborate and beautiful friezes. Its scale, like that of Kuelap, can be only described as titanic. In fact the whole area is covered in ruins, almost every prominent hilltop in the immediate vicinity has at least a watchtower of some sort. As yet there is no official accommodation as such in Levanto, although plans are being made to build a small *alojamiento*. However, small groups of travellers are very welcome and beds and bedding are provided in the mayor's office and village meeting hall. Sr Torres Mas, in Chachapoyas, will put the traveller in touch with César Torres Rojas, in Levanto, with regard to all the above. César is entertaining and very friendly, as well as being the official guardian and archaeological supervisor of Levanto. There is one small shop and bar in the village. Using Levanto as a staging point, many beautiful and interesting walks can be done in the area." Taxi from Cachapoyas to Levanto and back, including driver waiting while you look around, US$20.

About 65 km. SW of Chachapoyas, the largest ruined complex yet discovered in South America, Gran Vilaya, was found in 1985 by Gene Savoy. There are 80 inter-connected city-type layouts, comprising some 24,000 structures. It faces the Río Marañón at 2,850 metres.

Another Sachupoyan site is Cerro Olán, reached by colectivo to San Pedro (near Tingo), then a ½-hr. walk; here are the remains of towers which some archaeologists claim had roofs like mediaeval European castles.

50 km. from Chachapoyas, between Cheto and Soloco, are the pre-Inca ruins of **Monte Peruvia Lamud** (known locally as Purunllacta), hundreds of white stone houses with staircases, temples and palaces. Take a colectivo or bus to Pipus, 28 km. from Chachapoyas, then walk 11 km. to Cheto, then walk 2 hrs. to the ruins (take guide). Nearby are the Pueblos de los Muertos of the same culture, one near Luya (daily bus from Chachapoyas), another near Tingirobamba. "8 km. from Monte Peruvia is Puente de Conica, where you can see preColumbian burial figures in niches on the cliffside, known as the Purumachus de Aispachaca" (John Streather).

From Chachapoyas the next stretch of the road is 2-3 hrs. through more of the beautiful river canyon (US$1, by truck) to a small crossroads, Pedro Ruiz, where you continue on to Yurimaguas or return to the coast. There is basic accommodation (*Hostal Marginal* with good, cheap restaurant) there but advisable to stay the night if you arrive late as most trucks to Rioja leave at 0500-0700, the road on this stretch is very bad. Pedro Ruiz to Rioja is about 14 hrs. US$5.

From **Rioja** (an attractive, friendly town, 2 hotels, *Hostal San Martín* and *Restaurante Los Olivos* recommended) there is a road to Naranjillo and Aguas Verdes, with a 5-hr. walk to Venceremos, a pleasant way to see the jungle in good weather (don't attempt otherwise), and a good road with plenty of transport (colectivo, trucks from in front of *Hotel Cobos*, US$3, 6 hrs., beautiful valley journey, although in the rainy season the road may become impassable) via **Moyobamba**, capital of San Martín district (ruins of Pueblo de los Muertos nearby) (915 metres, 14,000 people, *Hotel Monterrey*, F; *Hotel Cobos*, F, good, friendly; many others). Tourists must register with the P.I.P.; tourist office on plaza. AeroPerú flights from Lima to Chiclayo stop at Rioja, two flights per week (Wed. and Sun.). Moyobamba is a pleasant town, in an attractive valley. Mosquito nets can be bought cheaply. Baños Termales (4 km. from Moyobamba), and Puerto Tahuisco (2 km.) at Río Mayo, worth a visit. The more adventurous can hike to the Jera waterfalls in the jungle near Moyobamba. Take a truck in the direction of Tarapoto; alight at the restaurant at km. 218. Take a good path through a well-populated valley (cross 2 bridges), then along the river, through dense jungle, with 3 more river crossings (no bridges—dangerous). A local guide is necessary to find the falls.

682 PERU

To **Tarapoto** (colectivo US$7.50, truck, 5 hrs., US$5), a busy town with several hotels. The whole journey from Rioja to Tarapoto costs about US$ 5.75 and it is best to carry food because of endless delays and road problems.

Tarapoto Hotels *Turistas* (D, with bath, excellent meals US$3.50) 1 km. out of town, non-residents can use the swimming pool for a small fee; *Juan Alfonso*, F, with shower, noisy, Jr. Pedro de Urzúa. *Hostal Residencial Grau*, Plaza de Armas, G, communal, cheap (in both senses of the word) shower. *Edinson*, near Plaza de Armas, E, clean and comfortable; *Tarapoto*, E; *Hostal Americano*, E, fan and private bath with each room. *Oriente*, F. *Hostal Victoria*, F, not recommended.

Restaurants *Río de Janeiro, Sadel, Tiveli, Chalet Venecia, La Pascana* and *Achín* good; *Heladería Tip Top* and *Cream Rica* for ices. *Las Terrazas*, poor service. Coconut water is recommended as coconuts abundant. Jirón Gregorio Delgado 268 sell excellent liquor at US$0.50 a glass (*uvachado* and *siete raices*).

Banks Banco de Crédito, Maynas 134, efficient, no commission on travellers' cheques.

Air Transport US$1.50 per taxi airport to town (there is no bus service from the airport). Flights by Faucett and AeroPerú to Lima (US$40, 50 mins.), Iquitos, Juanjui and Yurimaguas, but book in advance, particularly in rainy season. Those visiting Tarapoto and Iquitos would be advised to visit Tarapoto first, as aircraft leaving Iquitos tend to overfly Tarapoto; possible to be stuck there for days. AeroPerú flies to Tarapoto from Lima, Iquitos, Chiclayo, Trujillo (US$50), Juanjui and Yurimaguas. Faucett has similar routes, and daily flights to and from Trujillo and Chiclayo. Many smaller airlines operate, for example, flights to Yurimaguas (US$125).

Between Tarapoto and Moyobamba a road leads off to **Lamas** (colectivo from Tarapoto, US$1.20, 35 km.), where there is a picturesque Indian community completely unspoilt by tourism; also a small museum, with exhibits on local Indian community (Lamistas), ask at the café opposite if museum shut, and a new restaurant en route, *El Mirador*, recently opened by Tom, an American, and his Peruvian wife. Market in the early morning. Interesting journey also from Tarapoto to Tingo María (see page 745), not advisable in the rainy season. From Tarapoto to Yurimaguas (136 km.) the road can be very bad in the wet season; taking at least 13 hrs.; there are trucks (at 0800 or earlier, US$6), also colectivos (check the quality of the jeeps), US$8. A Swiss runs a quick jeep service to Yurimaguas, leaving early a.m., arrives 4 hrs. later, returns at noon same day from Plaza de Armas. At km. 96 (US$4) there is a bridge over the Shanusi river and the small village of Shanusi. It is possible to leave your truck here and take a 4½ hour (US$1.15) boat ride down the river, meeting the Huallaga at Yurimaguas. There is no accommodation at Shanusi, take a hammock, but boats run daily at about 0800. From Yurimaguas (see page 746), on the Huallaga River, launches ply to Iquitos.

Further N from Trujillo are three ports serving the Chiclayo area. The more southerly is **Etén,** an open roadstead 21 km. by road from Chiclayo; Panama hats are local industry. **Pimentel**, N of Etén, is larger, a favourite summer bathing place, with a broad sandy beach (very crowded on Sundays). Reached from Chiclayo (14½ km.) by road branching off from the Pan-American Highway. Coastal steamers call at both ports. Also worth seeing is **Santa Rosa**, situated between the two; excellent *ceviche* (small hotel, *Perú*, restaurant *Bello Horizonte*). The 3 ports may be visited on a pleasant ½ day trip. A red bus leaves Chiclayo market place every ½ hr. for Pimentel and Santa Rosa. Colectivos run frequently from Pimentel to Santa Rosa, and on to Etén and back to Chiclayo. To avoid paying excess luggage charges for weight above 15 kg, buy ticket in advance, and catch bus outside terminal (no scales!).

Chiclayo, on a plain near the coast, is capital of Lambayeque Department, which is the largest rice producer and the second largest sugar producer in Peru; wheat and cotton are also grown. Population, about 348,000. Nothing much for the tourist to see, but it is the liveliest of all the northern cities, with many parks and gardens. The most interesting spot is the new market place; the market is the best on the coast of Peru; well worth a visit: best buys are saddlebags (*alforjas*), woven goods such as hats, and baskets, and props for the local witch-doctors. The new Cathedral, principal club, and Municipal Palace front the Plaza de

PERU 683

Armas. Sunday is the day for horse racing. Hacienda Batán Grande, with its sugar plantations, is worth a visit.

Hotels *Turistas*, D, with bath; E, without, meals included, some distance from business centre, but there is much traffic noise, swimming pool, dirty, safe car park, cars may be hired for US$15 a day (check their condition first); *Hostal El Sol*, D, Elías Aguirre 115, Tel.: 232120, recommended (safe car park, and Chinese restaurant on 1st floor); *Costa de Oro*, E, central, good; *Americano* (E, with bath), on Calle Balta; *Ronald*, Calle Balta, G, poor; *Royal*, Plaza de Armas, F, clean, comfortable, basic; *Mediterráneo*, Balta 635, near Plaza, F, friendly, noisy, check the bill; *Mundial*, Calle Balta, near Plaza de Armas, basic, F, without bath; *Inca*, E with bath, clean, new and good; *Central*, near Plaza, F, cheap; *Madrid*, Calle Balta, near Plaza, F, not recommended, unfriendly, not clean. Several cheap hotels on Calle Balta, near bus offices; *Hostal Europa*, Elías Aguirre, G without bath, good value, clean, friendly, some hot water. Some hotels prohibit clothes-washing in rooms because of the high cost of water.

Restaurants First-class and very reasonable food (especially good breakfast) at *Roma*, Balta 512; *Bristol*, Calle Balta, good and cheap. Special dish: Alfajor King Kong (pie crust and manjarblanco—better in Lambayeque). *Nápoli*, Balta 951, recommended; also *El Tauro*, reasonable prices, and *Cruz de Chalpón* (good breakfasts) on same street; *Cordano*, on Plaza de Armas, good food, reasonably priced, friendly; *El Patio*, recommended, excellent regional food, but service can be poor, cheap and basic (Leoncio Prado, 1427); *Plaza Real*, between *Turistas* and Plaza de Armas, good food and value; *Los Paisanos* is recommended, has take-away service; *Imperial*, Calle Balta; *Maracaibo*, in market, good, cheap; *Las Américas*, on Plaza; *Chifa Julio*, good Chinese food; *Chifa Mymy*, near *Hostal Europa*, popular, OK; *Don José*, also serves Chinese dishes.

Exchange Change travellers' cheques at Banco Popular on corner of Plaza de Armas and Balta, or at Banco del Norte. Be prepared to wait. The travel agency next to *Hotel Royal* will change cash or cheques at reasonable rates out of banking hours. Several *casas de cambio* on 600 block of Balta, and street changers nearby.

Post Office on Aguirre, 6 blocks from Plaza.

Tourist Office Sáenz Peña 838, helpful. Touring y Automóvil Club de Perú, Huancavelica 280, of. 406.

Air Service Coronel Ruiz airport 2 km. from town. Daily Faucett and AeroPerú (except Tues.) jet flights from Lima; flights to Rioja (Aero Perú, Weds., and Sat.), 1130, US$38.15), Tarapoto, and to Iquitos and intermediate stops. Faucett flies to Chachapoyas.

Buses and Colectivos To Lima, Nor Pacífico, 2100, US$10. To Trujillo (Empresa Emtrafesa on Bolognesi) leave eight times a day, 0530 onwards, US$3. Bus to Piura, US$2.40, 2½ hrs., six a day (El Dorado, Av. Sánchez). *Micros* to Lambayeque leave from 200 block of Balta, US$0.10, frequent. Direct bus to Cajamarca, Empresa Díaz, El Cumbe, and Tepsa, Chinchay-Suyo, Empresa Cajamarca, US$3.15, US$ 3 with El Cumbe, twice daily (but tickets in advance), 5½ hrs. To Chachapoyas, D. Olano company (Vicente de la Vega 101, Tel.: 236310), US$10, 1300, except Sun., 18-25 hrs. depending on breakdowns; goes via Olmos and Jaén (see below), thereafter road is appalling to Pedro Ruiz, then O.K. to Chachapoyas. Bus to Huancabamba leaves Tues. and Fri., 1500, arrives 0530 next day, US$7.75 (Civa and Tepsa office, Balta 114b)—very rough ride, impossible to sleep. Tepsa to Tumbes, 0100 daily, US$6, 9½ hrs.; also Continental (Ormeño), Roggero (1930), Olano (recommended), and others (Nor Pacífico not recommended), all night buses US$6, 12 hrs., some continue to Aguas Verdes, but foreigners have to get off at Zarumilla for passport control. Trucks going in all directions leave from Calle Pedro Ruiz 948 and from the market.

Excursions To El Purgatorio about 30 km. N, near the town of Tucumé, with an unforgettable view from the top of the large adobe pyramid; Apurlec, 60 km. N: stone wall surrounding hill and pyramids dating from Tiahuanaco period, as well as irrigation canals and reservoirs; the system was enlarged during Mochica, Chimú and Inca occupation of the site, and the ruins of the town of Zaña (destroyed by floods in 1726). A minor road runs to **Chongoyape** (bus from Chiclayo, US$0.85, 1½ hrs., leaves from Leticia, just off Balta on N. of Plaza de Armas; hotel, F, on Plaza de Armas, with restaurant, limited menu, beware mosquitoes), a quaint old town 77 km. to the E. (3 km. west are the Chavín petroglyphs of Cerro Mulato). Batán Grande, a site consisting of nearly fifty adobe pyramids where many precolumbian gold artefacts, notably the 915-gram Tumi, were found, is reached by a branch turning left off the Chongoyape road after Tumán, about 30 km. from Chiclayo. Also near Chongoyape are the aqueduct of Racarrumi, the hill fort of Mal Paso and the ruins of Maguín. The road goes to **Chota**, an attractive town with a fine Sunday market (several hotels, F, *Plaza* the best, new and clean; *Continental* has deteriorated; *Hostal Elisabeth*, on plaza, cheap rooms with balcony, dirty bathrooms. *Restaurant San Juan*, good) where weavings are cheaper than in Cajamarca: cheap, friendly shops at 27 de Noviembre 144 and 246. Daily bus to Chiclayo a.m., 12-14 hrs.; bus to Cajamarca Wed., Fri., 9-10 hrs., return Tues. and Thurs. Occasionally buses, and many trucks, run on to **Bambamarca** (*Hotel Bolívar*, best; *Hotel Velásquez*, G, *Hotel Perú* has bugs; *Restaurant Pollos a la Brasa*, very good) which has an attractive Sunday morning market (truck from Chota US$1; Empresa Díaz to Cajamarca daily at 0600, 9 hrs., frequent stops, US$4, on Sun, there is a 2 hr. stop in Bambamarca for the market, some days also with Peregrino). Two buses a day pass through Chongoyape to Chota, 8 hrs., US$4. From there it goes on to **Hualgayoc** (a beautifully situated, quaint old mining town) and Cajamarca; a very interesting and beautiful journey, but few buses. The stretch from Bambamarca, about 90 km., to Cajamarca is exhilarating; the road climbs to about 4,000 metres through the Andean highlands with beautiful scenery of a *puna* landscape, nearly uninhabited, no gasoline supply; it takes about 6 hrs. in a 4-wheel drive car. The whole trip between Chongoyape and Cajamarca takes about 2 days in a car, the road is particularly bad between Chongoyape and Chota, max. speed 25 kph. The Chiclayo—Chota bus passes through Cochabamba (no hotels, not a friendly place, police searches for drugs), 34 km. from Chota, from where you can hitch in a truck to **Cuterva**, a town of 6,000 people at 2,800 metres in green meadows. Cattle and vegetables are raised here. Hotels: *San Juan* on plaza, cheap but has bugs; nicer one by Ciné San Juan, several more. Restaurants: *Salón Azul*, very good; *Central*, very dirty. A very friendly town which tourists rarely visit—don't be surprised if the local radio station wants an interview. Many trucks to Cuterva, Tues.-Sat., return Mon.-Fri., bus from Chiclayo Sat., returns Sun. 2000. Local market Thurs. and Sun.

Branching off the Pan-American Highway to Piura at Olmos (885 km. from Lima) is a poor road (being improved) which runs eastwards over the Porciulla Pass (2,150 metres); at km. 257 is a restaurant, but there are better ones at Jaén and Bagua Chica. A road branching from Chamaya, N of Hualgayoc, leads to the towns of Jaén and Bellavista. N of Chamaya, travelling via Aramongo and Oracuza, one finds a symmetrical hill of niche tombs.

Jaén (population: 3,600), an old settlement, has recently been revived as a rice-growing centre. The annual festival of the patron saint, Our Lord of Huamantanga, is on September 14. Hotels at Jaén: *Danubio*; *Hostal Lima*, not recommended. A road has been built N from Jaén to San Ignacio (114 km.), near the frontier of Ecuador. It crosses the valley of the Chinchipe, renowned for its lost Inca gold. San Ignacio has a *fiesta* on August 31. Another branch road from Jaén has been built SE to Chachapoyas, 263 km. from Olmos (see page 679), and has now been completed another 359 km. to Yurimaguas, on the Huallaga River (see page 746). A road also goes to Aramongo (280 km.), on the Marañón; it has been extended to Nazareth. From Nazareth two roads branch: one to Oracuza, via Puente Huabice and Puerto Delfus, and the other to **Sarameriza**, the most westerly point on the Marañón with a regular boat connection to Iquitos—it is 1 hr. downstream from Puerto Delfus. To reach Sarameriza, take a bus to Bagua (from Chachapoyas or Chiclayo, US$5.50, 12-15 hrs.), from where pick-ups run twice daily to Imasa. Get out at Campamento Mesones Muro, 15 mins. before Imasa (US$2.55, 7 hrs.), where you must register with the police (this can take time). For 150 km. from Mesones Muro to Sarameriza, you must wait for a pick-up (one should be along in 3-6 days) and then be prepared for a 2-3 day journey because of poor roads and missing bridges. The m/n *Fernández* makes the journey from Sarameriza to Iquitos every second week: downstream US$26 (inc. meals), 4 days, only a few cabins (US$2.50 extra), so take a hammock; upstream, US$30, 6 days. If you can't wait for the boat, it is possible with local help to make a raft and sail downstream, camping at night, until the *Fernández* catches you up (Peter Legaard Nielsen and Niels Pedersen, Copenhagen).

Ten km. to the N of Chiclayo is **Lambayeque,** population 20,700, well worth a visit. The narrow streets are lined by adobe houses, many retaining their distinctive wooden balconies and wrought iron grill-work over the windows. The town's most interesting feature is the well-known, recommended Bruning Museum, relocated in an impressive modern building. It specializes in Cupisnique, Lambayeque and Vicus cultures, has a fine collection of Mochica and Chimú ceramics, household implements, and gold artefacts, open 0830-1230 and 1500-1930 on weekdays, 0900-1300, Sat., Sun. and holidays. Admission, US$0.60. A hotel is soon to be opened. At Lambayeque the new Pan-American Highway branches off the old road (which skirts the Sechura desert to the E) and drives 190 km. straight across the desert to Piura. There are a few restaurants along its length. There is also a coast road, narrow and scenic, between Lambayeque and Sechura via Bayovar.

A large area of shifting sands—the Sechura Desert—separates the oasis of Chiclayo from that of Piura. Water for irrigation comes from the Chira and Piura rivers, and from the Olmos and Tinajones irrigation projects which bring water from the Amazon watershed by means of tunnels (one over 16 km. long) through the Andes to the Pacific coast. They will eventually water some 400,000 hectares of desert land. The northern river—the Chira—has usually a superabundance of water: along its irrigated banks large crops of Tangüis cotton are grown. A dam has now been built at Poechos on the Chira river, to divert water to the Piura valley. In its upper course the Piura—whose flow is far less dependable—is mostly used to grow subsistence food crops, but around Piura, when there is enough water, the hardy long-staple Pima cotton is planted. In 1983 the Niño current brought heavy rains and turned the Sechura desert into an inland sea. Damage to crops, roads, bridges and buildings was estimated at around US$1bn and it will be several years before the region is back to normal again.

Piura, an oasis in the hot and parched desert, is a proud and historic city, 264 km. from Chiclayo. Population, 293,000. Founded in 1532, three years before Lima, by the *conquistadores* left behind by Pizarro (whose statue is in the Parque Pizarro). There are two well kept parks, Cortés and Pizarro, and public gardens, old buildings are kept in repair and new buildings blend with the Spanish style of the old city. Its special dish is the delicious *natillas*, made mostly of milk and sugar.

A few blocks from the Plaza de Armas, where the cathedral stands, is the San Francisco church, where the city's independence from Spain was declared on January 4, 1821, nearly 8 months before Lima. The colonial church of Las Mercedes has ornately carved balconies, three-tiered archway, hand-hewn supports and massive furnishings. San Sebastián, on Tacna near Bolognesi, is also worth seeing. Birthplace of Admiral Miguel Grau, hero of the War of the Pacific with Chile, whose house Casa Museo Grau, on Jirón Tacna opposite the Centro Cívico, has been opened as a museum; it contains a model of the *Huáscar*, the largest Peruvian warship in the War of the Pacific, which was built in Britain. Interesting local craftwork is sold at the Model Market. The museum on the 3rd floor of the modern Municipalidad building is open Mon.-Fri. a.m. only.

Cotton has been grown mainly on medium-sized properties, which have changed hands frequently in recent years and which now form communal or co-operative farms, sponsored by the agrarian reform programme. Worth seeing as an example of a fine old plantation is the former Hacienda Sojo, in the lower Chira valley, which was the centre of the properties of the Checa family.

Hotels *Turistas*, D, faulty air conditioning, food and service poor, the city's social centre, facing Plaza de Armas. *Hispano*, Calle Ica, F, service poor, crickets; *La Terraza*, G, Jr. Loreto, noisy, not recommended (peeping toms), basic, near bus station, two blocks from Plaza Grau, as is *Residencial Piura*, Calle Loreto, unfriendly, traffic noise, E; opposite is *Hostal Las Palmeras*, F, warm water, fan, recommended, English owner; *San Martín*, Av. Cuzco, E; *San Jorge*, F with bath, clean and good value, Jr. Loreto, 3 blocks from Plaza Grau, recommended; *Tambo*, E, good, clean; *Palermo*, F, with bath, clean, recommended; *Bolognesi*, E, with private bath, near Roggero bus terminal, good. On Pan-American Highway are *El Sol*, F, bath, snack bar, will change travellers' cheques at official rate; *Vicus*, D, with bath, restaurant. *Oriental*, F without bath, E with, clean but very noisy, Jr. Callao; *Hostal Lelo*, near Plaza Grau, cheap, clean, shower; *Colón*, G, cheapest. It is extremely difficult to find a room in the last week of July because of independence festivities. The city suffers from water shortages.

Restaurants and Night Clubs *Tiburón*, 2 km. out of Piura on Panamericana Sur. In town; *Tres Estrellas*, Av. Arequipa; *Club Grau*; *Ganso Azul* restaurant recommended, it's a group of steak houses just out of town. *Las Tradiciones*, Ayacucho 579, high quality, reasonable prices, slow service; *García*, near Chinchay-Suyo terminal, quite good; *La Cabaña* serves pizzas and other good food; *Café Concierto*, Cuzco 933, pleasant; *Snack Bar*, Callao 536, good fruit juices. Good little cheap restaurants on Jirón Junín: *Chalán del Norte* at 722, *Bianca* at 732, *El Capri* at 715. A good ice cream shop is *Venezia* on the main square. Excellent Chinese fruit-juice and breakfast place, without name, at Av. Loreto 676, near Plaza Grau. *La Huerta*, Libertad 801 on corner of Plaza de Armas, sells 19 fresh juices, *quesillo con miel* (cream cheese and honey) and *natillas*.

Bank Banco de Crédito recommended. Banco Continental, Plaza de Armas, charges travellers' cheques with commission. Casa de Cambio in Plaza gives good rates.

Post Office on Plaza de Armas.

Tourist Offices Lima 575, 1st floor, friendly but not very helpful; Av. La Libertad 945-951 and at airport. Touring y Automóvil Club del Perú, Huancavelica 280.

Air Faucett daily jet flights to and from Lima; AeroPerú to and from Lima on Tues., Thurs. and Sun. (US$40); both companies fly always in evening, always late.

Buses Tepsa buses leave daily from Lima to Piura, US$8.50 en route to Tumbes. To Trujillo, 8 hrs., buses run day (not a.m.) and night, US$5 (Chinchay-Suyo on Calle Libertad 1117-27, leaves at 2200 and 2400, also at 1300 to Chiclayo-Trujillo-Chimbote-Huarás). To Trujillo in daylight, take 0800 Empresa Chiclayo bus to Chiclayo then change to Empresa Emtrafesa. To Tumbes, 7½-12 hrs., at least, owing to flood-damaged road, US$4.50 (El Dorado, Sánchez Cerro, 4 a day, Compañía Petrolera, same location, 2130, continues to Aguas Verdes, or Empresa Chiclayo), with

686 PERU

Tepsa, leaving at 1200 (coming from Lima, no reservations), or Sudamericana at 0400 (cheaper), colectivo US$9.50; to Chiclayo, US$2.40, 3 hrs., leave 1400; colectivo to Chiclayo US$5.10 each, leaves from near La Terraza, 4 hrs; to Paita, colectivo US$1.50. **N.B.** To the north of Piura, buses are subject to military checks.

Excursions A few km. to the SW of Piura is the village of **Catacaos** (colectivos leave from Avenida Tacna, US$0.35, bus US$0.25) famous for its *chicha* (maize beer, be careful, quality not always reliable), *picanterías* (local restaurants, some with music), tooled leather, gold filigree jewellery, wooden articles, the best straw hats in Peru and splendid celebrations in Holy Week. Also from Piura, one can visit **Sechura**, a coastal town with a fine 17th-century cathedral (splendid west front) and the Hospedaje de Dios (usually full of workmen from the oil terminal at Bayovar--forbidden to visitors). One can visit the coastal villages (no accommodation in any of them) of San Pedro (with a huge lagoon, edible crabs, flamingoes, a superb beach and a fierce sun—best visited in the week; take bus or colectivo to the right fork past Vice, then hitch); Yacila, La Tortuga, Parachique, Matacaballo (which has the best beach of these four places); Chullachay (the nearest beach to Sechura), Los Puertos and Angostura. Balsa reed-boats are common on the coast.

Chulucanas, 50 km. SE of Piura and 10 km. off the Pan-American Highway, is the centre of the lemon and orange growing area. *Hotel Ica,* Ica 636, F; *Restaurant Cajamarquino,* Ayacucho 530, good. *Canchaque* (*Hostal Don Félix,* central square, F, just tolerable; otherwise simple clean accommodation for about US$2 on right hand side of church), is a delightfully-situated small centre for coffee, sugar-cane and fruit production. The difficult and tiring road, impossible for ordinary vehicles in the wet season, continues over a pass in the Andes of more than 3,000 metres to **Huancabamba** (*Hotel El Dorado,* F, good, clean, with restaurant, on the main square; also, *Andino, Grau* and *Minerva*). Local specialities: *rompope,* a rich and strong drink made of egg, spices and *cañazo* (sugar-cane spirit); roast *cuy* (guinea-pig); and local cheeses. This very pretty town in a wonderful setting has three claims to fame (apart from a certain hostility among the young towards visitors). First, the predominance of European features, due to the fact that it was an important Spanish settlement in colonial times. Second, it is called "the walking town" (*"la ciudad que camina"*) as it is built on irregularly slipping strata which cause much subsidence. There are curious evidences of this fact for the tourist, such as the fall of the bridge over the Río Huancabamba some years ago. Third, and by far the most remarkable element, it is the base for reaching Las Huaringas, a series of lakes at about 4,000 metres. Around here live the most famous witch-doctors of Peru, to whom sick people flock from all over the country and abroad.

Horses to the lakes can be hired, US$5; village of San Antonio below Lake Carmen, village of Salala below Lake Shumbe (*Hotel San José,* G, very basic, take own food).

Transport from Piura A bus to Canchaque and Huancabamba leaves daily at 1030 if you're lucky (except Sun.; for Huancabamba, US$6.50) from the Civa office, Av. Ramón Castilla 155 (buy ticket early on day before travelling) and takes a minimum of eight hours to reach its destination, the same as by car in good weather. Take the Pan-American Highway south of Piura for 66 km. where there is a signpost to Huancabamba. Canchaque is about 70 km. along this same road (in miserable condition) and then there are 50 km. more of steep and winding road to Huancabamba.

By lorry from Piura, or bus from Sullana, to **Ayabaca**. John Streather writes: In the Andean summer—roughly the end of May till mid-September—it is worth making the long trip by lorry or bus (about 0600 from Piura market square, enquire the day, or days, before) to Ayabaca, whence many trips can be made to surrounding ruins, caves, petroglyphs and lakes. Mules are usually essential as are guides; mules about US$4 per day, guides the same. The one man to contact in Ayabaca is Sr. Celso Acuña Calle, Jr. Cáceres 161. Buy food and medicine in Piura (enough for the guides too) before leaving, as it is in short supply in Ayabaca. The little town is near the Ecuadorean border in a lovely situation, but is unfortunately a centre of cocaine smuggling. Therefore be sure to carry passport and visa on all trips (in a waterproof bag) and, of course, stop whenever asked to by police. In summer one can usually get a lift to the village of Yanchalá where most trips begin. It is a long muleback journey from there to the petroglyphs of Samanga (booklet purchasable at Piura Catholic University), and another long muleback ride to the Inca fortress town of Aypate—large but very overgrown. Other places of interest are: the pre-Inca cemetery of Hualcuy, Inca ruins and good view from Cerro Granadillo; pre-Inca ruins of Potrero de los Chaves; mummies in the pre-Inca cave cemetery of Potrero de los Jiménez at Cerro Pajonal; 4 or 5 days by mule to the Cuatro Lagunas Sagradas—all different colours. Near Chicuate is the Ciudad Encantada which still awaits explorers or indeed any visitors at all, as it is in a very isolated region, beyond Laguna Shimbe, and the few locals are frightened to visit it. It is said to be a ruined Inca town. There are at least three hotels in Ayabaca; the best, nameless, is in the first street parallel to the square and directly behind the Banco de la Nación (which will almost certainly refuse to change money). Various restaurants too: the *Trébol* is probably the best of a mediocre bunch. A torch is essential for trips outside Ayabaca, as there is no electric light in the region. No one should attempt to journey outside Ayabaca without a guide; there is danger from drug smugglers as well as of getting lost in the trackless bush. The way to the lost Inca city of Chicuate is particularly dangerous: lightning in the pass that gives access, and thick fog descending over the 100 metres of narrow road that lead between two lakes. Easier to reach from Chulucanas (see above) is Frías, where there is a pre-Inca cemetery and more caves can be reached if you have enough time (few locals know of them), rough road, no facilities, beautiful countryside.

The port for the area is **Paita,** 50 km. from Piura (colectivos and buses near Plaza Grau, US$1.50), which exports cotton, cotton seed, wool and flax. Population 51,500. Built on a small beach, flanked on three sides by a towering, sandy bluff, it is connected with Piura and Sullana by paved highways. The Paita-Piura road is notoriously dangerous (straight, narrow and potholed); better to do the journey via Sullana (colectivo US$0.80).

The Paita hotel has closed down; there is a guest-house which must be booked in Lima. Restaurant: *Marino*.

Fishing and whaling (at Tierra Colorada, 6½ km. S of Paita) are prosperous industries.

On a bluff looming over Paita is a small colonial fortress built to repel pirates. A short distance up the coast is Colán, a summer resort, reached by driving down a large, sandy bluff; near the base is a striking and lonely church over 300 years old. There is a good beach, but Colán is rather derelict since the agrarian reform; it used to be the favourite resort of the estate-owners.

Bolívar's mistress, Manuela Sáenz, lived the last 24 years of her life in Paita, supporting herself until her death in 1856 by weaving and embroidering and making candy after refusing the fortune left her by her husband.

Sullana (population 151,000), 39 km. N of Piura, is built on a bluff over the fertile Chira valley. Here the Pan-American Highway bifurcates. To the E it crosses the Peru-Ecuador frontier at La Tina and continues via Macará to Loja and Cuenca, but the road is poor, though marvellously scenic, and little used (walk over the bridge, pick- ups run from the border to Macará). The better route is the W road which passes through Talara and Tumbes, crossing the border at Huaquillas and on via Machala to Guayaquil; it is asphalted and has excellent bus services. Large stretches of this road and many bridges were damaged by the heavy floods in January 1983; although passable, much of the road has to be rebuilt and long delays can be expected.

Hotels *Sullana* (rooms with bath), E; *Hostal y Restaurant San Miguel*, opposite bus companies, E, helpful, good showers, staff will spray rooms against mosquitoes. *Hostal Aypate*, Av. José de Lama, E, comfortable, showers; *Buenos Aires*, F, Av. Buenos Aires, 15 mins. from city centre, friendly but bathrooms dirty. *Hostal La Siesta*, Av. Panamericana 400-04 (Tel.: 2264), at entrance to town (direction Talara), E, 3-star, hot water, swimming pool, café, laundry.

Bus to Tumbes, US$2.10. Bus to La Tina, or trucks, US$2 p.p., 5 hrs. Sullana-Piura, US$0.45 bus, US$0.70 colectivo; Sullana-Chiclayo, Tepsa, 4 hrs., US$3. Sullana-Trujillo, Sudamericano, 1430. To Lima with Sudamericano, Tepsa (*presidencial*, US$10, 1820, ordinary, US$7.50, 1830, 16-17 hrs.), Panamericana, US$5, Roggero. Colectivos to Paita, Colán and Esmeralda leave from the main road parallel to the market; buses to Máncora and Talara (Empresa EPPO) from market area. Trucks to the border, about 5 hours.

Between Sullana and the Ecuadorean border (209 km.) lies the main coastal oil area. The main centre is **Talara** (135 km. from Piura, 1,177 km. from Lima), in a desert oasis, which has a State-owned 60,000 barrel-a-day oil refinery and a fertilizer plant. Water is piped 40 km. from the Chira River. Paved highways connect the town with the Negritos, Lagunitos, La Brea and other oilfields; buses run to Máncora (wayside fish restaurants superb, including lobster), a few rooms available in one of the restaurants, good beaches, water warm enough for bathing; Playa Sal about 20 km. to the north (hotel) is good. The city is a triumph over formidable natural difficulties, but was badly damaged in the 1983 floods. Population 44,500. La Peña beach, 2 km. from Talara, is still unspoilt.

Hotels There are 4 hotels, all overpriced and usually full by early afternoon because of the number of oilmen in the town. *Hostal Talara*, clean comfortable, E. If in trouble finding a bed, enquire at the police station.

Restaurants *La Colmena*; *Club de Golf*.

688 PERU

Transport Airport with daily flights to Lima by Faucett and AeroPerú (not Sat.). AeroPerú has a direct route to Miami; leaves Tues. at 1035, arriving 1500. Return flight departs Miami Tues. at 0130, arriving at 0550.

Of historical interest are the old tarpits at La Brea, 21 km. inland from Punta Pariñas, S of Talara, and near the foot of the Amotape mountains. Here the Spaniards boiled the tar to get pitch for caulking their ships. Near this site is the first Peruvian oil well, brought into production in 1850, by digging and not by drilling. Production on land from this area is declining, but there are hopes of offshore production.

N of Talara, 51 km., is the small port of **Cabo Blanco**, until recently famous for its excellent sea-fishing. Camping permitted free of charge at Cabo Blanco, by the Fishing Club Lodge, overlooking the sea (at least in the off-season June-December). A room in the Fishing Club Annex can be taken, F.

Tumbes, about 141 km. N of Talara, and 265 km. N of Piura, is the most northerly of Peruvian towns; it is a garrison town with 34,000 inhabitants (do not photograph the military or their installations—they will destroy your film and probably detain you). There is a long promenade along the high banks of the Tumbes River. There are some old houses in the centre and the main square is quite attractive—trees, flowers, pavement restaurants and the usual church. The water supply is not good.

Small buses and colectivos (some marked "Puente Internacional") leave about every 20 min. and take 30 min. to get to Aguas Verdes on the Peruvian side of the international bridge (the Peruvian departure office opens at 0830, is closed at lunch time and after 1800; try not to arrive within ½ hour of the border closing). On the way most of them pass by the airport. By taxi it costs about US$4, colectivo fare is US$1 and bus fare US US$0.65. N.B. The customs post is at Zarumilla, some km. from the border, so do not pay taxi driver until after you have passed through customs. Colectivos do not wait at customs. Some bus companies from Chiclayo and beyond go to the border, but will stop at Zarumilla for foreigners to get off. Colectivo, Zurumilla to Aguas Verdes, US$0.20, or 15 mins.' walk. Second check at border, then 5 minutes' walk to Ecuadorean immigration and buses. With a pass from the authorities at the border you can spend the day in Huaquillas, the Ecuadorean border town, as long as you are back by 1800. There is nothing much to see there, but Peruvians hunt for bargains. It is a thoroughly unscrupulous border, with chaotic opening hours; don't change money, the changers are all dishonest.

Hotels *Turistas*, C, high standard, good restaurant, parking, has nice garden, very good, provides some tourist information; *Toloa*, E, good; *Amazonas*, F, Av. Tnte. Vásquez 33, clean, friendly, showers; *Córdova*, J. R. Abad Puell 777, F, with bath, no hot water, safe, clean, friendly; *Amazonas*, F, clean, hot-water, recommended; *Hostal Estoril*, 2 blocks from main square, F, good, friendly, *Gandolfo*, noisy, F, near colectivos for Aguas Verdes; *Hostal Kikos*, on Plaza de Armas, D, with shower; *Lourdes*, one block from main square, F with bath, clean, good, recommended; *Cristina*, F; *Bolívar*, G, clean but noisy; *Pilsen*, on main square, F, clean; *Elica*, Av. Tacna 337 (behind Tepsa), F, with bath and fan, run-down, grubby; *Italia*, Grau 733, E, private showers, clean, friendly, good; *Chultos*, near bridge, G, basic; *Pensión Curich*, F; *Florián*, G, near El Dorado bus company, clean, fan, private bath, recommended. Many other cheap hotels. One is on corner of the Plaza, unsigned, G. Sr. and Sra. Olavarría, 6-room guest-house, Caleta La Cruz, F, the first you come to having crossed Ecuadorean border, on the sea side of the road. Hotels are often fully booked by early afternoon, so try to arrive early, and at holiday times it can be very difficult to find a vacant room.

Restaurants *Bolívar*, cheap, recommended, also near is *Mendoza*. *Pez Espada*, good for fish, as is *Curich* in the Plaza de Armas (the one next door is not as good). *La Blanquita* recommended. Good for seafood is *Tito's*, Alfonso Ugarte 212, about 2 blocks from park (will change money), recommended. For *criollo* dishes, *Pekos* acceptable and *Europa*, on main square, is good. *Brujos* also recommended; also *Chifa Chen Wha*. *Samoa*, on mall leading to Plaza, has overcharged. There are other good, inexpensive restaurants on the Plaza de Armas and near the markets.

Bank Banco Popular, in a new building on the edge of the main square, will change travellers' cheques; alternatively change dollars cash in *casa de cambio*, *farmacías*, or import shops.

Buses Daily to and from Lima by Sudamericano, (US$12, overbooked, often subject to long delays); Expreso Continental (Ormeño group), new buses, a/c, 1130, 1900, 22 hrs., US$13, recommended; also Tepsa (often full, leaves 1100, 1600); 1,333 km., 26 hrs., comfortable; for other companies, ask around (e.g. Roggero, not recommended); cheaper ones usually leave 1600-2100, dearer ones 1200-1400. All buses to Lima are very slow because of repeated police checks—no chance of sleep overnight. One can get tickets to anywhere between Tumbes and Lima with little difficulty, although buses are often booked well in advance; Piura is a good place for connections. To Sullana (terrible road), US$2.10. To Talara, US$1.50 with El Dorado. To Piura, US$4.50 with Tepsa, Empresa Chiclayo, up to 12 hrs. Colectivo, US$8.10. To Chiclayo, US$6

PERU 689

(Tepsa). To Trujillo, 5 a day, 15 hrs. from US$6.50. To Chimbote, 18 hrs., US$8 with Sudamericano, 16 hrs. Several bus stations in Tumbes, some for buses to Lima, others for Piura. Frequent buses to Aguas Verdes, from market at 0600 onwards, colectivo, US$1, 20 minutes (**N.B.** border closed between 1200-1400). On the bus to Lima try to get a seat on the right hand side in order to have a good view of the coast. Bus to Machala (Ecuador), US$4. Taxi to Lima US$30 per seat. Hitching slow.

N.B. Travellers who hold a Tumbes-Huaquillas-Guayaquil ticket with Panamericana Internacional (bought outside Peru as an onward ticket) should note that Panamericana does not have an office in Tumbes. However, this ticket can be used for a colectivo (but not a taxi) to the border, caught at corner of Piura and Bolívar; if colectivo is full, you will be transferred to another company. Connection with bus at the border.

Road The Pan-American Highway in this region was severely damaged by the rains and floods in 1983 and is not expected to be back to normal for several years. The storms destroyed nearly all the bridges and parts of the road were virtually obliterated.

Air AeroPerú and Faucett, Lima to and from Tumbes daily, US$42 single. Essential to reconfirm flights 24 hrs. before departure. Taxi to airport, US$1.

This is the only part of the Peruvian coast where the sea is at all warm in the cooler months of April to December. Two good beaches near Tumbes: one at Caleta La Cruz (guest house and 2 restaurants, one offering basic accommodation) about 24 km. S, is easy to get to with regular colectivos (US$0.60 each way), which go on to **Zorritos**, heavily damaged by the 1983 flooding but with a good beach (the water is not oily), *Hotel de Turistas*, E; the better of the 2 restaurants is *Arriba*. Camping recommended. Just north of Tumbes is **Puerto Pizarro**, a small disused port at the southern limit of the mangrove swamps. In spite of the mangroves, it has an attractive beach (though water sometimes muddy), colectivos from Tumbes (US$0.30). *Puerto Pizarro Motel*, D, no hot water, restaurant dear and slow but food good, swimming pool, which is usually empty; *Hotel Venecia*, E, dirty, poor. Plenty of fishing, swimming and water-skiing. Mosquito repellant is a must for Tumbes area.

Warnings Porters on either side of the border charge exorbitant prices: don't be bullied. Many "illegal" money changers at the border. The money changers on the Ecuadorean side give a better rate than the banks and *casas de cambio* in Tumbes; always try to check the rate beforehand. If you are going to change cheques into Ecuadorean sucres in Huaquillas, make sure you cross the border in the morning because the bank is closed after lunch. Do not change money on the minibus to Aguas Verdes, their rates are very poor.

Checks for goods smuggled into Peru are carried out, especially at Tepsa bus station as well as at Aguas Verdes. Checks are thorough, both of luggage and body. Checks also intermittently on road to Piura.

South-East from Lima

The group of oases south from Lima grow Pima cotton, sugar-cane and vegetables for Lima and Callao, but the more southerly valleys specialize in vines—Ica in particular is well known for this and its port, Pisco, has given its name to the well-known brandy sold all along the coast. The Pan-American Highway runs S from Lima through all the places now to be described to Tacna and Chile. The first 60 km. from Lima are dotted with a series of seaside resort towns and clubs, including **Pucusana**, which is a charming fishing village (*Hotel Bahía*, good seafood). Excellent panoramas from the cliffs above the village. Hire a boat for an hour (fix price beforehand and stick to it); don't go in the direction of the only, smelly factory, but to the rocks where you can see seabirds close at hand.

Resort town of **Santa María**, 40 km. from Lima, beautiful *Santa María Hotel*, A, meals included. Taxi to Santa María: US$30 per day.

Cañete (hotels and restaurants), about 150 km. S of Lima, on the Río Cañete, is a prosperous market centre amid desert scenery. There is a road (no buses) to Huancayo (see page 737).

At Cerro Azul, 13 km. N of Cañete, is a unique Inca sea fort known as Huarco, now much damaged. *La Malla* is an excellent fish restaurant.

35 km. N of Pisco, near Chincha Baja, is **Tambo de Mora**, with nearby archaeological sites at Huaca de Tambo de Mora, La Centinela, Chinchaycama and Huaca Alvarado.

Pisco, population 82,250, largest port between Callao and Matarani, 237 km. S

690 PERU

of Lima, serves a large agricultural hinterland. The town is divided into two: Pisco Pueblo, colonial-style homes with patios and gardens; and Pisco Puerto, which has been replaced as a port by the deep-water Puerto General San Martín, beyond Paracas. In Pisco Pueblo, half a block W of the quiet Plaza de Armas, with its equestrian statue of San Martín, is the Club Social Pisco, the H.Q. of San Martín after he had landed at Paracas Bay. There is an old Jesuit church hiding behind the new one. Pisco is an alternative airport when landing is not possible at Lima. A 364 km. road has been built to Ayacucho, with a branch to Huancavelica (see Tambo Colorado, next page).

Hotels *Pisco*, on Plaza, E, basic, breakfast good, friendly, clean, disco until 2400 some evenings, can book (hotel provides sandwiches) for Ballestas Islands (US$3), near Ormeño bus station. *Embassy*, E, clean, comfortable, recommended, nice bar on roof, has disco in Jr. Comercio just off Plaza de Armas; *Joseíto Moreno*, Ayacucho 250, F, with bath, dirty; *Callao*, Callao 163, F, basic; *Comercial*, F, dirty rooms but good restaurant. *Hostal Angamos*, one block from Plaza, tiny rooms but good beds, clean, friendly, F, economical with water and light. *Perú*, G, basic, unfriendly; *Residencial Moreno*, G. Mosquitoes are a problem at night in the summer. The town is full at weekends with visitors from Lima. At Pisco Puerto, *Portofino*, F, clean, in slum area on sea front, arranges day excursion to Paracas, US$4, but avoid the nearby peña which is poor and can be dangerous.

Restaurants *La Rinconada* recommended but expensive; *As de Oros*, on the Plaza de Armas, good restaurant, reasonable prices, for the adventurous try *tortuga encebollada* (turtle steak with onions and tomatoes) and pisco sour, closed Mons.; *Las Vegas*, on Plaza, very popular; *Roberto's*, always busy, near Plaza, recommended; *Candelabra*, next to *Hotel Embassy*, quite expensive; *Bill More* restaurant near *Hotel Embassy*, good, cheap seafood; *Turistas*, good cheap food. *Bar Piave*, on Plaza, excellent pisco sours, but lone women should beware of the owner. *Piccolo-Bar*, near Plaza, good breakfast and coffee; *El Norteño*, off Plaza de Armas, good, cheap, clean; a number of restaurants around M. de Mancera 160, but avoid *Los Mellizos*, filthy. Seafood restaurants along shore between Pisco and San Andrés, and in San Andrés (buses from Plaza Belén, near *Hotel Perú* there is *La Estrellita*, recommended. Good fried chicken place opposite Ormeño: save your foreign cigarette packets for their mural!

Bank Banco de Crédito on Plaza de Armas gives good rates, but only for Amex and cash. Only the *casa de cambio* will exchange other travellers' cheques.

Transport Bus to Lima, Ormeño, US$2.75, recommended, many departures, 4 hrs., San Martín, Callao 136, 4 a day; Roggero, US$2, twice a day. To Ayacucho, US$7.80 with Ormeño, 12 hrs., 1730, often delayed, wear warm clothes as the road reaches 4,600 metres near Castrovirreyna and is very cold at night; Oropesa (Calle Comercial) to Huancavelica, US$7, 1100 daily, 13 hrs., very tiring, many stops; colectivo to Ica US$2, bus to Ica, US$1.50 (Ormeño, Roggero). To Arequipa direct 1220 with Ormeño, arrive 0300, US$10.75. To Nazca by bus, US$2, Roggero, 1430 (3-4 hrs.), Ormeño, 5 daily, recommended (3½-4 hrs.). Reservations can be made here at Nazca Tours for flights over the Nazca lines for US$36 p.p.

Fifteen km. down the coast from Pisco Puerto is the bay of **Paracas,** sheltered by the Paracas peninsula. (The name means "sandstorm" - they can last for 3 days.) The peninsula is a National Park (entrance US$3 for 2 days, no less); it is one of the best marine reserves, with the highest concentration of marine birds, in the world. There are archaeological and natural history museums about 20 mins'. walk from the residential area along an isolated stretch of beach (no bus), but contents reported less interesting than the Ica museum. A new monument on the sands marks the spot where San Martín set foot in Peru. The area has been developed as a resort: a beautiful bay, good sands, bathing (some pollution from local fishing industry, and beware of jellyfish) and fishing and excursions by boat to offshore islands. The Paracas necropolis, the burial place of a civilization which flourished here between 700 and 300 BC, has been buried by shifting sands and archaeologists can no longer visit it. About 17 km. from the museum is the preColumbian "candelabra" traced in the hillside, at least 50 metres long, best seen from the sea, but still impressive from the land. Hitch along paved road which leads to Punta Pejerrey, get off at left fork and you will see a trail (1½ hrs. walk to Candelabra). La Mina, a small beach 2 km. from Lagunilla, and Punta El Arquillo are also worth visiting.

On the southern side of the peninsula there is a colony of sealions, with many species of birds (such as cormorants, gannets, gulls, terns, pelicans). On the northern side, in the bay, there are flamingoes (in June and July mainly)—only reached on foot from Paracas. Condors may be seen from the (bad) road between Paracas and Laguna Grande. Trips to the **Ballestas Islands** for US$7 p.p. can be arranged from *Hotel Pisco* in Pisco at 0700, *Hotel Perú* (same organization), or from *Hotel El Mirador* in Paracas (cheaper than from *Hotel Paracas*). The trip to the islands, which are now a national reserve, takes about 5 hrs. all together, and is highly recommended (although some boats do not have life jackets, and are very crowded). You will see thousands of inquisitive sealions, guano birds, pelicans (the book *Las Aves del Departamento de Lima* by Maria Koepcke is useful); the boat returns past the Candelabra to the bay of Paracas where flocks of flamingoes and pelicans can be seen. The *Hotel Paracas* offers similar but more expensive trips, taking less time. Taxi from Pisco to Paracas (return) US$4, but more if arranged by a hotel. Colectivo, one way, US$0.75 or less if you change at San Andrés. Small buses leave frequently from the market place in Pisco to Paracas (US$0.25, US$0.40 with stop at J. C. Tello museum; last bus from museum at 1630). A yellow bus for Enapu workers leaves Pisco main square 2300 for Paracas National Park; it may give you a lift. Good walking in Paracas peninsula, details available from Park Office or ask for "Hoja 28-K" map at Instituto Geográfico Militar in Lima. The Mirador de los Lobos is a cliff overlooking sealion beaches, 20 minutes by car from Hotel Paracas—no public transport and the road peters out after a while (make sure your car is in good repair), crossing salty sand flats and mountains.

Hotels *Paracas* (B, check your bill carefully, good hotel, bungalows on beach, Tel.: Pisco 2220 or Lima 464865) good food, wide selection of dishes, not cheap, good buffet lunch on Sun., US$6 low season, US$9 high, fine grounds facing the bay, is a good centre for excursions to the Peninsula and flights over Nazca; it has tennis courts and an open-air swimming pool (US$2 for non-residents); it also houses the Masson ceramics collection (worth seeing). *El Mirador*, E, at entrance to Paracas, rooms spartan, cockroaches, no hot water, slow service, boat trips arranged, meals available. Excellent fried fish at open-sided restaurants by the fishing boats. Camping is possible on the beach near the *Hotel Paracas*.

Up the Pisco valley, 48 km. from Pisco on the road to Huaytará and Ayacucho, is **Tambo Colorado**, one of the best-preserved pre-Inca ruins in coastal Peru (entrance US$0.60); apparently a palace with ancillary buildings; the wall paintings have survived from Inca times. Buses from Pisco, US$1.75 (1½ hrs.), by Huaytarino for Huaytará, leaves 1200, or Oropesa for Huancavelica, leaves Pisco 1000 (12 hrs.). Alight 20 mins. after stop at Humay; the road passes right through the site. Return by bus to Pisco in afternoon; for bus or truck back to Pisco wait at the caretaker's house, as the area is dangerous. Taxi from Pisco US$19.50. From Humay, go to Hacienda Montesarpe, and 500 metres above the hacienda is the band of holes known as "La avenida misteriosa de las picaduras de viruelas" (the mysterious avenue of smallpox spots) which stretches along the Andes for many kilometres (its purpose is still unknown).

Huaytará, on the Pisco-Ayacucho road, contains Inca ruins and baths, and the whole side of the church is a perfectly preserved Inca wall with niches and trapezoidal doorways.

From Pisco the Pan-American Highway runs 93 km. S to **Ica,** on the Ica river, a pleasant city with a charming centre; population 147,000. The image of El Señor de Lurén in a fine church in Parque Lurén draws pilgrims from all Peru for the twice-yearly festivals in March and October (15-21), when there are all-night processions. Ica is famous for its *tejas*, a local sweet of *manjarblanco* (sold behind Lurén church); it is also Peru's chief wine centre and has a harvest festival in March. The Bodega El Carmel (on the right-hand side when arriving from Lima) can be visited; it is a pisco distillery and has an ancient grape press made from a huge tree trunk. The Vista Alegre wine and pisco distillery can be also be visited (Spanish essential) and its wholesale rate shop is recommended. Local bus drops you at the entrance.

The waters of the Choclacocha and Orococha lakes from the eastern side of the Andes are tunnelled into the Ica valley and irrigate 30,000 hectares of land. The lakes are at 4,570 metres. The tunnel is over 9 km. long.

Hotels *Las Dunas*, B plus 13 % tax and service, about 20 % cheaper on weekdays, highly recommended, in a complete resort with restaurant, swimming pool, horseriding and other activities, own airstrip for flights over Nazca (US$80, 1½ hrs.); Lima offices: Las Magnolias 889, Oficina 208, San Isidro, Tel.: 424180; *Turistas*, large and modern, with swimming pool, C, with private bath, meals US$4.50, not recommended; *Colón*, Plaza de Armas, E (rooms with and without bath,

692 PERU

some shared), old, noisy, restaurant; *Grau*, F (with or without bath), Grau 175; *Olimpia*, Calle Lima, F, clean, cold shower; *Confort*, 4 blocks from square, E, clean; *Presidente*, E, with bath, clean; *Amazonas*, with bath, good; *Jacarandá*, Calle Salaverry, behind bus terminals, E, with bath. *Hostal Díaz, Royal*, and *Ica* (basic, noisy), all friendly, clean, F or G, and on Calle Independencia. Several good hotels on Castrovirreyna; *Las Brisas*, D and *Silmar*, D. *El Carmelo*, on the Pan-American Highway S of turn-off for *Las Dunas*, swimming pool. Hotels are fully booked during the harvest festival and prices rise greatly.

Restaurants *Colón*, next to Colón Hotel, is best value; *Sergio, San Remo, Flor de Canela*, and *La Casona*, good and reasonable, all along Lima; *Siesta*, Independencia 160; *Pizzería Venezia*, Lima 243, good value pizza and other dishes, but service very bad. *Macondo*, Jr. Bolívar 300, fish good, recommended. Good one at Ormeño bus terminal.

Warning Beware of thieves; there is an increasing amount of theft here.

Museo Regional One of the best archaeological museums in Peru. Bus 17 from Plaza de Armas, open 0800-1800, Sat.: 0800-1200, 1400-1800, Sun.: 0800-1200 (US$0.50). Houses mummies, ceramics, textiles and skulls from Paracas, Nazca and Inca cultures; Inca counting strings (*quipus*) and clothes made of feathers. Good and informative displays with maps of all sites in the Department. The attendant paints copies of motifs from the ceramics and textiles in the original pigments (US$1), and sells his own good maps of Nazca for US$1.65.

The museum on the Plaza de Armas, run by Dr. Javier Cabrera, has a collection of several thousand engraved stones. We are informed that some of these stones are fakes: people have talked to the craftsmen concerned. If authentic, the stones suggest the existence of a technologically-advanced people contemporary with the dinosaurs, but the archaeological establishment seems very reluctant to study them properly. If interested, contact Ms. Sophia Afford, 31 Harrowdene Gardens, Teddington,Mx., TW11 0DH, England, a geologist who has written several articles on the subject.

Exchange Casa de Cambio Avisa, Municipalidad 263, no travellers' cheques.

Tourist Office Jirón Cajamarca 179, reported to be very helpful and courteous. Touring y Automóvil Club del Perú, Manzanilla 523.

Buses To Lima, Ormeño (Lambayeque 180) and Tepsa, US$3, 5 hrs.; Roggero 4 a day; colectivo to Lima, US$8.15. Several buses daily in the evening to Nazca, US$1.75, 2-3 hrs. Colectivo to Nazca, US$2.15; to Pisco, US$2; bus to Pisco, US$1.50 (Ormeño or Roggero). Bus to Arequipa, US$10.25 with Ormeño (a very popular route at weekends). Ormeño go to Cuzco Wed. and Fri., leaving 1700, 30 hrs., US$17.25. To Abancay with El Cóndor de Aymarães at 1600, US$12.20, 20 hrs. (take blankets). Several departures to Tacna, e.g. 1700, arrive 0900.

Among the sand dunes 5 km. from Ica, on the shores of its lagoon, is the summer resort of **Huacachina**, flourishing again after some years of decline. The Hotel *Mossone* (4 hours' drive from Lima), D, full board, is at the eastern end of the lagoon. Another good hotel is the *Salvatierra* (under renovation). (Sleeping in the open is pleasant here, but swimming in the lagoon can be dangerous because of soft sand.) Local bus from the square in Ica to Huacachina, US$0.20, 10-15 mins.

The Southern oases, S of Ica to the Chilean frontier, produce enough to support themselves, but little more. The highlands grow increasingly arid and the coast more rugged. There are only thin ribbons of cultivable lands along valley bottoms, and most of these can be irrigated only in their upper reaches. However, there are a few exceptions: the cotton plantations between Ica and Nazca, the orange centre at Palpa, the large and well-watered oasis centring upon Arequipa, and the smaller oasis of the river Moquegua further S. In several places the Highway is not protected against drifting sand and calls for cautious driving.

From Ica the Pan-American Highway runs inland 141 km. S to **Nazca**, a small colonial town of 25,000 people set in a green valley amid a perimeter of mountains, 452 km. from Lima. Its altitude of 619 metres puts Nazca just above any fog which may drift in from the sea: the sun blazes the year round by day and the nights are crisp. **Warning** Beware of thieves if you arrive early in the morning off a bus.

Hotels *De La Borda*, C, a former *hacienda* with garden, 2 swimming pools, pleasant, clean, friendly, hot showers, set meals only for US$6, near airfield at Panamericana 447, Tel.: Lima 400506; *Turistas*, C, with bath (less without), clean, rooms with private patio, hot water, peaceful, recommended, good meals US$2.75; safe car park, swimming pool (guests only). *Nazca*, Calle Lima 438, warm showers (electric—beware), clean and friendly, parties in courtyard at night, luggage store, helpful (only hotel with good information on tours, they also run cheap tours), highly

PERU 693

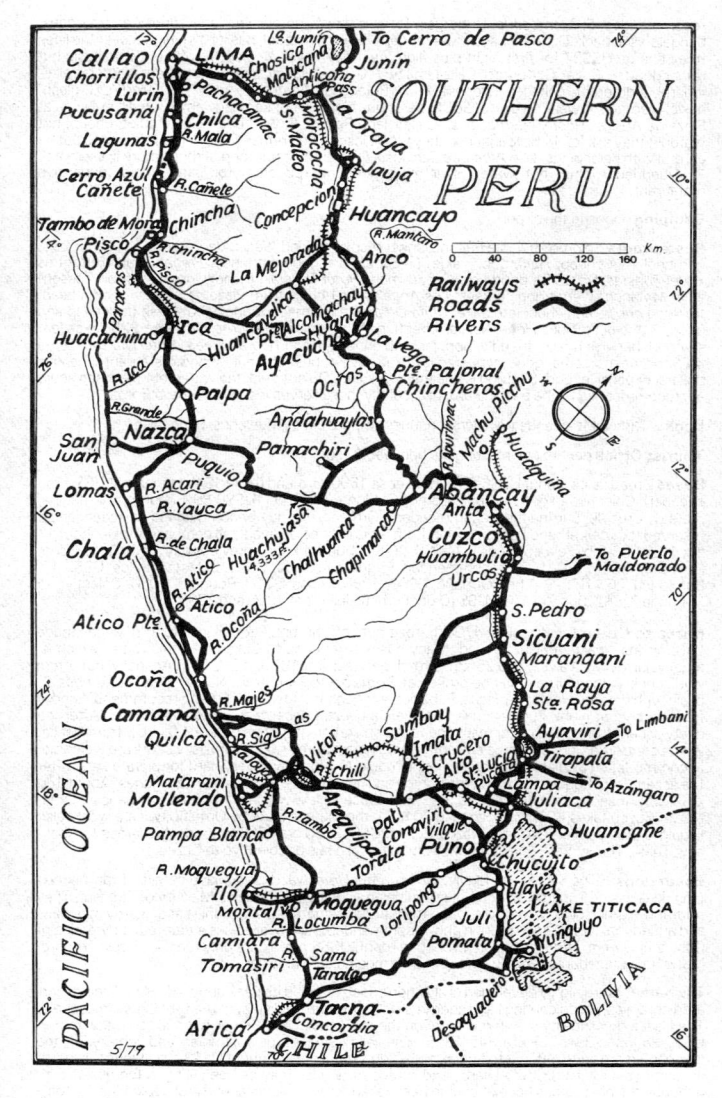

recommended, F; *Montecarlo*, D, bargain for less, noisy, unreliable water supply, cockroaches, bungalows at back, D, quieter and more modern, swimming pool, has its own flights over the lines (they charge US$31 for first night plus flight next day), near a colectivo office; *Lima*, basic but rather good, F; *Royal*, G; *Konfort*, Calle Lima 587, G, small, clean, safe, intermittent water (as elsewhere), indifferent manager; *Oropesa*, F, Jr. Bolognesi; *Central*, F, basic; *San Martín*, G, clean, basic, electric showers; *Hostal El Sol*, F, basic but friendly, hot showers, small, on Jirón Tacna at Plaza de Armas; *Hostal Internacional*, Calle María Reiche, F, with bath, clean, quiet, cheap, hot water (if they ask for 10% tourist tax, they won't insist if you refuse to pay), recommended but be careful with belongings; also *Albergue San José*, F. "Youth hostel" opp. airport, more like a motel, F, 4-bedded rooms, hot water, swimming pool, no reduction for cardholders, expensive restaurant.

Camping opposite the airport.

Restaurants *Colonial*, Jr. Lima 594, no longer recommended; *Selva Alegre*, good chicken; *Oasis*, unfriendly but cheap; *Haiti*, good value; *La Esperanza*, good set lunch; *Fragata* (same street as Hotel Turistas, No. 275), good fish; *Cañata*, near Hotel Turistas, friendly, good seafood, reasonable; *Marancha*, very filling courses; *Los Angeles*, half-block from Plaza de Armas, good, cheap, try *sopa criolla*, and chocolate cake. *Chifa Orlando*, on Lima, not original Chinese but cheap and good, 1¼ blocks from Hotel Nazca (direction Roggero); *La Taberna*, Jr. Lima 326, excellent seafood, bar, live music, friendly, popular with gringos; also *El Dorado*, near Hotel Nazca. *Fuente de Soda*, near cinema, good *almuerzo*; at Cruz del Sur bus terminal, gringo restaurant, changes dollars, expensive food. Seafood is cheaper than beef. Do not drink the water, but the pisco sours are recommended as the best in Peru, particularly those served in the *Hotel de la Borda*.

Bank Difficult to change travellers' cheques, impossible at weekends; bring cash.

Tourist Office next to cinema; enquire here about tours.

Buses Lima-Nazca, about US$6, 7½ hrs., Tepsa 1600, Ormeño (Lima 184) 3 times daily (8½ hrs., cheaper). Colectivo to or from Lima, Comité 3, Montevideo 581, US$8.80. Roggero to Arequipa, 3 a day, Cruz del Sur (neither recommended), Ormeño, 7 a day (recommended as seats can be reserved, but dearer, and buses coming from Lima may be delayed), all companies take about 11 hrs., US$4.50-6.50, except Tepsa at 2030, 10 hrs. Book ticket on previous day. Ormeño to Pisco, leaves at 0900, 1130, 1400, recommended; Roggero to Pisco, US$2. Colectivo to Ica, US$2.15. Bus to Ica, US$1.75, 3-4 hrs. Ormeño, 0900; 1830, Tepsa, 2200, Roggero, 2030. Colectivo to Marcona, US$2. Bus to Tacna, US$10.65; Ormeño leaves at 1900 and 2300.

Nazca to Cuzco A very rough 470 km. road cuts off through Puquío and NE to Abancay (page 740) on the Ayacucho-Cuzco road. Many buses from Nazca to Cuzco take this route, which is mostly narrow with a very bad 25-km. stretch between km. 187 and 212 from Abancay, but offers wild scenery; the journey may be broken at **Puquío**, (159 km. from Nazca, *Hotel Los Andes*, F, basic with garage; *Hostal Espinosa*, F, basic), although the town has little to recommend it and is freezing cold at night. Further on is Chalhuanca (*Hostal Zegarra* and *Hostal Porvenir*). After the dusty ascent from Nazca, you reach the research station at Pampa Galera, 89 km. from Nazca, which controls a vicuña reserve currently containing about 37,000 animals; visitors are welcome, accommodation available (3 rooms). From Puquío to Abancay is very hard for private cars: after the ascent from Puquío you reach the pampa and lakes where you can see flamingoes. About 160 km. from Abancay, you descend to the Pachachaca valley, which is followed to Abancay. Lima-Nazca-Cuzco takes 40 hours (can take 70 hrs.); the route is done by Ormeño twice a week, also Hidalgo. Cruz del Sur, Ormeño, Nazca-Cuzco, US$18, 30 hrs.; El Cóndor de Aymaráes to Abancay, Tues., Thurs., Sat., Sun., 21 hrs., from there take bus or colectivo to Cuzco.

Excursions The Fernández family, who run the *Hotel Nazca*, also have details of the Asociación de Guías de Turismo, a group of six guides trained by the Peruvian Ministry of Tourism. They offer three 2-hr. tours to the *mirador* on the pampa, cemetery at Chauchilla and nearby Inca ruins and aqueducts (US$3 each tour), highly recommended. Also available is a tour to the pyramids of Cahuachi (17 km. W of Nazca on a very bad road), US$6 p.p. Tours only run if 4 people or more. Mario Raúl Etchebarne, Tel.: 85, is a well-informed guide with a car.

The Nazcas had a highly developed civilization which reached its peak about AD 800. Their decorated ceramics, wood carvings and adornments of gold are on display in many of Lima's museums. The Nazca municipality's own museum, on the main plaza, has a small but fine collection (entry, US$0.25, open 0945-1300, 1345-1815). The valley is full of ruins, temples, and cemeteries; the last-named are quite difficult to find, but taxis do excursions for about US$3 p.p.; the trip is worth it, mummies, bones, pottery shards and scraps of textiles may be seen lying in the desert sun, although the best pieces have of course been taken by grave robbers and archaeologists. Recommended taxi-guides are Armando Denegri, office on Plaza de Armas by Aeroíca office, and José Barahona Calle, Jr. Bolognesi 282. At the edge of the town is the reservoir of Bisambra, whose water was taken by the Nazcas through underground aqueducts—many still in use—to water the land.

About 22 km. N of Nazca, along the Pan-American Highway, are the famous huge markings on the land, the Nazca Lines. Cut into the stony desert are large numbers of lines, not only parallels and geometrical figures, but also some forming the shape of a dog, an enormous monkey, birds (one with a wing span of over 100 metres), a spider and a tree. The lines can best be appreciated from the air; it is now forbidden to walk or drive on them, so climb the small hillock by the main road for views. The German expert, Maria Reiche, who has studied the lines (mostly from a step ladder!) for over 40 years, lives in the *Hotel de Turistas*; she maintains that they represent some sort of vast astronomical pre-Inca calendar.

The lines are thought to have been etched on the Pampa Colorada sands by three different groups: the Paracas people 900-200 BC, Nazcas 200 BC-AD 600 and the settlers from Ayacucho at about AD 630. For years Maria Reiche has presented a free lecture in the hotel every evening, but she is shortly handing over to Phyllis Pitluga, senior astronomer at the Chicago Planetarium. In 1976 she had a platform put up at her own expense, from which three of the huge designs can be seen—the Hands, the Lizard and the Tree (taxi, US$12 return). Her book, *Mystery on the Desert*, is on sale for US$10 at the hotel, or it may be obtained for US$10 from Dr. R. Reiche Grosse, Kohlgarten 7, 8726 Hohenpeisserberg, W. Germany. Another good book is *Pathways to the Gods: the mystery of the Nazca Lines*, by Tony Morrison (Michael Russell, 1978), obtainable in Lima. Another theory is that the ancient Nazcas flew in hot-air balloons; this is supported by the fact that the lines are best seen from the air, that there are burn (launching?) pits in many of the figures, and that there are pieces of ancient local pottery and tapestry showing balloonists, and local legends of flying men (which would be supported by the engraved designs on stones in Ica (see page 692) if these are proved authentic. See *Nazca, the flight of Condor 1*, by Jim Woodman, Murray, 1980 (Pocket Books, N.Y. 1977.) Georg A. von Breunig (1980) discounts both the above theories, claiming that the lines are the tracks of running contests. He bases his argument on the asymetrical surface level at curves in the designs and on the triangular fields which accord with human running characteristics, and with a number of runners starting from a straight line, then becoming an extended string of contestants. A similar theory was proposed by the English astronomer Alan Sawyer. Other theories are that the Nazca designs represent weaving patterns and yarns (Henri Stirlin) and that the plain is a map demonstrating the Tiahuanaco Empire (Zsoltan Zelko). *The Nazca Lines—a new perspective on their origin and meaning* (Editorial Los Pinos, Lima 18), by Dr Johan Reinhard, brings together ethnographic, historical and archaeological data on the lines, including current use of straight lines in Bolivia. Taxi-guides to the lines, 0800-1200, cost US$4 p.p., or you can hitch, but there is not always much traffic. Ormeño bus leaves for the lines at 0900 (US$0.60); hitch back, but have patience. Go by an early bus as the site gets very hot.

Small planes take 3-6 passengers to see the Nazca Lines; reservations can be made at the airport for flights with Aerocóndor: small planes, 3 passengers, good view (office opposite *Hotel de Turistas*, or can be booked at *Hotel Nazca*), Aeroíca (less good), or Aero Montecarlo (from hotel of that name; new planes and experienced pilots, good). Price for flight normally about US$40 in high season (July-August) and US$20 in low, travellers' cheques accepted; or apply at the Aerocóndor office in Lima (basement of *Hotel Sheraton*, Tel.: 329050, ext. 150-117; 471253; 453305, 460296). Sra. Fernández from *Hotel Nazca* can arrange flights by joining single travellers into group parties. Flights should last from 30 to 45 minutes, but are sometimes cut to 20, and are bumpy with many tight turns—many people are airsick. Aerocóndor offer the following round trips: Lima-Nazca-Lima, US$144; Lima-Nazca-Ica (lunch at *Las Dunas*) US$100 for 3; Nazca-Pisco, US$98; Ica-Nazca-Ica, US$60; all include a flight over the Lines, and other sights of interest (those from Lima involve a change of plane). The best time to fly is early in the morning, to benefit from the horizontal light. (Taxi to airport, US$1.10, bus, US$0.07). Many air companies (especially Aerocóndor) overbook early flights, then keep you waiting until later in the day when the light has deteriorated. Be careful with whom you fly; crashes are not unknown and they are probably due to poor maintenance. For photographs, be careful you do not find yourself in a middle seat (small planes are best). Nanaska Tours does a tour of the Nazca lines on land, operated by Sr. Carlos Santa Cruz and Sr. Josué S. Larcho (both students of ancient culture), recommended.

From a point 40 km. beyond Nazca along the Pan-American Highway a branch road (39 km.) runs to the ports of San Juan and San Nicolás, built to ship iron ore from the Marcona field, 29 km. inland, and Acarí, 53 km. E again, where a copper deposit is also being worked. San Juan, 553 km. S of Lima, has a beautiful deep-water bay.

After Nazca the Highway returns to the coast at Lomas (one hotel with only 3 rooms and *Restaurant Melchorita*) and passes by Chala, Atico and Ocoña, to Camaná (392 km. from Nazca).

Chala, 173 km. from Nazca, is a fishing village with beaches where condors may

696 PERU

be seen. Good fresh fish available in the morning and possibilities of fishing with the local fishermen. Electricity all day.

Hotels *Otero*, F, friendly, basic, clean; *Grau*, G, on the beach, basic, dirty, poor water supply. No good restaurants.

Excursion 10 km. N of Chala there are large precolumbian ruins on the coast. Go 6 km. N on the Pan-American; just after Km. 606 post is unpaved road on left. Follow this for 2 km., then take right fork another 2 km. to sea (bay with cliffs); on left there are ruins of a fishing village, on right tombs.

Camaná is a picturesque little town, 222 km from Chala, with a good food market and pleasant beaches 5 km. away at La Punta (hourly buses from Camaná); good bathing but little shade. Rice is the principal crop.

Hotels *Turistas*, E, poor; *Central*, F, just off main square, adequate; *Villa Mar*, F, basic.

Restaurant *Hong Kong*, Plaza de Armas, good. The fresh-water shrimps are delicious.

Buses Morales Moralitos to Chala, US$2.

Camaná sends its products to the small port of Quilca, S on the Río Quilca, in colonial times the unloading point for goods imported via Arequipa to Potosí (now in Bolivia). Now a seedy harbour. The village of Quilca is further along, perched on a cliff overlooking the Siguas river.

The Pan-American Highway swings inland from Camaná and runs along the top of a plateau with strange crescent-shaped dunes (see page 698). The sudden descents into the canyons of the Siguas and Víctor rivers are interesting. Before Repartición a branch to the left leads to Aplao and the valley of the Majes river. From there continue past Coropuna, the highest mountain in southern Peru, to Andagua, a village lying at the head of the valley of the volcanoes (bus from Arequipa, Sun., Wed., Fri., 1530, with Empresa Delgado; basic accommodation at the mayor's house in Andagua). The Arequipa-Andagua bus goes on to Orcopampa, from which the thermal springs of Huancarama can be visited. A mining lorry leaves Orcopampa for Cailloma on the 12th and the last day of each month; this enables one to make a round trip from Arequipa.

At Repartición, 134 km. from Camaná, the Highway bifurcates: one branch runs through Arequipa into the highlands (near Arequipa is a new 39 km. toll road, US$0.25, Camaná-Arequipa, 172 km); the other leads S to the Chilean border. From this latter road a branch leads off from La Joya W to Mollendo and Matarani.

Mollendo, 14,650 people, has now been replaced as a port by ***Matarani***, 14½ km. to the NW. Port workers still live mostly in Mollendo, where the main customs agencies are. Three beautiful sandy beaches stretch down the coast, small beach nearest town is safest for swimming (swimming pool on the beach open Jan.-March). Mollendo now depends partly upon the summer attraction of the beaches and partly upon the 15,000 hectares of irrigated land in the nearby Tambo valley. On the coast, a few km. SE by road, is the summer resort of Mejía.

Mollendo Hotels *Salerno*, 30 rooms, all with bath, excellent seafood. *Aller*, Arequipa 681, E; *Hostal Cabaña*, Comercio 240, F, clean, good; *Royal*, Tacna 155, basic, clean; *Moderno*, Tacna 179, F; *Verana*, Arequipa 337, cheap.

Restaurants *Salerno Bar*, good, excellent food; *Marco Antonio*, good; *Pizzería*, many gringos; *Sea Room*, Pasaje San Francisco, overlooking the Pacific; *Venezia*, Comercio 188; *Chifa Tun Fong*, good and cheap.

Bus to Arequipa (Empresa Agarón), 2 hrs., US$2 twice daily; colectivo to Arequipa, US$ 2.95. To Tacna, 3 hrs., US$3.40.

The Pan-American Highway runs S from La Joya through Moquegua to Tacna and Arica (Chile). ***Moquegua*** (200 km. from Arequipa), population 10,460, is a small town of winding cobblestone streets at 1,370 metres in the narrow valley of the Moquegua river. The plaza has llama-shaped hedges. The roofs are built with sugar-cane thatch and clay. Most of the valley below the city grows grapes and the upper part grows avocados (*paltas*), wheat, maize, potatoes, some cotton, and fruits. Climate: subtropical. Interesting cacti at Torata, nearby.

Hotels *Turistas* (5 km. from town), swimming pool, E, clean, friendly, hot water, restaurant fair; *Limoñeros*, E, basic rooms, showers, pretty garden, swimming pool (usually empty), few tourists.

Restaurants *La Sirena*, recommended for seafood and chicken dishes.

Buses Moquegua-Ilo, US$1, leaves at 1100. Returns from Ilo at 1700. Moquegua-Tacna, 0500, 3 hrs., US$1.25; Moquegua-Puno, San Martín, daily, about 10 hrs., US$5.

Moquegua's exports—avocados and wine—go by an excellent 96-km. road to the port of **Ilo** (population 95,000).

Ilo Hotel *Turistas*, D, with or without bath, meals US$3.20.

There are three Ilos: Ilo Viejo, in ruins after the earthquake of 1868; Ilo Nuevo, the present town, dirty, with a fishmeal factory, oil tanks, and dusty and sometimes cobbled streets and "half-door" saloons; and the spick and span village built by the Southern Peru Copper Corporation (hospital, cinema, playgrounds, etc.) for its engineers and their families.

The Southern Peru Copper Corporation is exploiting its copper property at Toquepala, SE of Moquegua (177 km. NE of Ilo) at an altitude of 3,050 metres, and is developing its property at Cuajone nearby (good view of valley, which is full of cacti). All exports are through Ilo, along the 183-km. railway and road from Toquepala. The SPCC smelter is on the coast, 18 km. from the port of Ilo.

Some 70 km. S of Moquegua a sign points to the Minas de Toquepala (64 km. by a good road); bus service from Tacna. **Toquepala** village, in a hollow, has a guest house (swimming pool), a church, club house and an American school, and is a pleasant place; however, it is a private mining community, and permission from the management must be obtained in advance to visit the village. A nearby cave contains paintings believed to date from 8000 BC. Helio Courier planes reach it from Moquegua (12 min.) and Ilo (26 min.). Taxis from Ilo. In the desert between Moquegua and Tacna, John Streather tells us that engraved stones dating from 10,000 BC have been discovered.

Tacna, at 550 metres, backed by the snow-capped peak of Tacora, is 156 km. S of Moquegua by Pan-American Highway, 42 km. from the Chilean frontier, and 64 km. from the international port of Arica, to which there is a railway. Above the city, on the heights, is the Campo de la Alianza, scene of a battle between Peru and Chile in 1880. Tacna is 1,292 km. from Lima by road, 987 by air.

Tacna was in Chilean hands from 1880 to 1929, when its people voted by plebiscite to return to Peru. There are good schools, housing estates, a stadium to seat 10,000 people, an airport suitable for jet planes, many military posts and one of the best hospitals in Peru. Population: 46,250.

Around the city the desert is gradually being irrigated. The local economy includes olive groves, vineyards and fishing. The waters of Laguna Aricota, 80 km. N, are now being tapped for further irrigation and hydroelectric power for industry. The cathedral, designed by Eiffel and begun in 1872 before the Eiffel Tower was built, was completed in 1954; it faces the main square, Plaza de Armas, which contains huge bronze statues of Admiral Grau and Colonel Bolognesi. The interior is austere but the round stained glass windows, each with a different motif, accent the fine, clean lines. The bronze fountain is said to be the duplicate of the one in the Place de la Concorde (Paris) and was also designed by Eiffel. The Parque Locomotiva (near city centre) has a British-built locomotive, which was used in the War of the Pacific. There is a very good railway museum at the station; the museum in the Casa de la Cultura has precolumbian pottery and war relics.

Hotels *Turistas*, Av. Bolognesi, tatty gardens, small swimming pool, tennis court, safe car park, D, with bath, meals expensive, large rooms, clean, can make telephone bookings for other Tourist Hotels; *Holiday Suite*, with swimming pool and safe car park, 10 minutes' walk from centre, follow Av. Bolognesi to the University, from where it's one block to the left; *Camino Real*, discotheque, modern; *Lima*, on main square, F, with bath, clean, cold water; *Chiclayo*, E (adequate); *Las Vegas Internacional*, F, without bath, clean, good restaurant; *Hostal Junín*, Junín, F, old house, hot water, good beds, clean; *Internacional*, E, with bath, no hot water or food but adequate; *Inclán*, F, no hot water. Cheaper hotels recommended are the *Gruta*, E, and *Luz, Hostal Comercio, Lido* (Calle San Martín, near Plaza, good), *Pensión Tauri, El Dorado Hospedaje*, Calderón de la Barca 476, *Tacna* and *San Cristóbal*, all F. *Las Vegas*, F, recommended. Accommodation is hard to find at Christmas-time because of Chileans on shopping sprees.

698 PERU

Restaurant *Sur Perú*, Ayacucho 80, recommended. *Viejo Almacén*, one of the best in Tacna; *Los Tenedores*, San Martín 888, good, clean, expensive; *Hostal Lido*, San Martín 876 A, good value; *El Sameño*, Arias Aráguez, near Ormeño bus terminal, good value fish restaurant.

Club Unión de Tacna. There is an exclusive Casino.

Tourist Office Av. Bolognesi 2088 and Complejo Fronterizo Santa Rosa. Touring y Automóvil Club del Perú, Av. 2 de Mayo 55.

Air Faucett daily jet flights to Lima, many cancellations; AeroPerú on Mon., Wed., and Sat. To Arequipa, US$18, ½ hr., almost same price to Cuzco (and cheaper than Arequipa-Cuzco).

Buses No bus station, companies are spread out over a 3-block area (colectivo from Arica will drop you at any company office). Tacna-Arequipa, US$3, Ormeño, about 5 hrs., 6 a day, from Aráguez 698 y Grohman. Berrios to Arequipa very slow, 5-6 police stops en route; better companies are harassed less, e.g. Ormeño. Colectivo to Arequipa, US$4.75, leave from plaza, opposite church. Expreso Tacna, San Martín 201, Tel.: 2642, will collect from hotel. Several to Lima, tickets can be purchased several days before departure; many passport checks; Tepsa at 1400, US$11.25, Ormeño 5 a day, US$11.25; all take 21-23 hrs. Bus to Ilave, US$6.50, about 13 hours. To Nazca, US$10.65. Bus Moquegua-Tacna, US$1.25, 3 hrs, Ormeño 7 a day, Sur Peruano (office, Jirón Callao 91, Tel.: 2802). To Arica, see below.

Warning Tacna is one of the worst towns for robberies, particularly around the bus station at night.

The road E to Bolivia—via Tarata (where Inca terraces are still in use) and Challapalca to Ilave, where it connects with the Puno-La Paz highway—is not too bad in the dry season, though difficult in the rains.

N.B. Soon after buses leave Tacna, passengers' passports and luggage are checked, whether you have been out of the country or not. Buses to Arica from Av. Miller 14; Empresa Adsublata recommended (US$1.50). Plenty of colectivos to Arica, US$3.20, Empresa Chasqui and Chiletur, which stop at both Peruvian and Chilean immigration; colectivos won't take passport-holders and border-card holders in the same car. There is also a train service Mon.-Sat. to Arica, at 0700, 0800, 1330 and 1530 (returning from Arica at 1130, 1200, 1630 and 1800, Chilean time-one hour ahead of Peru), US$0.75, 1½ hrs., customs and immigration at station. If you take this you must get your passport stamped at the station. Coming into Peru from Chile, you can only change pesos into intis with street money changers in Tacna (Banco de la Nación will not); the street rate is bad. Money changers line Av. Bolognesi. Better when leaving Peru to change intis to dollars at Banco de la Nación in Tacna and then buy pesos with dollars. You probably get a better rate for intis here than in Chile, but the money changers give a poor rate for pesos. Border closes at 2400, and Peruvian immigration is shut on public holidays.

For those travelling by car to Chile, ask the taxi drivers at the rank beside the Tourist Hotel for details of border formalities, and buy *relaciones de pasajeros* (official forms) from a bookshop.

Arequipa—Puno—Cuzco—Machu-Picchu

The Southern Railway no longer carries passengers between Mollendo and Arequipa, but there is a well-paved road from Mollendo to Arequipa via Matarani, about 130 km.

The ash-grey sand dunes near La Joya, on the Pan-American Highway and almost half way from the coast to Arequipa, are unique in appearance and formation. All are crescent shaped and of varying sizes, from 6 to 30 metres across and from 2 to 5 metres high, with the points of the crescent on the leeward side. The sand is slowly blown up the convex side, drifts down into the concave side, and the dunes move about 15 metres a year.

Arequipa, 1,030 km. from Lima by road, stands at 2,380 metres in a beautiful valley at the foot of El Misti volcano, a snow-capped, perfect cone, 5,822 metres high, guarded on either side by the mountains Chachani (6,096 metres), and Pichu-Pichu (5,669 metres). The city has fine Spanish buildings and many old and

PERU 699

interesting churches built of *sillar*, a pearly white volcanic material almost exclusively used in the construction of Arequipa. It was re-founded on August 15, 1540, by an emissary of Pizarro's, but it had been an Inca city.

Arequipa (870,000 people) is the main commercial centre for the south. Its people resent the general tendency to believe that everything is run from Lima; business travellers should know this. The climate is delightful, with a mean temperature before sundown of 23°C, and after sundown of 14½°C. The sun shines on 360 days of the year. Annual rainfall is less than 150 mm.

Because of the danger of earthquakes the churches are low, the houses have one storey only, patios are small with no galleries. Roofs are flat and windows are small, disguised by superimposed lintels or heavy grilles. In recent years, buildings with 2 or more storeys, and with large windows, have been constructed.

Interesting Holy Week ceremonies, culminating in the burning of an effigy of Judas on Easter Sunday and the reading of his "will", containing criticisms of the city authorities. On August 14, eve of the city's anniversary, there is a splendid firework display in the Plaza de Armas and a decorated float parade.

Points of Interest The twin-towered Cathedral on the Plaza de Armas, founded 1612, largely rebuilt 19th century; La Compañía church, whose main façade (1698) and side portal (1654) are striking examples of the florid Andean *mestizo* style: see the Royal Chapel to the left of the sanctuary, and its San Ignacio chapel with a beautiful polychrome cupola (admission, US$0.10, open 0900-1130, 1500-1730, recommended); Puente Bolívar, designed by Eiffel. Arequipa has several fine seignorial houses with large carved tympanums over the entrances. The Gibbs-Ricketts house (now offices, open to public 1700-2000), with its fine portal and puma-head waterspouts, and the Casa del Moral, or Williams house (Banco Industrial, with museum) are good examples. One of the oldest districts is San Lázaro, a collection of tiny climbing streets and houses quite close to the *Hotel de Turistas* at Selva Alegre. Behind the cathedral there is a very attractive alley with more handicraft shops. Churches are usually open 0700-0900 and 1800-2000. The churches of San Francisco, San Agustín, La Merced and Santo Domingo are all well worth seeing; San Francisco's fine old cloister is now open to the public (0900-1300, 1500-1800). Opposite the church is a handicraft centre, housed in a beautiful former prison. Next door is the municipal museum, open 0900-1600, most interesting; give donation as there is no admission charge. The archaeological museum at the San Agustín University has a good collection of ceramics and mummies (it is being restored and a donation is expected for entry); apply to Dr. E. Linares, the Director. Ask at Tourist Office for directions. La Recoleta, a Franciscan monastery on the other side of the river, is worth visiting, open 1000-1200, 1500-1700, entry US$0.30 (guide is not recommended). It contains several cloisters, a religious art museum, an Amazon museum and a library with many rarities.

By far the most interesting visit is to Santa Catalina Convent, opened in 1970 after centuries of mystery, the most remarkable sight in Arequipa; excellently refurbished, very beautiful, period furniture, kitchen utensils, and paintings. It is a miniature walled colonial town of over two hectares in the middle of the city; about 450 nuns used to live there in total seclusion, except for their women servants. The few remaining nuns have retreated to one section of the convent, allowing visitors to see a maze of cobbled streets, flower-decked cloisters and buttressed houses. These have been finely restored and painted in traditional browns and blues. Open 0900-1800, admission US$2, daily, including Sun. The many pictures of the Arequipa and Cuzco schools are worth seeing. Good Friday evening service particularly recommended. There is a small café, which sells cakes made by the nuns.

The flowered Plaza de Armas is faced on three sides by colonial arcaded buildings, and on the fourth by the Cathedral. The central San Camilo market (between Perú, San Camilo, Piérola and Alto de la Luna) is also worth visiting. At Selva Alegre there is a shady park in front of the *Hotel de Turistas*, which is within easy walking distance of all the famous churches and main plaza. Arequipa is

700 PERU

said to have the best-preserved colonial architecture in Peru, apart from Cuzco. A cheap tour of the city can be made in a Vallecito bus, 1½ hrs. for US$0.30; a circular tour going down Calles Jerusalén and San Juan de Dios. The country house of the founder of Arequipa, and a 17th-century mill close by, both restored by the same architect with great attention to detail, can be visited by excursion bus or private transport.

Hotels *Turistas*, Selva Alegre, C, with bath (less without bath), unsafe area, renovated 1982, swimming pool (cold), gardens, good meals, pub-style bar, cocktail lounge, tennis court, Wendy house for children; *Portal*, C, Plaza de Armas, excellent, wonderful views, expensive but food and service disappointing, roof top swimming pool; *Maison Plaza*, Plaza de Armas, D, with breakfast, clean, good value; *Jerusalén*, Calle Jerusalén 601 (Tel.: 222502/3), E, will change dollars, comfortable, modern with passable restaurant; *Crismar*, Calle Moral 107, opposite main Post Office, C, with shower, modern, central, civilized; *Posada del Puente*, Av. Bolognesi 101, Tel.: 21-74-44, D, good, restaurant, recommended; *Hostal Centenario*, on Mercaderes, no hot water, clean; *Hostal Las Mercedes*, end of Calle Consuelo, P.O. Box 417 (Tel.: 213601, or Lima 466196), D, clean, safe, restaurant, highly recommended; *Hostal Premier*, 50 rooms, Av. Quiroz 100, 2-star, restaurant, garage (Tel.: 221-791); *Hostal Selva Alegre*, Los Geranios 104, reasonable, clean; *Casa de Familia* (Av. Siglo Veinte 124), E, bed and board; *Villa Baden Baden* (Sra Bluemel de Castro), Manuel Ugarteche 401, Selva Alegre (Tel.: 222416), 6 rooms, D (F p.p.), breakfast included, German, French, English spoken, very informative about city's environs and children, recommended; *Arequipa Inn*, Rivero 412, modern hotel, D, with bath (US$4.60 for extra bed in room), garage, Tel.: 226077, slow service, owner unsympathetic; *Guzmán*, Jerusalén 408 (Tel.: 227142), F, hot water, friendly, small café, laundry, Sr. Guzmán will help with train tickets, very helpful, recommended; *Hostal Núñez*, Jerusalén 528 (Tel.: 218648), F, hot water, clean, laundry, comfortable, safe, recommended; *Casa de Mi Abuela*, Jerusalén 606, E, clean, friendly, safe, hot water, laundry, self-catering if desired, English spoken, breakfast on patio or roof terrace, recommended; *Royal*, Jerusalén, G, hot showers, clean, friendly, breakfast available; *Lira*, central (manager will buy train tickets for you), E. *Internacional*, 3 blocks from Plaza de Armas, located across the street from the market at Piérola 333 and can be noisy, clean, not recommended for women, ask for a room at the back, E, with bath; *El Conquistador*, Mercaderes 409, E, Tel.: 212916, clean, noisy, safe, 4 blocks from Plaza de Armas, colonial atmosphere, owner speaks English; *Excelsior*, Mercaderes 106, Tel.: 215241, F, 6 rooms with private bath, warm electric shower, central, some rooms noisy, others small, laundry facilities, safe for luggage and person, owner speaks German and English; *Hostal Mercaderes*, Mercaderes 142, F, shower and communal toilet, luggage safe, friendly, clean, English spoken; *Mirador* (on Plaza de Armas), clean but sagging beds, F, good, ask for room with view over Plaza (only singles overlook plaza), friendly, some English spoken, intermittent hot water; *Los Portales* (Calle Puente Grau 306, Tel.: 221547), F (with or without bath), smelly toilets, noisy, hot water, breakfast available, sun terrace; *Imperio* (by Cathedral), E, hot water, friendly; *Residencia Niza*, Calle Siglo Veinte 122, E (rooms, cabins and apartments), meals served, friendly; *Hostal Royal*, San Juan de Dios, F, hot showers but not enough (some rooms without water), very noisy; *Jorge's Hostal*, Santo Domingo 110, F; *Hostal Parra Residencial*, Av. Parra 97, Tel.: 223787, 5 mins. from station, clean, friendly, laundry facilities, F (some rooms with shower, US$1 more), recommended; *Grau*, Grau 126, E, with bath (F without), no hot water, reasonably clean; *Hostal Santa Catalina*, E or F, near Convent, clean, hot water, friendly, but some thieving by staff has been reported, popular with German travellers, light bulbs in short supply (take your own); *El Emperador*, Calle Moral, E; *Residencial Rivero*, Rivero 420, F, clean, with bath but not always hot water, friendly, helpful, washing facilities; *Crillón Serrano*, Calle Perú 109, F, with bath, hot water a.m., friendly to Germans, mice; *Americano*, Calle Alvarez Tomás (also called Ejercicios on maps), 4 blocks from the plaza, F, hot shower at any time, clean, beautiful geraniums; *Gran Hostal*, Cale Alvarez Tomás, friendly; *Tito*, Perú 105, F, clean, hot water. Also *Metro*, central (Alto de la Luna), E, showers, friendly, clean; *Residencial Bolívar*, Bolívar 202, E, with shower, clean and friendly. On San Juan de Dios are *Hostal Tacna*, F, no hot water; *San Juan de Dios*, F; *San Francisco*, F, good, hot showers, washing facilities; *Hostal Bolívar*, F (hot shower extra) and *Hostal Florida*, E, clean, modern, good beds, recommended. On Calle Nueva is *Residencia María*, E, clean, hot shower. *Hostal Extra*, Av. Olímpica, F, with bath, friendly; *Hostal El Dorado*, on Piérola, E, bath, hot water all day; *Palermo*, F, clean, quiet, laundry facilities; *Hostal Sucre*, Sucre 407, G without bath, friendly, clean; *Hostal Tradición*, Sucre 113, G, some hot water, mixed reports; *Hostal Cuzco*, Plaza de Armas, F, clean, modern communal baths, hot shower, not recommended, good views from 1st floor restaurant; *Hostal Vallecito*, Av. Lima 200, F, clean, comfortable, friendly staff; *Hostal Fernández*, Quesada 106, 10 mins. from centre, beautiful garden with parrot, views of El Misti, family affair, breakfasts, hot water, clean, recommended; *City Hotel*, Consuelo 211, F, quite good; *César's*, Consuelo 429, F, with bath, clean, good, friendly, safe; for family accommodation try Familia Ruiz Rosas, Vallarba 426, F, friendly, hot water.

Restaurants Many tend to close early—2030 or 2100. *The Royal Drink*, Centro Comercial Cayma, T 20-20A, clean, good local and Italian dishes; *Manolo*, San Francisco 135, clean, good, expensive, popular but poor service; *Astoria*, Calle Santo Domingo, local dishes, good service; *Chopería*, vaguely German, beer good, on road to airport, quite expensive; *La Taverna*, San Juan de Dios, *criollo* food, not good value; *André de París*, Santa Catalina 207, not as good as it used to be, holds *peñas* twice a week; *Cevichería El Pulpo*, Av. Agricultura 111, María Isabel, few foreigners, seafood, highly recommended; *Las Tejas*, Santa Catalina 206, cheap, recommended; *La Casona*, Calle Jerusalén; *Aranada*, Santo Domingo, cheap food; *Rodeo*, on O.M.Najar, Argentine-style grill, recommended. *1900 Pub Pizzería*, Claustros de la Compañía, excellent pizzas; *Balcón Arequipa*, popular with locals, good breakfasts and fruit juice, corner of Merced and Bolognesi; *Pizzería*, at Mercaderes 232, good; *Dolce Vita*, Plaza de Armas, good pastries; *Café Sunsin*, Plaza de Armas, excellent, cheap; *El Tambo*, Portal de la Municipalidad 124, Plaza de Armas, good breakfasts and *arequipeño* dishes; *Bonanza*, Jerusalén 114, one block from Plaza de Armas, expensive but food salty and service slow; *Salón de Té*, Jerusalén 207, good breakfasts, good tea; *Karlín*, Jerusalén 204A, good value, good food, good service; *Café Exposición*, Jerusalén 208, pleasant, young clientèle, live music, big choice of sandwiches, recommended; *El Quinqué*, opposite Santa Catalina convent, open evenings only, *peña*, Weds., Fri., Sat., US$1 entrance, clean, friendly, recommended, excellent grills, relatively expensive but worth it; *Monza*, Santo Domingo 1½ blocks from Plaza, good *menú económico*; *La Gran Vía*, Calle Bolognesi, cheap and friendly; *Chifa Liura*, Plaza de Armas, recommended; *Chifa Ha Wan Fe*, Calle Mercaderes, not so good, slow service; at Pasaje Catedral 108 is a small restaurant that is recommended for its excellent local food. Also Pasaje Catedral, 101, *La Chimenea*, simple, good food. *La Familia Café*, Calle Perú 105A, friendly, meals about US$1; *La Pizza Nostra*, on Plaza de Armas (open for breakfasts), safe dishes but no local ones; *Comedor de Gran Fraternidad Universal*, Jerusalén 400, cheap, good vegetarian food, friendly; *Govinda*, vegetarian Hindu food, Jerusalén 402; *La Vie Claire*, vegetarian, slow service, good brown bread, Pasaje Catedral 111; vegetarian food also at Calle Nueva 410A, cheap and good. Recommended café *Monaco*, Calle Mercaderes; *Café Granada*, Calle Santo Domingo, has several different types of coffee. There is a discotheque next door, *Piscín Club*, no entrance fee; *Hospedaje Cuzco*, corner of Plaza, balcony for drinking and watching the world go by, excellent (especially vegetable) tortillas but avoid the *ceviche*; *Aurelius*, San Francisco 125, cheap and friendly; *Las Vegas*, San Francisco, corner Moral, pricey, not too good; *Jaytuchaymi*, Calle Jerusalén, promises folk music during dinner and charges accordingly (food is dear), and musicians don't turn up. Bar at Portal San Agustín 133, Plaza de Armas (no name), recommended, unchanged since 1940s, run by elderly German lady, who makes excellent apple strüdel. *Mercaderes Pastelaría*, Calle Mercaderes, good cappucino. *La Esquina*, Morán and San Juan de Dios, café with good pisco sours; *Nenovi*, San Juan de Dios 301, good coffee; *Ice Palace*, Mercaderes, for ice cream. A score of *picanterías* specialize in piquant foods; try one called *El Pato*; *rocoto relleno* (hot stuffed peppers), *cuy chactado* (seared guinea-pig), *papas con ocopa* (boiled potatoes with a hot yellow sauce) and *adobo* (pork stew). Try them in Yanahuara suburb, or the well-known *Sol de Mayo*, Jerusalén 207, Yanahuara, just off airport road, noisy but serves excellent *arequipeño* lunches. *Arequipeño* food also at San Camilo market. Good cheap places down San Juan de Dios, but dodgy area for tourists. A good local speciality is Mejía cheese; try also the *queso helado* (frozen fresh milk mixed with sugar and a sprinkling of cinnamon), the chocolate (*La Ibérica*). Also, try the toffee (e.g. at *San Antonio Pizzería y Dulcería*, Jerusalén y Santa Marta), the chocolate (La Ibérica) and the fruit drinks called *papayada* and *tumbada*, local specialities in the market and restaurants.

Warning Thieves are active in Arequipa, and very few travellers seem to escape unscathed. Beware particularly well-organized women thieves in market. However, the police have been complimented as friendly, courteous and efficient.

Current 220 volts A.C., 50 cycles.

Clubs Club Arequipa; Golf Club; North American Cultural Institute; International Club; Club Hípico Los Leones (riding club).

Shopping Casa Secchi, Mercaderes 111, sells good arts, crafts and clothing; also Artesanías Peruanas, Puente Bolognesi 147. Empresa Peruana de Promoción Artesanal (EPPA), General Morán 120. The covered market opposite the Teatro Municipal in Calle Mercaderes is recommended for knitted goods, bags, etc. Arequipa is noted for its leather work; the street of saddlers and leather workers is Pte. Bolognesi. The handicraft shop in the old prison opposite San Francisco is particularly good for bags. At Fundo del Fierro shop 14, on Plaza San Francisco, alpaca-wool handicrafts from Callalli in the Colca canyon are sold. Sr. Fernando Delange, N-10 Urbanización Adepa, Tel.: 233120, repairs all kinds of electrical equipment as well as cameras. Foto Esperanza S. R. Ltda, Mercaderes 132-2, English spoken, cameras mended. Three antique shops in Calle Santa Catalina. Chocolate factory on Jerusalén (NE of Plaza de Armas) gives tours on weekdays only.

Bookshop Librerías ABC has a branch in Calle Santa Catalina 217, between the convent and the Plaza de Armas, which has a good stock of English books.

Laundry Jerusalén 311.

Taxi Fares US$2 an hr. within the town, US$0.30 minimum; US$2.10 in the country, US$2 airport to city (can be shared). US$1 railway station to centre.

Car Hire Dollar Rent-a-Car, Calle Jerusalén.

702 PERU

Entertainment Bar Romie, Plaza San Francisco, tiny bar with live music, Mon., Tues., *autóctono*, Wed.-Sat., *peña*. Excellent *peña* at El Sillar in the cloisters of La Compañía church, minimum charge of US$0.50, plus US$1 for the music, 1900-2300. Watch out for the local folk-music group Chachani, said to be one of Peru's best.

Banks (Beware of thieves.) Banco Internacional, Mercaderes 217, exchanges Citicorp dollar cheques. Banco de Crédito will change US$ travellers' cheques into US$ cash, allow about 30 mins. (accepts Visa Card and gives good rates, recommended). Others include Banco Popular, Banco Continental (will not change travellers' cheques) and Banco del Sur del Perú (Calle Jerusalén, close to Post Office, will change travellers' cheques, 2-3% commission, accepts Master Charge). *Casa de cambio*, Calle Morán, ½ block from Plaza de Armas, Peral 537, and Rivero 115-B (good rates for US cash). Lima Tours, Santa Catalina 120, Via Tours, Santo Domingo 114, Ideal Travel, Jerusalén 201, good rates. Parallel market down Calle Santo Domingo.

British Consul Mr. Roberts, Calle Quesada, Yanahuara.

English Library at Peruvian-North American Cultural Institute, Calle Melgar 109.

French Consul and Library Alianza Francesa, Santa Catalina 208.

Post and Cables At central Post Office, Moral 118 opposite *Hotel Crismar*. The central Post Office also provides a telex service. Letters can only be posted at the Post Office during opening hours. Telephone: Intel, San Francisco y Valdivia.

Sports Two public stadiums, a racecourse, several swimming pools, tennis courts and golf links (18 holes). The Arequipa Golf Club welcomes visitors from abroad. Riding is very popular. There are bullfights, and elaborate occasional firework displays (especially on August 14).

Climbing Club de Andinismo de Arequipa, Santo Domingo 416. Sr Zárate, who also runs a camera repair shop, is very helpful with maps and advice.

Tourist Office Opposite San Francisco church, next to the old prison. Complaints and suggestions are actively welcomed, information not always accurate but try to be helpful, open 0730-1500, free (but inadequate) street plans. Police may be contacted for information by phone: 226549, but not at all hours, Tourist police, office at Jerusalén 317, and at the bus station, are also helpful, Touring y Automóvil Club del Perú, Calle Sucre 209.

Travel Agencies Tony Holley takes small private groups by 12-seater Land Rover to interesting places in the area such as Toro Muerto, the Salinas borax lake, Chivay, the slopes of El Misti, cave drawings at Sumbay, the volcanoes Ubinas and Chachani, Caylloma where the Amazon rises, and rural Arequipa. Excursions cost from as little as $20 per person, providing there is a minimum of 6 people on tour. With fewer passengers the cost rises proportionally. Passengers are insured. Mr. Holley's postal address is Casilla 77, Arequipa, and his home address is Urb. Tahuaycani F-28, Umacollo, Arequipa (Tel.: 212525, Mon.-Fri. 0730-1600; 224452 daily after 1700, 24 hrs. Sat., Sun., and feast days.) When not on tour, Mr. Holley's car may be found near Santa Catalina between 0715 and 1230.

Turandes, Mercaderes 130, Tel.: 22962, specializes in tours, guides and equipment for climbing El Misti and other mountains, and trips to other local places of interest. They have very good maps. Continental Tours, Calle Jerusalén 402, good value, English and French-speaking guides. Conresa Tours, Jerusalén 409, Casilla 563, Tel.: 211847/ 223073/215820, specializes in trips to the Colca canyon, and to the Toro Muerto petroglyphs, Las Salinas and Mejía lakes, and city tours, *South American Handbook* users welcome. Happy Travels, Santa Catalina 106, offers tours of the city and surrounding area as well as the usual travel agency services, Tel.: 218592; English spoken. Not recommended for anything other than one-day trips is Hudel Tours, Jerusalén 400-D; similarly Martha Gómez, Jerusalén 300. Local office of Lima Tours reported reliable.

Roads Most bus companies have their offices in Calle San Juan de Dios (5-6 blocks from Plaza de Armas). To Lima, 1,030 km, colectivos take 18 hrs., rain damage to the road can cause delays; fare US$12.75 or more. Warning: need to book in advance to and from Lima in Jan.-March holiday season. Buses, de luxe Pullman, air conditioned with hostess, many daily, 16 hours or more, up to US$15.75 (Cruz del Sur, Arequipeño, Tepsa (toilet on board), Ormeño recommended; Roggero to be avoided because of breakdowns and poor timekeeping; Sudamericana is cheapest). Few buses stop at Pisco. Trucks to Lima take 3-4 days. To Puno and Cuzco both roads and buses are very bad; *a train would be better*. To Puno, US$4; San Cristóbal cheapest, up to 17 hrs., uncomfortable, cold; colectivo US$8.85. To and from Cuzco by bus (680 km.), San Cristóbal, 1600 (18 hrs.) US$8; Cruz del Sur, 21 hrs., US$8.50, 1600, Jacantaya at 1800. Colectivo-taxi to Cuzco US$20. Colectivo to Juliaca US$8.15 (office on Calle Salaverry) leaves 0900. Bus to Juliaca 8½-9½ hrs., US$4.90. Bus to Tacna (about 20 a day), Cruz del Sur, Ormeño, US$3; also Flores Hnos. Colectivo to Tacna, Expreso Tacna, San Juan de Dios 537, Tel.: 213281, will collect at hotel, US$4.75, 5 hrs. Moquegua by Angelitos Negros, leaves in the morning, US$2, interesting journey. Buses must be booked 24 hrs. in advance. Bus to Nazca, Sudamericana, 3 a day, US$6.50, Ormeño, 7 a day, 10 hours, US$4.50; also with Roggero and Tepsa.

PERU 703

Air New Rodríguez Ballón airport, 7 km. from town. To and from Lima, daily air service by Faucett and AeroPerú, about US$50. No direct flight to Iquitos; all go via Lima. To Miami via Lima and Panama; leaves on Wed. at 2340, arrives Miami 2155 folowing day. Return flight from Miami on Wed. at 0130 arriving 1045. To Cuzco, US$24, by Faucett and AeroPerú, daily at 0815 (except Sun.); to Puerto Maldonado with air force (Grupo 8), usually Friday. To Juliaca by AeroPerú daily (except Sun.). To and from Tacna, with AeroPerú; by Faucett on Mon., Thurs. and Sat. The plain-clothes police at the passport desk may arrange a taxi for you. Buses marked "Zamacola" go to about ½ km. from the airport. The offices of both Faucett and AeroPerú are on the Plaza de Armas.

Rail To Puno, 10 hrs., Mon., Wed., Fri., at 0740, and daily at 2100, with connections to Cuzco via Juliaca (arriving 0700); beautiful scenery. Fares: 1st class US$6, 2nd class US$4. Only the buffet (US$2 extra and US$3.20 for meals) and Pullman (well worth the extra as doors are kept locked by guards) cars are heated—important above 4,000 metres. Rail trip to Puno and Cuzco is spectacular, so try to travel this route by day (sit on right-hand side). It is also safer in the rainy season than by road. The night train arrives in Juliaca at about 0700, there is then a 3 hr. wait (time enough to visit the market) until the coaches for Cuzco leave. For a comfortable night book Pullman (US$2.50 extra) to Juliaca and re-book there for Cuzco. Take a blanket, the train is very cold at night in all carriages. If travelling 2nd class take a cushion as well. Fare to Juliaca is US$5 first class, US$3 second class; to Cuzco, US$12 first class, US$8 second class. If going to Puno, quicker to leave train at Juliaca and get colectivo from there to Puno. (The ticket office is open 0630-0830, 1000-1100, 1500-1700, 2000-2100, Sun. and holidays 1500-1800; queue at 1400 for 1st class tickets on day before morning departure, buy tickets for night train on day of travel. If you're out of luck try Sr. Guzmán of *Residencial Guzmán*, Jerusalén 408 (an ex-railway employee, fee US$0.35); Continental Tours charge US$ 0.60 extra to book for you) Train schedules and ticket office hours change frequently.

The buffet car ticket allows you to sit in the car throughout the journey but the fare does not include the lunch. The waiters will guard your luggage; no vendors are allowed in the buffet car. If you feel bad on train ask for the oxygen mask at once.

Warning Beware of thieves on Arequipa station, and especially when leaving the night train from Puno. Latest reports indicate that an increase in the police presence has made the station safer.

Excursions The hillside suburb of **Cayma,** with delightful 18th century church (open only until 1600). It also has many old buildings associated with Bolívar and Garcilaso de la Vega and is the home of contemporary Arequipeño poet, Manuel Gallegos Sanz. The Candelaria festival on February 2 is colourful. Many local buses marked Cayma. **Yanahuara,** also a suburb, with a 1750 *mestizo*-style church (opens 1500), with magnificent churrigueresque façade, all in *sillar;* the Tiabaya valley; Sabandia mill, built 1600, entrance fee US$0.50, swimming bath and countryside, well worth seeing (taxi, US$5 round trip); Yumina (adjoining Sabandia), many Inca terraces which are still in use; thermal baths of Jesús (½ hour by car, on the slopes of Pichu-Pichu), open 0500-1230. **Yura,** 29 km. from Arequipa (bus every 3 hours from San Juan de Dios, US$0.30) in a small, interesting valley on the W slopes of Chachani (*Yura Tourist Hotel*, D, wth bath, meals US$3, and an unsigned hotel opposite, F, good), has thermal baths open Tues.-Sat., morning only. **Socosani** (1½ hrs. by rail and road), now a spa owned by a mining consortium, can only be visited by appointment, 40 km. from Arequipa, in a beautiful small valley SW of Chachani, with a modern hotel providing meals and Socosani water, sports in Socosani include tennis, bowls. **Tingo,** which has a very small lake and 3 swimming pools, should be visited on Sun. (bus 7, US$0.15) for local food; *anticuchos* and *buñuelos.* 3 km. past Tingo on the Huasacanche road is *The Founder's Mansion*, with cafeteria and bar (and soon to provide accommodation); it is beside the Sabandía river. The interior of the church at Chiguita is well worth seeing.

Up a passable dirt road running through Cayma, Sumbay (4,150 metres) and Viscachani, between Misti and Chachani, is the village of **Chivay** (regular buses 5 hrs.) lying in the spectacular terraced valley of the Colca river. Local costumes still worn by women, and there is a beautiful swimming pool fed by hot springs. Water from this river is currently being diverted through a series of tunnels and canals to the desert between Repartición and Camaná, to irrigate the Siguas and Majes pampas. Further down the Colca valley, on both sides, (bridge—Puente del Inca—at Chivay only) unspoilt Andean villages are to be found, overlooked by the two volcanoes, Hualca-Hualca and Ampato. At one of these, Yanque (good

704 PERU

church, where two nuns from the Bronx sell handicrafts), walkers can cross the canyon by a colonial bridge (no vehicles—reached from the main square in Yanque via Av. Santa Rosa) and walk to villages on the other side: Coporaque and Ichupampa (about 2 hrs.), also with good churches; beyond Ichupampa is Lari, also with a fine church. On the opposite side of the river from Lari is Maca, whose church has an interesting interior. Beyond Maca is **Cabanaconde**, near where is Cruz del Cóndor, spectacular scenery, condors to be seen early a.m. and late p.m. The Colca (or Majes) Canyon is over 3,000 metres deep, twice as deep as the Grand Canyon. It was discovered from the air in 1954 by Gonzalo de Reparaz; the first descent was made in 1978 and the first descent by raft and canoe was made in 1981. AeroPerú and Aerocóndor have flights over it. It is possible to visit the canyon in one day, but if you do not get as far as Cruz del Cóndor, your money will not have been well-spent. A short circuit from Arequipa goes via Chivay, Yanque, Achoma, Maca, Cabanaconde, then on to Huambo and back to Arequipa. A longer route involves going to Callalli (beautiful alpaca-wool work at Centro Artesanal) from Viscachani, instead of to Chivay, then to Sibayo (possible detour to Cailloma), Tuti, and then to Chivay. This route adds an hour to the circuit, permitting views of fine landscapes with vicuña, Andean duck and llama, and a glance at the churches of Callalli and Tuti.

Bus to Cabanaconde from Arequipa (10 hrs.) via Chivay or Huambo. Transportes El Chasqui, at Pampita de Zevallos, Antiquilla, leave for Chivay (US$2, 5 hrs.) and Cabanaconde Mon., Tues., Thurs., and Fri., 0600; Transandino (no sign), Jerusalén 104 in Cayma, 15 min. walk from centre, leave daily at 0630. Via Huambo with Transportes Jacantaya, Víctor Lira 108, Tel.: 23258 leaves Arequipa daily at 0900, and Cabanaconde at 0700. Alternatively, a taxi can be hired for a day tour (US$80 for up to 5) at Expreso Chivay (Comité 10), Calle San Juan de Dios (if going by rented car, ask for an extra fuel can; no fuel in valley except at Chivay). Arequipa travel agencies run day tours to the canyon for US$10, but the one-day trip is very tiring and the viewing stops are short. Among the companies are Conresa Tours, Jerusalén 409 (Casilla 563., Tel.: 215820/223073), Arequipa, and Colca Tours. Buses leave Chivay for Cabanaconde at 1100, US$0.60, return from Cabanaconde to Chivay 0500. *Pensiones* in both Chivay (*Hotel Moderno*, F, basic, noisy, upstairs rooms best, no hot water; best food at unnamed restaurant at Calle Siglo 20 107, just off the plaza) and Cabanaconde (primitive *Alojamiento Bacilia*, one room with 6 beds, on main plaza, G; awful food at *Restaurant de Turistas*, eat at street vendors or take your own), but the best place to stay in the Colca valley is the *Albergue de Turistas* (E, bungalows for 6 are C) at Achoma, half an hour from Chivay along the Cabanaconde road: breakfast US$1.50, other meals US$2.50, only electricity, heating and hot water in valley; book through Receptur in Lima or Arequipa or Ricketts Turismo, Mercaderes 407, Arequipa, Tel.: 225-382. Valley best visited April-November, after rainy season, but never travel in mountains after dark. Whether travelling independently or on a tour, always take warm clothing.

El Misti volcano may be climbed. Start from the hydroelectric plant (first register with the police there), then you need one day to the Monte Blanco shelter (4,800 metres). Start early (take water) for the 4 hrs. to the top, to get there by 1100 before the mists obscure the view. If you start back at 1200 you will reach the hydroelectric plant by 1800. (Erick and Martine Perruche, of Montargis, who took this route, have left a map in the *Hotel Guzmán*). Alternatively, buses leave Arequipa for Baños Jesús, then on to Chiguata, where one can walk to the base of El Misti. Be sure to take plenty of food and water, it takes 2 days to reach the crater, guides may be available at Cachamarca.

The petroglyphs (hard to find on your own) at Toro Muerto (off the Majes canyon) can be reached by taking a bus (San Antonio, Calle Consuelo, 0700, returns Arequipa at 1300) to Corire, 3 hrs., US$4 return; get out 2 km. before Corire and walk 1 hr. to Toro Muerto (entry fee). Guide for US$3.

The early morning scene as the train from Arequipa winds its way up the valley towards Juliaca is enchanting. Winding around Misti and Chachani the train climbs steadily past Yura, Socosani and Pampa de Arrieros; after another 80 km. it reaches Crucero Alto, the highest point on the line (4,500 metres). Lakes Lagunillas and Saracocha are very pretty and both come into sight at the same time from opposite sides of the train, which skirts their margins for nearly an hour. As the descent continues streams become more plentiful. The scene changes in a few hours from desolate mountain peaks to a fertile pampa carrying a fairly populous agricultural community.

Road The rough dirt road from Arequipa to Juliaca reaches its highest point at Alto de Toroya, 4,693 metres. Train is more comfortable than bus.

PERU

Juliaca, 289 km. from Arequipa, at 3,825 metres (cold at night), has a population—mostly Indian—of 100,000. It is reported to be very poor and run down; you can buy good alpaca clothing here very cheaply, in the plaza in front of the railway station; fleeces can be purchased at about US$2.50 per kilo, but they sell very fast. On the huge Plaza Melgar, several blocks from the main part of the town, is an interesting colonial church. Large market in the Plaza, on Mondays, reported cheaper than Cuzco and Puno; there is another daily market in the Plaza outside the railway station, which is more tourist oriented. A first class hospital is run by the Seventh Day Adventists.

Warning Beware of pickpockets and thieves, especially at the station.

Hotels *Turistas,* good, D, but water turned off 2300, and extra for heating, meals US$4.50; *Royal,* E, clean, decent accommodation, restaurant O.K. *Benique,* opposite station, F, cold water in most rooms, hot showers in a few (more expensive) not recommended; *Hostal Sekura,* Jr. San Román 129, G, bath, dirty; *Hostal Loreto,* Loreto 237, F, bath, basic, little running water, dirty and smelly, not recommended; *Hostal Perú,* on main square, D, with bath, E, without, clean, comfortable, hot water sometimes; *Victoria,* F, cold water, clean but simple. *Yasur,* F, clean, safe, friendly, but no hot water, 500 metres from station, recommended, small bar and restaurant in evening. *Gran Hotel,* F, basic; *Alojamiento San Antonio,* G, basic but clean. In Juliaca water is only available generally between 0700 and 1900.

Restaurants *Ressi,* San Martín, good, but not cheap; *El Comedor del Sur,* adequate; Hole-in-the-wall breakfast parlour at corner of plaza opposite station, good.

Discotheque Aquarius, poor.

Transport Rail to Cuzco, US$6, 1st class, plus US$2 for seat in buffet car where good, reasonably-priced lunches are served, US$3.30, 2nd class; trains leave Mon.-Fri., 0850, Sat., 1025, 8½ hrs. Ticket office for first class tickets to Cuzco opens at 0700—tickets are hard to get. Trains to Arequipa daily at 2155, Tues. and Thurs. at 0835, Sat. at 1055. Jacantaya bus service, which is half the price of other buses, 11 hrs., to Arequipa. Bus to Cuzco, 3 companies, 12 hrs., US$5.50. Colectivo to Puno (from plaza outside rail station), US$1.50; US$0.50 bus. Taxi to Puno via Sillustani, US$15 per car. Daily bus to Moho, on east side of Lake Titicaca, from where it is possible to hitch into Bolivia.

Air To Lima, via Arequipa, with AeroPerú, daily, except Sun. 20 mins. to Arequipa. A new airport is being built. Taxi to airport, US$2, along a bad muddy road.

Excursion to thermal springs at village of Putina, 90 km. from Puno. Bus from Juliaca, US$0.50. About 32 km. NW of Juliaca (76 km. from Puno) is the unspoiled little colonial town of **Lampa,** known as the "Pink City", with splendid church, La Imaculada, containing a copy of Michelangelo's "Pietà". The area also has a chinchilla farm and a grove of *puya* plants. About 114 km. NE of Juliaca is the old town of **Azángaro** with another famous church, La Asunción, filled with *retablos* and paintings of the Cuzco school. Stone monoliths may be seen at Taraco and at Hatuncolla. The sheep farm of San Antonio, between Ayaviri and Chiquibambilla, owned by the Prime family (descendants of British emigrants), may be visited by those with a day to spare.

Puno, capital of its Department, altitude 3,855 metres, population 80,000 (with 8,000 at university), on the NW shore of Lake Titicaca, has a fine main square and an interesting, but dirty, lakeside quarter, largely flooded since the rise in the lake's water level. The austere Cathedral was completed in 1657. Puno gets bitterly cold at night: in June-August the temperature at night can fall to -25°C, but generally not below -5°C. Some guerrilla activity reported at night in early 1987.

Festival February 1-15, the very colourful Fiesta de la Virgen de la Candelaria, bands and dancers from all the local towns compete on two successive Sundays; better at night on the streets than the official functions in the stadium. May 3, Invención de la Cruz, exhibition of local art; June 29, colourful festival of San Pedro, procession at Zepita (see page 708). Also July 20. November 4-5, pageant on founding of Puno and arrival of Manco Capac from waters of Lake Titicaca.

Hotels *Isla Esteves* (Tourist Hotel), B, overpriced, cold, on an island linked by a causeway 5 km.

706 PERU

NE of Puno (taxi US$1.75), is built on a Tiwanaku-period site, with bath, telephone, bar, restaurant, discotheque, good service, inadequate sound-proofing, electricity and water, check bill carefully, *Sillustani*, C, including breakfast and dinner, good service, clean, friendly, hot water, recommended. *Ferrocarril*, Av. La Torre 185, Tel.: 409, opposite station, is modern, E, plenty of hot water, food fair, but good rooms, live folk music from 1915 in restaurant (food overpriced), central heating adequate, annex (F, not so good) but no hot water (will exchange Bolivian currency); *Hostal Nesther*, Deústua 268 (Tel.: 321), F (also 3-bedded rooms) with bath, hot water, 0730-0900, clean recommended, except for safety; *Internacional*, Libertad 161, Tel.: 25, E, with shower (extra bed US$2.70), hot water, clean, but not recommended, unfriendly, unhelpful, reservations not respected. *Torino*, La Libertad 126, near bus station, G, no hot water, but it is cheap and quiet, dirty. *Colonial*, Jr. Lima 345, F, dirty, dingy, sagging beds; *Roma*, La Libertad 115, F, is passable. *Motel Tambo Titikaka*, B, with half-pension, at Chucuito on the lakeside, 17 km. S of Puno; electricity only between 1800-2300, poor heating, rooms icy after sunset, food indifferent and bill charged in dollars, wonderful view, book in advance (travellers need own transport, local transport is scarce and expensive); *Hostal Embajador*, E, Los Incas 289 (Tel.: 592), clean; *Extra*, Calle Moquegua, F, hot water but none at night, dirty, laundry facilities; *Hostal Tumi*, Cajamarca 243, Tel.: 147, F (G in low season), negotiable, safe, cold at night, warm water limited (1830-2100), quiet; *Continental*, Alfonso Ugarte 161, F, cold water, dirty, friendly; *Hostal Lima*, Jr. Tacna 248, F, hot showers doubtful, clean, have breakfast at a booth on the street, egg sandwiches and hot chocolate or coffee; *Colón*, G, Tacna 290, Tel.: 180, hot water (cheaper the greater number per room) dirty, not safe even if room locked; *Don Miguel*, Av. Torre, Tel.: 177, E (negotiable), with restaurant, clean, service good, water intermittent; *Hostal Italia*, Teodoro Valcarcel 122 (Tel.: 640), E-F (negotiable), with shower and breakfast, good, safe, recommended; hot water except in cheap rooms on ground floor, good food, clean, electric heater, staff helpful, esp. Mario Alvarado. Many economy hotels; e.g. *Venecia*, Jr. Tacna 255, G, dirty but cheap. *Monterrey*, Lima 447A, G, "gringo hotel", reasonable, some rooms with bath, hot water after 1800, fairly clean, unsafe (has colectivo service to La Paz); and *Palace Puno*, Av. Tacna 786 Tel.: 167; *Los Uros*, Calle Valcarcel 135, Tel.: 644, G, clean, hot water unpredictable, plenty of blankets, breakfast available, quiet, safe for luggage, friendly, often full; *San Carlos*, F, near railway station, no hot water, no bath but nice room; *Europa*, Alfonso Ugarte 112, G, "gringo hotel", luggage may be stored, hot water in the common bathrooms in the evenings, all day in private bathrooms, dirty but friendly. *Hostal Posada Real*, Av. Titicaca 156, Tel.: 738, F, good, central, clean, friendly, warm water, rooms overlooking lake are also nearest to disco close by. Also *Hostal Real*, Av. El Sol 841, E, with bargaining, O.K. *Hostal de los Incas*, G, near centre, basic, fair. At Av. Circunvalación 470, good accommodation, F, in house of local priest run by Macericio and Nelly Rodríguez. Hotel rooms are difficult to find after trains arrive as everyone else is also looking. Clean public showers near the football stadium. Puno suffers from power and water shortages.

Restaurants *Isla*, Jr. Moquegua 152, one block S of railway station, cheap, food and service can be poor (musicians often play); *Sillustani*, Jr. Moquegua 199, service slow, cold food, meals about US$3, good *peña*; *Mesón del Corsario*, good, live music from 2000 (US$1.50); *Samary*, Jirón Deústua 323, wide variety, good service, trout reasonably priced; *Uros*, Plaza de Armas. Also try *Sale Caliente*, Tacna 381, or any of the *pollo* (chicken) places: ¼ chicken and french fries, US$1. *Ambassador*, Lima 347, recommended for cheap and varied food; reasonable *Bar Café Delta*, good for snacks, on La Libertad, try *flan de chocolate*; *Las Rocas*, Calle Teodoro Valcarcel, near *Hostal Italia*, good, cheap; *Café Internacional*, Melgar y Moquegua, "gringo", excellent service, good food, reasonable prices, recommended but service can be surly; *El Chalán*, Jr. Lima 144; *Peña Hostería*, Calle Lima, for music, serves only pizzas. *Club 31* on Moquegua, good cheap café; *Samaná*, Puno 334, inconsistent service, sometimes has live folk music from 2100, open fire and snacks and drinks (no minimum charge). *Café Dorado*, Jr. Lima 361, good service for breakfast, set lunches and dinners reasonably priced; *La Sirena*, in the lakeside quarter, for cheap breakfasts;

Colectur

Offers you tourist transport to:

PUNO – COPACABANA	US$ 5.-
PUNO – LA PAZ	US$ 10.-
PUNO – CUZCO	

daily service

WE OFFER TO GROUPS: SILLUSTANI, TAQUILE ISLAND, UROS,
train ticket reservations, and other destinations.

RESERVATIONS: In Puno:

COLECTUR
Jr. Tacna 232
Ph. 697

TUR COPACABANA
Jr. Arequipa 387
P.O. Box 615 - Ph. 317

In La Paz:

TURISBUS
Illampu 704 - P.O. Box 442
Ph: 325348 - 326531

Kimano, Calle Lima, very good cakes; *Café Copacabana*, Melgar y Av. del Sol, good pastries. Good coffee shop next to *Hotel Monterrey*, Grau y Lima. *Restaurant Monterrey*, behind hotel, good fish, only drink is pisco.

Shopping In the covered part of the market there are model reed boats, and attractive carved stone amulets and Ekekos (Bolivian household gods). One of the best places in Peru for llama and alpaca wool articles; many are still handmade, unlike in Cuzco. Artesanías Puno, on Calle Teodoro Valcarcel, has good quality alpaca goods with sizes for large gringos, but rarely open. Black market next to stadium; good for contraband imports; e.g. film. For good *artesanías*, take a bus to km. 20, Chinchera, where the *Trenza de Oro* has very good quality goods.

Museums The Municipal Museum has been combined with the private museum of Sr. Dreyer, Conde de Lemos 289, open Mon. to Sat. 1000-1800, entrance US$0.30.

Exchange Casa de Cambio on Jirón Lima. Very difficult to use credit cards anywhere: best not to try.

Post Office Jirón Moquegua, 2nd block.

Bolivian Consulate Moquegua 181, issues visas same day.

Tourist Information from Turismo Titicaca, and Kinjyo Travel Service, Calle Arequipa 401. Government Tourist Office, Moquegua 338 open Mon.-Fri., 1000-1300 (has maps). Check for details of village festivals. Touring y Automóvil Club de Perú, Arequipa 457. The booklet by Pedro Sueldo Nava on Puno, Arequipa and La Paz is informative and reasonably priced (includes maps), also available in Cuzco.

Travel Agencies Viajes El Sol, Jirón Arequipa 401, Tel.: 684, Sr. Ronald Zárate. Suri Tours, Av. La Torre 135, high commission charged. Cooperativa de Transportes Turísticos Dos de Febrero, Libertad 111, has received mixed reports. Turpuno next to *Hotel Sillustani* on Lambayeque recommended; also Andrés and Samuel López at *Hotel Don Miguel*.

Railways There is a 386-km. railway from Puno to Cuzco, via Juliaca. It is reported that the Puno-Juliaca section of line is sometimes closed (as in 1986 because of flooding); Puno passengers are taken to and from Juliaca by colectivos which leave from Jirón Pardo, 0630, US$1.50, arriving in good time to get Cuzco tickets in Juliaca station. When running, the Puno to Cuzco train leaves 0755 daily except Sun., arriving at 1800, 1st class US$7.70, 2nd US$5.10, buffet US$2.60 extra. Second class is usually to be recommended as thieves are less active than in 1st, and new carriages with padded seats have been introduced, but travellers with an extra-sensitive sense of smell, beware! Tickets either on sale only an hour before departure, or you can buy them the day before, after the train to Arequipa has departed (ticket office hours are very irregular—check in advance). Tour companies often buy up all the available tickets and you either have to queue for hours (or ask a young boy to do this for you, paying him half in advance), or pay the companies a premium. A magnificent run, with shopping possibilities at stations. Sit on right side on Puno-Cuzco train for best views. Hotel representatives join train near Cuzco to find customers.
Puno to Arequipa daily leaves 2215 and 0725. Buffet US$8, lunch US$3.20, 1st class US$6, 2nd class US$4 (no lighting), 8 hrs. splendid views. The train is not always reliable (daytime train Puno-Arequipa is sometimes withdrawn). Pullman class available on the night train (US$2.50 extra). Tickets can be booked in advance, before 1900, get to the station early to queue; if short of time get them through a travel agent (10%-20% commission).

Warning The night train from Puno to Arequipa is worked by professional thieves; strict measures are needed to ensure the safety of your valuables. The buffet car is usually full of tourists, which lessens the risk of theft. Beware of thieves in the Arequipa station and environs and at Puno station when train arrives. Although it appears that the number of police on the stations and greater security on the trains has improved the situation, great care should be exercised. One large bag is easier to watch than several smaller ones.

A good idea in Puno, Juliaca and other Andean towns, when moving about with heavy baggage, is to hire a 3-wheel cycle cart (about US$0.20 per km.)

Roads To Arequipa, road bad, few bridges and many streams. Several bus companies leave in the morning. Transportes San Cristóbal, cheapest, not recommended, 19 hrs. Jacantaya, Jr. Melgar, leaves at 0830, 10-11 hrs., US$4. Sur Peruano leaves at 1000, door-to-door service, about a 10-hr. journey by road. Colectivo (Comité 31 recommended; also Comité 3 Juliaca Express, Jirón Tacna) takes 9 hrs., US$8.50. To Cuzco, road first 44 km. (to Juliaca) and last 85 km. paved, other 260 km. very bad (the stretch Juliaca-Sicuani is appalling and very demanding for drivers of private cars), again several bus companies cover the route, from US$5, Sur Peruano, Transportes San Cristóbal. Cruz del Sur (1730), 11 hrs. Colectivo to Cuzco, US$10.75. To Lima, 18 hours, several companies. To Moquegua, for Chile, San Martín bus, US$5, 1800, 10 hrs., very cold, bad road.

708 PERU

Excursions from Puno Motorboats charging upwards of US$3.25 p.p. take tourists to the "floating islands"; prices usually depend on the number of islands visited, and are officially regulated—should not be over US$6. Boats go about every ½ hour from about 0700, or whenever there are 10 or more people to fill the boat, and take 3-5 hrs. Local boats may also be hired. They leave around the bay since the port suffered flood damage; buses go to the departure point. (Be careful where you walk on the floating islands.) The Uro Indians who used to live here are now intermarried with the Aymará and no pure Uros exist. The temptation to move ashore may soon deprive the floating islands of all residents (in 15 to 20 years, apparently). The present Puno Bay Indians do still practice some Uro traditions, but Aymará influence predominates. Many tourists report that though the people are friendly, they are very poor and consequently there are constant requests for money. However, the uniqueness of this way of life still makes the trip worthwhile (rather than money, give the children fresh fruit, pencils and paper, and buy their little reed boats!).

A much more interesting island to visit (quiet and hospitable) is **Taquile**, some 45 km. from Puno, on which there are numerous pre-Inca and Inca ruins, and Inca terracing. On the N side of the island is the warmest part of Lake Titicaca. Plentiful accommodation can be found in private houses but best to take warm clothes and a sleeping bag. No previous arrangements can be made; on arrival you walk up a steep path for 20 mins., are greeted by the Indians, sign the guest book and if wishing to stay are "assigned" a family to stay with (for US$0.50). Boats to Taquile leave daily at 0800 and 0915 (subject to change), but in low season there is only one a day, at 0830, return 1430, US$3.50 return, 4 hrs.; a day return is not recommended since one does not have enough time to see the island fully. Boats often stop at one of the floating islands on the way to Taquile, for about 20 mins. An entire boat can be hired for about US$50 to take 5-7 people to Taquile: 3 hrs. there, 3 back, 3 hrs. on island, so day trip possible this way. A sailing boat can be taken to Taquile for about US$1.50 p.p., departure time depends on the wind. There is a cooperative shop on the square that sells fine woollen goods. There are several small restaurants (El Inca recommended, check your change) on the island, but meat is rarely available and drinks often run out. You are advised to take with you some food, particularly fruit and vegetables, water, plenty of small-value notes and a torch. Take precautions against sunburn. June 7, July 25, August 1 and 2 are the principal festival days with many dances in between. Ask for Sr. Agustín, a dressmaker, who is very knowledgeable about the island. Another island worth visiting is **Amantaní**. Scarcely visited by tourists, it is very beautiful and peaceful and like Taquile, has ruins on both of the island's peaks: there are temples and on the shore there is a throne carved out of stone. There are no hotels or restaurants, but you can stay with local families, who like postcards: take some. Take fruit and vegetables as the Indians live on bread, rice and potatoes. Boats go most days at 0800, and Victoriano, with his boat Atún, will take you for about US$2.50 (4 hours), also recommended is Benito, who may be found at the docks; accommodation on the island for about US$1.50 p.p. (establish a price before leaving the dock). The festivities on New Year's Day have been reported as spectacular, very colourful, musical and hard-drinking.

Anybody interested in religious architecture should go from Puno along the western shore of Lake Titicaca to the churches of **Juli, Pomata** and **Zepita.** The church at Pomata has beautiful carvings, in Andean mestizo baroque, of vases full of tropical plants, flowers and animals in the window frames, lintels and cornices, and a frieze of dancing figures inside the dome (which is unusual in Peru), and alabaster windows (John Hemming). On the road to Juli is **Ilave,** where the road for Tacna branches off. (The Tacna road is unpaved, but in good condition and a worthwhile journey, not only in terms of scenery, but also because road conditions are better than on the alternative Juliaca-Arequipa route to the coast from Lake Titicaca.) Ilave is typical of a gaunt altiplano town; has a good Sun. market (woven goods). Many buses go there from Puno (US$1.15); Ilave-Tacna, US$6.50, 13 hrs., leaves at 1400 and 1700 (Transportes Ponce, best, and Transportes Gironda). You pass these places when travelling by road between Puno and La Paz. Near Juli there is a small colony of flamingoes and many other birds can be seen from the road.

Juli Hotels Only one, Hostal Tréboles, F, cold, dirty—best not to arrive in Juli at night looking for somewhere agreeable to stay. Bus Puno to Juli at 1430 from the market.

"Juli has four churches, two of them in ruins, that the visitor should see. The keys to two of these (Santa Cruz and San Juan Bautista) are kept by the couple who look after San Juan Bautista. San Pedro is now designated as the Cathedral. Juli's fourth church is La Asunción, now abandoned and its fine bell tower damaged by earthquake or lightning. The Peruvians have established a school of picture restoration at Juli to restore its mass of paintings" (John Hemming.)

All the Juli churches are being renovated. San Pedro has been extensively restored, it contains a series of superb screens, some in ungilded mahogany and others taken from other churches; also fine paintings, and a collection of coloured objects in the sacristy. San Juan Bautista has two sets of 17th century paintings of the lives of St. John the Baptist and of St. Teresa, contained in sumptuous gilded frames. San Juan is now a state museum, open a.m. only (US$0.15); it also has intricate *mestizo* carving in pink stone. Santa Cruz is another fine Jesuit church, partly roofless, so that it is easy to photograph the carvings of monkeys, papayas and grapes. La Asunción has an archway and atrium which date from the early 17th century.

Minibus Puno-Juli, 0800, US$1.80 (Colectur). A hydrofoil at 0800 from Juli to Bolivia operates most days as part of a Puno-La Paz package tour. Juli-La Paz costs US$115, lunch included, from Transportes El Sol (Sr. Ronald Zárate).

Pomata Hotel *Puma Uta*, F, water, electricity.

There are other excursions, near Puno, to the *chullpas* (precolumbian funeral towers) of **Sillustani** (admission, US$0.30) on a peninsula in Lake Umayo, 32 km. (excellent road) from Puno (colectivo US$6 p.p. for 3 hrs., bus from Puno, Plaza de Armas, 1400, US$2.50, 1 hr. at site—insufficient). Museum, reception area and restaurant now built. "Most of the towers date from the period of Inca occupation in the 15th century, but they are burial towers of the Aymará-speaking Colla tribe. The engineering involved in their construction is more complex than anything the Incas built—it is defeating archaeologists' attempts to rebuild the tallest "lizard" *chullpa*. Two are unfinished: one with a ramp still in place to raise blocks; the other with cut stones ready to go onto a very ambitious corbelled false dome. A series of stone circles to the east of the site are now thought to be the bases of domed thatch or peat living huts, rather than having any religious meaning. The quarry near the towers is also worth seeing." - John Hemming. Taxi, about US$12; tour with Transextour leaves plaza in Puno at 1430, US$1.50 or with Colectur (no guide), US$2.50 p.p. plus US$0.30 entrance fee, or US$5 with Suri Tours. Camera fans will find the afternoon light best; desert country, but impressive. There are Inca ruins at Tancatanca and Caluxo and an Inca sundial may be seen near the village of **Chucuíto** (which has an interesting church, La Asunción, a small useum in the church of Santo Domingo, and houses with carved stone doorways); cave paintings at Chichiflope.

Peru to Bolivia *By Road*. (See also under Bolivia, page 173).

1. The most remote route is along east side of Lake via Huancané and Puerto Acosta (Bolivia), recommended only on weekends when there is more traffic; after Puerto Acosta, the road is very bad.
2. The most direct route is the Puno-Desaguadero road (paved) passing through Chucuíto, Ilave, Juli and Pomata (see below). Bus to La Paz e.g. Chaski Andina (Sun., 0930). Bus from Titicaca 165 leaves 2000, arrives Desaguadero 0200. Bus from border to La Paz at 1130; whole journey Puno-La Paz takes about 8 hrs., costing US$6.40 overall by bus. Puno-Desaguadero by colectivo, 1 hr., US$4, leaving between 0600-0730. Colectivo, Juliaca Express, Puno-La Paz, twice daily, US$15. Offices: Puno, Tacna 298; Arequipa, Salaverry 111; Cuzco, Ruinas 407; Juliaca, San Román 129.
3. Transturin of La Paz runs a luxury service Puno-La Paz, for US$50, including hydrofoil and lunch, leaves Puno 0630, arrives La Paz 1800 on Mon. to Fri. stopping at Copacabana. Transturin has offices in both Puno (Jirón Tacna 201, Tel.: 737) and Cuzco (Portal de Panes 109, Of. 1, Plaza de Armas, Tel.: 222332) where tickets can be booked in advance. There is also a bus-hydrofoilbus route from Puno to La Paz run by Crillón Tours (the hydrofoil crossing from Juli to Copacabana, calling at the Island of the Sun), leaves Puno 0700, arriving La Paz at 1830. All luggage and formalities taken care of. Colectur/Turisbus runs a luxury bus service Puno-La Paz for US$12.
4. Puno-Yunguyo-Copacabana-La Paz: by far the pleasanter journey. Colectivos, leaving Puno 0800, ply to La Paz via Copacabana for US$10, but often ask you to pay ferry fare, US$0.20, in addition. You can take a bus Puno-Yunguyo (e.g. Cruz del Sur, leaving 0800, arriving 1000, US$1, colectivo, US$1.15), then bus (irregular service, US$0.30), truck or 11 km. walk to Copacabana for Immigration. There are three buses a day Copacabana-La Paz and you must book one or two days in advance (e.g. Pullman, US$1.50, reserve seats at *Hotel Ambassador*). Alternatively local buses and trucks go from Yunguyo to Copacabana, stopping at the frontier, for US$0.30. There are also direct buses from Yunguyo to La Paz, which stop at the border for both authorities to stamp passports. On Sun. there are many trucks carrying people between the markets. **Yunguyo** itself has improved: privet hedge on main square shows good examples of topiary. *Hotel Amazonas*, G, *Hostal Yunguyo*, also G, clean, but often no water or electricity. Passport sometimes stamped at Yunguyo, walk across bridge to Kasami—1 km., where passport must be stamped.

A few agencies in Puno, for example Colectur (Jr. Tacna 232, Tel.: 697), offer minibus services to the Bolivian border, with a lunch stop in Copacabana, stops at all necessary official posts, and at money changers in Yunguyo, with connection to La Paz, for US$5 up (the less expensive do not include lunch, US$2); depart Puno at 0800, arriving at the hotel of your choice in La Paz between 1500 and 1600. If you wish you can break your journey in Copacabana (US$1 bus, US$2.50 daily colectivo—you have to change buses at Copacabana regardless) and make a connection to La Paz next day. Coming into Peru at this point you can get an overnight truck to Puno for about US$1, though these are cold and uncomfortable. When entering Peru here, authorities ask to see an onward ticket. Many colectivos leave from the Laykakota market. La Paz-Copacabana-Yunguyo-Puno is possible in one day as a bus (2 de Febrero company) leaves La Paz at 0800 for Copacabana, leaving you time to catch an onward bus to Yunguyo and bus or colectivo to Puno. The road is unpaved from Yunguyo to Straits of Tiquina.

710 PERU

N.B. Delays and consequent expenses have been reported by travellers going from Puno to Bolivia by hired car. On the Yunguyo-Copacabana route Immigration, Customs and Police offices are all at different places on both the Peruvian and Bolivian sides: failure to check in at each usually means several hours wasted. When crossing Peru to Bolivia get an entry stamp in Copacabana (exit stamp in Peru of course). Bolivian authorities may want proof that you have US$10 for each day you intend to spend in Bolivia. There is no need to go to the Bolivian Consul in Yunguyo—he charges US$3 for a 10 day visa, whereas, at the border, a 90 day visa is free. If you go via Desaguadero (a miserable place; *Alojamiento Internacional*, dirty, F) there are two Peruvian offices to visit (colectivo drivers know where they are) and three Bolivian—at the frontier.

By Rail and Ferry 5. In 1985 the ferry service across Lake Titicaca was suspended; we have not received confirmation that this is permanent (but we suspect it is).

Puno to Cuzco On the way from Puno to Cuzco there is much to see from the train, which runs at an average altitude of 3,500 metres. At the stations, Indians sell food (roast lamb at Ayaviri and stuffed peppers at Sicuani) and local specialities such as pottery bulls at Pucará; fur caps, furs and rugs at Sicuani; knitted alpaca ponchos and pullovers and miniature llamas at Santa Rosa.

Ten km. after La Raya (where small boys throw snowballs into the train if they can!), the highest spot (164 km. from Juliaca; 4,321 metres), there is a research station for high-altitude animals, run by the University of San Marcos, Lima (whose permission is required); llamas, alpaca and vicuña may be seen here, and accommodation is available in the dining room at the research station, US$2.50 p.p. (there is an excellent hot-bath house). Up on the heights breathing may be a little difficult, but the descent along the river Vilcanota is rapid. Get out of the train at Aguas Calientes, the next station (4 km. from La Raya)— first class fare from Puno, US$3. To the right of Aguas Calientes station are steaming pools of hot water in the middle of the green grass; a startling sight. The temperature of the springs is 40°C, and they show beautiful deposits of red ferro-oxide. At Marangani, the river is wider, the fields greener, with groves of eucalyptus trees.

N.B. If cycling from Juliaca to Cuzco, a suitable path runs beside the railway line for 200 km. from Tirapata; it is preferable to the road, and there is no danger from trains—only one a day in either direction.

Sicuani, 38 km. beyond the divide (250 km. from Puno—a very tiring road— 137 km. from Cuzco), is an important agricultural centre, and an excellent place for items of llama and alpaca wool and skins; they sell them on the railway station and at the excellent Sun. morning market. Also known for its mineral baths at Uyurmiri.

Hotels *El Mirador*, E, basic, clean; *Raqchi*, F, basic; *Manzanares, Mollendo, Vilcanota*. *Turistas*, D, needs refurbishing, is poor and cold but best hotel in town (some way from centre).

Restaurants *Elvis* and *Vilcanota* in centre of town, recommended.

On the right, a few kilometres past the San Pedro stop, is the so-called Templo de Viracocha, grandiose, though almost unknown, with Inca baths 180 metres to the E. (For more information about various places between Sicuani and Cuzco, see page 722.)

Branch roads both S and N of Sicuani lead to a road past the Tintaya mines which forms an alternative route Cuzco-Arequipa. The surface is very bad in places, but it is a spectacular journey. Only one bus a day (Chasqui) passes, usually full. From Sicuani, a pretty lake is passed, then one climbs to a radio-transmission antenna; a few km. from the road is Yauri (primitive accommodation), isolated on a plateau by a canyon; the road leads to the Majes irrigation scheme and on to the Arequipa-Juliaca road.

The Vilcanota now plunges into a gorge, but the train winds above it and round the side of the mountain. At Huambutío we turn left to follow the river Huatanay—the Vilcanota here widens into the great Urubamba canyon, flanked on both sides by high cliffs, on its way to join the Ucayali, a tributary of the Amazon. We are now close to Cuzco.

Cuzco stands at 3,310 metres, a little lower than Puno. Its 143,000 inhabitants are mostly Indian, and the city is remarkable for its many colonial churches, monasteries and convents, and for its extensive Inca ruins. Respect the altitude; two or three hours' rest after arriving make a great difference; eat lightly and drink little alcohol, but suck glucose sweets the first day, and remember to walk slowly.

PERU 711

To see Cuzco and the surrounding area properly—including Pisac, Ollantaitambo, Chincheros and Machu-Pinchu—you need at least a week, allowing for slowing down because of altitude.

Almost every central street has remains of Incaic walls, arches and doorways. Many streets are lined with perfect Inca stonework, now serving as foundations for more modern dwellings. This stonework is tapered upwards; every wall has a perfect line of inclination towards the centre, from bottom to top. In the language of the stonemason, they are "battered", with each corner rounded. The circular stonework of the Temple of the Sun, for example, is probably unequalled in the world.

History Cuzco was the capital of the Inca empire—one of the greatest planned societies the world has known—from its rise during the 11th century to its death in the early 16th century. (See John Hemming's *Conquest of the Incas* and B.C.Brundage's *Lords of Cuzco* and *Empire of the Inca*.) It was solidly based on other Peruvian civilizations which had attained great skill in textiles, building, ceramics and working in metal. Immemorially, the political structure of the Andean Indian had been the *ayllu*, the village community; it had its divine ancestor, worshipped household gods, was closely knit by ties of blood to the family and by economic necessity to the land, which was held in common. Submission to the *ayllu* was absolute, because it was only by such discipline that food could be obtained in an unsympathetic environment. All the domestic animals—the llama and alpaca and the dog—had long been tamed, and the great staple crops—maize and potatoes—established. What the Incas did—and it was a magnificent feat—was to conquer enormous territories and impose upon the variety of *ayllus*, through an unchallengeable central government, a willing spiritual and economic submission to the State. The common religion, already developed by the classical Tiahuanaco culture, was worship of the Sun, whose vice-regent on earth was the absolute Sapa Inca. Around him, in the capital, was a religious and secular elite which never froze into a caste because it was open to talent. The elite was often recruited from chieftains defeated by the Incas: an effective way of reconciling local opposition. The mass of the people were subjected to rigorous planning. They were allotted land to work, for their group and for the State; set various tasks—the making of textiles, pottery, weapons, ropes, etc.—from primary materials supplied by the functionaries, or used in enlarging the area of cultivation by building terraces on the hill-sides. Their political organization was simple but effective. The family, and not the individual, was the unit. Families were grouped in units of 10, 100, 500, 1,000, 10,000 and 40,000, each group with a leader responsible to the next largest group. The Sapa Inca crowned the political edifice; his four immediate counsellors were those to whom he allotted responsibility for the northern, southern, eastern and western regions (*suyos*) of the empire.

Equilibrium between production and consumption, in the absence of a free price mechanism and good transport facilities, must depend heavily upon statistical information. This the Incas raised to a high degree of efficiency by means of their *quipus*: a decimal system of recording numbers by knots in cords. Seasonal variations were guarded against by creating a system of state barns in which provender could be stored during years of plenty, to be used in years of scarcity. Statistical efficiency alone required that no one should be permitted to leave his home or his work. The loss of personal liberty was the price paid by the masses for economic security. In order to obtain information and to transmit orders quickly, the Incas built fine paved pathways along which couriers sped on foot. The whole system of rigorous control was completed by the greatest of all their monarchs, Pachacutec (1400-48), who also imposed a common language, Quechua, as a further cementing force. After him the Incas conquered all Bolivia, northern Argentina, northern and central Chile, and Ecuador. The empire grew too large to be easily controlled from one centre, and the last of the great emperors, Huayna Capac, made the fatal mistake of dividing his realm between his two sons, Atahualpa reigning from Quito and Huáscar from Cuzco; the civil war that

712 PERU

ended just before the Spaniards' arrival resulted in Atahualpa's victory but weakened the empire. Resistance to the Spaniards was reduced by the fact that Huáscar's faction at first looked on the invaders as allies; the struggle was in any case a most unequal one because of the Spaniards' superiority in equipment, though Manco Inca almost recaptured Cuzco in 1536 and the Inca successor state of Vilcabamba, centred near Espíritu Pampa in the jungle foothills N of Cuzco, was held against the Spaniards until 1572.

Churches (*Note that the Compañía, Merced, San Francisco and Santa Catalina churches were closed after the earthquake of April 5, 1986.*) The heart of the city, as in Inca days, is the Plaza de Armas. Around the square are colonial arcades and four churches. To the N is the **Cathedral** (early 17th century, in baroque style), built on the site of the Palace of Viracocha. The high altar is solid silver; the original altar *retablo* behind it is a masterpiece of native wood carving. In the sacristy are paintings of all the bishops of Cuzco and a painting of Christ attributed to Van Dyck. The choir stalls, by a 17th-century Spanish priest, are a magnificent example of colonial baroque art. The elaborate pulpit and the sacristy are notable. Much venerated is the crucifix of El Señor de las Temblores, the object of many pilgrimages and viewed all over Peru as a guardian against earthquakes. (The Cathedral is open until 1000 for genuine worshippers, and thereafter 1000-1200, 1500-1800 with the combined entrance ticket—see below) The tourist entrance is through El Triunfo, which has a fine granite altar and a statue of the Virgin of the Descent, reputed to have helped the Spaniards repel Manco Inca when he besieged the city in 1536. It also has a painting of Cuzco during the 1650 earthquake (the earliest surviving painting of the city) in a side chapel. Doors from the Cathedral open into Jesús María.

On the E side of the plaza is the beautiful **La Compañía de Jesús**, built on the site of the Palace of the Serpents (Amaru-cancha) in the late 17th century; open only during regular services 1200-1800. Its twin-towered exterior is extremely graceful, and the interior rich in fine murals, paintings and carved altars. The cloister is also noteworthy.

Three outstanding churches are La Merced, San Francisco, and Belén de los Reyes. **La Merced,** almost opposite the *Tambo Hotel*, first built 1534, rebuilt late 17th century, attached is a very fine monastery with an exquisite cloister; open 0830-1200, 1430-1730 (admission US$0.75). Inside the church are buried Gonzalo Pizarro, half-brother of Francisco, and the two Almagros, father and son. Their tombs were discovered in 1946. The church is most famous for its jewelled monstrance, on view in the monastery's museum during visiting hours. The superb choir stalls, reached from the upper floor of the cloister, can be seen by men only (but you must persuade a Mercedarian friar to let you see them). **San Francisco** (3 blocks SW of the Plaza de Armas), is an austere church reflecting many Indian influences. Its monastery is being rebuilt (the first of the cloisters is now open to the public 0900-1200, 1500-1700—see the candelabra made from human bones and the wood carving). **Belén de los Reyes** (in the southern outskirts), built by an Indian in the 17th century, has a gorgeous main altar, with silver embellishments at the centre and goldwashed *retablos* at the sides (open 1000-1200, 1500-1700 except Thurs.) **Santa Catalina,** on the street of the same name, is a magnificent building; the church, convent and museum are included on the tourist ticket, open all day Fri., otherwise 0600-0800. (church), daily 0900-1200, 1500-1800, except Fri. (museum); both closed Sun. Delicious marzipan is sold next to the museum by the nuns through a revolving wooden door, US$1 for 200 grams. **San Pedro** (in front of the market) was built in 1688, its two towers from stones brought from an Inca ruin (open Mon.-Sat. 1000-1200, 1400-1700). The nuns' church of Santa Clara is unique in South America for its decoration, which covers the whole of the interior (but virtually impossible to visit). The smaller and less well-known church of **San Blas** has a fine carved *mestizo* cedar pulpit.

Santo Domingo (SE of the main Plaza) was built in the 17th century on the walls of the Temple of the Sun and from its stones; visit the convent to see the ancient walls of the Temple of the Sun, now restored. (Model of the Temple

PERU 713

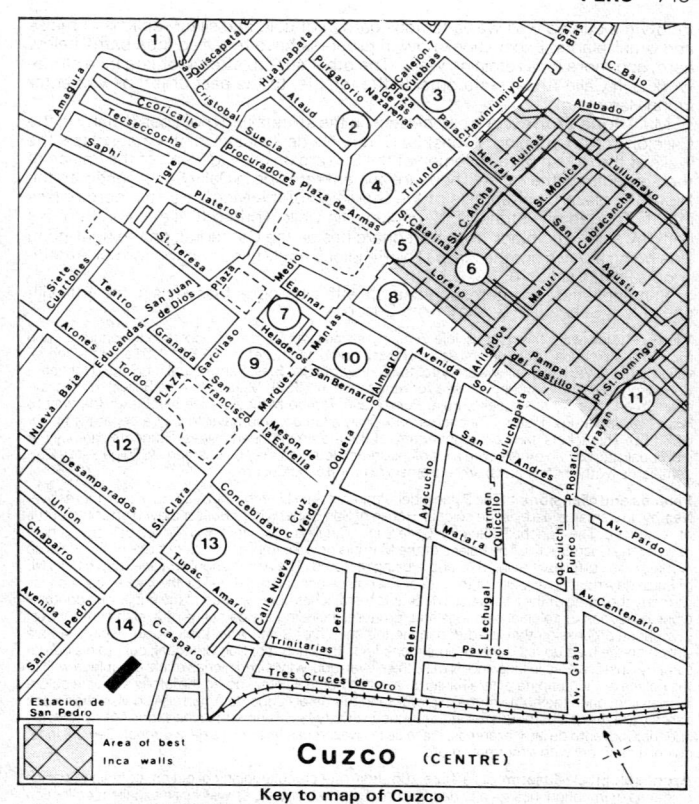

Key to map of Cuzco
1. Church of San Cristóbal; 2. Almirante Palace; 3. Church of San Antonio; 4. Cathedral; 5. Museum; 6. Church of Santa Catalina; 7. *Hotel Cuzco*; 8. Church of the Society of Jesus; 9. House of Garcilaso de la Vega; 10. Church of La Merced; 11. Church of Santo Domingo; 12. Convent of San Francisco; 13. Church of Santa Clara; 14. Church of San Pedro.

upstairs: ask to see it.) Current excavation is revealing more and more of the five chambers of the Temple of the Sun, which shows the best Inca stonework to be seen in Cuzco. The Temple of the Sun was awarded to Juan Pizarro, the younger brother of Francisco, who willed it to the Dominicans after he had been fatally wounded in the Sacsayhuamán siege. Open 0900-1200, 1500-1700.

The baroque cloister has been gutted to reveal four of the original chambers of the great Inca temple—two on the west partly reconstructed in a good imitation of Inca masonry. The finest stonework is in the celebrated curved wall beneath the west end of Santo Domingo (rebuilt after the 1950 earthquake, at which time a niche that once contained a shrine was found at the inner top of the wall).

714 PERU

Below the curved wall was a famous garden of gold and silver replicas of maize and other plants. Excavations now in progress have revealed Inca baths below here, and more Inca retaining walls. The other superb stretch of late Inca stonework is in Calle Ahuacpinta outside the temple, to the east or left as you enter (John Hemming).

Much **Inca stonework** can be seen in the streets and most particularly in the Callejón Loreto, running SE past La Compañía de Jesús from the main plaza: the walls of the House of the Women of the Sun are on one side, and of the Palace of the Serpents on the other. There are ancient remains in Calle San Agustín, to the NE of the plaza. The temples of the Stars and of the Moon are still more or less intact. The famous stone of 12 angles is in Calle Triunfo (Calle Hatun Rumioc) halfway along 2nd block from the square beside the Cathedral, on the right-hand side going away from the Plaza. The Religious Art Museum in the former Archbishop's Palace is nearby.

San Sebastián, an interesting church with a baroque façade, is in the little village of San Sebastián, 6½ km. from Cuzco.

Visitors' Tickets It is not possible to purchase individual entrance tickets to the churches and ruins in and around Cuzco; one must purchase a combined ticket for US$10 (US$5 for students), valid for ten days, which allows entry to: the Cathedral, San Blas, Santa Catalina, Santo Domingo-Coricancha, Museo Histórico (closed for renovation in 1986), Museo de Arte Religioso, Sacsayhuamán and the 3 ruins (Kenko, Puku Pukará and Tambo Machay—see below) on the way to Pisac, Pikillacta. For Pisac, Chincheros and Ollantaitambo, you have to buy a separate ticket, US$3.50. The tickets can be bought at any of the aforementioned places. Students can pay per individual site, as can others with a lot of insistence (but you may be charged US$5 per site). Student cards (with photographs) are extremely useful around Cuzco.

Palaces and Mansions The Palacio del Almirante, just N of the Plaza de Armas, is impressive. Nearby, in a small square, is the colonial House of San Borja, where Bolívar stayed after the Battle of Ayacucho. The Concha Palace (on Calle Santa Catalina), with its finely carved balcony, is now used by the Guardia Civil. The Palace of the Marquis of Valleumbroso (3 blocks SW of the Plaza de Armas) was gutted by fire in 1973 and is being restored. The Archbishop's Palace (two blocks NE of Plaza de Armas) was built on the site of the palace occupied in 1400 by the Inca Roca and was formerly the home of the Marqueses de Buena Vista; it has been opened to the public and contains a fine collection of colonial paintings and furniture, including the paintings of a 17th century Corpus Christi procession that used to hang in the church of Santa Ana. Well worth visiting. Above Cuzco on the road up to Sacsayhuamán, one finds the church of San Cristóbal, built to his patron saint by Cristóbal Paullu Inca and, N of it, the eleven doorway-sized niches of the great Inca wall of the Palace of Colcampata where Paullu Inca set up home. Further up, to the left, is a private colonial mansion, once the home of the explorer (and murderer) Lope de Aguirre. Also visit the palace called Casa de los Cuatro Bustos at San Agustín 400 (which is now the *Libertador-Marriott Hotel*) and the Convento de las Nazarenas, Plaza de las Nazarenas (alias Casa de la Sirena). See the Inca-colonial doorway with a mermaid motif.

Archaeological Museum Calle Tigre 165, first-rate precolumbian collection, contains Spanish paintings of imitation Inca royalty dating from the 18th century, as well as an excellent collection of textiles. Visitors should ask to see the forty miniature pre-Inca turquoise figures found at Piquillacta, and the golden treasures, all kept under lock and key but on display. Open Mon.-Fri., 0745-1300, January-March; 0745-1230, 1500-1800, April-December. Entry US$1.20. Closed after earthquake damage, April 1986.

Religious Art Museum at old Archbishop's Palace in Calle Hatun Rumioc (constructed over temple of Inca Roca), with religious paintings of the Cuzco School and Colonial furniture in beautiful rooms. Open Mon.-Sat., 0930-1200, 1500-1800. Sun. 1500-1800.

Regional History Museum, in the Palacio del Almirante on the street above the Cathedral, tries to show the evolution of the Cuzqueño school of painting. Open Mon.-Fri., 0900-1200, 1500-1800, Sat., 0900-1200. Contains Inca agricultural implements, colonial furniture and paintings and mementos of more recent times. Note the pillar on the balcony over the door, showing a bearded man and a naked woman. Closed after earthquake damage, April 1986.

Warning Thieves are numerous and persistent. Do not wear jewellery, watches or carry credit cards, leave valuables with hotel management. Don't change money on the streets. Be especially careful in the railway stations, the bus from the airport, the market (otherwise recommended) and at out-of-the-way ruins. More police patrol the streets and stations than in the past, but one should still be on the lookout for thieves. The tourist police station is at Portal de Belén 115, next to the Cathedral on the Plaza de Armas.

Hotels Book more expensive hotels well in advance through a good travel agency, for Cuzco is often very crowded, and particularly for the week or so around June 24 when the Inti Raymi celebrations take place. Prices given are for the high season in June-August though you can often bargain at other times, especially if you plan to stay a long time. On the Puno-Cuzco train there are many hotel agents for medium-priced hotels; prices can often be negotiated down to F category, but best to pay agent for one day only and then negotiate with hotel. Agents also provide transport to the hotel, which can be invaluable when arriving at the dimly-lit station. Best is *Libertador-Marriott* (5-star), in colonial palace (Casa de los Cuatro Bustos) at Calle San Agustín 400 (Tel.: 3842), A, plus 28 % tax, good, especially the service, but in July and August rooms in the older part of the hotel are cold and dark, restaurant overpriced; *Royal Inka*, Plaza Regocijo 299, A, 3-star, bar, dining room, good service, recommended, arranges trips to Machu Picchu; *Turistas*, B, good but overpriced; *Alhambra*, Av. Sol, B, modern, very good, prices negotiable for groups, but cold, and food disappointing; *Tambo*, Ayacucho 233, D, central, tatty rooms, hot water, restaurant fair; *Savoy* (Holiday Inn), A, group rate B, recently upgraded to Peruvian 5-star, good food, no coffee or food served after 2200, disappointing; *Marqués de Picoagua* on Calle Sta. Teresa, A, 70 rooms, central heating, private bathrooms, dining room, information in Lima Tel.: 286 314; *Viracocha*, Plaza de Armas, corner of Mantas, D, clean, hot water, restaurant opens at 0600 (P.O. Box 502); *Hostal Inti Raymi*, B, Matará 260, Tel.: 2833. *Espinar*, Portal Espinar 142, C, recommended but food poor, clean and helpful, and *El Inca*, Quera 251, D, F in low season (good, clean, heating, may have to ask for hot water after 0900 and before 0600, breakfast overpriced; Wilbur speaks English, and is helpful; *Colonial Palace*, Quera 270, one block from Av. Sol, C, hot water, restaurant, comfortable, some English spoken, helpful staff, luggage may be left for small fee (in a converted monastery); *Hostal El Dorado* (4-star) on Av. Sol, good but can be noisy in a.m., food good but a little expensive. Others: 1st class, *Cusco*, A, Heladeras 150 (Tel.: 2400), administered by Sociedad de Beneficencia Pública del Cusco, hot water, largest and best known, "old fashioned, not cheap and a little fusty", central; *Garcilaso de la Vega*, Garcilaso 233, C with bath, but in off-season can be negotiated lower (E), rooms dark, cold and not clean, "historic charm, but service poor", laundry expensive, noisy disco until 0300, overpriced in season, friendly; *Virrey*, small in Plaza de Armas, Portal Comercio 165, D, hot water, friendly but decrepit and overpriced, poor services; *Conquistador*, Santa Catalina Angosta 149, near Plaza de Armas, D (negotiable), safe, expensive meals, big ideas but small performance, money changing facilities helpful in getting rail tickets, etc (but commission charged); *Gran*, San Agustín, C, overpriced; *San Agustín*, Maruri y San Agustín, C, fine interior, clean, friendly, restaurant fair; *El Sol*, San Andrés, D, central, good service, rooms at the front noisy, locks insecure; *Cusi*, good, modern, all mod. cons.; *Ollanta*, Av. Sol, D, with bath, clean comfortable and fairly quiet; *Santa Catalina*, D; and *Los Marqueses*, Garcilaso 252, E, early colonial house, very helpful and comfortable, but not well kept, has a masseur, Douglas Chapman, recommended; *Del Angel*, Av. Afligidos 194, E, with bath and unreliable hot water, good breakfast but not served early, dirty, overpriced, not safe (nor is the electricity), beware of extra charges. *Hostal Corihuasi*, Calle Suecia, D, 4-room suites, colonial house, English-speaking owner; *Lennie's Lodgings*, Av. Pardo 820 (Tel.: 5436), D, including breakfast, clean, friendly, helpful, English spoken, now run by María, a Peruvian; *El Mesón*, Las Estrellas, E, good value; *Qoricancha*, opposite *Inti Raymi*, F, hot shower, being modernized, now recommended; *Internacional* (near San Pedro Station), E, with bath (out of season, more expensive in season), good, clean, safe; *Suecia*, Calle Suecia, F, shared rooms, cosy, clean, hot showers, safe, highly recommended; nearby is *Huaynapata*, Huaynapata 369, E, very safe, family-run, hot water, stores luggage. *Hostal Bolívar*, Tecsecocha 2, G, basic, dirty and noisy, but central and friendly, though watch out for clothes on washing line, gringo hotel, hot water; *Trinitarias*, Trinitarias 263, near San Pedro station, E, clean, hot water in shower, friendly, secure for left luggage; also near San Pedro station, *San Martín*, Trinitarias 232; and *Milán*, Trinitarias 237, E, with unreliable hot water in evening, safe, clean, a bit noisy; *Imperio*, Calle Chaparro, comfortable new extension, run by Elena and family, also near station, F, hot water, friendly, clean, safe to leave luggage; *Panamericano*, Calle San Agustín, F; *Palermo*, San Agustín 287, F, some Inca walls, good breakfast; *El Solar*, Plaza San Francisco 162, Tel.: 3645, D, with shower, friendly, helpful, safe, recommended; *Gran Hostal Machu Picchu*, Quera 274, pleasant, friendly, E or F in low season, will store luggage; *k'Ancharina*, E, with bath, hot water, not well recommended; *Samaná*, Nueva Baja 472, E, colonial mansion, good rooms with heaters and private baths, safe for luggage, helpful staff, laundry, restaurant slow but good; *Hostal Cabillado*, E with or without bath, worth bargaining here, safe; *Hostal El Arqueólogo*, E (rooms or dormitory), Ladrillos 425 not far from Sacsayhuamán, (Tel.: 232569), run by a Frenchman, hot water, highly recommended, clean, will store luggage, cafetería and kitchen; *Plateros*, Calle Plateros, off Plaza de Armas, F, triples available, simple but clean, friendly, recommended; *Cáceres*, Plateros 368, Tel.: 2809, G (ask for a receipt), recommended for hikers, clean, hot water available, safe to leave luggage, Juana is very helpful with tourist and other information, she speaks English and German; accommodation in *Convento Santo Domingo* (down an alley, behind the church), G, a sleeping bag p.p. in double rooms, hot showers, clean, friendly, safe to leave bags, must be in by 2200; *Hostal Familiar*, Saphi 661, F-E, with bath, cold, clean, attractive flower-filled patios, rooms around which are recommended (other rooms are not as good), can leave luggage here, with café, sister (Gloria) of owner works with Kantu Tours. Boarding house of Sra. de Angulo at Tullumayo 860 near Puno station, E, recommended; *Residencial Alfredo Paredes*, Quiscapata 250, near San Cristóbal, G, cooking facilities, will watch luggage, very nice people; *Alamo*, Av. Antonio Lorena

PERU

18, F, with bath and hot water if you ask for it, reasonably cheap, needs maintenance; *Hostal Familiar Las Esmeraldas* (Sra. Vega de Pineda), Av. de la Infancia 433, E, full board available, clean, hot showers, recommended; *Hostal Corona Real*, F, Av. Huáscar 226-228, Tel.: 4445, clean, friendly; *Bridge Hostal* (Av. Tacna 166), E; *Los Portales*, Matará 322, Tel.: 2191, clean, hot water unreliable, breakfast included, D, with bath (also 4-bedded rooms), has deteriorated; *Chavín*, F, Matará, dirty, poor service; *Chavín 2*, Av. Cuichipunco 299, F with bath, hot water, some rooms insecure; *Raymi*, Pardo 954, E, hot water, carpeting, safe; *Hostal Bellavista*, Av. Santiago 100, F, hot water, very friendly, safe (long walk from centre, not a safe area at night), breakfast available, will store luggage, recommended (particularly, rooms with view towards Estación San Pedro); *Hostal Cahuide y Saphi*, Saphi 845, F, cold, huge rooms with 4 beds; *Hostal Bambú*, on Av. Tullumayo near San Cristóbal bus station, F, hot water, laundry facilities, quiet, clean; *Hostal Cuichipunco*, Cuichipunco 231, F, clean, good; *Mantas*, Calle Mantas 115 (near Plaza de Armas), E, recommended, friendly, can leave luggage, has laundry service, good meals; *Hostal Tipón*, Calle Tecte, E, friendly and secure. *San Bernardo*, San Bernardo 136-154, no sign, 1 block from Plaza de Armas, F, with good bath and hot water, safe, can leave luggage, laundry facilities, clean, friendly; *Hostal Granada*, Teatro, F, modern rooms on patio better but more expensive, will wash clothes. *Loreto*, Pasaje Loreto 115, Plaza de Armas, Tel.: 2689, E (triples available— always full, but good value if you can get in), will look after luggage while you go to Machu-Picchu, clean, very friendly, rooms with Inca walls and electric heaters recommended; *Monte Carlo*, Av. Sol 138, F; *Residencial Carmen*, Av. Tullumayo 860, no sign (near Puno station), E, hot water, friendly, clean; *Inti Huatara*, Siete Cuartones 245, F, very clean; *Casona*, F, recommended three rooms overlook the Plaza de Armas (two others have no windows), entrance on Procuradores, no singles, luggage stored; *Residencial Las Rejas*, above main tourist office on Plaza de Armas, good value, hot water; *Tambo Real*, Av. Belén, E with bath and hot water, friendly but noisy (not to be confused with *Hotel Tambo*); *Santa Teresa*, Santa Teresa 364, F, hot water, may use washing machine for US$1.30, can leave luggage, but dirty and not recommended; *Richmond*, La Unión, expensive; *Hostal Alcázar*, F, with bathroom; *Hostal Perú*, Unión 140, near San Pedro station, hot water, private bath, breakfast; *Hostal Procuradores* on street of same name, F, cheap; also *Hotel del Procurador*, F, good beds, clean, hot water. Basic accommodation at *Restaurant La Ñusta*, F. *Central*, San Agustín 251, G, hot shower US$0.20 extra, safe for leaving luggage; *Hostal Royal*, San Agustín 256. There is a cheap dormitory on Calle San Cristóbal (under US$1 p.p.), hot water, friendly landladies. *Hotel Tigre* next to Archaeological Museum at Tigre 129, G, good value, friendly, safe, clean, hot water. Sra. Rosa de Calderón rents 2-3 rooms for E, full board and warm water, Almagro 131, 2 blocks from Plaza de Armas, very friendly and helpful. Hortensia de Velasco, Av. Pardo, Pasaje España, private accommodation in F range. Also Irma Rodríguez de Alarcón, Zarumilla 2A-101, 15-20 mins'. walk from Plaza de Armas, 2 rooms sleeping 4 people, safe, breakfast, recommended.

Hotels in Calle Procuradores are not safe and are subject to police raids when there is a drugs problem or a robbery.

Camping Permitted on hill above Cuzco museum, about ½ km. past museum on left; also permitted near Sacsayhuamán ruins, but arrive late and leave early so as not to interfere with the sightseeing. Vicuña Tours rent tents for 2 (which leak) for US$1.50, camping gaz US$5 (see also **Travel Agencies** below and page 727). If you use a spirit stove, "alcohol para quemar" can be bought in most pharmacies (bring your own bottle).

Restaurants Best are *Le Petit Montmartre*, Garcilaso 270, very well recommended; *Sumak*, Calle Mantas 117, *Mesón de los Espaderos*, Espaderos y Plateros, limited choice, but good and expensive; *Roma*, on Plaza de Armas (good food, bad service, folk music nightly without extra cost), and *Violines*, Plaza de Armas, very good, including *peña* show evenings. For a good meal and décor try *Inti Raymi* in the Libertador-Marriott, à la carte dinner for US$13. *Korikancha*, opposite Calle Loreto, recommended; *Café Cande*, Portal Corrizos in Plaza, recommended, local specialities. *El Fogón de las Mestizas* has been recommended for local food, best in the afternoon, has roast guinea-pig (*cuy*, known in Cuzco as *conejo*—rabbit). *El Aguador*, Garcilaso 252, good food through day, no smoking. The *Quinta* in Choquechaca serves good, typical food (including roast guinea-pig); vegetarian restaurant *Govinda* (Hare Krishna), Espaderos 128, just off NW corner of Plaza de Armas, excellent food and good value, always busy, you can buy bread here which will keep for days, ideal for Inca Trail (but order a day in advance), also samosas, cheese, etc. *Café Varayoc*, Espaderos 142, good meeting place, Dutch connection (coffee, pizzas and cakes). Good juice bar at Sta. Catalina Ancha 427. There is a good restaurant with stained glass lamps on Procuradores; same street at 365, *Chez Maggy*, pizzas (overpriced) freshly baked in wood-burning oven; also reasonable restaurants (e.g. *Qarawantana* at 297, *El Corsario*, Italian, excellent pasta; *Inti*, at 391, vegetarian, recommended; *Bar Kukuli*, good and cheap food and interesting local drinks, good music, also on Procuradores; *Los Almarios*, good food, nice atmosphere, *La Comida de Dioses*, on corner with Huaynapata, vegetarian, slow service, on the same street. A good and expensive pizzeria is *La Mamma* on Plaza Recojijo (service indifferent), in the *Hotel Turistas* building; *Bucaro*, Av. Sol 567, fair, reasonable service. Other restaurants and bars include: *La Gran Esquina*, corner of San Bernardo and Almagro, good Italian and local food, crowded, modern; *Piccolo Bar*, Plaza de Armas, popular and good; *Ayllu* (Portal de Carnes 208), also on Plaza de

Armas, Italian, classical music, good atmosphere, has a superb range of milk products and wonderful apple pastries, good breakfast, quick service; *Chef Victor*, Plaza de Armas, better food and fewer flies than *Roma*, almost next door; *Santa Clara*, Santa Clara 415; *Trattoria Adriano*, Calle Mantas y Av. Sol (just off SE corner of Plaza de Armas), recommended, nice atmosphere and fair but rather pricey Italian food, open for breakfast at 0700; *Incario*, in a courtyard off Av. Sol (opposite Industrial Bank), local food; *Hobby*, Av. Sol. good and cheap; *Maximum*, on Procuradores, good meal for less than US$1; *El Truco*, on Plaza del Cabildo (Regocijo), excellent stuffed green peppers, good trout, folklore some evenings (at extra cost), expensive; *Aqha Wasi*, near-by, good local food and music; *Tip-Top*, Palacio 122, good food, reasonable prices; also restaurant of *Hotel Palermo*, San Agustín 287, cheap. Restaurant of *Hotel El Solar*, good suppers for US$1. *Chifa HongKong*, Av. Sol, good, reasonable prices; *La Cabañita* and *Comedor Nacional*, off the Plaza, good cheap food; *Café Restaurant Rick*, opposite *Hotel Conquistador*, dish of the day US$1. *Café de París*, Plaza de Armas, good breakfasts and snacks, cakes and spaghetti recommended; *Café Citera*, Espaderos, good capuccino and cakes, nice atmosphere, not cheap; *Fuente de Soda San Antonio*, Plaza San Francisco, good, cheap, recommended; on same square is *San Agustín*, cheap and good local dishes; good *menú* at *El Tronquito* (also *peña*) and *Los Candiles*, Calle Plateros; *El Tacho*, near San Pedro railway station, for local food, especially soup; opposite *Bolívar* is a café that serves good breakfasts; *Paraíso*, Av. Sol 441, restaurant snack bar, reasonable prices, varied menu, small, friendly; *La Calesa*, Plateros 396, excellent, cheap bar; *Bar Retabillo*, good music, reasonably priced food. *Wiracocha*, on Procuradores, chocolate ice cream recommended. Peña *Do Re Mi*, Plaza de Armas (opp. La Compañía), good, no cover charge, but food is not cheap. *Posada*, on Plaza de Armas, has greatly improved. Several restaurants on Plateros do cheap 3-course *almuerzos* (US$0.50). You can eat cheaply in the market; a *saltado* (a mixture of meat and vegetables) costs about US$0.25, but be careful.

N.B. The Centro de Difusión Cultural Wasapay organizes "folklore evenings" in various restaurants which are supposed to be free, but which will be included as 15% extra on the bill—watch out for this if you don't want a more expensive meal.

Local Specialities Roast stuffed guinea pig (*cuy*). Order in advance at one of the *quintas* (inns in the suburbs). *Quinta Zárate*, Calle Tortera Paccha, recommended. Tel.: 2349. A good cheap *picantería-chichería* is *Mi Casa*, on 100 block of Choquechaca. Also *Quintas Eulalia*, Choquechaca 384, Tel.: 2421. Very rich and exotically spiced. The yoghurt is excellent. Also try *Quinta Tejada* and *Quinta Country Club*. Typical Cuzco *picantería*; *La Chola*, serving excellent *chicha* and delicious kidneys and other snacks in the inner courtyard (llamas often in courtyard) of a colonial house on Calle Palacio up the hill from the Nazarenas (this is not, however, a hygenic place), open only from 1500-1800. Try the *anticuchos* (roast beef hearts) cooked in side streets. The local drinks, herb tea with *caña* and hot milk with *pisco*, very warming in the cold evenings.

Folklore June 24; pageant of Inti Raymi (Indians outnumber tourists) enacted at 1300 at the fortress of Sacsayhuamán. (Try to arrive in Cuzco 15 days before Inti Raymi, there are many festivals, and get to Sacsayhuamán at about 1030 as even reserved seats fill up quickly.) Tickets for the stands can be bought a week in advance from the Town Hall, or for US$6 from travel agents the day before, otherwise standing is free. On Corpus Christi day statues and silver are paraded through the streets; colourful, everyone gets drunk by 1000. The Plaza de Armas is surrounded by tables with Indian women selling *cuy* and a mixed grill called *chiriuchu* (*cuy*, chicken, *tortillas*, fish eggs, water-weeds, maize, cheese and sausage). One week before the Inti Raymi, there is a dance festival in the village of Raqchi (see also page 722). (A special train leaves Cuzco early in the morning, or take a truck, US$ 1; 4 hours. At this festival dancers come to Raqchi from all over Peru; through music and dance they illustrate everything from the ploughing of fields to bull fights, reported to be most enjoyable.) On the Monday before Easter is the procession of the Lord of the Earthquakes, starting at 1600 outside the Cathedral. A large crucifix is paraded through the streets, returning to the Plaza de Armas around 2000 to bless the tens of thousands of people who have assembled there. On September 8 (day of the Virgin), there is a colourful procession of masked dancers from the church of Alundena, at the SW edge of Cuzco, near Belén, to the Plaza de San Francisco. There is also a splendid fair at Alundena, and a free bull fight on the following day (tourists should be very discreet at these celebrations, as they are not welcome—avoid pickpockets, too). Carnival at Cuzco very basic; flour, water, cacti, bad fruit and animal manure thrown about in streets.

Regular nightly folklore show at Qosqo Native Art Centre, Av. Sol. 604, at 1830 hours, for US$5 (students US$3), also Amanta Dances, Calle Unión 117, and Qoricancha Dances, San Juan de Dios 285 (US$4). Peña Folklórica in *Hotel Cuzco*, daily, 1830-1930. *La Taverna* bar on Plaza de Armas has folklore music nightly from 2100-0200, very crowded. Folk-dancing and music in the cellar of *Hotel Ollanta*, Av. Sol, nightly, US$2.50 p.p., 1845-2000. Also nightly at *Hotel Savoy*. Folk dancing at Teatro Central, US$4. There are good *peñas* at *Hatuchay*, on Plaza, and *Kamikaz*, just off Plaza, and folk music at *Restaurant Roma*, evenings.

Discotheques *El Muki* (opposite *Hotel Conquistador*) recommended. *Kamikaz*, many gringos, near Municipalidad, recommended; *Hatuchay*, on Plaza de Armas opp. Cathedral, also recommended for local music. *El Molino Rojo*, Av. de la Cultura; *El Gran Prise*, Av. Antonio Lorena 14;

cheap local bars. Also, *Las Quenas* in the basement of the *Hotel Savoy* and *Abraxas*, Calle Arequipa, recommended.

Local Crafts In the Plaza San Blas and the surrounding area, authentic Cuzco crafts still survive. Wood workers may be seen in almost any street. Leading artisans who welcome visitors include: Hilario Mendivil, Plazoleta San Blas 634 (biblical figures from plaster, wheatflour and potatoes); Edilberta Mérida, Carmen Alto 133 (earthenware figures showing physical and mental anguish of the Indian peasant); Víctor Vivero Holgado, Tandapato 172 (painter of pious subjects); Antonio Olave Palomino, Siete Angelitos 752 (reproductions of precolumbian ceramics and colonial sculptures); Maximiliano Palomino de la Sierra, Triunfo 393 (festive dolls and wood carvings); Santiago Rojas, near San Blas (statuettes). Museo Inca Art Gallery of Amílcar Salomón Zorrilla, Huancaro M-B—L8, Tel.: 231232 (P.O. Box 690), Telephone between 0900 and 2100. Contemporary art.

Shopping Market opposite Estación San Pedro (which also has the name Santa Ana) is the best Indian market for a variety of goods, but although less self-conscious and less expensive than Pisac is not very interesting. Empresa Peruana de Promoción Artesanal (EPPA), Plateros 359, and another good market on the corner of San Andrés and Quera.

Cuzco is the weaving centre of Peru, and excellent textiles can be found at good value. Artesanía La Paloma, Cuesta San Blas 552 and Plazuela Sta. Catalina 211, good but expensive. Sr. Aller, Plaza Santo Domingo 261, sells interesting antiques. Josefina Olivera, Santa Clara 501, sells old ponchos and carved soapstone items, without usual haggling. There is a good jewellery store beside the Cathedral in the Plaza de Armas and art shop at Instituto Americano de Arte, Av. Sol. However, be very careful of what you are buying in and around Cuzco; we have received many reports of sharp practices.

Sauna corner of San Bernardo and Quera Almagro, dry sauna, Mon.-Sat. 0900-2000, Sun. 0900-1300, US$0.90.

Laundry Service at Lavamatic on Procuradores, min. US$5 for 4 kg. (charges per item). Ironing extra. Very good service at Lavanderías Splendor, Suecia 328, just off Plaza de Armas (US$1.50 for 2 kg.), will also dry clean items such as sleeping bags, rucksacks etc.

Bookshop Near Plaza San Francisco (Mantas 191), a small shop sells used English, French, German and Spanish paperbacks—not cheap, but will trade paperbacks 2 for 1. Librería Studium, Mesón de la Estrella 144, stocks guide books. Los Andes, Portal Comercio 125, Plaza de Armas, large boxes of postcards, low prices.

Taxis Large cars parked in Plaza are more expensive. Airport-town; US$1.30 (bus, US$0.12); Railway-town, US$0.50; per hour in town, US$2.25, out of town, US$3. For many excursions, taxis have a fixed rate; ask the driver for a price list. A recommended taxi driver (also school teacher) is José Cuba, Urb. Santa Rosa, Pasaje R. Gibaja 182, Tel.: 226179, who is a guide and can organize tours, accommodation as necessary; he parks at the airport during flight hours, and at the station to await train arrival. Another is Angel Salazar, Saguán del Cielo B-11, Cuzco, English speaking, helpful, arranges good tours.

Car Rental Avis, Av. Sol 900, Volkswagens and Toyotas (poor reports on maintenance). Also, National Rentacar, Calle Santa Catalina near main plaza (cheaper). Never leave anything in a hired car, thieves have keys and may strike the same car again and again.

Banks Photocopy of passport sometimes required for changing travellers' cheques. Banco de Crédito is American Express agent, and good for changing travellers' cheques. Banco de los Andes has the best rates and is quickest for international money transfers. Many travel agencies also change money at favourable rates and remain open during civil disturbances. No bank in Cuzco will give out cash on credit cards. There are now a number of exchange houses on the Plaza de Armas; the one in the alcove by *Chef Víctor* is good. Lavamatic laundry on Procuradores give good rates, esp. for travellers' cheques. Money changers on Av. Sol give a worse rate than travel agents. Beware of people watching you when you change money.

Post Office Principal one on Av. Sol, hrs.: 0800-1900, 0800-1200 Sun. and festivals. Telephone and telegrams at Empresa Nacional de Telecomunicaciones, Av. Sol 386. To send packages over 1 kg., go first to Customs, near Plaza San Francisco (go early); buy sacking nearby to sew up the package, and then go to main post office.

Consulates West German, Av. Tullumayo 874. **French,** Calle Espinar (in a French-run hotel—may let French people leave luggage if going to Machu-Picchu).

Hospitals Hospital Regional, Av. de la Cultura, recommended.

Police Tourist police, Portal de Belén 115, next to Cathedral on Plaza de Armas (Tel.: 221961). If you are robbed and the thief has personal items of no commercial value but important to you, go to Radio Tawantinsuyo, Av. Sol 806, and place an *anuncio* offering an unspecified reward for their return. Tell the respondent to go through the radio station; do not reveal your hotel. The *anuncio*

PERU 719

costs about US$1 a run and about ten times is standard. They will help you write it; there is a standard etiquette (items are "strayed" never "stolen"). The local TV station will also broadcast the *anuncio* a few times free; enquire at your hotel or at the Policía de Turismo. If you need a crime report for insurance purposes, the Policía de Turismo will tell you what documents to buy (stamped paper) at the Post Office. The police will not normally investigate your complaint; getting things back is largely up to you and fate. Stolen cameras often turn up in the local market and can be bought back cheaply; remember the man selling them is not the thief and has got them at about fourth-hand.

Tourist Office (which has a complaints book): at airport (until 1200) and on Plaza de Armas (closed Sun.), next to La Compañía. Check all train information carefully. Maps available of Cuzco and Inca Trail to Machu-Picchu. Gives opening hours of churches in Cuzco. Other good guides to the area are the booklets by Víctor Angles (*Machu-Picchu, Ollantaytambo, Sacsayhuamán*) in Spanish and the Uniclam *Machu-Picchu* in French. Another office at Tecsecocha 474, 0745-1300 Mon.-Fri. Motorists beware; many streets end in flights of steps not marked as such. Very few good maps of Cuzco available; that of Cuzco and Puno Region by Zoila L. Vergara Valenza, available on train to Machu Picchu, is reasonable. The map of the Cuzco-Puno-La Paz route sold at the station can be bought more cheaply (US$0.50) in bookshops.

The book *Exploring Cuzco*, by Peter Frost, is very good; the updated and expanded 3rd edition was published by Bradt Enterprises in 1985 (£5.50).

Automóvil Club del Perú, Av. Sol, useful for maps.

Travel Agencies Exprinter and Dasatour are at the *Hotel Cusco*, Lima Tours at Av. Sol 567, next to Faucett office (no longer American Express). Cooks around the corner from the *Hotel Cusco*. Receptur and Universal Tours have offices in the *Hotel Savoy*. Kinjyo, at side of *Hotel Cusco*. Inca City Tours, Portal Nuevo 246, run by Elena Vargas (speaks English) and Angélica (speaks French), will arrange tours to local sites or further into the mountains with food, horses and porters. They also have tents, stoves and cooking pots for hire. Highly recommended. Andean Adventures, Procuradores 332, friendly, reliable (Aurelio is highly recommended mountain guide) also rent equipment, as do Walking Travel, Portal Confituría 257, Plaza de Armas. Dalfi, Plateros 354, Tel.: 222300, recommended for organizing trips on the Inca Trail. Expediciones Mayoc, Procuradores 354, Apartado 596, Cuzco, Tel.: 232666 (also at Av. Arequipa 4799, Lima, Tel.: 456493) organizes river-running and trekking expeditions on the Urubamba, Apurímac, Inanbari rivers, and to the National Parks near Cuzco (Mr. Frederic A. Schiller is the General Manager). Tambo Treks organize 7-21 day tours in the region (to Paucartambo, Pongo de Mainique, Salcantay, with local weavers) from US$490. For information write to Tambo Treks, Casilla 912, Cuzco, Peru, or Vicki Weeks, 5210, 12th NE, Seattle, WN 98105. International Service is a small, friendly organization with tours in and around Cuzco, including Machu-Picchu, their office is at Garcilaso 285, oficina 213, Cuzco, Tel.: 2735-4311. Kantu Tours, Portal Carrizos 258, recommended for local tours, competitive, Gloria Hermosa Tapiá speaks good English, helpful, highly recommended, guides speak Spanish only. Pisac Tours, Plaza de Armas, has comprehensive range of daily tours, but not recommended for private tours. Milla Turismo, Aptdo Postal 348, Tel.: 231710, run by Don Carlos Milla Vidal, excellent service, highly professional. Explorandes, Av. Pardo 987, recommended; Aries Tours, San Francisco 138, Tel.: 266001, satisfactory; Chincheros Tours (registered at the Cuzco Tourist office) is recommended for the Pisac-Urubamba-Ollantaitambo-Chincheros round trip. Sra. Luisa Bueno Hermosa offers tours of the Cuzco area at reasonable prices (in Spanish); Sr. Luis Vargas, Calle Triunfo 374, also is a recommended guide. Srta. Juana Pancorbo, Av. Los Pinos D-2, Tel.: 227482, is a guide who speaks English, recommended. Marco Bustamante, Casilla 720, Tel.: 225391, recommended. David Choque, Tel.: 224-327, English-speaking, good, but insist on itinerary first. The potter Nicolás Torre is also a good guide US$2 p.p. Puno-Cuzco Tours, Portal de Panes 137, are not recommended.

PERUVIAN ANDEAN TREKS LTD.
ADVENTURE TRAVEL SPECIALISTS

HIGH ANDES TREKS AND CLIMBS, HORSEBACKING, JUNGLE EXPEDITIONS TO MANU PARK, WHITEWATER RAFTING, WEAVING WORKSHOPS. WE DELIVER QUALITY, RELIABILITY AND PROFESSIONALISM. FIXED DEPARTURES AND CUSTOM EXPEDITIONS YEAR ROUND.

P.O. BOX 454, AVENIDA PARDO 575, CUZCO, PERU
TELEPHONE 22-5701; TELEX 52225PE PANTRKS

720 PERU

Minibuses that wait in front of cathedral take tourists to see the "Sacred Valley" (Pisac, Ollantaitambo and Chincheros), 0800, all-day tour, US$5; also Sacsayhuamán, Quenco and Tambo Machay, 1400, half-day, US$2.50. Other minibuses to these places, and further afield, from Av. Recoleta. An even cheaper "Sacred Valley" trip, at US$4, is given by César Silva Guzmán, Tel.: 226-627, who is often to be found in front of the tourist office on the Plaza de Armas.

Roads and Buses To Juliaca, Puno, La Paz, road in poor condition especially in the wet season, many parts are unsurfaced; Cruz del Sur, to Puno, leave at 1900 from Tullumayo, SE of centre, US$5, 12 hrs., recommended. Juliaca Express is not recommended. A direct bus Cuzco-La Paz, leaving Calle Belén 451 at 2000 on Mon., Tues. and Sat. at US$22, 22-24 hrs.; the Transturin luxury service with hydrofoil crossing of Lake Titicaca costs US$65. Taxi to Puno US$10.75 p.p., twice a week. Bus to Juliaca at 0900, US$5.50. To Lima (1,180 km.), road via Abancay, Andahuaylas, Ayacucho, Huancayo and Oroya is recommended for magnificent scenery and interesting towns, but sometimes closed by guerrilla action. The road is appalling in places and takes from 3 to 6 days by successive buses or colectivos; take a rug for the cold nights, and extra food. Approx. times of journeys from Cuzco: Abancay 8 hrs.; Andahuaylas 14 hrs.; Ayacucho 24 hrs.; Huancayo 36-45 hrs.; Lima 2-3 days. Those who tire of buses can transfer to a train at Mejorada, about 3 hrs. before Huancayo. Through fare Cuzco-Lima about US$23. Only Hidalgo run from Cuzco to Ayacucho, 0730 Thurs., US$15, 40 hrs., many passport checks, take sleeping bag and extra food. An alternative road to Lima goes SW from Abancay through Puquío and Nazca; this road is narrow, unpaved but spectacular. Ormeño (office at Plaza de Armas 177, depot, Av. Huáscar 128) to Lima via Abancay and Nazca, Tues., 0700, to Abancay 7 hrs., Puquío 22 hrs., Nazca 27 hrs., US$18, Lima 34-45 hrs. (US$22), also Hidalgo. Señor de Anima, Belén 537, to Lima via Abancay and Nazca (US$14, advertised as 13 hrs., more like 40, poor meal stops), Tues., Wed., Fri., Sun., 0600. By bus to Lima via Arequipa, 1,838 km., 3 days non-stop but the stretch Juliaca-Arequipa is poor, passing through a high arid plain at 4,700 metres before descending into Arequipa valley. Cruz del Sur, Av. Tullumayo, daily at 1800 to Lima via Arequipa, daily at 1900 to Puno, US$7, 11 hrs. San Cristóbal buses are less good (old and overcrowded), US$8, leave Cuzco at 0900, arrive Juliaca about midnight and depart Juliaca at 1000 for Arequipa next day. Better to take a more expensive minibus from one of the companies on the Plaza de Armas.

Rail To Juliaca and Puno, daily, except Sun., at 0730 (though delays common and schedules change) arriving at Juliaca 1630 and Puno 1800. To Juliaca, US$6. To Puno about 12 hrs., US$7.70, 1st, can be purchased on day before leaving, 2nd, US$5.10, can be booked, tickets on sale before, or from 0630; buffet car, comfortable, is 1st class fare plus US$2.60 (meals extra); beware of thieves in 1st class on this train. The advantage of the buffet car is that no one is allowed into it without a reserved seat ticket. Usually at stations the attendant keeps out vendors and doors are locked for security, although you are allowed out if you want to buy something. 1st class to Arequipa US$12, 2nd class US$8, extra on the train, heated buffet car, US$2. Train to Sicuani leaves at 1510, arriving at 2120 (US$3). To Lima, cheaper to go via Arequipa (bus from there to Lima) but make sure that your carriage does not detach at Juliaca. It is reported that the Juliaca-Puno stretch is sometimes closed; colectivos meet the train at Juliaca.

To Anta and Ollantaitambo (US$1) and Machu-Picchu. Trains Cuzco to Machu-Picchu and Quillabamba daily leave 0530 and 1325, arriving at Huarocondo at 0645 and 1575, Machu-Picchu at 0930 and 1755 (take a blanket on the early morning trains, very cold); train to Quillabamba costs US$3, special class (see page 728). The official name for Aguas Calientes station is "Machu Picchu"; the official name for the station at Machu Picchu is "Ruinas". Robberies are frequent on these trains, especially on the switchbacks, but 1st class coaches are locked on the switchback section. The afternoon local train is said to be the less dangerous since it is full of Peruvians, so robbers are less interested. The ticket office opens Mon.-Fri. 0900-1200, 1600-1700, Sat. 0500-0600, 1200-1430, Sun. 1200-1430. You can buy a ticket for the 0600 train the day before (it is not possible to reserve seats for return), the later one must be booked on the day of travelling.

Machu-Picchu trains leave from Estación San Pedro, opposite the market; those for Puno from Av. Sol station. Also, check all times as they change frequently, and that trains are running (especially the afternoon ones).

Air To Lima, Faucett has two flights a day, 0810, 0930, US$41 one way. AeroPerú also has 2 morning flights. There is a Sat. and sometimes Thurs. military flight to Lima, ask for next scheduled flight with Grupo Ocho de la Fuerza Aérea; book at airport several days in advance, be at airport at 0630 to check in at 0700, US$35, unpredictable in the extreme. Cuzco-Juliaca (for Puno), Fri. and Sun. Cuzco-Ayacucho, 2 a week, although this flight can be cancelled or diverted, so be prepared for long delays. AeroPerú and Faucett fly daily to Arequipa, US$24, often delayed. AeroPerú also flies to Iquitos (and on to Miami) Faucett flies to Iquitos, Tues., Thurs., Sat., 0730, US$104, calling at Pucallpa, 2½ hrs. N.B. in summer all flights to Iquitos go via Lima. To Puerto Maldonado: AeroPerú Mon., Wed., Fri., Sun.; Faucett Tues., Thurs., Sat.; airforce (Grupo 8) usually Thurs., US$18, enquire at office of Grupo Ocho de la Fuerza Aérea in airport. A new airport at Quispiquilla is in use. Taxi to airport, US$1.30, bus US$0.10, leaves from Tourist Office on Plaza de Armas. Book return well in advance, especially in the busy season and reconfirm 24 hours before departure. Flights between Lima and Cuzco tend to be heavily booked between July 29 and August 11 because of

PERU 721

school holidays. Shop around at travel agencies for seats if the airlines say they are full. The AeroPerú office is on Av. Sol opposite Faucett office at Av. Sol 391. There is no facility for buying tickets at the airport. There is a limited hotel booking service at the airport. In emergencies, for flights to Lima, try Sra Rossi at Lima-Tours, Plaza de Armas; Faucett are unhelpful in this respect. LAB has a flight to La Paz, leaving Cuzco on Tues. and Sat. at 0945, arriving La Paz at 1130. Flight from La Paz same days, leaves at 0900 (La Paz time), arriving 0845, US$105, cheaper when bought in La Paz.

Warning Cuzco-Lima, high possibility of cancelled flights during wet season; tourists sometimes stranded for 24 hrs. Possible for planes to leave early if bad weather. Sit on right side of aircraft for best view of mountains when flying Cuzco-Lima; it is worth checking in early to get these seats. Both Faucett and AeroPerú are unreliable on bookings: you must reconfirm your tickets but even then you cannot be sure of a seat. Baggage is often lost en route.

There is some magnificent walling in the ruined cult centre of **Sacsayhuamán,** on a hill in the northern outskirts, which is within walking distance (about ½ hr. walk, tiring because of the altitude). Take steps to San Cristóbal church (shorter than via Calle Saphi). The Incaic stones are bigger and even more impressive than at Machu-Picchu; huge rocks weighing up to 300 tons are fitted together with absolute perfection; three walls run parallel for over 360 metres and there are 21 bastions. Sacsayhuamán was thought for centuries to be a fortress, but the layout and architecture suggest a great sanctuary and temple to the Sun, which rises exactly opposite the place previously believed to be the Inca's throne—which was probably an altar, carved out of the solid rock; broad steps lead to it from either side. The hieratic, rather than the military, hypothesis was supported by the discovery in 1982 of the graves of priests: they would have been unlikely to be buried in a fortress. Zig-zags in the boulders round the "throne" are apparently "*chicha* grooves", channels down which maize beer flowed during festivals. Up the hill is an ancient rock slide for children: the Rodadero; near it are many seats cut perfectly into smooth rock. The temple and amphitheatre of Kenko (Quenco), with excellent examples of Inca stone carving, especially inside the large hollowed-out stone that houses an altar, are along the road from Sacsayhuamán to Pisac, past a radio station. On the same road are the Inca fortress of Puku Pukará and the spring shrine of Tambo Machay, which is in excellent condition; water still flows by a hidden channel out of the masonry wall, straight into a little rock pool traditionally known as the Inca's bath, but he would have had to be a pygmy to have used it as such. It seems much more likely that the site was a centre of a water cult.

The gates are manned from about 0700 but you can get in earlier if you wish and definitely try to get there before midday when the tour groups arrive. After seeing 3 sites you can catch truck back along road, 9 km., for US$0.25. Preferably, take the Pisac bus (from Calle Saphi) to Tambo Machay and walk back (downhill) to Cuzco, or taxi US$0.50 to Tambo Machay. Between Kenko and Puku Pukará is Cusillyuioc; caves and Inca tunnels in a hillside (take a torch/flashlight). Taxis to Inca sites outside Cuzco for 3 hrs. cost US$14, not including entry to the sites, and may be hired in the Plaza de Armas. A tour bus to all 4 sites costs US$4

Cuzco is at the W end of the gently sloping Cuzco valley, which stretches 32 km. E as far as Huambutío. This valley, and the partly isolated basin of Anta, NW of Cuzco, are densely populated. Also densely populated is the Urubamba valley, stretching from Sicuani (on the railway to Puno, at 3,960 metres) to the gorge of Torontoi, 600 metres lower, to the NW of Cuzco. There are several ruins of Inca buildings and fortresses in the Cuzco valley itself, especially at Piquillacta (also pre-Inca Huari) on the road to Andahuaylillas (45 mins. by bus from Av. Huáscar and Av. Garcilaso, US$0.10—ask driver to drop you off at the turning), the monkey temple (Templo de los Monos) NW of Piquillacta, the amphitheatre at Moray (three "colosseums", one large, two small, used by the Incas as a sort of plant breeding and acclimatization centre; remote, beautiful and worth visiting—by car to Maras, then 1½-hrs.' walk, or a bumpy 20-km. drive from Chincheros—Urubamba road; it is a 3½-hr. walk from Urubamba), the administrative and storage centre of Colcampata, and Rumicolca, on the shores of Lake Lucre. Interesting textile mill at Lucre village.

Andahuaylillas is a village 32 km. S of Cuzco, with early 17th century church;

722 PERU

beautiful frescoes, splendid doorway and a gilded main altar. Taxis go there as does Oropesa bus (Av. Huáscar, Cuzco) via Tipón, Piquillacta (pre-Inca ruins) and Rumicolca. There are other unexcavated ruins just beyond Andahuaylillas.

John Streather has most kindly given us information about more places south of Cuzco with interesting Inca remains and colonial buildings:

Tipón ruins, between the villages of Saylla and Oropesa, include baths, terraces and a temple complex, accessible from a path leading from just above the last terrace. ***Oropesa*** church contains a fine ornately carved pulpit. ***Huacarpay:*** ruins of the Inca town of Kañaracy, well-preserved, are nearby, reached from a path behind the Albergue. Also nearby are the ruins of Piquillacta, the monkey temple and the wall of Rumicolca. At Lucre, 3 km. from Huacarpay, there are many unexplored ruins; ask the local history teacher, Sr. Hernán Flores Yávar, for details. ***Tinta***, 23 km. from Sicuani, has a church with brilliant gilded interior and an interesting choir vault. Hotel: *Casa Comunal*, F, clean with good food. Frequent buses and trucks to Cuzco. ***Huaro*** has a church whose interior is covered entirely with colourful mural painting. ***Cusipata***, with an Inca gate and wall, is where the ornate bands for the decoration of ponchos are woven.

Raqchi, where the region's great folklore festival is held in June, has the ruins of the temple of Viracocha. There are also small Inca baths in the corner of a field beyond the temple and a straight row of ruined houses by a square. The landscape is extraordinary, blighted by huge piles of black volcanic rocks. John Hemming adds: The Viracocha temple is just visible from the train, looking from the distance like a Roman aqueduct. What remains is the central wall (adobe above, Inca masonry below) of what was probably the largest roofed building ever built by the Incas. On either side of the high wall, great sloping roofs were supported by rows of unusual round pillars, also of masonry topped by adobe. Nearby is a complex of barracks-like buildings and round storehouses. This was the most holy shrine to the creator god Viracocha, being the site of a miracle in which he set fire to the land—hence the lava flow nearby. (San Cristóbal bus to Raqchi from Av. Huáscar, Cuzco every hour, US$0.90, 4 hrs. Nearest hotel is in Tinta.) (See also page 717, under Folklore.).

Pacarijtambo is a good starting point for the 3-4 hr. walk to the ruins of Mankallajta, which contain good examples of Inca stonework. From there, one can walk to Pumaorco, a high rock carved with steps, seats and a small puma in relief on top; below are more Inca ruins. From Pumaorco walk back to the nearby hamlet of Mollepata (bus from Cuzco, US$1) and ask the schoolteacher the way to Pacarijtambo (a 2-3 hr. walk). One may seek lodging for the night in Pacarijtambo at the house of the Villacorta family and leave for Cuzco by truck the next morning. On the way back, one passes the caves of Tambo Toco, where the legend says that the four original Inca brothers emerged into the world.

Acomayo is a pretty village (*Pensión Aguirre*), which has a chapel with mural paintings of the fourteen Incas. From Acomayo, one can walk to Huáscar and from there to Pajlia; a climb beyond leads one through very impressive scenery. The canyons of the upper Apurímac are vast beyond imagination, great cliffs drop thousands of metres into dizzying chasms and huge rocks balance menacingly overhead. The ruins of Huajra Pucará lie near Pajlia; they are small, but in an astonishing position. John Hemming adds that the church at Checacupe is very fine, with good paintings and a handsome carved altar rail.

Paucartambo, on E slope of Andes, reached from Cuzco by a good road (one way on alternate days). In this remote though now popular tourist town is held the Fiesta de Carmen, usually on July 16, 17, 18, with masked dances. (*Fiesta* dates should be checked in Cuzco.) A family will usually provide lunch and with luck a bed for the night; to be certain of accommodation, camping is probably the best alternative. Private car hire for round trip on July 16: US$25, or the Tourist Office in Cuzco arranges an overnight trip (you sleep in the bus) for US$10.

From Paucartambo one can go 44 km. to Tres Cruces, along the Pilcopata road, turning left after 25 km.; Sr. Cáceres in Paucartambo will arrange trip. Tres Cruces gives a wonderful view of the sunrise and private cars leave Paucartambo between 0100 and 0200 to see it; they may give you a lift. One can walk from Paucartambo to the *chullpas* of Machu Cruz in about an hour, or to the *chullpas* of Pijchu (take a guide). Nearby is the Inca fortress of Huatojto, which has admirable doorways and stonework.

Travellers in the Cuzco area with plenty of time can visit the National Park of **Manu**, the biggest nature reservation in Peru, covering a huge jungle area around the River Manu. To go there, one must get permission from the Park's office, Jirón H. Capac, 146, Cuzco. Trucks leave Cuzco every Mon., Wed., and Fri. morning to Shintuya, via Paucartambo and Pilcopata. At Shintuya, a boat must be rented for a 2-day journey down the Río Alto Madre de Dios and then up the Río Manu to the Park's entrance at Palcitza (up to US$400 for 2 weeks). Buy all supplies (including food for the boatmen and petrol) in Cuzco. Lambayeque Tours organize expensive 2-week trips which do not

PERU 723

spend much time in the Park. Expediciones Manu, Procuradores 372, Cuzco, offer week-long trips beginning on the first Sundays of June, July and August (or you may be able to join a pre-organized tour), for US$500. It takes a day's driving and two on the river to reach the Reserve. At Tres Cruces in the Park there is an empty bungalow that may be used for the night. The National Park office at Salvación can also arrange your entry permit and with luck you might catch a lift in with park staff, or they will know of other people going in (*Hostal Salvación*, F, clean, basic bathrooms, swimming pool). Transport to Shintuya infrequent but possible although most boats are already fully laden and rarely carry tourists. *Quinta Erika*, small jungle lodge run by Sra. Gerlach, a German woman who has lived in the jungle since 1951, tranquil, few bugs, good food, animals, boat trips can be arranged with prior notice, transport from Cooperativa landing, 3 km. from Salvación.

Pisac, 30 km. N of Cuzco, is at the bottom of the Urubamba valley; high above it, on the mountainside, is a superb Inca fortress (admission by combined entrance ticket, see page 714, the ruins close at 1700). The masonry is better than at Machu-Picchu, the terraces more extensive and better preserved. When you climb it (a must), remember that there are 3 hill fortifications, but the third is the fortress proper, in which the actual temple is built: so go on to it and get the glorious view from the top. There is a 10-km. motor road up to the level of the ruins, upstream from Pisac town and then up a valley to the S of the spur containing the ruins. From the parking lot, enter along Inca roads and through Inca gates, seeing the fine view of terraces (which can be reached quite easily from the town). Quite a lot of walking is involved. The central part of the ruins is the Intihuatana group of temples and rock outcrops in the most magnificent Inca masonry. Above on the hilltop reached by a path along a vertiginous cliff are residential groups; there is a large Inca cemetery in caves on the valley opposite to the north; the curving group of houses called Pisallacta below the Intihuatana group; and more buildings, some with curious round towers, others of good Inca adobe, on the steep hillside above the town. It takes about 25 minutes to walk down. There is a path going right round the mountain, behind the main ruins; it has two tunnels. It takes 1-2 hours to walk.

Pisac has a Sun. morning market, described as totally touristy and expensive, after the arrival of tourist buses around 1000; it starts at 0900 and is usually over by midday. There are picturesque Indian processions to Mass. Pisac has another, poorer market on Thurs. morning. You can take in the market, then take taxi up to ruins, explore them, walk down and get last bus or truck back to Cuzco by 1630. You can continue the Sun. morning tour to Pisac along the Urubamba to Ollantaitambo, with lunch at the Tourist Hotel in Urubamba (US$4.25); Pisac Tours, Plaza de Armas, Cuzco, arrange trip for US$6 p.p. Splendid scenery. Apart from Sun., there are very few tourists. An alternative for lunch is the restaurant on the square in **Yukay** (open-air, good buffet and local dishes). On the N side of the square is the adobe palace built for Sayri Túpac (Manco's son) when he emerged from Vilcabamba in 1558. A pleasant old hotel, the *Alhambra 3*, B, is in Yukay, rather overpriced but very pretty and ancient. In Yukay monks sell fresh milk, ham, eggs and other dairy produce from their farm on the hillside. The tour by taxi costs US$40-45.

Pisac Hotels *Albergue Chongo Chico*, D, owned by Czechoslovakian, slightly decayed, also restaurant, good meal, most of the produce home-grown, à la carte about US$6, electricity only 1700-2400, ask owner to start generator at other times, cold water; camping allowed in garden; *Turistas*, E, pleasant, English spoken, meals US$5; *Hostal Pisac* on the square, F, above a handicraft shop, comfortable, breakfast only except on Sundays, good ceramics. The woman who owns the flour mill rents rooms for US$1.30 p.p. *Roma*, near the bridge by the Kodak sign, F, basic, quiet, cold shower, dreadful; camping allowed in its grounds for US$0.45 p.p. No good restaurants in town; better to take a packed lunch from Cuzco.

Buses Cuzco-Pisac road is paved. Early morning buses on Sunday, every ten min., from 0540 to 0700 (queue early or catch them on Huáscar before they fill up), colectivos to Pisac from Cuzco; they return all afternoon until 1715 and are always full. Fare US$0.70; try and book the previous day if possible. Tourist minibus leaves Cuzco Plaza de Armas outside Cathedral daily for Pisac and Ollantaitambo if there are more than five passengers, US$5 return. Minibus tours also Cuzco, Pisac, Urubamba, Ollantaitambo, US$10; taxi for this route, including Chincheros, US$30. Colectivos to Pisac and Ollantaitambo leave when full from Calle Recoleta, from 0600, Cuzco (past Calle Pumapacchai), to Pisac 45 mins., US$0.40, to Ollantaitambo, 2½ hrs., US$1. Return fare by truck, US$0.40, over 1 hr. Taxi fare (return) from Cuzco to the fortress costs US$8 and includes a visit to the market. Tours by agencies to Pisac on Thurs. and Sun. (market days) only. Two buses daily to

724 PERU

Urubamba. Bus stops in Pisac are brief, make sure you get on or off the bus quickly. Try hitching opposite the police checkpoint.

Calca Beyond Pisac (18 km.) is the village of Calca (Hotels: *Alojamiento Grau*, basic; *Alojamiento Alvarez*; *Alojamiento Central*, F, basic. Restaurants: *Sondar*, *Bolívar*, on Plaza; *Moreñitas* and *Café Calqueñita*, near post office). Mineral baths at Minas Maco (½ hr. walk along the Urubamba) and Machacama (8 km. E of Calca). If one continues past Minas Maco, one bears right up a small footpath leading by a clump of trees; the first house one comes to after crossing a small stream and climbing a hill is a precolumbian ruin. 3 km. beyond Machacama are the Inca ruins of Arquasmarca. The ruins of a small Inca town, Huchuy Cuzco, are across the river Vilcanota, and up a stiff climb. There are a two-storey house, paved with flat stones, and a large stone reservoir at Huchuy Cuzco. Bus to Pisac, or to Urubamba, US$0.50; bus to Cuzco, US$0.80. Market day: Sun. It is a two-day hike from Cuzco to Calca, via Sacsayhuamán, Kenko, Puka Pukará, Tambo Machay and Huchuy Cuzco; there are many places to camp, but take water. Between Calca and Quillabamba the road is narrow and subject to landslides.

Zurite is a little-known village north of Cuzco; Inca terraces of Patapata are only about an hour's walk from the village's main square. The construction of these terraces represents a Herculean effort as all of the earth is said to have been brought from elsewhere. A canal was built to bring water from the mountains. (John Streather.)

John Hemming recommends visiting to the W of Cuzco:

Chincheros; with an attractive church built on an Inca temple; recent excavations there have revealed many Inca walls and terraces. (On combined entrance ticket, see page 714.) It has become very tourist-oriented but nonetheless the Sunday market and Indian mass are more authentic than at Pisac (there is a small market on Thurs.). *Hotel Inca*, F, with restaurant; *Albergue Chincheros*.

At the market, there is a varied selection of handicrafts, including weaving, pottery and alpaca goods (nothing is cheap). Celebrations are held in Chincheros on September 8 (the day of the Virgin).

A new road Cuzco-Urubamba has been completed, which has cut the travelling time to Chincheros to 40 mins. from Cuzco by bus, leaving about 0700 from Av. Arcopata on Sun. mornings, US$0.60. Also colectivos from Av. Arcopata. Taxi, US$20 for 5-hr. trip. There is also a scenic path to Chincheros from Urubamba, about 4-5 hrs.

76 km. from Cuzco on the Abancay road, 2 km. before Limatambo (accommodation in *Albergue*, F; nice restaurant hidden from road by trees), at Hacienda Tarahuasi, a few hundred metres from the road, is a very well-preserved Inca temple platform, with 28 tall niches, and a long stretch of fine polygonal masonry.

100 km. from Cuzco along the Abancay road is the exciting descent into the Apurímac canyon, near the former Inca suspension bridge that inspired Thornton Wilder's *The Bridge of San Luis Rey*.

Also, 153 km. along the road to Abancay from Cuzco, near Carahuasi (restaurant on main road into town; camping possible on the football pitch, ask police), is the stone of Sahuite, carved with animals, houses, etc., which appears to be a relief map of an Indian village. (Unfortunately, "treasure hunters" have defaced the stone.) There are other interesting carvings in the area around the Sahuite stone.

For US$40 a taxi can be hired for a whole day (ideally Sun.) to take you to Cachimayo, Chincheros, Maras, Urubamba, Ollantaitambo, Calca, Lamay, Coya, Pisac, Tambo Machay, Kenko and Sacsayhuamán. (If you wish to explore this area on your own, Road Map (*Hoja de ruta*) No. 10 from the Automóvil Club del Perú is an excellent guide.)

N of Chincheros, on a new direct road from Cuzco via Chincheros, is **Urubamba;** one can stay at the *Hotel de Turistas*, E, clean, hot water, poor service, bungalows with neglected garden and swimming pool; the *Centro Vacacional Urubamba*, cabins (some with kitchen, must take own stove), 2 pools, E and F; *Hostal Naranjachayoc*, C, with antique furniture and swimming pool, 20 mins. walk from town, recommended, friendly, accommodating, will help with any problems, very clean and well-stocked restaurant and bar, even in low-season, car can be parked in locked patio, *Hotel Urubamba*, F, pleasant; *Hostal Vera*, beyond the Tourist Hotel; and *Hotel Retamanioj*, and *Restaurant Quinta los Geranios*, excellent lunch for US$3 with more than enough food; *Restaurant Norteñito*; *Comedor Aries* and *Andes*, both on Plaza; pleasant country surroundings. The Machu-Picchu tourist train can be caught at Pachar, about 20 minutes' drive away, at 0830; no fare reduction. Bus Cuzco-Urubamba, US$0.50.

Joanna Codrington writes: 6 km. from Urubamba on the Ollantaitambo road is the village of Tarabamba, where a footbridge crosses the Río Vilcanota. If one turns right after the bridge one comes to Piychinjoto, a tumbled-down village built under an overhanging cliff. Also, just over the bridge and to the left of a small, walled cemetery is a salt stream. If one follows this (there is a footpath) one comes to Salinas, a small village below which are a mass of terraced Inca salt pans, still in operation. A very spectacular sight.

The Cuzco-Machu Picchu train reaches the heights N of the city by a series of switchbacks (beware of thieves boarding train here) and then descends to the

PERU 725

floor of the Anta basin, with its herds of cattle. (In Anta itself, *Restaurant Dos de Mayo* is good; bus to Anta, US$0.25., felt trilby hats on sale). The railway goes through the Anta canyon (10 km.), and then, at a sharp angle, the Urubamba canyon, and descends along the river valley, flanked by high cliffs and peaks.

The railway and a 53-km. road also go to

Ollantaitambo, 70 km., a small town (alt.: 2,800 metres) built on and out of the stones of an Inca town, "which is a fine example of Inca *canchas* or corral enclosures, almost entirely intact. The so-called Baño de la Ñusta (bath of the princess) is of grey granite, and is in a small field between the town and the temple fortress. (Some 200 metres behind the Baño de la Ñusta along the face of the mountain are some small ruins known as Inca Misanca, believed to have been a small temple or observatory. A series of steps, seats and niches have been carved out of the cliff. There is also a water canal at shoulder level, some 6 inches deep, cut out of the sheer rock face.) The flights of terraces leading up above the town are superb, and so are the curving terraces following the contours of the rocks overlooking the Urubamba. These terraces were successfully defended by Manco Inca's warriors against Hernando Pizarro in 1536. Manco Inca built the defensive wall above the site and another wall closing the Yucay valley against attack from Cuzco, still visible on either side of the valley. Visitors should also note the Inca masonry channelling the river and the piers of the bridge of Ollantaitambo. (Entering Ollantaitambo from Pisac, the road is built along the long wall of 100 niches. Note the inclination of the wall: it leans towards the road. Since it was the Incas' practice to build with the walls leaning towards the interiors of the buildings, it has been deduced that the road, much narrower then, was built inside a succession of buildings.) The site opens at 0700.

"The temple itself was started by Pachacuti, using Colla Indians from Lake Titicaca—hence the similarities of the monoliths facing the central platform with the Tiahuanaco remains. The Colla are said to have deserted half-way through the work, which explains the many unfinished blocks lying about the site" - (John Hemming). Admission by combined entrance ticket, which can be bought at the site. The Sunday following Inti Raymi, there is a colourful festival, the Ollantay-Raymi. The guide book *Ollantaitambo* by Víctor Angles Vargas is available in Cuzco bookshops.

Accommodation *Parador Turístico*, off main street between Plaza and ruins, for groups by reservation but will sometimes take other groups or couples if not booked up, E-F, all renovated in 1985; offers travel info. and horseback/walking tours; for reservations write to María S. Martínez, Parador Turístico de Ollantaitambo, Cuzco, Peru or get your Cuzco hotel to phone the Ollantaitambo exchange as the Parador has no phone as yet. Russ Bentley writes: °a veritable oasis of comfort and excellent food (superb Italian cuisine)". *Albergue*, near the railway station, for groups by reservation only, but can occasionally be persuaded to take in stranded travellers, closed in the off-season; *Alojamiento El Tambo*, also known as *Alojamiento Yavar*, above main square, G, basic, friendly, has information on riding in the area, horses for hire at US$3 a day; *Hotel Panificadora*, G, tantalizing smell of fresh bread, very hard beds, basic, between main plaza and ruins.

Camping possible in eucalyptus grove, ½ km. from town, and along the river between the town and the railway station.

Horses can be hired for US$3 per day; a recommended trek is to La Marca, a gentle day's ride along the beautiful river valley; ask in the square for details.

Restaurants *Restaurant Ollantay* on Plaza de Armas, good. The *Café Alcázar* opposite *Parador Turístico* also has some rooms to let, G, hard beds, with breakfast at extra cost, good, cheap food, English spoken; *El Parador*, in converted barn, down from main square towards ruins, good pasta and garlic bread; *Restaurante Tanta Wasi*, by railway, has two rooms to let, run by Jaime and Pilar Paz. In restaurants, check your bill carefully.

Transport For those travelling by car, it is recommended to leave the car in Ollantaitambo (or the station previous on the road from Cuzco) for a day excursion by train to Machu-Picchu. (Park car in front of the local police station at Ollantaitambo. Much safer there than parked in Cuzco for US$1 a day. The local train starts here at 0800 and 1630 for Machu-Picchu.) Hourly bus from Calle Recoleta, Cuzco, 2½ hrs., US$1.15, to Urubamba, to Ollantaitambo, also to Pisac. Bus to Cuzco on Sat. at 0800 and 1200. Tourist minibus from outside Cuzco Cathedral to Pisac, Ollantaitambo, Cuzco, daily if over 5 passengers, US$5 (taxi tour costs US$40). Taxi to Cuzco, US$12. Train from Aguas Calientes costs US$0.80, 2 hrs.; to Cuzco, US$1, at 1000 and 1730. Bus to Urubamba, US$0.50 (truck US$0.15), from where one can return to Cuzco via Calca; Urubamba-Calca (21 km.), US$0.50.

A major excavation project has been carried out since 1977 under the direction of Ann Kendall in the **Cusichaca** valley, 26 km. from Ollantaitambo at the intersection of the Inca routes. (The Inca fort, Huillca Raccay, was excavated in 1978-80, and work is now concentrated on Llactapata, a site of domestic buildings).

From Ollantaitambo one can walk to the Inca Trail in about 5 hrs.: follow the railway in the direction of Machu Picchu until you come to a village where you can cross the river; climb up to a path that runs parallel to the river. This is an original Inca trail (still in use) that leads to Llactapata on the Inca Trail.

Pinculluna, the mountain above Ollantaitambo, can be climbed with no mountaineering experience, although there are some difficult stretches—allow 2-3 hours going up. Marvellous views from the summit.

The **Inca Trail** hike to Machu-Picchu makes a spectacular 3 to 5 day hike (take it slowly to appreciate it fully). It runs from Km. 88, Quoriwayrachi (about

---

VIDA TOURS
THE PERUVIAN ADVENTURES

Calle Ladrillos 425 San Cristobal CUSCO Tel. 227750
TELEX 52003 ó 52004 PE PB CUSCO
(At.: VIDA TOURS Tel. 227750)
WEEKLY DEPARTURES:
TREKS, RIVER RUNNING TRIPS
WILDLIFE SAFARIS AND OVERLANDING

PERU 727

2,600 metres), a point immediately after the first tunnel 22 km. beyond Ollantaitambo station. (Train to Km. 88 is US$1.10 first, US$0.90 2nd. Be ready to get out at Km. 88; easy to pass it.) A sturdy suspension bridge has now been built over the Urubamba River. An entrance ticket (US$8, US$4 for students) for the trail and Machu-Picchu must be bought at Km. 88. The trail is rugged and steep (beware of landslides), at one stage traversing a 4,200-metre high pass, but the magnificent views compensate for any weariness which may be felt. It is cold at night, however, and weather conditions change rapidly, so it is important to take not only strong footwear and warm clothing but also food, water, insect repellant, a supply of plastic bags, coverings, a good sleeping bag, a stove for preparing hot food and drink to ward off the cold at night. A stove using paraffin (kerosene) is preferable, as fuel can be bought in small quantities in markets, whereas camping gas is expensive and scarce. A tent is essential because walkers who have not taken adequate equipment have been known to die of exposure; caves mentioned on some maps are little better than overhangs, and are not sufficient shelter to sleep in. The trail is crowded in July and August. In the wet season (November-April) you don't have to worry about taking drinking water. At Puyopatamarca, on the Trail, there is a "tourist bathroom" where water can be collected (but purify it before drinking). Next place with water is Wiñay-Wayna (where there is a newly-built "tourist complex" with bunk beds (G p.p.), showers and a small restaurant, food and drink expensive), and then none till Machu-Picchu, where water supplies are turned off at 1530. A little-used variation to the Trail is to get off the train at Chilca, some 12 km. beyond Ollantaitambo, cross the bridge and walk 10 km. along the Urubamba River to join the trail at a point above Km. 88. This adds a day to the journey, but has the advantage of giving the body an opportunity to acclimatize itself before the very strenuous climb to the top of the first pass. Camping is possible on the bluff overlooking Llactapata and Km. 88 and this is an ideal starting point for the climb to the first pass, putting several hours between you and the other hikers who reach Km. 88 by train after 0900. **Warning** We have had a number of reports of armed robbery on the Inca Trail, the culprits being variously described as Sendero Luminoso or organized gangsters from Cuzco. For this reason alone, do not go singly or in couples, and if possible stay close to a tour group; avoid the July-August high season. Camp away from the sites on the main trail, and leave all valuables back in Cuzco.

All the necessary equipment can be rented from Sigui Tours (Portal de Panes 123, Plaza de Armas, Cuzco) who also sell good maps of the Trail and area, from Walking Tours, on Plaza de Armas, Portal Comercio, friendly, new equipment, or Vicuña Tours (cheapest) on the Plaza de Armas, Portal Comercio 141, good selection of equipment, this is essential. If you can't get a map at the tourist office, try for US$0.60 at the Club Andino, Calle Procuradores, or at Copias Vélez, Plaza San Francisco, Cuzco. Try to get the map prepared by the curator of Machu-Picchu Museum; it shows best sleeping places and drinking water. The guide Alberto Miori from Inca Trails is recommended, with many good reports. Remember there are no houses you can rush to if you get into difficulties; check carefully all equipment you hire before starting out. Robbers in the villages are on the increase.

Susan Whittlesey and Michael Young have prepared an excellent booklet on the Inca civilization and the Inca Trail (including a superb map), which is available for US$4 from Cin Co., 2912 E. 5th Avenue, Denver, Colorado 80206, USA.

The walk to Huayllabamba, following the Cusichaca river, needs about 3 hrs. and isn't too arduous. If planning a 2-4 day trip, carry on past Huayllabamba, which has become notorious for robberies. There is a camping place about an hr. ahead, at Llulluchayoc and another before the ascent to the first pass, Warmiwañuska, about 4 hrs. on in a meadow (highly recommended) 1½-2 hrs. from the summit. From Huayllabamba to the meadows is often discouragingly steep. Following the right path demands intuition more than orienteering knowhow, and the forest is occasionally very thick—but you should emerge towards 1600 hrs.

Leave early next day. The ascent to the first pass (4,200 metres) is the most taxing part of the walk. Afterwards take the path downhill, along left side of valley. You could camp by a stream at the bottom, or else about 80 % of the way up the second pass (a much easier climb) at Runkuracay (3,800 metres), an Inca ruin, where there are huts and caves. Magnificent views near the summit in clear weather. Good overnight place is past the Inca ruins at Sayajmarca (3,600 metres), about an hr. on after the top of the second pass.

Muddy jungle terrain leads gently up to the third pass, only about 2-2½ hrs.' walk, the gradient blissfully gentle. Near the top there's a spectacular view of the Urubamba river and the valley to the right. You descend to Inca ruins at Puyopatamarca, well worth a long visit.

From there steps go downhill to Wiñay-Wayna, reached by forking off to the right (it's marked by a sign) near the pylons, 3-4 hrs. or so on from Puyopatamarca. (A tourist complex has been built at the fork: there is no road. There is a shop selling drinks and nearby there is a shed where you can sleep if the weather is really bad, but better to go on to Wiñay-Wayna, 20 mins.) The ruins of Wiñay-Wayna are in an impressive location. The path from this point goes more or less level through jungle. You need about 2 hrs. to walk to the Intipunku (this part is littered very badly), where there's a magnificent view of Machu-Picchu, especially at dawn, with the sun alternately in and out, clouds sometimes obscuring the ruins, sometimes leaving them clear. Get to Machu-Picchu as early as possible, preferably before 0830 for best views but in any case before the tourist train arrives at 1030.

Four days would make a comfortable trip (though much depends on the weather) and you would not find yourself too tired to enjoy what you see. Walking the Trail has the advantage of putting Machu-Picchu in its true context: not a "lost city", but an integral part of a heavily populated valley. By the same token Machu-Picchu loses some of its uniqueness; the architecture and scenery are often better at several points along the trail. **N.B** It is not allowed to walk back along the trail, and you may not take backpacks into Machu-Picchu.

You can walk back from Aguas Calientes to Km. 107, cross the swing bridge from where Wiñay-Wayna can be reached by a switch-back path in 1½ hrs., back to Machu-Picchu. This round trip takes 5 hrs. Alternatively, coming from Cuzco, leave the train at km. 107 and walk the last few hours of the trail; you will reach Machu-Picchu just as the day visitors are leaving, but will have to walk the hour down to Aguas Calientes to stay the night. You can also leave the train at the second stop after Km. 88, called Cedrobamba (a brief stop), and walk from there to the swing bridge (1 hr.)

Littering along the Trail is a serious problem as 5,000 people are now using it each year. The Earth Preservation Fund now sponsors an annual cleanup July-August: volunteers should write to EPF, Inca Trail Project, Box 7545, Ann Arbor, Michigan 48107, USA.

Machu-Picchu, 42 km. from Ollantaitambo by rail (2,280 metres), is a complete city, set on a saddle of a high mountain with terraced slopes falling away to the Urubamba river rushing in great hairpin bends below. It is in a comparatively good state of preservation because the Spaniards never found it. For centuries it was buried in jungle, until Hiram Bingham stumbled upon it in 1911. It was then explored by an archaeological expedition sent by Yale.

The ruins—staircases, terraces, temples, palaces, towers, fountains, the famous sundial and the Museo de Sitio below the ruins—require at least a day—some say two (take an insect-repellant). The mountain overlooking the site, Huayna Picchu (on which there are also some ruins), has steps to the top for a superlative view of the whole but it is not for those who get giddy (don't leave the path); the walk up takes about 60 minutes but the steps are dangerous after bad weather (it is only possible to walk up in the morning and you must register at a hut on the trail; guards prevent you after 1300). The other trail to Huayna Picchu, down near the Urubamba, via the Temple of the Moon, in two caves, one above the other, with superb Inca niches inside (sadly blemished by idiots' graffiti), can only be undertaken with a guide to the Temple of the Moon, leaving Machu-Picchu at 0900; he will clear the path and kill poisonous snakes. After the Temple you may proceed alone to Huayna Picchu; round trip about 4 hours. An almost equally good view can be had from the trail behind the Tourist Hotel.

How to get there The most convenient way of seeing the ruins is to pay anything between US$25-60 (including lunch at Tourist Hotel) to an agency for a 1-day guided trip from Cuzco to Machu-Picchu by tourist train, which leaves at 0800 each day, enabling tourists to arrive at Machu-Picchu at 1015, visit the ruins and leave Machu-Picchu at 1600, arriving in Cuzco about 1930. The tourist train stops at Ollantaitambo. A day's round trip, including train and bus return fares and entrance fee, can be booked at the San Pedro station for US$15. Train journey takes 3½ -4 hours and costs US$5 each way, without lunch. Tickets may be bought one day in advance (returns available); office open 0600-0820, 1000-1100, 1500-1700; make sure you buy a single if staying overnight. A diesel railcar (autovagón), 1st class, leaves Cuzco 0700, returns 1505, 5hrs. an hour later. The local trains from Cuzco leave at 0530 and 1325, arrive Machu-Picchu 0930 and 1755. In the dry season there is also a night train from Cuzco at 2200, April-December. The fare is US$1.75 each way first class, US$1.35 each way second, though this class is very crowded; price does not include bus ride up to Machu-Picchu and entrance fee. The front coach of local trains is "special class" where meals are served and all seats numbered (US$2), book one day in advance in morning for the early train only (see page 720). The local trains return at 0800 and 1400, but are unreliable (on Sunday only the tourist train runs). Take a drinking mug on the train. Arrive early at station, and you will have to fight if you want a seat (1st class has reserved seat numbers on the way up, but not on return journey), particularly the left-hand side facing engine going (right on return) which gives a better view. Beware of thieves (bag-slitting is extremely common), particularly at the switch-backs when they can jump on and off the train (1st class coaches are locked on this stretch), and on the Urubamba stretch where there are many short tunnels. Police presence has been stepped up at the stations and on the trains. Buses from the station to Machu-Picchu start at 0800 (0630 buses for workers only) and meet both local and tourist trains, and charge US$1.25 each way for the trip to the ruins and back. There are theoretically enough seats on the buses for all the train passengers, but in practice you will have to wait for a seat (beware of drivers asking inflated prices). Last bus down to station goes at about 1500 (if you wish to stay longer, demand a single bus ticket). You can walk up in 1½ hrs. to 2 hrs., and down in 1 hr., if you have no luggage; there is a short-cut for walkers, said to take 45 mins. to 1 hr. Luggage can be deposited safely at the site entrance for US$0.45, where there is a self-service restaurant) but not at the station, nor at the museum (on opposite side of river from station, open Tues.-Sun. 1030-1530). Cost of entry to the ruins, US$5 (students, US$3); they are open 0630-1700. Tickets are valid for two days if you ask for them to be stamped appropriately. For the student reduction for groups, apply at Casa de Cultura. Post Office at Machu-Picchu station has special franking marks.

The cheapest way to visit the site is to take the "Indian train" from Cuzco at 1325, or a single ticket on the tourist train, stay overnight at one of the hotels offering basic accommodation at Aguas Calientes (see below), 1½ km. back along the railway (the town has electricity 24 hrs a day).
Note: In the rainy season trains are often delayed by landslides.

Permission to enter the ruins before 0630 to watch the sunrise over the Andes, which is a spectacular experience, may be obtained from the Instituto Nacional de Cultura in Colegio San Bernardo, Cuzco (near La Merced), but it is often possible if you talk to the guards at the gate. Sr. Quispe, a guard for many years (and of royal Inca descent), is friendly and informative.

Mon. and Fri. are bad days because there is usually a crowd of people on guided tours who are going or have been to Pisac market on Sun., and too many people all want lunch at the same time. Food is available around the station.

Camping Not permitted on the site, nor on Huayna-Picchu; may be possible on football field downstream of the station, or Aguas Calientes. Beware of thieves.

Accommodation and Food In season the Tourist Hotel at the ruins is heavily booked during the week; try Sunday night as other tourists find Pisac market a greater attraction. Book well in advance, through a reliable agency, or at the Enturperú office in Lima or Cuzco in this way you can spend 24 hrs. at the site. Often, however, though reportedly booked up weeks in advance, there are cancellations and you can obtain a room on arrival. Rooms with shower and breakfast (no singles) A, US$5 for meals in excellent self-service cafeteria. There is electricity and water 24 hours a day. Service and honesty not always good, but as they state in the English version of the rules card: "The grandeur of nature is such, that the conniving of man is overcome." The Tourist Hotel often does not have intis for exchange, make sure you have enough before setting out for Machu-Picchu; but the hotel will accept American Express travellers' cheques. Only hotel residents may eat in the restaurant; others have to use the self-service counter outside. It is recommended that you take food and soft drinks with you; prices are high.

At **Aguas Calientes**, the *Albergue Juvenil*, constructed by Copesco, the state tourism agency for the region, has 200 beds in dormitories and dining facilities (US$3 for a meal), for travellers and family groups, clean, comfortable, hot water, noisy with students, laundry, recommended, G p.p. (no IYHA card needed). *Hospedaje Los Camiones*, F, with bath, electric light from 1830-2200, basic, but clean; *Hostal Qoñi Unu* (run by William and Margarita Kaiser, who will act as guides to surrounding areas), third house to left of church, F, cheap, hot water, friendly, laundry and cooking facilities, money exchange, meals served (including 0530 breakfast), luggage stored, new huts built; *Hotel Sucre*, F, cheap and dingy; *Hostal Machu-Picchu*, F, in communal dormitory, clean, safe, rooms also F, quiet, friendly (esp. Wilber, owner's son, with travel info.), being extended, grocery store, recommended; *El Refugio*, cheap, good food, also *Samaná* and *Aiko*, recommended. At the *pizzería*, slow service, but reasonable food; *El Mirador*, run by Manuel, "the prince of the primus", near station, good food, friendly staff and cat, open 0500 for early starters to Machu-Picchu; *Huayna Picchu*, good value restaurant beside railway line. Despite reports that the standard of food and hygiene has improved, you are warned to be careful about what you eat and if in doubt about your constitution, take your own food. It may be difficult to get a room, so be prepared to sleep on a floor. Two new swimming pools have been built. The thermal baths (a communal pool), a 15-minute walk from the town, are particularly welcome to those who have walked the Inca Trail; officially they close at 2200 (US$0.40 per bath, no soap, bathing suits required, take torch if going by night, baths rather murky, but reported cleaner in morning).

From Machu-Picchu one can take the Inca Trail, which climbs up behind the Tourist Hotel, back to (2 hours' walk) the Inca settlement of Wiñay-Wayna, a village of roofless but otherwise well-preserved Inca houses where a basic "Complejo Turístico" for visitors has been opened. About 30 mins. along a well-marked trail on the other side of Machu-Picchu ruins is the famous Inca bridge. Both walks give spectacular views of the Urubamba River and the thickly wooded mountains, and the butterflies and flowers are beautiful. The tombs at Chaskapata, near Machu-Picchu, have recently been opened.

730   PERU

Note   Advisable to purchase paperback edition of *Lost City of the Incas* by Hiram Bingham, in Lima or Cuzco (more expensive), or *A Walking Tour of Machu-Picchu* (recommended) by Pedro Sueldo Nava, available in Cuzco. Choice of guide books in Cuzco much improved. The Tourist Hotel also sells guides, although at a rather inflated price. (The South American Explorers' Club in Lima has detailed information on walks in this area, and so has the Bradts' book.)

The railway goes on 79 km. through Chaullay to **Quillabamba** (24,000 people) in the Urubamba Valley at 1,054 metres, where there is a Dominican mission.

The train follows the Urubamba River much of the way from Machu-Picchu, and the improvised station at Quillabamba is right on the river. One crosses a foot bridge put up by the Lions Club and then climbs up a 100-odd flight of stairs to reach the town. Lots of colourful plants growing, the main plaza especially well decorated. Many *heladerías*, much needed in the heat, the best on the northwest corner of the square. Not many attractions for the tourist, but a place to unwind, bask in the sun or take a swim in the river, though ask the locals where the safe stretches are, as the current is quite rapid in places. Clean market building, and a football stadium.

Hotels *Don Carlos*, D-E, good, friendly, good, if limited meals, transport to station extra; *Hostal Alto Urubamba*, F, on Dos de Mayo, clean, good, with bath, or without, expensive restaurant; *Quillabamba* (unmarked entrance next to Quillabamba Autos behind market), roof terrace restaurant, recommended, D; *Urusayhua*, near market, F; *Progreso*, near market, F; *Hostal la Convención*, Plaza de Armas, F; *Comercio*, Libertad, D, with bath; *Hostal San Antonio*, cheap; *San Martín*, dirty, F; *Cusco*, very nice, E, with bath; *Thomas*, cheap; *Barrenechea*, cheap; *Turistas* expensive, though nice and modern, opposite the market, without sign. A good restaurant is on Dos de Mayo on the corner, in the same block as the *Hostal Alto Urubamba*, good inexpensive food (*almuerzo* and *comida* cost US$0.55 for three-course meal); though the best restaurants are to be found on Plaza de Armas.

Transport   The morning train from Quillabamba leaves at 0530 and arrives at Machu-Picchu about 0815, giving you 2½ hours at the ruins before the invasion from Cuzco starts with the arrival of the tourist train, but you may have to walk up: the buses may not be operating at that hour. Another train leaves Quillabamba at 1305, 6½ hrs. to Cuzco. There is a night train at 2200, which passes Machu-Picchu at 0100, arriving Cuzco 0500. Tickets must be bought one day in advance, from Enafer office off main plaza.

No buses to Cuzco but trucks go in the daytime, US$2. The road between Ollantaitambo and Quillabamba passes through Peña, a place of great beauty with snowy peaks already appearing on either side of the valley (taxis are very reluctant to go there). Once out of Peña, the climb to the pass begins in earnest—on the right is a huge glacier. Soon on the left, Salcantay begins to appear in all its huge and snowy majesty. After endless zig-zags and breathtaking views, one reaches Puerto Málaga (rudimentary *pensión*). The descent to the valley is alarming, highlighted by a series of dangerous curves. The hillsides are covered in lichen and Spanish moss. At Chaullay, the road meets the railway to Quillabamba, Machu-Picchu and Cuzco. One can drive from Chaullay to Santa Teresa (hot springs, ask the locals) from where the railway goes to Machu-Picchu, and can hike to Lucma and the village of Vilcabamba, from where one can descend to the valley of the River Concebidayoc where one comes to Espíritu Pampa, the site of the Vilcabamba Vieja ruins, a vast pre-Inca ruin with a neo-Inca overlay in deep jungle at 1,000 metres (the disputed last capital of the Incas); the site is reached on foot or horseback from Pampaconas. From Chaullay, take a truck to Yupanca, Lucma or Pucyura: there rent horses or mules and travel through superb country to Espíritu Pampa. Then continue to Cosireni, from where trucks go to Quillabamba. A permit from the National Cultural Institute is required to visit this area. Without one, you will be turned back at Pucyura. One can also go by boat to Kiteni and then by bus to Quillabamba (at 0400). There are daily buses from Quillabamba to Kiteni at 0900, Empresa Alto Urubamba, and *camionetas* leaving between 0700-1000, US$2, 5-6 hrs. (*Hotel Kiteni*, F, basic, several restaurants). At Kiteni you must register on arrival with the police station. Take torch, no electricity. Irregular boats to the Pongo de Maynique, where the river goes through the mountain with a rock wall of several hundred meters on either side, before descending into jungle, where you can see many varieties of animals, birds, butterflies, snakes etc. 14 hrs. from Quillabamba to Pongo. From Pongo you can get down through the jungle to Pucallpa if there is the right amount of water in the river; boats can be arranged at Kiteni. Price varies for number of people in the party, approximately US$15-$20 p.p. To hire a car in Cuzco for this area costs about US$50 per day, including insurance, mileage and fuel for about 250 km.

The South-Eastern Jungle

From Urcos, near Cuzco (bus US$0.50), a spectacular 484-km. road has been constructed over the Eastern Cordillera to Puerto Maldonado in the jungle. No buses, but several trucks do the journey every day. 47 km. after passing the snow-line Hualla-Hualla pass (4,820 metres) the super-hot thermal baths (US$ 0.05) of Marcapata provide a relaxing break. From here the road continues its descent through a tropical rain forest well stocked with orchids. 82 km. from Urcos, at the base of Mount Ausangate (6,600 metres), is the town of **Ocongate**, which has two hotels on the Plaza de Armas. The air force (FAP) provides a weekly air service from Cuzco and Puerto Maldonado to **Quincemil**, 240 km. from Urcos, a centre for alluvial gold-mining with many banks (*Hotel Toni*, F, friendly, clean, cold shower, good meals); ask the food-carriers to take you to visit the miners washing for gold in the nearby rivers. Quincemil marks the half-way point and the end to the all-weather road. Gasoline is scarce because most road vehicles continue on 70 km. to Masuco, another mining centre, where they fill up with the cheaper gasoline of the jungle region. Thirty more km. of sloshing mud and cascading waterfalls brings one out of the mountainous jungle and into the flat plains, for the 141 km. straight run to Puerto Maldonado.

Owing to the present gold rush on the Madre de Dios river, the flow of trucks to Puerto Maldonado has increased, and in Plaza Zimacpampa Chica in Cuzco there is a booking office for the 50-55 hr. journey; US$8-11 in the back, US$13 up front. As trucks pass each other, watch out for the exchanges of fire with fruit as the ammunition. The road has been widened. Times by truck: Urcos—Ocongate 6 hrs. (US$2), Ocongate—Quincemil 12 hrs. (US$5), Quincemil—Masuco—Puerto Maldonado 15-20 hrs. (US$5).

Puerto Maldonado is capital of the jungle Department of Madre de Dios. (Altitude, 250 metres; population of the department 31,000, of the capital 11,200—1981—but growing very rapidly.) Overlooking the confluence of the rivers Tambopata and Madre de Dios, this frontier town is the centre for development of Peru's southern jungle. The Plaza de Armas is very pleasant, and nearby is a new Banco de la Nación built to accommodate (and reflect) the prosperity that gold has brought. However, Puerto Maldonado is an expensive town and because of the gold mining and timber industries, much of the jungle (including most of the mahogany trees) has been destroyed. The temperature normally is between 30°-37°C during the dry season (May to October) and 28°-33°C in the rainy season (November to April); but *friajes* (cold winds that roll northwards along the foothills of the Andes from the South Atlantic region) can send the temperature plummeting, to about 7°C. Insect and reptile activity is greatly reduced; warm-blooded animals survive. Because of this climatic phenomenon, the fauna of the Madre de Dios include many unusual species not found in other jungle areas. Also unique to this area is the *rayo blanco* (white rainbow) that can be seen at sunset on the Madre de Dios River.

Madre de Dios has three superb jungle reserves, among the best in the world: Manu National Park, 1.5 million hectares to the N of the department; Tambopata Wildlife Reserve, 5,500 hectares, 40 km. up the Río Tambopata; and Río Heath Pampas Sanctuary, 100,000 hectares between the Río Madre de Dios and the Río Heath. A pair of binoculars is essential equipment for this area.

Hotels *Cuzco Amazonic Lodge* (*Albergue Cuzco Amazónico*), A, 45 mins. by boat down the Madre de Dios River, jungle tours and accommodation US$140 for 3 days, 2 nights, good food negotiable out of season; avoid in February when everyone goes on holiday including the mechanic. (Book at Av. Arequipa 4964, Lima, Tel.: 462775, or Procuradores 48, Cuzco, Tel.: 5047.) *Explorers Inn* (best booked through Peruvian Safaris,Garcilaso de la Vega 1334, Casilla 10088, Tel.: 313047 Lima, or through Peruvian Safaris, Plaza San Francisco 168, Cuzco—post to Puerto Maldonado is very bad but local *Casilla* is No. 48), A, located in middle of Tambopata wildlife reserve, 58 km. from Puerto Maldonado: an authentic jungle experience, a 4 hr. ride on Tambopata river (2 hours return, in early a.m., so take warm clothes), take food and drink for the journey, probably the best place in Peru (if not the world) for seeing jungle birds (547 species have been recorded here), butterflies (1,100-plus species), dragonflies (over 150 species) as well as tree species and mammals (including a giant otter) recommended more for serious naturalists than average tourists, all guides are graduate biologists (all vegetables and salads washed in iodised water), US$135-150 for 3 days, 2 nights (depending on season, 1½ days spent actually in the reserve), extra day US$30, flight from Puerto Maldonado not included; naturalists' programme at US$45 a night (minimum 6 nights). *Tambo Lodge*, bungalows 6 km. out on opposite bank of Río Madre de Dios, 2-day jungle programme US$35, 3-day US$75, 4-day US$115, recommended,

WILL YOU HELP US?

We do all we can to get our facts right in *The South American Handbook*. Each chapter is thoroughly revised each year, but Latin America and the Caribbean cover a vast area, and our eyes cannot be everywhere. A new highway or airport is built; a hotel, a restaurant, a cabaret dies; another, a good one is born; a building we describe is pulled down, a street renamed. Names and addresses of good hotels and restaurants for "budget-minded" travellers are always very welcome. We would especially like to receive maps and diagrams of towns and cities, walks, national parks and other interesting areas to use as source material for the Handbook and other forthcoming titles.

Your information may be far more up-to-date than ours. If your letter reaches us early enough in the year it will be used in the next edition, but write whenever you want to, for all your letters are used sooner or later.

Thank you very much indeed for your help.

**Trade & Travel Publications Limited
5 Prince's Buildings, George Street,
Bath BA1 2ED. England**

book through Cusco-Maldonado Tour, Portal de Panes 109 (Tel.: 222-332), Cuzco. *Turistas*, on the bank of the Tambopata River, D, with private bath, electricity and water sometimes cut, restaurant quite good.

In town; *Wilson*, D with bath, E without, well run, clean, no hot water, trucks coming from airport stop here; *Rey Port*, F with shower, secure, recommended; *Cross*, clean, generally recommended; *Oriental*, on the Plaza, G, dirty; *Chávez*, F, not recommended but cheap; *Toni, Central*, F and *Moderno*, F, (very clean and friendly but noisy, no hot water). *Tambo de Oro*, F. As there are many miners in Maldonado, it can be difficult to find a hotel room.

Restaurants There are several good restaurants in town. *Juanito's* on Plaza de Armas has been recommended, as has the unnamed restaurant opposite the AeroPerú office, and *Rulman*, round the corner from *Hotel Wilson*. Look for *pensiones* where meals are served at fixed times (lunch is at 1300). *Café Danubio Azul* on Plaza de Armas is good for information.

Typical Foods *Castañas* (Brazil nuts), try them chocolate-or sugar-coated. *Patarashca*, fish barbecued in banana leaves. Try *pescado sudado* as an appetizer. *Sopa de motelo*, turtle soup cooked and served in its own shell. *Mazato*, an alcoholic drink prepared from yuca and drunk by the Indians at their festivals. *Sangre de grado*, a thick deep-red sap collected from trees deep in the jungle which is a highly prized cure-all throughout Peru.

Excursions Motorcycles can be hired for local trips but are rather expensive at US$4 an hour. Bargain for reductions for longer. A very worthwhile one-or two-day excursion by motorcycle is to boat across the Madre de Dios River and follow the trail towards Iberia (*Hotel Aquino*, F). Along the trail are picturesque *caserios* (settlements) that serve as collecting and processing centres for the Brazil nut. Approximately 70% of the inhabitants in the Madre de Dios are involved in the collection of this prized nut. The beautiful and tranquil Lake Sandoval is a 1-hr. boat ride along the Madre de Dios River and then a 2-km. walk into the jungle. For fishing Lake Valencia, 60 km. away near the Bolivian border, is unsurpassed (2 days). Many excellent beaches and islands are located within an hour's boat ride; however, make sure you have a ride back at the end of the day. For the adventurous a one-or two-day trip can be planned to visit Indians still relatively unaffected by civilization; the Indians living nearer Puerto Maldonado, like those near Iquitos and Manaus, are strictly tourist Indians. Boats may be hired at the port for about US$36 a day to go to Lake Sandoval or visit the Indians. Barbara de Cárdenas from San Francisco and her Peruvian husband, Guillermo, organize interesting trips for photography, bird watching and fishing. They can be contacted at Puerto Tambopata, behind the Tourist Hotel (write to Correo Central, Puerto Maldonado). A recommended guide is Arturo Balarezo Revilla, who charges US$30 p.p. per day for a boat trip; contact him at his house near the Plaza de Armas, at the *Café Danubio Azul* or at the airport. Also recommended is Víctor Yohamona, Calle Cajamarca s/n, contactable at *Hotel Turistas*; his tours cost US$20 p.p., or less for groups, all inclusive (sleeping, eating, trekking gear). He speaks some English and has led several scientific expeditions. For guides meeting the plane, US$8- 10 p.p. per day is a normal fee. Alejandro and Héctor are recommended. **N.B.** All hunting in Amazonia is illegal. For those interested in seeing a gold rush, a trip to the town of **Laberinto** (one hotel, several poor restaurants) is recommended. The bus leaves Puerto Maldonado at 0900, 1000 and 1100 and returns in the afternoon daily.

Transport Taxi to airport US$1.70. The airport has a paved runway; flights are often cancelled because of rain. Faucett to and from Lima and Cuzco, Tues., Thurs., Sat., AeroPerú on the other days, US$38 return to Cuzco; flights to Lima US$97 one way; AeroPerú may cancel flights in Cuzco if not enough passengers. Once a week to Lima and Cuzco (usually Thursday) there is an airforce flight (Grupo Ocho) that goes in all but the worst conditions via Iberia and Iñapari, fare to Cuzco, US$18, to Iñapari, US$10. A weekly flight Arequipa-Puerto Maldonado (US$18 one way) is run by the air force, usually Friday, if demand is sufficient. Office of Grupo Ocho is in the airport at Cuzco. Open 0800- 1200.

Flight to **Iñapari** (½ hr.) on the Brazilian frontier, Thursday; this is a cargo flight and you must see the captain about a seat on the day of the flight. From the landing field it is 7 km. to the village (one hostel) where you must seek out the police for border formalities. Wade across the river to Brazil, to the village of Assis Brasil. Private boats can be contracted for travel into Bolivia; to Puerto Heath, at the border (US$28, one day); to Riberalta (US$90-120, 4 days). The trip by boat to Riberalta is very difficult, especially in the dry season. Boats are very few and far between. Some boats only go as far as Puerto Pardo (a Peruvian military post opposite Puerto Heath) for US$2.20, or US$52-64 *expresso*. The wife of one of the officers in Puerto Pardo offers meals for

734 PERU

US$0.80. From here one can cross to Puerto Heath, a Bolivian naval post, but boats into Bolivia are just as infrequent here. It should be noted that waiting for sailings in either Puerto Heath or Puerto Maldonado can take a lot of time.

Before leaving for Bolivia from Puerto Maldonado, one must first get a Bolivian visa (if needed) from the consulate (on Jirón Cuzco; very helpful), then a Peruvian exit stamp, before one can get a Bolivian entry stamp. Similarly if going to Brazil; if you have not obtained an exit stamp from the P.I.P. in Puerto Maldonado, you will be turned back at either border. The immigration office is opposite the Hotel Moderno.

Books *An Annotated Check List of Peruvian Birds*, by Theodore A. Parker, Susan Allen Parker and Manuel A. Plenge, published by Buteo Books, Vermillon, South Dakota, is particularly useful in this area. Also, *The Birds of Venezuela*, Princeton University, and *The Land Birds of South America*, by John Dunning.

Inland from Lima

The Central Railway from Lima to Oroya and on to Huancayo (420 km.) is one of the wonders of Latin America. It reaches its greatest altitude, 4,782 metres, inside the tunnel between Ticlio and Galera, 150 km. from Lima. The ruling grade is 4½&. Along the whole of its length it traverses 66 tunnels, 59 bridges, and 22 zig-zags where the steep mountainside permits no other way of negotiating it. It is by far the most important railway in the country, and the views during the ascent are beyond compare. Galera, the highest station in the world for a standard gauge railway (4,781 metres), is 158 km. from Lima. This masterpiece was the project of the great American railway engineer, Henry Meiggs, who supervised the construction from 1870 until his death in 1877; it was built by the Pole Ernesto Malinowski, with imported Chinese labour, between 1870 and 1893.

Chosica (40 km.), the real starting place for the mountains, is at 860 metres, and is a popular winter resort because it is above the cloudbank covering Lima from May to October. One train a day and frequent buses and minibuses. Beyond the town looms a precipitous range of hills almost overhanging the streets. Up picturesque Santa Eulalia valley off the Rímac valley are the Central Fruit Culture Nurseries. There is some dramatic scenery on the road up the valley, fairly good as far as the hydroelectric station at Callahuanca, but the road is afterwards quite nasty in places, narrow and rocky. Population: 31,200.

Hotels *Residencial Chosica*, D; *Residencial San Jorge*, Av. Lima Sur 401, with hot water, restaurant and bar.

Bus from Lima, No. 204, from 18th block of Calle Ayacucho (US$0.50).

N.B. The Lima-Chosica-Santa Eulalia-Huanza-Casapalca trip is the most impressive in the environs of Lima, and can be done in one day.

For a while, beyond Chosica, each successive valley seems to be greener, with a greater variety of trees and flowers. At **San Bartolomé** (1,513 metres), the platform is often crowded with local fruit sellers, the women in bright shawls, skirts, and black and white panamas. The first zig-zags begin. Then we pass through tunnels and over bridges to the next canyon, where there are more zig-zags. Sometimes the train seems airborne over the valley and the road far below.

Matucana, 27 km. beyond San Bartolomé, at 2,390 metres, is a small unattractive town set in wild scenery, where there are beautiful walks. Beyond it is Infiernillo (Little Hell) Canyon, to which car excursions are made from Lima. (Hotels: *Ritz*, F, fair, *Grau*, cheap.) At Tamboraque (3,009 metres) is the first of the mountain mines, with its overhead cables and smelter down a gorge. Climbing always, we pass San Mateo, where the San Mateo mineral water originates. From San Mateo a spectacular side-road branches off to the Germania mine. Between Río Blanco and Chicla the Inca contour-terraces can be seen quite clearly.

Casapalca (4,154 metres) has more mines; its concentrators are at the foot of a deep gorge. A climb to the dizzy heights beyond ends in a glorious view of the highest peaks. Soon we see a large metal flag of Peru at the top of Mount

PERU 735

Meiggs, not by any means the highest in the area, but through it runs Galera Tunnel, 1,175 metres long. Ticlio station, at the mouth of the tunnel, is on one side of a crater in which lies a dark, still lake. At Ticlio the line forks, one through the tunnel to La Oroya; the other line goes 14½ km. to Morococha, where there are important mines. The highest point, 4,818 metres, is reached on this latter line at La Cima. A siding off this line reaches 4,829 metres; higher than the peak of any mountain in Europe.

Beyond the tunnel zig-zags bring us down to Yauli (4,142 metres). Left is the ugliness inseparable from mining; right is a wide expanse of brown moors with cold, small mountain tarns and herds of grazing llamas.

La Oroya, the main smelting centre, with its slag heaps and black hills, is not attractive. Population: 36,000. It is at the fork of the Yauli and Mantaro rivers at 3,826 metres, 187 km. from Lima by a road which is paved throughout, though between the Anticona Pass at 4,843 metres and La Oroya the road is poor.

Hotels Hostal Martín, F, clean, friendly, no heating but plenty of blankets; Wilson; Lima.

Restaurants Las Vegas, recommended. Restaurant Huánuco, good, cheap food. El Tambo, 2 km. outside La Oroya, good trout and frogs.

Railway N to Tambo del Sol and Cerro de Pasco; SE to Huancayo and Huancavelica (when bridge is repaired); SW to Lima and Callao. Train to Cerro de Pasco leaving 1430 and arriving 1915. To Lima at 1005 and Huancayo at 1340, 3 days a week. (Local train to Huancayo on Sun.)

Roads SE to Huancayo, Ayacucho, and Cuzco, paved to Huancayo; N to Cerro de Pasco (US$0.75) and on to Pucallpa; 25 km. north along this road fork E for Tarma (US$1.50 by bus, US$1.85 by colectivo), San Ramón, the Perené colony, and Oxapampa; SW to Lima (6 hrs. by bus, 5 or less, US$2.95, by colectivo).

Huancayo, capital of Junín Department, is an old market town and commercial centre for central Peru; alt. 3,271 metres; pop. 359,000. The Indians flock in from far and wide with an incredible range of food, and rugs and blankets of llama and alpaca wool, for sale; fleeces can be bought (alpaca, US$2.50 per kilo), but arrive early before 1000. The market at the bottom end of the city in Av. Huancavelica, called the *feria*, sells handicrafts. The Sun. markets are primarily for food and fresh produce; the daily market sells typical clothes, fruit, vegetables, but especially traditional medicines and goods for witchcraft (don't take large bags or cameras, thieves abound; don't take photographs, or, worse still, offer to pay for a photograph). Huancayo is a good place to buy carved gourds, reputedly the lowest prices in Peru. Very impressive Good Friday processions. The colourful annual fiesta of the Virgin of Cocharcas starts on September 8 at Orcotuna, and there are a big early morning market and an afternoon bullfight on the same day as the parade of the Virgin; the feasting and dancing last a week. Costumes and dances are then at their best. In Huancayo, ponchos and various alpaca woollen goods are quite cheap, but often factory-made; most goods are reported to be cheaper than in Lima, particularly silver jewellery. Displays of folklore at the Coliseo, Calle Real, certain Sundays. For woven alpaca goods and other *artesanías*, much cheaper, go to outlying villages, such as San Jerónimo, or Hualhuas, 11 km. north of Huancayo (2 km. off the Huancayo-Jauja road, try Familia Meza, Jr. 28 de Julio 293); minibus from Huancayo, US$0.15 from Church of the Immaculate Conception (see Excursions below).

Warning Huancayo has a bad reputation for thieves, especially in the market and at bus stations. In particular, beware of locals who smear mustard (or something worse) on you, and while you are cleaning it off, steal your belongings.

Hotels Turistas, D, with bath, old building, some rooms small, quiet, but service can be unfriendly and theft is not unknown, good meals for US$3.50; Percy, E, with bath, hot water; Prince, Av. Calixto, F, with bath, no hot water, not recommended; Presidente, Calle Real 1138, Tel.: 231736, D, away from the centre, said to be better and cleaner than the Tourist Hotel, but has no restaurant; Confort, Calle Ancash 297, F, private bath, good; Hostal Dani, Giráldez 486 (Tel.: 235645/232762), F, small private hotel, hot water, clean, friendly, clothes-washing and cooking facilities, safe, English-speaking landlady Sra. María Carmela Barraza de Babilón, who goes out of her way to help travellers with problems, even if they are not staying at her hotel, someone from hotel meets the Lima train; Acolla, corner of Antonio Lobato and Real, Tambo district, F, private toilet, hot shower. *Residencial Inca Wasi*, Federico Villareal 106, clean and friendly, F (owner meets Lima train with car); *Residencia Huancayo*, Av. Giráldez, near railway station, F, all rooms with wash basin, hot showers; *Inca*, Calle Loreto, F, with bath (cold water), clean, but noisy; *Family Pensión Huanca*, Abancay 200, no sign, five blocks from railway station, F, small, English spoken, hot water, laundry and kitchen facilities, good food, typical Huancayo dishes; *Torre Torre*, F, hot shower, clean, poor value; *Residencia Baldeón*, Amazonas 543, G, with European-style breakfast, hot water, friendly; *Kiya*, Plaza de Armas (known nowadays as Constitución), C, with bath, hot water, restaurant does not serve breakfast, 'phones in rooms; *Felicitas*, next door, D; *Universal*, opp. railway station, F, reasonable. Señora Heidi from Switzerland rents rooms (some with bath, breakfast US$1) in her house, *Schweizer Haus*, San José 475, suburb of San Carlos, Tel.: 235578, 10 mins. walk from station, E, friendly, comfortable, recommended. Also private room at Pasaje San Antonio 113, in Club de Leones district, F, recommended; *Familia Jüng*, Huancas 463, F, breakfast served, clean, owners speak French, German and English and welcome Europeans; next door, *Hospedaje Suizo* (Marquino family), Huancas 473, Tel.: 231732, F, 10 mins. walk from railway station, comfortable, hot water, family atmosphere, warmly recommended. Luis Hurtado (see page 737) has 2 rooms (G), with hot water, washing and cooking facilities.

N.B. Prices may be raised in Holy Week.

Restaurants *Inca*, Calle Puno 530, recommended. On Av. Giráldez (Plaza de la Constitución) are *Olímpico*, *Lalo's*, and *Café Giráldez*, all good, Peruvian dishes at *Olímpico*, Av. Giráldez 199, recommended as the best in town. *Bianca* (opposite *Hotel Prince*) is good, as is *Saloon*. *Mil Osky*, in San Carlos quarter, on the Plaza Túpac Amaru, worth looking for, has music some nights after 2300; *Marisquería Mar Azul*, Ancash 578, excellent cheap seafood, opened 1986; many *pollo a la brasa* places. Street vendors sell delicious apple turnovers, and other delights, for about US$0.10. On Calle Real are *Santa Rosa*, and the *Panadería-Pastelería Imperial*, both recommended. *La Gran Chifa*, good Chinese food, connected with *Hotel Kiya*; *Chifa Porvenir*, Jirón Real 417, clean, reasonable. *Restaurant Florida*, Calle Ayacucho, reasonable, good for fish; *Comedor Vegetariano*, cheap. Also vegetarian *Hare Krishna*. Calle Real 356, cheap, good, clean, friendly. *Koky's*, Av. Huancavelica 109, English-speaking owners Adán and Gladys Camargo, good drinks, food, music, friendly, 10% discount to *South American Handbook* owners, information on sightseeing and travel, recommended. *José Antonio*, Av. Cuzco, average. Excellent pastries at *Chalet Suizo*, Huancas 473.

Peruvian-North American Cultural Institute, Jirón Guido 740, one block from old address.

The **museum** at the Salesian school has over 5,000 pieces, including a large collection of jungle birds, animals and butterflies, insects, reptiles and fossils. One can visit the historic house (containing picture gallery) of Sr. Guillermo Guzmán Mazaneda, a local painter of note (Amazonas 279).

The Country Club (very rural) is open to all, in very pleasant surroundings near the Mantaro River, to the north of town.

Crafts Visit Kamaq Maki, Centro Regional de Artesanías, Jirón Brasilia 200 in San Carlos, about 2 km. from centre, an artesans' cooperative (formerly the workshop of Sra. Francisca Mayer), selling woven goods, ceramics, carved gourds and much more; open Mon.-Fri., 0800-1200, 1400-1800, Sat.-Sun., 1000-1200, 1500-1700. Take minibus 5, 6, 13 to corner of San Carlos with P. Aurora, then walk. Woven goods available from Arequipa 463. For carved gourds visit Hermanos Leoncio y Pedro Veli Alfaro, Cochas Chicas, Km. 9, also Artesanías Kondor Kanki, a cooperative which sells gourds, and weaving is taught by Juan Velásquez Veli; also Florencio Sanabria Osores, excellent quality, high prices, Huancayo (Apartado 402); and Nicanor Sanabria Osores, Cochas Grandes, Km. 10, Huancayo (see under Excursions below). Also visit ***Izcuchaca***, 3-4 hrs. from Huancayo by truck to see pottery made. Hotel in main square, F, basic.

Discotheques *El Molino*, Calle Huancas, good; *El Dorado* (more Peruvian), *San Diego*, off Tambo (less good). In El Tambo district, three together, *Alpha 2001*, *El Infinito*, *El Rincón de los Recuerdos* ("boring romantic music and oldies").

Banks Banco de los Andes, near main plaza. For travellers' cheques, Sr. Miguel Velit, Calle Real 552, or Sr. Jung (*Chalet Suizo*, no commission); dollars cash no problem at exchange houses.

Tourist Information Sr. Oscar Alvarez, Huanamarca 270, Tel.: 232-760. Ministry of Industry, including Tourist Office, at Ancash 415. Huancayo Tours, Calle Real 543, organize tours of the surrounding countryside with English-speaking guides; they also rent cars and bicycles (deposit: US$250) and handle AeroPerú reservations. Touring y Automóvil Club del Perú, Calle Ancash 603. Luis Hurtado (see next page) also gives information at his house; if he's on tour, his American wife will help. He has maps, photographs of local crafts, slide shows every Sunday, 1900, and travellers may use his phone for national or international calls.

Rail Train to Huancavelica, *autovagón* US$2.30, 4 hrs. 0700, tickets from 0600, make sure to get off at second (smaller) station in Huancavelica (Sub Estación), since it is closer to Plaza; tourist trains leave every day except Sun. 0730 (6½ hrs.), more expensive (US$4), but quicker. Both leave

PERU 737

from Chilca station, which is not the station for Lima. Train from Huancayo to Lima 0700 Mon., Wed., Fri., 9-12 hrs., (suspended because of unsafe bridge; train ran to Lima only from La Oroya, from late 1986); 1st class US$4.20, 2nd class US$3.50, lunches in 1st class and buffet, US$1.50 (arrive early to ensure getting a seat), 1st class and buffet are bookable one day in advance for US$0.25 extra; ticket office open 1000-1200, 1430-1700.

Road Transport Bus to Lima, Etucsa—not recommended although their terminal does have a waiting room (several daily, US$4, 10 hrs.) Mariscal Cáceres (US$5, 8 hrs.), and other lines. Comité 30 and 22 colectivo to Lima, Av. Loreto 351, five a day, US$9, 5-7 hrs. (takes 5 passengers); also Comité 12 (Calle Montevideo 736, Tel.: 271283, Lima; Loreto 425, Huancayo), with services to Huanta. N. B. A new road to Lima is under construction, which will shorten the journey time. There are no morning buses to Ayacucho; evening buses go via Pampa; they are run by Molina (1800—worst), Empresa Ayacucho (1800, 1830) and Etucsa (not recommended) 1800, US$4.50, 12 hrs. if weather is good; if not, bus waits until daylight to cross pass. Colectivo to Ayacucho, US$20 p.p. (Comité 30). The only way to travel to Ayacucho in daylight is via Huancavelica, e.g. Hidalgo, 0600, 1500, US$2.50 (also, this route is best in rainy season); even so expect to move boulders and fill in the potholes. A beautiful drive, Andean flamingoes, llamas (especially near Huanta, *Gran Hotel*, F), alpacas, vicuñas, but snow and rain storms. Daily bus with Nor Oriente (Calle Huancavelica) to Cerro de Pasco and Huánuco at 1500; same company Mon., Wed., Fri., to Tingo María and Pucallpa at 1600. Ucayali bus company for Huánuco, Loreto 973. Direct buses to Tarma (see page 741; the departure point for La Merced) twice daily, US$2.40. Note: Huancayo and other towns in the area have a *fiesta* in January when it is impossible to get a colectivo to Ayacucho and buses are fully booked. If driving to Ayacucho, be careful with direction. Only three signposts, all to totally unknown villages.

Buses to Cuzco can be something of a problem; get a seat on a truck if stuck, lovely scenery. This road is often closed during wet season. Book as far ahead as possible, as buses tend to be heavily overbooked. They also frequently break down. Trucks are cheaper and offer better views—but take blankets against the cold on the mountains. The trip gives a fine view of the Sierra; one passes the site of the last battle against the Spaniards, near Ayacucho; some distance before Abancay one passes a bridge built by the Spaniards. The canyon of the Río Tomás is recommended for a visit. Those who have made this journey describe it as one of the most beautiful in Peru, but the road may be closed if guerrillas are active in the Ayacucho area. As long as you do not leave the main road to visit more remote villages, or take photographs, there should be no problem travelling from Huancayo to Ayacucho and Cuzco.

Excursions The Convento de Santa Rosa de Ocopa in Valle de Mantaro is worth a visit. W of Huancayo, past Chupaca (good Sat. market) and between Pilcomayo and Huayo is the Geophysical Institute of Huayo on the "Magnetic Equator" (12½° S of the geographical equator). Here meteorological, seismic and cosmic-ray observations are made. Six km. (standard taxi fare US$1.50) S of Huancayo the remarkable shrine of Wari-Willka (written "Warivilka" on buses), of the Huanca tribe of Inca times, has been reconstructed in a corner of the main plaza of **Auray** (often written "Huari"). Bus to Auray from Calle Real, US$0.10. Museum in the plaza, of deformed skulls, and modelled and painted pottery of successive Huanca and Inca occupations of the shrine. Open 1000-1200 and 1500-1700, US$0.15 admission. *Hotel Central*, G, good; *Hotel Sol*, G. Take a minibus to Cerrito de la Libertad, walk up hill to Torre Torre to see impressive eroded sandstone towers on the hillside (beware of begging children on the way up). Not far from here is a large park with a depressing zoo but also a beautiful, clean swimming pool (US$0.10, showers and changing rooms). Another pleasant excursion is to Cochas Chicas (beautiful views of Valle de Mantaro) or Cochas Grandes, where gourds are carved, highly recommended. Buses leave Huancayo every ½ hr. from Church of the Immaculate Conception, for 9 km. journey. In the hills beyond Cochas back-strap weaving of *mantas* for carrying babies can be seen. Back-strap weaving of beautiful *fajas* (belts) can also be seen at Víguez, 1½ hrs. S of Huancayo by colectivo from near the Mercado Modelo. There is a beautiful drive to Cañete (see page 689; the road crosses mountain landscape before following the Cañete river basin with its spectacular gorges (see the Instituto Geográfico Militar map). No bus service, trucks only.

Lucho (Luis) Hurtado (to whom thanks for much useful information) at Huancas 209, San Carlos (Apartado Postal 510, Huancayo, Tel.: 22-23-95), organizes 5-day and 7-day excursions to Indian villages in the low-lying jungle, with the possibility of living with the Indians, or to his father's farm near Chanchamayo in the high *selva*. He also organizes walking trips of 3 or more days into the mountains, to live with Indians. Trips cost about US$18 a day. He has been repeatedly recommended as a guide. Contact him only at his home (impersonators have been operating). He is English-speaking, has an American wife, and takes groups of up to eight people. Take old tennis shoes or something similar for walking in rivers; no other equipment necessary.

22 km. NW of Huancayo is the village of **Concepción**, which has a market on Sun. as well as a colourful bullfight later in the day during the season. Colectivos to Concepción from near *Hotel Turistas*, US$0.50, 30 mins. Other hotels, *El Paisanito*, 9 de Julio 641, G, clean; *Royal*, on Plaza, warm shower, G, pleasant; good restaurants, especially for pastries. From Concepción a branch road (5 km.) leads to the Convent of Santa Rosa de Ocopa, a Franciscan monastery in beautiful surroundings established in 1724 for training missionaries for the jungle, open 1000-1200 and 1500-1700, closed Tues. Tour costs US$0.65 (students US$0.25). It contains a fine library with over 20,000 volumes. The convent has a guesthouse, US$2.50 each. There is also a good restaurant. Bus from Huancayo (change at Concepción) takes 1½ hrs., US$0.35. Near Concepción is the village of **San Jerónimo**, renowned for the making of silver filigree jewellery (Wednesday market). The work of Sra. Nelly Vásquez, Calle Arequipa, 2 blocks from the Plaza de Armas, is particularly recommended; opposite is Sra. Porras, who also produces good pieces. Its fiesta is in August. There are ruins 2-3 hrs. walk above San Jerónimo, but the hike is dangerous in places. Buses from Plaza Amazonas, Huancayo, US$0.10. 45 mins'. walk from San Jerónimo is Hualhuas where beautiful tapestries of alpaca and sheeps' wool are made on rustic looms. (Luis Hurtado does day tours to these places, US$3 p.p., not incl. transport and food.)

18 km. beyond Concepción, on the road to La Oroya, is the old town of **Jauja**, Pizarro's provisional capital until the founding of Lima, where there is an interesting festival (San Fermín and San Fabián) begins on January 20 and lasts several days, enjoyable (but lone tourists should be careful). Also, a very colourful Wed. and Sun. market. Jauja is a friendly, unspoilt town, in the middle of a good area for walking, with ruins near a lake 3½ km. away. On a hill above Jauja there is a fine line of Inca storehouses, and on hills nearby ruins of hundreds of circular stone buildings from the Huanca culture (John Hemming). Bus from Huancayo, US$0.50, many daily, also colectivos (US$1). (*Hotel Jauja* and *Hotel Pizarro*, both E; *Hostal Santa Rosa*, on the square, F, some rooms with bath, poor water supply, restaurant, and on north side, *Turistas*, E, near pleasant Laguna de Paca.) *Hotel Huaychulo* is near Concepción and a 2 hr. walk from Ingenio where there is a government trout farm. The road to Satipo branches off near the Convento de Sta. Rosa de Ocopa, the village of Paca (2 km. further on) is very pleasant; easy to catch a taxi to Jauja; spectacular scenery, snow-capped mountains in the Paso de la Tortuga, followed by a rapid drop to the Caja de Silva in Satipo. (See page 742.)

Huancavelica, capital of its Department (altitude, 3,680 metres; population, 17,500), a friendly and attractive town, was founded over 400 years ago by the Spanish to exploit rich deposits of mercury and silver; it is predominantly an Indian town, and is still a major centre for mining. It is possible to visit the old mercury mine in the hill above the town—a stiff walk, or hire a car. The cathedral, located on the Plaza de Armas, has an altar considered to be one of the finest examples of colonial art in Peru. Also very impressive are the five other churches in town: the church of San Francisco has no less than 11 altars. (Sadly most of the churches are closed to visitors.) Lectures on precolumbian history and archaeology are given in the museum, 2nd floor.

Bisecting the town is the Huancavelica River. South of the river is the main commercial centre where fine leather and alpaca products can be purchased (especially on Calle Virrey Toledo). North of the river on the hillside are the thermal baths (US$0.15). There is a daily market. At the Sunday market, the men wear all black, with multicoloured woollen pom-poms dangling from their skullcaps, waists and knees; these are also used to decorate the livestock.

Hotels *Turistas*, D, for room with private bath, reasonable; *Perú*, near railway station, G, clean, good; *San Francisco*, G, basic; *América* (dirty), G; *Savoy*, G, clean rooms, adequate bathrooms. *Tahuantinsuyo* near Plaza de Armas, F, clean and well maintained; *Santo Domingo*, F; *alojamiento* at Santa Inés. Little water in cheaper hotels in evenings.

Restaurants *Hotel de Turistas*, food is expensive and only fair. *El Padrino*, expensive, not recommended. *Olímpica*, Virrey Toledo 303, good and cheap; *Cynthia*, cheap; *Fidel. Snake Bar Joy*, also *Ganso de Oro*.

Tourist Office In Correo building on Plaza da Armas, go up stairs from an entrance on the left-hand side of the building.

Transport Daily (except Sun.) to Huancayo (146 km.) are one train (0730) and one *autovagon* (US$2.30, 0700), and buses (7 hrs. Expreso Huancavelica leaves at 1700, Hidalgo, 0600 and 1500, US$2.50); sit on the right side for the best views. To Lima via Huancayo, US$5.75 (Expreso Huancavelica, 1700). To Pisco (267 km.), buses only, daily, US$7, 14 hrs. (Oropesa service leaves

PERU 739

at 0600, but be there by 0530 to get a seat, tickets can be bought the day before); route is via Santa Inés (4,020 metres), where there are ten restaurants. Half-an-hour's walk from Santa Inés are Lakes Choclococha and Orcococha, where llama herds can be seen; beautiful views; be prepared for sub-zero temperatures a.m. as bus passes snowfields, then for temperatures of 25-30°C as bus descends to coast p.m..

Getting to Ayacucho (257 km.) is a problem particularly in the rainy season. Take a bus (Oropesa) to Santa Inés, 0600, 4 hrs., US$2.20, then catch the Ormeño bus from Lima (Santa Inés-Ayacucho, 8 hrs., US$3. Alternatively catch a pick-up truck to Pilpichaca, via Santa Inés, 1330-1730, US$1.50, then a truck from Pilpichaca to Ayacucho, 2000 to 0500, US$2, very cold. The road (very bad) is the highest continuous road in the world, rarely dropping below 4,000 metres for 150 km. Out of Huancavelica one climbs steeply on a road that switchbacks between herds of llamas and alpacas grazing on rocky perches. Around Pucapampa (km. 43) is one of the highest habitable *altiplanos* (4,500 metres), where the locals claim the finest alpaca wool is grown; the rare and highly prized ash-grey alpaca can be seen here. 50 km. beyond Santa Inés, the rocks are all colours of the rainbow, and running through this fabulous scenery is a violet river (all caused by oxides). Eleven km. later one encounters Paso Chonta (4,850 metres) and the turnoff to Huachocolpa. By taking the turnoff and continuing for 3 km. one discovers the highest drivable pass (5,059 metres) in the world. Continuing on to Ayacucho one passes some very cold, fish-filled lakes before the road branches to Pisco at km. 77. Seventy km. later the high (4,750 metres) but unimpressive Abra Apachenta is reached, leaving a 98-km. descent into Ayacucho.

Ayacucho, capital of its Department, was founded on January 9, 1539. This old colonial city is built round Parque Sucre with the Cathedral, City Hall and Government Palace facing on to it. The city is famous for its religious processions and its splendid market (closed in 1985-86). There are no less than 33 churches—some long deserted—and a number of ruined colonial mansions. A week can be spent there and in the surroundings, which include La Quinua, site of the battle of Ayacucho, December 9, 1824, which brought Spanish rule to an end in Peru. Ayacucho has a very active student life. Altitude: 2,440 metres, with gently rolling hills around. A 364-km. road has been built to Pisco on the coast. Population: 30,800.

Visitors are advised to see the 17th century Cathedral (with Museum of Religious Art, closed indefinitely) and churches of San Francisco de Asís, La Compañía de Jesús, Santa Clara, Santo Domingo, and Santa Teresa, all with magnificent gold-leafed altars heavily brocaded and carved in the churrigueresque style. There is a small but surprising Museo Histórico Regional, in the Centro Cultural Simón Bolívar, at the outskirts of town, US$0.35 (many Huari artifacts). Tombs of the Huari nobles are being excavated along the road from Ayacucho to Quinua. The University, founded 1677, closed 1886, was reopened in 1958. Local craftsmen produce filigree silver, often using *mudéjar* patterns; others make little painted altars which show the manger scene, manufacture harps, or carry on the pre-Inca tradition of carving dried gourds. Good quality woven carpets can be found in the Santa Ana district (although Barrio Libertad is cheaper), where you can watch them being made; especially Alfonso Suka Chávez, Plaza Santa Ana 83. A charming Palm Sunday daylight procession of palm-bearing children accompanies a statue of Christ riding on a white donkey. This is the start of one of the world's finest Holy Week celebrations, with candle-lit nightly processions, daily fairs, horse races and contests among peoples from all central Peru. It was reported in early 1986 that very few of the churches were open, and if they are, it's early in the morning.

Warning Because of guerrilla (Sendero Luminoso) activity in this region, visitors are advised to seek information in advance and check whether a curfew is in force. Entry into the area has on occasion been prohibited for visitors.

N.B. Beware of thieves, even in the AeroPerú office.

Hotels *Turistas*, E, with bath, dirty, comfortable (meals, US$3.20, mediocre); *Colmena*, Jirón Cusco 140, just of Plaza de Armas, G, a beautiful building, nice rooms with table, wardrobe, not safe, noisy, dirty, good restaurant below; *Samari*, Jirón Callao, F, with toilet, very clean, friendly, recommended; *Hostelería Santa Rosa*, Jirón Lima 140, E, with bath, hot water mornings and evenings, friendly, car park, restaurant, recommended. *Sucre*, Plaza de Armas, F, 4-bedded rooms; *Wari*, G, hot showers, clean and friendly; *Alojamiento El Trocadero*, just off the Plaza, G, cheap, with shower, basic; *Crillonesa*, near market, G, hot showers, clean, good value; *Imperio*, Plaza de Armas, F; *Magdalena*, F, next to Etucsa bus station, clean, hot water; *Santiago*, near market (1½ blocks from Hidalgo bus), F, recommended. *Hostal El Marqués de Valdelirios*, Av. Bolognesi, F; *La Sixtina*, Jirón Callao, F, basic but friendly, hot water, clean, clothes washing facilities; and the private home of Sra. Ayala de Ruiz, Libertad 539, hot water, laundry facilities, personal attention. *Hostal Colonial*, Garcilaso de la Vega 252, F, clean, German-owned friendly, recommended, in an old colonial house, with small theatre and concert hall, *peña* in courtyard, restaurant, trips arranged to Huari and La Quinua. It is extremely difficult to find accommodation at Easter.

740 PERU

Restaurants *La Fortaleza*, Lima 169, 3 courses for US$1.20, very good meals; *La Victoria* (excellent french fries); *Chifa Oriental* on Jirón San Martín; *Mi Perú*, Jirón Grau 221, cheap, clean, good; good coffee and cakes at *El Turco*; *Chalán*, on same street as the *Fortaleza*, but not as good; *El Alamo* (next to *Hotel Colmena*), dirty, not recommended, folk music some evenings, and *El Agullo de Oro* for fish. Many good small cafés, one inside University buildings; *Cevichería* on block 500 of Grau, behind market, good fish dishes. On the Plaza, *Savory* café and *Los Portales* are good. The airport offers a good breakfast.

Sport There are public tennis courts in Ayacucho, and games may be booked at the police station.

Exchange Ayacucho Tours. Try *Hotel de Turistas*, AeroPerú, Morocucho Tours (Plaza de Armas).

Tourist Information Available from Ayacucho Tours, San Martín 406, near market, or from the AeroPerú office (Plaza de Armas, changes US$). State Tourist Information Office, Asamblea 138, has good free leaflets on Ayacucho.

Air To Lima by AeroPerú, 35 minutes, daily at 0720; no flights Ayacucho-Cuzco. In the rainy season expect cancellations. Taxi to airport, US$0.50 p.p., buses from 0600 from Plaza de Armas.

Buses Bus Ayacucho-Huancayo, none by day; via Pampas, Etucsa, 16 hrs., US$4.50, very cold and uncomfortable. Ordinary bus goes at night (1500 and 1800 daily), no wc on board; Ayacucho Transport and Molina, Calle Grau, have been recommended. Bus to Pisco (and Ica), US$7.80 with Ormeño (Jr. Libertad 257), 12-13 hrs.; and to Lima (1300, 1900), US$10.75, also Hidalgo (San Martín 330), at least once a day. Only one bus a week (Hidalgo on Mon.) to Cuzco; alternative is to take Ayacucho-Andahuaylas bus (Molina, daily at 0900, US$6) and change in Andahuaylas for Cuzco. Colectivo may be possible.

Excursions Inca ruins at **Vilcashuamán,** to the S, beyond Cangallo; "there is a five-tiered, stepped *usnu* platform faced in fine Inca masonry and topped by a monolithic two-seat throne. The parish church is built in part of the Inca sun temple and rests on stretches of Inca terracing. Vilcashuamán was an important provincial capital, the crossroads where the road from Cuzco to the Pacific met the empire's north-south highway" (John Hemming). Taxi trips can be arranged with Ayacucho Tours and Morocucho Tours, US$30 p.p., alternatively stay overnight; market day is Wed. A good road going N from Ayacucho leads to Huari (Wari), dating from the "Middle Horizon", when the Huari culture spread across most of Peru (US$0.50 by public transport). Trips can be arranged by Ayacucho Tours, recommended. They do a tour to Huari, La Quinua village and battlefield for about US$4.65. La Quinua village (recommended for handicrafts, especially pottery and guitars) has a charming cobbled main square and many of the buildings have been restored; there is a small market on Suns. Beautiful 18 km. walk downhill from La Quinua to Huari, where trucks leave for Ayacucho until about 1700. **San Francisco** in the jungle on the Apurímac River (3 basic hotels, *Suria*, E, the best but dirty) can be reached by bus from Ayacucho (junction of Av. Centenario and Av. Cavero) on Sat. (return Mon.), 10-12 hrs. on a very bad road often impassable in the wet season (very cold at night). Trucks travel daily leaving at about 0700 (wait at police control near airport), US$5 in driver's cabin, US$3 on back, or private cars, twice the price, bargain hard. From San Francisco you can take a morning canoe to **Luisiana**, about 2 hrs. upstream, to stay in Sr. Parodi's *Jungle Hotel*, Centro Vacacional de Luisiana, with swimming pool, C, on his large *hacienda*; trips are organized in the jungle but it is only open for 3 months in the dry season and Sr. Parodi is not always there. There is an airstrip at Luisiana with daily connections to Ayacucho, for over five passengers, US$29 single. Details in the Ayacucho Tourist Office. From San Francisco you can make excursions to nearby villages on cargo canoes, but it is very difficult to find transport all the way to Pucallpa unless you have a large group of people and are willing to pay handsomely.

From Ayacucho to Cuzco (Because of Sendero Luminoso guerrilla activity and army counter-measures, public transport is scarcer than it used to be, but travellers will be allowed through if they do not stray from the main road and do not take photographs.) The road to Cuzco goes through **Andahuaylas**, in a fertile, temperate valley of lush meadows, cornfields and groves of eucalyptus, alders and willows. It offers few exotic crafts, no comfortable accommodation, poor transport, but beautiful, largely undiscovered scenery. Bus Ayacucho-Andahuaylas 11-18 hours, about US$7.25 (Molina, Jr. Grau, daily at 0900; Transportes Hidalgo Mon. 0800, Wed. 1200, Fri. 1500. Buses stop between 2100 and 0530 if there is a curfew (very cold on board). Andahuaylas-Cuzco buses daily. The *road crosses three mountain ranges and is very rough in places but is definitely worthwhile*. **Abancay** is first glimpsed when you are 62 km. away by road, nestled between mountains in the upper reaches of a glacial valley. From Abancay a 470 km. road runs SW through Puquío and Chalhuanca (dirty *hostal*, F, in Plaza) to Nazca on the Pan-American Highway (see page 694). Trucks and buses leave Andahuaylas for Abancay at 0630-0700, take 6 hrs., US$1.25. There is one Hidalgo bus a week from Ayacucho to Cuzco, (Mon. 0800), US$15 (always overbooked); should take 24 hrs. but can take 3 days. The road is appalling in the rainy season. Sit on the left for best views. The bus is difficult to get on; people have been stuck in Ayacucho for days. Book at least 2 days in advance for a seat on the bus from Ayacucho to Cuzco or Andahuaylas; in the high season you have to wait and see if there is a spare seat. Buses from Abancay to Cuzco leave 0500 and 0700, US$4.55 (196 km.), minibus from near the market takes 7 hours to Cuzco, leaving 1200, US$5.35, colectivos also leave around 0800, arriving 1700, dramatic scenery especially in Apurímac valley, but most of the road between Abancay and Cuzco is very bad. See page 724 for sites of interest between Abancay and Cuzco, 10 hrs. Abancay to Machu-Picchu: take a truck to Izcuchaca (US$1.75) where the train can be caught to Machu-Picchu.

Andahuaylas Hotels *Turistas*, Jirón Dias Bárcenas 500, D with bath (E without), meals US$3 extra (no money exchange or credit cards accepted); *Gran*, Plaza de Armas, G, basic, and *Restaurant Las Palmeras*, meal for US$0.25, is possible; *Hermanos Chipuna*, G, basic, near bus station; *Delicias*, G, hot showers, basic but recommended, only 7 rooms, ask for extra blankets, cold at night; *28 de Julio*, cheap, G, adequate.

Abancay Hotels Discrimination against foreigners reported. *Turistas*, D, with bath, food good, US$3, comfortable, old-fashioned house, safe car park, camping permitted at US$3; *Hostal Grau*, F, with bath, clean; *Abancay*, F; *El Misti*, F, fair. *Alojamiento Centenario*, F. **Restaurant:** *Elena*, almost dop. *Hostal Grau*, good, plentiful and cheap portions.

Ronald Berg, of Cambridge, Mass., writes: Around Andahuaylas the old road by the river to Talavera offers some pleasant scenery. San Jerónimo is another picturesque town nearby. Most worth seeing is Pacucha, an hour's ride by truck from Andahuaylas. Pick-ups leave from the centre of Andahuaylas daily, most frequently on Sun., which is market day. Pacucha (pop. 2,000) is the largest of six villages on the shores of a large scenic lake, with a view of mountains to the NW. In the plaza, where the trucks stop, women sell bread, coffee and hot lunches, the only food for 16 km. There are dirt roads around the lake and the circumference can be done in an afternoon (but be back in Pacucha before dark to ensure transport back to Andahuaylas). The wildlife includes many types of wild duck and other birds, sometimes including flocks of green parrots and swallows. Opposite Pacucha, some 2km. past the lake, are the ruins of a Chanka fortress called Zondor. The trails into the jungle beyond the lake are not recommended: the area is very desolate. Except for Andahuaylas itself, this is a mainly Quechua-speaking region. It is one of the poorest parts of Peru, but as long as you do not display your wealth or eat in public, the people tend to be friendly to foreigners.

East of La Oroya The 60-km. surfaced road to Tarma follows the Cerro de Pasco road for 25 km., then branches off to rejoin the old road quite near Tarma, which is 600 metres lower than La Oroya.

Tarma, population 29,740; altitude 3,050 metres, was a nice little flat-roofed town, founded in 1545, with plenty of trees. It is now growing, and there are garish modern buildings, but it still has a lot of charm. It has a very colourful Easter Sunday morning procession in main plaza; Indians make fine flower-carpets. The surrounding countryside is beautiful.

Hotels *Turistas*, D, with and without bath, acceptable meals US$3.20, rather run down; *Plaza*; *Vargas*; *Ritz*; *Acahuantinsuyo*, G, basic; *Gran Hotel El Dorado*, E, with bath, warm water in a.m., secure; *América*, opp. market, F, clean and friendly; *Galaxia*, on square, E, with bath, modern, highly recommended;

Restaurants *Don Vale*, Jr. Callao, highly recommended; *Tradición*, Jr. Moquegua 350, also good. *Chavín Café*, beneath *Galaxia* hotel, on square, trout recommended. The *manjarblanco* of Tarma is famous.

An Englishman, Mr. V. J. Barnes, an authority on the area east of Oroya, would welcome visitors seeking information at his home in Lima. (Tel.: 287800).

Direct bus service, Huancayo-Tarma, twice daily 0600 and 1600, US$2.15. Daily colectivos from Jirón Huánuco 439 run almost hourly to Huancayo, US$2.40, 2½ hrs. bus to Oroya, US$1.50, colectivo, US$1.85; bus to La Merced, US$1.45; colectivos often leave for Chanchamayo, US$2.15. Passes over high limestone hills with caves. Visit the Grutas de Huagapo, 4 km. from town of Polcamayo—bus twice daily from Tarma US$0.20. Cave guide, Modesto Castro, lives opposite caves and is a mine of information. The precolumbian ruins of Tarmatamba, Shoguemarca, Yanamarca, Huayipirca, Cachicachi, Pichgamarca and Huancoy also lie nearby.

Eight km. from Tarma, the small hillside town of **Acobamba** has the futuristic Santuario de Muruhuay, with a venerated picture painted on the rock behind the altar. Festivities all May.

Dr. David Snashall writes: A road from Tarma via Acobamba goes through the village of Polcamayo to the Gruta de Huagapo ("*la boca que llora*°: the cave that weeps). Even without a guide you can penetrate the cave for some way with a torch. The road continues from Palcamayo (no buses, 3-hr. walk) to **San Pedro de Cajas**, a large village whence most of the coloured sheep-wool weavings for sale in Lima come. You can buy them here for half the price from the weavers

742　PERU

themselves. Basic hotel and 2 restaurants; no shops. The road continues on to rejoin the one from La Oroya to Cerro de Pasco below Junín; there is a bus at 0600 to La Oroya and Huancayo.

Hotel Oskanoa in San Pedro de Cajas, F, basic but friendly. Daily buses to Tarma, La Oroya and Huancayo; 3 buses a week direct to Lima (Coop. San Pedro).

Beyond Tarma the road is steep and crooked but there are few places where cars cannot pass one another. In the 80 km. between Tarma and La Merced the road, passing by great overhanging cliffs, drops 2,450 metres and the vegetation changes dramatically from temperate to tropical. A really beautiful run.
Some 11 km. before La Merced is **San Ramón** (population 7,000).

Hotels Turistas, D, is at the airport; ask there about journey to Pampasilva and Puerto Ubirique (see below). Chanchamayo, fairly cheap, Selva. Conquistador, E, with shower, parking, on main street. There is a recommended chifa on the main street, and the Hawaii is good for juices.

La Merced, population 10,000, lies in the fertile Chanchamayo valley. Sometimes Campa Indians come to town selling bows and arrows, and there is a small but interesting market selling snake skins, hides, armadillo shells, etc. Festival in the last week of September.

Hotels Rey and Christina, good, E, with bath; San Felipe, F, dirty; Chuncho, basic; Cosmos, opp. police station, E, fair, probably quieter than others; Hostal Mercedes, F, with bath, hot water, clean, recommended; Romero, Plaza de Armas, Tel.: 2106, F, good but noisy and water in evenings only. Best **restaurant** is Shambari-Campa, off Plaza de Armas; Hong Kong, restaurant; plenty of bars patronized by the coffee workers, who spend 6 months in the mountains each year.

Note that San Ramón and La Merced are collectively referred to as **Chanchamayo**. Many buses, both from Lima (e.g. Transportes Chanchamayo, best, Av. Luna Pizarro 453, La Victoria, Lima; Los Andes, Arellano, good, 10 hrs., US$4.85) and from Tarma (US$1.45, 3 hrs.). Bus La Merced-Puerto Bermúdez, 8 hrs., US$4, 1000 (Túpac Amaru). To get to Pucallpa, take a launch from Puerto Bermúdez to Laurencia (8 hrs., or more, US$4.50, be prepared for wet luggage), then truck to Constitución, 20 mins., thence colectivo to Zungaro, 1½ hrs., US$2. From Zunzaro, colectivos take 4½ hrs., to Pucallpa, US$3. Alternatively, you can take a truck from La Merced to Pucallpa, 3 days, between 0830 and 1400 any day you will probably be drenched by rain.
From La Merced you can take the Carretera Marginal de la Selva (a grandiose edge-of-the-jungle project of the mid-1960s, of which some parts have been built) to the jungle town of **Satipo** (Lobato or Los Andes buses from La Merced US$4.50 at 0800; Hostal Majestic, D, with bath, no clothes-washing facilities, electricity 1900-2300 only; many smaller hotels, all very basic, the best being Palmero, E, with bath, not very clean. Try Dany's Restaurant, surprisingly good food for such an out-of-the-way place). A beautiful trip. Halfway between La Merced and Satipo is Pichinaki, which has a good hotel, F, ideal for breaking one's journey (bus La Merced-Pichinaki, US$2.15). There are daily buses direct from Satipo to Huancayo and Lima at night, US$6, 12 hrs., Los Andes and Lobato (not as good), so no need to return from Satipo via La Merced. Satipo can also be reached from Concepción, following the Santa Rosa de Ocopa road (see page 738).

About 22 km. beyond La Merced is San Luis de Shuaro, but 3 km. before it is reached a road, right, runs up the valley of the Perené river. The Perené colony, a concession of 400,000 hectares, nine-tenths of it still unexplored, has large coffee plantations. The altitude is only 700 metres. Saturday and Sunday are colourful market days for the Indians. Beyond San Luis de Shuaro a branch road runs right to Villa Rica. It is no longer possible to take motorized canoes from Pampasilva on the River Perené to **Puerto Ubirique**, since the building of the new road.

The road has been extended from San Luis de Shuaro over an intervening mountain range for 56 km. to **Oxapampa,** 390 km. from Lima, in a fertile plain on the Huancabamba river, a tributary of the Ucayali. Population, 5,140; altitude, 1,794 metres. Logging, coffee, cattle are local industries, colectivo service from La Merced. A third of the inhabitants are descendants of a German-Austrian community of 70 families which settled in 1859 at **Pozuzo**, 80 km. downstream, and spread later to Oxapampa. There is much livestock farming and coffee is planted on land cleared by the timber trade. 25 km. from Oxapampa is Huancabamba, from where it is 55 km. to Pozuzo; the whole road between La Merced and Pozuzo is very rough, depending on the season, 30 rivers to be crossed. Sr. Luis Orbeza's mixto leaves from Oxapampa, opposite Hotel Bolívar, to Pozuzo at 0300, returning 1200, US$4.50, Tues., Thurs., Sat. Downstream 40 km. from

Pozuzo is Nuevo Pozuzo (local air service, or two-day walk); Padre Pedro has a collection of insects, weapons and stones in his office. There is a family near Padre Pedro's house who welcome guests for dinner (US$1), German spoken.

Oxapampa Hotel *Bolívar*, basic, good restaurant; *La Isabela*, F, cheap and clean, opposite church.

Pozuzo Hotels *Hostal Tirol*, E, full board, clean, recommended; *El Oriente*, basic.

There is an "air-colectivo" service from La Merced to **Puerto Bermúdez** on the Río Neguachi, US$10.50 single, 10 kg. baggage allowance, US$5 per kg. of excess luggage. The service continues to Atalaya, Satipo, Puerto Inca and Pucallpa. Bus service, La Merced-Puerto Bermúdez (see below). Air-colectivos go to Lima and to most places in the jungle region where there is an airstrip; flights are cheap but irregular, and depend on technical factors, weather and good will. Aero-taxis can be chartered (*viaje especial*) to anywhere for a higher price, maximum five people, you have to pay for the pilot's return to base. In Puerto Bermúdez there is accommodation (*Hostal Tania*, opposite dock where motorized canoes tie up, F, clean), an eating house opposite the airstrip; boat passages possible from passing traders.

North of La Oroya A railway runs 130 km. N from La Oroya to Cerro de Pasco. It runs up the Mantaro valley through narrow canyons to the wet and mournful Junín pampa at over 4,250 metres, one of the world's largest high-altitude plains; an obelisk marks the battlefield where the Peruvians under Bolívar defeated the Spaniards in 1824. Blue peaks line the pampa in a distant wall. The wind-swept sheet of yellow grass is bitterly cold. The only signs of life are the youthful herders with their sheep and llamas. The line follows the E shores of Lake Junín. The town of **Junín**, with its picturesque red-tiled roofs, stands beside its lake, whose myriads of water birds have made it famous for its shooting. At Smelter, the coal washing plant, the track branches to Goyllarisquisga, while the main line goes to the long-established mining centre of **Cerro de Pasco** (population 29,810, altitude 4,330 metres), 130 km. from La Oroya by road. It is not a pleasant town, having many beggars and thieves and much unemployment. The nights are bitterly cold. Copper, zinc, lead, gold and silver are mined here, and coal comes from the deep canyon of Goyllarisquisga, the "place where a star fell", the highest coal mine in the world, 42 km. N of Cerro de Pasco. A fine new town—San Juan de Pampa—has been built 1½ km. away (*Gran Hotel*, noisy, no hot water, poor service). A recommended excursion is to the precolumbian funeral towers at Cantamasia, reached on muleback.

Hotels *Gran Hotel Cerro de Pasco*, Av. Angamos in San Juan suburb, E, shower, little hot water, poor service, noisy; *América; Centromín Hotel*, emergency only; *El Viajero*, on the plaza, F, clean but no hot water; *Santa Rosa*, F, basic, very cold; *Restaurant Los Angeles*, near market, recommended.

Train Through tickets to Cerro de Pasco can no longer be bought at the Desamparados Station in Lima; one must change at La Oroya, where the train arrives at 1400. (The train leaves La Oroya for Cerro de Pasco at 1430, even if the Lima-La Oroya train has not arrived; it arrives at 1915.) The return train for Lima leaves at 0600 from the station, which is 20 min. out of town on foot. The *churrasco* served for breakfast on the train is a welcome defence against the cold.

Buses Bus to Lima, departs 0830 and 2000, 9 hrs., US$5. To La Oroya, bus from Plaza Arenales, 0900 and later, US$0.75; cars go when there are passengers, US$6. To Huancayo, US$2.95. Colectivos to Huánuco, US$4.50, from the central plaza. Buses to Huánuco leave between 0800 and 0900 from Plaza de Armas (5 hrs., US$1.20). A bus, connecting with the train from Lima, to Huánuco takes 3 hrs., at night.

Cerro de Pasco to Pucallpa

The Central Highway There are two roads from Lima to Cerro de Pasco. One goes via **Canta** (3 buses daily to and from Lima, US$2.25—El Canteño company, San Román 151-153, Lima). Two hotels and one good restaurant in Canta, from where one can visit the pre-Inca ruins of **Cantamarca**—many of the buildings still have roofs, supported by pillars; it is a 2-3 hour walk up to the ruins, from where there are extensive views. Continuing through the beautiful high pass of La Viuda (4,748 metres), one goes to the mines of Alpamarca (truck from Canta, 0200, take warm clothes, blanket, camping gear, food). From here there are 2-3 buses per week to Huallay, where there is the Bosque de Piedras (an outcrop of weathered limestone pinnacles which look from a distance like plantations of conifers). Thence to Cerro de Pasco.

The other road, the Central Highway, accompanies the Central Railway, more or less, over the Anticona Pass (4,843 metres) to La Oroya. From there it crosses the Junín pampa to Cerro de Pasco (130 km.), never far from the railway. From Cerro de Pasco it continues NE another 528 km. to Pucallpa, the limit of navigation for large Amazon river boats. The western part of this road (Cerro de Pasco-Huánuco) has been rebuilt into an all-weather highway (see map, page 747, for its contour). Buses run daily between Lima and Pucallpa, 847 km., taking 32 hrs., but ask about the state of the road during the rainy season from November to March, when the trip may take a week.

The sharp descent along the nascent Huallaga River (the road drops 2,450 metres in the 100 km. from Cerro de Pasco to Huánuco, and most of it is in the first 32 km.) is a tonic to travellers suffering from *soroche*, or altitude sickness. From the bleak vistas of the high ranges one drops below the tree line to views of great beauty. The only town of any size before Huánuco is Ambo.

Huánuco, on the Upper Huallaga (population: 82,240), is an attractive Andean town with an interesting market and the two old (but much restored) churches of San Cristóbal and San Francisco (16th century paintings). There is a small but interesting natural history museum at General Prado 495, called Museo de Ciencias; many of the displays have multiple language signs. Entrance, US$0.50. Visit ruin 5 km. on road to La Unión: Kotosh, the Temple of Crossed Hands, the earliest evidence of a complex society and of pottery in Peru (from 2000 BC). You must ford a stream to get there, and beware of the vicious black flies. The ruin has been sadly neglected since the original excavation in 1963. Main industry: sugar and rum. Altitude 1,812 metres.

Hotels *Turistas*, D, with bath, no hot water, meals US$6; *Hostal Residencial Huánuco*, Jirón Ayacucho (near Plaza de Armas) Tel.: 2050, F, with bath, hot water, more expensive than others in this range but excellent value, highly recommended; *Las Vegas*, on plaza, new, recommended, has good restaurant; *Real*, on Plaza, C, overpriced, has expensive café; *Nacional*, cheap but adequate; *Bella Durmiente*, near market square, cheap; *Cuzco*, near market, F, with bath, no hot water, expensive restaurant; *Astoria*, F, cheap and clean; *Imperial*, Ayacucho 581, F, with cold shower (intermittent water), reasonable value, clean, quiet; *La Cabaña*, F, friendly, safe but bathrooms dirty, *Internacional*, F, hot water in the common bathroom in the morning, good, clean and cheap. Hotels are often fully booked; arrive early.

Camping Camp by river, near stadium.

Restaurants *Las Palmeras*, good and cheap. *Tokio* and *El Imán*, off main square, both good. *El Café*, in the plaza is cheap and good. New Chinese restaurant also in plaza.

Tourist Information Plaza de Armas, opp. Post Office, above a bank. Huánuco Tours, Jirón General Prado 691.

Buses To Lima, US$4.60 with León de Huánuco, 14 hrs.; colectivo to Lima, US$12.75, leaves 0400, arrives 1400; book the night before at General Prado 607, one block from the main square. Daily buses to Cerro de Pasco, La Oroya and Huancayo, 0830, 1600, with Nororiente or Ucayali, Constitución 638, 11-12 hrs., US$4.60. "Mixto" Huánuco-Cerro de Pasco, half bus, half truck, departs 0400, 3 hrs., US$2.25; colectivo 1 or 12, US$ 4.50 at 0500. Frequent buses and colectivos to Tingo María, 3 hrs. (colectivo, US$2, many start from near river bridge, two blocks from main plaza). Bus to Pucallpa, US$6.50 (La Perla del Oriente, 0800 and 1600, recommended, unlike León de Huánuco); buses make stops for meals but it is wise to take your own food in case of breakdowns. To Huancayo, 10 hrs., US$3.

Air Huancapallac airport, 8 km. from town; AeroPerú (office at the Tourist Hotel) flights to and from Lima, Tues. and Sun.

To the north-west of Huánuco is **Tantamayo** (3,600 metres), a farming village in the Central Sierra; it is surrounded by precolumbian ruins which can be reached on foot (3-4 hrs., guides available) called Piruru, Susupillu, Japallan, and Castilla de Selinin; pictures and information from Huánaco Post Office. Hotel: *Turística*, where Don Cristián Ocaña and his Swiss wife, Theresa,

PERU 745

offer full board, D (F without food), they are very helpful, and Sra. de Ocaña speaks German, French, Italian and English. Bus from Huánuco, US$4.25, 12-14 hrs., departs 1800; returns at night. Tantamayo can also be reached by taking a truck to Tingo Chico, US$1.70, then another to Chavín de Pariarca (US$0.75) where there is a basic hotel (US$0.75 p.p.) and restaurants, then walk. This route, like the walks to the ruins, is arduous; take warm clothing, a hat, suntan lotion.

From Huánuco, road leads to **La Unión,** capital of Dos de Mayo district a friendly town, but electricity can be a problem (it gets very cold at night); 2 buses daily between 0700 and 1000 (including Acosta, 2 blocks from the market, returns to Huánuco about midnight, US$3, 8-9 hrs., truck, 10½ hrs., leaves late morning. La Unión-Tingo Chico, US$1.70. *Hostal Turista* and *Hostal Dos de Mayo*, at La Unión (G). Neither safe for left luggage. *Restaurant El Danubio*, near market, good home cooking, lots of garlic.

On the pampa above La Unión are the Inca ruins of **Huánuco Viejo**, a 2½ hr. walk from the town, a great temple-fortress with residential quarters. To get there, take the path starting behind the market and climb towards the cross, which is at the edge of a plateau. Continue straight through the village on the wide path (the locals are friendly, but some of their dogs are nasty); the views of the pampa, surrounded on all sides by mountains, are beautiful. Seemingly at the foot of a mountain, in front and to your right, is a silvery metalic roof of a little chapel, behind which are the ruins (about a 20-min. walk through herds of cattle). Take warm clothing and beware of thunderstorms. (Karin Kubitsch, West Germany).

Bus to Lima daily, crowded. Also possible to get to Callejón de Huaylas by taking 1600 bus to Conococha (US$3.25, 9 hrs.) and waiting there for a truck to Huarás (2-3 hrs.— see page 664). The wait is very cold, at 4,100 metres. La Unión-Huarás direct is very difficult because most transport does the route La Unión-Chiquián-Lima. You can take a truck from La Unión to Huansalla, then another to Pachacoto (some wait till 0100 for passengers), and from there it's 1 hr. to Huarás. The San Cristóbal bus to Lima at 1100 goes a few km. S of Catac; from there connections are easy to Huarás (1 hr.) and Chavín (via Catac). Salazar bus to Lima (3 a week at 1000-more like 1100), takes 9 hrs. To Conococha, US$4; this is supposed to connect with a Lima-Huarás bus at 1900-2000; if you miss it, hitch in the cold and dark (2 hrs., US$1.50 to Huarás). A night bus from Lima passes at 0300, but the restaurant at the Conococha crossroads closes at 2230.

The journey to Tingo María, 135 km., is very dusty but gives a good view of the jungle. Some 25 km. beyond Huánuco the road begins a sharp climb to the heights of Carpish (3,023 metres). A descent of 58 km. brings it to the Huallaga river again; it continues along the river to Tingo María. (The road is now paved from Huánaco to Tingo María, including a tunnel through the Carpish hills.) Landslides along this section are frequent and construction work causes delays.

Tingo María is on the middle Huallaga, in the Ceja de Montaña, or edge of the mountains, isolated for days in rainy season. Climate tropical; annual rainfall 2,642 mm. Population, about 20,560 and very mixed. The altitude (655 metres) prevents the climate from being oppressive. The Cordillera Azul, the front range of the Andes, covered with jungle-like vegetation to its top, separates it from the jungle lowlands to the E. The mountain which can be seen from all over the town is called La Bella Durmiente, the Sleeping Beauty. The meeting here of Sierra and Selva makes the landscape extremely striking. Bananas, sugar cane, cocoa, rubber, tea and coffee are grown. The main crop of the area, though, is coca, grown on the *chacras* (smallholdings) in the countryside, and sold legitimately and otherwise in Tingo María—plenty of police activity in this respect. As in many other places in Peru, watch out for gangs of thieves around the buses and do not leave luggage on the bus if you get off. A small university outside the town, beyond the *Hotel Turistas*, has a little museum-cum-zoo, with animals of that zone, and botanical gardens in the town, entrance free but a small tip would help to keep things in order. 6½ km. from Tingo is a fascinating cave, the Cueva de las Lechuzas, reached by car via the new bridge (or colectivo from garage, US$0.80); entrance to the cave is US$3 for foreigners, and a donation to the National Park is welcome; take a torch, and do not wear open shoes; the Cave can be reached by boat when the river is high. There are many nocturnal parrots in the cave and many small parakeets near the entrance. 13 km. from Tingo is the small gorge known as Cueva de las Pavas (no caves or turkeys, but good swimming).

Hotels *Turistas*, D, with and without bath, meals US$6 extra, including taxes, very good, swimming pool US$0.75, some way out of town; *Viena*, F, good value with private bathrooms, clean, near *Café Rex*; *Royal*, E, bed and private showers; *Marco Antonio*, E, clean, laundry service; *Imperial*, E, with bath, pleasant; *La Cabaña*, G, the cheapest, tolerably clean, good restaurant;

746 PERU

Cuzco, G, clean and good; *Raimundo*, G, (not to be confused with *Raimondi*, which is dirty, flea-ridden, and not recommended; *Palacio*, G, shower, but basic and not very clean; *Gran Hotel*, G. Hotels are often fully-booked. Rooms available at Av. Benavides 263, F, also meals; *Pensión* at Jr. Monzón 284, with 3 meals a day for US$ 1.50.

Restaurants *Pensión González*, expensive, but nice setting; *Café Rex*, Avenida Raimondi 500, cakes and ice cream, but rather run down; *Gran Chifa Oriental*, Chinese restaurant, on main street, cheap. Also 2 other restaurants of the same name elsewhere in the town— beware, they're not so good. *Restaurant Tingo*, on main street, recommended. Restaurant at *La Cabaña Hotel* good.

Transport Flights from Tingo María to Lima and Pucallpa. Normally 5 to 6 flights a week to Tingo María by Faucett and AeroPerú, but times often change. 4-seater plane flies to Juanjui, US$17.20 p.p. + US$0.35 for every kilo of luggage over 10 kilos. From Tingo María, on several transport services are run; the road is narrow and stony. Landslides and mud can be a problem. Some construction work is going on. Many Lima-Pucallpa buses go via Tingo, for example, Arellano, Av. Raimondi, whose buses leave between 0700 and 0900. Bus takes 18 hrs. From Tingo to Pucallpa, US$5, 8 hrs. Seats are hard to get on buses to Pucallpa; there are 4 booking offices: Huallaga, Tepsa, Arellano, Nororiente. Bus to Aguaytía, 3 hrs., US$1.70. León de Huánuco bus Tingo María-Huánuco takes 5-6 hrs., 0930, US$1.40; colectivos take 3 hrs. but beware of unauthorized colectivos, which charge the same as authorized ones but are smaller, slower and sometimes get into trouble with the police, US$2.

The Huallaga river winds northwards for 930 km. The Upper Huallaga is a torrent, dropping 15.8 metres per kilometre between its source and Tingo María. The Lower Huallaga moves through an enervation of flatness, with its main port, Yurimaguas, below the last rapids and only 150 metres above the Atlantic ocean, yet distant from that ocean by over a month's voyage. Between the Upper and Lower lies the Middle Huallaga: that third of the river which is downstream from Tingo María, upstream from Yurimaguas. The valleys, ridges and plateaux have been compared with Kenya, but the area is so isolated that less than 100,000 people now live where a million might flourish. The southern part of the Middle Huallaga centres upon Tingo María; down-river, beyond Bellavista, the orientation is towards **Yurimaguas,** which is connected by road with the Pacific coast, via Tarapoto and Moyobamba (see page 682). There is a fine church of the Passionist Fathers, based on the Cathedral of Burgos, Spain, at Yurimaguas; population 25,700. Market from 0400-0700. Tourist information from Consejo Regional building on main Plaza. Interesting excursions in the area include the gorge of Shanusi and the lakes of Mushuyacu and Sanango. **Warning:** there has been terrorist activity in the Yurimaguas region; visitors can expect attention from the police.

Yurimaguas Hotels *Yurimaguas*, F, with shower, toilet and fan, clean, reliable; *Estrella*, F, and shower, recommended; *Floríndez*, D, shower, air conditioning; *Florida*, F; *Camus*, no sign, Manco Capac 201, F, cheap; *Mache*, F, with bath and fan, recommended; *Felix*, D, not recommended; *Cheraton*, or *Leo's Palace*, G, Plaza de Armas 104-6, good, friendly, reasonably-priced, restaurant; *Heladería*, round corner from *Estrella*, serves good cheap lunch and dinner. Recommended restaurants, *El Naranjo, El Aguila, Chifa Coni* and *Copacabana*.

Exchange Banco Amazónico, near main plaza, good rates and service.

Air Yurimaguas, flights to Lima, Tarapoto and Iquitos, AeroPerú, Thurs. and Sun. When Yurimaguas-Tarapoto road is impassable, Grupo Ocho flies for civilians. Flights also to Juanjui. Faucett flights to Tarapoto and Lima on Mon., Thurs. and Sat. (highly unreliable). Planes may not land in rain.

River Travel Yurimaguas-Iquitos by regular ferry *La Libertad*, 60 hrs., US$15 on upper deck with meals (upstream takes longer). Ask at the harbour for smaller boats. You can break the journey at **Lagunas**, where you can ask the Indians to take you on a canoe trip into the swamps; you will see at very close range crocodiles, monkeys and a variety of birds, but only on trips of 4 days or so. Señor Lapiz has been recommended as a good guide; he seems to be well-known. Also Norberto Flores Rengifo, Janjui 703. Take water purifier and mosquito repellant on excursions that involve living off the land. *Hotel Montalbán* on the plaza (no sign), also accommodation at the Farmacia. The 45-foot river launch *Constante* plies to Lagunas 2-3 times a week, 12 hrs. downstream from Yurimaguas; from there US$10 to Iquitos if you can get a connection. A boat, *La Rosita*, runs regularly but stops at every village of any size. *Alfert* has been recommended, cabins, good food. Times of boats to Iquitos and Pucallpa very vague. The boats pass by the villages of Castilla and Nauta (*Residencial Olguita*, basic), where the Huallaga joins the River Ucayali and becomes the Amazon. You need a hammock, mosquito net, water-purification tablets, extra food and a good book.

PERU 747

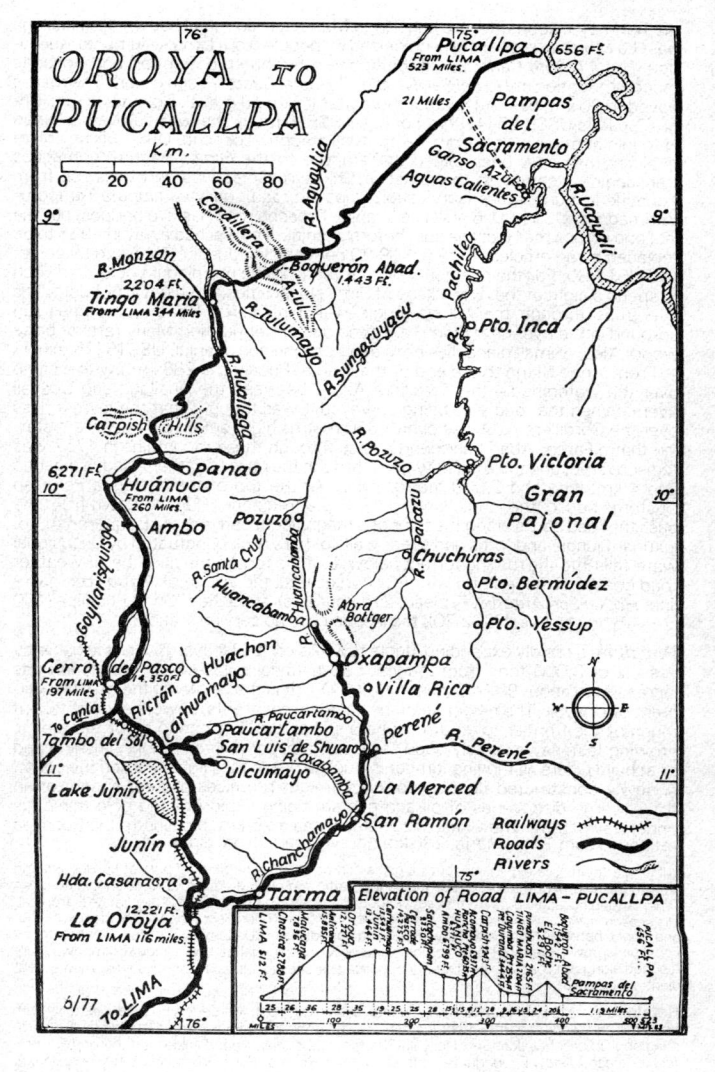

ROUGH SKETCH

748 PERU

At Tulumayo, soon after leaving Tingo María, a road runs N down the Huallaga past La Morada, successfully colonized by people from Lima's slums, to Aucayacu (*Hotel Monte Carlo*, E with bath; one other hotel, both poor) and Tocache (accommodation at *Hostal San Martín*, F; *Hostal Sucre*, F; one other). The road is paved to 20 km. past Aucayacu, thereafter it is good gravel. Colectivos run; Tingo-Tocache US$8.25 (4½ hrs.) or bus US$6 (6 hrs.). The road has been pushed N to join another built S from Tarapoto (Tarapoto-Tocache, US$4.65 by colectivo) and has now been joined at Tarapoto to the Olmos-Bagua-Yurimaguas transandine highway to the coast at Chiclayo. Colectivos and taxis run from Tocache to Yurimaguas (serviceable unpaved road); daily *camioneta* Tarapoto-Yurimaguas, US$4.90, 6 hrs. The Juanjui-Tocache road has five bridges, but the last one across the Huallaga, just before Juanjui, was washed away in 1983 to be replaced by an efficient ferry (US$9.20 per vehicle); Juanjui-Tarapoto by colectivo US$7.80. For the river journey, start early in the morning if you do not wish to spend a night at the river village of Sión. No facilities, but night is not cold. The river runs through marvellous jungle with high cliffs. Boats sometimes run aground in the river near Sión. Take food and water purifier. Many rafts of balsa wood. Also, a small plane flies between Tocache and Juanjui, US$16 (25 mins).

From Tingo María to the end of the road at Pucallpa is 288 km., with a climb over the watershed—the Cordillera Azul—between the Huallaga and Ucayali rivers. When the road was being surveyed it was thought that the lowest pass over the Cordillera Azul was over 3,650 metres high, but an old document stating that a Father Abad had found a pass through these mountains in 1757 was rediscovered, and the road now goes through the pass of Father Abad, a gigantic gap 4 km. long and 2,000 metres deep. At the top of the pass is a Peruvian Customs house; the jungle land to the E is a free zone. Coming down from the pass the road bed is along the floor of a magnificent canyon, the Boquerón Abad: luxuriant jungle and ferns and sheer walls of bare rock punctuated by occasional waterfalls into the roaring torrent below. At the foot of the pass the all-weather road goes over flat pampa with few curves until the village of **Aguaytía** (gasoline; *Hostal San Antonio*, F, clean; 2 restaurants) is reached. On to Pucallpa (160 km.—5 hrs. by bus, US$2.70); the last half has no service stations.

Pucallpa, a rapidly expanding jungle town, is on the Ucayali River, navigable by vessels of 3,000 tons from Iquitos, 533 nautical miles away. Population has increased to about 90,000 (district 130,000). It is the capital of the new Department of Ucayali. The newer sections have paved streets, sewers and lights, but much of the frontier town atmosphere still exists. The economy of the area is growing fast; sawmills, plywood factories, a paper mill, oil refinery, fishing and boat building are all thriving; timber is trucked out to the Highlands and the coast. A newly constructed floating dock for freight promises a great expansion in trade. Large discoveries of oil and gas are being explored, and gold mining is underway nearby. The Ganso Azul oilfield has a 75-km. pipeline to the Pucallpa refinery. From Tingo María, 286 km. (gravel road); from Lima, 847 km.

All jungle towns are expensive, but bargains can be found. The floating port La Hoyada and Puerto Italia are worth a visit to see the canoe traffic and open-air markets. Care should be taken when arranging jungle trips from street vendors in Pucallpa or at the ports. The climate is tropical: dry season in July and August, rainy seasons October-November, February-March; the town is hot and dusty between June and November and muddy from December to May. The centre of Pucallpa is now paved, but both the port and new commercial harbour, about 5 km. away, are reached along dirt roads. Expect plenty of police searches as this is a narcotics area. Also expect plenty of thieves.

Hotels *Turistas*, C with bath (taxes included), swimming pool; *Mercedes*, E, good, but noisy with good bar and restaurant attached; *Inambu*, C, with good value restaurant, a/c; *Komby*, E, swimming pool, excellent value; *Sun*, Ucayali, F, without bath, clean, good value next to *Komby*; *Comfort*, E, clean, *Sisley*, E, adequate, both on Coronel Portillo; *Perú*, Raymondi, E (try bargaining), dirty and not recommended, basic; *Europa*, at river end of 7 de Junio, F, dirty, unsafe; *Barbtur*, F, Raymondi 670 (Tel.: 6377), friendly, clean, central, obs. bus stop, good beds; *Alex*, F, private bath, dirty; *Hostal Mori*, Jr. Independencia 1114, G, basic; *Hostal Los Angeles*, on Ucayali, E, clean, communal shower, but noisy; *Tariri*, F, with air conditioning, food cheap and good, Calle Raymondi, near Calle Frederico Basadre; *Amazonas*, F, next door, good, secure, good dining room. If holidaying, better to stay at Lake Yarinacocha (see next page).

PERU 749

Restaurants Two chifas (Chinese restaurants) downtown, both said to be good: *Chifa Pucallpa* and *Chifa Hongkong*, Raymondi 650. *Jugos Don José*, quite cheap; *Restaurant San Isidro* recommended, also *Sabores Perú*, good food, poor service; *Jaricho*, under *Hotel Sun*, good; *Escorpión Cebichería*, Jr. Progreso, good, eat in rear garden; *Los Rosales*, expensive; *Puerto de Carlos*, best in the downtown area, expensive; *Jíbaros*, near *Hotel Amazonas*, good food and value; *Embutidos La Favorita*, Cnl. Portillo, good, cheap, friendly, US$1 for all 3 meals; *El Establo*, steak house on road to airport, excellent; *Sandwich Roma*, corner of Portillo and Ucayali, good snack bar; *Hotel Turistas* restaurant good. *La Baguette*, good bakery, cheap bottles of pisco. The local beer "San Juan" has been recommended. Brewery tours on Sat. but far out of city.

Small **motorcycles** for hire from Jr. Raymondi 654 and 7 de Junio 864, about US$1.50 per hour plus gasoline.

Bookshop Librería La Verdad and La Brisa Lodge have collections of English books on loan; a boon for stranded travellers.

Exchange Banco Continental, no commission. Importaciones Gutiérrez Padilla, Jr. Ucayali, Raymondi 601 (also good ice cream). Try also the owner of the *Barbtur Hotel*.

Air Faucett to and from Lima daily in the afternoons. Flights to Iquitos daily (except Fri.) with AeroPerú, 1500, US$52 (US$35 for Peruvians), try different agencies for lower price ticket (e.g. Pucallpa Tours, Jr. Coronel Portillo 747, Tel.: 6081); to Tarapoto on Thurs. and Sun. (US$33). Some seats are assigned, you need to arrive early. Departures must be confirmed 24 hrs. in advance. AeroPerú jet flights to and from Lima and Iquitos in the afternoon. Reconfirmation of tickets can only be done with any certainty at the office in town. Float plane from the airforce base at Yarinacocha, Sat, 0900 to Iquitos (check in Fri., be there at 0700), US$20. Grupo Ocho fly to Esperanza, San Ramón, Sepahua, Atalaya, with passengers—office in Pucallpa. The road to Brazil has not yet been opened. For connections by river see page 350 in Brazil section. SASA fly to Cruzeiro do Sul, US$35, minimum 4 passengers, if plane has no passengers booked for return, you'll have to pay US$70, very unreliable. Airport to town, bus US$0.25; taxi US$3.60.

N.B. Before entering Peru at Pucallpa by air from Cruzeiro do Sul check thoroughly that immigration facilities have been set up at Pucallpa. If you arrive and cannot get a stamp, the PIP in Pucallpa will (or should) send you back to Brazil; if they don't, you'll be in for a lot of hassles further on in Peru, including the possibility of arrest. To leave Peru from Pucallpa, you must get a special exit visa from the PIP in town or at the airport.

Buses Much of the Pucallpa-Lima road is now paved and there are regular bus services to Lima. Huallaga, Arellano, Tepsa (1410, 1510) and León de Huánuco (at 1730) from Lima to Pucallpa (US$10, 24 hrs. in good weather) via Huánuco (10 hrs., US$7 with León de Huánuco—1300 from Pucallpa, US$6.50 with La Perla del Oriente, 1200, or Tepsa, 1000, 11 hrs.). From Pucallpa Nororiente goes to Tingo María, US$5, 10-11 hours. Advised to take travelling rug or blankets as the crossing of the Cordillera at night is bitterly cold. Try to pick a bus crossing the mountains by day as the views are wonderful. It is also possible to get to Lima by truck.

Excursions The Hospital Amazónico Albert Schweitzer, which serves the local Indians, and Summer School of Linguistics (callers by appointment only) for the study of Indian languages are on picturesque Lake **Yarinacocha**, the main tourist attraction of the area. Yarinacocha is 20 mins. by colectivo or bus (line 6) from the market in Pucallpa (US$0.25), 15 mins. by taxi (US$3.60). The Indian market of Moroti-Shobo is a must. *Hotel La Cabaña*, C (price rises in high season), German owner, plane excursions (for instance to Indian villages). *La Brisa Lodge*, D, 5 rooms sharing 2 bathrooms, or 4-person bungalows, US-run (Connor and Mary Nixon), recommended, free information on jungle excursions and maps, plus their own excursions (3-day and 10-day); *Los Delfines*, F, rooms with bath, clean, noisy but best buy for budget traveller; *Los Pescadores*, in Puerto Callao, F, cheap, friendly, restaurant. Some small houses for rent on weekly basis. Restaurants: *La Brisa Lodge*, excellent but not cheap; *El Cucharón*, good food; *Grande Paraíso*, good view; local specialities include *tamales*, *humitas* (maize patties with meat and herbs), *junies* (rice with chicken and spices), *tacutacu* (banana and sauces). Here is bathing in clean water, but there is a lot of weed. It is a pleasant change after the mud of Pucallpa and the Amazon; you can camp, though there are no facilities and it is hot and insect-ridden. Motor canoes can be hired for about US$17 a day with guide, but guide not mandatory for lake trips. Trips into the canals and out to the river need a guide (Sr. Antonio has been recommended). Two types of excursions down river, recommended three days, can be arranged from the port in Yarinacocha directly with the boat owners, prices vary but approximately US$20 per boat a day, you buy food and some supplies. Boats hold up to 8 at reduced price. Recommended boats: *Amiguito*, *Veloz*, *Progreso*, *Akito* (of the García family, who also have accommodation, recommended, trustworthy)—beware, many boats are used for drug-running and tourists have come to grief. List of guides, maps and information available in *La Brisa Lodge*. Recommended guides Daniel Saavedra (B/M *Progreso*), Roberto C. Cenepo, Jorge Rucoba (navigator), who offer fishing, hunting, walks in the jungle along the rivers Aguaytía, Callena and Ucayali, and rivers and canals (especially the Chanchaguaya region of Contamaná). Also special excursions to Iquitos from Pucallpa. None of them

750 **PERU**

speaks English, but they can be found at Lake Yarinacocha, Puerto Callao, ask for B/M *Progreso*, prices are competitive. Also recommended for tours, Jorge Matos Grijalva of Selva Tours, also an English teacher and bar owner, great local character and most helpful, Coronel Portillo, next to *Hotel Amazonas*. **Note**: down-river trips visit numerous villages but much of the jungle is cultivated; up-river trips visit fewer villages but mostly virgin jungle. Certain sections of Lake Yarinacocha have been designated as a reserve.

River Service Bus Line 1 to the port, La Hoyada. To Iquitos, some better than others; only 3 boats with cabins, but don't count on getting one (hammocks are cooler). Travellers to Iquitos need confirmation from the PIP that their documents are in order, this must then be signed by the Capitanía otherwise no passenger can be accepted on a trip leaving Pucallpa. No such clearance is necessary when returning to Pucallpa. Passenger services are in decline owing to competition by air and priority for cargo traffic; it may be better to make journeys in short stages rather than Pucallpa-Iquitos direct. There's a risk of illness on the river, and public transport can be extremely uncomfortable. River water is used for cooking and drinking: none may leave afterwards for 4 to 6 weeks. Avoid boats that will be loading en route, this can take up to 6 days. The fare is about US$20 (bargain) a head with "cabin", rice, meat and beans. It is possible to hire a small boat from Pucallpa to Iquitos for US$89. Try at the north section of the port, but take care not to hire a boat running drugs. Further down the Ucayali river are Contamaná and Requena, from which launches sail to Iquitos, taking 12 hrs., US$7. Roroboya, a small Shipibo Indian village about 12 hrs. downstream from Pucallpa, should not be missed, as most other villages down to Iquitos are *mestizo*. You can go to Puerto La Hoyada and Puerto Italia (smaller boats) to find a boat going to Iquitos; the Capitanía on the waterfront may give you information about sailings, but this is seldom reliable. Do not pay for your trip before you board the vessel, and only pay the captain. (Captains may allow you to live on board a couple of days before sailing.) Boats going upstream on the Amazon and its tributaries stay closer to the bank than boats going down, which stay in mid-stream.

From Pucallpa to Cruzeiro do Sul overland requires plenty of time and money to organize, and even then is difficult. You can take a boat to Abojao (10 days), then walk to Brasiléia, from where buses go to Cruzeiro. Boats and guides are very expensive.

Iquitos, capital of the Department of Loreto and chief town of Peru's jungle region, is a fast-developing city of 175,000 people on the W bank of the Amazon, with Padre Isla island (14½ by 3 km.) facing it in midstream. It has paved streets and plenty of vehicles (including taxis) but roads out of the city go only a little way: Iquitos is completely isolated except by air and river. Some 800 km. downstream from Pucallpa and 3,200 km. from the mouth of the Amazon, it has recently taken on a new lease of life as the centre for oil exploration in Peruvian Amazonia. As one might expect from its use by the oil industry and its remoteness, it is an expensive town.

Local tourist literature talks of an iron house in the Plaza de Armas, designed by Eiffel in Paris and assembled in Iquitos. This is reputed to be the building on the corner of the Plaza de Armas and Calle Putumayo, which now houses several tourist agencies. It is said that the house was transported from Paris after the 1898 Exposition by a local rubber baron; it was constructed entirely of iron trusses and sheets, bolted together and painted silver.

Belén, the waterfront slum, is lively and colourful, and does not seem a dangerous place to visit, in daylight. Most of its huts are built on rafts to cope with the river's 10-metre change of level during floods. (Canoes may be hired on the waterfront to visit Belén; do not try paddling yourself as the current is very strong.) See in the city the Market, at the end of the Malecón, or riverside walk. Note that the principal street Jirón Lima has been renamed Jirón Próspero.

The University of Loreto (1962) specializes in engineering and agriculture. Of special interest are the older buildings, faced with *azulejos* (glazed tiles). They date from the rubber boom of 1890 to 1920, when the rubber barons imported tiles from Portugal and Italy and ironwork from England to embellish their homes. Werner Herzog's film *Fitzcarraldo* is a *cause célèbre* in the town; Fitzcarraldo's house still stands on the Plaza de Armas, and Herzog's boats are moored in the port.

A short drive S of the city is beautiful Lake **Quistacocha** in lush jungle, with a fish hatchery at the lakeside. Recommended is a visit to the Parque Zoológico de

PERU 751

Quistacocha, on the lake; the tourist office will supply a map of the zoo (take bus from Calle Octavio—also known as Ocho); also a truck (with pink frame, not green) from Abtao and Grau to the zoo and Quistacocha, US$0.20; taxi US$5.25, 2 hrs. We have heard that the animals (and particularly the fish) often depend on food from visitors to survive. See particularly the *paiche*, a huge Amazonian fish whose steaks you can eat in Iquitos' restaurants. The aquarium has been moved to Ramírez Hurtado.

Warnings As elsewhere, beware of thieves, especially of handbags, watches, jewellery, etc. Secondly, locals sell necklaces made with red and black rosary peas (Abrus pecatorius), which are extremely poisonous. Do not give them to children. They are illegal in Canada, but not in the U.S.A. If possible, avoid visiting Iquitos around Peruvian Independence Day (July 27 and 28) and Easter as it is very crowded and excursion facilities are overloaded.

Hotels *Los Bungalows*, Carretera Pampachica 1940 (P.O. Box 617, Telex 91034), free bus to town or 5 mins. by taxis from town (US$2), C, jungle bungalows, air-conditioned restaurant, bar, swimming pool, managed by Philippe Helsen, a Belgian, recommended, but noisy at weekends. *Amazonas Hotel Iquitos*, previously Holiday Inn, on Abelardo Quiñónez, 6 km. out of town (taxi US$1.75), A, plus 19% tax and service, swimming pool (free bus service hourly from airport in poor condition, not recommended); *Turistas*, Malecón Tarapacá, 2.7 km. out of town, C, with bath, meals US$4.50, with many good air-conditioned rooms US$1.50 extra (a few second-hand English books available in reception), does not accept travellers' cheques; *Hostal Acosta*, Ricardo Palma 252, C, hot and cold running water, shower, air conditioning, refrigerator and TV in room, very good café, central, recommended, but often full of oilmen; also *Acosta 2*, B, same good standard plus good restaurant and swimming pool; *Imperial Amazonas*, much cheaper, D, run down, no air conditioning, no restaurant; *Isabel*, F with bath, very good and clean; *Hostal Safari*, D, fair; *Hostal La Pascana*, Pevas 184, E with shower, clean, friendly, breakfast available, recommended; *Lima*, Próspero 549, F (triple rooms available), with bath and fan, very good; *Perú*, F (triples available), fan, clean, bathroom, café downstairs, good value; *Hostal Residencial Alfert*, García Sanz 03, F, with bath, good, friendly; *María Antonia*, Próspero 616, C, clean, air-conditioned, recommended; *Hostal Internacional*, Jr. Próspero 835, G without private bath (F with), very dirty, passable; *Hostal San Antonio*, Jr. Prospero 665, F, with bath, some fans, dirty; *Hostal Europa*, Brasil 222, very good, very helpful, D, a/c (cheaper with fan), shower, water if lucky; *Oriental*, D, large fan and showers, continental breakfast for under US$0.50; *Anita*, E, with shower, recommended; *Hostal Tacna*, on Tacna, F; *Excelsior*, E, with bath; *Hostal Residencial Ambassador*, Pevas 260, C, with shower, air-conditioning and snack-bar; *Hostal Residencial Loreto*, Jr. Próspero 311, E, with shower and air-conditioning (cheaper without air conditioning); *Tarapacá*, Calle Tarapacá, F, with plentiful water, fan; *Hostal Karina*, Av. Putumayo, F, good value, central, friendly, laundry, cheap food; *Maynas*, Próspero 388, E (triples available), with private shower and fan, very clean and friendly; *Hospedaje Las Neves*, unsigned, on 2nd block of Huallaga, F, cheap, friendly; *Residencial Wagner*, Coronel Portillo 687, opposite the Capitanía, F, friendly, cheap meals available, jungle tours of up to 6 days with groups of 4-6 people, US$ 40 p.p. a day.

Restaurants Best is probably *El Exclusivo*, well prepared local dishes, moderate prices; *Hostal Libertad*, Arica, US$1.30 for all 3 meals of the day, tasty, lots of vegetables; *El Mesón*, Jirón Napo, fish recommended; *El Dorado Inn*, Calle Huallaga near Plaza Veintiocho de Julio, good value and good menu; *Texas Snack Bar*, Calle Raymondi 390; *Maloca*, opposite Hotel Turistas on riverbank, average meal US$5, good food and service, recommended, no mosquitoes. Chinese restaurants include *Gran Chifa Central*, Av. Almirante Grau 1133; *Gran Chifa Chung Wa*, on the corner of Arica and San Martín; *Gran Chifa Wai Ming*, on Plaza Veintiocho de Julio at San Martín 462/6, good but quite expensive; *Chifa Pekin*, Av. Almirante Grau 837. For ice cream and snacks, try *Cohen's*, on Calle Próspero on corner with Calle Morona; *La Favorita*, next to Cohen's; restaurant of Kaya Tours at Jr. Pitumaco 139, good; *Snack Bar Jerez*, Próspero 127, on Plaza de Armas; for barbecued chicken the *Cocoroco* chain has a *Pollo a la Brasa* restaurant on the corner of Plaza Veintiocho de Julio. *Café* beneath *Res. Internacional*, Jr. Próspero, good, cheap. The best restaurants are on Plaza Veintiocho de Julio. Río Negro restaurants are to be avoided. Pineapples are good and cheap. Try the local drink *chuchuasi*, which is supposed to have aphrodisiac properties, and the alcoholic *siete raices*. You can eat cheaply, especially fish, at the market. Palm heart salad (*churro*) excellent.

Current 220 volts, A.C.

Clubs Club Social Iquitos, overlooking Plaza de Armas; Military Casino, for all classes; Centro Internacional.

Shopping Empresa Peruana de Promoción Artesanal (EPPA), Putumayo 128; Mercado Artesanal de Productores, 3 km. from the city in San Juan district, take colectivo; La Cocamita, Putumayo 120; Mocahua Juárez, Arica 1083. All sell handicrafts. Chemist shops: Del Correo, Arica 398; D'Onudio, Próspero 541; El Loretano, same street No. 355. Small selection of secondhand English books at the travel agent on Putumayo 184.

752 **PERU**

Discotheques *Costa Azul*, Requena 274; *La Pantera Rosa*, Moore 434; *Disco Pub Chich*, Condamine 771.

Cinemas Many cinemas (about US$0.50) show English-language films.

Museum Municipal Museum, has a large, old collection of stuffed Amazonian fauna which is rather disappointing. It has been incorporated into the Parque Zoológico.

Banks Banco Popular cashes travellers' cheques. Banco de Crédito, Plaza de Armas, good rates. Banco Amazónico changes cheques at the official rate without charging a commission or asking for a copy of your passport. *Cambio*, Calle Próspero, useful when banks are closed; Importaciones Lima on Próspero, good rates of exchange; *Cambio* next to Fénix Viajes, Pevas 216-20, good rates for travellers' cheques.

Post Office Entel Perú, corner of Calle Arica with Morona, near Plaza de Armas.

Brazilian Consul on Morona between Próspero and Arica.

Tourist Office Dirección Departamental de Industria, Turismo e Integración, Jr. Loreto 227; and at airport: town maps which vary from useful to illegible, maps of the Quistacocha zoo and literature from the main jungle tour operators. Also office on 500 block of Arica. Travel agents also have bad maps and information, but they always try to sell jungle tours. Town map also from Librería Mosquera, Jr. Próspero. (In the souvenir shop at the Tourist Hotel—the only place in town that has postcards— Jaime will give good information, especially on Amazon trips.)

Tourist Agencies arrange half-day, one-day, or longer trips to places of interest with guides speaking some English; packaged tours cost US$125-180 for three days when booked in Lima through a travel agency; it is much cheaper to book tours in Iquitos than in Lima. Launches for impromptu river trips can be hired by the hour or day (prices are negotiable); the tour operators are located on Calle Putumayo near the Plaza de Armas. Explorama Tours (recommended as the most efficient, including reconfirmation and reorganization of travel arrangements), Putumayo 150, has four sites: *Explorama Inn* on the Amazon, 25 km. below Iquitos, two-day trip, US$100 for 2; *Explorama Lodge* at Yanamono, 80 km. from Iquitos, US$110 for 2 days, US$200 for 3 days and US$40 for each additional day; *Explornapo Camp* at Llachapa, 160 km. from Iquitos; *Aventurama Camp* on the Napo River 300 km. from Iquitos, reached by Aerocóndor floatplane service (the last two are better for seeing fauna); Explorama's guide, Arí Arévalo, recommended. Amazon Lodge Safaris, Putumayo 165, owns the *Amazon Lodge*, which their powerful *Amazon Explorer* launch (100 passengers) services with day-trippers for US$45 p.p. Two-day, 1 night stay costs US$88 plus US$7 for lunch on second day. Paseos Amazónicos Ambassador, Putumayo 124, operates the *Amazon Sinchicuy Lodge* with day-trips at US$28.50 and 2 day, 1 night stays at US$60; they also organize visits to Lake Quistacocha and the zoo; *Jungle Amazon Inn*, about 10 km. further downstream from the *Amazon Lodge*, tour operators on ground floor of allegedly Eiffel-built house on corner of Plaza de Armas with Putumayo. Lima Tours offers 3 day, 2 night tours to Iquitos and the Amazon from Lima for US$250 p.p., flight included. Amazon River Lodge, S.A., Putumayo 184, Tel.: 233976, (Telex 91017): runs *Tamshiyacu Lodge*, US$40 for 2 days, 1 night, small, friendly, highly recommended, swimming, jungle walks, night-time canoe rides, the guide, Antonio is very good; their trips include the Yarapa River lodge, Tambo Safari Inn Camp and wilderness expeditions; tourists are met at the airport by Sr. Pedro Alava with information; Amazon Adventure Safari Trips run tours there (ask for Lucho de Cossio, the owner). Beware, though, it has been reported that different prices are charged to different clients, departure and arrival times are not always adhered to, and the owner is hard to approach. Trips to *Tamshiyacu Lodge* can be booked through Wilderness Expeditions S.A., 310 Washington Ave. SW., Roanoke, Va. 24016, Tel.: 703/342-5630. Amazon Selva Tours, Putumayo 133 (Daniel Ríos) highly recommended; they use *Selva Lodge* on Río Momón, and *Yarapa Lodge*, excellent food and able guides, US$32 a day. Sol Río Tours, owner Carlos Grández, who can be found at the airport, or agency on Jr. Napo (bookings also through Edificio La Torre de Lima, Centro Cívico, Lima), trips up to 5 people, 3 days or more, US$70 p.p. per day, no luxuries, recommended. Kaya Expeditions, Jr. Pitumaco 139, Jean-Pierre and Xavier speak most languages and run jungle tours, friendly, informal, informative, US$ 120 for 2 people for 3 days. Amazon Adventure Tours, Moore 1021, Tel.: 237306, run by Teodoro Valles Wing ("Lolo"), do 6-day jungle walking trips, US$30 a day with Lolo, who speaks English, and Adriano, warmly recommended. Queen Adventures, Calle Arica, jungle trips, about US$50 p.p. per day. For those who are tough, Freddie can be contacted opposite the iron Eiffel house; he organizes survival courses in the jungle and you learn to build your own camp, find your own food etc. Be warned, however: he has to approve of you and your level of fitness and stamina, not you of him. He speaks fluent English (US$400 for 3 for 5 days; longer would be better, mixed reports of his reliability). *Amazon Expedition Camp* on a tributary of the River Ucayali is run by Carlos Pérez (Tel.: 234529), US$260 for 2 nights. *Amazon Village*, opened in 1981. Tours there are operated by Exprinter; for details contact Amazon Village, c/o *Amazon Hotel* Iquitos, Miguel Drasso 167A, San Isidro, Lima, Tel.: 404-559. It is located on the River Momón, some hours away from the Amazon itself, so difficult river conditions can easily prevent visits to the Amazon. At the Village

PERU 753

there are clean, well-ventilated bungalows and good food; Philippe Itelsen, the manager, speaks many languages.

It is advisable to take a waterproof coat and shoes or light boots on such trips, and a good torch, as well as *espirales* to ward off the mosquitoes at night—they can be bought from drugstores in Iquitos. A recommended tour with a difference is the jungle survival excursion of Moisés Torres Viena (Jirón Brasil 217)—as taught to Peruvian soldiers—not cheap, but you will learn much about jungle botany and how to live off the plants. Artesanías La Chamita, Jirón Putumayo 157, offers week-long trips to different jungle villages. A bus from Jirón Lima takes you to Nanay river. Launches may do cruises to Leticia (Amazon Lodge Safaris have a 6-day trip to Leticia on the m/n *Adolfo*).

Excursions By bus to the village of Santo Tomás, about 20 km., a favourite week-end retreat of inhabitants of Iquitos; the village has a good restaurant and canoes may be hired. Launches also leave Iquitos for the village of Indiana; get off at the "varadero de Mazán" and walk through the banana plantations to the River Mazán. A trail leads from the village of Mazán through the jungle to Indiana (hotel), about a 2-hr. walk (steamy). Catch the launch back to Iquitos at 1300.

Naturalists should note that the area 50 km. around Iquitos is too inhabited to support much large wildlife; the Napo or Ucayali rivers have more to offer. Similarly the areas around the Lodges; however there is plenty of scope for seeing small fauna and learning about the flora. Trips to see Yagua Indians offer little but a chance to appreciate "a way of life which is not so much in transition as abandoned." (John C. O'Conor, Arlington, Va.)

Air International airport, Francisco Secada Vigneta, Tel.: 231501, 233094. Taxi to the airport costs US$2.50 (US$-5 at night); *motocarro* (motorcycle with 2 seats), US$1.50; bus, US$0.15, goes to market area, about 12 blocks from Plaza de Armas, taxi from there US$1.50. Automatic 90-day visa given on arrival on international flights. Faucett (Próspero 646), two daily jet flights (at 0600 and 1600) to Lima, one direct, the other via Pucallpa or Tarapoto on alternating days. Fare to Lima, US$83 foreigners, US$48 Peruvians. Faucett flies from Iquitos to Pucallpa, US$52. Mon., Wed., Fri., Sat., to Tarapoto; Tues., Thurs. Sun. AeroPerú (Jr. Próspero 248, Tel.: 232513) daily jet flights and extra on Tues., Thurs. and Sats., to Lima two flights daily via Tarapoto. To Trujillo, change planes at Tarapoto. Iquitos-Cuzco, Faucett, Mon., Wed., Fri., 0500 (via Lima in summer), also AeroPerú, Iquitos-Yurimaguas. No flights Iquitos-Ecuador. Faucett has three flights a week to Miami. TANS offices: Grupo 42 (for Brazil, Colombia), Sargento Flores 127; Grupo 8 (for Lima US$35, Trujillo US$30, Yurimaguas and Tarapoto US$19), Castilla 353, nr Plaza Sargento Flores; these flights are less than the cost of the commercial flights. TANS Catalina flying-boat to Ramón Castilla (about 2 hrs.) TANS DC6 flight to Ramón Castilla, US$13, Tues., Fri., Sun., and across Amazon by motor-boat to Leticia, Colombia, or Benjamin Constant, Brazil, for onward flights to Bogotá and Manaus, respectively. TANS also has a flight to Cabo Pantoja and other villages. TANS to Leticia (Tabatinga), but often booked up 2 months ahead for the aquaplane. The Brazilian airline Cruzeiro do Sul has two weekly flights on Wed. and Sat., at 1230, between Iquitos, Leticia (Tabatinga airport) and Manaus. Varig, Putumayo 188, Tel.: 234381 has flights to Manaus on Weds. and Sat., also to Tabatinga, US$75. It is also possible to fly from Tefé (Brazil—see page 346) to Iquitos, stopping at Tabatinga for border formalities. (Mark your luggage "Iquitos" or it will be unloaded at Tabatinga.) Flights Leticia-Iquitos on Sun., Wed., Fri., will have a connection flight to Pucallpa (exit tax Leticia airport US$10.), leaves Leticia 0800, leaves Iquitos for Pucallpa 1510; probably delayed (Pucallpa flight does not always operate). Iquitos flights frequently delayed. (Be sure to reconfirm your flight in Iquitos, as they are often overbooked.) Peruvian Air Force flies Pucallpa-Iquitos, US$20, but unreliable as seats in that plane may be requisitioned at short notice, and Iquitos-Leticia, US$12. The Air Force also flies to Andoas, an oil town in the jungle, on the river Pastaza. TANS hydroplane flies NNW along the river to Peneya, opposite Leguizamo in Colombia, or Gueppi, the military frontier post from where you can get to Puerto Asís (Colombia) by boat. On this flight, locals take precedence.

N.B. Travel agents sell flight tickets, but more expensive for foreigners than Peruvians; it helps if you can speak Spanish to bargain for the lower rate. Recommended is Fénix Viajes, Jr. Pevas 216-220, Tel.: 232417; not recommended is Laser, Jr. Próspero 213.

Shipping River boats to Pucallpa (infrequent) or Yurimaguas, 6-10 day trip (longer if cargo is being carried, which is usually the case), cheap, but beware of overcharging by gringos. Cabins are 4 berth and you have to buy both a first class ticket, which entitles you to food (whether you want it or not) and deck space to sling your hammock, and a cabin ticket if you want the "luxury" of a berth. Adequate washing and toilet facilities, but the food is rice, meat and beans (and whatever can be picked up *en route*) cooked in river water. Stock up on fruit and tinned food in Iquitos. There is a good cheap bar. Take plenty of prophylactic enteritis tablets; many contract dysentery on the trip. Also take insect repellant; one sold locally is called Black Flag and is quite effective. *Campeón* to Pucallpa, US$30 with food, 7 days; *Rosa* to Pucallpa, US$19, 7 days. Communications with Manaus by river are unreliable and the journey takes about 15 days (two boats doing this journey are *Clivia*, frequent, good food, and *Almirante Monteiro*, clean, reasonable food); best go first to Leticia, Tabatinga, Benjamin Constant, Ramón Castilla or Islandia. Ramón Castilla is a village before Islandia, opposite Tabatinga; Islandia itself is just a mud bank with an exchange shop on the Peruvian side of a narrow creek just a few yards from Benjamin Constant in Brazil. No boats from Iquitos go to Benjamin Constant, but all boats for Manaus start from there and a new hotel (*Benjamin*) has been built. Boats Iquitos-Islandia or Tabatinga, 36 hrs (2 days in other direction), about US$10; inc. food, US$2 extra for cabin. If a long wait is involved, then Leticia (Colombia) has the best hotels and facilities. Canoes put out from Leticia and will take off passengers from passing boats at another mud bank called Puerto Ancorade, just opposite. There are also ferries from Benjamin Constant to Tabatinga and Leticia, US$0.50, 1½ hrs. Information on boats for Pucallpa obtained on wharves, or at Meneses (Jirón Próspero), Bellavista (Malecón Tarapacá 596), Hurtado (Av. Grau 1223) and Casa Pinto (Sargento Flores 164). The *Oro Negro* boat is highly recommended for river journeys to Ramón Castilla, Leticia or Pucallpa. Avoid the *Rosa Angélica*, which is terrible. It is easy to find a boat, but difficult to get it to move, though you can stay on board. Details on exit and entry formalities seem to change frequently, so when leaving Peru, check in Iquitos first (Immigration, Arica 474, office hours 0900-1300); latest indications are that exit stamps are either given on the boat, or at Ramón Castilla, Puerto Alegría, or at the Peruvian Consulate in Leticia (0830-1430—the consul is elusive), while tourist cards for entry into Peru are given at Puerto Alegría, 2 hrs. upstream from Islandia, where the boat stops for police checks. Brazilian entry formalities are in Tabatinga, in town, 2 km. from the pier, or at the airport (taxis from riverfront to airport tend to overcharge). Boats to and across frontiers carry many smugglers and thieves.

The Inca Road

We have had great pleasure since 1979 in incorporating an account by Christopher Portway, the explorer and author, of the Andean Inca road. His most interesting book Journey along the Spine of the Andes *(Oxford Illustrated Press) was published in 1984. In view of space constraints, we have therefore shortened his account here.*

Basically, there were two great roads in the Inca system. One was the royal road between Cuzco and Quito, progressively extended to take in northern Ecuador, southern Colombia, and southwards, Bolivia and northern Argentina. A mind-boggling 5,230 km. in length, its remains have been best preserved (more through remoteness than any preserving agency) in Peru. Much of the 4,050 km. of the coastal road between Tumbes and the River Maule has been built over by the Pan-American Highway.

The standard width of the royal road varied between 5 and 6 metres (as against the 8 metres of the less-obstructed coastal road). It was unpaved, except where there was unavoidable water or when climbing steep hillsides necessitating the use of stone steps.

A good section, bordered by stone, may be seen some 13 km. east of the village of Shelby, served by the railway from Oroya to Cerro de Pasco. Its course is marked by the lonely ruins of Bonbón, an Inca community centre only recently identified, which in turn lies close to the modern dam holding back the Mantaro River as it flows out of the northern end of Lake Junín.

But perhaps the most astounding survival of Inca roads is the long stretch, displaying varied construction over differing terrain, between Yanahuanca and Huari.

Yanahuanca is situated in the incredibly beautiful valley of the same name. It is rarely entered by foreigners and thus a visitor has to contend with a retinue of a hundred or more curious inhabitants in his passage through the village. Its amenities include a few bars, a simple restaurant and a community social centre, but no hotel.

Two km. up the Yanahuanca Valley a lesser valley cuts northwards between the towering crags. The road, its paving uneven and disturbed by countless horse and donkey convoys, leads up the smaller valley, its course sometimes shared by a stream, to the village of Huarautambo, a community of some 220 people, about 4 km. distant.

This village is surrounded by many pre-Inca remains and the schoolmaster, Sr. Valentín Inga Castro, will be only too happy to show visitors the many ruins of the area, as well as the cave-tomb full of deformed skulls only recently discovered by him, a crop of cave paintings and numerous underground chambers.

For more than 150 km. the *Camino Incaico* is not only in almost continuous existence from the Yanahuanca Valley but is actually shown on the map issued by the Instituto Geográfico Militar. From Huarautambo, in company with lesser tracks, it winds up the head of the Huarautambo valley and across rock-scattered grasslands, over escarpments, following valleys, then veering away to utilize more valleys hidden by *saddles* over which the road triumphs even if the weary 20th-century traveller wilts along the way. At a spot known locally as Incapoyo, superb views of the Cordillera Huayhuash, with peaks soaring to 6,000 metres and more, are to be seen.

While the road fades from sight or has become muddled with present day tracks the route is marked by the ruins of *tampus*—or Inca rest houses—and, occasionally, larger sites. *Tampus* were official and utilitarian. Some of them consisted of a single structure, others had a series of smaller rooms opening on a large corral where the llamas were stabled. Each was maintained by the local *ayllu* as part of its labour tax.

Between Yanahuanca and Huari pre-Inca *tampus* and other remains provide landmarks for the road. Thereafter traces of the road become fainter though short sections can be identified in the hills behind San Luis, Piscobamba and Pomabamba. Behind Pomabamba, far up upon the final crest of the mountains to the west, the road is revealed by a chain of old forts older than the highway itself, but it is left to such disintegrating edifices to mark the route to Cajamarca and northwards into Ecuador.

Townships and villages along the way include the following: *Tamboccocha* and *Gashapampa*: One single shop with little to offer enlivens these two remote villages. *Pilcocancha*: A few km. north of the township of Baños, this village is notable for its hot thermal pools lying a kilometre south. *La Unión* (see also page 745): A "double town" with its main residential section across the River Vizcarra in the sheer-sided valley of the same name. Several small hotels, simple but adequate at about US$1 per night but no hot water, a farce of a cinema and half a dozen restaurants. On the grass plateau above the town are the spectacular ruins of *Huánuco Viejo* (see page 745). *Pomachaca*: A small village with a couple of shops at a road and river junction. The roads lead to Huari (*Hotel Ideal*, F), San Marcos and Llamellín. *San Luis*: A village in the shadow of the Cordillera Blanca. A few small restaurants and an occasional bus service to *Piscobamba*, with a basic, but clean hotel with friendly owner, and another, both F, and a few shops and small restaurants.

The staff of the mayor's office are helpful and from behind the town views across the valley are superb. Occasional buses to *Pomabamba*, a pleasant enough town, with several hotels (F), restaurants, a bank and a baker's shop that serves the best-value cakes in the province. On both sides of the valley in which Pomabamba stands are pre-Inca ruins of considerable interest. (There are 2 buses per week to Lima via Chavín, and 2 to Huarás via Sihuas, but you must book many days in advance.) *Sihuas*: A small township clinging to a hilltop. No hotel, but a couple of restaurants. *Huamachuco* (page 674). *Cajabamba* (see page 675). Lively little town with a hotel or two and a number of restaurants (not to be confused with the Ecuadorean town of the same name). *Ichocán*: Pleasant village with an interesting church and a few small restaurants. The council do not object to overnight camping in the plaza with its fountain and trees. *San Marcos*: Lively little town with a hotel or two. *Cajamarca* (page 675).

(**Warning** The Andean Inca road in the north of Peru passes through extremely remote mountain territory. Travellers are advised, therefore, to take full precautions against starvation and exposure. There is, apparently, some danger of attack by cattle rustlers).

The Economy

Revitalization of agriculture, which accounts for 14.1% of gdp and 37% of employment, is a government priority, with credits and improved prices being granted to farmers. While the Costa (which occupies 11% of the land area) has traditionally been the dominant economic region, with excellent crops of cotton, rice, sugar and fruit where the coastal desert is irrigated, the Sierra is being given preferential treatment with a view to restoring the self-sufficiency in food production of Inca times. It is hoped that, as the government's development plans gather momentum in 1987, food imports will be reduced. Irrigation of the coastal region using Andean waters is the key to improved yields of the main export crops, sugar and cotton. The other main export crop is coffee; these three make up 7.7% of total exports.

Although employing only 2% of the workforce, mining contributes 10.3% of gdp and the six major minerals and metals account for 40% of total export value. These are copper, iron, silver, gold, lead and zinc. Copper and iron deposits are found on the southern coast, but the principal mining area for all minerals is the Sierra. Low world prices, particularly for zinc and lead, strikes in the copper industry, rising costs and, since mid-1985, a fixed exchange rate have contributed to considerable losses for both public and private mining companies, and to reduced real output.

Peruvian oil accounted for over 50% of domestic energy consumption and 21% of export earnings in 1985. The northeastern jungle produced an average of 115,500 b/d in 1986, on and off the northwestern coast 55,000-65,000 b/d, while fields in the southern jungle are being explored. No major new reserves have been found since 1976, so Peru may become a net importer of oil by 1990. Local funds for investment have been falling in the 1980s, hence the need for foreign companies to invest in exploration, but in 1985 the García government rescinded the operating contracts of three major foreign firms, adversely affecting investment prospects, despite subsequent new agreements.

Manufacturing contributes 21.5% to gdp, employing 10% of the workforce.

756 PERU

After high growth rates in the early 1970s, industry slumped to operating at 40% of its total capacity as purchasing power was reduced, and the cost of energy, raw materials and trade credit rose faster than inflation. By the end of 1986, though, most of industry was working at full capacity following a consumer-led recovery. Similarly, construction returned to growth in 1986 as a result of government projects, after three years of recession. Construction accounts for 4.1% of gdp and 4% of employment.

Fishing, which accounts for 1.1% of gdp, suffered a dramatic decline in 1983 as the Niño current forced out of Peruvian waters the main catch, anchovy, whose stocks were already seriously depleted by overfishing in the 1970s. From being the world's leading fishmeal exporter, with exports accounting for 14% of the country's total, fishmeal sales fell to 4% in 1985, recovering in 1986 to 7%. The García government has partially reversed its predecessor's policy of closing fishmeal plants, in conjunction with promoting fish as a domestic food source.

Growing fiscal deficits in the 1980s led to increasing delays in payments of principal and interest on the foreign debt, which was US$14.7 bn at the end of 1986. As arrears accumulated to both multilateral agencies and commercial banks, the IMF declared Peru ineligible for further credits in 1986. On taking office, President García limited public debt service payments to 10% of foreign exchange earnings in order to maintain reserves to promote development. In 1986, the need to import food, the low level of exports and the fall in disbursements of foreign capital in fact caused international reserves to fall.

	1961-70 (av)	1971-80 (av)	1981-85 (av)	1986 (e)
Gdp growth (1980 prices)	5.7%	3.5%	-0.3%	8.9%
Inflation	9.9%	31.9%	104.9%	78.0%
Exports (fob) US$m	659	1,816	3,135	2,509
Copper	163	366	468	385
Crude petroleum	—	225	335	235
Zinc	33	139	291	222
Imports (fob) US$m	508	1,398	2,274	2,559
Current account balance US$m (cum)	-592	-4,109	-4,375	-1,155

Information for Visitors

Air Services from Europe Direct flights from Frankfurt, Paris, Amsterdam, Madrid and Lisbon by Lufthansa, Air France, KLM, Iberia, Viasa (who offer a cheap youth fare) and Avianca. Cheap flights from London; one way is to go via Madrid with Iberia, or standby to Miami, then fly with AeroPerú to Lima, or Faucett to Iquitos, Cuzco and Lima. Several low-price charters from Paris; apply to Jumbo (subsidiary of Air France), 60 rue Monsieur le Prince, Paris 75006 (Tel.: 325-93-75); or Uniclam-Voyages, 63 rue Monsieur le Prince, Paris 75006 (Tel.: 633-59-14, or Lima, Av. La Paz 744, Miraflores, Tel.: 467298), offices also in Arequipa, Cuzco and Puno; or Nouvelles Frontières, 63 av. Denfert-Rochereau, Paris 75014 (Tel.: 325-57-51) and Top Tours, Jirón A. Miró Quesada 247, of. 612, Lima (Tel.: 275152)—flights with Aeroflot to Luxembourg; or Le Point Mulhouse, 4 rue des Orphelins, Mulhouse 68200 (Tel.: (89)42-44-61); or Le Point, Vermittlung von Fernflügen, Rheinstrasse 165, Baden-Baden, West Germany (Tel.: 64017). Also Le Point flights with SATA, a Swiss company operating from Zurich to Lima weekly, Lima agent for Le Point; Promotora de Turismo, Nuevo Mundo, *Jirón Camaná 780, Oficina 506*; Le Point also at Nicolás de Piérola, 742, *Oficina 707* (Tel.: 271619, 271502). Sindbad Travel, another Swiss operator, has cheap charter flights with Balair, between Lima-Barbados-Paris/Brussels/ Zürich/Basle; office at Jirón Juan Fanning 480, Miraflores, Lima, Tel.: 47-7087, also in Zürich. Firma Setours, Jirón Unión 1011, Lima, has cheap flights to Brussels fortnightly. Sobelair, the charter subsidiary of Sabena, has flights leaving Brussels Sun., 16 hrs., stopover of 1 hr. in Martinique, return Mon. Tickets available throughout West Germany, France, Belgium and Holland. Cheap flights available from Zürich on same basis. Aeroflot fly from Frankfurt via Cuba with 3 hr. stopover in Havana including sightseeing. Tickets from Uniclam-Solmatur, La Paz 744, Miraflores, Lima (Tel.: 467298, 478764). To avoid paying Peru's 21% tax on international air tickets, take your used outward ticket with you when buying return passage. Students with a valid identity card can obtain a 7% discount on international flight tickets if they book through INTEJ, Av. San Martín 240, Barranco, Lima.

From USA and Canada Miami is the main gateway to Peru with flights every day. AeroPerú, Third Avenue, Miami (Tel.: 800-255-7378). Other direct flights from New York, Los Angeles, Washington, Vancouver, Toronto and Montreal by CP Air, Avianca, Aerolíneas Argentinas, Air Panamá, Varig, Lan Chile and Ecuatoriana. Faucett has an office in Toronto. Direct flights between Peru and USA, suspended in 1984, were restored in April 1987.

From South America Regular flights to all South American countries; in most cases, daily. Lloyd Aéreo Boliviano (LAB -non-IATA) is usually the cheapest airline for flights out of Lima but tickets bought in Peru are more expensive; try to get Lima-La Paz ticket in Colombia. LAB flies twice weekly between La Paz and Cuzco. Aerolíneas Argentinas and AeroPerú fly from Mexico. Beware of buying Viasa tickets in Peru, they often turn out to be false. AeroPerú has 30-day "Around South America" pass, recommended, US$759, cheapest available.

Trans-Pacific Flights from Tokyo by Varig and CP Air. From Australia and New Zealand to Tahiti by Air New Zealand, Qantas or UTA with a Lan-Chile connection to Lima via Santiago (stopover in Easter Island).

Trans-South Atlantic From South Africa to Rio de Janeiro by South African Airlines or Varig, with immediate connections.

Taxes There is a US$10 airport tax on international flight departures, payable in local currency or in dollars. Internal airport tax US$3. There is a 21% tax on economy international flights originating in Peru. There is a 9% tax on domestic flights. Tax should not be charged on an MCO, but 9% often is.

Shipping Services The most direct sea route from the UK is the PSNC's (freight only) from Liverpool. Another sea route from Europe is via New York, where transatlantic vessels connect with American vessels. European lines serving Peru are Norwegian Knutsen, the Swedish Johnson, the Italia Line, the French Compagnie Générale Maritime (from La Pallice/La Rochelle to Callao, US$1200 -4 weeks of luxury; enquire at Mundy Travel Ltd, 6-7 Rangoon St., London EC3 2PA, or Paseo de la República 3587, Lima), the Royal Netherlands Steamship Company, the German Hamburg Amerika Line, La Hanseática, Av. Enrique Canaval Moreyra 340 (Pisos 9-10), San Isidro, Lima and Hapag-Lloyd and the Westfal Larsen Line. Passenger services from France can be arranged through Continental Shipping and Travel, 179 Piccadilly, London W1V 9DB, Tel.: 01-491 4968. The Kawasaki Kisen Kaisha serves Peru from Australia, and the Bank Line from India. The Booth Line runs vessels to the Peruvian reaches of the Amazon. The Chilean Cía. Sudamericana de Vapores, CPV, and Flota Gran Colombiana ply between Peru and Europe but carry no passengers.

Consorcio Naviero Peruano, Paseo de la República 3587 (Piso 9), Lima, carries a few passengers to Le Havre and sometimes Hamburg; to Italy, Lauro, Av. Enrique Canaval Moreyra 328.

Documents No visa is necessary for citizens of Western European countries, South American countries (except Chile and Venezuela), Canada, the USA and Japan. Australians and New Zealanders must have visas. A Tourist Card (*Cédula C*, obligatory) may be obtained free from the immigration authorities on arrival in Peru for visits up to 90 days (insist on getting the full 90 days, at some borders cards valid for 60, or even only 30 days have been given). It is in duplicate, the original given up on arrival and the copy on departure, and may be renewed (see below). A new tourist card must be obtained for each re-entry or when an extension is given. An International Certificate of Vaccination against smallpox is no longer required. Declaration of foreign currency no longer required. All foreigners should be able to produce on demand some recognizable means of identification, preferably a passport. Officially, an exit ticket is required for entry into Peru to be allowed. At land frontiers, practices vary; an MCO may not be accepted as an onward ticket. One's best bet is a bus ticket Arequipa-Arica (Tepsa, valid for 6 months, sold as an onward ticket at the Ecuadorean border even though Tepsa have discontinued the route, and more expensive than Arequipa-Tacna, Tacna-Arica bus journeys) which may then be exchanged with persistence. Similarly, much persistence can get you through without a ticket and many travellers have reported that they have not been asked for a ticket at Aguas Verdes or Desaguadero. If you do not have one on arrival

758 PERU

at the border, you may be forced to pay US$15 minimum for an out-going bus ticket. Travellers arriving by air report no onward flight checks at Lima airport.

N.B. Tourist visas may be renewed for 60 days at the Ministerio del Interior, Paseo de la República at Av. 28 de Julio, Lima (also, we are told, in PIP offices in certain towns: check). On presentation of the visitor's passport, a valid return ticket to a destination outside Peru, a *solicitud* (written request for an extension) and on payment of US$20 or the equivalent in intis. If you wish to extend your entry permit after 90 days have already elapsed since your entry into Peru this is possible at the discretion of the authorities, but on payment of a fine of US$20. The maximum stay in such a case would be 150 days from the first entry. If you are in the Puno area when your visa expires, it is sometimes quicker and easier to cross the border to Bolivia for a day and return with a new visa, often for 90 days, which you would not get in Lima or Cuzco. To obtain a one-year student visa one must have: proof of adequate funds, affiliation to a Peruvian body, a letter of recommendation from your own and a Peruvian Consul, a letter of moral and economic guarantee from a Peruvian citizen and 4 photographs (frontal and profile). One must also have a health check certificate which takes 4 weeks to get and costs US$10. If your tourist card is stolen or lost, apply for a new one at Dirección General de Migración, Av. 28 de Julio 1118; very helpful.

Students are advised to take an international student's card in order to benefit from the many student reductions available, especially in and around Cuzco. To be any use in Peru, it must bear the owner's photograph. You can sometimes achieve benefits if "student" is on your tourist card as your occupation, but this can mean hours of haggling.

British business travellers are strongly advised to get "Hints to Exporters: Peru", from Export Services Division, Department of Trade, Sanctuary Buildings, Great Smith St., London SW1P 3DB.

Export Ban No object of archaeological interest may be taken out of Peru.

Duty-free Imports 400 cigarettes or 50 cigars or 500 grams of tobacco, 2 litres of alcoholic drinks, new articles for personal use or gifts up to value US$200.

Warnings Thieves are active in markets, streets, hotels, buses and trains, choosing especially tourists as their targets. Take care everywhere, but especially when arriving in or leaving from a town at night by bus or train. Don't get into conversation with locals at such times. Thieves normally work in groups. Don't wear jewellery on the street. Use of a capacious money-belt, worn beneath one's clothes, is repeatedly recommended. Don't pick up money in the street, it is often a ruse to rob you while you are off guard. If possible, lock your luggage when leaving it in your hotel room. Avoid staying in hotels too near to bus companies, as drivers who stay overnight are sometimes in league with thieves. The police and local people seem unwilling to help, although the police presence in Lima, Arequipa, Puno and Cuzco has been greatly stepped up. It is a good idea to inform your Embassy in Lima of your passport data, so that if the passport is stolen delays for replacement are minimized. As recommended in the Colombia section regarding personal safety, common sense is the best policy. Outside the July-August peak holiday period, there is less tension, less risk of crime, and more friendliness. A friendly attitude on your part, smiling even when you've thwarted a thief's attempt, can help you out of trouble.

Although certain illegal drugs are readily available anyone carrying any is almost automatically assumed to be a drug trafficker. If arrested on any charge the wait for trial in prison can take a year and is particularly unpleasant. Unfortunately, we have received reports of drug-planting, or mere accusation of drug-trafficking by the PIP on foreigners in Lima, with US$500 demanded for release. **Drugs use or purchase is punishable by up to 15 years' imprisonment**. Anyone wishing to visit fellow-countrymen in jail should contact Foreign Prisoners' Fellowship, Church of the Good Shepherd, Av. Santa Cruz 491 (Apartado 5152), Lima 18, Tel.: 457-908.

Another Warning The activities of the "maoist" guerrilla movement, *Sendero* Luminoso, are spreading. Avoid visiting places where they are reported as particularly active: they have no love for foreign tourists. Since Sendero Luminoso has been linked (supposedly) with the drugs trade, police and army searches have increased. Under state of siege legislation, be careful what you photograph. If possible carry an official letter stating your business. The following provinces are under martial law: Junín, Huancavelica, Ayacucho, Loreto, Apurímac, Huánuco, San Martín and Pasco. Lima and Callao were placed under state of siege in 1986. The Country Officer for Peru, Office of Andean Affairs, Dept. of State, Washington D.C. 20520, Tel.: 202-632-3360, will inform US citizens on the advisability of travel.

Important If your belongings are stolen: (1) If the value is over US$20, go to PIP International Police (ask for the *Extranjería* section if you encounter difficulties, the *comandante* or his second-in-command), if under US$20 go to the Guardia Civil. Alternatively, in Lima, one can go to the Tourist Police. (2) Make declaration of loss as soon as possible. (3) Buy *papel sellado* (stamped paper) on which to make statement. See also under Cuzco, page 718-719.

A *denuncia*—a statement of a theft signed by police—is valid in place of a student card if student card is taken, and is essential for insurance purposes. *Denuncias* (US$0.50) and *papeles sellados* (US$0.20) can be bought in the streets behind the Palacio de Justicia in Lima. If your credit card is stolen apply immediately to Lima Tours for American Express, who are represented in the major cities. For other credit cards, there is now a combined office in Lima, Tel.: 461545 (day and night service).

Internal Air Services link towns which are often far apart and can only be reached otherwise with difficulty. Virtually all the air traffic is in the hands of the Cía. de Aviación Faucett (who run bingo on board!) and AeroPerú. Tickets are not interchangeable between the two companies. See under Lima (page 653) for towns served, and above for taxes. Faucett and AeroPerú offer cheap unlimited travel within Peru; the ticket costs £140 and is valid for 60 days. You must decide which places you want to go to in advance, but you don't have to go to all of them, and you must fly to Peru with Faucett or AeroPerú and purchase the ticket outside South America. In the UK a £99 airpass is available for unlimited travel, but you can only fly standby; there is also a 4-flight, predetermined-itinerary pass for £165, and a 2-month, unlimited pass for £215. If you have a choice, remember timekeeping tends to be better early a.m. than later.

In 1985, the Government permitted foreigners to purchase air tickets at the rate charged to Peruvians (see text), but it is not known how long this arrangement will last.

N.B. Both companies are often criticized for frequent cancellations and poor time-keeping. The Andean area is dangerous for flying, and unpredictable weather contributes to poor time-keeping, but companies are also criticized for their passenger service, especially as regards information and overbooking. Note that flights into the mountains may well be put forward 1 hr. if there are reports of bad weather. Neither company has enough aircraft and both are in financial difficulties. Flights to jungle regions are also unreliable. See also warning on page 721.

Flights must be reconfirmed 24 hrs. in advance. Twenty mins. before departure, the clerk is allowed by law to let standby passengers board, taking the reserved seats of those who haven't turned up.

Air Freight (Internal) 16 kg. rucksack Lima-Tacna, US$4 including insurance. Packages must be secure so rucksack was enveloped in a flour sack that cost another US$4 (including paying someone to do the buying and work).

Motoring The Touring y Automóvil Club del Perú, Av. César Vallejo 699, Lince, Lima (Tel.: 403270), with offices in most provincial cities, gives news about the roads and hotels along the way (although for the most up-to-date information try the bus and colectivo offices). It sells a very good road map at US$2.25 (Mapa Vial del Perú, 1:3,000,000, Ed. 1980, reliable information about road conditions) and route maps covering most of Peru at US$0.40 (Hoja de Ruta, detail maps 1:1,000,000, very good but no information on road conditions). AAA maps sold at *Lima Times* office. Buy maps separately or in packages of 8. Cuadernos de Viaje are travel notebooks covering all Peru with valuable information and maps, in Spanish. Other maps can be bought from street vendors in Colmena and Plaza San Martín, Lima. "Westermanns Monatshefte; folio Ecuador, Peru, Bolivien" has excellent maps of Peru, especially the archaeological sites. Gasoline per US gallon: "extra" (84 octane), US$1.20; "importada" (95 octane), US$1.45, found in Lima, the coastal towns and Arequipa. Gasoline is cheaper in the Selva. In Lima never trust the green light; Peruvian drivers tend to regard traffic lights as recommendations, at most. When parking remove detachable accessories and screen wipers. No-parking signs are painted at the roadside: illegally parked cars are towed away.

Roads go to very high altitudes in Peru—make sure that the spark is properly adjusted and consider use of smaller carburettor jets if driving much at altitude. Avoid mountain travel between November and April. Take 2 planks of wood in case car gets stuck in soft soil when allowing other vehicles to pass. Never travel off the main roads without being self-sufficient. Always make sure your gasoline tank is full when branching off a major highway, fill up whenever possible and make sure you do not receive diesel or kerosene. If you need mechanical assistance in the mountains ask for the nearest mining or road construction camp. If you take your own car you are immediately a symbol of wealth and will be liable to have it broken into. Disadvantages of travelling in your own vehicle include the difficulties of getting insurance, theft, finding guarded parking lots, maintenance on appalling roads and nervous exhaustion, which may outweigh the advantages of mobility and independence.

Imported car spares available and cheaper than in neighbouring countries. Makes with well-established dealerships are easiest to obtain (e.g. Volvo, Peugeot, VW). VW Beetles, Toyota Coronas and Datsun Stanzas are assembled in Peru and therefore easier to get spares and service for. There is also a booming black market in motor parts involving both contraband and stolen parts. Must have international driving licence—especially with a number. If you don't have a number on your licence, improvise. (It has been reported that a UK driving licence is acceptable.)

Surface Transport Few roads in Peru, except for the Pan-American and Central Highways and the roads connecting Huarás and Carás with Pativilca, and Pacasmayo with Cajamarca, are paved. Paving of the important Puno-Desaguadero road to Bolivia is now reported complete. Toll roads in Peru include Aguas Verdes-Tumbes, Pativilca-Huarás, Lima-Pucusana, Ica-Nazca, Lima (highway around city), Variante-Pacasmayo, which vary from US$0.15 (for the roads around Cuzco), to US$0.25 for most others. Landslides are frequent, surfaces are usually very rough, and this makes for slow travel and frequent breakdowns.

Bus services along the coast and to Arequipa (best is Ormeño) are usually quite good; buses in the mountain areas generally are small, old, crowded and offer little comfort; Ormeño and Cruz del Sur thought generally to be the best. For long journey take a water bottle. Blankets and emergency food are a *must* in the mountains. Always possible to buy food on the roadside, as buses stop frequently. If your bus breaks down and you are transferred to another line and have to pay extra, keep your original ticket for refund from the first company. Colectivos not always much dearer; trucks not always much cheaper; they charge ¾ bus fare, but wholly unpredictable, not for long hops, and comfort depends on the load: the ideal is a half load of sugar. Colectivos go almost anywhere in Peru; most firms will have offices. Book one day in advance. They pick you up at your hotel or in main square. Always try to arrive at your destination in daylight: much safer.

Note for Hitch-Hikers: Hitch-hiking is difficult. Freight traffic has to stop at the police *garitas* outside each town and these are the best places to try (also, toll points, but these are further from towns). Drivers usually ask for money but don't always expect to get it. In mountain and jungle areas you usually have to pay drivers of lorries, vans and even private cars; ask the driver first how much he is going to charge, and then recheck with the locals (the Sierra Indians for whom it is normal method of travel). Private cars are very few and far between.

Taxis In most places taxi fares are fixed before the journey; therefore it is best to ask local advice on average charges before you bargain with taxi drivers. Taxis ordered at hotels are much more expensive than those hailed on the streets.

Walking Serious walkers are advised to get *Backpacking in Peru and Bolivia*, by Hilary and George Bradt. They describe 3-5 day treks in the Cordilleras Blanca, Vilcabamba and Vilcanota (Cuzco region), and in the Cajamarca area. Also Jim Bartle's book: *Trails of the Cordilleras Blanca and Huayhuash of Perú*, Ed. Gráfica Pacific, Lima, 1980 (Jim Bartle has also published a series of excellent postcards of various peaks, sold in many bookshops in Lima). John Richter's *Yurak Yunka* can be obtained from the South American Explorers' Club or from *Lima 2000* bookshop, J. Bernal 271, Lima.

Hotels The State Tourist Hotels (commonly known as *Hoteles de Turistas*) are run by Enturperú. They vary considerably but frequently offer the best accommodation in town in terms of cleanliness and reliable food. They provide safe *garaging* for cars at US$0.65 a night. Reservations can be made at Enturperú, Av. Javier Prado-Oeste 1358, San Isidro, P.O. Box 4475, Lima, Tel.: 287815, 282742, 274077, Telex: 20394.

Heating in rooms often unsatisfactory. Good local maps can usually be obtained at the Tourist Hotels; in some of the smaller towns they function as tourist offices. All de luxe, 1st class and State Tourist Hotels charge a high 18% in taxes, which includes service charges; lower category hotels charge 13-16%.

Most hotels have this surcharge included in their prices, but best check first. By law all places that offer accommodation now have a plaque outside bearing the letters H (Hotel), Hs (Hostal), HR (Hotel Residencial) or P (Pensión) according to type. Previously, in many cases, there was no indication that these places did in fact offer accommodation. Many hotels have safe parking for motor cycles. Check all bills most carefully. Bargaining is possible outside the peak July-August holiday season.

Note The Peruvian police seem to be sensitive about finding an unmarried Peruvian woman in a foreigner's hotel room after 1900 hours. They will charge her with prostitution, however innocent your intentions. (Non-Peruvian unmarried couples will not be bothered by the police.)

Camping Easy in Peru, especially along the coast. But following a number of attacks in the Andes on campers, it is not wise to camp in lonely places. Camping gaz bottles are available in Peru. Those with stoves designed for lead-free gasoline should use *ron de quemar*, available from hardware shops (*ferreterías*).

Swimming Between December and April the entire coast of Peru offers good bathing, but during the rest of the year only the northern beaches near Tumbes provide pleasantly warm water.

Climate The coast is at its most agreeable from December to April inclusive, but this is the period when most rain falls in the Sierra. Business is more active later, but climate does not interfere much with business. During the cooler months, June to November, there is little or no rain but Lima's humidity is from 90 to 98% —and there is little sunshine from Paramonga S to Arica. During this period the temperature rarely falls below 13°C, or rises above 27°C. For the high Sierra heavier clothing should be taken—difference between day and night temperatures is great. The jungles beyond are tropical.

N.B. Between mid-July and mid-September, a great many Europeans go to Peru on holiday (also, many young Peruvians are on holiday in July and the first half of August), so it is better to avoid the country at this time: prices rise, transport is difficult, and the Peruvians tend to be less friendly.

Health Drinking water from the tap is generally not safe in the cities of Peru (see also under Lima, page 645), but bottled water is available everywhere. Ask for drinks "sin hielo" (without ice) as the ice is likely to be made with ordinary tap water. Salads washed in tap water should be treated with caution on arrival in the country, but once accustomed, you are not likely to get "Inca Quickstep". Food at better hotels and restaurants is fine, even salads, but watch out for the typical dishes seasoned with highly spiced Peruvian peppers. In cases of diarrhoea, take "Colitina", an effective local remedy. There are frequent outbreaks of typhoid in Lima and in many other parts of Peru. Outbreaks of virus hepatitis occur and can be protected against by taking immunoglobulins; be careful when eating in markets. Be careful about buying gamma globulin in Peru as most pharmacists do not keep it under refrigeration, rendering it valueless. Buy a disposable syringe for US$0.25 to obviate risk of hepatitis from the clinic or doctor's needle. In Lima, there is a Centro de Antirabia if you are unfortunate enough to be bitten by a rabid dog; in other cities, hospitals give anti-rabies injections. Because of a TB epidemic, avoid non-pasteurized milk (i.e. most milk).

Altitude is often a problem in the mountain cities. Also, when walking at high altitude, the body needs sugar, which can be carried conveniently in the form of a block of *crystallized pure cane sugar*, called *chancaca*, and easily found in markets. (See also **Health Information** at front of book.)

Cost of Living Living costs in the Provinces are from 10 to 20% below those of Lima. Peru is not too expensive for those who want comfort and reasonable food; eat *table d'hôte* meals when possible; they are served more quickly. Hotel prices compare very favourably with those in other Latin American countries.

Tips Hotel 10% in addition to the 10% on the bill. Restaurants: medium to luxury class 5% in addition to bill which includes tax and 10% service unless otherwise stated. Taxi drivers, none (in fact, bargain the price down, then pay extra for good service if you get it). Cloakroom attendants and hairdressers (very high class only), US$0.50-$1. Railway porters, US$0.15 per bag, according to distance carried. Airport porters, US$0.50, or US$1 for 8 bags or more. Note: anyone who as much as touches your bag will expect a tip. Usherettes, none. Car wash boys, US$0.25, car "watch" boys, US$0.10.

Currency The monetary unit used to be the sol; there are still sol notes and

762 PERU

coins in circulation, probably to be withdrawn in 1989. On January 1, 1986, the inti was introduced, worth 1,000 soles, but people still think in terms of soles, or of "libras" (pounds) worth 10 soles (used for amounts under 1,000 soles only). The inti is divided into 100 céntimos. Coins are of 1, 5, 10, 25, and 50 céntimos; 1 and 5 intis. Notes are of 10, 50, 100 and 500 intis. It is extremely difficult to change currencies other than US dollars, and other currencies carry higher commission fees. The Banco de la Nación at Lima airport, and at large towns near the frontier, will repurchase intis from departing travellers, but don't leave it too late; you will not be able to buy dollars at the frontier itself. For repurchase, it is essential to retain Banco de la Nación exchange slips. Apparently, *casas de cambio* on Plaza San Martín in Lima give very good rates for sucres and Bolivian pesos (better than in those countries).

Warning We have been informed that a large number of forged notes are in circulation; check the numbers if possible, and hold notes up to the light to inspect the blank white space for silhouette portrait. We have also been told that there is a shortage of change in museums, post offices, railway stations and even shops, while taxi drivers are notorious in this regard—one is simply told "no change".

Foreign Exchange Banco de la Nación is now said to give only the official rate, therefore to be avoided by tourists. All banks close Sat., Sun., holidays, and June 30 and December 31 for balancing the books, except that the Jorge Chávez Airport branch is open 24 hrs. every day of the year. Always count your money in the presence of the cashier, particularly the "pre-counted" bundles of notes. It is possible to have US$ sent from your home country. Take the cheque to the Banco de la Nación and ask for a *liquidación por canje de moneda extranjera*. You will be charged 1% commission in US$ or intis. The main hotels, *casas de cambio* and other banks are now allowed to exchange foreign currencies; however, hotels usually only provide this service for their guests, and many commercial banks charge 4%-5% commission. The services of the Banco de Crédito have been repeatedly recommended.

Casas de cambio are recommended for their good rates, speed and honesty. All banks use the official exchange rate, but at *casas de cambio* the "financial" rate is normally used, which is about 20% higher than the official rate. However, not all exchange houses take travellers' cheques. American Express state that they will sell travellers' cheques and give out emergency money, but only in Lima. Travel agents are allowed to accept foreign currencies in payment for their services, and to exchange small amounts. Outside Lima, Arequipa and Cuzco changing travellers' cheques can be a long, slow process and a photocopy of your passport may be required. Travellers have reported great difficulty in cashing travellers' cheques in the jungle area, even Iquitos. Always sign travellers' cheques in blue or black ink or ballpen.

The parallel market rate, in January 1987 over 20 intis to the US$ against 13.90 official and 17.40 financial, is used by street money changers (in Lima around Plaza San Martín and in Arequipa along Calle Sto. Domingo).

Credit Cards Visa—most common—Diners Club, and Mastercharge (Access) widely accepted, including at State Tourist Hotels. Some shops only accept cards issued in Peru or South America, and we are told that in Puno it is virtually impossible to use any type of credit card.

Telephones Calls to Europe cost US$13 for 3 min., US$3.25 for each extra minute. Collect calls can now be made to North America and Europe (but not Switzerland) at the Entel offices, off the Plaza San Martín in Lima. Deposit for international calls is more in Cuzco than in Lima. Public telephone boxes need a token (*ficha*, 300 soles/30 céntimos called a *Rin*), often in short supply (there are street vendors who sell them, as well as news kiosks). Telephone directories found in most hotel rooms have a useful map of Lima and show itineraries of the buses. Telex to UK: US$15 for 3 minutes.

Mail Sending parcels abroad is subject to *a limit of 2 kg.* Customs for overseas mail is at Juan del Mar, corner of Bernedo, in Chacra Ríos. Staff in the post office help with all checking and then sew parcels into sacks for US$1. Try not to have articles sent by post to Peru; pilfering is very serious. Strikes are also very common. Letters to the UK, most European countries, USA and Canada all cost US$0.18; letters over 10 grammes cost US$0.55, increasing in line with weight. Letters of under 10 grammes within South America cost US$0.25 airmail. For a small fee letters can be sent "con certificado", which is recommended.

The **metric system** of weights and measures is compulsory.

Public Holidays

January 1: New Year.
March or April: Maundy Thursday (pm).
Good Friday.
May 1: Labour Day.
June 29: SS. Peter and Paul.
July 28, 29: Independence.

August 30: S. Rosa de Lima.
October 8: Battle of Angamos.
November 1: All Saints.
December 8: Immaculate Conception.
December 25: Christmas.

N.B. Everything closes on New Year's Eve, Christmas Eve, and other holidays designated "family holidays", especially July-August. At these times, expect prices to rise.

Hours of Business *Shops:* Jan. to March, 0900-1230 and 1600-1900 (0930-1245, 1615-1900 in Lima). Rest of year: 0900-1230, 1530-1900. Some are closed on Sat.; many close later in the evening. *Banks:* Jan. to March, 0830-1130. Rest of year: 0830-1200 (some have introduced afternoon opening). Closed Sat. **N.B.** All banks close on June 30 and December 31 for balancing; if it falls on Sat. or Sun., banks may close one day before or after. *Offices:* Jan. to March, 0830-1130, and 1500-1830. Rest of year: 0830-1230 and 1500-1830. Many now work a through day, 0800-1500, and most close on Sat. *Government Offices:* Jan. to March, 0930-1130, Sat. 0900-1230. Rest of year: 0930-1100, 1500-1700; on Sat. 0930-1130.

The Press Lima has 7 morning papers: *La Prensa, El Comercio, La República* (liberal-left) *La Crónica, Expreso, Ojo, El Diario.* There is a weekly paper in English, the *Lima Times,* and a monthly economic and political report, the *Andean Report.* The main provincial cities have at least one newspaper each.

Sports Association football is the most popular. Basketball and other sports are also played on the coast, particularly around Lima and Callao. There are many bathing resorts near Lima. Golf clubs and racecourses are mentioned in the text. Riding is a favourite recreation in the Sierra, where horses can be hired at reasonable rates. Cricket is played at the Lima Cricket Club. There is excellent deep-sea fishing off Ancón, N of Lima, and at the small port of Cabo Blanco, N of Talara (see text). In that part of the Andes easily reached from La Oroya, the lakes and streams have been stocked with trout, and fly fishing is quite good. Bullfights and cockfights are held in Lima.

For details about the best rainbow trout fishing in Peru (near Juliaca and in Lakes Arapa and Titicaca) write to Sr. José Bernal Paredes, Casilla 874, Arequipa.

Food The high-class hotels and restaurants serve international food and, on demand, some native dishes, but it is in the taverns (*chicherías*) and the local restaurants (*picanterías*) that the highly seasoned native food is often at its best. Generally found that the modest cafés are best value. Soups tend to be very good, and a meal in themselves. In the Lima area the most popular fish dishes are the *cebiche de corvina*—seasoned with lemons, onions and red peppers; the *escabeche de corvina*—with onions, hot green pepper, red peppers, prawns (*langostinos*), cumin, hard eggs, olives, and sprinkled with cheese; and *chupe de camarones*, a shrimp stew made with varying and somewhat surprising ingredients. *Parihuela* is a popular bouillabaisse which includes *yuyo de mar*, a tangy seaweed. *Yacu-chupe*, or green soup, has a basis of potato, with cheese, garlic, coriander leaves, parsley, peppers, eggs, onions, and mint. *Causa* and *carapulca* are two good potato dishes; *causa* is made with yellow potatoes, lemons, pepper, hard-boiled eggs, olives, lettuce, sweet cooked corn, sweet cooked potato, fresh cheese, and served with onion sauce. Favourite meat dishes are *ollucos con charque* (a kind of potato with dried meat), *caucau,* made with tripe, potatoes, peppers, and parsley and served with rice; *anticuchos,* hearts of beef with garlic, peppers, cumin seeds and vinegar; *estofado de carne,* a stew which often contains wine; *carne en adobo,* a cut and seasoned steak; *fritos,* fried pork, usually eaten in the morning; *sancochado,* meat and all kinds of vegetables stewed together and seasoned with ground garlic; *lomo a la huancaína,* beef with egg and cheese sauce; *lomo saltado* is a beef stew with onions, vinegar, ginger, chilli, tomatoes and fried potatoes, served with rice; and *sopa a la criolla* containing thin noodles, beef heart, bits of egg and vegetables and pleasantly spiced. Any dish described as *arequipeño* can be expected to be hot and spicy. *Mondonguito* is a boiled small intestine. The best beef is imported from Argentina and is expensive. Duck is excellent. For snacks, Peruvian *empanadas* are good. *Palta rellena* is avocado filled with chicken salad.

Among the desserts and confections are *cocada al horno*—coconut, with yolk of egg, sesame seed, wine and butter; *picarones*—frittered cassava flour and eggs fried in fat and served with honey; *mazamorra morada*—purple maize, sweet potato starch, lemons, various dried fruits, sticks of ground cinnamon and cloves and perfumed pepper; *manjar blanco*—milk, sugar and eggs; *maná*—an almond paste with eggs, vanilla and milk; *alfajores*—shortbread biscuit with *manjar blanco*, pineapple, peanuts, etc.; *pastellillos*— yucas with sweet potato, sugar and anise fried in fat and powdered with sugar and served hot; and *zango de pasas*, made with maize, syrup, raisins and sugar. *Turrón*, the Lima nougat, is worth trying. *Tejas* are sugar candies wrapped in wax paper; the pecan-flavoured ones are tastiest. The various Peruvian fruits are of good quality: they include bananas, the citrus fruits, pineapples, dates, avocados (*paltas*), eggfruit (*lúcuma*), the custard apple (*chirimoya*) which can be as big as your head, quince, papaya, mango, guava, the passion-fruit (*maracuyá*) and the soursop (*guanábana*).

The tea hour starts about 1800 at the good hotels. If asked to a party ask the hostess what time you are *really* expected unless the time is specified on the invitation card as *hora inglesa*—English time; Peruvians tend to ask guests for dinner at 2000, but don't expect them till at least 2130.

A normal lunch or dinner costs about US$4.50, but can go up to about US$25 in a first-class restaurant, with drinks and wine included. Lunch is the main meal: dinner in restaurants is normally about 1900 onwards. There are plenty of cheap and good restaurants around the centre of Lima and most offer a "business lunch" called *menú fijo* for no more than US$2 for a 3-course meal. There are many Chinese restaurants (*chifas*) in Peru which serve good food at reasonable prices. For really economically-minded people the *Comedores Nacionales* in most cities of Peru offer a standard 3-course meal for only US$0.50. Meals at this price, or little more, can be found under name of *menú económico* at many restaurants throughout Peru.

Drinks The usual international drinks with several very good local ones: *pisco*, a brandy made in the Ica valley, from which pisco sour is made; *chilcano*, a longer refreshing drink also made with *guinda*, a local cherry brandy; and *algarrobina*, a sweet cocktail made with the syrup from the bark of the carob tree, egg whites, milk, pisco and cinnamon. Wine is acidic and not very good, the best of a poor lot are the Ica wines Tacama and Ocucaje; both come in red, white and rosé, sweet and dry varieties. Viña Santo Tomás, from Chincha, is reasonable and cheap. Casapalca is not recommended. Beer is best in lager and porter types, especially the Cuzco and Arequipa brands (lager) and Trujillo Malta (porter). In Lima only Cristal and Pilsener (not related to true Pilsen) are readily available, others have to be sought out. *Chicha de jora* is a maize beer, usually homemade and not easy to come by, refreshing but strong, and *chicha morada* is a soft drink made with purple maize. Coffee is often brought to the table in a small jug accompanied by a mug of hot water to which you add the coffee. If you want coffee with milk, a mug of milk is brought. There are many different kinds of herb tea: the commonest are *manzanilla* and *herbaluisa*.

We wish to thank Martín Blum (Huancayo), M.Chiri (Huarás), Beverly Stuart de Hurtado (Huancayo), Warren L.Johns (C11R, c/o UK Embassy, Lima), Mari-Ann Roos and Charlotte Gottfries (Swedish Embassy, Lima), Nicolás Vexelman (Chosica), and the following travellers: Henk Aarts and Ine Chatrou (Eindhoven), Bill Addington (Warminster, Wilts), Sophia Afford (Teddington, Mx.), Richard and Sharon Alexander (Auckland 5), Susi Alexander and José Jacinto (Resedo, Ca.), David and Kathy Anderson (Chico, Ca.), Dr J.R.J. Asperen de Boer (Amsterdam), Stig Asterling (Halmstad, Swe.), Nigel L.Baker, Nicoline Beck (Doorn, Neth.), Russ Bentley (Longueuil, Québec) for an invaluable contribution, Trond Bergquist and Ian Gjertz (Oslo), Dr Michael Binzberger (Friedrichshafen), Michael Biró (Vienna 1090), Max Bleif (Gundenburg, W.Ger.), Christine Bräutigam (Basle), Joseph L.Breault (Bronx), Miss G.M.Brooke (Folkestone), Celia and Tom Bruneau (Westmount, Qué.), Stefan Brütt (Bonn), Klaus Bryn (Oslo), Jack Buckley (Rome), G.D.Claridge (East Grinstead, Sx.), John Clarke, Mark Collins (New York) good on Chimbote, R.D.Copley (Cheshunt, Herts), Malcolm Craven (Weston-super-Mare), Anke Cruse, Jonathan C.Curtis (Bury St Edmunds), Carina Dahlstrom and Ulf Carlsson (Gothenburg, Swe.), Lynne and Hugh Davies (Mill Valley, Ca.), Dr Sally Dealler (Leeds 8), Dagmar Drescher (Bad Kreuznach, W.Ger.), Robert Edge and Renate Kronemann (London SW4), Peter Ehrat and Rolf Ramsperger (Switz.), Julie Eisenberg and Andy Daitsman (Milwaukee), Christine Enkelaar and José Keldens (s'Hertogenbosch, Neth.), Kurt Farner (Köniz, Switz.), David Finn (Dallas) and Andrew Sherman (Los Angeles), Klaus Fritzsche (Dortmund) for a splendid update on Cuzco, Dr Gerry Frizzelle (London SE12), Pierre-Marie Gagneux (Taulignan) and Nathalie Baudouin (Bar-le-Duc), Mark Gfeller (Richterswil, Switz.), Thomas L Gire (Bethesda, Md.), Ulrich Gmünder (Mannheim), Harold Goldstein and Janet Young (Washington, DC.), Jean M.Guest (Banbury), Richard Guichard (Montreal), Helena Hagberg and Nils Allan Danielsson (Munkfors, Swe.) for a particularly fine contribution, Jürg Hangartner (Zürich), Thomas Harding (London NW3), Mrs Gerry Hardy (Alexandria, Va.), Silke Hartmann (Hannover), Kevin Healey (Balaclava, Vict.), Hans Hendriks (Maassluis, Neth.), Peter Hermans (Wageningen, Neth.), Ricardo Heyenn and Karin Kubitsch (Hamburg), Ronald Hijmans (Amsterdam), John E.Hildeburn (San Marino, Ca.), Bastian Hiss and Daniela Fleischhauer (Krefeld), Achim Holzenberger (Cologne 1), Catherine Hooper (Aptos, Ca.), Hessel van Hoorn (Amsterdam), Arlyne H.Johnson (Gatzke, Minn), Deborah Karp (London N3) and Karin Schamroth (London NW8), R.Kavenagh and Judy Connor (Liverpool), Todd Knutson (Pittsburgh), Dan and Sue Koenigshofer (Chapel Hill, NC), Jill Landers and Jeanne Gluesing (Minneapolis), Pete Larrett (Cheltenham), Roger Lemercier (Nice), Peter Lonsdale (Taupo, NZ), Jane Elizabeth Lunn (Killinghall, N Yorks), Shelly Lurie (Ramat Gan, Israel), Cindy McNamara (Santiago, Chile) for a most valuable contribution, Margaret McOnie (London W12), Suzanne Maillet (Montreal), Jason Malinowski (San Bruno, Ca.), Werner von Marinelli (Eindhoven), Anna-Mia Marks (Utrecht), Esther Meier (Switz.), Frans Mikkelsen and Karen Simonsen (Aarhus, Dmk.), Dermot Murphy and Kay Coombs (Twickenham, Mx.), Leona Nash and Max Green for new information on Chala, Paolo Nasuti (Venice), Hans and Ursula Niederndorfer (Lambach, Austria), Ane Cecilie Nordentoft (Risskov, Dmk.) and Michael Riis (Copenhagen), Mike O'Brien (Riverside, Ca.), Grace Osakoda (Hawaii), Martin J.Osborne (Toronto), Vaclav Penkava (Seattle), Erick and Martine Perruche (Montargis, Fr.) especially for information on climbing El Misti, Jens Plahte (Aas, Norway), Sally Purbrick (Berlin 21), Stefania Raspanti (Pistoia, It.), Annamarie Reichmuth and Roger Müller (Schwyz, Switz.), Annelies Roeleveld and Victor Kuijper (Amsterdam), Elliot Roseman (Arlington, Mass.), Trudy Rubingh and Gerry Metz (Amsterdam), Stephen Saks and Andrea Keir (Melbourne), Ulrich Schalt (Eschborn, W.Ger.), Joachim Schulz (Bad Soden, W.Ger.), Gillian Scourfield and Alastair Mitchell (Spalding, Lincs), D Seifert (London NW1), James Siever (Wiesbaden), Frampton Simons and Libby Black (Atlanta), Gustavo Steinbrun Bianco (Buenos Aires), Sophie Stirling and friends (Buchlyvie, Stirling), Evelien Stoutjesdijk and Monika Schmidt (Neth.), Catharine Strauss and Gregory Groth, Alse Strmsvaag (Steinkjer, Norway), Sean Stroud and Denise Wynne (London N19), Thomas Burnett Stuart (Huntly, Aberdeen), A.C.Tanswell (Walsall), Jon Taylor (Middlestown, W.Yorks.), Tina Tecaru (Burton-on-Trent), Brian and Christina Turner (Caazapá, Paraguay), Rose Vandepitte (Bruges), Dirk Vanmarcke (Bruges), Mrs Z.Verlinden (Huizen, Neth.), Andrew Waterworth and Kerrie Oldfield (Neutral Bay, NSW), Steve Wingfield (Toronto), Hubert Winston (Raleigh, NC), Rolf Würtz (Heidelberg), and Arthur Yeandle (Southampton).

URUGUAY

	Page		Page
Introductory	766	Up the River Uruguay	781
Montevideo	769	Routes to Brazil	784
East from Montevideo	777	Information for Visitors	787
West from Montevideo	780	Maps	767, 771

URUGUAY (area 186,926 square km.) is the smallest Hispanic country in South America, about the same size as England and Wales together, but its population, 2.93 million, is less than that of Wales alone. The rate of population growth at 0.5% pa. over the last fifteen years is low by the area's standards. Uruguay has Brazil to the north, the River Uruguay between it and Argentina to the west, and the wide estuary of the Plate to the south. The Atlantic Ocean washes its shores on the east.

Apart from a narrow plain which fringes most of the coast (but not near Montevideo), and an alluvial flood plain stretching N from Colonia to Fray Bentos, the general character of the land is undulating, with little forest except on the banks of its rivers and streams. The long grass slopes rise gently to far-off hills, but none of these is higher than 600 metres. The Río Negro, which rises in Brazil, crosses Uruguay from NE to SW, where it empties, amid dense forest, into the Uruguay River.

The black soil, rich in potash, produces grasses superior even to those of Argentina. About 90% of the land is suitable for agriculture but only 12% of it is used for arable farming.

History and Settlement The Spanish explorer, Juan Díaz de Solís, sailed up the River Plate in 1516 and landed E of the site of Montevideo, near what is now Maldonado. His second landing was in the present Department of Colonia, where he was killed by the Charrúa Indians. There was no gold or silver in Uruguay, and it was only after about 1580 that the Spaniards showed much interest in it. Military expeditions against the Indians were unsuccessful, but Jesuit and Franciscan missionaries, landing in 1624, founded a settlement on Vizcaíno Island. It is said that cattle were first introduced during an unsuccessful expedition by Hernando Arias in 1607; they were successfully established between 1611 and 1620.

By 1680, the Portuguese in Brazil had pushed S to the Plate and founded Colonia as a rival to Buenos Aires, on the opposite shore. It was the Portuguese who planned, but the Spaniards who actually founded, the city of Montevideo in 1726. It changed hands several times and was actually taken by the British in 1807, but after their failure to hold Buenos Aires, they withdrew altogether. In 1808 Montevideo declared its independence from Buenos Aires. In 1811, the Brazilians attacked from the N, but the local patriot, Artigas, rose in arms against them. In the early stages he had some of the Argentine provinces for allies, but soon declared the independence of Uruguay from both Brazil and Argentina. Buenos Aires invaded again in 1812 and was able to enter Montevideo in June 1814. In January the following year the Orientales (Uruguayans) defeated the Argentines at Guayabos and regained Montevideo. The Portuguese then occupied all territory south of the Río Negro except Montevideo and Colonia. The struggle continued from 1814 to 1820, but Artigas had to flee to Paraguay when Brazil took Montevideo in 1820. In 1825 General Juan Lavalleja, at the head of

URUGUAY 767

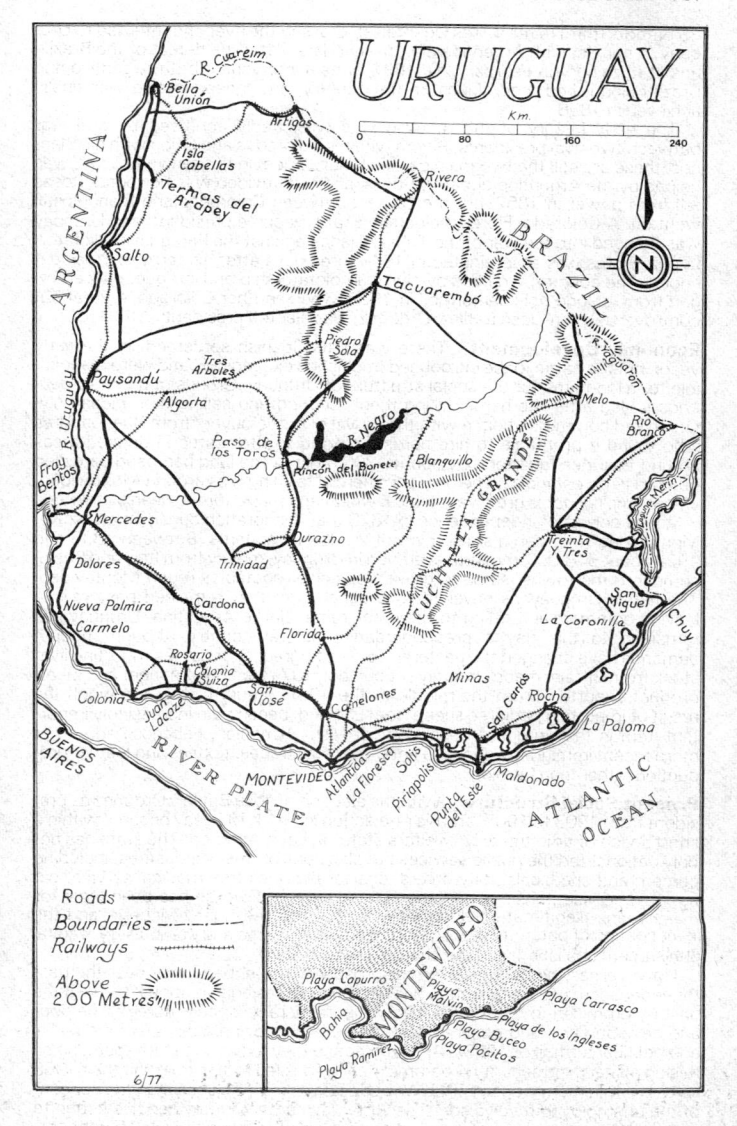

768 URUGUAY

33 patriots (the Treinta y Tres Orientales), crossed the river and returned to Uruguay to harass, with Argentine aid, the invaders. After the defeat of the Brazilians at Ituzaingó on February 20, 1827, Britain intervened, both Argentina and Brazil relinquished their claims on the country, and independence was finally achieved in 1828.

The early history of the republic was wretchedly confused by civil war between two rival presidents, Rivera with his Colorados and Oribe with his Blancos; these are still the two main parties today. Oribe, in this ten years' war, was helped by the Argentine dictator, Rosas, and Montevideo was besieged. Rosas fell from power in 1852, but the contest between Colorados and Blancos still went on. A Colorado, Flores, helped by Brazil, became president, and Uruguay was dragged into the war of the Triple Alliance against the Paraguayan dictator, López. Flores was assassinated in 1868 three days after his term as President ended. The country, wracked by civil war, dictatorship and intrigue, only emerged from its long political turmoil in 1903, when another Colorado, a great and controversial man, José Batlle y Ordóñez, was elected president.

Economic Development There was little Spanish settlement in the early years, but the cattle, once introduced, multiplied exceedingly and were responsible for a long time for the social structure of Uruguay. Groups of nomadic *gauchos* trailed after the herds, killing them for food and selling their hides only. Organized commerce began with the arrival of cattle buyers from Buenos Aires who found it profitable to hire herdsmen to look after cattle in defined areas around their headquarters. By about 1800 most of the land had been parcelled out into large *estancias*. The only commercial farming was around Montevideo, where small *chacras* grew vegetables, wheat and maize for the near-by town.

It was only after independence in 1828 that immigration began on any scale. Montevideo was then a small town of 20,000 inhabitants. Between 1836 and 1926 about 648,000 immigrants arrived in Uruguay, mostly from Italy and Spain, some into the towns, some to grow crops and vegetables round Montevideo. The native Uruguayans never took to agriculture: they remained pastoralists, leaving commercial farming to the immigrants. Unlike Argentina, Uruguay has remained to this day a preponderantly pastoral country, though modern demands have changed the pastoral life. The upgrading of cattle, importing livestock from Britain, made Uruguay second only to Argentina as a meat and meat-product exporter. From the middle of the 19th century high-grade wool, the result of importing pedigree sheep from England, became an increasingly important item in the Uruguayan economy. Jewish, Armenian, Lebanese and other more recent immigrants chose to enter the retail trades, textiles and leather production rather than farming.

Present Social Structure With the election of José Batlle y Ordóñez as president from 1903 to 1907, and his re-election in 1911, Uruguay became within a short space of time the only "welfare state" in Latin America. The state has not only nationalized the public services but also controls many industries, including cement and chemicals. Its workers' charter provides free medical service, old age and service pensions and unemployment pay. Divorce has been legal for many years; illegitimate children have status and the right to inherit, and the investigation of paternity is obligatory. Education is free and compulsory, capital punishment abolished, and the church disestablished.

However, as the country's former prosperity has ebbed away over the past three decades, the welfare state has become increasingly fictitious. In 1973 the military promised to reduce the massive bureaucracy, spend more on the poor and development, *and generally* get the country moving again after the social *and* political turmoil of 1968-1973. In practice they expanded state spending by raising military and security programs. Real wages fell to less than half their 1968 level (the minimum wage in 1985 was US$65 per month). Less than ten per cent of the unemployed receive social security payments. Montevideo has begun to sprout a few small shanty towns, once unheard of in this relatively affluent corner of the hemisphere. One of the most egalitarian countries in Latin America has increasingly come to resemble the rest of the continent, as only the very wealthy benefited from the military regime's attempted neo-liberal economic policies. Nevertheless, the country's middle class remains very large, if impoverished, and the return to democracy in 1985 has raised hopes that the deterioration in the social structure may be halted, if not quickly reversed. Almost ten per cent of the population emigrated for economic or political reasons during the 1960s and 1970s: the unemployed continue to leave, but the political and artistic exiles have returned en masse, to the great joy of most.

Allying himself with the Armed Forces in 1973, the elected President decreed the closure of Parliament, and stayed on to rule for the rest of his term as the military's figurehead. Scheduled elections were cancelled in 1976, and a serious wave of political and trade union repression instituted. Unable to convince the population to vote for a new authoritarian constitution in 1980, the military became increasingly anxious to hand back power to conservative politicians. However, moderate politicians refused to accept the harsh conditions the military continued to try and impose. Finally, in August 1984 agreement was reached on the legalization of most of the banned leftist parties and elections were held in November. The euphoria was spoiled by the fact that the strongest opponent of the regime was not allowed to stand. The new moderate government of Julio María Sanguinetti was inaugurated in March 1985 for a five year term of office. The process of national reconstruction and healing of political wounds began with a widespread political amnesty, but no new radical economic policies. Despite extraordinarily adverse conditions (such as the highest per capita debt in Latin America) Uruguay's former traditions and the innate conservatism of Uruguayans give grounds for hoping that the troubles will not return.

Population The population was 2.93m by mid-1985; just under half live in Greater Montevideo. Only some 15% are rural, and the drift to the towns is 1.6% per year. Both the death rate and the birth rate are low. The people are almost entirely white, mostly of Spanish and Italian stock, for there are no native Indians left, and only a few light-skinned "blacks" in parts of Montevideo and near the Brazilian border. Possibly 10% are mestizos. About 97% are literate. The natural population increase is low for Latin America: 0.5% per annum. So is infant mortality, 30.3 per thousand.

Montevideo, the capital and the only large city in the country, was founded in 1726. Population, in and near: 1,355,312 (1984). The original site on a promontory between the River Plate and an inner bay, though the fortifications have been destroyed, still retains a certain colonial atmosphere. The city not only dominates the country's commerce and culture—almost 90% of all the imports and exports pass through it—but is also a summer resort and the point of departure for a string of seaside resorts along the coastline to the E.

A major landmark, the Palacio Salvo on Plaza Independencia, has recently undergone exterior renovation which removed its formerly splendid *art-nouveau* mouldings. It is not open to visitors. On the same plaza, the Victoria Palace hotel has a rooftop restaurant with fine views. Otherwise, the best place to get a view of the city is from the top of city hall (La Intendencia); external glass elevators take you up to a viewing platform, where there is a pastry shop, and an expensive restaurant. Entrance at the back of the building on Soriano, between Ejido and Santiago de Chile.

Set between the old town (Ciudad Vieja) and the new is the grandest of Montevideo's squares, Plaza Independencia. On most sides it is surrounded by colonnades, and there are three pavement cafés at the eastern end. The other end has been spoiled by rebuilding, particularly to the N and S beside Government House. In 1986 the government of President Sanguinetti moved the executive offices to the Palacio Libertad far from the centre, which the Armed Forces had put up to house the Ministry of Defence. The old government house, known as the Palacio Estévez, is now used for ceremonial purposes only. The long unfinished modern block to the West was originally intended to be the Palace of Justice, then presidential offices, but its future use is in doubt. Just off the plaza to the West is the splendid Solís Theatre, a Museum of Natural History alongside. In the old town, a

770 **URUGUAY**

short distance west of Plaza Independencia, is the oldest square in Montevideo: the Plaza Constitución, also known as the Plaza Matriz. Here on one side is the Cathedral (1790-1804), with the town hall (1804-1810) opposite. Still further west along Calle Rincón is the small Plaza Zabala, with a monument to Zabala, founder of the city. N of this Plaza are four buildings well worth seeing: the Banco de la República (Cerrito y Solís), the Aduana (Rambla 25 de Agosto), and the houses of Generals Rivera (Rincón y Misiones, 1300-1900) and Lavalleja (around the corner in 25 de Mayo, Tuesdays and Fridays 1100-1900 only). Together, the latter two buildings form the National History Museum.

The Avenida 18 de Julio, whose pavements are always thronged, begins at the Palacio Salvo. Along this avenue is the Plaza del Entrevero (with a statue of a group of *gauchos* engaged in battle), between Julio Herrera and Río Negro, a very pleasant place to sit; and the Plaza Cagancha (or Plaza Libertad), with a statue of Liberty and the main tourist office. The Municipal Palace (Intendencia), with the viewing platform, is on the South side of Av. 18 de Julio, just before it bends N, at the statue of the local equivalent of a cowboy (*El Gaucho*). In front of the Municipality is a plaza with a copy of Michelangelo's David in one corner. The road which forks S from the *Gaucho* is Constituyente, and leads to the fashionable beachside community of Pocitos. There are two museums inside the Municipal Palace, entered around the corner in Ejido: Museum of Art History, and Museum of Precolombian and Colonial Art (1700-2100 except Mondays). The latter is the more interesting. Beyond is the University, and nearby are the National Library, the French *lycée*, and the Ministry of Health. The avenue ends at an intersection with Bulevar General Artigas. Here is an obelisk commemorating the makers of the 1830 Constitution, by José Luis Zorrilla de San Martín (born 1891), and here, too, one may enter the Parque Batlle y Ordóñez (see below). The immense Legislative Palace, built of native marble, is reached from Av. 18 de Julio along Av. del Libertador Brig. Gen. Juan Lavalleja (formerly Av. Agraciada), 5 blocks E of Plaza Independencia (buses 150, 173, 175 from Calle Mercedes).

At the western end of the bay is the Cerro, or hill, 118 metres high, (from which Montevideo gets its name), with an old fort on the top, now a military museum (0800-1800) with arms, flags and drums. The Cerro is surmounted by the oldest lighthouse in the country (1804). In the port (which one can visit on Sat.—see Tourist Office), opposite the Port Administrative Building, the ship's bell of H.M.S. *Ajax* has been set up to commemorate the scuttling of the *Graf Spee*. The anchor of the *Graf Spee* was set up at the entrance to the port area in 1964 to commemorate the 25th anniversary of the battle; the wreck itself lies about 3 km. offshore, but is no longer visible as it was dismantled some years ago. However, plates from its bulkheads have been used in the construction of the city stadium. One can still see the *Graf Spee*'s supply ship, listing but still afloat (used in the past as a prison hulk). Bus from centre to Cerro: 125 from Mercedes, and others.

Of the many parks, El Prado (about 5 km. from Av. 18 de Julio, along Av. del Libertador Brig. Gen. Juan Lavalleja) is the oldest. Among fine lawns, trees and lakes is a rose garden planted with 850 varieties; also in the Prado is La Diligencia (the stage coach). The two buildings of the Municipal Museums of Fine Art and History are in the grounds. During August, an annual farm show is held in the park. The largest and most popular park is Parque Rodó, on Rambla Presidente Wilson. Here are an open-air theatre, an amusement park, and a boating lake studded with islands. The National Museum of Fine Arts, with works by living artists, and a children's playground are at the eastern end. In Parque Batlle y Ordóñez (reached by a continuation eastwards of Av. 18 de Julio), are several statues: the most interesting group is the very well-known "La Carreta" monument, by José Belloni, showing three yoke of oxen drawing a waggon. In the grounds is the Estadio Centenario with a seating capacity of 70,000 and the main football pitch (Bus 177 from Av. 18 de Julio) but the 107 or 64 (a trolley-bus) are almost as convenient. There are a field for athletic sports and a bicycle racetrack as well. The Zoological Gardens are a few blocks E of this park (open until

Key to map of Montevideo

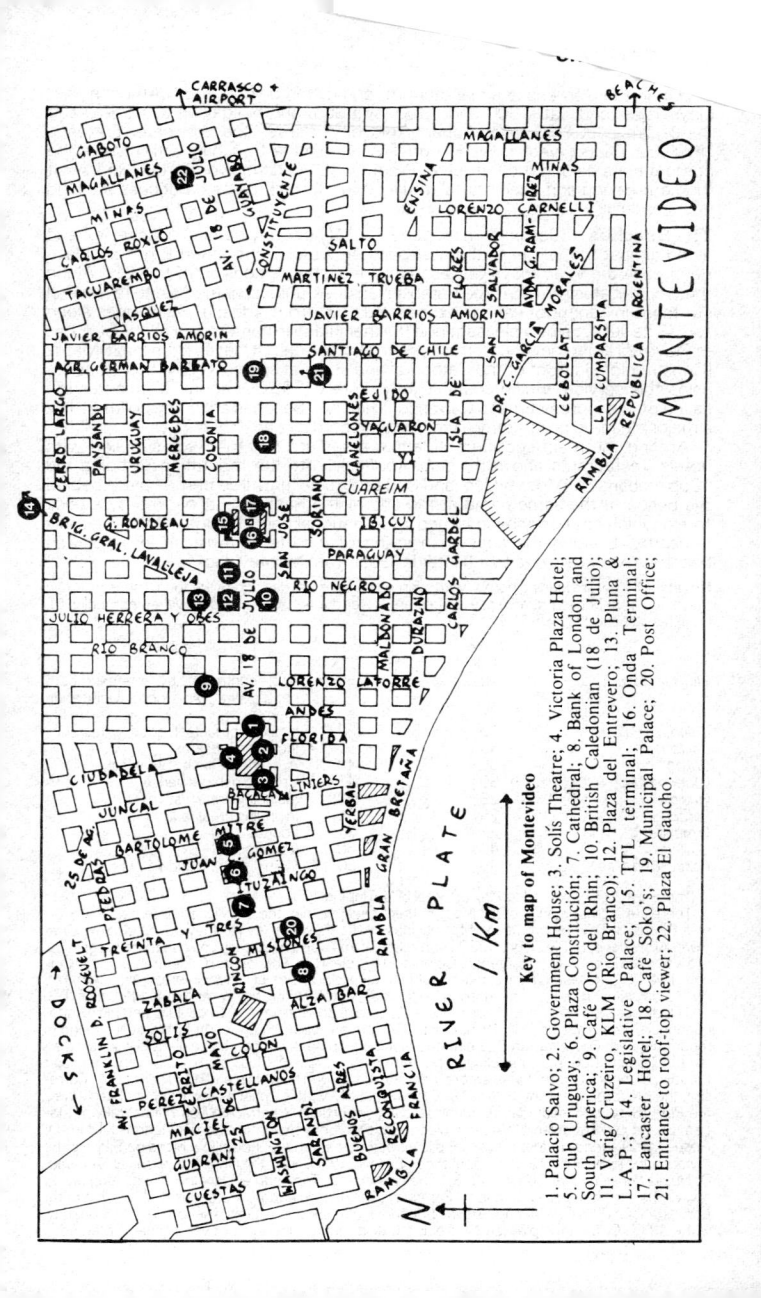

1. Palacio Salvo; 2. Government House; 3. Solís Theatre; 4. Victoria Plaza Hotel; 5. Club Uruguay; 6. Plaza Constitución; 7. Cathedral; 8. Bank of London and South America; 9. Café Oro del Rhin; 10. British Caledonian (18 de Julio); 11. Varig/Cruzeiro, KLM (Rio Branco); 12. Plaza del Entrevero; 13. Pluna & L.A.P.; 14. Legislative Palace; 15. TTL terminal; 16. Onda Terminal; 17. Lancaster Hotel; 18. Café Sokó's; 19. Municipal Palace; 20. Post Office; 21. Entrance to roof-top viewer; 22. Plaza El Gaucho.

URUGUAY

2000); in the Gardens is a planetarium, one of the best in South America, displays Tues. and Sat. 1800 and 1900, and Sun. and holidays 1700, 1800 and 1900. Trolleybus 60 from Aduana (old city) passes the zoo gate. Entrance US$0.80. Easter week is also Tourist Week (Fiesta Gaucha), with rodeo-type competitions held in the Parque El Prado (US$1.50 entry) or Parque Roosevelt (horse-breaking and handicrafts), music (mostly folk). Large barbecues are held in the open air.

The Beaches (See inset map, page 771) Nine sandy bathing beaches extend along almost the whole of the metropolitan water front, extending from Playa Ramírez in the W to Playa Carrasco at the eastern extension of the city. Along the whole waterfront runs the Rambla Naciones Unidas, named along its several stretches in honour of various nations. Bus 104 from Aduana, which goes along Av. 18 de Julio, gives a pleasant ride (further inland in winter) past all the beaches to Playa Miramar, beyond Carrasco. The express bus DI leaves from Plaza Matriz (Constitución) in front of the Cathedral and stops at special yellow bus stops; by using this service, which costs slightly more (US$0.30) about 30 minutes are saved on the journey time to Carrasco. The town beaches are badly polluted, but a major clean-up programme is to be completed by end-1987.

Among the main seaside residential areas are Pocitos, well supplied with hotels, restaurants and night-clubs (*boites*), with the reputation of being the "Copacabana" of Montevideo; and Carrasco, a delightful semi-rural place behind the beach of the same name at the end of the Rambla Sur, backed by a thick forest which has partly been turned into a national park. The international airport is nearby. E along the coast is a string of resorts, with much less polluted beaches, which are dealt with later in "East from Montevideo".

Hotels Below are leading hotels, with average charges per day during the tourist season, when they should be booked in advance. Prices are lower during other seasons. When not included, breakfast usually costs US$1-$2.

	Single US$	Double US$	Remarks
Victoria Plaza	48	60	A/c; controlled by interests connected with Mr Moon's Unification Church
Columbia Palace	32	50	Includes breakfast, good restaurant
California	36	50	Including breakfast
Crillón	35	48	A/c. and including breakfast
London Palace	30	42	Central, garage, parking
Iguazú	28	40	Including breakfast
Parque	25	35	Including breakfast
Ermitage	22	31	Pocitos
Cottage	42	60	Carrasco
Casino Carrasco	36	50	With breakfast and 7% tax

There is a 20% value-added tax on hotel bills. Tipping 10%.

There are a great many hotels, most of them cheaper than the ones listed. *Internacional*, Colonia 823/825, B, is recommended for business visits; however as yet they have no telex. *Gran Hotel Americano*, B, Río Negro 1330 (with telex). If you don't need a bill you can try to bargain for a lower price. For example, *Ateneo*, Colonia 1147, clean, E; *Presidente*, C, central; *Europa*, Colonia 1341, D; *Lancaster*, D, a/c, incl. breakfast, central; *Oxford*, D including breakfast; *Aramaya*, Av. 18 de Julio 1103, E, with bathroom, old, clean, comfortable, highly recommended, near TTL and Onda bus stop; *King's*, E, Andes 1491, 2½ blocks down from Av. 18 de Julio and Plaza Independencia; *Los Angeles*, Av. 18 de Julio 974, private bath, clean, central, old-style, friendly, recommended, D; *Balfer*, on Cuareim one block off 18 de Julio, good, excellent breakfast; *Cervantes*, Soriano 868, plain but clean room with bath, C; *Alcalá*, Río Branco 1105, very clean and friendly, C (without bath). *La Alhambra*, Sarandí 594, C with breakfast and good service. At Carrasco, the *Bristol*, E, pleasant, built in 1926 in true Louis-XV style, must be seen. Other cheap hotels are *Rex*, 18 de Julio, near Plaza Independencia, comfortable; *Central Río Negro*, near railway station, E; and *Gil*, Brandzen 2284, very clean. *Español*, Convención (ex-Coronel Latorre) 1317, D; *Hospedaje Diagonal*, near bus station, dirty, hot water shared, F, hot-pillow place on Sat. nights; *Americano*, 18 de Julio 1212, D; *Santander*, Ejido 1212, C. Near the Onda bus terminal: *Trinidad*, D; *Nueva Pensión Ideal*, Soriano 1073, F; *Residencial Tío Tom*, corner Canelones and Paraguay, F, noisy; *Residencial Ideal*, C, Soriano y Paraguay. *Residencial Litoral*, Mercedes 887, C, with bath; *Colón*, Rincón 620, C, with bath; *Royal*, Soriano, E, hot showers, clean, friendly. *Arosa*, Constituyente 1917, C, friendly, pleasant; *Cifre*, E (10% discount on stays of over 2 weeks) Mercedes

URUGUAY 773

1166, clean. *Libertad*, Ibicuy 1223, E, clean, quiet and food available; *Alojamiento Piedras*, E, Piedras 272; *Pensión Universal*, E, Piedras 270. Cheaper places along Av. San José or Soriano and around Plaza Independencia and behind the Onda bus terminal, e.g. *Casablanca*, San José 1039, central, friendly, E with bath; *Pensión del Este*, E, Ibicuy y Soriano, hot water, cold rooms, no clothes-washing allowed, nice cat, nosy *dueña*; *Pensión Trinidad*, San José 1220, F, clean, recommended. *Avenida*, 18 de Julio 973; *Sagaro*, 18 de Julio 2020; *Windsor*, Cuareim 1260. Plenty of cheap hotels (F-G) in and near the old city.

At the beaches many hotels offer full board only during the season. After April 1 prices are greatly reduced and some hotel dining rooms shut down. For Carnival week, on the other hand, prices are raised by 20%.

Information on hotels from tourist office on Plaza Cagancha (Libertad) and Centro de Hoteles y Restaurantes del Uruguay (Ibicuy 1213). **Hint**: cheap hotel rooms in Uruguay are invariably gloomy. Bring your own 220V Edison-screw bulbs and hope they don't put too much strain on the wiring. The booking situation at hotels can be found by ringing 90.04.53 (CIHTU) or 90.03.46.

Youth Hostel Canelones 935, 39 Río Branco, Telephone 98.13.24. US$2.20 first night; US$1.80 thereafter, about half for members, probably the best bargain, clean, dormitory style; you have to be out of your room between 1000 and 1700. Open Nov.-Feb.

Camping Parque Roosevelt, near Carrasco, free, hot showers, safe, no electricity, 15 km. from centre, open Dec.-March, or superb camping in the wild can be had to the west of the Cerro on the flanks of the hill below the fort, amid pine trees. Also, Hugo A. Morante has written to offer to rent a log cabin, 30 km. out in the woods (Tel.: 98.93.18/98.11.07). Reports please.

Restaurants The dinner hour is very late, from 2100 to 2400. (Less formal restaurants serve from 1930 onwards.) First-class restaurants at the centre are *El Aguila*, Buenos Aires 694, next to the Solís Theatre; *Victoria Plaza Hotel*, *La Lutèce*, French, excellent, in Mercado del Puerto, *Morini*, Ciudadela 12-29, serves excellent steaks and is one of the more expensive establishments.

In Pocitos are: *El Galeón*, Leyenda Patria 3096; *La Azotea*, Rambla Perú 1063; *El Panamericano*, Luis A. de Herrera y Rambla Armenia; *Hostal Suizo*, Ellauri y Pereira; *Tomasito*, Manuel V. Pagola y Pedro F. Berro; *Doña Flor* (classy French restaurant, limited menu but superb) Blvd. España y Artigas; *La Cigale*, Luis Alberto de Herrera; *Entrevero* (popular with Americans), 21 de Setiembre; *Tía Gretel*, German style, 21 de Setiembre y Mora. *Gatto Rosso*, good and cheap.

Other quite good restaurants are: *La Genovesa* (Spanish), San José 1242; *Dakel*, Gabriel Otero y Arocena; *Hong Kong Restaurant*, 8 de Octubre 2691; *Otto*, Río Negro 1301, warmly recommended, as well as *Soko*, 18 de Julio y Yí, for its food and cocktails, good value; *Sea Garden*, Rambla Perú 1402, pricey but good view; *El Fogón*, good value, San José 1080. *El David*, Gen. Rivera 2002, recommended. A good place for lunch is the *Golf Club*, good food, excellent surroundings and grand view. Typical local food is served at *Forte de Makale*, Parque Rodó; *Tahiti*, Bulevard Artigas; *Rovella*, Jackson 874, and *Las Brasas*, San José 909; *Aloha*, on Ibicuy, between San José and Soriano, close to the Onda bus station, cheap but cold food; *El Gran César*, also on Ibicuy, reasonable, recommended; *Empanadas 17*, San José 1166, very good eating spot. The Automóvil Club on Av. del Libertador Brig. Gen. Juan Lavalleja (ex Agraciada) between Uruguay and Paysandú serves extremely good food at reasonable prices, with excellent coffee. A good cheap place is restaurant on 6th floor of YMCA building, Colonia 1870, open for lunch and 1900-2200, US$2 (two courses) and plentiful with good views too. (Ask for the Asociación Cristiana de Jóvenes.) Worth a try is *Emporio de los Sandwiches*, Rondeau 1480, for its croissants, or *Cervecería La Pasiva* on Plaza Independencia or *Confitería Hamburgo*, Gen. Rival 2081, for cakes and ice-creams. *Bar 04* for good cheap *parrillada*. *Los Chivitos*, Río Branco y 18 de Julio, is a good cheap place to eat. *Gran Coco*, on Yí, offers a variety of good meat and vegetable dishes for about US$1.80 or *Centro Residentes de Artigas*, San José 885, cheap, clean and friendly. Vegetarians can try *Alimentación Integral*, Ituzaingó 1478, or *Macrobiótico*, Eduardo Acevedo 1513 or *Garafíos*, Yí 1334, esq. Av. 18 de Julio. Don't miss eating at the Mercado del Puerto, opposite the Custom House, on Calle Piedras, between Maciel and Castellanas, grills cooked on huge charcoal grates (menus are limited to meat); colourful atmosphere and friendly. There are about a dozen grills open during market hrs.; at night only *El Palenque* is open. *El Cabure*, Gen. Rivera 3450, is also good for grills. *Café y Bar Joselito* is open nearly all the time—Pérez Castellanos 1446. On Benito Blanco, at either end of the Plaza Rubén Darío, are the *Ocean Place* and the *Costa Azul* (meals), both are recommended and reasonably priced. The restaurant at the railway station is cheap, quick and good value. *Buen Ri*, on Andes, is also cheap while the *Cazuela de Mariscos* provides filling meals.

Discos *People*, on Cuareim; *Eros*, on Boulevard Artigas.

Night Clubs The Bar and the Záfiro Room at the *Victoria Plaza* with Tropicana Show US$12 (incl. food), also Lancaster Hotel. Other night-spots giving floor shows are *El Patio*, *Bonanza*, and *Porto Fino*. The best discotheques, called *boites*, are *Merek* and *Lancelot* in Carrasco (the former at lakeside, with swimming pool and chalet architecture, the latter a castle!); *Zum Zum* and *Privée* (Miguel Barriero and Rambla) in Pocitos are good too. They admit couples only and have taped

774 URUGUAY

music, US$15 a couple, entrance included on 1st drinks. They are open until very late (2230-0500). Reservations are recommended on Sat. night. There is a very good English-type "Pub", *Clyde's*, on Costa Rica and Riviera, in Carrasco, with loud music and good atmosphere. The delights of the tango are available at *Tanguería del 40* at *Hotel Columbia Palace* or *La Cumparsita* in Calle Gardel. For plain music try *Cantores*, Gonzalo Ramírez 1417, *Templo del Sol*, or *Pulpería* on Mercedes. For a good bar try the *Lighthouse* on Calle Piedras, Polish run seaman's bar near the old port.

Tea Shops, known locally as *confiterías*. Best is said to be *Sorocabana*, on Plaza Cagancha, traditional atmosphere, cakes and coffee. The most popular are along 18 de Julio, including *Latino*, *Facal*, *Manchester*, *Lusitano*, *Café del Rex*, *Soko's*, *Lion D'Or*, *Payaso*, *La Puerta del Sol*, *Hispano*. Good ones are *Taberna Portofino*, Ituzaingó 1325, and *Oro del Rhin* (0830-2100), Colonia y Convención (ex-Latorre). At Pocitos are *La Goleta*, *Haití*, *La Conaprole*, *Anrejo*, *La Castellana*, *El Vitral* and *Las Palmas*. At Puerto Buceo Yacht Club, where tourists are allowed in.

Coctelerías Cocktails served with lots of side dishes: *Soko's*, 18 de Julio; *Payaso*, Galería Yaguarón, 18 de Julio; *Giorgio's*, Scocería and Rambla, Pocitos. *Bar Hispano*, Av. San José, excellent vermouths with 28 varieties of *hors d'oeuvres*.

Heladerías Ice-cream parlours produce very good, unusual ice creams in the summer, and draw large crowds. Try *La Cigale*, Scocería, Pocitos, on Ejido, or on Brandzen. *Las Delicias*, Carrasco, or *Papitos*, at 18 de Julio 1054.

Information Dial "214" for the central bureau of information (in front of Onda bus terminal) about communications, the weather, pharmacies on night duty and anything you want to know about streets in the city. Dial "6" for exact time.

Electric Power 220 volts 50 cycles, A.C.

Shopping The main shopping area is Av. 18 de Julio. Excellent cheap leatherwork available; for this try Casa Mario, Piedras 641. Suede clothes cheaper than in Buenos Aires, but quality and fashion not quite as good. Amethysts and topazes are mined and polished in Uruguay and are good buys; see Topaz International, *Victoria Plaza Hotel*. For woollen wall hangings see Manos del Uruguay, which sells floor cushions, crafts, high quality woollen goods, etc. at Reconquista 616, and at San José 1111, and in the shopping centre in Carrasco near the Rambla. Other good craftwork (cheaper) in daily covered craft market on Plaza Cagancha, and Sat. a.m. craft fair in Villa Biarritz. On Sunday morning there is a street market on Tristán Narvaja (good for silver and copper) north of 18 de Julio. On Sats. there is one at Pocitos for fruit, leather and woollen handicrafts. Also in Galería Diri, 18 de Julio and Río Negro, which now has a branch in New York City. The Montevideo Shopping Center on the E edge of Pocitos (Herrera y Rivera) has wide range of shops including Manos del Uruguay as well as others selling leather goods. Best place for developing films is Photo Martín, Av. Libertador Lavalleja and Uruguay. Film developing and equipment is quite expensive in Uruguay; better to bring film from abroad. Antique shops on Plaza Independencia.

Bookshops English and American books: Librería Barreiro y Ramos, 25 de Mayo y J. C. Gómez; Ibana, International Book and News Agency, Convención (ex-Latorre) 1479, specializes in foreign publications. Librería Ingleson, Sarandí 580, specializes in language and children's books. Others include Librería Mosca Hermanos, Av. 18 de Julio 1578; Feria del Libro, Av. 18 de Julio 1308; Librería Papacito, Av. 18 de Julio 1415 and Heritage Internacional, Soriano 1610. There is a good one at Tristán Narvaja 1736.

Taxis US$0.30 for first 600 metres, and US$0.02 for each 140 metres afterwards; an additional 20% from midnight to 0600, charge for each hour of waiting, US$3.30. There is a small charge for each piece of luggage. Taxis can be hired, by agreement, by the hour within city limits. Taxis to Carrasco airport from the centre, US$9, also bus US$1.

City Transport City and suburbs US$0.20 (at night it costs a third more). There are many buses to all parts (104 to the beaches). Never ring the bell on bus to get off; ask the conductor (hiss—watch the locals) and he will ring it.

Car Hire without chauffeur, US$43 per 24 hrs., plus US$0.14 per kilometre; guarantee of US$100 required. The firms offering this are Hertz and National in Colonia, near Plaza Independencia; American International Budget and Sudamcar, La Paz 1523, National Fill Service, Rambla Rep. del Perú 815, Esq. 813, self-drive hire is not recommended. With chauffeur, US$35 per 8-hr. day plus US$0.12 per kilometre, and payment for a chauffeur's lunch or supper. Rogelio Martinelli, Canelones 1450; Luis Moro e Hijos, Camino Ariel 4737; Empresa Salhon, Av. 8 de Octubre 4199; F. Miramonte, Magallanes 1446; ARI, 18 de Julio 2142; Hertz, Calle Colonia near Paza Independencia; National, nearby; Snappy, Andes 1363; and Avis.

Casinos *Parque Hotel* at Playa Ramírez; *Hotel Carrasco* at Carrasco.

Museums Historical: Casa Lavalleja, Zabala 1464, and Casa Rivera, Rincón 437. *N.B. tie must* be worn. Natural History: Buenos Aires 562 1400-1800 Tues.-Sat. (has a well-preserved, half-unwrapped mummy). Botanical: 19 de Abril 1179. Art: Museo Nacional de Bellas Artes, in Parque Rodó. Worth a visit for the park alone. Municipal: in large rooms upstairs at the Cabildo. Zoological Museum, Rambla Chile 4215, on beach at Puerto Buceo. Gold Museum and Gaucho Museum in the sumptuous Banco de la República building, Av. 18 de Julio 996 (Mon.-Sat. 1300-1830). No entrance fees. The Sociedad de Amigos de Arqueología, Buenos Aires 652 (Casilla 6521) can provide professional advice. Museo Blanes, Millán 4015, has many Figari paintings, open 1400-2100. Naval museum by the Buceo in Pocitos; air force museum near municipal stadium on Av. Larrañaga. Museum schedules are indefinite: most are open Sun. and Tues. through Fri., but at times are open only in the afternoon, so make sure. Consult the newspaper *El Día* for current opening times of museums, exhibitions and libraries; also what's on generally.

Theatres Solís, housing the national theatre company and occasional visiting companies, worth seeing inside; cheap concerts on Mondays between March and November (US$0.25). El Galpón theatre company has now returned from exile. The Comedia Nacional plays at Sala Verdi, Soriano 914. Café Teatro "El Reloj"; Circular; Notariado; La Máscara, Río Negro 1180, Teatro del Anglo, San José 1426. The national ballet company Ossodre is said to outperform the Buenos Aires company. Stella d'Italia; Círculo; Centro. All these are more or less professional. Occasionally, small amateur or semi-professional groups put on plays in cinemas or other places. There is much interest in the drama and cinema-going is very popular. Price is almost the same in all cinemas, at US$1.25 (some half-price on Mons., Tues. and Weds.). Classic films at Cinemateca. Films are released quite soon after the UK and USA, and often before they get to Buenos Aires.

Music Concerts at Solís Theatre (see above) Jazz at Alíanza Francesa and Alianza Uruguay-Estados Unidos. Brazilian music: Clave de Fu, Pocitos. For tango clubs etc. see above under Night Clubs.

Sports The beach is more popular than the water. Uruguay has three important yacht clubs, the Uruguayo, the Nautilus and the Punta del Este. Both the Montevideo Rowing Club and the Club Nacional de Regatas have club houses on the Bay. The German Rowing Club is on the Santa Lucía River. Fishing is becoming popular. Association football is played intensively. Rugby football is also played, and there is a yearly championship. There are two good 18-hole municipal links. There are several lawn tennis clubs, and two for polo. Horse races at Las Piedras (see page 785). There is a national lottery. Massage is available at Suomi, Dr. José Scocería 2909.

Schools The British School at Carrasco and some 4 others, 1 French, 1 German, and the Crandon Institute, an American school for children up to 17. All have good scholastic ratings.

Churches The Roman Catholic Cathedral is known locally as the Iglesia San Juan. Anglican Church, Reconquista 522 (a national monument) Tel.: 908062 (English Service 1800 Sunday). Methodist services at Christ Church, Carrasco.
Holy Trinity Episcopal (British), and the Emanuel Methodist Church (American), hold regular services in English. The German Evangelical Church holds services in German at Calle J. M. Blanco 2. There is a synagogue.

Addresses

British Embassy, Marco Bruto 1073. Tel.: 780352/791033.
US Embassy and Consulate, Rambla Wilson 1776. Tel.: 409051/409126.
British Chamber of Commerce, Av. Libertador Lavalleja 1641, piso 2°, of.201. Tel.: 900936.
American Chamber of Commerce, Bartolomé Mitre 1337, esc. 108. Tel.: 906052.
The English Club, Treinta y Tres 1309. Tel.: 995605.
The British Council (Instituto Cultural Anglo-Uruguayo), San José 1426, 3° piso. Tel.: 908468.
The British Hospital, Av. Italia 2420. Tel.: 409011.
Goethe Institut, Canelones 1524. Tel.: 405813/404432.
The Apostleship of the Sea, Washington 274. Tel.: 952421.
West German Embassy, La Cumparsita 1417-35, Tel: 904958.
Spanish Embassy, Av. Brasil 2786.
Swiss Embassy, Ing. Frederico Abadie 2934-40; Tel.: 704315.
Youth Hostel, Pablo de María 1583, (1300-1900), Tel.: 404245.

Post Office, Misiones 1328 y Buenos Aires; postal services are cheaper than in Uruguay's neighbours.

Cables All America Cables & Radio Inc., Plaza Independencia; Italcable S.A., 25 de Mayo 400; Western Telegraph Co., Ltd., Cerrito 449; Telégrafo Nacional, Sarandí 472, or telephone 219 to send in Spanish or 90.14.55 in other languages. Public telex booths (open 0700-2300) are available at Antel, Mercedes 884 or Rincón and Treinta y Tres (open day and night).

Banks Bank of London & South America, Calle Zabala 1500, and 11 city agencies; Citibank, Cerrito 455 (corner Misiones); Banco Holandés Unido, 25 de Mayo 501; and Banco Comercial, Cerrito 400 and Banco Panamericano Uruguayo on Plaza Cajón. American Express, 18 de Julio near post office, no commission if buying US$ bills with Amex travellers' cheques. Open: 1300-1700, Mon.-Fri. Money-changing is done by banks and hotels. There are exchange houses, especially along 18 de Julio, e.g. Gales, at 1046. (1% commission on travellers' cheques.) However, do shop around for best rates. No restrictions on foreign-exchange transactions. i.e. an excellent place to stock up with U.S. dollar bills if travelling onward. Airport bank open every day 0900-2200; so is the Banco de la República exchange office on Plaza Cagancha.

Tourist Commission Headquarters is at Av. del Libertador Brig. Gen. Juan Lavalleja 1409, fourth floor. Information Centre is on Plaza Cagancha (Libertad); helpful but only carries information on Grade D hotels and above. For budget hotels and *pensiones* try Centro de Hoteles y Restaurantes, Ibicuy 1213. Also at Carrasco international airport.

Travel Agents Muritelli, Plaza del Entrevero, JP Santos, Colonia 951, and Jetmar, Plaza Independencia, all helpful. Wagon-Lits (Thomas Cook agents), Av. Gral. Rondeau 1392; Buemes Viajes, Colonia 997; COT, Sarandí 699; Exprinter, Sarandí 700; Turisport Ltda., Mercedes 942 (American Express); Viajes Cynsa, 18 de Julio 1120; Golden Tours, Colonia 1221, Tel.: 90 7500, English spoken.

Maps. An excellent map is produced by Ancap, the state oil company, US$1.50-2.00 depending on where you buy it.

Ferries To Buenos Aires: night (2100) service US$14.75 without sleeper and breakfast (about US$2.50 extra for sleeper) otherwise three daytime ferries. Car ferry, about US$37, via Colonia (bus leaves 0800 and Sunday 1615, ferry at 1300 and Sunday 2000, US$12.50), according to size of car, see also under Colonia (page 781).

N.B. Travel to Buenos Aires by Onda bus and plane, or hydrofoil (*Aliscafo*) 0315, 0615, 0915, 1015, 1615 (Tel.: 904608/905987) leaves from Rinconada de Plaza Libertad, costs US$21 and it breaks down frequently; by launch via Carmelo US$8; tickets available from Onda office, Florida 501.

Airport The main airport is at Carrasco, 21 km. outside the city; 30 mins. by taxi (US$ 9) to Montevideo or about 50 by bus from Av. 18 de Julio. Buenos Aires-Montevideo by air, US$40 single, plus US$2 airport tax. Arco and Lada from Colonia (US$22) are cheaper than the hydrofoil via Colonia, and they also land at Aeroparque (Buenos Aires). Weather permitting, they are also quicker. Flight to Rio, US$207 single. Internal flights are very cheap, e.g. US$25 to the Brazilian border at Rivera. Pluna will not accept credit cards. Tamu, the military airline, offers considerably reduced prices on many internal flights. If exchange facilities closed at airport, buses will accept dollars for fares to town. IBAT, Yaguarón 1318, runs the airport bus, leaves there at 1045 daily and calls at the Pluna office at 1100. Onda and COT services to and from Punta del Este call at the airport. Pluna airport bus, via Ramblas, starts at Plaza del Entrevero, US$0.75; Copsa bus goes along Paysandú and Av. Italia, US$0.30.

Rail Booking office and station at La Paz 1095. Information 914291/2/3. Trains to Salto and Paysandú, Mon., Wed., Fri. 0615, change to railcar at Paso de los Toros, arrive Paysandú 1800 and Salto 2100, poor track, crowded, buffet primitive; to Salto US$5.50 (US$8.40 with berth). Ganz service to Nico Pérez (daily), Melo (daily). Restaurant cars on all long-distance trains. To Rivera (off-season) night train. Weekly service to Artigas and Cuareim. Best to book sleeping berths beforehand. To Minas, US$1.75. There is a service to Maldonado (US$3.90 1st) on Hungarian railcars, off season one train a day (0815). Museum at the fine old central railway station. Besides the booking office at La Paz 1095, information and tickets on certain Ganz services can be obtained in the gallery at Plaza Cagancha 1322. Buses tend to be quicker but more expensive.

Buses Within Uruguay, good services to most towns; to Paysandú, US$8, 5½ or 7 hours, according to route; to Salto, 4 a day, 7½ hrs., US$10; to Punta del Este, 2 hrs., US$4. Piriápolis US$3 (slow). La Paloma US$4 (slow). Maldonado US$4.20. Carmelo US$5. Colonia US$3.50, by Onda. To La Coronilla US$6.25 (5 hours). During the summer holiday season buses are booked heavily; it is recommended to book in advance. All services to the east make a compulsory stop at Dante 1945/9; others at Terminal Goes, Av. General Flores y Domingo Aramburu. Services along Route 7 to Tala and San Jacinto are operated by Cita and leave from their office at Av. Libertador Brig Gen Lavalleja 1446.

Twice-weekly bus (Tues. and Fri.) to Asunción, Paraguay (24 hours, US$40). There are very comfortable buses to Porto Alegre and São Paulo via TTL company (Plaza Cagancha, opposite Onda), taking 11 hrs., with drinks service on the *coche cama* and luxury service: the buses run overnight; often booked very early. A cheaper alternative route is to Chuy (US$7), then catch an onward bus to Porto Alegre, either direct or via Pelotas. To Santiago (Empresa Gen. Artigas) US$90.25. TTL and Onda have the only direct Montevideo-Brazil services (same prices, four daily services between 2000 and 2230). To Santa Fe, Argentina, daily via Paysandú bridge; offers easy connection to Asunción. To Salto US$9 (via Trinidad) 7½ hrs. COT (generally cheaper than Onda) runs a daily service to Buenos Aires, leaving 2200 via Fray Bentos, US$12.50, taking about 10 hrs. Arco office for buses to Colonia on Plaza Cagancha. Onda runs services all over the country (the

URUGUAY

office is just off Av. 18 de Julio). The smaller competing services are just as fast and less expensive; differences in prices can sometimes be large. **N.B.** One needs a passport when buying international tickets.

East from Montevideo

The beach season is from December to the middle of April. This beautiful coastline, over 320 km. long, contains an endless succession of small bays, beaches and promontories set among hills and woods. There is a series of well equipped and modern camp sites all along the coast. Details are published in Friday's edition of *El Día* especially during the tourist season.

Two roads, both paved, go to Punta del Este. The northern branch (no tolls) via Pando and Soca, is Route 8; at Km. 75 Route 9 branches off NE towards Minas (see page 784); it continues to San Carlos (14½ km. N of Maldonado or 19 km. N of Punta del Este) through beautiful rolling country with views of the Laguna del Sauce (Willow Lake) and on to Chuy. The "Interbalnearia", runs largely along the coast, with short branches to some of the resorts, and is the one described in the text. There are toll posts at Arroyo Pando and at Arroyo Solís Grande. There is an alternative road to the Interbalnearia route, running parallel between it and the coast—its use is recommended during heavy traffic periods due to the frequency of dangerous road junctions. Route 9, the road to Chuy, is now completely paved. A spur of the road turn S to La Paloma, and there are secondary roads to some of the resorts further along the coast.

Atlántida (*Rex*, C, is main hotel; *Munday*, C, is clean and friendly; many good *residenciales* charging E off season; some good restaurants—try the *Banzai*), 45 km. from Montevideo, is ringed by fir forest and has a good country club. A short distance beyond, in groves of eucalyptus and pine, is the small and intimate beach of Las Toscas, followed by Parque del Plata, on the Solís Chico river. An *asado* on the beach (with wine) costs about US$12. Shortly before Atlántida, in an old fortress set in pine woods, is *El Fortín de Santa Rosa* hotel and restaurant, 2 mins. from a lovely sandy beach. Small zoo not far off.

At km. 64.5 on the Interbalnearia is Sr. Garabedian's **campsite**, with Youth Hostel. For bookings, telephone Sr. Garabedian at Montevideo 561230 (non-IYHA members pay slightly more).

Crossing by a (toll) bridge we come to

La Floresta (*Oriental*, highly recommended; *del Parque*), surrounded by woods. The chalets are pretty, the place reminds one of the villages of the Landes, near Biarritz. About 35 km. on, over a toll bridge, is **Solís** (*Solís Golf*; *El Chajá*), at the mouth of the River Solís. It has a very long beach, good fishing, delightful river and hill scenery. About 8 km. beyond Solís lies the small village of Las Flores, with a better beach than that at Solís. Accommodation is available at Edén Camping with room at US$3 p.p. or camping at km. 91 site.

Piriápolis, the next resort, 16 km. from Solís, 101 from Montevideo, may be reached either by turning south at the end of the Interbalnearia, and coming through Solís and then along the very beautiful R10, or by taking the original access road (R37) from Pan de Azúcar, which crosses the R93. It has a fine casino hotel and some 50 others, a good beach, a yacht harbour, a country club, a golf course, a motor-racing track and is particularly popular with Argentines. The town, set among hills, is laid out with an abundance of shade trees, and the district is rich in pine, eucalyptus and acacia woods. There are medicinal springs. Six km. to the N is Cerro Pan de Azúcar (Sugar Loaf), crowned by a tall cross with a circular stairway inside; there is only a path up to the cross. Just outside Piriápolis on the side road to Pan de Azúcar (town) by the entrance to the municipal park is a zoo and museum containing among other things live specimens of all snakes living in Uruguay. A recommended visit if you can endure proximity to reptiles, as they have "some freedom" to roam. The shortest route from Piriápolis to Punta de Este is by the Camino de las Bases which runs parallel to the R37 and joins the R93 some 4 km east of the R37 junction.

Hotels *Argentino*, C, with casino; *Neo*; *Esmeraldas*; *Gutiérrez*; *Ocean*; *City*; *Genovés*; *Rex*, next to Onda terminal, C, recommended; *San Sebastián*, D; *Juvencia*; *Cumbre*, D; *Colón*, open off-season, C; *Centro*, F, recommended. The Centro de Hoteles y Anexos de Piriápolis runs a reservation office at Edificio Piriá on Rambla de los Argentinos.

Restaurants *Argentino*; *Parador Punta Fría*; *Puertito Don Anselmo* (shellfish); *Entrevero*, in which vermouth is offered with about 20 side dishes, described as "a meal in itself"; restaurant of *Hotel Neo*, eood, friendly and reasonable.

Youth Hostel Close to beach, behind *Hotel Argentino*, at Simón del Pino 1136, US$3 a night. Mostly double bedrooms. For those wanting a beach holiday. There is also an international YMCA camp on the slope of Cerro del Toro, double rooms in bungalows, and tents.

Bus to Montevideo, US$3, 1½ hrs. Buses also to Rocha and Gen. José Artigas bridge (Argentina), US$17.

778 URUGUAY

Tourist Information Asociación de Fomento y Turismo, Rambla de los Argentinos 1348.

Portezuelo has good beaches with the Laguna del Sauce and the fine Lussich woods behind. At ***Punta Ballena*** there is a wide crescent beach, calm water and very clean sand. The *Solana del Mar Hotel* (opens mid-December, payment in dollars cash is demanded unless you protest) modern, is on the beach, A with full board. The place is a residential resort but is still quiet. Casa Pueblo, the house of Uruguayan artist Carlos Páez Villaro, can be visited; it is built in a Spanish-Moroccan style on a cliff over the sea; there are paintings, collages and ceramics on display, and for sale; season: Nov. 1 to April 1. The Arboreto Lussich (only open 1030-1700 in winter) on the West slope of the Sierra de la Balena (north of R10) contains a unique set of native and exotic trees. At the top of Punta Ballena there is a panoramic road with remarkable views of the coast. From Portezuelo it is possible to drive north towards the R9 by way of the R12 which then continues, unpaved, to Minas.

Maldonado, capital of Maldonado Department, 140 km. from Montevideo; population 6,000. This peaceful town, sacked by the British in 1806, has many colonial remains: the parish church, El Vigia watch tower, and fortifications on Gorriti Island in the semi-circular bay. Gorriti Island, densely wooded and with superb beaches, is an ideal spot for campers. See also the Mazzoni Museum and the windmill. *Hospedaje Ituzaingó*, E, on Ituzaingó, Irish owner, friendly, but charges for water for washing clothes. *Hotel Colonial*, D. *Hotel Dieciocho*, on Plaza, E with bath, recommended; *Hotel Santa Teresa* D, Rafael Pérez del Puerto y Santa Teresa. Restaurants: *Club Municipal*, *Matias*, good fish and meat US$10 p.p. *Ramón Guerra*, Ituzaingó and cheap *parrillada* at 2 Avenida on Santa Teresa. *Círculo Policial*, run by police, good cheap place to eat. Just after crossing the bridges to La Barra de Maldonado is the *Restaurant San Jorge* with its speciality of *tarta de mariscos*. Also *La Posta del Cangrejo* has a pleasant terrace, as well as rooms. About US$16 p.p. to eat there. Bus to Montevideo US$3.25. Bus to Minas, US$2.50. The railway track between Maldonado and Punta del Este has been turned into a road.

Camping Two sites: one free, in Parque El Placer; the other charges.

Punta del Este Seven km. on and 139 km. from Montevideo, facing the bay on one side and the open waters of the Atlantic on the other, lies the largest and best known of the resorts, Punta del Este. Prices seem to have come down since the recession in Argentina. The narrow peninsula of Punta del Este has been entirely built over; it has excellent bathing beaches, the calm *playa mansa* on the bay side, the rough *playa brava* on the ocean side. There are an excellent yacht marina, a yacht club, and a fishing club. There is good fishing both at sea and in three near-by lakes and the river Maldonado (which the main road crosses at Manantiales by a unique inverted-W-shaped bridge). The rest of the area consists of sand dunes covered with pines. On Isla de Lobos, which is a government reserve within sight of the town, there is a huge sea-lion colony; excursions to it every morning at 0800, return at 1115, US$7 p.p.; ticket should be bought at the harbour the day before. Direct daily Boeing 737 flights from Buenos Aires to Punta del Este airport during the high season. On the land side, Punta del Este is flanked by large planted forests of eucalyptus, pine and mimosa. A large country club (the *Cantegril*) lets cottages and hotel apartments at a high price, or one may hire from an "Inmobiliaria". There are a golf course and two casinos. After the Easter vacation the place is all your own and on sunny days it is still warm enough to swim. Many of the best hotels and restaurants close after the end of the season in March.

Hotels *Arenas*, B; *Oasis*, C; *Palace*, A, breakfast only, well kept but old, Calle 14; *Peninsula*, *London*, and *Playa Brava*, C; *Tamaris* (in the woods), very modern but only showers; *Kennedy*; *Santos Dumont*; *España*; *Iberia*; *Edén*; *Milano*; *Playa*, A, with breakfast. Very few low priced hotels but try *Hospedaje Isla de Gorriti*, Calle Isla de Gorriti 884, D; *Residencial Ituzaingó*, Ituzaingó 839, D; both OK and cheapest in town. *Colombia*, back of railway station, D, also *Shelton* (but bargain and examine your final bill) and *Charrúa*, near transport terminals. *Puerto* (near Onda bus station), C, clean and friendly, English spoken; *Tourbillón*, Calles 9 and 12, basic, no hot water, E, in the off season. *L'Auberge*, near golf course, air-conditioned, "lo más refinado". Hotel rates are down by a sixth in the winter months. In the high season, it is better to find a hotel in Maldonado and commute, or look for a hotel that is rebuilding, so that you can negotiate on prices. To stay at a hotel in the woods you will need a car; no public transport to beach or town.

Restaurants The most expensive restaurants are the *Tabla del Rey Arturo*, Pedragosa Sierra y Los Eucaliptos, and *La Floreal* (both in the woods) and *La Bourgogne*, excellent, French-run, Pedragosa Sierra, with gourmet shop in basement, about US$40 a head. *Bungalow Suizo*; *Las Tablitas*; *Piccolo*; *Picasso*; *Puertal del Sol*; *Tío Paco*; *Las Casitas*; *Mariskonea*, one of the oldest established and most expensive, US$25 p.p.; *El Mastil* (behind port); *El Ciclista*, inexpensive Italian

URUGUAY 779

cooking; *El Metejón*, Gorlero y 17, steak, US$6, simple; *Forte di Makalle*, Calle 8-828 y 11, US$7, recommended; *Cala Mayor*, Calle 11 y 10, US$16, well recommended; *Los Caracoles*, US$2 p.p.; *El Cacique*, Calle 28, No. 620; *El Sargo*, on Av. Gorlero. *Andrés* on a terrace at the Edificio Vanguardia, about US$13 p.p. Many enticing ice-cream parlours, such as *Confitería Gorlero* or *Concorde* in Gorlero.

Crafts Manos del Uruguay in front of the Casino Nogaró. Best sweaters from San Carlos.

Tourist Information Liga de Fomento, Parada 1, or Onda at Av. Gorlero and Calle 27, Tel.: 40023.

Banks Both Amex and Diner's Club have offices. Best rates of exchange from Banco de la República, which opens earlier and closes later than the other banks. Also *casas de cambio*.

Buses New terminal on Calle Sarandí (served by local bus No. 7). To Montevideo, COT or Onda (recommended) buses, US$4, less than 2 hrs., plenty of buses in the summer; to Piriápolis, US$1.50. To San Carlos (US$1.50) for a connection to Porto Alegre (US$30) or Onda services. To Gen. José Artigas bridge (Argentina) US$20.

Airport El Jagüel (full customs facilities) as well as the airport on the southern shore of the Laguna del Sauce, Capitán Curbelo, which handles the Pluna and Aerolíneas Argentinas flights to Buenos Aires, US$66. Airport tax US$6 and bus to town US$1. Exchange facilities, but no tax-free shopping yet.

Near Punta del Este, to the E, **Playa San Rafael**, where there is an 18-hole golf course, is growing rapidly. (*Casino San Rafael*, L, incl. full board, good, much used for conferences, Telex 1117, Tel.: 042-82161; *San Marcos*, B, incl. 2 meals; *L'Auberge*, A). Punta del Diablo has a beautiful beach, camping, restaurant (expensive) and a picturesque fishing village. Not far away is the village of Faro José Ignacio, with the well-known restaurant *Parador Santa Teresita*, where seaweed omelette is a speciality.

Rocha is 211 km. from Montevideo and 28 km. from the sea at La Paloma. Population: 20,000. Two casinos located at *Costas del Mar* and *Cabo Santa María* hotels. *Hospedaje Plaza* on the plaza, budget, D/E (3 rooms only). Cheap food at *Las Vegas* on Ramírez. Groves of palms dotted about the fields give it an unusual beauty.

Hotels at Rocha: *Arrate*; *Trocadero*, C; *Roma*; *Municipal*, very good and cheap.

Camping Sites at Parque Andresito, Rocha, and Rancho Pucará, Barra de Valizas. There are also cabins for rent at US$6 (4 beds).

La Paloma (Hotels *del Cabo*; *Barceló*; *Ocean*; *Viola*; *Trocadero, Bahía*, B; *Parque*; *Puertas del Sol*, C. *Youth Hostel*, G, clean, friendly, meals available, kitchen facilities.) A good port for yachts as it is protected by two islands. There is attractive scenery and good sea and lake fishing. Buses run between La Paloma and Rocha. An oil refinery is in operation, and a fishmeal plant can smell bad, if the wind is in the wrong direction. Horses can be hired. Some 10 km. beyond Paloma near the sandy beach is the *Hotel La Pedrera*, D, with swimming pool, tennis and comfortable rooms, recommended.

Beyond Rocha lies the colonial fortress (converted into a museum) of Santa Teresa, begun by the Portuguese and finished by the Spaniards in the 1750s. (It was the other way round with the fortress of San Miguel—see below— neither smelt battle.) It is set in the Parque de Santa Teresa, with avenues of palms, a bird sanctuary, and fresh-water pools to bathe in. The fortress is very impressive; free admission. Open 0800-2000, closed Tuesdays. There are cottages to let for the summer season, beside the sea and excellent "wild" camping in the north of the park, so get off the bus at the Fortaleza steps, *not* at the main entrance. There is a small supermarket, a butcher's and a bar in the commercial area where campers are expected to register. Nine km. beyond is the bathing resort of **La Coronilla** (no restaurants, hotels closed in off-season) with excellent ocean fishing for sharks, skate and black *corvina* from the rocks: there is an annual competition in January. Tour by taxi or Onda bus (US$9, daily) from La Coronilla to the Santa Teresa fortress and the strange and gloomy Laguna Negra,

780 URUGUAY

and the collection of native and exotic plants under glass. The beach stretches for many km., but there are too many waves for swimming.

Hotels Parador La Coronilla, C; El Pescador; Costas del Mar, C; Oceanía, C (highly recommended), family runs restaurant close by; both Rivamar and Las Cholgas claim to have heating.

Restaurants Buretche (recommended) and Las Cholgas, less good.

From the road between La Paloma and Castillos one can walk down to many pleasant fishing villages along the coast; accommodation is very basic. Visits to the islands of Castillos and Wolf can be arranged. Lookout for the sea-lions and penguins along this coast, for instance at Cabo Polonia. Local buses do not run at weekends.

At **Chuy,** on the Brazilian frontier, 340 km. from Montevideo (Hotel Iramar, E, recommended, Pensión Frontera, E, Internacional, D (incl. own bath); Hotel Plaza, D; Hotel Chuy, E, includes breakfast), the road branches off towards the elongated Laguna Merín; the frontier is along its middle. Buses stop to allow immigration formalities. On the Uruguayan side, overlooking the lagoon, stands the fortress of **San Miguel,** also set in a park in which many plants and animals are kept. A museum is attached to the fortress. (A must, but it is closed Tues.) A casino, open until 0400, recently began operations nearby. There is an excellent hotel, the Parador San Miguel, and good bathing on the sea-shore of the nearby Barra del Chuy; buses (US$0.38) every two hours, bathing excellent, many birds. Tourists arriving from Uruguay may cross the border to the Brazilian side of the town, and purchase a certain amount of Brazilian manufactured goods without formalities (but see below). At present it is much cheaper to stay in Brazil for the night but the food is better on the Uruguayan side. Uruguayan taxis are allowed 25 km. beyond the frontier, and vice versa. Onda runs an excursion bus daily from La Coronilla to Barra del Chuy beach, and Chuy to San Miguel fort, US$9 (4 hrs. trip). Bus Chuy-Porto Alegre, US$6 or 7 express. Bus to Montevideo US$7, cheapest by Ruta del Sol, US$5, frequent stops; otherwise by Onda or Cita.

The coastal road, now excellent, goes on to Pelotas and Porto Alegre, in Brazil. Ordinary (not international) buses ply the route. The border runs down the middle of the main street in Chuy. Passengers from Montevideo are set down at the bus company's office. You can immediately get passport clearance at the Uruguayan immigration, over one km. back on the way to Montevideo. Money exchange not far from hotel (no facilities on Sunday), bank won't change travellers' cheques. All except one restaurant (on the Uruguayan side) close at 2030; the one closes at 2300. The Brazilian immigration office is about 2 km. from Chuy on the road to Pelotas. It is necessary to take a taxi or the local bus marked "Chuí-Santa Vitória". The office for the Pelotas bus is across the road from the Hotel Quarain. Make sure your passport is stamped, or you may have difficulty in leaving Brazil. Getting a car into Brazil is no trouble. There is even less hassle if driving a car not registered in Brazil or Uruguay.

West from Montevideo

There is a toll on Route 1 (Montevideo-Colonia) at the Santa Lucía bridge (Km. 22.5). There are no tolls on Routes 2 to Fray Bentos and 3 to Paysandú and Salto.

Route 1, part of the Pan-American Highway, runs from Montevideo westwards for 177 km. to Colonia del Sacramento. There is a nice beach near the disused bull-ring, which is passed by regular buses. Much traffic from Argentina flows along this busy road; the surface has continued to deteriorate.

About 119 km. from Montevideo, a 5 km. branch leads N to **Colonia Suiza**, originally a Swiss settlement, with some 4,500 people. The Swiss national day is celebrated on August 1 with considerable zest. There are several hotels, the Bungalow Suiza restaurant and a Youth Hostel (three meals US$3.50). Quite near is Nueva Helvecia, where the tourist can buy locally made Swiss musical boxes. At 120 km. along the main road, and just S, is **Colonia Valdense**, another colony, this time of Waldensians, who still cling to some of the old customs of the Piedmontese Alps. There is little for the budget traveller in either Nueva Helvecia or Colonia Valdense.

Hotels at Colonia Suiza Nirvana, A, with full board, good; Suizo; del Prado (Youth Hostel).

Hotels at Colonia Valdense Brisas del Plata; Parador los Ceibos.

About 6½ km. further on, a paved main road branches off right to Rosario (5 km.), Mercedes (164 km.), and Fray Bentos (34 km. further). **Rosario** is a typical agricultural town given over to dairying and grain production. Its port, Juan Lacaze, lies 22 km. SW. Population: 8,000.

Hotels *Ricardi* and *Riviera*, E, good.

Clubs Club Cyssa, a social, cultural and sporting club, with a stadium, football field and basketball ground. Two fishing clubs.

Colonia (del Sacramento), a charming small town with an interesting historic section jutting into the River Plate, was founded by Portuguese settlers from Brazil in 1680. It contains rebuilt city walls and quite a number of colonial buildings and narrow streets in the older part of the town; all the more interesting because there are few such examples in this part of the continent. Worth seeing are the Parochial Church, the Municipal Museum in the old house of Almirante Brown (open Thurs., Sat. and Sun. 1300-1700), the Mansion of the Viceroy, the house of General Mitre, and the Farola (lighthouse). The plaza is particularly picturesque. The tourist office in the town hall offers good maps. Buenos Aires, to which there is a ferry service, is only 50 km. A "free zone" has been created here. Pop.: 10,000. At Real San Carlos, just out of town (take the blue bus from the centre) are the racecourse (Hipódromo) and bull-ring (out of use). The best beach is Playa Ferrando, with campsite, 2 km to the east.

Hotels *Rincón del Río*, C (with shower); *Onda*, D, good; *Esperanza*, A; *El Mirador*, A, Av. Roosevelt, Km. 176½; *Ciudadela*, Washington Barbor 164, E, clean; *Colonial*; *Avenida*, Calle Artigas 384, good, D; *Italiano*, D; *Español*, Henrique de La Peña, D, with shower; *Leoncia*, Rivera 216, modern, good, C (owns the *Nuevo Galpón* restaurant). Several cheap *hospedajes* near the Plaza. *Hospedaje* at General Flores 311, F, no bath.

Restaurant *Nuevo Galpón*, cheap and good. *La Casona* (coffee bar).

Camping Site at Playa Ferrando.

Ferries Three ferries a day to Buenos Aires, three hours crossing, US$14.40 p.p. To Tigre (Argentina) by ferry costs US$13 and takes about 4 hours; leaves Mon-Sat. 0430, 1000, 1200, 1800, Sun. 0100, 0630, 1330, 1630, student and YHA card holders get a 10% discount. (Tel.: Montevideo 900045 or 906617).

Hydrofoil 5 daily services, each way, to Buenos Aires (4 hours), 0315, 0615, 0915, 1015, 1615, US$16.60 (limited luggage allowance). It is substantially cheaper to buy ticket from office (Flores 256) than from a tourist agency.

Air Service Arco and Lada to Aeroparque, Buenos Aires, 3 times a day, US$22. It is generally quicker than the hydrofoil.

Bus to or from Montevideo, US$3.50 (2½ hrs.), Onda, five a day. US$1.50 to Carmelo, three times daily.

Up the River Uruguay

The road swings N and NW to reach the sleepy resort town of **Carmelo,** 74 km. from Colonia, on the shores of Las Vacas river. Population: 15,000. Across the bridge is a white restaurant on the left-hand side of the road: friendly, recommended. The port harbours several hundred yachts during the season. There is a launch service to Tigre, across the delta, a most interesting ride past innumerable islands (leaves Mon.-Sat. 1100, 1030, Sun. 1200, 1400, 1500, 4 hrs., US$8.15). You can pay at the Onda bus station in Montevideo for both bus and launch, US$10. There is a free zone at the port. Bus to and from Montevideo US$5.

Hotels *Casino Carmelo*; *Comercio*; *La Unión*, Uruguay 368, E, very good value. *Centro*, next door, E. The bank will only exchange bills and not travellers' cheques. **Bus** to Fray Bentos and Salto from the main square at 1500.

Some 30 km. up the river, by road, is ***Nueva Palmira*** (population 3,500). Worth visiting in the town are the Pirámide de Solís, the Calera, the Camacho, the Capilla de la Concepción, and the Convento de la Reducción Jesuítica (1780). A free zone at the port.

782 URUGUAY

Some 20 km. away is the historic beach of La Agraciada, famous for the landing of the Thirty-Three patriots on April 19, 1825, which led to Uruguayan independence. On the beach is a statue to General Juan Lavalleja, leader of the Treinta y Tres. A festival is held on each anniversary.

The road continues through the small river port of **Dolores** (population: 13,000), 32 km. up-river from the confluence of the Río San Salvador with the Río Uruguay, to

Mercedes, a livestock centre and resort best reached by road from the main Colonia-Montevideo highway, or by railway from the capital (275 km.). It is set on the S bank of the Río Negro, 48 km. above its confluence with the Río Uruguay. This pleasant town of 34,000 inhabitants is a yachting and fishing centre during the season.

The charm of the town derives from its Spanish-colonial appearance, though it is not as old as the older parts of Colonia. There is a pleasant *costanera* (riverside drive).

Hotels *Brisas del Hum*, C; *Comercio*; *Petit Hotel*, D; *Himalaya*, D, with bath; *Martín*, D; *Universal*, D, recommended. *Hospedaje Hotelcito*, Giménez 703, E. Good food at *La Brasa*, Calle Castro y Careaga, and at *Círculo Policial*, Calle 25 de Mayo.

Camping Site at Mercedes, and beside Rivers Negro and Uruguay.

Museums Palaeontology and Natural Sciences; the Museum of Eusebio Giménez, with a gallery of paintings.

Bus to Paysandú, 2½ hrs., US$4.

Excursions To the islands in the Río Negro—the largest has an inn. To the small town of **Santo Domingo** (Soriano), first town to be founded in Uruguay, to see a fine colonial church and an old house. Difficult to do this trip easily in one day.

The road continues westwards (34 km.) to

Fray Bentos, a port on the Uruguay River, 193 km. above Buenos Aires. An international bridge has been built across the Río Uruguay to Puerto Unzué (Argentina); toll US$2.10 per car, 3 buses a day to Gualeguaychú, Argentina, 0700, 1230, 1800. Main industry: meat packing and canning. Population: 14,000.

Hotels *Colonial*, close to main Plaza and ETA bus office, hot water, E; *Gran Plaza* (satisfactory); **Restaurant** *Club Armonía*.

River Boats Launch services four times a week to Gualeguaychú.

There is an ETA bus service to Rivera.

Paysandú, on the E bank of the Río Uruguay, 122 km. by good paved road from Fray Bentos (Route 2), and 480 by paved road via Trinidad from Montevideo (Route 3), has a population of about 80,000. Temperatures in summer can rise as high as 42°C. There is a golf club, and a rowing club which holds regattas. The cathedral is 19th century with cannon balls embedded in its walls from the 1865 Brazilian siege (at the time the town was held by the Paraguayans). The attached Salesian college has an interesting museum, opens 1700. The cemetery on the outskirts is worth a look. Also worth a visit is the Museo de la Tradición, with *gaucho* articles, at the Balneario Municipal beach, north of town. A historical museum has been opened at Florida 930. There is an international bridge (no buses on Suns.) to Colón (Argentina) (US$1.90 per car for crossing). It is about 8 km. to Colón. Airport with daily Tamu flights to Montevideo.

Hotels *Gran Hotel Paysandú*, D, 18 de Julio y 19 de Abril, Tel.: 3400, a/c, best; *Onda*, D, "super suites", good restaurant (one can reserve through Onda in Montevideo), recommended; cheapest is *Pensión Popular*, E, with shower; *Concordia*, 18 de Julio, E, clean; *Rafaela*, 18 de Julio 1181, E, large rooms, modern and friendly, no food but surrounded by cafés; *Lobato*, Leandro Gómez 1415, E, good. A good hotel, but not in the centre, is *Hotel Bulevar* at Bulevar Artigas and República Argentina. *Victoria*, 18 de Julio 974, F, highly recommended.

Youth Hostel Liga Departamental de Football, Gran Bretaña 872, US$2.70 a night. Cabins for 5 or more people.

Camping Free facilities available in a municipal park by the river.

Restaurant *Artemio,* Plaza de Constitución, 18 de Julio, "best food in town". *Parrillada de Asturias,* good and cheap. *Don Diego's,* 19 de Abril, serves cheap *parillada,* good value.

Tourist Bureau Plaza de Constitución, 18 de Julio 1226.

Travel Agency Viñar Turismo, Artigas 1163, helpful.

Bus to Montevideo, 7 hrs., US$8, by Onda, four buses daily. Other lines are cheaper and just as good. To Salto US$3.65. For drivers, Route 3 via Mercedes is only 38 km. longer than the direct Route 2 via Trinidad, but in much better condition.

Train to Salto US$1.90 (2nd) and Montevideo US$5.50 (2nd), three times a week, very slow. Change at Paso de los Toros.

Excursions To the waterfalls of the River Quequay, a few km. to the N; the Termas del Guaviyú thermal springs 50 km. away (1½ hrs. by bus) with cheap camping, and to the Meseta de Artigas, 90 km. N of Paysandú, 13 km. off the highway to Salto. The Meseta, where General Artigas lived (statue), is 45 metres above the Uruguay river, which here narrows and forms whirlpools at the rapids of El Hervidero. A terrace commands a fine view, but the rapids are not visible from the Meseta. The statue, with the general's head topping a tall shaft, is very original. There are some pleasant, somewhat primitive, chalets available from Erwin Frey, 90 Estación Chapieny, Dept. Paysandú. Early booking recommended. Bus to Km. 462 on Paysandú-Salto road.

Salto, 120 km. by rail or paved road N of Paysandú, has a population of 80,000. It is a centre for oranges and other citrus fruit and now processes them. See the beautiful park of Solari; the municipal park with an open air theatre and a well-kept, free zoo; the fine-arts museum in the donated mansion, French style, of a rich *estanciero,* Uruguay 1067, well worth a visit (the locals are justifiably proud of it); and the promenade along the River Uruguay. Across the river is Concordia, in Argentina, to which there are four ferries (US$1, 15 mins.) on weekdays, three on Sat. but none on Sun. The ferry service has been reduced with completion of the international highway and railway across the Salto Grande dam. There is a four-train-a-day shuttle service.

Hotels *Gran Hotel Salto,* best; *Los Cedros,* a/c, newest, D, Uruguay 657 (Tel.: 3989); *Girard,* D, basic; *Gran Biasetti,* D; *Uruguay,* D; *Magnolias,* C; *Plaza,* Plaza Treinta y Tres, near bus station, simple, clean, good food, D; *Rosa, Delma* and *Pensión Sabarros,* D, are also fairly cheap. *Pensión 33,* Treinta y Tres 269, D, basic, central. *Pensión Santa Catalina,* Brasil 1633 or *Pensión Jasil,* General Rivera 1155, cheaper, basic, E; *Artigas Plaza,* Plaza 18 de Julio next to Onda bus station, F with bath, hot water, very clean.

Youth Hostels Club de Remeros Salto (by the river) or Club de Leones, Uruguay 1626, if you can find a student to sign you in.

Camping Site at Salto.

Restaurants *Los Pingüinos,* Uruguay 702; *Chef Restaurant,* Uruguay 639; *Sigo* at La Rueda, in the E, for *parrillada,* 10 blocks from the cathedral; *Club de Remeros de Salto.* Good breakfast and cheap beer from *Bar Papá Castillo,* opposite post office.

Tourist Office Calle Uruguay 1052, helpful. Free map.

Bank of London & South America, two agencies: Uruguay 585 and Blandengues y 8 de Octubre. Open 1300-1700, Mon.-Fri. National banks. Cambio Pensotti has been recommended as helpful.

Anglican Church Calle República de Argentina, close to Calle Uruguay.

Bus to Montevideo, US$10 (Onda); to Termas del Arapey, 2 hrs., daily, US$3.50. Paysandú US$3.65, four a day.

Air Service Daily to and from Montevideo via Paysandú, by Tamu. To Buenos Aires.

Rail To Montevideo, railcar (*tacataca*) Mon., Wed., Fri. 0420, arrive Paso de los Toros 1200, then 8-hour train journey to the capital. Five times a week railcar (Brill) to Artigas (6½ hrs.) and once weekly to Bella Unión.

Excursions A favourite excursion from Salto is by launch to the Salto Chico; another is to Salto Grande, where a ranch-style guest house for anglers is run by

784 URUGUAY

the Tourist Commission. The most popular tourist site in the area is the large *Salto Grande* dam and hydroelectric plant 20 km. from Salto, built jointly by Argentina and Uruguay. A road and railway run along the top of the dam, giving connection to Concordia (Argentina). Medicinal springs at Fuente Salto, 6 km. N of the city. There are frequent bus services to *Termas de Daymán*; beautifully laid out and many swimming pools, with Youth Hostel and campsite (US$1 p.p.).

The road to *Termas del Arapey* branches off the partially paved highway to Bella Unión, 61 km. N of Salto, and then runs 35 km. first E and then S. Pampa birds, rheas and metre-long lizards much in evidence. Termas del Arapey is on the Arapey river S of Isla Cabellos (Baltazar Brum). The waters at these famous thermal baths contain bicarbonated salts, calcium and magnesium. There is a new hotel with pool (*Hotel Termas del Arapey*, A), also a motel (very small bungalows with kitchens, no sheets provided), a nice swimming pool and a very simple *parador* (meals only). Book ahead in Salto or Montevideo. Camping US$2 p.p.

Both road (148 km.) and railway run N to the little town of *Bella Unión*, 5,000 people, (with free campsite, ask at Prefectura Naval, insect repellant needed), near the Brazilian frontier.

From Isla Cabellos on the line to Bella Unión, a railway runs NE to *Artigas*, a frontier town in a cattle raising and agricultural area (excellent swimming upstream from the bridge). There is a bridge across the Río Cuaraim to the Brazilian town of Quaraí opposite. Population: 14,000.

Hotels *Concordia; Oriental. Pensión Uruguay* and *Hawaii*, basic but clean.

Camping US$0.24 p.p. a day, or at Agua Corriente—chance of camping at the yacht club on the river.

Youth Hostel Club Deportivo Artigas, Pte. Berreta and L.A. de Herrera.

Restaurants *Maricarmen*, Calle Lecueder 302, and *Municipal*, Lecueder y Berreta.

Bus service to Salto, 225 km. **Airport** at Bella Unión.

Montevideo North-east to Brazil

The Pan-American Highway, 486 km. long, runs NE into the hills away from the coast. Route 8 is paved to about 30 km. beyond Minas, 120 km. from Montevideo; beyond it is all-weather.

Minas, with 34,000 inhabitants, is a picturesque small town set in the wooded hills, which supply granite and marble. Juan Lavalleja, the leader of the Thirty-Three who brought independence to the country, was born here (equestrian statue). The church's portico and towers, some caves in the neighbourhood, and the countryside around are worth seeing. The Parque Salus, on the slopes of Sierras de las Animas, is only 8 km. to the S and very attractive; take the town bus marked "Cervecería Salus" from plaza to the Salus brewery, then walk 2 km. to the mineral spring and bottling plant. (*Parador Salus*, acceptable.) The Cascada de Agua del Penitente waterfall, about 11 km. out of town, off the Minas-Aigue road, is interesting and you may see wild rheas (protected) nearby. It is difficult to get to the falls in the off-season. Good confectionery is made in Minas; the largest firm, opposite *Hotel Verdun*, shows tourists round its premises. Museum in the Casa de la Cultura.

Hotels *Garibaldi; Verdun. City.* Avoid *Hotel Touring*. About five budget hotels in main plaza. All overcharge in the off-season.

Restaurant *San Francisco*, 25 de Mayo 586, is recommended as is *El Portal*, Aníbal del Campo 743, for *parrillada*. The best pastry shop is *Irisarri*, Calle Treinta y Tres 618, known for *yemas* (egg candy) and *damasquitos* (apricot sweets).

Bank of London and South America, and national banks, open 1300-1700 Monday-Friday.

Youth Hostel In small village of Villa Serrana, US$1.80 a night, 28 km. beyond Minas on road to Treinta y Tres; most attractive, but take plenty of food and drink as the last shop has now shut. Direct bus from Montevideo or Minas, ask driver to set you down and walk 3 km. to Villa Serrana; ask for Sra. Graciela (if the *Hotel Chatar* is closed) for the key to the Hostel.

Air Service Daily flight by Tamu from Montevideo.

Railway from Montevideo.

Bus To Montevideo, US$3.

The next centre of any importance, 286 km. from Montevideo, is

Treinta y Tres, 15,000 people, picturesquely placed a little way from the Olimar River. Some 20 km. beyond, a dirt road, left, runs 19 km. among and over hills to a rocky region with small streams—the Quebrada de los Cuervos— now a beautiful and quite unspoilt national park. Free camping and swimming at Municipal Park at Río Olimar. Main plaza has all the main restaurants and grills.

Hotel *Central*, and pensions *Jorgito* or *Mota*.

Air Service Daily by Tamu from Montevideo.

Railway On the line from Montevideo through José Batlle y Ordóñez to Río Branco.

Railway and road go on through **Melo** (111 km. from Treinta y Tres; *Hotel Internacional*, acceptable) to the border town of **Río Branco,** 88 km. from Melo, founded in 1914, on the Yaguarón River. The 1½ km.-long Mauá bridge across the river leads to the Brazilian town of Jaguarão.

Hotel *Italiano*, D, with bath.

Restaurant *Oasis*, good, *pollo a la brasa*.

This is where most international traffic used to cross the frontier; now the road via Chuy is better. Customs officials are at the international bridge, passport officials at the police station at Jaguarão. From Jaguarão buses run several times daily to Pelotas and Porto Alegre. There is usually a better rate of exchange at Melo than at the frontier.

Montevideo North to Brazil

This 509 km. road (there is also a railway) from Montevideo to the border town of Rivera runs almost due north, at first over rolling hills through cattle country, vineyards, apple orchards, orange, lemon and olive groves. Further N, hilly cattle-range land is crossed.

Las Piedras, 24 km. from Montevideo, in vineyard country, has a Gothic Chapel of the Salesians. Race meetings (pari-mutuel betting) Thurs., Sat. and Sun.

Bank of London and South America, Calle General Artigas 652. Open 1300-1700, Mon.-Fri.

Canelones, 45 km. from the capital, is a typical small town of 10,000 people in a grain growing area. Travellers then pass through the pleasant country towns of Florida, Durazno, **Paso de los Toros** (close to the huge lake created by the Rincón del Bonete dam on the Río Negro) and Tacuarembó. There is a toll on Route 5, going north, 67.8 km. from Montevideo; the road is dual carriageway as far as Canelones. Daily train Paso de los Toros-Montevideo at 1300, 8 hrs. E of Paso de los Toros (1½ hrs by Onda bus at 1700) is San Gregorio, cheap camping and bathing in Río Negro. Bus returns to Paso de los Toros 0245.

Florida Famous for a folklore festival on Independence Day each year.

Hotel *Español*, D.

Rivera is a town of 40,000 people, on the Brazilian frontier. It is divided by a street from the Brazilian town of Santa Ana do Livramento, which has a good golf course, and a daily bus to Porto Alegre. (To get to Foz do Iguaçu you must go to Porto Alegre first). Points of interest are the park (free camping facilities), the Plaza Internacional, and the dam of Cañapirú. There are an airport and a casino.

Hotels *Mabé* (near station); *Casino*; *Nuevo*.

Trains to Montevideo leave at 0510 (16 hours) and 2200 (10 hours) US$11 (1st) US$9.50 (2nd).

Bus to Montevideo, US$9 or less, there is also a service to Fray Bentos and Durazno, US$1.50.

The Economy

Although accounting for only 10.5% of gdp (less than either manufacturing or commerce and catering), agriculture is the dominant sector of the economy, as a supplier and a consumer. It employs 17% of the workforce. 90% of the land

URUGUAY

area is suitable for farming, and only about 3% of that is unused. Over three-quarters is given over to livestock rearing, the rest for crop production.

In the early 1980s, the beef-cattle sector suffered from low world prices and high interest rates, with the result that much of the herd was slaughtered. Slaughtering, domestic consumption and exports all declined in the 1983-85 period, but picked up thereafter, exports particularly in response to increased Brazilian demand. The number of sheep has risen in the 1980s, despite increased demand for exports of live and slaughtered animals. This reflects the lower prices for meat than for wool, of which Uruguay accounts for about 3% of total world production. Livestock and its manufactures contribute the major proportion of exports: in 1985, raw wool and manufactures' share was 31%, beef and veal 12%, and hides, skins and leather goods 13%. The only cereal exported is rice, accounting for 9.5% of the total. Others grown are maize and wheat. Also important are oilseeds (sunflower and linseed) and citrus fruits, of which oranges and tangerines are the main crops. The fishing industry has been expanded in the 1970s and 1980s, but catches and exports have fluctuated since 1981.

Manufacturing, which contributes 28% to gdp and employs 23% of the workforce, is concerned largely with agroindustrial activities. The most important of these are meat packing, drinks, tobacco, textiles, clothing and footwear. There are also some medium-technology industries such as oil refining, plastics, rubber products, electrical appliances and motor vehicle assembly. Import substitution behind tariff barriers encouraged growth until the 1960s, to be followed by stagnation until more export-oriented policies were introduced in the late 1970s. Various factors have contributed to mixed results in the 1980s, not the least of which have been economic problems in Argentina and Brazil. Construction accounts for 3% of gdp and 6% of employment. In the late 1970s, it benefitted from Argentine investment, which was curtailed as the Uruguayan peso appreciated against its Argentine counterpart. Further depression occurred as funds ran out for government housing programmes, although in 1985 another house-building scheme was launched.

Uruguay has no major mining industry, apart from the extraction of marble and various construction materials. It also has no known reserves of oil or natural gas. Its coal deposits are of poor quality and are not suitable for commercial mining. Almost 100% of electricity generation comes from hydroelectric plants, of which there are four. The combined installed capacity of their 14 turbines is 1,890 MW.

In the 1970s and 1980s, controlling inflation has been a high priority. Some success was achieved before the floating of the peso and the lifting of price controls in November 1982, since when consumer prices have climbed by over 70% a year. An expanding money supply and the growth in international reserves in 1986 meant that the government was unable to comply with IMF-imposed inflationary targets for the two years to June 1985. Other targets, set in an 18-month stabilization programme agreed with the IMF and commercial bank creditors in July 1985, were largely met in 1986. These covered growth, central bank net assets, public sector and publicly guaranteed debt and foreign exchange. Uruguay's external position was strengthened in 1986 by export-led recovery and by a multiyear rescheduling agreement with international banks. This included a rescheduling of maturities due between 1985 and 1989, with a repricing of these liabilities, and US$45 m in new money as part of a US$90 m loan cofinanced with the World Bank. At the end of 1986, Uruguay's total external debt stood at US$5.1 bn.

	1961-70 (av)	1971-80 (av)	1981-85 (av)	1986 (e)
Gdp growth (1980 prices)	1.8%	3.1%	-3.0%	6.3%
Inflation	34.2%	63.2%	45.9%	70.7%
Exports (fob) US$m	182	519	1,013	1,080
Meat	51	111	194	200
Wool	82	106	187	165
Hides	18	28	69	75
Imports (fob) US$m	160	607	939	840
Current account balance US$m (cum)	-0.1	-1,709	-988	55

Information for Visitors

Routes from Europe By air: direct flights by Pluna (Madrid), Air France, Iberia, KLM, Lufthansa, Varig and SAS. Flying by other carriers, a change must be made at Rio or Buenos Aires.

From the U.S.A. Pan American World Airways (2 a week), Varig, and Lan-Chile, and (as far as Buenos Aires) by Canadian Pacific Airlines, Avianca and Aerolíneas Argentinas.

From Argentina Car ferry, three times daily, single-class service (once daily in winter) between Buenos Aires and Colonia, about 2½ hrs. Hydrofoil passenger vessels (*aliscafos*) ply between Buenos Aires and Colonia 5 times a day and more in the holiday season; they carry 100 passengers and cross in 50 mins. About half the price: short crossing by launch between Carmelo and Tigre. Aerolíneas Argentinas and Pluna have several flights a day between Aeroparque in Buenos Aires and Carrasco Airport. Service intensified during holiday period. Also frequent flights to Punta del Este from Buenos Aires. Arco and Lada fly between Colonia and Buenos Aires. From Colonia there is a fast bus service by Onda to Montevideo. Foreign airlines connect Carrasco with the Buenos Aires international airport at Ezeiza. Buses run across the Paysandú and Fray Bentos bridges; a railway shuttle is operating across the Salto Grande dam, and there is also a road connection across the dam. Direct bus between Buenos Aires and Montevideo by one of these routes takes about 10 hours.

From Brazil Direct connection between Brazil and Uruguay by all the international airlines landing at Montevideo. Varig flies 3 times a week from Rio de Janeiro to Montevideo, via Buenos Aires. Cruzeiro do Sul has daily flights Rio de Janeiro, São Paulo, Porto Alegre and Montevideo. By road: the Pan-American Highway runs 2,880 km. from Rio de Janeiro to Montevideo and on to Colonia. It is poorly surfaced in parts. There are several bus services.

From Chile Only KLM direct; Lan-Chile flies thrice a week and Avianca twice. Lan-Chile flies between Santiago, Buenos Aires and Montevideo and between Montevideo and Lima.

From Paraguay Twice weekly by Pluna, thrice weekly by Líneas Aéreas Paraguayas (LAP) and weekly by Iberia. Twice-weekly buses Asunción-Montevideo.

Airport Tax of US$6 on all air travellers leaving Uruguay for South American republics or Mexico; US$7 for all other countries, and a tax of 3% on all tickets issued and paid for in Uruguay.

Documents A passport is necessary for entry except for nationals of other American countries, who can get in with national identity documents. Visas are not required by nationals of American and Western European countries, Israel and Japan. Tourist cards are valid for 3 months, extendable for a similar period. For extensions go to Migraciones office in Calle Misiones. A small fee is charged. Duties are not usually charged on a reasonable quantity of goods (such as tobacco and spirits), brought in obviously for the traveller's own use: 200 cigarettes or 50 cigars or 3 small packets of tobacco are admitted duty-free; so is 1 bottle of alcoholic drink, 3 little bottles of perfume and gifts up to the value of US$5.

Hours of Business Most department stores generally are open 0900 to 1200, 1400 to 1900, but 0900 to 1230 on Sat. Business houses vary but most work from 0830 to 1200, 1430 to 1830 or 1900, according to whether they open on Sat. Banking hours are 1300 to 1700 in Montevideo; there are special summer hours (Dec. 1-March 15) in Montevideo (1330-1730), in the interior (0730-1130) and in Punta del Este (1600-2000); banks are closed on Sat. Government departments, mid-March to mid-November, 1300 to 1830 from Mon. to Fri.; rest of the year, 0700 to 1230, but not Sat.

British business travellers are strongly advised to read "Hints to Exporters: Uruguay", obtainable from the Department of Trade, Sanctuary Buildings, 16-20 Great Smith Street, London SW1.

Best times for visiting Most tourists visit during the summer (December-mid March), though hotels have to be booked in advance. Business visits can be paid throughout the year, but it is best to avoid the tourist months. In June, July, and August, orders are placed for the winter season 12 months ahead.

Roads There are 45,000 km. of roads, 80% of them paved or all-weather. The Comisión Nacional de Turismo will help to plan itineraries by car. Onda buses radiate into the interior from Montevideo, using comfortable American (they even use the Greyhound logo) long-distance coaches; other companies do not run the same extensive network, but are often cheaper and as fast. All hotels display Onda timetables. Hitch-hiking can be difficult as drivers have memories of the Tupamaro urban-guerrilla movement of the early 1970s: at that time many

788 URUGUAY

hitch-hikers became hi-jackers. Gasoline prices are very high at US$1 a litre for super. Route 5 as far as Canelones is now dual-carriageway.

Motoring Carnet required. Vehicles do not stop, nor is there a right of way, at uncontrolled intersections. Traffic manners in Montevideo have improved recently, but the pace is slow because there are so many ancient cars on the road; all the same, driving standards are reckoned to be the most suicidal in South America. **Automóvil Club del Uruguay,** Av. Libertador General Lavalleja (ex Agraciada) 1532, Montevideo, publishes road maps of the city and the country at large. Uruguay is said to be better than Argentina or Brazil to ship a car to.

Railways converge upon Montevideo and have a total length of 2,993 km. They were mainly built by the British from 1868 on but were all sold to Uruguay in 1948. They are all of standard (1.435 metres) gauge. Services are very much slower (but cheaper) than buses. Railway buffs should do these trips soon, as the trend seems to be towards closing uneconomic (i.e. most) sections of line.

Internal Flights Internal air transport is provided by Tamu, an arm of the air force, which uses Brazilian "Bandeirante" and Fokker "Friendship" F-27s. Tickets from Colonia 1021, Montevideo. Provincial airports are mentioned in the text.

Climate Temperate, if somewhat damp and windy, and summer heat is tempered by Atlantic breezes, but there are occasional large variations. In winter (June-September), when the average temperature is 10° to 16°C, the temperature can fall now and then to well below freezing. It is generally humid and hardly ever snows. Summer (December-March), with an average temperature of 21° to 27°C, has irregular dry periods. There is always some wind and for the most part the nights are relatively cool. There are normally 120 sunny days in the year. The rainfall, with prolonged wet periods in July and August, averages about 1,200 mm. at Montevideo and some 250 more in the N, but the amount of rain varies markedly from year to year.

Youth Hostels Asociación de Alberguistas del Uruguay, Calle Pablo de María 1583 (open 1400-1900), Montevideo (Tel.: 981324) operates hostels at Montevideo (Canelones 935), Carmelo, Paysandú, Piriápolis, Salto, Los Titanes (Km. 64.5 on Interbalnearia), La Paloma and Villa Serrana, near Minas. Holders of YHA cards can get a 10% rebate on the price of the launch between Carmelo and Tigre; the ticket must be brought in Carmelo. A 10% rebate is available on Arco plane tickets between Colonia and Buenos Aires—obtainable at the Onda terminal in Montevideo.

Camping Several good sites in Montevideo and outside; see references in main text.

Shopping Bargains See under Montevideo, page 774.

Food and Drink Beef is eaten at almost all meals; it is good and now always available. The majority of restaurants are *parrilladas* (grills) where the staple is beef. *Asado* (barbecued beef) is popular; the main cuts are *asado de tira* (ribs); *pulpa* (no bones), *lomo* (fillet steak) and entrecote. To get a lean piece of *asado*, ask for *asado flaco*. *Costilla* (chop) and *milanesa* (veal cutlet) are also popular; usually eaten with mixed salad or chips. *Chivito* is a sandwich filled with slices of meat, lettuce, egg, etc. (normally over US$2). Two other good local dishes are *puchero* (beef with vegetables, bacon, beans and sausages) and the local varieties of pizza, fast becoming a staple. Other specialities are barbecued pork, grilled chicken in wine, *cazuela* (or stew) usually with *mondongo* (tripe) or sea foods (e.g. squid). The sausages are very good and spicy (*chorizos, morcillas, salchichas*). *Morcilla dulce*, a sweet black sausage, made from blood, orange peel and walnuts, has been highly praised; so has the *morcilla salada*, which is salty. An excellent dessert is *chajá*, a type of sponge-cake ball with cream and jam inside; others are *messini* (a cream sponge) and the common lemon pie. Pastries are very good indeed, and crystallized egg-yolks, known as *yemas*, are popular sweets.

The local wines are very varied: the Editor recommends a good red, Santa Rosa Cabernet, and an excellent one, Santa Rosa Anticuario, also known as "The Old Museum". Herbert Levi, a connoisseur from Buenos Aires, recommends Castel Pujol Rosé. The beers are good. Imported drinks are freely available, in Montevideo, e.g. whisky, US$2.50-3.00. *Mate* is a favourite drink between meal hours. The local spirits are *caña* and *grappa*; some find the locally-made whisky and gin acceptable. Try the Clérico, a tasty mixture of wine, fruit juices and fruits.

URUGUAY 789

Milk is always available, either in bottles or plastic sacs. The dinner hour is late, usually from 2100 to 2400.

Health Milk and fresh water can be drunk and fresh salads eaten fairly freely throughout the country. Medical services maintain a high standard, but they are expensive; so are medicines and drugs.

Tipping Normally all hotel and restaurant bills include a percentage service charge plus 20% value-added tax, but an additional small tip is expected. In other cases give 10% of the total bill. Porters at the airport expect about US$0.20 per piece of luggage; although there is an official rate of tips for porters at seaports, the actual charges are mostly higher. Taxi drivers are tipped 10% of the fare. Tips at cafés are about 10%. Cinema ushers get a small tip, as do cloakroom attendants and hairdressers (10%-15%).

Local Information Centres The Comisión Nacional de Turismo central office, at Plaza Cagancha, Montevideo, issues tourist literature. It has built a number of good guest houses at the various resorts and gives information about them at the Information Office. There is a good information kiosk at Montevideo's main bus station. The local papers publish "what's on" columns on Friday evenings and on Saturdays. Tourist section in Friday's *El Día*.

Media Of the 20 colour-TV stations, 4 transmit from Montevideo (channel 12 is the most popular). There are also 35 radio stations (8 private FM) in Montevideo and 65 in the rest of the country.
There are 5 Montevideo newspapers: *El País*, *El Día* and *La Mañana*, and *El Diário* and *Mundo Color* which come out in the evening. *Búsqueda*, is published weekly. The town of Paysandú has the *Telégrafo*. At noon the main Buenos Aires papers can be had in Montevideo.

Holidays Jan. 1, 6; Carnival (see below); Easter week; April 19; May 1, 18; June 19; July 18; August 25; October 12; November 2; December 8, 25.

Carnival Week is officially the Monday and Tuesday immediately preceding Ash Wednesday, but a great many firms close for the whole of the week. Carnival in Montevideo is no longer as lively as it was; festivities are mainly along the Av. 18 de Julio.
Business comes to a standstill also during Holy Week, which coincides with La Semana Criolla (horse-breaking, stunt riding by cowboys, dances and song). Department stores close only from Good Friday. Banks close all week. Easter Monday is not a holiday.

Currency Bank notes issued are for 50, 100, 500; 1,000, 5,000 and 10,000 new pesos, and coins for 10, 20 and 50 centésimos and 1, 2, 5 and 10 new pesos. Hotels tend to give unfavourable exchange rates. Any amount of currency can be taken in or out.

Exchange Rates change frequently because of a floating exchange rate and inflation differentials against the US dollar; see the "Latest Exchange and Inflation Rates" table near end of book. Many exchange houses *(casas de cambio)* will give you US$ cash for US$ travellers' cheques with a 1% commission charged, and US$ cash against a credit card. Dollars cash can be purchased when leaving the country. Exchanges from Brazilian and Argentine currency receive much worse rates than straightforward deals between dollars and pesos. Banks are closed on Saturday throughout the year; hours Monday-Friday 1300-1700.

Credit Cards Argencard is a member of the Mastercard organization, so one may use Access at outlets displaying their sign. Many shopkeepers are unaware of this but a phone call will confirm it.

Weights and Measures Metric units alone are legal. Odd fact: the timber trade still uses inches for the cross section of lengths of timber.

Postal services, both international and local, have improved since it was made illegal for postal employees to strike, but all items should be registered and sent by air mail to avoid delay. Rates are low, *e.g.* US$0.10 for postcard to Europe, US$2 for 1 kg. surface-mail package, US$3.50 for 1 kg. air-mail package.

Telecommunications Western Telegraph Co. Ltd. (British), ITT Comunicaciones Mundiales S.A., and Italcable provide communication with all parts of the world through their cable stations at Montevideo.
The Government-owned Cerrito station supplies international radio-telegraph communication service. Press wireless service is provided by Press Wireless Uruguaya Ltda. Radio-telephone conversations with the United States and Europe, etc., are routed through Buenos Aires. The telephone service still has a poor reputation.

We are deeply grateful to the following travellers: Richard and Sharon Alexander (Auckland 5), Susi Alexander and José Jacinto (El Paso, Tx.), Bruno Baumann and Franziska Hartmann (Zürich), Barbera Bot and Bob Domburg (Maasland, Neth.), Jürgen Bredtmann (Frankfurt), Malcolm Craven

URUGUAY

(Weston-super-Mare), Lynne and Hugh Davies (Mill Valley, Ca.), Julie Eisenberg and Andy Daitsman (Milwaukee), Toñi García and Diego Caña (Barcelona), Klaus Gresser (Bad Sassendorf, W.Ger.), Ricardo Heyenn and Karin Kubitsch (Hamburg), Bastian Hiss and Daniela Fleischhauer (Krefeld), Achim Holzenberger (Cologne 1), Alban Johnson (Hobart, Tas.) and Luci Montesinos Aguilar (Mexico City), Leo Joseph (Adelaide), José Kiska (Pullman, Wash.), Carmen Kuczma (Powell River, BC), Roger Lemercier (Nice), Herbert S. Levi (Buenos Aires), Arnold MacReave (Datchet, Bucks), Werner von Marinelli (Eindhoven), Mrs J.G.Morgan (Fareham, Hants), Paolo Nasuti (Venice), Nora Pope (Toronto), John and Stephen Roberts (Brandon, Mo.), Gustavo Steinbrun Bianco (Buenos Aires), and Doris Vaterlaus and Daniel Froelicher (Thalwil, Switz.).

WILL YOU HELP US?

We do all we can to get our facts right in *The South American Handbook*. Each chapter is thoroughly revised each year, but Latin America and the Caribbean cover a vast area, and our eyes cannot be everywhere. A new highway or airport is built; a hotel, a restaurant, a cabaret dies; another, a good one is born; a building we describe is pulled down, a street renamed. Names and addresses of good hotels and restaurants for "budget-minded" travellers are always very welcome. We would especially like to receive maps and diagrams of towns and cities, walks, national parks and other interesting areas to use as source material for the Handbook and other forthcoming titles.

Your information may be far more up-to-date than ours. If your letter reaches us early enough in the year it will be used in the next edition, but write whenever you want to, for all your letters are used sooner or later.

Thank you very much indeed for your help.

**Trade & Travel Publications Limited
5 Prince's Buildings, George Street,
Bath BA1 2ED. England**

VENEZUELA

	Page		Page
Introductory	791	Eastern Venezuela	817
Caracas	794	The Economy	829
West from Caracas	804	Information for Visitors	830
Maracaibo	809	Maps	792, 796

WHEN the Spaniards landed in Venezuela in 1498, in the course of Columbus' third voyage, they found a poor country sparsely populated by Indians who had created no distinctive culture. Four hundred years later it was still poor, almost exclusively agrarian, exporting little, importing less. The miracle year which changed all that was 1914, when oil was discovered near Maracaibo. Today, Venezuela is said to be the richest country in Latin America and is one of the largest producers and exporters of oil in the world. The oil revenues have been used to rebuild Caracas and Maracaibo and other cities, and to create the best network of roads on the continent. In view of recent new discoveries and the cutback of production, at the present rate of extraction oil reserves will last for about 40 years. Vast investments have been poured into state industry and agrarian reform and into tackling the problems of education, housing and unemployment.

Venezuela has 2,800 km. of coastline on the Caribbean Sea. To the east is Guyana, to the south Brazil, and to the west Colombia. Its area is 912,050 square km., and its population is over 17 million. It was given its name— "Little Venice" - by the Spanish navigators, who saw in the Indian pile dwellings on Lake Maracaibo a dim reminder of the buildings along Venetian waterways.

The country falls into four very different regions: the Venezuelan Highlands to the west and along the coast; the Maracaibo Lowlands around the fresh water lake of Maracaibo; the vast central plain of the Llanos of the Orinoco; and the Guayana Highlands, which take up over half the country.

The Venezuelan Highlands are an offshoot of the Andes. From the Colombian border they trend, at first, towards the NE to enfold the Maracaibo Lowlands. This section is known as the Sierra Nevada de Mérida. Beyond they broaden out into the Segovia Highlands N of Barquisimeto, and then turn E in parallel ridges along the coast to form the Central Highlands, dipping into the Caribbean Sea only to rise again into the North-Eastern Highlands of the peninsulas of Paria and Araya.

The general outline of each area will reveal that natural obstacles to farming, cattle breeding, and communications are formidable. It explains why the country was poverty-stricken for so long.

History At the beginning of the 16th century, Venezuela was inhabited by various tribes of Caribs and Arawaks, who could make no effective resistance against the Spaniards. The first permanent Spanish settlement was at Cumaná, in 1520. Soon afterwards settlers reached Coro, at the foot of the Paraguaná Peninsula. Indian slaves were used to mine and pan for gold, but the results were disappointing and the settlers turned to agriculture, forming settlements at Barquisimeto in 1552, at Valencia in 1555, and at Caracas in 1567. It was not until after a century of consolidation in these areas that they began to occupy the rest of the country, intermarrying freely with the Indians and later introducing black slaves to work the sugar plantations. Centralized colonial control from Spain was

792 VENEZUELA

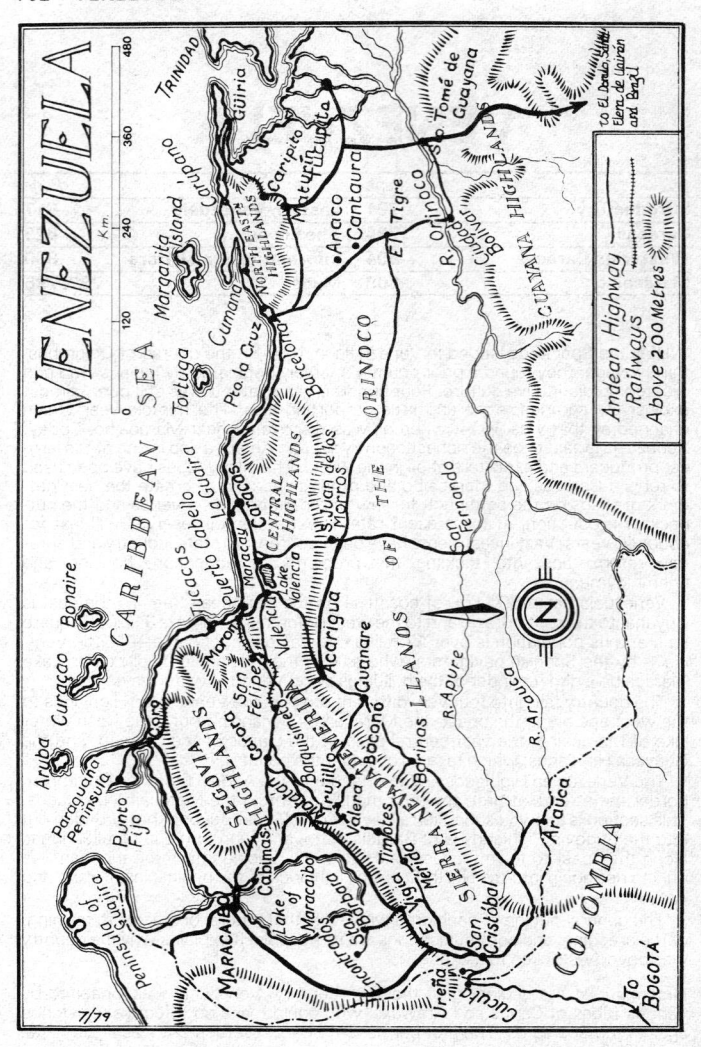

as irksome here as in the rest of Latin America: three risings reflecting these discontents took place in 1749, 1775 and 1797, and there were two abortive attempts by Francisco Miranda to achieve independence in 1806 and 1811. After Miranda had been captured, the movement was led by Simón Bolívar, a *criollo* with a touch of Indian blood, born in Caracas in 1783. He met with mixed success until his capture of Angostura, now Ciudad Bolívar, in 1817. There he was joined by a contingent of experienced Peninsular veterans recruited in London. At their head, together with the horsemen of the *llanos* commanded by Gen. José Antonio Páez, he undertook a dramatic march over the Andes in 1819 to win the battle of Boyacá and capture Bogotá. Three months later, the revolutionary congress at Angostura—with most of Venezuela still in Spanish hands—declared the independence of Gran Colombia, a union of what is now Ecuador, Colombia, Venezuela, and Panama. Bolívar returned from Bogotá, and on June 24, 1821, the revolutionaries routed the Spanish forces at Carabobo. There was some desultory fighting for two more years, but the last of the Spanish forces surrendered at Puerto Cabello in 1823.

Before Bolívar's death in 1830 Páez declared Venezuela an independent republic. Other presidents of note were Guzmán Blanco, Juan Vicente Gómez (1909-1935), a brutal but efficient dictator, and Isaías Medina Angarita, who introduced the oil laws. There was much material progress under the 6-year dictatorship of Gen. Marcos Pérez Jiménez (1952-58), but his Gómez-like methods led to his overthrow in January 1958. A stable democracy has been created since, with regular presidential elections every five years. Sr. Carlos Andrés Pérez of the centre-left Democratic Action party took office in 1974, presiding over a period of rapid development following the first great oil-price rise, and was succeeded in 1979 by Sr. Luis Herrera Campins of the Christian Democratic party, Copei. The elections of December 1983 were won by Dr. Jaime Lusinchi of Democratic Action, who will be President until 1989.

Population 53% are under 18. A large number are of mixed Spanish and Indian blood. There are some pure Indians, mostly in the Guayana Highlands and in the forests west of Lake Maracaibo. There are some pure-blooded Africans and a strong admixture of African blood along the coast, particularly at the ports. The arrival of 800,000 European immigrants since the war, mostly in the 1950s, has greatly modified the racial make-up in Venezuela. One in 6 of all Venezuelans is foreign born. Total population was 17,554,077 on December 31, 1985.

About 81% of the population is urban. Annual growth: 2.9%; urban growth: 4.2%. Birth-rate (1984) 29.9; mortality per 1,000 inhabitants: 4.6; expectation of life, 58.6 years.

Venezuela, despite its wealth, still faces serious social problems. About 12% are unemployed; about 14% are illiterate. Many rural dwellers have drifted to the cities; one result of this exodus is that Venezuelan farmers do not provide all the food the nation needs and imports of foodstuffs are necessary, even for items such as beans and rice.

Education Elementary schools are free, and education is compulsory from the age of 7 to the completion of the primary grade. Primary school enrolment is 76%, secondary school registration 21% and university entries 3% of the total.

Government Venezuela is a federal republic of 20 states, a Federal District, and two territories. The current Constitution is dated January 23, 1961. Voting is now compulsory for all over 18.

The Central Highlands

The Central Highlands are the most important upland area in Venezuela; they contain the capital, Caracas, and the cities of Valencia and Maracay. The mountains here rise abruptly from a lush green coast to heights of from two to three thousand metres. The capital, Caracas, lies in a small basin, a rift in the thickly forested mountains which runs some 24 km. east and west. This historic colonial town has been transformed into one of the most astonishing modern cities in Latin America.

A hundred km. W of Caracas is the great basin in which lies the Lake of Valencia and the towns of Maracay and Valencia. The basin, which is only 450 metres above sea-level, receives plenty of rain and is one of the most important agricultural areas in the country; sugar, cotton, maize, beans and rice are the main crops. In the other valleys and depressions in the Central Highlands are also

794 VENEZUELA

grown manioc, bananas, cocoa and the superb local coffee (very little of which is now exported).

Caracas, the capital, founded in 1567, has a population of around 4 million. It lies at 960 metres, but the southern parts of the city are 120 metres lower. Temperatures are moderate (a maximum of 32°C in July and August, and an occasional minimum of 9°C in January and February) and it is always cool at night.

A comparatively low pass (1,040 metres) in the mountains gives Caracas access by road to its port, La Guaira, and its international and domestic airports nearby at Maiquetía. The distance by a magnificently engineered road is 28 km. or 30 mins. by car (toll US$0.85 when going down; going up is free). Much longer should be allowed, however, for anyone with a plane to catch, as there are often delays arising from heavy traffic.

The proportionate growth of Caracas since the war has been greater than that of any other Latin American capital. Colonial buildings have given way to modern multi-storeyed edifices, many of which are architecturally impressive. Excellent examples are the University City, the twin towers of the Parque Central, the Centro Simón Bolívar, and the Círculo Militar.

Starting in Catia, an industrial area in the W where both roads from La Guaira enter, Avenida Sucre goes past the 23 de Enero workers' flats to join Av. Urdaneta between Palacio Miraflores and the Palacio Blanco, housing government offices. Later come the Post Office and Santa Capilla Church, looking like a wedding cake by a Parisian master pastrycook. Turn right here for Plaza Bolívar and the Capitol (the National Congress), or carry straight on down the Av. Urdaneta to San Bernardino (Colonial Museum). Here, we enter Av. Andrés Bello, which passes just below the cable railway station to join Av. Libertador to the Country Club and the E, or we can turn down the Av. La Salle to the eastern end of Los Caobos park, with the fine mahoganies which give it its popular name. From the Plaza Venezuela intersection at the eastern end of the park, the Avenida Abraham Lincoln leads E through Sabana Grande and continues as the Avenida Francisco Miranda to the residential section of Altamira, with its fine plaza and obelisk (unfortunately a construction site for a new Metro station in 1986). Sabana Grande, a modern shopping, hotel and business centre, is now a pedestrian mall closed to vehicular traffic: a very popular place to take a stroll.

Alternatively, forking right out of Avenida Sucre and crossing the viaduct, we reach El Silencio, and thence pass through the Centro Simón Bolívar, with its twin skyscrapers and underground parking and shopping centre (with an interesting mosaic at the lowest level), and finally along the Avenida Bolívar past Nuevo Circo bullring towards University City, the Sports Stadium, the *Tamanaco Hotel* and La Casona, residence of the President. S of the Nuevo Circo is the Helicoide, planned as a commercial centre under the Pérez Jiménez regime but left uncompleted at his fall in 1958. From the viaduct, we can also take Av. Universidad past the National Library (former University), Capitol and San Francisco church. Two corners later, we glimpse, left, Bolívar's birthplace, before continuing to the Art Museum and on round Los Caobos park, or by the Av. Libertador, to the east.

Another west-east route is along the Avenida Boyacá from Avenida Baralt in the west to Petare in the east, connecting with the main road east to Barcelona (Route 9), which skirts the Cordillera de la Costa, including ávila mountain, and gives fine views along the length of the city. Towards the E end is a monument commemorating the battle of Boyacá, and a viaduct strides majestically over the recently remodelled park in Los Chorros suburb, to which access is signposted.

To the SW from El Silencio the Avenida San Martín leads towards the factories of Antímano. This area can also be reached direct from Catia by the Planicie tunnel. In the SW is also the older residential section of El Paraíso.

The shady Plaza Bolívar, where sloths can be seen in the trees, with its fine equestrian statue of the Liberator and pleasant colonial cathedral, is still the official centre of the city, though no longer geographically so (it was under repair in 1986). In fact, several centres (Plaza Bolívar, Plaza Venezuela, Sabana Grande,

Chacaíto, La Floresta, Boleíta) are strung along the valley with residential areas between.

Parks Jardín Botánico, near Plaza Venezuela. Parque Nacional del Este has a zoo and is a peaceful place to relax, except at weekends, entrance free (show passport), closed on Mon. There is a boating lake and playground for children; many of the birds fly freely and there is an interesting collection of exotic flora. Parque El Pinar also has a large zoo. The Parque Los Chorros at the foot of the mountain and the Parque Los Caobos are also recommended; El Calvario, west of Plaza O'Leary, is quiet and pleasant with a good view of Centro Simón Bolívar. A new park, Parque Vargas, is to replace the Nuevo Circo bus station. See page 802 for El Avila National Park.

National Monuments

Panteón Nacional Open Mon.-Fri., 0900-1200 and 1430-1730, Sat.-Sun., 1000-1300 and 1400-1700. This was designed as the resting place of Bolívar, the Liberator, and Miranda, the Precursor of Independence. The remains of Bolívar lie there, but the tomb of Miranda, who died in a Spanish prison, has been left open to await the return of his body. There is a small military ceremony at 1430 daily.

Capitolio Nacional The Elliptical Salon has some impressive paintings by the Venezuelan artist Martín Tovar y Tovar and a bronze urn containing the 1811 Declaration of Independence. One of the paintings on the ceiling shows a British regiment fighting in the Battle of Carabobo, and the names of the officers appear on the wall; in acknowledgement of this assistance Bolívar granted the British armed forces the right to march through any city in Gran Colombia (Colombia, Ecuador, Panama and Venezuela) with bayonets fixed, drums beating and flags flying.

Museums

Museo de Bellas Artes, Plaza Morelos in Parque Los Caobos: open Tues.-Fri., 0900-1200, 1500-1730, Sat.-Sun., 1000-1700. Pictures include an El Greco among works by mainly Venezuelan artists. Adjacent is the Galería de Arte Nacional, which also houses the Cinemateca Nacional.

Museo de Ciencias Naturales, also in Plaza Morelos in Parque Los Caobos; open 0900-1200, 1500-1730 except Mon.

Museo de Arte Colonial, Quinta Anauco, Av. Panteón, San Bernardino: open Tues.-Sat. 0900-1200, 1400-1700, Sun., 1000-1700. Admission by guided tour only, last at 1130. A delightful house built in 1720. Chamber concerts most Saturdays at 1800. The beautiful suburb of San Bernardino glories in tropical flowers and whole avenues of forest trees, smothered in blossom in season.

Casa Natal del Libertador Open 1000-1300 and 1400-1700 daily except Mon. The present house is a reconstruction of the house where Bolívar was born. The first, of adobe, was destroyed by an earthquake. The second became a stable, and was later pulled down. The present building of stone was built by order of Gómez (whose birthday was the same as Bolívar's) in the early 1920s; it contains interesting pictures and furniture.

The Museo Bolivariano is alongside the Casa Natal and contains the Liberator's war relics.

House of Arturo Michelena, four blocks north of Miraflores palace, in the La Pastora section, is a typical 19th century home, now a museum. Open 0900-1200 and 1500-1700 (closed Mon. and Fri.).

Museo de Transporte, Parque Nacional del Este, includes a large collection of locomotives and old cars, as well as a fascinating series of scale models of Caracas a century ago. Open Wed., Sat., Sun., 0900-1800. Admission US$0.50.

VENEZUELA

Key to map

3. Central Post Office; 5. Capitol; 6. National Library; 7. Bolívar's House and Historical Museum; 8. Cathedral; 9. Centro Simón Bolívar; 10. Road to University; 12. Museo de Bellas Artes; 13. Museo de Ciencias Naturales; 14. Plaza Bolívar; 15. Plaza Candelaria; 16. Parque Carabobo; 17. Plaza Miranda (minibus station nearby); 18. Plaza La Concordia; 19. Road to Museo de Arte Colonial (Quinta Anauco).

VENEZUELA 797

In the Parque Central, between Av. Lecuna (E end) and the elevated section of Av. Bolívar there are four museums in a complex which includes 2 octagonal towers (56 floors each) and four large apartment buildings with shopping below.

Museo de Arte Contemporáneo, Parque Central, Cuadra Bolívar, near the Caracas Hilton, very good, European and Venezuelan painters represented. Open Tues.-Fri. 1200-1900, Sat. 1100-1900, Sun. 1100-1900.

Museo de los Niños, Parque Central, next to East Tower, is open to the public Wed.-Sun. and holidays, 0900-1200, 1400-1700, otherwise is for school visits; a science museum, well worth a visit and extremely popular, US$0.75 (adults). Also in the Parque Central complex, **Museo Audiovisual,** Tues.-Fri., 0900-1700, US$1, includes a library of Venezuelan television programmes, and **Museo del Teclado** (keyboard instruments).

Museo Histórico Militar, near Metro Gato Negro.

The Ministry of Foreign Relations contains pictures mostly of national heroes and historical events. Check museum schedules in *El Universal, El Nacional* or the *Daily Journal*.

The Concejo Municipal (City Hall) on Plaza Bolívar contains three museums: a collection of the paintings of Emilio Boggio, a Venezuelan painter; the Raúl Santana Museum of the Creole Way of Life, a collection of miniature figures in costumes and poses characteristic of Venezuelan life, all handmade by Raúl Santana and extremely realistic; and the Sala de Arqueología Gaspar Marcano, exhibiting ceramics, mostly discovered on the coast. All three open Tues.-Fri., 0930-1200, 1500-1800; Sat. and Sun., 0930-1800.

Those with a deeper interest in archaeology might like to contact the Junta Nacional Protectora y Conservadora del Patrimonio Histórico y Artístico de la Nación, Palacio de Miraflores, Av. Urdaneta.

Churches The Cathedral should be seen for its beautiful façade, and pictures including alleged Rubens and Murillo. San Francisco should be seen for its colonial altars.

Modern Caracas Visitors should see the Avenida de los Próceres with its twin monoliths and other monuments to the heroes of independence (it also has flowers and gardens); the magnificent Officers' Club on the same avenue, the Cuadra Bolívar near the *Caracas Hilton;* and the University City, an enormous and coherent complex of great buildings in which paintings, sculpture and stained glass are completely integrated with the architecture (which is now showing signs of wear).

Warning It is advisable not to arrive in Caracas at night and not to walk down narrow streets after dark. Fighting frequently breaks out and thefts and attacks are common on tourists and residents alike.

Hotels Prices are no longer high, in view of the 1983 devaluation. Cheap *pensiones* are usually full of long-stay residents and have very few rooms available for travellers. Hotels marked with an asterisk (*) are bookable through Anahoven (see next page).

The *Tamanaco** is the best hotel in Caracas and the most pleasant, but it is difficult to get rooms as it is normally fully booked, changes travellers' cheques for guests only (poor rate) A (US$100d). *Hotel de las Mercedes* (US$28d), Las Mercedes is almost next door to the *Tamanaco.* The *Caracas Hilton**, A (US$55-75d), is more central but noisy (traffic and air conditioning) and although the rooms are excellent and clean, the service has also been criticized; connected with the *Hilton* are the *Residencias Anauco Hilton**, Parque Central, an "apartotel", B; another apartment hotel is the *CCT Venantur** in the Centro Ciudad Comercial Tamanaco, luxury, C; furnished flats also at *Crillón**, Av. Libertador, between Las Acacias and Los Jabillos, D; the *Avila** is in San Bernardino on the higher levels of the city, set in park-like gardens and very pleasant, C; *Aventura**, Av. Fco. Fajardo, San Bernardino, C. *La Floresta**, Av. Avila, Sur Plaza Altamira, Tel.: 2844111, D, is recommended as clean, friendly, helpful, but restaurant not very good. Also good, *Continental Altamira**, D, Av. San Juan Bosco (there is also *Altamira,* Av. J. F. Sosa, D). *Montpark,* E, Los Cerritos, recommended; *Nostrum,* Av. Orinoco con final Calle París, Las Mercedes (near *de las Mercedes),* Tel.: 92-76-46, 92-66-46, a/c, hot water, clean, recommended, E; *Caroni,* near Cathedral, E, popular, good value; *Beethoven,* Av. Beethoven, Colinas de Bellomonte (½ block

798 VENEZUELA

from Sears), D with bath, TV, good, clean; *Centro Uslar*, 2a Av., Calles 1 y 2, Sector B, Urb. Montalbán, C, good but a long way from centre; *El Paseo*, Av. Los Ilustres, Urb. Los Chaguaramos, Tel.: 661-3438/3547/3315, D, good, clean; *Miami*, at Candilito, D, with shower; *Maracaibo*, Av. 6 and Calle 94, E; several cheap hotels on Calle 94; *Niteroy*, E, on Av. Baralt (Balconcito a Truco); *Bakistan*, E, Quebrado a Pescador 23, San Juan; *Pon Pen*, E, basic, Este 8; *ABC*, F, Av. Lecuna, 2 blocks from old Nuevo Circo bus station, with shower, very noisy (less so on higher floors, which are good value); *Inter**, Animas a Calero on corner of Av. Urdaneta, E, very clean, shower and toilet with each room, friendly, English spoken, very popular so be sure to make a reservation, the queues for rooms begin before 0700 and the hotel is full by 0800, poor restaurant; *Ausonia*, Norte 8 and Urdaneta, D, with bath, hot-water, TV, central, clean; *Plaza Catedral**, Blvd. Plaza Bolívar, next to Cathedral, D, a/c, TV, phone, excellent, some English spoken; *Grand Galaxie**, Truco a Caja de Agua, between Av. Baralt and Norte 4 on Salas Sta. Bárbara, Tel.: 83-90-11/83-90-44, D, deluxe, a/c, TV, phone, restaurant, central, comfortable; *El Pinar*, Av. La Paz, El Paraíso, E, quite nice; *K*, F, Sur 2 and Oeste 10, men only, basic, clean; *MS*, same address, E, prostitutes; *Melina*, E, Velásquez a Santa Rosalía No. 116, and *Pensión Carballino*, E, secure but little else. For other cheap hotels look on Calle Sur 2. The *Mara*, E, *Conde**, D, and *Veroes*, D, Av. Urdaneta, are in the centre, convenient for banks and business houses, but noisy; also *Cervantes*, Av. Urdaneta, Norte 5, F, cheap but spartan, safe, very noisy. *La Atlántida*, next to Archbishop's Palace, N of Plaza Venezuela, C. *Posada Turística Andrés Bello*, Av. La Salle, Quinta Bucaral, Los Caobos, Tel.: 782-29-25, F, good safe, friendly, shared rooms, segregated, showers, meals available; similar is *Posada Turística Cecilio Acosta*, Calle Los Abogados, Quinta Sta. María, Los Chaguaramos, Tel.: 661-12-26, F, good—both are run by Ontej, see page 832.

If you arrive in Caracas in doubt, ask a taxi driver to take you to Las Acacias in Sabana Grande, where you can choose a hotel from the very large number in that area. There are various grades all close together so you can walk from one to another until you find one suitable. However, many of the numerous small hotels on Av. Las Acacias do not cater for singles or for couples staying more than a few hours. (The weekend is not a very good time to look for a room.) If not using a taxi, take metro to Sabana Grande (for example). On Av. Las Acacias are *Bruno**, D, a/c, air conditioning, fair, Peruvian restaurant with live entertainment, unremarkable; *Everest*, D; *Myriam*, E, few single rooms, off-street parking, clean but noisy; *Embassy* (recommended by Tourist Office); *Ariston*, Av. Sur Las Acacias, is very unfriendly; *Tanausú*, E. On Av. Casanova are *Luna*, D (with Calle El Colegio); *Coliseo**, D; *Capri-Casanova*, D, spartan but clean and friendly; *Broadway**, No. 4, convenient for Chacaíto metro station, D, private bathroom, TV, friendly, clean, a bit noisy, Italian specialities in restaurant. Others in Sabana Grande include *El Cóndor**, (3a Av. Las Delicias), D, TV, air conditioning, businessmen on their own need to take suites because single rooms have no desks; *Plaza Palace*, Av. Los Mangos, Las Delicias, very good, friendly, good atmosphere, C-D; *Las Américas**, Los Cerritos, end of Casanova, D, warm water, food passable but unexciting; *City** (Av. Bolivia, Los Cabos), D, all rooms have TV and private bath; *Cristal*, D, a/c; *Madrid**, F, Av. Chacaíto, small, hot water, showers in all rooms; *Capri*, F, Calle Las Flores, clean; *The King's Inn Hotel**, D, Calle Olimpo, near Av. Lincoln; *Tampa**, F, Av. Francisco Solano López, D; *Savoy*, Av. Francisco Solano López, Las Delicias, C, without food, good, efficient, clean, secure vehicle park.

Hotel Reservations Anahoven, in Plaza Venezuela, Centro Capriles, will book hotel rooms in Caracas and also in 102 hotels in the rest of the country; telephone: 782-8888/8277/8433/8688/8077. The airport tourist office is very helpful and will book hotel rooms. Finding a hotel, particularly in the middle-price range, is always difficult. If you book from abroad (e.g. Thomas Cook in England) make sure you receive confirmation before beginning your journey or you may turn up and find yourself without a room. **Economy tip**: most hotel rooms have a TV set for which you will be charged; if you don't want it, ask for it to be removed. For apartment rental, consult *El Universal* daily paper, small ads. columns.

Restaurants There is such a profusion of eating places in Caracas that we give the following general advice, with a mention of just a few places currently reported reliable, rather than attempt the impossible task of keeping up to date with all the changes. Don't be shy about asking the price before you order in a bar as beer in one will cost three times as much as in another, and a modest portion of *manchego* cheese will cost more than a good steak. Food on display in a bar is free with your drink if they offer it as a *pasapalo*, but will be charged for if offered as a *ración*. You can save on the service charge by eating at the bar and not at a table. Coffee in a café is at government-controlled price if taken at the counter, but not if served at a table. Milk is subsidized and is cheaper than soft drinks. By decree, restaurants must put up a list of prices on or near the front door, and are prohibited from charging for place settings (*cubiertos*) or bread, butter, condiments etc. (*guarnición*). For dining out, here is a selection of good restaurants around Avenida Urdaneta (*Bar Pas de Calais* for paella, *El Parador* and *Politena*), La Castellana (*La Estancia*), Plaza Altamira (*Mayfair Station*), Las Mercedes (*Piccolo Mundo*, *Hereford Grill*, *Farms Grill*, *Mr Ribs*, Av. Valle Arriba, barbecued ribs etc., very fashionable; *Era de Acuario*, vegetarian), El Rosal (*La Barba Roja*, Calle Venezuela, *El Jabaguero*, Calle Pichincha, both seafood) and Sabana Grande (see below). In the Parque Central (Edificio Anauco—basement) is *El Parque*, good food and service; *Tarzilandia*, 10th Transversal Altamira, San Juan Bosco, international food; *Dog and Fox Pub*, Río de Janeiro, Las Mercedes, British-owned, cheap, good music, popular with European residents and travellers. Excellent pastries and cheese from *Panadería y Pastelería Madona*, Av. Sur, near corner with Camejo

VENEZUELA 799

(0800-2300). The *Sol y Sombra*, Sur 7 No. 110 at Velásquez, doubles as a betting shop on race days. Guides to eating are published in the VAAUW Guide to Caracas and the magazine *Ve Venezuela*. Also *Gourmet Dining out in Caracas*, available at travel agencies and good hotels. Advertisements appear in the *Daily Journal* and the Yellow Pages of the telephone directory.

Although it is not practicable to cover the whole of Caracas, the following description of the Sabana Grande area will give an idea of what is available. Breakfast in your hotel is likely to be poor (poor bread or none, insipid coffee and orange juice which is half artificial). It is better and cheaper in a *fuente de soda*, and cheaper still in a *pastelería* or *arepería*. (One correspondent recommends *La Ermita* on Plaza Venezuela.) Tables in the open air on the boulevard, however, are expensive, e.g. US$0.40 for a *batido* which costs US$0.25 down a side street or US$0.20 at a greengrocer, yet it is exactly the same fruit drink. (The boulevard waiters overcharge. Check prices on the displayed list.) Mid-day is the most economical time to eat the main meal of the day and about the only opportunity to find fresh vegetables. Look for "menú ejecutivo" or "cubierto", which is a three-course meal for US$1.50, e.g. at *Ventas de Madrid* on San Gerónimo and *O'Gran Sol* on Villa Flor.

Good, economical meals in the evening at *Sorrentino* and *Jabillos* on Francisco Solano, *Coraveña* (next to *La Bússola*, one block east of Torre La Previsora), *La Soledad* (next block south on Casanova) and *Tropical Room* (two blocks east on Casanova). For business and similar occasions: *La Bússola* (see above—try *carpaccio*), *Rugantino* in *Hotel Tampa* (speciality *cartuccio*), *El Chicote* behind La Previsora, and *Villa D'Este* in *Hotel Cóndor*. For variety: *Floridita* in La Previsora and *Esquina de Tejas* in *Hotel Kursaal* (both Cuban), *Hotel Kristal* (Chilean), *Le Coq d'Or*, Av. Los Mangos (French), *Hotel Bruno* (Peruvian), *Mario's* on Casanova (Brazilian—noisy), *Dragón Verde*, Ciné París, Av. Maturín (Chinese), *Berlín*, top floor, Centro Comercial ønico, Chacaíto Metro exit (German), and *Buffet Vegetariano*, Av. Los Jardines. Roast lamb at *La Taberna*, Torre Capriles, Plaza Venezuela. Fast foods: there is a plethora of burger and pizza places, as well as the ubiquitous hot dog stalls of doubtful hygiene (when the police don't close them down).

Prices: a modest *fuente de soda* offers *solomo* steak at US$1; meat dishes in restaurants and *cervecerías* from US$1.75 and at expensive places from US$3. *Langostinos* cost over twice as much. A *tercio* of beer (see page 834) is normally US$0.35 but can be up to US$1.50. Whisky starts at US$1.25.

Clubs The Country Club in the eastern part has an 18-hole golf course. The Social Centre of the British Commonwealth Association, Quinta Alborada, Avenida 7 with Transversal 9, Altamira, Caracas, with bar and swimming pool; British and Commonwealth visitors only; entry fee according to length of stay; Tel.: 261-30-60. Membership of the better clubs is by the purchase of a share, which can run to thousands of dollars. An exception is the sports club run by the *Tamanaco Hotel*, open to non-guests and suitable for people staying a short time. The Military Club (Círculo de las Fuerzas Armadas) is well worth seeing and, if the visitors are soberly dressed, permission to view the premises is often granted. Flying Club, at La Carlota, near *Tamanaco Hotel*. Robert and Daisy Kunstaetter of Richmond Hill, Ontario (call sign VE300G) tell us the Radio Club Venezolano is a very welcoming, efficient organiztion of amateur radio operators which is eager to meet amateurs from around the world (address: P.O. Box 2285, Caracas 1010-A, Tel.: 781-4878, 781-8303—Av. Lima, Los Caobos; branches around the country).

Shopping For gems and fine jewellery, visit the H. Stern shops at the Hotels *Hilton* and *Tamanaco* and at the International Airport. Pro-Venezuela Exposición y Venta de Arte Popular, Gran Avenida at Calle Olimpo, between Plaza Venezuela and beginning of Av. Casanova (opp. Torre La Previsora), for Venezuelan crafts. Indian and Andean crafts can be found at the market in Las Mercedes. The CCCT shopping centre is worth a visit. From Chacaíto, along Av. Abraham Lincoln, Sabana Grande, to Plaza Venezuela, is a pedestrian precinct, with good shops, street traders and cafés.

Bookshops English language ones include: *English Bookshop*, Concresa, Prados del Este; *American Bookshop*, Plaza Altamira; *Lectura*, Centro Comercial Chacaíto, and *Steele's Bookstore*, Calle Baruta, Sabana Grande. *Librería del Este*, Av. Francisco de Miranda 52, Edif. Galipán, *Librería Multilingua*, Torre Británica, Altamira Sr, and *Librería Unica*, Centro Capriles, ground floor local 13N, Plaza Venezuela, all have foreign language books. A French bookshop is *Librería La France*, Centro Comercial Chacaíto, Italian bookshop, *El Libro Italiano*, Pasaje La Concordia (between Sabana Grande pedestrian street and Av. Fco. Solano López), and for German books, *Librería Alemana* (Oscar Todtmann), Centro El Bosque, Avenida Libertador.

Buses and Taxis Starting from the bus station at Nuevo Circo (being replaced in 1987— see page 801), there are many buses, overcrowded in the rush hours, urban fare usually US$0.15. *Por puesto* minibuses running on regular routes charge up to US$0.30 depending on the distance travelled. Many *por puesto* services start in Silencio. Taxis are required by law to instal and use taximeters. The initial flag fee is US$0.30 plus US$0.10 for each km. and US$0.05 for each 30 seconds of the ride (hourly rate US$3). Taxi drivers are authorized to charge an extra 20% on night trips after 2200, on Sun. and all holidays, and US$0.45 for answering telephone calls. Beware of taxi drivers trying to renegotiate fixed rates because your destination is in "a difficult area". There are pirates, however, with possibly a taxi sign, but without yellow licence plates/

800 VENEZUELA

registration-number plate, which are to be avoided. If you get in a taxi with no meter you must negotiate the price in advance.

The Metro, opened in 1983, has one east-west line; it operates 0600-2300, Sun. 0900-1800, and costs US$0.15 for journeys up to five stations, US$0.20 for six to ten stations, and US$0.25 for eleven to fourteen stations (20 journey tickets available). It is air-conditioned, more comfortable and quicker than any other form of city transport; no smoking, no large bags.

Driving Self-drive cars (Hertz, National, Avis, Volkswagen) are available at the airport and in town. They are cheaper than guided excursions for less than full loads. Driver's licence from home country accepted. Major credit card or US$210 cash deposit required. The Government has fixed the rates and the cheapest available is US$19 per day plus US$0.19 per km. for a Volkswagen Beetle or Brasilia or a Ford Fairmont or Cherry Nova. For medium-sized cars, Hertz, National, Avis, US$21 per day plus US$0.21 per km. Auto and personal insurance strongly recommended as you will be lucky to survive two or three days as a newcomer to Caracas traffic without a dent or a scrape. Carry spare battery water, fan belts, the obligatory breakdown triangle, a jack and spanners. Some cars have a security device to prevent the engine being started and this is recommended. Don't run out of fuel; you can incur a Bs. 500 fine by so doing. Beware of potholes even in the best roads and avoid driving fast, particularly at night; a nationwide speed limit of 80 kph was imposed in 1982. The best road map can be bought from CVP petrol stations; it shows the distances between towns and is generally reliable. Many roads may be marked as dirt tracks but have been paved since the map was produced. Beware of the traffic-reduction system in Caracas, under which the Government has prohibited the use of cars with number plates ending in 1 or 6 on Mondays, 2 or 7 on Tuesdays, 3 or 8 on Wednesdays, 4 or 9 on Thursdays, 5 or 0 on Fridays, between the hours of 0700 and 2000.

Motorcycles may not be ridden in Caracas between 2300 and 0500. Pillion passengers are only permitted if of the opposite sex from the driver.

Night Clubs Caracas is a lively city by night, and there are many and varied discotheques and night clubs. Caraqueños dine at home around 2000, and in restaurants from 2100 to 2300, so night clubs don't usually come to life until after 2300, and then go on to all hours of the morning. Naiguatá (*Hotel Tamanaco*), expensive; best show in town. El Greco, Av. Principal de Macaracuay (also restaurant in same building). Hipocampo, Plaza Chacaíto. Mon Petit, Plaza Altamira Sur (there are many small clubs, restaurants and bars on Plaza Altamira Sur). México Típico, on Av. Libertador, said to be excellent, a Mexican band alternates with a Venezuelan band: no cover charge and drinks only double normal bar prices. The "Noches Caraqueñas" show put on by the *Hilton* each Mon. evening makes a pleasant introduction to Caracas night-life. Juan Sebastian Bar, Av. Venezuela, El Rosal, is a jazz club (closed Sun.) and Feelings, Av Tamanaco, El Rosal, is a popular *salsa* club. *Cervecería Nueva Esparta*, Av. los Marquitos (Sabana Grande) is cheap, provides good music, but is another couples-only venue. Two gay clubs are Ice Palace at Altamira Sur (not exclusively gay, non members admitted for US$4) and Zigzag restaurant and piano bar, Av. Libertador, Ed. La Línea.

Discotheques Water Point, Centro Comercial, El Parque de Los Palos Grandes, and Blow-up, Plaza Altamira Sur, have been recommended; also Teorema, La Jungla, Eva, The Flower, and many others. Couples only seems to be the norm.

Sports and Recreations Golf, tennis, riding, fishing, horse-racing every Sat. and Sun. at La Rinconada (a truly magnificent grandstand), bull fights (in season; go to the *Bar-Restaurant Los Cuchilleros* on Av. Urdaneta next to Plaza Candelaria to meet bullfighters and *aficionados*; tickets sold there on bullfight Sunday mornings, ticket sales end 1400, bar closes 1530, bullfight starts 1600), baseball (October-January), football, swimming, etc. Horse-racing commences at 1300, admission price to grandstand US$1.10. Several buses go to La Rinconada. There are numerous cinemas; in those charging Bs. 15 men are sometimes required to wear jackets (enquire beforehand if a jacket is required) but not in the equally comfortable ones charging Bs. 10 (half price Mon.). Parque del Este (Av. Francisco Miranda) has a planetarium. The recreational event of the year is the two days of Carnival.

Cultural Events There are frequent Sun. morning concerts in the Teatro Municipal, 1100, usually US$2.25. Concerts, ballet and theatre at the Ateneo de Caracas, Paseo Colón, Plaza Morelos; and similar events, including foreign artists, at the Complejo Cultural Teresa Carreño, on Paseo Colón, just E of *Caracas Hilton* (an interesting building, too). For details of these and other events, see the newspapers, *El Universal, El Nacional* and *Daily Journal*, and the Sunday issue of *El Diario de Caracas*.

Banks and Exchange Banco de Venezuela; Banco Caracas; Banco La Guaira Internacional; Banco Royal Venezolano; Banco Continental; Citibank; Banco Latinoamericano de Venezuela; Banco Mercantil; Banco Unión for Visa transactions. For exchange go to Italcambio offices: esquina Veroes and Urdaneta, Av. Casanova (Sabana Grande), Av. L. Roche (Altamira Sur) Simón Bolívar Airport. Cambio La Guaira (good for cruzados) in Sabana Grande, and on Av. Urdaneta; Cambios Caracas in Torre Capriles, Plaza Venezuela. Confinanzas, Centro Comercial Paseo Las

VENEZUELA 801

Mercedes, Local PA-CI, open 0800-1200, 1400-1700. Commission of 1 bolívar charged per US$1 changed in travellers' cheques. American Express cheques, Banco Consolidado, Av. San Francisco, Edif. Torre California, piso 9, Urb. Colinas de La California; AmEx rep is Turisol, Centro Comercial Tamanaco, level C-2, also in *Hotel Tamanaco*.

Addresses In the centre of Caracas, each street corner has a name, and addresses are generally given as, for example, "Santa Capilla a Mijares", rather than the official "Calle Norte 2, No. 26". Maps can be bought at *Caracas Hilton*, and Lagovén service stations. Good street maps of Caracas can be bought in kiosks, or be found at the back of the yellow pages telephone directory.

British Embassy, Consulate and British Council, Torre Las Mercedes, 3rd floor, Ciudad Comercial Tamanaco, Chuao (Tel.: 911255). Apartado 1246 for letters.
Instituto Cultural Venezolano-Británico, Edificio Torre la Noria, 6th floor, Las Mercedes. Modest library for members.
USA Embassy and Consulate, Av. Francisco Miranda, La Floresta, Tel.: 284 6111.
Centro Venezolano-Americano, Av. Las Mercedes, good free library of books in English, and free concerts. Also good for Spanish courses, US$195 for 2 months.
Colombian Consulate, Av. Luis Roche entre 6a y 7a Transversal, Quinta 53, Altamira (Tel.: 324318). Open Mon.-Fri. 0800-1130 for visas, can take anything from 2 hrs. to one day.
Anglican Church, Plaza Urape, San Román section of Las Mercedes (near *Tamanaco*; Tel.: 914727).
The United Christian Church, interdenominational, Av. Arboleda, El Bosque.
Australian Embassy, Torre C, piso 20, Centro Plaza (Tel.: 283-34-87).
Canadian Embassy, Edificio Torre Europa, piso 7, Av. Francisco de Miranda, Chacao (Tel.: 33-97-76).
West German Embassy, Edificio Panavén, piso 2, Av. San Juan Bosco.
Asociación Cultural Humboldt (Goethe Institut), Edif. Pigalle, 1° piso, Av. Leonardo da Vinci, Urb. Colinas de Bello Monte, library, lectures, films, concerts, Spanish courses.
Brazilian Consulate, visas same day if requested at 0900, returned 1800.
Suriname Embassy, 4a Avenida, between 7a and 8a Transversal, Urb. Altamira, Tel.: 324490.
Swedish Embassy, Av. San Juan Bosco.
Swiss Embassy, Torre Europa, piso 6, Av. Francisco de Miranda (Tel.: 951-4064/4453/4166/4606/4273/4816).

Telecommunications are operated by the state company, CANTV, from El Silencio building in West Caracas, Centro Simón Bolívar, or Centro Plaza on Francisco Miranda in the east. Open 24 hrs., latter opens at 0700.

Tourist Office Anahoven address: Apartado 6966, Caracas, Tel.: 782-8888/8277/8433/8688/8077. Information from floors 35-37, Torre Oeste, Parque Central (for hotel bookings go to Plaza Venezuela, Centro Capriles, ground floor). Very helpful, especially if you speak Spanish. No maps. There is a smaller office at the airport, which has been highly praised and where English is spoken. See page 832 for further recommended reading.

Travel Agents: Agencia Candes, Edificio Roraima, Av. Francisco de Miranda; Tel.: 33-93-46. Club de Turismo Venezolano, Conde a Carmelitas No. 4; Tel.: 81-02-66. Exprinter, *Hotel Tamanaco*; Tel.: 91-45-55. Molina Viajes, Av. Andrés Bello, Edif. San Bosco, Los Palos Grandes, recommended, branch director Daniella Harr speaks English, French, German and Italian; Viajes Vintur have staff speaking English, German and Italian, Plaza Altamira Sur, Av. San Juan Bosco, Tel.: 324-931/35.

Airport Maiquetía, for national flights, Simón Bolívar for international flights, adjacent to each other, 28 km. from Caracas, near the port of La Guaira. Taxi fares from airport to Caracas cost on average US$5 (fares are controlled— buy ticket from office in the airport); more by night when a 20% surcharge is added after 2200, also on Sundays and holidays. If you think the taxi driver is overcharging you, make a complaint to Corpoturismo or tell him you will report him to the Departamento de Protección del Consumidor. If you walk about 200 metres to the highway you can catch a Caracas or El Silencio *por puesto*, or a bus for US$0.50 will take you to the bus terminal (but they are often unwilling to stop if you have a suitcase). They stop running after 1900. *Por puesto* directly from Maiquetía airport to El Silencio, US$0.85, but much less if you walk out of the airport to the main road. The Tourist Office at the airport is very helpful; hotel bookings can be made there. *Casa de cambio* open 24 hrs. (Italcambio, outside duty-free area). Check your change. Always allow plenty of time when going to the airport, whatever means of transport you are using; the route can be very congested. Another way: Metro to Gato Negro, take the "Macuto Sheraton" bus to La Guaira, then airport bus, or taxi.

Long Distance Buses The Nuevo Circo bus station in the city centre was due to be closed in 1987, and replaced in 1987 by two new ones, at the E and W ends of the city (the latter near La Rinconada race track). Aerobuses maintain regular services by air-conditioned coaches with reclining seats between Caracas and the main towns in eastern and western Venezuela, and also to Cúcuta, in Colombia. The fares of other good companies are a third less. Fare to Maracaibo,

802 VENEZUELA

US$4, 10 hrs., *por puesto*, US$7; Maracay, US$0.75, 2 hrs., *por puesto*, US$1.80; Valencia, US$1.20, *por puesto*, US$2.70; Coro US$3.30 (overnight), *por puesto*, US$5.60; to Barquisimeto US$2.40. Overnight to Valera, US$4.50, 9 hrs. (Aerobuses). Buses to Mérida, Expresos Mérida, US$6, 12 hrs., *por puesto*, US$10; overnight to Mérida, via Panamericana or Los Llanos (12 hrs.) to San Cristóbal. Expresos Alianzas Caracas to Cúcuta, US$7.20, 8 hrs., daily at 1900. Get passport exit stamp at San Antonio; bus will stop there. Bus to San Antonio, US$5.50, *por puesto*, US$11.25. To Barinas, US$4.10, 8 hrs. To Puerto La Cruz, US$2.75, 5 hrs., *por puesto*, US$3.50; to Cumaná, US$2.75-5.50, 8 hrs., *por puesto*, US$6, to Margarita, US$6 including ferry; to Maturín, US$3.75, *por puesto*, US$5.55. To Ciudad Bolívar, US$4, 7 hrs. *por puesto*, US$6; Ciudad Guayana, US$4.50, *por puesto*, US$8.25; to Tucupita, US$4.50; Tumeremo, 1800, 14 hrs., US$6.30; El Dorado, US$7.25, 11½ hrs; San Fernando de Apure, US$5.25. Tepsa agents in Caracas: Rayco, Av. Olimpo, Edf. Anuncia, San Antonio, Sabana Grande, Tel.: 782-8276, reported to be very helpful and friendly. Always take identification when booking a long-distance journey. To avoid theft it is advisable not to sleep on the buses.

Long-distance bus travel varies a lot in quality. However, buses from Caracas to Maracaibo, Mérida and San Cristóbal are usually in excellent condition; buses to Guayana are of poorer quality. Frequent service to Maracay, Valencia and Barquisimeto, but buses are often in bad shape; the Panamericana route is not recommended because it takes the old road on which there are many accidents. The best lines are: to Maracaibo, Expresos los Llanos; to Guayana, Providencial; to the eastern coast, Responsable. Buses stop frequently but there will not always be a toilet at the stop. Long distance *por puesto* services are twice as expensive as buses, less comfortable, but generally faster. On public holidays buses are usually fully booked leaving Caracas and drivers often make long journeys without stopping.

Excursions The cable railway (*teleférico*) up Mount Avila gives a stupendous view of the city and the coast. It operates on Wednesdays to Sundays and public holidays, 0900-2400 from the city to the summit only—not from the summit to the coast (US$2 for adults, US$1 for children—reservations necessary). It is planned to operate every day except Monday once the future of the *Humboldt Hotel* on the summit has been decided. It has been refurbished, but not reopened. Camping is possible with permission. At the summit there is a restaurant and an ice rink. A recommended trip is to take the cable car up and hike back down (note that it is cold at the summit).

Good hiking: the three principal entrances to the Avila park are (a) 100 metres W of the restaurant *Tarzilandia* in Altamira (the easiest climb); (b) the car park on the N side of Av. Boyacá above Urbanización Los Chorros (where there is a crude map)—8 hrs. to Pico Oriental, 2,650 metres; and (c) the entrance to Av. Boyacá from El Marqués (this route well signposted)—7 hrs. to Pico Naiguatá, 2,750 metres. A map of the paths (and entrance permit— US$2.85) is available from the Instituto Nacional de Parques at the north entrance to Parque del Este, price US$1. A description of the park is included in *Backpacking in Venezuela, Colombia and Ecuador*, published by Bradt Enterprises. Essential to carry your own drinking water. Serious danger of bush fires in the dry season January-April, so be careful with cigarettes, etc.

Maximum rates for excursions and transport are published by the Ministry of Development's Tourist Department, which solicits complaints in case of non-compliance. The list of published prices should be shown to the driver *before* he quotes the price.

La Guaira is Venezuela's main port, only 20 mins. by road to Caracas, if the volume of traffic permits. Population: 20,775. Mean temperature: 29°C.

In the area are many seaside resorts and residential districts with a total population of about 70,000. There is a small museum (Museo Fundación John Boulton) in Calle Bolívar, open Tues.-Fri., 0930-1200 and 1500-1700, Sat.-Sun., 0900-1200. Old La Guaira is worth visiting and a short bus ride up the hill to the lighthouse gives a fine view of the port and its surroundings. A pleasant drive can be made along the Avenida Soublette eastwards to Macuto, Laguna Beach, Caraballeda and so on to Los Caracas (45 km.), a government holiday resort for workers. (All these places can be reached quite cheaply by bus). Westward, on the way to Caracas, is the international airport. Taxi to airport, US$1.50.

The town of ***Maiquetía*** is not spoilt by proximity to the airport. *Hotel Salamanca*, Calle Real; *Hotel Senador*, Plaza Los Maestros, both F. The *Avila* is a good restaurant, near Los Maestros.

VENEZUELA 803

Macuto is a pleasant seaside resort with a fine, tree-lined promenade (the Paseo del Mar), a splendid yacht marina and a "pigeon housing estate". An ideal place to stay if "stopping-over" between flights to and from Caracas. The beach is dirty and the sea floor sharply shelving. The bus ride to Macuto from Caracas costs US$0.60 and takes 1 hr. The bus to the airport (domestic terminal) is US$0.20. The taxi fare from the airport is US$4. Anyone attempting to get on a *por puesto* back to Caracas at rush hour (weekend afternoons, etc.) is advised to walk to the *Macuto Sheraton*.

Hotels On the coast, not too far from Maiquetía airport: *Macuto-Sheraton**, A, luxury, at Caribe, 7 Km. away; *Meliá Caribe**, B, luxury, Caraballeda; *Macuto**, C, 5 min. walk to beach, comfortable, nothing special. *Riviera*, D, clean, good food (French), recently reported temporarily closed, Boulevard Caraballeda; *Las Quince Letras**, C, Av. La Playa, recommended, good seafood in restaurant; *Palm Beach*, Av. Principal del Caribe, D; *Bahía*, C, Avs. La Playa y Costanera, Urb. Los Corales; *Fioremar*, D, Av. Principal, Urb. Caribe; *Royal Atlantic*, D, Urb. Caribe; *Puerta del Sol*, E, bathless on weekdays, but friendly. *Alamo*, Av. La Playa, D (possible to bargain), with shower and fan, good value, good restaurant on the shore, not cheap; *Diana*, D, close to *Riviera*, on the beach, bath, clean, a/c, helpful; *La Alemania*, Paseo del Mar, E, pleasant; *Isaibel*, corner of Isaibel and Calle 3, 2 mins. from sea, F, small, quiet, good; also *Colonial*, *Pensión Guanéttez*, E, simple accommodation with three meals. (* = bookable through Anahoven)

Restaurants Recommended for paella is the *Solimar* in Urb. Caribe-Caraballeda. *Neptuno* also recommended. Good cheap restaurant is *La Esquina*, near Hotel Alamo. Panadería Apdo. 8, on Alamo, good.

Beaches Fishing (boats for hire at *Macuto-Sheraton* marina) just N of La Guaira (mostly marlin).

There are three beaches, with all facilities, along 27 km. of Caribbean seashore: one, Catia La Mar, W of La Guaira, and two—Macuto and Naiguatá—E of it. Catia La Mar is not recommended because it is industrial, very littered and the sea is heavily polluted, but it is very convenient for Maiquetía airport (taxi, US$2-3 depending on time of day). (*Hotel Bahía La Mar*, D, very comfortable and clean, food quite good, *por puesto* minibus to Caracas 35 metres from door (US$0.35), handy for airport, only problem is that it is under flight path for airport; *Scorpio*, F, clean, modern, cockroaches; *Aeropuerto*, E, shower, a/c, O.K.). New beaches are being prepared. The beaches themselves are enclosed by breakwaters as the currents can be very strong. From Caracas, by car, it takes 30 mins. to the 1st, 45 mins. to the 2nd, and 1 hr. to the 3rd, provided there are not too many traffic jams. West of Catia La Mar are beaches at Puerto Carayaca (*Casa Francisco*, hotel and restaurant), Oricao (small, private beach), and Chichiriviche, no hotels or restaurants (not to be confused with the resort W of Puerto Cabello); hitch or take taxis to these beaches. Far better beaches are three or four hrs. by car from Caracas: Cata and Ocumare de la Costa (see page 805), Chichiriviche (see page 807) and several others in the Puerto Cabello area. These more distant beaches are recommended, but a day trip is tiring because of traffic jams, particularly when returning to Caracas.

The overnight trip to **Los Roques** islands, directly N of La Guaira, is well worth it. These islands are truly beautiful, with long stretches of white beaches and mile upon mile of coral reef. There is a small hotel. You can also reach the islands by hitch hiking a lift from the Aeroclub at La Carlota airport. It is best to go in the morning or weekends; several planes leave then and often have spare places if you ask. Helicópteros del Caribe at Maiquetía sells flights at US$30 (one day) and US$60 (more than one day). Be prepared to wait at the airport. You can take a small boat to other islands. Take care for sunburn as there is no shade.

Other Excursions Further afield, in **Yare**, a celebration is held on Corpus Christi day; the dance before the church of the enormously masked red devils, and of most of the villagers. It lasts the whole day. Yare is about 90 km. from Caracas; the road to it is through Petare and down the Río Guaira as far as Santa Teresa, and then up the Río Tuy. From Santa Teresa a detour may be made to the beautiful and little frequented Guatopo National Park on the road to Altagracia de Orituco, but you must return to Santa Teresa to continue your journey to Yare.

804 VENEZUELA

At the Parque Guatopo are various convenient places to picnic on the route through the forest. Take insect repellant. To stay the night in the park a permit must be obtained. There are a number of good nature trails in the park, for instance a 3-km. trail from Santa Crucita Recreation Area (well-signposted).

Another good excursion is into the mountains to **Colonia Tovar** (1,890 metres), a village so isolated that a few of its blond, blue-eyed people still speak the Black Forest German of their ancestors who settled there in 1843. They now grow strawberries, coffee, garlic, rhubarb and flowers for the Caracas market. See their Scandinavian-style ceramics. Ask in Colonia Tovar for the *petroglifos*, rock paintings. The 1½-hr. drive from Caracas is delightful. Along the road are small parks where picnic lunch can be taken (now in bad condition), but at weekends there are long traffic queues and you have to be early just to find a roadside spot to picnic and there are similar problems finding accommodation—no such difficulties in the week. Prices can be very inflated.

The road to Colonia Tovar passes through **El Junquito**, a picturesque small town with roadside stands selling fruit and barbecued meat. You see Caracas from one side of the road, the Caribbean from the other. 29 km. beyond El Junquito, a paved road with beautiful views winds down the mountain to the sea: it branches right to Oricao (see above), and Catia La Mar, or left to El Limón and Puerto Cruz (nice beach), from where one can go E, or W to Puerto Maya, a beautiful bay with nice swimming (there is another branch right to Puerto Cruz nearer Colonia Tovar). Another road, 34 km. (well-paved, but hair-raising), leads through glorious mountain scenery from Colonia Tovar to La Victoria on the Caracas-Valencia highway (4 buses a day).

Hotels in Colonia Tovar: *Bergland* (good, cheap breakfasts); *Selva Negra**, *Cabañas Baden*; *Edelweiss* (not recommended), *Freiburg*, *Kaiserstuhl*, all C; *Alta Baviera*. All serve German-style food in good restaurants. There is said to be a good spot for camping just below the town's cemetery, if you don't mind the company.

It is generally easy to get a lift if there are no buses. Taxi fare for the round trip from Caracas to Colonia Tovar (driver will wait) is about US$10. A minibus leaves Plaza Chita, Caracas, daily at 0700, 1100 and 1600 (be there early for seat), fare US$0.75 one way. *Por puesto* from Plaza Catia or O'Leary (more frequently), Caracas, 1 hr., US$0.60. Alternatively, take a *por puesto* from Plaza Capuchino to El Junquito, then one from there to Colonia Tovar, US$0.40.

West from Caracas

The Pan-American Highway, which links Caracas by road with the other capitals of South America, follows closely the route of Gómez' Great Andean Highway as far as Lake Maracaibo, though many sections have been widened and straightened. At the start, we have the choice of a direct toll motorway to Valencia (with exit to Maracay), toll US$1.25, or the old road called, familiarly, "La Panamericana" and known for its dangerous bends. (Hotels on "La Panamericana": *Colonial*, D, San Antonio de los Altos; *Cutlas*, D, Km. 10; *Panorama*, E, Km. 13; *Las Vegas*, D, Km. 14.) It leaves La Rinconada race course to its left, and climbs steadily but easily towards **Los Teques**, capital of Miranda state (pop.: 44,000, *Hotel Los Alpes*, E, very good; *Alemán*, E, Plaza Miranda). This passes on its way the park of Las Colinas de Carrizal (collections of local fish and birds, and pleasant paths). Twenty-four km. beyond Los Teques on the way down into the fertile valleys of Aragua, we can either join the Caracas-Valencia tollway or take the older road through several attractive little towns such as La Victoria (see above). The Quinta de Bolívar is at San Mateo, between La Victoria and Maracay. A little nearer Maracay, a good road leads off to **San Juan de Los Morros** where a cock-fighting tournament is held each year (Hotels: *Motel Santa Mónica*, E; *Gran Hotel Los Morros*, E, on Carretera Nacional towards Villa de Cura; *Excelsior*, E, Calle Marino; *Ana*, E). It has natural hot springs. Nearby are mountains with vertical cliffs, on which several climbing routes have been opened. The road divides

VENEZUELA 805

later: S to the Guárico dam, the *llanos* and San Fernando de Apure, and E to Valle de la Pascua (*Hotel Venezuela*, D, Plaza Bolívar; *San Marcos*, D, Carretera Nacional towards El Socorro) and El Tigre.

The Panamericana to Maracay should be taken at least once, for views and local colour, but winding up and down the mountains behind slow, smelly trucks is not much fun. The toll road also offers good views.

The new highway avoids city centres, so all that is seen of Maracay, Valencia and Barquisimeto are factories plus the huge concrete Barquisimeto Fourth Centenary Monument. Beyond Barquisimeto there are mountains like slag heaps, until we reach the green of the Andes.

Maracay, capital of Aragua State, has a population of 322,000, and is at an altitude of 455 metres. In its heyday it was the favourite city of General Gómez and some of his most fantastic whims are still there: the former *Hotel Jardín* (now a Government centre) with its beautiful zoo, park and fountain, built for his revels; the unfinished opera house opposite; his modest little house for personal use, and the bull ring, an exact replica of the one at Seville. The Gómez mausoleum, built in his honour, has a huge triumphal arch. Maracay is the centre of an important agricultural area, and the school and experimental stations of the Ministry of Agriculture are worth visiting; it is also important industrially and militarily.

Hotels *Byblos**, D, Av. Las Delicias, high standard; *Maracay**, C, Las Delicias, swimming pool, gymnasium, night club; *Micotti*, E, Av. Bermúdez; *San Luis*, Carabobo Sur 13, off the main shopping street, D, clean, showers, friendly; *Bermúdez*, D, Av. Bermúdez 22; *Wladimir*, E, Av. Bolívar Este 27, friendly, good restaurant at reasonable prices; *Caroní*, D, Av. Ayacucho (Norte) 19; *Cristal*, E, Av. Bolívar Oeste 206; *Italo*, D, Av. 6, Urb. La Soledad, service uninterested, ask for quiet side of building; *Pipo**, C, Av. Principal, El Castaño, swimming pool, discotheque, recommended restaurant (*parrillas* a speciality). in hills above the city; *Triani*, D, Pérez Almarza Norte 83-85; *Turístico*, E, Calle El Tierral, La Providencia (*-bookable through Anahoven).

Restaurants *Tosca El Pescador*, Av. Sucre Norte 75, recommended, especially for seafood; *El Dragón de Plata*; *Paella Valenciana*, recommended; *Italo*. There are many Chinese restaurants which are reliable.

Bank Banco Consolidado (American Express), Av. Bolívar y Fuerzas Aéreas.

Chris and Josephine Walker write: The FAV (Fuerza Aérea Venezolana) Museum in Maracay is open on Sun. mornings from 1000 to 1200. About two dozen aircraft are displayed, including Second World War fighters and bombers, later jets and earlier aircraft from between the wars. The most celebrated plane is Jimmy Angel's G-2-W Flamingo, "El Río Caroní", which he landed on top of Auyan-Tepuy mountain on October 9, 1937. It remained there, embedded in a bog, until it was dug out by the FAV in 1970 and restored in Maracay.

Excursions Lake Valencia; to Las Delicias, Gómez' country house, where he died, with its adjoining zoo. The huge 100,000-hectare Henri Pittier park (a birdwatcher's paradise) stretches from 24 km. N of Maracay to the Caribbean on both sides of the Andes. A road runs from Maracay over the 1,130-metre high Portachuelo pass, guarded by twin peaks, to three places by the sea: **Ocumare de la Costa** 37 km. from Maracay; the naval base of Turiamo; and **Cata**, once the most beautiful beach in Venezuela, now overdeveloped (Cuyagua beach, unspoilt, is 10 km. further on). The road was built by Gómez as an escape route if things grew too hot for him. Near the pass is Rancho Grande, the uncompleted palace Gómez was building when he died; it is in the shape of a question mark and is worth visiting. It houses a natural history museum, which appears to be closed to the public, although permission may be given to serious naturalists. A taxi can be hired at Maracay for a day's outing in the park for about US$12. The nearby town of **Victoria** has the oldest bullring in Venezuela and an interesting old hotel, *Hotel El Recreo*, D, originally a colonial house built in 1724 (also *Omni*, B). In the hills nearby is the *hacienda* formerly occupied by Simón Bolívar and now a museum. Another excursion to the coast, also through the Henri Pittier National Park, goes over a more easterly pass (1,830 metres), on a paved but winding road to **Santa Clara de Choroní**, a beautiful colonial town (bus from Maracay, US$0.65, 1 hr. 20 mins.). About 10 km. before Choroní are 2 waterfalls known as El Dique, where one can bathe; ask anyone for directions. Just beyond the town is the beach of Puerto Colombia (camping possible on the beach), from where launches may be taken to the otherwise inaccessible colonial village of Chuao, famous in the past for its cocoa.

Fifty km. to the west of Maracay the road reaches Valencia, through low hills thickly planted with citrus, coffee and sugar.

806 VENEZUELA

Valencia (population, about 495,000), the capital of Carabobo State, stands on the W bank of the Cabriales river, 5 km. before it empties into Lake Valencia (rather polluted). It is the third largest city in the republic, the centre of its most developed agricultural region, and the most industrialized. Annual mean temperature 24°C; altitude 490 metres; rainfall, 914 mm. a year. The atmosphere of the older and narrower streets is that of old Spain. The interesting 18th century Cathedral (open 0630-1130, 1500-1830 daily, 0630-1200, 1500-1900 Sun.) is on the central Plaza Bolívar. The statue of the Virgen del Socorro in the left transept is the most valued treasure; on the second Sunday in November it is paraded with a richly jewelled crown. See the Capitol, the Municipal Theatre, the old Carabobo University building and the handsome bullring, which holds the world record for takings at a single *corrida*. Also the Museo de Arte e Historia, Calle 98 and Av. 104 (open Tues.-Sun., 0800-1200 and 1400-1730), and the Aquarium de Valencia at the west end of Calle 107 beyond the *autopista*, featuring a dolphin show at 1630 (open Tues.-Sun., 0930-1800, admission US$0.25). There is a small zoo behind the aquarium. Like its Spanish namesake, Valencia is famous for its oranges. There is a nice country club.

Hotels *Residencias Ucaima**, Av. Boyacá, Centro Comercial La Viña, B; *Excelsior*, E, Av. Bolívar 129-33; *Carabobo*, E, Plaza Bolívar; *Don Pelayo**, D, in town centre, Av. Díaz Moreno, recommended, good restaurant; *Le Paris*, E, Av. Bolívar 125-92; *Intercontinental Valencia**, B, Av. Juan Uslar, swimming pool, night club; *Astor*, Calle Colombia, D, a/c, bath, clean, safe parking, good; *Camoruco*, Av. Bolívar 110-161, E; *Central*, E, near main square, nice patio, quiet and clean, English spoken; *Continental*, E, Av. Boyacá 101-70; *El Panal*, E, Calle Independencia 101-91; *De Francia*, D, Av. Bolívar 110-161; *Bilboa*, E, Calle 100 (Colombia), 96-10, clean and quiet; *Metrópole*, E, central but dingy, Calle Comercial 103-47; *Palermo*, Calle Colombia, E, clean and friendly with laundry, other *residencias* on same street for the same price (*-bookable through Anahoven).

Restaurants *Asociación de Ganaderos*; *Mar Chica*; *La Grillade*; *Venezuela*, recommended; *Fego*, Av. Bolívar 102-75, recommended.

British Vice-Consul (Hon.): Corporación Mercantil Venezolana, Av. 100, 93-7.

Exchange Banco Consolidado (American Express), Av. Bolívar, Edif. Exterior; Turisol (also AmEx); Italcambio, Av. Bolívar, Edif. Talia, Loc. 2.

Buses To Caracas, US$1.20; to San Cristóbal, 10 hrs., US$3.65; Barquisimeto, US$1.50, 3 hrs.

Excursions At the Safari Carabobo Reserva Animal, on the road from Valencia to Campo de Carabobo, you can see many wild animals, not all of them South American, in well-planned and quite spacious surroundings. Cars with roof racks are not permitted to enter. To the monument on the battlefield of Carabobo, southwards on the road to San Carlos, to see the battle story told in bronze: the British soldiers who helped Bolívar are particularly realistic. Buses to the battlefield leave from La Sanidad (Health Centre), US$0.20, 1 hr.

The Caracas-Valencia motorway continues down the mountains, reaching the sea near El Palito (refinery and pier). Here we turn right to Puerto Cabello. 18 km. from Valencia, the road passes Las Trincheras, a decaying spa with the second hottest springs in the world (98 °C); there are three baths (hot, hotter, very hot), a mud bath and a Turkish bath. Entrance US$1. Hotel* for cures only (D).

Puerto Cabello, 96 km. W of La Guaira, is the port for Valencia, 55 km. away by modern highway; it is in itself a large industrial centre. This, the second most important Venezuelan port, has an excellent harbour with a lighthouse, and a shipyard with dry dock. Average temperature, 28°C; population, 71,200. A standard-gauge 175-km. railway runs to Barquisimeto.

Hotels *Riviera*, with good restaurant. (Other good restaurants are *El Parque*, *Mar y Sol*, *Venezuela*, near the harbour and *San Antonio del Mar*.) Best hotels near are the *Cumboto*, D, Av. La Paz, Urb. Cumboto, swimming pool; *La Sultana*, E, Av. Juan José Flores; *El Ejecutivo*, E, good, friendly; *La Hacienda* (good German food).

About half an hour E of Puerto Cabello over a rough road is a beautiful horseshoe-shaped beach shaded by palms called La Bahía. It is well worth the drive, has a refreshment stand, changing rooms, toilet facilities and lifeguards, but take your

VENEZUELA 807

own lunch. You can buy oysters from little boys who open them for you and douse them with lemon juice.

Puerto Cabello has another beach, Quizandal, with a coral reef, near the naval base. (Taxi fare, US$2.75 but you may find it hard to get one on the way back.) The nearby Country Club also has a beach with coral reefs within reach by boat. There are two Spanish forts at Puerto Cabello, one on the water (which can be reached by a small ferry boat), the other on a hill over the city (in a military zone and it is difficult to get permission to enter).

N.B. The beach to the W of Puerto Cabello is not so attractive; be careful of going beyond the bathing area as the beach is notorious for armed robbery.

Twenty-four km. W of Puerto Cabello, at the junction of the Pan-American Highway and the road to Tucacas, is **Morón**, where there is a government petrochemical plant.

Quite near Morón is the lovely beach of **Palma Sola**, 16 km. long and deserted save at Easter time when Venezuelans camp out there in crowds. The water can be dangerous but the sands and palms are superb. There are hotels, many closed in the off season (Balneario Canaima, C, swimming pool; Balneario Caribe, D), restaurants and changing rooms. A road has been built from Morón to Coro via Tucacas, an hour from Puerto Cabello. **Tucacas** (Hotel Manaure-Tucacas, D, Av. Silva, a/c, hot water, clean, restaurant; La Palma, E; Centuca, E) is a small, dirty town of wooden shacks where bananas and other fruit are loaded for Curaçao and Aruba, but offshore is the national park of Morrocoy, where there are hundreds of coral reefs, palm-studded islets, small cosy beaches and calm water for water-skiing and skin-diving. (The Park is reached on foot from Tucacas; camping allowed, no facilities.) The largest and most popular of the islands is Cayo Sombrero. Boats are for hire. Venezuelan skin-diving clubs come here for their contests. This is one of the two main fishing grounds of Venezuela; the other is off Puerto La Cruz. A few km. beyond, towards Coro, is the favourite beach resort of **Chichiriviche**; the town is dirty but offshore are numerous lovely islands and coral reefs. Hotel Mario*, B including 3 meals, swimming pool; La Garza*, B (including 3 meals) or D, pool (both used by Canadian tour groups); Náutico, D with breakfast and dinner, friendly, not very clean, fans but no a/c; Capri, near docks, E, shower and a/c, good restaurant and supermarket, bakery opposite. It is possible to hire a boat to any one of the islands; recommended for a weekend away from Caracas. You may camp on the islands, but there are no facilities or fresh water, and you may require a permit from Inparques (National Parks). Nearby is a vast nesting area for scarlet ibis, flamingoes and herons.

From Tucacas it is 177 km. to **Coro** (population 80,000), capital of the State of Falcón (por puesto, US$4)—a charming town, with some interesting colonial buildings (the town is a national monument), surrounded by sand dunes (médanos). The isthmus north of Coro, leading to the Paraguaná Peninsula, is a National Park. There is an interesting xerophytic garden open to the public. Museo Diocesano, Calle Zamora 69 (open Tues. and Sun. 0900-1200, Wed.-Fri., 1600-1900), Museo de Cerámica, Calle Zamora 98 (open Tues., 0900-1200, Wed.-Fri., 1600-1900, Sat. 1000-1300 and 1600-1900, Sun., 1000-1300). At Puerto Cumarebo, just before Coro, is a hotel, Balneario Bella Vista, E, private bath, restaurant, with beach, but not recommended (dirty, facilities non-operational). From Coro, there is a good but uninteresting road to Maracaibo and another paved road along the narrow strip of land leading to the Paraguaná Peninsula, along whose beaches men fish, 15 to 20 a net. Near the village of La Vela along the Morón road the local handicraft is the production of rocking chairs of all sizes made from cactus wood. Airport has a direct service to Caracas and Las Piedras. Bus from Coro to Caracas US$3.30.

Hotels at Coro Miranda*, D, Av. Josefa Camejo, opposite airport, swimming pool; Arenas, opp. bus terminal, D-C, restaurant; Caracas, E, Calle Toledo 17, very good, a/c; Coro, D, Av. Independencia, friendly, clean, good value; Venezia, D, expensive food, sporadic water supply; Valencia, D, with private shower; Maracén, E, with private shower; Capri (friendly). The Bella Nápoli is good, F; the Italia is cheaper, with bath, fan, friendly, patio. Manaure, E, avoid.

808　VENEZUELA

Restaurant *Don Camilo*, by *Hotel Miranda* and airport; very good food and reasonable prices.

Bank Banco Consolidado, Calle Federación con Buchivacoa (for American Express).

The **Paraguaná Peninsula** is connected by pipelines with the oilfields of Lake Maracaibo. The Maravén (ex-Shell) and Lagovén (ex-Esso) groups have refineries, the former at Cardón, and the latter at Amuay. The airport, which has services to Maracaibo (30 min.), Coro and Maiquetía, is known as Las Piedras, the town itself as **Punto Fijo** (Hotels: *Luigi*, D, Judibana, swimming pool; *Jardín*, D, Centro Comercial Judibana; *Caribe*, D, Calle Comercio 120; *Del Este*, E, Av. Táchira; also *Victoria*, *Cardón*, D, Miami). Eventually, all four places will merge into one large town. There is a seaport, Las Piedras-Paraguaná, between Amuay and Cardón, which also serves the town of Coro. The villages on the peninsula have interesting colonial churches, notably that of Santa Ana.

There is a ferry service (Ferrys del Caribe) from La Vela de Coro and Punto Fijo to Aruba and Curaçao. The schedules are continually being changed, so apply to the company's offices. Buy tickets on morning of departure. The journey to both Aruba and Curaçao usually takes 4-6 hrs., but the bureaucracy can lengthen this period to 8-12 hrs. Fare to Curaçao US$59 return, plus US$16.50 for cabin. It is necessary to have ticket out of Curaçao before entering, even if you are Dutch. It is advisable to arrive at the terminal at least 4 hours in advance, because the immigration officers often leave their posts before the boat departs. The tourist office can provide more information. The office for the boat in Coro is at Av. Independencia, beside Supermercado Victoria (Tel.: 068-519676); there are also offices in Caracas at Av. Urdaneta esq. Ibárrez, Edificio Riera (Tel.: 5611300). *Por puesto* between La Vela de Coro and Coro itself costs US$1.25 per seat, bus costs US$0.25; taxi from La Vela to the ferry dock (3 km.) is US$1.35; *por puesto* from Maracaibo to ferry terminal, US$6.

The Segovia Highlands, lying N of Barquisimeto, suffer from droughts, and are only sparsely settled along the river valleys. From Morón the Pan-American Highway strikes up into the hills, reaching 550 metres at **San Felipe** (population 30,750), capital of Yaracuy State (Hotels: *Turístico Río Yurubi**, E; *Hostería Colonial**, E, Av. La Paz, pool; *El Fuerte*, E, Av. La Patria; *La Fuente*, E, Av. La Fuente).

If you do not want to go to Puerto Cabello and the coast, a newer section of the Highway from Valencia via Carabobo to just beyond San Felipe is 56 km. shorter.

Barquisimeto, capital of Lara State, has a population of 504,000. Altitude 565 metres, mean temperature 25°C. It stands on one of the alluvial fans so frequent in the Andes, and is Venezuela's fourth largest city, with the University of Lara. The Cathedral, an ultramodern structure of free-form concrete and glass, is very interesting. The Palacio Municipal at Carrera 17 with Calle 25 is an attractive modern building. Across the street is a large well-shaded plaza with a bronze equestrian statue of Bolívar. On Carrera 15 (Av. Francisco de Miranda) between Calles 41-43 there is a charming park, resplendent with lush vegetation, paths, fountains and another bronze statue of Bolívar. There is a road from Barquisimeto to Acarigua (see page 817) on the alternative route from Caracas to Mérida.

Hotels The *Motel El Parador*, B, excellent, near El Obelisco, a great roundabout in the northern suburbs of the town in the middle of which stands a tower; *Hilton**, B, Carrera 5, Nueva Segovia; *Hostería El Obelisco*, D, Av. Panamericana, American motel-style, swimming pool, always full; *Gran Hotel Barquisimeto*, D, Av. Pedro León Torres, pool; *Comercio*, D, Av. 20 between Calles 35-36; *Curumato*, E, Av. 20, esq. Calle 34; *Del Centro*, E, Av. 20, between Calles 26-27, good value; *Hevelin*, D, Av. Vargas, between 20-21, with or without a/c; *La Casona*, E, Carrera 17 con Calle 27 near Plaza Bolívar, a/c, clean, hot water, excellent, parking; *Miny*, D, Av. 20, between Calles 11-12; *Principe**, D, Carrera 19, esq. Calle 23, swimming pool, good; *Sport*, E, Calle 25, between 19-20; *Yacambú*, D, Av. Vargas, between Carreras 19-20, swimming pool. *Santa Lucía*, opposite bus station; *Avenida*, E, Av. Vargas, No. 21-124, 2nd floor, clean, economical.

Restaurants *Mesón de la Campaña*, *El Obelisco*; *Guido's*, good, expensive; *Terminal Vargas*, food average, service good, expensive; railway station restaurant, excellent.

Exchange Banco Consolidado, Av. Vargas entre Calles 20 y 21, also Turisol (Tel.: 516743), both American Express.

Transport Railway to Puerto Cabello, and an airport. (No bus from airport, only taxis. There is a single bus terminal on the edge of the city.) Bus to Mérida, only one a day, leaves at 0315, 8 hrs. via Agua Viva and El Vigía, US$3.85. For renting cars (Volkswagen best), Av. Pedro León Torres y Calle 56, or agency in lobby of *Hotel Curumato*, Calle 34 with Av. 20, also at airport. To Acarigua by bus, US$0.50, one hr.

West of Barquisimeto, about half an hour's drive, is **El Tocuyo** with a good hotel in a delightful colonial setting, *La Posada Colonial*, D, with moderately priced restaurant. Between Barquisimeto and El Tocuyo is the main grape-growing area.

About 24 km. SW of Barquisimeto is the small town of **Quíbor.** There is an interesting museum, Centro Antropológico de Quíbor, with exhibits of the Indians who used to live in the region. Stop in the plaza for a *chicha de maíz* or *arroz*, a refreshing traditional drink of the local Indians. About 18 km. from Quíbor is the mountain village of Cubiro (two hotels) which stands at 1,600 metres, ideal for walking. Direct buses from Barquisimeto or change at Quíbor. Turn right a few km. before Quíbor to get to a tiny *rancho* in the village of El Tintoreto where "blankets" are made from local wool. These are in bright coloured stripes or plaids and serve well as colourful rugs, but not as what we call blankets. The single blanket can be bought at Quíbor for US$5-6.50 and the double size for US$10-12. You won't get more than US$1 or so off by bargaining. They are well worth the price. Near Quíbor is the *Posadas Turísticas de Sahare**, E.

About 60 km. east of Barquisimeto is the little town of **Chivacoa**. Passing sugar-cane fields you reach the mountain of Sorte which is the holy region for the María-Lionza cult (similar to Voodoo) practised throughout Venezuela. Celebrations are held there mostly at weekends with October 12 (Día de la Raza) being the most important day. It is interesting to walk up the mountain when the pilgrims are camping beside the river and waterfalls, but do not go unless you are prepared to take it seriously, and use only the parking lot to park your car; other places are unsafe because of robbery.

Another pleasant excursion from Barquisimeto by bus or car is to **Río Claro,** about 28 km. inland, "where the Andes begin". You follow a lush river valley through the mountains. There are banana plantations in the area and many dirt trails you can follow on horseback or in a 4-wheel drive vehicle. From Río Claro a gravel road (dry season only) goes to Buena Vista and on to Quíbor; good views and pleasant villages.

Some 75 km. past Barquisimeto the Lara-Zulia motorway to Maracaibo forks off to the right (Caracas-Maracaibo 660 km.), through **Carora** (*Complejo Turístico Katuca*, C; *Motel* and *Restaurant Indio Mara*, E, reasonable; *Motel Posada Madrevieja*, E, both on Av. Francisco de Miranda; *Irpinia*, E, and *Parrilla Italia*, E, both on Av. 14 de Febrero).

The **Lowlands of Maracaibo**, lying in the encircling arms of the mountains, are more or less windless and extremely humid. Average annual temperature is higher than anywhere else in Latin America. Rainfall decreases steadily from the foothills of the Sierra Nevada to the coast. In these lowlands is the semi-salt Lake Maracaibo, of about 12,800 square km., 155 km. long and in places over 120 km. wide. It is joined to the sea by a waterway, 3 to 11 km. wide and 55 km. long, at the mouth of which is the bar of Maracaibo.

The area was once dependent on fishing and the transport of coffee across the lake from the Sierra. Since the discovery there of one of the world's greatest oilfields in 1914, there has been a great transformation, both in appearance (a forest of oil derricks covers the shore swamps and some of the lake), and in prosperity. The Lara-Zulia motorway reaches Maracaibo by the beautiful 8-km. long General Rafael Urdaneta bridge, which has the longest pre-stressed concrete span in the world.

Maracaibo, on the north-western shore of Lake Maracaibo, capital of the State of Zulia, is Venezuela's oil capital: 70% of the nation's output comes from the Lake area. Maracaibo, which is 55 mins. by jet from Caracas, is the country's second largest city. Population: 1.7 million. The airport is at La Chinita. The bus terminal is on the edge of the city.

The climate is damp and hot, but healthy. The hottest months are July, August and September, but there is usually a sea breeze from 1500 until morning. The mean temperature of 28°C and average humidity of 78% are most felt at sea

VENEZUELA

level. The new part of the city round Bella Vista and towards the University is in vivid contrast with the old town near the docks; this, with narrow streets and colonial style adobe houses, is hardly changed from the last century (parts, especially around Santa Lucía church, have been well-restored). A trip across the lake through the oil derricks is difficult to organize as the oilfields are a long way from Maracaibo. The zone begins at Cabimas (*Cabimas Internacional**, B, luxury, pool, discotheque) on the E shore of the lake and you can get a good view of the oil rigs from there (boat to Cabimas, US$1, semi-legal trip in fishing boat among the derricks, US$2-4, ask behind the market) and from other towns further down, such as Lagunillas (*Hotel Lagunillas*, D, pool)—though don't take pictures without asking permission.

From the port you can take a ferry to Altagracia for US$0.30, 25 mins., and either return the same way or take a minibus for US$0.30, travelling through exotic scenery for almost an hour and crossing the General Urdaneta bridge.

Hotels It is difficult to obtain rooms without making reservations well in advance. *Hotel del Lago Intercontinental**, C, B in new wing, non-residents may use the pool but will be charged; *Gran Hotel Delicias**, D, Av. 15 esq. Calle 70, swimming pool, night club; *Motel Granada* (*Mogranca*), D, room service only, outside town on road to La Concepción; *Aparthotel Presidente*, D, Av. 11, 68-50, pool; *Costa Azul*, D, Av. Bella Vista 74-49; *Cantaclaro**, E, Calle 86A (Santa Elena); *Maruma**, Circunvalación No.2, C, old and new sections, hotwater, a/c, TV, good value, reasonable restaurant; *Roma*, D, Calle 86, 3F-76, popular with Italians, food is very good; *Kristof**, C, Av. 8 (Santa Rita), swimming pool, night club; *Londres*, Calle 94, Av. 6, E, with bath; *Carrizal*, D, Av. 5 de Julio 17-104; *San José*, E, Av. 3Y (San Martín) 82-29; a/c, bath, good beds, friendly, Italian restaurant, recommended; several others nearby, e.g. *Matos*, E, a/c, bearable; *Venecia*, E, Av. 3Y 80-23; *Astor*, E, Calle 78, 3H-37, Plaza República; *Caribe*, E, a/c and shower; *Palace*, E, Calle 99, Esq. Av. 10; *Yacambú*, F, Av. Libertador, central and clean, fair; *Aurora*, E, Calle 96, near waterfront. *Santa Ana* is the cheapest, F, poor but friendly, opposite Occidente garage near main banking area on Av. 3, between Ciencias and Venezuela.

Restaurants *Chez Nicolás*, excellent food, highly recommended; *El Chicote* (seafood), Av. Bellavista, corner with Calle 70; *Rincón Boricua*, Av. 23, between Calles 66 and 67 (good meat); *El Pozo* (Spanish dishes); *El Pescadito* (Av. 2, 76-A-209), by lakeside, with agreeable breeze; *Mi Vaquita* (Av. 3H, Calle 76), steak house, very good; *La Carreta del Ché*, Av. 13A, No. 76-54; *Saint George*, Av. 12, No. 75-80, dear; *El Delfín*, Calle 75 and 3H, recommended, especially for seafood; *Central Lunch*, Calle 98, Chinese run, good helpings, cheap for Maracaibo, open when other places are shut. *La Friulana*, Calle 95, Av. 3. for good cheap meal at US$2.

Taxis US$1 fixed fare.

Banks Banco de Venezuela; Banco de Maracaibo; Banco Consolidado, Av. Bella Vista Con Calle 67 (American Express, also Turisol AmEx rep., Tel.: 70611); Banco Royal Venezolano; Banco Holandés Unido; Banco Latinoamericano de Venezuela; Citibank. *Cambio* at bus terminal will change Colombian pesos into bolívares.

Colombian Consulate Av. 3Y (San Martín) 70-16, 10 km. from centre, take bus or *por puesto* (Bellavista) out of town on Av. 4 to Calle 70; open Mon.-Fri., 0800, 90-day visa in 5 hrs., no questions, no tickets required (better than Caracas).

U.S. Consulate Edificio Matema, Av. 15 entre Calles 78 y 79.

British Vice-Consul (Hon.): Apartado 285, Edificio Gómez Castro, Av. El Milagro.

Anglican Church Christ Church, Av. 8 (Santa Rita) a Calle 74.

Telecommunications Servicio de Telecomunicaciones de Venezuela, Calle 99, esquina, Av. 3.

Transport Air services, to Maiquetía (US$14), Mérida, Valera, Barquisimeto, Las Piedras (for Amuay and Cardón), San Antonio (US$11.50, be early to guarantee seat) and other towns. Other airlines connect Maracaibo with Barranquilla (five flights a week), Curaçao, Trinidad, Miami, New York and Europe. Taxis have a set fare of about US$4. Bus station is 15 mins. walk from centre, 1 km. S of the old town (no beer available). There are several fast and comfortable buses daily to Valencia (US$3 by Expresos del Lago), San Cristóbal (US$4.50, 8 hrs., *por puesto*, US$9.75), Barquisimeto (US$2.10) and Caracas (US$4, 10 hrs.). Bus lines, other than Aerobuses de Venezuela, recommended are Occidente and Alianza, whose fares are cheaper. To Mérida, 5 hrs. (US$4.50). Bus to Caracas costs US$4. Minibus to Maracaibo from Maicao, US$5.75, 3 hrs., 6 police checks en route.

On the W side of the lake, between the rivers Santa Ana and Catatumbo, a large area of swampland is crossed by the road to La Fría. The swamp is inhabited by the Motilones, who, until 1960, refused to have dealings either with white men or other Indians. The southern border of the Motilones' territory, the River Catatumbo, is famed for its almost nightly display of lightning for which there is, as yet, no accepted explanation and which caused it to be known in the old days as "The Lighthouse of Maracaibo". There are various missions you can visit: the easiest to reach is Los Angeles del Tocuco, 51 km. from Machiques, where they welcome visitors; it helps to take a present, such as dried milk. There is a priest at the mission who was attacked, and they now preserve in their museum the arrow head they took from his body. From here you can do a 5-day trek to Picci Cacao, recommended by Manfred W. Frischeisen for the beautiful scenery and the friendliness of the Yuspa Indians. Take them rice and blankets if you can carry them. Ask the padre for a guide and mules, take your own food and camping equipment. **Machiques** is on a fast road from San Cristóbal via La Fría to Maracaibo, and has the good *Motel Tukuko*, E.

The best sightseeing trip is north about 1 hr. to the Río Limón (it has another local name). Take a bus (US$0.30) to El Moján, riding with the Guajira Indians as they return to their homes on the peninsula. Another bus or taxi (US$1) can be taken to the river. Alternatively, take a Sinamaica bus from the new station, US$0.75 (*por puesto*, US$1.50), then a colectivo to Puerto Cuervito, a small port on the Sinamaica lagoon, US$0.30. Hire a boat (bargaining recommended as the price is around US$30 for a boat holding 10 people; fix price, duration and route in advance to ensure full value), and go up the river for an hour to La Boquita (2,500 inhabitants) to see Indians living in houses made of woven reed mats built on stilts; the only place where they can be seen. Excursions by boat to the Sinamaica lagoon from Maracaibo charge about US$8 per hour, but if you think you are being overcharged, ask for *el libro de reclamaciones* which should give the maximum official price. By crossing the bridge over the river you come, in the north, to a paved road that leads to Riohacha, in Colombia, where border formalities are quick and easy, a recommended route, but the Colombian border town, Maicao, has a most unsavoury reputation; best not to stop there. Along the way you see Guajira Indians, the men with bare legs, on horseback; the women with long, black, tent-shaped dresses and painted faces, wearing the sandals with big wool pom-poms which they make and sell for US$2, as against the US$7-10 in the tourist shops. The men do nothing: women do all the work, tending sheep and goats, selling slippers and raising very little on the dry, hot, scrubby Guajira Peninsula. If you don't do this trip, you can see these Indians in the Ziruma district of Maracaibo. There is an interesting Guajira market at Los Filuos, a mile beyond Paraguaipoa, where you can buy the local tent-dress (*manta*) for about US$7-12, depending on the quality, but much cheaper than in Maracaibo.

Those who wish to go on to the Sierra Nevada de Mérida or the State of Trujillo should return over the lake and turn sharp right through Cabimas, Lagunillas, Bachaquero and Mene Grande, all unattractive oil towns, to rejoin the Pan-American Highway at Agua Viva. For the Colombian frontier or San Cristóbal we follow the Pan-American Highway.

The Pan-American Highway from Agua Viva is a splendid asphalt speed track, but devoid of much scenic or historical attraction. It runs along the foot of the Andes through rolling country planted with sugar or bananas, or park-like cattle land. At Sabana de Mendoza, 24 km. S of Agua Viva, is a possible stopover—*Hotel Panamérica* (good; air-conditioned). This road has plenty of restaurants, hotels and filling-stations, especially at Caja Seca and El Vigía, both rather new and raw looking towns. At **El Vigía** (*Hotel Gran Sasso*, D; *Hostería El Vigía*, D), where the road from Mérida to Santa Bárbara (Zulia) crosses the Río Chama, there is a fine bridge over 1 km. long. Santa Bárbara (56 km. NW) is a milk, meat and plantain producing centre, with air and boat services to Maracaibo and an important annual cattle show.

From El Vigía, the road continues fairly flat until **La Fría,** with a large natural-gas fuelled power station, where it is joined by the road along the west side of Lake Maracaibo and begins to climb to San Cristóbal. La Fría has two hotels; the family-run *Hotel Turística*, F, on main square, basic but clean, is recommended.

The **Sierra Nevada de Mérida**, running from S of Maracaibo to the Colombian frontier, is the only range in Venezuela where snow lies permanently on the higher peaks. Near Mérida itself there are five such snowcaps of almost 5,000 metres. Several basins lying between the mountains are actively cultivated; the inhabitants are concentrated mainly in valleys and basins at between 800 and 1,300 metres above sea level. The three towns of Mérida, Valera and San Cristóbal are in this zone. There are two distinct rainy and dry seasons in any year. Two crops of the staple food, maize, can be harvested annually up to an elevation of about 2,000 metres.

Those who wish to visit the Sierra Nevada should turn left at Agua Viva to **Valera**, the most important town in the State of Trujillo, with a population of 117,000 and an airport with connections to Caracas and La Fría. The bus terminal is on the edge of the town. The US$4.90 trip to Mérida across the Pico del Aguila pass (5½ hrs.) is well worth taking.

812 VENEZUELA

Hotels *Motel Valera**, E, Urb. La Plata; *Haack*, E, with private cold shower; *Victoria*, E, with bath, basic, noisy; *Pensión Lara*, F, good, friendly. *Albergue Turístico*, E, Av. Independencia, good value; *Camino Real*, nearby, D; *Aurora*, E, Av. 7 (Bolívar), Edf. Rangel; *Imperial*, D, Av. 4 esq. Calle 14. *Hidrotermal San Rafael*, 4 km. off road between Valera and Motatán, notable for its hot water springs and the thermal bath.

From Valera a visit can be made to the state capital, **Trujillo** (43,000 people), at 805 metres; a *por puesto* from Valera costs US$0.40. This politically important town is losing ground commercially to Valera. Trujillo runs up and down hill; at the top, across from the university, is a park (sadly rundown) with waterfalls and paths. The Centro de Historia de Trujillo is a restored colonial house, now a museum. Bolívar lived there and signed the "proclamation of war to the death" in the house. A monument to the Virgen de la Paz was built by the wife of President Herrera Campins in 1983; it stands on a mountain, at 1,608 metres, ½-hr's walk from town; open 0900-1700, good views. (*Hotel Roma*, F, good, clean, owner's daughter speaks English).

From Trujillo there is a high, winding, spectacular paved road to **Bocono**, a town built on steep mountain sides. (*Hotel Vega del Río**, E, offers most services and food and is clean; *Colonial*, E, Av. Miranda; *Colina*, where the river is bottom of town, D, motel-style, clean, comfortable, restaurant; *Italia*, E, Calle Jáuregui.) From there you can continue down to Guanare in the *llanos* via Biscucuy (where a very difficult road through Guárico leads to Barquisimeto).

We are now in the Sierra Nevada de Mérida, the Western Andes of Venezuela. The people are friendly, and very colourful in their red and navy blue *ruanas*. Forty km. beyond Trujillo on a good paved road we come to **Timotes** (hotels: *Las Truchas*, D, very nice, good food; *Aliso*), a mountainous little place set high in the cold grain zone. Near Timotes are La Mesa de Esnujaque (*Hotel Tibisay**, E; *Miraflores*, E) and La Puerta (*Guadalupe**, D, a fine hotel; *Chiquinquirá*, D, Av. Bolívar 34; *Valeralta*, E, on road to Timotes; *Los Andes*, E, Av. Bolívar), both places hill resorts for Maracaibo and district. The road now climbs through increasingly wild, barren and rugged country and through the windy pass of Pico del Aguila (4,115 metres, best seen early in the morning, frequently in the clouds). This is the way Bolívar went when crossing the Andes to liberate Colombia, and on the peak is the statue of an eagle. In the pass is the very pleasant little *Restaurant Páramo Aguila* in chalet style. Behind it there is a small road leading up to the antenna and down towards the village of Piñango where there is trout fishing. The breath-taking scenery and the old village are worth the hardship of the 40 km. road; 4-wheel drive vehicles recommended if the road is wet. The road then dips rapidly through **Apartaderos**, 12 km. away (*Hotel Parque Turístico*, D, clean, beautiful house); over the centuries the Indians have piled up stones from the rocky mountainside into walls and enclosures, hence the name. On Sunday they all stand and watch the tourists; the children sell flowers and fat puppies called *mucuchíes* (a variant of the Grand Pyrené) after a near-by town. Only 3 km. from Apartaderos is Laguna Mucubají, and a 1-hour walk takes you to Laguna Negra for trout fishing; a further 1½-hour's walk from Laguna Negra is the Laguna Los Patos (very beautiful if the weather is fine). Guides (not absolutely necessary) can be found at Laguna Mucubají or at the hotels in Santo Domingo (*Hotel Moruco**, D, reservations can be made through *Hotel Río Prado* in Mérida; *Santo Domingo**, E, hot water, clean, good restaurant but beware of overcharging; rooms for rent opp. *Restaurante Familia*, F). This quaint little hamlet lies a few km. away on the road which leads off to Barinas in the *llanos* and then on to Valencia. Between Santo Domingo and Laguna Mucubají is the *Hotel Los Frailes**, D, said to be one of the best in Venezuela, dinner is excellent but breakfast is appalling. Book well ahead. *Mucubají* restaurant, at the highest point of the road that passes Laguna Mucubají, is very good for trout.

From Apartaderos the road to Mérida leads up to San Rafael de Mucuchíes, at 3,140 metres (stay at the house of Sra Crys, a French artist, clean, hot shower, E, breakfast and dinner extra), from where you can walk up to a high valley where Indians tend cows and sheep (beware of the dogs that protect the houses), then down to **Mucuchíes**, (*Hotel Los Andes*, F, old house above plaza, 4 rooms, clean hot water, shared bathrooms, excellent; *Hotel Faro*) where there is a trout

VENEZUELA 813

farm. An old colonial trail, El Camino Real, can be taken from Apartaderos to Mucuchíes (3-4 hrs.), sometimes joining the main road, sometimes passing through small villages; below San Rafael is an old flour mill still in operation. We descend through striated zones of timber, grain, coffee and tropical products to reach level land at last and the city of Mérida. All through this part of the country you see a plant with curious felt-like leaves of pale grey-green, the *frailejón* (or great friar), which blooms with yellow flowers from September to December.

The patron saint of Mucuchíes is San Benito; his festival on December 29 is celebrated by participants wearing flower-decorated hats and firing blunderbusses continuously.

Mérida (173 km. from Valera and 674 km. from Caracas), founded 1558, is the capital of Mérida State. Its white towers are visible from far along the road, and it stands at 1,640 metres (mean temperature 19° C) on an alluvial terrace 15 km. long, 2½ km. wide, surrounded by cliffs and plantations and within sight of Pico Bolívar, the highest in Venezuela (5,007 metres), crowned with a bust of Bolívar. Mérida still retains some colonial buildings which contrast with the fine modern buildings, such as those of the University of the Andes (founded 1785). The main square with rebuilt Cathedral is pleasant, but is no longer colonial. The *fiesta* is the week of December 8; hotels will only let for the whole week. Mérida is also well known for its Feria del Sol, held on the week preceding Ash Wednesday. Population: 125,000, including 22,000 students.

Mérida is known for its many parks (twenty-one): the Parque de las Cinco Repúblicas (Calle 13, between Avs. 4 and 5), beside the barracks, has the first monument in the world to Bolívar (1842) and contains soil from each of the five countries he liberated; the peaks known as the Five White Eagles can be clearly seen from here. The Parque Los Chorros de Milla has a zoo (some cages disgracefully small) in a hilly setting with a waterfall, closed Mon., it is some distance from the centre (minibus, US$0.25); the Parque La Isla contains orchids, basketball and tennis courts, an amphitheatre and fountains; Jardín Acuario, besides the aquarium, is an exhibition centre, mainly devoted to the way of life and the crafts of the Andean peasants, admission US$0.50, closed between 1200 and 1400. There is fishing and mountaineering in the neighbouring Sierra Nevada.

Hotels *Prado Río**, D, Cruz Verde, 1, private bath, swimming pool, main building and individual cabins; *La Pedregosa**, Vía la Pedregosa, C; *Belensate**, D, Urb. La Hacienda, La Punta; *Park Hotel**, Parque Glorias Patrias, D; *Caribay**, Final Av. 2, D, good restaurant; *La Terraza**, D, Los Chorros de Milla; *Hostal Madrid*, F, Calle 23, Av. 7-8, good value; *La Sierra*, E, Calle 23, No. 2-31, private bath, friendly, clean, parking, good restaurant; *Luxemburgo*, E, Calle 24 (Rangel), between Avs. 6-7, private bath; *Tinjaca*, Av. 5 Independencia, E, hot water, will store luggage; *Chama*, E, Av. 4 con Calle 29, private bath, pleasant, friendly, recommended; *Mucubají*, E, Av. Universidad, clean and pleasant; *Frailejones*, Av. Independencia 3, D, with bath; *Gran Balcón*, E, Paseo Domingo Peña, private bath; *Italia*, Calle 19 between Avs. 2 and 3, F, with bath, hot-water (cheaper rooms available), clean, friendly; *Plaza*, Av. 5 between C. 23 and 24, E with bath, good value , noisy (laundromat next door); *Santiago de los Caballeros*, E, Av. 3, between Calles 24-25, private bath; *Llanero*, E, basic; on Avenida Obispo Lora; *Hostería El Llanito*, E, La Otra Banda; *Nevada Palace*, E, Calle 24 No. 5-45; *Oviedo*, F, Av. 3 No. 34-37; *Anaca*, D, Av. 5, family run; *Rose's*, Av. 2 y Calle 25, F, good value, English spoken; *Altamira*, Calle 25, No. 7-48, E; *Budapest*, Av. 3, Calles 18-19, E; several hotels on Av. 2 between Calles 17 and 20. *Don Cándido*, Av. 2, F, good but noisy TV; *El Andinito*, Plaza Bolívar, clean and friendly, E, good restaurant; *Montecarlo*, Av. 7 with Calles 24 and 25, Tel.: 52-66-88, F, clean, safe, hot water, restaurant poor (located between *teleférico* station and Plaza Bolívar); *Teleférico*, beside *teleférico* station, E, noisy, clean, hot water, good restaurant. It is difficult to get rooms during school holidays. Recommended to book in advance.

Restaurants *Casa Vieja*, decorated as 19th-century Andean home, very good food, moderately priced, expect to pay about US$10 for two people; good food at *Chama Hotel*; *El "13"*, next to Hostal Madrid, good value; *Marisquería Vargas*, good steak, flamenco; *Pekín*, Av. 3, good *menú fijo* for US$3; *Hong Kong*, Av. 5, good Chinese, reasonable prices; *Chipen*, good cheap food; *La Paellera*, Av. 5, good food, reasonable prices; *El Gaucho Martín*, Argentine food; *Pabellón Criolla*, Calle 18 and Av. 8, good, cheap local food as well as hamburgers; *Pizzería Monte Carlo*, Av. 3, recommended; *Hotel Europa* for cheap, good meals. Vegetarian restaurants: *Comida Vegetariana*, Calle 24, No. 8-205, opp. Parque Las Heroínas, excellent; *Anfora de Acuario*, Av. 2, Calles 24 and 23; *Acro Iris*, Av. 4 and Calle 19, very nice; *Pizzería Vegetariano*, Av. 5 and Calle 26, good, cheap; one at Av. 2 near Calle 23; *Gran Fraternidad*, Av. 4, Calle 26; *Macro-Mérida*, Av. 4, Calles

814 VENEZUELA

18 and 19; two cheap and filling restaurants are *Los Nevados*, Av. 2, No. 18-57 (recommended) and *Comedor Popular*, Calle 23, No. 6. *Restaurante Estudiantil Cuarta Avenida*, Av. 4 between C. 18 and 19, cheap. Good *arepas* at *Arepa Andina*, Av. 5, No. 21-46, and *La Arepera*, Plaza Bolívar. *La Fresa*, Calle 26 near Av. 5, for desserts. The *Heladería* on Av. 3 offers 185 choices of ice cream.

Museum Colonial Art Museum and Museum of Modern Art, Av. 3 No. 18-48, three blocks from Plaza Bolívar (open Tues.-Fri., 0900-1200, 1500-1800; Sat. and Sun., 1000-1200, 1600-1800). Instituto Municipal de Cultura, Av. 4, half block from Parque Bolívar, stages poetry readings, art shows etc.

Banks None accepts travellers' cheques, except Banco Consolidado for American Express, Av. Andrés Bello, Centro Comercial Las Tapias; hotels do and there is one *casa de cambio* (poor rates). Turisol, AmEx representative, Tel.: 63 1085.

Colombian Consulate Calle Ciejo, street opp. Night Club Las Vegas, 4 km. West of Centre; take *por puestro* to La Parroquia and ask at the end of the line. Visas free, take 10 mins.

Bullfights Mérida is a famous centre.

Tourist Offices Near the airport and near *Hotel Mucubají*. At Terminal Sur, helpful, map and hotel list. At Oficina de Turismo Aeropuerto, Manuel, is very informative about excursions in the mountains, Tel.: 639330. Club de Turismo, Calle 24, No. 8-107 (opp. Teleférico), good advice on excursions, ask for Fanny.

Air Services Airport is on the main highway, buses into town US$1. Aeropostal and Avensa. To Caracas (US$16.50), 1¼ hrs., also to San Antonio at 1730 (US$7.50).

Bus The bus terminal is about 3 km. out of town on the W side of the valley, connected by frequent minibus service. To Caracas, US$6 (11-15 hrs.), *por puesto*, US$10; daily bus to Maracaibo, US$4.50, or *por puesto* service US$7.25, by Unión de Conductores, Tel.: 24.364. Bus to San Cristóbal, US$1.80, 5 hrs., 4 a day, leaving 0400 onwards, *por puesto* US$3.60. Buses to Barinas, US$1.70, 6 hrs. *Por puesto* to Apartaderos, US$1.20. Those hitchhiking east from Mérida should take a minibus to Tabay (US$0.30) and try from there. *Por puesto* to Valera, US$4.90.

The world's highest aerial cable car runs to Pico Espejo (4,765 metres) in four stages. The trip up and down takes three hours and costs US$5.50, children US$2.75, 50% discount for holders of any student card; check beforehand that the cable car is operating; it runs Tuesday to Sunday, except holidays, starting up at 0730, last trip up at 1200, last trip down at 1400 (very crowded at weekends and children are affected by the thin air, which makes them vomit). This is a "must", best done early in the morning (before 0830 ideally), before the clouds spoil the view, and from November to June. (In summer the summit, with its statue to Our Lady of the Snows, is clouded and covered with snow and there is no view.) The glacier on Pico Bolívar can be seen clearly, so can Picos Humboldt and Bonpland, forming the Corona, and to the E, on a clear day, the blue haze of the *llanos*. Electric storms in the mountains are not uncommon. If the peak is slightly clouded when you start, stop at the Loma Redonda station (4,045 metres) the last station but one. From this station there is a path (6 or more hours' walking down, not recommended for the inexperienced or the ill-equipped, 7 hours up) to Los Nevados (2,711 metres), a pretty little place, accommodation G (must book), but no restaurant. Mules do the journey Weds.-Sun., US$3, 4 hrs. Take your own food. From Los Nevados you can continue downhill to El Morro (9 hours, not easy) where you may be able to get a jeep early in the morning to Mérida (2 hrs., very rough). It is possible to get a room to stay overnight. There is also an ice cave with dazzling crystal ice stalactites two hours' rough walk from the last station. Only those in good heart can make this high trip. The Andean Club in Mérida organizes trips to the top and guides will provide all equipment; enquire at the *teleférico* station at the end of Calle 24, beyond Av. 8. Travellers should book in advance (on previous day at or before 0700) for "white" tickets as there is now a quota of 200 people per hour. In the station in Mérida one can buy warm jackets, gloves and caps, although there is a restaurant at the top to which you don't have to leave if you feel the cold—temperatures can be as low as 0°C. At Aguada station you can see the *frailejón* plant and throughout the area there is a great variety and quantity of flora. A description of the Sierra Nevada is included in *Backpacking in Venezuela, Colombia and Ecuador*, published by Bradt Enterprises.

Note The management of the Pico Espejo cable car will not let you walk in the mountains unless you sign a responsibility discharge. You need a permit which must be obtained from the Inparques (National Parks) ranger's office next to the *teleférico* free; a mediocre topographical map is on sale. Permits are not given to single hikers: a minimum of 2 people is required. Camping gas may be bought in Mérida from a household shop near Plaza Bolívar. If camping, remember that the area is between 3,500 and 4,200 metres so acclimatization is necessary as is warm clothing for nighttime. Water purification is also recommended.

Excursions Visits to other resorts near Mérida: to Laguna de Mucubají, Laguna Negra or Pico del Aguila (see page 812). To Plaza Beethoven where a different melody from Beethoven's works is chimed every hour. The Museo de Arte

Moderno on the same square has a nice small collection with paintings by local artists. *Hotel Valle Grande**, D, good, nearby, chalets for 5 or 6 people. To ***Jaji***, 43 km. (good picnic spot en route overlooking Mérida), by *por puesto* (US$1), famous for its colonial architecture, including a nice main square, but over twenty. Tourists can get advice from the Club Andino (P.O. Box 66) or Casa del Turista, La Compalla; Tel.: 3391. Recommended hotel and restaurant *Posada de Jají*, good food. Continuing for 62 km.—narrow, but mostly paved—beyond Jají, the Pan-American Highway is reached (several gas stations on the way). From La Azulita, between Jají and the Pan-American, one can visit La Cueva del Pirata. Through splendid scenery to Lagunilla, with pleasant lakeside restaurant, but the lake is tiny and drying up. Thirty mins. beyond Lagunilla lies the little church of Estanques (seldom open except on Christmas Day) with a stupendous gold colonial altar. Near Estanques is the colonial village of Chiguará (*Posada Colonial Cantarranos*, F, friendly), visited by exchange students; *por puesto* from Mérida, US$0.75.

After Mérida the road passes on through the Chama valley to Lagunilla. Ninety-six km. beyond Mérida comes **Tovar** (population 19,000; *Hotel Junín*, F, *Hostería Sabaneta*, E, private bath), a nice little town with pleasant excursions, whence we can rejoin the Pan-American via Zea or tackle the wild and beautiful old mountain road over La Negra to San Cristóbal. 15 km. from Tovar is Bailadores (*Hotel La Cascada*, D, modern— Wilfredo plays electric organ in the bar on Sat. night, and at Mass on Sun. in the beautiful church, entertaining on both occasions); from Bailadores the road climbs up into the mountains. The *Hotel de Montaña*, E, private bath, Tel.: 077-82401/2, is recommended, 7 km. before La Grita on the road from Mérida. Daily buses between Tovar and La Grita on the old road. **La Grita** is a pleasant town, still not entirely Americanized; Hotels: *La Casona*, F, Carrera 2A, No. 6-69; *Capri*, E, Carrera 3, good value, bargain. Hard to find a reasonable restaurant.

San Cristóbal, capital of Táchira State, is on a plateau 55 km. from the Colombian border, at 830 metres. Average temperature 22°C, population 230,000. The city is on three levels, running N-S: a 1½ km. wide level zone along the Torbes river, which flows S into the Orinoco basin, and two terraces, one of them 200 metres above the river, and 5°C cooler. This, and the La Concordia sector to the S, are the "select" suburbs. The city was founded in 1561, and the Spanish colonial appearance—the appearance only—is preserved. The Cathedral, finished in 1908, had its towers and façade rebuilt in colonial style for the 400th anniversary of the foundation. There is a good road over the mountains, with beautiful Andean views, to San Antonio.

Hotels *De Ferias El Tamá**, D, Av. 19 de Abril, overlooking the town, has an Olympic-size swimming pool; *Korinu*, D, Carrera 6 bis, recommended, with good restaurant; *Bella Vista*, E, Calle 9, esq. Carrera 9; *Círculo Militar*, Av. 19 de Abril, E, all services including swimming pool and gymnasium; *El Cid*, E, Carrera 6, Edificio San Ignacio; *El Parador del Hidalgo*, Calle 7, No. 9-35, E; *Machirí*, E, Calle 7 No. 4-30, bath, hot water, clean, friendly, central, recommended; *Firenze*, Carrera 6, E; *Hamburgo*, Av. Libertador, F, clean; *Horizonte*, F, Av. 5, iced water provided; *Hospedaje El Almendro*, opp. old bus station, E, cheap and homely, near to *El Amparo* restaurant; *Incret*, Av. Libertador, E; *Jardín**, E, Av. Libertador 48; *Motel Las Lomas**, E, Av. Libertador; *Prados del Torbes*, E, Carrera 9, esq. Calle 11; *Ejecutivo*, E, old and basic but clean and central; *Mara*, F, Carrera 4 No. 5-29; *Valencia*, D, Calle 3, No. 4-28; *Americano*, Calle 8, F, basic and good; *del Sur*, F, noisy, no room key provided, near the old bus terminal; *Tropicana*, E, clean, spacious, just across the street behind the old bus terminal (billiard hall next door). There are several cheap hotels on Avenida 6A, just off the central plaza, in F category; *Residencia Hilton*, clean and friendly, is probably the most expensive.

Bank Banco Consolidado (American Express), 5a Av., Edif Torre E.

Launderette in Cada shopping centre next to *Hotel El Tamá*, open 0800-1200, 1400-1800.

Airports for San Cristóbal: at San Antonio (1 hr.) and La Fría (90 mins.).

By Road To Maracaibo, 8 hrs., US$4.50, *por puesto*, US$9.75. To Mérida, US$3.60 by *por puesto* or bus, US$1.80, 4 a day. To Caracas, US$5, 12 hrs. by Llanos route. To Valencia, US$3.65, 10 hrs.; to San Antonio, 2½ hrs. by bus, US$0.50, or *por puesto*, which continues to

816 VENEZUELA

Cúcuta, US$1, stopping at Immigration in both countries, runs every 20 mins. San Cristóbal now has a new bus terminal.

San Antonio, the frontier town (not a tourist attraction), is connected by international bridge with Cúcuta, Colombia, distant about 16 km. (bus US$0.50—in bolívares or pesos—to international bridge), whence you can continue by road or air to Bogotá. Be sure to get your Venezuelan exit stamp from the immigration office on Calle 7, Carrera 9, 10 blocks from the border, or Colombian officials will send you back (unless you are only visiting Cúcuta). Taxi San Antonio-Cúcuta, including stops for all exit and entry formalities, US$3. Once you are in Colombia go straight to the DAS office in Cúcuta, Calle 17, No. 2-60, to complete formalities there (closed on Sundays and holidays). If driving to Colombia, you must have your *carnet de passages* stamped at both the border and the DAS office. (The DAS office at the airport is for air passengers only.) Entry charge, US$1.50. Entering Venezuela in your own car presents no problems as long as you have obtained a visa and *carnet* in advance. You must visit Immigration in town, pay Bs. 5 for a form on which to pay exit tax and have your passport photocopied. Once in Venezuela, you may find that local police are ignorant of documentation required for foreign cars. Thirteen km. N on the Venezuelan side lies the spa of Ureña, with natural hot springs (*Hotel Aguas Calientes**, C, overpriced, private bath, swimming pool).

Hotels At San Antonio: *Don Jorge*, E, a/c dining room expensive; *Táchira*, D, with bath, recommended; *Neveri*, D, Calle 3, No. 3-11, Esq. Carrera 3, private bath, parking nearby, by border; *La Villa*, E, clean, fan; *Los Andes*, E, cheap; *San Antonio*, F, fan, clean, cheap meals available; *Frontera*, not too clean, E; many hotels near town centre.

Exchange, at the Banco de Venezuela on main square. *Casas de cambio* near the international bridge will not all change cheques and some will only change Colombian pesos, not even US dollars cash. The exchange rate for changing bolívares to pesos is better in San Antonio than in Cúcuta.

Colombian Consulate Carrera 6, No. 3-29, for visas, open until 0200.

Airport Has exchange facilities. Taxis run to DIEX (emigration) in town, and on to Cúcuta airport.

Llanos of the Orinoco This area of flat grasslands, 1,000 km. by 320 km., lies between the Andes and the Orinoco River. It is veined by numerous slow running rivers, forested along their banks. The vast flatland is only varied here and there by *mesas*, or slight upthrusts of the land. About 5 million of the country's 6.4 million cattle, many of the Zebu type from Brazil and India, are in the *llanos*, 30% of the country's area, but holding no more than 13% of the population. When the whole plain is periodically under water, the *llaneros* drive their cattle into the hills or through the flood from one *mesa* to another. When the plain is parched by the sun and the savanna grasses become uneatable they herd the cattle down to the damper region of the Apure and Orinoco. Finally they drive them into the valley of Valencia to be fattened for slaughter.

Parts of the area are coming under cultivation. The Guárico dam has created thousands of hectares of fertile land by controlling flood and drought. The *llanos* State of Portuguesa has now the largest cultivated area of any: rice and cotton are now produced.

There are several roads to the *llanos*. Sixteen km. E of Maracay, a good road leads off to San Juan de los Morros, with natural hot springs (see page 804). Later it divides S to the Guárico dam, the *llanos* and Puerto Miranda and E to Valle de la Pascua and El Tigre. Going S, keep an eye open for the egrets, which were almost exterminated early in the century for their feathers, once a valuable export. Crossing the bridge over the River Apure at Puerto Miranda we come to San Fernando de Apure. From there towards Puerto Ayacucho the route is only passable in the dry months of Feb.-May, and with a 4-wheel drive vehicle.

Manfred W. Frischeisen recommends a detour from the Guárico dam: San Fernando road, turn left at Calabozo along a gravel road (being paved) to Paso del Caballo (81 km.). A little trail goes on to Cazorla (85 km.); on the swamps one can see egrets, parrots, alligators, monkeys (and hear howlers). Turn left in Cazorla to Guayabal, back on the main road, 21 km. from San Fernando. From San Fernando, fair, interesting road goes over Guasdualito to San Cristóbal (take spare gasoline). Peter

VENEZUELA 817

Straub recommends taking the bus from San Cristóbal to Guasdualito, then the mail plane to San Fernando, continuing to Cuidad Bolívar. Most travel agents do not know of this method: insist on seeing the timetables.

San Fernando de Apure is the capital of the western llanos. Bus to Caracas, US$5.25, two a day to Barinas. Hotels: *Boulevard*, E, Av. Boulevard; *La Torraca*, E, Paseo Libertador; *La Fuente*, E, Av. Miranda; *Trinacria*, E, Av. Miranda; *El Río*, E, Av. Miranda; *Europa*, F, Paseo Libertador; all with a/c, water spasmodic.

Banco Consolidado for American Express, Av. Miranda, Res. 19 de Abril.

From San Fernando you can drive W towards Barinas, the road is beautiful between Mantecal and Bruzual. In the early morning, many animals and birds can be seen, and in the wet season alligators cross the road. At Bruzual, just S of Puente Nutrias over the Apure river, there are 3 primitive inns (e.g. *Los Llaneros*, F, you eat with the family).

Alternative route from Caracas to Mérida

There is a splendid road to the western llanos of Barinas, from Valencia through **San Carlos**, capital of Cojedes State (uninteresting, *Hotel Italo*, F, Av. Carabobo, a/c, private bath), **Acarigua**, a thriving agricultural centre (*Motel Payara**, D, on road to Guanare, pool, a/c; *Parigua*, D, Calle 30; *Motel Rancho Grande*, D, on road to San Carlos; *Miraflores*, D, swimming pool; *New York*, F; *Las Majaguas*, D, Calle 28), and **Guanare**, a national place of pilgrimage with an old parish church containing the much venerated relic of the Virgin of Coromoto, Patron of Venezuela. Population 32,500 (*Hotel Italia*, D, Carrera 5, No. 19-60, the most expensive; *Internacional Los Cortijos*, D; others, all E, include *Coromoto*, swimming pool; *Motel Portuguesa*, E, a/c, hot water, clean, good restaurant, pool; *Motel Victoria*; *Motel Arpe*; *Betania*).

After the first appearance of the Virgin, Chief Coromoto failed to be baptized, though he did hedge by getting other members of the tribe baptized. When the Virgin reappeared he made a grab at her and told her gruffly to be gone, but she vanished leaving in his hand a likeness of herself on the inner surface of a split stone now on display in the church. For years little attention was paid to the image, and it was only in 1946 that this Virgin was declared the Patron of Venezuela.

The road continues to **Barinas** (population 92,000), the capital of the cattle-raising and oil-rich State of Barinas. Fishing and game-watching excursions into the llanos. The rivers are full of *caribes* (*piranha*) and many kinds of fish good to eat. The local music at *La Terraza* bar near the bus terminal has been recommended; harp *cuatro*, singing, informal and very good.

Hotels *Motel El Cacique*, D, swimming pool; *Valle Hondo**, D, little service; *Bristol**, Av. 23 de Enero, D; *Comercio*, E, Av. Marqués del Pumar, cooking facilities; *Internacional*, E, Calle Arzobispo Méndez; *Motel Turístico Varyna**, D, Av. 23 de Enero; *Plaza*, D, a/c, shower, good restaurant; *Hostería Los Guasimitos*, E, a/c, clean, good restaurant, standard motel, on road to Guanare, swimming pool; *Suine*, quiet, E, with shower, no hot water, restaurant; *Lisboa*, opp. bus station, F, good.

Bank Banco Consolidado (American Express), Av. Libertador con Calle Camejo.

Bus, 4 a day for Mérida, US$1.70, magnificent ride through the mountains, 6 hrs. *Por puesto* costs US$2.10. Bus to Caracas, US$4.10, 8 hrs; to San Antonio, US$2.75. To Acarigua, US$0.75, 3 hrs; San Cristóbal, US$1.25, 4½ hrs. The bus terminal is on the edge of the town.

Airport, with local services and to Caracas (US$13).

From Barinas there is a beautifully scenic road to Apartaderos, in the Sierra Nevada de Mérida (see page 812).

Eastern Venezuela

The eastern part of the North-Eastern Highlands, with summits rising to 2,000 metres, has abundant rainfall in its tropical forest. The western part, which is comparatively dry, has most of the inhabitants and the two main cities, Cumaná and Barcelona.

818 VENEZUELA

Eastern Venezuela, with the Highlands in the NE, the great *llanos* of the Orinoco to the south, and south of the Orinoco again the range of Guayana Highlands, was until quite recently not of much account in the Venezuelan economy. Some coffee and cacao are grown on the eastern slopes of the north-eastern highlands in the tropical forest, but the western slopes are subject to drought. Cattle roam the *llanos*, and the Guayana Highlands produce gold and diamonds. The picture has now been changed, as about 30% of Venezuelan oil now comes from this area. South of the Orinoco vast iron ore deposits are mined. The area can most conveniently be divided into three zones: the oil zone, the Orinoco zone, and the coastal zone.

It is now only five hours from Caracas to Barcelona by road through Caucagua, from which there is a 47-km. road NE to Higuerote, which has a number of beaches, currently the focus of large-scale tourist projects.

Higuerote can also be reached by a road, which is being paved, along the coastal mountain range from Los Caracas (92 km., see page 802)—beautiful views, beaches everywhere, 4-wheel drive vehicles recommended (Higuerote hotels: *Campomar*, D; *Sol Mar*, D). One beach is at La Sabana (turn off after 37 km.); private rooms for rent, San Juan drum (*tambores*) festival at end-June. 4 km. beyond is Caruao, rebuilt in an old style (ask for Josefa, who cooks delicious seafood); follow the road for El Pozo del Cura, a waterfall and pool.

14 km. before Higuerote on the road from Caucagua is Tacarigua de Mamporal, where you can turn off to the Laguna de Tacarigua National Park. The road passes a Tunnel of Vegetation (almost 3 km. long), cocoa plantations, the towns of San José and Río Chico (excellent natural fruit ice-cream). In the fishing village of Tacarigua de la Laguna, you can eat delicious *lebranche* fish; an unmotorized ferry crosses the lagoon, which has many water birds (including flamingoes), to the beach on the Caribbean.

41 km. from Barcelona is Píritu, which has an interesting Franciscan church, and the fishing village of Puerto Píritu (*Casacoima Puerto Píritu**, D).

Barcelona, population 112,000, mean temperature, 27°C, capital of Anzoátegui State, is on the W bank of the Neveri River, 5 km. from the ocean. You can see the ruins of the Casa Fuerte, grim relic of the War of Independence. (Hotels: *Barcelona*, D; *Neveri*, D.) Ships from La Guaira call at **Guanta**, 22 km. away, now connected with the 4-lane highway which goes through Puerto La Cruz and an airport with services to Caracas.

Barcelona has been surpassed commercially by **Puerto La Cruz,** 22 km. away by an asphalted highway skirting the pleasant residential and bathing resort of Lechería. Puerto La Cruz, once a fishing hamlet, is now a thriving town of 180,000 with two oil refineries. Its seaport is also Guanta, with regular lines to U.S. and European ports. Bus to Caracas, US$2.75, 6 hrs.

On the highway from Puerto La Cruz to Barcelona is the Polideportivo sports stadium seating 10,000 people: covered gymnasium, velodrome, tennis, volleyball, and basket-ball courts and two swimming pools. A new Institute of Technology, part of the Universidad del Oriente, is near the stadium.

Hotels *Meliá**, B, on Paseo Colón, luxury hotel with all services and facilities; *Doral Beach**, D, swimming pool, beach, nearer Barcelona than Puerto La Cruz; *Europa*, D, Calle Sucre, esq. Plaza Bolívar; *Neptuno*, D, Paseo Colón, a/c, good restaurant; *San Remo*, D, Calle Simón Rodríguez 55, recommended, near bus station; *Comercio*, D, Calle Maneiro 9; *Riviera**, E, Paseo Colón, not good value, no restaurant; *Sorrento**, E, Av. 5 de Julio, shower, comfortable; *Regis*, D, on sea-front, basic; *Miramar*, Paseo Colón, E, beware of overcharging; *Noray*, Av. Libertad, E with a/c, good friendly; *Playa*, men only, F; *Monte Carlo*, Paseo Colón, F with bath and a/c, unfriendly. Plenty of eating and drinking places on Paseo Colón.

Exchange Banco Consolidado (American Express), Av. 5 de Julio, Local No. 43; Turisol, Am Ex rep., Tel.: 662161/669910. Banco Royal Venezolano. Casa de Cambio: Oficambio Oriente, Calle Maneiro 17, Edif. Latina; also *cambio* in Hotel Riviera.

Post Office and Telecommunications, corner of Freitas and Bolívar, one block from Paseo Colón.

The Coastal Zone Starting east from Puerto La Cruz, the road passes through the most beautiful coastal scenery in Venezuela, the Mochima National Park—a Côte d'Azur without people—to the seaport of Cumaná, 84 km. from Puerto La Cruz. On the way it passes Playa Arapito, the popular palm-fringed

VENEZUELA

beach at Playa Colorado with its red sands, 26 km. E of Puerto La Cruz; *por puesto* US$0.60; there are buses and it is easy to hitch. Boys sell oysters on the beach; there is a restaurant. Camping is allowed for a small fee. Also Playa Santa Cruz further E. From Mochima, a village in the Park, beyond Santa Fe (ask at police station for the only house that rents rooms), boats can be taken around the islands and to lonely beaches—very beautiful; fares negotiable, about US$25 per day for 6 people.

Cumaná, population 155,000, capital of Sucre State, founded 1520, is the oldest Hispanic city in South America. It straddles both banks of the Manzanares, 1½ km. from Puerto Sucre. The castle of San Antonio is worth a visit, although it has been damaged by an earthquake and is being restored, and there are good walks along the tree-lined Manzanares; San Luis beach, short local bus ride, recommended, but the water is somewhat dirty. Cumaná has an important sardine canning industry. Airport. Average temperature 27°C. Car ferry to Margarita Island. Famous for its carnival. A new museum was built in 1974 to commemorate the 150th anniversary of the battle of Ayacucho; mainly portraits, relics and letters of Bolívar and Sucre. There is also a maritime museum (Museo del Mar) with good exhibits of tropical marine life, at the old airport, Av. Universidad, open Fri.-Sun. 0900-1200, 1400-1800.

Hotels *Cumanagoto**, C, Av. Universidad, swimming pool, beach; *Los Bordones**, C, Final Av. Universidad, 8 km. from the bus station, recommended, beautifully situated on a good beach with good food and a swimming pool; *Villa Mar*, D, Av. Universidad, clean, comfortable, but all facilities closed, inc. restaurant; these three are a long way from the centre of town. *Gran Hotel*, D, Av. Universidad, beach, mid-way between *Cumanagoto* and town centre; *Master*, E, Boulevard Urdaneta, Pasaje Tobía; *Minerva*, D, clean, modern, Av. Cristóbal Colón, US$1 taxi ride from centre; *Savoia*, D, Av. Perimetral; *Turismo Guaiqueri*, Av. Bermúdez 26, D, comfortable, clean, a/c, bath, friendly, no restaurant; *El Río*, F, Av. Bermúdez, a/c, bath, phone, reasonable restaurant; *América*, E, Calle Comercio, Edif. Papín; *Residencias Trevi*, E, with bath and fan, facing airport on Av. Universidad, 2 km. from San Luis beach. *Miranda*, F with fan, but share bathroom, clean and friendly; *Mariño*, E, near centre on Av. Mariño with Junín, private bath, a/c, clean; *Astoria*, F with bath, clean and friendly; *Hospedaje La Gloria*, opposite Sta. Inés church, F.

Restaurants Good food at *El Colmao* restaurant in the centre as well as *El Teide* (seafood); *Parrilla Vittorio*, *Parrilla Ribera* on Av. Las Palomas, *El Bucanero; Fuente de Soda Monumental*. Lobster recommended at *Jardín de Sport. El Ilustre*, Av. Humbolt (opp. Plaza Sucre), for sandwiches, hamburgers, juices; *Pastelería Sucre*, Calle Mariño, breakfasts, cakes, coffee.

Bank Banco Consolidado, Av. Bermúdez. Perimetral. Edif. Ajounián.

Panamanian Consulate in a one-way street, next to Grupo Escolar José Silvero Córdova in Parcelamiento Miranda Sector D, Tel.: 663525; take a taxi.

Bus *Por puesto* to Puerto La Cruz, US$1.50, 1¼ hrs. To Güiria (see page 821), US$2.50 (5 hrs.). To Caracas, US$2.75-5.50 depending on company (7 hrs.), frequent service; 4 daily to Ciudad Guayana and Ciudad Bolívar (7 hrs.)

Excursion The Parque Nacional Cueva del Guácharo (see page 821) can be visited from Cumaná by taking a daily bus at 0730 hrs. to Caripe (US$1.75, 4 hrs.) or frequent *por puestos* (US$3.50, try bargaining, 2 hrs.). 44 km. East of Cumaná is the beautiful beach of Cachamaure , on the Golfo de Cariaco. To the Araya Peninsula, either by road, turning off the Cumaná-Carúpano road at Cariaco: the road on the peninsula soon becomes very rough; last chance to eat at Chacopata; or by ferry Cumaná-Araya (return ferries haphazard and difficult to get on as more cars than spaces). *Hotel Turístico* in Araya, E, with bar, restaurant, discotheque.

The road goes on to the port of **Carúpano,** on the Paría Peninsula. (The coastal route from Cumaná to Carúpano is beautiful, first passing the Gulf of Cariaco, then crossing to the shores of the Caribbean). It is famous throughout Venezuela for its pre-Lenten Carnival celebrations, and becomes a focus for tourists at that time. Population 80,000; airport.

Hotels *San Francisco*, F, Av. Juncal 87A (try the mussels: *mejillones*); *Bologna*, F, a/c, owner speaks German, recommended; *El Yunque*, E, Av. Perimetral, beach; *Lilma*, E, Av. Independencia 161, good restaurant; *Victoria**, E, Av. Perimetral, beach, swimming pool; *Boulevard*, D; *Carúpano*, F.

Bus to Caracas, Responsable de Venezuela, US$4.75, 8 hrs; Cumaná, US$3.

820 VENEZUELA

10 km. E of Carúpano is the fishing village of El Morro de Puerto Santo, in itself not very interesting but in a beautiful setting. On the coastal drive W of Carúpano are Cereza (famed for its basket-making) and Guaca, where clams packed with peppers are sold.

Margarita Island, off the N coast, is a popular holiday and weekend resort. Properly speaking, it is one island whose two sections are linked by the spit of land which separates the sea from the Laguna Arestinga. Most of its people live in the developed eastern part; the western part, the Peninsula de Macanao, hotter and more barren, is the roaming place of wild deer, goats, hares and the occasional huntsman. The entrance to the Peninsula de Macanao is guarded by a pair of hills known as Las Tetas de María Guevara, a National Monument covering 1,670 hectares. The climate is exceptionally good but rain is scanty. Water is piped from the mainland. The roads are good.

Most of the hotels are at **Porlamar** (22,500 people), 11 km. from the airport and about 28 km. from Punta de Piedras (where most of the ferries dock, *por puesto*, US$0.60); it has a magnificent cathedral. Not far N lie the capital, **La Asunción** (8,000 people), full of colonial buildings: the Castle of Santa Rosa, with a famous bottle dungeon, and a cathedral whose Virgin wears robes covered with pearls (*por puesto*, Porlamar-La Asunción, US$0.25). Further N lie the fishing port of Puerto Fermín, the windswept beach of El Agua with a tremendously powerful surf, and Manzanillo, peaceful and charming but the water gets deep rather suddenly. The bay of Juan Griego, to the W, is also attractive. NE is the picturesque Pedro González with its *mirador* on a sleepy little bay. To the S lies La Guardia; W of this town a long narrow dyke of broken sea-shells stretches over 20 km. to the Peninsula of Macanao: on its right a spotlessly clean long beach, on its left the lagoon. At the far end is a cluster of fishermen's huts with landing stages from which motor boats take visitors on trips through the labyrinth of canals in the heart of the lagoons. Margarita Island has splendid beaches: long white stretches of sand bordered by palms, but rather hot, with little shade (sunscreen essential), except at El Agua, where there are palm trees. The beach opposite *Hotel Bella Vista* in Porlamar is crowded with foreign tourists; for a more Venezuelan atmosphere go NW to Pampatar (*por puesto* US$0.10) where there are a number of quieter beaches. A full-scale model of Columbus' *Santa María* is used for taking tourists on trips.

The islanders are mainly occupied in fishing and fibre work, such as hammocks and straw hats. Margarita is a duty-free zone and goods of all kinds can be bought cheaply; Venezuelan shoppers go there in droves. The best way of getting round the island is by hiring a car, an economic proposition for any number above one. There are *por puesto* services over most of the island, most leaving from within a few blocks of the main square in Porlamar.

Hotels at Porlamar *Bella Vista**, Av. Santiago, B-A, swimming pool, beach; *Margarita Concorde**, A, pool, beach; *Boulevard*, C, Calle Marcano; *Real Flamingo**, D; *Caribbean*, Via El Morro, D; pool, beach; *For You**, C, recommended; *Le Parc**, E, pool; *Colibrí*, Av. Santiago Mariño, C; *Bahía*, E, beach; *Dos Primos*, Calle Nariño entre Zamora y San Nicolás, E, clean and modern, recommended; on the Boulevard, *Brasilia*, F, quiet, clean; *Central*, E; *Indian*, F without bath. *Cardón*, E, opposite old airport at Playa Cardón, peaceful, good rooms and restaurant, swimming pool, diving and snorkelling trips organized; *Evang*, D; *Granada*, D; *Gran Avenida*, D; *Internacional*, D; *María Luisa**, E, beach; *Chez David*, E, a/c, on beach, modern; *Evdama*, holiday flats with parking; *Vista Mar*, D, Urb. Bella Vista, on the way to El Morro, beach; *Punto Libre*, D; *Tama*, E (more with a/c, hot water, TV, etc.), very nice: *Paseo Rómulo Gallegos*, beach; *Porlamar*, D; *Marítimo*, E, Calle Maneiro Este 6; *Nueva Casa*, F with bathroom and fan, clean and friendly.

Café de París, outside *Hotel For You* is a good meeting place; discotheque for singles (the only good one), *Village Club*.

Bank Banco Consolidado (American Express), Boulevard Guevara with Calle San Nicolás.

Communications Easily reached by air from Caracas (US$10), or by air or ferry from Puerto La Cruz or Cumaná to Punta de Piedras. (Airport: General Santiago Marino, between Palamar and Punta de Piedras; taxi US$4). Ferry boats leave Puerto La Cruz for the island at 0600, 1300 and 2000 (4 hrs., US$4.60 first class, US$2.70 second) and from Cumaná at 0700 and 1600; the *Gran Cacique II* is a hydrofoil from Cumaná taking only 2 hrs., US$3; (0730 and 1600), compared with 3½ hrs. on the ferry; the *Gran Cacique I* from Puerto La Cruz takes 2½ hrs., US$7; return from Punta de Piedras at 0800, 1200, 1600 and 2000 for Puerto La Cruz and at 0700 and 1800 (ferry),

VENEZUELA 821

1030 and 1730 (hydrofoil) for Cumaná (check all ferry times in advance). There is also a ferry from Carúpano to Porlamar (near *Hotel Concorde*), US$4. Several bus companies in Caracas sell through tickets (US$6) from Caracas to Porlamar, arriving about midday.

From Puerto La Cruz a toll road goes inland, skirting Barcelona. At Km. 52 (where there is a restaurant) a road forks left to (near) Santa Bárbara (airport) and goes on to Jusepín, Quiriquire, and Caripito, all Lagovén oil camps.

Maturín, capital of Monagas State, an important commercial centre, is 16 km. beyond Jusepín. Population 152,000.

Hotels *El Cacique*, D, Av. Bolívar; *Pensión El Nacional* and *Latino*, both E, are recommended as simple and clean. Also *Emperador*, E, on Av. Bolívar; *Hostería Juanico*, D, swimming pool; *Friuli*, E, Carrera 9 with Calle 30; *Trinidad*, E, clean, English speaking, recommended; *Europa*, E, recommended as being as good as the *Trinidad* but with larger rooms; *Astrolobia*, E, good food, near bus station; *Paris*, D, Av. Bolívar; *Tamanaco*, E, is reasonable; *Mallorca*, E, Calle Mariño, reasonable with good food; *Comercio*, E with bath, not too clean, English spoken, central; *Asturias*, F, with cheap restaurant which serves excellent rice pudding. All hotel rooms have private bathroom and a/c.

Bank Banco Consolidado (American Express), Av. Raúl Leoni, Edif. D'Amico.

Transport Air services to Caracas (US$12), and to Ciudad Bolívar (Aeropostal, US$7, 20 mins.). Buses leave three times a day for Caracas from the central bus terminal, 2030, 2200 and 2245 hrs. (US$3.75, 8 hrs.); buses for Ciudad Guayana (US$3.75) and El Dorado leave from the terminus near the airport. No bus services to Puerto La Cruz or Barcelona; only *por puestos* at US$3.80. *Por puestos* only to Ciudad Bolívar. Colectivos Nos. 1, 5 and 6 to and from the airport (US$0.10) with a five-minute walk from the road. Bus US$0.05. Taxis from the Reponsable de Venezuela office will try to charge much more. The bus leaves from the main road outside the airport when going into town.

There are no exchange facilities in the airport except at the Aeropostal desk or the bar in the departure lounge, and they give a very bad rate.

In Santa Bárbara can be bought the native *chinchorros*, hammocks made by hand of woven *moriche* palm leaves, decorated with coloured yarn. They can also be found in Tucupita (see page 825). They "give" when you lie on them and do not absorb moisture when used on the beach. Very good for camping.

Just beyond Jusepín an unpaved 32-km. road, left, joins the Maturín-Cumaná road; 30 km. NW is San Francisco, from which a branch road runs 22½ km. NE to **Caripe**, a small town set in a mountain valley. 12 km. away is the remarkable **Cueva del Guácharo** National Monument; open 0700-1700 hrs., entrance US$0.30. (A bus from Cumaná to Caripe takes 4 hrs. and costs US$1.75, or take the *por puesto*, 2 hrs., US$3; from Maturín, take a *por puesto* from the bus terminal to Caripe, US$2, 2 hrs., and ask the driver to carry on to the Cave, only US$0.05 more; if staying in Caripe, take the Caracas bus at 0800 at *San José Hotel* to the Cave for nothing). The cave was discovered by Humboldt, and has since been penetrated 8 km. along a small, crystal-clear stream. First come the caves in which live about 30,000 of *guácharos* (oil birds) with an in-built radar system for sightless flight. Their presence supports a variety of wildlife in the cave: blind mice, fish and crabs in the stream, yellow-green plants, crickets, ants, etc. For two hours at dusk (about 1900) the birds pour out of the cave's mouth, continuously making the clicking sounds of their echo-location system, coming back at dawn with their crops full of the oily fruit of certain local palms. Through a very narrow entrance is the *Cueva del Silencio* (Cave of Silence), where you can hear a pin drop. About 2 km. in is the *Pozo del Viento* (Well of the Wind). No backpacks, torches (flashlights), cameras, etc. allowed in the caves (but tape recorders are permitted). Guides are compulsory (US$0.10); permits and special equipment are needed to go further than 1½ km. into the caves. The streams are now bridged, but there is still quite a lot of water around; wear old clothes and be prepared to take off your shoes and socks. In the wet season it is very muddy, and tours into the cave may be shortened. (Hotels at Caripe: *Samán*, excellent value and atmosphere, good restaurant; *Caripe*, F; *Venecia*, D; *Guáchero*, E) There is a huge *samán* tree in purple glory when the orchids which cover it bloom in May.

There is an interesting journey from Maturín to **Güiria** by bus, US$3, 6 hrs. (Also flights from Isla de Margarita or Tucupita each morning, US$5.50, best booked in advance). Güiria is very hot and dress is more casual than is common elsewhere. (*Hotel Nayade*, F. The general store opposite is helpful with travel information. There are a couple of small places to eat on the main square.) In one of the coves E of Güiria (exactly which one is not known) Spaniards of Columbus' crew made the first recorded European landing on the continent on August 5, 1498, and took formal possession the following day.

A good excursion from Güiria is to **Macuro**, a village of 1,000 people on the tip of the Paria Peninsula. It is accessible only by boat, being surrounded on its landward sides by jungle. Boats leave Güiria daily at 1000 (US$2.10, take protection against sun), returning 0530, taking 1½-2 hrs., passing dense jungle which reaches down to the sea, and deserted, palm-fringed beaches.

822 VENEZUELA

Macuro is friendly, with a good beach, a few understocked shops, one restaurant, but no hotel (easy to camp or sling your hammock somewhere). Eduardo (who speaks English, French and German) is planning to open a museum of the history of the area; he is knowledgeable about trips into the jungle. Boats may be hired to explore the coast. (Moshe Pinsly, Israel).

You can visit the Orinoco delta from Güiria; there are occasional motor boats trading between Güiria and **Pedernales** in the delta. The trip takes about 5 hrs., check for boats at the harbour or the *Hotel Fortuna*. 3 weekly flights Güiria-Pedernales, daily flights to Tucupita (US$10). Pedernales is a small village only a few km. from the south-western point of Trinidad. It is only accessible by boat from Güiria, Tucupita (much easier—page 826), or contraband boats from Trinidad costing perhaps US$200. (Unless you avoid Trinidadian or Venezuelan immigration controls you will find this method both difficult and very risky.) Only one hotel, *Gran Arturo*, F, very basic, bar and restaurant, take your own hammock. For a shower, ask Jesús, who runs a fish-freezing business. Only Indians live in the northern part of the village. Boat trip to Tucupita recommended as the boat stops in some of the Indian villages, where you can buy the best hammocks (*chinchorros*) and some beautiful carved animal figures made of balsa wood (see also page 826).

Continuing straight on from Km. 52, the road passes W of **Anaco** (*Motel Bowling Anaco*, D; *Motel Canaima*, D; *Internacional*, D). It has an airport, is an important centre for oil-well service contracting companies. Beyond Anaco a branch road leads to the oilfields of San Joaquín and San Roque.

The main road passes near Cantaura, a market town, and goes on to **El Tigre** (Hotels: *Arichuna*, D; *Caribe*, E; *Internacional Gran Hotel*, D, swimming pool, night club; *Tamanaco*, E; *Santa Cruz*, F; nearby Chilean restaurant serves excellent Chilean food and salads), and El Tigrito (*Hotel Rancho Grande*, D); two important trading centres within 20 km. of one another.

About 8 km. along the road is San Tomé (airport), the eastern headquarters of Menevén, the former Mene Grande oil company.

From El Tigre a good asphalt road leads off to Caracas; the one we are following leads, straight and flat, 120 km. over the *llanos* to the Angostura bridge over the Orinoco to Ciudad Bolívar, 282 km. from Puerto La Cruz.

The Guayana Highlands, lying S of the Orinoco River, constitute half of Venezuela. They rise, in rounded forested hills and narrow valleys, to flat topped tablelands on the borders of Brazil. These lands are very sparsely populated; but the savannas (interspersed with semi-deciduous forest), would make better cattle country than the *llanos*. So far, communications have been the main difficulty, but a road has now been opened to Santa Elena de Uairen on the Brazilian frontier (see page 828). This road can be followed to Manaus, and thence, by a suitable vehicle, to Brasília and southern Brazil. The area is Venezuela's largest gold and diamond source, but its immense reserves of iron ore, manganese and bauxite are of far greater economic importance.

Ciudad Bolívar, on the S bank of the Orinoco, is 400 km. from its delta and 640 by road from Caracas. Average temperature 29°C, but a cool and refreshing breeze usually springs up in the evening. It still has much colonial building but is changing rapidly. Population 115,000. River craft bring to the city the *balatá*, chicle, tonka beans, skins, gold and diamonds in which it trades. It stands by the narrows of the Orinoco, with its Cathedral, on a small hill, and the Zanuro hill fort (1902), on another hill in the centre, dominating the city.

The narrows, not more than 300 metres wide, gave the town its old name of Angostura. It was here that Bolívar came after defeat to reorganize his forces, and the British Legionnaires joined him; it was at Angostura that he was declared President of that Gran Colombia which he had yet to build, and which was to fragment before his death. When the town was still known as Angostura a physician invented the famous bitters there in 1824; the factory moved to Port of Spain in 1875.

It is a busy place, with a constant coming and going of the most varied rivercraft. It has a floating pontoon dock where ocean-going cargo boats discharge. A walk along the river bank is recommended at dusk when the sun is setting. Launches take passengers across the river.

You can buy baskets and items made by the Indians. It is also the best place in Venezuela for anything made of gold. There are beautiful hand-made charms for charm bracelets and, most typical of all, the Venezuelan orchid, made by hand, of red, yellow and green gold. The gold orchid pin or earrings, or a gold nugget (known as *cochano*), are the best souvenirs of Venezuela. There are many jewellers on Pasaje Guayana, which runs off Paseo Orinoco. A feature is the netting of *sapoara*, a delicious fish 30 to 35 cm. long which pours from the inlets when the river begins to swell in late June at the start of the rainy season and swims up stream to spawn. During its short season this is the favourite dish of the town.

Hotels *Don Salo*, Av. Bolívar, nr. Av. Táchira, D, very good apart from a disappointing restaurant; difficult to find, though quite near the airport; *Gran Hotel Bolívar**, Paseo Orinoco, D, surly staff, reports of theft, comfortable, good restaurant; *La Cumbre*, Av. 5 de Julio, good view of town but rather run down, D, without food; *Valentina*, D, Av. Maracay, far from centre, a/c; *Canaima*, E, Av. Upata (even further from centre), noisy, a/c, bath, clean; *La Redoma*, E, Av. Upata; *Del Sur*, D, Prolongación Paseo Orinoco; *Flórida*, E, Av. Táchira, *Morichal*, D and *Táchira*, E, both also on Av. Táchira; *República*, E, Av. República; *Mimo*, E, on the corner of Paseo Orinoco and Calle Amazonas, not secure, some rooms run down, unfriendly, but superb views of the river and suspension bridge and sunsets; *Residencias Delicias*, near *Mimo*, good value; *Italia*, on the riverfront, recommended except a bit run down, F, a/c and bath, a few single rooms with fan, no bath, food excellent, try *dulce de merey* for dessert; *Sicilia*, Paseo Orinoco, F, with shower, a/c, friendly, recommended, view of Orinoco; *Pensión Panamericana*, Calle Rocía 6, F, clean, good restaurant; *Pensión Boyacá*, Calle Babilonia, F, central, basic, friendly, a bit grubby, one shower for all, hourly rentals; *Río*, Paseo Orinoco, F, with a/c, friendly, clean, bar and restaurant; *Brasilia*, D, ¾ km. from bus terminal; *Terminal y Adriana*, E, Av. Moreno de Mendoza, near bus terminal, friendly. It is often difficult to find rooms in hotels here. For the cheaper hotels, take a red bus from the airport to Paseo Orinoco; at the eastern end there are many to choose from.

Restaurants *Alfonso*, Av. Maracay; *Almanola*, Av. Cumaná; *La Cabaña*, Paseo Meneses; *Las Cibeles*, Paseo Orinoco; *La Cumbre*, Av. 5 de Julio; *La Paragua*, Av. La Mariquita; *Mirador*, prettily situated on the Orinoco, relaxed atmosphere, good at the expensive end of the menu; *La Playa*, Paseo Orinoco 84, fish. Chinese restaurant on Av. Upata, opp. *Hotel Canaima*, good, open late. Cheap food at the market at the east end of Paseo Orinoco, need to bargain. Restaurants are closed on Sundays.

Museum The Museo Soto on the outskirts of the town has works by Venezuela's José Rafael Soto and other artists, open Tues.-Sun. 1000-1800, good. Museum at Casa del Correo del Orinoco, modern art and some exhibits of history of the city, including the printing press of the newspaper which spread the cause of independence; Tues. Sat. 0900-1200, 1600-1900, Sun. 0900-1200. Has free town map and booklet on Ciudad Bolívar (better than Tourist Office).

Taxis Under US$1 (Bs. 15 to 20) to virtually anywhere in town.

Bank Banco Consolidado (American Express), Edif. Pinemar, Av. Andrés Bello, Centro Comercial Canaima; Banco Royal Venezolano (Calle Orinoco 38) and Banco Mercantil y Agrícola (Av. Jesús Soto); show marginal interest in changing dollars. No banks will cash cheques. Filanbanco handles Visa tranactions.

Post Offices Av. Táchira, 15 mins' walk from centre.

Tourist Offices The small offices at the airport and the bus station in particular are very friendly and helpful. You will need a map: the town has a rather confusing layout.

Airport Served by Avensa, and Aeropostal which flies 4 times a week to Sta. Elena de Uairen for connections to Manaus and Brazil. Also flights to Tucupita. Minibuses to town centre and to bus station (in other direction). Three flights daily to Caracas (US$13).

Buses Several daily to Caracas 7 hrs., US$4, and to the coast: to Puerto La Cruz, US$2, 4½ hrs.; to Cumaná, US$2.75; Tumeremo US$2.80; Tumeremo bus through to El Dorado US$3, 3 daily. To Santa Elena de Uairen direct with Línea Orinoco, US$8, 18 hours. To Ciudad Guayana every 30 mins. from 0700 by Expresos Guayanera, US$1, 1½ hrs., *por puesto*, US$2.25, 1½ hrs. Terminal at junction of Av. República and Av. Sucre. Bus to Caicara, 7½ hrs., including 2 ferry crossings.

Bird-watching expeditions may be made into nearby swamps; look out for the primitive *hoatzi*; monkeys can also be seen.

Motorists travelling West from Ciudad Bolívar to Mérida can either go across the *llanos* or via El Tigre, Valle de la Pascua and El Sombrero, which route requires no ferry crossings and has more places with accommodation, see pages 816, and 822. Manfred W. Frischeisen suggests the following route across the *llanos* to Ciudad Bolívar: from Chaguaramas on the road to Valle de la Pascua, turn S through Las Mercedes and flat cattle land to **Cabruta** (179 km., daily bus to Caracas, US$4, there is no ferry to Puerto Ayacucho, but you can take a barge, US$10; 3-day trip, fix price with boat captain. Ask for Coronel Tefero about travelling on the river). There is a small hotel, infested with rats and cockroaches, but better accommodation in **Caicara**—ferry from Cabruta, about 1 hr., US$2 for car, passengers US$0.35. Hotels: *Diamante*; *Central*, E; *Italia*, F; *Buenos*

824 VENEZUELA

Aires, E; *Miami,* D; *Venezuela,* F; *Bella Guayana,* F. By bus from Caicara to Ciudad Bolívar, US$4, on a paved road which crosses the rivers Cuchivero (ferry, US$1.50) and Caura (ferry, US$2.50), takes 7 hrs. An all-weather road is under construction from Caicara to Puerto Ayacucho; the present road is only passable in the dry season, and although interesting for the Indians and the mining nearby, it is extremely hard going. There is a regular jeep service to Puerto Ayacucho, US$6. Ask for Asociación Civil de Conductores. There are two flights a week (Wed. and Sat.) to Puerto Ayacucho. Cargo boats take three days to Puerto Ayacucho but are unwilling to take passengers; better from Cabruta (see above).

Puerto Ayacucho is the capital of the Federal Territory of Amazonas, which has an area of 175,000 square kilometres and a population of only 15,000, a large proportion of whom live in Puerto Ayacucho. It is 800 km. up the Orinoco from Ciudad Bolívar, deep in the wild, but no direct boats do the five day journey up river. The town has daily air service (*Hotel Amazonas,* B; *Italia,* E, with fan, run down; *Residencia Internacional,* F; *Maguari,* F, friendly, will store luggage, recommended, next door to a restaurant.)

Tobogán Tours, Av. Río Negro 44, Puerto Ayacucho (Tel.: (48)21700), owner Pepe Jaimes, arranges trips on the Orinoco, to Indian villages and to the Paraguena river through waterfalls, untouched jungle with fascinating wildlife. A jungle camp is soon to be opened.

Beyond Puerto Ayacucho are rapids, but smaller launches on the upper Orinoco can reach the Casiquiare and the Río Negro which flows into the Amazon. It is very difficult to find boats willing to take passengers. For information on travelling by boat to Manaus, ask for Alejandro. In 1955/56 two Americans successfully canoed to Amazonia, continuing from the Amazon by way of the Tapajós, Paraguay and Paraná. The trip took about one year. The journey up the Amazon to the Casiquiare and Orinoco has also been successfully negotiated by a hovercraft with a British crew. Trips up the Amazon tributaries are organized in Caracas by Italcambio (Tel.: 820611) and Turismo Colorama (Tel.: 337326) otherwise it is impossible to go without a permit, e.g. for a scientific expedition. Permits are available from the Bureau of Indian Affairs (ORAI) in Caracas, or in Puerto Ayacucho itself. Buy your provisions here; nobody lives on the Casiquiare despite what the maps say. Do not travel alone. If you want to cross the border into Colombia at Puerto Ayacucho or further north at Puerto Carreño, you can expect difficulties with the local authorities. You will probably be asked for proof of how much money you have and where you are going; some travellers have had to obtain Colombian visas to enter the country when only a passport and ticket out of the country were strictly necessary. Money, offered tactfully, might help.

For trips anywhere from Puerto Ayacucho check at the central service station. Try Tobogán Tours (see above). Some recommended trips include by *por puesto* to Samariapo and waterfalls at Tobogán de la Selva. From Samariapo boat to Isla de Ratán and Santa Rosa; also to Vichada and Santa Rita and thence bus to Villavicencio (Colombia). From Puerto Ayacucho there is a cargo boat to Puerto Páez, 4 hrs., for crossing to Colombia. Check with Guardia Nacional and insist on exit stamp (they are strangely reluctant). Ferry to Puerto Carreño US$0.75. By air to San Fernando de Apure, US$15. Jeep from Caicara, US$8.

Manfred Frischeisen writes: coming from Ciudad Bolívar, after 73 km. you get to La Encrucijada (junction). To the left is the freeway to Ciudad Guayana (37 km.); straight on is the road to Upata via the Paso Carnachi (Caroní ferry); to the right is the road to Ciudad Piar (97 km.) and the iron ore mountain (Cerro Bolívar). Following this route through typical Guayana landscape you reach the village of La Paragua (107 km.) on a good, paved road. If you like adventure and untouched nature, take two ferries crossing the Río Paragua, towards El Paúl (4-wheel drive vehicles Dec.-May). There is usually transport available. From El Paúl you can get a ride towards the nearest river to Canaima, which you can cross on a *curiara* (passengers only), and from there hike about 15 km. to Canaima. Alternatively, from La Encrucijada, on the right hand road (in the direction of La Paragua) turn left after 8 km., past enormous black rocks, on to an almost hidden trail. After a further 2 km. is the Cueva del Elefante, where precolumbian relics were found and rock paintings can be seen. Following the track (10 km.) one comes to Playa Blanca on the Río Caroní, where miners dive for gold and diamonds. Mario Venarusso does boat trips.

In an area rich in natural resources 105 km. down-river from Ciudad Bolívar an entirely new metropolis, known as **Ciudad Guayana,** is still being built. It is forging into the one the four separate centres of San Félix, Palúa, Puerto Ordaz and Matanzas. Its population is already more than a quarter of the planned million, on the south bank of the Orinoco on both sides of the Caroní river before it spills into the Orinoco. East of the Caroní are the commercial port of **San Félix** (extensive work in progress to make a riverside walk and park) and the Palúa iron-ore terminal of the railway from El Pao. Crossing the Caroní by the 470-metre concrete bridge we come to **Puerto Ordaz** (airport), the iron-ore loading port connected by rail with the famous Cerro Bolívar open-cast iron mine (see below). The iron-tinted waterfall, which looks like a beerfall, in the pretty Parque Cachamay is worth a visit. To the west are the government-owned Siderúrgica del Orinoco whose production is being raised to 4.8m tonnes of steel a year, and an

VENEZUELA 825

aluminium plant, Venalum. Just up the Caroní is the Macagua hydroelectric plant with a capacity of 370,000 kw.; there are some truly beautiful cataracts called Salto Llovizna as you enter the grounds (known as Parque La Llovizna, reached by boat from *Hotel Intercontinental Guayana*, or by bus from San Félix most of the way, then hitch). Higher up the river is the Guri dam and hydroelectric undertaking with a capacity of 1,750,000 kw., being raised in its final stages to 6 million kw. (The trip to Guri takes 90 minutes by taxi; for a conducted tour (0900, 1030, 1400) phone Edelca, Puerto Ordaz 20-80-66 (Relaciones Institucionales del Guri); the area gets very full during holidays, Easter or carnival. *Por puesto* from Ciudad Bolívar, Route 70, US$12 one way; for return, ask at Alcabala Río Claro (gatehouse) if they can get you a free lift.) About 3 km. away, across bare savanna, is an area reserved for smaller industries; half a dozen plants are already built.

Hotels *Intercontinental Guayana**, Parque Punta Vista, C-B, all facilities, swimming pool; *Dos Ríos*, E, swimming pool, Av. Las Américas; *El Rasil**, D, Centro Cívico, with all comforts, swimming pool, good; *Embajador*, D, Carrera La Urbana; *Saint George*, E, on same street; *Tepuy*, E, a/c, Carrera Upata, Edif. Arichuna; *La Guayana*, F, Av. Las Américas, clean, a/c, no hot water; *La Habana*, same street, E; *Residencias Puerto Ordaz*, Vía Caracas, E with bath; *Jardín*, F, Italian run, friendly, fan, will store luggage, not too safe. Many cheaper hotels in San Félix, the historical town, have been removed or closed down in the restoration works. Only *Aguila* (D) and *Yoli* (F, no hot water, otherwise o.k.) in San Félix have decent restaurants. It is difficult to find hotels because of the influx of workers, who live in them for lack of other housing.

Restaurants In Puerto Ordaz: *Hotel Guayana Restaurant*, under different management from hotel, good service but expensive; near *Hotel Guayana* are *Casa del Roti*, Calle Tumeremo, good, inexpensive, *Siria-Lebanon*, Calle Ciudad Piar, Arab food, *Archie's Soda Fountain*, Tumeremo below *Casa del Roti*, and beyond is a Chinese restaurant; the market at the intersection of Tumeremo and Guasipati has many cheap food stalls; two *areparías* on Vía Las Américas above *Hotel Guayana*, and reasonable restaurants at corners of Las Américas with Calle Upata and Calle El Palmar, further up the hill. More expensive on Las Américas is *Rincón Bavaria* (German); two steak restaurants on Calle La Urbana (one next to cinema is best); Italian restaurants: *Paolos*, Calle Guasipati, *Romanino's*, Calle Ciudad Piar and, opposite but cheaper and less good, *Mario's*; *The Key Club*, via Caracas (opp. Banco Royal), good seafood, expensive; good seafood also at *Porrua*, but further from centre.

Car Hire Hertz, Puerto Ordaz, rents 4-wheel drive vehicles, US$25 a day with unlimited mileage. This is the best way to visit the Cerro Bolívar mine and Guri dam.

Banks Banco Consolidado (American Express), Calle Urbana, Edif. Don Andrés, Banco Royal Venezolano and Banco Provincial at Puerto Ordaz.

Transport Bus station at San Félix (can be a dangerous place). Bus from Ciudad Guayana to El Dorado US$3.75, 5 hrs., 3 times daily; jeep to Santa Elena, US$10.50, 12 hrs.; *por puesto* to Ciudad Bolívar US$2.25; to Maturín US$3.75, 3 hrs., 0800 every day; to Caracas, US$4.50, 10½ hrs.

General Airport, with daily flights to Caracas (US$14), walk 600 metres to main road for buses to San Félix or Puerto Ordaz; taxi to centre or bus station, US$3. Minibuses in town are fast, frequent and cheap; fare San Félix-Puerto Ordaz, US$0.25—0.35; buses run until about 2100. A stadium. The Casa Machupicchu, Calle Guasipati, sells a city map for US$0.70.

Excursions To Cerro Bolívar mine, take a *por puesto* or hitchhike to Ciudad Piar, or go with guided tour organized by Ferrominera Orinoco at their headquarters building in Ciudad Guayana. Tours are free, and leave at 0930 and 1400. To visit industries in the area, ask at the Corporación Venezolana de Guayana, Departmento de Relaciones Públicas.

From San Félix or Puerto Ordaz take a *por puesto* down the Orinoco to Los Castillos (1 hr., US$0.80, difficult to get there by boat). It is possible to camp on the beach. Candes Tours run an excursion from Puerto Ordaz but only if there are four people. There are two old forts here: one on a huge rock near the water, the other on top of a hill and both in good condition. A tiny village lies at their feet. It is said to have been here that Sir Walter Raleigh's son was killed in battle while searching for El Dorado. From Los Barrancos, on the N bank of the Orinoco, opposite San Félix, *curiaras* and other boats can be taken to the delta; settle prices before setting out, take hammock, mosquito net and repellant, and canned food (in the rainy season, take a raincoat).

Alan Rosenberg, of Homebush, Australia, writes as follows: "The most interesting excursion I was able to make in Venezuela was to **Tucupita** in the Orinoco delta. Transport from Ciudad Guayana is available, and the roads are asphalted. Tucupita is a river town, and one can bargain with the many boat operators for river trips through country of outstanding beauty." Flights are

826 VENEZUELA

also available from Caracas, Ciudad Bolívar, Porlamar and Güiria with Aeropostal. Taxi from airport to village US$2.50. *Por puesto* from Maturín or Ciudad Guayana about US$3.75, 2-3 hrs. Tucupita-Caracas by bus, 10 hrs., 2000, US$4.50.

Hotels at Tucupita *Gran Hotel Amacuro*, F, a/c, Calle Bolívar 23; *Delta*, F, a/c, Calle Pativilca 28; *Astoria*, F with bath, fan, not too clean, Av. Arismendi 64, couples only, and weather permitting; and a few cheaper *hospedajes*; *Wanauré*, F.

For a 3-4 day trip to see the delta and the Indians, boats may be arranged by asking for help at the information office near Plaza Bolívar, or contact Juan Carrión (all the taxi drivers know him), but they are not easy to come by and are expensive except for large groups. Be warned, if the river level rises after a downpour, arrangements may be cancelled. Take enough food for yourselves, the guide and the Indians, and plenty of water. Hammocks and mosquito repellants are mandatory. It is hard going but worth the effort. If you go to a *ranchería* take gifts such as fresh fruit, needles, thread, knives and only give them individually. You can buy hammocks and local handicrafts; always ask permission to take photographs and do not pay for them. For shorter excursions by boat, ask at gas station (*bomba*) by the river. Alternatively, take a *por puesto* from Plaza Bolívar to the village of La Horqueta (US$0.40), where it is easier to get a boat and where there are many Indians. The climate is very humid and Tucupita often suffers from flooding and subsequent loss of electricity. The cafés on the edge of the plaza are recommended and are said to be "especially interesting at night, without electricity, with your feet virtually awash in the Orinoco.°

An interesting dead-end village is **Barrancas** on the Orinoco, reached by road from Tucupita, 63 km. (*por puesto* to San Félix US$4) or from Maturín. *Hospedaje El Carmen*, F, Calle Carabobo 20, shower, clean, no fan. From Barrancas you can take a boat to Curiapo (Indian village) and Amacuro (near Guyana border), check at the harbour. It is also possible to go to Georgetown from here; ask for boats to Amacuro and then on to Mabaruma (only for the adventurous) or check with the lady at the *librería* on the river at the bottom of the village, she is from Georgetown and travels there occasionally.

Angel Falls, the highest fall in the world (979 metres) and **Canaima,** a nearby tourist lodge and hotel, are best reached from Caracas or from Ciudad Bolívar. Avensa airline has inclusive charges for tours which leave daily from Maiquetía airport (0600). The daily flights stop at Ciudad Bolívar, which can be the starting point for the trip. A Boeing 727 takes passengers from there to Canaima arriving in the morning, and will fly over the Angel Falls before landing, weather permitting. Trips to the falls may have to be booked in advance. From Caracas the return flight, two nights' accommodation, six meals and a free boat trip around the lagoon costs about US$100; from Ciudad Bolívar the return flight with two night's accommodation is about US$88 (US$70 for one night and 3 meals). All arrangements are made through Avensa, direct or through travel agencies. You cannot board the flight without a voucher from Avensa for at least one night's accommodation at Canaima; obtaining refunds is very difficult if you do not want to stay at the camp. One-night trips are possible, as are longer stays (open flights can be booked from Ciudad Bolívar). Reductions are available for parties. At Canaima there is a small shop, but no alternative accommodation or restaurant. Camping is possible with a permit from Inparques in Caracas (there is a representative at Canaima).

At Ciudad Bolívar airport Aerotaxis Tanca arranges Cessna flights for 3 persons for a whole day at Angel Falls and Canaima; the one-day excursion includes lunch at Canaima, a boat tour of the lagoon and the Falls. The return flight is usually after lunch (flight alone is US$20 one way). Canaima is on the edge of a tannin-stained lagoon with soft beige beaches; the Río Carrao tumbles over seven splendid falls into the lagoon below. The country is very beautiful. Lodging is in quite comfortable cabins; each is complete with shower and toilet: there are no hardships whatsoever. If travelling independently, one night's accommodation with 3 meals costs about US$25; the meals are basic, self-service, no choice. You could save yourself some money by taking food with you. Drinks are also expensive.

There are various excursions from Canaima, which are all worthwhile (and usually crowded): upriver to the Angel Falls costs between US$90-120 p.p. (more if less than 4 going); 5 operators organize this trip at short notice, including Isidoro Sandoval of Excursiones Churun-Vena S.R.L. (recommended, he has a video of a Japanese expedition which climbed the Falls in 1980), and "Jungle Rudy", the most expensive (he has his own hotel, US$35 with 3 meals, at Campamento Ucaima, just above the Hacha Falls, 2 hrs. walk from Canaima). All *curiaras* (dug-outs) must have 2 motors, by law, and carry first aid, life jackets, etc. Take wet weather gear, mosquito net for hammock and insect repellant. Trips by boat to the Falls only go June-November, leaving usually in the afternoon, staying the first night at Isla Orquídea, continuing to the Falls next day. Depending on the river, the trip takes on average 3 days (best to go Mon.-Wed. as everything is fully booked at weekends). You can also make walking expeditions into the jungle to Indian villages with a guide (e.g. Tomás), but bargain hard on the price. A highly recommended flight by Cessna 5-seater costs US$25 p.p., takes 40 mins. and does some circuits over and alongside the falls (better than organized flights is to go to the airstrip and ask around the pilots waiting there on business if they will fly over the Falls for the same price as a tour). Other excursions to Mayupa (US$5, half day), to Yuri Falls (US$5, half day); to Isla Orquídea (US$10, full day, good). The flat-topped Auyan-Tepuy, from which spring the Angel Falls, was the setting for W. H. Hudson's *Green Mansions*. The sheer

VENEZUELA 827

rock face of the Falls, named after Jimmy Angel, the US airman (see page 805) who discovered them in 1937, was climbed in 1971 by three Americans and an Englishman, David Nott, who recounts the ten-day adventure in his book *Angels Four* (Prentice-Hall).

Auyan-Tepuy can also be reached by a 2-3-hr. hike from the village of **Kamarata**, reached only by air from Ciudad Bolívar (with Aeropostal or Rutaca, 2½ hrs., book at least a week ahead in Ciudad Bolívar or Caracas, flights 4 times a week). In the dry season you can take a 3-4 day excursion to Kamarata from Canaima by boat. A friendly village with no hotels or restaurants; either camp (mosquito nets necessary) or, when it is not in session, sling your hammock in the mission school. It may also be possible to use the school's kitchen if you have no stove, otherwise ask around for who may sell you dinner. Several good day-long hiking trips; guides to Auyan-Tepuy, waterfalls and the Cuevas de Kavac, US$10.

In Caracas contact *Hotel Tamanaco*, Tel.: 914555, or Caribex Tours, Tel.: 728271/2, for trips to Falls. Italcambio, Tel.: 820611, organizes camping trips up the River Paragua for parties of four at a cost of US$220 for three days, or US$325 four days. The travel agency at the *Caracas Hilton* has also been recommended. Tours can usually be booked on the spot, with no reservation problems.

Warning Credit cards are not accepted by the people who take you on excursions, except on some of the flights. Travellers' cheques can be cashed, but at a poor rate.

Another Warning Necklaces of poisonous red and black seeds are on sale here, see page 311.

Travelling South from Ciudad Guayana to the Brazilian border is becoming an increasingly popular excursion for Venezuelan tourists, as well as for overland travellers heading for Manaus and the Amazon.

South from Ciudad Guayana there is a 285-km. paved road to **El Dorado,** where stands the regional prison made famous by Papillon's stay there. There is a gas station, open 0800-1900 daily. Bus from Caracas to El Dorado, Expresos del Oriente, at 1830 daily, US$7.25, 14½ hrs., return at 1400 (925 km.). The Orinoco bus line connects Ciudad Bolívar with El Dorado, 6 hrs. On the way to El Dorado the road goes through Upata (Hotels: *Yocoima, Comercio, Adriático*, and *La Palma*, which also has a restaurant, all E); El Callao (Hotels: *Italia* and *Ritz*, both F, on Calle Ricaurte), which has a good carnival, and is a good place to buy gold nuggets (8 km. away are the underground goldmines of El Perú); then on another 40 km. to **Tumeremo** (Hotels: *Leocar*, 3 blocks from plaza, F, fair, with shower and toilet, fan, restaurant recommended; *Central*, near plaza, good (but may be "full", try again later), bakery and snackbar, clean, F; *Florida*, E, not too good; restaurant *El Esturión*, good, friendly, Calle El Dorado, Edificio Bolívar). Tumeremo is recommended as the best place to buy provisions, there is Banco de la Unión, for Visa cash and cheque transactions, and gasoline (all grades) at a normal price (better than El Dorado; see also next page). 5 km. from Tumeremo towards the Fuerte Tarabay is the beautiful artificial lake of San Pedro with an attractive campsite. From Tumeremo to El Dorado is 108 km. By jeep from Santa Elena, US$11 (8-10 hrs.); bus to Ciudad Bolívar, US$3, 6 a day, 6½ hrs. (via San Félix and Puerto Ordaz, 5 hrs, US$2); *por puesto* to San Félix (Ciudad Guayana), US$3.75; bus Tumeremo-Caracas, US$6.30.

Hotels in El Dorado: *El Dorado*, next to gas station, E, fair; *San Agustino*, main plaza; *Hospedaje Portugal*, F, only six rooms, the Portuguese owner also runs the store next door. *Campamento Turístico*, run by Richard Sidney Coles (speaks English and German), F, with bath, basic. He arranges tours in motorized canoes.

The road is paved to Km. 145 (graded thereafter) and four-wheel drive is only necessary if one wanders off the main road, particularly in the rainy season. Beyond Tumeremo, only 83 octane gasoline is available; it is forbidden to travel beyond Km. 88 without a spare 20 litres of gasoline (spare tanks are available there, but better and cheaper to get one earlier); it is also advisable to carry extra water and plenty of food. There are police checks at the Río Cuyuní and at Km. 126; all driving permits, car registration papers, and identification must be shown.

At Km. 83 (from the bridge over the Río Cuyuní which is 6 km. from El Dorado), is Barquilla de Fresa, where tropical fish are bred (Henry Cleve speaks English and German). From Km. 85 (La Clarita, small hotel, restaurant; big market for food and gold) it's a 1½-hr. walk to gold-digging village of Santo Domingo, restaurant, easy to sling hammock, malaria. At Km. 88 (also called San Isidro), there is gasoline, a café and small hotel, F, basic, dirty, not recommended. Gold is sold here; ask Francisco Vargas at the grocery store and restaurant. Bus Km. 88-Caracas, US$10. Frequent *por puestos* from El Dorado to Km. 88, 1 hr., US$2.10. At Km. 88 you can catch a pick-up truck with seats in the back going from Tumeremo to Santa Elena, US$2. Jeep from Km. 88 gas station to Santa Elena leaves when full, 5 hrs., US$6.75. Ask here if stuck for the night at Km. 88. After Km. 88 there is no further public transport, but you can get a ride with passing jeeps and trucks (very little passes after 1030). The 40 km. beyond Km. 88 up to the Gran Sabana are very steep and must be driven in first gear (hard on a standard car—in the wet, friendly lorries may oblige with a tow). At Km. 100 is the huge, black Piedra de la Virgen; from here the steep climb begins up to La Escalera and the beginning of the beautiful Gran Sabana National Reserve. The road is graded from Km. 145 to Santa Elena and a stream must be forded. Characteristic of this area are the large abrupt *tepuyes* (flat-topped mountains or *mesas*) and the hundreds of waterfalls.

At Km. 123 a short trail leads to the 40-metre Danto Falls. If you are paying for your ride, try to persuade the driver to make a short stop at the falls; they are close to the road (about 5 mins.' slippery walk) but not visible from it. Near the Monumento al Soldado Pionero (Km. 141) is a popular camping place (4 km. beyond the monument); 6 km. beyond is the military checkpoint at Ciudadela. At Km. 148 is a bad road leading to Kavanayén (food, lodging, airport); off this road after 25 km. are the falls of Torón Merú (17 km.) and, further on, the falls of Chinak-Merú, 100 metres high and very impressive (take the trail to the Río Aponguao and the Pemón Indian village of Iboribó, tip someone to ferry you across the river and walk 30 mins. to the falls; 30-min. boat trips to the falls cost US$15. 18 km. before Kavanayén is a road to the *Hotel Chivaton*, D. Beyond Kavanayén a beautiful but risky trail leads along flat-topped mountains to the Karuai-Merú Falls. For the remaining 200 km. to Santa Elena de Uairen few people or villages are seen. The impressive falls at the Cama river should not be missed (Km. 211). At Km. 259 is the Río Yuruaní, free ferry from 0600-1800 (a tip asked for), from where it is a 15-minute hike to the Yuruaní waterfall—leave the main road 250 metres after the ferry, turn left; then comes the Pemón village of San Francisco de Yuruaní, then the checkpoint at San Ignacio de Yuruaní (excellent regional food). A trail at Km. 289 leads to the Quebrada de Jaspe where a river falls over red rocks.

Santa Elena de Uairen is a growing, pleasant frontier town. *Hotel Fronteras*, E, very nice and modern, good food, with bath (N.B. if you pay a deposit to hire a fan, you may have difficulty in getting the money back when you leave in the early morning to catch the Boa Vista bus); *Hospedaje Uairen*, German-owned, good and helpful with tourist information; *Hospedaje Roraima*, noisy, mosquitos, not recommended; all E; *Hotel MacKing*, with private bathroom, very clean, and restaurant attached, service slow, F; *Aurantepuy*, F, basic, clean, recommended; *Mini Hospedaje*, F, 2 blocks from *Fronteras*, clean, some rooms with private shower. Opposite airport rooms to let at Sergio's *granja*, friendly, due open in 1987. The best restaurant is *Gran Sabana*. Rooms are difficult to find around August 9-19, which is the *fiesta* of Santa Elena (if stuck, ask for Charlie at the *Hotel Fronteras*, he may be able to find you somewhere else to stay). There is a bank now at Santa Elena where you can change US dollars or cruzados (less easy) cash, not cheques; to obtain better rates for exchange you must wait until Ciudad Guayana. If the service station is dry, ask for Sr. Lucca who sells gasoline out of barrels. Grocery store: *Tienda Mixta El Gordito*, opp. *Hotel MacKing*, English and French spoken. Passports and car documents must be stamped here if leaving or entering the country; the immigration office is on the north edge of the town on a hill opposite the Corpoven gas station (open 0900-1700 except Sun., and holidays). All regular transport appears to call at the Immigration office when leaving Santa Elena. There is a daily União Cascavel bus to Boa Vista (Brazil) between 0600 and 0800, calling at Immigration soon after, 8 hrs., US$5 (US$4 in cruzados). The new road to Brazil is said to link Caracas with Manaus in three days if you drive hard, although it is only a dirt road with gravel on top.

Transport to and from Santa Elena From Caracas either take 1800 daily bus to Tumeremo (936 km., US$6.30); 0800-0900 next morning for Santa Elena, from Cooperativa de Conductores on main square, 9 hrs., 394 km., US$11; most jeeps bypass El Dorado if they are full. Alternatively, go to Ciudad Bolívar and take the Línea Orinoco bus straight through to Santa Elena, US$8, 18 hrs., returns from Santa Elena at 0500, take food and a large polythene sheet to cover yourself for the first 6 hours, otherwise you'll alight as a "walking desert". Anti-malaria pills are given out free at the military checkpoint before El Dorado. Regular jeep service Santa Elena-Tumeremo also US$11, 0700, takes 8-10 hrs., calls at Immigration en route for stamping passports (from Tumeremo you can get a bus to San Félix, 4 hrs., or colectivo to Maturín, 2 hrs.). Aeropostal has flights to Tumeremo and Ciudad Bolívar (US$15) but the planes when flying are fully booked in advance in the high season (timetable uncertain, check on arrival). On Wednesdays there is an interesting flight available to Tumeremo via Icabarú and the Indian villages of Uriman, Wonkin, and Kamarata. Book a week in advance.

116 km. W of Santa Elena is Icabarú, a diamond-producing centre (daily jeep from Santa Elena, US$5). 58 km. from Santa Elena is a Guardia Nacional checkpoint at Parai-Tepuy, with a waterfall nearby. At **El Pauji** (Km. 85, US$3 by jeep from Santa Elena), ask for Luigi, an Italian at El Cajón mine (he speaks English). 25 km. from the town is the *Canta Rana* tourist camp with basic accommodation (owners, Alfonso and Barbara Borrero, speak German, English and Spanish); waterfall and lovely surroundings; they have a private plane that collects people from Puerto Ordaz (Tel.: 086-22-68-51 or 22-07-09, Sr. Haissan Al Atrache). 15 km. from El Pauji, at Solís, Arquimedes and Philippe have a tourist camp; they organize tours. In El Pauji, Danielle operates *El Caminante* tourist camp, just after the bridge, coming from Santa Elena; just before the bridge is *El Merendero* restaurant. At *La Bodega* general store, Victoriano has information on guides for tourists.

Mount Roraima Robin Parish and Karin Hessenberg write: One of our most exciting trips was walking to Mt. Roraima (2,810 metres), which it has been suggested was the "Lost World" made famous by Arthur Conan Doyle's novel (although conflicting evidence points to the Brazilian Serra Ricardo Franco near the Bolivian border west of Cuiabá as the site). Supplies for a week or more should be bought in Santa Elena or El Dorado. You can start walking from San Francisco de Yuruaní, an Indian village (built of concrete and corrugated iron!) on the main road 60 km. north of Santa Elena, and 10 km. north of the San Ignacio police check post (by jeep prices vary from US$2.25 to

US$5.50!). Coca-cola and biscuits (very little else) can be bought in San Francisco. Follow the virtually unused dirt road to Parai-Tepuy across open savanna with patches of jungle in the river valleys. Parai-Tepuy is the nearest village to the mountain but has no shops. Short cuts can be taken—ask the friendly and interested local people. Beyond Parai-Tepuy it is probably best to take a guide from the village. If you do not, it is easy to get lost as there are many trails criss-crossing. (If you find yourself in Chirimata, a guide should be available.) Looking from the village, Roraima is the mountain on the right facing you, the other massive outcrop on the left is Mata Hui (sometimes known as Mt. Kukenaan after the river which rises within it). It is about a 2-day walk to the jungle at the foot of Roraima and then it is possible to climb to the plateau along the "easy" gully which is the only route to the top.

This gully is the more central of two which run diagonally up the cliff face. The ascent takes 3-5 hrs. and it is possible to camp on the eerie plateau, but beware of lightning from the frequent electrical storms which the mountains attract.

There is plenty of water en route (too much in the rainy season) but no accommodation. Full camping equipment is essential, and wear thick socks and boots to protect legs from snakes, also essential is effective insect repellant. The whole trip can take anywhere between one and two weeks.

The Economy

Venezuela's economy has been dominated by petroleum, despite contributing only 8% to gdp. Oil exports have inflated foreign exchange receipts and government fiscal revenues. Oil revenues have shaped the rest of the productive sector, even though employment creation has been minimal, and inter-industry links have been relatively underdeveloped. High earnings from oil have caused a tendency to overvalue the exchange rate, which has discouraged export-based production and hindered import substitution. Non-oil industry and agriculture are now being targeted for expansion as oil's role has diminished since the early 1980s.

Venezuela has vast natural resources, and is especially rich in energy, possessing 55.52 bn barrels of proved oil reserves. Apart from proved and exploitable reserves, there are another 1.2 trillion barrels in potential reserves of very heavy oil in the as yet unexploited Orinoco belt. There are 2.65 trillion cubic metres of natural gas reserves (plus 5 trillion probable), and 500 m tonnes of coal (9 bn estimated) in the provinces of Zulia and Táchira. There is believed to be a hydroelectricity potential (HEP) of 80,000 MW. The new hydroelectric generating capacity around Ciudad Guayana in the east is designed to act as the hub of economic growth. It includes the 10,300 MW Guri dam poject, the largest complete HEP station in the world, and which in July 1986 provided just over half the country's generating capacity.

Venezuela is Opec's third largest oil producer, with a capacity of 2.6 m barrels a day. Oil production is concentrated in three major sedimentary basins: the Maracaibo, the eastern, and the Apure-Barinas basins. Petróleos de Venezuela (PDVSA), the state-owned oil company created out of the nationalization of oil companies in 1976, has been relatively successful in keeping its market share because of its forward-looking marketing strategy based on forming partnerships with refineries and marketing chains in Europe and the USA.

The mining sector has been probably the most buoyant part of the economy since 1984, and is likely to continue in this vein with important mining ventures in bauxite, iron ore and coal. Venezuela could become the world's leading aluminium producer by the end of the century.

Only about 20% of the land surface is devoted to agriculture, and about three-quarters of this is pasture. Like mining, it is a small sector of the economy, accounting for 8% of gdp and employing 15% of the workforce, but it too is showing strong growth thanks to the government's encouragement. The main grain staples are maize and sorghum, while sugar and rice are also important. The main export crop is coffee, with other cash crops being cocoa and cotton.

Venezuela is Latin America's fourth largest debtor, and despite huge foreign reserves of over US$20 bn accumulated by the mid-1980s from oil wealth, the country became unable to service its external debt normally from 1982 because of a bunching of maturities. A US$21 bn debt rescheduling agreement was signed with commercial banks in 1986 but was almost immediately renegotiated,

830 VENEZUELA

with longer repayment terms and lower interest rates, as falling oil prices that year caused unexpected foreign exchange constraints; oil revenues fell by 44% in 1986. By running down foreign exchange reserves in the 1980s, Venezuela became the only Latin American country able to reduce its external debt, from US$34 bn in 1981 to US$31 bn in 1986, of which nearly US$1 bn was paid to commercial banks and the rest to other creditors.

	1961-70 (av)	1971-80 (av)	1981-85 (av)	1986 (e)
Gdp growth (1980 prices)	6.1%	4.1%	-1.3%	3.1%
Inflation	1.0%	8.4%	11.1%	10.6%
Exports (fob) US$m	2,436	9,228	15,582	8,686
Crude oil and products	2,240	8,743	14,048	7,218
Imports (fob) US$m	1,294	6,307	9,092	7,700
Current account balance US$m (cum)	1,217	5,114	12,685	-1,628

Information for Visitors

Travel from UK and Europe British Airways direct flights from London to Simon Bolívar, the international airport for Caracas, twice a week each way. There are also services from Europe by Air France, KLM, Viasa, Iberia, Alitalia, Lufthansa, Swissair and Avianca. A cheap route from London (twice a week) is by Caribbean Airways to Barbados, where you can get connections with Viasa or BWIA to Caracas. Caribbean Airways are represented in Venezuela by Interavia Marketing, 3rd floor, Torre a Veroes 11, Edificio 11, Caracas, Tel.: 812638. Iberia has a weekly service to Las Palmas, Canary Islands, from where connections can be made to various North and West African countries.

By sea, French Line (CGM) has passenger sailings to and from Southampton. Italian and Spanish ports are served by Sidarma and other Italian and Spanish passenger services. Scandinavia and Belgium have direct passenger cargo-service by Johnson Line. From Holland there are passenger ships of the KNSM. The Italian "C" Line (Costa) to and from Italy calls at Miami. Royal Mail Lines has a cargo service only from the UK to Venezuelan ports. There are direct cargo sailings (no passengers) by Harrison Lines also.

From the USA By air, passengers may reach Venezuela by KLM, Pan American, Air Panama (via Panama City) Varig and Viasa. Jets fly from New York to Caracas in 4 hrs. 15 mins. There are cargo services, some with limited passenger space, from Atlantic and/or Gulf ports by Alcoa, CAVN, P and O, Insco, KNSM, Lykes & Torm, and from the Pacific by Moore-McCormack.

From Colombia There are direct flights by Viasa, British Airways, Air France and Avianca. Caracas can also be reached from Bogotá by Pan-American Highway, and from the north coast, by the Caribbean coastal highway.

From Argentina, Brazil and Uruguay There are direct air services by Viasa, Aerolíneas Argentinas, Pan American and Varig. By sea, the Argentine State Line maintains a passenger liner service, every two or three weeks. Caracas may now be reached by a very rough road from Brazil, via Manaus, Boa Vista and Santa Elena de Uairen.

Others Lacsa flies from San José (Costa Rica), Panama and Barranquilla (Colombia) to Maracaibo and Caracas. Aeropostal has services to Port of Spain (3 times a week from Caracas or Isla Margarita, US$144 return, valid one year, or US$94 if staying less than 9 days), Curaçao and Aruba. Difficulties have been reported in entering Trinidad unless with a UK, US or Canadian passport. Viasa also flies to Bridgetown, Barbados but it is often difficult to get a seat. There is direct air service from Chile (Viasa has a weekly flight with extra flights Dec.-March; connections can also be made via Bogotá on Avianca), Peru (Air France via Bogotá, Viasa—Viasa tickets purchased in Peru should be checked most carefully), Ecuador (Ecuatoriana, Lufthansa and Viasa), Santo Domingo (Viasa, Dominicana de Aviación), Puerto Rico (Pan American), Curaçao (KLM, Viasa), Trinidad (Aeropostal, BWIA, Pan American). As yet, Venezuela has no road connection with Guyana, except through Brazil. Ferry from Curaçao, three times a week; also from Aruba.

Documents Entry is by passport and visa, or by passport and tourist card. Tourist cards (*tarjetas de ingreso*) are valid only for those entering by air and are issued by most airlines to visitors from 25 countries including the USA, Canada, Japan and all Western European countries except Spain and Portugal. If you enter the country overland, you will be required to obtain a visa from a Venezuelan consulate prior to arrival. Visas are free, but you will need your passport, return ticket and letter of reference from your employer and bank. You must fill in an application form and the visa will take about three working days to come through, sometimes longer if authorization has to come from Venezuela. There may be difficulties if you come in overland from Colombia, as this new ruling is designed to prevent illegal immigration from that country, so you are strongly advised to obtain your visa before leaving your country of origin. A tourist card issued by Viasa in Bogotá is only valid for arriving in Caracas by air from Bogotá, not if you travel overland. Officials will make it difficult for you to obtain a new visa and you may be given only 72 hrs. to stay in Venezuela. It is possible to renew it at the immigration office (Diex) on Plaza de Miranda (metro Capitolio) at no cost, with a wait of a few hours, but you must present two passport photographs. To change a tourist visa to a business visa, or to extend the latter, costs Bs. 1,000 (about US$50). A business visa costs about US$25. Visas are valid for one entry only. Transit passengers to another country can stay only 72 hrs.

N.B. Carry your passport with you all the time you are in Venezuela as the police are increasing spot checks and anyone found without identification is immediately detained.

Information for business visitors is given in "Hints to Exporters: Venezuela", issued by the Export Services Division, Dept. of Trade, Sanctuary Buildings, 16-20 Great Smith Street, London SW1. Businessmen on short visits are strongly advised to enter the country as tourists, otherwise they will have to obtain a tax clearance certificate (*solvencia*) before they can leave.

Taxes All non-tourists leaving the country, except nationals of Denmark and transit passengers who stay for 7 days or less (who pay one bolívar), must pay Bs. 105 at the airport or port of embarkation. Minors under seven years of age do not pay the exit tax. There is also an airport tax of Bs. 10 for those passengers leaving from Maiquetía.

Customs You may bring into Venezuela, free of duty, 25 cigars and 200 cigarettes, 2 litres of alcoholic drinks, 4 small bottles of perfume, and gifts at the inspector's discretion.

Shipping a car from the USA From Miami: Venezuelan Line (agent Oceanic Steamship Co.) and Delta Line, US$500-650 for a VW minibus; no passengers. From New Orleans: Delta Line, VW minibus, US$1,400-1,700, passengers carried, but for US$1,200. Alternatively, agent Hansen and Tiedemann charges same price as Delta for vehicle, but you can accompany it for US$190 p.p. (5 days, including meals). Also recommended: Coordinadora del Caribe Transmodal C.A. (CCT) Calle Veracruz, Ed. Torreón, Piso 7, Las Mercedes, Caracas, Tel.: 92-71-33. Also Seaboard Marine, agent in Venezuela, Conavén, US$650 for a VW Kombi; their route is advertised as La Guaira-Miami, but actually goes to West Palm Beach, 80 miles North of Miami; almost impossible to travel with your vehicle.

On arrival in Venezuela (La Guaira), you must go to the Tourism Department at Simón Bolívar airport where you must obtain a document identifying your car (serial and engine number, registry, etc.). With this you can get your car out of the port.

Motoring A tourist can bring in his/her car without paying duty, and the only documentation required is a visa for overland entry (this is necessary despite what Consulates may tell you) and a *carnet*. See also page 816. For vehicles with Venezuelan registration leaving Venezuela the following documents are required: an Automóvil passport book from the Touring y Automóvil Club de Venezuela, Apartado 68102, Centro Integral Santa Rosa, Locales 11 y 12, Calle A, Av. Principal, Santa Rosa de Lima, Caracas, Tel.: 914879; the original car papers; the registration document; a police *revisión* obtained from the Policía Técnica Judicial; and a temporary import/export licence for a vehicle obtainable from the Ministerio de Hacienda, Caracas, or from a customs agent in San Antonio de Táchira (border town) for about US$100. The export/import licence and the passport book must be signed and stamped by the Customs Administrator. If possible, check all details on bringing in/taking out a car in advance.

All visitors to Venezuela can drive if they are over 18 and have a valid driving licence from their own country. It is a good idea to hire a car (see page 800); many of the best places are off the beaten track. If planning to hire a car for any length of time it is worth the trouble to obtain a *licencia temporal para conducir*; for this you require a medical certificate (eye examination, blood pressure, Bs.50), photocopy of your home driver's licence and *carta médica* plus two black-and-white passport photos which must be presented at the Dirección General Sectorial de Transporte y Tránsito Terrestre in El Paraíso (by the jail)—full details in Venamcham's *Executive Newcomer's Guide*. If you have an accident and someone is injured, you will be detained as a matter of routine, even if you are not at fault. Be careful of motor cyclists; if you injure one, others will surround you in a threatening and dangerous manner. Motor cyclists also drive very dangerously, sometimes even on the pavements, and are responsible for many assaults on pedestrians. Do not drive at night if you can help it. In 1982 a nationwide speed limit of 80 k.p.h. was imposed. Venezuelans are aggressive drivers and use their horns whenever possible. The roads in Venezuela are very good, all major routes are fully paved and even the dirt and gravel roads are reliable. There is a "día de parada" in Caracas which prohibits motorists from driving one day a week (see page 800). Other motoring restrictions in Caracas include a ban on parking in front of a bank; motorcycles may not

832 VENEZUELA

be driven at night; pillion passengers may not be carried on motorcycles if of the same sex as the driver. You are more likely to be penalized for infringing these rules than for driving through a red light; they are designed to improve security for banks and pedestrians. In addition, motorcyclists are obliged to wear a crash helmet but it must not be of a type which obscures the face.

There are 5 grades of petrol: "normal", 83 octane (Bs.1.30 a litre); 87 octane (Bs.1.36 a litre); 89 octane (Bs.1.40 a litre); 91 octane (Bs.1.43 a litre); and "alta", 95 octane (Bs.1.50 a litre). Diesel (US$0.35 a litre). Service stations are open 0500-2100, Mon.-Sat., except those on highways which are open longer hours. Only those designated to handle emergencies are open on Sun. In the event of breakdown, Venezuelans are usually very helpful. There are many garages, even in rural areas; service charges are not high, but being able to speak Spanish will greatly assist in sorting out problems. Road maps are available for US$0.20 at most service stations.

Hitch-Hiking (*Cola*) is not very easy but the Venezuelans are usually friendly and helpful if you know some Spanish.

Tourist Information may be obtained from Corpoturismo, Apartado 50.200, Caracas, main office for information is floors 35-7, Torre Oeste, Parque Central; for booking hotels go to Plaza Venezuela, Centro Capriles (ground floor). A useful publication is the *Guía Turística y Hoteles de Venezuela, Colombia y el Caribe*, published every July by Corpoturismo, which includes not only hotel details, but also road maps and tourist attractions. For businessmen setting up home in Caracas, the Venezuelan American Chamber of Commerce publication, *Executive Newcomer's Guide, Welcome to Venezuela*, is recommended, with useful chapters on housing, employment, schools, services, recreation facilities and legal matters. Also useful is the *Atlas Geográfico y Económico—Venezuela Visualizada* by Levi Marrero, Ed. Cultural Venezolana, 1977, which contains maps, tourist information and statistics of every state, available in all good bookshops. The *Guide to Venezuela* (1981), by Janice Bauman, Leni Young and others, in English (freely available in Caracas) is a mine of information and maps, although prices are out of date.

For information on the National Parks system, and to obtain necessary permits, visit the Ministerio del Ambiente y de los Recursos Naturales Renovables (MARNR) at Parque del Este in Caracas. The book: *Guía de los Parques Nacionales y Monumentos Naturales de Venezuela*, obtainable in Audubon headquarters, Las Mercedes (formerly Holiday Inn) shopping centre, Las Mercedes, Caracas.

Hotel Reservations Anahoven (the hoteliers' association) will book hotel rooms both in Caracas and in other towns, where they have 102 hotels on their books, not all of which are mentioned in these pages. Hotels marked with an asterisk (*) are bookable through Anahoven.

Students If you possess a valid international student's card you may find the Organización Nacional de Turismo Estudiantil y Juvenil (Ontej) useful; Parque Central, Edificio Catuche, Nivel Bolívar, Caracas, Tel.: 572-7621. They will help you with visas, documents and half-price air tickets (contract for these with Aeropostal was terminated in 1987, but a new one was under negotiation).

Tipping Taxi drivers are tipped if the taxi has a meter (Caracas only, so far), but not if you have agreed the fare in advance. Usherettes are not tipped. Hotel porters, Bs.2; airport porters Bs.2 per piece of baggage. Restaurants, between 5 and 10% of bill.

Hours of Business Banks are open from 0830 to 1130 and 1400 to 1630, Mon. to Fri., but are no longer open on Sat. Government office hours vary, but 0800-1200 are usual morning hours. Government officials have fixed hours, usually 0900-1000 or 1500-1600, for receiving visitors. Business firms generally start work about 0800, and some continue until about 1800 with a midday break. Shops, 0900-1300, 1500-1900, Mon. to Sat. Generally speaking, the Venezuelan begins his day early, and by seven in the morning everything is in full swing. Most firms and offices close on Sat.

Holidays There are two sorts of holidays, those enjoyed by everybody and those taken by employees of banks and insurance companies. Holidays applying to all businesses include: January 1, Carnival on the Monday and Tuesday before Ash Wednesday, Thursday-Saturday of Holy Week, April 19, May 1, June 24, July 5, 24, October 12, December 25. Holidays for banks and insurance companies only include all the above and also: March 19 and the nearest Monday to January 6, Ascension Day, June 29, August 15, November 1 and December 8. There are also holidays applying to certain occupations such as Doctor's Day or Traffic Policeman's Day. On New Year's Eve, everything closes and does not open for at least a day; public transport runs, but booking offices are not open. Queues for tickets, and traffic jams, are long. Business travellers should not visit during Holy Week or Carnival.

Local: La Guaira: March 10. Maracaibo: October 24, November 18.

Health conditions are good. Water in all main towns is heavily chlorinated, so safe to drink, although most people drink bottled water. Medical attention is good, but extremely expensive (the Clínica Metropolitana in Caracas has been recommended). Inoculation against typhoid and yellow fever, and protection

VENEZUELA

against malaria, is recommended for the Orinoco and other swampy or forest regions. Malaria tablets may be obtained only from Hospital Padre Machado (left-hand building as you face it), Tel.: 61-8211, no charge; alternatively, bring malaria tablets with you. It is as well to carry some remedy in case of gastric upsets.

Climate is tropical, with little change between season and season. Temperature is a matter of altitude. Mean annual temperatures are given in the text. At Caracas it is 20°C, but during the dry season (December to April), there is a great difference between day and night temperatures, and during the whole year there is a burst of heat around mid-day. Rainfall in mm.: Caracas, 762; Maracaibo, 573; Barcelona, 660; Mérida, 1,295; Amazonas and parts of Barinas state 2,540.

Clothing Tropical weight in normal city colours is best for business in Caracas, otherwise clothing is less formal, but smart jackets and ties are required in the most exclusive restaurants and clubs. In Maracaibo and the hot, humid coastal and low-lying areas, regular washable tropical clothing is used. For women: blouse and trousers (shorts quite acceptable on the coast); cotton dresses, with a wrap for cool evenings, and for air-conditioned restaurants and cinemas. Shoes are very good value.

Railways The only passenger traffic of any importance is on the Barquisimeto to Puerto Cabello line. The 110-km. Yaritagua-Acarigua-Turén electric railway line was opened at the beginning of 1983 but was closed after the inaugural run because of damage to the track. It is intended mostly to transport agricultural products.

Road Transport There are excellent (but slow) bus services between the major cities, but the colectivo taxis and minibuses, known in Venezuela as *por puesto*, seem to monopolize transport to and from smaller towns and villages. Outside Caracas, town taxis are relatively expensive.

Camping is popular, and plenty of equipment is available at Tienda Scout (Las Acacias), Maxy's (ex-Sears) and sports-goods shops in Caracas. Camping in Venezuela is a recreation, for spending a weekend at the beach, on the islands, in the *llanos* and in the mountains. (People pitch their tents on Mount Avila overlooking Caracas.) Camping is not however used by travellers as a substitute for hotels on the main highways, and no special camp sites are yet provided for this purpose. If camping on the beach, for the sake of security, pitch your tent close to others, even though they play their radios loud. For information on hiking, climbing and relevant equipment, telephone Alexander on (02)573-00-56 (Spanish only).

Air Services Most places of importance are served by Avensa (private) and/or Aeropostal (government-owned, both heavily overbooked always). International services are operated by another government-owned line, Viasa. Both internal airlines offer special family discounts. Aeronaves del Centro runs daily services to Puerto Cabello, Maracay, Anaco, Barquisimeto and Barcelona. Beware of overbooking during holiday time, especially at Caracas airport; it is recommended that you check in two hours before departure, particularly at Easter. If you travel with Viasa or any other airline for which Viasa is agent, it is possible to check in the night before at any Viasa office in town if your flight leaves before noon. To avoid overbooking the Government now obliges airlines to post a passenger list, but it is important to obtain clear instructions from the travel agent regarding confirmation of your flight and checking-in time. Passengers leaving Caracas on international flights must reconfirm their reservations not less than 72 hours in advance; 24 hours for national flights. Beware of counterfeit tickets; buy only from agencies. If told by an agent that a flight is fully booked, try at the airport anyway. International passengers must check in two hours before departure or they may lose their seat to someone on a waiting list. Read carefully any notice you see posted with the relevant instructions. Handling charge for your luggage US$0.50. All flights are subject to delays or cancellation.

Currency The unit of currency is the bolívar, which is divided into 100 céntimos. There are nickel alloy coins for 5, 25 and 50 céntimos and 1, 2 and 5 bolívares, and notes for 5, 10, 20, 50, 100 and 500 bolívares. The 1,000-bolívares note no longer circulates, because of extensive counterfeiting. The free rate of exchange, which tourists use, was about Bs.22.70 per US$1 in March 1987. Change travellers' cheques or US dollar notes in a *casa de cambio* for optimum rates; of the banks, Banco Unión and Banco de Venezuela change cheques and cash, but the latter usually only change money after 1500. The majority of banks do not cash travellers' cheques; in major towns, one or two banks may, but this

834 VENEZUELA

varies from branch to branch. American Express cheques are widely accepted as is the Visa card (Banco Consolidado is affiliated with American Express, no commission, some branches cash personal cheques from abroad on an AmEx card; Banco Unión handles Visa transactions). When changing dollars cash in banks, it is best to go in the morning. It is impossible to change sterling in Ciudad Guayana or Ciudad Bolívar. Have money sent to you by telex and not by post, which can take weeks.

Popular names for coins: Fuerte. Bs.5; Real, Bs.0.50; Medio, 0.25; Puya or Centavo, 0.05.

Weights and Measures are metric.

Voltage   110 volts, 60 cycles, throughout the country.

Shopping Goods in shops bear a label "PVP" followed by the price. This is the maximum authorized price; you may be able to negotiate a discount but should never pay more than the PVP price.

Warnings Cameras and other valuables should not be exposed prominently. The police are increasing spot-checks and may confiscate pocket knives as "concealed weapons" if they find them, although they are sold legally in the shops. Always carry handbags, cameras etc. on the side away from the street as motor-cycle purse-snatchers are notorious and they often even drive up on to the pavement to assault a pedestrian. Motor cyclists are also very adept at snatching chains from necks in Caracas. Hotel thefts are becoming more frequent, even in the best hotels.

Food   Both in Caracas and to a lesser extent in Maracaibo there are excellent restaurants specializing in foreign regional cuisines. Venezuelan beef is comparable with Argentina's and, surprisingly, portions are larger. There is excellent local fish (we recommend *pargo* or red snapper), crayfish, small oysters and prawns, though sole, trout and large oysters are imported. Sometimes there is turtle, though it is a protected species. For those without a conservationist conscience, turtle may appear on menus in the Peninsula de Paraguaná as *ropa especial*. The *Tarzilandia* restaurant in Caracas also serves it. Of true Venezuelan food there is *sancocho* (a stew of vegetables, especially yuca, with meat, chicken or fish); *arepas*, a kind of white maize bread, very bland in flavour; toasted *arepas* served with a wide selection of relishes, fillings or the local somewhat salty white cheese are cheap, filling and nutritious; *cachapas*, a maize pancake (soft, not hard like Mexican *tortillas*) wrapped around white cheese; *pabellón*, made of shredded meat, beans, rice and fried plantains; and *empanadas*, maize-flour pies containing cheese, meat or fish. At Christmas only there are *hallacas*, maize pancakes stuffed with chicken, pork, olives, etc. boiled in a plantain leaf (but don't eat the leaf). The nearest thing to a boiled egg in most places is a *huevo tibio*. It comes without the shell because there are no eggcups. A *muchacho* (boy) on the menu is not a sign of cannibalism; it is a cut of beef. *Ganso* is also not goose but beef. *Solomo* and *lomito* are other cuts of beef. *Hervido* is chicken or beef with vegetables. *Caraotas* are beans; *cachitos* are croissants of bread. *Pasticho* is what the Venezuelans call Italian *lasagne*. The main fruits are bananas, oranges, grapefruit, mangoes, pineapple and pawpaws. Excellent strawberries are grown at Colonia Tovar, 90 minutes from Caracas. A delicious sweet is *huevos chimbos*—egg yolk boiled and bottled in sugar syrup. There is no good local wine though some foreign wines are bottled locally. Local wine is used only in cooking or in *sangría*. There are four good local beers: Polar (the most popular), Regional (with a strong flavour of hops), Cardenal and Nacional (a *lisa* is a glass of keg beer; for a bottle of beer ask for a *tercio*), mineral waters, gin and excellent rum. The citizens of Mérida sometimes drink a cocktail of beer and milk. The coffee is very good; visitors should also try a *merengada*, a delicious drink made from fruit pulp, ice, milk and sugar; a *batido* is the same but with water, not milk. A *plus-café* is an after-dinner liqueur. Water is free in all restaurants even if no food is bought. Bottled water in *cervecerías* is often from the tap; no deception is intended, bottles are simply used as convenient jugs. Insist on seeing the bottle opened if you do not want a mouthful of chlorine with your whisky. *Chicha de arroz* is a sweet drink made of milk, rice starch, sugar and vanilla; fruit juices are very good. The Caracas *Daily Journal* (in English) lists many reliable restaurants in Caracas and Maracaibo. Venezuelans dine late.

VENEZUELA 835

Film Kodak (La Trinidad) and Agfa have a regional plant in Caracas and colour-slide film can be developed in 3-4 days (go direct to the plant). Photographic laboratories in Caracas frequently scratch negatives when developing film. Travellers passing through are recommended to have the work done in some other city. Film is quite cheap to buy.

Postal Services The postal service is extremely slow and unreliable. Air mail letters to the USA or Europe can take from one to six weeks and registered mail is no quicker. Internal mail also travels slowly, especially if there is no P.O. Box number. If you want money sent to you from abroad, have it sent by telex. Avoid the mail boxes in pharmacies as some no longer have collections. Airmail to Europe: Bs.6.75 for letters, Bs.5 for postcards.

Telephone Service All international and long distance calls are operated by CANTV from El Silencio building in west Caracas, Centro Simón Bolívar or Centro Plaza on Fco. Miranda near US Embassy in east Caracas, open 24 hrs. Most major cities are now linked by direct dialling (*Discado Directo*), with a 3-figure prefix for each town in Venezuela. Otherwise CANTV offices deal with all long-distance and international calls in the cities outside Caracas. Collect calls unavailable. Calls out of Venezuela are more expensive than calls into it and are subject to long delays. Local calls are troublesome and the connection is often cut in the middle of your conversation; calls are best made from hotels or CANTV offices, rather than from booths. Local calls in Caracas cost US$0.06.

Warning Cables into Venezuela are very slow, sometimes taking longer to be delivered than air mail. If it's urgent, telephone or telex is far preferable. Ask your hotel for use of its telex machine.

Official Time in Venezuela is 4 hrs. behind G.M.T.

Press: Caracas: *El Universal*, *El Nacional* and *El Diario de Caracas*, *La Religión*, *Ultimas Noticias*. *The Daily Journal* (English), *El Mundo* and *2001* (evening), *Número* (weekly), *Resumen* (weekly), *Elite* (weekly), *Momento* (weekly), *Venezuela Gráfica* (weekly), *Páginas* (weekly), *Semana* (weekly), *Ve Venezuela*, tourist bi-monthly. Maracaibo: *Panorama*, *La Crítica*. Puerto La Cruz: *El Tiempo*.

Radio Write to Radio Nacional, Caracas 101, Apartado 3979, for details about their plans for English-language broadcasts.

Our thanks for help in revising this section go to Paul Millgate who revised the Economy section, to Michael Davison, former resident in Caracas, who has been extremely helpful as ever; and to the following travellers: Richard and Sharon Alexander (Auckland 5), Pierre-Yves Atlan (Paris 18e), Trond Bergquist and Ian Gjertz (Oslo), Dr Michael Binzberger (Friedrichshafen), Erik Bloom (Davis, Ca.), Peter Cohen (Australia), Malcolm Craven (Weston-super-Mare), Jonathan Curtis (Bury St. Edmonds), Lynne and Hugh Davies (Mill Valley, Ca.) for a most useful contribution, Ulrich Gmünder (Mannheim), Rhoda and Ron Greenwood, Stig Hagstad (Boden, Swe.), Alban Johnson (Hobart, Tas.) and Luci Montesinos Aguilar (Mexico City), Leo Joseph (Adelaide), Nils Kaltenborn (Lillestrm, Norway), Robert and Daisy Kunstaetter (Richmond Hill, Ont.), Jean Laberge (Montréal), Andrew Lawrence (Vancouver) and John Easterbrooke (Shaftesbury), Roger Lemercier (Nice), Micheline Levesque and Carol Côté (Montréal), John McCartney (Fairview Park, Ohio), Claus Mayer (Stuttgart), Françoise Novel (Montréal), Moshe Pinsly (Beit Yanai, Israel), Jens Plahte (Aas, Norway), Annamarie Reichmuth and Roger Müller (Schwyz, Switz), Jane Rowland (Ont.), David Snyderman (Chevy Chase, Md.) and Lila Cabrera (Rochester, NY), Alastair Speare-Gore (London SW6), Christine Summerville (Uphall, W.Lothian), Tina Tecaru (Stoke-on-Trent), Wubbo and Conny Tempel (Oss, Neth.), Jeff White (La Habra, Ca.), and Arthur Yeandle (Southampton).

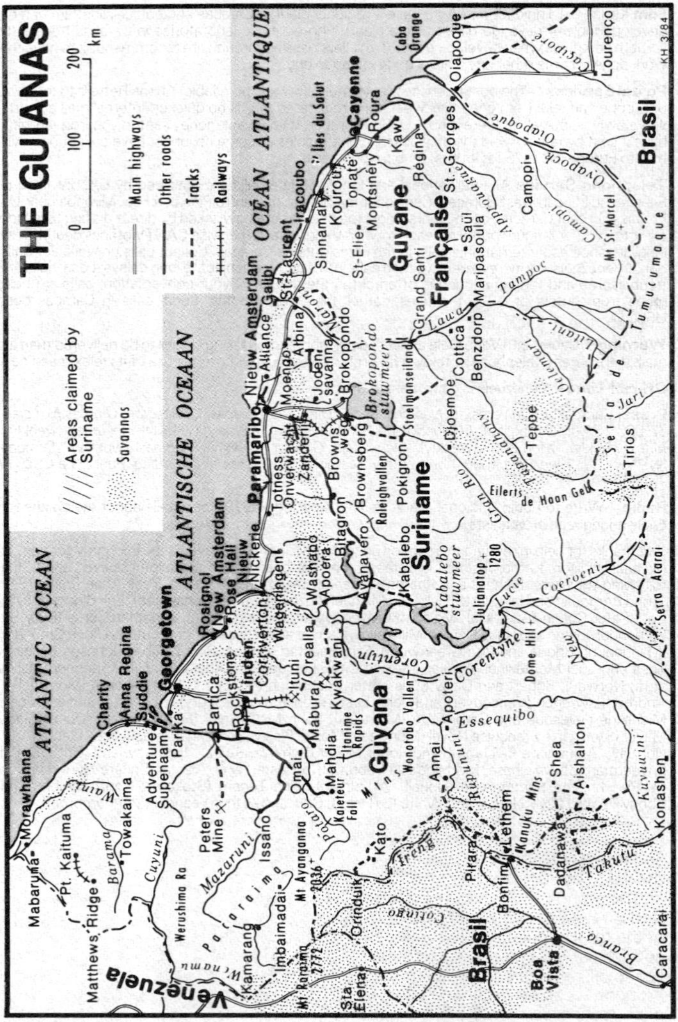
THE GUIANAS
0 100 200 km
Main highways
Other roads
Tracks
Railways
Areas claimed by Suriname
Savannas
ATLANTIC OCEAN
ATLANTISCHE OCEAAN
OCÉAN ATLANTIQUE
Venezuela
Guyana
Suriname
Guyane Française
Brasil
Georgetown
Paramaribo
Cayenne
Morawhanna
Mabaruma
Matthews Ridge
Pt. Kaituma
Towakaima
Charity
Anna Regina
Suddie
Adventure
Supenaam
Parika
Bartica
Rockstone
Linden
Corriverton
Rosignol
New Amsterdam
Rose Hall
Nieuw Nickerie
Wageningen
Totness
Onverwacht
Zanderij
Moengo
Nieuw Amsterdam
Alliance
Galibi
Albina
St-Laurent
Iracoubo
Sinnamary
Kourou
Tonate
Montsinéry
Roura
Kaw
Régina
St.-Georges
Oiapoque
Cabo Orange
Lourenço
Camopi
Saül
Maripasoula
Grand Santi
Cottica
Benzdorp
Djoemoe
Stoelmanseiland
Tepoe
Tirios
Eilerts de Haan Geb
Pokigron
Raleighvallen
Brownsberg
Browns weg
Brokopondo
Joden savanna
Brokopondo stuwmeer
Bitagron
Apoera
Washabo
Ayanavero
Kabalebo
Kabalebo stuwmeer
Julianatop 1280
Lucie
Coeroeni
Dome Hill
New
Corentyne
Orealla
Ituni
Mabura
Kwakwani
Mahdia
Omai
Itanime Rapids
Kaieteur Fall
Potaro
Peters Mine
Issano
Mazaruni
Cuyuni
Werushima Ra
Barama
Waini
Pakaraima
Kamarang
Imbaimadai
Mt Ayanganna 2036
Mt Roraima 2772
Wenamu
Sta. Elena
Orinduik
Kato
Ireng
Cotingo
Wonotobo Vallen
Annai
Apoteri
Essequibo
Rupununi
Pirara
Lethem
Bonfim
Kanuku Mtns
Shea
Aishalton
Dadanawa
Takutu
Kuyuwini
Konashen
Boa Vista
Caracaraí
Branco
Serra Acaraí
Serra de Tumucumaque
Mt St.-Marcel
Jari
Oelemari
Litani
Lawa
Tampoc
Tapanahony
Gran Rio
Marowijne
Approuague
Oyapock
Camopi
Oiapoque
Cassiporé
Îles du Salut
KH 3/84

THE GUIANAS

LIKE the West Indians, the people of the three Guianas, Guyana (formerly British Guiana), Suriname (formerly Dutch Guiana) and French Guyane, are not regarded as belonging to Latin America. The explanation of these three Northern European possessions on the South American continent goes back to the early days of the Spanish conquest of the New World. There was no gold or any other apparent source of wealth to attract the attention of the Spanish discoverers. This part of the coast, which Columbus had first sighted in 1498, seemed to them not only barren but scantily populated and seemingly uninhabitable. The English, the French and the Dutch, anxious to establish a foothold in this part of the world, were not so fastidious.

All three countries have much the same surface: along the coast runs a belt of narrow, flat marshy land, at its widest in Suriname. This coastland carries almost all the crops and most of the population. Behind lies a belt of crystalline upland, heavily gouged and weathered. The bauxite, gold and diamonds are in this area. Behind this again is the massif of the Guiana Highlands. They reach a height of 3,000 feet in the Tumac-Humac range, the divide between French Guyane and Suriname, and Brazil, and 9,219 feet (2,810 metres) at flat-topped Mount Roraima (see page 828), where Guyana, Venezuela and Brazil all meet.

N.B. You need to have your own shoe-cleaning equipment; there seem to be no shoeshine boys in any of the Guianas.

Thanks and acknowledgements for help with the Guianas sections will be found at the end of the chapter on French Guyane.

GUYANA

GUYANA has an area of 83,000 square miles, nearly the size of Britain, but only about 0.5 % (or 280,000 acres) is cultivated. The population numbers some 810,000, of whom about 86 % are literate; about one-third of the population lives in towns.

Some 10 % of the country is the upland savanna of the Rupununi and Kanaku mountains, in the remote hinterland of the SW. A huge tract of thick, hilly jungle and forest—85 % of the country—slopes down from this high plateau towards the sea. The soil is poor and sandy; there is little cultivation, but the bauxite, gold and diamonds are in this area. The rest of the country—3.5 %—is a narrow belt, seldom 8 miles deep, running 200 miles along the coast. It contains some 90 % of the total population (just under a third of the population work on sugar estates and farms), and grows all the sugar and rice. Much of this belt, which is below sea-level, is intersected by great rivers and suffers from both deluge and drought; it can be maintained only by a complicated system of dykes and drains, a permanent costly burden on agriculture but rather picturesque to travel through. Nearly all the cultivated land is in this belt.

From 80 to 110 inches of rain fall mostly in two well defined seasons: April to August and November to January. Less rain falls as one moves southward; here rainfall is 60 inches a year, mainly between April and September. A little natural drainage is given by the rivers; the Corentyne, along the Suriname border to the E; the Berbice and Demerara, 30 and 100 miles respectively to the W; and the Essequibo, which drains most of the country and enters the sea midway along

838 GUYANA

the coast. Falls and rapids hinder their use for communication with the interior, but 60 miles of the Demerara river are navigable by shallow-draft ocean craft up to the Mackenzie bauxite mines.

The original Dutch and English settlers at the beginning of the 17th century established posts up-river, in the hills, mostly as trading points with the Amerindian natives. Plantations were laid out and worked by slaves from Africa. Poor soil defeated this venture, and the settlers retreated with their slaves to the coastal area in mid-18th century: the old plantation sites can still be detected from the air. Coffee and cotton were the main crops up to the end of the 18th century, but sugar had become the dominant crop by 1820. In 1834 slavery was abolished. Many of the slaves scattered as small landholders, and the plantation owners had to look for another source of labour. It was found in indentured East Indians, a few Chinese, and some Portuguese labourers from the Azores and Madeira. About 240,000 had come from India by 1914. At the end of their indentures many settled in Guyana.

Sugar and rice are largely dependent for labour on the Guyanese of Indian descent. The Africans, who prefer town life, are outnumbered and will progressively be more so as the population increases. Europeans comprise below 1%, East Indians 51%, Africans 37%, Creoles (mixed race) 4%, and the others 7%. As for religion, 46% are Christian, 37% Hindu, 8% Muslim, 9% others. Unemployment is estimated to be 40%-50%.

Nearly 25% of the population lives in Georgetown or close by. Density per square mile in the coastal belt is over 1,700, compared with 9.87 average over the whole country. Until 1920 there was little natural increase, but the suppression of malaria and other diseases has since led to a large growth of population especially among the East Indians. The country is overpopulated in relation to its readily exploitable resources; whether the interior could support more people if it were opened up is debatable. The few remaining Amerindians, of the Arawak and Carib groups, are rapidly losing their isolation.

History

The country was first partially settled between 1616 and 1621 by the Dutch West India Company, who erected a fort and depot at Fort Kyk-over-al (County of Essequibo). The first English attempt at settlement was made by Captain Leigh on the Oiapoque River (now French Guyane) in 1604, but it failed to establish a permanent settlement. Lord Willoughby, famous in the early history of Barbados, founded a settlement in 1663 at Suriname, which was captured by the Dutch in 1667 and ceded to them at the Peace of Breda in exchange for New York. The Dutch held the three colonies till 1796 when they were captured by a British fleet. The territory was restored to the Dutch in 1802, but in the following year was retaken by Great Britain, which finally gained it in 1814, when the three counties of Essequibo, Berbice and Demerara were merged to form British Guiana. In 1899 a commission arbitrating on a boundary dispute between Britain and Venezuela awarded over half the present territory of Guyana, consisting of the territory to the W of the River Essequibo, to Britain. Venezuela is claiming the land then ceded.

On May 26, 1966, Guyana was granted independence, and on February 23, 1970 it became a co-operative republic within the Commonwealth; the President is Mr. Desmond Hoyte, who took office in August 1985 following the death of his predecessor Forbes Burnham. The bauxite and sugar industries have been nationalized, and the country appears to have been set firmly on a co-operative path. A Prime Minister and Cabinet are responsible to the National Assembly, which has 53 members elected under a single-list system of proportional representation for a maximum term of five years. President Hoyte has been elected unopposed as leader of the governing People's National Congress (PNC) as well as President General of the Guyana Labour Union. The party won elections, widely described as fraudulent, in December 1985. The main opposition to the PNC is the People's Progressive Party (Marxist) led by Dr. Cheddi Jagan.

GUYANA 839

Georgetown, the capital, and the chief town and port, is on the right bank of the River Demerara, at its mouth. Its population is 185,000, or roughly a quarter of the total population. The climate is tropical, with a mean temperature of 80.5°F. Georgetown, with 19th-century wooden houses supported on stilts, and charming green boulevards laid along the lines of the old Dutch canals, has a character of its own; protected by a sea-wall and a system of dykes opened at low tide, it is set on an alluvial flat below the high-water mark. All that is seen of it from the sea are the masts of the wireless station, the lighthouse (which may be visited by arrangement with the Harbour Master), the Gothic tower of Stabroek Market, the twin dishes of the radio-telephone system, the tower of the *Pegasus Hotel* and the twin square towers of the Church of the Sacred Heart. Most of the older buildings are of wood and some are shabby; since the disastrous fire of 1945 many concrete buildings have been put up in the commercial centre. Some of the most impressive wooden buildings from the colonial past are: the City Hall (Avenue of the Republic) constructed in 1887 in Gothic style; St. George's Cathedral (North Road) dating from 1892, which at a height of 143 feet is one of the tallest wooden buildings in the world; the Law Courts (High Street), finished in 1878 with mock Tudor framing; the President's residence at Guyana House (Main Street), built in 1852; and the imposing Parliament Building (Avenue of the Republic). Other important public buildings are the Roman Catholic Cathedral (Brickdam); the Bishop's High School; St. Stanislaus College (Jesuit); Queens College; the Technical Institute; the Stabroek Market (Water Street), a focal point of the city; the Public Free Library; the Guyana Museum (Company Path); and several churches. The Playhouse Theatre, seating 216, is in Parade Street. The historical museum opposite the post office no longer has Amerindian exhibits. Modern architecture is represented by the *Pegasus Hotel,* the Bank of Guyana and Telephone House. At the head of Brickdam, a main street, is an aluminium arch which commemorates independence. Across the road is a monument to the 1763 slave rebellion surmounted by a striking statue of Cuffy, leader of the rebellion. Adjacent to the Botanic Gardens on Homestretch Avenue is the new Cultural Centre. This is a magnificent theatre, probably the best in the Caribbean, air-conditioned, comfortable, with a large stage and fine acoustics. All it needs now is a regular schedule of performances; for the most part it is closed.

The Georgetown Cricket Club at Bourda, with its pavilions and club rooms, has one of the finest cricket grounds in the tropics. The old Dutch sea-wall (now being rebuilt) is cool in the evening. The mud makes it undesirable to swim in the sea but many locals do so, then go home for a bath. The racecourse has been closed. The international airport is at Timehri, 25 miles S of Georgetown on the first piece of solid ground in the coastlands—a hill rising to the phenomenal altitude of 40 feet. There is an airstrip for local flights at Ogle, six miles from the city.

Things to See The Botanic Gardens (entry free), covering 120 acres, have a fine collection of palms, as well as orchids and ponds of Victoria Regia and lotus lilies. There are thousands of birds in the shrubberies. The Zoo has a fine collection of local animals, including several manatees in lakes surrounding the area. It appears that about half of the gardens is now closed to the public: do not enter or go near the fenced-off part, as you may be attacked by muggers or arrested by the police. The police band gives a free concert on Thursdays, 1730-1830, in the gardens. Entry to Zoo, adults 50 cents, children 25 cents, but it was reported closed in January 1987, because of a chemical accident which killed several animals.

The University of Guyana is at Turkeyen, near the city. The Promenade Gardens on Middle Street (entry free) have many beautiful tropical plants and flowers, including the rare cannonball tree (*Couroupita guianensis*), so named for the appearance of its poisonous fruit.

Hotels Air-conditioned, private bathrooms, *Guyana Pegasus,* L, swimming pool (non residents wishing to swim must pay G$50 for a month's bathing), restaurant (G$45, lunch, G$50+ dinner). The following have a/c, and non a/c rooms which are cheaper; all have restaurants: *Tower,* A, run down, depressing atmosphere, theft no longer a problem, swimming pool closed for repairs, also

840 GUYANA

3-course meals at G$20 p.p., staff courteous and friendly; *Country Pride*, "soon to be opened, looks good"; *Belvedere*, Camp Street, C; can be very noisy; *Park*, C without a/c, good security (new annex recommended); *Penthouse*, D; *La Chalet*, D expensive for what it is; *Le Grille*, 176 Middle Street, P.O. Box 744, Tel.: 57593, C, incl. breakfast (beware of robbers); *Demico* (opposite Stabroek Market, over cafeteria, recommended), C, book a month ahead, recommended. *Chinese Dragon*, D (a/c and non a/c rooms same price), with restaurant. *Palm Court*, D, with breakfast; *Roma*, C with breakfast; *Aunt Aggie's*, 69 Main Street—if you don't mind the prostitutes, E; *Waggon Wheel*, E, a bit noisy; *German's*, F, w.c. in every room, flush before use. All in main business area. Several comfortable and central boarding houses, e.g. *Bill's Guest House*, 46 High Street, E, highly recommended, but it is a rough area of town, and the owner is reported to have emigrated, meals not available; *Elizabeth Guest House*, Wellington Street, E; *Rima Guest House*, Middle Street, D, with breakfast, no a/c, modernized and good; *Water Chris*, D, friendly, good restaurant. If in doubt, go to a larger hotel for first night and shop around in daylight. Prices are rising rapidly and frequent water cuts make for a troubled stay.

Restaurants Generally eating out has suffered from food shortages; even bread and butter may be unavailable except in street markets. At *Pegasus* and *Tower* Hotels, good Anglo-American food; the *Pegasus* puts on Sunday lunch for G$45—there is a steel band; *Palm Court*, quite good; *Belvedere Hotel*, "The Hut", Anglo-American and French; *Qik-Serv*, good and clean self-service; *Arawak Steak House* (US$10) and roof garden (over *Demico Hotel*) with "wild meat" (game) served Thurs. evenings; *Park Hotel* now only serves food upstairs; lunch and dinner must be ordered in advance. A new restaurant for those who can afford the best is *Del Casa*, Middle Street (US$20). *Kwang Chow*, Camp St. and Regent St., and *Chinese Dragon*, Robb St. and Av. of the Republic, both good Chinese; there are several Chinese places along Sheriff Street (nickname Noodles Boulevard). Indian/Chinese/Creole fare provided at the *Rice Bowl/Doc's Creole Corner* on Robb Street, recommended; also *Country Pride* with excellent fish either fried or curried. *Hack's Hallal*, though still serving quality fare, is no longer cheap. Two other recommended Chinese restaurants are *Diamond Food House*, 9 Camp St., Werk-en-Rust, and *Double Happiness* at 88 Sheriff St. near the town centre, which both have the same owners. Chinese restaurant, *Double Dragon*, on Avenue of the Republic, on site of the old *Local. Grub Inn*, good cheap Creole food and dancing. Also good for cheap food are *Sip 'n Chat*, *The Coalpot* (recommended, US$8), *Yamin's Eatwell Centre*, Camp St., *King Creole* (fast food) plus a cheap Chinese restaurant in virtually every block.

Tipping Hotel and restaurant staff, 10%; taxis, same; airport porters, 25 cents a bag; hairdressers, 50 cents; cloakroom attendants and cinema usherettes, no tip.

Current 110 volts in the city and 220 volts outside.

Shopping The East Indian shops have a fine assortment of the beaten brasswork commonly known as Benares ware. They sell Indian jewellery, knick-knacks and items made of native hardwood (best buy). Other possible buys are fragrant kus-kus grass, guava jelly, cassava cakes, many Amerindian curios such as bead aprons, bows and arrows, blowpipes, basket work and bright plumed head-dresses. Buy these in souvenir shops in Water Street, Margarita Gift Shop in Middle Street, or in the *Tower Hotel* or at the Guyana Crafts Co-operative in High Street or at "Houseproud", 6 Ave. of the Republic, tho' expensive, recommended. Guyana Stores (Amex representative) and Fogarty's (cheaper) are the two big department stores in the centre of town, both have small book sections and are good for clothing. Regent Street is the major shopping area. (Jaigobind recommended for hammocks.) Guyana Stores carries photographic supplies (Kodak), Acme in Regent Street carries Agfa. Developing film takes time and is not always reliable. A more interesting way of getting curios is to go into the Bush (special permit needed) among the Amerindians. Note that Stabroek Market can be dangerous for travellers. Credit cards are accepted at the *Pegasus* and *Tower* hotel shops.

Bookshop Guyana National Trading Corporation on Camp Street. 2nd hand available on Regent Street at "Argosy" and Kharg, some paperbacks. Guyana Stores has some books (Robb St. branch).

Motoring Self-drive from Sankar Bros., Main Street (Tel.: 61058), daily charge, then free for 30 miles, then a mileage charge, reported to be rising rapidly. Allied Services, Croal Street (Tel.: 63851) and Ammo Taxis, Charlotte Street (Tel.: 63687). Try to book one month in advance. Gasoline: G$10 for Imperial gallon of "regular" (G$20 on black market at night). **Beware**: serious gasoline shortages can make this a difficult way to travel.

Taxis G$12 per fare in city limits, double night fares on longer trips. Shared taxis in city during daytime (between 10-12 people) cost G$1.00 pp. The system can be difficult to figure out; often impossible to get a seat during rush hours.

Banks National Bank of Industry and Commerce (7 branches); Barclays Bank International (2 branches); The Republic Bank; Bank of Baroda (2); Bank of Nova Scotia; are all good for receiving money from abroad. Guyana Co-operative Bank (10). Open: 0800-1200, but 0800-1100 on Sat.

GUYANA 841

When the amount exceeds G$100 the transaction becomes very time consuming. Amex will hold mail and process loss claims.

Post Office Main one at North Road, open 0730-1600.

International Telecommunications: Telegraph, telephone and telex: Guyana International Telecommunications Corp., Bank of Guyana building. No "collect" telephone calls may be made. Local telephone service is sporadic and the telephone book is out of date. Generally the interior is not served although a few places have radio telephone links.

British High Commission 44 Main Street, P.O. Box 10849. Tel.: 658814. Telex: GY2221.

Travel Agency Guyana Overland Tours, P.O. Box 10173, 6 Avenue of the Republic, (above "Houseproud" shop), first floor, Tel., 69876, cables Gotours, offer a number of tours of one, two and more days in the interior, including Kaieteur Fall, and will send details on request; they also sell good maps and their guide (G$4.95) is one of the only sources of current tourist information and maps. Extremely helpful. Frandec Travel Service (Main St.), Neil Mendoza (the manager) is very helpful and informative. Joe Chin on Main St. is also recommended.

Churches. Anglican: St. Georges Cathedral, Christ Church, Waterloo Street; St. Andrews (Presbyterian), Avenue of the Republic; Roman Catholic Cathedral, Brickdam.

Bus Service In the city and long distance, unreliable: shortage of spares. Main terminal at Stabroek Market Square. City services run 0600-2200, US$0.50. Linden US$5.30, Parika US$2.15. For New Amsterdam and Springlands; bus to Rosignol G$8.40, then 95-cent ferry to New Amsterdam, then bus to Springlands, G$6 (2½ hrs). Taxi to Springlands, US$50 for vehicle, leave by 0730 to catch ferry to Suriname.

Ferries Service reduced since bridge built over Demerara River 4 miles upstream from Georgetown. The *Makouria* crosses the Demerara River between Georgetown's Ferry Stelling and Vreeden-Hoop on weekdays only (Sunday, bus G$1.50). Single fare: G$1. Weekly ferry direct to Bartica.

Roads There is a good road between Linden (Mackenzie) and Georgetown; four miles south of Georgetown on the East Bank Demerara road is the Demerara harbour bridge (cars G$24 return toll) leading to Parika on the Essequibo and Wales, a sugar growing area, south of the bridge after seven miles of the West bank of the Demerara. A twice-daily ferry from Parika (cars G$11.90 one way toll) to Adventure connects with the Essequibo road system. Supenaam to Charity about 40 miles. There are no other paved roads, but a number of trails (4WD necessary) radiate from Bartica and Linden. The EEC have put up ECU12m to finance a Guyana-Suriname car ferry and the Brazilians are planning a bridge over the Takutu at Lethem. Also planned is a laterite road from Lethem-Annai-Kurupukari on to the Essequibo and then Mabura (new timber complex) to connect to the existing laterite road to Linden.

Air Services Guyana Airways (*Tower Hotel*) has many scheduled and non-scheduled passenger and freight services to airfields in Guyana, which have recently improved following assistance from Romania with planes and pilots, and Ireland with pilots. Fuel shortage is leading to a further curtailment of flights. To Lethem on the Brazilian frontier, daily except Monday and Tuesday, 1145, G$90 single (tickets for this service can only be got at the airline's office and not through travel agents, see also page 846). Try to book as far ahead as possible; local people do it four weeks in advance. Scheduled flights to Brazil, Suriname, French Guyane and nearby Caribbean islands (e.g. Port of Spain, G$336.50. Exit tax G$50). Shared taxi (arranged by travel agent with Loy's Taxi Service on booking flight) between Georgetown and airport, G$40 (day/night) per seat or G$140 per taxi; you may get a seat for less *from* airport *into* town; bus, G$3.80 (Timehri bus, stops outside airport terminal) uncertain timing, runs sometimes on the hour into town. Do not use pirate taxis as they charge much more. Guyana Airways international bookings are not reliable. Check that the flight you want is operating. Offers in foreign currency can sometimes help clear two-week average waiting lists. Tickets purchased with local currency may not be exchanged abroad. All tickets out of Guyana attract 50% travel tax. Onward tickets after a stop-over if you buy your ticket in Guyana may have to be purchased on arrival. Check with airlines for details.

Warnings Georgetown has acquired an unpleasant reputation for assaults and robberies, especially after dark. Do not wear jewellery or watch, or carry cameras, handbags or wallets, etc. in easily accessible places and take particular care at night by travelling in a taxi. Recent visitors stress, however, that the atmosphere has improved since Desmond Hoyte took over the Government. Frequent and prolonged water and power cuts continue. Water pressure is low except in the best hotels, and typhoid has become a risk. Do not photograph public buildings—or even the market—without permission; this can lead to police confiscation of your camera.

Linden (pop. 30,000), the bauxite centre 70 miles S of Georgetown on the

842 GUYANA

Demarara River, is made up of three towns: Mackenzie, Wismar and Christianburg. The latter two are separated from Mackenzie by the river on whose banks they all lie, in secondary jungle. There is a golf club; visitors are welcome. The river is navigable right up to the mine, and it is disconcerting on rounding its bends to meet large ocean-going ships. Linden is the second largest community in Guyana, but accommodation is scarce and expensive (*Mackenzie Hotel*, D, Tel.: 04-2183). There are also several other guest houses at a price. There is a bridge across the river, and a road to Georgetown (taxi, about G$30 pp). To visit the interior from here you need a permit from Georgetown. Lifts are sometimes available from gold prospectors.

Current 220 volts, 60 cycles. Same at New Amsterdam and Bartica, below.

New Amsterdam, capital of Berbice, the most easterly county of Guyana, is on the right bank of the Berbice River near its mouth. It is 65 miles SE of Georgetown, from which there is a good road to Rosignol, ferry point (95 cents) for New Amsterdam, across the river. Pop. 20,000. The foliage gives the town a picturesque air. Poor roads; water should be boiled before drinking.

Hotels *Penguin* (Tel.: 03-2012) B-C, a/c. *Church View Guest House*, D, incl. meals. At Rose Hall: *Hotel Embassy*.

Banks National Bank of Industry and Commerce; Barclays Bank International; Bank of Baroda.

Bus To Georgetown, none-direct, but eight ferries a day to Rosignol and then bus (G$8.40) or taxi (shared) to Georgetown; also to Springlands (G$9.30 a seat).

Springlands, near the mouth of the Corentyne River (can be smelly), is a small port frequented by sailing vessels. There is a daily ferry (Sf7.50 one-way Sf12.50 return—counts as onward ticket in both countries) run by Suriname (not Sundays or national holidays of either country) to and from Nieuw Nickerie (Suriname), which involves a 24 hour wait. Booking office open at 0730 Mon.-Sat. in small yellow building 100 feet before ferry; passport and G$2 needed for booking but you can buy the actual ticket on the ferry. If travelling in a group, one member with all the group's passports could travel ahead and book onto the ferry, thus saving time and possibly a wasted trip. Then from 0900 onwards Immigration stamp you out, keeping your passport until about 1200 when you go to Customs with your money declaration. Border formalities at Springlands are very thorough and slow; the waiting list can take a week to clear, and it can take two to ten hours to cross the river. (A new ferry, being installed with EEC funds, should be ready in 1988.) Before you leave check whether you require a visa to visit Suriname -it can take as long as six weeks to get one. A transit visa on the other hand can be obtained right away. Local advice to save time is to fly. The town is officially referred to as ***Corriverton,*** as it has been joined with Skeldon to form the Corentyne River Town (population 17,000). The road from Springlands to New Amsterdam has been rebuilt.

Hotels *Ambassador*, close to point for ferry to Nickerie; *Parpark*, E, opposite ferry; *Arawak* (Room 27, the best) honest, opposite ferry, F, good value; *Liberty*; *Mahogany*, with colour TV (Suriname programme). Also *Swiss Hotel* (Pakistani run), rough but helpful. Good Chinese restaurants within a few blocks of town centre.

Banks National Bank of Industry and Commerce; Barclays Bank International.

Transport To Georgetown via New Amsterdam, ferry and Rosignol (not a through service) G$18. Shared taxi to Georgetown, G$50 pp. ***Morawhanna*** (Morajuana to the Venezuelans), on the Waini River near the Venezuelan frontier, is another small port.

Bartica, at the junction of the Essequibo and Mazaruni rivers, is the "take-off" town for the gold and diamond fields, Kaieteur Fall, and the interior generally. Here an Amazonian mass of waters meets, but vastly more beautiful, for they are coloured the deep indigo purple of all Guyanese rivers and not the dull mud-brown of most of the Amazon. Swimming very good.

A boat takes you between Bartica and ***Parika*** (36 miles) twice a week on Mondays and Thursdays at 0930, 0815 on Sats., returns a day later at 0800 (1330 on Sats.), G$12.50. Stops at Fort Island, food available, but better to take your own as choice is limited to sweetcorn and pastries. A faster

GUYANA 843

service is available by speedboat G$50. There is a weekly direct ferry to Georgetown. Buses ply between Parika and Vreed-en-Hoop, connecting with the bridge and ferry for Georgetown. (You travel with the *Glory Halleluya*, a wooden boat, at your own risk—it is always overcrowded and has already sunk twice.) Buses also connect with the Parika-Adventure ferry, dep. 1700 daily and 0830 Weds. and Fridays and returning from Adventure 0300 and 1330 Weds. and Fridays. One sailing at 1200 Sunday. From Parika there are 3 ferries a day to Leguan Island (30 minutes, G$ 1.35) where the new *Hotel President* has opened. Parika-Adventure G$6; Parika-Bartica G$7.20. The m.v. *Malili* plies daily between Parika and Adventure (Essequibo Coast area)—see *Three Singles to Adventure*, by Gerald Durrell.

Hotels *Marin; The Nest* on Fifth Avenue, E, unsafe, very noisy, meals to be had from disco after 1730, or "Robbie's". *Modern*, near ferry, good food. Book ahead if possible. Mrs Payne, near Hospital, basic, clean.

Airstrip Flights on Monday, Wednesday (2) and Saturday to Timehri, Georgetown.

The Essequibo is navigable to large boats for some miles above Bartica. The Cuyuni flows into the Mazaruni 3 miles above Bartica, and above this confluence the Mazaruni is impeded for 120 miles by thousands of islands, rapids and waterfalls. To avoid this stretch of treacherous river a road has been built from Bartica to Issano, where boats can be taken up the more tranquil upper Mazaruni. To visit the diamond fields there are regular air trips by Guyana Airways to Kurupung on the Mazaruni river. From there it is just a walk (with a permit) to the diamond fields.

The **Kaieteur Fall,** on the Potaro River, ranks with the Niagara, Victoria, and Iguazú Falls in majesty and beauty. This Fall, nearly five times the height of Niagara, with a sheer drop of 741 ft., pours its waters over a channel nearly 300 ft. wide. Guyana Overland Tours starts a six-day trip on the first Tues. of the month, about G$400 p.p., for groups of ten (or more); they require four weeks' notice. Air fare G$120. There is a once-a-week air service, most seats reserved for residents (Friday, G.A.S., G$75) but no time for sightseeing. Instead larger groups often charter G.A.S. planes on Sundays, or small parties a light aircraft, for the day. It is rumoured that G.A.S. personnel expect G$30/40 to get you on the scheduled service.

The overland route to the Fall takes 7 days and requires a special permit. This takes at least two weeks to obtain from the Secretary of Home Affairs. The first day's journey is from Georgetown to Bartica: either take the ship round the coast and see the island of Leguan (*Hotel President*) at the mouth of the Essequibo or cross the Demerara by bridge or ferry to Vreed-en-Hoop and on by road to Parika, there to join the ship for Bartica at the confluence of the Essequibo and Mazaruni (cost about G$7.) The second day is a 113-mile journey via Garraway Stream with its fine suspension bridge across the Potaro, over a jungle road to Kangaruma where the night is spent at a government rest house (reservations can be made by radio from Georgetown). The next day a boat is taken to Tukeit (rest house, F, bring your own food) with portages at the Amatuk and Waratuk Falls. There is a rest house at Tukeit and good bathing. The climb to the top of the Kaieteur Fall takes at least two hours (but is worth it) to watch the blue, white and brown water tumbling into a stupendous gorge. There is a rest house at the top of the falls but it has been closed for repairs. Avoid April and October, the dry season, as the flow of the falls is reduced. The height of the wet (June) season should also be avoided if attempting to walk from Mahdia (4-6 days). Alternatively the gold prospectors have boats going up river or one can pay to travel by jeep, or the plane to the Fall leaves on Friday, cost G$25.

The Kaieteur Fall lies within the Kaieteur National Park, where there is a variety of wildlife—tapirs, ocelots, monkeys, armadillos, anteaters, and jungle and river birds. The Pakaraima Mountains stretch from Kaieteur westwards to include the highest peak in Guyana, Mt. Roraima (9,219 feet), the possible inspiration for Conan Doyle's *Lost World* (see page 828).

Kaieteur continues to be where most people want to go, but now that there is very little tinned food available locally, planning five days' food is a headache. The boatman has doubled his hire rates for the 3-day Kangaruma (guesthouse, F)-Tukeit leg and chartering a Britten-Norman Islander costs G$430 each for a return flight to Ogle for eight people. Alternatively in Bartica one can ask around for trucks or prospectors going to the Mahdia area. Even if there is an immediate lift, leave your name at the hotel beside the docks. Other people will be looking to share the cost of transport "down under". The road between Kangaruma and Mahdia is very bad indeed during the

844 GUYANA

rainy season and can take over seven hours, so take sufficient food. The cost of a rented truck for the journey is just over US$200 but divided between six it is reasonable. There are also plenty of gold prospectors above Amatuk falls and they frequently go to Kangaruma and Mahdia. Instead Guyana Overland Tours are suggesting Imbaimadai which is accessible, enjoyable and also has a waterfall, not as high but as beautiful a setting. You will also see Mt. Roraima on landing and take-off. Tues. and Sats. by Guyana Airways, try to pick a clear day, book outside Guyana and confirm on arrival in Georgetown.

Precautions Book accommodation at Bartica and the Rest House if at all possible (if not, do not worry too much as few people seem to be visiting the area at the moment), and arrange for boats on the Potaro in advance. Take what food and drink you need, a sleeping bag, a sheet and blanket, a mosquito net, and kerosene for the Tilley lamps.

Elizabeth Allen writes: The south-western area of Guyana is known as the Rupunuri Savanna. 13,000 sq. km. lie in Guyana and 47,000 sq. km. more in Venezuela and Brazil. The Kanuku Mountains divide the Rupununi from west to east, and rise to 3,143 feet at Mt. Ilamikipang. The savanna is a dry grassland region covered with native grasses, scattered scrub, and termite hills. Since the late nineteenth century it has been settled by cattle ranchers and Jesuit missionaries. It is one of the more densely settled Amerindian areas. Special permits must be obtained to visit, from the Secretary of Home Affairs, 6 Brickdam, Georgetown. Malaria is prevalent and prophylactic should be taken.

Mr J. Dalzell of Guyana Overland Tours writes: There is one major tourist centre in the Rupunuri, Karanambu Lodge which is about 40 miles north of Lethem (10 miles north of Yupukari). This was featured in David Attenborough's *Zoo Quest in Guyana* and Gerald Durrell's *Three Singles to Adventure*. It is a cattle ranch, founded by Tiny McTurk in 1926 and now run by his daughter Diane as a ranch and tourist centre. Marvellous situation on the Rupununi River, fishing (including the famous arapaima), hunting, excellent accommodation in small guest houses with running water, showers etc. Food is always superb and the whole place is fabulous. The problem is getting there. The latest arrangement is a package trip involving charter flight from Ogle Airstrip direct to Karanambu, and then returning in a Land Rover (usually via Yupukari) to Lethem, overnight at Manari and back to Georgetown. Wendela Jackson (300 New Garden Street, Georgetown) is Diane's town agent and will make all the necessary arrangements and get permits etc. There is the perennial problem that having made all the arrangements planes aren't always available.

Yupukari is an Amerindian village in the savannah on a breezy hilltop, the centre for Anglican mission work in the Rupununi (begun in 1840). The Alan Knight Training Centre is a theological college for training Amerindians for the Anglican priesthood, and consists of twelve small houses, a thatch and brick library cum-lecture room, wooden church and brick vicarage. It is a unique venture, the first of its kind in the world, and they are always glad to see visitors who may be passing through, and if anyone should get stranded in the savanna will happily provide a bed and food!

Lethem, on the Brazilian frontier in the SW, has no reliable road connection as yet with the rest of the country. Guyana Airways flies Weds. (twice) and Sats. (irregular) from Georgetown, usually direct but sometimes flying via Kato in the Pakaraima Mountains where tomatoes are being produced. The flight takes one hour and costs G$115 (returns only sold). To purchase an airline ticket in Lethem one must first complete passport and customs formalities at the police station ½ mile from the airstrip, then buy an open ticket, then make a reservation; the flights are often full as Lethem is where Georgetown's street traders come to get their goods (via Bom Fim and Boa Vista), and flights are generally booked up two or three months in advance. Reconfirmation (repeated) of your flight is therefore essential. Taxi to Lethem airport from town, G$100, is a worthwhile investment. Alternatively one can hitch. There are 3 buses a day from Bom Fim to Boa Vista, starting 1½ miles from the Lethem border crossing (G$1 in canoe). The plane from Georgetown is usually late (it leaves Georgetown at 1430) so an overnight stay in Lethem is often necessary. There are tracks NE to Manari and Annai, and the Takutu river can easily be crossed to enter Brazil (rowing boat, or ford in dry season; there is now a vehicle pontoon, G$2 p.p., one way). The Boa Vista-Manaus bus leaves at 1730. If you think you have malaria you will be given an *injection*. Foot-and-mouth dip for boots.

Elizabeth Allen writes: Lethem supports hotels, 3 bars (the coldest beer is sold nearest the airstrip) a military post, telegraph office and a number of small stores. If you need to cool off, there is a stream 15 minutes out of town on the road with the guest house and the army barracks. (There is no one much interested in foreign exchange dealing. Mr. Jardin, who owns a shop, will change travellers' cheques at a reasonable rate.) It is the centre of the ranching economy (as well as Guyana's parallel economy). The first Jesuit mission to be established in Guyana is at the village of St. Ignatius, about 1½ miles from Lethem—it was founded in 1911 by the famous Jesuit Cary Elwes. There has been an attempt to settle blacks from the coast on agricultural land near Lethem.

Hotels Mr. Arthur M. Bobb's *Takutu Hotel*, near airfield (he organizes trips into Brazil and will advise and arrange passage to Boa Vista), C, full board, other arrangements possible (very pleasant indeed); *Manari Guest House and Ranch*, 10 km. from airport by jeep, C, with bath and full board, very good, riding, fishing and swimming; *Roy's Bar*, about 1 km. from the airport, allows one to sleep on the tables or in your hammock if you've got one. No charge; his excellent food is G$10 p.p. Alternatively ask for Mrs. Matthews, or Mr. Ching who may allow one to stay in the Government rest house (G$6); breakfast G$10; a good evening meal can be had from Mrs. Matthews for G$8 (advance warning essential).

Elizabeth Allen writes: The creek at the rear of the ranch-house is safe for swimming, and horses may be hired for riding, and there is good fishing nearby. Day trips can be arranged to the Kanuku Mountains, about 2 hours' drive by jeep, appearing blue, clad in forest and occasional cloud in the distance. A half-day visit can be made to the Moco-Moco Falls to bathe and eat lunch by the cascading river after walking for about a mile through the rich jungle vegetation. G$50 each up to eight people, then G$120. To Manon, same prices.

Border Crossing Exit stamp, customs forms and currency declarations and all immigration procedures must be conducted at the police station before leaving Guyana for Brazil. One can hire a taxi and get it to wait while the form filling is carried out. From the police station to the river is about 1½ miles. There are boats there if a flight has come in. (More easygoing than it sounds, but the red tape requires patience). The Brazilian military post at Bom Fim is some 1½ miles inside Brazilian territory or 15 minutes walk. It closes at 1800 each evening. The bus leaves at 1730. There is no public transport from the Takutu River crossing to the village; given time and patience a vehicle can be arranged in Lethem with "Selino". (Brazilian time at this point is one hour behind Guyanese time.) Beware inebriated immigration officers on Sun., otherwise few problems with border crossing.

The Economy

Apart from instant, temporary prosperity brought about by the brief non-oil commodities boom in the mid-1970s, which raised gdp growth to 10.4% in 1975, Guyana's economy has been in almost permanent recession in the last two decades, despite considerable, unexploited potential in hydroelectric power, minerals and forestry. While Venezuela's long standing claim to the Essequibo region, within which most of these resources are situated, has discouraged investment, other factors are more to blame. Inefficient management in the dominant state sector covering vital sugar and bauxite industries, an investment climate discouraging both domestic and foreign savings, and an acute foreign exchange shortage, have resulted in poor performances from the key agricultural and mining sectors, and a largely moribund manufacturing sector.

Most agriculture is concentrated on the coastal plain, and many sugar plantations are below sea level, necessitating an extensive system of dams, dykes, canals and pumps to prevent inundation. Sugar is the main crop, and has vied with bauxite and alumina as the most important source of export earnings. Rice is the second most important crop, and a useful foreign exchange earner, though significant quantities of rice production are bartered or export proceeds are undeclared through trade with South American neighbours, especially Suriname and Brazil.

Guyana is the world's largest producer of calcined bauxite, the highest grade of the mineral, and currently has roughly half the world market, though competition from China is becoming stronger. The East Montgomery mine in Pakarima is expected to produce 50% of total calcined bauxite output from its 80-m tonne reserve by 1989. Production is currently concentrated at Linden, on the Demarara river, and at Kwakani in Berbice county. No alumina (refined bauxite) has been exported since 1982 because the Linden refinery still awaits investment for refurbishment.

In January 1987 the government devalued the Guyanese dollar, hoping to break out of a balance of payments vice that has prevented a current account surplus since 1963, pulling reserves down to only US$6.5 m by November 1986—enough for just a few days' imports. The government also hopes that the devaluation will persuade the US government to relax a hardline stance on World Bank and Inter-American Development Bank (IDB) loans to Guyana: in 1983 the USA vetoed three IDB loans, and has not resumed bilateral lending. The IMF declared Guyana ineligible for further assistance in May 1985, because of payment arrears.

846 **GUYANA**

	1961-70 (av)	1971-80 (av)	1981-85 (av)
Gdp growth (1980 prices)	3.3%	1.7%	n.a.
Inflation	2.2%	10.2%	n.a.
Exports (fob) US$m	142	258	239
Sugar	47	91	81
Bauxite	35	84	96
Alumina	22	25	8
Rice	16	25	23
Imports (fob)US$m	105	247	259
Current account balance US$m (cum)	-102 (a)	-602	-677

(a) = 1963-70

Information for Visitors

Air Services: From Europe: flights via Antigua and Barbados (BA recommended route), which connect with British Airways flights to London. Guyana Airways operates 3 times a week to Barbados to connect with the BA London flights; connections from other points via Curaçao, Trinidad, Guadeloupe or Martinique. Paramaribo is not good for connections with Europe—a night-stop is always incurred.

From North America: by Tropical Air from New York taking 5 hrs.; or from Miami (2 a week) via Caracas and Port of Spain. Connections three times a week via Port of Spain by BWIA (this ticket entitles you to two free stops over on Antigua, St Kitts, St Lucia, Barbados or Trinidad) or Guyana Airways via Miami (Wed., Fri.).

Regional Services: From Paramaribo by Guyana Airways twice a week. From Port of Spain and other islands by Cubana. Curaçao-Georgetown-Paramaribo services are now operated by Guyana Airways. Cruzeiro do Sul flights terminate at Paramaribo. Connecting flights to Paramaribo and Cayenne for Belém leave weekly (Thurs.). Return flights also weekly, leaving Belém on Fri. Cubana fly Havana-Barbados-Trinidad-Georgetown. Guyana Airways has a slightly cheaper link flight to Barbados, Tues., Thurs. and Sat. Boa Vista twice a week. The flight from Georgetown to Boa Vista (if you can get on) is a fairly cheap link into the excellent Brazilian air network. Best to consult your travel agent as flight timetables change frequently. Check over-weight charges in town so as to have enough G$ to pay at the airport. Exchange facilities frequently closed.

Internal Guyana Airways run scheduled flights to 22 places within the country, from Timehri airport (25 miles south of Georgetown). Only military and charter flights operate from the Ogle airstrip (6 miles out). Flights have been curtailed because of shortages of fuel. Book early and make sure that the service is operating.

Sea Transport Up to 12 passengers are carried by cargo vessels run by the Royal Netherlands Steamship Co. (agents: Phs. Van Ommeren, Ltd., Avenfield House, 118/121 Park Lane, London W1).

Exit Tax Visitors pay a tax of G$50 on leaving, if they stay more than 24 hrs, either to Immigration Officer or the firm with whom booking has been made. On payment of the tax a voucher is issued which must be produced for cancellation at the time of embarkation.

Documents and Customs All visitors must carry passport and all require visas, and must have an interview before travelling with the relevant Consul or High Commission (in London at 3, Palace Court. W.2. Tel.: 01-229-7684). Take 2 photos when you attend for your visa interview. Visitors without visas lose their passports and have to collect them from Immigration in Georgetown at Camp Street on the next working day before 1030. Travel regulations are liable to change at short notice and visitors are advised to check with their travel agents and Guyanese overseas representatives. Vaccination for yellow fever required by passengers arriving from most tropical countries (check). It is *not* recommended to describe oneself as a journalist as this can entail being

GUYANA 847

ensnared in red tape. Normally the time given at the airport for a visit is 3 days, unless you are staying with friends. Stays can be extended by going to the Home Department with your documents: they will approve the application and send you to have it stamped at Immigration.

A through or return ticket to a destination outside the country is essential; a ticket out from Suriname or French Guyane is accepted (a ticket from Georgetown to Lethem is often sufficient for this purpose). In the absence of such a ticket you may be required to pay a deposit. A permit is required from the Home Department at 6 Brickdam to visit Rupununi. (Three weeks' notice is required before an application can be considered). Tourists may bring in duty free one-sixth of a gallon of spirits and of wine, 200 cigarettes or 50 cigars or half a pound of tobacco; due to shortages, foreign cigarettes and drink are unobtainable and much sought after and surpluses can be easily disposed of. Baggage examination is very thorough but has been speeded up recently. You may be required to show you have enough money for your stay and fill in forms declaring money and jewellery that you may have with you, both when you arrive and when you leave. Keep your copy as you will need it to get your foreign currency out of Guyana. Foodstuffs generally may *not* be imported but one can import food for personal use (any surplus will make very acceptable gifts for hard pressed Guyanese householders). The best place to fill out a departure card is at the airline office, as the cashier's office for the payment of exit tax is frequently shut, especially when international flights are departing.

Railways None for passengers. Buses cover the old railway route.

Riverways The Transport and Harbours Department operates: (1) Ferries across the Demerara (also bridge), Berbice, and Essequibo; (2) Georgetown to Morawhanna and Mabaruma, on the Barima and Arika rivers, N.W. District; (3) Georgetown to Adventure on the Essequibo coast; (4) Georgetown to Bartica at the junction of the Essequibo, Mazaruni, and Cuyuni rivers; (5) Georgetown to Pickersgill and other stations on the upper reaches of the Pomeroon river; (6) Parika to Adventure and Bartica; (7) New Amsterdam to Kwakwani, the bauxite town; (8) Launch service from New Amsterdam to Ikuruwa, up the Canje Creek; (9) Daily ferries up Mahaica and Mahaicony creeks. There are 607 miles of navigable river in all. No vehicle ferry across the Corentyne.

Roads A rebuilt 185-mile road runs along the coast from Springlands on the Corentyne to Charity on the Pomeroon; the Berbice and Essequibo rivers are crossed by ferries and the Demerara by a new bridge (toll G$5 return). In the interior the road from Bartica to Garraway Stream on the Potaro River (102 miles) links up with the old Potaro road system, leading to the gold fields, and a branch road to Issano, Mazaruni River, gives easy access to the principal diamond areas. The new road from Georgetown to Linden will, if linked with the Ituni road, open a new route to the interior. A very rough old trail runs between Bartica to Mahdia in the deep interior, but the "self-help" road from Mahdia to Annai has reverted to forest. A new road is being built along the Upper Mazaruni river; this will eventually link up with another road being built north along the Essequibo river, which is already open between Wismar and Rockstone. Roads and trails usable by vehicles total 1,810 miles. Motor spares are impossible to come by and people fly out of the country to obtain parts.

Clothes Above all avoid wearing shorts; the locals see this as a remnant of colonialist behaviour.

Food, Drink and Restaurants The variety of races which constitutes the population has led to the emergence of a variety of local food specialities—Indian, Portuguese, African, English and Creole food. Of the latter, the best known is pepper-pot, a meat dish cooked in cassava juice with peppers and herbs. (Guyanese hot pepper sauce is *very* hot.) Most meals are accompanied by rice, when available. Hotels often do not have bread and butter. There are street traders everywhere, and if you want anything you have to bargain hard. The Government lacks the foreign exchange to import powdered milk, and interruptions of electricity supply make it risky to keep milk in liquid form. Seafood, found in restaurants near the Stabroek Market in Georgetown, is good, as are the wide variety of tropical fruits such as mangoes, papayas, oranges, bananas, etc. in season. Generally foodstuffs may not be imported for sale. Personal-use quantities are allowed (e.g. 10 lb of flour max.). Additionally yellow peas, white sugar, canned butter, cooking oil, toilet paper, soaps, yeast and canned food make excellent gifts in return for hospitality. Alternatively most of these items are available at a price on the black market.

Rum is the most popular drink. Produced locally it is quite cheap (XM Gold

848 GUYANA

Medal Rum, G$15 a bottle). Other recommended brands are XM Liquid Gold (10 years old) and Eldorado Bonded Reserve. High Wine is a strong local rum. Local gin, vodka and whisky are worth a try. The local beer, Banks, is acceptable. There are about 20 different types of fruit brew; try Mauby, made from the bark of a tree.

Health There is some risk of malaria, especially in the interior. Both types are present. Blood-smear tests are carried out at Georgetown airport. Take prophylactics and sleep under a mosquito net, and vaccinate against typhoid too. Boil milk and sterilize drinking water. Water pressure is very low in Georgetown and there have been outbreaks of typhoid when locals have broken the pipes to increase their supply. Yellow fever vaccination certificate required for landing from Suriname and Venezuela. Medical treatment is free at Georgetown Hospital but the hospital is run-down, understaffed and without equipment. Readers are advised to seek treatment at St. Joseph Hospital run by the Sisters of Mercy (USA), or the small but efficient Davis Memorial Hospital. Doctors expect G$40-G$50 for an appointment. If admitted to hospital you are expected to provide your own sheets and food (St. Joseph's provides all these). Travellers should examine shower pipes, bedding, shoes and clothing for snakes, especially in the interior.

The **climate**, although hot, is not unhealthy. Mean shade temperature throughout the year is 80°F; the mean maximum is about 87°F and the mean minimum 75°F. The heat is greatly tempered by cooling breezes from the sea and is most felt from August to October. There are two wet seasons, from the middle of April to the middle of August, and from the middle of November to the end of January. Rainfall averages 91 inches a year in Georgetown.

Cost of Living Shopping and entertainments are expensive, though you can sometimes get a meal for G$15 in one of the cheaper restaurants.

Hours of Business Shops and offices, 0930-1800; there is some late shopping on Monday and Friday while some stores close half day on Weds. and are open on Saturday afternoon. Banks, 0800-1200 Mon. to Fri., 0800-1100 Sat., Government offices, 0800-1130, 1300-1600 Mon. to Fri., 0800-1200 Sat., British High Commission, 0800-1145, 1300-1615 Mon. to Fri.

Currency The unit is the Guyana dollar (G$) divided into 100 cents. The official exchange rate (March 1987) was G$10 to the US$, though you could get G$20 on the black market for US$1 notes. There is a "grey" market for travellers' cheques which now appears to operate from *Pegasus* and *Tower* Hotels. The black market is illegal, but seems to be tolerated as long as one is discreet. Notes: 1, 5, 10, and 20 dollars. Coins: 1, 5, 10, 25, and 50 cents. Only G$40 in local currency may be taken in or out, and money-changing procedures at the banks are laborious because of strict controls. If you have more, only declare the G$40 as the balance can be confiscated. The airport bank is not always open and local currency must be changed back into foreign currency at a named bank. Banks in the city are only open in the mornings 0800-1200. (Travellers' cheques are not recommended as you may only change them into local currency and will have difficulties in getting the balance out of the country.) Few credit cards accepted, and then with a surcharge. A 50% tax on airline tickets for foreign flights purchased locally is in operation, but a good deal on the black market could still save money on a ticket bought locally. Hence the increasing restrictions on the sale of tickets to destinations other than those directly connected with Guyana.

Weights and Measures Electricity: 110v in Georgetown, but some however also have 220 volt 50 cycle A/C. The rest of the country is 110v (50/60 cycles) plug fittings are 2 pin square for radios, lights etc. and 3-pin for heavier apparatus. Guyana went metric in 1982 but the old Imperial system remains in general use.

Telecommunications A radio telephone service connects with a number of Government and private radio telephone stations in the interior. Overseas telegrams are transmitted via Guyintel, formerly Cable and Wireless Ltd., at Bank of Guyana Building, Georgetown. Cable to U.K. costs G$0.34 per word up to 22, or G$3.74 for a minimum of 22 words, and G$0.17 for each additional word. Local calls in Georgetown cost twelve cents. There are no longer any functioning telephone booths or post-boxes. Radio telephone calls to the U.K. cost G$20 for three minutes and G$7 for each additional minute. Telex costs the same.

SURINAME 849

G.B.C. (state controlled) runs Channels One and Two (radio). Both take commercial advertising. There is no TV service, apart from Suriname's.

Diplomatic Representatives The British High Commission is at 44 Main Street, Georgetown; the US Embassy is at 31 Main Street.

Time 4 hrs. behind GMT.

Press *The Chronicle* (state owned) publishes seven days a week, although most locals rely on the *Catholic Standard* (a news sheet), which is sold in all R.C. churches and at 1 Brickdam. *The New Nation* (PNC) and *Mirror* (PPP) are Sunday papers. There are 2 weeklies. The Georgetown Chamber of Commerce issues a monthly *Commercial Review*, and *Caribbean Contact* normally carries extensive reports on Guyana.

Public Holidays

January 1: New Year
February 23: Republic Day
March: Holi Phagwah
Easter: Good Friday, Monday
May 1: Labour Day
Eid ul-Fitr
July 1: Caribbean Day

Eid ul-Azha
August 4: Freedom Day
October: Deepavali
Youm um-Nabi
December 25: Christmas Day
December 26: Boxing Day

Precise dates for Holi Phagwah and Deepavali depend on specific phases of the moon. The Moslem holidays fall 11 days earlier each year: in 1988 Eid ul-Fitr is May 17, Eid ul-Azha is July 14 and Yaum un-Nabi is October 23. The precise dates should be checked with Consulates or High Commissions during the month preceding a holiday.

SURINAME

SURINAME has a coast line on the Atlantic to the N; it is bounded on the W by Guyana and on the E by French Guyane; Brazil is to the S. Its area is 163,820 sq. km.

The principal rivers in the country are the Marowijne in the E, the Corantijn in the W, and the Suriname, Commewijne (with its tributary, the Cottica), Coppename, Saramacca and Nickerie. The country is divided into topographically quite diverse natural regions: lowland, savanna, and highland.

The northern part of the country consists of lowland, with a width in the E of 25 km., and in the W of about 80 km. The soil (clay) is covered with swamps with a layer of humus under them. Marks of the old sea-shores can be seen in the shell and sand ridges, overgrown with tall trees.

There follows a region, 5-6 km. wide, of a loamy and very white sandy soil, then a slightly undulating region, about 30 km. wide. It is mainly savanna, mostly covered with quartz sand, and overgrown with grass and shrubs.

South of this lies the interior highland, almost entirely overgrown with dense tropical forest and intersected by streams. At the southern boundary with Brazil there are again savannas. These, however, differ in soil and vegetation from the northern ones. A large area in the SW is in dispute between Guyana and Suriname. There is a less serious border dispute with Guyane in the SE.

Population The 1980 census showed that the population had declined to 352,041, because of heavy emigration to the Netherlands. By 1985 it was estimated to have grown to 396,000, or at an annual overall rate of 0.4% a year between 1970 and 1985. The 1980 population consisted of Creoles (European-African and other descent), 35%; East Indians (known locally as Hindustanis),

850 SURINAME

35%; Indonesians, 15%; Chinese, 3%; Amerindians, and Bush Blacks (descendants of escaped slaves), 10%; Europeans and others, 2%. About 90% of the existing population live in or around Paramaribo or in the coastal towns; the remainder, mostly Carib and Arawak Indians and Bush Blacks, are widely scattered. Life expectancy 64.5 years; birth rate, 29.7 per 1,000; death rate, 7.4 per 1,000; infant mortality 32.5 per thousand; literacy, 78.8%.

The Asian people originally entered the country as contracted estate labourers, and settled in agriculture or commerce after completion of their term. They dominate the countryside, whereas Paramaribo is a predominantly Creole city. One of Suriname's main problems is the racial tension between Creoles and East Indians.

The official language is Dutch. The native dialect, called negro English (Sranan Tongo or Taki-Taki) originally the speech of the Creoles, is now a *lingua franca* understood by all groups, and standard English is widely spoken and understood. The Asians still speak their own languages among themselves.

History Although Amsterdam merchants had been trading with the "wild coast" of Guiana as early as 1613 (the name Parmurbo-Paramaribo was already known) it was not until 1630 that 60 English settlers came to Suriname under Captain Marshall and planted tobacco. The real founder of the colony was Baron Willoughby of Parham, governor of Barbados, who sent an expedition to Suriname in 1651 under Anthony Rowse to find a suitable place for settlement. Willoughbyland became an agricultural colony with 500 little sugar plantations, 1,000 white inhabitants and 2,000 African slaves. Jews from Holland and Italy joined them, as well as Dutch Jews ejected from Brazil after 1654. On February 27, 1667, Admiral Crynssen conquered the colony for the states of Zeeland and Willoughbyfort became the present Fort Zeelandia. By the Peace of Breda—July 31, 1667—it was agreed that Suriname should remain with the Netherlands, while Nieuw Amsterdam (New York) should be given to England. The colony was conquered by the British in 1799, and not until the Treaty of Paris in 1814 was it finally restored to the Netherlands. Slavery was forbidden in 1818 and formally abolished in 1863. Indentured labour from China and the East Indies took its place.

Political System On November 25, 1975, the country became an independent republic, which signed a treaty with the Netherlands for an economic aid programme worth US$1.5bn until 1985. A military coup on February 25, 1980 overthrew the elected government. A state of emergency was declared, which still continues, and there is censorship for press, radio and TV. The military leader, Col. Desi Bouterse, and his associates have come under pressure from the Dutch and the USA as a result of dictatorial tendencies. After the execution of 15 opposition leaders on 8th December 1982, the Netherlands broke off relations and suspended its aid programme.

The ban on political parties was lifted in late 1985. A new constitution and Assembly were to have been installed in April 1987. Opposition parties have participated in discussions on the future political system. According to the draft constitution the military will be represented on the National Security Council, the county's highest decision making body, and will participate in all the country's developmental projects. As a result of these movements towards redemocratization the Dutch Government announced the resumption of partial economic aid early in 1986, but later in that year, anti-government rebels, led by a former bodyguard of Bouterse, Ronny Brunswijk, mounted a campaign to overthrow the government, disrupting both plans for political change, and the economy.

Warning: Those caught taking pictures of Fort Zeelandia, the People's Palace, police stations, military installations etc. face confiscation of their film, at least. Be careful also when taking pictures from ferries.

Paramaribo, the capital and chief port, lies on the Suriname river, 12 km. from the sea. It has a population of about 178,500, mainly Creoles.

The People's Palace (the old Governor's Mansion) is on Eenheidsplein (formerly Onafhankelijkheidsplein, and before that, Oranjeplein) and many beautiful 18th and 19th century buildings in Dutch (neo-Normanic) style are in the same area. The recently restored Fort Zeelandia used to house the Suriname Museum, but the fort has been repossessed by the military (the whole area is fenced off); some exhibits are still in the old museum in the residential suburb of Zorg-en-Hoop. Look for Mr. F. Lim-A-Po-straat if you wish to see what Paramaribo looked like only a comparatively short time ago. The nineteenth-century Roman Catholic cathedral is built entirely of wood and is well worth a visit. Much of the old town and its churches have been restored, and date only from the nineteenth century. Other things to see are the colourful market and the waterfront, Hindu temples in

SURINAME 851

Koningstraat, a mosque at Keizerstraat and the Synagogue (1854) at Herenstraat. A new harbour has been constructed about 1½ km. upstream. Two pleasant parks are the Palmentuin and the Cultuurtuin (with zoo)—but the latter is quite a distance from the town and there are no buses to it. National dress is normally only worn by the Asians on national holidays and at wedding parties, but some Javanese women still go about in sarong and klambi. A university was opened in 1968. There is one public swimming pool at Weidestraat, US$0.60 p.p. There is an exotic Asian flavour to the market and nearby streets. Cinemas show US, Indian and Chinese movies, with subtitles.

Hotels *Krasnapolsky*, (Tel: 74050) A, swimming pool and shops, launderette on 1st floor, and bank (open until 1430); *Torarica*, A-L, swimming pool, casino, nightclub, tropical gardens, fully air conditioned, central, the largest breakfast US$2 (Tel: 71500); *Ambassador*, A (Tel: 77555); *Riverclub*, at Leonsberg (8 km. from city), B (motel annex), swimming pool; *Lashley*, B-D. All have a/c. Service charge at hotels is 10-15%.

For budget travellers, best is still the recently refurbished YWCA Guesthouse at Herenstraat 11, E, or cheaper weekly rates. Best to book in advance but if it's full try the *Graaf Van Zinzendorff-Herberg* at Gravenstraat 100, the same price as the YWCA. Advance booking advisable. Otherwise, try *Continental Inn*, *Fanna* (Princessestraat 31), *If's Palace* (Keizerstraat 68), *Blue Moon* or *Au Soleil Levant*; they have more or less similar prices, E. *La Vida* on the way in from the airport is "cheap but nice". *Balden*, Kwathweg 183, 2 km. from centre on the road to Nickerie is probably the cheapest available accommodation; its Chinese restaurant serves cheap meals. Beware: many cheap hotels not listed above are "hot pillow" establishments. The *Salvation Army* will give the hard up a bed for Sf4.50 a night (Saramaccastraat).

Restaurants There are some good restaurants, mainly Indonesian and Chinese dishes for as little as Sf3. Try a *rijsttafel* in an Indonesian restaurant, best is *Sarinah* (open-air dining), Verlengde Gemenelandsweg 187. A good restaurant is the *Bali*, Dr J. F. Nassy Laan 5; *Fa Tai*, Maagdenstraat 64, air conditioned; *Tai Toong* (good and interesting); *Iwan's*, Grote Hofstraat, for the best Chinese food. Many other Chinese restaurants: *Chi Wan* (Sf5-12) for its egg foo yung and won ton soup, Keizerstraat and Zwartenhovenburgstraat 16. The YMCA Cafeteria has good, cheap breakfasts and lunches. Meat and noodles from stalls in the market costs Sf3.00. In restaurants the cost rises to Sf5-7. Along the river there are cheap Javanese foodstalls, lit at night by candles. Try *barri* for Sf1 and *petjil* (vegetables) for Sf0.50. Especially recommended on Sundays when the area is busiest. In restaurants a dish to try is *gadogado* (an Indonesian vegetable and peanut concoction) available for about Sf5. Good places for lunch include *Orlando's* opposite the Post Office and *Hola's Terrace*, Domineestraat. A nice place for a drink and dance is *Old Inn Cassiri Club* off the road to Afobakka.

Shopping Arts & Crafts, Neumanpad 13a, for Amerindian goods, batik prints, carvings, basket work.

Bookshops The two main bookshops are Vaco and Kersten, both on Domineestraat, and both sell English-language books. Also Hoeksteen (Gravenstraat 17) and the kiosk in *Krasnapolsky Hotel*. Boekhandel Univers N.V., Gravenstraat 61, is recommended for nature, linguistic and scholarly books on Suriname (it also sells the Handbook). Most bookshops sell a large map of Paramaribo, price Sf12. The souvenir shop in Neumanpad has one for free, showing city centre streets.

Taxis generally have no meters. The price should be agreed on beforehand to avoid trouble. A trip inside the city costs about Sf5-6. Fare for one to Zanderij Airport is Sf50; by minibus or shared taxi Sf25. Cheap local buses (route PZB and POZ fairly frequent), but only run in the day, Sf1.50. Try telephoning 79600 (De Paarl) who will arrange pick-up or set down from airport (US$9).

Self-Drive Cars City Taxi charges Sf34 a day plus Sf0.30 per km. after the first 100 km. Other rental agencies with similar prices: Purperhart, Kariem, Intercar, Kentax (Tel.: 72078) is open 24 hours a day. All driving licences accepted, but you need a stamp from the local police and a deposit of Sf250-750. Gasoline costs Sf0.84 a litre for "regular" and Sf0.93 for "extra".

Bicycles Can be bought for about Sf80 from A. Seymonson, Rijwielhersteller, Rust en Vredestraat. Recommended rides include to Nieuw Amsterdam, Marienburg, Alkmaar and back via Tamanredjo in the Javanese Commewijne district or from Rust en Werk to Spieringshoek to Reijnsdorp (3½ hours) and return to Leonsberg via ferry, whence it is a 30 minute ride to Paramaribo.

Banks Algemene Bank Nederland (Kerkplein 1), Surinaamse Bank and Hakrin Bank, 0700-1400. Surinaamse branch in *Hotel Krasnapolsky* open 0700-1430; 0800-1200 Sat, the bank charges Sf1.30 flat rate commission on each travellers cheque exchanged.

Current 127 volts AC, 60 cycles.

Church The Anglican Church is St. Bridget's, Hoogestraat 44 (Sunday 0900 service in English).

852 SURINAME

Golf Club Introduction from a member required.

Tourist Bureau On waterfront, Tel.: 71163/78421. Has useful handouts on lodgings in town and rural areas as well as restaurants. Sometimes friendly and helpful; organizes tours (4 days at Sf275) and bus journeys. Does Travel Service, Domineestraat.

Tourist Agency Stinasu, the Foundation for Nature Preservation in Suriname, Jongbawstraat 10, offers reasonably priced accommodation and provides tour guides on the extensive nature reserves throughout the country. One can see "true wilderness and wildlife" with them. (See page 853.) Mrs. W. J. Robles-Cornelissen, Rosenveltkade 34, telephone 74770, organizes excursions to the interior.

Bus services on the 376 km. East-West Highway: E from Paramaribo through the bauxite town of Moengo to Albina, on the French Guyane border; and W through Coronie and Wageningen to Nickerie, Sf10 (plus Sf5 per item of baggage), leaves hourly or when full. Many buses of different companies leave in the morning for Albina (Sf5). Transport from the border on to Cayenne is more difficult (shared taxi, one bus daily 0500 except Sundays) and more expensive. One Suriname company runs direct buses from Paramaribo to Cayenne, but not regularly. Transport to Georgetown can take up to five days (night stop at Nieuw Nickerie). Buses to Nickerie leave from Waaldijkstraat and Sophie Redmondstraat (0500, 1100 and 1300, Sf10). Get there early for a seat. For all details enquire at Tourist Office. To Afobakka via Brokopondo from Saramaccastraat (0700 and 0800, Sf3) and to Groningen from in front of Drugstore Singh, Maagdenstraat (0800, 0900, 1100 and 1200, Sf1.25). When someone tells you to take a "numbered bus" they are referring to the "wild buses", not the yellow Straat bus.

Most people use so-called "wild buses" running on fixed routes in and around Paramaribo. Not very comfortable, but very cheap (20 cents) and fast. Most towns and villages are served by private buses.

Local Shipping The three ferries across the main rivers operate only in daytime (the Paramaribo-Meerzorg ferry until 2200). Two bridges have been built. The Suriname Navigation Co. (SMS) has a daily service, leaving 0700, on the Commewijne river (a nice four-hour trip; one can get off—see below—at De Nieuwe Grond, a plantation owned by an English couple, and stay overnight). The SMS has a daily service to Reynsdorp, leaving Paramaribo early in the morning. SMS also has infrequent services on other rivers (Wayombo and Cottica). The coastal service to Nieuw Nickerie has been discontinued, but there is a weekly (Mon.) 36-hour run over inland waterways (see page 854).

Airports The international airport is Zanderij, 45 km. S. of Paramaribo (bus to town Sf15, return Sf20) There is a taxi, US$28, and there is a regular minibus, marked PZB, which leaves from the service station 15 minutes walk from the centre on the south highway, Sf1.25. De Paarl minibus recommended as cheaper.

Airline minibus or shared taxi cost US$5.60 a seat. Money exchange facilities (now compulsory—see page 858): Hakrin Bank between Customs and Immigration (closed Sundays). There is a new guest house near Zanderij airport. Internal flights leave from Zorg-en-Hoop airfield in a suburb of Paramaribo—twice daily (except Sunday) to Nieuw Nickerie (Sf60), to Stoelmanseiland in the interior 3 times a week, Sf55, and to Washabo (twice weekly, Sf75), Djoemoe (twice weekly, Sf70), Ladoani (weekly Sf55) and Botopasi (weekly Sf60).

Excursions Powaka, about 90 minutes outside the capital, is a primitive village of thatched huts but with electric light and a small church. In the surrounding forest one can pick mangoes and other exotic fruit. By bus (Route 4) or taxi and ferry to Nieuw Amsterdam, the capital of the predominantly Javanese district of Commewijne. There is an open-air museum inside the old fortress (open only in mornings except Fri. 1700-1900), which guarded the confluence of the Suriname and Commewijne rivers. There are some old plantation mansions left in the Commewijne district which are of interest; Mariënburg is the last sugar estate in operation in Suriname. Accommodation for 6-8 persons with own cooking facilities is available on an old citrus plantation, *De Nieuwe Grond*, which is owned by an English couple; details: Tel.: 76872, or by mail to Mr. Jenkins, de Nieuwe Grond, district Commewijne.

By private car to **Jodensavanne** (Jews' Savanna, established 1639), S of Paramaribo on the opposite bank of the Suriname river, where part of one of the oldest synagogues in the Western Hemisphere has been restored. Small museum. Interesting Amerindian villages nearby. You need permission from the Forestry Department (LBB), in Jongbawstraat, to use the ferry to Jodensavanne. There is a new guesthouse, D (with six rooms), at Blakkawatra, nearby. Accommodation is available through Stinasu (see page 852) and camping is possible. Near Zanderij Airport there is a resort called Kola Kreek, with swimming area.

SURINAME 853

By bus (Sf3) or car to Afobakka, where there is a large hydro-electric dam on the Suriname river. There is a government guesthouse, C (including 3 meals a day) in nearby Brokopondo. Victoria is an oil-palm plantation in the same area. The Brownsberg National Park is one hour by car from here.

There is also a 70-year-old narrow-gauge railway, originally built for the Lawa goldfields, which leaves from the village of Onverwacht (½ hour from Paramaribo by bus, Sf1, route PBO) for Brownsweg (87 km.) and passes through savanna and jungle. The complete journey to Brownsweg is done twice a week, on Mon. and Fri., returning the same day, Sf5 pp. There is no hotel at Brownsweg, but transport (14 km. up hill) to **Brownsberg,** where there is accommodation, can be arranged, Sf30 (telephone Paramaribo 75845, Ext 34). The return bus is supposed to leave at 1100. Guest house, C. A bus to Paramaribo leaves Brownsweg every morning (price doubles between low and high seasons—see page 827).

Stinasu arranges trips to the Brownsberg Park (entry Sf1) as well as the Raleigh Falls/Voltzberg Nature Reserve on the Coppename river (good swimming), the Wia-Wia reserve on the northeast coast where giant sea-turtles nest, and the Galibi reserve on the Marowijne river, another nesting place for turtles. There is accommodation of sorts in all these places. Soft drinks are generally available from Park offices. See below for more details on Nature Reserves.

Suriname Airways (SLM) has organized tours to **Stoelmanseiland** on the Lawa River (guest house with full board, C, including meals) in the interior, and to the Bush Black villages and rapids in that area. Price Sf240 pp for 3 days (5 persons, minimum).

Nature Reserves *Raleighvallen/Voltzberg Nature Reserve* (57,000 hectares) is one of the more accessible rain-forest parks. You can fly via Gum-Air or SLM from Paramaribo (40 mins. Sf555 return) to Foengoe Island in the Reserve. For a more scenic trip, you can take a three-or four-hour car ride from Paramaribo to Bitagron, a colourful Bush-Black village on the Coppename River (swimming good, but do not swim at Moedervallen because of electric fish), where the car can be left with the guard of the Government Geological Service. From there a four-hour boat trip (Tues. and Fri.) up the Coppename to the reserve costs (round-trip) Sf50 per adult and Sf25 per child. There is no electricity, refrigerator, beds or tents at Voltzberg Camp. However, climbing Voltzberg peak at the sunrise is unforgettable. The camp is 6 km. from the lodge. *Lolopasi Lodge*—with a secluded beach and view of the rapids—accommodates twelve, and can be rented for Sf60-70 per night. The *Foengoe Island Lodge* has accommodation for 64 people with complete kitchen facilities (drinks may be purchased from the manager, but you must bring linen and food), electricity, and shower. Group accommodation with kitchen privileges (twelve people, three rooms) available for US$14 per room; or you may stay for US$1.60 per person per night without kitchen privileges. Bedding is extra. Boat excursions Sf20 per hour (high season) Sf15 (low) and guided tours can be arranged with the manager; otherwise there are huts at Gonini (8 people at Sf65-55), Koejaké (20 persons at Sf140-120 per night) Tamanoea (24 at Sf110-95 per night) or Sonloir, 12 beds at Sf20 p.p. and 10 hammocks, Sf4 per night.

Only two or three hours by car from Paramaribo is the *Brownsberg Nature Park* (6,000 hectares). Alternative methods of transport from the city include a combination bus and van (schedule irregular, Sf4) and a scenic, six-hour, wood-burning steam train ride. In this tropical rain-forest park live giant toads, communal spiders, monkeys, jaguars, peccaries, agoutis, and a variety of birds. Admission for car and driver is US$2 with 57c per extra adult, and 15c per child. Rooms in the *Central Lodge* rent from US$9 to US$15. Group accommodation available for US$2 a night. A cottage or bungalow sleeping eight to ten people—with toilet, shower, and complete kitchen facilities (again, bring your own food)—would be US$58-53. Rates may be slightly higher at weekends and holidays. They are up to one-third cheaper in the low seasons. Hiking maps are available at the Park office, and a guidebook to the birds of Brownsberg can be purchased in the Stinasu office in Paramaribo. A useful contact is Lesley Hattun (English speaking) Stinasu, P.O.B. 436, Paramaribo. Tel.: 75845/71856, who is the organization tour organizer. A native canoe (for six people) can be rented for US$25 for fishing and/or sightseeing on the Brokopondo Reservoir.

Two reserves are located on the northeast coast of Suriname. Known primarily as a major nesting site for sea turtles—five species including the huge leatherback turtle come ashore to lay their eggs—*Wia-Wia Nature Reserve* (36,000 hectares), also has nesting grounds for some magnificent birds. The nesting activity of sea turtles is best observed February-July. Since the beaches and consequently the turtles have shifted westwards out of the reserve, accommodation is now at Matapica beach, not in the reserve itself. The turtle nursery was scheduled to close by end-1984 due to lack of funds. (After a visit to the reserves please send any comments to Hilde Viane at Stinasu. Your support is needed to keep the reserve functioning.) There may also be mosquitoes and sandflies, depending on the season. A riverboat leaves Paramaribo daily at 0700, and arrives in Alliance by way of the Commewijne River at 1100. You then transfer to a Stinasu *piaka* (launch) for

854 SURINAME

a one-hour ride to Matapica. The launch holds twelve people and costs US$22.40 per person, round trip. Suitable waterproof clothing should be worn. Two beach huts accommodate five people each at a cost of US$5 per person, high season; bring your own bedding.

The *Galibi Nature Reserve*, where there are more turtle-nesting places, is near the mouth of the Marowijne River. There are Carib Indian villages. From Albina one takes a 3-hour (incl. ½ hr. on the open sea) boat trip at US$4.25 to Galibi where the beach hut holds 12 people at US$9 (high season) per person; or one bed in group accommodation or to Eilanti, US$9 (high season), where the beach hut holds six people at US$2.30 each. Boat travels Fri. and Tues. to Baboensanti and back; there is an extra charge of Sf35 for travel on other days of the week.

Note It is advisable to check the weather conditions and probabilities of returning on schedule before you set out on a trip to the interior. Heavy rains can make it impossible for planes to land in some jungle areas; little or no provision is made for such delays and it can be a long and hungry wait for better conditions.

Nieuw Nickerie, on the S bank of the Nickerie River (new bridge opened end-1984), 5 km. from its mouth, is the main town and port of the Nickerie district and is distinguished for the number and voraciousness of its mosquitoes. The town has a population of more than 8,000, the district of 35,000, mostly East Indian. Paramaribo is 237 km. away by road. Buses leave hourly or when full, Sf10 (plus Sf5 for large bag) and take less time (5 hrs.) with the opening of the bridge than they did before. Sit on the left-hand side of the bus to get the best views of the bird-life in the swamps. SLM has two daily flights to the capital (Sf35). The coastal ferry service has been discontinued, but once a week the SMS company makes an interesting water trip, using inland waterways, to Nieuw Nickerie taking 36 hours; it leaves Paramaribo on Mondays at 0800, departs Nieuw Nickerie 1200 Weds. Food and drink sold on board.

Hotels *Blue Hawaii*, E, clean, central, recommended; *Dorien*, C, bed and breakfast; *Amer Ali*, B; *Ashoko*, F; *Nickerie Logeergebouw*, B; *Sjiem Fat*, C, without meals; *Luxor*, E-F, among the cheapest; *Nemelo*, E, 3 blocks from the ferry, recommended friendly; *Oasis* (men only), F, basic. Restaurant: *Tokyo*, rather basic. The *Ajai* (E) guest house runs a free minibus to and from the ferry and takes passengers the next morning to catch the Paramaribo bus (dirty and noisy). Good food at the Asanredjo foodstand (unmarked), ask to be directed, two blocks east of *Ajai*, on Oranjenassaustraadt. Cheap filling meals can be obtained on the street for as little as Sf2 p.p.

Banks Algemene Bank Nederland, Hakrin Bank, Post Office Savings Bank, People's Credit Bank, Surinaamse Bank.

Ferry to Springlands, Guyana, Sf7.50, Sf12.50 return. For the following day's ferry, go to police station at 0630, some 200 metres below ferry point. It is essential to be in the first 80-100 and the ferry is always crowded. If the police take your passport you are on. Currency declaration forms are handed in at the ferry. Baggage weigh in from 0700 takes two hours and the ferry leaves about 0830-0900. A return ferry ticket to Guyana will suffice as an onward ticket; without one you can be sent back on the next ferry. You reclaim your passport when boarding the ferry. Customs will demand duty on your luggage—don't pay but insist that you are only carrying clothes (i.e. no food). No service on Sun., or national holidays of either country; foot passenger service only. The EEC has approved a grant of ECU 12m to finance the provision of a new ferry service to Guyana; a new terminal for the ferry is to be constructed 25 km up river from Nieuw Nickerie; it should be operational by 1988.

Totness is the largest village in the Coronie district, along the coast between Paramaribo and Nieuw Nickerie. There is a good government guesthouse, E. The road leads through an extensive forest of coconut palms. Bus to Paramaribo Sf5 at 0600.

Wageningen is a modern little town, the centre of the Suriname rice-growing area. The road from Nickerie has recently been renewed. One of the largest fully mechanized rice farms in the world is found here. (*Hotel de Wereld*, C.)

Moengo, 160 km. up the Cottica River from Paramaribo, is a bauxite mining and loading centre for the Suriname Aluminium Company (Suralco) a subsidiary of Alcoa. (*Government Guesthouse*, B, annex D.) Paranam, another loading centre for the Company, is on the left bank of the Suriname River. It can be reached by medium draught ships and by cars. Near Paranam is Smalkalden, where bauxite is loaded by the Billiton company on the road to Paramaribo.

Vast reserves of bauxite have been discovered in the Bakhuis Mountains, in

SURINAME 855

the northern part of Nickerie District. A road has been built from Zanderij to the Bakhuis Mountains and on to the Kabalebo River, where a large hydro-electric station is planned. Camping is possible at several beautiful sites along this road. Gasoline available at Bitagron and Apoera only. A road and railway have been built from the mountains to **Apoera** on the Corantijn, which can be reached by sea-going vessels. **Blanche Marie Falls**, 320 km. from Paramaribo on the Apoera road, is a popular destination. There is a guesthouse, *Dubois*, B, contact Eldoradolaan 22, Paramaribo Tel.: 76904/2. Camping is Sf30 tent/day. There is a good guesthouse at Apoera (C, with 3 meals, advance booking from Paramaribo advisable). **Washabo** near Apoera, which has an airstrip, is an Amerindian village. There is no public transport from Paramaribo to the Apoera-Bakhuis area, but many private cars and trucks go there and there are frequent charter flights to the Washabo airstrip. SLM also flies to Washabo on Tuesdays and Saturdays (Sf75). Irregular small boats go from Apoera to Nieuw Nickerie and to Springlands (Guyana).

Albina, the eastern frontier village, is 140 km. from Paramaribo, 29 km. from the mouth of the Marowijne River—the boundary with French Guyane. Albina is the centre for trips by powered dugouts to Amerindian and Bush Black villages on the Marowijne, Tapanahoni and Lawa rivers (about Sf50 plus). It takes 1½-2 days to get to the beautiful Stoelmanseiland (see Excursions, page 853). There is a park along the Marowijne river (about 15 minutes walk from the town centre) called Het Park with free hammock places. Opposite Albina, in French Guyane, is St.-Laurent (see page 861), with good restaurants and the old penal settlement to see (ferry Sf2, every three hours from 0600); bank at Albina ferry terminal will change money. The French authorities will sometimes ask for yellow-fever vaccination certificates and cars must have at least "pink card" insurance; this card is purchased in Paramaribo. Shops in Albina will not accept or change French francs, whereas the French will sometimes change Suriname guilders at black market rates. Some shops will change money. Don't forget to get passports stamped at the post near the landing stages (close to the Esso gas station).

Hotels *Albina Government Guesthouse*, E; *Marowijne*, E; *Happy Day Inn*, D (swimming and boating), *Albina*, E; *Rorico* (good), D, *Riverside*, D. If these are full, enquire at the police station; they'll let you camp in the park.

Bus Paramaribo-Albina, Sf5 and Sf0.25 for a ferry, 3½ hrs. Buses leave from Paramaribo at 0630 and noon at the ferry on Paramaribo side daily; many trucks carry passengers US$1.50 daily. Post-office buses are cheaper but slower. Hitchhiking can be attempted. The taxi service is expensive.

The Economy

Agriculture is restricted to some districts of the alluvial coastal zone, covering about 0.8m hectares and employing about 8.6% of the labour force. At least two-thirds of permanent crop and arable land is under irrigation. Farming accounts for 9.4% of gdp and 10% of exports. The main crops are rice (the staple), sugar cane and citrus fruits, all of which are exported to Europe, along with small quantities of coffee and bananas. Apart from rice, Suriname is a net importer of food; priority is being given to rice and livestock. Since 1981, the sector has registered annual declines in output, recovering only in 1984; in 1985 production fell by 3.2%, compared with 2.4% growth in 1984. Suriname has vast timber resources, but exports account for only 1.1% of the total and development has been hampered by a lack of investment. There is a small fishing industry, the chief catch being shrimps.

Manufacturing's contribution to gdp is 16.0%, employing 8.3% of the workforce. Import substitution, using both imported goods and local raw materials, is the main activity, with food processing accounting for 60% of the total.

Suriname is the world's sixth largest producer of bauxite, with reserves estimated at 1.9% of the world's total. The country has the capability to process the extracted ore into alumina and aluminium ingot. The bauxite/aluminium industry accounts for 79.5% of exports (1985), while the mining sector as a whole contributes 6.6% of gpd and employs 5.0% of the workforce. Two companies control the industry, the Suriname Aluminium Company (Suralco), a subsidiary of Alcoa, and Billiton Maatschappij, part of Royal Dutch Shell. Production of both bauxite and aluminium remained static in 1984 and 1985 (at 3.4 m tonnes and 23,000 tonnes respectively), but labour problems, the overvaluation of the Suriname guilder and falling world prices contributed to substantial losses for both companies. Since 1983, they have been progressively merging operations to improve competitiveness on world markets. Government revenue from bauxite has been declining in line with reduced sales, but in 1986 it agreed to drop the bauxite levy in return for Suralco and Billiton carrying out a US$155 m investment programme.

Oil production from the Tambaredjo heavy oil deposit, operated by the state oil company, Staatsolie, was 2,000 bpd in 1986. Exploratory wells in the Saramacca district have also yielded oil, raising hopes for achieving Staatsolie's 5,000 bpd target by 1990. Installed electricity generating capacity is 415 MW, of which 54% is thermal, 46% hydroelectric.

The tying of the Suriname guilder to the US dollar, at a rate of 1.785 to US$1, meant that inflation fell with the strength of the dollar to 3.7% in 1984. Shortages of essential goods and rapid increases in the money supply and domestic credit reversed the downward trend in 1985, when inflation was estimated at 12.5%. The suspension of Dutch aid in 1982 has had a catastrophic effect on government finances; the government's reluctance to slow down development programmes prompted it to borrow heavily from domestic sources and the central government deficit rose from 6.9% of gdp in 1980 to an estimated 22% in 1985. Without foreign aid or strong foreign exchange earnings from bauxite, international reserves have dwindled. Fortunately, Suriname does not have the added burden of a high foreign debt, which at end-1985 was US$24 m, with a debt service ratio of about 0.5% of exports of goods and services.

	1961-70 (av)	1971-80 (av)	1981-85 (av)
Gdp growth	10.3%	11.5%	3.2% (a)
Inflation	4.1%	9.9%	7.3%
Exports (fob) US$m	82	298	388
Alumina	35	142	217
Aluminium	16	44	45
Bauxite	40	61	38
Imports (fob) US$m	79	266	388
Current account balance US$m (cum)	-113 (b)	250	-311

(a) = 1981-84
(b) = 1965-70

Information for Visitors

Air Services Zanderij airport is served by SLM (Suriname Airways), Guyana Airways and Cruzeiro do Sul. SLM flies to Caracas and Miami (twice weekly) and Belém (weekly), and direct to the Netherlands, twice a week during holiday periods and weekly in low season. Cruzeiro do Sul flies to Cayenne and Belém once a week while Guyana Airways provides a twice-weekly flight to Georgetown. This means that there are now only seven or eight flights a week out, and many people now go to Cayenne to take advantage of cheap Air France tickets to Europe as well as increased seat availability. There is an exit tax of Sf30. Internal services are maintained by SLM and two small air charter firms.

Sea Services Three shipping companies have regular sailings to and from Paramaribo: Kroonvlag (former Royal Netherlands Steamship Co., KNSM), Alcoa Steamship Co. and Scheepvaart Maatschappij Suriname (SMS), all with freighters with limited passenger accommodation only. Kroonvlag has a regular service from Europe and from many ports in the Western Hemisphere. Alcoa has

SURINAME 857

sailings from different ports in the USA. SMS has a service to and from New Orleans, via some Caribbean ports. In addition there are many freighters of different companies, which take passengers but have no regular service. Flying is generally cheaper than coming by ship.

Tourism Points of interest are: some colonial architecture, especially in and around Paramaribo; and the tropical flora and fauna in this very sparsely populated country. There are no beaches to speak of; the sea and the rivers in the coastal area are muddy, and mosquitoes can be a worry in places. Hotels and restaurants are rare outside the capital, and you usually have to bring your own hammock and mosquito-net, and food. A tent is less useful in this climate. By using your own hammock and food, travelling can become quite cheap. Hitchhiking is not common, but it is possible. The high seasons, when everything is more expensive, are March 15-May 15, July-September and December 15-January 15.

Documents Visitors must have a valid passport (issued by any government other than those of the communist countries or Hong Kong), a visa or tourist card (cost Sf25, valid 30 days) in most cases (see below) and a through ticket to another country or a return ticket home from any of the Guianas. If the visitor wants to stay longer than 30 days he must report to the Immigration Office in Paramaribo (van 't Hogerhuysstraat, Nieuwe Haven) as soon as he arrives and take with him two passport-size photographs. Europeans and citizens of the USA and Canada are required to have a visa or a tourist card. Any foreign currency must be declared on entry and exit; don't lose the double entry form. No consulate to give visas in Boa Vista, Brazil: nearest is in Caracas.

Customs Duty-free imports include (if declared) 400 cigarettes or 100 cigars or ½ kg. of tobacco, 2 litres of spirits and 4 litres of wine, 50 grams of perfume and 1 litre of toilet water, 8 rolls of still film and 60 metres of cinefilm, 100 metres of recording tape, and other goods up to a value of Sf40. Personal baggage is free of duty. Customs examination of baggage can be very thorough.

Communications Roads are being built all over the country. There are 2,500 km of main roads, of which 850 km are paved. The main east-west road, 390 km in length, links Albina with Nieuw Nickerie. Driving is on the left. Most settlements have an airstrip for the internal air services.

Clothing Except for official meetings, informal tropical clothing is worn, but no shorts. An umbrella or plastic raincoat is very useful.

Climate Tropical and moist, but not very hot, since the north-east trade wind makes itself felt during the whole year. In the coastal area the temperature varies on an average from 23° to 31°C, during the day; the annual mean is 27°C, and the monthly mean ranges from 26° to 28°C. The mean annual rainfall is about 2,340 mm. for Paramaribo and 1,930 mm for the western division. The seasons are: minor rainy season, November-February; minor dry season, February-April; main rainy season, April-August; main dry season, August-November. None of these seasons is, however, usually either very dry or very wet. The degree of cloudiness is fairly high and the average humidity is 82%. The climate of the interior is similar but with higher rainfall.

Health No special precautions necessary except for a trip to the malarial interior; for free malaria prophylaxis contact the Public Health Department (BOG). Mosquito nets should be used at night over beds in rooms not air-conditioned or screened. Outside Paramaribo drinking water should still be boiled despite protestations. In some coastal districts there is a risk of bilharzia (schistosomiasis). Vaccinations: yellow fever and tetanus advisable, typhoid only for trips into the interior. Swim only in running water because of poisonous fish. There is good swimming on the Marowijne river and at Matapica beach and on the Coppename river.

Working Hours Shops: Mon.-Thurs and Sat., 0700-1300 and 1600-1800 or 1900 on Saturday; 0730-1300 and 1700-2000 Friday. Business houses: 0730-1700. Government departments: 0700-1400, but 0700-1130 on Sat. Banks are open 0800-1230 weekdays, 0800-1100 Sat.

Electricity Supply 127 and/or 220 volts AC, 60 cycles. Plug fittings are usually 2-pin round (European continental type). Lamp fittings are screw type.

Post, Telegraph, Telephone Telegrams can be sent from 0700 until 2200 and from Government Telegraph Service, Gravenstraat, in urgent cases. Night rate Sf7.26 (min). ordinary Sf5.25 (min).

There is a telephone and telegraph office on Vaillantplein. Calls can be made to the US and UK via satellite, Sf18 for 3 mins. The office is open 0700-2000; calls booked before 2000 can be made up till midnight. Censorship is reported to be in operation on telephones and mail.

Currency The unit of currency is the Suriname guilder (Sf) divided into 100

858 SURINAME

cents. There are notes for 1, 2½, 5, 10, 25, 100 and 1,000 guilders. Since end-1982 only notes showing the revolutionary symbol have been legal tender: do not accept the old ones. Coins are for 1 guilder and 1, 5, 10 and 25 cents (the 25-cent coin is usually known as a *kwartje*). Suriname's monetary system is quite independent of Holland's; the Suriname guilder is valued against the US dollar; US$1 = Sf1.78 (fixed), which has resulted in the country becoming expensive for the tourist. There has been a crackdown on the black market in cash US dollars, which operates mainly from cheap hotel rooms. Don't go looking for dealers; they will approach you.

Currency Regulations Everybody has to fill out a foreign currency declaration when entering and leaving. On departure, the imported foreign currency can be exported again provided a validated exchange permit is presented. Travellers' cheques can only be exchanged into guilders at banks. Only Sf100 in local currency and up to Sf5,000 (eq) in foreign currency may be imported or exported without currency declaration.

Persons arriving at Zanderij airport are required to exchange money to the equivalent of Sf500 per person at official rates. At land borders the sum may be reduced to Sf200 or Sf20 per day for less than 10 days stay (or ignored altogether); for children, half these rates. Exchange facilities are now situated at exit-entrance points.

Time is 3 hrs. behind GMT.

Public Holidays January 1, New Year; February 25, Revolution Day; Holi Phagwa (1 day in March); Good Friday; Easter (2 days); May 1 (Labour Day); July 1 (National Unity); November 25 (Independence Day); Christmas (2 days). For Moslem holidays see note under Guyana (page 849).

The **metric** system is in general use.

Newspaper in Dutch: *De Ware Tijd*.

Broadcasting There are several stations in Paramaribo and in the districts, broadcasting in Dutch, Hindi, Negro English and Javanese. There is also one state-controlled television station called Surinaamse Televisie Stichting (STVS), transmitting for 4 hours daily in colour on channel 8 (in Dutch).

Embassies USA, Netherlands, Belgium, Brazil, Cuba, France, Mexico, Venezuela, South Korea, India, Indonesia, Guyana, India, Japan, China (People's Republic), USSR.

Consulates There are consuls-general, vice-consuls or consular agents for Canada, Denmark, Dominican Republic, Ecuador, Finland, W. Germany, Haiti, UK, Mexico, Norway, Spain, and Sweden—all in Paramaribo.

Visa for Guyana Nearly everyone now needs a visa and an interview to enter Guyana. The application form costs Sf1 and one needs to show an outward ticket and take two passport photos to Lim-A-Po-straat to apply.

Information about Suriname can be had from: Suriname Tourist Bureau, 105 Rockefeller Plaza, New York, N.Y. 10020, and from the Suriname Embassy, Alex. Gogelweg 2, The Hague, Netherlands or the Tourist Board, P.O.B. 656 (Tel.: 72267; telex 292), Paramaribo, or Stinasu, Cornelis Jongbawstraat 14, P.O.B. 436 (Tel.: 75845) Also from embassies.

GUYANE

GUYANE, an Overseas Department of France, has its eastern frontier with Brazil formed partly by the River Oiapoque (Oyapoc in French) and its southern, also with Brazil, formed by the Tumuc-Humac mountains. The western frontier with Suriname is along the River Maroni-Itani. To the north is the Atlantic coastline of 320 km. The area is estimated at 89,941 square km., or one-sixth that of France. The land rises gradually from the coastal regions to the higher slopes and plains or savannas, about 80 km. inland. Forests cover some 8 million hectares of the hills and valleys of the interior, and timber production is increasing rapidly.

The territory is well watered, for over twenty rivers run to the Atlantic. Besides those named above, there are the Mana, Cayenne, Sinnamarie (with its tributary the Coureibo), Maroni, Oyack, and Approuage. Smaller rivers are the Inini, Ardoua, and Camopi.

The only mountain range of importance is the Tumuc-Humac. Among the higher peaks are Mounts Mitarka, Temorairem, Leblond, and Timotakem; this last in the extreme S on the Brazilian frontier. The mountains reach a height of 800 metres.

The total population is 73,022, the work force 26,423. The basic population consists of Creoles, the descendants of non-indigenous blacks (66%), Asians and whites (12%), and tribal natives (10%). There are an estimated 20,000 migrant workers from Haiti and nearby countries. Their presence has resulted in a rise in the school age population from 13,215 in 1973 to 21,432 by 1983. The Amerindian villages in the Haut-Maroni and Haut-Oyapoc areas may only be visited if permission has been obtained from the Préfecture in Cayenne *before* departure to Guyane.

History Awarded to France by the Peace of Breda in 1667, Guyane was twice attacked, first by the British in 1654 and later by the Dutch in 1676. In the same year the French retook possession and remained undisturbed until 1809. In that year a combined Anglo-Portuguese naval force captured the colony, which was handed over to the Portuguese (Brazilians). Though the land was restored to France by the Treaty of Paris in 1814, the Portuguese remained until 1817. Gold was discovered in 1853, and disputes arose about the frontiers of the colony with Suriname and Brazil. These were settled by arbitration in 1891, 1899, and 1915. By the law of March 19, 1946, the Colony of Cayenne, or Guyane Française, became the Department of Guyane, with the same laws, regulations, and administration as a department in metropolitan France. The seat of the Prefect and of the principal courts is at Cayenne. The colony was used as a prison for French convicts with camps scattered throughout the country; Saint-Laurent was the port of entry. After serving prison terms convicts spent an equal number of years in exile and were usually unable to earn their return passage to France. Those interested should read *Papillon* by Henri Charrière. Majority opinion seems to be in favour of greater autonomy: about 5% of the population are thought to favour independence.

Cayenne, the capital and the chief port, is on the island of Cayenne at the mouth of the Cayenne River. It is 645 km. from Georgetown (Guyana) and 420 km. from Paramaribo (Suriname) by sea. Population 34,000. There is an interesting museum (open daily, Monday-Saturday 0900-1300, additionally Mon. and Thurs. 1630-1830 and Sunday 0900-1200; free admission); the Jesuit-built residence (circa 1890) of the Prefect (L°Hôtel-de-Ville) in the Place de Grenoble; the Canal Laussant built by Malouet in 1777; the Place des Armandiers (also known as the Place Augusto Horth) by the sea; Botanical Gardens; the Place des Palmistes, with assorted palms; a swimming pool; a municipal library and four cinemas. There are bathing beaches (water rather muddy) around the island, the best is Montjoly (no bus), but watch out for sharks.

860 GUYANE

Trips by motor-canoe up-river into the jungle can be arranged. Every week the boat *São Pedro* leaves for St. Georges (75F single); tickets sometimes available from STMG, 136 Monnerville (Tel: 311388). Six-and-a-half km. outside Cayenne is a restaurant with paintings of prison life by an ex-convict whose work can also be seen in the church at Iracoubo. Ten km. out, near the bridge to the mainland, is an American shrimp-packing plant. The road to Iracoubo is narrow and badly surfaced. There is a road to St.-Laurent (now paved) and another inland. Camp on the beach, or put a hammock between two trees.

Hotels *Novotel Cayenne*, on beach, A, restaurant, a/c; *Le Polygone*, a/c, TV, A; *Du Montabo*, pleasantly situated 60 metres up on Montabo hill, 5 km. out of town; most rooms air-conditioned; very good, booking advisable, A-B, breakfast US$2 (taxi to town 10F) (Tel.: 31-25-75). *Chez Matilde*; C; *Guyane Studio Kitchenettes*, C. *Amazonia*, Av. Gen. de Gaulle (100 rooms central location, Tel.: 30-03-02), a/c. *Neptima*, Rue F. Eboué 21 (15 rooms), C, best value, breakfast 7.50F, a/c, friendly. *Ajoupe*, a/c, D; *Ket-Tai*, D, still cheap, mixed rooms, but a good view. *Kima-Lae*, E, 12 Rue La Louette in town; *Madeleine*, B, a/c, no breakfast, will book Raffinel bus to St.-Laurent, 1 km. out of town, friendly. About 9 km. from Cayenne is the *Beauregard*, C. Also *Hotel M*, a motel with air conditioned rooms and a small swimming pool; the owner hires out small cars. Recommended for businessmen— 15F breakfast; Tel.: 35 4100, Telex 010 310. Most hotels do not add tax and service to their bill, but stick to prices posted outside or at the desk. Great shortage, even in off-seasons; arrive early or book ahead. Amex cards often not accepted but Visa O.K.

Restaurants and Bars Main hotels. *L'Auberge des Amandiers*, excellent, good value; *Cap St. Jacques*, Rue Docteur E Gippet, excellent Vietnamese food, reasonable. *La Bonne Casserole*; *Les Heures d'Antan*; *Maxim'um*, Av. Estrée. *La Croix du Sud*, Av. de Gaulle; *Le Snack Créole*, 7 Rue Eboué; *T-A-Hing (Huguette)*; *Le Viet Nam*; *Club 106*, about 4 km. outside Cayenne; *Montjoly Bar*; *Beaurivage*; *Palmiste*, central and spacious; *Frégate*, Av. de Gaulle; *Tatou* (Creole), Av. Pres. Monnerville; *La Baie D'Alang*. Along the Canal Laussant there are Javanese snack bars; try *bambi* (spicy noodles) or *saté* (barbecued meat in a spicy peanut sauce). Vans around Place des Palmistes in evenings sell cheap, filling sandwiches.

Bookshops Librairie AJC, 31 Boulevard Jubelin, has some stock in English. Also old maps and prints. Current map sold at Librairie Alain Pion, Av. de Gaulle and in most bookshops.

Car Hire R. Desmond & Cie, Hertz International licensee, Route de La Madeleine, BP 148. Cables: Hertzcars. Avis, Esso-Baduel, BP 853. Tel.: 31-17-70. Europcar, Tel.: 31.16.23. Budget. An international driving licence is required.

Bank Banque de la Guyane, Place Schoelcher. Open 0715-1130 and 1445-1730, and Sat. a.m., but no exchange facilities on Sat., and will only give cash on a Visa card against a personal cheque. There are no exchange facilities at the airport; if in extreme need on Sat. you may be able to change money at Air France office in Place des Palmistes. Central drugstore may help when banks closed. Buy francs before arrival if possible.

Laundromat Corner of Rue F. Roosevelt and Rue Eboué, US$5 load all in.

Tourist Office Office de Tourisme de la Guyane, located near zoo (open 0900-1200 and 1600-1800) and botanical gardens (Tel.: 910356). Free map and tourist guide (Guyane Poche). The SLM manager is reported to be very helpful with advice.

Travel Agent Takari Tour, *Hotel du Montabo*, Tel.: 31-19-60 (BP 513). Somarig, Place L. Heder, is reported to be good for South American and European airline tickets. It also sells boat tickets to Ile Royale as well as meal tickets for the Auberge which are recommended.

Post Office, 2 km out from town (15F by taxi or 20 minutes on foot). Poste Restante letters are only kept for one month maximum. P.O. annex opp. Préfecture open a.m.

Bus Only westbound bus is run by Ruffinel & Cie (Tel.: 31-17-36) (Kourou 30F, St Laurent 100F) leaves 0530; will pick up at hotel if ticket bought day before. Otherwise transport is by shared taxis (collectifs), which leave from Av. de la Liberté, near the fish market early in the morning (Kourou 40F, St. Laurent 140F.) Ferry or dugout to Albina, Sf1.50. Bus leaves Albina for Paramaribo 0700 and 1230, 3½ hrs. No money exchange at the border. To Paramaribo direct 84F. Transport John (proprietor, John Hector, speaks English), Route Baduel, Tel.: 31-16-69, runs taxis to Paramaribo, 125F per seat, leaves 0200, arrives 1000. It is much cheaper to buy a bus ticket to St.-Laurent and another from Albina to Paramaribo than to buy a through ticket.

International Airport Cayenne-Rochambeau is 16 km. from Cayenne, 20 mins. by taxi. (See Routes to Guyane, page 862.) Local air services: Air Guyane to all main centres, circular flights twice a month. No public transport; only taxis (80F daytime, 100F night, but you can bargain or share). No exchange facilities. Cheaper taxi: Richard Lugret, Tel.: 31-29-89.

Kourou, 56 km. W of Cayenne, where the main French space centre (Central

GUYANE

Spatial Guyanais), used for the European Space Agency's Ariane programme, is located, is referred to by the Guyanais as "white city" because of the number of metropolitan French families living there; its population is about 6,000. It has two excellent hotels and a number of good restaurants, but the project and population have been substantially reduced. Tourist attractions include bathing, fishing, sporting and aero club, and a variety of organized excursions. The space centre occupies an area of about 4 km. deep along some 30 km. of coast, bisected by the Kourou river. It is open to the public on Wednesday mornings. Phone 33-44-82 to reserve a place on the tour of the centre, often booked up days ahead; closed during Carnival. Kourou has its own port facilities. Boats to Iles du Salut (120F return) depending on tide, but around 0800, returning at 1600. The port is 4 km. out of town. There are no buses, but one can sometimes hitch a lift with the Space Centre bus to the cross roads 1 km. from the port. *Taxis collectifs* leave for Cayenne at 0600 and 1400 from Shell petrol station. A bank operates daily.

Hotels *Diamant*, A; *Des Roches* (restaurant) topless beach, pool, C (incl. breakfast, service and taxes). In the old part of town one can find some rooms for about half the price found in the new.

Restaurants *Guinguette Pim-Pum* (dinner only); *Le Saramacca*; *Viet Huong* (behind the Church; Vietnamese cooking); *Le Mandarin* (Chinese cuisine); *Le Cactus*; *Le Bretagne*; *L'Estrambord*; *Au Bon Accueil*, *Resto* and *Le Catouri* (Creole specialities).

The **Iles du Salut** islands, opposite Kourou, include the Ile Royale, the Ile Saint-Joseph, and the Ile du Diable. They were the scene of the notorious convict settlement built in 1852; the last prisoners left in 1953. The Ile du Diable ("Devil's Island"), a rocky palm-covered islet almost inaccessible from the sea, was where political prisoners, including Alfred Dreyfus, were held. There is a 60-bed hotel on Ile Royale, *Auberge Iles du Salut*, D (recommended for a night at least); former guard's bungalow, lunch (excellent) US$8, breakfast US$2.50, (ex-mess hall for warders, with good food). You can also see monkeys and agoutis, and sharks patrolling the water separating the two islands. Paintings of prison life are on show in the tiny church. Boat from Kourou 110F (120F weekends) return, leaves 0830, returns from island at 1700, 4 hrs. each way. Tickets may be obtained from Somarig Voyager, Place L. Heder 1. Boat owners are very reluctant to visit Devil's Island: pleading with them can sometimes change their minds. An hour on the island should enable you to see everything.

St.-Laurent du Maroni (population 7,000) is a quiet colonial town 250 km. from Cayenne on the River Maroni, bordering Suriname. (Nearby is St.-Jean du Maroni, an Indian village.) There are three acceptable hotels and several restaurants. *Hotel Toucan*, adequate and cheapest, E; they will accept some Surinamese money in payment of bills. *Hotel Bacadel*, E, airy; the owner, Mme. Bacadel, is friendly. *Star Hotel* (air conditioned) C. We are informed that the restaurants (*Chez Casimir* near fish market, *Vietnam*, and *Le Point d'Interrogation*, near the hospital) are better than Albina's (good market here for FFr), on the other side of the river, and that the old Camp de Transportation (the original penal centre but now full of squatters) can be wandered round at will (an absolute must if visiting the country), though if you want to see the cells you will have to apply to the local *gendarmerie*. The bank in St.-Laurent is open limited hours a.m., will not change Suriname guilders. The brasserie with the orange trim on corner when coming into town from Cayenne has been recommended, English spoken, friendly. There is a bank in Albina. Ferry to Albina (every two hrs.) costs 7.50F or Sf1.70; a dugout can be hired for a bit more. Get your passport stamped at the ferry terminals on both sides of the river. Bus to Cayenne, 100F, 0500 daily; *taxis collectifs* to and from Cayenne, 140F a head, 3½-hr. trip. Buses for Paramaribo leave the Albina ferry terminal up until 1230. They will pick up at the *Star Hotel* if booked before 1700 the previous day. Hitch-hiking is also quite easy.

Jef D Boeke of Boston, Mass., writes: I spent 6 weeks in the Saül area, which I think is interesting. **Saül** (population 52) is a remote gold-mining settlement in the "central massif". The main attractions are for the nature-loving tourist—beautiful undisturbed tropical forests are accessible by a very well-maintained system of 90 km. of marked trails, including several circular routes. The place has running water, a radiotelephone, and electricity. A hostel (*Gîte d'Etape*) is run by Michel Modde (who also runs the tourist office); the price is 50-70F per day with 3 meals. Own hammock and bedding useful but not essential. Air service MWF with Air Guyane from Cayenne or via Maripasoula (215F one way). Try at the airport even if flight said to be full; Air Guyane office in Cayenne very unhelpful. Motor canoe (*pirogue*) from Mana up Mana River; 9-12 days, then one day's walk to Saül. Restaurant: *Chez Joseph*. Tourist Office: Syndicat d'Initiative, 97314 Saül, Guyane Française.

40 km north of St. Laurent du Maroni is **Mana**, a delightful town with rustic architecture. 16 km south of Mana along the river (via a single-track access road) is Les Hattes, an Amerindian village: 4 km further on is beach where turtles lay their eggs.

Aonara, an Amerindian village with hammock places, is a few kilometres south of Les Hattes. Aonara is well known for the mainly leather turtles that came at night between February and July to lay their eggs; they take about three hours over it. Take mosquito nets, hammock and insect repellant.

St.-Georges de l'Oyapoc is 15 min. down river from Oiapoque (Brazil) US$2 p.p. (canoe), *Hotel Damas*, *Hotel Modestina*, E, restaurant, also *Theofila*, lunch US$3, other restaurants and a night club. Several duty-free shops with French specialities. Immigration ½ km. from docks—only French spoken. GAT flies Mon.-Sat. US$26 single to Cayenne. Normally booked up a week ahead. No banks but try Post Office. There is a beautiful 19 metre waterfall one day up the Oyapoc River at Saut Maripa.

Air Guyane has daily flights to Régina and regular flights to St. Georges (US$27, their office in St. Georges is practically the only place that will exchange money into French francs) and Maripasoula: the latter may also be reached by *pirogue* in 2-4 days. There are also freight canoes which take passengers (200F) or private boats (750F) which leave from St.-Laurent.

Economy

Guyane has renewable natural riches in its timber forests (about 80,000 sq km.) with 15 sawmills and mineral resources. Farming employs only 13% of the population and the country is very sparsely populated. An estimated 42 million tons of extractable bauxite have been located in the Kaw mountains to the E of Cayenne by Alcoa and Pechineys. Some 40m tonnes of kaolin have been located at St.-Laurent du Maroni and it is thought that other minerals including gold may again be mined.

Guyane imports most of its foodstuffs and manufactured goods, of which about 50% come from France. The value of exports, mainly shrimps, rum, essence of rosewood, hardwoods and gold, is very low; France buys just over 20% and the USA about 50%.

At end-1982 the Mitterand administration announced plans to step up the Department's development in consultation with local parties: the so-called Green Plan (Plan Vert), backed by the Société Financière de Développement de la Guyane. Under the plan local production of basic foodstuffs, such as meat and eggs, was to be raised, and areas of timber plantations doubled to 22,000 hectares. In recent years new building has taken place and facilities for visitors have been much improved.

Information for Visitors

Routes to Guyane Air France has flights on Mon. and Thurs. the year round and on Sat. between Jan. 19 and Oct. 20 from Paris to Manaus and Lima (return flight Mondays), via Pointe-à-Pitre (Guadaloupe) and Cayenne. The Air France Vacances flight has been recommended as one of the cheapest flights from Europe. You have to confirm your return trip—which must be within a year. A change of booking may be made once free, thereafter it costs 270F. SLM and Cruzeiro do Sul fly to Belém on Mon., Thur. (3 week excursion fares available), US$120. There is an Air France 737 to Guadeloupe and Martinique on Mondays and Thursdays. On Monday, Thursday and Friday there are flights to Paramaribo. The Suriname Navigation Company has a fortnightly service between Cayenne and Suriname. The Compagnie Générale Maritime runs a passenger service to France once a month, via Martinique, and a freight service every three months. **N.B.** Do not accept verbal confirmation of flights from Air France: get a time/date stamped confirmation to avoid later misunderstandings.

Transport There are no railways, and only 462 (over 75% asphalted) km. of road. The main road, narrow but now paved, runs for 130 km. from Pointe Macouris, on the roadstead of Cayenne, to Iracoubo. Another 117 km. takes it to Mana and St.-Laurent. One-to three-ton boats which can be hauled over the

GUYANE

rapids are used by the gold-seekers, the forest workers, and the rosewood establishments. There is a twice-a-month shipping service which calls at nearly all the coastal towns of Guyane. Ferries are free except those at the frontier. Internal air services by Air Guyane; bookings are made through Air France. There are 0815 and 1500 Air Guyane flights to St. Georges—on Sunday it leaves in the afternoon and on Saturday there is only a morning flight. This flight is always heavily booked, so be prepared to wait or write or telephone Air Guyane in Cayenne (Tel: 317200).

Transport to Brazil by motorized dugout from St. Georges to Oiapoque; no customs or immigration post, and foreigners are still sometimes returned to Guyane if their papers and visas are not in order. Be sure to get an exit stamp from Gendarmerie. The other way round is said to be possible (see above).

Travellers Passport not required by nationals of France and most French-speaking African countries carrying identity cards. No visa (45F) required for most nationalities (except for those of Guyana, the communist bloc and Asian—not Japan—and other African countries) for a stay of up to 3 months, but an exit ticket out of the country (a ticket out of one of the other Guianas is not sufficient) is essential; a deposit is required otherwise. If one stays more than three months, income tax clearance is required before leaving the country. Inoculation against yellow-fever officially required only for those staying in Guyane longer than 2 weeks, but advisable for all; you must have it if entering Guyane from Suriname across the river. Travel to certain Amerindian villages is restricted (see page 859). Malaria prophylaxis recommended.

Climate is tropical with a very heavy rainfall. Average temperature at sea-level is 27°C, and fairly constant at that. Night and day temperatures vary more in the highlands. The rainy season is from November to July, with (sometimes) a short dry interruption in February and March. The great rains begin in May. The dry season is from July to mid-November. The best months to arrive are February and March, while trips to the jungle are normally made in the dry season. Tropical diseases, dysentery, malaria, etc., occur, but the country is fairly healthy.

Public Holidays In addition to the feasts of the Church: January 1, New Year's Day and July 14, Fête Nationale. Moslem holidays are observed, but the dates vary because of the shorter Moslem year; see note under Guyana, page 849.

Communications There is telephone communication throughout the territory. International telephone calls via STD to Europe and French Antilles. Foreign telegraph communication is via Paramaribo or Fort-de-France, from the TSF station at Cayenne. There are about 10,000 TV sets in use.

Consulates British, 16 Av. Monnerville (B.P. 664, Cayenne 97300); Brazilian, 12 Rue L. Helder, at corner of Place des Palmistes, near Air France offices (closed Sats.). Suriname, 38 rue Christophe Colombe.

General The language is French, with officials not usually speaking anything else. The religion is predominantly Roman Catholic. Weights and measures are metric. The currency is the French franc. It is virtually impossible to find a hotel single room under 65F a night or a 3-course meal for under 45F. Food, most of which is imported (except seafood), is very high quality but expensive. La Presse de la Guyane is the daily paper (circ. 1,500). France-Guyane-Antilles is a weekly newspaper with a good information page for the tourist. There is a lack of public transport; car hire can be a great convenience. Gasoline costs 5F a litre and most major car hire firms have an operator in Guyane. It is advisable if at all possible to arrive in Guyane with a supply of French francs, as many banks do not offer exchange facilities.

The French Government tourist offices generally have leaflets on Guyane; there is a special office in Paris, L'Office du Tourisme des Antilles et de la Guyane, 12 rue Amber, 75009 Paris, Tel.: 268-11-07. The Cayenne office is at Jardin Botanique BP 801, 97303 (Tel.: 910356, Telex 300900). In 1980 there were 5 hospitals with 868 beds, and 11 midwives and 14 dentists as well as 287 nurses.

We are most grateful to Sarah Cameron and Paul Millgate of Lloyds Bank Economics Department for updating the economic sections and to Lynne and Hugh Davies (Mill Valley, Ca.), Madge Ferrand (St.-Georges, Guyane) and J. Thomas Kutta (Takoma Park, Maryland).

FALKLAND ISLANDS
ISLAS MALVINAS

(In accordance with the practice suggested by the UN, we are calling the Islands by both their English and their Spanish names.)

The Falkland Islands (Malvinas) comprise two groups: East Falkland (Isla Soledad), with its adjacent islands, has an area of 2,580 square miles; West Falkland (Gran Malvina), with its islands, 2,038 square miles. These two groups lie between latitudes 51° and 53° S and between longitudes 57° and 62° W, approximately 480 miles north-east of Cape Horn. The land fighting during the 1982 hostilities was all on the northern half of East Falkland; the southern half, known as Lafonia, and West Falkland were not affected. The 1,800 inhabitants are almost exclusively of pure British descent. Half of them live and work on the sheep farms.

Early History The islands were visited in 1592 by the English navigator Captain John Davis. Captain Strong landed upon them in 1690 and gave them their present name, but earlier in the 17th century seafarers from St. Malo had visited the islands, and called them Iles Malouines in French, hence Islas Malvinas in Spanish.

In 1764 they were taken by France and Bougainville planted a small colony at Port Louis. Two years later France admitted Spain's prior claim and ceded its rights. In 1767 Britain asserted its dominion, and a post was established to survey the group. This was closed by the Spaniards in 1770 and restored in the following year, after threat of war. The post was abandoned in 1774, and there was no further formal occupation until 1820, when the United Provinces of South America (Argentina, later) hoisted their flag at Port Louis (Soledad). This settlement was broken up in 1831 by an American warship owing to the illegal imprisonment, by a German in charge of the settlement, of some American sealers. In 1833 British warships were sent to reassert Britain's claim. Argentina refused to leave; its flag was struck, the British flag raised, and the Argentine garrison expelled. In April 1982 Argentina occupied the islands, which were repossessed by Britain in June 1982.

Administration The islands' Constitution provides for a Governor, an Executive Council, and a Legislative Council. **Education** A Junior and Senior school in Stanley cater for the needs of the children in the town and those that board in the School Hostel. The other settlement children are trained by specialist travelling teachers who use radio tuition as a homework reminder and to contact the more isolated farms.

Climate The islands are in the same latitude South as London is North. Mean monthly temperatures are uniformly lower than in London but London has both higher and lower extremes. The Islands are exposed and persistent strong winds spoil many otherwise pleasant days, especially in winter. (The wind reaches gale force one day in five). The annual rainfall is rather higher than in London. Spring, autumn and winter clothing, as used in the United Kingdom, is suitable. The normal temperature range is from 20°F to 70°F, with a annual mean of 42°F. The annual rainfall is about 28 inches.

Stanley, on East Falkland, the only place of importance, has a fine inner and outer harbour. The population is about 1,100 and the houses are mostly of wood and iron. The bay, surrounded by hills covered with a brownish vegetation, looks somewhat like home to the native of Northern Scotland.

Accommodation *Upland Goose Hotel*, £31 full board, £20 bed and breakfast; *Emma's Guest House*, £20.50 full board, £14.50 bed and breakfast; *Malvina House Hotel*, 3 Ross Road £28 full board, £20 bed and breakfast. *Sparrow Hawk House* (previously *Byron House*), bed and breakfast

FALKLAND IS. (MALVINAS) 865

£18.50. A handful of private homes take in paying guests. Meals at *Emma's*, *Malvinas House*, or at *Woodbine* fish and chip shop.

The town has a hospital (damaged by fire early 1984), and a town hall, which also houses the Library and the Post Office. There are overseas telephone, telegram and telex services. There are some fairly well-stocked stores, open mainly Monday to Friday. The few pubs, such as *The Globe* and *Rose*, are good meeting places during their strict drinking hours (Sundays only from 1200 to 1300, the "Glory hour"!).

The small Museum, in the Falkland Islands Company buildings near the dockyard, is worth a visit. Mr. John Smith, the curator, is extremely knowledgeable on most aspects of the Islands' history, particularly maritime. If the museum is closed, ask at the Falklands Islands Co. if it can be opened. The roads are electrically lit but not all are paved. There is a race course. Government House and the little Cathedral (the most southerly in the world, built in 1890; it contains interesting woodcarvings) are worth looking at, and so is the monument commemorating the battle of 1914.

Travel Agent Outward Bound Tours, P.O. Box 178, Stanley. Falklands Camp and Tramp, P.O. Box 146 Stanley.

Tourists The Islands offer endless interest to keen wildlife enthusiasts. The best months to visit are October to March. Allowance must always be made for unpredictable changes in the weather. There are virtually no roads outside Stanley except for the one to the new airport; only tracks which require Land Rovers.

Visitors are warned that there still may be unexploded mines in the neighbourhood of Port Stanley.

Travel outside the neighbourhood of Stanley is mainly by air. The Falkland Islands Government Air Service (Figas) operate three Islander aircraft to farm settlements and settled outer islands according to bookings, seat availability and weather conditions.

Points of Interest Sparrow Cove, Kidney Cove and adjacent areas, only a short distance across Stanley Harbour by boat and out into Port William, are good areas to view Gentoo and Magellan penguins; shore birds and sealions can also be seen and dolphins or porpoises may well follow in the wake of your boat near The Narrows.

Kidney Island, a very small island densely covered with tussock grass, is a Nature Reserve. Contrary to popular belief, it is suitable only for hardy and dedicated bird lovers. Rockhopper penguins nest here in a small colony, as do King cormorants and many other species. Kidney Island is accessible by boat, 1½ hours from Stanley.

Rookery Valley, not too far from Stanley and accessible by Land Rover as well as by boat-plus-walk, holds breeding Rockhopper penguins.

Land Rover and boat hire from Dave Eynon, South Atlantic Marine Services—also diving and fishing trips. If stuck for a boat, enquire of Ron at the *Globe* bar.

Stanley Common, in areas surrounding the old airport, lighthouse and, to the south of the town, Eliza Cove and nearby ponds, offers rewarding walks for the keen naturalist. These areas have not been grazed by sheep and many of the original flowering plants and grasses remain. Several of the small birds, e.g. black-throated finch, pipit, siskin, dotterel, as well as snipe, may be observed.

Of particular interest are the hulls of old sailing ships in and around the harbours at Stanley and Darwin. Examples at Stanley are the *Jhelum* in front of the Governor's house (built 1839 for the East India Company), on board, the stern section is very well preserved, the *Charles Cooper* (the last US sailing packet to sail out of New York harbour; in the islands since 1866), the iron-built *Lady Elizabeth* at the far end of the harbour (228 ft. long, with three masts still standing) and the *Snow Squall* (a survivor of the famous American clipper ships). At Darwin are the *Vicar of Bray* (the last survivor of the California Gold Rush fleet) and another old iron ship, the *Garland*. Many of these hulls are still used for storage. There are interesting old French buildings at Port Louis.

Volunteer Point, north of Stanley, is a wild animal and bird sanctuary. Permission to visit must be obtained from the owner, Mr. O. Smith, resident at Johnsons Harbour. Trips run by Dave Eynon in 48-ft. schooner MV *Penguin*, also to Kidney Island, or arrangements made with Mr. Smith for possible overnight stay at the shepherd's house on Volunteer Point (you must take your own food and sleeping bag). Volunteer is the only area in the islands where King penguins nest in any numbers. Gentoo penguins, Magellan penguins and geese, ducks and seals can also be observed and photographed.

The smaller islands to the West of West Falkland are the most spectacular and attractive for their wildlife and scenery. New Island, on the extreme west of the archipelago, is run as a nature reserve. Enquiries from naturalists and bird lovers are most welcome and should be addressed to Mr. T. Chater, The Pink Shop, Stanley, or to Ian or Maria Strange, New Island. The island offers an excellent cross-section of the archipelago's breeding species of birds and has large colonies of Rockhopper penguins, black-browed albatross, Gentoo and Magellan penguins, King and Rock cormorants and many other birds, as well as a fur-seal colony.

FALKLAND IS. (MALVINAS)

Communications The RAF operates two Tri-Star flights a week from Brize Norton, Oxfordshire, to the new airport. Enquiries about passages can be addressed to the Falkland Islands Co. Tourist visits are being resumed by British Airways flights at a cost (return, all-in) of about £1,450, and Twickers World are arranging holidays from November 1986 at a new prefab. hotel on Sea Lion Island at an expected cost of £2,500 per person.

Entry Requirements All travellers must have passports. Citizens of the USA, and some other countries which do not have reciprocal visa abolition agreements with the UK, still require a British visa.

There are no buses or taxis at the airport. The hotel collects expected guests; others will have no trouble getting a lift. A new airport, both military and civil, has been built W of Stanley; regular flights began in mid-1985.

Economy In East Falkland the country is wild moorland, interspersed with rocks and stones. The soil, mostly soft peat, makes travel difficult. The islands are so well adapted for sheep-farming that the whole area has been devoted to that industry. The tussac, which grows to the height of 7 ft., yields fattening food for cattle; it has disappeared from the two main islands, but abounds on the smaller islands. There are only a few trees.

The poverty of the soil, isolation, and the intemperate climate make progress difficult. Re-grassing schemes are in progress. Sheep-farming is the only important activity, and there are some 600,000 sheep. Wool is the only important export. Small quantities of oats and potatoes are grown.

Cost of living is about the same as it is in Britain. Freight necessarily adds to the prices of groceries, all imported. There is, however, no value-added tax, and only tobacco, wines, spirits and beer pay import duty. Small luxury goods on which the freight is correspondingly low are therefore much cheaper than in the UK.

Mails New air-mail arrangements have been made following the 1982 repossession. Heavy parcel mails come direct from the UK four or five times a year. The inter-island service for mails is carried out by the inter-island vessels *Monsunen* and *Forest* and by the local Government Air Service.

Currency The local £ is on a par with sterling. Local notes and coins. UK notes and coins also legal tender. Foreign currency changed at local Treasury (Secretariat Building), or at the Falkland Islands Company offices, Crozier Place. There is a branch of the Standard Chartered Bank in Stanley.

South Georgia

South Georgia, in latitude 54½° S and longitude 36° to 38°W, has an area of about 1,450 square miles, and a small population composed entirely of scientists of the British Antarctic Survey, who man the scientific station. Communications are supported entirely by the Survey. Government and private boats calling at Stanley will often take passengers to the island, but there are no passenger ships as such. Also, there is no accommodation except for survey personnel. Anyone intending to visit the island must be self-sufficient and must submit a request through the Colonial Secretary, Stanley. The island was occupied by Argentina in April-May 1982.

The island is a mass of high mountains covered with snow where not too precipitous. Observations extending over three years point to snowfall upon 124 days per annum. The valleys are filled with glaciers which descend in many cases to the sea. The coastal region is free from snow in summer when it is partially covered by vegetation. Reindeer have been introduced, and are doing well; other points of interest are the 5 abandoned whaling stations, the little white church, and many sailing-ship hulks.

MEXICO

	Page		Page
Introductory	867	Mexico City to Acapulco	942
Roads from USA:		Mexico City to Guatemala	953
From Laredo	870	Yucatán	967
From Eagle Pass	876	Baja California	991
From El Paso	880	Economy	997
From Nogales	889	Information for Visitors	998
Mexico City	910	Maps	874, 911, 934
Mexico City to Veracruz	929		

CORTES, asked what the country looked like, crushed a piece of parchment in his fist, released it and said: "That is the map of Mexico." This crumpled land is so splendid to the eye, and so exotic to the other senses, that millions, mainly from the USA, visit it each year.

Mexico is the third largest and the most populous Spanish-speaking country in Latin America (78.5m. people). Its geography ranges from swamp to desert, from tropical lowland jungle to high alpine vegetation above the tree line, from thin arid soils to others so rich that they grow three crops a year. Over half the country is at an altitude of over 1,000 metres and much at over 2,000 metres; over half is arid and another 30% semi-arid. Only about 30m. hectares (16% of the total land area) can be cultivated, and of these 33% are irrigable.

Mexico has an area equal to about a quarter of the United States, with which it has a frontier of 2,400 km. The southern frontier of 885 km. is with Guatemala and Belize. It has a coast line of 2,780 km. on the Gulf of Mexico and the Caribbean, and of 7,360 km. on the Pacific and the Gulf of California.

The structure of the land mass is extremely complicated, but may be simplified (with large reservations) as a plateau flanked by ranges of mountains roughly paralleling the coasts. The northern part of the plateau is low, arid and thinly populated; it takes up 40% of the total area of Mexico but holds only 19% of its people. From the Bolsón de Mayrán as far S as the Balsas valley, the level rises considerably; this southern section of the central plateau is crossed by a volcanic range of mountains in which the intermont basins are high and separated. The basin of Guadalajara is at 1,500 metres, the basin of México at 2,300 metres, and the basin of Toluca, W of Mexico City, is at 2,600 metres. Above the lakes and valley bottoms of this contorted middle-land rise the magnificent volcano cones of Orizaba (5,700 metres), Popocatépetl (5,452 metres), Ixtaccíhuatl (5,286 metres), Nevado de Toluca (4,583 metres), Matlalcueyetl or La Malinche (4,461 metres), and Cofre de Perote (4,282 metres). This mountainous southern end of the plateau, the heart of Mexico, has ample rainfall. Though only 14% of the area of Mexico, it holds nearly half of the country's people. And here, in a small high intermont basin measuring only 50 km. square, is Mexico City, with 12 million inhabitants.

The two high ranges of mountains which rise E and W of the plateau, between it and the sea, are great barriers against communications: there are far easier routes N along the floor of the plateau to the United States than there are to either the east coast or the west. In the W there are rail and road links across the Sierra Madre Occidental from Guadalajara to the Pacific at the port of Mazatlán; both continue northward through a coastal desert to Nogales. The Sierra Madre Oriental is more kindly; in its mountain ramparts a pass inland from Tampico

868 MEXICO

gives road-rail access to Monterrey (a great industrial centre) and the highland basins; and another from Veracruz leads by a fair gradient to the Valley of México.

South of the seven intermont basins in the south-central region the mountainland is still rugged but a little lower (between 1,800 and 2,400 metres), with much less rainfall. After some 560 km. it falls away into the low-lying Isthmus of Tehuantepec. Population is sparse in these southern mountains and is settled on the few flat places on which commercial crops can be grown—subsistence crops are sown on incredibly steep slopes. The Pacific coast here is forbidding and its few ports of little use. Very different are the Gulf Coast and Yucatán; half this area is classed as flat, and 75 % of it gets enough rain the year round, leading to its becoming one of the most important agricultural and cattle raising areas in the country. The Gulf Coast also provides most of Mexico's oil and sulphur. Geographically, North America may be said to come to an end in the Isthmus of Tehuantepec. South of the Isthmus the land rises again into the thinly populated highlands of Chiapas.

Climate and vegetation depend upon altitude. The *tierra caliente* takes in the coastlands and plateau lands below 750 metres. The *tierra templada*, or temperate zone is at 750 to 2,000 metres. The *tierra fría*, or cold zone, is from 2,000 metres upwards. Above the tree line at 4,000 metres are high moorlands (*páramos*).

The climate of the inland highlands is mostly mild, but with sharp changes of temperature between day and night, sunshine and shade. Generally, winter is the dry season and summer the wet season. There are only two areas where rain falls the year round: S of Tampico along the lower slopes of the Sierra Madre Oriental and across the Isthmus of Tehuantepec into Tabasco state; and along the Pacific coast of the state of Chiapas. Both areas together cover only 12 % of Mexico. These wetter parts get most of their rain between June and September, when the skies are so full of clouds that the temperature is lowered: May is a hotter month than July. Apart from these favoured regions, the rest of the country suffers from a climate in which the rainy season hardly lives up to its name and the dry season almost always does.

Population is growing at the rate of 1½ millions a year, or 2.8 %. Birth rate per thousand, 35; death rate, 9. Urban growth is 4.7 %; 50 % of the population is under 20. About 5 % consider themselves pure white and about 25 % pure Indian; about 60 % are *mestizos*, a mixture in varying proportions of Spanish and Indian bloods; some 10 % are a mixture of black and white or black and Indian or *mestizo*. Mexico also has infusions of other European, Arab and Chinese blood. About 24 % are still illiterate; 59 % live in towns or cities; 41 % are rural. There is a national cultural prejudice in favour of the Indian rather than the Spanish element. Mexicans of Spanish descent sometimes use Indian surnames instead of Spanish. There is hardly a single statue of Cortés in the whole of Mexico, but he does figure, pejoratively, in the frescoes of Diego Rivera and his contemporaries. On the other hand the two last Aztec emperors, Moctezuma and Cuauhtémoc, are national heroes.

Among the estimated 17 million Indians there are 56 groups or sub-divisions, each with its own language. The Indians are far from evenly distributed; 36 % live on the Central Plateau (mostly Puebla, Hidalgo, and México); 35 % are along the southern Pacific coast (Oaxaca, Chiapas, Guerrero), and 23 % along the Gulf coast (mostly Yucatán and Veracruz): 94 % of them, that is, live in these three regions.

The issue of access to the land has always been the country's fundamental problem, and it was a despairing landless peasantry that rose in the Revolution of 1910 and swept away Porfirio Díaz and the old system of huge estates. Since 1927 the Partido Revolucionario Institucional (PRI), the party which incorporates the social-democratic ideal of the revolution, has been in power. Its accomplishments have been mixed. Life for the peasant is still hard. His minimum wage barely allows him a simple diet of beans, rice, and *tortillas*. His home is still, possibly, a shack with no windows, no water, no sanitation, and he may still not be

MEXICO

able to read or write, but something has been done to redistribute the land in the so-called *ejido* system, which does give the peasant either communal or personal control of the land he cultivates, though the purely economic benefit of the system is in doubt. At least the peasant is freed from the landowner, and his family receives basic health and educational facilities from the state.

Constitution Under the 1917 Constitution Mexico is a federal republic of 31 states and a Federal District containing the capital, Mexico City. The President, who appoints the Ministers, is elected for 6 years and can never be re-elected. Congress consists of the Senate, elected every 6 years, and the Cámara de Diputados, elected every 3 years. There is universal suffrage, and one Deputy for 60,000 inhabitants. The President for 1982-88 is Lic. Miguel de la Madrid Hurtado.

Local Administration The States enjoy local autonomy and can levy their own taxes, and each State has its Governor, legislature and judicature. The President appoints the Chief of the Federal District.

Religion Roman Catholicism is the principal religion, but the State is determinedly secular. Because of its identification firstly with Spain, then with the Emperor Maximilian and finally with Porfirio Díaz, the Church has been severely persecuted in the past by reform-minded administrations, and priests are still not supposed to wear ecclesiastical dress (see *The Lawless Roads* and *The Power and the Glory*, by Graham Greene).

History Of the many Indian nations in the vast territory of Mexico, the two most important before the Conquest were the Aztecs of Tenochtitlán (now Mexico City) and the Mayas of Yucatán. The Aztecs, a militarist, theocratic culture, had obtained absolute control over the whole Valley of México and a loose control of some other regions. The Mayas (whose early history is given in the Central American chapter) were already in decline by the time the Spaniards arrived. The 34-year-old Cortés disembarked near the present Veracruz with about 500 men, some horses and cannon, on April 21, 1519. They marched into the interior; their passage was not contested; they arrived at Tenochtitlán in November and were admitted into the city as guests of the reigning monarch, Moctezuma. There they remained until June of the next year, when Pedro de Alvarado, in the absence of Cortés, murdered hundreds of Indians to quell his own fear of a rising. At this treacherous act the Indians did in fact rise, and it was only by good luck that the Spanish troops, with heavy losses, were able to fight their way out of the city on the Noche Triste (the Night of Sorrows) of June 30. Next year Cortés came back with reinforcements and besieged the city. It fell on August 30, 1521, and was utterly razed. Cortés then turned to the conquest of the rest of the country. One of the main factors in his success was his alliance with the Tlaxcalans, old rivals of the Aztecs. The fight was ruthless, and the Aztecs were soon mastered.

There followed 300 years of Spanish rule. In the early years all the main sources of gold and silver were discovered. Spanish grandees stepped into the shoes of dead Aztec lords and inherited their great estates and their wealth of savable souls with little disturbance, for Aztec and Spanish ways of holding land were not unlike: the *ejido* (or agrarian community holding lands in common), the *rancho*, or small private property worked by the owner; and that usually huge area which paid tribute to its master—the Spanish *encomienda*—soon to be converted into the *hacienda*, with its absolute title to the land and its almost feudal way of life. Within the first 50 years all the Indians in the populous southern valleys of the plateau had been christianized and harnessed to Spanish wealth-getting from mine and soil. The more scattered and less profitable Indians of the north and south had to await the coming of the missionizing Jesuits in 1571, a year behind the Inquisition. Too often, alas, the crowded Jesuit missions proved as fruitful a source of smallpox or measles as of salvation, with the unhappy result that large numbers of Indians died; their deserted communal lands were promptly filched by some neighbouring *encomendero*: a thieving of public lands by private interests which continued for 400 years.

By the end of the 16th century the Spaniards had founded most of the towns which are still important, tapped great wealth in mining, stock raising and sugar-growing, and firmly imposed their way of life and belief. Government was by a Spanish-born upper class, based on the subordination of the Indian and *mestizo* populations and a strict dependence on Spain for all things. As throughout all Hispanic America, Spain built up resistance to itself by excluding from government both Spaniards born in Mexico and the small body of educated *mestizos*.

The standard of revolt was raised in 1810 by the curate of Dolores, Miguel Hidalgo. The Grito de Dolores: "Perish the Spaniards", collected 80,000 armed supporters, and had it not been for Hidalgo's loss of nerve and failure to engage the Spaniards, the capital might have been captured in the first month and a government created not differing much from the royal Spanish government. But eleven years of fighting created bitter differences. A loyalist general, Agustín de Iturbide, joined the rebels and proclaimed an independent Mexico in 1821. His Plan of Iguala proposed an independent monarchy with a ruler from the Spanish royal family, but on second thoughts Iturbide proclaimed himself Emperor in 1822: a fantasy which lasted one year. A federal republic was created on October 4, 1824, with General Guadalupe Victoria as President. Conservatives stood for a highly centralized government; Liberals favoured federated sovereign states. The tussle of interests expressed itself in endemic civil war. In 1836, Texas, whose cotton-growers and cattle-ranchers had been infuriated by the abolition of slavery in 1829, rebelled against the dictator,

Santa Ana, and declared its independence. It was annexed by the United States in 1845. War broke out and US troops occupied Mexico City in 1847. Next year, under the terms of the treaty of Guadalupe Hidalgo, the US acquired half Mexico's territory: all the land from Texas to California and from the Río Grande to Oregon.

A period of reform dominated by independent Mexico's great hero, the pure-blooded Zapotec Indian, Benito Juárez, began in 1857. The church, in alliance with the conservatives, hotly contested by civil war his liberal programme of popular education, freedom of the press and of speech, civil marriage and the separation of church and state. Juárez won, but the constant civil strife wrecked the economy, and Juárez was forced to suspend payment on the national debt. Promptly, Spain, France and Britain landed a joint force at Veracruz to protect their financial rights. The British and the Spanish soon withdrew, but the French force pushed inland and occupied Mexico City in 1863. Juárez took to guerrilla warfare against the invaders. The Archduke Maximilian of Austria became Emperor of Mexico with Napoleon III's help, but United States insistence and the gathering strength of Prussia led to the withdrawal of the French troops in 1867. Maximilian, betrayed and deserted, was captured by the Juaristas at Querétaro and shot on June 19. Juárez resumed control and died in July 1872. He was the first Mexican leader of any note who had died naturally since 1810.

The distinguished scholar who followed him was soon tricked, very easily, out of office by General Porfirio Díaz, who ruled Mexico from 1876 to 1910. But Díaz's paternal, though often ruthless, central authority did introduce a period of 35 years of peace. A superficial prosperity followed upon peace; a real civil service was created, finances put on a sound basis, banditry put down, industries started, railways built, international relations improved, and foreign capital protected. But the main mass of peasants had never been so wretched; their lands were stolen from them, their personal liberties curtailed, and many were sold into forced labour on tobacco and henequen plantations from which death was the only release.

It was this open contradiction between dazzling prosperity and hideous distress which led to the upheaval of November, 1910 and to Porfirio Díaz's self-exile in Paris. A new leader, Francisco Madero, who came from a landowning family in Coahuila, championed a programme of political and social reform, including the restoration of stolen lands. The reactionaries rose and Madero was brutally murdered, but the great new cry, *Tierra y Libertad* (Land and Liberty) was not to be quieted until the revolution was made safe by the election of Alvaro Obregón to the Presidency. Later, President Lázaro Cárdenas fulfilled some of the more important economic objectives of the revolution; it was his regime (1934-40) that brought about the division of the great estates into *ejidos* (or communal lands), irrigation, the raising of wages, the spread of education, the beginnings of industrialization, the nationalization of the oil wells and the railways. Later presidents nationalized electric power, most of the railways, the main airlines and parts of industry, but at the same time encouraged both Mexican and foreign (mainly US) entrepreneurs to develop the private sector. All presidents have pursued an independent and non-aligned foreign policy. One of the remarkable things about this transformation is that it has been able to express itself as successfully in terms of painting, poetry and architecture as it has in economic progress.

Laredo to Mexico City: the Gulf Route

We are concerned here with the four great road routes from the US border to Mexico City: the Gulf Route from Laredo (by Pan-American Highway), the Eagle Pass/Piedras Negras route, the Central Route from El Paso and the Pacific Route, from Nogales. The first of these to be opened was the Gulf Route: Nuevo Laredo-Mexico City: 1,226 km. (760 miles).

Traffic from the central and eastern parts of the United States can enter northeastern Mexico through four gateways along the Río Bravo; at Matamoros, opposite Brownsville (which has 90% Mexican population, despite being in the USA; cheap hotel, *Hotel Bienvenidos*, about 200 metres from Río Grande bridge, D, if you don't want to cross the border at night); at Reynosa (*Hotel San Carlos*, on Zócalo, D, recommended) opposite McAllen; at Ciudad Miguel Alemán, opposite Roma; and at **Nuevo Laredo,** opposite Laredo—by far the most important of them. The roads from these places all converge upon Monterrey, though there are alternative roads from Reynosa and Matamoros which join the Laredo-Mexico City highway at Montemorelos and Ciudad Victoria, respectively: the latter runs along the tropical Gulf coastal plain and then climbs sharply through the Sierra Madre Oriental to Ciudad Victoria, at 333 metres.

Hotels at Nuevo Laredo, *Dos Laredos,* F, Matamoros y 15 de Junio; *Motels: Hacienda,* Prol. Reforma 5530, C; *El Río,* Reforma y Toluca, D; *Reforma,* Av. Guerrero 822, D; *Texas,* on Av. Guerrero, F, cheap and not bad.

Crafts Shop Centro Artesanal Nuevo Laredo, Maclovio Herrera 3030. Tel.: 2-63-99.

MEXICO 871

Buses Buses to Mexico City with Tres Estrellas de Oro, mid-afternoon, from the Trailways bus station, about 17 hrs.; get there by 1400. Transportes del Norte is generally recommended by travellers through this area to the N and NE of Mexico, and extending S to Guadalajara and Mexico City. It is fast, efficient and clean and the drivers are courteous. Buses for Monterrey (4 hrs, US$5.50, leave at 0800), Mexico City (15 hrs., US$25, leave at 1400) and intermediate points may be taken from the Greyhound bus station in Nuevo Laredo. Buses direct to Mexico City leave the Greyhound bus station at 1600 from Laredo, Texas; this saves crossing the border and then getting a bus. The Nuevo Laredo bus station is not near the border; you need a bus to get there. (Connecting tickets from Houston via Laredo to Monterrey can be obtained at a cost of US$35, 14 hrs. Overland Greyhound bus New York-Laredo, US$85 with as many stops as you want, but only valid for 15 days.) Bus Laredo-Tampico leaves at 1600, US$13, arrives in the middle of next day. Bus Laredo-Morelia 17 hrs., US$26, leaves at 1730. If pressed for time, avoid November 20 and other national holidays as there are delays at customs owing to Mexicans visiting the USA in large numbers. Border formalities can take 2 hrs. or more. We have been informed that at the border crossing at Matamoros guards have demanded bribes of from US$5 to US$20.

Train Aguila Azteca to Mexico City from Nuevo Laredo, US$17 *primera especial*, a/c, US$13 1st, US$8 2nd class, daily at 1855, 24 hrs., no difference between 1st and 2nd classes.

Matamoros (151,000 people), has a bright and unforbidding museum, designed to let a prospective tourist know what he can expect in Mexico. It is well worth a visit. Several lines run first-class buses to Mexico City in 18 hrs. for US$28. Transportes del Norte to Ciudad Victoria for US$6 (4 hrs.). Craft shop: Centro Artesanal Matamoros, Calle 5a Hurtado and Alvaro Obregón (Tel.: 2-03-84).

Hotels *Holiday Inn*, Av. Obregón 249, C; *Ritz*, Matamoros y Siete, F. There are 4 motels on the road to the beach, all D.

Visas can be obtained in Brownsville from the Mexican Consulate at 940, E Washington. About 8 km. outside Matamoros there is an immigration check-point; to cross this point a visa must be shown which must be signed at the bus station by an immigration official. Without this signature you will be sent back.

After 130 km. of grey-green desert, the road from Nuevo Laredo climbs the Mamulique Pass, which it crosses at 700 metres, and then descends to

Monterrey, capital of Nuevo León state, third largest city in Mexico, 253 km. S of the border and 915 km. from Mexico City. The city, which is dominated by the Cerro de la Silla from the E, has increased its population (1,300,000) by a third since 1960 and is still growing fast in spite of its unattractive climate—too hot in summer, too cold in winter, dusty at most times—and its shortage of water. It now turns out (using cheap gas from near the Texas border and increasingly from the new gas fields in the South), over 75% of Mexico's iron and steel, and many other products accompanied by an almost permanent industrial smog. Its people are highly skilled and educated, but its architecture is drab. In its main centre, Plaza Zaragoza, there is a pleasant 18th century Cathedral badly damaged in the war against the US in 1846-47, when it was used by Mexican troops as a powder magazine. Its famous Technological Institute has valuable collections of books on 16th century Mexican history, of rare books printed in Indian tongues, and 2,000 editions of Don Quixote in all languages. Altitude: 538 metres, and evenings are cool.

Students of architecture should see the remarkable church of San José Obrero built in a working-class district by Enrique de la Mora and his team. Daily flights from Mexico City take 1¼ hrs. The road link (915 km.) can be covered in a day.

Hotels It is difficult to obtain accommodation because of the constant movement of people travelling north/south. *Holiday Inn Crowne Plaza*, Av. Constitución 400 Oriente, near Plaza Zaragoza, A, best, Tel.: (91-83) 44-60-00; *Holiday Inn*, Universidad 101, A; *Ancira*, Hidalgo y Escobedo, C; *Ambassador*, Hidalgo y Galeana, B; *Ramada Inn*, Av. Almazán, B; *Río*, Padre Mier 194, C; *Colonial*, Escobedo y Hidalgo, C; *El Paso*, Zaragoza y R. Martínez, C; *Victoria*, E, with shower, hot water only in day time, 2 blocks from railway station, clean, safe, but do not get room opposite station (less 10% if you show student card); *Monterrey*, Morelos y Zaragoza, B; *Plaza*, Corregidora 519, F; *Nuevo Amado*, F, with bathroom. *Reforma*, Av. Universidad, 1132, F, one of the better cheap ones; *Mary Car*, opp. bus station, D, clean, a/c; *Pino Suárez*, nr. bus station, F, filthy, not recommended. Many hotels between Colón and Reforma, 2 blocks from the bus station. **Motels** *El Paso*

872 MEXICO

Autel, B, Zaragoza y Martínez; on Laredo highway: *Alamo,* D; *Regina,* E; *Royal Courts,* E; *Dorado,* D; *Nevada del Norte,* D

Restaurant *La Cabaña,* Calle Pino Suárez, meals and snacks. 23 eating places around the "Pink Zone" and Plaza Zaragoza in the heart of town.

British Consulate (Honorary) Mr Edward Lawrence, Privada Tamazunchale 104, Colonia del Valle, Garza García. Tel.: (91-83) 56-88-29.

Railways To Mexico City (US$6.30 2nd class, US$10.60 1st) and the port of Tampico. Day trains are slow but a night express does the trip to Mexico City in 15 or 16 hrs.

Bus Monterrey-Mexico City, US$25, 12 hrs. To San Luis Potosí, US$7.

Airport Aeropuerto del Norte, 24 km. from centre.

In the hills around are the bathing resort of Topo Chico, 6½ km. to the NW; water from its hot springs is bottled and sold throughout Mexico; and 18 km. away Chipinque Mesa, at 1,280 metres in the Sierra Madre, with magnificent views of the Monterrey area.

Leaving Monterrey, the road threads the narrow and lovely Huajuco canyon; from Santiago village a road runs to within 2 km. of the Cola de Caballo, or Horsetail, Falls. (First-class hotel on the way.) Our road drops gradually into lower and warmer regions, passing through a succession of sub-tropical valleys with orange groves, banana plantations and vegetable gardens.

At **Montemorelos,** just off the highway, 79 km. S of Monterrey, a branch road from the Matamoros-Monterrey highway comes in. On 53 km. is **Linares** (13,518 people), a charming small town. (*Hotel Guidi,* E, nr. bus station; *Escondido Court,* motel, D, clean, air-conditioned, pool and restaurant, recommended, 1½ km. N of Linares on Highway 855.)

Bus Linares to San Luis Potosí, US$7.

A most picturesque 96 km. highway runs west from Linares up the lovely Santa Rosa canyon, up and over the Sierra Madre after Iturbide, turn S on top of the Sierra Madre and continue on good road through the unspoilt Sierra via La Escondida and Dr. Arroyo. At San Roberto, N of Matehuala (see page 877) join the Highway 57 route from Eagle Pass to Mexico City.

(Km. 706) **Ciudad Victoria,** capital of Tamaulipas state, a quiet, unhurried city with a shaded plaza and a tiny church perched on the top of a hill. It is often used as a stop-over. Alt.: 336 metres; pop.: 70,000.

Hotels *Sierra Gorda,* E, garage US$0.70 a night; *Condesa,* F, bath, dirty, no water at night. *Trailer Park,* Libramiento 101-85, follow signs, good service, hot showers. Owner has lots of travel information, US$5 for 2 plus vehicle. **Motels** *Panorámica,* Lomas de Santuario, C; *Los Monteros,* Plaza Hidalgo, downtown, D.

Buses Omnibuses Blancos to Ciudad Valles (see below) for US$4. Bus Ciudad Victoria-Mexico City 12 hrs., US$23.

After crossing the Tropic of Cancer the road enters the solid green jungle of the tropical lowlands.

Monterrey trains run via Ciudad Victoria to the Caribbean port of **Tampico,** definitely not a tourist attraction, reached by a fine road from (km. 570) El Mante, in a rich sugar-growing area, a deviation of 156 km. Tampico is on the northern bank of the Río Pánuco, not far from a large oilfield: there are storage tanks and refineries for miles along the southern bank. The summer heat, rarely above 35°C, is tempered by sea breezes, but June and July are trying. Cold northerlies blow now and again during the winter. Fishing (both sea and river) is excellent. The Playa de Miramar, a beach resort, is a tram or bus-ride from the city, but is reported dirty. Population: 260,000. The Museo de la Cultura Huasteca in Ciudad Madero is worth visiting (Instituto Tecnológico, Av. 1 de Mayo y Sor Juana Inés de la Cruz); take a colectivo, "Madero", from the centre of Tampico to the Zócalo of Ciudad Madero, then another to the Instituto; open 1000-1500, except Mon., small but select collection.

A second paved road from Tampico joins the Laredo-México highway further S at Ciudad Valles. Trains west to San Luis Potosí. There are direct buses to

Brownsville (Texas), leaving at 2400 and 0545, US$12. Ferry to Villa Cuauhtémoc, wait to board between 2-6 hours; better to come off Gulf Route 180 and take Route 70 to Bypass 105 or to plan to get the ferry before 0600. The long wait applies in both directions.

Hotels *Camino Real*, Av. Hidalgo 2000, C; *Impala*, Mirón 220 Pte., C; *Inglaterra*, Mirón y Olmos, B; *Imperial*, Aurora Sur 201, E, clean, shower, fan, but noisy; *Tampico*, Carranza 513, E; *Rex*, a little run down, F, no hot water; *Nuevo León*, E, Aduana N. 107, a/c, shower, clean; *Ritz*, on Miramar beach, F, beautiful beach, deserted at night.

Restaurant To the N of Tampico on the Pan-American Highway, at Soto de Marina, *Colonial*—recommended. Also, 4 good Chinese places in town.

West German Consul Av. Madero, Hon. Consul Dieter Schulze. Postal Address: Apdo. 775. Also deals with British affairs.

(Km. 548) Antiguo Morelos. A road turns off W to San Luis Potosí (see page 878) 314 km., and Guadalajara (see page 897).

(Km. 476) **Ciudad Valles,** on a winding river and a popular stop-over with many hotels (*San Fernando*); *Valles*, Carretera México-Laredo, E). Museo Regional Huasteco, Calles Rotarios y Artes (or Peñaloza), open 1000-12000, 1400-1800, Mon.-Fri., centre of archaeological and ethnographic research for the Huastec region. Omnibus Oriente to San Luis Potosí for US$3 (4 hrs.). The road to Tampico (145 km.) goes through the oil camp of El Ebano.

(Km. 370) **Tamazunchale** (alt. 206 metres), with riotous tropical vegetation, is perhaps the most popular of all the overnight stops. (*San Antonio Hotel*; *Mirador*, E, good, but passing traffic by night is noisy; *Hotel OK*, F, cheapest but not recommended; *Pemex Tourist Camp*, US$ 2 p.p., nice position, poor plumbing.) S of this little place begins a spectacular climb to the highland, winding with a steady grade over the extremely rugged terrain cut by the Río Moctezuma and its tributaries. The highest point on the road is 2,502 metres. From (km. 279) Jacala there is a dizzying view into a chasm. **Zimapán** (*Posada del Rey*, out on the highway), with a charming market place and a small old church in the plaza, is as good a place as any to stay the night. From (km. 178) **Portezuelo** a paved road runs W to Querétaro (see page 878), 140 km. In an area of 23,300 sq. km. N and S of (km. 169) **Ixmiquilpan,** just off the highway, 65,000 Otomí Indians "live the bitterest and saddest life". The beautifully worked Otomí belts and bags may sometimes be bought at the Monday market, and also in the Artesanía shop in the main street almost opposite the government aid offices.

See early Indian frescoes in the main church, which is one of the 16th century battlemented Augustinian monastery-churches; the monastery is open to the public. John Streather writes: "At sunset each day white egrets come to roost in the trees outside the church; it's worth going up on to the battlements to see them swoop down. The church of El Carmen is worth a visit too, lovely west façade and gilded altars inside. There is also a 16th century bridge over the river; beautiful walk along the ahuehuete-lined banks". (*Hotel Diana*, F, rear buildings slightly dearer rooms but much cleaner, recommended, safe parking.)

Near Ixmiquilpan are several warm swimming pools, both natural and man-made—San Antonio, Dios Padre, Las Humedades, and near Tephé (the only warm-water bath, clean, entry US$0.40) and Tzindejé (this is about 20 mins. from town). The Otomí villages of La Lagunita, La Pechuga and La Bonanza, in a beautiful valley, have no modern conveniences, but the people are charming and friendly.

Actopán (km. 119) has another fine 16th century Augustinian church and convent. From Actopán a 56 km. branch road runs to one of Mexico's great archaeological sites: Tula, capital of the Toltecs (see page 929).

On the way to Tula there is an interesting cooperative village, **Cruz Azul.** Free concerts on Sun. mornings at 1000 in front of main market. At (km. 85) Colonia, a road runs left for 8 km. to

Pachuca, one of the oldest silver-mining centres in Mexico and capital of Hidalgo state. Pop.: 70,000; alt.: 2,445 metres. The Aztecs mined here before the Spaniards came and the hills are honeycombed with old workings and terraced with tailings. Even today the silver output is one of the largest of any mine in the world. A large number of colonial buildings among its narrow, steep and

874 **MEXICO**

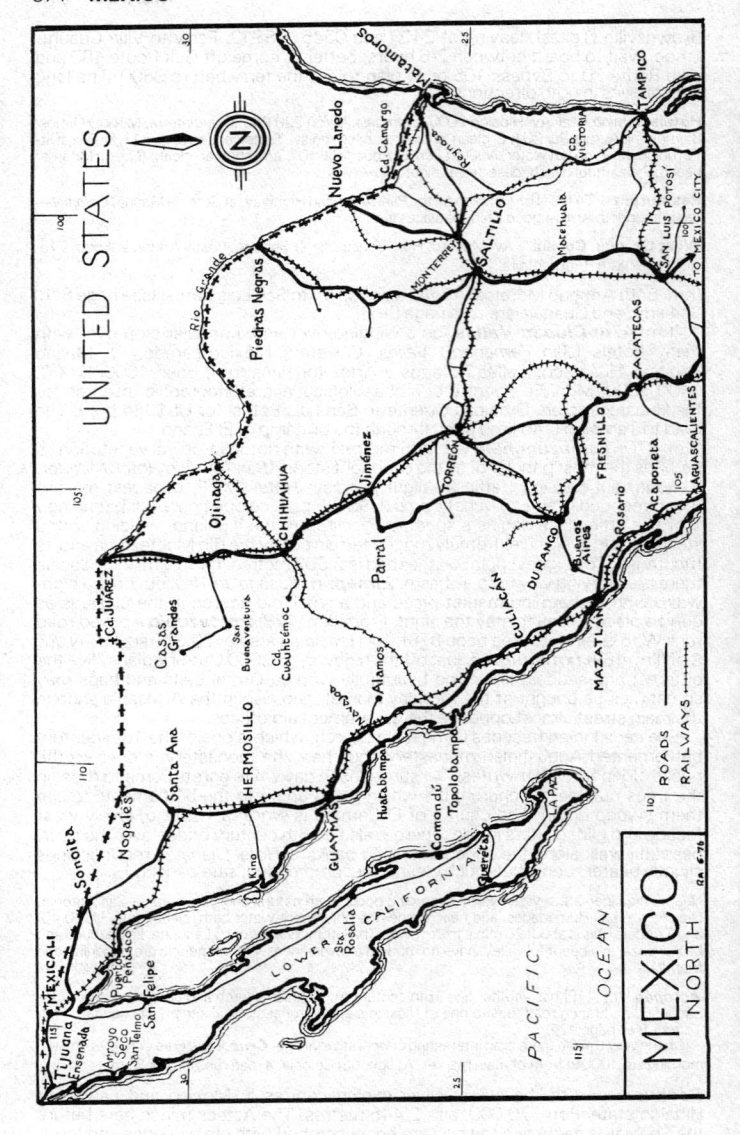

ROUGH SKETCH

crooked streets include the treasury for the royal tribute, La Caja, in Calle Cajas (1670), now used as offices; Las Casas Coloradas (1785), now the Escuela Vicente Guerrero; and a former Franciscan convent (1596) on Plaza Bartolomé de Medina, 5 blocks S of the Zócalo at Arista y Hidalgo, now a Regional History Museum displaying chronological exhibits of the state's history. It is known as the Centro Cultural Hidalgo (open Tues.-Sun., 1000-1400, 1600-1900—may close early on Sun. p.m.). An outstanding photographic museum is in the large cloister on the far side of the convent. In the complex there are a souvenir shop with reproductions of ceramic and metal anthropological items and recordings of indigenous music. Casa de las Artesanías for Hidalgo state is at the junction of Avenidas Revolución y Juárez. The modern buildings include a notable theatre, the Palacio de Gobierno (which has a mural depicting ex-President Echeverría's dream of becoming Secretary-General of the UN), and the Banco de Hidalgo. An electric railway and a road run 10 km. to the large mining camp of Real del Monte, picturesque and with steep streets. Collective taxis also run frequently from beside La Caja in Pachuca (US$0.40 p.p.). The mine turns out 10% of Mexico's silver production.

Hotels *De los Baños*, E, good but unreliable water supply; *Grenfell*; *América*, F, one block from Zócalo, quiet; *Colonial*, Guerrero 505, central, E; *Juárez*, Barreda 107, F, with bath, some rooms without windows. just before Real del Monte, in superb wooded surroundings. Modern Youth Hostel at the turn off to El Chico.

Restaurant *Casino Español*, Matamoros 207, 2nd floor, old-time favourite.

British Vice-Consul, Av. de la Revolución 1209. Tel.: (91-771) 2-27-77.

Cornish miners settled at Real del Monte in the 19th century; their descendants can be recognized among the people. The Panteón Inglés (English cemetery) is on a wooded hill opposite the town.

N of Pachuca via Atotonilco el Grande, where there are a chapel and convent half-way down a beautiful canyon, is the impressive Barranca de Metztitlán which has a wealth of different varieties of cacti, including the "hairy old man" cactus, and a huge 17th century monastery. Farther N (difficult road) is Molango, where there is a restored convent. 34 km. NE of Pachuca is **San Miguel Regla**, a mid-18th century *hacienda* built by the Conde de Regla, and now run as a resort, fine atmosphere, excellent service. A road continues to Tulancingo, on the Pachuca-Poza Rica road, Route 130. 17 km. from Pachuca, and a further 4 km. off Route 130 to the right is Epazoyucan, a village with an interesting convent. After Tulancingo, Route 119 branches off to the right to **Zacatlán**, famous for its apple orchards and now also producing plums, pears and cider. Its alpine surroundings include an impressive national park, Valle de las Piedras Encimadas (stacked rocks), camping possible. Nearby is *Posada Campestre al Final de la Senda*, a ranch with weekend accommodation, horse riding, walks, E, p.p. full board, Tel.: Puebla 413 821 for reservations. Some 16 km. S. of Zacatlán is Chignahuapan (about 1½ hrs. from Puebla), a leading producer of *sarapes*, surrounded by several curative spas.

30 km. from Tulancingo on Route 130 is *La Cabaña* restaurant, of log-cabin construction, cheap; thereafter, the road descends with many bends and slow lorries, and in winter there may be fog. At Huauchinango, an annual flower fair is held in March; 22 km. from here is Xicotepec de Juárez (*Mi Ranchito*, one of the nicest small hotels in Mexico; *Italia*, near main square, F). Along the route are the villages of Pahuatlan and San Pablito, where sequined headbands are made, and paintings are done on flattened *amate* bark. The entire route from desert to jungle is 190 km., taking 5 hours.

Poza Rica is an oil boom town, with unpaved dusty roads, an old cramped wooden market and great temperament.

Hotels *Fénix*, basic, F, opposite ADO bus station; *San Román*, 8 Norte 5, F; *Aurora*, Bolívar 4, basic but quiet and fairly clean, F; *Nuevo León*, opp. market, E, rooms quite spacious, fairly clean and quiet, recommended. *Poza Rica*, 2 Norte, E, fairly comfortable. *Juárez*, Cortines y Bermúdez, E, average.

Bus All buses leave from the few streets between the Zócalo and the market (including about 100 a day to Mexico City, 5 hrs., US$5). To Veracruz, 4 hrs., US$6.25. To Pachuca, Estrella Blanca, 4½ hrs., US$2, change in Tulancingo. To Tecolutla (see below), US$1, 1¼ hrs.

From Poza Rica you can visit the Castillo de Teayo, a pyramid with the original sanctuary and interesting carvings on top, buses every ½ hr., change halfway. Some 45 km. N is Tuxpan, tropical and humid, 12 km. from the sea on the River Tuxpan. Essentially a fishing town (shrimps a speciality). Interesting covered market, but beware of the bitter, over-ripe avocados; fruit sold on the quay. Beach about 2 km. E of town, reached by taxi or bus (marked "Playa"), at least 10 km. long. White

876 MEXICO

sands; hire deckchairs under banana-leaf shelters for the day (US$2). Bus to Mexico City (Terminal del Norte), US$6, 6½ hrs. via Poza Rica.

Some 20 km. SE of Poza Rica is **Papantla** (which is easily reached from Veracruz, 4 hrs., by ADO bus, US$4.80, good road, Jalapa, by ADO bus, US$2.60, 6 hrs., and Mexico City). Men and women come to market in the local costume and there are *voladores* at 2000 at weekends in the churchyard. Mariachi bands play in the *cervecerías* near Zócalo on Sundays. Papantla is also the centre of the vanilla-producing zone, and small figures and animals made in vanilla are for sale, as well as the essence.

Hotels Pulido, Enríquez 215, modern, recommended, clean, F, with bath, parking; Papantla, on Zócalo, F, very clean, hot showers, friendly; Trujillo, Calle 5 de Mayo 401, F, rooms with basin, but other facilities dirty, friendly; Totonacapán, 20 de Noviembre and Olivo, D, bar, restaurant, TV, best in town; Tajín, Calle Dr. Núñez 104, restaurant and bar, F, reasonable. (It is better to stay in Papantla than in Poza Rica if you wish to go to El Tajín.)

Restaurant Las Brisas del Golfo, Calle Dr. Núñez, reasonable and very good.

Tourist Office at Papantla is in municipal offices in the Zócalo; it is rarely open, mostly mornings.

About 12 km. away, in the forest, is **El Tajín**, the ruined capital of the Totonac culture (6th to 10th century AD) entry, US$0.30, ½ price on Sun. Guidebook US$1.25, available in Museum of Anthropology, Mexico City. At the centre of this vast complex is the Pyramid of El Tajín, whose 365 squared openings make it look like a vast beehive. On Corpus Christi, Totonac rain dancers erect a 30-metre mast with a rotating structure at the top. Four *voladores* (flyers) and a musician climb to the surmounting platform. There the musician dances to his own pipe and drum music, whilst the roped *voladores* throw themselves into space to make a dizzy spiral descent, sometimes head up, sometimes head down, to the ground. This colourful ceremony of the *voladores* also takes place every Sun., between 1100 and 1400, free, but contributions asked by performers. There are buses from both Poza Rica marked Martínez or San Andrés, US$0.50, frequent departures near market and Papantla; to reach Tajín from Papantla take a local bus to the crossroads of El Chote (½ hr.) then another local bus to the ruins (10 mins.); otherwise take a taxi. The tourist office near the Zócalo will show you bus schedules.

E of Papantla and on the coast, on the road to Nautla which divides to Jalapa or Veracruz, is **Tecolutla**, a small resort on the river of that name. Hotels Playa, F, good, Tecolutla, F, best, and Marsol (run down) are on the beach. Posada Guadalupe and Casa de Huéspedes Malena (F, basic but clean) are on Avenida Carlos Prieto, near the river landing stage. Newer hotels, D-E, on road to Nautla. Restuarant Paquita, next to Hotel Playa, recommended.

A 4-lane highway now runs from Pachuca to Mexico City via (km. 27) Venta de Carpio, from which a road runs E to Acolman, 12 km., and Teotihuacán, another 10 km. Neither of these places should be missed (see page 928); buses are available from Pachuca; get them at the tollbooth on the highway to Mexico City.

At Santa Clara, 13 km. short of the Capital, the road forks. The right-hand fork (easy driving) goes direct to the City; the left fork goes through Villa Madero, where you can see the shrine of Guadalupe.

Eagle Pass—Piedras Negras to Mexico City

This route, 1,328 km. (825 miles), is 102 km. longer than the Laredo route, but is very wide, very fast and much easier to drive. It is by now the most popular route, but is far from being the most interesting. Take in enough gasoline at Monclova to cover the 205 km. to Saltillo.

Piedras Negras, pop. 27,578, altitude 220 metres, is across the Río Bravo from Eagle Pass, Texas. (Artesanía shop—Centro Artesanal Piedras Negras, Edificio la Estrella, Puerta México, Tel.: 2-10-87.) Beyond (137 km.) Hermanas the highway begins to climb gradually up to the plateau country.

Monclova (243 km.) has one of the largest steel mills in Mexico. The first big city is **Saltillo** (448 km.; alt.: 1,600 metres; population: 238,000), capital of Coahuila state, a cool, dry popular resort noted for the excellence of its *sarapes*. Its 18th century cathedral is the best in northern Mexico and it has a grand market. Indian dances during May 30 and August 30; picturesque ceremonies and bullfights during October *fiestas*. *Pastorelas*, the story of the Nativity, are performed in the neighbourhood in Christmas week. Good golf, tennis, swimming. College students from the US attend the popular Summer School at the Universidad

MEXICO 877

Interamericana. Good views from El Cerro del Pueblo overlooking city. An 87-km. road runs E to Monterrey. You turn right for Mexico City.

Saltillo Hotels Several hotels a short distance from the plaza at the intersection of Allende and Aldama, the main streets, e.g. *San Jorge*, Manuel Acuña 240, D; *Ramos Arizpe Sainz*, Victoria 418, E; *Poza Rica*, F, Allende 436, basic, with shower, a little dark but adequate, quiet. *De Avila*, on main plaza, F, basic, cold water, safe motorcycle parking. Cheaper are *Hidalgo* and *Baños* on Padre Flor, F, without bath, not worth paying for bath in room, cold water only. *Saade*, Aldama 397, E; *Premier*, Allende 556, run down, E, outside centre; *Urdinola*, Victoria 211, reasonable, E. Several good motels in this area, e.g. *Huizache*, D; *La Fuente*, C, Blvd. Fundadores; *Camino Real*, Carretera 57, Km. 865, B.

Restaurants *Victoria*, next to *Hotel Baños*, has reasonable *comida*; *Dik-Dik*, Aldama 548. Drinks and night-time view can be had at the *Rodeway Inn* on the N side of town; *Kentucky Fried Chicken*, Victoria Pte. 358.

Tourist Office Near crossroads of Allende and Blvd. Francisco Coss. Map with all useful addresses, incl. hotels.

Bus to Monterrey and Nuevo Laredo with Transportes del Norte.

(581 km.) San Roberto junction, where a 96-km. road runs E over the Sierra Madre to Linares, on the Gulf Route (see page 872).

At about 720 km. we reach **Matehuala** (*Motel Las Palmas*, on the N edge of town, clean, reasonably priced, English spoken and paperbacks sold, bowling alley and miniature golf, tours to Real de Catorce (see below) arranged; *Hotel Matehuala*, F, rooms shocking pink, full of furniture, adequate), an important road junction; *Motel Palapa*, on highway, C, excellent dining room (*fiesta*, January 6-20).

Chris and Miyuki Kerfoot write: From Saltillo to Matehuala by 2nd class bus, Estrella Blanca, 1½ hrs., US$2 to San Roberto, which is no more than a road junction with a Pemex petrol station, hitch to the junction of Highways 58 and 68 and catch a bus (Transportes Tamaulipas) to Matehuala (US$3, 4 hrs.). From these junctions near Caleana to La Soledad the scenery is worthwhile, as the road winds its way up and down through wooded valleys. The final section to Matehuala is pretty dull as it passes through undulating scrub country.

Bus To San Luis Potosí, with Estrella Blanca, 2½ hrs., US$3.50. Flecha Amarilla, the main bus company in the regions bounded by San Luis Potosí, Mexico City, Guadalajara and Pachuca, should be avoided if alternative is possible; its nickname is "mejor muerto que tarde" - better dead than late.

56 km. W of Matehuala is one of Mexico's most interesting "ghost towns", **Real de Catorce,** founded in 1772.

Tim Connell writes: Four minibuses a day go there from the agency by the *Hotel Matehuala* (US$3 return, journey 1½ hrs., with 2 hrs. to wander around). A taxi can be hired nearby for US$12.50—economic for 4 people. Tours can be arranged with Turismos del Altiplano, Bustamante 128, Tel.: 3-40. (Real de Catorce is also easily reached from Saltillo or San Luis Potosí by train. Jeeps collect passengers from the station (US$8-10 per jeep) and follow a more spectacular route than the minibuses.)

Route: turn left along the Zacatecas road (not signposted) through Cedral. After 27 km. turn left off the paved road, on to a gravel one—which is actually due to be properly paved. The road passes through Potrero, a big centre for nopal cactus. Some people live in the old mine workings and old buildings. Huichol Indians are seen here occasionally. A silver mine is still being worked at Santana.

Real de Catorce is approached through Ogarrio, an old mine gallery widened (only just) to allow trucks through. It is 2½ km. long, and very eerie, with the odd tunnel leading off into the gloom on either side. There is an overtaking bay half way through. A small chapel to the Virgen de los Dolores is by the entrance. The tunnel opens out abruptly into the old city, once a major mining centre with its own mint and nearly 40,000 inhabitants. About 700 people still live here, mainly round the Zócalo, looking for silver. The cockpit and the 16 chapels are worth seeing; the Church of San Francisco is believed to be miraculous. There is a pilgrimage here, on foot from Matehuala, overnight on October 4. The floor of the church is made of wooden panels, which can be lifted up to see the catacombs below. In a room to one side of the main altar are *retablos*, touchingly simple paintings on tin, as votive offerings to the Saint for his intercession. This remarkable city, clustering around the sides of a valley, is so quiet that you can hear the river in the canyon, 1,000 metres below. Next to the church is a small museum (entry US$0.10) showing mining equipment, etc., worth a visit. (Hotels in Real de Catorce: one in the main street, very comfortable with restaurant and bar, expensive, another, *Hotel Real*, in a side street, clean, E.)

878   MEXICO

Huizache (785 km.) is the junction with the Guadalajara-Antiguo Morelos-Tampico highway. At 901 km. we come to San Luis Potosí.

San Luis Potosí, 423 km. from Mexico City, capital of its state, is the centre of a rich mining and agricultural area, which has expanded industrially in recent years. Alt.: 1,880 metres; pop.: 380,000. Glazed, many-coloured tiles are a feature of the city: one of its shopping streets, the main plaza, and the domes of many of its churches are covered with them. It became an important centre after the discovery of the famous San Pedro silver mine in the 16th century, and a city in 1658. The Cathedral is on Plaza Hidalgo. See the churches of San Francisco, with its white and blue tiled dome and suspended glass boat in the transept; Carmen, in Plaza Morelos, with a grand tiled dome, an intricate façade, and a fine pulpit and altar inside (the Teatro de la Paz is next door); the Capilla de Aránzazu, behind San Francisco inside the regional museum; the Capilla de Loreto with a baroque façade; and San Agustín, with its ornate baroque tower. The Palacio de Gobierno, begun 1770, contains oil-paintings of past governors. The Casa de la Cultura, Av. Carranza 1815, to the W of the centre, houses a good collection of colonial paintings. Other points of interest are the pedestrian precinct in Calle Hidalgo and the Caja del Agua fountain (1835) in Av. Juárez. The modern railway station has frescoes by Fernando Leal. The Teatro Alarcón is by Tresguerras (see under Celaya, page 888). Locally made *rebozos* (the best are from Santa María del Río) are for sale in the two markets. The University was founded in 1804. A scenic road leads to Aguascalientes airport.

Hotels   Many between the railway station and the cathedral. *Panorama*, Av. Venustiano Carranza 315, E; *Gran*, Bravo 235, F; *Posada de la Reina, Gante, Roma, Royal, Príncipe*, all F, not recommended; *Progreso*, Aldama 415, F; *Posada España*, Calle Aldama, F. *Jardín*, Los Bravos 530, F, good; *María Cristina*, F, with swimming pool on roof (Juan Sarabia 110, Altos); *Tampico*, nr. railway station, F, not too clean. CREA Youth Hostel on the SW side of the Glorieta Juárez, 5 min. walk from central bus station. F. **Motels** all along Highway 57: *Hostal del Quijote*, B, five-star, convention facilities, 6 km. S on the San Luis Potosí-Mexico City highway, one of the best in Mexico; *Santa Fe*, C; *Cactus*, C; all with pools.

Restaurants *Panorama*, roof-garden restaurant, Plaza de la Universidad, good; *Tokio*, Los Bravos 510, excellent *comida*. *La Lonja*, Aldama 300, and *La Virreina*, Carranza 830, both popular eating places; *Café Versalles*, Madero 145, excellent coffee and yoghurt; *El Girasol*, Guerrero 345, vegetarian; good cafeteria at bus station.

Museum   Museo Regional de Arte Popular, open 1000-1300, 1600-1800; Sats. 1000-1300. La Casa de la Cultura on Av. Carranza, halfway between the centre and university, is a converted mansion with frequent art displays and musical recitals.

Tourist Office   Jardín Hidalgo 20.

Shopping   Local sweets and craftwork at Plaza del Carmen 325, Los Bravos 546 and Escobedo 1030. The famous local painter, Vicente Guerrero, lives in a modest neighbourhood at Plata 407, Colonia Morales (Tel.: 3-80-57) where he also has his studio.

Buses   Station on outskirts of town 1½ km. from centre. Bus to centre US$0.10. Flecha Amarilla to Querétaro, US$3.50, 2 hrs. (50-odd km. of 4-lane highway have been built N of Querétaro, about half the way, and 40 km. have also been completed to the S of San Luis Potosí; to Nuevo Laredo, US$20. To Mexico City, US$6.10, 6 hrs.

Train to Querétaro, US$1.75 2nd class, leave at 1015; to Mexico City, 10-11 hrs.; to San Miguel de Allende, 3-4 hrs.

Excursions   Hot springs at Ojocaliente, Balneario de Lourdes and Gogorrón. Balneario de Lourdes (hotel, clean, nice atmosphere, small pool, D) is S of San Luis Potosí. Gogorrón is clean and relaxing, with pools, hot tubs, picnic grounds and campsites. There is a restaurant. A day trip or overnight camp-out is recommended in the lightly wooded hills and meadows near the microwave station (at 2,600 metres) 40 km. E of San Luis Potosí: go 35 km. along the Tampico highway and continue up 5 km. of cobblestone road to the station. Good views and flora.

(1,021 km.) **San Luis de la Paz,** the junction with Highway 110 leading west to three of the most attractive towns in Mexico: Dolores Hidalgo, Guanajuato, and San Miguel de Allende. (See pages 886-889.) No one who yields to the temptation of this detour can hope to get back to the main route for three or four days.

(1,105 km.) **Querétaro,** pop.: 140,000; alt.: 1,865 metres (can be quite cold at night); now an important industrial centre and capital of Querétaro state, an antique and beautiful city, dotted with attractive squares. (No buses in the centre.) Hidalgo's rising in 1810 was plotted here, and it was also here that Emperor Maximilian surrendered after defeat and was shot, on June 19, 1867, on the Cerro de las Campanas (the Hill of Bells), outside the city.

La Corregidora (Doña Josefa Ortiz de Domínguez, wife of the Corregidor, or Mayor), a member of the group of plotters for independence masquerading as a society for the study of the fine arts, was able, in 1810, to get word to Father Hidalgo that their plans for revolt had been discovered. Hidalgo immediately gave the cry (*grito*) for independence. Today, the Corregidor gives the Grito from the balcony of the Palacio Municipal (on Plaza Independencia) every September 15 at 1100 (it is echoed on every civic balcony thoughout Mexico on this date). La Corregidora's home may be visited.

Buildings to see: the Santa Rosa de Viterbo church and monastery, remodelled by Francisco Tresguerras; his reconstruction of Santa Clara, one of the loveliest churches in Mexico, and that is saying much; the church and monastery of Santa Cruz, which served as the HQ of Maximilian and his forces (view from the bell tower); the church of San Felipe, now being restored for use as the Cathedral; the damaged but still splendid Federal Palace, once a monastery; the important Museum of Pío Mariano, on Plaza Obregón (not all its galleries are always open); the Museum in Convento de San Francisco on the Zócalo, which contains much material on the revolution of 1810 and the 1864-67 period; the aqueduct, built in 1726. Several *andadores* (pedestrian walkways) have been developed, greatly adding to the amenities of the city; prices are high here. The *andadores* replace particular roads in the centre—e.g. Av. 16 de Septiembre becomes Andador de la Corregidora in the centre, and then reverts to its original name. There are local opals, amethysts and topazes for sale; remarkable mineral specimens are shaped into spheres, eggs, mushrooms, and then polished until they shine like jewels (US$10-30, cheaper than San Juan del Río, but more expensive than Taxco). Recommended is Lapidaría Querétaro, Pasteur Norte 72 (Hermanos Ramírez), for fine opals. City tour plus execution site and Juárez monument, excellent value, from museum daily at 1100, US$4.45. There is a *feria agrícola* from 2nd week of December until Christmas; bull fights and cock fights. On New Year's Eve there is a special market and special performances are given in the main street. Try local Hidalgo Pinot Noir wine.

Hotels *Impala*, E, poor; *Mirabel*, D, Constituyentes 2, good value, garage, restaurant; *Corregidora*, Corregidora 138, F, reasonable but noisy; *Del Marqués*, Juárez Norte 104, F, clean, basic; *Plaza*, airy, modernised, quite comfortable, E; *El Cid*, F, more of a motel, clean, good value, close to bus station (left out of bus station and first left); *Hidalgo*, near Zócalo, F, quite helpful; *San Agustín*, off Zócalo, F, clean, quiet, recommended; *Posada del Carmen*, F; *Avenida*, Invierno 21, G CREA Youth Hostel, adjoining Convento de la Cruz, F, running water a.m. only. **Motels** *Holiday Inn*, near highway junction, C; *La Mansión*, C, 6½ km. S of town, excellent dining facilities, gorgeous grounds; 5 km. on opp. side of highway 3 km. is *Mansión Galindo*, B, exquisite former *hacienda*, vast; *Flamingo*, on Constituyentes Poniente 138, E, comfortable; *Azteca*, km. 57, E; *Jurica*, edge of town, B, former *hacienda*, with gardens, squash, golf-course; opulent.

Restaurants *Fonda del Camino*, on Highway 57; *Fonda del Refugio*, Jardín Corregidora; *Pizza La Rondine*, Jardín Corregidora; *Flor de Querétaro*, on Plaza de Armas, Juárez Norte 5; *Salón del Valle*, Corregidora 91; *El Mirador*, roadhouse on highway 57, overlooking city, popular.

Tourist Office Casa de Acala, on Plaza Independencia.

Post Office (Palacio Federal) on Allende, nr. San Agustín church.

Bus Mexico City (Terminal del Norte) frequently 2nd class with Estrella Blanca or Flecha Amarilla, US$2.90, 3 hrs.; to San Miguel de Allende, 1 hr., hourly with Flecha Amarilla, US$1. To Guadalajara, US$4.45. To San Juan del Río, US$0.70, ½ hr. with Flecha Amarilla. To Tula US$2.30. To Guanajuato, US$1.60, 3½ hrs. (Flecha Amarilla); to Pachuca, US$2.20, 4½ hrs. (Estrella Blanca, poor buses).

Rail To Guadalajara US$3 1st class, US$1.80 2nd.

There is now a 215 km. 4-lane motorway (US$1.20 a car) from Querétaro to Mexico City. Along it (Km. 1,152) is **San Juan del Río** (several picturesque hotels, E), near where the best fighting bulls are raised; the town is a centre for

880 MEXICO

handicrafts, and also for polishing gemstones—opals and amethysts. There is one friendly and reasonable shop: La Guadalupana, 16 de Septiembre 5; others are expensive and less friendly. A branch road runs NE from San Juan to the picturesque town of **Tequesquiapán,** with thermal baths, fine climate, good and cheap hotels (*Los Virreyes*; *El Reloj*, etc.), and between San Juan del Río and Tequesquiapán, a small track leads off the main road 4 km. to the village of La Trinidad, near which lie some of the opal mines which are still in operation. Then at 1,167 km., Palmillas, 153 km. to Mexico City.

Bus San Juan del Río-Tequesquiapán US$0.30, 20 mins.

The Querétaro-Mexico City motorway passes close to Tula and Tepozotlán (see page 928). There are various country clubs along the road: *San Gil Ciudad Turística* 7 km. along the road to Amealco; *El Ocotal*; *Bosques del Lago*.

Ciudad Juárez to Mexico City: the Central Highway Route

Ciudad Juárez, opposite El Paso, Texas, to Mexico City: 1,866 km. Buses connect Ciudad Juárez with El Paso hourly from the Greyhound terminal. Ciudad Juárez is at an altitude of 1,150 metres; population, 436,000; Airport.

Hotels *Calinda Quality Inn*, B, Calz. Hermanos Escobar 3515, downtown; *El Presidente*, Centro Comercial Pronas, C; same price *Camino Real*, *Rodeway Inn*, Lincoln y Coyoacán, C, *La Quinta Colonial* Av. de las Américas, 1355, C. *Central*, Corona 151, E.

Restaurants *Denny's*, Lincoln 1345, modern; many reasonable Chinese places.

Rail Train from Ciudad Juárez to Mexico City (1,970 km.), 36 hrs, US$20.80 1st class. Reverse journey leaves at 1950 from Mexico City. The route is through Chihuahua, Torreón, Zacatecas, Aguascalientes, León, Silao (for Guanajuato), Celaya and Querétaro. There are daily pullman trains.

Road Pemex Travel Club, Chamber of Commerce Building, El Paso. A.A.A. office: 916 Mesa Avenue, El Paso. By bus the trip to Mexico City takes about 26 hrs., US$30. To Chihuahua, 5 hrs., about US$7.45.

Juárez, like Tijuana on the California border, attracts a nightly horde of tourists to be fascinated by a swarm of bead and spinach-jade peddlers, strip joints, doll shops blazing in magenta and green, dubious book stores, and "native dance" halls, mitigated by nightly bouts of that swift and beautiful ball game, *jai-alai*. It has a famous race course, too. There are pleasant markets. A monument in the form of a giant head of Father Hidalgo, who sparked off the 1810 revolution, surmounts a hill. See the cheerful Museum which acts as a Mexican "shop window" - well worth it for the uninitiated tourist.

The road is wide, mostly flat, easy to drive, and not as interesting as the Gulf and Pacific routes. From Ciudad Juárez, for some 50 km. along the Río Bravo, there is an oasis which grows cotton of an exceptionally high grade.
The first 160 km. of the road to Mexico City are through desert sand; towns en route are Salamayuca (restaurant), at 58 km.; Villa Ahumada (131 km.). *Dunas Motel*, E, scruffy. At 180 km. is Moctezuma (restaurant). The road leads into grazing lands and the valley of Chihuahua. This is the country of the long-haired, fleet-footed Tarahumara Indians, able, it is said, to outstrip a galloping horse and to run down birds.

About 225 km. S of Juárez, near the village of El Sueco (restaurant), is the turnoff to the **Casas Grandes** ruins. Follow paved State Highway 10 for about 105 km. W, then turn NW for about 55. The place is spectacular: pyramids, a large ball court, an irrigation system and a great number of large adobe-brick houses. The ruins are signposted from the plaza in Casas Grandes, about 1 km. No accommodation in the Casas Grandes village, but in the nearby Nueva Casas Grandes, *Motel Casa Grande* has air-conditioning, good dining room, fair accommodation; *Hotel California*, F; cheap hotels between the two bus stations.

Bus There are frequent buses from Nueva Casas Grandes to Casas Grandes village, leaving from near the railway station. Two bus companies go from Casas Grandes to Chihuahua, passing through pleasant landscapes.

(Km. 1,638) **Chihuahua,** capital of Chihuahua state; alt.: 1,420 metres; pop.: 375,000; centre of a mining and cattle area. Worth looking at are the Cathedral on Plaza Constitución, begun 1717, finished 1789; the old tower of the Capilla

MEXICO 881

Real (in the modern Federal Palace on Calle Libertad) in which Hidalgo awaited his execution; the Museo Regional, Bolívar 401, with not only exhibits but also extremely fine Art-Nouveau rooms: child's room features Little Red Riding Hood scenes; bathroom, frogs playing among reeds, etc.; and the murals in the Palacio de Gobierno. Good Sunday market. The famous Santa Eulalia mining camp is 16 km. away; 8 km. from town is one of the largest smelting plants in the world. Pancho Villa operated in the country around, and once captured the city by disguising his men as peasants going to market; the Quinta Luz, Calle 10 No. 3014, where Pancho Villa lived, is now a museum. Summer temperatures often reach 40°C. Rain falls from July to September. The local hairless small dog has a constant body temperature of 40°C (104°F)—the world's only authentic "hot dog".

Hotels *El Presidente*, Av. Libertad 9, C; *Exalaris Hyatt*, Independencia y Niños Héroes, B; *San Francisco*, Victoria 504, B, restaurant good for steaks; *Victoria*, Juárez y Colón, courtyard, E; *Balflo*, Niños Héroes 321, modern, E; *San Juan*, Victoria 823, in old colonial house, E, nice atmosphere, reasonable food; *Plaza*, behind cathedral, Calle 4, No. 206, clean, F, recommended; *Maceyra*, Ocampa Antigua 302, F, with shower, simple but clean, despite occasional beetles; *Reforma*, Calle Victoria 809, F, good, friendly, recommended but room cannot be locked from outside; *Cortez*, simple, good, quiet, F, 3 blocks from Plaza Constitución; *El Cobre*, E, Calle 10A y Progreso, with bathroom, beside bus terminal, restaurant, bar and laundry; *Alojamiento Fátima*, Doblada 113, and *Cuauhtémoc*, nearby, F. *Turista*, Juárez 817, E, with bath, very clean. *Roma*, Libertad 1015, very basic, F, to be avoided, The cheaper hotels are in Calle Juárez and its crossstreets, but are not very good. **Motel** *Mirador*, Universidad 1309, C; *Nieves*, Tecnológico y Ahuehuetes, D.

Restaurants Best: *Los Parados de Tomy Vega*, followed by *La Calesa* and *La Olla*, excellent steaks. *Pam-Pam*, in the centre, recommended; *Orsini's Pizzaría*, 2 locations; *Casita de Paja*, Libertad 402, cheap and good; *Mi Café*, Victoria 807, good, friendly; *La Parrilla*, same building, good steaks. Corn (maize) is sold on the streets, excellent with cheese, lime, salt and chile.

Taxis work on a zone system. Agree price before boarding, to avoid unpleasant surprises.

Tourist Office Avenida Universidad 505, very helpful, books rooms. Sr. Molina at Av. Cuauhtémoc 1800, 3rd floor, is very helpful.

Buses Bus station is out beyond the airport (US$1 shuttle from the port). To El Paso, Texas, US$7.95 first class, 5 hrs. Change buses at Ciudad Juárez (get a seat number) at Customs. One meal stop. Zacatecas, US$6.45 1st, US$3.45 2nd class, Omnibus de México, several a day, 12 hrs. 2nd class bus, to Hidalgo del Parral, US$4, 5 hrs. To Mexico City, 1,488 km., US$21, 21 hrs., every 2 hours; Silao, US$13. León US$16, Durango, US$7. Bus to Ciudad Cuauhtémoc, 1½ hrs.; this is where the Mennonite order from Germany established its headquarters in 1920.

Airport 20 km. from centre, airport buses collect passengers from hotels, fare US$1.50. Also minibuses.

Chihuahua may also be reached from the border at *Ojinaga* (*Hotel Parral*, cheap; cheap meals at *Lonchería Avenida*, across from bus station) an easy crossing, used infrequently by foreigners. On the way to Chihuahua from Ojinaga is Ciudad Delicias (*Hotel Delicias*, nr. market, several others of similar quality nearby). If leaving Mexico here, make sure they stamp your papers.

Railway There are two railway stations: the station for Ciudad Juárez and Mexico City is 35 mins. walk along Av. Niños Héroes, left at Av. Colón, which becomes Av. Tecnológico, past the river and right along Av. División Norte. Train to Mexico City, daily at midnight, US$5.95 2nd, US$9.90 1st class reserved, US$7.40 ordinary first, sleeper US$12.20, plus US$12.20 for bed or US$20 for private cabin, 30 hours, no food provided, soft drinks available. Train to Zacatecas about 16 hrs.

The station for the Chihuahua-Pacífico railway is one block behind the prison (nr. Av. 20 de Noviembre and Blvd. Díaz Ordaz—take bus marked C. Rosario, or walk up Av. Independencia, then right along Paseo Bolívar or Av. 20 de Noviembre). Train journey to Los Mochis is very spectacular and exciting: book seats in advance. Sit on left hand side of carriage going to Los Mochis. As the train weaves through the mountains it crosses over 30 bridges and passes through 45 tunnels. It crosses the Sierra of the Tarahumara Indians, who call themselves the Rarámuri ("those who run fast"), and were originally cave-dwellers and nomads. They now work as day-labourers in the logging stations and have settled around the mission churches built by the Spanish in the 17th century. The train stops about 15 mins. at Divisadero Barrancas (*Cabañas Divisadero*, on edge of canyon next to station, good cabins, good food, friendly, bookable at Aldama 407, Chihuahua, Tel.: 12-33-62), the watershed between the Pacific and Atlantic (spectacular views), in the Urique Canyon, comparable to the Grand Canyon in the USA. At Carocahui is *Misión-Urique Canyon*, A. Deep in the canyon are orange, banana and avocado trees, and jungles inhabited by pumas and parrots. High above, turning green in July, are the rocky mountain sides. The most beautiful part of the trip

882 MEXICO

is between Creel (just east of the Barranca) and Los Mochis. Local women sell their handicrafts at bargain prices.

The *vistatrén* leaves daily at 0700, supposedly arriving at Divisadero at 1340 and Los Mochis at 2045, local time; double check all details as they are subject to frequent change. There can however be up to 4 hrs. delay in departure, which means you will reach Divisadero as it is getting dark. Fares are US$10 special first class with English-speaking hostess (but windows do not open for photography). The train has a dining car (about US$2.60 a meal, poor value, better take own supplies) but there is food at 2-3 stations along the way. An ordinary train to Los Mochis leaves at 0830 (1st and 2nd class, US$5.50 and US$4.00), reaching Divisadero at 1900 and Los Mochis at 0400, therefore useless for tourism. There is a time change on arrival. The *autotrén* runs to Creel only (1st class only), on Mon., Wed., Fri., Sat. and Sun., leaving at 0815, arriving at 1325; returning at 1430 to Chihuahua, arriving 1935. The fare is US$2.50. If you break the journey at Creel and decide to take the 1300 train from Creel to Los Mochis, you will probably pass through the canyon in darkness. (For return journey, and for alternative route to Los Mochis, see page 891.)

On the Chihuahua-Los Mochis line is **Creel**, at 2,300 metres (very cold in winter), the centre of the Tarahumara region, an important timber centre and an upcoming tourist resort, colourful and pleasant. Maps of the region (simple) and other good buys (such as excellent photographs of Indians) available at mission, which acts as a quasi-tourist office (none in town, in spite of sign). Several hotels: *Motel Parador La Montaña*, expensive, will exchange foreign currency at reasonable rates (horses can be hired here, US$5 and a tip for guides—2 hrs. are necessary to get anywhere; spectacular countryside); *Nuevo*, E, meals overpriced, but nice and clean; *Casa de Huéspedes Margarita*, López Mateos 11, no sign, between two churches, friendly, good food, recommended, F, organizes tours to waterfalls and thermal springs, horses can be hired; *Korachi*, F, opp. railway, not particularly clean, only 1 blanket; *Creel*, F, basic, but friendly, 3 blankets, no running water (jug and basin), buses leave from outside hotel, filthy toilets; *Santa Fe*, F, only for the desperate; *Ejido*, very basic but nice people, F. Cheap meals at *Café El Manzano* next to railway station; other cheap restaurants nearby. A few km. out of town is *Cabaña de las Barrancas de Urique*, B, with 3 meals, with minibus service to and from station. About 40 mins. drive from station is *Copper Canyon Lodge* (Apdo 3, Creel, Chihuahua, A, full board), which has a minibus to collect travellers, rustic woodstoves and oil-lamps, basic cuisine; set in high grassland near waterfall, considerable distance from Barranca del Cobre; other lodges include *Posada Barrancas Hotel*; but only *Hotel Cabañas Divisadero* is situated on the edge of the canyon. There is a bank in Creel, Serfín, next door to the mission, very friendly, does not change travellers' cheques; hotels cash travellers' cheques at poor rates.

N.B. There is a time change (one hour back) between Creel and Los Mochis.

Buses daily at 0700 and 1300, 5 hrs., US$2.50, from *Hotel Creel* to Chihuahua. **Guachochi**, 156 km. (ask for times at *Korachi Hotel*) twice a week; buses, return on following days. Hotels of questionable quality; try *Hotel Ejidal*, E, clean, friendly, belongs to the Creel-Guachochi bus driver. From Guachochi one can walk 3 hrs. to the impressive Barranca de Sinforosa. Marlen Wolf and Markus Tobler of Switzerland write: "You will reach a point several hundred metres above the Río Verde where you can see an unforgettable extended system of immense canyons, grander than you can see from the Divisadero or on crossing the Barranca del Cobre. You can descend to the river on a path". **San Juanito**, 30 km. NE, a little larger than Creel, dusty, has an annual *fiesta* on June 20-24, one hour away by train; bus from Creel at 0700, returns at 2000, paved roads. The Laguna is a little lake 7 km. S of Creel, but is polluted, hire a truck to get there, horses for hire once there, caves. S of Creel is **Cuzarare** ("Place of the Eagles") 20 km. from Creel with Jesuit church (1767) painted by Indians; *Norogachi* (80 km. away), with Tarahumara school and authentic costumes worn on Sun., typical *fiestas*; El Tejabán (Copper Canyon); **Basihuara** ("Sash") village, surrounded by pink and white rock formations (40 km. from Creel); Puente del Río Urique, spans the Urique canyon, ideal camping climate. **Samachique**, where the *rari-pame* race, consisting of kicking a wooden ball in a foot-race of 241 km. without rest, often takes 2-3 days and nights in September. **Kirare**, 65 km. from Creel and on the road to La Bufa mine, offers sights of Batopilas canyon, of great beauty. At the T junction Creel-Guachochi-Bufa is a small restaurant/hotel, *La Casita*, very primitive and romantic, F. **Batopilas** (on a 150-km. dirt road from Creel after La Bufa) is a village of 600 inhabitants, quiet, palm-fringed, subtropical and delightful, hemmed in by the swirling river and the cactus-studded canyon walls. Horses, pigs, goats and chickens wander freely along the cobblestone streets; the town now has electricity, and private rooms for rent. Try *Restaurant Clarita* (basic accommodation, F) and Sra. Monsé—ask prices first—at plaza (curio shop), rooms with gas lamps, who can give information in English (which she likes to practice on tourists) and can change travellers' cheques at a worse rate than in Creel. One hotel on the main road, 1 block from the plaza, not marked, clean, next to the river, with a garden, F, run by owners of *Motel Parador* in Creel, opp. the church. *Carmen's Youth Hostel*, basic accommodation, good food, friendly. In the village there are only basic supplies in shops, no bread or alcohol. Pleasant unnamed restaurant in the top right-hand corner of the little plaza beyond the main Zócalo, fixed, good menu. (Bring insect repellant against locally-nicknamed "assassin bug" or bloodsucking insect.) There is a 350-year-old, bat-infested church in Satebó, a 7-km. walk from Batopilas along the river, a poor place with 15 houses. The area is inhabited by the Tarahumaras known as Gentiles

MEXICO 883

(women don't look at, or talk to, men). **Chomachi**, famous for its caves, some 10 km. deep, inhabited in the past by Apaches. **Basaseachi**, with highest (over 300 metres) single-jump waterfall in North America. Tours arranged by the more expensive hotels to the places mentioned above require a minimum of 4 people and cost from US$8 p.p. to Cuzarare to US$28 p.p. to places further away such as La Bufa. Buses leave for Batopilas from outside Hotel Creel (a two-storey building in Creel) daily at 0800, (8 hrs.), returning at 0400 from the Plaza to catch, with luck, the Los Mochis and Chihuahua train, US$10 return, best take own food, rough ride. The gruelling 120 km. journey depends on road conditions and passes through or close to Cuzarare, Basihuare, Urique Canyon, Samachique, Kirare, before awesome 14 km. descent into Batopilas Canyon at La Bufa. The road ends 30 km. later at Batopilas. **N.B.** If you leave the train at Creel you may not get a train back next day, but on most days there are 1 or 2 services to Los Mochis and Chihuahua. No heating on Creel train. The train Creel-Chihuahua may take up to 27 hrs. instead of the scheduled 13; be prepared. Watch your luggage and cameras, thefts occur.

Ciudad Camargo (Km. 1,484), a small cattle town in a green valley, quiet save for its eight days of *fiesta* for Santa Rosalía beginning on Sept. 4, when there are cockfights, horse racing and dancing. Black bass fishing at the dam lake, and warm sulphur springs 5 km. away.

Hotel *Santa Rosalía Courts*. **Motel** *Baca*.

From Ciudad Jiménez (km. 1,225; *Motel Florido*, E, hot water) there are two routes to Fresnillo and Zacatecas: the Central Highway through Durango or a more direct route via Torreón (290 km. from Ciudad Jiménez), passing Escalón (restaurant), Ceballos (*Hotel San José*, F, basic), Yermo (restaurants) and Bermejillo (restaurant), on Highway 49.

Torreón, is the principal city of La Laguna cotton and wheat district. Population, 283,000, and shrinking. Here is the Bolsón de Mayrán (altitude 1,137 metres) an oasis of about 28,500 square km. which might be irrigated, but only about 2,000 square km. have been developed and much of that is stricken with drought. On the opposite side of the mostly dry Nazas river are the two towns of Gómez Palacio (61,000 people; *Motel La Cabaña*, E, hot water) and Lerdo (18,000 people).

Hotels *El Presidente*, Paseo de la Rosita y Fuentes, B; *Paraíso del Desierto*, Independencia y Jiménez, C, resort; *Río Nazas*, highrise, very good, D, on Av. Morelos y Treviño; *Palacio Real*, Morelos 1280, E; *Galicia*, Cepeda 273, D; *Laguna*, Carrillo 333, D; *Casa del Viajero*, Av. Morelos 772, cheap.

Restaurant *La República*, Musquiz 360, abundant *comida corrida*, cheap; *Kentucky Fried Chicken*, good, 2 locations.

Buses To Chihuahua, 10 hrs.; to Tepic, US$12; to Ciudad Juárez, US$11. There is also an airport.

From Ciudad Jiménez it is 77 km. to (Km. 1,138) **Hidalgo del Parral,** an old picturesque mining town of 70,000 people with mule waggons in its steep and narrow streets. See the parochial church and one dedicated to the Lightning Virgin (Virgen del Rayo). The Museum of Pancho Villa, which is also the public library, is worth seeing for the many old photos and newspaper clippings related to the 1910 revolution and Villa, who was assassinated in Parral on July 20, 1923 on the orders of Obregón and Calles.

Hotels *Moreira*, Maclovio Herrera 2, E, modern, clean, good value, large restaurant meals for US$2.50, recommended. Near the Estrella Blanca terminal are 3 F-range hotels; *Internacional*, *Pinos Altos*, basic, and *La Fe*, *Viajero*, near main square, F. *Fuente*, Herrera 79, F, basic but clean. **Motel** *Camino Real*, Pan-American Highway, C. **Restaurant** *Tupinamba*, Jesús García 5, excellent food and service at reasonable prices.

Buses Each company has its own terminal. To Durango, Transportes Chihuahuenses US$5.75, 6 hrs. To Zacatecas, Omnibuses de México, US$8, 9 hrs.

Between Gómez Palacio and Zacatecas are Cuencame (*Motel la Posta*, F, hot water), Río Grande (*Hotel Río*, F); Fresnillo (*Motel La Fortuna*, E, comfortable, hot water, *Hotel Cuauhtémoc*, F, basic).

(Km. 926) **Durango,** capital of Durango state: alt.: 1,924 metres; pop.: 137,000; founded in 1563. It is a pleasant city, with parks, a Cathedral (1695)

884 MEXICO

and a famous iron-water spring. Presa Victoria can be reached by bus from Durango; there is a new dam and one can swim there.

Hotels *Casa Blanca*, 20 de Noviembre 811, E, nice, big old hotel in the centre, unguarded parking lot; *El Presidente*, 20 de Noviembre 257, C; *Posada Durán*, *Metropolitano*, *Campo México Courts*, all on 20 de Noviembre, F (good but restaurant service poor); *Gallo*, 5 de Febrero, F, with bath, good. *Reyes*, 20 de Noviembre 220, clean, E; *Elizabeth*, 1 block W of cathedral, beautiful colonial house, clean, good, F. *Casa de Huéspedes Fénix*, F, nice family environment, Calle Pino Suárez. *Del Valle*, F, to be avoided, noisy, brothel-like. Cheap hotels around the cathedral. CREA Youth Hostel.

Restaurants Only *La Bohemia* recommended so far, reasonable food, good breakfasts.

Durango is on the Coast-to-Coast Highway from Mazatlán to Matamoros. The 320 km. stretch of road from Durango W to Mazatlán is through splendid not-to-be-missed mountain scenery. Durango is some 260 km. SW of Torreón.

Buses Several buses a day cross the Sierra Madre Occidental to Mazatlán (Transportes Chihuahuenses, 1st class, 7 hrs., US$5.40). This is recommended if you cannot do the Los Mochis-Chihuahua journey, sit on left side. Second class buses for camera buffs stop more frequently. Guadalajara, US$6; Chihuahua, US$7. Second class bus to Hidalgo del Parral, 7 hrs., US$5 with Transportes Chihuahuenses. Zacatecas, Omnibus de México, 4½ hrs., US$4.25. Chihuahua 10 hrs., US$7.

Airport 5 km. from centre.

(Km. 636) **Zacatecas,** founded 1548, capital of Zacatecas state; alt.: 2,495 metres; pop. 120,000; picturesque up-and-down mining city built in a ravine, pink stone houses towering above one another and sprinkled over the hills. The largest silver mine in the world, processing 10,000 tonnes of ore a day or 220 tonnes of silver, is at Real de Angeles. Places to see are the Cathedral (1730-52), the Jesuit church of Santo Domingo and the little houses behind it, the Pedro Coronel museum on Plaza Santo Domingo, Plaza Hidalgo and its statues, the Casa Moneda (better known as the Tesorería), the Calderón Theatre, and the Chapel of Los Remedios (1728), on the Cerro de La Bufa (cablecar, US$1.20 return, starts at 1230, crowded Sun.) which dominates the city, through which an old aqueduct runs, the market, and the Museo Francisco Goitia, housed in what was once the Governor's mansion, near the aqueduct and park, with modern paintings by Zacatecans, free admission. La Mina Edén (admission US$0.80) is accessible from the upper end of the Alameda, behind the Seguro Social hospital. Visit also the Chicomostoc ruins 56 km. S by taking the Línea Verde bus to Adjuntas (about 45 mins.), on the Villanueva road. Then walk ½ hr. through beautiful, silent, nopal-cactus scenery to the ruins, which offer an impressive view. Admission US$0.20. Women are advised to keep at a distance from the caretaker! Zacatecas is famous for its *sarapes* and has two delicacies: the local cheese, and *queso de tuna*, a candy made from the fruit of the nopal cactus (do not eat too much, it has laxative properties). Visit the small *tortilla* factories near the station, on the main road.

Zacatecas Fiesta spreads over most of September, a rainy month here. There are bullfights on Sundays.

Hotels *Aristos*, Lomas de Soledad, D; *Calinda*, near bus station, very comfortable, D; the cheap hotels are all within 5 minutes walk of the bus station, towards Av. Hidalgo. *Barranca*, F, opp. bus terminal, pleasant, but not a safe area; *Río Grande*, opp. bus terminal, 150 metres uphill, G, nice and clean, share bath; *Colón* and *Reina Cristina* on Zócalo, E, run down, with bath, clean; *Posada de La Moneda*, nr. Cathedral, Av. Hidalgo 415, nice and clean, E; *Posada del Conde*, Juárez 18, good-looking, D. *Condesa*, opp. *Posada del Conde*, E, OK. *Avenida* and *Baños*, F, with bath, no hot water, at Hidalgo 203. *Casa de Huéspedes*, Av. Hidalgo 304, F, with hot shower, miserable; *Zamora*, off Plazuela del Vivar, F. Cheap: *Río Grande*, F, noisy, musty. **Motels** *Del Bosque*, D, *Fortín de la Peña*, *Parador Zacatecas*, excellent, D, Pan-American Highway.

Restaurants *La Parroquia*, beautiful colonial house, excellent food and wines and inexpensive for its class. *El Jacalito*, Juárez 18, excellent *comida corrida*. *Don Parroquín*, Av. Hidalgo, good pizzas; *El Fortín*, near Cathedral, good, nice coffee shop. *El Carnerito*, Av. Juárez 110, good and cheap. *Café Nevería*, good cappuccino.

Tourist Office behind Cathedral in Palacio del Gobierno, friendly, helpful. Ask here for language classes at the University.

MEXICO 885

Trains To Mexico City at 0500 and at 1600, 1st class US$4.90, 2nd US$3.25 (bus from Mexico City at 1940 daily); to Chihuahua 1030, US$6.45, 1st class, US$3.65, 2nd class to Aguascalientes, 4 hrs. US$1.60 2nd class.

Bus New terminal outside town; buses from Plaza Independencia. To Chihuahua via Torreón, 12 hrs., US$12.50; Jiménez, US$9; San Luis Potosí with Estrella Blanca; Ciudad Juárez 1st class with Omnibus de México at 1930, 11 hrs; to Guadalajara, 6½ hrs., several companies, US$4, but shop around for different journey times. To Mexico City, 8 hrs., US$10.

Beyond Zacatecas lies Guadalupe with an interesting church; about 45 km. further on are a motel and restaurant.

(Km. 508) **Aguascalientes** was founded in 1575 and is capital of its state; alt.: 1,190 metres; pop.: 380,000; its name comes from its many hot mineral springs. An oddity is that the city is built over a network of tunnels dug out by a forgotten people. It has pretty parks, a pleasant climate, delicious fruits, and specializes in drawn linen threadwork, pottery, and leather goods. Places to see are the Government Palace (once the castle of the Marqués de Guadalupe, with colourful murals round inner courtyards), the churches of San Marcos and San Antonio (somewhat odd) and the Municipal Palace.

On items of interest in Aguascalientes, Tim Connell writes:
Museo de la Ciudad, Calle Zaragoza 505, is by Church of San Antonio. The José Guadalupe Posada museum is in a gallery, by the Templo del Cristo Negro, close to a pleasant garden—Díaz de León (known locally as the Jardín del Enciso). A remarkable collection of prints by the lithographer Posada, best known for his *cadaveras*, macabre skeletal figures illustrating and satirizing the Revolution and events leading up to it. Admission free, Tues.-Sun. 1000-1400, 1700-2100. Shut Mon. Cultural events in the courtyard on Sat. and Sun. The Casa de las Artesanías is near main square. The Casa de la Cultura, on Venustiano Carranza and Galeana Norte, is a fine Colonial building. Display of *artesanía* during the *feria*.

Hacienda de San Blas, 34 km. away, contains Museo de la Insurgencia. Murals by Alfredo Zermeño. The area is famous for viticulture—22,000 acres are under vines. The local wine is called after San Marcos, and the *feria* in his honour lasts for 3 weeks, starting in the middle of April (ends May 3), with processions, cockfights (in Mexico's largest *palenque*, seating 4,000), bullfights, agricultural shows etc. The Plaza de Armas is lavishly decorated. The *feria*, covered by national TV networks, is said to be the biggest in Mexico. Accommodation can be very difficult and prices double during the *feria*.

Teatro Morelos next to Cathedral; Tel.: 5-00-97. The University is ½ hr. from the city centre. Its administrative offices are in the ex-Convento de San Diego, by the attractive Jardín del Estudiante, and the Parián, a shopping centre. The market is not far away. There is carp fishing at El Jocoqui and Abelardo Rodríguez. The bull ring is on Avenida López Mateos.

Hotels *Francia*, Plaza Principal, E, airy, colonial style; good restaurant (*El Fausto*) for breakfast and lunch; near bus station, *Posada Reforma*, E; *Praga*, F, with TV, Zaragoza, 214, Tel.: 5-23-57; *Parador San Marcos*, Chávez 701, F; *París*, Plaza Principal 20, E. *Las Américas* and *Continental*, Av. 5, No. 307, nr. Zócalo. At Rep. de Brasil 403, *Casa de Huéspedes*, nr. main square, F. Also near main square, *Señorial*, F, helpful lady speaks English; *Rosales*, F; *Maser*, 3 blocks from Cathedral on Montaro, F, *comedor* for breakfast. CREA Youth Hostel. **Motel** *El Medrano*, Chávez 904, D; *La Cascada*, Chávez 501, D.

Restaurants *Mitla*, Madero 220, cheap and clean, good Mexican menu; *Cascada*, main plaza; *Bugambilia*, Chávez 102, quite plush, reasonable menu, but service can be morose. *Café de los Artesanos*, Calle José María Chávez 122, good atmosphere and coffee, friendly owners welcome foreigners.

Tourist Office In outskirts of town Av. López Mateos Oriente, 1500.

Taxis There is a ticket system for taxis from the Central Camionera, with the city divided into different fare zones. There is no need to pay extra; a phone number for complaints is on the ticket.

Transport Trains: twice a day to Mexico City, due from Ciudad Juárez at 1840 and from Torreón at 0815. Bus: to Guadalajara, 5 hrs. US$3.55 1st, US$3.40 2nd class, but 0900 and 1415 bus take 4 hrs. To Guanajuato from Aguascalientes US$2.60 with Flecha Amarilla. Aguascalientes-Zacatecas: US$1.90. There is an airport. Some 170 km. to the E is San Luis Potosí (see page 878).

Encarnación de Díaz (hotel and restaurant) is halfway to **Lagos de Moreno** (km. 425), a charming old town with fine baroque churches. A road turns off right to Guadalajara, 197 km. away; the same road leads, left, to Antiguo Morelos via San Luis Potosí. Lagos de Moreno has a hotel and restaurant.

After about 1,600 km. of desert or semi-arid country, we now enter, surprisingly, the basin of

886 MEXICO

Guanajuato, known as the Bajío, greener, more fertile, higher (on average over 1,800 metres), and wetter, though the rainfall is still not more than 635 to 740 mm. a year. The Bajío is the granary of central Mexico, growing maize, wheat, and fruit. The agricultural towns we pass through, León, Irapuato, and Celaya, have grown enormously in population and importance.

(Km. 382) **León** (de los Aldamas), in the fertile plain of the Gómez river. The business centre is the Plaza de Constitución. There are a striking municipal palace, a cathedral, many shaded plazas and gardens. León is the main shoe centre of the country, and is noted for its leather work, fine silver-trimmed saddles, and *rebozos*. Alt.: 1,885 metres; pop.: 306,000. Frequent buses to Torreón (10 hrs.).

Hotels *León*; Madero 115, F; *Gema*, L. Mateos 613, F; *Hidalgo*, Av. Miguel Alemán 304, opp. market, F; *Condesa*, D, main square; others near market in F category.

Airport San Carlos, 15 km. from centre. (Km. 430) Silao (24,000 people, hotel). Between León and Silao, left off Highway 45 at Km. 387 (going S) are the famous swimming pools of Comanjilla fed by hot sulphurous springs (rustic, semi-tropical with hotel and restaurant at moderate rates). Eleven km. beyond Silao, at Los Infantes, a short side road through the picturesque Marfil canyon leads to Guanajuato.

Guanajuato, capital of Guanajuato state, has been important for its silver since 1548. Population, 70,000 in 1880, now only 45,000, altitude, 2,010 metres. It stands in a narrow gorge amid wild and striking scenery; the Guanajuato river cutting through it has been covered over and an underground street opened—an unusual and effective attraction. The streets, steep, twisted and narrow, follow the contours of the hills and are sometimes steps cut into the rock: one, the Street of the Kiss (Callejón del Beso), is so narrow that kisses can be—and are—exchanged from opposite balconies. Over the city looms the shoulder of La Bufa mountain. A most interesting building is the massive Alhóndiga de Granadita, built as a granary, turned into a fortress, and now an attractive museum (US$0.35, theoretically closed Mon.). Guanajuato contains a series of fine museums, as well as the most elegant marble-lined public lavatories in Mexico. The best of many colonial churches are San Francisco (1671); La Compañía (Jesuit, 18th century); San Diego (1663) on the Plaza de la Unión; and the exquisite church of La Valenciana, one of the most beautiful in Mexico, 5 km. out of town and built for the workers of the Valenciana silver mine, once the richest in the world (a local "Valenciana" bus goes to it, US$0.07 from centre, 10 minutes ride; 10 mins. walk between church and mine pit-head; don't believe anyone who tells you a taxi is necessary). A gruesome sight shown to visitors is of mummified bodies in the Museo de las Momias, arranged in glass cases along one wall (US$0.10). Buses go there ("Momias", US$0.06, 10 mins., along Av. Juárez), but you can walk. Do not go on expensive "guided" tour to mummies—costs US$13! The Cathedral (Basilica) and the church of San Roque should also be visited. Local pottery can be bought at the Hidalgo market and the street the potters frequent. Good bargaining for *rebozos* in the plaza opposite the *Hotel San Diego*. The University was founded in 1732. The painter Diego Rivera was born in Calle de Pocitos; visit the museum there with permanent collection of his drawings, paintings and Popol Vuh collection. On the E side of the city is the Presa de la Olla, a favourite picnic spot; several parks and monuments in the vicinity, frequent buses (US$0.08). The area is being industrialized.

When Father Hidalgo took the city in 1810, the Alhóndiga was last to surrender, and there was a wanton slaughter of Spanish soldiers and royalist prisoners. When Hidalgo was himself caught and executed, along with three other leaders, at Chihuahua, their heads, in revenge, were fixed at the four corners of the Alhóndiga. There is a fine view from the monument to Pipila, the man who fired the door of the Alhóndiga so that the patriots could take it, which crowns the high hill of Hormiguera. Look for the "Al Pipila" sign. Steep climb. Local buses go from *Hotel Central*, on the hour, to the Pipila.

Hotels Bus station very helpful in finding hotels. Check hotel prices, as cheaper central hotels try to put up prices when foreigners appear, and they also try to insist on a room with two beds, which is more expensive than with a double bed. Hotel rooms can be hard to find after 1400. There are frequent water shortages, so that hotels with no reservoirs of their own have no water on certain days. On Jardín de la Unión are *Posada Santa Fe*, No. 12, E, and *San Diego*, No. 1, D, good bar,

MEXICO 887

dearer but better run; *Real de Minas*, at city entrance, C; *Parador San Javier*, Plaza Aldama 92, C; *La Abadía*, San Matías 50, D. *El Presidente San Gabriel de Barrera*, C, 2 km. out in Marfil suburb, former *hacienda Hostería del Frayle*, Sopeña 3, D; *Reforma*, Av. Juárez 113, E, with bath, clean and quiet; *Castillo de Santa Cecilia*, Dolores road, tourist-bus haven, C; *Parador San Javier*, opp. side of Dolores road, genuine hacienda style, D; *Central*, Juárez 11, by bus station, restaurant, good value but noisy, F; several others on same street: *El Insurgente* (No. 226) E, pleasant and quiet, poor restaurant service; *Posada San Francisco*, Av. Juárez y Gavira, E, on Zócalo, good value, lovely inner patio; *Granadita* (No. 109) clean and friendly, F; *Posada del Comercio* (No. 210) F, filthy avoid; *Posada del Rosario* (No. 31) F; *Posada Dos Ríos*, Alhóndiga 29, F. *Alhóndiga*, Insurgencia 49, good, E; and *Murillo* at No. 9, F; *Dos Ríos*, San Clemente 1, F; *Mesón de la Fragua*, Tepetapa 46, E. *Molino del Rey*, Campañero 15, simple and quaint, F; *Hacienda de Cobos*, Padre Hidalgo 3, D. At Calle Alonso 32 is *Casa Kloster*, F; very friendly, rooms for 4 (although few with private bath), very good value, laundry facilities, recommended, gardens. On the main square between the bus terminal and market is *Posada Juárez*, F, noisy but otherwise all right; near the bus terminal is *Mineral de Rayos*, Alhóndiga 7, F, with bath, small rooms, clean linen, running down; *Posada Hidalgo*, Juárez 220, F, with bath, run down. *Posada Condesa*, Plaza de la Paz, filthy, very cheap, F. Very close to the main street is a street full of *casas de huéspedes*. **Motels** Many on Dolores Hidalgo road exit: *Valenciana*, E; *Villa de Plata*, D; *El Carruaje*, D. *De Los Embajadores*, Paseo Embajadores, Mexican décor, D, restaurant, famous Sun. lunch. Trailer Park just off the road to Valenciana, clean bathrooms and hot showers, US$1.40 for tent and 2 people. 20 mins.' walk from centre.

Restaurants Good coffee and reasonable food at *El Retiro*, Sopeña 12, is in Jardín de la Unión. Student-frequented. *Pizza Piazza*, Plaza San Fernando; *4 Ranas*, Jardín Unión 1, most popular; *Casa Kloster* on Calle Alonso, cheap and good value; *La Bohemia*, Calle Alonso, cheap, good sandwiches; *BBQ chicken* on Av. Juárez about 200 metres up from Mercado Hidalgo; *Las Palomas*, near post office, reasonable *comidas*. *El Granero*, good *comida*, US$1.50, until 1700. *El Figón*, open after 1830 (closed 2-3 days a week), family run, small, on same street as Teatro Principal, heading towards Teatro Cervantes. *La Antorcha*, perched on the hillside with good views of the town, restaurant and disco, quite a way out and not really worth it. *Hamburguesa Feliz*, Sopeña 10, good value.

Entertainment Sketches from classical authors out of doors in lovely old plazas from April to August. Programme at Teatro Juárez (a magnificent French-type Second Empire building, US$0.25 to view), on Friday and Saturday nights. The Teatro Principal is opposite this. A band plays in Jardín de la Unión (next to the theatre) thrice weekly. Arts festival, the Festival Cervantino de Guanajuato (in honour of Cervantes), is an important cultural event in the Spanish-speaking world, encompassing theatre, song and dance. *Viernes de las Flores* is held on the Friday before Good Friday—starting with the Dance of the Flowers on Thurs. night at about 2200 right through the night adjourning at Jardín de la Unión to exchange flowers. Very colourful and crowded.

Tourist Office Excellent, 5 de Mayo y Juárez near bus terminal. They have all hotel rates and give away folders. American Express, Av. Juárez 36.

Bus San Miguel de Allende, 1st class, US$6, 0700 and 1715, 2 hrs; Flecha Amarilla, 2nd class, ½ hourly between 0630 and 2300, 2 hrs. via Dolores Hidalgo (most of them go on to Mexico City), US$2; to Guadalajara 1st class US$5.50, three buses, most around 1500 but via León and Lagos de Moreno with Flecha Amarilla, 2nd class, hourly (0550-2235) US$4 (7 hrs.). Also daily at 1500 with Omnibus de México, US$5. Flecha Amarilla to León (1¼ hrs.), US$1; hourly service to Morelia (6 hrs.) US$ 2.20. To Mexico City, 1st class, Estrella Blanca, 5½ hrs. US$4.80, book well in advance. To San Luis Potosí, US$3. To Querétaro, US$1.60, 3½ hrs. by Flecha Amarilla.

Rail One train a day to Irapuato, at 0820.

Excursion A very good round trip is through Dolores Hidalgo to San Miguel de Allende, taking in Atotonilco (see page 889). See also the three local silver mines of La Raya (you can walk up from town; it is still operating), La Valenciana and La Cata. It is possible to visit the separating plant at La Cata, but visitors are not admitted to mines. At odd side of La Cata mine (local bus near market), a church with a magnificent baroque façade, also the shrine of El Señor de Villa Seca (the patron of adulterers) with *retablos* and crude drawings of miraculous escapes from harm, mostly due to poor shooting by husbands. 30 km. from Guanajuato is Cerro Cubilete, with a statue of Christ the King, local buses take 1½ hrs., spectacular view of the Bajío, US$1, hourly from Guanajuato (also from Silao for US$0.60). Dormitory at the site (US$1.50) food available; last bus up leaves at 1600 from Silao and Guanajuato. Visit the *Rancho de Enmedio* midway between Guanajuato and Dolores Hidalgo. Good dried meat specialities and beautiful scenery. A profusion of wild pears is sold from the roadside by children. Go also to San Gabriel de Barrera with the bus to Marfil, beautiful garden and *hacienda*, 15 patios, quiet. Tours to local sights leave from the main square.

(Km. 315) **Irapuato,** 176,000 people (*Hotel Real de Minas*, overpriced, with equally overpriced restaurant, on Portal Carrillo Puerto, quiet rooms on church side; *Restaurant El Gaucho*, Díaz Ordaz y Lago), noted for delicious strawberries,

888 MEXICO

which should on no account be eaten unwashed. (Km. 265) **Celaya,** population, 59,000; altitude, 1,800 metres; famous for its confectionery, especially a caramel spread called *cajeta*, and its churches, built by Mexico's great baroque architect Tresguerras (1765-1833), a native of the town. His best church is El Carmen (1807), with a fine tower and dome; see also his fine bridge over the Laja river.

From Celaya to Querétaro, where we join the route from Eagle Pass (see page 876), there is a 56-km. limited-access toll motorway (US$0.40 a car), or the old road through Apaseo el Alto. Between Celaya and San Miguel de Allende is Comonfort; from there go 3 km. N to Rancho Arias: on a hilltop to the W are precolumbian pyramids. Cross the river N of the church and climb to ruins via goat-tracks.

San Miguel de Allende, a charming old town at 1,850 metres, on a steep hillside facing the broad sweep of the Laja River and the distant blue of the Guanajuato mountains, is 50 km. N of Querétaro by paved road. Population, 15,000. Its twisting cobbled streets rise in terraces to the mineral spring of El Chorro, from which the blue and yellow tiled cupolas of some 20 churches can be seen. It has been declared a national monument and all changes in the town are strictly controlled. In recent years there has been an influx of Americans, with a consequent rise in prices.

Social life centres around the market and the Jardín, or central plaza, an open-air living room for the whole town. Around it are the colonial city hall, several hotels, and the parish church, adorned by an Indian mastermason in the late 19th century, Zeferino Gutiérrez, who provided the austere Franciscan front with a beautiful façade and a Gothic tower; see also mural in chapel. The church of St. Philip Neri, with its fine baroque façade, is on a hill just S of the town. Notable among the baroque façades and doors rich in churrigueresque details is the Casa del Mayorazgo de Canal, and San Francisco church, designed by Tresguerras. The Convent of La Concepción, built in 1734, is now an art school, the Instituto Allende (which has an English-language library; Spanish courses, US$70 a week, US$230 a month, without accommodation). Handicrafts are the traditional tin, silver, and leather work, *sarape* weaving and hand embroidery. The city was founded as San Miguel in 1542, and Allende added in honour of the independence patriot born there. Local US women's committees run house and garden tours for charity: ask at the hotel. (They start at noon every Sun., and cost US$6.)

Fiestas One every 10 days or so. Main ones are Independence Day (Sept. 15-16); Fiesta of San Miguel (Sept. 28-Oct. 1, with Conchero dancers from many places); Day of the Dead (Nov. 2); the Christmas Posadas, celebrated in the traditional colonial manner (Dec. 16-24); the pre-Lenten carnivals, Easter Week, and Corpus Christi (June).

Hotels Many weekend visitors from Mexico City: book ahead if you can. *Posada La Aldea*, D, beautiful, colonial style, spotless, quiet, swimming pool, gardens, wood fire in lounge, highly recommended. *Posada de San Francisco*, main square, D; *Parador San Miguel Aristos*, at Instituto Allende arts centre, students given priority, D; *Vista Hermosa Taboada*, Allende 11, D, very popular, nice old colonial building with plant-filled patio, some ground floor rooms dark and noisy; *Rancho-Hotel El Atascadero*, Querétaro road entrance, in an old colonial *hacienda*, very satisfactory, D; *Posada de las Monjas*, Canal 37, E, with shower, includes breakfast, clean and attractive, very good value. *Misión de los Angeles*, de luxe, 2 km. out on Celaya road, colonial style, swimming pool, convenient facilities, C. Near Jardín, on Calle Vinaron, *Posada La Fuente* has a few rooms, good food (by arrangement), D. *Posada de Allende*, generally clean, with bath, central F; *Posada Lourdes*, Morelos Norte 340, F, hot shower. *San Sebastián*, nr. market, recommended, F, large rooms with fireplace, clean, courtyard. *Quinta Loreto*, Loreto 13, modern rooms, swimming pool, pleasant garden, E, splendid value, good food (but beware of mosquitoes); *Hidalgo*, Hidalgo 22, F, no hot water, good value, but rooms vary in quality. *La Huerta*, F, nice and quiet at the bottom of a dead-end street 4 blocks from the market. *Posada Carmina*, Cuña de Allende 7, E, colonial building, courtyard for meals, recommended; *Mansión del Bosque*, Aldama 65, B, half-board; *Mesón San Antonio*, E, Mesones 80, renovated mansion, clean, friendly, quiet; *Villa Jacarandá*, Alameda 53, B; *Sierra Nevada*, A, French elegance; *Sautto*, Dr. Macías 59, E, a bargain, rustic, pleasant but little hot water; *Huéspedes Feliz*, small, E, incl. breakfast. **Motels** *Villa del Molino*, Mexico City road entrance D; *Siesta*, road to Guanajuato, with trailer park, D, gardens; KAO campgrounds further out on same road.

Restaurants *Mama Mía*, near Zócalo, jazz evenings, good, overpriced; *Señor Plato*, Jesús 7, pricey, but has amazing 1920s atmosphere piano bar, and colonial-style patio filled with plants and parrots, excellent steaks, free garlic bread. *Guacamaya*, Jesús y Pila Seca, home cooking; *El Circo*, Insurgentes by the library, Italian, singing waiters, fancy; *Icabala*, Calle Aldama, near Cathedral, good; on same street, *Posada Carmen*, OK but more expensive; *Café Colón*, San Francisco 21, smart, clean and inexpensive. *Pepe Pizza*, Hidalgo 15, *strudel* too. *Vegetarian* restaurant at Correo

MEXICO 889

4 1/2 (on right-hand side as you walk away from centre), clean, cheap. Try the *licuados* (fruit-shakes) in the market; ask for a *campechana*!

Bookshop El Colibrí, near Zócalo, French and English books.

Tourist Office on Plaza, helpful with finding hotels, English spoken.

Communications The crack Aguila Azteca through train between Laredo and Mexico City stops here. The El Paso train stops at Celaya and Querétaro. Frequent buses to Guanajuato (2 hrs.) with Flecha Amarilla and Estrella Blanca, via Dolores Hidalgo, US$2. San Miguel-Dolores Hidalgo, US$0.50. Spectacular scenery between Dolores Hidalgo and Guanajuato as the road corkscrews up to a watershed from which you look down to oak-covered hills on the east and tree-covered slopes on the west. Buses to Mexico City every 2 hrs., US$4, 2nd class, crowded but interesting. Buses to Morelia until 2040 daily, 4 hrs., US$3, 2nd class. Morelia-Pátzcuaro, US$0.90, 1 hr. Bus San Miguel-Atotonilco US$0.30, plus short walk.

Excursions A good all-day hike can be made to the Palo Huérfano mountain on the S side of town. Take the road to just before the radio pylon then take the trails to the summit, where there are oaks and pines. Twenty mins. away is the small village of **Atotonilco,** where there is a church built around 1740 whose inside walls and ceiling are covered with frescoes done in black, red and grey earth: unrivalled anywhere for sheer native exuberance. An interesting local wine is made here from oranges. There is a spa, the Balneario Taboada (admission US$1.70), between San Miguel and El Cortijo (about 20 mins. bus ride on the way to Dolores Hidalgo very near Atotonilco), a warm and hot pool, a fine swimming pool and good fishing in a nearby lake—very popular. **Dolores Hidalgo,** the home of Father Hidalgo, is 29 km. on, another most attractive small town; celebrations are held there on September 16. Visit Hidalgo's house, Casa Hidalgo, Morelos 1, entry US$0.30. Traditional Talavera tiles still made there. (*Hotel María Dolores*, between by-pass and centre coming from San Miguel de Allende; *Posada Las Campanas*, Guerrero 15; *Posada locomacán*, on the plaza.)

Nogales—Mexico City: the Pacific Highway

From Nogales-Santa Ana (a feeder entry) to Mexico City via Guadalajara is 2,043 km. (1,492 miles).

Rail Pacific Railway as far as Guadalajara, and on by National Railways of Mexico. Guadalajara, 1,759 km. away, is reached in 29 hrs., at a speed of 60 k.p.h., and Mexico City (after changing) in 40 hrs. (Mexicali-Mexico City costs US$20, 2nd, US$40, 1st class). Conditions vary in both 1st and 2nd class carriages, several unpleasant experiences reported, e.g. lack of air conditioning, dirt, overcrowding, etc. 1st class trains go only to Guadalajara and journey on to Mexico City has to be made in slower 2nd-class train.

Road Journey It takes 18 hrs., driving at an average of 65 k.p.h., to get to Mazatlán, 1,202 km. from Nogales. There is a good road—Highway 2—from Tijuana (entry from San Diego), going through Mexicali (see page 991), Sonoita (*Desert Sun Motel; Motel Sono Inn*, F, American style, others nearby; customs inspection and immigration check), and Caborca to Santa Ana, where it joins the West Coast Highway (Highway 15) route to Mexico City. Between La Rumerosa and Mexicali, the road descends about 1,200 metres in fantastic, panoramic serpentines from the coastal highland to the desert (organ-pipe cacti in abundance). Between Mexicali and Sonoita is **San Luis** (25,000 people), in the "free zone" and serving cotton country: summer bullfights, small night-life district like those of the "open towns of the old west". Coming from Lukeville, Arizona, make sure you take the road to San Luisito and not San Luis; they are both on Route 2, but 320 km. apart in opposite directions. 9 km. S of San Luis is Pozos, which 40 years ago had 60,000 inhabitants, now only 2,500 and ruins of large buildings, churches, no hotels.

For transport from Tijuana, see page 992. Customs stop at Sonoita, then 18 hours on at Guaymas, then Los Mochis. Best to take food and make use of toilet facilities at stops, though they are reported filthy.

Motel *Naranjo* (first class); *El Rey* and others. Economy hotel: *Capra*.

Between San Luis and Sonoita is the Mexican Sahara, 200 km. with only three houses in the whole stretch. There are sand dunes and volcanic hills on the way. The desert has interesting vegetation, peculiar formations and few stopping places, but Caborca has the Motel *Posada San Cristóbal*. Sonoita is a good place for exploring the famous Kino missions, and there are recently discovered and very interesting archaeological ruins. Transportes Norte de Sonora and Tres Estrellas have first class services (the former is slightly better). Water and snacks should be carried, the tank kept full and replenished whenever possible. This feeder road can also be entered at Sonoita on the border S of Organ Pipe National Monument (Arizona). The very good highway from Tijuana to Hermosillo is patrolled by the Free Assistance Service of the Mexican Tourist Department, whose green jeeps patrol most of Mexico's main roads. The drivers speak English, are trained to give first aid and to make minor auto repairs and deal with flat tyres. They carry gasoline and have radio connection. All help is completely free. Gasoline at cost price.

890 MEXICO

In summer, west coast drivers prefer the Central Route from El Paso, Texas, unless they love heat. It is dangerous to drive on retread tyres over the hot desert. Do not drive at night and never park or sleep along the road.

The road down the coast to Acapulco has now been completely paved but does have military searches in the State of Guerrero (for narcotics and arms). The coast road goes on from Acapulco to Puerto Angel and Salina Cruz.

Note The amount of accommodation along the Pacific Highway has increased greatly in recent years. There are many motels along the whole route, so that each town of any importance has one or more. All available accommodation is listed in the American Automobile Association's *Mexico by Motor*.

From Nogales to Guaymas on the Gulf, the road runs along the western slopes of the Sierra Madre, whose summits rise to 3,000 metres. From Guaymas on to Mazatlán it threads along the lowland, with the Sierra Madre Occidental's bold and commanding escarpment to the E. Like the W coasts of all continents between latitudes 20° and 30°, the whole area is desert, but fruitful wherever irrigated by water flowing from the mountains. Summers are very hot, sometimes rainy, but winters are mild and very dry. Within the Sierra Madre nomadic people hunt the many wild animals; along the coasts available water determines the spots of concentrated settlement and of agriculture. Mexico gets most of its wheat from the southern part of Sonora state, and the irrigated valley bottoms (around Hermosillo) are also used for maize, cotton and beans. Farther S, in frost-free Sinaloa and Nayarit, sugar, rice, winter vegetables, tomatoes, and tobacco are grown. The three coastal states we pass through make up 21% of Mexico's area, but include only 6% of its population.

(Km. 2,403) **Nogales,** half in Mexico, half in Arizona, lies astride a mountain pass at 1,180 metres. It is a mining centre, with walnut groves and cattle ranches. It has the usual border night life. Through Nogales and Mexicali the winter vegetable crops of southern Sonora and Sinaloa are exported. Population, 38,000.

Festival Cinco de Mayo festival, lasting four days, celebrates the defeat of the French army at Puebla on May 5, 1862.

Hotel *Fray Marcos de Niza*, Campillo 91, C, not too good. **Restaurant** *Caverna Greca*, Elias 3, in a cave.

Train Nogales to Mexico City, US$40 (Pullman compartment), daily at 1600, arr. two days later at 1200. Food on train good (dining car only open a few hours) until Guadalajara, then becomes overpriced. If coming from the US, book seat and ticket at Nogales station by telephone, pay day you leave, much cheaper. 2nd class train to Guadalajara 48 hours, crowded. Train Nogales-Hermosillo, daily at 1000, continues to Mazatlán.

Bus to Mexico City, 42 hrs. with Transportes de Pacífico or Norte de Sonora, US$40, Tres Estrellas de Oro, 36 hrs. To Guadalajara 1st class, US$15, 26 hrs., very clean, fold-down seats, many food stops, leaves 1600, arrives 0700. Bus from Nogales to Tepic, 24 hrs., US$20. Nogales-Obregón via Hermosillo, US$8.50. There is a customs check after Nogales.

The highway passes through the Magdalena Valley. The Cocospera mines are near Imuris and there are famous gold and silver mines near Magdalena, which has a great Indian *fiesta* in the first week of October. Beyond, the cactus-strewn desert begins. At 120 km. from Nogales is Santa Ana.

(Km. 2,123) **Hermosillo,** capital of Sonora state, is a modern city, a winter resort town, and centre of a rich orchard area. The La Colorada copper mines are to the E. It has a colonial cathedral, a traditional quarter round an old plaza, and houses the University of Sonora. Altitude, 237 metres; population, 206,600. Golf course. Airport.

Hotels Generally poor standard of hotels; *San Andreas*, Oaxaca 16, E, with bath. *Internacional*, Rosales y Morelos, D; *Washington*, Dr. Noriega, E, with bath, but gloomy; *Kino*, reasonable, Pino Suárez 151, F; *San Alberto*, Serdán y Rosales, E; *Monte Carlo*, Juárez y Sonora, F; *Lourdes*, F, with bath, very dirty; *Guaymas Inn*, 5½ m. N, air-conditioned rooms with shower, E. **Motel** *Motel Valle Grande*, Padre Kino and Ramón Carral, B; *Bugambilia*, Padre Kino 712, C.

Restaurants *Henry's Restaurant*, across the road from *Motel Encanto*, nice old house, good.

Bus to Nogales US$3.80, 4 hrs. dull; 2nd class to Agua Prieta, 7 hrs., US$4; to Los Mochis, 1st class, US$9, 2nd, US$8.50, 7½ hrs. through scrubland and wheat fields. Bus to Tijuana, US$14.50 1st class, 11 hrs. Bus to Mazatlán 10-12 hrs., US$ 12 1st, US$11.50 2nd class. The bus station is on the outskirts.

Train overnight to Mazatlán at 1945, arrives 0730, worth taking a sleeper (US$13).

MEXICO 891

Excursion A dry-weather road, 106 km., goes W to Bahía Kino, on the Gulf. (bus US$1, from Autobuses de la Costa, Calle Plutarco, 1 block from Rosales). The Seri Indians, who used to live across El Canal del Infiernillo (Little Hell Strait) from the port on the mountainous Isla del Tiburón (Shark Island), have been displaced by the navy to the mainland, down a dirt road from Bahía Kino in a settlement at Punta Chueca (no east access). They come into Kino on Sat. and Sun. to sell their ironwood animal sculptures (non-traditional) and traditional basketware (not cheap). They may usually be found at the *Posada del Mar Hotel*. A fine Museo Regional de Arte Seri has opened in new Kino, Calle Puerto Peñasco, 3 blocks from the main beach road.

At Km. 1,988 the road reaches the Gulf at the port of **Guaymas**, on a lovely bay backed by harsh desert mountains; excellent deep-sea fishing, and sea-food for the gourmet. Miramar beach, on Bocachibampo bay circled by purple mountains, its blue sea sprinkled with green islets, is the resort section. Water sports on May 10. The climate is ideal in winter but unpleasant in summer. The 18th century church of San Fernando is worth a visit; so also, outside the town, is the 17th century church of San José de Guaymas. Excursions to the cactus forests. Some 22 km. N of Guaymas is the Bahía San Carlos, very touristy, where "Catch 22" was filmed; there is free camping on a good beach at the end of the runway made for the film; also good fishing. Both Miramar and San Carlos beaches are easily reached by bus. Nice little beach 1 km. past Miramar beach with pleasant cafés, at the end of F bus line. Airport.

Hotels *Club Mediterranée*, end of beach. *Rubi*, Serdán, and Calle 29, wrong end of town with shower and w.c., E, overpriced; *Playa de Cortés*; on Bocachibampo bay, D; *La Posada de San Carlos*, Bahía San Carlos, C. *Leo's Inn* on Miramar beach, D; *Casa de Huéspedes La Colimense*, very basic, rooms on the inside best, F, with fan, near bus station; *Rolyat* on the main street. **Motels** *Flamingos*, Carretera Internacional, E; *El Tular*, E, 15 min. walk from beach, convenient; *Malibu*, D, Carretera Internacional N; *Bahía Trailer Court*, 6 kms. NW of town on Bahía San Carlos road and *Los Playibos*, motel/restaurant/trailer park, 7 km. N on Highway 15 with pool and all facilities. Those who feel like fleeing high prices in Guaymas and can make Ciudad Obregón 129 km. S will find the *Costa de Oro* (see below).

Restaurant *Del Mar*, Aquiles Serdán and Calle 17, excellent seafood, expensive.

British Vice-Consul Apartado 88 for letters. Casa 3, Av. 11.

Tourist Office Av. Serdán, lots of pamphlets.

Rail *Autovía* from Guaymas to Nogales leaves at 1000, 6 hrs., US$9, daily except Sat.; book in advance.

Ferry Transbordadores sail from Guaymas to Santa Rosalía, Baja California, at 1100 every Sun., Tues. and Thur., and return on the same days at 2300, 7 hr. trip. To La Paz, Baja California Sur, Thur. and Sat. 1500, return Fri. and Sun. 1400, 16 hrs.

Buses 2nd class bus Guaymas-Hermosillo (1½ hrs., US$2). Guaymas-Mazatlán, frequent, 12 hrs., US$13; Guaymas-Tijuana, 2nd class, 18 hrs., US$19. Bus to Empalme will allow you to take the train at 1400 (very full at times) coming from Mexicali to Sufragio, to catch the Los Mochis-Chihuahua train the next morning (seats usually no problem).

From Guaymas to Mazatlán is 784 km. First comes **Ciudad Obregón** (*Motel Valle Grande*, *Costa de Oro*, well-kept and pleasant; *Dora*, E), mainly important (68,000 people) as the centre of an agricultural region. **Navajoa** (31,000 people) has the *Motel El Rancho* and *Motel del Río* and a trailer park in the N of town on Route 15; 52 km. E into the hills is the delightful old colonial town of **Alamos** (accommodation in short supply; *Los Portales Hotel*, with beautiful frescoes, D, on plaza; *Somar*, on the road into Alamos, F; *Enriques*, F, basic but O.K.) now declared a national monument. (Bus Navajoa-Alamos every hour on the ½ hr. from 0630, about US$0.30, until 1830, 45 mins—bus station can be reached from main bus station by going right out of the front door, again take first right and then walk six blocks to the terminal on the left.) It is set in a mining area fascinating for rock enthusiasts. About 10 mins. by bus from Alamos is Minas Nuevas, once an important source of silver, very photogenic, bus US$0.25. West of Navajoa, on Huatabampo bay, are the survivors of the Mayo Indians; their festivals are in May.

Los Mochis, in a sugar-cane area, is a fishing resort with a US colony and a US-style layout and facilities. A stairway leads up the hillside behind La Pérgola,

892 MEXICO

a pleasant public park near the city reservoir, for an excellent view of Los Mochis. Km 1,636.5; 100,000 people.

Hotels Book well in advance, especially if arriving late at night. *Holiday Inn*, Carretera 15, C; *Beltrán*, Hidalgo 281, F, recommended, has all travel time-tables for Los Mochis; *América*, E, Allende Sur 655, clean, a/c, near bus station, has restaurant with good, cheap sandwiches. *Santa Anita*, B, Leyva and Hidalgo, comfortable, clean dining room, noisy a/c, not very friendly or efficient, has own bus service to station; *Lorena*, Prieto y Obregón, run down, a/c, F; *Hidalgo*, F, Av. Hidalgo 260, not recommended. *Casa de Huéspedes Chavela*, Av. Melgar, F, primitive; *Montecarlo*, F, a/c, Independencia y Flores. **Motel** *Santa Rosa*, López Mateos 1051 N, D.

Restaurants *El Farallón*, Flores and Obregón, good seafood and service; *Los Globos*, near TNS bus station, reasonable.

A railway trip to Chihuahua (see page 881) and back from Los Mochis (station—called Sufragio—reached by "peso" taxi, US$2.50, 15 mins.; or regular bus from city centre). The *vistatrén* leaves daily at 0600 (arrives 2000, special 1st class, US$10 with English-speaking hostess, no limit on number of passengers). Tickets can be bought at Flamingo Travel the day before, avoiding the queue at the station (but you pay a 10% commission—well worth it owing to station distance; find out if you can get a ticket the day before departure at between 1300 and 1600 from the station). An ordinary train, US$5.50 1st class, US$3.50 2nd, leaves at 0700 (ten hours) for Chihuahua (this is the cheapest way to see the canyon in daylight); cold as you get to Creel, photographing possible. Train timetables bear little relation to actual departure times, so check at Los Mochis and Chihuahua. There is a time change (one hour forward) between Los Mochis and Creel. If you do not want to take the train all the way, go to Bahuichivo (simple hotel, F, a few shops), and return to there. Pick-ups go to Urique (except Sun.) in the Urique Canyon (a bus from the *Misión Urique Canyon* meets the train in Bahuichivo). 2 simple hotels (F) in Urique.

Connexion with the Nogales-Guadalajara train at Sufragio (see also page 992).

Air To La Paz, Baja California Sur.

Bus Mexico City-Los Mochis US$24. Ciudad Obregón-Los Mochis, US$6. Los Mochis-Tijuana, US$18, several daily up to 24 hrs. Los Mochis-Mazatlán US$6.50, 1st class, leaves 2100, arrives 0345; with Tres Estrellas de Oro or Transport Norte de Sonora. Los Mochis-Nogales, 2nd class, US$14, 12 hrs. No reservations can be made for buses N or S at the terminal of Tres Estrellas de Oro and it is difficult to get on buses. Try instead Transportes de Pacífico, 3 blocks away and next to TNS terminal. First class bus to Guaymas 5½ hrs., US$5.

An hour NE by train from Los Mochis is **El Fuerte**. This town has recently been renovated and has interesting colonial architecture. The station is a few miles from the town; taxis. *Hotel San Francisco*, good value. Good restaurants, nice plaza.

About half an hour's drive along a side road SW takes us from Los Mochis to **Topolobampo**, on the beautiful bay-and-lagoon-indented coast. It is difficult to find a beach unless one pays for a private launch. Now that a railway—take food with you—has been opened to Ojinaga (Chihuahua), Topolobampo is being developed as a deep-water port.

Hotels *Yacht Hotel*, modern, clean and good food, quiet, D, but seems to close for the winter; *Casa de Huéspedes* not recommended.

Ferry Topolobampo-La Paz, Baja California Sur, see page 995.

Some 240 km. beyond Los Mochis (at km. 1,429) is the capital of Sinaloa state, **Culiacán** (358,800 people), chief centre for winter vegetables. No longer a colonial city; it has a university. Hotels: *Del Valle*, Solano 180, D; *Executivo*, Madero y Obregón, C. Motels: *Los Caminos*, Carretera Internacional, C; *Los Tres Ríos*, 1 km. N of town on highway 15, trailer park, pool, resort style. The safe beaches of Altata are 30 minutes by dirt road.

Airport 10 km. from centre.

Culiacán is suitable for connections to Los Mochis (see page 882 on trips to the Copper Canyon). Take one of the several daily Mexico City-Culiacán flights and then rent a plane (US$360 for five), hire a car (3 hrs.' drive), or take a bus. Whichever you do, try to arrive before the train at 2100, as hotel reservations are not always honoured.

Another 208 km. bring us to a roadside monument marking the Tropic of Cancer. Beyond, 13 km. is (km. 1,204) **Mazatlán,** spread along a peninsula at the foot of the lofty Sierra Madre. It is the largest Mexican port on the Pacific Ocean and the

MEXICO

main industrial and commercial centre in the W. The beauty of its setting and its warm winters have made it a popular resort, but unfortunately with expansion it has lost some of its attraction. It overlooks Olas Altas (High Waves) bay, which has a very strong current. Tourism is now concentrated on Gaviota beach, which is solidly built up. On one side of the peninsula, the beach is fringed with groves of coconut palm; on the other a fine promenade overlooks a number of picturesque islands. There are more islands in the nearby lagoons, which teem with wild life. A great promenade lined by hotels, with a long slender beach at its foot, curves round the bay; fine for watching the famous sunsets. The local carnival is almost as good as at Veracruz. The best beaches, 3 to 5 km. from the city, are easily reached by taxi. Boats ply between the shore and the island beaches. The crooked streets can be explored in reasonably cheap three-wheeled taxis. On top of the only hill in the city is a park. The lighthouse, on El Faro island, is 157 metres above sea-level. Its light is visible 50 km. away. Population, 174,000. Airport 26 km. from centre. (Taxi, fixed fare US$6.60 airport-Mazatlán.)

Fishing is the main sport (sailfish, tarpon, marlin, etc.). Shrimp from the Gulf are sent, frozen, to all parts of Mexico. Its famous fishing tournament follows Acapulco's and precedes the one at Guaymas. In the mangrove swamps are egrets, flamingoes, pelicans, cranes, herons, and duck. Nearby at Camarones there is "parachute flying", drawn by motorboats. **N.B.** Always check with the locals whether swimming is safe, since there are strong rip currents in the Pacific which run out to sea and are extremely dangerous. There is a free Red Cross treatment station 9 blocks along the avenue opposite the Beach Man on the right. There are bull-fights at Mazatlán, US$4.50 for a general seat in the shade (*sombra*). Good view here, although you can pay up to US$15 to get seats in the first 7 rows—Sundays at 1600.

Firmly rooted and extremely popular in the State of Sinaloa is a type of orchestra known as the Banda Sinaloense, which can be seen and heard at almost any time of day or night in restaurants, dance halls, bars, at family parties or on the street. It usually has from 14 to 16 musicians: 4 saxophones, 4 trumpets, clarinets, tuba, 3-4 men on drums and other percussion instruments, including *maracas*, *guiro*, and loud, strong voices. It is unabashed, brutal music, loud and lively, sometimes very fast.

Hotels Along the northern beach Sábalo-Camarón are: *Los Sábalos*, A, Health Club facilities; *Playa Mazatlán*, B, good atmosphere; *Torres Mazatlán Condominiums*; *El Cid*, A, with *El Caracol* nightclub; *Camino Real*, A; *Oceano Palace*, A; *Holiday Inn*, A; *Azteca Inn*, D. Along Av. del Mar beach are: *De Cima*, B; *Hacienda*, B; *El Dorado* D; *Playamar*, D, with TV, air-conditioned; *Las Brisas*, recommended, C, with shower, swimming pool and on sea front, air-conditioned. Along Olas Altas Beach are: *Freeman*, D, old, highrise; *Belmar*, modernised but old, D. Along Paseo Centenario are: *Olas Altas*, D, efficiently run and clean. Most of the others are in the downtown area away from the beach front: *Posada Colonial*, N of south docks, D, well-kept, good food; *Del Centro*, modern, E, behind main church; *Alberto*, Calle Luis de Zubido, F, with shower; *Roma*, Av. Juan Carrasco 127, very clean and friendly 2 blocks from beach, recommended, F, with bath but some rooms noisy; *Zaragoza*, Zaragoza 18, old and pretty, F, with bath; *Esperanza*, nr. bus station, F, fairly clean, but noisy; *Pensión María Luisa*, Mariano Escobedo, F, no fans, friendly but hot, quiet; *San Jorge*, near market modern, F, with shower, dusty, local bus No. 2 to bus station passes outside; *Lerma*, Simón Bolívar 5, near beach, F, friendly, simple, but quiet and cool; *Vialta*, three blocks from market, F, with bath; *Casa de Huéspedes Sonora*, close to market, F, noisy, basic, facing university student house. *Villa del Mar*, nice and clean, with car park, D, with fan and private facilities; *Económico*, E, with bath and fan, noisy, dark but very clean, next to bus station, ½ km. from main beach; *Sands*, E, pool, near bus station. Although N of the city there are undeveloped beaches with free overnight camping, they are only recommended if you are in a group for security—travellers have warned against it: e.g. *Isla de la Piedra*, friendly, huts for US$1.50 or camping permitted if you have a meal there, good food. Beware of sandflies! At least 10 trailer parks on Playa del Norte/Zona Dorada and on towards the N, including *Casa Blanca Disco*, F, cheapest, on beach side, dirty. Much better is *La Posta*, ½ block off beach, with swimming pool and tent space, E, lots of shade. Big hotels rapidly expanding all along N beach seashore to Mármol. **Motels** are strung all along the ocean front: *Agua Marina*, D, not recommended; *Las Palmas*, B; *Marley*, C; *Las Gaviotas*, B; *San Juan*, B; *Azteca Inn*, C; *Del Sol*, C. On Highway 15: *Papagayo*, D; *Flamingos*, D. Downtown: *Maity*, E; *Mazatlán*, F. *Mar Rosa Trailer Park*, N of *Holiday Inn* on northern beach, F, hot water, safe, recommended.

Restaurants *Doney's*, M. Escobedo 610, downtown, good home cooking; *El Bistro*, in craft centre in Zona Dorada, good steaks and seafood; *Shrimp Bucket* and *Señor Frog*, Olas Altas 11 and Av. del Mar, same owners, very famous, popular, good; *Lobster Trap*, Camarón Sábalo, good chicken(!); *Joncol's*, Flores 254, downtown, popular; *Mamucas*, Bolívar 73, best seafood in town. *La Red*, Av. del Mar 112, reasonable lunches. *El Ostión Feliz*, Flores y Villa, seafood; *Pekin*, Juárez 4, good Chinese, inexpensive; *Pizza Hut*, Av. del Mar, good salads too; *Balnearios Mazatlán* and

894 MEXICO

Miramar, on Playa Norte, good cheap Mexican fare. *Casa del Naturista*, Zaragoza 809, sells good wholegrain bread.

Tourist Office on road to northern beach, past *Señor Frog*.

Bus Station at Centro Colonia, 10 mins. walk from beach or take yellow bus from centre marked "Insurgentes"; safe luggage store. Bus fare Mazatlán-Mexico City about US$13 (2nd class). Mazatlán-Guadalajara, with Transportes Norte de Sonora, several times a day, US$7 (10 hrs.). Mazatlán-Tepic US$4.60 (5¼ hrs.), with Estrella Blanca, efficient, clean buses); bus (frequent) to Los Mochis (7 hrs.), US$6.50 with Transportes Norte de Sonora. Mazatlán-Navajoa, US$5. 1st class; 1st class bus Mazatlán-Durango, US$5.40; Mazatlán-Guaymas, 12 hrs., US$13, 2nd class. Bus to Rosario US$0.80, can then with difficulty catch bus to Caimanero beach, nearly deserted. Terminal Alamos, Av. Oeste Guerrero 402, 2 blocks from market, buses to Alamos every hour on the half hour.

Ferries La Paz (Baja California Sur), daily at 1700, 16 hrs., car (one way), US$30-40, Tourist class is a small room with two bunks and a sink, US$3.60, recommended, cabin class has showers, US$7.25, salon seat US$1.70 in a very crowded room. Deck gets wet during the night, toilets quickly get blocked up, so make an early call. Allow plenty of time for booking and customs procedure. Quite a way from centre to dock (take bus marked "Playa Sur"). **N.B.** Ticket office for La Paz ferry opens 1200-1300 only, on day of departure. Don't expect to get vehicle space for same-day departure. Ferry returns from La Paz also at 1700.

Rail Take bus out to Morelos railway station. Train Mazatlán-Guadalajara, 12 hrs., departs 0800, very comfortable, air-conditioned scenic trip with a variety of topography and agriculture. From Tepic it climbs gradually through the hills to 1,650 metres at Guadalajara, passing through some 30 or 40 tunnels. Best travel 1st class US$6 or pullman US$10.50; 2nd class dirty and uncomfortable, US$3, leaves before dawn. Buy tickets at *Hotel Hacienda*, on the seafront near centre. Train to Tepic, special 1st US$3.50, 2nd class US$2.10, about 6 hrs. 1st class train fare to Mexico City, US$12.50.

Air Daily flights to La Paz and San José del Cabo (Baja California Sur), and the USA.

Excursions to Islas de Piedras, 30 km. of now littered beach. Take a small boat from S side of town from Armada (naval station near brewery), regular service, US$0.20, walk across island (10 mins.). Local *comedores* on beach provide primitive accommodation. Try smoked fish sold on a stick. About 100 km. N of Mazatlán is a turn-off to the town of La Cruz, with two hotels: *Las Palmitas*, F, off the main street, quiet. Few tourists. A boat excursion on the *Yate Fiesta* cruises out at 1000 or 2000 (with dancing), from second last bus stop in the direction of Playa del Sur. Refreshments included, and you can see the wildlife in the day time; US$4.40.

Twenty-four km. beyond Mazatlán, the Coast-to-Coast Highway to Durango, Torreón, Monterrey and Matamoros turns off left at Villa Unión (at about 25 km. from Mazatlán on this road there is a good German hotel with excellent restaurant serving German food; roof has good view over Moctezuma pines, down the mountain to the sea). Before reaching Tepic both road and railway begin the long climb from the lowland level over the Sierra Madre to the basin of Jalisco, 1,500 metres above sea-level. Eleven km. short of Tepic a road on the right descends 900 metres to a pretty South Sea-type beach.

The resort of **San Blas** is 69 km. from Tepic and is overcrowded during US and Mexican summer holidays. It has an old Spanish fortress and a smelly harbour. In August it becomes very hot and there are many mosquitoes but not on the beach 2 km. from the village; few tourists at this time. Seven km. from San Blas is the beach of Matanchén, where dark, menacing jungle comes down to the shore, good swimming. 16 km. from San Blas is the beautiful Los Cocos beach. **N.B.** Don't wander too far from public beach; tourists have warned against attacks and robberies.

Hotels *Marino Inn*, Bataillon, a/c, friendly, pool, fair food, D; *Las Brisas*, Cuauhtémoc Sur 106, very clean, D, highly recommended, excellent restaurant; *Bucanero*, Juárez Poniente 75, E w/bath and fan, frequented by US people, food good, lizards around, noisy discos twice a week; *Posada del Rey*, very clean, swimming pool, excellent value E; *Posada de Morales* also has a swimming pool, more expensive, ½ block from *Posada del Rey*. *Flamingos*, Juárez Poniente 105, F, clean, friendly, being improved; *Vallarta*, very basic with fan, 50 m. from beach, F; *María's*, fairly clean with cooking, washing and fridge facilities, F, with shower, hot rooms. *Mueblería Popular*, has rooms available, F. No camping or sleeping permitted on beaches but several pay campsites available. *San Blas Motel*, near Zócalo, E, patio, fans, good value. Sometimes free camping possible behind *Playa Hermosa Hotel* (old house, only partly occupied, occupied rooms clean, 2 km from town, F, recommended).

MEXICO 895

Restaurants *Tony's* and *La Isla* now said to be best. *Tropicana*, try its *sopa marinera*, fish soup; *La Diligencia*, on Calle Juárez near Zócalo, good food, especially fish, clean, friendly and cheap but slow service; turtle *tacos* at *MacDonald* just off Zócalo. *Bar-Restaurant Torino*, steaks, seafood, pasta, wine by glass, very reasonable.

Bank Banamex just off Zócalo, exchange 0830-1000 only. Comercial de San Blas on the main square will change money at 10% commission.

Bus To Tepic, 1st class, US$1.75, 3 a day, 2nd class, 5-6 a day, US$1, 1½ hrs. To Guadalajara, US$5, 1st class, US$3.90 2nd class, 8½ hrs.

It is possible to take a 4-hr. jungle trip in a boat (bus to launching point, US$0.50) to **La Tovara**, a small resort with fresh-water swimming hole and not much else, or walking, to do. Tour buses leave from the bridge 1 km. out of town and cost US$28 for canoe with six passengers. Competition is keen between guides so some bargaining is possible, although official prices are posted. Guides tend to speed along so you must restrain them if you want to photograph (or even see!) the wildlife. There are coatis, raccoons, iguanas, turtles, boat-billed herons, egrets and parrots. Twilight tours enable naturalists to see pottos and, if very lucky, an ocelot. La Tovara is crowded at midday during the summer. A cheaper 1½-2 hr. cruise is also possible. When arranging your trip make sure you are told the length of journey and route in advance; the longer trip is more worthwhile than the direct 25-min. trip. You can take a bus from San Blas towards Santa Cruz (see below) and get off at Matanchén beach (see above). From here, a boat costing US$10 for ½-day hire includes the best part of the jungle cruise from San Blas.

Quaint tiny towns just off the highway between Mazatlán and Tepic: Acaponeta (turnoff for Novillera beach), Rosario, Tuxpan and Santiago.

(Km. 909) ***Tepic***, capital of Nayarit state, altitude 900 metres, population 111,300, founded in 1531 at the foot of the extinct volcano of Sangagüey. The Huichol and Cora Indians of the Sierra come to town in very picturesque dress; their craftwork—bags (carried only by men), scarves woven in colourful designs and necklaces (*chaquira*) of tiny beads and wall-hangings of brightly coloured wool—is available from souvenir shops, but best to let Indians approach you when they come to town. (These handicrafts are reported to be cheaper in Guadalajara, at the Casa de Artesanías.) There are many little squares, all filled with trees and flowers. The Cathedral, with two fine Gothic towers, in Plaza Principal, has been restored. Worth seeing are the Municipal Palace; the Casa de Amado Nervo (the poet and diplomat); the Regional Museum, Av. México 91 Norte (open 1000-1400 and 1700-2000 hrs., closed Mon.); and the Convento de la Cruz, on the summit of a wooded hill. The landscape around Tepic is wild and mountainous. Nearby are the Ingenio and Jala waterfalls, good places for picnics. Tombs in cemetery worth seeing.

Hotels *Sierra de Alicia*, Av. México Norte 180, E; *San Jorge*, Lerdo 124, E, very comfortable, good value; *Avenida*, Lerdo 260, F; *Ibarra*, Durango 297 Norte, luxurious noisy rooms, E, with bath, and slightly spartan, cheaper, cooler rooms without bath, very clean. *Fray Junípero Serra*, Lerdo Poniente 23, D, main square, a/c, good restaurant, friendly, good service; *Casa de Huéspedes Grijalva*, F, on Zócalo, hot water; *Tepic*, F, with bath, near bus station outside town, clean, friendly; *Mayo*, near bus station, E, clean and bright; *Corita*, Insurgentes 298, modern, F, free parking in locked yard, good reasonable restaurant, attractive gardens; *Pensión Morales*, Insurgentes y Sánchez, 4 blocks from bus station, F, clean and friendly. *Villa de las Rosas*, Insurgentes 100, E, fans, friendly, but not too clean; *Pensión Marí*, 3 blocks off Zócalo, F, with hot water, friendly, clean, very good value. Others on Zócalo, E. *Central*, E; *Juárez*, F, near Palacio de Gobierno, on Juárez 116, for clean room with bath, locks on room doors not very effective, limited parking in courtyard; *Altamirano*, near Palacio del Gobierno, F, noisy but good value; *Sarita*, Bravo 112 Poniente, clean, good, F; *Nayarit*, *Bravo*, spartan, F. **Motels** *La Loma*, Paseo la Loma 301 (swimming pool), D, run down; *Cora Motel Apartamentos Koala*, La Laguna, Santa María del Oro, has units for up to 3 people with kitchen and bathroom, and snack bar, US$6.50 per unit. Fishing and waterskiing on nearby lagoon.

Restaurants Two restaurants in Tepic, both on the outskirts of town, sell *carne en su jugo estilo Guadalajara*, delicious meat and bacon stew with beans in a spicy sauce, served with stewed onions. Restaurant in bus terminal. The local *huevos rancheros* are extremely *picante*.

Tourist Office At Convento de la Cruz, English spoken.

Transport Bus to San Blas from Central Camionera: TNS, US$1, 5 or 6 a day; Tres Estrellas three a day, US$1.75. To Guadalajara, US$3, 1st class, 4-4½ hrs.; Mazatlán, 4½ hrs., US$4.60 (2nd class); Mexico City, US$10.50; Torreón, US$12. Train to Guadalajara, US$1.75 (2nd class),

MEXICO

US$4.50 (1st) leaves at 1130, arrives at 1800, sit on left-hand side for best views. Train to Mexicali, 22-27 hrs., special 1st class, a/c, US$18; to Nogales, 19-23 hrs., ditto, US$16. (Same train to Benjamín Hill, leaving Tepic 1400, then divides). Airport.

Time Change There is a time change, forward one hour, between Tepic and most places inland, such as Guadalajara.

Excursions One can visit Huichol villages only by air, as there are no real roads, takes at least two days. Flight to a village, US$10 return. To various beaches along the coast, some of them off the Nogales highway we have come along. A road runs through Compostela, a pleasant small town with an old church (1539) (1½ hrs. by bus from local bus station at Tepic), to **Santa Cruz**, about 37 km. from Tepic (rocky beach). 2½ hrs. ride by open-sided lorry, difficult to leave the town again, check for transport. No hotels, but accommodation at *Peter's Shop*, F, basic but pleasant and friendly. Simple food available, *Restaurant Belmar*, fish and rice, all reminiscent of the South Seas. (2 buses a day from San Blas to Santa Cruz, US$0.70) From Compostela one can also catch an old bus to **Zacualpan**, 1½ hrs. over a very rough dirt road, to visit a small enclosed park with sculptures that have been found in the area, two blocks from main square. Gate to the park must be unlocked by caretaker; inside there is a small museum. Zacualpan is a pleasant village, knock on a door to ask for the caretaker. About 1½ to 2 hrs. by bus from Tepic on the main road to Guadalajara is **Ixtlán del Río**. Two km. out of town along this road are the ruins of a Toltec ceremonial centre. The main structure is the Temple of Quetzalcoatl, noted for its cruciform windows and circular shape. The journey from Tepic to Guadalajara can easily be broken at Ixtlán with a couple of hours' sightseeing. There are a few souvenir shops and a museum.

Other beaches between Santa Cruz and Puerto Vallarta include Rincón de los Guayabitos, which is being developed as a tourist resort with holiday village and trailer park; Chacala, lined with coconut palms and reached by an unsurfaced road through jungle; and Canalán, near Las Varas, reached only on foot, isolated and beautiful.

Puerto Vallarta (population 70,000), near where "Night of the Iguana" was filmed, is reached by plane from Tepic, Tijuana, Los Angeles and Mexico City. The town is divided by the River Cuale and on one side are the expensive hotels, many shops, the airport and the port where the ferry arrives from San Lucas. On the other side of the river are the bus terminal and some cheaper hotels. It offers aquatic sports, particularly fishing and hunting for sharks. From the public beach you can hire parachuting equipment to be pulled by motor-boat (US$10). The Malecón is the waterfront drive. The beach at Puerto Vallarta is not particularly good but there are better ones about 8-10 km. south along the coast, e.g. Mismaloya (reached by bus, US$0.30). There is now a paved road from Tepic to Puerto Vallarta, continuing down the coast to Barra de Navidad and Manzanillo with excellent *Hotel Careyes*, A, en route, and several cheaper ones, including *El Tecuán* (D) and *Hotel Tenacatita* (B) near the village of the same name (see page 902), and further to Zihuatanejo and Acapulco, and finally to Salina Cruz.

Hotels Puerto Vallarta is divided naturally into 3 sections: N of town are: *Playa de Oro*, B; *Posada Vallarta*, L; *Fiesta Americana*, L; *Pelícanos*, B; *Las Palmas*, B; *Plaza Vallarta*, A; *Bugambilias Sheraton*, L; *Puerto Vallarta Holiday Inn*, Av. de las Garzas, A. In town are: *Buenaventura*, C; *Rosita*, very pleasantly situated, 5 min. bus ride to beaches on other side of town, where the sandy beach begins, D; *Océano*, 31 de Mayo, E; *Río*, F, good value; *Cuatro Vientos*, C, lots of stairs; *Belmar*, E; *Central*, F, off main square; *Las Cabañas*, *Marlyn*, both F; *Paraíso*, Paseo Díaz Ordaz, on the sea but stony beach, F. South of Río Cuale are: *Camino Real*, L; *Garza Blanca*, Playa Palo María; *Oro Verde*, Gómez 111, A, a/c, recommended as clean, pleasant, friendly; *Posada Río Cuale*, excellent food, Serdán 242, swimming pool, a/c, D; *Eloísa*, F; *Fontana del Mar*, Diéguez 171, D, attractive; *Tropicana*, D, Amapá 227, Mexican families; *Molino del Agua*, Vallarta 130, B, beautiful, beside the new bridge, clean, a/c, good service, pool, recommended; *Playa los Arcos*, Olas Altas 380, D; *Villa del Mar*, Cárdenas 444, F, good; *Posada de Roger*, C, Badillo 237, good value, near two main city beaches, beware of thieves, popular with students. *Playa de Bucerías*, Carretera Tepic Km. 154, D. Several *casas de huéspedes* in town, F. Cheap apartments: *La Peña*, F, Rodríguez 174.

Camping 8 km. S of Puerto Vallarta at Playa Mismaloya, popular with North Americans travelling by car; not a proper campsite but showers operate during the day, as do toilets, but women's toilets are locked at night. *Chico's Paradise*, in the village of Mismaloya, is a restaurant with water cascading down forming fresh-water pools where one can swim.

Restaurants The *Mercado Restaurant* is good and very cheap. *Mismaloya Beach* restaurant, excellent, US$2-4 for dinner (8 km. S of Puerto Vallarta). *Ostión Feliz*, Libertad 177, excellent seafood. *El Coral*, Olas Altas, good breakfast and *comida corrida*. *Carlos O'Brians*, beautifully

MEXICO 897

decorated, popular, young clientèle. *Tony's Please*, Encino y Hidalgo, near bridge, good, reasonable food. Very good ice-cream and frozen yoghurt is sold along the Malecón. Puerto Vallarta has an active night life, with many bars and discotheques.

Shopping *Plaza Malecón*, near *Hotel Río*, end of Malecón, has 28 curio shops, restaurant, music, etc.

Tourist Office In the government buildding on the main square, very helpful.

Ferries To Cabo San Lucas, Baja California Sur, Sat. and Tues., 1600., one way fare US$5.50 (reclining seat), US$10 p.p. in cabin for 4, 18 hrs. Return Fri. and Sun., 1600; Transbordadores, run by Caminos y Puentes Federales. No advance booking for foot passengers; try to pay for cabin or sleeper tickets on board. Poor food. Also to La Paz, Fri. 1200, 21 hrs., back from La Paz Thurs. 1600.

Buses By Sonora del Norte, Estrella Blanca and Autobuses del Pacífico, to Mexico City, 15 hrs. US$13. Puerto Vallarta to Guadalajara, US$7 1st class, 7 hrs.

Air Travel International airport 7 km. from centre.

Excursions To Yelapa, beautiful tropical village with waterfall; by boat or car.

Warning Those confined to wheelchairs are warned that Puerto Vallarta is a bad place, with its high kerbs and cobblestone streets.

Tequila (58 km. from Guadalajara), on the Tepic-Guadalajara road, is the main place where the famous Mexican drink is distilled, from *maguey*. Free tours of tequila factories along the highway. Half-way between Tequila and Guadalajara, in the mountains, is the British-run *Rancho Río Caliente*, 8 km. from the highway, a vegetarian thermal resort.

Tequila and Guadalajara are in the State of Jalisco. The State's cultural life has been helped by an economy based on crafts, agriculture, and livestock, with fewer pockets of abject poverty than elsewhere in Mexico. Many villages have traditional skills such as pottery, blown glass, shoemaking, and a curious and beautiful form of filigree weaving in which miniature flower baskets, fruit and religious images are shaped from *chilte* (chicle, the raw substance from which chewing-gum is made). The State is the original home of Mexico's *mariachis:* roving musical groups dressed in the gala suits and *sombreros* of early 19th century rural gentry.

Guadalajara, capital of Jalisco state; altitude 1,650 metres, and slightly warmer than at the capital; population, 2,500,000, and 696 km. from Mexico City, was founded in 1530. It used to be a fine, clean city, not unlike the towns of southern Spain, but pollution has now grown. Graceful colonial arcades, or *portales*, flank scores of old plazas and shaded parks. The climate is mild, dry and clear all through the year. A pedestrian mall, Plaza Tapatía, has been installed between the Cabañas Orphanage and the Degollado Theatre, crossing the Calzada Independencia, covering 16 square blocks. It has beautiful plants, fountains, statuary, a tourist office, and is designed in colonial style. The best shops are all found in or near the Plaza Mayor and the Avenida Juárez. The Plaza del Sol shopping centre, with over 100 shops, is located at the S end of the city, while the equally modern Plaza Patria, with as many shops, is at the N end near the Zapopán suburb. The Plaza Mayor is flanked by the Government Palace (1643) where in 1810 Hidalgo issued his first proclamation abolishing slavery (plaque). Orozco's great murals can be seen on the central staircase. In the main University of Guadalajara building, on Av. Juárez Tolsa, is the dome in which is portrayed man asleep, man meditating, and man creating. Other works by this artist can be seen at the University's main Library, at Glorieta Normal, and at the massive Cabañas Orphanage near the Mercado de la Libertad (now known as Instituto Cultural Cabañas, housing, among other cultural attractions, Orozco's stunning "Man of Fire") take bus 49 or 53 from F. Madero, alight at Glorieta La Minerva. The Orphanage is a beautiful building with 22 patios, which is floodlit at night (entry US$0.40). The contents of the former Orozco museum in Mexico City have also been transferred to Guadalajara. On the Plaza Mayor also is the Cathedral, begun in 1561, finished in 1618, in rather a medley of styles; there is no longer admission to the tower (the structure has been declared dangerous), where remarkable frescoes were recently discovered half-way up. There is a

898 MEXICO

reputed Murillo Virgin inside (painted 1650), and the famous La Virgen del Carmen, painted by Miguel de Cabrera, a Zapotec Indian from Oaxaca. NE of the Cathedral is the State Museum (US$0.50, closed Sat.-Tues.) in an old monastery (1700) with a good, prehistoric section and interesting display of "hidden" tombs, excellent display of Colima and Jalisco terracotta figures, colonial art section (religious); and two blocks E is the enormous and fantastically decorated Degollado Theatre (1866), half-price for students on Sats. There is an Archaeological Museum of Western Mexico on Plaza Juárez, open Mon.-Sat. 0900-1300 and 1600-1800, free. A school of crafts (ceramics, glass weaving, leatherwork) is on Alcalde and Avila Camacho; and there is also the Albarrán hunting museum, Paseo de los Parques 3530, Colinas de San Javier, Sat. and Sun. 1000-1400, with a collection of rare animals from all over the world.

The best churches are Santa Mónica (1718), with a richly carved façade; El Carmen, with a main altar surrounded by gilded Corinthian columns, San José, with a fine gilded rococo pulpit, the Belén, enclosed in the Hospital Civil and facing a fine botanic garden, which contains three fine late C.18 *retablos*, and San Francisco (1550). To the N of this last church is the quite exquisite Jardín San Francisco, and to the W the old and quaint church of Our Lady of Aránzazu, with two fantastic churrigueresque altarpieces (now closed for renovation). There are 3 universities (visit architectural faculty near Parque Mirador, 20 mins. by car from centre, or take bus 45 overlooking Barranca de Oblatos, a huge canyon), a Cultural Institute with contemporary arts displays and a film theatre (US$0.50), and a ticket office for Teatro Azul, and an open-air theatre, Auditorio Gonzalo Cunel. Other sights worth seeing are the Agua Azul park near the Sheraton hotel (swimming pools dirty); dances on Sun. at 1700, flower market, handicrafts shop. The markets, in particular the Libertad (San Juan de Dios) market which has colourful items for souvenirs with lots of Michoacán crafts including Paracho guitars and Sahuayo hats, and delicious food upstairs on the 1st level (particularly goat meat, *birria*, also *cocada*), but expensive soft drinks (check prices before sitting down or you will be grossly overcharged as tourists); the Tianguis (Indian market) on Av. Guadalupe, Colonia Chapalita, on Fri. is of little interest to foreigners, bus 50 gets you there; the Tianguis near the University Sports Centre on Calzada Tlaquepaque on Sundays; the Plaza de Los Mariachis, Obregón and Leonardo Vicario, near La Libertad; the Templo Expiatorio, gothic style, still unfinished after most of a century. There is a new, large park, zoological garden and planetarium just past the bullring going out on Av. Independencia.

Festivals March 21 commemorates Benito Juárez' birthday and everything is closed for the day. Ceremonies around his monument at the Agua Azul park. At the end of October there is also a great *fiesta* there with concerts, bullfights, sports and exhibitions of handicrafts from all over Mexico. October 28-December 20, *fiesta* in honour of the Virgin of Guadalupe; Av. Alcalde has stalls, music, fair etc. In December there is one at Parque Morelos and hand-made toys are a special feature.

Hotels *Fiesta Americana*, López Mateos at Minerva circle, L; *Exaralis Hyatt-Regency*, López Mateos opp. Plaza del Sol, L; *Guadalajara-Sheraton*, 16 de Septiembre, A; *Quinta Real*, Av. México y López Mateos, small, A, good but slow restaurant; *Camino Real*, Vallarta 5005, A, some way from the centre; *Fénix*, Calle Corona 160, reasonable, B, modernized; *Roma*, Av. Juárez 170, C; *El Tapatío*, Bld. Aeropuerto 3275 (in Tlaquepaque, fine view of city), A; *Mendoza*, V. Carranza 16, C; *Holiday Inn*, Av. López Mateos opp. Plaza del Sol, B. *Suites María Isabel*, Circun. Providencia 1140, D; *Lafayette*, Av. La Paz 2055, C; *Del Parque*, Juárez 845, F, deteriorating, limited parking; *Tres Estrellas*, cheap, noisy, all rooms with bath, restaurant and garage, Calzada Independencia Sur 667 near bus station (restaurant closed in January), F. There are many cheap hotels in the two blocks N of the bus station, Calle 28 de Enero and Calle 20 de Noviembre (where there is a small market, good for breakfasts) and the side streets (although rooms can sometimes be filthy, so check), and near Mercado Libertad. Between the bus terminal and market is *Gran Hotel El Aguila*, F, with bath, very hot water, very basic; *Reno*, Calle Independencia 482, F, clean, front rooms a bit noisy otherwise recommended; *San José*, opp. bus terminal, F, good value, fills up fast, can be noisy, be there early in the morning. Large, noisy but good value *Continental*, E, and *Morales*, both on Calle Corona, E, recommended (but others of similar quality cheaper), often fully booked. *Celta*, on Balderas, B; but friendly, F; *Emperador de Occidente*, opp. bus terminal, good but noisy, Av. 5 de Febrero, F; *Madrid*, 20 de Noviembre, nr. bus station, F, good value, quiet; *Calzada*, Calzada Independencia Sur, good value but loud TV and Space Invaders, F; *Hamilton*, F, clean and central at Madero 381; *González*, behind Mercado Corona, near cathedral, González Ortega 77, good

MEXICO 899

value, F, often full, recommended; *Americano*, Av. Hidalgo, behind theatre, E, clean, very nice but noisy traffic; *Posada de la Plata*, López Cotilla y Ocho de Julio, in centre, F, large rooms, shower, clean, friendly; *Praga*, near bus station and across from *San Carlos*, both F, noisy, clean, no comfort, nice people; also *Morelia* on 28 de Enero, F, shabby, unsavoury; *Nueva Galicia*, E, older style, Av. Corona 610; *Balderas*, Calle Balderas, near bus station, F, dirty. *Pensión Jalisco*, Obregón 833, F, with bath, spotless, comfortable, but in horrible district. *Sevilla*, Prisciliano Sánchez 413, good, clean (2 blocks from centre), owner speaks English, good restaurant, F. *Monaco*, opp. bus station's side exit (tunnel), F, clean and friendly; open late, near Calzada Independencia Sur; *Pacífico*, Los Angeles 27, nice clean rooms, F. *Lisboa*, Huerta 20, near Mercado Libertad, F, with bath, not clean. *Las Américas* E, Calle Hidalgo, friendly and clean. *Señorial*, ½ block from bus station, F, pleasant. *Janeiro*, Obregón 93, by market, clean, F, good value, clean; *Central* (No. 739), F, and *Cónsul* (a bit run down), F, both near bus terminal on 28 de Enero, clean; *Azteca*, 1½ blocks from Mercado Libertad, clean, F; *León*, Calzada Independencia Sur 557, D, clean, shower, ask for room at back. 2 blocks from bus station, in direction of centre, *Casa de Huéspedes Norteña*, Calle 28 de Enero, F, without bath, clean, room to wash clothes in patio. Also *Oriental*, F, Estadio 21, basic; *Nayarit*, F, not very clean, some rooms better than others, in the block N of bus station; Los Angeles 231A; *Manzanillo*, Calle Estadio 2074, near bus station, G; *Mexicali*, Independencia, F; *Camino*, on the road from Mazatlán. **Motels** *Rose*, D; *Chapalita*, F; *Del Bosque*, C; *Posada del Sol*, C; *Las Américas*, C; *Colonial*, D. There are additional ones at the end of Vallarta: *Vallarta*, D; *Guadalajara*, C; *California*, D; *Real Vallarta*, F. There are 16 more around town. Many along López Mateos near the edge of town, before the *periférico* road.

Youth Hostel CREA at Prolongación Alcalde 1360, Sector Hidalgo, Tel.: 24-62-54. Bus from centre: Mezquitera, from bus terminal, No. 133, or No. 16 from Cathedral.

Restaurants *Gerardo*, on Calle La Paz, main dish about US$5, and *La Vianda*, just off López Mateos Sur by Plaza del Angel, as reported best. *La Concordia*, P. Moreno 1679, good seafood; *El Tío Juan*, Independencia Norte 2246, local meat dishes including goat; Mexican specialities also at *Caballo Blanco*, López Mateos Sur 700; local country fare at *Ahualulco Campestre*, 20 de Noviembre 122A; *Jacques* (in Lafayette Park); *Guadalajara Grill*, López Mateos Sur, excellent meat and music; *El Tirol* on Duque de Rivas, Sector Hidalgo, excellent steak. *Holiday Inn* does grills on Sun., 1300-1700. *Carnes Asadas Tolsa*, Tolsa 510 and Chapultepec 189, recommended; *Copa de Leche*, and *El Balcón*, smart and reasonable on Juárez 414; *Las Margaritas*, one at López Cotilla 1477, and one at Ruben Darío and M. Acuña, good and cheap vegetarian dishes. *Bazar de la Salud*, López Cotilla 608, good vegetarian *lonchería*; round the corner on Juárez is *La Naturaleza*, also vegetarian, both closed Sun. Vegetarian restaurant opp. Hotel Sevilla on Prisciliano Sánchez. Good but expensive Japanese restaurant, *Suchiro*. *Restaurant and Pastry Shop Suiza*, Vallarta 1519, good breakfast and coffee, recommended; *Don Tomasito*, Vidrio 1688 y Argentina, Jaliscan dishes, very good, unpretentious. *Hong Kong*, opp. Hotel Fénix, set meals from US$3 but not very good. *El Nuevo Polo Norte del Parque*, N side of Parque de la Revolución, excellent chicken, esp. in *pepián*; *Agora*, in ex-Convento del Carmen, on Juárez, good for fish. *Mesón de Sancho Panza* on park where Calzada Federalismo and Av. Juárez bisect, good five-course meals and Mexican wines. *Las Banderillas* on Av. Alcalde, excellent *carnes asadas* (roast meat), always open, try *cerdo adobado* (marinated pork) *guacamole* and *cebollitas* (onions). Cheap meals at *El Bordo*, Calle Independencia and at the *Fonda Vieja Mexicali* at No. 391 (Sur) of the same street. Many cheap restaurants in the streets near the bus stations, esp. in Calle de Los Angeles. *Nino's*, Av. México and Manuel, reasonable and good; *Alpes*, Calle López Cotilla, German food, inexpensive; *Nueva Galicia*, not recommended, short-changing. *La Herredura*, Calle Estadio next to Hotel Terminal across from bus terminal, good *carne asada*. In Tlaquepaque, Dayton Herzog runs *El Restaurant sin Nombre*, on Fco. Madero, excellent food and drink out of doors, with singing waiters. Many bars serve snacks, *botanas*, with drinks between 1300 and 1500, free, e.g. *Pancho S.A.* (best) on Maestranza 179, several blocks from the Libertad market. Most of these bars are for men only, though. **N.B.** The bars in the centre have become pick-up points for the city's growing gay population, who may be very pressing in their attentions.

Crafts Two glass factories at **Tlaquepaque** where the blue, green, amber and amethyst blown-glass articles are made with recycled glassware which is ground down by hand before being melted down; visit the shop of Sergio Bustamante, who sells his own work: expensive but well worth a look. Also, the Casa de los Telares (Calle de Hidalgo 1378), where Indian textiles are woven on hand looms. Potters can be watched at work both in Guadalajara and at Tlaquepaque; you may find better bargains at Tonalá (pottery and ceramics), 15 km. SW of Guadalajara on the road to Mexico City, but no glass there; take bus 110, bumpy ½ hr. journey. Overall, Tlaquepaque is the cheapest and most varied source of the local crafts; best buys: glass, papier mâché goods, leather (cheapest in Mexico), and ceramics. Guadalajara is the home of Ornelas cigars, smoked by Churchill, available on Av. México 2467, closed 1300-1600. Casa de Artesanías, edge of Agua Azul park, high quality display (and sale) of handicrafts. There is another shop-cum-exhibition at the Instituto de Artesanía Jaliscense, México 54, extension of the Avenida Alcalde and Avila Camacho. Look out for leather belts with sewn-on tapestry. Parián is a covered commercial area with a whole variety of restaurants and handicraft shops, Calle Grecia, off Juárez. See also the Tienda Tlaquepaque, at Av. Juárez 267-B, in Tlaquepaque, Tel.: 35-56-63.

900 **MEXICO**

Car Rental Niños Héroes opp. *Sheraton*: Quick, Budget, National, Avis, Ford and Odin. Others scattered throughout the city.

Entertainment Folk dances every Sun. at 1000 in the Degollado Theatre; concert every Thurs. and Sun. at 1830 in the Plaza de Armas, in front of the Palacio de Gobierno, free. *Charreada* (cowboy show) near Agua Azul Park at Aceves Calindo Lienzo, Sun. at 1200. *Peña Cuicalli*, Sector Juárez, López Cotilla 1225 with Atenas, opens 2000, small cover charge, food and drink available, fills up fast—local groups perform folk and protest songs. Music also at *La Peña* on Avenida Unión.

Sport Bullfights: October to March; football throughout year; *Charreadas* are held in mid-September at Unión de San Antonio; baseball, April-Sept.; golf at: Santa Anita, 16 km. out on Morelia road, championship course; Rancho Contento, 10 km. out on Nogales road; San Isidro, 10 km. out on Saltillo road, noted for water hazards; Areas, 8 km. out on Chapala road.

British Vice-Consul near Niños Héroes, Lerdo de Tejada 2264 and Unión. Tel: 151406, open from 1100.

Cultural Institutes US at Tolsa 300; British at Tomás V. Gómez 125, Sector Hidalgo, Tel.: 160268, closed between 1200 and 1600. Benjamin Franklin Library, Libertad 1492, US papers and magazines.

Post Office and Customs at Independencia 226, near theatre.

Spanish Language Schools much more expensive here than further S.

Tourist Office Regional one is at Calle Juárez 638, at ex-Convento del Carmen, helpful, has maps, ask about free open-air events in courtyard in the evenings. Municipal Tourist Office in the Plaza Tapatía Mall, information on everything. Ask for official free tourist guides outside the bus station (they have documentation), useful. American Express-Convisa S.A., 16 de Septiembre 730, 100 metres from the *Sheraton Hotel*, open Sat. at 0930.

Rail Ticket office in town, Av. Libertad and Colonias, near the US Consulate (but not for trains to Mexico City). National Railways to Mexico City and Manzanillo. Mexico City-Guadalajara "pullman" at 2030 daily, 12 hrs., US$30 for a private double compartment. The ordinary train from Mexico City to Guadalajara leaves at 0945 and 1900 daily, 14-18 hrs., US$6.50 (1st class), US$3.85 (2nd class). There is a first and special first class; only the latter is better than 2nd class. Train Guadalajara-Irapuato (US$1.70 2nd class) leaves at 0700, which connects there with the train to Mexico City from the north. Train to Mexicali, 0945 "Pullman", 28 hrs., US$21; ordinary 1200, 44 hrs. Daily trains to Los Reyes (change at Yurecuaro) and Manzanillo. Train to Mazatlán (book well in advance) 1st class and Pullman at 0910, US$3 and US$6 respectively. All classes on 1330 train, 2nd class US$2 (price difference really shows). Journey Guadalajara-Colima, US$1.20, 2nd class, 7 hours, worth taking because scenery between Ciudad Guzmán and Colima is spectacular.

Airport Miguel Hidalgo, 20 km. from town; fixed rate for 3 city zones and 3 classes of taxi: *especial, semi-especial* and *colectivo*—no tip necessary. Bus No. 71 from 1st class entrance at Terminal de Autobuses, US$0.20; VW buses, Calle Federalismo Sur No. 915, "servicio terrestre", US$2.50 p.p. Eight flights daily to and from Mexico City, 50 mins.

Bus Central station 3 blocks from railway station. To Uruapan, US$3, 2nd class, 6 hrs., with Estrella de Oro before 0900 and at 1500, with Flecha Amarilla about 7 hrs.; departures every hour until midnight; with Norte de Sonora to Mazatlán, 9½ hrs., US$6, Ciudad Obregón, 15 hrs., US$13, Hermosillo, 19 hrs., US$17; Mexicali, 32 hrs., US$25; Tijuana, 36 hrs., US$28 and Ciudad Juárez, US$30, 1st class (15 hrs.) with Omnibus de México; Mexico City, US$7.70 1st class, US$6.80 2nd class, leave every hr., 8 hrs., much of road under repair; Nogales, US$15, 26 hrs.; Zihuatanejo, US$8, 12 hrs. (2nd class). Guanajuato 3 1st class, US$5.50, 2nd class hourly, US$4. To Durango, US$6. To Morelia, every hour until midnight, 1st class US$6, 2nd class US$4. Manzanillo, US$5, 6 hrs.; Pátzcuaro, US$3.50, Flecha Amarilla at 1400, 6 hrs. Interesting journey to Zacatecas, but Autobuses de México front window is half painted. To Pátzcuaro at 1125, 1325 and 1525 (US$6.75 1st class); to Querétaro, US$5, 7 hrs.; to Colima, US$3; to Chapala US$1.

Excursions 8 km. to the great canyon of Barranca de Oblatos, 600 metres deep, reached by bus 45 from the market to end of line (admission US$0.05), with the Río Santiago hurling and cascading at the bottom (except in dry season): a stupendous sight. Guides to the bottom. See especially the Cola de Caballo waterfall and the Parque Mirador Dr Atl. Park crowded on Sunday; Balneario Los Comachos, a beautiful large swimming pool with diving boards set on one side of the Barranca de Oblatos, has many terraces with tables and chairs and barbecue pits under mango trees; drinks and snacks on sale. Entry US$1.30. Also to Barranca de Huentitán, in the canyon of the River Lerma, access via the Mirador de Huentitán at the end of Calzada Independencia Norte, interesting flora, tremendous natural site. Take bus 54 from Calzada Independencia. It follows the same route as route 45 but turns off at Carros Chocados (car dump) and continues 4 km. At the end of the line one can walk down the winding, rock-strewn path. 1 hr. to the bottom (no guide

MEXICO 901

needed) and the River Lerma which is straddled by the historic bridge of Huentitán. Drinks at bottom, recommended before return! All budding Jaliscan marathon runners train here. An alternative route to Huentitán is bus 133 from Av. Alcalde or 16 de Septiembre, but route 132 takes you back the same way. All buses cost US$0.05. In a NW suburb of Guadalajara are also the Basílica de Zapopán, with a miraculous image of Nuestra Señora on the main altar, given to the Indians in 1542, and a museum of Huichol Indian art (agricultural fair in Nov.). Zapopán is reached by a system of underground trolley buses, known as the *metro*, which also goes to Tlaquepaque. En route for Tepic is the Bosque de Primavera, reached by town buses. Pine forests ideal for picnics, although increasingly littered; US$0.50 for a swim.

"From Guadalajara to Irapuato: via Tepatitlán (79 km, on the León road), a small unfinished market town with a *charro* centre, in an impressive setting with steep hills all around; Arandas has a curious neo-gothic church and a pleasant square with a white wrought-iron bandstand; the road then winds tightly up over a range of hills and then down into a long and heavily cultivated valley. Five-hour journey." Tim Connell.

Lake Chapala, 64 km. to the south-east, is near the town of Sayula from which D. H. Lawrence took the name when he wrote about Chapala in "The Plumed Serpent" (return 1st class bus fare to the lake US$2, every ½ hr, 1 hr. journey). There is an *Aldea India*, Indian settlement, on the Chapala road, with murals of the history of Jalisco. **Chapala** town, on the northern shore of Lake Chapala (113 km. long, 24 to 32 wide), has thermal springs, several good and pricey hotels, 3 golf courses, helpful tourist office at Hidalgo 227, and is a popular resort particularly with moneyed North Americans. Watch women and children play a picture-card game called *Anachuac*. "The house in which Lawrence wrote his novel still stands at Zaragoza 307, although a second floor and some modernization have been added. The church that figures in the last pages of "The Plumed Serpent" still stands on the waterfront, its humble façade and interior now covered by a handsome veneer of carved stone," writes Robert Schmitz, of Chapala. The lake is set in beautiful scenery. There are boats of all kinds for hire, water-fowl shooting in autumn and winter, sailing, and the lake teems with freshwater fish. Not much swimming because the water isn't very clean. On the Fiesta de Francisco de Asís (Oct. 2-3) fireworks are displayed and excellent food served in the streets. Horses for hire on the beach, bargain.

Hotels *Camino Real*, C; *Chulavista*, Km. 3 Chapala-Jocotepec, E; *Villa Montecarlo*, exclusive; *Nido*, E, clean, pleasant, good swimming pool; *Chapala Haciendas*, Km. 40, Chapala-Guadalajara highway, F; *Las Palmitas*, Juárez 531, F, good. Good discotheque, *Pantera Rosa*.

Ajijic, 7 km. to the W, a smaller, once Indian village, has an arty-crafty American colony. *Posada Ajijic* is a pleasant place to stay, from D, some rooms with fireplace, nice garden; *Las Casitas*, apartments, E (just outside Ajijic, at Carretera Puente 20); *Hotel Real de Chapala*, Fracción la Floresta; very cheap basic accommodation at *La Playita*, Calle Hidalgo 12B, large bed-bugs included. Try the *Teheban* bar for entertainment. Restaurant: *Italo*. Bus from Chapala, US0.45. Beyond Ajijic is the Indian fishing village of **Jocotepec**, a sizeable agricultural centre (recently invaded by more cosmopolitan types) on the lake; there is a local *fiesta* on January 11-18. Stay at *La Naranjita*, built 1828 as coaching inn, good food, and an art shop. *Hotel Olmedo*, E, opposite police chief's house. *Casa de huéspedes* on Calle Matamoros 83 (same street as bus station), F, with bath, modern facilities. *Ramón's Bar*, popular drinking place. Jocotepec can be reached from Ajijic or, right, from the Mexico-Guadalajara highway. Bus Chapala-Jocotepec US$1, at 1030, 1230 and 1730. The Indians make famous black-and-white *sarapes*. Nearby is the *Motel El Pescador*. Between Ajijic and Jocotepec lies the small town of **San Juan Cosalá**, with thermal springs at *Balnearios y Suites Cosalá*, which has private rooms for bathing with large tiled baths. Sunbathing in private rooms also possible. Rooms to let at *Balneario Paraíso*, F. *Hotel Kikos*, nearby, not so good. Bus service from Chapala.

About 130 km. S of Guadalajara off the road to Sayula and Ciudad Guzmán (*Hotel Flamingo*, nr. main square, E, excellent value, very modern, very clean, and quiet), is **Tapalpa**, very pretty indeed. 3½ hours' drive from Guadalajara. The bus has several detours into the hills to stop at small places such as Zacoalco (Sunday market) and Amacueca. The road up to Tapalpa is winding and climbs sharply; the air becomes noticeably cooler and the fresh invigorating atmosphere is a contrast to the contamination in Guadalajara; it is becoming increasingly popular as a place for weekend homes. The town itself, with fewer than 1,000 inhabitants, shows ample signs of this influx of prosperity. There are two churches (one with a curious atrium) and an imposing flight of stone steps between them, laid out with fountains and ornamental lamps. Being set in cattle country, the rodeo is a popular sport at weekends.

The main street is lined with stalls, selling *sarapes* and other tourist goods on Sundays and fresh food the other days of the week. The more expensive restaurants have tables on balconies overlooking the square—the *Restaurante Posada Hacienda* (which has a US$1 cover charge) is perhaps best placed, with views behind overlooking the sloping hillside. Others are the *Buena Vista* (which also has rooms) and *La Cabaña*, and all are visited by the mariachis. Less grand is the *Hotel Tapalpa*, but clean and fairly cheap to eat in; rooms seem slightly expensive (E). Some rooms are for hire (*Bungalows Rosita*). The only local speciality is *ponche*, an improbable blend of tamarind and mescal which is sold in gallon jars and recommended only for the curious or foolhardy. If you

902 MEXICO

are planning a day trip get your return ticket as soon as you arrive as the last bus back to Guadalajara (1800 on Sundays) is likely to be full.

Manzanillo has become an important port on the Pacific, since a spectacular 257-km. railway has been driven down the sharp slopes of the Sierra Madre through Colima. The road from Guadalajara is via Jal. 33 to Ciudad Guzmán and on to Manzanillo. Occupations for tourists at Manzanillo (population, 26,000) include deep-sea fishing, bathing, and walking in the hills. There is a bullring on the outskirts on the road to Colima. Tourist Office at Juárez 111. The best beach is the lovely crescent of Santiago, 8 km. N, but there are three others. Airport.

Hotels *Roca del Mar*, Playa Azul, vacation centre, A; *Las Brisas Vacation Club*, E, Av. L. Cárdenas, some a/c, good restaurant; *La Posada*, C, US manager. At Santiago beach: *Playa de Santiago*, C; *Parador Marbella*, D, including breakfast and dinner; *Club Las Hadas Camino Real*, A; *Anita*, D. At the port: *Colonial*, good restaurant, México 100, E, friendly; also *Colonial*, 10 de Mayo, E; *Flamingos*, 10 de Mayo y Madería, F; *Emperador*, Davalos 69, E. *Medina*, México 133, F; *Pacífico*, F, with bath, also on Calle México. Camping at Miramar and Santiago beaches. *Vida del Mar*, B, at Miramar.

Transport Bus to Miramar, US$0.20, leaves from J. J. Alcaraz, "El Tajo". Autocamiones del Pacífico bus, 1st class to Guadalajara, US$4, 6 hrs. To Mexico City with Autobus de Occidente, 19 hrs., 2nd class, US$8.80. To Guadalajara, US$5, 6 hrs.; to Barra de Navidad, US$0.80, 1½ hrs.; to Colima, US$1.50; to Tijuana, bus US$48, 1st class, 36 hrs. Bus terminal in Av. Hidalgo, local buses go there. Train to Guadalajara daily at 0800, US$1.50.

Another Route to Manzanillo Turn off Mexico City highway 35 km. S of Guadalajara and continue 270 km. S to Melaque Bay and the village of **Barra de Navidad** (commercial but still pleasant; *Hotel Barra de Navidad*, with balcony on beach, E or bungalows, US$6.60, where you can cook (free camping); at *Alice's Restaurant*, E, simple food; *Hotel Jalisco*, F, hot water, safe and clean; fish restaurants e.g. *Antonio* on beach), where there is a monument to the Spanish ships which set out in 1648 to conquer the Philippines. Avoid oil spillages on beach. This road is paved. Pretty seaside villages near Barra de Navidad include La Manzanilla (*Posada del Cazador*) and Tenacatita, with perfect beach complete with palm huts, tropical fish among rocks. *Hotel* (no name) in village near beach, F, or you can sleep on the beach under a palm shelter— but beware mosquitoes. **Melaque** bay is one of the most beautiful on the Pacific coast but the place has become very commercialized. (Hotel: *Melaque*, quite satisfactory; *Bungalows Azteca*, 23 km. from Manzanillo airport, E for 4 at Calle Avante, San Patricio, Tel.: (333) 7-01-50, with kitchenette, pool, parking.) The road, paved, goes on to Manzanillo. S of Manzanillo is **Tecomán**, a small town with delightful atmosphere. Unnamed *pensión* on the corner of the Zócalo, if you face the church it is on your left, F. Try the local deep-fried *tortillas* filled with cheese.

A beautiful hilly road runs from Manzanillo to **Colima**, 96 km., capital of Colima state, at an altitude of 494 metres, and with a population of 160,000. Colima is a most charming and hospitable town with gothic arcade on main square and strange rebuilt gothic ruin on road beyond Cathedral; the museum at Colima University is well worth a visit. *Hotel América*, Morelos 162, E, a/c, good restaurant, new (1984), central, friendly; *Ceballos*, Portal Medellín 16, main square, fine building, good value; *Flamingos*, pleasant rooms, Av. Rey Colimán 18, near Jardín Núñez, E; another *Flamingos*, near Jardín Torres Quintero, not very clean, F; *Núñez*, Jardín Núñez, basic, dark, F with bath; *San Cristóbal*, near centre, run down, F. Many *casas de huéspedes* near Jardín Núñez. *Motel Costeño* on outskirts is recommended. *Hotel Madero*, basic F, may not have water. Nice, cheap restaurant *La Fuente* in centre. Good tourist office on Hidalgo near Jardín Torres Quintero but no info. on climbing local volcanoes. Public swimming pool in park on Calle Degollado. Airport. Grand views of Colima volcano (3,842 metres), one of the most exciting climbs in Mexico, which erupted with great loss of life in 1941, and of El Nevado (4,339 metres). They can be climbed from Ciudad Guzmán (formerly Zapotlán), by taking a bus to the village of Fresnito. Bus, Ciudad Guzmán-Colima, Flecha Amarilla, US$1.40, 2 hrs.; train Colima-Ciudad Guzmán, US$0.55, 2nd class, 3 hrs., daily at 1035. Train Colima-Guadalajara at 0830. Comala is a pretty village near Colima, worth a few hours' visit, bus US$0.10.

Continuing to Mexico City We go round the southern shores of Lake Chapala, and after 154 km. come to Jiquilpan (a road leads off, right, to Manzanillo). There are frescoes by Orozco in the library, which was formerly a church.

The State of Michoacán, where the Tarascan Indians live, is a country of deep woods, fine rivers and great lakes. Climates vary from tropical through temperate to cold according to altitude. Fruit, game, and fish are abundant. It has some of the most attractive towns and villages in the country. The Tarascans are among the more interesting Indians of Mexico; visitors are attracted by their customs, folklore, ways of life, craft skills (pottery, lacquer), music and dance. The dance is of first importance to them; it is usually performed to the music of wooden drum, flute and occasionally, a fiddle. Masks are often worn and since the dance is part of a traditional ritual, it is done intently and seriously. The dances which most impress outsiders are the dance of Los Viejitos (Old Men; at Janitzio, January 1); Los Sembradores (The Sowers; February 2); Los Moros (The Moors; Lake

Pátzcuaro region, *fiestas* and carnival); Los Negritos (Black Men; *fiestas* at Tzintzuntzán); Los Apaches (February 4, at the churches); Las Canacuas (the crown dance; Uruapan, on Corpus Christi). At the weddings of fisherfolk the couple dance inside a fish net. In the local *fandango* the woman has fruits in her hand, the man has a glass of *aguardiente* balanced on his head, and a sword.

Zamora (58 km. beyond Jiquilpan), with 88,000 people, is an agricultural centre founded in 1540. There is an interesting ruined gothic-style church in the centre, and a market on Calle Corregidora by the bus station.

Hotels *Fénix*, near bus station, E, run down but clean, swimming pool, pleasant balconies; *Amelia*, Hidalgo 194, D. **Motel** *Jérico*, C, Km. 3 on La Barca road just N of town, swimming pool, restaurant.

On 40 km. is Carapán, from which a branch road runs 72 km. S through pine woods to **Uruapan** ("Place where flowers are plentiful"), a town of 130,000 set among streams, orchards and waterfalls at 1,610 metres in the Parque Nacional Barranca del Cupatitzio; a little cool at night. The most attractive of its three plazas is the Jardín de los Mártires, with the 16th century church facing it. In the *portales* or at the market can be bought the local lacquered bowls and trays, or the delicate woodwork of the Paracho craftsmen, Patamban green pottery and Capácuaro embroideries. Restored hospital, built by Fray Juan de San Miguel in the 16th century; now a well-arranged ceramics museum. Adjoining the museum is a 16th-century chapel now converted into a craft shop. There is also a church of the same period, and a public park, Eduardo Ruiz, 1 km. from the centre, full of streams and waterfalls at the top of Calle Venustiana with a good handicraft shop at the entrance, selling wooden boxes and bracelets. Walk there or catch a bus at the Zócalo marked "El Parque". Airport.

Festivals In the first week of April the Zócalo is filled with pottery and Indians from all the surrounding villages. Around September 16, in nearby village of San Juan, to celebrate the saving of a Christ from the San Juan church (see below) at the time of the Paricutín eruption. Endless fireworks that week in Uruapan, too.

Hotels *Victoria*, Cupatitzio 13, D, good value, quiet, restaurant and garage; *Hernández*, main square, D, older, noisy; *Mi Solar*, Juan Delgado 10, E; *El Tarasco*, Independencia 2, D, pool, lovely; *Progreso*, 5 de Febrero 17, adequate, some rooms noisy, E; *Oseguera*, main square, F, clean, hot water spasmodic; *Santa Fe*, Constitución 20, F, without bath, adequate, beside open-air food stalls; *Moderno*, by main square and market, F, with bath, dark rooms; *Capri*, by market, friendly, F. *Concordia* on main square has nice restaurant, C; *México*, in main square, F; *Casa de las Maravillas*, very pretty and clean, E, with shower, no hot water until 0700; *Cairo*, Calle Pino Suárez 28, F; *Económico*, F, 3 blocks from Zócalo, Calle N. Bravo 25; *Posada Uruapan*, F, share bath, very clean, daily change of sheets, friendly, Calle 16 de Septiembre 43; *Casa de Huéspedes Guadalajara*, Av. Independencia 42. **Motels** *Mansión del Cupatitzio*, on the road to Guadalajara, nice; *Paraíso*, D, entrance from Pátzcuaro; *Pie de la Sierra*, D, good moderately-priced restaurant; *Paricutín*, Juárez 295, F, well-maintained. *Las Cabañas*, near the bus terminal, clean, F, local bus until 2200.

Restaurants One with English menu near bus station at back of church, reasonably priced; *Oriental*, on the Plaza, near *Hotel Moderno*, reasonable and clean. Locals eat at open-air food stalls under one roof at back of church, very picturesque; *Typ's*, Madero 16, is quite good, but expensive; recommended is *La Estrella*, near the square. *La Palma* behind Cathedral, good and cheap, student clientèle. For some of the best *tostadas* in Mexico go to *La Carmelina*, next door to Farmacia Lister on Calle García Ortiz, between the main square and Odeon cinema, excellent value. Local speciality, dried meat, *cecina*.

Laundry at Emilio Carranza 51.

Tourist Office in main square, in courtyard of a *juguería* (address please), good map.

Train Two daily to Mexico City: *rápido* at 0635 and Pullman at 1915, US$4.90 special 1st, US$4 1st, US$2.40 2nd class. First class tickets from *Hotel Victoria*.

Bus Travellers have recommended ADO and other companies in preference to Flecha Amarilla, whose security and safety are said to be poor. Bus station on the NE edge of town, necessary to get a city bus (US$0.07) into town, finishing at about 2100, or a taxi to the Plaza, US$0.90. To Mexico City, 9¼ hrs., 2nd class, Flecha Amarilla via Toluca leaves 0845 and then every hr., US$6.10, many stops; 1st class less frequent but quicker, US$7.50. Omnibus de México has night buses and Tres Estrellas morning departures. To Morelia, 2nd class (Flecha Amarilla) US$1.60 (2½ hrs.), nice ride. To Colima with Flecha Amarilla US$3.30, 5 hrs. and to Los Reyes, US$0.90,

904 MEXICO

1¼ hrs. with same company. To Zihuatanejo (Galeana or Occidente) 2nd class, several a day along winding, intermittently wooded road, which turns off just before Playa Azul (pop. 6,000) at La Mira (pop. 12,500) from where there are frequent local buses. Fare Uruapan-La Mira US$3.20 (6 hrs.). Local bus from La Mira to Lázaro Cárdenas on the River Balsas and from there frequent buses to Zihuatanejo (see page 950). The ride along the coast is rather uninteresting. Also direct buses to Zihuatanejo every hour, US$6.45 1st class, 8 hrs., rather hot and hot. Bus to Guadalajara, several companies, US$3, 2nd class, 6 hrs. Bus to Pátzcuaro, Flecha Amarilla every hour, US$ 1.05, 45 mins; also with Galeana.

Excursions Through coffee groves and orchards along the Cupatitzio (meaning Singing River) to the Zararacua Falls; restaurateurs at bus stop where you can hire a horse for US$2 to the falls. Good camping some 300 metres below the village under the shelter on the top of a rim, with a view down into the valley to the waterfall (1 km. away) and a small lake. A bus (marked Zararacua) will take you from the Zócalo at Uruapan to Zararacua, US$0.30, about every 40 mins. Beautiful rose gardens at Pie de Serrán on road W out of town.

To the volcano of **Paricutín**, 64 km.; it started erupting in the field of a startled peasant on February 20, 1943, became fiery and violent and rose to a height of 1,200 metres above the 2,100-metre-high region, and then died down after several years into a quiet grey mountain surrounded by a sea of cold lava. The church spires of San Juan, a buried Indian village, thrusting up through cold lava is a fantastic sight. Paricutín is best reached by taking a bus over rough track to Angahuán, US$0.65 return, 1½ hrs., 9 a day each way (check as sometimes they don't run) with Galeana; then hire a mule. (Cars suitable for rough terrain can, we are told, also get there.) Sr. José Gómez in Angahuán has mules for hire, but he is expensive; Sr. Juan Rivera and Sr. Francisco Lázaro are recommended, but there are a host of other guides (it is definitely worthwhile to have a guide—essential for the volcano). Up to US$3 per mule, US$1 for a guide—bargain—to San Juan, about 3 hours' journey there and back past a Tarascan village, and if you include also Paricutín the price is US$6.75 in total. Distance Angahuán-San Juan ruins, 3 km., an easy walk: go from the bus stop on the main road, then take right-hand road (with your back to the church) from the plaza, which will lead you to the new hostel, F, from where you can see the buried church. To the peak of the volcano is 12-13 km. Wear good walking shoes with thick soles as the lava is very rough and as sharp as glass; bear in mind the altitude too, as the return is uphill. There are no hotels at Angahuán, although one is under construction. Chris Kerfoot writes: One can continue on to the volcano itself; it takes about 7 hrs. there and back and costs from US$9 each. The cone itself is rather small and to reach it, there is a stiff 30 min. climb from the base. A path goes around the tip of the crater, where activity has ceased. Take something to drink because it is pretty hot and dusty out on the plains. Best to leave Uruapan by 0800 so that you don't have to rush. Take sweater for evening. Last bus back to Uruapan at 1900 (but don't rely on it).

Past Angahuán and Peribán, after the volcano, over a terrible road is the little town of **Los Reyes**; good swim above the electricity generating plant in clear streams (take care not to get sucked down the feed pipe!). Hotels: *Arias* behind Cathedral, E, best, clean, friendly; *Fénix*, clean, between bus station and plaza; *Villa Rica*, F (hot water a.m. only) opp. side to *Fénix* just off plaza, not recommended; *Casa de Huéspedes*, clean, basic, F, lovely courtyard, a little further along the same road as *Villa Rica*, F, often no water; *Plaza*, not as good as *Arias* but nice, clean, E, on street facing Cathedral; *Oasis*, with pool, Av. Morelos 229, good. Restaurant: *La Fogata*, in main square. Buses from Uruapan to Los Reyes go via Angahuán (so same frequency as above). Bus to Los Reyes from Guadalajara with Ciénaga de Chapala 4 a day, 14 hrs., US$2.80 2nd class. Train Guadalajara-Mexico City connects at Yurécuato for Los Reyes, almost no wait, beautiful ride up fertile valley. Bus to Tijuana with Tres Estrellas de Oro at 1800. Bus from Los Reyes, on Av. 5 de Mayo, to Angahuán, US$0.55, 1½-2 hrs.

Paracho, reached by bus from Pátzcuaro, is a quaint, very traditional Indian village of small wooden houses; in every other one craftsmen make guitars worth from US$10 to 1,000 according to the wood used. The town is virtually traffic free. Try local pancakes.

(Km. 400) Zacapu, 22,000 people. See Franciscan church (1548). (Km. 357) **Quiroga,** where a road turns off right for Pátzcuaro, heart of the Tarascan Indian country. The town is named after Bishop Vasco de Quiroga, who was responsible for most of the Spanish building in the area and for teaching the Indians the various crafts they still practise: work in wool, leather, copper, ceramics and canework; many Indians, few tourists. Fair and craft exhibitions in December. Good place to buy cheap leather jackets—most shops in town sell them.

Hotels (all on outskirts) *Posada de Vasco, Motel los Nogales, Hostal Residencia Mesón, Motel San Felipe, Motel Apo Pau, Fonda del Sol, San Diego,* F.

We pass through **Tzintzuntzán,** also touristy, the pre-conquest Tarascan capital; the fascinating ruins just above the town have almost been restored. In Calle Magdalena is a monastery built in 1533 but closed over 250 years ago,

MEXICO 905

which has been restored, but its frescoes have deteriorated badly. The bells of its church, now burnt down, date from the 16th century; a guard will show you round the monastery. A most interesting Passion play is given at Tzintzuntzán. Beautiful and extensive display of hand-painted pottery, very cheap but also brittle. (It is available in other markets in Mexico.) Good bargaining opportunities.

Pátzcuaro is 312 km. from Guadalajara and 23 km. from Quiroga; altitude 2,110 metres; population 24,300, one of the most picturesque small towns in Mexico, with narrow cobbled streets and deep overhanging eaves. It is built on Lake Pátzcuaro, about 50 km. in circumference, with Tarascan Indian villages on its shores and many islands. The Indians used to come by huge dugout canoes (but now seem to prefer the ferry) for the market, held in the main plaza, shaded by great trees. There is an interesting *fiesta* on December 12 for the Virgin of Guadalupe; on October 12, when Columbus discovered America, there is also a procession with the Virgin and lots of fireworks. There are several interesting buildings: the unfinished La Colegiata (1603), known locally as La Basílica, with its much venerated Virgin fashioned by an Indian from a paste made with cornstalk pith and said to have been found floating in a canoe (behind the Basílica there are remains of the precolumbian town and of a pyramid in the precincts of the Museum of Popular Art); the restored Jesuit church of La Compañía (and, almost opposite, the early 17th-century church of the Sagrario) at the top of Calle Portugal; behind this street are two more ecclesiastical buildings: the Colegio Teresiano and the restored Templo del Santuario; on Calle Lerín is the ancient monastery, with a series of small patios. (Murals by Juan O'Gorman in the Library, formerly San Agustín.) On Calle Allende is the residence of the first Governor. On Calle Terán is the church of San Francisco; nearby is San Juan de Dios, on the corner of Calle Romero. Visit also the Plaza Vasco de Quiroga. Fifteen minutes' walk outside the town is the chapel of El Calvario, on the summit of Cerro del Calvario, a hill giving wide views; good views also from the old chapel of the Humilladero, above the cemetery on the old road to Morelia. The very well arranged Museum of Popular Art is in the Colegio de San Nicolás (1540) entrance US$0.40, English speaking, friendly guide: ask there for the Casa de los Once Patios, which contains the local tourist office and boutiques selling handicrafts. See also the attractive Jardín de la Revolución and, nearby, the old church of the Hospitalito in Calle Codallos. Excellent Fri. and also Sat. markets, often much cheaper than shops. Some stalls open daily on the main square, selling handicrafts, and there is a friendly handicraft shop on the road down to the lake, Vicky's, with very funny toys. There is a free medical clinic, English-speaking, on the outskirts of Pátzcuaro.

Fiestas Nov. 1-2: Día de los Muertos (All Souls' Day), ceremony at midnight, Nov. 1, on Janitzio island, but mostly a tourist event, heavily commercialized; Dec. 6-9, Virgen de la Salud, when authentic Tarascan dances are performed in front of the *basílica*. Carnival in February when the Dance of the Moors is done.

Hotels *Posada de don Vasco*, attractive, colonial-style hotel on Av. de las Américas (halfway between lake and town) presents the Dance of the Old Men on Wed. and Sat. at 2100, no charge, non-residents welcome but drinks very expensive to compensate, and then the men come round for money. Also mariachi band. *Las Redes*, Av. Américas 6, D, near lake, popular restaurant; *Posada La Basílica*, Arciga 6, E, nice restaurant with good views, and *Mesón del Gallo*, Dr. J. M. Coss 20, D, both central; *Mesón del Cortijo*, Obregón, just off Américas, D, recommended, but often fully booked at weekends. *Los Escudos*, Portal Hidalgo 74, E, colonial style, good restaurant; *Posada San Rafael*, Plaza Vasco de Quiroga, E, clean, safe, very nice, restaurant, parking in courtyard; *Gran Hotel*, Portal Regules 6, on Plaza Bocanegra, small rooms, good restaurant, E; *Mansión Iturbe*, Portal Morelos 59, restored mansion on main square, E, good food; *Misión San Manuel*, Portal Aldama 12 on main square, restaurant, highly recommended, E; *San Agustín*, above restaurant, F, with shower and toilet, not very clean; these are all central. *Posada Lagos*, Zaragoza 14, F, clean; *Posada de la Salud*, Benigno Serrato, clean, quiet, pleasant, excellent value, some rooms with individual fireplaces, F; *Valmen*, Lloredo 34, F, with bath, charming colonial building but noisy. *Pito Pérez*, on the second main plaza, F, without bath, shower facilities inadequate. *El Artillero*, nice, clean, with hot water, F, with bath, friendly, near Zócalo, Ibarra 22. *Posada de la Rosa*, Portal Juárez 29, F, hot water a.m. only, noisy electronic games downstairs; next door is

906 MEXICO

Concordia, F. There are many *hospedajes* and hotels near the bus station. **Motels** *Chalamu*, Pátzcuaro road Km. 20, trailer park too, C; *San Felipe*, Cárdenas 321, D, trailers; *San Carlos*. Muelle Col. Morelos, E; *Pátzcuaro*, Cárdenas 506, bathrooms but no showers, F, not recommended.

Camping Camping and caravan site at *Motel Pátzcuaro*, spotless, lush green grass, flowering trees, showers with hot water, toilets, tennis court and pool, cheap.

Restaurants *El Patio*, on main square, clean, friendly, try *pescado blanco* (white fish), regional dish, it tends to be expensive. *El Cayuco Café Cantante*, French owner, music Sat. and Sun., open 1600-2300. *Mansión Iturbe*, Portal Morelos 59, good, cheap, delicious coffee. Pizzas from *pizzería* on Plaza Vasco de Quiroga. Make sure you don't get overcharged in restaurants—some display menus outside which bear no resemblance to the prices inside. *Gran Hotel*, filling *comida corrida*; good chicken and *enchiladas* over the market. Several interesting eating places by the jetty for Janitzio.

Tourist Office Casa de las Once Patios, off Plaza Vasco de Quiroga.

Transport New bus station out of town. To Mexico City, Tres Estrellas de Oro and Autobuses de Occidente— ADO (which also runs once a day from Pátzcuaro to Guadalajara), 1st (US$8.50) and 2nd class buses. Very enjoyable and cheaper, though slower, train ride around lake and plateau to Mexico City. Train leaves daily at 0655, from Mexico City to Pátzcuaro, arrives at 1920, beautiful views between Uruapan and Acámbaro (*fiesta*, July 4), 1st class US$4. Train to Mexico City at 0905 (*rápido*) and 2145 (Pullman). Take pullover. Trains to Uruapan: 0756, pullman; 1856, *rápido*; 1222, *normal* (slow, 2½ hrs., US$0.40 1st class).

Regular bus service to Morelia, 1 hr., US$1 with ADO and Flecha Amarilla (latter departs every ½ hr.). Buses to Guadalajara go through Zamora, with Occidental US$6.75 1st class (beware of the bus drivers if you're the only—and female— passenger) 6 hrs.; no trains to Guadalajara. Local buses from corner of market in town to lakeside.

Excursion Pátzcuaro-Ario de Rosales-Nueva Italia-Uruapan-Pátzcuaro takes about 6 hrs., beautiful tropical countryside. An excursion can be made into the hills to the village of Santa Clara del Cobre (fine old church), where all the hand-wrought copper vessels are made. (*Fiesta*: August 12-15.) Nearby is the pretty Lake Zirahuen. Past Santa Clara, on the La Huacana road, after Ario de Rosales, one descends into the tropics; fine views all along this road, which ends at Churumuco. From Pátzcuaro one can also visit Tzintzuntzán (see page 904) and Quiroga by regular bus service.

Bus to lake (marked Lago) from corner of market. The best-known island is **Janitzio**, although it has become overrun by tourists and filled with cheap souvenir shops and beggars, which has made its local people hostile and the place lose its charm (45 mins. by motorboat, US$0.75, tickets from dock, including fisherman's show, most picturesque, but an unfortunate monument to Morelos crowning a hill). Winter is the best time for fishing in the somewhat fish-depleted lake, where Indians throw nets shaped like dragonflies. White fish from the lake was a delicacy, but the lake is now polluted, so beware (still plenty of places sell white fish). The Government is planning to improve the lake. On a lakeside estate is the Educational Centre for Community Development in Latin America, better known as Crefal (free films every Wed. at 1930). For a truly spectacular view of the lake, the islands and the surrounding countryside, walk to Cerro del Estribo; an ideal site for a quiet picnic. It is 1½ hrs. walk to the top from the centre of Pátzcuaro. Follow the cobbled road beyond El Calvario, don't take either of the 2 dirt tracks off to the left. Cars go up in the afternoon, the best time for walking. No buses, 417 steps to the peak.

(Km. 314) **Morelia**, capital of Michoacán state, population 280,000, altitude 1,882 metres, is a rose-tinted city with attractive colonial buildings (their courtyards are their main feature), rather quiet, founded in 1541. The Cathedral (1640), set between the two main plazas, with graceful towers and a fine façade, is the only large church in Mexico in the plateresque style; there are paintings by Juárez in the sacristy. Other important churches are the Virgin of Guadalupe (also known as San Diego) with a most ornate Pueblan interior, the modernized Iglesia de la Cruz, and the churches in the charming small Plaza de las Rosas and Plaza del Carmen. The oldest of Morelia's churches is the San Francisco. Even more interesting than its five colonial churches are the many beautiful colonial houses still standing. The revolutionary Morelos, Melchior Ocampo, and the two unfortunate Emperors of Mexico (Agustín de Iturbide and the Archduke Maximilian of Austria) are commemorated by plaques on their houses. The Colegio de San Nicolás (1540) is the oldest surviving institution of higher education in Latin America. (It has a summer school for foreign students.) The fine former Jesuit college, now called the Palacio Clavijero, is the town hall, with a helpful tourist office on the ground floor (corner of Madero Poniente y Nigromante). Also notable are the law school, in the former monastery of San Diego, next to the Guadalupe church; the Palacio de Gobierno (1732-70), facing the Cathedral; the Palacio Municipal; and the Palacio Federal. Visit also the churches of La Merced, with its lovely tower, and Santa María, on a hilltop S of the city. Thursday and Sunday are market days: specialities are pottery, lacquer, woodcarving, jewellery, blankets, leather sandals; in this connection see the Casa de Artesanías de Michoacán, in the former convent of San Francisco, next to the church of the same name; it is full of fine regional products for sale, not cheap. Shops close early. Food and drink specialities in the plaza in front of San Agustín: fruit jams (*ates*), candies, and *rompope* (a milk and egg-nog). Free weekly concerts are held in the municipal theatre. On the outskirts, on the road to Mexico City, are the 224 arches of a ruined aqueduct, built in 1788 (walk 11 blocks W from Cathedral along Av. Madero). Visit the Museo de Michoacán and the new Casa de la Cultura, Av. Morelos Norte, housed in the ex-Convento del Carmen, which has a good collection of local masks, crucifixes and archaeological remains. The Museo de Estado has been opened in the house of Iturbide's wife (Casa de la Emperatriz), SE corner of Jardín de las Rosas. Many good language schools. Fairly good zoo in Parque Juárez, S of the centre (25 mins. walk S along Galeana). Planetarium. Airport with daily flights to Mexico City.

Hotels Some of the cheaper hotels may have water only in the morning; check. *Virrey de Mendoza*, Portal Matamoros, C, superb old-style building, poor restaurant, service could be better, could be cleaner, ask for room at front with balcony. Off the Plaza de Armas and much quieter is the *Posada de la Soledad*, Zaragoza and Ocampo, fine courtyards, converted chapel as dining room, D, good value; *Catedral*, Zaragoza 37, close to Plaza, spacious, D, recommended; *Presidente*, Aquiles Serdán 647, C, often lacks water, not well run; *Calzada*, Fray Antonio de San Miguel 173, E; *Posada Familiar*, Morelos Norte 340, dark, stuffy rooms, F; *Alameda*, main square, D; *Casino*, main square, E, clean, hot water, private bath; *Florida*, Morelos 161, D; *Concordia*, Farias 328, E; *Orozco*, Madero Poniente 507, central, clean, shower, E; *Posada San José*, Av. Obregón 226 beside Templo de San José, F, rooms like cells, clean; *Posada Morelia*, F, with bath, dirty, Santiago de Tapiá 31. *Posada La Muralla*, León Guzmán 50, F, a bit shabby, with bath. *Señorial*, basic, F, Santiago Tapiá 543, being improved; *Casa de Huéspedes Margarita*, Antonio Alzate 53, and another next door at 51; *Carmen*, F, good value, overlooks the Casa de la Cultura, no hot water. Cheap hotels on Morelos Norte: *Colonial*, corner with 20 de Noviembre 15; *Casa de Huéspedes Lourdes*, Morelos Norte 340, 5 blocks E of bus station. Hotel (no name) on Eduardo Ruiz 298, 2 mins. from bus station. *Gran Hotel*, 1 block from bus station, very basic, not very clean, F. *Calinda Quality Inn*, C, Av. Acueducto, colonial-style, modern. On Santa María hill, S of the city, with glorious views, are hotels *Villa Montaña* (each room a house on its own, run by French aristocrats, very expensive but value for money), *Vista Bella* and *Villa San José* next door and much cheaper, reached only by car. CREA youth hostel at corner of Oaxaca and Chiapas, 1 km. SW of bus station (walk W to Calle Cuautla, then S along Cuautla to Oaxaca) F, p.p. Camping possible in a forest about 4 km. S of centre on unnumbered Pátzcuaro-signposted road. **Motels** *Villa Centurión*, Morelos road, good antiques, pool, TV; *Las Palmas*, Guadalajara road, also trailer park, F; *El Parador*, Highway 45, with trailer park, F.

Restaurants Superb food at the *Villa Montaña* hotel. *La Huacana*, García Obeso behind cathedral, regional, pleasant, *mariachis*; *Fonda de Cachamay*, Santiago Tapiá y Zaragoza, friendly and interesting; *Rey Sol*, recommended by locals; Restaurant of low Woolworth's is in a 17th-century episcopal chapel. *Rincón de Tarasco*, good. *Govinda*, vegetarian, Av. Morelos Sur 39, opp. cathedral, delicious meal for US$1.20. *Comidas corridas* at the *Paraíso*, Madero Poniente 103 facing the cathedral, and at *Café El Viejo*, Madero Oriente and Quiroga, US$1. Down Calle León Guzmán opposite the church of La Merced there is, on the right, a market for local sweets and egg-nog. *Café y Arte*, round corner from Hotel Catedral, coffee and drinks, good atmosphere.

Tourist Office Nigromante 79, helpful, has local hotel information list and map, open 0900-2000. Also kiosk at bus terminal.

Rail Morelia-Mexico City at 2311, US$2.35 2nd class, US$3.90 1st, train starts at Uruapan.

Bus Terminal on Eduardo Ruiz, between Guzmán and Farias, has luggage office and tourist kiosk; 3 blocks W of plaza, then 3 W. Many buses to Guanajuato, 6 hrs., US$2.20. Guadalajara, US$4. Uruapan, US$1.60 2nd class; Irapuato, US$1.80 2nd class, rough ride. Mexico City, 2nd class every hour or ADO, every 20 mins., 6½ hrs., US$4.60. Bus Morelia-Acapulco US$14, 15 hrs. Bus to Pátzcuaro every ½ hr., 1½ hrs., US$1. Also about 15 a day to Zihuatanejo on the coast, US$5.50.

Diversion Just after Morelia there is a good road to two villages on beautiful Lake Cuitzeo, the second largest in Mexico. At *Cuitzeo*, the first one (hotel, *Restaurant Esteban*, by post office), there is a fine Augustinian church and convent, a cloister, a huge open chapel, and good choir

908 MEXICO

stalls in the sacristy. From here one can go to Valle de Santiago (*Hotel Posada de la Parroquia*, E), attractive mountain scenery. The second village, 23 km. to the N, **Yuriria**, has a large-scale Indian version of the splendid church and convent at Actopán (see page 873). The road continues to Salamanca (hotel, appalling traffic), where one turns left for Irapuato or right for Celaya and Querétaro. Near Morelia is Zinapécuaro, and near this is the large swimming pool of San Miguel Taimeo. Beyond Zinapécuaro is Acámbaro, and between there and Toluca is the old mining town of **Tlalpujahua** with a museum, several churches, and cobblestoned streets, very picturesque among forests and hills. (*Casa de Huéspedes*.)

The road soon climbs through 50 km. of splendid mountain scenery; forests, waterfalls, and gorges, to the highest point at (km. 244) Mil Cumbres (2,886 metres), with a magnificent view over mountain and valley, and then descends into a tropical valley. Between Morelia and Ciudad Hidalgo is Queréndaro, where the pavements are covered in *chiles* drying in the blazing sun, and all the shops are filled with large bags of *chiles* in the season. Worth a glance with the façade of the 16th century church at **Ciudad Hidalgo** (km. 212)—*Hotel Fuerte*, F, some rooms have no keys, clean, showers, no water in the afternoon; *Restaurant Manolo*, inexpensive, good; and the old colonial bridge and church at **Tuxpan** (km. 193—a few expensive hotels parallel to the river; *Hotel Colón*, reasonable, fan, F, not very quiet, friendly management, can store luggage; *Hotel Florida*, F, damp rooms, garage US$0.50 a night). At km. 183 a side road runs, right, to the spa of *San José Purúa* at 1,800 metres, in a wild setting of mountain and gorge and woods. The radioactive thermal waters are strong. First-class hotel. Smaller, cheaper hotels lie on the road past the spa and in the town of Jungapeo.

(Km. 86) A branch road, right, goes to the mountain resort of **Valle de Bravo**, a charming old town on the edge of an attractive artificial lake. This area gets the week-end crowd from Mexico City.

Hotels *Montiel*, central, pool, restaurant, satisfactory, Independencia 404; *Hotel del Lago*; *Refugio del Salto*; *Los Arcos* (expensive but good) is several km. beyond, in pine woods, excellent restaurant. **Motels** *Avándaro*, Fraccionamiento Avándaro, D, pleasant.

If you want to avoid the Mil Cumbres pass go via Maravatio from Morelia. The road is at first flat then climbs and descends again to Maravatio (hotel) and then climbs steeply, towards Tlalpujahua (see above). Road climbs steeply and then descends to Atlacomulco. There are plenty of places to stop at on the way to Toluca.

(Km. 75) A road branches off to the volcano of Toluca (Nevado de Toluca; 4,583 metres, the fourth highest mountain in Mexico) and climbs to the deep blue lakes of the Sun and the Moon in its two craters, at about 4,270 metres, from which there is a wide and awe-inspiring view. During winter it is possible to ski on the slopes; 5 km. from the entrance is an *Albergue* (US$1) with food and cooking facilities. From here it is 10 km. to the entrance to the crater, where there is a smaller *albergue* (cooking facilities but no food, US$1.50). Trips to the volcano are very popular at weekends; no problem getting a lift to the lakes. If walking remember the entrance to the crater is on the far left side of the volcano. This route, the Mil Cumbres route, is by far the most difficult. There are two other routes between Morelia and Toluca and they all join together or are connected at some point.

(Km. 64) **Toluca**, population 220,200, altitude 2,639 metres, about 4¾ hrs. from Morelia by bus, is the capital of the state of México. It is known mostly for its vivid Friday market—reportedly less colourful than it used to be— where tourist-conscious Indians sell colourful woven baskets, *sarapes, rebozos*, pottery and embroidered goods (beware of pickpockets and handbag slashers). See churches of Tercer Orden and Vera Cruz, convent of Carmen and chapel of S. María de Guadalupe, the new Cathedral, the Palacio de Gobierno, the Museo de Bellas Artes, the botanical garden, called the Cosmo Vitral because of its unique stained-glass decor, Chamber of Deputies, all in centre of city near or on the Zócalo. Also Museo de Arte Popular and Casa de las Artesanías, with excellent display of local artistic products for sale, at corner of Paseo Chamizal and Paseo Tollocán. The new Market is at Calle Manuel Gómez Pedraza Oriente, open daily, big day is Friday. Famous for textiles.

MEXICO 909

Hotels *San Carlos*, Madero 210, D, remodelled; *La Mansión*, E, with bath, simple; *Morelia*, Hidalgo 615, F without bath, noisy; *Rex*, Matamoros 101, E; *Bravo*, Bravo 105, F, near old bus terminal in centre; *Hidalgo*, Hidalgo 615, F, without private bath, noisy; *Azteca*, Pino Suárez and Hidalgo, F; all the above are in the centre, not many cheap hotels. *Terminal*, adjoining bus terminal, E. **Motels** *Del Rey Inn*, Mexico City road entrance, C, resort facilities.

Tourist Office In the *portales* behind the Cathedral, on the Zócalo, helpful.

Bus To Mexico City, US$0.65. Bus to Pátzcuaro, 6 hrs., US$3.10, several daily. Many buses to Tenango de Arista (US$0.25, ½ hrs.), Tenancingo (US$1); also regular buses to Calixtlahuaca US$1.50 (1 hr.) from platform 7. Bus station away from centre.

Excursions A side road runs S of Toluca. Along the road, or reached from it, are a number of most interesting "art and craft" producing villages, all with old churches. The first village is **Metepec**, the pottery-making centre of the valley, 1½ km. off the road to Tenango. The clay figurines made here—painted bright fuchsia, purple, green and gold—are unique. This is the source of the "trees of life and death", the gaudily-painted pottery sold in Mexico. Market is on Mon. Interesting convent. Also off the main highway near Tenango, turning right at La Marquesa, you will come to a sign pointing to Gualupita to the right; just beyond that is the village of **Santiago Tianpuistengo**. Lovely *cazuelas*, *metates*, baskets and *sarapes*. Between July and early November displays of wild mushrooms for sale. Try *gordas* or *tlacoyos*, blue corn stuffed with a broad bean paste. If you are brave try *atepocates*; embryo frogs with tomato, *chile*, boiled in maize leaves. Try restaurant *Mesón del Cid*, good regional food, go to kitchen to see choice. Try *sopa de hongos*, mushroom soup. Market day is Tuesday. The town is crowded at weekends.

The main road descends gradually to **Tenango de Arista** (Toluca-Tenango bus, US$0.25), where one can walk (20 mins.) to the ruins of **Teotenango** (Matlazinca culture, reminiscent of La Ciudadela at Teotihuacán, with 11 ball courts). There is an interesting museum covering Teotenango (entry to museum and ruins US$0.45; to enter go to the end of town on the right hand side. Restaurant in Tenango: *María Isabel*, cheap, good local food). 48 km. from Toluca the road descends abruptly through gorges to **Tenancingo**, still at 1,830 metres, but with a soft, warm all-the-year-round climate. Nearby is the magnificent 18th century Carmelite convent of El Santo Desierto, making beautiful *rebozos*. The townspeople themselves weave fine *rebozos* and the fruit wines are delicious and cheap. Market day is Sun. Recommended hotels at Tenancingo are *Lazo*, with clean rooms in annex with shower, E, and *San Carlos*, F, good value. *Hotel Casa Juana* on main plaza, F, good value. There is a small waterfall near the bus station.

About 11 km. to the E over an improved road is **Malinalco**, from which a path winds up 1 km. to Malinalco ruins (Matlazinca culture, with Aztec additions), certainly one of the most remarkable pre-Hispanic ruins in Mexico, now partly excavated. Here, after a substantial climb, is a fantastic rock-cut temple in the side of a mountain which conceals in its interior sculptures of eagle and jaguar effigies. Visit also the Augustinian convent to see the early frescoes. There is a *fiesta* in Malinalco on January 6. (Camping. Two hotels, one expensive, one cheap. Ester at Ferretería La Provincia in Malinalco arranges accommodation, F, p.p. Swiss-run, open-air restaurant serves local trout, about US$2.50, superb, bring own supplies of beverages, bread, salad.) (Buses Tenancingo-Malinalco, take about 1 hr. and are not cheap). You can get to Malinalco from Mexico City by taking a 2nd class bus to Chalma (see below), which takes about 2 hrs. and costs US$0.95— Malinalco is the next village along and can be reached by shared taxi for US$0.25 p.p. (Terminal in Mexico City, Central de Buses Oeste, opp. Observatorio, ½ hr. frequency, at least two companies go there.) You can also go to Malinalco from Toluca by leaving the Toluca-Tenancingo road after San Pedro Zictepec, some distance N of Tenancingo, which is gravel surfaced and 28 km. long. Journey will take 45 mins. By public transport from Toluca, take a bus to **Chalma**, then a shared taxi. Chalma is a popular pilgrimage spot, and is also where you make connections if coming from Cuernavaca (take a Cuernavaca—Toluca bus to Santa Marta, then wait for a Toluca—Chalma bus).

On 32 km. from Tenancingo is **Ixtapan de la Sal**, a pleasant forest-surrounded leisure resort with medicinal hot springs. In the centre of this quiet whitewashed town is the municipal spa, adult admission US$0.30. At the edge of town is Parque Los Trece Lagos. For the hedonist there are private "Roman" baths, for the stiff-limbed a medicinal hot-water pool, mud baths for the vain, an Olympic pool for swimmers, rowing boats and a water slide for the adventurous. The latter is 150 metres long, prohibited to those over 40, US$0.55 for a 30 minute stint, which can lead to plenty of bruises and some nasty clashes with any larger bodies hurtling around. "The Thirteen Lake Park" is privately run and has a train running around; there are numerous picnic spots. Market day: Sun. *Fiesta*: second Fri. in Lent. (*Hotel Ixtapan*, Nuevo Ixtapan, A, food and entertainment included; *Kiss*, C; *Casablanca*, D; *Bungalow Lolita*; *Guadalajara*, F, clean, with bath; plenty of reasonable restaurants on Av. Benito Juárez.) Ixtapan de la Sal can also be reached in 2 hrs. by car from Mexico City on Route 55 (turn left off Toluca highway at La Marquesa). The road goes on to Taxco (see page 946).

From Toluca take bus to pyramids and Aztec seminary of **Calixtlahuaca**, 2 km. off the road to Ixtlahuaca; pyramids are to Quetzalcoatl (circular) and to Tlaloc; they are situated just behind the village, 10 mins. walk from the final bus-stop. Entry US$0.10.

910 MEXICO

The basin of Toluca, the highest in the central region, is the first of a series of basins drained by the Río Lerma into the Pacific. To reach Mexico City from Toluca—64 km. by road—it is necessary to climb over the intervening mountain range. The centre of the basin is swampy. (Km. 50) **Lerma,** a small city, is on the edge of the swamp, the source of the Lerma river. The road climbs, with backward views of the snow-capped Toluca volcano, to the summit at Las Cruces (km. 32; 3,164 metres). There is a good Bavarian restaurant, *La Escondida*, about 100 metres to the left of the Toluca-México road at 38 km., on a beautiful site. There are occasional great panoramic views of the City and the Valley of México during the descent.

Mexico City

Mexico City, the capital, altitude 2,240 metres, is the oldest capital of continental America, built upon the remains of Tenochtitlán, the Aztec capital, covering some 200 square km. The Valley of México, the intermont basin in which it lies, is about 110 km. long by 30 km. wide. Rimming this valley is a sentinel-like chain of peaks of the Sierra Nevada mountains. Towards the SE tower two tall volcanoes, named for the warrior Popocatépetl and his beloved Ixtaccíhuatl, the Aztec princess who died rather than outlive him. Popocatépetl is 5,452 metres high, and Ixtaccíhuatl (Eestaseewatl) 5,286 metres. Both are snow-capped, but you need to get up early in the morning to see them from the city, because of the smog. To the S the crest of the Cordillera is capped by the wooded volcano of Ajusco.

About 14 million people (one in five of the total population) live in this city, which has over half the country's manufacturing employment, pays 82% of all wages, has half the telephones, radios and television sets, 230 cinemas, 30 radio stations, 18,000 taxis, 2,500,000 other vehicles and much of the nation's industrial smog. The last-mentioned makes the eyes of the unaccustomed sore (contact-lens wearers take note).

The city suffers from a fever of demolition and rebuilding, especially since the inflicting of heavy damage by the September 1985 earthquake. Of late years it has burst its ancient boundaries and spread; the new residential suburbs are most imaginatively planned, though some of the outskirts are shabbily blatant. Like all big centres it is faced with a fearsome traffic problem, despite the building of a new inner ring road. The noise can be deafening; Elizabeth Allen tells us that the definition of a split second in Mexico City is the amount of time between the traffic-lights going green and the first horn sounding. To relieve congestion seven underground railway lines are now operating, and are being extended. There is also a large traffic-free area E of the Zócalo.

The 1985 earthquake damage was concentrated along the Paseo de la Reforma, Avenida Juárez, the Alameda, and various suburbs and residential districts. About 20,000 people are believed to have lost their lives, largely in multi-storey housing and government-controlled buildings, including Juárez hospital in which there were about 3,000 fatalities.

Mexico's architecture ranges from Spanish-Baroque to ultra-modern: it is, indeed, fast becoming a city of skyscrapers. The tallest is now the *Hotel de México* in Insurgentes Sur, with a restaurant; US$2.30 just to go up, but the ticket lets you see *son et lumière* in the Siqueiros Polyforum next door (daily exc. Sun., at 1800 in English and 1600 and 1930 in Spanish). The Polyforum includes a handicraft shop, a "museum of the evolution of man", and huge frescoes by Siqueiros, including the largest mural in the world, inside the huge ovoid dome. Entrance for frescoes, US$1.

Key to Map of Mexico City

1. Independence Monument; 2. Institute of Mexican Art; 3. Carranza and Bolívar Monuments; 4. "La Madre" Monument; 5. Cuauhtémoc Monument; 6. National Museum of Anthropology; 7. Tlaloc Monolith; 8. Museum of Modern Art; 9. Castle of Chapultepec; 10. Palacio de Minería, and "El Caballito" (Carlos IV) Monument; 11. Monument to the Revolution; 12. Santo Domingo Church; 13. National School of Plastic Arts; 14. San Fernando Church; 15. San Hipólito Church; 16. Santa Veracruz; 17. Palace of Fine Arts; 18. Viceregal Art Gallery (San Diego); 19. Chinese Clock; 20. Morelos Monument; 21. Latin American Tower and House of Tiles; 22. Aztec Ruins; 23. Hospital of Jesus; 24. Salto del Agua Fountain; 25. Palace of the Counts of Valaparaíso; 26. Monte de Piedad; 27. Church of Tlaxcoaque; 28. College of the Vizcaínas; 29. Cathedral; 30. Iturbide Palace.

MEXICO 911

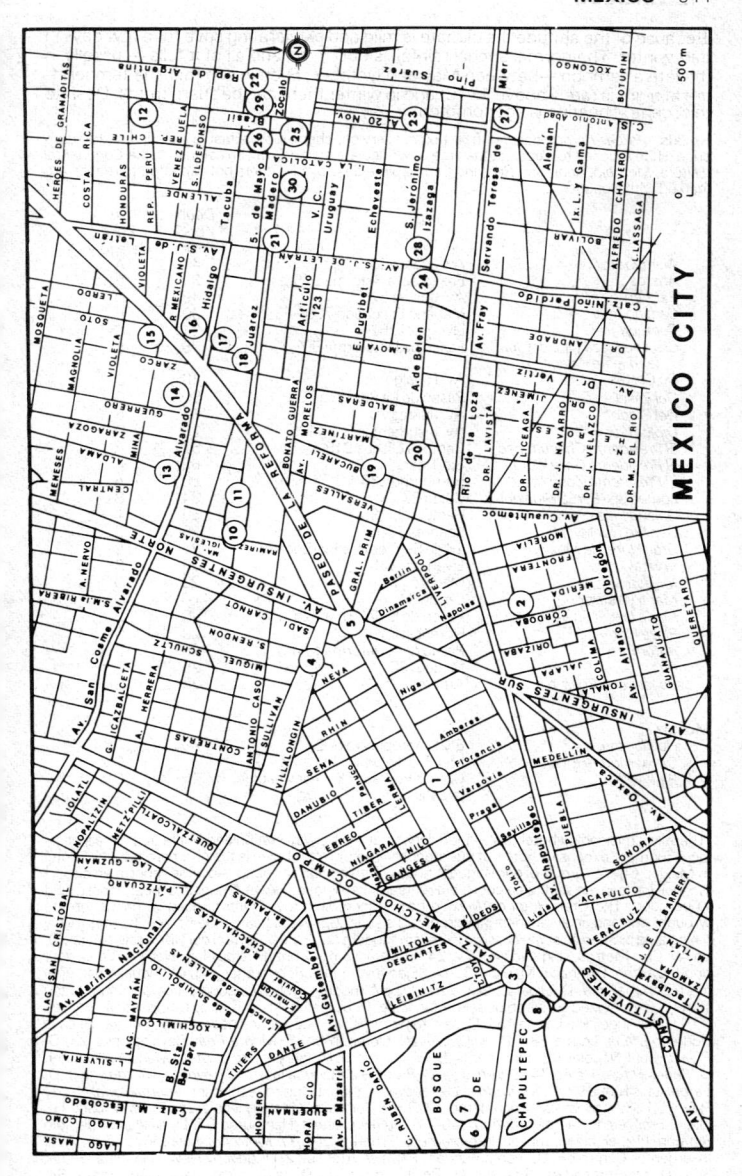

912 MEXICO

Because of the altitude the climate is mild and exhilarating save for a few days in mid-winter. The normal annual rainfall is 660 mm., and all of it falls— usually in the late afternoon—between May and October. Even in summer the temperature at night is rarely above 13°C, and in winter there can be sharp frosts. Despite this, central heating is not common.

Hotels Prices do not include 15 % tax and service; check if breakfast is included in the room price. Hotels closed for repair at the time of writing are marked with an asterisk *; the *Continental* (*Hilton*), *Montejo*, *Regis* and *Romano Centro* were destroyed. Others not expected to reopen are marked with a dagger †.

		Double US$ from	Our Price Category
Alameda†	Av. Juárez 50	47	A
Aristos	Paseo de la Reforma 276	31	B
Barnen	Av. Juárez 52	19	D
Camino Real	Mariano Escobedo 700	90	L
Century	Liverpool 152	24	C
Crowne Plaza (Holiday Inn) (ex-Fiesta Palace)	Paseo de la Reforma 80	78	L
De Cortés	Av. Hidalgo 85	19	D
Del Paseo†	Paseo de La Reforma 208	20	C
Del Prado*	Av. Juárez 70	33	B
Diplomático	Av. Insurgentes Sur 1105	28	D
El Presidente Chapultepec	Campos Elíseos 218	57	A
El Presidente Galerías	Río Tiber	60	A
El Presidente Zona Rosa†	Hamburgo 135	60	A
Fontan (ex-Purúa Hidalgo)	Colón 27	34	B
Galería Plaza	Hamburgo 195	68	A
Genève Quality Inn	Londres 130	28	C
Gran Hotel de México	16 de Septiembre 82 (Zócalo)	36	B
Krystal	Liverpool 155	36	B
Majestic	Madero 73	20	D
María Cristina	Lerma 31	20	D
María Isabel Sheraton	Paseo de la Reforma 325	90	L
Plaza Florencia	Florencia 61	29	C
Reforma	Paseo de la Reforma y París	85	L
Ritz	Madero 30	25	C
Royal Zona Rosa	Amberes 78	25	C

Motels

Holiday Inn	Blvd. Aeropuerto 502	80	A
Dawn Motor Hotel	Mex 57 Highway		C
Park Villa	Gómez Pedraza 68 (near Chapultepec Park)		C

There is a misleading hotel reservation service at the railway station and at the airport; also services for more expensive hotels at bus stations. The *Cortés*, above, is the only baroque-style hotel in Mexico City, a former pilgrims' guest house, with a pleasant patio. Adverse reports on airport *Holiday Inn* (service said to be poor), but restaurant still good. *Fiesta Americana*, near airport, said to be good. The *Gran Hotel de México* has an incredible foyer with birdcages, palms, ornate wrought iron and an all-stained-glass roof, 30's style. *Genève* is being modernized, but has lovely dining area in Spanish style. *Brasilia*, excellent modern hotel, near Central del Norte bus station, D, on Av. Cien Metros, king size bed, TV, 24-hr. traffic jam in front. *Bristol*, Plaza Necaxa 17, D, very good; *Carlton*, E, Ignacio Mariscal 32-bis; *Ejecutivo*, Viena 8, overcharging, earthquake damage, not recommended, D; *Hidalgo*, Sta. Veracruz 37, modern, good, C, good 5-course lunch. In the same street, owned by same people, *Mariscala*, D, by Bellas Artes metro; *Compostela*, Sullivan 35, D; *Del Angel*, Río Lerma 154, D, said to be run down and service poor; *Doral*, Sullivan 9, D; *El Romano Diana*, Lerma 237, D; *Milán*, Alvaro Obregón 94, E; *Monte Real*, Revillagigedo 23, D; *Palacio Real*, Nápoles 62, apartments, D; *Principado*, J. M. Iglesias 55, D; *Stella Maris*, Sullivan 69, D; *Suites Havre*, Havre 74, E; *Versalles*, G. Prim 59 and Versalles, C; *Virreyes*, J. M. Izazaga 8, D; *Estoril*, Luis Moya 93, D; *Metropole*, Luis Moya, C, touristy, good restaurant; *Internacional Havre*, Havre 21, C; *Lisboa*, Av. Cuauhtémoc 273, C; *Del Valle*, Independencia 35, D, with bath; TV, clean; *Francés*, Paseo de la Reforma 64, E; *Suites Orleans*, Hamburgo 67, D; *Mallorca*, Serapio Rendón 119, D, clean, reasonable; *Marbella*, Frontera 205, D; *Metropol*, Luis Moya 39, E; *Pisa*, Insurgentes Centro 58, D, recommended; *Premier*, Atenas 72, D; *Beverly New York*, Nueva York 301, D, recommended; *Guadalupe*†, Revillagigedo 36, D, fairly good; *Jardín Amazonas*, Río

Amazonas 73, D; *Regente*, París 9, D, clean, friendly, noisy at front, restaurant; *Vista Hermosa*, Insurgentes y Sullivan, damp, decaying, F; *La Riviera*, Aldama 9, E, with shower, TV and restaurant; *Royal Plaza*, Baja California y Medellín, E; *Viena*, Marsella 28, D. Recommended: *Cónsul*, on Insurgentes Sur, Tel.: 546-93-70, E; and *El Greco*, San Antonio 22, Colonia Nápoles, D. Cheaper hotels are clustered together N of the Plaza República and can also be found in the oldest part of the city near the Zócalo. Reasonable hotels we can recommend are: *Paraíso*, Ignacio Mariscal 99, E; *Ensenada*, Alvaro Obregón, D; *Polanco*, Edgar Poe 8, near Chapultepec, dark, quiet, D, good restaurant; *Emporio*, Paseo de la Reforma 124, C, recommended, good service, clean rooms, good restaurant; *Fleming*, on Revillagigedo, C, sometimes noisy; on the same street, *Alffer Century*†, extremely noisy because of adjacent car park and club, C; *Sevilla*, Serapio Rendón and Sullivan, D, restaurant, garage, reasonable; *Iberia*, Mina 186 and Zaragoza, E, with private bath, recommended, sheets changed every other day, good for buses and trains; *Nueva Estación*, Zaragoza 114, E, with bath; *Detroit*, Zaragoza 55, D, has parking; *Savoy*, Zaragoza, F with shower, clean, good value; *Mayaland*, Maestro Antonio Caso 23, E, with bath, good value; *Alvarado*, next to metro Revolución, F; *Fornos*, Revillagigedo 92 (renovated), E, with bath and phone. *Monte Carlo*, Uruguay 69 (D. H. Lawrence's hotel), clean, friendly, F, with bath; good about storing luggage, bit noisy at front; car park inside the hotel premises—small fee; cooking facilities. *Moneda*, Moneda 8, just off Zócalo, good value, E, with bath, stay in rooms on street and not too close to TV lounge; *Yale*, Mosqueta 200 (near main railway station), F, recommended; or *Suiza*, Aldama 99 in Guerrero district, near Delegación de Cuauhtémoc (near bus and railway stations), F, shower, recommended, except for noise; *Pontevedra*, Insurgentes Norte opp. railway station, F, clean, helpful, will store luggage; *Isabel la Católica* (street of the same name, No. 63) is good, central, quite good restaurant, D, with bath, luggage held; *Torreón*, next to Isabel la Católica metro station, clean, E, with bath; *Gillow*, 5 de Mayo e Isabel la Católica, E, central, large, clean, attractive; *Ambassador*, Humboldt 38, central, from D, good service; *Las Américas*, on Magnolia, E, has small free enclosed parking, rates double at weekend; *Santander*, Arista 22, F, with bath, good and clean; *Buenavista*, Bernal Díaz 34, F, basic, quiet, friendly; *Concordia*, Uruguay 13, nr. Niño Perdido, excellent, E, lift, phone. *Casa de Huéspedes la Asturiana*, Uruguay 117, in early 17th century house, with cars parked in courtyard, central, near Pino Suárez metro, F, with bath, very good value, cheap 5-course meals for US$2; *Toledo*, López 24, E, shower, can be noisy, otherwise recommended; *Reyna*, on Isabel la Católica, handy, F; *Ontario*, Uruguay 87, F, nice exterior but run-down rooms, telephone; on same street, one block away, *Roble*, Uruguay y Pino Suárez, F, with shower, recommended; *Pensylvania*, Ignacio Mariscal 15, esq. Puente Arriga, E, with bath, within walking distance of railway station and close to Revolución monument, will keep luggage, good value; *Casa de los Amigos*, Mariscal 132, near train and bus station, F, use of kitchen, max. 15-day stay, separation of sexes, run by Quakers, breakfast and laundry facilities, safe-keeping for luggage, advance booking recommended; nearby is *Imperial*, Edison 52 (metro Hidalgo), fairly clean, telephone, F, overpriced restaurant, unfriendly, sometimes known to overcharge; *Niza*, near Isabel la Católica and Mesones, F, dreary, basic, clean; *La Paz*, Mina 141, close to bus stations on Insurgentes, E, with bathrooms. *Frimont*, E, Jesús Terán 35; *El Salvador*, Rep. de El Salvador 16, good value E; *American*, Avenida Buenavista, F, near ADO terminal and ½-km. from railway station, clean and safe; *De Carlo*, Plaza República, 35, C, private bath, TV, very good, catch bus to airport outside this hotel, every 45 mins till 0100; *Conde*, Pescaditos 15, off Luis Moya, 10 mins. walk from Alameda (Balderas metro), excellent value, E, with bath, heavily booked, clean, friendly; *República*, Cuba, E, a few blocks from Zócalo, central, clean; *Coliseo*, F, with bath, no windows, clean, luggage held, Bolívar 28, near metro Allende; *Habana* on República de Cuba, NW of Zócalo, E, good value; also *Cuba*, deteriorating but very quiet, F; *Pensión Francesa*, 5 de Febrero 33, 1st floor, book well in advance; *La Fuente*, Orozco y Berra 10 (near ADO bus station and Hidalgo metro), E, with bath. *San Pedro*, Mesones and Pino Suárez, F, clean and friendly. *Congreso*, good, central, F, at Allende 18; *Avenida*, Eje Lázaro Cárdenas (ex S. Juan Letrán) 38, F, with shower, central but dirty; *León*, Calle Brasil 5, F, clean, noisy bar downstairs, round the corner from the Zócalo; *Jardines de Churubusco*, Calzada de Tlalpan 1885, nr. General Anaya metro, excellent value, F; *San Francisco*†, Luis Moya 11, D, with bath, good rooms but surly management, best ask for top back rooms. *Capitol*, Av. Uruguay 12, F, with shower, noisy but clean, some gloomy rooms; *Principal*, Bolívar 27, F, with bath, noisy and cramped, but clean, some rooms without baths at half price; *Antillas*, B. Domínguez 34, E, hot shower, TV, clean, friendly, restaurant; *Dormitorio*, B. Domínguez Palma, F, men only. *María Angelo*, Lerma 11, E, with private bath, weekly rates possible, quite pleasant; *Imperio*, Correo Mayor 94, near Zócalo, F, with bath, old fashioned with Mexican residents, sheets changed daily, but noisy early morning and late at night. Very good value and near Allende metro is *Rioja*, Av. 5 de Mayo 45, share bath, fairly clean, well placed, F; *Galveston*, Insurgentes Sur 50, F, cheap, clean, safe; *Pensión Chacón*, Nayarit and Monterrey, F, clean and good. *Pensión Costa Rica*, Tonalá 260, F, good, friendly; *Hospedaje Estadio* on Coahuila, nr. Insurgentes Sur, F, very clean; *Londres*, F, Buenavista 5, clean, friendly, occasionally noisy. *España*, Pte. Alvarado 100, F; *Lafayette*, Motolinia 40 and 16 de Septiembre in the Zona Rosa, E, with bath, and TV, clean, quiet (pedestrian precinct), but check rooms, there's a variety of sizes, watch your luggage; *Lepanto*, Guerrero 90, E, set lunch, 6 courses, very good value, modern; *Ambasad*, F, with bath, telephone, TV room, clean, very good value, beside Pino Suárez metro station; also nearby *Ambar*, F, shower, TV, cockroaches. *Meave*, on Meave, 4 blocks from

914 MEXICO

Torre Latinoamericana, F, safe, clean, friendly; *Azores*, Brasil 25, E, helpful, TV, phone; *Casa González*, Lerma y Sena (near British Embassy), D, full board, shower, English spoken by Sr. González, clean, quiet and friendly; *El Porvenir*, on Bernal Díaz, 400 metres from Revolución metro station, cheap; on same street is *Estaciones*, F, reasonable but singles grim; *Lido*, Av. Brasil 208, near Zócalo, *Oxford*, Mariscal 67, E, very clean, radio and TV; *Moderno*, F/E, with bath, clean, not too noisy but not all rooms have windows, on Calle de los Incas 9 (metro Allende) off Honduras 2 blocks from Plaza Garibaldi; *Atlanta*, corner of B. Domínguez and Allende, F, good, quiet, clean and friendly, recommended; *Patria*, Rep. de El Salvador, nr. Pino Suárez metro, clean, E, but area a bit rough; *Apartamentos Azteca*, Hamburgo 29, F; *Encino*, Av. Insurgentes, 1 block from the railway station, E, clean, private bath; *Managua*, on Plaza de la Iglesia de San Fernando, near Hidalgo metro, E, with bath, very friendly; *Cima*, Av. Alfonso Cevallo 12, 1 street from metro Moctezuma, convenient for Oriente bus terminal, F, clean, shower; *Suites Quinta Palo Verde*, Cerro del Otate 20, Col. Romero de Terreros (Mexico 21 DF) Tel.: 554-35-75, C, diplomatic residence turned guest house, near the University; run by German owner/manager, Sr. Günter Böhm, who also conducts personalized tours and expeditions.

Camp Sites Mexico City has two camp sites, for addresses see American Automobile Association's "Mexico by Motor". There is a trailer-park on Calle Hortensia adjacent to the Av. Universidad, US$4 for 2 plus van, hot water and other facilities. Also *El Caminero*, on Route 99 in the Tlalpan suburb. Or try the parking lot of the Museum of Anthropology.

Youth Hostels Asociación Mexicana de Albergues de la Juventud, Madero 6, Of. 314, México 1, D. F. Write for information. Mexico City Hostel at Cozumel 57, Colonia Roma, not far from Chapultepec Park (Sevilla metro station, Line 1). Requires Mexican *and* IHS card, very basic, G, not recommended. There is a similar organization, CREA, in Serapio Rendón. There is a CREA *albergue* (hostel) in Pedregal on S side of the city (bus on Insurgentes to next stop after the Olympic Village), in pleasant surroundings, but noisy. Agencia Nacional de Turismo Juvenil on Plaza Insurgentes.

Restaurants All the best hotels have good restaurants. *Ambassadeurs*, Paseo de la Reforma 12 (swank and high priced); *Prendes*, 16 de Septiembre 12, murals (good European food, moderate); *La Cava*, Insurgentes Sur 2465 (excellent French food and steaks, lavishly decorated as an old French tavern, moderate); *Del Lago*, in exciting modern building in Chapultepec Park, excellent; *Tibet-Hamz*, Av. Juárez 64 (Chinese restaurant specializing in Cantonese and Mexican national dishes, centrally located, nice atmosphere, moderate); *Chalet Suizo*, Niza 37 (very popular with tourists, specializes in Swiss and German food, moderate); *Shirley's*, Reforma 108 (real American food, moderate); *Focolare*, Hamburgo 87 (swank and high priced); *Rivoli*, Hamburgo 123 (a gourmet's delight, high priced); *Jena*, Morelos 110 (deservedly famous, à la carte, expensive); *Sanborn's*, 36 locations (known as the foreigners' home-from-home: soda fountain, drugstore, restaurant, English language magazines, handicrafts, chocolates, etc.); *Delmonico's*, Londres 87 and 16 de Septiembre, elegant; *Mesón del Cid*, Humboldt 61, Castilian with medieval menu; *Chipp's*, Génova 59; *Café Konditori*, Génova 61, Danish open sandwiches; *Mesón del Castellano*, Bolívar y Uruguay, good, plentiful and not too dear, excellent steaks; *Alex Cardini's*, Madrid 21, home of the famous Caesar Salad. French cuisine at *La Lorraine*, San Luís Potosí 132 (home style), *Les Moustaches*, Río Sena 88, and *La Madelon*, Río Plata 55, home style. *La Marinera*, Liverpool 183, best seafood restaurant in Mexico City.

Reasonable in centre: *Centro Castellano*, Uruguay 16, one flight up; *Café Rosalía*, Eje Lázaro Cárdenas 46. *Reforma*, Reforma 27-1, cheap and good; *Pensión Francesa*, 1st floor, 5 de Febrero 26A, delicious, abundant meals. Cheap lunches at *Pensión Española* at Isabel la Católica 10, off 5 de Mayo, 1st floor. *Anderson's*, Reforma 400, very good atmosphere, reasonable, excellent local menu. *Sírvase Vd. Mismo*, on Iturbide, near Av. Juárez, fine smorgasbord lunch with choice of 4 hot meals, plus salads and dessert. *Mesón del Perro Andaluz*, Copenhague 26, very pleasant, US$5 for Spanish all-inclusive meal. Many economical restaurants in Calle 5 de Mayo: the *Cinco de Mayo*, *Latino*, *La Blanca*, and *El Popular*; La Nueva Opera there has Spanish and Mexican food. *Vasco*, Madero 6, 1st foor and *Español*, Calle López 60, good Spanish food, including roast kid. *Varsovia*, Paseo de la Reforma, Yugoslav food, very good value, also suitable for vegetarians. *Las Fuentes*, Tíber 79 and Liverpool 169, more quantity than quality. *Casa de Huéspedes la Asturiana* at Uruguay 117 has enormous *corridas* at US$2; *París* at El Salvador 91, is good value. *Pastelería Madrid* on 5 de Febrero 25 has especially good cakes.

El Vegetariano, Filomeno Mata 13, open 0800-2000, closed Sun.; 4-course meal US$3.50. Other vegetarian restaurants: *Carlos Mario*, Dolores 52, between Victoria and Ayuntamiento, open 1200-1800, inc. Sun., in spite of generally good reports some travellers report sickness after eating here; *Chalet Vegetariano*, near Dr. Río de la Loza; *El Bosque*, Hamburgo 15 between Berlín and Dinamarca, recommended. Vegetarian restaurant at Motolinía 31, near Madero, is open Mon.-Sat. 1300-1800, reasonably priced. *Yug*, Varsovia 3, excellent and cheap vegetarian, 4-course set lunch US$1.50. Wholewheat bread at *Pastelería Ideal* on 16 de Septiembre 14 (near Casa de Los Azulejos-Sanborns).

Rincón Gaucho, Insurgentes Sur 1162, Argentine food; *La Pérgola*, Londres 107B, in the Zona Rosa, Italian; *Humboldt*, Humboldt 34, off Juárez, friendly and good value; *La Casserole*, Insurgentes Sur near Núcleo Radio Mil building, French; *Rhin*, Av. Juárez, cheap, good, German décor;

MEXICO 915

Lonchería la Torta, Av. de la Independencia 16, clean, cheap and very friendly; *El Caminero*, behind *María Isabel Sheraton Hotel*, is an excellent open-air *taco* restaurant. Many US chain fast-food restaurants. Reasonable *ostionería* (oyster bar) at Bolívar 56, try Baja California Chablis. *Vero's*, Tolstoy 23, Col. Anzures, off Reforma and near Chapultepec Park, very reasonable *corridas*; many cheap restaurants on Chapultepec, e.g. *El Rico Menudo* at No. 481, *comida corrida*; *Presente y Futuro*, corner of Independencia and Revillagigedo, good and cheap; also *Anna Capri*, Balderas 91, *La Casa del Naturismo*, good vegetarian food, you can eat under a "pyramid", on Dolores 10, near Alameda. *Buffet Coyoacán*, on Allende, 50 metres from Frida Kahlo museum, fixed price (about US$4) for unlimited helpings. *Taquería Lobo Bobo*, Insurgentes Sur 2117, mushrooms a speciality; *Beverley Grill*, Reforma 382.

San Angel Inn, in San Angel, is excellent and very popular, so book well in advance. (San Angel may be reached by bus from Chapultepec Park or by trolley bus from Metro Taxqueña.) The *Piccadilly Pub*, Copenhague 23, is dear but serves British food at its best, especially steak and kidney pie; very popular with Mexicans and expatriates alike. Similar (and dearer), is *Sir Winston Churchill*, Avila Camacho 67.

Others recommended are *Normandia*, López 16; *Bellinghausen*, Londres y Niza (Mexican, not German); *Passy*, Amberes 10; *El Nuevo Acapulco*, López 9 (excellent sea food, inexpensive); *Lar*, Río Lerma 86 (opp. British Embassy); *Casa Regional Valenciana*, López 60, 3rd floor; *Restaurante Ehden*, Correo Mayor 74, 1st floor, open Sun., authentic and reasonably priced Arab food; *Centro Asturiano*, Orizaba and Puebla, Spanish; *Napoleón*, French, and *Viena*, Viennese, in Plaza Popocatépetl; *Café Restaurant Elsa*, Bolívar 44, good vegetable dishes. *Casa Zavala*, on Uruguay between Isabel la Católica and Bolívar, very good, clean and cheap (better than *Elsa* nearby). *El Buen Café*, Sonora 9, has chess sets to lend. *Pastelería Madrid* on 5 de Febrero, one block from *Hotel Isabel la Católica*, good pastries. Also on 5 de Febrero, *Café Blanca*, friendly, reasonably priced food, open till midnight. *Azteca*, Pino Suárez 68, good food. *Fonda del Recuerdo* for excellent *mole poblano*, Bahía de las Palmas 39A, 17DF, with music. Very good, *Club de Periodistas de México*, F. Mata 8, near Calle 5 de Mayo, open to public. More expensive but still good value, *Las Delicias*, Venezuela 41; *El Parador*, Niza 17, good local and international; *Lory's de México*, Génova 73, and *La Calesa de Londres*, Londres 102, good meat at both; *Le Gourmet*, Dakota 155, said to be most expensive restaurant in Mexico, and also said to be worth it! Good small restaurants in Uruguay, near *Monte Carlo Hotel*. Another centre for small restaurants is Pasaje Jacarandas, off Génova: *Llave de Oro* and many others. *Lady Baltimore*, good, cheap and clean, on F. I. Madero. *Francis Drake* on Av. Juárez, reasonable and good. *Gaby*, cheap, friendly, on Calle Palma, near Zócalo. *Lim* on Bucarelli before Morelos, good value *comidas*. *Grand Chose*, Moya 62, family atmosphere, cheap three-course meals.

A very old restaurant with interesting tile décor and not touristy is the *Café Tacuba*, Tacuba 28; it specializes in Mexican food, very good *enchiladas*. Cheap cafeterias in Calle Belisario Domínguez. Good breakfasts at *Coliseo*, Bolívar 28. *La Bombi*, corner of Tacuba and Brasil, recommended; Typical, non-touristy snack-bar, *Poblanos*, at Heliópolis and Allende in the Tacuba area. Health food shop, *Alimentos Naturales*, close to Metro Revolución, on P. Arriagal. There are over 2,000 others.

Bars *Opera Bar*, 5 de Mayo near Bellas Artes, good atmosphere, see Pancho Villa's bullet-hole in ceiling. *Bar Jardín*, in the *Hotel Reforma*; *Montenegro* and *Nicte-Ha*, in *Hotel del Prado*; *El Colmenar*, Ejido y Eliseo; *Cavalier*, on top of Torre Latinoamericano skyscraper, for sunsets and views at night. *Morrocco*, Club Marrakesh, Calle Florencia.

Cabarets and Night Clubs Every large hotel has one. *El Patio*, Atenas 9; *Passepartout*, Calle Hamburgo, *La Madelon*, Florencia 36; *Gitanerías*, Oaxaca 15, wild gypsy show; *Capri*, on the tourist guided route, to be avoided. *Hotel de Cortés* has Mexican Fiesta incl. meal Sat., entertainment. *El 77*, Calle Londres, Flamenco show. There are many discotheques in the better hotels and scattered throughout town.

Folk Music *Peña El Cóndor Pasa* is a cafeteria, open 1900-0100, closed on Tues., on Rafael Checal, San Angel; it has different folk-music groups every night; get there early. A fine place for light refreshments and music is the *Hostería del Bohemio*, formerly the San Hipólito monastery, near Reforma on Av. Hidalgo 107, next to the church of that name. Look hard for the entrance: no sign, poetry and music every night from 1700 to 2200, light snacks and refreshments US$1, no cover charge.

Clubs *Sports* Reforma Athletic Club, Hacienda de los Morales, Lomas de Chapultepec; Churubusco Sports Club (golf, tennis, swimming); French Club in San ángel; British, Mexican, and Spanish boating clubs, in Xochimilco, near Mexico City; Polo Club in Lomas de Chapultepec. Club Suiza, Borja 840.
General American Legion, Lucerna 71; Spanish Club, Isabel la Católica 29; YMCA, Av. Ejército Nacional 253; YWCA, corner of Humboldt 62 and Artículo 123 (US$4.80 for single room with bath, good restaurant and laundry); Lions Club, Ures 13; Rotary Club, Londres 15; Automobile Club (Asociación Mexicana Automovilística-AMA), Av. Chapultepec 276; Women's International Club, Humboldt 47; University of Mexico, Paseo Reforma 150; Junior League Library, Iturbide Building, Av. Madero.

916 MEXICO

Shopping Mexico's "West End", the Zona Rosa (Pink Zone), where most of the fashionable shops and many restaurants are found, is bounded by the Paseo de la Reforma, Av. Chapultepec, Calle Florencia and Av. Insurgentes Sur. Note that most streets in the Zone are called after foreign cities—Londres, Liverpool, Hamburgo, Niza, Amberes (Antwerp), Génova, Copenhague, etc. The handicrafts section is between Liverpool and Hamburgo. There are also many handicraft shops on Av. Juárez. There are also good shops on 5 de Mayo, 16 de Septiembre, Insurgentes, Colonia Juárez. Mexican jewellery and hand-made silver can be bought everywhere. Among the good silver shops are Sanborn's, Calpini, Prieto, and Vendome. There are also good buys in perfumes, quality leather, and suede articles.

San Juan market, Calle Ayuntamiento and Arandas, nr. Salto del Agua metro, good prices for handicrafts, especially leather goods (also cheap fruit); some bargaining acceptable. Check whether restoration work, which closed the premises, has finished. The Ciudadela market just off Balderas (metro Juárez), government-sponsored, reasonable and uncrowded (Plaza Ciudadela) is cheaper, but not for leather, than San Juan; craftsmen from all Mexico have set up workshops here. Mercado Lagunilla on Calle Allende near Plaza de Sta. Cecilia (formerly Garibaldi) has everything from antiques to typical Mexican tourist wares, open Sun. El Mercado Central de Artesanías, at Balderas and Ayuntamiento (metro Revolucion), open 0900-1800 weekdays, Sun. 0900-1400. Market in Calle Londres (Zona Rosa) good for silver. There is a market in every district selling pottery, glassware, textiles, *sarapes* and jewellery. Try also San Angel market, although expensive, many items are exclusive to it; good leather belts; open Sat. only from about 1100. Mexican tinware and lacquer are found everywhere. You can bargain in the markets and smaller shops.

Government Artesanía shop in basement of Siqueiros Polyforum, on Insurgentes Sur. Other sponsored shops: Arts and Crafts of Michoacán and Querétaro, Glorieta del Metro de Los Insurgentes, Locales 14 and 17 (Tel.: 525 01 37). Tienda del Arte e Industrias Populares at Juárez 44. Try also Decorask, Pino Suárez 28. Try Fonart, Fondo Nacional para el Fomento de las Artesanías, Av. Patriotismo 691, main office and branches at Av. Juárez 93 and 70, Londres 136, Altos A in the Zona Rosa, Londres 6 in Colonia Roma, Av. de la Paz 37 in San Angel, Insurgentes Sur 1630 and at Manuel Izaguirre 10 in Ciudad Satélite, with items from all over the country, recommended. The Mercado de Artesanías Finas Indios Verdes is at Acueducto 13, corner of Insurgentes Norte (metro Indios Verdes): walk out on to Calle Tenochtitlán, head N 500m. and Acueducto is on your left; good prices and quality but no bargaining. There is an annual national craft fair in Mexico City, 1st week in Dec. Good selection of onyx articles at the Brunner shop, in Calle Dolores. For first class luxury leather goods, go to Arias, in Av. Juárez near Turismo building, and in Florencia, Antil. Víctor, at Av. Madero 10/305, 2nd floor, has genuine, and high quality craft articles. With the extension of the ring roads around the city, hypermarkets (suburban shopping malls) are being set up: there are two, Perisur at the extreme S end of the city (with Liverpool, Sears, Sanborn's and Palacio de Hierro), with quite futuristic designs, open Tues.-Fri. 1100-2000, Sat. 1100-2100; and Plaza Satélite at the extreme N end of the city (with Sumesa, Sears and Liverpool), open on Sunday. Luggage repairs (moderate prices) at Rinconada de Jesús 15-G, opposite Museum of the City of Mexico on Pino Suárez, but opening times can be unreliable; better try the shop in Callejon del Parque del Conde off Pino Suárez opp. Hospital de Jesús Church.

Bookshops Many good ones, e.g. American Book Store, Madero 25, excellent selection of Penguins and Pelicans, low mark-up; Libros, Libros, Libros, Monte Ararat 220, Lomas Barrilaco, Tel.: 540-47-78, hundreds of hardback and paperback English titles; Librerías CIPSA, Polanco branch and a concession at the Anthropology Museum; Librairie Française, Reforma 250A, for French selection; Librería Británica, Av. de la Paz 23, San Angel; the British bookshop on Río Ganges has a second-hand section where you can trade in old books (as long as they're neither even slightly damaged nor "highbrow") and buy new ones, but at poor rates; Librerías de Cristal (Ediapsa) has a branch on Horacio near corner with Newton in Polanco district—excellent selection. Antigua Librería Robredo, Paseo de la Reforma 234, new and old books in Spanish, mainly Mexican history and culture. *México Desconocido* by Harry Möller, is no longer obtainable as a book but is now a series of seperate booklets following a TV series of the same title. These tell you about all kinds of off-the-beaten-track places which are mostly accessible by bus. Available at better bookshops. Libros y Discos, Madero 1. (Librería Bellas Artes, Av. Juárez 18, sells the *South American Handbook*, as do all the bookshops mentioned above.) The Sanborn chain has the largest selection of English-language paperbacks, art books and magazines in the country. Good second-hand bookshop, *Librería Minerva* on Calle Artículo 123.

Traffic System The city has two ring roads, the Anillo Periférico around the city outskirts, and the Circuito Interior running within its circumference. In the centre, the system of Ejes Viales has been developed in recent years. It consists of a series of freeways laid out in a grid pattern, spreading from the Eje Central; the latter serves as a focal point for numbering (Eje 2 Poniente, Eje I Oriente etc.). Norte, Sur, Oriente, Poniente refer to the roads' position in relation to the Eje Central. The system is remarkably clear in its signposting with special symbols for telephones, information points, tram stops, etc. Beware of the tram lines—trams, buses, emergency services and plain simple folk in a hurry come down at high speed; and as often as not this lane goes against the normal flow of traffic! **N.B.** Eje Lázaro Cárdenas used to be called Calle San Juan de Letrán.

City Buses Buses have been nationalized and coordinated into one system: odd numbers run

MEXICO 917

North-South, evens East-West. Fares about US$0.06. There are 60 direct routes and 48 feeder (SARO) routes. We are informed that thieves and pickpockets haunt the buses plying along Reforma and Juárez. Be careful of your valuables! A most useful route for tourists (and well-known to thieves, so don't take anything you don't require immediately) is No. 76 which runs from the Zócalo along Paseo de la Reforma, beside Chapultepec Park. A new *Peribus* service goes round the entire Anillo Periférico (see Traffic System). The 100 bus line also insures its passengers: collection of insurance requires presentation of the ticket.

Taxis Taxis are fitted with taximeters, but they are often not used. Cabs called by radio charge from the time of the call. So-called "peso taxis" (*peseros*) go back and forth on Reforma and its eastern extensions as far as the Zócalo, and on Insurgentes. Number of fingers held out indicates number of seats left. Fares about US$0.25, at driver's discretion. Wave down at special stops on kerb or even from kerb itself. Up to 17 fixed routes. No tip necessary. Fixed-route taxis have to be identified by a lime-green colour, rank taxis by coral and those with no fixed route by yellow. The *peseros* are to be replaced by the new "midibus", which carry 22 passengers.

Agree fares in advance, on basis of time and distance, outside the city. Taxis are very cheap, but the drivers often do not know where the street you want is; try and give the name of the intersection between two streets rather than a number, because the city's numbering can be erratic. When it is raining or dark you may have to agree to pay up to twice the normal amount. There are special tourist taxis, called "Turismo", which are dearer because they have English-speaking drivers, outside the main hotels, but they have no meters: arrange the prices beforehand. VW taxis are very cheap, but make sure they put the meter on (if they say it is broken, they are lying, no cab is allowed on the streets with a broken meter): they should be tipped. Unmarked taxis may work out more expensive than marked ones. At all four bus terminals you must buy taxi-tickets at a booth near the door, five persons a taxi. Hired cars with driver are dear.

Metro Maps of the network are usually available from ticket offices and from tourist offices and are displayed at most stations since lines have been extended; at the Zócalo metro station there is a map showing the whole network. There is a metro information service at Insurgentes station on Pink Line which dispenses maps and most interchange stations have information kiosks. (The *Atlas de Carreras*, US$1.65 has a map of Mexico City, its centre and the metro lines marked. Good metro and bus maps at the Anthropology Museum, US$1.25.) All the stations have a symbol, e.g. the grasshopper signifying Chapultepec. There are seven lines in service. 1 (Pink), from Observatorio (by Chapultepec Park) to Pantitlán in the eastern suburbs. It goes under Av. Chapultepec and not far from the lower half of Paseo de la Reforma, the Mercado Merced, and 3 km. from the airport. 2 (Blue), from Tacuba in the NW to the Zócalo and then S above ground to Taxqueña; 3 (Green), from Indios Verdes SE to the University City (free bus service to Insurgentes); 4 (Light Blue), from Zaragoza, via Terminal Aérea (which is close to gate A of the airport), Pantitlán, crossing the green line at La Raza, up to Politécnico; 5 (Orange), from El Rosario to Terminal Aérea; 6 (Red), from Santa Anita on the SE side to Martín Carrera in the NE; 7 (Purple), from Tacuba in the NW to Barranca del Muerto in the SW. Trains are noiseless on rubber wheels. Music is played quietly at the stations. Tickets about US$0.04. Originally a splendidly modern service (virtually impossible to get lost), it is still clean and efficient, although overcrowded at some times: the Pink Line, 1, is impossible to get on or off between 1500 and 2000. Beware thieves, and women should avoid using the metro when alone at night, severe attacks of "roving-hand syndrome" are common—between 1700 and 2100 men are separated from women and children at Pino Suárez, direction Zaragoza. Also beware: no heavy luggage or large back-packs permitted (although at off-peak times the station security guard may allow you on with a back-pack if you carry it in your arms), but medium-sized rucksacks OK. To airport: Go to "Terminal Aérea" station, right outside, and take No. 4 line to La Raza, then No. 3 down to Hidalgo for the centre. At the Zócalo metro station there is a permanent exhibit about the metro, interesting. At Pino Suárez, station has been built around a small restored Aztec temple. **N.B.** Metro opens 0500 weekdays, 0700 on Sundays. Do not take photos or make sound-recordings in the metro without obtaining a permit and a uniformed escort from metro police, or you could be arrested.

Car Hire Agencies Budget Rent Auto, Reforma 60; Hertz, Revillagigedo 2; Avis, Medellín 14; VW, Av. Chapultepec 284-6; National Car Rental, Insurgentes Sur 1883; Auto Rent, Reforma Norte 604; quick service at Av. Chapultepec 168, Tel.: 533-5335 (762-9892 airport); Pamara, Hamburgo 135, Tel.: 525-5572—**N.B.** 200 km. free mileage; Odin, Balderas 24-A; and many local firms, which tend to be cheaper. Gasoline is reassuringly cheap.

Entertainments Theatres: Palacio de Bellas Artes (for ballet, songs, dances, also concerts 2-3 times a week), Fábregas, Lírico, Iris, Sullivan, Alarcón, Hidalgo, Urueta, San Rafael and Insurgentes in town and a cluster of theatres around the Auditorio Nacional in Chapultepec Park (check at Tourist Office for details of cheap programmes). Spectaculars (e.g. presidential inauguration) are often staged in the Auditorio Nacional itself. Also in Chapultepec Park is the Audiorama (behind the Castle on the Constituyentes side) where one may listen to recorded classical music in a small open ampitheatre in a charming wooded glade. A request book is provided, for the following day. There may be a free performance of a play in one of the parks by the Teatro Trashumante (Nomadic Theatre). Variety show nightly with singers, dancers, comedians, magicians and ventriloquists, very popular with locals, at Teatro la Blanquita, on Av. Lazaro Cárdenas Sur near Plaza

918 MEXICO

Garibaldi. On Sundays there is afternoon bull-fighting in a vast ring (see page 925) and morning football at the stadium. The balloon sellers are everywhere. Especially recommended, the Ballet Folklórico de México, at Palacio de Bellas Artes (see page 922). The Teatro de la Ciudad, Donceles 36 (Tel.: 510-2197 and 510-2942) has the Ballet Folklórico Nacional Aztlan.

Football Sun. midday, Aztec and Olympic stadia; also Thurs. (2100) and Sat. (1700).

Horse Races Hipódromo de las Américas, every Tues., Thurs., Sat. and Sun. almost all the year. Pari-mutuel betting (minimum bet US$1). Races begin at 1400, and may be watched from Jockey Club restaurant. Beautiful track with infield lagoons and flamingoes, and plenty of atmosphere. Free entry with a tourist card, just pay the tax.

Jai-Alai Events with the foremost players in the world every day except Friday at the Frontón México across from Monumento a la Revolución, at 1800. It seats 4,000. Theoretically, jackets and ties are needed for admission. The people in the red caps are the *corredores*, who place the bets. Pari-mutuel betting. US$1.

Golf at Chapultepec Golf Club and Churubusco Country Club. These are private clubs, open to visitors only if accompanied by a member. Green fees are high (US$20 upwards).

Hiking Every weekend at the Alpino and Everest clubs. Club de Exploraciones de México, Juan A. Mateos 146, Col. Obrero, DF 06800, Tel.: 1930-2400 Wed. or Fri. 578-5730, organizes several walks in and around the city on Sats. and Suns.

Swimming Agua Caliente, Las Termas, Balneario Olímpico, Elba, Centro Deportivo Chapultepec and others.

Charreadas (Cowboy displays), Rancho Grande de La Villa, at very top of Insurgentes Norte, Sun. 1100-1500, US$1.30.

Banks 0900-1330 (closed Sat.); Banco de Comercio (Bancomer), Venustiano Carranza y Bolívar; Banco Nacional de México (Banamex), Av. Isabel la Católica 44 (entrance for exchange on Calle Palmas), (said to give best exchange rates (this branch is a converted baroque palace, ask the porter for a quick look into the patio; another worthwhile building is the bank's branch on C. Madero 17 with Gante); Banca Serfín, corner of 16 de Septiembre y Bolívar; Citibank, Uruguay e Isabel la Católica. Apparently many banks carry the Eurocard symbol but will not in fact recognize the card. These include at least some of the branches of the Banco del Atlántico. American Express office at Reforma 234 is the only place one can change cheques on Sats., 0930-1330. Open Mon.-Fri. until 1800; and many others. One can change money into pesos at the airport 24 hrs. a day, and only US$500-worth back into dollars after you have passed through customs when leaving. Impossible to exchange Guatemalan quetzales, Belizean dollars, cruzados and other "exotics".

Addresses Always check location of embassies and consulates; they tend to move frequently. Most take 24 hrs. for visas; check to make sure you have a visa and not just a receipt stamp.
British Embassy, Calle Río Lerma 71, 511-48-80 (Apartado 96 bis, Mexico 5). Consular Section at Calle Usumacinta 30, immediately behind main Embassy Building. Reading room in main building. Visa to Belize US$8.90, takes 2 days, pay in advance. Poste restante for 1 month.
British Chamber of Commerce, Río Tíber 103, 6th floor, Cuauhtémoc, Tel.: 533-24-53.
Guatemalan Consulate, Vallarta 1-501 A (i.e. 5th floor); tourist card costs US$1; visa issued on the spot, must be used within one month from date of issue, now costs US$5 payable only in US currency, no photo (check whether visa and photograph required) for UK passports. Tel.: 546-89-84, open 0900-1330. Other Guatemalan consulates are cheaper than in Mexico City. No visa required by Canadian citizens.
Nicaraguan Consulate, Nuevo León 144, nr. Parque España, 1st floor (Tel.: 553-9791), visas for 30 days from date of issue, 2 photographs, US$11, one-day wait. Embassy is at Sierra Villa, Gran Ahumada 36, Tel.: 520-2270.
Honduran Consulate, Juárez 64 (9th floor), visas issued on the spot (no waiting) valid up to one year from date of issue.
Salvadorean Embassy, Galileo 17.
Panamanian Embassy, Campos Eliseos 111.
Costa Rican Embassy, Darwin 142 (4th floor).
USA Embassy, Reforma 305.
American Chamber of Commerce, Lucerna 78.
Benjamin Franklin Library, Londres 116.
Anglo-Mexican Cultural Institute (with British Council Library), Maestro Antonio Caso 127. Tel.: 566-61-44. Keeps British newspapers.
Canadian Embassy, Schiller 529 (corner Tres Picos), nr. Anthropological Museum. Tel.: 254-3288.
Australian Embassy, Paseo de la Reforma 195, 5th Floor. Tel.: 566-30-55.
New Zealand Embassy, Homero 229, 8th floor.
West German Embassy, Byron 737, Colonia Rincón del Bosque. Tel.: 545-66-55.

French Embassy, Havre 15, near the Cuauhtémoc Monument, Tel.: 533-13-61.
Netherlands Embassy, Monte Urales 635-203 (near Fuente de Petróleos).
Swedish Embassy, Blvd. M. Avila Camacho 1-6, Tel.: 540-63-93.
Danish Embassy, Tres Picos 45, near Canadian ditto.
Swiss Embassy, Hamburgo 66, 5th floor. Tel.: 533-07-35.
Colombian Consulate will request visa from Bogotá by telegram (which you must pay for) and permission can take up to a month to come through.
Chief Telegraph Office for internal telegrams, Palace of Communications and Transport, Plaza Senado de la República, off Calle Tacuba. For international telegrams, see page 1004.
Mountain Rescue, Socorro Alpino, Eje Lázaro Cárdenas 80-305. Open after 1900 weekday evenings.
American Community School of Mexico, complete US curriculum to age of 12, Observatorio and Calle Sur 136, Tel.: 516-67-20.
Instituto Mexicano Norteamericano, Hamburgo 115; 4-week intensive and painless courses in Spanish, US$80 a course, less intensive, US$40; free, excellent concerts, art exhibits, reading-room, bulletin board advertising rooms. Instituto Italiano has the same courses, but less crowded, US$95 including books. The Universidad Nacional Autónoma de México (Unam) offers cheap 7-week courses which include history lectures.
Setej (Mexican Students' Union), Hamburgo 273, Zona Rosa, Metro Sevilla, only office to issue student card, which is required to buy a hostel card, Tel.: 514-42-13 or 511-66-91, deals with ISIS insurance. Student cards not available at Youth Hostel on Calle Cozumel 57.
Instituto Francés de la América Latina, Nazas 43, free films every Thurs. at 2030.
Goethe-Institut, Tonalá 43 (metro Insurgentes), 0900-1300, 1600-1930.

International Post Office Calle Aldama 218, open until 1800.

Spanish Classes See above under *Instituto Mexicano Norteamericano*.

English-Speaking Churches Roman Catholic—St. Patrick's, Calle Bondojito; Evangelical Union—Reforma 1870; Baptist—Capital City Baptist Church, Calle Sur 136; Lutheran—Church of the Good Shepherd, Palmas 1910; First Church of Christ Scientist— 21 Dante, Col. Anzures. Jewish—Beth Israel, Virreyes 1140.

American British Cowdray Hospital, or the ABC, to give it its popular name, at Observatorio and Calle Sur 136. Tel.: 277-5000 (emergency: 515-8359); very helpful

Medical Services C. German, Calle Eucker No. 16-601, Tel.: 545-94-34. Dr. César Calva Pellicer (who speaks English, French and German), Copenhague 24, 3° piso, Tel.: 514-25-29. Dr Smythe, Campos Elíseos 81, Tel.: 547-78-61, recommended by US and Canadian Embassies. For any medical services you can also go to the Clínica Prensa, US$ 1.20 for consultation, subsidized medicines. Hospital de Jesús Nazareno, 20 de Noviembre 82, Spanish-speaking, friendly, US$4 to consult a doctor, drugs prescribed cheaply. It is a historical monument (see page 922).

Vaccination Centre Benjamín Hill 14, near metro Juanacatlán (Pink Line), near Soviet Embassy. Open Mon.-Fri. 0830-1430, 1530-2030, avoid last half hour, also open on Sat. from 0830-1430; typhoid free (this is free all over Mexico), cholera and yellow fever (Tues. & Fri. only) US$2. For hepatitis shots you have to buy gamma globulin in a pharmacy (make sure it's been refrigerated) and then an injection there (cheap but not always clean) or at a doctor's surgery.

Pharmacies *Farmacía Homeopática*, on Calle Mesones 111-B. Twenty-four hour pharmacy at *Farmacía Arrocha* off the Periférico next to Hospital de Seguro Social. *Sanborn's* chain and *El Fénix* discount pharmacies are the largest chains with the most complete selection.

Laundromat on Río Danubio, between Lerma and Panuco and at Chapultepec and Toledo, nr. Sevilla metro. Lavandería Automática Atoyac, Atoyac 69, near Chapultepec Metro station, one block N of Reforma, corner C. Elba. Also at Parque España 14.

Telephones The LADA system provides a range of useful services: Long distance— Dial 91 + town code + the number. There is a 25% discount between 1900 and 2200, and a 50% one between 2200 and 0700. International—Dial 95 for US and Canada. Discounts of 11%-34% are available depending on when you ring and where to. Dial 04 for exact information. Dial 98 for the rest of the world. Other services—92 person to person; 01 Directory enquiries; 02 Long distance; 03 Talking clock; 04 Ex-Directory; 05 Engineers; 09 International. Calls overseas can be made from Victoria 59, 0800-2200 and from Victoria 14, 24 hrs., 3 mins. minimum; also from Parque Via 198 from 0800-2130 and at the International Airport.

The **Mexican Secretariat of Tourism** is at Calle Masaryk 172, between Hegel and Emerson, Colonia Polanco (reached by bus No. 32), Tel.: 250-85-55. In the past it has given the best tourist service in Latin America, and was genuinely anxious to investigate any complaints. Visitors feel the tourist service is no longer so efficient. Booking of hotels in other parts of the country possible here. You may also refer your problems to the tourist police, in blue uniforms, who are

920 MEXICO

reported to be very friendly. Articles from the various craft displays can be bought. Free maps not always available, but try Mexico City Chamber of Commerce, Reforma 42, which provides maps and brochures of the city; may otherwise be got from Department of Public Works; or buy in bookshops. Bus maps available. Office hours: 0800-1900, closed Sat. and Sun. Information bureau outside Insurgentes metro station. Tourist information can be dialled between 0800 and 2000 (bilingual operator) on 250-01-23. Incidentally, museums are closed Mon., except Chapultepec Castle, which is open daily, as are the Acolman monastery and the Churubusco museum. A weekly magazine, *Tiempo Libre*, covers what's on in Mexico City.

Geographical Maps Centro de Asesoría y Distribución de Información Estadística y Cartografía, Balderas 71 (mezzanine), México 1, D.F. Tel.: 585-70-55, ext. 287. Three times a year it publishes an Inventario de Información Geográfica with a list of all maps published.

Travel and Tourist Agencies Corresponsales de Hoteles will make reservations for high-category hotels in other Mexican towns, Av. Morelos 20, 7th floor, very friendly. Trailways, Londres 161, No. 48, Tel.: 525-20-50; Excursiones y Viajes (Evisa), Reforma 76, 4th floor; Garza López Tours, Juárez 64; Mexamérica, Reforma 92; Turismo Mundial Iter, Reforma 104; Viajes Panamericanos, Reforma 20-103; Viajes Felgueres, Florencia 17; Viajes Meliá, Madrid 21; Hadad y Asociados Professionales de Viajes, Insurgentes Sur 605, 705A, Tel.: 536-47-40, arranges mileage tickets; Wells Fargo & Co. Express, Calle Niza 22; Wilfer Tours, Morelos 37-201; Viajes Bojórquez, Av. Juárez 98, very good tours arranged; Thomas Cook, about 11 branches, main office Av. Juárez 88; Uniclam agent in Mexico City is Srta. Rosa O'Hara, Río Pánuco 146, Apto 702, Col. Cuauhtémoc, Tel.: 525-53-93. American Express, Reforma 234 y Havre, open Mon.-Fri. 0900-1800, Sat. 0900-1300, charges US$3-4 for poste restante if you do not have their travellers' cheques and US$1 if no card or cheques are held for other services. Service slow and you must be firm if you want something. Turistoria, Insurgentes Centro 114, Room 209 (Tel.: 535-94-88) takes people to *fiestas* in different parts of the country, tours from ½ day to a few days—speaking Spanish an advantage. Recommended guide/taxi driver: Raúl Méndez Guerrero, Frontera 80, Dpto. 6, Tel.: 536-88-97.

Railways The central station is on Insurgentes Norte, junction Alzate with Mosqueta, nearest metro Revolución or Guerrero. For details of train services, see destinations in text.

International Airport, 13 km. from city. There are five access points: A. Aeroméxico arrivals; B. Departure for internal flights (US$4.50 tax); C. Internal arrivals; D. International departures (US$10); E. International arrivals. The Instituto Nacional de Bellas Artes has a permanent exhibition hall and there is an interesting mural *La Conquista del Aire por el Hombre* by Juan O'Gorman. Tourist shops (including meat, wine, books, souvenirs, clothes, a hairdresser and a juice bar) 2 bars and restaurants, banks, line the ground floor. Telephone calls abroad from booth 19 (0600-2200) and booth 8 (0700-2300). Mexicana bookings in annex by C and Aeroméxico bookings and timetable booklets from near A. Opp. point E, cars are rented. Fixed-price taxis from despatcher's office at exit; about US$4 to Alameda. Buy pesos opp. D and B, open 24 hrs. Purchase foreign exchange once through immigration for outward international flights. Near C is a post office, with telegraph and telex. Left luggage on 1st floor. Journey about 20 mins. from town centre if there are no traffic jams. Línea Gris, Londres 166 (Tel.: 533-15-40 and 533-16-65), does hotel pick-up service for airport at US$6 per head. (A traveller has recommended Taxi Mex.) Taxi to airport US$10; marked taxis usually cheaper than unmarked. There are regular buses to the airport (e.g. No. 20, along N side of Alameda) but the drawback is that you have to take one to Calzada Ignacio Zaragoza and transfer to trolley bus at the Boulevard Puerto Aéreo (i.e. at metro station Aeropuerto). Buses to airport may be caught every 45 mins. until 0100 from outside *De Carlo Hotel*, Plaza República 35. It takes an hour from downtown and in the rush hour— most of the day—it is jam-packed. But you can take baggage if you can squeeze it in. See under "Metro" on how to get to airport cheaply, if you have no heavy luggage. The Mexican Hotel Association desk at the airport will call any hotel and reserve a room for you, also has a collective taxi which will drop you at your hotel, but it does not open until 1000.

Long-distance Buses For details of bus services, see destinations in text. Buses to destinations in N. Mexico, including US borders, leave from Central del Norte, Avenida Cien Metros 4907 (34 bus companies in all), where there is also a tourist information kiosk (Spanish-speaking only, closed at 1630) which at times issues street plans and will make reservations for the more expensive hotels. The bus station is on metro line 5 at Autobuses del Norte. City buses marked Cien Metros or Terminal del Norte go directly there. Central Autobuses del Sur, at corner of Tlalpan 2205 across from metro at Taxqueña (line 2), serves Cuernavaca, Acapulco, Zihuatanejo areas. Direct buses to centre (Donceles) from Terminal del Sur, and an express bus connects the Sur and Norte terminals as well as taxis, for which tickets can be purchased at a fixed price of US$2 in the terminal. It is difficult to get tickets to the S, book as soon as possible; the terminal for the S is chaotic. The Central de Autobuses del Poniente is situated opposite the Observatorio station of

MEXICO 921

line 1 of the metro (pink line), to serve the W of Mexico; check luggage in 30 mins before bus departure. You can go to the centre by bus from the "urbano" terminal outside the Poniente terminal (US$0.08). The Central del Oriente is on Zaragoza opp. metro San Lázaro (pink line), Calzada Ignacio Zaragoza, for buses to Yucatán and South East, incl. Oaxaca (it has a tourist information office open from 1000). All bus terminals operate taxis with voucher system and there are long queues. It is much easier to pay the driver. However, make sure you don't part with the voucher until you're safely in the taxi. In the confusion some drivers move each other's cabs to get out of the line faster and may take your voucher and disappear. About US$2.20 to Zócalo area, US$3 to Zona Rosa. Advance booking is recommended for all trips, and very early reservation if going to *fiestas* during Holy Week, etc. At Christmas, many Central American students return home via Tapachula and buses from Mexico City are booked solid for 2 weeks before, except for those lines which do not make reservations. You must go and queue at the bus stations; this can involve some long waits, sometimes 2-2½ hrs. Even if you are travelling, you may sometimes be required to buy a *boleto de andén* (platform ticket) at many bus stations, it usually costs 1 peso.

Bus Companies: (tickets and bookings) Going N: Transportes del Norte, at Av. Insurgentes Centro 137, nr. Reforma (Tel.: 5460032 and 5355084); dep. from Central Norte. Omnibus de México, Insurgentes Norte 42, at Héroes Ferrocarrileros (Tel.: 5676756 and 5675858). Greyhound bus, Reforma 27, closed Sun.; information at Terminal Norte from 1100-1500, Tel.: 5678444 and 5678426. Going to Central States: Autobuses Anáhuac, Bernal Díaz 8 (Tel.: 5468382 and 5910533); Central Norte departures. Going NE: ADO, Av. Cien Metros 4967 (Tel.: 5678364 and 5678076). Going NW: Tres Estrellas de Oro, Calzada de Niño Perdido 19A (Tel.: 5789888), Central Norte. Going S (incl. Guatemala) Cristóbal Colón, Blvd. Gral Ignacio Zaragoza 38. Tel.: 5424354; from Central del Oriente; also ADO, Buenavista 9 (Tel.: 5660055 and 5467448). Going SW: Estrella de Oro, Calzada de Tlalpan 2205 (Tel.: 5498520 to 29).

Excursions in and around the city can easily take up ten days. The main places of interest are listed below.

You will find, as you explore the city, that you use two thoroughfares more than any others. The most famous is Paseo de la Reforma, with a tree-shaded, wide centre section and two side lanes; it runs somewhat diagonally NE from Chapultepec Park. At the Plaza de la Reforma it bends eastwards and becomes Avenida Juárez, still fairly wide but without side lanes. Beyond the Palacio de Bellas Artes this becomes Av. Madero, quite narrow, with one-way traffic. The other and longer thoroughfare is Av. Insurgentes, a diagonal north-south artery about 25 km. long. The two avenues bisect at a *plazuela* with a statue of Cuauhtémoc, the last of the Aztec emperors.

The Zócalo, the main square, or Plaza Mayor, centre of the oldest part, always alive with people, and often vivid with official ceremonies and celebrations. On the north side, on the site of the Great Teocalli or temple of the Aztecs, is

The Cathedral, the largest and oldest cathedral in Latin America, designed by Herrera, the architect of the Escorial in Spain, along with that in Puebla; first built 1525; rebuilding began 1573; consecrated 1667; finished 1813. Singularly harmonious, considering the many architects employed and time taken to build it. At present only certain parts can be visited, as restoration work is being carried out. There is an underground crypt reached by stairs in the W wing of the main part of the building. Next to the Cathedral is the **Sagrario Metropolitano,** 1769, with fine churrigueresque façade. Behind the Cathedral at the corner of Av. Guatemala and Calle Seminario are some Aztec ruins known as the **Templo Mayor** or **Teotitlán**, which were found in 1978 when public works were being carried out. They are open to the public between 1000 and 1300, a very worthwhile visit, especially since the Aztecs built a new temple every 52 years, and 7 have been identified on top of each other. The sculptured head of the Aztec goddess of the moon, Coyolxauhqui, was found here. Archaeologists also were then able to confirm that the major temple was not under the Metropolitan Cathedral, as previously thought. On the W side of the Zócalo are the Portales de los Mercaderes (Arcades of the Merchants), very busy since 1524. North of them, opposite the Cathedral, is

The Monte de Piedad (National Pawnshop) established in the 18th century and housed in a 16th-century building. Prices are government controlled and bargains are often found. Monthly auctions of unredeemed pledges.

Palacio Nacional (National Palace), takes up the whole eastern side of the Zócalo. Built on the site of the Palace of Moctezuma and rebuilt in 1692 in colonial baroque, with its exterior faced in the red volcanic stone called *tezontle;* the top floor was added by President Calles in the 1920s. It houses various government departments and the Juárez museum (open Mon.-Fri., 1000-1800), free. Over the central door hangs the Liberty Bell, rung at 2300 on September 15 by the President, who gives the multitude the *Grito* - "Viva México!" The thronged frescoes around the staircase are by Diego Rivera. Open daily; guides. Other murals by Rivera can be seen at the Ministry of Education, four blocks N of Zócalo, on corner of Cuba and Argentina. In the Calle Moneda and adjoining the back of the Palace is the **Museo de las Culturas,** with interesting international archaeological and historical exhibits. Open 0930-1800; closed Suns. Also in Moneda are the site

922 MEXICO

of the first university in the New World (building now dilapidated), the Archbishop's Palace, and the site of the New World's first printing press.

Wax Museum in Av. República Argentina, a few blocks N of Zócalo on righthand side, US$0.05.

Museo de Artes e Industrias Populares de México is in Av. Juárez 44, in the old Corpus Christi Church, next to *Hotel Alameda*. Open Tues.-Sat. 1000-1400 and 1500-1800, shop 1000-1800 Mon.-Sat. Free. Operated by Instituto Nacional Indigenista (INI). It has well-arranged permanent exhibitions and the articles are for sale, although you may prefer to find cheaper goods at San Juan market (20% cheaper).

Supreme Court, opposite Palacio Nacional, on SE corner of the Zócalo, see frescoes by Orozco.

Palacio de Bellas Artes, a large, showy building, interesting for Art Deco lovers, houses a museum and a theatre, and a *cafeteria* at mezzanine level (light, average continental food at moderate prices). Open Tues.-Sun., 1100-1900. Its domes are lavishly decorated with coloured stone. The museum has old and contemporary paintings, prints, sculptures, and handicraft articles. The fresco by Rivera is a copy of the one rubbed out in disapproval at Radio City, New York, and there are spirited Riveras in the room of oils and water-colours. Other frescoes are by Orozco, Tamayo and Siqueiros. Daily, 1000-1730; Sun., 1000-1400. The most remarkable thing about the theatre is its glass curtain designed by Tiffany. It is solemnly raised and lowered—for a fee—on Sun. mornings between 0900 and 1000. The Palace is listing badly, for it has sunk 4 metres since it was built. Operas are performed; there are orchestral concerts and performances by the superb Mexican Folklore Ballet on Wed., Sat. and Sun.—one must book in advance. Tickets from US$5 to US$10 (top balcony seats are good value as they provide a good vantage point to see formations from above). Tickets on sale from 1100. Don't buy tickets from touts, who also short-change. Cheap concerts at 1200 on Sun., and also at Teatro Hidalgo, behind Bellas Artes on Hidalgo, at the same time.

Across the road, on the 41st floor of the Torre Latinoamericana, is a good restaurant and bar with splendid views of the city, especially at sunset and after dark (entry fee US$1.30). This great glass tower dominates the **Alameda Gardens,** once the Aztec market and later the place of execution for the Spanish Inquisition. Beneath the broken shade of eucalyptus, cypress and ragged palms, wide paths link fountains and heroic statues.

On the northern side of the Alameda, on Av. Hidalgo, is the Jardín Morelos, flanked by two old churches: Santa Veracruz (1730) to the right and San Juan de Dios to the left. The latter has a richly carved baroque exterior; its image of San Antonio de Padua is visited by those who are broken-hearted for love.

Escuela Nacional Preparatoria, near church of Jesús Nazareno (see below) built 1749 as the Jesuit School of San Ildefonso in splendid baroque. There are some exciting frescoes by Orozco and (in the Anfiteatro Bolívar) by Diego Rivera and Fernando Leal.

Ministry of Education, on Argentina, 3 blocks from Zócalo, built 1922, contains frescoes by a number of painters. Here are Diego Rivera's masterpieces, painted between 1923 and 1930, illustrating the lives and sufferings of the common people.

Plaza Santo Domingo, two blocks N of the Cathedral, an intimate little plaza surrounded by fine colonial buildings: (a) a beautiful palace; (b) on the west side, the Arcades of Santo Domingo, where public scribes and small hand-operated printing presses still carry on their business; (c) on the north side, the church of Santo Domingo, in Mexican baroque, 1737. Note the carving on the doors and façade; (d) the School of Medicine, where the tribunals of the Inquisition were held. There is a remarkable staircase in the patio, and striking Siqueiros murals above it. The nearby streets contain some fine examples of colonial architecture.

Two blocks E of Santo Domingo are the church and convent of **San Pedro y San Pablo** (1603), both massively built and now turned over to secular use. A block N of it is the public market of Abelardo L. Rodríguez, with striking mural decorations.

Church of Loreto, built 1816 and now tilting badly, but being restored, is on a square of the same name, surrounded by colonial buildings.

La Santísima Trinidad (1677, remodelled 1755), to be seen for its fine towers and the rich carvings on its façade.

The Mercado Merced (Metro Merced), said to be the largest market in all the Americas, dating back over 400 years. Its activities spread over several blocks. In the northern quarter of this market are the ruins of La Merced monastery; the fine 18th century patio is almost all that survives; the courtyard, on Avenida Uruguay, between Calle Talavera and Calle Jesús María, opposite No. 171, is nearly restored.

The oldest hospital in the New World, **Jesús Nazareno**, 20 de Noviembre 82, founded 1526 by Cortés, was remodelled in 1928, save for the patio and staircase. Cortés' bones have been kept since 1794 in the adjoining church, on the corner of Pino Suárez and República de El Salvador, diagonally opp. Museum of the City.

MEXICO 923

Avenida Madero leads from the Zócalo W to the Alameda. On it is **La Profesa** church, late 16th century, with a fine high altar and a leaning tower. The 18th century **Iturbide Palace,** Av. Madero 17, once the home of Emperor Iturbide (1821-23), has been restored and has a clear plastic roof—wander around, it is now a bank head office. To the tourist the great sight of Av. Madero, however, is the **Casa de los Azulejos** (House of Tiles) at the Alameda end of the street. Now occupied by Sanborn's Restaurant, it was built in the 16th century, and is brilliantly faced with blue and white Puebla tiles. The staircase walls are covered with Orozco frescoes. (There are further Orozco frescoes at Biblioteca Iberoamericana on Cuba between 5 de Febrero and Argentina.) Over the way is the **Church of San Francisco,** founded in 1525 by the "Apostles of Mexico", the first 12 Franciscans to reach the country. It was by far the most important church in colonial days. Cortés' body rested here for some time, as did Iturbide's; the Viceroys attended the church.

Beyond San Francisco church, Eje Lázaro Cárdenas, formerly Calle San Juan de Letrán, leads S towards **Las Vizcaínas,** at Plaza Las Vizcaínas, one block E. This huge building was put up in 1734 as a school for girls; some of it is still so used, but some of it has become slum tenements. In spite of neglect, it is still the best example of colonial secular baroque in the city. Visiting hours: Sat. 0800-1400 only.

Museo San Carlos, Puente de Alvarado 50 (Metro Revolución), a 19th-century palace (open to visitors 1000 to 1700, closed Mon.), has fine Mexican colonial painting and a first-class collection of European paintings by Titian (3), Tintoretto (3), Ingres, Poussin, Daumier, Pisarro, Delacroix, El Greco (2), Goya, Zurbarán, Ribera, the 14th century Catalan Luís Borrasa, Rubens, Breughel, and Lawrence and Opie of the English school. The **Escuela Nacional de Artes Plásticas** at the corner of Academía and Calle Moneda, houses about 50 modern Mexican paintings. There is another picture gallery, the **Pinacoteca Nacional de San Diego,** in the former church of San Diego in Calle Dr. Mora, at the Juárez end of the Alameda. (Cheap concerts on Thurs. at 2000.)

Moving eastwards along Av. Hidalgo, before the Palace of Fine Arts, on the right is the **Post Office,** built 1904, open for letters 0800-2400 Mon.-Fri., 0800-2000 Sat., and 0900-1600 Sun. For parcels open 0900-1500 Mon.-Fri. only; parcels larger than 2 kilograms not accepted and difficult to send things other than books, records and cassettes. Mail kept for only 10 days. Poste restante at window 19, not recommended (see page 1004).

North from the west side of the Post Office leads to the Calle Santa María la Redonda, at the end of which is **Plaza Santiago de Tlatelolco,** next oldest Plaza to the Zócalo, heavily damaged in the 1985 earthquake. Here was the main market of the Aztecs, and on it, in 1524, the Franciscans built a huge church and convent. This is now the Plaza of the Three Cultures (Aztec, colonial and modern): (a) the Aztec ruins have been restored; (b) the magnificent baroque church of Santiago Tlatelolco is now the focus of (c) the massive, multi-storey Nonoalco-Tlatelolco housing scheme with school, shops, and tall blocks of flats stretching from Reforma to the unusual triangular office building on Insurgentes Norte, a garden city within a city, with pedestrian and wheeled traffic entirely separate. It sustained serious earthquake damage.

About 4 blocks N of the Post Office off Eje Lázaro Cárdenas is **Plaza Garibaldi,** a must, especially on Saturday night, when up to 200 *mariachis* in their traditional costume of huge sombrero, tight silver-embroidered trousers, pistol and *sarape,* will play your favourite Mexican serenade for US$4. If you arrive by taxi you will be besieged. The whole square throbs with life and the packed bars are cheerful, though there is some danger from thieves and pickpockets. The Lagunilla market is held about 4 blocks NE of the plaza, a hive of activity all week. Inexpensive nearby bar is *Guadalajara:* good drinks (but no soft drinks), dancing to *mariachi* band, entrance US$1, not dear. If very crowded, try *Tenampa,* somewhat dearer. On one side of Plaza Garibaldi is a gigantic eating hall, different stalls sell different courses, very entertaining.

Palacio de Minería, Calle Tacuba 9 (1797), is a fine old building, now restored, and once more level on its foundations. (Cheap concerts on Sun. at 1700, upstairs.) Moved from the Plaza de la Reforma to Plaza Manuel Tolsa opposite the Palacio is the great equestrian statue, "El Caballito", of King Charles IV cast in 1802; it weighs 26 tons and is the second-largest bronze casting in the world.

Along the S side of the Alameda, running E, is Av. Juárez, a fine street with a mixture of old and new buildings. In the *Hotel del Prado* vestibule (may be closed for repair after the earthquake), facing the Alameda, Diego Rivera's "scandalous" fresco, "Sunday in the Alameda", is now exhibited (an explanation, in English, is given at 1700 daily; you are expected to buy a drink). A stroll down Calle Dolores, a busy and fascinating street, leads to the market of San Juan. The colonial church of Corpus Christi, on Av. Juárez, is now used to display and sell folk arts and crafts. The avenue ends at the small Plaza de la Reforma. At the corner of Juárez and Reforma is the National Lottery building. Drawings are held three times a week, at 2000: an interesting scene, open to the public. Beyond Plaza de la Reforma is the Monument to the Revolution of 1910: a great copper dome, now rather tarnished, soaring above supporting columns set on the largest triumphal arches in the world.

South of this area, on Plaza Ciudadela, is a large colonial building, **La Ciudadela,** put up in 1700. It has been used for all kinds of purposes but is now a library.

The wide and handsome but earthquake-damaged Paseo de la Reforma, 3 km. long, continues to Chapultepec Park: shops, offices, hotels, restaurants all the way. Along it are monuments to

924 MEXICO

Columbus; to Cuauhtémoc and a 45-metre marble column to Independence, topped by the golden-winged figure of a woman, "El Angelito" to the Mexicans. Just before entering the park is the Salubridad (Health) Building. Rivera's frescoes in this building cannot be seen by the public, who can view only the stained-glass windows on the staircases.

Museo Nacional de Arte, Tacuba 8, opp. Palacio de Minería, nr. main Post Office. Open Tues-Sun., 1000-1800; paintings, sculptures, objects from pre-hispanic times to modern artists. Entry US$0.20.

Chapultepec Park, at the end of Paseo de la Reforma, with its thousands of ahuehuete trees, is one of the most beautiful in the world but is becoming spoiled by constant littering. It contains a maze of pathways, a large lake, a marvellous botanical garden, shaded lawns, a zoo with giant pandas (closed Mon. and Tues.), a large amusement park (there is a section for children and another for adults) with huge roller-coasters (open Wed., Sat. and Sun., entry US$0.90, all rides free, except roller-coaster; on Sat. and Sun. only, US$0.22), bridle paths and polo grounds. Just below the castle and a little to the left are the remains of the famous Arbol de Moctezuma, known locally as "El Sargento". This immense tree, which has a circumference of 14 metres and was about 60 metres high, has been cut off at a height of about 10 metres. In this park too, are the Don Quixote fountain, the Frog's fountain, the Niños Monument, and Monkey Island, a replica of Cacahuamilpa caves. At the top of a hill in the park is Chapultepec Castle, with a view over Mexico Valley from its beautiful balconies, entry US$0.02. It has now become the **National Museum of History,** open 0900-1700 (closed in 1985 for renovation). Its rooms were used by the Emperor Maximilian and the Empress Carlotta during their brief reign. There is an unfinished mural by Siqueiros and a notable mural by O'Gorman on the theme of independence. Entrance US$0.20; US$0.12 on Sun. Halfway down the hill is the new **Gallery of Mexican History.** On Sun. mornings large numbers of people gather round the lake for open-air extension classes in a great variety of subjects (e.g. hairdressing, artificial flower-making, guitar-playing) organized by the University and open to all.

The crowning wonder of the park is the **Anthropological Museum** built by architect Pedro Ramírez Vásquez to house a vast collection illustrating pre-conquest Mexican culture. It has a 350-metre façade and an immense patio shaded by a gigantic concrete mushroom, 4,200 square metres—the world's largest concrete expanse supported by a single pillar. The largest model (8½ metres high, weighing 167 tons) is Tlaloc the rain god, removed—accompanied by protesting cloud bursts from near the town of Texcoco— to the museum. Open Tues.-Sat., 0900-1900 and Sun., 1000-1800. Only Mexican student cards accepted. Entrance is US$0.25 except Sun. (free), and holidays, when all museums charge US$0.10. Guides in English cost an additional US$0.20; ask for the pieces you want to see as each tour only visits two of 23 halls; guided tours in Spanish free. Audio-visual introduction US$0.10. If you want to see everything, you need two days. Permission to photograph with tripod, free, from INAH, Córdoba 45, if you are professionally interested, date must be fixed in advance; otherwise cameras not allowed. The most fanatical museum hater will enjoy this one, particularly the display of folk costumes upstairs. There is an excellent collection of English, French, German and Spanish books, especially guides to Mexican ruins, including maps. Restaurant on site is expensive and not very good.

Warning We are told that when the Museum of Anthropology closes in the evening, Chapultepec park abounds with thieves. Also, some tourists have been robbed at knife point in the underpass between Chapultepec metro and the Archaeological Museum.

There are now four other museums in Chapultepec Park: the Tamayo Museum, and in the new section the museums of Natural History, Technology and **Modern Art** (US$0.50, students US$0.25). The last shows Mexican art only in two buildings, pleasantly set among trees with some sculptures in the grounds. The smaller building shows temporary exhibitions. The delightfully light architecture of the larger building is spoilt by a heavy, vulgar marble staircase, with a curious acoustic effect on the central landing under a translucent dome, which must have been unplanned; open 1100-1800 daily except Mon. The Gallery of Mexican History has dioramas, with tape-recorded explanations of Mexican history, and photographs of the 1910 Revolution. The **Tamayo Museum's** interior space is unusual in that you cannot tell which floor you are on or how many there are. Excellent international modern art. Warhols, Picassos, etc. It is situated between the Modern Art and Anthropology Museums. US$0.25 entry, ½ price to students with international card (only place in Mexico). There is also a Diego Rivera fountain in this new section of the park. The **Museum of Technology** is free; it is operated by the Federal Electricity Commission, has "touchable" exhibits which demonstrate electrical and energy principles. It is located beside the roller-coasters.

Natural History Museum Open 1000-1700, Tues to Sun. Entry 2 pesos.

Not far from the Anthropological Museum in Chapultepec Park is the Sala de Arte Público Siqueiros, Calle Tres Picos 29, which has a large collection of items associated with the artist in addition to a number of his works. Open Mon.-Fri., 1000-1400, 1700-2100, Sat. 1000-1400, free.

Further places of interest to tourists are as follows:
Museum of the City, on Av. Pino Suárez and República de El Salvador, shows the geology of the city and has life size figures in period costumes showing the history of different peoples before

MEXICO 925

Cortés. In the attic above the museum is the studio of Joaquín Clausell, with walls covered with impressionist miniatures. Free admittance, Tues. to Thurs. Two blocks S on Misioneros from this museum is the **Anglican (Episcopal) Cathedral**, called the Cathedral of San José de Gracia. Built in 1642 as a Roman Catholic church, it was given by the Benito Juárez government to the Episcopal Mission in Mexico. Juárez himself often attended services in it.

Museo Nacional de las Culturas, Moneda 13, open 0930-1800, closed Sun. Exhibits of countries from all over the world and some historical information.

Museo de Arte Carrillo Gil, Av. Revolución esq. Los Leones, near San Angel; paintings by Orozco, Rivera, Siqueiros and others.

Instituto Nacional Indigenista, Av. Revolución 1297.

Escuela Nacional de Ingeniería, next to the main post office on Calle Tacuba, houses a permanent exhibition of meteorites found all over Mexico (up to 14 tonnes).

Museo Universitario de Chopo, E. G. Martínez 10, opp. Metro San Cosme, nr. Insurgentes Norte. Contemporary international exhibitions (photography, art) in a church-like building. Saturday music market, records, cassettes, books, instruments, clothes traded and exchanged, particularly popular with young Mexicans.

Museo Arqueológico del Sitio (ruins of main pyramid of Tenochtitlán), Seminario 4 y Guatemala, open 0900-2000, Sat. and Sun. 0900-1800, closed Mon.

Museo del Convento de Carmen, Av. Revolución 4, San Angel, open 1000-1700. Two other museums worth visiting are the Museo Nacional de Culturas Populares, Hidalgo 289, which focuses on livelihoods in Mexico (open 0900-1600, Tues., Thurs., Sat.; 0900-2000, Weds. and Fri., and 1100-1700, Sun.), and the Museo de las Intervenciones, concentrating on foreign intervention in Mexico (20 de Agosto y General Anaya, about 4 blocks from Gen. Anaya metro, next to ex-Convento de Churubusco, open Tues.-Sun., 0900-2100).

Art Galleries *Arvil*, Cerrada Hamburgo 9, contemporary Mexican and international art; *Artmex*, Mexican Popular Gallery, Sabino 13; permanent exhibition of over 100 paintings of well-known Mexican artists, open 0900-1900. *Central Art Gallery Migrachi*, Av. Juárez 4, sculptures, drawings, also *Galería de Arte Migrachi*, on Génova 20. *Galería Lanai*, Hamburgo 151. *Galería Merkup*, Moliere 328. *Galerías Rubens*, Independencia 68. *Galería Tere Haas*, important contemporary artists, Génova 2-C. *Summa Artis*, Hotel Presidente Chapulteped, Campos Elíseos 218, contemporary Mexican art. *Val-Ray Gallery*, Reforma 412, Zona Rosa.

The Bull Ring is said to be the largest in the world, and holds 60,000 spectators. Bull fights are held every Sunday at 1600 from October through March. Buy tickets on Saturday or on Sunday 2 hrs before spectacle: seat in sun US$0.32, in shade US$ 0.48. The Bull Ring is in the Ciudad de los Deportes (City of Sports), Plaza México, reached from Paseo de la Reforma by Av. de los Insurgentes. (A little to the W of where Los Insurgentes crosses Chapultepec, and on Av. Chapultepec itself between Calles Praga and Varsovia, are the remains of the old aqueduct built in 1779.) Besides the Bull Ring, the Sports City contains a football stadium holding 50,000 people, a boxing ring, a cinema, a *frontón* court for *jai-alai*, a swimming pool, restaurants, hotels, etc.

Modern Buildings On Avenida Insurgentes Norte is a remarkable building by Alejandro Prieto: the Teatro de Los Insurgentes, a theatre and opera house seating 1,300 people. The main frontage on the Avenida consists of a high curved wall without windows. This wall is entirely covered with mosaic decoration, the work of Diego Rivera: appropriate figures, scenes, and portraits composed round the central motif of a gigantic pair of hands holding a mask, worth going a distance to see.

The most successful religious architecture in Mexico today is to be found in the churches put up by Enrique de la Mora and Félix Candela; a good example is the chapel they built in 1957 for the Missionaries of the Holy Spirit, in a garden behind high walls at Av. Universidad 1700. (An excellent Candela church, and easy to see, is the Church of La Medalla Milagrosa, just to the E of Avenida Universidad at the junction of Avenida División Norte, Metro station División del Norte.) "All the churches and chapels built by this team have such lightness and balance that they seem scarcely to rest on their foundations." One of the seminal works of one of Mexico's greatest modern architects, Luís Barragán, is at Los Clubes, Las Arboledas bus from Chapultepec bus station. See also the *objet trouvé* mural at the Diana cinema in the centre of the city, and Orozco's great thundercloud of composition, the "Apocalypse", at the Church of Jesús Nazareno. Both the *Camino Real Hotel* and the IBM technical centre were designed by Ricardo Legorreto; very well worth seeing. Consult Max Cetto's book on modern Mexican architecture. In this connection, University City (see next page) is also well worth a look.

Sullivan Park (popularly known as Colonia Park or Jardín del Arte) is reached by going up Paseo de la Reforma to the intersection with los Insurgentes, and then W two blocks between Calles Sullivan and Villalongín. Here, each Sunday afternoon, there is a display of paintings, engravings and sculptures near the monument to Motherhood, packed with sightseers and buyers; everything is for sale.

Reino Aventura, S of the city near the Mall del Sur, amusement park for children along Disneyland lines, clean, orderly, popular with families.

The **Basilica of Guadalupe**, in the Gustavo A. Madero district, often called La Villa de Guadalupe, in the outer suburbs to the NE, is the most venerated shrine in Mexico, for it was here, in December 1531, that the Virgin appeared three times, in the guise of an Indian princess, to the Indian Juan Diego and imprinted her portrait on his cloak. The cloak is preserved, set in gold and protected by a 27-ton railing of silver, at the centre of the magnificent altar. A chapel stands over the well which gushed at the spot where the Virgin appeared. The great day here is December 12, the great night the night before. A new basilica has been built next door, impressive and worth visiting; it holds over 20,000 people. The original basilica is being converted into a museum and is half open, entrance US$0.40. Mostly representations of the image on the cloak, but interesting painted tin plates offering thanks for cures, etc., from about 1860s. There are, in fact, about seven churches in the immediate neighbourhood, including one on the hill above; most of them are at crazy angles to each other and to the ground, because of subsidence; the subsoil is very soft. The Templo de los Capuchinos has been the subject of a remarkable feat of engineering in which one end has been raised 3.375 metres so that the building is now horizontal. There is a little platform from which to view this work. Buses marked La Villa go close to the site, or you can go by underground to Basílica and walk 3 mins to the site (Green Line).

Suburbs of Mexico City

Churubusco, 10 km. SE, reached from the Zócalo by Coyoacán or Tlalpan bus, or from General Anaya metro station, to see the picturesque and partly ruined convent (1762), now become the National Interventions museum (open 1000-1700, closed Mon.). Seventeen rooms filled with mementoes, documents, proclamations and pictures recounting invasions, incursions and occupations since independence. The site of the museum was chosen because it was the scene of a battle when the US Army marched into Mexico City in 1847. There is a golf course at the Churubusco Country Club. Churubusco has the principal Mexican film studios. The new Olympic swimming pool is here. Near enough to Coyoacán (see page 927) to walk there.

Tlalpan, 6½ km. further, or direct from Villa Obregón (see page 927), a most picturesque old town on the slopes of Ajusco, an extinct volcano: colonial houses, gardens, and near the main square an early 16th century church with a fine altar and paintings by Cabrera. Reached by bus or trolley bus from the Taxqueña metro station. Two-and-a-half km. W is the village of Peña Pobre, near which, to the NE, is the Pyramid of **Cuicuilco**, believed to be the oldest in Mexico (archaeological museum on site, Insurgentes Sur Km. 16, intersection with Periférico, open 0800-1800, closed Mon.). The pyramid dates from the 5th or 6th century B.C.; it is over 100 metres in diameter but only 18 high. On the road from Mexico City to Cuicuilco there is a pre-classic burial area under the lava flow, at Copilco, which is closed to the public.

Another excursion can be made to **Ajusco**, about 20 km. SW of Mexico City. Catch a bus on Calzada Tlalpan direct to Ajusco (US$0.30). Get out at terminal and ask for directions to Volcán Ajusco, which is very close to the village. It's a 2 hr. walk to the summit, excellent views on a clear day. Foothills around the area are also pleasant.

Xochimilco, to the SE, in the Valley of México. Take metro to Taxqueña (terminus) and catch a tram or bus No. 140 (US$0.05) to the market. Turn left out of the station to catch the bus. The bus back leaves from the street left of the main church (don't believe taxi drivers who say there is no bus back). The bus stops some distance away beside the market (cheap fruit) in Xochimilco; bad signposting, but often tours from the *embarcaderos* will meet the buses and escort you to the boats. Otherwise keep to the right of the large church on the square, on Nuevo León, carry on until Violeta then turn right for 1 block and then turn left into Embarcadero. Xochimilco has a maze of canals, originally part of the canal system of Tenochtitlán, which wander round fruit and flower gardens. Punts adorned with flowers, poled by Indians, can be hired for about 1½ hrs for US$7-10 weekdays (one per "family", so arrange to join others beforehand) and US$0.25 at weekends only on "public" boats. Make sure you bargain hard before boarding and ensure you get all the time you paid for as many of the boats are punted by boys without watches. At the canal-side restaurants there is music and dancing. The canals are busy on Sundays, quiet midweek. There is a fine market on Saturday; Indians come from miles around. It has a 16th century fortified monastery, San Bernardo, built on Xochimilco's main square by the Franciscans in the 16th century, one of the finest of its kind in Mexico and has escaped heavy-handed restoration. The main altar is a masterpiece of painting and sculpture. Only one hotel, basic, F. Many cheap souvenirs; fruit and flowers sold from boats in canals. **Ixtapalapa** (2 good churches) is at the foot of the Cerro de Estrella, whose top is reached by a bad road or a path for a good view. One of the most spectacular of Mexican passion-plays begins at Ixtapalapa on Holy Thursday. Note that it is virtually impossible to get on to the Mexico City-Cuernavaca toll road from Xochimilco.

University City, world-famous, is 18 km. via Insurgentes Sur on the Cuernavaca highway. Perhaps the most notable building is the 10-storey library tower, by Juan O'Gorman, its outside walls iridescent with mosaics telling the story of scientific knowledge, from Aztec astronomy to molecular theory. The Administrative Building has a vast, mosaic-covered and semi-sculptured mural by Siqueiros. Across the highway is the Olympic Stadium, with seats for 80,000, in shape, colour, and situation a world's wonder. Diego Rivera has a sculpture-painting telling the story of Mexican sport. A new complex is being completed beyond the Ciudad Universitaria, including the newspaper library, Hemeroteca Nacional, Teatro Juan Ruiz de Alarcón, Sala Nezahuacoyotl (concerts etc.) and the Espacio Escultórico (sculptures). In the University museum there is an exhibition of traditional masks from all over Mexico. Beyond the Olympic Stadium is also a Botanical Garden which shows all the cactus species in Mexico (ask directions, it's a ½ hr. walk). The University of Mexico was founded in 1551, 85 years before Harvard. Bus (marked C.U., one passes along Eje Lázaro Cárdenas; also bus 17, marked Tlalpan, which runs the length of Insurgentes); gets you there, about 1 hr. journey; *peseros* also take you there. Another way to the university is on metro line 3 to Universidad metro, walk 15 mins. to university entrance and library. At the University City there is a free bus going round the campus. The University offers cheap 6-week courses.

In the same direction as the University but further out is **Anahuacalli** (usually called the Diego Rivera Museum, open Tues.-Sun. 1000-1800, closed Holy Week). Here is a very fine collection of precolumbian sculpture and pottery, effectively displayed in a pseudo-Mayan tomb built for it by Diego Rivera. View of southern rim of mountains from the roof. In some ways it beats the Anthropological Museum. Reached by bus from the Taxqueña metro station to Estadio Azteca, or take the bus marked División del Norte from outside Salto del Agua metro. Calle Museo crosses Div. del Norte.

Villa Obregón (popularly known as **San Angel**) 13 km. SW, has narrow, cobble-stone streets, many old homes, huge trees, and the charm of an era now largely past. See the triple domes of its church, covered with coloured tiles, and the former Carmen monastery, now a museum (open 1000-1700). See also the beautifully furnished and preserved old house, Casa del Risco, near the market, and the church of San Jacinto and its adjoining monastery. One of the more macabre sights of Mexico is the severed hand of Alvaro Obregón, preserved in a bottle inside his monument on the spot where he was assassinated in 1928. See also the Museo de Arte Carrillo Gil, Av. Revolución 1608, with excellent changing exhibits. In San Angel also, there is a *bazar sábado*, a splendid Saturday folk art and curiosity market, and the Parroquia, a Dominican convent church dating from 1566. Reach San Angel by bus from Chapultepec Park or by metro line 3 to M.A.Quevedo. Excellent restaurants: the *San Angel Inn* is first class. Desierto de los Leones (see below) is reached from Villa Obregón by a scenic road.

Coyoacán, an old and beautiful suburb adjoining Villa Obregón, and also reached via line 3, is the place from which Cortés launched his attack on Tenochtitlán. The Casa de Cortés, now the Municipal Hall, was built 244 years after the Conquest. The rose-coloured house at Francisco Sosa 383 is said to have been built by Alvarado. The San Juan Bautista church and the nearby Franciscan monastery are both early 16th century. Friday market. The Frida Kahlo Museum at Allende y Londres, preserved as lived in by Diego Rivera and Frida Kahlo, is fascinating and well worth any afternoon, reached by metro line 3 to Tres Manos then by colectivo. Drawings and paintings by both. Free guided tours Sat. and Sun. at 1100. Nearby, Trotsky's house is now open at 1000-1400 and 1500-1730, Tues.-Fri., and 1030-1600, Sat.-Sun. (students man it), as a museum at Viena 45 (with Morelos). The Museo Nacional de Culturas Populares, Hidalgo 289, should be seen: open Wed. and Fri. 0900-2000, Tues., Thurs. and Sat. 0900-1600, Sun. 1100-1700. The new market and the remarkable Chapel of Our Lady of Solitude are by Enrique de la Mora and Félix Candela. *El Coyote Flaco* is a good restaurant; night club *Peña Nahuatl*, fine folk singing and poetry readings.

The Pyramid of **Tenayuca,** 10 km. to the NW, is about 15 metres high and the best-preserved in Mexico. The Aztecs rebuilt this temple every 52 years; this one was last reconstructed about 1507; well worth seeing, for it is surrounded with serpents in masonry. The easiest way to get there by car from Mexico City centre is to go to Vallejo, 11 km. N of the intersection of Insurgentes Norte and Río Consulado. Admission US$0.08. By metro, take the line to the Central de Autobuses del Norte (see page 920), La Raza, and catch the bus there. By bus from Tlatelolco; ask driver and passengers to advise you on arrival as site is not easily visible. An excursion to Tula may go via Tenayuca. It is not far from the old town of **Tlalnepantla:** see the ancient convent (ask for the *catedral*) on the Plaza Gustavo Paz and the church (1583), which contains the first image, a Christ of Mercy, brought to the New World. Two-and-a-half km. to the N is the smaller pyramid of Santa Cecilia, interesting for its restored sanctuary.

Los Remedios, a small town 13 km. NW of Mexico City, has in its famous church an image, a foot high, adorned with jewels. See the old aqueduct, with a winding stair leading to the top. It can be reached by car or by taking the Los Remedios bus at Tacuba metro. Fiesta: September 1 to the climax September 8.

At Tlatilco, NW of the city (just outside the city boundary on Querétaro road), pre-classic Olmec-influenced figurines can be seen.

Excursions from Mexico City

Desierto de los Leones, a beautiful pine forest made into a national park, can be reached from Mexico City (24 km.) by a fine scenic road through Villa Obregón. In the woods is an old Carmelite convent, around are numerous hermitages, inside are several subterranean passages and a secret hall with curious acoustic properties. Take a torch. Take an hour's bus ride from Observatorio metro to La Venta and ask bus-driver where to get off for the path to the monastery (about 4 km. walk). One can either get there via the paved road or via the beautiful conifer-forest path, but the latter splits frequently so stick to what looks like the main path; or take the fire-break road below the row of shops and cheap restaurants near the main road. Food stalls abound, particularly at weekends when it is crowded.

Acolman has the formidable fortress-like convent and church of San Agustín, dating from 1539-60, with much delicate detail on the façade and some interesting murals inside. Note the fine portal and the carved stone cross at the entrance to the atrium. Closed Fri. Reached by bus from Indios Verdes metro station, or from the Zócalo. It is 42 km. NE of the city.

Teotihuacán, 45 km. from Mexico City, has some of the most remarkable relics of an ancient civilization in the world. The old city is traceable over an area of 3½ by 6½ km. The Pyramids make the largest artificial mounds on the American continent: the Pyramid of the Sun (64 metres high, 213 metres square at the base) covers almost the same space as the Great Pyramid of Cheops in Egypt. The sides are terraced, and wide stairs lead to the summit; unfortunately its surface was restored in the wrong materials to wrong specifications around 1910. The Pyramid of the Moon, 1 km. away, is only half its size. There are temples of agriculture, of Tlaloc (the Rain God), of the Plumed Serpent, of Quetzalcoatl (Lord of Air and Wind), and the broad Highway of the Dead. There are subterranean buildings with large halls and coloured decorations, and many superimposed buildings of a later epoch. The pyramids, buildings, courts, etc., are now completely restored and well worth a visit; but beware the fake "idol" sellers and the flute-players who lurk everywhere and play you an awful tune! The Palace of Quetzalpapalotl, where the priests serving the sanctuaries of the Moon lived, has been restored together with its patio. Visit also the cactus garden, with every type of cactus imaginable. Site open 0800-1800. (Entrance near the bus stop only opens at 1000 despite the sign; try entrance near the Pyramid of the Moon.) Entrance, US$0.25, US$0.10 per car. Entrance US$0.10 on Sundays. Reckon on about 5-8 hrs to see the site properly. Tetitla and Atetelco, two smaller sites to the W of the perimetral road, are worth seeing; they are about 1 km. N of the main entrance from the *autopista*; to get to them from the museum, exit W and walk right up to main road, turning left after crossing stream. NE exit from main site brings you to Tepantitlán, superb frescoes. There is a run-down, pseudo-colonial "castle", *Charlie's Restaurant*, with outdoor tables and good, although rather expensive food, overlooking the buildings. There is a small museum below the restaurant. Easily reached from the bus terminal (platform E, bus shelter marked for Teotihuacán) at Indios Verdes metro station (green line 3) where the buses to and from Teotihuacán make a stop (US$0.75, 45 mins.-1 hr.), or from Terminal del Norte, Gate 8 (Autobuses del Norte metro). Bus returns from Door 1 at Teotihuacán site, supposedly every ½ hr. Interesting restaurant, *La Gruta*, in cave, costume waitresses, *mariachis*, dancers on Sun., reasonable prices, but takes a long time serving. *Son et lumière* display, costs US$4 per person (good *lumière*, not so good *son*); lasts 45 mins., starts at 1900. English commentary. Shown between January and end-April; take blanket or rent one there. You can ride back to town with one of the tourist buses for about US$2. Note that the site is more generally known as "Pirámides" than as "Teotihuacán". The craft shops at the site are recommended for good variety and reasonable prices.

Hotel *Villas Arqueológicas*, C.

Tepozotlán, about 43 km. NW of Mexico City just off the route to Querétaro, has a splendid Jesuit church in churrigueresque style. There are fine colonial paintings in the convent corridors. The old Jesuit monastery has been converted into a colonial art museum (Museo Nacional del Virreinato, open 1000-1700, closed Mon., entry US$0.40, US$0.20 Sun.) and tourist centre with restaurants: the *Hostería del Monasterio* has very good Mexican food and a band on Sun.; try their coffee with cinnamon. *Restaurant Artesanías*, opp. church, recommended, cheap. Also good food at *Brookwell's Posada*. Well worth a visit for the paintings alone. Bus from Tacuba metro station, US$0.50, 1 hr. ride. Many buses from Terminal del Norte pass the turn-off at "Caseta Tepozotlán" from where one can take a local bus or walk (30 mins.) to the town. (Do not confuse Tepozotlán with Tepoztlán, which is S of Mexico City, near Cuernavaca).

In the third week of December, *pastorelas*, or morality plays based on the temptation and salvation of Mexican pilgrims voyaging to Bethlehem, are held. Tickets are about US$10 and include a warming punch, the play, a procession and litanies, finishing with a meal, fireworks and music. Tickets from Viajes Roca, Neva 30, Col. Cuauhtémoc, Mexico City.

Another splendid one-day excursion is to **Tula,** some 65 km., the most important Toltec site in Mexico; two ball courts, pyramids, a frieze in colour, and remarkable sculptures over 6 metres high have been uncovered. There are four huge warriors in black basalt on a pyramid, the great Atlantes anthropomorphic pillars. The museum is well worth visiting and there is a massive fortress-style church, dating from 1553, near the market. Admission to site and museum, US$0.40 weekdays, US$0.22 Sun. and holidays. Multilingual guidebooks at entrance. All the guided tours have left by 1600; as the site is open until 1800 the best visiting time is in these 2 hrs. of comparative calm. The town itself is dusty, however, with poor roads; *Restaurant la Cabaña*, on main square, local dishes, also *Nevería*, with good soup. If driving from Mexico City, take the turn for Actopán before entering Tula, then look for the Zona Arqueológica sign (and the great statues) on your left.

Transport 1½ hrs. by train from Buenavista station; leaves at 0800, returns at 2035, US$0.20, but sometimes can be several hours late; it follows the line of the channel cut by Alvarado to drain the lakes of Mexico Valley, visible as a deep canyon. One can take bus back, which leaves earlier. It can also be reached by 1st class bus, "Valle de Mesquital", from Terminal del Norte, Avenida de los Cien Metros, goes to Tula in 1½ hrs.; US$1.70 each way, 15-min service; bus terminal is 3 km. from the site (badly signposted, an alternative route is: 200m. to the Zócalo, to Calle Quetzalcoatl, to small bridge, sandy road to the right, and opening in the fence). Also bus or car from Actopán, on the Pan-American Highway (see page 873). Tula-Pachuca US$1.30; safe to leave belongings at bus station.

Mexico City-Veracruz-Mexico City

By Road A round tour by way of Cholula, Puebla, Tehuacán, Orizaba, Córdoba, Veracruz, Jalapa, Tlaxcala, and Alvarado. Paved all the way (no Pemex service station between Puebla and Orizaba, a distance of about 150 km.); total distance: 924 km., or 577 miles. A toll *autopista* (motorway) from Mexico City to Veracruz has been finished as far as Córdoba. From there on you take the regular highway. Our description is a trip along the old road.

We go E along the Puebla road, past the airport and swimming pools, and some spectacular slums. At (km. 19) Los Reyes, a road runs left into a valley containing the now almost completely drained Lake Texcoco, a valley early settled by the *conquistadores*. Along it we come to **Chapingo,** where there is a famous agricultural college with particularly fine frescoes by Rivera in the chapel. Next comes **Texcoco,** a good centre for visiting picturesque villages in the area. Bus from Mexico City, from Emiliano Zapata 92, near Candelaria metro station. Near Chapingo a road runs right to the lovely village of **Huexotla** (see the Aztec wall and the old church). Another road from Texcoco runs through the very beautiful public park of Molino de las Flores. From the old *hacienda* buildings, now in ruins, a road (right) runs up the hill of Tetzcotingo, near the top of which are the Baths of Netzahualcoyotl, the poet-prince. All the nearby villages are charming to stroll through. Another village worth visiting is (San Miguel de) **Chiconcuac** (road to San Andrés and left at its church), only 4 km. away. Here Texcoco *sarapes* are woven. Tues. is their market day and there is a rousing *fiesta* in honour of their patron saint on September 29.

At km. 29, Santa Bárbara, a road on the right leads to the small town of **Amecameca** (60 km. from Mexico City), buses go every 10 mins. (1½-2 hrs'. journey, US$0.50) from the Terminal del Oriente, slow, unreliable, crowded service, so get there early; if hitching, take the Calzada Zaragoza, very dusty road. By train at 0700, 2½ hr. trip, US$0.20. It is at the foot of the twin volcanoes **Popocatépetl** and Ixtaccíhuatl; the saddle between them, reached by car via a paved road up to

930 MEXICO

the Paso de Cortés (25 km. from Amecameca), gives particularly fine views. Just before the pass, cars (but not pedestrians) pay US$0.10 entry to the national park. A road reaches the sanctuary of El Sacromonte, 90 metres above the town (magnificent views), a small and very beautiful church built round a cave in which once lived Fray Martín de Valencia, a *conquistador* who came to Mexico in 1524. It is, next to the shrine of Guadalupe, the most sacred place in Mexico and has a much venerated full-sized image of Santo Entierro weighing 1½ kg. only. Population of Amecameca: 10,000; altitude: 2,315 metres; market day is Saturday. (On the way to Amecameca, see the restored 16th century convent and church at Chalco, and the fine church, convent and open-air chapel of the same period at Tlalmanalco.) Rooms at the *San Carlos* restaurant on the main square, F, clean, good, modern, good food, but no hot water; another hotel, one block N of Zócalo on the same street as *San Carlos*, F, basic, shared bathroom.

Popocatépetl is not easy to climb; experienced climbers may wish to climb up to the refuge at 3,800 metres (Las Cruces—so named for all the graves—safest route), no hot water or heating, about 11 hrs.' climb. The best time to climb the volcanoes is between late Oct. and early March when there are clear skies and no rain. From May to October the weather is good before noon; in the afternoons it is bad. Climbers are advised to spend at least a day at **Tlamacas** (3,950 metres) to acclimatize, reached from Paso de Cortés via the paved road which turns right (S), 5 km. on. It is also possible to take a taxi (or hitchhike from the turn-off 2 km. S of Amecameca, morning and early afternoon, best at weekends, no public transport) from Amecameca to Tlamacas, US$5, up to 5 people, 26 km. There are a few houses and a tourist lodge *Albergue de Tlamacas*, catering for day trippers from the capital, with cafeteria (open 0930-1700), limited food, and a restaurant which opens at weekends. You're not supposed to eat your own food within the hostel; sheets and pillow provided; book in advance, US$2 a night in mixed dormitories (sleeping bag recommended); beautiful house in wooded enclosure, plenty of hot water. 1½ km. below Tlamacas is a camping and picnic area. Minibuses charge US$2 p.p. and run only Sat. and Sun. (from the E to Tlamacas: a bus from Cholula goes as far as San Nicolás de los Ranchos—the remaining 10 km. to Paso de Cortés must be covered on foot or by hitching). From Tlamacas a path goes up to the hut at Las Cruces at 4,400 metres and the snowline; from there it is two hours (spikes and ice axe) to the rim of the crater and thence another hour's easy walk round the rim to the top. Equipment hire US$3 for crampons and ice-axes at the hostel, or in Amecameca, but preferable to hire from Mountain Club in Mexico City. The Brigada de Rescate del Socorro Alpino de México, A.C., in Mexico City (Lázaro Cárdenas 80, Tel.: 521 18 13) will provide information and free guides. If you wish to go to the top of Popocatépetl (5,400 metres) leave at 0400, as the ground is more solid early on (take warm clothes and a flashlight, and sunglasses for the snow-glare. Alternative routes from Paso de Cortés: straight down dirt road to reach eventually Puebla; or turn left (N) along another dirt road which leads past TV station for 12 km. to nearest parking to summit of Ixtaccíhuatl. From there you find various routes to summit (12-15 hrs. return) and 3-4 refuges to overnight (no furniture, bare floors, dirty).

Beyond Santa Bárbara our road climbs through pine forests to reach 3,196 metres about 63 km. from Mexico City, and then descends in a series of sharp bends to the quiet town of San Martín **Texmelucan**, km. 91. The old Franciscan convent here has a beautifully decorated interior, and a former *hacienda* displays weaving and old machinery. Market day is Tuesday.

From here a side-road leads NE for 24 km. to the quaint old Indian town of Tlaxcala; a remarkable series of precolumbian frescoes are to be seen at the ruins of **Cacaxtla** near San Miguel de los Milagros, a steep 25-minute climb up from the main highway, between Texmelucan and Tlaxcala. The colours are still sharp and some of the figures are larger than life size. To protect the paintings from the sun they are only shown from 1000-1300 (closed Mon.), admission US$0.20. Then there is **Tlaxcala**, with its simple buildings washed in ochre, pink and yellow, capital of small Tlaxcala state whose wealthy ranchers breed fighting bulls, but whose landless peasantry is still poor. To see: the church of San Francisco, the oldest in Mexico (1521), from whose pulpit the first Christian sermon was preached in the New World—its severe façade conceals a most sumptuous interior; the extremely colourful murals (1966) depicting the indigenous story of Tlaxcala in the Palacio de Gobierno; and the ruins of the pyramid of San Esteban de Tizatlán, 5 km. outside the town. There is an hourly bus from the Central Camionera in Tlaxcala or take a city bus to La Garrita from which the ruins are a 15 min. walk. Most interesting relics are two sacrificial altars with original colour frescoes preserved under glass. The pictures tell the story of the wars with Aztecs and Chichimecs. The annual fair is held Oct. 29-Nov. 15 each year. Population 10,000. Altitude 2,240 metres.

The **Sanctuary of Ocotlán** (1541), on a hill outside the town, described as "the most delicious

MEXICO

building in the world", commands a view of valley and volcano. "Its two towers are of lozenge-shaped vermilion bricks set in white stucco, giving an effect of scarlet shagreen, while their upper storeys are dazzlingly white, with fretted cornices and salomonic pillars. . . . A pure-blooded Indian, Francisco Miguel, worked for 25 years on the interior, converting it into a kind of golden grotto." - Sacheverell Sitwell.

(Km. 106) **Huejotzingo.** It has the second-oldest church and monastery in Mexico, built 1529; now a museum. Market: Sat., Tues. Dramatic carnival on Shrove Tuesday, portraying the story of Agustín Lorenzo, a famous local bandit.

(Km. 122) **Cholula** is a small somnolent town, but one of the strangest-looking in all Mexico. When Cortés arrived, this was a holy centre with 100,000 inhabitants and 400 shrines, or *teocallis*, grouped round the great pyramid of Quetzalcoatl. In its day it was as influential as Teotihuacán. In fact there were a series of pyramids built one atop another. When razing them, Cortés vowed to build a chapel for each of the *teocallis* destroyed, but in fact there are no more than about seventy. There is a very helpful tourist office opposite the main pyramid: Cholula map and guide book for US$1; the site is open 1000-1730.

Places to see are the excavated pyramid, admission US$0.45 on weekdays, US$0.23 on Sun. and holidays, guide US$2.25, it has 8 km. of tunnels and some recently discovered frescoes inside, but only 1 km. of tunnel is open to the public, which gives an idea of superimposition. The entrance is on the main road into Cholula; the chapel of Los Remedios on top of it, for the view; the Franciscan fortress church of San Gabriel (1552), in the plaza (open 0600-1200, 1600-1900, Suns. 0600-1900); and next to it, the Capilla Real, which has 48 domes (open 1000-1200, 1530-1800, Suns. 0900-1800).

See also the Indian statuary and stucco work, newly repainted, of the 16th century church of Santa María de **Tonantzintla,** outside the town; the church is one of the most beautiful in Mexico (open 1000-1300, 1500-1700 daily, or get someone to open it for you for a small tip), and may also be reached by paved road from San Francisco **Acatepec** (see its 16th century church also, supposedly open 0900-1800 daily, but not always so) off the highway from Puebla to Cholula. Cholula has the University of the Americas. Population 13,000.

Hotels in Cholula *Villa Arqueológica*, 2 Poniente 501; *Los Sauces*, Km. 122, Carretera Federal Puebla-Cholula; *Motel de la Herradura*, Carr. Federal; *Trailer Park Las Américas*, 30 Oriente 602; *Hotel de las Américas*, 14 Oriente, near pyramid, actually a motel, modern with rooms off galleries round paved courtyard (car park), small restaurant, clean, good value, D; *Super Motel* on the road from Puebla as you enter town, each room with private garage, very secure, E. *Restaurant Choloyan*, also handicrafts, Av. Morelos, good, clean, friendly.

Buses Second-class bus from Puebla to Cholula from 8 Poniente 713, 9 km. on a new road, US$0.20. From Mexico City, leave for Cholula from Terminal del Oriente with Estrella Roja, every 30 mins. 1st class buses to Mexico City every 10 minutes, US$1, 2½-3 hrs., 2nd class every 20 mins., a very scenic route through steep wooded hills. Good views of volcanoes.

One can visit Tonantzintla and Acatepec from Cholula main square with a "peso-taxi". Or one can take a bus from Cholula to Acatepec for US$0.25 from junction of Av. 5 and Av. Miguel Alemán. This is 2 blocks from Zócalo, which is 3 blocks from tourist office. You can walk back to Tonanzintla to see church, 1 km., and then take bus Tonantzintla-Puebla US$0.30. John Hemming says these two churches "should on no account be missed; they are resplendent with Poblano tiles and their interiors are a riot of Indian stucco-work and carving." Both churches, though exquisite, are tiny. Some visitors note that regular visiting hours are not strictly observed at Cholula, Acatepec, Tonantzintla and Huejotzingo.

Just before Puebla one comes to the superb church of **Tlaxcalantzingo,** with an extravagantly tiled façade, domes and tower. It is worth climbing up on the roof for photographs.

(Km. 134) **Puebla,** "The City of the Angels", one of Mexico's oldest and most famous cities and the capital of Puebla state, is at 2,060 metres. Unfortunately, its recent industrial growth—the population has risen to 750,000—is rapidly destroying its colonial air and filling it with smog, and the centre, though still beautifully colonial, is cursed with traffic jams, except in those shopping streets reserved for pedestrians. On the central arcaded plaza is a fine Cathedral, notable for its marble floors, onyx and marble statuary and gold leaf decoration (closed 1230-1530). There are statues flanking the altar which are said to be of an English king and a Scottish queen. The bell tower gives a grand view of the city

932 MEXICO

and snow-capped volcanoes. There are 60 churches in all, many of their domes shining with the glazed tiles for which the city is famous. Earthquake damage in 1973. Craft shop sponsored by the authorities: Tienda Convento Sta. Rosa, Calle 3 Norte 1203, Tel.: 2-89-04. *Feria* in mid-April for two weeks.

In the Rosario chapel of the Church of Santo Domingo (1596-1659), the baroque displays a beauty of style and prodigality of form which served as an exemplar and inspiration for all later baroque in Mexico. There is a strong Indian flavour in Puebla's baroque; this can be seen in the 16th century churches of Tonantzintla and Acatepec (see above); it is not so evident, but it is still there, in the opulent decorative work in the Cathedral. Beyond the church, up towards the Fort of Loreto, there is a spectacular view of volcanoes.

Other places well worth visiting are the churches of San Cristóbal (1687), with modern churrigueresque towers and Tonantzintla-like plasterwork inside; San José (18th century), with attractive tiled façade and decorated walls around the main doors, as well as beautiful altar pieces inside; the Congreso del Estado in Calle 5 Poniente, formerly the Consejo de Justicia, near the post office, is a converted 19th century Moorish style town house—the tiled entrance and courtyard are very attractive—it had a theatre inside (shown to visitors on request), and is now the seat of the state government; and the Museum of Santa Rosa has a priceless collection of 16th century Talavera tiles on its walls and ceilings. The Patio de los Azulejos should also be visited; it has fabulous tiled façades on the former almshouses for old retired priests of the order of San Felipe Neri; the colours and designs are beautiful; it is at 11 Poniente 110, with a tiny entrance which is hard to find unless one knows where to look. One of the most famous and oldest local churches is San Francisco, with a glorious tiled façade and a mummified saint in its side chapel. Santa Catalina, 3 Norte with 2 Poniente, has beautiful altarpieces; Nuestra Señora de la Luz, 14 Norte and 2 Oriente, has a good tiled façade and so has San Marcos at Av. Reforma and 9 Norte. The Maronite church of Belén on 7 Norte and 4 Poniente has a lovely old tiled façade and a beautiful tiled interior. Worth visiting is also the library of Bishop Palafox, by the tourist office, 5 Oriente No. 5, opposite the Cathedral.

Besides the churches, the fragile-looking and extravagantly ornamented Casa del Alfeñique (Sugar Candy House), a few blocks from the Cathedral dominating the centre of the town, is worth seeing (entry US$0.40). Nearby is Plaza Parián, with onyx souvenir shops (6 Norte and 4 Oriente). Onyx figures and chess sets are attractive and cheaper than elsewhere, but the *poblanos* are hard bargainers; another attractive buy is the very tiny glass animal figures. A former convent is now the Museum of Santa Mónica; generations of nuns hid there after the reform laws of 1857 made the convent illegal, at Av. Poniente 18, No. 203. The Cinco de Mayo civic centre, with a stark statue of Benito Juárez, is, among other things, a regional centre of arts, crafts and folklore and has a very worthwhile Regional Museum, Natural History Museum, auditorium, planetarium, fairgrounds and an open air theatre all nearby. In the same area, the forts of Guadalupe and Loreto have been restored; they were the scene of the Battle of Puebla, in which 2,000 Mexican troops defeated Maximilian's 6,000 European troops on May 5, 1862 (although the French returned victorious ten days later). Inside the Fort of Loreto (excellent view of the city) is a small museum depicting the battle of 1862. May 5 is a holiday in Mexico.

Other places worth seeing are the church and monastery of El Carmen, with its strange façade and beautiful tile work; the Teatro Principal (1550), possibly the oldest in the Americas; the grand staircase of the 17th century Academia de las Bellas Artes and its exhibition of Mexican colonial painting; a magnificent library, one of the oldest in the Americas, access through the Casa de la Cultura and the Jesuit church of La Compañía, where a plaque in the sacristy shows where China Poblana lies buried. This mythical figure, a Chinese princess captured by pirates and abducted to Mexico, is said to have taken to Christianity and good works and evolved a penitential dress for herself which has now become the regional costume; positively dazzling with flowered reds and greens and worn with a strong sparkle of bright beads. Also worth visiting is the house of Aquiles Serdán, a leader of the Revolution, preserved as it was during his lifetime. The tiled façade of the Casa de los Muñecos, 2 Norte No. 1 (corner of the main square) is famous for its caricatures in tiles of the enemies of the 17th century builder.

The famous Puebla tiles may be purchased from factories outside Puebla, or from Fábrica de Azulejos la Guadalupana, Av. 4 Poniente 911; D. Aguilar, 40 Poniente 106, opposite Convent of Sta. Mónica, and Casa Rugerio, 18 Poniente 111; Margarita Guevara, 20 Poniente 30.

Barrio del Artista The artists' studios are near to *Hotel Latino* and adjoining Mercado El Parián, with tourist shops. Live music and refreshments at small *Café del Artista*. The University Arts Centre offers folk dances at various times, look for posters or enquire direct—free admission.

Museums Museo de Bello—the house of the collector and connoisseur Bello—has good displays of Chinese porcelain and Talavera pottery; the building is beautifully furnished (entry US$0.40, guided tours, closed Mon.). Museo Regional de Puebla, in the Centro Cívico 5 de Mayo, is open 1000-1700; Museo de Santa Mónica (convent) at 18 Poniente 103, open 1000-1800, closed Mon.; and Museo de la No Intervención, in the Fuerte de Loreto, open 1000-1700, closed Mon.

Hotels *Gran Hotel de Alba*, Serdán 141, C; *Lastra*, Calz. de Los Fuertes, B; *Royalty*, Portal Hidalgo

MEXICO 933

8, D, good, central, quiet; *San Miguel*, 3 Poniente 721, D; *Misión de Puebla*, 5 Poniente 2522, C, delightful; *Hostal de Halconeros*, Reforma 141, C; *Palace*, 3 Oriente 13, D; *Del Portal*, Portal Morelos 205, very good, but ask for room away from Zócalo side (noisy), restored colonial, C; *Colonial*, 4 Sur 105, old-fashioned and charming, has excellent restaurant and accepts American Express cards; ask for back room, E, with bath; *Señorial*, 4 Norte 602, E; *Imperial*, 4 Oriente 203, F, basic, shower, parking; *Cabrera*, 10 Oriente 6, E, with shower and phone, clean, quiet and reasonably priced restaurant, don't be put off by outward appearance, near bus terminal; *Latino*, 6 Norte 8, E, with bath, hot water, F, without bath, next ADO bus station, noisy, dirty; *San Miguel*, 3 Poniente 721, clean and quiet, E; *Avenida*, F, Calle 5 Poniente 336; *Mar*, 3 Av. Sur 707, F, very basic. *Teresita* (near San Agustín church), 3 Poniente 309, F, with shower, awful but cheap; *Ritz*, 2 Norte 207, F, basic, all rooms have showers, no parking, not recommended; *San Francisco*, F, reasonable; *Augusta*, Calle 4 Poniente, F; *San Agustín*, 3 Poniente 531, F, basic, clean, quiet; *Victoria*, near Zócalo, 3 Poniente 306, basic, F; *Venecia*, 4 Poniente 716, G, without bath; *Casa de Huéspedes*, 3 Poniente 725, F; several basic *casas de huéspedes*, near market. *Mesón del Angel*, B, good, near first Puebla interchange on Mexico-Puebla motorway, possibly best in town. **Motel Panamerican**, Reforma 2114, E, restaurant, bar, recommended.

Camping Possible in the extensive university grounds about 8 km. S of centre.

Food Speciality *Mole poblano* (meat or chicken with sauce of *chiles*, chocolate and coconut). Cheap *mole* at *Fonda la Mexicana*, 16 Sept. 706; best *mole* at *La Poblanita*, 10 Norte 1404-B, and *Fonda Sta. Clara*, 3 Poniente 307, good for local specialities. Also on Zócalo, at *Hostería de los Angeles*, but no dinner. Also good, *Iberia*, Portal Juárez. 101, 1st floor; *La Bola Roja*, 17 Sur 1305. *Posada del Coyote*, 4 Norte and 4 Oriente has cheap and original *comidas* in a lovely courtyard. *Camotes* (candied sweet potatoes) and *dulces* (sweets). Also *nieves*—drinks of alcohol, fruit and milk—worth trying, and excellent *empanadas* bought from a lady just outside the ADO station. Also noted are *quesadillas* - fried *tortillas* with cheese and herbs inside.

Other Restaurants *Monza's*, Calle Reforma, reasonable, good food. *China Poblana*, 6 Norte; *Que Chula es Puebla*; *Parián*, 2 Oriente 415. Cheap *comidas* at *Las Cazuelas del Chato*, 2 Oriente 209. *Alianza Francesa*, 2 Poniente, 101-402. Many cheap places between ADO depot and main square with menus prominently displayed. *Hostería del Virrey*, 11 Sur and 15 Poniente, live music and good atmosphere. *La Chiesa Veglia*, Swiss, good cheese fondue, attached to *Hotel San Andrés*, 2 Norte, slow service. *Antojitos Aries*, 5 Sur and 5 Poniente, serves a good, cheap *comida corrida* at lunchtime and *à la carte* menu for dinner, reasonable. *Teorema* on Reforma and 7 Norte is a cold-store with a *cafetería*, good.

Tourist Office 4 Oriente 3, Av. Juárez behind the Cathedral, Tel.: 46-09-28.

Road A 4-lane highway, 70 mins., to Mexico City, toll US$1.30 (ADO buses every 15 mins., seats bookable, 2 hrs., US$2.20; Mexico City-Puebla buses every 10 mins. but 2½ hr. queue); Estrella Roja from Terminal del Oriente. 2-lane highway to Orizaba, toll US$1.85. For the road from Puebla S through Oaxaca to Guatemala, see page 953. Bus from Puebla to Oaxaca costs US$7 (9 hrs.). Bus Puebla-Veracruz 1st class, US$3.50.

Rail Trains from Mexico City, 1st class US$2.30, US$1.35 2nd class to Puebla via Cuautla at 0704, a very slow (10-11 hrs.) Puebla train at 0815; train to Oaxaca (1st class) leaves Puebla 0640, US$3, 12 hours. Beautiful journey as the line weaves through cactus laden gorges recalling the Wild West. On clear days one gets a good view of Popocatépetl. A train from Mexico City leaves at 1730 and stops at 2230 at Puebla on its way to Oaxaca. Train Puebla-Jalapa leaves at 0910, US$1.25, 2nd class, takes 7-8 hrs. The ride from Oriental to Jalapa is very enjoyable, excellent view, sit on left-hand side.

Excursions Interesting day-trip to **Cuetzalán** market (via Tetela-Huahuaztla) which is held on Sun. in the Zócalo (3 hr walk up.). On October 4 each year dancers from local villages gather and *voladores* "fly" from the top of their pole. Nahua Indians sell cradles (*huacal*) for children; machetes and embroidered garments. Big clay dogs are made locally, unique stoves which hold big flat clay plates on which *tortillas* are baked and stews are cooked in big pots. Also available in nearby Huitzitlán. *Casa Elvira Mora*, Hidalgo 54, cheap, friendly place to stay in Cuetzalán. Women decorate their hair with skeins of wool. You can also go via Zaragoza, Zacapoaxtla and Apulco, where one can walk along a path, left of the road, to the fine 35-metre waterfall of La Gloria.

Direct buses from Puebla (Tezinteco line at Av. 12 Oriente and Calle 4 Norte) leaves 0830. Leaves Cuetzalán at 1520, back at Puebla at 2100. ADO has a night-bus, 1915 arrives 2245; returns 0700, arriving 1030. There are many buses to Zacapoaxtla with frequent connections for Cuetzalán.

15 km. S of Puebla lies Lake Valsequillo, with Africam, a zoo of free-roaming African animals. Entry US$1, open Mon.-Fri. 1000-1730, Sat., Sun. and holidays 0900-1800. Take a bus from Terminal Autobuses Unidos (AU), 4 Norte, Puebla. Information from 11 Oriente, Tel.: 460888.

(Km. 151) **Amozoc,** where tooled leather goods and silver decorations on steel are made, both mostly as outfits for the *charros*, or Mexican cattlemen. Clay toys are also made. Beyond Amozoc lies **Tepeaca** with its late 16th century

934 MEXICO

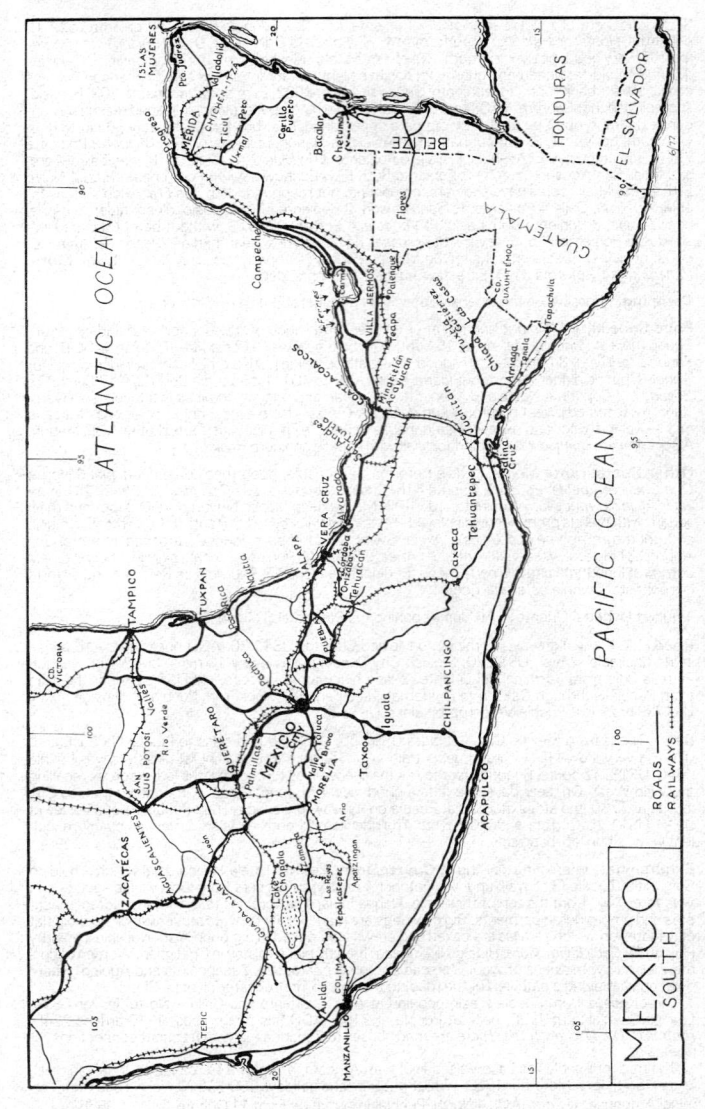

ROUGH SKETCH

monastery, well worth a visit—its weekly market is the 2nd largest in the whole of Mexico. An old Spanish tower or *rollo* (1580) stands between Tepeaca's main square and the Parroquia. Beyond Tepeaca, 57½ km. from Puebla, lies **Tecamachalco** with its vast 16th century Franciscan monastery church with beautiful murals on the choir vault, in late medieval Flemish style, by a local Indian.

Beyond, the road leads to **Tehuacán** (population 85,000, altitude 1,676 metres), a charming health resort with an equable climate. It has some old churches. Water from the mineral springs is bottled and sent all over the country by Garci Crespo and Peñafiel, who also have baths at the spas where people come to bathe for health reasons. From the small dam at Malpaso on the Río Grande an annual race is held for craft without motors as far as the village of Quiotepec. The central plaza is pleasant and shaded; the nights are cool. A paved road has been completed to Oaxaca passing through the Salado Grande irrigated zone, the arid Cañada area studded by cacti, and up over the mountains; it takes 3½-4 hrs. of driving. Railway junction for Oaxaca and Veracruz. Wild maize was first identified by an archaeologist in caves nearby. There is an airport.

Hotels *Hotel-Spa Peñafiel*, old, reasonable, long term rates, resort facilities, just out of town, on the way to Puebla; *Garci-Crespo*; *México*, Reforma Norte and Independencia Poniente, one block from Zócalo, garage, TV, restaurant, renovated colonial building, pool, quiet; *Villa Grañadas*; *Ibero*, nr. Zócalo, F. Several *casas de huéspedes* along Calle 3 (Norte and Sur) but low standards, and generally a shortage of decent cheap accommodation and restaurants. Cafés on Zócalo serve snacks and drinks, and some meals, but the main meal is served at midday in Tehuacán. Try *Restaurant Santander*, good and inexpensive, and *Peñafiel*, good.

Buses ADO bus station on Av. Independencia (Poniente). Bus direct to Mexico City, 3 hrs., US$2.40; to Oaxaca and the Gulf: Autobuses Unidos, 2nd class on Calle 2 Oriente with several buses daily to Mexico City and Oaxaca. Local bus to Huajuapan 3 hrs., US$2; from there, frequent buses to Oaxaca (4 hrs., US$2.50).

Above Tehuacán, in the hills, is the Indian town of Huautla de Jiménez, where the local Mazatec Indians consume the hallucinogenic "magic" mushrooms made famous by Dr. Timothy Leary. Foreigners going up this road are stopped and turned back by the army.

Beyond, our road soon begins to climb into the mountains. At Cumbres we reach 2,300 metres and a wide view: the silvered peak of Citlaltépetl (or Orizaba) volcano to the E, the green valley of Orizaba below. In 10 km. we drop down, through steep curves, sometimes rather misty, to Acultzingo 830 metres below. The road joins the main toll road from Puebla to Orizaba at Ciudad Mendoza, where it has emerged from the descent through the Cumbres de Maltrata, which are usually misty and need to be driven with care and patience. (The toll road Puebla-Orizaba is a much safer drive than the route we have described.)

(Km. 317) **Orizaba**, the favourite resort of the Emperor Maximilian (population 81,000, altitude 1,283 metres), lost some of its charm in the 1973 earthquake, when the bullring, many houses and other buildings were lost. In the distance is the majestic volcanic cone of Orizaba. The town developed because of the natural springs in the valley, some of which are used by the textile and paper industries and others are dammed to form small pools for bathing beside picnic areas; Nogales (restaurant) is the most popular, Ojo de Agua is another. The Cerro del Borrego, the hill above the Alameda park, is a favourite early-morning climb. The Zócalo at one time lost much of its area to permanent snack bars, but these have been removed. On the N side is the market, with a wide variety of local produce and local women in traditional dress, and the many-domed San Miguel church (1690-1729). There are several other quite good churches, and there is an Orozco mural in the Federal School on Av. Colón. The Palacio Municipal is the actual cast-iron Belgian pavilion brought piece by piece from France after the famous 19th century Paris Exhibition—an odd sight.

Hotels *De France*, F and US$0.25 for parking in courtyard, clean, comfortable, shower, reasonable if uninspiring restaurant; *Aries*, Oriente 6 No. 265, E (nightclub on top floor). *Trueba*, Oriente 6 and Sur 11, D, resort facilities.

Restaurants *Romanchu* and *Paso Real*, on the main street, have excellent cuisine. Hare Krishna vegetarian restaurant, *Radha's*, on Sur 4 between Oriente 1 and 3, excellent. In the market, try the local morning snack, *memelita picadita*.

936 MEXICO

A road leaves Orizaba southwards, up into the mountains of Zongolica, a dry, poor and isolated region, cold and inhospitable, inhabited by various groups of Indians who speak Nahuatl, the language of the Aztecs. Zongolica village is a good place to buy *sarapes*; take early bus from Orizaba (ask for direct one) to get clear views of the mountains.

Beyond Orizaba the scenery is magnificent. We descend to coffee and sugar-cane country and a tropical riot of flowers. It is delectable country except when a northerly blows, or in the intolerable heat and mugginess of the wet season.

(Km. 331) **Fortín de las Flores,** a village devoted to growing flowers and exporting them. Sometimes Indian women sell choice blossoms in small baskets made of banana-tree bark.

Hotels *Ruiz Galindo,* now run down (swimming pool, over-elaborate for some tastes). *Posada la Loma,* very attractive, moderately expensive. There are others, slightly cheaper, which also offer a tropical garden for relaxation.

Near Fortín there is a viewpoint looking out over a dramatic gorge (entry free). The *autopista* from Orizaba to Córdoba passes over this deep valley on a wide four-lane concrete bridge.

Córdoba (population 60,000, altitude 923 metres), 8 km. on in the rich valley of the Río Seco, an old colonial city, is also crazy with flowers. Its Zócalo is spacious and leafy, but is being allowed to deteriorate; three sides are arcaded; two of them are lined with tables. On the fourth is an imposing church with a chiming clock. There are several hotels in the Zócalo, which is alive and relaxed at night. In one of them, the *Hotel Zevallos,* Gen. Iturbide signed the Treaty of Córdoba in 1821, which was instrumental in freeing Mexico from Spanish colonial rule. There is a local museum at Calle 3, 303, open 1000-1300 and 1600-2000. Córdoba has the highest rainfall in Mexico, but at predictable times. The area grows coffee.

Hotels *Hostal de Gorbeña,* Calle 11, 308, modern, clean, really hot water, some traffic noise but good value, D. *Virreynal,* Av. 1 y Calle 5, D; *Mansur,* Av. 1 y Calle 3, D; *Vigo,* E. Near the ADO terminal is *Palacio; Marina, Iberia, Riscado* and *Casa de Huéspedes Regis* are all on Avenida 2. *Casa de Huéspedes La Sin Rival* and *La Nueva Querétana* are at 511 and 508 of Avenida 4, respectively. *Los Reyes,* F, with bath.

The direct road from Córdoba to Veracruz is lined, in season, by stalls selling fruit and local honey between Yanga and Cuitláhuac. Yanga is a small village named after the leader of a group of escaped black slaves in colonial times. A slightly longer but far more attractive road goes from Córdoba northwards through Huatusco and Totutla, then swings E to Veracruz.

(Km. 476) **Veracruz,** the principal port of entry for Mexico (population 245,000), lies on a low alluvial plain bordering the Gulf coast. Cortés landed near here on April 17, 1519. The town is a mixture of the very old and the new; there are still many picturesque white-walled buildings and winding side-streets. In spite of the occasional chill north winds, it has become a great holiday resort, and is reported touristy, noisy and expensive. Some of the beaches in and around Veracruz are polluted from the many ships. The food is good, the fishing not bad, and the people lively: there is much marimba and guitar playing, café life and dancing. (The most famous dances, accompanied by the Conjunto Jarocho, are the Bamba and Zapateado to harp and guitar, with much stamping and lashing of feet.) At night the Malecón is very lively, and sometimes fire-eaters and other performers entertain the public. The heart of the city is Plaza Constitución; make at once for the excellent *La Parroquia* café, cool and tiled. (The newer café of the same name on the Malecón does not have the same atmosphere.) The local craft is tortoiseshell jewellery adorned with silver, but remember that the import of tortoiseshell into the USA and many other countries is prohibited. There are two buildings of great interest: the very fine 17th-century Palacio Municipal, on Plaza Constitución, with a splendid façade and courtyard, and the castle of San Juan de Ulúa (1565), on Gallega Island, now joined by road to the mainland; take bus marked Ulúa. It failed to deter the buccaneers and later became a political prison. Mexico's "Robin Hood", Chucho el Roto, was imprisoned there, and escaped three times. (Entry US$0.45.) There is a city historical museum with good collection of photographs, poorly maintained and exhibits now visible with difficulty, traces history from Conquest to 1910; it is at Zaragoza 397. The Baluarte de Santiago, a small fort which once formed part of the city walls, is at Francisco Canal y Gómez Farias, open 0900-1800, Suns. and holidays, 1600-1900, closed

MEXICO 937

Tues. On the southern arm of the harbour breakwater is a small aquarium (admission US$0.10). The people are called *Jarochos*. Helpful tourist office on Zócalo, in Palacio Municipal, has no hotel price list. Airport at Las Bajadas, 3 flights daily to the capital. *Antigua*, a small colonial town outside Veracruz (good atmosphere), is where Cortés is said to have first landed in 1519.

The Zócalo, white-paved, and with attractive cast iron lampstands and benches, and surrounded by the impressive cathedral, governor's palace and colonial-style hotels, comes alive in the evening at weekends. An impressive combination of the crush of people, colour and marimba music in the flood-lit setting.

The beach along the waterfront, and the sea, are filthy, but a short bus ride from the fish market takes you to Mocambo beach, which has a good swimming bath (with restaurant and bar, admission US$0.40), beach restaurants, Caribbean-style beach huts and the water is quite a bit cleaner through still rather uninviting in colour. There are crabs and mosquitoes. The Gulf is even warmer than the Caribbean. The beach is crowded. At holiday time cars race up and down, there are loud radios, etc. Deckchairs are expensive and there is little shade near the beach.
NB: Travellers are warned to be particularly wary of thieves in Veracruz.

Hotels *Exalaris Hyatt*, Mocambo 4300, A, fanciest on the entire Gulf coast; *Mocambo*, Boca del Río, C, 8 km. out on Mocambo beach, palatial, good service and food, mostly empty; *Veracruz* on Plaza de Armas, C, a/c with pool and night club; *Emporio*, C, overpriced, with bath, swimming pool, inexpensive *comida corrida*, rather old-fashioned, on Paseo del Malecón; a block before the *Emporio* when approaching from the Zócalo is *Hotel Puerto Bello*, good; *Villa del Mar*, Blvd. M. Avila Camacho, C; *Impala*, on Orizaba, E, with bath, cold water, mosquitoes but clean, near bus station; *Colonial*, D, on Zócalo, swimming pool, indoor parking, recommended; *Imperial*, on Zócalo, E, with bath. *El Sol*, Carlos Cruz 320 (off Av. Allende) C, with bath. Many hotels in port area, including *Royalty*, E, nice and clean, near beach, 20 min. walk from Zócalo; *Palma*, Av. González Parges, F, with bath, cockroaches, fan. *Asturias*, Calle Juan Soto, F, with bath; *La Carmelita*, Av. Serdán, F, 2 blocks from Zócalo; *Ortiz*, on Zócalo, good value, F, family-owned; *La Paz*, Av. Díaz Mirón 1242, nr. bus station, E, with bath, highly recommended, cheap, clean and helpful; *Cheto*, near bus station, overpriced; *Cielo*, also near terminal, G; *Amparo*, A. Serdán 68, F, adequate. *Mar y Tierra*, on Malecón, F, good value, some rooms with balconies overlooking the harbour. *Central*, Mirón 1412, E, clean, get room at back, esp. on 5th floor, laundering facilities; *Oriente*, F, on Zócalo, friendly; *Ruiz Milán*, E, on seafront, good; *Príncipe*, Collado 195, F, some distance from centre, very clean with hot shower and toilet; *Vigo*, Av. Landero y Casa, F; and on same street *Santillana*, F, very noisy all night, luggage not safe, both in the port area, and reached by bus from the bus terminal. Two more on Miguel Lerdo, near the Portales: *Rías* and *Concha Dorada*. CREA Youth Hostel.

Trailer Parks Several along the ocean side. Two at Mocambo, side by side, bus marked Boca del Río goes there from corner of Zaragoza and Serdán. *Los Arcos* has hot showers, laundry tubs, lighting and plugs, owner speaks English. The other is *Los Arcos Fiesta*; noisy from main beach road, and a bit shabby, but well supervised, esp. at night. Nearest supermarket is on the road into Veracruz at the modern shopping centre.

Restaurants The local gourmet speciality is *langosta loca* (mad lobster). *La Parroquia* (original) has fans, white tiled walls, cement floors and waiters in white jackets, overlooks town square; wonderful coffee, scrambled eggs and steak *tampiqueña*. Also *El Chato Moya* on the Malecón and the market for excellent fish, opp. is an unnamed restaurant, good seafood, and *El Azteca de Cayetano* where *mondongos de fruta* (a selection of all the fruits in season) are prepared on one plate. *Torros* are the local drinks made of eggs, milk, fruit and alcohol—delicious and potent. Try a Tequila Sunrise in one of the restaurants on the Zócalo. *La Paella*, Plaza Constitución, has its name written into the concrete of the entrance floor, no sign otherwise, good *comida corrida*; *El Unico*, cheap Mexican dishes. There is a good local fish restaurant, *Olympica*, near the fish market in the street running parallel to Av. 16 de Septiembre, 2 blocks from the Zócalo. Tim Connell recommends two places: *Pescadores*, for fish, on Zaragoza (not evenings); and the steakhouse *Submarino Amarillo*. Good shellfish at Boca del Río.

British Consul The Hon. Consul, Sr. A. Castro Soto, Av. Morelos 145. Tel.: (91-293) 2-43-23.

Transport Rail: to Mexico City, at 0725 via Jalapa, at 0800 and 2130 via Córdoba; *alcoba* (sleeper for 2) US$9.40, for 3 US$11.80, for 4 US$14.20; *camarín* (small sleeper) US$5.60 for one, US$8.50 for 2; 1st class, *primera especial numerada*, US$ 2.40; *primera general* US$1.95; 2nd class, US$1.20. (Train from Mexico City at 2100, arr. 1230.) The majority of buses are booked solid for three days in advance throughout summer; at all times queues of up to 2 hrs. possible at Mexico City booking offices of bus companies (best company: ADO, Buenavista 9, Mexico City). Book outward journeys on arrival in Veracruz, as the bus station is some way out of town and there are often long queues. For local buses, get accurate information from the tourist office. Buses to the main bus station along Av. 5 de Mayo. Bus to Mexico City, US$4.30 (6 hrs.),

938 MEXICO

via Jalapa, misses out Orizaba, Fortín and Córdoba; to Villahermosa US$12 (10 hrs.); to Puebla, US$3.50.

Connections with Guatemala There are no through buses to Guatemala, but there are connecting services. Train leaves Veracruz 0915 daily for Ixtepec and Tapachula; 1st class (recommended), US$9.50, 2nd US$2. Take your own toiletries and food. No sleeping accommodation. The connecting railway from the border to Guatemala City no longer carries passengers. (Mexican 1st-class railway accommodation quite good.) Local bus services run Tapachula-Tecún Umán-Guatemala City; quicker than the much more mountainous route further N. Alternatively, take ADO bus to Oaxaca, then carry on to Tapachula (11½ hrs.) by bus. Another bus to frontier at Hidalgo, US$0.25. This route allows you to stop at intermediate points of your choice, but has few "comfort" stops. Buy bus tickets out of Veracruz well in advance.

Bus daily (ADO) at 0800 to Oaxaca, 11 hrs. via Orizaba, Tehuacán and Huajuapan de León, essential to book in advance, US$8.50. Road very winding from Orizaba so take travel sickness tablets if necessary. Philippe Martin, of the Touring Club Suisse, writes: "The road from Veracruz to Oaxaca is spectacular but tiresome to drive and will take about a day. The road from Veracruz to La Tinaja and Tierra Blanca is good and fast although there are many lorries. From there to Miguel Alemán the road is bad, speed reasonable, still many lorries. The Tuxtepec area has lovely lowland, jungle areas, charming villages, and the traffic is sparser between Tuxtepec and Oaxaca, while there are no more gasoline stations. The road is very bad and winding and the fog only lifts after you leave the pines at 2,650 metres above sea level. After a descent and another pass at 2,600 metres you enter the bare mountainous zone of Oaxaca. Very few eating places between Tuxtepec and Oaxaca." This route is possible by bus but is a long, tiring journey, not recommended; also the Tuxtepec-Oaxaca stretch has been reported dangerous because of drug-traffickers.

Excursions Isla de Sacrificios, half an hour from the harbour, beautiful beach (trip US$2.20 return). Trips Sundays and holidays, every hour between 0900 and 1400. Excursion to Zempoala (see page 942), buses from ADO terminal 1½ hrs. each way, via Cardel, or less frequent direct 2nd class buses. On Sunday, to Mandinga for cheap fresh sea food (big prawns), and local entertainment. By car or bus (US$1, 1½ hrs.) S to Puerto Alvarado on the tip of a peninsula, claimed to be the most modern fishing port in the world.

The Papaloapan Region At **Puerto Alvarado** (Hotel del Pastor, F, avoid next-door restaurant), cross the Río Papaloapan (Butterfly River) by a toll bridge (US$0.50), go along Route 180 into the sugar-cane area around Lerdo de Tejada and Angel R. Cavada. At El Trópico a dirt road turns left to some quiet beaches such as Salinas and Roca Partida. Only at Easter are the beaches crowded: they are normally the preserve of fishermen using hand nets from small boats. In the dry season (Dec.-May) the road is passable around the coast to Sontecomapan.

At Tula, a little further along the main road, is a spectacular waterfall, El Salto de Tula; a restaurant is set beside the falls. The road then climbs up into the mountainous volcanic area of Los Tuxtlas, known as the Switzerland of Mexico for its mountains and perennial greenness.

Santiago Tuxtla, set on a river, is a small town of colonial origin. In the main square is the largest known Olmec head carved in solid stone, and also a museum (open 0900-1500, Sat.-Sun. 0900-1200 and 1500-1800), containing examples of local tools, photos, items used in witchcraft (brujería), and the first sugar-cane press used in Mexico and another Olmec head. (Hotel Central, E, cold shower, clean.)

The archaeological site of **Tres Zapotes** lies to the west; it is reached by leaving the paved road south towards Villa Isla and taking either the dirt road at Tres Caminos (signposted) in the dry season (a quagmire from May-Dec.), or in the wet season access can be slowly achieved by turning right at about km. 40, called Tibenal, and following the dirt road north to the site of the Museum which is open 0900-1700 hrs. (If it is closed, the lady in the nearby shop has a key.) There is another Olmec head, also the largest carved stela ever found and stela fragments bearing the New World's oldest Long Count Date, equal to 31 B.C. Not far from Tres Zapotes are three other Olmec sites: Cerro de las Mesas, Laguna de los Cerros, and San Lorenzo Tenochtitlán.

Overlooking Santiago Tuxtla is the hillside restaurant El Balcón, which serves excellent langostino (crayfish) for US$4 and horchata de coco, a drink made from the flesh and milk of coconut.

15 km. beyond lies **San Andrés Tuxtla**, the largest town of the area, with narrow winding streets, by-passed by a ring road. This town is also colonial in style and has a well-stocked market with Oaxacan foods such as totopos, carne enchilada, and tamales de elote (hard tortillas, spicy meat, and cakes of maize-flour steamed on leaves). It is the terminus for trains (daily) from Rodríguez Clara to the south (see page 940) and it is the centre of the cigar trade. One factory beside the main road permits visitors to watch the process and will produce special orders of cigars (puros) marked with an individual's name in ½ hr. Near the town centre is the restaurant La Flor de Guadalajara; it appears small from the outside but is large and pleasant inside, well recommended; sells tepachue, a drink made from pineapple, similar in flavour to cider, and agua de Jamaica. Hotels: Colonial, Figueroa, del Parque, Madero 5, E, a/c, very clean, good restaurant; Casa de Huéspedes la Orizabana, in the centre of town, F, without bath, clean hot water, friendly; Ponce de León, primitive, pleasant patio, F. (Bus San Andrés Tuxtla-Villahermosa US$5.50, 6 hrs.)

At Sihuapan, 5 km. towards Catemaco, is a turning to the right on to a very bumpy dirt road which leads to the impressive waterfall of Salto de Eyipantla. Bridge toll payable at Comoapan, US$0.10, plenty of small boys offer themselves as guides.

Catemaco is a pleasant little town (15,000 people) with large colonial church and picturesque situation on lake, 13 km. from San Andrés Tuxtla. Beware of thieves at all times. At weekends there is a stall selling handicrafts from Oaxaca, and boat trips out on the lakes to see the shrine where the Virgin appeared, the spa at Coyame and the Isla de Changos, and to make a necklace of lilies, are always available (about US$5). The town is noted for its *brujos* (sorcerers) and the Monte del Cerro Blanco to the north is the site of their annual reunion. Catemaco can be reached by bus from Veracruz, changing to a local bus at San Andrés Tuxtla. Catemaco is about 120 km. NW of Minatitlán (see page 968). Catemaco is synonymous throughout Mexico with picturesque, vulgar language.

Hotels and Restaurants *Catemaco*, E, excellent food and swimming pool, and *Berthangel*, similar prices; both on main square of Catemaco town. *Tio Tin*, with views of lake, F, no food, but close to good restaurants. *Motel Playa Azul*, some km. away, C, modern, a/c; in a nice setting, comfortable and shady, with water-skiing on lake. A number of hotels are situated at the lakeside; *Posada Komiapan* (swimming-pool and restaurant), very comfortable, E; *Brujos*, F, fan, a/c, shower, nice clean rooms, balcony overlooking the lake; *Los Arcos*, F, clean, fan, good value. On the promenade are a number of good restaurants—*María José*, best; *La Julita* (*anguilla* and *tacholgolo*), *La Ola* (*payiscadas*, *anguilla*, *tegogalso*, *carne de chango*, and *cesina*) built almost entirely by the owner in the local natural materials, and *La Luna*, among others. Best value are those not directly on the lake e.g. *Los Sauces*, which serves *mojarra*.

The Gulf Coast may be reached from Catemaco by car or by bus along a dirt road (which can be washed out in winter). It is about 18 km. to Sontecomapan, crossing over the pass at Buena Vista and looking down to the Laguna where, it is said, Francis Drake sought refuge. The village of **Sontecomapan** (1,465 pop., *Hotel Sontecomapan*) lies on an entry to the Laguna and boats may be hired for the 20-min. ride out to the bar where the Laguna meets the sea (US$10 return). A large part of the Laguna is surrounded by mangrove swamp, and the sandy beaches, edged by cliffs, are almost deserted except for local fishermen and groups of pelicans. Two good restaurants in Sontecomapan. Beaches are accessible to those who enjoy isolation—such as Jicacal and Playa Hermosa. **Jicacal** can be reached by going straight on from the Catemaco-Sontecomapan road for 9 km. on a good dirt road to La Palma where there is a small bridge which is avoided by heavy vehicles; immediately after this take left fork (dirt road) for Monte Pío and watch out for a very small sign marked Playa Escondida; road impassable when wet, about 12 km., and then continuing for about 4 km. from there. Playa Jicacal is long and open, the first you see as you near the water. The track reaches a T-junction, on the right Jicacal, to the left Playa Escondida. It is not recommended to sleep on the beaches (assaults and robberies) although at Easter time many people from the nearby towns camp on the beaches.

At **Acayucán** (*Hotel Joalica*, Zaragoza 4, E; *Hotel Ritz*, F, adequate), 267 km. from Veracruz, turn right for Route 185 if you want to go across the Isthmus to Tehuantepec, Tuxtla Gutiérrez and Central America, but continue on Route 180 for Minatitlán, Coatzacoalcos and Villahermosa (Tabasco). The road across the Isthmus is straight but is not always fast to drive because of high winds (changing air systems from Pacific to Atlantic). Gasoline and food both on sale at the half-way point, Palomares, where there is a paved road to Tuxtepec (see page 940), 2½ hours' drive. A few kilometres south of Palomares a gravelled road enters on the eastern side; this passes under an imposing gateway "La Puerta de Uxpanapa" where some 24,500 families are being settled in land reclaimed from the jungle. An hour's drive further south the road crosses the watershed and passes across the flat coastal plain to Juchitán.

About 15 km. from Alvarado a new bridge replaces the old ferry-crossing at Buenavista over the Papaloapan River and the road heads southwards to the fishing village of **Tlacotalpan** where the Papaloapan and San Juan rivers meet. It has many picturesque streets with one-storey houses all fronted by stuccoed columns and arches painted in various bright pastel colours. Two churches in the Zócalo, and a Casa de las Artesanías on Chazaro, 1½ blocks from the Zócalo. There is a famous *fiesta* there on January 31 which is very much for locals rather than tourists (accommodation is impossible to find during *fiesta*). The *Viajero* and *Reforma* hotels are good; so is the *Posada Doña Lala*, E with a/c and TV, restaurant expensive. Excellent *sopa de mariscos* and *jaiba a la tlacotalpina* (crab) at the *Restaurant La Flecha*. Buses go to Veracruz via Alvarado (US$0.35, 45 mins.), to San Andrés, Tuxtla Gutiérrez, Santiago Tuxtla (US$1, 1½ hrs.) and Villahermosa.

Cosamaloapan, some 40 km. beyond Tlacotalpan, is the local market centre with a number of hotels, and the staging point for most bus lines from Veracruz, Orizaba and Oaxaca. One of the largest sugar mills in Mexico is situated just outside the town—Ingenio San Cristóbal—and there is a local airstrip. From Cosamaloapan to Papaloapan the banks on either side of the river are lined with fruit trees. Chacaltianguis, on the east bank of the river, reached by car ferry, has houses fronted by columns.

40 km. beyond Cosamaloapan is a ferry to **Otatitlán**, also on the east bank of the river (it leaves whenever there are sufficient passengers, US$0.08 the ride). The town, also known as El Sanctuario, dates back to early colonial times, its houses with tiled roofs supported by columns, but most

interesting is the church. The padre maintains that the gold-patterned dome is the largest unsupported structure of its kind in Mexico, measuring 20 metres wide and 40 high. El Sanctuario has one of the three black wooden statues of Christ brought over from Spain for the son of Hernán Cortés. During the anti-clerical violence of the 1930s attempts to burn it failed, although the original head was cut off and now stands in a glass case. The first weekend in May is the saint's day and fair, for which pilgrims flock in from the *sierra* and from the Tuxtlas, many in local dress. (*Restaurant-Bar Pepe* serves delicious local, but unusual food; *Restaurant-Bar Ipiranga III* also offers excellent cooking; both by embarkation point.)

At **Papaloapan** on the eastern bank of the river, the main road from Orizaba to Rodríguez Clara crosses the main road from Alvarado to Oaxaca; the railway station has services to Yucatán and Chiapas, and to Orizaba or Veracruz. On the west bank is the bus terminal of Santa Cruz (almost under the railway bridge) where all second class buses stop. A passenger ferry may be taken from here to Papaloapan (US$0.08). Although Papaloapan is the route centre for the area the most convenient centre is Tuxtepec, 9 km. further south (see next page).

The river basin drained by the Papaloapan and its tributaries covers some 47,000 sq. km.— about twice the size of the Netherlands—and is subject to a programme of regional development by the Comisión del Papaloapan, which includes the construction of two large dams to control the sometimes severe flooding of the lower basin. The lake formed behind Presidente Alemán dam at Temascal is scenically very attractive and boats may be hired to go to Mazatec Indian settlements on the islands or on the other side. There is also a daily ferry passing round the lake. **Soyaltepec** is the closest settlement, situated high above the water on an island, the peak crowned by a church. **Ixcatlan** lies on a peninsula jutting into the lake on the SE side; it has one hotel and one restaurant, as well as a large beer repository. Ixcatlan may also be reached by dirt road from Tuxtepec, but it is less nerve-racking to take a ferry.

Temascal (Sun. is the most active day) may be reached by taking Route 145 from Papaloapan through Gabino Barreda, Ciudad Alemán (no facilities, centre of the Papaloapan Commission), Novara (petrol and 3 restaurants of varying prices, 1 air-conditioned), as far as La Granja where the turn to Temascal is clearly marked. Route 145 continues paved and straight past **Tres Valles** (cheap, good regional food; annual fair mid-Nov.), and on to **Tierra Blanca** (hotels *Balun Canán*, cheap, hot, F; *Principal*, F, own shower and fan, clean, just above bus station, noisy; *Bimbis* restaurant by ADO bus station, good; shopping centre, market, car repairs, e.g. Volkswagen agent). Mérida train from Tierra Blanca leaves late although scheduled for 0530 (2nd class, US$2.90, crowded, sleeper for 1—or two small people—US$11) stops at Palenque, 15½ hrs. later. Train also stops at Ciudad Alemán on the way. Route 145 passes under a sign saying "La Puerta del Papaloapan", to join the main Orizaba-Veracruz road (Route 150) at **La Tinaja**, a second-class bus junction, also gasoline, and restaurants (1 air-conditioned at service station). Papaloapan to La Tinaja takes about 1 hr., the road often has a lot of lorries and in the cane-cutting season great care should be taken at night for carts travelling on the road without lights. There are three railway crossings on the road, also poorly marked, two near La Granja and one near Tierra Blanca. The tarmac is often damaged in the wet season (June-Dec.).

From Papaloapan a paved road runs eastwards as far as Rodríguez Clara (planned to continue to Sayula on the Trans-Isthmian road). This road passes through the main pineapple-producing region of Mexico, which has encouraged the development of towns such as **Loma Bonita** (local airstrip, hotels, restaurants and gasoline) and **Villa Isla** (hotels, *La Choca* restaurant good, railway station, ADO bus terminal, and centre for the rich cattle-producing area that surrounds it).

From Villa Isla a good dirt road runs south to **Playa Vicente** (6,974 pop.), another ranching town, located beside a wide river; excellent crayfish may be eaten at the *Restaurant La Candileja*, while the café on the central plaza serves tender steaks. Another dirt road leaves the Villa Isla-Playa Vicente road for Abasolo del Valle (2,000 pop.), but only reaches to within 7 km. The last few kms. can be impassable by vehicle in the wet season. The town is set beside a lagoon and the houses are surrounded by fruit trees (no hotels or restaurants). Gasoline can be bought—ask at a shop who has some to sell.

At the cross-roads of the Papaloapan-Sayula road about 80 km. from Papaloapan, where the S turn is to Villa Isla, the N turn is a paved road which in about ½ hour will take you past two turnings to Tres Zapotes and up to Santiago Tuxtla.

The road from Papaloapan continues E to a point just N of **Rodríguez Clara,** which is reached by branching off S down a dirt road. This is a compact, thriving town, also with a railway station. There are 2 hotels, the better is in the centre of the town, *Hotel Roa*, F; *Restaurant Mexicana* recommended. The railway line from Papaloapan is the only all-year means of transport to visit the villages and towns E of Rodríguez Clara.

Tuxtepec is the natural centre for a stay in the Papaloapan area. It is a small market town some 9 km. south of Papaloapan (toll for Caracol bridge, US$0.40). Consequently the streets are alive every day in season with Indians who have come from surrounding villages to buy and sell, and there is a fascinating mixture of the music and exuberance of Veracruz with the food and handicrafts of Oaxaca. The town is built on a meander of the Santo Domingo River and a walk past the main shops in Calle Independencia will allow two halts at viewpoints for the river.

Hotels *El Rancho*, restaurant, bar, evening entertainment, most expensive, accepts travellers' cheques as payment, recommended; *Tuxtepec*, good value; *Sacre*, also good, quiet, F; *Catedral*, Calle Guerrero, nr. Zócalo, F, very friendly, fan and ventilator. *Miramar*, F, hot showers, safe car park, with view of filthy river. Very good value is the *Avenida* in Independencia round the corner from ADO bus station, F, with bath and ventilator, basic, clean but restaurant below not very good value. *Posada del Sol*, basic and noisy, opp. Fletes y Pasajes bus station, F.

Restaurants *El Estero* across from the street from ADO (fish dishes and local cuisine excellent), *El Mino* (near Fletes y Pasajes bus terminal), *Mandinga* for fish dishes, *Queso Fundido* in Independencia. *Ostionería Pata-Pata*, on the street beside *Hotel Avenida*, good *mojarra*. *Ronda*, Calle Independencia, cheap and good; *La Mascota de Oro*, 20 de Noviembre 891, very friendly, cheap. Beer from the barrel can be bought from the bar next to the Palacio Municipal, and the best ices are found in *La Morida*.

Transport There are four bus terminals in town, clear street signs for each one. ADO bus services to Mexico City (Thurs., US$7), Veracruz and regular daily minibus (taking 5-6 hrs.) to Oaxaca leaving at 0800 and 1230. AU (Autobuses Unidos, on Matamoros, ½ block from Libertad) daily to wide variety of destinations. AU to Oaxaca, US$4 2nd class, 8 hrs., slow, not recommended; 3 buses a day from 2nd class terminal to Oaxaca, first at 0800, worth leaving early for the scenery, 7 hrs., US$3.20, from Calle Libertad 1684. Fletes y Pasajes to local villages and Juchitán, and a 2nd class, wild journey to Oaxaca, 6 hrs.; Cristóbal Colón, which has its own terminal near the Cultural Centre, sometimes stop by the ADO office to find passengers for Chiapas or Mexico City. The Tuxtepec-Palomares road provides a short cut to the Transístmica; it passes through many newly cleared jungle areas. Bus to Acayucan, ADO, 4 hrs., US$1.50. There are scattered villages, the main halt being at María Lombardo (some 2 hrs. from Tuxtepec where food is sold); Zócalo is attractive. Gas station 4 km. further on at Cihualtepec junction, a village of Indians moved from the area flooded by the Temascal dam.

Excursions To Temascal to see the dam (see previous page); also a visit to the Indian villages of Ojitlán and Jalapa de Díaz (bus leaves from the end of Calle 20 de Noviembre, US$2.20, 2½ hrs.; hotel, F and food stores, good and cheaper *huipiles* from private houses) is well worth the ride; easily reached by car, along semi-paved road and also by AU bus service (from Mercado Flores Magón, 20 de Noviembre y Blvd. Juárez, every hour on the half hour). The Chinantec Indians' handicrafts may be bought on enquiry; hotels non-existent and eating facilities limited but some superb scenery, luxuriant vegetation and little-visited area. Ojitlán is best visited on Sunday, market day, when the Chinanteca *huipiles* worn by the women are most likely to be seen. Part of the area will be flooded when the Cerro de Oro dam is finished and the lake will join that of Temascal. Heavily armed checkpoint on the road from Tuxtepec to Tierra Blanca (bus 1½ hrs., US$0.50), non-uniformed men, very officious, do not get caught with any suspicious goods.

The road from Tuxtepec south to Oaxaca (Route 175) is now well paved, and a spectacular route. Many people avoid it; it is said to have become dangerous for travellers because of drug plantations along its length. It takes about 5 hrs. to drive, up Valle Nacional. This valley, despite its horrific reputation as the "Valle de los Miserables" in the era of Porfirio Díaz, for political imprisonment and virtual slavery from which there was no escape, is astoundingly beautiful. The road follows the valley floor, on which are cattle pastures, fruit trees and a chain of small villages such as Chiltepec (very good bathing in the river), Jacatepec (reached by ferry over the river, produces rich honey and abounds in all varieties of fruit, there are no cars at all), Monte Flor (where swimming and picnicking are possible beside natural springs, but *very* cold water, and an archaeological site) and finally Valle Nacional. (Bus to Valle Nacional from Tuxtepec, 1½ hrs., basic hotel, restaurants, stores, and gasoline available; river swimming.) The road climbs up into the Sierra, getting cooler, and slopes more heavily covered with tropical forest, and there are panoramic views.

San Pedro Yolox lies some 20 minutes' drive W of this route down a dirt road; it is a peaceful Chinantec village clustered on the side of the mountain, while Llano de Flores is a huge grassy clearing in the pine forest with grazing animals and cool, scented air. Wood from these forests is cut for the paper factory in Tuxtepec. Ixtlán de Juárez has gasoline. While houses in the lowlands are made of wood with palm roofs, here the houses are of adobe or brick. From Guelatao (see page 959) it is about 1½ hours' drive, mainly downhill, to Oaxaca (see page 954), with the land becoming drier and the air warmer.

By the road followed to Veracruz, the driving time from Mexico City is about 9 hrs. One can return to the capital by a shorter route through Jalapa which takes 6 hrs.; this was the old colonial route to the port, and is the route followed by the railway.

Jalapa, capital of Veracruz state, 132 km. from the port, is in the *tierra templada*, at 1,425 metres. There was a passion for renovation in the flamboyant gothic style during the first part of the 19th century. It is yet another "City of

Flowers", with walled gardens, stone-built houses, wide avenues in the newer town and steep cobbled crooked streets in the old. The 18th century cathedral, with its sloping floor, has been recently restored. Population 200,000. Just outside, on the road to Mexico City, is a modern museum showing archaeological treasures of the Olmec, Totonac and Huastec coastal cultures, open daily. The three colossal heads dating from the 2nd to the 5th centuries A.D., and displayed in the grounds of the museum, are Olmec. Jalapa (spelt Xalapa locally) has a University; you can take a pleasant stroll round the grounds, known as El Dique.

Festival Feria de Primavera, mid-April.

Hotels Cheaper hotels are up the hill from the market, which itself is uphill from Parque Juárez (there is no Zócalo). Many hotels are overpriced; no price-lists displayed and not available at tourist office. *Del Pardo*, probably the best, but noisy; *María Victoria*, Zaragoza 6, C, first class; *Limón*, E, with shower; *Regis*, E, without bath; *México*, E, clean, with shower; *Salmones*, on Zaragoza, E, recommended; *Dulcilandia*, on Revolución. *Amoro*, nr. market, F, no shower but public baths opp., very clean. *Continental*, on Enríquez, F, friendly; *Suites Los Lagos*, good for longer stays, E.

Restaurants *La Parroquia*, Zaragoza 18, recommended, good strong coffee (you tap your glass with a spoon for a refill); *La Barranquilla*, expensive but good; *Quinto Reyno*, Juárez 67 close to Zócalo, lunches only, excellent vegetarian with health-food shop, very good service. *Chino's*, on Enríquez, very friendly and pleasant; *Enrico*, good value; *El Mayab*, next to *Hotel Regis*, for *antojitos* and good *carne tampiqueña*; *La Tasca*, a club, good music, recommended.

Theatre Teatro del Estado, Av. Avila Camacho; good Ballet Folklórico Veracruzano and fair symphony orchestra.

Communications Radio-telephone available opposite *Hotel María Victoria*. Letters can be sent to the Lista de Correos in Calle Diego Leño, friendly post office.

Airport 15 km. SE, on Veracruz road.

Transport 2nd class bus station, Autobuses Unidos, uphill from Parque Juárez. 1st class buses (ADO) leave from the terminal 1 km. away. Frequent ADO service Jalapa-Veracruz. Railway station on outskirts, buses from near market to get there. Train to Mexico City at 1140, to Veracruz at 1530 (4 hrs.).

Excursions To ruins of **Zempoala** (hotel, *Chachalaca*, near sea, spotless, recommended), the coastal city which was conquered by Cortés and whose inhabitants became his allies. The ruins are interesting because of the round stones uniquely used in construction. (Entry US$0.40, small museum on site.) Take 2nd class bus to Zempoala via Cardel, which will let you off at the ruins, or take a taxi from the Plaza de Zempoala, US$1.20 return. You can also get there from Veracruz. To Texala waterfalls, some 15 km. away near the neighbouring town of Coatepec, famous for its ice-cream.

Tim Connell writes: "**Naolinco** is ½ hr. ride, 40 km. NE of Jalapa up a winding hilly road, *Restaurant La Fuente* serves local food; has nice garden. Las Cascadas, with a *mirador* to admire them from, are on the way into the town: two waterfalls, with various pools, tumble several thousand feet over steep wooded slopes. Flocks of *zopilotes* (buzzards) collect late in the afternoon, soaring high up into the thermals. Baños Carrizal: 8 km. off main road, 40 km. from Veracruz. Chachalacas is a beach with swimming pool and changing facilities in hotel of same name, US$0.70 adults. Thatched huts; local delicacies sold on beach, including *robalito* fish." **La Antigua**: dilapidated Spanish garrison, plus colonial church, near the main coast-road toll booths for Veracruz (US$0.50 toll). Also, to El Tajín, see page 876.

The road towards the capital continues to climb to Perote, 53 km. from Jalapa. The San Carlos fort here, now a military prison, was built in 1770-77; there is a good view of Cofre de Perote volcano. A road branches N to **Teziutlán** (*Hotel Valdez*, hot water, car park, F), with a Friday market, where good *sarapes* are sold, continuing to Papantla (see page 876). The old convent at **Acatzingo**, 93 km. beyond, is worth seeing. Another 10 km. and we join the road to Puebla and Mexico City.

Mount Orizaba From Acatzingo one can go via a paved road to Tlachichuca (35 km.) and contact the Reyes family to get a four-wheel drive car to go up an appalling road to a hut on Mount Orizaba (Citlaltépetl), the highest peak in Mexico (5,700 metres). There is no hut custodian; it's usually fairly empty, except on Sat. night. No food or light, or wood; provide your own. There is a glacier some 150 metres above the hut. Water close at hand, but no cooking facilities.

Mexico City-Cuernavaca-Taxco-Acapulco

A 406-km. road, beginning as a 4-lane toll motorway, connects Mexico City with Acapulco. (The 4-lane ends at Iguala, 209 km. from Acapulco.) Driving time is

MEXICO 943

about 6 hrs. The highest point, La Cima, 3,016 metres, is reached at km. 42. The road then spirals down through precipitous forests to (Km. 75):

Cuernavaca, capital of Morelos state (originally Tlahuica Indian territory); at 1,542 metres: 724 metres lower than Mexico City. Population 340,000 and growing because of new industrial area to the S. The temperature never exceeds 27°C nor falls below 10°C, and there is almost daily sunshine even during the rainy season. The city has always attracted visitors from the more rigorous highlands and can be overcrowded. The Spaniards captured it in 1521 and Cortés himself, following the custom of the Aztec nobility, lived there. The outskirts are dotted with ultra-modern walled homes. The Cathedral, finished in 1552, known as Iglesia de la Asunción, stands at one end of an enclosed garden. 17th-century murals were discovered during restoration; also, on the great doors, paintings said to have been done by an Oriental convert who arrived by a ship from the Philippines, relating the story of the persecution and crucifixion of 24 Japanese martyrs. The Sun. morning masses at 1100 are accompanied by a special *mariachi* band. *Mariachis* also perform on Sun. and Wed. evenings in the Cathedral. By the entrance to it stands the charming small Church of the Tercera Orden (1529), whose quaint façade carved by Indian craftsmen contains a small figure suspected to be one of the only two known statues of Cortés in Mexico. (The other is a mounted statue near the entrance of the *Casino de la Selva* hotel.) The palace Cortés built in 1531 for his second wife stands by the city's central tree-shaded plaza; on the rear balcony is a Diego Rivera mural depicting the conquest of Mexico. It was the seat of the State Legislature until 1967, when the new legislative building opposite was completed; it has now become the Regional Cuauhnahuac museum (second only to the Anthropology Museum in Mexico City), showing everything from dinosaur remains to contemporary Indian culture (closed Thurs., as are other museums in Cuernavaca). The 18th century Borda Gardens, on Calle Morelos, were a favourite resort of Maximilian and Carlota, but have now more or less run wild (small fee). The weekend retreat of the ill-fated imperial couple, in the Acapantzingo district, is being restored. Other places worth seeing are the three plazas, Calle Guerrero, and, some distance from the main plaza, the new market buildings on different levels. The house of David Alfaro Siqueiros, the painter, is now a museum at Calle Venus 7 and contains lithographs and personal photographs. The very unusual Teopanzolco pyramid is to be found near the railway station. Remarkable frescoes have recently been found in the old Franciscan church of La Parroquia. There are occasional concerts at the San José open chapel. Many spas in surrounding area, at Cuautla, Xocitepec, Atrotomilco, Oaxtepec and others. Cuernavaca is called Cuauhnahuac, the original Aztec version of its name, in Malcolm Lowry's *Under the Volcano.*

Hotels *Papagayo,* Motolinia 13, 5 blocks from Zócalo, D, incl. breakfast, pool, gardens, clean, convenient, noisy, suitable for families, parking; *España Colón,* Av. Morelos 200C, restaurant E; *Las Mañanitas,* Linares 107, A (one of the best in Mexico), Mexican colonial style, many birds in lovely gardens, excellent food. *Hacienda de Cortés,* Atlacomulco suburb, 16th century sugar *hacienda,* magnificent genuine colonial architecture, garden, suites, pool, restaurant, A, access by car; *Posada Jacarandas,* Cuauhtémoc 805, B, garden, restaurant, parking; *Suites Paraíso,* Av. Domingo Diez 1100, family accommodation, D; *Posada Xochiquetzal,* Francisco Leyva 200, near Zócalo, restaurant, pool, garden, C. *Posada San Angelo,* Privada la Selva 100, restaurant, gardens, pool, C; *Posada San Antonio,* Av. Morelos Sur 1100, F; *Casino de la Selva,* C, Leandro Valle 26, with huge mural by Siqueiros on the future of humanity from now till A.D. 3000, shops, restaurant, bars, gardens; *Hostería Las Quintas,* Av. las Quintas 107, A, built in traditional Mexican style, owner has splendid collection of bonsai trees, restaurant, pool, magnificent setting, fine reputation; *Hostería Peñalba,* Matamoros 204, B, beautiful courtyard with exotic birds and a monkey, restaurant with famous Spanish food, was once Zapata's H.Q. during the Revolution, very atmospheric and friendly, warmly recommended except for the plumbing; *Casa de Huéspedes,* Morelos Sur 702, good value, D including 3 good meals; for economy, *Roma,* Calle Matamoros 405, F, good value, with hot water and shower, but now reported dirty. Probably cheapest is *Casa Blanca,* on Arista, 2 blocks from bus station, simple, F. Rooms from US$75 a month on Calle Degollado 104, quite clean, but heavy bus traffic outside; communal kitchen and bath. Furnished flat US$200 per month. *Royal,* Matamoros 19, F. Several cheaper hotels in Calle Aragón y León, recommended is *Colonial,* E, clean, friendly, secure; *El Buen Vecino, Casa La Paz, Marilú, Posada*

944 MEXICO

San José, Francés, and *América,* E, noisy (couples only, but clean, basic; some rent rooms by the hour).

Near Cuernavaca is the *Hacienda de Cocoyoc,* an old converted *hacienda* with a swimming pool backed by the mill aqueduct. Glorious gardens, 18-hole golf-course, tennis and riding, A. Also *Hacienda Vista Hermosa,* another converted *hacienda,* from C; **Motels** *Los Canarios,* Morelos 711, F, old, crumbling; *El Verano,* Zapata 602, D; *Posada Cuernavaca,* Paseo del Conquistador, view, restaurant, grounds, D; *Suites OK Motel* with *Restaurant Las Margaritas,* Zapata 71, special student and long-term rates, apartments, trailer park; swimming pool and squash courts; Tel.: (731) 3-12-70. *Torrell,* Jesús Preciado 414, nr. San Antón suburb, student discounts, E.

Restaurants *Las Mañanitas,* beautiful but expensive, Ricardo Linares 107; *Sumiya,* Barbara Hutton's oriental mountain-top retreat, in the suburbs, exquisite decor, must be seen; *Hosteria Las Quintas,* Las Quintas 107, excellent; *Harry's Grill,* on Hidalgo, excellent Mexican food, good service and prices; *Harry's Bar,* Gutemberg 3-1 (New York style); *Los Arcos,* opp. post office in Zócalo, good, prices reasonable, foreigners meeting place in a.m., full at weekends. *Casa de Gardenias,* opp. Cortés' palace, open air, food good at US$2 a dish; *Villa Roma* on Zócalo, good *chilaquiles* for breakfast, good service, pricier; *Château Renee,* Swiss-European cuisine, Atzingo 11, in woods above town. *Mister Grill,* entrance to town, steak house; *Eric Pup,* 2nd floor on main square, German-Mexican food; *Baalbek,* Netzahualcoyotl 300, gorgeous garden, best Lebanese food in town; *Vienés,* Lerdo de Tejada 4, German-Swiss food, very good; *La Parroquía,* main square, very popular, sidewalk café; *Madreterra,* vegetarian, in pretty patio near Cortés' palace, Sunday lunch with live music. *Portal,* nearby, in Calle Galeana, has good cheap breakfasts. Mexican food at *Los Comales,* Morelos Sur 1321; *Tizoc,* Carretera a Cuautla 2½ km.; *Las Cazuelas,* Galeana 104; *El Tapatío,* Rayón 104; *Chipitlán,* Av. Morelos Sur 79; *Hacienda Los Ocampo,* recommended for *mariachi* music, at 1400 the house-band plays, Av. Plan de Ayala 310 and at No. 616 *Nuevo Comedor Pachuquilla; Mi Ranchito,* Domingo Diez 1518; vegetarian food at *La Remolada* on Matamoros, good, classical music; bar with live music at the *Parrilla Danesa* (guitar); seafood at *Moby Dick,* Av. Plan de Ayala 383; *Pancho's Place,* Morelos Sur 1004; *Playa Bruja,* Galeana 104; *Rancho Cortés,* Margarita 2; Yucatán specialities at *Merendero Yucateco,* F. Villa 112.

Language Schools There are about 12 Spanish courses on offer. These start from US$45 per week at the University, 4 hrs. daily; private schools charge US$80-100 a week, 5-6 hrs. a day and some schools also have a US$80 registration fee. The peak time for tuition is summer; at other times it may be possible to arrive and negotiate a reduction of up to 25%. There is a co-operative language centre, Cuauhnahuac, with Spanish courses, at 1414 Av. Morelos Sur. Intensive courses also at Instituto Panamericano, Morelos Sur 712 (nearest school to centre), good teachers, friendly, US$85 a week, staying with family, US$10 extra a day, no registration fee, free excursions; Instituto Fénix, San Jerónimo 304, which also has excursions and minor courses in politics, art and music (arranges board with families); at Cale, Nueva Tabachín, 22-A bis, Col. Tlaltenango, friendly; at Cemanahuac, Calle San Juan 4, Las Palmas, which includes weaving and pottery classes; at Experiencia, which encompasses all these features and will arrange lodgings with Mexican families in the area, Registro Público 16, Colonia Burocrática; at Cidoc, Av. Río Balsas 14, Colonia Vista Hermosa; at Ideal (small classes, friendly atmosphere), Privada de la Pradera 107; and Idel, Las Palmas 101, Colonia Jiguilpan. Staying with a family will be arranged by a school and costs US$10-15 a day or US$100-250 a month incl. meals; check with individual schools, as this difference in price may apply even if you stay with the same family.

Telephones Long-distance calls can be made at Farmacia Central, on the Zócalo.

Tourist Office Av. Morelos Sur 900, very helpful, many maps. For cultural activities, go for information to the university building behind the Cathedral on Morelos Sur.

HOMESTAY WITH MEXICAN FAMILY ARRANGED BY SCHOOL

Cuauhnahuac

instituto colectivo de lengua y cultura

OFFERS: ★ **Intensive Spanish classes**
★ **Maximum of 4 students per teacher**
★ **5 hours per day, 5 days per week** ★ **Emphasis on oral communication**
★ **Excursions & other Cultural Activities** ★ **Classes begin every Monday**
For more information contact: **CUAUHNAHUAC, APDO 26-5, CUERNAVACA, MORELOS, 62051, MEXICO Tel: 12-16-98, 12-36-73 Or visit us at Morelos Sur 1414**

MEXICO 945

Railway Station on Calle Amacuzac; only passenger service is daily train to Iguala.

Buses Terminal on Av. López Mateos, adjacent to main market. To Mexico City 0600-2200, every 15 mins.: Estrella de Oro, 1st class, US$1.15, more comfortable than Flecha Roja, 2nd class, 1 hr. journey, US$0.65. To Acapulco, 6 hrs. with either. To Taxco, Flecha Roja, 2nd-class buses from Calle Morelos, US$0.80, 1½ hours, fairly comfortable, about every hour, or Estrella de Oro, 1st class, Las Palmas-Morelos Sur. Cuautla (page 953) via Yautepec every hour, 1 hr., interesting trip; go there for long-distance buses going South.

Warning Theft of luggage from waiting buses in Cuernavaca is rife; don't ever leave belongings unattended.

Excursions To the Chapultepec Park, W end of town, with boating facilities, small zoo, water gardens, small admission charge. To the potters' village of **San Antón**, perched above a waterfall, a little W of the town, where divers perform Sun. for small donations. To the charming suburb of **Acapantzingo**, S of the town, another retreat of Maximilian. To the village of **Tepoztlán**—24 km.—at the foot of the spectacular El Tepozteco national park, picturesque steep cobbled streets, wild view, with Tepozteco pyramid high up in the mountains (US$0.10, open 0900-1600), the climb is an hour long, and strenuous, but the view is magnificent) and a remarkable 16th century church and convent (entry US$0.45, site closes at 1630): the Virgin and Child stand upon a crescent moon above the elaborate plateresque portal; now sporting a noticeably "hippy" population (*Posada del Tepozteco*, a very good inn, C, with swimming pool and excellent atmosphere; *Casa de Huéspedes Las Cabañas*, D, overpriced; budget travellers would do better to stay in Cuernavaca. *Restaurant Carmen*, S of convent, recommended). There is a small archaeological museum behind the church. This was the village studied by Robert Redfield and later by Oscar Lewis. Local bus from Cuernavaca market bus terminal takes 40 mins., US$0.40; bus to Mexico City, US$0.90.

Near Cuernavaca is Chalcatzingo, where there are interesting Olmec-style rock carvings. Near Jojutla is the old Franciscan convent of Tlaquiltenango (1540), frequent bus service.

Km. 100) **Alpuyeca,** whose church has good Indian murals. A road to the left runs to **Lake Tequesquitengo** (*Paraíso Ski Club*) and the lagoon and sulphur baths of Tehuixtla. Near the lake a popular resort—swimming, boating, water skiing and fishing—is *Hacienda Vista Hermosa,* Hernán Cortés' original *ingenio* (sugar mill), and several lakeside hotels (also at Jojutla, above). From Alpuyeca also a road runs right for 50 km. to the **Cacahuamilpa** caverns, (known locally as "Las Grutas") some of the largest caves in North America, open 1000 to 1700 (well lit); strange stalactite and stalagmite formations; steps lead down from near the entrance to the caverns to the double opening in the mountainside far below, from which an underground river emerges (entry, US$0.60, up to 1600). Buses going to Cacahuamilpa from Cuernavaca leave every 20 mins. between 1000 and 1700 (1 hr.); they are usually overcrowded at weekends; enquire about schedules for local buses or buses from Taxco to Toluca, which stop there (from Taxco, 40 minutes). At 15 km. is the right-hand turn to the **Xochicalco** ruins (36 km. SW of Cuernavaca), topped by a pyramid on the peak of a rocky hill, dedicated to the Plumed Serpent whose coils enfold the whole building and enclose fine carvings which represent priests. The site is large: needs 2-3 hrs. to see it properly.

Xochicalco was at its height between 650 and 900 AD. It is one of the oldest known fortresses in Middle America and a religious centre as well as an important trading point. Xochicalco means "place of flowers" although now the hilltops are barren. It was also the meeting place of northern

---

Come to **EXPERIENCIA**

BILINGUAL AND CULTURAL EXCHANGE PROGRAMS

★ Intensive Spanish classes, maximum of 4 students per teacher, 5 hours per day, 5 days per week. Emphasis on oral communication.
★ Exchange programs with Mexican participants, round table discussions, folk music programs, sports, parties, excursions.
★ Home stay with Mexican family arranged by school.

FOR FURTHER INFORMATION, WRITE TO
EXPERIENCIA APDO. POSTAL C-96 CUERNAVACA, MORELOS, MEXICO
Tel. (73) 12-70-71 ADRESS: PASEO COSUMEL 16 COL QUINTANA ROO

CUERNAVACA

946 MEXICO

and southern cultures and both calendar systems were correlated here. The sides of the pyramid are faced with andesite slabs, fitted invisibly without mortar. After the building was finished, reliefs 3-4 inches deep were carried into the stone as a frieze. There are interesting underground tunnels; one has a shaft to the sky and the centre of the cave. There are also ball courts, an avenue 18.5 metres wide and 46 m. long, remains of 20 large circles and of a palace and dwellings. Xochicalco is well worth the 4 km. walk from the bus stop; take a torch for the underground part to save employing a guide, entry US$0.10. (Flecha Roja bus to Xochicalco from terminal at Av. Morelos y Arista, marked Las Grutas, passes the turn-off to Xochicalco—same bus schedule as Cacahuamilpa, above.) Alternatively take bus from Cuernavaca to Cuentepec (infrequent), which passes by the entrance gate to Xochicalco ruins. This bus passes through Alpuyeca, which is also easily reached from Taxco by bus.

Leave the toll road at Amacuzac (Km. 121) and take the old road (39 km.) to **Taxco,** a colonial gem, population 60,000, with steep, twisting, cobbled streets and many picturesque buildings. The first silver shipped to Spain came from the mines of Taxco. A Frenchman, Borda, made and spent three immense fortunes here in the 18th century; he founded the present town and built the magnificent twin-towered, rose-coloured parish church of Santa Prisca which soars above everything but the mountains. There are magnificent mirrors at the back of the church, which is in the main square. Well worth a visit are the Casa Humboldt, where Baron von Humboldt once stayed, and the Casa Figueroa, the "House of Tears" (closed Sun.), so called because the colonial judge who owned it forced Indian labourers to work on it to pay their fines. Museo Guillermo Spratling, behind Santa Prisca, is a fascinating silver museum, entry US$0.20. Large paintings about Mexican history at the Post Office. The roof of every building is of red tile, every nook or corner in the place is a picture, and even the cobblestone streets have patterns woven in them. It is now a national monument and all modern building is forbidden. Gas stations are outside the city limits. The plaza is 1,700 metres above sea-level. A good view is had from the Iglesia de Guadalupe. The climate is ideal, never any high winds (for it is protected by huge mountains immediately to the N); never cold and never hot, but sometimes foggy. Silverwork is a speciality and there are important lead and zinc mines. The processions during Holy Week are spectacular. The most tourist-free part is up from the main street where the taxis can't go; day trippers fill the town in the early afternoon. Wear flat rubber-soled shoes to avoid slithering over the cobbles. Vendors will not bargain. Cheaper silver items can often be found in less touristy towns including Mexico City—beware of mistaking the cheapish pretty jewellery, *alpaca*, which only contains 25% silver, for the real stuff. By law, real silver must be stamped somewhere on the item with the number .925. The downtown shops in general give better value than those on the highway. On the 2nd Sunday in December there is a national silversmiths' competition. Colourful produce market near the Zócalo. Beware of handbag snatchers.

N.B. All silver jewellers must be government-registered. Remember to look for the 925 stamp and, if the piece is large enough, it will also be stamped with the crest of an eagle, and initials of the jeweller. Where the small size of the items does not permit this, a certificate will be provided instead.

WILL YOU HELP US?

We do all we can to get our facts right in *The South American Handbook*. Each chapter is thoroughly revised each year, but Latin America and the Caribbean cover a vast area, and our eyes cannot be everywhere.

Your information may be far more up-to-date than ours. If your letter reaches us early enough in the year it will be used in the next edition, but write whenever you want to, for all your letters are used sooner or later.

Thank you very much indeed for your help.

Trade & Travel Publications Limited
5 Prince's Buildings, George Street,
Bath BA1 2ED, England

One of the most interesting of Mexican stone-age cultures, the Mezcala or Chontal, is based on the State of Guerrero in which Taxco lies. Its remarkable artefacts, of which there are many imitations, are almost surrealist. The culture remained virtually intact into historic times.

Hotels *De la Borda*, on left as you enter Taxco, largest, all facilities, B; dearest and best, *La Cumbre Soñada*, 1.5 km. or so towards Acapulco on a mountain top, colonial, exquisite, B. *La Hacienda del Solar*, Acapulco exit of town, B, best restaurant in Taxco. *Monte Taxco*, on a hill top, 400 metres above the city, restaurant, special buses to town, B; *Rancho Taxco-Victoria*, Soto la Marina 15, walk to centre, B; *Posa Don Carlos*, Cerro de Bermeja 6, converted old mansion, restaurant, good view, C; *Los Arcos*, Juan Ruiz de Alarcón 2, magnificently reconstructed 17th century ex-convent, charming, friendly, good restaurant, C; *Posada de los Castillo*, Alarcón 7, off main square, Mexican style, friendly, excellent value, D. *Meléndez*, D, clean, no hot water, somewhat noisy as it is near market, good breakfast, other meals available; *Agua Escondida*, near Zócalo at Calle Guillermo Spratling 4, D, with bath, very good value and nice view, restaurant indifferent; *Casa Grande*, Plazuela San Juan, nr. Santa Prisca church, 2 mins. from Zócalo, small clean rooms with shower (hot water in mornings only) ask for top floor, E, good views; *Del Monte*, 2nd block from Zócalo, E, colonial, with bath, dilapidated; *Posada Santa Anita*, F, with bath, basic, very dirty, many insects, near bus station; *Posada de la Misión*, Cerro de la Misión 84, Juan O'Gorman mural, restaurant, good, pool, C; *Colina del Sol*, F, clean, nice rooms, on the Kennedy Highway between Estrella de Oro and Flecha Roja terminals. *Posada del Jardín*, 6 rooms, cheap, clean, friendly, view from patio, F, Celsa Muñoz 2, left of Santa Prisca. Also near Zócalo good *Casa de Huéspedes*, unnamed, Pajaritos 23, F, with bath; *Colonial*, G, sometimes no water.

Restaurants *La Ventana* of the *Hacienda del Solar* hotel, renowned. *Alarcón*, overlooking Zócalo, very good meal for US$3.60, with everything included. *Sr. Costilla*, next to church on main square, good drinks and grilled ribs. *Cielito Lindo*, on Zócalo, good food, service and atmosphere; Next door is *Papa's Bar*, a discotheque and a small pizza place in an arcade. *Paco's Bar*, at other end of square for drinks and people-watching. Good drinks at *Berta's Bar*. *Mi Oficina*, straight up hill from where buses from Cuernavaca arrive. Good food at *Los Arcos* and *Victoria* hotels. Argentine *empanadas* at unnamed restaurant opp. Casa Humboldt, cheap, excellent breakfast. *Lonchería Liliana*, Juan Ruiz de Alarcón 13, recommended; *Pozolería Betty*, Mora 20 (below bus station), good food including the local beetle (*jumil*) sauce. Many small restaurants just near *Hotel Meléndez*, good value. Good snacks in small shop on NW corner of Zócalo. Excellent *comida corrida* at *Restaurant Santa Fe*, under Hotel Sta. Prisca. **Nightclub:** *La Jungla*, set in a jungle-like location (somewhat frightening 15-min. drive out of town), cover charge includes a show and dancing.

Buses Book onward tickets (e.g. to Acapulco) the day prior to departure. (Taxis meet all buses and take you to any hotel, quite cheaply.) Taxco is reached from Mexico City from the Terminal Sur, Estrella de Oro, 1st class US$2.50, only two stops, quick, no overcrowding, five a day (3 hrs.); also five 2nd class, Flecha Roja, a day for US$2, up to 5 hrs. Buses to Cuernavaca; 1st class buses at 0900, 1600, 1800 and 2000 (Estrella de Oro), 2nd class hourly at a quarter to the hour, but can be erratic. Little 24-seaters, "Los Burritos", take you up the hill from the bus terminal on main road. Spectacular journey from Toluca, missing out Mexico City. To Acapulco 1st class, Estrella de Oro, US$2.50, 5 hrs. To Cacahuamilpa for caverns, 40 minutes.

Excursions Visit *Posada Don Carlos*, Bermeja 6, for best panoramic view; also Ventana de Taxco in *Hacienda del Solar* for a panoramic view. "Combi" to Panorámica every 30 mins. from Plaza San Juan, US$0.10. Take a funicular just off the Mexico City entrance to town for a spectacular aerial ride to the *Monte Taxco Hotel*. About 20 km. out of Taxco a rodeo is held on Sat., guides available, admittance US$0.50. 12 km. from Taxco to Acuitlapán waterfalls, with Flecha Roja bus; hire a horse to travel down 4 km. path to large clear pools for swimming. Taxis about US$4.50 per hour. Visit the villages where *amate* pictures are painted (on display at Casa Humboldt and in the market). Xalitla is the most convenient as it is on the road to Acapulco, take 2nd class bus there. Other villages: Maxela, Ahuelicán, Ahuehuepán and San Juan, past Iguala and before the River Balsa.

Warning Travellers have stressed that people should *not* wander alone in isolated places, especially women; there have been violent attacks, e.g. in Acuitlapán.

The road descends. The heat grows. We join the main road again at Iguala, 36 km. from Taxco. Beyond the Mexcala river, the road passes for some 30 km. through the dramatic canyon of Zopilote to reach **Chilpancingo,** capital of Guerrero state, at Km. 302. Population 32,000, altitude 1,250 metres. The colourful reed bags from the distant village of Chilapa are sold in the market. The Casa de las Artesanías for Guerrero state is on the right-hand side of the main highway proceeding from Mexico City to Acapulco. It has a particularly wide selection of lacquerware from Olinala. Its *fiesta* starts on December 16 and lasts a fortnight. It has a University. Hotel: *La Posada Meléndez*. Not far from Chilpancingo are Oxtotitlán and Juxtlahuaca, where Olmec cave paintings can be seen. The road goes down to Acapulco (about 420 km. from Mexico City).

948 MEXICO

Warning Avoid travelling by car at night in the State of Guerrero, even on the Mexico City-Acapulco highway. *Guerrilleros* have been active in recent years.

Acapulco (population 240,000) is the most popular resort in Mexico, particularly in winter and spring. During Holy Week there is a flight from the capital every 3 mins. The town stretches for 16 km. in a series of bays and cliff coves and is invading the hills. The hotels, of which there are 250, are mostly perched high to catch the breeze, for between 1130 and 1630 the heat is sizzling; they are filled to overflowing in January and February. It has all the paraphernalia of a booming resort: smart shops, night clubs, red light district, golf club, touts and street vendors and now also air pollution. The famous beaches and expensive hotels are a different world from the littered streets, dirty hotels and crowded shops and buses which are only two minutes walk away. There are some twenty beaches, all with fine, golden sand; deckchairs on all beaches, US$0.50; parachute skiing in front of the larger hotels at US$7 for 5 mins. The two most popular are the sickle-curved and shielded Caleta, with its smooth water and now dirty sands, and the surf-pounded straight beach of Los Hornos. One can swim, and fish, the year round. Best free map of Acapulco can be obtained from the desk clerk at *Tortuga Hotel*.

Acapulco in colonial times was the terminal for the Manila convoy. Its main defence, Fort San Diego, where the last battle for Mexican independence was fought, still stands in the middle of the city and is worth a visit. (Open 1000-1800, closed Thurs., free admission.)

There are numerous excursions. The lagoons can be explored by motor boats; one, Coyuca Lagoon, is over 110 km. long; strange birds, water hyacinths, tropical flowers. Daily, in the morning and after dark, amazing 40-metre dives into shallow water by boys can be watched from the Quebrada (5 times a day, the first at 1300, the last, with torches, at 2200). There is a *jai-alai* palace. At Playa Icacos there is a marineland amusement park *Ci-Ci*, with a waterslide, pool with wave-machine and arena with performing dolphins and sea-lions, US$1.50. Pleasant boat trip across beach to Puerto Marqués, US$ 0.80 return; one can hire small sailing boats there, US$6.50 an hr. Bay cruises, 2½ hrs., from Muelle Yates, US$3, at 1100, 1630 and 2230. Visit island of La Roqueta, glass-bottomed boat, US$2.50 return, 2 hrs., overpriced. Take local bus to Pie de la Cuesta, 8 km. (now preferred by many budget travellers to Acapulco itself), several bungalow-hotels and trailer parks (see below), nice lagoon and big beaches (warning: the surf is dangerous), where you drink *coco loco*—fortified coconut milk—and watch the sunset from a hammock. Beware at all times of thieves.

Hotels can cost up to US$120 a night double; cheaper for longer stays, but this also means less expensive hotels insist on a double rate even for 1 person and for a minimum period. In the off-season (May-December) you can negotiate lower prices even for a single for one night. *Acapulco Plaza*, Costera 22, 3 towers, 2 pools, 5 bars, 4 restaurants, a city in itself, A; *Exalaris Hyatt Regency*, next to naval base, and *Exalaris Hyatt Continental*, at Fuerte Diana, both with all services, A; *Villa Vera Raquet Club*, luxurious celebrity spot, A; *Los Flamingos*, Gran Vía Tropical 73, in the hills, D; *El Cid*, a/c, swimming pool; *El Mirador*, C; *Caleta*, Playa Caleta, remodelled, B; *El Presidente*, Costera near Condesa beach, A; *Elcano*, Costera near golf club, B; *Casa Blanca Tropical*, Cerro de la Pinzona, D, with swimming pool, is recommended; *Ritz*, Auto Hotel Ritz, Magallanes y Costera, C; *Aloha*, Gran Vía Tropical 7, E; *Las Hamacas*, Costera 239, C; *Condesa del Mar*, Costera at Condesa beach, all facilities, A; *Acapulco Imperial*, Costera 251, B; *Fiesta Tortuga*, B, and *Romano's Le Club*, both on Costera, many groups, B; *Maralisa*, Enrique El Esclavo, B, smallish and elegant, Arab style, recommended; *Tropicano Best Western*, Costera 510, C; *San Francisco*, Costera 92, old part of town, E; *Maris*, C, very good value and among the cheapest along the Costera; *Liverpool*, minimum 3-night stay, E. The fabulous *Club Residencial de las Brisas*, L, a hotel where the services match the astronomical price. (It begins at sea-level and reaches up the mountain slope in a series of detached villas and public rooms to a point 300 metres above sea-level. Guests use pink jeeps to travel to the dining-room and recreation areas.) The *Acapulco Princess Country Club*, part of the *Acapulco Princess*, 20 km. away on Revolcadero beach, is highly fashionable. *Fiesta*, clean and nice, D, with bath, fan, 2 blocks NW from Zócalo; *Lindavista*, Playa Caleta, D; *Vilia*, Av. Roqueta, D; *La Condesa*, Morro 57, D; *Belmar*, Gran Vía Tropical, D; *Marlyn*, Av. de la Suiza, D; *Miami Acapulco*, Vasco Núñez de Balboa, C; *Vacaciones*, Caleta zone, E, good value. Most cheaper hotels are grouped around the Zócalo, especially Calles La Paz and Juárez; about 15 mins. from the 2nd class bus station (Flecha Roja) on Av. Cuauhtémoc. *Sutter*, Juárez 12, E, with bath, in the high season. *Casa García*, E, clean, cold shower, pleasant, 3 blocks SW of Zócalo; *Isabel*, La

MEXICO 949

Paz y Valle, F with fan, reasonable, near Zócalo. Other cheaper hotels recommended include *El Faro*, next to *El Mirador*, very clean, E; *Felmar*, Teacapanocha 5, E; *Mallorca*, D, with swimming pool, and *Acapulco*, E, with shower, both on Calle Benito Juárez, off Zócalo, noisy, no air conditioning; *La Estrella*, two blocks off main beach behind *de Gante* is recommended, E, use of kitchen and fridge available; *California*, 1½ blocks W of Zócalo, D, good value, fan. Many cheap hotels on La Quebrada, basic but clean with fan and bathroom. *Casa de Huéspedes La Tía Conchita*, Quebrada 32, F (cheaper if staying more than 2 nights), friendly, clean, relaxed. *Guadalajara*, La Quebrada, F with bath, recommended; *Casa de Huéspedes Aries*, F, Quebrada 30, recommended; *Amueblados Orozco*, near Quebrada, friendly, clean, E, with shower; *Alta Mar*, near Caleta beach and bus station, F, convenient but dirty; *Posada del Sol*, clean, friendly, on the beach, pool, good food, C, *Playa del Coco* opp. new convention center; *Alameda*, Plaza Alvarez and B. Juárez, D; *Los Siete Mares*, Agua and Pozo del Rey, E; *Los Virreyes*, Playa Langosta, E; *Añorve*, 2 blocks off Zócalo, clean, E, with bath; *Colimense*, E, off Zócalo, pleasant; *Jungla*, Miguel Alemán, towards Caleta beach; *Morales*, behind new Artesanía buildings, cheap; *Hotel Inn*, Ing. Walter Massieu, round corner from Estrella de Oro bus station, 4 mins. from beach, modern but simple, C; *Santa Cecilia*, Francisco Madero 7, off Zócalo, E with bath and fan, noisy, but otherwise fine; *Villa Lucía*, built around pretty swimming pool, with kitchens in rooms, mostly frequented by Mexicans, a/c, one block from sea and one block from *Ritz*. Probably cheapest in town, *La Casa del Río*, 1½ blocks from the 2nd class bus terminal towards Los Hornos beach, cabins with stretchers and sheets, F. *María Cristina's*, E; in bungalows for 4, clean and comfortable, shower and cooling facilities, at Pie de la Cuesta (Km. 11), near fresh water lagoon and sea; also there is *Villa Rosita*, E for bungalow and primitive accommodation next to *Restaurant Tres Marías*, F. Several other nice places at Pie de la Cuesta, E/D, in clean rooms with shower, *Quinta Karla*, *Quinta Blanca*, *Puesta del Sol*, expensive places for hammocks, *Quinta Dora Trailer Park*, E for hammock, managed by American, helpful. The student organization Setej offers dormitory accommodation, F, if one has a valid international student card, at Centro Vacacional, Pie de la Cuesta, hours, 0700-2400. For longer (1 month plus) stays, try *Amueblados Etel*, Av. la Pinzona 92 (near Quebrada) for self-catering apartments, cheap off-season (before November), *Apartamentos Maraback*, Costera M. Alemán, D. The Tourist Bureau is helpful in finding a hotel in any price range. **Motels** *Impala*, *Bali-Hai*, *Costera*, *La Joya*, *Monaco*, *Playa Suave*, *Villas del Sol* and *Gran Motel Acapulco* all along the Costera, C; *Ofelia*, *Victoria*, *Cristóbal Colón*, 1 block behind Costera, D. *Trailer Park El Coloso*, in La Sabana, small swimming pool, and *Trailer Park La Roca* on road from Puerto Márquez to La Sabana, both secure.

Restaurants There are a number of variously-priced restaurants along and opposite Condesa beach; many inexpensive restaurants cluster in the blocks surrounding the Zócalo; another group along the Caleta beach walkway; yet another group of mixed prices on the Costera opp. the *Acapulco Plaza Hotel*. *Antojitos Mayab*, Costera y Avilés, is a favourite for Mexican dishes; *Hong Kong*, near *Ritz Hotel* on Costera, best for Chinese food; *Madeira*, on the hill to *Hotel Las Brisas*, best fixed priced, elegant meal in town, delightful; *Carlos and Charlie's*, opp. Condesa beach, 2nd floor, "fun place for the young at heart"; *Emmas*, next to *Playa Suave Motel*, local favourite for chicken; 250 more to select from.

Night Clubs There are 22 discos including *Baby 'O*, *Magic*, *Tiffany's*, *UBQ*, etc. Every major hotel has at least one disco plus bars; *El Fuerte*, famous Flamenco show; *La Perla*, renowned cliff divers, and at least 3 gay transvestite shows, plus a *Voladores de Papantla* native pole dancers show. Superb varied night-life always.

City Transport Taxis US$8 an hour. Several city bus routes, with one running the full length of Costera Miguel Alemán linking the older part of town to the latest hotels, another operating to Caleta beach. Buses to Pie de la Cuesta, 8 km., US$0.15.

Buses Mexico City, 406 km., 6½ hours; de luxe air-conditioned express buses, US$8; ordinary bus, about US$6, all-day services from Estación Central de Autobuses del Sur by the Taxqueña underground station, with Estrella de Oro or Flecha Roja (part of Líneas Unidas del Sur). 1st class bus depot at Av. Cuauhtémoc 1490. Taxi to Zócalo, US$2; bus, US$0.12. To Oaxaca by continuation of the scenic highway from the beach and naval base at Icacas, 402 km.: 6 hrs. on main road, 264 km., of which 170 km. unpaved, 6 hrs. on rough dirt road through mountains by bus, change at Pinoteca Nacional; caught close to where highway from Mexico City joins the beach. One 1st class bus at 0900, US$4.75 and 2nd class (Flecha Roja) bus a day to Taxco at 1730, US$2.50, 4½ hrs.; alternatively take bus to Iguala (4 hrs., US$3) and then on to Taxco with local bus (1 hr., US$0.35). Bus to Puerto Escondido, 2nd class, Flecha Roja, US$6, seats bookable, advisable to do so the day before, 7½ hrs.

Air Services Airport, Plan de los Amales, 26 km. from Acapulco. Direct connections with New York, Philadelphia and Toronto, by Aeroméxico. Acapulco-Cancún, 3¾ hrs., via Mexico City. Acapulco-Guadalajara, 55 mins.; Acapulco-Mérida, via Mexico City, 3¾ hrs. Acapulco-Oaxaca, 45 mins. Acapulco-Villahermosa, 2 hrs. Acapulco-Mexico City, 45 mins. Transportación Aeropuerto taxi service charge return trip (*viaje redondo*) when you buy a ticket, so keep it and just call for a taxi when required, US$24. Airport bus takes 1 hr., US$0.50 and *does* exist!

Coast NW of Acapulco

Between Acapulco and Zihuatanejo are Coyuca de Benítez, a lagoon with little islands 38 km. from Acapulco, also a market town selling exotic fruit, cheap hats and shoes. Pelicans fly by the lagoons, there are passing dolphins and plentiful sardines, and young boys seek turtle eggs; El Carrizal, a village of some 2,000 people, a little paradise with a beautiful beach (many pelicans) with dangerous waves; *Hotel-Bungalows El Carrizal*, on Route 200 just after Coyuca, left by the hammock vendors at the "Bungalows" sign and continue to the beach—F, owned by Armando and Teresa Chávez, very friendly and helpful, swimming pool, access to lagoon, good restaurant opposite. A couple of km. SE of El Carrizal is El Morro on an unpaved road between the ocean and the lagoon. El Morro is a small fishing village (carp) reminiscent of African townships as it is constructed entirely of *palapa* (palm-leaf and wood). Every other house is a "fish-restaurant". San Jerónimo, 83 km. from Acapulco, has 18th century parish church, you can make canoe trips up river to restaurants; Tecpan de Galeana, 108 km. from Acapulco, is a fishing village; there is a beach further on at Cayaquitos where a series of small rivers join the ocean and there is a large variety of birds and dense vegetation; three restaurants offer fish dishes, there is a reasonable modern hotel, *Club Papánoa*, with lovely views, and a camping site; and one can also visit the lovely bay of Papanda.

Playa Azul, 350 km. NW of Acapulco (bus US$3.50) and 122 km. from Zihuatanejo, is basically a coconut-and-hammock small beach town with a few large hotels, e.g. *Costa de Oro*, E, clean, with fan. *Posada Marilyn*, clean, run by La Mira schoolteacher, F, cold showers (hard to find; ask in main street). *Hospedaje Casa Silva*, F, very basic but adequate, restaurant around the corner. Excellent but expensive restaurant under a modern hotel near the road into Playa Azul. Many small fish restaurants along beach. 40 km. of excellent deserted beaches N of Playa Azul.

N.B.: Beware of the large waves at Playa Azul and of dangerous currents; always check with locals if particular beaches are safe.

Zihuatanejo is a beautiful fishing port and tourist resort 237 km. NW of Acapulco by the paved Route 200, which continues via Barra de Navidad along the Pacific coast to Puerto Vallarta (see page 896); 1st class bus from Acapulco, 4 hrs. (This road goes through coconut plantations where you can buy *tuba*, a drink made from coconut milk fermented on the tree, only slightly alcoholic.) There are 3 beaches: one in the natural harbour and one 20 min. walk from centre (Playa de la Ropa) with the *Sotavento* and some beach restaurants. Another is the Playa de la Madera. Las Gatas beach is secluded, a haven for aquatic sports and can be reached by boat from the centre (US$0.50 return) or a 20-min. walk from La Ropa beach over fishermen-frequented rocks. Watch out for coconuts falling off the trees! The chief attraction, apart from beaches, is clam fishing; there is also a small shark-processing factory. The desert islands off the coast may be visited. Difficult to find accommodation in March.

Hotels *Las Tres Marías*, very pleasant with large communal balconies overlooking town and harbour, E; *Villa del Sol* and *Villas Miramar*, both on Playa la Ropa, B; *Irma* (Playa la Ropa), very warmly recommended, D; *Catalina*, Playa la Ropa, C; *Sotavento*, Playa la Ropa, C. *Bungalows Calpuli*, *Bungalows Palacios*, both on Playa la Ropa, E; *Posada Caracol*, *Bungalows Pacíficos* and *Allec* all on Playa de la Madera, D. Medium hotels: *Casa la Mariana*, pretty, on seafront; *Bahía*, by town pier; *Avila*, behind *Belmar*; *Corona*, in coconut plantation on the road to other beaches; *Casa Lulu*, at end of main beach. *Casa Minam*, clean, E. *Casa Elvira* hotel-restaurant, F, in older part of town, very basic but clean, noisy from 0730, share bath, the restaurant is on the beach front (*the* place to watch the world go by), good and reasonable. Several hotels along the beach, D: try *Del Mar*; *Playa de la Madera*; *Safari* (by bus station, expensive); *Casa La Playa*, similar to *Elvira*, E, but not as good; *Belmar*, all rooms face sea; *Sinar-Bahagra*, very good value; *Imelda*, clean, recommended, E.

Camping on Playa la Ropa, US$0.60 p.p. and US$0.60 per car.

Restaurants On Playa la Ropa, cheap: *Elvi*, *La Perla*. In Zihuatanejo, *La Bocana*, favourite for seafood; *Cantamar*, downtown, "cute"; *La Mesa del Capitán*, owned by an Englishman, good; *Don Juan*, downtown, English decor, fancy; *Coconuts*, downtown, "Hollywood tropical", nice but somewhat expensive garden restaurant; *Elvira*, *La Perla*, *Gitano's*, thatched roof beach spots, reasonable; *Kon Tiki*, road to La Playa, pizzas and oriental; *Kapi Kofi*, downtown, a/c, breakfast.

Night Clubs *Adán y Eva*, *Ibiza Disco*, *Chololo*, *Captain's Cabin*, *Joy Disco*, *Kan Kan*.

Skin Diving US$15 an hour and hire of all equipment and guide from Oliverio, on Playa de las Gatas, off which is an underwater wall built by the Tarascan king Calzonzin, to keep the sharks

MEXICO 951

away while he bathed; the wall is fairly massive and can be seen clearly while skin diving. Many fish too. US$2.50 a day for mask, snorkel and flippers.

British Vice-Consul at Zihuatanejo: D. B. Gore, *Hotel Las Brisas*, Aptdo. Postal 281. Tel.: (91-748) 4-15-80 and 4-16-50.

Buses Four direct buses a day from Mexico, Estrella de Oro, US$10, at Central Camionera del Sur (by Taxqueña underground station), a good 12 hrs. 5 times a day from Mexico City via Morelia, by Autobuses de Occidente. Bus to Acapulco, US$6.50 1st, US$3.75 2nd class, 4 hrs, at least 20 times a day with Flecha Roja. To Tijuana with Estrella de Oro at 1530, 50 hrs.; to Manzanillo, at 2000 with Estrella de Oro, 16 hrs. To Guadalajara, US$8 overnight 2nd class, 12 hrs., frequent stops and people standing in the aisles, or with Autobuses de Occidente, US$11 at 1320 and 1720. To Morelia (see page 906) at least 15 a day, US$5.50 with Norte de Sonora. To Puerto Escondido, US$4.

Airport Daily service to and from Mexico City. Frontier Airlines flies from locations in Western USA.

From Zihuatanejo one can drive 5 km. or take a bus (US$0.20) or taxi (US$ 2.50, colectivo, US$0.45) to ***Ixtapa***, "where there are salt lakes". The resort, being developed on a large scale, boasts 14 beaches: La Hermosa, del Palmar, Don Juan de Dios, Don Juan, Don Rodrigo, Cuata, Quieta, Oliveiro, Linda, Larga, Carey, Pequeña, Cuachalate and Varadero. There are turtles, many species of shellfish and fish, and pelicans at El Morro de los Pericos, which can be seen by launch. There is a famous island a few metres off Quietas beach; boats go over at a cost of US$1.50. Ixtapa is a new resort and has ten large luxury hotels and a Club Méditerranée (all obtain food-supplies from Mexico City making food more expensive, as local supplies aren't guaranteed); a shopping complex, golf course, water-ski/parachute skiing and tennis courts. There are a yacht marina and an 18-hole golf club, Palma Real. Isla Grande is being developed as a nature park and leisure resort. **N.B.** The beach can be dangerous (strong undertow).

Hotels *Camino Real*, spectacular, A, in a small jungle; *Kristal*, *Dorado Pacífico*, *Sheraton*, with panoramic lift, *El Presidente*; *Aquamarina*; *Aristos*, A; *Holiday Inn*, B; *Riviera del Sol*.

Restaurants Besides those in every hotel, there are *Montmartre*, *Villa Sakura*, *Villa de la Selva*, *Baffone*, *Carlos y Charlie's*, *Hacienda de Ixtapa*, all more costly than in Zihuatanejo.

Nightclubs Every hotel without exception has at least one night club/disco andd two bars.

Transport Many flights from Mexico City and others from Mazatlán, Guadalajara, Los Angeles, Houston, Albuquerque, etc. By road from Mexico City via the Toluca-Zihuatanejo highway (430 km.) or via the Acapulco-Zihuatanejo highway (405 km.). Also via Uruapan and Playa Azul from Michoacán.

Coast E of Acapulco

Highway 200, E from Acapulco along the coast, is paved all the way to Puerto Escondido; the stretch is known as the Costa Chica. "From ***Pinotepa*** Nacional (*Hotel Carmona*, restaurant, good value but poor laundry service, F), you can visit the Mixtec Indian village of Pinotepa de Don Luis by *camioneta*. These leave from the side street next to the church in Pinotepa Nacional, taking a dirt road to Don Luis. The women there weave beautiful and increasingly rare sarong-like skirts (*chay-ay*), some of which are dyed from the purple of sea snails. Also, half-gourds incised with various designs and used both as caps and cups can be found. The *ferias* of Don Luis (January 20) and nearby San Juan Colorado (November 29-30) are worth attending for the dancing and availability of handicrafts." (Dale Bricker, Seattle)

Puerto Escondido is on a beautiful bay south of Oaxaca: very popular and getting very touristy, good surfing; camping with showers US$1 a day, also trailer facilities. Palm trees line the beach, which is well provided with good-quality reasonably-priced restaurants. There are plans afoot to develop the SE end of town, in the words of one developer "to make it the next Acapulco". A new resort is also to be built in Huatusco Bay on the Pacific, with 1,300 hotel rooms in 1988 rising eventually to 21,000, and a planned population of 200,000.

952 MEXICO

N.B. There can be dangerous waves, and the cross-currents are always dangerous; non-swimmers should not bathe except in the bay on which the town stands. Also, a breeze off the sea makes the sun seem less strong than it is—be careful. Do not stray too far along the beach; armed robbery by groups of 3-5 is becoming more and more frequent, take as little cash and valuables as possible, US$ sought after. Also at La Barra beach 10 km. away.

Hotels Very crowded during Holy Week. Many cheaper hotels have no hot water. *Viva*, most expensive; *Bugambilias*, very pleasant, A, lovely gardens, pool, path to beach, attentive, a/c, good service, food included (*à la carte*, also lobster); *El Rincón del Pacífico*, E, very popular, always full, on beach, with restaurant, hot water, much stealing, not always friendly. Next door to this is a camping site; *Las Palmas*, very clean, on the beach, poor restaurant, D, with bath; *Paraíso Escondido*, noisy a/c, not on beach but with own swimming pool, management cool, but recommended, C, colonial style; *Ranchero El Pescador*, a/c, D, free minibus service, good restaurant, pool; *Los Crotos*, F, damp-smelling rooms, on the beach, cockroaches, overpriced restaurant; *Nayar*, E, with bath and fan, restaurant, recommended; *La Posada Económica*, one big dormitory, F, attached to restaurant, but also runs hotel across the road, ask for a room opp. the flat; good huachinango; *Alojamiento Las Cabañas* has dormitories with bunks, F, on main road (S side), friendly, very nice, food is good, you will be charged for all beds regardless of whether they are occupied, unless you share the cabin. *Cabañas Neptuno*, US$2 per cabin, on the beach, clean; camping, US$0.75 p.p.; *Cabañas Coco Beach*, in the town near the church, US$3 per cabin (6 or 7 available), family-run. *Bungalows Villa Marinero*, on beach, clean, own cooking possible, friendly, D, restaurant a little dear but good. *Norma*, F, dark room, no fan, shower, in town above bus station. Most hotels are on the beach, little air-conditioning.

Camping If camping, beware of clothes being stolen, especially after washing; 3 sites available. *Carrizalillo Trailer Park*, near old airport on W side of town, on cliff top with path leading down to secluded beach, swimming pool and bar, very pleasant. All facilities, US$4.45 for 2 plus car, US$1.35 p.p. Campsite for vehicles, tents and hammocks on water front in centre of town, vehicles and tents accepted, swimming pool, US$1.10 p.p.

Restaurants *Lolys*, try *pescado a la parrilla*, with sweet onion sauce; *Da Ugo*, good pizzas, popular; *El Papagallo*, best value in town, excellent fresh food, prepared by taciturn Austrian cook, every dish a meal. Not always open. *San Martín* on main street, good fish; *Lisa's Restaurant*, nice location on beach but expensive and very poor service. *Restaurant San Angel*, on main street, good fish dishes, and nearby *El Tubo*, cheaper. Good *licuados* at *Bambú Loco*, also fish. *La Estancia* is good but expensive. *Las Palapas*, good, heading up it is just over the stream (sewer) on the right.

Bookshop *Paperback Shack*, owner speaks English, second-hand books, English and Spanish. Long distance calls can be made from here.

Banks Bancomer. Open 0900-1330.

Transport Bus to Oaxaca, 5 or 6 a day, US$3, advertised as 7 hr. trip, but can take up to 17 hrs, very bad road and many accidents; also Estrella del Valle (1st class, from 2nd class terminal) and Auto Transportes Oaxaca-Pacífico, better, journey through spectacular cloud forest, goes via Puerto Angel, stops in Pochutla, 10-18 hrs. (depending on roadworks)—leaves at 0700, 2nd class, 2300 1st class; all have bookable seats. Puerto Escondido-Oaxaca, 2nd class at 2200, 1st at 2230. Puerto Escondido-Pochutla, US$1.50, and on to Salina Cruz, US$5. The road to Salina Cruz is now paved. It is now best to go from Oaxaca to Puerto Escondido by the road to Puerto Angel, turning off at Pochutla (see below). The direct highway to Oaxaca is being upgraded. Bus to Acapulco, 2nd class, Flecha Roja (near La Solteca terminal), 7½ hrs., US$6, not exciting. The 1030 bus stops for 2 hours' lunch at Pinotepa, 1st class from Acapulco US$11, book tickets at least one day in advance. First bus to Acapulco at 0400, hourly on to 2100 thereafter. To Zihuatanejo, US$4. Transport to Puerto Angel from Puerto Escondido consists of VW bus or pick-up truck caught on main road, every hour, 1 hr.

Flights Airline offices will arrange VW bus to pick you up for your departure when you reconfirm or book your outward flight, US$0.75 p.p. Airport 10 minutes drive from town, orange juice and coffee sold; improvement programme under way. Puerto Escondido-Mexico City, with Aerolíneas Unidas, Wed., Fri. and Sun. at 1710 and 1825 (Mexico City-Puerto Escondido on same days at 1400 and 1515); also Puerto Escondido-Oaxaca, US$40 return. CV-580 plane, seats 20. Aerolíneas Unidas is at Reforma 157-B, México 5, Tel.: 592-57-77.

Also S of Oaxaca (240 km, paved road, but many curves) is **Puerto Angel,** a coffee port on the Pacific with a good safe beach, 69 km. from Puerto Escondido, with road connection. It is 8 hrs. by bus from Oaxaca, nine a day, US$3.40, nearest exchange at Pochutla (taxis). Luxury hotel on a hill away from the beach, *Angel del Mar*, D, friendly, helpful, bookings not always honoured; for *cabañas* and hammock places ask at *Susanna's Restaurant*, near the football pitch; *Hotel Soraya*, E, fan, bath, very clean; *Casa de Huéspedes Gladys*, just above *Soraya*, F, owner can prepare food; *Casa de Huéspedes* (Gundi and Tomás López), clean, rooms or hammocks, good value, snacks and breakfast, F; similar is the *casa de huéspedes* run by Harald and Maria Faerber, with restaurant. *Pensión Puesta del Sol*, F on road to Playa Panteón, clean, friendly, recommended. *Noah's Arc*, at the end of the beach, for the "flower-powered"; hammocks at *Gustavos*, F; *Posada Cañón de Vata*, on Playa Panteón, E, also hammocks, F, lovely setting, booked continuously; good restaurant *Capís* has 5 rooms above). Three km. N is Zipolite beach (name means "the killing beach" - reached by taxi), dangerous for bathing, hammocks for rent, food available. "About 25 km. from Zipolite (also known as Puerto Angelito) on a dirt road is a sign to Ventimilla beach; follow the rough track until you find a thatched ranch and ask for Hilario Reyes, who is building huts for tourists. The beach is long and empty and there are 2 lagoons with fresh water, a lost paradise", writes Janet Westgarth.

You can go to Salina Cruz from Puerto Angel via Pochutla: take taxi to **Pochutla** (US$ 0.85, beware overcharging) and catch 0930 or 1430 bus to Salina Cruz (US$3, 3½ hrs.), to which a new road is finished. Pochutla-Oaxaca (a safer route than Puerto Escondido-Oaxaca) bus US$4, 8 hrs. The service between Pochutla and Puerto Escondido is in VW buses and pick-up trucks (US$0.75) which link with the bus to Puerto Angel. At Pochutla there is a prison; you can buy black coral necklaces made by prisoners very cheaply.

Pan-American Highway: Mexico City to Guatemala

The National Railway runs daily from Mexico City to Tapachula. Taxi to Talismán, on the Guatemalan border, for bus to Guatemala City (also accessible from Puebla). There is a new bridge which links Ciudad Hidalgo with Tecún-Umán (formerly Ayutla) in Guatemala. Cristóbal Colón bus Mexico City-Guatemala City, 23 hrs., US$24, leave at 1045; at border change to Rutas Lima. Bus Mexico City-Tapachula, 20 hrs., US$15. Bus, Tecún-Umán-Guatemala City US$3.

Note Motorists who know the area well advise that anyone driving from Mexico City to Tehuantepec should go via Orizaba-La Tinaja-Papaloapan-Tuxtepec-Palomares. This route is better than Veracruz-Acayucán and far preferable to the route which follows, via Matamoros and Oaxaca, if drivers are in a hurry. The reason is that between Oaxaca and Tehuantepec the road, although paved throughout and in good condition, serpentines unendingly over the Sierras and it is villainously hot, windy and dry in winter. But as the Oaxaca route is far more interesting and spectacular we describe it below. For the alternative journey through the Papaloapan region, see page 938.

This road through southern Mexico is 1,355 km. long. It can be done in 3 or 4 days' driving time. There are bus services from Mexico City along the route through Oaxaca to Tehuantepec and on to the Guatemalan frontier through San Cristóbal de Las Casas to Ciudad Cuauhtémoc or through Arriaga to Tapachula. A road now runs (still rough in places) from Paso Hondo near Ciudad Cuauhtémoc via Comalapa and Porvenir to Huixtla on the S road, and from Porvenir to Revolución Mexicana.

From Cuernavaca to Oaxaca: take Route 160 via Yantepec to the semi-tropical town of **Cuautla** (80,000 people), with a popular sulphur spring (known as *aguas hediondas* or stinking waters) and bath, a week-end resort for the capital. Tourist Cuautla is divided from locals' Cuautla by a wide river, and the locals have the best bargain: it is worth crossing the stream. From Cuautla go to Atotonilco by bus for a swim. Buses from Mexico City to Cuautla from Terminal del Oriente. Buses from Cuautla at Cristóbal Colón terminal, 5 de Mayo and Zavala, to Mexico City hourly; 2nd class buses to Cuernavaca hourly, 1 hr, US$0.65; to Oaxaca, US$5.80. There is a market in the narrow streets and alleyways around 5 de Mayo. Hotel Colón in Cuautla is on the main square, E, good; *Hotel Vasco*; *Hotel del Sur*, F, recommended; *Hotel Madrid*, F. *Jardín de Cuautla* in Dos de Mayo, nr. bus station, modern, clean, but bad traffic noise, pool, E; *Hotel España* in same street. The tourist office is opp. *Hotel Cuautla*, on Av. Obregón, satisfactory. CREA Youth Hostel. Try the delicious *lacroyas* and *gorditas*, tortillas filled with beans and cheese. At least 2 good restaurants in main square. A road leads to Amecameca (page 929).

Then take Route 140 with long descent and then ascent to **Izúcar de Matamoros**, famous for its clay handicrafts, 16th-century Dominican convent of Santo Domingo, and two nearby spas, Los Amatitlanes (about 6 km. away) and Ojo de Carbón. A side road leads from Izúcar to Axochiapan (Morelos state), leading to a dirt road to the village of Jolalpan with the baroque church of Santa María (1553). Route 190 heads N from Izúcar to Puebla via Huaquechula (16th-century renaissance-cum-plateresque chapel) and **Atlixco** ("the place lying on the water"), with interesting baroque examples in the Chapel of the Third Order of St. Augustine and San Juan de Dios. There is an annual festival, the Atlixcayotl, on San Miguel hill (*Hotel Colonial* behind parish church, F, shared bath; nearby—20 mins.—are the curative springs of Axocopán). Thence to Acatepec (page 931) and, 30 km., Puebla. Route 190 S switchbacks to Tehuitzingo (*Hotel Mónica*, F, very basic). Then fairly flat landscape to **Acatlán** (hotel) where black and red clay figures, and palm and flower hats are made. Carry on to Petlalcingo (restaurant), then descend to Huajuapan (page 958) and Tamazulapan (hotel, restaurant). Road climbs slowly at first, then more steeply and eventually flattens to Nocluxtlán (*Hotel Sarita*, E).

The major route from Mexico City first runs generally eastwards to Puebla, where it turns S to wind through wooded mountains at altitudes of between

954 MEXICO

1,500 and 1,800 metres, emerging at last into the warm, red-soiled Oaxaca valley.

Oaxaca (population 230,000, altitude 1,546 metres) is 413 km. from Puebla, 531 km. from Mexico City. It is a very Indian town, of airy patios with pink arcades, famous for its colourful market, its *sarapes,* crafts, dances and feast days. On Sat. Indians of the Zapotec and Mixtec groups come to market near the 2nd class bus station on the outskirts of town, which starts before 0800; prices are rising because of tourists' interest. Specialities: black earthenware, tooled leather, blankets, ponchos, shawls, embroidered blouses, the drink *mescal.* Beware pickpockets. The Zócalo with its arcades is the heart of the town; its bandstand has a nice little market underneath. Since the streets surrounding the sides of the Zócalo have been closed to traffic it has become very pleasant to sit there at all times of day. In the daytime vendors sell food, in the evening their tourist wares and gardenias in the square.

On the Zócalo is the 17th century cathedral with a fine baroque façade, but the best site, about 4 blocks from the square, is the church of Santo Domingo with its adjoining monastery, now the Regional Museum (see below). The church's gold leaf has to be seen to be believed. There is an extraordinary vaulted decoration under the raised choir, right on the reverse of the façade wall: a number of crowned heads—kings and queens—appear on the branches of a tree. It is a genealogical tree of the family of Santo Domingo de Guzmán (died 1221), whose lineage was indirectly related to the royal houses of Castile and Portugal. By making a donation (say US$1) to the church you can get the lady at the bookstall on the right of the church to light up the various features after 1800. The Capilla del Rosario in the church is being restored, and no flash pictures are allowed.

The massive 17th century church of La Soledad has fine colonial ironwork and sculpture (including an exquisite Virgen de la Soledad); there are elaborate altars at the green-stone church of San Felipe Neri, and Indian versions in paint of the conquest at San Juan de Dios; a museum of religious art behind the church is open in the morning. The church of San Agustín has a fine façade, with bas-relief of St. Augustine holding the City of God above adoring monks.

The Regional Museum (entry US$0.50, US$0.25 on Sun., open 1000-1800, 1000-1700 Sat.-Sun., closed Mon.) has displays of regional costumes, and pottery, glass, alabaster, jewellery and other treasures from Monte Albán, whose jewellery is copied with surprising skill in several home factories near Oaxaca. Museo Rufino Tamayo, Av. Morelos 503, has a beautiful display of precolumbian artefacts dating from 1250 BC to AD 1100 (1000-1400, 1600-1900, closed Tues.); entry for US$0.25. Teatro Macedonio Alcalá, 5 de Mayo with Independencia, beautifully restored theatre from Porfirio Díaz' time. Visit also the Street of the Little Arches, a picturesque, narrow, cobbled street with archways along the sides. There is a grand view from the monument to Juárez on Cerro de Fortín hill. D. H. Lawrence wrote parts of "Mornings in Mexico" here, and revised "The Plumed Serpent"; the house he rented is in Pino Suárez, a block S of the Llano (the main park), NE corner. The Zapotec language is used by over 300,000 people in the State as a first or second language (about 20% of Oaxaca State population speaks only an Indian language).

Warning Travellers have reported that men asserting they are local Indians sometimes get into conversation, especially near the Zócalo, invite you to a drink, order several things and then claim they have no money and leave the tourist to pay the bill!

The best *mescal* in the region is El Minero, made in Mitla. *Mescal* sours are good at the bar of Misión Los Angeles. The poor man's drink is *pulque.* Local *sarapes* are more varied and cheaper than in Mexico City. Buy at the market (which will come down a third) or at Casa Cervantes. The Zapotec Indians, who weave fantastic toys of grass, have a dance, the *Jarabe Tlacolula Zandunga* danced by barefooted girls splendid in most becoming coifs, short, brightly coloured skirts and ribbons and long lace petticoats, while the men, all in white with gay handkerchiefs, dance opposite them with their hands behind their backs. Only women—from Tehuantepec or Juchitán—dance the slow and stately *Zandunga,* costumes gorgeously embroidered on velvet blouse, full skirts with white pleated and starched lace ruffles and *huipil.*

MEXICO 955

Fiestas Carnival in February. Los Lunes del Cerro, on the first two Mondays after July 16 (the first is the more spontaneous, when Indian groups come to a hill outside the city to present the seven regional dances of the State in a great festival, also known as La Guelaguetza). Hotels book up early. Upper seats free, getting expensive near the front, be there 1½ hrs. in advance to get a good seat, tickets from Tourist Office, Calle García Vigil 105, 3 blocks from the Cathedral (has free maps, brochures and information, open Mon.- Sat. 1000- 1300). Nov. 2, the Day of the Dead, is a mixture of festivity and solemn commemoration; the decoration of family altars (competition in the Zócalo) is carried to competitive extremes; traditional wares and foods, representing skulls, skeletons, coffins etc. are sold in the market. Ask before photographing. Dec. 8, 12, 18 (Soledad), and 23 (Rábanos) with huge radishes carved in grotesque shapes sold for fake money; *buñuelos* are sold and eaten in the streets on this night, and the dishes ceremonially smashed after serving. Night of Dec. 24, a parade of floats (best seen from balcony of *Merendero El Tule* on the Plaza; go for supper and select a window table). Posadas in San Felipe (5 km. N) and at Xoxo, to the S, the week before Christmas. Bands play in the Zócalo every evening except Sat., and there are regional folk dances twice a week.

Hotels *El Presidente/Parador Santa Catalina*, Plazuela Bastida, magnificently restored convent circa 1690, true colonial with all services, street rooms noisy, avoid expurgated menu offered to gringos in restaurant, B; *Calesa Real*, García Vigil 306, modern colonial, good *Los Arcos* restaurant recommended, parking, central, good value, D; *Marqués del Valle*, C, on Zócalo, noisy, deteriorating; *Margarita Courts*, at N entrance to city, good and reasonable, C; *Misión Oaxaca*, San Felipe del Agua, some way out, attractive, C; *Misión de Los Angeles* (formerly Oaxaca Courts), Porfirio Díaz 102, C, motel-style, 2 km. from centre, quiet and most attractive, with swimming pool, good food, but cockroaches in rooms; *Victoria*, C, colonial house turned into hotel, bedrooms with showers built round the garden, many tour groups, but out of town (around 15-min. walk) at Km. 545 on Pan-American highway; *Santo Tomás*, Abasolo 105, clean, private shower, friendly, kitchen for use of guests, some comfort, washing facilities, E, quiet, recommended; *Francia*, 20 de Noviembre 212, around enclosed courtyard, good food, popular, E; *Plaza*, Trujano 112 (D. H. Lawrence once stayed there); near centre, reasonable, friendly; *California*, Chapultepec 822, near 1st class bus station, E, with bath, friendly, pleasant, restaurant; *Veracruz*, next to ADO bus station, spotless, E. *San Fernando*, Díaz Ordaz 307, F, a bit shabby; *Lupita*, also on Díaz Ordaz, F with bath; *Virginia*, Periférico 205, E, reasonable. *Del Bosque*, exit road to Mitla, modern, restaurant, D; 2 blocks from the Zócalo at 5 de Mayo 208 is *Principal*, F, colonial house, very clean, friendly, private shower with hot and cold water, English spoken, heavily booked. *Vallarta*, Díaz Ordaz 309, E, clean, good value, enclosed parking. *Mansión Imperial*, facing Juárez park, E, good value. *María Luisa*, J. García Tinoco 507, F, with bath, good, hot water a.m. only; *Rex*, Las Casas 308, F, with shower, clean, friendly, secure, close to market, narrow entrance; *Ninivé*, overlooking bus terminal, clean, shower, F; *Donají*, Calle Hidalgo, F, basic; *Plaza*, Portal de Flores 6, unpleasant, will store luggage, suites or rooms, D, with bath, swimming pool, on main square, some rooms rather noisy, regular folk dance performances are given here, photography permitted, poor restaurant; *Isabel*, Av. Murguia 104, near 5 de Mayo, D, with bath, rather dirty; *Monte Albán*, E, friendly, opp. Cathedral; *Virreyes*, Av. Morelos 1001, E, overpriced, noisy, hot; *Ruiz*, just off Zócalo, E, nice and clean, quiet, hot water only very early morning, don't leave valuables lying around, otherwise recommended; *Asunción*, Aldama and 20 de Noviembre, F, with bath, clean, nr. market; *Central*, 20 de Noviembre 104, F, private bathroom, best bet for hot water a.m., good value but very noisy, also reports of peeping toms; *Modelo*, Portal de los Mercaderes; *Antequera*, near Zócalo, not so good value, E, with bath; *Reforma*, F, Morelos 1004, annex cheaper; *Fortín*, Díaz Ordaz 312, nr. south side of main market, clean, very basic, noisy at ground floor level, F, with bath, hot water a.m. only; *San José*, Trujano 412, 5 mins. from Zócalo, F; *La Reyna*, Trujano 414, F; *Yalalag*, Mina 105, F, hot water, restaurant, noisy from market, not too clean; *El Típico*, 20 de Noviembre, F; *Pasaje*, Mina 302, near market, F, no private bathrooms, clean, very friendly; *Yagul*, F, on Mina near market and Zócalo, use of kitchen on request, very clean; *Casa de Huéspedes Mixteca*, on Mina, F; *Chayo*, 20 de Noviembre, F, cheap, basic; *Rivera* in same block, same price tange; *El Valle*, Aldama, F, quite good; *Casa de Huéspedes Arnel*, three blocks to the right of ADO station, Aldama 404, Col. Valatlaco, F, very clean. There is also accommodation in private houses which rent rooms (*casas de huéspedes*); *Posada Las Palmas*, Av. Juárez 516, F, without bath, restaurant, recommended; *Residencial*, students, F; *Pacífico*, Trujano 420, clean, F; *Del Arbol*, Calzada Madero 131, modern, comfortable, bath, E; *Aldama*, Aldama, F, clean; *Casa de Huéspedes Farolito*, Calle de Las Casas 508, F, more expensive with bath. *Posada Margarita*, Calle Abasolo, 3 blocks from Zócalo, F, with bath, not clean, friendly. *Villa Alta*, Cabrera 303, 4 blocks from Zócalo, friendly service, F, clean. On the road to Tehuantepec (Km. 9.8), *Hotel Posada Los Arcos*, Spanish-style motel at San Sebastián Totla.

N.B. Hotels near the corner of 20 de Noviembre and Mina are in the red light district.

Camping Oaxaca Trailer Park on the N fringe of town (corner of Calles Pinos and Violetas), US$4.80 for 1-2 persons, secure, clothes washing facilities; bus "Carmen-Infonavit" from downtown.

Restaurants *El Asador Vasco*, 2nd floor overlooking Zócalo, best food in the state, not cheap but worth it; *Flor de Oaxaca*, Armenta y López 311, delicious hot chocolate; *Casa de Doña Elpidia*, M.

956 MEXICO

Cabrera 413, lunch only (there is no sign, don't be put off by exterior, US$3 for 6-course meal; it is reputed to be so good that advertising is not necessary, menu changes are infrequent, good cheap wine); *Guelatao*, on main square, good for breakfast and snacks, cheap beer; *Portal*, next door, similar to *Guelatao* but better, local dishes US$1-1.50; *Montebello*, good, at Trujano 307; *Colón*, Colón 111; *La Catedral*, corner of Gral. García Vigil and Morelos, 1 block from Cathedral, local specialities— steaks, good *tamales*, classical music. *Alameda*, Calle Trujano, 2 blocks from Zócalo, excellent regional food, crowded Sun. Vegetarian restaurant reported disappointing; *Piscis*, Hidalgo 119, 6 blocks from Zócalo on the right. Pizzeria *Alfredo da Roma*, good and friendly, Bustamente near Plaza Santo Domingo; *Gino's Pizza*, pleasant café, inexpensive in Independencia, 500 block; RCHS Pizza next door; *El Sol y la Luna*, on Murguia, good although not cheap, live music some nights, now open evenings only; *Típico de Antequera*, has excellent national and regional food; *Café Fontana*, excellent, opp. *Hotel Presidente*; *Café ADO*, ADO Terminal; unmarked small restaurant in Calle Abasolo, between 212 and 218, cheap light meals, clean; *Colonial*, 20 de Noviembre, cheap *comidas corridas*, recommended. However, the best Oaxacan food is found in the *comedores familiares* such as *Clemente*, *Los Almendros*, *La Juchita*, but they are way out of town and could be difficult to get to. Some restaurants lining the Zócalo are reported to be overpriced, also very slow service, up to 1½ hrs to get complete order; *Café Tito*, near Zócalo on García Vigil, good value for breakfast; *Cafetería Quickly*, clean, friendly, cheap; *El Hipocampo*, Hidalgo 505, cheap, good; *Levenda*, M. F. Fiallo 116 y Hidalgo, good, clean, reasonable prices; *El Tecolote*, a few blocks from Zócalo, open air eating, good *quesadillas* and *tacos*; *Casa de Chocolate*, quiet, pleasant, near to Tourist Office on Av. Independencia, coffee and home-made cakes; *Café Fontana*, good food but dear; *Cafetería Alex*, Díaz Ordaz y Trujano, good *comida corrida*, coffee and breakfasts; *Restaurant El Tube*, on Zócalo, nothing special; *El Merón*, Hidalgo 803, cheap. *El Patio*, 1 block from Zócalo, has mainly good fish and seafood dishes, moderate prices and good service. Cheap and clean café *Las Palmas* (near *Hotel Pasaje*) on 20 de Noviembre. Good *dulcería* (sweet shop) in the 2nd class bus station.

Entertainment *La Luna y el Sol*, good bar with music.

Shopping There are endless temptations such as green and black pottery, baskets and bags made from cane and rushes, embroidered shirts, skirts, and blankets of all colours and designs; Saturdays are the best for buying woollen *sarapes* cheaply. A group of Zapotecs can be seen weaving on Zaragoza between 20 de Noviembre and Tinoco y Palacios on Sunday, selling wall hangings and *sarapes*. Also daily on Zaragoza and García, between 0800-2000, but more expensive than elsewhere. Unfortunately some of the woven products are of a different quality from the traditional product—more garish dyes and synthetic yarns are replacing some of the originals; but you can still find these if you shop around. *Aripo*, on García Vigil, cheaper and better than most, service good. *Artesanías Cocijo*, interesting collection of handicrafts, a little expensive, English spoken and will ship goods, García Vigil 212. *Pepe*, Avenida Hidalgo, for jewellery; cheap local crafts. Good for silver, *Plata Mexicana*, 20 de Noviembre 209-C. *Yalalag*, Alcalá 104, has good selection of jewellery, rugs and pottery, somewhat overpriced; *Victor*, Porfirio Díaz 111; cheapest and largest selection of pottery plus a variety of fabrics and sandals at *Productos Típicos de Oaxaca*, Av. Dr. B. Dominguez 602; city bus near ADO depot goes there. *Casa Aragón*, J. P. García 503, famous for knives and *machetes*. Fine cream and purple-black pottery (Zapotec and Mixtec designs) available at *Alfarería Jiménez*, Zaragoza 402; further along Zaragoza is a small straw market with all kinds of baskets and bags. Other potteries at Las Casas 614, makers of the Oaxacan daisy design, and Trujano 508, bold flower designs. Many excellent fixed-price bargains to be had at *El Gran Bazaar*, Av. Independencia. Large selection of cotton and wool. Bargain for up 50% reduction. The old market sells fruit, vegetables, meat and some handicrafts (good, cheap meals here); Mercado de Abastos, open daily, which sells mostly food and flowers next to the 2nd class bus station, where the old Saturday market has also moved and caters mainly to the tourist trade. Those disappointed with it should go to the Sunday market at Tlacolula.

Dr. Robin Hoult adds: "Some of the local clothing factories are worth visiting (e.g. for cloths, tablecloths and blankets), and the work is attractive, of good quality and reasonably priced. Also well worth driving out of town (or bussing) to buy unique black pottery, e.g. at San Bártolo de Coyotepec; it's quite special."

Library English lending library with very good English books, a few French and Spanish, also English newspapers (*The News* from Mexico City) at Calle Pino Suárez 802 (open Mon.-Fri., 1000-1300, 1600-1800). *The News* is also sold round the Zócalo by newsboys, from mid-morning.

Banks It's difficult to change travellers' cheques at weekends but if you get stuck try some of the more expensive restaurants in the Zócalo. Bancomer, 1 block from Zócalo, exchanges travellers' cheques, 0900-1330, on García Vigil. *Hotel Señorial* will change travellers' cheques.

Laundromat E.L.A., Super Lavandería Automática, Antonio Roldán 114, Col. Olímpica, washes and irons. Another one at Francisco Zarco, off the Periférico, and another in Av. Juárez 900, open until 1900, corner with Niños Héroes de Chapultepec. Good laundry on Calle 20 de Noviembre, 2½ blocks S of the market. All about US$1.50 for 7 lbs.

Local Buses There is a bus marked "Circular' or "Circular Panteón" which connects the C.

Colón and ADO first class bus stations on the N of town with the Zócalo, the market, C. Colón second class terminal, the modern 2nd class bus station (on the other side of town) and the railway station.

Railway Station on Calzada Madero at junction with Periférico, 15 min. walk from Zócalo. From Mexico City, 563 km., 17 hrs., take food, magnificent scenery, US$4 1st class, US$3 2nd, at 1720 daily. To Mexico City daily at 1820, only one sleeper. Tickets must be bought the same day. Seats scarce in 2nd class, quite a scramble! To Puebla 0710, 11 hrs., US$3. Derailments at times.

Buses 1st class terminal is NW of Zócalo (no luggage office); 2nd class is W of Zócalo, has left-luggage office. Beware of double-booking and short-changing, especially when obtaining tickets from drivers if you have not booked in advance. ADO to Mexico City, 10 hrs., about 15 a day, mostly evenings, US$8, 2nd class by Fletes y Pasajes, 9 hrs., comfortable; 1st class to Cuautla, US$6 (change there for Cuernavaca); Puebla (2nd class, 11 hrs., US$4, at 0800, 1200 and 1900 with Fletes y Pasajes); to Tuxtepec (2nd class, 6 hrs., US$ 1.20, road regarded as dangerous because of drug plantations) and other towns; Cristóbal Colón to Villahermosa, US$10, book well ahead, 13½ hrs., daily at 1200 and 1700 (arrives in time to connect with 0645 bus to Palenque, and good for connecting with ADO buses to Mérida—for alternative, awkward route, see below). 1st class; San Cristóbal de Las Casas (US$7.50, at 0700, 13-16 hrs.) book 1-2 days in advance with C. Colón (not very good, better to go with ADO on Mon.); and Tapachula, 11 hrs., US$8.40. Also Fletes y Pasajes and Transportes Tuxtla (2nd class). Book well in advance as buses often come almost full from Mexico City. 2nd class bus to Tuxtla Gutiérrez, 11 hrs., US$8 at 1030, 1730 and 2100, ¾ hr. wait in Juchitán (see page 960). To Tehuantepec, scenic, almost every hour, 2nd class US$2.20, 5 hrs. To Ciudad Cuauhtémoc, US$9, 12 hrs. To Arriaga US$8, 5 a day. To Tapachula, US$7. To Puerto Escondido, US$3, gruelling 13 hrs. journey (can be longer) at 1300, partly along dirt roads, interesting scenery. Night bus 5 hrs. faster. La Solteca is reputed to have had some very bad accidents in recent years. Oaxaca-Pacífico has good 2nd class buses (several to Pochutla, nine a day to Puerto Angel). Estrella del Valle run 1st class buses from 2nd class terminal, 8-10 hrs., at 0500. Buses to most local villages go from this terminal.

To Mérida from Oaxaca: bus to Juchitán (2nd class), 6 hrs., bus to Ixtepec, ¾ hrs., then train to Coatzacoalcos, 9 hrs., food sold on train by sellers. In Coatzacoalcos you have to go to another station, about 5 km. by bus, named Puerto Libre, then 19 hrs. to Mérida! Toilets filthy, dirty train.

Air Services The airport is about 8 km. S, direction Ocotepec. The airport taxis (*colectivos*) cost US$1.50 p.p. Book at Transportaciones Aeropuerto Oaxaca on the Alameda (Tel.: 67878) for collection at your hotel to be taken to airport. From Mexico City (US$28) daily by Aeroméxico in less than an hr., leaves at 0755, or Mexicana four daily and Mon., Wed., Fri., and Sun. at 1100 (Tues., Sat. and Thurs. also 1120); Tues., Thurs., Sat. at 1235 with Mexicana to Tuxtla Gutiérrez; Tapachula flights with Aeroméxico, daily, 0820 (US$52); Aeroméxico also flies daily to Acapulco, 0930, to Villahermosa daily at 1700 (US$42), 50 mins; and Mérida daily at 1700. Daily flights to Guadalajara with Aeroméxico at 0930 and 1100, 3 hrs., to Ixtapa/Zihuatanejo at 1100, to Chihuahua at 1100 (with Mexicana at 1630), to Manzanillo at 1100; to Mazatlán at 0740 with Mexicana daily (Tues., Thurs., and Sat. at 1500), to Reynosa at 0740, to San Antonio at 0855, to Tijuana at 1100. Mexicana daily to Denver at 0740 (Tues., Thurs., Sat. at 1500), to Los Angeles daily at 0740 via Mexico City and on Fri. at 1100. Daily flights to Puerto Escondido, 40 mins, Aerovías Oaxaqueñas at 1100, returns at 0730 or 1200; Líneas Aéreas Oaxaqueñas fly at 1030 Mon.-Sat. and 0830 Sun. Costs US$40 return, but all Puerto Escondido planes (DC-3s) break down frequently, and for several days, rough ride back if no plane, 9 hrs. Daily flights also to Puerto Angel (2), and Pochutla. Oaxaca-Salina Cruz, Mon.-Sat. at 0830, Salina Cruz-Oaxaca Mon.-Sat. at 0920; Oaxaca-Pinotepa Nacional Mon.-Sat., two flights, one at 0630, returning 0720. Líneas Aéreas Oaxaqueñas office at Av. Hidalgo 503. Tel.: 65362, airport 61280. There is a Mexicana office next to *Hotel Señorial* on the Zócalo, helpful.

Excursions To **Monte Albán** (open 0800-1800) about 10 km. (20 mins.) uphill from Oaxaca, to see the pyramids, walls, terraces, tombs, staircases and sculptures of the ancient capital of the Zapotec culture. The place is radiantly colourful during some sunsets. Beware of fake "antique" sellers. Guide US$1. Take a torch for later visits. Autobuses Turísticos (office at Trujano 607, but departure from behind *Hotel Mesón del Angel*, Mina nr. Díaz Ordaz; bus tickets available from hotel lobby) from Oaxaca at 0930, 1130, 1330 and 1545, fare US$1.20 return; 2 hrs. at the site, allow not quite enough time to visit ruins before returning (you are not allowed to come back on another tour on one ticket, but you can arrange to buy a separate return for a later bus in addition to the mandatory round trip). On the last go straight to tombs first, before closing time. Good tours also from *Hotel El Presidente*, US$6 each with excellent guide. You can also also get a city bus from the new market to Colonia Monte Albán and then walk about 4 km. (1 hr.) up the road to the ruins. The city bus does not leave on Sun. for Col. Monte Albán until 0930. Entrance to ruins US$0.10, free on Sun. Most people go in the morning, so it may be easier to catch the afternoon bus. A private museum in an old colonial house is worth visiting. To the right, before getting to the ruins, is Tomb 7, where a fabulous treasure trove was found in 1932; most items are in the Regional Museum in the convent of Santo Domingo. The remarkable rectangular plaza, 300 by 200 metres, is rimmed by big ceremonial platforms: the Ball Court, and possibly a palace to the E, stairs rising to an unexcavated platform to the S, several platforms and temples to the W and one—known as Temple of

958 MEXICO

the Dancers but in reality, probably a hospital—with bas-reliefs, glyphs and calendar signs (probably 5th century B.C.). A grand wide stairway leads to a platform on the N side. Most of the ruins visible are early 10th century, when the city was abandoned and became a burial place. There is a footpath down to Oaxaca, ask for information. Informative literature is available at the site. (Recommended literature is the Bloomgarden *Easy Guide* to Monte Albán or *Easy Guide* to Oaxaca covering the city and all the ruins in the valley, with maps. In major hotels or the bookshop at Guerrero 108, and all the ruins. Restaurant near site is expensive; no food actually at site, but warm drinks. Just before the ruins is a swimming pool, Granja Tita; San Juanito buses take you there.

A paved road leads to **Teotitlán del Valle**, where Oaxaca *sarapes* are woven, which is now becoming rather touristy. If you knock at any door down the street, you will get them only a little cheaper than at the market, but there is greater variety. The best prices are to be had at the stores along the road as you come into town. (Make sure whether you are getting all-wool or mixture.) Buses leave every 2½ hrs. from 0800 from Miguel Cabrera nr. corner with Mina (US$0.30). *Juvenal Mendoza*, Buenavista 9, will make any design any size into a rug to order (daily at 1100). Opposite the turning for Teotitlán, turn right for **Dainzu**, another important ruin recently excavated. Its pyramid contains figures, probably ball players, similar to the Monte Albán dancers. The nearby site of **Lambytieco** is also well worth visiting, to see several fine and well-preserved stucco heads. Only 72 km. from Oaxaca is **Yanhuitlán**, with a beautiful 400-year-old church, part of a monastery. NW of Yanhuitlán is **Huajuapan de León**, with *Hotel García Peral*, on the Zócalo, good restaurant, *Hotel Casablanca*, Amatista 1, Col. Vista Hermosa, also good restaurant (just outside Huajuapan on the road to Oaxaca), and *Hotel Bella Vista*, F, and *Colón*, F, very good. 2nd class bus from Oaxaca to Huajuapan at 0730, 1030, 1445, 1730, US$1.75.

To Mitla, paved road, 42 km. from Oaxaca past (1) **El Tule** (12 km. from Oaxaca) which has what is reputed the world's largest tree, a savino (*Taxodium Mucronatum*), estimated at 2,000 years old, 40 metres high, 42 metres round at base, weighing an estimated 550 tons, fed water by an elaborate pipe system, in churchyard (bus from Oaxaca, 2nd class bus station, every ½ hr., US$0.40, buy ticket on bus, sit on the left to see the Tule tree; bus El Tule-Mitla US$0.30); (2) **Tlacochahuaya**, 16th century church, vivid Indian murals, carpets and blouses sold in market nearby, admission US$0.45 to church; and (3) **Tlacolula**, with a good Sunday market and the renowned Capilla del Santo Cristo in the church, elaborate decorations and gruesome figures of saints; can be reached by bus from Oaxaca, from the 2nd class bus station every 30 mins. but every 15 mins. on Sun., US$0.25. Taxi costs US$4 each to Mitla for 4 sharing, with time to take photographs at Tule and Mitla and to buy souvenirs at ruins. A band plays every evening in the plaza, take a sweater, cold wind most eves, starts at 1930. Tours to Tule, Mitla and Tlacolula on Sunday from *Hotel Señorial*, US$4, in VW buses. Fletes y Pasajes bus from Oaxaca, 2nd class bus station, every 30 mins. to Mitla, 1 hour, US$0.50; the ruins are 10-min. walk across the village (from the bus stop).

From the main road a turn left leads 4 km. to **Mitla** (whose name means "place of the dead") where there are ruins of four great palaces among minor ones. Entry US$0.10, no literature available on site. See in particular the magnificent bas-reliefs, the sculptured designs in the Hall of Mosaics, the Hall of the Columns, and in the depths of a palace La Columna de la Muerte (Column of Death), which people embrace and measure what they can't reach with their fingers to know how many years they have left to live (rather hard on long-armed people); Indians gather on New Year's day to embrace it. There is a soberly decorated colonial church with three cupolas, and a rash of guides and pedlars. Beautiful traditional Indian clothes and other goods may be bought at the new permanent market. Also good *mescal*.

Hotel Mitla, E, clean, local food (*comida corrida*, US$4.80), beautiful garden. *Hotel La Zapoteca*, on road to ruins, F, friendly. The University of the Americas has a small guest-house, and runs the small Frissell museum in the Zócalo at Mitla, with restaurant, *La Sorpresa*, in a patio; restaurant opp. site, *Santa María; María Elena* restaurant 100m. from site towards village, good *comida corrida* for US$0.90. The local technical college provides accommodation, showers and a bathroom; good shopping too.

Fletes y Pasajes buses and taxis from Oaxaca go to the ruins of **Yagul** (on the way to Mitla, ask to be put down at the turn-off to Yagul, entry, US$0.05), an outstandingly picturesque site where the ball courts and quarters of the priests are set in a landscape punctuated by candelabra cactus and agave. Yagul was a large Zapotec and Mixtec religious centre; the ball courts are perhaps the most perfect discovered to date; also fine tombs (take steep path from behind the ruins) and temples. You will have to walk some 2 km. from the bus stop to the site, and you can return the same way or walk 3 km. to Tlacolula to catch a bus (signposted). The 2 km.-long side road off the main road is paved.

There are 2 national parks in Oaxaca State: Benito Juárez in the municipality of Huayapan, some 5 km. from the capital, with pine forests, comprising 2,737 hectares; and the Lagunas de Chacacahua (14,187 hectares), which includes tropical vegetation and a 28-km. coastline on the Pacific, at Tututepec, 77 km. from Pinotepa Nacional.

Friday trips from Oaxaca to market at San Antonio Ocotlán on the road to Puerto Angel, with good prices for locally woven rugs and baskets, also excellent fruit and veg.; buses leave every 30 mins. for San Antonio from the co-operative bus station opposite Oaxaca Mercado de Abastos (½ hr. journey). Stop in San Bártolo Coyotepec to see Doña Rosa's black pottery (she's been dead for years but her name survives) and don't try to bargain (also red and green ceramics in the village), and in San Tomás Jaliezа, where cotton textiles are made.

17 km. SW of Oaxaca is **Cuilapan,** where there is a vast earthquake-shattered 16th-century convent with a famous nave and columns. The last Zapotec princess was buried at Cuilapan. Reached by bus from Oaxaca from 2nd class bus station, take bus to Zaachila which leaves every 30 mins., then walk to unexcavated ruins in valley. **Zaachila** is a poor town, but there are ruins, with two Mixtec tombs, with owls in stucco work in the outer chamber and carved human figures with skulls for heads inside. Admission US$0.13, no restrictions on flash photography. There is an Indian market on Thursday.

To San Pablo de **Guelatao** (65 km. from Oaxaca), the birthplace of Benito Juárez. The town is located in the mountains NE of Oaxaca and can be reached by bus (3 hrs.) along a paved but tortuously winding road. There are a memorial and a museum to Juárez on the hillside within the village (entry, US$0.17), and a pleasant lake with a symbolic statue of a shepherd and his lambs.

We are approaching a more traditional part of Mexico; Tehuantepec peninsula and the mountains of Chiapas beyond, a land inhabited by Indians less influenced than elsewhere by the Spanish conquest. Only about 210 km. separate the Atlantic and the Pacific at the hot, heavily-jungled Isthmus of Tehuantepec, where the land does not rise more than 250 metres. There are a railway (to be renewed) and a Trans-Isthmian Highway between Coatzacoalcos and Salina Cruz, the terminal cities on the two oceans.

N.B. In southern Mexico the name "Zócalo" is not often used for the main square of a town: "Plaza (Mayor)" is much more common.

Salina Cruz is a booming and evil-smelling port with a naval base, extensive oil-storage installations and an oil refinery. Bathing is dangerous because of the heavy swell from Pacific breakers and also sharks. Ten km. to the S is a picturesque fishing village with La Ventosa beach which, as the name says, is windy. Buses go to the beach every 30 mins. from a corner of the main square.

Accommodation: *champas,* or hammocks under thatch shelters by the beach, US$0.25-US$0.40 a night. The owners serve drinks and food (fish, shrimps, crabs just caught) from early morning on. Prices often high.

Warning Do not wander too far off along the beach as many people have been attacked and robbed. Do not sleep on the beach or in your car.

Hotels *Fuente,* F, bath, basic. *Río,* reasonable, nr. Cristóbal Colón bus station. Avoid the *Magda,* overpriced, unfriendly; *La Posada de Rustrian,* with restaurant, overlooking the sea, F, with bath in new block, half in old block. Friendly family at the top of the dirt road coming from Salina Cruz (on the right) and 200 metres after the first path that leads down to the beach, rents hammocks, US$0.20 a night, fried fish US$1.

Restaurant *Costa del Pacífico,* hires shower cabin, stores luggage.

Buses Buses from Salina Cruz to San Cristóbal all come from Oaxaca and are very often full (2nd class, US$5.25); take instead a 2nd class bus to Juchitán, then to Arriaga and from there to Tuxtla and San Cristóbal. A long route. To Coatzacoalcos, US$5, 6 hrs. Salina Cruz-Pochutla, US$3, 3½ hrs. Frequent buses to Tehuantepec, US$0.75.

(Km. 804). **Tehuantepec** (population 15,000, altitude 150 metres) is 257 km. from Oaxaca and 21 km. inland from Salina Cruz. A colourful place, it is on the bend of a river around which most of its activities are centred and which makes it very humid. The plaza has arcades down one side, a market on the other, and many stands selling *agua fresca,* an iced fruit drink. Houses are low, in white or pastel shades. The Indians are mostly Zapotecs whose social organization was once matriarchal: the women are high-pressure saleswomen, with some Spanish blood; their hair is sometimes still braided and brightly ribboned and at times they wear embroidered costumes. The men for the most part work in the fields, as potters or weavers, or at the nearby oil refinery. Hammocks made in this area are of the best quality. The town is divided into 15 wards, and each holds a *fiesta,* the main one at the end of Holy Week, when the women wear their finest costumes and jewellery. There is another splendid *fiesta* in honour of St. John the Baptist on June 22-25. January and February are good months for the ward *fiestas.*

Hotels *Tehuantepec,* on the road to Juchitán; *Oasis* (central and good atmosphere), F, with bath,

960 MEXICO

good value, near Plaza; *Tehuanita*, F, adequate; *Donaji*, Juárez 10, reasonable, fan, nr. market, F; *Posada Colonial*; *Calli*, C; *Posada Villa Real*, F, nice courtyard; *Posada Inn*, E. A guest house on the same street as Cristóbal Colón bus terminal is basic, but reasonable, friendly, with lovely patio, F.

Restaurants *Café Colonial*, near the *Hotel Oasis*, and *Kike* under *Posada Colonial* have reasonable *comidas corridas* for about US$2. Cheap food on top floor of market. The local *quesadillas* made of maize and cheese are delicious; sold at bus stops.

Bus There is no bus station, so getting information about 2nd class buses is difficult (the buses park by the Plaza)—get information from office around the square—but there are a few a day in all directions. Cristóbal Colón buses stop just round the corner from the Plaza, 1st and 2nd class tickets, one bus a day to San Cristóbal at 1255 (7½ hrs.) plus other destinations. To Coatzacoalcos at 0730, 9-10 hrs. Bus to Arriaga at 0600, 0800, 1800 to connect to Tonalá. To Tuxtla Gutiérrez, 1000 and 1500 (6 hrs.) 2nd class at 0130, and Tapachula. Bus to Tonalá (Cristóbal Colón) at 0030 and 0130. To Oaxaca, US$5 with Istmo at 1000 and 2200; to Salina Cruz, US$0.20. (**N.B.** Some buses from Salina Cruz do not stop at Tehuantepec.)

Train to Coatzacoalcos daily at 0700, about 11 hrs.

Excursions To neighbouring villages for *fiestas*. Near the town are the ruins of Criengola, apparently not very accessible.

27 km. beyond Tehuantepec on the road to Tuxtla Gutiérrez is **Juchitán** (*Hotel Don Alex*, F, noisy, but better than *Hotel Modelo*, same price but filthy, no safety whatsoever, no service either; *Hotel Casa Río*, has an Indian name, not posted, next to Casa Río shop, F, nr. market, clean; be prepared to bargain in cheap hotels), very old, Indian, with an extensive market, many *fiestas* and a special one on June 19 (2nd class bus Oaxaca-Juchitán, US$3.75, 6 hrs., frequent). A road runs 6 km. N to **Ixtepec** (airport) (Hotels: *Panamericano*, noisy from railway station, F; *San Juan*, F, bath, acceptable; *Colón*) train Ixtepec-Coatzacoalcos at 0800. At Las Cruces (restaurant), a road runs right to **Arriaga** (12,000 people; Hotels: *El Parador*, clean with swimming pool; *Juchitán*, E, with bathroom; *Restaurant Xochimilco* near bus stations), through **Tonalá**, formerly a very quiet town but now reported noisy and dirty, with a small museum; good market (bus Tonalá-Tapachula, 5 hrs., US$3, hot and boring. Also buses to Tuxtla and, opp. the market street, local bus to disappointing Puerto Arista— the latter every hour, 45 mins.). By Route 200 to **Tapachula**, a pleasant and neat, but expensive, hot commercial town (airport) and the Talismán bridge to Guatemala. Beyond Tonalá the road is mostly straight, smooth and fast. (North of Arriaga a road is now open paralleling the railway and by-passing Las Cruces, so avoiding dozens of sharp curves on a steep road.) This is by far the better road for travellers seeking the quickest way from Mexico City to Guatemala.

Tonalá Hotels *Galilea*, E, with bath, air-conditioned, good, basic shape rooms on 1st floor, balconies, on main square, with good restaurants; *Casa de Huéspedes El Viajero*, Avenida Matamoros, near market, F, with bath, rough but OK; *Faro*, near Plaza, F; *Tonalá*, opposite museum, E; *Sta. Elena Restaurant*, at the S end of town, near Cristóbal Colón bus station on outskirts, good. On the Plaza, try *Restaurant Nora* but avoid *Liz* next door. Numerous Chinese-named restaurants.

Tapachula Hotels *Internacional*, good, with restaurant; *Central*, E, with shower, clean; just around the corner is *Tazacapec*, F; *San Francisco*, good, air-conditioned, C; *Rochester*, 2a Avenida Norte; *Nina*, E, with bath, comfortable; *Colombo*, near Plaza, E, shower but no fan, OK but overpriced; *Colonial*, reasonable, F, with shower; *Colón*, Central Norte Juárez, F, with shower, near bus station; *San Gerónimo*, F; *Casa de Huéspedes Mexicana*, 8a Avenida Norte, F, basic, with a little zoo in the courtyard. Many hotels along Avenidas 4, 6, 8 (near Plaza). *Pensión Mars* (Av. 4) has cheap *comidas*; *Granada*, F, near Plaza, rather dark and dire; *Tayopec*, F, friendly; *Motel Loma Real*, 1 km. N of city, D, operates as a 1st class hotel, use of swimming pool, cold showers. *Cinco de Mayo* near market and 1 block from buses to the border, F, with bath. *Tapachula*, friendly but dirty, F, not recommended; *Cervantes*, nr. *Hotel Central*, F, with bath. Good restaurant next to Cristóbal Colón terminal.

Travel Agent Viajes Tacaná, operated by Sr Adolfo Guerrero Chávez, 4a Av. Norte, No. 6, Tel.: 63502/63501/63245; trips to Izapa ruins, to mountains, beaches and can gain entry to museum when closed.

Into Guatemala 2nd class buses from Tapachula (taking 50 mins.) include Cristóbal Colón, which leaves at noon (US$0.30), and Unión y Progreso near the market (1st class leave 0900 and 1100, US$0.40—stating "Col. Juárez" as its destination, US$ 0.30) to the frontier (open 24 hrs. a day) at the Talismán bridge (8 km.) but no through buses. Taxi Talismán-Tapachula, US$6, exit tax

US$0.25. The Guatemalan customs post is 100 metres from the Mexican one. No immigration services between 1200 and 1400, exchange cash dollars for quetzales with men standing around customs on the Guatemalan side (there is a bank on the Guatemalan side, near customs). Crossing into Guatemala by car may take more than 2 hours. If you don't want your car sprayed inside it may cost you a couple of dollars. Guatemalan buses (Galgos) leave Talismán bridge about every two hours for Coatepeque, Quezaltenango and Guatemala City (fare US$6, entry tax US$1).

It is difficult to get a bus from the Talismán bridge to Oaxaca or Mexico City (though they do exist); advisable therefore to travel to Tapachula for connection. Buses to Mexico City, US$10.50, five a day, all p.m., take 12 hrs. to reach Oaxaca (US$7), and same again to Mexico City. Two additional buses to Oaxaca, 0730 and 1800. The train from Mexico City to Tapachula leaves daily at 2100, it costs US$12.50 1st class but takes 37 hours to complete the journey, changing at Veracruz (Veracruz-Tapachula, 29 hrs., 887 km., US$3.50 2nd class), stops to get food on the way. If travelling in the reverse direction, board train at Tapachula hours in advance of departure to get seats, and guard them. Tickets on sale only in Tapachula at 1630. Train departs daily at 1800 for connection to Mexico City but again requires change at Veracruz and tends to miss evening train to Mexico City. Best to stay overnight at Veracruz and catch morning train. Don't get off at Tierra Blanca to change to the Mérida-Mexico train; you arrive after it has gone. Hitch-hikers should note that there is little through international traffic at Talismán bridge. Tapachula—Salina Cruz, 9 hrs. with Flecha Roja, US$6.40.

Consulates It is possible to get a visa for El Salvador at the Salvadorean Consulate in Tapachula (Calle 2a Sur, No. 10) without any delay. There is a Guatemalan Consulate in Tapachula at 2 Calle Oriente and 7 Av. S., Tel.: 6-12-52. (Open Mon.-Fri. 0700-1400, also Sat. a.m.; visa US$3.50, friendly and quick.)

Off the road between Tonalá and Tapachula are several fine-looking and undeveloped beaches (although waves are dangerous). **Puerto Arista** is now being built up and spoiled; bus from Tonalá US$0.25, taxi US$0.50—one hotel or hammocks on beach, US$0.85 a night (many sandflies), also several guest houses, US$24 a month, 3 or 4 restaurants (closed by 2000) with rooms to rent, e.g. *Restaurant Turquesa; Hotel Vacacional* for cheap but dirty accommodation, only for the desperate, no locks; new small hotel/restaurant 3 blocks down on the right from where the road reaches the beach coming from Tonalá and turns right, next to bakery, no fan, basic, F. Buses also from Tonalá to Boca del Cielo further down the coast, which is good for bathing but has no accommodation or other attractions, and similarly Cabeza del Toro. **Paredón,** on the huge lagoon Mar Muerto near Tonalá, has excellent seafood and one very basic guest house. One can take a local fishing boat out into the lagoon to swim; the shore stinks. Fishermen clean fish on the beach among dogs and pigs. Served by frequent buses. En route for Tapachula one passes through Pijijiapan where there is the *Hotel Pijijilton* (!) next to the Cristóbal Colón bus station. Also **Puerto Madero,** 20 km. from Tapachula (bus US$0.80), worse than Puerto Arista because built up and stench on beaches from rubbish being burned. Intense heat in summer. (*Hotel Puerto Madero,* accommodation in what are really remains of cement block room, F.) Water defences are being built. Many fish restaurants on beach.

45 km. (16 km. to turn-off) beyond Tapachula, on the way to Guatemala, is **Unión Juárez** (*Hotel Colonial,* F; *Restaurant Carmelita* on the square is modest with fair prices). Visit the ruins of **Izapa** (proto-classic stelae, small museum) on the way to Unión Juárez; the sector of the site on the N is easily visible but a larger portion is on the S side of the highway, about 1 km. away, ask caretaker for guidance. These buildings influenced Kaminal Juyú near Guatemala City and are considered archaeologically important as a Proto-Mayan site. In Unión Juárez one can have one's papers stamped and proceed on foot via Talquián to the Guatemalan border at Sibinal. Take a guide.

A worthwhile and easy hike can be made up the Tacaná volcano (4,150 m.), which takes 2-3 days from Unión Juárez. Ask for the road to Chiquihuete, no cars. Jorge de León will guide you, or the Club Andinista at the Tapachula tourist office can help, on the Plaza Mayor.

Beyond Las Cruces we enter the mountainous Chiapas state, mostly peopled by Maya Indians whose extreme isolation has now been ended by air services and the two main highways. Chiapas ranks first in cacao production, second in coffee, bananas and mangoes, and cattle-grazing is important. Hardwoods are floated out down the rivers which flow into the Gulf.

Mike Shawcross writes: Anyone with a vehicle who has time to visit or is looking for a place to spend the night would find it well worth while to make a 4-km. detour. 50 km. beyond Las Cruces a gravel road leads north (left) to the beautiful waterfall El Aguacero (small sign), which falls several hundred feet down the side of the Río La Venta canyon. There is a small car-park at the lip of the canyon. 986 steps lead down to the river and the base of the waterfall.

From Las Cruces to Tuxtla Gutiérrez, Route 190 carries on to Cintalapa (restaurant) whence there is a steep climb up an escarpment. Carry on to Ocozocoautla (airport for Tuxtla, hotel, F), make a long ascent followed by descent to

(Km. 1,085) **Tuxtla Gutiérrez,** capital of Chiapas; pop.: 200,000; alt.: 522

962 MEXICO

metres, 301 km. (183 miles) from Tehuantepec. It is a hot, modern city of no great interest to the tourist except during the fair of Guadalupe, on December 12. The market is worth a look. There is a State Archaeological Museum, open daily, at the E end of town, near the botanical garden (on a wooded hillside near the Teatro de la Ciudad). There is a zoo some 3 km. W of town, worth a visit because it contains only animals from Chiapas (the best zoo in Mexico—good for birdwatchers too) about 100 metres from *Hotel Bonampak* on the main thoroughfare (open Tues.-Sun., 0700-1730, free; the buses "Zoológico" and "Cerro Hueco" pass the entrance). Tourist office at E end of town.

The street system here is as follows: Avenidas run from E to W, Calles from N to S. The Avenidas are named according to whether they are N or S of the Avenida Central and change their names if they are E or W of the Calle Central. The number before Avenida or Calle means the distance from the "Central" measured in blocks.

Hotels *Bonampak*, Bld. Belisario Domínguez 180, W end of town, the social centre, E, clean, good restaurant; *Gran Hotel Humberto*, C; *Posada del Rey*, D, a/c; *La Mansión*, E, a/c, bath; *Esponda*, D; *Esperanza*, E; *Serrano*, E—all centrally located; *Hotel Mar-Inn*, E, pleasant, clean, 2a Av. Norte Oriente 347; *Balun Canan*, Av. Central Oriente 922, E; *Brindis*, not very clean, Av. Central Oriente, F. *Posada Muñiz*, opposite cooperative bus station, F, not very clean; opp. Cristóbal Colón bus station: *María Teresa* and *Santo Domingo*, each F with shower, good if you arrive late, but noisy; *Canadá*, near market, F, without bath. Cheap: *Serrano*, F, with bath; *Ofelia*, 2a Av. Sur Oriente, between 5a and 6a Calle Oriente Sur, clean, not very friendly, noisy on street side, F. **Motels** *Paraíso*, Pan-American Highway, E; *La Hacienda*, trailer-park-hotel, Belisario Domínguez 1197, E.

Restaurants *Los Cazadores*, good, regional, expensive; *Mina*, Av. Central Oriente 525, nr. bus station, good cheap *comidas*; *Parrilla La Cabaña*, excellent *tacos*, very clean; *Las Pichanchas*, pretty courtyard, *marimba* music between 1400-1700 and 2000-2300, on Av. 14 de Septiembre Oriente 837, worth trying; *Central*, on Plaza, reasonable; many others; *Las Calandrias*, 2a Av. Norte Poniente, 20 metres from Cristóbal Colón terminal, open 0700-2400, good and cheap. Coffee shop below *Hotel Serrano* serves excellent coffee.

Travel Agency Carolina Tours, Sr José Narváez Valencia (manager), Av. Central Pte. 1138, Tel.: 2-42-81; reliable, recommended; also coffee shop at Av. Central Poniente 230.

Roads and Buses 35 km. E of Tuxtla, just past Chiapa de Corzo (see below), a road runs N, 294 km., to Villahermosa via Pichucalco (see page 970), paved all the way. There is a gas station before Pichucalco at Bochil (80 km. from Tuxtla). Cristóbal Colón 1st class bus terminal is at 2 Av. Norte Poniente 268, Transportes Tuxtla 1st and 2nd class terminals are at 2 Av. Sur Oriente 712. Cristóbal Colón has buses daily to Villahermosa (for Palenque) at 0620, 1300 and 1730, 8½ hrs., US$6; to Oaxaca at 1100 and 2245, 12 hrs., US$7; 4 a day to Mexico City, US$19, plus frequent buses to San Cristóbal de Las Casas, US$2, superb mountain journey. Tuxtla-Tapachula, US$5, 4 a day; one (1st class) to the Talismán bridge daily at 0300. Take travel sickness tablets for Tuxtla-Oaxaca road if you suffer from queasiness. Transportes Tuxtla 2nd class buses to Oaxaca, 5 a day, US$8, and 1st class buses to Pichucalco, 6 a day, US$4 (Pichucalco-Villahermosa and Villahermosa-Campeche (6 hrs.) have frequent services); to Villahermosa at 0500 and 1330, US$5; to Palenque (via Villahermosa) at 0500, 10 hrs., US$6.50; to Mérida at 1330, US$15. The scenery between Tuxtla and Mérida is very fine, and the road provides the best route between Chiapas and Yucatán. There are VW taxis at the bus station but they will not drive to the airport unless they have a full passenger load and may tout hotels before going there.

By Air The new airport for Tuxtla is way out at the next town of Ocozocoautla, a long drive to a mountain top. It is often shrouded in cloud and has crosswinds. There are times when aircraft do not leave for days! Good facilities, including restaurant. Tuxtla Gutiérrez to Oaxaca, 1 hr., Tues., Thurs., Sat. US$40; to Tapachula, daily, 35 mins., US$28; to Villahermosa daily, US$20, 25 mins.; to Veracruz, Mon. and Fri., 1 hr. 25 mins.; to Monterrey daily via Mexico City, 4 hrs. 15 mins.; to Minatitlán Mon. and Fri., 30 mins.; frequent to Mexico City, direct 1 hr. 15 mins.; to Acapulco daily, 2 hrs. 40 mins.; to Chihuahua daily; to Guadalajara daily; to Ixtapa/Zihuatanejo daily. There is a 40 min. flight by Britten-Norman Islander to Palenque, very exciting, no reservations or tickets available. You must be at the airport before dawn, flights leave at about 0700, Sumidero canyon can be seen during flight.

Excursions Two vast artificial lakes made by dams are worth visiting: the Presa Netzhualcoyotl, or Mal Paso, 77 km. NW of Tuxtla, and La Angostura, SE of the city. Information from the tourist office. Mal Paso can also be visited from Cárdenas (see page 969). By paved road, which starts at zoo gates (23 km.), in excellent condition, to the rim of the tremendous El Sumidero Canyon, over 1,000 metres deep (taxi fare US$20 return; minibus daily from *Hotel Bonampak*, US$9 p.p. or from *Hotel Posada del Rey*, US$12.25 p.p.). Indian warriors galled by the Spanish conquest hurled themselves into it rather than submit. Excursions by air to Bonampak and Yaxchilán cheaper from

San Cristóbal (see below). Transportes Tuxtla has a 1st class bus from Tuxtla to Palenque at US$6.50 one way, which leaves Tuxtla at 0500; 9-hr. journey via Pichucalco and Villahermosa.

Chiapa de Corzo, 15 km. on, a colonial town of about 7,000 people on a bluff overlooking the Grijalva river, is more interesting than Tuxtla: see a lovely 16th century crown-shaped fountain, a church whose engraved altar is of solid silver, and famous craftsmen in gold and jewellery and lacquer work who travel the fairs. Painted and lacquered vessels made of pumpkins are a local speciality. There is a small lacquer museum. The *fiestas* here are outstanding: January 20-23 with a pageant on the river and another, early February. *Hotel Los Angeles*, on Plaza, E, good value, fills up quickly; few other places to stay so make alternative arrangements if necessary. Plaza filled with bars playing jukeboxes. Chiapa de Corzo was a preclassic and proto-classic Maya site and shares features with early Maya sites in Guatemala; the ruins are behind the Nestlé plant, and some restored mounds are in a field near modern houses. Ask the householders' permission to climb over the fence as the ruins are on private property.

Bus to San Cristóbal at 1000 and 1200.

Mike Shawcross tells us: The waterfall at the Cueva de El Chorreadero is well worth a detour of 1 km. The road to the cave is 10 km. past Chiapa de Corzo, a few km. after you start the climb up into the mountains to get to San Cristóbal.

You can take a boat from Chiapa de Corzo into the Cañón del Sumidero, very impressive, US$20 for four.

(Km. 1,170) **San Cristóbal de Las Casas** (40,000 people), 85 km. beyond Tuxtla Gutiérrez, was founded in 1528 by Diego de Mazariegos and was the colonial capital of the region. It stands in a high mountain valley at 2,110 metres. It was named after Las Casas, protector of the Indians, its second bishop. There are many old churches; two of them cap the two hills which overlook the town. Santo Domingo, built in 1547, has a baroque façade, a gaily gilt rococo interior and a famous carved wooden pulpit (see below). Other churches include San Nicolás, with an interesting façade, El Carmen, La Merced, and La Caridad (1715). From the Temple of Guadalupe there is a good view of the old colonial city and surrounding wooded hills. Various kinds of craftwork are sold in the new market, open daily, and in the Sunday markets of the local Indian villages. At the ex-convent of Santo Domingo (now a handicrafts centre, Sna Jolobil, open 0800-2000) there are occasional concerts featuring music by players from local tribes on traditional instruments. There is a small American colony. July 25 is *fiesta* day, when vehicles are taken uphill to be blessed by the Bishop. There is also a popular spring festival on Easter Sunday and the week after. There is a remarkable cemetery on the road to Tuxtla Gutiérrez, 2-3 km. from the centre of town. Most Indian tribes here are members of the Tzotzil and Tzeltal groups. The Tenejapans wear black knee-length tunics; the Chamulans white wool tunics; and the Zinacantecos multicoloured outfits, with their men exhibiting marital status by wearing ribbons on their hats; bachelors allow ribbons to flow freely. The Chamula and Tenejapa women's costumes are more colourful, and more often seen in town, than the men's.

N.B. The neighbourhood is acquiring a reputation for having hostile inhabitants. Check on the situation before you visit the villages. Travellers are strongly warned not to wander around on their own, especially in the hills surrounding the town where churches are situated, as they could risk assault. Warnings can be seen in some places frequented by tourists. Heed the warning on photographing, casual clothing and courtesy (see page 966). Note also: international connections are difficult: only one public trunk telephone line; 30 mins.-2 hrs. wait.

Na Bolom, the house of the archaeologists Frans (died 1963) and Trudi Blom, has become a museum, open 1600-1800 (except Mon.); address: Vicente Guerrero 33, and a beautiful individual guest house (previous reservation necessary, double room with 3 meals, US$46 a day), with good library, run by Mrs Trudi Blom. It is well worth visiting: beautifully displayed artefacts, pictures of Lacandón Indians, with information about their history and present way of life (in English). Also only easily-obtainable map of Lacandón jungle. At 1630 guides take you round display, rooms of beautiful old house, and garden. Entrance US$0.50, at 1600. The Na Bolom library opens as follows: Mon., 1430-1830; Tues.-Fri., 0900-1330; Sat., 0800-1200. We have been told that travellers can sometimes stay there free, in exchange for voluntary work.

964 MEXICO

Hotels *Motel Alcanfores,* on side of mountain W of city, two-bedroom bungalows (sleep 6), US$45 per day; *Posada Diego de Mazariegos,* María A. Flores 2, Tel.: 8-06-21, 1 block N of Plaza, C, warmly recommended, restaurant and bar; *Parador Ciudad Real,* Diagonal Centenario 32, W edge of city; *Bonampak,* Calzada México 16, Tel.: 8-16-21, fairly expensive; *Español,* 1° de Marzo 16 (with "aircraft-hangar" restaurant), D; *Rincón del Arco,* 8 blocks from centre, fireplaces, Ejército Nacional 66, D, warmly recommended, bar, restaurant, discotheque; *Molino de La Alborada,* Periférico Sur Km. 4, S of airstrip, modern ranch-house and bungalows, D; *Santa Clara,* on Plaza, D; *Palacio de Moctezuma,* Juárez 18, colonial style, E, good Mexican food; *Posada Los Morales,* Ignacio Allende 17, F, cottages with open fires and hot showers; *Real del Valle,* Av. Guadalupe, next to Plaza, F, very clean, friendly, recommended, parking; *Parador Mexicano,* Av. 5 de Mayo 38, E, tennis court, quiet and pleasant; *Posada Capri,* Insurgentes 54, near Cristóbal Colón bus terminal, E; *Ciudad Real,* on Plaza, clean, good value, good restaurant, attractive rooms, but noisy parrot talks a lot, D; *Molino de Las Casas,* small bungalows in spacious grounds near Pan-American Highway, E; *San Martín,* Calle Real de Guadalupe 16, near Plaza, E, clean, good value, hot water, left-luggage, check you have enough blankets; *Posada Del Cid,* on Pan-American Highway, adjoining restaurant, E; *Fray Bartolomé de Las Casas,* Insurgentes and N. Héroes, F, with bath, nice rooms and patio, can be noisy, cold at night but extra blankets available; *San Francisco,* Insurgentes, F, run down, noisy from fake "churchbells" ringing; *Casa de Huéspedes Chamula,* Calle Julio M. Corzo, clean, hot showers, washing facilities, friendly, parking, F, recommended; *Posada del Abuelito,* quiet location 9 blocks from Plaza at Tapachula 18, cooking and washing facilities, F, run down; *Casa de Huéspedes Lupita,* on Av. Juárez, F, without shower; opp. is *Casa de Huéspedes Pola,* 1 block from Cristóbal Colón bus station, and close to other bus stations, small rooms and thin walls and blankets, cold at night, F, clean, hot water, adjoining restaurant; *Posada Insurgente,* Av. Insurgentes 5, clean, basic, but cheap; *Casa de Huéspedes Santa Lucía,* 1 block from bus station, F; *Casa de Huéspedes Margarita,* Real de Guadalupe 34, F, popular with young tourists, free purified water, communal sleeping, washing and toilets, clean, friendly, hot water, laundry possible, restaurant serves breakfast and dinner, slow service, wholefood, horse-riding arranged; *Posada Tepeyac,* one block from Margarita, friendly, not very clean, F; *Pensión* at Av. Gen. Utrilla 13, F, rooms vary greatly in quality; *Posada El Cerillo,* G, hot showers, washing facilities, not very clean, Av. B. Domínguez 27, *Parador Ciudad Real,* 1 km. from centre, friendly, new, E. Ask at Tienda Santo Domingo at Av. Gen. Utrilla and Calle Flavio A. Paniagua (2 blocks down Utrilla from Plaza), for *La Carpintería,* at Paniagua 2B, rooms round carpenter's courtyard, F, not clean, secure, rooms furnished and fitted individually by the carpenter; *Baños Mercederos,* Calle 1° de Marzo 55, F, shared quarters, good cheap meals, steam baths ($0.80 extra) (*Baños Torres* next door has no rooms.) At No. 25 and No. 59 of the same street, pleasant rooms with families, quiet, clean, friendly, E, also good food. Several unmarked guest houses.

Camping *Rancho San Nicolás,* at end of Calle Francisco León, 1½ km. E of centre, beautiful, quiet location, is a camping and trailer park, but do take warm blankets or clothing as the temperature drops greatly at night. Hot showers, US$1.60 p.p., children free. *La Amistad* trailer park and campground is 27 km. from San Cristóbal (4 km. before Teopisca) on the Pan-American Highway towards Comitán. Hook-ups, hot showers, fresh vegetables, US$2.25 for a VW van plus US$0.45 p.p.; up to US$4 for larger recreational vehicles.

Restaurants Restaurants close quite early. *La Galería,* S of Plaza at Av. Miguel Hidalgo 3, now rather expensive, also sells quality art-work and handicrafts, frequented by young US people, coffee shop, carrot cake, German and US magazines to read. *Baños Mercederos* (Los Baños), Calle 1° de Marzo 55, meals US$1.10, showers US$0.35, steam baths US$0.65. *El Fandango,* ex-*Olla Podrida,* US-run and frequented, international menu, poor value for money, slow service, handicrafts, English book exchange, Diego de Mazariegos 24. *El Mural,* further along same street, and *Café Torreón* in Plaza outside La Merced church. *La Plaza,* upstairs, SW corner of Plaza, clean, good, rather dear. *El Bazar,* also American-run, Gen. Utrilla 10 (left side of Plaza, towards market) good, excellent coffee, not cheap, live music some nights. *El Patio,* next to *Posada Diego de Mazariegos,* try their coffee with liqueur, very exotic, e.g. Diablo with kahlúa and rum. *La Parroquia,* large and airy restaurant, on Guadalupe Victoria nr. 16 de Septiembre, the haunt of the local middle class. *Normita,* Av. Benito Juárez, good Mexican food, open 1300-1500 and for supper, owner plays guitar and his wife and daughter sing, bill-board with cheap accommodation. *El Tuluc,* Calle F. Madero, good value esp. steaks, highly recommended, near Plaza; also recommended is *Capri* on Insurgentes; *La Casa Blanca,* on Guadalupe, cheap; *El Punto,* Domínguez y Madero, good pizza. *Los Arcos,* varied menu, on Madero; *El Trigal,* 1° de Marzo, restaurant and shop, vegetarian, good; Wholemeal bread at health-food shop marked with star-shape near post office. Good cake at *Pan y Arte,* Ignacio Allende 5, amber jewellery for sale. *El Jardín,* S of Benito Juárez, good meat and Mexican dishes, worth the expense. Many others. San Cristóbal is not lively in the evenings: main meeting place is around *ponche* stall on Plaza.

Shopping Part of the ex-convent of Santo Domingo has been converted into a cooperative, *Sna Jolobil,* selling handicrafts from many Indian villages (best quality, so expensive). For purchases of local goods try *Miscelánea Betty,* Gen. Utrilla 45, good value. Leather goods purchases recommended in San Cristóbal. A good place to buy handicrafts is at *Doña Paula,* Calle Real de Guadalupe 25, just off the Plaza (there are craft shops all along the Guadalupe; the farther along,

MEXICO 965

the cheaper they are) and *El Quetzal* for costumes from local villages. Variety of Mexican and Guatemalan handicrafts at *La Galería* restaurant. (See also under Tenejapa, page 966) Main market is worth seeing as well. Bookshop *El Sol y La Luna* has good 2nd-hand stock and postcards.

Laundromat Lava Sec, Av. Rosas near Niños Héroes. Close to Plaza on Calle B. Domínguez, 5-hour service, 3 kg. for US$1.

Foreign Exchange *La Galería* restaurant will change travellers' cheques at a reasonable rate if banks are closed (also into Guatemalan quetzales). Banks charge a commission for each cash transaction on travellers' cheques and are open for exchange purposes between 1100 and 1330 only; this leads to long queues.

Guidebook in English *San Cristóbal de Las Casas, Chiapas, Mexico: City and Area Guide,* by Mike Shawcross, obtainable from the author at Apartado Postal 1, Antigua, Guatemala, with much interesting information on the area.

Tourist Office helpful, at the Palacio Municipal, W side of main Plaza; maps of San Cristóbal US$0.20, some English spoken. Ask here for accommodation in private house of mother of one of the staff (E, excellent).

Into Guatemala Cristóbal Colón, S end of Av. Insurgentes (left luggage facilities open 0600-2000 exc. Sun. and holidays), clean station has direct 1st class buses to the Guatemalan border of Ciudad Cuauhtémoc at 0800, 1630 and 2130, 2½ hrs., US$1.90, 87 km. all tickets can be booked up to 4 days in advance. Cristóbal Colón to Comitán (if you can't get a bus to the border, take one to Comitán and get a pick-up truck there—about US$1), 8 a day from 0800 (tickets may be bought ½ hr. in advance), US$2, 87 km (a beautiful, steep route). Transportes Tuxtla, S end of Av. Ignacio Allende, has several 1st and 2nd class buses, 4½ hrs., to the border daily, though these do not continue through to the Guatemalan customs post (3.7 km., uphill, taxi sometimes available, US$0.65 p.p., minimum 3 people). The 0800 Cristóbal Colón makes connections at the Guatemalan border at 1200 with El Cóndor for Huehuetenango and Guatemala City. Note that it is cheaper to pay initially only to Huehuetenango and buy a ticket onwards from there (no change of bus necessary). Do not buy a ticket at the border until a bus leaves as some wait while others come and go.

Buses Beware of pickpockets at bus stations. Cristóbal Colón 1st class bus to Oaxaca, about 12 hrs., at 1645 daily, book well in advance, monotonous trip, US$9.50, 622 km. To do the trip in daytime, you need to change at Tuxtla Gutiérrez (0745 Cristóbal Colón to Tuxtla, then 1100 on to Oaxaca); to Mexico City, via Tuxtepec, about 18 hrs., 1,169 km. at 2200, US$13; to Tapachula, 9 hrs., at 1200, US$5.25, 483 km.; to Puebla at 1400, US$11.25, 1,034 km.; to Tuxtla Gutiérrez, 1½ hrs., 10 a day, US$0.90. Book tickets as far in advance as possible—during Christmas and Holy Week buses are sometimes fully booked for 10 days or more.

Transportes Tuxtla (often strikebound) has several 1st (US$2) and 2nd class (US$1.50) buses daily to Tuxtla Gutiérrez, and a 2nd class bus to Tapachula at 1330; to Tapachula via Motozintla: Transportes Tuxtla at 0800 and 0900, 5 hrs., then connections take about 3 hrs. to Tapachula. Cristóbal Colón 1st class; to Arriaga, at 1200 via Tuxtla Gutiérrez, 235 km., US$2.55; to Coatzacoalcos at 0630, 576 km., US$6.25; to Orizaba 845 km.; to Chiapa de Corzo, 64 km. There is a new road with fine views to Palenque, 210 km., of which some 25 km. are not yet paved; direct Lacandonia 2nd class bus to Palenque from 2nd class bus station on Calle Allende (where the 1st class bus station is also) at 0730 (arrives at 1330), US$2.80; First-class bus to Palenque, Trans. Tuxtla, 0600, 5½ hrs.; rough ride, expecially in rainy season. Other buses leave one at Ocosingo, US$2, 4 hrs. Refunds of fares to Palenque when reaching Ocosingo are not rare, and you then have to make your own way. Transportes Tuxtla has a 1st class service to Palenque via Villahermosa, 0900, 9 hrs., US$8.50, but road to Villahermosa described as treacherous.

Hitchhiking The San Cristóbal-Palenque road is not easy to hitch along. Part of it is still rough and unpaved, so not too many cars pass. It is served by *camionetas*, which charge whatever the market will bear.

Air Services No major aircraft can land here. San Cristóbal-Tuxtla Gutiérrez Tues., Thurs., Sat. at 1345, US$14.30, 84 km. (Tuxtla is the major local airport but see page 962). Regular daily flights, except Sundays, to Palenque, 0715 (some crashes); booking only at airport. Charter flights to see Lacanjá, Bonampak and Yaxchilán on the Usumacinta River, 7 hrs. in all (US$100 p.p.). All with Aerochiapas at airport; office Tel.: 80037. Office in Real de Guadalupe has closed. Santa Ana travel agency can book flights for Tuxtla (off Plaza). Also Jobel.

Excursions You are recommended to call at Na Bolom before visiting the villages, to get information on their cultures and seek advice on the reception you are likely to get. Photography is resisted by some Indians (see below) because they believe the camera steals their souls, and photographing their church is stealing the soul of God. Many Indians do not speak Spanish. On Sun. you can visit the villages of San Juan Chamula (horses can be hired near Na Bolom, to go here for a morning, at corner of Calle Comitán and Av. Vicente Guerrero, US$6.50 for horse and US$9

966 MEXICO

for guide, or from Julio González, who may be found at El Recoveco bookshop at 1900 each evening, US$4.50 per horse and the same for a guide), **Zinacantán** and Tenejapa. (Zinacantán is reached by VW bus from market, US$0.20, ½ hr. journey, sometimes frequent stops while conductor lights rockets at roadside shrines. The men wear pink/red jackets with embroidery and tassels, the women a vivid pale blue shawl and navy skirts. Main gathering place around church; the roof was recently destroyed by fire. Do *not* photograph anywhere or anything in Zinacantán.) You can catch a VW bus ride to **Chamula** every ½ hr., last at 1700, US$0.20 p.p. (or taxi, US$4) and visit the local church; a permit (US$0.30) is needed from the village tourist office and photographing inside the church is absolutely forbidden. (Two tourists were killed for ignoring the warning.) There are no pews but family groups sit or kneel on the floor with rows of candles lit in front of them, each representing a member of the family and certain significance attached to the colours of the candles, chanting. The religion is centred around the "talking stones", and three idols and certain Christian saints. Pagan rituals held in small huts at the end of August. Pre-Lent festival ends with celebrants running through blazing harvest chaff. Just after Easter prayers are held, before the sowing season starts. Festivals in Chamula should *not* be photographed. The men wear grey, black or light pink tunics, the women bright blue blouses with colourful braid and navy or bright blue shawls. Interesting walk from San Cristóbal to Chamula along the main road to a point one km. past the crossroads with the Periférico ring road (about 2½ km. from town centre); turn on to an old dirt road to the right—not sign-posted but 1st fork you come to between some farmhouses. Then back via the road through the village of Milpoleta, some 8 km. downhill, 5 hrs. for the journey round trip (allow 1 hr. for Chamula). Best not done in hot weather. The Sun. market at **Tenejapa** (pleasant small *pensión*) is very colourful, mainly fruit and vegetables, excellent woven items can be purchased from the weavers' cooperative near the church (and in San Cristóbal from the house at Calle 28 de Agosto 19). They also have a fine collection of old textiles in their regional ethnographic museum adjoining the handicraft shop. The cooperative can also arrange weaving classes. Buses leave from San Cristóbal market at 0700 and 1100 (1½ hr. journey). We were warned in mid-1983 that there was much violence in Tenejapa; probably best avoided for the moment. Market thins out by noon. Two other excursions can be made, by car or local bus, from San Cristóbal S on the Pan-American Highway (½ hr. by car) to **Amatenango del Valle**, a Tzeltal village where the women make and fire pottery in their yards, and then SE (15 min. by car) to Aguacatenango, picturesque village at the foot of a mountain. Continue 1 hr. along road past Villa las Rosas (hotel) to **Venustiano Carranza,** women with fine costumes, extremely good view of the entire valley. SE of San Cristóbal, 10 km., are the Grutas de San Cristóbal, caves with entrance in a beautiful park.

Get to outlying villages by bus or communal VW bus (both very packed); buses leave very early, and often don't return until next day, so you have to stay overnight; lorries are more frequent. To Zinacantán catch also VW bus from market. Buses from the market area to San Andrés Larrainzar (bus at 1000, 1100, 1400, overnight stay required, return at 0600) and Tenejapa. Transportes Fray Bartolomé de Las Casas, behind Transportes Tuxtla, has buses to Chanal, Chenalhó (US$13 with taxi, return, one hr. stay), Pantelhó, Yajalón and villages en route to Ocosingo. Transportes Lacandonia on Av. Crescencio Rosas also go to the interior villages of Huistán, Oxchuc, Yajalón, on the way to Palenque, Pujiltic, La Mesilla and Venustiano Carranza. If you are in San Cristóbal for a limited period of time it is best to rent a car to see the villages.

Warning Remember that locals are particularly sensitive to proper dress (i.e. men or women should not wear shorts, or revealing clothes) and manners; persistent begging should be countered with courteous, firm replies. It is best not to take cameras to villages: there are good postcards and photographs, e.g. at La Galería restaurant. Drunkenness is quite open and at times forms part of some of the celebration rituals—best not to take umbrage if accosted.

Follow the 170-km. paved road via Teopisca (*pensión*, F, comfortable), past **Comitán** (85 km.), a lively town at 1,580 metres above sea level with a large, shady Plaza, to the border (many pick-up trucks from Comitán) at Ciudad Cuauhtémoc (not a town, despite its name; just a few buildings and a small restaurant with basic rooms). A road branches off the Pan-American Highway 16 km. after Comitán to the very beautiful region of vari-coloured lakes, the **Lagunas de Montebello**; there are no restaurants or shops, but you can stay in Sra. Gloria's *cabañas*, cheap, pleasant, friendly. Frequent buses and VW Combis *from Comitán*. On the road to Montebello, 30 km from the Pan-American Highway, lie the ruins of Chinkultic, with temples, ballcourt, carved stone stelae and *cenote* (deep round lake); from the signpost they are about 4-5 km. along a dirt road and they close at 1600. Watch and ask for the very small sign and gate where road to ruins starts, worth visiting when passing, but difficult to get to without private transport.

Hotels in Comitán Accommodation inferior in quality and almost twice the price of San Cristóbal. *Robert's,* 1 Av. Poniente Sur, D, restaurant. *Los Lagos de Montebello*, on Pan-American

Highway, noisy but good, D; *Internacional*, E, near Plaza, decent restaurant. *Delfín*, on Plaza, F, fairly clean, as are *Hospedaje Santo Domingo*, Calle Central B. Juárez 45, F; *San Francisco*, F, and *Ideal*, F, both centrally located. *Morales*, main square, very comfortable, parking, restaurant and bar, F. *Casa de Huéspedes Río Escondido*, next to *Robert's*, F. *Posada Panamericana*, F, basic, and *Posada Maya*, F, both on 1 Av. Poniente Norte. *Hospedaje Comitán*, and *Posada Las Flores*, near Transportes Tuxtla bus terminal, basic, F. *Lety*, near Transportes Tuxtla bus station, clean. *Casa de Huéspedes Villa* is to be avoided.

Restaurants *Nevelandia*, clean, recommended, and *Café Casa de La Cultura*, on the Plaza. *L'Uccello*, Italian, 1 Av. Poniente Norte, recommended. *Cancún*, 2 Calle Sur Poniente. *Puerto Arturo* on the Pan-American Highway is good. Several small *comedores* on the Plaza.

N.B. It is very difficult to exchange Amex travellers' cheques in Comitán.

Buses marked Tziscao to the Lagunas de Montebello (60 km. from Comitán, about 2 hrs.), via the Lagunas de Siete Colores (so-called because the oxides in the water give varieties of colours) leave from 2 Av. Poniente Sur between 2 and 3 Calles, 4 blocks from Plaza in Comitán, the buses go as far as Laguna Bosque Azul; Tziscao is 9 km. along the road leading right from the park entrance, which is 3 km. before Bosque Azul; two buses a day Comitán-Tziscao, last at 1200, bumpy ride; the last bus back is at 1500 and connects with the 1930 bus to San Cristóbal. (Costs US$0.90.) VW Combis from Comitán bus station take half the time and cost only 10% more. The Bosque Azul area is now a reserve: there are, as well as picnic areas, a basic hostel at Lake Tziscao, (10 km., F, rooms for 4-6, no hot water, US$2.50 p.p., dirty kitchen facilities, camping US$1.60 per site incl. use of hotel facilities; boats for hire) small *comedores* and 2 very basic food shops, and there are small caves. The area is noted for its orchids and birdlife, including the famous *quetzal*; very crowded at weekends and holidays; better to stay at *Posada Las Orquídeas*, on the road to Montebello near Hidalgo and the ruins of Chinkultic, dormitory or cabin, F, family-run, very basic but friendly, small restaurant. 2 basic shops at Hidalgo.

N.B. Because of the Guatemalan refugee camps, it is now forbidden to travel further E by bus than Tziscao.

From Comitán the road winds down to the Guatemalan border at La Mesilla via La Trinitaria (restaurant but no hotel) and Ciudad Cuauhtémoc. Beyond, the El Tapón section, a beautiful stretch, leads to Huehuetenango, 85 km. This route is far more interesting than the one through Tapachula; the border crossing at La Mesilla is also reported as easier than that at Tapachula. A tourist card for Guatemala can be obtained at the border, normally available for 30 days, renewable in Guatemala City, US$1. Holders of most European passports do not need visas (note that the British do), only tourist cards. Visas are also available at the border but buses do not wait for those who alight to obtain them. You pay US$1 to enter Guatemala. Have your Mexican tourist card handy as it will be inspected at the Río San Gregorio, about 20 km. before the border. Don't change money with the Guatemalan customs officials: the rates they offer are worse than those given by bus drivers or in banks (and these are below the rates inside the country).

Buses The Cristóbal Colón bus (book seats in advance) leaves Comitán at 0930, 1800 and 2300 daily for the Guatemalan border at Ciudad Cuauhtémoc, fare US$1.50. Frequent 2nd-class buses also by Transportes Tuxtla. Another line leaves at 0745 for La Mesilla on the border. From here take a taxi to the Guatemalan side and get your passport stamped to allow entry for a month. Cristóbal Colón (terminal on the Pan-American Highway) has 1st class buses to Mexico City at 0900, 1100 and 1600 (which leave the border 2½ hrs. earlier), fare US$24; to Oaxaca at 0700 and 1900, US$14; to Tuxtla Gutiérrez at 0600 and 1600, US$3.50, and to Tapachula (via Arriaga) at 1200 and 1800, US$9. Transportes Tuxtla, 3 Calle Norte Poniente and 1 Av. Poniente Norte, has 6 1st class (US$3.50) and 8 2nd class (US$3.40) buses daily to Tuxtla Gutiérrez; a bus to Tapachula, via Arriaga, at 1100, US$11; to Arriaga at 1215; and 7 buses daily to Motozintla (connections to Tapachula), US$3.30.

Airport Flights available from Comitán to Lacanjá, Bonampak, Yaxchilán, contact Capitán Pérez Esquinca, Tel.: Comitán 4-91.

Travellers report that the Lacandón Indians at Lacanjá are rude and threatening if one doesn't buy their tourist wares.

N.B. Entering Mexico from Guatemala, it is forbidden to bring in fruit and vegetables; rigorous checking at two checkpoints to avoid the spread of plant diseases.

Yucatán Peninsula

Many tourists come to Yucatán, mostly to see the ancient Maya sites. The places which attract most visitors are Mérida, Palenque, Chichén Itzá and

968 MEXICO

Uxmal. A good paved road (four ferries) runs from Coatzacoalcos through Villahermosa, Campeche and Mérida (Route 180). All the great archaeological sites except Palenque are on or just off this road and its continuation beyond Mérida. An inland road has been built from Villahermosa to Campeche to avoid the ferries; it gives easy access to Palenque. A train from Mexico City to Mérida goes through Palenque; Pullman passengers can make the whole trip without leaving the car in 2 nights, US$20. Route 307 from Puerto Juárez to Chetumal is all paved and in very good condition; there is very little traffic. Air services from the USA and Mexico City are given under Mérida. Details of the direct road route, with buses, between Guatemala and Yucatán are given on page 981. The state of Quintana Roo is on the eastern side of the Yucatán Peninsula and has recently become the largest tourist area in Mexico with the development of the resort of Cancún, and the parallel growth of Isla Mujeres and Cozumel.

The peninsula of Yucatán is a flat land of tangled scrub in the drier north-west, merging into exuberant jungle and tall trees in the wetter south-east. There are no surface streams. The underlying geological foundation is a horizontal bed of limestone in which rainwater has dissolved enormous caverns. Here and there their roofs have collapsed, disclosing deep holes or *cenotes* in the ground, filled with water. Today this water is raised to surface-level by wind-pumps: a typical feature of the landscape. It is hot during the day but cool after sunset. Humidity is often high. All round the peninsula are splendid beaches fringed with palm groves and forests of coconut palms. The best time for a visit is from October to March.

The people are divided into two groups: the pure-blooded Maya Indians, the minority, and the *mestizos*. The Maya women wear *huipiles*, or white cotton tunics (silk for *fiestas*) which may reach the ankles and are embroidered round the square neck and bottom hem. Ornaments are mostly gold. A few of the men still wear straight white cotton (occasionally silk) jackets and pants, often with gold or silver buttons, and when working protect this dress with aprons. Carnival is the year's most joyous occasion, with concerts, dances, processions. Yucatán's folk dance is the Jarana, the man dancing with his hands behind his back, the woman raising her skirts a little, and with interludes when they pretend to be bullfighting. During pauses in the music the man, in a high falsetto voice, sings *bambas* (compliments) to the woman.

The Mayas are a courteous, gentle, strictly honest and scrupulously clean people. They drink little, except on feast days, speak Mayan, and profess Christianity laced with a more ancient nature worship. In Yucatán and Quintana Roo, the economy has long been dependent on the export of *henequén* (sisal), and chicle, but both are facing heavy competition from substitutes and tourism is becoming ever more important.

The early history and accomplishments of the Mayas when they lived in Guatemala and Honduras before their mysterious trek northwards is given in the introductory chapter on Central America. (See page 1006.) They arrived in Yucatán about A.D. 600 and later rebuilt their cities, but along different lines, probably because of the arrival of Toltecs in the ninth and tenth centuries. Each city was autonomous, and in rivalry with other cities. Before the Spaniards arrived the Mayas had developed a writing in which the hieroglyphic was somewhere between the pictograph and the letter. Bishop Landa collected their books, wrote a sinfully bad summary, the *Relación de las Cosas de Yucatán*, and with Christian but unscholarlike zeal burnt all his priceless sources.

In 1511 some Spanish adventurers were shipwrecked on the coast. Two survived. One of them, Juan de Aguilar, taught a Maya girl Spanish. She became interpreter for Cortés after he had landed in 1519. The Spaniards found little to please them: no gold, no concentration of natives, but Mérida was founded in 1542 and the few natives handed over to the conquerors in *encomiendas*. The Spaniards found them difficult to exploit: even as late as 1847 there was a major revolt, mainly arising from the inhuman conditions in the *henequén* plantations.

N.B.: Travellers have found that guards will not permit use of tripods for photography at sites.

Coatzacoalcos, 350,000 people, the gateway for Yucatán, was 1½ km. from the mouth of its wide river, but now has expanded down to it. It is hot, frantic and lacking in culture, and there is not much to do save watch the river traffic (river too polluted for fishing and swimming—less than salubrious discos on the beach by the pier at the river-mouth; beach is dangerous at nights, don't sleep there or loiter). Ocean-going vessels go upriver for 39 km. to **Minatitlán**, the oil and petrochemical centre (200,000 people; airport), whose huge oil refinery sends its products by pipeline to Salina Cruz. The road between the two towns carries very heavy industrial traffic. The offshore oil rigs are serviced from Coatzacoalcos. Sulphur is exported from the mines, 69 km. away.

Coatzacoalcos Hotels Very difficult as all hotels are used by oil workers. Don't spend the night on the street if you can't find lodging. Prices double those of hotels elsewhere. *Lemarroy; Oliden; Ritz; Tubilla; Palacio; Margón; Valgrande, Hotel Doce* (renamed *Carilla*), F, with shower,

MEXICO 969

basic. *Motel Colima* at km. 5, Carretera Ayucan-Coatzacoalcos, may have rooms if none in Coatzacoalcos; it is clean, in a quiet position, but does have a lot of red-light activity.

Restaurants Meals at *Gloria Café*; *Los Lopitos*, Hidalgo 615, good *tamales* and *tostadas*. Cheap restaurants on the top floor of the indoor market near the bus terminal. There is a 24-hr. restaurant in one of the streets just off the main Plaza, good *empanadas* with cream.

British Vice-Consul (also Lloyd's agent), Lerdo 202.

Bus to Mexico City, US$11; to Mérida US$12.25. To Veracruz (312 km, US$3.65, 7¼ hrs.), Ciudad del Carmen (US$7.35), Salina Cruz (US$2); to Minatitlán, to which taxis also ply. To Villahermosa, US$3.

Rail Railway station is 5 km. from town at Cuatro (for Mexico City and Mérida) at end of Puerto Libre bus route and on Playa Palma Sola route, smelly and dingy, the through train is swept out here; irregular bus services. Better walk about ½ km. to the main road and get a bus there, US$0.10. Train to Tehuantepec takes 13 hrs. (208 km.). Train to Mérida (at 1240). Train to Palenque, 1600. Coatzacoalcos-Campeche at 2030. Another station, in the city centre, serves Salina Cruz, small and dingy. The train to Salina Cruz leaves daily at 0700, costs US$2.50 for the 12 hr. journey 2nd class.

Air Services Minatitlán airport, 30 mins.

Cárdenas 116 km. from Coatzacoalcos and 48 km. from Villahermosa, is headquarters of the Comisión del Grijalva, which is encouraging regional development. Between Cárdenas and Villahermosa are many stalls selling all varieties of bananas, a speciality of the area, and the road passes through the Samaria oilfield. (From Chontalpa there is irregular transport to Raudales on the lake formed by the Netzahualcoyotl dam.) It is very hard to find accommodation in Cárdenas, *Hotel Xol-Ou*, cheapest, E, with bath, a/c, parking, clean, on main plaza.

Villahermosa, capital of Tabasco state, is on the River Grijalva, navigable to the sea. It is very hot and rainy. The Centro de Investigaciones de las Culturas Olmecas is set in a new modern complex with a restaurant, airline offices and souvenir shops, a few minutes' walk S out of town along the river bank. Three floors of well laid out displays of Mayan and Olmec artefacts. Entry US$1, opens at 0900. The cathedral, ruined in 1973, is to be rebuilt. Paved road to Coatzacoalcos and another S to the railway at Teapa, 50 km.; paved road to Tuxtla Gutiérrez (page 961). Population, over 110,000. The tourist office is in the 1st class bus station and there is another close to the La Venta park, at Paseo Grijalva and Paseo Tabasco, closed 1300-1600. Villahermosa is heaving under pressure from the oil boom, which is why it is now such an expensive place. Buses to Mexico City are often booked up well in advance, as are hotel rooms, especially during the holiday season (May onwards). Overnight free parking (no facilities) in the Campo de Deportes. It is hard to find swimming facilities in Villahermosa—Ciudad Deportiva pool for cardholders only. There is a bull ring. There is a warren of modern colonial-style pedestrian malls throughout the central area. Warning: Ash Wednesday is celebrated from 1500 to dusk by the throwing of water in balloon bombs and buckets at anyone, regardless of dress, who happens to be on the street.

Hotels The price difference between a reasonable and a basic hotel can be negligible, so one might as well go for the former. Best is *Exalaris Hyatt*, Juárez 106, all services, L; *Aristos, Maya-Tabasco, Presidente*, are all on Paseo Tabasco, all services, A; *Manzur*, C, Madero 422, central, slightly faded, good restaurant (accepts American Express card— one of the few that do) nearby parking; *San Rafael*, Constitución 232, F, with bath, no hot water, clean; *Pino Suárez*, Pino Suárez y Magallanes, bath and fan, F; *Olmeca*, D, Reforma 304, central, good, fridge in room, restaurant; *El Choco*, Merino 100, E, friendly, clean, a/c; *La Paz*, near ADO bus station, basic, F; *Ritz*, Madero 1013, fairly smart, a/c, E; *Orient*, E, Madero 441, central; *Madero*, Madero 301, E, hot water, good value; *San Francisco*, Madero 604, D, near a small park; *Buenos Aires*, Constitución 216, D; *María Dolores*, Aldama 104, a/c, E, hot showers, excellent restaurant (closed Sundays); *Palma de Mallorca*, Madero 516, quiet, a/c, E, parking lot 2 blocks N of hotel on Madero run by family. *Caballero*, Lerdo 307, clean, good, E; *San Miguel*, Lerdo 315, good value, but some rooms damp, no hot water p.m., E; *Aurora*, Av. 27 de Febrero 623, cheap for Villahermosa, basic, hot showers, E; *Sofía*, Zaragoza 408, D, central, tolerable but overpriced, a/c. *Viva*, near La Venta, very good, D. There is a CREA youth hostel at the Ciudad Deportiva, but it doesn't accept travellers arriving in the evening (4 km. SW of the bus station).

N.B. Tourists are often wiser to go directly to Palenque for rooms; cheaper and no competition from business travellers. Villahermosa can be difficult for lone women: local men's behaviour said to be aggressive because of eating iguanas.

970 MEXICO

Camping at the old airport, near Parque La Venta, mosquitoes.

Restaurants *El Mural*, highly recommended, 4-course lunch with drink included, US$4, dinner US$8, with band; *La Embajada*, good local food, suckling pig is the best, open for lunch only; *La Rueda* serves good local specialities; the *Casino* for odd dishes like turtle steaks and dogfish; *Los Azulejos* serves good lunch for US$2.40; *Restaurant Kathy*, Av. Constitución 204, reasonable prices; avoid the bad and expensive tourist eating places on and near the river front.

Airport Daily services to Mexico City, Tuxtla Gutiérrez, Mérida, and one to Oaxaca-Acapulco-Guadalajara, from airport 15 km. SE, out along the Palenque road, VW bus to town US$3 p.p., taxi US$7 for 2. Local flights to Palenque and Bonampak.

Local Transport Taxis now mainly on a fixed-route collective system, which can be a problem if you have a different destination in mind. You may have to wait a long time before a driver without fares agrees to take you. Bus station (ADO) with restaurant, but very uncomfortable owing to poor ventilation, 20 min.-walk to centre; has lockers for left luggage for 24 hrs., US$1. Information office at this station unhelpful. The 2nd class bus station is only 5 mins. walk from centre and 2½ blocks from 1st class station but is usually in disarray and it is difficult to get a ticket. Mind your belongings.

Buses Several buses (1st class) to Mexico City, US$16, 15 hrs., direct bus leaves 1730, expect to wait a few hours for Mexico City buses and at least ½ hr. in the ticket queue; to Campeche, US$5 (6 hrs.); to Coatzacoalcos, US$2; to Tapachula, US$9, 14 hrs.; to Mérida 8 hrs., 1030, US$9.50 (ADO) (extremely difficult to book, better go 2nd class from Palenque, see page 971) leaves at 0920; to San Cristóbal, US$4.50, 9 hrs.; also 2nd class bus with one change at Tuxtla, leaves 0800, arrives 2100, fine scenery but treacherous road. Cristóbal Colón from ADO terminal to Oaxaca via Coatzacoalcos and Tehuantepec at 0800 and 1900, 1st class, stops at about 7 places, US$10. Bus to Veracruz, US$7, 8 hrs.; to Chetumal US$8.50, 7 hrs., four buses. To Catazaja, US$2, 1½ hrs. To Palenque 2nd class several, one direct but crowded at 1230, 2½ hrs.; Circuito Maya, US$2.60; 1st class 1000 (buy ticket day before) and 1700.

Excursion NW of Villahermosa are the Maya ruins of **Comalcalco**, easily reached by bus (3 a day by ADO, US$1.20, or local Zimillera bus, US$0.90 over dirt roads). The ruins are unique in Mexico because the palaces and pyramids are built of bricks, long and narrow like ancient Roman bricks, and not of stone. From Comalcalco go to **Paraíso** on the coast, frequent buses from town. Interesting covered market, good cocoa. *Centro Turístico* beach hotel, D, clean, no hot water, food and drink expensive. Also hotel in Paraíso main square.

In 1925 an expedition discovered huge sculptured human and animal figures, urns and altars in almost impenetrable forest at La Venta, 96 km. from Villahermosa. About 1950 the monuments were threatened with destruction by the discovery of oil nearby. The poet Carlos Pellicer got them hauled all the way to a woodland area near Villahermosa, now the Parque La Venta with scattered lakes, next to a children's playground and almost opposite the old airport entrance on the edge of town. There they are dispersed in various small clearings. The huge heads—one of them weighs 20 tons—are Olmec, a culture which flourished about 1150-150 B.C. Be sure to take insect-repellant for the visit. It takes 1 hr. to walk around, excellent guides, speak Spanish and English. There is also a zoo of lonely, dispirited and wretched creatures from the Tabasco jungle: monkeys, alligators, deer, wild pigs and birds. Open 0830-1700, entrance US$1, bus, marked "Gracitol", Villahermosa-La Venta from bus terminal US$0.40. Bus Circuito No. 1 from outside 2nd class bus terminal goes past La Venta.

Further Travel If the Villahermosa-Mexico City bus is booked up, try taking the train from **Teapa** (buses run between Teapa and Villahermosa), 1st class pullman fare, US$25. The dining car is good but very expensive. Check in rainy season whether bridges are OK. (It took one passenger 56 hrs. to travel some 950 km. after being diverted). Vendors ply the train with local foods and drinks. Journey 14 hrs. Teapa is a nice, clean little town with several cheap hotels (*Casa de Huéspedes Mija*, F, in the main street) and beautiful surroundings. The square is pleasant, and you can swim in the river or in the sulphur pool, El Azufre and cavern of Cocona (dear). From Teapa, Tapijulapa on the Chiapas border can be visited, beautiful views. Bus to Chiapa de Corzo at 0730, 7 hrs., US$4, lovely, mountainous landscape (see page 963).

80 km. SW of Villahermosa on Route 195 is **Pichucalco**, a very quiet town with some interesting tiles in the main Plaza. *Hotel México*, on left turn from bus station, E, with bath, fan, clean but musty; *Vila*, on Plaza, *Jardín*, F, noisy, *La Selva*. Buses almost every hour to Villahermosa, US$1.50.

From Villahermosa you can fly to Campeche, or sometimes by a small plane carrying 3 passengers, to Palenque, which can also be reached by the new paved road from Villahermosa to Campeche (no gas stations until the Palenque turn-off; if you look like running out, turn left half-way for Macuspana, where there is one). This road has a turning at 117 km. from Villahermosa for Palenque, 26 km. away on a good paved but winding road. (If short of time you can fly Mérida-Villahermosa at 0655, hire car at Villahermosa airport, drive to Palenque and back with 3½ hrs. at ruins, and catch 2205 flight from Villahermosa to Mexico City. The Editor did it.) Palenque can also be

MEXICO 971

reached by an almost fully-paved road from San Cristóbal de Las Casas, a beautiful ride via *Ocosingo* (25 km. of unpaved road to be used with caution during rainy season in summer as mud makes it impassable for any vehicle). Ocosingo (not particularly attractive) has many new hotels (two E, of which the best is on the main street across from the Plaza, *Central* on Plaza, F, shower, clean, verandah, and several others F) and clean restaurants. Road to ruins of **Tonina,** 12 km. away, is unpaved but marked with signs once you leave Ocosingo (jeep recommended); well worth visiting the ruins excavated by a French government team. Temples are in the Palenque style with internal sanctuaries in the back room. Stelae are in very diverse forms, as are wall panels, and some are in styles and in subject unknown at any other Mayan site. Ask guardian to show you second unrestored ballcourt and the sculpture kept at his house. (Take drinks with you; nothing available at the site.) The Agua Azul waterfalls (see page 973) are between Tonina and Palenque, on your left. The improved road to Palenque from San Cristóbal (Route 195) is dangerous because of mudslides and subsidence. Excellent road from Campeche, 5 hrs.' drive, only rough stretch about 1 hr. from Palenque; toll bridge US$0.60.

Palenque, 143 km. from Villahermosa (public transport difficult Sun.), is a splendid experience, with its series of hilltop temples in remarkably good condition. It is best to visit the ruins early in the morning. The site is in a jungle clearing (with interesting wildlife, mainly birds, but also including mosquitoes) on a steep green hill overlooking the plain and crossed by a clear cascading brook (swimming allowed at pools downstream from the museum). The ruins are impressive indeed, particularly the Pyramid of the Inscriptions, in the heart of which was discovered an intact funerary crypt with the Sarcophagus of the Sun God (you walk from the top of the pyramids into a staircase, descending to ground level, before having to walk up again, very humid; illuminated 1000-1600 only), the temples around, with fantastic comb-like decorations on their intact roofs, and the sculptured wall panels, undoubtedly the most exquisite achievement of the Mayas. Check time of opening of crypt. A path behind the Temple of Inscriptions leads through jungle to a small ruined temple—if you continue for 8 km. the path leads to a friendly village, the only means of access. A small museum at the ruins has some excellent classical Mayan carvings (open 1000—more like 1100—to 1700). Entry to ruins, US$0.20 (Sun. US$0.10), charge for car parking. Special permission required for videos and super-8 cameras. The site opens at 0800 and closes at 1700 (guide, up to 10 people). Beware of thieves at all times. The ruins are 8 km. from the village. A restaurant by the cascades serves a limited range of food (stores luggage—compulsory on entering the ruins, no receipt—for US$0.40); shops quick to overcharge.

Bus service from station to town, 5 km. goes to local bus station, but unhelpful, be prepared to wait. Taxi from station to ruins US$1.35 p.p. with 4 people. Taxi, ruins to town US$1.20. Bus to the ruins from 2nd class bus station every 3 hrs. from 0600, 20 mins, US$0.25 until 1630. From the village to the ruins: either take a taxi, or a white VW minibus from Pemex gas station, or corner of Hidalgo and Allende, or the Plaza end of 5 de Mayo, or the Mayan head near 2nd class terminal, US$0.20, 15 mins., from 0600-1700, every ½ hr. or so. Some buses have been seen at 0600, 0930 and 1330 (marked "Ruinas") from *Hotel León* or at Pemex gas station at the top of the village. It is convenient to stay at hotels near this gas station, as they are also nearer the ruins and the 2nd class bus station.

Hotels near Palenque Ruins (Prices treble around *fiesta* time.) *Misión Palenque,* far end of town in countryside, complete resort, C; *Motel de Las Ruinas* within walking distance of the ruins, D, very clean and good, has swimming pool, waterfall just above. *Motel La Cañada,* very rustic, E, with fan, lovely garden, good restaurant, the owner, Sr. Morales, is an expert on the ruins. *Motel Chan Ka Inn,* at Km. 31, halfway between village and ruins, D, swimming pool fed from river, beautiful gardens, perfectly clean; *Centro Turístico Tulijá,* D, car park, satisfactory and convenient; hot water if you make them turn it on; also bungalows, 10 km. from ruins, first as you enter village; reasonable restaurant; pool, book local flights here. *Hotel and Trailer Park Tulipanes,* Calle Cañada 6, D, a/c, or fan, garage, bar, restaurant and pool; *Lacroix,* 2 blocks from Zócalo, F, will charge full room price for one or two, lazy fan, no hot water, friendly, clean, good for motorcyclists; *Palenque,* off Zócalo, E, with bath, a/c restaurant, vast, rambling menage, poor plumbing and service, has good rooms, pool, night-time robberies reported, usually through bathroom windows, management unhelpful; long-distance telephone office here. *Casa de Pakal,* 1 block from Zócalo, D, a/c, TV, very good; next door is *Mi-Sol-Ha,* fan, very clean, well-booked, with bath, E. *Avenida,* opp. 2nd-class bus station above cinema on 20 de Noviembre, with restaurant, clean, large rooms, F, but does not display price in rooms so ask for government list to check, no hot showers, some rooms with balcony. *Regional,* 2 blocks from Plaza, F, 100 m. from bus station, no hot showers, get an upstairs room with fan, clean. *Vaca Vieja,* 5 de Mayo, 3 blocks from Plaza, popular with

972 MEXICO

gringos, good value, hot showers, E, cafeteria; *Pensión Chapito*, Av. 20 de Noviembre, F. *Posada Alicia*, Av. Manuel Velásquez Suárez, G, clean and cheap, owner unfriendly, mixed reports, rooms on left as you enter are cooler.

Camping *Trailer Park Palenque* nr. entrance to town, good, US$4 p.p. *Trailer Park Mayabel*, a bit scruffy, on road to ruins 2 km. before entrance (bus from town US$0.20) for caravans and tents, hammocks permitted, also for rent, US$1 for tent or to sling hammock, palmleaf huts, clean toilets and showers, good restaurant; many ticks in long grass. Watch your belongings. At night, around 0100, one can often hear the howler monkeys screaming in the jungle; quite eerie. *Camping El Tucán*, 500 metres before *Mayabel*, F, cheap food and drink, can be muddy, Canadian-run, beer. Good swimming at *Balneario and Hotel Nututún*, 3 km. along Palenque-Ocosingo road, US$1.10 camping site per night, no tent rentals, showers, toilets, disco bar, at restaurant with laughable service; and beautiful lake and waterfall open to the public for a small fee. Misolhá, 2 km. off same road at km. 19, large paved car-park for camping, good bathing; small cave, with bats, where water springs from.

Restaurants *Maya*, on plaza, good value; at moderately priced *Tarde*, or rough restaurant *El Jade* in town. Water is often hard to get in the area. There is a good and friendly restaurant on Av. Juárez, *Los Trota Mundos*, opp. *Hotel Avenida*, French owner, slow and rather expensive, less on offer than on menu, has tourist information. *Artemio*, Av. Hidalgo, nr. Plaza, good, reasonably-priced food. *Las Carmelitas*, good service, reasonably priced; At Av. Benito Juárez 77, *Nicte-Ha* on the plaza, unfriendly, interminable service, but good food. *Comedor La Terminada*, off the main street, good value. *Tertulia*, opp. *Hotel Regional*, good steaks, recommended.

N.B. We are told that the large influx of young "hippie-like" people has put off the locals, and visitors may be given misleading information. Also, the Federal police are very strict on tourist cards—*always* keep it with you, even when eating in your hotel. The penalty is searches and jail, with large fines. Visitors should respect the local customs and dress in such a way as not to offend—men should wear footwear and always a shirt; women wearing shorts are unwelcome.

Tourist Office in the municipal offices on plaza, open 0900-1300 and 1700-2000 (maybe). Post Office in the same building, on left-hand side.

Banks Exchange rate only comes through at 1030, until then yesterday's rate prevails. At weekends travellers' cheques will not be changed but the owner at Farmacia Central will change US$ at a reasonable rate.

Buses 1st class bus to Mexico City, at 1600 and 1800, 14 hrs., 1,006 km., US$17. First-class bus goes daily from the ADO terminal at Villahermosa at 0800, arriving at 1030, and returns from ruins at 1600, take food and drink, return fare US$5. Also at 1700 1st class bus to Villahermosa. Buy return ticket from the ruins on arrival, otherwise the driver may not let you get on for the stretch ruins-Palenque. 2nd class bus to Villahermosa at 0800 and 1230, from the bus depot in the suburbs (on 20 de Noviembre, opp. *Hotel Avenida*). Bus 2nd class, to Campeche, US$5, 6 hrs., daily at 1700, overcrowded, arrive early. One direct bus a day from Campeche, leaves 0200, US$2 (2nd), but if you wish to travel in the daytime there is a bus to Emiliano Zapata 0900 and 1400 (*Hotel Ramos*, opp. bus station, F, reasonable restaurant, friendly, bad mattresses; at least 4 other hotels in town, F and E—one by the entrance to town near the Pemex station. No alcohol on Sun.). From Emiliano Zapata you can make connections to Campeche and Mérida. Daily 2nd class bus to Mérida only at 1700 (566 km.), numbered seats bookable from 0730, US$8.80, 8 hrs., scheduled to arrive at Campeche 2300, arrives in Mérida in the middle of the night (perhaps better to take 0800 to Villahermosa or 0900 to Emiliano Zapata and travel on from there). (Also to Francisco Escárcega, 3 hrs.).

To San Cristóbal de Las Casas via Villahermosa by 1st-class minibus, 8 hrs. or more, leaves at 0800 and 1230, US$6; 1st class buses at 0700 and 1030, US$2.30; four second class buses a day to San Cristóbal direct (6 hrs.), US$2.80 via Ocosingo, also goes to Tuxtla Gutiérrez, or 1230 via Pichucalco, 9 hrs. Tuxtla Gutiérrez (no 1st class buses) at 0800, 9 hrs., 377 km., US$3, and San Cristóbal de Las Casas (and not far from the railway station either). The San Cristóbal-Villahermosa road has been described as "treacherous". Some buses go 63 km. past ruins to the beautiful Agua Azul waterfalls (see below). Palenque-Flores: two routes, one via River San Pedro, 5-8 hrs., the other via the River Usumacinta (see also page 981) going to Chancalá with the 1200 bus and continuing by bus (evening or early morning) to Frontera Echeverría. From Echeverría boats go up the river in Guatemala, to Sayaxché. No direct bus Palenque-Tuxtepec, but can be done using 7 different buses, staying overnight at, say, Acayucan.

Trains There are trains daily from Mexico City at 2010, US$35 in sleeper, US$10 1st class, US$3.50 2nd class (filthy toilets), up to 31 hrs. (book Palenque hotel in advance). Tickets on sale from Estación de Ferrocarril Buenavista on day of departure after a certain hour, no numbered seats; it is apparently impossible to buy 1st class tickets in Palenque for Mexico City but you pay 1st class because from Coatzacoalcos the carriages are treated as 1st class—this is accepted practice. Railway station for Palenque is 10 km. outside town (bus goes from in front of *Posada Alicia* at 2000). Taxi, railway station to Pemex service station US$1 for 2. The slow train from Campeche to Palenque leaves at 2030 (beware of thieves), arrives at 1100. *Rápido* train to Mérida at 0500

MEXICO 973

hrs., daily, usually late, takes about 11 hrs., keep your luggage with you, US$5, 1st (only one car) very comfortable, US$3, 2nd, dirty and smelly. Tickets on sale one hour before train arrives. The train may be crowded so it may be necessary to stand all the way. Your best bet is to arrange for the *dormitorio* (only one) ahead of time or, if permitted, to pay for *dormitorio* when on train, without purchasing seating ticket first. It is reported that the train is sometimes unreliable with delays of up to 11 hrs. Slow, 2nd class only train to Mérida at 1400 and 1900, at least 16 hrs., no light (beware of thieves). Make certain you catch the right train as there are two stopping very close together. **N.B.** If returning from Palenque to Mérida on the night train, bear in mind that in Dec. and Jan. it is nearly impossible to make reservations.

Air Travel Light aircraft Palenque-San Cristóbal (watch for Agua Azul falls 5-10 mins into flight) with Aerochiapas, Tel.: 80037, 8 people, supposed to leave at 0715, but more like 0830, provided there isn't a better offer to fly into the jungle. Tickets either at airstrip (shed only), or from Arrendadora de Carros Ik, two doors away from *Restaurante Maya* (on Plaza) in Palenque town. Aviacsa flies from Palenque to Villahermosa and Tuxtla, Tel.: 50210.

Other Sites Flights from Palenque to **Bonampak** and **Yaxchilán** (no hotel or refreshments), in light plane for 4, US$200 p.p., to both places, whole trip 6 hrs. Prices set, list available; Aviación de Chiapas at Av. Benito Juárez and Allende, open 0800-1330 and 1600-1800, Sat. 0800-1400, to Bonampak; book at airport (visitors report that the journey is less worthwhile since the famous murals are being damaged by insects and water and are practicably unrecognizable); Yaxchilán more interesting. Do not visit ruins at night, it is forbidden. Otherwise hire a jeep at Palenque and drive there yourself, but since there is greater demand than supply of jeeps, make arrangements as soon as possible; new road to Yaxchilán; day tours from Palenque by road for US$20 p.p. Bonampak is 12 km. from Frontera Echeverría (food, gasoline and accommodation) and can be reached only on foot from the crossroads with the road to Echeverría and then with great difficulty (all maps are inaccurate, directions must be asked frequently). Beware of sandflies, black flies which cause river blindness, and mosquitoes— there is basic accommodation at the site, take hammock and mosquito net. Sturdy boots are needed for the 3½ hr. walk to the ruins. The workers are not to be trusted. There are many new roads criss-crossing the Selva Lacandona (jungle), most going to Echeverría.

The Río Usumacinta, on the Chiapas border with Guatemala, is being dammed. Three dams are projected just downstream from Piedras Negras ruins. The ruins are accessible only by white water rafts, no road, no airstrip, unspoiled jungle (NW of Yaxchilán).

Agua Azul, a series of beautiful waterfalls aptly named for the blue water swirling over natural tufa dams that have over the ages created the cascades over 7 km. of fast-flowing river, is a popular camping spot reached by an exceptionally bad 4-km. dirt road from the junction with the road to San Cristóbal (this stretch is paved), 65 km. from Palenque. Best visited in dry season as in the rainy season it is hard to swim because of the current (don't visit if it was raining the day before). It is extremely popular at holiday time. Some direct buses (and minibuses from Palenque at 1000, returning at 1300) daily, e.g. 0730, US$1, 2nd class, 2 hours., about 5 buses at 1000 and 1200, though you may be deposited at the junction; otherwise take bus to Ocosingo and get out at the junction (US$0.35, 1½ hours), and walk the 4 km. downhill to the falls. The Palenque minibus stops a few minutes at Mi Sol Ha waterfalls. There are one or two buses daily between San Cristóbal de Las Casas and Palenque (to 2nd class bus station, Transporte Maya) which will stop there, but a number of others need changing at Temo, over 20 km. away, N of Ocosingo, which may require a fair wait. Entrance fee to this *ejidal* park US$0.15 on foot, US$0.50 for cars, US$0.50 per tent for camping, parking a trailer or using a hammock. There are a few restaurants (not very good) and also a *cabaña* for hammocks. The village to one side has, as its main street, the Agua Azul airport runway.

Beware of ticks when camping in long grass, use kerosene to remove them. Watch out carefully for thieves; bring your own food, etc. Flies abound during the rainy season (June-November).

Villahermosa to Guatemala by car is by route 195 and 190 to Ciudad Cuauhtémoc via San Cristóbal de Las Casas. Highway 195 is fully paved, but narrow and winding with landslides and washouts in the rainy season, high altitudes, beautiful scenery. If this route is impassable, travel back by route 180 to Acayucan, to 190, via 185 and go to Ciudad Cuauhtémoc or by route 200 to Tapachula.

Villahermosa to Chetumal, on the Belize frontier: Highway 186 (paved), branches off to the SE from **Francisco Escárcega** with interesting ruins at Chicana (145 km.), Becán (watch for very small sign— 146 km.), X-Puhil (153 km.), via Francisco Villa (217 km.); see below. The road is in excellent condition and there is very little traffic. There are a couple of military checkpoints en route where documents must be shown.

Francisco Escárcega hotels are expensive because of the oil boom; *Motel Ah Kim Pech*, F, reasonable restaurant, nice rooms; good restaurant across from the motel; *Casa de Huéspedes Lolita* on

974 MEXICO

Chetumal highway at E end of town, F, pleasant; *Hotel Bertha*, E, with bath, fairly clean; *Escárcega*, F, good value. Restaurant at ADO terminal is hot, slow and overpriced. Also bank, market and motor repairs. Beside Highway 186, near Km. 231, W of Escárcega (near the turnoff for Candelaria) is a roosting spot for white ibis, also known as Ojo de Agua. Bus Escárcega to Palenque at 0430, US$4.75, 3 hrs.; the town is on the Mexico City-Palenque-Mérida railway line. Only train leaves at 0300, crowded. Bus, Escárcega-Chetumal, 3½ hrs.

Chetumal, the capital of the state of Quintana Roo, now being developed for tourism (albeit slowly), is a free port with clean wide streets, and a greatly improved waterfront with parks and trees. Good for foreign foodstuffs—cheaper at covered market in outskirts than in centre. Some travellers have warned that there are many drunks roaming the streets; also many mosquitoes and high prices. Villahermosa to Chetumal by car, 6-7 hours. Airport.

N.B. Now that Quintana Roo is no longer a territory but a state, it is illegal to sell cars and other imported goods there. Visas to Guatemala can be obtained in Chetumal (Consulate, Alvaro Obregón 342, US$10 for 30 days, one entry open) but not in Belize City. Hitching is difficult to the Belizean border. Cars with light-green licence plates are a form of taxi and want payment.

Hotels at Chetumal (accommodation may be a problem during the holiday season); most are 4 blocks from bus terminal, turn right as you leave. *Continental Caribe*, D; *El Presidente*, rather scruffy and poorly equipped, quiet, overpriced restaurant, D; *Real Azteca*, E, cheerful, friendly and clean, but no hot showers; *San Jorge*, E, car parking, highly recommended; *Ucum*, 1 block from bus station, F, not too friendly but clean, good value; *Pensión Tabasco*, check for cleanliness, fan, F, with bath; *El Dorado*, Av. 5 de Mayo 21, D, hot water, a/c, overpriced (no restaurant); *América*, F, on Juárez, 1 block from Héroes, basic, but friendly, six blocks downhill from bus station on the right; *Tulum*, F, beside bus terminal; *Bahía* on sea front, F. *Luz María*, friendly but not very clean, F, owner speaks English; *Brasilia*, opp. bus station, F, with bath and fan; *Baroudi*, Obregón y Héroes, cheap, basic, small rooms with cockroaches, sometimes no water, good value; *María Dolores*, Alvaro Obregón 206, both F; *Dorys*, Avenida Héroes 41a, F, dirty, rats, never any water for shower; opp. is *Big Ben*, E, clean, pleasant and safe, but a bit overpriced. Plenty more. CREA Youth Hostel, corner Gen. Anaya and Obregón, hot water.

Restaurants   Near and at bus station, clean and cheap, also one next door to *Hotel Ucum*, which is reasonable. *Grijalva* on Lázaro Cárdenas. *Hadad*, corner of Héroes and Blanco, reasonable, open on Sun., vegetarian meal of the day, homemade yoghurt. Cheap snacks at *Lonchería Ivette* on Mahatma Ghandi 154 (left out of bus station and right on 1st street). *La Charca de las Ranas Verdes*, opp. bandstand, cheap and good; *Sergio Pizza*, same block as *Hotel Baroudi*, good drinks too. Generally difficult to find restaurants Sunday night. *Caribe*, near park, with bandstand, near water, recommended. *Viky* on Isla Cancún, ½ block W of the N side of the market, good local dishes, good value. The *Vaticano*, on the same street has good *tamales*. *Los de Colores*, Zaragoza and Juárez, good fish.

Shopping   Shops are open from 0800-1300 and 1800-2000. For exchange, Banamex (0900-1330) on corner of Juárez and Obregón, may need to wait till 1100 for rates.

Garage   Talleres Barrera, helpful, on Primo de Verdad; turn right off main street that passes market, then past the electrical plant.

Buses   Bus station is on Héroes y Aguilar. Bus companies won't take US dollars as payment. Many buses going to the border, US$0.15; taxi from Chetumal to border, 20 minutes, US$4 for two. ADO to Mexico City, 22 hrs., US$28, leaves at 0900, 1300, 2000, 2230 daily via Villahermosa (8 hrs.); bus to Francisco Escárcega, 3½ hrs., US$3, 2nd class (2 in the morning, then at 1700 and 2100); from Chetumal to Palenque, better connections at Emiliano Zapata (bus there at 0900) than Francisco Escárcega, more buses daily, but must take bus from E. Zapata to Catazaja, thence minibus or cheap taxi to Palenque. Bus to Mérida, 6 a day, US$6.60 1st class, about 5½ hrs. To Felipe Carrillo Puerto, US$1.75, 1½ hrs., many, on excellent road. To Cancún, 6 hrs., boring road, about 8 daily, between 0630 and 2400. To Tulum, five (2nd class) a day, 4 hrs., US$2.90.

Batty Bus and Venus Bus to Belize, several daily taking 3½-4½ hrs on new road (0500 or 0630 Batty bus to make direct connection with Guatemalan frontier), US$3.50 in pesos or Belize dollars. Be there at least one hour before to get a seat—pay on bus. If avoiding travel at night on the first day in Belize take an afternoon bus as far as Corozal, continuing the next morning to Belize City. Bus Chetumal-Orange Walk, US$1.40. Money checked on entering Belize. Excess Mexican pesos are easily changed into Belizean dollars with men waiting just beyond customs on the Belize side. West German and Austrian citizens *must* have a visa to enter Belize, obtainable at Mérida for US$8, takes two days. To hitch once inside Belize, it is best to take the *colectivo* from in front of the hospital (1 block from the bus station, ask) marked "Chetumal-Santa Elena", US$0.30. You can change US for Belizean dollar bills in the shops at the border, at a rather poor rate. Note that on the Mexican side border guards can be rather offhand and indolent. **N.B.** If travelling by car be at

MEXICO 975

the border before 1500 to have your papers checked. On entering Belize you must purchase car insurance. The road Chetumal-Belize is now largely paved.

W of Chetumal, just before turn to Belize, a restaurant. Just N of Chetumal is Laguna de los Milagros, a beautiful lagoon, and 34 km. N of Chetumal, on the road to Tulum (page 989), is Cenote Azul, over 70 metres deep, with an expensive waterside restaurant serving good regional food and a new and well-equipped trailer park (Apartado 88, Chetumal). About 3 km. N of Cenote Azul is the village of Bacalar (nice, but not special) on the Laguna de Siete Colores; swimming and skin-diving. There is a frequent minibus service from the street alongside the electricity generating plant in Chetumal, US$0.35 s. There is a Spanish fort there; hotel and good restaurants on the Laguna. *Buk-Halot*, E, and a cheap but comfortable *casa de huéspedes* near the fort on the park. Camping possible at the end of the road 100 metres from the lagoon, toilets and shower, US$0.10, but lagoon perfect for washing and swimming; gasoline is sold in a side-street. About 2 km. S of Bacalar (on left-hand side of the road going towards the village) is *Hotel Las Lagunas*, very good, swimming pool and opp. a sweet-water lake, E; restaurant is, however, overpriced.

From Chetumal one can visit the fascinating Mayan ruins that lie on the way to Francisco Escárcega. Buses leave at 0600 (2nd class) from Chetumal to Francisco Villa and X-Puhil; there is no direct transport to Kohunlich, Becán and Chicana, so from X-Puhil the following journey must be done privately. Just before Francisco Villa lie the ruins of **Kohunlich** (entry US$0.40), about 7 km. S to the main road, where there are fabulous masks (early classic, A.D. 250-500) set on the side of the main pyramid, still bearing red colouring; they are unique of their kind. Seven km. further on from **X-Puhil**, 8th century A.D., (all that remains of one large pyramid, recently restored, beside the road), lies the large Maya site of **Becán**, shielded by the forest with wild animals still wandering among the ruins, surrounded by a water-less moat and a low wall, now collapsed, with vast temples and plazas and a decayed ball court. Two km. further on and 10 mins. down a paved road lies **Chicana,** with a superb late classic Maya temple with an ornate central door which has been formed in the shape of the open-fanged jaws of the plumed serpent. Buses return from X-Puhil at 1300 and 1700. Across the bay from Chetumal, at the very tip of Quintana Roo is **Xcalak**, which may be reached from Chetumal by boat (2 hrs., about US$10) or by a long, scenic (recent) unpaved road from Limones (3½ hrs., 120 km., suitable for passenger cars but needs skilled driver). Xcalak is a fishing village (250 pop.) with a few shops with beer and basic supplies—no hotels, no nightlife. Rent a boat and explore Chetumal Bay and Banco Chincherro, unspoiled islands. N of Chetumal are also 3 unexcavated archaeological sites. Ichpaatun (13 km.), Oxtancah (14) and Nohochmul (20).

Maps of roads in Quintana Roo are obtainable in Chetumal at Junta Local de Caminos, Secretaría de Obras Públicas. The road from Chetumal through Tulum to Mérida (via Cancún) is paved.

Travelling from Villahermosa to Campeche one can follow either the old coastal route, Highway 180, which takes 10 hours to drive and has 4 ferries (total cost for one car US$6.60) or the inland Highway 186, via Francisco Escárcega, with 2 toll bridges (cost US$1.35). Gasoline in Champotón, an attractive fishing village where the coastal and inland roads converge.

Ciudad del Carmen (pop. 80,000), on the coastal route, is hot, bursting at the seams since the oil boom, and spoilt by the new conditions. *Fiestas* at the end of July. There is a lot of shipbuilding here now and there are many trawlers in the harbour. The port is to be developed to become one of the biggest and most modern on the Mexican Gulf. The 3.2 km. Puente de la Unión, built in 1982, is considered the longest bridge in Mexico, linking Ciudad del Carmen with the mainland. There is a bull ring.

Hotels *Ll-re*, near ADO station, best in centre, a/c, expensive restaurant, D; *Zacarias*, Calle 24, 60-B, overpriced to D, and does not permit backpackers; *Gloria*, Calle 22 No. 100, a/c, F; *Internacional*, near ferry, Calle 20 No. 39, E; *Acuario*, Calle 51 No. 60, a/c, comfortable, D; *Isla del Carmen*, Calle 20 No. 9, a/c,restaurant, bar, parking, D; *Lino's*, Calle 31 No. 32, a/c, pool, restaurant, D; three others on Calle 22. If you can't find accommodation, there are 3 buses between 2100 and 2200 to Campeche and Mérida. Ciudad del Carmen is renowned for its sea-food: giant prawns, clams, *ceviche* and baby hammerhead shark are all tasty.

Bus To Villahermosa at 1930, arriving 2300-0100; it depends how long one has to wait at the ferry. A connection can be made to Palenque at 2330 or 0400; slow but worthwhile trip.

Campeche, capital of Campeche state, population 120,000, is beautifully set

976 MEXICO

on the western coast of Yucatán. It was the very first place at which the Spaniards set foot in 1517. In the 17th century it was fortified against pirates; seven bastions of the old walls and an ancient fort (now rather dwarfed by two new big white hotels on the sea-front) near the crumbling cathedral remain. In some of the bastions are housed: Baluarte Soledad (N of the plaza), a small room of Mayan stelae, free (open Tues.-Sat., 0800-2000), Baluarte San Carlos (NW corner), museum of the fortifications (open Tues.-Sat. 0900-1300, 1600-2000, Sun. 0900-1300, free), Baluarte Santa Rosa (W side), Biblioteca Histórica, open 0830-1400, 1600-1900. The Museo Regional is at Calle 59, No. 35, containing archaeology and history sections, open Mon.-Sat., 0900-1300, Sun. 0900-1300. There are several 16th and 17th century churches. The most interesting are San Francisquito (16th century with wooden altars painted in vermilion and white), Jesús, San Juan de Dios, Guadalupe and Cristo Negro de San Román, and there is a historical museum on the Plaza (admission US$0.10). There is also a museum in the former church of San José, which changes its exhibits frequently, near the SW corner of the old town. The old houses are warmly coloured, but the town is now in a sad state of repair. The nearest beaches are Playa Bonita (which is no longer fit for swimming and is generally dirty, being next to oil storage tanks) and San Lorenzo. The people fish, trawl for shrimp, carve curios and make combs from tortoiseshell. The new market building is attractive. The bathing and fishing resort of Lerma is quite near; take a rickety bus marked Lerma or Playa Bonita; beach strewn with glass and other debris.

Hotels In general, beware of overcharging. *Baluartes*, Av. Ruiz Cortines, reported badly maintained, parking for campers, who can use the hotel washrooms, D, good meal US$2.40-3.20, waiters apt to short-change, pool; *López*, Calle 12, No. 189, E, clean if a bit musty, with bath, better food; *Señorial*, Calle 10, comfortable, D, with bath, no restaurant; *Campeche*, F, basic, with cold shower and w.c. on Plaza, can be unfriendly; *Castelmar*, Calles 8 y 61, colonial style, F, large rooms with bath, recently refurbished, clean, friendly; *Cuauhtémoc*, F, clean (except downstairs rooms which are damp and smelly), with bath, in old house near the square (Calle 57); on Calle 10: *América* and *Roma*, opp. *México* (F and not recommended), No. 329; *Posada San Francisco*, No. 331. *El Presidente*, near the *Baluartes* on the seafront, Av. Ruiz Cortines 100; *Colonial*, clean, good, Calle 14 No. 122, not very friendly, F; *Autel El Viajero*, E, overcharges, but often only one left with space in the afternoon. *Central*, opp. bus terminal, Av. Gobernadores 462 (no sign), clean, fan and bathroom, F, front rooms somewhat noisy; *Roma*, F, with balconies; *Misión Si-Ho Playa*, km. 35 on road to Champotón, E p.p., with small beach, pool, take bus from 2nd-class bus station; 20 km. S of Campeche is *Hotel Selho*, F, excellent, beautiful setting on Gulf coast, swimming and other facilities. CREA Youth Hostel in the S suburbs, nr. University, bus from market US$0.12, clean and friendly. It is virtually impossible to get hotel rooms around the Mexican holiday period, starting May.

Camping There is a trailer park with camping signposted in town. Can be reached by taking a Samula bus from the market place. Owner speaks English; US$1.50 p.p.

Restaurants *Campeche*, good value; cafeteria next door sells good yoghurt and fruit juices; *Miramar* (good seafood, reasonable); *La Perla*, Calle 10 No. 329 (good fish, busy and popular), venison, squid; locals' haunt, sometimes erratic service, off Plaza; *Lonchería* Calle 8 No. 53, open 0700, recommended; *Pizzería Gato Pardo*, corner of Calle 10 and 49, on Jardín San Martín, outside the wall, excellent pizzas, loud music. Two doors away, *La Cava*. It is hard to find reasonably-priced food before 1800; try the restaurant at the ADO terminal.

Shopping Excellent cheap Panama hats (here they are called jipi hats, pronounced "hippie"). Handicrafts are generally cheaper than in Mérida. The new market (just outside the city wall) is worth a visit. Plenty of bargains here, especially Mexican and Mayan clothes, hats and shoes, fruit, vegetables; try some delicious ice-cream—though preferably from a shop rather than from a barrow.

Tourist Information New centre near waterfront, close to Palacio de Gobierno, good (open 0800-1430, 1600-2030, Mon.-Fri.).

Excursions Two km. S. of Campeche is the 18th-century fort of San Miguel, containing museums and worth visiting for its archaeological pieces. Entry, US$0.15. Between Campeche and Champotón is Playa Seyba, a fishing village with good camping possibilities (but no facilities) N of the village. Eighty km. N of Campeche is Becal, centre of the panama hat trade. The hats are made in man-made limestone caves, whose coolness and dampness facilitate the weaving.

Maya Sites in Campeche State About 40 km. beyond Campeche on the road to Uxmal (see page 982), there is a deviation, right, along a white stone road for 20 km. near Cayal to the pyramid of Edzná, worth a visit (entry, US$0.22, bus from Campeche at 0800 but may leave hours later; possible to take 0800 bus to Cayal and hitch from there). SE of Edzná are Dzibilnocac and Hochob sites, with elaborately decorated temples and palaces. For these sites you need a car as the bus returns to Campeche almost at once after arrival at Dzibilnocac, and there is nowhere to stay. For those with a car, continue beyond Edzná on Route 261 to the very picturesque villages of Hopelchen and Bolonchen de Rejón (Dzibalchen, for Hochob ruins, is on a road 40 km. from Hopelchen, may be reached by early morning bus from Campeche, 80 km., but again no return buses or accommodation guaranteed). Santa Teresa is a tiny village W of Hopelchen; turn off the main road S for ½ km.; very quiet and simple, excellent bakery with tall beamed ceiling and colourful tiled floor. There are Mayan ruins on the islands of Jainu and Piedra, 3 hrs. by boat off the coast. Written official permission is required to visit as the islands are Federal property and guarded.

Transport You can go to Mérida by rail, 4 hrs. or by road, 252 km. (158 miles). First class buses go by the Camino Real ("Via Corta"), which does *not* pass through Uxmal, Kabah, etc. Take a really quite comfortable 2nd class bus from the same terminal ("Via Ruinas"), have 3 hours at the ruins, and catch the next bus to Mérida, but don't buy a through ticket to Mérida; you'll have to pay again when you board the bus. Check bus times, as there are fewer in the afternoon. Bus Campeche-Mérida direct, US$3.30, 2nd class. Bus Campeche-Uxmal, US$3, 2nd class, 3 hrs., 5 a day. Buses along new inland road to Villahermosa; take posted times with a pinch of salt, 2nd class, 5 a day, US$7, 1st class US$8; 6½ hrs., 2300 bus comes from Mérida but empties during the night. Train Campeche-Palenque, 2nd class, US$2.50, 9½ hrs., leaves at 2310. Bus via Emiliano Zapata (2 hrs. before Villahermosa) to Palenque, change at Emiliano Zapata, see page 972. ADO bus to Mexico City, US$23. Train to Mexico City, 30 hrs., comfortable, US$19 1st class. Mexico City-Campeche train leaves at 2000 daily, very crowded in holiday times.

Mérida, capital of Yucatán state, population 285,000, is one of the most interesting cities in Mexico, but suffers from pollution caused by heavy traffic, narrow streets and climatic conditions favouring smog-formation. It was founded in 1542 on the site of the Mayan city of Tihoo. Its centre is the Plaza Mayor, green and shady; its arcades have more than a touch of the Moorish style brought by the Spanish conquerors. It is surrounded by the severe twin-towered 16th century Cathedral, the City Hall, the State Government Palace, and the Casa Montejo, originally built in 1549 by the *conquistador* of the region, rebuilt around 1850 and now a branch of the Banco Nacional de México (Banamex), open to the public during banking hours. The Casa de los Gobernadores, on Paseo de Montejo, is an impressive building in the turn-of-the-century French style of the Porfirio Díaz era. A small museum well worth a visit, the Museo de Arqueología, closed on Mon. (open 0800-1400 Sun., 0800-2000 all other days, US$0.10), in the Casa de los Gobernadores, Paseo Montejo and Calle 43 (has good bookshop). The Museum of Peninsular Culture, run by the Instituto Nacional Indigenista (INI), a contemporary crafts museum, is well worth visiting. There are several 16th and 17th century churches dotted about the city: Tercera Orden, San Francisco, San Cristóbal, and La Mejorada. Along the narrow streets ply horse-drawn cabs of a curious local design. In all the city's parks you will find *confidenciales* or S-shaped stone seats in which people can sit side by side facing each other. All the markets, and there are several, are interesting in the early morning. One can buy traditional crafts: a basket or *sombrero* of sisal, a filigree necklace, also a good selection of Maya replicas. Tortoiseshell articles are also sold, but cannot be imported into most countries, as sea turtles are protected by international convention. The Mérida market is also particularly good for made-to-measure sandals of deerskin and tyre-soles, panama hats, and hammocks of all sizes and qualities. Some of the most typical products are the *guayabera*, a pleated and/or embroidered shirt worn universally, its equivalent for women, the *guayablusa,* and beautiful Mayan blouses and *huipiles.* In the Park of the Americas is an open-air theatre giving plays and concerts. There are monuments to Felipe Carrillo Puerto, an agrarian labour leader prominent in the 1910 revolution. Redevelopment is rapid; many of the old houses are being pulled down. Mérida is a safe city at night, but the large influx of visitors in recent years is creating "mostly quiet hostility" towards them.

In Paseo de Montejo (part of Calle 62), together with many shops and restaurants, there are many grand late 19th century houses. Calle 65 is the main shopping street and the Plaza Mayor is between Calles 61/63 and 60/62. Odd-number streets run E and W, even numbers N and S. In colonial times, painted or sculpted men or animals placed at intersections were used as symbols for

978 MEXICO

the street: some still exist in the small towns of Yucatán. The houses are mostly of Spanish-Moorish type, painted in soft pastel tones, thick walls, flat roofs, massive doors, grilled windows, flowery patios. The water supply, once notorious, is improved. Begging and much molestation from car-washers, shoe-shiners and souvenir-peddlers. All streets are one-way. Free town map at tourist kiosk on the Plaza Mayor, or the Secretaría de Obras Públicas, almost opposite airport at Mérida (cheap bus from centre). Enquire at hotels about the house and garden tours run by the local society women for tourists to raise money for charity. Every Thursday evening there is free local music, dancing and poetry at 2100 in the Plaza Santa Lucía, two blocks from the Plaza Mayor (Calles 55 and 60), chairs provided. The Ermita, an 18th century chapel with beautiful grounds, is full of impressive preColumbian sculpture; a lonely, deserted place 10-15 mins. from the centre.

In the State Government Palace, on the Plaza Mayor, there is a series of superb symbolic and historical paintings, finished 1978, by a local artist, Fernando Castro Pacheco. The Palace is open evenings and very well lit to display the paintings. Tourist information from Ministerio de Fomento, Calle 59 opp. Centenario park.

Fiesta Carnival on Tuesday before Ash Wednesday. Floats, dancers in regional costume, music and dancing around the Plaza and children dressed in animal suits. **N.B.** Banks closed Monday following carnival.

Hotels *Los Aluxes*, Calle 60 No. 444, delightful, pool, restaurants, C; *Bojórquez*, D, a/c, pool, restaurant, service a little offhand, Calle 58/57, near main square; *Cayre*, Calle 70, No. 543, rooms a little dilapidated but clean, good pool, a/c, very convenient for bus station, friendly, recommended, E; *Hacienda Inn*, Av. Aviación 709, C; *Holiday Inn*, Av. Colón and C.60, B; *María del Carmen*, C, Calle 63, No. 550, breakfast reported poor; *Casa de Balam*, Calle 60, No. 488, B; *Montejo Palace*, Paseo del Montejo 483, C, noisy on 1st floor, lots of cooking smells, pool; *Latino*, Calle 66 and 63, E, with fan and shower (water supply problems), friendly and scrupulously clean; *Mérida Misión*, Calle 60, No. 491, C; *Colón*, Calle 62, No. 483, C, good value, pool, being remodelled; *Grande*, E, good, fine restaurant; *Lord*, Calle 63, No. 516, E; *Casa Bowen*, restored colonial house (inside better than out), corner of Calle 66, No. 521-B, and 65, recommended, friendly, stores luggage, F, excellent value, near ADO bus station, as is *Posada del Angel*, Calle 67, No. 535, between Calle 66 and 68, E, clean, excellent value; *Caminante*, also nearby at Calle 64, No. 539, F, clean, friendly; *Reforma*, Calle 59, No. 508, E; *México*, Calle 60, No. 525, E, good restaurant, attractive; *Milo*, Calle 63, basic but very clean and friendly, E; *Gran Hotel*, Calle 60 No. 496, just off the Plaza, is clean and good value, poor plumbing, E, with shower, recommended; *San Luis*, Calle 61, No. 534-68, E, with fan and shower (and US$2.25 for noisy a/c), basic, friendly, patio pool, restaurant; *Gobernador*, on the corner of Calle 59 and 66, E, a/c, big rooms, quite good; *Posada Cristóbal*, about 5 blocks from market on Calle 69, F, with bath, clean and quiet; *San Clemente*, Calle 58 and 71, E, with bath; *Rossana Pastora*, Calle 58, No. 563, E, very clean, excellent value, sells cold drink; *Príncipe Maya Airport Inn*, E, noisy from night club, convenient for airport. *El Presidente*, Calle 59, No. 455, good, expensive, with elaborate courtyard in the Porfirian style, very spacious and airy, with swimming pool, 5 blocks from centre, C; *Castellano*, Calle 57, No. 513, modern, clean, friendly, pool, C; *Montejo*, Calle 57 and 60, E (bargain), recommended; *Sevilla*, Calle 62, No. 511, E, with bath; *Casa de Huéspedes*, F, Victorian showers, will keep luggage for small fee, mosquitoes, so take coils or net, pleasant and quiet except at front, Calle 62, No. 507, better value than *América*, simple, private shower and toilet, noisy, will look after luggage, F, Calle 67, No. 500, between 58 and 60, about 10 mins. from bus station and near centre, recommended. *San Fernando*, opp. ADO bus terminal, E, overpriced. Recommended: *Posada Toledo*, Calle 58, No. 487, Tel.: 3-16-90, E, good, central, in charming old house, has paperback exchange; *Del Mayab*, Calle 50, No. 536A, F, with bath, reasonable, swimming pool and car park; *Flamingo*, Calle 58 and 59, F, near Plaza, with private shower, swimming pool, noisy, so get room at the back; *Caribe*, clean, central, convenient, E, on Calle 59; *Rodríguez*, Calle 56, F, rooms open off interior, quiet, adequate; *Autel*, Calle 59, No. 546, C; *Peninsular*, Calle 58, No. 519, near Plaza, D, pool, a/c, clean, friendly; *Nacional*, Calle 61, No. 474, E; *Parque*, Calle 60 No. 495, E, with bath and fan, clean, friendly, recommended; *Segovia*, F, with bath; *Alamo*, F, with bath, next to bus station, storage; *Margarita*, Calle 66, No. 506 (with Calle 63), F, clean, recommended; *Dolores Alba*, Calle 63 No. 464, E, good, pool, tame monkey; *Del Arco*, Calle 63, 452, cheap and basic but with bath, beware overcharging; *La Paz*, Calle 62, No. 522, F; *Regis*, Calle 63, No. 438, between 59 and 61, nr Plaza, basic, shared cold shower, F; *San Jorge*, across from ADO bus terminal, E, clean, but take interior room as the street is noisy; *San José*, F, with bath, basic, restaurant, W of Plaza on Calle 63, one of the cheapest, will store luggage; *Mucuy*, Calle 57 between 56 and 58, F, friendly, good, with shower, use of fridge, washing facilities, efficient; *Centenario*, F with bath, friendly, clean, safe on Calle 84, between 59 and 59A; *Hotel del Faraóu*, above textile shop near Post Office, F, big rooms, not too clean, noisy; rooms on Calle 66 Norte, No. 386 (with private bath). *Hospedaje Casbillio*, Calle 56, between 53 and 55, clean and friendly. Cheaper hotels tend to be S of the main Plaza (odd streets numbered 63 and higher), near the market or bus station; latest recommendation is *María Teresa*, Calle 64 No. 529 (between Calles 65 and 67), clean, friendly, safe, central, E with bath. More expensive hotels are on the N side of the city and near the Paseo Montejo. *Maya Paradise Trailer Park*, recommended, good pool, pick a site away from the water towers; right opp. the airport; *Trailer Park Rainbow*, Km. 8, on the road to Progreso, US$1.80 for car and US$1.20 for one or two, basic facilities.

MEXICO 979

Restaurants *Jaraneros Patio*, Montejo Circle, regional food and entertainment from 1600; *Pancho Villa's Follies*, very friendly, try abalones, owner speaks English, overpriced; and *Soberanis*, on Plaza with two branches elsewhere, serving delicious fish dishes, seafood cocktails highly recommended, but expensive, one on Calle 60, No. 503 between 63 and 65 (slow service), and another on Calle 56, No. 504. *Los Almendros*, Calle 50A, No. 493 at Calle 59, in high-vaulted, whitewashed thatched barn, for Yucatán specialities, recommended but mind the peppers, esp. the green sauce! *Mesón del Mestizo* (Plaza Sta. Lucía), *Pórtico del Peregrino* (Pop), Calle 57, between 60 and 62, excellent snacks, popular with foreigners; *Méson del Quijote*, Calle 62 No. 519, cheap and excellent, try their fish dishes with garlic; *Los Portales*, Calle 60 (charming patio) and *Yanal-Luum* are medium-price; *Las Palomas*, very expensive, not recommended; the *Patio Español*, inside the *Gran Hotel*, well cooked and abundant food, local and Spanish specialities, moderate prices; *Express*, Calle 60 and 59, has good huachinango a la veracruzana; *Louvre*, lazy staff but large meals, on Plaza; *David*, Calle 62, No. 468A (Arab food—closes before 2100); *La Prosperidad*, Calle 53 and 56, good Yucateca food, live entertainment at lunchtime; *Los Pájaros*, Calle 69 near ADO bus station, cheap and good; *Yannig*, Calle 62, No. 480, best, cheapest French food. *Cedral del Libano*, Calle 59 No. 529, good family-style Arabic food. *El Mariachi Hacienda*, Calle 60 No. 466, regional food, loud local music, dancing and cock-fighting, cover charge US$2. *El Faisán y El Venado*, Calle 59 No. 617, inexpensive, regional food, Mayan dance show, near zoo. Cheap comidas at *Los Cardenales*, Calle 69, ½ block from bus station; *La Carretera*, Calle 62 and 59, a little expensive but very good. Good food at *Flamingo*, Calle 51; *Leo's*, good value for meat dishes, pleasant, Calle 60, just N of Plaza Santa Lucía; *Café de Guaya*, Calle 60, between 53 and 55, vegetarian; *Pizzería Vito Corleone*, near Gran Hotel and Plaza, good; *Les Balcons* on Calle 62, No. 497, part-vegetarian, recommended, go through to the back of *Hotel El Parque* and up the stairs; *Jugos California*, good, expensive fruit juices, Calle 60, also in Calle 65 and at the main bus station; *Jugos de Caña*, Calle 62 between 57 and 59, very good; *Jugos Michoacán*, good milkshakes on Calle 57. *Dulcería Colón*, on Plaza Mayor, for excellent, if expensive, ices. *Café Alameda*, nr. Correos, Arab food, closes at 1900, cheap and good; *Santa Lucía*, Calle 60, good Arab food. Cold sliced cooked venison (*venado*) is to be had in the Municipal Market. *Cafetería La Giralda El Rey*, in the shoe section of the market place, excellent coffee. Good coffee in *Café* on Calle 60, between 65 and 67, traditional coffeehouse where locals meet; *Mil Tortas*, very good and cheap sandwiches, Calle 62 with 65 and 67. *La Pérgola*, warmly recommended (both drive-in and tables), at corner Calles 56A and 43, good veal dishes. *Cafetería Erik's*, ½ block from Plaza, meals and snacks. Banana bread and wholemeal rolls at health shop on Calle 59 between 60 and 62, and good juice bar close by.

Shopping Guayaberas: *Canul*, Calle 59, No. 496; *Genuina Yucateca*, Calle 50, No. 520. At *Mayalandia* on Calle 61, before Calle 48 archway, one can bargain. *Jack* in Calle 59, near Canul, makes guayaberas to measure in 4 hrs., expensive.

The best hammocks are the so-called 3-ply, but they are difficult to find, about US$13 (cheaper than in Campeche); also mosquito nets. Try *Mayoreo de Mérida*, Calle 65, or *La Poblana* (see below) both near Post Office; or *Claudia*, Calle 58 and 89 (US$10). There are three sizes: single, matrimonial and family. Count the end-strings yourself; 50 end-strings for a small single, 150 strings and over for a comfortable double. At least 130 strings required for two people. *La Poblana*, Calle 65, No. 492, is one place to buy (outside the market), fixed prices; and across the street by *El Tigre del 65*; bargain like mad if buying more than one, but wherever you buy, you must count the strings yourself or you may be cheated. (Most hammocks are made in Tixkobob, 20 km. from Mérida: you can take a bus, US$0.40, 45 min., ask at the houses on the edge of the village.) Mosquito nets are obtainable from *Mosquiteros de Luxe*, one block W from the market but not very good quality; no bargaining, but cheaper than hammock shops. The ones at *La Poblana* are charmingly sold but the one available size is too small for larger hammocks. Embroidered *huipil* blouses US$3-6. Good panama hats at *El Bombín* next to 511b (tailor's shop) on Calle 67, between 60 and 62. Bargain. Also *Nipis Becal*, buy by market. Sr. Raúl Cervera Sauri has a reasonable souvenir shop on Calle 59, No. 501 and will charge a fair price for mailing souvenirs and anything else you care to send, taking care of customs forms, etc. *Uncle Sam's* on main square, run by retired American, reasonably priced hammocks, panama hats. Next door to restaurant *Los Almendros* on Calle 59 is the Cordamex (sisal products) outlet—don't go to the factory 8 km. from town as they won't sell there. Good buys in black coral, jewellery and tortoiseshell (may not be imported into several countries—check) in the markets, particularly the 2-storey one on Calles 56 and 67. There is a big supermarket, *Blanco*, on Calle 67 and 52, well stocked.

Tourist Office Corner of Calles 57 and 60, also corner of Calles 61 and 54, and on N side of Plaza Mayor in the Palacio de Gobierno. Has list of all hotel accommodation with prices.

Travel Agents and Car Hire *Wagon-Lits* (Cooks), helpful, Av. Colón 501 (Plaza Colón), Tel.: 554-11; *Cozumel Travel Service*; *Yucatán Trails*, Calle 62, No. 482, is very helpful, run by Canadian, Denis Lafoy. Car reservations should be booked well in advance wherever possible; there is a tendency to hand out cars which are in poor condition once the main stock has gone, so check locks, etc., on cheaper models before you leave town. The all-inclusive cost (inc. gasoline) for a one-day 250 km. trip is about US$50 in a VW. *Avis* in Hotel Mérida; *Hertz*, Calle 55, No. 479; *Budget*, Calle 62, No. 588-3; *Volkswagen*, Calle 60, No. 486; *Alquiladora de Autos Sureste*, Calle

MEXICO

60, No. 481, and at airport; Mexico Rent-A-Car in the lobby of *Hotel del Parque*, Calle 60, No. 495, has good rates, new VW Beetles; Odin, Calle 59, No. 506-3.

Taxis We are warned that taxi drivers are particularly prone to overcharge by taking the long route, so always establish the journey and fare in advance.

Exchange Banamex in Casa de los Gobernadores on PLaza, and at Calles 56 y 59. Many banks on Calle 65, off the Plaza. Jugos California on the main square may change dollars and travellers' cheques at good rates.

Post Office Calle 65, Poste restante held for ten days only. Generally crowded, use branches at airport (also for quick delivery) or on Calle 58, instead. Telegrams from Calle 56, between 65 and 65A, open 0800-2100.

International Calls Possible from main telephone exchange at Calle 59 and 64, open until 2200 hrs. Signposted "Larga Distancia", difficult to see; in a small yard.

British Vice Consul Corner Calles 58 and 53. Tel.: (91-992) 1-679-9. Postal address Apdo. 89.

English-Speaking Doctor Dr. A. H. Puga Navarrete (also speaks French), Calle 13 No. 210, between Calles 26 and 28, Colonia García Gineres, Tel.: 25-07-09, open 1600-2000.

Cameras and Film Repairs by Señor Riera, Calle 62 Altos, between 65 and 67. Many processors around crossing of Calles 59 and 60.

Trains Fees for red-capped porters posted at the station (Calles 48 and 57). From Mexico City at 2010. Sometimes only sleeper and 2nd class available but no 1st class or restaurant car. Two sizes of room on sleeper, one not much larger than closet. Larger ones have two bunks, very comfortable with a/c, clean; they sell out quickly, book early. To Mexico City, Pullman US$37, 1st class US$17.25, 2nd class US$10.30, leaves Mérida at 2200 (37 hrs. but often more like 45 to 72); book ticket from 1100 on same day of departure at station. 2nd class not recommended, dirty. Difference between 1st and 2nd class in age of carriages, no seats assigned on either, with live animals in 2nd. Even though boarding not supposed to be before 1900, most people get on on arrival of the train, at 1830. Queuing for 2nd class starts hours before. No clean running water, lavatory dirty. Beggars get on at every stop; thieving. Best to take Special 1st Class, reserved seats, comfortable (take blanket, a/c is cold), or Pullman if you can afford it and don't mind small cabins. No food except for vendors at stations, stock up. Many breaks up to Coatzacoalcos. Possible to break journey at Palenque but not on one ticket. Mérida-Palenque (on same train as to Mexico City), takes 12 hrs., book *dormitorio* in advance (from 1100 to 1300), non-refundable, US$8 for two in a single *camarín*, cosy, if you are not large, otherwise cramped, US$11.50 in double, i.e. two bunks; own lavatory and sink and safest way to travel as doors can be locked. Old-fashioned 1940 North American coaches, but very comfortable. Passengers may not enter *dormitorio* before 1930. Track recently improved, train rocks rather than jerks as it did, speed about 50 km. an hour. Air conditioning improves as you leave the station, but not spectacular. Conductor brings drinks round, and coffee and sandwiches early a.m. Fruit near station, bread and cheese a couple of streets away from station, better bought before leaving centre. Mérida-Valladolid, at 1510, 5 hrs., US$2. There are two picturesque narrow-gauge railway lines SE of Mérida—one to Sotuta and the other to Peto via Ticul and Oxcutzcab. One train on each line leaves daily at 1400 from Mérida, returns at 0400. The journey takes 5 hrs., covers 150 km., US$0.50 to Peto. You can return by bus from Oxcutzcab (see also page 983).

Buses Almost all buses except those to Progreso leave from terminal on Calle 69 between Calles 70 and 72. The station has lockers. To Mexico City, US$21.75, 24-28 hrs.; to Coatzacoalcos, US$12. To Puerto Juárez, US$4 1st, US$3.50 2nd class, 5 hrs. Bus to Veracruz, US$18, 16 hrs.; to Chetumal, 1st class, 6 a day, US$6.60, 6 hrs. To Ciudad del Carmen at 0600, 1st class, ADO, US$5, 9 hrs. Three buses to Tulum: at 0700, 1100 and 2300, 8 hrs., US$6.50, drops you off at the ruins. Excursions to Uxmal and Chichén Itzá by 1st and 2nd class buses from ADO terminal on Calle 69 and 68. To Uxmal, 6 2nd class buses a day from 0600 (none early p.m.), returning from 0830 (unreliable), 1½ hrs., US$0.80 each way; regular buses to Campeche (US$3, 4½ hrs.) also pass Uxmal. Last bus from Uxmal to Campeche (US$1.50, 3 hrs.) at 2315 is quite crowded. To Chichén Itzá (US$1.35, 1½ hrs.) 2nd class buses leave every hour, 1000-2000. Round trip 1st class leaves at 0830 and returns at 1500. Buses to Puerto Juárez every hour until midday, can be booked 3 days in advance. Bus to Cancún US$4.40 1st class, US$4 2nd. Buses to Progreso (US$0.45) passing the road to Dzibilchaltun (see next page), leave from the bus station on Calle 62, between Calle 65 and 67 every 15 mins. from 0500-2100. To Valladolid, US$1.80. One direct bus daily at 1300 via Villahermosa and Pichucalco to Tuxtla Gutiérrez, 8 hrs., US$10. Autotransportes del Sureste de Yucatán, at 0600. One can arrange to visit Kabah (20 mins.), Sayil (30 mins.), X-Lapak (10 mins.) and Labná (30 mins.) with the J. González company Calle 59, No. 476 (Tel.: 10197, 19710, 10865), VW buses, daily round trip at 0900, US$13-20 (admission not included) including Uxmal (90 mins.) often price includes meal and sometimes *son et lumière*. Very tiring,

MEXICO 981

especially since Uxmal last, but soft drinks available at sites. Entry cheaper on Sun. and holidays. Book preferably a day in advance.

Bus to Palenque from Mérida leaves 2330 from ADO terminal, arrives 0830, US$6.60, rather a grim proposition, better to travel in daytime via Emiliano Zapata and local bus (see page 972). Bus to Mérida via Campeche from Palenque, with Líneas Unidas de Chiapas, leaves Palenque at 1700 hrs., daily. Buses to Celestún and Sisal from corner of Calle 50 and 67.

Route 261, Mérida-Francisco Escárcega, paved and in very good condition. Buses.

To Guatemala by public transport from Yucatán, take train from Mérida to Pichucalco; it gets in about 1300. Take a small bus downtown and catch the bus to Tuxtla Gutiérrez. Road is slow, so it is probably quicker to cut across from Coatzacoalcos. Alternatively travel on the México-Mérida railway line to **Tenosique**, 1 hr. E by train from Palenque (*Hotel Garage*, E, a/c, on main square with restaurant, very clean, and *Azuela*, F, a block away, also clean). From Tenosique (pleasant, friendly, but no money exchange), at 0600, 0800, 1300 and 1600 buses leave to La Palma (1300, 45 mins.), whence boats leave to El Naranjo (Guatemala) at 1400, returning 0800, about 5 hrs., US$5. Make sure the boat takes you beyond the border, where there is only a customs office. From El Naranjo there is a new dirt road through the jungle to Flores; hitchhiking apparently possible. Beautiful trip. One can take a boat from La Palma (rather than San Pedro, which is more expensive) and go for US$2.50 to El Martillo. Autotransportes del Sureste de Yucatán bus from Mérida to Tuxtla, via Palenque and Ocosingo to either San Cristóbal or Comitán; 2 or 3 changes of bus. Bus from Mérida direct to Tuxtla at 1330 hrs., then direct either Tuxtla-Ciudad Cuauhtémoc or to Tapachula; although the journey may not be as pretty, it saves changing. **Road to Belize**: paved all the way to Chetumal. Bus Mérida-Chetumal US$6, 2nd class. Leaves at 1200 and takes 7½ hrs. Bus station on corner of Calle 68 and 69.

By Air Mexicana office at Calle 58 and 61. From Calle 67 and 60 bus 79 goes to the airport, marked Aviación, US$0.10. Taxi US$2, voucher available from airport, you don't pay driver direct. Mexicana and Aeroméxico both have about 6 flights to Mexico City daily, 1½ hrs., 2½ hrs. from New Orleans (five days a week on Aviateca); 1¾ hrs. from Miami via Tampa with Eastern Airlines; Aeroméxico Miami-Mérida daily at 1955; 2 hrs. from Mexico City, 960 km.; Pan-American World Airways flies the routes Miami-Tampa-Mérida-Mexico City and Miami-Mérida-Central America. Vega flies every other day to Oaxaca, on to Acapulco. Aeroméxico flies to Acapulco, via Veracruz and Monterrey to Los Angeles, 3 times a week. Acapulco, via Oaxaca and Villahermosa, 3 hrs.; Cancún, 35 mins.; Cozumel, 35 mins., US$20 one way; Monterrey, 1¾ hrs.; Oaxaca, 2 hrs.; Tuxtla Gutiérrez, 2½ hrs.; Villahermosa, 50 mins. (Aeroméxico leaves at 0655 and returns to Mérida at 2205, making it easier to visit Palenque in a rented car in a one-day tour). The airport is splendid; direct flights also to Guatemala City by Aviateca on Tues. and Thurs., US$96. Mexicana to Cuba, Sun. and Wed., US$179 return, payable in pesos. A package tour (one week) Mérida-Havana-Mérida is available, US$213, including flight, hotel and half-board (MAP). For return to Mexico ask for details at Secretaría de Migración, Calle 60, No. 285. The smaller airlines tend to offer cheaper flights, on older aircraft. Food and drinks at the airport are very expensive.

Excursions North-west of Mérida is first Hunucma, like an oasis in the dry Yucatán, about ½ hr. from the Central Camionera bus station, US$0.30. Then about 52 km. (buses). is Sisal beach (frequent buses 0500-1700, from Calle 50, between Calle 65 and 67), with an impressive lighthouse, where one can hire a boat and go to the reef of Los Alacranes where many ancient wrecks are visible in clear water. West of Mérida regular buses (US$1.10) serve **Celestún** beach, a resort frequented by Meridans, with a huge lagoon with flamingos; hire a boat (US$18 for one big enough for 6-8). There are several hotels here, and you can camp on the beach or pitch a hammock at *Las Palapas*, a restaurant at the N end of town, along the beach. You can drive to Celestún by a narrow road parallel to the beach. It is quite pretty, but beware of a few patches of soft sand; best to maintain good speed so as not to get stuck.

Halfway to Progreso turn right for the Maya ruins of **Dzibilchaltun**, open 0800-1700. This unique city, according to carbon dating, was founded as early as 1000 B.C. The most important building is the Temple of the Seven Dolls (partly restored). The Cenote Xlaca contains very clear water and is 44 metres deep. Buses from Mérida to Progreso pass the junction to the ruins, 8 km. from the main road, taxis wait at the bus stop; buses pass in either direction every 15 mins. Apparently one can swim in the *cenote*.

Progreso, the port (now decaying as the glamour has moved to Cancún and Cozumel), 39 km. away, is reached by road or railway. Population 14,000; temperatures range from 27° to 35°C. Main export: *henequén*. It claims to have the longest stone-bridge pier in the world. Hotel on the once lovely but now filthy beach. If bathing, women in bikinis can be expected to be surrounded by men within minutes of arrival, even if accompanied by a man. Impossible to deter.

Hotels *Miralmar*, E, seedy, owner speaks English; better value is *Malecón*, on sea front; hotel of

982 MEXICO

Mayan-type bungalows on road, not beach, fairly dirty, F. *Posada Familiar* and *Casa de Huéspedes Bonanza*, *Río Blanco*, F, by market, basic. Good **restaurants** and quite cheap are *Capitán Pescado*, *Charlie's* and *El Cordobés*, but latter has slow service, expensive but good; *Soberanis*; *La Terraza*, variable results, expensive. *Salón Familiar* is overpriced, unfriendly and of poor quality. Police permit free beach camping. Many homes, owned by Mexico City residents, available for rent; typical prices, US$350-650 a month (4 beds) services included. Sr. A. Morán, at Calle 22 and 27 (speaks English) can arrange furnished accommodation (cheapest unfurnished). Good local market with lowest food prices in Yucatán, esp. seafood. You can buy fresh shrimps cheaply in the mornings on the beach. Bus, Progreso-Mérida US$0.50 every 15 mins.

The beach front by the pier is devoted to cafés with seafood cocktails as their speciality. They also have little groups performing every weekend afternoon in summer; and the noise can be both spirited and deafening.

A short bus journey from Progreso are Puerto Yucalpetén and Chelem, an expensive and dusty resort. Balneario Yucalpetén has a beach with lovely shells. Yacht marina, changing cabins, beach with gardens and swimming pool. Near to Chelem is a small, unspoilt fishing village, Chixachib, about 4 km. from Progreso. Between the Balneario and Chelem there is a nice hotel of small Mayan-hut type bungalows, *Hotel Villanueva*, and also *Costa Maya*, on Calle 29 y Carretera Costera, with restaurant. Fish restaurants in Chelem, *Las Palmas* and *El Cocalito*, reasonable, also other small restaurants.

Uxmal is 74 km. from Mérida, 177 km. from Campeche, by a good paved road. If going by car, there is a new circular road round Mérida: follow the signs to Campeche, then Campeche via *ruinas*, then to Muna via Yaxcopoil (long stretch of road with no signposting). Muna-Yaxcopoil about 34 km. The Mayan ruins (entrance US$0.10), are quite unlike those of Chichén-Itzá (see below), and cover comparatively little ground. Uxmal, the home of the Xiu tribe, was founded in 1007. Its finest buildings seem to have been built much later. See El Adivino (the Sorcerer, pyramid-shaped, topped by two temples with a splendid view); the Casa de las Monjas (House of Nuns), a quadrangle with 88 much adorned rooms; the Casa del Gobernador (House of the Governor), on three terraces, with well preserved fine sculptures; the Casa de las Tortugas (Turtle House) with six rooms; the Casa de las Palomas (House of Doves), probably the oldest; and the cemetery. Ruins open at 0800, close at 1700. Drinks at entrance of ruins, may not be taken inside; also guide books here. Many iguanas (harmless) wandering about, watch out for occasional scorpions and snakes. There is a *son et lumière* display at the ruins nightly—English version (US$0.50) at 2100, Spanish version (US$0.15) 1930 (check for times), highly recommended (bus leaves at 1400). 2nd class bus from Mérida to Campeche ("Via Ruinas") passes Uxmal, US$0.80 one way, can buy tickets on bus, 1½ hr. journey, 2 hrs. enough to see ruins. Bus stops just under ½ km. from entrance to ruins on main road, just follow sign. Return from *Restaurant Bar Nicté-Ha* (open 1230-1900) across the road. From Mérida go with Autotransportes from the main bus station at 1715, return at 2015 with same bus. Return ticket US$ 2.75. Return to Mérida after the show is only possible with tourist buses. (There may be spare seats for those without return tickets.) Good service with Yucatán Trails (see page 979). For best photographs early morning or late afternoon arrival is essential. Overnight parking for a van US$0.50.

Hotels *Hacienda Uxmal*, 100 metres from ruins, is quite good but very expensive (B-A, restaurant open 0800-2200). Swimming pool. It has a less expensive dependency *Posada Uxmal*, C, meals in either part cost US$4.35 and US$6 depending on restaurant. *Misión Uxmal*, A, 1-2 km. from ruins on Mérida road. Club Méditerranée *Villa Arqueológica*, D-B, beautiful, close to ruins, good value, swimming pool, breakfast US$3 but worth it. *Lapalapa*, A, nothing special. From the *Hacienda Uxmal* jeeps visit the four ruins of Kabah, Sayil, X-Lapak and Labná (see page 976) daily, US$20 p.p., incl. box lunch. **N.B.** There is no village at Uxmal, just the hotels. Camping possible beside the parking lot (watch out for scorpions), using public lavatories for washing dishes etc. after asking permission from the guard. Ordinary daytime buses leave opp. *Posada Uxmal*.

On the road from Uxmal to Mérida (with good restaurant, *Rancho*, a few km. from Uxmal) is Muna (15 km. from Uxmal, 62 from Mérida; delightful square and old church), with the nearest railway station to Uxmal.

By the main road a few km. S of Uxmal and often included in tours of the latter (about 5½ km. before the sign for Sayil), are the ruins of **Kabah** where there is a fascinating Palace of Masks, whose façade bears the image of Chac; mesmerically repeated over and over again about six hundred times. (The style is classic Puuc. Watch out for snakes and spiders.) Bus: Campeche-Kabah, US$2.40.

Further South of Uxmal, about half-way between Mérida and Campeche, a paved road branches off to the left to the Sayil ruins (5 km.), **X-Lapak** (about 13 km.) and **Labná** (about 22 km.). The palace at Sayil (admission US$0.40) is a good 2 hrs.' walk from the main site. Labná has a most astonishing arch. Both Sayil and Labná are in low, shrubby bush country. From Labná, continue to immense galleries and caves of Bolonchen (bus from Mérida). You *must* take a guide and a powerful torch. If visiting Sayil, X-Lapak and Labná, you can take a taxi from the village of Santa Elena at the turn-off (no hotels or restaurants), costing US$20 for 1-3 persons. By hire-car one can continue to Oxcutzcab (see below).

Recommended reading for the area: *The Maya*, by M. D. Coe (Pelican Books). The ruins of Labná, X-Lapak, Sayil, Kabah and Uxmal can now be reached by 2nd class bus from Mérida. One can connect with the 2nd class bus tours from Mérida from Campeche if one takes the 0600 bus to Kabah. Guided tours from Mérida US$11-13.

The road from Mérida (and also from Uxmal) to Chetumal is through Muna, **Ticul** (where pottery, hats and shoes are made; *Los Almendros* restaurant, opp. Cinema Ideal, recommended), Peto (best avoided, via Tzucacab-Santa Rosa bypass, no restaurant) and Felipe Carrillo Puerto. Between Ticul and Peto is **Oxcutzcab**, with a hotel, F, at W end of town, opp. Pemex station, clean, fan, a little run-down. No beds, hammocks provided, clean, quiet rooms with bath. Also *Hotel Bermujo*, by Pemex station on road to Muna, 4-5 blocks from bus station, F, some a/c, fans, good. Nearby, to the S, are the fantastic caverns and pre-columbian vestiges at **Loltún** (supposedly extending for 8 km.). Caves are open Tues.-Sun., admission at 0930, 1130, 1330 and 1500 (US$0.25). Caretaker may admit tours on Mon., but no lighting. Take pickup or truck from the market going to Cooperativa (an agricultural town). For return, flag down a passing truck. Alternatively, take a taxi. Oxcutzcab is a good centre for catching buses to Chetumal, Muna, Mayapán and Mérida. It has a lot of character with a large market on the side of the Plaza and a church with a "two-dimensional" façade on the other side of the square. The area around Ticul and Oxcutzcab is intensively farmed with citrus fruits, papayas and mangos. Between Oxcutzcab and Peto is **Tekax** with restaurant *La Ermita* serving excellent Yucateca dishes at reasonable prices. From Tekax an unpaved but perfectly acceptable road leads to the ruins of Chacmultun. From the top one enjoys a beautiful view; there is a caretaker. All the towns between Muna and Peto have large old churches. Beyond Peto the scenery is scrub and swamp as far as the Belizean frontier.

Mayapán is a large, peaceful late Mayan site easily visited by bus from Mérida; also two large pyramids in village of Acanceh en route. Before Acanceh, on the road to Mayapán, is a restaurant at Kanasin, *La Susana*, to which there are frequent buses. It is known especially for local delicacies like *sopa de lima, salbutes* and *panuchos*. Clean, excellent service and abundant helpings at reasonable prices. Between Acanceh and Mayapán is Tecóh, with the caverns of Dzab-Náh; you must take a guide as there are treacherous drops into *cenotes*.

Chichén-Itzá is 120 km. by a paved road running SE from Mérida. The scrub forest has been cleared from over 5 square km. of ruins. The city was founded in 432, and taken over by the Toltecs in the 10th century; the major buildings in the N half are Toltec. Dominating them is El Castillo, its top decorated by the symbol of Quetzalcoatl, and the balustrade of the 91 stairs up each of the four sides is decorated by a plumed, open-mouthed serpent. There is also an interior ascent to a chamber lit by electricity where the red-painted jaguar which probably served as the throne of the high priest burns bright, its eyes of jade, its fangs of flint (see below for entry times). There is a ball court with grandstand and towering walls each set with a projecting ring of stone high up; at eye-level is a relief showing the decapitation—death was the penalty for defeat—of the losing captain. El Castillo stands at the centre of the northern half of the site, and almost at right-angles to its northern face runs the sacred way to the Cenote Sagrado, the Well of Sacrifice. The other *cenote*, the Xtoloc Well, was probably used as a water supply. It requires at least one day to see the many pyramids, temples, ballcourts and palaces, all of them adorned with astonishing sculptures, and excavation and renovation is still going on. Old Chichén, where the Mayan buildings of the

984 MEXICO

earlier city are, lies about ½ km. by path from the main clearing. The famous observatory (the only one known among the Maya ruins) is included in this group as is the Nunnery. A footpath to the right of the Nunnery takes one to the House of the Three Lintels after ½ hr. walking. Entry to Chichén-Itzá, 0800-1700, US$0.10 (Sun. half price); check at entrance for opening times of the various buildings. Best to arrive before 1030 when the mass of tourists arrives. Entry to see the jaguar in the substructure of El Castillo along an inside staircase at 1130-1300 and 1600-1700. Try to be among the first in as it is stuffy inside and queues form when the season is busy. Entry to Cámara de los Tigres at 1000-1100 and 1500-1600. Convenient luggage store by ruins entrance, US$0.10. Drinks and snacks available at entrance, also guidebooks, clean toilets. Also toilets on the way to old Chichén, and a drinks terrace with film supplies. The badly translated guide-book of José Díaz Bolio provides useful background comment; the little Bloomgarden booklet is also interesting. The Catholic church has walls built on a boulder and older foundations, and incorporates old Mayan stones, some with carvings (step to the side door); there are even two serpents over one of the doors. *Son et lumière* (US$0.50) at Chichén every evening, in Spanish at 1900, and then in English at 2100.

Into the Cenote Sagrado were thrown valuable propitiatory objects of all kinds, animals and human sacrifices. The well was first dredged by Edward H. Thompson, the U.S. Consul in Mérida, between 1904 and 1907; he accumulated a vast quantity of objects in pottery, jade, copper and gold. In 1962 the well was explored again by an expedition sponsored by the National Geographical Society and some 4,000 further artefacts were recovered, including beads, polished jade, lumps of copal resin, small bells, a statuette of rubber latex, another of wood, and a quantity of animal and human bones. The bottom of the well is paved with the ruins of a fallen temple. There are several tours daily to the Balancanchén caves, 3 km. E, just off the highway (caretaker turns lights on and off, answers questions in Spanish); minimum 3, maximum 15 persons. Worth the trip: there are archaeological objects, including offerings of pots and *metates* in a unique setting; it is very damp and you may have to go through narrow openings, so dress accordingly. Not for claustrophobics. Open 0900-1100 and 1400-1600 on the hour, US$0.10 (allow about ½ hr. for the 300-metre descent), closed Sun. afternoons.

Hotels The only two hotels close to the ruins are *Hacienda Chichén*, B, once owned by Edward Thompson with charming bungalows; *Villas Arqueológicas*, D, 1st class, pool, tennis, good value. Most other hotels are at the nearby village of Pisté. *Mayaland Hotel*, B, incl. breakfast and dinner, pool, but sometimes no water in it, no a/c, just noisy ceiling fans, but good service and friendly; *Pirámide Inn*, C, with food, swimming pool, well run; also *Pirámide Inn Trailer Court*, 1½ km. from ruins, camping, book swapping facility at desk, clean toilets and showers, lots of trees for hammock hanging (US$2 p.p. per night) and grass space for small tents, electricity and water outlets, US$1.30 p.p., allows use of *Pirámide Inn* swimming pool, watch out for snakes and tarantulas; *Lapalapa Chichén*, C, with breakfast and dinner, a few km. from the ruins, excellent restaurant, modern, park with animals; *Dolores Alba*, small hotel (same family as in Mérida), 2½ km. on the road to Puerto Juárez (bus passes it), good and comfortable, F, with shower; has swimming pool and serves good meals, English spoken. Other hotels at **Pisté** about 2 km. from ruins: *Posada Novelo*, F, near *Pirámide Inn*, sparse but clean, run by José Novelo who speaks English, restaurants nearby, not very good value, sanitation in poor condition. *Hotel Cunanchén*, on Plaza, prices negotiable with owner, not recommended; ask to see private *cenote*. There is a small pyramid in village opp. the *Hotel Misión Chichén Itzá*, B, not easily seen from the road; it has staircases with plumed serpents and a big statue facing N on top; close by is a huge plumed serpent, part coloured, almost forming a circle at least 20 metres long. There is no sign or public path, climb over gate into scrubland, the serpent will be to right, pyramid to left (a traveller believes these to be the remains of a hotel built by a French concern in the 1940s—further reports please!). Although Pisté is growing there is no bank; the nearest is in Valladolid. Bus Pisté-Valladolid US$1.40.

Restaurants Mostly poor and overpriced in Chichén itself. *Hotel Restaurant Carrousel* (rooms E); cheap meals at *Las Redes*.

Shopping Hammocks are sold by Mario Díaz, excellent quality, huge, at his house ½ km. up the road forking to the left at the centre of the village. Worth visiting as he is a great character. A few km. from Chichén is Ebtún, on the road to Valladolid. A sign says "Hammock sales and repairs": it is actually a small prison which turns out 1st class cotton or nylon hammocks—haggle with wardens and prisoners; there are no real bargains, but good quality.

Taxi Chichén Itzá-Valladolid, US$8.90.

If driving from Mérida, follow Calle 65 (off the Plaza) out until the dirt section, where you turn left, then right and right again at the main road, follow until hypermarket on left and make a left turn at the sign for Chichén-Itzá. Chichén-Itzá is easily reached (but less easily during holiday periods) from Mérida by 1st (ADO) and 2nd class buses (US$1.35 one way), about 1½-2½ hours' journey; buses now take you direct to the ruins. Tours (0830, bus returns 1445) charge about US$3.75. You can often also negotiate a fare with some of the VW buses that park in the lay-bys off the main road opp. the site entrance; the journey can later be continued to Puerto Juárez and Isla Mujeres (again, this can be over-crowded at holiday times), which is reached by launches (45 min. crossing), US$0.50. 10 buses a day go to Cancún and Puerto Juárez, last at 1700, US$3.30. The first bus from Pisté to Puerto Juárez is at 0730, 3 hrs. Budget travellers going on from Mérida to Isla Mujeres or Cozumel should visit Chichén from Valladolid (see below). Buses from Valladolid go every hour to the site and you can return by standing on the road at the ruins and flagging down any bus going straight through. Bus Chichén Itzá—Tulum, US$3.

On the way back, turn to the right at Kantunil (68 km. from Mérida) for a short excursion to the charming little town of **Izamal** (basic hotel on one of the two main squares, and a restaurant next door), to see the ruins of a great mausoleum known as Kinich-Kakmo pyramid, right at the centre of Izamal, with an excellent view of the town and surrounding *henequén* plantations from the top; a huge old convent, and the magnificent early Franciscan church, built on the ruins of a Mayan pyramid (1553). This church was founded by Fray Diego de Landa, the historian of the Spanish conquest of Mérida.

Train Mérida-Izamal leaves at 0600, returns 1500, US$0.30.

From Izamal one can go by the 1630 bus to **Cenotillo,** where there are several fine *cenotes* within easy walking distance from the town (avoid the one *in* town), especially U-Cil, excellent for swimming, and La Unión. From Mérida, take 1530 train to Tunkas, and then bus to Cenotillo. Lovely train ride, US$0.20. Past Centotillo is Espita and a road forks left to Tizimín (see below). Take a bus from Mérida (last bus back 1700) to see extensive ruins at Aké, unique structure.

Beyond Chichén-Itzá, and easily reached from Mérida (bus, US$1.80) is **Valladolid** (pop. 30,000), a pleasant Mayan town with another large Franciscan church, on the paved road between Mérida and Puerto Juárez.

Hotels *María de la Luz*, Plaza Principal, Tel.: 6-20-71, good, swimming pool (non-residents, US$0.50) and small night-club, poor restaurant, closes at 2230, E; *San Clemente*, Calle 41 and 42 No. 206 (Tel.: 62208), E, with air conditioning, has car park, swimming pool, opposite Cathedral, in centre of town. *Mesón del Marqués*, E (air-conditioned), with bath, on square, with good restaurant and shop, excellent value. *Oso Río*, on W side of Plaza, 2 blocks N, small, clean, friendly, E; quiet and excellent is *María Guadalupe*, Calle 44, No. 198, F, with hot water, but uncertain water supply. *Lili*, Calle 44, F, hot shower, fan, basic, safe motorcycle parking, friendly; next to it is *Osorno*, G, hot water (but only very early a.m.), dirty and full of cockroaches; *Don Luis*, Calle 39 (same street as bus station) 1 block E of 26 Calo, quiet, friendly, pool, a/c, F, mosquitoes; *Mendoza*, Calle 39, No. 204C, good, clean, near bus station, F. *Alcócer*, F, with bath if you bargain, fairly clean. *Zaci*, Calle 44, E (F with fan rather than a/c), good. In *Casa de Caminero*, 6 blocks W from bus station, hammocks US$0.80 a night. **Restaurant** *Los Arcos*, near plaza, set lunch US$1.20.

Post Office Calle 46, almost opp. bus terminal, 1½ blocks S from square on E side (does not accept parcels for abroad); telegraph office 1½ blocks S on W side of same block.

Bank Bancomer on E side of square (to the right of church).

Tourist Office on Plaza next to Bancomer, not very helpful, but willing.

Buses To Chichén-Itzá, take Mérida bus, US$0.80, every ½ hr., 1 hr. ride, also to Balancanché; many buses go to Mérida, US$2.45; and to Puerto Juárez, US$2.45, from 0800 and Cancún, US$2.45. To Playa del Carmen at 0430 and 1400 (via Cobá and Tulum) US$3.20; fare to Tulum, US$3.50, 2½ hrs.; to Chetumal, at 0600, 1500 and 2000, 2nd class US$5.30, 5 hrs. Many buses to Mérida. Taxi to Puerto Juárez (160 km.), US$31.10, takes seven passengers. N.B. beware of harassment by beggars at the bus station.

One can swim in the very clean electrically-lit *cenote* of Dzit-Nup (entry US$0.30, taxi, return plus wait, US$3 from Valladolid) outside Valladolid. Also lovely *cenote* at Zací, with a restaurant and lighted promenades, 2 blocks N of *Don Luis*, but you cannot swim in it because of the algae. Road turns left from Puerto Juárez road a couple of blocks from main plaza.

A paved road heads N (buses) from Valladolid to **Tizimín**, a very pleasant town with a 16th-century church and convent, open squares and narrow streets, and a few hotels, E and F; it has a famous New Year *fiesta*. There is a good restaurant, *Tres Reyes*. There is also a local *cenote*, Kikib. The road continues N over the flat landscape to **Río Lagartos**, itself on a lagoon, where the Mayas extracted salt. (*Hotel Nefertiti*, E, hot shower, also room for hammocks upstairs, fish

986 MEXICO

restaurant.) There are a number of small eating-places. Swimming from island opposite Río Lagartos, where boats are moored. Bus from Río Lagartos to **San Felipe** (13 km.), can bathe in the sea; good cheap seafood at *El Payaso* restaurant. On a small island with ruins of a Maya pyramid, beware of rattlesnakes. One can also go from Río Lagartos to **Los Colorados** (15 km.) to swim and see the salt deposits with red, lilac and pink water. Boat trips (US$4, expensive, bargain the price before embarking) can be arranged in Río Lagartos to see the flamingoes (often only a few pairs) feeding in the lagoons E of Los Colorados. Not a lot else here, but if you are stuck for food, eat inexpensively at the *Casino* (ask locals). Road on to El Cuyo, rough and sandy, but passable. El Cuyo has a shark-fishing harbour. Fishermen cannot sell (co-op) but can barter fish—fry your shark steak with garlic, onions and lime juice.

Also N of Valladolid, turning off the road to Puerto Juárez after Xcan, is **Holbox** Island. Buses to Chiquilá for boats, 3 times a day. If you miss the ferry a fisherman will probably take you quite cheaply (say US$2). You can leave your car in care of the harbour master for a small charge; his house is E of the dock. Take water with you if possible. Totally unspoiled, take blankets and hammock (ask at fishermen's houses where you can put up), and lots of mosquito repellant. Best camping on beach E of village (N side of island). Fish expensive but bread very good. Wonderful shell-hunting. Five more uninhabited islands beyond Holbox. Beware of sharks and barracuda, though few nasty occurrences have been reported.

Off the rough and mostly unpopulated bulge of the Yucatán coastline are several islands, once notorious for contraband. Beware of mosquitoes in the area. A paved road runs from Mérida to **Puerto Juárez** (*Hotel Caribel*, F with bath and fan; *Hotel Isabel* at ferry terminal, not clean, with restaurant, F; *Posada Zuemy*, 100 metres from bus terminal, on road to Cancún, F; another unsigned hotel a bit further along this road, F; *Hotel Los Faroles*, F, with bath, small, hot cabins less good; opp. is *Hotel Jannette*, E, dearer, and better. *Restaurant Puerto Juárez* at bus terminal, friendly, good value). Camping/trailer park *Almirante de Gante*, new, hot showers, right on the beach, 4 km. from army camp and 1 km. from Punta Sam. *Cabañas Punta Sam*, clean, comfortable, on the beach, E with bath; also *Meco Loco* campsite at Punta Sam. Irregular bus service there, or hitchhike from Puerto Juárez. Check to see if restaurant is open evenings. No shops nearby. Take mosquito repellant. Tourist kiosk, open 0900-1700, at passenger ferry to Isla Mujeres which leaves from the jetty opposite the bus terminal at Puerto Juárez seven times a day (at same time each way); can be erratic and sometimes leaves early (US$0.75). Also small boats, US$0.45. Ferry from Punta Sam to Isla Mujeres, which takes cars (about 15), 5 km. by bus from Cancún via Puerto Juárez (facilities to store luggage), US$0.25; check for times as time-tables at Punta Sam and Isla Mujeres differ, and may not even give correct information either end. Our information is that it leaves six times a day between 0830 and 2300, returning between 0715 and 2200 (45-min. journey). For early morning ferry from Isla Mujeres, tickets sale anytime from about 0615. Get there early as it is popular. The bus from Mérida (US$4) stops at the ferry and there are hourly buses from Puerto Juárez from 0500. The boat trip across is US$2.20 for car, US$4.45 for trailer, US$0.22 p.p.

Buses go from Puerto Juárez to Tulum (see page 989), Felipe Carrillo Puerto and Chetumal. Bus to Chetumal, 1st class US$7, 2nd class, US$4.80, 5 a day, 6 hrs. To Palenque 2nd class, US$4. To Chichén Itzá, 2nd class, 4 hrs., US$3.30. To Cancún US$0.25. All regular buses from Puerto Juárez stop at Tulum, US$2, 2 hrs. If driving from Puerto Juárez to Tulum, turn right by the Pemex station on to Route 307—it is badly signposted. "You can travel to Emiliano Zapata (40 km. from Palenque) in a day," write Dirk Noordman and Mieke Jansen of the Netherlands, "taking a launch from Isla Mujeres at 0700, take 0800 bus from Puerto Juárez (very few seats available as the vehicle comes from Cancún) to Chetumal, take 1330 bus from Chetumal to Villahermosa (or later bus at 1430) to Tuxtla Gutiérrez) reach Emiliano Zapata at 1900, good hotels and restaurants; 2nd class buses hourly from Zapata to Plaza, at the crossing of the Palenque and Chetumal road."

Isla Mujeres (which got its name from the large number of female idols first found by the Spaniards) once epitomized the Caribbean island: long silver beaches, palm trees and clean blue water at the N end (although the large *El Presidente* hotel spoils the view there) away from the beach pollution of the town, and the naval airstrip to the SW of the town. There are limestone (coral) cliffs and a rocky coast at the S end. A lagoon on the W side is now fouled up. The island is suffering from competition from Cancún and many hotels are now looking rather run-down; however, Isla Mujeres is reported to be still a pleasant place. The main activity in the evening takes place in the square near the church, where there are also a supermarket and a cinema. Between December 1-8 there is a fiesta for the Virgin of the island, fireworks, dances until 0400 in the Plaza. If driving, respect speed limits, roads with new gravelling are tricky.

There is public transport on Isla Mujeres, i.e. taxis at fixed prices, e.g. US$1.20 to N beach, and US$0.10 bus service. You can walk from one end of the island to the other in 1½ hrs. Worth hiring a bicycle (wonderfully rickety), by the hour, US$0.35, or US$2.50 a day (about US$7 deposit), or a Honda 50 hourly or for a day (US$15), to explore this tiny island in about 2 hrs. Do check if there is any damage to the bicycle *before* you hire. Bicycles for hire from several hotels. Try Ciro's Motorrentor by *Hotel Caribe*. You can rent skin and scuba diving equipment, together with guide, from Divers of Mexico, on the waterfront N of the public pier. They can set up group excursions to the Cave of the Sleeping Sharks; English spoken. It is cheaper to hire snorkel gear in town than on the beach. Deep sea fishing US$89 for 10 in a boat from *Aguamundo*. Diving is not in the class of Cozumel and Mexico Divers, with slapdash attitude to safety, not recommended.

At Garrafón beach, 7 km. (mind your belongings, entry US$0.75) there is a tropical fish reserve (fishing forbidden) on a small coral reef. Take snorkel (rental US$3 a day from shop opp. the ferry (need tourist card for security), but US$2 an hour and US$0.75 for locker at Garrafón where drinks are twice the price of those in town) and swim among an astonishing variety of multicoloured tropical fish—they aren't at all shy. At peak times, however, there can be more snorkellers than fish. Worth walking on from here up a track to the lighthouse. (Taxi to Garrafón US$2.75; there is a bus which goes half-way there.) One can cycle down to the southern end of the island to the curious remains of a pirate's domain, called Casa de Mundaca, a nature reserve with giant turtles at El Chequero, and a little Mayan lighthouse or shrine of Ixtel. It is not signposted—mind you don't walk into the army firing range. Fine views. The island is best visited April to November, off-season (although one can holiday here the year round); beaches are then empty and the town is not overcrowded. It is best to go before 1000. The northern beach has dazzling white sand, so wear sunglasses. **N.B.** Travellers are warned that there is a very dangerous beach on the ocean side near the north with strong undertows and cross-currents; there have been numerous drownings. It is just behind the *Bojórquez Hotel*. Trip to unspoilt Isla Contoy (bird and wildlife sanctuary), US$15, two hours of fishing, snorkelling (equipment hire extra, US$2.50) and relaxing (see also under Cancún). Boats may not leave until full.

Hotels At Christmas hotel prices are increased steeply and the island can heave with tourists, esp. in January. The island has several costly hotels and others, mainly in the D category, and food is generally expensive, but fish is cheaper than on the mainland.

Reasonable hotels to stay at on Isla Mujeres are *Posada Zorro*, unpretentious, E; *Osorio*, E, 1 block from waterfront, bath, fan, with bath and hot water, recommended, excellent bakery nearby. *El Presidente Caribe*, private lagoon, spectacular (changes travellers' cheques), very fancy, C; *Caribe Maya*, central, modern, fans, E; *Carmelina*, E, central with bath, good, hires out bicycles; *María José* nr. seafront, E with bath. *Martínez*, D, doors locked at 2200; *El Paso*, D, with bath, clean, facing the pier, 2nd floor; *Posada San Luis*, E, with bath, good, 1 block to ocean side of island in coconut plantation, 4 bungalows; *Xul-Ha*, 1 block to N beach, baths, D; *Caracol*, E, central, clean, good value; *María de los Angeles*, ½ block from naval base, E, with bath; *Rocamar*, D, Caribbean side, restaurant, sea views, thunderous wave noise (especially at night), clean but overpriced; *Posada del Mar*, B (including meals) has pleasant drinks terrace but expensive drinks, restaurant for residents only; *Rocas del Caribe*, B, 100 metres from ocean, cool rooms, big balcony, clean, good service; *Isla Mujeres*, D, next to church, E, with bath, being renovated late 1986; one of cheapest is *Las Palmas*, E with bath, clean and friendly, across from the market, with good little restaurants nearby. *Berny*, C, with bath, good, long-distance calls possible, residents only, but does not even honour confirmed reservations if a deposit for one night's rate has not been made. Try, however, at the cheaper end the *Hostal Poc-Na*, F, dormitory style (mixed, 8 beds), bunks or hammocks, hot water upstairs, very clean, pet room with fan, American-run; breakfast and sandwiches, central sitting area with juke box. Good for meeting fellow back-packers. One block from *Poc-Na* is *Marcionita*, F with bath, recommended. (As ever, have plenty of mosquito repellant or pyrethrum coils.) There is a trailer park on the island, with a restaurant. At S end of island is *Camping Los Indios* where you can put up your hammock. In town nobody seems to know (or want to know) about this place. **N.B.** If you arrive late, book into any hotel the first night and set out to find what you want by 0700-0800, when the first ferries leave the next morning.

Restaurants Many beach restaurants close just before sunset. *Ciro's*, good, but beware of overcharging; *Caracol*, also good, slightly cheaper; *Super Tortas*, delicious sandwiches served by young Jenny, a real character. *Villa del Mar*, recommended, about US$2.70-3.20. At Garrafón Beach: *El Garrafón, El Garrafón de Castilla, French Marías*, all 3 cater for tour boats from Cancún, pricey lobster on magnificent tropical beach. *Gomar*, in town, probably best value and slowest service, possible to eat outside on verandah or in the colonial-style interior, popular; *Eric's*, 1 block inland, very good inexpensive Mexican snacks; *Tropicana*, 1 block from pier, simple, popular, cheap; *Cielito Lindo*, waterfront, open air, good service; *La Langosta*, 3 blocks S, good Mexican dishes, lovely view; *Bucanero*, downtown, steak, seafood, prime rib, classy for Islas Mujeres. *Sergio's* on main square, expensive, very good. *Dhaymaru*, inexpensive, good lentil soup; *Giltri*, in town, good value. Small restaurants round market are good value; try the local Poc-Chuc (pork and vegetables) dish.

Opposite the restaurant *Gomar* is a souvenir shop that sells good stone Maya carvings (copies), macramé hangings and colourful wax crayon "Maya" prints. *El Paso Boutique*, opp. ferry, trades a small selection of English novels.

There is a road from Puerto Juárez to Belize via Chetumal (paved all the way to

988 MEXICO

Chetumal, fast). About 40 km. before Chetumal there are seven *cenotes* which are ideal for swimming.

The much-talked about resort of **Cancún**, near the north-eastern tip of the Yucatán peninsula, can be reached by bus from Puerto Juárez, which also connects with ferry services from the islands. Cancún (whose site is said to have been selected by a computer) is a thriving resort complex and town with skyscraper hotels, basically for the rich, and many smaller hotels with cheaper accommodation. Prices are higher on Cancún than elsewhere in Mexico because everything is brought in from miles outside. Hotels in Cancún town are much cheaper than on the beach and there are buses running every 5 minutes for US$0.05. The population is about 30,000, almost all dedicated to servicing the tourist industry. There is an archaeological museum next to the Convention Centre with local finds, which also houses the Ballet Folklórico shows in air-conditioned splendour. There are 3 supermarkets (one of them, Bodego El Teniente on Av. Tulum, is good place for changing US dollar cash or cheques) and 5 interconnecting shopping malls. Excursion to Isla Contoy daily, once a day, US$55, including boat, food and snorkelling equipment. The computer seems to have failed in two respects: (a) there are sharks; (b) there are undercurrents. So swimming in the sea is discouraged on several beaches.

Hotels *Camino Real; Sheraton, Exalaris Hyatt, Cancún Caribe* and *Exalaris Hyatt Regency; Fiesta Americana* and *Krystal.* Slightly less expensive: *Aristos, Quality Inn, Club Lagoon Caribe, Viva* (B), *El Presidente, Miramar Mansion.* Less expensive still: *Bahía de Mujeres, Caribe Mar* and *Playa Blanca;* at the far end of the island is the *Club Mediterranée* with its customary facilities. Youth hostel, *CREA,* on the beach, dormitory style, 12 people per room, F p.p. Hotels in Cancún town: *América, Atlantis, Reifa;* slightly less expensive: *Antillano, Batalo, Carillo, Colonial, Handall, Konvasser* (a Mayan, not German name), *María de Lourdes, Parador, Plaza Caribe, Plaza del Sol, Rivemar, Caribe Internacional, Soberanis, Tulum, Villa Maya.* Least expensive but acceptable still: *Arabe, Bonampak, Canto, Coral, Mar y Mar, Marufo, Villa Rossana, Yaxchilán,* and *La Carreta Guest House.*

Camping is not permitted in Cancún except next to the CREA youth hostel. It is otherwise restricted to a magnificent stretch of beach just past Puerto Juárez and before Punta Sam, a few km. N of town.

Restaurants There are about 200 restaurants apart from those connected with hotels. They range from hamburger stands to 5-star, gourmet places. The best buys are on the side streets of Cancún town, while the largest selection can be found on the main street, Av. Tulum. The ones on the island are of slightly higher price and quality and are scattered along Kukulkan Blvd., the main island drive, with a high concentration in the 5 shopping centres. The native Mexican restaurants in the workers' colonies are cheapest. Very popular is *El Establo* with *El Granero* disco, just off Av. Tulum on Claveles.

Buses Local bus (Route No. 1), US$0.10. Within easy reach of the new resort are Chichén-Itzá (bus, 3½ hrs., US$2.75), Tulum, and many lesser known Maya centres such as Cobá and Tablé. The road to Tulum is completely paved. Local bus to Puerto Juárez US$0.25, about 4 hrs., hourly between 0600-2300. To Chetumal, US$6.45 1st class, 0800-1600 hourly, takes 5 hrs. To Tulum US$1.65, 4 daily 1st class, 5 daily 2nd class, walk 1 km. from bus stop. To Valladolid, US$2.45 1st, US$2 2nd class; To Mexico City, ADO, 1st class at 0615, 1215 and 1815. It is possible to get to Isla Mujeres direct from Cancún with hydrofoil, 20 mins., up to 5 trips a day planned.

Puerto Morelos (bus US$0.50), not far S of Cancún, is not special. It has 3 hotels, two expensive, one basic, *Amor,* F, near bus stop; also free and paying camping. Popular with scuba divers and snorkellers, but beware of sharks.

Boat Services See Cozumel, below; boats leave from the pier near *Calinda Quality Inn* in Cancún.

Air Services Cancún (very expensive shops and restaurant), Cozumel and Isla Mujeres have airports. Aeroméxico, Av. Tulum 3, Tel.: 42758; Mexicana, Av. Cobá 13, Tel.: 41090; American Airlines, Aeropuerto, Tel.: 42947; United Airlines, Centro El Pavaín, Tel.: 42340. Mexicana has direct flights Mexico City-Cancún-Miami; also daily flights Mexico City-Cancún-Mérida. From Cancún to Mérida US$24; Monterrey US$81; Mexico City US$153; Houston US$135; Los Angeles US$237; New York US$250, by Aeroméxico. Lacsa flies Cancún-Costa Rica, US$190 one way, US$10 more to Panama. Bookable only at *Hotel María de Lourdes,* closed during siestatime. Nouvelles Frontières fly charter Zürich-Cancún, 66 Blvd. St. Michel, 75006 Paris, France. Flight Cozumel-Mexico City via Mérida with Mexicana. Taxi-buses from airport to Cancún town US$2. Irregular bus from Cancún to the airport four times a day. Ordinary taxi US$3-3.50.

Paamul, about 90 km. S of Cancún, is a fine beach with chalets and campsites (recommended) on

MEXICO 989

a bay, with good restaurant. Good snorkelling and diving. 2nd-class buses from Cancún and Playa del Carmen pass.

Playa del Carmen, which is under development, has nice beaches; 68 km. or one hour by bus from Tulum (US$1), but also buses from Mérida, Cancún (US$1) and Pto. Juárez. From Mérida 1st class buses go via Cancún, 4 a day (co-ordinate with ferry to Cozumel), 2nd class buses 7 a day, 5 hrs. Campsite, avoid *Hotel Molcas* (A), but *Posada Lily*, F, with shower, recommended, 1 block from first class bus station; *Hotel Nuevo Amanecer*, C, very attractive; *Hotel Balam Ha*, beside the pier, complete resort, C; at km. 297/8, before Playa del Carmen, *Cabañas Capitán Lafitte*, rustic, on barren beach, E; at km. 296 and similar, *El Marlín Azul*, A, swimming pool, better food; *Sian Ka'an*, Calle Siyan Can, 100 m. from bus station, F/G, simple, clean, recommended; *Cabañas La Ruina*, on beach, F, popular, recommended. Restaurants: *La Nena* and *Pizza Moluscas* (expensive, good service); *Balam*, good breakfasts; *Chac Mool*, good, reasonable, near airstrip. *Chateau Las Palmas*, across from school, good, especially breakfast. Avoid *Hueva del Coronado*, complaints about overloaded bills. Ferry for Cozumel, US$2.50, 1¼ hrs., journey, leaves at 0600, 1000, 1200, 1600, last at 1800, returns at 0400, 0700, 0930, 1300, and 1600; dirty old ship. The luxurious catamaran sails once a day for US$4. Bus to Tulum and Chetumal, US$4.50, 0530, 0700, 0900.

Best value for money on **Cozumel** island are the *Hotel Pepita-Bungalows*, E; *Maya Cozumel*, clean, friendly, pool, on Calle 4, D; *Barracuda*, C; *Aguilar*, D, pool, clean, central, a/c, recommended; *Posada Martín*, E; *Mesón San Miguel*, Plaza, D; *Posada Cozumel*, a/c, E; *López*, D, hot showers, clean, main square, no meals; *El Pirata*, E, with private bath; *Capitán Candela*, inland, pool, good value, E. First class (A) hotels: *Cabañas del Caribe, Cozumel Caribe, El Cozumeleño, El Presidente, Fiesta Americana, La Ceiba, Mayan Plaza*. The first-class hotels on the island charge about US$50-110 d a day and all are directly on the beach except the *Fiesta Americana*, which has a tunnel under the road to the beach. The best public beaches are some way from the town: in the N of the island they are sandy and wide, in the S narrower and rockier. All these hotels are on the sheltered W coast. The E coast is rockier and has only one, rustic *Hotel Cupido*, more like bungalows. Swimming and diving on the unprotected side is very dangerous owing to ocean underflows. Camping is not permitted although there are two suitable sites on the S shore. Try asking for permission at the army base.

Restaurants *Las Palmeras*, at the pier (people-watching spot), recommended; *Pizza Rolandi*, waterfront; *Grip's*, on waterfront, good; *Morgans*, main square, elegant; *Café del Puerto*, 2nd floor by pier, South Seas style; *Super Tortas Los Moros*, Mexican, popular; *Costa Brava*, good seafood and breakfast, good value, recommended. *Carlos and Charlie's* restaurant/bar, popular, 2nd floor on waterfront.

Nightclubs *Joman's, Scaramouche, Grip's*, all downtown, apart from hotel nightclubs.

Boat Service The *Carnaval Cozumel* catamaran, seating almost 400 in comfort, sails in the morning and again in the afternoon from the main pier in Cozumel for Cancún. A very popular day trip; US$12 p.p. each way. Get reservations early, always full; Tel.: 215-08.

Paved road on Cozumel but no bus service round island; best to hire push-bike (quiet) when touring around the island so one can see wildlife—iguanas, turtles, birds—but if taking motorbike beware of policemen who take unguarded ones and then claim they were parked illegally; local police are strict and keen on fining so avoid illegal parking, U-turns, etc. Snorkel 9 km. S of San Miguel de Cozumel at Parque Chankanaab, with restaurants and hire facilities: equipment US$4 a day. Deportes Acuáticos Damián Piza on Calle 8 Norte, US$40 p.p. includes all equipment, 2 dives with diligent guide separated by a cooked lunch and sunbake on Playa San Francisco—fascinating. Restored ruins of Maya-Toltec period at San Gervasio (7 km. from Cozumel town, then 6 km. to the left).

There are some Mayan ruins, unrestored (the Pole ruins) at **Xcaret**, a turnoff left on Route 307 to Tulum, after Playa del Carmen. You can go to a hand-forged chain over a 2 km. bad road and pay whoever comes out of the house 20 pesos entry and proceed down the road a few metres on foot. The ruins are near three interlocking *cenotes*, to their left; there are also lovely sea water lagoons—one can swim. Pole was the departure point for Mayan voyages to Cozumel. There is a roadside restaurant which despite its looks is very clean (accepts Visa).

Akumal, a luxury resort, is 20 km. N of Tulum. Cove owned by Mexican Skin-Divers Society, 110 km. S from Puerto Juárez. *Hotel Caribe*, B, not very special food so don't take full board (there is a small supermarket nearby at Villas Mayas), no entertainment, excellent beach, linked to two buildings separated by Villas Mayas, with coral reef only 100 metres offshore. In addition at *Villas Mayas*, bungalows B, with bath, comfortable, some with kitchens, on beach, snorkelling equipment for hire, US$6 per day, good restaurant with poor service. Recommended as base for excursions to Xelhá, Tulum and Cobá. Not far from Akumal are Chemuyil and X-Cacel down new roads, with restaurants.

Tulum The Tulum ruins, Maya-Toltec, are 128 km. S of Cancún, 1 km. off the

990 MEXICO

main road; they are 12th century, with city walls of white stone atop seashore cliffs (frescoes still visible on interior walls of temples). The temples were dedicated to the worship of the Falling God, or the Setting Sun, represented as a falling character over nearly all the West-facing doors (Cozumel was the home of the Rising Sun). The same idea is reflected in the buildings, which are wider at the top than at the bottom. Open 0800-1700, about 2 hrs. needed to view at leisure (entry US$0.25). Tulum is these days crowded with tourists. The village is not very large and has neither a bank nor post office (nearest at Playa del Carmen or Felipe Carrillo Puerto, 132 km. away); there is no accommodation here, so you must leave the bus at the ruins. Shops at the ruins are expensive and locals can be unfriendly. Beaches are beautiful but sometimes dirty, and there is thieving from beach camping spots and *cabañas*, so be careful.

The ruins are just off the paved road, restaurant at turning will store luggage for US$0.40 per bag, between Felipe Carrillo Puerto (*Hotel Carrillo Puerto* has been recommended; *Hotel Esquivel*, just off Plaza, F, not good, dirty, no locks on doors, noisy; *Restaurant Addy*, on main road, S of town, good, simple) and Puerto Juárez (133 km.), and can also be visited by boat from Cozumel.
There is a large car-park at the entrance to the ruins (here you can leave luggage), which is ringed by small shops (selling dresses, etc). and restaurants of which only one sells beer and liquor and closes at 1700. Soft drinks expensive. There is a newly-laid road linking Tulum with the large but little-excavated city of Cobá (see below) with the turn-off to Cobá 1½ km. along the main road in the direction of Chetumal, which joins the Valladolid-Puerto Juárez road at X-Can, thus greatly shortening the distance between Chichén-Itzá and Tulum. On the paved road to the right of the parking lot, along the coast, you will find a whole string of beach places with hammock and tent space and rooms with meals, F. Hammock space may also be rented in the village of Tulum, 2 km. from ruins (minibus to ruins at 0900, US$0.50); *Motel Crucero*, F; about 1½ km. from the ruins down the beach is *Santa Fe* where *cabañas* are rented for US$3, noisy (cars, music), has poor restaurant, no toilets, littered, not recommended; again along the beach nearby is *Cabañas El Mirador*, small, quiet, cabins US$1.60, no sanitation, and *El Paraíso*, very casual, agree rates in advance. Mosquito-net supplies are very limited so take good repellant lotion with you. Water at *El Mirador* and *Santa Fe* a bit smelly because well-water is used for washing and suds have spoiled it, but good water at a spot on the road between ruins and the path to the camp sites. One restaurant on the road and two restaurants next to the Navy camp, worth trying. Walk past the restaurants to the shops and main centre (15-20 mins.), where you can stock up on supplies which are cheaper than at the ruins. Continue on the road out of town past the village well and then some beehives, then take a well-worn path to the beach. *Pablo's House* (the village is 3 km. away from Pablo's), is cheaper with own hammocks, meals, no w.c. or showers, only a well, fairly basic, beware of overcharging. Watch your belongings. Trailer Park next door. *Chac Mool*, 7 km. S from ruins, again wooden huts (E), good showers, restaurant, nice, F. You can cook over open fires along the beach about ½ km. from the ruins, so take your own food. A new hotel is being built at crossroads where buses stop to let people off for the ruins, and there is a restaurant there, which will hold luggage while you visit the site. *Hotel Posada Tulum*, 8 km. S of the ruins on the beach, has an expensive restaurant and is not served by public transport. About 6 km. from ruins are *Cabañas de Tulum*, E, also with restaurant and camping, Swiss owner; take taxi there, empty white beaches, no bus to ruins. The road from Tulum to Felipe Carrillo Puerto is paved. Gasoline stations at Cancún near Tulum, Nuevo Xcan and Felipe Carrillo Puerto, but one only between Tulum and Cancún (140 km.). Late arrival at Tulum is not recommended, as everything closes at dusk and it is difficult to find accommodation. Ruins of Chumyaxche, three pyramids (partly overgrown), on the left-hand side of this road, 18 km. S of Tulum, worth a visit.

Parking or camping possible on beach S of lighthouse, whose keeper also rents huts along beach for US$1.20 a day, and at *Cabañas El Mirador*. Good swimming locally; divers bring in lobster from a coral reef about 400 metres offshore.

N of Tulum (12 km.) at km. 245 is a beautiful clear lagoon (**Laguna Xelhá**) full of fish, but no fishing allowed as it is a national park (open 0800-1700), entry US$0.40. Snorkelling gear can be rented at US$3.15 for a day, but it is often in poor repair; better to rent from your hostel. Arrive as early as possible to see fish as later buses full of tourists arrive from Cancún. Bungalows being built. Very expensive hotel. There is a marvellous jungle path to one of the lagoon bays. Xelhá ruins (known also as Los Basadres) are located across the road from the beach of the same name. You may have to jump the fence to visit. Small ruins of Ak are near Xelhá. N of Tulum, at Tancáh, are newly-discovered bright post-classical Maya murals but they are sometimes closed to the public.

Bus to Mérida, three daily via Puerto Morelos, 6 hrs.; from Felipe Carrillo Puerto to Mérida via Muna, US$4, 4½ hrs. To Felipe Carrillo Puerto, 1 hr., US$1.50, few buses; to Chetumal, US$2.90, 4 hrs.; to Puerto Juárez, 2 hrs., 2nd class, US$2; to Cancún, US$1.65, 2 hrs.; to Playa del Carmen, US$1. To Cobá at 0600 and 1200, goes on to Valladolid (US$1.30); at 1700 goes only to Cobá; bus to Cobá from Valladolid passes X-Can (no hotel but the owner of the shop where the road

MEXICO 991

branches off to Cobá may offer you a room); to Valladolid, US$3.50, 2½ hrs., few buses (it is easier to reach Valladolid via Cancún than direct).

Cobá, the ancient political capital of the area, with the largest ruins (entry US$ 0.20), about 50 km. inland from Tulum, still unspoiled, is also being developed and has one of the *Villa Arqueológica* hotels belonging to the Club Méditerranée, open to non members, clean and quiet, B-D, swimming pool, good food; *Isabel*, 6 double rooms, F, separate bathrooms, cool, mosquito-free; go via Valladolid, Chemax on Puerto Juárez road—or bus from Cancún or daily from Playa del Carmen via Tulum to Cobá. Bus, Cobá-Tulum, 1500. Few buses, but two daily to Valladolid at 0730 and 1230 (from Valladolid, 0430, 1400, US$1.90, 2 hrs.). Good, cheap restaurant in the village, *El Bocadito*. Beware of ticks and snakes when rummaging through the brush. 1½ km. from the extensive ruins of Cobá lies a huge pyramid called Nohoch-Mul. The entire archaeological zone encompasses about 6,500 structures and covers many square kilometres.

Baja California

Baja California (Lower California) is that long narrow arm of land which dangles southwards from the US border between the Pacific and the Gulf of California for 1,300 km. It is divided administratively into the states of Baja California Norte and Baja California Sur, with a time change at the state line. The average width is only 80 km. Rugged and almost uninhabited mountains split its tapering length. Only the southern tip gets enough rain: the northern half gets its small quota during the winter, the southern half during the summer. Most of the land is hot, parched desert. There are some Indians still, but without any tribal organization. Not only the northern part, bordering the USA, but also the southern tip is attracting increasing numbers of tourists. The US dollar is preferred in most places north of La Paz.

Hitch-hiking is difficult, and there is very little public transport off the main highway. The local population is not particularly friendly towards tourists, especially those from the USA. There is no immigration check-point on the Mexican side of the border—immigration authorities are encountered when boarding the ferry to cross the Gulf. Ferries ply to La Paz, Santa Rosalía and Cabo San Lucas from various places on the mainland coast (see text). As a car needs an import permit, make sure you get to the ferry with lots of time and preferably with a reservation if going on the La Paz-Mazatlán ferry.

Recommended guide: the Automobile Club of Southern California's "Baja California", which contains plenty of information on the peninsula. Also excellent AAA maps. The value-added tax (IVA) is only 6 % in Baja California compared with 15 % on the mainland. Stove fuel is impossible to find in Baja California Sur. Beware of overcharging on buses and make a note of departure times of buses in Tijuana or Ensenada when travelling S; between Ensenada and Santa Rosalía it is very difficult to obtain bus timetable information, even at bus stations. Don't ask for English menus if you can help it—prices often differ from the Spanish version. Always check change, overcharging is rife.

Cortés paid a brief visit to La Paz, in the S, soon after the Conquest, but the land had nothing but its beauty to recommend it and it was left to the Missions to develop. The first Jesuit settlement was at Loreto in 1697. Other orders took over when the Jesuits were expelled in 1768. The results were tragic: the Indians were almost wiped out by the diseases of the Fathers. Scattered about the Sierras are the beautiful ruins of these well-meaning but lethal missions.

Baja California's population has increased by two-thirds in the past decade through migration from Mexico's interior and Central Pacific coast. The development of agriculture, tourism, industry, and migrant labour for California has caused a great upsurge of economic growth and consequently of prices, especially in areas favoured by tourists.

The Morelos dam on the upper reaches of the Colorado river has turned the Mexicali valley into a major agricultural area: 400,000 acres under irrigation to grow cotton, and olive groves are also succeeding. Industries are encouraged in all border regions by handsome investment incentives.

Mexicali (pop. 500,000), capital of Baja California Norte state, isn't much of a tourist attraction but the neighbourhood around the *Rivera Hotel* is pleasant. There are *charreadas* (rodeos), in season, on Sundays, around April to October—check times.

Hotels *Cecil*, OK, not too dear, avoid Chinese restaurant next door; *Capri*, in centre, E, acceptable; *Motel Aztec de Oro*, E, with shower, a bit scruffy but convenient; *Rivera*, near railway station, E, a/c, tolerable; *Frontera*, F, with bath. *Playa*, F, next to Banca Serfín, no fan; CREA Youth Hostel, Av. Salina Cruz y Coahuila, new, clean, friendly, ask for mattress on floor if full; reasonable Chinese

992 MEXICO

restaurant nearby. **Motels** *Holiday Inn*, Juárez 2220, C; *Bel Air*, on road to Coahuila, D; *Regis*, San Felipe road, D; *La Siesta*, Calzada Justa Serra, C; 11 more around town.

Train The railway station to the S is about 3½ km. from the tourist area on the border and Calle 3 bus connects it with the nearby bus terminal. There is a passport desk at the station. The ticket information office closes at 1230 but there are timetables on the wall. There is no direct service between Mexicali and Mexico City, every trip requires changing in Guadalajara. Slow train (leaves 2145, has regular 1st and 2nd class cars) to Guadalajara and Mexico City takes 57 hrs.; fast train 44 hrs. (36 hrs. to Guadalajara) at 1045, has only sleepers and special 1st class (although at times it is as slow as the slow train owing to breakdowns), little price difference. Be sure to take your own food. Make sure you are on the right car as some are disconnected—guards not always reliable. Thorough police luggage searches for drugs and guns possible. Mexicali to Mazatlán, 23 hrs. Toilets in each class are inefficient and therefore unpleasant. There is no air conditioning except in *dormitorio* cabins for 1-2 persons. Price difference between cabins and roomettes minimal, but cabin vastly preferable. If there are dining cars they can run out of food, when there are delays. Very hot and dusty in desert part of trip, though train is cleaned twice. Food and drink sold on station platforms. Passengers not on sleeping cars on fast train change at Benjamín Hill to the train from Nogales which is often very full on arrival (on the slow train only the special 1st class car and the dining car are detached, the rest go all the way to Guadalajara). If you come from the N on the slow train and want to go to Chihuahua you'll arrive at 2005 at the junction, Sufragio (the fast train arrives at 0250). For a hotel, go to San Blas, 5 mins. away by local bus, where there are 3 hotels: *Santa Lucía*, *San Marco*, both often full; *Pérez* dirty but adequate, F. If the next morning you are refused a ticket because the train is full, try getting in and getting a ticket on the train.

Bus Tijuana, 3 hrs., US$2.20 1st class, US$1.15 2nd class, leave from the bus terminal outside town, sit on right for views. To Sufragio US$5.40. Mexico City US$35. San Felipe, 3 hrs.; one departs at 1700, US$3. Hermosillo, 10 hrs., US$9. To Mexicali from San Diego (California), take the Greyhound bus from San Diego to Calexico via El Centro (US$8) and cross the border; this eliminates the need to go to Tijuana and then Mexicali. From near Mexican-US border take No. 33 local bus to main bus station. The bus station is two rather long blocks from the railway station.

The road to Tijuana leads from below-sea-level desert in endless serpentines over the coastal ranges. About 10 km. beyond Rumorosa a breathtaking panorama of the desert is one of the most dramatic views in the continent.

Tijuana (pop. 900,000), on the Pacific, is where millions of US tourists a year pop across the border for a quick visit. Besides countless bars, about 90 nightclubs and tourist bars range from the extremely stark to the respectable, with top class international entertainment. Daily horse or dog races at Caliente track; *jai-alai* games Fri. to Wed. Bullfights on most Suns. from April to October. One of its two bull rings is unique in the world for being set on an ocean beach. **N.B.** There are many good and inexpensive English-speaking dentists in the town, who attract Americans with their low fees. The road from Tijuana to La Paz is all paved. Although one crosses the border here there is no passport check and no granting of tourist visa until you get to Sonoita.

Hotels and Motels, first rate: *El Conquistador*, Blvd. Agua Caliente 700, B; *Fiesta Americana*, Blvd. Agua Caliente, A; *Calinda Quality Inn* and *El Presidente* on same street, both B, and *La Mesa Best Western Inn*, C; *Motel León*, Calle 7 No. 144, E; *Motel Alaska*, Calle 1, No. 125, E; *Country Club*, far out on same street, good value, C; *Caesar's*, Revolución y Zapata, a/c, restaurant, TV, good, D; *Machado*, Calle 1 A No. 1724, restaurant, E. CREA youth hostel; *La Posada*, Calle 1A (Artículo 123) No. 1956, just off Av. Revolución, F, dirty but central; *St. Francis*, Benito Juárez 2A, F, recommended, safe and pleasant area. There are more than a hundred others to choose from.

Restaurants *Capri*, cheap; *Tijuana Tilly's*, excellent meal, reasonably priced. Many more of every category imaginable.

Night Clubs recommended: *Flamingos*, S on old Ensenada road; *Chantecler*.

Flight Bargains from Tijuana airport (20 mins. from San Diego, California); Mexico City and Acapulco, round trip with stopovers in La Paz, Mazatlán, Guadalajara and Puerto Vallarta, or without stop-overs, 30 days, depending on day of departure, by Aeroméxico. Acsa airline offers a round trip to Mérida (Yucatán). Flight to La Paz, 1¼ hrs., leaves at 0950. "Expreso de Lujo" round trip to Puerto Vallarta.

Buses The shuttle bus to the new bus terminal (18 km. from town) beyond the airport, US$0.15. To Mexico City (about every hour) by first-class bus lines, US$40, about 48 hrs. Mexicali, 3 hrs., 1st class, US$2.20. La Paz at 1400 and 1800, two others daily, Tres Estrellas, 10 min. walk from US border (22 hrs., US$27), buses often not clean, slow journey because of bad road stretch between El Rosario and Guerrero Negro, book well in advance. In January and February the road is often flooded and then closed, so you may have to wait up to 5 days until it reopens. The bus to the Tijuana main bus station (marked Buena Vista) from the Tres Estrellas terminal, which is in the centre of Tijuana, is US$1 (US$2 return), caught from Calle Constitución and 3rd. Don't buy your internal ticket at the Tres Estrellas terminal but at the main station as it is cheaper; all companies there charge the same prices but the quality of buses varies. Bus to Mazatlán, US$25, 28 hrs., not recommended (only two rest stops and numberless customs stops). Bus to Hermosillo, 11 hrs.; to Guadalajara 36 hrs., US$28; to Los Mochis, US$15, 18 hrs. Avoid an expensive taxi ride between the bus station and the US border by taking a local bus from the end of the bus terminal. Tram from the border to downtown San Diego US$1. Greyhound terminal on the US side is 20 metres from the U.S. immigration office.

A dramatic 96-km. toll road (US$2.40) leads along cliffs overhanging the sea to **Ensenada**, whose Todos Santos bay on the Pacific, a gigantic curve with dolphins swimming in it, underlines the austere character of a landscape reduced to water, sky and scorched brown earth. Fishing for sport and commercial fishing, canning, wineries, olive groves and agriculture. The port serves deep-sea vessels, primarily for cotton export. In general, the town is of no great interest. Several hotels, many motels, good to modest; cheap hotels around Miramar and Calle 3. (*Hotel Pacífico*, F, clean and hot shower; *México*, Calle 4A and Av. Ruiz, F, satisfactory value; Restaurant: *Domico's*, Av. Ruiz 283, also Chinese restaurants in same avenue.) Handicrafts at Centro Artesanal Ensenada, Av. López Mateos 1306, Tel.: 9-15-36. Many shops competing so very reasonable clothes, blankets, pottery, etc. Population 113,000.

N.B. There is a police block on the highway S of town, visas or tourist cards needed.

La Bufadora, the largest blowhole on the Pacific coast, is located 16 km. S of Ensenada. Take the paved road which heads W from Mancadero, and follow it to the end (12½ km.). Spectacular scene of solid rock shuddering underfoot with each wave.

Rosarito, between Tijuana and Ensenada along the old "free" road, is a fast growing, informal and drab seaside resort. *Rosarito Beach Hotel*, de luxe. Other hotels: *Ensenada*; *Rosita*, F, adequate. Many economy motels.

San Felipe, a fishing village on the Gulf of California, 196 km. by paved road from Mexicali, has fine beaches, good fishing, and facilities for camping, but is now becoming dirty and noisy as a result of mass tourism.

Motels *Augie's Riviera*; *Del Mar*; *El Cortez*; *Los Cirios*, Calle 8a and Avenida B, E, pleasant.

The 1,556-km. road from the border, via Ensenada, San Quintín, Punta Prieta, Guerrero Negro, San Ignacio, Santa Rosalía, Mulegé, Loreto, Villa Insurgentes and Ciudad Constitución to La Paz is now completed, and services en route are adequate. Gasoline is now in ample supply. The road passes through a land of astonishing beauty and grotesque ugliness. At Cataviña, SE of Punta Baja, are *La Pinta* (ex-*El Presidente*) (D) and *Rancho Santa Inés* (F); it is an excellent base from which to explore desert fauna and flora. Half-way down the peninsula, at parallel 28°N, there is a time-change; Baja California Sur is one hour ahead of Baja California Norte. The latter is one of the few places in the world where you can see the *cirio* (candle) tree, which grows to heights of 6 to 10 metres, mainly between Rosario and Rosarito. It is also known as "boojum" and has a long slim trunk with short spiny branches that come out only after rain. There are also huge *cardón* cacti, and elephant trees in the central desert, a short thick, white tree, leafless in summer.

At **San Quintín,** an ugly town with an even uglier reputation, 193 km. S of Ensenada, is *Ernesto's Resort Motel*, 9 km. out of town, on beautiful beach. On an even more beautiful, deserted beach, many clams, 15 km. out of town, is *Cielito Lindo Hotel*, C, very clean, bad restaurant; trailer park (not recommended) in town near *El Presidente* (B, unfriendly); no cheaper places to be found. At **Guerrero Negro,** 400 km. S of San Quintín, there is a motel *El Presidente*, C, very clean. These motels are found at about every 150 km. along the route. Also *Las Dunas*, C, and *Motel California*, E. From late Nov. until late March whales can be seen at the grey whale national park 8 km. from town, 3¼ km. S on highway 1; turn at signpost, carry on 27 km. to park entrance. Watch between 0700 and 0900 and again at 1700, saves hiring a boat. At Scammon's Lagoon whale watchers have a good view of the breeding animals from December to January, 29 km. from Guerrero Negro. As there are few gas stations on the way, fill up wherever you can. **San Ignacio,** 144 km. by road SE of Guerrero Negro (pop. 1,000) is a charming oasis with a well-preserved church (founded 1728). This mission was begun by Jesuits who were recalled to Spain, and finished in

MEXICO 993

994 MEXICO

1786 by Juan Crisóstomo Gómez, of the Dominican order. Beautiful woodwork. Local dates are the best in Baja California. *Hotel La Pinta-Presidente* (D, overpriced) and *Motel La Posada* have very good restaurants (but latter's service deteriorates if you order the cheaper items on the menu); *Cuartos Glenda*, E, with shower, basic but cheapest in town, excellent simple restaurant beside highway less than 350 metres beyond turn to San Ignacio travelling SE, on the right: Difficult to change any money other than US dollars cash. Camp site on main road near gas station. The manager at *La Posada* can arrange visits to the painted caves in the nearby Sierra de San Francisco: 1-day jeep trip to the only cave accessible by "road" (called Cuesta Palmarito) or 2-week horseback journey through the Sierra staying at ranches and visiting a number of spectacular caves decorated with humans, whales, deer, etc. At **Santa Rosalía** are *Hotel El Morro*; *Francés*, bad restaurant service; *Central*, F, no locks on doors, hot showers, restaurants, old building, beware of gross overcharging; *del Real*, E, with bath, cheap; *Luque*, by bus terminal, F, with bath, clean; *Playa, Blanco y Negro, Anita*. Santa Rosalía, a fascinating planned town built by a French mining company, has a dirty beach and sparse accommodation, but helpful tourist office by ferry station. The ferry runs to Guaymas Tues., Thur. and Sun., 2300, 7 hrs., returns same days at 1100. There are an anthropology museum at the Casa de Cultura Federico Galaz Ramírez and an industrial museum on Route 1 to the N. The church of Santa Bárbara here was designed by the French engineer Gustave Eiffel and built in 1887. Just outside town some old mining machinery can be viewed. Close to Santa Rosalía are the cave paintings known as "El Pollo" and others at Santa Agueda.

Bahía de Los Angeles, reached from a turnoff (50 km.) at Punta Prieta (no public transport), is a village on the Gulf side, popular with fishermen; hotel: *Mama and Papa Díaz*, B, with full board. Lynn and Walt Sutherland from Vancouver write: "Bahía de los Angeles (pop. 600) is worth a visit for its sea life. There are thousands of dolphins in the bay June-December. Some stay all year. In July and August you can hear the whales breathe as you stand on shore. There are large colonies of seals and many exotic seabirds. Fishing is excellent. A boat and guide can be rented for US$40 a day; try Raúl, a local fisherman, who speaks English." Camping free and safe on beach.

Loreto is where the first California Jesuit mission church was founded in 1697; it is a drab town with a poor beach which boasts a fine museum and has few cheap hotels: *Oasis*, A with full board, and *El Presidente*, *Misión Loreto*, C, good value, on seafront, no keys on doors, nice swimming pool; *Club Deportivo de Vuelos*, all local class A; Class B includes *Fray Junípero Serro*, D and a motel with the same price opposite the Pemex station, a/c, clean, *Restaurant Don Luis*, bus stops there and is Tres Estrellas ticket office. Loreto is very crowded with US tourists who fly in for a fortnight, and prices are very steep. It is proposed to develop Loreto on a larger scale, like Cancún and Ixtapa, by 1988. W of Loreto along a very bad road (not suitable for ordinary cars) but with lovely scenery is Comondú (no hotels), an oasis, then on to San Javier, Loreto-San Javier takes 1-2 hrs., for 30 km. distance. There is a Jesuit mission, San Francisco Javier, built in 1699. Near San Javier is Piedras Pintas, close to Rancho Las Parras; there are eight prehistoric figures painted here in red, yellow and black. Past Comondú the road is straight to Ejido Insurgentes. The last 15 km. or so are paved. Loreto-Ejido Insurgentes takes about 9 hrs. **Mulegé** (pop. 4,000) is a lovely oasis on the Gulf N of Loreto, although the town itself is drab, reached by good roads. It has several luxury beach hotels just outside town: the *Mulegé* and *Serenidad*, with their own airstrips; *Las Terrazas*, most rooms clean, comfortable, a/c, D, shower and fine view over town; *Casa Nachita*, F with fan, basic and pleasant; nearby is *Casa de Huéspedes Manuelita*, sloppily run but reasonably clean, F; *Hacienda*, untidy, carelessly run but with good bar, E; *La Palma*, D, with bath, E without food. *Restaurants Tandil* and *Las Casitas*. The Pemex station at Mulegé is sometimes closed. There is a mission, Santa Rosalía de Mulegé, built in 1705 by the priest Juan Manuel Basaldúa. There are also prehistoric cave paintings at San Borjita, on the cliff of Arroyo San Baltazar, nr. Mulegé, 30 km. on the way to Santa Rosalía and then down a dirt track which requires 4-wheel drive. Nearby are Bahía Coyote and Bahía Concepción, with very varied marine life. You can camp on the beach for US$1 a day (although some coves are free); the only problem is fresh water, which is obtainable in Pemex station near Mulegé. Lovely walk along the palm-lined river to the sea (5 km.), with pelicans and other birds fishing at the river-mouth. There is spectacular scenery over the pass through the Sierra de la Giganta just S of Loreto, but the road is very dangerous. To the W of Loreto are Villa Insurgentes and Ciudad Constitución. **Villa Insurgentes** is 120 km. from Loreto; on the way is San Javier (30 km.), the second well-preserved Jesuit mission. On to Puerto Escondido, a popular camping and fishing resort. The road then swings west over the mountains and crosses a plain to Insurgentes where there are a gas station and shops. (Villa Insurgentes to La Paz 238 km.) About 25 km. from Villa Insurgentes is **Ciudad Constitución,** a town which supplies the farming community in the Santo Domingo valley. Gas station. Hotels: *Maribel*, D; *Conchita*, clean, on Ruta 1, E; *Casius, Santo Domingo*; *Julia, Reforma*, F; *El Conquistador*, E, clean, to the right of Ruta 1, coming from La Paz.

La Paz, the capital of Baja California Sur, is a peaceful town (and a free port, although some goods, like certain makes of camera, are cheaper to buy in the USA). The mild winter climate is attracting more and more tourists; it has consequently become rather expensive. There are many beaches: El Comitán, El

MEXICO

Mogote, El Coromuel, El Caimancito, El Tesoro, Pichilingüe, Balandra, El Tecolote, facing Espíritu Santo Island and El Coyote, facing the Gulf of California. The best beaches are in the S. The famous pearling industry, which had died, is reviving. There is a helpful tourist office opp. the cathedral at Av. 5 de Mayo (maps with good descriptions and services in Baja California) and a Centro Artesanal La Paz, on Parque Cuauhtémoc, between Bravo and Rosales; other craft shops are *Mercado Madero*, Av. Revolución and Degollado; *Taller de Artes Regionales* on Chiapas and Encinas. Orphans do painting and carpentry at the Ciudad de los Niños y Niñas on 5 de Febrero, between A. Serdán and Revolución. Historical and cultural library of the three Californias at Madero and 5 de Mayo, unique volumes. Mission of Our Lady of La Paz in Plaza Constitución, founded 1720 by the Jesuit Jaime Bravo. There is a Museo Antropológico de Baja California Sur, on Altamirano and 5 de Mayo (closed Mon.), which contains photographs of prehistoric paintings, the geological history of the peninsula, fossils and different art exhibits. There is a carved mural depicting the history of Mexico at the Government Palace on Isabel la Católica, between Bravo and Allende. Population 100,000. On the way to Cabo San Lucas are the wood carving centre of San Pedro and leather work at Miraflores (2 km. off road).

Hotels Great lack of cheap accommodation. *Gran Hotel Baja*, on Rangel, B; *El Presidente Sur*, Playa Caimancito, Km. 3 to Pichilingüe, A; *María Cristina*, E, Revolución 80-A, shower, recommended, washing done cheaply. *Posada San Miguel*, Blvd. Domínguez Norte 45, E, good and cheap, near Plaza; *La Aldea*, 5 de Febrero and Topete; *Los Arcos*, Obregón 498, B; *La Posada*, Reforma y Plaza Sur, B; *Calafia*, Carr. Transpenínsular Km. 3; *El Príncipe*, 16 de Septiembre and Prof. Rubio Ruiz; *María Dolores Gardenias*, C, Aquiles Serdán and Vicente Guerrero, excellent, good food and pool; *Lori*, Bravo 110, D/E, with shower, pleasant, a/c; *Jalisco Yeneka*, F. Madero 1520, close, some comfort, D, with bath; *Guadalajara*, E, with bath (opp. bus station), basic; *Central*, on plaza, 5 de Mayo y Francisco Madero, probably cheapest, F, with bath; *Clark*, Bravo 265; *Prado*, Bravo and Lic. Verdad; *Cintya*, nice, very clean, Madero 2060, E; *Moyron*, Av. 16 de Septiembre, 3 to 5 blocks from sea, reasonable; *La Purisima*, very friendly, clean, restaurant next door, D, with bath. *Valadez*, 16 de Septiembre and Altamirano, F, 6 blocks from sea front. Various *casas de huéspedes*: *Palencia*, 16 de Septiembre and Blvd. Domínguez; *Flores*, Madero 275 Norte; *Yo-Ya*, Morelos and Lic. Verdad; *Playa*, Lerdo and Mutualismo; *Convento*, Madero and Degollado; *San Bernadino*, clean, good, reasonably priced. CREA Youth Hostel, clean. Trailer park near airport, US$2 a day. *El Cardón*, Km. 4 on Highway to N. Cheapest accommodation probably available at the language school in Edificio Biblioteca across street from Servi-Centro food market, 4 blocks from the bus station—cots for renting.

Camping On beach at El Mogote (hotel and restaurant there, too) and Pichilingüe (near ferry terminal, parking, toilets restaurant). Avoid Balandra beach (bugs). El Coyote beach, good.

Restaurants *Mazatlán*, Mutualismo and Bravo 106, seafood, good but slow. *Palapa Adriana*, on beachfront, open air, excellent service. *La Tavola Pizza*, good value. *Okey* disco good: US$2.50 cover charge, a beer costs US$1.20.

Buses La Paz bus station is a long walk from town, taxi essential; on Jalisco and Josefa Ortiz de Domínguez. Tres Estrellas de Oro (1st class) La Paz-Tijuana, US$21.50, 22½ hrs., 5 a day, stops at Loreto (5 hrs.), Santa Rosalía (8), Guerrero Negro (11), San Quintín (16), Ensenada (21)—beautiful trip; US$8 for La Paz-Santa Rosalía bus, stops at Ciudad Constitución, Villa Insurgentes, Loreto, Mulegé at 0900 and 1200. To Mexicali at 1600. *La Paz-San José del Cabo and Cabo San Lucas* at 0700, 1000 and 1400, 3½ hrs., US$4, crowded at times. Bus La Paz-Todos Los Santos leaves daily between 1300 and 1500, US$2.50, buy your ticket in the morning, leaves from different terminal.

Air Services Aeroméxico from Los Angeles, Tijuana and Mexico City. Hughes Air Corporation from Tucson. La Paz to Los Mochis with Aero California, US$20, daily, early a.m. La Paz international airport is 10 km. from centre. Taxi from airport US$1.85 each, fixed rate.

Ferry Services Book in town or at the ferry terminal for daily (1700) ferry to Mazatlán; allow plenty of time for this as there are long queues and there may not be room until the next day as a great many heavy trucks (which have loading priority) take produce across; the trip takes 16 hours, US$1.70 reclining chair (not very comfortable, but a/c, and luggage can be locked up safely), US$7.25 cabin (double room with private bath), or a *turista* compartment with 4 beds, US$3.60, goes daily, at 1700 hrs. each way. Restaurant, US$4 for set meal. Customs clearance is necessary if taking a car (US$27.70), allow plenty of time; ticket available in La Paz, not at ferry terminal which is about 15 km. out of town. Bus from bus station on beach front, Auto Transportes Aguila,

996 MEXICO

to terminal leaves at 1300 and 1400, US$0.50. Long queue at customs, allow about 3 hrs. before scheduled sailing time. Ferry to Topolobampo, Sun., Tues., and Thurs. at 2000, reclining seat US$1.50; also *cabinas* and *turista* compartments on some sailings; car US$29, 8 hrs. Ferry also available to Guaymas Fri., Sun., 1400, 16 hrs., US$5, reclining chair (single fare), car US$18.50. La Paz-Puerto Vallarta Thurs. 1600 returns Fri. at 1200 (21 hr. journey). Addresses for reservations: La Paz: Av. Madero 910, Tel.: 20109; Puerto Vallarta: Muelle Marítimo (Tel.: 20476); Cabo San Lucas: Muelle Marítimo (Tel.: 30079); Guaymas: Muelle Patio (Tel.: 22324); Sta. Rosalía: Muelle de la Aduana (Tel.: 20013/14). Topolobampo: Atracadero de los Transbordadores, Av. Juárez 125 Pte. Tel.: 35. Los Mochis: Tel.: 25642. Mexico DF: Niños Héroes 150, Local 20 and 21, Col. Doctores, Tel.: 588-0077. **N.B.** On all ferry crossings, delays can occur from September if there is bad weather, which could hold you up for up to 3 days.

Excursions Espíritu Santo Island is suitable for camping and water sports, fishing; natural pools of clear water, wildlife. Beautiful beaches facing Cerralvo Island along the Highway to Cabo San Lucas, turning left at the San Juan de Los Planes sign, then on to the signs to El Sargento, La Ventana and La Cueva del León beaches. Punta Arenas beach also faces Cerralvo Island; camping, watersports, hotels, restaurant, bar, boats and fishing equipment available. *Hotel Las Arenas*. Cerralvo Island has good beaches, fishing, wildlife, camping. Along 5 de Mayo up to Colonia de San Guelatao and by dirt road to the left is the private club and airstrip of Las Cruces beach; Puerto Mejía, with bungalows for hire and good beach is just along. Excursions to Cabo San Lucas (see below) organized by travel agency next door to *Hotel Yeneka* on Av. Madero, US$30. This includes: breakfast at the travel agency, transport by mini-bus and lunch at Cabo San Lucas, and a motor-boat excursion to see the marine life. Assembly at 0700, return 1900.

Beyond Los Planes is **El Triunfo**, one of the most important towns in Baja California Sur at the end of the 19th century. Its population grew to 10,000, in search for gold and silver; now only abandoned old houses remain. There is a craft shop at the town entrance where young people make palm-leaf objects. Further along is San Antonio, with a gasoline station, restaurant, shops, sited on the side of a canyon, and some of the beaches can be viewed from the road. Next is San Bártolo, a beautiful town surrounded by fruit trees, including oranges, mangoes, avocadoes. Sugar-cane is produced, and jam. There is a natural spring arising from a rock shaded by palms and banana plants.

At extreme tip of peninsula, 201 km. S by air from La Paz, is **Cabo San Lucas**, not a resort for the budget conscious. *Hotel Mi Ranchito*, D, with shower, dirty, unfriendly, another 2 hotels in this price bracket. *Marina*, D, quiet, clean, hot shower, swimming pool; *Mar de Cortés*, clean, C; *Sol Mar*, slow service, A, on the beach (but beware of rip surf, no swimming), with beautiful view; *Finisterra*, built on rocks, A (American Plan), superb view; *Cabo San Lucas*, B; *Las Cruces Palmilla*, A; *Camino Real*, A, very exclusive apartments on beach attractive in industrial area; *El Presidente Los Cabos*, good view, modern, B; *La Hacienda*, L, on beautiful beach, recommended. *Casa Blanca*, clean, shower, friendly, at E probably cheapest in town. Campsite *Alfonso Loves You*, US$ 1 p.p. A 60-hectare marine tourist complex in Cabo San Lucas consists of a cruise vessel landing pier, ferry terminal, two hotels, condominiums, civic centre, yacht clubs, and other facilities. All the better hotels offer safaris in the desert, diving gear, fishing boats, etc. Entertainment only in hotel bars and *Oasis Disco* (cover charge US$2). Cheap *taquerías* and several good restaurants on main street. Tourist office in Plaza Central also offers tours to the desert, a pirate creek, etc. Bank hours: Mon.-Fri., 0830-1300 hrs. Only one bank, Banco de México, changes travellers' cheques. The rainy months are Sept.-Oct., but also occasional rain at the end of January. Plenty of beaches between Cabo San Lucas and San José del Cabo, the further E, the more sheltered. Playa Tropical just outside the latter is very popular. Boat trip to further beaches and beautiful Los Arcos rocks, US$3 p.p., 30 mins. round trip—you can see seals and pelicans.

Ferries Cabo San Lucas-Puerto Vallarta, Fri., Sun., 1600, 18 hrs. officially but 21 in reality. Returns from Puerto Vallarta Tues. and Sat. 1600. Cabin only US$4.

La Paz can also be reached from Cabo San Lucas via **Todos Los Santos** (*Hotel California*, E, friendly, no running water; beach dangerous—better go 5 km. S to El Pescadero for the day, good surfing, no accommodation); there is a 80 km. dirt road, but you must be careful when passing another vehicle as the shoulders are very sandy. Todos Los Santos is very dull. Bahía Las Palmas on the way to La Paz has *Camping R. V. Park*, near sea front, shady, clean, US$4 with water and electricity. Between Todos Los Santos and El Pescadero (25 km.) is Sierra de la Laguna National Park, pine forest and clear springs, whose flora and fauna contrast with the dry desert and the ocean around it. Cabo San Lucas can also be reached from the airport of **San José del Cabo** (46 km., good for everyday shopping needs, now being developed on a large scale; *Hotel Costa Aquamarina*, *Hotel Ceci*, F, hot shower, good, in centre, and *Castel Cabo Hotel*) with minibuses (*colectivos*) or taxis: prices are fixed and posted at the airport. Air services from San José del Cabo to Mazatlán, Los Angeles and San Francisco.

The Economy

Mexico has been an oil producer since the 1880s and was the world's leading producer in 1921, but by 1971 had become a net importer. This position was reversed in the mid-1970s with the discovery in 1972 of major new oil reserves. Mexico is now the world's fourth largest producer, 65% of crude output coming from offshore wells in the Gulf of Campeche, and 28% from onshore fields in the Chiapas-Tabasco area in the southeast. Proven reserves of 48.6bn barrels in the mid-1980s were sufficient to last 54 years. Mexico depends on oil and gas for about 85% of its primary energy supply and exports of crude oil, oil products and natural gas account for half of exports and about two-fifths of government revenues.

Mexico's mineral resources are legendary. Precious metals make up about 36% of non-oil mineral output. The country is the world's leading producer of silver, fluorite and arsenic, and is among the world's major producers of strontium, graphite, copper, iron ore, sulphur, mercury, lead and zinc. Mexico also produces gold, molybdenum, antimony, bismuth, cadmium, selenium, tungsten, magnesium, common salt, celestite, fuller's earth and gypsum. It is estimated that although 60% of Mexico's land mass has mineral potential, only 25% is known, and only 5% explored in detail.

Agriculture employs 27% of the labour force but has been losing importance since the beginning of the 1970s and now contributes only 9% of gdp. About 12% of the land surface is under cultivation, of which only about one-quarter is irrigated. Over half of the developed cropland lies in the interior highlands. Mexico's agricultural success is almost always related to rainfall and available water for irrigation. On average, four out of every ten years are good, while four are drought years. In the 1970s and early 1980s Mexico's population rose by about 3.5% a year but then slowed to about 2% a year, while agricultural output, including fishing and forestry, rose by only 2.6% in 1981-85.

Manufacturing, including oil refining and petrochemicals, contributes nearly a quarter of gdp. Mexico City is the focal point for manufacturing activity and the metropolitan area holds about 45% of the employment in manufacturing and 30% of the country's industrial establishments. The government offers tax incentives to companies relocating away from Mexico City and the other major industrial centres of Guadalajara and Monterrey; target cities are Tampico, Coatzacoalcos, Salina Cruz and Lázaro Cárdenas, while much of the manufacturing export activity takes place in the in-bond centres along the border with the USA.

Tourism is the second largest source of foreign exchange, after oil, and the largest employer, with about a third of the workforce. About 4.5m tourists visit Mexico every year, of whom about 85% come from the USA. The government is actively encouraging new investment in tourism and foreign investment is being welcomed in hotel construction projects.

During 1978-81 the current account of the balance of payments registered increasing deficits because of domestic expansion and world recession. Mounting public sector deficits were covered by foreign borrowing of increasingly shorter terms until a bunching of short-term maturities and a loss of foreign exchange reserves caused Mexico to declare its inability to service its debts in August 1982, thus triggering what became known as the international debt crisis. Under the guidance of an IMF programme and helped by commercial bank debt rescheduling agreements, Mexico was able to improve its position largely because of a 40% drop in imports in both 1982 and 1983. In 1986, however, the country was hit by the sharp fall in oil prices, which reduced export revenues by 28%, despite a rapid growth of 37% in non-oil exports through vigorous promotion and exchange rate depreciation policies. Agreement was reached in 1986 on further debt rescheduling and a new money package totalling US$12.5 bn, mainly from the banks, the IMF, the World Bank and the Japanese government. Mexico's external debt was expected to rise to US$113 bn and become the largest of the developing countries once the money had been disbursed. The financing package was hailed as a landmark because of the IMF's acceptance of the need for economic growth rather than austerity.

MEXICO

	1961-70 (av)	1971-80 (av)	1981-85 (av)	1986 (e)
Gdp growth (1980 prices)	7.0%	6.6%	1.6%	-3.1%
Inflation	2.7%	16.6%	60.7%	86.2%
Exports (fob) US$m	1,140	5,097	21,908	15,759
Petroleum	32	2,343	16,536	6,259
Coffee	74	327	440	752
Shrimp	51	192	397	450
Imports (fob) US$m	1,574	7,091	14,347	11,384
Current account balance US$m (cum)	-4,947	-32,139	-9,920	-1,930

Information for Visitors

Travel by Air Several airlines have regular flights from Europe to Mexico City. *Air France* from Paris via Houston; *Iberia* from Madrid non-stop or via Montreal; *Aeroméxico* from Paris and Madrid; *KLM* from Amsterdam via Houston; *Canadian Pacific* from Amsterdam via Montreal; *Lufthansa* from Frankfurt via Montreal to Mérida, Monterrey and Mexico City; also via Dallas; *Pan Am* from Europe via New York, Houston or Miami.

Mexico City from New York, under 4 hrs.; from Chicago, 4 hrs.; from Los Angeles, 3 hrs. with *Mexicana* ("Moonlight Express", cost about 60% of normal); from Houston, 3 hrs.; from Brownsville (Texas), via Tampico, 2½ hrs.; from St. Louis or Washington (by connecting air lines through Houston), 6¾ hrs. and 9 hrs. respectively. Aeroméxico, again, cut its fares by 50% for flights from the NW of the USA and Canada in Feb. 1983. *Mexicana* does a round trip Los Angeles-Guadalajara ("Moonlight Express") nightly. There are direct *Pan-Am* and *Aeroméxico* flights connecting Miami with Mérida, 1½ hrs., and direct *Aeroméxico* flights daily connecting New York with Tijuana and Cancún, Miami-Mexico City, 2½ hrs. *Eastern Airlines* flies between Atlanta and Acapulco, Mérida and Cancún. Round-trips Atlanta-Cancún or Mérida-Miami-Cancún. Cheapest way to get to San Diego is to fly from Mexico City to Tijuana, walk across border and take the train to downtown San Diego (15-20 min. journey). Quito-Mexico City with *Ecuatoriana*. *Aerolíneas Argentinas* and *AeroPerú* fly to and from Lima. Many direct cheap charter flights from continental European airports to Mexico City and Mérida, for instance, try Le Point, 4 rue des Orphelins, 68200 Mulhouse, France, or Uniclam-Voyages, 63 rue Monsieur-le-Prince, 75006 Paris.

Airport Departure Tax US$10 on international flights; US$4.50 on internal flights (February 1987).

By Sea All the following shipping services are for cargo, carrying a limited number of passengers.

Mexican Line, from New York to Veracruz, sailing every Fri., 7 days. North-bound ships leave Tampico every Sun. via Philadelphia to New York, 7 days. Commodore Cruise Lines from Miami to Cozumel, sail every Sat. night (November-Spring). Cruise continues on Mon. to Haiti, Jamaica and back to Miami. Naviera Turística Mexicana makes 2 round trips a month between Los Angeles, Mazatlán, and Acapulco.

Hapag-Lloyd, Bremen, 2 to 3 sailings a month from Hamburg, Bremen, Antwerp to Veracruz and Tampico.

Harrison Line: from Liverpool, every fortnight. Sidarma Line: monthly from Genoa to Veracruz. Spanish Line: from Spain to Veracruz. S.A. Armement Deppe: from Antwerp to Tampico and Veracruz.

Norwegian Caribbean Lines occasionally take one-way passengers with about 2 weeks advance booking at a flat rate of US$67 a night.

Overland Toronto to Mexico City, via Chicago-St. Louis-Dallas-San Antonio Laredo-Monterrey, with Greyhound bus (74 hrs.) on a 15-day pass. Montreal-Laredo via New York, Washington, Atlanta, New Orleans, Houston and San Antonio, 60 hrs., US$132. Both Greyhound and Trailways provide services from Miami to the Mexican border and on to Mexico City. It's cheaper to make booking outside the US, but the information is hard to come by in Mexico City. Trailways in London, c/o Holiday Inn, Heathrow Airport, Stockley Rd., West Drayton, Middlesex, UB7 9NA. Los Angeles-Mexico City, US$58, 44 hrs.; New York-Mexico City, US$120.50, 70 hrs.; San Antonio-Mexico City, US$27, 20 hrs. If coming from the US it is usually cheaper to travel to the border and buy your ticket in the Mexican border town from the Mexican company.

To Cuba Return flight to Cuba, Sun. and Wed., with stop at Mérida (US$179) if plane is not fully booked. Cuba package tours US$285 for seven day all-inclusive stay and return flight from Mexico City or US$213 from Mérida.

To Guatemala Daily flights to Guatemala City.

N.B. VAT is payable on domestic plane tickets bought in Mexico.

Travel in Mexico Promotional packages for local tourism exist, with 30-40% discount, operated by hoteliers, restaurateurs, hauliers and Aeroméxico and Mexicana (the latter is more punctual). Their tickets are not interchangeable. Aeroméxico has all-inclusive travel (*VTI*) and journey-inclusive hotel (*VHI*) rates; the former includes 3 nights lodging, half-board and return flight, the latter transport and lodging only. Mexicana has similar arrangements with the initials *VIP* and *VHP*. Check whether you qualify for the dozen or so destinations. The two local airlines offer 15% discounts to foreigners for their domestic air services; 20% if the foreigners arrive on their own flights. Discounts must be claimed within one week of arrival.

Book ahead for buses when possible, and try to travel from the starting-point of a route; buses are often full at the mid-point of their routes. Buses in the country will not stop on curves—walk until you find a straight stretch.

There are three kinds of buses, first and second class, and local. Terminals for each are usually distinct, and may not be in one bus station. First-class buses assign you a seat and you may have to queue for 1-2 hrs. to get a ticket. It is not easy to choose which seat or to change it later. No standing, and you may have to wait for the next one (next day, perhaps) if all seats are taken. You *must* book in advance for buses travelling in the Yucatán Peninsula, but it is also advisable to book if going elsewhere. Be especially careful during school holidays, around Easter and August and the 15 days up to New Year when many public servants take holidays in all resorts; transport from Mexico City is booked up a long time in advance and hotels are filled, too. Beware of "scalpers" who try to sell you a seat at a higher price, which you can usually get on a stand-by basis, when somebody doesn't turn up, at the regular price. Sometimes it helps to talk to the driver, who has two places to use at his discretion behind his seat (don't sit in these until invited). First-class buses often have toilets and air-conditioning which does not work, but are nevertheless recommended for long-distance travelling. If going on an overnight bus, book seats at front as toilets get very smelly by morning. Second-class buses are often antiques (interesting, but frustrating when they break down) or may be brand new (the passengers are invariably more entertaining and courteous than in other types of buses). They call at towns and villages and go up side roads the first-class buses never touch. They stop quite as often for meals and toilets as their superiors do and—unlike the first-class buses—people get on and off so often that you may be able to obtain a seat after all. Seats are not bookable, except in Baja California. In general, it is a good idea to take food and drink with you on a long bus ride, as stops may depend on the driver. First class fares are usually 10% dearer than 2nd class ones. There seem always to be many buses leaving in the early morning. Buses are sometimes called *camiones*, hence *central camionero* for bus station. A monthly bus guide is available for US$1 (year's subscription) from Guía de Autotransportes de México, Apartado 8929, México 1, D.F.

As for trains, apart from one narrow gauge line, most of the passenger equipment in use now dates from the forties or fifties, including a number of *autovías*. In some cases they are slow, but there are now completely modern trains between Mexicali and Guadalajara in 36 hours, and overnight good Pullman trains between Mexico City and Monterrey, Guadalajara, Veracruz and Mérida. The railways claim that you can see more from a train than from any other form of transport; this may well be true, but trains tend to be slower (though generally cheaper if you take 2nd class and carriages are empty at non-holiday periods) than the buses; they generally have comfortable sleeper cars with *alcobas* (better berths) and *camarines* (small sleepers). The special first class has air-conditioning and reclining seats and costs about 10% more than the regular 1st class, which costs about twice the 2nd class fare. A condensed railway timetable may be obtained from the Mexican railways' office at 500 Fifth Ave. (Room 2623), New York, N.Y. 10036. (For extensive information about the Mexican railway network consult *Makens' Guide to Mexican Train Travel*, compiled by James C. Makens and published by Le Voyageur Publishing Co., 1319 Wentwood Drive, Irving, Texas 75061, at about US$6.)

If you should get caught during the holiday season try to book a 2nd class train, but this may involve queuing 12 hrs. or more if you want a seat. More first-class tickets are sold than the total number of first-class seats; first-class passengers are allowed on first, so you may still find a 2nd class seat. Some travellers have remarked that the last carriage of a 2nd class train is often half full of soldiers, who might deter would-be thieves from taking one's personal belongings if one shares their carriage. We have received a report of conductors turning out lights on night trains, enabling thieves to operate with impunity; take care of your belongings under these circumstances.

1000 MEXICO

Walking Walkers are advised to get *Backpacking in Mexico and Central America*, by Hilary Bradt and Rob Rachowiecki. Do not walk at night on dark, deserted roads or streets.

Hitch-hiking is usually possible for single hikers, but apparently less easy for couples. The most difficult stretches are reported to be Acapulco to Puerto Escondido, Santa Cruz-Salina Cruz and Tulum-Chetumal.

Camping Beware of people stealing clothes, especially when you hang them up after washing. Paraffin oil (kerosene) for stoves is called *petróleo para lámparas* in Mexico; it is not a very good quality (dirty) and costs about US$0.03 per litre. It is available from an *expendio*, or *despacho de petróleo*, or from a *tlalalperia*, but not from gas stations. Alcohol for heating the burner can be obtained from supermarkets. Repairs to stoves at Servis-Coliman at Plaza de San Juan 5, Mexico City.

Youth Hostels CREA *albergues* may be found in most large towns. All US$2.00 with Youth Hostel card, US$2.50 without.

Documents A passport is necessary, but US and Canadian citizens need only show birth certificate (or for US, a naturalization certificate). Tourists need the free tourist card, which can be obtained from any Mexican Consulate or Tourist Commission office, at the Mexican airport on entry, from the offices or on the aircraft of airlines operating into Mexico, ask for at least 30 days; if you say you are in transit you may be charged US$8, with resulting paper work. Best to say you are going to an inland destination. (Airlines may issue cards only to citizens of West European countries, most Latin American countries—not Cuba, Chile or Haiti—the USA, Canada, Australia, Japan and the Philippines.) Also at border offices of the American Automobile Association (AAA), which offers this service to members and non-members. There is a multiple entry card valid for all visits within 6 months for US nationals; the normal validity for other nationals is 90 days, but sometimes only 30 days are granted at border crossings; insist you want more if wishing to stay longer. Renewal of entry cards is quick and easy at visa office, Insurgentes Sur 1388, Mexico City (Bus 17). Take travellers' cheques as proof of finance. Best to collect visa, not have it forwarded by post, as it often gets lost. Travellers not carrying tourist cards need visas. Tourist cards are not required for cities close to the US border, such as Tijuana, Mexicali, etc. Businessmen who want to study the Mexican market or to appoint an agent must apply for the requisite visa and permit.

At border crossings make sure the immigration people don't con you to pay a dollar for the card or visa. It is free and the man typing it out is only doing his job. We would warn travellers that there have been several cases of tourist cards not being honoured, or a charge being imposed, or the validity being changed arbitrarily to 60 days or less. In this case, complaint should be made to the authorities in Mexico City. Some border stations do not issue tourist cards; you are therefore strongly advised, if travelling by land, to obtain a card before arriving at the border. Above all, do not lose your tourist card—you cannot leave the country without it and it takes at least a week to replace. There is an airport tax of US$3 on all international flights from Mexico and of US$1 on internal flights within the country; these taxes are not charged at Cozumel (a free zone).

At the land frontiers with Belize and Guatemala, you may be refused entry into Mexico if you have less than US$200. (This restriction does not officially apply to North American and European travellers.) Persuasion, whether verbal or financial, can sometimes remedy this.

British business travellers are strongly advised to read *Hints to Exporters: Mexico*, obtainable from the Department of Trade, Export Services Division, Sanctuary Buildings, 16-20 Great Smith Street, London SW1P 3DB.

Customs Regulations The luggage of tourist-card holders is often passed unexamined. If flying into Mexico from South America, expect to be thoroughly searched (body and luggage) at the airport. US citizens can take in their own clothing and equipment without paying duty, but all valuable and non-US-made objects (diamonds, cameras, binoculars, typewriters, etc.), should be registered at the US Customs office or the port of exit so that duty will not be charged on returning. Radios and television sets must be registered and taken out when leaving. Tourists are allowed to take in duty-free 1 kg. of tobacco and 400 cigarettes (or 50 cigars), 2 bottles of liquor, US$80 worth of gifts and 12 rolls of film, but the US will allow them to take out only a quart of duty-free liquor. There are no restrictions on the import or export of money apart from gold but foreign gold coins are allowed into the US only if they are clearly made into jewellery (perforated or otherwise worked on). On return to the US a person may take from Mexico, free of duty, up to US$100 worth of merchandise for personal use or for personal gifts, every 31 days, if acquired merely as an incident of the trip. Alcoholic drinks may not be taken across the border from Mexico to California. Archaeological relics may not be taken out of Mexico. US tourists should remember that the US Endangered Species Act, 1973, prohibits importation into the States of products from endangered species, e.g. tortoise shell. The Department of the Interior issues a leaflet about this. Llama, alpaca, etc. items may be confiscated at the airport for fumigation and it will be necessary to return to the customs area on the Mexico City airport perimeter 2-3 days later to collect and pay for fumigation. Production of passport will be required and proof that goods are to be re-exported otherwise they may also be subject to import duties. Duty-free goods from Aeroboutiques at Mexico City, Mazatlán, Puerto Vallarta, Guadalajara, Monterrey, Mérida and Acapulco airports.

MEXICO 1001

Automobiles These may be brought into Mexico on a Tourist Permit for 180 days (don't overstay—driving without an extension gets a US$50 fine for the first five days and then rises abruptly to *half the value of the car!*). No fee is charged for the permit, and the AAA always writes "free" across the preliminary application form it gives its clients because, apparently, some Mexican border officials absentmindedly forget this fact. If you don't have proof of ownership (certificate or title of registration) you will need a notarized statement that you own the vehicle or drive with the permission of the owner. Your US car insurance does not cover you while driving in Mexico, but agencies on both sides of the border will sell you Mexican automobile insurance, so only buy 1-day US insurance if crossing the border. Sanborn's Mexican Insurance Service, with offices in Texas, New Mexico, Arizona and 6 Mexican cities, will provide insurance services (about US$3 a day) within Mexico and other parts of Latin America, and provide "Travelogs" for Mexico and Central America with useful tips. British AA members are reminded that there are ties with the AAA, which extends cover to the US and entitles AA members to free travel information including a very useful book and map on Mexico. Holders of 180-day tourist cards can keep their automobiles in Mexico for that time. Luggage is no longer inspected at the checkpoints along the road where tourist cards and/or car permits are examined. Gasoline—regular and medium (92 or *extra* and 81 or *nova*) octane (no high octane)—can be got throughout Mexico. Make sure you are given full value when you tank up, that the pump is set to zero before your tank is filled, that the pump is correctly calibrated, and that your filler cap is put back on. Government road patrols using green jeeps ("*Angeles Verdes*") offer helpful service to motorists. Parking: Multi-storey car parks are becoming more common but parking is often to be found right in city centres under the main square.

Motorbikes All Japanese parts are sold only by one shop in Mexico City at extortionate prices (but parts and accessories are easily available in Guatemala at reasonable prices for those travelling there). Robert S. Kahn recommends Señor Romano's shop, Av. Revolución 1310, Mexico City, for bike repairs. Sr. Romano, a Belgian-Mexican, speaks French and English. Some motorbike travellers have warned that particularly in Mexico City groups of plain clothes police in unmarked cars try to impound motorbikes by force of arms. Uniformed police are no help here.

Warnings When two cars converge on a narrow bridge from opposite directions, the driver who first flashes his lights has the right of way. Don't drive fast at night; farm and wild animals roam freely. In fact, it is advisable to drive as little as possible at night. Some motorists report that it is better not to stop if you hit another car, as although Mexican insurance is proof of your ability to pay, both parties may sometimes be incarcerated until all claims are settled. "Sleeping policemen" or road bumps can be hazardous in towns and villages as there are no warning signs; they are sometimes incorrectly marked as *vibradores*.

On the west coast, the Government has set up military checkpoints to look out for drug-smugglers and gun-runners, almost as far south as Puerto Angel. Papers will be checked at these points and your car searched. The degree of search is apparently linked to general appearance; young people travelling in VW vans can expect thorough searches all the way. Watch searchers carefully; sometimes they try to make off with tools, camping gear and the like, especially if there are two or more of them.

If you are stopped by police for an offence you have not committed and you know you are in the right, do not pay the "fine" on the spot. Take the number of the policeman from his cap, show him that you have his number and tell him that you will see his boss at the tourist police headquarters instead. It is also advisable to go to the precinct station anyway whenever a fine is involved, to make sure it is genuine.

When entering Mexico from Belize by car point out to the authorities that you have a car with you, otherwise they may not note it and you could be arrested for illegally importing a car.

Tourists' cars cannot, *by law*, be sold in Mexico. This is very strictly applied. You may not leave the country without the car you entered in, except with written government permission with the car in bond.

Warning The number of assaults is rising, especially in Mexico City. Never carry valuables in easily picked pockets.

Local Information All Mexican Government tourist agencies are now grouped in the Department of Tourism building at Avenida Masaryk 172, near corner of Reforma. A few cities run municipal tourist offices to help travellers. The Mexican Automobile Association (AMA) is at Chapultepec 276, México, D.F.; they sell an indispensable road guide, with good maps and very useful lists of hotels, with current prices. The ANA (Asociación Nacional Automobilística) sells similar but not such good material; offices in Insurgentes (Metro Glorieta) and Av. Jalisco 27, México 18 D.F. For road conditions consult the AMA, which is quite reliable. A calendar of *fiestas* is published by *Mexico This Month*.

Maps The Mexican Government Tourist Highway map is available free of charge at tourist offices (when in stock). If driving from the USA you get a free map if you buy your insurance at AAA or Dan Sanborn's in the border cities. The official map printers, Detenal, produce the only good large-scale maps of the country.

1002 MEXICO

The Dirección General de Oceanografía in Calle Medellín 10, near Insurgentes underground station, sells excellent maps of the entire coastline of Mexico. Good detailed maps of states of Mexico and the country itself from Dirección General de Geografía y Meteorología, Av. Observatorio 192, México 18, D.F. Tel.: 515-15-27 (go to Observatorio underground station and up Calle Sur 114, then turn right a short distance down Av. Observatorio). Best road maps of Mexican states, free, on polite written request, from Ing. Daniel Díaz Díaz, Director General de Programación, Xola 1755, 8° Piso, México 12 D.F. Building is on the corner of Xola with Av. Universidad. Mapas Turísticos de México has Mexican (stocks Detenal maps) and world-maps, permanent exhibition at Río Rhin 29, Col. Cuauhtémoc, Mexico 5, Tel.: 566-2177. Good road maps of Mexican states also available from Sanborns at US$1.30.

Guidebooks Travellers wanting more information than we have space to provide, on archaeological sites for instance, would do well to use the widely available Easy Guides written by Richard Bloomgarden, with plans and good illustrations.

Photographs The Instituto Nacional de Antropología e Historia (INAH), Córdoba 44, Colonia Roma, Mexico City, will grant teachers, archaeologists, etc. written permission to take any type of photograph at sites and museums, including photos which general public may not take. Also issue admission discounts.

Hours of Business in Mexico City are extremely variable. The banks are open from 0900 to 1300 from Mon. to Fri. and (head offices only) 0900 to 1230 on Sat. Business offices usually open at 0900 or 1000 and close at 1300 or 1400. They reopen at 1400 or 1500, but senior executives may not return until much later, although they may then stay until after 1900. Other businesses, especially those on the outskirts of the city, and many Government offices, work from 0800 to 1400 or 1500 and then close for the rest of the day. Business hours in other parts of the country vary considerably according to the climate and local custom. In Monterrey they are roughly as in Britain.

Standard Time The same as US Central Standard Time, 6 hrs. behind GMT. In Sonora, Sinaloa, Nayarit and Baja California Sur, 7 hrs. behind GMT; and in Baja California Norte 8 hrs. behind GMT.

The **best season** for a business visit is from late January to May, but for pleasure between October and early April, when it hardly ever rains in most of the country.

Hotels Maximum rates are registered with the Government and advertised in the press. There are six rate zones: I: Guadalajara, Monterrey, Mexico City; II: Most seaside resorts, incl. Acapulco; III: Port zones, like Veracruz; IV: State of Yucatán, and several states surrounding the state of México; V: Most border zones, incl. the state of Baja California Sur; VI: The rest, including Chiapas. Rates are set on May 15 and December 15. Complaints about violations to be reported to the Department of Tourism, Presidente Masaryk 172, Colonia Polanco, Mexico City. Tel.: 250-1964 and 250-8555. English is spoken at the best hotels.
Beware of "helpfuls" who try to find you a hotel, as prices quoted at the hotel desk rise to give them a commission. If backpacking, best for one of you to watch over luggage while the other goes to book a room and pay for it; some hotels are put off by backpacks. During peak season, it may be hard to find a room and clerks do not always check to see whether a room is vacant. Insist, or if desperate, provide a suitable tip. When using a lift, remember PB (*Planta Baja*) stands for ground floor.

Airport Taxis To avoid overcharging, the Government has taken control of taxi services from airports to cities and only those with government licences are allowed to carry passengers from the airport. Sometimes one does not pay the driver but purchases a ticket from a booth on leaving the airport. No further tipping is then required. The same system has been applied at bus stations but it is possible to pay the driver direct.

Tipping has been standardized at 15% everywhere except perhaps lunch counters and the like where 10% is acceptable; the equivalent of US$0.25 per bag for porters, the equivalent of US$0.10 for bell boys, theatre usherettes, and nothing for a taxi driver unless he gives some extra service. It is not necessary to tip the drivers of hired cars.

Health The Social Security hospitals are restricted to members, while the Centros de Salud and Hospitales Civiles found in most centres are very cheap and open to everyone. Water in the cities is potable, but you are recommended to use bottled or mineral water for drinking. Tehuacán mineral water is sold all over Mexico; both plain and flavoured are first class. Raw salads and vegetables, and food sold on the streets and in cheap cafés, especially in Mexico City, may be dangerous. Advisable to vaccinate against typhoid, paratyphoid and poliomyelitis if visiting the low-lying tropical zones, where there is also some risk of malaria. Heavy eating and drinking of alcohol is unwise in the capital because of its

MEXICO 1003

altitude; so is overdoing it physically in the first few days. Some people experience nose-bleeds in Guadalajara and Mexico City because of pollution; they cease with fresh air. Locals recommend Imecol for "Montezuma's Revenge" (the very common diarrhoea).

Drink The beer (best brands: Bavaria, Bohemia, XXX, Superior and Tecate) is quite good. Negra Modelo is a dark beer, it has the same alcohol content as the other beers. Local wine, some of it of good quality, is cheap; try (Domecq, Casa Madero, Santo Tomás, etc.—the white sold in oyster restaurants *ostionerías*) is usually good. The native drinks are *tequila*, made mostly in Jalisco and potent, and *pulque*, also powerful. *Mescal* from Oaxaca is another drink to be careful with. Imported whiskies and brandies are expensive. Rum is cheap and good but drunkenness is detested in Mexico. There are always plenty of non-alcoholic soft drinks (*refrescos*) and mineral water. Water-purifying tablets can be bought in Mexico City. Herbal teas, e.g. camomile, are available. There are few outdoor drinking places in Mexico except in tourist spots.

Food Usual meals are a light breakfast, and a heavy lunch between 1400 and 1500. Dinner, between 2100 and 2300, is light. Many restaurants give foreigners the menu without the *comida corrida* (specials of the day), and so forcing them to order *à la carte* at double the price; watch this! Try to avoid eating in restaurants which don't post a menu (their prices are always higher). Meals cost about US$1-2 for breakfast, US$3-5 for lunch and US$4-10 for dinner (about US$7-17 a day on meals, depending on lavishness). In resort areas the posh hotels include breakfast and dinner in many cases.

What to Eat *Tamales*, or meat wrapped in maize and then banana leaves and boiled. Turkey, chicken and pork with exotic sauces—*mole de guajolote* and *mole poblano* (*chile* and chocolate sauce with grated coconut) are famous. *Tacos* (without *chiles*) and *enchiladas* (with all too many of them) are meat or chicken and beans rolled in *tortillas* (maize pancakes) and fried in oil; they are delicious. Try also spring onions with salt and lime juice in *taquerías*. Indian dishes are found everywhere: for instance, *tostadas* (toasted fried tortillas with chicken, beans and lettuce), or *gorditas*, a fried, extra-thick tortilla with sauce and cheese. Black kidney beans (*frijoles*) appear in various dishes. Try *crepas de cuitlacoche*, best during rainy season—this consists of a pancake stuffed with maize fungus, which has a delicate mushroomy taste— very moreish. In the Pátzcuaro area ask for *budín de cuitlacoche*, with tomato, cream and *chiles*. Red snapper (*huachinango*), Veracruz style, is a famous fish dish, sautéd with *pimientos* and spices. Another excellent fish is the sea bass (*robalo*). Fruits include a vast assortment of tropical types—avocados, bananas, pineapples, *zapotes*, pomegranates, guavas, limes and *mangos de Manila*, which are delicious. Don't eat fruit unless you peel it yourself, and avoid raw vegetables. Try *higos rebanados* (delicious fresh sliced figs), *guacamole* (a mashed avocado seasoned with tomatoes, onions, coriander and *chiles*) and of course, *papaya*, or pawpaw. Mexico has various elaborate regional cuisines. Chinese restaurants, present in most towns, generally give clean and efficient service. Milk is only safe when in sealed containers marked *pasteurizado*. Fried eggs in Mexico are known as *huevos estrellados*. On January 6, Epiphany, the traditional *rosca*, a ring-shaped sweet bread with dried fruit and little plastic baby Jesuses inside, is eaten. The person who finds a baby Jesus in his piece must make a crib and clothes for Him, and invite everyone present to a *fiesta* on February 2, Candelaria.

Clothing People are usually smartly dressed in Mexico City. Women visitors should not wear shorts other than at the seaside, though trousers are quite OK. There is little central heating, so warm clothing is needed in winter. Four musts are good walking shoes, sun hats, dark glasses, and flip-flops for the hot sandy beaches. Women are always escorted, except in the main streets of the larger cities. Topless bathing is now accepted in parts of Baja California, but ask first, or do as others do.

Currency The monetary unit is the Mexican peso, divided into 100 centavos. Owing to the rapid devaluations of the past few years both coins and notes are being reissued. The smallest note is for 500 pesos, then 1,000, 2,000, 5,000 and 10,000, with the largest at 20,000. Coins have all been changed from silver and bronze to strange alloys that have various colours. The tiny 5-peso piece is gold-coloured, as is the 100-peso coin. The 10-peso piece is octagonal; there is a

1004 MEXICO

small 20-peso coin as well as an older, larger one, similarly with the 50-peso coins. It is wise to check the number on coins.

Exchange In the border states such as Baja California Norte, the most-used currency is the US dollar, and the Mexican peso is often accepted by stores on the US side of the border. Travellers' cheques from any well-known bank can be cashed in most towns if drawn in US dollars; travellers' cheques in terms of sterling are harder to cash, and certainly not worth carrying outside Mexico City. The free rate of exchange changes daily and varies from bank to bank even though all are government-owned. Until the new day's rate is posted, yesterday's rate prevails. Many banks, including in Mexico City, only change foreign currency during a limited period (often between 1000 and 1200), which should be remembered, especially on Fridays. Telegraphic transfer of funds *within* Mexico is not reliable. Beware of short-changing at all times. American Express, Mastercard and Visa are generally accepted in Mexico and cash is even obtainable with these credit cards at certain banks. 25% tax is payable on the use of credit cards. N.B. An American Express card issued in Mexico states "valid only in Mexico", and is used only for peso transactions. All other American Express cards are transacted in U.S. dollars even for employees living in Mexico.

Weights and Measures The metric system is compulsory.

National Holidays Sunday is a statutory holiday. Saturday is also observed as a holiday, except by the shops. There is no early-closing day. National holidays are as follows:

January 1: New Year.
February 5: Constitution Day.
March 21: Birthday Of Juárez.
Maundy Thursday.
Good Friday.
Easter Saturday.
May 1: Labour Day.

May 5: Battle of Puebla.
September 1: President's Annual Message.
September 16: Independence Day.
October 12: Discovery of America.
November 20: Day of the Revolution.
December 25: Christmas Day.

Nov. 2, All Souls' Day, and Dec. 12, Our Lady of Guadalupe, are not national holidays, but are widely celebrated.

Press The more important journals are in Mexico City. The most influential dailies are: *Excelsior, Novedades, El Día* (throughout Mexico), *Uno más Uno; The News* (in English); *El Universal* (*El Universal Gráfico*); *La Prensa*, a popular tabloid, has the largest circulation. *El Nacional* is the mouthpiece of the Government; *El Heraldo; Uno más Uno* publishes a supplement, *Tiempo Libre*, on Fridays, listing the week's cultural activities. A number of monthly and weekly magazines have a wide circulation and outweigh the influence of the dailies. The most influential are the two weekly magazines *Siempre* and *Sucesos*, both left of centre, very nationalistic. The political satirical weekly is *Los Agachados*.

Postal Services Rates are raised periodically in line with the peso's devaluation against the dollar. They are posted next to the windows where stamps are sold. Air mail letters to the US take about six days, and to the UK (US$0.25) via the US one to two weeks. Weight limit from the UK to Mexico: 22 lb., and 5 kg. in the reverse direction. About 3 months to Europe. Small parcel rate cheaper. Parcel counters often close earlier than other sections of the post office in Mexico. As for most of Latin America, send printed matter such as magazines registered. International parcels must be examined by the Customs Office at Oficina de Correos at Dr. Andrade, 25 Río de la Loza (Metro Salto de Agua); or the Correo Central at Calle Tacuba, open 0800-1300, window No. 48 from which only books or records can be sent; parcels with books in them must be less than 5 kg. (US$5 air mail to Europe per kg., US$1 surface mail to Europe per kg.) before posting. Dr. Andrade post office open 0800-1400 Mon.-Fri. for parcels by air only (max. 2 kg.). No more than 3 parcels may be sent at a time; maximum parcel size: 40 cm. X 60 cm.; registered letters received here. Surface parcels from Aduana Postal, Ceylán 468 (open 0800-1400, Mon.-Fri.); take metro to La Raza, catch bus marked "Ceylán" on Calle Cuitlauac to Colonia Cosmopólita (extremely complicated and long way N from centre). Bus No. 13 marked "Canal 13-Industrial Vallejo" also goes there. We have heard that the Customs Department at the airport hold up registered parcels coming in from abroad. Many travellers have also recommended that one should not use the post to send film or cherished objects as losses are frequent. A permit is needed from the Bellas Artes office to send paintings or drawings out of Mexico. Not all these services are obtainable outside Mexico City; delivery times in/from the interior may well be longer than those given above. *Poste restante* is not recommended, but if you wish to use this facility it is known as *lista de correos*; mail is sent back after ten days. Address "*favor de retener hasta llegada*" on envelope.

Telecommunications Telégrafos Nacionales maintains the national and international telegraph systems, separate from the Post Office. There is a special office at Balderas 14-18, just near corner of Colón, in Mexico City to deal with international traffic (open 0800-2300, Metro Hidalgo, exit Calle Basilio Badillo). There are three types of telegraph service: *extra urgente, urgente* and *ordinario*; they can only be prepaid, not sent collect. A telegram to Britain costs US$0.20 a word, and US$15 for 21 words including flat fee and taxes. Telex US$13-20 for 3 mins, will hold messages.

MEXICO 1005

Telephone service to USA, Canada and Europe. There is a telegraph and telex service available at Mexico City airport. There is a heavy tax levied on all foreign long-distance calls originating and paid for in Mexico, so it is better to call collect. Calls to Britain are more expensive per min. from 0500 to 1700, but cheaper per min. from 1700 to 0500 and all day on Sun. It costs US$15 to the US for 3 minutes. Again, not all these services are available outside the capital.

Cost of Living Manufactured goods and clothing are cheaper than in the USA. Film is usually expensive. Food is cheaper. Services are abundant and cheap: there are armies of waiters, waitresses, chauffeurs, maids, gardeners, night watchmen, etc. Rent for living quarters outside Mexico City and the beach resorts is very low compared to US and European levels.

We are most grateful to Ben Box for updating the Economy section, and to Lindsay Maginn (Mexico City); we also wish to thank the following travellers: Bill Addington (Warminster, Wilts), Hans Altmann (Seekirchen, Austria), Deborah Berlin, Stefan W. Berther (Geneva), Dr Michael Binzberger (Friedrichshafen, W. Ger.), Dale Bricker (Seattle), Larry Cebula (Vernon, Ct.), Anke Cruse, Alexander Daughtry (Vancouver), Jack Davis, Dagmar Drescher (Bad Kreuznach, W. Ger.), Christine Enkelaar and José Keldens ('s-Hertogenbosch, Neth.), Jill Ennever (Avalon, NSW), Dr Gerry Frizzelle (London SE12), Jorge Guimarães (São Paulo), Wayne Hedenschoug (Springfield, Ill.), John E. Hildeburn (San Marino, Ca.), Bastian Hiss and Daniela Fleischhauer (Krefeld), Alan Hoffman (Tallahassee, Fla.), Steve and Iona Hudson (London SW6), Tomas and Kristina Jäderkvist (Gävle, Swe.), Edith A. Kapuscinski (Portland, Ore.), Deborah Karp (London N3) and Karin Schamroth (London NW8), Roy Kellett (Middlesborough) for an outstanding contribution, Dr Paul Kelly and Jenny Gallagher (Perth, W. Aust.), Dr J Kleinwachter (Hamburg), Carmen Kuczma (Powell River, BC), Mme. C. Lapostolle (Paris), Pete Larrett (Cheltenham) for a most useful contribution, Daniel Le Goffe (Montreuil, France), Annette Lees and Shane Wright (Whakatane, NZ), Roger Lemercier (Nice), Herbert S. Levi (Buenos Aires), Trevor Long (London NW6), Suzanne Maillet (Montréal), Jason Malinowski (San Bruno, Ca.), Annette Morris (Redhill), Steve Morris (St John, NB, Canada), and Christiane Fischer (Frankfurt), Karl G. Olson (New York 10009), Vaclav Penkava (Seattle), Robert E. Pugh (Napanee, Ont.), Kristen Rasmussen and Ann Thordrup (Aarhus, Dmk.), John M. Raspey (Santo Domingo, DR), Helma Rausch (Darmstadt), Annamarie Reichmuth and Roger Müller (Schwyz, Switz.), George Ridenour (New York 10016) for some most useful observations, Christer Robertson (Stockholm) and Patricia Galvin (Galway), Ann K. Rodzai (Ithaca, NY) and Doug Hanauer, William C. Rynecki (Tuscaloosa, Ala.), Chesley and Carole Schart (Teton Village, Wyo.), Frank Scheenmann (Heusenstamm), Beat Schmutz (Münchenstein, Switz.), Gillian Scourfield and Alastair Mitchell (Spalding, Lincs), Sophie Stirling and friends (Buchlyvie, Stirlingshire), Clemens Streicher (W. Ger.), Carla Tromp and Douwe van Dijk (Meppen, Neth.), Dirk Vanmarcke and Liesbet Chielens (Bruges), Alan Wagman (Washington, DC), Anne Welsh (Nepean, Ont.), Paul Whitfield (Auckland, NZ), Gisela Willems and Uwe Thieme (Aachen), and Rolf Würtz (Heidelberg).

WILL YOU HELP US?

We do all we can to get our facts right in *The South American Handbook*. Each chapter is thoroughly revised each year, but Latin America and the Caribbean cover a vast area, and our eyes cannot be everywhere.

Your information may be far more up-to-date than ours. If your letter reaches us early enough in the year it will be used in the next edition, but write whenever you want to, for all your letters are used sooner or later.

Thank you very much indeed for your help.

Trade & Travel Publications Limited
5 Prince's Buildings, George Street,
Bath BA1 2ED, England

CENTRAL AMERICA

CENTRAL AMERICA comprises seven of the smallest countries of Latin America: Panama, Costa Rica, Nicaragua, Honduras, El Salvador, Guatemala and Belize (formerly British Honduras). Together they occupy 544,700 square km., which is less than the size of Texas. The total population of Central America in 1986 was about 24 million and it is increasing by 2.8% each year.

The degree of development in these countries differs sharply. Costa Rica and Panama have the highest standard of living, with two of the highest rates of literacy in all Latin America. At the other end of the scale, Honduras has one of the lowest standards of living.

Geographically, these countries have much in common, but there are sharp differences in the racial composition and traditions of their peoples. Costa Ricans are almost wholly white, Guatemalans are largely Amerindian or *mestizo*; Hondurans, Nicaraguans and Salvadoreans are almost entirely *mestizo*. Panama has perhaps the most racially varied population, with a large white group. Some of these countries also have a black element, the largest being found in Panama and Nicaragua.

Early History The best known of the pre-Conquest Indian civilizations of the area was the Maya, which is thought to have evolved in about A.D. 100 in the Pacific highlands of Guatemala and El Salvador. After 200 years of growth it entered what is known today as its "classic" period when the civilization flourished in Guatemala, Belize and Honduras, and in Chiapas, Campeche and Yucatán (Mexico). This period lasted until A.D. 900-1000, after which time the Mayas, concentrated into Yucatán after a successful invasion of their other lands by non-Maya people (this is only one theory; another is that they were forced to flee after a peasants' revolt against them), came under the influence of the Toltecs who invaded that area. From that time their culture declined. The Maya civilization was based on independent and antagonistic city states, including Tikal, Uaxactún, Kaminal Juyú, Iximché, Zaculeu and Quiriguá in Guatemala; Copán in Honduras; Altún Ha in Belize; Tazumal and San Andrés in El Salvador; and Palenque, Bonampak (both in Chiapas), Uxmal, Chichén Itzá, Mayapán, Tulum and the Puuc hill cities of Sayil, Labná and Kabah (all on the Yucatán peninsula) in Mexico.

The cities were all meticulously dated. Mayan art is a mathematical art: each column, figure, face, animal, frieze, stairway and temple expresses a date or a time relationship. When, for example, an ornament on the ramp of the Hieroglyphic Stairway at Copán was repeated some 15 times, it was to express that number of elapsed "leap" years. The 75 steps stand for the number of elapsed intercalary days. The Mayan calendar was a nearer approximation to sidereal time than either the Julian or the Gregorian calendars of Europe; it was only .000069 of a day out of true in a year. They used the zero centuries in advance of the Old World, plotted the movements of the sun, moon, Venus and other planets, conceived a cycle of more than 1,800 million days, achieved paper codices and glyphic writing, were skilled potters and weavers and traded over wide areas, though they had not discovered the wheel and had no beasts of burden. Their tools and weapons were flint and hard stone, obsidian and fire-hardened wood, and yet with these they grew lavish crops, hewed out and transported great monoliths over miles of difficult country, and carved them over with intricate glyphs and figures which would be difficult enough with modern chisels.

The Mayan cities were principally ceremonial centres controlled by a theocratic minority of priests and nobles in whom was vested the entire cultural activity of each state. The Toltecs, who had firm control in Yucatán in the 10th century, gradually spread their empire as far as the southern borders of Guatemala. They in turn, however, were conquered by the Aztecs, one of whose revolutionary principles was the private ownership of land, but they did not penetrate into Central America.

CENTRAL AMERICA

At the time of the coming of the Spaniards there were several other isolated groups of Indians dotted over the Central American area: they were mostly shifting cultivators or nomadic hunters and fishermen. A few places only were occupied by sedentary agriculturists: what remained of the Maya in the highlands of Guatemala; a group on the south-western shores of Lakes Managua and Nicaragua; and another in the highlands of Costa Rica. The Spanish conquerors were attracted by precious metals, or native sedentary farmers who could be christianized and exploited. There were few of either, and comparatively few Spaniards settled in Central America.

It was only during his fourth voyage, in 1502, that Columbus reached the mainland of Central America; he landed in Panama, which he called Veragua, and founded the town of Santa María de Belén. In 1508 Alonso de Ojeda received a grant of land on the Pearl Coast east of Panama, and in 1509 he founded the town of San Sebastián, later moved to a new site called Santa María la Antigua del Darién. In 1513 the governor of the colony at Darién was Vasco Núñez de Balboa. Taking 190 men he crossed the isthmus in 18 days and caught the first glimpse of the Pacific; he claimed it and all neighbouring lands in the name of the King of Spain. But from the following year, when Pedrarias replaced him as Governor, Balboa fell on evil days, and he was executed by Pedrarias in 1519. That same year Pedrarias crossed the isthmus and founded the town of Panamá on the Pacific side. It was in April 1519, too, that Cortés began his conquest of Mexico.

Central America was explored from these two nodal points of Panama and Mexico. Cortés' lieutenant, Alvarado, had conquered as far south as San Salvador by 1523. Meanwhile Pedrarias was sending forces into Panama and Costa Rica: the latter was abandoned, for the natives were hostile, but was finally colonized from Mexico City when the rest of Central America had been taken. In 1522-24 Andrés Niño and Gil Gonzales Dávila explored Nicaragua and Honduras. Many towns were founded by these forces from Panama: León, Granada, Trujillo and others. Spanish forces from the north and south sometimes met and fought bitterly. The gentle Bartolomé de Las Casas, the "apostle of the Indies", was active as a Dominican missionary in Central America in the 1530s.

Settlement The groups of Spanish settlers were few and widely scattered, and this is the fundamental reason for the political fragmentation of Central America today. Panama was ruled from Bogotá, but the rest of Central America was subordinate to the Viceroyalty at Mexico City, with Guatemala City as an Audiencia for the area. Panama was of paramount importance for colonial Spanish America for its strategic position, and for the trade passing across the isthmus to and from the southern colonies. The other provinces were of comparatively little value.

The comparatively small number of Spaniards intermarried freely with the local Indians, accounting for the predominance of *mestizos* in Central America today. In Guatemala, where there were the most Indians, intermarriage affected fewer of the natives, and over half the population today is pure Indian. On the Meseta Central of Costa Rica, the Indians were all but wiped out by disease; today, as a consequence of this great disaster, there is a buoyant community of over 2 million whites, with little Indian admixture, in the highlands. Blacks predominate all along the Caribbean coasts of Central America; they were not brought in by the colonists as slaves, but by the railway builders and banana planters of the nineteenth century and the canal cutters of the twentieth, as cheap labour.

Independence and Federation On November 5, 1811, José Matías Delgado, a priest and jurist born in San Salvador, organized a revolt in conjunction with another priest, Manuel José Arce. They proclaimed the independence of El Salvador, but the Audiencia at Guatemala City quickly suppressed the revolt and took Delgado prisoner.

It was the revolution of 1820 in Spain itself that precipitated the independence of Central America. When on February 24, 1821, the Mexican general Iturbide announced his Plan of Iguala for an independent Mexico, the Central

American *criollos* decided to follow his example, and a declaration of independence, drafted by José Cecilio del Valle, was announced in Guatemala City on September 15, 1821. Iturbide invited the provinces of Central America to join with him, and on January 5, 1822, Central America was declared annexed to Mexico. Delgado refused to accept this decree, and Iturbide, who had now assumed the title of Emperor Agustín the First, sent an army south under Vicente Filísola to enforce it in the regions under Delgado's influence. Filísola had completed his task when he heard of Iturbide's abdication, and at once convened a general congress of the Central American provinces. It met on June 24, 1823, and established the Provincias Unidas del Centro de América. The Mexican republic acknowledged their independence on August 1, 1824, and Filísola's soldiers were withdrawn.

The congress, presided over by Delgado, appointed a provisional governing *junta* which promulgated a constitution modelled on that of the United States on November 22, 1824. The Province of Chiapas was not included in the Federation, for it had already adhered to Mexico in 1821. No federal capital was chosen, but Guatemala City, by force of tradition, soon became the seat of government.

Breakdown of Federation The first President under the new constitution was Manuel José Arce, a liberal. One of his first acts was to abolish slavery. El Salvador, protesting that he had exceeded his powers, rose in December, 1826. Honduras, Nicaragua, and Costa Rica joined the revolt, and in 1828 General Francisco Morazán, in charge of the army of Honduras, defeated the federal forces, entered San Salvador and marched against Guatemala City. He captured the city on April 13, 1829, and established that contradiction in terms: a liberal dictatorship. Many conservative leaders were expelled and church and monastic properties confiscated. Morazán himself became president of the Federation in 1830. He was a man of considerable ability; he ruled with a strong hand, encouraged education, fostered trade and industry, opened the country to immigrants, and reorganized the administration. In 1835 the capital was moved to San Salvador.

These reforms antagonized the conservatives and there were several risings. The most serious revolt was among the Indians of Guatemala, led by Rafael Carrera, an illiterate *mestizo* conservative and a born leader. Years of continuous warfare followed, during the course of which the Federation withered away. As a result, the federal congress passed an act which allowed each province to assume what government it chose, but the idea of a federation was not quite dead. As a result, Morazán became President of El Salvador. Carrera, who was by then in control of Guatemala, defeated Morazán in battle and forced him to leave the country. But in 1842, Morazán overthrew Braulio Carrillo, then dictator of Costa Rica, and became president himself. At once he set about rebuilding the Federation, but was defeated by the united forces of the other states, and shot on September 15, 1842. With him perished any practical hope of Central American political union.

The Separate States Costa Rica, with its mainly white population, is a country apart, and Panama was Colombian territory until 1903. The history of the four remaining republics since the breakdown of federation has been tempestuous in the extreme. In each the ruling class was divided into pro-clerical conservatives and anti-clerical liberals, with constant changes of power. Each was weak, and tried repeatedly to buttress its weakness by alliances with others, which invariably broke up because one of the allies sought a position of mastery. The wars were rarely over boundaries; they were mainly ideological wars between conservatives and liberals, or wars motivated by inflamed nationalism. Nicaragua, for instance, was riven internally for most of the period by the mutual hatreds of the Conservatives of Granada and the Liberals of León, and there were repeated conflicts between the Caribbean and interior parts of Honduras.

Of the four republics, Guatemala was certainly the strongest and in some ways the most stable. While the other states were skittling their presidents like so many ninepins, Guatemala was ruled by a succession of strong dictators:

Rafael Carrera (1838-1865), Justo Rufino Barrios (1873-1885), Manuel Cabrera (1896-1920), and Jorge Ubico (1931-44). These were separated by intervals of constitutional government, anarchy, or attempts at dictatorship which failed. Few presidents handed over power voluntarily to their successors; most of them were forcibly removed or assassinated.

Despite the permutations and combinations of external and civil war there has been a recurrent desire to reestablish some form of *la grande patria centroamericana*. Throughout the 19th century, and far into the 20th, there have been ambitious projects for political federation, usually involving El Salvador, Honduras and Nicaragua; none of them lasted more than a few years. There have also been unsuccessful attempts to reestablish union by force, such as those of Barrios of Guatemala in 1885 and Zelaya of Nicaragua in 1907.

Rapid change is now coming to Central America. During colonial times the area suffered from great poverty; trade with the mother country was confined to small amounts of silver and gold, cacao and sugar, and cochineal and indigo. During the present century the great banana plantations of the Caribbean, the growing coffee and cotton trade and industrialization have brought some prosperity, but its benefits have, except in Costa Rica and Panama, been garnered mostly by a relatively small landowning class and the middle classes of the cities. Nicaragua is now a case apart, with extensive and radical reforms carried out by a left-leaning revolutionary government. Poverty, still the fate of the great majority, has brought about closer economic cooperation between the five republics, and in 1960 they established the Central American Common Market (CACM). Surprisingly, the Common Market appeared to be a great success until 1968, when integration fostered national antagonisms, and there was a growing conviction in Honduras and Nicaragua, which were doing least well out of integration, that they were being exploited by the others. In 1969 the "Football War" broke out between El Salvador and Honduras, basically because of a dispute about illicit emigration by Salvadoreans into Honduras, and relations between the two were not normalized until 1980. It seems likely that nationalist feeling and ideological differences will continue to block attempts to re-establish economic integration. Political integration, when the wide disparities in political behaviour between the different countries is considered, is at present virtually impossible.

For revising the Central American sections, we are most grateful to Simon Ellis (San José) for essential airline information, and for the region in general to the following travellers: Hans Altmann (Seekirchen, Austria), Eberhard Baer (Koenigsbrunn, W.Ger.), Tania Brown and Keith Kimber (World Motor Cycle Journey 1983-88), Klaus Bryn (Oslo), Larry Cebula (Vernon, Ct.), Daniel D'Andrea (Calif.) and Lisbeth Sivertsen (Denmark), Jack Davis, Dr Sally Dealler (Leeds 8), Christine Enkelaar and José Keldens ('s-Hertogenbosch, Neth.), Michael J.Finnerty (Indianapolis), Dr Gerry Frizzelle (London SE12), John E. Hildeburn (San Marino, Ca.), Tomas and Kristina Jäderkvist (Gävle, Swe.), Andrew Lawrence (Vancouver) and Jon Easterbrooke (Shaftesbury, Dorset), Alban Johnson (Hobart) and Luci Montesinos Aguilar (Mexcio City), Deborah Karp (London N3), and Karin Schamroth (London NW8), Daniel Le Goff (Montreuil, Fr.), Robert Le Riche (Longueuil, Qué.), Trevor Long (London NW6), Dr Horst Müller (Pulheim, W.Ger.), David Rehe (E. Doncaster, Vict.), David Ridges (Caldy, Wirral), William C.Rynecki (Tuscaloosa, Ala.), Sophie Stirling and friends (Buchlvyie, Stirlingshire), Dirk Vanmarcke and Liesbet Chielens (Bruges), Paul Whitfield (Auckland), and Rolf Würtz (Heidelberg).

Travellers who have made particularly valuable contributions to updating individual Central American country sections are listed at the end of the sections concerned.

GUATEMALA

GUATEMALA (109,000 square km., 8.19 million people), is the most populous of the Central American republics and the only one which is largely Indian in language and culture. It still has large areas of unoccupied land, especially in the north; only about two-thirds is populated. Two-thirds of it is mountainous and 62% forested. It has coastlines on the Pacific (240 km.), and on the Caribbean (110 km.). The population of Guatemala City amounts to 1,330,000, more than ten times as large as that of any other town.

A lowland ribbon, nowhere more than 50 km. wide, runs the whole length of the Pacific shore. Cotton, sugar, bananas and maize are the chief crops of this lowland, particularly in the Department of Escuintla. There is some stock raising as well. Summer rain is heavy and the lowland carries scrub forest.

From this plain the highlands rise sharply to heights of between 2,500 and 3,000 metres and stretch some 240 km. to the N before sinking into the northern lowlands. A string of volcanoes juts boldly above the southern highlands along the Pacific. There are intermont basins at from 1,500 to 2,500 metres in this volcanic area. Most of the people of Guatemala live in these basins, drained by short rivers into the Pacific and by longer ones into the Atlantic. One basin W of the capital has no apparent outlet and here, ringed by volcanoes, is the splendid Lake Atitlán.

The southern highlands are covered with lush vegetation over a volcanic subsoil. This clears away in the central highlands, exposing the crystalline rock of the E-W running ranges. This area is lower but more rugged, with sharp-faced ridges and deep ravines modifying into gentle slopes and occasional valley lowlands as it loses height and approaches the Caribbean coastal levels and the flatlands of El Petén.

The lower slopes of these highlands, from about 600 to 1,500 metres, are planted with coffee which is some 60% by value of the total exports. Coffee plantations make almost a complete belt around them. Above 1,500 metres is given over to wheat and the main subsistence crops of maize and beans. Deforestation is becoming a serious problem. Where rainfall is low there are savannas; the middle Motagua valley is so parched that it can only bear xerophytic plants like cactus, but water for irrigation is now drawn from wells and the area is being reclaimed for pasture and fruit growing.

Two large rivers flow down to the Caribbean Gulf of Honduras from the highlands: one is the Río Motagua, 400 km. long, rising among the southern volcanoes; the other, further N, is the Río Polochic, 298 km. long, which drains into Lake Izabal and the Bay of Amatique. There are large areas of lowland in the lower reaches of both rivers, which are navigable for considerable distances; this was, and may be again, the great banana zone.

To the NW, bordering on Belize and Mexico, in the peninsula of Yucatán, lies the low, undulating tableland of El Petén, 36,300 square km. of almost undeveloped wilderness covered with dense hardwood forest. Deep in this tangled rain-forest lie the ruins of Maya cities such as Tikal and Uaxactún. In the Department of Petén, almost one-third of the national territory, there are only 40,000 people. In some parts there is natural grassland, with woods and streams, suitable for cattle.

Settlement When the Spaniards arrived from Mexico City in 1523 they found little precious metal: only some silver at Huehuetenango. Those who stayed settled in the intermont basins of the south-eastern parts of the southern highlands around Antigua and Guatemala City and intermarried with the groups of native subsistence farmers living there. This was the basis of the present

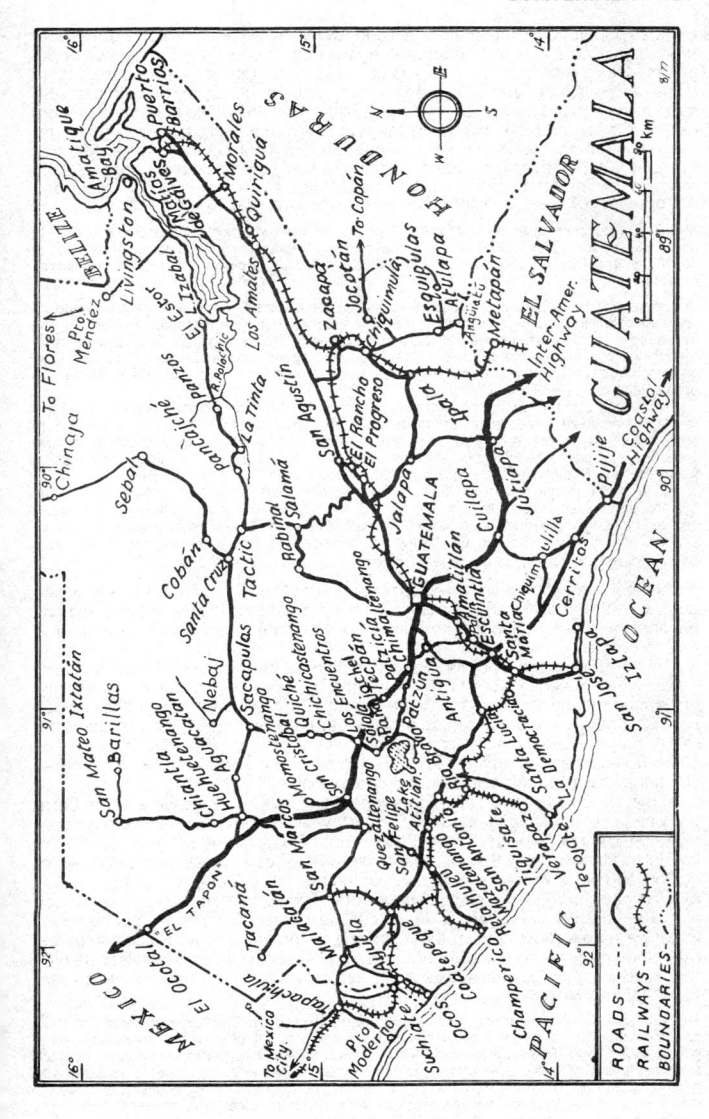

GUATEMALA 1011

ROUGH SKETCH

1012 GUATEMALA

mestizo population living in the cities and towns as well as in all parts of the southern highlands and in the flatlands along the Pacific coast; the indigenous population—more than half the total—is still at its most dense in the western highlands and Alta Verapaz. They form two distinct cultures: the almost self-supporting indigenous system in the highlands, and the *ladino* commercial economy in the lowlands. At first sight the two seem to have much in common, for the Indian regional economy is also monetary, but a gulf opens between the two systems when it is realized that an Indian will carry an article a hundred km. and ask no more for it than he would at home. To him, trade seems to be a social act, not done out of need, and certainly not from any impulse to grow rich.

N.B. The word *ladino*, used all over Central America but most commonly in Guatemala, applies to any person with a "Latin" culture, speaking Spanish and wearing normal Western clothes, though he may be pure Amerindian by descent. The opposite of *ladino* is *indígena*; the definition is cultural, not racial.

The scenery of the Indian regions W of the capital is superb and full of colour. In the towns and villages are colonial churches, some half ruined by earthquakes but often with splendid interiors. The Indians speak some 20 languages and 100 or more dialects. The coming of the Spaniards transformed their outer lives: they sing old Spanish songs, and their religion is a compound of image-worshipping paganism and the outward forms of Catholicism, but their inner natures remain largely untouched.

Their markets and *fiestas* are of outstanding interest. The often crowded markets are quiet and restrained: no voice raised, no gesture made, no anxiety to buy or sell; but the *fiestas* are a riot of noise, a confusion of processions, usually carrying saints, and the whole punctuated by grand firework displays and masked dancers. The chief *fiesta* is always for a town's particular patron saint, but all the main Catholic festivals and Christmas are celebrated to some extent everywhere.

Indian dress is unique and attractive, little changed from the time the Spaniards arrived: the colourful head-dresses, *huipiles* (tunics) and skirts of the women, the often richly patterned sashes and kerchiefs, the hatbands and tassels of the men. It varies greatly, often from village to village. Unfortunately a new outfit is costly, the Indians are poor, and denims are cheap. While men are adopting western dress in many villages, women are slower to change.

Cochineal and indigo were the great exports until 1857, when both were wiped out by synthetic dyes. The vacuum was filled by cacao, followed by coffee and bananas, and essential oils. The upland soil and climate are particularly favourable to coffee.

Only coffee of the Bourbon variety is planted below 600 metres, and until 1906, when bananas were first planted there, the low-lying *tierra caliente* had been used mostly for cane and cattle raising. The first plantations of the United Fruit Company were at the mouth of the Motagua, near Puerto Barrios, then little more than a village. Blacks from Jamaica were brought in to work them. The plantations expanded until they covered most of the *tierra caliente* in the NE—along the lower Motagua and around Lake Izabal.

In the 1930s, however, the plantations were struck by disease and the Company began planting bananas in the Pacific lowlands; they are railed across country to the Caribbean ports. There are still substantial plantations at Bananera, 58 km. inland from Puerto Barrios, though some of the old banana land is used for cotton and *abacá* (manila hemp). Despite the fall in banana exports, overall exports have increased greatly, because of the growth of other export lines such as coffee, cotton and sugar. As a result of the increase in cotton-growing, many Indians are now moving from the highlands to the *ladino* lowland cotton areas; other Indians come to the southern plains as seasonal labourers whilst retaining their costumes, languages and customs and returning to the highlands each year to tend their own crops.

The equitable distribution of occupied land is a pressing problem. The Agrarian Census of 1950 disclosed that 70% of the cultivable land was in the hands of 2% of the landowners, 20% in the hands of 22%, and 10% in the hands of 76%—these figures corresponding to the large, medium and small landowners. A quarter of the land held by the small owners was sub-let to peasants who owned none at all. There were over 417,000 farms according to the 1964 census, and 10,000 land titles have been given to landless peasants since 1970; this means that there has been some spread of land ownership since the 1950s. Under the present government a peaceful movement of *campesinos* (farm labourers) was formed in 1986 to speed land distribution.

Roads There are now 13,632 km. of roads, 2,638 of which are paved.

GUATEMALA 1013

Railways The only railway (apart from a few private branch lines on the United Brands estates) was bought by the State from a US company, International Railways of Central America, in 1968. This system links the Caribbean seaboard with the Pacific, running from Puerto Barrios up the Motagua valley to Guatemala City and on to the port of San José. From Santa María a branch line runs W through Mazatenango to the port of Champerico and the Mexican frontier (passenger services to Mexico were suspended in 1982). From Zacapa, halfway from Puerto Barrios to the capital, a branch line runs S to San Salvador. There are 867 km. of public service railways and 290 km. of plantation lines.

Population Birth rate: 38.0 per 1,000 (60% born to unmarried mothers); infant mortality, 75 (1985); population growth: 3.1%; urban growth: 8%. Some 65% of the people live at elevations above 1,000 metres in 30% of the total territory; only 35% live at lower elevations in 70% of the total territory.

Government Guatemala is administratively divided into 22 Departments. The Governor of each is appointed by the President, whose term is for 5 years. The latest constitution was dated May 1985.

Recent History For early history see the introductory chapter to Central America. Jorge Ubico, an efficient but brutal dictator who came to power in 1931, was deposed in 1944. After some confusion, Juan José Arévalo, a teacher, was elected President. He set out to accomplish a social revolution, paying particular attention to education and labour problems. He survived several conspiracies and finished his term of six years. Jacobo Arbenz became President in 1950, and the pace of reform was quickened. His Agrarian Reform Law, dividing large estates expropriated without adequate compensation among the numerous landless peasantry, aroused opposition from landowners. In June 1954, Colonel Carlos Castillo Armas, backed by interested parties and with the encouragement of the United States, led a successful insurrection and became President. For the following 29 years the army and its right-wing supporters suppressed left-wing efforts, both constitutional and violent, to restore the gains made under Arévalo and Arbenz; many thousands of people, mostly leftists, were killed during this period. In August 1983 General Oscar Mejía Víctores took power; he permitted a Constituent Assembly to be elected in 1984; among its major tasks were to draw up a new constitution and to work out a timetable for a return to democratic rule. This proceeded successfully, with presidential elections held in November 1985. The victor was Vinicio Cerezo Arévalo of the Christian Democrat party (DCG); he took office in January 1986.

Cities and Towns

Note Although security in general has improved, conditions in the Northern territories of Alta Verapaz and El Petén should be checked prior to travelling because of sporadic guerrilla and military activities. Chichicastenango and Tikal, however, are safe.

Guatemala City, at 1,500 metres, was founded by decree of Charles III of Spain in 1776 to serve as capital after earthquake damage to the earlier capital, Antigua, in 1773. The city lies on a plateau, a gash through the high Sierra Madre. The lofty ranges of these green mountains almost overhang the capital. To the S looms a group of volcanoes. Population, 1,330,000.

The climate is temperate, with little variation around the year. The average annual temperature is about 18°C, with a monthly average high of 20° in May and a low of 16° in December-January. Daily temperatures range from a low of 7°C at night to a high of about 29° at midday. The rainy season is from May to October but rainfall (every afternoon) is not heavy; it averages about 1,270 mm. a year, and sunshine is plentiful. The city has a serious smog problem.

The city was almost completely destroyed by earthquakes in 1917-18 and rebuilt in modern fashion or in copied colonial; it was further damaged by earthquake in 1976. Houses are mostly of one storey, but several high multi-storey buildings have now been put up. A plaza called Parque Central lies at its heart: it is intersected by the N-S running 6 Avenida, the main shopping street. The E half has a floodlit fountain; on the W side is Parque Centenario, with an acoustic shell in cement used for open-air concerts and public meetings. To the E of the plaza is the Cathedral; to the W are the National Library and the Banco del Ejército; to the N the large Palacio Nacional. Behind the Palacio Nacional, built of light green stone, is the Presidential Mansion.

1014 GUATEMALA

Guatemala City is large. Any address not in Zona 1—and it is absolutely essential to quote Zone numbers in addresses—is probably some way from the centre. Addresses themselves, being purely numerical, are easy to find. 19 C, 4-83 is on 19 Calle between 4 and 5 Avenidas.

Many of the hotels and boarding houses are in the main shopping quarter between 2 and 11 Avenidas and between 6 and 18 Calles, Zona 1. The railway station is in the southern part of Zona 1, at 10 Av., 18C, facing the Plaza named for Justo Rufino Barrios, to whom there is a fine bronze statue on Av. las Américas, Zona 13, in the southern part of the city. To see the finest residential district go S down 7 Avenida to Ruta 6, which runs diagonally in front of Edificio El Triángulo, past the Yurrita chapel (Zona 4), into the wide tree-lined Avenida La Reforma. Just south are the Botanical Gardens (open Mon.-Fri., 0800-1200, 1400-1600) and the Natural History Museum of the University of San Carlos at Calle Mariscal Cruz 1-56, Zona 10 (same hours as the Botanical Gardens). Admission free. Parque El Obelisco (also known as Próceres or Independencia), with the obelisk to Guatemalan independence, is at the S end of the Avenida. La Aurora international airport, the Zoo (free, newer areas show greater concern for the animals' well-being), the Observatory, the Archaeological and the Modern Art Museums and racetrack are in Parque Aurora, Zona 13, in the southern part of the city.

Museums The National Museum of Archaeology and Ethnology, Salón 5, Parque Aurora, Zona 13, contains stelae from Piedras Negras and typical Guatemalan costumes, and good models of Tikal, Quiriguá and Zaculeu, and other Mayan items. (Open 0900-1600, Tues.-Fri., Sat. and Sun., 0900-1200, 1400-1600.) Admission US$0.50, Sun. free for Guatemalans only. Contains sculpture (including stelae, murals, etc.), ceramics, textiles, and a collection of masks. Take bus No. 5.

The Museum of Modern and Contemporary Arts has replaced the National Museum of History and Fine Arts in Parque Aurora, "modest, enjoyable collection". Open Tues.-Fri., 1000-1600, Sat.-Sun., 1000-1200, 1400-1600, US$0.12.

Museum of Natural History, collection of stuffed birds and animals as well as butterflies, geological specimens etc., in Parque Aurora, 7 Av. 6-81, Zona 13 (take bus 5 or 6 from 8 Av. in Zona 1); open Mon.-Fri., 0900-1630, free; rebuilt and reorganized in 1983.

National Museum of Arts and Popular Crafts, 10 Av. 11-72, Zona 1, small exhibition of popular ceramics, textiles, silversmiths' work etc. Hours Mon.-Fri. 0900-1530, Sat. and Sun. 1000-1200, 1400-1600 (US$0.12).

Museo Ixchel del Traje Indígena, 4 Av. 16-27, Zona 10, has a collection of over 4,000 examples of Indian costumes. Open Tues.-Sat., 0900-1700, entrance US$0.35; Bus 14 from city centre; get off at Av. La Reforma and 16 C.

Popol Vuh Museum of Archaeology, Edificio Galerías Reforma, Av. La Reforma 8-60, Zona 9 (6th floor, Tel.: 318921). Extensive collection of precolumbian and colonial artefacts; said to be best archaeological museum in Guatemala. Has a replica of the Dresden Codex, one of only 3 Mayan parchment manuscripts in existence. Open Mon.-Sat., 0900-1730. Admission US$0.35 (students and children half price). As the showcases bear numbers only, one must pay US$0.25 for a catalogue. US$1 charge to take photographs. The research library of FLAAR (see page 1019) is on long-term loan to the Popol Vuh Museum. Take bus 2 or 14 (red numbers).

National Museum of History, 9 C. 9-70, Zona 1 (Mon.-Fri., 0900-1600), US$0.12, historical documents, and objects from independence onward; and colonial furniture and arms.

It could be noted here that each museum has a sign in 4 languages to the effect that "The Constitution and Laws of Guatemala prohibit the exportation from the country of any antique object, either preColumbian or colonial". The USA in fact prohibits the import of such items and penalties are severe.

There is a magnificent view all the way to Lake Amatitlán from Parque de Berlín at the S end of Av. las Américas, the continuation of Av. La Reforma.

In the northern part (Zona 2) is the fine Parque Minerva, where there is a huge relief map of the country made in 1905 to a horizontal scale of 1 in 10,000 and a vertical scale of 1 in 2,000 (open 0800-1700). Buses 1 (from Av. 6, Zona 1) and 18 run to the park, where there are basketball and baseball courts, two swimming pools, bar and restaurant and a children's playground.

The most notable public buildings built 1920-44 after the 1917 earthquake are the National Palace (the guards have keys and may show you round the rooms of state), the Police Headquarters, the Chamber of Deputies and the Post Office. The modern civic centre includes the City Hall, the Supreme Court, the Ministry of Finance, the Banco de Guatemala, the mortgage bank, the social-security commission and the tourist board.

GUATEMALA 1015

The University of San Carlos was founded in 1680; it has archaeological and natural history museums and a botanical garden, Mcal. Santa Cruz 1-56, Zona 10, entrance free, Mon.-Fri. 0800-1200, 1400-1800 (gardens close 1700).

The National Theatre dominates the hilltop of the W side of the Civic Centre. An old Spanish fortress provides a backdrop to the Open Air Theatre adjoining the blue and white mosaic-covered National Theatre; open Mon.-Fri.

On the W outskirts in Zona 7 (easily reached by buses 7, 17 and 21), are the Mayan ruins of Kaminal Juyú (Valley of Death). About 200 mounds have been examined by the Archaeological Museum and the Carnegie Institute. The area is mainly unexcavated, but there are three excavated areas open to the public, and a sculpture shed.

Churches

Cathedral Begun 1782, finished 1815, damaged by the 1976 earthquake. Paintings and statues from ruined Antigua. Solid silver and sacramental reliquary in the E side chapel of Sagrario. Next to the Cathedral is the colonial mansion of the Archbishop.

Cerro del Carmen a copy of a hermitage destroyed in 1917-18, containing a famous image of the Virgen del Carmen, situated on a hill with views of the city, was also severely damaged in 1976.

La Merced (11 Av. and 5 C, Zona 1), dedicated in 1813, which has housed beautiful altars, organ and pulpit from Antigua as well as jewellery, art treasures and fine statues, also damaged in 1976.

Santo Domingo church (12 Av. and 10 C, Zona 1), 1782-1807, is a striking yellow colour, reconstructed after 1917, image of Our Lady of the Rosary and sculptures.

Santuario Expiatorio (26 C and 2 Av., Zona 1) holds 3,000 people; colourful, exciting modern architecture by a young Salvadorean architect who had not qualified when he built it. Part of the complex (church, school and auditorium) is in the shape of a fish.

Las Capuchinas (10 Av. and 10 C, Zona 1) was another victim of the earthquake. It has a very fine St. Anthony altarpiece, and other pieces from Antigua.

Santa Rosa (10 Av. and 8 C, Zona 1) was used for 26 years as the cathedral until the present building was ready. Altarpieces again from Antigua (except above the main altar). Now damaged.

San Francisco (6 Av. and 13 C, Zona 1) has a sculpture of the Sacred Head, originally from Extremadura.

Capilla de Yurrita (Ruta 6 and Vía 8, Zona 4), built in 1928 on the lines of a Russian Orthodox church as a private chapel. It has been described as an example of "opulent 19th century bizarreness and over-ripe extravagance." There are many wood carvings. Seldom open but worth seeing.

Carmen El Bajo (8 Av. and 10 C, Zona 1) built in the late 18th century; façade severely damaged in 1976.

Warning Thieves and handbag snatchers operate openly around 7 Av. and 16 C. Do not park on the street, either day or night, or your car may well be broken into. There are plenty of lock-up garages and parking lots (*estacionamientos*).

Hotels (Av.=Avenida; C.=Calle). *More Expensive.* Zona 1: *Ritz Continental,* 6 Av. "A" 10-13, C; *Del Centro,* 13 C. 4-55; *Pan American,* 9 C. 5-63, D, central and recommended as quiet and comfortable with good and reasonable food (US$1.25 and US$2 for the set meals), parking; *Suites Córdoba,* 6 Av. "A' 10-52, C; *Guatemala Internacional,* 6 Av. 12-21, C; *Maya Excelsior,* 7 Av. 12-46, D, crowded, noisy and commercial.

Zona 2: *La Gran Vía,* Av. Simeón Cañas 7-23, C, fully-equipped apartments.

Zona 4: *Conquistador-Sheraton,* Vía 5, 4-68, A, luxurious, good; *Motel Plaza,* Vía 7, 6-16, D, outdoor pool, squash court, satisfactory.

Zona 9: *Cortijo Reforma,* Av. La Reforma 2-18, A, recommended; *El Dorado Americana,* 7 Av. 15-45, A; *Alamo Apart-Hotel,* 10 C. 5-60, C; *Carillon,* 5 Av. 11-23, D; *Villa Española,* 2 C., 7-51, Tel.: 65417, restaurant, bar, parking, colonial atmosphere, D.

Zona 10: *Camino Real,* Av. La Reforma and 14 C., A; *Guatemala Fiesta,* 1 Av. 13-22, A; *Residencial Reforma,* Av. La Reforma 7-67, near American Embassy, C; *Apartamentos Las Torres,* 1 Av. 12-70; *Biltmore Internacional,* now part of *Camino Real; Alameda Guest House,* 4 Av. 14-10, C; *Suites Reforma,* Av. La Reforma 12-51.

Medium price, all in Zona 1 unless otherwise stated: *Centenario,* 6 C. 5-33, E, commercial but reasonable, good facilities; *Posada Belén,* 13 C. "A' 10-30, with bath in a colonial-style house, D, quiet, extremely friendly, Francesca and René Sanchinelli speak English, highly recommended, good dining room (Tel.: 29226, 534530, 513478); also offers 8-day, 7-nights escorted package (starting Sats.), including tours, transfers, meals, taxes, tips, etc., for US$599—please enquire. *Hogar del Turista,* 11 C. 10-43, E, clean, friendly; *Brasilia,* 2 Av. 4-20, D, with bath (10% discount if staying a week or more); *Lessing House,* 12 C. 4-35, E, run-down, dangerous electric bathroom facilities, no hot water; *Mansión San Francisco,* 6 Av. 12-62, E, gloomy, overpriced; *Colonial,* 7 Av. 14-19, D, reasonable restaurant, quiet and recommended, although ground floor rooms are

1016 GUATEMALA

small and poorly ventilated, ask for 2nd floor; *Casa Shaw*, 8 Av. 12-75, D, with bath, recommended; *Plaza Bolívar*, 20 C. 3-40; *San Juan*, 16 C. 2-51, E, with bath, clean, quiet, convenient; *International Boarding House*, next door, a little cheaper; *Las Ninfas* 7 C. 3-11; *Embajador*, 19 C. 11-34; *Posada Real*, 12 C. 6-21, E; *Hernani*, 15 C. 6-56, E; *Royal Home*, 13 C. 2-52, E, with bath; *La Quinta Bayou*, 5 Av. 3-58, E; *Montecarlo*, 9 Av. 5-37.

Inexpensive, all in Zona 1 unless otherwise stated: *Posada Guatemala*, 8 Av. 13-30, G, not incl. meals; *Ritz*, 6 Av. 9-28, 2nd. floor, E, central, hot water, friendly; *El Virrey*, 5 Av. 13-52, F, meals US$1.25; *13 Calle Inn*, 13 C. 9-08, 2nd. floor, F, with hot shower, cheaper without, clean; *Spring*, 8 Av. 12-65, E, with shower and hot water, cheaper without, recommended; *Pensión Patricia*, 13 C. 2-30, E, full board; *Mansión Española*, 6 Av. 'A' 14-31, F, good; *San Juan*, 16 C. 2-51, E; *Bristol*, 15 C. 7-36, F, shared bath, pleasant, back rooms are brighter; *Bilbao*, 8 Av. 15 C., F, clean, pleasant, helpful, some English spoken, shared showers, good toilets; *San Diego* 15 C. 7-37, G, with bath (cheap breakfast and meals, annex opp., F, good value, full by 1000); *Centro-América*, 9 Av. 16-38, E, with 3 meals, US$1 extra with bath, clean, bright; *Capri*, 9 Av. 15-63, F, with shower, a bit noisy, clean, hot water, recommended; *Belmont*, 9 Av. 15-30 and 46 (there are two houses), E, with bath (no singles available); *La 14*, 14C. Avs. 9-10, G, noisy, short-stay; *Le Petit Parisien*, 2 C. 6-77, E, with bath, clean, friendly; *Chalet Suizo*, 14 C. 6-82, F, with or without shower, (US$ 2.25 for extra bed) popular, often crowded, clean, friendly, locked luggage store US$0.10/day, German-speaking owner; *Pensión Pérez*, 7 Av. 15-46, F, with bath, doors closed at 2100, meals US$1.50; *Fénix*, 7 Av. 16-81, F, some rooms with bath, clean, safe, corner rooms noisy, good meals US$1.25 and 1.50; *Pensión Meza*, 10C. 10-17, G, popular, helpful staff, hot showers, noisy (loud music all day), inhabited mainly by young travellers, basic, beware of petty theft; *Meza Annex*, 13 C., 10 Av. 'A', G; *Hospedaje San José No.2*, 16 C. 9 Av., G; *Washington*, 16 C. 6-17, F; *Mundial*, 16 C. 6-23, F with or without bath (hot water in communal bathroom), take own lock, dirty, meals US$1 each; *Hostal Biskaia*, 8 Av. No. 16-14, G, hot shower a.m. only, very pleasant, safe, will store luggage, Basque owners; on 7 Av. *Santa Ana No. 2*, G, hot water, friendly; *Tranquilidad*, 14 C. 9-59, F, without shower, quiet, hot water; *Karen Inn*, 17 C. 8-58, F, reasonable; *Mi Hotel*, 17 C. 9-45, G, dirty; *Pensión San Antonio*, 17 C. between 8 and 9 Av. (near Rutas Orientales), G, or F in new block (rooms with bath, good); *Europa*, 13 C. 9-65, G; *Santa Rafaela No. 1*, C. 13/53 and *Santa Rafaela No. 2*, C. 14/64, both G; *Marte*, 11 Av. 11-48, F; *Luna*, 6 Av. 15-50, 2nd. floor, F; *Gran Central*, 9 Av. 15-31, F, without bath; *Casa Real*, 11 C. 10-57, F, hot water, not safe; *Estación*, 17 C. 9-49, G, very basic; opposite bus terminal on 6 Av.; *Maya*, G, dirty, and two cleaner *hospedajes* next door. *Venecia*, 4 Av. 'A', 6-90, Zona 4, very comfortable, E, with bath, reasonable meals; *La Felicidad*, Zona 4 near bus station, G, clean, basic, used for prostitution. *Turicentro Santa Anita*, Blvd. Liberación 15-66, Zona 13; *Turicentro Las Amacas*, 34 C., 7-42, Zona 11.

N.B. The water supply in hotels tends to be spasmodic, and water for showering is often unobtainable between 1000-1800. At the cheaper hotels it is not always possible to get single rooms. Most hotels charge a 10% room tax. There are many other cheap *pensiones* near bus and railway stations and market; those between Calles 14 and 18 are not very salubrious.

Camping For campsites within easy access of Guatemala City see page 1035 under Amatitlán. Parking is available free at the Airport from 1900-0700. Camping-gas cartridges hard to find (they are stocked at Supermercado Norte, 6A Av., 2-47, and at 11 C., 7-75, Zona 1).

Electric Current 110 volts A.C., 60 cycles.

Restaurants (Restaurants at hotels. Food prices vary less than quality.)
In the capital, the tourist can easily find everything from the rather unsophisticated national cuisine (black beans, rice, meat, chicken, soup, avocado, cooked bananas - *plátanos* -, and tortillas with everything) to French, Chinese, Italian and German food (and pastries). A simple, but nourishing, three-course meal can be had for US$1 at any *comedor*. Fashionable places, such as *Hola* (French and Italian), Av. Las Américas, Zona 14, *Romanello* (Italian), 1 Av. 13-38, Zona 10, *Estro Armonico* (French), Vía 4, 4-36, Zona 4, *Puerto Barrios* (seafood), 7 Av. 10-65, Zona 9, or *Grischun* (Swiss), 14 Av. 15-36, Zona 10, charge on average US$10 for a three-course meal. Wine and other alcoholic drinks are expensive, beer good and inexpensive. *Europa* (German and Austrian), 11 C. at 5 Av., Zona 1, English and German spoken, is recommended. Fast food is available in all parts of the city, and is relatively safe; e.g. *Picadilly*, 6 Av., C.12, good; *Las Cebollines*, several locations in Zona 1, Mexican, inexpensive, good. Recommended vegetarian restaurants: *El Arbol de la Vida*, Ed. Reforma Montúfar, 12 C. y Av. Reforma, Zona 9; and *Comida de Vegetales* chain, several branches, also take-away.

The best cafeterias for pies, pastries and chocolates (German, Austrian and Swiss styles) are *Zurich*, 4 Av. 12-09, Zona 10; *Los Alpes*, 10 C. 1-09, Zona 10; *Jensen*, 14 C. 0-53, Zona 1. *American Doughnuts*, 5 Av. 11-47, Zona 1, and several other branches in the capital. (With thanks to Rainer Gruss of Guatemala City, and other travellers' recommendations.)

Clubs Guatemala Club; the American Club (introductions can be arranged for temporary membership). Lions Club. Rotary Club. Von Humboldt (German). Italian Club. Club Caza, Tiro y Pesca.

GUATEMALA 1017

Shopping The Central Market was destroyed in the 1976 earthquake but a new one has been opened, from 7 to 9 Av., 8 C., Zona 1; one floor is dedicated to native textiles and crafts, and there is a large, cheap basketware section on the lower floor. Many stalls selling vegetables etc. and pottery goods were moved to Parque Colón between 8 and 9 C. and 11 and 12 Av. Of the markets mentioned the one likely to be of most tourist interest is behind the Cathedral, between Avs. 8 and 9 in Zona 1, selling mainly native textiles and crafts. Apart from the Mercado Terminal in Zona 4, there is the Mercado del Sur, 6 Av. 19-21, Zona 1, primarily a food market though it has a section for popular handicrafts. There is also a new *artesanía* market in Parque Aurora, near the airport, where marimba music is played, and which is strictly for tourists; there is yet another food market in the Parque Colón. *La Placita* by the Church of Guadalupe at 18 C. and 5 Av. is good for conventional clothes, leather suitcases, etc. Silverware is cheaper at the market than anywhere else in Guatemala City, but we are told that a better place for silverware is Cobán. The market is, however, recommended for all local products. Bargaining is necessary at all markets in Guatemala. Also, *4 Ahau*, 11 C. 4-53, Zona 1, very good for huipiles, other textiles, and crafts and antiques; hand-woven textiles from *Miranda* factory, 8 Av. 30-90, Zona 8; *La Tinaja*, 12 C. 4-80, Zona 1; *El Patio*, 12 C. 3-57, Zona 1; *Rodas Antiques*, 5 Av. 8-42, Zona 1 and *Barrientos Antigüedades*, 10 C. 4-64, Zona 1, have high quality (and priced) silver and antiques. *Mayatex*, 12 C. 4-46, good choice, wholesale prices. *Maya Exports*, 7 Av. 10-55, credit cards accepted. Opposite is *Sombol*, Av. Reforma 14-14 and Calle 7-80, good for handicrafts, dresses and blouses. *La Momosteca* has a stall in Plaza Barrios and a shop at 7 Av. 14-48, Zona 1, and sells both textiles and silver. Pasaje Rubio, 9 C. near 6 Av., is good for antique silver charms and coins. *The Modern India*, 9 C. 6-23, Zona 1 (will mail goods abroad). *Supermercado Norte*, 6A Av., 2-47, well-stocked for fresh and tinned food, gas cylinders, etc. Shop hours 0830-1230, 1500-1930 weekdays; may open all day on Sats.

Bookshops *Arnel*, Edificio El Centro No. 108, 9 C., 6 Av., Zona 1, excellent selection; *Geminis*, 6 Av. 7-24, Zona 9 (good selection); both have new English books; *La Plazuela*, 12C. 6-14, Zona 9, large selection of 2nd hand books (very poor re-sale value, better to buy); *Vista Hermosa*, 2 C. 18-48, Zona 15; *V.H. II* (English, German, Spanish); *Cervantes*, Av. La Reforma 13-70, Zona 9; *El Palacio de la Revista*, 12 C. 5-42, Zona 1, and 7 Av. 7-16, Zona 4, has wide selection of magazines and US newspapers. Museo Popol Vuh bookshop, Av. La Reforma 8-60, Zona 9, has a good selection of books on precolumbian art, crafts and natural history; also *Plaza* and *Janés*, 6 Av. 11-73, Zona 1. *Librería Bremen*, Pasaje Rubio, 6 Av. between 8 C. and 9 C., Zona 1, has material in German plus old books on Guatemala. Instituto Guatemalteco Americano (IGA), Ruta 1 and Vía 4, Zona 4 (also library).

Car Rental *Hertz*, 19 C. 7-07, Zona 1, Tel.: 510202; *Avis*, 12 C. 2-73, Zona 9, Tel.: 316990; *Budget*, Av. Reforma y 15 C., Zona 9, Tel.: 316546; *National*, 14 C. 1-42, Zona 10, Tel.: 680175; *Dollar*, 6 Av. "A" 10-13, Zona 1, Tel.: 23446 (at *Hotel Ritz*—US$200 all inclusive, unlimited mileage for a week, Nissan March); *Tikal*, 2 C. 6-56, Zona 10, Tel.: 316490; *Ambassador*, 6 Av. 9-31, Zona 1, Tel.: 85987; *Tabarini*, 2 C. "A" 7-30, Zona 10, Tel.: 316108 (have Toyota Land Cruisers); *Jerry*, 7 Av. 14-60, Zona 1, Tel.: 536238 (also rent motorcycles, US$10 a day); *Tally*, 7 Av. 14-74, Zona 1, Tel.: 514113 (have Nissan and Mitsubishi pick-ups). The last two offer the lowest rates (US$13 a day + mileage), but these vehicles are not always available. Insurance rate (extra) varies from US$4-6 a day.

Local Buses in town, US$0.05 per journey. Not many before 0600 or after 2000.

Taxis are from US$0.50 for a short run to US$3 for a long run inside the city. Hourly rates are from US$4 to US$5. Taxis of the Azules, Concordia and Palace companies recommended. Agree fares in advance; no meters. Taxis always available in Parque Central and Parque Concordia (6 Av. and 15 C., Zona 1) and at the Trébol (the main crossroads outside city if coming from Pacific or Highlands by bus, convenient for airport).

Traffic Traffic lights operate only between 0800 and 2100; at all other times Avenidas have priority over Calles (except in Zona 10, where this rule varies).

Night Clubs *La Quebrada*, 6 Av. 4-60, Zona 4; *Plaza Inn*, Motel Plaza, Vía 7, 6-16, Zona 4; *Brasilia* in *Hotel Ritz Continental*. Discothèques: *After Eight*, Ed. Galerías España, Zona 9; *Kahlúa*, 1 Av. 13-21, Zona 10; *Manhattan*, 7 Av. opp. *Hotel El Dorado*, Zona 9; *El Optimista*, Av. La Reforma 12-01, Zona 10; *La Petite Discothèque*, La Manzana, Ruta 4, 4-76, Zona 4. *El Establo*, Av. La Reforma 11-83, Zona 10, is a bar with excellent music.

Guatemala is the home of marimba music. It can be heard nightly at *El Gallito* club, 9 C. 8-43, Zona 1 (min. charge US$0.75 p.p.). The marimba is a type of xylophone played with drum sticks by from one to nine players. Up country the sounding boxes are differently sized gourds, the *marimbas de tecomates*. The city ones are marvels of fine cabinet work.

Theatres National Theatre. Teatro Gadem, 8 Av. 12-15, Zona 1; Antiguo Paraninfo de la Universidad, 2 Av. 12-30, Zona 1; Teatro Universidad Popular, 10 C. 10-32, Zona 1; Teatro Artistas Unidos, 3 Av. 18-57, Zona 1. Occasional plays in English, and many other cultural events, at Instituto Guatemalteco Americano (IGA), Ruta 1 and Vía 4, Zona 4. List of current offerings outside

1018 GUATEMALA

Teatro del Puente, 7 Av. 0-40, Zona 4, and in local English-language publications and city newspapers.

Cinemas are numerous and often show films in English with Spanish subtitles. Prices are US$2. Alianza Francesa, 4 Av. 12-39, free film shows on Monday evenings.

Concerts Concerts of the Philharmonic Orchestra take place in the Teatro Nacional, Civic Centre, 24 Calle, Zona 1. During the rainy season at the Conservatorio Nacional, 5 C. and 3 Av., Zona 1, and occasionally in the Banco de Guatemala.

Sports There is an 18 hole golf course at the Guatemala Country Club, 8 km. from the city, and a 9 hole course at the Mayan Club. The Guatemala Lawn Tennis Club and the Mayan Club are the chief centres for tennis.

Swimming Pools Apart from those at the Parque Minerva (page 1014) there are pools at Ciudad Olímpica, 7 C., 12 Av., Zona 5 (monthly membership only, US$2.50 a month— photograph required; you may be allowed in for a single swim); Piscina Ciudad Vieja, Zona 15; Baños del Sur, 13 C. "A" 7-34, Zona 1, has hot baths for US$0.50, saunas for US$1.50. Try the hotels and the campsites near Amatitlán also.

Bowling Ten-pin variety and billiards at Bolerama, Ruta 3, 0-61, Zona 4, 2 blocks from *Conquistador-Sheraton* hotel.

Banks Lloyds Bank International (8 Av. 10-67, Zona 1); agencies at Plazuela 11 de Marzo, 7 Av. 4-87, Zona 4; Autovía Mixco 4-39, Zona 11 and C. Marti 14-57, Zona 6. Open weekdays, 0900-1500 (special cash facilities 1500-2000, Sat., 0900-1200). Banco de Guatemala (7 Av. and 22 C., Zona 1) open Mon.-Thurs. 0830-1400, Fri. 0830-1430, will change foreign cash and travellers' cheques after 1000. Banks now change US dollars into quetzales at the free rate. There is a bank open 7 days a week at the airport, weekdays 0730-1830, Sat., Sun. and holidays 0800-1100, 1500-1800 (only place to change foreign banknotes). When shut, try airport police or porters who may be able/willing to change US$ cash for quetzales. All banks mentioned above cash travellers' cheques, although some travellers have experienced difficulties. Try also the Banco Industrial. Banco del Café (American Express), Av. La Reforma, 9-00, Zona 9, Tel.: 311311, good rates.

The legal street exchange for cash and cheques may be found on 6 Av., 12-14 C. near the Post Office (Zona 1), although it is better to go direct to the exchange offices to avoid paying the street dealers' commission (for example, in the basement of the big shopping centre between 6 and 7 Av. behind the car park, opp. Post Office). Good place for exchange, *Le Point* shoe shop, C. 14 between Avs. 4 and 5. When changing travellers' cheques, always keep the receipt. Be careful when changing money on the street; never go alone. Quetzales may be bought with Visa or Mastercard in the basement of Av. 7, 6-22 (open until 2000, Mon.-Fri.).

Embassies and Consulates Addresses change frequently.

U.S.A., Av. La Reforma 7-01, Zona 10 (Tel.: 311541-55). *Canada*, Galería España, 7 Av. and 12 C., Zona 9. *Mexico* Consulate, 13 C. 7-30, Zona 9 (closes 1430 for tourist cards). *El Salvador*, 12 C. 5-43, Zona 9, Tel.: 325848. *Honduras*, 15 Av. 9-16, Zona 13., Tel.: 373921. *Nicaragua*. 2 C. 15-95, Zona 13, Tel.: 65613 (open 0800-1300, visas in 24 hrs.). *Costa Rica*, Edificio Galerías Reforma Oficina 320, Av. Reforma, 8-60, Zona 9, Tel.: 325768. *Panama*, Edificio Maya, Vía 5, 7 Av., Suite 717, Zona 4.

Argentina, 2 Av. 11-04, Zona 10. *Bolivia*, 12 Av. 15-37, Zona 10. *Brazil*, 18 C. 2-22, Zona 14, Tel.: 37-09-49. *Colombia*, Edificio Gemini 10, 12 C., 1 Av., Zona 10, unhelpful. *Chile*, 13 C. 7-85, Zona 10. *Ecuador*, Diagonal 6, 13-08, Zona 10. *Paraguay*, 7 Av. 7-78 (8th floor), Zona 4. *Peru*, 2 Av. 9-48, Zona 9. *Uruguay*, 20 C. 8-00, Zona 10. *Venezuela*, 8 C. 0-56, Zona 9.

Israel, 13 Av. 14.07, Zona 10. *Japan*, Ruta 6, 8-19, Zona 4. *South Africa*, 6 Av. 14-75, Zona 9.

Austria, Trade Council, 6 Av. 20-25, Zona 10; Consulate, 6 Av. 11-00 (Tel.: 64314, 0900-1100). *Belgium*, Av. La Reforma 13-70 (2nd floor), Zona 9. *Denmark*, 7 Av. 20-36 (Apartment 1, 2nd floor), Zona 1. *Finland*, 10 C. 6-47, Zona 1. *France*, 14 C. 5-52, Zona 9, Tel.: 66-336. *West Germany*, 6 Av. 20-25, Edificio Plaza Marítima 2nd floor, Zona 10, Tel.: 370028, 370031 (bus 14 goes there). *Netherlands*, Consulate General, 15 C. 10-19, Zona 10 (open 0900-1200). *Italy*, 8 C. 3-14, Zona 10. *Norway*, Vía 5, 4-50 (4th floor), Zona 4. *Portugal*, 5 Av. 12-60, Zona 9. *Spain*, 10 C. 6-20, Zona 9. *Sweden*, 8 Av. 15-07, Zona 10.
Switzerland, Edif. Seguros Universales, 4 C. 7-73, Zona 9 (Tel.: 65726, 31-3725); *British Consulate*, C. 7 y Av. 4, No. 13, Zona 19, Tel.: 63302.

Immigration Office 12 C and 8 Av., Zona 1 (for extensions of visas, take photo to "Inspectoria").

Central Post Office 7 Av., 12 C., Zona 1. 2nd floor for overseas parcel service. This is the only post office in country from which parcels over 2 kg. can be sent abroad. Poste restante keeps mail for 2 months (US$0.03 per letter). Open Mon.-Fri. 0800-1630. Free marimba concert at post office every Fri. at 1500. Alternative: American Express, for its customers only.

GUATEMALA 1019

Telecommunications Empresa Guatemalteca de Telecomunicaciones (Guatel), 7 Av. 12-39, Zona 1 (international); 24-hr national and international telephone service; collect calls to N and Central America only. Local telegrams from central post office.

Non-Catholic Churches Episcopalian Church of St. James, Av. Castellana 40-08, Zona 8, and the Union Church of Guatemala (Plazuela España, Zona 9). Sun. morning service in English at the first: 0930; at the second: 1100.

Synagogues 7 Av. 13-51, Zona 9. Service at 0930 Sat.

Health Centro Médico Hospital, 6 Av. 3-47, Zona 10, private, but reasonably priced, all senior doctors speak English; very helpful. Dr Mariano A. Guerrero, 5 Av. 3-09, Zona 1, German-speaking, understands English (US$10 for treatment). Dentist: Dr Freddy Lewin, Centro Médico, 6 Av. 3-69, Zona 10, Tel.: 325153 (German, English).

Spanish Classes Instituto Guatemalteco Americano (IGA) offers 6-week courses, 2 hours a day, for US$60. Several other schools in the city.

Laundromats Lava-Centro Servimatic, Ruta 6, 7-53, Zona 4 (opposite Edificio El Triángulo) sometimes has hot water; Express (dry cleaners), 7 Av. 3-49, Zona 4; El Siglo (dry cleaners), 7 Av. 3-50, Zona 4, 11 Av. 16-35, Zona 1, and 12 C. 1-55, Zona 9. 4 Av., just up from 13 C., Zona 1. Dry cleaner also at Vía 2, 4-04, Zona 4, open Mon.-Fri., 0730-1830.

Car Insurance for Mexico Granai y Townson, 7 Av. 1-82, Zona 4.

Car Repairs Christian Kindel, 47 Calle 16-02, Zona 12. Honda **motorcycle** parts from F.A. Honda, Av. Bolívar 31-00, Zona 3; general manager and chief mechanic are German, former speaks English. In Guatemala City, parts available for most motorcycles.

Camera Repairs Sertecof Panamericana, 10 C. 9-68, Zona 1, Edif. Rosanza, Of. 105, Tel.: 537-533, 537-613, expensive but work guaranteed 3 months.

Tourist Information Inguat, 7 Av. 1-17, Zona 4 (Centro Cívico); Tel.: 311333/47. Very friendly. Hotel lists, will ring hotels. Open Mon.-Fri. 0830-1800, Sat. 0800-1200, accurate map of city, other maps, information, major tourist attractions and will book tours.
Travellers wishing to get to know Guatemala should contact Yvonne Martínez, 11 Avenida, 25-04, Zona 12, who very kindly offers to provide information and a meeting place for young visitors.

Maps Good maps of all sorts can be bought from the Instituto Geográfico Nacional, Av. Las Américas 5-76, Zona 13, open 0800-1630 Mon. to Fri., closed Sat. and Sun.; some of the more detailed maps can only be obtained by post, and permission must be obtained from the Ministry of Defence before buying maps of "sensitive areas". Other maps from bookstores, US$0.33-$0.50. Also good map of city on back of map of country, from Hertz at airport.

Travel Agents Clark Tours (agents for American Express), 6 Av. y Vía 7, no exchange, in Edificio El Triángulo, Zona 4; Maya Tours, Hayter Travel (Edificio El Prado, 9 C., 4 Av.), Flamingo, King's Tours, Guatemala Sightseeing, ECA, Guatemala Travel Advisors, Turismo Kim'Arrin, Panamundo, Setsa Travel, 8 Av., 14-11, very helpful, tours arranged to Tikal, Copán, car hire; Aire, Mar y Tierra, Plaza Marítima, 20 C. y 6 Av., Zona 10, and Ed. Herrera, 5 Av. y 12 C., Zona 1; Tourama, Av. La Reforma 15-25, Zona 10, both recommended, German and English spoken.

Archaeological Tours Anyone interested in genuine archaeological (or botanical, ornithological and zoological) expeditions should contact Foundation for Latin American Anthropological Research (FLAAR), 6355 Green Valley Circle, No. 213, Culver City, CA 90230 and Apartado Postal 1276, Guatemala City. (There is no Guatemalan research centre; the foundation's library is on long-term loan to the Popol Vuh Museum.) This organization runs trips to well-known and almost unknown areas of interest (including Yaxchilán, Piedras Negras, Tonina, Comalcalco, El Tajín, Xochicalco, and all of Yucatán, Campeche and Quintana Roo, and the archaeology of Belize). FLAAR, formerly EPANS, has published *Tikal, Copán Travel Guide*, by Nicholas Hellmuth, on all the Mayan sites in Central America and Mexico. It costs US$25 (available from the Popol Vuh museum, the museum at Tikal, and from California address above) and gives useful tips on how to get to each of the sites. Turismo Kim'Arrin, Edificio Maya, Office No. 103, Vía 5, 4-50, Zona 4, and Panamundo Guatemala Travel Service also arrange tours to Maya sites.

Airline Agents Local airlines: Aviateca, 10 Calle 6-30, Zona 1, and at airport; Aerovías, 18 C., Zona 13 (Tel.: 81463/316935); Tapsa at airport. In Edificio El Triángulo, 7 Av. and Ruta 6, Zona 4, are offices of Copa, SAM and Avianca. Agencia de Viajes Mundial, 5 Av. 12-44, Zona 1, is very good. Aviateca office is on 3rd floor of shopping centre, corner 6 Av. y 10 C., Zona 1. KLM, Pan Am, Iberia (Ed. Galerías Reforma, Av. La Reforma, 8 C., Zona 9), Mexicana, and the Central American airlines all have offices, so has Lufthansa, Plaza Marítima, Av. 20-25, Zona 10.

Airport At La Aurora, 8 km. S; restaurant with cheap "meal of the day" (more appetizing than it looks); all prices marked up in the shops. Taxi to town, US$2.50 one way, US$5 return (airport tourist office supplies official taxi-fare chits—drivers may try to charge new arrivals US$8 to

1020 GUATEMALA

town). Nos. 5 (in black not red) 6 and 20 buses from 8 Av., Zona 1, and the Zona 4, 4 Av., 1 C, bus terminal, run the ½ hour's journey between airport and centre (US$0.05). (Bus 20 runs from Centro Cívico to Aeropuerto Local.) There is also a bus to 7 Av. C. 18 (US$0.08 at night). Domestic flights to Flores (see page 1031) leave from the international airport. All other domestic flights must be chartered.

Rail Guatemalan Railways to Puerto Barrios, 0700, Tues., Thurs., Sat. 13 hrs., US$3 (an excellent, if slow, opportunity to get a first impression of the country, trains are usually delayed). Trains to San José (US$0.38) leaving at 0730 (arriving 1845). Trains to Tecún Umán (290 km.) 0715 Tues. and Sat. No cooked meals are served in trains, although sandwiches and light refreshments, iced beer and soft drinks can be bought at inflated prices. Station at 18 C. 9 and 10 Av., Zona 1, on east side of Plaza Barrios. No passenger connections to El Salvador. All earthquake damage to railways now repaired.

Buses Ticabus international services were suspended in 1984. To San Salvador: Inter-Futuro Express, 8 Av. 15-69, Zona 1, daily at 0700, 1300, US$2.50 (not recommended; may desert you at the border). With this service one arrives in San Salvador early enough to catch a bus to the El Salvador-Honduras border. (Don't trust phone reservations.) Mermex, 20 C. 6-39, Zona 1, daily except Sun., 0800, small, uncomfortable and unreliable. Transportes Centroamérica, 9 Av. 15-06, Zona 1, Tel.: 23432 (minibus service to hotel on request), daily, 0730 after all passengers have been collected. Melva, 7 buses daily from 0800, US$2.50, Pezzarossi 7 departures daily, 6 hrs.; both recommended, own terminal in Zona 4 (office at 4 Av. 1 C., Zona 9, at edge of bus station at 4 Av. 7 C.—all except Pezzarossi go also to Santa Ana). To Honduras avoiding El Salvador, take bus to Esquipulas (see below), then minibus to border. To Mexico: Moreliana (from bus terminal) to Talismán, US$2.25, from 0600 to 1600, also to Tecún Umán; Galgos, 7 Av. 19-44, Zona 1, 4 buses daily to Talismán, US$3, connections with Cristóbal Colón bus line— rebookings at the border may be necessary (local buses to Talismán take 7 hrs., involve 3 changes, and cost US$2.25). El Cóndor, 2 Av. 19 C., and Rutas Lima, 8 C. 3-63 (note some complaints about this service), both Zona 1, each have several buses daily to La Mesilla, connections with Cristóbal Colón; El Cóndor cheaper, recommended, US$2. Unión Pacífica, 9 Av. 18-38, Zona 1, go to El Carmen and Tecún Umán; at both one can get connections to Tapachula, 0630, 0845, 1245 daily. No Guatemalan bus goes into Mexico. Through tickets to Mexico City are available, but don't be tempted to buy one; purchase tickets as you go along because of poor connections and full buses from the border into Mexico.

To Flores (for Tikal and Belize), Fuente del Norte, 17 C. 8-46, Zona 1, 3 in the early morning (e.g. 0430), book the day before, first on the list is first on the bus, US$4.60 (from 12 to 20 hrs. over dreadful roads). To Huehuetenango, El Cóndor (5 a day, US$2.10), Los Halcones, 7 Av. 15-27, Zona 1 (reliable, reserved seats) 0700, 1400 and Rutas Lima (en route to La Mesilla); from 6 Av. "A" 20-66, Zona 1, from 0800 every ½ hr. To Quezaltenango, Marquensita, 21 C. 1-56, Zona 1, 0430 and 0630, US$1.75, Rutas Lima, 4 a day, US$1.75; Galgos, 5 a day, recommended, US$2. To Panajachel, Rebuli, 20 C. 3 Av., Zona 1, terminal C.1 and C.4, Zona 9, take city bus No. 17 (continues to Sololá), 5 a day, US$1.25 (3 hrs., 1st class), To Chichicastenango, Rebuli, throughout the day, US$1.50 (3½ hrs.). To Puerto Barrios, Litegua, 15 C., 10-40 Av., Zona 1, about 10 a day until 1700, US$3.50, 6 hrs.; Fuente del Norte, Unión Pacífica y Las Patojas, 9 Av., 18-38, Zona 1 (Zona 4 terminal), 4 a day, US$2. To Esquipulas, via Chiquimula, Rutas Orientales, 19 C, 8-18, Zona 1, every ½ hr., 0400-1800, 4 hrs. (US$1.50 "Pullman". Transportes Guerra to Chiquimula, US$1.25, 3½ hrs., 0700. To Santa Cruz del Quiché, via Los Encuentros and Chichicastenango, Reyna de Utatlán, Zona 4 bus terminal, 0600 to 1600, 4 hrs., US$1. To Cobán (US$1.75) and San Pedro Carchá (US$2.25), Cobanerita, 9 C. 11-46, Zona 1, 0600 and 1100; to Biotopo del Quetzal, Transportes Monja Blanca, 7 Av. 20-07, Zona 1, US$2.

The Zona 4 bus terminal between 1-4 Av. and 7-9 C. serves the Occidente (West), the Costa Sur (Pacific coastal plain) and El Salvador. The area of 19 C. 8-9 Av. Zona 1, next to the Plaza Barrios market, contains many bus offices and is the departure point for the Oriente (East), the Caribbean Zone, Pacific coast area toward the Mexican border and the north, to Flores and Tikal. First class buses often depart from company offices in the south-central section of Zona 1.

To Antigua, the shortest route is 45 km. via San Lucas by paved double-lane highway passing (25 km. out) El Mirador (1,830 metres), with fine view of the capital. Road then rises to 2,130 metres and gradually drops to 1,520 metres at Antigua.

Antigua was the capital city until it was heavily damaged by earthquake in 1773. Population today: 30,000. Founded in 1543, after destruction of a still earlier capital, Ciudad Vieja, it grew to be the most splendid city in Central America, with a population of 60,000, numerous great churches, a University (1680), a printing press (founded 1660), and famous sculptors, painters, writers and craftsmen. Centre of the city is Plaza de Armas, the old Plaza Real, where bullfights and markets were held. The Cathedral (1534) is to the E, the Palace of the Captains-General to the S (1769), the Municipal Palace (Cabildo) to the N (all have been repaired since the 1976 earthquake) and an arcade of shops to the

GUATEMALA 1021

west. Alvarado was buried in the Cathedral, but whereabouts is not known. All the ruined buildings, though built over a period of three centuries, are difficult to date by eye, partly because of the massive, almost Norman architecture against earthquakes: cloisters of the convent of Capuchinas (1736), for example, look 12th century, with immensely thick round pillars (entrance, US$0.12). The most interesting ruins (apart from those mentioned) are of the monastery of San Francisco (which has a superb monument to Hermano Pedro), the convent of Santa Clara (1723-34, entrance US$0.12), El Carmen, San Agustín (the last two may only be viewed from outside), la Compañía de Jesús (being restored with a Unesco grant), Santa Cruz, Escuela de Cristo church, La Recolección (1703-17) off the road, set among coffee groves, Colegio y Hermita de San Jerónimo (Real Aduana), open every day except Mon., 0800-1700, La Merced (being restored, said to have largest fountain in the New World), the Hospital*(badly damaged, and no longer functioning), and the Museum. John Streather tells us that other ruins, such as Santa Isabel, San Cristóbal, El Calvario and San Gaspar Vivar, all south of the town, are well worth visiting. Many sculptures, paintings and altars have been removed to Guatemala City.

N.B. Buildings marked * were badly damaged by the 1976 earthquake, and parts of those which are open have not yet been rebuilt.

Antigua is so restored that only convents and churches are in ruins, and San Francisco church has been rebuilt. The old cobblestones are being replaced in the original pattern. Indian women sit in their colourful costumes amid the ruins and on the Plaza, and sell handicrafts. Most picturesque, and the goods are not expensive if you bargain. Good views from the Cerro de la Cruz, 40 mins'. walk N of town.

Finding your way around: Agua volcano is due S of the city and the market is to the W. Avenidas are numbered upwards running from East (Oriente) to West (Poniente), and Calles upwards from Norte to Sur. Avenidas are Norte or Sur and Calles Oriente or Poniente in relation to the central Plaza; however, unlike Guatemala City, house numbers do not give one any clue towards how far from the central Plaza a place is. There are authorized guides whose tours of Antigua and surroundings are good value.

Fiestas Holy Week. The most important and colourful processions are those leaving La Merced at 1500 on Palm Sunday and 0800 on Good Friday (best) and Escuela de Cristo and the Church of San Felipe de Jesús (in the suburbs) at 1630 on Good Friday. Gay carpets, made of dyed sawdust and flowers, are laid on the route. The litter bearers wear purple until 1500 on Good Friday afternoon, and black afterwards. Only the litter bearing Christ and His Cross passes over the carpets, which are thereby destroyed. Holy Week in Antigua is claimed to be one of the finest in the New World. Also July 21-26 and Oct. 31-Nov. 2 (All Saints and All Souls, in and around Antigua).

Hotels Antigua (best), de la Concepción (4 C. Or., 1 block E of Plaza) B, beautiful gardens, non-residents may use the pool for US$1; Ramada Antigua, 9 C. Poniente and Carretera Ciudad Vieja, B, pool (US$5 per month for non-residents), riding, tennis courts, discotheque, sauna; Suites Santa Isabel, self-contained, spotlessly clean suites in pleasant rural setting, 1 km. SE of town centre by Santa Isabel church, B, one-bedroom suite, US$35, two-bedroom suite, sleeps 6, US$55; Posada de Don Rodrigo, 5 Av. Norte 17, D, very agreeable, good food, in Colonial house (Casa de los Leones), recommended, marimba music p.m.; Casa El Patio, 5 Av. Norte 37, by Merced church, D, beautifully renovated, well-kept, American run, book in advance; Casa de San Felipe, 2 km. N, E, pleasant gardens and restaurant; Aurora, 4 C. Oriente 16, E (full board available, the oldest hotel in the city, recommended); El Rosario, 3 Av. Sur 4, pleasant apartment lodge motel complex in a coffee and orange farm round the corner from the Antigua, small pool, E, proprietress speaks English and will tell you all about Antigua and the area, house-keeping apartments by the month US$150-160, not as secure as it claims; Los Capitanes (ex-Contreras), 5 Av. Sur 8, F, with bath (no hot water), good cheap restaurant; El Descanso, 5 Av. Norte 9, 2nd floor, F, with private bath, clean, pleasant; Casa de Santa Lucía, Alameda de Santa Lucía 5, near bus terminal, highly recommended, F (no singles), with bath, good value; close by, Hospedaje El Pasaje, Alameda de Santa Lucía, F, clean, quiet, friendly, recommended; Posada Colonial, 2 C. Poniente 2, picturesque, F, without bath (beware of dog); El Sínodo, 6 Av. Norte, F; Posada San Francisco, 3 C. Oriente 19, F, friendly, with bath, highly recommended; Pensión El Arco No. 1, 4 C. Oriente 27, G, hot water, friendly, breakfast (also for non-residents) for US$1; El Arco No. 2, 5 Av. Sur. 6 C. Poniente, 7, F; Posada El Refugio, 4 C. Poniente 28, F, with bath, or full board, G, without, showers, no hot water, clean, serves good cheap meals, popular, cooking facilities; Posada La Antigüeñita, 2 C. Poniente, F, new and clean;

1022 GUATEMALA

Casa Brañas, 5 Av. Norte, 31, F, clean, friendly, cheap meals; *Posada de Doña Angelina*, 4 C. Poniente 33, F, with shower, G without (rooms in new part more expensive but good), near market; friendly, clean, safe, good dinner available, US$1.50. *Placido*, Calle del Desengaño, 7 blocks from Parque Central, F, good, not all rooms have hot water, beautiful courtyard, cooking facilities. Rooms, from about US$50 per month, and houses, from about US$150 per month, are sometimes advertised in the Tourist Office and in Doña Luisa's café. Recommended is Familia Juárez Méndez, 5 Av. Norte 33. For room rental also contact sculptor José Tinoco (speaks English), 7 Av. Norte No. 64; for weekly stays Juan Cuéllar (fire chief) at *Zeus* or *Madison Rock* stores, 4 C. Poniente 23, or Candelaria 38, US$50 d for room and board. The buses are often met by men who press to show you around the unmarked *pensiones* for a tip of about US$0.25. During Holy Week hotel prices are generally double.

Restaurants In several of the more expensive hotels. *El Sereno*, 6 C. Poniente 30 (Tel.: 0320-073), well-prepared meals in beautifully-reconstructed colonial-style house, open 1200-1500, 1830-2200 Wed. Sun. highly recommended, reservations advised, especially Sun. lunch (children under 8 not served), chamber music recitals often on Mon. and Tues., art exhibitions, handicrafts and old books on display and for sale. *Panadería y Pastelería Doña Luisa Xicotencatl* ("*Doña Luisa's*"), 4 C. Oriente 12, 1½ blocks E of the Plaza, a popular meeting place, serves superb pies and bread, breakfasts, *chile con carne*, etc.; at the back of *Doña Luisa's* is *El Tarro*, a popular bar (closed Mons.) with draught beer and free U.S. films on Tues and Wed. night; 1 block E is *Dixie Deli*, run by an American, outdoor dining, popular. Near Plaza are *La Estrella*, 5 C. Poniente No. 6, Chinese and other food, recommended, and *El Churrasco*, steakhouse, 4 C. Poniente. *Zen* (Japanese), closed Weds. after 1200, 3 Av. Sur, No. 3, popular, recommended, closed Wed.; in same street, *Mío Cid*, Canadian owned, good food and music, meeting place for foreigners; *Los Capitanes* (ex-*Contreras*, belongs to hotel); *Fonda de la Calle Real*, 5 Av. Norte No.5, speciality is queso fundido, guitar trio on Sun. evenings; *Emilio* and *Emilio 2*, both on 4 C. Poniente, and *Gran Muralla* opposite, all sell reasonable Chinese food; *Casa de Café Ana*, adjoining *El Rosario* lodge, serves all meals, and sells fine ice-cream, closed Weds.; *San Carlos*, on main square, sells reasonably-priced meals; *Jardín*, on main square, nice atmosphere; *Comedor Veracruz* in the market, good; *Lina*, near market on Alameda de Santa Lucía, serves good, cheap meals; *El Prado*, in San Felipe, 2 km., limited menu, good food, pleasant atmosphere; *El Capuchino*, 6 Av., between C.5 and 6, excellent Italian food and salads, friendly English-speaking owner. *Pastelería Okrassa*, 6 Av., C. 1-2, for meat and fruit pies.

Bars *Los Encuentros*, 4 C. Oriente 29 C, at crossing with 1 Av., popular, bar, American and Chinese food, live music at weekends, dancing; *Lanai*, 3 Av. y 5 C., open at 1200; see also *El Tarro*, above under Restaurants.

Shopping *Casa de Artes* for traditional textiles and handicrafts, antiques, jewellery, etc. 4 Av. Sur. *Casa de los Gigantes* for textiles and handicrafts, and *Concha's Footloom*, both opposite San Francisco Church. *Fábrica de Tejidos Maya*, 1 Av. Norte, C. 1-2, makes and sells good cheap textiles, wall hangings, etc. The *Atatlán* cooperative on 5 Av. Norte specializes in good handicrafts and antiques (expensive). Doña María Gordillo's sweet (candy) shop on 4 C. Oriente is famous throughout the country. There are many other stores selling textiles, handicrafts, antiques, silver and jade on 5 Av. Norte and 4 C. Oriente (*Ixchel* on 5 Av. Norte sells blankets from Momostenango). A number of jade-carving factories may be visited, e.g. *Jades, S.A.*, 4 C. Oriente 34, open 0900-1700, *La Casa de Jade*, 4 C. Oriente 3 or J.C. Hernández, 2 Av. Sur, No. 77. Jade is sold on the Parque Central on Sats. more cheaply. Painted ceramics can be obtained from private houses in 1 Av. del Chajón (C. San Sebastián) near C. Ancha, and glazed pottery from the *Fábrica Montiel*, N of Calle Ancha on the old road to San Felipe. Various local handicrafts at *Hecht House* in the same area. *Calzado Fase*, 6 Av. Norte 61, makes made-to-measure leather boots.

Bookshops *Un Poco de Todo*, on W side of Plaza, sells English language books, postcards, maps. Shawcross Book Service, Casa Andinista, 4 C. Oriente No. 3.

Market There is an extensive daily market, particularly on Mon., Thurs. and Sat. (best) next to the bus terminal at end of 4 Calle Poniente, W of Alameda de Santa Lucía. Good handmade textiles, pottery and silver.

Car Rental Hertz.

Bathing Non-residents may use the pool at the *Hotel Antigua* for a charge of US$1; also, at *Ramada Antigua* for US$5 a month. Both hotels have special Sunday prices of US$3.75 for buffet lunch, swimming and marimba band (the *Ramada* also has children's shows). At the latter, weekly and monthly rates for use of sports facilities can be negotiated. Also *El Viejo Club*, 1 Av. Sur. US$0.75 per session, also has table tennis, same price per hour. Warm mineral springs (public pool and private cubicles) at San Lorenzo El Tejar: Chimaltenango bus to San Luis Las Carretas (about 8 km.) then 2½ km. walk to "Balneario". Public saunas US$0.75, massage US$2.50, health foods, medicinal herbs in Jocotenango, 2 km. N and at the Institute in Santa Lucía Milpas Altas, 500 metres to the left at Km. 35 (10 km. out of Antigua) on the way to Guatemala City. Open Sun.-Thurs., 0730-1730.

GUATEMALA 1023

Museums Colonial Museum in the old University of San Carlos Borromeo (1680), facing Cathedral, includes colonial sculptures and paintings. US$0.12 to get into museum (open 0900-1200, 1400-1800) and other ruins around the town. Museo de Santiago in Municipal Offices to N of Plaza, contains replica of 1660 printing press (original is in Guatemala City), old documents, collection of 16th-18th-century books (1500 volumes in library, open afternoons), and representations of the colonial way of life, and the Museo de Armas weapons collection. Open Mon.-Fri. 0900-1600, Sat. and Sun. 0900-1200, 1400-1600. Admission US$0.12 (free Sundays). Also small museum in Convento de Capuchinas.

Cinemas Imperial, on the Plaza, Los Capitanes on 5 Av. Sur. Showings several days a week. English films with Spanish subtitles often shown. US$0.20.

Concerts Music festival in November, excellent. The Alianza Francesa, 3 C. Oriente 19, has French music on Fridays between 1600 and 2000, also French newspapers.

Banks Lloyds Bank International, 4 C. Oriente 2 on NE corner of Plaza, Mon.-Fri. 0900-1500; Banco del Agro, N side of Plaza, same times; Banco de Guatemala, W side of Plaza, Mon.-Thurs. 0830-1400, Fri. 0830-1430. Try also 4 Av. Sur No. 01, good rates. US dollars not obtainable.

Spanish Language Schools Proyecto Lingüístico Francisco Marroquín, 4 Av. Sur No. 4, Tel.: 320-406, Apartado 237, Antigua. This school provides up to 7 hrs. individual tuition a day and places students with local families. The fee for one week incl. 7 hrs. study, board and lodging is Q250 (it is more expensive than the other schools because it helps language research in the country). Atabal, weekly rates available, Q80 a week. Maya, 5 C. Poniente 20, fees, Q165 for first week, reduction of Q10 for each consecutive week up to 4, good (6 hr. day)—must be paid in advance; Tecún Umán, 6 C. Poniente 34, good individual tuition, recommended (rates from US$250-400 per month, depending on number of hours per day); Español Dinámico, Q75 for 30 hrs., Q35 extra for accommodation with a family; Jiménez, near La Merced, 1 C. Poniente No. 41, small, 5 teachers, US$70 a week staying with family. Cooperativa de Lengua Española Antigua, recommended; contact Vinicio Muñoz, Colonia Candelaria No. 9; also Marco Tulio's Centro Lingüístico Antigua, 6 C. N., No. 33, US$65 for 5 days, tuition and lodging. Also check advertisements in Doña Luisa's and the Tourist Office for private lessons (about Q5 per hour). There are guides who take students around all the schools and charge a commission; avoid them if you don't want this extra cost.

Post Office, Telephone, Cables International cables in Guatel building, 5 Av. Sur. Post office at Alameda de Santa Lucía and 4 C., near market (local cables from here); *lista de correos* keeps letters for a month, air mail parcel service.

Research Library The Centro de Investigaciones Regionales de Mesoamérica (Cirma), 5 C. Oriente 5, offers good facilities for graduate students and professional scholars of Middle American history, anthropology and archaeology.

Public Library On E side of Plaza, open evenings only. The Banco de Guatemala library, on W side of Plaza, is open to the public, Mon.-Fri. 1000-1200, 1400-1900.

Doctor Dr. Julio R. Aceituno, 2 C. Poniente (Calle Santo Domingo), No. 7, Tel.: 0320-512, speaks English.

Tourist Office, at E corner of Palace of the Captains-General, S side of Plaza, is helpful (free street plan available). Open: 0900-1600 (except Monday). The tourist office can arrange guides for visits to monuments for between US$3 and US$6 per day. Ask here for campsite details (there are no caravan parks).

Guide Book *Antigua, Guatemala, City and Area Guide,* by Mike Shawcross.

Travel Agent Agencia de Viajes above art gallery on W side of the main square, very friendly and helpful (owner, Leslie from California).

Buses Half-hourly from Guatemala City, from 0700 to 1900, US$0.35, 45 mins, from 15 C., 3-37, Zona 1 (La Preciosa). Buses to Guatemala City leave from Alameda de Santa Lucía near the market, with the same time and schedules as buses to Antigua. To Chimaltenango, on the Pan-American Highway, hourly, US$0.10, for connections to Los Encuentros, Sololá and Panajachel (Lake Atitlán), also for the Guatemala City—Chichicastenango bus. To Escuintla, US$0.38. Buses and microbuses also to nearby villages.

Excursions To *Ciudad Vieja*, 5½ km. SW at the foot of Agua volcano. In 1541, after days of torrential rain, an immense mud-slide came down the mountain and overwhelmed the city. Alvarado's widow, newly elected Governor after his death, was among the drowned; you can see the ruins of the first town hall. Today it is a mere village (*Hospedaje Shigualita* (cheap) at S end of village), but with a handsome church, founded 1534, one of the oldest in Central America. *Fiesta:* December 5-9. Small early market, busiest Sundays; bus US$0.10. At **San Juan del Obispo**, not far, is the restored palace of Francisco Marroquín, first bishop of Guatemala, now a convent. The parish church has some fine 16th century images.

1024 GUATEMALA

Behind San Juan del Obispo, on side of Agua volcano, is the charming village of **Santa María de Jesús**, with a beautiful view of Antigua. In the early morning, there are good views of all 3 volcanoes 2 km. back down the road towards Antigua. Beautiful *huipiles* are made and sold in the houses. Frequent buses from Antigua on main market days, US$0.10 (Mon., Thurs., Sat.). *Fiesta* on Jan. 10, accommodation at *municipalidad* for US$0.30; *Hospedaje y Comedor El Oasis* on road to Antigua has clean, pleasant rooms, F.

About 9 km. SE of Antigua (bus service, US$0.10) is **San Antonio Aguas Calientes**, a village with many small shops selling locally made textiles. Carmelo and Zoila Guarán give weaving lessons for US$1 per hr., as does Rafaela Godínez, very experienced, and Sra Felipa López Zamora, on the way to the church, 30 metres from bus station (bring your own food and she will cook it with you), US$2 daily. *Fiestas*: first Sunday in January; June 13; November 1.

Volcanoes The three nearby volcanoes provide incomparable views of the surrounding countryside and are best climbed on a clear night with a full moon or with a very early morning start. Altitude takes its toll and plenty of time should be allowed for the ascents. Plenty of water must be carried and the summits are cold. Descents take from a third to a half of the ascent time. There have been reports of robberies on the volcanoes. Tourist Office in Antigua helpful. There is a volcano-climbing club: Club de Andinismo, Chicag, Volcano Tours, Daniel Ramírez Ríos, 6 Av. Norte, No. 34, Antigua; members are informative, enthusiastic, will act as guides for a small fee, and Daniel speaks English.

Agua Volcano 3,760 metres, the easiest of the three, is climbed from Santa María de Jesús (directions to start of ascent in village). Crater (with football field!) with small shelter and 5 antennae at top. Fine views of Volcán de Fuego; 3 to 5 hours' climb. To get the best views before the clouds cover the summit, it is best to camp overnight at the shelter ¾ of the way up, or stay at the radio station at the top. Bus from Antigua to Santa María de Jesús at 0530 allows you to climb the volcano and return to Antigua in one day.

Acatenango Volcano 3,976 metres. The best trail (west of the one shown on the 1:50,000 topographic map) heads south to La Soledad (15 km. west of Ciudad Vieja on Route 10) 300 metres before the road (Route 5) turns right to Acatenango (good *pensión*, G, with good cheap meals). A small plateau, La Meseta on maps, known locally as El Conejón, provides a good camping site two-thirds of the way up (3-4 hrs.). From here it is a further 3-4 hrs. harder going to the top. Excellent views of the nearby (lower) active crater of Fuego. To reach Acatenango, take a bus heading for Yepocapa or Acatenango (village) and get off at Soledad, or from Antigua to San Miguel Dueñas, and then hitch to Soledad. Alternatively, take a bus, or walk, from Dueñas to Finca Concepción Calderas; take a track just before entry to village on left, and it is about 5 hrs. to the peaks. Be sure to take the correct track going down (no water on the way up, hut at top in reasonable repair).

Fuego Volcano 3,763 metres, for experienced hikers only. Can be climbed either via Volcán de Acatenango (sleeping on the col between the two volcanoes), up to 12 hrs. hiking, or from Finca Capetillo in village of Alotenango (south of Ciudad Vieja), 9 km. from Antigua. One hour to reach base of mountain, then 7 hrs. ascent with an elevation gain of 2,400 metres. A very hard walk, both up and down, and easy to lose the trail. Steep, loose lava slopes in places. Danger of eruptions and sulphur fumes.

At the village of San Felipe (US$0.05 by bus, or 15 min. walk from Antigua) is a figure of Christ which people from all over Latin America come to see. *Restaurant El Prado* is recommended.

Three Indian villages N of Guatemala City are easily reached by bus. At Chinautla (9½ km.), the village women turn out hand-made pottery. Eight km. beyond is another small village, San Antonio las Flores: good walking to a small lake (70 mins.) for bathing. Santo Domingo Xenacoj can be reached by bus from the Zona 4 terminal, Guatemala City. It has a fine old church and produces good *huipiles*.

At **San Lucas Sacatepéquez**, the Fábrica de Alfombras Típicas Kakchikel at Km. 29½, Carretera Roosevelt (usually known as the Pan-American Highway) will make rugs for you. Restaurants: *La Parrilla*, *La Cabaña*, *Nim-Guaa*, *La Diligencia*, and *El Ganadero*, all good for steaks; *Delicias del Mar* for seafood. 5 km. beyond San Lucas is Santiago Sacatepéquez, whose *fiesta* on Nov. 1 is characterized by colourful kite-flying.

A most interesting short trip by car or bus from the capital is to **San Pedro Sacatepéquez**, 22½ km. NW. Good view over Guatemala valley and mountains to the N. Its inhabitants, having rebuilt their village after the 1976 earthquake, are returning to the weaving for which the village was renowned before the disaster. The Cooperative (a member of Artexco, the Federation of Artisans' Cooperatives) is San José Caben. Bus from Guatemala City, Zona 4 bus terminal, US$0.15, 1 hr.; bus to Rabinal, 5½ hrs., a beautiful, occasionally heart-stopping ride. *Hotel Samaritano*, near Plaza, F with bath, clean, hot shower. *Fiestas*: Carnival before Lent; June 29 (rather rough, much drinking) and great ceremony on March 15 when passing the Image of Christ from one officeholder to the next, and in honour of the same image in May.

GUATEMALA 1025

6½ km. beyond, through flower-growing area, is **San Juan Sacatepéquez,** where textiles are also made.

San Raimundo beyond is a friendly town. Buses go N through Rabinal to Cobán (see page 1026).

28 km. N of San Juan Sacatepéquez is **Mixco Viejo,** the excavated site of a post-classic Mayan fortress, which spans 14 hilltops, including 12 groups of pyramids, but was almost ruined by the earthquake. It was the 16th century capital of the Pokomam Maya; there are a few buses a day from the Zona 4 bus terminal in Guatemala City, departures at 1000 and 1700. The bus goes to Pachalum; ask to be dropped at the entrance to the site—it's an 8 km. walk from the main road (the area is quite remote, take provisions).

The village of **Rabinal** was founded in 1537 by Las Casas as the first of his "peaceful conquest" demonstrations to Charles V. It has a handsome 16th century church (under reconstruction), Sun. market interesting; brightly lacquered gourds, beautiful *huipiles* and embroidered napkins, all very cheap. The local pottery is exceptional. (*Pensión Motagua*, F, friendly, has bar attached).

The town of **Salamá** can be reached from the capital direct, or from San Juan Sacatepéquez and Rabinal through San Miguel Chicaj along another road which offers stunning views (Rabinal-Salamá US$0.75, ½ hr.). Its church contains very fine carved gilt altarpieces. Market day is Monday; worth a visit. *Pensión Juárez*, F, not recommended; *Hotel Tezulutlán*, F, better.

Another popular excursion is to the still active **Pacaya** volcano. Tours are available for US$8. It can be reached by private car, the road from Antigua is unpaved, but suitable for all vehicles. Alternatively take a bus from the central bus station in Zona 4 to San Vicente de Pacaya (US$0.30); then one must walk to San Francisco (2 hrs.), and walk up the mountain (1-2 hrs. and a hard climb). Buses go to both villages from the turn-off on the Guatemala City-Escuintla road. Last bus back from San Vicente is at 1630. However, it is well worth staying overnight to get the full visual benefit of the eruptions. Take a torch, camping equipment, warm clothing and a handkerchief to filter the dust and fumes. The best view is to be had from the top of the old cone of the volcano, which is above the new one. Guides in San Francisco (for example Pedro, who charges US$2.50 for 5 people) are recommended because it is easy to miss the best parts. There is also a bus from Palín (see page 1036), US$0.10. If you miss the last bus back to Palín or San Vicente, you can sleep in the porch at the school in El Cedro, the village below San Francisco. **Warning:** There have been several reports of armed robbery and equipment being stolen from campsites on the slopes of Pacaya volcano.

Guatemala City to San Salvador The paved Pan-American Highway through Fraijanes, Barberena and Cuilapa keeps to the crest of the ridges most of the way to the border, 166 km. Beyond Cuilapa it crosses the Río de los Esclavos by a bridge first built in the 16th century. Fifty km. on is Jutiapa (population 9,200). Beyond, it goes through the villages of Progreso and Asunción Mita, where another road runs to Lake Güija. Before reaching the border at Cristóbal it dips and skirts the shores (right) of Lake Atescatempa, an irregular sheet of water with several islands and set in heavy forest. From the border to San Salvador is 100 km.

A right turn after Barbarena towards Chiquimulilla (road No. 16, with old trees on either side, some with orchids in them) leads after 20 km. to a sign to Ixpaco. A 2-3 km. steep, difficult and narrow road goes to the Laguna de Ixpaco, an impressive, greenish-yellow lake, boiling in some places, emitting sulphurous fumes, set in dense forest.

The quickest way of getting to San Salvador is to take a paved highway which cuts off right from this route at Molino, beyond the Esclavos bridge. This cut-off goes through El Oratorio and Valle Nuevo to Ahuachapán and San Salvador. (Try *Motel Martha*, 15 km. from frontier on Guatemalan side, F, excellent breakfast, swimming pool.) A third paved road, in less good condition, runs from Guatemala City through Escuintla and Guazacapán to the border bridge over the Río Paz at La Hachadura, then through the coastal plain to Sonsonate and on to San Salvador, 290 km. in all; this road gives excellent views of the volcanoes. At Pedro de Alvarado (formerly Pijije) there are several *hospedajes* (all G, basic).

If stuck at La Hachadura (the last bus for Sonsonate leaves at 1800), you can get food at the service station restaurant and there is a very basic *hospedaje*, G, nearby—not recommended for lone women.

Guatemala City to the Caribbean

The Atlantic Highway from Guatemala City to the Caribbean port of Puerto Barrios is fully paved and gives access to the Honduran border, Cobán and the Petén. Note that the distances between filling stations are greater than in other parts of the country.

1026 GUATEMALA

At km. 54 a paved, winding branch road, 203 km. long, runs through fine scenery, E by way of San José Pinula, Mataquescuintla, Jalapa, San Pedro Pinula, San Luis Jilotepeque, and Ipala to Chiquimula (see page 1028). It was the route to the great shrine at Esquipulas, but visitors now use the Atlantic Highway to Río Hondo and the new road to Honduras past Zacapa and Chiquimula.

Jalapa, capital of Jalapa Department, 114 km. from Guatemala City, is particularly attractive. It is set in a lovely valley at 1,380 metres; average to capital, which can also be reached by bus on road NW to Jalapa station on Guatemalan Railway and thence by train, but this route takes longer. Population 42,000.

Hotel *Pensión Casa del Viajero*, F.

The branch road to Cobán is at Km. 85; this is a better alternative to the route through Rabinal and Salamá (see page 1025).

Between Cobán and Guatemala City, 4 km. S of Purulhá (Km. 166), is the **Biotopo del Quetzal**, a reserve for the preservation of the quetzal bird and its cloud-forest habitat; camping (free, good, lots of mosquitoes) and beautiful trails in the jungle. Entrance is restricted in the breeding season (Bus Cobán-Purulhá, US$0.50.).

Mike Shawcross writes: "I saw my first quetzal late in 1980, and consider the sighting a highlight of all my time here; it really is an incredibly beautiful bird. The Quetzal Sanctuary recently created by biologists from San Carlos University is at Km. 163 (53 km. from Cobán) on the highway to Guatemala City. A series of trails, taking up to 3 hrs. to cover on foot, lead more than 300 metres up the mountainside. At Km. 156 is the new hotel and restaurant *Posada Montaña del Quetzal*, D, highly recommended (phone 31-41-81 in Guatemala City for reservations)." Free camping at entrance. 100 metres N of the entrance to the Biotopo is the *Hospedaje Los Ranchos*, F in 10-bed cabins, fairly basic, restaurant, cafetería, bar, swimming pool and gardens. The *farmacía* at Purulhá has rooms to let, G. *Comedor San Antonio* in Purulhá, simple meals.

Tactic, on the main Guatemala City-Cobán road, is famous for beautiful *huipiles* and for its "living well", in which the water becomes agitated as one approaches. (Ask for the Pozo Vivo; it is along a path which starts opposite the gas station on the main road.) Colonial church with Byzantine-influenced paintings, well worth a visit. (*Hotel Sulmy*, G, nice, clean, meals, US$0.75; *Pensión Central*, G, clean, hot showers, cheap meals; and *Hospedaje Cocompchi*, less good, G.) Doña Rogelia sells *huipiles* made in the surrounding area, and the silversmith near her shop will make silver buttons etc. to order. Market days are Thursday and Sunday (very few people now wear traditional costume). To the W of Tactic is **San Cristóbal Verapaz**, which has a large colonial church with interesting altar silver and statue of San Joaquín (*Pensión Central* and *Pensión Torres*, both G). The lake is popular for fishing and swimming. Markets: Tuesday and Sunday; festival July 21-26. From Tactic the road (paved) runs 25 km. N to Cobán, past Santa Cruz Verapaz, which has a fine old 16th century church and a festival May 1-4. (*Tico's Hotel and Restaurant*, opp. turn off to Santa Cruz on road to Cobán, E, hot showers, English spoken, good food, recommended.)

Cobán, capital of Alta Verapaz Department, is the centre of a rich coffee district. Population 59,307, altitude 1,320 metres, climate semi-tropical. Road S to El Rancho (buses), on Guatemalan Railway and the highway to Guatemala City. Founded by Apostle of the Indies, Las Casas, in 1544. See church of El Calvario (1559), now completely renovated, original façade still intact. Daily market (local costume no longer in evidence). *Fiestas*: Holy Week (which is said to be fascinating) and August 3 (procession of saints with brass bands, pagan deer dancers and people enjoying themselves), followed by a folklore festival, August 22-28.

Hotels: *La Posada*, 1 C., 4-12, E, (full board available); *Central*, 1 C., 1-79, F, with hot shower; *Pensión Norte*, 3 C., 4-51, G; *Chipi Chipi*, F; *Oxib Peck*, 1 C., 12-11, F, with bath; *Pensión Minerva*, F, friendly, but a little far from the centre; *Pensión El Portillo*, very good, F; *Hospedaje Maya*, opp. Ciné Norte, F, rooms with showers available, hot showers, friendly, recommended; *Valenciana*, G (you can sleep on the balcony for US$0.50), basic; *El Carmen*, on main square, G, clean; *Pensión Apolo*, 3 blocks from main square, G; *Monterrey*, G, recommended; *La Paz*, 6 Av. 2-19, F, with extension which is recommended; *Pensión Familiar*, Diagonal 4, 3-36, Zona 2, 1 block N of Parque Central, G, warm water, fairly basic, friendly; nameless *pensión* at 1-12 Av. Estado (near *Hotel La Paz*), clean; *Central* has a good restaurant but mealtimes are rigidly fixed; *Comedores Chinita*, *El Refugio* (Parque Central, good *comidas corridas*), *Café Norte* (good fast food), and *Las Delicias* serve meals for less than US$1; *Restaurant Chapín*, good. It has been recommended not to use standard electrical appliances in Cobán as the voltage is high. Accommodation is hard to find in August.

Electric Current 110 volts.

Buses from Guatemala City: US$1.75 from 9 C. 11-46, Zona 1. The bus from El Estor takes 9 hrs., 3 services a day (0600, 0800, 1000). Return buses leave at 0400 and 0800. The trip from the capital via Rabinal, along an old dirt road, takes about 12 hrs. (change buses in Salamá). Cobán can also be reached from Sacapulas and Quiché (page 1042) and from Huehuetenango (page 1047).

Excursions Near Cobán is the old colonial church of San Juan Chamelco, well worth a visit. *San Pedro Carchá* (5 km. east of Cobán, bus US$0.10, 15 mins. frequent; *Hotel Shanghai*, F; *Delgado*, G; *Pensión Central*, G, cheap, basic, dirty, serves good meals—all close at 2200) used to be famous for its pottery, textiles and wooden masks, and silver, but only the pottery seems to be available at the Tuesday market. Truck to Sebol (see page 1034), 7 hrs., US$1.20. Good swimming and walks at Balneario Las Islas, just outside the village, well signposted; crowded at weekends, good camping.

Tamahú, on the road down the Polochic valley to El Estor, and Tucurú, beyond Tamahú on the same road, produce fine *huipiles* market days are Thurs. and Sat. and there are interesting images in the Tucurú church. Also worth visiting is Senahú, though the journey takes 7 hrs. from Cobán takes 7 hrs. (Autotransportes Valenciano, departures from Cobán at 1030, bus goes through Telemán (US$1.25), particularly crowded on Sundays); its *huipiles* are particularly sought after. Climb to the cemetery for good views. (*Pensiones* at Senahú: *González*, G, good meals for US$0.60, at entrance to village, and another in centre).

From Cobán a rough road runs 70 km. to **Lanquín** cave, in which the Lanquín river rises. If you want to visit the cave ask at the police station in the village (2 km.) to turn the lights on (this cost US$5, however many, or few, people in the group); the entrance fee is US$0.50 (a guide costs US$2.50). The cave is very slippery, so wear appropriate shoes and take a torch for additional lighting. Outside the cave you can swim in the deep, wide river, and camp or sling a hammock under a large shelter. From Lanquín one can visit the natural bridge of Semuc Champey stretching 60 metres across the Cahabón gorge. A new road runs to the footbridge over the river, 20 minutes' walk from Semuc Champey. At the end of the road, which is very steep in places, is a car park. A steep track heads down to the new bridge half-way along the road (the route is not signposted so ask frequently for the shortest route). There are a number of shortcuts between Lanquín and this spot, any locals walking this way will be taking them. The natural bridge has water on top of it as well as below, and the point where the river Cahabón goes underground is spectacular. One can swim in the pools on top of the bridge, but foot protection is needed as the edges of the pools are very sharp. At Semuc Champey is a place where you can camp. (Thoughtless littering has made the place dirty.) If planning to return to Lanquín the same day, start early to avoid the midday heat. At Lanquín there is *Hospedaje Mary*, pleasant, G, cheap, basic, and a small restaurant. The church has fine images and some lovely silver. Bus from Cobán at 0530, 4 hrs., US$0.75 including breakfast stop en route; returns at 0700; also to and from San Pedro Carchá, 0530 (you can try hitching from San Pedro Carchá, from the fumigation post, where all trucks stop). There are buses at 0500 and 0730 from Lanquín to Pajal (12 km., 1 hr., US$0.30) from where one can go to Sebol, US$0.75, 5½ hrs. (page 1034); Pajal is just a shop. Pick-up Lanquín-Sebol, US$1.

To the W of Cobán is Nebaj which can be reached by taking the Huehuetenango bus to Sacapulas and either hitching from there or waiting for the bus from Quiché. See pages 1043 and 1047 for places en route to Sacapulas, Nebaj and Huehuetenango.

At Río Hondo, 138 km. from Guatemala City (town 1-2 km. from the Atlantic Highway), a road runs S to **Zacapa**. Population 15,000, altitude 187 metres. Sulphur springs for rheumatic sufferers at Baños de Agua Caliente, well worth a visit (closed on Mon.); tobacco grown. It is an attractive town with a colourful market, 148 km. from Guatemala City. Climate hot and dry. *Fiestas:* June 29, Dec. 1-8. April 30-May 1, small local ceremony. Just outside the town is Estanzuela (minibus, US$0.30), a village whose museum houses a complete skeleton of a prehistoric monster.

Hotels *Wong*, F, with bath; *De León*, G; next to station is *Ferrocarril*, D; other *pensiones* (basic) opposite; *Pensión Central*, opposite market, G, clean, friendly, very good, swimming pool, delightful setting. *Posada Doña María*, E of Zacapa at Km. 181 on road to Puerto Barrios, F, with bath, recommended.

Bank Granai y Townson, near central market, changes travellers' cheques.

Transport Bus from Guatemala City to Zacapa, US$1 with Rutas Orientales, every ½ hr., 3½ hrs. Train to Quiriguá and on to Puerto Barrios 1330, Tues., Thurs., Sat., usually late. Zacapa is the junction for the railway to San Salvador, but there are no passenger services across the border.

1028 GUATEMALA

From Zacapa there is a road S to Chiquimula and Esquipulas. **Chiquimula** (21 km.) is capital of its Department. Population 42,000. It has a colonial character; see church ruined by 1765 earthquake. Bus from Zacapa US$0.12, from Quiriguá, US$0.55, and from Cobán via El Rancho (where a change must be made) US$1.65. Daily market. The town has a historic ceiba tree. A road, 203 km., runs W through splendid scenery to the capital (see page 1026). *Fiestas*: August 12-18, Virgen del Tránsito, December 12.

Hotels *Posada del Oriente*, few blocks from centre, restaurant, E, recommended; *Pensión Hernández*, F, recommended, good cheap food; next door is *España*, G; *Chiquimula*, E, with bath; *Casa de Viajeros*, G, basic but clean; *Darío*, 8 Av., 4-40, ½ block from main square, F, with bath, recommended. *Hospedaje Oriental*, G. *Pollo Frito* for a good meal. The town's water supply is often cut off.

Exchange possible at Almacén Nuevo Cantón on the Plaza, will change quetzales into lempiras.

At Vado Hondo (10 km.) on road to Esquipulas, 51 km. from Chiquimula, a good-quality dirt road branches E to the great Mayan ruins of Copán (see Honduras section, page 1104). It goes through the small town of **Jocotán** (*Pensión Ramírez*, G, showers, clean, pleasant, very friendly, recommended; *Pensión Sagastume*, bus will stop outside, good meals on request; meals at the bakery; exchange at *farmacia*, with 10% commission, *fiesta* July 25) which has hot springs 4 km. from town, and to the border at **El Florido**, where there is now a good bridge. From El Florido to Copán there is a 14-km. dirt road, improvemed in 1982, but fording the many streams after heavy rain can still be hazardous. The drive to Copán takes 4-5 hrs. from Guatemala City, or 2 from Vado Hondo, including the frontier crossing.

There is a through bus from Chiquimula to El Florido at 0600 and 1100 (Transportes Vilma, US$1, 3-4 hrs.); at 0900, 1430, 1730 a bus goes as far as Jocotán (no connection to border on last 2); Transportes Rutas Orientales buses from 19 C. 8-18, Zona 1, Guatemala City run to Chiquimula from 0400, ½ hourly (US$1.25, US$1.75 Pullman), any one before 0730 should make this connection. Also Transportes Guerra from Guatemala City to Chiquimula. Alternatively there are pick-up trucks which meet the morning bus from Zacapa to Jocotán and run to the border for US$0.50-1.50 each. The last bus from Jocotán to Zacapa is at 1400. Bus Jocotán to the border, US$0.50, taxi, US$5. There is a Vilma bus from Zacapa to the border at 0530, US$0.75, which will enable you to spend 2-3 hours at Copán and return the same day. From the border to Copán there are minibuses, US$2 (one leaves at 1400). Those travelling by bus will find that it is impossible to look at Copán properly and return to Guatemala in one day. If you can find somewhere to stay, you can spend the night at El Florido and catch the 0500 bus from there to Chiquimula (although there may be delays in Honduras) or spend the night in Copán village. Bus to border at 0800, which is met by a pick-up truck to Jocotán (last bus from Copán to El Florido 1300 for connecting bus from Jocotán to Chiquimula at 1700). Bus goes from Jocotán to Chiquimula at 1400 arriving at 1600, in time for a connection to Guatemala City, although not to Puerto Barrios (only as far as Río Hondo, from where one can hitch or stay at the motel). Taxi Chiquimula to the border, US$10; Chiquimula to Copán and back in same day, US$20. If you are coming in to Guatemala at this point you must carry a visa or tourist card as there are absolutely no facilities for obtaining one. There is no transport from the border after 1700. If returning to Guatemala remember that you must have a new visa or tourist card (see page 1053). **Documents**). The customs officials may try to claim that you must have a tourist card and not a visa; we are not aware that this is the case, and if you do have undue difficulties at this crossing, ask to speak to the *delegado*. Make sure that the customs official stamps your papers. There is a Q 3 charge to leave Guatemala (similar entry tax) and a 10 lempiras entry charge for Honduras. Motorists crossing this border are asked for all sorts of "fees"; ask for a receipt or bargain! (Visas may be bought at the border if you need one for Honduras.) Unfortunately the border officials of the two countries do not keep the same hours: Guatemalan hours are 0800-1200, 1400-1800; Honduran hours 0800-2100. If you leave Guatemala outside business hours there is an extra charge of US$0.50. You can sometimes get a lift to Guatemala City with tourist agency guides whose minibuses are not full—cost about US$2. Travel agents do a one-day tour from Guatemala City to Copán and back, for about US$35 p.p.

To visit the Mayan ruins of El Petén, take a bus from Chiquimula to Río Hondo (US$0.25, 1 hr.) to connect with the 0730 bus from Guatemala City to Flores which leaves Río Hondo at 1030, cost US$2.50.

Esquipulas (population: 7,500) is a typical market town in semi-lowland, but at the end of its 1½-km. shabby street is a magnificent white basilica, one of the finest colonial churches in the Americas. In it is a black Christ carved by Quirio Catano in 1594 which draws pilgrims from all Central America, especially on

GUATEMALA 1029

January 27-30 and during Lent and Holy Week. The image was first placed in a local church in 1595, but was moved in 1758 to the present building.

The Benedictine monks who look after the shrine are from Louisiana and therefore speak English. They show visitors over their lovely garden.

Hotels *Payaquí*, D; *Los Angeles*, F; *Montecristo*, 3 Av., 9-12, F; *Rosas*, F; *Zacapa*, 3 Av. 9-51, G; *Pensión Modelo*, 3 Av. 2-81, G; *Hotel San Carlos*, 3 Av. 10-37, G; *Pensión Lemus*, G; *Pensión Mi Hotelito*, 2 Av. 10-30, F; *París*, 10 C., 1 Av., G; *La Favorita*, 3 Av. 10-16, G; *Santa Rosa*, F *Hospedaje Colonial*, G.

Restaurants Plenty, but watch overcharging.

Honduran Consulate in the lobby of the *Hotel Payaquí*, very helpful.

Transport Buses from (and to) the capital every 30 mins. US$1.50 (4½-5 hrs). The road goes on to Atulapa, on the Honduran border (minibuses every few hours, US$0.25, plus US$0.25 across border), and continues to the Honduran town of Nueva Ocotopeque and S to San Salvador. El Salvador may be reached direct by taking the road from Concepción Las Minas and then on to the Salvadorean border at Anguiatú. From there a good road goes to Metapán.

On the Atlantic Highway, at Km. 181 is *Motel Longarone*, D (higher prices for a/c), swimming pool, in a delightful setting.

Quiriguá, about 4 km. from some remarkable Mayan Old Empire remains: temple, carved stelae, etc. In 1975 a stone sun-god statue was unearthed here. Try to visit the ruins in the morning as the afternoon sun casts shadows on many of the stelae. The tallest stone is over 8 metres high. Many of the stelae are now in a beautiful park, where refreshments are served. Open 0800-1800.

From main highway to ruins, ride on back of motorbike, US$0.50, walk or take a taxi. *Hospedaje Blanqui*, G, without bath or running water, no mosquito netting, no door locks, clean, near station; *Hotel Royal* recently opened, F, with bath; clean; mosquito netting on all windows, good meals US$1.60. Reached by road from Guatemala City to Los Amates, then a 3½-km. dirt road (ask to be put down at the "ruinas de Quiriguá", 10 km. after Los Amates), Velázquez bus at 0700, US$1.25, 3½ hrs. If driving the road branches off the Atlantic Highway at Km. 207. Take insect-repellant. The best reference book is S. G. Morley's *Guide Book to Ruins of Quiriguá*, which should be obtained before going to the ruins.

Puerto Barrios, on the Caribbean (population 23,000), 297 km. from the capital by the Atlantic Highway (toll, free for motorcycles) and with rail connections also, has now been largely superseded as a port by Santo Tomás. It is the capital of the Department of Izabal. The beach of Escobar on the northern peninsula is recommended. Toll, US$0.25. The launch to Livingston leaves from here, and one can take a boat to Puerto Modesto Méndez, on the Sarstún river.

Hotels *Del Norte*, 7 C. and 2 Av., "rickety old wooden structure" on sea front, E (rooms 5 and 7 have bath), pleasant, clean, recommended, huge breakfasts, mainly seafood dinners, US$4; *Motel Canadá*, on sea front behind *Del Norte*; *San Marcos*, 7 C. 7 Av. 63, F, with bath, 3 good meals, US$4.25; *El Dorado*, 13 C. between 6 and 7 Av., F, with bath, clean, friendly; *Hospedaje Los Arbolitos*, 9 C. and 5 Av., G, basic; *Gran Hotel Quinto*, 8 Av. and 15 C., F, with bath; *Europa*, 8 Av., 8 and 9 C., new, clean, F, with bath, restaurant; *Español*, 13 C. between 5 and 6 Av., E with bath, clean, friendly; *Caribeña*, 4 Av., between 10 and 11 C., F, recommended; *Hotel Xelajú*, 9 C. between 6 and 7 Av., G, clean, friendly, by market and bus station, noisy; *Pensión Xelajú*, 8 Av., between 9 and 10 C., quiet, clean, G; *Hospedaje Atlántico*, G; *Tivoli*, nice, open; *Hotel del Norte*, backs on to railway station, G, very basic. There are other cheap hotels on 7 and 8 Calles between 6 and 8 Avenidas (e.g. *Canadá*, 6 C., between 6 and 7 Av., F), and on and near 9 Calle towards the sea.

Restaurants Most hotels. *Cafesama*, 8 C., and 6 Av., open 24 hours, reasonable. *Ranchón La Bahía*, good, reasonable prices; *Guana Chapi*, on 9 C. near landing stage for Livingston ferry, very cheap and good. *Copos* and *Frosty* ice-cream parlours, 8 C. between 6 and 7 Av., both good and clean. Numerous others, undistinguished, in centre and on 9 Calle. *Monte Carlo* has a floor show.

Market In block bounded by 8 and 9 C. and 6 and 7 Av. Footwear is cheap.

Banks Lloyds Bank International, 7 C. and 2/3 Av., open 0900-1500, Mon.-Fri., (will not cash American Express travellers' cheques). Banco de Guatemala on seafront, opens and closes ½ hr. earlier (will cash Amex cheques).

Post Office 3 Av. and 7 C., behind Bandegua building.

Cables/Telephones Guatel, 10 C. and 8 Av.

1030 GUATEMALA

Buses to capital, 6 hrs., US$3.50, first class, Litegua office; 6 Av., 9-10 C, last bus at 1600. Unión Pacífica y Las Patojas has 4 2nd-class buses a day to capital, and one semi-pullman a day, with luggage on top, to Pacific coast (US$4.75). There are good road connections to the Honduran frontier, but one must go as far south as Copán to cross into Honduras by car, though there is a walking route to a border crossing near Puerto Barrios (passable only in the driest of weather).
Train from Guatemala City dep. Tues., Thurs., Sat. 0700, scheduled to arrive 2000, but hardly ever does; return 0700, arr. 1930. Fare US$3 single.

Santo Tomás de Castilla is a few km. S of Puerto Barrios on Santo Tomás bay. Its port works have been completed, and it is now the country's largest and most efficient port on the Caribbean, connected with the capital by a paved road. It handles 77% of the exports and half the imports as well as 20% of El Salvador's imports and 10% of its exports. Cruise ships are beginning to put into Santo Tomás and before long the town will become more expensive. However, at present, it is still being built. Apart from *Hotel Puerto Libre* (see below), no good hotel or eating place as yet, and no shops, and nothing to do save sea bathing.

Hotel *Puerto Libre*, 25 rooms, at highway fork for Santo Tomás and Puerto Barrios, D, a/c and bath, TV, phone for international calls, restaurant and bar, swimming pool.

Shipping A motor-boat service is maintained with Livingston and Puerto Cortés (Honduras). To ship a car to New Orleans costs US$300-400, depending on size of car.

Transport To Guatemala City one has either to take a local bus to Puerto Barrios to connect with the train, or to Puerto Barrios or the highway fork by the *Hotel Puerto Libre* to catch the Pullman bus.

Puerto Barrios to Río Dulce Launch to **Livingston** (22½ km.), at mouth of Río Dulce, leaves twice daily, 0600 and 1000, arrive 1 hour in advance to ensure a seat (1000 Sun.), cost US$0.40 (private dugout, US$4-8). (Launch returns at 0400 and 1400 plus 1700 on Sat. and Sun.) Very quiet, now little trade save some export of famous Verapaz coffee from Cobán, and bananas. Population: 3,026, mostly blacks of Jamaican origin, many Carib-speaking, a few English-speaking. Beach is reported to be dirty; many young travellers congregate here. There is a bank, but it is hardly ever open. Some hotels will change travellers' cheques, as will the Chinese shop. No phone service between 2000 and 0700.

Warning Don't stroll on the beach after dark as there is a risk of rape and robbery.

Hotels at Livingston: *Tucán Dugú*, C (Fri.-Sun., less in week), new, sea view, swimming pool, expensive, to book, Tel.: 321259, Guatemala City, Telex 5139; *Casa Rosada*, 300 metres first left from dock, 5 thatched cabins for 2-3 persons each on the beach, F, breakfast and bar, boat trips to Río Dulce or just for swimming can be arranged, recommended, call Guatel in Livingston for reservations, hotel will call back, American owner, Jean Swanson. *Hotel del Mar*, at top of hill from dock, D, air-conditioned; *Río Dulce*, G, good views, basic, popular but dirty and not very safe; *Casa Azul* (on main street, no sign), damp, unfriendly; *Caribe*, 100 metres first left from dock, F with bath, cheaper rooms without, good; *Ramón's Place* (no proper name), very basic, sling your hammock for US$1; *Flamingo*, Playa de París D-823, E, with garden, clean, comfortable cottages, safe, German owner. Camping is said to be good around Livingston. Beware of theft from hotel rooms.

Restaurants *El Malecón*, 100 metres from dock, on right; *The African Place*, left on paved road at top of hill; both reasonable. Near *African Place*, *Café Margoth*, recommended. Good meals can be obtained in private houses; try *New York Greenhouse* where Peter serves delicious meals that must be ordered one day in advance. **N.B.** Too much coconut bread, although delicious, can cause constipation.

Río Blanco beach can be reached by *cayuco*, and Los Siete Altares, beautiful waterfalls and pools during the rainy season, some 6 km. from town, on foot or by *cayuco*. Beware of theft when leaving belongings to climb the falls. Also paddle up the Río Dulce gorge. *Cayucos* can be hired near Texaco station, US$2.50 per day.

Boats Government passenger boat to Punta Gorda, Belize, Tues. and Fri. 0830, starting from Puerto Barrios, US$5; return same days at 1500. Ticket office and immigration on Calle 9, near landing; immigration opens 0700, then buy ticket (can be done day in advance). There is a service on Sat. and Sun. Puerto Barrios-Livingston-Río Dulce, US$4.25 one way (it will not leave Puerto Barrios if there aren't enough passengers; it should arrive at Livingston about 0900). Return from Río Dulce to Livingston at 1400. One can get the mail boat from Livingston up to the new bridge at Río Dulce at 1030, Tues. and Fri., (0600 in the other direction) but schedules subject to change, US$1.50—2.50 depending on number of passengers. Boats may be hired for Livingston-Río Dulce trip for US$10-80 (depending on your situation and on the hirer).

GUATEMALA 1031

Near *Río Dulce*, 23 km. upstream at entrance to Lake Izabal (site of new bridge, toll US$1), is *Turicentro Marimonte*, 500 metres to right at Shell station, C for bungalows (phone Guatemala City 324493/334511 for reservations), restaurant, pool; camping site US$3, use of showers and pool; *Marilú*, El Relleno on N side, G, basic: The US-owned *Catamaran*, C, in bungalows, pool, meals about US$2, is reached by outboard canoe (US$1.50 from Río Dulce, 2 km. or 10 mins. downstream, phone 324-829, Guatemala City, for reservations). *Hotel Del Río*, a few km. downstream, B, incl. 3 meals (Guatemala City 310-016 for reservations). *Hotel Santa Isabel*, dirty and expensive. There are yachting facilities at Río Dulce.

At the entrance to Lake Izabal, 2 km. upstream, is the old Spanish fort of San Felipe in an attractive setting (boat from El Relleno, Río Dulce— below the new bridge—US$2.50 return for one, US$0.50 p.p. in groups; it is a 5 km. walk, practically impossible after rain). (*Hotel Don Humberto*, at San Felipe, E; also basic *pensión*, G.) Lake Izabal is a habitat for the manatee (sea cow). A reserve, the Biotopo del Manatí, has been set up halfway between San Felipe and Livingston at El Golfete. It covers 135 sq. km., with both a land and an aquatic trail. (The Park, like the Biotopo del Quetzal, is run by Centro de Estudios Conservacionistas—Cecon—and Inguat.). Sr. Cambell in Livingston runs boat trips to the reserve (and up rivers) for about US$12 for 6 people—bargain. On the NW shore is **El Estor**—its name dates back to the days when the British living in the Atlantic area got their provisions from a store situated at this spot—where nickel-mining has now begun. We have heard that one can hire a boat from Río Dulce to El Estor, which can be alternatively reached by taking two buses to Mariscos on the south side of Lake Izabal, then crossing on the afternoon boat (1300) to El Estor, to which there is no direct road. *Hotel Los Almendros*, F; *Hospedaje El Milagro* G, and *Santa Clara*, G (friendly), others at similar prices. Also restaurants (a very good one at ferry point for Mariscos). A ferry leaves El Estor at 0600 for Mariscos (US$0.75, 1 hr. 50 mins., returns 1300) from where there are buses to **Bananera** (officially called **Morales**) US$0.50 and Puerto Barrios, US$0.75; from Bananera there are buses to the Río Dulce crossing (road paved, 30 km.), Puerto Barrios and the Petén (US$4.80, 10 hrs. to Flores; return buses from Río Dulce to Bananera start at 0600; train to Guatemala City is supposed to leave at 0915). At Bananera, *Hospedaje Liberia, Simon's*, both G and basic but OK. *Cauca* (dory) trips can be arranged to Livingston, via San Felipe, from Mariscos, 5 hrs., US$18 for 3 people. At **Mariscos**, *Hospedaje Karilinda*, G (per room, regardless of number of occupants), recommended, good food; *Cafetería/Hospedaje Los Almendros*, G, good. From El Estor there is a reasonable and very beautiful unpaved road through Panzós (guest house, bus to El Estor p.m. and 2030), via Teleman, La Tinta, Tucurú and Tamahú to Tactic. Just after the Río Cahabón crossing a road branches off to Cahabón (no buses, and not much traffic). A road runs through Cahabón, starting at El Estor and continuing to Lanquín(page 1027).

El Petén: the Maya Centres and the Jungle

El Petén Department in the far N, which was so impenetrable that its inhabitants, the Itzáes, were not conquered by the Spaniards until 1697, is now reached by road either from Km. 245, opposite Morales, on the Atlantic Highway, or by the overland route from Cobán, through Sebol and Sayaxche, or by air. The local products are chicle and timber—and mosquitoes in the rainy season; take plenty of repellant, and re-apply frequently.

Driving from Guatemala City or from Puerto Barrios, the road from the Atlantic Highway, is being paved to Modesto Méndez. Never drive at night. Some drivers suggest driving in front of a truck and, if you break down, do so across the road, then you will be assured of assistance. Alternatively after rain, it is advisable to follow a truck, and do not hurry. A new bridge has been built over the Sarstún River. Then 250 km. along narrow, winding, dusty or muddy potholed road.

Flores, the Department's capital, lies in the heart of the Petén forests, and is built on an island in the middle of Lake Petén Itzá. It is linked by a causeway with Santa Elena (airport). Its population is 5,000. From Flores the ruins of Tikal and other Mayan cities can be reached. (For description of Maya culture see page 1006). There is a collection of stelae, altars, etc., from Naranjo and other remote

1032 GUATEMALA

Mayan sites, in a park W of the airport; no labels or guide book. *Fiesta*: January 1-14.

Hotels in Flores: *Yum Kax*, E, with bath and a/c, comfortable, new; *El Itzá*, E, no hot water (the owner is a good doctor); *Petén*, Tel.: 0811-392, F with cold water, E with hot, comfortable, clean, friendly, recommended, breakfast a little extra; *Pensión Universal*, F, hot shower, friendly, pleasant; *El Jade*, F, clean, basic, just by the dyke leading to Flores; *Santana*, on the lake, G, friendly, basic, shared showers and toilets, serves cheap meals, boats may be hired for rowing to "Radio Petén" Island. At Santa Elena; *El Patio*, D, restaurant and bar, simple; *Maya Internacional*, under same management, Sr. Rafael Sagastume, E, + tax, recommended, beautifully situated, good restaurant, used by package tours from the capital; *Monja Blanca*, F; *Ahauna-Ula*, G, good restaurant; *Santa Teresa*, G, basic, nothing special; *San Juan* at bus stop, clean, G without bath, F with; *San Juan 2*, F, very basic, dirty, not recommended; *Santa Elena*, G; *Hospedaje Esquipulas*, G.

Restaurants Restaurant of *Ahauna-Ula* Hotel recommended. *La Mesa de los Mayas*, poor food, slow service. Also *Restaurant Santana*, meals, US$0.75 but slow service; *Gran Jaguar*, pleasant, very good; *La Jungla*, reasonably priced, recommended; *Restaurant Típico*. At Santa Elena, *Cafetería Oriental* is said to be good and cheap, as is *Comedor Los Angeles*.

Dugouts can be hired to paddle yourself around the lake (US$0.50 per hour from Don Rosso, house before *Hotel Petén*, ask in *Restaurant Santana*). You can swim from "Radio Petén" island, the small island which used to have a radio mast on it, US$0.12 by boat. La Guitarra island in the lake is being developed for tourism; there is a small zoo of local animals, birds and reptiles and a water toboggan slide; plant-lined walks will be made. Dugout to island, US$2.50.

San Benito, a US$0.05 (US$0.10 after 1800) ride across the lake, has a better selection of fruit and vegetables and some small restaurants (e.g. *Santa Teresita*), which are cheaper but less inviting than those in Flores. *Hotel Holiday Inn*, G, basic; *Diplomático*, G without bath, F with, clean, but damp, friendly; *Dany*, G; *Hospedaje Pabellón*, G; *Hospedaje Hernández*, G; *Bella Guatemala*, G, dirty, poor value, at bus stop; *San Juan*, G, clean; *Hotel Rey*, G, friendly, untidy, noisy; *Hotel Miraflores*, F, good, private showers; *Hospedaje Favorito*, G, and *Palermo*. A dirty village. Regular launch service from San Benito across the lake to San Andrés (US$0.12) and San José (US$0.15) on NW shore. *Hospedaje El Reposo Maya*, at San Andrés, G.

Car Hire at airport, mostly Suzuki jeeps; Jade recommended.

Banking Flores is the only place in the Petén where one can reliably change travellers' cheques. Banks close December 24-January 1. The major hotels change cash and travellers' cheques.

Airport 3 companies fly from Guatemala City to Flores: Aviateca, Aerovías and Tapsa; all charge US$35 one way. The schedules appear to change frequently, but there is at least one flight a day in each direction, including a tourist flight which is met by buses for Tikal (latest information, 0700 from Guatemala City with Aviateca). If returning from Flores by plane, reconfirm flight on arrival; most flights back leave around 1630, but check. Don't buy air tickets at *Hotel San Juan*; they add on all sorts of extras. You must have passport (or identity documents) to pass through Santa Elena airport and all bags will be searched. Beware of people who say no buses are running to Tikal, and then offer to take you for US$5 from the airport; as likely as not, the public bus will be running. Taxi airport-Flores, US$0.50 p.p., a free bus to Santa Elena village then walk. Airport to Flores is 3 km.

Buses The Flores bus terminal is in Santa Elena, a 10-min. walk from Flores (taxi, US$0.40 by day, US$0.80 at night). Daily (Fuente del Norte, 17 C 8-46, Zona 1) buses leave Guatemala City in the early morning for the 13-22 hr. run via Morales-Río Dulce-Puerto Modesto Méndez to Flores (US$4.60, 1st class; one way, take food); return buses to Guatemala City at 0530, 1100, 2300 from centre of Santa Elena; Pinita to Guatemala City from *Hotel San Juan 1* (don't believe them if they tell you Pinita is the only company to the capital), 1100, not as good; Flores-Morales, US$4.80. Bus Flores to Río Dulce, US$4.50, departs 0400. Bus between Flores and Quiriguá (see page 1029), US$5, 11 hrs. In the rainy season the trip can take as much as 28 hrs., and in all weathers it is very uncomfortable (flights warmly recommended).

Mayan ruins fans wishing to economize can travel to Copán by bus from Flores (La Pinita, 0500) to Río Hondo, then from Río Hondo to Chiquimula, then from Chiquimula to El Florido (see page 1028) or La Entrada, and finally from either of these places to Copán. La Pinita also has a service to Flores from Guatemala City via Sebol, El Pato and Sayaxché, see below.

Those who wish to break the journey could get off the bus and spend a night in Morales, Río Dulce, San Luis (*Pensión San Antonio*, G, nice; *Comedor Oriente*, cheap, good) or Poptún. **Poptún** is 100 km. from Flores (5 minibuses a day from Flores, US$2 or take Fuentes del Norte bus, US$1.15, 4 hrs; bus Poptún-Guatemala City at 0900, 11 hrs.; it can be reached by air for US$16). *Pensión Isabelita*, F, clean, recommended; *Pensión Gabriel*, G. *Restaurant Gil-town*, best. Also at certain times of the year delicious mangoes are on sale in this area. Good view of the town from Cerro de la Cruz, a 15-minute walk from the market. 3 km. S of Poptún is *Finca Ixobel*, a working farm owned by Mike and Carole De Vine; here one may camp for US$0.50 p.p., recommended ("a paradise"). There are shelters, showers, free firewood, swimming, farm produce for sale; family-style meals available, and there is a small guest house; they have a restaurant-bar (also called

GUATEMALA 1033

Ixobel, excellent too, with *hospedaje* next door) in the centre of Poptún where the buses stop. Three cave expeditions are organized, the most spectacular being a 3-day mule hike to the Cueva de las Inscripciones, once used by Maya; inside are marvellous glyphs (US$5 p.p. per day). Bus travellers should alight at the large signpost on the main road.

Buses leave Santa Elena for Tikal from *Hotel San Juan* daily at 0600 (does a tour of town looking for passengers, passing *San Juan* again about 0620) and 1300, US$1.50 return (70 km., 1½-2 hrs. on good paved road). Buses return at 0600 and 1300 (Pinita). *Jungle Lodge* minibus from Tikal at 1400, US$2. Minibuses meet Guatemala City-Flores flights to take visitors to Tikal for US$3.85.

In 1982, the Cerro Cahui Conservation Park was opened on the northern shore of Lake Petén Itzá; this is a lowland jungle area where one can see 3 species of monkeys, deer, jaguar, peccary, some 450 species of birds; run by Cecon and Inguat.

Tikal The great Mayan ruins of vast temples and public buildings are reached by plane to Santa Elena, from where buses run (see above). Tikal lasted from the 4th century A.D. until the tenth. An overall impression of the ruins (a national park) may be gained in 4-5 hrs., but you need two days to see everything, and detailed study needs much longer. Guides are available near the Plaza Mayor. A Land Rover trip through the ruins costs US$2.50. Marvellous place for seeing animal and bird life of the jungle. *Birds of Tikal* book available at the museum. Wildlife includes spider monkeys, howler monkeys (re-established after being hit by disease), three species of toucan (most prominent being the "Banana Bill"), deer, foxes and many other birds and insects. Mosquitoes can be a real problem even during the day if straying away from open spaces (use repellant and cover up).

Hotels (Note: It is advisable to book a hotel room or camping space as soon as you arrive.) *Jaguar Inn*, C, full board, triple room E (without board: E, US$12.50 for a bungalow), and will provide picnic lunch at US$1.30. Its electricity supply is the most reliable (1800-2200); will store luggage, very friendly. *Tikal Inn*, E p.p., cheap accommodation without electricity also available, not recommended, meals said to be good (US$1 for dinner); *Posada de la Selva* (Jungle Lodge—reservations may be made at Edificio Villa Real, 6 Av., in the capital), from F (communal shower) to E p.p. in bungalows, D full board (mixed reports about the food) (roofs of cheapest accommodation leak badly) has its own campsite where you can sling your hammock for US$0.50. Jungle Lodge's Tikal tours (US$5) have been recommended; runs bus to meet incoming flights, US$2.50 one way. Three *comedores*, *Comedor Tikal*, *Corazón de Jesús*, and *Imperio Maya* (opens 0530); quality and service better nearer the airstrip. Economical travellers are best advised to bring their own food, and especially drink.

Wear light cotton clothes, a broad-brimmed hat and take plenty of insect repellant. The nights can be cold, however; at least one warm garment is advisable. There is one campsite (free), by the airstrip, good, rents small hammocks for US$0.50 and a deposit of US$5. Mosquito netting is recommended. Take your own water as the supply is very variable, sometimes rationed, sometimes unlimited, depending on season. Bathing is possible in a pond at the far end of the airstrip (check first). Beware of jiggers in the grass. Soft drinks are available near the Plaza Mayor and Temple IV (US$0.25). There are no fresh fruit or vegetables available. No banking services available. Ruins (open 0600-1730) charge US$0.40, but museum at Tikal is free (open Mon.-Fri. 0900-1700, Sat. and Sun. 0900-1600). Extended passes to see the ruins at sunrise/sunset (until 2100) are easy to obtain (especially good for seeing animals). It is best to visit the ruins after 1400 (fewer tourists). There is nowhere to store luggage at Tikal while you are visiting the ruins. Recommended guide book is *Tikal*, by W. R. Coe,—with essential map, price US$4.20 in the capital or Antigua or slightly more at the Tikal Museum. Without a guide book, a guide is essential (Clarence has been recommended), as outlying structures can otherwise easily be missed. Take a torch, electricity at Tikal is only available 1800-2200. It is now possible to visit Tikal in a day: take 0600 bus from Santa Elena (Flores), arrive by 0830, return at 1300, allowing 5 hrs. at the site. You may hitch back with a tourist bus 1 hr. later. Tour from *Hotel Maya Internacional* in Santa Elena: dep. 0900, return 1600, transport only US$6, guided tour US$18. *Hotel Petén* also runs tours from 0600-1700.

Note Heavy rains and flooding can close the roads between Tikal and Flores.

For Belize there are 4 buses daily from Flores to **Melchor de Mencos** (US$1.15) on the border (take the 0500 Pinita bus from *Hotel San Juan* 1 (they promise to wake you up, but don't count on it), to be sure of making a connection in San Ignacio for Belize City). This can be caught at El Cruce if coming from Tikal. The 0600 or 1300 bus from Tikal gives you a 1 hr. wait at El Cruce (US$0.50) for the Flores-Melchor de Mencos bus, one leaves El Cruce at 1500 (El Cruce-Melchor de Mencos, US$1). Pinita bus to Flores leaves Melchor de Mencos 4 times a day, with a 2-4 hr. wait at El Cruce for the bus to Tikal. Journey takes about 3 hrs. and the bus tours town, including the border, for passengers. Pick-up Melchor de Mencos-Flores, US$3.85; taxi from the border to Tikal, US$35 for up to 6 passengers. About 3 km. from El Cruce on the Tikal road, if one turns off to the left along the north shore of Lake Petén-Itzá, is *El Gringo Perdido*, with a restaurant, cabins, camping (US$0.55 a night) and good swimming in the lake, meals available at US$1.25. The road from El Remate to *El Gringo Perdido* is often flooded (latest reports suggest that this is not a safe area,

1034 GUATEMALA

owing to robbers). For onward connections, it is best to take a taxi from the border to San Ignacio (Cayo), BZ$3. From there you can catch a bus to Belize City. Hitching is not easy as there is little traffic on these roads. Taxis to Belize City can be hired, about US$10 p.p. Banco de Guatemala at the border, also black market in Belizean dollars. If driving from Flores/ Tikal to Belize, be prepared for police checks (watch out for drugs being "planted" in your vehicle) and take spare fuel. **N.B.** If you need a visa to enter either Belize or Mexico, get it before crossing from Guatemala at this point.

Hotels at Melchor de Mencos: *Maya*, G (sells bus tickets and acts as bus stop, small rooms); *Zacaleu*, F, clean, good value, sells bus tickets to Flores; *Mayab*, F, clean, comfortable, shared showers and toilets, hot water, recommended, safe parking. *Pensión Central*, G, dirty; *Esquipulas*, G, basic. Will sometimes change Belizean dollars for quetzales and vice versa; Tienda Unica will change travellers' cheques. *Restaurant Damarco*, very good, US$1 for meal, usually closed in evening; *La Chinita*, 1 block from *Maya*, good dinner under US$2.

To Mexico From Flores or Tikal to Chetumal in a day is reportedly possible if the 0500 bus Flores—Melchor de Mencos, or 0600 from Tikal (change at El Cruce), 4 hrs., connects with a bus at 0930 from the border to Belize City, from where you can take an afternoon bus to Chetumal. A rough, unpaved road runs 160 km. to **El Naranjo** on the San Pedro River—a centre for oil exploration, unfriendly—on the Mexican border (US$10). There are daily buses from Santa Elena at 1300 and 1500 from *Hotel San Juan* (US$2.70, 5½ hrs. at least; bus from El Naranjo to Flores at 0200). At *Posada San Pedro*, F, basic, (under same ownership as *El Patio* and *Maya Internacional* in Santa Elena) there is information, group travel, guides, and arrangements for travel as far as Palenque; reservations can be made through travel agencies in Guatemala City. Also bungalows in El Naranjo, which has an immigration office. On arrival in El Naranjo, your luggage will be searched; next morning, go to immigration and have your passport stamped (if not travelling alone, make sure everyone gets a stamp). From El Naranjo, it is about 4 hrs. (US$9.50) by boat to the military post on the Mexican border, then a daily ferry at 0600 (US$2.50) to La Palma in Mexico, from where buses go to Tenosique and on to Palenque. Mexican tourist cards can be obtained at the border. Expect thorough searches on either side of the border.

Sayaxché is a good centre for visiting the Petén, whether your interest is in the wild life or the Mayan ruins. The *Hotel Guayacán*, known locally as *Hotel de Godoy* after the owner Julio Godoy, is a good source of information on the area, F, excellent value, on S bank of river, close to ferry; *Hotel la Montana*, G, has its own, separate restaurant (at which Carlos is very informative); *Hotel Mayapán*, S bank near ferry, F, no water or electricity after 2200; or *Hotel Sayaxché*, G, basic, dirty, food not bad. No money-changing facilities.

There are buses to and from Guatemala City via Sebol and Raxruhá, and to and from Santa Elena, Flores, 4 a day (US$0.80, 2½ hrs.); La Pinita has a through bus, Guatemala City-Flores, via Sayaxché. On August 24, all-night mass is celebrated in **Sebol** (free food at 0100) with games played on the church lawn in the daylight hours. 10 km. from Sebol is Las Casas (*Hospedaje Rallos*, F, better than the other hotel here), a village which has a *fiesta* (parade and rodeo) on May 1. A rough dirt road links Sebol with Sayaxché via Raxruhá (*Pensión Aguas Verdes*, G, new); many *comedores*, e.g. El Ganadero, quite good) and El Pato (2 *comedores* and 1 basic *pensión*, G). Besides the direct Guatemala City-Sebol-Sayaxché-Flores bus, local buses connect most of these towns: Sayaxché-Raxruhá, 6 hrs., US$1.20; El Pato-Raxruhá (minibus 0500 daily); Raxruhá-Sebol, 1 hr., US$0.40 or El Pato-Sebol; Sebol-Cobán, 0500, 9 hrs., US$1.50 (Cobán-Sebol at 0530). You can also go from Lanquín to Sayaxché via Pajal, Las Casas, Sebol and Raxruhá (see page 1044) (not recommended as a 1-day journey, better to rest in Raxruhá).

From Sebol, there is an 0300 bus to Poptún (see page 1032), via Las Casas and San Luis (on the Morales-Río Dulce-Poptún-Flores road). This route is impassable in the rainy season. From San Luis there is an 0630 bus to Flores, stopping at Poptún (4½ hrs.). It is easy to get a ride on one of the many trucks which run on all these routes.

Downriver from Sayaxché is **El Ceibal**, where the ruins were excavated by Peabody Museum and Harvard. There is now a difficult road linking Sayaxché with El Ceibal—impassable in the wet (leave bus at El Paraíso on the main road—local pick-up from Sayaxché US$0.20.—then walk to the ruins, a further 8 km., 1½ hrs.) so the trip can be made either by road or by river (*pensión* G). You can sling a hammock at El Ceibal and use the guard's fire for making coffee if you ask politely—a mosquito net is advisable, and take repellant for walking in the jungle surroundings. From Sayaxché the ruins of the Altar de Sacrificios at the confluence of the Ríos de la Pasión and Usumacinta can also be reached. Further down the Usumacinta river is Yaxchilán, just over the border in Mexico (temples still standing, with sculptures and carved lintels—see page 973). Still further down the Usumacinta in the west of Petén department is **Piedras Negras**, with little standing architecture, and most sculpture removed to the National Museum in Guatemala City, which can be reached by special rafts suitable for light rapids, at some considerable expense (can be arranged through FLAAR, see page 1019). The Usumacinta river has been dammed by Mexico below Piedras Negras; so no longer are river trips possible. From Sayaxché one can go down river to the border post at Echeverría, thence on to Palenque in Mexico. The Río de la Pasión is a good route to visit other, more recently discovered Maya ruins. From Laguna Petexbatún (46 km.), a fisherman's paradise, which can be reached by outboard canoe from Sayaxché (US$10 or more for 6 people and luggage) excursions can be made to unexcavated ruins **Dos Pilas** (many well-preserved stelae), **Aguateca** (excursion over only known Mayan bridge and down into huge chasm) and **Itzán**—discovered only in 1968. Lagoon fishing includes 150-lb. tarpon, snoek and local varieties. Many interesting birds, including toucan and *guacamayo*. On W side of Laguna Petexbatún is the *Posada del Mundo Maya*, set in a jungle wilderness. Rooms F (E incl. 3 meals). Camping US$0.50 per day. Hire of hammock US$0.50 per day. Meals US$1.25 each. (Enquire at Sayaxché for the *posada*. Reservations through the owner Ana Smith, Panamundo Travel Agency, or *Hotel Camino Real*, Guatemala City, where she is manager.) Jungle guides can be hired for US$1.50-2.50 per day.

(On the foregoing information, Mr. John Streather comments that the ruins are spread over a large area and that the non-specialist could well content himself with seeing El Ceibal and, possibly, Dos Pilas.)

About 30 km. from Flores, on the road towards the Belize border, is Lake Yaxhá. On the northern shore is the site of **Yaxhá**, the third-largest known classic Maya site in the country, accessible by causeway (little excavation has yet been done). In the lake is the site of Topoxte. (The island is accessible by boat.) The site is unique since it flourished between the 12th and 14th centuries, long after the abandonment of all other classic centres. Twenty km. further north lies **Nakum,** with standing Mayan buildings. It is possible to drive part of the way (dry season, April-May) only, or else to walk, but since there are numerous forks in the track, it is essential to hire a guide (no overland transport or flights in the off-season).

The largest Maya site in the country is at **El Mirador,** 36 km. direct from Carmelita, very many more by jungle trail from Flores (a 2-4 day trek—a guide is essential, take plenty of food). It was being excavated by archaeologists from Brigham Young University, but work had stopped temporarily in 1983. The larger of the two huge pyramids, called La Danta, is probably the largest pyramid in the world. There are paintings and other treasures; guards at the site will show you around if no one else is on hand. Camping is possible. Tom Courtenay-Clack (of New York City) writes: Permission, in the form of a letter from the Governor of El Petén, is required. He is to be found at the FYDEP complex on the mainland near Flores. Free water purification tablets for the trip can be obtained at the pharmacy of the army barracks by the airport. Drive or hitch-hike to Carmelita (no bus service); a hard 35 km. that can take 5 hrs.—after rain four-wheel drive, a winch and shovel are necessary. At Carmelita, ask around for space to sling your hammock or camp. Also ask for guides to El Mirador (Victor is recommended), they provide mules: US$1 per mule per day and the same per day for the guide. Allow 2 days each way unless you want a forced march. Take water, food; hammocks, mosquito nets, tents and torches; cooking gear is not essential because guides will make a fire and the guards may let you use their kitchen if you're polite (they also appreciate gifts, e.g. a giant can of peaches).

In the same direction as El Mirador, though much nearer Tikal, is **Uaxactún,** which has a stuccoed temple with serpent head decoration. Uaxactún is one of the longest-occupied Maya sites. Conflicting reports say either that there is no public transport to Uaxactún, or that there is a direct bus from Flores (same times as for Tikal), US$2 return. The hardy might consider walking the 24 km. through the jungle from Tikal, as the dirt road is impassable to vehicles from June to February, but December to April can be driven by a standard vehicle. (Guides ask about US$8 for a 2-day trip from *Posada de la Selva* in Tikal.) No *pensiones*, but the signalman at the airfield will let you sling your hammock in his home for US$0.25. Excavation recommenced in 1983. Nearby is **El Zotz**, another large site, reachable by a reasonable dirt road. In the far north of El Petén is **Río Azul**, which has impressive early tomb murals and Early Classic standing architecture (seasonally being studied) All the sites are accessible by jeep and FLAAR runs tours to them in the dry season.

Guatemala City to San José

Amatitlán is 37 km. by rail and 27 by road SW of the capital, on attractive Lake Amatitlán, 12 by 4 km. Fishing and boating; bathing is not advisable, as the water has become seriously contaminated. Beware of people offering boat trips on the lake, which last no more than 10 minutes. The thermal springs on the lake side, with groves of trees and coffee plantations, feed pools which *are* safe to bathe in. Lake surrounded by picturesque chalets with lawns to the water's edge. Altitude 1,240 metres, population 12,225. Grand view from the United Nations Park, 2½ km. N, above Amatitlán. A road goes round the lake; a branch runs to the slopes of Pacaya volcano, US$0.15 by bus (see page 1025). The town has two famous ceiba trees; one is in Parque Morazán. Buses from Guatemala City (every ½-hr., US$0.20) go right to the lakeside.

Fiesta Santa Cruz, May 2-3.

Hotel *Los Arcos*, E.

Camping The by-road to the U.N. Park (turning at 19½ km. from Guatemala City) ends at camping sites and shelters; it is rather steep and narrow for caravans. View, US$0.12 entrance

1036 **GUATEMALA**

fee. On the main highway S of Amatitlán, accessible by any bus going to Palín, Escuintla or beyond, is Automariscos (km. 33.5, Tel.: (0)330479), English-speaking owner, electric and water hookups, large swimming pool (thermal), good toilets. A second, next door in the direction of Escuintla, is La Red, which has swimming pools fed by hot, volcanic springs (US$0.50 each); restaurant/bar and good toilet facilities. Las Hamacas, on the same road, but closer to the Amatitlán turn-off, with hot, volcanic swimming pool and good café; charge is US$0.75 each. Bus, Guatemala City to any of these 3, US$0.20.

Road and rail continue S to the Pacific port of San José through Palín.

Palín, 14½ km. from Amatitlán, has a Sunday Indian market in a square under an enormous ceiba tree. Grand views to E, of Pacaya, to NW, of Agua volcano, to W, of Pacific lowland. Power plant at Michatoya falls below town. Road runs NW to Antigua through Santa María de Jesús (see page 1024). See old Franciscan church (1560). *Fiestas:* December 8, first Sunday January, June 3, and movable feasts of Holy Trinity and Sacred Heart. Textiles here are exceptional, but are becoming hard to find. *Pensión Señorial,* G, basic.

Escuintla, 18 km. from Palín on the road to San José, is a market town in a rich tropical valley at 335 metres. Population 62,500. Famous for its medicinal baths and fruits. There is a large market on Sunday, and a daily market over 2 blocks. Agua volcano looms to the N. Road N to Antigua. Beyond Escuintla a railway branches W at the station of Santa María to Mexico (no passengers).

The Pacific Highway to the Mexican border at Tecún Umán (paved all the way, 200 km.) and E to El Salvador (first 25 km. bad, then only fair) runs through it. As a route to Mexico, it is shorter, faster and easier to drive, but much less picturesque, than the El Tapón route to the N. There is a meat packing plant. *Fiesta:* December 8 (holiday) to 12. Many buses to the capital (US$0.38, Veloz Porteño) also direct to Antigua at 0730 and 1500, US$0.50 (poor road).

The Department of Escuintla, between the Pacific and the chain of volcanoes, is the richest in the country, producing 80% of the sugar, 20% of the coffee, 85% of the cotton, and 70% of the cattle of the whole country.

Hotels (each with acceptable restaurant) *Metropol; Tahormina; Motel Sarita,* km.59, CA2 road, E; *Motel Texas,* km. 59, CA9 road, E. *Hospedaje San Vicente,* G; *Pensión México,* G; *Hospedaje El Aguila,* G; *Mansión La Paz* and *Pensión Marina,* both G, on Calle 10; *Hospedaje Comodidad,* near market, G; *Shing Chi Rest,* G; *Restaurant Deliciosas Tony,* meals for US$0.75; also several Chinese restaurants.

Banks Lloyds Bank International (agency) 7a Calle 3-09, Zona 1. Open 0830-1200, 1400-1600.

Between Escuintla and Santa Lucía **Cotzumalguapa** is **La Democracia** (7 km. off the Pacific highway), where sculptures found on the Monte Alto and Costa Brava estates (fincas) are displayed. These are believed to date from 400 BC or earlier and have magnetic navels or temples. Visit the Museo del Pueblo on the main square. At Cotzumalguapa (an unfriendly town which charges tourists for the privilege of visiting) is the 9th century site of Bilbao (or Cotzumalguapa), which shows Teotihuacán and Veracruz influences. El Baúl, a pre-classic monument (stelae) which dates back to Izapán, is 6 km. from Cotzumalguapa: cross bridge, keep left and follow the road to the timberyard where numerous interesting stelae are displayed. From this early art, the classic Mayan art developed. El Castillo, between Bilbao and El Baúl, has some small sculptures dating back to Mayan times. On the Las Ilusiones and Finca Pantaleón estates are ruined temples, pyramids and sculptures, and there are other stelae to be found in the area. More detailed information and a map can be obtained from FLAAR in Guatemala City (page 1019). N. Hellmuth's *Maya Archaeology Travel Guide* and M. Coe's *The Maya* are the best books on these remains. Hotels at Cotzumalguapa: *El Camino,* E; *Galeano, El Carmen,* both G. Hotel at La Democracia, *El Reposo,* F. Buses from the Zona 4 terminal in the capital run to both places.

San José, 52 km. beyond Escuintla, 109 km. by road (fully paved, bus US$1.50, Reyna del Pacífico) and 121 by rail from the capital, is the country's second largest port; it handles nearly half the imports. Population 8,000. Hot climate. Fishing, swimming, though beware the strong undercurrent. *Fiesta:* March 19, when town is crowded and hotel accommodation difficult to get. Interesting trip can be taken through Chiquimulilla canal by launch from the old Spanish port of **Iztapa,** now a bathing resort a short distance to the E. At Iztapa you can camp

GUATEMALA 1037

on the beach (dirty), but as it is only possible to get there by launch, one cannot take a car.

Hotels at San José *Club Chulamar*, C; *Balneario Chulamar*, bungalows, D upwards; *Casetas San Jorge*, F p.p.; *Viñas del Mar*, on the beach, E, with bath, run down, unfriendly; *Turicentro El Coquito*, D, on the road to Escuintla; *Motel La Roca*, at km. 71, F; *Veracruz* (Calle Principal), G, clean. *Posada Roma Linda*, G, extra for sheet), no shower, basic, good fish meals with family.

Rail To Guatemala City and Puerto Barrios; also to Champerico via Retalhuleu. Train for the capital leaves at 0500, arriving at 1200. Fare, US$0.75.

Bus San José-Guatemala City hourly from 0600; from Iztapa to San José US$0.12. To Escuintla, US$0.50. Reyna del Pacífico to the capital, US$1.25.

Beyond San José is the smart resort of *Likin,* which fronts on both the Chiquimulilla canal and the Pacific. (Hotel: *Turicentro Likin*, C, per bungalow.) Further on is the less expensive resort of Monterrico.

West from Guatemala City

The Pacific Highway goes W from Guatemala City to Tapachula and Arriaga in Mexico. The Pan-American Highway (fully paved) cuts off NW at San Cristóbal Totonicapán and goes into Chiapas by the El Tapón, or Selegua, canyon. This is a far more interesting route, with fine scenery.

The highway to Tapachula will be followed first. It and its many offshoots to N and S lead to many highland towns and villages of great interest.

A railway also runs through south-western Guatemala from Guatemala City to Mexico.

Some 6½ km. W of the capital a road (right) leads to San Pedro Sacatepéquez (see page 1024) and Cobán (see page 1026). Our road twists upwards steeply, giving grand views, with a branch to Mixco (16½ km. from Guatemala City). About 14 km. beyond, at San Lucas Sacatepéquez, the road to Antigua turns sharp left. *Sumpango*, which is a little over 19 km. beyond this turn-off, has a Sun. market, and *huipiles* can be bought from private houses; they are of all colours but preponderantly red, as it is believed to ward off the evil eye. Good font in church. At **Chimaltenango**, another road runs left, 20 km., to Antigua; this road is served by a shuttle-bus (US$0.10), so Antigua can be included in the Guatemala-Chichicastenango circuit. Chimaltenango is the capital of its Department (*Pensión La Predilecta*, G, pleasant rooms with bath, rooms without bath not so nice, poor water supply, unfriendly; tends to overcharge, rebuilt since the earthquake). Excellent views at 1,790 metres, from which water flows one side to the Atlantic, the other side to the Pacific. Thermal swimming pool at San Lorenzo El Tejar, which can be reached by bus from Chimaltenango. *Fiesta*: January 18-20. Buses to Antigua pass the famous park of Los Aposentos, 3 km. (lake and swimming pool). Bus to Panajachel, US$1.

A side-road runs 21 km. N to San Martín **Jilotepeque** over deep *barrancas*; markets on Sun., Thurs. Bus from Chimaltenango, US$0.40. *Fiesta*: November 11. Fine weaving. Striking *huipiles* worn by the women. Ten km. beyond Chimaltenango is Zaragoza, former Spanish penal settlement, and beyond that (right) a road (13 km.) leads N to the interesting village of **Comalapa:** markets 1000-1430, Tues. and Fri., bright with Indian costumes. Fine old church of San Juan Bautista (1564). *Fiestas*: June 24, Dec. 8, 12.

There are several local artists working in Comalapa; no studios, so best to ask where you can see their work (Artexco cooperative, *Figura Antigua*). There is a *pensión* here, G.

Six km. beyond Zaragoza the road divides. The southern branch, the old Pan-American Highway, goes through Patzicía and Patzún to Lake Atitlán, then N to Los Encuentros. The northern branch, the new Pan-American Highway, much faster, goes past Tecpán and over the Chichoy pass, also to Los Encuentros. From Los Encuentros there is only the one road W to San Cristóbal Totonicapán, where the new road swings NW through El Tapón and La Mesilla to Ciudad

1038 GUATEMALA

Cuauhtémoc or El Ocotal, as it is sometimes called, the Mexican border settlement; and the old route goes W through Quezaltenango and San Marcos to Tapachula, in Mexico.

The northern road to Los Encuentros: from the fork the Pan-American Highway runs 19 km. to near **Tecpán**, which is slightly off the road at 2,287 metres. It has a particularly fine church: silver altars, carved wooden pillars, odd images, a wonderful ceiling which was severely damaged by the 1976 earthquake. The church is being slowly restored: the ceiling is missing and much of its adornment is either not in evidence, or moved to a church next door. The women wear most striking costumes. Market: Thursdays. *Fiestas:* May 3 (Santa Cruz), October 1-8, and December 8. *Hotel Iximché; Restaurant de la Montaña*, 1 km after the road to Tecpán; the owner of *Zapatería La Mejor* has a guest house, G; 1 km. before the Tecpán turn-off is the *Restaurant Alemana* (recommended). Buses from Guatemala City (Zona 4 terminal), 2¼ hrs., every hour; easy daytrip from Panajachel.

Near Tecpán are the very important Mayan ruins of **Iximché**, once capital and court of the Cakchiqueles, 5 km. of unpaved road from Tecpán, open 0900-1600 (admission US$0.20). Iximché was the first capital of Guatemala after its conquest by the Spaniards; followed in turn by Ciudad Vieja, Antigua and Guatemala City. A museum was due to open in 1986.

Beyond Tecpán the road swings up a spectacular 400 metres to the summit of the Chichoy pass. The pass is often covered in fog or rain but on clear days there are striking views. Some 14 km. from Tecpán, at km. 101, is the *Café Chichoy*, with cheap accommodation (recommended); 58 km. from the fork is Los Encuentros (and the road to Chichicastenango) and 3 km. further the new northern road joins the old southern one from Sololá.

Sololá, at 2,113 metres, 11 km. from the junction, has superb views across Lake Atitlán. Population 4,000. Fine Monday, Tuesday and Friday markets, to which many of the Indians go. Good selection of used *huipiles*. Note costumes of men. Great *fiesta* around August 15. Hot shower 500 metres from market on Panajachel road, behind Texaco station, US$0.18.

Tightly woven woollen bags are sold here: far superior to the usual type of tourist bags. Prices are high because of nearness of tourist centres of Panajachel and Chichicastenango.

Hotels *Letona*, G, communal, cheap food, not clean, outdoor washing facilities; *Pensión Salas*, G, basic, meals US$0.50, not recommended; *Posada Santa Elena*, G; *Pensión Paty*, on road to Panajachel, very basic, G. Also good cheap restaurant, *Santa Rosa*.

Bus to Chichicastenango US$0.25, 2 hrs. Bus to Panajachel, US$0.15, or 1½-2 hour walk. Colectivo to Los Encuentros, US$0.15.

From Sololá the old Pan-American Highway drops 550 metres in 8 km. to Panajachel: grand views on the way. Take the bus up (US$0.15, they stop early in the evening), but quite easy to walk down (the views are superb), either direct by the road or via San Jorge La Laguna. The walk is highly recommended. You can return to Panajachel from San Jorge along the lake, if you take the southern road from the plaza, go through the woods and down to the flats. Ask permission at the house on the lake shore to follow the trail; a 3-hour walk.

The southern road to Los Encuentros (much more difficult than the northern, with a very poor surface, steep hills and hairpin bends, bus, US$0.30) goes through **Patzicía**, a small Indian village founded 1545 (no accommodation). Market on Wed. and Sat. *Fiesta* for the patron, Santiago, on July 23-26. The famous church, which had a fine altar and beautiful silver, was destroyed by the 1976 earthquake; some of the silver is now in the temporary church. Fourteen km. beyond is the small town of **Patzún**; its famous church, dating from 1570, was severely damaged; it is still standing, but is not open to the public. Sun. market, which is famous for the silk (and wool) embroidered napkins worn by the women to church, and for woven *fajas* and striped red cotton cloth. *Fiesta:* May 17-21 (San Bernardino). Lodgings at the tobacco shop, G, or near market in unnamed *pensión*.

Road descends, then climbs to Godínez, 19 km. W of Patzún, where there is a

GUATEMALA 1039

good place for meals (no bus Patzún-Godínez after 1730). A branch road runs S to village of San Lucas Tolimán and continues to Santiago de Atitlán; both can be reached by a lake boat from Panajachel. The high plateau, with vast wheat and maize fields, now breaks away suddenly as though pared by a knife. From a viewpoint here, there is an incomparable view of Lake Atitlán, 600 metres below; beyond it rise three 3,000-metre-high volcano cones, Tolimán, Atitlán and San Pedro to the W. The very picturesque village of San Antonio Palopó is right underneath, on slopes leading to the water.

Occasional guerrilla activity and armed robbery have been reported in this area.

Lake Atitlán, 147 km. from the capital via the northern road and Los Encuentros, 116 km. via the southern road and Patzún, and 1,562 metres above sea-level, about 7-10 km. across and 18 km. long, is one of the most beautiful and colourful lakes in the world. It changes colour constantly— lapis lazuli, emerald, azure— and is shut in by purple mountains and olive green hills. Over a dozen villages on its shores, some named after the Apostles, house three tribes with distinct languages, costumes and cultures. The lake is the only place in the world where the *poc*, a large flightless water grebe, may be seen. Beware of robbers (armed) at the lake.

Six hotels are actually on the lakeshore: *Atitlán, Visión Azul, Monterrey, Del Lago, Playa Linda* and *Tzanjuyu*. Apart from them, visitors to the lake stay at or near **Panajachel,** 1 km. from the lake; the main attraction is the scenery. (Visitors planning to travel round the lake should be warned that the only bank here is here.) The town is a popular tourist resort and inhabited by many *gringos* ("Gringotenango"). There is water-skiing (at weekends), private boating (kayaks for hire) and swimming in fresh clear water (but the beach is dirty). Good market on Sun. mornings, especially for embroidery; you are expected to bargain (despite the amount of tourism, prices are reasonable). Visit La Galería (near *Rancho Grande Hotel*), where Nan Cuz, an Indian painter, sells her pictures which evoke the spirit of village life. The village church, originally built in 1567, was restored, only to be badly damaged by the 1976 earthquake. *Fiesta:* Oct. 2-6.

Hotels *Del Lago*, luxury hotel on lakeshore, B, pool, has boat to Santiago Atitlán, 0915 daily, US$5 return; *Atitlán*, C, 3 meals US$10, 1 km. W of centre on lake, excellent; *Tzanjuyu*, C, 3 meals US$10, a bit disappointing, balconies and private beach; *Monterrey*, D, discounts for longer stay, 3 meals US$9, restaurant fair; *El Aguacatal*, near *Hotel del Lago*, has bungalows, C, for 4, Tel.: 0621482; *Turicentro Los Geranios*, also near *Hotel del Lago*, has fully-equipped new bungalows which sleep 6, B, on Sat. and Sun., C, on other days, outdoor pool; *Bungalows Guayacán*, beautifully located among coffee bushes 700 metres from centre on road to Santa Catarina Palopó, D; *Rancho Grande*, cottages in charming setting, 4 blocks from beach, popular for long stay, good, simple food, D, includes breakfast, recommended; *Cacique Inn*, D (full board available), swimming pool, garden, English spoken, good food, recommended; *Regis*, E, well-kept house, friendly people, recommended; *Playa Linda*, above public beach, E, slow service in restaurant; *Visión Azul*, near *Hotel Atitlán*, D, and *Mini Motel Riva Bella*, bungalows, E, with bath; *Galindo*, on main street, E, with bath, unfriendly, good set meal, US$1.50; *Fonda del Sol*, on main street, F, with bath, noisy but comfortable, good restaurant; *Mayan Palace*, on main street, E, with shower, clean; *Maya Kanek*, near market, has annex, F, with bath, hot water, some rooms better than others, no food; *Las Casitas*, E, with private bath, noisy, not clean; *Del Viajero*, on main street, F, basic; *Panajachel*, near market, simple, F, hot water rarely, clean, lots of other travellers; *Casa Loma*, opp. *Hotel del Lago*, F; *Viajero Annex*, F, camping US$0.75 p.p.; *Hospedaje San Francisco*, G; *Rooms Santa Elena*, G, with bedding, beds uncomfortable, cheaper without, all facilities charged extra, friendly, clean, recommended; has annex which is O.K.; 2nd-hand English books on sale. There are a number of cheap *pensiones* on same road to the beach as Guatel building, including *Santander*, F (US$0.20 for shower), hot water, clean, friendly, lovely garden, recommended; *Villa Martita*, G, friendly, will do washing, recommended; *Hospedaje Ramos*, close to lake shore, G, run by an Indian family, friendly, safe, repeatedly recommended (despite some noise from nearby cafés); nearby *Bungalows El Rosario*, F, safe, clean, run by Indian family, hot water 0700-1100; *Hospedaje García*, same street as *Last Resort*, opp. *Galería*, G, clean, friendly, family atmosphere; *Casa Santizo Galindo*, Av. Los Arboles, F, hot shower (US$0.25), clean, quiet, friendly; *Pensión Londres*, G; *Casa Marcos*, G; *Mario's Rooms*, F, Tel.: 621313, with garden, clean, hard beds, noisy from *Last Resort*, hot water (sheets US$0.35, good breakfast US$0.55), *Chico's*, *Vista Hermosa* (basic, but very pleasant family, hot showers) all G. For long stay, ask around for houses to rent; available at all prices from US$10-75 a month, but almost impossible to find in November and December. The water supply is generally bad, with water usually only available 0630-1100.

1040 GUATEMALA

Camping No problem, but campsites (US$0.50 p.p.) are dirty. Camping on the lakeshore is currently allowed in a designated area; some distance from the beach is Parque Panajachel Trailer Park on same road as Guatel, charges US$0.50 p.p. (intermittent water); also laundry and sauna. Camping gas for sale in supermarket on main street.

Restaurants Many of the higher priced hotels have restaurants open to the public. *Las Brasas*, on main street, pleasant dining, reasonable prices; *Restaurant de La Laguna*, patio dining, good value; *Fonda del Sol*, large varied menu, reasonable prices, all on same road as Guatel. *The Last Resort*, on left after Guatel building, "gringo bar", good food (especially breakfast), bar (open 1800). On Guatel road, *Villa Martita*, recommended, and *Ranchón Típico Atitlán*, good. *Blue Bird*, on side street to market, specials recommended US$0.75, good yoghurt and fruit salad (closed Thursdays). *El Cisne*, opposite *Hotel del Lago*, good cheap meals. *Brisas del Lago*, good meals at reasonable prices, all on main street. *El Paraíso*, large meals, inc. vegetarian, in lane, off main street, to lake. *Atitlán Fiesta* near market. On the side street to the market are a number of vegetarian restaurants: *Comedor Hsieh*, nearest to market, great variety of dishes, recommended, *Casa de Pays* (pie shop, also known as *La Zanahoria*), good food, good value, clean and friendly (shows English language videos in evening US$0.60). Two small *comedores* on the public beach and others on the Guatel road to the lakeshore. *Copo's*, opposite Texaco station, has ice-cream. Go to *Panadería San Martín* at 1500 for fresh brown and banana bread. *El Bistro*, Swiss-owned, "overpriced, bland food", near beach on same road as Guatel; *Restaurant Sicodélico*, near *Mario's Rooms*, is pleasant but grubby (good yoghurt and crêpes). The yoghurt dishes at *Mario's* restaurant are highly recommended; also serves pizza or lasagne on Sat. and Sun. night. *Jebel* (same management as *Blue Bird*), on road to beach, good yoghurt, avocado omelette, recommended. *Munchies*, good snacks, chocolates and cakes. *El Unico Deli*, coffee shop, dear, but nice food.

Entertainment *Poco Loco*, has video films for US$0.50 (one must buy a drink to enter), loud music, food, bar; *Posada del Pintor*, same street, bar and restaurant, cheap beer and steaks, owner is a Swiss couple; *Shell Station Bar*, on site of old gas station, often has live music and dancing, and films on T.V. *Past Ten* discotheque, open till 0400, Q3 entry. Opp. *Hotel del Lago*, *Circus Bar*, good live music; *The Last Resort*, bar and restaurant, popular, table tennis, foreign magazines; next door, *Los Techos*, above *Cakchiquel* restaurant, English language films on video twice daily.

Shops Many small stores selling local handicrafts including *Tomás Xon*, on Guatel road, and *Mundo Real* which has jewellery and authentic weaving (they also buy, sell and swap used books), and *Caramba*, both on main street. Also on road to San Andrés Semetebaj is the *Idol's House*, an antique shop where you must bargain. (Indians sell their wares cheaply on the lakeside.)

Motor Bike Hire From opposite *Poco Loco*, US$6 per day; check lights and fill up before setting out. Hiring of bicycles, US$2-3 a day.

Health There are good clinics at Santiago Atitlán and San Lucas Tolimán, which specialize in treating dysentery. Amoebic dysentery and hepatitis are less common than in the past. Treatment free, so a donation is appropriate.

Bank Mon.-Thurs. 0900-1500. Fri. to 1530. Exchange after 1000. Prefers to change smaller denomination travellers' cheques. Better rates at Toro Pinto exchange office (0900-1800). The barber's shop near the bank will change travellers' cheques.

Post Office Will not arrange for parcels to be sent, or received from, abroad.

Tourist Office Open Wed.-Fri., 0800-1200 and 1400-1800, Mon. and Sat. 0800-1200, Tues. closed; has maps. (Sells flight tickets for Flores.)

Bus Rebuli, first class to Guatemala City, 3 hrs. US$1.25; run 5 direct buses to the capital daily. There are direct buses to Los Encuentros on the Pan-American Highway (US$0.25). To Chichicastenango direct 4 in morning and on Sun. at 0730 (US$1). Change at Los Encuentros for other buses to Guatemala City, Chichicastenango, or Quezaltenango. Direct bus to Quezaltenango 0600. There are direct buses to Cuatro Caminos, US$0.40 (see page 1045) from 0530, for connections to Totonicapán, Quezaltenango, Huehuetenango, etc. (No buses from Los Encuentros to Panajachel after 1830). Bus to Chimaltenango (for Antigua), US$0.75. Bus to Sololá, US$0.15.

Excursions To **Santiago Atitlán** by mail boat from the pier at the *Hotel Tzanjuyu* at 0845 and 1135 daily (check at hotel for times of services), US$1.25 single, US$2 return (back to Panajachel at 1200 and 1700). From the beach, many between 0900-0930, returning between 1200 and 1700, US$1 single. By bus to San Lucas Tolimán, and from there by bus, US$0.65. The road is very rough for private cars after San Lucas. The women wear full costumes and the men wear striped, half-length embroidered trousers. There is an Artexco cooperative: *Flor del Lago*. There is a daily market, best on Friday, Fiesta: June 5 and July 25. The Franciscan church dates back to 1568. Nearby were the ruins of the fortified Tzutuhil capital on the Cerro de Chuitinamit (nothing now to see). *Pensión Rosita*, near the church, F, dirty. *Brisas del Lago*, on way to market, G (pay extra US$1 for sheets); *Hospedaje Chi-Nim-Ya*, G, hot water but problematic supply (good café

GUATEMALA 1041

opposite). Houses can be rented, but be extremely careful to check for, and protect against, scorpions and poisonous spiders in the wooden frames. *Santa Rita* restaurant good and cheap. Bus to Guatemala City, US$1 (5 a day, first at 0300). Buses back to Panajachel 0600, 4 hrs.

At **San Lucas Tolimán** there is cheap basic accommodation at *Café Tolimán* (poor sanitary conditions, but good yoghurt), and *Jorge's Pensión*, at water's edge, G, in 4-bedded room, excellent breakfasts. San Lucas is well-known for the making of sisal ropes. There is a market on Tues., Fri., and Sun. From San Lucas the cones of Atitlán, 3,535 metres, and Tolimán, 3,158 metres, can be climbed. Warm clothing and sleeping gear are essential, as the climb takes 2 days (less if you are very fit); maps available at *American Pay* (pie) restaurant. There is a good cheap *pensión*, *Santa Ana*, G, and restaurants *American Pay* and *Jorge's* on the lakeside. Bus to San Lucas from Panajachel at 0700 and 0830 daily, US$0.50. A bus leaves San Lucas for Santiago at 0900, 1200 and 1500, 1 hr., (US$0.25, returning at the same times). It is difficult to return to Panajachel the same day, unless one gets the bus at 1200. Direct buses back to Panajachel along paved road one km. out of San Lucas (one passes at noon). Bus San Lucas to Quezaltenango, US$1, frequent; a few start at Santiago. Between Santiago and San Lucas is Cerro de Oro, a small village on the lake.

Ferries leave from *Hotel Tzanjuyu* at Panajachel for **San Pedro La Laguna**, daily at 0400, Tues., Fri. and Sun. at 1500, returning at 0630 on Mon., Wed., Sat., and at 1600 daily (US$0.75 one way). There is a ferry from Santiago to San Pedro at 1200 and 1700 (45 mins., US$0.75) locals pay less (ferry to Santiago at 0700 and 0800). 0300 bus to Guatemala City, US$1.50, 7 hrs. San Pedro is at the foot of the San Pedro volcano (which can be climbed in 4-5 hrs., but after 1000 the top is usually smothered in cloud) and is surrounded by coffee plantations. Canoes are made here (hire, US$0.50 a day) and a visit to the rug-making cooperative on the beach is of interest. Backstrap weaving is taught at *Casa Felipe*, and other places, about US$0.50 per day. Market days Thurs. and Sun. (better). There are many *pensiones*, including two on the public beach, at about US$0.50. (*Pensión Balneario*, G, good, *Pensión Chuazanahi*, G (known as the Colonel's Place), bedding US$0.50 p.p., boating and swimming, you can sling your hammock for US$1; *Johanna*, near landing stage for Panajachel mail boat, G, nice rooms without bath, cold water only, friendly; *Hotel Felix* and *Hotel Felipe*, both G, clean and friendly, all are basic; houses can be rented on a weekly basis for US$2.50). Pizzas and fresh wholemeal bread can be obtained from *Panadería El Buen Gusto*. Good food is available at *Restaurant Chez Michel*, for US$0.75 (some French spoken), turn right from landing stage along beach road, past *Pensión Chuazanahi; Lucky; La Carolina*; *Pirámides*, in the village, run by gringos, very slow service, also good food but slow service at *Comedor Francés* on lake shore, and at *Casa Felipe* for US$0.65. Village café, meals US$0.30. Dugouts can be hired for US$0.50 per day. From San Pablo (on the way to San Pedro) you can walk to San Marcos and Santa Cruz (a difficult track), where there is a 16th century church, you can get beautiful views of the lake and volcanoes in the early morning light. Sisal bags and hammocks are made at San Pablo. If hiking around the lake, remember there are no hotels between San Pedro and Panajachel.

Warning Not a safe area for women to go walking alone; rape is not uncommon. Beware of theft, including of clothes hanging out to dry, in the Lake Atitlán area. Also beware of overcharging on private boats crossing the lake: practices include doubling the price half-way across and if you don't agree, out you get.

Santa Catalina Palopó is within walking distance of Panajachel (about 2 hrs.; truck US$0.12). The town has an attractive adobe church. Reed mats are made here, and you can buy *huipiles* and men's shirts. Must bargain for articles. (Houses can be rented here.)

San Antonio Palopó (6 km. beyond Santa Catalina) has another splendid church; it lies at the head of the lake in an amphitheatre formed by the mountains behind. The village is noted for the costumes and headdresses of the men, and *huipiles* and shirts are cheaper than in Santa Catalina. *Fiesta*: June 14. The Artexco cooperative is called by the name of the village. *Hotel Casa de don Félix* (or *Casa del Lago*), superb views and good bathing, E, only a few rooms but gradually being expanded, good restaurant. A good hike is to take the bus from Panajachel to Godínez, walk down from there to San Antonio Palopó (1 hr.) and then along the new road back to Panajachel via Santa Catalina Palopó (3 hrs.).

San Andrés Semetebaj, about 6½ km. from Panajachel, has a beautiful ruined early 17th-century church. Market on Tues.

All the villages around the lake can be reached by bus or car, on rough roads.

Los Encuentros The old and new Pan-American Highways rejoin 11 km. from Sololá. 3 km. E is Los Encuentros, the junction of the Pan-American Highway and the road 18 km. NE to Chichicastenango. Altitude 2,579 metres. (Very poor accommodation available, G, if you miss a bus connection, easy to do as they are all full.)

Chichicastenango (also known as Santo Tomás) is the hub of the Maya-Quiché highlands, and is very popular with tourists. Altitude 2,071 metres, and nights cold. About 1,000 *ladinos* in the town, but 20,000 Indians live in the hills

1042 GUATEMALA

near-by and flood the town, almost empty on other days, for the Thursday and Sunday markets. The town is built around a large square plaza of 180 metres a side, with two churches facing one another: Santo Tomás parish church and Calvario. Santo Tomás is now open again to visitors, although restoration work is still going on; photography is not allowed, and visitors are asked to be discreet and enter by a side door. Groups burn incense and light candles on steps and platform before entering. Inside, from door to high altar, stretch rows of glimmering candles, Indians kneeling beside them. Later they offer copal candles and flower-petals to the "Idolo", a black image of Pascual Abaj, a Mayan god, on a hilltop 1½ km. SW of the plaza. Next to the church are the cloisters of the Dominican monastery (1542) where the famous Popol Vuh manuscript of Mayan mythology was found in 1690; Father Rossbach's jade collection can be seen in the municipal museum on the main square and is well worth a visit (open 0800-1200, closed Tues.), and so is the house of a mask-maker on the way up to the "Idolo", who rents masks and costumes to the dancers and will show visitors the path to the idol. This is a little difficult to find even then, and clear instructions should be obtained before setting out.

Derivation of town's name: *chichicas*—a prickly purple plant like a nettle, which grows profusely—and *tenango*, place of. The town itself is charming: winding streets of white houses roofed with bright red tiles wandering over a little knoll in the centre of a cup-shaped valley surrounded by high mountains. Fine views from every street corner. The costumes are particularly splendid: the men's is a short-waisted embroidered jacket and knee breeches of black cloth, a gay woven sash and an embroidered kerchief round the head. The cost of this outfit, over US$200, means that fewer and fewer men are in fact wearing it. Women wear *huipiles* with red embroidery against black or brown and skirts with dark blue stripes. The Sun. market is more colourful than the one on Thurs.: more Indians, brighter costumes and dancing to marimba bands, but it certainly becomes very touristy after the buses arrive from Guatemala City (bargains may be had after 1530 when the tourist buses depart). In fact the markets begin, and are better, on the previous p.m. Sololá and Panajachel shirts are cheaper, and better, here than in their own markets. You must bargain hard. It is said one can shop around and get things more cheaply on Sat. or Wed. afternoon.

Fiestas Santo Tomás, December 17-21: processions, dances, marimba music (well worth a visit); Holy Week; November 1; January 20; March 19; June 24 (shepherds). There is also a *fiesta* at the end of May.

Hotels *Mayan Inn*, C (charges in US dollars), with beautiful colonial furnishings (mixed reports): a museum in itself; 3 meals US$7.50, bar, marimba music; *Santo Tomás*, C (often full at weekends), very good, friendly service, helpful owner (Sr. Magermans), good restaurant and bar, marimba music p.m., same day laundry, old building with home patio, meals US$2.50; nearby *El Salvador*, 10 C. 4-47, 2 blocks from main square, E with sheets but no bath, friendly, noisy; *Maya Lodge*, 6 C. 4-08, E with bath and up, with breakfast, good; *Martita*, F, with bath and sheets (G without either); guest house of Señora Jenny Taylor, F, with hot water (Sra. Taylor is English, and has lived in the town for over 35 years); *Pensión Chigüilá*, 5 Av. 5-24, clean, good, E, with bath and breakfast, F without, meals another US$3.85 (some rooms have fireplaces, wood costs US$0.90 a day extra), F, without sheets, *Pensión-Restaurant Katokok* serves good meals; *Posada San Antonio*, F (less without sheets), good but basic; *Cantina Claveles*, G, for a poor room, but US$0.35 for a good meal. There is a bakery attached. *Pensión Girón*, F (G without sheets), opp. vegetable market, good, ample parking. Local boys will show you other cheap lodgings, G.

Restaurants *Tapena*, 5 Av. 5-21, clean, good value; *Las Marimbitas; El Samaritano* (reasonable).

Buses Rutas Lima bus leaves Guatemala City four times daily for Quezaltenango, connecting at Los Encuentros for Panajachel (US$0.25) and Chichicastenango. The slower Reyna de Utatlán bus from the capital, 4 hrs. (Zona 4 Terminal) costs only US$1.50, several daily. For return, take local bus (US$0.25) to Los Encuentros where you can pick up another for the capital. One direct bus to Panajachel on Sun. at 1330 from *Hotel Santo Tomás*, US$1, and others in week. For Antigua, change at Chimaltenango. Beware of overcharging on buses in the Panajachel/Chichicastenango area. To Huehuetenango, via Los Encuentros, US$1.12. 2 weekly buses Chichicastenango-Nebaj, US$1, may have to change at Sacapulas, otherwise take a bus to Quiché and change there.

The Quiché Region (see warning on page 1013.) 19 km. N by road from Chichicastenango is Santa Cruz del **Quiché**, a quaint town at 2,000 metres, colourful market on Sun. and Thurs. There are few tourists here and prices are consequently reasonable. Good selection of local cloth. Quiché's speciality is palm hats, which are made and worn in the area. Population 7,750. Remains 5 km. away of palaces of former Quiché capital, Gumarcaj, sometimes spelt Kumarkaah and known also as Utatlán, destroyed by Spaniards; the ruins consist of

GUATEMALA

adobe mounds, their chief attraction being the setting. They can be reached on foot (¾-hr. walk W along 10 Calle from bus station) open 0700-1800, entry US$0.20. *Fiestas:* about August 14-20 (but varies around Assumption), May 3. Serious earthquake damage.

Hotels *San Pascual*, 7 C. 0-43, F, with hot showers, clean, quiet, locked parking; *Hospedaje Hermano Pedro*, F, friendly, clean, private shower, close to bus terminal so arrive early; *Posada Calle Real*, 2 Av. 7-36, parking, F, clean, friendly, recommended; *Pensión Santa Clara*, G, hot water, plus US$0.50 for good meals; *Pensión Xelajú*, at bus terminal, G, bargain, dirty; *Tropical*, 1 Av. 9 C., G. Basic accommodation near bus terminal. Restaurant: *Lago Azul*, 2 Av. 6-45, quite good, pricey; *Musicafé* and one next to it, with bookshop, reasonable; most are dirty. Thermal baths at Pachitac, 4 km. away, and beside the market building.

Electric current 220 volts.

Cinema 3 Av. y 6 C.

Bank Banco de Guatemala, 3 C. y 2 Av.

Buses Terminal at 10 C. y 1 Av. Reyna de Utatlán from Guatemala City (US$1). ½ hr. from Chichicastenango, US$0.20, every ½ hr. from *Pensión Chigüilá*. At 1030 to Nebaj, US$1.15, 5 hrs.; a rough but breathtaking trip (may leave early if full). At 1000, 1130 and 1330 to Uspantán, 5 hrs., US$1.20. Bus to Joyabaj, 0930 daily, US$0.50, 1½ hrs. 0300 bus Uspantán to Cobán and San Pedro Carchá, about 5 hrs., the best part is done in darkness.

There is a paved road E from Quiché to (8 km.) Santo Tomás Chiche, a picturesque village with a fine rarely-visited Indian Sat. market (*fiesta*, December 21-28). Buses and vans (US$0.15) run from Quiché. (There is also a road to this village from Chichicastenango. Although it is a short-cut, it is rough and should be attempted in dry weather only, and even then only in a sturdy vehicle.)

On 32 km. from Chiche is **Zacualpa**, where beautiful woollen bags are woven. There is an unnamed *pensión* near the square; on the square itself is a private house which has cheap rooms and meals. (Mosquito coils are a must.) Market: Sun., Thurs. Church with remarkably fine façade. On another 11 km. is **Joyabaj**, where women weave fascinating *huipiles*; there is nowhere to stay, but the mayor may have some ideas. This was a stopping place on the old route from Mexico to Antigua. During *fiesta* week (the second in August) Joyabaj has a *palo volador*—two men dangle from a 20-metre pole while the ropes they are attached to unravel to the ground. The villages of San Pedro and San Juan Sacatepéquez (see page 1025) can be reached from Joyabaj by a dry-season road suitable only for strong vehicles. The scenery en route is spectacular (Joyita bus, Guatemala City 3-4 Av. 7-9 C. Zona 4, to Joyabaj, US$1.).

Road N from Quiché, 48 km., to **Sacapulas**, 1,220 metres, at foot of Cuchumatanes mountains, highest in the country. Bus from Quiché, at 1000, very crowded, US$1, 3 hrs. for rough journey; 6 buses to Quiché. Bus to Huehuetenango via Aguacatán (see below), at 0500, 4½ hrs, road can be closed in rainy season. Remains of bridge over Río Negro built by Las Casas. Primitive salt extraction. Market under large ceiba tree on Sunday. The only *pensión* is *Comedor Gloris* near the bridge (G), which is basic, cheap and friendly, poor meals, US$0.65. British travellers are made very welcome at *Comedor Central* near the market. Colonial church with surprising treasures inside, built 1554, and there are communal hot springs.

The road E to Cobán from Sacapulas is one of the most beautiful, if rough, mountain roads in all Guatemala, with magnificent scenery in the narrow valleys. Truck to Cobán, 5 daily a.m., US$1, 5 hrs. There is no direct bus to Cobán; instead, take one of the three Quiché-Uspantán buses (passing Sacapulas at about 1230, 1400, 1600) to Uspantán, *fiesta* May 6-10 (US$0.60) stay the night at the *Viajero* (3 blocks E of Plaza, basic, G, fleas), then take early morning bus (0300-0400, you can spend the night on the bus before it leaves) or hitch-hike to Cobán. (Truck Uspantán-San Cristóbal Verapaz, US$1.25.) Buses to Quiché at 0530, 0700, 1530. A morning bus starts at 0200 in Quiché, with a change at Cunén (*fiesta* February 1-4).

Branching off this road, about 5 km. N of Sacapulas, is a spectacular road to the Indian villages of Nebaj and Chajul. It is easy enough to get by truck to Nebaj

(US$0.50) and there is a daily bus from Quiché, passing through these villages. It is not so easy to Chajul and San Juan Cotzal. There are no lodging or restaurant facilities in Chajul or other small villages and it is very difficult to specify what transport facilities are in fact available in this area as trucks and the occasional pick-up or commercial van (probably the best bet—ask, especially in *Las Tres Hermanas*, Nebaj) are affected by road and weather conditions. For this reason, be prepared to have to spend the night in Chajul, Cotzal or other villages, even though there is no accommodation. Chajul has a pilgrimage to Christ of Golgotha on the second Friday in Lent, beginning the Wednesday before (the image is escorted by "Romans" in current-issue, Guatemalan camouflage fatigues!) Also hunting with blowpipes.

Nebaj has *Las Tres Hermanas*, G (friendly, very basic), good food available for about US$0.50; *Las Gemelitas*, nice, basic, cheap meals (book in advance), recommended. Alternatively you can get a room in a private house for slightly less. There is also an army camp. Chajul has market Tues. and Fri. In Cotzal it is possible to stay in the monastery, market Sat. *Huipiles* may be bought from María Santiago Chel (central market) or Juana Marcos Solís (Cantón Simacol), who gives weaving lessons from 1 day to 6 months. This village has a very good Sun. market (also on Thurs.). Nebaj has a *fiesta* on August 15. There are magnificent walks from Nebaj along the river or in the surrounding hills. Although the weather is not very good at this altitude, the views of the Cuchumatanes mountains are spectacular. From Nebaj, bus to Sacapulas and Quiché 0100, 0200, and on Sun. 0600, 2½ hrs. to Sacapulas (US$0.60), a further 3 to Quiché.

2 hours' walk from Nebaj is Acul, one of the new villages settled by the government to control guerrilla activity. It has water, electricity, a doctor and school, but "the people obviously are not happy there."

The views are also fine on the road which runs W from Sacapulas to (36 km.) **Aguacatán** at 1,670 metres (*Pensión La Paz*, G, unsigned *Hospedaje*, 2 blocks E of market and 1 North, G) and to Huehuetenango (another 32 km.—see page 1047). Aguacatán has an interesting market on Sunday (beginning Saturday night) and Thursday (excellent peanuts). The women wear beautiful costumes and head-dresses. There are buses to Huehuetenango at 0530 and 1630 daily, with returns from Huehuetenango at 0345 and 1600 daily, US$0.50. Bus to Chichicastenango at 0400, very crowded, or take a truck.

Western Guatemala

The stretch of Pan-American Highway between Los Encuentros and San Cristóbal Totonicapán runs past **Nahualá**, at 2,470 metres, a most interesting Indian village where *metates*, or stones on which maize is ground to make *tortillas*, are made. The inhabitants wear distinctive costumes, and are considered by other Indians to be somewhat hostile. Good church. Market on Thursdays and Sundays, at which finely embroidered cuffs and collars are sold, also very popular *huipiles*, but check the colours, many run. No accommodation except perhaps with Indian families at a small cost. *Fiesta* (Santa Catalina) on November 25. Population 1,369.

There is another all-weather road a little to the N and 16 km. longer, from Los Encuentros to San Cristóbal Totonicapán. In 40 km. it reaches Totonicapán.

Totonicapán, 14½ km. E of Cuatro Caminos (see below), is the capital of its Department, at 2,500 metres. Population 52,000, almost all Indian. There are sulphur baths, but they are dirty and crowded. Market (mind out for pickpockets) considered by Guatemalans to be one of the cheapest, and certainly very colourful, on Tues. (small), and Sat. (the main market noted for ceramics and cloth—very good); annual fair September 26-30; *fiestas* on September 29 and July 25. The school of handicrafts in the centre of town is well worth a visit. *Chuimekená* cooperative is at 3 C. between 7 and 8 Avs., Zona Palín. Frequent buses to Quezaltenango along a paved road (fine scenery), US$0.25, and there are buses from Quiché at 0400 and 0500 daily on a little-travelled but spectacular route (bus returns at 1030, US$0.50, 4 hrs). Bus to Los Encuentros, US$1.25.

GUATEMALA 1045

Hotels On 4 Calle: *Pensión Rosario*, G, basic and dirty; *Hospedaje San Miguel*, 2 blocks from town square, F, clean, comfortable.

San Cristóbal Totonicapán, 1 km. from the Cuatro Caminos road junction (Pan-American Highway, with the roads to Quezaltenango, Totonicapán, Los Encuentros and Huehuetenango; *Hotel y Restaurant Reforma*, F, Tel.: 066-1438) has a huge church, built by Franciscan friars, of which the roof has recently been renovated. The silver lamps, altars and screens, all hand-hammered, and Venetian glass altars are worth seeing. Noted for textiles (and *huipiles* in particular) sold all over Guatemala; they are cheap here because the town is off the main tourist circuit. Also well known for ceramics. Market, Sunday, on the other side of the river from the church (only 2 blocks away), spreading along many streets. Annual fair, July 20-26. Altitude 2,340 metres, population 3,186. Two hotels. Bus service to Quezaltenango.

Excursion Two km. W of the Cuatro Caminos junction a road runs N to San Francisco El Alto (3 km.) and Momostenango (19 km.). **San Francisco El Alto,** at 2,640 metres (also reached by a new paved road 5 km. W of Cuatro Caminos, at Km. 151), stands in the mountain cold, above the great valley in which lie Totonicapán, San Cristóbal and Quezaltenango. Church of metropolitan magnificence. Crammed market on Friday; Indians buying woollen blankets for resale throughout country, and fascinating cattle market. An excellent place for buying woven and embroidered textiles of good quality, but beware of pickpockets. Colourful New Year's Day celebrations. It is a pleasant walk from San Francisco down to the valley floor, then along the river to San Cristóbal. There is a bus from Totonicapán at 0800 on Fri. Bus from Quezaltenango on Fri., 20 mins., from market terminus, US$0.25 (go early if you wish to avoid staying overnight).

Hotel *Hospedaje Central San Francisco de Asís* on main street near market, G. *Buena Vista*, F, clean but cold, no hot water.

Momostenango, at 2,220 metres, is the chief blanket-weaving centre. Indians can be seen beating the blankets on stones to shrink them. The Feast of the Uajxaquip Vats (pronounced "washakip") is celebrated by 30,000 Indians every 260 days by the ancient Mayan calendar. Frequent masked dances also. Momostenango means "place of the altars", and there are many on the outskirts but they are not worth looking for; there is, however, a hilltop image of a Mayan god, similar to the one outside Chichicastenango. There are said to be 300 medicine-men practising in the town; their insignia of office is a little bag containing beans and quartz crystals. Outside town are three sets of *riscos:* eroded columns of sandstone with embedded quartz particles, which are worth visiting. The most striking are the least accessible, in the hills to the N of the town. The town is quiet except on Wed. and Sun., the market days (the latter being larger, and interesting for weaving; also try Tienda Manuel del Jesús Agancel, 1 Av., 1-50, Zona 4; on non-market days, ask for weavers' houses). It has a spring-fed swimming pool; also a sulphur bath (5 in all) at Palo Grande, near town; the water is black, but worth experiencing. Bus service from Cuatro Caminos (US$0.25) and Quezaltenango, US$0.38.

Accommodation *Hospedaje Roxane*, G, bad; *Hospedaje Paclom*, G, basic, hot water, cheap meals. *Comedor Tonia*, friendly, cheap.

At San Cristóbal the old and the new routes of the Pan-American Highway, which joined at Los Encuentros, part again. The new route to the Mexican border at Ciudad Cuauhtémoc (not a town, despite its name: just a few buildings) goes NW, by-passing Huehuetenango before entering the Selegua canyon stretch, known as El Tapón, now in very good condition. The old route, running W to Tapachula, in Mexico, reaches, 5 km. from San Cristóbal, the small *ladino* town of

Salcajá, well worth a visit. Jaspé skirt material has been woven here since 1861. Yarn is tied and dyed, then untied and warps stretched around telephone poles along the road or along the riverside. Many small home weavers will sell the

1046 GUATEMALA

lengths—5 or 8 *varas*—depending on whether the skirt is to be wrapped or pleated. The finest, of imported English yarn, cost US$40. The Artexco cooperative is *San Luis*, Calle Capitán Juan de León y Cardona, Zona 2. Market, Tues.; it is early, as in all country towns. The church of San Jacinto behind the market is 16th century and also worth a visit. (Good restaurant, *Cafesama*.) The taxi rate is US$2.50-3 per hour. Several minibuses a day from new commercial centre, 10 Av. and 8 C.

Quezaltenango, 14½ km. SW of Cuatro Caminos, over 100,000 people, is the most important city in western Guatemala. Altitude 2,335 metres, and climate decidedly cool (particularly November to April, and there is no heating anywhere). Set among a group of high mountains and volcanoes, one of which, Santiaguito, the lower cone of Santa María (which can be easily climbed), destroyed the city in 1902 and is still active sometimes. A modern city, but with narrow colonial-looking streets, a magnificent plaza (between 11 and 12 Av. and 4 and 7 Calle), and a most varied daily market. Especially interesting is the stately but quaint Municipal Theatre (14 Av. and 1 C.); there is also a small museum on the S side of the Plaza. There is a modern gothic-style church, the Sagrado Corazón, on the Parque Juárez near the market; other churches include San Juan de Dios on 14 Av. and La Transfiguración, from which there is a good view. The cathedral is modern with a 17th-century façade. A National Artisan Park has been built but is almost abandoned; there are a textile museum, warehouses, a craft school, showrooms, shop and restaurant. Festivals March 30-April 5, Sept. 12-18 and Holy Week (very interesting). There is a museum on the S side of the Parque Central, open Mon.-Fri., 0900-1700. A good centre for buses to all parts of the Indian highlands. Airfield. Tourist cards (free) for Mexico can be obtained from the Mexican consulate at the *Pensión Bonifaz*. (All addresses given are in Zona 1, unless otherwise stated.)

Warning Local people always call the town by its old name of Xelajú, or "Xela" (pronounced "Shayla").

Hotels *Pensión Bonifaz*, 4 C. 10-50, D, 3 meals US$7, good restaurant (really not a *pensión* but an excellent hotel), clean, comfortable, quiet; *Del Campo*, at city limits (4 km.) on road to Cuatro Caminos, D, good meals; *Los Alpes*, Zona 3, Swiss-owned, private bath, recommended; *Quetzalcoatl Inn*, Boulevard Minerva 14-09, Zona 3, D; *Modelo*, 14 Av. 'A', 2-31, D, good, with good restaurant; *Casa Suiza*, 14 Av. 'A', 2-36, F, without bath, constant hot water; *Casa Kaehler*, 13 Av. 3-33, F without bath; *Kiktem-Ja*, 13 Av. 7-18, E, all with bath, recommended; *Canadá*, 4 C. 12-22, F, helpful but dirty, humid, overpriced; *Pensión Andina*, 8 Av., 6-01, F with bath, no hot water; *Casa del Viajero*, F, with bath, recommended; *Capri*, 8 C., 11-39, F, with bath, dirty, basic; *Pensión Altense*, 9 C. and 9 Av., G, meals US$0.75, good and clean, hot water extra; *Fénix*, 9 Av. 6-73, G; *El Aguila*, 12 Av. and 3 C., F, friendly, hot water extra; *Residencial*, nearby, F, good; *Victoria*, 6 C. 14-09, G, clean, hot water early a.m., shared rooms, good meals US$0.75 p.p.; *Hospedaje Central*, G, *Pensión Regia*, 9 Av. 8-26. *Oriani*, 12 Av. and 2 C., F, friendly, not very clean.

Restaurants *Bikini*, 10 C., behind municipal offices, *Shanghai*, expensive and poor; Chinese restaurant next to Hotel *Canadá*; *Kopetin*, 1 block from Hotel *Canadá*, friendly, good, meat and seafood dishes; *Maruc*, near brewery, good but expensive; *Pájaro Azul*, E side of central Plaza; *Taberna de Don Rodrigo*, 14 Av. 2-42, hamburgers and beer, cakes and coffee; *Delicadezas La Polonesa*, 14 Av. 'A' 4-71, snacks, cold meats, sausage, etc.; *Acuario Zurich*, 14 Av. 3-11, Swiss-owned, coffee, tea and good pies (no meals); *La Rueda* (new name of *Bonanza*), by University in Zona 3, good snacks, somewhat expensive; *Buena Vista* on square, reasonable; *El Portalito*, Av. 12 just above the square, good, cheap; *Pollo Chivo*, US$1 for chicken meals; Hotel *Modelo* restaurant (open earlier than most others); *Restaurant Capri*, next to Hotel *Capri*, poor meals from US$1.50; *La Oropendola*, 3 C., good light meals; *Bombonier*, 14 Av. 2-20, new, snacks, excellent pastries and ice-cream.

Shopping *Artexco*, the National Federation of Artisans' Cooperatives, has its headquarters at 7 Av. 15-97, Zona 5, and at Local No. 12, Centro Comercial Municipal; also at *Luna de Xelajú*, 9 C. 9-36, Zona 1; prices are fixed and quite high; for local items better to try the markets. In the same area you can have clothes made up very cheaply. Fine small boutique selling local handicrafts, handmade textiles and traditional costumes of excellent quality in *Los Mangos* restaurant. *Curiosidades La Chivita* makes up locally produced woollen blankets into jackets.

Laundry Minimax, Av. 12, No. C-47, 0730-1930, US$0.75, wash and dry.

Banks Many on the central plaza. Banco de Guatemala, W side, Mon.-Thurs. 0830-1400, Fri. to 1430.

GUATEMALA 1047

Cinemas Cadore, 13 Av. and 7 C., Roma, 14 Av. 'A' and Calle 'A'; from US$0.15.

Communications Post and Telegraph Office, 15 Av. and 4 Calle, Telephone (Guatel) 15 Av. 'A' and 4 Calle.

Spanish Language Schools KIN (a cooperative); another cooperative, Instituto Cooperativa Azumanche, 3 Calle, 15-16, Zona 1, recommended. International School of Spanish, 8a. Avenida 6-33, Zona 1, Aptdo Postal 265 (Tel.: 061-4784), cost for 5 hrs: tuition, room and 3 meals a day: 2 weeks US$225, 3 weeks, US$325, 4 weeks, US$425. Proyecto Lingüístico Xelajú, 1 C, 16-87, Zona 1, Tel.: 2631.

Tourist Office SW corner of the Plaza, Mon.-Fri., 0900-1200, 1430-1700. Helpful. Free maps of city and leaflet on local villages and markets. Ask here for the Club de Andinismo for information on mountain climbing in the area.

Buses Rutas Lima, NE corner of Plaza (11 Av. and 4 C.), 4 a day to Guatemala City (US$1.75, 3½ hours). The 0800 bus has connections to Chichicastenango, Panajachel and Sololá (US$1.50, 2½ hrs.). Galgos, E side of Plaza, 1st class buses to Guatemala City, 5 a day (US$2, 4 hrs; will carry bicycles.). For Antigua, change at Chimaltenango (Galgos, US$1.75). Rutas Lima to Huehuetenango 0500 and 1530, US$0.50; to frontier at La Mesilla, 0500, US$2 (cheaper if change at Huehuetenango); to frontier at Talismán bridge 0500 via Tecún Umán (US$2, 3 hrs.). Rutas Lima to San Pedro (see page 1050) at 1200. Regular buses from 10 Av., 8 C. to Cuatro Caminos US$0.75 (where buses for Guatemala City and Huehuetenango stop on the highway; bus Guatemala City-Cuatro Caminos, US$1.50), Totonicapán, 1 hr. (US$0.25) San Francisco El Alto (US$0.25) and Momostenango (0600, US$0.38). Also many second class buses to many parts of the country from Zona 3 market (13 Av. 4 C. ° A'); e.g. Transportes Velásquez to Huehuetenango, US$0.50; to Malacatán, US$1; to Los Encuentros, US$0.75; to Chichicastenango, US$0.50, 1200, 2 hrs.; to Zunil, US$0.20; also to La Mesilla at 0800.

Excursions Many places of interest around on roads N to Huehuetenango, W to San Marcos and Mexico, S to Ocós and Champerico. Six km. SE is **Almolonga**, which is noted for its fine 16th-century church and beautiful costumes, especially skirts, which are hard to buy. There is also an interesting vegetable market. *Fiesta* June 29. Good swimming pool (entrance, US$0.25). About 1 km. further on are the thermal baths of Cirilo Flores (US$0.50 for large pool, US$1 to soak for an hour, hot, soothing water but heavily cleaned— frequently cleaned) and El Recreo (entrance, US$0.30); bus from Quezaltenango, US$0.12. The Fuentes Georginas hot springs, 15 km. from Quezaltenango, are mentioned under Zunil (page 1051). Take picnic or barbecue equipment, but it might be best to avoid Sundays when the Guatemalans descend on the springs. There are also hot steam baths at Los Vahos, reached by a dirt road to the right (3 km.) on the outskirts of town on the road to Almolonga; a taxi will take you there and back with a one-hour wait for US$1.50. El Baúl, a hill to the E, may be reached by winding road, or direct trail to the top where there is a cross (visible from the city), monument to Tecún Umán. To reach the Santa María volcano you can take a bus from the market in Quezaltenango to Palajunoz, from where it takes 4½ hours to walk up the N side of the volcano (the only side you can climb) to watch the still active crater, Santiaguito, on the Pacific side. Superb views of the Pacific from here. Alternatively, take bus to Llano del Piñal (at 0630 from Calvario, or at 0900 from Minerva), from where it is also a 4½-hr. climb: tracks are hard to find in summer (1,435 metres).

Travellers on to Huehuetenango normally go via Cuatro Caminos and the Pan-American Highway, but there is a direct road N through mountainous farmland.

According to folklore, at Olintepeque, an Indian town 6 km. from Quezaltenango (on a road parallel to the main road), the greatest battle of the conquest was fought, and Alvarado slew King Tecún Umán in single combat. Its river is still known as Xequizel, the river of blood. Market, Tuesday; *fiestas*, June 24, August 29 (beware of theft). The local idol, San Pascual Baillón, has its own little church. The direct road climbs 18 km. to San Carlos Sija, at 2,642 metres, with wide views. The Spanish strain is still noticeable amongst the inhabitants, most of whom are tall and fair. A climb through conifers for another 10 km. to Cumbre del Aire, with grand views behind of volcanoes, and ahead of Cuchumatanes mountains. Another 25 km. to the junction with the Pan-American Highway.

From Cuatro Caminos the Pan-American Highway climbs for several km. before dropping down past the *ladino* town of Malacatancito (48 km.) and swinging NW through the Selegua (El Tapón) gap to Mexico.

A 6½ km. spur from this road leads to **Huehuetenango**, a mining centre in farming country, with Indians from remote mountain fastnesses coming in for the daily market and especially Thurs. and Sun. Fair, July 12-18. Racecourse. Population, 20,000; altitude, 1,905 metres. The Honorary Mexican Consul at the Farmacia del Cid (5 Av. and 4 C.) will provide you with the Mexican tourist card

1048 GUATEMALA

for US$1 (but it's free at the border); Huehuetenango is the last town before the La Mesilla border post, on the Pan-American Highway into Mexico.

Hotels *Centro Turístico Pino Montano*, recently opened at Km. 259 on the Pan-American Highway, 2 km. past the fork to Huehuetenango on the way to La Mesilla (swimming pool); *Zaculeu*, best, but poor food in restaurant, 5 Av., 1-14, Zona 1, E; *Gran Shinula*, 4 C., E with bath, negotiate for cheaper rate, restaurant; *Pensión Astoria*, 4 Av., N of Plaza, F, good meals; *Palacio*, 2 C. 5-49, E, incl. 3 meals; *Central*, 5 Av., 1-33, G, excellent meals for US$0.65-$0.75, recommended, clean, washing facilities; *Auto Hotel Vásquez*, 2 C. 6-67, 2 blocks W of Plaza, F, with bath, new, clean; *Nueva Posada Familiar*, F with bath, clean and good; *Maya*, 3 Av., 3-55, F, with bath, hot water, clean, good value; *Venecia*, 6 Av. and 6 C., F, all with bath; *Hospedaje El Viajero*, 2 C., 5-20 Zona 1, G, basic but friendly; *Mansión El Paraíso*, 3 Av. 2 C., G; *Posada La Española*, 5 C., 4-13, G, with bath, no hot water; *Nancy*, 5 Av., S of Plaza, G. There are a number of cheap *pensiones* on 1 Av., by the market, including *Pensión San Román*, G, basic, friendly, convenient for bus stations; near market, *Tikal 2*, G, friendly, hot shower extra; *Tikal*, G (reasonably clean), *San Antonio*, next door, G, and *Centroamericana*, 1 Av., 4-85, G.

Camping at the ruins, or further on the same road at the riverside.

Restaurants All hotel restaurants are open to the public (*Hotel Central* is best; *Hotel Damascus* gives savouries with each drink). *Los Alpes*, 2 C., good. *Superlyckoss*, 2 C., quite good; *Buen Samaritano*, 4 C. and *Las Magnolias*, 4 C. and 6 Av. are probably the best of the central restaurants; *Cafetería Las Palmeras*, very good, close to Plaza; *Pizza Hogarena*, 6 Av. between 4C and 5C, recommended; *Damasco*, 4 Av., N of Plaza, new; *Taberna del Conquistador*, ½ km. S of town, peaceful location; *Snoopy's Helados*. *Tienda Santa Marta*, 6 C. is good café; *Rico Mac Pollo*, 3 Av., for chicken; numerous cheap *comedores* on E side of market including *Ideal*, and W side of Plaza; *Doña Estercita's*, 2 C., coffee and pastries, recommended.

Shopping Artexco, Local No. 10, Centro Comercial Xinabajul. In the Huehuetenango area are two Artexco cooperatives: *La Jacaltequita*, at Jacaltenango, and *La Guadalupana*, at San Miguel Acatán.

Cinema Lili on 3 Calle, W of Plaza, often has films in English.

Swimming Pool Known as Brasilia, entry US$0.50, ½ hr. walk SE of town.

Banks Banco de Guatemala, 4 C. and 5 Av., Mon.-Thurs., 0830-1400, Fri., 0830-1430, will exchange Mexican pesos for quetzales. Several local banks, some open Sat. a.m. All change travellers' cheques. Try also the hairdresser near Banco Café for good rates for pesos.

Postal, telephone and cable services on 2 Calle, 1 block E of Plaza.

Spanish Language Schools Fundación XXIII, 7a C., 6-27, Zona 1, is recommended highly, and is good value (one month: Q 360 with family accommodation). Instituto El Portal, 1 Calle, 1-64, Zona 3, US$70 per week living with a family, recommended also.

Buses To Guatemala (about 5 hrs.): US$2.10. Rutas Lima have 2 buses daily to Guatemala City, 0330 and 1530, but note that these go via Quezaltenango (US$1 or US$1.25 Pullman) and that the afternoon bus waits there for 3 hrs., arriving in the City at 2330; Los Halcones, 7 Av., 3-62, Zona 1, 0700, 1400, reliable; El Cóndor, 5 a day; Zaculeu, 3 Av. 5-25, 0600 and 1500. Los Flamingos, S side of market, 0445. To La Mesilla: (1½-3 hrs.), El Cóndor, 0600 (Pullman), 1100, 1300 (Pullman), 1730, 1900 (US$0.50; US$0.75 Pullman). Rutas Lima, 0800, US$1. Los Verdes, 1 Av. 1-34, 0500 and 1300. Osiris, 1 Av. and 3 C., 0430, 1030, 1230, US$0.50. López, 2 C. 2-39, 0630, US$0.50. To Cuatro Caminos, for Quezaltenango, Momostenango and Totonicapán, US$0.50; to Los Encuentros, for Lake Atitlán and Chichicastenango, US$1.25; to Sacapulas, US$0.50, 1200 (Rutas Zaculeu, returns 0600); direct bus to Nebaj at 1200; to Nentón, Cuilco and other outlying villages, enquire on 1 Av. near market. Beware of touts at the bus station who tell you, as you arrive from the border, that the last bus to wherever you want to go is about to leave; it's probably not true.

Ruins of ***Zaculeu***, old capital of the Mam tribe, pyramids, a ball court and a few other structures, completely reconstructed, concrete stepped forms, devoid of any ornamentation (museum), 5 km. NW on top of a rise ringed by river and *barrancas* (admission US$0.50, closes 1600). Yellow Alex bus runs at 1030, 1330 and 1530 as long as at least 5 people are going (fare US$0.05) and regular minibuses (US$0.15) to the ruins from *Hotel Maya*. It is possible to walk to the ruins in about 60 mins.

Car Insurance for Mexico and Guatemala can be arranged at Granai & Townson, next door to Mexican Consulate (see above).

Chiantla, 5 km. N of Huehuetenango, has a great pilgrimage to the silver Virgin of La Candelaria on February 2. Another *fiesta* on September 8. Daily market, largest on Sun. Buses leave regularly from 1 Av. and 1 Calle. Road runs N 117 km. to **San Mateo Ixtatán**, at 2,530 metres, in the Cuchumatanes mountains. The *huipiles* made there are unlike any others produced in Guatemala, and are much cheaper than in Huehuetenango. The road passes through San Juan Ixcoy (*Pensión*, G), Soloma (*Mansión Katty* recommended; *Hospedaje San Ignacio*), and Santa Eulalia (*Pensión*, G, recommended; *Hospedaje El Cisne*, G). San Mateo itself (very basic *pensión*, G, bring own sheets or sleeping bag) is a colourful town, with an interesting old church and black salt mines nearby. Bus from Huehuetenango to San Juan Ixcoy, Soloma, Santa Eulalia, San Mateo Ixtatán and Barillas leaves at 0200, very crowded, be early and get your name high up on the list as passengers are called in order. The bus returns to Huehuetenango from San Mateo (at least 5 hrs.) at 1330, but it is advised to take two days over the trip. Solomerita buses (1 Av. and 2 C.) run as far as Soloma, at 0500 and 1300.

After San Mateo the road runs 27 km. E to Barillas: a fine scenic route. Some 13 km. N of Chiantla is a viewpoint with magnificent views over mountain and valley. (Several cheap *pensiones* in Barillas, *Terraza* recommended, G.)

The village of **Todos Santos Cuchumatán** (*Hospedaje Lucía*, G, friendly, good, opposite market, meals, US$0.50; *Hospedaje Tres Olquitas*, G, friendly, basic, cheap meals; *Hospedaje La Paz*, G, cold; three cheap *comedores*) is very interesting; some of Guatemala's best weaving is done there, and fine *huipiles* may be bought in the cooperative on the main street and possibly at the makers' huts. There are also embroidered cuffs and collars for men's shirts, and colourful crotcheted bags made by the men. There is an Artexco cooperative, *Estrella de Occidente*. A fair selection of old woven items can be bought from a small house behind the church. The Sat. market is fascinating. One can learn backstrap weaving here; a recommended teacher is Srta. Santa Jiménez J. *Fiesta*: Nov. 1, characterized by a horse race in which riders race between two points, having a drink at each turn until they fall off. There are buses from Huehuetenango at 1100 and 1300 (Díaz Alva, Av. 1-37) 2½ hrs., US$0.65, crowded on Fri. (return at 0500 and 1200). Sat. bus at 1100 arrives after market has finished, and there is no afternoon return. The drive is spectacular, but much of the land has been overgrazed and there is much soil erosion. See also the village of Aguacatán (see page 1044, 26 km. E on the road to Sacapulas.

The source of the Río San Juan is about 2 km. past the centre of town (signposted); there is a small admission charge to the park, which is a delightful place for a freezing cold swim. Camping is permitted. Los Verdes, 1 Av. 2-34, has buses to Aguacatán at 1300 (last return bus at 1500, 3½-hr. journey), US$0.25, and buses for Sacapulas, Quiché, Nebaj and Cobán pass through the village. Zaculeu, 1 Av. 2-53, to Sacapulas, 1400, 2 hrs. US$0.50 (truck at 1630, arrives 2000, US$1), and from the same place Alegres Mañanitas has a bus to Quiché at 0415. The Campo Alegre company has buses to Nebaj from the *Hospedaje San José*, 1 Av. and 4 C. 'A', and buses for Cobán leave from the same area. From Todos Santos, one can walk to San Juan Atitán, 5 hrs., (more interesting costumes; Artexco cooperative *Atiteca* and from there the highway, 1 day's walk). Also, walk to San Martín (3 hrs.), or Santiago Chimaltenango (7 hrs., stay in school, ask at Municipalidad; the Artexco cooperative here is *Flor de Pascua*), then to San Pedro Necta, and on to the Pan-American Highway for bus back to Huehuetenango. **N.B.** Remember the warning on violence in this region.

The Pan-American Highway runs W to La Mesilla, the Guatemalan border post, and on 3.7 km. to Ciudad Cuauhtémoc (just a few buildings, sometimes known as El Ocotal), the Mexican border point, a very good and interesting route. Rooms at Ciudad Cuauhtémoc and La Mesilla (both very basic); best to avoid having to stay at either, by leaving Huehuetenango early. There is nowhere to change dollars into pesos at the border and the quetzal-peso rate is very poor but, coming into Guatemala, the peso-quetzal rate is better than the dollar-quetzal rate (don't change dollars until Huehuetenango or, better still, Guatemala City). The Guatemalan authorities charge Q3 exit tax and require a visa or tourist card on entry. Outside the hours of 0800-1200, 1400-1800, an extra US$0.50 is charged. A US$0.20 "bridge tax" (!) may also be demanded. From Ciudad Cuauhtémoc, Cristóbal Colón and Transportes Tuxtla buses go to Comitán and San Cristóbal de Las Casas (the Cristóbal Colón buses leave the La Mesilla border post at 0900, 1100 and 1600; there is a taxi, US$0.40 p.p., between the border posts during the day; Mexican officials charge exorbitant fees for transport between the border posts).

Buses from La Mesilla to Huehuetenango (El Cóndor) US$0.50, US$1.50 (first class) and US$1.75 (Rutas Lima). Wait until a bus is about to leave before buying a ticket as some wait for up to 4 hrs.

1050 GUATEMALA

at the border. Rutas Lima charges US$2 to Quezaltenango (by changing in Huehuetenango and Cuatro Caminos this can be done for US$1.12). Change at Los Encuentros for Lake Atitlán and Chichicastenango, and at Chimaltenango or San Lucas for Antigua. Express buses go to Guatemala City.

Quezaltenango W to Mexico Eighteen km. to San Juan Ostuncalco, at 2,530 metres, noted for good twice-weekly market and beautiful sashes worn by men. *Fiesta,* Virgen de la Candelaria, Feb. 2. See below for road S to Pacific town of Ocós. The road, which is paved, switchbacks 60 km. down valleys and over pine-clad mountains to a plateau looking over the valley in which are San Pedro and San Marcos, also known as La Unión. Interesting town hall, known as the Maya Palace. **San Marcos,** at 2,350 metres, is 2 km. or so beyond San Pedro. **San Pedro** has a huge market every Thurs. Its Sun. market is less interesting. The Indian women wear golden-purple skirts. (Weaving lessons from Rosa Cruz, who is good and patient, US$1). Tajumulco volcano, 4,200 metres (the highest in Central America), can be reached by taking the road from San Marcos to San Sebastián; after the latter, several km. on is the summit of a pass at which a junction to the right goes to Tacana, and to the left is the start of the ascent of Tajumulco, about 5 hours' climb. Once you have reached the ridge on Tajumulco, turn right along the top of it; there are two peaks, the higher is on the right. The one on the left is used for shamanistic rituals; people are not very friendly, so do not climb alone. Tacana volcano may be climbed from Sibinal village. About 15 km. W of San Marcos the road begins its descent from 2,500 metres to the lowlands. In 53 km. to **Malacatán** it drops to 366 metres, one of the toughest stretches in Central America—even for 4-wheel drive vehicles. It is a tiring ride with continuous bends, but the scenery is attractive.

Hotels At San Marcos: *Pérez,* with good dining room, G, meals US$0.50; *Palacio,* G, without bath; *Pensión Minerva,* G, basic. At San Pedro: *El Valle,* G, said to be good. *Bagod,* G. At Malacatán: *América,* F, lunch, US$1, good; *Pensión Santa Lucía,* G; *Hospedaje Santa Emilia,* G; *Hospedaje La Predilecta,* G; *Hospedaje Rodríguez,* G, good.

The international bridge over the Suchiate river at Talismán into Mexico is 18 km. W of Malacatán. Beyond the bridge the road goes on via Tapachula and Tonalá to Arriaga and Las Cruces (195 km.), where it joins the Pan-American Highway to Mexico City; most of the motor traffic from Mexico comes down this road. From Quezaltenango to Tapachula: take 1200 Rutas Lima bus from Quezaltenango to San Pedro; from bus terminal on 4 Av. in San Pedro, frequent local buses from 0430 to 1630 to Malacatán, from where colectivos will get you to the border with ease, arriving Tapachula about 1800.

There is a Mexican consular service at the border, and at Malacatán (closed after 1300). Travelling by bus to Mexico is quicker from Quezaltenango than from San Marcos. Most traffic seems to go via Coatepeque and Quezaltenango and not via San Marcos; the former road is longer but is reported very good. There is one direct bus from the border to Quezaltenango in the early morning (Rutas Lima, US$2). Otherwise you must make your way to Malacatán (only one bus a day, at 1500, US$0.15) from where there are 3 buses a day to Quezaltenango. Beware of overcharging on buses from the border to Quezaltenango. Bus Talismán-Guatemala City, US$3, 6½ hrs. because of checkpoints.

Quezaltenango to Ocós After San Juan Ostuncalco (see above) S for 1½ km. to **Concepción Chiquirichapa,** one of the wealthiest villages in the country. It has a small market early every Thursday morning where some of the most beautiful *huipiles* in Guatemala are to be seen. 5½ km. to **San Martín** (sometimes known as Chile Verde; this village appears in Miguel Angel Asturias' *Mulata de Tal*), in a windy, cold gash in the mountains. *Huipiles* and shirts from the cottage up behind the church. Accommodation next door to the Centro de Salud (ask at the Centro), US$0.50. Food in *comedor* opposite church, US$0.20. Indians speak a dialect of Mam not understood by other Maya tribes, having been separated from them during the Quiché invasion of the Guatemalan highlands. The men wear very striking costumes. *Fiesta,* November 11 (lasts 5 days). Primitive ceremonies of witchdoctor initiation held on May 2 at nearby Lake Chicabal, in crater of volcano. The walk to the lake from San Martín takes about 2 hrs; there are two paths. Ask the way to the "Laguna", not Chicabal which the Indians do

GUATEMALA 1051

not understand. The last bus to Quezaltenango leaves at 1900. Road descends to lowlands. From Colomba a road branches S (28 km.) to Retalhuleu; the road to Ocós runs 21 km. W from Colomba is **Coatepeque,** at 700 metres, with a population of 13,657; one of the richest coffee zones in the country; also maize, sugar-cane and bananas, and cattle. Fair, March 10-15.

Hotels at Coatepeque: *Europa*, 6 C., 4-01, E; *Virginia*, at km. 220, E; *Beachli*, 6 C., 5-35, E; *Posada Santander*, 6 C., 6-43, F. Bus from Quezaltenango, US$0.38.

Both railway (no passenger service) and paved Pacific Highway go to

Tecún Umán (Ayutla), 34 km. W, on the Mexican frontier, separated by the Suchiate river from the Mexican town of Suchiate. This is an alternative crossing point to the Talismán bridge and many buses run to it from Guatemala. It is quite a quick border crossing. Buses run from Tecún Umán to Tapachula, ½ hr., cheap (beware of overcharging). (Be warned, however, that you have to walk across a very long bridge (toll, US$0.20) over the river between the two border posts.) The bus to the capital costs US$3. Colectivo from Coatepeque, US$0.50. Road N to Malacatán for international road bridge into Mexico. Population 4,250. Hotels: *La Perla; Pensión Rosita.*

Ocós, a small port now closed to shipping, is served by a 22-km. road S from Tecún Umán. Across the river from Ocós is **Tilapa,** a small resort; buses from Coatepeque and ferries from Ocós (*Pensión Teddy*, G, friendly, but said to have deteriorated). The swimming is good, but both here and at Ocós there are sharks, so stay close to the shore.

Quezaltenango to Champerico, via Retalhuleu: a 53-km. link between the old Pan-American Highway and Pacific Highway, paved all the way. A toll (Quezaltenango-Retalhuleu, US$0.25) is collected. The first town (11 km.) is **Cantel,** which has the largest textile factory in the country. There are three Artexco cooperatives: *Ixchel,* at Xecán; *Monja Blanca,* Barrio Centenario Antiguo; *Copavic,* a cooperative of glassblowers. Market, Sunday; *fiestas,* August 15 and a passion play at Easter. Nine km. from Quezaltenango is **Zunil,** picturesquely located in canyon of Samalá river. Market, Mon. (beware pickpockets); *fiesta,* November 25, and a very colourful procession on Palm Sunday. Striking church, inside and out. The local idol is San Simón, described by one traveller as a plastic tailor's dummy, dressed in suit, shoes and hat; the statue is lodged in a greenhouse on the far side of the river. Behind the church is a cooperative (*Santa Ana,* a member of Artexco) which sells beautiful *huipiles,* and shirt and skirt materials. Zunil mountain, on which are the thermal baths of Fuentes Georginas 6 km. to the E (entrance US$0.50; rooms for night with individual hot spring baths, E), in attractive surroundings. They can be reached either by walking the 8 km., uphill (300 metres' ascent; take right fork after 4 km.) to south of Zunil, or by truck (US$2.50 to hire). Alternatively, take the bus from Quezaltenango to Mazatenango, but get out at the sign to Fuentes Georginas, from where it is 8 km. to the springs. The springs are 13 km. from Almolonga (see page 1047). Our road descends through Santa María de Jesús (large hydro-electric station) to **San Felipe,** at 760 metres, 35 km. from Zunil. Tropical jungle fruits. Spur line to Mulua, on Guatemalan Railways. Beyond, 3 km., is San Martín, with a branch road to Mazatenango. The thermal baths of Aguas Amargas are also on Zunil mountain, below Fuentes Georginas; they are reached by a road E before Santa María de Jesús is reached. **N.B.** The main road by-passes San Felipe, which has a one-way road system (delays of up to 1½ hrs. if you go through the town).

Mazatenango, 18 km. from San Martín, is chief town of the Costa Grande zone. Altitude 380 metres, population 21,000. Chitalón airfield 3 km. away. The Pacific Highway passes through. Road paved to Quezaltenango.

Hotels *Jumay,* G; *Alba,* E; *La Gran Tasca,* F; *Roma,* F; *Costa Rica,* G; *Pensión Mejía,* G, without bath. **Motel** *Texas.*

SW 11 km. from San Martín is **Retalhuleu,** at 240 metres, a town of 42,000 people on the Pacific Highway and on Guatemalan Railways to Champerico. It serves a large number of coffee and sugar estates. *Fiesta,* December 6-12.

1052 GUATEMALA

Hotels *Astor, Modelo*, both on 5 C. and 4 Av, and both F; *Pacífico*, G, next to new market; *Posada de Don José*, 3 Av. "A', 5-14, E. **Motel** *La Colonia* (swimming pool), 1½ km. to the N, is good, E.

Trains 2 a day to and from the capital.

Champerico, 43 km. SW of Retalhuleu by a paved road, is the third most important port in the country, although it remains open and unprotected, shipping having to lie offshore. Population 4,500. Good beach, though the sand is black and there is a strong undercurrent; good fishing.

Hotels *Martita*, F, without private bath; *Miramar*, F.

Bus Last bus to Quezaltenango departs at 1700.

The Economy

In international trade the accent is still heavily on agriculture, which accounts for some 65% of total exports. Coffee accounts for about 40% of exports, followed by bananas and cotton about 7% each, but sugar, soya, sorghum and cardamom are also important crops. There has been an attempt to diversify agricultural exports with tobacco, vegetables, fruit and ornamental plants, and beef exports are increasing.

The industrial sector has been growing steadily; the main activities, apart from food and drink production, include rubber, textiles, paper and pharmaceuticals. Chemicals, furniture, petroleum products, electrical components and building materials are also produced. Local industries, encouraged by tax remissions and tariff barriers, are gradually eliminating the need for imported consumer goods. Guatemala's exports (mostly industrial) to the other Central American countries account for about 25% of its total exports.

Petroleum has been discovered at Las Tortugas and Rubelsanto in the Department of Alta Verapaz. The Rubelsanto find is estimated to have proven and probable reserves of 27.3 m barrels, with production from this field and from West Chinajá running at 6,600 bpd. First oil exports in 1982 were valued at US$28m. A pipeline to transport oil from Rubelsanto to the port of Santo Tomás de Castilla has been completed. Exploration is continuing in both the Rubelsanto area and in the nearby department of El Petén. New wells, for prospects are good, are at Yalpemech, Xan and Caribe. Offshore exploration has so far been unsuccessful. In order to lessen imports of petroleum, US$1.7 bn. is to be invested in five hydroelectricity projects. Aguacapa (90 mw) and Chixoy (300 mw) are already completed and could satisfy electricity needs until the 1990s.

Guatemala's poor growth record in the 1980s can be attributed to the world recession bringing low agricultural commodity prices, particularly for coffee, and political instability both at home and in neighbouring Central American countries. It was hoped that the return to democracy would bring confidence and higher rates of growth into the 1990s as inflows of foreign funds were renewed. Other factors improving the balance of payments included moderate imports, rising exports, a rebound in tourism and debt rescheduling arrangements.

	1960-71 (av)	1971-80 (av)	1981-85 (av)	1986 (e)
Gdp growth (1980 prices)	5.5%	5.6%	-1.3%	0.0%
Inflation	0.8%	9.6%	7.5%	32.0%
Exports (fob) US$m	198	804	1,149	1,119
Coffee	81	283	364	-
Sugar	6	57	71	-
Cotton	30	100	81	-
Imports (fob) US$m	195	848	1,128	966
Current account balance US$m (cum)	-265	-974	-1,819	-38

GUATEMALA 1053

Information for Visitors

By Air From London, fly British Airways, Pan Am, or Virgin Atlantic to Miami, from where Pan Am flies direct daily to Guatemala City, and Taca via San Salvador and Sahsa via Honduras. From other US cities: Los Angeles, Lacsa and Taca; Mexicana flies Los Angeles—Mexico—Guatemala—San José. New Orleans, Taca and Sahsa; Houston, Taca and Sahsa. From Europe, KLM fly to Guatemala on Sunday from Amsterdam (via Netherlands Antilles, Panama and San José); Iberia from Madrid (Mon. and Fri.) via Santo Domingo and Panama. Taca, Mexicana and Sahsa fly from Mexico City; Copa from Panama, San José, Managua and San Salvador; Sahsa from Tegucigalpa; KLM, Mexicana, Lacsa and SAM from San José. Aviateca flies to San Salvador (as does Taca). Direct flight Guatemala-Belize City, daily (except Sat.) with Toucan Air (Ed. Maya, 1° nivel, Vía 5, 4-20, Zona 4, Tel.: 320288). SAM and Sahsa both fly to Bogotá, (SAM, at least, stops at Medellín, US$206, Cali, US$215, or Cartagena via San Andrés, US$179, all + 15 % tax). **N.B.** You will have to have an outward ticket for Colombia to be allowed a visa. There are no direct flights to Peru or Ecuador; connections via Panama or Colombia. Round-trips Miami-Guatemala are good value, and useful if one does not want to visit other Central American countries.

By Sea There are passenger services between Antwerp, Göteborg and Stockholm and Puerto Quetzal, and between Rotterdam, New York (6½ days) and New Orleans (4 days) and Santo Tomás de Castilla. None of the freight lines represented in Guatemala City makes passenger reservations; the only way to get passage on a freighter is to see the captain.

Taxes There is a 13 % ticket tax, single or return, on all international tickets sold in Guatemala. A stamp tax of 2 % is payable on single, return, baggage tickets and exchange vouchers issued in Guatemala and paid for in or out of the country. A US$5 tourism tax is levied on all tickets sold in Guatemala to Guatemalan residents for travel abroad. There is also a US$7 (Q20) airport departure tax, and an entry and departure tax of Q3/US$3 if travelling overland. An additional US$0.50 is charged outside official working hours (0800-1200, 1400-1800).

British Business Travellers should read "Hints to Exporters: Guatemala", obtainable from Dept. of Trade, Export Services Division, Sanctuary Buildings, 16-20 Great Smith St., London SW1P 3DB.

Business and commercial offices are open from 0800-1200, and 1400-1800 except Saturdays. Shops: 0800-1200, 1400-1800, but 0800-1200 on Saturday. Banks in Guatemala City: 0900-1500. In the interior banks tend to open earlier in the morning and close for lunch, and be open later. Government offices open 0700-1530.

Documents Necessary, a passport and a tourist card, issued free by the airlines or at the border, or a visa issued before arrival, but very few nationalities need a visa. Among those that do are the UK, Ireland and Australia (valid for 30 days, US$10, must be used within 30 days). It is advised that identification should always be carried. Tourist cards (US$1) are valid for 30 days from day of issue, then 6 months from entry into Guatemala (they allow the tourist to leave the country and return once provided that the time outside Guatemala is not more than 30 days). They must be renewed in Guatemala City after 30 days at the Migración office, on the corner of 12 C. and 8 Av., Zona 1, open weekdays 0800-1630. This office extends visas and renews tourist cards on application (before noon) for 30 days at a time (up to 90 days maximum)—takes 1 day. Renewing a visa takes 14 days, costs US$10, fingerprints and photograph required, and you may not be given the full 90 days. Those wishing to make more than one visit should get a multiple-entry visa (there are, apparently, no multiple-entry tourist cards). If you wish to stay longer than 90 days, you must have a Guatemalan guarantor whose financial resources must be vouched for. Tourist cards are not issued to nationals of communist countries, nor to black people unless they are citizens of the USA. Visitors staying less than 30 days, and holders of tourist cards, do not need an exit permit, which costs US$2.50. There is a fine of US$10 per day for overstaying a visa, payable as you leave the country. Borders are open 24 hours, but outside the official border crossing hours 0800-1200, 1400-1800, weekdays and 0800-1200 Sat., a small surcharge of US$0.50 is charged. Although not officially required, some airlines may not allow you to board a flight to Guatemala without an outward ticket (e.g. SAM in Colombia). Bribery is rife at border crossings; the Government is trying to eliminate overcharging for tourist cards and entry and exit taxes. Always ask for a receipt and, if you have time and the language ability, do not give in to corrupt officials.

Tourists can get an entry permit from the customs to take their cars into Guatemala for 30 days (US$10 or Q10), renewable at the Aduana, 10 C. 13-92, Zona 1. There is an exit tax for cars of US$1.50, and to take a car across the Mexico-Guatemala border costs US$5.50. There is also a charge of US$2.50 when the whole car is fumigated on entry. Spare tyres for cars and motorcycles must be listed in the vehicle entry permit, otherwise they are liable to confiscation. It is better not to import and sell foreign cars in Guatemala as import taxes are very high.

1054 GUATEMALA

You are allowed to take in, free of duty, personal effects and articles for your own use, 2 bottles of spirit and 80 cigarettes or 100 grams of tobacco. Once every 6 months you can take in, free, dutiable items worth US$100. Temporary visitors can take in any amount in quetzales or foreign currencies; they may not, however, take out more than they brought in, and quetzales may not be reconverted into US dollars when you leave.

Warning Be prepared for frequent police checks between the Mexican border and Quezaltenango. See also under **Clothing** below.

Information Instituto Guatemalteco de Turismo (Inguat), 7 Av. 1-17, Zona 4, Guatemala, provides bus timetables, hotel lists and road maps. Tourist information is provided at the Mexican border for those entering Guatemala. Recommended reading: Loraine Carlson, *A Traveller's Guide to Yucatán and Guatemala*, Paul Glassman's *Guatemala Guide*, and *Guatemala for You* by Barbara Balchin de Koose. Maps include Belize as Guatemalan territory. Roads marked in the Petén are inaccurate.

Road Travel The paved roads are very bad in places and generally poor, and the dirt roads are often very bad. Identification should be carried at all times. Stopping is compulsory: if driving your own vehicle, watch out for the "ALTO" sign. When driving, keep at least 200 metres in front of, or behind, army vehicles; their drivers are concerned about attacks on military personnel. Most buses are in a poor state of repair and breakdowns can be expected; they are often overloaded. Although recent government legislation has reduced problems of overcrowding, it is still difficult to get on buses in mid route. When travelling on them, resist overcharging. The correct fare should be posted up; if not, ask your neighbours. Hitchhiking is comparatively easy, but increasingly risky, especially for single women, also beware of theft of luggage, especially in trucks. The only way to retrieve "lost" luggage is by telling the police the vehicle registration number. Gasoline costs US$1.10 "normal", US$1.15 "extra" for the U.S. gallon. All Japanese motorbike parts and accessories are available at decent prices in Guatemala. Guatemalan driving is atrocious.

Hired cars may be taken into neighbouring countries except Mexico; rental companies charge US$7-10 for the permits and paperwork. Only credit cards accepted for car hire. Tourists involved in traffic accidents will have to pay whether the guilty party or not. If someone is injured or killed, the foreigner will have to pay all damages.

Note Many long names on bus destination boards are abbreviated: Guate = Guatemala City, Chichi = Chichicastenango, Xela = Xelajú = Quezaltenango, Toto = Totonicapán, etc. Buses in the W and N are called *camionetas*. Regarding pronunciation, "X" is pronounced "sh" in Guatemala, as in Yucatán (compared with "h" in central, and "k" in N, Mexico).

Railways The railways operate from Atlantic to Pacific and to San Salvador (no passenger service) and close to the Mexican border. Service is neither luxurious nor reliable.

Walkers should get a copy of *Backpacking in Mexico and Central America* by Hilary Bradt and Rob Rachowiecki.

Clothing Men and women should wear dark clothes in the evening. Trousers are OK for women. It is illegal to bring in, or wear, military-style clothing and equipment; such items will be confiscated.

Shopping Woven goods are normally cheapest bought in the town of origin, or possibly even cheaper at big markets held nearby. Try to avoid middlemen and buy direct from the weaver or from a member-cooperative of Artexco, to be found in all main towns. Guatemalan coffee is highly recommended, although the best is exported.

Kerosene is called "Gas corriente", and is good quality, US$0.80 per U.S. gallon; sold only in gas stations.

Film is very expensive, and film for transparencies is very hard to find (it is available at Calle 9, 6-88, Zona 1, Guatemala City, US$15 for 36 exposures).

Health Guatemala is healthy enough if precautions are taken about drinking-water, milk, uncooked vegetables and peeled fruits; carelessness on this point is likely to lead to amoebic dysentery, which is endemic. In Guatemala City the American, Bella Aurora, and Centro Médico hospitals are good. Herrera Llerandi is a good private hospital. Most small towns have clinics. At the public hospitals you may have an examination for a nominal fee, but drugs are expensive. There is an immunization centre at Centro de Salud No. 1, 9 C., 2-64, Zona 1, Guatemala City (no yellow fever vaccinations). In the high places avoid excessive exertion. If going to the Maya sites and the jungle areas, prophylaxis against malaria is strongly advised; there may also be a yellow fever risk (it is available at Calle 9, 6-88, Zona 1, Guatemala City, US$15 for 36 exposures).

GUATEMALA

Hotels The tourist office in Guatemala City will deal with complaints about overcharging if you can produce bills etc. Room rates should be posted in all registered hotels.

Tipping Hotels, about 10%; hotel staff: bell boys, US$0.25 for light luggage, US$0.50 for heavy. Chamber maids at discretion. Restaurants: 10%, minimum US$0.25. Taxi drivers: US$0.25 to US$0.50, according to time and distance. Airport porters: US$0.25 per piece of luggage. Cloakroom attendants and cinema usherettes are not tipped.

Climate, which depends upon altitude, varies greatly. Most of the population lives at between 900 and 2,500 metres, where the climate is healthy and of an even springlike warmth—warm days and cool nights. The pronounced rainy season in the highlands is from May to October; the dry from November to April.

Currency The unit is the *quetzal,* divided into 100 centavos. There are coins of 25, 10, 5 and 1 centavos. The paper currency is for 50 centavos and 1, 5, 10, 20, 50 and 100 quetzales. If you have money sent to Guatemala, you will only be given half in US dollars. In January 1985, the Banco de Guatemala authorized the establishment of exchange houses, effectively legalizing the black market, but not preventing street-trading in dollars. In April 1987, the quetzal was officially pegged at par with the US dollar, but the authorized parallel rate, at which prices in the *Handbook* have been converted, and which is used by banks, was about Q2.60 to the US$ while the flourishing free rate was about Q2.73. Rates vary around the country; the best being in the capital, the worst in Livingston, Puerto Barrios, Tikal and Panajachel. Miami airport is sometimes a good place to buy quetzales at favourable rates. **Warning:** Torn notes are not always accepted, so avoid accepting them yourself if possible. There is often a shortage of small change. Credit cards are very expensive to use; all (except American Express, apparently) are charged at the official rate.

The quetzal, a rare bird of the Trogon family, is the national emblem. A stuffed specimen is perched on the national coat of arms in the Presidential Palace's ceremonial hall and others are at the Natural History Museums in Guatemala City, Quezaltenango and in the Historical Exhibit below the National Library. (Live ones may be seen, if you are very lucky, in the new Biotopo on the Guatemala City-Cobán road.)

Cecon (Centro de Estudios Conservacionistas) and Inguat are setting up Conservation Areas (Biotopos) for the protection of Guatemalan wildlife (the quetzal, the manatee, the jaguar, etc.); 3 have been opened (see text), more are planned. Those interested should see Thor Janson's book *Animales de Centroamérica en Peligro.*

Weights and Measures The metric system is obligatory on all Customs documents: specific duties are levied on the basis of weight, usually gross kilograms. United States measures are widely used in commerce; most foodstuffs are sold by the pound. The metric tonne of 1,000 kg. is generally used; so is the US gallon. Old Spanish measures are often used; e.g. *vara* (32.9 inches), *caballería* (111.51 acres), *manzana* (1.727 acres), *arroba* (25 lbs.), and *quintal* (101.43 lbs.). Altitudes of towns are often measured in feet.

Public Holidays

January 1.
January 6: Epiphany
Holy Week (4 days).
May 1: Labour Day.
June 30.
August 15 (Guatemala City only).
September 15: Independence Day.
October 12: Discovery of America.
October 20: Revolution Day.
November 1: All Saints.
Dec. 24: Christmas Eve: from noon.
Dec. 25: Christmas Day.
Dec. 31 (from noon).

October 12 and Christmas Eve are not business holidays. During Holy Week, bus fares may be doubled.

Although specific dates are given for *fiestas* there is often about a week of jollification beforehand.

Time Guatemalan time is 6 hours behind GMT; 5 hours during Summer Time (May-August).

Posts and Telecommunications Urgent telegrams are charged double the ordinary rate. The cable companies are given under the towns. Sea mail from Europe takes about 40 days. Airmail to

GUATEMALA

Europe takes 6-12 days (letters cost 30 centavos for first 5 grammes, 15 centavos for each additional 5 gm). Telephone calls to other countries can be made any day at any time; to Europe, these are slightly cheaper between 1900 and 0700 (personal calls to Europe cost Q60 for minimum 3 mins.; station to station calls to Europe Q45); at least an hour's wait for calls to USA or Europe. Collect calls may be made only to North and Central America. All telephone services and the international cable service are in the hands of Guatel, but local telegrams are dealt with at the post office. Mail to the US and Canada on average takes twice as long as to Europe. Airmail parcel service to the U.S. is reliable (4-14 days); 2-3 months by boat. Post to Europe, several rates. Parcels up to 20 kg. can be sent by sea mail to Europe cheaply (3-4 months). Parcels sent abroad must be checked before being wrapped for sending; take unsealed package, tape and string to the appropriate counter at the back of the Central Post Office. Parcels by air to Europe cost about US$1.50/kg.; a good service. Note, though, that parcels over 2 kg. may only be sent abroad from Guatemala City; in all other cities, packets under 2 kg. must be sent registered abroad. Mail from Mexico is specially slow. **N.B.** The Lista de Correos charge US$0.03 per letter received. Correos y Telégrafos, 7a Av. 12 C., Zona 1; Guatel next door. Also, no letters may be included in parcels: they will be removed.

Press The main newspapers are *Prensa Libre* and *El Gráfico* in the morning; *La Razón* and *La Hora* in the afternoon.

We are grateful for information on Guatemala as follows: Rainer Gruss (Guatemala City) for a particularly useful contribution, Floretine Kramer (Quezaltenango) for information on that city, and the following travellers: Paul Aster (Los Angeles), Ian Beharell and Georgina Howes (Oxford), Stefan W. Berther (Geneva), Dr Michael Binzberger (Friedrichshafen), Dr Klaus Busch (Touristik Service, Osnabruck), Dagmar Drescher (Bad Kreuznach, W.Ger.), Gerardo Dutto (Vancouver), Richard Ebright (Brookline, Mass.), Jill Ennever (Avalon, NSW), Pierre-Marie Gagneux (Taulignan, Fr.) and Nathalie Baudouin (Bar-le-Duc, Fr.), Thomas Harding (London NW3) and members of the Intermediate Technology World Cycle Tour team, Arthur Judson (Fort Collins, Colo.), Dr Paul Kelly and Jenny Gallagher (Perth, W.Aust.), Torlief Larsen (Solna, Swe.), Roger Lemercier (Nice), Charles Luttman (Portland, Ore.), Annette Morris (Redhill), Tony Palios (London W3), Annamarie Reithmuth and Roger Müller (Schwyz, Switz.), Rev. Jamie Robbins (Seattle), Christer Robertson (Stockholm) and Patricia Galvin (Galway), Ann K. Rodzai (Ithaca, NY) and Doug Hanauer, Bill Rotecki (Ketchikan, Alaska), Jonas Sandberg (Stockholm) and Per Lindell (Västerås, Swe.), Chesley and Carole Schart (Teton Village, Wyo.), Frank Scheenmann (Heusenstamm), Beat Schmutz (Münchenstein, Switz.), Ingo Thor (Berlin), Carla Tromp and Douwe van Dijk (Meppen, Neth.), Alan Wagman (Washington DC), and others whose names will be found at the end of the general Central America section.

The decision is easy...

FORT GEORGE HOTEL

Call Utell, 01-741 1588 or write to Paul Hunt, P.O. Box 321, Belize City for brochures and tariffs.

BELIZE

BELIZE, formerly known as British Honduras, borders on Mexico and Guatemala, and has an area of about 8,900 square miles, including numerous small islands. Its greatest length (N-S) is 174 miles and its greatest width (E-W) is 68 miles. Forests occupy some 65% of the area.

The coastlands are low and swampy with much mangrove, many salt and fresh water lagoons and some sandy beaches. In the north the land is low and flat, but in the south-west there is a heavily forested mountain massif with a general elevation of between 2,000 and 3,000 ft. In the eastern part are the Maya Mountains, not yet wholly explored, and the Cockscomb Range which rises to a height of 3,681 ft. at Victoria Peak. To the west are some 250 square miles of the Mountain Pine Ridge, with large open spaces and some of the best scenery in the country.

From 10 to 40 miles off the coast an almost continuous line of reefs and cayes (meaning islands, pronounced "keys") provides shelter from the Caribbean and forms the longest coral reef in the Western Hemisphere. Most of the cayes are quite tiny, but some have been developed as tourist resorts. Many have beautiful sandy beaches with clear, clean water, where swimming and diving are excellent. (However, on the windward side of inhabited islands, domestic sewage is washed back on to the beaches, and some beaches are affected by tar.)

The most fertile areas of the country are in the northern foothills of the Maya Mountains: citrus fruit is grown in the Stann Creek valley, while in the valley of the Mopan, or upper Belize river, cattle raising and mixed farming are successful. The northern area of the country has long proved suitable for sugar cane production. In the south bananas and mangoes are cultivated; the lower valley of the Belize river is a rice-growing area as well as being used for mixed farming and citrus cultivation.

N.B. A wildlife protection Act was introduced in 1982, which forbids the sale, exchange or dealings in wildlife, or parts thereof, for profit; the import, export, hunting or collection of wildlife is not allowed without a permit; only those doing scientific research or for educational purposes are eligible for exporting or collecting permits.

Climate Shade temperature is not often over 90°F even in the hotter months of February to May. Inland, in the W, day temperatures can exceed 100°F, but the nights are cooler. Between November and February there are cold spells during which the temperature at Belize City may fall to 55°F.

There are sharp annual variations of rainfall—there is even an occasional drought—but the average at Belize City is 65 inches, with about 50 inches in the N and a great increase to 170 inches in the S. Hurricanes can threaten the country from June to November, but there have been only four in the past thirty years. An efficient warning system has been established and there are hurricane shelters in most towns and large villages.

The **population** is estimated at 162,000. Half of them are of mixed ancestry, the so-called Creoles, a term widely used in the Caribbean. They predominate in Belize City and along the coast, and on the navigable rivers. About 17% of the population are Indians, mostly Mayas, who predominate in the north between the Hondo and New rivers and in the extreme south and west. About 10% of the population are Black Caribs, descendants of the Black Caribs deported from St. Vincent in 1797; they have a distinct language, and can be found in the villages and towns along the southern coast. Another 10% are of unmixed European ancestry (the majority Mennonites, who speak a German dialect, and are friendly and helpful) and a rapidly growing group of North Americans. Birth rate (1984), 38.0 per 1,000; death rate, 4.9; annual population growth, 2.8%; adult literacy 90%. Free elementary education is available to all, and all the towns have secondary schools.

About 75% speak fluent but mostly "Creole" English. Spanish is the mother tongue for about

1058 BELIZE

15%. About 30% are bilingual, and 10% trilingual. Spanish is widely spoken in the northern and western areas.

History Deep in the forests of the centre and S are many ruins of the Old Mayan empire, which flourished here and in neighbouring Guatemala from the 4th to the 9th century and then somewhat mysteriously emigrated to Yucatán. It has been estimated that the population then was ten times what it is now.

The first settlers were Englishmen and their black slaves from Jamaica who came about 1640 to cut logwood, then the source of textile dyes. The British Government made no claim to the territory but tried to secure the protection of the wood-cutters by treaties with Spain. Even after 1798, when a strong Spanish force was decisively beaten off at St. George's Cay, the British Government still failed to claim the territory, though the settlers maintained that it had now become British by conquest.

When they achieved independence from Spain in 1821, both Guatemala and Mexico laid claim to sovereignty over Belize as successors to Spain, but these claims were rejected by Britain. Long before 1821, in defiance of Spain, the British settlers had established themselves as far south as the river Sarstoon, the present southern boundary. Independent Guatemala claimed that these settlers were trespassing and that Belize was a province of the new republic. By the middle of the 19th century Guatemalan fears of an attack by the United States led to a *rapprochement* with Britain. In 1859, an Anglo-Guatemalan Convention was signed by which Guatemala recognized the boundaries of Belize while, by Article 7, the United Kingdom undertook to contribute to the cost of a road from Guatemala City to the sea "near the settlement of Belize"; an undertaking which was never carried out.

Heartened by what it considered a final solution of the dispute, Great Britain declared Belize, still officially a settlement, a Colony in 1862, and a Crown Colony nine years later. Mexico, by treaty, renounced any claims it had on Belize in 1893, but Guatemala, which never ratified the 1859 agreement, renews its claims periodically.

Belize became independent on September 21, 1981, following a United Nations declaration to that effect. Guatemala refused to recognize the independent state, but in 1986, President Cerezo of Guatemala announced an intention to drop his country's claim to Belize. A British military force has been maintained in Belize since independence.

Communications Formerly the only means of inland communication were the rivers, with sea links between the coastal towns and settlements. The Belize river can be navigated by light motor boats, with enclosed propellers, to near the Guatemalan border in most seasons of the year, but this route is no longer used commercially because of the many rapids. The Hondo River and the New River are both navigable for small boats for 100 miles or so. Although boats continue to serve the sugar industry in the north, the use of waterborne transport is much diminished.

Some 400 miles of all-weather roads, with bus and truck services, connect the eight towns in the territory. There are road links with Chetumal, the Mexican border town, and the Guatemalan border town of Melchor de Mencos.

Heavy rain can often play havoc with the road system, making roads impassable, bridges unsafe and ferries unmanageable. There are no railways in Belize.

Government There are a ministerial system and a National Assembly, with a House of Representatives of 28 members elected by universal adult suffrage, and a Senate of 8: 5 appointed by the advice of the Premier, 2 on the advice of the Leader of the Opposition, 1 by the Governor-General after consultation. General elections are held at intervals of not more than 5 years. Dr. Minita Gordon was named Governor-General of the new state in 1981. Mr. George Price, of the People's United Party, who had been reelected continuously as Prime Minister since internal self-government was instituted in 1964, was defeated by Mr Manuel Esquivel, of the United Democratic Party, in general elections held in December 1984 (the first since independence).

Belmopan is the new capital since the seat of government was moved there from Belize City in August 1970. It is 50 miles inland to the west, near the junction of the Western Highway and the Hummingbird Highway to Dangriga (Stann Creek Town—rough, but very scenic). It has a National Assembly building (which is open to the public), two blocks of government offices (which are copies of Mayan architecture), police headquarters, a public works department, a hospital, over 700 houses for civil servants and a market. The Department of Archaeology in the government plaza has a vault containing specimens of the country's artefacts, as there is no museum to house them. Guided tours are offered on Mon., Wed. and Fri. (prior appointment advisable). Recent additions have been a cinema and a civic centre, but no non-civil-service residential area as yet. The Western Highway from Belize City is now good (one hour's drive), continuing to San Ignacio, and an airfield has been completed. Hotels: *Belmopan Convention Hotel*, Bliss Parade (opp. bus stop and market), A, a/c, hot water, swimming pool, restaurant, bars; *Circle A Lodgings*, 35/37 Half Moon Avenue, D-C,

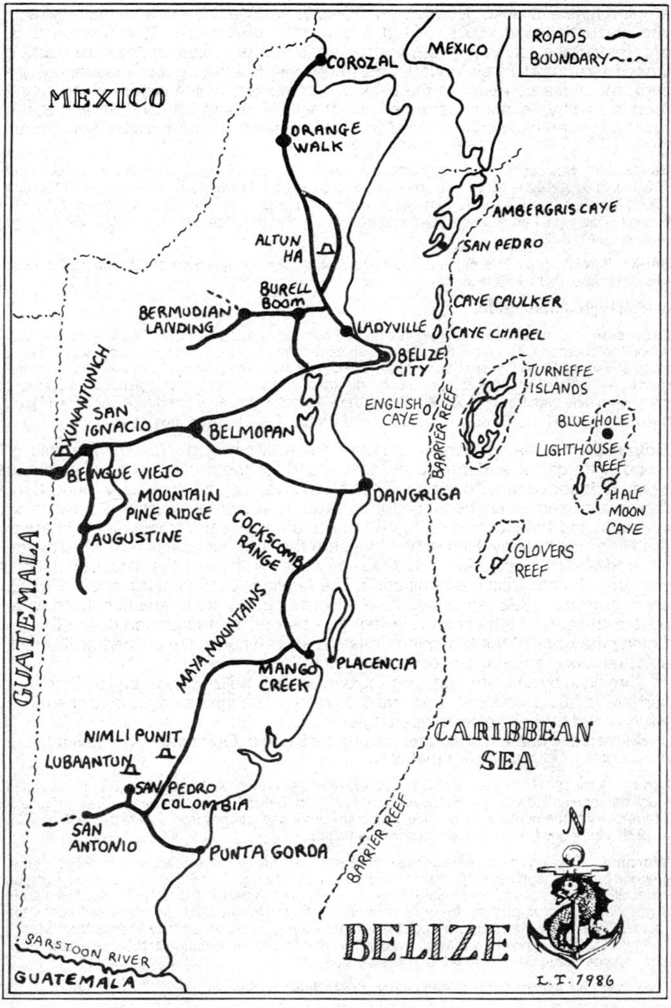

ROADS
BOUNDARY
MEXICO
MEXICO
COROZAL
ORANGE WALK
AMBERGRIS CAYE
SAN PEDRO
ALTUN HA
BURELL BOOM
BERMUDIAN LANDING
CAYE CAULKER
LADYVILLE
CAYE CHAPEL
BELIZE CITY
XUNANTUNICH
TURNEFFE ISLANDS
ENGLISH CAYE
SAN IGNACIO
BELMOPAN
BARRIER REEF
BLUE HOLE
LIGHTHOUSE REEF
BENQUE VIEJO
MOUNTAIN PINE RIDGE
DANGRIGA
HALF MOON CAYE
COCKSCOMB RANGE
AUGUSTINE
GLOVERS REEF
GUATEMALA
MAYA MOUNTAINS
MANGO CREEK
PLACENCIA
CARIBBEAN SEA
NIMLI PUNIT
LUBAANTUN
SAN PEDRO COLOMBIA
SAN ANTONIO
PUNTA GORDA
BARRIER REEF
N
BELIZE
SARSTOON RIVER
GUATEMALA
L.T. 1986

1060 BELIZE

a/c and fans available, despite sign, friendly, breakfast is extra, dinner also served, and bath (laundry BZ$3.75); *Bull Frog Hotel*, 23/25 Half Moon Avenue, D-B, a/c, restaurant, laundry. There are two restaurants (*Caladium*, next to market, limited fare, moderately priced, small portions; *Bullfrog*, good, reasonably priced); there is a *comedor* at the back of the market, which is very clean. Local food is sold by vendors, 2 stands in front sell ice cream (closed Sat. and Sun.), fruit and vegetable market open Mon.-Sat., limited produce available Sun. Shops close 1200-1400. No cafés open Sun.

Buses Batty Bus service to San Ignacio, 45 mins.—1 hr., BZ$1.50 (28 miles), daily 1000 and 1130, plus 0730 Mon., 0930 Sat. and 0830 and 0930 Sun. Novello's hourly between 1100 and 1700 Mon.-Sat. (to 1500 on Sun.) to San Ignacio and Benque Viejo; also Transportes del Carmen. Buses to Dangriga, Punta Gorda, see under Belize City. Bus to Belize City, 1 hr., BZ$2.75. Truck to Mango Creek, BZ$5.

Bank Barclays Bank International (0800-1300, Mon.-Fri.); Royal Bank of Canada (0800-1300 Mon.-Fri., also 1500-1700 Fri. only).

British High Commission.

Excursion 13 miles from Belmopan along a bad road is the Blue Hole. This is a natural pool which lies about 100 ft. below the road. It can be reached by steps and swimming is possible. 2 miles SW of the Blue Hole are St. Hernan's Caves, which are magnificent (they are ½ mile off the road from the Blue Hole to Belmopan along a dirt track). A torch is essential; you can walk for more than half a mile underground. At Mile 30 on the Western Highway is the Belize Zoo (The Place), open daily 1000-1700, BZ$5, many local species, tours, T-shirts, postcards on sale.

Belize City is the old capital and chief town. Most of the houses are built of wood, with galvanized iron roofs; they stand for the most part on piles about seven feet above the ground, which is often swampy and flooded. Ground-floor rooms are used as kitchens, or for storage. A sewerage system is now being installed, and the water is perfectly safe to drink. For the tropics the climate is both cool and healthy. Humidity is high, but the summer heat is tempered by the NE trades. The population—42,000—is nearly a third of the total population, with the African strain predominating. The Anglican Cathedral (founded in 1812, consecrated in 1826) and Government House nearby are interesting; both were built in the early 19th century. In the days before the foundation of the Crown Colony the kings of the Mosquito Coast were crowned in the Cathedral. There is an attractive memorial park on the sea front.

Coming in by sea, after passing the barrier reef, Belize City is approached by a narrow, tortuous channel. This and the chain of mangrove cayes give shelter to what would otherwise be an open roadstead.

Belize is the nearest adequate port to the State of Quintana Roo (Mexico), and re-exports mahogany from that area.

Note Hurricane Hattie swept a 10-ft. tidal wave into the town on October 31, 1961, and caused much damage and loss of life. Hattieville, 16 miles from Belize City on the road to Cayo, originally a temporary settlement for the homeless after the hurricane, still has from 2,000 to 3,000 people. In 1978, Hurricane Greta caused extensive damage.

Warning Take good care of your possessions or they will be stolen. Cars should only be left in guarded carparks (such as Majarrez in N. Front St., BZ$10 a night). The city is not safe by night; be especially careful in side streets. Safest streets are Regent, Albert and Queen Streets. The market is notorious for drug-pushing (beware of drug-planting). Do not trust the many self-appointed "guides" who also sell hotel rooms, boat trips to the Cayes, drugs, etc. (Many operate from *Mom's Triangle*). The Government is making every effort to improve the situation in the interests of tourism. Outside Belize City, there is much less tension.

The whole city, except Mom's Triangle Bar, closes down on Sunday.

Hotels All hotels are subject to 5% government tax. *Fort George Hotel*, 2 Marine Parade (P.O. Box 321, Tel.: 7242/3, Telex 220), has much the same tariff as luxury Caribbean hotels, and rooms are air-conditioned, L, helpful staff, reservations must be made, good restaurant, good pool (non-residents may use pool for BZ$5). Other hotels: *Villa*, 13 Cork St., L, a/c, 7 restaurant, bar; *Bellevue*, 5 Southern Foreshore, A, including 2 meals, a/c, and private bath, nice bar; *El Centro*, 4 Bishop St., B, good; *Venus*, Magazine Rd., at Venus Bus Station, B; *Bliss*, 1 Water Lane, C, with a/c and private bath, clean, safe; *Mopan*, 55 Regent Street, C, with bath, breakfast, a/c, very clean, in historic house, has restaurant and bar (owners Tom and Jean Shaw); *International Airport Hotel*, at Ladyville, 9 miles on Northern Highway, 1½ miles from airport, C, restaurant and bar;

BELIZE 1061

Chateau Caribbean, 6 Marine Parade, from D to A, with bar, restaurant and discotheque; *Vinat's*, 53 Regent St. West, F, friendly, good, and *Vinat's II*, on North Front Street, E, better, clean; *Las Palmeras*, corner George and Bishop Sts., E-D; *Dianne*, 65 George St., F; *Belcove*, 9 Regent St. West, E-D; *Mona Lisa*, Regent St., next to market and Tourist Office, modern, clean, C with bath; *Jane's*, 64 Barrack Rd., E; *Dominique II*, Douglas Jones St., E, dirty, rooms rented by the hour; *Bel-Prince*, 33 Prince St., E; *Golden Dragon*, 29 Queen St., E-D, with bath and a/c, cheaper rooms with bath and fan, cheaper still without bath, hot water, good, clean but noisy; *Simon Quan's "Luxury" Hotel*, 16 and 26 Queen St., E with fan, and D, private shower, hot water, a/c, good value; *Belice*, corner Orange and West St., E, with shower, secure (luggage may be left for US$1), clean, unpleasant area; *North Front Street Guest House*, 1 block N of Post Office on North Front St., F, hot water, book exchange, T.V., clean, friendly; *Riverview*, 25 Regent St. West, F, basic; *Mar's Riverside Resort*, 44 Regent St. West, F, no fan, friendly, basic; *Dominique*, 8 Gabourel Lane, E; *Bon Aventure*, Pickstock and Front Sts., E with bargaining, clean, helpful, Spanish spoken; *Marin Travel Lodge*, 6 Craig St., F, good, fans, shared hot showers, safe, laundry facilities; *Golden Star Guest House*, 114 New Rd., E, fan, clean, shower, simple, facilities leave something to be desired, not very friendly; *Freddie's*, 86 Eve St., E, with shower and toilet, fan, hot water, clean, very nice; *Hans Guest House*, 53 Queen St., F, little or no English spoken by Chinese owners, basic. Rooms at *Mom's Triangle*, see below.

Warning Self-appointed tourist guides will offer to take you to a hotel, then demand payment.

Camping There is a caravan trailer park about 20 miles from Belize on the road to Orange Walk, BZ$2 per vehicle, regardless of number of passengers. In the city itself is the *Caribbean Trailer Court*, at the end of Eve St., caravan park with 2 dilapidated showers and toilet, cold drinks available; some supervision, but no fence, beware of thieves; BZ$2. Camping on the beach is not allowed. **N.B.** Camping Gaz is not available in Belize and there are no campsites for tents.

Restaurants *Golden Dragon*, disappointing; *Macy's*, 18 Bishop Street, recommended for well-prepared local game, different fixed menu daily, charming host; *Mom's Triangle Bar*, US, Chinese, and Creole food, a very popular meeting place, has lots of information and safe deposit boxes (beware the touts), 11 Handyside Street, P.O. Box 332, also has 6-room *Inn* at same address, D (with bath and fan); *Hong Kong*, near police station, Chinese, reasonably priced; *China Village*, Regent and Dean Sts., quite good; *Archie's*, Albert St., Chinese; *Upstairs Café*, Queen Street, by bridge, for seafood; *Play Boy Restaurant*, King St., good sandwiches; *Pizza House*, King St., closed Mon., inexpensive, good also for juices and shakes; *New York, New York*, Queen St. near Post Office, delicatessen-style restaurant, good food, friendly, popular with Peace Corps; *Katy's*, Gabourel Lane, good and cheap, breakfasts; *Michelles*, opposite hospital, cheap and clean; *Belicean Roast Chicken*, S end of swing bridge, cheap; *Sandy's*, New Road, cheap and popular. *Blue Bird*, Albert St., cheap fruit juices; *Babb's Saloon*, Queen and Eve Sts., good pastries, meat pies, juices, friendly; *Pete's Pastry*, Queen St., opp. *Babb's*, good pastries. Lots of bars some with juke boxes and poolrooms. *Buccaneer Bar*, Mile 4½ on Northern Highway, on seafront, expensive drinks but you can sit outside. Try the local drink, anise and peppermint, known as "A and P"; also the powerful "Old Belizeno" rum. The local beer, Belikin, is unremarkable, but the "stout" strong and free of gas, is good.

Clubs and Discos *The Pub*, North Front St., bar and disco, admission charged, taped music, frequented by British soldiers; *The Big Apple*, same street, live music at weekends, good; *Bellevue Hotel* has live music at weekends, respectable, recommended. *The Gate Club*, and the *Old Belize Club* on E Canal Street, are reported not to be safe; the *Old Louisville Democratic Bar*, though recommended by Richard West of *The Spectator*, has been described as dangerous by a woman visitor.

Electricity 110/220 volts single phase, 60 cycles for domestic supply.

Shopping Handicrafts, woodcarvings, straw items, good jewellery in pink and black coral, and tortoiseshell (not to be imported into the USA) are all good buys. Try National Craft Centre, Cemetery Rd., near cemetery, very high quality workmanship; Cottage Industries, 26 Albert Street. The Book Centre, close to bridge and Catholic church, very good. Cathedral Bookshop, Regent St. (opp. *Mopan Hotel*), sells *South American Handbook* (also available in some expensive hotels). Zericote (a type of tree found only in Belize) wood carvings can be bought in Belize City, for example at Brodies Department Store, which also sells postcards, or in the *Fort George Hotel*. (At the Art Centre, near Government House, the wood sculpture of Charles Gabb, who introduced carving into Belize, can be seen.)

Taxis within Belize, BZ$3 for one person; each additional passenger BZ$1 if all going to same place, BZ$1 for each extra stopping place. Check fare before setting off. No meters. No tips necessary.

Car Hire Smith's, 18 Central American Blvd., Tel.: 02-3779; Elijah Sutherland, 127 Neal Pen Rd., Tel.: 02-3582; Royal Rentals, 5 Berkeley St., Tel.: 02-3063; Pancho's, 47A Kelly St., Tel.: 02-4554; S and L Rental, 69 West Collet Canal. Rates US$50/day; some offer tours. Land Rovers at

1062 BELIZE

about BZ$90 a day (BZ$400 deposit, no credit cards) at Belize. It is impossible to hire a car with insurance.

Banks Royal Bank of Canada; Barclays Bank International, facilities to arrange cash advance on Visa card (has copies of *The Times*), both with some country branches. Atlantic Bank buys and sells Honduran lempiras, and exchanges travellers' cheques; Bank of Nova Scotia. Banking hours: all except Atlantic Bank, 0800-1300 Mon.-Fri., 0800-1100 Sat.; Atlantic Bank, 0800-1200, 1300-1500 Mon.-Tues., Thurs.-Fri., 0800-1200 Wed., 0800-1100 Sat. It is easy to have money telexed to Belize City. Guatemalan quetzales are very difficult to obtain. American Express at Global Travel, 41 Albert Street (no service charge for changing Amex cheques). Money changers at Batty Bus terminal just before departure of bus to Chetumal (the only place to change Mexican pesos). The black market is not recommended.

Baron Bliss Institute Maya remains (3 stelae), and public library.

Churches There are an Anglican Cathedral, a Catholic Cathedral, a Methodist and a Presbyterian church. The Baptist Church on Queen St. is interesting for the sermons (very vivid).

Cinemas Two cinemas with a daily change of film, BZ$2-2.50.

Consulates U.S.A., 20 Gabourel Lane; Canada, South Foreshore; Mexico, 20 North Park St. (open 0900-1230, Mon.-Fri., when shut the man at the gate may get you a tourist card for a fee); Honduras (Front St., above *The Pub*), El Salvador (13 Eve St.), Panama, Cork St., Belgium, Eve St.; Norway and the Netherlands (Regent St.). No Guatemalan Consulate; Guatemalan visas must be obtained in Chetumal (Calle Alvaro Obregón 342), Mexico.

Post Office Letters held for one month. Beautiful stamps sold.

International Telecommunications Telegraph, telephone, telex services, Cable & Wireless Ltd., Albert Cattouse Building, Regent Street.

Tourist Information Belize Government Tourist Board (next to *Mopan Hotel*), 53 Regent Street, Belize, P.O. Box 325, Tel.: 02-7213, provides complete bus schedule as well as list of hotels and their prices. Also has a list of recommended taxi guides and tour operators. Excellent maps of the country for BZ$4. Mon.-Fri. 0830-1200, 1300-1700. Suggested reading is *Formerly British Honduras* (Setzekorn), or *Hey Dad, this is Belize*, by Emory King, a collection of anecdotes, available in bookshops. Maps, books on Belizean fauna etc. available at Angelus Press, Queen St.
Caribbean Charter Services, P.O.Box 521, Belize City, Tel.: 011-501-4-5841, Telex 263 Rebco Bz. Attn. Princess Charters, is a tourist information centre and agency for boat charters, inland resorts and other facilities. The owners (Americans George and Ruha'mah Baguette) operate M.V. *Princess* for fishing, diving and sightseeing trips to the Cayes.

Tours International Zoological Expeditions, 210 Washington Street, Sherborn, MA 01770, USA, offer guided trips to the rainforests and coral reefs of Belize; recommended.

Transport There are bus services to the main towns and to Chetumal, Mexico (see page 974), several daily each way, BZ$7, 4-5 hrs., with 2 companies: Batty Bus, 54 East Collet Canal, Tel.: 2025—courtesy taxi will collect you from your hotel, and Venus, Magazine Rd., Batty Bus, 5 a day, 4 on Sun., Venus Bus, 4 a day, 3 on Sun. Batty Bus to Belmopan and San Ignacio, 2½ hrs., BZ$3.75, Mon.-Sat. 0900, 1030, plus 0630 on Mon., Sun. 0730, 0830, 0930, 1030; to San Ignacio and Benque Viejo via Belmopan, Novello's, West Collet Canal, BZ$4.25 to Benque, 3 hrs., hourly Mon.-Sat., 1100 to 1700 (to 1500 on Sun.); Transportes del Carmen, East Collet Canal, to Benque, Mon.-Sat. 1230, 1530, 1630, Sun. 1230. To Dangriga, via Belmopan and the Hummingbird Highway. Z-line, from Venus bus station, Mon.-Sat. 1000, 1300, 1600, plus 0600 Mon., Sun. 1400-1500 (the 1000 bus connects with the 1430 Z-line bus to Punta Gorda); James Bus Line, Pound Yard Bridge (Collet Canal), unreliable, slow, "a real adventure", 10-12 hrs., BZ$16.50, to Punta Gorda via Dangriga, Mango Creek, Tues., Wed., Fri. 0600, Mon. 0800, Sat. 0900. Within the city the fare is BZ$1. Take a taxi to town from the bus stations at night. Trucks are a cheaper mode of transport; enquire about them near the market.

Airport There is a 9-mile tarmac road to the Belize International Airport; collective taxi BZ$20; make sure your taxi is legitimate. Any bus going up the Northern Highway passes the airport junction (BZ$1), then 1½ mile walk. There is a municipal airstrip for local flights (safe to leave cars here if going to the Cayes). To Corozal, 30 mins., BZ$62; to Punta Gorda, BZ$82.50; to San Pedro, BZ$35; Caye Chapel, BZ$25; Dangriga, BZ$36.

Airline Offices Taca (Belize Global Travel), Albert St.; Sahsa/Tan, just off Queen St. Maya Airways, 6 Fort St., Tel.: 2312/7215.

Shipping The only boat to Guatemala goes from Punta Gorda. Obtain all necessary exit stamps and visas before sailing (remember, nearest Guatemalan consulate is in Chetumal). For Dangriga and Punta Gorda boats must be chartered.

BELIZE 1063

Fishing The rivers abound with tarpon and snoek. The sea provides game fish such as sailfish, marlin, wahoo, barracuda and tuna. On the flats, the most exciting fish for light tackle—the bonefish—are found in great abundance.

Skin Diving The shores are protected by the longest barrier reef in the Western Hemisphere. Old wrecks and other underwater treasures are protected by law and cannot be removed. Spear fishing, as a sport, is discouraged in the interests of conservation. The beautiful coral formation is a great attraction for scuba diving. Fishing boats (no motor) can be rented at flat rate of BZ$30 a day, for boat and crew, for trips to reef.

The Cayes off the coast are most attractive. They are used by holiday campers from February to May and in August. From many of the holiday villas stretch pens or "crawls" to protect the bather from sharks or barracudas, and to keep the water clean.

There are 212 square miles of cayes. St. George's Caye, 9 miles NE of Belize, was once the capital and was the scene of the battle in 1798 which established British possession. The larger ones are Turneffe Island and Ambergris, Caulker, and English Cayes. Fishermen live on some cayes, coconuts are grown on others, but many are uninhabited swamps. The smaller cayes do not have much shade, so be careful if you go bathing on them. Sandflies infest some cayes (e.g. Caulker), the sandfly season is December to beginning of February; mosquito season June, July, sometimes October. On Big Caye Bokel, at the southern end of the Turneffe group, are 3 "Caribbean Lodges" for big-spending fishermen and skin-divers, each holding 12 guests (*Turneffe Island Lodge*, bar, restaurant, diving and snorkelling trips; *Turneffe Island Flats*, less expensive). Caye Chapel has a large hotel and a private airstrip, and Caye Caulker several guest rooms and hotels. Boats leave from fishing cooperative up Belize river a few blocks from bridge (BZ$12 p.p.). Connections between Ambergris, Caulker and Chapel Cayes are quite frequent though it may be harder to hop between the other cayes, making it necessary to return to Belize City first. For cheap boats to the cayes ask (rather, you'll be "asked") around the market pier, or at *Mom's Triangle Bar*. Most leave from 0930 onwards, BZ$10-15 each way, from the swing bridge. 5-day trips to the Turneffe Islands costs BZ$500 for 10 people; to Puerto Cortés, BZ$720, 2-4 days, for 8 people.

On Caye Chapel is the *Pyramid Island Resort*, B without a/c, A with, American or European Plan available, diving packages, air transfers to Belize City (P.O.Box 192, Belize City, Tel.: 4-4409). Caye Chapel is free of sandflies and mosquitoes and beaches are cleaned daily. 40 mins. by boat from Belize City.

Ambergris Caye This island, with its village of San Pedro, is being rapidly developed as a tourist resort and is expensive. *Ramon's Reef Resort*, a diving and beach resort, US$85 p.p. per day for double room, all meals and all diving, highly recommended even for non-divers (fishing, swimming, boating, snorkelling), very efficient. Hotels: *San Pedro Holiday Hotel*, L, including meals; *Coral Beach*, C, incl. meals; *Ambergris Lodge*, C and B; *Casa Solana*, B; *San Pedrano*, C; *El Pescador*, on Punta Arena beach, L, a/c; facilities for sailing, diving etc. *Tomas Hotel*, D (more if reserved in advance) with bath, clean, trips to reef. There are other expensive hotels, several in the BZ$20-45 range, and some basic hotels. *Big Daddy's Disco*, recommended. At Coral Beach, the Forman, Gómez, González and Paz families provide rooms and meals for BZ$18 each. At Sea Breeze, the Paz and Núñez families offer the same accommodation at the same price. It is possible to camp on the beach. Four flights daily to and from Belize City, BZ$35 one way, BZ$60 return. Cargo boats leave Customs Wharf Mon., Wed., Fri. 1500, 5 hrs., BZ$8; motor boats BZ$15, 1 hr., ask for departure point. Sailing and snorkelling trips with Ray (an English expatriate), for BZ$5, BZ$3 for hire of equipment. Boats, irregular, from Ambergris to Caye Caulker, US$10. From San Pedro one can hike along the beach (camping on the way) to enter Mexico at Xcalak (about 20 miles). It is a beautiful hike beside the barrier reef on white sand; two rivers have to be waded. Boats cross the river border at the end of the Caye; easy to find just before the river. Bus service from Xcalak to Chetumal on Sunday, easy to hitch, though; entry and exit at Xcalak at Port Commandant's office. Exit stamp from Police Station in San Pedro.

Caye Caulker A lobster-fishing island, which used to be relatively unspoilt, but the number of tourists is now increasing and the shoreline has become dirty. There are no beaches, but you can swim at the channel ("cut") or off one of the many piers. There are several boats for about BZ$24 return, 1½ hrs. one way (boats depend on weather and number of passengers, they leave from the swing bridge between 0930 and 1100); return boat at 0700 (if booked in advance at *Edit's Hotel*, BZ$10). (Ask for "Chocolate" at *Mom's Triangle*, he returns daily, except Sun., at 0730, or Reuben—who charges BZ$10 on the way back if you go both ways with him—or opposite *Poppy's Bar*, on North Front St.) Hotels: *Tom's Hotel*, F, with fan, basic, clean, friendly, excellent value; Tom's boat trips cost BZ$7. *Mira Mar*, E, bargain if staying longer, helpful owner Melvin Badillo, he owns liquor store, his family runs a pastry shop and grocery store; *Shirley's Guest House*, E; *Martínez Caribbean Inn*, E, basic, but nice disco 5 nights a week, with live reggae bands, the new part is better, E, with bath, poor service, poor meals for BZ$5.50; *Edits*, E, good; *Marin*, F, with bath, recommended (the proprietor will take you out for a snorkelling trip on the reef for BZ$6), good meals; *Riva's Guest House*, F, basic accommodation, excellent meals for BZ$6 (also for non-residents if booked in advance), highly recommended. Their reef trips in an attractive schooner are the longest; snorkelling equipment hire, BZ$3. Tony Vega (*Vega's Far Inn*) rents 7

1064 BELIZE

rooms, all doubles, E with ceiling fan and fresh linen, flush toilets and showers (limited hot water) shared with camping ground, which is guarded, has drinking water, hot water, clean toilets, barbecue, can rent out camping gear (camping costs BZ$5.30). Mr. Vega is an expert on the reef and arranges snorkelling trips; a 3-hr. trip costs BZ$10. *Ignacio Beach Huts*, small huts or hammocks just outside town, E for a hut for 3-4, recommended, camping space (Ignacio's reef trips cost BZ$4). Beach houses can also be rented for BZ$100-300 a month. Camping on the beach is forbidden. For dinner, seek out Mrs. Rodríguez, who serves meals at 1700/1730 for BZ$7-8 for 2, very good (limited accommodation available). Also Evelyn (near the Post Office), order meal by 1500, curried lobster BZ$6.50. Priscilla's (*Pris Kitchen*) is recommended for lobster salad; order in the morning, meals 1800-2100. *Tropical Paradise* for excellent seafood. Cakes and pastries can be bought at houses displaying the sign, recommended are *Daisy's, Jessie's* (open 0830-1300, 1500-1700, behind *Riva's*); *Emma*, on path to co-op, sells delicious lobster pies, and chocolate-coconut pies. Many private houses serve food; baked lobster at Post Office costs BZ$4 (make a reservation). International telephone connections available on Caye Caulker.

Reef trips, BZ$6-8 each for 3-7, hours as long as there are 3 or more in a group. Protect against sunburn on reef trips. Ask for Crispin if you are interested in snorkelling. Mervin, a local man, is also reliable for snorkelling trips, he will also take you to Belize City. Also Gamoosa, who will spend all day with you on the reef and then invite you to his house to eat the fish and lobster you have caught, prepared deliciously by his wife, BZ$9. Chuck, an American, has a snorkelling shop next to the football field; courses offered, trips for experienced divers; to rent equipment, BZ$37 a dive, BZ$10 each extra dive, BZ$60 to rent the boat. A 3-day course US$150, with certificate at the end. Cap'n Ray charters boat trips to the reef and atolls for BZ$20 per day p.p., to San Pedro for BZ$10, and to other National Island Parks along the Barrier Reef. His trip to the reef for snorkelling (recommended as reliable) leaves at 1000, BZ$7 (BZ$10 inc. gear). Also recommended is Alfonso Rosardo, a Mexican, reef trips for up to 6 people, 5-6 hrs., BZ$9, sometimes offers meals at his house afterwards. Also recommended is Lawrence (next to Riva's Guest House) and Obdulio, BZ$6 p.p. for 3 hr trip (or BZ$40 for a full day's fishing, inclusive). Lobster fishing and diving for conch is also possible. Mask, snorkel and fins for BZ$3-6 (for instance at the post office). Windsurfing equipment hire: BZ$8 an hour, BZ$20 ½ day, BZ$40 a day, lessons, BZ$10 exc. equipment. Allen Hively's scuba tuition is reasonably priced and great fun. Frank and Janie Boulting (P.O.Box 667, Tel.: 44307, ext. 143 mainland side, past the football pitch) charge BZ$60 for 2 scuba dives, good value; they also offer a 3-day P.A.D.I. certificate course. It may be possible to hire a boat for 6-8 people to Chetumal.

English Caye, 12 miles off Belize City, is beautiful, with no facilities; take a day trip only. It is part of the reef so you can snorkel right off the beach.

Half Moon Caye at Lighthouse Reef, 45 miles E of Belize City, is the site of the Red-Footed Booby Sanctuary, a national monument. The Belize Audubon Society maintains the sanctuary; there is a lookout tower and trail. A lighthouse on the caye gives fine views of the reef. No facilities.

Other Excursions Bargain with local drivers for a visit to Tikal ruins, in Guatemala (page 1033). Mr. Richard Smith has his own station waggon. There are buses from Belize to the Guatemalan border; for connections to Flores see page 1066 under Benque Viejo.

The Mayan remains of *Altun Ha*, 31 miles N of Belize City and 3 miles off the old Northern Highway, are worth a visit (insect repellant necessary); they are deserted after 1800 hours. Since there is so little transport on this road, hitching is not recommended, best to go in a private vehicle. A vehicle does leave Belize City in the early afternoon, but does not return until 0500 next day; camping not permitted at the site, although the helpful caretaker may allow it (Mr Gardener). No accommodation in nearby villages. Tourist Board provides a good booklet on the ruins for BZ$1.25, and a guide book for BZ$12. Entry BZ$1. The largest piece of worked Mayan jade ever found, a head of the Sun God weighing 9½ pounds, was found here in 1968. It is now in the vaults of the Royal Bank of Canada in Belize City.

Truck transport at 1230 from George St. goes to Bermudian Landing, a small Creole village 25 miles from Belize City; there is a howler monkey (called baboons locally) sanctuary. Details from the Belize Audubon Society, 49 Southern Foreshore.

Two roads penetrate the country from Belize City: one to the N and another to the SW. The Northern Highway, well paved to the Mexican border, misses Altun Ha and runs to (66 miles) the Orange Walk district, where about 17,000 Creoles, Mennonites and Mayan Indians get their living from timber, sugar planting, general agriculture and chicle bleeding. In the Orange Walk District is a large Old Mayan ceremonial site, **Nohochtunich**; enormous masonry slabs were used in a stairway up one of the pyramids.

The population of **Orange Walk,** a bustling agricultural centre, is 8,500. A toll bridge (BZ$1) now spans the New River. Spanish is the predominant language, and this is one of the drug-growing centres of Belize.

Hotels *Chula Vista Hotel*, at gas station just outside town, safe, clean, helpful owner, D. *Mi Amor*, 19 Belize-Corozal road, E with shared bath, and more expensive rooms, restaurant; *Jane's*, 2

Baker St., E; *La Nueva Ola*, 73 Otro Benque Rd., E; *Paradise* restaurant, very expensive; *Rocky's Restaurant*, rather dear, and others.

Banks Barclays Bank International; Royal Bank of Canada; Bank of Nova Scotia; same hours as Belize City (see page 1062).

Bus Urbina Bus (Cinderella Plaza) from Belize City to Orange Walk: daily at 1100, 1300, 1400, 1800 (except Sun.), Sun., 1900, returning 0500, 0630, 0700 (all except Sun.), 1 hrs., BZ$5. All Chetumal buses pass Orange Walk Town.

The Northern Highway continues to Corozal (96 miles from Belize) then for 8 miles to the Mexican frontier, where a bridge across the Río Hondo connects with Chetumal. Border crossing formalities are relatively relaxed. Driving time, Belize-frontier, 3 hours (Taxi, BZ$8 Corozal-border, BZ$17 Corozal-Chetumal). One can no longer acquire a tourist card at the border; you must get one at the Mexican Consulate in Belize City. If entering Belize for only a few days, you can ask the Mexican officials to save your tourist card for you (but don't depend on it). If you want a new tourist card for a full 30 days you must get it in Belize City. It is possible to buy pesos at the border with either US or Belizean dollars (outside office hours, try the shops). If coming from Mexico it is better to change pesos than US dollars. Bargain for good rates of exchange at the border, better here than with money changers in Orange Walk Town or Corozal.

Corozal, with a population of 7,000, is the centre of the growing sugar industry. Both Corozal and Orange Walk Town are economically depressed because of low world sugar prices; there has been a greater dependence on marijuana as a result. It is open to the sea with a pleasant waterfront.

Hotels *Don Quixote*, Consejo Shore, A; also at Consejo Shore, *Adventure*, D, 7 miles from town, bar and restaurant (no public transport); *Maya*, South End, D; *Capri*, 14 Fourth Ave., F. Two motels: *Caribbean*, South End, E-D, basic; *Tony's*, South End also, D (C, with a/c), superb. Both have restaurants. Other restaurants: *Club Campesino*, decent bar, good fried chicken after 1800; *Rexo*, North 5th St., Chinese.

Camping *Caribbean* Motel and Trailer Park, on Barracks Road, camping possible, has 12 cottages, shaded sites, laundry, restaurant, swimming pool, beach, recreation room.

Banks Barclays Bank International, Bank of Nova Scotia, Royal Bank of Canada, open same hours as Belize City (see page 1062).

Buses There are 5 buses a day from Belize to Corozal by Venus Bus, Magazine Road and Batty Bus, 54 East Collet Canal, 3-3½ hrs., BZ$6. Both continue to Chetumal; because of the frequency, there is no need to take a colectivo to the Mexican border unless travelling at odd hours (BZ$5). The increased frequency of buses to Chetumal and the number of money changers cater for Belizeans shopping cheaply in Mexico—very popular, book early. It is also possible to cross Belize from San Ignacio Town (see below) to Corozal by bus, BZ$6, 8 hrs.

Excursion 8 miles N of Corozal, on the road to Chetumal, is 4 Miles Lagoon, about ¼ mile off the road (buses will drop you there). Clean swimming, better than Corozal bay, some food and drinks available; it is often crowded at weekends.

The south-western road runs through savanna, pine ridge and high canopied forest to **San Ignacio** (capital of Cayo District, 72 miles) and the Guatemalan frontier. About 60 miles along this road is Ontario Village. There is camping space and a trailer to rent. San Ignacio, known locally as Cayo, has a population of about 5,600. It stands at 200-250 feet, with a pleasant climate, and is a good base for excursions into the Mountain Pine Ridge, some 120 square miles of well-watered, undulating country rising to 3,000 feet. (Bus to Belize City, Mon.-Fri., 1100, 1330, 1530, plus 1230 on Mon., Sat., and Sun., 1300, 1400, 1500, 1600 BZ$3.75, with Batty Bus; also Novello's, 4 daily Mon.-Sat., 1030 on Sun.)

Hotels *Belmoral*, 24 Burns Ave., E with bath; *Hi-Et Hotel*, 12 West St., E, very friendly, good, clothes washing permitted; *San Ignacio Hotel*, on road to Benque Viejo, new, D, with bath, fan, hot water, clean, helpful staff, swimming pool, excellent restaurant, highly recommended, disco at weekends, bar opens at 1000 (good place for meeting British soldiers); around the corner is *Piache Hotel*, E-D in either thatched cottages with bath or room without bath, cold water, basic, bar in p.m. Doña Elvira Espat serves meals at her house (inc. breakfast), she requires advance notice and will prepare special requests, she is very friendly, and an excellent cook (no sign at her house, corner of Galvez Street and Bullet Tree Road). *La Fuente*, Eve St. and West St., good juices and pastries; *The Place*, small pastry shop on Burns Ave., good; *Maxim's*, Bullet Tree Rd. and Far West St., Chinese, good food, poor service. George, at the *Club Shangrila*, serves a good cup of tea, and offers assistance of all sorts. Also informative is Bob at *Eva's Bar*, Burns Ave. (good, inexpensive local dishes). *Farmers Emporium*, Burns Ave., a shop selling wholewheat bread, raisins, juices, fresh milk. Fruit and vegetable market every Sat. a.m. Note that all shops and businesses close 1700-1900.

Bank Barclays Bank open same hours as Belmopan (see page 1058). Venus Stores, 23 Burns Av. (09-2186) gives better rates of exchange for quetzales than you can get at the border with Guatemala.

Tours Jungle View Tours, No. 26 18th St., San Ignacio, Tel.: 092-2012, recommended. Local taxis which offer tours of Mountain Pine Ridge in the wet season probably won't get very far; also, taking a tour to Xunantunich is not really necessary. Mountain Equestrian Trails, Mile 8, Mtn. Pine Ridge Rd., Cayo District, or P.O. Box 1158 Belize City (Tel.: 02-2331), offers ½-day, full-day or 7-8 day adventure tours on horseback in western Belize.

The British Army's Holdfast camp is about 12 miles from the border.

San Ignacio is on the eastern branch of the Old, or Belize River, known as the Macal, navigable almost to the Guatemalan frontier. The river journey of 121 miles from Belize, broken by many rapids, needs considerable ingenuity to negotiate the numerous "runs".

Chaa Creek Cottages, on the Macal River, 5 miles upstream from San Ignacio, has rooms for E (no meals), D (b. and b.), C (all meals), set on a working farm in pleasant countryside. Trips on the river, to Xunantunich, to Benque Caves (with Mayan remains), to Mountain Pine Ridge and Hidden Valley Falls organized. If coming by road, turn off the Benque road at Chial; hotel will collect you by boat from San Ignacio (US$25 for 4); reservations P.O. Box 53, San Ignacio, or New Hope Trading Co., San Ignacio, Tel.: 092-2188.

Jamal Cottages, also on the Macal River, ¾ mile from San Ignacio at 9 Cristo Rey Road, E-D, camping US$6, special weekly and monthly rates and for families, Tel.: 092-2164 (The Farm Store), P.O. Box 46, San Ignacio, restaurant, laundry, postal service, swimming, hiking, riding, canoeing, fishing, tours in the region and beyond—also Maya Mountain Language School, Spanish courses, from US$20 for 6 hrs. to US$100 for 40 hrs. intensive tuition (US$10 registration).

Blancaneaux Lodge, in the Mountain Pine Ridge reserve at 1,600 ft., has 6 cabins, and 6 rooms in the lodge hotel, D and A, with meals (not open all year round). Airstrip (rarely used) and a campsite with lights, showers, toilets, BZ$10 (this is the only permitted camping in the Mountain Pine Ridge reserve). A good area for sightseeing, bird-watching, cave exploring (Mayan remains), horseback riding. Nearby is the Hidden Valley waterfall, among the world's highest—1,665 ft., and the Río Frio Caves, where the river passes beneath a hill; one can walk along its banks. (For bookings, write P.O. Box 32, Belize.). Also near is Barton's Creek, a Mennonite community, from which one can buy produce. Five miles away, on the road to *Blancaneaux Lodge*, is Georgeville, where one can try the Mennonites' ice cream and cheese. **N.B.** Between January and June, the risk of fire in the reserve is very great, please take extra care; camp fires are strictly prohibited.

Tropical Jungle Paradise, Mile 88, Western Highway, Cayo District, Tel.: 092-2060, D in cabins, meals extra, riding, tours and expeditions on the Belize River or on land in Belize and Guatemala, US-owned and operated (Tom Dale). Closed during some of the year (e.g. August).

El Indio Suizo, a farm/guest house (recommended), is 1½ miles N of the Western Highway (turn-off 5 miles from San Ignacio, 2 from Benque Viejo), D with shared shower, C with shower, B with private bath, meals US$3-7.50; activities include swimming, boating (US$5-15), riding (US$5-15), walking, trips to Xunantunich, Tikal (Sats.), the Caves and Mountain Pine Ridge. The farm is on the Mopan River, near Xunantunich. Address: Marco and Colette Gross, Benque Viejo del Carmen, Cayo District, Belize, Tel.: 092-2025 or VHF 8450.

Nine miles up-river from San Ignacio is **Benque Viejo del Carmen,** near the Guatemalan frontier (road not sealed, very dusty in the dry season). Population, 2,500. Visas and tourist cards can, it appears, be obtained at the border. Exchange at the border (or in the central plaza in San Ignacio, poorer rates), black market for BZ$.

Hotels *Okis*, George St., E; *Roxi*, 70 St. Joseph St., F, vermin, unsavoury; *Hospedaje Castellanos*, 45 Church St., very unpleasant, F; next door is *Restaurant Los Angeles*. (Hotels on Guatemalan side of the border are better.) Meals at *Riverside Restaurant*, on main square, or at one of picturesque huts.

Four miles away, at **Xunantunich,** now freed from heavy bush, there are Classical Mayan remains, particularly a fine carved astronomical frieze from the roof façade of the spectacular main temple. (A booklet on the area is available from the Tourist Board for BZ$0.65.) Xunantunich can be reached by walking along the Cayo road for about 10 mins. until you reach the landing stage for a ferry; this will take you across the river (BZ$1, does not run 1200-1400); taxi from San Ignacio, BZ$2. On the far side turn right for Xunantunich (open 0800-1700, entry, BZ$1).

South of San Ignacio is the rediscovered Mayan city of Caracol, "six times the size of ancient Rome in the classic period".

Transport Novello's and Transportes del Carmen run daily buses from Belize City to Benque Viejo; frequent buses from San Ignacio to Benque Viejo, or colectivo from central plaza, BZ$2 (or BZ$3 to Melchor de Mencos in Guatemala, 20 minutes). To Guatemala from Benque Viejo by taxi, BZ$2. Free passage of border only weekdays, 0800-1100 and 1400-1700; at other times a fee is charged (US$0.50). The bridge over the Río Mopán has been rebuilt. On far side someone will carry the luggage to Melchor de Mencos (hotels, and money change possible—see page 1033), where there is a landing strip with flights, for example, to Flores. There is also a road (very rough) on to Santa Elena, for Flores (4 daily buses from Melchor de Mencos, 3½ hrs., US$1). By catching an early bus (0530) it is possible to go to Tikal without first going to Flores; change at El Cruce, bus leaves for Tikal at 1300 (see page 1033). Taxi from the border to Tikal, US$35 (takes 6).

Along the south-western road, at Belmopan, some 48 miles from Belize City, the good 52-mile Hummingbird Highway branches off SE through beautiful jungle scenery to **Dangriga** (chief town of the Stann Creek District), some 105 miles from Belize City. Road is one bus wide with passing places, 1¾-2½ hours drive from Belmopan. Dangriga's population is 2,500. In this, the most fertile area in the country, are grown citrus fruits, bananas, cassava, and general food crops. The town is on the seashore, and has an airstrip and cinema. Houses built of wood, on piles. Mosquitoes and sand flies are a nuisance.

Local Holiday Nov. 19, Garifuna, or Settlement Day, re-enacting the landing of the Black Caribs (Garinagu) in 1823.

Hotels *Riverside*, 135 Commerce St., E, not always clean, expensive restaurant; *Pelican Beach*, outside town (P.O. Box 14), on the beach, L, with private bath and a/c; both have good restaurants. *Chameleon*, 119 Commerce St., E, owned by Don Carmelo, good and friendly (close by, towards the bridge) is an excellent Chinese restaurant. Cheaper lodgings in *Catalina*, 35 Cedar St., F, good, and in private homes (basic). Unfurnished houses are rented out for BZ$40-60 a month.

At Mile 25.5 on the Hummingbird Highway, N of Dangriga, is *Hummingbird Café*, owned by Ron and Louise Lines (Canadians—mailing address P.O. Box 120, Belmopan); excellent meals and very helpful.

Banks Royal Bank of Canada, Bank of Nova Scotia; Barclays Bank International. Same hours as BelizeCity. (See page 1062.)

Bus from Belize City, Z Line, Magazine Street, Mon. to Sat. at 1000, 1300 and 1600, Sun. at 1400 and 1500, returning daily 0530, 0930, 1000, Sun. at 0900, 1000, 1500, BZ$8, 4 hrs. (buy ticket in advance to reserve seat), or truck, BZ$2. Two buses daily to Punta Gorda, one is the James Line bus from Belize City and the other (Z line), at 1430, 4-5 hrs., BZ$8.50, stops at Independence, near Mango Creek.

Placencia, a quiet, unspoilt little resort S of Dangriga, reached by dugout (BZ$10 each way, 3 hrs., or by bus or truck to Mango Creek (BZ$5), and a boat from there (20 min., BZ$5 by dugout, or BZ$25-30, chartered on a per boat, not per person, basis), boats meet the 1430 bus from Dangriga; return to Mango Creek early a.m., from Fishing Cooperative. A road to Placencia was due for completion in December 1986. Maya Airways fly 3 times a day Belize City-Dangriga-Placencia/Big Creek (dugout Placencia-Big Creek arranged at *Sonny's*, where flight tickets are also sold), BZ$63 one way. Accommodation: *E-Lee Placencia*, E, full board BZ$15 extra (single meals available), creole cooking, run by Dalton Eiley and Jim Lee; they offer reef fishing, snorkelling, excursions to the jungle, Pine Ridge, Mayan ruins and into the mountains. If arriving by air at Big Creek, first contact Hubert Eiley, 3 Richard Sidewalk, Belize City (Tel.: 3567) who will arrange for a boat to take you to Placencia; *Ran's Travel Lodge*, F, shower, toilet, clean, friendly, safe; Carla, who looks after the place, lives next door and cooks breakfast (BZ$3), and dinner (BZ$6); *Maya Beach Tropical Lodge*, C (P.O. Box 23); *Placencia Cove* and *Rum Point Inn* (both A); *Hilltop*, F; Miss Jackson rents rooms, E-F, BZ$7 for 3 meals (book in advance if non-resident), cooking facilities, friendly (contact Bill, an American, here, for trips to the reef); she also at the Post Office rents houses at BZ$40 per day (4-6 people, fridge and cooker); she also has hammock space for 3, BZ$5 per night (noisy); Mrs Leslie's son Charles makes all arrangements for the boat to Puerto Cortés, Honduras (see below), and occasionally changes travellers' cheques; he also, organizes trips to the reef, etc. (expensive). Mr. Clive rents 2 houses, one at BZ$4.50, one at BZ$5 p.p. per day; Mr. Zabari's house (rented by Mr. Leslie), BZ$20 per day, 3 large rooms, all facilities.

1068 BELIZE

Camping on the beach or under the coconut palms. There are three restaurants (*The Galley*; *Jennie's*—ask here for lodgings at *Seaspray*, F, without bath, good value, by post office; and *Sonny's*), at least 5 shops (fresh fruit and vegetables supplied to *The Market* once a week, mostly sold out the same day), a video-cassette movie theatre, four bars (*Cosy's* is recommended, disco every night, good hamburgers), the fishing cooperative, open Mon.-Sat., a.m., sells fish cheaply, and supplies the town's electricity. There is a police station. The people are very friendly (a pleasant change after Belize City) and excursions can be made to the coral reef, 16 km. off-shore (US$75-100 for 6 people). The only 'phone is at the Post Office. Nearest bank in Mango Creek (Bank of Nova Scotia) open Thurs. only 0900-1200, but shops change travellers' cheques. Visa extensions obtainable in Mango Creek.

Mango Creek exists for the banana export trade; it is 20 miles S of Dangriga. Bus Belize City-Mango Creek, Southern Transport, James Bus Service, from Pound Yard Bridge, Mon. at 0800, Tues., Wed., Fri. at 0600, Sat. at 0900; return Tues., Thurs., Fri. and Sun., 0830, arrives 1530, BZ$11.50 (insect-repellant imperative). 1000 Z-line bus from Belize City to Dangriga connects with another Z-line bus to Mango Creek, 2 hrs., BZ$5. Hotel above *People's Restaurant*, F, bad food; better at the white house with green shutters behind it (book 2 hrs. in advance if possible); *Hello Hotel* (at Independence) run by Antonio Zabaneh at the shop where the Z-line bus stops, F, clean, comfortable, helpful. Motorized canoe from Mango Creek to Puerto Cortés, Honduras, no fixed schedule, but mostly Thurs.-Sun. (Antonio Zabaneh at his store—phone 06-2011—knows when boats will arrive), US$50 one way, 7-9 hrs. (rubber protective sheeting is provided—hang on to it, usually enough to go round, nor lifejackets—but you will still get wet unless wearing waterproofs, or just a swimming costume on hot days; it can be dangerous in rough weather). Remember to get an exit stamp (preferably in Belize City), only obtainable at the police station in Mango Creek, not Placencia (the BZ$20 departure tax demanded here is not official). Glover's Reef, about 45 miles off Dangriga, is an atoll with beautiful diving, cottages for rent (BZ$10-25 p.p., bring own food); boats BZ$40-80.

A hundred miles down the coast by road (very bad, often impassable in wet season) from Dangriga is **Punta Gorda,** port of the Toledo District. Population 2,500. Rainfall is exceptionally heavy: over 170 inches. The coast, which is some 10 feet above sea-level, is fringed with coconut palms. The main products are beans, rice, cattle and pigs.

Hotels *Foster's*, 19 Main St., E; *Lux Drive Inn*, 17 Front St., D with bath, best, but often full, cockroaches, noisy, damp, good food; *Mahung's Hotel*, 11 Main St., E; *Isabel*, 52 Front St. E sharing, basic. *Mira Mar*, 95 Front St., C-A, overpriced, noisy disco, restaurant. *Toledo*, opp. police station, F, cheapest but absolutely filthy. The town has a cinema.

Bus from Belize, 10-12 hrs., BZ$16.50, daily except Thurs. and Sun. (times as for Mango Creek); returns Tues., Thur., Fri., Sun. at 0600, with a 1700 bus on Fri. for passengers from Guatemala ferry. To Dangriga, Z-line daily at 0530, arriving in time to catch 1000 bus to Belize City.

Ferry to Guatemala The ferry has superseded all the dugout passages to Livingston and Puerto Barrios, Tues. and Fri. at 1630, 3 hrs. to Puerto Barrios, ticket must be purchased before 1400, costs BZ$11 (US$5.50) or Q6 (US$2.50). Ferry ticket agent is at *Mira Mar Hotel* (closes 1400); he will insist that you have a visa for Guatemala. If you do not need a visa, insist on being sold a ticket without one; if you do need a visa, the nearest place to obtain one is Chetumal, Mexico. Police station for exit stamp is near the ticket office. Leaving Belize City by 0600 bus on Tues., Wed. or Fri., theoretically you can be in Guatemala on the same day, but with changes of bus in Dangriga and delays it is usually impossible; besides it's a tiring journey (to be sure, fly to Punta Gorda). In the other direction, two days are needed.

As there is nowhere to change Belizean dollars into quetzales in Guatemala, try *Mira Mar Hotel* or Vernon's grocery in Punta Gorda (he changes travellers' cheques).

About 9 miles N of Punta Gorda, about ¾ mile off the Southern Highway, is the Mayan site of Nimli Punit.

There is a road inland to two villages in the foothills of the Maya mountains; **San Antonio** (21 miles), with Maya ruins of mainly scientific interest (*Hotel Indita Bonita*, with *comedor*, good, clean; picturesque accommodation at Tacho's, BZ$2; may be allowed use of an army hut); medical centre nearby. About 3 miles along the road to San Antonio is a branch to **San Pedro Colombia**, a Kekchi village. (Kekchi is a sub-tribe of Maya speaking a distinct language.) The Maya and Kekchi women wear picturesque costumes. There are many religious celebrations, at their most intense (mixed with general gaiety) on San Luis Rey day (August 5). No bus; pick-up vans for hire in Dangriga, or get a ride in a truck from the market or rice co-operative's mill in Punta Gorda (one leaves early p.m.); alternatively, go to the road junction, known as Dump, where the northern branch goes to Independence/Mango Creek, the other to San Antonio, 6 miles, either hitch or walk. Transport daily from San Antonio to Punta Gorda at 0500, 0530 punctually; if going to Dangriga, take the 0500, get out at Dump to catch 0530 Z-line bus going N.

Turn left, just after crossing the new bridge at San Pedro Colombia, for one mile to reach the Mayan remains of **Lubaantum,** excavated by Cambridge University in 1970 and found to date from the 8th to 9th centuries A.D., late in the Mayan culture and therefore unique. According to latest reports, however, the site is fast reverting to jungle. Local food at a hut and swimming in a river nearby. If hiking in the jungle in this area, there are plenty of logging trails and hunters' tracks, but do not go alone.

The Economy

Belize's central problem is how to become self-sufficient in food: imports of food are still some 25% of the total imports. Necessity is forcing the people to grow food for themselves and this is gathering pace. One difficulty is that the territory is seriously under-populated and much skilled labour emigrates. Three immigrant Mennonite communities have already increased farm production, and new legislation provides for the development of lands not utilized by private landowners.

Agriculture is by far the most important sector of the Belizean economy, employing more than half the population, and bringing in 75% of the country's total foreign exchange earnings. The main export crops, in order of importance, are sugar, citrus and bananas. Maize, beans and rice are grown, and attempts are also being made to increase the cattle herd.

Forests cover about 65% of the country, and timber is extracted during the first six months of the year. Forest products were for a long time the country's most important export, but their relative importance has fallen. Fish is an important export item, though some of the traditional grounds have been overfished and restrictions necessary for conservation are enforced.

The Government is encouraging the development of tourist facilities. There is also some light industry; items of clothing have been exported. Oil was discovered, near the Mexican border, in April 1981; the search for oil is being intensified.

The slowing down of economic growth at the beginning of the 1980s was attributable to decline in the sugar industry and pressures on Belize's international accounts. Prudent financial policies in the mid-1980s led to the elimination of external debt arrears, the increase of foreign exchange reserves and the reduction of the balance of payments deficit to 3.7% of gdp in 1986.

	1971-75 (av)	1976-80 (av)	1981-85 (av)	1986 (e)
Gdp (1980 prices)	3.9%	4.4%	1.0%	4.0%
Exports (fob) US$m	37.7	76.1	94.3	95.0
Imports (fob) US$m	50.0	100.1	120.0	91.0

Information for Visitors

How to get there There is no regular sea passenger service (but see under Belize City). There is a first-class airport, 9 miles from Belize, served by TAN/Sahsa Airlines, Taca International and Challenge Airlines; there are daily flights from Miami (reached by British Airways, Pan Am, or Virgin Atlantic). Other US points served: New Orleans, Houston, Los Angeles. Also daily flights to San Pedro Sula and Tegucigalpa and less frequent flights to San Salvador, San José, Panama, Guatemala City, Mexico City, San Andrés and Jamaica (with Challenge).

Documents and Customs British and Canadian visitors who begin their journeys in their own countries and stay for not more than 6 months do not need passports. Proof of citizenship, adequate funds for stay and an onward ticket are the only requirements. Other nationalities do need passports (including U.S. citizens), as well as sufficient funds and an onward ticket, but visas are usually not required from nationals of the Commonwealth, Western European countries (although Swedes, W. Germans and Austrians do need a visa, which can be obtained from the Belizean Consulate in Chetumal, Mexico, for US$10—may also be charged the price of a telex to Mexico City, US$40), Mexico, Turkey, Tunisia and Uruguay, although this can depend on the length of stay. Visas may not be purchased at the border. Those going to other countries after leaving Belize should get any necessary visas in their home country. Visitors are initially granted 30 days' stay in Belize; this may be extended up to 90 days, but anyone staying over 30 days must secure a release from the Income Tax Office, Barrack Rd., Belize City, before departure. Travellers should note that the border guards seem to have complete power to refuse entry to people whose looks they do not like. There have also been reports that tourists carrying less than US$30 for each day of intended stay have been refused entry. Visas may be extended in Belize, though once again a show of funds may be requested. Drivers must report to a police station soon after entry to get a

1070 BELIZE

"circulation permit" - they must also have a BZ$5 a day, BZ$25 a week insurance policy, which can be obtained at the Mexican border.

Clothing and articles for personal use are allowed in without payment of duty, but a deposit may be required to cover the duty payable on typewriters, dictaphones, cameras and radios. The duty, if claimed, is refunded when the visitor leaves the country. Visitors can take in any amount of other currencies. No fruit or vegetables may be brought into Belize; searches are very thorough.

Sellers of American cars must pay duty (if the buyer pays it, he may be able to bargain with the customs official), but prices are quite good particularly in Orange Walk (ask taxi drivers in Belize City).

Departure tax of BZ$20 on leaving by air, but not for transit passengers who have spent less than 24 hrs. in the country, nor for children of under 12.

Language English is the official language, but Spanish is widely spoken. Radio Belize devotes about 40 per cent of its air-time to the Spanish language. A Low German dialect is spoken by the Mennonite settlers (hard for present-day German speakers to understand).

Internal Transport Traffic drives on the right. Hitch-hiking is not easy. The Belize stretch of the road to Mexico has been improved, and the Belize-Belmopan road is good with some unpaved stretches. Gasoline costs about BZ$4 a gallon. In Belize there is a BZ$10 per week compulsory road insurance. Most roads are in reasonable condition, but are narrow.

Maya Airways flies daily to each of the main towns (see under Belize City) and offers charter rates to all local airstrips of which there are 25. 5 other companies have charters from Belize City to outlying districts. (Belize Aero Company, Tel.: 44102; Cari Bee Air Service, Tel.: 44253; Flight Service Ltd, Tel.: 7049; National Air Service, Tel.: 3727; Tropical Air Service, Tel.: 7049). Charter rates: Cessna 3-seater, BZ$240; 4/5-seater, BZ$320; 9-seater, US$560.

Passenger transport between the main towns is by colectivo or bus, and trucks also carry passengers to many isolated destinations. Enquire at market place in Belize City. By law, buses are not allowed to carry standing passengers; some companies are stricter than others. Hitch hiking is very difficult as there is little traffic.

Health Europeans leading a normal life and taking common precautions find the climate pleasant and healthy. Malaria is on the increase as a result of the influx of refugees infected with the disease from other Central American countries; prophylaxis is advisable. Inoculation against yellow fever and tetanus is advisable but not obligatory. The Tourist Board advises visitors to use boiled water. Out-patients' medical attention is free of charge.

Official time is 6 hrs. behind GMT.

Clothing The business dress for men is a short-sleeved cotton or poplin shirt or *guayabera* (ties not often worn) and trousers of some tropical weight material. Formal wear may include ties and jackets, but long-sleeved embroidered *guayaberas* or bush jackets are commoner. Women should not wear shorts in the cities and towns; acceptable only on the cayes and at resorts.

The **monetary unit** is the Belizean dollar, stabilized at BZ$2=US$1. Currency notes (Monetary Authority of Belize) are issued in the denominations of 100, 20, 10, 5, and 1 dollars, and coinage of 50, 25, 10, 5 and 1 cent is in use. Notes marked Government of Belize, or Government of British Honduras, are only redeemable at a bank. The American expressions Quarter (25c.), Dime (10c.) and Nickel (5c.) are common, although 25c. is sometimes referred to as a shilling. There is a BZ$1.00 charge for cashing travellers' cheques. Good rates for Mexican pesos in Belize. Best rates of exchange at the borders.

Weights and measures Imperial and US standard weights and measures. The US gallon is used for gasoline and motor oil.

The **Cost of Living** is high. Retail shops are open 0800-1200, 1300-1600 and Fri. 1900-2100, with a half day from 1200 on Wed. Small shops open additionally most late afternoons and evenings, and some on Sundays 0800-1000.

Government and commercial office hrs. are 0800-1200 and 1300-1600 Mon. to Fri.

Public Holidays

January 1: New Year's Day.
March 9: Baron Bliss Day.
Good Friday and Saturday.
Easter Monday.
May 1: Labour Day.
May 24: Commonwealth Day.

Sept. 10: St George's Caye Day.
Sept. 21: Belize Independence Day.
Oct. 12: Pan American Day.
  (Corozal and Orange Walk).
Nov. 19: Garifuna Settlement Day.
December 25: Christmas Day.

EL SALVADOR 1071

Warning Most services throughout the country close down Good Friday to Easter Monday: banks close at 1130 on the Thursday, buses run limited services Holy Saturday to Easter Monday, and boats to the Cayes are available. St. George's Caye Day celebrations in September start 2 or 3 days in advance and require a lot of energy.

Telephone and Cable There is a direct-dialling system between the major towns and to Mexico and USA. Cable and Wireless, open 0730-2100 Mon.-Sat., closed Suns. and holidays, has an international telephone, telegraph and telex service. To make an international call from Belize costs far less than from neighbouring countries. BZ$26.25 for 3 min. to UK and Europe (a deposit of BZ$30 required first); BZ$15.75 to most of USA and Canada; BZ$10.50 to Florida and US South-East; BZ$8 per min. to Australia. Collect calls to just about anywhere.

Airmail Postage to UK 4-5 days. BZ$0.75 for a letter, BZ$0.45 for a postcard; BZ$0.60 for a letter to U.S.A, BZ$0.25 for a post card.

Press Belize: *Belize Times; Amandala, Beacon, Reporter* (weekly). *The Belizean Tourister* (monthly) offers useful information for tourists.

We are grateful for most useful information from Ian Beharell and Georgina Howes (Oxford), Dr Michael Binzberger (Friederichshafen), Caribbean Charter Services (Belize), Dave Duckett (Jackson, Miss.), Thomas Harding and members of the Intermediate Technology World Cycle Tour team (London NW3), Wayne Hedenschoug (Springfield, Ill.), Walter Kilbourne (Seattle), Annette Morris (Redhill, Sy.), Chesley and Carole Schart (Teton Village, Wyo.), and Lisa Tenuta (Kenosha, Wis.) for a particularly valuable contribution; also several travellers listed at the end of the general Central America section.

EL SALVADOR

EL SALVADOR is the smallest, most densely populated, most industrialized and most integrated of the Central American republics. Its intermont basins are a good deal lower than those of Guatemala, rising to little more than 600 metres at the capital, San Salvador. Across this upland and surmounting it run two more or less parallel rows of volcanoes, 14 of which are over 900 metres. The highest are Santa Ana (2,365 metres), San Vicente (2,182), San Miguel (2,130), and San Salvador (1,943). One important result of this volcanic activity is that the highlands are covered with a deep layer of ash and lava which forms a porous soil ideal for coffee planting.

The total area of El Salvador is 21,200 square km. Guatemala is to the W, Honduras to the N and E, and the Pacific coastline to the S is 260 km. or so.

Lowlands lie to the N and S of the high backbone. In the S, on the Pacific coast, the lowlands of Guatemala are continued to just E of Acajutla; beyond are lava promontories till we reach another 30-km. belt of lowlands where the Río Lempa flows into the sea. The northern lowlands are in the wide depression along the course of the Río Lempa, buttressed S by the highlands of El Salvador, and N by the basalt cliffs edging the highlands of Honduras. The highest point in El Salvador, Cerro El Pital (2,730 metres) is part of the mountain range bordering on Honduras. After 160 km. the Lempa cuts through the southern uplands to reach the Pacific; the depression is prolonged SE till it reaches the Gulf of Fonseca.

The population of 4.96 million is far more homogeneous than that of Guatemala. The reason for this is that El Salvador lay comparatively isolated from the main stream of conquest, and it had neither the precious metals nor the agriculturally active Indians that acted as magnets for the Spaniards. The small number of Spanish settlers intermarried with the Indians to form a group of mestizos

1072 EL SALVADOR

herding cattle in the valley of the Lempa and growing subsistence crops in the highlands. There were only about half a million people as late as 1879, but soon afterwards coffee was planted in the highlands; easy access to the coast made this crop profitable. The population grew quickly and the prosperity of the coffee planters fertilized the whole economy, but the internal pressure of population has led to the occupation of all the available land. Several hundred thousand Salvadoreans have emigrated to neighbouring republics because of the shortage of land and the concentration of landownership, and more lately because of the high level of violence.

Of the total population only some 10% are purely Indian; less than 10% are of unmixed white ancestry; the rest are *mestizos*. Birth rate: 29.8; death rate, 6.0 per 1,000; infant mortality, 35.1 per 1,000 live births. Annual growth rate 1.6% (1980-86); urban growth: 3.2%; and 41.8% live in the towns. Expectation of life at birth, 56 years.

El Salvador is fortunate in that its temperatures are not excessively high. Along the coast and in the lowlands it is certainly hot and humid, but the average for San Salvador is 23°C with a range of only about 3°. March, April, May are the hottest months; December, January, February the coolest. There is one rainy season, from May to mid-November, with only light rains for the rest of the year: the average is about 1,830 mm. Occasionally, in December and March there is a spell of continuously rainy weather, the *temporal*, which may last from two or three days to as many weeks. The pleasantest months are from November to January. From time to time the water shortage can become acute.

Recent History There has been a marked increase in political unrest and violence. On October 16, 1979, the President, General Carlos Humberto Romero, was overthrown in a military coup and replaced by a reformist civilian-military junta. In December 1980 a civilian member of the Junta, the Christian Democrat Sr. José Napoleón Duarte, was appointed President. A decline in popular support and the founding of an opposition front, the Frente Democrático Revolucionario (FDR), and attempted reforms to shift power away from the landowning and banking families, have increased political tension to the proportions of civil war. Sr. José Napoleón Duarte again became President after elections in May 1984. Political killings perpetrated by both left and right wings have resulted in an average death toll of 30 per day. The leftist guerrilla forces have maintained their strength, and exploratory meetings have been held between the guerrillas and President Duarte, but the initiative was lost until Duarte's Christian Democrats unexpectedly won a majority over the right-wing parties in the Congressional elections of April 1985. This, however, did not revive the dialogue between the Government and the insurgents. Guerrillas have continually interfered with traffic along the main highways and with economic activities generally, but visitors have been interfered with rather less in 1986/87 than in previous years.

The People With a population of 234 to the square km., El Salvador is the most densely peopled country on the American mainland. Health and sanitation outside the capital and some of the towns leave much to be desired, and progress has been very limited in the past few years because of the violence. The illiteracy rate is 50%. Education is free if given by the Government, and obligatory. There are two universities, one national and the other Catholic, and a National School of Agriculture. Roman Catholicism is the prevailing religion.

Cities and Towns

San Salvador, the capital, is in an intermont basin at 680 metres, on the Río Acelhuate in the Valle de las Hamacas and with a ring of mountains round it; the population is 1.5 million. It was founded by Pedro de Alvarado in 1525, but not in the valley where it now stands. The city was destroyed by earthquake in 1854, so the present capital is a modern city, most of its architecture conditioned by its liability to seismic shocks. However, in the earthquake of October 10, 1986, many buildings collapsed; over 1,000 people died. As a result, many government offices have been temporarily relocated until reconstruction has been completed. The climate is semi-tropical and healthy, the water supply pure. Days are often hot, but the temperature drops in the late afternoon and nights are always pleasantly mild. Since it is in a hollow, the city has a smog problem, caused mainly by traffic pollution.

Four broad streets meet at the centre: the Av. Cuscatlán and its continuation the Av. España run S to N, Calle Delgado and its continuation Calle Arce from E to W. This principle is retained throughout: all the *avenidas* run N to S and the *calles* E to W. The even-numbered *avenidas* are E of the central *avenidas*, odd numbers W; N of the central *calles* they are dubbed Norte; S of the central

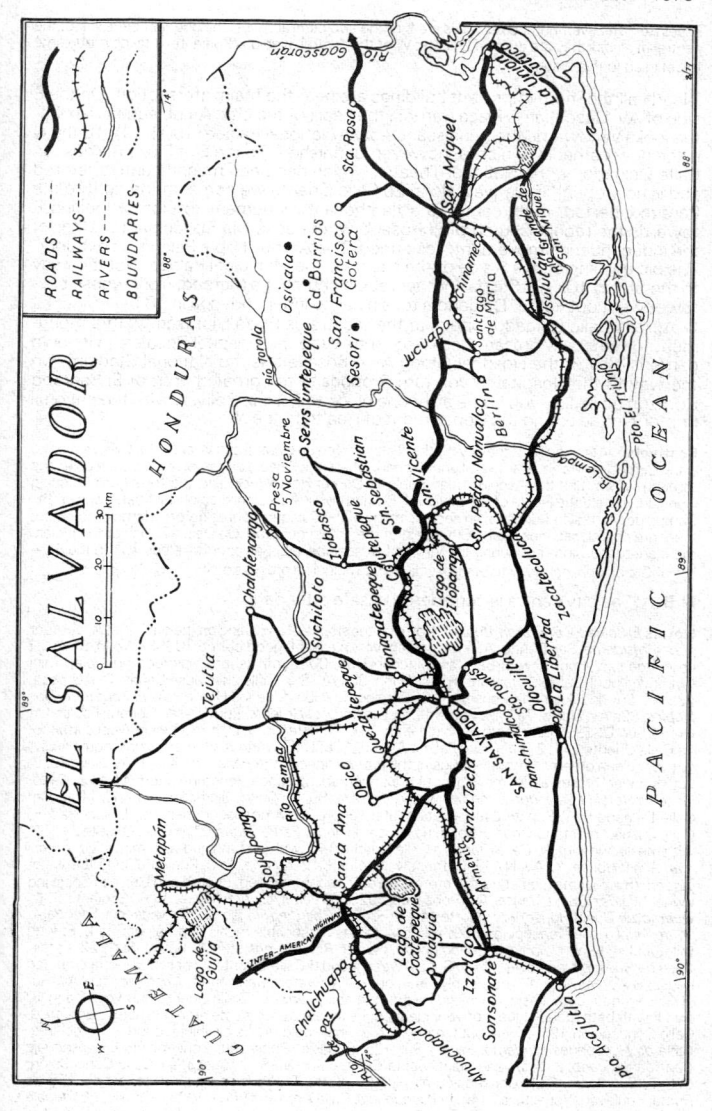

EL SALVADOR 1073

ROUGH SKETCH

1074 EL SALVADOR

calles Sur. The even-numbered *calles* are S of the two central *calles*, the odd numbers N. E of the central *avenidas* they are dubbed Oriente, W of the central *avenidas* Poniente. It takes a little time to get used to this system.

Nearly all the more important buildings are near the main intersection. On the E side of Av. Cuscatlán is Plaza Barrios, the heart of the city. A fine equestrian statue looks W towards the Renaissance-style National Palace (1904-11). To the N is the new cathedral which is, however, unfinished. To the E of Plaza Barrios, on Calle Delgado, is the National Theatre (which has been magnificently restored and is now open). If we walk along 2a Calle Oriente we come on the right to the Parque Libertad; in its centre is a flamboyant monument to Liberty looking E towards the rebuilt Church of El Rosario where José Matías Delgado, father of the independence movement, lies buried. The Archbishop's Palace is next door. The big building on the S side of the square is the Municipal Palace. Not far away to the SE (on 10a Av. Sur) is another rebuilt church, La Merced, from whose belltower went out Father Delgado's tocsin call to independence in 1811.

Across Calle Delgado, opposite the theatre, is Plaza Morazán, with a monument to General Morazán. Calle Arce runs W to the Hospital Rosales, in its own gardens. SW of the Hospital, along Av. Roosevelt, is the National Stadium. On the way to the Hospital, if you turn S opposite the great church of El Sagrado Corazón de Jesús, you come after one block to Parque Bolívar, with the national printery to the S, and the Department of Health to the N.

Festivals At the edge of the city (to the N along Avenida España and W along 9a Calle Poniente) is the Campo de Marte, a large and popular park where the Palacio de Deportes has been built, and through which runs the Avenida Juan Pablo II. During Holy Week, and the fortnight preceding August 6, is held the Fiesta of the Saviour ("El Salvador"). As a climax colourful floats wind up the Campo de Marte. On August 5, an ancient image of the Saviour is borne before a large procession; there are church services on the 6th, Feast of the Transfiguration. On Dec. 12, Day of the Indian, there are processions honouring the Virgin of Guadalupe in El Salvador (take bus 101 to the Basilica of Guadalupe, half-way to Santa Tecla, to see colourful processions).

N.B. The city centre is considered unsafe after dark.

Hotels *El Salvador Sheraton*, 89a Av. Norte on the slopes of a volcano on the outskirts, A, outdoor pool; *Presidente*, San Benito, A, pool, garden, very pleasant, good buffets (US$8); *Novo*, 61 Av. N (in cul-de-sac), rooms with bath and kitchen US$500/month (shorter periods possible), mini swimming pool, garden, pleasant; *Ramada Inn*, 85a Av. Sur, Calle Juan José Cañas, C; *Alameda*, 43a Av. Sur and Alameda Roosevelt, C; *Camino Real*, Blvd. de los Héroes, A; *El Parador de los Nobles*, 89a Av. Norte, 7a Calle Poniente, C; *Escalón Apartments*, 3689 Paseo General Escalón at Av. 71 Sur, US$300 per month double; *Fénix*, 1a C. Oriente 2319, D, free parking. *Nuevo Mundo*, 1a Calle Oriente 217, E; *Internacional*, 8a Av. Sur 108, D (E, without shower), front rooms noisy, not very clean otherwise good. Opposite the *Internacional* is the *Panamericano*, 8 Av. Sur 113, E, with shower, closes early, meals from US$2 and parking space, recommended; *Motel El Patio*, close to Hotel El Salvador, E, no hot water. *Terraza*, 85 Av. Sur, Calle Padre Aguilar, C-B; *León*, Calle Delgado 621, F, with bath, erratic water supply, dirty, not recommended; *La Libertad*, Calle Castillo, nr. station, basic. Boarding houses include: *Parker House*, 17a Calle Oriente 217 (D, with meals, without E); *Casa Clark*, 7a Calle Oriente 144 (without bath and with meals, D); *American Guest House*, 17 Av. N 119, C, friendly, helpful; *Casa Austria*, 1a C. Poniente 3843 (between 73 and 75 Av.), small, quiet, family atmosphere, D, recommended, English and German-speaking owner; *Valdez Guest House*, Av. Roosevelt 1925, C; *Family Guest House*, 1a C. Poniente, D; *Oberholzer Guest House*, 9 Av. Norte 144, E; *España Boarding House*, Col. Providencia, Escorial 4, D; *Imperial*, Calle Concepción 659, friendly, serves reasonable meals and has car park, E, with toilet and shower. *Colonial* boarding house, next to Ramírez bus station, 6a Av. Sur 322, F, fair; *Casa de Huéspedes Venvier*, 6 Av. Sur between 4 and 6 Calle Oriente, F, basic; *Barletta* boarding house, 8 Av. Sur 129, F, reasonably clean but noisy, water intermittent; *Custodio*, 10a Av. Sur 109, F, without bath, basic, clean and friendly but noisy; *Bruno*, 1 Calle Oriente, between 8 and 10 Av., F with bath, good value, not very clean, quite safe (but not a safe area of town); *San Carlos*, Calle Concepción 121, F with bath, early morning call, cold drinks available, good; in same area *Casa de Huéspedes Moderno*, 8a Av. Sur 125, F, basic. *Roosevelt*, Concepción, E; *Hospedaje Centroamericano*, E, clean and quiet; *Santa Clara*, 6 Av. N 18, C; *Cuscatlán*, Calle Concepción, 675, F; *San Jorge*, Calle Concepción and 20 Av. Norte, F; *América*, Av. Independencia 125, E; *Roma*, Boulevard Venezuela 3145, F; *Lucedencia*, Calle Arce and 9 Av. Norte, G, basic; *Hospedaje Yucatán*, Calle Concepción 673, F, basic, friendly; excellent restaurant downstairs; *Hospedaje Latino*, same street, F with bath, filthy, noisy; *Hospedaje Rex*, 10a Av. N, 1a Calle Oriente, F. Prices are without meals unless otherwise stated. Hotel tax: 10%. **Motels** *Boulevard*, E, with shower, very clean, with parking, 2 km. from centre, but good bus service. *Siesta*, on Autopista Sur, off

EL SALVADOR 1075

Pan-American Highway, west of the city, C. Several motels exist on all main roads leading out of the capital.

Restaurants   At hotels. All close between 2000 and 2100. *Siete Mares*, Paseo Escalón, very good seafood; *La Fonda*, Paseo Escalón y 85 Av. Norte; *El Greco*, Paseo General Escalón, Colonia Escalón; *Diligencia* (for good steaks) and *El Bodegón* (Spanish style) both on Paseo Escalón, are excellent; also on Paseo Escalón: *Gran Tejano*, *La Ponderosa* (famous for steaks with *chirimol*, near Plaza Beethoven); *Le Mar* (seafoods), *Beto's* (Italian); *Pip's Carymar* (also in Santa Tecla— good, cheap typical food), *Rancho Alegre* (cheap, also opp. Metrocentro shopping mall), and *tacos* and *pupusas* at Redondel Masferrer, good view over city. *Texas Meats*, Calle La Mascota, good for steaks. *München*, Av. Roosevelt, German; opp. is *China Palace*, excellent value (oldest Chinese restaurant in San Salvador); *Romano*, Av. Roosevelt 45 y 47 Av. Norte; *Chez Balta*, Av. Roosevelt 3104; *El Café Don Pedro* (drive-in in Av. Roosevelt); *Benihana of Tokyo*, Paseo Escalón, 89 Av. Sur; *Balam Quitzé*, Japanese, good; *Café Cathay* (good Chinese); *Chung Sam*, nr. Supermarket La Mascota, Chinese, road to Santa Tecla; also on this road, *Pupusería Margot*, opp. Estado Mayor, good; *El Coche Rojo*, Calle Santa Tecla km. 4; *La Carreta*, 45 Av. Sur 116; *Royal*, 8a Av. Norte 342. In Blvd. Hipódromo (Zona Rosa): *Marcelino's*, *Mediterráneo* (good *ceviche*), *La Ola*, *Chili's*, *Paradise* (all popular); *Basilea/Schäffer's*, also in Zona Rosa, restaurant and excellent cakes, nice garden atmosphere. *Rosal*, El Mirador, near Sheraton, Italian, good. *Hardees Hamburgers* on Blvd. Los Héroes, and other branches; also branches of *MacDonalds*; *Pollo Campero* (branches throughout the city); *Café Palacio*, 4 Calle Poniente, good cheap local food, popular and has opened a new branch near the Mercado Cuartel; *Comedor Colonial*, 4 C. Poniente; *Comedor Mercedes*, around corner from Hotel Internacional, reasonable. Vegetarian restaurants: *La Zanahoria*, Calle Arce 1199, *El Tao*, 21 Av. Norte y Calle Arce, and Centro de Gobierno, 19 C.P.; *Govinda*, 25 Av. Norte, next to Super Selectos, *Catay*, Metrocentro, *Actoteatro*, 1 Calle Poniente (between 15 and 13 Av. N), good atmosphere, patio, music, good buffet lunch, cheap, central. Try some of the delicious and very popular *pupusas*, or savoury pancakes. They are particularly good at a cave restaurant in Puerta del Diablo. *Victoria*, bakery, good for pastries. The food market, one of the biggest and cleanest in Latin America, has many stalls selling cheap food. *Pops*, near Bruno Hotel on 1 Calle Oriente and Av. 4, is a good ice-cream parlour; there is another branch on Escalón, near the British Club. Coffee shops: *Shaw's*, chocolates and coffee; *Flashback*, Blvd. Hipódromo (Zona Rosa), good coffee.

Electric Current   110 volts, 60 cycles, A.C. (plugs are American, 2 flat pin style).

Clubs   Club Salvadoreño, admits foreigners, owns a fine Country Club on Lake Ilopango called Corinto (with a golf course), and has a seaside branch at Km.43 on the coast road, near La Libertad, much frequented during the dry season, November to May. The Automobile Club of El Salvador has a chalet for bathing at La Libertad. International Rotary; Lions; British Club (Paseo Escalón 4714—approx), has British newspapers and swimming pool. (Temporary visitors' cards if introduced by a member.) Club Deportivo Internacional (Calle Santa Tecla), The Country Club Campestre (Paseo Escalón), admits foreigners with cards only. Club Náutico, at the Estero de Jaltepeque, famous for its mud boat races.

Shopping   Mercado Cuartel, crafts market, 8 Av. Norte, 1a C. Oriente, a few blocks SE of the National Theatre. One can buy towels here with various Maya designs. A large new shopping precinct with ample parking (Metrocentro) is on Boulevard Los Héroes, NW of city centre. Metrocentro and the Zona Rosa have handicraft shops, but at least twice as dear as Mercado Cuartel.

Bookshop   Librería Cultural Salvadoreña, new address not known. A few English books at Librería Quixaje, Calle Arce, and a few at Shaw's Chocolate shop, 1 block past Parque Beethoven on Paseo Escalón.

Local Buses   Flat fare of US$0.10.

Taxis   Plenty (all yellow), very few have meters. Fares: from centre to outskirts or *Hotel El Salvador Sheraton*, US$1.60; central runs, US$1. Double fare after dark. Taxis from Taxis Atayco (Tels.: 218870 and 216644) and Taxis Santa Fe (Tel.: 217500 and 215044). Self-drive cars cost US$6 to US$16 per day or US$40 to US$80 per week according to size of car plus a rate per km. of US$0.08.

Complaints   Director General of Police, 6a Calle Oriente. Tel.: 216605.

Night Clubs   Club Salvadoreño (for members and guests only). *El Buho*, *Camelot*, both on Plaza Suiza; *Mario's*, *Café-Concert*, both on Blvd. Hipódromo, Zona Rosa, latter with good live music; *Faces on the Top*, double-disco, Calle El Mirador, near *Sheraton*. *Club M*, also near Sheraton; *Deportivo* (members and guests only).

Entertainments   Many cinemas, with Cinerama at the Grand Majestic (best quality cinemas cost US$1.60, films in English with sub-titles), or ballet and plays at the National Theatre of Fine Arts, and music or plays at the Cámara Theatre. Bowling at Bolerama Jardín and Club Salvadoreño. Kermesses are held pretty nearly every Sun. Football is played at the Stadium on Sun. and some week nights. Motor racing at new El Jabalí autodrome on lava fields near Quezaltepeque.

EL SALVADOR

Basketball, tennis, international swimming, fishing, target shooting, wrestling, boxing and boat and sailing boat races, but in private clubs only.

Museum Museo Nacional David J. Guzmán, on the outskirts of the city, has a small but good archaeological exhibition. Open Tues.-Fri. and Sun. 0900-1200 and 1500-1700, Sat. 1500-1700.

Banks Citibank, in Torre Roble, Blvd. de los Héroes; and national banks. Open 0900-1600; some banks have a late night counter until 1900. Banks charge 1 colón for changing money and cheques; cashing travellers' cheques involves lengthy paperwork. Foreign currency is difficult to obtain. At the Central Post Office is a window where dollars are bought at the parallel rate. Black market can be found outside the Centro Gobierno, and on the W side of Parque Infantil for dollars cash, travellers' cheques and quetzales.

Immigration Department Owing to earthquake damage, temporarily at Antiguo Plantel I.V.U., Col. Monserrat.

British Embassy The British Embassy and Consulate is at 17C. Poniente No. 320, Centro Gobierno, Gibson y Cía., Tel.: 71-1050. **US Embassy** and Consulate-General are at 25 Av. Norte, 1230, in front of Fuente Luminosa, Tel.: 267100. **Dutch Consulate** Of. La Curazao, Edif. Lotisa 2° piso, Final C. La Mascota y Av. Masferrer (Tel.: 23-4000, 0800-1200, 1330-1630). **Guatemalan Embassy** 15 Av. Norte 135 y C. Arce (0900-1200). **Nicaraguan Embassy** 27 Av. Norte No. 1134 (Tel.: 25-7281, 0900-1400); **Honduran Embassy** 9a C. Poniente 4612 y 89 Av. Norte, Col. Escalón (Tel.: 24-6662, 0800-1300); **Mexican Embassy** Paseo Gral. Escalón 3832 (Tel.: 24-0162, 0900-1400); **Belize** 15C. Poniente 4415 (½ block behind *Sheraton*, Tel.: 23-5271, 0830-1200); **West German Embassy** 3a C. Poniente 3832, Col. Escalón (Tel.: 23-6173, 0800-1400); **French Embassy** 1a C. Poniente 3718 y 73 Av. Norte, Col. Escalón (Tel.: 23-0728, 0900-1200).

Churches Anglican Centre (St. John's Episcopal Church), 63 Av. Sur and Av. Olímpica, services on Sun., 0900 in English, 1000 in Spanish; American Union Church, C. 4 off Calle La Mascota, has services in English on Sun., at 1000, and also has a gift shop (local crafts and textiles) and an English paperback library (both open Weds. and Sat.). Jewish Synagogue, 23a Av. Norte 215.

International Industrial Fair, held in November, every two years (even dates), in Calle Santa Tecla, near the Monument of the Revolution. Site is also used for other functions such as the August traditional fair.

National Tourist Institute Instituto Salvadoreño de Turismo, Calle Rubén Darío 519, Tel.: 217445/214845 (closed at weekends), and at Cuscatlán airport. They will advise on the security situation in the country. They give away a map of the country and city, but the Texaco and Esso maps (obtainable from their respective service stations) are more accurate. The office is very helpful. Also "Advice to Tour Guides", a recommended booklet. Good map of the country is available from the Instituto Nacional de Geografía, Av. Juan Bertis, 59 and Librería La Ibérica, 1 Calle Oriente, 127.

Tourist Agents El Salvador Travel Service, 23 Av. Sur 201. Ibalaca Tours, Edificio La Reforma, 4a Calle Oriente; Avia, la Calle Poniente, at junction with 73a Av. Norte in Colonia Escalón, are recommended. Also, Maya Av. Olímpica, and Morales, Paseo Escalón, near Plaza Beethoven.

Airport The new international airport, Cuscatlán, is 40 km., from San Salvador, near La Libertad. Minibus to airport from 1a Diagonal near U.S. Embassy (Taxi Acacya, Tel.: 26-0888, 25-7768, 25-9137), 0600, 0700, 1200, 1500, US$2. Taxi, US$20 (for foreigners, US$12 for locals). The airport tax is US$9, plus US$1 boarding tax. The old airport is at Ilopango, 13 km. away. It is primarily used by the airforce. However, from Ilopango small planes fly to San Miguel (30 mins., good, US$25), Usulután, Santa Rosa de Lima and La Unión; tickets from the civilian traffic offices (TAES, Taxis Aéreos El Salvador, or Gutiérrez Flying Service). There is a sales tax of 10% on all air tickets bought in or outside El Salvador for all journeys beginning in that country. No internal air lines but charter flights are easily arranged. The prices in the gift shops at the airport are exorbitant, and there is no post office.

Rail W to Santa Ana, Sonsonate and Acajutla. There are no pasenger services.

Long-Distance Buses Terminal del Occidente, down an alleyway off Boulevard Venezuela, opposite No. 2963 (dangerous area; take city buses 4, 27 or 34). Most international buses pass through if not starting from here. About 5 buses a day (various companies) to Guatemala City (5 hrs.), leave at 0800. Single, US$5; return, US$8. By car to Guatemala City takes 4 hrs. To Tegucigalpa, Transportes El Salvador, 7a C. Poniente y 14 Av. Norte 322, on Mon., Thurs. and Sat. at 0630. Mermex (6 Av. Sur 333) US$5, 10 hrs., Transportes Centro América (2a C. Oriente y 8a Av. Sur 129, Tel: 216480), use minibuses on this route. Melva y Pezarrossi, Onda and Futuro-Express

EL SALVADOR 1077

(518a Pasaje Alcaine, Av. Sur 13) also go to Guatemala. One bus a day to Puerto Barrios (Guatemala) via Santa Ana with Rutas del Atlántico from central terminal (leave this bus at Morales, Guatemala, and take bus next morning to Flores for the Petén). The only way to Managua and further S is by taking local buses beyond Choluteca or Tegucigalpa. Good bus services to other main cities: from Terminal Oriente, end of Av. Peralta (take city buses 7, 33 or 29): to San Miguel every half hr., US$1.40, and to La Unión, US$1.75, five times a day.

N.B. The Honorary British Consul in El Salvador advises, "If buses are running regularly, the route is probably reasonably safe." Bus routes most frequently attacked by guerrillas are the Troncal del Norte to Chalatenango and El Poy and the eastern Pan-American Highway between San Vicente and San Miguel, and San Miguel and Goascarán.

A good **sightseeing tour** of from 2 to 3 hrs. by car is along Av. Cuscatlán, past the Zoo (which though small, is quiet and attractive) and the Casa Presidencial and up to the new residential district in the mountain range of Planes de Renderos. This place, reached by bus 12 from the centre, is crowned by the beautiful Balboa Park (good view of city from El Mirador at foot of Park). From the park a scenic road runs to the summit of Cerro Chulo, from which the view, seen through the Puerta del Diablo (Devil's Door), is even better. The Door consists of two enormous vertical rocks which frame a magnificent view of the San Vicente volcano. At the foot of Cerro Chulo is Panchimalco (see below). There are local buses (12, US$0.20 and 17, and 12 minibus marked "Mil Cumbres") to Puerta del Diablo about every hour. The Teleférico on the hill overlooking the city and Lake Ilopango has good views, cafeterias and a children's funfair. Reached by 43 bus from centre, US$1.60. Open Mon. and Wed.-Fri. 1400-2000, Sat. 1000-2100 and Sun. 0900-2100.

For a quick "taste" of San Salvador, Taca airlines take passengers in transit through San Salvador to the *Sheraton Hotel* from the airport, provide a free lunch, and a room for US$5 (this generally applies to flights between Managua/San José and Tegucigalpa/Guatemala City, which involve an 8-hour wait in El Salvador for connecting Taca flights).

Excursions can be made by road to Panchimalco and Lake Ilopango; to the crater of San Salvador volcano; and to the volcano of Izalco (1,910 metres) and the near-by park of Atecosol, and Cerro Verde (see Sonsonate, page 1082); to the garden park of Ichanmichen (see Zacatecoluca, page 1081); to Lake Coatepeque (lunch at *Hotel del Lago*) and to Cerro Verde in 90 minutes. The excavated site of San Andrés, on the estate of the same name, 32 km. west of San Salvador, is unimpressive (take bus 201 from Terminal del Occidente). Bus 495 from the Terminal del Occidente goes to Costa del Sol, Sihuatehuacán, the pyramid of Tazumal (page 1084) and Los Chorros (bus 79 from Calle Ruben Darío—see below), where there are swimming pools. Buses from the Oriente terminal go to Quezaltepeque, near which is La Toma, a popular inland resort, to Amapulapa, where there are gardens and a swimming pool, and to Lake Apastepeque (see page 1080).

Panchimalco is 14½ km. S by a paved road. Around it live the Pancho Indians, pure-blooded descendants of the original Pipil tribes; they have retained more or less their old traditions and dress. Streets of low adobe houses thread their way among huge boulders at the foot of Cerro Chulo (rolled down the hill to repel the Spaniards, according to local legend). A very fine baroque colonial church with splendid woodcarvings in the interior and a bell incised with the cypher and titles of the Holy Roman Emperor Charles V. An ancient ceiba tree shades the market place. Bus 17 from Mercado Central at 12 Calle Poniente, San Salvador, every 45 min., US$0.30, 1½ hrs.

Lake Ilopango A 4-lane highway, the Ilopango Boulevard, runs E for 14½ km. from San Salvador to Ilopango airport, quite near Lake Ilopango, 15 km. by 8, in the crater of an old volcano, well worth a visit. Pre-Conquest Indians used to propitiate the harvest gods by drowning four virgins here each year. The water is reported to be polluted. There are a number of lakeside cafés and bathing clubs, some of which hire dug-outs by the hr. Pete's Yacht Club accepts day visitors for boating, swimming etc. *Hotel Vistalgo*, D. A number of private chalets make access to the lake difficult, except at clubs and the Turicentro. Bus 15, marked Apulo, runs from the bus stop on 2a Av. Norte y Plaza Morazán to the lake (via the airport), 70 minutes, US$ 0.30. Entrance to the Turicentro camping site costs US$0.18 and is recommended; showers and swimming facilities.

Santa Tecla, 13 km. W of the capital by the Pan-American Highway, is 240 metres higher and much cooler, in a coffee-growing district. Population, 52,563.

1078 EL SALVADOR

The huge crater of San Salvador volcano (known as Boquerón by the locals)—1½ km. wide and 1 km. deep—can be reached from Santa Tecla, road starts 1 block E of Plaza Central, going due N (very rough). Bus (101) leaves 3 Av. Norte, near the junction with Calle Ruben Darío, San Salvador, every ten mins. for Santa Tecla (US$0.12). There is a bus (103) from there to Boquerón hourly, last one back at 1500 (US$0.30) and from there you must walk the last 1½ km. to the crater. There is also a daily bus from San Salvador at 0600 (details from Tourist Office). A walk round the crater is rather rough going and can take 3-4 hrs. The views are magnificent. The inner slopes of the crater are covered with trees, and at the bottom is a smaller cone left by the eruption of 1917. The path down into the crater starts at the last of a row of antennae studding the rim, 45 mins. down (don't miss the turn straight down after 10 mins. at an inconspicuous junction with a big, upright slab of rock 20 metres below), 1 hr. up. There are a number of army checkpoints on the way to the summit. A road further North leads also to/from San Salvador volcano through extensive coffee plantations. Santa Tecla, also known as Nueva San Salvador, has a training school for factory technicians, set up with British funds and technical help.

The National Museum, with Indian relics, is now in a new building off the road to Santa Tecla. At **Los Chorros**, in a natural gorge 6 km. N of Santa Tecla, there is a beautiful landscaping of 4 pools below some waterfalls. The first pool is shallow, and bathers can stand under the cascades, but there is good swimming in the other three. Visit at night for the lighting effects. Entry, US$0.15. Car park fee: US$0.40. Camping is allowed, US$1 for two people. There is a trailer park at Los Chorros, with restaurant and showers.

Just before Santa Tecla is reached, a branch road turns S for 24 km. to

La Libertad, 37 km. from San Salvador, now only a fishing port. Population 14,500. It is also a popular seaside resort during the dry season, with good fishing and surf bathing, but watch out for undercurrents and sharks. The beaches are black volcanic sand; they are dirty but the surf is magnificent. (The Automobile Club and the Club Salvadoreño have beach chalets.) Bus 102 from San Salvador leaves from 4 Calle Poniente, 17 Av. Sur, US$0.62. Bus from Santa Tecla, US$0.30.

The Costa del Bálsamo (the Balsam Coast), stretching between La Libertad and Acajutla (see page 1082), is now rather a myth, but on the steep slopes of the departments of Sonsonate and La Libertad, scattered balsam trees are still tapped. However, few pure-bred Indians of the Tunalá tribe, who traditionally tapped the trees, are left in the area, and the pain-relieving balsam, once a large export, has almost disappeared. Bus along the coast to Sonsonate at 0600 and 1300, about 4 hrs.

Hotels Hotels charge for 12 hrs. only. *Don Rodrigo*, C; *Don Lilo*, D; *Puerto Bello*, E, good; *Rich*, 5 Av. 375 (near beach), E. *Hosdepaje Familiar*, F, filthy; *Pensión Peace and Love*, F, very basic and friendly; *Tropicana Inn and Trailer Park*. *Bar Gringo* on the beach front lets rooms, F, so does the *Miramar* restaurant (E, negotiable); *Pensión San Miguel*, F. **Motel** *Siboney*, nearby, good.

Restaurant Food is good in the town, especially at *Punta Roca* (American-owned, by Don Bobby), try the shrimp soup, and *Altamar* for seafood. *Pupusería*, specializes in snacks, recommended. *Los Mariscos*, good, reasonable prices, popular, closed Mons. Cheap restaurants near the pier; also cheap food in the market.

Excursions To the large village of Jicalapa, on high rockland above the sea, for its magnificent festival on St. Ursula's day (October 21). 8 km. to the north is **Zunzal**, which has superb surf (*Hospedaje El Pacífico*, F, 1 km. towards La Libertad; *Surfers' Inn*, F, not recommended, share room with bats, filthy; restaurant next door—the only one in town—is grim); buses 102 and 192, from La Libertad. 15 km. away is the *Atami Beach Club*, with pool, private beach, restaurant, 2 bars, gardens, a beautiful place, tourists may enter for US$2, prices are reasonable.

Eastern El Salvador

E to La Unión/Cutuco There are two ways of reaching the port of La Unión/Cutuco on the Gulf of Fonseca from the capital now that rail services have been discontinued: (i) by the Pan-American Highway, 185 km., through Cojutepeque, San Vicente (road being repaved either side of this city), the 15 de Septiembre dam (since the destruction of the Cuscatlán bridge) and San Miguel; (ii) by the Coastal Highway, also paved, running through Santo Tomás de Aquino, Olocuilta, Zacatecoluca, and Usulután. The roads have frequently been cut by guerrilla action against bridges and traffic.

EL SALVADOR 1079

By Pan-American Highway Some 5 km. from the capital a dry-weather highway branches N to Tonocatepeque, Suchitoto, and Chalatenango.

Tonocatepeque, 13 km. from the capital, is an attractive small town on the high plateau, in an agricultural setting but with a small textile industry. There has been some archaeological exploration of the town's original site, 5 km. away.

Suchitoto is quite near the Lempa River, and the Cerrón Grande reservoir, under which is the old road to Chalatenango. The new road to Chalatenango branches right off the Troncal del Norte beyond the Cerrón Grande (see page 1085). There has been much guerrilla and counter-insurgency activity in this northern area: visitors are advised to take care.

Continuing along the Pan-American Highway: a short branch road (about 2 km. beyond the airport) leads off right to the W shores of Lake Ilopango. The first town is **Cojutepeque,** capital of Cuscatlán Department, 34 km. from San Salvador. (Reached by bus 113 from Oriente terminal in San Salvador, US$0.75.) Population 18,347. Lake Ilopango is to the SW. Good weekly market. The volcano of Cojutepeque is nearby. The town is famous for cigars, smoked sausages and tongues, and its annual fair on August 29 has fruits and sweets, saddlery, leather goods, pottery and headwear on sale from neighbouring villages, and sisal hammocks, ropes, bags and hats from the small factories of Cacaopera (Dept. of Morazán).

Hotels *Jovel*, E; *Motel Edén*, E, with shower; *Comedor Toyita*, good value.

Cerro de la Virgen, a conical hill near Cojutepeque, dominates Lake Ilopango and gives splendid views of wide valleys and tall mountains. Its shrine of Our Lady of Fátima draws many pilgrims.

Excursion From San Rafael Cedros, 6 km. E of Cojutepeque, a 16-km. paved road N to Ilobasco has a branch road E to Sensuntepeque at about Km. 13. **Ilobasco** has 26,703 people, many of them workers in clay; its decorated pottery is now mass-produced and has lost much of its charm. The area around, devoted to cattle, coffee, sugar and indigo, is exceptionally beautiful. Annual fair: September 29. An all-weather road leads from Ilobasco to the great dam and hydroelectric station of Cinco de Noviembre at the Chorrera del Guayabo, on the Lempa River. Bus to Cojutepeque. Another road with fine views leads to the Cerrón Grande dam and hydroelectric plant; good excursion by bus or truck. Permission is given in normal times to enter the dam area and one can climb the hill with the Antel repeater on top for a view of the whole lake created by the dam. The whole Lempa valley is now a security zone and there has been much guerrilla activity there.

Four km. further S along the Pan-American Highway at San Domingo (km. 44 from San Salvador) an unpaved road leads in 5 km. to **San Sebastián** where colourfully patterned hammocks and bedspreads are made. You can watch them woven on complex looms of wood and string, and can buy from the loom. The 110 bus from the Oriente terminal runs from San Salvador to San Sebastián (US$1.50). There are also buses from Cojutepeque.

Sensuntepeque, 35 km. E of Ilobasco, *is an attractive small town at 900 metres,* in the hills S of the Lempa valley. It is the capital of Cabañas Department, once a great source of indigo. There are some interesting ceremonies during its fair on December 4, the day of its patroness, Santa Bárbara. It can be reached from the Pan-American Highway from near San Vicente. Population: 30,000.

N.B. San Vicente and San Miguel have been the centres of intense guerrilla activity in Eastern El Salvador and consequently there is a strong military presence.

San Vicente, 61 km. from the capital, is a little SE of the Highway on the Río Alcahuapa, at the foot of the double-peaked Chinchontepec volcano, with very fine views of the Jiboa valley as it is approached. Population: 48,000. Its pride and gem is El Pilar (1762-69), most original church in the country. It was here that the Indian chief, Anastasio Aquino, took the crown from the statue of San José and crowned himself King of the Nonualcos during the Indian rebellion of 1833. In its main square is the *tempesque* tree under which the city's foundation

1080 EL SALVADOR

charter was drawn up. Bus 116 from Oriente terminal, San Salvador. Carnival day: November 1.

Hotels *Pensión Vicentina*, E. Better is *Casa Romero*, which is near the bridge but has no sign, so ask for directions, E; good meals for US$0.80. *Hospedaje Viajero*, F; *Hospedaje Rivoly*, E, good food.

Two km. E of the town is the Balneario Amapulapa, one of a number of recreational centres developed by the National Tourist Board. There are three pools at different levels in a wooded setting. Small entry and parking charges. Reached by bus 174 from San Vicente.

Excursion Lake Apastepeque, near San Vicente off the Pan-American Highway, is small but picturesque. The Tourist Board has built a pier and bathing cabins. Hotel: *París*.

The Highway used to cross the Río Lempa by the 411-metre-long Cuscatlán suspension bridge (destroyed by guerrillas in 1983), and now crosses the 15 de Septiembre dam at the San Lorenzo hydroelectric plant, and goes on (in very poor condition) to

San Miguel, 142 km. from San Salvador, capital of its Department, founded in 1530 at the foot of the volcanoes of San Miguel (Chaparastique—which erupted in 1976, and Chinameca). It has some very good parks and a bare 18th century cathedral. Some silver and gold are mined. It is an important distributing centre. Population, 112,600. Bus 301 from Oriente terminal, San Salvador (US$1.40, return every ½ hr. from 0500 to 1630). Fiesta of the Virgen de la Paz: November 20. There is a charming church with statues and fountains in its gardens about 16 km. away at Chinameca.

Hotels Very few in centre, most on the entrance roads: *Trópico Inn*, C, clean, comfortable, reasonable restaurant; *Hispanoamericano*, 6A Av. Norte B, F, with toilet and shower, air-conditioned (cheaper in older rooms without a/c); *Motel Milián* (pool), D, recommended, good food; *El Motelito*, F, dirty; *Central*, G, English spoken. *Pensión El Carmen*, F; *San Luis*, G, clean and quiet. Plenty of cheap places near the bus station. *Comedor Divina Providencia* for good meals; 3 Chinese restaurants.

Banks Local banks. Open: 0830-1200, 1430-1800.

From San Miguel a good paved road runs S to the Pacific Highway. Go S along it for 12 km., where a dirt road leads to Playa El Cuco, a pleasant long beach; a small motel 1 km. from El Cuco village. There are lots of *pensiones* in the village quite near the bus stop, E/F. Bus 320 from San Miguel, US$1. The climate in this area is good. Another interesting excursion is to Sabanetas (10 km.) on the Honduran border. The road from San Miguel runs to Jocaitique (there is a bus) from where an unpaved road climbs into the mountains through pine forests. Accommodation at both Jocaitique and Sabanetas. (This trip is not possible while guerrilla activity continues.) A mainly paved, reasonable road goes to San Jorge—Usulután: leave the Pan-American Highway 5 km. W of San Miguel. The road goes through hills and coffee plantations with superb views of San Miguel volcano. Accessible only by private car from San Miguel are two places worth a visit: **Laguna de Alegría** is in a crater of an extinct volcano and is fed by both hot and cold springs; good swimming. To the N are the Indian ruins of **Quelapa** (bus 326).

It is another 42 km. to the port of La Unión/Cutuco. Before it gets there the Pan-American Highway turns N for the Goascarán bridge to Honduras. Bus San Miguel-Goascarán, US$0.80, 2½ hrs. (may be disrupted by guerrillas). There is a tourist office at the border (El Amatillo).

To save time when travelling eastwards, take the Ruta Militar NE through (34 km.) Santa Rosa de Lima to the Goascarán bridge on the border with Honduras, 56 km. (There are plenty of money changers, accepting all Central American currencies and travellers' cheques, but beware of short-changing on Nicaraguan and Costa Rican currencies.)

Santa Rosa de Lima (15,770 people) is a charming small city with a wonderful colonial church, set in the hills. There are gold and silver mines. Don't miss the excellent *sopa de apretadores* (crab soup, the best in El Salvador), near the town centre—everyone knows the place.

La Unión/Cutuco, on the Gulf of Fonseca, is the only port in El Salvador except Acajutla at which ships can berth. Population, 22,500. The port handles half the country's trade. There is good fishing and swimming, but much mud during the

EL SALVADOR 1081

rains. It is a holiday resort during the dry season, but nearest really good beach is at Playitas. Bus 304 from Oriente terminal, San Salvador.

Hotels *Centroamérica*, E, with fan, more with a/c; *Miramar*, G, good; *Hospedaje Annex Santa Marta*, F, basic, dirty, unfriendly; *San Carlos*, opposite railway station, E, good meals available; *Hospedaje Santa Rosa*.

Restaurant *La Patia*—fish; *Comedores Gallego* and *Rosita* recommended. *Comedor Tere*, Av. General Menéndez 2.2, fairly good.

Exchange at *Cafetín Brisas del Mar*, 3 Av. Norte y 3 Calle Oriente.

Customs at 3 Av. Norte 3.9; **Immigration** at 3 Calle Oriente 2.8.

Ferry There is no longer a ferry to Puntarenas (Costa Rica). A number of boatowners run regular, but not scheduled, crossings by dugout to Potosí (Nicaragua); first get your Salvadorean exit stamp, then go to wharf and ask around, best before 1400, for a boat leaving next day (usually at 0500). Negotiate fare (about US$5) and give the captain your passport, which he will return on the boat. Crossing takes 4-5 hrs.; be prepared to get wet (plastic sheet for baggage advisable). We have received details of the route by cargo boat from Nicaragua to El Salvador (see page 1127).

Bus terminal is at 3 Calle Poniente (block 3); to San Salvador, US$1.75, 4 hrs., many daily, direct or via San Miguel, one passes the harbour at 0300. Bus to Honduran border at El Amatillo, No. 353, US$0.50.

Excursions To Conchagua to see one of the few old colonial churches in the country; Conchagua volcano can also be climbed and a hard walk will be rewarded by superb views over San Miguel volcano (good bus service). One can take an early morning boat to the islands in the Gulf of Fonseca: to Zacatillo (about 1 hr.) and Meanguera (more), where there are many secluded little beaches. Take plenty of provisions, as afternoon boats can be uncertain and one may have to spend the night in a fishing hut. To El Tamarindo (bus 383, US$0.25, service not good so best start early), a small, attractive fishing village with beautiful white beaches. No accommodation, but the place is popular and huts to sling a hammock are US$2 a day. Also from La Unión, the ruins of Los Llanitos can be visited.

By Coastal Highway This is the second road route, running through the southern cotton lands. It begins on a 4-lane motorway to Cuscatlán airport. The first place of any importance after leaving the capital is (13 km.) Santo Tomás de Aquino. There are Indian ruins at Cushululitán, a short distance N.

Beyond, a new road to the E, rising to 1,000 metres, runs S of Lake Ilopango to join the Pan-American Highway beyond Cojutepeque.

Ten km. on from Santo Tomás is **Olocuilta,** an old town with a colourful market on Sunday under a great tree. Good church. (Both Santo Tomás and Olocuilta can be reached by bus 133 from San Salvador.) From the airport, the road becomes a 2-lane toll-road, going E across the Río Jiboa to

Zacatecoluca, capital of La Paz Department, 56 km. from San Salvador by road and 19 km. S of San Vicente. Bus 133 from Occidente terminal, San Salvador. José Simeón Cañas, who abolished slavery in Central America, was born here. Population, 56,400. Quite near are the small towns of San Pedro Nonualco and Santa María Ostuma (with an interesting colonial church and a famous *fiesta* on February 2); both are worth visiting, but not easy to get to.

Near the town is the garden park of Ichanmichen ("the place of the little fish"). It is crossed by canals and decorated with pools: there is, in fact, an attractive swimming pool. It is very hot but there is plenty of shade.

Hotel *América*, E. *Hospedajes América* and *Popular* clean, E. *Comedor Margoth* (beware high charging).

Both road and railway cross the wide Lempa River by the Puente de Oro (Golden Bridge) at San Marcos. (The road bridge has been destroyed; cars use the railway bridge.) A branch road (right) leads to tiny Puerto El Triunfo on the Bay of Jiquilisco, with a large shrimp-freezing plant. About 110 km. from the capital is

Usulután, capital of its Department. Population, 40,350. Bus 302 from San Salvador.

Hotels *Hotels and Restaurant España*, on main square, recommended, nice patio, bar and discotheque. *Millions*, D; *Motel Usulután*, D; *Central*, E.

1082　EL SALVADOR

A road branches NE from Usulután, some 45 km. to San Miguel (see page 1080) On this road is Lake Jocotal, a national nature reserve supported by the World Wildlife Fund, which can be visited by arrangement with the warden.

The Coastal Highway goes direct from Usulután to La Unión/Cutuco.

Western El Salvador

The route from the capital S to La Libertad has already been given. Both a paved road and the railway connect San Salvador with Sonsonate and the port of Acajutla. The road goes W through Santa Tecla (see page 1077) to Sonsonate, and then S to the port. 6 km. W of Santa Tecla on the main road is Los Chorros (see under Santa Tecla); 3½ km. beyond, the Pan-American Highway runs NW past Lake Coatepeque to Santa Ana.

Acajutla, Salvador's main port serving the western and central areas, is 85 km. from San Salvador (bus 207 from Occidente terminal, US$2.80), 58 km. from Santa Ana (it is 8 km. S of the Coastal Highway). It handles about 40% of the coffee exports and is a popular seaside resort (good surf riding) during the summer, though not an attractive town. Population: 15,635.

Hotels Miramar; California, E. Brisas del Mar, F. Good, cheap pensión at back of La Campana store.

The nearby beaches at El Espino, El Cuco, Jaltepeque and Barra de Santiago are recommended.

Sonsonate, 19 km. N on the road to the capital (64 km.) produces sugar, tobacco, rice, tropical fruits, hides and balsam. An important market is held each Sun. Sonsonate is in the chief cattle-raising region. Population: 48,200. It was founded in 1552. The beautiful El Pilar church is strongly reminiscent of the church of El Pilar in San Vicente. The Cathedral has many of the cupolas (the largest covered with white porcelain) which serve as a protection against earthquakes. The old church of San Antonio del Monte, just outside the city, draws pilgrims from afar. Capital to Sonsonate by bus 205, US$1.50, 90 mins.

Hotels Sonsonate, 6 Av. Norte with Calle Obispo Marroquín, D, with a/c, meals available; Orbe, D; Centroamericano, near centre, E; Hospedaje Taplán, near bus station, G, basic; del Viajero, opposite bus station, F.

Restaurants Milkbar; Comedor Santa Cecilia.

Roads　N to Santa Ana, 39 km., a beautiful journey through high, cool coffee country, with volcanoes in view; NW to Ahuachapán, 40 km., and on to Guatemala (road paved from Ahuachapán through Apaneca and passes through some spectacular scenery); S and W to the Guatemalan frontier points of La Hachadura and Ciudad Pedro de Alvarado at the bridge over the Río Paz. Border crossing is straightforward, but if in a private vehicle requires a lot of paperwork (about 2 hrs.). Many buses ply between La Hachadura and Sonsonate, US$0.60 to Ahuachapán, US$0.50, 4 hrs.

At the foot of Izalco volcano, 8 km. from Sonsonate, is the villlage of **Izalco,** which has resulted from the gradual merging of the ladino village of Dolores Izalco and the Indian village of Asunción Izalco. Festivals, August 8 to 15 and during the Feast of St. John the Baptist from June 17 to 24. Near Izalco, on the slopes, is the spacious swimming pool of Atecozol, in the middle of a beautiful park with a restaurant. The park is shaded by huge mahogany trees, palms, aromatic balsam trees and amates. There is a battlemented tower; a monument to Tlaloc, god of the rain; another to Atonatl, the Indian who, on this spot, shot the arrow which lamed the conquistador Pedro de Alvarado; and a statue to the toad found jumping on the spot where water was found. Izalco village and Izalco volcano are not directly connected by road. A paved road branches from the highway 14 km. of the turning for Izalco village (about 22 km. from Sonsonate) and goes up towards Lake Coatepeque (see below); when you reach the summit, an all-weather road branches for **Cerro Verde** with its fine views down into the Izalco crater. A camping ground and car park at 1,980 metres overlook the crater. The road to Cerro Verde has fine views of Lake Coatepeque; ¾ of the way to Cerro Verde, a track branches off to the right to Finca San Blas. From there it is a 1 hr. walk straight up Santa Ana volcano. There are four craters inside one another; the newest crater has a lake and fuming columns of sulphur clouds. You can walk around the edge and down on to the ledge formed by the third crater (beware of the fumes). The main paved road goes on to the lakeshore. The fine Hotel Montaña (C) at the top of Cerro Verde was originally built so that the international set could watch Izalco in eruption; unfortunately, the eruptions stopped just as the hotel was completed and it was empty for years. Good food is provided at fairly reasonable prices. There is a

EL SALVADOR 1083

US$0.25 charge for parking, but none for camping. There is a bus (No. 209B) twice daily from Santa Ana to a junction 14 km. from the top of Cerro Verde (US$1). From Sonsonate to the turn-off for Cerro Verde costs US$0.30; from there it is easy to hitch a lift (tip expected).

Just below the car park on Cerro Verde, a path goes down towards the saddle and on to Izalco volcano. The ascent is quite difficult because of loose debris.

There is an Indian village at **Nahuizalco,** north of Sonsonate. The older women still wear the *jaspé corte* (a doubled length of cloth of tie-dyed threads worn over a wrap-round skirt), and various crafts are still carried on, although use of the Indian language is dying out.

The Pan-American Highway runs through Santa Tecla to Santa Ana. A new dual carriageway road parallels the old Pan-American Highway, bypassing Santa Ana; toll: US$0.40. (Keep your ticket if turning off to Coatepeque, as it serves for the return.) The road, with turnoffs for Sonsonate and Ahuachapán, carries on to San Cristóbal on the Guatemalan frontier.

There is an archaeological site at San Andrés, half-way between Santa Tecla and Coatepeque. Exhibits from it and from Tazumal are at the National Museum.

Some 13 km. short of Santa Ana a short branch road leads (left) to **Lake Coatepeque,** a favourite week-end resort with good sailing, swimming, and fishing near the foot of Santa Ana volcano. There are good hotels, restaurants, and lodging houses. The surroundings are exceptionally beautiful. (Bus 201 from San Salvador to Santa Ana, where one changes to a 220 for the lake, or take a bus from San Salvador to El Congo on Pan-American Highway, US$1, then another to the lake, US$0.20.) Cerro Verde is easily reached in 90 mins. by good roads through impressive scenery.

Tourists are put up free in cabins with mattresses and showers at Balneario Los Obreros (a resort for workers). When you reach the lake shore from the rim of the crater follow the road a little. Permission to stay must be obtained from the Departamento de Bienestar, Ministerio de Trabajo, 2a Av. Norte, San Salvador. Restaurant and supervised swimming. Otherwise, water difficult to reach because of the number of weekend homes.

Hotels Hotels charge per 12 hrs. *Del Lago* (try the crab soup), D, overpriced; *Torremolino,* E; *Casa Blanca,* F, dirty; *Lido,* E; *Costa Azul,* near telegraph office, F, dirty, meals available.

Santa Ana, 55 km. from San Salvador and capital of its Department, is the second largest city in the country (bus 201 from Terminal del Occidente, San Salvador). The intermont basin in which it lies at 656 metres on the NE slopes of Santa Ana volcano is exceptionally fertile. Coffee is the great crop, with sugar-cane a good second. The city is the business centre of western El Salvador. There are some fine buildings, particularly the classical theatre, the neo-gothic cathedral, and several other churches, especially El Calvario, in colonial style. Population: 416,878.

Hotels *La Libertad,* near cathedral, C with bath, good meals for about US$2; *Roosevelt,* E, good meals for US$1.60; *Florida,* room with bath, E, recommended, serves excellent meals for US$2; *Hospedaje Carao,* Av. José Matías Delgado, F, with bath, basic, quite clean; *Pensión Lux,* on Parque Colón. *Colonial,* F, 8 Av. Norte 2, clean, helpful, good breakfasts for less than US$1, a little noisy; *Hospedaje Livingston,* 10 Av. Sur, 29, F, with bath, clean, friendly; *Pensión Monterrey,* F, without bathroom, and *Hospedaje El Santaneco,* F, without bath, basic, on same street. Restaurants are expensive so it is best to eat in *comedores*. Everything closes at about 1900.

Banks Local banks. Open 0830-1200, 1430-1700.

The border with Guatemala is 30 km. by paved road from Santa Ana (the fastest road link from San Salvador to Guatemala City is via the Santa Ana bypass, then to Ahuachapán and on to the border at Las Chinamas—tourist office here). Buses (Melva) leave from the *Pensión Lux* on the east side of Parque Colón for Guatemala City, US$3, 5½ hrs. including meal and border stops. Also Inter Futuro Express, Transportes Centro América, and Mermex, US$5, unreliable. Alternatively there are local buses to the border for US$0.30; they leave from the market. Bus 406 from the capital (Terminal del Occidente), goes direct to the frontier at Las Chinamas.

Excursions To Lake Coatepeque, 19 km. (bus to *Hotel del Lago* US$0.40). **Chalchuapa,** 16 km. from Santa Ana, on the road to Ahuachapán, population 34,865, is at 640 metres. President Barrios of Guatemala was killed in battle here in 1885, when trying to reunite *Central America by force. There is some good colonial-style domestic building;* the church of Santiago is particularly striking. See the small but picturesque lake; the very interesting church, almost the only one in El Salvador which shows strong indigenous influences, and the **Tazumal** ruin just E of Chalchuapa,

1084 EL SALVADOR

built about A.D. 980 by the Pipil Indians but with its 14-step pyramid now, alas, restored in concrete. The site has been occupied since 5000 B.C. and in the simple museum are the artefacts found in the mud under the lake. There are very interesting bowls used for burning incense, intricately decorated with animal designs. The ruin, which is open 0900-1200 and 1300-1730, is free of entry and only 5 minutes' walk from the main road. Minibus (No. 218) from Santa Ana, 20 mins., US$0.30. On the west of the town is the El Trapiche swimming pool. Bus 51 or 55 goes to Turicentro Siuatehuacán, on city outskirts; US$0.13 admission to pools, café, park, etc.

Hotel at Chalchuapa: *Gloria*, E.

Guatemalan consul in Chalchuapa (Av. Club de Leones Norte, between Primero and Calle Ramón Flores—unmarked blue house, knock for attention).

Ahuachapán, capital of its Department, is 35 km. from Santa Ana, at 753 metres. Population, 53,260. It is a quiet town with low and simple houses, but an important distribution centre. Coffee is the great product. Like many places in the area, it draws the mineral water for its bath-house from some hot springs near the falls of Malacatiupán, near-by. Power is from the falls of Atehuezián on the Río Molino, which cascade prettily down the mountain-side. See also the *ausoles*—geysers of boiling mud with plumes of steam and strong whiffs of sulphur, which are now being harnessed to produce electric power. A road runs NW through the treeless Llano del Espino, with its small lake, and across the Río Paz into Guatemala. There are two other small lakes, Laguna Verde and Apaneca, whose crater-like walls are profusely covered in tropical forest, in the Cordillera de Apaneca, part of the narrow highland belt running SE of Ahuachapán; they are popular with tourists. It is possible to swim in the former, but the latter is too shallow and reedy. Local buses run some distance away, leaving one with a fairly long walk. Laguna Verde can also be reached by road via Cantón Tulapa, from a turn off on the CA-8 road east of Apaneca. Ahuachapán is 116 km. from the capital by bus 202 from San Salvador (US$2.75). Buses direct to the border, US$0.80.

The *ausoles* are interesting—an area of ground which is warm to the touch. They are used for generating electricity and are being covered by drums and pipes; only the smallest will soon remain untouched. One can take a bus from Ahuachapán to El Barro, take a taxi or walk the 5 km. to the area. Permission to visit the power station can be obtained from the office in town, near the police station.

Hotel *Astoria*, E; *La Ahuachapaneca* guest house, E; *Hospedaje San Juan*, E. One can get good meals at *Restaurant El Paseo*.

Metapán (32 km. N of Santa Ana) is about 10 km. NE of Lake Güija. Its colonial baroque cathedral is one of the very few to have survived in the country. The altarpieces have some very good silver work (the silver is from local mines) and the façade is splendid. Lots of easy walks with good views to the lake. There are many lime kilns and a huge cement plant.

Hotels *Gallo de Oro*, G; *Ferrocarril*, G.

A mountain track from Metapán gives access to Montecristo National Nature Reserve, El Salvador's last remaining cloud forest. There is an abundance of protected wildlife; permits to visit have to be obtained in San Salvador (and are not given during the breeding season, thought to be Feb. to May).

A good paved road runs from Metapán to the Guatemalan frontier.

Lake Güija, on the Guatemalan border, 16 km. by 8, is very beautiful and dotted with small islands, but it is not easy to reach. A new dam at the lake's outlet generates electricity for the western part of the country.

Northern El Salvador

There has been much guerrilla and counter-insurgency activity in the northern areas; visitors are required to have a permit to travel in this region unless they have a visa (soldiers may ask for a permit regardless).

Steven Edwards writes: The main road north (Troncal del Norte) is paved throughout, and runs due North through Apopa (junction with a good road to Quezaltepeque) and Aguilares to the western extremity of the Cerrón Grande reservoir. A branch to the right skirts the northern side of the reservoir to Chalatenango, capital of the department of the same name. **Chalatenango,** 55 km. from San Salvador, is a quaint little town with an annual fair and *fiesta* on June 24. (Bus 125 from Oriente terminal, San Salvador.) Population, 15,137. It is the centre of an important region of traditional livestock farms.

The main road continues north through Tejutla to **La Palma,** a charming village set in pine clad mountains, and well worth a visit. It is famous for its local crafts, particularly the brightly-painted wood carvings and hand-embroidered tapestries. There are a number of workshops in La Palma where the craftsmen can be seen at work and purchases made. (The products are also sold in San Salvador.) Buses run from San Salvador to La Palma (No. 119, US$1).

The road continues north to the frontier at El Poy, for western Honduras (at least 5 buses a day—No. 119—from Terminal del Oriente in San Salvador). 2 km. before El Poy is *Hotel Cayahuanca,* F, clean, friendly. Travellers' cheques exchanged at El Poy. Exit tax ¢3, plus a ¢5 "tourist tax" (stamp affixed to passport).

The Economy

Agriculture is the dominant sector of the economy, accounting for 75% of export earnings as well as employing some 30% of the population. Coffee and cotton are the most important crops, but attempts have been made at diversification and now sugar and maize are becoming increasingly important as foreign exchange earners. Land ownership has been unevenly distributed with a few wealthy families owning most of the land, while the majority of agricultural workers merely lived at subsistence level; this led to serious political and social instability despite attempts at agrarian reform by successive governments, of which the latest (and most determined) was in 1980.

With the expansion of the industrial sector in recent years, there has been a rapid growth in the middle and industrial working classes. The most important industry is textiles; others include shoes, furniture, chemicals and fertilizers, pharmaceuticals, cosmetics, construction materials, cement (and asbestos cement), food and drink processing, rubber goods. A small quantity of petroleum products, including asphalt, is also produced. Exports of manufactured goods, mostly to other Central American countries, account for some 24% of foreign exchange earnings.

There are small deposits of various minerals: gold, silver, copper, iron ore, sulphur, mercury, lead, zinc, salt and lime. There is a gold and silver mine at San Cristóbal in the Department of Morazán. In 1975 a geothermal power plant came into operation at Ahuachapán, with capacity of 30 mw. The plant was expanded by 60 mw in 1978. Hydraulic resources are also being exploited as a means of generating power and thermal plants have been shut down, thus affording an even greater saving in oil import costs.

The country's agricultural and industrial production, and consequently its exporting capability, have been severely curtailed by political unrest. In 1986 further economic and social damage was caused by an earthquake; damage to housing and government property alone was estimated at US$311m, while the total, including destruction and disruption of businesses was put at US$2bn. El Salvador is heavily dependent upon aid from the USA to finance its budget. Total US assistance was estimated at US$2.5bn in 1979-86 and was expected to be US$600-US$800m in 1987.

1086 EL SALVADOR

	1961-70 (av)	1971-80 (av)	1981-85 (av)	1986 (e)
Gdp (1980 prices)	5.6%	3.2%	-2.1%	-0.5%
Inflation	0.7%	10.7%	14.7%	30.0%
Exports (fob) US$m	182.1	662.9	743.1	800.0
Coffee	90.2	346.9	435.3	na
Cotton	26.5	64.8	39.9	na
Imports (fob) US$m	175.5	623.3	897.9	970.0
Current account balance US$m (cum)	-131.7	-452.2	-572.3	81.0

Information for Visitors

Warning Prices in El Salvador are sometimes quoted in US dollars. Make sure which currency is being used.

How to get there From London: To Miami with Pan Am, British Airways or Virgin Atlantic, thence to San Salvador with Taca (direct) or Sahsa via Honduras. Other connecting cities in the USA with flights to San Salvador are: Houston, New Orleans (both served by Taca and Sahsa), Los Angeles (Pan Am, Taca, Lacsa) and San Francisco (Pan Am, Taca). Taca flies to all Central American capitals and to Mexico City (also served by Lacsa). Copa flies to the other Central American capitals, except Belize City and Tegucigalpa, which are served by Sahsa. Aviateca flies to Guatemala City, Aeronica (on Sat.) to Managua, and Lacsa to San José. From Europe, San Salvador can be reached with Taca connecting flights from Guatemala City, to which Iberia (twice weekly) and KLM (once a week) fly. Alternatively, go KLM to Mexico City, and Taca from there.

Royal Netherlands Line, the Johnson Line, Royal Mail Lines, Hapag-Lloyd and Marina Mercante Nicaragüense operate cargo-passenger services between North Sea ports and El Salvador.

By sea from the USA: from New Orleans, a United Brands cargo boat on to Santo Tomás (Guatemala). This company also plies from New York and Philadelphia to Santo Tomás; it also has a service from New Orleans to the Panama Canal, where transshipment is made to the ports of El Salvador.

N.B. There is a 10% tax on international air tickets bought in El Salvador and a US$1 boarding tax. There is also an airport tax of US$9 if staying more than 6 hours.

Documents Necessary: a passport (not necessary for citizens of any country who have been issued with 90-day tourist cards, costing US$2, by airlines or Salvadorean consulates). At the border a visa for 8 days is obligatory for many countries (cost US$5), but not for citizens of most Western European, Latin American (but see below) or Commonwealth countries, or of Ethiopia, Egypt, Israel, Japan, Jordan, Lebanon, Malagasy, Morocco, Philippines, South Africa and Turkey. US citizens need a visa (free). French nationals need a visa, US$5, one entry only, 8 days only. Travellers doing business directly in the country must get an ordinary (non-immigrant) visa at a cost of US$1.60, and visit the Immigration Bureau (25a Av. Norte 11-57) within 48 hours of arrival and get a permit to stay for 30 days. It costs US$4. They must get an exit permit from the same place, at the same price, before they leave the country. Business travellers are sometimes assessed for income tax during their stay. Border formalities tend to be relatively brief, although thorough searches are common. A baggage charge of US$0.50 is made at borders. There is an entrance tax of and an exit tax of 3 colones. There are restrictions on entry by citizens of Belize and Cuba.

Up to 200 kilograms of personal luggage is allowed in free of duty. Also allowed in free: 1 kg. of tobacco products, or 100 cigars or 400 cigarettes, and 2 bottles of liqueur. There are no restrictions on export or import of any currency. **N.B.** Customs do not like woollen goods from Peru; they will treat them with 'formaline' against disease.

"Hints to Exporters: El Salvador" can be obtained from Dept. of Trade, Export Services Division, Sanctuary Buildings, 16-20 Great Smith Street, London SW1P 3DB.

Warning Do not try to enter El Salvador carrying literature that may be regarded as subversive or left-wing, for example books from Nicaragua, or by Russian authors. At best, it will be confiscated, or you may be refused entry. Furthermore, it is advisable not to say that Nicaragua is on your itinerary. Army-style clothing will also be confiscated. It is wise not to camp out, but generally travellers report no problems; just be prepared for plenty of police checks and body searches on buses. It is best not to mention politics.

Motoring At the border, after producing a driving licence and proof of ownership, you are given a permit to stay for 15 days. This can be extended at the National Tourist Institute, Calle Ruben

EL SALVADOR

Darío 519, San Salvador (Tel.: 217445 and 214845) or you can simply cross the border, turn round and get another permit to stay another 15 days. In any case the formalities for bringing in a car involve considerable paperwork. There is a US$0.50 charge for compulsory tyre fumigation. There is also a US$0.40 departure tax for cars. Insurance is not compulsory in El Salvador, but you should arrange cover. A good map, both of republic and of capital, can be obtained from Texaco or Esso, or from the Tourist Institute.

Local Information can be got from the National Tourist Institute, Calle Ruben Darío 519, San Salvador, or from the capital's three big hotels, *El Salvador Sheraton, Presidente* and *Camino Real*. The Tourist Institute provides a small map of the country with at least ten campsites or "Turicentros" marked on it.

The **best months** for a business visit are from February to May, when there is least rainfall and most business. August is the holiday season. Business is centralized in the capital, but it is as well to visit Santa Ana and San Miguel.

Language Spanish, but English is widely understood. Spanish should be used for letters, catalogues, etc.

Clothing White suits and white dinner jackets are not worn.

Food Try *pupusas*, savoury pancakes, cheap and tasty; also *garobo* (iguana) and *cusuco* (tatou—armadillo). They are sold at many street stalls and in fact are better there than in restaurants. On Sat. and Sun. nights local people congregate in *pupuserías*.

Tips at hotels and restaurants: 10%, but 15% for small bills. Nothing for taxi drivers except when hired for the day; airport porters US$0.20 a bag; haircut, US$0.20.

Health The gastro-enteric diseases are the most common. Visitors should take care over what they eat during the first few weeks and should drink *agua cristal* (bottled water). Specifics against malaria should be taken if a night is spent on the coast. Warning of the existence of dengue fever has been reported from that part of the main road running north from San Salvador between Suchitoto and Tejutla, where a large area of land has been flooded for the Cerrón Grande dam. The San Salvador milk supply is good.

Internal Transport Buses are excellent (if sometimes crowded). San Salvador has plenty of taxis. Hitchhiking is comparatively easy. There are no longer any real passenger services.

Currency The unit is the colón (¢), divided into 100 centavos. Banknotes of 1, 2, 5, 10, 25 and 100 colones are used, and there are nickel coins for the fractional amounts. The colón is often called a peso. The official rate in April 1987 was 5 colones to the US dollar. At that time there were also a free rate of ¢5.5 to the US$. See adverts in the papers and shop windows for the rates. When leaving El Salvador, one may only change US$80-worth of colones back into dollars if one has overestimated one's needs. Money sent to El Salvador will be paid out in colones only and then only US$40-worth when leaving by plane. **N.B.** Change all colones before entering Guatemala or Honduras, where they are not accepted or changed anywhere (except at borders).

The **metric system** of weights and measures is used alongside certain local units such as the *vara* (836 millimetres, 32.9 inches), *manzana* (7,000 square metres, or 1.67 acres), the *libra* (0.454 kilogramme, about 1 English pound), and the *quintal* of 100 *libras*. Some US weights and measures are also used. US gallons are used for gasoline and quarts for oil.

Posts and Telegraphs Sea-mail to and from Britain takes from 1-3 months; air mail to or from Europe takes up to one month. The correct address for any letter to the capital is "San Salvador, El Salvador, Central America". Lista de Correos is at new post office building on 11a Av. Norte. Letters to Europe ¢0.60; parcels ¢12 half kilo, ¢30, kilo; surface mail, ¢15 each kilo.

The charge for a local telephone call is ¢0.10 for 3 mins. A private telephone call or telex to Europe costs US$5 per minute (if made from the state telecommunications company, Antel), with a small surcharge for the first 3 minutes. Calls made from hotels cost US$6-7 per minute. Direct dialling is available to Europe (US$5 per minute), U.S.A. (US$2 per min.) and other parts of the world.

Radio Inc. communicates with all parts of the world through local stations. Public telex at Antel. British businessmen can use the telex system at the Embassy.

Time in El Salvador is 6 hrs. behind GMT.

1088 HONDURAS

Hours of Business 0800-1200 and 1400-1800 Mon. to Fri.; 0800-1200 Sat. Banks in San Salvador 0900-1600 Mon. to Fri.; different hours for other towns given in text. Government offices: 0730-1230 and 1500-1730 Mon. to Fri. Department of Migration also open on Sat. from 0900-1200.

Public Holidays The usual ones are January 1, Holy Week (3 days), April 14, 17, May 1, 10, Corpus Christi (half day), August 1-6, September 15, October 12, November 2 and 5 (half-day), December 24 (half-day), and Christmas Day. Government offices are also often closed on religious holidays. Little business in weeks ending Easter week, the first week of August, and the Christmas-New Year period. Banks are closed for balance June 29, 30, and December 30, 31.

Press In San Salvador: *Diario de Hoy*, *La Prensa Gráfica*, every day, including Sunday (both right wing). *Diario Latino* and *El Mundo*, afternoon papers, but not on Sunday. There are provincial newspapers in Santa Ana, San Miguel and elsewhere. Weekly bilingual newspaper (English and Spanish), *El Salvador News Gazette*, available from foyer of *Sheraton Hotel*.

There are 39 radio stations, at least 4 of which cover the whole country, and all but one accept advertisements. There are 3 commercial television stations, one of which has a national coverage, and a government-run educational channel.

We are grateful for updating material to Andreas Halbach (San Salvador) for a very useful contribution, Carla Tromp and Douwe van Dyk (Meppen, Neth.), Alan Wagman (Washington DC), and to various travellers listed under the general Central America section.

HONDURAS

HONDURAS is larger than all the other Central American republics except Nicaragua, but has a smaller population than El Salvador, less than a fifth its size. Bordered by Nicaragua, Guatemala, and El Salvador, it has an area of 112,088 square km.—rather less than England. It has a narrow Pacific coastal strip, 124 km. long, on the Gulf of Fonseca, but its northern coast on the Caribbean is some 640 km. long.

Much of the country is mountainous: a rough plateau covered with volcanic ash and lava in the S, rising to peaks such as Cerro de las Minas in the Celaque range (2,849 metres), but with some intermont basins at between 900 and 1,400 metres. The volcanic detritus disappears to the N, revealing saw-toothed ranges which approach the coast at an angle; the one in the extreme NW, along the border with Guatemala, disappears under the sea and shows itself again in the Bay Islands. At most places in the N there is only a narrow shelf of lowland between the sea and the sharp upthrust of the mountains, but along two rivers—the Aguán in the NE, and the Ulúa in the NW—long fingers of marshy lowland stretch inland between the ranges. The Ulúa lowland is particularly important; it is about 40 km. wide and stretches southwards for 100 km. From its southern limit a deep gash continues across the highland to the Gulf of Fonseca, on the Pacific. The distance between the Caribbean and the Pacific along this trough is 280 km.; the altitude at the divide between the Río Comayagua, running into the Ulúa and the Caribbean, and the streams flowing into the Pacific, is only 950 metres. In this trough lies Comayagua, the old colonial capital. The lowlands along the Gulf of Fonseca are narrower than they are along the Caribbean; there is no major thrust inland as along the Ulúa.

The prevailing winds are from the E, and the Caribbean coast has a high rainfall and is covered with deep tropical forest. The intermont basins, the valleys, and the slopes sheltered from the prevailing winds bear oak and pine down to as low as 600 metres. Timber is almost the only fuel available. There is a little coal near the capital but no oil has been found. In the drier areas, N and E of Tegucigalpa, there are extensive treeless savannas.

The Spaniards, arriving in the early 16th century, found groups of Indians of the Mayan and other cultures. Pushing E from Guatemala City they came upon silver in the SE, and in 1578 founded Tegucigalpa near the mines. The yield was

HONDURAS 1089

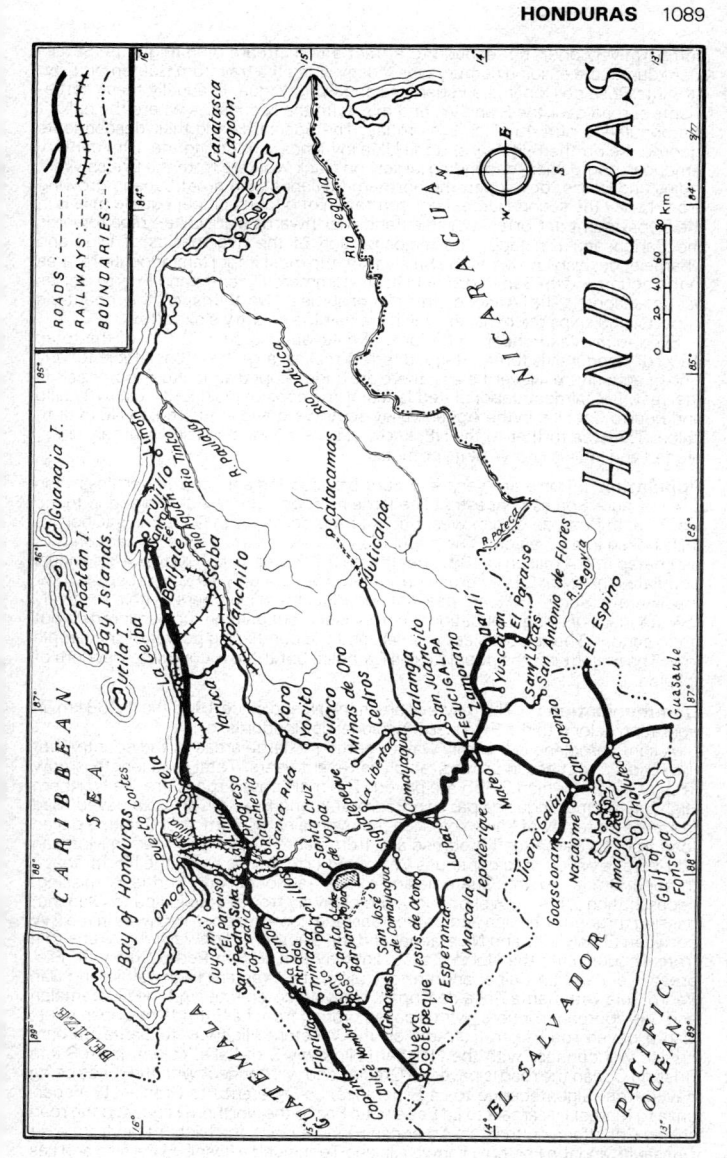

ROUGH SKETCH

comparatively poor, but enough to attract a thin stream of immigrants. Settlement during the ensuing century was mostly along the trail from Guatemala City: at Santa Rosa de Copán, La Esperanza and Comayagua. Gradually these settlements spread over the S and W, and this, with the N coast, is where the bulk of the population of 4.4 million lives today. The Spaniards and their descendants ignored the northern littoral and the Ulúa lowlands, but during the 19th century American companies, depending largely on black workers from the British West Indies and Belize, developed the northern lowlands as a great banana-growing area. Today the second largest concentration of population per square mile is in the Department of Cortés, which extends northwards from Lake Yojoa towards the Caribbean; it includes the major portion of the river basins of Ulúa and Chamelecón, also known as the Sula valley: the most important agricultural area in the country, with San Pedro Sula as its commercial centre and Puerto Cortés as its seaport. The Atlantic littoral consumes two-thirds of the country's imports, and ships the bananas which are half the country's exports.

Even today, land under some form of cultivation is only 22.4% of the total; 45% of Honduras is forest. Rugged terrain makes large areas unsuitable for any kind of agriculture. Nevertheless, there are undeveloped agricultural potentials in the vast, flat, almost unpopulated lands of the coastal plain E of Tela to Trujillo and Puerto Castilla, in the Aguán valley southward and in the region NE of Juticalpa. The area further to the NE, known as the Misquitia plain, is largely unexploited and little is known of its potential.

Population   There are very few pure-blooded Indians, and fewer (less than 1%) of pure Spanish ancestry. The largest proportion of Indian blood is found from Santa Rosa de Copán westwards to the border with Guatemala (Chortí is still spoken in this region). The population is 90% *mestizo*. The population was estimated at 4.4 million in 1987; death rate 8.3% per 1,000; birth, 44%; annual population growth: 2.9%; urban growth, 5.7%, but only 40% is urban; 40.5% are illiterate. Some 53% are peasants or agricultural labourers, with a relatively low standard of living. Education is compulsory, but half the rural children do not go to school. The middle class is small, and the purchasing power of the people low. The majority of the population is Catholic, but there is complete freedom of religion.

Communications   The railways are in the N, and since 1975 the 1,268 km. in operation belong to the Ferrocarril Nacional de Honduras.

A light aeroplane is the only way of getting to large areas of the country, but the road system has improved rapidly in recent years. Total road length is now 18,577 km., of which 2,155 are paved. The main paved roads are the Northern Highway linking Tegucigalpa, San Pedro Sula and Puerto Cortés; a paved road from Las Flores (N of Lake Yojoa) to the hydroelectric dam at El Cajón; a paved road from La Barca to El Progreso and from Santa Rita on this road to Morazán and Yoro; a paved road continues W from Puerto Cortés along the North Coast, through Omoa, to the Guatemalan frontier (although one bridge is missing, necessitating 2 hrs.' travel on foot); the highway from Tegucigalpa to Olancho, passing through Juticalpa and Catacamas; the Pan-American Highway in the SW between El Salvador and Nicaragua, and the Southern Highway which runs to it from Tegucigalpa; the North Coast Highway joining San Pedro Sula with Progreso, Tela and La Ceiba, and on to Trujillo; the Western Highway linking San Pedro Sula with Santa Rosa de Copán, Nueva Ocotepeque and the Guatemalan and Salvadorean frontiers, with a paved branch from La Entrada to Copán ruins; also a paved road from Cofradia on the Western Highway to Santa Bárbara (which will connect with the Northern Highway S of Lake Yojoa); from Santa Rosa de Copán the road is paved to Gracias and will connect with the roads being paved from Siguatepeque to La Esperanza, La Esperanza to Gracias, La Esperanza to Marcala, Marcala to La Paz and La Paz to the Northern Highway; the road linking Choluteca on the Pan-American Highway with the Nicaraguan frontier at Guasaule; and the Eastern Highway linking Tegucigalpa, Danlí, El Paraíso and Las Manos (Nicaraguan frontier). Travel is still by oxcart and mule in many areas. Tegucigalpa, La Ceiba and San Pedro Sula all have international airports.

HONDURAS 1091

Government The Legislature consists of a single Chamber. Deputies are elected by a proportional vote. Executive authority rests with a President, elected for 4 years. No President may serve two terms in succession. The Constitution was revised by a Constituent Assembly elected in April 1980.

In 1957 free and authentic popular elections brought a Liberal Government into power with Ramón Villeda Morales as President. He was deposed in October 1963, and a military junta took over. A constituent assembly elected Gen. Osvaldo López Arellano (head of the junta), as President. A civilian, Ramón Ernesto Cruz, was elected President in June 1971 at the head of a coalition government; he was ousted by the military in December 1972, and Gen. López Arellano resumed the presidency, which he retained until April 1975 when he was ousted by another military man, Gen. Juan Melgar Castro. Gen. Melgar was in turn deposed on August 7, 1978 by a military junta headed by Gen. Policarpo Paz García. In April 1980, elections for a new Constituent Assembly were won unexpectedly by the Liberal Party. The successor to General Paz García as President was Dr. Roberto Suazo Córdoba of the Liberal Party, elected in November 1981. Elections, held in November 1985, brought José Simón Azcona del Hoyo, also of the Liberal Party, to the Presidency.

The National University is centred in Tegucigalpa though it also has departments in San Pedro Sula and La Ceiba. Also in Tegucigalpa is the Universidad José Cecilio del Valle; there is also a university in San Pedro Sula.

Cities and Towns

Tegucigalpa, the capital, a city of over 800,000 inhabitants, stands in an intermont basin at an altitude of 975 metres. No railway serves it. It was founded as a mining camp in 1578: the miners found their first gold where the N end of the Soberanía bridge now is. The name means "silver hill" in the original Indian tongue. On three sides it is surrounded by sharp, high peaks. It is an amalgam of two towns: the almost flat Comayagüela and the hilly Tegucigalpa built at the foot and up the slopes of El Picacho. A steeply banked river, the Choluteca, runs between the two towns, now united administratively as the Distrito Central. Tegucigalpa has not been subjected to any disaster by fire or earthquake, being off the main earthquake fault line, so retains many traditional features. Many of the stuccoed houses, with a single heavily barred entrance leading to a central patio, are attractively coloured. However, the old low skyline of the city has now been punctuated by several modern tall buildings.

Its altitude gives it a reliable climate: temperate during the rainy season from May to November; warm, with cool nights, in March and April, and cool and dry, with very cool nights, in December to February, although hot breezes can make the atmosphere oppressive. The annual mean temperature is about 74°F (23°C).

The Carretera del Sur (Southern Highway), which brings in travellers from the S and from Toncontín Airport, 6½ km. from Plaza Morazán, runs through Comayagüela into Tegucigalpa. It goes past the obelisk set up to commemorate a hundred years of Central American independence, and the Escuela Nacional de Bellas Artes, with a decorated Mayan corridor and temporary exhibitions of contemporary paintings and crafts.

The market in Comayagüela is very interesting. There is a large handicrafts market (open Wed.-Sun.) on the south side of the park adjoining the obelisk in Comayagüela. In Colonia Palmira, is the Boulevard Morazán, an elegant shopping and business complex, with restaurants, cafeterias, discotheques, etc. (worth a visit on Fri. or Sat. evening). You can get a fine view of the city from the Peace Monument on Juana Laínez hill, near the football stadium.

Crossing the river by the colonial Mallol bridge, on the left is the Presidential Palace (1919), with a beautiful interior courtyard which, unfortunately, is no longer open to the public. If we go by Calle Bolívar we pass through the area containing the Congress building and the former site of the University, founded in 1847. Calle Bolívar leads to the main square, Plaza Morazán (commonly known as Parque Central). The eastern side of the square takes us to the City Hall, and to the domed and double-towered Cathedral built in the late 18th century. (See the beautiful gilt colonial altarpiece, the fine examples of Spanish colonial art, the cloisters and, in Holy Week, the magnificent ceremony of the Descent from the Cross).

Av. Paz Barahona, running through the northern side of the square, is a key

1092 HONDURAS

avenue. On it to the E is the church of San Francisco, with its clangorous bells, and (on 3a Calle, called Av. Colón) the old Spanish Mint (1770), now the national printing works. If, from Plaza Morazán, we go along Av. Paz Barahona westwards towards the river, by turning right along 4 Av. we come to the 18th century church of Virgen de los Dolores. Two blocks N and 3 blocks W of the church is Parque Concordia with copies of Mayan sculpture and temples.

Back on Av. Paz Barahona and further W are the Ministerial Palace, the National Theatre, with a rather grand interior (1915) and, across the square, the beautiful old church of El Calvario. If we cross the bridge of Carías (quite near the theatre) we can visit Comayagüela's market of San Isidro.

One is always conscious, in Tegucigalpa, of the summit of El Picacho looming up to the N (at the top is a zoo of indigenous animals, open Thurs.-Sun., US$0.25). From Plaza Morazán go up Calle 7a and the Calle de la Leona to Parque Leona, a handsome small park with a railed walk overlooking the city. Higher still is the reservoir in El Picacho, also known as the United Nations Park. The park can be reached by bus from behind Los Dolores church, Sun. only, US$0.15; camping is allowed here. Parque La Libertad in Comayagüela (where one can find cheap enjoyable entertainment in the evening, e.g. *mariachi* bands) and Parque Central in Tegucigalpa are also pleasant.

N.B. If you have anything stolen, report it to Dirección General de Investigación Nacional, DIN, ½ block N of Los Dolores church.

Hotels *Honduras Maya*, Av. República de Chile, Colonia Palmira, Tel.: 32-31-91, A-L, rooms and apartments, casino, swimming pool, sauna, bars, cafeterias (*Cafeteria 2000*), restaurant (*El Candelero*), conference hall, view over the city (only from uppermost rooms), in central location; *La Ronda*, 6 Av., 11 C., 5 blocks from cathedral (Tel.: 22-8151/55), a/c, TV, recommended, A/B, cafeteria (*Rondalla*) and night club; *Alameda*, Blvd. Suyapa, A, comfortable, pool, good restaurant *Le Chalet* (Tel.: 32-69-20); *Prado*, Av. Cervantes, 7 y 8 Av., A/B, *La Posada* restaurant; *Istmania*, 5 Av., 7 and 8 Calle (Tel.: 22-1638/39, 22-1460) near Church of Los Dolores (poor location), C-A, *Versalles* restaurant; *Plaza* (ex-Holiday Inn), in Av. Paz Barahona (Tel.: 22-0182/84), A, *Papagallo* restaurant; *Madero*, Barrio La Hoya, Tel.: 22-3637, D/E; *Granada*, Av. Gutemberg 1401, Barrio Guanacaste, E (hot water on 2nd floor only), good, table tennis, Tel.: 22-23-81, annex 1½ blocks uphill, turn right at sign for Cinés Tauro and Aries, also E (but a bit more than old building), better beds, hot water in all rooms; *Marichal*, 5 Av., 5 Calle, D/E (Tel.: 22-00-69) (ask for a back room), noisy, clean, centrally located; *Nuevo Boston*, Av. Jérez No. 313, Tel.: 22-9411, D (E without bath), hot water, central, clean, laundry, restaurant, recommended; *MacArthur*, 7 Av., 1225, D/E, good, reasonably-priced restaurant; *Nuevo Hotel MacArthur*, C/D, 8C., 4 y 5 Av., under same management; *Santa Eduviges*, 7C., 3-4 Av. Barrio Abajo, Tegucigalpa, Tel.: 22-07-76, F/D; *San Francisco*, Av. Cervantes, Tegucigalpa, D, fan, T.V., restaurant, bar, Tel.: 22-71-01; *Boarding House El Príncipe*, 3 Av., 3-4 C., No. 346, Comayagüela, D; *Imperial* (opposite *Istmania*) F, with or without bath, Chinese run. *Hedman y Alas*, Av. 4, Calle 9, Comayagüela, E-C, poor value; *Ritz*, 4a C., and 5 Av., Comayagüela, E-D, cold shower, clean but noisy; *Eden House*, on winding road to Parque La Leona, D, with food, poor value. *Centenario*, 6 Av., 9-10 Calles, Comayagüela, E-D (Tel.: 22-1050), recommended; *Mallorca*, Blvd. Comunidad Europea, Comayagüela (Tel.: 33-3929), D/E; *Bristol*, 5 Calle, 4 and 5 Av., Comayagüela, E; *Alcázar*, C. 5, Av. 4 and 5, E; *Real de Oro*, Av. Cabañas, 11 and 12 C., Comayagüela, D/E, clean, friendly; *Astoria*, la Calle, 3 and 4 Av., Comayagüela, E/F; *Regis*, 4a Av., 1 and 2 Calle, Comayagüela, E, recommended, clean, friendly; *Central*, 4a Calle, Av. 4 and 5, Comayagüela, E-D; *Cádiz*, 4 Av., C. 4 and 5, Comayagüela, D/E; *Royalton*, Barrio Morazán, E, clean, good food. Lots of cheap *pensiones* and rooms in Comayagüela but most are not suitable for travellers; *San Pedro*, Calle 9, Av. 6, Comayagüela, E with bath, F without or with private cold shower, popular, recommended but for cockroaches, restaurant; *Jupiter*, Av. 5, 5 and 6 Calles 509, Comayagüela, E-D, clean and comfortable; *Ticamaya No. 1*, Av. 6, Calle 9, Comayagüela, E/D, nice, quiet, good restaurant with US cable TV, open to non-residents, popular with Americans, breakfast from 0600, recommended; *Ticamaya No. 2*, Av. 7a, 4 and 5 Calle Comayagüela, E, clean, friendly, noisy, restaurant below; *Teleño*, Av. 7, Comayagüela, F, clean, friendly; *Entrada*, 3-4 Avs., Comayagüela, 50 metres from Transportes El Rey, F, friendly, not too clean; *Rainieri*, 10 Calle, E, fan, safe, very good value; there are 5 *Hospedajes El Nilo*, No. 4 is clean, but the rest are to be avoided; *Hospedaje Pacífico*, near Comayagüela market, F, basic; *Royal*, Av. 7, Comayagüela nr. market, F, noisy but cheap; *Hospedaje España*, between 4a and 5a Calle, Comayagüela, F, dirty, noisy (chicken farm), not recommended; *Hotel Richard No. 1*, 4a Calle, 6 and 7 Av., Comayagüela, F/E, "laundry" on roof; *Hotel Richard Nos. 2, 3, 4* and 5 at 5a Calle, all between 5 and 7 Av., Comayagüela, fewer facilities, all F, with or without bath. *Hospedaje 515*, Av. 6, No. 536, Comayagüela, F, quiet, clean; *Hospedaje Familiar*, Av. 6, No. 812, F, clean, noisy, Comayagüela. A 5% sales tax is added to hotel bills.

Restaurants A meal in a good restaurant costs betweem US$20-25; for hotel restaurants, see

HONDURAS 1093

above. International food: *El Arriero*, Av. República de Chile, near *Honduras Maya*; *Kloster*, Blvd. Morazán; *Marbella*, 6 C., 3-4 Av., central. Seafood: *Hungry Fisherman*, Av. República de Chile 209, Col. Palmira. Italian: *Roma*, near Av. Rep. de Chile, Col. Palmira; pizzerias: *Tito*, Callejón Los Dolores, and Blvd. Morazán, Col. Palmira, both branches recommended; *Vicente*, near *Honduras Maya*. Spanish: *Mesón de Castilla*, Av. Rep. de Chile 1802, Col. Palmira; *Rincón Español*, Blvd. Morazán; *Cafetería La Gran Vía*, good paella; French: *Jardín de París*, Blvd. Morazán, highly recommended. Latin American: *Rincón Tapatío*, Blvd. Morazán; Mexican: *Gauchos*, Av. de La Paz, near U.S. Embassy; Uruguayan: *El Jacal*, Blvd. Morazán, Honduran style. Chinese: *La Gran Muralla*, Barrio Guanacaste, good; *Pekín*, 3 C. No.525, Barrio San Rafael, 1 block from *Hotel Maya*; *Lin-Nan*, Blvd. Morazán; *China Palace*, Barrio La Plazuela, Tegucigalpa; *Mei-Mei*, Pasaje Midence Soto, central, recommended; *Ley-Hsen*, Pasaje Fiallos Soto, also central and recommended. Meat: *El Patio 2*, Blvd. Morazán; *La Granja*, same street. Burgers: 3 *Burger Hots*, next to *Holiday Inn*, 2 C. north of Parque La Merced, and Centro Comercial Los Castaños. Plenty of *comedores* near market. *Todo Rico*, vegetarian, 3 C., 4 Av. *Salmans*, branches throughout the city, excellent bread and ice cream. *Pops*, and *Kibom*, ice cream, hamburgers, coffee, etc. *Dunkin Donuts*, several outlets. *Keops*, near Congress building, good sandwiches and milkshakes. *Pastelería Francesa*, opp. French embassy - recommended. Many cheap restaurants on 2 Av., Comayagüela. Fried chicken is sold at small lunch counters all over Honduras, providing an excellent, cheap meal.

Clubs and Institutes Country Club (golf, tennis, swimming); many private clubs with swimming pools, tennis courts, etc. Alliance Française, end of 4 Av., Barrio Abajo, cultural events Fri. p.m., French films Wed. p.m., Tel.: 22-04-45; Centro Cultural Alemán, 8 Av., Calle La Fuente, German newspapers, cultural events, Tel.: 22-15-55; Instituto Hondureño de Cultura Interamericana (IHCI), Calle Real de Comayagüela has an English library and cultural events, Tel.: 22-75-39.

Market Mercado Colón or San Isidro, Avenida 6 at Calle 1, Comayagüela; many things for sale; food available. Saturday is busiest day. Good supermarkets: La Colonia, Sucasa, Plaza Más x Menos.

Fair at Comayagüela Fair of La Concepción, December 7 to 24.

Bookshops Book Village, Centro Comercial Los Castaños, Blvd. Morazán, English books, both new and secondhand, for sale or exchange. Librería Panamericana, 6a Av., 2a Calle, stocks English books and magazines, expensive. Secondhand bookstalls in Mercado San Isidro (Av. 6 y 2 Calle, Comayagüela), good value.

Car Rentals Car rentals Avis, Tel.: 32-00-88; Toyota, Col. El Prado, Tel.: 33-52-10; at Toncontín airport: Molinari, Tel.: 33-13-07, Blitz, Budget, Tel.: 33-51-70, National, Tel.: 33-49-62.

Car Repairs Emil Bohnet, 1 Av., Comayagüela. Metal Mecánica, 4 blocks above U.S. Embassy.

Taxis Flat rate, US$1.50 p.p. (no reduction for sharing); more after 2000 hrs.

Local buses Cost US$0.10, stops are official but unmarked (no minibuses).

Cinemas Ciné Maya on Blvd. Morazán in Palmira; a double cinema on Av. La Paz, 2 blocks below U.S. Embassy; Plaza 1, 2 and 3 in Centro Comercial Plaza Miraflores; Regis and Real at Centro Comercial Centroamérica, Blvd. Miraflores; Alfa and Omega in Av. de La Paz (all have good US films). In city centre, double cinemas Lidia and Palace, Clamer and Variedades.

Entertainment Casino Royal in *Hotel Honduras Maya*, all types of gambling. In front of the National University is a *peña*, where people dance and sing; also a discotheque and restaurant. *El Metro* Disco, Blvd. Morazán, good; *El Tulipán*, same street; *Chico Lara*, near airport for organ music.

Museum Museo Nacional Villa Roy, in home of a former President, has an exhibition of archaeological finds. It is situated on a hill top above the beautiful Parque Concordia (open 0830-1540, closed Mon.).

Bank Banco de Londres (Lloyds Bank) 4a Calle y 5a Av. Tegucipalga. Open 0900-1500; closed Sat. Banco Atlántida, 5C. in front of Plaza Morazán; Banco de Honduras (Citibank), Edif. Midence Soto, Tegucigalpa; Banco de Ahorro Hondureño, 5C. in front of Plaza Morazán. All accept American Express travellers' cheques, and cash travellers' cheques which are accredited to them, but not for US$. Visa cash advances and travellers' cheques, Credomatic de Honduras, Blvd. Morazán. American Express: Transmundo Tours, Calle 5a, Costado Norte Ministerio; do not always have stocks of new cheques, otherwise good. Black market outside *Hotel Plaza*.

Embassies *British* (also *Belize* and *Canada*), Edificio Palmira, 3rd floor, opp. *Hotel Honduras Maya* (Apartado Postal 123); *USA*, Av. La Paz (0800-1100, Mon.-Fri.— take any bus from Parque Central in direction "San Felipe", Tel.: 32-31-20); *West German*, Ed. Paysen, Blvd. Morazán. *French*, Av. Juan Lindo 416, Colonia Palmira. *Guatemala*, Calle Juan Lindo 419, Colonia Palmira, Mon.-Fri., 0900-1300; *El Salvador*, Colonia San Carlos—one block from Blvd. Morazán, friendly, helpful; *Nicaragua*, Colonia Las Minitas, on steep hillside of Colina Tepeyac (Tel.: 329025), 10

1094 HONDURAS

blocks SE of Ciné Maya, Blvd. Morazán (or take "Alameda" bus from Parque La Merced, alight 1 block above "Planificación de familia", walk left up side street and turn up 4th street on right, a dirt road, with the consulate on a steep hillside on the right), 0800-1200, visas issued at 1300 on same day if applied for in early a.m. (but may take 5 days); *Costa Rica*, Colonia Palmira, Primera Calle Casa 704, Tel.: 32-1054 (Near Mas x Menos supermarket); *Mexico*, 3 Av., 2 C. No. 1277, Col. Palmira; *Spain*, Col. Matamoros 103; *Israel*, Ed. Midence Soto 4° piso; *Italy*, Col. Reforma; *Netherlands* (also *Portugal*), Carretera a Suyapa, desvío a Lomas del Mayab; *Switzerland*, Cosude, 4 Av., 7 C. No. 403, Col. Alameda. *Jamaican* consul, Mr George Schofield, *Hotel Boston*, Calle Jérez. To get to Colonia Palmira where most Embassies are, take buses marked "San Miguel" and "Lomas". Take "San Felipe" bus from Central Park for the following consulates: Costa Rica, Guatemala, USA and El Salvador.

Immigration Dirección General de Migración, Edificio Viera, 6 C., 11-12 Av., Tegucigalpa.

Post Office on Av. Paz Barahona, 3 blocks from Parque Central.

Telephone, Telex Hondutel, Calle 5 and Av. 4, Tegucigalpa.

School American and Elvel School, on US lines with US staff.

Non-Catholic Churches Episcopal Anglican (Col. Florencia—take Suyapa bus) and Union Church, Colonia Lomas del Guijarro, with services in English.

Peace Corps has an office with library and photographic dark room, on Av. República de Chile, up hill past *Hotel Honduras Maya*; open Mon.-Fri. 0800-1600.

Tourist Office Under Congress Building (Plaza La Merced), opp. Banco Central, also at Toncontín airport. Very helpful; good maps of city available. Provides lists of hotels and sells posters, postcards and slides. Information on cultural events around the country from Teatro Manuel Bonilla, better than at regional tourist offices. The best map of the country is produced by the Instituto Geográfico Nacional and may be bought from the Institute on production of passport and map request, typed, in triplicate (it is a long process, involving a trip to the Treasury). Open weekdays 0730-1200, 1230-1530. (Texaco also do a good map of the country, available at Texaco stations.)

Motorists Note that Tegucigalpa is appallingly badly signposted and is a nightmare for motorists. Motorists leaving Tegucigalpa for San Pedro Sula or Olancho can avoid the congestion of Comayagüela market by driving N down to Barrio Abajo, crossing the river to Barrio Chile and taking the motorway up the mountainside, to turn right to Olacho, or left to rejoin the northern outlet to San Pedro Sula (at the second intersection, turn right for the old, winding route, go straight on for the new, fast route.

Airport Toncontín, 6½ km. from the centre. Checking-in takes a long time; generally standard is poor. Buses to airport from Comayagüela, Loarque Ruta No. 11, catch it on 4a Av. between 6 and 7 Calle; into town US$0.10, 20 mins. from outside the airport; yellow cabs, US$6, smaller colectivo taxis, US$3.20.

Airlines For national flights: Aero Servicios, Toncontín airport, Tel.: 33-12-69 (private); Lansa, Toncontín, Tel.: 33-18-14; TAN/Sahsa, Toncontín, Tel.: 33-10-10, in town, Tel.: 22-86-74. Taca International, Ed. Banfinan; SAM, Blvd. Morazán, Tel.: 32-08-08; Challenge International, Ed. La Interamericana, Blvd. Morazán, Tel.: 32-08-08; Pan Am, Ed. San Miguel, Barrio La Plazuela, Tel.: 22-01-57; Alitalia, Centro Comercial Los Castaños, Blvd. Morazán, Tel.: 32-18-82; Iberia, Ed. Palmira, opp. *Honduras Maya*, Tel.: 31-52-53; KLM, Ed. Lanach, 4 piso, No 401, Tel.: 22-69-48; Lufthansa, Ed. Midence Soto, 5 piso, No.503, Tel.: 22-69-00.

Buses To San Pedro Sula on Northern Highway; 4 hrs. (5 companies: Sáenz, 4a Calle, 5 and 6 Av., El Rey, Av. 6, Calle 9, Comayagüela, Hedmán Alas, 13-14C., 11 Av., Comayagüela, Tel.: 229333, 7 a day, Norteño and San Cristóbal, all charge US$3.50, except Hedmán Alas, US$4, excellent). Mi Esperanza, Comayagüela, to Choluteca, 3 hrs., US$2, every 2 hrs. from 0600 onwards; to San Marcos de Colón for Nicaraguan border at El Espino, and direct to frontier at 0400, US$3.50, 5 hrs. (0730, 0900 buses best for onward connections). To La Esperanza, Empresa Joelito, 4 Calle No. 834, Comeyagüela, 8 hrs, US$2.30. To Comayagua, US$1.50, Transportes Catrachos, Comayagüela, every 30 mins., 1½-2 hrs. To Guatemala, go to San Pedro Sula and take either Impala or Congolón to Ocotepeque and the frontier at Agua Caliente, or take the route via Copán (see page 1104). To San Salvador, via San Miguel on Tues., Fri. and Sun., Transportes El Salvador, US$10, book 2 days in advance, 0700 from opp. *Hotel Calle Real*, Calle Real (Av. 2a), Comayagüela; direct bus to border at El Amatillo, US$2.50; alternatively from San Pedro Sula via Ocotepeque and El Poy. If you choose to avoid El Salvador when travelling N, take a bus to San Pedro Sula, and from there go to Guatemala.

For travellers leaving Tegucigalpa, take the "Villa Adela" bus in Calle Jérez, by Cine Pálace, and alight in Comayagüela at Cine Centenario (Av. 6a) for nearby Empresa Aurora buses (for Olancho) and El Rey buses (for San Pedro Sula or Olancho); 3 blocks S is Ciné Lux, near which are Empresas Unidas and Maribel for Siguatepeque (to town centre, US$0.50 cheaper but 1 hr. slower than San

HONDURAS 1095

Pedro Sula buses which drop you on the main road, a US$0.50 taxi ride from Siguatepeque). By the Mamachepa market are Sáenz and Norteño bus lines for San Pedro Sula; also nearby are buses for Nacaome and El Amatillo frontier with El Salvador. "Villa Adela" bus continues to Mi Esperanza bus terminal (for Choluteca and Nicaraguan frontier). Take a "Belén" or "Santa Fe" bus from Tegucigalpa for the hill ascending Belén (9a Calle) for Hedman Alas buses to San Pedro Sula and for Comayagua buses (to town centre, cheaper but slower than main line buses to San Pedro Sula which drop passengers on main road, a taxi ride away from the centre).

Excursions Eight km. NE to the church at Suyapa, which attracts pilgrims to its wooden figure of the Virgin, a tiny image about 8 cm. high set into the altar. Excursions to Copán (1 hr. by air, US$295 for a plane taking 5 passengers), visits to the Agricultural School at Zamorano, and sightseeing tours of Tegucigalpa and Comayagüela are arranged by several tour operators. It is about a ½ hour drive to **Valle de Angeles,** 1,310 metres (old mines, many walks possible in surrounding forests, picnic areas, swimming pool; *Hotel San Francisco,* F; *Comedor La Abejita,* recommended; several others. Hospital de los Adventistas, in the valley, a modern clinic, sells vegetables and handicrafts; there are many handicraft shops in town—a visit to the Artisans' School is recommended) and on to San Juan de Flores (also called Cantarranas) and San Juancito, an old mining town. (Bus to Valle de Angeles hourly from beginning of Av. de los Próceres, Tegucigalpa, US$0.50; bus to San Juan de Flores from Mercado San Pablo, Barrio El Manchen, 1000, 1230, 1530.) On the way to Valle de Angeles take a right turn off to visit the quaint old mining village of **Santa Lucía,** perched precariously on a steep mountainside overlooking the wide valley with Tegucigalpa below. The town has a beautiful colonial church with a Christ given by King Philip II of Spain in 1592; there is a festival in the 2nd and 3rd weeks of January. Delightful walk down old mule trail across pine-clad ridges to the city (1½ hrs.). Bus to Santa Lucía from Mercado San Pablo, US$0.40.

There are bracing climbs to the heights of Picacho; don't take left fork at summit; take right fork to El Hatillo and on 24 km. to visit the rain forest (small buses from North of Parque Herrera, Tegucigalpa). Jeeps and 4-wheel drive vehicles can go on in dry weather to San Juancito (*Hospedaje Don Jacinto;* simple meals in the village). Above San Juancito is La Tigra rain forest, a National Park (a stiff, 1-hr. uphill walk to park offices and trail, Sendero Bosque Nublado); a few quetzal birds survive here, but do not leave paths when walking as there are precipitous drops. Bus from San Pablo market, Tegucigalpa, 1½ hrs., US$1; passes turn-off to Santa Lucía and goes through Valle de Angeles.

From Parque Herrera a bus at 1200 goes to the village of El Peleguín; a delightful 40-min. walk down the pineclad mountainside leads to El Chimbo (meals at *pulpería* or shop—ask anyone the way), then take bus either to Valle de Angeles or Tegucigalpa.

A half-hour drive from Tegucigalpa to **Ojojona,** another quaint old village; turn right 24 km. down Southern Highway. The village's pottery is interesting (but selection reported to be poor). There is a small, but interesting museum. *Fiesta* Jan. 18-20. There are 3 well preserved colonial churches in Ojojona (notice the fine paintings), plus two more in nearby Santa Ana which is passed on the way from Tegucigalpa. Ojojona is completely unspoiled, and has no organized accommodation. (Bus hourly from Calle 4, No. 825, Comayagüela, US$0.50, 1½ hrs.) From same location, buses go to Lepaterique ("place of the jaguar"), another colonial village, over an hour's drive through rugged, forested terrain. Distant view of Pacific on fine days from heights above village.

Minas de Oro, on a forested tableland at about 1,060 metres, is a centre for walking in wooded mountains, 3-hrs. bus ride with Transportes Díaz-Donavil, 10 Av. 11 C. Barrio Belén, Comayagüela at 0630 and 1300 (US$ 2.50). It is a picturesque old mining town, N of Talanga on the Olancho highway. Several *pensiones,* incl. *Los Pinares* (F, meals US$1) and *Hospedaje Mi Esperanza* (F, clean, basic). Robert Millar writes: Climb Cerro Grande (beware of snakes); walk to Malacatán mountain and Minas de San Antonio; follow old mule trail to San José Potrerillos. Strenuous climb, 3 hrs., over forested mountain range to lovely old colonial village of **Esquías,** with church, *cabildo* (town hall), tree-shaded plaza; bus from Esquías to Tegucigalpa (irregular), otherwise hitch from Minas de Oro or Comayagua (via Rancho Grande). Also nearby are the villages of San Luis, San José del Potrero, and Victoria and the Montana de la Flor, in a remote area, inhabited by the Xicaquels tribe. Bus Minas de Oro-Comayagua (daily) passes through **Cedros,** one of Honduras' earliest settlements, dating from Pedro de Alvarado's mining operations of 1536. It is an outstanding colonial mining town, with cobbled streets, perched high on an eminence, amid forests. The festival of El Señor del Buen Fin takes place in the first two weeks of January.

Swimming at thermal springs of Balneario San Francisco Támara; 32 km., along road to San Pedro Sula, turn off right 8 km. N of Támara. Parque Aurora, midway between Tegucigalpa (about 50 km. N) and Comayagua, has a small zoo and picnic area among pine-covered hills, a lake with rowing boats (hire US$1 per hour), a snack bar and lovely scenery. Camping US$0.50 p.p.; admission US$0.75.

At km. 17 on Zamorano road (at summit of range overlooking Suyapa church) take dirt road left to TV tower. From here a delightful 2-hour walk over forested ridges leads to Santa Lucía. At km. 24 on Zamorano road, climb the highest peak through the Uyuca rain forest, information from Pan-American Agricultural School at Zamorano from their office in the Edificio Guillén in Tegucigalpa.

1096 HONDURAS

The school has rooms for visitors. On the NW flank of Uyuca is the picturesque village of Tatumbla.

The North Coast

Puerto Cortés, the Republic's principal port, at the mouth of the Ulúa river, is 58 km. by road and rail from San Pedro Sula, 333 from Tegucigalpa, and only two days' voyage from New Orleans. About half of Honduran trade passes through it. The climate is hot, tempered by sea breezes; many beautiful palm-fringed beaches nearby; rainfall, 2,921 mm. It has a small oil refinery, and a free zone was opened in 1978. Population 42,200. Festival, in August, including "Noche Veneciana" on 3rd Saturday.

Hotels *Craniotis*, 4 C., 1-2 Av., B (suite with a/c, D with fan, not perfect); *International Mr. Ggeerr*, Barrio El Centro, B, hot water, recommended; *Cosenza*; *Los Piratas*, F, basic but friendly; *Colón*, F, pleasant, hot water, but in red-light district; *Formosa*, F, dirty, but good food; *Las Vegas*, E, clean, unfriendly.

Restaurants *La Playa*, on outskirts, fish dishes excellent, others O.K. *Miramar* on sea front, excellent seafood. *Hotel Craniotis*. *Restaurant-Cafe Kalúa* in centre of town. *Restaurant Formosa*, expensive, but good. *La Roca*, Av. Ferrocarril; *Príncipe Maya* on road to Omoa.

Protestant Church Anglican/Episcopal.

Bank of London (agency), 2a Av. y 3a Calle; Banco Atlántida and other local banks. Banco de Comercio cashes travellers' cheques. Banco de Occidente, Calle Principal; Bancahsa, 2 Av. 2 Calle. Open 0800-1130, 1330-1600; Sats. 0800-1100.

Shops There are two souvenir shops in the customs house at the entrance to the National Port Authority, which sell hand-embroidered clothes. A shop on the main street sells mahogany wood carvings and the market in the town centre is quite interesting.

Rail Daily train to San Pedro Sula (departs 0815) and Potrerillos, 95 km., 1.067 metres gauge. Two daily trains to Tela, change at La Junta, one at 0700 (US$1, second class, US$1.75 first).

Road To San Pedro Sula and Potrerillos and on to the capital. Bus service several times an hour to San Pedro Sula, US$1, 2 hrs., Citul and Impala lines.

Shipping Continental Line (Miami-Panama) operates passenger cruises. No regular passenger sailings to New Orleans, or Santo Tomás de Castilla (Guatemala). A *goleta* (canoe) leaves Pueblo Nuevo, Puerto Cortés, every Tues. a.m. for Mango Creek, Belize, US$20, 7 hrs.; can be dangerous in rough weather. Also ask for large cement or timber boats to Belize City, US$30. Remember to get your exit stamp. The Immigration Office is near the Plaza Central (it is not noted for its efficiency). If entering Puerto Cortés by boat, one must go to Immigration immediately. Passports are sometimes collected at the dock and you must go later to Immigration to get them; you must pay US$1 entry fee, make sure that you have the stamp. This is the only official payment; if asked for more, demand a receipt.

Excursions W to Tulián, along the bay, for picnics and freshwater bathing. Minibuses (US$0.35 each way) ply along the tropical shoreline past Tulián W to Omoa (or 3-hr. walk—15 km. from Puerto Cortés), with its restored 18th century castle (admission, US$0.25); *Motel Vitanza-Omoa*, B-A. There is a paved road through Omoa, continuing to the Guatemalan border. Other buses go E to beaches of coconut palms and white sands at Travesía, Baja Mar, etc., which are beautiful, and unspoilt. Café at Travesía, but none at Baja Mar. The black fishing communities are very friendly. Beware of sunburn, and mosquitoes at dusk. From November to May, because of tourist ships arriving two or three times a week, there are tours to La Lima to visit the banana plantations, trips to Copán to visit the Mayan ruins and tourist parties at the Ustaris Hacienda.

Tela, another important banana port some 50 km. to the E, is reached from Puerto Cortés by sea, rail, road, or from San Pedro Sula by rail and by bus service via El Progreso. It is pleasantly laid out, with a magnificent sandy beach (although the beach is not as safe as it used to be). Population 27,800. *Fiesta*: San Antonio in June.

Hotels *Villas Telamar*, a complex of wooden bungalows, set on a palm-fringed beach, rooms A, villas from A-L, restaurant, bar, golf club, swimming pool; *Paradise Hotel*, in a palm grove about 3 km. W of Tela, beside magnificent beach, cabins, C-B, restaurant, insecure; *Tela*, Calle El Comercio, E, good, with restaurant; *La Playa*, F, friendly, English-speaking owner, good value, next door is *Atlántico* (C, with a/c, E without, both on beach); *Maribú Inn*, on same street, D, with a/c, good, good but expensive food; *Atlántida*, nearby, E. The *hospedaje* owned by Doña Sara is quite good, E, with bath; *Hotel Robert*, F, recommended, in red light district, noisy, close to bus and railway

HONDURAS 1097

stations. *Royal*, noisy; next door is *Taurino*, equally noisy, basic; *Balderach*, in Central Park, old, basic, cheap; *París*, also cheap. Plenty of cheap *hospedajes* n₁ ar railway station, e.g. *Valencia*, recommended (on R-hand side of tracks as you arrive). *Gina Boarding House*, E, with bath and fan, parking. *Pensión Muñoz* on beachfront, F, meals extra, basic; *Pensión Iris*, both budget. During Easter week, the town is packed; room rates double and advance booking is essential.

Camping at municipal site next to beach, US$1. Also possible, but not safely, on beach.

Restaurant *Northern Lights* (*Luces del Norte*), Canadian owned (Slim Jim), one block towards beach from Parque Central, excellent value, also English book exchange; *César's*, on the beach, serves good seafood, beware of short-changing. *Bahía Bar/Restaurant*, overpriced. *China*, on main street. *Bambo Bar*, Av. México.

Protestant Church Anglican.

Banks Banco Atlántida, Bancahsa, Banadesa.

Buses Cati or Tupsa lines from San Pedro Sula to El Progreso (US$1.20) where you must change to go on to Tela and La Ceiba (last bus at 1900), or express bus through from San Pedro Sula which costs an extra US$1, 2 hrs. Bus from Tela to El Progreso every 45 mins., US$1.25; to La Ceiba, 2½ hrs., US$1.75.

Rail The National Railways 1.067-metre gauge line W to Puerto Cortés; two trains per day US$1 2nd class, 4 hrs. A branch of this line runs south along the eastern bank of the Ulúa River to Progreso and Potrerillos. Train to San Pedro Sula via Baracoa, 3 hrs. There is no longer a rail link with La Ceiba but frequent buses run from San Pedro Sula or Tela (US$1.75) on paved roads.

Excursion It is interesting to go by road to the tropical experimental farm at Lancetilla (established 1926), 5 km. inland; open Mon.-Fri., 0800-1400; Sat., Sun. and holidays 0800-1700, admission US$0.50. *Hospedaje* and *comedor*, full at weekends, and camping facilities. Either take employees' bus from town centre at 0700, or local bus to entrance and walk back or hitch the 3 km. to the botanical gardens. Ask for Víctor Gámez for a good guided tour. Local buses and trucks from beside the cinema go E to the Black Carib village of Triunfo, site of the first Spanish settlement on the mainland, in a beautiful bay, in which a sea battle between Cristóbal de Olid and Francisco de las Casas (2 of Cortés' lieutenants) was fought in 1524. Truck to Triunfo, US$0.40 (about 5 km.). Also, W to the Carib villages of Tornabé and San Juan (4 km. W of *Villas Telamar*), worth a visit, beautiful food (fish cooked in coconut oil). Further NW, along palm-fringed beaches and blue lagoons, is Punta Sal, a lovely place.

El Progreso, on the Río Ulúa, an important agricultural and commercial centre (no longer just a banana town) is less than an hour's drive on the paved highway SE of San Pedro Sula en route to Tela. Population, about 61,000. Local *fiesta*: Las Mercedes, end of September. Visit the Santa Elizabeth handicraft centre, where women are taught wood carving.

Hotel *Municipal*, Calle de Comercio, E to C with a/c and bath, clean, comfortable restaurant. *Honduras*, F p.p. with bath, run down, meals US$1.25; *Imperador*, attractive, F with bath; other cheap *pensiones*.

Restaurants *Maya*, 1 Av., 4-5 C.; *La Posta*, Calle del Comercio.

Banks Bancahsa, Banco Atlántida, Banco del Comercio, Banco Sogerín, Banadesa.

The highway is paved 25 km. S of El Progreso to Santa Rita; if one continues towards the San Pedro Sula-Tegucigalpa highway, one avoids San Pedro Sula when travelling from the N Coast to the capital. The highway is paved from Santa Rita to Yoro. (See also page 1108.) 10 km. S of El Progreso on the paved highway to Yoro or Santa Rita, at the village of Las Minas, is El Chorro (1 km. off the highway), a charming waterfall and natural swimming pool. A rugged hike can be made into the mountains and on to El Negrito from here.

La Ceiba, the country's busiest port for the export of bananas and pineapples, is 100 km. E of Tela, from which it is reached by sea, road or rail (85 km.). The capital of Atlántida Department, it lies in a green valley at the foot of Pico Bonito (2,580 metres). The climate is hot, but tempered by sea winds. There are some fine beaches nearby (La Barra and Miramar are the most popular), though some are dirty. Beyond La Ceiba is the old colonial village of Jutiapa. The Bay Islands are usually visited from La Ceiba. Population 66,000. *Fiesta*, Feria Isidra, in May; main day is the 3rd Saturday of the month.

Hotels *Gran Hotel París*, C, a/c, with good cafeteria, swimming pool, parking, and small night club; *Ceiba*, Av. San Isidro, 5 C., D with fan and bath, C with bath and a/c, restaurant and bar; next door is *Iberia*, D, a/c; and *San Carlos*, good, F, with shower; *Italia*, Av. 14 de Julio, 7-8 C., D; *Los*

1098　HONDURAS

Angeles, Av. La República, E, good value; *Príncipe*, 7 Calle, E, with bath, better than average; *Ligero's*, Av. San Isidro, 5 C., E; *La Isla*, next to bus station, F, nice rooms; *El Paso*, Av. La República, F; *Royal*, same Av., 2-3 C., E; *Pensión Tegucigalpa*, F, clean, basic. Many cheap hotels beside railway line leading from central plaza to pier: *Arias*, F without bath, good value. **Camping** at the airport for US$0.20.

Restaurants *Maxim's*, Av. San Isidro; *Atlántico*, Av. 14 de Julio; *Deportivo*, Blvd. Las Américas; *Partenón*, *Le Petit Café* (Gran Hotel París), *Lido, Ricardo's* (American-owned), good food, garden setting and a/c tables, *La Piraña, Rex's, Berlín. Mini Café* (near *Pensión Tegucigalpa*), reasonable, helpful owner. *Hotel San Carlos'* cafeteria is assembly point for the predominantly European Bay Islands.

Rent a Car　Molinari.

Night Clubs　Emperador, Rex, Pigalle, Flamingo. New World Discotheque, Av. 14 de Julio.

Non-Catholic Churches　Anglican, Methodist, Mennonite, Evangelical and Jehovah's Witnesses, among others.

Banks　Bank of London, Av. San Isidro y 10a Calle; Banco Atlántida; Bancahsa, 9 C., Av. San Isidro; Bancahorro, Av. San Isidro, 7 C.; Banco Sogerín, Av. San Isidro. Open 0830-1130, 1330-1600; Sats. 0800-1200.

Travel Agencies　Pasajes y Viajes Lafitte, Viajes Transmundo.

Buses　Most leave from a central terminal, 8 blocks from centre (taxi US$0.50). Regular bus service to San Pedro Sula, US$4 (7 a day, 3 hrs.). Alternatively, take bus to Tela (2 hrs.), then another to El Progreso, then another to San Pedro Sula, cost in all US$3.10, but much slower. To Trujillo, 5-8 hrs., US$5; to Olanchito, US$4, 3 hrs.; also regular buses to Sonaguera, Tocoa, Jutiapa, Balfate, Isletas and Iriona and San Esteban.

Airport　Golosón, with direct jet services to Miami and New Orleans as well as internal destinations. Sahsa flies to Tegucigalpa, and Lansa to Roatán, Utila, and Guanaja (Bay Is.). To Puerto Lempira, Isleña (Ed. Hermanos Kawas, Tel.: 42-01-79), Tues. and Sun., Lansa on Sun. US$93 return, both booked up 2-3 weeks ahead (Tel.: 42-26-83). Taxi to town US$10 per car, share with other passengers.

The Hog Islands (Cayos Cochinos), with lovely primeval hardwood forests, NE of La Ceiba: owned by a private U.S. consortium with reserved accommodation at Cayos del Sol. On the Isla de Cochino Grande is a dive resort; very beautiful. Resident managers are Jim and Gae McDonald; write in advance for reservations.

The **Bay Islands** (Islas de la Bahía) lie in an arc which curves NE away from a point some 30 km. N of La Ceiba. The three main islands are Utila, Roatán, and Guanaja. At the eastern end of Roatán are three small ones: Morat, Santa Elena, and Barbareta; there are other islets and 65 cays. Their total population, trading mostly in coconuts, bananas and plantains, with boat-building as the only and dying industry, is 8,863. There are some blacks and Black Caribs; the majority are fair-skinned people originally of British stock and still English-speaking. The culture is very un-Latin American. Columbus anchored here in 1502, on his fourth voyage. In the 18th century they were bases for English, French and Dutch buccaneers. They were in British hands for over a century but were finally ceded to Honduras in 1859. The government schools teach in Spanish, and the population is bi-lingual. The islands are very beautiful, but beware of the strong sun (the locals bathe in T-shirts) and sand gnats and other insects, especially away from the resorts.

The underwater environment is rich and extensive; reefs surround the islands, often within swimming distance of the shore. Caves and caverns are a common feature, with a wide variety of sponges and the best collection of pillar coral in the Caribbean. The islands are destined to become a major diving centre within a few years.

Utila (population 1,500) is only 32 km. by launch (US$5) from La Ceiba (Mon. p.m., 3 hrs., and irregularly through the week) or Puerto Cortés. Lansa flights La Ceiba-Utila, US$16 (frequently cancelled). Isleña flights leave La Ceiba as soon as there are 4 passengers; several flights daily. Utila, the main town, known locally as East Harbour, is a 40-minute boat ride from the Cays, a chain of small islands populated by fisherfolk off the S coast. On the main Cay, a few families live; they are very friendly to foreigners, but there is nowhere to put a tent. 3

HONDURAS 1099

islands further out is Water Cay where you can camp, sling a hammock or, in emergency, sleep in the house of the caretaker; take food and fresh water. It is a coconut island with "white holes" (sandy areas with wonderful hot bathing in the afternoon) and some of the most beautiful underwater reefs in the world. Ask around for a boat going there. Utila is the cheapest of the islands to visit. Take plenty of insect repellant in the rainy season. Do not pick coconuts, even in the remotest places; you may well be fined. Sunbathing and swimming are not particularly good, but there are caves, tropical vegetation, and some evidence of earlier Paya Indian culture. Snorkelling and diving equipment for hire. Lempiras or dollars accepted on the island, which is a little more expensive than the mainland.

Hotels on Utila *Captain Spencer*, E-D, with bath, and restaurant, diving equipment for hire; *Trudy's*, B, E without bath, good meals, diving equipment and boats for hire. *Gran View Gallery*, owned by Günter, an Austrian, gourmet seafood, diving expeditions and plenty of information. Good, reasonable food from *Big Mama's Cook Shop* (she organizes good picnics on the Cays, US$2 p.p. and US$1.50 for food, "unforgettable"). *Monkey Tail Inn*, F, basic, rats, but water all the time (beyond the *Bucket of Blood Bar*). There are plenty of houses and rooms for rent: e.g. at Willy Bodden, US$6 for 4 people (snorkelling equipment for hire).

N.B. Beware of theft, especially at night if you sleep with your windows open to reduce the heat.

There are a bank, a post office and a nurse. Local crafts include wood-carving (see Marc Coburn, called Tom).

The *Caribbean Pearl* sails to Utila from La Ceiba on Mon. or Tues., US$4 single, 3 hrs., and returns overnight to Puerto Cortés (bunks available), US$5, times posted in main street. Take food and torch. Captain Juni Cooper sails from La Ceiba to Utila from Mon. p.m. to Tues. a.m., US$4 for the 2½-3-hr. trip; sailings posted in *Hotel San Carlos*. He sails to Roatán a day or so later. From Utila to Roatán he charges US$5, 3½ hrs., irregular sailings. Launch La Ceiba-Roatán, US$15.

It is a few hours' sail to **Roatán**, the largest of the islands. The capital of the department, Roatán (locally known as Coxen's Hole), is on the south-western shore. It was from here that William Walker set sail in 1860 to conquer Honduras, and met his death at Trujillo. Port Royal, towards the eastern end of the island, and famous in the annals of buccaneering, is now almost deserted. Archaeologists have been busy on the islands but their findings are very confusing. Take a plane to Coxen's Hole (airport is 15 mins.' walk from town) and launch up coast to French Harbour and Oak Ridge. Flights to La Ceiba with Sahsa or Lansa, several daily; Lansa flies frequently to Utila and Guanaja. Also flights San Pedro Sula-Roatán (airport being extended to take jets).

From Coxen's Hole it is an hour's walk to Flowers Bay, or US$1 by bus. Mr. Lambert rents rooms an hour's walk W along the coast. West End, on the opposite coast, can be reached by a stiff walk over the hills (more than an hour). There are many buses on the unmade roads, but those that charge US$1-1.50 on set routes daily at nightfall or on Sunday charge US$10 for express journeys. Frequent bus service from Coxen's Hole to French Harbour (US$1.50), with its shrimping and lobster fleet. At Brick Bay, just before French Harbour, the Caribbean Sailing Club has a modern hotel (A with breakfast) and rents a fleet of 30 sailing boats for US$200 per day. From French Harbour to Oak Ridge by bus, on a rough road, is US$1.50; Oak Ridge, situated on a cay (US$0.50 crossing in dory), is built around a deep inlet. Hire a boat for an hour's sail up the coast to Port Royal (also reached by good road from Oak Ridge); Old British gun emplacements on Fort Cay. Lord Nelson visited here in 1780 as a young captain. No regular bus from Port Royal to Oak Ridge, and it's a tough 3-hr. walk. Note the Black Carib village of Punta Gorda (probably the first non-Indian settlement on the islands).

Boats go irregularly from Puerto Cortés to Roatán, US$10 plus US$0.50 dock charge for tourists. Boats most days at 1400 for La Ceiba. *Caribbean Pearl* sails irregularly from Puerto Cortés, via Utila, to Roatán; also fishing boats for US$10 p.p. Jeeps across island to Sandy Bay (US$0.50). Beaches excellent but Roatán is expensive, twice as dear as the mainland.

Hotels on Roatán At Roatán: West End, *Roberts Hill*, C-A, without meals, diving, etc., good value; *Lost Paradise of the West End*, B-A, full board (D without), delicious meals, snorkelling equipment, transport back to airport (to *Lost Paradise*, take bus from Coxen's Hole to Sandy Bay,

1100 HONDURAS

and walk ½ hr.); at Sandy Bay, *Anthony's Key Resort*, L (US$150 full board), glorious situation, launch and diving facilities included; *Pirate's Den*, D-A, full board, poor service, beware of overcharging (well named); *Bamboo Inn*, E-D, a few km. outside the town, clean and good (nice restaurant next door); *Quinn's*, reasonable; at French Harbour, *Coral Reef Inn*, E-D; *Caribinn*, D; *French Harbour Yacht Club*, C-B; *Buccaneer Inn*, C-A; at Oak Ridge, *Reef House Resort*, B-L, inc. meals and boats; *San José Hotel*, Oak Ridge, D, clean, pleasant, good value, good food, English-speaking owner, Louise Solórzano; *Gran Hotel Ronnie*, cafeteria nearby; *Clear View Hotel*, B; at Port Royal, *Camp Bay Resort*, A; *Roatán Lodge*, Port Royal, D, accommodation in cabins, hosts Brian and Lisa Blancher provide scuba diving and snorkelling expeditions; *Miss Merlee's Guest House*. *Coco View Resort*, A/L, French Cay; *Caribbean Sailing Yachts*, A/L, Brick Bay. Also, *Hotel Coral*, E, Coxen's Hole, and *Welcome*, D; *Solbod House*, D; *Spyglass Hill Resort*, L, overlooking Punta Gorda village, an hour's walk from Oak Ridge, lodge or bungalow accommodation. There are other, cheaper, places to stay (for example, Miss Effie's, near *Anthony's Key Resort*) and houses to let (about US$20 per month at West End, Half Moon Bay, or Punta Gorda).

Barbareta Beach Club on Barbareta Island; excellent diving, but expensive. The adjacent Pigeon Cays are ideal for snorkelling, shallow scuba; picnics. There are stone artefacts on the island, and you can hike in the hills to caves which may have been inhabited by Paya Indians. The island was once owned by the descendants of Henry Morgan.

Columbus called **Guanaja**, the easternmost of the group, the Island of Pines, and the tree is still abundant. The locals call the island Bonacca. Much of Guanaja town, covering a small cay off the coast, is built on stilts above sea water: hence its nick-name, the "Venice of Honduras". An airport on Bonacca Island, boat to Guanaja, US$1; Lansa flight from Roatán daily except Sun. at 0930, 1430; also to La Ceiba. Bathing is made somewhat unpleasant by the many sandfleas. The *Suyapa* sails between Guanaja, La Ceiba and Puerto Cortés. The *Miss Sheila* also does the same run and goes on to George Town (Grand Cayman). Cable Doly Zapata, Guanaja, for monthly sailing dates to Grand Cayman (US$75 one way). Also boats to the islands from Trujillo. Irregular but frequent sailings in lobster boats for next to nothing to Puerto Lempira in Caratasco Lagoon, Misquitia, or more likely, only as far as the Río Plátano (see page 1111).

Hotels on Guanaja *Bayman Bay Club* (beautiful location) and *Posada del Sol* (on an outlying cay), both A-L; *Miller*, D-C (cheaper without a/c or bath); *Harry Carter*, E-D.

A roundabout railway and a direct road run from La Ceiba to **Olanchito**, in the hills to the SE. It was founded, according to tradition, by a few stragglers who escaped from the destruction of Olancho el Viejo, between Juticalpa and Catacamas, then a wealthy town. (Olanchito is prosperous, but also hot and ugly.) They brought with them the crown made of hides which the Virgin still wears in the church of Olanchito. Population: 13,400.

Bank Banco Atlántida.

Bus To La Ceiba, 2½ hrs., US$4 via Jutiapa and Sava; to Trujillo, 3 hrs., US$5 via Tocoa and Sava.

Trujillo, 90 km. to the east again, is a port and former capital. The population now is fewer than 5,000. The town was founded in 1525 (the oldest in Honduras) by Juan de Medina; Hernán Cortés arrived there after his famous march overland from Yucatán in pursuit of his usurping lieutenant, Olid. It was near here that William Walker (see under Nicaragua) was shot in 1860 (a commemorative stone marks the spot); the old cemetery where he is buried is interesting, giving an idea of where early residents came from. El Castillo (Santa Bárbara), a ruined Spanish fortress overlooking the Bay, is worth a visit. Ask the caretaker to show the relics found there. To the S, and E to the Río Segovia, lies a huge territory of jungle swamps and mountains lived in by a few Indians and timber men (see page 1111). Nearby is Guaymoreto lagoon, which has a bird island (Isla de Pájaros) and monkeys. Flying in is best—Lansa has flights to La Ceiba. The town can be reached by bus from San Pedro Sula, Tela and La Ceiba now that a road (appalling apart from 40 km. from Trujillo) has been built from La Ceiba (a dull journey, 5 hrs. via Tocoa, 3 direct buses early a.m. from Trujillo, US$5). In this area, many people speak English, so if answered in English, do not continue in Spanish.

Local holiday: San Juan Bautista in June, with participation from surrounding Garifuna (Black Carib) settlements.

Hotels *Villa Brinkley*, B, private beach, good view, recommended; *Colonial*, F, E with bath, near plaza, opp. El Castillo, good; *Central*, E, with bath, basic, no water during the day (*Rubens Restaurant*, good, in the hotel). *Roxi*, D. *Turismo*, E; *Emperador*, F; *Imperial*, F, basic, noisy. Excellent seafood at *Cocopando*, set in a coconut grove on western beach (room for rent); *Comedor Albita*, near telephone office, good; *La Cueva del Pirata*, beside airstrip, excellent restaurant and bar, cabins F-C. Also good food in the market. Many fish restaurants along the beach; *pan de coco*, delicious, is baked almost daily.

Bank Banco Atlántida.

There are interesting villages of Black Caribs (Garifuna) at Santa Fe, 10 km. W of Trujillo (US$1 by bus), San Antonio and eastwards to Limón. At Puerto Castilla near Trujillo, Columbus landed in 1502 and the first mass on Central American soil was said. It is a meat-packing station and active shrimping centre; a new port is being built. A military training centre operates here. The beach between the port and the spit of land that forms Trujillo Bay is deserted. There are some pleasant beaches around the magnificent Bay. Twenty minutes' walk from Trujillo plaza is Riveras de Pedregal (known as *la piscina*), a series of swimming pools filled from the Río Cristales. The owner, Sr. Rufino Galán, has a collection of precolumbian, colonial and modern artefacts and curios. The pools are usually open at weekends and holidays, but not during the Nov.-Feb. rainy season.

San Pedro Sula

San Pedro Sula, 58 km. S of Puerto Cortés by road and railway, is the second largest city in Honduras and one of the most rapidly growing cities in Latin America. It is a centre for the banana, coffee, sugar and timber trades, a focal distributing point for northern and western Honduras, and the most highly industrialized centre in the country. Industries include a small steel rolling mill, textiles and clothes making, margarine, furniture (wooden and metal), zinc roofing, cement and concrete products, and plastics. Its business community is mainly Arab. The population is 422,100.

The city was founded by Pedro de Alvarado in 1536 but nothing remains of the old city and there are no old buildings of interest. The large neo-colonial-style cathedral, started in 1949, is now completed. San Pedro Sula is situated in the lush and fertile valley of the Ulúa (Sula) river, beneath the forested slopes of the Merendón mountains and, though pleasant in the cooler season from October to March, reaches very high temperatures in the summer months with considerable humidity levels.

The higher and cooler suburb of Bella Vista with its fine views over the city affords welcome relief from the intense heat of the town centre. The cafeteria and foyer swimming pool of *Hotel Sula* provide a cool haven for visitors. The city's main festival is in the last days of June.

Hotels *Gran Hotel Sula* (the best), 1 C., 3 and 4 Av., A/L, pool, restaurant (upstairs, very good, reasonably priced) and café, also good, 24-hr. service; *Copantl Sula*, very modern, A/L in Col. Las Mesetas, free bus to city centre, Telex IT5584; *Bolívar*, 2a C., 2 Av., N.O., D/A, cabins beside pool, with a/c, restaurant; *El Rey*, at bus station; *San Pedro*, 3 C., and 2 Av., S.O., F-D, with bath and a/c, also cheaper rooms, inexpensive restaurant; *Palmira*, 6-7 Av., 6 C., with a/c, E-A; : *Manhattan*, 7 Av. 3-4 C., E-D, with a/c; *Terraza*, C with a/c, E without, good dining room, friendly staff, 6 Av., 4-5 Calle S.O.; *Colombia*, 3 Calle, 5-6 Av., E/D, with a/c, E without; *Colombia Annex*, a few blocks away, F; *Moderno*, 7 Av., 5-6 C., E, opp. Empresa el Rey buses; *Brisas del Occidente*, a 5-storey building on Av. 5, E, with fan, friendly, comfortable, recommended (do not confuse with nearby *Brisas de Copán*, a dive which rents rooms by the hour); *Castillo*, 8 C., 5-6 Av. S.O., F/E; *Siesta*, 2 Av. S.E., 7 C. (Tel.: 522650), F, cheaper without bath, clean, safe, friendly, recommended; *Hospedaje Castro*, by market square, F; *Colonial*; *Monte Cristo*; *París*, near bus station for Puerto Cortés, F, shared bath, clean but noisy; *San Juan*, 6 C., 6 Av. S.O. No. 35, E; *Ritz*, 1 C., 5-6 Av., E; *El Centro*, E, with bath, good breakfasts. 5 km. south, on the road to Tegucigalpa, *Tropical* has opened, a good stopping place for motorists.

Other, cheaper, hotels are the *Continental*, 3 Av., 7 C., S.O. No. 57 (E), *Copán* (E with fan, clean), *Nueva España* (F). *Lucky*, hotel/restaurant (Oriental), near bus station; *Motel Vitanza* and *Mesón Español* (near *Hotel Manhattan*), good typical dishes available; *Pizza Don Corleone*, several throughout the city; *Italia*, near *Gran Hotel Sula*, good; *Vicente* and *Nápoli* restaurants, centre of town, Italian food available at reasonable prices; *Salón Marte*, near market, good, cheap light meals in evening;

1102 HONDURAS

others include *El Rincón Gaucho, Westphalia*; *La Cesta*, good for chicken; *Pops* and *Ka-Boom* for ice cream. Many good fried chicken stands in market.

Clubs The private Casino Club in the centre of town has a swimming pool, tennis courts and a dance hall.

Night Clubs There is a "roaring" red light area on the E edge of the city, open day and night, bus No. 3 from centre, US$0.10.

Discotheques Fondo del Recuerdo and Sancho Panza, good; Don Quijote; San Fernando (small); Genesis (bad).

Theatre The Círculo Teatral Sampedrano puts on plays at the Centro Cultural Sampedrano, 3 Calle N.O., No. 20, which also has an art gallery and an English and Spanish library. There are five air-conditioned cinemas.

Shopping Excellent wood and leather products are sold at CDI, in the old US Consulate building.

Taxis Cheap; ask the price first and bargain if necessary (US$1-1.50 per journey).

Bank of London at 4a Av. S.O. 26, between 3a and 4a Calle, Banco Atlántida; Banco de Honduras (Citibank); Banco de Ahorro Hondureño, has a beautiful mural in its head office, 5 Av., 4 Calle S.O. Bancahsa, 5 Av., S.O., No. 46; and all other local banks. Open 0830-1500, closed Sat. Black market at *Hotel Gran Sula*.

Belize Consulate Sr. Antonio E. Canahuati, Edif. Plásticos Sula, Km. 5, Tel.: 52-61-91, open 0800-1100, 1300-1600. Also **Guatemalan Consulate**, 8 C., 5-6 Av. No. 38.

Schools and Institutes La Escuela Internacional (English-speaking). On US lines with US and some British staff. Alianza Francesa, Ed. Bermúdez, 3 Calle S.O. No. 38, Tel.: 53-11-78, has a library, French films on Wed., and cultural events on Fri.

Churches Episcopal Church, round corner from Sports Stadium, English service, Sun., 1000. High Mass on Suns., 1030, at Orthodox church at Río Piedras is picturesque and colourful.

Telphone, Telex and Cables from Hondutel.

Tourist Office Edificio Inmosa, 3-4 C., 4 Av. and at airport.

Airport Ramón Villeda Morales, 13 km. from city centre, US$7.50 p.p. by taxi; US$3 by colectivo. Buses do not go to the airport terminal itself; you have to walk the final 1½ km. from the La Lima road (bus to this point, US$0.30). Flights to Tegucigalpa (35 mins.) 4 times daily. Twice daily to La Ceiba and to Belize. Direct flights every day to Guatemala, New Orleans and Miami. Irregular flights to other Honduran cities and to the Copán ruins.

Buses To Tegucigalpa, 4½ hrs., 250 km. by paved road. Main bus services with comfortable coaches and terminals in the town centre are Hedmán Alas, 7-8 Av. N.O., 3 C., Casa 51, Tel.: 531361 (US$4), which is the best, and Transportes Sáenz (station is 20 mins. walk or US$1 taxi ride off Av. Las Leones, Calle 9, S.O., 10 mins. walk W towards hills), San Cristóbal and El Rey (all US$3.50), last bus at 1730. Small friendly buses run by El Norteño. Other services operate with less comfortable buses. The road to Puerto Cortés is paved, a pleasant 1-hr. journey down the lush river valley. Train journey takes two hours at least to cover the same distance and there are two or three trains a day. Buses run N to Puerto Cortés (Empresa Impala, 2 Av., 4-5 C., several each hour, US$1), E to La Lima, El Progreso (US$0.60), Tela and La Ceiba (7 a day, US$4, 3½ hrs.), S to Lake Yojoa and Tegucigalpa, and SW to Santa Rosa and then through the Department of Ocotepeque with its magnificent mountain scenery to the Guatemalan border (US$4.50 to the border by bus). Transportes Impala, 2 Av., 4-5 Calle S.O. No. 23, has 6 buses a day to Nueva Octepeque and Agua Caliente on the Guatemalan border; Empresa Torito and Transportes Copanecos go to Santa Rosa de Copán every 45 mins. from 0430 to 1830 (5 Av., 5-6 Calle S.O. and 6 C., 4-5 Av. S.O., respectively). Road paved all the way.

Excursions One can take a taxi up the mountain behind the city for US$1-1.50; good view, a restaurant, and interesting vegetation on the way up. Lake Ticamaya, near Choloma, is worth visiting between June and December. The head office of the former United Brands subsidiary is at **La Lima** (4,000 inhabitants), 15 km. to the E by road (bus frequent, US$0.25), where the banana estate and processing plants can be seen. There is a club (golf, tennis, swimming) which takes members from outside. A little to the E, near the Ulúa river, is Travesía (not the Travesía near Puerto Cortés), where Mayan pottery remains have been found, but no ruins as such. Buses run E to El Progreso and on N to Tela on the coast, and to La Ceiba. (The train to Tela goes via Baracoa at 1500, 3 hrs.) A bus from 2 Av. goes to Las Vegas-El Mochito mine where there is a cheap *pensión* (F) and walks along W side of Lake El Rincón.

The waterfall at Pulhapanzak is on the Río Lindo, off the main San Pedro Sula-Tegucigalpa road; by car it's a 1½ hr. drive, longer by bus. Take a Mochito bus from San Pedro Sula (hourly 0500-1700) and alight at the sign to the falls, US$1.25. Alternatively stay on the bus to Cañaveral (take

HONDURAS 1103

identification because there is a power plant here), and walk back along the Río Lindo, 3-4 hours past interesting rock formations and small falls. The waterfall (42 metres) is beautiful in, or just after the rainy season, and, in sunshine, there is a rainbow at the falls. There is a picnic area and a small overpriced restaurant, but the site does get crowded at weekends and holidays; there is a small admission charge (US$0.50). *Pensión* at Peña Blanca, 4 km. from the falls.

Copán and Western Honduras

The Western Highway (171 km.) runs from San Pedro Sula SW along the Río Chamelecón to Canoa (from where there is a paved road S to Santa Bárbara) and Santa Rosa de Copán; it goes on to San Salvador. **Santa Bárbara** (6,000 inhabitants) is 32 km. W of Lake Yojoa, in hot lowlands. Panama hats and other goods of *junco* palm are made in this pleasant town. Carlos Rivera, director of the high school, speaks English and has much information on the area. In the vicinity the ruined colonial city of Tencoa has recently been rediscovered. The road goes on to join the Northern Highway S of Lake Yojoa (being paved).

Hotels *Herrera, Santa Marta*, both on La Independencia, F; *Hospedaje Rodríguez*, F, with bath, recommended; *Pensión Moderno*, E, with hot shower, reasonable dining room. **Restaurants** *Brasero*, the best; also *Majestic* and *Oasis*; *Comedor Estudiantina*, for good, cheap, basic meal (US$1).

Bank Banco Atlántida.

Bus from Tegucigalpa, Tues., Thurs., Sat. at 0600, return Mon., Wed., Fri., at 0500, US$4.50, 7 hrs. (passing through remote villages in beautiful mountain scenery); from San Pedro Sula, 3½ hrs., US$2.50, 7 a day between 0500 and 1630.

A branch road from the road to Santa Bárbara goes to **San Luis**, a coffee town of 3,000 people in beautiful scenery. *Hospedaje San José*, F, clean, friendly; *Hospedaje San Isidro*. Several *comedores*. Bus from San Pedro Sula, US$2.50, twice daily. (Electricity 1800-2130 only.) Near Santa Bárbara is Ilama with one of the best small colonial churches in Honduras (no accommodation).

In the Department of Santa Bárbara is an area known as El Resumidero, in which are the Quezapaya mountain, and six others over 1,400 metres, and a number of caves (Pencaligüe, Los Platanares, El Quiscamote, and others). From Santa Bárbara, go to El Níspero and thence to El Quiscamote; or go to San Vicente Centenario (thermal springs nearby), and on to San Nicolás, Atima, Berlín, and La Unión, all of which have thermal waters, fossils, petrified wood and evidence of volcanic activity.

Santa Rosa de Copán, 153 km. by road from San Pedro Sula, is the centre of a rich agricultural and cattle-raising area. Altitude 1,040 metres, population 20,500. Much maize and tobacco is grown in the area. Excellent *sombreros de junco* (Panama hats) are made here. Santa Rosa is a colonial town with most attractive narrow cobbled streets. The central plaza and church are perched on a hilltop. It holds a festival in the last 10 days of August.

Hotels *Elvir* (the best), Calle Real Centenario O., 2 Av. O, D, all rooms have own bath, good meals in cafeteria or restaurant; nearby: *Hotel Maya* (not to be confused with *Hospedaje Maya*, see below), 1 C. N.O. y 3 Av. N.O., F, next door is *Castillo* (1 C. N.O. No. 111), E with bath, F without, dirty, simple; *Suyapa*, 2 C. N.E. y 2 Av. N.E. F; *Hospedaje San Pedro*, C.N.E. No. 243, F; *Rosario*, 3 Av. N.E. No. 139, E with bath, F without; next door is *Hospedaje Guillén*, F, No. 193; *Hospedaje Santa Rosa*, 3 Av. N.E. No. 119, F, simple, clean; *Copán*, 3 Av. N.E. y 1 C. N.E., E, and next door, *Hospedaje Maya*, F. *Hospedaje Calle Real*, Real Centenario y 6 Av., F, clean, quiet, friendly, sometimes water failures, good cheap meals; *Pensión Rivera*, 2 Av. No. 131, F, very basic; *Hispano*, on main square, 1 C. N.E. y 1 Av. N.E., F; *Hospedaje Santa Eduvigis*, 2 Av. N.O. y 1 C. N.O., F, with reasonable restaurant; *Erick*, 1 C. N.E. No. 362, E with bath; *Mayaland*, opp bus station on Carretera Internacional, E, parking, restaurant.

Restaurants *Danubio Azul*, 1 Av. S.E., No. 040, 1 block from Plaza; *Cafetería Elvir*, fair value. *Miraflores* in Col. Miraflores.

Bank Banco de Occidente and Atlántida, both on main plaza. Banadesa, Calle Real.

Bus from Santa Rosa to Tegucigalpa via San Pedro Sula leaves at 0400 from main square, US$4.50, 7-8 hrs. 4 buses daily to Gracias between 0930 and 1600, 3 hrs., US$1.10. To San Pedro Sula, US$2, 4 hrs. every 45 mins. (Empresa Torito, and Transportes Copanecos), bus to La Entrada, US$0.50. Copanecos bus San Pedro Sula-La Entrada-Santa Rosa de Copán every 90 mins. Frequent service of small buses S to Nueva Ocotepeque. Local bus from bus station to centre ("El Urbano"), US$0.10, taxi US$0.50.

1104 HONDURAS

Excursions Robert Millar writes: There is a bus from Santa Rosa at 1000 and 1400, west to the small town of Dulce Nombre de Copán (US$0.65). Hardy hikers can continue west through forested mountains to stay at the primitive village of San Agustín (take hammock or sleeping bag), continuing next day to emerge a few kms. from Copán ruins. From Santa Rosa there is a 3-hr. bus ride to Lepaera (cheap, simple *pensión* and *comedores*, perched on a lovely mountainside (also reached from Gracias). One can scale the peak or descend on foot by an old mule trail heading back to Santa Rosa, crossing the river on a swingbridge (*hamaca*), then hitch-hiking.

Numerous daily buses go to Corquín (US$1, 2 hrs.)—2 good *pensiones*, one with a charming garden. From here take a rough, dusty, 2½-hr. ride in a pick-up truck (US$1) to Belén Gualcho, 1,850 metres up in mountains, amid coffee plantations. There are 3 simple *pensiones* (F, cheap meals); it is a fine centre for walking in the dense rain forests of the Celaque mountains; colourful Sunday Indian market. A steep descent east from Belén by mule trail leads in 5 hrs. to San Manuel de Colohuete, with a magnificent colonial church whose façade is sculpted with figures of saints. There is an equally fine colonial church 5 hrs. to the south-west at San Sebastián, continuing then by mule trail via the heights of Agua Fría to reach the bus route near the frontier at Tomalá. Alternatively, one can walk 5 hrs. east from San Manuel to La Campa (colonial church) where there is irregular transport to Gracias.

There are buses from Santa Rosa to Mapalaca and villages bordering El Salvador.

From San Pedro Sula there are regular buses via Santa Rosa south to **Nueva Ocotepeque** (6 hrs., US$4); road is well paved. From Nueva Ocotepeque, buses to San Pedro Sula stop at La Entrada (US$2.25), first at 0030, for connections to Copán. There are splendid mountain views. The Salvadorean border S of Nueva Ocotepeque is open again. Colectivos, US$0.50, and the occasional bus run to El Poy, and you can cross into Guatemala at Atulapa, just after Agua Caliente (tourist office here). There are several buses a day from San Pedro Sula to Agua Caliente, first at 0300 (e.g. Congolón, Impala, US$5, 6-7 hrs. (can be even longer owing to frequent military checks); the Honduran and Guatemalan migration offices are about 2 km. apart, minibuses do the trip for US$0.25). You can get into El Salvador via Esquipulas, Guatemala (see page 1028). Before you reach Nueva Ocotepeque there is a police checkpoint, where Guatemalan currency can be bought as well as at the border (though probably cheaper to buy at banks in the cities) and an army checkpoint on the continental divide at 2,130 metres. Make sure all documents are in order and to hand. There are Guatemalan consuls in San Pedro Sula and Nueva Ocotepeque from whom visas or tourist cards may be obtained (preferable to trying to get one at the border). There are also, of course, excursions to Copán (see below), and to the beautiful Lake Yojoa (page 1105) on the Tegucigalpa road (1½ hours). There is an old colonial church, La Vieja (or La Antigua) between Nueva Ocotepeque and the border.

Hotels in Nueva Ocotepeque *Gran*, F-D; *Ocotepeque*, F (by Transportes Impala); restaurant *La Cabaña*.

The magnificent Mayan ruins of **Copán** are 225 km. by air from Tegucigalpa or 186 by air or paved road from San Pedro Sula, and 1 km. from the village, called Copán Ruinas. The road runs SW for 125 km. to La Entrada, where it forks left for Santa Rosa and right for Copán, 60 km. away (the road from La Entrada to Copán is paved). Copán can also be reached by road from Guatemala City. The Honduran immigration office is now at the border; one can get exit stamps there. For one route from Guatemala, see page 1028.

How to get there One can charter flights from Tegucigalpa and Guatemala City. There are also regular buses (Copanecos, Impala or Torito lines) from San Pedro Sula to La Entrada, US$1.50 (2 hrs.); from La Entrada to Copán, US$1.50 by bus, US$3 by minibus (3 hrs.), every 40 mins.; last bus from La Entrada to Copán apparently leaves at 1530. Some direct. (If going by bus, and returning, from San Pedro Sula, it is impossible to see Copán in one day. But if going on to Guatemala, one can take the 0445 San Pedro-La Entrada bus, 0600 La Entrada-Copán, arriving 0900, then the 1300 bus from Copán to the border.) Etuni bus from San Pedro Sula direct to Copán, at 1030 and 1300, 5-6 hrs. Direct bus also from 6 Av. S. O. y 7 C. S. O., at 1100 daily, US$2.50, 5-6 hrs. Return to San Pedro Sula direct at 0400 and 0500, 3 early a.m. buses from Copán to Santa Rosa, 4 hrs., US$2.50. King's Tours in Guatemala City run a one-day tour from there to Copán and back (US$60), recommended. To return to San Pedro Sula, minibuses will collect you from your hotel and take you to La Entrada, from where buses go to San Pedro Sula.

La Entrada is a hot, dusty little town (*Hospedaje Copaneco*, 1 Av. No. 228, F; Hospedajes *Alexandra*, *Mejía*; Hotel *Tegucigalpa*; *Hospedaje María*, F, clean, good, limited food also; eat in the market or at the bus station). A few km. beyond is the small town of Florida (primitive accommodation). The owner of the gas station here will advise archaeologists about the many Maya ruins between Florida and Copán. (Minibus Florida-Copán at 1800.) There are a number of hilltop stelae between the border and Copán. At Jihua, 3 km. to the left from Km. 4 from La Entrada, is a restored colonial church. The road from La Entrada to Copán is paved but in poor condition.

Another route from Guatemala City is by Rutas Orientales bus to Chiquimula (efficient buses leaving from 19 Calle 8-18, every hour from 0500-1830, buy ticket—US$1.50 - in advance, 4 hr.

journey), take 0700 bus in time to catch 1000 Transportes Velásquez bus to Copán. Bus from Chiquimula to the border, US$1.50. Minibuses from Copán back to the border leave at 0700 and 1300, US$2. Truck to Guatemalan border leaves Copán when full, US$1. From the border there is a bus at 1630 to the Atlantic Highway, which connects Guatemala City and Puerto Barrios—change at the highway to arrive in Guatemala City at 2000. No buses from border into Guatemala on Sunday, and little traffic to hitch a lift.

To enter (or return to) Guatemala an alternative route is via Nueva Ocotepeque (see above); every 40 mins. a bus leaves Copán for La Entrada (US$3, 2¼ hrs., longer in rain). From there, there are several buses a day to Santa Rosa (US$0.50, 1 hr.). Minibuses run from Santa Rosa to Nueva Ocotepeque (US$2, 2½ hrs.). Trucks take you across the Agua Caliente border into Guatemala (US$1) and minibuses run on to Esquipulas (US$0.25, ½ hr.) from where there is a regular bus service to Chiquimula (US$0.25, 1½ hrs.). A first class bus to Guatemala City runs from the junction of CA10 and the Copán road, south-east of Chiquimula (US$1.25).

Exit tax from Guatemala is Q3, entry to Honduras US$2.50. If you are leaving Honduras make sure to get your passport stamped at the police check point just outside Copán on the road to the border. The nearest Guatemalan consulate is in San Pedro Sula, so if you need a visa, you must get one there.

Hotels in Copán: *La Posada*, tourist hotel at the ruins, 80 rooms. *Maya Copán*, E, with bath, restaurant; *Marina*, on the Plaza, E, with bath, meals US$3, breakfast US$1.50, cheaper annex, F, excellent value; *Hotelito Brisas de Copán*, E, with bath (F without, quiet, recommended); *Hospedaje Los Gemelos*, F, without bath, nice, good value; *Hotelito Peña*, F, clean. *Pensión Hernández*, G, food available, noisy and unfriendly; *Hotel-Restaurante Paty*, friendly, under the same ownership as one of the mini-bus companies, has good meals (a bit dear) and 10 clean rooms, G p.p. without bath, E in newer rooms with bath. *Paty* and *Hernández* are noisy from buses after 0400. *Restaurant El Sesteo*, opposite *Brisas de Copán*. *La Llama del Bosque*, comedor 2 blocks W of central Plaza. Good meals at the market. There is a small museum in the plaza, which is worth seeing (open 0800-1200, 1300-1700). There is also a cinema (films at 1930, daily except Tues. and Wed.), which leaves much to be desired. Horses for hire near the square, US$1 per day (if you look around and bargain).

Postage stamps available at the Post Office. Only travellers' cheques of US$20 or less may be changed at the bank. Guatemalan currency is rarely accepted at Copán; it is impossible to change quetzales. Change dollars at the better hotels. There is a service station at Copán.

N.B. It is advisable to get to the ruins (open 0800-1700) as early as possible; this way you will miss the guided tours. However, the site is very crowded only at weekends. There is a cafeteria by the entrance to the ruins, and also a shop. Guided tours available all year. Take a torch for the passageways and tunnel. There is a tourist office in the Parque Arqueológico, next to the shop.

When Stephens and Catherwood examined the ruins in 1839, they were engulfed in jungle. In the 1930s the Carnegie Institute cleared the ground and rebuilt the Great Stairway, and since then they have been maintained by the Government. Entry to ruins US$1.50 and museum (open 0800-1600) US$0.50 for foreigners.

Some of the most complex carvings are found on the 21 stelae, or 3-metre columns of stones on which the passage of time was originally believed to be recorded, and which are still in their original sites among the buildings. Under each stela is a vault; some have been excavated. The stelae are deeply incised and carved with faces and figures and animals. (John Streather tells us that the stelae are not chronologies but in fact "are royal portraits with inscriptions recording deeds and lineage of those portrayed as well as dates of birth, marriage(s) and death".). (Some of the finest examples of sculpture in the round from Copán are now in the British Museum or at Boston.) Ball courts were revealed during excavation, and one of them, with the stone seats of its amphitheatre, has been fully restored. The Hieroglyphic Stairway leads from the lower level to an upper. A temple, approached by more steps and guarded by heraldic beasts, was on the upper level.

The last stela was set up in Copán between A.D. 800 and 820, after less than five centuries of civilized existence. That no further developments took place is attributed now to revolt by the common people against an increasingly distanced nobility and priesthood, rather than outside invaders (John Streather). The nearby river has been diverted to prevent it encroaching on the site when in flood. (See general account of Maya history on page 1006.)

South from San Pedro Sula to Tegucigalpa

Potrerillos (*Hotel Alvarez*), the railhead, is 37 km. S of San Pedro Sula. From Potrerillos the paved Northern Highway (288 km.) climbs some 37 km. from the hot lowlands to **Lake Yojoa**, 600 metres high, 22½ km. long and 10 km. wide, splendidly set among mountains. To the E rise the Jicaque mountains; to the W some lower hills, with Los Naranjos and other villages along the shores or set back towards the hills. Pumas, bears and jaguars range the forests and pine-clad slopes. There are two islands in the lake. The road follows the eastern margin to the lake's southern tip at Pito Solo, where sailing boats and motor boats can be

1106 HONDURAS

hired. The road is mostly out of sight of the lake: the side-road to the lake itself is not signposted and can be easily overlooked. (Bus to Lake from San Pedro Sula, US$1.50, 1½ hrs.; bus from Lake to Tegucigalpa, US$3, 3½ hrs.).

Accommodation *Hotel Los Remos* has cabins and camping facilities at southern end of the lake, C and up; *Motel Brisas del Lago*, on N shore, A including breakfast; *Motel Agua Azul* (at N end of lake), B, meals for non-residents (reports vary); facilities for swimming and boating. *Comedores* on the road beside the lake serve the bass that is caught there. Buses between Tegucigalpa and San Pedro stop to let passengers off at Los Remos, and at Peñas Blancas, 5 km. from the turning for Agua Azul. At Peña Blanca Córtez on N side of Lake is *Comedor El Cruce*, very good home cooking. 10 km. N of the lake is the turn off for the village of Santa Cruz de Yojoa, and at 24 km. is the El Cajón hydroelectric project (to visit the dam, apply at least 10 days in advance by phone—22-21-77, or in writing to Oficina de Relaciones Públicas de la ENEE, 1 Av., Edificio Valle-Aguiluz, Comayagüela, D.C.) Accommodation can be booked at El Mochito mine of the Honduras Rosario Mining Company (US-owned), near Lake Yojoa.

Thirty-two km. beyond Pito Solo is **Siguatepeque**, a little town (population 26,400) with a cool climate. It is the site of the Escuela Nacional de Ciencias Forestales and, being exactly half-way between Tegucigalpa and San Pedro Sula, a collection point for the produce of Intibucá, La Paz and Lempira departments. The beautiful Cerro and Bosque de Calanterique, behind the Evangelical Hospital, is ¾ hour's walk from town centre.

Hotels and Restaurants *Boarding House Central*, F, reasonable; *Versalles*, F; both have restaurants; *Mi Hotel*, 1 km. from main road, E, with bath, parking, restaurant; *Hospedaje Elena*, *Hospedaje San Cristóbal*, *Hospedaje San José*, all F, none recommended; *Cafetería Ideal*, hamburgers and light lunches; *China Palace*, Chinese and international; *Pizzería y Restaurante Fiallos*, clean, varied menu, or eat in the market; on the Northern Highway there are several restaurants, best are *Nuevo* and *Antiguo Bethania*, good, abundant, inexpensive meals.

Banks Bancahsa, Banco Atlántida, Banco de Occidente.

Bus to San Pedro Sula, ½ hourly, US$2.50; Tegucigalpa with Empresas Unidas or Maribel, US$2, 3 hrs.; to Comayagua, Transpinares, US$0.75, 45 mins.

From Siguatepeque through lovely forested mountainous country, 5 buses daily go SW to **La Esperanza** (98 km.), capital of Intibucá Department, at 1,485 metres (bus from La Esperanza to Siguatepeque 0700, 0900, last at 1000 Trans, 3 hrs.; La Esperanza, Siguatepeque, Comayagua at 0600, buses from La Esperanza to the Salvadorean border). This old colonial town set in a pleasant valley has an attractive church in front of the park, and there are simple but pleasant *pensiones* (e.g. *Hospedaje Mina*, F, adequate, 1 block E of market; *Hotel Solís*, 1 block E of market, E, recommended; *Rosario*, on road to Siguatepeque; *San Cristóbal*, F; *San José*, 4 Av. Gen. Vásquez No. C-0005, F; *La Esperanza*, F; *Pensión Mejía Paz Batres*, 1 block W of Plaza, E with bath, F without, hot water, overpriced; *San José*, in same building as Farmacia La Esperanza, 2 blocks S of Plaza, F; *Hotel y Comedor San Antonio*, F). Market: Sun., at which Lenca Indians from nearby villages sell wares and food, including *junco* blankets. 2 craft centres: Tejedoras Intibucanas, 4 C., ½ block S of park, and Centro Indígena de Capacitación Artesanal Intibucano, 1 Calle N.E. Nearby is Yaramanguila, an Indian village. The area is excellent for walking in forested hills, with lakes and waterfalls. In Dec.-Jan. it is very cold. An unpaved road, bus 1 hr. 20 mins., runs from La Esperanza E to **Marcala**, Department of La Paz (a paved road is under construction); *Ideal*, E; *Hospedaje Margoth*, E; *Hotel y Cafetería La Sureña*, E; *Motel Montana*, E. Daily bus to Tegucigalpa (0400, US$3.50), via La Paz (bus from Tegucigalpa at 1000, except Sun., Empresa Lila, 4-5 Av., 7 C., No. 418 Comayagüela); bus to La Paz only, 0800. Plenty of *comedores*. The Marcala region is one of the finest coffee-producing areas of Honduras, and this road gives access to markets. Transport goes to La Florida (stay with priest, who has a collection of Indian artefacts) where there is good walking to Indian village of Opatoro and climbing Cerro Guajiquiro.

NW from La Esperanza a very bad road runs to **Gracias**. It is one of the oldest and most historic settlements in the country, dominated by the highest mountains in Honduras, Montañas de Celaque. There are 3 colonial churches, San Sebastián, Las Mercedes, San Marcos (a fourth, Santa Lucía, is 2½ km. SW of Gracias), and a restored fort, with two fine Spanish cannon, on a hill in the outskirts. Some 5 km. from Gracias swim in a hot thermal pool in the forest, Agua Caliente.

Gracias was the centre from which Montejo, thrice Governor of Honduras, put down the great Indian revolt of 1537-38. Cáceres, his lieutenant, besieging Lempira the Indian leader in his impregnable mountain-top fortress at Cerquín, finally lured him out under a flag of truce, ambushed him and treacherously killed him. When the Audiencia de los Confines was formed in 1544 Gracias became for a time the administrative centre of Central America.

From Gracias buses go through coffee plantations to San Rafael (makeshift accommodation) from where one can walk to El Níspero (*pensión*) and catch a bus to Santa Bárbara. A strenuous 6-hr. hike east from Gracias by mule trail through a wilderness of forest and mountain leads to La Iguala, a tiny village attractively set between 2 rivers, magnificent colonial church. Irregular transport from/to Gracias. The Celaque mountains can be climbed from Gracias. (Robert Millar).

Hotels in Gracias: *Herrera*, G, clean, basic; *Rosario*, F, with bath; *Hospedaje San Antonio*, on main street, N edge of town, F, good, clean; *Pensión Girón*, 2 Av. No. 76, F, basic; *Iris*, 2 Av. 40, opp. San Sebastián church, E, with restaurant. Many *comedores* and cafeterias. *Comedor Elizabeth. La Nasa*, at bottom of the hill, O.K.; *Odiseo 2000*, one block from plaza, good, cheap, friendly; excellent *tacos* ½ block from main square.

Bank Banco de Occidente, changes money.

Buses One bus per day to La Esperanza, wakes you at your hotel; bus La Esperanza-Gracias at 1400 daily, US$2.30, 7 hrs. An alternative to La Esperanza is to take the daily 0800 bus to San Juan, get off at El Crucero, 1 km. beyond San Juan, then hitch, or rides can be taken on pick-up trucks for US$2; a plane trip costs US$8. There is also a bus service from Gracias to Santa Rosa de Copán, US$1.10, 4 per day, 3 hrs. (see page 1103); beautiful journey through majestic scenery. Cotral office is 1 block N of Plaza. A new road is under construction between Siguatepeque, La Esperanza, Gracias and Santa Rosa de Copán; it is due for completion in 1991.

Alban Johnson of Sandy Bay, Tasmania, and Jorge Valle-Aguiluz write: Roughly half way between Gracias and La Esperanza is San Juan del Caite, from where a rough track runs 45 km. S to **Erandique** (*Pensiones*, of Reginaldo Muñoz, and Doña Bárbara Cruz, F; meals at the house of Doña María Felix de Inestroza). Set high in pine-clad mountains not far from the border with El Salvador, Erandique is a friendly town, and very beautiful. Lempira was born nearby, and was killed a few km. away. The third weekend in January is the local *fiesta* of San Sebastián. Best time to visit is at the weekend. Each of the three *barrios* has a nice colonial church. For the visitor there are lakes, rivers, waterfalls, springs and bathing ponds, but most are hard to find. Nearby is San Antonio where fine opals are mined and may be purchased. There is only one road in the area, and it is impassable from July to October; transport to the many hamlets in the surrounding mountains is on foot or by horse (beware, it is very easy to get lost on the multitude of tracks). Despite what people say, there are minibuses to Erandique, but most people go by truck from Gracias or La Esperanza (US$3, very dusty).

Thirty-two km. beyond Siguatepeque the road dips into the rich Comayagua plain, part of the gap in the mountains which stretches N from the Ulúa lowlands to the Gulf of Fonseca. In this plain lies

Comayagua, a colonial town of 31,200 people at about 300 metres, 1½ hrs. drive N from the capital. It was the capital for 333 years until Tegucigalpa, 120 km. away, displaced it in 1870. It was founded in 1537 on the site of an Indian village by Alonzo de Cáceres, Francisco de Montejo's lieutenant, and there are many old colonial buildings: the former University, the first in Central America, founded in 1632, closed in 1842 (it was located in the Casa Cural, Bishop's Palace, where the bishops have lived since 1558); the Cathedral (1685-1715); the churches of La Merced (1550-58) and La Caridad (1730); San Francisco (built in 1584); San Sebastián (1585). San Juan de Dios (1590, destroyed by earthquake in 1750), the church where the Inquisition sat, is now the site of the Santa Teresa Hospital. El Carmen was built in 1785. The most interesting building is the Cathedral in the Central Park, with its square plain tower and its decorated façade with sculpted figures of the saints, which contains some of the finest examples of colonial art in Honduras. The clock in the tower was originally made over 800 years ago in Spain; it was given to Comayagua by Philip II in 1582. At first it was in La Merced when that was the Cathedral, but moved to the new Cathedral in 1715. There are two colonial plazas shaded by trees and shrubs. A stone portal and a portion of the façade of *Casa Real* (the viceroy's residence) survives. It was built 1739-41, but was damaged by an earthquake in 1750 and destroyed by tremors in 1856. The army still uses a quaint old fortress built when Comayagua was the capital. There is a lively market area.

There are two museums nearby: the ecclesiastical museum (a small contribution is expected) and the anthropological museum (housed in the former presidential palace) with Indian artefacts (closed Monday). The latter is the less interesting of the two.

The US military base at Palmerola, 8 km. from Comayagua, exerts a strong socio-economic influence over the entire Comayagua Valley, and the city itself. The base has English-language radio and TV stations.

Hotels *Libertad*, on Parque Central, E-D, much choice of room size, noisy, clean, *Libertad Annex*, E with bath, F without, as good as main hotel; *Halston*, Barrio El Centro, E-D; *Emperador*, E-C, good but overpriced, cafeteria, on the boulevard leading into town from the Tegucigalpa-San Pedro Sula highway; *Hospedaje Primavera*, F, opposite market, noisy, basic, not recommended. *Hospedaje San Cristóbal, Hospedaje y Comedor Libertéño*, both F; *Imperial*, Barrio Torondón, E

1108 HONDURAS

with bath and fan, attractive, parking; *Moderno*, opp. municipal market, F, rudimentary; *Los Lirios*, Barrio Torondón, F. *Boulevard*, F, small, clean, economic, dark rooms; *Comayagua*, F, one block from Plaza Central, basic, cheap, restaurant; *Motel Quan*, 8 C. N.O., 3 y 4 Av., excellent, E, with private bath, popular; *Quan Annex*, E; *Motel Puma*, off the same Boulevard, garage parking, hot water, E with bath (catering for short-stay clientèle); *Bueso*, Barrio Arriba, F.

Camping possible 2 km. N of town, beside the stream; beware of sandfleas.

Restaurants Central Park is surrounded by restaurants and fast food establishments. *Casa Vieja*, near new cinema, good but overpriced; *China*, 3 blocks W of Plaza, good, but beware of the overpriced "tourist" menu; *Gran Muralla*, Chinese and international food; *Restaurant Central*, *Sayvic* and *Flipper* in the central park serve ice cream, tacos, etc.; *Padrino* (2 blocks from centre, pizzas, lasagne) and *Gourmet*, both clean, good; *Urbano's*, private house, 4 blocks SW of façade of the Cathedral, excellent meals and value. *Cafetería Central* (not to be confused with *Restaurant* on central park), *Palmeras*, S side of Central Park; some food in the market. In the Centro Turístico Comayagua is a restaurant, bar, disco, and swimming pool; good for cooling off and relaxing; on the road to the stadium.

Banks Banco Atlántida, Banco de Occidente, Bancahsa, Bancahorro, Banco Sogerín.

Bus To Tegucigalpa, US$1.50, every 45 mins., 2 hrs. (Catrachos—or walk 1¼ km. to highway and catch a quicker San Pedro Sula-Tegucigalpa bus); to Siguatepeque, US$ 0.50 with Transpinares. To San Pedro Sula, either catch a bus on the highway or go to Siguatepeque and change buses there.

Excursion To the coffee town of La Libertad (hourly bus, 2 hrs., US$1), several *hospedajes* and *comedores*; a friendly place. Before La Libertad is Jamalteca (1½ hrs. by bus US$0.75), from where it is a 40-minute walk to a large, deep pool into which drops a 10 metre waterfall surrounded by lush vegetation. Here you can swim, picnic or camp, but it is on private property and a pass must be obtained from the owner (ask at Supermercado Carol in Comayagua). Best to avoid weekends, when the owners' friends are there.

A paved road runs S of Comayagua to **La Paz**, capital of its Department in the western part of the Comayagua valley. Population: 4,000. From the new church of the Virgen del Perpetuo Socorro, on the hill, there is a fine view of the town, the Palmerola military base, and the Comayagua Valley. A short road runs E from La Paz to Villa San Antonio on the highway to Tegucigalpa. 5 km. from La Paz is Ajuterique, which has a fine colonial church. Bus from Comayagua, Cotrapal (opp. Iglesia La Merced), every hour from 0600, passing Ajuterique and Lejamaní.

Hotels In La Paz: all F: *Córdoba* (with restaurant), *Pensión San Francisco* (cheaper, but nicer). *Hotelito Ali* (5 rooms), eat at Ali's Restaurant.

Banks Bancahsa, Banco Atlántida, Banadesa.

A road (being paved) runs SW from La Paz to Marcala (see previous page). Along this road lies **Tutule**, the marketplace for the Indians of Guajiquiro (one of the few pure Indian communities in Honduras). Market: Thurs. and Sun. There are two minibus services a day from Marcala (US$1).

We are grateful to Robert Millar for the following description of the road from San Pedro Sula to Tegucigalpa: 46 km. S of San Pedro there is a paved road leading E through banana plantations to Santa Rita, thence either E to Yoro, or N to Progreso and Tela, thus enabling travellers between Tegucigalpa and the North Coast greatly to shorten their route by avoiding San Pedro Sula. An unpaved road right, at Caracol, leads up to Ojo de Agua (a pretty bathing spot), then on to El Mochito, Honduras' most important mining centre. This same turnoff at Caracol, marked "Río Lindo", also leads to Peña Blanca and Pulhapanzak with some unexcavated ceremonial mounds adjacent. On the northern shore of Lake Yojoa (see page 1105) a paved road skirts the lake for 5 km. and a further 11 km. (unpaved) to Pulhapanzak. The main highway S skirts the eastern shore of the lake. 16 km. S of the lake at Taulabé is the turnoff northwest of a road (being paved) to Santa Bárbara (see page 1103).

1 km. S of Taulabé uphill on the highway South are the caves of Taulabé (illuminated and with guides, open daily). The road now ascends an enormous forested escarpment of the continental divide to reach cool, forested highlands around Siguatepeque (see page 1106). Proceeding S, the highway descends to the vast hot valley of Comayagua, skirting the old capital of Honduras with its colonial churches. At the southern end of the valley the road ascends another forested mountainous escarpment. After about 5 km. climb a track leading off to the left (ask for directions), with about half-an-hour's climb on foot to a tableland and natural fortress of Tenampua where Indians put up their last resistance to the *conquistadores*, even after the death of Lempira. Visitors last century rated Tenampua of equal importance archaeologically with Copán, but sadly it has now been looted of its treasures, except for an interesting wall and entrance portal.

The road continues its ascent through lovely forested heights to Zamorano and Parque Aurora (see page 1095)—this spot would be perfect for caravans, which need to avoid the narrow streets and congestion of Tegucigalpa. The road then descends to the vast intermont basin of Támara; a turning right at the village leads to San Matías waterfall, another delightful area for walking in cool forested mountains. There is another entry to San Matías when the road S has once more climbed about 9 km. north-east of the capital.

From Tegucigalpa to the Pacific

A paved road runs S from the capital through fine scenery. Just off the highway is Sabanagrande, with an interesting colonial church. Further S is **Pespire,** a picturesque colonial village with a beautiful church. At **Jícaro Galán** (92 km.) the road joins the Pan-American Highway, which enters Honduras from El Salvador over the Santa Clara bridge at Goascarán and runs through **Nacaome,** where there is a 16th-century colonial church, to Jícaro Galán (40 km.). A temporary pass can be purchased in Honduras for US$1.50 for a visit to the Salvadorean village of El Amatillo for an hour or so (many Hondurans cross to purchase household goods and clothes; towels are the best buy. Bus Tegucigalpa—El Amatillo, US$2.50, 4 hrs.). This border is very relaxed. On the Pacific coast nearby is **San Lorenzo,** on the shores of the Gulf of Fonseca (9,300 people). The climate on the Pacific littoral is very hot, but healthy.

Hotels The only good modern hotel is the *Miramar* at San Lorenzo, 26 rooms, 4 air-conditioned, E. Also *Paramount,* E, and *Hospedaje Perla del Pacífico,* F, very basic. There are hotels of a sort at Goascarán (pop.: 2,190), Nacaome (pop. 4,474). At Jícaro Galán (pop.: 3,007) is *Oasis Colonial,* B, and an unnamed, basic guesthouse. Restaurants at all these places.

Frequent service of small *busitos* from Tegucigalpa to San Lorenzo (US$1) and to Choluteca (US$1.50).

The Pacific port of **Amapala** (5,600 people), on Tigre Island, has been replaced by Puerto de Henecán in San Lorenzo, reached by a 3.5 km. road which leaves the Pan-American Highway on the eastern edge of San Lorenzo. Amapala has a naval base, but otherwise it is moribund. Fishermen will take you—but not by motor launch— to San Lorenzo at a low charge: the trip takes half a day. It is possible to charter boats to La Unión in El Salvador. There is an airport, and a plane for the capital (35 mins.) can be chartered. The deep-sea fishing in the gulf is good. There is a passable bathing beach. *Hotel Internacional* on the harbour, F, pleasant; *Tino's Restaurant,* owned by Sr. Tino Monterrosa who has recently opened two bungalows (US$25 for 4, rooms at D); he also arranges fishing trips. Swimming at beautiful Playa Grande. The volcano on the island may be climbed, best early in the day.

There is a daily direct bus service between Tegucigalpa and Tigre Island, except on Sunday, with Transportes CHE; leaving Tegucigalpa at 1130, 3-4 hrs. A new 31 km. road leaves the Pan-American Highway 2 km. W of San Lorenzo, signed to Coyolito. It passes through scrub and mangrove swamps before crossing a causeway to a hilly island, around which it winds to the jetty at Coyolito (no facilities). Motorized dugouts and a small car ferry cross to Amapala. Return journey starts at 0400 from Tigre Island.

The Pan-American Highway runs SE from Jícaro Galán past Choluteca to the Nicaraguan border at El Espino, on the Río Negro, 111 km.

Choluteca, 34 km. from San Lorenzo in the plain of Choluteca, has a population of 63,700, expanding rapidly. Coffee, cotton and cattle are the local industries; a visit to the sawmill is interesting. The town was one of the earliest foundations in Honduras (1535) and has still a fascinating old colonial centre. The church of La Merced (1643) is now the Casa de la Cultura. The local feast day, of the Virgen de la Concepción, is December 8. The climate is very hot; there is much poverty here.

Hotels *Pierre,* Av. Valle y C. Williams, Tel.: 82-0676, C, with bath and a/c, D, with fan, central, free protected parking, cafetería, very central, English-speaking owner (Glyn M. Harris), credit cards accepted; *Lisboa,* Av. Rosa (by Transportes Mi Esperanza), E, recommended, good restaurant; *Pacífico,* also near Mi Esperanza terminal, outside the city, clean, quiet, E, breakfast US$1.50; *Tomalag,* moderately priced with bath and fan; *La Fuente,* Carretera Panamericana, C, with bath, recommended, swimming pool, a/c, meals; *Rosita,* E, with bath, basic, friendly, good food; *Camino Real,* road to Guasaule,D, good steaks in restaurant; *Copacabana,* next to bus station, G, friendly; *San Carlos,* F with shower, pleasant, Paz Barahona 757, Barrio El Centro; *Hibueras,* F,

1110 HONDURAS

with bath and fan, clean, purified water, *comedor* attached, Av. Bojorque; *Motel Fraternidad*, E, on Panamericana. Local specialities are the drinks *posole* and *horchata de morro*.

Salvadorean Consulate, opposite entrance to infantry barracks, visas given immediately.

Banco de Honduras (close to market), as is Post Office and Banco Atlántida. Good rates of exchange on the black market at Choluteca bus station (a fascinating place!). There is also a black market in Jícaro Galán. The Texaco service station, which is known as *Gringa Patricia's*, is very helpful in case of car trouble. Trailer Park, laundry, groceries and propane on sale. The campsite here is run by a Canadian, Elvin; shaded camping, showers, swimming pool, peaceful, pleasant, safe water supply, US$1. Mosquito repellant or netting may be needed.

Bus to El Espino from Choluteca, US$1.50, 1½ hrs., 0700 (this is the only crossing to Nicaragua since the Guasaule crossing is closed). Mi Esperanza buses regularly to Tegucigalpa (US$2.50); bus station is 5 blocks from market.

An hour's drive from Choluteca over an excellent road leads to Cedeño beach, very basic accommodation (inc. *Hotel Coco*) and meals. A lovely though primitive spot, but avoid public holiday crowds. In the dry season, there is little fresh water, often none for bathing. Turning for Cedeño is 13 km. W of Choluteca. Hourly bus from Choluteca, US$1 (1¼ hrs.). A turn off leads from Choluteca—Cedeño road to Ratón beach, also lovely, bus from Choluteca early p.m., returns early next morning.

Beyond Choluteca is a long climb to San Marcos de Colón, 915 metres in the hills (a clean, tidy town with plenty of eating places). Two *pensiones* in San Marcos, neither very nice; the better of the two is up the hill from the central square. Bus from Choluteca at 0700, US$1, 1½ hrs., one bus back at 1130; bus from Tegucigalpa, Mi Esperanza, 6 Av. 23 C., Comayagüela (office in San Marcos near Parque Central), 12 a day. 6 km. beyond San Marcos the road enters Nicaragua at El Espino—a ghost town—(altitude 890 metres; *Motel Fraternidad*, 1 km. from border); then it is 5 km. to the Nicaraguan checkpoint at La Playa. There is transport between the border posts, but if you are refused entry to Honduras (see page 1114), you will have to walk back. Taxis/minibuses run from Choluteca to the border. Entry and exit tax in Honduras, US$2.50, but on Sat. and Sun. officials may try to charge extra: ask for a receipt and/or bargain. Exchange is easy at the border for dollars, córdobas (essential to get them here if you want to take advantage of black market rates, but see page 1136), Costa Rican colones, even Salvadorean colones. (See also page 1136.) The Pan-American Highway from the border of El Salvador to the border of Nicaragua is 151 km. (bus between the two, US$2). Border formalities tedious at El Espino. American citizens and Europeans travelling N through Central America are advised to check with their embassy in San José, Costa Rica, to see if there are any restrictions on entering Honduras from Nicaragua. **N.B.** After floods in May 1982, the border bridge at Guasaule was washed away and the road Choluteca-Chinandega (Nicaragua) is closed; the only crossing-point is at El Espino.

East of Tegucigalpa

A good road runs E from Tegucigalpa to Danlí, 121 km. away, in the department of El Paraíso: good walking country. Some 40 km. along, in the Zamorano valley (see page 1095), is the Pan-American Agricultural School run for all students of the Americas with US help: it has a fine collection of tropical flowers. At Zamorano turn off up a narrow winding road for about 5 km. to the picturesque old mining village of **San Antonio de Oriente,** much favoured by Honduran painters such as Velásquez (it has a beautiful church). A little further along our road branches S to **Yuscarán,** in rolling pine-land country at 1,070 metres (*Hospedaje Monserrat*, F, good value). The climate here is semi-tropical. Yuscarán was an important mining centre in colonial days and is a picturesque, typically Spanish colonial village, with cobbled streets and houses on a steep hillside. The Yuscarán distillery is considered by many to produce the best *aguardiente* in Honduras (tours possible). Cardomom plantations are being developed here. The Montserrat mountain which looms over Yuscarán is riddled with mines; the disused Guavias mine is about 4 km. along the road to Agua Fría, 10 km. to the SE by a steep, narrow, twisting and very picturesque road. Population, 1,250. For information, ask the lady who owns the *comedor* opposite the church in Yuscarán. From Zamorano, a road goes to Güinope (one hotel, F, several *comedores*) famed for its oranges and jam. Good walking in the area.

Danlí (19,500 people), a pleasant town, uses the sugar it grows for making *aguardiente* and is a centre of the tobacco industry. There are 7 cigar factories; visit the Honduras-América S.A. factory (opposite Ciné Aladino) and purchase export quality cigars at good prices. Its *fiesta* at the last weekend of August (Fiesta del Maíz, with cultural and sporting events, all-night street party on the Saturday) is very crowded with people from Tegucigalpa. There are regular buses (Empresa Discua Litena, from N side of Mercado Jacaleapa on boulevard to Colonia Kennedy, Tel.: 32-79-39, 8 per day) which take 2 hrs. (US$2) between Tegucigalpa and Danlí. One road continues from Danlí to Santa María, crossing a mountain range with panoramic views. Another goes S to **El Paraíso** (124 km. from the capital, hourly bus, US$1.80, 2 hrs.; 3,805 people), from which a connecting paved road links with the Nicaraguan road network at Ocotal. This border crossing was closed in 1986.

Hotels at Danlí *La Esperanza*, Gabriela Mistral, E, adjoining restaurant; *Danlí*, Calle del Carral, E; *Apolo*, del Canal, E, with bath; *Maya Ejecutivo*, C, with bath; *Pensión San Cristóbal*; *Regis*, F, with bath, basic. **Restaurants:** *Pepy Lu's*, very good food at reasonable prices; *McBeth's*, snackbar, good ice cream. *Nan-kin 2*, Chinese.

Hotels at El Paraíso *Eva*, E; *Florida*, F; *Recreo*, F.

Banks in both towns, Bancahsa, Banco Atlántida, Banadesa, and other local banks.

North-east of Tegucigalpa

The Carretera de Olancho runs from the capital to the Río Guayape, 143 km., and continues another 50 km. to **Juticalpa** (capital of Olancho department), at 820 metres above sea-level in a rich agricultural area, herding cattle and growing cereals and sugar-cane. There is a gravel road N to Olanchito and a paved road NE through the cattle land of Catacamas to the coast at Cabo Camarón. Population 14,000. Airfield.

Hotels at Juticalpa *Antúñez*, Barrio El Centro, E-D; *Las Vegas*, E; *Boarding House Honduras*, F.

There is an adventurous bus service from Juticalpa to Trujillo (see page 1100), via San Francisco de la Paz and San Esteban (*Hotel San Esteban*, F, expensive but clean; *Hospedaje Henríquez*), the last part being on a good, unpaved road; it passes through interesting scenery. The road is being paved; it passes through San Jerónimo, the setting of Paul Theroux's *The Mosquito Coast*.

Bus Tegucigalpa to Juticalpa/Catacamas, Empresa Aurora (8C. 615, Av. Morazán) 8 times a day, 3½ hrs. to Catacamas, US$3.50. Bus Catacamas-Dulce Nombre de Cumli (see below), 3 hrs., US$1.75, several daily; bus Juticalpa-San Esteban from opp. Aurora bus terminal at 1200, 6 hrs., US$3, very difficult in rainy season.

The route by road from Tegucigalpa to Trujillo through Olancho is 413 km. via Talanga, San Diego (restaurant *El Arriero*), Los Limones and Juticalpa (fill up with fuel here as there is none available until Trujillo). After Juticalpa, take the turn off, where the paved road ends, to San Francisco de la Paz. Beyond San Francisco is Gualaco, which has an interesting colonial church; from here to San Esteban you pass Agalta mountain and some of the highest points in Honduras, and the waterfalls on the Babilonia river. The road from San Esteban to Bonito Oriental (via El Carbón, a mahogany collection point while Paya Indian communities in the vicinity) is being paved. The final 38 km. from Bonito Oriental to Trujillo are paved, through Corocito.

Misquitia is the name given to the region in the far NE of the country, which is forested, swampy and almost uninhabited, but well worth visiting. Apart from the one road that stretches 100 km. from Puerto Lempira to Leymus and a further 100 km. to Ahuasbila, both on the Río Coco, there are no roads in the Honduran Misquitia. The Government has built the last stage of the Tegucigalpa-Puerto Lempira road, between Catacamas (*Hotel Moderno*, F, excellent value) and Mocorón; it is a two-day rough ride to Puerto Lempira, capital of Honduran Misquitia, on Caratasco Lagoon. Lansa flies from La Ceiba on Wednesday, and Isleña on Friday (cheaper, US$46, 1¼ hrs.), to Ahuas, Brus Laguna and Puerto Lempira. Coastal vessels leave several times a week from La Ceiba to Brus Laguna and Puerto Lempira and back (2-3 day journey), carrying passengers and cargo. There are also refugee boats which are quicker. From Puerto Lempira to Tegucigalpa you may be able to get a flight on a US or Honduran Air Force plane, but this means listening for the aircraft, going to the airfield with your luggage, and asking permission every time. A surer way is to hitch to Mocorón, from where a refugee plane to Tegucigalpa costs US$50. Essential equipment: torch.

Communication between Honduras and Nicaragua is not possible in Misquitia; there has been guerrilla and counter-insurgency activity on both sides of the border and tourists are currently advised not to visit the border area.

Robert Millar writes (with additional information from Grace Osakoda of Hawaii): Numerous large *cayucos* (canoes) with outboard motors cross the large Caratasco Lagoon from Cauquira to Puerto Lempira for about US$2.50. *Pensión Modelo*, F (good, friendly, electricity 1800-2230), and inferior *Pensión Santa Teresita*, F, at **Puerto Lempira**; *La Perla* restaurant, next to dock, fish meals US$1.75; *Restaurant Quinto Patio*, good breakfasts and information on refugee boats;

generous meals at Doña Marina's for US$1.25 (Isleña flight tickets for La Ceiba may be bought here; Lansa tickets at *La Perla*). Contact helpful Reverend Stanley for almost daily flights in tiny Moravian mission plane to the Evangelical hospital at Ahuas; a 15-minute (US$15) scenic flight above Caratasco Lagoon and grassy, pine-covered savannas to **Ahuas**, one hour's walk from the Patuca River (fabled for gold). *Hospedaje y Comedor Suyapa*, F, basic, no electricity, meals, US$1.25; mosquito repellant and coils absolutely essential here. Irregular *cayucos* sail down to **Brus Laguna** (Brewer's Lagoon) for US$ 2.50, at one mouth of the Patuco River, or US$12.50 (15-mins.) scenic flight in the mission plane. George Goff rents rooms (good but basic, no electricity, F,) and has meals for US$1, he speaks English and runs the Lansa agency (flights to La Ceiba—he will also help with mission-plane flights). Behind his house is a *hospedaje* being built by the "Medio-Francés" (who speaks English, German, French, "Scandinavian" and Spanish); he plans to operate tours. Meals with Sarah de Eden, but plague of mosquitoes for all but 5 months of the year (winter and spring). Two tiny hilly islands near the entrance to the wide lagoon were hideouts where pirates once lurked. It is better to fly direct from Ahuas for US$15 via Brus and the mouth of the Plátano River to mosquito-free **Cocobila** (Belén), picturesquely situated on a sandspit between the ocean and huge, sweetwater Ibans Lagoon. (Nicaraguan refugee settlements S of here may be visited). Excellent meals (US$1.25) with Miss Erlinda, and room with Alfonso Molina who has a motor boat for **Paplaya** at the mouth of the Río Negro or Sico (bad mosquitoes), or walk the distance in over two hours along the beach. Malaria is endemic in this area; take antimalaria precautions. Room and meals with Doña Juana de Woods at Paplaya. Boats to La Ceiba (US$11), or up the Río Sico (US$5) to Sico. Paplaya is the Western terminal of the Honduran Misquitia. Plátano village at the mouth of the Río Plátano can be reached by lobster boat from Guanaja or by the supply ships from La Ceiba to Brus Laguna (in all cases *cayucos* take passengers from ship to shore); Plátano-Brus Laguna, 1½ hrs., US$ 2.50, Plátano-La Ceiba, US$17.50.

Palacios, situated in the next lagoon west of Paplaya, is mosquito-free; cannons are relics of an old English fort. Room for US$2.50 with Felix Marmol and meals for US$1. Lansa's Wednesday 6-seater plane (often booked up) flies for US$ 28 to La Ceiba or East to Bruis/Puerto Lempira. When sea is calm, irregular sailings of the *Baltimore* or *Douglas*, US$11, go to La Ceiba. One can also cross the lagoon by *cayuco* (US$0.50) from Palacios to Black Carib village of Batalla, from which it is 112 km. W along beach to Limón where, in dry months March to May, there are buses to Tocoa, Trujillo and La Ceiba. The beach route is gruelling, past *morenales*, or Black Carib villages (honest, friendly) of Tocamacho (Reverend Donald Grable is a godsend to benighted travellers), Sangrelaya (Catholic mission), Siraboya (dry weather walk from here across forested mountain to Sico River, and downriver to Sico village); further W along the beach to Iriona Casuna and interminable stretch of 48 km. along the beach to Limón (this stretch is now inadvisable because of recent murders and robberies when crossing the beautiful forested headland at Farellones). One can take a picturesque *cayuco* trip from Paplaya up the Río Sico for US$4-5 to Sico village (possible food and meals with Edmund Jones—insist on paying him). A strenuous 32 km. walk from Sico (only in dry months from March to May) up forested Río Paulaya Valley to stay with Ray Jones, who has mined gold here for 60 years (insist on paying him too). One can also descend the Paulaya River from Dulce Nombre de Cumli, Olancho (*Hospedaje Tania*, G, very basic, on main street; several *comedores* on main square), 34 km. in the pick-up of "el Indio", then on foot or muleback over the Cerro de Will, staying en route with the *campesinos*, arriving in about three days at Mr. Ray's. (Local police say there is a footpath in the dry season from Dulce Nombre de Cumli to San Esteban). The fabled lost White City of the Mayas is thought to be about 4 days' march from here on a ridge between the headwaters of the Plátano and Guampu rivers. (For notes on Nicaraguan Misquitia see page 1133.)

The Economy

Honduras has the poorest economy in Central America and one of the lowest income rates per head in all Latin America. Unemployment is about 25% of the working population, owing to low investment, and poor harvests and labour disputes in the agricultural sector. Inflation has dealt less severely with Honduras than with some other Central American countries: the rate has been less than 10% a year in the 1980's.

About 75% of the population live by the land: coffee and bananas are the main export crops. Cotton, once important, is now far less so. Tobacco, maize, beans, rice and sugar are grown mostly for domestic use but small quantities are sometimes exported. Cattle raising is important and exports of both meat and livestock are growing. Some 45% of the land is forested and timber is the third leading export; it is to become more important as the development of forestry reserves in the Department of Olancho is carried out. This project includes the installation of a vast paper and pulp complex and is expected to have a considerable impact on the whole economy, once implemented.

Honduras has considerable reserves of silver, gold, lead, zinc, tin, iron, copper, coal and antimony, but only silver, gold, lead and zinc are mined and

HONDURAS 1113

exported. Considerable offshore exploration for petroleum is in progress. There is an oil refinery at Puerto Cortés and exports of petroleum derivatives are becoming significant. The US$600m. hydroelectric scheme at El Cajón was expected greatly to reduce the country's oil bill.

Local industries are small, turning out a wide range of consumer goods, besides being engaged in the processing of timber and agricultural products. The more important products are furniture, textiles, footwear, chemicals, cement and rubber.

Honduras' total external debt amounts to some US$2.5b, nearly three times the size of merchandise exports, or US$580 per person. The government has been negotiating since 1982 to reschedule its debt to commercial banks, but unlike most other Latin American countries, no agreement had been signed by the beginning of 1987. Interest arrears built up as the economy deteriorated and hopes of paying them off declined as the coffee price fell.

	1961-70 (av)	1971-80 (av)	1981-85 (av)	1986 (e)
Gdp growth (1980 prices)	5.0%	4.8%	0.9%	2.0%
Inflation	2.3%	8.1%	6.9%	5.0%
Exports (fob) US$m	129	446	748	850
Bananas	57	123	217	-
Coffee	18	107	162	-
Imports (fob) US$m	127	473	834	990
Current account balance US$m (cum)	-194	-1,186	-1,315	-250

Information for Visitors

How to get there From London: British Airways, Pan Am, or Virgin Atlantic to Miami, then Tan Airlines (direct), Challenge Air or Taca via San Salvador to Tegucigalpa. Other US cities from which you can reach Honduras: to Tegucigalpa from New Orleans and Houston with Sahsa and Taca, from New York with Challenge, from Los Angeles via San Salvador with Taca; San Pedro Sula can be reached from Miami (same carriers as to Tegucigalpa) and Houston (Sahsa). Lacsa flies to San Pedro Sula from Los Angeles (once a week) and from New Orleans via Cancún (three times weekly). Sahsa flies from Tegucigalpa to all Central American capitals, and to Mexico City (direct), San Andrés Island, and to San José from San Pedro Sula (also Lacsa on this route direct); Taca flies to Mexico City and Belize City direct as well as to San Salvador. From Europe: Iberia twice weekly to Guatemala City, connecting with Sahsa; KLM the same connection once a week; alternatively, fly to Mexico City (5 per week) and on from there.

There are airstrips in the larger and smaller towns. Sahsa, Aero Servicios and Lansa have daily services between Tegucigalpa, San Pedro Sula and La Ceiba.

There is an airport tax and hospital tax of 3% on all tickets sold for domestic journeys, and a 10% tax on airline tickets for international journeys. There is an airport departure tax of US$10. Note that the border offices close at 1700, not 1800 as in most other countries; there is an extra fee charged after that time.

N.B. If you are flying from Honduras to a country that requires an onward ticket, Sahsa will not let you board their planes without it.

By Sea The French Line sails regularly from London, the Hapag-Lloyd, the Royal Netherlands Steamship Co. and others run regular cargo vessels with limited passenger space from North Sea ports to the Atlantic ports of Honduras; 3 or 4 weeks. Hapag-Lloyd, N.G. Lloyd and Johnson Line have cargo/passenger services from North Sea ports to Amapala, on the Pacific coast of Honduras. The United Brands Line and the Standard Fruit Co. have services from continental and US ports.

Documents Citizens of the U.S.A., Canada, Australia, New Zealand require a visa and a tourist card which can be bought from Honduran consulates for US$2-3, at border. Holders of the card must show proof of nationality. Visa not required, nor tourist card, for nationals of West European countries (except France, West Germany—tourist card only, Austria—visa, and Portugal) and Japan. The price of a visa apparently varies per nationality, and according to where bought. Officials at land borders and airports allow only 30 days for visitors, regardless of arrangements made prior to arrival. Make sure border officials fill in your entry papers correctly and in accordance with your wishes. Extensions of 30 days are easy to obtain (up to a maximum of 6 months' stay, cost US$5). There are immigration offices for extensions at Tela, La Ceiba, San Pedro Sula, Santa Rosa de Copán, Siguatepeque, La Paz and Comayagua, and all are more helpful than the Tegucigalpa

1114 HONDURAS

office. A valid International Certificate of Vaccination against smallpox is required only from visitors coming from the Indian subcontinent, Indonesia and the countries of southern Africa. A ticket out of the country is necessary for air travellers (if coming from USA, you won't be allowed on the plane without one); onward tickets must be bought outside the country. An entry and exit tax is charged to all but travellers in transit, US$2.50 each (and sometimes requested in dollars). An additional US$1 "baggage inspection charge" is levied on bus passengers. Customs charge US$3.50 for "special Sunday service". It is advisable always to carry means of identification, since spot-checks have increased. Some motorists have been charged an exit fee of US$2.50. Bicycles must pay the same entrance taxes as motor vehicles. There are no Customs duties on personal effects; 200 cigarettes or 100 cigars, or ½ kg. of tobacco, and 2 quarts of spirit are allowed in free. No fresh food is allowed to cross the border and the interiors of cars are fumigated (US$1 on entry, plus US$5 for entry, with receipt). Note for those entering overland from Nicaragua: your baggage will be searched very thoroughly and *all* literature concerning Nicaragua will be confiscated. You will not be allowed to enter Honduras if you have a Cuban stamp in your passport. There is a fair amount of bribery at border crossings.

British business travellers planning a visit should get a copy of "Hints to Exporters: Honduras", on application to Dept. of Trade, Export Services Division, Sanctuary Buildings, 16/20 Great Smith Street, London SW1P 3DB.

Hours of Business Mon. to Fri.: 0900-1200; 1400-1800. Sat.: 0800-1200, and some open in the afternoon. Banks in Tegucigalpa 0900-1500; 0800-1100 only along the N coast on Sat. In San Pedro Sula and along the N coast most places open and close half an hour earlier in the morning and afternoon than in Tegucigalpa. Post Offices: Mon.-Fri. 0700-2000, Sat. 0800-1200.

Language Spanish, but English is spoken in the N, in the Bay Islands, by West Indian settlers on the Caribbean coast, and is understood in most of the big business houses. Trade literature and correspondence should be in Spanish.

Tipping Normally 10% of bill.

Electric current generally 110 volts. U.S.-type flat-pin plugs.

Internal Transport Hitch-hiking is relatively easy. The best map of the country is produced by the Instituto Nacional de Geografía, open weekday mornings. Take your passport when you go to buy one. Another map is issued by Texaco; the tourist office may provide one. If hiring a car, make sure it has the correct papers, and emergency triangles which are required by law. Petrol costs US$2 per US gallon. **N.B.** There are frequent police searches on entry or exit from towns and villages.

Climate Rain is frequent on the Caribbean littoral during the whole year; the heaviest occurs from September to February inclusive. In Tegucigalpa the dry season is normally from November to April inclusive. The coolest months are December and January but if a traveller visits the Caribbean littoral he should avoid these months because heavy rains impede travel; the best months for this area are April and May, though very hot.

Clothing Western; on the north coast, which is much hotter and damper, dress is less formal. Laundering is undertaken by most hotels.

Health Dysentery and stomach parasites are common and malaria is endemic in coastal regions, where a prophylactic regime should be undertaken and mosquito nets carried. Inoculate against typhoid and tetanus. Drinking water is definitely not safe; drink bottled water. Salads and raw vegetables must be sterilized under personal supervision. There are hospitals at Tegucigalpa and all the larger towns. Excellent ointments for curing the all-too-prevalent tropical skin complaints are Scabisan (Mexican) and Betnovate (Glaxo).

Currency The unit is a lempira. It is divided into 100 centavos and its par value is half the United States dollar. There are copper coins of 1 and 2 centavos and nickel or silver coins of 5, 10, 20, and 50 centavos. US visitors will find that many coins are exactly the same size and material as US coins of equivalent value; hence the 20 centavos is a "dime". A *real* is 12½ centavos (there are no coins of this value, but the term is much used). Bank notes are for 1, 2, 5, 10, 20, 50 and 100 lempiras. Any amount of any currency can be taken in or out. **N.B.** U.S. dollars are hard to obtain in Honduras. There is a parallel market, particularly active at borders, which stood at about L2.10 to the US$ in April 1987.

The metric system of weights is official and should be used. Land is measured in *varas* (838 mm.) and *manzanas* (0.7 hectare).

Shopping The best articles are those in wood; straw baskets, hats, etc., are also highly recommended. Leather is cheaper than in El Salvador and Nicaragua, but not so cheap as in Colombia. The coffee is good. Note that film is expensive.

Food Cheapest, meals are the *comida corriente* or (sometimes better prepared and dearer) the

HONDURAS 1115

comida típica; these usually contain some of the following: beans, rice, meat, avocado, egg, cabbage salad, cheese, *plátanos*, potatoes or yuca, and always tortillas. Pork is not normally recommended as pigs are often raised on highly insanitary swill. *Carne asada* from street vendors, charcoal roasted and served with grated cabbage between tortillas is good, though rarely sanitarily prepared. *Tajadas* are crisp, fried *plátano* chips topped with grated cabbage and sometimes meat; *nacatamales* are ground, dry maize mixed with meat and seasoning, boiled in banana leaves. *Sopa de mondongo* (tripe soup) is very common.

Cheap fish is best found on the beaches at Trujillo and Cedeño and on the shores of Lake Yojoa. While on the north coast, look for *pan de coco* (coconut bread) made by *garifuna* (Black Carib) women.

Soft drinks are called *refrescos*, or *frescos*, the name also given to fresh fruit blended with water; *licuados* are fruit blended with milk. *Horchata* is rice water and cinnamon. Coffee is thick and sweet. (Don Moore, ex-Peace Corps volunteer, Bellefonte, Pa.).

Sea-Mails from London to Tegucigalpa take 1 to 3 months. Parcels from the United States for Tegucigalpa arrive via Puerto Cortés.

Air Mail takes 4 to 7 days to Europe and the same for New York. Airmail costs 85 centavos for a letter to N America (1 lempira to Europe), 60 centavos for a postcard (80 centavos to Europe); aerograms (not easy to find), 75 centavos.

Telephones Hondutel provides international telephone and telex services from their stations at Tegucigalpa, San Pedro Sula, Puerto Cortés, Tela, La Ceiba, Comayagua, Siguatepeque, Santa Rosa de Copán, Danlí, Choluteca, Juticalpa, La Paz, La Lima, El Progreso, Valle de Angeles, El Paraíso, Catacamas and Marcala.

Telephone service between Honduras and Britain costs about L40 for a 3-min. call; calls to USA L22 for 3 mins. Local Standard Time is 6 hrs. behind GMT. Collect calls to N America can be made from Hondutel office in Tegucigalpa.

The principal **newspapers** in Tegucigalpa are *El Heraldo* and *La Tribuna*. In San Pedro Sula: *El Tiempo* and *La Prensa* (circulation about 45,000). None is of very high quality.

There are 6 television channels and 167 broadcasting stations.

Public Holidays Most of the feast days of them Roman Catholic religion and also

January 1: New Year's Day.
April 14: Day of the Americas.
Holy Week: Thurs., Fri., and Sat.
before Easter Sunday.
May 1: Labour Day.

September 15: Independence Day.
October 3: Francisco Morazán.
October 12: Discovery of America.
October 21: Army Day.

We are deeply grateful to Jorge E. Valle-Aguiluz, resident in Tegucigalpa, for a thorough revision of the entire Honduras chapter and also to Philipp Cadario (Tegucigalpa), Jeff Fenley (Santa Barbara, Ca.), Robert Millar (Tela, Hond.) for another invaluable contribution, Tony Palios (London W3), Christer Robertson (Stockholm) and Barbara Galvin (Galway), and to travellers whose names are listed in the general Central America section.

NICARAGUA

NICARAGUA (148,000 square km.), the same size as England and Wales, is the largest Central American republic. It has 541 km. of coast on the Caribbean and 352 km. on the Pacific. Costa Rica is to the S, Honduras to the N. Only 8% of the whole country, out of a possible 28%, is in economic use and population density is low: 12.2 persons to the square km., as compared with El Salvador's 157.3. Nine-tenths of its 3.4m. people live in the west. An odd feature for a country so slightly industrialized is that 55% of its people live in towns.

There are three well-marked regions. (1) A large triangular-shaped central mountain land whose apex rests almost on the southern border with Costa Rica; the prevailing moisture-laden NE winds drench its eastern slopes, which are deeply forested with oak and pine on the drier, cooler heights. (2) A wide belt of eastern lowland through which a number of rivers flow from the mountains into the Atlantic. (3) The belt of lowland which runs from the Gulf of Fonseca, on the Pacific, diagonally across the isthmus to the Caribbean. Out of it, to the E, rise the lava cliffs of the mountains to a height of from 1,500 to 2,100 metres. Peninsulas of high land jut out here and there into the lowland, which is from 65 to 80 km. wide along the Pacific.

In this diagonal plain are two large sheets of water. The capital, Managua, is on the shores of Lake Managua, 52 km. long, 15 to 25 wide, and 39 metres above sea-level. The river Tipitapa drains it into Lake Nicaragua, 148 km. long, about 55 km. at its widest, and 32 metres above the sea; Granada is on its shores. Launches ply on the Río San Juan which drains it into the Caribbean.

There has been great volcanic activity at the north-western end of the lowland, from Lake Nicaragua to the Gulf of Fonseca. Three volcano cones rise to 1,500 metres or so in Lake Nicaragua itself, and one, the famous Momotombo, on the northern shore of Lake Managua. From Momotombo NW to the truncated cone of Cosegüina, overlooking the Gulf of Fonseca, there is a row of over 20 volcanoes, some of them active. Their ash makes a rich soil for crops. The wet, warm winds of the Caribbean pour heavy rain on the basin of the San Juan river, which is forested as far as Lake Nicaragua, but rains are moderate in the rest of the lowlands running NW to the Gulf of Fonseca.

Settlement The Spanish *conquistadores* reached the lowland from Panama as early as 1519. On the south-western shores of Lake Nicaragua they found an area comparatively densely settled by peaceful Indians, who lavished gold ornaments on them. Five years later another expedition founded colonies at Granada and León, but the flow of gold soon stopped and most of the Spaniards moved elsewhere. In 1570 both colonies were put under the jurisdiction of Guatemala. The local administrative centre was not rich Granada, with its profitable crops of sugar, cocoa, and indigo, but impoverished León, then barely able to subsist on its crops of maize, beans and rice. This reversal of the Spanish policy of choosing the most successful settlement as capital centre was due to the ease with which León could be reached from the Pacific. In 1858 Managua was chosen as a new capital.

Nine in ten of the people of Nicaragua live and work in the lowland between the Pacific and the western shores of Lake Nicaragua, the south-western shore of Lake Managua, and the south-western sides of the row of volcanoes. It is only of late years that settlers have taken to coffee-growing and cattle-rearing in the highlands at Matagalpa and Jinotega. Elsewhere the highlands, save for an occasional mining camp, are very thinly settled.

The densely forested eastern lowlands fronting the Caribbean were neglected, because of the heavy rainfall and their consequent unhealthiness, until the British settled several colonies of Jamaicans in the 18th century at Bluefields and San Juan del Norte (Greytown). But early this century the United Fruit Company of America opened banana plantations inland from Puerto Cabezas, worked by blacks from Jamaica. Other companies followed suit along the coast, but the bananas were later attacked by Panama disease and exports today are small. Along the Misquito coast there are still English-speaking communities in which African, or mixed African and indigenous, blood predominates.

NICARAGUA 1117

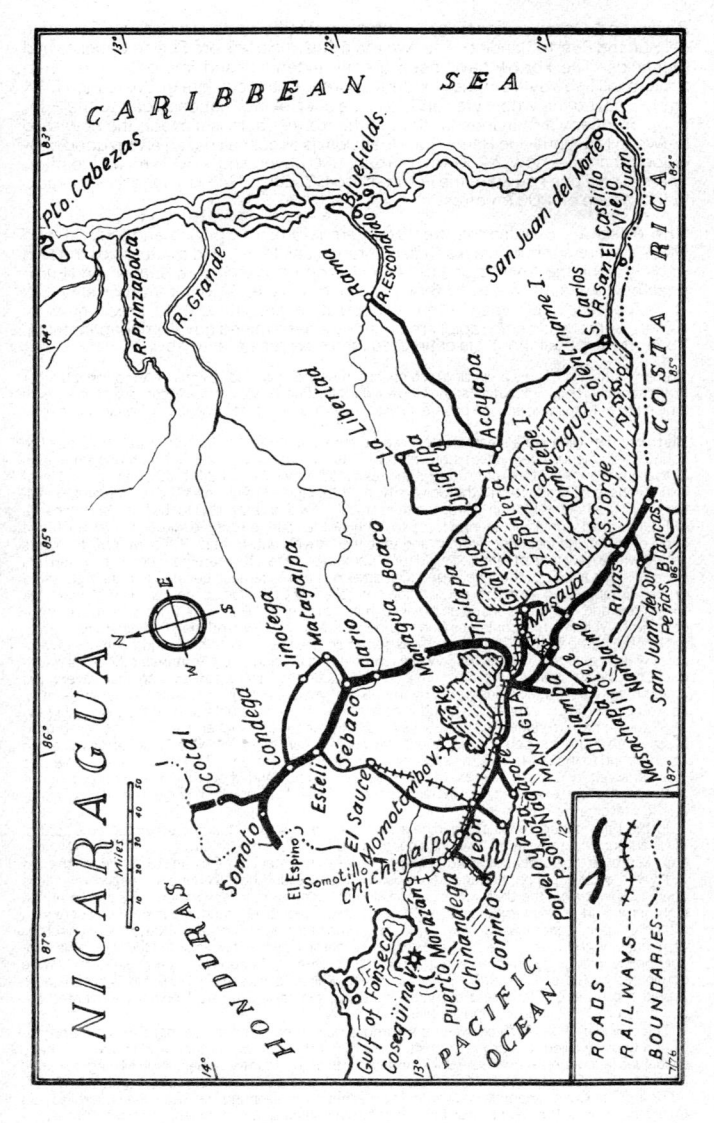

ROUGH SKETCH

1118 NICARAGUA

Ports and Communications The main Pacific ports are Corinto, San Juan del Sur and Puerto Sandino. The two main Atlantic ports are Puerto Cabezas and Bluefields. The **roads** have been greatly extended and improved. The Pan-American Highway from the Honduran border to the borders of Costa Rica (384 km.), is paved the whole way and so is the shorter international road to the Honduran frontier via Chinandega (though the frontier here is closed); the new road between Managua and Rama (for Bluefields) is almost all paved and in good condition. There are now 2,260 km. of road, 900 paved and 1,300 km. all-weather. There is only one **railway**, the Ferrocarril del Pacífico, 349 km. long, single track, with a gauge of 1.067 metres.

The People Besides the *mestizo* intermixtures of Spanish and Indian blood (77%), there are pure blacks (9%), pure Indians (4%), and mixtures of the two (mostly along the Atlantic coast). A small proportion is of pure Spanish and European blood. Death rate is 10.6 per 1,000; birth rate, 44.6; infant mortality, 87; life expectancy, 60 years. Annual population growth: 3.4%; urban growth: 4.5%. Illiteracy is being rapidly reduced by a determined government campaign: 88% of the population, it is estimated, can now read and write.

Roman Catholicism is the prevailing religion, but there are Episcopal, Baptist, Methodist and other Protestant churches. Education at the Universidad Nacional Autónoma de Nicaragua at León, with 3 faculties at Managua, and the private Jesuit Universidad Centroamericana at Managua is good.

History For Nicaragua's early history, see the introductory chapter to Central America. The country became an independent state in 1838. The famous (or infamous) filibustering expedition of William Walker is often referred to in the text. William Walker (1824-1860) was born in Nashville, Tennessee, graduated at the University in 1838, studied medicine at Edinburgh and Heidelberg, was granted his M.D. in 1843, and then studied law and was called to the bar. On October 5, 1853, he sailed with a filibustering force to conquer Mexican territory, declared Lower California and Sonora an independent republic and was then driven out. In May 1855, with 56 followers armed with a new type of rifle, he sailed for Nicaragua, where a belligerent faction had invited him to come to its aid. In October he seized a steamer on Lake Nicaragua belonging to the Accessory Transit Company, an American corporation controlled by Cornelius Vanderbilt. He was then able to surprise and capture Granada and make himself master of Nicaragua. Rivas was made President, with Walker in real control as Commander of the Forces. Two officials decided to use him to get control of the Transit Company; it was seized and handed over to his friends. A new Government was formed and in June 1856 Walker was elected President. On September 22, to gain support from the southern states in America he suspended the Nicaraguan laws against slavery. His government was formally recognized by the US that year. A coalition of Central American states, backed by Cornelius Vanderbilt, fought against him, but he was able to hold his own until May 1857, when he surrendered to the US Navy to avoid capture. In November 1857, he sailed from Mobile with another expedition, but soon after landing near Greytown, Nicaragua, he was arrested and returned to the US. In 1860 he sailed again from Mobile and landed in Honduras. There he was taken prisoner by Captain Salmon, of the British Navy, and handed over to the Honduran authorities, who tried and executed him on September 12, 1860. Walker's own book, *The War in Nicaragua*, is a fascinating document.

In 1911 the United States pledged help in securing a loan to be guaranteed through the control of Nicaraguan customs by an American board. In 1912 the United States sent marines into Nicaragua to enforce the control. Apart from short intervals, they stayed there until 1933. During the last five years of occupation, nationalists under General César Augusto Sandino waged relentless guerrilla war against the US Marines, who failed to suppress it. In November 1932 the American high command appointed Anastasio Somoza García supreme commander of the Nicaraguan National Guard. General Sandino was killed by Somoza's men in February 1934. American forces were finally withdrawn in 1933, when President Franklin Roosevelt announced the "Good Neighbour" policy, pledging non-intervention. From 1932, with brief intervals, Nicaraguan affairs were dominated by General Anastasio Somoza until he was assassinated in 1956. His two sons both served a presidential term and the younger, Gen. Anastasio Somoza Debayle, dominated the country from 1963 until his deposition in 1979.

The civil war of 1978-79 between the Somoza government and the Sandinista guerrilla organization (loosely allied to a broad opposition movement) resulted in extensive damage and many casualties (estimated at over 30,000) in certain parts of the country, especially in Managua, Estelí, León, Masaya, Chinandega and Corinto. After heavy fighting General Somoza resigned on July 17, 1979 and the Government was taken over by a Junta representing the Sandinista guerrillas and their civilian allies. Real power was exercised by nine Sandinista *comandantes* whose chief short-term aim was reconstruction. A 47-member Council of State formally came into being in May, 1980; supporters of the Frente Sandinista de Liberación Nacional had a majority. Elections were held on 4 November 1984; the Sandinista Liberation Front won 69% of the vote (82% of those

NICARAGUA

eligible voted). Daniel Ortega Saavedra, who had headed the Junta, was elected president. The Democratic Conservatives and the Independent Liberals took 11% of the vote each, but the failure of the Sandinista government to meet the demands of a right-wing grouping, the Democratic Coordinating Board (CDN), led to this coalition boycotting the elections and to the US administration condemning the poll as a "sham". The Sandinista government has brought major improvements in health and education. With the end of the fighting, Nicaragua is again a safe place to visit, but keep away from the frontier areas, where US-supported anti-Sandinista guerrillas (the "contras") are active.

Cities and Towns

Managua, the nation's capital and commercial centre since 1858, is on the southern shores of Lake Managua, at an altitude of 55 metres. It is 45 km. from the Pacific, but 140 km. from the main port, Corinto, though a new port, Puerto Sandino (formerly Puerto Somoza), is only 70 km. away. Managua was destroyed by earthquake in March 1931, and part of it swept by fire five years later; it was completely rebuilt as an up-to-date capital and commercial city (population 650,000) but the centre was again completely destroyed, apart from a few modern buildings, by another earthquake in December 1972. There was further severe damage during the civil wars of 1978-79.

The Government has now decided that it will rebuild the old centre, adding parks and recreational facilities (one such has opened E of Avenida Central, the tourist office is located here), although it is anticipated that this project will take years to complete. Present-day Managua has no centre as such, but rather consists of a series of commercial developments which have been built in what used to be the outskirts of the old city. No street names are in evidence, and the overall effect can be disconcerting. Directions are given according to landmarks; in place of cardinal points, the following are used: Lago (N), Arriba (E), Montaña (S), Abajo (W).

The principal commercial areas of Managua are now situated on the Masaya road and the two bypass roads S of the city. These centres contain a wide variety of shops, modern cinemas and discothèques.

In the old centre of Managua, one can still see examples of colonial architecture in the Palace of the Heroes of the Revolution (previously the National Palace) and the Cathedral. The Cathedral is open, although its interior is in ruins, and its exterior cracked. These buildings are situated on the Parque Central and provide a striking contrast with the modern Ruben Darío theatre on the lake shore (good plays and musical events, entry US$2-5; also Teatro Experimental) and the Banco de América building in the background. At the Iglesia Santa María de los Angeles a Catholic/secular/revolutionary mass is held each Sunday; it is recommended to attend to savour the atmosphere of present-day Nicaragua.

Points of Interest There are several volcanic-crater lakes in the environs of Managua, some of which have become centres of residential development and also have swimming, boating, fishing and picnicking facilities for the public. Bathing is possible in the Laguna de Tiscapa, behind the *Intercontinental Hotel*. Among the more attractive of these lakes is Laguna de Xiloá, situated about 16 km. from Managua just off the new road to Léon. At Xiloá a private aquatic club (El Náutico) has recently opened; here boats can be rented. (On Sat. and Sun., the only days when buses run, Xiloá gets very crowded, but it is quiet during the week, when you must walk there. You can camp there. Take bus 113 to Piedracitas for bus to Xiloá.) Other lakes within a ¾ hr. drive of Managua are the Laguna de Apoyo and Laguna de Masaya, situated respectively at Kms. 35 and 15 on the Masaya road.

The Huellas de Acahualinca are Managua's only site of archaeological interest. These are prehistoric animal and human footprints which have been preserved in solidified lava, and are assumed to have come into existence as a result of flight from a volcanic eruption about 5,000 years ago. The Huellas are located close to the old centre of town, near the lakeshore at the end of the South Highway. Bus No. 102 passes the site, on which there is also a small museum which exhibits a variety of prehistoric artefacts.

1120 NICARAGUA

A 10-km. drive down Carretera Sur—this is the Pan-American Highway—through the residential section of Las Piedrecitas takes us by the US Ambassador's residence to Laguna de Asososca, another small lake (the city's reservoir) in the wooded crater of an old volcano. Piedrecitas Park is to one side of the lake: there is a beautiful 3½-km. ride, playgrounds for children, a café, and splendid view of Lake Managua, two smaller lakes—Asososca and Xiloá—and of Momotombo volcano. Beyond again is the little Laguna de Nejapa (medicinal waters). The Pan-American Highway to Costa Rica passes through Casa Colorada (hotel), 26 km. from Managua, at 900 metres, with commanding views of both the Pacific and of Lake Managua, and a delightful climate.

Boats can be hired on the shores of Lake Managua for visiting the still-smoking Momotombo and the shore villages (see also page 1125). At its foot lies León Viejo, which was destroyed in 1609 and is now being excavated. It was in the Cathedral here that Pedrarias and his wife were buried. Near the large volcano is a smaller one, Momotombito. A fine drive skirts the shores of the lake. Volcano fans can also visit the Santiago volcano (page 1128). The Las Mercedes international airport (now renamed César Augusto Sandino) is near the lake, 9 km. E of the city, reached by bus No. 115. Do not swim in Lake Managua, as it is polluted in places.

Fiesta Santo Domingo is the patron saint of Managua. His festival is held at El Malecón from August 1 to 10: church ceremonies, horse racing, bull-fights, cock-fights, a lively carnival; proceeds to the General Hospital. August 1 (half day) and August 10 are local holidays.

Voltage 110 A.C., 60 cycles.

Hotels Hotel bills must be paid in US dollars, except where indicated. Several hotels have been built along the highway that bypasses the old part of the city, but there is still a shortage. Try to choose a central hotel (i.e. near *Intercontinental* or Plaza España) since transport to the outskirts is so difficult to get on. There is regular water rationing. *Intercontinental*, just N of Calle Colón, L, service poor, sauna, use of swimming pool for non-residents US$3, do not take photographs in vicinity as it is surrounded by military areas; *Camino Real*, A; *King's Palace*, B, Km. 5. on road to Masaya, rooms with bath, a/c, Tel.: 80115/80015, unfriendly, not recommended; *Managua*, B; *Aeropuerto*, C; *Casa Serrano*, 3 streets N of Sears (Tel.: 2-52-64), C b. and b., a/c, pleasant, friendly; *Ticomo* at Km. 8½, Carretera Sur, has parking facilities, rents apartments, C with maid service and kitchenette, C breakfast extra, good for longer stay; *Estrella*, D, a/c, swimming pool, with breakfast, long way from centre, book in advance as it's very popular; *Nuevo Siete Mares Hotel* and Chinese Restaurant, one block from *Intercontinental*, C with a/c, bath, cold water only, clean, noisy, unfriendly, overpriced; *Casa de Fiedler*, 8a Calle Sur-Oeste 1320, C, with bath and a/c, D with fan, comfortable, good breakfasts; *Colonia Residencial Pereira*, small and quiet, D, meals US$2.50; *Palace*, C, with a/c and bath, comfortable, helpful, TV lounge, quiet and good value; *residencias* in D range are *Casa Skandia*, *Bolonia Inn* (unfriendly, dirty), *Pataky Residence*. *Colón*, near Sirca bus terminal, D, with bath and fan, a bit run down, secure, good restaurant; *El Pueblo*, in the old centre, F with bath, good; *Familia Lesbia*, E, with bathroom, F, without; *Sultana* (basic) E, noisy, clean, recommended, if full, staff will arrange for you to stay at *Mi Siesta* on the other side of town (E with bath and a/c, F no a/c), good, friendly, laundry facilities; *Casa de Huéspedes Santos*, in a green house on street leading to *Intercontinental Hotel*, G p.p., basic, friendly, clean; one block away on same street is *Hospedaje Meza*, same rates, very basic, TV and drinks available, friendly, popular; *Casa de Huéspedes Gladys*, in same area, F; *El Colibrí*, single-storey, thatched, clean, with shower, good value, often fully-booked, F, 4 blocks from *Intercontinental*; *Royal*, near railway station, F (payable in córdobas), always full; next door is *Pensión Norma*, on road N of Supermercado in Ciudad Jardín, F, basic, friendly, popular; *Pensión Guerrero*, F, friendly; *El Dorado*, 8 blocks from *Intercontinental*, F, clean, basic, safe but noisy; *El Almendro*, opp. *Almond Tree Lodge*, F, bargain; *Hospedaje Oriental*, near eastern market, F, clean; *Ensueño*, near Mercado Periférico, F with bath, pleasant, clean; *Residencia Los Pinos*, close to *Hotel Lido* (see below) F (can pay in córdobas), with bath, basic but friendly, safe, much "passing trade", has curfew; *Pensión Molinito* (no sign), Calle Pablo Corese, tiny partitioned rooms, basic but clean, F, noisy, not safe, cheap food available. Many others in same area, e.g. *Azul* (blue doors, no sign), east of Portinal, and *Tres Laureles*, D, recommended, clean, friendly, private bath and fan; nearby is *El Portal*, F, shower, cheap. *Hospedaje Atlántico No. 2*, 4 km. from centre, F (payable in córdobas); *Mascote* also accepts córdobas, F, opp. Mercado Huembes, often full; *Hospedaje Fuente*, 2 blocks behind this hotel, G (córdobas accepted), friendly, safe. Many cheap hotels W of *Intercontinental Hotel* have very thin walls and are therefore noisy. This district, which also has a number of good eating places, is where many gringos congregate. At Km. 3.5 on Carretera Sur is *Hotel Lido*, C + 10%, use of swimming pool by non-residents, US$1.

Camping 13½ km. from the centre, W of Managua on Route 12 is the Nica Trailer Park.

Another 5 km. N of Nica, 2½ km. after the junction with Ruta 2. Free, good camping at Laguna de Xiloá.

Restaurants *The Lobster's Inn* (Km. 5½ South Highway), good for guess what; *Lacmiel*, Km. 4½ on road to Masaya, recommended, good value, real ice-cream; *Los Ranchos*, US$7.50 p.p (Km. 3 South Highway), behind it is Eskimo ice cream factory where you can eat; *El Corral* (Km. 8½ North Highway), and *Los Gauchos* (Km. 3 Masaya Highway), for steaks; *El Ternero* and *La Fonda*, open air, good, also good for drinks and snacks, both located in Camino Oriente, Managua's entertainment centre (containing 2 cinemas, bowling alley, 2 discos and a *Macdonalds*—an appalling local version since it lost its US franchise); *El Mesón*, good; *El Coliseo* (Km. 8 Masaya Highway), Italian; *El Rincón Español* (Av. Monumental, old Managua), Spanish, fair; *Peppers* (Drefus Centre), pizzas; *Pizza Deli* (Km. 6 Masaya Highway); *Faisán Dorado*, in Ciudad Jardín L-3, meals for US$6; *Antojitos* (opposite *Intercontinental Hotel*), open at 1200, Mexican, a bit overpriced, but has interesting photos of Managua pre-earthquake, good food and garden; *La Marseillaise* (Colonia los Robles), excellent French food, and *Zummen Cafetería* (Bypass South) for cheap eating; *El Rubi* (Chinese, good food, poor service); *Café Flamingo*; *Gambrinus*; *Chips* (snack bar at Ciné Dorado). *Costa Brava*, 200 metres up road from Ciné Dorado, excellent seafood. Self-service at Plaza España, US$2.10 p.p., nearby, *La Terraza*; *La Rondilla*, on park near Plaza España; *Cafetería Bolonia*, next to *Panadería* on Plaza España, a/c,good; *Yerba Buena*, Pista Benjamín Zeledón, 2 blocks E of Plaza España, open 1700-2400 except Sun., coffee house, good recorded music and chocolate cake; *Gran Marisquería Maxim's*, C.S.T., 6 C. Av. Sur. The second café on right from old Ticabus station serves good meals for US$1-2. The *Hotel Intercontinental* serves enormous breakfasts (US$0.70), and an excellent lunch between 1200 and 1500, US$1.40 for as much as you want (best to dress smartly). Several *comedores* behind *Hotel Intercontinental*. *Nuevo Siete Mares*, Chinese, one block W of *Intercontinental*, unfriendly, overpriced. *Comedores Sara* and *Victoria*, another in same street with "Victoria beer" sign, are cheap, former is O.K., latter not so good. *Mirador Tiscapa*, overlooking Laguna Tiscapa, good meat and seafood, reasonably-priced, dancing to the band Fri. and Sat. p.m. *Los Nopales*, good food and service, recommended. *Soya Restaurant*, vegetarian, Pista de la Resistencia, off Carretera a Masaya (119 bus line); health food bakery near Tiscapa (take 109 bus to Supermercado del Pueblo, then 2 blocks S). *Jicote*, excellent, and *Naturales Margarita*, Carretera a Masaya, several blocks from *casa de cambio* towards lake, vegetarian and other dishes, good *refrescos* (closed Tues.).

Shopping Some handicrafts (goldwork, embroidery, etc.) are available in the Centro Comercial de Managua; good general shopping here and at Mercado Huembes, both on Pista de la Solidaridad (buses 110 or 119). Worth a visit is the Casa del Lagarto, where alligator handbags and shoes are sold at reasonable prices but US visitors had better make sure first whether they can be imported; the Endangered Species Act is very stringent. Also, a visit to the handicrafts market in Masaya (30 km. away) is worthwhile. Universidad Centroamericana (UCA) bookshop (sells maps of Nicaragua) and coffee house. Ciudad Jardín for books, records, etc.; also Ministry of Culture (near Plaza España), the lobby of the *Intercontinental* (also has expensive gift shop) and the CST building, Ho Chi Minh Way. Managua Centro has a wide range of shops. Most ordinary shops are in private houses without signs. Centro Sandinista de Trabajadores has an excellent selection of books and postcards, on Carretera Sur. Diplotienda (diplomatic shop), opp. *Los Gauchos* restaurant on Carretera a Masaya, offers Western-style goods, take your passport, accepts dollars and travellers' cheques if to value of purchase.

Local Transport Bus service in Managua is cheap and as good as can be expected under the circumstances. All buses are packed. Fixed fare, C$3 (except on some *rápido* buses, e.g. No. 119, C$6, and yellow microbuses, C$20). Last services begin their routes at 2200; buses are regular but it is difficult to fathom their routes. Beware of pickpockets on the crowded urban buses. A map from the Tourist Office (poor), and a couple of days riding the buses will help you orient yourself. Bus map available from the Ministry of Transport, near Plaza España. Taxis can be flagged down along the street, but they run mostly on set routes, so you have to know where you're going. Most *taxis are colectivos*, charging at most US$0.05; bargain on those that aren't (fares range from US$0.10-US$1). One pays per zone. Every taxi is required to have a price list; check this before making your journey. Taxis stationed at the *Intercontinental Hotel* and the airport are relatively more expensive. US$3 for a short trip, US$8 from the airport to downtown. For the airport take Tipitapa bus from Mercado Huembes; this bus is very crowded, better to hitch (very easy) or take a taxi.

Car Hire There are three rental firms in Managua: Hertz, Avis and Budget. Rates are US$25 per day plus US$0.25 per km., or US$60 per day with unlimited mileage— only foreign exchange or credit cards accepted; special weekend rates available. Given the poor public transport and the decentralized layout of Managua, renting a car is often the best way to get around. Gasoline is US$0.95 the US gallon. Alternatively hire a taxi for long-distance trips, about US$1.50-2 per hour for the car; for journeys out of Managua, taxis need a special permit from an office opp. *Hotel Intercontinental* (opens 0930).

Discothèques Lobo Jack, La Nueva Managua, Frisco Disco, Casa Blanca, Pantera Rosa. 2 discos in Camino Oriente centre. Live music is offered at La Vista, Torre Blanca, Tiffany's Saloon and

1122 NICARAGUA

El Arroyito, Plaza 19 de Julio, Pista de la Resistencia opp. Universidad Centroamericana, two live bands, crowded, festive, great dancing.

Cinemas 2 in Camino Oriente entertainments centre; Dorado; Cabrera on same street as *Intercontinental*. Most films in English with Spanish sub-titles (US$0.30). Cinemateca, on Av. Bolívar (behind Cine González), Government theatre with good programmes (only US$0.10 on Sun. a.m.).

Sport Baseball—between Plaza de España and Plaza 19 de Julio on Sunday mornings (the national game), basketball, cockfighting and bullfighting (but no kill), swimming, sailing, tennis, golf.

Museums The National Museum is near the lakeshore, to the E of the railway station (closed Sun.). Museo de la Alfabetización (closed Mon.) near Parque Las Palmas in W section of city commemorates the Sandinista Government's literacy programme. Museum of the Revolution, behind bus station near Mercado Eduardo Contreras; fascinating collection of photographs, weapons and documents from 1880s to the struggle against the Somozas (open Tues.-Sat., 0900-1200, 1400-1700, Sun., 0900-1200; admission free). Centro Cultural Ruinas del Gran Hotel, near Palacio Nacional, permanent display of "revolutionary" art and visiting exhibitions; small cafeteria (expect to have to deposit your bag at the door).

Banks Banco Central de Nicaragua, Km. 7, Carretera del Sur. The only bank that gives dollars cash is Banco Central de Nicaragua, Edificio Oscar Pérez Cassar, Plaza de Compras, Ruta de Masaya (bus No. 119): tell them you need dollars to pay your hotel bill. Bank of London & South America, Plaza de Compras, Colonia Centro América. Citibank, Banco de América (up to US$100 in cheques may be changed here at C$50 charge, US dollars are obtainable; also will change quetzales). Open Mon.-Fri. 0900-1500, Sat. 0830-1130. Local banks all nationalised in July 1979. Travellers' cheques may be exchanged at Banco de América, or in branches of Banco Nicaragüense in Centro Comercial Zumen, Centro Comercial Linda Vista and Plaza de Compras on Carretera Norte. The bank at Plaza España changes both bank notes and travellers' cheques. *Casas de cambio* at Km. 4.5 on road to Masaya, opp. *Sandy's* restaurant (Bus 119), open 0900-1200, 1400-1600; at terminal for Granada buses, several in Ciudad Jardín; much quicker than banks. It is advisable to change money in Managua as it is very difficult elsewhere. The illegal "parallel" market offers far better rates of exchange; ask discreetly for the "coyotes" in Ciudad Jardín suburb. Otherwise change money at the parallel rate at the Costa Rican or Honduran border. Beware of shortchanging. (See page 1136.)

Immigration Km. 7 Carretera del Sur, bus No. 118, open till 1400.

Customs Km. 5 Carretera del Norte, bus No. 108.

Embassies *U.S.A.*, Km. 4½ Carretera del Sur (Tel.: 23881); *W. German*, off Plaza España; *French*, Km. 12 Carretera del Sur, Tel.: 26210/27011; *British*, Calle Princalle, 2a Casa a la Derecha, Primera Etapa, Los Robles postal address 700,34/Apdo Aéreo 169, it is located on a R-turn off Carretera a Masaya; Honorary *British Consul* at Viajes Griffiths, No. C8, Centro Comercial San Francisco, Tel.: 72365/74785; letters to Apdo. Postal 13, Managua; *Swedish*, Apartado Postal 2307, Tel.: 66778/60085; *Panamanian* Consulate, near UCA, Plaza 19 de Julio; *Costa Rican*: near Plaza de Compras, 15-min. walk from Mercado Huembes, or Bus 108; *Honduran* Consulate, Carretera del Sur, Km. 15, Colonia Barcelona, open Mon.-Fri., 0800-1400 (bus 118 from *Hotel Intercontinental*); *Guatemalan*, just after Km. 11 on Masaya road, visa US$10 (for British citizens, cash only), fast service.

General Post Office 3 blocks W of Palacio Nacional and Cathedral, 0700-1600 (closed Sat. p.m.). Separate entrance and exit, luggage searched on entry. Poste Restante (Lista de Correos) keeps mail for 1 month.

Cables Telcor, Radio Nacional, Mercado Roberto Huembes (Eduardo Contreras), on Ruta 109 from *Hotel Intercontinental*.

Tourist Information Inturismo occupies a kiosk in Parque Luis Alfonso Velásquez (behind the Biblioteca Infantil), just N of the Banco de América building. Hours: 0800-1700, Mon.-Fri. (Administration office, 1 block E of *Hotel Intercontinental*, gives information reluctantly, enter by side door.) Standard information available. Maps of Managua (almost up-to-date), with insets of León and Granada and whole country on reverse, US$2 (paid in dollars). Inturismo will help with finding accommodation with families at US$5 per day including 3 meals. Day trips can be arranged for US$50. Post cards for sale at Tourist Office and *Intercontinental* Hotel (more expensive), also at Tarjetas Gordión. The best map of the capital and country can be bought from the Instituto Nacional Geográfico, or from the Tourist Board (where it is cheaper). The Esso map is also good. Nica-tours on Plaza España sells maps of Managua and of the country.

Airlines Pan Am, Taca International, Copa, Sahsa, Aeronica, Aeroflot, SAM, Varig. All airline offices are around Plaza España, except KLM (very helpful), in a small house just off road to Masaya, on opp. side from *Sandy's* Restaurant. Copa accepts córdobas from residents only; foreigners have to pay in dollars for all flight tickets.

NICARAGUA 1123

Rail Pacific Railway to port of Corinto via León (branch to El Sauce) and Chinandega (Managua-León 1100 and 1800 daily, US$0.07, 3 hrs.); 3 a day to Granada, via Masaya (1 hr. 25 mins., US$0.15); to Masaya one a.m. and one p.m., continuing to Jinotepe; also to Masatepe, San Marcos, Diriamba. Always very dusty in the dry season, and there are no windows to close.

Roads to León and Chinandega and then (when frontier bridge is repaired) to Choluteca in Honduras; to Masaya and Granada; Pan-American Highway N to Honduras (to Tegucigalpa is 444 km.), and SE to Costa Rica. Good paved roads from Casa Colorada to Masachapa, Managua to Granada and Nandaime.

Buses Good connections by bus or taxi between city centre and bus stations. The Comandante Casimir Sotelo bus station by the Mercado Roberto Huembes (adjacent to Mercado Eduardo Contreras), by Museo de la Revolución, on Pista de la Solidaridad, is for Granada, Masaya, Estelí, Somoto, Matagalpa, etc., and all destinations in the N, including the Atlantic Coast. Take bus 109, which runs past *Hotel Intercontinental* and terminates near railway station, or bus 118 and alight at San Juan Bosco church and walk 2 blocks. Bus to Granada, Ruta 4, 0530-2200, every 10 minutes, US$0.05, 1 hr. (luggage extra). To Masaya, US$0.03. To Ocotal US$0.50 (with Lestram). To Estelí US$0.15, every 20 mins, 3 hrs. For other destinations, e.g. to León, Corinto and Pacific Coast, Chinandega and Rivas, the terminal is beside Mercado Israel Lewites, Pista de la Resistencia, on SW side of city (bus 118). To get from the first to the second, take bus 109, then change at *Intercontinental* to bus 118. Bus to León, US$0.20, 1½ hrs., or take Interlocal taxi from bus station, 1½ hrs., US$0.45; to Rivas, 3 hrs., US$0.20, 1400; to Peñas Blancas on Costa Rican border, 3½-4 hrs., US$0.40; to Chinandega, 3 hrs., US$0.30.

International Buses In 1985 Ticabus suspended its services to Managua. Look in *El Nuevo Diario* for buses running to San Salvador, Tegucigalpa and Guatemala City. Sirca Express leaves 0600 Wed., and Fri. or Sat. for Costa Rica and Panama (office near *Sandy's* restaurant, taxi for 0600 departure very expensive, US$2). Sirca Bus to San José, US$2.65, 12-15 hrs. (inc. 4-6 at border). Sirca office and terminal reached by bus 119 from Plaza España to 4-5 km. past Masaya road, alight at Supermercado de Nicaragua, turn left, pass Shell petrol station, turn left again and continue for some blocks (hotel at terminal, E with bath). International buses are always booked-up many days in advance and tickets will not be sold until all passport/visa documentation is complete. However, the Sirca Bus journey to San José (can be picked up in Granada or Rivas) avoids a 5-km. walk between the Nicaraguan and Costa Rican border posts.

Tours of city by private car, 1 or 3 persons, about US$10. All-day tour to Granada and León, US$30. A 2-day round trip by motor bus and riverboat from Managua to Bluefields costs US$50. Bus tours are available Managua-Tegucigalpa-Copán-Guatemala City for US$28. All must be paid in US dollars. Few tours of the country are available.

Beaches There are several beaches on the Pacific coast, about an hour's drive from Managua. The nearest are Pochomil and Masachapa (54 km. from Managua, side by side, regular bus service from terminal in Israel Lewites market) and Casares (69 km. from Managua, dirty, thorns on beach; one hotel—*Casino Casares*, clean, simple—and 2 restaurants). A few km. from Casares is La Boquita, visited by turtles from Aug. to Nov. Because of their proximity to the capital, these are very popular during the season (Jan.-April) and tend to be somewhat crowded. Out of season (except at weekends) Pochomil is deserted (don't sleep on the beach, mosquitoes will eat you alive). Very slow bus journey from Managua. A visit to the broad, sandy El Velero beach (turn off at Km. 60 on the old road to León and then follow signs) is recommended despite the US$3.50 entrance charge. All facilities controlled by the INSSBI, for the benefit of state employees, and at weekends is fully booked for weeks in advance. You may be able to rent a cabin (F for 2) in the week, pay extra for sheet and pillows. You can eat in the restaurant (*Pirata Cojo*), at the INSSBI cafeteria (bring your own utensils, buy meal ticket in advance, or take your own food). However, the beach itself is beautiful, and the sea is ideal for both surfing and swimming. El Tránsito is a beautiful, undeveloped Pacific beach; bus from Managua at 1300 (from end of No. 107 bus route behind Ciné México), return at 0600 or 0700. Good cheap meals from Sra Pérez on the beach (possible accommodation); *Restaurant Yolanda*; beach flats for 4-6 people normally available midweek at N end (Centro Vacacional de Trabajadores, good value).

Pan-American Highway from Managua to Honduras: 214 km., paved the whole way. Also paved are the branch roads to Matagalpa and Jinotega. The first stretch of 21 km. to Tipitapa is along the southern edge of Lake Managua. **Tipitapa**, on the SE shore of the lake, is a tourist resort with hot sulphur baths, a casino, a colourful market, and a *fiesta* of El Señor de Esquipulas on January 13-16. (The border with Honduras on the more easterly route, by road from Ocotal via Las Manos to Danlí, and the more westerly Chinandega-Río Guasaule-Choluteca link are both closed.)

Hotel *Aguas Calientes*, F with shower; the thermal bath still functions.

1124 NICARAGUA

Restaurant *Salón Silvia*, unpretentious, but excellent lake fish. Slightly cheaper, but good, is the a/c restaurant attached to the thermal baths.

Bus from Managua (minibus), US$0.05. Bus to Estelí, US$0.30.

From San Benito, near Tipitapa, the Atlantic Highway runs E through Juigalpa (25,000 people; 109 km. from Managua). Here is one of the best museums in Nicaragua, with a collection of idols resembling those at San Agustín, Colombia. Staying here overnight on the way to Bluefields (e.g. at *Hotel Mayales*, G, close to Cathedral, best of a bad lot), one can avoid staying in Rama. Restaurant at *Mayales* or *La Plancha*. Small zoo in the valley below town. The road continues to La Libertad, a goldmining town at 600 metres, to Cara de Mono, on the Río Mico, and finally to Rama, on the Río Escondido or Bluefields River, 290 km. from Managua. River boats ply from Rama 100 km. downstream to Bluefields (see page 1131).

The Pan-American Highway goes N through Tipitapa to Sébaco, 105 km. Fourteen km. before reaching Sébaco is Ciudad Darío (off the main road, turning N of town, is not signposted), where the poet Ruben Darío was born; you can see the house, which is maintained as a museum. E of the Highway is Esquipula, 100 km. from Managua, 2½ hrs. by bus, a good place for hiking, fishing, riding; *Hotel Oscar Morales*, G, clean, shower, friendly. From Sébaco a 24-km. branch road leads (right) to **Matagalpa** at 678 metres, in the best walking country in Nicaragua, population 40,000. Matagalpa has an old church, but it is about the only colonial style building left; the town has developed rapidly in recent years. It was badly damaged in the civil war, but is undergoing reconstruction, retaining much of its original character. While *Contra* activity continues, visitors can expect frequent police checks. There is a small zoo in the northern suburbs along the river. The main occupation is coffee planting and there are cattle ranges; the chief industry is the Nestlé powdered-milk plant. A 32-km. road runs from Matagalpa to the Tuma valley. September 24, Día de La Merced, is a local holiday.

Hotels *Selva Negra*, 10 km. on road to Jinotega, F, good, but poor restaurant; *Soza*, opp. river, good; *Ideal*, E, with bath, same range without (but C for those not on a work brigade); *Bermúdez*, reasonably clean, friendly, no meals; *Monteleón*; *Plaza*.

Restaurants *Comedor San Martín*, main street, good breakfasts; *San Diego*, opp. cinema near plaza, good; *Los Pinchitos Morenos*, near the centre, good and cheap; *Corona de Oro*, *Monte Sol*, *Oriental*, *Cantón*, *Royal Bar*, *El Establo*.

Bank Four national banks.

Souvenir shop Next to *Hotel Ideal*.

Buses every half hour to Managua, 127 km., take 2½ hrs. (US$0.32). Buses for the local area leave from Guanuco, a long way from the centre in the E suburbs.

There is a fine 34-km. highway from Matagalpa to **Jinotega**, and on another 80 km. (unpaved), via the picturesque villages of San Rafael del Norte and La Concordia, to join the main highway at Condega, 51 km. from the Honduras border (*pensión*, F). Jinotega (altitude 1,004 metres) is served by buses from Managua and Matagalpa. Population 20,000; famous images in church. Excellent coffee grown here and in Matagalpa. Road (18 km.) to El Tuma power station; another to Estelí.

The 134-km. section from Sébaco to the border at El Espino is through sharp hills with steep climbs and descents, but reasonably well banked and smooth.

The Pan-American Highway goes through **Estelí** (839 metres), a rapidly developing departmental capital of about 20,000 people (heavily damaged during the civil wars of 1978-79). It is the site of prehistoric carved stone figures. Worth visiting are the Casa de Cultura and the Salvadorean cooperative for crafts (off main square). Also ask at the Reforma Agraria Office (above Banco de América) if you wish to see any local farming cooperatives. Tourist information at Cathedral Plaza. Bus Estelí-Managua, first at 0700, none after dark, every 30 mins., US$0.15 plus a charge for luggage.

Hotels *Mesón*, 1 block N of Cathedral and plaza, F with shower, good value, but not very clean, restaurant; *Alpino* (G, poor but friendly), *Adela* (dirty, G), *El Chalet*; *Bolívar*, unmarked, 2 blocks S on main street from *Restaurant La Plancha*, good, G; *Moderno*, F, with shower, good, safe parking, slow service in restaurant; 3 *hospedajes* on Av. Bolívar, all G: *La Florida* (not recommended),

Juárez, and San Francisco; Barlop, edge of town opp. bus station, 4 blocks from main square, 12 rooms, 6 of which good, 6 basic, former have hot showers, Tel.: (071) 2486, G, good; several on main road a few blocks SW from main square; they are often full. Restaurant La Plancha nearby, and opp. Sorbetería Estelí, is Colectivo de Soja vegetarian restaurant; El Mesero, on street which joins main street at hospital, opp. an open field, very good despite appearance.

Bathing near Estelí at Puente La Sirena, 200 metres off the road to Condega, or Salta Estanzuela, 5 km. S of Estelí, a waterfall of 25 metres, with a deep pool at the bottom, surrounded by trees and flowers (inc. orchids—only worth it in the rainy season), at least 5 km. off the Managua road, four-wheel drive recommended. Take the dirt road, starting ½ km. S of Estelí on Pan-American Highway, through San Nicolás.

Highway then goes to Condega (2,000 people) and to Somoto (7,000 people), centre of pitch-pine industry, thence to El Espino (20 km.), a ghost town 5 km. from Honduran border at La Playa. The Nicaraguan checkpoint at El Espino is where luggage is checked and financial formalities are undertaken (US$60 to be changed into córdobas, proof of US$200 when entering Nicaragua). Walk, hitch or take colectivo taxi (US$0.07) between the border posts. For private cars only, Customs is at Somoto where luggage is checked and financial formalities are carried out. Minibuses run between Somoto and the border (US$0.05, plus US$0.20 per bag), and 3 or 4 buses daily between Somoto and Estelí (US$0.10); Somoto-Managua, 5 hrs., US$0.25 plus US$1 for luggage. The border opens at 0800 on each side, Nicaraguan side closes at 1530, and 1200-1300 for lunch (if you arrive at the border after 1530, there are no buses back to Somoto and nowhere to stay in El Espino). (There is food bar on the Nicaraguan side.)

Just before reaching Somoto a road leads off from Yalagüina right (18 km.) to **Ocotal**, an attractive small town of 3,863 people at 600 metres on a sandy plain near the Honduras border, to which a road runs N (bus—marked Las Manos—but this border is closed; bus Ocotal-Somoto, US$0.05). Close by, at San Albino, there are many gold mines and gold is washed in the river Coco (bus only from Ciudad Sandino—formerly Jícaro, 50 km. from Ocotal; a dangerous area). Friendly, helpful Tourist Office 2 blocks from main square, opposite the market. Bus Estelí-Ocotal, US$0.05, 2 hrs., beautiful views.

Hotels at Ocotal El Portal, G, reasonable; El Castillo, G, basic, quiet; Pensión Centroamericana, G, not as dirty as most others. For eating, Restaurant La Cabaña; Brasilia, very good, ask for directions.

Hotels on Pan-American Highway At Somoto: Panamericano and Internacional, both only fair, G; small, clean hospedaje close to bus station, G (will arrange meals); Las Americanas, on plaza opp. church, dormitory accommodation, G, friendly, basic; 4 others; restaurant Zetaponat in Somoto; Somotillo, F (7 km. from frontier, no sign, on right just before sign on left to Cine Karla), communal showers, adequate, meals. At Ciudad Darío: Grande.

A fine new highway leads off the Pan-American Highway near San Isidoro, about 20 km. SE of Estelí, to join the Pacific Highway near León. This is an attractive alternative route to Managua through the Chinandega cotton growing area, past the spectacular chain of volcanoes running W from Lake Managua, and through León. (Bus Estelí-San Isidoro, US$0.05, San Isidoro-León, 2½ hrs., US$0.20, all on good roads.)

Managua to Corinto 140 km. The first city of note along the railway is León, 88 km. from Managua, reached in 2¼ hrs. The Pacific Highway between the two cities goes on to Chinandega and has been continued to Corinto and to the Honduran border (border bridge destroyed by floods early in 1982, and frontier crossing closed).

About 60 km. down the new road to León lies the village of La Paz Centro. It is from here that one can gain access to the volcano **Momotombo**, which dominates the Managua skyline from the West. Although it is possible to drive halfway up the volcano, access to the crater itself involves a further 2-3 hr. hike. Proper preparations should be made if this expedition is undertaken as the terrain is rough and dry and there are poisonous snakes in the area. During the ascent of the mountain, you can see geysers being tapped for thermal energy. Another interesting active volcano, easier to visit, is Santiago (see page 1127).

1126 NICARAGUA

One now has to have a permit from Empresa Nacional de Luz y Fuerza in Managua to climb Momotombo; they have built a geothermal power station on the volcano's slopes; alternatively ask police in León Viejo for a permit. Permits are very difficult to get.

León, with a population of 63,000, was founded by Hernández de Córdoba in 1524 at León Viejo, 32 km. from its present site, at the foot of Momotombo. It was destroyed by earthquake on December 31, 1609 (the ruins can be reached by boat from Managua), and the city moved to its present site the next year. It was the capital from its foundation until Managua replaced it in 1858; it is still the "intellectual" capital, with a university (founded 1804), religious colleges, the largest cathedral in Central America, and several colonial churches. It is said that Managua became the capital, although at the time it was only an Indian settlement, because it was half-way between violently Liberal León and equally violently Conservative Granada.

The city has a traditional air: narrow streets, roofs tiled in red, low adobe houses and time-worn buildings everywhere. The old Plaza de Armas, in front of the Cathedral, is now Parque Jérez; it contains a statue of General Jérez, a mid-19th century Liberal leader. There was heavy fighting in the town during the civil wars of 1978-79, and it is badly damaged and, in parts, impoverished.

The Cathedral, begun in 1746 and not completed for 100 years, is an enormous building. It has a famous shrine, 145 cm. high, covered by white topazes from India given by Philip II of Spain, which is kept in a safe in the vestry, and the bishop holds the key; a very fine ivory Christ; the consecrated Altar of Sacrifices and the Choir of Córdoba; the great Christ of Esquipulas, a Colonial work in bronze whose cross is of very fine silver; and statues of the 12 Apostles. At the foot of one of these statues is the tomb of Ruben Darío, the 19th-century Nicaraguan poet, guarded by a sorrowing lion.

The western end of the city is the oldest, and here is the oldest of all the churches: the parish church of Subtiava (1530) where Las Casas, the Apostle of the Indies, preached on several occasions. It has a fine façade, the best colonial altar in the country and an interesting representation of the sun ("El Sol") revered by the Indians. Near the Subtiava church are a small town museum (entrance free) and the ruins of the parish church of Vera Cruz, now crumbling. Other churches well worth visiting include El Calvario (beautifully decorated ceiling), La Recolección (fine façade), La Merced, San Felipe, Zaragoza, San Francisco and El Laborío. There is a pleasant walk S across the bridge, past the church of Guadalupe, to the cemetery. The house of Ruben Darío, one of the greatest Latin American poets, the famous "Four Corners" in Calle Ruben Darío, is now the Museo-Archivo Ruben Darío; he died in 1916 in another house in the NW sector marked with a plaque. The Holy Week ceremonies are outstanding. Visit the Casa de Cultura in the suburb of Subtiava.

Local Holidays June 20 (Liberation by Sandinistas), September 24, November 1 (All Saints' Day).

Hotels *Europa,* best, D (córdobas accepted), with bath, G without, excellent, good breakfasts (US$0.35); *América,* Av. Santiago Argüello, central, F, with bath and fan, clean and friendly, restaurant (good breakfast); *Teluca,* G with shower, clean, 4 blocks from railway station; *Hospedaje de la Primavera,* Calle 9N, 3½ blocks W of railway station, G with shower, nice but women travelling alone should take one of the more expensive rooms close to reception as drunken men are a problem here, also has rats; Several cheap *pensiones* near the railway station (e.g. *Hospedaje Blando,* G, or *Pensión Cortez,* basic).

Restaurants *La Cueva del León,* good seafood and steaks, two blocks N of Parque Jérez, opp. 2 cinemas; *Pizza Caliente,* 2-3 blocks from Cathedral towards station; *Fortuna,* good Chinese food, also *Cantón* and *Hong Kong,* close to station in market square. *Central,* Calle 4 Norte, good service. *Cuerva,* Av. 1 Poniente, good value; *Metropolitano, Los Angeles,* both behind Post Office. *Club de León,* good food, disco in youth centre, restaurant on roof. Cheapest (and good) food in market by behind Cathedral.

Shopping Market square at the railway station and a market with some handicrafts behind the Cathedral. Good bookshop next to city hall at Parque Jérez.

Cinemas 3 in centre.

Banks National banks.

NICARAGUA 1127

Post Office Parque Jérez, opposite Cathedral. Phone calls abroad possible.

Bus Managua-León, Route 12, 1½ hrs., US$0.20. Colectivo, US$0.45; to San Isidro, US$0.20; buses leave from market by railway station.

Train Managua-León, US$0.07, 2 hrs.; train from León to Managua departs 0500 and 1200; rough, dusty, colourful, real experience! Trip gives good view of lakes and volcanoes. A branch railway runs to El Sauce (64 km.), where there is an old church, and a riotous fair in February.

There is a good road (20 km.) to the sandy Pacific beach (large waves, strong currents, very dangerous) at **Poneloya** (Hotel Lacayo, basic, G, meals, beware of insects at night, bring coils; good fish restaurant down the road); the local minibus from Southern part of town, not the same place as Managua buses (US$0.06, 50 mins.) finishes at Las Peñitas at the S end of Poneloya beach. It gets crowded at weekends; camping possible on the beach.

Chinandega is about 35 km. beyond León. Population 37,000. This is one of the main cotton-growing districts, and also grows bananas and sugar cane. Horse-drawn cabs for hire, and a crocodile in the fountain in the main square. Not far away, at Chichigalpa, is Ingenio San Antonio, the largest sugar mill in Nicaragua, with a railway to its own port on the Pacific. From Managua, by road, 3 hrs., US$0.30. Hourly buses to Managua from main square from 0500. From León, 1 hr. by bus, US$0.12. Local holiday: July 26.

Hotels Glomar, F (shower extra), friendly, safe, may be closed Sun. p.m., owner (Filio) will change dollars; Salón Carlos, F, with breakfast, share shower; Pensión Cortés, S of Parque Central, G, basic. Pensión Urbina, G, basic; Hospedaje Aguirre, G. On the road to Honduran border, Cosigüina, 50 rooms, 2 restaurants, shops, cinema and discothèque.

Restaurants Corona de Oro, Chinese, 1½ blocks E of Parque Central, Tel.: 3511; Central Palace, same street; Caprax Pizza, one block E of Parque Central.

Banks National banks.

Post Office in new building opp. Caprax Pizza.

A road runs NE to Puerto Morazán. This passes through the village of El Viejo (US$0.05 by bus from Chinandega, 5 km.) where there is an ancient church. (Restaurant: El Retoño, on main street, N of market; bars close to market.) Puerto Morazán (hotel), 26 km. from Chinandega (bus at 1030 and 1600, 1½ hrs., US$0.05), is a modern town on a navigable river running into the Gulf of Fonseca. From Chinandega there is a bus at 1400 daily to Potosí, at least 3 hrs., US$0.10 (return 0330). Comedor Adela, 24-hr. service, cheap. You can sling your hammock in the comedor 150 metres past immigration for US$0.15. Ask Héctor for permission to stay in the fishing cooperative. The fishermen are very friendly. Although the passenger ferry from Potosí to La Unión (El Salvador) has been suspended, you can take a cargo launch for US$4, 4 hrs. (be prepared for sun, spray and serious overloading). Entering Nicaragua from La Unión takes about ½ hr.; travellers are not usually asked to change US$60 into córdobas here. Apparently launches also go from Puerto Morazán, 5-6 hrs. It is a 4-hour hike to the cone of Cosigüina volcano. On January 23, 1835, one of the biggest eruptions in history blew off most of the cone, reducing it from 3,000 metres to its present height of 870 metres. Michael Tesch and Leone Thiele of Cape Paterson, Australia, tell us: There are beautiful views of the lake inside the cone and over the islands of Honduras and El Salvador. There is plenty of wildlife in the area, including poisonous snakes, so take a machete. There are pleasant black sand beaches; the sea, although the colour of café con leche, is clean. In the centre of the village are warm thermal springs in which the population relaxes each afternoon. From Chinandega a paved road goes to the Honduran border at Somotillo, on the Río Guasaule, where it is continued by an equally good road to Choluteca, Honduras. **N.B.** The bridge over the Río Guasaule was washed away in floods in May 1982 and the bridge over the Río Negro was destroyed by guerrillas in the same year. The border here was closed at the time of going to press (1987).

Jiquilillo beach, 42 km. from Chinandega, is reached by a mostly-paved road branching off the El Viejo-Potosí road. It lies on a long peninsula; small restaurants (e.g. Fany) and lodgings.

Corinto, 21 km. from Chinandega, is the main port of entry, and the only port at which vessels of any considerable size can berth. About 60% of the country's commerce passes through it. The town itself is on a sandy island, Punto Icaco, connected with the mainland by long railway and road bridges. Population: 10,000. On the Corinto-Chinandega road is Paseo Cavallo beach (Restaurante Buen Vecino).

Hotels Costa Azul; Restaurant Imperial on Calle Mario Izaguirre has double rooms, G.

Managua to Granada There are two routes, one by rail and one by a very good 61 km. paved road with a fast and comfortable bus service; both run through Masaya.

Santiago Volcano The entrance to Masaya National Park is at km. 23. The road is paved up to the crater (6 km.). Taxi from Managua to top of volcano, US$7 return. The volcano is double-crested, but half (Masaya) is dormant. The other crater (Santiago) is spectacular and best seen at dawn or twilight (which means arriving before opening time, or staying in the park after closing time): colourful rock dropping 60 metres to the lava plug with steaming red hot vents and encrustations of multi-coloured sulphur (latest reports say there is only smoke now). Many squawking green parakeets dive and wheel in and out of the sulphurous clouds emitted by the crater. The best view of the crater itself is from the far side, opposite the approach road. Do not walk on the lava cinders or go down the crater, unless you have strong boots and climbing experience. There is a beautiful picnic area half-way up. Take something to drink. There is no public transport, although you can alight from the Managua-Masaya bus at Km. 23, from where hitch-hiking is easy, especially at weekends. Park rangers pick up stragglers after 1700; they may also give you a lift up before 0900. Luggage may be left at the gate lodge safely; open at 0800, closed at 1630 Tues.-Fri., 0900-1630 Sat. and Sun.; closed all day Mon. Cars have to pay US$1 to get in; pedestrians 1 centavo.

Masaya (population 38,000), 30 km. SE of Managua, is the centre of a rich agricultural area growing tobacco. Small Laguna de Masaya (at the foot of Masaya volcano), and Santiago volcano are near the town. Interesting Indian handicrafts and a gorgeous *fiesta* on September 30, for its patron, San Jerónimo. (Indian dances and local costumes.) The market (Sunday at railway station) is reportedly commercialized now. There is a new Centro de Artesanías, near the hospital and overlooking Laguna de Masaya; big selection, high quality. The best place for Indian craft work is Monimbo, and 15 minutes from Masaya is Villa Nindirí, which has a rich museum and an old church with some even older images. A branch railway runs SW to Jinotepe and Diriamba in the small highland between the two lakes. The town suffered severely in the civil wars of 1978-79.

Hotels *Motel El Nido*, D, expensive, not too good. *Victoria*, G; *Rex*, G, dark, dirty but friendly, near the church; *Cailagua* (Km. 29.5, Carretera a Granada), clean, F, good, reasonably priced. *Pensiones* are hard to find, and dirty when you've found them.

Restaurants *El Jade*, near 2nd market, good Chinese food. *Alegría*, nr. main square, good, expensive; *El Arabe* at station; *Mini 16*, W end of town, nr. hospital.

Transport from Managua, 3 trains daily, Managua-Masaya, 1½ hrs. (0800, 1300, 1800, return 3½ hours later); trains to Jinotepe (Mon., 1415, Tues., 1300, return Tues., 0405, Wed. 0425, 2½ hrs.); train to León at 0600, US$0.05, time of arrival is anyone's guess; by car to Managua, ½ hr.; taxi, US$2.85; bus every 10 mins., US$0.03; bus and train to Granada, US$0.07. Entering Masaya by bus, do not wait for the end of the line as there are no hotels near the market terminal.

Excursions Just outside Masaya, on the road from Managua, is an old fortress, Coyotepe, also called La Fortillera. It was once a torture centre, and is now deserted, eerie "with a Marie Celeste feel to it".

To Niquinohomo, Sandino's birthplace. James N. Maas writes: Take a bus from Masaya (or Granada) to San Juan de Oriente, a colonial village with an interesting school of pottery (products are for sale). It is a short walk to neighbouring Catarina, and a 1 km. walk uphill to El Mirador, with a wonderful view of Laguna de Apoyo (good for weekend visits; get out of bus at Km. 38 on Managua-Granada road, walk 1½ hrs. or hitch—easy at weekends), Granada and Volcán Mombacho in the distance. Follow the Jinotepe branch railway down to Masaya.

For Masaya volcano, take the Masaya-Granada bus, get off at the entrance, from where it is 1 hr. 15 mins. to the volcano.

Another 18 km. by road (bus, US$0.05) and rail is

Granada, on Lake Nicaragua, the terminus of the railway from the port of Corinto (190 km.). It is the third city of the republic, with a population of 45,200, and was founded by Hernández de Córdoba in 1524 at the foot of Mombacho volcano. The rich city was three times attacked by British and French pirates coming up the San Juan and Escalante rivers, and much of old Granada was burnt by filibuster William Walker in 1856, but it still has many beautiful buildings and has faithfully preserved its Castilian traditions. The Cathedral has been rebuilt in neo-classical style; also of interest are the church of La Merced (1781-3), the church of Jalteva in the outskirts, and the fortress-church of San Francisco: its Chapel of María Auxiliadora, where Las Casas, Apostle of the Indies, often preached, is hung with Indian lace and needlework. Granada is more traditional than León: horse-drawn cabs for hire (bargain over the price), many oxcarts and a fine cemetery. The lake beach is popular, but a little dirty; marimba bands stroll the

NICARAGUA

beach and play a song for you for a small charge. Roads to Managua (61 km.), Diriamba and Nandaime. Launches to the islands on the lake leave from a pier about 2 km. from the city centre (taxi, US$0.10). Take the road along the lake shore from Guadalupe church. Launches cost US$10 for 30 mins., but that is for the launch, which can carry 15 or 20 people, so find a group (arrive early in the morning). The island vegetation is unusual and different, so are the Indian idols found there on display in the Instituto Nacional del Oriente, next door to the San Francisco church. (The Instituto is a school; teachers will open the door for you.) Worth visiting.

Fiestas Holy Week: Assumption of the Virgin, August 14-30; and Christmas (masked and costumed mummers).

Hotels *Granada*, Calle La Calzada (opp. Guadalupe church), B, new, luxury, swimming pool, a/c, breakfast only served, very good, only US$ accepted, Tel.: 2974; *Alhambra*, Parque Central, Tel.: 2035, pleasant, comfortable rooms with bath, B (dollars only), large restaurant serves good food, often has good, live music, parked cars guarded by nightwatchman. *Pensión Cabrera*, Calle Calzada, E with bath, G without, clean, meals available, pleasant; opposite and of same standard is *Pensión Vargas*, G, basic. These three hotels are on the road from the main square to the wharf. *Pensión Cigarro*, G (short stay, thieves). There is a shortage of hotels and restaurants in Granada.

Restaurants *Pingüín*, good, expensive; *Drive Inn El Ancla*, opp. *Hotel Granada*, clean; *Restaurant Asia*, good steaks, and Chinese food, expensive (Tel.: 2969); *El Sombrero*, Calle del Comercio, Tel.: 2876; *Interamericano*, road to Masaya next to Esso, clean, dear. *La Cabaña Amarilla*, on lakeshore. *Chupi's Ice Cream Parlour*. A tourist complex on the lakeside (S of Plaza España) includes restaurants and bars. 1 km. further along the beach are 3 restaurants which have launch trips for US$2.50 p.p. for an hour to some of the islands. Good breakfasts at the market.

Bus Buses leave from an area 200 metres beyond the market. Many fast minibuses to Managua, US$0.05, 1 hr. (these do not stop in Masaya). Bus to Nandaime, US$0.08. Bus to Masaya, US$0.05, 15 mins. Express bus to Rivas, 1130, 1½ hrs., US$0.50, other, slower buses every ½ hr., US$0.16. To Costa Rican border: if you ask around the Cathedral you may find someone to drive you to the border for US$10-note, taxis are not allowed out of town. Sirca Bus from Granada or Masaya to San José twice a week (Tues., Thurs.) 0600.

Rail To Managua, via Masaya, 3 a day, US$0.15, journey times vary from 1hr. 25 mins., to 2 hrs. 5 mins.; ½-¾ hr. to Masaya, US$0.07.

Lake Nicaragua, the "Gran Lago", 148 km. long by 55 at its widest, is a fresh-water lake abounding in salt-water fish, including sharks, which swim up the San Juan river from the sea and later return. Terrapins can be seen sunning themselves on the rocks and there are many interesting birds. There are about 310 small islands, Las Isletas, which can be visited either by hired boats or motor launches, from *La Cabaña Amarilla*, about 3 km. along the beach from Granada, for US$1 p.p. for 1½ hrs. Alternatively, take the morning bus from Granada to Puerto de Aseses (pleasant restaurant with fine view) and hire a rowing boat for US$1.50 per day. (No buses back p.m. though.) People live on most of the Isletas. Most of the Indian idols in the Instituto Nacional del Oriente come from one of two larger islands: the Isla Zapatera (Cobbler's Island).

The largest island, Ometepe (population 20,000), has two volcanoes, one of them a perfect cone rising to 1,610 metres. There are two villages on the island— **Moyogalpa** (population 4,500) and Alta Gracia, which are connected by bus (1 hr. US$0.60). Boat from Granada to Alta Gracia, US$1, 4½ rough hrs., the public service is on Tues., at 1000; returning the following day. Moyogalpa is pleasanter than Alta Gracia which has several unnamed *hospedajes* of varying quality); *Pensión Ali* and *Pensión Moyogalpa*, both G, recommended, cheap (latter best but noisy). Cheaper, *Pensión Jade*. Cock-fights in Moyogalpa on Sunday afternoons. One can stroll to the base of Volcán Concepción for good views of the lake and the company of howler monkeys (*congos*).

Moyogalpa can be reached from **San Jorge** on the lake's SW shore (boats at 1100 and 1700, returning at 0700 and 1400, schedules can be checked at the Tourist Board in Managua, US$1). From San Jorge a road runs through Rivas (bus service every 10 mins., US$0.03, 30 mins.) to the port of San Juan del Sur. The Río San Juan, running through deep jungles, drains the lake from the eastern end into the Caribbean at San Juan del Norte. Launches ply down the river irregularly from the lakeside town of **San Carlos** (1,500 people, not a pleasant place) at the SE corner of the Lake. Several boats run from Granada to San Carlos: three slow passenger/cargo boats leave on Mon., Wed. and Fri. at 1400, taking 15-20 hrs.; they start the return journey next day. Fare is US$2.50 (plus US$1.20 for a hammock— be early; tickets from near the pier). Two fast boats leave Granada on Mon., Wed. and Fri. at 1200, 8 hrs. returning next day at 1800, costing US$13 (a noisy trip, anything left on deck will get wet). Tickets must be bought from the office by *Hotel Granada*, open at 0800 but be there earlier. The slower boats stop at San Miguelito (one primitive *pensión*). On Mon. a launch leaves Granada at 1200 for Punta Pato, Monito and San Miguelito, arriving at 1630 and leaving for San Carlos Tues. 0600, arrives 0700. Leaves for Granada via above ports at 1000

1130 NICARAGUA

(Tues.); fare US$8.50. Take your own food and a hammock if you want to get some sleep. (Bus Granada-San Miguelito, Mon., Tues., Wed., Thurs. 0830 from the pier, 8 hrs.) At San Carlos (*Restaurant Río San Juan*, good meals, rooms for rent, G, dirty, noisy; also *San Carlos* and 2 more *pensiones*; vacancies hard to find; parallel market exchange in some stores, one bank) are the ruins of a fortress built for defence against pirates. Some 6 hrs. down river (9 hrs. back, US$0.25) are the ruins of another Spanish fort, Castillo Viejo (*Pensión Merlot*, G, no sign). This is the furthest point down the Río San Juan that non-military travellers are allowed to go. Boats also run from San Carlos to the Solentiname Islands in the Lake. A special permit is required to visit this area, see page 1135. The only hotel on the islands is *Hotel Isla Solentiname*, on San Fernando island, safe, acceptable but basic (you wash in the lake), cost including meals D (at official rate); on Mancarrón island, the largest, is a library and an interesting church. Ernesto Cardenal (the poet and Minister of Education) lived and worked here. The islands are home to many primitive painters and are pleasant to hike around.

About 40 km. S of San Carlos, on the Río Frío, is Los Chiles, over the border in Costa Rica (see also page 1151). No foreigners are allowed into this area.

Warning The lake is not only shark-infested but dirty, even contaminated in some places, so do not swim in it. Swimming is possible in nearby Laguna de Apoyo (see page 1128).

By Pan-American Highway from Managua to Costa Rica: 148 km.; bus services all the way to San José of Costa Rica. The road, in good condition, runs into the Sierra de Managua, reaching 900 metres at Casa Colorada, 26 km. from Managua. Further on, at El Crucero, a paved branch road goes through the Sierra S to the Pacific bathing beaches of **Masachapa,** a popular playground of Managuans. Hotels: *Summer*, F; *Teraza*, F; *Rex*, G (all serve meals). Masachapa is very crowded and noisy at weekends. The Highway continues through the beautiful scenery of the Sierras to

Diriamba, 42 km. from Managua, at 760 metres, in a coffee-growing district. Population 26,500. Hotel: *Diriangén*, G with bath. Good fish at restaurant *2 de Junio*. Its great *fiesta* is on January 20. There is a 32-km. dirt road direct to Masachapa (no buses), and another NE to Masaya, on the Managua-Granada highway. Being on a through route, it is impossible to get on buses to Managua or Rivas. Five km. beyond Diriamba is

Jinotepe, capital of the coffee-growing district of Carazo, is joined by railway with Diriamba and Masaya. It has a fine neo-classical church with modern stained glass windows from Irún, in Spain. The *fiesta* in honour of St. James the Greater is on July 24-26. Altitude 760 metres; population 17,600; hotel, *Imperial*; local holiday, July 25.

From **Nandaime,** 21 km. from Jinotepe, altitude 130 metres, a paved road runs N to Granada (bus US$0.06). Nandaime has two interesting churches, El Calvario and La Parroquia (1859-72). About 45 km. beyond Nandaime (US$0.10 by bus) is

Rivas, a town of 21,000 people. The Costa Rican national hero, the drummer Juan Santamaría, sacrificed his life here in 1856 when setting fire to a building captured by the filibuster William Walker and his men. The town has a lovely old church. (In the dome of the Basilica, see the fresco of the sea battle against the ships of Protestantism and Communism.) Rivas is a good stopping place (rather than Managua) if in transit by land through Nicaragua. The road from the lake port of San Jorge joins this road at Rivas; 11 km. beyond Rivas, at La Virgen on the shore of Lake Nicaragua, it branches S to San Juan del Sur. Buses to the frontier: every 2 hrs.: 0545 and 0700 good for connections for buses to San José (US$0.05, 1 hr.) (taxis available, about US$2). Bus to Managua, from 0400 (last one 1700), 3 hrs., US$0.20; taxi, US$20. One fast bus to Granada, US$0.50; other, slower buses, frequent. Regular bus to San Jorge on Lake Nicaragua (taxi to San Jorge, US$0.10).

Hotels *Hospedaje Delicia*, on main Managua-border road, G, basic and dirty, friendly; *Pensión Dalia*; *Nicaragua*, on street behind bank on main square, F, clean, well-equipped, hot water, good restaurant (cinema next door); *Pensión Primavera*, F, basic; *El Coco*, G near where bus from frontier stops; *Hospedaje El Mesón*, basic; several on Highway, *Hospedaje Lidia*, near Texaco, G, clean, unfriendly, service not too good. *Restaurant Chop Suey* on Parque Central.

NICARAGUA 1131

San Juan del Sur is 34 km. from Rivas (regular minibus from market, crowded, 45 mins., US$0.05), 93 from Granada. There are roads from Managua (a 2½-hr. drive) and Granada. Population 4,750. It has a beautiful bay with a sandy beach and some rocky caves reached by walking round the point past the harbour. Best beaches (Playa del Coco, Playa del Tamarindo) are 15 km. away on the road to Ostional, but ask the local authorities if they are safe to visit (*Contra* activity). Sunsets here have to be seen to be believed. Check tides with officials at the Customs Office, who will give permission to park motor-caravans and trailers on the wharves if you ask them nicely.

These vehicles may also be parked on Marsella beach, about 5 km. from San Juan; coming S, turn right on entering San Juan, by shrimp-packing plant.

Hotels *Estrella*, on Pacific, F, with balconies overlooking the sea, breakfast extra, partitioned walls, toilet facilities outside, rooms must be shared as they fill up; *Irazú*, one block from beach, some rooms with bath, very run down; *Buengusto*, opposite, F. *Hospedaje Casa No. 28*, 40 metres from beach, near minibus stop for Rivas, G p.p., shared showers, TV lounge, kitchen and laundry facilities, clean. 2 other *casas de huéspedes* near market.

Restaurant *Salón Siria*, good. *Soya*, vegetarian, good and cheap. AMNLAE (national women's organization) has a good vegetarian restaurant, one block from beach; good *panadería* on same street. Good cafés along the beach for breakfast and drinks. Food in the evening from a stall in street running W from the market; good fish restaurant at N end of bay beyond the river.

Post Office   2 blocks S along the front from *Hotel Estrella*.

The road reaches the Costa Rican boundary at Peñas Blancas, 37 km. beyond Rivas (no gasoline for sale between border and Rivas; no hotels at the border). It is easy to exchange money on the Costa Rican side of the border, which is closed from 1300-1400 and 1800-0800. Duty-free shop on each side of border. It is 3½-4 hrs. by bus to Managua, 4 to San José, but through journeys are longer because of slow border formalities (last bus to Liberia, 1715). You must walk or hitch the 4 km. from the Nicaraguan to the Costa Rican border posts (avoid early morning and evening, though, because of *Contra* activity at these times). To avoid the walk, take a Sirca bus although the queues are longer when they pass through; if not on a Sirca bus, arrive at border before 0800 to miss the queues. This border presents no problems for motorists, but remember that it is compulsory to buy insurance in Costa Rica (see page 1163).

The Caribbean Coast has more rain than the Pacific coast. Its economy is based on the export of bananas, cocoa, mahogany, black walnut, rosewood, and other high-class timbers. There are gold mines in the interior.

Warning *In the border area with Honduras there has been much fighting; tourists are advised not to go there. In any event, permits are needed; see page* 1135.

This area, together with about half the coastal area of Honduras, was a British Protectorate from 1780 to 1885, and was known as the Miskito kingdom. It was populated then, as now, by Miskito Indians, but today there is a predominance of African blood. They still speak English and in spite of hispanic influence at school and elsewhere, they maintain their special way of life. (Protestant missions played a most important role in the making of Bluefields and are still significant in the social *organization of the* town, where there is a Protestant cathedral.)

Bluefields, the most important of Nicaragua's 3 Caribbean ports, gets its name from the Dutch pirate Bleuwveldt. It stands behind the Bluff at the mouth of the Bluefields river (Río Escondido), which is navigable as far as Rama (96 km.). From Rama an improved highway runs through Santo Tomás (*Hotel Rosaura* and two others, F, good food at *Rosaura*) and Juigalpa to Managua, 290 km. away. Bananas, cabinet woods, frozen fish, shrimps and lobsters are main exports. Population 17,700. Flights with state airline Aeronica from Managua (1 hr.) on Sat., returning Wed., US$27.50 (double-check bookings made in Managua for this flight). For a free lift on a military plane, book ahead at Consejo Militar. It used to be possible to get to San Andrés, a Colombian island in the Caribbean, but Nicaragua is now disputing its ownership with Colombia: boats there are now very infrequent, there are no air services, and the customs officials are not always willing to give an exit stamp.

1132 NICARAGUA

N.B. To visit Bluefields, the Corn Islands and the Atlantic Coast, a permit is required in Managua. See page 1135.

From Managua to Bluefields Take a bus from Managua to **Rama** along the now-completed road (in poor condition near Rama). Minibus, several companies (e.g. Cotrán, on Carretera Norte), US$0.60, 8½ hrs. They leave from Mercado Huembes terminal. (There is an express bus to Rama which leaves at 0500, 5 hrs., US$0.70, which connects with the express boat to Bluefields.) Or take your car and park it in the compound at the Chinaman's store (opposite *Hotel Amy*) for US$0.30 a day. Buses back to Managua leave Rama from 0300 onwards (tourist bus, US$0.40, minibuses, same price, but quicker). *Hotel Amy* (F and good, inexpensive food), near main jetty. *Hotel Lee Cor*, G, noisy, sometimes no water, has good, reasonably priced restaurant; *Pensión Rama*, G, no water or electricity but very good food. There is a boat daily (1000, 6 hrs.) down the Escondido river to Bluefields, and an express or *rápido* at 0545 (returning 1000), which costs US$5, 3-4 hrs. (tickets can be bought between *Hotel Amy* and the wharf); take your own food and drink.

Hotels at Bluefields: *Cueto*, E-C (reserve rooms with a/c), good; *Veneral*, F; *El Dorado*, F, good; *Crowdell*, F; *San Cristóbal*, E; *Cheque*, F, with bath, good value; *Hollywood*, opp. *Cueto*, G, clean, reasonable, basic; *Dipp*, G, cheap, popular, but no running water and plenty of cockroaches and rats; several decrepit *pensiones* on street leading to market. *Hospedaje Urbina*, G, basic. *Darío*; *Pensión Sylvia G.*, unsavoury. There is a *pensión* next to *Darío*, above shoe shop, G. *El Velero*, hotel upstairs, F, clean, friendly, good seafood restaurant below on main street. Several other good seafood restaurants. All hotels are full on Fri., Sat. and Sun.; try in Barrio Fátima for an *hospedaje* (dirty and noisy). Water is scarce in afternoons and evenings.

Consulate Colombian Vice-Consulate just up the road from *Hospedaje Hollywood*.

Cables Tropical Radio; Radio Nacional.

Corn Islands (Islas del Maíz), in the Caribbean opposite Bluefields, are two small beautiful islands fringed with white coral and slender coconut trees. The larger is a popular Nicaraguan holiday resort; its surfing and bathing facilities make the island ideal for tourists (best months March and April). For fishing (barracuda, etc.), contact Ernie Jenkie (about US$5/hour). If you climb the mountain, wear long trousers, as there are many ticks. The language of the islands is English. Empresa Nacional de Cabotajes (ENCAB) boat from Bluefields to the Corn Islands leaves Weds. 0800 (ticket must be bought on Tuesday), returning Thurs.; journey takes 5 hrs., can be rough. Cargo boats sail on an irregular basis. It is possible to hitch a lift on a fishing boat, usually from El Bluff; you have to ask for "The Company". Air services twice a week, US$7.50, book well in advance and book return immediately on arrival. Also, check your reservation continually; there is a waiting list and your chances depend on the size of the plane (either 22- or 26-seater). Return flights to Bluefields at 0930, continuing to Managua, US$28; timetable seems to change weekly, so check. Local industries: coconut oil, lobsters, and shrimp-freezing plants.

Hotels and Restaurants *Isleño*, Government-owned, beach huts D, or C with breakfast and dinner, good food. More expensive is *Hotel Morgan*, B, with bath, including full board (less with fewer meals), at North End; hotel above Mr. Morgan's store is best value at F (opp. entrance to fish factory). *Residencia Bryan*, D, with shower, in same area; *Hotel de la Punta*, F; *Hotel Coco Playa*, F, not recommended; one can find rooms for about US$2 (recommended is Miss Florence's house—*Casa Blanca*—at Playa Coco). The chief problem in all the hotels is rats, which may not be dangerous, but neither are they pleasant to see. Miss Maree's house, near airstrip, for good food. Sally Beaches, US$1 per meal. Doña Quita's *comedor* on the quay. Good restaurant next to *Coco Playa*. Ask around for where meals are available. Try banana porridge and sorrel drink (red, and ginger-flavoured). Disco opp. airport office; also *Artistas*, nicer.

The best beach for swimming is Long Beach on Long Bay; walk across the island from Playa Coco.

Boat every 2 days from Bluefields to Laguna de las Perlas, US$2, 5 hrs.; express boat from Rama Wed., Fri., 0700, return same day, one hotel (F), clean, new, no electricity; ask at the only 2-storey house for meals. Boats from Rama en route to La Cruz de Río Grande on Sat., return Mon., stop at Laguna de las Perlas.

From El Bluff, on the headland opposite Bluefields (regular boats from market, US$1, 15 mins.), you can hitch a lift on a fishing boat to Monkey Point and from there another to Cocal. From Cocal it is about 30 km. to **San Juan del Norte,** a small village of 400 inhabitants who live from fishing and coconut-growing. From San Juan it is possible to go up the river of the same name to Lake Nicaragua or cross lagoons to a sandbar in Costa Rica. From this bar it is a 2-hr. walk to where canoes go to Barra del Colorado, Costa Rica—a further hour's journey—(see page 1151). **N.B.** Owing to cross-border fighting between government forces and anti-Sandinista *Contras* based in Costa Rica, this area (including San Juan del Norte) is at present out of bounds to foreigners.

Puerto Cabezas (Bragman's Bluff), is N of the Río Grande. Population: 11,850. There are air services 3 days a week to Managua (US$32). The Standard Fruit Company and Nipco have guest-houses for business visitors. Boats from Rama sail to Puerto Cabezas, and S to Monkey Point, Punta Gorda and Atlanta (Río Maíz) with no fixed schedule. Two trucks a day to Waspam, ask anyone for details of times.

Hotels and Restaurants *Costeño*, cheap, but filthy toilets, permanent water shortage; *Hospedaje Carutón*, F, friendly, serves breakfast; one block away from the bus stop and Anglican Church. There are at least three Chinese restaurants: *Tung Moi* is the best.

Note that there has been guerrilla activity in the Nicaraguan Misquitia; communications with the Honduran side are now closed.

2 flights weekly (usually cargo) connecting Waspam and Puerto Cabezas with Managua; Mon., Wed., US$32.70. Also service to Siuna and Bonanza. For notes on Honduran Misquitia, see page 1111.

Accommodation in the Misquitia is sometimes a problem as there are few facilities for the tourist. In villages, and as a last resort in the town, the Baptist, Moravian and Catholic US missionaries and local clergy are very helpful to stranded travellers.

The Economy

Nicaragua's economy showed a fairly stable annual growth rate over the two decades up to 1977, despite sharp fluctuations from year to year as agricultural production and world commodity prices varied. The economy is based on agriculture, principal export items being cotton, coffee, sugar, beef, seafood and bananas. The Government is encouraging a diversification of exports, and exports of tobacco and other agricultural products are gaining in importance. At present agriculture constitutes 24% of gdp but employs 48% of the economically active population and is responsible for by far the largest proportion of exports. Land reform has been actively undertaken by the Sandinistas; in 1987, 16,000 families were expecting to receive land. In the 1970s however, substantial industrialization developed, mainly through foreign investment. Main industries are food processing (sugar, meat, shrimps), textiles, wood, chemical and mineral products. There are few mineral resources in Nicaragua: although gold, copper and silver are mined, they are of little importance to the overall economy.

Since the late 1970s gdp growth rates have ranged from the extremes of −29% in 1979 to +10% in 1980. The huge variations have been caused by guerrilla insurgency, fluctuations in Central American Common Market trade, floods, drought and changing commodity prices. Growth has usually been led by agriculture when weather, international prices and political conditions have been favourable.

Inflation, which had been traditionally low, has been a problem since the 1972 earthquake; the rate shot up by 84.3% in 1979 as a result of the civil war, moderating to an average of 30% in 1980-84. As an effect of insurgency and *other difficulties, the rate shot up* to an estimated 300% in 1985 and 800% in 1986. Nicaragua is dependent upon foreign aid, which has averaged US$600m a year since 1980, of which the USSR is believed to have granted nearly half. There have been no new investment projects for several years and consumption fell by 42% in 1984-86. The government aims to manage carefully the distribution and rationing of scarce resources and increase production and productivity, but while the country is at war, inflation and other economic problems will continue and the black market will persist. Nicaragua's foreign debt, including arrears, amounts to some US$5bn, but reduced foreign exchange earnings in the mid-1980s (partly because of the US blockade) made it impossible for the government to service the debt.

	1961-70 (av)	1971-80 (av)	1981-85 (av)	1986 (e)
Gdp growth (1980 prices)	6.9%	1.1%	1.2%	−0.4%
Inflation		17.8% (a)	54.4%	778.0%

1134 **NICARAGUA**

Exports (fob) US$m	133	436	434	216
Cotton	46	99	112 (b)	-
Meat	12	46	28 (b)	-
Coffee	22	105	133 (b)	-
Imports (fob) US$m	130	468	803	850
Current account balance US$m (cum)	-280	-976	-2,441	-690

(a) = 1973-80
(b) = 1981-84

Information for Visitors

Air Services From London: British Airways or Pan Am to Miami and connect to Taca for Managua, via San Salvador; Taca also flies from Houston, New Orleans and Los Angeles; Sahsa flies from these destinations (except Los Angeles), but via Tegucigalpa. Aeronica flies to Mexico City direct, San Salvador, San José and Panama City; Taca to Guatemala City, Belize City, San José, Mexico City, Panama as well as San Salvador; Sahsa, in addition to Tegucigalpa, flies to Belize, and Copa flies to Guatemala City, San José, San Salvador and Panama. From Europe, with Iberia to Managua on Tues., or connect with KLM in Panama City. Aeroflot and Cubana (once a week) fly to Havana, and Aeroflot continues via Shannon to Moscow. Aeronica flies from Managua to Puerto Cabezas, Bluefields and the gold-mining centres of Siuna and Bonanza; also to the Corn Islands. All flight tickets purchased by non-residents must be paid in US dollars.

All passengers have to pay a sales tax of 12% on all tickets issued in and paid for in Nicaragua; a transport tax of 1% on all tickets issued in Nicaragua to any destination; a consular fee of US$1.50 from all passengers who arrive, and an airport tax of US$11 on all departing passengers (except on Aeroflot and Cubana flights).

By Sea There are good shipping services from the United Kingdom to Cristóbal (14 to 16 days), including those of the PSNC and Royal Mail Lines (no passengers). The port of Corinto, on the Pacific Coast, is served by vessels from Cristóbal, and also from San Francisco and Los Angeles.

Both the Royal Netherlands Steamship Company and the local Mamenic Line run monthly services from Europe to San Juan del Sur, Corinto or Puerto Sandino: the former from Amsterdam and the latter from Antwerp. The Mamenic Line also serves most other central and north American ports.

Documents Visitors must have a passport with 6 months validity (at least), and proof of US$300 (or equivalent in córdobas) in cash or cheques for their stay in the country (according to the Nicaraguan Consulate in London—but see below). No visa is required by nationals of Central American countries, USA, Belgium, Denmark, Liechtenstein, Luxembourg, Netherlands, Norway, Spain, Sweden, Switzerland or the United Kingdom for a 90-day stay. Citizens of all other countries need a visa. A visa, which should be bought before arriving at the border, is valid for arrival within 30 days, and for a stay of up to 30 days (90 days if working in an International Brigade); it costs US$25; 6 months validity on passport, 2 passport photographs and an onward ticket are required. Visas can take 24 hrs. to be processed. Extensions are difficult to obtain. W. Germans can obtain visas (DM 70) from Generalkonsulät von Nicaragua, 2 Hamburg, P.O. Box 32 33 54, or in Central America. Ensure that your visa runs from the day you enter the country, not from the day of issue: ask the Generalkonsulät to give a written statement, in Spanish, to this effect. Commercial travellers should carry a document from their firm accrediting them as such. Only those visitors who have no tourist cards and require visas for entry need an exit permit. 72-hour transit visas cost US$20, from embassies, or at borders. A transit visa, obtained at a land border, cannot be converted into a full visa within the country. An air ticket can be cashed if not used, especially if issued by a large company, but bus tickets are sometimes difficult to encash. It is reported, however, that the Nicaraguan Embassy in a neighbouring country is empowered to authorize entry without the outward ticket, if the traveller has enough money to buy the ticket. (In Costa Rica, visas for Nicaragua can be obtained in San José, Liberia or Puntarenas.) Also, if you have a visa to visit another Central American country, you are unlikely to be asked to show an outward ticket (this applies to all Central American countries: be two visas ahead!). An exit stamp costing US$10 is required for visitors who have stayed over 30 days in the country.

In 1983, a regulation was introduced stating that all visitors, whether arriving by air or land, *must* change US$60 into córdobas at the official rate; this demand is maybe made on exit as well. If turned back from Honduras (or Costa Rica) for any reason, get your Nicaraguan exit stamp cancelled, not a new entry stamp, otherwise you will have to change another US$60. Motorists and

NICARAGUA

motorcyclists must pay US$20 in cash on arrival at the border; allow plenty of time for border facilities (especially when coming from Honduras)—average is 4 hours—because vehicles not cleared by 1700 are held at customs overnight. Make sure you get all the correct stamps on arrival, or you will encounter all sorts of problems once inside the country. You will also be asked on arrival to show that you have US$200 to cover your stay in Nicaragua. Hotel bills must be paid in dollars (except in the lowest categories and in *hospedajes* outside Managua).

Warning Nicaraguan customs and border formalities can take up to 8 hours (but sometimes much less).

Customs Duty-free import of ½ kg. of tobacco products, 3 litres of alcoholic drinks and 1 large bottle (or 3 small bottles) of perfume is permitted. There is a duty-free shop at the border with Costa Rica.

Much detailed commercial information is given in "Hints to Exporters: Nicaragua", obtainable on application to the Dept. of Trade, Export Services Division, Sanctuary Buildings, 16-20 Great Smith Street, London SW1P 3DB.

Motoring Low octane gasoline costs US$2.60 (at official rates) a US gallon. Cars will be fumigated on entry. For motorcyclists, the wearing of crash helmets is compulsory. Petrol is very cheap, but only available with coupons, which are obtained at INE offices in all cities and at borders (free except in Managua where they cost C$100 per gallon).

Climate and Dress There is a wide range of climates. According to altitude, average annual temperatures vary between 15°C and 35°C. Mid-day temperatures at Managua range from 30° to 36°C, but readings of 38° are not uncommon from March to May, or of 40° in January and February in the West. It can get quite cold, especially after rain, in the Caribbean lowlands. Maximum daily humidity ranges from 90% to 100%. Dress is informal; business men often shed jackets and wear sports shirts, but shorts are never worn. The wearing of trousers is perfectly OK for women. The dry season runs from December to May, and the wettest months are usually June and October. Best time for a business visit: from March to June, but December and January are the pleasantest months.

Warnings Visitors to Nicaragua must carry their passports with them at all times. Border officials do not like army-type clothing on travellers, and will confiscate green or khaki rucksacks (backpacks), boots, parkas, canteens. They also inspect all luggage thoroughly on entering and leaving Nicaragua. Do not photograph any military personnel or installations.

The whole of the Atlantic Coast, the Corn Islands, almost all the Honduran and Costa Rican border zones and the Solentiname Islands are "special regions" (i.e. fighting is possible). To visit them (and this includes the towns of Bluefields, Puerto Cabezas and San Juan del Norte), you must apply to Mar y Sol agency (name above door is "Trapos") Plaza Libertad 12, Managua, although some say you have to apply at Migración in Managua, near the Israel Lewites Market, Km. 7 Carretera del Sur (bus 118); the special permit takes a minimum of 3 days to issue if given at all (sometimes permission for organized tours only is given), costs US$5, payable in dollars only.

The standard form of address is "compañero/-a", rather than "señor/-a".

If you wish to work in Nicaragua (for instance coffee picking), go straight to the place of work; information can be found in the area of Managua west of the *Intercontinental Hotel*, near the old Ticabus terminal.

Internal Transport Hitchhiking is easy (except at night). Local buses are the cheapest in Central America, but are extremely crowded owing to a lack of vehicles and fuel. Baggage that is loaded on to the roof or in the luggage compartment is charged for, usually twice the rate for passengers.

Health The usual tropical precautions about food and drink. Tap water is reasonably safe but avoid uncooked vegetables and peeled fruit. Malaria risk especially in the wet season; take regular prophylaxis.

Food There is still a food shortage in some parts of the country, and it can be difficult to find items such as eggs and rice outside Managua. Sugar and salt are rationed to one packet each per purchase. Many staples (rice, milk, bread) are subsidized. Note the government-owned *Colectivo de Soja* which encourages the use of soya as an alternative source of protein; vegetarian restaurants of this chain in San Juan del Sur, Rivas, Masaya, Managua, León, Granada and Estelí.

Tipping in Nicaragua: 10% of bill in hotels and restaurants (many restaurants add 10% service and 15% tax to bills); C$5 per bag for porters; no tip for taxi drivers.

1136 NICARAGUA

Hours of Business 0800-1200, 1430-1730 or 1800. Banks: 0830-1200, 1400-1600, but 0830-1130 on Sat. Government offices are not normally open in the afternoon.

Standard Time Six hours behind GMT.

Cost of living Imported goods tend to be expensive. There are shortages of various items such as toilet paper, toothepaste and film. A 10% tax is levied on all hotel and restaurant bills, nevertheless, outside Managua, hotel accommodation is extremely cheap.

Currency The unit is the córdoba (C$), divided into 100 centavos. There are notes for 1,000, 500, 100, 50, 20, 10, 5, 2, and 1 córdobas (rare) and coins of 5, 10, 25, 50 centavos, 1 and 5 córdobas (7-sided, with the head of Sandino on the obverse). Some notes and coins have popular names; the córdoba is often known as a *peso*, 25 centavos as a *chollina* or *peseta* and 10 centavos as a *real*. Exchange controls are fairly stringent. The official commercial rate is C$70 to the US$, but there is also an official "casa de cambio" exchange rate, authorized by the Central Bank which in April 1987 was C$900-US$1, and on the free market at the borders higher still (best in Costa Rica); this rate has been used for converting prices in the chapter. However, the state of economic emergency declared in September 1981 has led to tightening up in this area of exchange. The black market for exchange, which is illegal and therefore dangerous, can be found with difficulty in Managua, in Ciudad Jardín, or in Granada. Money changers are called *coyotes* (but some are government officials). It has been reported that dollars exchanged on the black market are destined for the *Contras*.

Remember, when changing money at the border, that in Managua, and in larger hotels outside, bills are in most cases charged in dollars; so do not overstock with córdobas.

Weights and Measures The metric system is official, but in domestic trade local terms are in use; for example, the *medio*, which equals a peck (2 dry gallons), and the *fanega*, of 24 *medios*. These are not used in foreign trade. The principal local weight is the *arroba*=25 lb. and the *quintal* of 101.417 English lb. Random variety of other measures in use include US gallon for petrol, US quart and pint for liquids; *vara* (33 ins.) for short distances and the lb. for certain weights.

Mail By Sea: from the UK to Nicaragua is sent via Panama, and takes 4 to 5 weeks. There are delays in forwarding between the western ports and the interior owing to poor communications. Air-mail from London takes 4 to 6 days. Airmail letters: C$30 per 5 grams; C$50 to Europe; postcard to USA C$20, to Europe C$30. Airmail to Australia C$30. Sea mail: 5 kg., C$250, 8 kg., C$150, must be passed through customs at Telcor building, Managua. Poste restante charges 6 córdobas per letter; mail kept for 1 month.

Telegraph and Telephone lines are owned by the Government. Rather unreliable automatic telephone services between Managua, León, Chinandega and Corinto. Plenty of public telephones in Managua of the Brazilian "big-ear" type. The cable and telegraph companies are given under the towns. There are wireless transmitting stations at Managua, Bluefields and Cabo Gracias a Dios, and private stations at Puerto Cabezas, El Gallo, and Río Grande.

Telephone calls from Managua to Europe: 0700-2100 weekdays, 0800-1100 and 1700-1900 on Sun. (cheaper on Sun.) International phone calls must be paid for in dollars and prices have been increased steeply. You may have to wait a long time for a line.

Telex As with telephones, prices have been greatly increased.

Press Managua: *La Prensa* (anti-government), *Nuevo Diario* (the best—close to government line). *La Barricada*, official organ of the Sandinista Front (has a weekly international edition). León: *El Centroamericano*. *La Gaceta* is the official gazette. *Ya Veremos*, monthly, covering international subjects. *Revista Conservadora* is the best monthly magazine. Other magazines: *Envío* (monthly, English and Spanish editions, Jesuit); *Pensamiento Propio* (current affairs, monthly); *Soberanía* (Nicaraguan affairs, Spanish/English bilingual). *El Pez y la Serpiente* is a monthly magazine devoted to the arts, poetry and literature.

Public Holidays

January 1: New Year's Day.
March or April: Thursday of Holy Week and Good Friday.
May 1: Labour Day.
July 19: Revolution of 1979.
September 14: Battle of San Jacinto.
September 15: Indepedence Day.
November 2: All Souls' Day (Día de los Muertos).
December 25: Christmas Day.

Businesses, shops and restaurants all close for most of Holy Week; many companies also close down during the Christmas-New Year period. Holidays which fall on a Sunday are taken the following Monday. Local holidays are given under the towns.

Broadcasting   There are about 50 radio stations, and 2 television channels of the Sistema Sandinista de Televisión.

We are deeply grateful for updating material to Alexander Daughtry (Vancouver), E.A.Domoney, Carmen Kuczma (Powell River, BC), Keith Mundy (Bangkok), Grace Osakoda (Hawaii), Jerry Rathbone (London NW5), and David Ridges (Caldy, Wirral) for a most valuable contribution, and to travellers listed in the general Central America section.

COSTA RICA

COSTA RICA is the smallest but one—El Salvador—of the Central American republics, and only Panama has fewer inhabitants, but it is known throughout Latin America as the continent's purest democracy. The Army was abolished in 1949, though it should be stressed that there is a very efficient-looking khaki-clad Civil Guard. Costa Rica has the highest standard of living in Central America, the fastest population growth and the greatest degree of economic and social advance. Area, 51,100 square km. Population in 1986 was 2.59 million—a density of 51 to the square kilometre.

Costa Rica lies between Nicaragua and Panama, with coastlines on both the Caribbean (212 km.) and the Pacific (1,016 km.). The distance between sea and sea is from 119 to 282 km. A low, thin line of hills between Lake Nicaragua and the Pacific is prolonged into northern Costa Rica, broadening and rising into high and rugged mountains in the centre and S. The highest peak, Chirripó Grande, SE of the capital, reaches 3,820 metres. Within these highlands are certain structural depressions; one of them, the Meseta Central, is of paramount importance. To the SW this basin is rimmed by the comb of the Cordillera; at the foot of its slopes, inside the basin, are the present capital, San José, and the old capital, Cartago. NE of these cities about 30 km. away, four volcano cones soar from a massive common pedestal. From NW to SE these are Poás (2,704 metres), Barba (2,906 metres), Irazú (3,432 metres), and Turrialba (3,339 metres). Irazú and Poás are intermittently active. Between the Cordillera and the volcanoes is the Meseta Central: an area of 5,200 square km. at an altitude of between 900 and 1,800 metres, where two-thirds of the population live. The north-eastern part of the basin is drained by the Reventazón through turbulent gorges into the Caribbean; the Río Grande drains the western part of it into the Pacific.

There are lowlands on both coasts. The Nicaraguan lowland along the Río San Juan is continued into Costa Rica, wide and sparsely inhabited as far as Puerto Limón. A great deal of this land, particularly near the coast, is swampy; below Puerto Limón the swamps are continued as far as Panama in a narrow belt of lowland between sea and mountain.

The Gulf of Nicoya, on the Pacific side, thrusts some 65 km. inland; its waters separate the mountains of the mainland from the 900-metre high mountains of the narrow Nicoya Peninsula. From a little to the S of the mouth of the Río Grande de Tárcoles, a lowland savanna stretches NW past the port of Puntarenas and along the whole north-eastern shore of the Gulf towards Nicaragua.

Below the Río Grande the savanna is pinched out by mountains, but there are other lowlands to the S. From Puerto Quepos, built by the United Fruit Company (now United Brands), 188 km. of railway run through banana-growing lowlands, which are not now as productive as they were. Small quantities of African palm and cacao are now being grown in these lowlands. In the far S there are swampy lowlands again at the base of the Peninsula of Osa and between the Golfo Dulce and the borders of Panama. Here there are 12,000 hectares planted to bananas;

1138 COSTA RICA

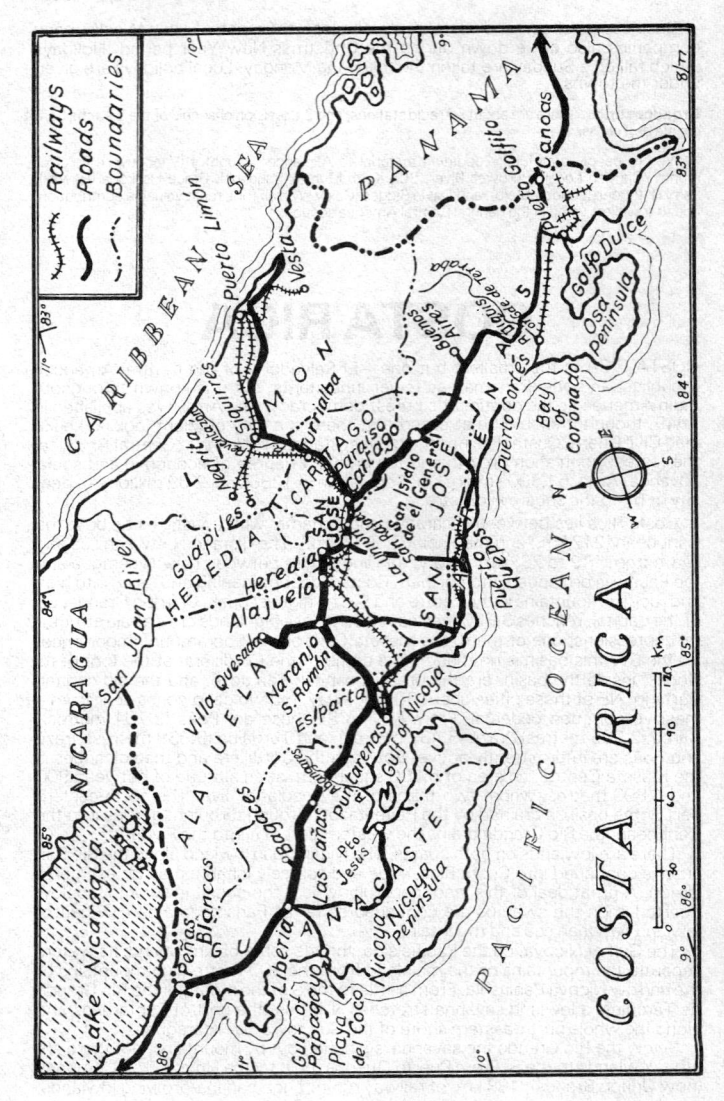

ROUGH SKETCH

COSTA RICA 1139

317 km. of railway run to the United Brands banana port of Golfito. The Río General runs through a southern structural depression almost as large as the Meseta Central; this is now being occupied.

Altitude, as elsewhere in Central America, determines the climate, but the *tierra templada* and the *tierra fría* start at about 300 metres lower on the Pacific than on the Atlantic side. The Pacific side is the drier, with patches of savanna among the deciduous forest; the Atlantic side has heavy rainfall— 300 days a year of it—and is covered far up the slopes with tropical forest: about two-fifths of Costa Rica is forested. On the Cordillera Talamanca, the average temperature is below 16°C.

National Parks Tourists will particularly enjoy the many well-kept and well-guarded national parks and nature reserves which protect some samples of the extraordinarily varied Costa Rican ecosystems. Some of the last patches of dry tropical forest, for instance, can be found in the Santa Rosa National Park, and other parks protect the unique cloud forest.

The first step is to visit the Servicio de Parques Nacionales (SPN) in San José (Calle 17 y Av. 9; write in advance to Apartado 10094, or Tel.: 33-50-55), to get permits if necessary. Persistence may be sometimes needed to get permits, particularly in the case of the Corcovado park, where visitors' facilities are officially considered inadequate. To contact park personnel by radio link, Tel.: 33-54-73.

Bird watchers and butterfly lovers have long flocked to Costa Rica to see some of the 900 species of birds (the whole of the United States counts only about 800 species) and untold varieties of butterflies. All of these can be best seen in the parks, together with monkeys, deer, coyotes, armadillos, anteaters, turtles, coatimundis, raccoons, snakes, wild pigs, and, more rarely, wild cats and tapirs. Bird lists can be purchased from the Organization for Tropical Studies (in San Pedro, near the University; take the "San Pedro" bus from Av. 2 and Calle 1 and get off in San Pedro at the church—on the left—, the OTS is 2 blocks S and 3 blocks E); they will have a breakdown by park. You can also get plant and butterfly lists from them, and other valuable natural history information as well. Good field guides are Petersen, *Birds of Mexico* and *Birds of North America*; Ridgely, *Birds of Panama*; Golden Guide, *Birds of North America*; Daniel H.Janzel, *Costa Rican Natural History*; Philip J. de Vries, *Butterflies of Costa Rica*. Cheap maps and all information for the parks are available at the CIDA office of the SPN in Parque Bolívar (the zoo), Av. 11 just E of Calle 7, open Mon.- Fri., 0800-1530 (on Mon. ask zoo guard to let you in as zoo grounds are closed Mon.). The map annex to the SPN office in San José has all the parks marked in the excellent Instituto Geográfico maps, and the latter can be purchased at various places.

Nature guides can be found at The Bookshop in San José, and there is also available an illustrated book, *The National Parks of Costa Rica*, by Mario A. Boza (1986), which gives a good impression of what the different parks are like. (Descriptions of the individual parks will be found in the text.)

Settlement Costa Rica was discovered in September 1502, during Columbus' last voyage. Rumours of vast gold treasures (which never materialized) led to the name of Costa Rica (the Rich Coast). The Spaniards settled in the Meseta Central, where there were some thousands of sedentary Indian farmers (whose numbers were soon greatly diminished by the diseases brought by the settlers). Cartago was founded in 1563 by Juan Vásquez de Coronado, but there was no expansion until 145 years later, when a small number left Cartago for the valleys of Aserrí and Escazú. They founded Heredia in 1717, and San José in 1737. Alajuela, not far from San José, was founded in 1782. The settlers were growing in numbers but were still poor and raising subsistence crops only. Independence from Spain was declared in 1821 whereupon Costa Rica, with the rest of Central America, immediately became part of Mexico. This led to a civil war, during which, two years later, the capital was moved from Cartago to San José. After independence, the government sought anxiously for some product which could be exported and taxed for revenue. It was found in coffee, introduced from Cuba in 1808, which Costa Rica was the first of the Central American countries to grow. The Government offered free land to coffee growers, thus building up a peasant landowning class. In 1825 there was a trickle of exports, carried on mule-back to the ports. By 1846 there were ox-cart roads to Puntarenas. By 1850 there was a large flow of coffee to overseas markets: it was greatly increased by the opening of a railway from San José and Cartago to Puerto Limón along the valley of the Reventazón in 1890.

From 1850, coffee prosperity began to affect the country profoundly: the birth rate grew, land for coffee was free, and the peasant settlements started

1140 COSTA RICA

spreading, first down the Río Reventazón as far as Turrialba; then up the slopes of the volcanoes, then down the new railway from San José to the old Pacific port of Puntarenas.

Much of the Caribbean coastland, more especially in the N, is still unoccupied. Bananas were first introduced in 1878; Costa Rica was the first Central American republic to grow them. Labour was brought in from Jamaica to clear the forest and work the plantations. The industry grew and in 1913, the peak year, the Caribbean coastlands provided 11 million bunches for export, but the spread of disease lowered the exports progressively. The United Fruit Company then turned its attentions to the Pacific littoral especially in the S around the port of Golfito. However, although some of the Caribbean plantations were turned over to cacao, abacá (Manilla hemp) and African palm, the region has regained its ascendancy over the Pacific littoral as a banana producer (the Standard Fruit Company is an important redeveloper of the region).

On the Pacific coastlands a white minority own the land on the *hacienda* system rejected in the uplands. About 46% of the people are *mestizos*. To the N, most of the country's cattle come from the large estates of the savannas, and timber is exploited along the northern coast. The mountainous Peninsula of Nicoya is an important source of coffee, maize, rice and beans. Its population has risen sharply. Rainfall is moderate: 1,000 to 2,000 mm. a year, but there is a long dry season which makes irrigation important.

Population   In all provinces save Limón over 98% are whites and *mestizos* but in Limón 33.2% are blacks and 3.1% indigenous Indians, of whom only 5,000 survive in the whole country. Although officially protected, the living conditions of the indigenous Indians are very poor. But even in Limón the percentage of blacks is falling: it was 57.1 in 1927. Many of them speak Jamaican English as their native tongue. Some 50% are urban. Population growth rate is 2.6%; urban growth rate 4.6%. Illiteracy, at 10%, is among the lowest in Latin America. Contact with the rural population is easy since the people are friendly and enjoy talking. (The national adjective, *costarricense*, is rather a mouthful: the universal short form is *tico/a*.)

Roads   Costa Rica has a total of 27,494 km. of roads. The route of the Pan-American Highway (now wholly paved) is described on page 1159. A new highway is being built from San José to Caldera, a new port on the Gulf of Nicoya which has replaced Puntarenas as the principal Pacific port, and another has been completed from San José via Guápiles and Siquirres to Puerto Limón. Also a new road is being built to improve access to the Pacific beaches, from Playas de Jacó to Puerto Quepos and Puerto Cortés. All 4-lane roads into San José are toll roads (US$0.03-0.10).

Railways   There are 1,286 km., all of 1.067-metre gauge; 967 km. are plantation lines—336 km. of the Northern Railway and 631 km. of the United Brands Company. The formerly British-owned Northern (Atlantic) Railway has 525 km.: its main line is between Puerto Limón and San José (166 km.), and it has a branch line (21 km.) between San José and Alajuela. The government-owned Ferrocarril Eléctrico al Pacífico between San José and Puntarenas has 132 km. of track; this line has been lengthened by the new branch to Caldera, with Caldera as its western terminus. New track has been laid in the Río Frío banana plantation zone; these trains are electric. Plans exist for electrification of the entire Atlantic railway.

Constitution and Government

Legislative power is vested in a Legislative Assembly of 57 deputies, elected for four years. Executive authority is in the hands of the President, elected for the same term by popular vote. Men and women over 20 have the right to vote. Voting is secret, direct and free. The President (1986-1990) is Sr. Oscar Arias Sánchez of the Liberación Nacional party (Social Democrat).

Main Towns

San José, with a population estimated at over one million, stands in a broad, fertile valley at an altitude of 1,150 metres, which produces coffee and sugarcane. It was founded in 1737 and is a pleasant mixture of traditional Spanish and modern. The climate is excellent, though the evenings can be chilly. The lowest and highest temperatures run from 15° to 26°C. Slight earthquake shocks are frequent. Rainy season: May to November. Other months are dry.

Streets cross one another at right-angles. Avenidas run E-W; the Calles N-S. The three main street are Av. Central, Av. 2 and the intersecting Calle Central:

COSTA RICA 1141

the business centre is here. The best shops are along Av. Central. It is best not to take a car into San José between 0700 and 2000, since traffic is very heavy. Many of the narrow streets are heavily polluted with exhaust fumes.

Avenidas to the N of Av. Central are given odd numbers; those to the S even numbers. Calles to the W of Calle Central are even-numbered; those to the E odd-numbered. The Instituto Costarricense de Turismo has an excellent map of the city, marking all the important sights and business houses. **N.B.** Few buildings have numbers, so find out the nearest cross-street when getting directions (200 metres means 2 blocks).

Sightseeing Many of the most interesting public buildings are near the intersection of Avenida Central and Calle Central. The Teatro Nacional (1897)—marble staircases, statuary, frescoes and foyer decorated in gold with Venetian plate mirrors—is just off Av. Central, on Calle 3 (US$0.75 to look around). Functions (ballet, concerts, etc.) take place most Tuesdays. Closed on Sundays. It has a good coffee bar. Nearby is Plaza de la Cultura, Av. Central, C. 3/5. The Palacio Nacional (Av. Central, Calle 15) is where the Legislative Assembly meets; any visitor can attend the debates. Along Calle Central is Parque Central, with a bandstand in the middle among trees (bands play on Sun. mornings). To the E of the park is the Cathedral; to the N are the Raventos and Palace theatres, interesting; to the S are the Rex Theatre and a branch of the Banco Nacional. N of Av. Central, on Calle 2, is the Unión Club, the principal social centre of the country. Opposite it is the General Post and Telegraph Office. The National Museum, with a good collection of precolumbian antiquities, is the reconstructed Vista Buena barracks, E along Av. Central (open 0830 to 1700; from 0900 on Suns. and holidays; closed Mons.). Two blocks N of it is Parque Nacional, with a grandiloquent bronze monument representing the five Central American republics ousting the filibuster William Walker (see Nicaraguan chapter) and the abolition of slavery in Central America. There is also a statue donated by the Sandinista Government of Nicaragua to the people of Costa Rica. To the N of the park is the National Library.

Still further N is Parque Bolívar, now turned into a recreation area, with zoo (sloths in the trees), entrance, US$0.30. Along Av. 3, to the W of Parque Nacional, are the four gardens of Parque Morazán, with another bandstand at the centre. On Sun. there is an art market here. A little to the NE, Parque España—cool, quiet, and intimate—has for neighbours the Casa Amarilla (Yellow House), seat of the Ministry of Foreign Affairs, and the Edificio Metálico, which houses several of the main schools. In Parque Carrillo opposite the church of La Merced is a huge carved granite ball brought from the archaeological site at Palmar Norte.

The attractive Paseo Colón continues the Av. Central W to the former La Sabana airport (now developed as a sports centre, which is worth visiting) with a colonial-style building with frescoes of Costa Rican life in the Salón Dorado, on the upper floor. Further W is La Sabana, which has the National Stadium, seating 20,000 spectators at (mainly) football matches, basketball, volleyball and tennis courts, a running track, lake and swimming pool.

Local Holiday December 28 to 31. Festivities last from December 18, with dances, horse shows and much confetti-throwing in the crowded streets. Also parades during Easter week in the streets.

Warning Pickpockets are on the increase in San José, especially in the centre, in the market and on buses—the same applies throughout the country; be careful. We have also received reports of travellers (in particular backpackers) being detained or harassed by the police in a drive against illegal immigration, although few explanations are given. You must carry your passport with you at all times and make sure your papers are in order. To report theft: Policia Judicial-Detectives, Av. 6, C. 17/19.

Hotels

	Address	Tel.	US$ Single	Price Double	Range
Alameda	C.12 Av.Ctl	23-63-33	18	22	C
Ambassador‡	C.26 P.Colón	21-81-55	20-45	25-55	A
Amstel*	C.7 Av.1	22-46-22	20-25	25-30	C-B
Aurola Holiday Inn	C.5 Av.5	33-72-33	72-98	92-108	L

1142 COSTA RICA

Balmoral	C.7 Av.Ctl	22-50-22	44	58	A
Bougainvillea‡	Barrio Tournon	33-66-22	23-39	32-42	B
Cariari† ‡	Near Airport	39-00-22	73	87	L
Corobici	Sabana Norte	32-81-22	43	49	A
Don Carlos	C.9 Av.7-9	21-67-07	22	27	C
Gran Hotel Costa Rica	C.3 Av.2	21-40-00	36-39	48-52	A
Diplomat	C.6 Av.Ctl-2	21-81-33	11-13	18-24	D-C
Europa†	C.Ctl Av.3-5	22-12-22	34-97	45-108	B-L
Royal Crown*	C.4 Av.Ctl	22-15-38	32-39	45-52	B-A
Sheraton Herradura‡	Near Airport	39-00-33	57	65	A
Irazú†	La Uruca	32-48-11	45	52	A
La Gran Vía	C.3 Av.Ctl	22-77-37	20	24	C
Posada Pegasus‡	S.Antonio de Escazú	28-41-96	14-17	15-19	D
Plaza	C.2 Av.Ctl	22-55-33	18	22	C
President	C.7-9 Av.Ctl	22-30-22	19-29	24-34	C-B
Talamanca	C.8-10 Av.2	33-50-33	18	22	C
Torremolinos‡	C.40 Av.5	22-52-66	48	54	A
Tennis Club	Sabana Sur	32-12-66	20-38	24-38	C-B
Apartotels (With kitchen, etc.)					
Apartotel San José	C.17 Av.2	22-04-55	25	30	C
Apartotel Los Yoses‡	Los Yoses	55-00-33	23-60	41-67	B-A
Apartotel Conquistador‡	Los Yoses	25-30-22	23	27	C
Apartotel Castilla‡	C.24 Av.2-4	22-21-13	23-25	30-40	B
Apartotel Lamm§	San José	21-47-20	26-51	29-56	C-A
Apartotel Ramgo‡	Sabana Sur	32-38-23	25-30	30-35	B
Apartotel Napoleon‡	C.40 Av.5	23-32-52	25-28	30-33	B
Gran Hotel Costa Rica Anexo	C.9 Av.1	21-72-72	365 per month		
Los Chalets‡	Montalegre, San Rafael de Escazú	28-18-06	20	20	C

* Food recommended, book in advance †Swimming pool
‡ Out of town § 10% discount given for monthly stays

These rates are per day, without food. Others include: *Príncipe*, C. Central/2, Av. 6, Tel.: 22-79-83, E, friendly, clean; the *Gran Hotel Costa Rica* has been reported as incredibly noisy, but otherwise recommended. The *Ambassador* is recommended, clean, modern, TV and phone in rooms, travel agency next door, restaurants and cinemas opposite. The *Herradura Sheraton*, on the other hand, has had some unfavourable reports.

Cocori, C. 16, Av. 3, Tel.: 33-47-87, D with bath; *Boruca*, C. 14, Av. 1/3, Tel.: 23-00-16, E without bath, restaurant; *Bristol*, C. Central 2133, Tel.: 22-08-49, E with bath; *Capital*, C. 4, Av. 3/5, Tel.: 21-84-97, E with bath, phone, hot water; *Chorotega*, C. 29, Av. 2, Tel.: 25-21-55, E with bath; *De Montaña Atravia*, C. 11, Av. 6, Tel.: 22-68-22, C with bath and 3 meals; *Fortuna*, C. 2/4, Av. 6, Tel.: 23-41-90, C-B with bath, phone; *Pensión Canadá*, C. 9, Av. 3/5, Tel.: 21-67-07, D with bath and breakfast, clean, comfortable, convenient; *Los Angeles*, C. 10/12, Av. 12, Tel.: 22-84-09, E without bath; *Vista Palace*, C. 25, Av. 8/10, Tel.: 23-32-38, D with bath. *Park*, C. 2/4, Av. 4, B, clean, with bar (Tel.: 21-69-44); *Ritz*, C. Central, Av. 8 and 10, Tel.: 224103, D with bath and hot water, friendly, manager helpful, good breakfast, clothes washing facilities, 2nd-hand book exchange, recommended; *Pensión Centro Continental*, Av. 8-10, C. Central (Tel.: 33-17-31), F, Japanese hospitality, clean, friendly, laundry, helpful, coffee available, highly recommended; *Terminal*, C. 12, Av. 3/5 (Tel.: 22-54-25), F, with bath. *Galilea*, Av. Central, C. 13 (Tel.: 22-69-56), C, hot water, English spoken, friendly, comfortable; *Canadá*, 5 Av. and C. 6, F, recommended; Tel.: 22-86-07, hot showers (but in the red light district); *Colón*, C. 8, Av. 5-7, (Tel.: 23-88-58), F, with bath, no hot water, cheaper rates for stays over 1 week; *Roma*, C. 14, Av. Central and 1, Tel.: 23-21-79, uphill from Alajuela bus station, E, clean, safe, good value but windowless rooms; *Boston*, C. Central, Av. 8 (Tel.: 21-05-63), E, with or without bath, good, but noisy; *Centroamericano*, Av. 2, C. 6/8 (Tel.: 21-33-62), restaurant, E, very clean, hot water, very noisy; *Johnson*, C. 8, Av. Central (Tel.: 23-76-33), D; *Napoleón*, C. 6, No. 339 (Tel.: 21-06-94), E, bath, friendly, cockroaches, free safe parking for motorcycles; *Residencial Balboa*, Av. 10, C.6, F, safe, cold shower thin walls, basic, cheap; *Pensiones* are: *Araica*, Av. 2 No. 1125, Tel.: 22-52-33, F without bath, clean, dark, thin walls, friendly; *Americana*, C.4, Av. 7, F, clean, safe, poor water supply; *Bonilla*, C 7 No. 653, Tel.: 22-43-74, C with bath; *California Inn*, C.27, Av. No. 1039, Tel.: 21-73-78, E; *La Unica*, C. 8, Av. 3/5, Tel.: 22-02-84, F no bath; *Melva*, C. Central/2, Tel.: 22-48-57, C with bath, laundry included; same at *Reforma Hilton*, C. 11, 20, No. 105, Tel.: 21-97-05, restaurant, and *Moreno*, C. 12, Av. 6-8, Tel.: 21-71-36, both E with bath. *Costa Rica Inn*, C. 9, Av. 1/3, Tel.: 22-52-03, D, without breakfast, safe to leave luggage; *Morazán*, C. 9/11, Av. 3, Tel.: 21-90-83, E; *Astoria*, Av. 7, No. 749, Tel.: 21-21-74, F, clean, hot showers, uncomfortable beds, thin walls, noisy; *Villa Blanca*, Av. 7 between C. 2 and C. 4, F, noisy but friendly; *Poás*, Av. 5, Calles 3-5, F, friendly, hot water, laundry facilities, soda attached; *Illimani*, near Tica Bus terminal, C. 9/11, Av. 2, Tel.: 22-06-07, F, friendly, will change money; *Managua*, C. 8, Av. 1/3, F, small rooms, cold showers, friendly; *Musoc*, C. 16, Av. 3/5 (Tel.: 22-94-37), E, with private bath (F without), very clean, hot

COSTA RICA 1143

water, luggage stored, near to (and somewhat noisy because of) bus stations, but recommended (popular with Peace Corps); *Bella Vista*, Av. Central, C. 19 (Tel.: 23-00-95), E without bath, also rooms with bath, TV, D; *Asia*, C. 11 No. 63N (between Avs. Central and 1), Tel.: 23-38-93, F, clean, friendly, but paper-thin walls, lots of noise from rapid turnover, hot showers, Chinese-run, English spoken; *América*, Av. 7, C. 4, F, clean, good value; *Corobicí*, Av. 1, between C. 10 and 12, F, clean, cold showers; *Pensión Otoya*, C. Central, Av. 5-7 (Tel.: 21-39-25) F, pleasant, popular with foreigners, English spoken; *Pensión Familiar* (also called *Hotel Delca*), Av. 6, C. 6-8), F, bath, clean, good value; *Pensión Niza*, Av. Central No. 4043, Tel.: 21-22-30, E, in need of renovation; *Rialto*, Av. 5 and C. 2, F, bath, clean, hot water, noisy, good value; *Nuevo Hotel Rialto*, Av. 1, C. 8/10, E with bath; *Jomalu*, Av. 5, C. 10-12, F; *Gran París*, Av. 1, C. 12, F; *Nicaragua*, Av. 2, No. 1167, F, clean, friendly, safe to leave luggage, partitioned rooms, near Tica Bus station; *San José*, C. 14 and Av. 5, E, with shower, clean, friendly, near bus station; *Pensión Palma*, Av. 6, C. 11/13, F, basic, opp. Tico Times office, near Tica Bus station; *Ticalinda No. 1*, Av. 2, No. 553, F, friendly, noisy, little privacy, cheap laundry, good information, "gringo" place, often full; *Ticalinda No. 2*, C. 1, No. 858, Avs. 8 and 10, G, shared rooms, quieter but no food (neither is signed); *Moderno*, C. 8, Avs. 1 and 3, opposite market, G; *Lincoln*, C. 6 between Avs. 10 and 12, Tel.: 22-27-31, F, clean, friendly, with hot water, recommended, free transport to Tica Bus station. *El Faro*, Av. 3, C. 8, No. 153, is central, F, noisy, but clean and friendly, the food is reasonable; *Pensión Salamanca*, C. 9/11, Av. 2, Tel.: 23-16-05, F. There are several new hotels near the various markets, such as the *España*, Av. 3/5, C. 8, F, run by a Spanish family; *Comerciante* annex (C. 10, Av. 3/5) and *Valencia* (C. 8, Av. 1, Tel.: 21-33-47, in F range) which are quite clean. Cheaper hotels usually have only wooden partitions for walls, so they are noisy. Also, they usually only rent by the hour. E.g.: *La Rivense*, C. 10, Av. 6/8, with bath, not very good, *Sevilla*, C. 12, Av. 6/8 (Tel.: 21-76-61), no bath, *Tokio*, C. 6/8, Av. 6, (Tel.: 22-15-37), no bath, *Unión*, C. 10, Av. 3, (Tel.: 23-11-32), with bath, all F. *Toruma Youth Hostel*, Av. Central between Calles 29 and 33, spacious, kitchen, clean, recommended, hot water not always available, F p.p. more expensive for those who do not hold International Student Identity Card (which can be purchased here); music, free for guests, on Fri. and Sat. nights; a good place for meeting other travellers to arrange group travel (ask for Fred Morris, editor of *Meso America* journal. Students are taken in as guests in private houses at low rates.

Electric Current 110, 60 cycles, A.C.; (U.S. flat-pin plugs).

Campsites A few km. S on Pan-American Highway, 1 km. S of Tres Ríos.

Restaurants Apart from the hotels, the best ones are the *Bastille*, French type, on Paseo Colón; *L'Escargot*, also French, on Av. 5; 2 further good French restaurants are *Le Mirage*, Ed. Metropolitano, Av. 2 (Tel.: 22-22-82), expensive, and *Ile de France*, C. 7, Av. Central and 2 (Tel.: 22-42-41), both have good French chefs; next door is *La Hacienda Steak House*, expensive but good; *Los Anonos*, in Escazú area, grills; *Las Cascadas de Pavas*, 3 km. from centre, very good. *El Chalet Suizo*, poor service and value. Others are: *Ana* (Italian food), recommended; *La Nonnina*, Av. 1, C. 2/4; and *Soda Palace* Av.2, C.2, (good breakfasts). *Café Mallorquina*, C. 9, is good and cheap; so is *El Caudil. Corona de Oro. Plaza de España*. Av. 3, excellent value midday meals; *Comedor* beneath "Dorado" sign, C. 8, Av. 4-6, very cheap; *Las Condes*, Av. Central/1, C. 11, inexpensive; *Café H.B.*, C.2, Av. 5 for breakfast; *Lido Bar*, C.2, Av. 3., for *casado*. A good Chinese retaurant is *Kuang Chaou* on C. 11 between Av. Central and Av. 2; another is *Fortuna*, Av. 6, C. 2/4; yet another is *Lung Mun* on Av. 1, between C. 5 and 7, reasonably priced. Also recommended, *Kung Fu*, Av. 5, C. 1. *Fu Su Lu*, C. 7, Av. 2, Chinese, Korean, very good; *Tin Hao*, Av. 10, C. 4, Tel.: 21-11-63, Chinese, good; *Young*, opp. *Hotel Lincoln* (C.6, Av. 10-12), Chinese; *Morazán*, near park of same name, cheap; *La Crêperie*, good (but no *crêpes*), corner of 2 Av. and 6 C.; *La Flecha*, Centro Colón Building, Paseo Colón, superb. The following are recommended: *La Casa de los Mariscos*, Los Yoses; *Italiano*, Carretera a Sabanilla, 1 block N. of Av. Central; *Goya*, Av. 1, C. 5/7, Spanish food (in the centre); *La Mazorca*, in San Pedro, near University of Costa Rica (Rodrigo Facio site), vegetarian and health foods; in same area, *Chi-Chi's*, Tex-Mex; *Macrobiótica*, C. 2, Av. 3/5, vegetarian and take-away. *Casa de España*, in Bank of America, C. 1, good lunches; *Gourmet*, C. Central, Av. 3/5, lunches US$2, good value, menu changes daily; also at *El Escorial*, Av. 1; nearby *Sina*, good Tico food. *Masia de Triquell*, Av. 2, Calle 38/40, Barra 1, Catalan, warmly recommended.

Piccolo Roma, Av. 2, Calle 24, highly recommended; *Churrería Manolo*, Av. Central, C Central and 2, good sandwiches and hot chocolate; *Los Lechones*, Av. 6, C. 11 and 13, good food, live music Fri. and Sat., reasonable prices; *Castro*, C. Central, Av. 12, economical; *La Perla* (name on doormat), C. Central y Av. 2, 24 hr., recommended; *El Balcón de Europa* (Italian, good), also *Alpino* and *Italia*; *Los Yoses*, drive in; *Dos Pinos Auto Soda*, drive in (C. 21 and Av. 12) has gigantic banana splits made from pasteurized ice-cream, and large hamburgers; another good drive-in "Soda" is *Tapia* (Mercado Central, C. 6 and 8, Av. Central and 1); *Finisterre*, Av. Central, reasonable, cheap food; *MacDonald's*, Av. Central, C. 4, near Banco Central, opp. Plaza de la Cultura, and in Sabana, and Guadalupe, also for hamburgers; *Kentucky Fried Chicken*, Paseo Colón, Calle 32, also Av. 2, C. 6, and Av. 3, C. 2, and Los Yoses, Av. Central; *Pollo Obay*, Av. 10, 6 C., good fried chicken; *Antojitos*, on Paseo Colón and Centro Comercial Cocorí (road to suburb of San Pedro), serves excellent Mexican food at moderate prices; *La Fánega*, in San Pedro, for excellent hamburgers, folk music some nights; *Orléans*, also in San Pedro, serves crêpes; *Arturo's*, C. 5 between Av. 1 and Central, American-style bar; *Key Largo*, Av. 3, C. 7, is a friendly bar with live music; *El Prado*, C. 8,

1144 COSTA RICA

Av. 3-5, good cheap breakfasts; *El Floridito*, Av. 1, just E of post office, good, clean, inexpensive, excellent breakfasts; *Mr. Pizza*, Av. 1, C. 7/9; *Pizzalegre*, Av. 1, C. 1/3, reasonable (but note tax and service charges added); *Pizza Hut*, Escazú, *Omni* (Av. 1, C. 3/5), Barrio California (Av. Central), Paseo Colón and Av. Central, C. 4, US$3; *Pizza Expresso*, has vegetarian pizzas; *Don Taco*, Av. 1, C. 2, Mexican food in MacDonald's style; *Billy Boy*, Av. Central, snacks; *Pops*, near Banco Central, and other outlets, for ice cream (excellent); also for ice cream *Mölnpik*, Av. Central, C. Central; *Soda Central* on C. Central, good local dishes; *Soda Familiar*, C. 8, Av. 4 and 6, very cheap and good; *Soda Coliseo*, Av. 3, C.10/12, next to Alajuela bus station, recommended; *Soda Amon*, C.7, Av. 7/9, good, cheap *casados*; *Soda Nini*, Av. 3, C. 2/4, cheap; *La Geishita*, C. Central, Av. 14, cheap *casado*; *Soda Maly*, Av. 4, C. 2/4, Chinese and *tico*, good; *Las Cuartetes*, 2 C., 1 block N of Post Office, excellent pastries and expresso; *Heladería Italiano*, excellent ice cream; *El ABC*, Av. Central between Calles 11 and 9, self-service, good, clean, cheap; *Salón París*, Av. 3, C.1/3, recommended; *La Tranquera* (parking space) on the highway to Cartago at Curridabat, 6-8 km. E of San José, serves good steaks and other foods (orchestra for dancing at weekends). On N side of old La Sabana airport on Av. 3 and about C. 50 are two good restaurants, *El Chicote* (country-style; good grills) and *El Molino*. *La Selecta* bakeries recommended. *Café del Teatro*, reasonably priced, *belle époque* interior, popular meeting place for poets and writers. Restaurants are decidedly expensive in San José; the budget traveller is advised to stick to the bars W of C. 8, *i.e.* in even-numbered Calles with a number larger than 8. Food bars in restaurants in the Mercado Central (C.6/8) are good for breakfast and lunch, high standards of sanitation. At lunchtime cheaper restaurants offer a set meal called a *casado*, US$1-1.50, which is good value; e.g. in the snack bars in the *Galería* complex, Av. Central-2, C. 5-7. Try *Chicharronera Nacional*, Av. 1, C.10/12, very popular, or *Popular*, Av. 3, C.6/8, good *casado*.

Bars Quiet places to have a drink include *Arturo's Bar*, C. 5, Av. Central and 1. *El Cuartel de la Boca del Monte*, Av. 1, C.21-23, recommended, nice atmosphere; *Ye Pub* (C. Central, Av. 7, Tel.: 220337)—almost a genuine English pub!

Shopping Market on Av. Central, Calles 6/8, open 0630-1800 (Sun. 0630-1200), good leather suitcases, wood and leather rocking chairs (which dismantle for export). Mercado Borbón, Avs. 3/5, Calles 8/10, fruit and vegetables in abundance. More and more *artesanía* shops are opening, e.g. Mercanapi (C. 11, Av. 1) and Mercado Nacional de Artesanía (C. 11, Av. 4), and others on Av. Central, C. 1 and 3. La Casona, a market of small *artesanía* shops, Av. Central-1, C. Central. In Moravia (8 km. from centre) El Caballo Blanco and H.H.H. are good for leather work. Coffee is good value and has an excellent flavour (although the best quality is exported). Automercados are good supermarkets in several locations (e.g. C.3, Av. 3). Cosiña de Lena, new shopping centre (good regional food available).

Bookshops The Bookshop, Av. 1, Calle 1 and 3, good selection of English language books (double US prices), also in Pavas, opp. new American Embassy under construction; Universal, Av. Central, Calles Central and 1, for Spanish books and maps. Lehmann, Av. Central and C. 3, maps, Spanish, a few English and German books; Librería Italiana/Francesa, C. 3, Av. Central/1, English, French, Italian books; Staufer, nr. Centro Comercial, Los Yoses, also in San Rafael de Escazú and Plaza del Sol shopping mall in Curridabat, English and German books; Apple, Barrio California; Airport shop; Casey's, C. Central between Av. 7 and 9, second-hand books (English only), good.

Photography 1 hr. colour processing available at all IFSA (Kodak) branches (15% discount for ISTC cardholders). Fuji processing in 1 hr. at Universal stores. Minor camera repairs undertaken. Film prices are similar to Europe.

Fares Bus fares in San José: large buses: US$0.10, small: US$0.15 from the centre outwards. Hand baggage in reasonable quantities is not charged, but no trunks of any kind are taken.

Taxis Usual fares US$0.50-2; very difficult to get taxis in afternoon rush hour. Beware of overcharging. Cabs now have electronic meters (called "Marías"); make sure they are used. Hiring a taxi for a full day (0700-1800) costs US$80, for half a day (to 1330), US$60 (cheaper than taking a tour). Cooperativo taxis recommended.

Car Rentals Prices generally US$16-18 with US$0.20 per km. Free mileage rates about US$60-80 per day. Avis, C. 38, Av. 7 (Tel.: 21-65-69); Budget, C. 30, Paseo Colón (Tel.: 23-32-84); Dollar, C. Central, Av. 9 (Tel.: 33-33-39); National, C. 38, Paseo Colón (Tel.: 33-44-06); Ada, C. 4, Av. 4/6 (Tel.: 22-79-29). All the above also at the Airport. Rent-a-Jeep, C. 38/40, Paseo Colón (Tel.: 21-22-31); Poas Rent-a-Car, C. 26/28, Paseo Colón (Tel.: 23-42-49); Rentacar, *Balmoral Hotel* (Tel.: 21-71-16), not recommended, cars badly maintained. Hertz, Paseo Colón, C. 30 (Tel.: 21-18-18); Continental Rent-a-Car, Barrio Mexico (Tel.: 23-39-63); Elegante Rent-a-Car, Av. 5-7, C. 24 (Tel.: 22-89-20). Check *Tico Times* for special offers and free km. with Nissan 120/Toyota Starlet compacts.

Ask for special rates with unlimited mileage; reservations must be made abroad (much cheaper if reservation made in North America). No car is of very good quality; check your vehicle carefully as the rental company will try to claim for the smallest of "damages". You must have public liability

COSTA RICA 1145

insurance (US$350-1,000 always at the owner's risk). Cars are not very powerful so you may have difficulties climbing steep gradients.

Night Clubs, one at the *Hotel Balmoral, Grill La Orquídea; Les Moustaches* in Centro Colón, Paseo Colón, C. 38, expensive. Many restaurants and bars with varying styles of music at El Pueblo centre on road to San Francisco (take "Calle Blancos" bus from C. 1, Av. 5-7, alight 500 m. after river); also 3 discos here, *Cocoloco, Infinito* and *La Plaza* (very luxurious and expensive). *Le Club* is considered to be the liveliest night spot. Discos in the centre: *Kamakiri*, on the way to Tibas; *Top One* (U.S. rock music); *La Rueda* (for the over 30's). Other nice, less expensive dance spots downtown: *El Túnel del Tiempo, Talamanca* and *Disco Salsa 54*. Night spots W of Calle 8 are in the red light district. Topless clubs between Avs. 4 and 10 on C. 2, none open before 2200; check drinks prices before ordering. *La Copucha*, C. 9, Av. Central-2 has good, live folk music on Fri. nights.

Theatres All are closed on Monday. Teatro Carpa, outdoor, alternative; plays, films, C. 9, opp. Parque Morazán. Teatro Tiempo (also called Sala Arlequín), C. 13 between Av. 2 and Central. Compañía Nacional de Teatro. Teatro del Angel, Av. Central, between C. 13 and 15. Teatro Nacional, Av. 2, C. 3/5, behind it is La Plaza de la Cultura, a large complex. 3 modern dance companies. All good.

Cinemas Sala Garbo, Av. 2 at C. 28 (high-quality foreign films). Many excellent modern cinemas showing latest releases from Hollywood. Prices, US$1.30.

Swimming Pools The best is at Ojo de Agua, 5 minutes from the airport, 15 minutes from San José. It is open up to 1700 hours; direct bus from Parque Carrillo, Av. 2, C. 14, US$0.65 or take bus to Alajuela via San Antonio de Belén. There is also a pool in La Sabana (at western end of Paseo Colón), entrance US$3, open 1200-1400, about 2 km. from the city centre. Open air pool at Plaza González Víquez (south-eastern section of city).

Museums Museo Nacional, Calle 17, Av. Central and 2, very interesting, open Tues.-Sat., 0830-1630, Sun. and holidays, 0900-1630; replicas of precolumbian jewellery may be bought at reasonable prices (entrance, US$0.20). Gold Museum in the Plaza de la Cultura complex adjoining the Teatro Nacional, Av. Central, C.3/5, excellent, open Mon.-Fri., 0800-1100, free 1½-hr., bilingual guided tour available (get ticket in advance); Museo de Arte Costarricense at the end of Paseo Colón, Calle 42, in La Sabana park in the old airport building (Tues.-Sun. 1000-1630, US$0.20). In the INS building, Av. 7, C. 9/ 11, is the Jade Museum on the 11th floor (open 0900-1500, Mon.-Fri.), with jade carvings, very interesting, a "must", and a beautiful view over the city. Museo de Ciencias Naturales, Colegio La Salle, Mon.-Fri., 0730-1500; Sat., 0730-1200, US$0.10 (in the grounds of the Ministry of Agriculture; take "Estadio Sabana" bus from Av. 2, C.2/ Central to the gate). Entomology Museum, in School of Agronomy of the University of Costa Rica, Wed.-Thurs. 1300-1800, only museum of its kind in Central America. Museo Criminológico, 2nd floor, Supreme Court Building, Av. 6, C. 17-19, Mon., Wed., Fri., 1300-1700, "pretty grisly"; Museo de Entomología in Agronomy Faculty of University, Carretera a Sabanilla, Wed., Thur., 1300-1800, many beautiful insects.

Zoo There is a pleasant small zoo in Parque Simón Bolívar (Av. 11, just E of C.7), near INS building. Entrance US$0.40, open 0830-1530, Tues.-Fri., 0900-1600, Sat. Go down C. 11 about 3 blocks from Av. 7.

Banks Opening times: Mon.-Fri., 0900-1500 Banco Nacional, head office, Av. 3, C. 2/4; office in Plaza de la Cultura for changing dollars on weekdays and at weekends (0900-1500, Sat., 0900-1300, Sun. and holidays); Banco de Costa Rica, Av. Central, C. 4., changes travellers' cheques for colones and for dollars, but must present a ticket out of Costa Rica—take passport. Banco de San José, C. Central, Av. 3-5. Money can be sent through Banco de San José or Banco de Costa Rica at 4 % commission. Banco Anglo Costarricense, Av. 2 near Teatro Nacional, very good service for *travellers' cheques* and *Mastercharge*. Credit card (Visa, Mastercharge) holders can obtain cash advances from Banco de San José in colones or US dollars; minimum cash advance: US$50, maximum US$500. Banco Crédito Agrícola de Cartago, S side Parque Central, also makes advances on Visa, no limits. Since August 1986, banks may charge whatever commission they please on foreign exchange transactions and other services: shop around for the best deal. Dollars are available at banks and hotels (for guests only), but a commission is payable when cashing any cheque and there is a maximum limit of US$50-worth (much paperwork and at least 1-hr. wait involved); you have to show your ticket out of the country and the dollars can only be obtained when you are leaving). All *casas de cambio* have been closed down, and exchange transactions on the street are now illegal.

Embassies and Consulates *British*, Centro Colón, 11th floor, end of Paseo Colón with C. 38 (Apartado 10056), Tel.: 21-55-66 (also serves Nicaragua); *West German*, Av. 3 and Calle 36, Aptdo 4017; *Swiss*, Paseo Colón, Centro Colón, 4th floor, Calles 34/36, Tel.: 21-48-29; *Canada*, Av. Central, C. 3, Cronos Building, 6th floor, Aptdo 10303 (Tel.: 23-04-46); *U.S.A.* Av. 3, C. 1, 2nd floor, Tel.: 22-55-66, open Mon.-Fri. 0800-1130, 1230-1500 (a new embassy is under construction in the western suburb of Pavas—the consulate will remain at present address), on July 4, U.S.

1146　COSTA RICA

ambassador's home hosts the American Legion of Costa Rica's annual party: all U.S. citizens welcome (bring passport); *Colombian*, corner Av. 5 and C. 5, La Viña building, 2nd floor, Tel.: 21-07-25 (Mon.-Fri. 0800-1230) issues free tourist cards for Colombia, but onward ticket must be shown and 2 photos provided. *Venezuela*, 1 block S of Automercado de Yoses (on Av. Central, C.35/37), consulate open Mon.-Fri. 0900-1230, Tel.: 25-13-35, visa takes 48 hrs.; *French*, Curridabat, 200 metres S, 25 metres W of Indor Club, Tel.: 25-07-33. *Belgium*, C. 35-37, Av. 3, Tel.: 25-62-55; *Holland*, Av. 2, Edif. Metropolitano, 7th floor, Tel.: 22-73-55; *Italy*, C. 29, Av. 8-10, Tel.: 25-20-87; *Spain*, Paseo Colón, C. 30, Tel.: 21-19-33; *Japan*, Bo. Rohrmoser, Tel.: 32-12-55. *Nicaraguan*, Av. Central, Calles C.25-27, Mon.-Fri., 24-hr. wait for visa (better in Liberia or Puntarenas); *El Salvador*, Los Yoses, opposite Venezuelan Embassy; *Guatemala* (Embassy and Consulate), Centro Comercial, Guadalupe, closes at 1200, Tel.: 33-52-83, visa given on the spot, US$10 (dollars only); *Panama*, La Granja (100 metres S of Banco Popular), San Pedro district (Tel.: 25-34-01); *Honduras*, Av. 5, C. 1, Tel.: 22-21-45; *Mexico*, Consulate, Av. 7, C. 15, open 0800-1000, 1400-1500; *Ecuador*, Av. 5, C. 1, Tel.: 23-62-81; *Brazil*, Av. Central-1, C. 4, Tel.: 23-43-25.

Immigration Irazemi Building, C. 21, Av. 6-8; you need to go here for exit visas, extensions, etc. (or a travel agent can obtain them).

Churches Protestant: The Good Shepherd, Av. 4, Calles 3-5 (Anglican), Union Church, Moravia; bus service to downtown hotels Sun. a.m., times and locations given in Friday *Tico Times*. Services in English. International Baptist Church, in San Pedro, 150 metres from Banco Anglo Costarricense corner, English services at 0900 on Sun. Roman Catholic services in English at *Sheraton Herradura* Hotel, 1600 every Sun. Centro de los Amigos para la Paz, Quaker, English books, US periodicals, information, Tel.: 21-03-02.

Libraries Centro Cultural Costarricense Norteamericano (Calle Negritos—good films, plays, art exhibitions and English-language library), University of Costa Rica (in San Pedro suburb), and National Library (opp. Parque Nacional; has art and photography exhibitions), all entry free. Alianza Franco Costarricense, Av. 7, C. 5, French newspapers, French films every Thursday evening, friendly.

Language Schools Conversa, Apartado No: 17, Centro Colón (Tel.: 21-76-49), 12 monthly programmes. Centro Cultural Costarricense Norteamericano, C. Negritos, Tel.: 25-93-47; Instituto Lengua Española, San Francisco suburb, Tel.: 26-92-22. Instituto de Idiomas, Av. 3, C. 3-5, Edif. Victoria, piso 3, Tel.: 23-96-62, Spanish lessons and lodging with Costa Rican families. Intensa, C. 33, Av. 5-7, Barrio Escalante, Tel.: 25-60-09, P.O. Box 8110, 1000 San José.

British School San Pedro, Av. Central, C. 33 (Tel.: 34-22-66).

Post Office Av. 1 and 3, C. 2.

Cables Internal, from main post office, abroad from Compañía Radiográfica Internacional de Costa Rica, Av. 5, C. 1, 0730-1000, collect calls available from special booths.

Hospitals and Inoculations Social Security Hospitals have good reputations (free to social security members, few members of staff speak English), free ambulance service run by volunteers: Dr Calderón Guardia (Tel.: 22-41-33), San Juan de Dios (Tel.: 22-01-66), México (Tel.: 32-61-22). The Clínica Bíblica C. 1, Av. 14, (Tel.: 23-64-22) and Americana (C. Central-1, Av. 14 (Tel.: 22-10-10) have been recommended; both offer 24-hr. emergency service at reasonable charges and have staff who speak English; better than the large hospitals, where queues are long. Bíblica also has addresses for emergencies it cannot handle. Free malaria pills at office on C. 16, Av. 8/6.

Dentist Clínica Dental Dr. Francisco Cordero Guilarte, Tel.: 323645, Sabana Oeste, opposite Colegio La Salle. Take bus marked Sabana Estadio. Dra. Fresia Hidalgo, corner C. 10, Av. 15, 1400-1800, English spoken, reasonable prices, recommended (Tel.: 22-16-53).

Laundromat General Dry Cleaning y Lavandería, Av. Central and C. 11-13. Sixoala, branches throughout San José. 2-hr. dry cleaning available.

Travel Agencies Swiss Travel Service, *Hotel Corobici*, Tel.: (506) 31-40-55, P.O. Box 7-1970, with branches in Hotels *Sheraton*, *Irazú*, *Amstel* and *Balmoral*, large agency, good guides, much cruise business, railway excursions, warmly recommended. Tikal, Av. 2, C. 7-9, Tel.: 23-28-11, recommended. Panorama Tours, C. 9, Av. Central/1, P.O. Box 7323, Greyhound agent; Blanco Travel Service, Av. Central, C. 7/9, P.O. Box 4559; Viajes Rodan, Calle 1, 75 yards (*varas*) S of American Embassy. French-speaking owner. American Express, TAM, only open Mon.-Fri., Edif. Alde, 2nd floor, Calle 1, Av. Central/1, good service. Costa Rican Expeditions, Av. 3, C. Central/2, offer tropical forest adventure tours, white water rafting, etc., rent camping equipment (P.O. Box 6941), Tel.: 23-99-75; Mundo Acuático, 200 metres N of *Mas X Menos*, San Pedro, rents snorkelling gear. Tursa, *Gran Hotel Costa Rica*, Tel.: 336194/214000, all types of tour offered; Cosmos Tours, German-speaking owner.

COSTA RICA 1147

Tourist Office Instituto Costarricense de Turismo, information office: below Plaza de la Cultura, C. 5, Av. Central/2, Tel.: 23-1733, ext. 277, and 22-1090 (Mon.-Sat. 0900-1700, closed Sun.). Also at Juan Santamaría airport (very helpful) and borders. Head office is at Av. 4, C. 3/5 (open at 0900). Excellent service. Free guide: *Gran Pequeño Guía de San José*, good. An4099R Otec, youth and student travel office and cheap lodgings, Edif. Victoria, 2nd floor, Av. 3, C. 3-5, Tel.: 22-08-66, for ISTC and FIYTO members (has discount booklet for shops, hotels, restaurants; also good fares on Aeronica). The Instituto Geográfico, Av. 20, C. 9/11 at Ministry of Public Works and Transport, supplies very good topographical maps for walkers (which can easily be bought at Librerías Universal and Lehmann). The national park service (SPN, office: Calle 17, Av. 9) can provide very interesting material on the flora and fauna of the parks, brochure with descriptions and how to reach the parks, US$0.50 from its CIDA information office in the zoo grounds at the N end of Av. 11 (see page 1139). American Express office has good, free maps of San José. **N.B.** It is much cheaper to take tours aimed at the local rather than the tourist market.

Airports The Juan Santamaría international airport is at El Coco, 16 km. from San José by motorway (5 km. from Alajuela). Taxi US$7-8, or minibus from Av. 2, C. 10/12, or Av. 2, C. 12/14, every 10 mins., US$0.30, or by Alajuela bus via the motorway from C. 14, Av. 5 and 7. Taxis Unidos run a colectivo for US$1-2 each. Sansa runs its own bus service to the airport. If catching an early flight it is a good idea to stay in Alajuela, taxis run all night from the main square to the airport. Bank at the airport open 0800-1600; at other times try car rental desks, or the restaurant cash desk. Light aircraft use the Tobias Bolaños airport at Pavas, about 5 km. W of San José.

Airlines Addresses (and telephone numbers) of major airlines: Copa, Av. 5, C. 1-3 (23-70-33); SAM, Av. 5, C. 1-3 (33-30-66), and in Escazú; Lacsa, Av. 5, C. 1 (31-00-33); Challenge International, next door, Av. C. 1, Av. 5 (22-11-66); Aeronica, Av. 2, C. 1-3 (23-02-26); Sansa, Paseo Colón (21-94-14); Sahsa, Av. C. 1-3 (21-55-61); Taca, Av. 3, C. 1 (22-17-90); Mexicana, Av. 2-4, C. 1 (22-17-11); Varig, Av. 1, C. 2 (22-47-37); Viasa, Av. 5, C. 1 (23-34-11); TWA, Av. 1-Central, C.2 (22-13-32); Pan Am, Av. 3, C. 5 (21-89-55); Eastern, Paseo Colón, next to *Ambassador Hotel*, C. 26, Tel.: 22-56-55 (to cash an MCO takes 6 weeks, must be sent to Miami); British Airways, Av. 5, C. 1 (23-56-48); British Caledonian, Av. 10, C. 26-28 (22-51-86); Iberia, Av. 2-4, C. 1 (21-33-11); KLM, Av. Central, C. 1 (21-30-81); Lufthansa, Av. 3-5, C. 5 (22-73-11); Air France, Av. 1, C. 4-6 (22-88-11); Swiss Air, Av. 1-3. C. Central (21-66-13). Apparently, MCOs are hard to obtain from any airline in San José.

Internal Flights Sansa operate internal flights throughout the country at reasonable prices from Juan Santamaría airport, Mon.-Sat. only. Check-in is at Sansa office on Paseo Colón one hour before departure (free bus to and from airport). Check schedules on 21-94-14. Flights operated to Golfito (US$18), Río Frío (US$13), Puerto Limón (US$ 13), Puerto Quepos (US$10), Tamarindo, Mon., Wed., Fri. only, US$20.

Railway Services On the NE side of Parque Nacional is the main station of the Northern Railway to the Atlantic port of Limón and to Heredia and Alajuela in the Meseta Central, Av. 3, C. 21 (Tel.: 26-00-11). The main station of the Ferrocarril Eléctrico al Pacífico to the Pacific ports of Puntarenas and Caldera in the extreme S of the city C. 2, Av. 20, Tel.: 26-00-11 (take bus marked Paso Ancho). The two 1.067-metre gauge lines are connected. The trains are slow, noisy, dusty, but comfortable; recommended for beautiful views.

There is one train a day from San José to Puerto Limón (166 km.) at 1130; train from Limón to San José at 0600. Journey takes about 7-8 hrs. to Limón (on a good day) and 9 back. Fare: US$1.70. Train times should be checked in advance since the timetable varies. Light refreshments are served on all trains except the local service, which operates once a day between San José, Heredia and Alajuela on the Northern Railway. A luxury, 1st class coach may be taken to Puerto Limón for US$55 (bookable through Swiss Travel Service).

The journey to Limón is one of the most beautiful railway journeys anywhere. On the way to Limón, sit on the right-hand side. From the continental divide near Cartago the line follows the narrow, wooded Reventazón valley down past Turrialba and Siquirres (2 hrs. from Limón). One can shorten the journey by transferring to a bus at Siquirres. The 40 km. of line in the lowlands near Limón cost 4,000 lives during building in the 1870s, mostly from yellow fever. The last 16 km. into Limón run along the seashore, amid groves of coconut palms. Train splits at Siquirres, front half to Puerto Limón, rear to Guápiles. Beware of robberies on trains after dark and in the crush while boarding.

Between San José and Puntarenas there are two trains daily, this also is a very scenic journey; from Puntarenas to San José leaving at 0600 and 1500 and from San José to Puntarenas leaving at 0630 and 1300 (the timetable changes sometimes). Journey takes about 4 hrs. Fastest train (*directo*) 3 hrs. Fare US$1 one way. Last return train on Sundays is overcrowded. Passengers can buy light refreshments at wayside stations and stops. There are also services to the new port of Caldera.

Buses There are services to most towns. *Cartago*, every 20 mins., 0500-2300, *Turrialba* buses start from Sacsa station behind Service Station (Bomba), Av. Ctl, Calle 13. *Puntarenas* every hour from 0600-1900 (US$1.40), Av. 7-9, Calle 12. *Heredia*, every 30 mins., Av. 5, Calle 1. Minibuses from Av. 2, C. 12. or Av. 7, C. 1. *Alajuela* (including airport), 30 mins, (US$0.30) Av. 2, Calle 12-14 every 10 mins. *Quepos*, from Coca Cola bus station, Calle 16, Av. 1-3, 4 buses daily, 5 hours. Direct bus to Manuel Antonio, 0600, 1200, US$4.15, from Coca Cola station. Many buses for nearby towns and villages to the west of San José leave from the main Coca Cola bus station or the streets nearby. (eg: *Santa Ana, Escazú, Acosta, Puriscal, Santa María Dota, San Marcos, San Ramón*). *Escazú* minibuses from Av. 4, Calle 12-14; buses from front of Coca Cola terminal. *San Isidro de El General*, regular buses, near Coca Cola. *Liberia, Nicoya, Sta. Cruz, Cañas* buses, Empresa Alfaro, Coca Cola bus station. *Grecia*, bus Calle 6, Av. 5-7. *San Carlos*, bus, in Coca Cola terminal. *Guápiles*, Calle 0, Av. 7-9. *Puerto Viejo*, by Puntarenas terminal, Av. 7-9, Calle 12. *Siquirres*, Av. Ctl, Calle 11-13. *Limón*, hourly service, 3½-4 hours, good views, leaving on time. You may buy ticket the day before. US$2.10, Calle 19-21, Av. 3 Transportes Unidos/ Coope Limón. *Paso Canoas, Golfito, Ciudad Neily*, (Zona Sur) buses, Tracopa, Calle 2-4, Av. 16 (21-42-14). Service to David, Panama. Bus to Paso Canoas (Panama-Costa Rica border) US$5.25.

Minibuses run on most routes to nearby towns offering better service, never crowded like the regular buses. Fares about US$0.20-$0.25.

International Buses Sirca (Av. 2, Calle 11, Tel: 22-44-80) runs a scheduled service along the Pan-American Highway from San José to Peñas Blancas, on the Nicaraguan frontier, and on to Managua (US$10), dep. 0600 (schedules appear to change frequently), reports of unreliability with this company (book on Fri. for following week). Tica buses run to Panama City, but their services northward to Guatemala City, Tegucigalpa, Managua and San Salvador have been suspended. The terminal is at Calle 9-11 and Av. 2 (Tel.: 21-89-54). It is to this office that all refund claims have to be made (take 10 days and have to be collected in person). The Ticabus journey from San José to Panama City now takes 18 hrs. (with at least 3 hrs. at the border), US$15 (at official exchange rate and much cheaper than in Panama), at 2200 daily (book at least 3 days in advance); by Ticabus to David, US$14. To get a Panamanian tourist card one must buy a return ticket. Tracopa, opposite Pacific railway station on C.2/4, Av.18, (Tel.: 21-42-14) goes as far as David, US$10 (buses daily at 0800, 13 hrs.); fare to border US$3.30; book in advance.

Excursions San José is a good centre for excursions into the beautiful Meseta Central. The excursions to the Orosí valley and volcano of Irazú are given under Cartago. Poás volcano (described on page 1153) can be visited from Alajuela (see page 1153). Enquire first about the likely weather when planning a visit to Poás or Irazú. From Barba take a bus to San José de las Montañas (see page 1153). A road runs NE of San José to (11 km.) San Isidro de Coronado, a popular summer resort (bus from Terminal Coronado, Av. 7, C. Central and 1); its *fiesta* is on February 15. Those interested in medical research can visit the Instituto Clodomiro Picado snake farm, open Mon.-Fri. 0800-1600 (snake feeding, Fri. only 1330-1600), take Dulce Nombre de Coronado bus from C.3, Av. 5/7, 30 mins., or San Antonio Coronado bus to end of line and walk 200 metres downhill. The road goes on through fine countryside to (32 km.) Las Nubes, a country village which commands a great view of Irazú.

From San José to the Atlantic Coast

Cartago, 22½ km. from San José, stands at 1,439 metres at the foot of the Irazú volcanic peak and is encircled by mountains. It was founded in 1563 and was the capital until 1823. It has a population of only 25,000, though the neighbourhood is densely populated. Earthquakes destroyed it in 1841 and 1910, and it has been severely shaken on other occasions. That is why there are no old buildings, though some have been rebuilt in colonial style.

The most interesting church is the Basilica, rebuilt 1926 in Byzantine style, of Nuestra Señora de Los Angeles, the Patroness of Costa Rica; it houses La Negrita, under 15 cm. high, an Indian image of the Virgin which draws pilgrims from all over Central America because of great healing powers attributed to it. The feast day is August 2, when the image is carried in procession to other churches in Cartago and there are celebrations thoughout Costa Rica. In the shrine is a bubbling spring surrounded by the gifts of devotees. Worth seeing is the old parish church (La Parroquia), ruined by the 1910 earthquake and now converted into a delightful garden retreat with flowers, fish and humming birds. There is an impressive procession on Good Friday.

Hotels *Tarsis*, E; *Casa Blanca* in Barrio Asís, E; *Venecia*, F, next to railway station, basic, run down; *Valencia*, F, clean; *Familiar Las Arcadas*, at railway station, F (rents rooms hourly late into the night). Also near station, *Pensión Torre de Lully*, F, not too good.

Restaurants *Salón París*, very good food. Restaurants, among other places, are closed on the Thursday and Friday of Holy Week, so take your own food.

Excursions Best is by a road (40 km., paved) to the crater of Irazú (3,432 metres). Michael J.

Brisco of Cambridge writes: Irazú crater is a half-mile cube dug out of the earth, and all around is desolate grey sand, with little wildlife (apart from the ubiquitous Volcano Junco, a bird like a dunnock) other than the few plants which survive in this desert. The phrase "it's like the surface of the moon" describes Irazú quite well. Entrance to Irazú in season, US$0.10, out of season free. There is a small museum. Cartago buses to Irazú from 1 block N of Cartago ruins at 0600 and 1300 on Mon., Thurs. and Sat., and 0700 on Sun. (but check in advance if bus is running), 1¾ hrs. up, the first bus arrives long before the tour buses and private cars, but returns after about 30 minutes, so you must either hitch down, or wait until the afternoon bus goes down at about 1500, US$2 return; taxi is US$24 return (it is very difficult to get taxis to return for you in the morning if you have stayed at the crater overnight). (The clouds come down early, obscuring the view.) Alternatively you can take a bus from Cartago to Sanatorio. Ask the driver at the crossroads just outside the village. From there you walk to the summit, 16 km.; on the way up are the *Hotel Montana* (D inc. 3 meals) and the *Bar-Restaurant Linda Vista*. 1½ km. from the crater a road leads to Laguna Verde and a camping site; the road is paved, but steep beyond the Laguna. Tourist minibuses go to Irazú from San José, about US$24. If driving from San José, take the road signed "Plantel M.O.P.T. Cartago, 3 kms.", just after Río Taras, which goes directly to Irazú, avoiding Cartago. The walk down, on a dirt road through Pinchas, is also recommended. On Sat. and Mon. a bus from Cartago to San Juan, 12 km. from the summit (0630 and 1300); *Hotel Gran Irazú*, E, comfortable, clean.

National Park rules forbid visitors to walk around the crater; on the tourist track on the North side is a "Prohibido pasar" sign, which can be passed only at your own risk, there are some very dangerous drops, and the rim is cracking (we advise obeying the rules). There is an easier walk on the southerly side, which ends before the high crest; J. Douglas Porteous of the University of Victoria, B.C., writes: "Stupendous views: you look down on mountain tops, clouds, light aircraft. Wear good shoes and a hat, the sun is strong. Those with sensitive skins should consider face cream if the sulphur fumes are heavy. By 1300 (sometimes by even 0900 or 1000) clouds have enveloped the lower peaks and are beginning to close in on Irazú; time to eat your picnic on the far side of the crater before returning to the tourist side."

Mike Marlowe, of Blacksburg, Virginia, writes as follows: "In the afternoon the mountain top is buried in fog and mist or drizzle, but the ride up in the mist can be magical, for the mountainside is half-displaced in time. There are new jeeps and tractors, but the herds of cattle are small, the fields are quilt-work, handcarts and oxcarts are to be seen under the fretworked porches of well-kept frame houses. The land is fertile, the pace is slow, the air is clean, there is no (great) poverty. It is a very attractive mixture of old and new. Irazú is a strange mountain, well worth the two-plus hours' bus ride up.°

Aguas Calientes is 4 km. SE of Cartago and 90 metres lower. Its *balneario* (warm water swimming pool) is a good place for picnics. 4 km. from Cartago on the road to Paraíso is the Jardín Lancaster orchid garden (run by the University of Costa Rica), 10 mins.' walk from the main road (ask bus driver to let you out at Campo Ayala—Cartago-Paraíso bus); the best display is in April. Open 0830-1530, entry usually on the hour, US$0.50. 1 km. further on is Parque Doña Ana (La Expresión), a lake with picnic area, basketball courts, exercise track and bird watching, open 0900-1700, US$0.50. Get off bus at Cementerio in Paraíso and walk 1 km. south. **Ujarrás** (ruins of a Colonial church and village) is 6½ km. E of Cartago by a road which goes from Paraíso through a beautiful valley to the small town of **Orosi**, in the enchanting Orosi valley, down which flows the tumultuous Reventazón (*Motel Río*, D, and *Restaurant Río Palomo*). Bus from Cartago, US$0.15. Here are magnificent views of the valley, a 17th century mission with colonial treasures, and just outside the town two *balnearios* (bathing, US$1.60) and restaurants serving good meals at fair prices. The *miradores* of Ujarrás and Orosi both offer excellent views of the Reventazón valley. There are buses from Cartago to all these places. A beautiful one-day drive from Cartago is to Orosi, then to Ujarrás, and on to Cachi where there is a dam with artificial lake (very popular with residents of San José, Charrarra buses from 1 block N of Cartago ruins, several daily). The Charrarra tourist complex, with a good restaurant, swimming pool, boat rides on the Orosi river and walks, can be reached by direct bus on Sun., otherwise ½-hr. walk from Ujarrás.

12 km. beyond Orosi is the Tapanti Wildlife Refuge (Refugio Nacional de Vida Silvestre Tapanti, owned by the Forest Service), on the headwaters of the Reventazón. It is a 6,000 hectare reserve of mainly cloud forest and pre-montaine humid forest with over 300 species of birds, 3 of monkeys, orchids and ferns. There are picnic areas, a nature centre with slide shows (ask to see them) and good swimming in the dry season (Nov.-June), and trout fishing (April 1 to October 31). Open daily 0600-1600, US$0.10. From June to Nov.-Dec. it rains every afternoon. To get there take 0600 bus from Cartago to Orosi which goes to Puricil by 0700, then walk (5 km.), or take any other Cartago-Orosi bus to Río Macho and walk 9 km. to the refuge, or take a taxi from Orosi (ask for Julio who, for US$7 round trip, will take 6 passengers). By the refuge is the *Pensión Tapanti* with 8 beds (E p.p.), meals included, reserve in advance (Tel.: 51-34-52), U.S.-owned, discounts for group reservations and biologists doing research (address: David Lockshin, Pensión Tapanti, C.P. 7107, Orosi, Cartago, Costa Rica).

The Turrialba volcano may be visited from Cartago by a bus to the village of Pacayas, where horses may be hired to take you to the top (fine view and a guesthouse).

Turrialba (57 km. from San José, 40,000 people, altitude 625 metres), on the

1150 COSTA RICA

railway between Cartago and Puerto Limón, has the Inter-American Institute of Agricultural Sciences (rooms for visitors) and many fine coffee farms. Also very good cheese. The railway runs down to Limón on a narrow ledge poised between mountains on the left and the river on the right.

Hotels *Central*, F with restaurant, no bath; *Chamanga*, F, no bath; *Interamericano*, F with bath (all opp. railway station); *Pensión Primavera*, F, 1 block away; opp. is *Restaurant Kingston*, reasonable, cheap food.

At Turrialba, a naturalists' and birdwatchers' lodge offers 3-7 day packages at low cost, including airport to San José collection; advance reservations required. Write to TBC, P.O. Box 14, Reigate, RH2 9PW, Surrey, England, for brochure.

From Turrialba you can get to the village of Moravia del Chirripó, where guides and horses can be hired for an excursion into the jungled, trackless area of the Talamanca Indians, where there are legends of lost goldfields (bus from Turrialba takes 4 hrs., only certain in dry season; in wet season go to Suiza and get out at Gran d'Oro, from where it's one hr. walk—no accommodation in Moravia, stay put at *pulpería* in Gran d'Oro). About 30 km. E of Turrialba, near Guayabo, an Indian ceremonial centre has been excavated and there are clear signs of its paved streets and stone-lined water-channels. This area is now a National Park. There are buses daily at 1100 from Turrialba (US$0.45) to Guayabo from where it is a 1½ hour walk to the site (several buses each day pass the turn-off to Guayabo, the town is a 2-hr. walk uphill). It is possible to camp at the park (water and toilets, but no food); entry US$0.05. Further along this road (1½ hours' drive) is Santa Cruz, from which the Turrialba volcano can be reached. Bus from Cartago to Turrialba, 1 hr., US$0.60 (all Limón-San José buses stop at Turrialba for a 15-min. coffee break).

Puerto Limón is on a palm-fringed shore backed by mountains and is the country's most important port. It was built on the site of an ancient Indian village, Cariari, where Columbus landed on his fourth and last voyage. Much of the population is black. Visitors should see the palm promenade and tropical flowers of the Parque Vargas (where sloths live in the trees); the nightlife is good, particularly for Caribbean music and dancing. The road to the capital (190 km.) is fully paved. Population 49,600. Some 2.8 million bunches of bananas are exported each year. New docks are being built. Moín, just outside Puerto Limón, has docks for tankers, container and ro-ro ships, and is also the departure point for barges to Tortuguero and Barra del Colorado (8 hrs.). There is now much drilling for oil around Puerto Limón.

Warning Beware of theft at night.

Hotels *Acón*, C. 3, Av. 3, Tel.: 58-10-10, D with bath, a/c, clean, safe, good restaurant, discotheque *Aquarius*; *Puerto*, C. 7, Av. 5/6, D, a/c, restaurant, bar; *Lincoln*, Av. 5, Calle 2-3, F, with bath, excellent value; *Caribe*, Calle 1, Av. 2, E; *Park*, C. 1/2, Av. 3, Tel.: 58-04-76, D, with bath (cold water), overpriced, damp, dining room; *Pensión Los Angeles*, Calle 6-7, Av. 7, F, with bath, cheap, average; *Miami*, Calle 4-5, Av. 2, near station, D, a/c, with bath, cold water, a little dirty, unfriendly; *Internacional*, Av. 5, Calle 3, D, a/c, grubby, overpriced restaurant; *Fung*, E, by market, modern; *El Cano*, C. 4/5, Av. 3, F, very hot and steamy; also C. 4/5, Av. 3 *Pensión Niza*, F; *Miramar*, 3 blocks from old railway station, clean; *Pensión Hotel Costa Rica*, near central park, F, pleasant, spacious rooms; *Pensión El Sauce*, one block from main square, F, reasonably clean; *Río*, C. 3/4, Av. 2/3, F, no bath; *Paraíso*, C. 5, Av. 5/6, F, no bath, clean, noisy; *Cariari*, Av. 3, F, small; *Palace*, F; *Hong Kong*, on main street, F, clean but noisy; *Hawaii*, on main square, F, basic, not very clean; *Nuevo Oriental*, F, nice, cold showers; *Centro*, F, clean, basic, noisy, cold showers; *Venus*, C. 2/3, Av. 4/5, F, very basic. Pensiones: *Libia*, C. 2/3, Av. 4; *Pensión Dorita*, C. 3/4, Av. 4, fairly clean, friendly, basic, close to bus stop for Cahuita; *Rosemary*, C. 3/4, Av. 4, all F, first 2 no bath. *Balmoral*, near market, G, basic; *Linda Vista*, Parque Vargas, F, basic, friendly, noisy.

In Portete nearby, *Matama*, B, bath, a/c, restaurant, tennis, pool, boats for rent to Tortuguero; *Las Olas*, B, a/c, bath, good, with pool and sauna, set on rocks in the sea (buses every 1½ hr.), own water supply, no protection against insects, expensive restaurant; *Cabinas Getsemaní*, cabins, C, bath, a/c, restaurant, pleasant (Tel.: 58-11-23).

Restaurants Several Chinese restaurants. *Park Hotel* does good meals, US$2.25; *American Café Springfield* (try the *tortuga*); good West Indian food available from place near hospital. Also *Restaurant La Chucheca* serves good *comidas* for US$1 and breakfast US$0.75. *La Hacienda*, for steaks, cheap. *Soda/Restaurant Roxie*, opp. hospital, some way out of town, good value *casado*. *Harbour Restaurant*, good value meal of the day. *Mölnpik* for good ice cream; *Milk Bar La Negra Mendoza* at the central market has good milk shakes and snacks. *Casados* in market in the day, outside it at night.

Swimming Japdeva, the harbour authority, has a 25-metre pool open to the public for a small fee in the harbour area.

COSTA RICA 1151

Cables Radiográfica maintain offices in Limón.

Protestant Church Baptist, with services in English.

Hospital A new Social Security Hospital was opened in January 1982.

Rail One train daily to San José, 0600, US$1.70 (sit on left); the new station is on the edge of town (bus from centre, US$0.03).

Buses Town bus service is irregular and crowded. Service to San José with Transportes Unidos del Atlántico, every hour on the hour between 0500-1400, then 1730; leave from the street between Central Plaza and Parque Vargas (ignore the old signs for the departure point), US$2.10, 3½-4 hrs. with stop in Turrialba and Cartago. To Cartago, US$2.

Airport 5 km. from centre (Viajes bus, US$0.75 one way). Sansa services once daily (except Sun.) to San José, US$13; check-in next to *Hotel Park*, C. 1/2, Av. 3.

The Atlantic Coast Once the border has been reopened (it has been closed since 1981 because of guerrilla activity), the enterprising might care to travel by motorized dugout canoe along the Río Frío between San Carlos, on Lake Nicaragua (in Nicaragua) and Los Chiles (Costa Rica). The Río San Juan forms the border between Costa Rica and Nicaragua; the frontier is not in mid-river but on the Costa Rican bank. The river trip, between thickly wooded banks, offers absorbing interest. **Los Chiles** itself has cheap accommodation (F range) and restaurants; the principal traffic is on the river, but a road has been built to Los Chiles (bus to Quesada, US$1). English is spoken widely along the coast.

Northward from Limón, past **Siquirres** (a clean, friendly town; hotels include *Colerón*, *Wilson*, *Garza*, *Cocal* and *Vidal*, all E), trains run to **Guápiles**, centre of the new Río Frío banana region. One flight daily from San José to Río Frío. There is also a good new road to Siquirres, and from there to San José. Standard Fruit have built about 75 km. of new railway lines on from Guápiles (Hotels *Hugo Sánchez Cheng* and *Alfaro* (with bath), both F). On the coast N of Limón, there is a good beach (but strong currents) at Playa Bonita; buses every ½ hr. from Limón; train from San José.

6½ km. N of Limón is Moín, with a pleasant beach and *Hostal Moín* (E, 15 mins. from railway and docks—runs "24-hr. service" for sailors off the banana boats), buses run every 40 minutes from 0600-1740, ½ hr., US$0.14. From Moín one can go to **Tortuguero**, a National Park protecting the Atlantic green turtle egg-laying grounds and the Caribbean rain forest inland. The turtles lay their eggs at night from July to September, but before going to watch, contact the National Park administration, or the scientists at Casa Verde (very helpful), Km. 0.6, for instructions, otherwise you may disturb the protected turtles (take a torch if going at night). No permission is needed to enter the park. There are several hotels: *Tortuga Verde*, Tel.: 71-85-85, B p.p. with bath and 3 meals; *Tortuga Lodge*, Tel.: 71-81-56 (owner Alex Mehneri); *Pensión Tortuguero*, F, not recommended; *Sabina's Cabañas*, 30 units, from US$2 p.p., good food is limited, but good at *Miss Juni's* with Mona Lisa painting (book in advance) and at *Tío Leo's*. Don't dally on arrival if you want cheap accommodation. Park rangers friendly and make trips into the jungle waterways; particularly recommended for viewing tropical rain forest wildlife (birds, crocodiles, tapirs, jaguars, anteaters, manatees, sloths, monkeys, lungfish); their trips are quite short, about US$2 p.p. for 3-4 hr. trip. Ricardo in the *pulpería* in Tortuguero has a motor boat for rent (US$5 p.p. for 3 hrs.); his boatman, Fernando (Pepito), is good at finding birds, monkeys, etc. Seek out the German, Pete, who owns a fishing boat (Tortuguero-Puerto Limón, US$20-25 p.p.). Take insect repellant against the ferocious mosquitoes, ticks and chiggers. Tours to Tortuguero are expensive and disappointing; best to go on your own. From Moín, a regular boat goes to Tortuguero, Thurs., 0700, Sat., 1030, returning Fri., 0600 and Sun., 1000, US$4 one way, 7 hrs. (locals are always given preference, ask one to get tickets for you; the boat is noisy, take protection against rain). Other boats (every 2 days or so) go to Barra del Colorado and take 9 hrs. through the natural canals to Tortuguero. If excursion boats have a spare seat you may be allowed on. A road is under construction between Moín and Guápiles.

Michael J. Brisco writes: "The canals pass many small settlements, and for many of them the barge is their only means of communication. The canals are part artificial, part natural; they were originally narrow lagoons running parallel to the sea, separated from it by ¾ km. of land. Now all the lagoons are linked, and it is possible to sail as far as **Barra del Colorado**, in the extreme NE of Costa Rica, 25 km. beyond Tortuguero." The passenger launch from Moín to Tortuguero continues to Barra del Colorado on Thurs., returning early Fri. a.m., US$2. There is a luxury hotel lodge operated by Swiss Travel Service; *Río de Colorado Lodge*, C p.p. inc. 3 meals and fishing with guide, reservations preferred (P.O. Box 5094, San José 1000); *Pensión Acapulco* (F p.p., fairly dirty). There is an annual tarpon fishing competition. Flight Barra del Colorado-San José up to US$50 p.p.

Southward from Limón, travellers can catch a train to Penshurst or can drive; the road is paved. Here the road branches to Valle de Estrella, a large Standard Fruit banana plantation; camping is easy in the hills and there are plenty of rivers for swimming. Small buses leave Limón (C. 4, Av. 6) for Valle de Estrella/Pandora at 0500, 0700, 0900, 1100, 1300, 1500, 1800, 1½ hrs. (returning from Pandora at similar times).

1152 COSTA RICA

From Penshurst it is 11½ km. to **Cahuita;** this stretch of the road is paved to the edge of Cahuita. There is a bus service direct from Puerto Limón, in front of Radio Casino (4 a day each way—2 in a.m., 2 in p.m., US$0.60, 1-3 hrs., and continue on paved road to Bribri, two basic *residencias*, and on to Sixaola on the Panamanian border (bus, US$1 from Puerto Limón, 4 hrs.; not a pleasant place, 2 *pensiones, Castaneda* and *Dorita*). The Cahuita National Park is a narrow strip of beach (1,780 hectares) and a unique coral reef off shore; an old Spanish wrecked ship may be seen (both can be reached without a boat; take snorkelling equipment, but the undercurrent is strong). The Park extends from Cahuita town to Puerto Vargas further SE. Best access to the Park is from Puerto Vargas where there are the Park headquarters, a nature trail, camping facilities, drinking water, toilets (take the bus to Km. 5, then turn left at the sign; the road from the Cahuita-Bribri road to Puerto Vargas is muddy; take a torch if walking it after dark). The length of the beach can be walked in 2 hrs., passing endless coconut palms and interesting tropical forest, through which there is also a path, including fording the shallow Perezoso River, which is brown with tannin (it is hot and humid, but a wide range of fauna can be seen, including howler monkeys, white face monkeys, coatimundis, snakes, butterflies and hermit crabs—torch essential if walking at night, assaults and rape have been reported on the path and some of the jungle has been cleared for safety reasons). No permission is necessary from SNP to enter the Park. Cahuita hotels: *Buchanan's Cabins; Winston's* cabins on the black beach; *Jenny's Cabinas,* F, cooking area, rustic, basic, recommended; *Pepe's Place,* pleasant owner, but beware of theft; *Grant's Cabins,* F, good water service, Señorita Letty Grant (blue house on right of track to black beach) rents rooms (F) and *cabañas,* clean, nice, friendly; *El Atlántido,* next to football ground, clean bungalows in nice gardens, F with bath, fan, mosquito screen, pleasant, free safe parking for cars and motorcycles (also known as Canadian John's); *Hotel Cahuita,* F, without bath, D with, clean, also cabins with fan and bath, pricey but good food; *Samwell's,* F, clean, friendly, recommended. There are also empty rooms to let, so take a hammock or sleeping bag. Camping: US$0.25 p.p., good facilities but no meals. *Soda Sol y Mar,* opp. *Hotel Cahuita,* recommended. *Daisy's Café,* for breakfast, and dinner if ordered in advance, 100 metres past ball ground, good view of beach, poor service, also book exchange and snorkelling equipment hire, very expensive. Ask at *Bar Vaz* (good food), next to bus stop, for private rooms for rent (*Cabinas Vaz,* opp. *Hotel Cahuita,* D with fan and bath, cold shower). Other restaurants: *Sands,* cheap, *Típico,* good. On public holidays Cahuita is very crowded; the remainder of the year it is a favourite resort of backpackers (don't bathe or sunbathe naked). Money can be changed in the store in same building as *Bar Vaz.* Tony Mora runs glass-bottomed boats over the coral reef. The National Park services have warned against muggings in the park at night; also beware of theft on the beach. The beaches at **Puerto Viejo,** 13 km. from Cahuita, unpaved (bus US$1, 1½ hrs.; 3 hotels in F range (*Rafa's,* dearest, *Maritza,* F, clean, friendly, English spoken; *Maiti,* cheapest, best of several restaurants; electricity in town 1700-2200), also rooms to let) are also worth a visit. It is possible to walk along the beach from Puerto Viejo to Cahuita in one day; there is a bus, US$0.45. Take road from Cahuita to Hone Creek where one road (dirt) goes to Puerto Viejo and another (paved) to Bribri, one of the villages at the foot of the Talamanca range, which has been declared an Indian Reserve. From Limón, Aerovías Talamaqueñas Indígenas fly cheaply to Amubri in the Reserve (there is a *Casa de Huéspedes* run by nuns in Amubri). Villages such as Bribri, Chase, Bratsi, Shiroles and San José Cabécar can be reached by bus from Cahuita. (For a good introduction to the Talamanca Mountains, read *Mamita Yunai* by Fallas, or *What Happen* by Palmer.) Continuing S from Cahuita is **Sixaola,** on the border with Panama. 2 hotels just before the bridge: *Central,* Chinese run with good restaurant, and *pensión.* There are no banks in Sixaola, but it may be possible to change money in one of the shops before the bridge. A narrow-gauge railway runs to Almirante (Panama) from Guabito, on the Panamanian side (shops will accept colones). If crossing to Panama take the earliest bus possible to Sixaola (see page 1184).

From San José to the Pacific Coast

A paved road and a railway run from the capital to the two other main towns of the Meseta: Heredia and Alajuela.

Heredia, capital of its province, 10 km. from San José, is a great coffee and cattle centre. It looks a little like the towns of southern Spain: church towers above red-tiled roofs, iron grilles at the windows, and bright gardens set among whitewashed adobe and stone walls. There is a statue to the poet Aquileo Echeverría (1866-1909). The Tourist Institute will arrange a visit to a coffee finca. Altitude 1,137 metres, population 23,600.

Hotel *Herediana,* E, Calle 6; 2 *pensiones* in the centre (usually full).

Excursion Beautiful views from road across mountains to town of **Puerto Viejo de Sarapiquí** (3 small hotels including *Monteverde,* Tel.: 71-20-85, ext. 236) on river with good fishing. There is a spectacular waterfall here. There is a bus service from San José, C. 12, Avs. 7-9, via Heredia, US$2.50, at 0600, 1200, 1400, returning at 0700, 0930 and 1500. Buses from Puerto Viejo to Río Frío and San Carlos. Nearby is the Organization of Tropical Studies station at Finca La

COSTA RICA

Delva on the Río Sarapiquí. To visit, phone in advance to book. Visitors are provided with maps of the superb primary rain forest and a bunk in a co-ed dormitory; rates are US$55 a day inc. all meals for ordinary visitors, US$26 for students, researchers or interested journalists (proof required). Try to avoid the rainy season. To get there by car, take Route 9 from San José, one day's driving; park at the suspension bridge then walk. Buses run from Puerto Viejo. The river flows into the San Juan, which forms the northern border of Costa Rica. In the mountains near Heredia is *San José de la Montaña.*

Braulio Carrillo National Park. This large park was created to protect the high rain forest north of San José from the impact of the new Guápiles-San José road and it also includes Barba volcano. The latter is accessible from Heredia; take a bus to San José de la Montaña; from there it is 4 hrs.' walk to Sacramento, but some buses continue towards Sacramento, halving the walk time (otherwise walk, hitchhike, or arrange a ride with the park director). Ranger station nearby, from which 3 km. of easy climb to the top. Good views; no permit needed here. Easter Week is a good choice. The views down the Patria River canyon are impressive. Bird watchers will also get their fill. The park is also widely known among (illegal) birdcatchers. Alternatively, you can take one of many buses to San Jerónimo de Moravia (1 hr. from San José).

Alajuela, 13 km. beyond Heredia (5 km. from Juan Santamaría international airport), capital of its province, stands at 952 metres, and is a midsummer resort for people from the capital. It is famous for its flowers and its market days (Sat. market is good value for food); an interesting craft cooperative produces pictures in relief metalwork; the unusual church of La Agonía in the E part of town has murals done from life. The national hero, Juan Santamaría, the drummer who fired the building at Rivas (Nicaragua) in which Walker's filibusters were entrenched in 1856, is commemorated by a monument. The Museo Histórico Juan Santamaría (Tues.-Sun. 1400-2100) tells the story of this war. Just outside the town is the Ojo de Agua swimming pool (good restaurant) in beautiful surroundings: a popular bathing and boating resort. Entrance, US$0.60 p.p., plus US$0.80 per vehicle. The gushing spring which feeds the pool also supplies water for Puntarenas. Population 28,700.

Hotels *Alajuela,* C. 2, Av. Central and 2, E, with shower, clean, friendly (best to book in advance). *Chico,* C. 10/12, Av. Central, F with bath (hourly rental only).

Restaurant *Antarcha,* Av. 2, C. 2 and Central, good.

Language School Centro Lingüistico Latinoamericano, Apartado 151, Tel.: 41-02-61, recommended (located in San Antonio).

Excursion From Alajuela a paved road runs to 2,704-metre volcano Poás (57 km. by road from San José). In the National Park of Poás, the still-smoking volcano is set in beautiful tropical forest. The crater is 1½ km. across (said to be the second largest in the world). Within one area of its sharp-sided walls is a lake of very hot water. In another area geysers throw steam 600 metres or so occasionally. One km. away is a still, forest-fringed water lake in another crater. A 30-min. jungle trail to the crater starts from the car park. Clouds often hang low over the crater permitting little to be seen. Entrance to Park, US$0.40. The volcano can be reached by car from San José. (Tours from San José, US$24, are not worth it since they tend to arrive after the cloud has come down and include neither lunch nor the entrance fee.) On Sunday there is a regular excursion bus from the main square of Alajuela right up to the crater, leaving at 0900 (be there early for a seat), US$3 return. The bus waits at the top with ample time to see everything, returning at 1500. Daily bus Alajuela-Poasito 1200 (US$1). From Poasito hitch a lift as it is a 10 km walk. The visitors' centre offers shelter, electricity outlets and good water even when closed (hours claim to be Mon.-Fri. 0800-1200, 1300-1500, Sat., Sun. and holidays 0800-1600); further up the road are good toilets. There is a restaurant near the parking area. If you spend the night there, a ranger might take you down to the water's edge on a clear night to watch and listen to the dome. The volcano is very crowded on Sun., go in the week if possible.

Campsites Trailer park nearby, with hookups: the Inca.

San Carlos, also known as Villa Quesada, lies some 25 km. from the Pan-American Highway and can be reached by a road which branches off the highway near Naranjo. It is the main town of the lowland cattle and farming region. Between San Carlos and the Highway is the mountain town of Zarcero, known for its beautiful park and church. There are buses every hour from San José (US$2.50).

San Carlos Hotels *La Central Recepción,* B, with bath, restaurant, not recommended; *Conquistador,* E with bath; *El Retiro,* E with bath; *Lily* and *Riviera,* F with bath and restaurant; *Cristal,* F with bath; *Porfirio Rojas,* F, restaurant; *Diana, Ugalde, Tesika,* all F.

1 hour from San Carlos by bus (US$0.60) is *Venecia* (3½ hrs., US$2.50 by bus from San José);

1154　COSTA RICA

one hotel, F, clean, friendly. Nearby is Ciudad Cutris, preColumbian tumuli (a good road goes to within 2 km. of Cutris, from there walk or take 4-wheel drive vehicle; get a permit to visit from the *finca* owner). A difficult road goes from San Carlos to Fortuna (3½ hrs. US$1.50). Arenal volcano can be reached by taking the road S for 20 km. (buses every 1-2 hrs. from San Carlos); here are the lake and dam for hydroelectric power and irrigation. Hot baths near the dam; one cannot climb the volcano because the slope is cut off by lava flows but it is nevertheless a dramatic mountain, with jets of steam and explosive noises. La Selva, a private forest research centre, has a cafeteria and accommodation (which is often fully-booked), Tel.: 71-85-27 for information and reservations; prices US$30 for students, US$60 others. The S side of Lake Arenal is very difficult to drive, with many fords; the longer N side is safer but four-wheel drive is still a must. From San Carlos there are buses to the Río Frío district and to towns on the San Carlos and Sarapiquí rivers (incl. Puerto Viejo) where launches can be taken via the Colorado river, to the Canales de Tortuguero and Moín, about 10 km. by road and rail from Puerto Limón. **Warning** In the last two years there has been guerrilla activity in this border region.

Beyond Alajuela the Pan-American Highway divides into a toll highway and a *vía libre*, which is the old road. Though it is rough, it passes through attractive countryside and the towns of Naranjo, Sarchí and Grecia. At **Sarchí** one may visit the factory that produces the traditional painted ox-carts, which are almost a national emblem. Also, hand-made cowhide rocking chairs and wooden products may be purchased at Fábricas de Carretas; there are many shops at the roadside (prices are half those in San José). Travel agents in San José charge US$20 or more; Tuasa buses every 15 mins. from Alajuela bus station. Grecia is the centre for the pineapple-growing area. Two very attractive towns in this region are **San Ramón** (76 km. from San José—*Hotel Nuevo Jardín*, E, with bath, hot water; *El Viajero*, F; *Hotel Central*, F, dirty; *Restaurant Tropical*) and, 7 km beyond, Palmares (one hotel). (The people in this region are friendly and like talking to foreigners.)

Puntarenas (population 30,829) is on a 5-km. spit of land thrusting out into Nicoya Gulf and enclosing the Estero lagoon. It is hot (mean temperature 27°C); the beaches are dirty, and are crowded on Suns. There is a new public swimming pool on the end of the point (US$ 0.35 entrance). Good surfing off the headland. Across the gulf are the mountains of the Nicoya Peninsula. In the gulf are several islands, the Islas Negritos, to which there are passenger launches. The chief products around Puntarenas are bananas, rice, cattle, and coconuts. Puntarenas is connected with San José by a road (1½ hrs., by hourly buses), and a railway (116 km.; 4 hrs., see page 1147). It is being replaced as the country's main Pacific port by Caldera.

Hotels *Tioga*, Barrio El Carmen, near beach, C with bath, including continental breakfast, swimming pool, very good indeed. Next best is *Cayuga*, Calle 4, Av. Central, D., with shower, a/c, also rooms at D, restaurant. Others are *Las Brisas*, on the waterfront, C, good restaurant, swimming pool; *Chorotega*, Calle 3, Av. 3, D, with bath and fan, clean, central, recommended (one block east of river); *Las Humacas*, Calle 5/7, Av. 4, D with bath; *Gran Hotel Imperial*, opp. the S beach pier, 5 mins.' walk from bus and rail stations, F, no bath; *La Riviera*, D, with bath; *De Verano*, C. 3, Av. Central/1, E with bath; *Ayicón*, C. Av. 1/3, E with bath; *La Eureka*, C Central, Av. 3/5, E with bath; *Cóndor*, C. 2/4, Av. Central, F, no private bath; *Viking*, C. 32, Av. 2, new, on the beach, D; *Choluteca*, F, clean; *Río*, Av. 3, C. Central/2, near market, F, with shower, basic and noisy, but clean and friendly; *Cabinas Thelma*, very good, friendly (ask at Holman Bar, Calle 7); *Colonial*, Calle 72/74, Av. Central, B, with breakfast, recommended; *Ayi-Con*, F, a/c available, one block from market. *Pensión Costa Rica*, near market, F. *Cabinas Orlando* at San Isidro de Puntarenas, with bath and kitchen, D; *Río Mar Hotel* at Barranca 15 km. from Puntarenas, D with bath, restaurant, good, pricey. Accommodation difficult to find Dec.-April, especially at weekends. *Pensión Cabezas* and *Pensión Puntarenas* (C. 1, Av. 1), both in the centre, F.

Restaurants Next to *Hotel Tioga* is Aloha Restaurant (good). Porto Bello, luxurious, not cheap, but good, shady. A number of Chinese restaurants on the main street (e.g. Mandarín, good value). The majority of restaurants in town are Chinese and not too good. Soda Parada and Soda La Nación are both good, as is Soda Internacional. Fonda Brisas del Pacífico, near wharf, good value casado. There is a lively night life in the cheaper bars. On the beach, Bierstube, good for sandwiches, hamburgers and spaghetti. Recommended bars: Pier 14, near wharf, good pizza and hamburgers made by Captain Ed from Mobile (Alabama) and his wife; Yate Bar, friendly, English-speaking owner (no girls at either).

Ferry to Playa Naranjo, US$1 p.p., US$7 per car, 1¼ hrs., crossings Mon.-Fri. 0700 and 1600, returning 0900 and 1800; Sat. and Sun. 0700, 1100 and 1600, returning 0900, 1400 and 1800.

COSTA RICA 1155

Buses meet the ferry for Coyote, Bejuco, Nicoya and Jicaral. Launches to Paquera (for Cóbano, Playa Montezuma, etc.) daily 0600, 1500, returning at 0900 and 1800, 2 hrs., US$1.20). Take bus "Barrio Carmen" from centre for ferry.

Cables   ICE and Radiográfica.

Nicaraguan Consulate   Calle 27-25, Av. 2 Barrio del Carmen, Tel.: 61.19.71, open 0800-1300.

Warning   Thieves abound on the beach.

On the San José-Puntarenas railway, near the new port of Caldera is **Mata de Limón,** which has a beach. It is on a lagoon surrounded by mangroves, peaceful. Bus from Puntarenas market every hour (marked to Caldera); train back to Puntarenas passes through at about 1615. (Hotels: *Casablanca,* full board C, or cabins; *Manglares,* reasonable, good restaurant; *Dormitorios de Mata de Limón,* next to railway.)

Monteverde   The site of a 1,600-hectare private nature reserve, mainly primary cloud forest with hundreds of species of birds (including the quetzal, best seen between January and May, which are the dry months, especially near the start of the Nuboso Trail, and the three-wattled bellbirds), monkeys, reptiles, amphibians (including orange toads) and orchids and other flowers. Too many visitors have frightened most of the wildlife out of sight. Entry, US$2.50 (students US$1.65), a 7-day pass costs US$15. At any time of year protective rainwear and boots are a must; also take food and drink. The entrance is at 1,500 metres, but the maximum altitude in the Park is over 1,800 metres. The best months to visit are January to May, particularly March and April. There are two rather run down shelters in the reserve, 2 and 2½ hrs.' walk from the office (US$2.50 for their use, take sleeping bag). A free map is available from the office. An experienced guide to the reserve is Gary Diller, Apdo. 10165, 1000 San José (Tel.: 61-0903); he charges US$10 p.p. for half-day tours, US$25 for a full, 6-hr. day. Donations to the reserve can be made at the park centre, or to the Tropical Science Centre, C. 1 No. 442 (apply here for information), Apdo. 8-3870, San José.

Take bus which runs from Puntarenas, opposite the bus station, to **Santa Elena**, one a day, 1400 (3½ hrs., US$1.40) which is about 4 km. from Monteverde. Bus from Santa Elena to Puntarenas at 0600 only. From San José, take any bus in the direction of Tilarán, Las Cañas or Liberia to the turn off to Santa Elena, at Río Lagartos, about 150 km. from the capital (US$1.50 from turn off to San José). From here you can take a bus at about 1530 (Puntarenas—Santa Elena) or hitch to Santa Elena. *Pensión Quetzal*, D, with or without bath, full board only, fresh bread baked on the premises for residents only, American-run (very popular so reservations must be made, Tel.: 61-19-29; Apdo. 10165, 1000 San José). Also *Pensión Flor Mar*, E, full board (less without food), excellent value, very friendly and helpful, American owner, rubber boots for hire; it is 3 km. from Santa Elena, 4 km. from Monteverde; Arnold's jeep meets Puntarenas bus, taxi US$4.70, 2 km. from Monteverde; for bookings, Tel.: 61-09-09. *Hotel de Montaña*, between Santa Elena and Monteverde, B, overpriced, restaurant (with poor food and service according to latest reports), horses for hire (US$1 per hr.); located just outside Santa Elena, excellent birdwatching around the hotel (reservations can be made through San José travel agents, or Tel.: 61-18-46); *Bel Mar*, B, Swiss-chalet style, good, new. *Pensión Santa Elena*, in Santa Elena, E, pleasant (except room 8—very hot), cheap, clean, good food; and *Pensión de Franklyn Vargas*, F, with shower, clean; *Restaurant Irene*, opp. church, good *casado. Restaurant Iman*, opp. bus stop, will let you eat your Quaker cheese on its toast; under same ownership, *Pensión Iman*, inexpensive, clean, spartan, room 6 has shower. In Santa Elena there is a cooperative gift shop, Casem, which sells embroidered shirts, T-shirts, wooden and woven articles and baskets. Also Banco Nacional which changes travellers' cheques.

The settlement at Monteverde was founded by American Quakers in the 1950s; it is essentially a group of dairy farms and a cheese factory run by a cooperative. Excellent cheeses of various types can be bought; also fresh milk and *cajeta* (a butterscotch spread) are sold. The land has only been partially cleared. The Quakers have an English library at Monteverde. A number of Christian sects can be found at Santa Elena.

From Puntarenas a road runs to the Pan-American Highway at **Las Cañas.** (5 buses daily from Coca Cola terminal, San José. Hotels: *Cañas Cabinas*, C, 2, Av. 1, E; *El Corral*, C, 4, Av. Central, D; *Guillén*, C, Central, Av. 2, F; *El Faro del Norte*, F, all with bath; *Oriental*, F without, beside bus station, also *Luz*.) From there are buses to Tilarán (and from San José, 0730, 4 hrs.). (Hotels *Grecia*, F with shower, cheaper without, and *Cabinas El Sueño*, both 1 block from bus station.) Two buses leave each afternoon for Arenal on the N side of the lake formed by the new Arenal dam (check return times if you want to go back same day). Further round the lake are the villages of the Guatuso Indians near the Nicaraguan border, Upala and Caño Negro. There is now a direct bus from San José to Upala (from Av. 5, C. 14 at 1445, 4 hrs., US$2.80), where there are the *Hotel Rigo, Pensión Isabela, Pensión Buena Vista,* basic, F, food available. 5 km. N of Las Cañas is a very good campsite, *La Pacífica*, run by a Swiss family, with restaurant, cottages, cabins, small zoo, medical service, workshop, spare parts, etc.; camping US$1 per day, cabins D. There is free camping along the river. Good camping is also reported at a beach 2 km. north of Brasilito.

Also S of San José one can visit Aserrí, a village with a beautiful white church; further along the

COSTA RICA

same road is the *Mirador Ram Luna*, a restaurant with a fine panoramic view. At the end of the road is San Ignacio de Acosta, again with a good church containing life-size Nativity figures for use in Christmas processions.

SW of San José is the Santa Ana valley, which includes the popular weekend centre of Lagos de Lindora. The road goes on through lovely scenery to Puriscal and Puerto Quepos (see next paragraph). Before Quepos, at Parrita, is a fine beach, Playa Palma; Hotels *El Nupal* and *La Orquídea*, both F with bath and restaurant.

Some 155 km. S of San José, in Puntarenas province, is **Puerto Quepos**, built by United Brands as a banana exporting port, but now rather run down. The road is beautiful but mostly unpaved; the last hour goes through United Brands' palm oil plantations. There are 4 buses a day from the capital, book a day in advance, 3½ hrs., US$2.50, and there is a daily except Sun.) flight (Sansa) to the international airport, 20 mins., US$10. *Hotel Viña del Mar*, D with bath, fan, restaurant; *Hotel Quepos*, E; *Linda Vista*, F with bath; *Ceciliano*, E; *Luna*, F with bath. *América*, G p.p., basic, clean; *Imperial*, *Majestic*, also G p.p.; *Ramu's* and *Allan* both F p.p. Accommodation is impossible to find on Sats., Dec.-April. The *Jardín Cervecero Los Arcos* sells good food; *El Gran Escape*, central, good food, cheap; *Soda Nido* and *Restaurant Ana*, cheap cazados. A few km. E of Quepos (½ hr.) lie the 3 beautiful beaches of **Manuel Antonio** which have been declared a National Park (entrance US$0.40, good hiking in the area; camping, US$0.25 p.p., beware of theft); the beach on which the hotels stand has dangerous rip tides, the 2 inside the park are safest. There is a regular bus service from Quepos, 7 a day (US$0.25; taxi, US$2.50), and a twice daily bus from San José, 3½ hrs (0600, 1200). There are many new sets of *cabinas*; the *Mar y Sombra*, F, without bath, food and bar, friendly, generous owners, contact Sr. Ramírez (hammocks and camping free), guests can help with cooking in exchange; *Vela*, C in season, D out of season, excellent, clean, good restaurant; *Manuel Antonio Cabinas*, F, private showers, no hot water, or US$15 for family cabin; *Costa Linda*, cheapest, F, quite noisy; very basic rooms behind *Soda El Grano de Oro*; *Karahue*, D; *Los Almendros*, good fish restaurant, has rooms for 1-4 people, D, quiet, pleasant. On beach, just S of *Mar y Sombra*, is a shop renting surf boards, selling drinks and light meals, has a collection of English novels to read in the bar. Also, *Hotel Mariposa*, 3 km. from Manuel Antonio on way to Quepos, L, exclusive, but non-residents may use restaurant, good meals (book in advance), and swimming pool for US$1. Nearby is *Barba Roja* restaurant/bar, US-style, popular, not cheap (closed Sept.- Nov.). Good surfing, but there could be dangerous currents. The Park is of 490 hectares with swamps as well as beaches, and a rich variety of bird life. No permit is needed to enter. A paved road runs from Quepos to Manuel Antonio and to a pleasant beach at Dominical, which has simple cabins for rent. The beach at Jacó (with many small pebbles and rip tides, 50 km. from Quepos, 40 km. paved), which now has a good hotel *Jaco's Beach*, A; *San Antonio Cabinas*, D, with bath, clean, and the *Hotel Austral*, C full board, *Cabinas Heredia*, E with bath, can be reached from San José (bus service, from C. 1, Av. 18/20, 1500 daily plus 0845 at weekends, US$1.60) by taking the highway via Alajuela and turning off at Atenas to Orotina and the Río Tárcoles (bridge) and then on to Jacó. A coastal road is being built from Esparta (on the Pan-American Highway) through Orotina, Jacó, Quepos, Playa Dominical and thence on to San Isidro de El General. Much paving remains to be done and many bridges are still missing.

To get to the Panamanian border from Puerto Quepos take the direct bus to San Isidro de El General at 0500 and 1330 daily from the cinema (5-5½ hrs.). Motorists can do a round trip from San José via San Isidro de El General and the Pacific Coast in a day in the dry season.

Isla del Coco is a thickly-wooded island and National Park of 24 square km., 320 km. off the Peninsula of Osa, in the S. It has a 2-man outpost. Contact Michael Kaye of Costa Rican Expeditions for reasonably priced tours; also Otec in San José, see page 1147. Arrangements for reaching it by chartered boat can be made in Puntarenas, after a permit has been got from the Government. It was at one time a refuge for pirates, who are supposed to have buried great treasure there, though none has been found by the 500 expeditions which have sought it. Treasure seekers make an initial cash payment, agree to share any treasure found with the Government, and are supervised by Costa Rican police. The offshore waters are a fisherman's paradise.

Isla San Lucás is a prison island, but you may visit its beautiful beaches on Sunday. The prisoners are friendly and sell arts and crafts very cheaply. You can buy them or exchange them for items such as toothpaste, soap, etc. There is a shop selling refreshments. Launch leaves Puntarenas Sun. 0900, but arrives by 0800; returns 1500, US$1.50.

Guanacaste Province, in the NW, includes the Peninsula of Nicoya and the lowlands at the head of the gulf. The Province, with its capital at Liberia, has a distinctive people, way of life, flora and fauna. The smallholdings of the highlands give way here to large *haciendas* and great cattle estates. Maize, rice, cotton, beans and fruit are other products, and there is manganese at Playa Real. The rivers teem with fish; there are all kinds of wildlife in the uplands.

The people are open-handed, hospitable, fond of the pleasures of life: music, dancing (the Punto Guanacasteco has been officially declared the typical national dance); and merry-making (cattle and jollity often go together). There are many *fiestas* in January and February in the various towns

COSTA RICA 1157

and villages, which are well worth seeing. There are no hotels worthy of the name, and the lowlands are deep in mud during the rainy season. From San José to Nicoya, one can go via Liberia; or one can take the Pan-American Highway to a point between Puntarenas and Cañas, at a sign to Río Tempisque ferry. After crossing on this ferry (hourly, US$0.50) one can drive to Nicoya. A third route is: San José to Puntarenas, then take the ferry across the Gulf of Nicoya to Playa Naranjo (see below). Buses ply along the road from Playa Naranjo (due W across the Gulf from Puntarenas) to Nicoya (40 km. unpaved, 30 km. paved road, crowded), US$1.25, 2¼ hrs. and to Sámara, US$1.30. At Nicoya there are connections for Liberia (US$1.30, 2 hrs., US$6 from Playa Naranjo) on the Pan-American Highway. All the beaches on the Nicoya Peninsula are accessible by road in the dry season.

Nicoya, on the Peninsula, is a pleasant little town distinguished by possessing the country's second-oldest church. 5 buses a day to San José, and to nearby towns. Daily buses to Liberia.

Hotels At Nicoya: *Curime*, D with bath, restaurant; *Las Tinajas*, near bus station, E with bath, modern, clean, good value; *Chorotega*, F with bath, very good; *Yenny*, E with bath; *La Elegancia*, F; *Martín Ali*, F, both with bath; *Pensión Venecia*, opp. old church, G p.p. A good restaurant is *Chop Suey* (Chinese).

Beaches on the Nicoya Peninsula At Playa Naranjo is *Playa Oasis del Pacífico*, D, and at Playa Nandayure are *El Banco*, F, and *Hotel San Marcos*, F. On the Gulf of Nicoya is Jicaral (*Hotel Guamale*, F with bath, restaurant). At Playa de El Ocotal is *Hotel El Ocotal*, A, Tel.: 66-01-66. The beaches of Tambor and Cóbano can be reached by road from Nicoya or launch from Puntarenas, 1½ hrs. (Fri. and Sun.); Cóbano can also be reached by bus from Paquera ferry terminal, 2 hrs., US$1.50; *La Hacienda* at Tambor, B, built around a cattle farm, excellent, good restaurant, the beach is 14 km. long, grey sand, rolling surf, 1½ hrs. on a boneshaking road from ferry; *Hotel Playa de Tambor* at Cóbano, C (other *pensiones*, F). From Cóbano it is a ½-hr. ride by taxi (US$4.50, or hitch) to Montezuma, a small village on the sea (*Hotel Montezuma*, D, and another, both with restaurants; also Doña Karen lets rooms, F, she is Danish, speaks English, is very friendly, and permits use of her kitchen; one other restaurant). 20 mins.' walk from the village is a beautiful waterfall; offshore is the Island of Death; there are beautiful walks along the beach. Horses for hire from the hotels. The beach at **Sámara**, 37 km. from Nicoya, is recommended as probably the safest major bathing beach in Costa Rica. Tourists are spoiling this, and other beautiful beaches, by leaving litter. Bus from Nicoya, US$1.15, 2 hrs., twice daily (bad road, poor bus). *Cabinas Manolo*, C per cabin, good restaurant. *Cabinas Punto Guanacasteco*, not recommended. Camping on the beach possible. North of Sámara is Nosara (one bus daily from Nicoya, US$2, 2 hrs., 31 km.), with 2 beaches, Guiones, which is safe for swimming, and Peladas; a colony of North Americans has formed the Nosara Association, to protect its wildlife and forests, and prevent exploitation. There is the *Hotel Playa de Nosara* (B), expensive restaurant, and a condominium. 12 km. S of Nosara is *Hotel Villaggio Aquario Morada*, at Punta Guiones de Garza, A, a luxury beach hotel (30 bungalows, Italian restaurant, club house, bars, pool, disco, Tel.: 68-07-84).

A number of beaches are reached by unpaved roads from the Nicoya-Liberia road. They can be reached by bus from the Liberia bus station. Playa de Panamá and **Playa Junquillal** are reached by taking a bus from Liberia to Santa Cruz (on the Nicoya road), then bus at 1000 or 1415 from Guillermo Sánchez store to Paraíso (US$0.80), from where it is a 4 km. walk to Playa Junquillal, or take a car from one of the *cantinas* (*Hotel Antumalal*, L, Tel.: 68-05-06; *Villa Serena*, A, Tel.: 68-07-37; *Junquillal*, F, nice, friendly, good food; *Tortuga Inn*, 2 rooms for rent, F, meals, US$1/3, tent, and hammock space, run by Californian Bill Lauer who has plenty of information for travellers, also riding, fishing, hiking, surfing—and beautiful sunsets) glorious camping and a good beach. At Playa de Panamá is *Los Bananos*, cabins, restaurant and bar, D with bath, friendly, English spoken, good hiking, swimming, horseriding can be arranged, recommended (address is Apdo. 137, Liberia, Guanacaste). Buy food inland in **Santa Cruz**, NW of Nicoya. Hotels in Santa Cruz: *Palenque Diria*, D, bath, restaurant; *Sharatoga*, D, bath (Tel.: 68-00-11); *La Uvita*, same street as Post Office, F, clean, friendly. Cheap *pensiones*, all G and basic: *Santa Cruz*, *Isabel*, *Palmares*. La Tortillera tortilla factory is an excellent place to eat. Bus San José-Santa Cruz, 0730 direct, US$2.80; bus Santa Cruz-Tamarindo at 1500, US$0.85; Santa Cruz-Nicoya, US$0.30. Another good beach is **Playa Tamarindo**, which has an airport (plane Mon., Wed., Fri. (US$20) to San José), and is served by several buses from Liberia. *Hotel Tamarindo Diria*, B with bath, excellent; *Pozo Azul*, cabins, C (all rooms), cooking facilities, clean, good; two small *pensiones*: *Cabinas Zullymar*, D, recommended (free, protected camping nearby), and *Dolis Bar*, F, basic. *Tamarindo Diria* has a good restaurant and there are several bars and a good fish restaurant, next to Zullymar. *Boutique New York*, good French clothing and waffles. The beaches go on for many km. (one, to the left is covered in small shells). At Playa Hermosa is *Playa Hermosa Cabinas*, run by an American couple, E, clean, good reasonably-priced food; also cheaper cabins (F p.p.); 3 small restaurants on the beach. Also *Condovac La Costa*, A (Tel.: 67-02-83), luxury, and nearby *Condominio Hotel El Sitio*, B, Tel.: 66-05-74. Walking either to the left or the right you can find isolated beaches with crystal-clear water. At Playa Potrero, *Hotel Potero*, D, Tel.: 68-06-69. Popular (so noisy and very dirty) is **Playa del Coco** in an attractive islet-scattered bay hemmed in by rocky

1158 COSTA RICA

headlands; to reach it one should leave the bus at Comunidad. There are bars, restaurants and one or two motels along the sandy beach: *Hotel Flor de Itabo*, B, Tel.: 67-00-11; *Casino Playa del Coco*, E with bath; *Luna Tica* D, also has a dormitory, F (friendly, clean), both usually full at weekends. Bus to San José 0800 (Arata company), US$4, 4 hrs.; bus from San José at 1000 and from Liberia at 1230 (US$0.50).

Barra Honda National Park Small park in the midst of the Nicoya Peninsula. No permit required. Created to protect some caves (in particular Terciopelo) on a *mesa* and small remainders of dry tropical forest at the *mesa's* foot. First go to Nicoya (frequent buses from Liberia, or take the Tempisque ferry if you come from San José). There are several buses a day to Quebrada Honda, a settlement one hour away. The park office is there, at the foot of the *mesa*, and there are two different trails to the top; two hours hiking. Also noteworthy are the *cascadas*, bizarre limestone fountains built by sedimentation on a seasonal riverbed. You'll need a guide to get here, as the trails are hopelessly muddled by cowpaths; arrange in advance for the visit to the cave. Avoid coming in the rainy season (May to November), but the dry season is exceedingly hot in the open fields. Bring your own food from Nicoya.

Also on the Nicoya Peninsula, is the **Palo Verde National Park** of marshes and many water birds. Getting there is rather complicated.

Liberia (pop.: 13,700) is a neat, clean, cattle town with a church in the most modern style and a small meticulous market. There is a tourist office at the junction of the Pan-American Highway and the road leading to the town. There are regular buses (7 a day, US$2.30) to and from the capital. A well paved branch road leads SW into the Nicoya Peninsula.

Hotels at Liberia: *La Siesta*, Calle 4, Av. 4-6, E with bath, clean, good, swimming pool, helpful owner who speaks English; *Las Espuelas*, 2 km. South, C, expensive but good, swimming pool, American Express accepted (Tel.: 66-01-44; *La Ronda* (Tel.: 66-04-17), E with bath, restaurant; *El Sitio*, just off highway on road to Nicoya, D, bath, a/c, good; *Intercontinental*, D, new, good; *Bramadero Motel*, E, not all rooms have bath, good, open air restaurant and bar but somewhat noisy, swimming pool; *Liberia*, 50 metres from main square, F with shower (less without), noisy, reasonable; *Margarita*, F, basic but nice; *Casa del Ganadero Hotel*, D, bath, restaurant, also *Boyeros* (also has swimming pool) and *Centroamericano*, same price and facilities; *Oriental*, F, bath, restaurant; *Daisita*, F with bath, not very clean; *Motel Delfín*, 5 km. N of Liberia on the Pan-American Highway, E, with bath, run down, with excellent campsite and large swimming pool. Good Chinese restaurants: *Pekín*, *Cuatro Mares* (just off main square), *Cantón*. *Elegante* restaurant opp. *Hotel Liberia*. On the west side of the Plaza is a *soda* that specializes in *refrescos*. There is also a photographic studio.

Nicaraguan Consulate (6 blocks E of the main square), open Mon.-Fri. 0800-1300; 15 minutes to process a visa; take 2 photos (no onward ticket required).

37 km. north of Liberia, about half-way to the Nicaraguan border, is the **Santa Rosa National Park.** Together with the Murciélago Annex, which lies north of the developed park, it preserves some of the last dry tropical forests in Costa Rica, and shelters abundant and relatively easy-to-see wildlife. During the dry season, the animals depend on the water holes for their drinks, and are thus easy to find (except at the end of the season when the holes dry up). Santa Rosa (16,000 hectares) is of easy access from San José, as it lies west of the Pan-American Highway, about one hour north of Liberia. Any bus going to Peñas Blancas on the Nicaraguan border will drop you right at the entrance. There is a pleasant campground about 7 km. from the entrance with giant strangler figs that shade your tent from the stupendously hot sun, and very adequate sanitary facilities, picnic tables, and so forth. Bring your own food, although meals available for US$3 from kitchen at administration; a tent is useful—essential in the wet season. Bring a mosquito net and insect repellant against gnats. (If the water is not running, ask at Administration. Administration hires horses for US$1.50 per hour; if you want to make a one-way journey, ask for a *vuelvo automático*, horse which will make its own way home.) In the park is the Santa Rosa *hacienda* (*Casona*), at the start of the nature trail and close to the camp. There the patriots repelled the invasion of the filibuster Walker, who had entrenched himself in the main building.

Michael Tesch and Leone Thiele of Cape Paterson, Australia, write "**Playa Naranjo** (3 hrs.' walk) and Playa Nancite (20 mins. further) are major nesting sites of Leatherback and Ridley sea turtles. The main nesting season is between August and October (although stragglers are seen up to January regularly) when flotillas of up to 60,000 Ridley turtles arrive at night on Playa Nancite. Females clumsily lurch up the beach, scoop out a 2-foot hole, deposit and bury an average of 100 ping-pong-ball sized eggs before returning exhausted to the sea." Playa Nancite is a restricted access beach; you need a written permit to stay there free, otherwise, US$1 per day to camp, or US$1.50 in dormitories. Permits from SPN in San José.

Rincón de la Vieja National Park (20,000 hectares, NE of Liberia) was created to preserve the area around the Volcán Rincón de la Vieja, including dry tropical forest and various geothermal curiosities: mudpots, hot sulphur springs, hot springs of various other kinds. The ridge of which the volcano is the highest peak can be seen from a wide area around Liberia; it is often enshrouded in clouds. The area is cool at night and subjected to strong, gusty winds and violent rains; in the day it can be very hot, although always windy. These fluctuations mark all of the continental divide, of which the ridge is a part. To get there: a bumpy 2-hr. ride from Liberia in a truck leaving at irregular hours; alternatively, inquire when the park's truck will visit Liberia; a frequent occurrence. You can stay for free in an old, spacious, refurbished *hacienda* 2 km. inside the park. Bring your own food and bedding. From the old *hacienda* you can hike to the boiling mudpots and come back in the same day; the sulphur springs are on a different trail and only 1 hr. away. Horses can be rented from the park for US$0.60 per hour. The climb to the volcano requires camping near the top (need a tent) in order to ascend early in the morning before the clouds come in. Permission required from the SPN for visiting the park. Warning: millions of tiny ticks can be picked up in a short time of strolling in the apparently innocuous grass. Bring masking tape and a flashlight for those midnight tick hunts.

The Pan-American Highway to the Nicaraguan border, 332 km., completely paved and good. From San José it leads past El Coco airport, Heredia and Alajuela, on a new dual-carriageway section, to San Ramón (79 km.) in the middle of a coffee area, where there are good hotels (see page 1154). From San Ramón to Cañas, now resurfaced, is 98 km.; this stretch includes the sharp fall of 800 metres from the Meseta Central between San Ramón and Esparza (34 km.). (Beware of fog on this stretch if driving or cycling.) Beyond Esparza there is a left turn for Puntarenas. From Esparza through Cañas to the frontier (198 km.) the road runs through the low hills of northern Guanacaste Province; the likeliest stopover is Liberia (see page 1158), 119 km. from Esparza and 79 from Peñas Blancas on the Nicaraguan border. (Bus Liberia-Peñas Blancas, US$1.25, usually very crowded at 0900, very few between late a.m. and late p.m.; Bus Peñas Blancas-San José, Tralopa, 1030 and 1500, from San José—Coca Cola terminal—at 0445 and 0745, 6 hrs, US$2.50.) The last town before the border is La Cruz, with eating places and 3 small hotels, lovely views over the bay. At Peñas Blancas there is a duty-free shop and a thriving black market for córdobas. There is a good bar and restaurant adjoining the Costa Rican immigration offices; a good map of Costa Rica is available from the tourist office at the border (the desk opposite the counter where one pays entry tax). It's a 5 km. walk from Costa Rican immigration to the Nicaraguan side of the border. The Nicaraguan border is closed 1200-1300. Crossing to Nicaragua can be a slow process (up to 6 hrs.).

The Pan-American Highway to the Panama border runs 352 km. from San José. First to Cartago (toll road, US$0.10), and southwards over the mountains between Cartago and San Isidro de El General (124 km.). (This is a spectacular journey. The climate is ideal for orchids.) At Cartago begins the ascent of Cerro Buena Vista, a climb of 1,830 metres to the continental divide at 3,490 metres; this is the highest spot on the Highway (with an interesting *páramo* ecosystem). For 16 km. it follows the crest of the Talamanca ridge, with views, on clear days, of the Pacific 50 km. away, and of the Atlantic, over 80 km. away.

5½ km. S. of the highest point (at Km. 95, 3,335 metres, temperatures below zero at night) is *Hotel Gregorina*, F, clean, hot shower, good food; before you get there a side road leads off to the peaceful mountain villages of **Santa María de Dota** (*Hotel Santa María*, E with bath) and San Marcos de Tarrazú (Hotels: *Marilú*, F, restaurant; *Continental*, E with bath; *Zacateca*, F with bath). Santa María is quiet, and beautifully situated; it is in a good area for walking, and 8 km. away is a small lake where many waterbirds nest. From Santa María one can hike (10 hrs.) to the Pacific coast of the Puerto Quepos district, or go by road (3 hrs. in a 4-wheel drive vehicle).

The road then drops down into **San Isidro de El General**, 760 metres above sea-level in a fertile valley in the centre of a coffee and cattle district. The town is growing fast and now has several hotels: *Amaneli*, with restaurant, *Manhattan*, both E with bath; *Lala*, F with bath, restaurant, recommended; *Astoria*, *Del Sur*, D with bath, comfortable, swimming pool, good restaurant; *Hotel Balboa* in the centre, F, bath; *Hotel Chirripó*, E with bath, near bus office, modern, clean, good; *El Jardín* hotel, F, and good restaurant (especially the yoghurt); *Restaurant Wu Fu* is good, as is *Soda El Parque*, one block from Parque Central, reasonable prices.

From San Isidro de El General one can go to the highest mountain in Costa Rica, El Chirripó (3,820 metres). **Chirripó** is a large (at 72,000 hectares, the second largest), well-visited National Park including the highest peaks of Costa Rica and a considerable portion of cloud forest. Splendid views from the mountaintops; interesting alpine environment on the high plateau.

At San Isidro de El General, get food and take the Pueblo Nuevo bus to San Gerardo (0500 or 1400; be early; it leaves from the NE corner of the central plaza, but enquire carefully or you may miss it). Highly interesting trip up the Chirripó River valley; San Gerardo offers no lodging and little food; but it is situated in a cool, pleasant landscape at the confluence of two rivers. You can camp at or near the park office, 500 metres further up the road from the bus stop. Horses can be rented. Start in the early morning for the 8- to 10-hr. hike; no special skills are needed. The first shelter, where the horses will take you, is barely adequate and located in a windy spot; the second, 40 min. away, is better built, larger, and more convenient for reaching Cerro Chirripó the next morning before the clouds come in. Plan for at least two nights on the mountain, and bring warm sleeping bags and clothing. It can be hot in the daytime, though. In the rainy season trails up the plateau are uncomfortably slippery and muddy, and fog obscures the views. Time your descent to catch the 1530 bus to San Isidro. Permission from SPN necessary for this park.

Near the border is the town of **San Vito**, built by Italian immigrants among denuded hills; it is a prosperous but undistinguished town. *Hotel San Vito*, F, noisy, between 2 discos, water problems; *Pitier*, 2 blocks off main street, new, clean, F with bath. Tracopa bus from San José, 0630 daily, book previous day. Hotels also in the nearby village of Cañas Gordas. At Las Cruces there is a botanical garden run by an American couple; it has been established since the early 1950s in an old coffee plantation, 8 km. from San Vito. It consists of 50 hectares of tropical plants, orchids, other epiphytes, and tropical trees. Many birdwatchers come here. It is possible to spend the night here if you arrange first with the Organization of Tropical Studies in San José. Buses from San Vito at 0530 and 0700; return buses pass Las Cruces at 1510.

Thirty-two km. N of the border a road (26 km.) branches S at Río Claro to **Golfito**, the banana port (fuel available at the junction on the Pan-American Highway). Many of the banana plantations have been turned over to oil palm, others are diseased, so much of Golfito's business has disappeared. Golfito is really two towns: the banana company community and the town itself—about 2½ km. apart. (Hotels: *Delfina*, E with bath; *Golfito*, F; *Miramar*, *Cabinas El Tortugo*, *El Puente*, E with bath—D with a/c—clean, friendly, recommended. *El Uno*, above restaurant of same name, G, basic, friendly.) About 6 km. (1½ hr. walk) from Golfito is the Playa de Cacao and Captain Tom's place, where you can sling your hammock or camp for US$5 a day (he also has accommodation: boat, caravan or shed—the cheapest—and sells pricey drinks), but take your own food as local shopping is poor. A taxi boat from Golfito will take you there for US$0.50 (1½ km.), or you can drive (if it hasn't rained too heavily) along an inland road, starting at the left of the police station in Golfito, and left again a few km. later. 0630 bus from San José (US$3.50) with Tracopa; from San Isidro de El General, take 0730 bus to Río Claro and wait for bus coming from Ciudad Neily. Flights San José-Golfito, US$8. Bus Golfito-Paso Canoas, US$0.70.

At the southern end of the country is the **Osa Peninsula,** reached by public boat from Golfito. A boat leaves at 0700 and 1200 for Puerto Jiménez, the only town on the Peninsula (1 hr., US$1; returning 0500 and 1000, all times subject to the tide). At the same time a smaller boat leaves for Rincón (boat is called *Rincón*, 4 hrs., US$1.75). *Pensión Quintero*, Puerto Jiménez, G p.p., clean, good value; *Pensión Valentín* to be avoided. Plenty of deserted beaches (tide goes out a long way, plenty of sandflies at high tide). Puerto Jiménez is full of North Americans because of the gold mines near Carate on the Pacific coast and elsewhere on the Peninsula. Several buses a day to Dos Brazos to see the gold mines; ask for the road which goes uphill, beyond town, for the mines. Last bus back from Dos Brazos at 1530 (often late). Trucks, called "taxis" run daily between Puerto Jiménez and La Palma (several, 1 hr., US$1.50); from the small settlement of La Palma an all-weather road goes to Rincón. Another road from Rincón to the Pan-American Highway, and one is under construction from Sierpe (on the Sierpe River) to Agujitas on the Pacific coast. To reach Puerto Jiménez from the Pan-American Highway (70 km.), turn R at the restaurant about 30 km. S of Palmar Sur; this is a dirt road, impassable in the wet, otherwise best tackled with four-wheeled drive as a few rivers have to be forded (high clearance essential). Bus Puerto Jiménez-Ciudad Neily 0500 and 1400, 3½ hrs., US$2.50. There is a police checkpoint 47 km. from the Pan-American Highway.

From Agujitas boats go to the **Corcovado National Park** (closed in 1986). Including the Isla del Caño, it comprises 86,000 hectares, making it the largest park in the system. It consists largely of tropical rainforests, and it includes swamps, miles of empty beaches, and some cleared areas now growing back. It is located at the western end of the Osa Peninsula, on the Pacific Ocean. The SPN plane will fly you in (Wednesdays US$47 round trip) if they have room. Reserve well in advance. You may also arrange to eat meals and lodge at Sirena (where the plane leaves you). There is a reasonable fee for these services; lodging is US$1.20, in the open and relatively cool attic of the main building at Sirena; bring mosquito netting.

From Sirena you can walk north along the coast to the shelter at Llorona (adequate; plenty of water), from which there is a trail to the interior with another shelter at the end. Waterfalls at Llorona. From Llorona you can proceed north through a forest trail and then along the beach to the station at San Pedrillo on the edge of the park. You can stay here, camping or under roof, and eat with the friendly rangers, who love company. From San Pedrillo you can take the park boat (not cheap) to Isla del Caño, a lovely park outpost with 2 men. Continue north to the village of Agujitas, outside the park. Frequent trips with the park boat from San Pedrillo to Agujitas. From Agujitas you can get a boat to Sierpe on the Sierpe River (4 hrs.; perhaps 2 boats a week); Sierpe is connected by bus with the town of Palmar on the Pan-American Highway. Also from Sirena you can walk along the beach to Madrigal on a southern direction (excellent tidepools on the way; 2 hrs.' walking) and continue along the coast to Carate.

You can head inland from Sirena on a trail past three conveniently spaced shelters to the park border (6 hrs. of walking); then, crisscrossing the Río Rincón to La Palma, a settlement near the opposite side of the Peninsula (six more hours); from which there are several "taxis" making the one-hour trip to Puerto Jiménez. An offshoot of this trail will lead you to a raffia swamp that rings the Corcovado Lagoon. The lagoon is only accessible by boat, but there are no regular trips. Caymans and alligators survive here, sheltered from the hunters. Horses can be rented cheaply at Sirena. Chiggers (*coloradillas*) infest the horse pastures and can be a nuisance; bring spray-on insect repellant.

Avoid the rainy season. Bring umbrellas (not raincoats—too hot), because it will rain. Shelters can be found here and there, so only mosquito netting is indispensable. Bring all your food if you haven't arranged otherwise; food can only be obtained at Puerto Jiménez and Agujitas in the whole peninsula, and lodging likewise. The cleared areas (mostly outside the park, or along the beach) can be devastatingly hot. Get the Instituto Geográfico maps, scale 1:50,000. Remember finally that, in any tropical forest, you may find some unfriendly wildlife, like snakes (fer-de-lance and bushmaster snakes may attack without provocation), and herds of wild pigs.

At **Palmar Sur** (gas station), 99 km. from the border, a banana plantation has stone spheres, 1½ metres in diameter and accurate within 5 mm., which can also be seen in other places in Costa Rica. They are of precolumbian Indian manufacture, but their use is a matter of conjecture; among recent theories are that they were made to represent the planets of the solar system, or that they were border markers. 96 km. from the border at Río Claro are Hotels *Palmar Norte* and *Ximia* (F). At **Ciudad Neily,** about 18 km. from the border, are the *Motel Rancho*, *Hotel Villa*, F, simple, clean, cheap; *Hotel Museo*, new; *Las Vegas*, F with bath; *El Viajero*, F rough; and 6 km. from the border is the *Camino Real* where it is possible to camp. Here and there on the road *cantinas* sell local food. Bus Ciudad Neily to border; US$0.25. Daily bus to San José, Tracopa, from main square, US$2.70, 7 hrs. (on Sunday buses from the border are full by the time they reach Ciudad Neily). Panamanian Consulate behind Tracopa terminal. The road goes on for a bumpy 2 hrs. (plenty of buses) to **Paso Canoas** (*Hotel Azteca*, in free zone at border, E; with bath, unfriendly; *Las Cabañas El Hogar*, opp. Customs, F) on the Panama border. No fruit or vegetables can be taken into Panama. At Paso Canoas shops sell luxury items brought from Panama at prices considerably lower than those of Costa Rica (e.g. sunglasses, stereo equipment, kitchen utensils, etc.); banks either side of border close at 1600. No difficulty in getting rid of surplus colones with money changers. Bus San José-Paso Canoas, US$5.25, Tracopa terminal Av. 18, C. 4 at 0500, 0800 and 1700, not all buses go to border; Paso Canoas-San José at 0700 and 1400. Those motoring N can get insurance cover at the border for US$6 ensuring public liability and property damage. Border open 0700-1200, 1300-1700, 1800-2200. **N.B.** If you need a tourist card only to enter Panama, you are strongly advised to get it before the border, as Panamanian border officials often do not have them (see page 1190).

The Economy

The country's economy is based on the export of coffee, bananas, meat, sugar and cocoa. The Meseta Central with its volcanic soil is the coffee-growing area: here too are grown the staple crops: beans, maize, potatoes and sugar cane, and the dairy farming is both efficient and lucrative. Some 22% of the land area is planted to crops, 36% to pasture and 40% is forested. The country's timber industry is very small and its resources have yet to be commercially utilized.

High growth in the industrial sector has led to considerable economic diversification, and industry accounts for 20% of gdp, compared with 21% in the case of agriculture. Industry is largely concerned with food processing but there is also some production of chemicals (including fertilizers—also exported), plastics, tyres, etc. Current major industrial projects include aluminium processing, a petrochemical plant at Moín, and a tuna-fish processing plant at Golfito.

There are small deposits of manganese, mercury, gold and silver, but only the last two are worked. Deposits of iron ore are estimated at 400m. tons and sulphur deposits at 11m. tons. Considerable bauxite deposits have been found but have not yet been developed. In 1980, the Arenal hydroelectric plant was opened; when operating at full capacity it can supply 98% of the country's electricity needs. The Government is presently involved in developing the Corobicí and other hydroelectric complexes as well as improving the port of Caldera on the Pacific coast and encouraging manufacturing through the state agency Codesa. Oil companies are interested in offshore concessions in the Pacific. The State has recently taken over the oil refinery at Puerto Limón.

Despite several IMF-supported austerity programmes, the Costa Rican economy still suffers from large public sector deficits, partly because of a high level of government spending on social welfare. The country is burdened with a large foreign debt, which including accumulated arrears, amounts to nearly US$5bn and is one of the highest per capita (pop. 2.6m est.) in the developing workld. In the late 1980s, Costa Rica turned to the IMF and the World Bank for help in adjusting its economy, and proposed several radical means by which it could begin again to service its debt to commercial banks.

COSTA RICA

	1960-71 (av)	1971-80 (av)	1981-85 (av)	1986 (e)
Gdp growth (1980 prices)	6.1%	5.6%	0.2%	3.0%
Inflation	2.3%	10.8%	34.8%	12.0%
Exports (fob) US$m	137	601	922	1,114
Coffee	52	180	255	-
Bananas	35	126	231	-
Beef	79	45	53	-
Imports (fob)m	164	765	959	1,092
Current account balance US$m (cum)	-407	-2,823	-1,503	-160

Information for Visitors

Air Services From London: British Airways, Pan Am or Virgin Atlantic to Miami, then by Lacsa to San José. British Caledonian, TWA, etc. to other US gateway cities: carriers from the USA are: from Houston, Sahsa, Taca; from San Francisco, Taca (Sat., direct); from Los Angeles, Taca, Lacsa, Mexicana; from New Orleans, Lacsa, Taca, Sahsa; from New York/Miami, Challenge International; from Los Angeles/San Francisco/ Miami, Pan Am (5 days a week); from Miami, Lacsa (direct), Taca and Sahsa. Lacsa flies to the following Central and South American destinations (other airlines on these routes in brackets): Mexico City (Mexicana, Taca, Aeronica), Cancún, San Pedro Sula (Sahsa), San Salvador (Copa, Taca, Aeronica), Panama City (Copa, Taca, Aeronica), Cartagena (SAM) and Barranquilla, Maracaibo and Caracas, Quito and Guayaquil, Rio de Janeiro, San Juan (Puerto Rico). Aeronica excursion from Panama City, US$200 including 3 free nights in a good hotel and free airport transfers. Other connections from San José: Belize City (Sahsa, Taca), Tegucigalpa (Sahsa), Managua (Copa, Taca, Aeronica), San Andrés Island (SAM), Bogotá and Medellín (SAM), Quito with Varig every Saturday. From Europe: KLM from Amsterdam twice a week via Caracas, Curaçao and Panama; Iberia from Madrid on Sunday via Santo Domingo, on Thursday via San Juan (Puerto Rico), continuing to Lima (returning to San José before flying back to Madrid).

There is an airport tax of about US$7 for tourists, and if you obtained an extension on your tourist card or visa, you need an exit visa, US$6. There is an 8% tax on airline tickets purchased in the country. Tickets bought in San Andrés (Colombia) carry no tax.

Shipping Services The quickest and cheapest freight route from the United Kingdom is by vessels of the Pacific Steam Navigation Co., with transshipment at Cristóbal: thence by local service to Limón or through the Canal to Puntarenas. Hapag-Lloyd and the Horn Line have services from European ports to Puntarenas and Puerto Limón. Royal Mail Lines and PSNC carry no passengers.

Documents Passports are required, except for holders of tourist cards, who must also hold proof of identity. Visas are not required for visits of up to 90 days by nationals of Western European countries, USA, Canada, Colombia, Panama, Brazil, Japan, and Yugoslavia. Tourist cards can be got from airlines or bought at San José airport; they are valid for 30 days but may be extended to 6 months, and cost US$2. Sometimes it is difficult to get an extension, which costs US$1.20 and involves a lot of "red tape". Australians, Israelis, Central American countries except those given above, and others require a visa, costing US$5 (payable only in US dollars, one report said US$20 for a visa for Australians), valid for only 30 days. For extensions it is apparently quicker to go to Migración in Puntarenas than queue in San José. However, it appears that extensions for visas are very costly, about US$30; they are valid for 30 days. Then you have to get an exit visa when you leave (US$6). Alternatively you can just get an exit permit, which is valid for one month. This involves going to Tribunales in San José to declare that you are leaving no dependants in Costa Rica. There is an emigration tax of US$2. Travel agents can arrange all extension and exit formalities for a small fee. An onward ticket (a bus ticket—which can be bought from the driver on Tica international buses—or an MCO will do) is asked for, but cashing in an air ticket is difficult because you may be asked to produce another ticket out of the country. Also, tourists may have to show at least US$300 in cash or travellers' cheques before being granted entry (especially if you have no onward ticket). There is an entrance tax of 10 colones and an exit tax of 20 colones for overland travellers (except those in their own vehicle). On international bus trips, departure tax is paid before leaving and is paid in US dollars. Half a kilo of manufactured tobacco and 3 litres of liquor are allowed in duty-free. Any amount of foreign or local currency can be taken in or out.

COSTA RICA 1163

Always carry a passport, or photocopy, for presentation at spot-checks. Failure to do so may mean imprisonment.

N.B. At the land borders with Nicaragua, travellers have had to show that they are taking anti-malaria tablets. If you have been more than a few days in Nicaragua (for example, working on a brigade), you may be refused entry into Costa Rica. Nicaraguan literature is likely to be confiscated.

N.B. also Entrance and exit taxes, by air or land, and legislation regarding visa extensions, are subject to frequent change and travellers should check these details as near to the time of travelling as possible.

Warnings Those arriving by air from Colombia can expect to have their persons and baggage carefully searched because of the rampant drug traffic in the area. In Costa Rica, particularly on the Atlantic coast, do not get involved with drugs: many dealers are undercover police agents.

There has been much illegal immigration into Costa Rica: this explains why Migración officials sometimes grill visitors in their hotels.

The information offices of the **Instituto Costarricense de Turismo** are by the Plaza de la Cultura, entrance on C. 5, Av. Central/2, San José (tel.: 22-10-90). There is a branch office at Cartago. All tourist information is given here. Take complaints about hotel overcharging to the Instituto. There is a free weekly magazine, *The San José Gourmet*, dealing with tourism and restaurant news.

Shopping Best buys are wooden items, ceramics, leather handicrafts and coffee.

British business travellers going to Costa Rica are strongly advised to get a copy of "Hints to Exporters: Costa Rica" from Export Services Division, Dept. of Trade, Sanctuary Buildings, 16-20 Great Smith Street, London SW1P 4DB.

Business Hours 0800 or 0830 to 1100 or 1130 and 1300 to 1700 or 1730 (1600, government offices), Mon. to Fri., and 0800 to 1100 on Sat. Shops: 0800 to 1200, 1300 to 1800 Mon. to Sat.

Standard Time is 6 hrs. behind Greenwich Mean Time.

The climate varies from the heat and humidity of the Caribbean and Atlantic lowlands to warm temperate on the Meseta Central and chilly temperatures at the greater heights. There are dry and wet seasons: the dry runs from December to April, the wet from May to November, when the rainfall in the Meseta Central averages 1,950 mm. and roads are often bogged down. The hottest months are March and April. Between December and April is the best time to visit.

Clothing Shorts are worn just about everywhere, except in San José, by both men and women. Strapless sun-dresses are never worn in San José, but trousers are quite OK. Women need hats only for weddings and official functions.

Health Drinking water is safe in all major towns; elsewhere it should be boiled. Intestinal disorders and Chagas disease are prevalent in the lowlands although malaria has to a great extent been eradicated; malaria prophylaxis is advised for visitors to the lowlands, all the same. Uncooked foods should not be eaten. The standards of health and hygiene are among the best in Latin America. Ice cream, milk, etc. are safe.

Food Stefaan Platteau, resident in San José, tells us: *Sodas* (small restaurants) serve local food, which is worth trying. Very common is *casado*, which includes rice, beans, stewed beef, fried plantain and cabbage. *Olla de carne* is a soup of beef, plantain, corn, yuca, *ñampi* and *chayote* (local vegetables). *Sopa negra* is made with black beans, and comes with a poached egg in it; *picadillo* is another meat and vegetable stew. Snacks are popular: *gallos* (filled tortillas), *tortas* (containing meat and vegetables), *arreglados* (bread filled with the same) and *empanadas*. *Pan de yuca* is a speciality, available from stalls in San José centre. A *soda* in Moravia (8 km. from San José), Soda San Martín, is highly recommended for local fare. Best ice cream can be found in *Pops* shops in San José. *Schmidt* bakeries are highly recommended; they also serve coffee. Also *La Selecta* bakeries. Eating in Costa Rica is cheap on the whole.

There are many types of cold drink, made either from fresh fruit, or milk drinks with fruit or cereal flour whisked with ice cubes. The fruits range from the familiar to the exotic; others include *cebada* (barley flour), *pinolillo* (roasted corn), *horchata* (rice flour with cinnamon), *chan*, "perhaps the most unusual, looking like mouldy frogspawn and tasting of penicillium" (Michael J. Brisco). All these drinks cost the same as, or less than, bottled fizzy products. Excellent coffee.

Motoring Car hire firms are not covered by tourist regulations and many complaints have been made to the authorities concerning their operations. If hiring a car, be very cautious. Tourists who come by car pay US$10 road tax and can keep their cars for an initial period of 30 days. This can be extended for a total period of 6 months at the Instituto Costarricense de Turismo, or at the Customs office if you take your passport, car entry permit, and a piece of stamped paper (*papel sellado*) obtainable at any bookshop. Cars are fumigated on entry (US$1). It is now mandatory for

COSTA RICA

foreign drivers to buy insurance stamps on entry for a minimum of 3 months; e.g. motorcycle, US$6 and car, US$6. If you want to travel on from Costa Rica without your car, you should leave it in the customs warehouse at the international airport at San José. For a longer period than 60 days, however, it is necessary to leave it in a private bonded warehouse. The cost is about US$10 a week, plus US$60 to arrange it through a customs agent, plus a considerable amount of paperwork. San José is the best place to get Land Rover spares. To sell a car in Costa Rica you must pay a duty which is equivalent to four times the market value of the car. **Important Note:** Only regular-grade gasoline is available (but of good quality), US$0.50 per litre; high-compression engines need to be adjusted before entering Costa Rica. Tyres without rims are confiscated and burnt by the Customs. Motorcyclists must wear crash helmets. Gas-oil is available, as are spares for Japanese makes in San José.

Hitch-hiking is easy. Walkers should obtain a copy of *Backpacking in Mexico and Central America* (1982), by Hilary Bradt and Rob Rachowiecki.

Currency The unit is the colón, sub-divided into 100 céntimos. The old coins of 5, 10, 25 and 50 céntimos and 1 and 2 colones, and notes of 5, 10 and 20 colones are being phased out. New coins in use are for 25 and 50 céntimos and 1, 2, 5, 10 and 20 colones. Public telephones now use 2, 5, and 10 colon coins. Paper money in use: 50, 100 and 1,000 colones. (5,000 and 10,000 colon notes have not yet been issued, although they are planned).

Exchange of US dollars (etc) must be effected in a bank, and for bank drafts and transfers a minimum of US$7.50 commission is charged (Central Bank regulation). Some hotels (e.g. *Austral, Gran*) are permitted to change dollars. A small black market exists although it is illegal to exchange in the street, and is hardly worth the risk. In April 1986 the official exchange rate was 54.70 colones per US$, and the free market on the Panamanian side of the frontier offered 57.50 colones per US$. Sterling is not officially exchangeable, but Barclays cheques are negotiable at Banco Lyon, S.A.

Tips A 10% service charge is automatically added to restaurant bills, as well as 10% government tax. Ten colones per bag for porters; same for hairdressers. Taxis and cinema usherettes, nil; 10% at hotels, restaurants, cafés, bars; Ten colones for cloakroom attendants.

Mail by sea from the UK takes from 2-3 months and 3 to 5 days by airmail. Airmail letters to Europe cost 18 colones; to North/South America, 16 colones; to Australia, Africa and Asia, 20 colones. "Expreso" letters, 14 colones extra, several days quicker to USA and N. Europe. Registered mail, 25 colones extra. All parcels sent out of the country by foreigners must have clearance from the Banco Central de Costa Rica. Lista de Correos charges 8 colones per letter, and will keep letters for 4 weeks.

Cable Offices and long-range radio-telephone service are run by the Instituto Costarricense de Electricidad and by Cía. Radiográfica Internacional de Costa Rica, whose HQ is at San José (Av. 5, Calle 1). Local cables, though are sent from the main post office in San José, Av. 1/3, C. 2. A telephone system connects San José with the country's main centres. The Government's wireless station at San José communicates with Mexico, Guatemala and El Salvador. A Radio and Telephone Ground Satellite Station was opened at San Pedro in January 1982. Calls abroad can be made from phone booths; collect calls abroad may be made from special booths in the telephone office, Av. 5, C. 1, San José. A daytime telephone call to the UK costs US$3 a minute, US$2 at night and weekends (no reverse charge calls to Europe); to USA, US$1.60-2.40 per min., night and weekends US$0.65-1 per min., depending on to which state; to Canada, US$2.80-3.80 per min. depending on which province; to Australia, Africa, Asia, US$5 per minute. Public telex booth at Radiográfica S.A., Av. 5, C. 1 (telex CR 1050); the telex must show your name and Tel. no. or address for them to advise you. There is a public telex service run by Canon Copying Centres (Av. 2, C. 11/13—Telex No. CR 2913) who charge US$1 for receiving; telex to UK, US$3 per minute. Facsimile charge (FAX), US$8 to North America, US$10 to Europe.

For Customs the metric system of **weights and measures** is compulsory. Traders use a variety of weights and measures, including English ones and the old Spanish ones.

Public Holidays

January 1: New Year's Day
March 19: St. Joseph.
Easter: 3 days.
April 11: Battle of Rivas.
May 1: Labour Day.

June: Corpus Christi.
June 29: St. Peter and St. Paul
July 25: Guanacaste Day.

August 2: Virgin of Los Angeles.
August 15: Mothers' Day.
September 15: Independence Day.
October 12: Columbus Day.
December 8: Conception of the Virgin.
December 25: Christmas Day.
December 28-31: San José only.

COSTA RICA 1165

N.B. During Holy Week, nearly everyone is on holiday. Everywhere is shut on Fri., Sat., and Sun., and most of the previous week as well (in San José and Cartago only a small percentage of businesses and services close Mon.-Wed. and Sat. of Holy Week; almost all transport stops on Good Friday only).

Association football is the **national sport** (played every Sunday at 1100, May to October, at the Saprissa Stadium). There are golf courses at San José and Puerto Limón. There is sea-bathing on both Atlantic and Pacific coasts (see text). The Meseta is good country for riding; horses can be hired anywhere. Most *fiestas* end with bullfighting in the squares, an innocuous but amusing set-to with no horses used. Bullfights are held in San José during the Christmas period. There is no kill and spectators are permitted to enter the ring to chase, and be chased by, the bull. Much wildlife in the Guanacaste and northern jungle areas. There is good sea-fishing off Puntarenas and in the mouth of the Río Chirripó, on the Caribbean side near the Nicaraguan border; inland river-fishing has been ruined by dynamiting.

Newspapers The best San José morning papers are *La Nación* and *La República*. *La Prensa Libre* is a good morning and evening paper. *Libertad*, weekly newspaper (socialist). *El Debate* is another good weekly. *La Gazette* is the official government weekly paper. *Tico Times* (Fri.) in English.

Broadcasting 6 local TV stations, many MW/FM radio stations throughout the country. Local Voz de América (VOA) station. Many hotels and private homes receive one of the 4 TV stations offering direct, live, 24-hr TV from the USA (Canal 19, Supercanal, Cable Color and Cable Yudu—all US cable TV can be received in San José on the 2 cable stations).

We are deeply grateful for the assistance received from Simon Ellis, and Chris Rosene, resident in San José, and from the following travellers: Mary Lou Benoit (Trenton, NJ), Alexander Daughtry (Vancouver), David Finn (Dallas) and Andrew Sherman (Los Angeles), Sara S. Hradecky (Ottawa), the Very Revd. Michael Napier (London SW7), Susan L. Niemayer (Ankeny, Iowa) for a most useful contribution, C.Nooteboom (Amsterdam), Martin J. Osborne (Toronto) for a most valuable contribution, Ken Robinson (Johannesburg), Judy L. Schneider (Tucson, Ariz.), Gustavo Steinbrun Bianco (Buenos Aires), Pauline Williams (St. Feock, Cornwall) for another fine contribution, Roman Zukowski (Karlsruhe) and other travellers listed in the general Central America section.

PANAMA

THE S-SHAPED ISTHMUS OF PANAMA, 80 km. at its narrowest and no more than 193 km. at its widest, is one of the great cross-roads of the world. Its destiny has been entirely shaped by that fact. To it Panama owes its national existence, the make-up of its population and their distribution: two-fifths of the people are concentrated in the two cities which control the entry and exit of the canal. Panama covers 82,860 square km. The Canal Area, formerly Zone, is being gradually incorporated into Panamanian jurisdiction; this long process began in 1964, when Panama secured the right to fly its flag in the Zone alongside that of the USA, and is due for completion and Panamanian operation of the Canal by 2000.

Only about a quarter of the country is inhabited and most of it is mountainous, with shelvings of lowland on both its 1,234 km. of Pacific and 767 km. of Atlantic coastlines. The country's axis is, in general, SW to NE, but the mountain chains do not conform to this and run NW to SE. At the border with Costa Rica there are several volcanic cones, the boldest of which is the extinct Barú, 3,383 metres high. The sharp-sided Cordillera de Talamanca continues SE at a general altitude of about 900 metres, but subsides suddenly SW of Panama City. The next range, the San Blas, rises E of Colón and runs into Colombia; its highest peaks are not more than 900 metres. A third range rises from the Pacific littoral in the SE; it, too, runs into Colombia and along the Pacific coast as the Serranía de Baudó.

Good fortune decreed a gap between the Cordillera de Talamanca and the San Blas range in which the divide is no more than 87 metres high. The ranges are so placed that the gap, containing the Canal, runs from NW to SE. To reach the Pacific from the Atlantic we must travel eastwards, and at dawn the sun rises over the Pacific.

Rainfall is heavy along the Caribbean coast: more than 3,800 mm. a year in some places, with huge but brief downpours between April and December. Temperature in the lowland ranges from 21°C (70°F) at night to 32°C (90°F) by day. The result is deep tropical forest along the coast and far up the sides of the ranges: most of the land surface of Panama is forested. The rain begins to shade off towards the crests of the mountains (10° to 18°C), and is much less along the Pacific, though there is no scarcity of it anywhere. At Balboa it is only 1,727 mm. a year, and the tropical forest gives way to semi-deciduous trees and areas of savanna between the Pacific and the mountains.

Most of the rural population live in the 6 provinces on the Pacific side, W of the Canal. Only 16% of the total land area is farmed; 7.3% is pasture, nearly all of it in the 6 provinces; 3.1% only is under crops, almost all in the same provinces. There are some very large estates but the land-reform process has begun. There is only one rural population centre of any importance on the Caribbean: in Bocas del Toro, in the extreme NW.

Population The population (2.23 million in 1986) is mostly of mixed blood but there are communities of Indians, blacks and a few Asians. About 40% live in or near Panama City and Colón, at opposite ends of the Canal. Annual population growth is 2.2%. Of the sixty Indian tribes who inhabited the isthmus at the time of the Spanish conquest, only three have survived: the Cunas of the San Blas Islands, the Guaymíes of the western provinces and the Chocóes of Darién.

The birth-rate is 26.5 and the death-rate 3.9 per thousand, 57% is urban; in the countryside 43%, and in the towns 6% are illiterate; 65.5% of the children are born to unmarried mothers. In Bocas de Toro half the population speaks Spanish, half speaks English. Only a few of the indigenous Indians can speak Spanish.

Numbers of African slaves escaped from their Spanish owners during the 16th century. They

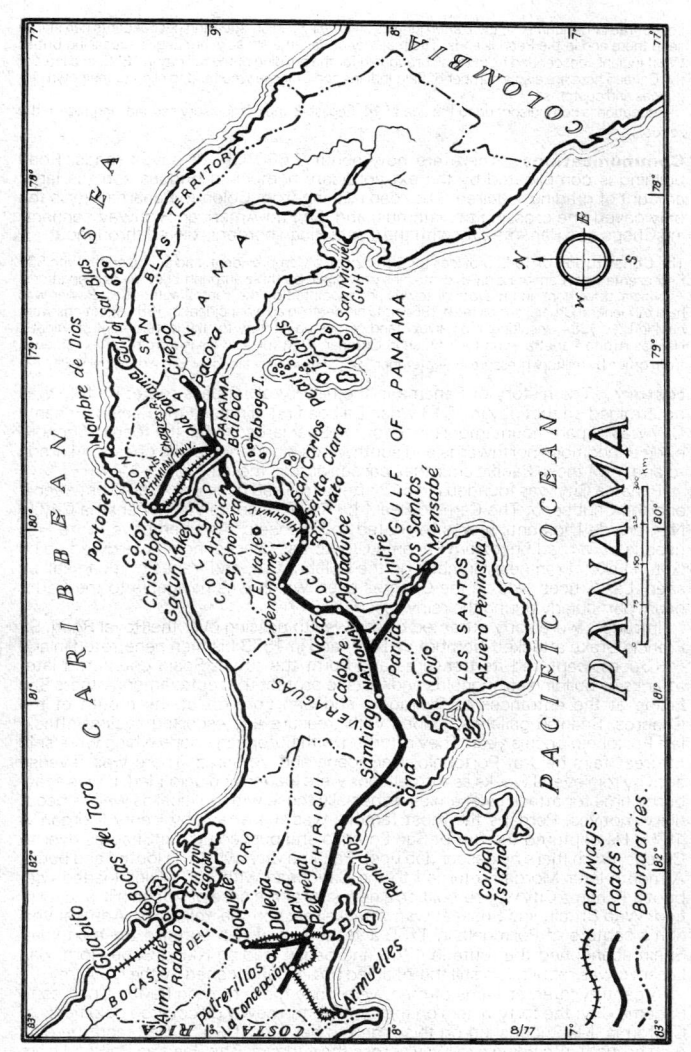

PANAMA

1168 PANAMA

set up free communities in the Darién jungles and their Spanish-speaking descendants can still be seen there and in the Pearl Islands. The majority of Panama's blacks are English-speaking British West Indians, descended from those brought in for the building of the railway in 1850, and later of the Canal. There are also a number of East Indians and Chinese who tend to cling to their own languages and customs.

Education is compulsory up to the age of 14. English is the compulsory second language in the schools.

Communications   There are now about 7,680 km. of paved roads. Road building is complicated by the extraordinary number of bridges and the large amount of grading required. The road running from Colón to Panama City is the only paved one crossing the isthmus, and the Pan-American Highway connecting Chepo and Panama City with the Costa Rican border is paved throughout.

The **Constitution** of 1972 provides for a president, a vice-president, and an Assembly with 505 Representatives. Panama is divided into nine provinces and three autonomous Indian reservations. Provincial governors and mayors of towns are appointed by the central authorities. Power was held by General Omar Torrijos from 1968 until his death in an air accident in 1981. Elections were held in May 1984, resulting in a narrow (and contested) victory for the government candidate, Nicolás Ardito Barletta, who took office in October 1984 for a six-year term but was removed from office by military pressure in September 1985. He was replaced by Eric Arturo del Valle.

History   The history of Panama is the history of its pass-route; its fate was determined on that day in 1513 when Balboa first glimpsed the Pacific. Panama City was of paramount importance for the Spaniards: it was the focus of conquering expeditions northwards and southwards along the Pacific coasts. All trade to and from these Pacific countries passed across the isthmus.

Panama City was founded in 1519 after a trail had been discovered between it and the Caribbean. The Camino Real (the Royal Road) ran from Panama City to Nombre de Dios until it was re-routed to Portobelo. An alternative route was used later: a road built from Panama City to Las Cruces, now swallowed up by Gatún Lake; it ran near Gamboa on the Culebra Cut, and traces of it can still be seen. Las Cruces was on the Chagres river, which was navigable to the Caribbean, particularly during the rainy season.

Intruders were early attracted by the wealth passing over the Royal Road. Sir Francis Drake attacked Nombre de Dios, and in 1573 his men penetrated inland to Cruces, captured its treasures and burnt the town. Spain countered later attacks by building strongholds and forts to protect the route: among others San Felipe at the entrances to Portobelo and San Lorenzo at the mouth of the Chagres. Spanish galleons, loaded with treasure and escorted against attack, left Portobelo once a year. They returned with European goods which were sold at great fairs held at Portobelo, Cartagena and Veracruz. There was feverish activity for several weeks as the galleons were loaded and unloaded. It was a favourite time for attack by enemies, especially those with political as well as pecuniary motives. Perhaps the most famous was the attack by Henry Morgan in 1671. He captured the fort of San Lorenzo and pushed up the Chagres river to Cruces. From there he descended upon Panama City, which he looted and burnt. A month later Morgan returned to the Caribbean with 195 mules loaded with booty. Panama City was re-built on a new site, at the base of Ancón hill, and fortified. With Britain and Spain at war, attacks reached their climax in Admiral Vernon's capture of Portobelo in 1739 and the fort of San Lorenzo the next year. Spain abandoned the route in 1746 and began trading round Cape Horn. San Lorenzo was rebuilt: it is still there, tidied up and landscaped by the US Army.

A century later, streams of men were once more moving up the Chagres to Panama City: the forty-niners on their way to the newly discovered gold fields of *California. Many* perished on this "road to hell", as it was called, and the gold rush brought into being a railway across the isthmus. The Panama Railroad from Colón (then only two streets) to Panama City took four years to build, with great loss of life. The first train was run on November 26, 1853. The railway was an enormous financial success until the re-routing of the Pacific Steam Navigation Company's ships round Cape Horn in 1867 and the opening of the first US transcontinental railroad in 1869 reduced its traffic.

Ferdinand de Lesseps, builder of the Suez Canal, arrived in Panama in 1881, and decided to build a sea-level canal along the Chagres river and the Río Grande. Work started in 1882. One of the diggers in 1886 and 1887 was the painter Gauguin, aged 39. Thirty km. had been dug before the Company crashed in 1893, defeated by extravagance and tropical diseases (22,000 people died). Eventually Colombia (of which Panama was then a Department) authorized the Company to sell all its rights and properties to the United States, but the Colombian Senate rejected the treaty, and the inhabitants of Panama, encouraged by the States, declared their independence on November 3, 1903. The United States intervened and, in spite of protests by Colombia, recognized the new republic. Colombia did not accept the severance until 1921.

Before beginning the task of building the Canal the United States performed one of the greatest sanitary operations in history: the clearance from the area of the more malignant tropical diseases. The name of William Crawford Gorgas will always be associated with this, as will that of George Washington Goethals with the actual building of the Canal. On August 15, 1914, the first passage was made, by the ship *Ancón*.

The former Canal Zone was a ribbon of territory extending 8 km. on either side of the Canal and including the cities of Cristóbal and Balboa. The price paid by the United States Government to Panama for construction rights was US$10m. The French company received US$40m. for its rights and properties. US$25m. were given to Colombia in compensation for the transfer of the French company's rights. The total cost at completion was US$387m. Panama long ago rejected the perpetuity clause of the original Canal Treaty. In April 1978 a new treaty was ratified and on October 1, 1979 the Canal Zone, now known officially as the Canal Area, was formally transferred to Panamanian sovereignty, including the ports of Cristóbal and Balboa, the Canal dry docks, the trans-isthmus railway and the naval base of Coco Solo, but the US still retains extensive military base areas. Until the final transfer of ownership in 2000 the Canal administration is in the hands of the Comisión del Canal, on which the USA retains majority representation.

Landfall on the Caribbean side for the passage of the Canal is made at the twin cities of Cristóbal and Colón, the one merging into the other almost imperceptibly and both built on Manzanillo Island at the entrance of the Canal; the island has now been connected with the mainland. Colón was founded in 1852 as the terminus of the railway across the isthmus; Cristóbal came into being as the port of entry for the supplies used in building the Canal.

Cristóbal Ships usually dock at Pier No. 9, five mins. from the shops of Colón. Vehicles are always waiting at the docks for those who want to visit Colón and other places. Cristóbal Yacht Club has a good restaurant.

Colón, population 68,000, the second largest city in Panama, was originally called Aspinwall, after one of the founders of the railway. Despite its fine public buildings and well-stocked shops, it has some of the nastiest slums in Latin America, and is generally dirty. It has been described as having a "rough, but wonderful honky-tonk atmosphere." Annual mean temperature: 26°C.

Warning Mugging, even in daylight, is a real threat in both Colón and Cristóbal. We have received repeated warnings of robbery in Colón, often within 5 minutes of arrival.

There is a Free Zone at Colón which offers facilities for the import, free of duty, of bulk goods for re-export to neighbouring countries after packaging; it is not possible to take your purchases out of the zone; you must arrange for them to be taken to the airport before you leave (or you must smuggle them out). The zone is closed on Saturdays and Sundays.

There are good roads to Coco Solo nearby, to France Field, and to Fort Davis and the Gatún Locks, some 11 km. away.

The tourist should see the Cathedral between Herrera and Av. Amador Guerrero (open afternoons only), and the statues on the promenade known as the Paseo Centenario. The historic *Hotel Washington* is worth a look. For local products, try Isthmian Curio Shop, between Calle 10 and 11, and Sombrería Aldao for panama hats.

The beach drive round Colón, pleasant and cool in the evening, takes 30 minutes or longer.

Hotels *Washington*, A, there is a small casino; *Sotelo*, B, also has casino; *Andros*, C; *Plaza*, C; *García*, C; *Astor*, D. These rates are without meals, whose average price is US$5-8. *Pensión Plaza*,

1170 PANAMA

Av. Central, is clean, cheap, D. *Pensión Acrópolis*, E, clean and comfortable; *Pensión Andros Annex*, E, comfortable and safe; *Pensión Kingston*, E. If destitute try the Salvation Army.

Principal Restaurants *Cristóbal Yacht Club; La Nueva China*, Av. Central and Calle 8, a/c; *VIP Club* in Front Street; YMCA restaurant, right across from the railway station.

Taxi Tariffs vary, but are generally not high and may be agreed on in advance. Most drivers speak some English.

Cabarets Club 61, Av. Bolívar. No cover charge. Three shows nightly at 2000, 2300 and 0100. Club Florida, 3 shows nightly. Café Esquire.

Cinemas Non-stop performances on Av. Central.

Fishing The Panama Canal Tarpon Club (entrance US$15, annual subscription US$15) has accommodation for anglers at the Gatún Spillway at a charge of US$5 per day. Live bait is provided, tackle is loaned. The sleeping cots are not furnished with bedding. The kitchen has facilities for cooking foods bought from the club attendant. The hut is a few yards only from the Spillway, a torrent teeming with large fish.

Clubs Golf (18 holes) at Brazos Brook Country Club. Rotary Club, weekly lunches.

Cables Tropical Radio Telegraph Co., Av. Roosevelt.

Post Office On corner of Av. Bolívar and Calle 9.

Banks Chase Manhattan Bank; Citibank; Banco Nacional de Panamá; Caja de Ahorros; Lloyds Bank International (Bahamas)—ex BOLSA—agency in Colón Free Zone, at Calle 15 & D. Open 0800-1300, Mon. to Fri.

British Consulate P.O. Box 1108, Cristóbal. Tel.: 7-3075.

Shipping a vehicle to Colombia, see page 1187.

Bus Service At least every hour to Panama City: US$1.75, 2 hours including express bus from Av. Amador Guerrero.

Trains On weekdays there are 4 trains a day and on Sat and Sun. and holidays 3, to Panama City from Colón. Journey time 1 hr. 25 mins., US$1.25. Colón station is at Calle 11 and Front Street, near the shopping area. The journey is interesting, with views (not all the time) of Canal, ships and jungle.

Air Services Local flights to Panama City.

Trips from Colón: *Portobelo* is 48 km. NE of Colón by sea or by road. Colombus used the harbour in 1502 and it was a Spanish garrison town for more than two centuries. Drake died and was buried at sea off the Bay of Portobelo. Three large stone forts face the entrance to the harbour. There can be seen old Spanish cannon, and the treasure house where gold from Peru brought over the Las Cruces trail from Panama City was stored until the galleons for Spain arrived. There are ruins of various forts, a waterfall, and mountain views (no information available locally). In the Cathedral is a statue of the Black Christ; it was being shipped from Spain to the Viceroy of Peru, but the ship was wrecked in the bay and the statue salvaged by the natives. The image is carried through the streets at 1800 on October 21; afterwards there is feasting and dancing till dawn. Local rainfall, 4,080 mm. a year. Population 1,980.

Buses from Colón to Portobelo, every hour from 0700; leave from corner Calle 11 and Av. Domingo Díaz, US$1.30 single. Portobelo can be visited from Panama City in a day by taking an early train to Colón, then go straight to the bus for Portobelo: on the return, take a bus from Portobelo to Sabanitas, at the junction with the Transisthmian Highway (US$1) and catch a bus back to Panama City (US$0.90). Many beaches on the way from Colón, such as Cangrejo, about 8 km. Playa Langosta, 8 km. from Portobelo, is also recommended, though facilities there are basic. María Chiquita beach has a bathing pavilion managed by the government tourist bureau, 45 minutes from Colón, US$0.60.

From Colón, visit also the old French canal, modern Canal township of Margarita, Gatún Locks (one hour). The locks are open to visitors every day 0800-1600; they can enter the lock area and take photographs, while guides explain the Canal operation. (Bus from Colón to Gatún locks, US$0.20.) Visitors can cross the locks at Gatún, and also ride through virgin jungle where wild pigs, iguanas, land crabs and snakes scuttle across the road.

Fort San Lorenzo, on the other side of the Canal at the mouth of the Chagres river, is a 16th-century fort with 18th-century additions, reached from Gatún locks by road to Fort Sherman in the

Canal Area. From Fort Sherman one must drive, hitch-hike or walk 10 km. to the fort; the 18th-century part, on the top of cliffs, commands a fine view of the mouth of the Chagres river and the bay below. It was sacked by Henry Morgan and by Admiral Vernon; one of Vernon's cannon with the GR monogram can be seen.

Isla Grande, just off the coast, can be reached by boats hired from a car park, and a bus service; there are two hotels: *Isla Grande*, A p.p. in huts scattered along an excellent sandy beach, meals extra, and *Jackson's*, cheaper, also huts. The island is a favourite of scuba divers and snorkellers.

San Blas Islands An interesting trip can be made to the San Blas archipelago, which has 365 islands ranging in size from tiny ones with a few coconut palms to islands on which hundreds of Cuna Indians live. The islands, off the Caribbean coast E of Colón, vary in distance from the shore from 100 metres to several kilometres.

The Cuna are the most sophisticated and politically organized of the country's three major tribes. They run the San Blas Territory virtually on their own terms, with internal autonomy and, uniquely among Panama's Indians, send their representative to the National Assembly. The women wear gold nose- and ear-rings, and costumes suggestive of ancient Egyptians. They are outside the Panamanian tax zone and negotiated a treaty perpetuating their long-standing trade with small craft from Colombia.

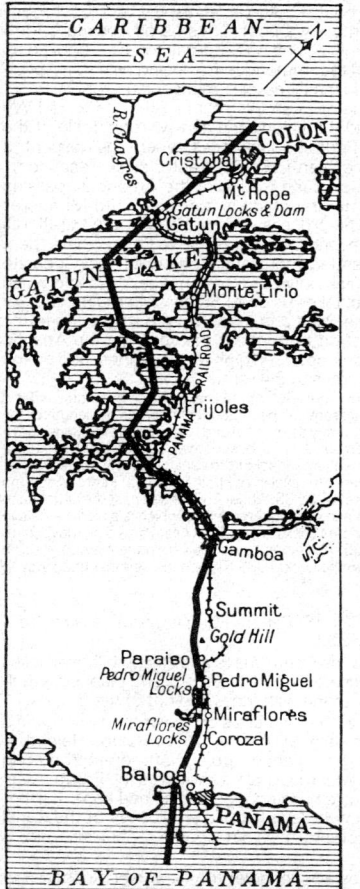

Photographers need plenty of small change, as set price for a Cuna to pose is US$0.25. *Molas* (decorative handsewn appliqué for blouse fronts) cost upwards of US$5 each (also obtainable in many Panama City and Colón shops). Agencies run trips to Wichub Wala island, which is next to El Porvenir where the planes land (US$100 for weekend, one night at *Hotel Anai*, US$40 for each additional night), bookable at the major Panama hotels. One night is not really sufficient. These trips are inclusive of food and sightseeing. Take your own drinks, beer costs US$1. Flight leaves Paitilla airport at 0600, returning next day at 0630; if you can collect 9 people to fill the plane, you can leave at 0800 and return next day at 1600. The airline serving the islands, Aviones de Panamá (Tel.: 64-1677), can provide further information, and also runs trips to the Chocó Indians of the Darién jungle. Ansa flies at 0800, returning same day at 1630, US$49.35.

There are occasional boats to the San Blas islands from Colón, but there is no scheduled service and the trip can be rough.

Through the Canal to Panama City As the crow flies the distance across the isthmus is 55 km. From shore to shore the Canal is 67½ km., or 82 km. (44.08 nautical miles) from deep water to deep water. It has been widened to 150 metres in most places. The trip normally takes 8 or 9 hours for the 42 ships a day passing through.

About 10 km. from Cristóbal, up the Chagres river, is the Gatún Dam, built to impound its waters. The 422 square km. Gatún Lake serves as a reservoir to hold sufficient water in the channel and for use in the locks during dry spells. A high level reservoir, Lago Alajuela (formerly the Madden Dam), feeds the lake and maintains its level, 26 metres above the sea. A ship ascends into Lake Gatún in three steps or lockages. Each of the twin chambers in each flight of locks has a usable length of 305 metres, a width of 33½ metres, and is about 21 metres deep. The flights are in duplicate to allow ships to be passed in opposite directions simultaneously. Passage of the Gatún Locks takes about an hour. Gatún may be reached by bus or train from Colón.

The largest section of the Canal is in Gatún Lake. In the lake is **Barro Colorado** island, to which the animals fled as the basin slowly filled. It is now a biological reserve for scientific research. (Visits can be arranged with the Smithsonian Institute in Ancón, US$10 including boat, audio-visual display and lunch; take 0700 train to Frijoles where you are met by a boat. Trips go on Tuesdays for 5 people—booked up 2 weeks in advance—, and on Saturday for 10—booked up months ahead. The excursion is highly recommended for seeing wildlife, especially monkeys. For longer stays, write to the Director, Smithsonian Tropical Research Institute, Box 2072, Balboa, Panamá. Administration, Tel.: 22-02-11.) We travel through the lake for 37 km. and then along the narrow rock defile of the Gaillard or Culebra Cut for 13 km. to Pedro Miguel Locks, where the descent to sea-level is begun. Culebra Cut can be seen from Contractor's Hill, reached by car (no buses) by turning right 3 km. past the Bridge of the Americas, passing Cocoli, then turning left as signed. The first stage is a descent into Miraflores Lake, 16½ metres above sea-level. The process is completed at the Miraflores Locks, 1½ km. further on. The road beyond Cocoli goes on to Posa, where there are good views of the locks, the cut and former Canal Zone buildings. Opposite Miraflores Locks is a swing bridge which only operates on weekdays and when canal traffic is light. The Canal channel takes us on to Balboa and the Pacific. An odd fact is that the mean level of the Pacific is some 20 cm. higher than the Atlantic, but the disparity is not constant throughout the year. On the Atlantic side there is a normal variation of 30 cm. between high and low tides, and on the Pacific of about 380 cm., rising sometimes to 640 cm.

Most people are surprised by the Canal. Few foresee that the scenery is so beautiful, and it is interesting to observe the mechanics of the passage. Since no tourist boat runs the length of the canal, and since the Panama City-Colón train journey does not afford full views, travellers are advised to take a bus to the Miraflores Locks (open 0900-1700, best between 0600-1000 and 1430-1800 if you want to see shipping—the museum and model of the canal, formerly in the Department of Transport at Ancón, is being moved here). If travelling by train, get out at Pedro Miguel (no station at Miraflores), and take a bus from there, US$0.35. About 250 metres past the entrance to the Locks is a road (left) to the filtration plant and observatory, behind which is a picnic area and viewing point. Bus from Panama City to Miraflores Locks leaves from near Plaza 5 de Mayo (direction Paraíso or Gamboa), 15 mins., US$ 0.35. Ask driver to let you off on the main road, from where it's a 10-min. walk to the Locks. Taxi to the Locks, US$10 per hour. Another good way to see the Panama Canal area is to rent a car.

Balboa The ship usually berths at Pier 18. Panama City is about 3¼ km. from the docks, an average of 10 minutes by taxi.

Balboa stands attractively between the Canal quays and Ancón hill, which lies between it and Panama City. It has been described as an efficient, planned, sterilized town, a typical American answer to the wilfulness and riot of the tropics.

The Canal administration building (with fine murals on the ground floor) and a few official residences are on Balboa Heights. At the foot of Balboa Heights is Balboa, with a small park, a reflecting pool and marble shaft commemorating Goethals, and a long parkway flanked with royal palms known as the Prado. At its eastern end is a theatre, a service centre building, post office and bank. Farther along Balboa Road are a large YMCA (where only male employees of the Canal Company can stay, but where all comers may eat), various churches and a Masonic temple.

It is possible to traverse the canal as a linehandler (no experience necessary) on a yacht; the journey takes an entire day, and the yacht owners need the help. Put your name and address on the bulletin board at Balboa Yacht Club, inside

PANAMA 1173

Fort Amador (unrestricted entry), and make every effort to meet yacht owners. The Club offers good daily lunch special for US$ 2.15. Good place to watch canal traffic from, if you can get in.

Banks Citibank; Chase Manhattan Bank.

Telegrams INTEL; Tropical Radio & Telegraph Co. Public Telex booth.

Post Office Av. Balboa and El Prado.

Ancón curves round the hill N and E and merges into Panama City. It has picturesque views of the palm-fringed shore. The following walk, proposed by Andrew M. Smith of Panama City, takes in the sights of Ancón: walk to the top of the hill in the morning for views of the city, Balboa and the Canal (conveniences and water fountain at the top); the entrance is on Av. 4 de Julio (Av. de los Mártires). Return to Av. 4 de Julio and take a clockwise route around the hill, bearing right on to Balboa Road (Av. Estado de Jamaica), passing YMCA, Chase Manhattan and Citibank, until you reach Stevens Circle where Cuna Indians sell *molas*. Here is the Post Office and a cafeteria. Then walk down the Prado lined with royal palms to the Goethals Memorial and up the steps to the Administration Building to see the murals of the Construction of the Canal (entrance free, identity must be shown to the guards). Follow Heights Road until it becomes Gorgas Road. You will pass the headquarters of the Smithsonian Tropical Research Institute (where applications to visit Barro Colorado Island are made) and, among trees and flowers, the famous Gorgas Hospital for tropical diseases. Gorgas Road leads back to Av. 4 de Julio, but look out for the sign to the Museo de Arte Contemporáneo (open Mon.-Fri. 0800-1230, 1430-1800, Sat. 0800-1200), before Av. 4 de Julio. 2 libraries are open to the public: that of the Smithsonian Tropical Research Institute in the Canal Area, opp. Plaza 5 de Mayo, and that of the Panama Canal College, underneath the Bridge of the Americas.

At the foot of Ancón Hill the Instituto Nacional stands on the 4-lane Avenida 4 de Julio (Tivoli). The University City is on the Transisthmian Highway. Opposite the campus is the Social Security Hospital.

Excursions There is a launch service to ***Taboga Island,*** about 20 km. offshore (return fare US$4). Taboga is reached in about an hour from Pier 18 in Balboa (check the times in advance). There are 2 boats daily during the week and 3 boats on Sat. and Sun. The island is a favourite year-round resort; its pineapples and mangoes have a high reputation and its church is the second oldest in the western hemisphere.

Hotels *Taboga* and *Chu*, B, beautiful views, restaurant, own beach and bar.

The trip out to Taboga is very interesting, passing the naval installations of the Pacific end of the Canal, the great bridge linking the Americas, tuna boats and shrimp fishers in for supplies, visiting yachts from all over the world at the Balboa Yacht Club, and the 4-km. Causeway connecting Fort Amador on the mainland with three islands in the bay. Part of the route follows the channel of the Canal, with its busy traffic. Taboga itself, with a promontory rising to 488 metres, is carpeted with flowers at certain seasons. There are few cars in the meandering, helter-skelter streets, and only one footpath as a road. Swimming is fine, though you may have to pay US$0.25 to use the beach in front of the hotel.

The first Spanish settlement was in 1515, two years after Balboa's discovery of the Pacific. It was from here that Pizarro set out for Peru in 1524. For two centuries it was a stronghold of the pirates who preyed on the traffic to Panama. Because it has a deep-water, sheltered anchorage, it was during colonial times the terminal point for ships coming up the W coast of South America. El Morro, at low tide joined to Taboga, is at high tide an island; it was once owned by the Pacific Steam Navigation Company, whose ships sailed from there. For a fine view, walk through the town and up to the top of the hill with a cross at the summit, to the right of the radar station (there is a shady short cut, ask locals). When surveying the view, don't miss the pelican rookery on the back side of the island; it is an easy walk down.

It is a longer trip by launch—some 75 km.—to the **Pearl Islands,** visited mostly by sea-anglers for the Pacific mackerel, red snapper, corvina, sailfish, marlin, and other species which teem in the waters around. High mountains rise from the sea, but there is a little fishing village on a shelf of land at the water's edge. There was much pearl fishing in colonial days. **Contadora,** one of the smallest Pearl Islands, has become quite famous since its name became associated with a Central American peace initiative; it has *El Galeón Hotel*, A, and the very luxurious chalet complex known

1174 PANAMA

as *Hotel-Casino Contadora*. Return air ticket from Paitilla, US$12.75 by Aeroperlas, Tel.: 69-4555. Good skin-diving and sailing, 3-hour boat trip. Beware the sharks. Three day package tour to Contadora, US$150 for 2, recommended.

Argonaut Steamship Agency, Calle 55 No. 7-82, Panama City, Tel.: 64-3459, runs launch cruises.

Panama City, capital of the Republic, has a population of 1.2 million. It was founded on its present site in 1673 after Morgan had sacked the old town, now known as Panamá Viejo, 6½ km. away by road. Most of Panama City is modern; the old quarter of the city—the part that Spain fortified so effectively that it was never successfully attacked—lies at the tip of the peninsula; both it and Panamá Viejo are being extensively restored.

Note Some of the street names have recently been changed, which may make finding your way around a little difficult. The locals are likely still to refer to the streets by their old names, so if in doubt ask. Also, few buildings display their numbers, so try to find out the nearest cross street.

Panama City is a curious blend of old Spain, American progress, and the bazaar atmosphere of the East. It has a polyglot population unrivalled in any other Latin American city. For the sober minded, the palm-shaded beaches, the islands of the Bay and the encircling hills constitute a large part of its charm. The cabarets and night life (very enterprising) are an attraction to those so inclined.

Most of the interesting sights are in the old part of the city and can easily be reached by foot, taxi, or bus. A good starting place is the Plaza de Francia, in the extreme S. In this picturesque little Plaza, with its red poinciana trees, is a memorial obelisk (topped by a cock) to the French pioneers in building the Canal, and a monument to Carlos Finlay, the Cuban who discovered the cause of yellow fever. Facing the Plaza are several colonial buildings and the Palace of Justice, where the Supreme Court meets. Behind it runs part of the old sea wall—Las Bóvedas (The Dungeons)— built around the city to protect it from pirates. There are steps up this old wall to the promenade—the Paseo de las Bóvedas—along its top, from which there is a fine view of the Bay of Panama and the fortified islands of Flamenco, Naos, and Perico. Beyond are Taboga and Taboguilla, tinged with blue or violet. Just beyond the end of the promenade is the Club de Clases de la Guardia Nacional, a barracks, previously the Club Unión, the city's leading club, which is now housed in a new building in the residential area.

Flush under the wall, at the side of the Palace of Justice, are the old dungeons, with thick walls, arched ceilings and tiny barred windows looking on to the Bay (they have been converted into art galleries and a handicraft centre by IPAT, the tourist authority). Behind the French monument, in a recess in the walls, is a series of large tablets recording, in Spanish, the early attempts to build the Canal. The French Embassy faces the Plaza.

A little way from the Club de Clases, along Av. A and to the right, are the ruins of Santo Domingo church, which has been restored and is now open to the public at times. Its flat arch, made entirely of bricks and mortar, with no internal support, has stood for three centuries. When the great debate as to where the Canal should be built was going on, a Nicaraguan stamp showing a volcano, with all its implications of earthquakes, and the stability of this arch—a proof of no earthquakes—are said to have played a large part in determining the choice in Panama's favour. At the Santo Domingo site is the interesting Museum of Colonial Religious Art, open Tues.-Sat. 1000-1530, Sun. 1500-1730 (adults US$ 0.50, children US$ 0.25, closed for extensive rebuilding in 1987).

Panama City's main street, the Av. Central, runs W from the old city and sweeps right and almost parallel with the shore through the whole town (its name changes to Av. Central España and finally to Vía España). On the right, at the intersection with Calle 3, is the National Theatre, built in 1907, and recently restored. Up Calle 3 on the right is San Francisco Church (colonial, but modernized), and the Instituto Bolívar, where the Liberator proposed a United States of South America during the Bolivarian Congress of 1826. On Av. Norte, running along the Bay, is the President's Palace (La Presidencia), the most impressive building in the city. It is locally known as Palacio de las Garzas, or herons, which are kept in a fountain area there and can be seen up to 1500 hrs. It was the residence of the Spanish Governor during colonial days, and is well worth visiting to see its patio with a fountain and strolling birds and a fine yellow salon. Av. Norte goes on to the colourful public market, on the waterfront. On Av. Norte are the wharves where coastal boats anchor and fishermen land their catches.

Av. Central runs on to the Plaza Independencia, or Plaza Catedral. This Plaza, with busts of the Republic's founders, is the heart of the colonial city. Facing it are the Cathedral, the old Cabildo (which has now become the Central Post Office), the venerable *Hotel Central* and the Archbishop's Palace. The Cathedral has twin towers and domes encased in mother-of-pearl. The Post Office was the headquarters of the French during their attempt to build the Canal. Also in the Plaza Catedral is the Museo de Historia de Panamá from colonial times to Torrijos' days in power, US$0.25 (open Tues.-Sat., 1000-1600, Sun. 1500-1800, closed for lunch). Beyond the Cathedral, Calle 8a runs S to the church of San José, which has a famous organ and a magnificent golden baroque altar, originally installed at a church in Panamá Viejo and resourcefully painted black by monks to disguise it during Morgan's famous raid.

On Av. Central, to the right, in the second block beyond the Cathedral, is the church of La Merced, burnt in 1963 and now completely restored. It was near here that the landward gate of the fortified city stood. Further along the now curving Av. Central is the small Plaza Santa Ana, a favourite place for political meetings. Its church is colonial. Not far away is Sal si Puedes, "Get out if you can", a narrow street swarming with vendors.

Some blocks E is the Caledonia district, where live the descendants of the British West-Indian blacks brought in to build the railway and the Canal. Caledonia is the Harlem of Panama City, exotic and unassimilated; whites are said to be unwelcome. Mugging is very frequent, even in daylight.

Much farther along Av. Central, on Plaza 5 de Mayo (at Calle 22A Este), is the old railway station, now the Museo Nacional del Hombre Panameño, with a good display showing the origins of the populations of Panama (Tues.-Sat., 1000-1530, Sun. 1500-1800, US$0.50), and almost opposite is the Plaza De Lesseps. This part of the city is known as La Exposición because of the International Fair held here in 1916 to celebrate the building of the Canal. Calle 30 Este leads down to the Av. Balboa along the waterfront. The Santo Tomás hospital is here and on a promontory jutting out from this popular promenade is a great monument to Balboa, who stands on a marble globe poised on the shoulders of a supporting group, representing the four races of man. Many of the best hotels are in Bella Vista, also one of the main business areas, and the chief restaurant area is, appropriately, El Cangrejo ("the crab").

On Independence Day, November 3, practically the whole city seems to march in a parade lasting about 3½ hours, centred in the old part of the city. Colourful, noisy, spectacular. Another parade takes place the following day.

Hotels

	Address	Telephone	US$ Single	Double	Our Price Range
Holiday Inn	Winston Churchill y Vía Itaiad, Punta Paitilla	69-1122	90	96	L
El Marriott Panamá	Vía Israel	26-4077	110	120	L
El Panamá	Vía España, 111	23-1660	78	89	L
El Continental*	Vía España	64-6666	81	88	L
Europa	Vía España y Calle 42	63-6911	45	52	A
El Ejecutivo	Calle Aquilino de la Guardian	64-3333	65	70	A
La Siesta	Near Tocumen airport	20-1400	50	55	A
Gran Hotel Soloy	Av. Perú	27-1133	65	70	A
Granada	Av. Eusebio Morales	62-4900	65	71	A
Internacional	Plaza 5 de Mayo	62-1000	45	54	A
Caribe	Av. Perú y Calle 28	25-0404	42	48	A
Monteserín	Calle Monteserín	62-5144	36	40	B
Roma	Av. Justo Arosemena	27-3844	38	44	B

1176 PANAMA

Centroamericano	Av. Ecuador	27-4555	32	36	B
Gran Hotel Lux	Av. Perú	25-1950	33	38	B

*noisy till 2230 from organ music

Note a 10% tax on all hotel prices. All hotels are air-conditioned. *Caesar Park; Verz Cruz*, Av. Perú, B, without breakfast, new, clean, good, but rooms at front noisy; *Colón*, Calle 12, Oeste and Calle "B", C with shower (cheaper without), a/c, erratic water supply; *Acapulco*, Calle 30 Este (near *Hotel Soloy*), Tel.: 25-3832, between Avs. Perú and Cuba, C, a/c, clean, comfortable, TV, private bath, restaurant, conveniently located, recommended; also around corner from *Soloy*, *Residencia Turístico Volcán*, Calle 29, D with shower, a/c, clean; *Central*, Plaza Catedral (22-6080), E, not very clean, safe motorcycle parking, good cheap meals in restaurant, lots of South American travellers; *Colonial*, Plaza Bolívar, D, dirty, old rooms without bath or toilet; *Bella Vista*, Vía España, B; *Caracas*, Plaza Santa Ana, C, with bath, a/c, TV, central, convenient, unprepossessing area at night; *Ideal*, Calle 17, above Ticabus terminal, C, with a/c and private bath, not recommended; *Ideal* annex, cheaper at D, but not recommended for women travelling alone, some rebate for Ticabus travellers; *Riazor*, Calle 16 Oeste, near *Ideal*, D, a/c with bath, good value, cheap restaurant downstairs. Ten mins. from airport (nearest) on right is *El Continental*, D, air conditioned, shower, bar, excellent and easy to reach from the city, the docks, or Panamá Viejo; *Parador*, 5 km. from airport at first traffic lights, D, clean; *Herrera*, Plaza Herrera, basic, noisy but quite clean, E, good meals in restaurant downstairs at about US$1.50 p.p. *María Victoria*, C, friendly but front rooms are a little noisy.

Cheaper accommodation can be found in *pensiones*: *América*, Av. Justo Arosemena and Av. Ecuador, D, back rooms best to avoid street noise, communal bathrooms, safe, clean and pleasant; *Chiriquí*, Santa Ana district, E; *Las Palmeras*, Av. Cuba between C.38-39, Tel.: 250811, E, safe, clean; *Darling*, E, Calle 6, 3-22 near President's Palace, scruffy; *David*, Av. 7, 13-63, E; *Foyo*, Calle 6, No. 825, near Plaza Catedral, clean (but there are mice—hang up food), E, good and central, the restaurant nearby is OK and cheap but closes at 1700 and on Sun.; *Panamá*, Calle 6, 8-40, F, fan, noisy, reasonable, but cockroaches. *Las Tablas*, Av. Perú 28-30, E; *Lila*, Vía Brasil, E; *Mi Posada*, Calle 12 y Av. Central (dangerous area), E, unfriendly, noisy, overcharges; *México*, Av. México 3-69, between Calles 41E and 42E, D, near sea, owner speaks English; many others (unlisted here) on same street; *Nacional*, Av. Central 22-19, near Plaza 5 de Mayo, E with fan, basic, no hot water, many permanent residents; *Panamericana*, Av. A, 8-15 with Calle 10 E; *Pacífico*, Calle Carlos Mendoza (dangerous area), E; *Riviera*, Vía España, C; *Residencias Sevilla*, Av. Justo Arosemena, C; *Santa Ana*, Calle 12, 7B-45, F; *Tiza*, Av. B, 13A-18 (dangerous area), E; *Tropical*, Calle 8, 8-31, E; *Universal*, Av. Central, 8-16 (between Calles 8 and 9), E, no fan, very basic, no hot water, not very clean but friendly; *Vásquez*, Av. A, 2-47, close to the Palace of Justice, quiet, friendly, nice rooms and view of ocean and sand, E; *María Isabel*, E for a room with 2 double beds and cold shower; *Rivera*, Av. Calle 11 Oeste, 8-14, off Av. A, pleasant and friendly, but noisy, E (monthly rates available). *Pensión Catedral*, Calle 6, 3-48, scruffy and no locks on doors, E; *Velázquez*, E, clean and friendly.

N.B. It may not be easy to find accommodation just before Christmas, as Central Americans tend to invade the city to do their shopping.

Warning Thieves abound, and muggings are frequent. It is not safe to walk on any streets alone after dark (i.e. after 1730). Keep valuables in money belt, or otherwise hidden, and don't carry a bag of any sort if possible. Also you shouldn't take a taxi which has 2 people in it as you may get mugged or robbed. Be careful when putting luggage into a car. (All the same, most Panamanians are friendly and helpful.) Marañón (around the market), El Chorillo (W from Santa Ana to Ancón hill) and Caledonia can be particularly dangerous; never walk here at night. For this reason, do not book into a hotel or *pensión* between Calles 9 and 30, i.e. W of Plaza Herrera.

Camping There are no official sites but it is possible to camp on some beaches or, if in great need (they agree, but don't like it much) in the Balboa Yacht Club car park. It is also possible to camp in the Hipódromo grounds (11 km. E of the city, on Avenida España) where you can use the swimming pool showers; this is allowed if you are waiting to ship your vehicle out of the country. Also possible, by previous arrangement, at La Patria swimming pool nearby, and at the Chorrera (La Herradura) and La Siesta beaches on the Pan-American Highway.

Electricity In modern homes and hotels, 220 volts. Otherwise 110 volt 3 phase, 60 cycles A.C.

Restaurants (apart from hotels). Good are: *Pana China* (Chinese and international food), Vía España, *Sarti's* (Italian food), Calle Ricardo Arias 5; *Panamar*, end of Calle 50, specializes in seafood; *Pez de Oro* (Peruvian) superb *mariscos*, and fish, and good wine, Calle 2, El Cangrejo; *Las Rejas*, Vía Brasil, just off Vía España; *Las Américas*, Calle San Miguel, Obarrio. *La Casa del Marisco* (sea food) on Av. Balboa, is open-air. *Cocina Vasca* (sea food) Calle D, in El Cangrejo, really excellent, US$18-20 for a full meal. Also in El Cangrejo, *El Cortijo*, between Eusebio A. Morales and Vía Argentina on Calle D; *Tinajas*, on Calle 51, near *Ejecutivo Hotel*, Panamanian food and entertainment, recommended. *El Pavo Real*, Calle 51, expensive lunches; *Rincón Suizo*, Vía Argentina 17,

PANAMA 1177

Le Bistrot, Centro Comercial La Florida, Calle 53, both expensive. *Montigo Bay*, good rum punches, but food poor value and quality.
Other restaurants include: *Manolo*, Vía Argentina; *Piscolabis*, Transisthmian Highway, Vista Hermosa district, local food, reasonable; *El Jorrón*, Vía Fernández de Córdoba, Vista Hermosa district, local food, reasonable and good; *La Tablita*, Transisthmian Highway, Los Angeles district, reasonable; *Nápoli*, Av. Estudiante, corner with Calle 16, Italian, good and cheap; *Gran China*, Av. Balboa, between Calles 26 and 27, Chinese, good value; *Madrid*, Vía España near UK Consulate, Spanish and local food, *comida* daily for US$ 2.60; *Marbella*, Av. Balboa y Calle 39, Spanish, small; *La Cascada*, Av. Balboa and Calle 25, reasonably-priced, open air; *El Dorado*, Calle Colombia 2, good service, excellent seafood, recommended; *La Mascote*, above Ticabus terminal (Chinese), good and cheap. There are good pavement cafés along Av. Balboa. Many other good Chinese and Italian places; also the *Azteca* (Mexican) on the Transisthmian Highway at Las Cumbres. *Matsuei*, Japanese, excellent, pricey; *Mandarin*, Chinese, excellent, fair prices; *Peng Sun* (Chinese) good from US$2.50. *Krispy, Macdonalds, Dunkin Donuts, Frutilandia, Dairy Queen, Taco Bell, Pizza Hut, Hardee's, Burger King* and *Kentucky Fried Chicken* all have their branches; *La Viña*, close to central Post Office (good and cheap); unnamed *café*, corner C. 6 Oeste and Av. A, behind Post Office, good, cheap; also *Popular*, Av. A y C. 12 Oeste; *Cafetería Jaime*, Plaza Santa Ana; *La Conquista*, Calle J, up Av. Central. *La Cresta* (good food from US$1), Vía España and Calle 45, or *The Balboa Clubhouse* in Balboa (*cafetería*). Two good restaurants on Avenida Central are *A & P* and *Yirny*, the first opposite the National Museum, the second near Chase Manhattan and Bank of America. *Café El Exagerado* serves very good meals at reasonable prices. *Café Coca Cola*, Av. Central and Plaza Santa Ana, pleasant, reasonably-priced. *Café Jaime*, corner of Calle 12 and Av. Central, for good *chichas* (natural drinks). *Delmonico Steak House*, Calle Manuel M. Icaza 5 (US$15-$17).

Shopping *Casa Salih*, Av. Central 125, try local perfume Kantule from San Blas islands; *Casa Fastlich*, Av. Central at Plaza 5 de Mayo, good local jewellery; *Nat. Méndez*, Calle Jota 13, near Av. Tivoli, for Colombian emeralds and pearls; *Curiosidades Típicas de Panamá*, Av. 4 de Julio y Calle J. B. Sosa, for local craft work; *Mercado Artesanal Gago*, next to Gago supermarket on corner of Vía España y Vía Brasil, competitive prices; *Curiosidades Panameñas*, Calle 55 near *Hotel El Panamá Hilton*, local crafts; *Panamá Típico*, Vía España y Calle La Perejil, same again; *Inovación* is a gift shop in the *Hotel El Panamá Hilton* complex on Vía España, has wide selection of new and used *molas*; *Crossroads*, Calle E. A. Morales, by Granada Hotel, more "typical" goods; *Joyería La Huaca*, Av. Central y Calle 21, genuine precolumbian ojects for sale upstairs Good selections also in main hotels. Gago, El Rey, Super 99 and Machetazo (on Central) supermarkets are said to be the best. There is a store (Army-Navy) on Av. Central, near Plaza 5 de Mayo, which sells camping and hiking equipment. There are many laundromats around Plaza Catedral, where wash and dry will cost about US$2.
Duty-free imported luxuries of all kinds from all nations. Panamanian items include *molas* (embroidered blouse fronts made by Cuna Indians); straw, leather, wooden and ceramic items; the *pollera* circular dress, the *montuno* shirts (embroidered), hats, the *chácara* (a popular bag or purse), the *chaquira* necklace made by Guaymí Indians, and jewellery; good selection at Artesanías Nacionales, in Panamá Viejo.

Bookshop English books at Librería Argosy, Vía Argentina y Vía España; Gran Morrison shops, Vía España (near Calle 51 Este and *Hotel Continental*), Av. 4 de Julio, Transisthmian Highway, El Dorado, limited selection of English books.

Photographic Equipment Camera Center, on Tivoli at 4 de Julio (P.O. Box 7279); Foto Internacional, on main street. Panafoto, Av. Central by Plaza 5 de Mayo. Regular prices of cameras and other luxury goods sold in the USA are lower than the duty-free prices in Panama! Some deliver goods to airport, or to transit passengers staying 30 mins., at 5% less than Panama City price. Parcels can be collected in customs shed. Developing in one day in Foto El Halcón, alongside the Panama Hilton. In some places you will get a free film. Shortwave radios can also be bought cheaply at the airport.

Local Transport Taxis have no meters; charges are according to how many "zones" are traversed. Try to settle fare beforehand if you can. Note that there are large taxis (*grandes*) and small ones (*chicos*); the latter are cheaper. Taxis charge US$12 for a 2½-hr. tour to Miraflores locks and the Canal Area. The adventurous will board one of the numerous small buses nicknamed *chivas* (goats). These charge US$0.15, are not very comfortable but run along the major streets (e.g. Av. Central as far as Calle 12, Av. Perú and Av. Justo Arosemena; all buses go to Bella Vista—the business section—except those marked Tumba Muerta or Transístmica). Travel into the suburbs costs more. Yell "*parada*" to stop the bus.

Car Rental At the airport (Hertz, Avis, Econorent); special rates if reservations made abroad (e.g. Toyota, 1 day, unlimited mileage, US$13 inc. insurance). Cars in good condition.

Motorcycle Club Road Knights, at the Albrook Air Force base (Tel.: 86-3348), very welcoming; allows international motorcyclists to stay for free for up to 2 weeks, has repair and maintenance workshop.

1178 PANAMA

Cabarets and Discothèques Hotels *El Panamá Hilton, Holiday Inn* and *El Continental*; Playboy de Panamá, Calle 55, El Cangrejo; Zebra, Vía España; Bunny Club, Jerónimo de la Ossa; Oasis, Vía Brasil; Los Cuatro Ases, Calle L. Recommended discos: *Open House*, near Ejecutivo Hotel, *Bacchus*, Vía España and *Magic*, Calle 81.; Las Molas, entrance to Chase Manhattan Bank, Vía España, Los Angeles district, small band, rural decor, drinks US$1.50; Unicornio, Calle 50 y R. Arías 23 is night club with discothèque and gambling; reasonable prices, will admit foreigners for US$3 a week. El Bon Ton and Camelot, Río Abajo. Caballo de Hierro, Av. 11 de Octubre in Hato Pintado district, is a restaurant in a railway carriage with a discothèque in a neighbouring carriage. Discothèque also at Fiesta Yatch on Av. Balboa.

Theatres There are occasional performances at the National Theatre (folklore sessions every other Sun., 1600, check dates). Atlapa Convention Centre. The usual air-conditioned cinemas (US$2.50 except the University and Balboa cinemas, near Stevens Circle, US$2). Foreign films must, legally, have Spanish sub-titles.

Casinos In the main hotels, at Unicornio on Calle 50, and at airport.

Bathing Piscina Patria (the Olympic pool), take San Pedro or Juan Díaz bus, US$0.15. Piscina Adán Gordon, between Av. Cuba and Av. Justo Arosemena, near Calle 31, 0900-1200, 1300-1700 (except weekends to 1700 only). Admission US$0.25, but beards and long hair frowned on (women must wear bathing caps). Hotels *El Continental, Ejecutivo, Holiday Inn, El Panamá Hilton, Granada* and *La Siesta* have pools. Many beaches within 1½ hours' drive of the city. Fort Kobbe beach (US$0.50, bus from Canal Area bus station US$0.40) and Naos beach (US$1, Amador bus from same station, US$0.30, then 2 km. walk along causeway) have been recommended; both have shark nets, but at low tide at the former you must go outside it to swim! Vera Cruz beach is not recommended as it is both dirty and dangerous.

Golf Panama Golf Club; courses at Summit, Amador and Horoko; Coronado Beach Golf Club (open to tourists who get guest cards at Coronado office on Calle 50).

Fishing Mackerel, red snapper, sailfish and other species. Boats for charter at *Hotel El Panamá Hilton*.

Horse Races (pari-mutuel betting) are held Sat., Sun. and holidays at the Presidente Remón track (bus to Juan Díaz, entry from US$0.50 to 2.50). Cockfights are held on Vía España, near the road that leads to Panamá Viejo, every Sun., same bus but get out at crossing with Calle 150.

Instituto Panameño de Arte, Av. de los Mártires near Palacio Legislativo, art gallery. Open 0900-1200, 1500-1800 except Sun.

Banks The Chase Manhattan Bank (US$0.65 commission on each cheque); Citibank; Lloyds Bank International (Bahamas) Ltd. (ex-BOLSA) Av. José María Icaza 8 (also El Cangrejo agency), offers good rates for sterling (the only bank which will change sterling cash, and only if its sterling limit has not been exhausted); Bank of America; Banco de Colombia; Swiss Bank Corporation. Thomas Cook travellers' cheques only exchangeable at Banco Sudameris and Alegemene Bank Nederland; Deutschmarks exchanged at Deutsch-Südamerikanische Bank. Panamanian banks. Open 0800-1300. Closed Sat., except for Banco General which takes Bank of America travellers' cheques. American Express, 1½ blocks from *Hotel Continental*, opp. Banco de Colombia. There is a US$100 limit per day for cashing travellers' cheques.

If travelling N stock up on dollars as they are hard to obtain, but essential for exchange, in the rest of Central America.

Exchange Free market for almost all currencies, and good rates for all South American currencies. *Cambio* on Av. Central near *Hotel Internacional*. Coin and stamp dealer one block behind Plaza 5 de Mayo on left side of Av. Central.

British Consulate Vía España 124 (Banco Continental building), Panama City, P.O. Box 889, Zona 1, Panama R. P. Tel.: 23-0451/2/3. Telex, Panama 3620.
U.S. Embassy Av. Balboa and Calle 37; P.O. Box 1099. Tel.: 27-1777.
French Embassy Plaza Francia. Tel.: 22-0024.
W. German Embassy Edificio Altamira, piso 11, Vía Argentina 5. Tel: 23-0202.
Netherlands Embassy Vía Argentina y Erick del Valle. Tel.: 64-6793.
Swedish Consulate Edificio Melinda, Vía Argentina 25, Panama 5; Tel.: 64-7655.
Swiss Embassy Av. Cuba (2 Sur) y Calle 29. Tel.: 25-0732.
South African Consulate Edificio Las Vegas, P.O. Box 7010. Tel.: 23-1834.
Colombian Consulate Calle 52 (E. A. Morales) No. 5, 2 blocks from Vía España, open 0800-1200.
Guatemalan Consulate Vía España 128, about Calle 55, open 0800-1300.
Costa Rican Embassy Edif. Plaza Regency, Piso 2, Vía España, Tel.: 642980.
Salvadorean Consulate Vía España 125.
Nicaraguan Embassy Av. Federico Boyd y Calle 50, Tel.: 23-0981.

Customs for renewal of permits and obtaining exit papers for vehicles in Ancón, off Curundu Road, near Albrook U.S. airbase.

Hospitals Gorgas Hospital, Balboa is only for canal workers, except in emergency. The private clinics charge high prices; normally visitors are treated at either the Clínica San Fernando or the Clínica Paitilla (both have hospital annexes). For inoculations buy vaccine at a chemist, who will recommend a clinic; plenty in La Exposición around Parque Belisario Porras.

Post Office Plaza Catedral, Calle 6 and Avenida Central. Also Calle 30 E, nr. Av. Balboa, and at the University. Parcels sent "poste restante" are delivered to Encomiendos Postales Transístmicos, behind the Sears store on Simón Bolívar; tax has to be paid on the value of the goods. If asked for a tip, feign inability to understand!

Cables All America Cables & Radio, Inc., Calle 228, No. 12-17; Tropical Radio Telegraph Co., Calle Samuel Lewis. Tel.: 3-7474. Intel, Edificio Aresa, Vía España (close to *Hilton*, open 0700-2300 weekdays, from 0800 Sat and Sun.) Public telex booth available TRT office. Excellent long-distance telephone by Intel and Tropical Radio. Charges can be transferred to UK.

Worship Services in English at St. Luke's Episcopalian Cathedral, Ancón. Bahai temple, 11 km. N of Panama City on Transisthmian Highway, in the Ojo de Agua district. Modern; worth seeing for its architecture. Taxi round trip for US$5, with an hour to see the temple, should be possible to arrange.

Travel Agency Viajes Panamá S. A., Av. Justo Arosemena 75, Tel.: 25-1838/4466, 27-4166, recommended, English spoken, helpful with documentation.

Tourist Bureau Information office of the Instituto Panameño de Turismo (IPAT), in the Atlapa Convention Centre, Vía Israel open (0900 to 1600) issues a list of hotels, pensiones, motels and restaurants. One list is for Chiriquí, and the other for the central provinces. Worth getting. They issue a free *Focus on Panama* guide (available at all major hotels, and airport). Best maps from Instituto Geográfico Nacional Tommy Guardia (IGNTG), on Vía Simón Bolívar, opp. the University (footbridge nearby, fortunately), take Transístmica bus from C. 12 in Santa Ana: physical map of the country in 2 sheets, US$3.50 each; Panama City map in many sheets, US$1.50 per sheet (travellers will only need 3 or so). At the back of the Panama Canal Commission telephone books are good maps of the Canal Area, Panama City and Colón.

Buses Ticabus, with office on ground floor of Hotel Ideal, Calle 22 B, run air-conditioned buses to San José, about US$30. Air conditioners rarely work. (Tickets are refundable; they pay on the same day, minus 15 %.) Impossible to do Panama City-San José in one day on public transport. Buses going north tend to be well booked up, so make sure you reserve a seat in advance, and never later than the night before you leave. Buses to the W of the country (including David and Chepo) leave from a terminal at the corner of Av. A and Av. Balboa (Av. 6 Sur), behind a 13-storey block of flats (no sign). Buses to all Canal Area destinations (Balboa, Summit, Paraíso, Kobbe, etc.) leave from Canal Area bus station (SACA), behind Plaza 5 de Mayo. Bus Panamá-Chepo US$1.20. Panamá-Colón 1½ hrs., US$1.75, from Calle 26 Oeste y Av. Central in Caledonia, opp. San Miguel church. To Kobbe Beach by bus ½ hr., US$0.40 on US military territory (Pacific side). Panamá-David, 6 hrs., US$10.60, express US$15, 5 hrs. (Transchiri, from Calle 17 Este and Balboa).

Rail Four trains daily, except 3 on Sat. and Sun., and holidays (check timetable in advance), to Colón from Panamá. Station now on Av. de los Mártires, 1 km. NW of Plaza 5 de Mayo, not a pleasant area at night. Comfortable steel-car trains run roughly parallel to the Canal, of which there are excellent views, especially of Gatún Lake, crossed by a causeway. Journey takes 1 hr. 25-50 mins. Single costs US$1.25. For information, Tel.: 52-7720.

Airport at Tocumen, 27 km. Taxi fares about US$20, colectivo US$8 p.p. (if staying for only a couple of days, it is cheaper to rent a car at the airport, e.g. from Econorent). For about US$3 (should only be US$1.20) driver takes you by Panamá Viejo, just off the main airport road. Travellers whiling away hours at the airport can visit the delightful nearby village of Pacora, a few km. off the Pan-American Highway. Bus marked Tocumen, every 15 mins., from Plaza 5 de Mayo, US$0.35, one hour's journey. Bus ("El Chirrillo") to Panama City from the crossing outside the airport (US$0.30), 45 min. There is a 24 hour left-luggage office near the Avis car rental desk for US$1 per article per day. There are duty-free shops at the airport but more expensive than those downtown. There is a small airport at La Paitilla, nearer Panama City, for domestic and private flights.

Excursion A visit is usually paid to **Panamá Viejo** and its ruins, 6½ km. away. A concrete highway to it runs parallel to the sea. On the way you can visit the Justo Arosemena Institute in the Paitilla district. Panamá Viejo, founded in 1519 by Pedrarias, was the point where gold from Peru was unloaded and kept in the King's store-house. There it was loaded on to mules and transported across the Isthmus to Nombre de Dios and Portobelo for shipment to Spain. In January,

1180 PANAMA

1671, Henry Morgan looted and destroyed the city. Because the old site was hard to defend, the city was refounded on its present site.

Today the visitor can wander among the ruins of the Cathedral, its plaza with moss-covered stone pillars and what remains of the old government buildings. The King's Bridge, the starting point of the three trails across the Isthmus, still stands. Past the Plaza and near the sea is what remains of San José, where the golden altar was. At one side are the dungeons where prisoners were drowned by the rising tide. The whole area is attractively landscaped and floodlit. Taxi from the centre, US$1.50; bus US$0.15 from Vía España or Av. Balboa, Nos. 1 and 2.

In Panamá Viejo is the Artesanía Nacional shop, for handicrafts (more expensive than elsewhere). There is also a free display of folk dancing on six Saturdays in the dry season, which is well worth seeing.

On the way back to Panama City you can see the fine outlying residential districts, which include Bella Vista (also the business section, with banks, shops, cinemas and *Hilton* and *Continental* hotels), La Cresta, Golf Heights, Campo Alegre and El Cangrejo. There is a fine view of the sea and bay from the summit at La Cresta. There is an excellent drive along the beach past the United States Embassy, the Santo Tomás Hospital, and the monument to Balboa.

Other Excursions See Balboa (page 1172) for trips to Taboga Island and Pearl Islands. A good excursion—a 2-hr. drive through picturesque jungle—is to Lago Alajuela (formerly Madden Dam). The drive runs from Balboa along the Gaillard Highway and near the Canal. Beyond Fort Clayton there is a fine view of the Pedro Miguel and Miraflores locks. Beyond Pedro Miguel town a road branches off to the left to Summit (Las Cumbres), where there are experimental gardens containing tropical plants from all over the world (closed Mondays) and a small zoo containing native wild life. (The trip to Summit may be made by buses marked Gamboa, every 1-1½ hrs., from near Plaza 5 de Mayo (US$0.35); the Paraíso bus will also take you to the Miraflores and Pedro Miguel locks.) The road to Lago Alajuela (37 km.) crosses the Las Cruces trail (old cannon mark the spot), and beyond is deep jungle (if walking the trail, take machete and compass and arrange boat across the Chagres river at the end of the trail well in advance). A large area of rain forest between Gatún Lake and Lago Alajuela has been set aside as Parque Nacional Soberanía (trails for walking). The Park has an information centre at the Summit Garden. For excursion to Portobelo, see page 1170.

The Madden Dam (Lago Alajuela) is used to generate electricity. A trip through part of the Canal by launch *Fantasía del Mar* costs US$16 for adults, US$8 for children, and lasts about 4 hours. A trip to Lago Alajuela by taxi is only worth while if there are enough people to fill the taxi.

The return from Lago Alajuela to Panama City can be made by the Transisthmian Highway. In Las Cumbres the restaurant *La Hacienda* serves native dishes, and *La Azteca*, Mexican food.

West from Panama City

The Pan-American Highway runs westwards from Panama City through Concepción to the Costa Rican border (489 km.), and is well graded and completely paved. The Highway begins at the Puente de las Américas across the Canal at the Pacific entrance. The bridge, 1,653 metres long and high enough to allow all ships to pass under it, has 3 lanes, a 4-lane approach from Panama City and a pedestrian pavement all the way (muggings have occurred on the bridge in broad daylight, so be careful!).

Where the road W crosses the *savannas*, there are open pastures and fields where *clumps of beautiful trees*—largely mangoes and palms—alternate with grass.

The first place you reach, 23 km. from Panama City, is the small town of Arraiján (2,200 people). On 21 km. by 4-lane highway (toll US$0.50) is La Chorrera (26,317 people); an interesting store, Artes de las Américas, has items in wood, etc. A branch road (right) leads 1½ km. to a waterfall. On 20 km., among hills, is the old town of Capira (12,744 people). We pass through the orange groves of Campana (where a 10-km. road climbs to Cerro Campana and the 6-room *Hotel Sulin*, B, with full board), and then twist down to Río Sajalises (bathing) and the low-level plains. On through Bejuco and Chame to the town of **San Carlos** (7,289 people; Hotels: *Playa Coronado; Río Mar*, C; *El Palmar*, B), near the sea; good river and sea-bathing. Not many restaurants in San Carlos, but there are plenty of shops where food can be bought. Near San Carlos are the Nueva Gorgona (*Cabañas Ocean Blue*, C) and Coronado (*Golf Club* villas, B) beaches, both with restaurants. The Coronado beach is between San Carlos and Chamé and is the most popular in Panama, even so it is never crowded (it is about 4 km. from the main road). Minibus Panama City-San Carlos, US$2.70, San Carlos-David, US$9.30. Beyond San Carlos is the Río Mar beach, with a good seafood restaurant. Five km. on a road (right) leads after a few km. to a climb through fine scenery to the summit of Los Llanitos (792 metres), and then down 200 metres to a mountain-rimmed plateau (7 by 5½ km.) on which is comparatively cool **El Valle**, a small summer resort. 4 km. before El Valle is a parking spot with fine views of the village. (*Hotel Campestre*, C; *Cabañas El Potosí*, friendly; *El Greco Motel*, D; *Pensión Niña Delia*, E, no single rooms; private houses nearby rent rooms, F with meals; accommodation hard to find at weekends.) Soapstone carvings of animals, and straw birds, for sale. The town's Sunday market has become touristy and expensive, but the town itself is a good example of what life away from the cities is like. Gold coloured frogs can be seen here, including at the main hotel. There are many good walks in the vicinity, for instance to the cross in the hills to the W of town.

We leave Panamá Province at La Ermita and enter Coclé, whose large tracts of semi-arid land are used for cattle raising.

Santa Clara, with its famous beach, 115 km. from Panama City, is the usual target for motorists: fishing, launches for hire, and riding (Hotels: *Muu Muu*, B; *Vista Bella*, A, per cabin, for weekend). About 13 km. beyond is Antón (20,561 people): it has a special local type of *manjar blanco*. There is a crucifix here which is reputed to be miraculous. (*Hotel Rivera*, D, Km. 129.) On 20 km. is the capital of Coclé: **Penonomé** (30,913 people), an old town even when the Spaniards arrived. An advanced culture here, revealed by archaeologists (things found are in National Museum, Panama City, also Museo Conte here), was overwhelmed by volcanic eruption (*Hotel Dos Continentes*, C with shower, a/c, restaurant; *Pensión Motel; Pensión Ramírez*, E with bath, Calle Juan Arosemena near church and Parque; *Pensión Dos Reales*, Calle Juan Vásquez, E, basic, noisy). Just under a km. N of town is Balneario Las Mendozas, on street of the same name, an excellent river pool for bathing in deep water. In another 18 km., passing a number of anthills, 1½-2 metres high and as hard as cement, we come to **Natá** (9,318 people), an important place in colonial days; old church (Iglesia de los Caballeros, 1522) and other colonial buildings. A few km. beyond we enter the sugar area and come to (10 km.) **Aguadulce**, 30,000 people (bus from Panamá, US$4.50); its port is 5 km. from the town; native pottery for sale; large salt-beds nearby. Hotels: *El Interamericano* (D, a/c); *Pensión Sarita*, E p.p., and others (it may be possible to sleep by the fire station). On the way to (22½ km.) Divisa, just beyond the large Santa Rosa sugar plantation, a road leads off right to the mountain spa of Calobre, 37 km. from Aguadulce; the hot springs are, however, a good hour's drive away, on a very rough road; grand mountain scenery.

From Divisa a road leads (left) into the Azuero Peninsula through Parita (25 km., 6,554 people; colonial church), and **Chitré** (40 km., 14,635 people), capital of Herrera Province (bus from Panama City, US$6, 4 hours); Herrera museum in centre of town.

Hotels: *El Prado*, D, friendly; *Hong Kong*, D; *Rex*, D (good restaurant next door), on main plaza; *Santa Rita*, D; *Pensión Rodríguez*, noisy, F; *Pensión Azuero*, Calle Manuel Correa, F, usually full; *Pensión Granada*, E (bargain), on road to Los Santos, basic; *Pensión Lilly*, E with bath, road to Monagrillo; *Versalles*, D; *Toledo*, C. *Restaurant Popular*, Manuel Correa, good, cheap; *Restaurant Las Tejas*, on main square, small, good juices. Swimming pool on road to Monagrillo, US$0.25 (closed lunchtime). Tourist agencies in Panama City can arrange trips to La Arena, ¾-hr. walk from the centre of Chitré, which is the centre for Panamanian native pottery.

Los Santos (13,999 people), an old and charming town in Los Santos Province, has a fine church containing many images. The History Museum on plaza is small but interesting, in lovely house and garden. Feria de Azuero, held late each April, is worth seeing. (*Pensión Deportiva*, E (no single rooms), private showers; *Hotel La Villa de Los Santos*, C, a/c caravans, with swimming pool and good restaurant). **Las Tablas** (19,323 people), capital of Los Santos (Hotels: *Oria*, out of town, C; *Piamonte*, C; *Pensión Mariela*, opposite, Calle Belisario Porras, E, basic,

1182 PANAMA

O.K.; *Pensión Marta*, E; swimming pool near National Guard barracks, US$0.25), has a picturesque and famous *fiesta* at Carnival time, just before Lent. Bus from Chitré (US$ 0.90) 1 hr. From Divisa to Las Tablas is 67 km.; the road runs on nearly 13 km. to the port of Mensabé. From Las Tablas it is possible to take a taxi to **Pedasí** (leaves when full, US$2 p.p., 1½ hrs.) which has beautifully empty beaches with crystal clear sea 3 km. from town. *Pensión Moscoso*, E, good, friendly (only place in town), meals arranged by owner at nearby bar. Most things in Pedasí, a peaceful colonial town, are run by the Moscoso clan. You can drive from Las Tablas to Pedasí by an inland route: take the unsigned road to Flores, a small tropical village (no hotel), after which the road deteriorates to Tonosí and thence to Cañas. Between Cañas and Pedasí the road is good again; a sign points to the black-sand beach of Puerto Venado (small restaurant). After Pedasí, heading back to Las Tablas, a right turn at a white house goes to a beautiful, quiet beach.

About 53 km. W of Chitré, by road into the mountains, is **Ocú** (12,722 people), an old colonial town whose inhabitants wear traditional dress during the *fiesta* for its patron saint, San Sebastián, January 19-24.

Hotel *Posada San Sebastián*, E.

Travel Ocú can be reached from David (see below) by taking a bus to the Ocú turning on the Pan-American Highway (US$4) and a colectivo from there (US$0.50). One bus a day to Chitré, and several minibuses from Chitré to Panama City, US$6. From Chitré, a bus can be taken to Las Minas in the mountains, and then another to Ocú, stay the night and take a bus on to Santiago.

Our road from Divisa to Santiago, the next town, 37 km., runs across the Province of Veraguas, the only one which has seaboards on both oceans. **Santiago** (28,866 people), capital of the Province (bus from Penonomé, US$3, from Aguadulce, US$2), is well inland; one of the oldest towns in the country, in a grain-growing area (very good—and cheap—macramé bags are sold in the market here). Nearby is San Francisco; it has a wonderful old church with wooden images, altar pieces and pulpit.

Hotels in Santiago: *Motel Sanson*, B; *Motel Gran David*, on Pan-American Highway, D, a/c, TV, shower, clean, recommended; *Pensiones Continental, Central* and *Jigoneva*, all on Av. Central, close together, all E; *Pensión San José*, Av. Central, E; *Magnolia*, E; *Santiago* near the Cathedral, clean, D with a/c, T.V. and shower. *Fortuna*, D, Chinese-run, safe, a little unfriendly. Swimming pool near town centre, US$0.75.

The bad road through Soná (43 km., 19,372 people) in a deep fertile valley to Guabalá, near Remedios (4,809 people), the country's largest stock-raising centre, has been replaced by a direct paved highway from Santiago to Guabalá. This saves a couple of hours. From Guabalá to David is 92 km.

17 km. W of Guabalá, on the highway, is a hotel just outside Las Lajas, D, with restaurant. No hotels in Las Lajas itself. *Hotel Playa Corona*, D, 2½ km. S of Pan-American Highway at 100 km., has camping (secure, clean, showers, pleasant beach, bar, US$5 for 2; also has good seafood restaurant). Las Lajas has good beaches. To get there take a bus from David to the turn off (US$2), then walk 3 km. to the town, from where it is 10 km. to the beach (taxis only, US$5).

David, 45,000 people, capital of Chiriquí Province, rich in timber, coffee, cacao, sugar, rice, bananas and cattle, is the third city of the Republic. It was founded in colonial times and has kept its traditions intact while modernizing itself. The town has a fine park and beautiful neighbourhoods. Pedregal, its port, is 8 km. away. Airport. International fair and *fiesta*, March 19.

Hotels *Siesta Motel*, on edge of town on the Pan-American Highway, recommended; *Nacional*, C, restaurant, pizzería, swimming pool, tennis court; *Palacio Imperial*, D; *Saval*, D; *El Camino Real*, D; *Pensión Fanita*, a/c rooms with bath, F, basic, food fair. *Iris* in central square, E, recommended; *Pensión Chiriquí*, Av. 4 Este, W of Calle Central, clean, but very noisy, E; *Pensión Colonial*, clean, E; *Pensión Irazíú*, E; *Pensión Anita*, E; *Pensión Punta Arenas*, F, basic; *Pensión Costa Rica*, near Tica-bus terminal, F-E, not recommended; *Hotel Valle de la Luna*, E, reasonable food; *David* and *Madrid* also E. Most cheap hotels are on Av. 5 Este.

Restaurants *Oriente*; *Don Dicky*, very good 24-hr. café, meals, friendly. Good cheap food at *Rocío*, Av. 5 Este. A few cheap places round bus station and the market. *Balneario Risacua*, on the Pan-American Highway, N end of town (follow Av. 6 Este to the river), has restaurant, very nice.

PANAMA 1183

Tourist Office   IPAT at *Hotel Nacional*, friendly but not too helpful; ask for details of hot springs in the vicinity.

Bus from Panama City: apart from Ticabus, ordinary buses, US$10.60 (7 hrs.), about every hour from 0700 to 1900, plus express buses at 1200 and at midnight, 5½ hrs., US$15 (try Transchiri, Calle 8, 7A-23). The municipal bus terminal is in Av. 3 de Noviembre. An alternative way to Panama City is to Santiago (US$6) and then to Panama City (US$6). There is a bus to San Isidro (Costa Rica) at 0600 and 1300, 6 hrs., US$8, and to San José (Costa Rica), five buses a day from 0500 to 1430, US$10, that leave from outside the *Pensión Costa Rica*. Regular minibus to Boquete from bus station (US$1.20) 1 hr., Frequent "*frontera*" buses, US$1.50. 1½ hrs.

Note: If driving S, stock up with food in David: it is much cheaper than in Panama City. It is difficult to change Costa Rican colones in David. The Store Romero in main square gives a good rate of exchange.

Inland from David are the deeply forested highlands of Chiriquí, rising to 3,383 metres at the extinct Barú volcano. The region favours coffee, fruit and flowers and is very beautiful, with delightful mountain streams for bathing and fishing. A great variety of wildlife flourishes in the area. There is some camping. There is a road from David to the mountain village of **Boquete,** at 900 metres, on the slopes of Chiriquí. It enjoys a spring-like climate the year round and has many attractions: good lodging and board, excellent river bathing, fishing, riding, and mountain climbing, but it is an expensive place. Around is a beautiful panorama of coffee plantations, orange groves, and gardens which grow the finest flowers in the country. Plenty of good walks, including paved road to summit of Barú volcano. It is possible to cash travellers' cheques in the small bank in plaza.

Hotels *Panamonte*, A, full board, in very attractive surroundings, recommended. Cheaper hotels: *Fundadores* and *Central*, both D; *Pensión Marilos*, D, English spoken, very clean and well run with excellent, cheap food; *Pensión Wing*, F; *Pensión Virginia*, F for cheapest rooms, clean, friendly, English spoken, good and cheap restaurant downstairs. *Coffee Bean*, a café on road into town, very friendly, English-speaking owner. Plenty of cheap eating places.

After David, a dirt road turns off to the right to Las Palmas, a pleasant orange-growing village which welcomes tourists. Just before the village is a waterfall where a single column of water falls into a pool, delightful for swimming and camping.

The road (and a railway) goes on from David to **Concepción** (24 km.; 6,532 people), from where one can visit the beautiful Highlands to the N (US$11 bus fare—Transchiri—from Panama City). A road runs 29 km. N to **El Hato del Volcán** (Hotels: *Dos Ríos*, C; *California*, D; *Pensión Omaya*, E; *Pensión Hung Wang*, F—no singles. Plenty of cheap eating places) and on to Río Sereno (no hotel) or to **Cerro Punta** (Hotel *Cerro Punta*, A-B; *Pensión La Primavera*, E-D, no singles; several restaurants). There are mountain lakes nearby. Bus David-Volcán, US$2.30. At Bambito there is a luxury hotel which serves good but expensive meals, it has swimming pool, horse-riding, trout farm (in the off-season very good bargains can be had here). From Volcán to Cerro Punta (US$0.95 by bus) the road follows the Chiriquí Viejo river valley. Just beyond Cerro Punta lies the Finca Rogelio Rodriguez Argüello (only a 4-wheel drive vehicle can get to it), where Sr. José will show you the haunts of the quetzal. Cerro Punta itself, in a beautiful valley at 2,130 metres devoted to vegetables and flowers, has many fine walks in the crisp mountain air. Concepción is 30 km. from the Costa Rican border at Paso Canoas by road (the border is open 0700-1200, 1400-1800, 1900-2200— remember Panama is 1 hr. ahead of Costa Rica). The railway goes on to

Puerto Armuelles (10,712 people), the port through which all the bananas grown in the area are exported. Puerto Armuelles and Almirante (Bocas del Toro) are the only ports in Panama outside the Canal area at which ocean-going vessels habitually call and anchor in deep water close inshore; there is now an oil transit pipeline across the isthmus between the two places.

Hotels *Pensión Balboa*, on waterfront, E, pleasant; *Pensión Trébol*, E, 1 block from waterfront. Plenty of cheap eating places.

Chiriquí Railway, S from Concepción to Puerto Armuelles, with passenger trains, one a day in each direction, irregular. There is also a "Finca Train", 4 decrepit, converted banana trucks, leaving at 1500 for the banana fincas, returning, by a different route, at 1800. No charge for passengers. Minibuses also leave all day for the fincas. Freight service only to David and to Pedregal.

Across the Cordillera from David, on the Caribbean side, are the once thriving but now depressed banana ports of **Bocas del Toro,** on the SE tip of Colón Island, and Almirante, on the SW side of Almirante Bay, the central office of the Chiriquí Land Company (the Panamanian subsidiary of United Brands). Some of the plantations, destroyed by disease, have been converted to abacá and cacao, but are now being planted again, especially near **Changuinola** (airfield). Unlike Almirante, which is a busy port, dirty and disorganized, Bocas del Toro deserves a visit: clean, peaceful, quiet, mostly English-speaking, as are the nearby islets and coastal settlements. The protected bay offers all forms of water sport and diving, beautiful sunrises and sunsets, and, on land, tropical birds, butterflies and wild life. For more information: Ligia (Lee) Paget, Turismo y Artesanías Bocatoreñas, Apdo Postal 5, Bocas del Toro (Tel.: 78-9309/9248). Boat Almirante-Bocas del Toro, at least once a day, but none on Wed., US$0.50, Isla Colón. From Almirante, take Almirante launch (Mon., Wed., Fri. 0930) to Chiriquí Grande, 5 hrs. if lucky, US$7.50, from where a spectacular road runs over the mountains to connect with David, bus 2½ hrs., US$6 (ferry Chiriquí Grande-Almirante Tues., Thurs., Sat. 1100; pensión in Chiriquí Grande if stuck). Alternatively Bocas del Toro and Changuinola can be reached by Aeroperlas, Alas Chiricanas, Aviones de Panamá both from Paitilla Airport and David. There is a road from Changuinola to Almirante (no buses, taxi, US$3), and a road is planned from Almirante to Chiriquí Grande.

Hotels At Concepción: Rocio, some a/c rooms and a/c bar and dining rooms, very reasonable; Pensión Caribe. At Bocas del Toro; Bahía (D); Pensión Peck, F (Miss Peck is a charming hostess); Botel Thomas, on the sea. At Changuinola: Changuinola, D, near airport; restaurant near market has rooms, also D. At Almirante: Hong Kong, D with a/c, cheaper without, San Francisco, D with bath, both very clean; Pensión Colón, F, uncertain water supply, friendly English-speaking owner; Viajero, E—all hotels noisy. Bocas del Toro province is about 25 % more expensive than the rest of Panama.

Railways The banana railways provide links between Guabito on the Costa Rican frontier, Changuinola and Almirante. Trains leave Guabito 0500 and 1400, arriving Almirante 0730 and 1630; extra train Changuinola—Almirante 1130, arr. 1330. Train Almirante-Changuinola, 0745, 1400, 1700, US$0.35, delightful.

On Thurs. and Sun. the Isla Colón ferry leaves Bocas del Toro at 1300 for Bastimentos Island, a small community of blacks with a marvellous beach; good snorkelling about ½-hrs'. walk from the jetty. Return 1800, no charge.

Entering Panama from Costa Rica The border at Sixaola-Guabito is open 0700-1100, 1300-1700, but only on Mon.-Thurs. can you guarantee with any certainty that officials will be on hand. Malaria test on entering Panama, entry charge US$10 (receipt given), 5 days' entry card only given (extensions at Changuinola airport immigration, opens 0830—5 passport photos, photographer nearby charges US$7 for 6, another US$ charge). Advance clocks 1 hr. entering Panama.

No accommodation in Guabito; bus to Changuinola US$0.75, ¾ hr. If seeking cheap accommodation, cross border as early as possible in order to get as far as Almirante.

How to get to Colombia

The Pan-American Highway runs E 60 km. to the sizeable town of **Chepo,** full of friendly blacks. From Chepo the Highway has been completed to Yaviza, 240 km. from Panama City; it is gravel from Chepo until the last 30 km. which are of earth. 35 km. E of Chepo it crosses the new Lago Bayano dam by bridge (the land to the N of the Highway as far as Cañazas is the Reserva Indígena del Bayano). The road will eventually link Panama with Colombia. (Bus to Chepo from Panama City leaves from Plaza 5 de Mayo.)

Darién East of Chepo is Darién, almost half the area of Panama and almost undeveloped. Most villages are accessible only by air or river and on foot. At Bahía Piñas is the Tropic Star Lodge, where a luxury fishing holiday may be enjoyed on the sea and in the jungle for over US$1,000 a week. (Information from Hotel El Panamá.)

The Darién Gap road will not be open for some years, so the usual way of getting to Colombia is by sea or air. It is possible to go overland: the journey is in fact more expensive than going by air, and while still challenging, the number of travellers going overland is increasing. The main villages (Yaviza, Pucuro, Paya and Cristales) have electricity, radios and cassette decks, canned food is available in Yaviza, Pucuro and Paya, only the Chocó Indians and the Cuna women retain traditional dress. Prices are rising steeply and friendliness is declining. Venturers are advised to get Backpacking in Mexico and Central America (Bradt Publications), which contains special maps covering the whole route and background information on Indians, fauna and flora. Maps of the Darién area can be purchased from the Ministro de Obras Públicas, Instituto Geográfico Nacional Tommy Guardia, in Panama City (US$5). The best time to go is in the dry months (Jan.-mid April); in the wet season (from May) it is only recommended for the hardy. Organized jungle tours to Cuna Indians, Chocó Indians and the Río Bayano costing from US$65 to over US$300 can be purchased through Mar Go Tours, Aptdo 473, Balboa. The journey as described below takes about 7 days to the first house in Colombia.

There is a daily bus from Panamá to Yaviza, US$14. Alternatively there is an irregular boat, about three times a week. The only sleeping accommodation is the deck and there is one primitive toilet for about 120 people. The advertised travel time is 16 hours, but it can take as much as 28. There is only one hotel at **Yaviza** (*Three Américas*, D). From Yaviza it is an easy walk, with two river crossings by dugout, US$1 each, to Pinogana, 2 hrs on foot (small and primitive) and by motor dugout from Pinogana to Boca de Cupe (US$60). Or you can take a boat from Yaviza to El Real (US$10), stay at the Touricenter of Gringo Gery (very nice and friendly people) and from there a motor dugout to Boca de Cupe (if possible, take a banana dugout, otherwise bargain hard on boats). Stay the night at Boca de Cupe with a family. You can go with Chocó Indians to Unión de Chocó, stay one or two days with them and share some food (they won't charge for lodging). Chocós are very friendly and shy, better not to take pictures (US$5 after bargaining). In Boca de Cupe get your exit stamp and keep your eye on your luggage. From Boca de Cupe to Pucuro, dugout US$30 (bargain). Pucuro is a Cuna Indian village and it is customary to ask the chief's permission to stay (he will ask to see your passport). People are unfriendly there; stop with your luggage. A missionary couple live there: Jim and Polly Browne. From Pucuro you can walk through lush jungle to Paya, 8½ hrs. (guide costs US$20, not really necessary, do not pay in advance), which was the capital of the Cuna empire. From Pucuro to Paya you have to cross the river 4 times. After the third crossing you have to look carefully for the trail. It continues on the right-hand side of a little creek which runs into the river. In Paya you will meet Alberto (chief's son); they will not let you stay in the village and you will be taken 2 km. away eastwards to the barracks across the river. You can stay there (passport check and baggage search), and for a small fee you will get meals. The Cuna Indians in Paya are more friendly than in Pucuro. Paje is a similar village, with a chief (be sure to ask his permission on everything). From Paya, the next step is a 4-6 hrs walk to Palo de los Letras, the frontier stone; at every bifurcation, take the left-hand trail. On reaching the left bank of the Tulé river (in 3 hrs.), you follow it downstream, which involves 7 crossings (at the third crossing the trail almost disappears, so walk along the river bed—if possible—to the next crossing). About ½ hr. after leaving this river you cross a small creek; 45 mins. further on is the abandoned camp of the Montadero, near where the Tulé and Pailón rivers meet to form the River Cacarica. Cross the Cacarica and follow the trail to the Inderena (Colombian National Parks) hut at Cristales. If you insist on walking beyond Montadero, a machete, compass and fishing gear (or extra food) are essential; the path is so overgrown that it is easier, when the river is low, to walk and swim down it (Cristales is on the left bank, so perhaps it would be better to stick to this side). The rangers at Cristales may sell you food, will let you sleep at the hut and will take you by dugout to Bijao (or Viajado), 1½ hrs., for US$10 (they will try to charge US$30). At Bijao ask for the Inderena station, where you can eat and sleep. From Bijao a motor dugout runs to Puerto América (also called Travesía) for US$15 (3 hrs.), from where motorboats go to Turbo for US$5. Get your Colombian entry stamp at the DAS office in Turbo.

You can get some food along the way, but take enough for at least 5 days. Malaria pills, mosquito netting, salt tablets and insect repellants are a must as are water sterilization tablets—you cannot be too careful about the water, and watch out for solitary big black ants (*congo*), especially along river banks. The worst insect pests are ticks, which can be removed with kerosene—or masking tape if you find them before they attach themselves. In all other respects travel as light as possible because the heat and humidity can make the going difficult.

It is highly recommended to travel in the dry season only, when there is no mud and fewer mosquitoes. If you have time, bargains can be found. There is nothing frightening about the jungle, it is as penetrable as any forest in the US or elsewhere (at least in the dry season). Follow tourist regulations, ask for inspectors of migration in Yaviza, Boca de Cupe, Pucuro and Paya. If taking a motorcycle through Darién, do not entrust it to a small dugout; the large ones, though, can take 2 easily.

The Katíos National Park, extending in Colombia to the Panamanian border, can be visited with mules from the Inderena headquarters in Sautatá. In the park is the Tilupo waterfall, 125 metres high; the water cascades down a series of rock staircases, surrounded by orchids and fantastic plants. Also in the park is the Alto de la Guillermina, a mountain behind which is a strange forest of palms called "mil pesos", and the Ciénagas de Tumaradó, with red monkeys, waterfowl and alligators. (We are grateful to José Serra-Vega of Lima for help with updating this section.)

There are about two boats a week from Colón for San Andrés Island (see page 473), from which there are connections with Cartagena; the *Johnny Walker* takes 30 hours, costs US$20, including food, but the service is very irregular and travellers have sometimes waited over a week in vain. Boats also leave, irregularly, the Coco Solo wharf in Colón (minibus from Calle 12, 15 mins., US$0.30) for Puerto Obaldía, via the San Blas Islands. There is also a light plane at 0600 from Panama City to Puerto Obaldía 3 times a week (Mon., Wed., Fri.) for US$37 single, Aerovías Nacíonales (ANSA). There are boats from Puerto Obaldía (after clearing Customs) to Turbo, on the Gulf of Urabá (see page 473), US$15 p.p., 10-18 hrs. (take shade and drinks), from which Medellín can be reached by road. Walk from Puerto Obaldía to Zapzurro for a dugout to Turbo, US$10. It seems that most of the boats leaving Puerto Obaldía for Colombian ports are contraband boats. There are also (contraband) boats from Dock 3 at the end of Calle 5, Colón, to Barranquilla. 3-day journey, US$25, uncomfortable, and entirely at your own risk; captains of these boats are reluctant to carry travellers. A passenger travelling in a contraband boat had some problems in the DAS office about getting an entrance stamp: they wanted official papers from the boat's captain showing that he brought him in. You have to bargain for your fare on these boats. Accommodation is a little primitive. There is a good pension in Puerto Obaldía: *Residencia Cande*, nice and clean (E) which also serves very good meals for US$1.50. Book in advance for meals. Also in Puerto Obaldía are shops, Colombian consulate, Panamanian immigration, but nowhere to change travellers' cheques until well into Colombia (not Turbo). Alternatively one can get from Puerto Obaldía to Acandi on the Colombian side of the border, either by walking nine hours or by hiring a dugout or a launch to Capurgana (US$60), thence another launch at 0715, 1 hr., US$3. Several *pensiones* in Capurgana. To walk to Capurgana takes 3-4 hrs.; guide not essential (they charge US$20); first to go to La Miel (2 hrs.), then to Zapzurro (20 mins.), where there are shops and cabins for rent, then 1-1½ hrs. to Capurgana. Most of the time the path follows the coast, but there are some hills to cross (which are hot—take drinking water). From Acandi frequent but irregular boats go Turbo (US$8, 3 hrs.).

Dale de Graaf of Grand Rapids, Minn. and Paul K. Kirk of Stockton, Calif. have sent us details of an alternative route through the Darién Gap to Colombia: Although not quick, it is relatively straightforward (spoken Spanish is essential). Take a bus from Panama (Plaza 5 de Mayo) to Santa Fe, a rough but scenic 6-8 hours (US$8, 3 a day, check times). In Santa Fe it is possible to camp near the national guard post (no *pensiones*). Then hitch a ride on a truck (scarce), or walk 2 hrs. to the Sabanas River at Puerto Lardo (11 km.) where you must take a dugout or launch to La Palma, or hire one (US$5, 2 hrs.; also reached by boat from Yaviza, US$3, 8 hrs.). This is the capital of Darién; it has one *pensión* (friendly, English-speaking owners, F, pricey, with cooking and laundry facilities, or see if you can stay with the *guardia*). Wait for a flight to Jaque (US$25, you may have to return to Panama City with the plane first—no one seems to know), near

Puerto Piña, 50 km. N of the Colombian border. Alternatively, at the Muelle Fiscal in Panama City (next to the main waterfront market, near Calle 13), ask for a passenger boat going to Jaque.

The journey takes 18 hours, is cramped and passengers cook food themselves, but costs only US$10. Jaque (pop. 1,000) is only reached by sea or air (the airstrip is used mostly by the wealthy who come for sport fishing); there are small stores with few fruit and vegetables, a good *comedor*, one *hospedaje* (but it is easy to find accommodation with local families), and camping is possible anywhere on the beautiful 4 km. beach. The guard post is open every day and gives exit stamps. Canoes from Jaque go to Jurado (US$20) or Bahía Solano (US$45, 160 km., with two overnight stops) in Chocó. The first night is spent in Jurado (where the boat's captain may put you up and the local military commander may search you out of curiosity). There are flights from Jurado to Turbo. Bahía Solano is a deep-sea fishing resort with an airport and *residencias*. Get your Colombian entry stamp here. Flights from Bahía Solano go to Quibdó, US$18, connecting to Cali, US$30 (with Satena), or Medellín (Aces also fly to Bahía Solano, but all flights have to be booked in advance; the town is popular with Colombian tourists). On this journey, you sail past the lush, mountainous Pacific coast of Darién and Chocó, with its beautiful coves and beaches, and you will see dolphin, flying fish, dorado, bio-luminescent plankton and tuna, to name but a few.

It is not easy to get a passage to any of the larger Colombian ports as the main shipping lines rarely take passengers. Those that do are booked up well in advance. The Agencias Panamá company, Muelle 18, Balboa, represents Delta Line and accepts passengers to Buenaventura (US$90). Anyone interested in using the Delta Line ships should book a passage before arriving in Panama. The only easy way of getting to Colombia is to fly. Copa, SAM and Avianca fly to Medellín, Cartagena and Barranquilla.

Shipping agencies have not the authority to charge passages. Many travellers think they can travel as crew on cargo lines, but this is not possible because Panamanian law requires all crew taken on in Panama to be Panamanian nationals.

Colombia officially demands an exit ticket from the country. If you travel by air the tickets should be bought outside Panama and Colombia, which have taxes on all international air tickets. If you buy air tickets from IATA companies, they can be refunded. Copa tickets can be refunded in Cartagena (Calle Santos de Piedra 3466—takes 4 days), Barranquilla—2 days, Cali or Medellín. Refunds in pesos only. Copa office in Panama City, Av. 3 Sur, Calle 39 Este. One traveller has told us that the Colombian consulate at Panama City required him to buy a Miscellaneous Charges Order (US$100) which was not required at Cali airport (Colombia). Those who do not want to go to Panama can fly from San José (Costa Rica) to San Andrés and on to Cartagena cheaply.

Shipping a Vehicle from Panama to Colombia is not easy or cheap. The cheapest we have heard of is US$500, but this was arranged in the home country (Netherlands). Inair, Tel.: 66-11-98, are very helpful and offer a variety of destinations, e.g. Curaçao (US$2,000 for Land Rover and driver). The following agencies can be contacted: Agencia Motonaves (Colón); Prudential Line; Litres; Pacific Ford; French Line; Lauro Line. The Italian Line takes vehicles but tends to be booked well in advance. It has an office opposite the Post Office in Cristóbal, or you can book through a travel agent. If going on one of the large lines it is recommended to ship to Guayaquil rather than Buenaventura, thereby avoiding the hassles of Colombia's paperwork, also taxes make it more expensive to ship to Colombia. Cheaper than the Italian line is the Unif. Trading Company in Colón (contact Captain Gilberto Pavis, Tel.: 47-3867). (For the return journey contact the Remar Agency in Buenaventura.) With a great deal of luck you might get one of the sugar boats bringing cargo to Aguadulce (page 1181) to ship you and your car to Colombia. One traveller was lucky and it cost him only US$100.

Sometimes, if enough vehicles are collected together, it is possible to charter a boat to Buenaventura from the Zócalo (Nuevo Panamá). One secret here is to go to the Hipódromo in Panama City because there are usually enough cars there to form a party at least once a month. The groups will then rent a local freighter (a customs agent is necessary for the group, and this is included in the price). It is considered the best way to go south, and drivers and cars arrive at the same time. The regular shipping companies are not interested in this business, so they raise prices to discourage customers. In addition to freight charges there are, of course, handling charges of about US$25. Very few lines take passengers; if you do succeed in getting a passage it may cost as much

1188 PANAMA

as US$180. (A plane ticket to the port of arrival can cost up to US$150.) Lykes Line (head office: New Orleans) runs a fortnightly ship to Cartagena (preferable) and Barranquilla in Colombia. Lykes takes passengers but it is more expensive than flying.

A cheaper alternative to the above-named lines is to try to ship on one of the small freighters that occasionally depart from Pier 3 in Colón, which allow you to travel with your car. Obviously there is a considerable element of risk involved though the financial cost is far lower. In Balboa shipping arrangements can be made at Agencias Panamá, whose office is located just outside the entrance to Pier 18; they act as agents for most shipping lines. It is possible to sleep in your car when loading at Pier 18; there is a good and cheap restaurant inside the dock.

Once you have a bill of lading, have it stamped by a Colombian consulate. The consulate also provides tourist cards. They require proof, in the form of a letter from your Embassy (or the Embassy representing your country in Panama) that you do not intend to sell the car in Colombia, though this requirement is usually dispensed with. Then go to the customs office in Panama City (Calle 80 and 55) to have the vehicle cleared for export. After that the vehicle details must be removed from your passport at the customs office at the port of departure. In Colón the customs office is behind the post office. The utmost patience is needed for this operation as regulations change frequently, so do not expect it to be the work of a few minutes.

Some small freighters go only to intermediate ports such as San Andrés, and it is then necessary to get another freighter to Cartagena; a couple had to wait for a week in San Andrés to make the connection. From Colón to San Andrés takes 2 days and from San Andrés to Cartagena takes 3 days. There are two boats plying regularly between Colón (Pier 3) and San Andrés that are big enough for vans, but there is no schedule; they leave when they finish loading. There are also two regular boats between San Andrés and Cartagena; each stays in port about 15 days, but it can be longer.

Customs formalities at the Colombian end will take at least a full day to clear (customs officials do not work at weekends) even if you have a *Carnet de Passages*. Make sure the visa you get from the Colombian consulate in Colón is *not* a 15 day non-extendable transit visa, but a regular tourist visa, because it is difficult to get an extension of the original visa. Clearance from the Colombian consul at the Panamanian port of embarkation may reduce the bureaucracy when you arrive in Colombia, but it will cost you US$10. In Colombia you can pay an agent US$15 to deal with the paperwork for you, which can reduce the aggravation if not the waiting time. It is understood that Cartagena is much more efficient (and therefore less expensive) as far as paperwork is concerned.

Do not ship or fly your vehicle to Ecuador without the *Carnet*, or you may be held up for up to two weeks at customs, and only allowed to continue to Peru with a police escort!

Warning The contents of your vehicle are shipped at your own risk—generally considered to be a high one!

Air-freighting a Vehicle: Most people ship their vehicles from Panama to South America but some find air-freighting much more convenient. Generally it is faster and avoids many of the unpleasant customs hassles, but is more expensive. Prices vary considerably. The major carriers (Avianca, Ecuatoriana) charge about US$3,000 for a VW bus, US$1,500 for a 4-wheel drive Subaru station wagon, but the cargo lines and independents can offer more reasonable prices (US$800 to US$1,250). Prices and availability change from month to month depending on the demand by regular commercial shippers. You are generally not allowed to accompany the vehicle. Taking a motorcycle (BMW R100RS) from Panama to Medellín by Copa: driver US$111, bike US$0.67 per kg. Drain oil and gasoline, and remove battery before loading; the bike goes in with just an inch to spare so you must expect a scratch or two. Mr Barham at the Copa office is most helpful. Having brought your passenger ticket, take your airweigh bill to the Colombian Consolate for stamping, then have it stamped at Customs (in Ancón, see page 1179: US$4.05 per vehicle); with luck this will only take a few hours. Retrieving the bike in Colombia, although costing very little, will take at least a day of paperwork and pleading.

The Economy

Panama's economy has traditionally been founded on income derived from services rendered to incoming visitors, taking advantage of its geographical position, and Canal employees and US military personnel spending money in the Republic. However, this contribution is *lessening* proportionately as the country *develops new sources* of income: tourism, industry, copper, etc.

Apart from the Canal, the other traditional mainstay of the Panamanian economy is agriculture, which contributes about 10% of gdp. About 25% of the population works in agriculture. Agrarian reform has begun, and has brought the post-1968 governments much support from tenant-farmers and squatters. Most of the land is forested, and development here could also bring added wealth into the country, at the same time helping to reduce the country's dependence on the Canal. Recently the Government has taken a more significant role in

PANAMA

industry and now owns sugar mills and cement plants. The main industry is food processing and there are textile and clothing concerns and chemicals, plastics and other light industries. Petroleum products are the only industrial export.

Mining should also help to lessen the Republic's dependence on the Canal. Vast deposits of copper have been found at Cerro Colorado and if fully developed the mine could be the largest in the world. There is also copper at Petaquilla, Cerro Chorca and Río Pinto. Large coal deposits have been found at Río Indio. The country also has gold and silver deposits. So far no oil has been discovered, but exploration is taking place.

One of the most dynamic sectors of the economy is banking. Since 1970 offshore banks have increased from 20 in number to 130 with the establishment of liberal conditions and the abolition of currency controls. In the mid-1980s, total assets amounted to over US$40bn, while deposits were around US$35bn. It is hoped that as well as becoming an important financial centre, Panama will also attract international reinsurance business.

Following a rapid accumulation of foreign debt by the public sector in the late 1970s and early 1980s, the debt service burden became intolerable. Panama has received assistance since 1983 from the IMF and the World Bank in support of its fiscal and structural adjustment programme, while commercial banks have both rescheduled existing loans and provided new money on easier terms.

	1961-70 (av)	1971-80 (av)	1981-85 (av)	1986 (e)
Gdp growth (1980 prices)	7.7%	5.5%	2.6%	2.8%
Inflation	1.3%	7.0%	3.2%	1.9%
Exports (fob) US$m	94	451	2,052	2,136
Bananas	40	63	72	-
Shrimp	8	26	39	-
Sugar	3	26	36	-
Imports (fob)m	211	933	2,759	2,750
Current account balance US$m (cum)	-295	-1,836	203	141

Information for Visitors

Air Services Airlines flying to Panama from North America include: from New York City, Air Panamá, Challenge International; from Washington, Challenge; from Miami, Air Panamá, Challenge, LAN-Chile, Ecuatoriana; from Los Angeles and San Francisco, Air Panamá; from Dallas, Challenge; from New Orleans, Challenge, Taca; from Houston, Challenge. From Mexico, Air Panamá, Aeroméxico. From Central America, Taca, Iberia (Guatemala City; also to Santo Domingo), Copa, Lacsa (to San José, to connect with its Central American network, and Los Angeles/Mexico/Miami/New Orleans routes), Sahsa and Aeronica (to Managua, San Salvador, Mexico, San José). From South America, Air Panamá, Lacsa (Barranquilla, Maracaibo, Caracas, and San Juan, Puerto Rico), Copa, LAN-Chile, Aeroméxico, Avianca, Ecuatoriana, Varig, Viasa, Lloyd Aéreo Boliviano, KLM (to Lima, Quito, and to the Netherlands Antilles), SAM. From Europe, Iberia, KLM, Viasa.

There are local flights to most parts of Panama by the national airlines Copa and Adsa. There is a service between Paitilla airport (Panama City) and the Comarca de San Blas by Sasa. To Barranquilla, Cartagena and Medellín by Copa, who also fly to Port au Prince, Santo Domingo and Kingston, Jamaica. To Bogotá via Medellín by SAM, it leaves Panama City at 1230 and arrives Bogotá 1430, but be at airport very early because it can leave before time; also to Cali with SAM. Student flights Panama-Guayaquil for those with valid student cards, US$88, are a cheap way to South America, but you will be on a waiting list behind those who have paid full price.

An airport tax of US$15 has to be paid by all passengers, except those in transit who do not pass customs. If you stay for a short period (6 hrs. maximum), make sure you put "transit" on your arrival card, so as to avoid the airport tax.

There is a US$8 tax on air tickets purchased in Panama.

1190 PANAMA

Shipping Services From Panama there are frequent shipping services with the principal European and North American ports; with the Far East, New Zealand, and Australia, with both the E and W coast ports of South America and Central America, regularly with some, irregularly with others. Freighters carrying a limited number of passengers operate in all trades. The Italian Line serves Cristóbal from Mediterranean ports. For service from France contact Continental Shipping and Travel, 179 Piccadilly, London W1V 9DB, Tel.: 01-491 4968 (passengers taken).

Documents Visitors must have a passport, together with a tourist card (issued for 30 days and renewable for another 60) or a visa (issued for 90 days). Holders of visas require exit permits unless they stay in Panama less than 48 hrs.; holders of tourist cards (US$3 from Panamanian consulates, Ticabus or airlines, valid 30 days, renewable in Panama City) do not need exit permits. Customs at Paso Canoas, at the border with Costa Rica, have been known to run out of tourist cards; on one occasion they told some people to go to Golfito (Costa Rica) to get visas from the consulate of Panama there. If not entering Panama at the main entry points (Tocumen airport, Paso Canoas), expect more complicated arrangements. Travellers overland may be asked to show US$150 in cash (or a proportion in travellers' cheques with persuasion). Neither visas nor tourist cards are required by nationals of Costa Rica, the Dominican Republic, El Salvador, Western Germany, Honduras, Spain, Switzerland and the UK, but if the stay in Panama exceeds 30 days they must obtain an exit permit from the authorities in Panama City. The procedure is: take your passport to the Ministerio de Hacienda y Tesoro, Av. Perú y Calle 35 E, to obtain a *Paz y Salvo* form (US$0.25); then go to Oficina de Migración, Av. Cuba y Calle 28 E, where the *Paz y Salvo* will eventually be stuck into your passport, and you are given an exit stamp covering the week beginning on the date you went to the office. US and Japanese citizens need a visa (free to the former, US$20 for the latter, produced in the same day); Australians need a visa (US$10). Tourist cards may not be issued to citizens of Communist countries, India and Pakistan, who must have visas. Onward tickets are required, with the exception of travellers in their own vehicles. Once in Panama, you cannot get a refund for an onward flight ticket unless you have another exit ticket. Copa tickets can be refunded at any office in any country (in the currency of that country).

Customs Even if you only change planes in Panama you must have the necessary papers for the airport officials. Cameras, binoculars, etc., 500 cigarettes or 500 grams of tobacco and 3 bottles of alcoholic drinks for personal use are taken in free. The Panamanian Customs are strict; drugs without a doctor's prescription and books deemed "subversive" are confiscated. In the latter case, a student's or teacher's card helps. **Note:** Passengers leaving Panama by land are *not* entitled to any duty-free goods, which are delivered only to ships and aircraft. **Another Note:** You may be asked to show that you have at least US$150, or US$10 for each day of intended stay if that exceeds 15 days, before being allowed in. (However, several people have told us that the Panamanian customs are not always that strict in this respect. On the other hand, young Europeans have been strip-searched on arrival by air.)

Motoring Coming in by car visit Customs and Immigration in the same building for a 20-day visa, entry documents for your car. Passport is stamped for 2 weeks' entry for a car, 3 days for a motorcycle, given at frontier. Entry costs US$4.05, plus US$1 for fumigation. Exit calls for 4 papers which also cost US$4.05 (obtainable, as are extensions for entry permits, from Customs in Ancón, off Curundu Road, near Albrook air base. Entering Panama by sea with a car is time-wasting—at least at Colón. Low octane gasoline costs US$1.90 per gallon, super grade US$1.98. For motorcyclists, note that a crash helmet must be worn. **Note** that you may not take dogs into Panama by car, though they may be flown or shipped in if they have general health and rabies certificates; dogs and cats now have to spend 40 days in quarantine after entry.

Warning It is virtually impossible for a tourist to sell his car in Panama unless he can show (with help from his Consulate) that he needs the money for his fare home. He will in this case have to pay import duty on the sale. The only alternative is to sell the car in Costa Rica, but the level of tax incurred is very high. It is also impossible to leave a vehicle in Panama while travelling on.

British business travellers are advised to get "Hints to Exporters: Panama", on application to the Export Services Division, Department of Trade, Sanctuary Buildings, 16-20 Great Smith Street, London SW1P 4DB.

Hours of Business Government departments, 0800-1200, 1230-1630 (Mon. to Fri.). Banks: open and close at different times, but are usually open all morning, but not on Sat. British Embassy: 0800-1330 and 1430-1630 Mon. to Fri. Shops and most private enterprises: 0700 or 0800-1200 and 1400-1800 or 1900 every day, including Sat.
Business interests are concentrated in Panama City and Colón.

Climate The Isthmus is only 9°N of the equator, but prevailing winds reduce the discomfort, especially in the cool evenings of the dry season, though the humidity is high. The mean temperature in the city is 26°C with a maximum temperature record of 36°C and a minimum of 17°. The average rainfall in the area is 1,524 mm. a year (the wet season is called *invierno*—winter, the dry *verano*—summer).

Clothing Light weight tropical type clothes for men, light cotton or linen dresses for women, for whom the wearing of trousers is quite OK. The dry season, January-April, is the pleasantest time. Heavy rainfall sometimes in October and November.

Health No particular precautions are necessary. Water in Panama City and Colón is safe to drink.

Language Spanish (hard to understand), but English is widely understood.

Living is costly, although food is much the same price as in Costa Rica. US Canal employees and military personnel buy their supplies at low prices in special stores. These facilities are not available to tourists of course, but checks on users' status are said to be few and far between! These privileges will of course be reduced as the Canal is gradually handed back to Panama under the new Treaties. The annual average increase in consumer prices fluctuates in line with US trends.

Festivals The *fiestas* in the towns are well worth seeing. That of Panama City at Carnival time, held on the four days before Ash Wednesday, is the best. During carnival women who can afford it wear the *pollera* dress, with its "infinity of diminutive gathers and its sweeping skirt finely embroidered", a shawl folded across the shoulders, satin slippers, tinkling pearl hair ornaments in spirited shapes and colours. The men wear a *montuno* outfit: native straw hats, embroidered blouses and trousers sometimes to below the knee only, and carry the *chácara*, or small purse. There is also a splendid local Carnival at Las Tablas, west of Panama City.

At the Holy Week ceremonies at Villa de Los Santos the farces and acrobatics of the big devils—with their debates and trials in which the main devil accuses and an angel defends the soul—the dance of the "dirty little devils" and the dancing drama of the Montezumas are all notable. The ceremonies at Pesé (near Chitré) are famous all over Panama. At Portobelo, near Colón, there is a procession of little boats in the canals of the city.

There are, too, the folk-tunes and dances. The music is cheerful, combining the contagious rhythms of the African with the melodic tones and dance-steps of Andalusia, to which certain characteristics of the Indian pentatonic scale have been added. The *tamborito* is the national dance. Couples dance separately and the song— which is sung by the women only, just as the song part of the *mejorana* or *socavón* is exclusively for male voices—is accompanied by the clapping of the audience and three kinds of regional drums. The *mejorana* is danced to the music of native guitars and in the interior are often heard the laments known as the *gallo* (rooster), *gallina* (hen), *zapatero* (shoemaker), or *mesano*. Two other dances commonly seen at *fiestas* are the *punto*, with its promenades and foot tapping, and the *cumbia*, of African origin, in which the dancers carry lighted candles and strut high.

The Guaymí Indians of Chiriquí province meet around February 12 to transact tribal business, hold feasts and choose mates by tossing balsa logs at one another; those unhurt in this contest, known as Las Balserías, are allowed to select the most desirable women.

What to Eat Best hors d'oeuvre is *carimañola*, cooked mashed yuca wrapped round a savoury filling of chopped seasoned fried pork and fried a golden brown. The traditional stew, *sancocho*, made from chicken, yuca, dasheen, cut-up corn on the cob, plantain, potatoes, onions, flavoured with salt, pepper and coriander. *Ropa vieja*, shredded beef mixed with fried onions, garlic, tomatoes and green peppers and served with white rice, baked plantain or fried yuca. *Sopa borracha*, a rich sponge cake soaked in rum and garnished with raisins and prunes marinated in sherry. Panama is famous for its seafood: lobsters, corvina, shrimp, tuna, etc. Piquant *seviche* is usually corvina or white fish seasoned with tiny red and yellow peppers, thin slices of onion and marinated in lemon juice; it is served very cold and has a bite. *Arroz con coco y titi* is rice with coconut and tiny dried shrimp. Plain coconut rice is also delicious. For low budget try *comida corriente* or *del día* (US$1.50 or so). Corn (maize) is eaten in various forms, depending on season, e.g. *tamales*, made of corn meal mash filled with cooked chicken or pork, olives and prunes; or *empanadas*, toothsome meat pies fried crisp. Plantain, used as a vegetable, appears in various forms. A fine dessert is made from green plantain flour served with coconut cream. Other desserts are *arroz con cacao*, chocolate rice pudding; *buñuelos de viento*, a puffy fritter served with syrup; *sopa de gloria*, sponge cake soaked in cooked cream mixture with rum added; *guanábana* ice cream is made from sweet ripe soursop.

Tipping at hotels, restaurants: 10% of bill. Porters, 15 cents per item. Cloakroom, 25 cents. Hairdressers, 25 cents. Cinema usherettes, nothing. Taxi drivers don't expect tips; rates should be arranged before the trip.

Currency Panama is one of the few countries in the world which issues no paper money; US banknotes are used exclusively, being called balboas instead of dollars. It has silver coins of 10 balboas, 50c (called a *peso*), 25c, 10c, nickel of 5c (called a *real*) and copper of 1c. All the silver money is used interchangeably with US currency; each coin is the same size and material as the US coin of equivalent value. You can take in or out any amount of foreign or Panamanian currency.

PANAMA

Both metric and the US system of weights and measures are used.

Foreign Postage Great care should be taken to address all mail as "Republic of Panama" or "RP", otherwise it is returned to sender. Air mail takes 3-5 days, sea mail 3-5 weeks from Britain. Rates (examples) for air mail (up to 15 grams) are as follows: Central, North and South America and Caribbean, 30c; Europe, 37c up to 10 grams, 5c for every extra 5 grams; Africa, Asia, Oceania, 44c; all air letters require an extra 2c stamp. Parcels to Europe can only be sent from the post office in the El Dorado shopping centre in Panama City (bus from Calle 12 to Tumba Muerta).

Telecommunications The radio station at Gatún is open to commercial traffic; such messages are handled through the Government telegraph offices. The telegraph and cable companies are given under the towns in which they operate.

Telex is available at the airport, the cable companies and many hotels. Rate for a 3-minute call to Britain is US$14.40, and US$4.80 for each minute more.

Telephone calls can be made between the UK and Panama any time, day or night. Minimum charge for 3 min. call: US$10 station to station, but person to person, US$16 on weekdays, US$12 on Sun. plus tax of US$1 on each call. To the USA the charge is US$4 for 3 mins. Difference in time: GMT minus 5 hrs. Phone to Australia costs US$16 for 3 mins. (US$13 on Sunday).

Inter-continental contact by satellite is laid on by the Pan-American Earth Satellite Station. The local company is Intercomsa.

Public Holidays

Jan. 1: New Year's Day.
Jan. 9: National Mourning.
Shrove Tuesday: Carnival.
Good Friday.
May 1: Labour Day (Republic)
Aug 15: (Panama City only, O)
Oct. 11: National Revolution Day
Nov. 1: National Anthem Day (O)

Nov. 2: All Souls (O).
Nov. 3: Independence Day.
Nov. 4: Flag Day (O).
Nov. 5: Independence Day (Colón only).
Nov. 10: First Call of Independence.
Nov. 28: Independence from Spain.
Dec. 8: Mothers' Day.
Dec. 25: Christmas Day.

O=Official holiday, when banks and government offices close. On the rest—national holidays—business offices close too. Many others are added at short notice.

Press The *Star and Herald* and *La Estrella de Panamá*, *La República*, *La Prensa* (oppositon) (Spanish) are the largest daily newspapers. Other papers are: *Crítica*, and *Matutino* (daily Spanish); *Colón News* (weekly—Spanish and English).

We are deeply grateful to the following travellers for new information: Max van Arnhem (Huissen, Neth.), Mary Lou Benoit (Trenton, NJ), Hans Hendriks (Maassluis, Neth.), Ruth Kamm (Munich 19), James Maas (London W3), Ken Robinson (Johannesburg), Josyane Sechaud (San Salvador), Gustavo Steinbrun Bianco (Buenos Aires), Stefan Thommen (Liestal, Switz.), and Thomas Meier (Schaffhausen, Switz.) for valuable new information on Darién; also to various travellers listed in the general Central America section.

CUBA

THE ISLAND OF CUBA, 1,250 km. long, 191 km. at its widest point, is the largest of the Caribbean islands and only 145 km. S of Florida. Gifted with a moderate climate broken only occasionally by hurricanes, not cursed by frosts, blessed by an ample and well distributed rainfall and excellent soils for tropical crops, it has traditionally been the largest exporter of cane sugar in the world. The population is about 9.8 million.

About a quarter of Cuba is fairly mountainous. To the W of Havana is the narrow Sierra de los Organos, rising to 750 metres and containing, in the extreme W, the strange scenery of the Guaniguánicos hill country. S of these Sierras, in a strip 145 km. long and 16 km. wide along the piedmont, is the Vuelta Abajo area which grows the finest of all Cuban tobaccos. Towards the centre of the island are the Trinidad mountains, rising to 1,100 metres, and in the E, encircling the port of Santiago, are the most rugged mountains of all, the Sierra Maestra, in which Pico Turquino reaches 1,980 metres. In the rough and stony headland E of Guantánamo Bay are copper, manganese, chromium and iron mines. About a quarter of the land surface is covered with mountain forests of pine and mahogany. The coastline, with a remarkable number of fine ports and anchorages, is about 3,540 km. long.

History Cuba was discovered by Columbus during his first voyage on October 27, 1492, and he paid a brief visit two years later on his way to the discovery of Jamaica. Columbus did not realize it was an island; it was first circumnavigated by Sebastián de Ocampo in 1508. Diego Velázquez conquered it in 1511 and founded several towns, including Havana. The first African slaves were imported in 1526. Sugar was introduced soon after but was not important until the last decade of the 16th century. When the British took Jamaica in 1655 a number of Spanish settlers fled to Cuba, already famous for its cigars, made a strict monopoly of Spain in 1717. The coffee tree was introduced in 1748. The British, under Lord Albemarle and Admiral Pocock, captured Havana and held the island in 1762-63, but it was returned to Spain in exchange for Florida.

The tobacco monopoly was abolished in 1816 and Cuba was given the right to trade with the world in 1818. Independence elsewhere, however, bred ambitions, and a strong movement for independence was quelled by Vives, the Captain General, in 1823. By this time the blacks outnumbered the whites in the island; there were several slave rebellions and little by little the Creoles (or Spaniards born in Cuba) made common cause with them. A slave rising in 1837 was savagely repressed and the poet Gabriel de la Concepción Valdés was shot. There was a ten-year rebellion against Spain between 1868 and 1878, but it gained little save the effective abolition of slavery, which had been officially forbidden since 1847. From 1895 to 1898 rebellion flared up again under José Martí and Máximo Gómez. The United States was now in sympathy with the rebels, and when the US battleship *Maine* was blown up in Havana harbour on February 15, 1898, this was made a pretext for declaring war on Spain. American forces (which included Colonel Theodore Roosevelt) were landed, a squadron blockaded Havana and defeated the Spanish fleet at Santiago de Cuba. In December peace was signed and US forces occupied the island. The Government of Cuba was handed over to its first president, Tomás Estrada Palma, on May 20, 1902. The USA retained naval bases at Río Hondo and Guantánamo Bay and reserved the right of intervention in Cuban domestic affairs, but granted the island a handsome import preference for its sugar. The USA chose to intervene several times, but relinquished this right in 1934.

From 1925 to 1933 the "strong man" Machado ruled Cuba as a dictator. His

1194 **CUBA**

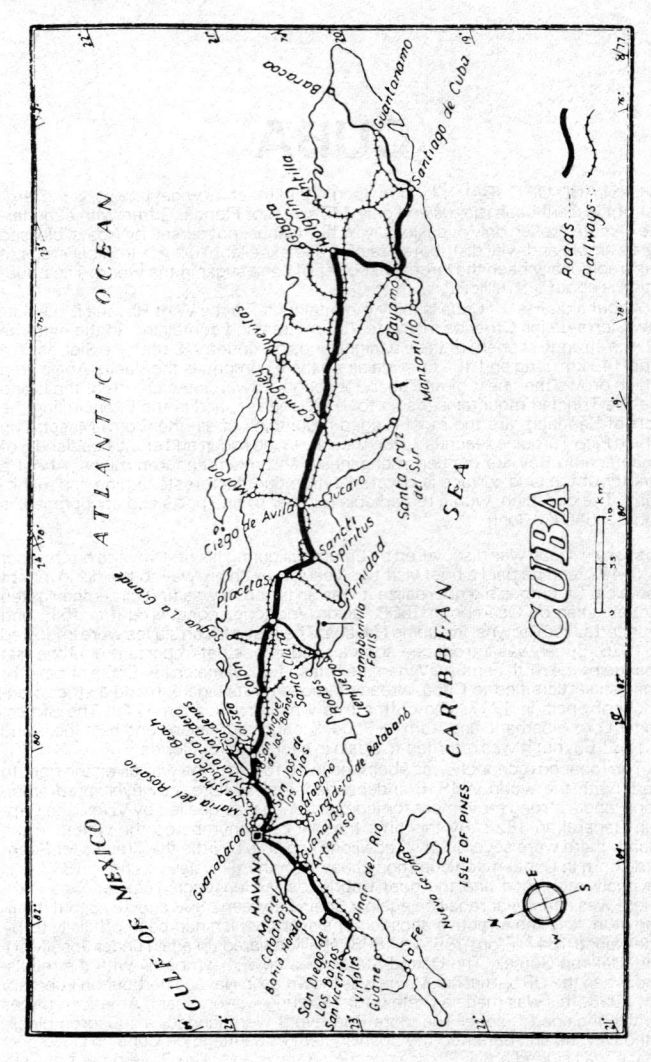

CUBA 1195

downfall was brought about by Fulgencio Batista, then a sergeant, whose increasingly corrupt dictatorship was brought to an end by Fidel Castro in January 1959, after an extraordinary and heroic three years' campaign, mostly in the Sierra Maestra, with a guerrilla force reduced at one point to twelve men.

From 1960 onwards, in the face of increasing hostility from the USA, Castro led Cuba into communism. All farms of over 67 hectares have been taken over by the state. Rationing is still fierce, though less so than formerly, and there are still shortages of consumer goods. However, education, housing and health services have been greatly improved. Considerable emphasis is placed on combining productive agricultural work with study: there are over 400 schools and colleges in rural areas where the students divide their time between the plantations and the classroom. Education is compulsory up to the age of 17 and free.

Before the Revolution of 1959 the United States had investments in Cuba worth about 1,000 million dollars, covering nearly every activity from agriculture and mining to oil installations; it took 66.8% of Cuba's exports and supplied 69.8% of the imports in 1958. Today all American businesses, including banks, have been nationalized; the USA has cut off sugar imports from Cuba, placed an embargo on exports to Cuba, and broken off diplomatic relations. Cuba's sugar is today sold largely to Communist countries, which are now granting Cuba over US$500m. in aid each year. Of recent years, though, sugar sales to non-communist countries, for instance Japan, have increased appreciably, and it was hoped that relations with the USA might soon be normalized, though promising moves in this direction have been aborted as a result of Cuban military activities in Africa.

Government In 1976 a new constitution was approved by 97.7% of the voters, setting up municipal and provincial assemblies and a National Assembly of 481 members, elected by the members of the municipal assemblies. As a result of the decisions of the First Congress of the Communist Party of Cuba in December 1975, the number of provinces was increased from six to fourteen. Dr. Fidel Castro was elected President of the Council of State by the National Assembly and his brother, Major Raúl Castro, was similarly elected First Vice-President.

The People Some 73% of Cubans firmly register themselves as whites: they are mostly the descendants of Spanish colonial settlers and immigrants; 26% are black, now living mostly along the coasts and in certain provinces, Oriente in particular; about 1% are Chinese; the indigenous Indians disappeared long ago. Some 50% live in the towns, of which there are 9 with over 50,000 inhabitants each. The population is estimated at 9,800,000; a third lives in Havana province, a fifth in Havana itself, though recent population movements have swelled the rural population at the expense of the urban. It is claimed that illiteracy has been wiped out.

Communications Cuba has 18,115 km. of railway and over 20,000 km. of roads. They are shown on the map. An 8-lane highway along the length of the island, between Pinar del Río and Santiago, is being built. Internal flights link Havana with Santiago, Varadero and other towns. Tourism, which had long been more or less confined by the authorities, in practice, to Havana and environs, is being extended to other parts of the country.

Havana, the capital, was before the Revolution the largest, most beautiful and the most sumptuous city in the Caribbean. Today it is rather run-down, but thanks to the Government's policy of developing the countryside, it is not ringed with shantytowns like so many other Latin American capitals. With its suburbs it has 1,933,000 people. Some of it is very old—the city was founded in 1515—but the ancient palaces, plazas, colonnades, churches and monasteries merge agreeably with the new. The old city is being substantially refurbished with Unesco's help, as part of the drive to attract tourists.

The oldest part of the city, around the Plaza de Armas, is quite near the docks. Here are the former palace of the Captains-General, the temple of El Templete, and La Fuerza, the oldest of all the forts. From Plaza de Armas two narrow and picturesque streets, Calles Obispo and O'Reilly, go W to the heart of the city: Parque Central, with its laurels, poincianas, almonds, palms, shrubs and gorgeous flowers. To the SW rises the golden dome of the Capitol. From the NW corner of Parque Central a wide, tree-shaded avenue, the Paseo del Prado, runs

1196 CUBA

to the fortress of La Punta; at its northern sea-side end is the Malecón, a splendid highway along the coast to the western residential suburbs of Vedado and Marianao. Calle San Lázaro leads directly from the monument to Gen. Antonio Maceo on the Malecón to the magnificent central stairway of Havana University. A new monument to Julio Antonio Mella, founder of the Cuban Communist Party, stands across from the stairway. Further out, past El Príncipe castle, is Plaza de la Revolución, with the impressive monument to José Martí at its centre. The large buildings surrounding the square were mostly built in the 1950s and house the principal government ministries. The long grey building behind the monument is the former Justice Ministry (1958), now the HQ of the Central Committee of the Communist Party, where Fidel Castro has his office. The Plaza is the scene of massive parades and speeches marking important events. From near the fortress of La Punta a tunnel runs eastwards under the mouth of the harbour; it emerges in the rocky ground between the Castillo del Morro and the fort of La Cabaña, some 550 metres away, and a 5-km. highway connects with the Havana-Matanzas road.

The street map of Havana is marked with numerals showing the places of most interest to visitors.

1. Castillo del Morro was built between 1589 and 1630, with a 20-metre moat, but has been much altered. It stands on a bold headland; the flash of its lighthouse, built in 1844, is visible 30 km. out to sea. The castle is open to the public, Tues.-Sun., 1000-1800, as a museum. On the harbour side, down by the water, is the Battery of the 12 Apostles, each gun named after an Apostle. It can be reached by bus through the tunnel to the former toll gates.

2. Fortaleza de la Cabaña, built 1763-1774. Fronting the harbour is a high wall; the ditch on the landward side, 12 metres deep, has a drawbridge to the main entrance. Inside are Los Fosos de los Laureles where political prisoners were shot during the Cuban fight for independence. Visitors are no longer allowed inside La Cabaña as it is used as a barracks; there are plans to convert it into a hotel.

The National Observatory and the railway station for trains to Matanzas are on the same side of the Channel as these two forts.

3. Castilla de la Punta, built at the end of the 16th century, a squat building with 2½-metre thick walls, is open to the public, daily 1400-2200. Opposite the fortress, across the Malecón, is the monument to Máximo Gómez, the independence leader.

4. Castillo de la Fuerza, Cuba's oldest building and the second oldest fort in the New World, was built 1538-1544 after the city had been sacked by buccaneers. It is a low, long building with a picturesque tower from which there is a grand view. Inside the castle is the Museo de Armas, open Tues.-Sat., 1315-2030, Sun., 0900-1200. *Note:* There are two other old forts in Havana: Atarés, finished in 1763, on a hill overlooking the south-west end of the harbour; and El Príncipe, on a hill at the far end of Av. Independencia, built 1774-94, now the city gaol. Finest view in Havana from this hill.

5. The Cathedral, built in 1704 by the Jesuits, who were expelled in 1767. Belltowers flank the Tuscan façade; there is a grand view from the E tower. The church is officially dedicated to the Virgin of the Immaculate Conception, but is better known as the church of Havana's patron saint, San Cristóbal, and as the Columbus cathedral. The bones of Christopher Columbus were sent to this cathedral when Santo Domingo was ceded by Spain to France in 1795; they now lie in Santo Domingo (see page 1214). The bones were in fact those of another Columbus. The Cathedral is open Mon-Fri. 0900-1130 and Sat. 1530-1730.

6. Plaza de Armas (now known as Plaza Carlos Manuel Céspedes), has been restored to very much what it once was. The statue in the centre is of Céspedes. In the NE corner of the square is the church of El Templete; a column in front of it marks the spot where the first mass was said in 1519 under a ceiba tree. A sapling of the same tree, blown down by hurricane in 1753, was planted on the same spot, and under its branches the supposed bones of Columbus reposed in state before being taken to the cathedral. This tree was cut down in 1828, the present tree planted, and the Doric temple opened. There are paintings by Vermay, a pupil of David, inside.

7. On the W side of Plaza de Armas is the former palace of the Captains General, built in 1780, a charming example of colonial architecture. The Spanish Governors and the Presidents lived here until 1917, when it became the City Hall. It is now the Historical Museum of the city of Havana. Open Tues.-Sat., 1430-1800, 1900-2200; Sun. 1500-1900. The arcaded and balconied patio is well worth a visit. The former Supreme Court on the N side of the Plaza is another colonial building, with a large patio.

8. The church and convent of San Francisco, built 1608, reconstructed 1737; a massive, sombre edifice suggesting defence rather than worship. The three-storeyed tower was both a landmark for returning voyagers and a look-out for pirates. No longer open to the public.

CUBA 1197

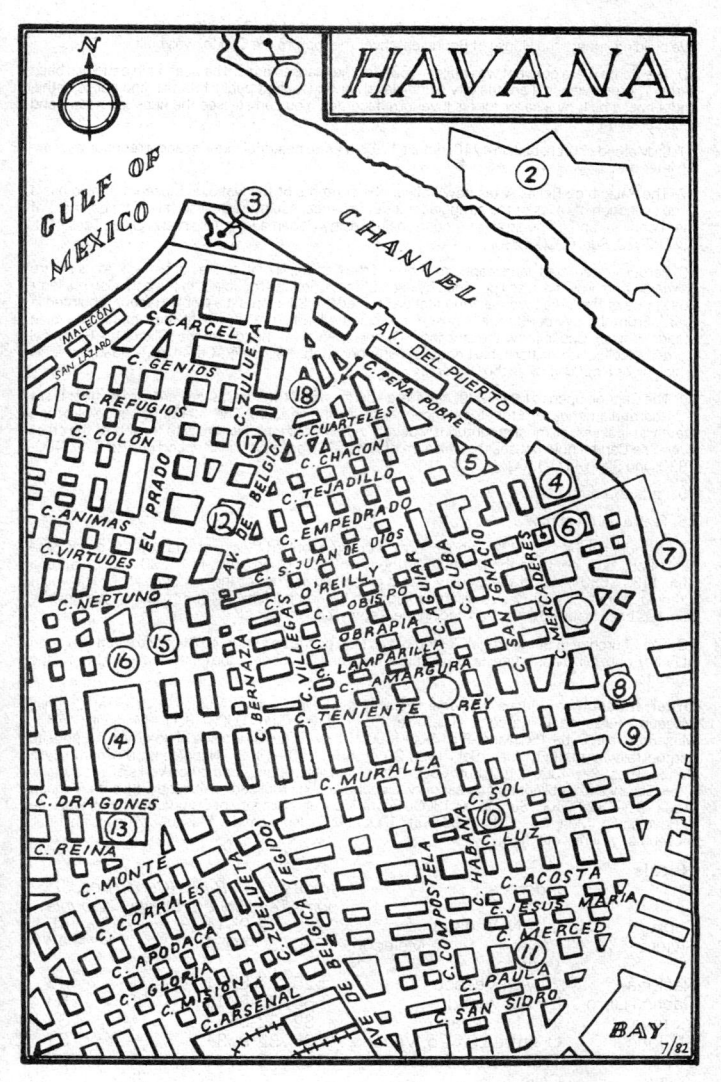

CUBA

9. The Corinthian white marble building on Calle Oficinas S of the Post Office was once the legislative building, where the House of Representatives met before the Capitol was built.

10. The Santa Clara convent was built in 1635 for the Clarisan nuns. The quaint old patio has been carefully preserved; in it are the city's first slaughter house, first public fountain and public baths, and a house built by a sailor for his love-lorn daughter. You can still see the nuns' cemetery and their cells.

11. La Merced church, built in 1746, rebuilt 1792. It has a beautiful exterior and a redecorated lavish interior.

12. The Palacio de Bellas Artes now houses the contents of the National Museum. It also has a large collection of relics of the struggle for independence, sculptures, classical paintings (most of them copies), and a fine array of modern paintings by Cuban and other artists. Open Tues.-Sat. 1300-2030, Sun. 0900-1230.

13. Parque Fraternidad, landscaped to show off the Capitol, N of it, to the best effect. At its centre is a ceiba tree growing in soil provided by each of the American republics. In the park also is a famous statue of the Indian woman who first welcomed the Spaniards: La Noble Habana, sculpted in 1837. From the SW corner the handsome Avenida Allende runs due W to the high hill on which stands Príncipe Castle (now the city gaol). On this avenue, at the foot of the hill, are the Botanical Gardens (collection of flora, bird houses, fish-ponds, etc.). N, along Calle Universidad, on a hill which gives a good view, is the University.

14. The Capitol, opened May 1929, has a large dome over a rotunda; at the centre of its floor is set a 24-carat diamond, zero for all distance measurements in Cuba. The interior has large halls and stately staircases, all most sumptuously decorated. Entrance for visitors is to the left of the stairway. The Capitol now houses the Museum of Natural Science, which is open Tues. to Sat. 1400-1930, and Sun. 0900-1300.

15. Parque Central.

16. Teatro García Lorca.

17. Presidential Palace (1922), a huge, ornate building topped by a dome, facing Av. de las Misiones Park, now contains the Museum of the Revolution. Open Tues.-Fri. 1230-1930, Sat. and Sun. 1130-1630. A bit of the old city wall is preserved in front of the front entrance. The yacht *Granma*, from which Dr Castro disembarked with his companions in 1956 to launch the Revolution, has been installed in the park facing the S entrance.

18. The Church of El Santo Angel Custodio was built by the Jesuits in 1672 on the slight elevation of Peña Pobre hill. It has white, laced Gothic towers and 10 chapels, the best of which is behind the high altar.

Other Museums Museo Nacional, Palacio de Belles Artes, Animas y Zulueta; Colonial Museum, Plaza de la Catedral (Tues.-Sat. 1300-2100, Sun. 0900-1300); Medical Science Museum, Calle Cuba 460 (Mon.-Fri. 0900-1200, 1300-1700); Birthplace of José Martí, opposite central railway station (Tues.-Sat. 1300-2000, Sun. 0900-1300); Napoleonic Museum, Calle Ronda (Tues.-Sat. 1300-2100; Sun. 0900-1300), houses paintings and other works of art, a specialized library and a collection of weaponry; Decorative Arts Museum, 17th and E Streets, Vedado (Tues.-Sat. 1300-2100; Sun. 0900-1300); Postal Museum, Ministry of Communications, Plaza de la Revolución (Mon.-Fri. 1000-1800, Sat. 1000-1400); Numismatic Museum. Admission to all museums, galleries etc. free.

Hotels

	Address	No. of rooms	Telephone	Rates (Cuban pesos)* Single	Double
Capri	21 y N, Vedado	220	32-0511	-	45
Riviera	Paseo y Malecón, Vedado	360	30-5051	-	49
Nacional	21 y O, Vedado	525	7-8981	19	43
Habana Libre	L y 23, Vedado	568	30-5011	35	53
Victoria	19 y M, Vedado	32	32-6531	-	31
St. John's	O, entre 23 y 25, Vedado	96	32-9531	-	31
Sevilla	Trocadero y Zulueta	196	6-9961	-	27
Colina	Calle 1			18	25
Deauville	Galiano y Malecón	140	61-6901	-	37
Bristol	San Rafael y Amistad	124	61-9944	15	17
Alamac	Galiano 308	50	61-6971	3	5

* Official rate: US$1=0.85 peso.

CUBA 1199

The Vedado hotels (the best) are away from the centre; the others reasonably close to it. Other hotels are the *Inglaterra*, Parque Central, C, recommended for its colonial atmosphere; *New York*, Dragones 156, E, water outside; *Presidente*; *Packard*, Prado, Paseo Martí, D; *Plaza*, D, no running water; *Caribbean Regis*, Paseo Martí 154, E, clean, central; *Bruzón*, D; *Isla de Cuba*, Máximo Gómez 169, E; and *Clara*. All the better hotels are bookable only in dollars.

The cheaper hotels are usually hard to get into; often full. To pay in pesos at cheaper hotels involves presenting yourself in the morning to be listed at the hotel selected and then going back in the afternoon to collect a registration card. Some are reserved for Cuban tourists, most have two tariffs, one for nationals and another (higher) for foreigners. If price is no object, George Raft's penthouse suite at the *Capri* is available for 103 pesos a night. Foreign tourists must obtain a reservation from Cubatur, the government tourist agency, before proceeding to the hotels (all government-owned). *Posadas* are legal, short-term lodgings designed for couples, they charge 3-5 pesos a night. A Cubatur hostess is always on duty in the immigration area at José Martí International Airport to receive incoming flights, and visitors arriving on their own should get her to book them a room at one of the hotels at that time. You will not, in fact, be allowed to leave the airport unless you have a hotel room booked. The main Cubatur office is at Calle 23, No. 156 between N and O, La Rampa, Vedado (open Mon.-Fri. 0800-1700, Sat. 0800-1200), and reservations for all Cuban hotels, restaurants, and night clubs can be made here. Always tell the hotel each morning if you intend to stay on another day.

Restaurants are not cheap. The choice of food is very restricted by rationing. Book a table between 2200 and midnight the evening before, if you can, in the main ones, where meals are about US$10-15, usually paid in US dollars. The *Bodeguita del Medio*, near the Cathedral, made famous by Hemingway and worth a visit if only for a drink, and *The Patio*, nearby, are recommended for national dishes; so is *Rincón Criollo*, on the outskirts of town, which is most easily reached by taxi; try to persuade the driver to come back and fetch you, as otherwise it is difficult to get back; the same applies to *Las Ruinas* in Parque Lenín, Cuba's most exclusive restaurant—and aptly named for its prices. *La Floridita*, near the Parque Central, is reputedly the original home of the *daiquiri*. The *Sevilla Hotel* has the best hotel restaurant. Visit *Dulcería Doña Teresa* (end of Obispo) for the caramel pudding. Reasonable cafeteria-style meals are available at *Wakamba*, opposite *St. John's* hotel; nearby is the *Pizzeria Milán*; *Caracas* restaurant near Parque Central, and nearby, also good and cheap, *Los Parados*. In Vedado, *El Cochinito*, Calle 23 (national *criollo* dishes); *El Conejito*, Calle N, and *La Torre* (at top of Edificio Fosca), are quite expensive. Also expensive, *"1830"* on Malecón. Along and near La Rampa there are some cheaper pizzerias and self-service restaurants. At Marianao beach there are also some cheaper bars and restaurants.

A visit to the *Coppelia* ice-cream parlour, 23 y L, Vedado, is recommended. It tends to be very crowded in the evenings as it and La Rampa are very popular with young people. To get an ice-cream (0.50-1.50 pesos), pay first, collect a dish and then the ice. This process can take more than an hour.

Tipping Visitors are not allowed to tip in hotels and restaurants. Taxi drivers are not tipped. If you want to express gratitude, offer a packet of American cigarettes.

Shopping Local cigars, cigarettes and rum are excellent. Original lithographs and other works of art can be purchased directly from the artists at the Galería del Grabado, Plaza de la Catedral (Mon.-Fri. 1400-2100, Sat. 1400-1900). Just opposite this is the Galería de Arte (Mon.-Fri. 1030-1800, Sat. 1700-2200), where a variety of works of art are on sale. On Saturday afternoons there are handicraft stalls in the Plaza. There is a special boutique in the old mansion at Calle Cuba 64 where the largest selection of Cuban handicrafts is available; the artisans have their workshops in the back of the same building (open, Mon.-Sat. 1230-1930). All the larger hotels have boutiques where visitors can make purchases on presentation of their white currency-exchange papers. Shops in hotels insist on being paid in dollars; essential in Intur shops which stock necessities for the traveller. The best boutiques are those located in the *Riviera*, *Habana Libre*, *Nacional* and *Deauville* hotels. The large department stores are along Galiano (Av. Italia) near San Rafael and Neptuno. Rationed goods are distinguished by a small card bearing the code number and price but a great deal is now sold freely and these articles bear only the price. Most stores are open only in the afternoon.

Night Club The *Tropicana* is a must; book with Cubatur for US$15. Despite being toned down to cater for more sober post-revolutionary tastes, it is still a lively place with plenty of atmosphere. Admission is free, but the drinks are expensive: minimum charge is 5 pesos a head; again, may demand payment in dollars. Foreigners showing their exchange paper at the door may be admitted without booking if there is room. All the main hotels have their own cabarets. Best to reserve through Cubatur.

Theatres *Teatro Mella*, Vedado, specializes in modern dance; more traditional programmes at *Teatro García Lorca*. Havana has some very lively theatre companies.

1200 **CUBA**

Cinemas Best are *Yara* (opposite *Habana Libre* hotel); *América/Jiqüe*, Galiano 253; *Duplex/Rex*, San Rafael 161; *Payret*, Prado 505.

Zoo Av. 26, Vedado (open Tues.-Sun. 0900-1800).

El Bosque de la Habana is worth visiting. From the entrance to the Zoo, cross Calle 26 and walk a few blocks until you reach a bridge across the Almendares. Cross this, turn right at the end and keep going N, directly to the Bosque which is a jungle-like wood.

Aquaria National Aquarium, Calle 60 and Av. 1, Miramar, specializes in salt-water fish (open Tues.-Fri. 1300-1730, Sat. and Sun. 1000-1730) while the Parque Lenín aquarium has fresh-water fish on show.

Banks Banco Nacional and its branches.

British Embassy is on the 8th floor, Edificio Bolívar, Capdevila 101-103, Havana. Telegraphic address: Prodrome, Havana. Tel.: 61-5681/4.
Canadian Embassy, Calle 30 (No. 518) and Av. 7, Miramar (Tel.: 2-6421).
Mexican Embassy, Calle 12, 518 and Av. 7, Miramar.
Swiss Embassy, on the Calzada, Calle L and M, Vedado. Includes the United States Interest section, Tel.: 320551 and 329700.

Cables Calle Obispo 351. Tel.: 6-9901/5. Obispo y Aguiar. Ministerio de Comunicaciones, Plaza de la Revolución, Tel.: 70-5581.

Electric Current 110-230 V. 3 phase 60 cycles, A.C.

Transport Taxis tend to be scarce. Some are only allowed to operate in a restricted area (indicated by a sign in the window). If you want to go further afield look for one without a sign. The newer taxis have meters which should be set at No. 1 during the daytime and at No. 2 at night (2300-0700). Normal charge: 60 centavos per person for 500 metres, then 10 centavos for each 300 metres thereafter. In the older taxis there are no meters and there is normally a fixed charge between points in or near the city. The fare should be fixed before setting out on a journey. Most taxis are not allowed to accept US dollars (Special Tourist taxis will try to insist on dollars), so be sure to have pesos on you. There is a new type of taxi in operation, Turistaxi, taking US$ only, metered and slightly more expensive. Beware of unofficial taxis at the airport arrival gate who will overcharge. Town buses are frequent and cheap (5 centavos flat rate fare), though crowded, and run hourly through the night as well. Destinations are indicated above or behind windshield. There are long queues for all buses; you must get a waiting number.

Bus to Santiago, "especial" (a/c), 25 pesos. The out-of-town bus services leave from the central terminal; buses nos. 67 and 84 go there from the hotel area. Trains leave from the station in Av. de Bélgica, Havana, to the larger cities. It is sometimes easier to get a seat on a train than on a bus, but all public transport out of Havana is overcrowded and difficult to get on.

Car Hire Minimum US$25 a day plus US$0.20 each km after the first 100 km. Petrol must be paid for in US$, Visa accepted for the rental. Havana Autos, *Hotel Capri*.

Airport José Martí, 18 km. from Havana. No departure tax.

Suburbs The western sections of the old city merge imperceptibly into **Vedado.** W of it, and reached by a tunnel under the Almendares river, lies **Marianao,** some 16 km. W of the capital, and easily reached by bus. Population: 235,492. Marianao was where the wealthy lived before the Revolution; today there are several embassies and government buildings, and also many old, abandoned villas. The former Havana Country Club has become quite overgrown.

The project housing 3,000 families in Havana East is worth seeing. The houses are functional, economic, and pleasant. An even larger and more impressive project is underway, further east past Cojimar, at Alamar.
The Cuban pavilion, a large building on Calle 23, Vedado, is a combination of a tropical glade and a museum of social history. It tells the nation's story by a brilliant combination of objects, photography and the architectural manipulation of space.
The new Arts Centre, a series of buildings in Marianao to house schools for different arts, was designed by Ricardo Porro. Architects will be interested in this "new spatial sensation".

Beaches The beaches in Havana, at Miramar and Marianao, reached by No. 132 bus, are generally very crowded in summer. Those to the E, El Mégano, Santa María del Mar and Bacuranao, for example, are much better. Buses going along the Vía Blanca to these places leave from near the central railway station in the old city. To the W of Havana are Arena Blanca and Bahía Honda, which are good for diving and fishing but difficult to get to unless you have a car.

Guanabacoa is 5 km. to the E and is reached by a road turning off the Central Highway, or by the Hershey Railway, or by No. 162 bus or by launch from Muelle

CUBA 1201

Luz (not far from No. 9 on the map) to the suburb of Regla, then by bus direct to Guanabacoa. It is a well preserved small colonial town; sights include the old parish church which has a splendid altar: the monastery of San Francisco; the Carral theatre; and some attractive mansions. The Historical Museum of Guanabacoa, a former estate mansion, has an unusual voodoo collection in the former slave quarters at the back of the building. Open: Tues.-Sat., 1600-2200; Sun., 0900-1300.

A delightful colonial town, **Santa María del Rosario,** founded in 1732, is 16 km. E of Havana. It is reached from Cotorro, on the Central Highway, or by 97 bus from Guanabacoa, and was carefully restored and preserved before the Revolution. The village church is particularly good. See the paintings, one by Veronese. There are curative springs nearby.

Cayo Largo, a westernized island resort reached by air from Havana (US$69 return), has pleasant *cabañas* (cheaper) as well as the main hotel.

West from Havana along the northern coast road is some beautiful countryside: sugar and tobacco plantations. Near *Viñales* (Hotels: *Rancho San Vicente,* E; *Motel Los Jazmines,* E, are several caves in the limestone which are open to the public. In *Piñar del Río,* the major city W of Havana, near Viñales, is the modern *Hotel Piñar del Río,* swimming pool, night club etc., B. Also the *Vuelta Abajo,* D, and the *Hotel Occidente,* Calle Gerardo Medina, clean but old, D.

Hemingway fans may wish to visit the house in San Francisco de Paula where he lived from 1939 to 1960. Bus 7 from the Capitolio. Open Tues.-Sat. (closed Mon. and on rainy days) 0900-1200 and 1300-1700, Sun. 0900-1300. There is a bust of the author in the village of Cojimar.

Some 60 km. E of Havana is *Jibacoa* beach, which is excellent for snorkelling as the reefs are close to the beach. To get there take bus 70 to Santa Cruz del Norte and from there either a 126 or "La Matancera" - be warned, though, that the journey takes some time. From the bus stop walk to the beach. (Camping de Jibacoa, D for a cabin for four, F for 2. Food is rather expensive: 1.40 pesos for breakfast, 5 for lunch; 5 for dinner.)

The old provincial town of **Matanzas** lies 104 km. E of Havana along the Vía Blanca, which links the capital with Varadero beach, 34 km. further E. There are frequent buses but the journey via the Hershey Railway is more memorable (six trains daily from the Casablanca station, which is reached by public launch from near La Fuerza Castle, 0.50 peso). Those who wish to make it a day trip from Havana can easily do so, or one can continue on to **Varadero** (Hotels *Kawama,* B; *Internacional,* B; *Oasis,* C; the *Siboney,* C and the *Caribe,* D, which is the country's most important beach resort and has many facilities. Other hotels: *Ledo,* Av. Playa, D; *Playa Azul,* D; *Villa La Herradura,* Av. Playa, D; *Los Delfines,* Av. Playa, D. *Solymar Cabines* (near Hotel *Internacional*), C, recommended, pool and restaurant. Each November a festival is held in Varadero, lasting a week, which attracts some of the best artists in South America. Entrance US$2-10 per day. Good restaurants: *Bodegón Criollo* and *Mi Casita* (book in advance). In Varadero all hotels, restaurants and excursions must be paid in US dollars. Book excursions at Hotel Internacional, Av. Las Américas. From Varadero it is possible to explore the interesting town of **Cárdenas,** where the present Cuban flag was raised for the first time in 1850.

In Matanzas one should visit the Pharmaceutical Museum (Mon.-Sat. 1400-1800, 1900-2100), the Matanzas Museum (Tues.-Sun. 1500-1800, 1900-2200), and the cathedral, all near Plaza La Libertad. There is a wonderful view of the surrounding countryside from the church of Montserrat. Bellamar Cave is only 5 km. from Matanzas.

Cienfuegos, on the S coast, is a popular resort. Many of the hotels are out of town or booked solid by Cubans. *Hotel Pascabello* and *Rancho Luna,* both D, are seaside complexes with cafeteria etc. The *Hotel Jagua,* C, is nearer to town.

Trinidad, 133 km. south of **Santa Clara** (*Motel Los Caneyes* and *Santa Clara Libre Hotel,* both C; *América,* Calle Mujica, F; *Central,* Calle Cuba), further E, is a perfect relic of the early days of the Spanish colony, with many fine palaces and churches. (Hotels in Trinidad: *Motel Las Cuevas,* C; *Hotel Costa Sur,* 10 km. out of town, D). Camping at Base Manacal in the mountains: tent or small hut for US$5 per day; take No. 10 bus from Cienfuegos.

The Museo Ignacio Agramonte in the large city of **Camagüey** is one of the biggest and most impressive museums in the country. Adequate food and lodging is at the *Gran Hotel*, C, or *Hotel Camagüey*, C.

Holguín, a provincial capital in the E, near Santiago, has the *Hotel Pernik*, B; *Motel El Bosque*, D; and *Motel Mirador de Mayabe*, C. *Hotel Puerto Príncipe*, Av. de los Mártires, C; *Hotel Colón*, República 472, D; *Hotel Isla de Cuba*, Oscar Primelles, D.

Santiago, near the E end of the island, is Cuba's second city. Excellent excursions can be made to the Gran Piedra and along the Ruta Turística to the Morro Castle, and to Playa Bacanao, a wonderful amusement park and beach. There are buses Nos 14, 35 & 62 to the public beaches. In the city there is a number of museums, the best of which are the Colonial Museum located in Diego Velázquez' house, the Museo Bacardí and the Moncada barracks museum. The national hero, José Martí, is buried in Santa Efigenia cemetery, just W of the city.

The Festival de Caribe runs from 16 to 19 April, with traditional African dancing and beautiful costumes. There is singing every weekend at the junction of Calle Heredia and Casa de la Trova.

Hotels *Leningrado* (out of town), C; *Motel Versalles*, near airport, B; *Balcón de Caribe*, C; *Casa Grande*, recommended, opposite the cathedral, D; *Motel El Rancho*, E; *Las Américas*, C. *Libertad*, E; *Rex*, Av. Garzón; *Venus*, near Parque Céspedes. Hotels charging 20 pesos plus are bookable in dollars only.

The Economy

Following the 1959 revolution, Cuba adopted a Marxist-Leninist system. Almost all sectors of the economy are state controlled and centrally planned, the only significant exception being agriculture where some 12% of arable land is still privately owned by 192,000 small farmers. Cuba assumed full membership of the Council for Mutual Economic Assistance (Comecon) in 1972.

The Government has made diversification of the economy away from sugar the prime aim of economic policy. Some progress towards this has been made. The overwhelming reliance on sugar remains and there is little expectation of achieving balanced and sustained growth in the foreseeable future. Aid from the USSR is estimated about 25% of gnp. Apart from military aid, economic assistance takes two forms: balance-of-payments support (about 84%), under which sugar and nickel exports are priced in excess of world levels and oil and other imports priced below world levels; and assistance for development projects. There is, however, a trend towards more trade credits, which are repayable, rather than trade subsidies.

Cuba recorded impressive rates of economic growth during the 1981-85 five-year plan, averaging 6.7%. After a 7.4% increase in 1984, gross social product (gsp) grew by 4.8% in 1985 and by 1.5-2.0% (est.) in 1986.

Construction and industry have been the main growth motors in recent years; the sugar industry (70% of export earnings in 1985) has consistently failed to reach the targets set. Cuba's dream of a 10m tonne raw sugar harvest has never been reached, but output is targeted to rise from the 8.0m tonnes of 1984/85 to 9.3m tonnes by 1990 and 14m tonnes by 2000. Cuba is expected to remain the world's second-largest producer after Brazil and will probably retain its position as the world's leading exporter (3.7m tonnes out of total world exports of 7.2m tonnes in 1985). Cuba has no difficulty in selling its sugar to the Comecon countries; it receives subsidized prices (850 roubles per tonne), but is paid in inconvertible roubles or by barter. The collapse of world sugar prices has thwarted its attempts to raise hard currency.

In 1986 hard currency sales of sugar were US$275m, but the largest source of dollars was the resale of unneeded supplies of Soviet-supplied crude oil, which amounted to US$574m in 1985 but to only half that in 1986. The USSR's production difficulties, combined with the collapse of the oil price in early 1986, increases Cuba's incentive to save energy. The use of sugar cane bagasse helped to cut total energy consumption by 2.1% in 1985: the economy now uses 20% less in oil-based energy imports than in 1980.

Cuba became a member of the International Coffee Agreement in February 1985, and was allocated an export quota of 160,000 bags of 60 kg (1985/86). In that period production was 375,000 bags; exports were 250,000 bags.

Citrus has become the second-most important agricultural export. Annual production rose from 289,000 tonnes average in 1976-80 to 600,000 tonnes in 1981-85. Production rose by 25% in 1985, to 743,500 tonnes.

The fish catch increased by 10.8% in 1985, 221,000 tonnes, and the value of output is over 400m pesos.

Tourism is set to expand considerably. Comarco, of Argentina, is building 8 hotels, providing a total of 2,000 rooms, at Varadero beach, for a total cost of US$120m. Cuba hopes to add another 3,000 rooms, and tourism earnings could rise by US$75m annually (US$87.3m from 206,000 visitors in 1984).

Under the 1986-90 plan some minor profit incentives are likely to be introduced, as well as an element of decentralization, in that provincial and municipal planners will be allowed to retain more tax revenues. Since July 1985 consumers have been allowed to obtain housing mortgages.

Most trade is with Comecon: 85.5% of exports and 80.5% of imports in 1985. In that year Cuba recorded a US$73m surplus in convertible currency trade.

Cuba's foreign debt in convertible currency was about US$4.4bn end-1986, including US$175m arrears on interest payments and US$427m on principal. Cuba's first US$125m (eq) repayment to the USSR, originally due in 1986, has been rescheduled to 1990. The debt with the USSR is a secret: estimates range from US$8.5bn (eq) to US$23bn (eq).

Foreign Trade (US$m)

	1981	1982	1983	1984	1985
Exports (fob)	1,799	1,627	1,431	1,283	1,356
Imports (fob)	-1,435	-900	-919	-1,201	-1,283

	1961-70(av)	1971-80(av)	1981-85(av)
Global social product at constant prices (%)	2.8	5.7	6.7

Information for Visitors

How to Get There Soviet, Cuban, Czechoslovak and East German airlines have direct flights from East Berlin, Frankfurt, Moscow, Prague and Rabat (Morocco), and anyone thinking of going that way should contact the Czechoslovak National Airlines, Cubana de Aviación, Interflug or Aeroflot for further information. Cubana fly charters from Vienna and Cologne; they also fly from Berlin-Schöneberg Tuesdays, from Prague Fridays and from Paris-Orly Saturdays. Aeroflot operate from Moscow and Luxembourg Mondays and Wednesdays.

Cubana operates a twice weekly service between Havana and Mexico City, normally on Mon. and Fri. but often subject to delay. Cubana and Aeroflot fly to Havana from Lima and Georgetown. Cubana also flies weekly to Barbados, Trinidad and Jamaica. Cubana flies twice a week between Madrid and Havana; Balair, a Swiss company, also has regular flights from Switzerland to Cuba and Haiti. Cubana also has flights to Montreal; Air Canada flies between Toronto and Havana. Mexicana de Aviación flies from Mexico to Cuba calling at Mérida (Yucatán), and organizes package tours. From Mérida, 7 nights in Havana (tourist class) US$213, good value, 4 nights (first class). Similar from Mexico City (US$256). Some Latin American countries will not admit anyone carrying a passport stamped by the Cuban authorities. It is advisable to book your flight out of Cuba before actually going there as arranging it there can be time-consuming. Unitours (Canada) run package tours to Cuba for all nationalities.

No passenger ships call regularly, but the East German line DSR of Rostock runs periodic passenger-carrying freighters (London agents: Cory Bros., World Trade Centre, London E1 9AB, Tel.: 01-480 6321).

1204 CUBA

Documents Citizens of Denmark, France, Italy, Norway, Sweden, Switzerland, Liechtenstein, Yugoslavia and most East European countries only need a valid passport. A visa is required by Austrians, Canadians and British subjects, travelling in Cuba in transit for a period of 30 days, or as tourists or temporary visitors for up to 6 months (renewable for a like period). Visa requirements tend to alter: check well in advance. In the USA, the Czechoslovak Embassy in Washington, D.C. will process applications for visas for US$5. Visas can take several weeks to be granted, and are apparently difficult to obtain for people other than businessmen, guests of the Cuban Government or Embassy officials, or those going on package tours. When the applicant is too far from a Cuban consulate to be able to apply conveniently for a visa, he may apply direct to the Cuban Foreign Ministry for a visa waiver.

Visitors must go in person to the Immigration Office for registration the day after arrival. The office is on the corner of Calle 22 and Av. 3, Miramar. (Bus 132 from the old city centre, get off at second stop after the tunnel; also bus 32 from La Rampa or Coppelia ice-cream parlour in Vedado, alight at same stop.) When you register you will be given an exit permit. Restrictions on travellers going to Mexico from Cuba have been lifted.

Travellers coming from or going through infected areas must have certificates of vaccination against cholera and yellow fever.

British business travellers should get "Hints to Exporters: Cuba", from the Dept. of Trade, Export Services Division, Sanctuary Buildings, 16-20 Great Smith Street, London SW1P 4DB. US citizens on business with Cuba should contact Foreign Assets Control, Federal Reserve Bank of New York, 33 Liberty St., NY 10045. Another useful leaflet "Tips For Travelers to Cuba" is available from the Passport Office, US Dept. of State, Washington DC 20524.

Customs Personal baggage and articles for personal use are allowed in free of duty; so are 200 cigarettes, or 25 cigars, or 1 lb. of tobacco, and 2 bottles of alcoholic drinks. Many things are scarce or unobtainable in Cuba: take in everything you are likely to need other than food (say razor blades, medicines and pills, reading and writing materials and photographic supplies).

Hotel Reservations It is advisable to book hotel rooms before visiting any of the provinces. This can be done through the Cubatur office, Calle 23, No. 156, Vedado, La Habana 4; telex 051-243; telephone 32-4521. It is still necessary to book the first night's hotel at the airport on arrival. It's also a good idea to book hotel rooms generally before noon. In the peak season, July and August (carnival time), it is essential to book in advance.

Note Cuba is an expensive place and is geared more to package tourism than to independent visitors. It is impossible to lodge with local families and camping out on the beach or in a field is forbidden. Because of rationing it is difficult to buy food in the shops. Do not take photographs near military zones. Also be prepared for long waits for everything: buses, cinemas, restaurants, shops etc.

Language is Spanish, with local variants in pronunciation and vocabulary. Some English is spoken.

Hours of Business Government offices: 0830-1230 and 1330-1730 Mon. to Fri. Some offices open on Sat. morning. Banks: 0830-1200, 1330-1500 Mon. to Fri., 0830-1030 Sat. The Banco Nacional de Cuba is the only bank in the country. Shops: 1230-1930 Mon. to Sat.

Internal Air Services Cubana de Aviación services between most of the main towns. (Camagüey, Cienfuegos, Holguín, Baracoa, Guantánamo, Manzanillo, Moa, Nueva Gerona and Santiago all have airports.)

Buses From Varadero: to Havana 2.60 pesos (2 hrs.); to Santa Clara (1.95 pesos). From Santa Clara to Santiago 12 pesos. From Holguín to Santiago 3.50 pesos (six departures daily, there are four to Havana). There are buses at 1330 and 0130 from Camagüey to Santiago. The 20-hour journey from Santiago to Havana costs 25 pesos, and leaves daily at 0500 and 1930. (It is best to travel on weekdays and at night.) From Havana to Santiago 1320 and 1930. Havana to Metanzas (1.20 pesos), 2 hrs.; Varadero to Sta. Clara (2.25 pesos), 4 hrs.; Sta. Clara to Cienfuegos (0.55 peso), 2 hrs.; Cienfuegos to Trinidad (1.05 pesos), 2 hrs.; Trinidad to Sancti Spiritus (0.80 pesos), 2 hrs.; Sancti Spiritus to Santiago (12.00 pesos), 10 hrs.

Trains Santiago to Havana, 13.75 pesos, 12 hrs. (The same journey is 43 pesos by air).

Excursions Cubatur, the national tourist office, offers day trips to Soroa, Viñales, Trinidad, Cienfuegos, Varadero (particularly recommended) and Guamá as well as tours of colonial and modern Havana. It is also possible to go on a "Vuelta a Cuba", 7-day round-trip of the island, travelling by bus to Santiago and returning by air. Details from the Cubatur office.

Health
Sanitary reforms have transformed Cuba into a healthy country, though tap water is not safe to drink; bottled and mineral water are recommended. Medical service is free to all but prescription drugs must be purchased.

Climate NE trade winds temper the heat. Average summer shade temperatures rise to 30°C

CUBA 1205

(86°F) in Havana, and higher elsewhere. In winter, day temperatures drop to 19°C (66°F). Average rainfall is from 860 mm. in Oriente to 1,730 mm. in Havana; it falls mostly in the summer and autumn, but there can be torrential rains at any time. Hurricanes come in the autumn. The best time for a visit is during the cooler dry season (November to April). Walking is uncomfortable in summer but most offices, hotels, leading restaurants and cinemas are air-conditioned. Humidity varies between 75 and 95%.

Dress is generally informal. Summer calls for the very lightest clothing, such as cotton or cotton-terylene mixture. Cuban men mostly wear the *guayabera* (a light pleated shirt worn outside the trousers). Men should not wear shorts except on or near the beach. Trousers are quite OK for women, if preferred.

Currency The monetary unit is the peso, US$1=0.85 peso. There are heavy penalties for those caught exchanging money on the black market, though a tourist will frequently be approached, especially on the east side of La Rampa, in front of the Hotel Colina and, at night, in the Parque Central in Havana, going rate US$1 = 5 pesos: watch out for pre-1949 green notes, no longer valid. There are notes for 1, 5, 10, and 20 pesos, and coins for 1, 5, 20, and 40 centavos. The 5 centavo coin is known as a *medio* and you must have a supply if you want to use the Havana buses. The 20 centavo coin is called a *peseta*. Essentials—rent and most food—are cheap, but non-essentials tend to be very expensive. US dollars are accepted by hotels and other official institutions. Major credit cards seem to be acceptable in most places.

Currency Control The visitor should be careful to retain the white exchange paper every time money is changed; this will enable Cuban pesos remaining at the end of the stay to be changed back into foreign currency. It is better not to change too much money into pesos. Expensive items tend to be payable only in dollars anyway and you may not be allowed to cash in all remaining pesos on exit.

Travellers' cheques expressed in US or Canadian dollars or sterling are valid in Cuba. Don't enter the place or date when signing cheques, or they may be refused. It is often easier to change money in the big hotels than in banks.

Black Market As in the Soviet Union, tourists willing to take risks can earn extra spending money by taking along bluejeans, aviation-style sunglasses, perfume, etc. to sell to Cubans. Any foreigner sitting in the Parque Central with a flight bag at his side is soon approached by buyers. One can usually get about 3 times what was paid for the articles, but every visitor will have to change at least some money legally as most hotels, tourist restaurants, and bars insist on seeing an exchange paper which covers the amount of the bill. It's inadvisable to bring in too many of a single item (example, jeans) or you may have trouble at Customs. And with the prices the Cubans are willing to pay, you wouldn't be able to spend the money anyway (David Stanley).

Post, Telegraph and Telephone When possible correspondence should be addressed to post office boxes (Apartados), where delivery is more certain. Telegraphic services are adequate. You can send telegrams from all post offices in Havana. Telegrams to Britain cost 35 centavos a word. The night letter rate is 3.85 pesos for 22 words. Local telephone calls can be made from public telephones for 5 centavos. A telephone call to Britain costs 15 pesos for the first 3 mins. "Collect" calls are not permitted. Air mail rates to Britain are 31 centavos for half an ounce and 13 centavos to Canada. All postal services, national and international, have been described as appalling. Letters to Europe, for instance, take at least 4-5 weeks. Cuban time is 5 hrs. behind Greenwich Mean Time.

Weights and Measures The metric system is compulsory, but exists side by side with American and old Spanish systems.

Newspapers *Granma*, mornings except Sunday; and *Juventud Rebelde*, evening paper. No foreign newspapers are on sale, but *Granma* has a weekly English edition.

Holidays

January 1: Liberation Day
January 2: Victory of Armed Forces
May 1: Labour Day.

July 26: Revolution Day.
October 10: Beginning of War of Independence.

We are most grateful to Dorothy Millgate for editorial work, to Paul Millgate for revising the Economy section, and to Achim Holzenberger (Cologne 1), Steve and Iona Hudson (London SW6), Deborah Karp (London N3) and Karin Schamroth (London NW8), Mme C. Lapostolle (Paris), Keith Munday (Bangkok), Karl G. Olson (New York 10009), Beat Schmutz (Münchenstein, Switz.), Rolf Würtz (Heidelberg), Gustav-Adolf Yunge (Cologne), and finally Helmut Zettl (Ebergassing, Austria) for most useful updating information.

HISPANIOLA

One might expect that a relatively small island such as Hispaniola (from Spanish "Isla Española" - the Spanish island) lying in the heart of the Caribbean would be occupied by one nation, or at least that its people should not demonstrate great ethnic and cultural differences. This is not so. Hispaniola, with an area of just over 76,900 square km., not much more than half the size of Cuba, is shared by two very different countries, the Dominican Republic and Haiti. The original indigenous name for the island, Quisqueya, is still used in the Dominican Republic as an "elegant variation".

The Haitians are almost wholly black, with a culture that is a unique mixture of African and French influences. Haiti was a French colony until 1804 when, fired by the example of the French Revolution, the black slaves revolted, massacred the French landowners and proclaimed the world's first black republic. Throughout the 19th century the Haitians reverted to a primitive way of life, indulging in a succession of bloody, almost tribal wars. Even today, nowhere else in the Caribbean do African cults, particularly voodoo, play such a part in everyday life. The standard of living is the lowest in the New World.

The Dominicans are a mixture of black, Amerindian and white, with a far stronger European strain. Their culture and language are Spanish and their religion Roman Catholic. Economically, the country is much more developed, despite a stormy political past and unsavoury periods of dictatorship, particularly under Generalissimo Trujillo (1930-61). Nevertheless, in a material sense the country prospered during the Trujillo era and the standard of living is much higher than it is in Haiti.

Both countries have been occupied by the United States: Haiti in 1915-1934 and the Dominican Republic in 1916-1924. The Spanish-speaking part was also ruled by France from 1795 to 1808 and, unbelievable as it might seem today, by Haiti between 1822 and 1844, after just one year, 1821-22, of what the Dominicans call their "Independencia Efímera" under José Núñez de Cáceres. In 1844 the Haitians were driven out by a national movement led by the writer Duarte, the lawyer Sánchez and the soldier Mella, and the Republic of Santo Domingo was proclaimed. In 1861, however, following various tribulations, the country reannexed itself to Spain for four years; finally dissatisfied with this, in 1865 it applied unsuccessfully to join the USA. It was, therefore, as a kind of third best that the Republic settled for independence for the third time. The country must be one of the very few where a Roman Catholic archbishop has served as head of state: Archbishop Meriño was President from 1880 to 1883.

Hispaniola is mountainous and forested, with plains and plateaux. The climate is tropical but tempered by sea breezes. The cooler months are between December and March.

Haiti, with 27,750 square km., has a population of just over 5 millions increasing at an annual rate of 1.7%. The Dominican Republic is much larger—about 48,422 square km.—but its population is only slightly larger at 5.6 millions, growing at 2.8% a year.

HAITI

The Republic of Haiti occupies the western third of the island. French is the official language, though the common speech of all classes is a Creole patois. Nine-tenths of the people are of pure African descent, and the remainder are mulattoes, the descendants of French settlers. Haiti means "high ground" and indeed it is the most mountainous country in the Caribbean. There are three mountain ranges, the main one stretching right across the northern peninsula. In this range the highest peaks are about 3,000 metres above sea-level. In its mountains Haiti has a wealth of timber, including mahogany and pine.

Government The dictatorship of the Duvaliers (father and son) was brought to a swift and unexpected end when the President-for-Life, M. Jean-Claude Duvalier, fled to France on February 7, 1986. Several months of unrest and rioting gradually built up into a tide of popular insistence on the removal of M. Duvalier, during the course of which several hundred people were killed by his henchman.

The Duvaliers' power had rested on the use of an armed militia, the "Tontons Macoutes", to dominate the people. This private army became the focus of wrath for a population suddenly confident. Discontent began to grow with the May 1984 riots in Gonaives and Cap Haitien, and resurfaced after the holding of a constitutional referendum on 22 July, 1985, which gave the Government 99.98% of the vote.

The removal of the Duvaliers has left Haitains hungry for radical change. The leader of the interim military-civilian Government, Lt.-General Henri Namphy, promised presidential elections for November 1987.

Haiti is tourist conscious, and the tourist is well looked after by people eager to give good service and guidance (in English, but a knowledge of French is helpful). It is especially fascinating for the tourist who is avid for out-of-the-way experience. Prophylaxis against malaria is essential. Tap water is not to be trusted and take care when choosing food. The local herb tea can help stomach troubles.

Port-au-Prince, capital and chief port of Haiti, population 700,000, is set at the end of a beautiful deep horseshoe bay, with high mountains behind and a small island across the bay protecting it from high seas and tidal waves. The town, with its fascinating "gingerbread" houses, is built in the form of an amphitheatre. In the lower part, at sea-level, is concentrated the business section, with a palm-shaded sea-front known as the Exposition which unfortunately has become very dirty. On the heights are the private houses, generally surrounded by shady gardens. The heat is some degrees less at several summer resorts easily reached from the city. Port-au-Prince is a friendly and safe place, but it is very poor, apart from a few "swank" areas. The centre of the town is quite small and nearly everything of interest is within walking distance.

The Protestant Episcopal Cathedral of Sainte-Trinité has naive biblical murals painted by Haitian artists. The Musée Nationale is in the former presidential mansion in the Bois Patate area of Port-au-Prince, some distance from the centre. It houses Haitian relics, early costumes, paintings and historic documents and also boasts the anchor of Columbus' ship, the *Santa María*. The Musée d'Art Haitien du Collège St.-Pierre, on Rue Capois, not far from the French Embassy, contains the works of Haiti's leading artists. The Musée Archéologique is on the southern side of the Place de l'Indépendance.

Carnival in Haiti takes place on the three days before Ash Wednesday. It is not nearly as lavish as the Brazilian or Trinidadian carnivals. On Sunday afternoons before carnival there are practice parades in the main streets and the atmosphere is exuberant. Carnival attracts many tourists: it is best to book a flight and hotel well in advance if you plan to visit Haiti at this time.

Guides Young men and boys offer their services as guides at every turn and corner. It seems that it's worthwhile taking one (for about US$4 a day) just to prevent others pestering you. If you

1208 HAITI

hire a guide you can also visit places off the beaten tourist-track and avoid some of the frustrations of the public transport system. However, if you take guides you must realize that they expect you to buy them food if you stop to eat.

Secondly, and more important, the guides are often "on commission" with local shop-and stall-keepers, so that even if you ask them to bargain for you, you will not necessarily be getting a good price; nor will they necessarily go where you want to go. If you don't want a guide a firm but polite "non, merci" gets the message across.

Hotels *Castel Haiti* (most rooms air-conditioned, swimming pool), B; *Beau Rivage* (swimming pool), B; *Sans Souci* (best for businessmen, good cuisine, swimming pool), A; *Oloffson* (swimming pool), A, in interesting Victorian house, very good food but less good drinks, both expensive; *Splendide* (swimming pool), B recommended; *Plaza*, A; *Park*, A; *Chatelet*, C; *Prince*, Rue 3, B, small and friendly; *Coconut Villa*, C; *El Dorado*, B; *Excelsior*, C; *Palace*, rue Champ-de-Mars 55, C;

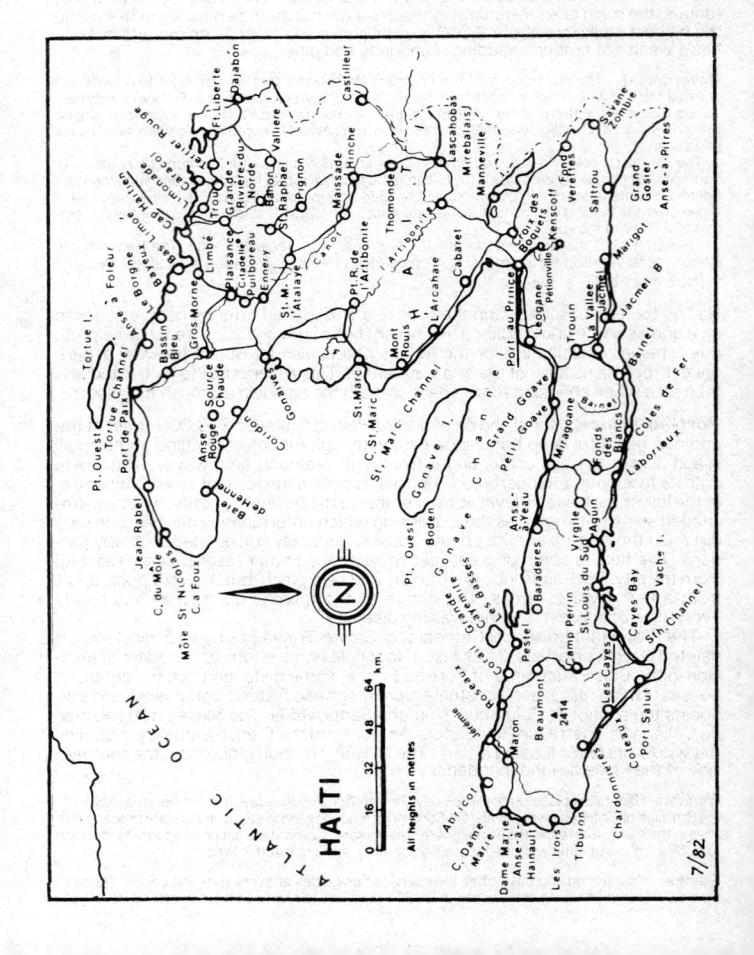

HAITI 1209

Paloma, B; *Simbic*, B; *Royal Haitian Club*, A; *Central*, rue du Centre 78, central, D, very basic; good cheap restaurant below.

Guest Houses *Margot*, Lalue 270, prop. Mme J. P. Grenier, 5 mins from town centre (D with 3 meals—E if just breakfast); *Hillside*, Av. M. L. King, C; on same street *Le Triangle* is new and recommended, D, food available, possible to leave luggage; *L'Auberge Port-au-Prince*, Rue du Centre, near Iron Market, D, basic but clean, cheap restaurant downstairs; *Hotel Acropolis*, on road S, electric fan, swimming pool, D; *Holiday*, on main street, D, restaurant below; *Haiti Chérie*, near drive-in cinema en route for airport, run by Haitian/American couple, D; *Villa Carmel*, Av. J. C. Duvalier (name changed?) 40, D, meals available, swimming pool. Other guest houses recommended as both cheap and good: the *Santos Guest House*, Rue Pacot, colonial building with excellent view, highly recommended, C, including 2 meals; *La Griffonne*, Rue Jean-Baptiste 21, Canapé Vert (Tel.: 5-4095), C, including 2 meals, in the hills above the main part of the town and so slightly cooler, yet within walking distance of the centre, and near to *publique* run to centre, swimming pool, clean, comfortable and friendly and very highly recommended; *May's Villa*, Debussy district, B, with a/c, price includes taxes and 2 meals, clean, swimming pool and panoramic view of the city; *My Dream Hotel*, Bvd. J. J. Dessalines and Rue Champs de Mars (on *tap-tap* route from airport), E, reasonably priced restaurant downstairs. There are a number of other guest houses whose prices vary from C to E.

Note There is a 10% service charge and 5% tax added to all hotel bills. Most hotels and guest houses do not have full air-conditioning, so aim for the US$50 plus range if you prefer something cool.

Restaurants There are some very good but very expensive eating places in Port-au-Prince. *Aux Cosaques* (local food); *Au Rond Point* (local food); *Le Carillon* (local food); *Chandler*, opposite Banque d'Haiti, has US$2.50 lunch (several restaurants on both sides of Grand' Rue to S have meals for US$1); *Château Caprice*, at Mousseau (Continental and American food); *Chez Noelle*, Rue Pavée; *Chez Tony*, Rue Ponce in town centre, good, cheap meals; there are two *Kentucky Fried Chicken* restaurants: one on the seafront, and another on John Brown, near the junction with Jérémie.

Clubs include the Turgeau Club; society clubs such as the Bellevue and the Port-au-Princien; the American Colony Club at Bourdon and sports clubs.

Shopping There are many tourist shops in Port-au-Prince, but be warned that they charge high prices for items which can be bought for far less in the market. Always bargain hard when shopping. Hand-carved wooden goods are a typical Haitian product; embroidered shirts, skirts and dresses can also be bought at reasonable prices. Copper jewellery is another speciality. Shops are open 0800-1600 in the summer and 0800-1700 in winter. On Sat. they are open 0800-1200. Probably the best place to buy sculptures is from the "United Sculptors of Haiti" on the road to Kenscoff. There are many craft shops and stalls, and many of the products are of high quality. Many good bargains to be had at the Iron Market.

Art Centres Commercial galleries include the Néhémy, Nader's (Place Geffrard 92) and Issa's (Rue Chile 17), very good quality for buyers. Local art can be seen at the Cathedral of S. Trinité, the Airport, and Exposition buildings, and in the principal hotels. Olivier has a gallery near the *Hotel Oloffson* and is very knowledgeable about local artists. There is a gallery at Rue Champs de Mars 29, run by Raoul Michel, which is one of the least expensive and has a good variety of work.

Warning Watch out for pickpockets in the market and bus-station areas.

Night Clubs *La Lambie*, just S of Port-au-Prince (take a taxi, or *tap-taps*—pick-up trucks—run past until about midnight), good national food and music, open to the ocean. *Byblos*, and others on the beach at Carrefour. *Le Bistro*, Ave. John Smith. Good local music, and reasonably priced.

Voodoo Voodoo ceremonies are open to visitors in Port-au-Prince and Cap Haitien. Arrangements to see them can be made through hotels.

Cinemas are cheap and interesting.

Banks Royal Bank of Canada, and others. Banque d'Haiti reported to have best rate for £. Commission is charged on the exchange of currencies other than the US dollar.

Library Alliance Française, opposite Pan-Am., open 0830-1200, 1430-1900 except Mon. and Sat. p.m. Book: *You can learn Creole*, from Caravelle bookshop (US$1.25).

Tourist Office Provides good maps of the city and is very helpful. It is worth checking bus and taxi fares to avoid being overcharged.

Airport Aéroport François Duvalier (name changed?), 13 km. out of town. Taxi into town, US$10, or a seat in a *tap-tap* (open-sided truck), US$0.16. Tourist bureau at the airport is very helpful, but the snackbar is expensive and service unfriendly. The so-called "supervisors" at the airport are in fact taxi-drivers, touting for business.

1210 HAITI

Taxis *Publiques*, shared taxis, charge US$0.20-$0.40 a trip (double after 1900). They are identified by a red cloth in the window. *Camionettes* (Peugeot station wagons) charge the same for a trip to Pétionville. *Tap-tap* (open-sided truck) fares are US$0.10 anywhere in town. Taxis are scarce early in the morning, and along the Rue Dessalines; *tap-taps* are difficult to manage with luggage.

Beaches To the N of Port-au-Prince is Ibo beach (entrance fee US$2 p.p.). To get there take the *tap-tap* going to St. Marc and tell the *driver where you want to get off. You will probably have a* half-hour walk from the turnoff. The same *tap-tap* will take you to Kyona beach, about 1 hr. from Port-au-Prince (entrance US$1.50, good diving) and Kaloa beach (entrance again US$1.50). The fare to Kaloa is US$1. Further on still are Ouanga bay, Mai-Kai and Amani-Y. To the SW are Taino and Sun. When available, food and drink on the beaches are expensive.

Excursions A few km. out in Port-au-Prince harbour is Sand Cay, said to be one of the most beautiful coral reefs in the world. To visit it take a US$10 trip on a glass-bottomed boat which leaves the pier opposite the *Beau Rivage* hotel at 0800 on days when a cruise ship is in port. The boat makes an additional pickup at the cruise ship wharf at 0900.

A paved road leads to (10 km.) **Pétionville**. Hotels and guest houses include: *Choucoune, Montana* (B); *Majestie Dambala, Villa Creole* (A); *Ibo Lele* (A, recommended as probably best in town); *Villa Quisqueya; Marabou, El Rancho*, "Mexican-style" hotel with good facilities (A); *Doux Séjours*, cheaper and delightfully eccentric, 460 metres above sea-level. An excellent sea food restaurant is *La Recife* in Route de Delmas; also good are *Le Picardie* (French), the moderately-priced *Belle Epoque* (French/Creole), *Chez Gerard* (also French/Creole) and *Le Papyrus* at 52 Rue Foubert (French, dinner with wine costs US$10-15 per head). *Publique* from Iron Market to Pétionville, US$0.30. *Publiques* in Pétionville run along the Rue des Miracles, US$0.20 any distance. Just outside the town, at Boutilliers, is *Le Chateaubriand*.

A good paved road, 16 km. runs from Pétionville to the holiday resort of **Kenscoff** (*Hotels Dereix, Florville*; *publique* from Pétionville market, US$0.40), 1,370 metres above sea-level, where climatic conditions are excellent all the year round. From the 19th century Fort Jacques, there is an excellent view across Port-au-Prince harbour. There is a market here every Tues. and Fri. which is well worth a visit. Good quality local crafts can be purchased at the Baptist Church. If you have time, a drive through the fertile Cul-de-Sac plain, about 30 km. each way, is well worthwhile for those interested in agriculture and local life.

At La Boule, about 5 km outside Pétionville, visit the Jane Barbancourt Castle. One can sample an unlimited quantity of the company's 17 differently-flavoured rums, which include coffee, mango, coconut, orange. Rum is sold at US$3 a bottle. From the castle one can visit the bottlers and get an excellent view of Port-au-Prince. A Peristyle Voodoo show open every evening at 2200 on road west of Pétionville.

At **Gonaives**, on the road to Cap Haitien, there is a motel, *Chez Frantz*, C with 2 meals; recommended is the *Pensión Elias*, Rue L'Ouverture, clean, friendly and safe. The restaurant in town lets rooms above. Bus from Port-au-Prince, US$2, no fixed schedule. Most leave between 0700 and 1200. Buses from Gonaives to Cap Haitien also leave mornings only.

Cap Haitien, 258 km. from the capital, is the second city, locally known as Le Cap. Population 30,000. It is on the N coast and is linked to Port-au-Prince by a fairly new highway which has some hair-raising bends but also affords breathtaking views. *Tap-taps* and *camionettes* leave from the Mahogany Market, near the waterfront in Port-au-Prince. The journey to Le Cap can take as little as 4 hours but usually it is much longer, even as much as 10 hours. Fares vary as to whether you sit in the front or back. Public transport stops short of the town, at the police checkpoint, and from there it is an easy 15 min. walk. The official bus fare is US$5. Turks and Caicos Airways have flights from the capital. Cruise ships visit Mon. and Thurs. Tourist bureau at Rue 24, Esplanade. Banque Union Haitien changes travellers' cheques, open until 1800. The city is poor and scruffy, but not without interest. It is from here that many of the would-be refugees set out for the wonders of Miami.

Hotels *Beck*, a long way from town, but has a pool and attractive grounds, B, may be amenable to bargaining; *Mont Joli*, A (MAP); *Roi Christophe* (patronized by Pauline Bonaparte Leclerc while her own home was being built near Port-au-Prince), B; *Le Gite*, Rue 11, E, restaurant attached; *Congo*, B including 2 meals, excellent food and friendly staff. *Pension Colon*, on seafront opposite Post Office, E, without food (not recommended); *Dupuy*, D, very pleasant; *Bon Dieu Bon*, E, reasonably priced restaurant; *A à Z*, on main square opposite Cathedral, E, rambling, delightful colonial building with friendly management and good views from the balcony; *Pension Colomb*, Av. C and Rue 19-20, E, clean but basic. At W end of town, on beach, *Brise de Mer*, B, with 2 meals, excellent

HAITI 1211

food, private bathroom, pleasant atmosphere, but not very safe. Mme. Manoir runs an unmarked *pension* in a rambling old colonial house on Av. E between Rues 24 and 25, D, including 2 meals, rather run down.

Restaurants *Sacade*, Rues 18 et B, near *Pension Dupuy*; *San Raison*, near market, cheaper; *Universelle*, 2 blocks from *Sacade*, bakery with restaurant, friendly, cheap and good value. Unnamed restaurants on corner of 6 and I and on 11 between F and G, cheap meals. Fresh and cold fruit juices served on Av. A, between Rues 23 and 24.

Beaches There are many beautiful beaches near Le Cap but most are difficult to get to. The *Mont Joli* hotel has a beach at Rival which is about 15 minutes walk from the public beach near the *Brise de Mer* hotel. Cormier beach is 9 km. from Le Cap (hotel, A, including 2 meals) and can be reached by bus from the *Mont Joli* hotel (US$1.50) or taxi (more expensive at up to US$15). At weekends it is easy to hitch a lift to Cormier and you may be able to get a lift back in the hotel minibus. Admission to the beach is US$1. At Cormier, where boats are built, you can buy freshly-caught lobster very cheaply and you can hire someone to row you to **Labadie**, a fine, deserted beach from where there is excellent snorkelling over coral reefs. Some hotels can arrange transport to Labadie. The village of Labadie itself is worth a visit and bungalows can be rented there for about US$5. Coco Beach and Rat Island are other beaches in the area, but you have to find your own means of getting there. Fishermen on the beach near the *Brise de Mer* hotel can be hired to sail you to beaches further afield.

Excursions The Citadelle is a vast ruined fortress built for King Henri Christophe in the 1800s. Haitians claim that it is the eighth wonder of the world and it is indeed very impressive and has breathtaking views. Restoration work is being carried out. To get there take a *publique* or *tap-tap* from Le Cap to **Milot**, the fares being US$1 and US$0.30 respectively. (*Tap-taps* leave from outside the *Hotel Bon Dieu Bon* in the morning.) From Milot it is an interesting but rugged two-hour walk uphill to the fortress. You can however hire a horse and with it two men—one to push and one to pull!—for about US$4. Guides are also available. The men expect, if not a drink at each stage of the journey, then at least a tip. If you have your own transport you can drive 5-6 km. along a very rough road from Milot to a parking area and thence have a much shorter walk up to the fortress. Admission to the Citadelle costs US$1.25. It is advisable to take refreshments with you: prices charged at the Citadelle are exorbitant. It is also essential to go protected against the sun and to wear stout shoes. In Milot itself are the ruins of the Sans Souci Palace which was built in the early 19th century to rival Versailles. Even though it has been devastated by an earthquake, it is well worth a visit. Admission is US$ 0.50. Try to avoid visiting the Citadelle and Sans Souci on Mon. and Thurs. when up to 4 cruise ships are in Le Cap. There are no buses or *tap-taps* back to Le Cap after 1700.

Inland from Le Cap is Hinche with the nearby waterfall of Bazim Zim. Hinche can be reached from Port-au-Prince (by bus 5½ hrs.; also by *tap-taps* for US$11 round trip) but from Le Cap the journey is more difficult: there are buses to Pignon (US$1.50) and from there you can hitchhike to Hinche. The waterfall is a 3-hour walk from Hinche but it is also possible to hire horses. There is a guesthouse behind the church in the main square in Hinche, but no accommodation in Pignon.

Rent-a-Bike Cap Rent-a-Bike at 11-D-D (Tel.: 3-8831) rent bicycles and motorcycles. The cost is US$15-20 per day.

Jacmel, a port on the S coast, is 2-3 hours by *tap-tap* on a new road from Port-au-Prince—seat by driver US$2.50, in back US$2, they leave from behind the customs house on the corner of Rue du Quai and Rue des Césars, every hour. The road takes you through some spectacular scenery. The town itself has some interesting old architecture and many buildings are being restored. The town's Congo beach has black sand and although it is free, it is rather dirty. A new and expensive hotel has been built on the beach. Sat. is market day and at weekends local bands play on the beach in the evening.

Hotels The luxury *La Jacmélienne sur Plage*, 30 rooms, Haitian cuisine (Tel.: 2-4899). *Guy's Guesthouse*, Av. François Duvalier 52 (Tel.: 8-3421), friendly and clean; *Pension Craft*, B, room with 2 meals, quaint and clean, recommended; *Hotel Alexandra*, also recommended, opposite, C, including 2 meals; *Chez Madame Luc*, F; *Aux Zombis*, hotel and restaurant, Swiss owner, C incl. 2 excellent meals, clean. Several discothèques, including *La Ruine*.

Near Jacmel, Raymond-les-Bains has a good beach and near the village of Cayes Jacmel is a beautiful white-sand beach (*tap-tap* from Jacmel, US$0.20). Cyradier Cove has a small but protected white sand beach. It is best to take your own provisions with you to the beaches. A visit to the Bassin Bleu is well worthwhile. Horses are provided for the day's excursion; choose one that looks sound as part of the journey is steep and rocky. You have to walk the last kilometre and climb down a rope to the first waterfall. From there you can see a series of other

1212 **HAITI**

cascades and enjoy the view out across the Bay of Jacmel. The cost is US$5 for the horse and US$2 per person for the guide. There are buses to Les Cayes, the other main town in S. Haiti.

Jérémie, reached by overnight boat from Port-au-Prince, US$2 passage, plus US$3 for bunk in bridge-house. *Take food and drink. Pension Frankel,* D with food. Road to Les Cayes.

Les Cayes is a pleasant town with several hotels including *Les Relais, Pension Condé* and *Pension Mme. Bayard,* which charges D, with 2 meals. In Cayes Bay is Vache Island, which can be visited by taking the boat leaving between 1600 and 1700 and spending the night there or by hiring a motorboat for a day (about US$30). There are several beaches on the island. Buses leave Port-au Prince for Les Cayes every morning (US$3-5). The road has recently been paved and is very good.

About 1½ hrs. drive from Les Cayes is **Port Salut,** with beautiful beaches. There are 2 Swiss-owned *pensions* here: "Deck's" and "Sylvie's". The St. Dominique and Althania bus companies go to Port Salut from Port-au-Prince.

A trip round this south-western corner of Haiti is recommended for the adventurous. From Les Cayes you can get transport to see Les Anglais and thence walk through the attractive town of Tiburon to Les Trois; alternatively it is possible to get on one of the sloops which sail from port to port round the coast. From Les Trois the road goes to Dame Marie and Jérémie, and from there a spectacular but rugged mountain route takes you back to Les Cayes. The round trip can take about 5-7 days; the missionaries in the larger villages sometimes have accommodation.

Economy

Haiti is the poorest country in the Western hemisphere and is among the thirty poorest countries in the world. It suffers from overpopulation, lack of communications, lack of cheap power and raw materials for industry, and mountainous terrain that cannot provide an adequate living for the farming population. Life expectancy at birth is only 54 years and the infant mortality rate 11%. Haiti's recent economic problems have been caused by historical low productivity in the vital agricultural sector, compounded by the world recession which depressed commodity prices and therefore export earnings, and the continuing effects of hurricane damage. Deforestation has seriously damaged agriculture and watersheds, in the south in particular: some 70% of all fuel needs are met by charcoal.

Agriculture provides about a third of gdp and employs two thirds of the workforce. Coffee is the most important crop, providing over a quarter of total exports and a livelihood for 2m people. Production of sugar and sisal has been declining because population pressure has encouraged many farmers to plant subsistence crops.

The industrial and commercial sectors are small and are heavily concentrated in the Port-au-Prince area. There are assembly operations producing baseballs, electric and electronic parts and clothing for export to the USA, and domestic operations producing vegetable oils, footwear and metal products. Manufacturing wage rates average below US$3 a day and manufactured goods make up a third of total exports.

Business was seriously disrupted after the fall of the Duvalier regime, but the new government managed to reduce its fiscal deficit and achieve a balance of payments surplus in the 1985-86 fiscal year, although gdp declined by about 2%. Haiti is now receiving aid or soft loans from the USA, the World Bank and the IMF, among others, and its adjustment programme aims for gdp growth of 4.5% a year, a balance of payments surplus and an inflation rate similar to that of its trading partners.

	1961-70 (av)	1971-80 (av)	1981-85 (av)
Gdp growth (1980 prices)	1.1%	4.7%	-1.0%
Inflation	2.8%	10.7%	9.1%
Exports (fob) US$m	37	101	180 (a)
Imports (fob) US$m	39	151	331 (a)
Current account balance US$m (cum)	-44	-296	583 (a)

(a) = 1981-84

HAITI

Information for Visitors

Air Services From USA: Air France, Eastern Airlines, American Airlines, Haiti Air and ALM all fly direct from New York or Miami, or San Juan, Puerto Rico. ALM also flies from Curaçao (4 times a week); Kingston and Aruba; Dominicana flies from Santo Domingo. British Airways flies to Kingston; enquire about connecting flights. Air Canada, Air Jamaica and Bahamasair also serve Haiti, which can often be reached by making a stop-over between Miami and S. America. No extra charge, depending on the routing of the ticket. Copa flies the route Panama City-Kingston-Port au Prince twice weekly. Balair has regular flights from Switzerland to Cuba and Haiti. Travellers to Haiti report problems with flights, so check thoroughly. There are also flights from Grand Turk and Bahamas to Cap Haitien and Port-au-Prince on Mon., Wed. and Fri. Turks and Caicos Airways have a franchise for internal flights; they fly every weekday from Port-au-Prince to Jacmel, Cap Haitien, Jérémie and Les Cayes and back. They also fly to Port de Paix. Fares are low.

Shipping Port-au-Prince is served by several cruise lines from the USA.

Transport Public transport services between towns are mainly operated by collective taxis known as *publiques* (they have a "P" on registration plate) and by open-backed pick-up trucks, known as *tap-taps*. *Camionettes* are a type of minibus (actually Peugeot station wagons) with fares similar to *publiques*. Cars can be hired at the airport, in Port-au-Prince and in Pétionville. Driving in Haiti is extremely impulsive, and it is not easy to get gasoline outside Port-au-Prince.

Tipping Though there are an increasing number of tours visiting Haiti, budget travellers, particularly outside Port-au-Prince, are a rarity. Expect to be the subject of much friendly curiosity, and keep a pocketful of small change to conform with the local custom of tipping on every conceivable occasion. Hotels generally add 10% service charge. Baggage porters at hotels and airports usually get 50 cents per bag. Nobody tips taxi, *publique*, *camionette* or *tap-tap* drivers.

Documents All visitors apart from North Americans need passports, and visas are required for all except nationals of Austria, Belgium, Denmark, Western Germany, Israel, Luxembourg, Netherlands, Switzerland and the UK; US and Canadian visitors need only proof of citizenship. (It is however advisable to check this information.) Visitors are advised to have an onward ticket but may be able to get in without one. It is no longer necessary to have a *laissez-passer* before visiting the interior, but you must have some form of identification to satisfy the many police controls. It may also be wise to obtain a letter from the Tourist Office or police in Port-au-Prince confirming that you are a tourist. To travel to the Dominican Republic, you must call at the Dominican consulate (on the corner of Av. J. Brown and Rue Beane). A permit to travel there by land must be obtained several weeks in advance, either from the Haitian consulate in your country of origin or from the ministry in Port-au-Prince. These permit requirements seem to change constantly and we strongly recommend a last-minute check on any information concerning entry to Haiti.

Tax There is a "head tax", payable when leaving Haiti, of US$10 for non-residents. It is not payable by those who stay in Haiti less than 24 hrs.

Climate The climate is generally very warm but the cool on-and off-shore winds of morning and evening help to make it bearable. In coastal areas temperatures vary between 20° and 35° C, being slightly hotter in April-September. The driest months are Dec.-March. In the hill resorts the temperature is cooler.

Clothing As in most other countries in the Caribbean beachwear is restricted to the beach and poolside.

Electricity 110 volt, 60 cycle AC.

Currency The unit is the Gourde, divided into 100 centimes (kob); it is supposed to be exchangeable on demand and without charge at the fixed rate of 5 gourdes to the US dollar, but can vary, and a black market, with a 12% premium, has been reported. US notes and coins co-circulate with local currency. Always double-check whether you are dealing in gourdes or dollars. There is no exchange control. Travellers' cheques are widely accepted and credit cards are accepted in most hotels and larger tourist shops. Weights and measures are on the metric system.

Banks International banks in Haiti include Bank of Nova Scotia, First National Bank of Chicago, Banque Nationale de Paris, First National Bank of Boston, Citibank and Royal Bank of Canada. Hours: Mon.-Fri. 0900-1300.

Tourist Office The one in Port-au-Prince (on the corner of Rues Marie-Jeanne and Roux) gives information on hotels and guest-houses (very helpful and sells maps of Haiti for US$0.25). In New York: 30 Rockefeller Plaza, NY 10020. In Montreal: 44 Fundy/Floor F, Place Bonaventure, Montreal H5A 1A9.

Radio There are broadcasts in English from 1100 to 1400 on 1,035 KHz, MW.

1214   DOMINICAN REPUBLIC

Embassies and Consulates   Canada, Rue Camille Léon 6 (Tel.: 2-4231/2-2358); France, Champs de Mars (Tel.: 2-0951); UK, Av. Marie Jeanne 21, P.O. Box 1302 (Tel.: 2-1227); Netherlands, Rue D. Destouches (Tel.: 2-1321); West Germany, Cité de l'Exposition (Tel.: 2-0634). The Haitian consulate in W. Germany at D-8000 München 12, Landsbergerstrasse 79, has good information. In the UK the Haitian Embassy is at 33 Abbots House, St. Mary Abbots Terrace, London W14.

(Acknowledgements to informants on Haiti will be found at the end of the Dominican Republic section).

DOMINICAN REPUBLIC

The Dominican Republic occupies the eastern two-thirds of Hispaniola. Its population is mostly a mix of black and white, and is Spanish-speaking. The country is mountainous, though less so than Haiti, and is reasonably prosperous with large sugar plantations and widespread food production.

Government   The Republic has the conventional type of presidential system, with separation of powers, but in practice for many years anarchy alternated with dictatorship. Though President Trujillo was killed in 1961, his associates retained power until 1978, except for a few months in 1963. In 1978 and again in 1982 the Dominican Revolutionary Party won free elections. President (1986-90): Dr. Joaquín Balaguer.

The Dominican Republic is building up its tourist trade, and has much to offer in the way of natural beauty, old colonial architecture and native friendliness. The climate is tropical. The rainy months are May and June, September to November. The temperature shows little seasonal change, and varies between 18° and 32°C.

Santo Domingo, the capital and chief seaport, population now about 1.6 million, was founded in 1496 by Columbus' brother Bartholomew and hence was the first capital in Spanish America. For years the city was the base for the Spaniards' exploration and conquest of the continent: from it Ponce de León sailed to discover Puerto Rico, Hernán Cortés launched his attack on Mexico, Balboa discovered the Pacific and Diego de Velázquez set out to settle Cuba. In the old part of the city, on the W bank of the River Ozama, there are many fine early 16th-century buildings: some of them have been restored by the Government and others are in ruins. Of the greatest interest are:

Catedral Basílica Menor de Santa María, Primada de América, Isabel La Católica esq. Nouel, the first cathedral to be founded in the New World. First stone laid by Diego Columbus, son of Christopher, in 1514. Architect: Alonzo Rodríguez. Finished 1540. Alleged remains of Christopher Columbus found in 1877 during restoration work. In 1892, the Government of Spain donated the tomb in which the remains now rest, behind the high altar.

Torre del Homenaje inside Fortaleza Ozama, reached through the mansion of Rodrigo Bastidas (later the founder of Santa Marta in Colombia) on Calle Las Damas, which is now completely restored. Oldest fortress in America, constructed 1503-07 by Nicolás de Ovando, whose house in the same street has been restored and turned into a splendid hotel.

Museo de las Casas Reales, on Calle Las Damas, in a reconstructed early 16th-century building which was in colonial days the Palace of the Governors and Captains-General, and of the *Real Audiencia* and Chancery of the Indies. It is an excellent colonial museum (often has special exhibits); entry US$0.50; open 0900-1200, 1430-1730; closed Mon.

Alcázar de Colón at the end of Las Damas, constructed by Diego Colón (Columbus' son) 1510-14. For six decades it was the seat of the Spanish Crown in the New World. Sacked by Drake in 1586. Now completely restored, it houses the interesting Viceregal Museum (Museo Virreinal). Open 0900-1200, 1430-1730; Alcázar closed Tues., Museum closed Mon.

DOMINICAN REPUBLIC 1215

Casa del Cordón, Isabel La Católica esq. Emiliano Tejera, built in 1509 by Francisco de Garay, who accompanied Columbus on his first voyage to Hispaniola. Named for the cord of the Franciscan Order, sculpted above the entrance. Now the offices of the Banco Popular; free guided tours during working hours.

Monasterio de San Francisco (ruins), Hostos esq. E. Tejera, first monastery in America, constructed in the first decade of the 16th century. Sacked by Drake and destroyed by earthquakes in 1673 and 1751.

Reloj de Sol (sundial) built 1753, near end of Las Damas, by order of General Francisco de Rubio y Peñaranda; by its side is

Capilla de Nuestra Señora de Los Remedios, built in the early 16th century as the private chapel of the Dávila family. It has recently been restored.

La Ataranza, near the Alcázar, a cluster of 16th-century buildings which served as warehouses. Now restored and contains shops, bars and restaurants.

Hospital-Iglesia de San Nicolás de Bari (ruins), Hostos between Mercedes and Luperón, begun in 1509 by Nicolás de Ovando, completed 1552, the first stone-built hospital in the Americas. Sacked by Drake. Probably one of the best constructed buildings of the period, it survived many earthquakes and hurricanes. In 1911 some of its walls were knocked down because they posed a hazard to passers-by; also the last of its valuable wood was taken.

Convento de San Ignacio de Loyola, Las Damas between Mercedes and El Conde. Finished in 1743, it is now the National Pantheon. Restored 1955 and contains memorials to many of the country's heroes and patriots. It also contains an ornate tomb built before his death for the dictator Trujillo, the "Benefactor of the Fatherland", but his remains do not lie there.

Iglesia de Santa Bárbara, off Mella to left near Calle J. Parra, near end of Isabel La Católica. Built in 1574. Sacked by Drake in 1586, destroyed by a hurricane in 1591. Reconstructed at the beginning of the 17th century. Behind the church are the ruins of its fort, where one can get good views.

Convento de los Dominicanos, built in 1510. Here in 1538 the first university in the Americas was founded, named for St. Thomas Aquinas; it now bears the title of the Universidad Autónoma de Santo Domingo. It has a unique ceiling which shows the medieval concept that identified the elements of the universe, the classical gods and the Christian icons in one system. The Sun is God, the 4 evangelists are the planetary symbols Mars, Mercury, Jupiter and Saturn. The University itself has moved to a site in the suburbs.

Iglesia de la Regina Angelorum, built 1537, contains a wall of silver near one of its altars.

Iglesia del Carmen, built around 1615 at side of Capilla de San Andrés, contains interesting wooden sculpture of Christ.

Puerta del Conde (Baluarte de 27 de Febrero), at the end of El Conde in the Parque Independencia. Named for the Conde de Peñalva, who helped defend the city against William Penn in 1655. Restored in 1976, near it lie the remains of Sánchez, Mella and Duarte, the 1844 independence leaders.

Puerta de la Misericordia, Palo Hincado and Arzobispo Portes. So named because people fled under it for protection during earthquakes and hurricanes. It forms part of the wall that used to surround the colonial city, into which are now built many of the houses and shops of Ciudad Nueva. It was here on February 27, 1844 that Mella fired the first shot in the struggle for independence from Haiti.

Capilla de La Virgen del Rosario, on the other side of the Río Ozama, near the Molinos Dominicanos at the end of Av. Olegario Vargas. It was the first church constructed in America, restored in 1943.

Museo Duartiano, Isabel La Católica 308. Contains items linked with the Independence struggle and Duarte, the national hero, whose home it was.

Other old buildings are the Iglesia de las Mercedes, dating from 1555; the Puerta de San Diego, near Alcázar; the Palacio de Borgella, Isabel La Católica, near Plaza Colón; the ruins of Fuerte de la Concepción, corner Mella and Palo Hincado, built in 1543; the ruins of Fuerte de San Gil, Paseo de Pte. Billini, near end of Calle Pina; and the ruins of Iglesia de San Antón, off Mella, near V. Celestino Duarte.

There are fine avenues in the outer city, especially Av. George Washington (also known as the Malecón), Av. Independencia, Av. Bolívar, Av. Abraham Lincoln and Av. Winston Churchill. The old gate at Calle Pina and Arzobispo Portes lends itself to photography. Among the attractive parks are the Central Olímpico in the city centre, with excellent athletic facilities, Parque Independencia, Parque

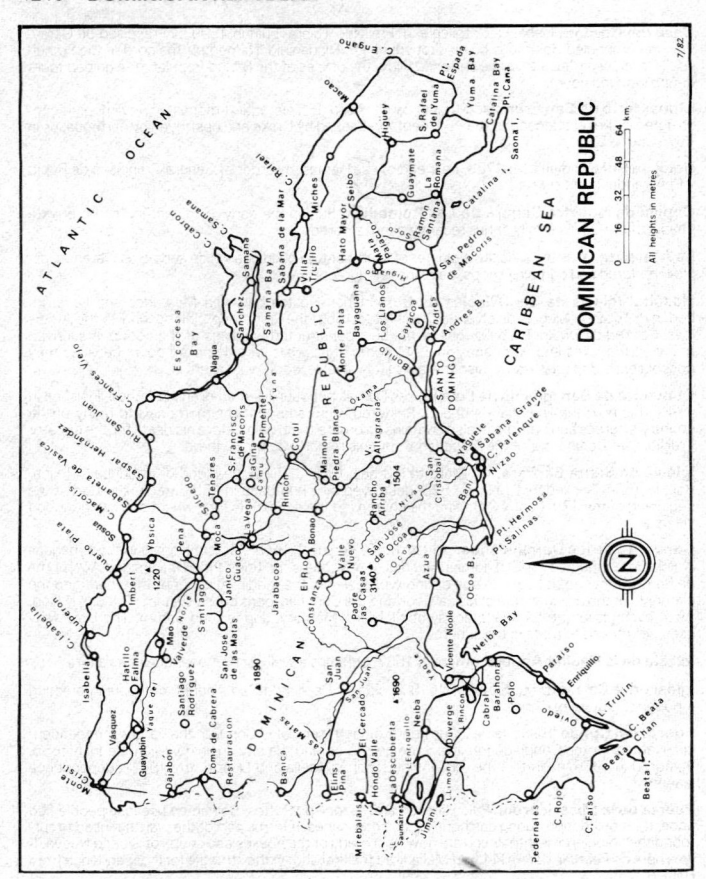

Colón and Paseo de las Indios at Mirador Sur, the Botanical Gardens at Marmolejos (open Tues.-Sun. 0900-1200, 1400-1800) and the National Zoo (Zoodom) at Arroyo Hondo (open 0900-1800). Admission to the Botanical Gardens and the Zoo is US$0.15; children US$ 0.10; for information call 566-8151. The 1955/56 World's Fair buildings now house the Senate and Congress and other government offices. The national museum collection, which includes a wonderful display of Taino artefacts, has been moved to the Museo del Hombre Dominicano (closed on Mon.), which forms part of a new cultural centre also including the ultra-modern national theatre and national library; there are also the Gallery of Modern Art, Museo de Historia Natural and Museo de Historia y Geografía. The Museum of the Dominican Family is housed in the Casa de Tostada (Calle Padre Billini, esq. Arzobispo Meriño), an early 16th century mansion. On the Carretera Duarte (km. 4½) the Fundación García Arévalo has an exhibition of pre-hispanic art and civilization. For archaeologists there is the Instituto de Investigaciones

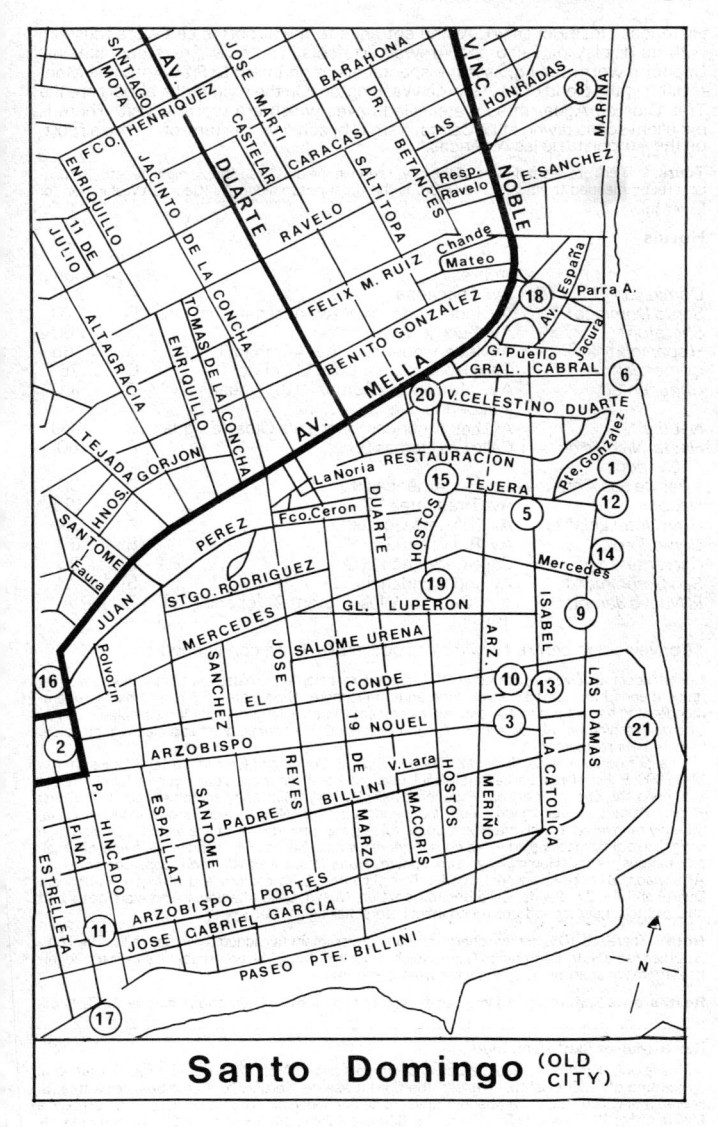

DOMINICAN REPUBLIC 1217

Santo Domingo (OLD CITY)

1218 DOMINICAN REPUBLIC

Históricas, José Reyes 24. At the entrance to the airport is La Caleta museum with its display of Taino and Arawak artefacts. The new pink stone National Capitol is worth seeing, as is the spectacular monument to Fray Antón de Montesinos at the E end of Av. George Washington. On the road to the airport are the Tres Ojos de Agua, three water-filled caves which are worth a visit. There is excellent scuba diving at La Caleta, a small beach near the turn-off to the airport, on the Autopista de las Américas.

Tours. There are several tours of the city, taking in the duty-free shops, nightlife, etc. Particularly recommended (from 2100 to 0200) is the ritual *paseo* along Av. George Washington (or Malecón).

Hotels

	Address	Price Range	Rooms
Dominican Concorde†	Av. Anacaona	A	316
Santo Domingo†	Av. Independencia y Av. Abraham Lincoln	D	220
Sheraton†	Av. George Washington	A	260
Hispaniola†	Av. Independencia y Av. Abraham Lincoln	A	165
Comercial*	Calle Hostos, near Calle El Conde	C	75
Continental*†	Av. Máximo Gómez 16, near Av. Independencia	B	100
Nautilus	Av. Las Américas, near Tres Ojos de Agua	D	100
Hostal Nicolás de Ovando*†	Calle Las Damas 53	A	60
Villas de Las Américas	Av. Las Américas 96	D	36
Naco†	Av. Tiradentes 22	B	105
Gran Hotel Lina*†	Av. Máximo Gómez	A	200
Comodoro†	Av. Bólivar 193	B	87
Cervantes*†	Calle Cervantes 202	C	96
San Gerónimo*†	Av. Independencia	B	72
El Nuevo Jaragua†	Av. George Washington 2 (opening in 1987)	2	A

*Convenient to centre † Swimming pool and fully air-conditioned.

Hostal Nicolás de Ovando, a restored 16th-century mansion in the oldest part of the city, is warmly recommended for comfort, quiet, food and atmosphere. *Gran Hotel Lina* is also highly recommended and has a good restaurant, and has recently been enlarged. Other hotels include: on Av. George Washington, *Napolitano*, B*†; and *Neptuno*, C; *Cervantes*, quiet and clean, good value, with 24-hour restaurant.

Cheaper hotels include *Radiante*, clean, E; *Aida*, El Conde and Espaillat, C, and *La Fama*, Av. Mella 609, E. *Estrella*, Isabel La Católica 59, near cathedral, looks basic but is central for old city, at E, among the cheapest accommodation available, very quiet and recommended; *Villy Guest House*, Pasteur 4, very good value; *Independencia*, Arz. Nouel, near Parque Independencia, recently renovated, E incl. breakfast, soap, towels etc. provided, also has a club, bar, language school, a roof terrace and art exhibitions. *Señorial*, Vinicio Burgos 58, friendly, clean and informal, and famous for its "Hemingway" atmosphere. *Hotel Restaurant Alameda*, opp. *Cervantes*, C; *Arcaonada*, D, opp. Puerto del Conde; *Tres Gigantes*, E, at eastern end of Mella. *Caribbean*, Duarte and Av. 27. *Benito*, Calle Benito González; *Nuevo*, Calle Altagracia. There are dozens of cheap hotels; have a good look round them before making any decision.

Note There is a 10% service charge and 5% government tax added to all room bills. The Tourist Office has a Hotel Information Guide which is worth getting. The newspaper *Listín Diario* advertises rooms or apartments to let by the week or month.

Restaurants *Lina* in hotel of same name, excellent Spanish and international cuisine; *Le Diplomat*

Key to Map of Santo Domingo

1. Castle of Columbus (Alcázar de Colón); 2. Independence Arch (Altar de la Patria); 3. Cathedral (with tomb of Columbus); 5. House of the Cord (Casa del Cordón); 6. Columbus' ceiba tree; 8. Fountain of Columbus; 9. Pantheon (Convento de San Ignacio); 10. Plaza Colón; 11. Puerta de la Misericordia; 12. Puerta de San Diego; 13. Borgella Palace; 14. Sundial; 15. Church and Monastery of S. Francisco (ruins); 16. Fort of La Concepción (ruins); 17. Fort of San Gil (ruins); 18. Fort of Santa Bárbara (ruins); 19. Hospital of San Nicolás de Bari (ruins); 20. Church of San Antón (ruins); 21. Tower of Homage (Torre del Homenaje).

DOMINICAN REPUBLIC 1219

(*Hotel El Embajador*); *Alcázar* (*Santo Domingo*); *La Canasta*, open till dawn; *Antoine* (*Sheraton*); *Rincón Argentino*, for beef, and *Vesuvio I* on Av. George Washington and also *Vesuvio II* on Av. Tiradentes, Italian and international cuisine; *Mesón de la Cava*, Mirador Sur, near *Hotel El Embajador*, situated in a natural cave, good steaks, dancing, very popular so reserve in advance; *Cantábrico*, *Jai-Alai*, and *La Mezquita Taverna* on Av. Independencia for excellent seafood; *El Bodegón*, *Il Buco* (Italian, Arz. Meriño 152A, reserve on 685-0884), and *Chez François* on Arzobispo Meriño and Padre Billini near the Cathedral are recommended. Many good ones, but usually expensive, on the Malecón (Av. George Washington) along the seafront, including *Le Café*, *El Gaucho*, good value for steaks, and 3 blocks east of *Hotel Napolitano*, *Llave del Mar*, which has a stuffed dolphin hanging outside, a weird and wonderful collection of curios inside and serves good seafood at reasonable prices. *Fonda La Ataranza*, in La Ataranza, popular for creole and international cuisine; *Gerd's Hofbrauhaus*, Palo Hincado, unpretentious, good German food; *D'Agostini*, Máximo Gómez; *Lucky Seven*, Av. Pasteur, good for seafood and steaks, popular haunt for baseball fans. Also worth visiting are *Via Veneto* on Av. Independencia, *La Tratoria*, Embajador gardens and *Da Ciro* on Av. Pasteur (Italian cuisine) and *La Fromagerie*, also on Av. Pasteur, *Cafe St. Michel* on Av. Lope de Vega and *Café De La Gare* on Av. Winston Churchill (French cuisine). *Mesón de Castilla*, on Dr. Báez near the National Palace; and *Juan Carlos*, Gustavo Mejía Ricart (Spanish cuisine). For good Chinese food try *Marios* on Calle Mercedes opposite Parque Independencia, very popular, *La Gran Muralla*, Av. 27 de Febrero, *Jardín de Jade* in the *Hotel El Embajador*. For local food at reasonable prices try *El Buren* on Padre Billini, *Pacos Café*, *Comedor Independencia* and *Freidura Nacional*, all near Parque Independencia. Two good vegetarian restaurants are *Ananda*, Casimiro de Maya 7, and *Vegetariano*, Calle Luperón 9 (open 0800-1500). There are numerous pizzerias whch are good value; also try a *chimichurri* (spiced sausage) from the stalls along the Malecón. *La Plaza Argentina* near the Cathedral, *Drakes Pub* opposite the Alcázar, *Mary*, Plaza Colón (good breakfast), *Raffles Pub*, *Mesón de Bari* and *The Village* in Calle Hostos, opposite the ruins of Hospital San Nicolás de Bari, are good places for snacks and drinks in a pub-type atmosphere, in the colonial city.

Shopping Duty free at Centro de los Héroes, La Ataranza, shops in *Embajador*, *Sheraton* and *Santo Domingo* hotels; departure lounge at airport; all purchases must be in US dollars. Mercado Modelo, on Av. Mella esq. Santome, includes gift shops; you must bargain to get a good price. Sunday morning market on Paseo Pte. Bellini, near Montesinos monument. There are also "speciality shops" at Plaza Criolla, 27 de Febrero y Máximo Gómez. The native amber is sold throughout the country. Larimar, a sea-blue stone, and red and black coral are also available. Calle El Conde is the oldest shopping sector in Santo Domingo, and go to Av. Mella at Duarte for discount shopping and local colour. In contrast are the modern complexes at Plaza Naco and at Av. 27 de Febrero and Av. Abraham Lincoln; also the new US style shopping mall at the corner of Av. 27 de Febrero and Winston Churchill. Shops in the capital are open 0830-1200 and 1430-1800/1830.

Buses Public transport buses (Onatrate) run throughout the city, fares are US$0.20, but best avoided as the service is limited therefore crowded. Exact change is needed. Private companies operate on some routes.

Taxis *Públicos* or *conchos* are shared taxis normally operating on fixed routes, 24 hours a day, basic fare US$0.35, though more on longer routes. *Públicos* can be hired by one person, if they're empty, and are then called *carreras*. They can be expensive (US$4-5); settle price before getting in. Fares are higher at Christmas time. *Públicos* also run on long-distance routes; ask around to find the cheapest. Most hotels have a taxi or limousine service with set fares throughout the city and to the airport.

Car Rentals Avis, Budget, Hertz, Via, Neily, El Mundo, National, Dial, City; McDeals, Av. George Washington 105, has the most reasonable rates (ask for Mike). Car hire costs from US$30 a day and is on a free mileage basis. Pueblo Renta Car, recommended, on Av. Independencia (esq. *Jaragua* hotel), also provides the best road map of the country. Avoid going for the cheapest: it is better to pay more with a well-known agency. Watch for "sleeping policemen" (ramps on highways) at entrances to towns to discourage speeding.

Library Instituto Cultural Dominico-Americano, corner of Av. Abraham Lincoln and Calle Antonio de la Maza. English and Spanish books. Biblioteca Nacional, in the Plaza de la Cultura, has a fine collection and is a good place for a quiet read.

Concerts and other cultural events are often held at the National Theatre, the Casa de Francia, corner of Las Damas and El Conde, where Cortés lived for a while, and the Casa de Teatro on Arzobispo Meriño.

Theatres Teatro Nacional, Plaza de la Cultura, Av. Máximo Gómez; Palace of Fine Arts, Av. Independencia and Máximo Gómez; Casa de Teatro, small drama workshop, Arzobispo Meriño.

Night Clubs *Embajador*, *Napolitano*, *San Gerónimo*, *Sheraton* (El Yarey); *Dominican Concorde*, *Santo Domingo* and *Comodoro* hotels all have nightclubs; *Sexto Sentido*, on Padre Billini corner of Isabel la Católica, and *José Night Club*, Av. George Washington, have nightly shows. Maunaloa, Centro de los Héroes; *Le Petit Chateau*, Autopista 30 de Mayo; *La Voz de Santo Domingo*;

1220 DOMINICAN REPUBLIC

Morocco, in the new Cinema Centro which has six cinemas and a wine bar; Sui Generis on the Malecón; Teatro Agua; Luz (Jockey Club); Mesón de la Cava. The Safari is the best place to see locals dance and to listen to leading *merengue* bands; The Herminias, a colourful nightclub, is best left to the sophisticated male visitor. **Bars:** La Pipa; Moulin Rouge; El Bodegón Bar-Lounge, Arz. Meriño 152, live jazz Monday nights.

Discotheques in Hotels *Sheraton* and *Hispaniola,* also *Jet Set,* Av. Independencia 184; *Morocco,* Av. G. Washington; *Tropicalia,* Av. Independencia 624; *Alexanders,* Av. Pasteur; *Imagen,* Av. Independencia. *Bella Blue,* next to *Vesuvio I* on George Washington.

Casinos in *Hotel Dominican Concorde, San Gerónimo, Sheraton, El Embajador, Naco,* and Maunaloa, Centro de los Héroes.

Sports Golf: Country Club Santo Domingo; *Casa de Campo Hotel* in La Panamana; some hotels including the *Santo Domingo* can arrange guest passes. Polo matches at weekends at Sierra Prieta, Santo Domingo. Baseball at Quisqueya stadium, water skiing/deep-sea fishing at Náutico Club, Boca Chica beach. Basketball, boxing and wrestling matches can also be seen in Santo Domingo. Snorkelling and scuba-diving tours are operated by Mundo Submarino at Gustavo Ricart 99, and by Bucco Dominicano, Av. A. Lincoln 960. Tennis at Country Club.

Exchange Houses Vimenca, Av. Lincoln 306; Lacinio Pichardo, Av. Nouel 58; Alcántara y Asoc., Arz. Meriño 251; El Tesoro, París 101; La Nacional, Isabel La Católica; Chicot, Av. Duarte 138.

Post Office Calle Emiliano Tejera, opp. Alcázar de Colón. Open 0700-1200, 1400-1800, Mon.-Fri. Also certain hours on Sat. There is a post office on the 2nd floor of the government building El Haucal, tallest building in the city.

Episcopal Church Av. Independencia 253. Service in English, 0830 Sunday.

All America Cables and Radio Inc. Julio Verne 21 (Tel.: 682-3115). Telegrams may be sent through RCA Global Communications, El Conde 203, open 24 hrs., 7 days a week.

Health Clínica Abreu, Av. Independencia and Beller, and adjacent Clínica Gómez Patiño are recommended for foreigners needing treatment or hospitalization. Fees are high but care is good. 24-hour emergency department.

Tourist Office Centro Dominicano de Información Turística, now at Av. George Washington (Malecón) near the Obelisk, friendly but not very useful except for providing essential bus map. Also in arrival area at airport, and on Arzobispo Meriño, opposite the cathedral. Haitian Tourist Office is on Calle Padre Billini (an overland entry permit takes at least 3 weeks to get).

Travel Agents Viajes Internacionales, El Conde 15; Servicios Turísticos, Av. George Washington 67; Metro Tours, Av. Winston Churchill; Santoni, José Joaquín Pérez 6. Amber Tours and Prieto Tours, Av. Francia 125, both offer a variety of sightseeing tours around the country. Thomas Tour, Pedro Henríquez Ureña 170-E 1, Tel.: 688-2562; Cesintur, Av. Independencia 301, Tel.: 685-4655 (highly recommended, near *Hotel Cervantes*); Fantasy Tours, Tel.: 533-2131 ext. 746; Dorado Travel, Tel.: 688-3913; Vimenca Tours, Av. Abraham Lincoln 306, Tel.: 533-9362; Diana Tours, Plaza Criolla. Consult your hotel reception or yellow pages for others.

Airport 23 km. out of town. Taxi to town US$12 (max. 5 people) or less if you bargain with drivers in the car park (though this is not easy) or telephone Radio Taxi in advance. Bus or *público* to town from *Restaurante La Caleta*; turn right out of airport compound along main road; cross over main highway; turn left to restaurant (about 25 mins. walk). Bus passes every ½ hr., until 2000, or walk down the airport road to the highway, Avenida de Las Américas, and flag down anything that passes! To get to the airport cheaply take a *público* at Av. Duarte and París (to Savanna Larga). Get off before the car turns on to Savanna Larga, walk 50 metres and there are *carros* to the airport, US$4-7. Expresos Dominicanos have a regular service to the airport from Av. Independencia, US$2.75. Various tour agencies also run minibuses to the airport; check with your hotel. Herrera airport for internal flights to Santiago, Puerto Plata, Barahona and La Romana (allow plenty of time).

Long-Distance Buses See page 1226.

To the north of Santo Domingo, along the Carretera Duarte, is **Bonao** (Hotels: *El Viejo Madrid,* D; *Yaravi Rooms,* D; *Jacaranda,* D; *Elizabeth,* F, with bath, and other cheap hotels near the market such as *Granada* and *Copacabana,* F). Further N is **La Vega**, a quiet place in the heart of the Cibao valley. (Hotels: *América,* D; *Guaricano,* D; and *Royal, San Pedro,* and *Astral,* all F.) Further along the road from La Vega on the right is the turn for Santo Cerro. From there one can get a view of the valley of La Vega Real. If one continues along the road to the other side of the hill and into the valley the ruins of La Vega Vieja can be seen. It was

DOMINICAN REPUBLIC 1221

founded by Columbus but destroyed by an earthquake in 1564; it is presently undergoing restoration. (*Hotel Mariza*, E, very basic with fan; *Pensión Ana*.)

Further along the highway, on the left, is the turn for **Jarabacoa**. The road winds through some beautiful pine forests to the town itself, which is a popular summer hill resort with warm days and cool nights. *Público* from La Vega, US$1.25; bus from Santo Domingo, US$2.50. (Hotels in Jarabacoa: *Nacional*, E, friendly and clean; outside town, *La Montaña*, D, and *Pinar Dorado*, C, which has cottages. *Dormitorio*, basic, clean, friendly, with a good *comedor*, *Carmen*, nearby. The town has several restaurants; try the *Rincón Montañés* on Calle El Carmen; other good-value ones are run by shopkeepers.) There are several clubs offering golf, tennis and riding, and the *balneario* (swimming hole) of La Confluencia is nearby. Further along the road which goes to Jarabacoa is **Constanza,** where the scenery is even better than in Jarabacoa, with rivers, forests, waterfalls, etc. The valley is famous for its strawberries, mushrooms and ornamental flowers. (Hotels: Nueva Suiza, C; *Mi Cabaña*, E. *Margarita* and *Casa de Huéspedes*, both on Calle Luperón.) Constanza can be reached by taking a bus to Bonao from either Santo Domingo or Santiago, then a *público* to Hatney, and finally another *público* for the rough 1½ hr. trip to the town through the finest scenery in the Republic. *Público* from Jarabacoa, US$3.50.

In the Cordillera Central near both of these towns is **Pico Duarte**, the highest peak in the Caribbean, measuring 3,075 metres in altitude. Before climbing it one must obtain the permission of the army in Jarabacoa. (When doing this you will be told that mules are necessary at 6 pesos daily for the ascent, but it can be done without them.) The climb takes two days and the walk from the tropical rain forest of the National Park through pine woods is pleasant. There are two huts on the path, which is clearly marked; they are lacking in "facilities". Take adequate clothing with you; it can be cold and wet. The last *carro* leaves Manatao for Jarabacoa at 1600, so aim to climb the peak well before lunch on the second day. The National Park itself is a 4 km. walk from La Ciénaga, which is reached by a road passing through some magnificent scenery from Jarabacoa.

Santiago de Los Caballeros is the second largest city in the Republic and chief town of the Cibao valley in the north-central part of the country. It is much quieter, cleaner, cooler and "slower" than Santo Domingo, from where it is easily reached by bus (US$3.25). Places worth visiting are the Universidad Católica Madre y Maestra (founded 1962), the new tobacco museum (opposite the Cathedral), the Catedral de Santiago Apóstol, and the Monumento a los Héroes de la Restauración, which was originally constructed by Trujillo on a hill as a monument to himself. The Instituto Superior de Agricultura is in the Herradura on the other side of the Río Yaque del Norte (km. 6). A carriage ride around the city should not be missed.

Hotels *Camino Real*, B, Del Sol and Mella, has good restaurant and night club; *Don Diego*, B, Av. Estrella Sadhalá, has restaurant and night club; *Don Carlos*, B; *Ambar*, C, also on Av. Estrella Sadhalá; *Matun*, B, Las Carreras (altos) has night club. Also *Corona*, C, away from centre. A recommended *pensión* is the *Diri*, F (Las Carreras and Juan Pablo Duarte).

Restaurants The best are the *Pez Dorado* (Chinese and international), the restaurant of the Hotel *Don Diego*; *Oriente*, Calle 30 de Marzo, good meals for about US$3.50; *El Dragón* (Chinese). Excellent sandwich and pizza places are *Olé* (Av. Juan Pablo Duarte, esq., Independencia), *Dinós* (formerly *Capri*, Del Sol). Others include *Las Antillas* (Parque Duarte), meals from US$4 upwards; *El Mexicano* (Ensanche El Ensueño); *Yaque* (Restauración), US$4 plus for a good meal; and *La Suiza*.

Buses in Santiago US$0.20. *Públicos* charge US$0.25-0.35 in the city. There is a Tourist Office on the 2nd floor of the Town Hall (Ayuntamiento), Av. Juan Pablo Duarte; it has good maps and brochures. The markets are located at Del Sol and España, Av. J. Armando Bermúdez and near the lower part of 16 de Agosto.

To the SW of Santiago is the pleasant town of San José de las Matas, (Hotels, *Oasis* and *La Modenza*, F.) and to the NW of Santiago a road runs through the Yaque del Norte valley to Mao (*Hotel Cahoba*, D) and on to

1222 DOMINICAN REPUBLIC

Monte Cristi, a dusty little town on the coast. One can visit the house of Máximo Gómez, a Dominican patriot who played an important role in the struggle for Cuban independence and in the Dominican Restoration. Very near Monte Cristi is a peak named El Moro which has a beach (very rocky) at the foot of its east side. There are a couple of decent hotels there (*Montechico*, on Bolaños beach, E; *Roalex*).

Puerto Plata, the chief town on the Atlantic coast (which is also known as the Amber Coast) was founded by Columbus and has some fine colonial architecture. It is reached by bus from Santo Domingo (US$ 6.00 by Metrobus, 3½ hrs. by Expresos Dominicanos (only US$2.50)), or by *público* (US$10). The older scenic road from Santiago to Puerto Plata is now in excellent condition. A visit to the colonial San Felipe fortress, at the end of the Malecón, and a ride in the *teleférico* are recommended. The latter goes some 1,000 metres up behind the town to the summit of Isabel de Torres, with a statue of Christ, craft shops, a café and some fine gardens with a view of the coast and mountains. (Cost US$1 for cable-car round trip; from town to *teleférico* station is US$2 by taxi, US$1 by colectivo. The cable-car does not run on Tues. or Wed.) The Museum of Dominican Amber, Duarte 61, houses a collection of rare amber; open Mon.-Sat. 0900-1700. The town is already a stop for cruise-ships, thus attracting hordes of beggars and overly persistent small boys, and is being developed as the hub of a major tourism project on the N coast. There is a tourist office on the Malecón which has plenty of useful information. Fishing: contact Santiago Camps (Tel.: 586-2632) for equipment and boat hire. A new international airport has been built to serve the area (Flights Mon., Fri. and Sun to San Juan; also to USA). At the E end of town is Long Beach, US$0.15 by bus, but it is crowded at weekends and rather dirty. To the W is the new Costambar resort area (cottages, sports facilities) and Cofresí beach (cabins, US$30 p.p. and more at weekends). Further W is Punta Rucio which has a beautiful beach not yet developed for tourism.

Hotels *Montemar*, on beach, A, all facilities; *Dorado Naco*, EP, A (add US$20, MAP) Tel.: 586-2019. *Castilla*, in centre of town, D, splendid atmosphere; *El Condado*, Av. Circunvalación Sur, D. *Caracol*, on sea front, C, modern; *Costatlántica Resort*, on the seafront, B; *Palacio*, Av. J. F. Kennedy, D, bar and restaurant below, friendly, good value; *Ilra*, Calle Villa Nueva, Tel.: 586-2337, good food and *Alfa*, all in F range; some houses also available from US$22 a week.

Restaurants: *Los Pinos*, international cuisine; *Pizzería Portofino*, Hermanas Mirabel; *La Isabella* (Hotel Montemar); *La Carreta*, Calle Separación; *Oceánico* on sea front; *El Canario*, 12 de Julio; Hotel *Castilla* restaurant, all have good food at relatively low prices. *China*, Av. Hermanas Mirabel; *D'Amico*, Luis Ginebra 150; *El Sombrero*, Autopista Santiago-Puerto Plata; *Terraza La Carpa*, Av. John F. Kennedy; *Madrid*, very good value; *Cafetería Los Bonilla*, La Javilla, highly recommended, *merengue* players visit it most evenings. Also popular are *Café Terminus*, *El Cable* and the *Beach Club Restaurant*, all at Long Beach.

Just E of Puerto Plata is the new beach resort of **Playa Dorada** with an exceptional golf course. Recently opened is *Jack Tar Village* hotel, A, all inclusive, Tel.: 586-3800, US style and US prices. *Playa Dorada Holiday Inn*, (use the Club Playa snack bar next door to save money), *Dorado Naco Resort*, B; *Villas Doradas Resort Hotel. Villas Caraibe*, B.

Still further E is **Sosúa,** which has an excellent beach in a small bay, very good for diving and water sports; *público* from Puerto Plata, US$1. The unusually European atmosphere stems from the Jewish refugees who settled here in 1940.

Hotels: *Sosuamar*, in the hills overlooking Sosúa; *Club Náutico*; *Los Charamicos*, B; *Sosúa*, C; *Los Coralillos*, C; *Ninos*, D; *Sosuasol*, D, in El Batey.

Restaurants: *La Roca*, *El Coral*, *El Oasis*, *Pizzería Roma III*, *Sosuasol* in El Batey and *Le Bistró* in Charamicos.

At one point the old road passes La Cumbre, which used to be a Trujillo mansion, but is now the property of the Secretariat of Agriculture. Still further to the east is **Río San Juan,** which has a lagoon called Gri-Gri and a beach. *Público* from Puerto Plata, US$2.50. Best hotel *Río San Juan*, C, on main street, also has a good restaurant. Cheaper hotels: *San Martín* and *Caridad*. **Playa Grande**, 60 km. from Puerto Plata, is another new resort which is being developed, in conjunction with Playa Dorada, at a cost of many millions of dollars. Between Playa Grande and Samaná, on the coast, is **Nagua** (Hotel-Restaurant China; Hotel Corazón de Jesús, F). Público from Río San Juan to Nagua, US$1.50. The scenery along the northern coast from Sosúa to Samaná is exceptionally beautiful.

On the peninsula of **Samaná** is the city of the same name. Recently the entire city was reconstructed. Many new restaurants and hotels have been built. (Hotels: Bahia Beach Resort, A, reservations: World Travel Center, Av. Bolivar 260, Santo Domingo, Tel.: 687-5053/5033; accommodation can be found in private homes; El Portillo Beach Club at Las Terrenas, a beautiful beach on N coast, C, has bungalows, quite basic but friendly. Some cheaper hotels near the market.) A new airport for the peninsula was recently opened and the city should be fully functional soon. There are several beautiful offshore islands here too; Cayo Levantado and Las Galeras are particularly worth a visit. In fact, the whole peninsula is beautiful but many beaches are accessible only by boat (the boatmen at Samaná charge the earth to take visitors out). Others are reached by a dirt road, negotiable by ordinary saloon cars. La Mariscada, good restaurant, Sta. Bárbara 4, run by a Canadian couple, Juan Dutreuil and Raymonde Corbeil. Next door is an hotel (F) with air conditioning. Chez Paco is an outstanding beach restaurant at Las Terrenas; dine on lobster caught same day. Club Las Terrenas is also outstanding for seafood. For dancing go to the Diny Restaurant on the beach at Las Terrenas.

Communications with the capital either by bus direct, via Nagua and Sánchez, or by bus or público to Sabana la Mar (Hotel Brisas de la Bahía, E), and cross by boat (3 return trips a day) from Sabana to Samaná, last trip from Samaná at 1500. Visits by launch can also be arranged to the Parque Nacional de Haitises. Alas del Caribe now has flights to the airport from Santo Domingo. Road Puerto Plata-Samaná excellent, bus US$4, 3½ hrs (daily 0530). Road to Hato Mayor is bad, but from Hato Mayor to San Pedro de Macorís (see next page) it is excellent.

To the west of Santo Domingo is Haina, the country's main port. Further W one can visit **San Cristóbal** in the interior, the birthplace of the dictator Trujillo. Trujillo's home, the Casa de Caoba (now rapidly disintegrating, but open 0900-1700) may be reached by a Land-Rover bus from behind the market, though you may have to walk the last km., uphill. Nearby are La Toma pools for scenery and swimming. Hotels: San Cristóbal, D; Constitución, E.

From San Cristóbal the road runs W to Bani, "a much richer town than any other in Santo Domingo". Cheaper hotels to be found near the market on Máximo Gómez. Don't bother with the beach, better to carry on to Las Salinas and Barahona. At **Barahona** Hotel Guarocuya is particularly recommended, being cheap, clean and on the beach, E for double room with fan; D with a/c, also Hotel Barahona on Calle Jaime Mora, and Fenicia, Palace and Victoria, all F; Hotel Caribe, E, basic, with an excellent open-air restaurant (La Rocca) next door. Those with a car can visit other, more remote, beaches from Barahona (public transport is very basic): all along the southern coast are many white sand beaches which offer the best snorkelling and scuba diving in the Republic. One such is San Rafael (about 40 mins. from Barahona) where there is a fresh-water swimming hole in the river at the end of the beach. There is a small, pleasant restaurant on the beach and it is possible to camp there. At weekends it gets very crowded. There are cool, fresh-water lagoons behind several of the other beaches on this stretch of coast. One must explore for oneself: the area is not developed for tourism.

Inland from Barahona, near the Haitian border, is the salt-water, below-sea-level Lake Enriquillo with a wealth of wild life including crocodiles (best seen in the morning), iguanas and flamingoes. The iguanas can, however, only be seen on the largest island in the lake; it is possible to hire a boat. To visit the lake it is best to have a car, though it is possible to get there by bus from Santo Domingo to Jimaní (US$5, La Experiencia and Riviera companies; the journey takes 8 hours) and getting off either at Los Ríos or at La Descubierta, where there is a swimming hole (balneario). From these places walk or hitch a lift to the lake. At Jimaní there are Hotel Jimaní, E, and Hotel Baoruco, basic and friendly.

1224 DOMINICAN REPUBLIC

William E. Rainey, of Berkeley, Calif., writes: "The highway south from Barahona deteriorates considerably after Baoruco but is passable by passenger car. Between Baoruco and Enriquillo there is wet tropical forest with rushing mountain streams and fruit stands in little roadside settlements. At Enriquillo you enter the Barahona Peninsula lowlands and the terrain grows markedly drier. Continuing west from Oviedo to Pedernales the road is in good condition and the surrounding habitat, particularly near Pedernales, is tropical thorn scrub with abundant cacti growing on karstic limestone.

"The entire country is dotted with checkpoints adjacent to roadside military installations; at most of these the traffic is simply waved through. At checkpoint in Pedernales (perhaps because gringos were an anomaly there) there were brief interrogations each time we passed (with automatic weapons pointed at us by uniformed teenagers). The last time we passed this point, one of them initiated a detailed search of our gear. Fortunately, this entertainment was cut short by a senior officer who apologized. It was, on balance, a minor aggravation, but one likely to be experienced by travellers near the Haitian border."

San Juan de la Maguana is further from the Haitian border (*Hotel Maguana*, D). Visit the Corral de Los Indios, an ancient Indian meeting ground several km. north of the town.

About 25 km. E of Santo Domingo is the beach of Boca Chica, the principal resort for the capital. It is a reef-protected shallow lagoon, and has an excellent restaurant, *L'Horizon*. The Guayacanes and Embassy beaches, further E, are also popular, especially at weekends. Further E again is Juan Dolio (*Palmas de Mar*, US$60-80 for chalets; *Punta Garza* bungalows, B; *Hotel Playa Real*, C). Buses going to **San Pedro de Macorís,** a quiet town on the coast which is now being developed for tourism (*Hotel Macorís*, D, *Hotel Brisas de Higuamo*, central, cheap and clean) will drop you, and pick you up again, at the turn-off to the beaches. E of San Pedro is **La Romana** (*Casa de Campo*, hotel, villas and country club with many sporting facilities in 7,000 acres, prices start at US$155; *Club Dominicus*, a 2,000-acre beach resort with cottages, villas and sports facilities; cheaper is the brand-new *Puerto Laguna*. *Hotel Romana*, A; *Roma*, much cheaper, E; *Pensión de Aza*, Parque Duarte; *Pensión Verónica*, Calle Santa Rosa). Nelly Veerman from Volendam, Holland says that the village of Bayahibe is well worth a visit. La Romana can be reached by air and by bus from Santo Domingo (US$2). An international artists' village in mock-Italian style has been established at Altos de Chavón, near La Romana, in a spectacular hilltop setting, but there is no public transport and it's a long walk from La Romana. There are a hotel here, and two restaurants. Further E is **Boca de Yuma,** an interesting fishing village which is the scene of a deep-sea fishing tournament every year. A recently repaved road runs from Boca de Yuma inland to Higüey; along this, about 2 km. N of San Rafael de Yuma, is the restored residence of Ponce de León (1505-1508).

Higüey has the Basílica de Nuestra Señora de la Altagracia (patroness of the Republic), a very impressive modern building to which every year there is a pilgrimage on Jan. 21; the old 16th-century church is still standing. Plenty of cheap hotels on Calle Colón. Due E from Higüey, on the coast again, is **Punta Cana** which has some beautiful beaches; a new Club Méditerranée, A, has recently been opened here. Continuing round the coast, there are many other beaches to be visited, with white sand and reef-sheltered water.

NB The staff of the *Santo Domingo News* recommend visiting the many swimming holes, *balnearios*, both in the towns and surrounding countryside. Among others try *Bayaguana* about 1 hr. NE of Santo Domingo; *La Descubierta* north of Lake Enriquillo near the Haitian border; *Loma de Cabrera* south of Dajabón; and *La Confluencia* in the attractive town of Jarabacoa in the centre of the island.

Economy

The land area is 4.8m hectares, of which 12% is forest and woodland, 30% arable land and 44% pasture. There are six main agricultural regions: the north, the Cibao valley in the north central area, Constanza and Tiero, the east, the San Juan valley, and the south. Cibao is the most fertile and largest region, while the eastern region is the main sugar producing area. Sugar is the main crop and largest export item. Until 1984, the US sugar import quota system, of which the Dominican Republic was the largest beneficiary, provided a preferential market for over half the country's sugar exports as well as a cushion against the slump in world sugar prices. Major adjustments in

DOMINICAN REPUBLIC

US consumption patterns, particularly the switch by Coca Cola and Pepsi to High Fructose Corn Syrup, prompted the USA to cut quotas drastically. By 1986/87, the Dominican Republic's quota had been cut to 30% of previous levels. The government is encouraging diversification of some cane lands to other crops.

Since 1975 gold and silver mining has been of considerable importance. The Pueblo Viejo mine, on the north coast, is run by Amax of the USA. The mine's oxide ores are expected to be exhausted by 1990, but there are undeveloped reserves of sulphide ores, believed to contain 60m tonnes of gold-bearing ore. The country also produces ferronickel, which is the third largest export earner. Proven and probable reserves at the end of 1982 were estimated at 46m tonnes of laterite ore grading 1.78% nickel.

In the first half of the 1980s, a combination of fiscal and external account problems brought about a sharp decline in the rate of gdp growth and led the government to turn to the IMF for financial assistance. The government agreed to reduce its fiscal deficit and take a number of other austerity measures, including a gradual devaluation of the peso. It failed to meet targets, so the programme was suspended in early 1984. Government measures to remove subsidies, as part of the austerity package agreed with the IMF, led to riots in Santo Domingo in April 1984. Negotiations with the Fund were finally resumed and a one year standby loan facility worth SDR78.5 m was approved in April 1985. The government also successfully renegotiated its debts to foreign commercial banks, although persistent low world prices for its major export commodities made debt servicing commitments increasingly burdensome.

	1961-70 (av)	1971-80 (av)	1981-85 (av)
Gdp growth (1980 prices)	5.0%	6.9%	1.5%
Inflation	1.9%	10.4%	16.2%
Exports (fob) US$m	170	657	869
Sugar	88	262	318
Doré	-	100 (a)	156
Imports (fob)m	165	747	1,307
Current account balance US$m (cum)	-419	-2,158	-1,269

(a) = 1975-80

Information for Visitors

How to get there There are cargo and passenger shipping services with New York, New Orleans, Miami and South American countries. There is a daily ferry from San Pedro de Macorís to Mayagüez, Puerto Rico US$80 round trip (call Viajes Tiradentes 562-3732/3868). American and Dominicana fly to Miami; and American and Dominicana to New York. Dominicana and ALM fly to San Juan, and Iberia, Viasa, ALM and Dominicana fly to Central and South America. Copa and Iberia fly to Panama twice weekly. From the new international airport at Puerto Plata there are flights to Miami, New York and Puerto Rico by American and Dominicana. ALM flies to the Netherlands Antilles six times a week. Vaughan Travel, 52 Perrymount Road, Haywards Heath, Sussex, offers package holidays in the Dominican Republic.

Documents Citizens of the US, Canada, Mexico, Jamaica and Venezuela need only adequate identification and a tourist card (US$5, valid for 60 days.) extensions obtainable from Immigration, Huacal Building. Citizens of Austria, Belgium, Denmark, France, Finland, West Germany, Israel, Italy, Japan, Luxembourg, Netherlands, Norway, Panama, Spain, Sweden, Switzerland and the U.K. need passports and a tourist card (not needed for W. German citizens) which can be purchased from the airlines or on arrival for US$5. All others must have a valid passport and a visa. Entry may be refused to nationals of communist countries. In some places visas can be obtained instantly, but in others you must allow at least 15 days for them to be granted.

All visitors should have an outward ticket. The airport police are on the lookout for illegal drugs. Backpackers especially may expect a thorough search of person and property. There is no longer a departure tax. If travelling to Haiti overland you must get a permit, which involves considerable delay and much paper work.

Currency The effective rate of exchange of the Dominican peso (RD$) to US dollar is approximately US$1 = RD$2.75. Hotels will give approx. 15% less on travellers' cheques. US and Canadian dollars are freely exchangeable on the official or parallel market. There are many exchange houses and most banks and some travel agencies change money at the parallel market rate. Dominican currency may not be imported nor exported. Remember that if you use the free market you will not be able to change back into US$ at the official rate: that can only be done if you produce bank exchange slips.

Internal Travel Alas del Caribe has a daily air service from Santo Domingo to Barahona, Cabo Rojo, Puerto Plata, San Juan de Maguana and Santiago. Ambar Air also flies daily from Herrera airport (Santo Domingo) to Barahona and Puerto Plata. Air taxi services are also available. Hitchhiking is perfectly possible, through *público* services between most towns are efficient and inexpensive.

DOMINICAN REPUBLIC

There are usually fixed *público* rates between cities, so inquire first. Many drivers pack a truly incredible number of passengers in their cars, so the ride is often not that comfortable. If travelling by private taxi, bargaining is very important.

Buses Autobuses Metro operates from Av. Winston Churchill near Av. Abraham Lincoln and has buses to Bonao, La Vega, Santiago, Puerto Plata, San Pedro de Macorís, the airport, La Romana, Jarabacoa, San Cristóbal and other points. Terrabus, a new company, offers the most luxurious service for only slightly higher fares. Their service to Santiago comes complete with hostesses and refreshments. A third company, Caribe Tours, operates from Av. 27 at Leopoldo Navarro. In the capital buses leave from Parque Enriquillo (Av. Duarte and Ravelo) for Higüey, Nagua, San Francisco de Macorís, Miches, etc. For really cheap travel try the *guaguas*, which go everywhere. Board at Parque Independencia intersection, Av. Duarte and París.

Driving A valid driving licence from your country of origin or an international licence is accepted. Dominicans drive on the right. The speed limit for city driving is 60 kph and on main roads 80 kph. Service stations close at 1800. Cars driven by tourists are often stopped by the police; a bribe is expected. Local drivers can be erratic; be on the alert.

Customs Duty-free import of 200 cigarettes or one box of cigars, plus one opened bottle of alcoholic liquor, is permitted. Military-type clothing and food products will be confiscated on arrival. Currency in excess of US$5,000 may not be taken out of the country without special permission.

Health It is not advisable to drink tap water. All hotels have bottled water. It is also advisable to avoid the midday sun.

Electricity 110 volts, 60 cycles A.C. current. There are frequent power cuts, so take a torch with you when you go out at night.

Tipping A 10% service charge is added to all hotel and restaurant bills, however it is customary to give an extra tip in restaurants, depending on service. Porters receive US$0.50 per bag; taxi drivers, *público* drivers and garage attendants are not usually tipped.

Food and Drink Local beers, Presidente, Bohemia and Quisqueya, are excellent. There are also many good rums. Imported drinks are very expensive. Local dishes include *sancocho* (a type of stew made of local meats and vegetables, often including *plátanos*, *ñame* and *yautia*), *mondongo* (a tripe stew), *cocido* (a soup of chickpeas, meat and vegetables), *chivo* (goat). The salads are often good; another good side dish is *tostones* (fried and flattened *plátanos*). *Quipes* (made of flour and meat) and *pastelitos* (fried dough with meat or cheese inside) can be bought from street vendors; can be risky. Also try *pipián*, goats' offal served as a stew. The traveller should be warned that Dominican food is rather on the greasy side; most of the dishes are fried. There are excellent cigars at very reasonable prices.

Folklore The most popular dance is the *merengue*, which dominates the musical life of the Dominican Republic; other dances are the *mangulina*, the *salve* and the *carabiné*. The traditional *merengue* is played by a 3-man group called a *perico ripiao* which consists of a *tambora* (small drum), a *guirra* (a percussion instrument scraped by a metal rod) and an accordion. There is a *merengue* festival in the last week of July and the first week of August.

Banks Bank of Nova Scotia at Santo Domingo, Santiago, and Puerto Plata. The Chase Manhattan Bank, Santo Domingo and Santiago. Citibank, Santo Domingo and Santiago; Banco Universal, Banco Popular, Banco de Reservas, nationwide.

Business Hours Shops: 0800-1200/1300; 1400/1500-1800 Mon.-Fri.; 0800-1300 Sat. Banks: 0800-1300 Mon.-Fri. Government offices 0730-1430.

Newspapers The best daily papers are *Listín Diario*, *El Caribe* and *Hoy*, the afternoon tabloids *Ultima Hora* and *Nacional* have the widest circulation. English-language *Santo Domingo News*, published every Wednesday and available at hotels.

Broadcasting There are many local radio stations and 5 television stations. Also 2 cable TV stations broadcasting in English.

Maps Arco (Tel.: 565-7756) has map of Hispaniola; Esso (Tel.: 565-6641) Santo Domingo and Dominican Republic. Texaco also produce a good map of the country.

US Embassy and Consulate, César Nicolás Penson; Tel.: (embassy) 682-2171; (consulate) 689-2111.

Public Holidays

Jan. 1: New Year's Day
Jan 6: Epiphany
Jan 21: Our Lady of Altagracia

Corpus Christi (60 days after
   Good Friday
May 1: Labour Day

Jan 26: Duarte Day
Feb. 27: Independence Day
Good Friday

Aug 16: Restoration Day
Sept 24: Our Lady of Las Mercedes
Dec 25: Christmas Day

Fiestas Santo Domingo, Carnival between Feb. 26 and 2 March; Year-end celebration Dec. 22-Jan. 2.

Churches Roman Catholicism is the predominant religion. There are also Episcopalian, Baptist, Seventh Day Adventist, Presbyterian and Methodist Churches in the main towns. There is a synagogue on Av. Sarasota, Santo Domingo; call Israeli Embassy (533-2379/7359) for details of services. Voodoo, technically illegal, is tolerated and practised mostly in the western provinces.

Telephones are operated by the Compañía Dominicana de Teléfonos. All local calls and overseas calls to the Caribbean, US and Canada may be dialled directly from Santo Domingo.

Weights and Measures Officially the metric system is used but business is often done on a pound/yard/US gallon basis.

Our thanks to Dorothy Millgate for editorial work on the countries of Hispaniola, to Michael Hirschhorn, Clifford Groome and the staff of the *Santo Domingo News*, and to John M Raspey (Santo Domingo); and we express our gratitude to the following travellers in Haiti*, the Dominican Republic† and both countries‡: Pierre-Yves Atlan† (Paris 18e), Herbert S Levi* (Buenos Aires) and Gustav-Adolf Yunge‡ (Cologne).

PUERTO RICO

THE COMMONWEALTH OF PUERTO RICO, the smallest and most easterly island of the Greater Antilles, is the first Overseas Commonwealth Territory (defined as a "free and associated State") of the USA. Spanish is the first language but the citizenship is US and English is widely spoken. Puerto Rico lies at the north of the Caribbean sea about a thousand miles south-east of Miami between the island of Hispaniola and the Virgin Islands, which give it some shelter from the open Atlantic, and is between longitudes 66° and 67° west and at latitude 18°30 north.

Almost rectangular in shape, slightly smaller than Jamaica, it measures 153 km. in length (east to west), 58 km. in width, and has a total land area of some 8,768 square km.

Old volcanic mountains, long inactive, occupy a large part of the interior of the island, with the highest peak, Cerro de Punta, at 1,325 metres in the Cordillera Central. N of the Cordillera is the karst country where the limestone has been acted upon by water to produce a series of small steep hills and deep holes, both conical in shape. The mountains are surrounded by a coastal plain with the Atlantic shore beaches cooled all the year round by trade winds, which make the temperatures of 28-30°C bearable in the summer. Temperatures in the winter drop to the range 21-26°C and the climate all the year round is very agreeable.

History Puerto Rico was discovered by Columbus, accompanied by a young nobleman, Juan Ponce de León, on November 19, 1493. Attracted by tales of gold, Ponce obtained permission to colonize Borinquén, as it was called by the natives. In 1508 he established the first settlement at Caparra, a small village not far from the harbour of San Juan (museum). A year later the Spanish Crown appointed him the first Governor. In 1521, however, the settlement was moved to the present site of Old San Juan as the former site was declared unhealthy. In that year Ponce de León was mortally wounded in the conquest of Florida.

Because of Puerto Rico's excellent location at the gateway to Latin America, it played an important part in defending the Spanish empire against attacks from French, English and Dutch invaders until the Spanish-American war, when Spain ceded the island to the United States in 1898. The inhabitants became US citizens in 1917, with their own Senate and House of Delegates, and in 1948, for

1228 PEURTO RICO

the first time, they elected their own Governor, who is authorized to appoint his Cabinet and members of the island's Supreme Court. In 1952 Puerto Rico became a Commonwealth voluntarily associated with the United States.

Government The Governor (1984-88) is Sr Rafael Hernández Colón of the Popular Democratic Party, which favours the island's existing Commonwealth status. The other main party is the New Progressive Party, which favours Puerto Rico's full accession to the USA as the 51st state. Pro-independence groups receive little support. Puerto Ricans do not vote in US federal elections, nor do they pay federal taxes, when resident on the island.

The population is 3.3 million, of whom all speak Spanish and a large majority English; half of them live in urban areas. The country is a strange mixture of very new and very old, exhibiting the frank, open American way of life yet retaining the sheltered and more formal Spanish influences. The people are very friendly and hospitable but there is much crime, probably because of economic difficulties and unemployment.

San Juan Founded in 1510, San Juan, the capital (population about 850,000) spreads several km. along the N coast and also inland. The nucleus is Old San Juan, the old walled city on a tongue of land between the Atlantic and San Juan bay. It has a great deal of charm and character; the Institute of Culture restores and renovates old buildings, museums and places of particular beauty. The narrow streets of Old San Juan, some paved with small grey-blue blocks which were cast from the residues of iron furnaces in Spain and brought over as ships' ballast, are lined with colonial churches, houses and mansions, in a very good state of repair.

Some of the restored and interesting buildings to visit include La Fortaleza, the Governor's Palace, built between 1533 and 1540 as a fortress but greatly expanded in the 19th century (open 0900-1100, 1330-1615 Mon.-Fri.; tours every hour); the Cathedral, built in the 16th century but extensively restored in the 19th and 20th, in which the body of Juan Ponce de León rests in a marble tomb; the tiny Cristo Chapel with its silver altar, built after a young man competing in 1753 in a horse-race during the San Juan festival celebrations plunged with his horse over the precipice at that very spot; El Morro, built in 1591 to defend the entrance to the harbour (open daily 0800-1700, admission free, good guided tours at 1100 and 1430, US$0.50), the 11-hectare Fort San Cristóbal, completed in 1772 to support El Morro and to defend the landward side of the city, with its five independent units connected by tunnels and dry moats, rising 46 metres above the ocean (open daily 0800-1700, admission free, guided tours at 1100 and 1430, US$0.50); the Dominican Convent built in the early 16th century, later used as a headquarters by the US Army and now the office of the Institute of Culture, with a good art gallery; the 16th-century San José church, now being restored; the early 18th century Casa de los Contrafuertes, now containing specialized museums (open 0900-1700); the Casa Blanca, built in 1523 by the family of Ponce de León, who lived in it for 250 years until it became the residence of the Spanish and then the US military commander-in-chief, and is now a historical museum which is well worth a visit (open 0900-1700, except Mon.); the Alcaldía, or City Hall, built 1604-1789 (open Mon.-Fri. 0800-1615 except holidays); the Intendencia, formerly the Spanish colonial exchequer; the naval arsenal, now closed for restoration, which was the last place in Puerto Rico to be evacuated by the Spanish in 1898; and the Casa del Callejón, a restored 18th-century house containing two colonial museums, the architectural (open 0900-1700) and the Puerto Rican Family (open 0900-1200, 1300-1630, entry for adults US$0.25, for children free). The university campus has beautiful gardens and architecture.

Old San Juan is an excellent shopping area for goods from all over the world and particularly popular with visitors from Latin America and the United States. It is also the centre for night life unless one visits the hotels. Discotheques and dance clubs abound and Spanish flamenco dancing is a great attraction.

Museums Apart from those in historic buildings listed above, there are the Children's Museum in an 18th-century powder-house in El Morro grounds (Tues-Sun. 0900-1200, 1300-1700); the

PEURTO RICO

Pablo Casals Museum beside San José church, with Casals' cello and other memorabilia (Tues.-Sat. 0900-1200, 1300-1600, Sun; 1200-1700); the Museum of Puerto Rican Art (daily 0900-1700); the Casa del Libro (Mon.-Sat. 1100-1700); and the Museum of the Sea on Pier One (daily 0900-1700).

Other museums include a military museum at Fort San Jerónimo (open 0900-1700, 25 cents, free Sat.); the Ponce de León Museum at Caparra, Puerto Rico's first Spanish settlement, which has many exhibits from the period when the Taino Indians inhabited the township (open 0900-1700, closed Sun.); and the Adolfo de Hostos archaeological museum behind the Tapiá theatre on Plaza Colón (in the old public baths, open Tues.-Sat. 1000-1700, Sun. 1200-1900).

Directions Up until the 1950s tramcars ran between Río Piedras and Old San Juan along Avs. Ponce de León and Fernández Juncos. To this day directions are given by Paradas, or tram stops, so you have to find out where each one is.

Excursions A 10-cent ferry ride crosses every 15 mins. to Cataño where minibuses (45 cents) go direct to the gates of the Bacardi rum distillery. There are conducted tours around the plant every hour on the hour, travelling from one building to the next by a little open motor train.

The University of Puerto Rico at Río Piedras is in a lovely area. (Bus from Río Piedras to Fajardo for a train journey, US$1—see below.) The University Museum has archaeological and historical exhibitions, and also monthly art exhibitions.

On Sun. and holidays at 1430 and 1630 there are trips around the bay lasting 1½ hours. The boat passes the city wall, the San Juan gate and La Fortaleza. Another boat trip is around the Torrecilla Lagoon, which takes 2 hours and shows passengers the mangrove forests and the bird sanctuary. This runs daily, except Mon., at 1430.

The Interior Out of the metropolitan area "on the island" are a variety of excursions; as it is a small island it is possible to see forested mountains and desert-like areas in only a short time. However, because the public transport system is rather limited, it is difficult if not impossible to visit some places without your own car. The cool climate in the mountains has caused resort hotels to be built in several towns inland.

An interesting round trip through the eastern half of the island, starting E from San Juan, is as follows: San Juan-Río Piedras (there are *públicos* between these two places, US$1.85)-Fajardo-El Yunque-Vieques-Culebra-Humacao-Yabucoa-Guayama (again it seems that you can get from Humacao to Guayama by a series of *públicos*, the whole journey costing about US$2.50)-Cayey-Aibonito-Barranquitas-Bayamón-San Juan.

El Yunque (also called the Caribbean National Forest) is a tropical forest of 11,200 hectares with some 240 varieties of trees. The whole area is a bird sanctuary. Trails (very stony) to the various peaks: El Yunque (The Anvil) itself, Mount Britton, Los Picachos. In view of the heavy rainfall, another name for the forest is Rain Forest. Visitors need not worry unduly, as storms are usually brief and plenty of shelter is provided. (No buses through the national forests, unfortunately; El Yunque is reached via Route 3 from San Juan towards Fajardo, and then right on Route 191.) A narrow-gauge steam railway offers a different mode of travel from Fajardo to El Yunque on Sun., taking an hour for the return journey. Adults US$1.75 and children US$1.25. From Fajardo beach launches ply (US$2) to the comparatively unspoilt islands of Vieques and Culebra. One of the prettiest parts of Puerto Rico, which should be visited, lies S of Humacao, between Yabucoa and Guayama. Here are the villages of Patillas (*público* from Guayama, US$0.50) and Maunabo (*público* from Patillas, US$0.65 and from Yabucoa, US$0.65) where you can camp on the beach. There is a bar which sells good, cheap food.

A round trip through the western half of the island would take in Ponce, the second city (reached by motorway from San Juan via Caguas), Guánica, Parguera, San Germán, Boquerón, Mayagüez (the third city), Aguadilla, Quebradillas and Arecibo, with side trips to the Maricao State Forest and fish hatchery, the Río Abajo State Forest and Lake Dos Bocas (launch trips all day), the precolumbian ceremonial ball-park near Utuado (open 0900-1700, free), and the Arecibo observatory (open Sun. p.m., but there is no public transport, so you have to hitchhike from Arecibo).

Off the motorway which runs from San Juan to Ponce is Baños de Coamo, which was once the island's most fashionable resort. (Take Route 153 and then 546 from the motorway.) It has been redeveloped by Paradores Puertorriqueños

1230 **PEURTO RICO**

and still has a thermal bath. About 45 mins. SE of Coamo is Salinas, a fishing and farming centre. Several good seafood restaurants on the waterfront.

Ponce has a very fine art museum, donated by a foundation established by Luis A. Ferré (Governor 1968-72) in a modern building now famous. It contains a representative collection of European and American art of the last five centuries. (Open 1000-1200, 1300-1600, Mon. and Wed.-Fri., 1000-1600 Sat., 1000-1700 Sun. and holidays, closed Tues.; entry US$1 for adults, US$0.25 for children under 12.) The cathedral is also worth a look, and so is the polychromatic fire-station, built for a fair in 1883 and now used by the information office. *Público* to Guayama, US$2.50.

Going W from Ponce is Parguera, a fishing village, and nearby is Phosphorescent Bay, an area of phosphorescent water, occurring through a permanent population of minescent dinoflagellates, a tiny form of marine life, which produce sparks of chemical light when disturbed. A 1 hr. boat trip round the bay costs US$2, hourly departures, the experience is said to be rather disappointing, however. Further W is Guánica, the place where American troops first landed in the Spanish-American war. It has an old fort from which there are excellent views.

Mayagüez has fine botanical gardens: well worth visiting, free admission, open daily 0900-1600. The city also has an interesting zoo. *Públicos* leave from a modern terminal in Calle Peral. The tourist office is in the Municipalidad on Plaza Colón.

San Germán has much traditional charm; it was the second town to be founded on the island and has preserved its colonial atmosphere. The beautiful little Porta Coeli chapel on the plaza contains a small museum of religious art. (Normally open 0900-1200, 1400-1600 but reported closed for restoration.) A university town: it can be difficult to get cheap accommodation in term time.

As there is a large forest area, there are several excursions to various countryside resorts. The Maricao State Forest (Monte del Estado) is open from 0600 to 1800, and is a beautiful forest with magnificent views. Also the views are marvellous at the Toro Negro State Forest, open from 0800 to 1700, and at Río Abajo State Forest (open 0600-1800) where there is a swimming pool and various picnic spots. It is approached through splendid views of the karst hills and the Dos Bocas Lake. Free launch trips are offered on this lake at 0700, 1000, 1400 and 1700; they last two hours and are provided by the Public Works Department.

On the southern side of the W coast is **Boquerón** which has a good beach; there are cottages for rent and restaurants serving the local speciality, *ostiones*, a type of oyster. This is one of the cheapest spots on the island. Going N from here, through Mayagüez, you come to **Rincón**, on the westernmost point of the island. Here the mountains run down to the sea, and the scenery is spectacular. The town itself is unremarkable, but the nearby beaches are beautiful and the surfing is a major attraction. There are cottages to rent (about US$200 a month) and there is also accommodation in Rincón and the neighbouring village of Puntas (see below). There are also some small bars and restaurants, including *Danny's Café* in Rincón, a health-food restaurant in Puntas and a pizzeria just N of Puntas. Rincón can be reached by *público* from Mayagüez or (less frequent) from Aguadillas. Public transport is scarce at weekends.

Hotels in Puerto Rico Most of the large San Juan hotels are in Condado or Isla Verde and are built on modern lines, overlooking the sea, with swimming pools, night clubs, restaurants, shops and bars. The summer season runs from April 18 to December 15 and is somewhat cheaper than the winter season, for which we give rates where possible. A 6% tax is payable on rooms costing more than US$5 a day. A full list is given in the monthly tourist guide, *Qué Pasa*, published by the Puerto Rican Tourism Company, but listed below is a selection. To get value for money, it may be advisable to avoid the luxury hotels on the sea front. There is plenty of cheaper accommodation within walking distance of the beaches. *Caribbean Beach Club*, Loíza and Jupiter, Isla Verde, A; *Continental*, A; *Borinquén*, Fernández Juncos 725, Miramar, A; *Howard Johnson's Nabori Lodge*, 1369 Ashford, A; *Caribe Hilton*, Ocean Front, Puerta de Tierra, A, set in 17 acres of gardens, many sporting facilities; *Dutch Inn*, 55 Condado Av., Condado, A; *El San Juan*, Ocean Front, Isla Verde, A; *Du Pont Plaza*, 1309 Ashford Av., Condado, A; *Joffre*, Condado, C, swimming pool, a/c, 2nd floor particularly noisy, reasonable bar and restaurant; *Condado Holiday Inn*, 999 Ashford Ave., Condado, A; *The Duffy's*, 9 Isla Verde Road, popular for its pub-like bar, B; *El Palmar*, Route 187,

PEURTO RICO 1231

km. 0.3, Isla Verde, B, swimming pool. *La Casa Mathieson*, Uno Este 14, Isla Verde, near airport, B, swimming pool, cooking facilities, friendly, free transport to and from airport; *El Patio*, Tres Oeste 87, Bloque D-8, Villamar, swimming pool, use of kitchen, B, recommended; *Green Isle*, 36 Uno Este, Isla Verde, B, airport transport service. *Capri*, Fernández Juncos 902, basic and not very safe. In Old San Juan, try Calle Luna for cheap accommodation. One block on the corner of San Justo, where a room can be rented from US$25 a week. Enquire at the launderette next door. *El Convento* is a charming hotel with a Spanish atmosphere and the dining room is in the former chapel, A. Guest house at Calle San Francisco 260, US$50 per week; Tel.: 723-3973. Information from Joyería Sol, Tanca 207. Fan, cooking and washing facilities, friendly and helpful. Also in Old San Juan is *La Fortaleza*, Fortaleza 252, B and *Central*, Plaza de Armas, C. *Linda*, Calle Tetuán, D; *La Bahia Guesthouse*, Sol 320, most rooms rented by the month but empty rooms can sometimes be taken on a daily basis, E, clean, hot water, recommended (telephone first, 722-4050). *Buena Vista Guesthouse by the Sea*, Gral. Valle 2218, Sta. Teresita, English, French spoken, A-B with bath and kitchen, near beach, airport pickup for US$1. In Miramar, *Villa Firenze*, Avenida Miramar, C, much cheaper if rooms taken on a weekly basis, basic and not very clean, but runs good Italian restaurant; nearby, *El Toro*, C, good value, there is an airport limousine to *El Toro*. In Santurce, *Los Dos Hermanos*, clean, bathroom shared with one other room, D, cheaper weekly rates. *La Vista*, C; *Castilla*, Calle Cruz, C; several hotels around Plaza de Armas are in D range. There is a guesthouse on Calle Tetuán, near the bus station, which charges B per week, basic but share kitchen and bathroom.

In Ponce, *El Coche* and *Hotel Meliá* can be recommended (C and B respectively), also the *Holiday Inn Ponce*, A, where there are tennis courts, pools, and golf arrangements made. Cheaper hotels round main square. *Hotelito Argentino*, Calle Luna, D, basic; *Hospedaje Mi Hogar*, F, very basic; *Hotel Comercio*, F. *Sta. Bárbara Guesthouse*, Calle Cristina, E. To the W of Ponce, at Guánica, *Cycle Center Youth Hostel*, E, cooking facilities.

At Barranquitas the *Barranquitas Resort Hotel*, 700 metres above sea level, offers a quiet mountain setting with golf, tennis, horse-riding and swimming in a heated pool, B. In San Germán, *Oasis Hotel*, C; for room on top of Giuseppi's shop on main plaza, F. In Parguera, *Posada Porlamar*, a/c, kitchen facilities, B, good; several other hotels, C. On Vieques, *Sportsman's House* and *La Casa del Francés*, near Esperanza, B; *Ocean View Guesthouse*, B, balconies on seafront; *Carmen*, C, very clean; *Hotel Alvarez*, D, and *Depakos* also reasonable. On Culebra, *Seafarer's Inn*, A; *Posada La Hamaca*, C, well kept; *Doña Coral* has four rooms, C. On the E coast, *Palmas del Mar Hotel*, A, swimming pools and other sports. At Guayama, *Hotel Caribe*, E, clean; *Hotel España*, near square, F, noisy, dirty and very little privacy. At Arecibo, *Hotel El Cid*, D, about cheapest of all the hotels and guesthouses which are situated around the main square. At Mayagüez, *Hotel Colón*, Plaza Colón, E, no bath, ask for a quiet room. *Hospedaje San Vicente*, Calle San Vicente, F, very basic. At Rincón, *Villa Antonio*, C, and at Puntas, Carmen's grocery store has rooms, basic, F, cooking facilities. At Utuado, *Riverside*, D, bargain with the manager. There are seven of the new Paradores Puertorriqueños to put you up while touring: one is at Baños de Coamo (high season price B, recommended) and another is the *Hacienda Gripiñas*, which lies in the mountains near Juyuya, N of Ponce, C.

Restaurants All major hotels. In old San Juan: *Galería*, Fortaleza; for Puerto Rican cuisine, *La Fonda del Callejón*, Fortaleza 319; *Bacardi*; *La Mallorquina*, San Justo 207, recommended; *La Zaragozana*, San Francisco 356, some Spanish specialities, highly recommended; *La Posada de San Luis Rey*, Fortaleza 317; *La Danza*, corner of Cristo and Fortaleza La Bombanera, San Francisco (in the 200s). *Sole Mio*, Av. Ponce de León 655, good, cheap Italian food; on same street *El Miramar*, good and cheap. *Taza de Oro*, Luna 254, near San Justo. *Cecilia's Place*, Rosa St. Isla Verde. *Atena*, on corner of Luna and San Justo. In Mayagüez the *Cacique Restaurant* is recommended, as is the *Drive-In Restaurant*.

Nightclub Jazz at The Place, Calle Fortaleza in old San Juan, no admission charge, drinks about US$2.

Warning Female tourists should avoid the Condado beach areas at night if alone.

Sports All the hotels provide instruction and equipment for water skiing, snorkelling, boating and day trips to areas of aquatic interest. Fishing-boat charters are available. At Puerta de Tierra, near the Caribe Hilton, is the sports complex built for the 1979 Pan-American Games.

Swimming from most beaches is safe; the best beaches near San Juan are those at Isla Verde in front of the main hotels; Loquillo to the E of San Juan is less crowded and has a fine-sand beach from where there are good views of El Yunque. There are twelve *balneario* beaches round the island where lockers, showers and parking places are provided; there are also deserted beaches.

Boating Puerto Rico's coastline is protected in many places by coral reefs and cays which are fun to visit and explore. Sloops can be hired at US$35 a day, with crew, and hold six passengers.
There are three marinas at Fajardo, the Club Náutico at Miramar and another at Boca de Cangrejos in Isla Verde (both in San Juan) and one near Humacao.

Deep-sea Fishing is popular and more than 30 world records have been broken in Puerto Rican

1232 PEURTO RICO

waters, where blue and white marlin, sailfish, wahoo, dolphin, mackerel and tarpon, to mention a few, are a challenge to the angler.

Surfing The most popular beaches for surfing are the Pine Beach Grove in Isla Verde (San Juan) and Punta Higuero, Route 413 between Aguadilla and Rincón on the west coast, where several international surfing competitions have been held.

Golf The *Cerromar* and *Dorado Beach* hotels in Dorado have excellent 36-hole championship golf courses, there are several 18-hole courses, and in Ponce the *Hotel International Ponce* makes arrangements for guests to play at a nearby country club's 9-hole course.

Cockfighting The season is from November 1 to August 31. This sport is held at the new, air-conditioned Coliseo Galístico in Isla Verde, near the Holiday Inn. Wed. and Fri. 2030; Sat. and Sun. 1400. Admission from US$4 to US$10.

Racing El Comandante, Route 3, Km. 5.5, is one of the hemisphere's most beautiful race courses. Races are held all the year round (Wed., Fri. and Sun.). First race is at 1415. Wed. is ladies' day. Children under 12 not admitted at any time.

Riding Rancho Borinquén, at Carolina, near San Juan, rents horses at US$7 an hour, or US$15 for half-day.

Car Hire and Taxis Hertz Rent-A-Car System, Isla Verde International Airport; Lease Division Caribe Motors, 519 Fernández Juncos; Metro Taxicabs, Km. 3.3, Route 3, Isla Verde; Metropolitan Taxi Cabs, 165 Quisquella; National Car Rental System, 1102 Magdalena Ave.; University Taxi, Río Piedras. Budget have a bus service from the airport to their office. It is advisable to reserve a car in advance, through your airline, as they tend to be heavily booked. A small car may be hired for US$24 for 24 hrs., unlimited mileage (national driving licence preferred to international licence). The Rand McNally road map is recommended. All taxis are metered and charge 40 cents for initial charge (80 in San Juan) and 10 cents for every additional ⅓ km.; 25 cents is charged for a taxi called from home or business. Taxis may be hired at US$6 an hour unmetered. Taxi drivers sometimes try to ask more from tourists, so beware, insist that the meter is used, and avoid picking up a taxi anywhere near a cruise ship. There are also shared taxis (*públicos*) which have yellow number plates and run to all parts of the island. Most of them leave from Río Piedras. They do not usually operate after about 1900.

Airport There are airport limousines to a number of hotels. There is also a bus service (T1), US$0.25 to and from Plaza Colón and the main road outside the airport; note that people take precedence over luggage if the bus is full. A van, marked with AA logo, runs a free shuttle service to and from the main road. The taxi fare to old San Juan is US$20; the Airport Limousine Service (shared taxi) is US$2.75.

Buses *San Juan:* There is a city bus (*guagua*) service with a fixed charge of 25 cents. They have special routes against the normal direction of traffic and the bus lanes are marked by yellow and white lines. Bus stops are marked by yellow posts or signs marked "Parada de Guaguas". The central terminal is at Plaza Colón and there is another at the San Juan main post office (for *públicos*). No. 10 passes near all the main hotels; No. 1 to the University of Puerto Rico. (No change given; make sure you have right money.) City buses are not very frequent, however; they run to a 30-, or 45-minute schedule and many do not operate after 2200. *Interurban:* Puerto Rico Motor Coach company has daily scheduled services between San Juan, Arecibo (US$2.50), and Mayagüez (6 per day, US$8, 4 hour drive) through Caguas and Cayey or through Salinas. Hitchhiking is possible, but slow. From Old San Juan buses Nos. 1 and 2 run to the Río Piedras bus station. Walk to the Plaza Colón for other buses. *Público* to Ponce takes 7 hours (US$5-7).

The Economy Income per head is high at over US$4,700. Life expectancy is now 71 years, and illiteracy has been reduced to about 10%. Great economic progress has been made in the past thirty years, as a result of the "Operation Bootstrap" industrialization programme supported by the US and Puerto Rican governments, which was begun in 1948. Accordingly manufacturing has become the most important sector of the economy, in place of agriculture. The principal manufactures are textiles, clothing, electrical and electronic equipment and petrochemicals. Dairy and livestock production is one of the leading agricultural activities; others are the cultivation of sugar, tobacco, coffee, pineapples and coconut. Tourism is another key element in the economy. Despite the progress made to industrialize the country, the economy has suffered from the budget cuts made by the Reagan Administration (some 30% of all spending on gnp originates in Washington) although growth began to pick up in the mid-1980s. Inflation is low, averaging only 1.1% a year in 1982-86.

Information for Visitors

Airlines *International:* BWIA (Tel.: 791.1190); Iberia (Tel.: 725.5630); Avianca (Tel.: 724.6900); Liat (Tel.: 791.1190); Mexicana (Tel.: 725.5450); Dominicana (Tel.: 725.9393); Air France (Tel.: 724.0500); ALM (Tel.: 724.3013); British Caledonian; Capitol Airlines from Brussels. *Domestic:*

PEURTO RICO 1233

American Airlines (Tel.: 725.8484); Delta (Tel.: 724.5221); Eastern (Tel.: 725.3131); Pan American (Tel.: 767.5447); Capitol Airlines. Several local airlines operate services within Puerto Rico and between the islands, including Antilles Air Boats, Caribair, Prinair, Air Best, Culebra Aviation, Crownair, Air Indies, Aero Virgin Islands and Vieques Air Link, and they all have offices at the International Airport. There are cheap Eastern and American Airlines night flights between New York and San Juan, and hourly flights between San Juan and Ponce (US$15). One of the cheaper ways of getting from Mexico to the Caribbean is to fly from, say, Mérida to San Juan and there get a connection. Lacsa and Iberia fly between San Juan and San José (Costa Rica).

Shipping Jennie Tours has a service to the Virgin Islands (in season daily; out of season weekends only; US$25). From Fajardo Beach to Vieques and Culebra, US$2-3. There are no boats to other Caribbean destinations, apart from cruise ships.

Documents All non-US residents need a US visa. (Canadians may not need one: check.)

Tourist Information can be obtained from the Puerto Rico Tourist Bureau, P.O. Box 3968, San Juan (and at international airport); the Puerto Rico Tourism Company, Banco de Ponce Building, Hato Rey, San Juan (GPO Box BN, San Juan PR 00936), with offices in New York, Chicago, Los Angeles, Washington D.C., Atlanta, Toronto and Frankfurt/Main. The San Juan office is apparently closed quite frequently. The Caribbean Travel Service, Av. Ashford 1300, Condado, are happy to help.

Qué Pasa, a monthly guide for tourists published by the Tourism Company, can be obtained free from the tourist office. It is very helpful, and we wish here to acknowledge our debt to it.

Health Dengue fever is endemic; any "common cold" syndrome should be investigated. Avoid swimming in rivers: bilharzia may be present.

Food and Drink Two good local dishes are the mixed stew, *asopao*, and a splendid risotto known as *yuquiyú*, a mixture of rice, sausage, pineapple, peppers, etc., cooked in a pineapple husk. Black bean soup is another local speciality. Corona beer is good and many restaurants pride themselves on their *piñas coladas*. *Maví* is a drink fermented from the bark of a tree and sold in many snack-bars.

Currency United States currency.

Newspapers and Periodicals *San Juan Star* is the only daily English paper. There are two Spanish daily papers of note, *El Mundo* and *El Día*.

Public Holidays

New Year's Day
Jan. 6: Three Kings' Day
Jan. 11: De Hostos' Birthday
Feb. 22: Washington's Birthday
March 22: Emancipation Day
Good Friday
April 16: José de Diego's Birthday
May 30: Memorial Day
June 24: St. John the Baptist

July 4: Independence Day
July 17: Muñoz Rivera's Birthday
July 25: Constitution Day
July 27: Dr. José Celso Barbosa's Birthday
Sept. 1: Labour Day
Oct. 12 Columbus Day
Nov. 11: Veterans' Day
Nov. 19: Discovery of Puerto Rico
Nov. 25: Thanksgiving Day
Christmas Day

Churches Roman Catholic, Episcopal, Baptist, Seventh Day Adventist, Presbyterian, Lutheran, Christian Science and Union Church. There is also a Jewish community. At the Anglican-Episcopal cathedral in San Juan there are services in both Spanish and English.

Everything is closed on public holidays. One of the most important is June 24, though in fact the capital grinds to a halt the previous afternoon and everyone heads for the beach. Here there is loud *salsa* music and barbecues until midnight when everyone walks backwards into the sea to greet the Baptist and ensure good fortune.

Medical Services Government and private hospitals. Hospital charges are high.

Banks Banco de Ponce; Banco de San Juan; Banco Mercantil de Puerto Rico; and branches of US and foreign banks.

Postal Service Inside the new Post Office building in Hato Rey, on Av. Roosevelt, there is a separate counter for sales of special tourist stamps. In Old San Juan, the Post Office is in an attractive old rococo-style building.

1234 PEURTO RICO

Telephone Operated by Puerto Rico Telephone Co., state-owned. Overseas calls can be made from the former ITT office at Parada 11, Av. Ponce de León, Miramar and from the airport. Three minutes to New York, US$2.35 and to the UK, US$14.

Broadcasting Two radio stations have English programmes.

Tipping Fixed service charges are not included in bills and it is recommended that 15% is given to waiters, taxi drivers, etc.

We are most grateful to Dorothy Millgate for editorial work on this section, and to Herbert S. Levi (Buenos Aires) and Gustav-Adolf Yunge (Cologne), for some most valuable updating.

WANTED: MAPS
ARGENTINA – BRAZIL – MEXICO GUATEMALA – EL SALVADOR – THE CARIBBEAN ISLANDS

We would much appreciate receiving any surplus maps and diagrams, however rough, of towns and cities, walks, national parks and other interesting areas, to use as source material for the Handbook and other forthcoming titles.

The above regions are particularly needed but any maps of Latin America would be welcome.

The Editor Trade & Travel Publications Limited
5 Prince's Buildings, George Street,
Bath BA1 2ED. England

THE WEST INDIES

We wish to express our gratitude to Paul Millgate and Jane Canovan for updating the British and ex-British Caribbean sections; and also to Angela Allen (Swansea) and Paul Stearns (Derby), Jens Plahte (Aas, Norway), Hans Schwegler (Lucerne), and Gustav-Adolf Yunge (Cologne). Travellers whose contributions refer to one territory only will be mentioned at the end of the relevant subsection.

JAMAICA

JAMAICA lies some 90 miles south of Cuba and 455 miles west of Haiti. With an area of 4,411 square miles, it is the third largest island in the Antilles. It is 146 miles from E to W and 51 miles from N to S at its widest, bounded by the Caribbean. Like other West Indian Islands, it is an outcrop of a submerged mountain range. It is crossed by a range of mountains reaching 7,402 ft. at the Blue Mountain Peak in the E and descending towards the W, with a series of spurs and forested gullies running N and S. Most of the best beaches are on the N and W coasts, though there are some good bathing places on the S coast too.

Jamaica has magnificent scenery and a tropical climate freshened by sea breezes. The easily accessible hill and mountain resorts provide a more temperate climate, sunny but invigorating. In the mountains, the temperature can fall to as low as 7°C during the winter season. Temperatures on the coast average 27°C, rising occasionally to 32° in July and August and never falling below 20°. The humidity is fairly high. The best months are December to April. Rain falls intermittently from about May, with daily short tropical showers in September, October and November. Light summer clothing is needed all the year round, with a stole or sweater for cooler evenings.

It would be hard to find, in so small an area, a greater variety of tropical natural beauty. Jamaica has been called the Island of Springs, and the luxuriance of the vegetation is striking. This is also a land of humming-birds and butterflies; seacows and the Pedro seal are found in the island's waters. There are crocodiles, but no wild mammals apart from the hutia, or coney (a native of the island and now an endangered species), the mongoose and, in the mountains, wild pig. The main products are bauxite, sugar and rum, tobacco, bananas, spices, coffee, coconuts, and palm products.

History When Columbus discovered Jamaica in 1494 it was inhabited by peaceful Arawak Indians. Evidence collected by archaeologists suggests that the tribe had not lived on the island much before the year 1000. Under Spanish occupation, which began in 1509, however, the race died out and gradually African slaves were brought in to provide the labour force. In 1655 an English expeditionary force landed at Passage Fort and met with little resistance other than that offered by a small group of Spanish settlers and a larger number of African slaves who took refuge in the mountains. The Spaniards abandoned the island after about five years, but the slaves and their descendants, who became known as Maroons, waged war against the new colonists for 140 years. The Cockpit Country, or "Look Behind Country," where the Maroons hid is still the home of some of their descendants, and may be visited (see page 1277).

JAMAICA

After a short period of military rule, the colony was organized with an English-type constitution and a Legislative Council. The great sugar estates, which still today produce an important part of the island's wealth, were planted in the early days of English occupation when Jamaica also became the haunt of buccaneers and slave traders. In 1833 complete freedom was declared for slaves and modern Jamaica was born. On August 6, 1962, Jamaica became an independent member of the Commonwealth.

Most of the earlier historical landmarks have been destroyed by hurricanes and earthquakes. Very few traces, apart from place names, therefore remain of the Spanish occupation. In 1692 an earthquake destroyed Port Royal which—because of being the base for English buccaneers such as Henry Morgan— had become famed as the most splendid town in the West Indies. In 1907 another disastrous earthquake damaged much of Kingston. Some of the historic buildings which are still standing, including the 18th century churches at Port Royal, St. Ann's Bay and Montego Bay, are now in the care of the National Trust Commission. The Great Houses are a reminder of the British settlers; some have been converted into hotels or museums.

The People Over 90% of Jamaicans are of West African descent, the English settlers having followed the Spaniards in bringing in slaves from West Africa. Because of this, Ashanti words still figure very largely in the local dialect, which is known as Jamaica Talk. There are also Chinese, East Indians and Christian Arabs as well as British and other European minorities. The population is approximately 2.1m. Their religion is predominantly Protestant, but there is also a large Roman Catholic community. The Jewish, Moslem, Hindu and Bahai religions are also practised as is Rastafarianism, a cult based on belief in the divinity of the late Emperor of Ethiopia, Haile Selassie (Ras Tafari). There is considerable poverty on the island, which has created social problems and some tension. The Jamaicans have a "Meet the People" programme which enables visitors to meet Jamaicans on a one-to-one basis.

Administration Governor-General, Prime Minister, Cabinet, House of Representatives and Senate. All citizens over 18 are eligible for the vote. The judicial system is on English lines. There is a two-party system; the Prime Minister is Mr. Edward Seaga, of the conservative Jamaica Labour Party, who defeated the socialist People's National Party, led by Mr. Michael Manley, in elections in October 1980 and again in December 1983, when the PNP boycotted the elections because a promised revised electoral register had not been completed.

Kingston, the capital since 1870 and the island's commercial centre, has a population of over 700,000 (part of St. Andrew's Parish is included in the metropolitan area, which helps swell the figure). It has one of the largest and best natural harbours in the world. Following the earthquake of 1907 much of the lower part of the city was rebuilt in reinforced concrete, but since then efforts have been made to improve the area's appearance and now it rivals New Kingston, some 2 miles away, where many hotels and restaurants are situated. There is interesting shopping of all kinds; the Jamaica Crafts Market and many shops at W end of Port Royal Street have local crafts. Shopping hours in Kingston are: downtown—0930-1600 except Sat. (0930-1730) and Wed. (0930-1300); uptown—0900-1700 except Thurs. (0900-1300). There are various duty-free concessions for visitors.

Amusements in Kingston include cinemas (the Carib is the most luxurious), and concerts and plays at the Ward Theatre and Little Theatre (St. Andrew) where the local Repertory Company performs regularly. At the Institute of Jamaica, in East Street, visitors can see Arawak carvings, old almanacs, many other historical relics and natural history and art sections. Another museum is now at Devon House, a former "great house" at the corner of Trafalgar and Hope Roads, with an open-air restaurant next door. Among buildings of note are Gordon House, which dates from the mid-18th century and houses the Jamaican legislature. Visitors are allowed into the Strangers' Gallery but must be suitably dressed (jackets for men and dresses for women). There is also the early 18th century parish church where Admiral Benbow is buried. The Parish Church at St. Andrew dates from 1700; here, too, is King's House, the official residence of the Governor-General and, nearby, Jamaica House, the Prime Minister's impressive residence.

JAMAICA 1237

Warning There are many thieves and pickpockets. Always guard your belongings and never wander around on your own. It is thoroughly inadvisable for whites to enter many areas of Kingston (especially the Trenchtown district) at any time. Unfortunately buses drop you in Victoria Square in the uneasy downtown area.

Hotels Lists available from Tourist Board: addresses on page 1241. *Mrs Johnson's Guest House*, 3, Holborn Rd, D, with breakfast and bath, in a safe area, has been recommended. Also: *Ivor Guest House*, Ivor Drive, Jack's Hill P.A., St. Andrew, B (including full breakfast and transport to and from Kingston), lunches US$3.60, dinners US$9.10 by reservation only, Reg and Sue Aitken (805) 927 8861.

Restaurants The *Blue Mountain Inn* has an excellent night club and restaurant; *Herb's Steak House; The Mill; Meemee; Jayjays; Victoria Grill; Trafalgar Square; Dynasty* (Chinese); *Bistro*, Manor Park Plaza; *Paul's 104*, 104 Harbour Street; *Cathay* (Chinese). In Half Way Tree area: *La France Continental; Bird-in-hand; Oriental, House of Chen*, and *Golden Dragon* (Chinese); *Tip Top* (German), and *Swiss Chalet*. At the Norman Manley Airport is the *Horizon Room*, where meals are served until midnight. At Liguanea, *Golden Dragon* (also Chinese) in Hope Road. For the impecunious, meat patties may be had at US$0.25 each. Out of town there are the *Rodney Arms*, Port Henderson, and *Morgan's Harbour Hotel*, Port Royal.

Night Life Most hotels have dancing at weekends, and there is a good discothèque, Epiphany, at Spanish Court, New Kingston. Tourists are strongly advised not to try, unless they have Jamaican friends, to probe deeply into real Jamaican night life, at least in towns. For genuine local dances and songs, see the advertisements in the local press.

Airport The airport for Kingston is the Norman Manley (with good tourist office, offering much information, maps and up-to-date hotel and guest-house lists), 11 miles away, about 30 minutes' drive. Bus No. X97 leaves West Parade every half hour for the airport, US$0.35, but the service is infrequent, so allow for waiting time. Taxis generally charge US$12-20 for the same trip. There is no sales tax on air tickets purchased in Jamaica, but tourists arriving by air are not allowed, generally, to visit the island unless they have an onward ticket. New arrivals are always besieged by hustlers, so make a speedy exit. There is a US$5 departure tax. Taxi fare to the railway station is US$5.50.

Internal Transport There are several flights each day between Kingston and Montego Bay (US$27.50), they are operated by Trans-Jamaican Air Service, which also flies to Mandeville, Ocho Rios, Port Antonio and Negril. Domestic flights leave from Tinson Pen airfield, 2 miles from the centre of Kingston on Marcus Garvey Drive. There is a train running Mon. to Fri. (called "The Diesel") between Kingston and Montego Bay, leaves Kingston (via Spanish Town and Springfield) at 1540, arrives Montego Bay at 2115; it leaves Montego Bay at 0645 and reaches Kingston at 1250, US$5, 1st-class return (but check the times in advance: the service is unreliable). The line between Kingston and Port Antonio was damaged in a hurricane some years ago, and has yet to be repaired. Country buses are slow and sometimes dangerous, but are a cheap mode of transport. They run, for instance, to Irish Town, Mavis Bank, Gordon Town and Red Hills for US$0.40. Bus X20 goes from Victoria Square to Port Henderson. There are also minibuses which ply all the main routes and operate on a "colectivo" basis, leaving (only when full) from the Parade in Kingston. Colectivo to Ocho Rios costs US$2, and takes 2 hours. Crossroads and Half Way Tree are the other main bus stops. Bus travel in Kingston costs between US$0.20 and 0.30. To Mandeville costs about US$2.25 and to Montego Bay about US$8.50. The buses are invaded by touts as they approach the bus station. A free map of Kingston bus routes is available from Jamaica Omnibus Services Ltd., 80 King St. Travelling by bus is not safe after dark. Taxis display red PPV plates; in Kingston many of the smaller ones have meters. Best way of exploring interior: hire a car; the interior is well worth it. There are several car hire firms based at the airport and in and around Knutsford Blvd., including Martins, Hertz and Avis. Fiesta Car Rentals is at South Avenue. The cheapest cars are about US$210 per week with 500 miles free, plus US$45 insurance. Daily rates are about US$30 plus US$0.30 per mile.

Excursions Kingston is a convenient centre for excursions. A little over five miles away, at the foot of the mountains at Hope, are the Royal Botanical Gardens with a splendid collection of orchids and tropical trees and plants. Not very far away, at about 4,000 ft., is the former British military station of Newcastle, which today is used as a training centre for the Jamaican army. It is reached by a scenic road with over 300 bends (some hairpin) before it reaches a pass in the Blue Mountains. From there the road runs on through spectacular country to Buff Bay on the N coast. For Port Royal and Spanish Town, see below.

More easily accessible on the way to Blue Mountain peak is the Flamstead area, with a modern cottage at 4,000 ft., overlooking Kingston and Port Royal;

1238 **JAMAICA**

US$22 per day for four. Write to Donald Lindo, Waterloo Road, Devon Place, Half-Way Tree, Kingston 10.

For the athletic, a walk (or muleback ride for US$10) to the Blue Mountain Peak is recommended. A bus goes from Kingston to Mount Charles, from where it is a steep 4-mile walk to the Whitfield Hall Hostel, where you spend the night (US$4; US$0.70 per person for camping). Then start early a.m. for the peak, which will show you most of the E half of the island on a good day. You will need your own food, torch, sweater and rainproof. There are two huts on the peak which are quite adequate for overnight shelter though it is easily possible to walk down again in a day. The next day walk down to Mavis Bank and catch a bus back to Kingston. Information from the Tourist Board, or from Mr John Allgrove (with transport if needed), 8, Armon Jones Crescent, Kingston 6. Tel.: 927-0986. For the less ambitious, a car trip into the Blue Mountains, to Newcastle, Hollywell or Clydesdale, is an interesting experience, as is the bus trip to Mount Charles.

Bathing The swimming at Kingston is not very good. The sea at Gunboat beach, near the airport, is dirty. "Hellshire", south of Port Henderson, is a locals' favourite, but is difficult to reach.

Port Royal, the old naval base, lies across the harbour from Kingston, beyond the international airport, some 15 miles by excellent road. It can also be reached by boat from Victoria Pier; they leave every 2 hours, take 20 mins. and cost US$0.15. Nelson served here as a post-captain from 1779 to 1780 and commanded Fort Charles, key battery in the island's fortifications. Part of the ramparts, known as Nelson's Quarterdeck, still stands. St. Peter's Church, though the restoration is unfortunate, is of historic interest, as is the Historical Archaeological Museum (admission US$0.30). *Morgan's Harbour* at Port Royal is a favourite holiday centre, with water ski-ing, a salt water swimming pool, beach cabins, a good sea-food restaurant, and dancing to calypso bands. Boats may be hired for a picnic bathing lunch at Lime Cay or Port Henderson.

Spanish Town, the former capital, some 14 miles W of Kingston by road or rail, is historically the most interesting of Jamaica's towns. Its English-style architecture dates from the 18th century. Well worth seeing are the Spanish Cathedral, the oldest in the anglophone West Indies; the fine Georgian main square with, of special note, the ruins of the King's House built in 1762; a colonnade and statue commemorating Rodney's victory at the Battle of the Saints; the House of Assembly and the Court House. There is a museum with interesting relics of Jamaican history and accurate portrayal of life of the country people. Restaurant: *Miami*, Cumberland Road, near the market area. Food is delicious, especially the pumpkin soup.

Mandeville About 40 miles further W again, high in the heart of the island, lies Mandeville, a beautiful, peaceful upland town with perhaps the best climate in the island. It looks New England with its village green on either side of which stand a Georgian court house and the church. There is a 9-hole golf course at the Manchester Club. There are interesting excursions to Christiana (about 2,800 ft.); the Santa Cruz Mountains; the Bamboo Avenue at Lacovia, and Alligator Pond on the south coast. Further round the coast is Treasure Beach which, with its black sands, is probably one of the best beaches in the south.

The main road W from Mandeville joins the coast at Black River and runs from there through Bluefields - near which there are several pleasant coves for bathing—and Savanna-la-Mar before reaching Negril.

Negril, on a seven-mile stretch of pure white sand on the western end of the Island, is far less formal than other tourist spots. The beach is "topless", which is quite rare in non-French Caribbean islands. Drug pushers gather here. Watersports are a particular attraction and there are facilities for tennis and riding. In the West End of the village are many fine caves.

Banks Bank and *bureau de change* in the shopping centre in town. The larger hotels in Negril also convert at the official rate. Do *not* patronize money-changers as any transaction not made at officially-approved facilities is illegal, thus you will have no legal rights if you are cheated.

Hotels Seven of categories L and A. Lists from Tourist Board, page 1241. *Tigress Cottages*, in the West End, C, cooking facilities available; *Jenny's Cakes*,

JAMAICA 1239

US$35 a week for two, nice rooms, bath, fan and kitchen. *Hilltop View Cottages,* D, fully equipped. In the "redground" area *Mrs. Ruby's Tip Top Cottages,* D; further up the same road, Grandma, who is known by everybody, has rooms, C, not very clean; *Croton Grove,* on the road to the West End, charges the same. Accommodation is available at the Yacht Club, C, and rooms can also be rented at Sunrise and other houses. Houses can be rented for about US$60 a month. Locals living along the beach will often let you camp on their property. *The Yacht Club* and *Wharf Club* both have restaurants, the latter being cheaper. *Falcon's Nest,* opposite the Yacht club, C, very good, with use of kitchen, own bath. *Chris Donemar's Hotel,* D, friendly, and can sometimes arrange tours for a good price. Hotels to the West of centre are about 10-20 minutes' walk, and are in a better area for mixing with the locals. For entertainment try the *White Swan,* where the locals go. *The Dolphin,* next to *New Providence Guest House,* is good. *Peewee's Restaurant,* in the West End of Negril, has excellent seafood and other dishes at reasonable prices. *Erica's* restaurant and *The Tigress,* both near West End; latter is cheaper than many and good. *Rick's Café,* the "trendy" place to watch the sunset, but pricey with it. The native restaurant-food stalls are good and relatively cheap; the local patties are delicious. *Cool Runnings,* with a chef/owner, is also recommended.

Transport The orange minibuses are the cheapest way to travel around the town.

There are buses to Negril from both Savanna-la-Mar (about ¾ hr.) and Montego Bay. From Montego Bay the fare is about US$3.75; there are also taxi and colectivo services. From the Donald Sangster airport minibuses run to Negril; you must bargain with the driver to get the fare to US$5-7. From Negril it is 29 miles to **Lucea**, via Green Island. Lucea is a charming spot on the N coast where the *Tamarind Lodge* serves excellent Jamaican food. Between here and Montego Bay (bus, US$0.88) is Tryall, with one of the best golf courses on the island.

Montego Bay About 120 miles from Kingston by road or rail, situated on the NW coast, is Montego Bay, Jamaica's principal tourist centre. It has superb natural features, sunshine most of the year round, a beautiful coastline with miles of white sand and deep blue water never too cold for bathing (20°- 26°C average temperature) and gentle winds which make sailing a favourite sport. There are underwater coral gardens in a sea so clear that they can be seen without effort from glass-bottomed boats at the Doctor's Cave, which is also the social centre of beach life (there is an admission charge). Montego Bay caters also for the rich and sophisticated. Visitors enjoy the same duty-free concessions as in Kingston. Instruction in scuba diving costs US$7-20 per session. Cricket is the most popular spectator sport. (Test matches are played at Kingston.) Of interest to the sightseer are an old British fort and an 18th century church in Montego Bay, the Arawak rock carving at Kempshot and the bird sanctuary at Anchovy. Constant importuning in the town's streets is a major problem.

Hotels There are 33 hotels, guest houses and apartment hotels of our price-range C and above; lists from Tourist Board, page 1241. The *Coral Cliff* (a US$7 cab ride from the airport) is recommended, with a beautiful veranda, restaurant and friendly service, off season B including tax.

Night Clubs The Rum Barrel, the Cellar and the Reef Club. Sands and Disco Inferno discoteques.

Diesel Train to Kingston, and stations en route, Mon.-Fri., getting there in 5½ hours. Highly recommended, scenic journey, costing US$5 first class return.

Airport The Donald Sangster international airport is only 2 miles from the town centre. For those landing here, instead of Kingston, there is a transfer service by Martins minibus which takes 5 hrs. It is also possible to get to the Norman Manley airport, Kingston, by taking the minibus from the town centre to West Parade, Kingston, from where the airport buses leave; US$4.50, 3 hrs. The airport officials' general courtesy and helpfulness apparently leaves much to be desired.

From Montego Bay the **Cockpit Country** can be visited. The tourist office in Montego Bay will recommend the best villages to visit. They recommend you to take a bottle of rum for the local head man, to guarantee that your visit is welcomed. (The "great houses" of Rose Hall and Greenwood can also be visited from Montego Bay.) Take a minibus from Maroon Town (near Montego Bay),

1240 JAMAICA

although the last five miles to Accompong Town, "capital" of the Cockpit Country, must be done on foot. For a guided tour, contact Mrs Richards, Cockpit Country Tours, Casa Montego Hotel, Montego Bay (Tel.: 952-4150 ext. 284). For lodging in the Cockpit Country contact Mr Samuel Clarke of Sam Sharpe Teachers' Training College, Granville (Tel.: 952-4000). They own *Pemco Hotel* (swimming pool, a/c—you can stay there E or F when the teachers are on holiday in July, August and at Christmas).

Seaford Town, nearby, was settled by Germans in the early 19th century, and much of the local population is still recognizably white. Write Francis Friesen, Lamb's River Post Office.

Falmouth, a charming small town, is about 20 miles E of Montego Bay. It has a fine colonial court house (restored inside), a church, some 18th century houses, and Antonio's, a famous place to buy beach shirts. There is good fishing (tarpon and kingfish) at the mouth of the Martha Brae, near Falmouth, and no licence is required. It is possible to go rafting from Martha Brae village. Expert rafters guide the craft for the 1-hr. trip to the coast. Jamaica Swamp Safaris (a crocodile farm). Some 10 miles inland is the 18th century plantation guest-house of Good Hope amongst coconut palms: horses for hire and its own beach on the coast.

Continuing E along the coast is **Runaway Bay,** an attractive and friendly resort. It is named for the Spanish governor Ysasi, who left quickly for Cuba in a canoe when he saw the English coming. Only 5 miles away is Discovery Bay where Columbus made his first landing. From Runaway Bay, the Runaway Caves can be visited with a boat ride on the lake in the Green Grotto.

Hotels Six of categories L and A. Lists from Tourist Board, page 1241.

Ocho Rios On a bay sheltered by reefs and surrounded by coconut groves, sugar cane and fruit plantations, is Ocho Rios, which has become increasingly popular, with many cruise ships making a stop here. It is 64 miles E of Montego Bay, and claims some of the best beaches on the island. The scenery of the surrounding area is an added attraction. Most spectacular are the beauty spots of Fern Gully, a marvel of unspoilt tropical vegetation, Roaring River Falls, which has been partially exploited for hydroelectric power, and Dunn's River Falls, tumbling into the Caribbean with invigorating salt and fresh water bathing at its foot.

Historical attractions in the area include Sevilla Nueva, some 9 miles to the W, which was where the Spanish first settled in 1509. The ruins of the fort still remain. Tours may be made of the plantations at Prospect and Brimmer Hall.

Beautifully sited, near Ocho Rios, is the *Upton Country Club*: golf links, tennis riding and swimming. The *Lion's Den* is a friendly club frequented by Rastafarians; rooms available, good food, clean.

W of Ocho Rios is Mammee beach, which is beautiful and less crowded than Ocho Rios, though there is no shade there. There is much fashionable night life in and around Ocho Rios.

Hotels Twelve of categories L and A. Lists from Tourist Board, page 1241.

Port Antonio Dating back to the 16th century, Port Antonio is now a major banana port. At the same time it is one of the island's older tourist resorts, and has some fine, and relatively uncrowded, beaches. It lies on the NE coast at the foot of the island's highest mountains, and has a splendid yachting harbour and excellent fishing. The annual International Marlin Tournament, which is held in October, attracts anglers from all over the world. This part of the island is particularly rich in tropical plant life. Boston Bay, San San Beach and the Blue Lagoon (also known as Blue Hole) are notable beauty spots (bus to Boston Bay, US$0.40). The mountains which lie inland are a great attraction as are the Nonsuch Caves. Expert guides take tourists on bamboo rafts down the rapids of the Rio Grande, an exhilarating but safe experience. Each raft carries two passengers and the trip takes over 2 hrs. through wonderfully luxuriant vegetation. A driver will take your car from the point of departure to the point of arrival.

Between Boston Bay and Kingston there are several other beaches: Bamboo Cove is delightfully secluded (a cottage for up to 6 people can be rented there for

JAMAICA 1241

US$22 a day from Donald Lindo, Devon Place, Waterloo Road, Half Way Tree P.O., Kingston). There are also good beaches at Prospect and Pera.

Hotels, Port Antonio Five of categories L and A, and *De Montevin Lodge*, D, EP. *Scotia*, E. Ask for *Miss Ruby's House*. You live with the family and use their facilities. Lists from Tourist Board, see below.

The Economy

Once one of the more prosperous islands in the West Indies, Jamaica has been in recession since 1973. By the mid-1980s gnp per head was only 65% of the 1973 level, in real terms. At the core of Jamaica's economic difficulties lies the collapse of the vital bauxite mining and alumina refining industries. Bauxite and alumina export earnings provided 46% of all foreign exchange receipts and 28% of gdp in 1980 but by 1984 these shares had fallen to 33% and 20% respectively. Nevertheless, Jamaica is the world's third largest producer of bauxite after Australia and Guinea, despite its falling share from 18% of the market in 1974 to 11% in 1984, largely because of higher production costs. By comparison with mining, agriculture is a less important sector in terms of contribution to gdp, though it generates far more employment. Sugar is the main crop, and most important export item after bauxite and alumina. Other export crops include bananas, coffee, cocoa and citrus fruits. Tourism is now the leading foreign exchange earner and Jamaica is the third most populous destination in the Caribbean after the Bahamas and the Netherlands Antilles. Stopover arrivals grew by an annual average of 8% and cruise visitors by 14% in the first half of the 1980s.

The government turned to the IMF for support in 1976 and has since been a regular customer. In compliance with IMF agreements, the government had to reduce domestic demand commensurate with the fall in export earnings, by devaluing the currency and reducing the size of its fiscal deficits. Jamaica has rescheduled its debt to creditor governments and also to foreign commercial banks. The IMF is Jamaica's largest single creditor, while total official lending makes up about 78% of the total foreign debt of around US$4 bn.

	1961-70 (av)	1971-80 (av)	1981-85 (av)
Gdp growth (1980 prices)	4.7%	-0.8%	1.3% (a)
Inflation	3.9%	18.1%	16.6%
Exports (fob) US$m	244	668	740
Imports (fob) US$m	284	749	1,133
Current account balance US$m (cum)	-575	-1,691	-1,461

(a) = 1981-84 (av)

Information for Visitors

Jamaica Tourist Board Circulates detailed hotel lists. Offices at Sheraton Complex, Knutsford Blvd., P.O. Box 360, Kingston. *New York*: 866 Second Avenue, 10th Floor (2 Dag Hammarskjold Plaza), New York, N.Y. 10017; *Chicago*: Suite 1210, 36 South Wabash Avenue, Chicago, Illinois 60603; *Miami*: 1320 South Dixie Highway, Coral Gables, Fla. 33146; *Los Angeles*: 3440 Wilshire Blvd., Suite 1207, Los Angeles, Ca. 90010; *Montreal*: Mezzanine Level, 110 Sherbrooke St. West, Montreal, Québec H3A 1G9; *Toronto*: 2221 Yonge Street, Suite 507, Toronto, Ontario M4S 2B4; *London*: Jamaica House, 50 St. James St., London SW1A 1JT; *Frankfurt*: Goetheplatz 5, 6000 Frankfurt/Main 1, West Germany. The Jamaica Association of Villas and Apartments, Pineapple Place, Ocho Rios, has information on villas available for rent. Accommodation tax payable per room per day as follows: Category A US$12, Category B US$10, Category C US$8. **N.B.** All hotel bills must be paid in local currency.

Air Services Air Jamaica has services to Canada, West Germany, UK and USA. British Airways and Air Jamaica fly direct between London, and Kingston and Montego Bay. Air Canada flies to Jamaica as do American Airways, Cayman Airways, Cubana, Eastern Airlines and Lufthansa. BWIA and ALM serve the island from the southern and eastern Caribbean. There is a weekly Cubana flight to Havana on Fridays, US$166 return. Copa flies Panama City-Kingston-Santo Domingo (Dominican Republic) twice a week.

JAMAICA

Documents Canadian and US citizens do not need passports or visas for a stay of up to six months, if they reside in their own countries and have some proof of citizenship (e.g. a birth certificate, certified by the issuing authority with an embossed seal, together with a voter's registration card). Residents of Commonwealth countries need only a birth certificate for entry. Other nationalities require passports; but people of West European countries, Bangladesh, Israel, Mexico, Pakistan, and Turkey do not need visas. All visitors need an onward ticket. All visitors must pay a US$10 departure tax when leaving Jamaica. Immigration may insist on your having an address, prior to giving an entry stamp. Otherwise you will have to book a hotel room in the airport tourist office (friendly and helpful.).

Currency In May 1987 the official rate for the Jamaican dollar was J$5.48 = US$1.

Banks The Royal Bank of Jamaica, at Kingston (8 branches), Montego Bay and Mandeville; Bank of Montreal (Jamaica) 111-115 Harbour St., Kingston, and Half Way Tree branch; National Commercial Bank Jamaica Ltd., 77 King St., Kingston and branches all over the island; the same applies to the Bank of Nova Scotia Jamaica Ltd. The Canadian Imperial Bank of Commerce (main office at 121 Harbour St., Kingston) has branches in the main towns. Citibank, 63-67 Knutsford Blvd., Kingston. First National Bank of Chicago (Jamaica) Ltd. In Kingston banking hours are 0900-1400 Mon.-Thurs., 0900-1200 and 1430-1700 Fri. Elsewhere 0900-1400, Mon., Tues., Wed., and Fri., and 0900-1200 Thurs. and Sat.

Cables International cable, telephone and telex services: Jamaica International Telecommunications Ltd., 15 North St., Kingston, and 36 North St., Montego Bay.

Royal Mail Lines Agency Grace Kennedy & Co. (Shipping) Ltd., New Port West, PO Box 86. It is extremely difficult to book a passage by ship to other Caribbean islands.

Electric Current 110 volts, 50 cycles, A.C.

Tipping Hotel staff, waiters at restaurants, barmen, taxi drivers, cloakroom attendants, hairdressers get 10-15% of the bill. In places where the bill already includes a service charge, it appears that personal tips are nonetheless expected.

Taxis All taxis have red PPV (Public Passenger Vehicle) plates in addition to the normal registration plates. In Kingston many of the smaller taxis have meters; elsewhere they do not. Those that do not should carry a schedule of rates but in any case it is wise to agree the fare with the driver before taking the taxi.

Food Local dishes, fragrant and spicy, are usually served with rice. There are many unusual and delicious vegetables and fruits such as sweetsop, soursop and sapodilla. National specialities include codfish ("stamp-and-go" are crisp pancakes made with salt cod) and ackee; curried goat; and jerked pork, highly spiced pork which has been cooked in the earth covered by wood and burning coals.

We are grateful for new information to Mrs Gerry Hardy (Alexandria, Va.), Wayne Hedenschoug (Springfield, Ill.), Douglas L. Saunders (Berkeley, Ca.), and various travellers whose names appear on page 1235.

BARBADOS

BARBADOS, the most easterly of the islands, has the pleasantest climate in the West Indies. Its charm and natural attractions have made it one of the most popular holiday resorts in the world. Barbados is 1,200 miles from Miami, 2,100 from New York, and 3,456 from London. It has only 166 square miles and lies 100 miles off-course from the main curve of the Windward Islands, which perhaps explains why it was missed by Columbus on his second voyage of discovery. It was missed by others too, including the Caribs, and when discovered had no native inhabitants. Its name is thought to derive from the word *barbudos*, the name the Portuguese gave to the bearded fig trees they found when they landed there briefly in 1536. It was the British who colonized the island and it remained under the British Crown from 1625 until, after a period of internal self government, Barbados achieved independence within the Commonwealth in November 1966. The Prime Minister is Errol Barrow of the Democratic Labour Party, which won 24 out of the 27 seats at the general election on May 28, 1986.

Although the island is so small (its greatest length is 21 miles and its extreme width only 14) there are nearly 140 hotels and guest houses, many with dancing and first-class floor shows. (Lists from Board of Tourism: for addresses see page 1245.) Tourism is of major importance, especially on the S coast. The E coast is beautiful and as yet relatively untouched by tourism. Inland, too, the island is still very quiet.

The People The population is about 300,000, of whom over 70% are black. Europeans account for about 8%. Annual rate of growth 2%. With 1,557 inhabitants per sq. mile, the island is one of the most densely populated in the world, part of the reason being the abundance of fresh water; the island covers a huge underground lake. There is little illiteracy.

Bridgetown, the capital, with a population of over 102,000, is on Carlisle Bay, an open roadstead exposed to the wind from the S and the W, but there is an inner harbour protected by the Mole Head. Larger ships land passengers and discharge and load cargo in the new deep-water harbour to the NW of Carlisle Bay and immediately W of Bridgetown. The old part of the town with its wooden houses is in marked contrast to the newer Bridgetown and is well worth exploring.

The main street is Broad Street, which leads into Independence Square, with the chief public buildings, Nelson's statue, 50 years older than the one in London, and nearby, the Cathedral which is worth a visit. The straw market is very interesting. Buses run at frequent intervals from Fairchild Street and Lower Green to the out-districts. The information bureaux at the Deepwater Harbour and at Grantley Adams Airport are helpful about places of interest, hotels, taxi fares, etc. The local daily newspaper, *The Nation* (*Sunday Sun* on Suns.), contains useful information on current entertainment.

Museum Barbados Museum, off Garrison Savannah, in old prison dating from 1817. Entry B$4, open 0900-1800 Mon.-Sat.

Excursions Places well worth a visit include Hackleton's Cliff (997 ft.) where there is a view of the eastern hills and the lovely beaches of Bathsheba. Also worthwhile for its view is St. John's Church (824 ft.). Codrington College (affiliated to the University of the West Indies) is interesting and from it one may walk up the E coast, along the abandoned railway track to the Atlantis Hotel beneath the Andromeda Gardens (admission B$4). Buses leave Pelican Village near the deepwater dock for Welchman Hall Gulley, an old plantation house with a tropical jungle garden (admission charge B$3). This, together with the Morgan Lewis Windmill (to which the bus goes on) belongs to the Barbados National Trust and the surrounding countryside is the most beautiful on the island. Nearby is Harrison's Cave, opened to the public in 1981. A 45 min. tour of the huge limestone cavern, riding on a special tram and trailer, should cost around B$10. Open 0900 to

1244 BARBADOS

1600 daily. Long wait if booking not made in advance (Tel.: 26048). At Farley Hill (B$4) there are the remains of an old plantation house. At Cherry Tree Hill, monkeys can be seen playing in the mahogany trees in the evening. Also worth a visit is the Christchurch Parish Church with its eerie Chase vault renowned for supernatural occurrences. At Sam Lord's Castle there are a beautiful garden and beach. Admission to the Animal Flower Garden, B$4. The Flower Forest (Richmond, St. Joseph, opened in December 1983), has 50 acres of flowering shrubs and fruit trees.

Plantation Houses Three houses can be visited: St Nicholas' Abbey, mid 17th cent., Mon.-Fri., 1000-1530, B$5; Sunbury House and Museum, Highway 5, St. Philip, 17th cent., carriage collection, Mon.-Fri., 1000-1600, B$6; Villa Nova (1834), Mon.-Fri., 1000-1600, B$4. Others are not normally open, but the Barbados National Trust has a programme of visits.

Visitors can see the manufacture of sugar at the larger factories, such as Searles, Foursquare, Bulkeley, or Corrington. A noted Barbadian rum is made at Mount Gay, parish of St. Lucy, and at two distilleries near Bridgetown.

To the SE of Bridgetown is **Oistins**, the principal fishing town. Here snapper, dolphin, kingfish and flying fish are the main delicacies. Fish Festival in April.

Climate Temperatures average 24° to 30°C. They rarely exceed 32° or drop below 20°. The island is cooled by NE trade winds which are strongest on the Atlantic coast. June to November is the rainy season, with heavy, short downfalls which soon drain away in the porous coral.

Local Crafts Pelican Village crafts centre on Princess Alice Highway; nearby is the Handicraft Division of the Industrial Development Corp. Best craft shops are at *Sandpiper Hotel, Hilton, Skyway Plaza* and *Sam Lord's Castle*.

Bookshops Advocate Bookshop, 34 Broad St., Bridgetown.

Sports and Entertainment Water sports, as well as swimming, surfing (on the E coast, though the sea can be dangerous), water skiing, skin-diving and snorkelling, deep-sea fishing, and sailing. Sea life among the coral reefs can be viewed from glass bottomed boats. Spear-fishing equipment can be bought (or broken parts replaced) at Fisherman's Corner, Lower Wharf, Carenage, or De Costa, Broad Street, Bridgetown. The *Jolly Roger Pirate Ship* offers 3-4 hr. cruises for B$40; the price includes a barbecue dinner. Camping on the beaches is *not* allowed. Sea urchins are a danger on the beaches and in the water.

Golf: The Rockley Golf and Country Club has an excellent 18-hole course and a splendid club house, to which visitors are cordially invited. Special subscription rates per day or per week. The Sandy Lane Golf Club, 7 miles from Bridgetown on the west coast, has a splendidly landscaped 9-hole course of 3,400 yards. There is a golf course at Durrants Golf and Country Club, Christ Church.

There are good tennis courts at the Yacht Club, Sandy Lane, Sam Lord's, Garrison Savannah, Sunset Crest and the Government Courts, Deepwater Harbour. There are 4 squash courts at the Rockley Country Club and 2 at Marine House, the home of the Barbados Squash Club. Riding can be arranged, through the hotels.

First class cricket matches are played at Kingston Oval from January to April (Shell Shield). Inter-club cricket is played from June to November. There is polo at the Garrison Savannah. Race meetings on some Sats., Jan.-April and Aug.-Nov., on Garrison Savannah.

Cinemas includes ordinary and 2 drive-ins. The night life is colourful and lively. The leading hotels provide a variety of first-class entertainment with steelbands, calypsos, flaming limbo dancers and floorshows. Each hotel has its special night.

Roads throughout the island are good and self-drive cars are available at B$315 a week (B$275 for Mini-Mokes); scooters at B$150 a week (B$50 deposit). Petrol B$1.15 a litre. Drive on the left. Most driving licences are valid in Barbados, but you must also acquire a Barbados permit, cost B$20. Bicycles can be hired on Garrison Savannah, where *Brigade House Hotel* used to be; the charge is about B$10 a day. Taxis are plentiful and charge about 90c per mile. Official taxi rates from the airport are posted in the customs hall. There is a speed limit in Bridgetown and Speightstown (on the west coast) of 20 mph; elsewhere 30 mph (not, apparently, that buses pay much heed to it!). The bus service is excellent but always crowded; there is a standard fare of 75c.

Economy Barbados is highly dependent on tourism, which accounts for 10% of gdp, and about 30% of all foreign exchange receipts. Between 1982 and 1985 US-source arrivals increased by 96% while visitors from Europe declined, resulting in falling hotel occupancy and lengths of average stay, as US tourists prefer to take only long weekends in the Caribbean. Barbados is actively encouraging European and up-market tourism to boost revenues. Sugar has traditionally been the mainstay of the economy, with rum and molasses being produced as by-products, but especially with the fall in world prices, there has been a tendency to diversify into other crops. Manufacturing has been encouraged in order to reduce the island's dependence on tourism and

BARBADOS 1245

agriculture, and employs about 13% of the labour force; exports of manufactures are now second to tourism for their foreign-exchange importance. Barbados produces about 700,000 barrels of oil a year, enough to provide 57% of its oil demand and hopes to be self-sufficient by the end of the century. Income per head was US$4,700 in 1985. The cost of living rose by an average of 7.7% a year in 1981-85.

	1966-70 (av)	1971-80 (av)	1981-85 (av)
Exports (fob) US$m	34	87	246
Imports (fob) US$m	82	239	540
Current account balance US$m (cum)	-127	-427	-148

Information for Visitors

Barbados Board of Tourism, Marine House, Hastings, Christ Church (P.O. Box 242), Bridgetown (Tel.: 72623/4), detailed hotel lists, very helpful; 6 Upper Belgrave Street, London, SWIX 8AZ (01-235 4607); 20 Queen Street West, Suite 1508, Toronto M5H 3R3 (416-979-2137); 666 Sherbrooke St. West, Suite 1105, Montreal H3A 1E7 (514-288-1200); 5920 Macleod Trail South, Suite 307, Calgary, Alberta (403-255-7585); 3440 Wilshire Blvd., Suite 1215, Los Angeles, CA; 199 South Knowles Ave., Winterpark, FL 32789 (305-645-4145); 800 Second Avenue, New York 10017 (212-986-6516). Steinweg 5, 6000 Frankfurt/Main (28-4451); Quinta Chapaleta, 9A Transversal entre 2a y 3a Avenidas, Altamira, Caracas (33-1518).

Hotels Barbados has a wide range of luxury, first-class and other relatively cheaper hotels, guest houses and furnished apartments. On the whole accommodation is more expensive than in many other Caribbean islands. The peak tourist season is from 16 December to 15 April, when rates are much higher than the rest of the year. Rooms can be booked from the tourist office at the airport. Electric current is 110 volts AC. Board of Tourism has detailed lists.

YMCA in Bridgetown has occasional vacancies; C for full board or E for bed and breakfast, not very clean. *Shonlan Guesthouse*, C, without breakfast. *Salvation Army Men's Hostel*, Bridgetown, F. The Youth Hostel, Worthing, E each in a double room or dormitory, full (vegetarian) board; alternatively, tents can be hired for US$5.50 each, which also includes the price of 2 meals; campers with their own tents and cooking facilities are charged US$3.50 per day; the hostel (which is on the bus route from the airport to Bridgetown and near the beach) incorporates an international language school as well as a vegetarian restaurant; yoga classes are free, but all guests are expected to put in 20 mins. work a day around the hostel and its garden. There are good supermarkets nearby. Note: An 8% sales tax is levied on all hotel and restaurant charges. Most hotels and restaurants also add an extra 10% for service.

Restaurants There are excellent independently-run restaurants, as well as good eating places at the leading hotels. As well as evening barbecues, many hotels offer sumptuous luncheon buffets: *Sam Lord's Castle*, *Sandy Lane*, *Paradise Beach*, *Atlantis* and the *Edgewater* are well known for their Sunday buffets. Visitors can sample local dishes, tropical fruits, vegetables and seafoods at many restaurants. Good places include: *Greensleeves* and *La Cage aux Folles*, both international cuisine, reckoned the two best; *La Bonne Auberge* (French specialities), *Bagatelle Great House* (international cusine), *Dolly's* (many local dishes including flying fish, good atmosphere); *Luigi's* (Italian food), the *Steak House*, the *Pelican*, in Pelican Village (lunch from US$1.50); *Ship Inn* at Worthing, limited but good, cheap menu. *Hotel School*, in same building as Tourist Board, US$5.50 for full lunch, 12-1330 Tues.-Fri.; *The Office*, Broad Street, Bridgetown, light lunches; *Hotel Abbeville* (Rockley) recommended for dinner; *Flying Fish*, corner of Fairchild St. and Bridge St., also has discotheque.

Food Fish is excellent, including flying-fish, dorado, kingfish, dolphin; also West Indian specialities such as cou-cou, blackpudding and souse, jug-jug, pepper-pot, sucking-pig. The usual tropical fruits. Try mauby, a soft drink made from the bark of a tree.

Beaches The Sandy Lane Hotel beach at St James is good. Small sailing boats can be hired for US$7 an hr. and glass-bottomed boats for about US$3.50 p.p. per hr. One beach which is well worth a visit is at Crane (take the Sam Lord's Castle bus) where there is excellent surfing. Just N of Speightstown is another good beach which is relatively uncrowded.

Documents You must have a return ticket to your country of origin, or an onward ticket to another destination. Sometimes people with backpacks have trouble with customs officials.

Passports are not required by nationals of Canada and the USA who have proof of identity, nor by residents of other British and ex-British Caribbean islands holding permits to travel. Passports, but not visas, are required by nationals of West European countries, Commonwealth countries, Bangladesh, Israel, Peru, Suriname, Turkey and Venezuela. Extensions to the visas given on arrival cost B$20, so make sure you ask for a long enough period when you first arrive.

BARBADOS

Customs Duty-free import: 200 cigarettes or ½ lb. of other tobacco products, one quart of alcoholic drinks and 150 grams of perfume.

Travel Agents Safari Tours, on corner of St. George and Prince Alfred Street, Bridgetown (Tel.: 427-5100), arrange combined land/sea tour of Barbados and tours to other Caribbean islands.

Festivals Holetown (3 days in Feb.), anniversary of first settlers; Crop Over (2 wks. June-July) with costume parade first Mon. in July; National Festival of Creative Arts (Oct.-Nov.) culminating in Independence Day celebrations on Nov. 30.

International Telecommunications Telegraph, telephone and telex services. Cable and Wireless (W.I.) Ltd., Gardiner Austin Building, Lower Broad St., Bridgetown. (Tel.: 63178—open 0700-1900 Mon.-Fri. and 0700-1300 Sat.) and St. Lawrence Gap, Christ Church (Tel.: 87187—acceptance of telegrams 24 hrs. a day) and Wilder, St. Michael (Tel.: 75200—open 24 hrs.). Cables can also be handed in at hotel desks. The telephone service is good and overseas calls can be dialled direct from most telephones on the island. Postal services are inexpensive and efficient. An airmail letter to Europe costs B$0.50, to USA B$0.45. Postcards to Europe are B$0.35 and to USA B$0.25.

Currency The Barbados dollar is at a fixed parity with the US dollar, of B$2 = US$1. Export of local and foreign currencies limited up to the amounts declared on arrival. Visa cards are widely accepted.

Banks Barclays Bank International, Royal Bank of Canada, Canadian Imperial Bank of Commerce, Bank of Nova Scotia, Bank of America, Chase Manhattan Bank, Citibank. Main offices in Bridgetown, but offices also in Hastings, Worthing, Holetown and Speightstown. Hours are 0800-1300 Mon.-Fri., and 1500-1700 on Fri.

Air Services *From Europe:* British Airways (5 a week) and BWIA (weekly) from London. *From North America:* From New York by American Airlines, Eastern Airlines, or BWIA; from Miami (daily) by BWIA and Eastern Airlines; from Toronto and Montreal by Air Canada or BWIA (up to 12 weekly). *Within Caribbean:* Links with many points by Liat (e.g. to St. Vincent, US$108 (3 flights daily) return and to Grenada, US$69 return. One way tickets are not sold.) BWIA (return to Trinidad costs US$47). British Airways, Eastern Airlines (San Juan-St. Maarten-Port of Spain, daily), Cubana (Havana-Kingston-Port of Spain-Georgetown, weekly), Air Jamaica (Kingston), Air Martinique (Martinique, with connections to the Windwards), and Viasa (Caracas and Port of Spain, four times weekly). Viasa is the only airline which will supply the required Venezuelan tourist card; the only other source is the Venezuelan embassy. BWIA flies to Caracas via Port-of-Spain where you can stop off at no extra charge. It also has a direct service to Tobago.

There are no left-luggage facilities at the airport. There is an airport tax of B$6 on flights within the West Indies and of B$16 to other places. There are taxis from the airport to Bridgetown (B$14), but it is much cheaper to walk to the main road and catch a bus (12A) from there. Many hotels are situated on this road.

Shipping Geest Industries have a weekly service of banana boats between Barry, Wales, or Preston, Lancs. and Barbados. The boats call at the Windward Islands and carry between 8 and 16 passengers. It is possible, though not easy, to get a passage to other islands on cargo boats. The *MV Perica* (Tel.: 65068) sails to St. Vincent, the *MV Hassell* (Tel.: 64047) to St. Lucia and Dominica. The *Stella* sails to St. Lucia and Dominica. Departure times can be checked at the Delice Joseph shipping agency. A ticket out of these places is required before you can buy the boat ticket, which is negotiable but costs about 75% of the airfare. Information about cargo boats going to Trinidad or the mainland of South America can be obtained from the customs house, shipping agents and harbour staff. However it is not easy to get a berth on one and if you succeed you may have to pay more than it costs to fly; it is also advisable to travel in numbers. You can advertise for crewing duties and other ways of getting trips at the Boat House on Highway 7 (Fore Street).

British High Commission, Barclays Bank Building, Roebuck Street, Bridgetown.

Embassy of the USA, Canadian Imperial Bank of Commerce Building, Broad Street, Bridgetown.

West German Consulate, 37 Roebuck Street, Bridgetown (Tel.: 61837).

We are most grateful to various travellers whose names appear in the main West Indies section, for helpful new information.

TRINIDAD AND TOBAGO

Trinidad, the most southerly of the Caribbean islands, lying only seven miles off the Venezuelan coast, is one of the most colourful of the West Indian islands. It is an island of 1,864 square miles, traversed by two ranges of hills, the northern and southern ranges, running roughly east and west, and a third, the central range, running diagonally across the island. Apart from small areas in the northern range, of which the main peaks are Cerro del Aripo (3,083 feet) and El Tucuche (3,072 feet), all the land is below 1,000 feet.

Tobago (116 square miles) is only 21 miles by sea to the North-East. It is 26 miles long and only 9 miles wide, shaped like a cigar with a central 18-mile ridge of hills in the North (highest point 1,890 feet) running parallel with the coast. The coast itself is broken by any number of inlets and sheltered beaches. These north-eastern hills are of volcanic origin; the South-West is flat or undulating and coralline.

Climate The climate on the islands is tropical, but, thanks to the trade winds, rarely excessively hot. Temperatures vary between 21° and 37°C, the coolest time being from December to April. There is a dry season from January to mid-May and a wet season from June to November, with a short break in September, but the rain falls in heavy showers and is rarely prolonged. Humidity is fairly high, however.

History The aboriginal name for the island of Trinidad was Iere (Land of the Humming Bird). Columbus landed there on his third voyage in 1498 and named the island Trinidad, supposedly after a "trinity" of prominent hilltops. The first Spanish settlement was established under Don Antonio Sedeño in 1532. In 1595 Sir Walter Raleigh destroyed the newly-founded Spanish town of San José (now St. Joseph). In 1797, when Spain was an ally of France against Britain, a British expedition resulted in the surrender of the island. In 1802 Trinidad was ceded to the British Crown by the Treaty of Amiens.

Tobago is thought to have been discovered by Columbus in 1498, when it was occupied by Caribs. In 1641 James, Duke of Courland (in the Baltic), obtained a grant of the island from Charles I and in 1642 a number of Courlanders settled on the north side. In 1658 the Courlanders were overpowered by the Dutch, who remained in possession of the island until 1662. In this year Cornelius Lampsius procured Letters Patent from Louis XIV creating him the Baron of Tobago under the crown of France. After being occupied for short periods by the Dutch and the French, Tobago was ceded by France to Britain in 1763 under the Treaty of Paris. But it was not until 1802, after further invasions by the French and subsequent recapture by the British, that it was finally ceded to Britain, becoming a Crown Colony in 1877.

In 1888 Tobago was amalgamated politically with Trinidad. Trinidad and Tobago achieved independence on August 31, 1962 and became a republic within the Commonwealth on August 1, 1976.

Government The National Alliance for Reconstruction (NAR), led by Mr A.N.R. Robinson, won a 33 seats to 3 victory in the general election of December 15, 1986. The vanquished People's National Movement had held power continuously for 30 years. The size of the NAR victory, which took many observers by surprise, was due to the breaking down of traditional voting patterns on racial lines by black former PNM supporters.

1248 TRINIDAD AND TOBAGO

The People Trinidad has one of the world's most cosmopolitan populations. The emancipation of the slaves in 1834 and the adoption of free trade by Britain in 1846 resulted in far-reaching social and economic changes. To meet labour shortages over 150,000 immigrants were encouraged to settle from India, China and Madeira. Of today's population of approximately 1,176,000, about 45% are black and 35% East Indian. French and Spanish influences dominated for a long time—Catholicism is still strong— but gradually the English language and institutions prevailed and to-day the great variety of peoples has become a fairly harmonious entity, despite some tension betwen blacks and those of East Indian descent. Spanish is still spoken in small pockets in the northern mountains and French patois here and there. Tobago's population, mainly black, numbers about 50,000. The people of both islands are, as a rule, very friendly but the country's economic problems may be starting to scratch at old scars of anti-white ill-feeling, especially in Trinidad.

Port of Spain, with a population of 350,000, lies on a gently sloping plain between the Gulf of Paria and the foothills of the Northern Range. The city has a pleasant atmosphere, but the streets and buildings are not well maintained. The streets are mostly at right-angles to one another and the buildings are of fretwork wooden architecture, interspersed with modern office towers. Within easy reach of the port (King's Wharf and its extension) are many of the main buildings of interest—the Red House, which contains the House of Representatives, the Senate and various government departments; the General Post Office; the fine Anglican Cathedral Church of the Holy Trinity, with an elaborate hammer-beam roof festooned with carvings. These buildings are around Woodford Square, named after Sir Ralph Woodford; the Cathedral was built during his governorship (1813-28) and contains a very fine monument to him. On the opposite side of the Square to the Cathedral is the Town Hall, with a fine relief sculpture on the front. The Square is Trinidad's equivalent to Speaker's Corner in London's Hyde Park; in fact it played an important part in Trinidad's path to independence, as it was here that the late Dr. Eric Williams, who was later Prime Minister for 25 years, gave a series of open-air lectures teaching the people to prepare for the future; it became known as "The University of Woodford Square". On the waterfront is the San Andres Fort built about 1785 to protect the harbour.

In Independence Square is the Roman Catholic Cathedral, built in 1832, and the modern Textel and Salvatori buildings. Behind the Cathedral is Columbus Square, with a statue of the island's discoverer. On Ethel Street is a large new Hindu temple.

To the north of the city are the Botanic Gardens, founded in 1818 by Sir Ralph Woodford. There is an amazing variety of tropical and sub-tropical plants from South-East Asia and South America, as well as indigenous trees and shrubs.

Adjoining the Gardens is the small Emperor Valley Zoo, which specializes in animals living wild on the island, but is rather ill-kept. Also next to the Gardens is the presidential residence—a colonial style building in an "L" shape in honour of Governor James Robert Longden. There are several other Victorian-colonial mansions along the seaward side of Queen's Park Savannah, north of the city, and the Anglican Church of All Saints here is worth a visit. The Savannah itself has many playing fields and a racecourse with grandstands. Just off the Savannah is Queen's Hall, where concerts and other entertainments are given.

Before leaving this area, pay a visit to the Lookout, 300 feet high, which gives superb views across the city to the Gulf of Paria.

Excursions There are pleasant drives in the hills around with attractive views of city, sea, and mountain: by Lady Chancellor Road to a look-out 600 ft. above sea-level and to the Laventille Hills to see the view from the tower of a chapel. From Fort George, a former signal station at 1,100 ft, there are also excellent views; to reach it take the St. James route taxi from Independence Square and ask to get off at Fort George Road; from there it is about 1 hour's walk uphill. Midway along the Western Main Road to St. Pierre a road runs off to the N. The Blue Basin waterfall is off this road but very difficult to find. (If you do leave your car to try and visit the fall, leave nothing of value in it.) Further on is Maraval where there is the 18-hole Moka golf course. At St. Pierre itself there is a remarkable little church on the waterside. The road runs on to Carenage, with many pretty views, especially of the Five Islands. For the adventurous there is a trail

through the jungle along the northern coast. Take a route taxi to Arima and then a bus, or hitchhike, to Paria (though apparently the latter does not appear on some maps). From here the trail runs to Paria Bay, which is possibly the best beach on the island (about 8 miles). There is a primitive shelter on the beach but no other facilities so take provisions with you. From the beach another path leads to Blanchisseuse (7 miles), where the track forks; take the fork closer to the shore. There is a spectacular waterfall half a mile inland. From Blanchisseuse there are two buses daily to Arima; off the road which connects the two places are the Aripo Caves with spectacular stalagmites and stalactites. Also along this road you can get (by car or taxi) to the Asa Wright nature trail, a must for bird-lovers. Rooms are provided at the Asa Wright Centre, US$60 per day for foreign tourists. There is swimming in a beautiful man-made pool, and guided tours to see, for example, humming birds and rare oil-birds. There is a small entrance charge.
Arima itself has a small but interesting Amerindian museum at the Cleaver Woods Recreation Centre, on the W side of town. From Arima the road runs either to Toco on the N coast (which is well worth a visit though its rocky shore defies bathing) or back to Port of Spain, via St. Joseph. At **St. Joseph**, which was once the seat of government, is the imposing Jinnah Memorial Mosque and nearby, high on a hill, is Mount St. Benedict monastery, which has a guest house. There are marvellous views over the Caroni Plain to the sea. Driving S you see dhoti-clad Indians in the rice fields, herds of water buffalo, Hindu temples and Moslem mosques. There are boat trips to the Caroni Bird Sanctuary, the home of scarlet ibis, whose numbers are dwindling as the swamp in which they live is encroached upon. The boats leave around 1600 so as to see the ibis returning to their roost at sunset (charge, TT$20). Egrets, herons and plovers can also be seen. Bus or route taxi to Chaguaramas, where the boats leave, TT$1.75. Ask to be dropped off at the Caroni Bird Sanctuary. Lawrence Marcano, 60D Clifton Hill EDR, Port of Spain, will arrange day trips on the island.

Beaches The nearest beach to Port of Spain is Carenage, but it is badly polluted. To the NW there are one or two pleasant swimming places at Chaguaramas, though the beach is owned by a hotel and you have to pay to use it. The clientele using beach and hotel can tend to be a little punchy, though. Maracas Bay on the north coast over the hills, 10 miles from the capital, has a sheltered sandy beach fringed with coconut palms (Try the "shark and bake," sold all along the beach for TT$5). There are buses to Maracas Bay on Sats., Suns. and holidays only, from the bus terminal. At other times a taxi from Port of Spain costs US$9 or there is a pick-up "route taxi" service from the centre of town, US$0.62. (Alternatively it is quite easy to hitch a lift from the Queen's Park Savannah roundabout.) Las Cuevas, also on the N coast (like Maracas Bay, surfing is good here), and Blanchisseuse and Balandra, near Toco, have lovely beaches but are more difficult to reach. The Atlantic coast from Matura to Mayaro is divided into three huge sweeping bays, with palm trees growing as high as 200 feet in some places. Of these bays Mayaro and Manzanilla both have beautiful sandy beaches. Maqueripe Bay has a sheltered beach. In general the beaches are difficult to get to except by taxi or hired car.

San Fernando on the SW coast is a busy little town, as yet not spoilt by tourism. In its neighbourhood are the principal industrial-development area of Point Lisas and the Pointe-a-Pierre oil refinery. For Chinese food, try *Soongs Great Wall*, 97 Circular Rd.

A famous phenomenon to visit on the south-west coast near San Fernando is **Pitch Lake,** about 110 acres of smooth surface resembling caked mud but which in fact is hot black tar. (In fact, it has been described by disappointed tourists, expecting something more dramatic, as looking like a parking lot!) If care is taken it is possible to walk on it, watching out for air holes bubbling up from the pressure under the ooze. The legend is that long ago the gods interred an entire tribe of Chayma Indians for daring to eat sacred humming-birds containing the souls of their ancestors. In the place where the entire Carib village sank into the

1250 TRINIDAD AND TOBAGO

ground there erupted a sluggish flow of black pitch gradually becoming an ever-refilling large pool. It provides a healthy, though recently decreasing, item in Trinidad's export figures. It can be reached by taking a bus from Port of Spain to San Fernando (TT$0.75—by taxi it costs TT$5) and then another from there to La Brea (TT$0.40).

Festivals Trinidad is the birthplace of the calypso and the steel band. Towards the end of the last war, the local inhabitants discovered that the empty oil drums left behind by the Armed Forces could be transformed into musical instruments. A crude musical drum, or "pan", was first played, so it is claimed, on Lady Day 1945. Since then it has become quite sophisticated. To tune a "pan" is a complicated business entailing heating and cooling and hours of pounding. Many leading steel bands will tackle the classics, and in fact, the test piece for steel bands in the annual music festival is a classical arrangement.

Carnival takes place each year on the two days before Ash Wednesday. The participants, good-humoured and colourful, dance to the rhythmic throbbing of the steel bands, converging from all parts of the island on Port of Spain. The festivities start with "J'ouvert" at about 0400 on the Monday. This is followed by "Ole Mas" which lasts until 0900. In the afternoon is "Lil Mas" when the bands start moving, followed by their lively and brightly dressed supporters. Tuesday is the more important day, however, when the bands all have their own troops of followers, there is a procession of floats and everyone is "jumping up" in the street. (Beware of pickpockets!) Some people say that the Trinidad carnival is better than Rio's. For the stadium parades and band play-offs, try the North Stand.

The Hosein Festival, commemorating the murder of two Moslem princes, starts ten days after the first appearance of the new moon in the Moharrun month of the Moslem calendar. Colourful processions, hauling 10-to 30-ft.-high miniature wooden temples, start the next day, heralded by moon dancers and accompanied by drum-beating. Divali, the Hindu festival of lights, takes place in October-November. Also in November is the Prime Minister's Best Village Folk Festival competition, at Queen's Park Savannah Grand Stand, price TT$3 per night. Villages throughout the island send artistes, troupes, bands etc. (usually two acts a night), with the aim of becoming the "Cream of the Crop".

On August 29 in Arima the feast of St. Rose of Lima is celebrated; the parish church is dedicated to her. Descendants of the original Amerindians come from all over the island to walk in solemn procession round the church.

Tobago is not as bustling as Trinidad but is ideal for those in search of relaxation. The tourist area is centred on the southern coast, near the airport, and about 10 miles from the capital, Scarborough. In Scarborough itself there are interesting Botanic Gardens. Roxborough is worth a visit, and Pigeon Point has the island's most beautiful beach, though TT$ 5 is charged for admission as the land is private; however, the beach is free and can easily be reached by walking along the shoreline. From Mount Irvine Bay, where there is an attractive, palm-fringed championship golf course (the hotel of the same name has a good beach) you can walk up to Bethel, the island's highest village, for excellent views across the island. At Store Bay, which is near the airport, are the ruins of Milford Fort, and brown pelicans frequent the beautiful beach. Two other beaches which are well worth a visit are Bacolet Bay and Turtle Bay. A trip to Charlotteville (2 hrs.; by bus TT$1, be sure to check there is a bus back to Scarborough in the afternoon) is recommended; there are magnificent views on the way and the village itself is on a fine horse-shoe bay with a good beach: fine swimming and snorkelling. From Charlotteville, it is a 15 min. walk to Pirate's Bay, which is magnificent and unspoilt. For the Forest Reserve, take a bus from Scarborough to Mount St. George and then walk or hitch to Hillsborough Dam; from there continue NE through the forest to Castara or Mason Hall. A map (obtainable in Port of Spain), compass and supplies, including water, are essential. Birdwatching is excellent, but look out for snakes. In the SW lies Buccoo Reef.

Buccoo Reef Glass-bottomed boats for visiting this undersea garden tend to be cheaper if rented at Buccoo Village rather than Scarborough or Pigeon Point: the charge is TT$20 for 2 hrs, and you can hire snorkelling gear. From Store Bay a 2½ hr. trip in a glass-bottomed boat including snorkelling gear costs TT$20 per person. The dragging of anchors and greed of divers have tarnished the glory of this once marvellous reef, though. Boats leave between 0900 and 1430, depending on the tide. Be selective, though, in choosing which boat—and captain—you take for the trip. Some are less than satisfactory. From Scarborough to Buccoo by bus is TT$0.20. Taxis also go to Buccoo.

Little Tobago, an islet off the NE coast, is a sanctuary for birds-of-paradise.

TRINIDAD AND TOBAGO 1251

Camping On Tobago you can camp on Store Bay. It is safe and highly recommended. Use of facilities (toilets and cold showers) costs TT$0.10 per day. The *Pelican Hotel* at Pigeon Point has a good supermarket. Camping is also possible near the Mt. Irvine beach. Ask the taxi drivers for advice on where to camp. Camping is often discouraged on Trinidad, is unsafe and is not recommended. Try the Boca Islands to the west.

Very frequent flights between Trinidad and Tobago; the crossing takes 20 mins. and costs TT$75 return, TT$38 single. Departures, however, are often subject to long delays and flights are heavily booked at weekends. Boats leave twice daily, at 1430 and 2300 in both directions, though the Friday timetable is different, TT$77 for a car and 4 people. Recommended for the crossing is the Danish ship *Gelting*, which sails 4 times a week. The trip takes 4½-6 hrs. and can be rough. Best to book 4-5 days in advance. TT$13 single, TT$26 return per person.

Buses on Tobago tend to be crowded. Buy tickets in advance as drivers will not accept money. Buses between Crown Point (airport) and Scarborough, TT$0.75.

Where to Stay There are a great many hotels on the islands and the better known ones are expensive, but there are very good guesthouses and smaller hotels which are reasonable. There is also a YWCA (TT$12 bed and breakfast). Information about accommodation can be obtained from Trinidad and Tobago Tourist Board, 56 Frederick Street, Port of Spain (for other addresses see page 1253). Their office at the airport is not helpful. If you intend to stay in Trinidad for Carnival, when prices rise steeply, you must book a hotel well in advance. Some are booked a year ahead. If arriving without accommodation arranged at Carnival time, the tourist office at the airport may help to find you a room with a local family, though this like hotels will be expensive, C. A 3% room tax is charged at all hotels and in most a 10% service charge is added to the bill. Guesthouses in the D-F range are few and far between in the capital, though the Hillcrest Haven guesthouse, D, is recommended (7A Hillcrest Rd.) Mrs Davies' Guest House in Scarborough, TT$ 60, includes 3 meals. Highly recommended. *Zollna House*, 12 Ramlogan Development, La Seiva, Maraval, Tel.: 809 628 3731, owned by Gottfried and Barbara Zollna, small guest house, food varied with local flavour, special diets catered for, C, breakfast and dinner per person US$5 and US$12 respectively. (The Zollnas also manage the *Blue Water Inn*, Batteaux Bay, Speyside, Tobago, A.) *Glenco Guest House*, Glen Road, Scarborough, E, clean, breakfast US$1. Tel.: 639 2912. A cheap room with two typical meals (about US$6) contact: Lawrence Marcano, 60D Clifton Hill EDR, Port of Spain. Trips on island also arranged. Rooms available at the *City Gate Pub* on South Quay, Port of Spain, TT$40 D.

Restaurants in Port of Spain: *The Greenhouse*, Dundonald St., Queens Park West, local dishes, inexpensive; *Hello Bob*, Duke St., native food at reasonable prices; *Mario's Pizza Place*, Tragarete Rd. and *Ciprian*; *Dairy Queen*; *Wimpy*, Independence Square and other places; *Kentucky Fried Chicken* also has several outlets; good Chinese restaurant near *Fabienne's Guest House*; many Chinese restaurants offer two-course meals at modest prices. *House of Chan*, Picton St., excellent Chinese food, not too expensive. In San Fernando: *Marsang's* and *New City* (Chinese) are good. *Shay Shay Thien* is a good, inexpensive Chinese restaurant on Cipriani Boulevard. On Tobago, the *Beach Bar* at Store Bay has music all day on Sun., and an excellent barbecue in the afternoon, for TT$15 per head. The *Pelican Inn*, Coblentz Ave., Cascade, has a good Indian restaurant upstairs, *Le Locrico*, Henry St., French, good, expensive. *The Waterfront*, West Mall, serves steaks and seafood in a congenial atmosphere. *Tiki Village* in the Kapok Hotel, Calton Hill, serves good Polynesian and Chinese food. Also in the Kapok is the *Café Savannah* (French). The self-service *Charbeque* on Tragarete road serves steaks cooked on an open fire. *Mangals*, Savannah East, has reasonable Indian food. The *Swiss Chalet* and *Fisherman's Wharf*, both in Long Circular Mall, are not good value. If you've a yen for the best pepper shrimps in the Caribbean, the *Peninsular Restaurant* in Carenage is the place. *Buddies Café* in the Mall, Scarborough, Tobago, is highly recommended. Eating out is considered fairly expensive in Trinidad and Tobago.

Entertainment Trinidad abounds in evening entertainment, with calypso dancing e.g. Sparrow's Hideaway, limbo shows and international cabaret acts. Monday's local song and dance at the *Hilton* is less authentic in atmosphere than the steel band concerts on Fridays at the same venue. Entrance TT$10. For those wishing to visit the places where the local, rather than tourist, population go, anyone in the street will give directions. Though the atmosphere will be natural and hospitality generous, it will not be luxurious and the local rum is likely to flow. *Chaconia* on Saddle Rd. has live music on Fridays and Saturdays. The *Pelican* bar on Coblentz Ave. is the "in" place for prosperous young Trinidadians. *JBs* discotheque in Valsayu has a good restaurant attached. The *Bel Air* near the airport has a good bar and restaurant. For spicier entertainment, go to the *Crab Hole*, or the *Bagshot* (*Cavalier Pub*), both off Saddle Rd. past the Country Club, the *International* (Wrightson Rd.) or the *21 Club*.

Though not as lively as Trinidad, Tobago offers dancing in its hotels and a variety

1252 TRINIDAD AND TOBAGO

of places to dine. The Buccoo Folk Theatre gives an attractive show of dancing and calypso every Thurs. at 2100, admission TT$5. In Scarborough, El Tropical is a club frequented mostly by locals. It has a live show every Sat. night at about 2330. Admission TT$8.00.

Taxis are not marked. Look for cars with first letter H on licence plates. Agree on a price before the journey and determine whether the price is in TT or US dollars. Taxis are expensive, although route taxis (similar to colectivos) are very cheap. These cannot be distinguished from ordinary taxis, so ask the driver. They travel along fixed routes, like buses, but have no set stops, so you can hail them and be dropped anywhere along the route. During rush hour it is not easy to hail them, however, and in general it takes time to master how they work. They usually set off from Independence Square. Fares in town TT$1, further out about TT$2. On long-distance journeys, let the locals pay first so that you know you're not overcharged. (Be warned that route taxis are not covered by insurance so you cannot claim against the driver if you are involved in an accident.) There are also "pirate" taxis with the P registration of a private car, which cost the same as the ordinary taxis, although you can sometimes bargain with the drivers. Maxi-taxis are an innovation; they are minibuses which charge the same as route taxis (TT$1.50 in town). Taxis to and from airport TT$60, and 50% more after midnight; route taxis charge about TT$3 to Arouca and TT$3 from there to Port of Spain; there are also buses between Arouca and Port of Spain (TT$1). Be careful if hitching on Tobago as the cars that stop often prove to be pirate taxis.

Car Rentals Small cars can be rented for TT$100 a day, unlimited mileage. Deposit TT$1,000, book in advance. Try Wongs in Belmont Circular Rd. Driving is on the left and the roads are narrow, winding, and in places rather rough. On Tobago the roads are good in the South but badly maintained further north. The road between Charlotteville and Bloody Bay is for four-wheel drive vehicles only. Insurance costs TT$6-7. US, Canadian and British driving licences are all accepted for up to 90 days. Taxi and car rental firms include Battoo Bros., Hub Travel Ltd (Hertz) and Rentex, and on Tobago there is Tobago Travel Ltd. Most companies, however, only rent for a minimum of 3 days. Hub Travel have a good map of Trinidad.

Scooter Rentals Mr. Mackenzie, at Scarborough bus station, can arrange scooter hire in Tobago for TT$20 a day. Bicycles can be hired at the Mount Irvine Bay hotel on Tobago.

Motorboat Tours for birdwatching or fishing are run by David Ramsahai and Sons, Tel.: 638-3162. Scuba diving tours and tuition are arranged by Teach-Tour Diving Co. at Bateaux Bay, Tobago. **Waterskiing:** On Tobago Joseph Alleyne has a speedboat for waterskiers and also gives tuition for about TT$20. He can be contacted through John Grant's bar-restaurant at Store Bay. **Horses** can be hired near Fort George.

Buses The bus service has been somewhat improved by the acquisition of new vehicles, but a shortage of drivers means that the service is still inadequate and buses are therefore very crowded. This is especially true for the out-of-town services. Fares on the blue buses, which tend to be unreliable, are TT$0.50 or TT$1, depending on destination. (The longest trip on the island is TT$5) At the PTSC office in the old railway station you can get information showing how to reach the various sights by bus.

Airports Piarco International, 16 miles SE of Port of Spain. There is a TT$20 exit tax. Chaos is the order of the day at the airport. Allow plenty of time to get there. The Airport Authority bus, stopping at major hotels, charges TT$17 per person, otherwise the taxi fare to Port of Spain is TT$60. Unlicensed taxis outside the main parking area charge TT$30. The cheapest way to get to the airport is to take a bus to Arouca (TT$1), then a route taxi to the airport (TT$3). There is a direct cheap bus, TT$1, 1 hr., from the airport to Port of Spain bus station, departing every 20 minutes. Between Tobago's Crown Point Airport and Scarborough there are plenty of buses which charge TT$0.30. Route taxis charge TT$4. Taxis to Buccoo Village cost about TT$11.

Bookshops Abercromby Bookstore on Abercromby St., good selection of West Indies-related books. Mills and Boor, 28 Dundonald St., used paperbacks, will trade.

Economy The economy of this prosperous country—gdp per head in 1984 was US$7,140—is firmly based on the petroleum industry, which in 1985 accounted for 23.8% of the gdp and 76.1% of total export earnings. Depressed world oil markets in the mid-1980s severely affected foreign revenues; the Government's subsequent deflationary policies, designed to help stem the supply of imports to preserve foreign exchange reserves, caused a sharp decline in gdp. The island has substantial reserves of natural gas, estimated at 13 trillion cubic feet, and these are used to power several new heavy industries such as an iron and steel mill, urea, methanol and ammonia plants. Although the soil is remarkably rich, the agricultural sector has been on the decline in recent years.

TRINIDAD AND TOBAGO

The output of sugar, traditionally the major export crop, has fallen and food production has demonstrably failed to keep pace with demand, making it necessary to import 75% of the islands' needs. Coffee, cocoa, citrus fruits and coconut oils are the main agricultural exports besides sugar; the most important export after oil products, however, is fertilizers.

	1961-70 (av)	1971-80 (av)	1981-85 (av)
Gdp growth (1980 prices)	4.3%	4.4%	1.1%
Inflation	3.0%	13.0%	12.6%
Exports (fob) US$m	297	1,036	2,260
Imports (fob) US$m	333	799	1,921
Current account balance US$m (cum)	-510	1,047	-2,034

Information for Visitors

Trinidad and Tobago Tourist Board, 56 Frederick St., Port of Spain (off Woodford Square), sells good street maps for TT$4. There are also offices in New York (400 Madison Ave., New York, N.Y. 10017); Miami (Suite 702, 200 S.E. First Street, Miami, Florida 33131); London (120 Lower Regent Street, London SW1Y 4PH) and Toronto (York Centre, 145 King Street West and University Ave., M5H 1J8). These offices all have up-to-date hotel lists.

Air Services BWIA links Trinidad with Tobago (daily flights); so do Trinidad and Tobago Air Services and ALM. *USA*: Pan American; BWIA; Eastern. *Canada*: Air Canada; BWIA from Montreal and Toronto. *Europe*: British Airways; Air France; KLM; BWIA; Jetsave. *Venezuela*: BWIA to Caracas; Aeropostal to Maturín. Book well in advance (it's very difficult to get a flight in December). *Guyana*: BWIA has daily flights to Georgetown. *Inter-Island*: BWIA, Leeward Islands Air Transport (Liat) and Cubana airlines connect Trinidad and Tobago with other Caribbean islands including Puerto Rico. There are direct flights between Tobago and Barbados (daily) with BWIA. Suriname: KLM flies this once a week to Paramaribo. BWIA, and possibly other airlines, is reluctant to let you leave unless you have an onward ticket from your immediate destination to the next one.

Airline Offices Pan-Am, Air India, ALM, British Airways, Eastern Airlines, American Airlines, KLM and Viasa all have offices in the Furness Building, Independence Square. Air Canada and Air France also have offices on Independence Square. BWIA is at 39-41 Pembroke Street and Aeropostal at 6 St. Vincent Street, but be prepared for a long wait and don't be afraid to queue-jump for service. There is a 5% tax on airline tickets purchased in Trinidad and Tobago.

Climate, though humid, is pleasant all the year with temperatures varying from 21-37°C. The wet months are June-November.

Clothing Beachwear should be kept for the beach. In the evening cocktail dresses and suits are usually worn.

Banks Barclays Bank International (National Republic Bank), Royal Bank of Canada, Canadian Imperial Bank of Commerce, Bank of Nova Scotia, Trinidad Co-operative Bank, Chase Manhattan Bank, Citibank, National Bank of Trinidad and Tobago. Open 0800-1230 Mon.-Thurs.; 0800-1200 and 1500-1700 Fri. All banks charge a fee for cashing travellers' cheques, some more than others, so check first. Apparently it is not possible to exchange Brazilian cruzados in Trinidad.

Useful Addresses (Port of Spain) Canadian High Commission, Colonial Bldg., 72 South Quay; US Embassy, 15 Queen's Park West; British High Commission, 3rd floor, Furness House, 90 Independence Square (P.O. Box 778). Tel.: 52861-6; New Zealand High Commission, same building; W. German Embassy, Wrightson Rd.; Brazilian Consulate, 6 Elizabeth St., St. Clair; Argentine Consulate, 2nd floor, 3a Queen's Park West.

Travel Agents Wong and Kahn Travel Service, Woodford Street, Newtown, Port of Spain. (Tel.: 62-25603.) Lazzari and Sampson, corner of Duke St., Pembroke St., Port of Spain, recommended. Mahons, Port of Spain and San Fernando.

Currency The Trinidad and Tobago dollar, fixed at TT$2.40 = US$1 since 1976, was devalued to TT$3.60 = US$1 on December 17, 1985. There has been an increase in prices owing to the devaluation. Notes are for TT$1, 5, 10, 20 and 100. Coins are for 1, 5, 10, 25 and 50 cents. Not more than £50 in sterling notes can be brought in by visitors from the UK, or TT$48 by visitors from other countries. When changing money keep the receipt so that what remains unspent can be changed back, as long as there is no more money taken out than was brought in. Travellers' cheques are accepted almost everywhere. There is a thriving black market in US$ (TT$4 = US$1).

Documents Passports are required by all visitors. Visas are not normally required by nationals of Commonwealth countries, West European countries (except Netherlands), Brazil, Colombia,

1254 TRINIDAD AND TOBAGO

Israel, Suriname and Turkey for visits of up to 3 months; for US citizens for visits up to 6 months; and for Venezuelans for stays of up to 14 days. Entry permits for one month are given on arrival; they can be extended at the immigration office in Port of Spain (at the Ross Building, Frederick Street) for TT$ 5. This is a time-consuming process, so try and get a 3-month entry permit if planning a long stay. After 6 weeks visitors must get a tax clearance from the Inland Revenue office on Edward St. All travellers need an onward ticket, dated, not open-ended, proof that they can support themselves during their stay, an address at which they will be staying in Trinidad (the tourist office at the airport can help in this respect but is unreliable as far as making bookings at hotels is concerned), and must pay the TT$5 embarkation tax (if staying over 48 hrs.) and the airport service charge of TT$1 each. Only those coming from an infected area need a yellow fever inoculation certificate. People going to Venezuela can obtain a tourist card (free of charge) at the Aeropostal office; this means buying a return ticket but this can be refunded or changed if an alternative ticket out of Venezuela is later purchased.

Warning: Some immigration officials do not take too kindly to those with a "hippy"-type appearance and may refuse them entry.

Customs Duty-free imports. 200 cigarettes or 50 cigars or ½ lb. tobacco, and 1 quart wine or spirits. Perfume may not be imported free of duty, but may be deposited with Customs until departure.

Post and Telephones The main Post Office is on Wrightson Road, Port of Spain, and is open 0700-1700, Mon.-Fri. The main Textel office on Independence Square and Edward St. operates international telephone, cable and telex, and is open 24 hrs. Cables can also be sent from the tourist bureau at Piarco airport and hotel desks. There is a Textel telephone office in Scarborough, Tobago. The service for international calls has apparently improved greatly, with direct dialling to Europe and the USA. Telegrams from Tobago to Venezuela and Trinidad take 5 *days*. The very poor internal telephone system is apparently being improved.

Food A wide variety of European, American and traditional West Indian dishes (these include pork souse, black pudding, roast sucking pig, salcoche and callaloo stews, and many others) is served at hotels and guest houses. Some also specialize in Creole cooking. There is also, of course, a strong East Indian influence in the local cuisine. Seafood, particularly crab, is excellent. Do not eat local oysters: their habitat has become polluted. The many tropical fruits and vegetables grown locally include the usual tropical fruits, and sapodillas, eddoes and yam tanias. The variety of juices and ice creams made from the fruit is endless. For those economizing, the *roti*, a pancake which comes in various forms, filled with peppery stew, for about TT$8, is very good. The best place for *roti* is probably the Hot Shoppe for Hot Roti, on Mucaripo St., W of downtown Port of Spain. *Pilau*, savoury rice and meat, is also good, but when offered pepper, refuse unless you are accustomed to the hottest of curries or *chile* dishes. A local drink is mauby, like ginger beer, and the rum punches are recommended. Fresh lime juice is also recommended; it is sometimes served with a dash of Angostura bitters.

Tipping If no service charge on bill, 10% for hotel staff and restaurant waiters; taxi drivers, 10% of fare, minimum of 25 cents; dock-side and airport porters, say 25 cents for each piece carried; hairdressers (in all leading hotels), 50 cents.

Holidays and Special Events Carnival Sunday, Monday and Tuesday, before Ash Wednesday, Good Friday; Easter Monday; Butler's Day (June 19); Corpus Christi; Whit Monday; Discovery Day (first Mon. in August); Independence Day (August 31); Republic Day (September 24); Divali; All Souls' Day (November 2); Christmas Day; Boxing Day. The Moslem festivals fall 10-11 days earlier each year: in 1988 Eid ul-Fitr will be on May 20, Eid ul-Azha on July 25 and Yaum um-Nabi on November 4.

Shopping Shops are open from 0800 to 1600, Mon.-Fri.; 0800-1200 Sat. The main Port of Spain shopping area is in Frederick Street. Nothing is open on Sunday. Purchases can be made at in-bond shops in Port of Spain and at the airport. Markets offer wide varieties of fruit. Handicrafts can also be purchased at markets. A good place for souvenirs is Lakhan's Bazaar, 32 Western Main Road, St. James. It has a branch at Piarco Airport. The Central Market is on the Beetham Highway.

Electricity 115 or 230 volts, 60 cycles A.C.

We express our gratitude to Dr. Michael Binzberger (Friedrichshafen), Lynne and Hugh Davies (Mill Valley, Ca.), Dr Thomas Herz (Cologne), Leo Joseph (Adelaide), Andrew Lawrence (Vancover) and Jon Easterbrooke (Shaftesbury, Dorset), and Bill and Tina; also various travellers listed at the end of the general West Indies section.

LEEWARD AND WINDWARD ISLANDS

This scatter of islands clustered in two main groups, together with the Virgin Islands, form the Lesser Antilles. The Leewards, in the NE of the Caribbean, comprise Antigua, Barbuda, Redonda, St. Christopher (commonly known as St. Kitts), Nevis, Anguilla and Montserrat. The Windwards (Dominica, St. Lucia, St. Vincent and the Grenadines, and Grenada) spread southwards across the path of the cooling trade winds which sweep over this area. (The French and Dutch islands in these groups are dealt with under French and Netherlands Antilles, and the Virgin Islands, both US and British, are also discussed separately.) These small islands, like so many others in the West Indies, depend heavily on holiday makers and they are doing all they can to build up their tourist industry. The best months are from January to May, January and February being the peak season. Summer is from April to December; winter from January to March (hotel seasons). At any time between June and October (the hurricane season) the weather can be blustery and unpredictable. The climate is best in the Leewards. There is little humidity and summer temperatures are around 28-29°C, falling to 24°C in winter.

Currency East Caribbean dollar (EC$), fixed at 2.70 to the US$. (Also known as a BWI (pronounced "bee-wee") dollar.) **Note:** When shopping make sure you establish which dollar you are dealing in.

LEEWARD ISLANDS

ANTIGUA

Antigua, with about 108 square miles, is the largest of the Leewards. It has a population of around 77,000, most of them of African origin although some are of English descent. It is also the most popular and the most developed of the Leewards, and for this reason is rather expensive for the budget-traveller. This popularity is largely thanks to its airport—Coolidge, some 4½ miles from St. John's, the capital—which is the centre for air traffic in the area and is served by British Airways, Eastern Airlines, Air Canada and Air France. There are frequent air services to neighbouring islands operated by Leeward Islands Air Transport (Liat).

Antigua (pronounced Anteega) was discovered by Columbus on his second voyage in 1493. It was occupied for brief periods by the Spanish and the French and finally by the British in 1667. The island became independent in November 1981. The Prime Minister is Mr. Vere Bird.

The island is low-lying and volcanic in origin; its highest point is 1,330 feet and there is nothing spectacular about its landscape, but its coast line, curving into coves and graceful harbours, once the craters of now dead volcanoes, with soft, white sand beaches (365 of them) fringed with palm trees, is among the most attractive in the West Indies. First sugar, and then cotton, used to be produced,

1256 LEEWARD ISLANDS

but output of both is now insignificant. Industrial development has taken place on a modest scale.

St. John's Built around the largest of the natural harbours is St. John's, the capital, with an estimated population of about 25,000. It is rather quiet and a little run-down, with interesting historical associations. Nelson served in Antigua as a young man for almost three years, and visited it again in 1805, during his long chase of Villeneuve which was to end with the Battle of Trafalgar. Some of the old buildings in St. Johns, including the Anglican Cathedral, were damaged by earthquakes in 1974.

On the other side of the island is **English Harbour**, which has become one of the world's most attractive yachting centres. Here "Nelson's Dockyard" has been restored and is one of the most interesting historical monuments in the West Indies. Near the Dockyard, Clarence House still stands where Prince William, Duke of Clarence, later to become William IV, stayed when he served as a midshipman.

At Shirley Heights, overlooking English Harbour, are the ruins of fortifications built in the 18th century. Here there is a small museum. Great George Fort, on Monk's Hill, above Falmouth Harbour (a 30-minute walk from the village of Liberta, and from Cobb's Cross near English Harbour) has been less well preserved than that of Goat Hill which also gives excellent views across Deep Bay. There is a museum of precolumbian artefacts in the Dow Hill tracking station building (formerly used in connection with the US Apollo space programme). It can be visited by prior arrangement, or on Thurs. afternoons there are tours, starting from Nelson's Dockyard and taking in Dow Hill (check the details at Nicholson's travel agency). If advance notice is given, the Antigua Rum Distillery welcomes visitors (phone 20458). At Mill Reef is the Old Mill Museum with a small but excellent collection of Amerindian artefacts; to see it you must either have an introduction, or contact the manager by telephone. There is spectacular cliff scenery, including a natural arch and blowholes, on a marked trail starting on the beach at Half Moon Bay. Fig Tree Drive between Old Road and John Hughes is a steep, winding road, through mountainous forest, in a most attractive part of the island.

Carnival Antigua's carnival, second only to Trinidad's in the Caribbean, is at the end of July and lasts until the first Tuesday in August. The main event is "J'ouvert", or "Juvé" morning when from 0400 people come into town dancing behind steel and brass bands. Hotels and airlines tend to be booked up well in advance.

Beaches The nearest beach to St. Johns is Fort James; further but better is Dickinson Bay. Also good is Deep Bay to which there is at present only a rough track, and which can only be reached by taxi or car. Near English Harbour is Galleon Beach, which is splendid, but again can only be reached by taxi or car. It has an excellent restaurant. There is good swimming at Freeman Bay.

Sport and Entertainment Antigua offers sailing (sailing week at the end of April is a major yacht-racing event), water-skiing, snorkelling, deep-sea fishing, golf (there are three courses, including the professional 18-hole one at Cedar Valley), tennis, riding, and of course cricket. (Test Matches at the Recreation Ground.) On public holidays there is horse racing at Cassada Park. "Cocktail" and "barbecue" cruises have recently been started and are reasonably priced. From Shorty's Watersports at Dickinson Bay, glass-bottomed boats take people out to the coral reefs; there are also excursions to Bird Island, food and drink provided. Dickinson Bay is the only beach with public hire of water-sports equipment but some hotels will hire to the public especially out of season, e.g. the *Jolly Beach* hotel near Bolan's Village (bus from West End bus station). At EC$13.50 per hour, windsurfing is only half as expensive as at Dickinson Bay. The largest hotels provide dancing, calypso, steel bands, limbo dancers and moonlight barbecues. There are cinemas and a casino. A free newspaper, *It's Happening, You're Welcome*, contains lots of information on forthcoming events.

Warning Finding your way around is not easy: street names are rarely in evidence.

Transport Minivans (shared taxis) go to some parts of the island from the West End bus terminal in St. John's. Buses, which are banned from the tourist area (N of the line from the airport to St. John's), run frequently between St. John's and English Harbour, EC$1.35. There are also buses

LEEWARD ISLANDS 1257

from the E terminal to Willikies, whence a 20 min. walk to Long Bay beach. There are no buses to the airport and very few to beaches though two good swimming beaches on the way to Old Road can be reached by bus (EC$1). Bus frequency can be variable, and there are very few buses after dark or on Sundays. Buses to Old Road are half-hourly on average, though more frequent around 0800 and 1600. There are no publicly-displayed timetables—you'll have to ask for one. Taxis between St. John's and Coolidge airport are EC$15; between English Harbour and Coolidge, EC$42. Taxis are not metered, so agree a price first. There is a list of government approved taxi rates published in *It's Happening, You're Welcome*. Hitchhiking is easy in daylight but at night you might fall prey to a taxi driver.

Car Hire (all in St. John's and some at airport): Antigua Car Rentals (*Barrymore Hotel*); Carib Car Rentals (*Michaels Mount Hotel*); Lapp's Rent-a-Car (Long and Cross Streets); Alexander Parris (St. Mary's St.); Prince's Rent-a-Car (Fort Road); Capital Rental (High St.); Dollar Rental (Nevis St.); E. J. Wolfe Ltd. (Long St.); National and, cheaper, Hustler Hires at The Toy Shop (Long St.). Rates are from US$25 a day (no mileage charge, petrol is EC$4.60 a gallon). A local driving licence, EC$25, must be purchased. Renting a car or motorcycle is probably the best way to see the island's sights if you have only a short time to spend, as the bus service is inadequate. Small motorcycles can be hired on St. Mary's St.

Tourist Office Antigua Tourist Office on the corner of High Street and Corn Alley. Postal address: P.O. Box 363, St. John's, Antigua, W. Indies. Tel.: 20029. Open 0830-1600 (Mon.-Fri.) and 0830-1200 (Sat.). Gives list of official taxi charges. Also has an office at airport, which is very helpful.

Hotels in St. Johns: in our range A, MAP bracket: *Barrymore*, Fort Road., *Beach-comber* and *Sugar Mill*, near airport. *Stevendale*, Fort Rd., B, EP; *Spanish Main*, Independence Ave., B, EP; *Silver Dollar Inn*, EP; *Palm View*, C, EP; *Shell Inn*, Clare Hall, D, EP, clean and friendly; *Montgomery's Guest House*, D, self-catering facilities, E, but in a rather seedy area, has bicycles for hire; *Roslyn's Guest House*, Fort Road., C, EP perhaps overpriced, but about 15 minutes' walk from the beautiful, secluded Fort James beach; *Cortsland*, Upper Gambles, A, MAP; *Skyline*, on airport road, C, EP, recommended; *St. Mary's Court*, 34 St. Mary's Street, B, including breakfast, good restaurant, recommended; *Sand Haven*, Piggotsville, C, EP; *Joe Mike's*, B; *Castle Harbour*, C, MAP; *Open View*, E, EP; *Main Road Guest House*, Otto's Main Road, E, basic but clean. At Dickinson Bay: *Halcyon Cove*, A, MAP. At English Harbour: *Admiral's Inn*, A, MAP. At Marmora Bay: *Holiday Inn*, A, MAP. At Falmouth Harbour: *Catamaran*, on beach, clean, friendly, good food, B, MAP. Cottages and apartments are available for rent, costing about US$60 per day for 4 people. 10 miles from St. John's, *Antigua Horizons*, private beach, A; *Hawksbill Beach*, incorporating a former Great House, in its own extensive grounds, A. *Long Island Resort*, P.O. Box 243, St John's, Tel.: (809) 463-2176. U.S. reservations: Resorts Management Inc., The Carriage House, 201 E. 29th St., New York, NY 10016 Tel.: (800) 225-4255 or (212) 696-4566. The resort does not accept credit cards.

Note There is a 10% service charge and 5% government tax at all hotels. There is also a 1% tax on currency exchange.

Restaurants *Admiral's Inn*, expensive but good. In St John's, *Mark's Restaurant*, Market St., local food. *Mill's Restaurant and Hotel*, Camacho Ave., good but rather pricey. *Darcy's*, Kensington Court, steel band at noon. *Spanish Main Hotel*, *Roots*, Upper St. George's St., *Golden Peanut Lounge*, Old Parham St., are all recommended. *Brother B's* good for local food and hamburgers. *Castle Harbour*, Indian curries. *Tropical Blend*, on Market St., offers local dishes at reasonable prices. *Barrymore's Restaurant* and the *Spaniard's* are recommended, there are 2 Chinese restaurants on Newgate St; *Sand Haven Beach Bar and Grill*, just outside St. John's. At English Harbour, there is a restaurant and bar on Shirley Heights, steel band and barbecue every Sun. afternoon. On Galleon Beach, *Colombo's* Italian restaurant, recommended. Near the airport, *Le Bistro*, excellent French food. At Falmouth Harbour *Catamaran* hotel has a good restaurant and the Antigua Yacht Club provides a moderately priced dinner on most nights of the week, though it is livelier at weekends.

Food In addition to a wide selection of imported delicacies served in the larger hotels, local specialities, found in smaller restaurants in St. John's, often very reasonable, should never be missed: saltfish, pepper-pot with fungi (a kind of cornmeal dumpling), goat water (hot goat stew), shellfish (in reality boxfish), and the local staple, chicken and rice. Imported wines and spirits are reasonably priced but local drinks (fruit and sugar cane juice, coconut milk, and Antiguan rum punches and swizzles, ice cold) must be experienced. There are no licensing restrictions. Tap water is safe all over the island. Most luxury hotels provide rain water.

Banks Bank of Nova Scotia, Barclays Bank International, Canadian Imperial Bank of Commerce, Royal Bank of Canada, Antigua Commercial Bank. Barclays are reported to charge less to cash travellers cheques than some others.

Hours of Business Banks: 0800-1300 Mon.-Thurs.; 0800-1300 and 1500-1700 Fri. Bank of

1258 LEEWARD ISLANDS

Antigua opens Sat. 0800-1200. Shops: 0800-1200, 1300-1600 Mon.-Sat. Thurs. is early closing day for most non-tourist shops.

Documents A valid onward ticket is necessary. American, Canadian and British nationals need only proof of citizenship. Passports but no visas are required by nationals of other Commonwealth countries, West European countries (except Austria and Portugal), Tunisia, Turkey, Uruguay and Venezuela. Nationals of almost all other countries may stay for up to 14 days without visa if travelling to a third country; this concession does not apply to citizens of communist countries and of Haiti. Visitors must satisfy immigration officials that they have enough money for their stay.

Cables Cable and Wireless Ltd., St. Mary's St., St. John's. Tel.: 20078.

Electricity 220 volts usually, but 110v in some areas.

Shopping Market day in St. John's is Saturday. There is a good supply of fruit and vegetables, which are easy to obtain on the island. There are two American-style supermarkets in St. John's as well as the Speciality Shoppe on St. Mary's St. which stocks a wide range of duty-free goods. Some tourist shops offer 10% reductions to locals: they compensate by overcharging tourists.

Overseas Information Eastern Caribbean Tourist Association, 200 E 42nd St., New York; Editorial Services Ltd., 980 Yonge St., 6th floor, Toronto; Eastern Caribbean Tourist Association, Rooms 238-250, 200 Buckingham Palace Road, London SW1W 9TJ.

Airport Tax There is an airport tax of US$3 for flights to destinations other than Montserrat, St. Kitts, Dominica, St. Lucia, St. Vincent and Grenada, for which a EC$6 tax applies.

Shipping There is a regular weekly service to Dominica (EC$72): tickets can be obtained from the shipping agents on Thames St. Occasional services to St. Kitts; see boat captains at Fisherman's Wharf.

Barbuda Some 30 miles to the North and easily reached by air (EC$40 return, taking 15 minutes), or (with some difficulty and at a high price) by boat from St. John's, is Barbuda, one of the two island dependencies of Antigua. The population is about 1,300 and most of them live in the only village on the island, Codrington, which stands on the edge of the lagoon. Barbuda, too, has some excellent beaches and its seas are rich with all types of crustaceans and tropical fish. This is one of the few islands in the area where there is still much wild life; duck, guinea fowl, plover, pigeon, wild deer and wild pig. There is an impressive frigate-bird colony (said to be the last in the Caribbean) in the mangroves in Codrington Lagoon. Wild donkeys also roam the island. Barbuda is being developed as a tourist resort with such attractions for snorkellers and skin-divers as exploring old wrecks. The only hotel is *Coco Point Lodge*, which charges in price range L (US$400 per night) to include all meals and drinks. It is possible to lodge with Eric Burton or at Dulcina. Do not expect many "mod. cons." on Barbuda. The local night spot is Jam City, with beer at EC$2—cheaper than Antigua. Paradise Tours, run by Lynton Thomas (Tel.: 24786-7), is highly recommended, as is his guest house. The island has a Martello Tower.

Excellent 1:25,000 maps are available from the Codrington post office, or from the map shop in Jardine Court, St. Mary's, St. John's (good 1:50,000 maps of Antigua as well). It is possible to hire jeeps or horses in Codrington, otherwise everywhere is a long hot walk, so take liquid refreshment with you. If you want to camp, Two Foot Bay provides possibly the best sites.

Redonda Antigua's second dependency, little more than a rocky islet, is uninhabited.

ST. KITTS-NEVIS

St. Kitts was discovered by Columbus in 1493 and became the first British settlement in the West Indies in 1623. For a time it was shared by France and England but it finally became a British colony in 1783. Reminders of those days can still be found in the old fortifications, the most famous of which is the Citadel on Brimstone Hill. Entry is EC$2 and it is well worth a visit for the views—take the minibus from Basseterre (EC$1) to the bottom of the Hill and walk up (40 minutes). Sir Thomas Warner, the founder of the British West Indian colonies, is buried here, in the graveyard of St. Thomas' Church near Old Roadtown. There

LEEWARD ISLANDS 1259

are also Carib remains. St. Kitts-Nevis became independent on September 19, 1983. The Prime Minister is Dr Kennedy Simmonds.

The highest point on the island is Mt. Misery, 4,314 ft, whose peak is usually hidden in clouds. There are sheltered beaches, especially at Salt Ponds, some of them of black volcanic sand. Inland, the valleys are ablaze with flowering shrubs and there are the green and white fields of sugar cane and cotton. Sugar production, on which the economy relies heavily, is now in the hands of the government. The people are very friendly.

The small port of **Basseterre** is the capital and chief town, with a population of about 16,000. (The population of St. Kitts and Nevis is about 49,000.) From the tower of St. George's Cathedral there is a fine view of the island. St. Kitts has good main roads (cars can be hired) and shops in Basseterre are well stocked. Local Sea Island cotton-wear and cane and basket work are attractive and fairly reasonable. Romney Manor, near Old Roadtown, is an old plantation house which is now the headquarters of Sea Island cotton producers. Food on the whole is good: apart from almost every kind of imported food and drink, there is a wide variety of local fish, pork, poultry and fruit and vegetables. The local "Cavalier" rum is excellent; it is also the cheapest drink available.

On the whole, St. Kitts is a quiet resort, but it has attracted the attention of US developers. Apart from swimming (Frigate Bay has a sandy beach and is good for swimming), there is tennis, riding, sailing, skin-diving and fishing. There are a few first-class hotels and also modest guest houses. Cottages can also be rented. It is advisable to book accommodation well in advance. A taxi tour of the island costs about US$40 for 5-6 hours. Information from St. Kitts Tourist Board, P.O. Box 132, Basseterre, St. Kitts, W. Indies. The tourist office by the landing stage in Basseterre has useful information. St. Kitts and Nevis also have a representative in the USA: Mel Henville, ECTA, 220 East 42nd St., New York, NY 10017 (Tel.: 212-986-9370).

Hotels In Basseterre: *Parkview*, A, (MAP); *Blakeney*, central, A (MAP), has a good restaurant; *Fort Thomas* (has a swimming pool which is open to non-residents for EC$2.50), and *Ocean Terrace Inn*, both near the University centre on the edge of town and both A (EP); *Ilan Pine Inn*, A (MAP), clean, comfortable with good food; *Canne à Sucre Guest House*, C, not good value for money; *Golden Lemon*, on NW coast, lovely building, excellent lunches; *Windsor* (the cheapest), clean and friendly, D, *Liburd's*; *Caine's*; *Roseate*. **Nightlife:** Discotheques at La Cabana, near *Royal St. Kitts* hotel near Frigate Bay. Buses are 5 cents a mile.

Airport is at Golden Rock, two miles from Basseterre; it can handle international jets, and a direct service to New York was inaugurated in 1983. There is a flight to San Juan, Puerto Rico (US$74 one-way). There is an EC$5 departure tax. Taxi from airport to Basseterre, EC$7. For boats to St. Maarten and Anguilla, enquire at Horsford Shipping Agency or Barker and Kelly on the quay. It is possible to hitch a lift with one of the freighters on the "flour run" to and from St. Vincent, whence St. Kitts-Nevis imports its flour. You may be asked to pay what you feel is "right" for the seven-day journey. (Perhaps EC$400—half the air fare.)

The climate is pleasant all the year round, but the best time is during the dry months from December to April.

Nevis Across a 3-mile channel—The Narrows—from St. Kitts lies Nevis (pronounced Neevis), with a population of only 12,770. Smaller than St. Kitts, in other respects it is very similar, although more rocky and less fertile. It has superb beaches (the beautiful 3-mile Pinney's beach is only 10 minutes' walk from Charlestown) and a treasure of historical relics. Here Nelson met and married Frances Nesbit; the marriage certificate is kept in Fig Tree church. The Nesbit plantation still exists today and is a guest house open all the year round (A, MAP). Here, too, in Charlestown, was born Alexander Hamilton, who helped to draft the American constitution. The former capital, Jamestown, was drowned by a tidal wave in 1680 and can still be visited by snorkellers and skindivers. At Morning Star, a converted sugar mill, there is a museum of Nelsoniana; riding can also be arranged there.

The main town and port is **Charlestown**. It was once famous for its thermal springs. Many of the buildings date back to the eighteenth century. Nevis is reached by boat, leaving at 0600 and 1500, daily from St. Kitts, except Thurs.

LEEWARD ISLANDS

(EC$7), or in a few mins. by air. There are also direct flights from Antigua and St. Croix. The airport is at Newcastle, about 8 miles from Charlestown. Local handicrafts, including red clay pottery, are on sale. There is a very helpful tourist office in Charlestown (Tel.: 494). Nevis is an altogether friendly and relaxed place.

Accommodation In Charlestown, *Austin Hotel*, D, with shower, MAP, not par-ticularly good; *Lyndale*, C; *Pinney's Beach Hotel*, A, AP, on a 3-mile stretch of sandy, palm-fringed beach. *Golden Rock Estate*, accommodation in cottages or the 19th century Sugar Mill tower, A; cars can be hired at the hotel as can boats and diving equipment. There are self-contained apartments for rent in and around Charlestown, cheaper than hotels: *Donna's Apartment* (2 rooms) owned by Mrs. Howell at the post office, charges EC$3.10 per person p.w. Also on an old estate are the *Zetland Plantation Inn* and *Montpelier Hotel*. *Old Manor Hotel*; *Rest Haven Inn*; *Cliff Dwellers Hotel*. *Long Stone* bar and restaurant in Charlestown; the *Qualie Beach Club*, near the airport, also has a restaurant.

ANGUILLA

In 1980 **Anguilla** formally ended its association with St. Kitts-Nevis, though a *de facto* separation had been in force since 1971. Anguilla is now a separately administered dependency of the UK. It is a small island, only about 35 square miles, with a population of about 8,000. It is low lying and unlike its larger sisters it is not volcanic but of coral formation. It has excellent beaches and good game fishing. The Valley, the administrative centre and principal village on the island, is near Wall Blake airport. The island's name is the Spanish word *anguilla* (eel)—a reference to its long, narrow shape. Taxis can be hired for a tour of the island. Off the E coast is the uninhabited Dogs Island which is excellent for swimming.

Accommodation In The Valley, *The Guesthouse*, C, about 30 metres from the main crossroads at the only traffic light on the island. Clean, with bath on the same floor, small bar in the house, and breakfast possible.

Government Since its secession from St. Kitts-Nevis in 1969, Anguilla has been governed by a Commissioner, directly responsible to London, assisted by an elected Council. Mr. Emile Gumbs is Chief Minister. There is no income tax; the UK meets 60 per cent of the normal budget and all capital needs.

Transport Weekday ferry from Marigot, Saint-Martin, periodic boats from St. Kitts, and daily air service from Sint Maarten and St. Thomas.

Documents St. Kitts-Nevis and Anguilla, see under Antigua (page 1255).

MONTSERRAT

Montserrat, a volcanic island, has a beauty of its own, with its black beaches and forested mountains. There are three main volcanic mountains on the island: Chance's Peak (3,000 ft.) is the highest point; it can be reached by a picturesque but steep path. The crater of Galway, with sulphur welling over its sides, can be reached by road. For the more energetic there is the charm and challenge of climbing to see the hot springs and to swim in high mountain pools. The Great Alps Waterfall is one of the more spectacular sights in the West Indies; it can be reached by following the river bed, and takes about 45 minutes from the sign by the road-bridge near Radio Antilles.

Montserrat, discovered by Columbus in 1493 and named for its likeness to the area around the monastery of that name near Barcelona, is also called the Emerald Isle, not only because of its greenness; some of its early settlers in the 17th century were Irish. It is about the size of Anguilla but has a population of around 13,000; it is a self-governing British colony. The Chief Minister is Mr John Osborne.

Montserrat is becoming a popular home for retired US citizens, Canadians and Britons, which has a positive effect on its economy, but also tends to make the island more expensive than some of its neighbours. Cotton, fruit and vegetables are grown and exported to neighbouring islands, as are cattle. In addition some small industries are being developed. There are four Liat flights a day from Antigua. Sometimes it is possible to get a boat to Montserrat from one of the nearby islands. The capital and only town is **Plymouth,** with a population of 2,500. The people are friendly and relaxed. The forts on St. George's Hill are worth a visit as are both the Anglican and Catholic churches. A walk N along the beach will bring you to a hot pond and, further on at Foxes Bay, to the mangrove swamp where the island's cattle egrets come in to roost at dusk (bird sanctuary). There is a splendid 100-acre golf-course where the fee is EC$6 per day. There are several black-sand beaches. Rendezvous Bay has a white-sand beach and can be reached by boat from Little Bay or Old Road Bay, or by mountain track. Cruises to Rendezvous Bay from Old Road Bay are arranged at *Vue Pointe* hotel.

Hotels All rates are for a double room and MAP unless stated. *Caribelle Inn*, A; *Coconut Hill*, B, very good value; *Hideaway*, B; *Letts Guest House*, B, recommended; *Olveston House*, A; *Sea Haven*, B; *Vue Pointe*, A; *Wade Inn*, B. *Rileys Kinsale*, D. There are a 10% service charge and 7% government tax on hotel bills.

Restaurants *The Anchorage* provides lunch for about EC$5 and dinner for EC$10. Night life is found at *The Cellar* bar/restaurant and at *Jerry's Drive-in Disco, Café Le Cabotin*, just outside Plymouth, pleasant.

Transport Taxi to airport from Plymouth (9 miles), EC$20. Airport departure tax US$5. There is a local minibus service which costs EC$1 but it is infrequent and the buses are hard to find. Cars can be hired from several local agencies but car hire agencies are not allowed to operate at the airport. (If you don't want to take a taxi, walk about 1½ miles towards Plymouth, to the junction of the Bethel Village-Plymouth road, where you can catch a bus.) Jefferson Enterprise hire cars for US$25 per day, US$100 per week. Presentation of a valid driver's licence at the Plymouth police station or airport enables you to obtain a temporary licence for EC$7.50. Hitchhiking is easy.

Tourist Information from Tourist Board, Plymouth, Montserrat, W. Indies, or Eastern Caribbean Tourist Association at 200 Buckingham Palace Road, London SW1W 9TJ, and Room 411, 200 East 42nd Street, New York, N.Y. 10017. The Plymouth tourist office has maps of the island.

Banks Royal Bank of Canada, Barclays Bank International. Open 0800-1200 Mon.-Thurs.; 0800-1200 and 1500-1700 Fri.

Shopping Shops are open 0800-1600 except Wed. and Sat. which are half-days.

Documents See under Antigua.

WINDWARD ISLANDS

We are most grateful to Andrew Lawrence (Vancouver) and Jon Easterbrooke (Shaftesbury, Dorset) for new information on the Windwards.

DOMINICA

Dominica (pronounced Domineeca) is the largest and most mountainous of the Windward Islands, with an area of 289 sq. miles. It is 29 miles long and 16 miles wide. (The highest peak, Mt. Diablotin, rises to 4,747 ft. and is usually covered in mist. It is recommended that you climb it with a guide. Ask at the National Parks Office in Roseau. Note that the mountains are much wetter and cooler than the coast.) Dominica is known as the Nature Island of the Caribbean: its principal attractions include the Boiling Lake, the second largest of its kind in the world and reached after a three-hour climb with a guide from the village of Laudat. There is also a freshwater lake which can be reached by road. The Emerald Pool is a grotto in the forest and there are the Trafalgar triple waterfalls in the Roseau Valley, 5 miles from the capital. It is a botanist's paradise, too, for in the valleys there are orchids and wild gardens of strange plant life. The island is self-sufficient in fruit and vegetables; its main products are bananas (the principal export), copra, grapefruit and limes. It is one of the poorest islands in the Caribbean, but the people are some of the friendliest.

WINDWARD ISLANDS

In Dominica, one can also meet the last remnants, about 2,500, of the original inhabitants of the Caribbean, the once warlike Caribs. They live in the Carib Reserve, a 3,700-acre reservation near the Melville Hall airport. The total population of Dominica, which is otherwise almost entirely of African descent, is around 90,000, of whom about 25 % live in and around **Roseau,** the capital, on the Caribbean coast. The Woodbridge Bay deep-water harbour is 1 mile from the capital and handles most of the island's commercial shipping, as well as accommodating tourist vessels. The Botanical Garden has a collection of orchids and numerous other plant species. The new market in Roseau on Saturday mornings is a fascinating sight. The second town is Portsmouth in the north-west with a natural yacht harbour, near the ruins of the 18th-century Fort Shirley on the Cabrits. Like St. Lucia, Dominica was once a French possession: although English is the official tongue and is spoken in some villages such as Marigot, many of the inhabitants speak a kind of creole French similar to that spoken in Haiti. The Catholic church is the most important, though there are some Protestant denominations. Straw goods are among the best and cheapest in the Caribbean; they can be bought in the Carib Reserve.

In September 1979 the island was devastated by Hurricane David and 60,000 people were left homeless. Since then much reconstruction has taken place, a new airport has been built, new hotels established and Dominica is developing its tourist trade.

Government Dominica became a fully independent member of the Commonwealth on November 3, 1978. In 1980 Miss Eugenia Charles became Prime Minister; she was reelected in July 1985. The official title, Commonwealth of Dominica, should always be used in addresses to avoid confusion with the Dominican Republic.

Accommodation There are a number of small, informal hotels, guest houses and apartment facilities on the island. *Papillotte; Continental Inn; Sisserou; Castaways; Anchorage*, on seafront, swimming pool, A, EP, food poor; *Castle Comfort Guesthouse; Kent Anthony Guesthouse*, C, good food, 3 Great Marlborough St., Roseau, Tel.: 2730; *Springfield Guesthouse; Vena's Guesthouse*, D, on the corner of the two main streets, near the Tourist Board; *Emerald Guesthouse*, part of a 20-acre plantation, from D for log cabin (add US$28 for MAP), island tours available; *Cherry Lodge Guesthouse*, historic and quaint, C, meals available to order; *Riviere La Croix; Douglas Guesthouse*, Portsmouth. At Laudat, a good base for walking or climbing; there is only one expensive guesthouse. However, Mr. Maglore (105 Bath Estate, Roseau, Tel.: 4107) takes guests for reasonable prices. There are a 10% service charge and a 10% government tax on hotel bills.

Restaurants *Papillotte, Sisserou, Ti Kai, Guiyave* and *La Robe Creole. Golden Fry* offers a fast food service.

Entertainment Mid-week entertainment at *Sisserou* hotel. Discos and live bands at weekends. Carnival takes place in the first half of February, before Lent: not commercialized like many in the Americas.

Sports Football and cricket are among the most popular national sports. There are also hard tennis courts. The *Anchorage* and *Castaways* hotels offer sailing and deep-sea fishing.

Climate and Clothing Daytime temperatures average between 70° F and 85° F, though the nights are much cooler, especially in the mountains and in December and January. The rainy season is from June to October though showers occur all through the year. Clothing is informal, though swimsuits are not worn on the streets. A sweater is recommended for the evenings.

Transport Public transport is almost non-existent and roads are bad. Return transport by open van from Salybia or Marigot to Roseau costs EC$14. It can be difficult to return to Roseau by van, except on Fridays. Cars can be rented from Connie Astaphans, 23 Queen St. (Tel.: 3296/2348); Jackson Pascal, c/o Government Printery, High St. (Tel.: 2561, ext. 11); Lockhart Sebastian, c/o Customs, Bay Front (Tel.: 2602); Emmanuel Guy, c/o General Post Office (Tel.:2601); Nicholas Ducreay, 7 Shop Lane, Goodwill (Tel.: 3070). Rates are about US$35 per day, unlimited mileage, and the vehicles are usually Mazda automatics. It may be preferable to rent a car as the taxi service is expensive.

Documents All visitors entering Dominica must be in possession of an outward ticket and a valid passport. Proof of citizenship only is required for US and Canadian citizens. Visas are required by nationals of communist countries: they can be obtained from the Ministry of Home Affairs, Government Headquarters, Roseau. You may have trouble in extending your stay on the island, so bring some good references if you intend to stay any length of time.

WINDWARD ISLANDS 1263

Banks Royal Bank of Canada, Barclays Bank International, National Commercial and Development Bank of Dominica, Banque Française Commerciale. Open 0800-1300 Mon.-Thurs.; 0800-1300 and 1500-1700 Fri.

Electricity 220/240 v. AC 50 cycles. There is no electricity or running water in any of the villages between Marigot and La Plaine.

Airport Liat, Air Guadeloupe and Air Martinique have daily flights to Dominica, linking it with Antigua, Guadeloupe, Martinique and Barbados. A return ticket from Guadeloupe will cost 450 francs with Air Guadeloupe and 550 by Liat. Some flights arrive at the newly-opened Canefield airfield, a 5 minute drive from Roseau (taxi to Roseau, US$6). Others land at Melville Hall airport, in the N, 38 miles from Roseau (taxi to Roseau, EC$35). Taxis go from Melville Hall airport through the Carib Reserve (new road) to Roseau, via Salybia. There is a departure tax of US$6.

Tourist Information The Dominica Tourist Board has an office at 37 Cork St., Roseau (P.O. Box 73, Tel.: 809-445-2351/2186). In New York information can be obtained from the Caribbean Tourism Assoc., 20 East 46th St., New York, NY 10017 and from Caribbean Holidays Inc., 711 Third Avenue, New York, NY 10017. In West Germany from Caribic Holidays Reisen, Regerstrasse 5, 8000 Munich 90.

Warning. The only drug that is widely available is marijuana, so bring your own medicines, and be warned that the police are strict in their enforcement of anti-narcotic laws. The present Government takes a strong stand on "moral" issues.

Telecommunications Telegraph, telephone and telex services at Mercury House, Hanover St., Roseau, open 0700-2000, Mon.-Sat.

ST. LUCIA

St. Lucia is another island which is becoming a holiday centre. Its total population is around 120,000, and the area is about 238 square miles.

St. Lucia (pronounced "Loosha") has all the attractions one has come to expect of these islands; sport, splendid beaches, a clear, warm sea (which can be dangerous) and sunshine. It also has some of the finest mountain scenery in the West Indies. (The island was the scene of the film *Dr Doolittle*.) The highest peak is Mt. Gimie (3,145 feet); the most spectacular are the Gros Piton (2,619 feet) and the Petit Piton (2,461 feet) which are old volcanic forest-clad plugs rising sheer out of the sea near the town of Soufriere on the W coast. A few miles away is one of the world's most accessible volcanoes. Here you can see *soufrières*: vents in the volcano which exude hydrogen sulphide, steam and other gases and deposit sulphur and other compounds. There are also pools of boiling water. Entry to sulphur springs, EC$5. The mountains are intersected by numerous short rivers; in places, these rivers debouch into broad, fertile and well-cultivated valleys. The scenery is of outstanding beauty, and in the neigbourhood of the Pitons it has an element of grandeur.

There is a dry season roughly from January to April, and a rainy season from May to August. Towards the end of the year it is usually wet. The island lies in latitudes where the north-east trade winds are an almost constant influence. The mean annual temperature is about 26°C. Rainfall varies (according to altitude) in different parts of the island from 60 to 138 inches.

Even though some St. Lucians claim that their island was discovered by Columbus on St. Lucy's day (December 6—the national holiday), neither the date of discovery nor the discoverer are in fact known, for according to the evidence of Columbus's voyage, he appears to have missed the island. As early as 1605, 67 Englishmen en route to Guiana touched at St. Lucia and made an unsuccessful effort to settle though a Dutch expedition may have discovered the island first. The island at the time was peopled by Caribs and continued in their possession till 1635, when it was granted by the King of France to MM. de L'Olive and Duplessis. In 1638 the first recorded settlement was made by English from Bermuda and St. Kitts, but the colonists were killed by the Caribs about three years later.

In 1642 the King of France, still claiming sovereignty over the island, ceded it to the French West India Company, who in 1650 sold it to MM. Honel and Du Parquet. After repeated attempts by the Caribs to expel the French, a treaty of peace was concluded between them in 1660. In all, St. Lucia changed hands fourteen times before it became a British Crown Colony in 1814 by the Treaty of Paris.

St. Lucia became a fully independent member of the Commonwealth on February 22, 1979. The Government is led by Mr. John Compton, returned to power in May 1982; he called fresh elections for April 30, 1987, following an unsatisfactory one-seat win on April 6. There is still a good

1264 WINDWARD ISLANDS

deal of French influence: most of the islanders, who are predominantly of African descent (though a few Caribs are still to be found in certain areas), speak a French patois, and there is still a French provincial style of architecture; a large proportion of the population are Roman Catholics. Apart from tourism the island's economy is based on agriculture, particularly bananas and also cocoa and coconuts. There is also some industry and an oil transshipment terminal has been built.

The capital, **Castries,** rebuilt after being destroyed by fire in 1948, is splendidly set on a natural harbour against a background of mountains. It has a covered market which is worth a visit, especially on Saturday morning. Basketware is a good buy. From the old Morne fortress (now a teacher training college), above the town, you get an excellent view of the town, coast-line and mountains. The highway from Castries to the other end of the island at Vieux Fort, now completely renovated, is a delightful drive. Leaving Castries, one gets an increasingly good view of the town and harbour as the road climbs to the "top of the morne", over a thousand feet, and then continues down and up and down for the 40 miles to Vieux Fort where the jet airport is situated. Another spectacular part of the road is the crossing of the Barre de l'Isle, the mountain barrier that divides the island. One passes the coastal villages of Dennery and Micoud, and can camp at Praslin bay. The road on the western side of the island leading from Vieux Fort to Laborie, Choiseul (a quaint old West Indian village indeed) and Soufriere is bad in parts, but approaching Soufriere it is very easy to walk to the volcano and even have a sulphur bath. Plenty of guides will offer to show you the way, and as it is possible to get lost it may be advisable to hire one. A more convenient set of baths is located within walking distance of Soufriere, and a stay in this town within view of the majestic Pitons is well worth while. Indeed, it is essential if you have no transport of your own and want to see the volcano and the Pitons, as there are no buses back to Castries after midday. Buses to Castries leave from the square. Of the beaches on the island Vigie (1½ miles from Castries) and Reduit are both beautiful, but heavily populated. The best is La Brelotte, with its quiet and secluded *East Winds* hotel. There is a yacht basin at Gros Islet. There is a boat trip to Soufriere on the brig *Unicorn,* cost US$40. At the swimming stop on the return journey local divers may try to sell you coral. Don't buy it—a reef dies if you do.

Airports St. Lucia has two airports—Vigie Airport (near Castries, taxi for EC$8 or walk across runway to town), and Hewanorra International Airport in the Vieux Fort district, where the runway was recently lengthened from 5,000 to 9,000 feet. Most international flights land there; there is an air link with Vigie (EC$80). Alternatively a taxi to Castries costs EC$100 (though, out of season, you can negotiate a cheaper rate). At both airports there is a departure tax of EC$20, or EC$10 for flights to countries within the Caribbean Commonwealth. Air services are maintained by BWIA, Liat, Pan-Am and British Airways. Inter-Island Air Services fly to St. Vincent, Grenada, Union Island, Carriacou, Canovan and Mustique. No baggage storage yet available at Hewanorra. Try to arrange it with one of the Vieux Fort hotels.

Shipping The island is served by the following shipping lines: Harrison Lines—cargo vessels only; Geest Industries—cargo and passenger vessels; local trading schooners. Yachts can be chartered at the Moorings, Marigot Bay.

Documents Regulations for St. Lucia and the other Windward Islands are similar to those for the Leewards, given under Antigua (page 1258).

There is a commercial radio station, Radio Caribbean, which broadcasts daily in French and English, and a government-owned station, Radio St. Lucia. A commercial television service operates in both languages.

Hotels *Leon Rojo* (Vigie Beach), A; *Hurricane Hole* (Marigot Bay), where much of the *Dr. Doolittle* film was made, is recommended, A (MAP add US$23 per person), children under 12 free; there is a pleasant beach 300 yds away by ferry, also by ferry you can get to Doolittle's bar and restaurant, excellent but expensive; nearby *Marigot Inn,* A; *Green Parrot,* A (add US$18-28 for MAP); *East Winds Inn* (La Brelotte), A, (MAP add US$20); *Harmony Apartel* (Reduit), A; *La Toc,* A, cottages, tennis courts, golf course; *Steigenberger Cariblue Hotel* (Cap Estate), A; *St. Lucian* (Reduit Beach), A; *Couples* (only for couples) (Vigie Beach) A; has some self-catering cottages also A, many facilities, recommended despite the noise of aircraft landing and taking off; *Halcyon Beach Club* (Choc Beach), A; *Morne Fortune Apartments,* A; *Villa Beach Cottages* (Choc Beach) A; *Anse Chastnet Hotel* (Soufriere), A; *Kimatria Hotel* (Vieux Fort), C; *Cloud's Nest Hotel* (Vieux Fort), B, also apartments; *Dasheen* (Soufriere), A, in spectacular setting, used to film *Superman II,* good restaurant.

Guesthouses Castries: *Lee's,* Chaussee Road, noisy and no fan, D; *Matthews,* High Street, C;

WINDWARD ISLANDS 1265

Elwins, La Chaussee, C, MAP; *Twin Palm Inn*, Morne Fortune, D; *Boots*, 36 Micoud St., C; *William's*, Chaussee Road; *Tropical Haven*, just outside Castries, C, 10 mins. from town, more than adequate, excellent food. Vieux Fort: *St. Martin*, D. Vide Bouteille (just outside Castries): *Creole Inn*, C, with bath, clean and simple; *Coconut Cove*, Soufriere: *Home Guesthouse*, D, EP; *Tropical Palm*, F. It is possible to bargain cheaper rates for longer stays. *Hippo's*, C. *Sunset Lodge Guesthouse*, near Vigie Airport, C, convenient, ask for a room away from the road. In the hills at Marisule, a 15 min. walk from La Brelotte Bay, the Zephirin family has cottages to let, D, self-catering, highly recommended. You can stay at the National Research and Development Foundation, at Bernards Hill, D. 20 mins walk from Vigie airport, 5 mins. to Castries. AP = All meals; MAP = breakfast and dinner; EP = no meals; CP = breakfast. There is a 10% service charge and a 7% government tax on all hotel bills.

Restaurants include the *Flamingo Restaurant*, Marigot; *Rain* and the *Green Parrot* (recommended) and *Kimian's*, Colombus Square, meal costs about EC$10, recommended. *Charles Bon Appetit*, Morne Fortune. *The Last Wagon*, Chaussee Road, serves good sandwiches. *Banana Split*, *Le Boucan*, *Wicki-Up*, *Pat's Pub*, all quite good; recommended is the *Edge Water Beach Hotel* restaurant at Vide Bouteille. Creole dishes are served at the *Pelican* (near the *Holiday Inn*) and local cuisine is the main feature of *The Still* (Soufriere); *The Humming Bird* (Soufriere) is a good place to eat and take a swim; *Pisces* (Choc Bay); *Le Bambou* has a discothèque (admission EC$8 at weekends) as well as a restaurant and pizza parlour. *Behind The Wall Club*, in Gros Islet, has live steel band Friday nights. Be prepared for a EC$20 taxi fare to get back to Castries.

Tourist Information Cars, mini-mokes and motorcycles can be rented, the latter from Happy Chappy Rentals for US$12 a day. Car hire costs about EC$80 a day. You get 45 free miles, then you are charged at EC$1 a mile. If you do not have an international driving licence a temporary licence can be obtained for EC$15 (or EC$10 for motorcyclists), if you have a national permit. Drive on the left. Taxi fares are supposedly set by the Government, but the EC$5 Castries-Soufriere fare turns into EC$10 on the return journey as unlucky tourists discover that there are no buses. Smugglers Village, in the extreme north, to Castries, about 10 miles away, costs EC$25 one way. If in doubt about the amount charged, check with the tourist office or hotel reception. A trip round the island by taxi, off season, can be arranged for about EC$150. Alternatively—and much cheaper—go by bus. St. Lucia's buses are usually privately-owned minibuses. Those going N leave from behind the market in Castries. Those going S leave from Bridge St. From Castries to Vieux Fort, EC$5; to Choc Beach, EC$0.75; to Soufriere, EC$5; to Dennery EC$2; to Gros Islet EC$1; to Morne Fortune EC$0.50. Water taxis and speedboats can be rented and there is also a ferry service. As some of the best views are from the sea, it is recommended to take at least one boat trip. *The Buccaneer* sails down the coast to Soufriere; the cost is US$30, which includes transport to the sulphur springs and volcano at Soufriere and lunch. Likewise (and better), the brig *Unicorn* leaves from near the *Coalpot* restaurant, Wed. and Fri., 0900, charging US$30 with unlimited rum punches. The tourist board map is expensive at EC$15. Friday nights, from 2100, there is a street fair in Gros Islet. Try the grilled conch from one of the booths selling local food.

Other attractions for visitors include a trip to Pigeon Island, which is connected to the mainland by a causeway. The day can be spent beachcombing and treasure hunting among the wrecks offshore; there is crab racing; a visit to a coconut oil factory; deepsea fishing; diving (scuba diving, snorkelling and fishing trips are run by Dive St. Lucia, P.O. Box 412, Vigie, Castries, who also provide tuition); sailing and shopping for local handicrafts.

Hitching is considered quite safe, though some drivers might expect a tip.

The address of the office of the British Government representative is: Micoud St. (P.O. Box 227), Castries. Tel.: 2484/5/6. Cable and Wireless (West Indies) Ltd., George Gordon Building.

Warnings One correspondent warns about harassment by locals, especially on the East Road between Marigot Bay and Soufriere, and in other remote areas. Roads to the waterfalls and sulphur springs on Soufriere lack signposts. "Guides" might expect large payments for their services. We have received more reports from St. Lucia of harassment and hostility towards tourists than from any other island in the Lesser Antilles.

Camping is allowed on most beaches.

Health Drinking water is safe in most towns and villages. The bilharzia fluke has apparently been totally eliminated from river systems.

Banks Bank of Nova Scotia, Barclays Bank International, Royal Bank of Canada, Canadian Imperial Bank of Commerce, and the St. Lucia Co-operative Bank. It is better to change currency at a bank than in a hotel where you can get 5-10% less on the exchange.

Business Hours Banks 0800-1200 Mon.-Thurs.; 0800-1200 and 1500-1800 Fri. Shops 0800-1200, 1300-1600, closed Wed. pm. Offices 0800-1600 Mon.-Fri.

Communications The island has an adequate telephone system, with international direct dialling. Intra-island calls are EC$0.25 for three minutes.

Electricity 220v. 50 cycles.

1266 WINDWARD ISLANDS

Tourist information is available from St. Lucia Tourist Board, Castries, St. Lucia, and New York City, USA. We are most grateful to Catherine Strauss and Gregory Groth for additional updating material.

ST. VINCENT & THE GRENADINES

St. Vincent, until fairly recently, was almost unknown to tourists. It is very picturesque, with its fishing villages, coconut groves and fields of arrowroot, of which the island provides 90% of world supply. Fruit and vegetables abound and account (especially bananas) for much of the island's exports. St. Vincent became fully independent on October 27, 1979 under the name of St. Vincent & the Grenadines: James "Son" Mitchell is Prime Minister.

About 133 square miles, it has a population of some 124,000, mostly of African and East Indian descent with some English blood. Many Caribs were deported to Belize in 1787; most of the remainder were wiped out by a volcanic eruption in 1902. Most Vicentians are Anglican though there are some Catholic and nonconformist churches. The capital, **Kingstown,** stands on a sheltered bay where scores of craft laden with fruit and vegetables add their touch of colour and noisy gaiety to the town.

The highest peak on the island, the Soufriere volcano, rises to about 4,000 feet. In 1970 an island reared itself up out of the lake in the crater: it smokes and the water round it is very warm. Hiking to the volcano, which erupted as recently as April 1979, is very popular, but one must leave very early in the morning. A jeep track runs 3 miles through banana plantations to where the trail begins. It takes about 3 hrs. to reach the crater edge.

There are few good roads, but cars, including self-drive, can be hired and most of the beauty spots are accessible by road. The drive along the W coast towards the Soufriere should not be missed; it has been described as a "tropical corniche". The Marriaqua Valley with its numerous streams is particularly beautiful. The Queens Drive takes you into the hills east of Kingstown and gives splendid views all around. The Leeward Highway is a dramatic drive, passing through Questelles and Layou. There are lush valleys and magnificent sea views. A boat trip to the falls of Baleine is recommended. There are some interesting petroglyphs and rock carvings dating back to the Ciboney, Arawak and Carib eras. The best known are just N of Layou.

In Kingstown itself the Botanical Gardens just below Government House are well worth a visit. There is a very interesting museum of Amerindian artefacts in the Gardens, open only Wed. a.m. and Sat. p.m. Here there is a sucker of the original bread-fruit tree planted by Captain Bligh of the *Bounty*, who brought the first bread-fruit here from the Pacific; it became a staple food item in the West Indies. St. Vincent also has splendid beaches, mostly with volcanic black sand. Some of them, however, are difficult to reach by public transport. (Sea urchins are a hazard, especially among rocks on the less frequented beaches.) There is excellent sailing; the island has a good yacht marina. Boats can be hired from several places, or CSY operate a charter service. They also have "sail-and-learn" cruises. There are also facilities for scuba-diving, snorkelling, deep-sea fishing, tennis and golf: the 9-hole Aqueduct course in Buccaneer Valley is very attractive. Fort Charlotte has an interesting museum of Carib artefacts and other items of local history. There are first-class hotels and more modest guest houses; St. Vincent is regarded as one of the cheaper islands to visit. Best months are December to May. There is an airport tax of EC$10 for non-nationals, EC$5 for nationals.

Buses Minibuses from Kingstown to Arnos Vale airport, EC$1, and all other places on the island, including a frequent service to Indian Bay, the main hotel area; they stop on demand rather than at bus-stops. Also to Layou in the N. Worthwhile to make a day trip to Mesopotamia (Mespo) by bus (EC$2). On the whole, though, buses are not a particularly good form of transport for the sightseer; if you do want to travel round St. Vincent, it is better to hire a car for about EC$65 a day. Car Rentals Ltd., Davids, Kings, De Freitas, Hillocks, Star Garage and Johnsons all hire cars.

Taxis Kingstown to Airport EC$12, Layou EC$30, Orange Hill EC$70, Blue Lagoon EC$25. Taxi fares are fixed by the Government.

WINDWARD ISLANDS 1267

Accommodation All prices are for a double room, MAP, unless otherwise stated: *Cobblestone Inn*, B; *Grand View*, A; *Haddon*, A; *Heron*, B. At Indian Bay, 3 miles from town, *Coconut Beach*, A; *Yvonette Apartments*, C, 2 mins. from beach, clean, friendly and highly recommended; *Treasure Island*, A, EP; *Villa Lodge*, A, 5 mins. from airport, recently refurbished, recommended; *Indian Bay Beach*, B. Also out of town, *Mariner's Inn*, A, MAP, attractive old colonial house with own beach and good restaurant; *Rawacou*, A; *Sugar Mill Inn*, B; *Grand View Beach*, A, EP; *Olives*, E, but not at all safe; *Sunset Shores*, A; *Tropic Breeze*, EP, A; *Valley Inn*, A; *Young Island*, AP; A; *Yvonette Beach*, EP, A; *Palm Leaf*, quite clean, D, EP. *Kingstown Park Guest House*, D; *Whaleback*, EP, D; *Sea Breeze Guest House*, near airport, D, cooking facilities, friendly, helpful, bus to town from the door. *Breezeville Apartments*, Arnos Vale. *Chubbies Dine-in and Live-in*, opposite Kingstown docks, D with bath. There is a 5% tax on hotel bills. At the *Bounty Café*, where local artists' paintings are exhibited, you can have a good light meal. For entertainment there is the *Aquatic Club*, Young Island Beach, open Tues. and Fri. (better). In the Villa area, *The French Restaurant*; the *Dolphin Restaurant*, Young Island, Tel.: (809) 458-4826. US reservations: Ralph Locke, 315 E. 72nd st., New York, NY 10021. Tel.: (212) 628-8149.

International Transport The Geest Line calls weekly at St. Vincent en route from and to Wales. Several flour ships ply between St. Vincent and St. Kitts via Montserrat, and it is possible to hitch a lift on these. Air Martinique has services direct to Fort-de-France, connecting with Air France to Paris. Liat flies to nearby islands. Interair services operate to St. Lucia and Grenada. There is a regular boat service to Grenada and the Grenadines (see page 1269).

Banks Barclays Bank International, Caribbean Banking Corporation, Bank of Nova Scotia, Canadian Imperial Bank of Commerce, National Commercial Bank.

Electricity 220/240 v. Power cuts occur fairly frequently.

We are most grateful to Alvin and Elsie Joubert for updating material.

GRENADA

Grenada, the most southerly of the Windwards, can be described as a spice island, for it produces large quantities of cloves and mace and about a third of the world's nutmeg. It also grows cacao and sugar. Some of its beaches, specially Grand Anse, a dazzling two-mile stretch of white sand, are considered to be among the finest in the world. The island's capital, **St. George's,** with its terraces of pale, colour-washed houses and cheerful red roofs, is picturesque; it was established in 1705 by French settlers, who called it Fort Royal; and much of its present-day charm comes from the blend of two colonial cultures: typical 18th century French provincial houses intermingle with fine examples of English Georgian architecture. There is a small museum in the centre of town which is worth a visit. In contrast to St. Lucia and Dominica, however, the French cultural influence in Grenada has completely died out. The town stands on an almost land-locked sparkling blue harbour against a background of green and hazy blue hills. Inland, the scenery is just as attractive; wooded hills, wild flowers, rivers, waterfalls and quiet crater pools and lakes.

Grenada (pronounced "Grenayda") is about the same size as St. Vincent, with a population of some 110,000. It is a predominantly Catholic island (visitors are welcome to visit the monastery on Mount St. Ervans in the afternoon) though there are various Protestant churches. Average temperature is 26°C. The weather is sunny and hot from December to May. The tourist season is at its height between Jan. and March. The rainy season runs from June to November.

Grenada did not opt for associated-state status when it was offered by the UK, and became independent in 1974. Following a bloody *coup d'état* in October 1983, in which the left-wing Prime Minister, Mr. Maurice Bishop (who had been in office since the revolution of March 1979), and several dozen followers were murdered, joint US and Caribbean forces invaded the island, displaced the new marxist regime and expelled the Cubans who had been advising the Bishop government. Grenada was then run by an interim advisory council until the holding of elections in December 1984, which resulted in Mr Herbert Blaize becoming Prime Minister.

Airport The old airport, Pearls, is just N of Grenville, the second most important town, and 18 miles from St. George's. Taxi from Pearls to St. George's, EC$50. Airport departure tax is US$15. The new Point Salines airport was completed with US help in October 1984. It is 5 km. from St. George's; taxis only, EC$30. Cheaper from town to airport, about EC$20.

1268 WINDWARD ISLANDS

Hotels St. George's: *Cinnamon Hill*, A, AP; *Crescent Inn*, A; *Ross Point Inn*, A,Q Grand Anse Beach: *Flamboyant* (cottages); *Hibiscus*, B; *12 Degrees North*, A; *Spice Island Inn*, A, AP; *Blue Horizon Cottage Hotel*, EP. Lance aux Epines: *Secret Harbour*, A and *Horseshoe Bay*, A; *Calabash*, A; *Silversands*, B, EP (with a/c); *Riviera Cottages*, B; *Rock Gardens Inn*, A, EP; *Hamilton Inn*, A, EP; *Sam's Inn* (near airport), A; *St. James's* A, AP; *Tropical Inn*, A, AP. *Renaissance*, now refurbished and renamed (formerly *Grenada Beach Hotel*) after housing US troops.

Guesthouses St. George's: *Tita's Guest House*, D; *Mitchell's Guest House*, D, recommended; *St Ann's Guest House*, beyond Botanic Gardens, B, MAP, very clean and friendly, highly recommended, meals good value; *Skyline*, Grand Anse Beach, B, recommended. Grenville: *St. Andrew's Guest House*, D, EP. There are also many furnished cottages available for rent from various agents; US$200 off season, US$300 in season.

Restaurants *Nutmeg*, delicious local dishes and its own famous rum punch, very popular; *Rudolph's* expensive, but good, local and international food; *The Greenery*, seafood, good drinks, recommended; *Turtle Back*, good view, discotheque; *Sand Pebble*, cheap and clean; *Red Crab*, an "English pub" and restaurant, near the Grand Anse beach; *The Pebble*; *Snug Corner*, *Pitch Pine Bar*; *Portofino*. *La Belle Créole*, at the Blue Horizons Cottage Hotel, is one of the island's best. Rum punches are excellent at EC$1.75, and be sure to try the local sea-moss drink. **Discotheques** include *Sugarmill*, *BBC* and *Grenada Yacht Services (GYS)*.

Transport Buses run to all parts of the island from the market place in St. George's. The public transport system has new Mitsubishi buses and there are also privately-run minibuses. Fares are EC$0.50-1.00 within St. George's and EC$4 to Grenville and Sauteurs. The last buses tend to be in mid-afternoon and there are very few on Sundays. The maximum taxi fare is EC$50. Hitchhiking is quite easy though the roads are not very good. Cars can be hired from Chasley David, Steeles, McIntyres as well as Avis and Hertz.

Excursions Tours of the local nutmeg factories at Charlotte Town or on the Douglasson Estate are worthwhile, can easily be arranged and are free. The village of Sauteurs, in the north of the island, is where some of the last Carib inhabitants are reputed to have leapt to their deaths in 1641, preferring suicide to surrender. To escape the heat, visit Lake Grand Etaing and go on the forest trail to Mt. Qua Qua. Henry, of Henry's Travel (Tel.: 5313) conducts tours of the island and is very well informed on all aspects of Grenada.

Shopping There is a national handicraft centre.

Tourist Office Carenage, St. George's. Open 0800-1600 and is helpful. Has information on the two Grenadines which are dependencies of Grenada: Carriacou and Petit Martinique (see below). Also excellent map of Grenada, EC$7.

Travel Agents (all in St. George's) Grenada International Travel Service, of Church St. (American Express representative), Huggins Travel Service, McIntyre Brothers, George Otway.

Banks Barclays Bank International, Commercial Bank of Grenada, Chase Manhattan, Canadian Imperial Bank of Commerce, Bank of Nova Scotia. They do not exchange European currencies other than sterling.

Business Hours Banks: 0800-1200 Mon.-Thurs; 0800-1200, 1500-1800 Fri. Shops: 0800-1145, 1300-1600 Mon.-Fri., 0800-1200 Sat. Government offices: 0800-1145, 1300-1600 Mon.-Fri.

Holidays

January 1: New Year's Day
February 7: Independence Day
Good Friday and Easter Monday
May 1: Labour Day
First Monday in August
December 25 and 26

Sports Tennis, golf (9 hole course), swimming, snorkelling, scuba diving and water-skiing.

Food Lambi (shellfish), sea-moss drink, callaloo soup, soue (a sauce made from pig's feet).

Newspapers *Grenadian Voice*, published weekly by the Trinidad Express; *The New Grenadian* (pro status quo); *Indies Times* (socialist); *Crucial Times* (Black Muslim).

Cables Cable and Wireless Ltd., Carenage, St. George's. Open 0700-1900 Mon.-Sat.; 1600-1800 Sun.

Electricity 220/240 volts, 50 cycles A.C.

International Transport Liat flies to Grenada from Barbados, Trinidad and St. Vincent. There are also flights to Maturín (Venezuela). There is a EC$5 tax on airline tickets purchased in Grenada. Chandris American Line, Royal Caribbean Cruise Line and Geest call at the island. There is a schooner, the *Alexis II*, to Trinidad every Tuesday afternoon (EC$75) operated by Paddy's Shipping (Tel.: 3261), as well as other unscheduled services. Also regular sailings to St. Vincent and the Grenadines (see below). It is easier to get a Trinidad-bound boat from Grenville, rather than St George's. Tel.: Isaac Joseph, St Andrew's 7512, for information about sailing on the *Fazeela*.

Documents An onward ticket is essential, though one from Barbados to the US (for example) is accepted. When you arrive in Grenada expect to have your luggage examined very thoroughly. You must be able to give an accommodation address when you arrive.

Information Write to Grenada Tourist Board, St. George's, Grenada, W. Indies; Grenada Information Office, 866 2nd Av., New York; Grenada High Commission, Driveway Place, Ottawa; Grenada Tourist Office, 200 Buckingham Palace Road, London SW1W 9TJ. We are most grateful to Dr. Thomas Herz (Cologne) for new information on the island.

THE GRENADINES

The **Grenadines** are divided politically between St. Vincent and Grenada, a string of tiny, rocky islands stretching across some 35 miles of sea between the two. With a combined population of about 18,000 they are still very much off the beaten track as far as tourists are concerned, but are popular with yachtsmen and the "international set". **Carriacou** (pronounced Carr-yacoo) and **Petit Martinique** are dependencies of Grenada. Carriacou, an attractive, sandy island, the largest of the Grenadines with an area of 13 sq. miles, has interesting underwater reefs. Visitors should see the oyster beds where "tree-oysters" grow. Big drum dances take place around Easter. The Tombstone Feasts are unique. An annual regatta takes place in early August which is a good time to visit. There is a small museum in Hillsborough and the woman who runs it can tell you about the Arawak ruins on the island. Buses go from Hillsborough, where boats are built, and to Tyrell Bay. There are also plenty of taxis. Out of season the island is quiet, and not all the hotels are open. Barclays Bank International has a branch on Carriacou. Food is limited in variety, especially fresh vegetables. "Jack's Iron" rum (180° proof) is a local hazard.
It is advisable to use insect repellant on the beaches, especially in the rainy season.

Hotels on Carriacou: *Silver Beach Cottages*, B, though for a longer stay a cheaper rate can be negotiated with the owner, Mr Delmar, who is very knowledgeable about the area; *Mermaid Tavern*, A, MAP; *Amigo Guest House*, D, AP; *Modern Guest House*, E, AP. *Traveller's Inn*, run by Mr. Prescott Simon at Hillsborough, D, 30 mins. walk along the coast from the airstrip, or by the not-very-regular bus service. There are some local bar/restaurants but they often run out of food quite early; *Peter's Place*, breathtaking views, water supply erratic. (Plus 10% service and 5% government tax). There are many fully equipped houses to rent, costing about US$100 a month. See Mr. Emmons or Mrs. Joseph or ask at the tourist office on the quay. A clean, modern apartment may cost EC$300 per week, but it is possible to find simpler accommodation for as little as EC$7 a night (per person). There are no hotels on Petit Martinique.

Bequia (pronounced Bek-*wee*) and **Mustique** are the largest of the St. Vincent dependencies. Bequia attracts quite a number of tourists, chiefly yachtsmen. Its main village is Port Elizabeth and here Admiralty Bay offers a safe anchorage. Experienced sailors can sometimes get a job crewing on boats sailing on from here to Panama and other destinations. Away from Port Elizabeth the beaches are empty; Hope beach is particularly pleasant. Hotels include: *Friendship Bay*, A, MAP; *Spring*, A, MAP; *Frangipani*, A, MAP; *Mitchells*, overlooking harbour, D, cooking facilities available; *Sunny Caribee*, A; *Julie's Guest House*, C, MAP. *Lucy's Guest House*, B, MAP, and *Lower Bay Guest House* at Lower Bay are recommended. *Mac's Pizza* is recommended. On Mustique: *Cotton House*, L, is the only hotel and is outrageously expensive Tel.: (809) 458-4621; *Basil's Beach Bar*. Other Vincentian islands are as follows: **Union Island**, which has two settlements, Clifton and Ashton. The beach at Chatham Bay is beautiful and deserted. Hotels: *Anchorage Yacht Club* with excellent French restaurant, A; *Clifton Beach*, B, MAP; *Sunny Grenadines*, C, and several other small hotels between Clifton and Ashton. Barclays Bank has a branch. **Canouan** is a quiet, peaceful island with very few tourists and excellent beaches; *Crystal Sands*, A, MAP, and *Silver Beach* hotels; *Villa de Bijou* (Mme Michelle Peroche), B, MAP; also possible to rent houses. **Mayreau** is a small island without any hotels though some tourist facilities are now being built at Salt Whistle Bay. **Petit St. Vincent** is a beautiful, privately-owned island with one of the best resorts in the Caribbean, the *Petit St. Vincent* which is open from November-May, L (US$130-200 d depending on time of year). Tel.: (809) 458-4801. U.S. reservations: P.S.V., P.O. Box 12506, Cincinnatti, Ohio 45212; Tel.: (513) 242-1333. Palm Island (*Beach Club*, Tel.: (809) 458-4804. A, MAP) on Prune Island.

Inter-Island Transport Every Mon. and Thurs. the *Grenadine Star* sails between St. Vincent, Bequia, Canouan, Mayreau, Union and Mustique. The *Friendship Rose* plies daily between St. Vincent and Bequia, leaving at 1330 from St. Vincent and returning at 0600, 1½ hr. crossing, and on Sun. at 1200 a sailing boat leaves St. Vincent for Bequia (EC$4). A car ferry leaves St. Vincent for Union Island at 1000 on Mondays and Thursdays (EC$15). Every Wed. and Sat. the trading schooners *Gliding Star* and *Success* sail from Grenada to Carriacou (EC$20), returning on Thurs.

and Mon. There are also unscheduled schooner services between these islands; by asking around you might be be able to get a passage on one. Carriacou is one hour by schooner from Union Island.

There are daily Liat flights (heavily booked) from Grenada to St. Vincent, via Carriacou and Union Island, EC$61. (The airline is sometimes forgetful where luggage is concerned, so make sure yours is loaded on and off the 'plane. Also be sure to reconfirm your flights.)

Inter-Island Airways (IAS) connects St. Vincent, Canouan, Mustique, Union, Carriacou and Grenada.

BAHAMAS

THE BAHAMAS is a coral archipelago consisting of some 700 low-lying islands, and over 2,000 cays (pronounced "keys"). Grand Bahama Island is only 60 miles from Florida. Nassau, the capital, on New Providence Island, is 184 miles by air from Miami.

About 15 island areas have been developed. They have a total population of about 235,000; about 135,000 live in New Providence and 27,000 in Grand Bahama. Thanks partly to the Gulf Stream, the climate is one of the finest in the world, and there are good hotels, good shops, picturesque buildings and a round of sport and entertainment. The other islands, known as the "Family Islands", include Grand Bahama, Bimini, the Abacos, Harbour Island, the Exumas, Andros, Eleuthera (the last two are particularly attractive), Berry Islands, Cat Island, Long Island, the Inaguas, San Salvador, Spanish Wells, Crooked Island and Ragged Island. They are all being transformed now; there are about 20 Family Island landing strips, and those that have none are served by amphibian aircraft as well as the normal inter-island surface vessels.

The total area of the islands is about 5,400 square miles, roughly the same as Jamaica. The whole archipelago extends for about 600 miles south-eastward from the Mantanilla shoal off the coast of Florida to 50 miles north of Cuba. Some of the smaller cays are privately owned but most of them are uninhabited and some possibly have never been visited. As such they make ideal havens for drug smugglers.

Thanks to the sunny climate visitors are attracted throughout the year; total arrivals normally exceed 2m.; spending about US$800m. However, there has been unfavourable publicity concerning alleged corruption and the drugs trade. Agriculture is less important than tourism, though it is growing. This is not restricted to the two main islands: on the Family Islands tourist facilities are being developed and agriculture extended. Some steps have been taken to encourage light industries, notably timber and salt production. As far as foreign trade is concerned, exports are mostly re-exports of oil products. Imports are of food, consumer goods and crude oil (mainly kept in bunkers for re-export).

History Columbus discovered the Bahamas in 1492. The island of Guanahani (renamed by him San Salvador) is generally credited with his first landfall in the New World. It was after founding their first colonies in Virginia that the English realized the strategic importance of the Bahamas, and in 1629 the islands received their first constitution as part of the Carolinas. In fact, the first settlers came from Bermuda with the aim of founding a colony free from the religious and constitutional troubles of Charles I's England. Then William Sayle, who had been Governor of Bermuda, published in London in 1647 *A Broadside Advertising Eleuthera and the Bahama Islands*. As a result of this publicity, a company of Eleutherian Adventurers was formed and a party of about 70, led by Sayle himself, set out for Eleuthera. Their ship was wrecked on the reefs. The party managed to land but most of the stores were lost and the settlers barely managed to survive by trading ambergris.

From this time on, the life of the Bahamas was largely influenced by their proximity to the North American mainland and their place on the sea routes. Piracy, buccaneering and the slave trade were features of the next two centuries. In 1919, with the advent of Prohibition in the United States, Nassau became a bootleggers' paradise, but with the repeal of Prohibition, this source of wealth dried up and the islands had little to fall back on. The Thirties, a time of severe depression, ended in disaster in 1939 when disease killed off the sponges which had provided some means of

BAHAMAS 1271

livelihood. Once again, it was war which brought prosperity back. This time, however, foundations were laid for more stable conditions in the future and the two bases of prosperity, tourism and the real estate business, became firmly established.

Political After three centuries of rule by the merchant classes of Nassau, an administration supported by the black majority came to power in 1967, led by Mr. Lynden Pindling. The Bahamas became independent, within the Commonwealth, in July 1973; Mr. Pindling, now Sir Lynden, is still Prime Minister. High levels of unemployment, particularly among the young, are a source of social tension and rising crime.

Nassau (population: 110,000), on New Providence Island, is the capital. It looks comfortably old-fashioned with its white and pink houses: by-laws forbid skyscrapers and there are few neon lights. Many of the hotels are designed for Americans who have come south for the sun and the sea, and are expensive. Gambling at *Paradise Island Hotel* (L, EP) in a casino as big as a large railway station, and at 2 casinos in Freeport.

Nassau has plenty to interest the tourist: fishing, skin diving, golf, water skiing, tennis, bowling, a visit to the flamingo gardens, a trip on a glass-bottomed boat, a sight-seeing tour of the old forts and churches, and attractive examples of early local architecture: houses built of limestone, with wide wooden verandas. There is a *son-et-lumière* show every night at Fort Charlotte; visit too the Versailles Gardens and Cloisters on Paradise Island, Straw Market, the Queen's Staircase and Woodes Rogers Walk. There is a seaquarium at Nassau; it costs US$4 to see a show there; this includes the return bus fare from the town centre. Nearby is Ardastra Gardens, with trained flamingoes (entry US$2). Five minutes across Nassau harbour is the famous Paradise Island, reached by an extremely ugly steel toll bridge (US$2), where you can eat in the *Café Martinique* or gamble in the Casino.

Hotels Note: There is a great variety of accommodation in the Bahamas, ranging from small guest houses, offering only rooms, to luxury hotels complete with swimming pools, private beaches, sailboats and skin-diving equipment, restaurant, dancing and entertainment. For information, write to Bahamas Ministry of Tourism, Nassau Court, Nassau, Bahamas, or at 23 Old Bond Street, London, W1 (Tel.: 01-629-5238); 30 Rockefeller Plaza, New York, NY 10020; 85 Richmond Street W, Toronto 1, Ont.

Restaurants At Nassau: *El Toro; Dirty Dick's; Pilot House;* the *Poop Deck* at the Nassau Yacht Haven serves lunch and dinner; *Green Shutters*, Parliament Street, good bar and restaurant; *Parliament Street Restaurant*, lovely setting, excellent salads and local dishes. Cheaper at midday. *Buena Vista Hotel*, restaurant recommended; *Grand Central Restaurant; Blackbeard's Tavern; Riviera*, Bay Street, near Charlotte Street, good for breakfast and quick lunches, cheap; nearby, *Bahamian Kitchen*, delicious meals for about US$3.50; *Sandpiper* and *Skan* cafeterias for quick, relatively cheap meals. Also *Kentucky Fried Chicken, Howard Johnson's, Macdonalds, Burger King, Pino's Pizza, Lums, Lofthouse* and *Mermaid Tavern*. To the W of Nassau, at Gambier, is *Travellers' Rest*. Near the *Pearl Cox Guest House*, on the beach, fish is cooked and makes a cheap meal.

Night-life Most of the large hotels have night clubs. Other night spots include King Eric's (good floor show), Peanut Taylor's (expensive), Dirty Dick's and Pino's. Some clubs have a cover charge or a two-drink minimum.

Clubs East Hill Club and Lyford Key Club at W end of island, with fine golf course.

Warning to young women. Beware the "beach bums" who earn a living picking up young female tourists.

Diving Equipment Boats and diving equipment can be hired at shops by the Paradise Island bridge. The cost of hire for a morning's dive is about US$25. Scuba-diving with an instructor costs about US$32 a day.

Tourist Office, Rawson Square, staff not particularly helpful. Ask for *What to Do* pamphlet. Another, *Best-Buys*, is in your hotel or at the airport. There is also an office at the airport which will help you find accommodation. The Ministry of Tourism is at Nassau Court. The tourist office has a list of churches (and church services).

Tourist Agencies Majestic Tours (Tel.: 2-2606) arranges day trips to "deserted" islands or cays. The cost is US$30 each which includes lunch. The many organized excursions offer the visitor an easy way of getting about. As well as drives to places of interest, tours include visits to

1272 BAHAMAS

beaches on the Family Islands and trips aboard a catamaran with stops for swimming and sunbathing. Details from hotels or Playtours, Tel.: 2-4018; Nassau Tours, Tel.: 2-2881; Mauras Tourist Services, Tel.: 2-8262; Triangle Tours, Tel.: 5-9603; Tropical Travel Tours, Tel.: 2-3802.

Airport Windsor Field, about 14 miles from Nassau. Taxi to Nassau, US$20. There is no public bus service to or from the airport, though some hotels have buses. If you ask politely and discreetly you might be able to get a lift on the bus which takes the luggage porters to town. Otherwise you can try getting a lift in the car park. For the return journey there is a bus from Nassau to Clifton (US$1.50); it leaves on the hour from Bay and Frederick Streets (Western Transportation Company) and will drop you 1½ miles from the airport. The airport departure tax is US$5. During the day US immigration and customs formalities for those going to the US are carried out at Nassau. Plenty of left luggage space is available.

Transport Taxis are abundant: the minimum charge is US$0.90, plus US$0.50 p.p. per mile. To avoid overcharging, agree a price beforehand, or check that the meter is used. Taxi drivers in Nassau may "take you for a ride" otherwise. There are very few public buses, but minibuses called "jitneys" go all over New Providence Island from Woodes Rogers Walk and Frederick Street.

Car Hire Avis, W. Bay St.; Hertz, *Sheraton-Colonial Hotel*; National, Bay St.; S. J. Humes, W. Bay St. All these have offices at the airport. Their rates range from US$25 to 40 a day. For two-wheelhire, see page 1274.

Communications Main post office is at East Hill. Air mail to UK and Europe, US$0.24 per ½ oz.; to USA and Canada, US$0.21 per ½ oz. Telephone calls and cables can be made from Bahamas Telecommunications Corp., East St., open 24 hours. There is now direct telephone dialling to North American cities (area code is 809-32).

US Embassy Mosmar Building, Queen St. Tel.: 2-4733.

British High Commission Bitco Building, East St. Tel.: 5-7471.

Grand Bahama Island, the nearest to the USA and, with Great Abaco, the most northerly of the Bahamas, is where the most spectacular development has taken place.

The island has several natural advantages over others in the group. It has miles of south-facing beaches sheltered from northerly winds and enjoys the full benefit of the Gulf Stream. Away from Freeport, there are good beaches at William's Town, Barbary and Fortune Beach. Thanks to a fresh water table under the island it has no water problem. The pinewoods which this natural irrigation supports were, indirectly, the beginning of the present prosperity. Early in the 1940s, an American financier, Wallace Groves, bought a small timber company and developed it into an enterprise employing 2,000 people. In 1955, the Bahamas Government entered into an agreement with him as president of the Grand Bahama Port Authority Ltd., granting to the specific area, called **Freeport,** owned by the Port Authority, certain rights and privileges which apply to that area only and to no other section of the Colony.

So successful was this that the population of the island grew from 9,500 in 1963 to 35,250 in 1967. In the same period, the total investment rose from US$150m. to US$577m. and the tonnage of cargo handled increased ten times to 1.25m. tons. In 1969, however, the Government decided to introduce controls on the expansion of Freeport, and the vertiginous growth process has since slowed down.

In Freeport the sights to see include the Garden of Groves, the Hydro Flora Gardens and the Museum of Underwater Exploration. The International Bazaar is an integrated shopping-complex with streets built in various assorted national styles; the English street is a Tudor-style courtyard. Nearby is El Casino, the largest in the western world. Away from Freeport are the villages of Seagrape, Pine Ridge and Water Cay. West End, 25 miles from Freeport, was a haven for rum-runners during the American prohibition era. Today there is a huge resort complex there, the *Grand Bahama Hotel and Country Club*. The Nature Centre, Settlers Way, is 2 miles out of town. B$2 entry, check when open. Guided tours 1330, 1400 and 1500. Highly recommended. 15 miles east, towards High Rock, is a newly-opened National Park, with caves, plus a path through a Mangrove swamp. This was built in March 1985 by volunteers from "Operation Raleigh". West of Freeport: Eight Mile Rock (8 miles from Freeport). Local bar, *The Ritz*, very friendly, dancing in the street, Wednesday nights. Sample Mr Wildgoose's tequila. Perfume factory open to visitors, as is Catholic church with walls shaped like praying hands. East of Freeport: High Rock (20 miles). Further East (10 miles) is Pelican Point, excellent deserted beach, road to Maclean's Town/East End, poor, but passable. On Discovery Day, October 12, Fair is held at Maclean's Town, including a conch-cracking competition started by a British couple in the 1940s.

Vintage motor car races around Freeport take place in December. New Year's Eve Junkanoo, drums, costumes, dancing outside *Bahama Princess Hotel* 0400-0500. Much smaller than Nassau's but worth seeing.

Hotels See note on Hotels under Nassau. Also, *Lucayan Beach Hotel*, reopened 1986, lovely patio bar, overlooking garden and beach, arrangements can be made to visit lighthouse, new

BAHAMAS

casino. *Xanadu Hotel*: Howard Hughes, the recluse, used to live on the top floor. There is a small study/library dedicated to him on the ground floor.

Restaurants The *Pub on the Mall*, *Scorpio's*, Explorers Way, *The Early Bird*, East Sunrise Highway, and *Pier One* all serve local food at reasonable prices. The *Bazaar* serves Chinese. The *Phoenix* (*Silver Sands Hotel*) serves kebabs and curries and has an unusual bar; *Club Caribe* (on the beach) is in a beautiful setting. *Buccaneer Restaurant* (West of Freeport), good food, reasonable prices, Wednesday night specials. *Jack Tar Village Holiday Complex* (West End), food/drink expensive; *New Beach Club* (East of Freeport) beach setting, good value food.

Bars Inexpensive: *The Main Mast*, opposite Holiday Inn, Freeport's cheapest bar; *The Rugby Club*, Pioneers Way (Friday—Happy Hour). Tel.: 3522952 for events. Also at High Rock (various), 20 miles East of Freeport. At West End: *Jack Tar Village Holiday Complex* (open to non-residents), expensive.

Discos *Panache*, at Holiday Inn, B$8 entrance includes 2 free drinks; *Sultan's Tent*, Bahama Towers Hotel, B$8, 2 free drinks; *Harbour Lobster House*, B$3, Sats. only; *Freeport Inn*, free entry, but drinks more expensive—recommended. Try the talent contest at the *Winson Churchill* pub, Wednesdays 2230. *El Galleón*, imitation galleon docked Lucayan Marina, disco B$10 includes 2 drinks; daily, moonlit cruises, dinner/dancing. *The Palace*, East Sunrise Highway, newest and most prestigious disco, 2 dance floors. *Electric City*, near the downtown area. Haunt of local teenagers.

Golf 18 holes at West End (fabulous sea views), Ruby Swiss, Bahama Reef (poor condition), Lucayan Country Club, Shannon (near Garden of Groves)—abandoned but playable. 9 holes: Fortune Hill.

Tourist Office In Freeport, Bazaar, along the Mall, next to the library, as well as in any large hotel.

The Family Islands' main attraction are their water sports with sailing, snorkelling, swimming and fishing being the most popular. The **Abaco** islands, the boat-building centre of the Bahamas, have several first-class hotels or there are cottages for rent. Development on **Andros** has been concentrated on the E coast facing one of the world's largest underwater reefs. Inland, birdlife is prolific. **Bimini** has North and South Islands, famous for game fishing. Ernest Hemingway lived here at Blue Marlin Cottage; a display of Hemingway memorabilia can be seen at the *Compleat Angler Hotel* bar and museum. There is a straw market in Alice Town, N. Bimini. On S. Bimini is the legendary site of the Fountain of Youth. **Eleuthera** was the first permanent settlement in the Bahamas. It has many facilities including a golf course. Ask the harbour master, or better, shopkeepers in streets near *Kemp's Guest House*, about mailboat sailings. Hotel in Eleuthera: *Cambridge Villas*, in Gregory Town, B.

Exuma is 16 hrs. from Nassau by mail boat. Cost B$25, bunk US$5 extra. Leaves Potters Cay at 1300. Hotels in George Town, Exuma: *Two Turtles*, 200 yds. from harbour, A, rooms large enough for 4, barbecue on Friday nights; *Peace and Plenty Hotel*, 300 yds. from harbour. Dances on Wednesdays, L, EP. The Scuba diving in Exuma is excellent. Exuma Divers, phone 336-2030 or 336-2710. Toll Fee (USA) (800) 327-0787.

Air Services to the mainland (Miami, Fort Lauderdale, West Palm Beach, New York, Toronto) Pan Am, Air Canada, British Airways, Bahamas Air, Flamingo Airlines, Mackey, Shawnee, Delta, Eastern Air Lines, New York Air and Gulf Air. To and from the U.K., Bermuda and Kingston: British Airways; and for other European cities, Sabena and Lufthansa. Air and sea services to the Bahamas are continually increased: for Haiti by Flamingo Airlines and Bahamas Air, for Jamaica by Air Jamaica, for Mérida, Mexico, by Lufthansa. Icelandic Airways flies daily from Nassau to Luxembourg, except Wed.; special youth fares apply throughout the year. International Air Bahamas also flies cheaply between Nassau and Luxembourg. There is a flying-boat service between Nassau and Miami.

Boats to USA *Sea Escape* boat return trip to Miami, including meals and entertainment, costs about B$96. Journey is 8 hours one way. Hydrofoil service to Fort Lauderdale B$59 return. No advance purchase possible at Freeport end: just turn up. Both run from Nassau port area.

Information for Visitors US, Canadian and British citizens do not need passports or visas but must carry some form of identification for stays of up to three weeks; for longer, a valid passport is required. Visitors must have sufficient funds for their stay and an onward or return ticket. Passports are required by all other nationalities, but visas are not needed by nationals of Commonwealth and West European countries, nor by most Latin American nationals if staying no longer than 14 days. To enter the Bahamas for business purposes the permission of the Immigration Officer, Nassau, must be obtained. It is advisable to apply in writing to: Chief Immigration Officer, Immigration Office, P.O. Box 831, Nassau.

Visitors are permitted to drive on a valid British licence or International Permit for up to 3 months. Beyond that they need a local licence issued by the Road Traffic Department in Nassau. Traffic keeps left. Strict speed limits: Nassau and Freeport 20 m.p.h.; elsewhere 30 m.p.h.

1274 BAHAMAS

Bahamas time is 5 hours behind GMT. A number of publications of interest to tourists can be obtained free from hotels.

Currency The unit of currency is the Bahamian Dollar (B$) which is at par with the US dollar. There is no restriction on foreign currency taken in or out; Bahamian currency may be exported up to B$70 p.p.; imports of Bahamian currency only by permission of the Central Bank. Notes of B$ 100, 50, 20, 10, 5, 3, 1 and 50c; coins of B$5, 2, 1, 50c, 25c, 15c, 10c, 5c and 1c.

Credit Cards Visa (Barclaycard) and Mastercard (Access) are more readily accepted than American Express.

Banks Royal Bank of Canada at Nassau, Bimini, Harbour Island, Hatchet Bay (Eleuthera Island), Lyford Key, and Spanish Wells. Lloyds Bank (Bahamas); Barclays Bank International; Bank of Nova Scotia; Canadian Imperial Bank of Commerce; Chase Manhattan Bank; Bank of America; Citibank.

Hours of Business in Nassau, Mon.-Thurs. 0930-1500, Fri. 0930-1700. In Freeport, Mon.-Fri. 0900-1300 and Fri. 1500-1700. Shops 0900-1700 Mon.-Sat. Govt. offices 0900-1730 Mon.-Fri.

Local Travel Bahamas Air, Mackey, Chalk's, Helda Air and Shawnee operate scheduled flights between Nassau and the Family Islands. Charter flights and excursions available through them and several private companies, including Greg of Nassau Air. The Family Islands can also be reached by regular ferry boat services timed to connect with arrivals by air in Nassau. The *Noel Roberts* sails from Nassau to Freeport at 1600 on Thurs., leaving again at 1400 on Sat. The fare for the 15-16 hr. trip is US$20 2nd class, or US$25 1st class (which includes a bunk). Tickets can be bought at City lumberyard on Bay Street. A colourful way of travelling to the islands is on the mail boats, which also carry merchandise. They leave from Potters Cay and Woodes Rogers Walk; their drawback is that they are slow and accommodation on board is very basic. The Bahamas Family Islands Association has a helpful brochure listing fares and schedules. Package tours to the Family Islands can be surprisingly good value, e.g. 3 days (2 nights) in Eleuthera for B$90, including free transport from hotel to beach. Meals not included. On New Providence Island the main out-of-town hotels provide frequent free bus transport for their guests to and from Rawson Square, Nassau Harbour. Taxis are usually available from ranks in the towns. A drive in a "surrey" horse-drawn carriage is a pleasant way of seeing Nassau; about US$5 per hour. The number of minibuses, or "jitneys", on the main islands is expanding fast: fare about US$0.50. For radio cabs in Nassau Tel.: 3-5111; Freeport 6666.

Vehicle Hire British and American cars are available for hire, the former more suited to the relatively narrow roads, B$25-40 a day, unlimited mileage according to type. Freeport: Five Wheels Car Hire, Tel.: 7001; Hertz, Tel.: 6288; National, Tel.: 7251. On some other islands cars can be hired through your hotel but on many of the Family Islands bicycles and mopeds are appropriate. These can be hired in Nassau, Tel.: 2-2374 or 2-3788; in Freeport, Tel.: 6090; in many other places through hotels. Approx. rates: bicycles US$8 per day, 20 per week; mopeds: US$6 per day, 25 per week. Scooters and light motorcycles can be hired from about US$18 per day. Remember, though, that rates for car and bike hire tend to vary, according to season. Scooter hire in Freeport: Honda Sales and Service, Queens Highway, Tel.: 7035. In Exuma: Out Island Inn, George Town, B$15 for 4 hrs. Minimum age for hiring in Exuma is 24.

Climate The sunshine and warm seas attract visitors throughout the year but winter, from December to April, is the high season. Temperatures are around 20°C (68°F). Summer temperatures average 30°C (86°F). Humidity is fairly high but is tempered by sea breezes and is not oppressive. Light rain showers occur throughout the year but heavy thunderstorms take place mainly in June, July and October.

Sport *Yachting:* There are now 30 official ports of entry for private boats; a continuous series of competitions is organized ranging from the Family Island Regatta to the Bahamas 500, a gruelling 500-mile race for high-powered craft from Miami to Nassau to Freeport. *Private Flying:* The Annual Flying Treasure Hunt, started in 1963, has attracted increasing number of private aircraft. There are 24 official ports of entry for sea or land aircraft. Light aircraft can be hired by licensed pilots. *Golf:* Splendid championship courses. The main golfing centre is Grand Bahama, followed by Nassau. A notable course is the Cotton Bay Club on Eleuthera. *Auto Races:* Grand Prix in Freeport and other events during winter season. *Water Sports:* The Bahamas have hundreds of miles of sunny beaches and comprise an area of about 100,000 square miles of warm, clear Atlantic ocean. Every conceivable type of water sport is available and the variety of deep-sea fishing is famous. *Scuba Diving.* Freeport, UNEXSO Diving, introductory 1-day resort course includes one dive B$59. Certification course, lectures, dives, skills etc. about B$250. More specialized diving catered for: nights, caves, photography. Also less busy centre at West End, trips arranged to Memory Rock, edge of shelf, 40 minutes. *Road Running Races.* Two 10 km. races plus some smaller ones. Bahama Princess attracts world's top runners. Held February and for B$10 anyone can enter. Guinness 10 km. Oct/Nov. Contact Dave Warren Tel.: 373 7683.

Food Conch, a shellfish meal, baked crab, grouper cutlets, red snapper fillets. The Bahamas have some good fruit: sapodilla, mango, breadfruit, sugar apple and pawpaw. Tap water is brackish; fresh water can be bought at the supermarket.

Tipping The usual tip is 15%, including for taxi drivers. Some hotels and restaurants, however, include a service charge on the bill.

Electricity 120 volt/60 cycles.

We are deeply grateful to K. E. Hillman, of Freeport, Grand Bahama for valuable new information.

TURKS AND CAICOS ISLANDS

THE TURKS AND CAICOS ISLANDS lie some 575 miles SE of Miami, Florida, directly east of the Bahamas and north of Hispaniola. They comprise about thirty low-lying islands covering 193 square miles, only eight of which are inhabited. The Turks and the Caicos groups are separated by the Turks Island Passage, a 22-mile channel over 7,000 feet deep which connects the Atlantic and the Caribbean, contributing to the area's profusion of marine life.

The smaller Turks group—the main islands are Grand Turk and Salt Cay—shelters half of the colony's nearly 8,000 "belongers," as the islanders call themselves. The rest of the population is scattered among the larger Caicos group to the west—South Caicos, Middle Caicos, North Caicos, and Providenciales, known locally as "Provo." East and West Caicos, inhabited from 1797 to the mid-19th century, are now the private domain of wild cattle. Most of the smaller cays are uninhabited.

The Turks and Caicos are a British Crown Colony, whose main income derives from tourism and fishing for conch and crayfish. However, tax laws modelled after those of the Cayman Islands are attracting businesses, and bulldozers have been busy on Providenciales, the fastest developing and most westerly of the inhabited islands. Club Méditerranée's 600-bed village on Provo, opened in December 1984 but was closed in April 1987 because of industrial relations problems. A US$40m Hyatt Hotels resort complex on Provo, including a 300-room hotel, will cause a great change in the islands, which seem no longer the preserve of seclusionists and escapists.

History The islands' first dwellers were probably the peaceful Arawaks, who left behind some ancient utensils and little else. Whether the first European to set foot here was Ponce de León or Christopher Columbus (a much disputed issue), by the middle of the 16th century not one Arawak, or Lucayan as Columbus named them, remained. The infamous Caicos Banks south of the Caicos group, where in the space of 1000 yards the water depth changes from 6000 to 30 feet, claimed many of the Spanish ships lost in the central Caribbean from the 16th to the 18th century.

The history of the islands has been tumultuous. The Bermudian traders who settled the islands of Grand Turk, Salt Cay, and South Caicos in the 17th century used slaves to rake salt for sale to British colonies on the American mainland, and fought pirates and buccaneers for over 200 years. Not surprisingly, it was probably pirates from the Mediterranean who gave the islands their name: they were referred to generally as "Turks" and their boats were called "*caicos (caiques)*." During the American Revolution, British loyalists found refuge on the islands, setting up cotton and sisal plantations with the help of imported slaves.

For a while, cotton and sisal from the islands were sold in New York and London, solar salt became the staple of the economy, and the Turks and Caicos thrived, but all these products encountered overwhelming competition from elsewhere. Following a chaotic alternation of Spanish, French and British control, the Turks and Caicos were annexed to Jamaica in 1874. After Jamaica's independence in 1962, they were loosely associated with the Bahamas for just over ten years until the latter became independent. At that point, the Turks and Caicos became a British Crown Colony. The "belongers" in the meantime have turned to the sea for sustenance, fishing mainly

1276 TURKS AND CAICOS ISLANDS

lobster and conch, while the Government is banking on tourism to help the islands support themselves. Mr Nathaniel Francis was appointed Chief Minister in March 1985, following the arrest of Mr Norman Saunders on suspicion of drugs smuggling in Miami. The islands are at the moment under UK direct rule pending an inquiry into alleged maladministration.

Grand Turk is the seat of government, largest population centre, and main port of entry for air travellers until the opening of the islands' second airport on Provo.

Cockburn Town, the capital, is a modern centre, with a Philatelic Bureau and nearby Numismatic Bureau of interest to collectors. Dive packages are available; dives are off the beach to leeward, as well as windward, sides of the island (limited to windward on the other islands, making windy days risky), but Grand Turk is not basically a resort island, and only relatively picturesque.

Accommodation in some old Bermuda-style buildings facing the beach: *Salt Raker Inn* (A-B, EP); *Turks Head Inn*, over a hundred years old (A-B, EP); *Hotel Kittina*, the newest (A-L, EP). In town is *Windjammer Guest House*, C. A new French restaurant has opened on the beach opposite the hotels, *Papillon's Rendez-Vous*.

Salt Cay, ten miles south of Grand Turk, is out of the past, with remnants of the old salt industry and little else. Rather relaxed guest houses are the *Mt. Pleasant Guest House* (A, AP) and remote *Balfour Beach Cottages* (A, EP). There is also the *Brown House* (A, AP).

South Caicos is the nearest Caicos island, 22 miles north of Grand Turk, and the most populous of the Caicos group with its thriving lobster/conch industry and popular annual regatta. Excellent diving. Here is the cliffside *Admiral's Arms* (A, EP); also *Coreen's Cottages* (restaurant nearby) and *Bassett's Apartments* (both C, EP).

East Caicos and **Middle** (also known as Grand) **Caicos** have splendid beaches, but accommodation for mosquitoes only. Bring repellant.

North Caicos, the lushest of the islands, has a 4,400-foot runway, 1,226 inhabitants, and the *Prospect of Whitby Hotel* (L, MAP), on a 6-mile wide sand beach with all amenities.

Providenciales ("Provo") is being vigorously developed for tourism. Apart from the Hyatt installations noted on the previous page, there are the *Third Turtle Inn* (L, AP) on a terrace built into the side of a coral cliff; overlooking it the 12-unit *Erebus at Latitude 22* (A, MAP); Lord David Brooke's villas (over US$2,000 a month, including maid and cook) at *Leeward-Going-Through*, on one of the best marinas in the colony; the duplexes (L) at *Treasure Beach*, some way from the *Third Turtle*; a car is a must. The *Island Princess* (A) is Provo's other beach hotel. Sheraton plans to open a 155-room hotel on Provo in November 1988, to include the island's first casino. Provo boasts a new international airport, several long beaches, three dive shops, a windsurfing and sailing centre, tennis, and record-breaking fishing (these are said to be the best bonefishing waters in the world). A new US$1.5m dock caters for increased roll-on-roll-off ferry traffic.

Pine Cay, an 800-acre privately-owned resort community with a resident population of 40, has the exclusive 11-room *Meridian Club* (L, EP). Snorkelling and diving programmes are run by neighbouring PRIDE, a non-profit public foundation. Research is currently being conducted there on wind and solar energy and the commercial farming of conch for future export.

Practical Information: US and Canadian citizens need only proof of identity to enter Turks and Caicos. All others need a valid passport, although visa is not necessary. The official currency is the US dollar. Most hotels will accept travellers' cheques, but neither credit cards nor personal cheques are widely accepted. There are banks (Barclays Bank International) on Grand Turk, South Caicos, and Providenciales. A 10% service charge is added to most hotel bills in lieu of tipping. There is no recognized rainy season, and temperatures average 75°-85°F from November to May, reaching into the 90s from June to October, but constant tradewinds keep life comfortable. Dress is extremely informal. On-island transport is restricted to expensive taxi service (US$10 for a ten-minute airport transfer). Rental cars are available on Grand Turk and Provo for equally high rates. Driving is on the left. Communications are limited to fairly erratic telephone and telex services on Grand Turk, North and South Caicos, and Provo.

Transport A full-scale international airport has opened on Providenciales. Bahamasair provides scheduled passenger service from Nassau to Grand Turk. Turks & Caicos National Airlines (TCNA) provides connecting flights to Salt Cay, South Caicos, North Caicos, Pine Cay and Providenciales for arriving passengers on Grand Turk. Flight time to the furthest island (Provo) is 45 minutes, but TCNA delays are notorious. Fairly regular charter flights connect Provo with Miami or Fort Lauderdale (usually 2 or 3 weekly). Private charters are readily available within the island group. Provo is

CAYMAN ISLANDS 1277

the only island with modern, full-service marinas (Turtle Cove adjacent to the *Third Turtle Inn* and *Leeward Marina*, both on the north-east or windward coast).

Further Information Turks & Caicos Islands Tourist Board: c/o Ministry of Tourism & Development, Grand Turk, Turks & Caicos Islands; Tel. 2300/2306; also at 48 Albemarle Street, London W1X 4AR; Tel. 01-629 6353; The West India Committee Representative in Germany, Lomerstrasse 28, Hamburg 70, West Germany; Tel. 696 8846; P.O. Box 592617, Miami, Florida 33159, U.S.A.; Tel. (305) 592-6183. Package holidays are available through Bye-Coastal, 4270 Main St., Bridgeport, CT. 06606; Tel. (203) 371-1119 or toll-free within continental US (800) 243-4954; and through Caribbean Holidays, 711 Third Ave., New York, N.Y. 10017.

CAYMAN ISLANDS

THE BRITISH CROWN COLONY of the Cayman Islands consists of Grand Cayman, Cayman Brac and Little Cayman, in the Caribbean Sea. **George Town,** the capital and financial and administrative centre, with a population of 19,350 (1984), is located in **Grand Cayman,** the largest of the three islands, lying S of Havana, Cuba, about 180 miles WNW of Jamaica and 480 miles S of Miami.

The beaches of the Cayman Islands are said to be the best in the Caribbean. On Grand Cayman, West Bay Beach, now known as Seven Mile Beach, has dazzling white sand and is lined by tall Australian pines. Beaches on the E and N coasts are equally good, and are protected by an offshore barrier reef. The Cayman Islands are world-famous for their underwater scenery. Many of the better reefs and several wrecks are found in water shallow enough to require only mask, snorkel and fins. A complete selection of diving equipment is available and there are several highly qualified instructor-guides.

Sightseeing Some of the many things of interest to visit in Grand Cayman include a tour round Cayman Turtle Farm, which houses giant green turtles. Located at North West Point, this is the only commercial turtle farm in the world. A trip to Gun Bay at the east end of the island will show you the scene of the famous "Wreck of the Ten Sails", which took place in 1788. On this trip you will pass the blow-holes—waterspouts that rise above the coral rock in unusual patterns as a result of water being funnelled along passages in the rock as the waves come rolling in. Hell, situated near West Bay, is an unusual rock formation worth visiting. Have your cards and letters postmarked "Hell, Grand Cayman" at the little sub-post-office situated there. Snorkelling at Eden Rock costs just CI$4 for a day's equipment hire; the swimming is easy and the fish are friendly. For a pleasurable day's outing, arrange a boat trip to North Sound. This will include snorkelling, fishing and a good look at marine life on a barrier reef. Your guide will cook fish and lobster for you by wrapping them in foil and roasting them on hot coals.

History The Cayman Islands were first sighted by Columbus in May 1503. At that time he named the islands Las Tortugas which means "The Turtles". The islands were ceded to the English Crown under the Treaty of Madrid in 1670; early inhabitants were mixed groups of shipwrecked sailors, debtors, buccaneers and beachcombers, and no serious settlement took place until the early part of the 18th century. Cayman Brac and Little Cayman were permanently settled as recently as 1833, when several families from Grand Cayman established themselves and lived in isolation until 1850. The Cayman Islands were relatively isolated from the world until the 1940s, when modern transport began to develop.

Political and Economic A Governor appointed by the British Crown is the head of Government. Major policies are studied and proposed by the Executive Council comprised of three official and four elected members, and laws are enacted by the Legislative Assembly, which is mostly elective. There is at present no intention to seek independence or even a greater degree of self-government. General elections are held every five years. The most recent, in November 1984, saw Mr Benson Ebanks become Chief Minister.

The standard of living is one of the highest in the Caribbean: per capita income was estimated at US$14,643 in 1985. Apart from a certain amount of meat, turtle, fish and a few local fruits and

CAYMAN ISLANDS

vegetables, almost all foodstuffs and other necessities are imported. The islands' economy is based largely on offshore finance and banking, tourism, real estate and construction, a little local industry, and remittances of Caymanians working on ships abroad. The cost-of-living rises in line with those of the main trading partners: 3.6% average for 1982-86.

Cayman Brac Cayman Brac (Gaelic for "bluff") gets its name from the high bluff rising from sea level to a height of 140 feet. The island is 89 miles ENE of Grand Cayman, about 12 miles long and a little more than a mile wide. Here are beaches lapped by calm waters, ideal for swimming, sunning and diving. Those who find Grand Cayman (population about 20,000) a little too "citified" will enjoy lingering on Cayman Brac, where the population is less than 2,000. Closely united, they are a warm and friendly people.

Little Cayman The oft-repeated legend that many Cayman Islanders have lived to the age of 115 or so can readily be accepted after a visit to Little Cayman, which is 74 miles NE of Grand Cayman. It is peaceful, but not dull, for here is exhilarating excitement for the dedicated pursuer of the bonefish and wahoo.

Ten miles long, two at its widest, with an area of approximately ten square miles, Little Cayman numbers only a few dozen in population. The friendliness and hospitality are legendary. Cayman Airways operates excursion flights.

Information for Visitors

Documents No passports are required for US, British or Canadian visitors. However, proof of citizenship such as voter registration or "British Visitor's Passport" is required, as well as an outward ticket. Passports but not visas are required for citizens of West European and Commonwealth countries, Israel, Japan and South Africa. A visitor from any of these countries may be admitted to the Cayman Islands for a period of up to six months providing he has proof of citizenship, sufficient resources to maintain himself during his stay, and a return ticket to his country of origin or another country in which he will be accepted. Visitors from other countries may enter without visa if staying only 14 days; this concession does not apply to nationals of communist countries—other than Yugoslavia. Luggage is inspected by customs officials on arrival; no attempt should be made to take drugs into the country.

Climate The Cayman Islands lie in the trade-wind belt and the prevailing NE winds moderate the temperatures, making the climate delightful all year round. Average temperatures in winter are about 24°C and in summer are around 26°-29°C. Most rain falls between May and October, but even then it only takes the form of short showers. The winter season, running from December to April, is the peak tourist season. Visitors intending to come to the island during this period are advised to make hotel and travel arrangements well in advance. **Note** Although Grand Cayman is sprayed regularly, it is advisable to bring plenty of insect repellant to combat mosquitoes and sandflies.

How to Get There Air communications are good. Grand Cayman is served from Miami by Cayman Airways and Republic Airlines; from Houston by Cayman Airways; from Tampa by Aerosun International; from Kingston, Jamaica by Cayman Airways and Air Jamaica. Cayman Airways also provides daily inter-island services from Grand Cayman to Cayman Brac and Little Cayman and return. Owen Roberts International Airport is situated less than 2 miles from the centre of George Town and only ten minutes' drive from most of the hotels on Seven Mile Beach. The average taxi fare from the airport to a Seven Mile Beach hotel will be about US$10. There is a departure tax of US$4 payable either in Cayman or US currency when you leave the Islands.

Where to Stay Accommodations are many and varied, ranging from resort hotels on the beach to small out-of-the-way family-run guest houses. There is also a wide variety of cottages, apartments (condominiums) and villas available for daily, weekly or monthly rental. Cottages, basic, may cost CI$300-400 a month. A full list of tourist accommodation and prices, including hotels, cottages, apartments and villas, is available from Cayman Islands Department of Tourism at the addresses shown at the end of this section. A government tax of 6% is added to the room charge and most hotels also add a 15% service charge to the bill in lieu of tipping.

Where to Eat Good restaurants include: *Cracked Conch*, Spanish Cove (buffet not recommended), *Almond Tree*, *Cayman Arms*, *Grand Old House*, *Lobster Pot*, *Ports of Call*, *Swiss Inn*, *Chez Jacques*, *Yorkshire Pudding*, an English restaurant, and *Kim's Caruso's* has good Italian

CAYMAN ISLANDS

food. *Welly's Cool Spot* has native food at reasonable prices. All of these restaurants are near George Town or are at the W side of Grand Cayman. Good sandwiches from *Coconut Place Delicatessen*. During the high season it is advisable to reserve tables for dinner. Probably the best-value place to eat on Grand Cayman is the *Wholesome Cafeteria* located above the Wonder Bakery on North Church Street (3 courses plus a drink for CI$6.50) Others in the same price range include *Champion House, Dominique's, Island Taste Bar-B-Que, Roger's Wreck. My Bar*, at the Sunset House hotel, does a good cheap lunch; it is also one of the cheapest places for drinking.

Currency The legal currency is the Cayman Islands dollar (CI$). The exchange rate is fixed at CI$1 to US$1.25, or CI$0.80 to US$1, although officially the exchange rate is CI$0.83 to US$1. US currency is readily acceptable throughout the Islands, and Canadian and British currencies can be exchanged at all banks. Personal cheques are not generally welcome and credit cards are accepted only in some places.

Banks Most of the major international banks are represented in George Town, Grand Cayman. These include Bank of Nova Scotia, Barclays Bank International, Canadian Imperial Bank of Commerce, Lloyds Bank (by a wholly-owned subsidiary, LBI Bank & Trust Co. (Cayman) Ltd.) and Royal Bank of Canada. Commercial banking hours are 0830 to 1300 Mon. to Thurs., and 0830 to 1300 and 1630 to 1800 on Fri.

Local Travel There is a regular bus and jitney service between West Bay and George Town that stops at all the hotels on Seven Mile Beach. The fare from the hotels to town is about US$1 each way. Taxis are readily obtainable at hotels and restaurants, and fares are based on a fixed place-to-place tariff rather than a meter charge. For going a long distance (i.e. across the island) they are expensive. From the airport to George Town is about US$5. A tour of the island by taxi costs US$50. For car hire, Budget, National, Avis and Hertz are represented and there are a number of good local companies as well. For small European cars daily rentals start at about US$20, or US$120 per week plus insurance for deductible waiver. Rental firms issue visitors with driving permits on production of a valid driving licence from the visitor's country of residence. Bicycles, mopeds and motorcycles can also be rented, from US$5 a day. Driving is on the left. Island tours can be arranged at about US$60 for a taxi, or US$10 p.p. on a bus with a minimum of 20 persons. Check with your hotel for full details.

Warning Care must be taken when walking on a highway, especially at night; highway shoulders are narrow and vehicles move fast.

Pirates' Week is the islands' national festival and takes place in late October. Parades, regattas, fishing tournaments and treasure hunts are all part of the celebrations, which commemorate the days when the Caymans were the haunt of pirates and buccaneers.

Time Eastern Standard Time (USA) for the whole year.

Telephone and Cable The Cayman Islands have a modern automatic telephone system which links them with the rest of the world. Telex facilities are available to the public at the Cable and Wireless offices and telegrams can be sent 0730-1800.

Medical Care on Grand Cayman is good and readily available.

Department of Tourism Further information may be obtained from the Cayman Islands Department of Tourism at: 250 Catalonia Ave., Suite 604, Coral Gables, Florida 33134, Tel.: (305) 444-6551; 333N Michigan Ave., Suite 1521, Chicago, Illinois 60601, Tel.: (312) 782-5832; 420 Lexington Ave., Suite 2312, New York, N.Y. 10170, Tel.: (212) 682 5582; 3440 Wilshire Blvd., Suite 1201, Los Angeles, California 90019, (213) 738-1968; 11 Adelaide St. W., Suite 406, c/o Earl B. Smith, Travel Marketing Consultants, Toronto, Ontario, Canada M5H IL9 (416) 362-1550; Hambleton House, 17B Curzon St., London W1Y 7FE, UK, 01-493 5161; P.O. Box 67, George Town, Grand Cayman, BWI, Tel.: 9-4844 Ext. 175.

BERMUDA

THIS GROUP of some 150 coral islands and tiny islets, of which only 20 are inhabited, lies in the western Atlantic, about 800 miles SE of New York and 750 miles NW of the Turks and Caicos Islands. Aircraft from London reach Bermuda in 7 hrs. and from New York in 1¾ hrs.

The islands are believed to have been discovered by the Spaniard Juan Bermúdez in 1503; they are the oldest British colony. Bermuda was first inhabited by the company of a British ship, the *Sea Venture*, bound for Virginia, she ran into a storm near the Islands and foundered on a reef in 1609. The ship's company, headed by Admiral Sir George Somers, remained there for nearly a year before resuming their voyage. A replica of the ship *Honey* built to carry on the voyage is moored in St. George harbour. In 1612 a charter was granted by King James I to the Virginia Company to include the Bermudas as part of its dominion, and the first party of settlers arrived from England. Shortly afterwards the Virginia Company sold the islands to the Governor and Company of the City of London "for the plantation of the Somers Islands", but in 1684 the Company's charter was annulled and the colony passed to the Crown. The Prime Minister is Mr. John Swan.

Today, the islands have one of the highest densities of population in the world. The score of them that are inhabited have a total area of slightly more than 22 square miles and a civilian population of 57,100 in 1984, of whom about two thirds are black; the remainder are mainly of English or Portuguese stock. Also, the standard of living is among the world's highest; gnp was an estimated US$16,522 per head in 1986. The ten largest islands, which comprise 21 square miles, form a narrow chain, linked by causeways and bridges. Some 2.3 square miles are leased to the United States Government for naval and military purposes. The Bermudas are hilly but lack rivers and streams. The water supply is derived from rainfall and the desalination of sea water.

Bermuda's chief source of income is the tourist industry. International business is another important part of the economy; insurance companies are the largest single group in this category. In 1986, 591,800 tourists, including those on cruise ships, visited the islands. There is a certain amount of small-scale industry: ship repairing and small boat building, cedar woodwork and the manufacture of handicraft souvenirs, perfume, pharmaceuticals, mineral water extracts and essential oils all help to support the population and in recent years the cultivation of Bermuda lilies, for export by air, has assumed importance. The time to see these is at Easter, when a Lily Queen is chosen. Easter is a favourite time for American student visitors. The season is a long one, from mid-March to autumn. Even in February, the coolest month, temperatures rarely fall below 15°C. The peak temperatures of July and August, about 30°C, are tempered by trade winds. In September, strong winds can reach hurricane force. The old town of **St. George** (pop. 1,800), the capital until 1815, is a delightful place with its old houses and walled gardens and picturesque alleyways leading to the harbour. The islands are said to be the scene of Shakespeare's *Tempest* (though they could hardly have been well known in London by the time the play was written) and Ariel's Cave is one of many beauty spots. The lighthouse at Gibb's Hill, in Southampton Parish, is one of the oldest in the world; for a superb view of the islands and lagoons, visit its gallery. A famous drive along the North Shore is past the Governor's Residence, with its 200-acre estate, while at Sandys Parish you can see the world's reputed smallest drawbridge. Ferry boats ply to Ireland Island and to Somerset, Paget and Warwick.

Hamilton, the capital (pop. 3,700) is a charming small town, laid out geometrically on rising ground. Most of the public buildings are built around a square near the wharf. Here is the seat of the second oldest British parliament, the Sessions House. The Cathedral, the Library and the Historical Museum are also well worth

BERMUDA 1281

visiting. There is a fine aquarium at Flatts, and the Crystal and Leamington caves and the Devil's Hole are enjoyable.

Transport Motor cars were not admitted until 1947 and they are limited as to size. The maximum speed limit is 20 m.p.h., and 15 m.p.h. in built-up areas (traffic keeps left). International driving licences are not valid. Visitors wishing to drive must hold a Bermudian licence, not issued until after a minimum stay of 30 days. There are no car hire facilities. The island is well served by bus routes and ferryboat connections to the main shoreline points, but the most popular form of transport is the moped, which can be hired for about US$42 a week. Pedal cycles can also be hired. Taxis are available and can also be hired by the day or week; there is a 25% surcharge between midnight and 0600. Horse-drawn carriages (single for 2 people, double for 4) charge about US$12-15 an hr.

What to Wear During the summer season, cool, informal clothing is suitable and Bermuda shorts are worn by both sexes. For evenings, men can wear Bermuda shorts with a white or black dinner jacket for dining and dancing. During the cooler months warmer clothing, with raincoats and cardigans, is needed.

Food and Drink. Tap-water is safe, though sometimes brackish, but on no account drink water from wells. Hotel cooking is usually international, but Bermuda specialities are sometimes served, especially in restaurants: lobster and fish chowder are favourites, and mussel pie, conch stew, shark and other fish delicacies are popular. Local desserts include sweet potato pudding, bay grape jelly and a syllabub of guava jelly, cream and sherry. All kinds of rum punches and cocktails are served.

Where to stay Probably no place of comparable size has so many hotels, guest houses, pensions and private homes taking in a few visitors. Most hotels are in the luxury class, but the very wide range of accommodation available makes it possible for tourists on a lower budget to stay in Bermuda. It is advisable to book accommodation well in advance. Be warned that it is not easy to find accommodation at less than our price range D. For a full list (indeed, so full and so readily available that it does not seem worth while for a book of this type to go into details), including board and lodging in private houses, write to the Bermuda Department of Tourism, at Old Town Hall, Front Street, Hamilton 5-23; or at 58 Grosvenor Street, London W1X 0JD (Tel.: 01-499 1777); 610 Fifth Avenue, New York 10020; 85 Richmond Street W., Toronto M5H 2C9. Alternatively, the information airport desk will help you find a hotel.

Sport and Entertainment Fishing is at its best between mid-April and mid-October. No fishing licence is required and all tackle can be hired.

Nine golf courses (6 or 18 holes) provide an interesting and challenging variety of play. An introduction can be arranged through the visitor's hotel or guest house. Green fees: US$7-12. Sailing dinghies (about 16 foot) can be hired by the day or half day. There are races twice a week. Swimming at beach clubs and hotel pools as well as public beaches. (Horse Shoe Bay is recommended.) The islands provide ideal conditions for underwater sports: helmet tours US$15 for 4 hrs.; skindiving on reefs US$20 per hr. Spear-fishing is prohibited within one mile of the coast and spear guns are banned. Water ski-ing from US$6 per lesson. Equipment for aqua-planing can also be hired. Tennis can be played at all-weather courts throughout the islands. Approximate fees at Bermuda Tennis Stadium US$2 an hr.; at Southampton, Princess Hotel and Elbow Beach Surf Club US$5 an hr. Rackets can be hired.

Currency The Bermudian dollar is valued at par with the US$. US and Canadian currencies are accepted everywhere. Sterling notes and travellers' cheques are no longer normally accepted, so should be changed into US or Bermudian currency at the banks. The import and export of Bermudian currency is prohibited. There is no limit to the amount of foreign currency which may be taken into Bermuda, but the amount taken out must not exceed that declared on entry. There is no income tax in Bermuda.

Banks Hours are 0930-1500 Mon.-Fri. and 1630-1730 Fri. only. Four banks operate: Bank of Bermuda, Front Street, Hamilton 5-31, with branches in Church Street, Hamilton, and in Somerset and St. George's; Bank of N.T. Butterfield, Front Street, Hamilton 5-24, with branches in Somerset and St. George's; Bermuda National Bank, Church Street, Hamilton 5-24, with branches in St. George's and Southampton Princess Hotel; and Bermuda Provident Bank, Church Street, Hamilton 5-24. Only the Bank of Bermuda (up to US$100) and the Provident Bank (Barclays cheques only) will normally cash foreign personal cheques.

Road Travel Bus services run to all parts along 150 miles of road. Bus from Hamilton to airport US$0.25; from Hamilton to St. George's US$0.30. Taxi from Hamilton to airport US$5. Taxis have meters and cost US$1 for the first mile and 50 cents each mile beyond. From midnight until 0600 they cost 25% more.

How to get to Bermuda

The international airport at Kindley Field is some 12 miles from Hamilton, about 35 minutes' drive across a causeway. It belongs to one of the US bases and is used by military and civil aircraft. British Airways operates direct services from London, New York and points in the Caribbean. Pan Am, Delta and Eastern also provide frequent services from New York and other cities in the USA. Air Canada operates flights from Toronto and Montreal and between Canada, Barbados, Antigua and Trinidad. Qantas calls at Bermuda on its flights from Sydney to London.

By Sea Holland America Home Lines operate a weekly cruise service between New York and Bermuda from April to October. Accommodation can sometimes be obtained via New York (Cunard) and then to Bermuda. Ships of the P. & O. occasionally call at Bermuda.

Cables International Cables, Telephones and Telex services. Cable and Wireless (West Indies) Ltd., Church Street, Hamilton.

Newspapers *The Royal Gazette* is the only daily (not Sun.) newspaper.

VIRGIN ISLANDS

THE VIRGIN ISLANDS are a group of about 1,600 small islands situated between Puerto Rico and the Leeward Islands; the total population is upward of 100,000. Politically they are divided into two groups: the larger western group, with a population of 102,410 (1984), were purchased from Denmark by the USA in 1917 and remain a US Territory; the smaller eastern group constitute a British Crown Colony, with a population of only 10,500 (1983). The climate in the Virgin Islands is very pleasant, with the trade winds keeping the humidity down. The average temperature varies little between winter (25°C or 77°F) and summer (28°C or 82°F).

The **US Virgin Islands** (USVI), in which the legacies of Danish ownership are very apparent, contain three main islands—St. Thomas, St. John and St. Croix. They have long been developed as holiday centres for US citizens, and the population, mainly black, has always been English-speaking, despite the nearness of Puerto Rico and the long period of Danish control.

Government The USVI are an unincorporated Territory under the US Department of Interior with a non-voting Delegate in the House of Representatives. The Governor is elected every four years; there are 15 Senators; judicial power is vested in local courts. All persons born in the USVI are citizens of the United States, but do not vote in presidential elections while resident in the islands. The present Governor is Mr. Alexander Farrelly.

History Columbus discovered the Virgin Islands on his second voyage to the New World in 1493. He first came upon St. Croix (Santa Cruz) and then moved on to St. Thomas and St. John. The islands remained almost forgotten for more than a century, but it is recorded that on St. Croix in 1625 both English and French colonists were engaged in agriculture. By 1650, only the English remained.

In that very year, the English were ejected by the Spanish from St. Croix; later that year the Spanish were usurped by the French. In 1653, St. Croix was willed to the Knights of Malta, but the Knights were unaccustomed to the rigours of the Caribbean and sold St. Croix to the French West India Company.

The Danes took possession of St. Thomas in 1666 and of St. John shortly thereafter. They divided St. Thomas into 125-acre plantations, which at their peak numbered more than 170, but the terrain was not especially suited for agriculture and by the middle 1700s commerce was the backbone of St. Thomas' economy. It was part of the triangular trade route that brought slaves from Africa and sent molasses and rum to Europe, and was also a haven for pirates who attacked Spanish, French and Dutch ships.

In 1733, St. Croix was purchased by Denmark. It was more suitable for agriculture, and today there are the ruins of numerous sugar plantations with their proud Great Houses and windmills. (Judith's Fancy is the best preserved from the time of the French; Whim Estate is restored to the way it was under Danish rule in the 1700s.)

From 1900 on, the sugar market declined, and Denmark became eager to dispose of the

VIRGIN ISLANDS 1283

islands. As a protection for the mainland in World War I, they were purchased on March 31, 1917 by the USA for US$25m.

The three US islands are connected by "Bomba" launches and seaplanes which charge about US$12 a trip. On the islands camping is easy and fruit and vegetables are cheap; other food is expensive, however.

St. Thomas lies about 75 miles east of Puerto Rico at 18°N, 40 miles north of St. Croix. Thirteen miles long and less than three miles wide, with area of 32 square miles and population of 46,630, St. Thomas rises out of the sea to a peak of 1,500 feet and a range of hills that runs down its spine. At Coki Beach, on the NE coast, a US$3.50 taxi ride from St. Thomas, is the Coral World underwater observatory (US$5 entrance). On the beach snorkelling equipment can be rented for US$2-3.

The harbour at **Charlotte Amalie,** capital of St. Thomas and also of the entire USVI, still bustles with colour and excitement. The town was built by the Danes, who named it after their King's consort, but to most visitors it remains "St. Thomas". Beautiful old Danish houses are a reminder of the island's history. There are also picturesque churches and one of the oldest synagogues in the western hemisphere. The island's principal source of income today is tourism. The Virgin Islands Museum, in the former dungeon at Fort Christian, is open Mon.-Fri. 0800-1630.

Hotels There are many hotels on St.Thomas, some of which are listed below. In or near Charlotte Amalie: *Bluebeard's Castle*, A; *Carib Beach*, A; *Island Beachcomber*, A, on pleasant beach, excellent service, taxi (US$2) and bus (US$0.25) to town; *St. Thomas Sheraton*, A; *Michele Motel*, B; *New Holiday Isles*, on waterfront, C, shower, hot water, a/c, good. *Domini Hus*, C, often full; *Beverley Hill Guesthouse*, on road to airport, C, basic but clean. At Hill Bay, *Larry's Hideaway and Campsite*, US$10 per person in shared tent, most other facilities available, good beach, taxi to town about US$6. *Poor Man's Bar*, friendly and cheap. *The Greenhouse*, on harbour front, attracts younger crowd, serves food and drinks, in season has a band.

Jewellery H. Stern have four shops selling high-quality jewellery at 12 Main Street, Havensight Shopping Mall, Frenchman's Reef Hotel and Bluebeard Castle.

Commerce The island is a major distiller and exporter of rum, and is also a free port, in common with the other USVI.

Transport Harry S. Truman international airport. Taxi to town US$2. There are open taxi-buses which charge US$1 for the trip from Red Hook to Market Place. Buses between Charlotte Amalie and Red Hook and Bordeaux. All types of wheels are available with rental firms plentiful. One popular idea, especially given the hilly terrain of St. Thomas, is to get about by motor bike. There are also group tours by surrey, bus or taxi. There are a number of ferry boats to various destinations, including one from Red Hook to nearby St. John (every hour from 0730 to 1900, takes 15 mins, costs US$1.50).

Festivals Carnival April 21-26. Most spectacular.

Nightlife St. Thomas offers the greatest variety of nightlife to be found in the Virgin Islands. Bands and combos play nightly at most hotels. Several of the hotels offer limbo dancing three or four nights a week and the ubiquitous steel bands remain a great favourite with both visitors and inhabitants.

Sports Magens Bay is considered to be the finest beach on the island. There is deep sea fishing with the next world record in every class lurking just under the boat; sailing of all types and cruises are available. The *St. Thomas Sheraton* hotel at Long Bay has a good yachting marina. The waters around the islands are so clear that snorkelling is extremely popular. Equipment and instruction for underwater photography are available. Ashore, tennis, golf (at the Herman Moore Golf Club), riding, and on nearby St. John, camping.

St. John is about 5 miles east of St. Thomas and 35 miles north of St. Croix. The population is only 2,570, mainly concentrated in the little town of Cruz Bay and the village of Coral Bay. Two-thirds of the island is a US National Park which is covered by an extensive network of trails. Several times a week a Park ranger leads the Reef Bay hike, which passes through a variety of vegetation zones, visits an old sugar mill and some unexplained petroglyphs and ends with a ferry ride back to Cruz Bay. Advisable to book. There are many other hikes. Off Trunk Bay, the island's best beach, there is an underwater snorkelling trail maintained

1284 VIRGIN ISLANDS

by the National Parks Service. Not surprisingly, the beach tends to get rather crowded.

Hotels *Caneel Bay Plantation*, A, with 2 meals; *Gallows Point*, A, EP. At Cinnamon Bay (frequent taxibuses from Cruz Bay, US$1) there is a campground and chalet site run by the National Park Service; space costs US$4 and tents, US$30 d, chalets, reported to be in poor state of repair, a few shared showers, food expensive in both the cafeteria and grocery store. At Maho Bay (8 miles fron Cruz Bay, regular bus service) a private-enterprise campground has been opened. "Tent cottages°" are available from US$25 a night. There is a restaurant; also facilities for scuba diving and snorkelling and evening lectures on diving, sailing etc. It is possible to stay in private homes; contact Havens with Ambiance, P.O. Box 635, Cruz Bay.

Carnival St. John's carnival is in the week of July 4.

St. Croix (population 53,210) is some 75 miles east of Puerto Rico and 40 miles south of St. Thomas. Columbus thought that St. Croix looked like a lush garden when he first saw it during his second voyage in 1493. It had been cultivated by the Carib Indians and the land still lies green and fertile between the rolling hills. Agriculture was long the staple of the economy, cattle and sugar the main activities. Today it has been surpassed by tourism and industry. The Hess oil refinery on the North Coast is one of the biggest in the world, with a throughput capacity of 545,000 barrels per day. Tourism, however, has suffered slightly from a rise in social and racial tension. St. Croix is dotted with vacant sugar mills, many of them restored as private homes. The Whim Great House is worth a visit; it houses a museum of the period of Danish rule. There is a distinct lack of road signs on St. Croix, so if you use a car, take a good map with you.

Christiansted The old town square and waterfront area of Christiansted, the old Danish capital, still retain the colourful character of the early days. Overhanging second-floor balconies designed by the Danes to shade the streets serve as cool arcades for shoppers. Red-roofed pastel houses built by early settlers climb the hills overlooking Kings Wharf and there is an old outdoor market.

Old Christiansted is compact and easy to stroll. The best place to start is the Visitors' Bureau, housed in a building near the Wharf which served a century ago as the Customs Scale House. Here you can pick up brochures.

Across the way is Fort Christiansvaern, which the Danes built in 1774 on the foundations of a French fort dating from 1645. Admission is free. See the punishment cells, dungeons, barracks room, officers' kitchen, powder magazine, an exhibit of how to fire a cannon, and the battery—the best vantage point for photographing the old town and harbour.

The Steeple Building is a minute's walk away. Built as a church by the Danes in 1734, then converted into a military bakery, storehouse and later a hospital, it is now a museum of the island's early history. There are displays of Indian ceremonial bowls and cooking vessels, a diorama of Christiansted as it was in 1800, and a layout of an early sugar plantation which shows the various steps of producing sugar, molasses and rum.

The area here is a treasury of old Danish architecture, and many of the original buildings are still in use. The West India and Guinea Co., which bought St. Croix from the French and settled the island, built a warehouse on the corner of Church and Company Streets in 1749 which now serves as a post office.

Across the way from Government House on King St. is the building where the young Alexander Hamilton, who was to become one of the founding fathers of the USA, worked as a clerk in Nicolas Cruger's countinghouse. Today the building houses the Little Switzerland shop and Hong Kong Restaurant.

Government House has all the hallmarks of the elegant and luxurious life of the merchants and planters in the days when "sugar was king". The centre section, built in 1747 as a merchant's residence, was bought by the Secret Council of St. Croix in 1771 to serve as a government office. It was later joined to another merchant's town house on the corner of Queen Cross St. and a handsome ballroom was added. Visitors are welcome to view the ballroom, stroll through the gardens and watch the proceedings in the Court of Justice.

Queen Cross St. leads into Strand and the fascinating maze of arcades and alleys lined with boutiques, handicrafts and jewellery shops. Along the waterfront there are bars and restaurant pavilions.

Frederiksted, 17 miles from Christiansted, is the only other town on St. Croix and although quiet, its gingerbread architecture has its own charm. The mahogany forest is worth a visit. Buses link the two towns and there are taxis from the airport to Frederiksted.

VIRGIN ISLANDS

Transport Alexander Hamilton international airport. Boat, cycle, plane or car, the scenery is consistently beautiful and all methods of getting to see it are easy to arrange. Cruises under sail around St. Croix or to Buck Island (there is an underwater US National Park here) are available through hotels or in either Christiansted or Frederiksted. The major car rental agencies are represented at the airport, in hotels and in both cities. Car hire costs from US$22 a day with free mileage. Driving is on the left hand side, though cars are left-hand drive.

Hotels *Buccaneer*, A; *Gentle Winds*, A; *St. Croix-by-the-Sea*, A; *King Frederik*, A; *Frederiksted, Cabret* and *Oriental*, all B; *Smithfield*, C; *Cottages-by-the-Sea*, B, fully equipped, good facilities; *Club Comanche*, B, and *King Christian*, A, both on waterfront; *Hotel on the Cay*, on an island in the harbour, A; *Sprat Hall*, A, a former Great House, has riding stables; *Hill View Apartments*, 1 Queen St., Christiansted, US$70 per week single, one week minimum; *Ackie's Guesthouse*, C, kitchen facilities, in peaceful, rural location, though rather difficult to get to and from: it is a 15 min. walk to the main road whence shared taxis run to Christiansted or Frederiksted, US$0.50, double after 1800. All price ranges quoted are EP.

Restaurants *Captain Weeks 10 Grand Restaurant*, West Indian cooking; *Heart of Palm*, a very good sandwich shop; *The Pig's Ear*, a good snack bar.

Shopping Biggest bargain in the islands is duty-free rum, cheap and good.

Nightlife Most hotels provide evening entertainment on a rotating basis, the custom of many of the Caribbean islands, so it is sometimes best to stay put and let the world of West Indian music and dance come to you. The Grandstand Play Bar has American-style entertainment. Restaurant life on St. Croix is rich but basic; charcoal-boiled steaks and lobsters, West Indian creole dishes and Danish and French specialities. Do not miss the open-air Crucian picnics.

Carnival St. Croix's carnival lasts from Christmas week to January 6. There is another festival on the Sat. nearest to March 17, St. Patrick's Day, when there is a splendid parade.

Sports St. Croix has it all—swimming, sailing, fishing, tennis, horse racing and riding, plus the only 18-hole golf course in the Virgins, at Fountain Valley. Above all, the island is famous for diving. At Buck Island there are guided tours on underwater snorkelling rails. Another attraction is the Salt River coral canyon. Diving trips are arranged by Teddy's Charter Service (which also charters boats out and offers sailing lessons) and the Virgin Islands Diving School. Both are located in the Pan-Am Pavilion in Christiansted. The latter, as well as the North Shore Dive Tours, run beach diving courses.

The **British Virgin Islands** (BVI) are much less developed than the US group, and number some 60 islands, islets, rocks, and cays, of which only 16 or so are inhabited. They are all of volcanic origin except one, Anegada, which is coral and limestone. The two major islands, Tortola and Virgin Gorda, along with the groups of Anegada and Jost Van Dyke, contain most of the total population of over 10,000. A nearly self-contained community, the islands are a Crown Colony with a Governor appointed by London, although to a large extent they are internally self-governing. The economy is based predominantly on tourism, and the clean, crystal-clear waters around the islands provide excellent snorkelling, diving, cruising and fishing. "Bareboating" (self-hire yacht chartering) has become extremely popular.

At the most recent general election, in September 1986, Mr Lavity Stoutt, of the Virgin Islands Party, became Chief Minister for the third time.

Tortola is the main island, with a population of nearly 9,000. **Road Town,** on the S shore, is the capital and business centre of the territory, with about 1,500 inhabitants. There are also communities at East End and West End (reached by bus from Road Town for US$1). From West End, regular "Bomba" launches provide a link to Virgin Gorda and the US islands. (The fare from St. Thomas is US$13.) Mount Sage, the highest point in the archipelago, rises to 1,780 ft., and traces of a primeval rain forest can still be found on its slopes. Josiah's Bay, near East End, has a pleasant beach as does Brewers Bay on N coast. Apple Bay and Smugglers Cove have fine sandy beaches; so has Cane Garden Bay. It is possible to hitch-hike on the island. A day's sailing excursion to Norman and Salt Islands can be arranged from Tortola. In and around Tortola there is a growing number of yachting marinas, where boats can be hired, including those at Wickham's Cay, Maya Cove, Nanny Cay, Marina Cay, Prospect Reef, Baughers Bay and Trellis Bay.

Hotels Rates apply to double rooms, EP in the peak season. *Fort Burt*, near Road Town, pool,

1286 VIRGIN ISLANDS

half board, A; *Treaure Isle*, pool, tennis, no meals, A; *Colonial Manor Hotel*, pool, gardens, A; *Sebastian's on the Beach*, pleasant, beach bar, US management, A-B; *Sugar Mill Estate*, a restored West Indian cottage, US management, gardens, pool, beach, A; *Smugglers Cove*, beach, A, also cottages; *Long Bay Hotel*, beach, pool, A; *Christopher's Guest House*, D; *Castle Maria Hotel*, Road Town, friendly, B; *Wayside Inn*, Road Town, D, clean and friendly, *Maya Cove*, on S coast, rooms with cooking facilities, restaurant, good value, D, depending on season; *Brewers Bay* campsite on N coast, site US$5, tent hire US$14, beach bar and simple restaurant, 3 buses a day along a bad road (US$3). *Prospect Reef Resort*, A; *Moorings-Mariner Inn*, A; *BVI Aquatic Hotel*, C; *CSY Yacht Club*, B; *Village Cay Marina*, B; *Sea View Hotel*, B; *Cane Garden Bay Beach Hotel*, *Tamarind Country Club Hotel*, B. Rates given are for peak season where possible. There is a 5% hotel tax in the BVI. The *Francis Drake Pub*, Road Town, reasonable prices, has steel band on Fridays.

Virgin Gorda was, over a century ago, the centre of population and commerce. It is now better known as the site of the geological curiosity called The Baths, where enormous boulders form a natural swimming pool and underwater caves. The island is 7 miles long and has a population of about 1,000. The northern half is mountainous, with a peak 1,370 ft. high, while the southern half is relatively flat. There are some 20 secluded beaches; the most frequented are Devil's Bay, Spring Bay, and Trunk Bay. North of the island is the Sound, formed to the S and E by Virgin Gorda, to the N by Prickly Pear Island, and to the W by Mosquito Island. On the SE tip is Copper Mine Point, where the Spaniards mined copper, gold and silver some 400 years ago; the remains of the mine can be seen. The rocky façade here is reminiscent of the Cornish coast of England. There is a 3,000 ft. airstrip. The amateur geologist will find stones such as malachite and crystals embedded in quartz. All land on Virgin Gorda over 1,000 ft. high is now a National Park, where trails have been blazed for walking. There are beautiful beaches on the W. coast. Bitter End and Biras Creek are good anchorages and both have a hotel and restaurant.

Hotels *Little Dix Bay*, Rockefeller's Rockresort hotel, pool, beach, full board L, AP; under same management is the *Virgin Gorda Yacht Harbour*, a large marina offering convenient facilities. *Biras Creek Hotel*, at North Sound, luxurious also, with Scandinavian architecture, pool, tennis, with full board, L, AP. *Ocean View Hotel*, only 12 rooms, B. *Guavaberry Spring Bay*, cottages, A. *Bitter End Yacht Club*, at North Sound, cottages and rooms, L, AP. *Tony Mack's Lord Nelson Inn*, in The Valley, 5 rooms, bar, with darts, croquet course, putting green, C. *Fischer's Cove Beach Hotel*, cottages at St Thomas Bay, A. *Olde Yard Inn*, The Valley, L, MAP. *Leverick Bay Hotel*, L; *Tradewinds Resort*, L, AP. *Castle Marina*, A. There is another small guest house by the cinema, said to be not too clean. (Rates quoted are for peak season where possible.) It is possible to camp at Spring Bay.

Beef Island was famed as a hunting ground for beef cattle during the buccaneering days. The island is linked to Tortola by the Queen Elizabeth bridge. The main airport of the BVI is here. Long Bay beach is on the northern shore. Off the N shore is Bellamy Cay.

Salt Island is the location of the salt ponds, which attract tourists during the gathering season (April-May). There is a small settlement on the N side as well as a reef-protected lagoon on the E shore. The population numbers about 20. The British mail ship *Rhone* was sunk off Salt Island and the site was used in the film *The Deep*.

Marina Cay is a tiny island of six acres just N of Beef Island. Here Robb White wrote his book *Our Virgin Isle*, which was made into a film starring Sidney Poitier and John Cassavetes. A charming cottage hotel, *Marina Cay Hotel*, comprises most of the island, which is encircled by a reef, L, MAP.

Norman Island is uninhabited, but reputed to be the "Treasure Island" of Robert Louis Stevenson fame. On its rocky west coast are caves where treasure is said to have been discovered many years ago.

Anegada is unique among this group of islands because of its coral and limestone formation. The highest point is only 28 ft. above sea level. There is an airstrip 2,500 ft. long and 60 ft. wide, which can handle light aircraft. There are still a few large iguanas, which are indigenous to the island. The waters abound with fish, and the extensive reefs are popular with scuba divers who also explore wrecks of ships which foundered in years past. Some were said to hold treasure, but to date only a few doubloons have been discovered. There are beaches on the N and W ends. The population numbers about 290. *Reefs Hotel*, L, AP, where there is a marina; *Wheatly Guest House*, and *Neptune Treasure*.

VIRGIN ISLANDS

Jost Van Dyke is mountainous, with beaches at White Bay and Great Harbour Bay on the S coast. It is surrounded by some smaller islands, one of which is Little Jost Van Dyke. Population about 130. *White Bay Sandcastle*, L, AP; *Foxy's Restaurant*, friendly and cheap. It is possible to get there by boat (about $10 return, minimum of 3 people) from West End or Brewers Bay on Tortola.

Camping *Tula's N and N Campground*, Little Harbour, 8' X 10' $25 per day, 9' X 11' US$35 (per couple).

Peter Island has a tiny population and offers isolated beaches and picnic spots. Dead Man's Bay has a palm-fringed beach and good anchorage. The *Peter Island Yacht Club* is built on reclaimed land jutting out into Sir Francis Drake Channel, forming a sheltered harbour with marine facilities. Built by Norwegians, there are 8 chalet-type cottages, a pool, tennis; with full board, A (high season). *Peter Island Hotel*, A, MAP. Daily ferry from Tortola (US$8 return). Tel.: (809) 494-2561. US reservations: Resorts Management Inc., The Carriage House, 201 ½ E. 29th St., New York, NY 10016; Tel.: (800) 225-4255 or (212) 696-4566.

Great Dog Island features marvellous views of frigate birds nesting.

Great Thatch, just off West End, Tortola, has a pleasant guest house.

Mosquito Island: *Drake's Anchorage*, L, AP.

Guana Island: *Guana Island Club*, L, AP (winter).

How to get there From the USA several airlines fly direct to St. Thomas or St. Croix (USVI). There are good connections for both the USVI and the BVI from Puerto Rico and Antigua: Aero Virgin Islands has 12 daily flights to St. Thomas from Puerto Rico, and other airlines operating on these routes include Liat (which connects with British Airways flights in Antigua), Air BVI, Prinair, Caribair, Coral Air, Trans Commuters Airlines, and Crownair. Linking the islands there are frequent flights (Air BVI, Eastern Caribbean Airways, and All Islands Air) between St. Thomas, St. Croix, Beef Island and Virgin Gorda. From St. Croix and St. Thomas, Virgin Island Seaplane Shuttle. Air Boats go to Beef Island.

There are regular services by *Bomba Charger* and *Native Son* launches between St. Thomas and Tortola (Road Town); if you telephone from St. John's the captain may call there to pick you up en route. A departure tax of US$2.50 for those leaving by air, US$1.50 by sea. Every weekend a boat sails from Fajardo, Puerto Rico, to Tortola, US$18 one way. Speedy Fantasy ferries operate between Virgin Gorda and Road Town (Mon., Wed, Fri. and Sat.) and between Virgin Gorda and St. Thomas on Tuesdays and Thursdays. *Sundance II* between Cruz Bay and West End. Nine boats daily between Peter Island and Tortola.

Self-Drive Cars Minimokes and jeeps can be hired on Tortola and Virgin Gorda. Jeeps may be more useful for exploring secluded beach areas. Car rental offices (or the Police Headquarters) provide the necessary temporary BVI driving licence (US$ 5) but you must also have a valid licence from your home country. Rates range from US$28 to US$60 per day. *Tortola*: Alphonso Car Rentals, Fish Bay; Budget, Wickams Cay; Hertz, Road Town; International, Road Town; Nibbs, opp. Police Station, Road Town; Anytime, Wayside Inn Guest House, Road Town. *Virgin Gorda*: Bomba, Yacht Harbour; Speedings, The Valley.

Documents US citizens do not of course require passports for visits to the US Virgin Islands. For the British Islands, an authenticated birth or citizenship certificate or voter's registration may suffice for US or Canadian citizens. British visitors to the US islands need passport and US visa. Visitors of other nationalities will need passports, visas and return/onward tickets.

Hotel Tax There is a 5% hotel tax. Departure tax is levied at the rate of US$5 per person leaving by air and US$3 by sea.

Banks Barclays International and Bank of Nova Scotia on the main islands.

Currency The US dollar circulates as the official medium of exchange in US and British islands alike.

Communications All telephone calls within the USVI are local. The service is poor; it is advisable, when trying to get a connection, to omit the first two 7s (which prefix all USVI numbers).

Tourist Information For USVI, there are offices of the USVI Division of Tourism in the USA at: 307 Michigan Ave., Chicago, 60601; 100 Biscayne Blvd., Miami 33132; 1270 Av. of Washington, New York; 1050 17th Street N.W., Washington DC, 20036; also in Denver, San Francisco and Seattle. In Canada: 11 Adelaide St. W., Toronto, Ontario M5H 1A9. In the UK: 25 Bedford Square, London WC1. In West Germany: Freiherr vom Stein Strasse 24-26, D-6000 Frankfurt am Main 1. In Puerto Rico: 1300 Ashford Ave., Condado, Puerto Rico 00902. There are also offices in

1288 VIRGIN ISLANDS

Charlotte Amalie, Cruz Bay, Christiansted and Frederiksted. Hotel and restaurant lists and descriptive leaflets available. Texaco issue a map of the US islands. For BVI, Tortola Travel Services, Main Street, Roadtown, have brochures on all the islands. There is a Tourist Board in Road Town. *This Week in St. Croix*, is a weekly publication containing much useful information.

Note Spearfishing is not allowed, hunting on land is also banned, and backpacking is actively discouraged. Camping is allowed only on authorized sites.

WANTED: MAPS
ARGENTINA – BRAZIL – MEXICO GUATEMALA – EL SALVADOR – THE CARIBBEAN ISLANDS

We would much appreciate receiving any surplus maps and diagrams, however rough, of towns and cities, walks, national parks and other interesting areas, to use as source material for the Handbook and other forthcoming titles.

The above regions are particularly needed but any maps of Latin America would be welcome.

The Editor Trade & Travel Publications Limited
5 Prince's Buildings, George Street,
Bath BA1 2ED. England

NETHERLANDS ANTILLES AND ARUBA

THE NETHERLANDS ANTILLES consist of the islands of Aruba, Bonaire, and Curaçao (popularly known as the ABCs) off the coast of Venezuela; and Sint Eustatius (Statia), Saba, and the southern part of Sint Maarten (St. Martin) in what are generally known as the Leeward Islands. There is some confusion regarding which islands are Leeward and which Windward: locals refer to the ABCs as "Leeward Islands", and the other three as "Windward", a distinction adopted from the Spaniards, who still speak of the *Islas de Sotovento* and *de Barlovento* with reference to the trade winds.

The Netherlands Antilles form two autonomous parts of the Kingdom of the Netherlands. The main part, less Aruba (see below), is a parliamentary federal democracy, the seat of which is in Willemstad, Curaçao. A Governor, appointed by the Queen of the Netherlands, represents the Crown, and each island has its own Legislative and Executive Council. The economy of the islands is based on oil refining (in Curaçao) and tourism. Industry is restricted to some petrochemical production and a few light manufacturing operations. The Netherlands Antilles form an important offshore financial centre. Lately the ABC islands have suffered as a result of the recession in Venezuela: many Venezuelan-backed building projects are still awaiting completion.

On January 1, 1986, Aruba was granted separate status from the other islands, but remains subject to the Dutch crown until full independence in 1996. No independence schedule has yet been agreed for the other islands. Mr Don Martina is Prime Minister of the five-island federation, and Mr Henny Eaman is Prime Minister of Aruba.

CURAÇAO

Curaçao, the largest of the six islands comprising the Netherlands Antilles, lies in the Caribbean Sea 60 km. off the Venezuelan coast at a latitude of 12°N, outside the hurricane belt. It is 65 km. long and 11 km. at its widest, with an area of 448 square km.

The landscape is barren, because of low rainfall (560 mm. a year) which makes for sparse vegetation (consisting mostly of cactus thickets), and mostly flat, except in the northwest where hills rise to 375 metres. Deep bays indent the southern coast, the largest of which, Schottegat, provides Willemstad with one of the finest harbours in the Caribbean.

Coral reefs surrounding the island, constant sunshine, a mean temperature of 27°C (81°F), and refreshing trade winds lure visitors the year round, making tourism the second industry; the first is the oil refinery dating back to 1917, now one of the largest in the world, to which the island owes its prosperity. That prosperity is now under threat since Shell has pulled out of the refinery; the island government purchased the plant, and leased it to Venezuela. Bunkering has also become an important segment of the economy, and the terminal at Bullenbaai is one of the largest bunkering ports in the world. Besides oil, other exports include the famous Curaçao liqueur, made from the peel of the native orange. The island's extensive trade makes it a port of call for a great many shipping lines.

1290 NETHERLANDS ANTILLES AND ARUBA

The population of 165,000 is truly cosmopolitan, and 79 nationalities are represented, of whom 16% were born outside the Netherlands Antilles. Dutch is the official language, and many islanders also speak English or Spanish, but the *lingua franca* of the ABC islands is Papiamento, which originated with the Portuguese spoken by Jewish emigrants from Portugal, who were the most numerous settlers in the 17th century. Since then it has developed into a mixture of Portuguese, Dutch, Spanish, English, and some African and Indian dialects. Papiamento has been in existence since at least the early 18th century, but has no fixed spelling, though it is becoming a written language.

History The first known settlers of Curaçao were the Caiquetios, a tribe of peaceful Arawak Indians. One of the clans of the Caiquetios were called "Curaçaos", seafarers who conducted a lively traffic with Venezuelan Indians in their log canoes. In 1499, Curaçao was discovered by Alonso de Ojeda, a lieutenant of Christopher Columbus, accompanied by Amerigo Vespucci. The Spaniards settled on the island in 1527 and, there being no gold, mainly raised livestock for hides. In 1634, the Dutch occupied and fortified Curaçao, which became the base for a rich entrepot trade flourishing through the 18th century. Other Spaniards and Portuguese, particularly Jews fleeing the Inquisition, sought shelter here among the tolerant Dutch, and became important in business. Peter Stuyvesant was Governor in 1642 before going off to become the governor of New York, at that time New Amsterdam. Following various slave uprisings, and attempts by the English and the French to take the island, it became a British protectorate in 1800. It was returned to the Dutch in 1802, was again captured by the British in 1807, and was returned to the Netherlands definitively by the Treaty of Paris in 1815. Slavery was finally abolished in 1863. The 19th century was a time of economic decline—alleviated only by ventures such as the cultivation of aloes for pharmaceutical products and oranges for Curaçao liqueur—until the discovery of oil in Venezuela and the consequent building of the Royal Dutch Shell refinery in 1917.

Willemstad, capital of the Netherland Antilles and of the island of Curaçao (population about 140,000), is full of charm and colour. The architecture is a joyous tropical adaptation of 17th-century Dutch, painted in storybook colours. Pastel shades of all colours are used for homes, shops, and government buildings alike. Rococo gables, arcades, and bulging columns evoke the spirit of the Dutch colonial burghers.

The earliest buildings in Willemstad were exact copies of Dutch buildings of the mid-17th century—high-rise and close together to save money and space. Not until the first quarter of the 18th century did the Dutch adapt their northern ways to the tropical climate and begin building galleries on to the façades of their houses, to give shade and more living space. The chromatic explosion is attributed to a Governor-General of the islands, the eccentric Vice-Admiral Albert Kikkert ("Froggie" to his friends), who blamed his headaches on the glare of white houses and decreed in 1817 that pastel colours be used. Almost every point of interest in the city is in or within walking distance of the shopping centre in Punda, which covers about five blocks. Some of the streets here are only five metres wide, but attract many tourists with their myriad of shops offering international goods at near duty-free prices. The numerous jewellery shops in Willemstad have some of the finest stones to be found anywhere. Shops are open Mon. to Sat. 0800-1200, 1400-1800.

The Floating Market, a picturesque string of visiting Venezuelan, Colombian and other island schooners, lines the small canal leading to the Waaigat, a small yacht basin. Fresh fish, tropical fruit, vegetables and handicrafts are sold with much haggling. Visit early in the morning.

In the new public market building nearby there are straw hats and bags, spices, butcheries, and a couple of modest restaurants upstairs offering a lunchtime view of the city (as out of a concrete tower) and genuine local food and live music.

Nearby is one of the most important historical sites on Curaçao, the Mikve Israel-Emanuel synagogue, which dates back to 1732, making it the oldest in the Western Hemisphere. Services are held Friday nights and Saturday. Open 0900-1145 and 1500-1700, free, no photographs allowed. Worth seeing for its big brass chandeliers (replicas of those in the Portuguese synagogue in Amsterdam), ritual furnishings of richly carved mahogany with silver ornamentation, blue windows and stark white walls. The traditional sand on the floor is sprinkled there daily, some say, to symbolize the wandering of the Israelites in the Egyptian desert during the Exodus. Others say it was meant to muffle the sound of the feet of those who had to worship secretly during the Inquisition period.

NETHERLANDS ANTILLES AND ARUBA 1291

In the courtyard is the Jewish Museum, occupying two restored 18th century houses, which harbours a permanent exhibition of religious objects. The Museum is open Mon.-Fri. and sometimes on Sun. if there are cruise ships in port; entrance fee is US$1. Incidentally the visiting cruise ships are themselves a tourist attraction.

The 18th century Protestant church, the Fortkerk, located at the back of the square behind Fort Amsterdam, the Governor's palace, still has a British cannonball embedded in its walls. It is presently being restored, and was not scheduled to re-open until 1987.

The swinging Queen Emma bridge spans St. Anna Bay, linking the two parts of the city, Punda and Otrabanda (the latter means "the other side" in Papiamento). Built on sixteen great pontoons, it is swung aside some thirty times a day to let ships pass in and out of the harbour. The present bridge, the third on the site, was built in 1939. While the bridge is open, pedestrians are shuttled free by small ferry boats.

The new Queen Juliana fixed bridge vaults about 50 metres over the bay and connects Punda and Otrabanda by a four-lane highway.

In Otrabanda is the Curaçao Museum—housed in an old quarantine station built in 1853—with an interesting collection of artefacts of the Caiquetio Indian culture, as well as paintings, furniture, and other items from the colonial era. The museum is open daily, except Mon. and the last Sunday of the month, admission NAf2, NAf0.50 for children (open 1000-1200 and 1400-1700).

West of the city, on the Schottegatweg Nord, is the Jewish cemetery, consecrated in 1659 and still in use. There are more than 1,700 tombstones from the 17th and 18th centuries, many still legible. The Octagon, where Simón Bolívar stayed during his exile in Curaçao in 1812, is near the *Avila Beach Hotel*.

On the island cactus plants grow up to 6 metres high, and the characteristic wind-distorted dividivi trees reach 3 metres, with another 3 metres or so of branches jutting out away from the wind at right angles to the trunk. The occasional thatched huts and adobe homes are in striking contrast to the restored country estate houses, or *landhuizen*, which emerge here and there in the parched countryside. Worth visiting are the Jan Kok, built in 1654, and the Santa Martha *landhuizen*. To visit them take the Lagun bus which leaves from beside the Rif Fort in Otrabanda, daily Mon.-Fri. Also worth a visit is the 18th-century fortified *landhuis* of Brievengat which now houses a gift shop. Open Mon.-Fri. 0900-1200 and 1500-1700, entry US$1. To reach it, take a Brievengat bus from the Wilhelminaplein in Punda to the Curaçao Sports Centre (US$0.40); there is a service every 30 mins. from 0645, Mon.-Sat. The *landhuis* lies behind the Sports Centre. The Savonet and the beautiful restored Ascension *landhuizen* are on the Otrabanda-Westpunt bus route. On the first Sun. in every month, the latter is open to the public. It contains some antique Curaçao furniture and at 1100 there is a display of Antillean dancing. Admission is free. In yet another old *landhuis*, at Chobolobo, is the Curaçao Liqueur Distillery where free samples are provided.

There are few really good beaches on Curaçao. The northeastern coast is rugged and rough for swimming, but the western coast offers some sheltered bays and beaches with excellent swimming, snorkelling, scuba diving, water-skiing, boating, and fishing. Southeast of Willemstad is Jan Thiel Bay, which has coral reefs and open sea (good snorkelling and scuba diving), as well as a snack bar with hot and cold food, changing facilities, and inexpensive apartments for rent. Entrance is free for visitors. For US$18 you can get a taxi to take you to the beach and return to fetch you at the time you specify. Santa Barbara, located at the mouth of Spanish Water Bay on the Mining Company property, is a favourite with locals and has recently received new changing rooms, toilets and snack facilities. Entrance free but NAf6 per car. Across the bay, which is one of the island's beauty spots, is the Curaçao Yacht Club, with a pleasant bar.

A good road leads northwest from Willemstad direct to the beach at West Point (Westpunt) at the northwestern tip of the island, about 45 mins. by car or an hour by bus. Smaller and more isolated beaches between Willemstad and Westpunt include Knip beach, which lies 1 km. off the Lagun-Westpunt road and thus can be reached on foot, the distance between the two places being only 6 km. It is advisable to take drinking water with you. There is good snorkelling at Knip. Only a 5-minute walk from Lagun (bus from Otrabanda, US$0.70) is Jeremi bay and in the same area are Port Marie, Daaibooi, Boca St. Cruz and Blauwbaai. Blauwbaai has changing facilities, showers, and food and drinks at weekends and charges an entry fee of about NAf3 per car, as do Jeremi and Port Marie. Beyond Westpunt is Kalki beach, which is particularly good for snorkelling and scuba diving as well as bathing. Back at Willemstad you can get to the beach near the *Curaçao Caribbean* or *Las Palmas* hotels by catching the hotel shuttle buses which leave regularly from beside the Rif Fort in Otrabanda. The only beach near town is the artificial one at *Avila Beach Hotel*. Non-residents pay a small entrance fee.

Near Westpunt is Mt. St. Christoffel, which at 375 metres is the highest point on the island. On a clear day you can see as far as Aruba, Bonaire and Venezuela. The 4,000 acre Christoffel Park offers interesting flora and fauna, including orchids, the indigenous *wayacá* plant and the tiny, shy Curaçao deer. One of the three caves in the park has paintings by Arawak Indians. The park is open daily, 0800-1500 (last admission is at 1400), entry NAf2 for adults, NAf1 for children, toddlers free. Also worth a visit, but probably dangerous to try and get into, is Boca Tabla, a cave in which the crashing waves make an awe-inspiring sight and sound. It is on the road from Christoffel Park. Entrance NAf10, at the entrance to Spanish Water Bay. Behind Spanish Water Bay rises Mt. Tafelberg, where phosphate mining used to take place. It can be visited on Tues. and Fri. when a special bus leaves the Mining Company entrance at 1400.

Among the hotels, the *Curaçao Caribbean* (ex-Concorde), *Las Palmas*, *Holiday Beach*, and *Princess Beach* have beaches and pools. The *Avila* is on a beach but has no pool, while the *Country Inn*, *Madeira Queen's*, *Plaza*, *Holland*, and *Madeira* have pools but no beaches.

Beware of a tree with small green apples that borders some beaches. This is the *manzanilla* and its sap causes burns on exposed skin.

Scuba diving gear can be hired, as can deep-sea fishing boats. There are also glass-bottom boats for the less sporty who wish to catch a glimpse of the fascinating underwater life surrounding Curaçao. Two ranches offer horses for hire by the hour, and there are tennis courts, a golf course, a squash court, and a bowling alley on the island. For "night-owls", there are four casinos as well. The Centro Pro Arte presents concerts, ballets and plays. While on the subject of entertainment, one of the most bizarre sights of Curaçao, not dealt with in the tourist brochures, is the government-operated red-light area, aptly named Campo Alegre. Close to the airport, it resembles a prison camp and is even guarded by a policeman. On a different level, the Coscora Zoo is well worth a visit.

Hotels Unless otherwise stated, the following ranges are for a double room without meals, to which a 5% government tax and 10% service charge must be added. Rates for Modified American Plan (MAP—breakfast and one meal), per day p.p., are indicated where available: *Curaçao Caribbean*, L (MAP add US$46 p.p. per day); *Holiday Beach* (MAP add US$52), L; *Princess Isles*, A (MAP US$20); *Curaçao Plaza*, L (MAP US$54, rather run down); *Coral Cliff Hotel*, between Willemstad and Westpunt, near Soto, expensive but recommended, every apartment faces the ocean, quiet and friendly (L, MAP US$56), tennis, windsurfing facilities, etc.; *Las Palmas*, A (MAP US$40). On a smaller scale: *Avila Beach* (charming, Dutch colonial style), A (MAP US$46); *Country Inn*, L; *Hotel Madeira*, B, low season; *Madeira Queen's*, B, low season; *San Marco*, B: *Park Hotel*, Fredrikstraat 84, B, recommended; *Pension La Creole*, Salinja 2, very hospitable, C; *Holland*, C, with breakfast; *Paris*, Breedestraat, C. Comparatively cheaper hotels (prices for one person) include: *Venezuela* and *Caracas*, on Van der Porandhofstraat, both C with food; *Central*, Scharlooweg 12, C; *Pensión Ida*, same street, D, also operates as a bordello; all of these are in Scharloo across the drawbridge from the market. In Otrabanda are *Pensión Estoril*, Breedestraat, C; *Stelaris*, D, clean but basic; *Carlos*, one of the cleanest in this price range, C; *Pensión Gratia*, Roodeweg, very simple, D; *Passangrahan Hotel Bellevue*, overlooking harbour, simple with good restaurant though possibly suitable only for men. Cheaper hotels are often full and sometimes none too clean, but taxi drivers will often be helpful in trying to find you one. There are some opposite the floating market. Check with Tourist Board for availability and latest prices.

Restaurants and Food International food at the major hotels. Historical *Fort Nassau* (view over town and harbour) is good and expensive; *Fort Waakzaamheid Tavern*, newly restored, international food, dancing, good bar too; *Bistro La Hacienda*, near *Princess Beach Hotel*, country house, features some local dishes and the best disco in Curaçao. *Restaurant Indonesia*, Mercuriusstraat 13, Dutch-run; *Rodeo Ranch*, van Staverenweg 6, *Cas Cora*, steakhouse with wild west atmosphere. *La Bistroelle* behind Promenade shopping centre, expensive but very good; *De Taveene*, Landhuis Groot Davelaar, is under the same management; *Golden Star* offers local food in unpretentious surroundings at modest prices (try *carco stoba* or conch stew; *bestia chiki* or goat stew; local fish with *funchi* which is the local staple made of corn meal; or *locrio*, a chicken rice dish); *Playa Forti* on Westpunt beach specialises in fish dishes; *Tom's Place*, friendly and cheap; *China Garden*, good Chinese food; *Bistro Le Clochard*, excellent French and Swiss dishes, reasonable prices, essential to book; *Tamarijn Bar*, on the Schottegat, is used mainly by locals; *Jaanchie's*, Westpunt, an open-air restaurant with excellent seafood (it is a guesthouse too); *Pisces*, another good fish restaurant at the end of the Caracasbaaiweg, near the Spanish Water; *San Marco*, rather staid, in the heart of town; *The Wine Cellar*, informal eating and drinking, recommended, as are *McDonald's Kentucky Fried Chicken* and *Pizza Hut*. In the Riffort, on the Otrabanda side, at the entrance to St. Anna Bay, are *Le Clochard* and *Le Recif*, both good, the latter for seafood. Cheap Chinese restaurants available: *Chung-King*, *Sun-Sing*, *Kowloon*, *Rose Garden Bar*, Oud Caracasbaaiweg, and *Bow Bon* for about US$3.50; *Gun Kook Yuen* (recommended) for US$4. In some small Chinese restaurants you can eat for even less. *De Fles* and *Le Papillon* provide good value eating.

While in the Netherlands Antilles, most visitors enjoy trying a *rijsttafel* (rice table), a sort of Asian *smörgåsbörd* adopted from Indonesia, and delicious. Because *rijsttafel* consists of anywhere from 15 to 40 separate dishes, it is usually prepared for groups of diners, although some Curaçao restaurants will do a modified version of 10 or 15 dishes for smaller parties of two or three couples. Unfortunately good *rijsttafel* is now quite difficult to find; that at *The Indonesia* is not recommended.

A limited selection of European and Californian wines is usually available in restaurants, although local waiters have little familiarity with them and it is advisable to examine your bottle well before allowing it to be opened. Curaçao's gold-medal-winning Amstel beer—the only beer in the world brewed from desalinated sea water—is very good indeed and available throughout the Netherlands Antilles. Some Dutch and other European beers can also be found. Curaçao's tap water is good; also distilled from the sea.

Health The climate is healthy and non-malarial; epidemic incidence is slight. Rooms without air-conditioning or window and door screens may need mosquito nets during the wetter months of November and December and sometimes May and June, and, although some spraying is done in tourist areas, mosquitoes are a problem. Mosquitoes don't like draughts, and it is often enough to leave two windows (or doors) open to discourage them with cross-ventilation.

Tourist Office Located on Plaza Piar, next to the *Curaçao Plaza Hotel*, as well as in the arrival and transit halls at the airport, offering helpful information, assistance in finding a hotel, brochures, maps, etc.

Carnival Curaçao, Aruba and Bonaire all hold the traditional pre-Lent carnival.

Self-drive Cars Hertz, Avis and Budget available in town, at airport, and major hotels. Also National, Ruiz, Lucky, Caribe Automotive, Curaçao U-Drive (at *Intercontinental*), Dijs, Drive Yourself N.V., Rent a Bug, Ric, and several other local agencies. Inquire at your hotel. Prices start at about US$25 daily, unlimited mileage, including insurance with US$150 deductible.

Ferry Service Car ferry service weekly to and from La Vela de Coro, Venezuela, but check first. There is also a ferry service to and from Aruba, leaving at 1000 on Tues. and returning at 2400 on Wed. Fares are US$30 p.p. each way for passengers on all ferries. Taxi to ferry terminal-centre, US$3.

Cable Offices All American Cables & Radio Inc., Keukenstraat; Kuyperstraat; Radio Holland N.V., De Ruytergade 51; Sita, Curaçao Airport.

Banks Algemene Bank Nederland, Banco Popular Antilliano, Banco Venezolano Antillano, First National Bank of Boston, Maduro & Curiel's Bank. Banking hours are 0830-1200 and 1300-1630 Monday to Friday.

Shops are open on Sun. morning if cruise ships are in port. Weekday opening is 0800-1200 and 1400-1800. Von Dorp/Endine stock the Handbook.

Taxis Taxis are easily identified by the signs on the roof and TX before the licence number. There are taxi stands at all hotels and at the airport, as well as in principal locations in Willemstad. It is not always possible to get a taxi to the airport early in the morning. Fares for sightseeing trips should be established at beginning of trip. Tipping is not strictly obligatory. There are collective taxis, called buses, and identified by an AC prefix on their licence plates.

Buses *Konvoois* are big buses which run to a schedule and serve outlying areas of Curaçao. Buses leave the Punda-Hato market for the airport hourly at fifteen minutes past the hour, US$0.40. They leave for Westpunt from beside the post office, two-hourly on the odd hour, return on the even hour in the afternoon, US$0.85.

Camping There are no campsites in Curaçao; camping is allowed on the beaches, but fresh water has to be obtained from restaurants or private houses. Perhaps not the ideal place for backpackers generally.

1294   NETHERLANDS ANTILLES AND ARUBA

Electricity   110/130 volts AC, 50 cycles.

ARUBA

Aruba, smallest and most westerly of the ABC group, lies 25 km. north of Venezuela and 68 km. west of Curaçao, at 12° 30´N, outside the hurricane belt. It is 31.5 km. long, 10 km. at its widest, with an area of 184 sq. km. The average yearly temperature is 27.5°C, constantly cooled by northeasterly trade winds, with the warmest months being August and September, the coolest January and February. Average annual rainfall is less than 510 mm., and the humidity averages 76%. Like Curaçao and Bonaire, Aruba has scant vegetation, its interior or *cunucu* a dramatic landscape of scruffy bits of foliage—mostly cacti, the weird, wind-bent dividivi trees, and tiny bright red flowers called *fioritas*—plus huge boulders and lots of dust.

Over 200,000 tourists visit Aruba each year, mainly East Coast Americans. A cluster of glittering luxury hotels has sprung up in the past two decades along the northern part of Eagle and Palm beaches, with smaller and less luxurious hotels further south.

Aruba is one of the very few Caribbean islands on which the Indian population was not exterminated. The Aruban today is a descendant of the indigenous Arawak Indians, with a mixture of Spanish and Dutch blood from the early colonizers. Of the total population of 68,000, including some 40 different nationalities, only about two-thirds were actually born on the island. The official language here, as in the other Netherlands Antilles, is Dutch, but Papiamento is the colloquial tongue. English and Spanish are widely spoken. On January 1, 1986, the island finally succeeded in its bid to be treated separately from the other islands. Mr Henny Eaman is Prime Minister and independence is to be granted in 1996.

History No written historical record of Aruba's discovery exists, though the island appears on maps dating back to 1494. In 1499 Alonso de Ojeda claimed Aruba for Spain, but because the Spanish found the island worthless, the Indians were saved from extermination. Charles V decreed that foreign colonists should not settle on Aruba. In 1636 the Dutch came in, near the culmination of the 80-year war between Spain and Holland. The English took over in 1805 during the Napoleonic wars, but in 1816 the Dutch returned to stay. Gold was discovered in 1825, but the mine ceased to be economic in 1916. In 1929, black gold brought real prosperity to Aruba when Lago Oil and Transport Co., a subsidiary of Exxon, built a refinery at San Nicolás at the eastern end of the island. At that time it was the largest refinery in the world, employing over 8,000 people. In March 1985 Exxon closed the refinery, a serious shock for the Aruban economy.

Aruba has three ports. San Nicolás was used for the import and transshipment of crude oil and materials for the refinery and for the export of oil products. There are also two sea-berths at San Nicolás capable of handling the largest tankers in the world. Oranjestad is the commercial port of Aruba, and it is open for day and night navigation. In 1962 the port of Barcadera was built to facilitate shipment of products from Aruba's new industrial zone on the leeward coast.

Oranjestad, the capital of Aruba, population about 17,000, is a bustling little freeport town where "duty-free" generally implies a discount rather than a bargain. Liquor rates are good, but prices for jewellery, silverware and crystal are only slightly lower than US or UK prices. The main shopping street is the 6-block Nassaustraat.

While the north coast is too rough for most swimmers—and can indeed be dangerous—there are two picturesque yet accessible coves for surf lovers, Andicouri and Dos Playas. Near the former is a natural bridge which has been carved by the waves out of the coral rock. At the site is a small souvenir shop and a snack bar. Further north are the abandoned gold mines at the Pirate's Castle, as well as the site where the island's garbage is dumped daily to the hungry jaws of local sharks. It is said that by being fed, the sharks are kept away from the calmer waters of the heavily touristed western coast. To date, no visitors have been lost to the sharks.

There are ancient Indian drawings on the walls and ceilings of the caves of Fontain and Canashito, and on the rocks of Arikok and Ayo. Frenchmen's Pass, near Spanish Lagoon on the south coast, is where the Indians fought the French

NETHERLANDS ANTILLES AND ARUBA

to protect the island from foreign invaders. Nearby is a breeding place for Aruba's parakeets. The village of Noord is known for St. Ann's church with its 17th-century hand-carved oak altar.

All around the countryside are cactus fences, and the Aruban cottages, colourfully surrounded by bougainvillea, oleanders, flamboyant, hibiscus and other tropical plants, are often protected from evil spirits by "hex" signs molded in cement around the doorways.

There is also a windmill which was shipped in parts from Holland in 1804 and assembled (now a restaurant) *De Olde Molen*, and a gigantic stone oven, the Rancho Kalk Kiln, which was employed in the 1900s to produce the lime or *kalk* used to plaster the walls of Aruban homes.

Water Sports For water-sports enthusiasts, facilities are available for snorkelling and scuba diving, and visibility in Aruban waters is about 30 metres in favourable conditions. Organized boat trips regularly visit the two wrecks worth exploring for the fascinating marine life which surrounds them. One is a German freighter, the *Antilla*, which went down just after World War II was declared and is found in 20 metres of water off the western coast between Playa Hadikurari and Malmok (where there is a good coral reef also). The other is nearby in 10 metres of water, the *Pedernales*, a flat-bottomed oil tanker which was hit in a submarine attack in May 1941, while ferrying crude oil from Venezuela to Aruba. For the less sporty there is little to do except get a glimpse of the marine life and wrecks from glass-bottom boats which cruise the same area.

Equipment is also available for water-skiing, water-bike paddling, sailing, and fishing (best sport fish here is sailfish, plus wahoo and blue and white marlin).

Near Spanish Lagoon is the Aruba Nautical Club complex, with pier facilities offering safe, all-weather mooring for almost any size of yacht, plus gasoline, diesel fuel, electricity and water. For information, write P.O. Box 161. A short sail down-wind from there is the Bucuti Yacht Club with clubhouse and storm-proofed pier providing docking, electricity, water, and other facilities. Write P.O. Box 743. For water sports equipment and instruction, contact also L. L. & S. Sports at the *Holiday Inn* and *Hotel Americana*.

Other Sports There is a 9-hole golf course near San Nicolás (green fees, US$5), as well as an 18-hole mini-golf course at the *Holiday Inn*, tennis courts at most major hotels, and horses for hire as well as riding instructions at Rancho El Paso, about US$12 an hour. At Boca Prins, "dune-sliding" is a popular sport. Arrangements for most sports (including horse-riding at Rancho El Paso) can be made through your hotel or De Palm Tours.

Hotels High season rates (Dec. 16 to Apr. 15) are roughly double the low season rates. The following are minimal high season ranges EP, to which a 5% government tax and 10% service charge must be added. Rates for Modified American Plan (MAP—breakfast and one meal), per day p.p., are indicated where available:

At Palm Beach (calmest sea): *Aruba Caribbean Hotel & Casino*, L; *Aruba Sheraton Hotel & Casino*, L; *Holiday Inn & Casino*, A; *Americana Aruba Hotel & Casino*, A; *Concorde Hotel* (further south on slightly rougher beach), A. On Manchebo Beach (between Oranjestad and Palm Beach): *Manchebo Beach Hotel*, A, all facilities interchangeable with *Talk of the Town Hotel* under same management. On Druif Beach: *Aruba Beach Club* (residential), A; *Divi Divi Beach Hotel*, A, all facilities interchangeable with *Tamarijn Beach Hotel*, A, just down the beach with same management. In or near Oranjestad: *Talk of the Town*, a comfortable, clean hotel, with pool, overlooking sea, A, facilities interchangeable with *Manchebo Beach*. In town: *Victoria*, B (service slow); *Central*, B; *Caribana*, C; *Bon Bini*, C; *Pension Colombia*; *Vistalmar*, Bucutiweg 28, new apartments, A, no service charge but a deposit is required; *Edges Guesthouse*, flatlets, C, summer, B, winter. In San Nicolás: *Astoria*, C. On Palm Beach, the once charming *Basi Ruti Hotel* is undergoing changes, no price available at time of writing. A list of apartments, guest houses, and rooms is available from the Tourist Office. Add an average US$45 for MAP on Aruba.

Restaurants With few exceptions, meals on Aruba are expensive and generally of the beef-and-seafood variety. Most tourists are on MAP at the hotels, many of which have a choice of formal or informal restaurants. For local dishes, particularly seafood, the *Trocadero Restaurant* on Nassaustraat in Oranjestad is highly recommended: try a turtle steak. A full meal with wine and service comes to about US$20 p.p. At the *Bali Floating Restaurant*, moored to the oldest pier in Oranjestad's harbour, you can try an Indonesian *rijsttafel* (see page 1293). There are several Chinese restaurants, including the highly recommendable *Kowloon* (offering a five-course meal for US$12), the *Dragon-Phoenix*, the *Beep-Beep*, the *Hong Kong* in Oranjestad, and the *Astoria Hotel* in San Nicolás. The new *El Gaucho* offers Argentine fare; *Alfredo's*, Italian food; and *De Olde Molen* has international food in an authentic windmill dating from 1804. Across the road from the *Americana Hotel* you can get a good breakfast for US$5. For wine and beer, see page 1293.

Tourist Office Arnold Shuttestraat 2, Oranjestad, just off L. G. Smith Boulevard near the harbour.

Taxis Telephone the dispatcher at Dakota Shopping Paradise, Tel.: 2116/1604. Drivers speak

1296   NETHERLANDS ANTILLES AND ARUBA

English, and individual tours can be arranged. Ask for flat rate tariffs (Oranjestad to Palm Beach is US$6 at time of writing). Taxi from airport to town, US$4; jitney from Nassaustraat, Oranjestad to St. Nicolás will drop you at the airport, US$0.75.

Buses   Roughly one every hour until 1800 between town and the hotels on Eagle and Palm Beach (schedules available at the hotels and the Tourist Office). One way fare is US$0.40. Otherwise there are "jitney cars" which operate like colectivos; the fare is US$0.40.

Self-drive Cars   Hertz, Avis, Budget, Jansen, National, Caribbean and Rentcar have offices in Oranjestad and at the airport. Prices begin at US$20 daily (some cars available at US$10 from Aru Rentals), US$96 weekly, with unlimited mileage, including insurance with US$150 deductible. Cost of full collision protection is about US$2.50 daily, US$15 weekly. Some motorcycles and scooters available from Marco's (Tel.: 2743/4971), from US$9; Aru Rentals are a bit cheaper. Beware the local drivers, who are aggressive.

Ferry   There is a ferry service to Curaçao, see page 1293.

BONAIRE

Bonaire, second largest of the six islands comprising the Netherlands Antilles, is 38 km. long and 6½-11½ km. wide. It lies 80 km. north of Venezuela, 50 km. east of Curaçao, 140 km. east of Aruba, at 12° 5 N and 86° 25 W, outside the hurricane belt.

The least developed and least populated of the ABC islands, Bonaire has a special appeal to devotees of the sea—whose treasures are unsurpassed in the Caribbean. Surrounding the island's beaches—with submarine visibility up to 60 metres—are coral reefs harbouring over a thousand different species of marine creatures. Ranked as one of the three top dive spots in the world, and number one in the Caribbean (followed by Grand Cayman Island and Cozumel), Bonaire is a leader in the movement for preservation of underwater resources. Stringent laws passed in 1971 ban spearfishing and the removal of any marine life from Bonaire's waters. It is a serious offence to disturb the natural life of the coral reefs, and the two local diving schools have set up permanent anchors in their dive spots to avoid doing any unwarranted damage.

History   When Amerigo Vespucci discovered Bonaire in 1499, he found a tribe of Arawak Indians, the Caiquetios, but by 1515, not one was left—some were brought to Spain and sold, the rest were all deported to Hispaniola where they were put to work in the copper mines. Some trickled back over the years, but by the early 19th century none remained. Indian inscriptions in several caves around the island can still be seen, particularly at Boca Onima, but they have not been decyphered.

The Spaniards eventually colonized Bonaire for a little over a century, but it was under the Dutch occupation that the salt industry was first developed and slaves brought in to work the salt pans, which were flanked by three 10-metre obelisks (still to be seen) that guided the early salt ships to their moorings. When slavery was finally abolished in 1863 the salt industry became unprofitable and the island was parcelled up and sold.

The Antilles International Salt Company recently reactivated this long dormant industry. Bonaire's constant sunshine (with air temperatures averaging 27°C and water 26°C), scant rainfall (less than 560 mm. a year), and refreshing trade winds so inviting for tourists are also ideal for the solar manufacture of salt.

Wildlife   The old salt pans of Pekelmeer, needed by the Salt Company, posed an ecological problem: Bonaire has one of the largest flamingo colonies in the western hemisphere, and these birds had built hundreds of their conical mud nests in the salt pans. Pleas from wild-life conservationists convinced the company that it should set aside an area of 56 hectares for a flamingo sanctuary, well away from access by car. The birds, initially rather startled by the sudden activity, have settled into a peaceful coexistence, so peaceful in fact that they have actually doubled their output and are now laying two eggs a year instead of their previous one. There are said to be over 6,000 flamingoes on the island, and they can also be seen wading in Gotomeer Bay in the northwest, in the salt lake near Playa Grandi northeast, and in Lac Bay on the southeast coast of Bonaire, feeding on algae which give them their striking rose-pink colour.

Population   The inhabitants of Bonaire, who number around 9,500 and are mostly of mixed Arawak, European and African descent, are a very friendly and hospitable people, undisturbed as yet by mass tourism. As in Curaçao and Aruba, Dutch is the official language, Papiamento the colloquial tongue, and Spanish and English are both widely spoken.

Kralendijk, the capital of Bonaire, is a small, sleepy town with a Folklore Museum on Helmundweg. Tourists, almost exclusively American, generally stick

NETHERLANDS ANTILLES AND ARUBA 1297

to the beaches or concentrate on water-sports, especially scuba diving. The interior has scant vegetation but the enormous cacti provide perching places for yellow-winged parrots and food for the island's wild goats. Flamingoes can be seen around the island (see above) and a sense of peace predominates.

Excursion Hire a car for the day. In the morning, take the drive north past the Water Distillation Plant along the "scenic" road, which offers several descents to the sea and some excellent spots for snorkelling or diving. See the Bonaire Petroleum Company where the road turns inland to Gotomeer Bay, the best place to see flamingoes, en route to Rincón, Bonaire's oldest village. Past Rincón is a side road to the Boca Onima caves with their Arawak Indian inscriptions. The road leading north from Rincón takes you to Washington National Park, which occupies the northern portion of the island and contains more than 130 species of birds. The park is open to the public daily (entrance fee US$1, children up to 15 free) from 0800 to 1700, except Wednesdays. No hunting, fishing, or camping is permitted, but an early morning drive along the 27-km. route through cactus forests and coral rock formations is a poetic experience—as long as you're not driving your own car. The return to Kralendijk is inland through the villages of Noord Salinja and Antriol.

The tour south passes the airport and Trans World Radio's towering 213-metre antenna which transmits 3 million watts, making it the hemisphere's most powerful radio station. Its shortwave broadcasts can be picked up in almost any part of the world. Further on are the snow-white salt piles and the three obelisks—blue, white, and orange—dating from 1838, with the huts that sheltered the slaves who worked the saltpans. Remember the flamingoes are easily startled, so move quietly if near them. At the southern tip of the island is Willemstoren, Bonaire's lighthouse, which dates from 1837. Pass Sorobon Beach and the mangrove swamps to Boca Cai at landlocked Lac Bay, with its clear water excellent for underwater exploration. What seem to be snow-capped hills from a distance are great piles of empty conch shells left by the local fishermen at Boca Cai. Take the road back to Kralendijk through the village of Nikiboko.

Diving Whether you dive or snorkel, you are certain to enjoy the underwater world of Bonaire. Most visitors are tempted to take at least the one-day "resort" or crash diving course (about US$65). This enables you to decide whether you'd like to continue, but one day will not make a diver of anyone.

The main schools are Aquaventure, Dive Bonaire and Bonaire Scuba Centre. Aquaventure, run by Don Stewart, has a base at Habitat, a diving community (see Hotels). Dive Bonaire is run by Peter Hughes and his wife Alicia, who teaches underwater photography. Their base is the *Flamingo Beach Hotel*. The Bonaire Scuba Centre is based in the *Hotel Bonaire* and is operated by Ady Everts and Eddie Statia. Prices are competitive.

Hotels High-season rates (Dec. 16 to two weeks after Easter) are roughly double low-season rates. The following are typical high-season ranges, without meals, to which a 5% government tax and 10% service charge must be added. Rates for Modified American Plan (MAP—breakfast and one meal), per day p.p., are indicated where available: *Hotel Bonaire*, A (MAP add US$35), is rambling yet low-keyed on its own artificial beach, with pool; dining is both outdoors and indoors (air-conditioned); there is a small casino which opens in the late evening. *Flamingo Beach Hotel*, A (MAP add US$ 35), 15% service charge, is the largest, best and busiest hotel on Bonaire, on a somewhat smaller artificial beach (but snorkelling or diving just off the beach is excellent); dining is outdoors); *Habitat*, Aquaventure's diving community, offers single rooms and bungalows for 2 to 6 persons, B. Some meals are self-service; the atmosphere is informal and functional, aimed at sportsmen and sportswomen, children discouraged. *Hotel Rochelaine*, C, low season, with bath, is in the centre of Kralendijk; new, functional, with bar facing sea and air-conditioned restaurant serving local specialities. Shops and car rental operations in the hotels are not always run by the hotels themselves; it is worth checking prices before doing business with them.

Restaurants International food at the two major hotels varies on different nights of the week with barbecues or Indonesian nights, etc. There are a few good Chinese restaurants in town, the best of which is probably the *China Garden* in an old restored mansion, which is open all day. Also in town is the tiny *Beefeaters* with English and Continental cooking; *Zeezicht* on the sea front is recommended, offering a complete meal for NAf24; *Den Laman* and *Bistro des Amis*, French style and good. Prices in all these restaurants are roughly comparable. Local cooking (try goat or conch stew) under neon lights at the very simple *Black and White Bar-Restaurant* near Tera Cora, southeast of Kralendijk. There are snack bars in Kralendijk and Rincón.

Entertainment is limited. There are a small disco and modest cinema in Kralendijk, as well as the casino at *Hotel Bonaire*.

Tourist Office Across from *Beefeater Restaurant* on Breedestraat, Kralendijk.

Cable and Phone J. A. Abraham Blvd., Kralendijk.

Banks Open 0930-1200, 1400-1600, Mon.-Fri.

Shops Open 0800-1200 and 1400-1800, Mon.-Sat. Bonaire is not a major shopping centre, though some shops do stock high quality goods.

1298 NETHERLANDS ANTILLES AND ARUBA

Taxis Tel.: 8100. Taxis do not "cruise" so you must telephone for one. Drivers carry list of officially approved rates, including touring and waiting time.

Self-drive Cars Hertz and Avis at airport and in town. Also Boncar. Check for current rates. At the busiest times of the year, it is best to reserve a car in advance.

Tennis Courts on outskirts of Kralendijk.

Camping is possible on the beach, though fresh water is hard to obtain; there are no campsites.

Electricity 127 volts, 50 cycles. Power cuts are quite common in parts of the island, including the hotels, so a torch (flashlight) is of benefit.

Water in the larger hotels and restaurants is safe to drink.

Klein Bonaire, a small (1,500 acres), flat, rocky and uninhabited islet one km. off Bonaire's shores, is frequented by snorkellers and divers.

SINT MAARTEN

Sint Maarten (Dutch) or St. Martin (French—see French Antilles, page 1309) lies 260 km. N of Guadeloupe and 310 km. E of Puerto Rico. The island is amicably shared by the Dutch, who have 41 square km., and the French, with 54 square km. The population of 19,520 (11,520 in St. Maarten and 8,000 in St. Martin) depends largely on tourism for a living, which they have found easier than the traditional occupation of extracting salt from the sea.
Dutch is the official language but English is widely spoken. French is also spoken, as is Papiamento on the Dutch side, and the melodious French Creole on the other. Netherlands Antillean guilders are the official currency (French francs are not accepted on the Dutch side), but the most common currency is the American dollar, which one need never change at all.

The Dutch side has the main airport and seaport and most of the tourists, and its capital, Philipsburg, is a busy little place. The French side is generally quieter and somewhat greener, and cherished for its Gallic restaurants. There are no border formalities between the two parts: only a modest monument erected in 1948 which commemorates the division of the island three centuries earlier.

Originally settled by the Caribs, the island was discovered by Columbus during his second voyage on Nov. 11, 1493, and named after the saint of the day, St. Martin of Tours. The Spanish never settled and the Indians, who had called it Sualouiga, meaning land of salt, had abandoned the island by the time the natural salt ponds attracted the first Dutch settlers in 1631. Spain reconsidered and occupied St. Maarten from 1633 to 1648, fending off an attack by Peter Stuyvesant in 1644 which cost him his leg. In 1648 the island was divided between France and the Netherlands with the signing of the Treaty of Mount Concordia. Since then, St. Maarten has changed hands 16 times, including a brief occupation by the British, but the Dutch-French accord has been peaceably honoured at least since it was last revised in 1839. The bays on the southern and western shores are best for swimming, diving and fishing. On the eastern side is Oyster Pond, a land-locked harbour which is difficult to enter because of the outlying reefs.

Philipsburg, the capital of Dutch St. Maarten, is built on a narrow strip of sandy land between the sea and a shallow lake which was once a salt pond. It has two main streets, Front and Back, which run parallel to Great Bay Beach, perhaps the safest and cleanest city beach anywhere. Front Street is lined with old wooden buildings, most of which house quaint shops offering duty-free goods at 10% less than the other islands. The historic Townhouse (court-house and post office) on De Ruyterplein faces the Pier, which is frequented by cruise ships, inter-island schooners, and fishing boats.

Hotels in St. Maarten (For hotels in French St. Martin, see page 1309.) There is a 5% government tax on all hotel bills, as well as 10% service. *Mullet Bay* (casino and 18-hole golf course), Mullet Beach, A, EP (add US$24 pp for MAP); *Great Bay*, Philipsburg, A (MAP; US$24) *Little Bay* (casino), Little Bay, A, EP; *Concord* (casino), Maho Bay, A, EP; *Oyster Pond Yacht Club*, Oyster Pond, A, EP (MAP US$22); *Caravanserai*, Maho Beach, A, EP (MAP US$30); *Pasangrahan*, Philipsburg, A, MAP; *Captain Hodge's Inn*, Philipsburg, B, EP; *Summit*, Simpson Bay, B, EP; *Mary's Boon*,

NETHERLANDS ANTILLES AND ARUBA 1299

Simpson Bay, A, EP; *Sea View*, Philipsburg, B; *Prince's Quarter*, Philipsburg, B, CP; *Caribbean*, Philipsburg, B, EP. Guesthouses include: *Josie's* Philipsburg, C; *Marcus*, Philipsburg, C (low season); *Tamarinde*, Pointe Blanche, C, CP; *Sea Side*, Philipsburg, D, EP; *Aambeeld*, Simpson Bay, B, EP; *Nina's*, Pointe Blanche, D, EP; *Beco's*, Philipsburg, C. *Lucy's*, D, is the cheapest, but is unfriendly and uncomfortable; *China Night*, also D, is far better.

Villas and Apartments Town House Apartments, Great Bay; *Lagoon Inn*, Cole Bay; *Beachcomber Villas*, Burgeaux Bay; *Naked Boy Apartments*, Pointe Blanche; *Blue Waves Apartments*, Pointe Blanche; *Seagrape Apartments*, US$100 a week off season; *Rama Apartment Hotel*, Pointe Blanche, US$130 per week or US$20 per day off season (US$35 a day in season), new, comfortable, friendly owners; also private homes leased through various agencies, contact St. Maarten Tourist Bureau.

Restaurants All the major hotels have restaurants with international cuisine. The *Frigate*, the best of Mullet Bay's five restaurants, serves excellent charcoal-broiled steaks and lobster. Highly recommended in Philipsburg for terrace dining overlooking the sea is *La Grenouille*, French and expensive, but with a reasonably priced *plat du jour*. The *West Indian Tavern* occupies the ruins of the 250-year-old synagogue. The *Rusty Pelican*, at the far end of Great Bay beach in town, serves unpretentious American food and good drinks, making it a popular, informal meeting place. *Le Panoramique*, at Oceanside Hotel, French, must book. *Nina's Cantina*, on road to Pointe Blanche, serves American food all night (also few rooms, D, EP). *Sea Grape Arbor*, West Indian food, reasonable prices. *Soerabaja* is a restaurant/night club near airport, also has some rooms. *Sam's*, E end of Front Street, good for breakfast and snacks. On Front Street is *Kallaloo*, a new and pleasant bar/restaurant, steaks, hamburgers and pizzas are served at reasonable prices, very popular. *The Greenery*, also on Front Street, is a good place for breakfast. Indonesian *rijsttafel* at the hotels or at the *Bilboquet* in Pointe Blanche. Pizzas at *Portofino*. Chinese fare at the *Mandarin* and *Majesty*. *St. Maarten Bar and Restaurant*, Back St., excellent Chinese or local cooking, good value. The *Phoenix* Chinese restaurant at the top end of town is relatively cheap, and will cash traveller's cheques. Also good value, *Harbour Lights Bar and Restaurant* on road to Pointe Blanche, delicious West Indian and Creole dishes. Americanized French at *L'Escargot*. On Front Street a good bar is *Pinocchio's*, where, during the happy hour (2200-2300) drinks cost only US$1.

Taxis Rather high fixed prices to airport (US$7) and the French side. Sightseeing tours can be arranged.

Buses Fairly regular service until 2000 hrs. to Marigot and Grand Case on the French side. Pick up along Front Street. There are frequent minibuses which charge a flat rate of US$0.50. Minibuses from Juliana Airport to Philipsburg cost US$6. Hitchhiking is easy.

Self-drive Cars Shortage in high season; advisable to request from hotel when booking room. Largest is Risdon. Others include Avis-Holidays, Hertz-Fleming, Budget, Carnegie, Lucky, Vlaun's, Carioca. Many meet flights at Juliana Airport and have offices in the major hotels. Motor-bikes at Carter's on Bush Road, Cul-de-Sac; mopeds can also be rented.

Telephones At telecommunications office in Back Street. It is easier to call New York than the French side of the island.

Excursions Island day tours by air to St. Eustatius, Saba, and St. Barthélémy; to Saba the cost is US$40. Charters available to St. Barthélémy, St. Eustatius, Saba, and Anguilla aboard *La Esperanza*. There are also day trips to St. Barthélémy as well as diving expeditions aboard the *Maho* (contact Maho Bay Watersports, Mullet Bay Beach Hotel) and aboard the schooner *Moby Dick*, cost about US$30. The *Moby Dick* also provides bed and breakfast for around US$12 each. Half-day cruises from Philipsburg to Marigot and back are made on the *Ovation*.

Transport to St. Maarten KLM and Eastern from New York, Air France from Miami. From Europe via San Juan, Puerto Rico, with Pan Am, via Curaçao with KLM, or Guadeloupe with Air France. Direct connections also from the Virgin Islands and Antigua. By cruise ship from N.Y., Florida, New Orleans, and San Juan. There are sailings to San Juan, Puerto Rico and Guadeloupe and St. Barthélémy. Embarkation tax at Juliana Airport, US$5 for all except French travellers returning to Guadeloupe or France. Travel agents ask for US$3 to confirm flights.

Tourist Bureau De Ruyterplein, behind the Little Pier. Tel.: 2337. Well supplied with brochures and guides to St. Maarten, St. Eustatius, Saba and St. Barthélémy, and the monthly *St. Maarten Holiday!* Sightseeing tours available by bus or by car.

Electricity 110 v., A.C.

Banks Bank of Nova Scotia, Windward Islands Bank, Barclays International, Banque des Antilles Françaises.

Shopping For those staying in self-catering apartments, fresh fish can be bought cheaply at the Saturday market in Marigot, on the French side. Good fresh bread at 1700 from baker 3 blocks from end of Back St.

1300 NETHERLANDS ANTILLES AND ARUBA

Warning Watch your possessions.

SINT EUSTATIUS (STATIA)

St. Eustatius, or *Statia,* 61 km. from St. Maarten, was originally settled by the Caribs, and the name Statia is probably a sound-imitation of an Indian word. Only during the last century was the little-known St. Eustatius proclaimed patron of the island.

Only 30 square kilometres, Statia was sighted by Columbus on his second voyage but never settled by the Spanish. The Dutch first colonized it in 1636 and soon built Fort Oranje which is still standing. Like St. Maarten and Saba, Statia changed flag many times—22—before finally remaining Dutch in 1816.

Besides Fort Oranje, which now serves as the seat of the island government, historical sites worth visiting are the Jewish synagogue, built in 1738 and restored after it was severely damaged by a hurricane in 1772, and the ruins of the Reformed Church which dates from 1776.

The island's principal town, Oranjestad, is situated on a cliff overlooking the long beach below. Lower Town, on the beach, was the site of warehouses full of sugar, tobacco, rum, and slaves awaiting shipment to other points in the Caribbean. The ruins of the warehouses, fort and castle are still there but more modern additions include a landscaped park, water-sports centre and luxury hotel.

Statia is quiet and friendly, with a population of about 1,500 given to farming and fishing, although the island has recently opened a 2m barrel oil terminal. It is dominated by the long-dead volcanic mountain called the "Quill", inside which is a lush rain forest where the locals hunt land crabs at night. Visitors are advised, however, to go there only during the day.

Hotels *The Old Gin House* and *Mooshay Bay,* both in Lower Town and under same management, prices from B range upwards. In town are *Gloria* and *Ocean View;* Miss Timber, 17 Kerkweg, has rooms, E. *Henriquez' Guesthouse,* cooking facilities, reasonable. Reasonable meals can be had at *Charley's* and the *Old Tea Room.*

Transport to St. Eustatius Windward Island Airways from St. Maarten and St. Kitts. Occasional cruise ships stop here. Boat charters available in the larger nearby islands.

SABA

Saba, pronounced "Say-bah", a mere 13 square km. and the smallest of this group of islands, 50 km. from Sint Maarten, was also inhabited originally by the Caribs, relics of whom have been found. Saba was sighted by Columbus in 1493 but not settled until around 1640 by the Dutch. It became for a time a dependency of St. Eustatius and changed hands 12 times until becoming definitively Dutch in 1816; despite this, English is the predominantly-used tongue. The population numbers about 1,000, half of them white (descendants of Dutch, English, and Scots settlers) and half black. The island is an extinct volcano which seems to shoot out of the sea, green with lush vegetation but without beaches. In fact there is only one inlet amidst the sheer cliffs where boats can come in to dock. The island has a particular charm of its own and is completely unspoiled to date: until 1947, with the advent of the jeep, the only "roads" were steps which were cut into the rock by the first colonists (there are 800 from Fort Bay to Windwardside). There is some local industry, which attracts inhabitants of other islands.

The Bottom, the main village and seat of government, is probably not "the bottom" of the crater, as often believed. Its name is believed to be a derivation of the Dutch Zeeland word *botte,* meaning bowl-shaped. Windwardside is a storybook village lying at 550 metres above sea level. Two other villages are St. Johns and Zions Hill (which is also known as Hellsgate). The volcanic crater, no trace of which has existed for 5,000 years, was probably near or at the top of Mount Scenery (870 metres above sea level). The airstrip is constructed on a solidified lava stream running into the sea.

The typical local drawn-thread work (also known as "Spanish Work" because

NETHERLANDS ANTILLES AND ARUBA 1301

it was learned by a Saban lady in a Spanish boarding school at the end of the last century) is sold at several shops on the island. There are several good places for scuba diving on the island and equipment can be hired.

Hotels Windwardside: *Captain's Quarters*, best known and largest with 13 rooms and some cottages, is a handsomely decorated restored sea captain's house with a pool, about A, with all meals; *Scout's Inn*, only 5 rooms, is the former government guesthouse, A, full board; another guesthouse with 10 rooms on Booby Hill. The Bottom: *The Bottom Guesthouse*, B, full board; *Caribe Guesthouse*, A, with full board; *Cranston Inn*, A; *Bugaloo*, beachside cottages, C, with breakfast; and several smaller pensions with cheap rooms. There is a good Chinese restaurant at The Bottom.

Transport to Saba By small aircraft from St. Maarten.

Transport on Saba Hire jeep or car for tour; take guide if hiking to top of Mount Scenery.

Information for Visitors

Climate Curaçao, Aruba and Bonaire. Despite their tropical position, humidity is low and the climate is pleasant all the year round. January is the coolest month with an average temperature of 28.5°C. The hottest month is September with temperatures at around 30°C. There is little rain; what there is falls mostly in November and December.

Sint Maarten, Saba and Sint Eustatius. Though tropical the climate is cool, thanks to the North-East Trade winds. January and February are the coolest months with temperatures around 24.5°C. August and September are the hottest months, temperatures are around 27.5°C. The rainy season is between May and December.

Travel by Air There are direct air connections from New York and Miami to Curaçao and Aruba (ALM and American Airlines) and to Sint Maarten by American and Eastern Airlines. ALM operates a full schedule between Curaçao, Aruba, Bonaire and St. Maarten. KLM flies from Amsterdam to Curaçao. Viasa and Aeropostal link Caracas and Curaçao, Avianca and ALM fly to Medellín, Colombia and SLM to Guyana and Suriname. ALM also flies to Caracas, Jamaica, Panama, Suriname, Haiti, Trinidad, the Dominican Republic, and Puerto Rico. Windward Island Airways have flights between St. Maarten, Saba, St. Eustatius, St. Kitts, Anguilla and St. Barthélémy. At Curaçao, Dr. Albert Plesman Airport has a good restaurant and is about 16 km. from Willemstad. International airports also on Aruba and St. Maarten. Airport tax in Curaçao is NAf 10 and at St. Maarten, NAf 5.30. For those travelling on a budget, the Curaçao-Miami connection is one of the cheapest flights between South America and the USA. KLM flies on Sun. from Curaçao to San José, Costa Rica (one flight early, another late), and Air Jamaica operates between Curaçao and Kingston, US$200. Other KLM destinations are Caracas, Guatemala and Panama.

Sea From New York: Grace Line; Home Lines. From New Orleans: Delta Line; Alcoa Steamship Co. From West Coast Ports: Interocean Line; French Line; Fred Olsen Line; Hanseatic Vasa Line; Mitsui OSK Line. (Royal Mail Lines Agency: Firma C. S. Gorsira, J. P. Ez., Kerkstraat 9, Helfrichplein, P.O. Box 161). Because so many ships call at Curaçao it is still possible to get passages to distant places by making enquiries locally but this apparently does not include Panama or Ecuador.

Ferries The ferry to Venezuela from Curaçao is weekly; it is worth checking departure times almost on a daily basis at Ferries del Caribe, on the waterfront. You will require a return ticket.

Documents All visitors require an outward ticket to a destination outside the Netherlands Antilles. US citizens and those of the EEC countries require only documentary proof of identity, for others a valid passport is necessary. Visas are not required by nationals of most countries (except Cuba), for a stay of less than 14 days. Exit tax US$5.75.

Currency The Antillean guilder (NAf, but sometimes also written Fl.) is divided into 100 cents with 1, 2½, 5, 10, 25 cent and 1 guilder coins. Banknotes in denominations of 1, 2½, 5, 10, 25, 50, 100, 250 and 500 guilders. Rate of exchange: NAf1.79 per US$ travellers' cheques; 1.77 per US$ cash. Aruba has its own currency, the Aruba florin (Af), at par with the Antillean guilder. US dollars are accepted everywhere, as are the major credit cards; sterling, Dutch guilders and other currencies must be changed in the banks. It is not possible to change Suriname guilders in Curaçao.

Postage Letters to USA cost US$0.45 and to Europe US$0.53.

1302 FRENCH ANTILLES

For information write to: Information Department, Office of the Minister Plenipotentiary of the Netherlands Antilles, 175 Badhuisweg, The Hague, The Netherlands, or Saba Tourist Information Office, 445 Park Avenue, Suite 903, New York City, NY 10022 (Tel.: (212) 688-8350).

We are grateful to Dorothy Millgate for editorial work, and to Pierre-Yves Atlan (Paris 18e), Lynne and Hugh Davies (Mill Valley, Ca.), Hans Hendriks (Maassluis, Neth.), Robert and Daisy Kunstaetter (Richmond Hill, Ont.), Jean Laberge (Montréal), H.L. Ravenwaaij (Curaçao), and Gustav-Adolf Yunge (Cologne), for valuable updating information.

FRENCH ANTILLES

THE FRENCH CARIBBEAN ISLANDS form two Départements d'Outremer: one comprises Martinique, and the other Guadeloupe with its offshore group—Marie-Galante, Les Saintes, La Désirade—and two more distant islands—Saint-Barthélémy and the French part of Saint-Martin (the Dutch have the other part; see page 1298).

Geographically, the main islands form the N group of the Windward Islands, with the ex-British island of Dominica in the centre of them. Saint-Barthélémy and Saint-Martin are in the Leeward group.

As the islands are politically Departments of France they have the same status as any Department in European France. There is a Prefect at the head of the local government of each Department, which also sends two senators and three deputies to the National Assembly in Paris. The inhabitants are French citizens. The currency is the French franc (F). The connection with France confers many advantages on the islands, which enjoy French standards of social legislation etc., but it also drives up the cost of living, which is rather higher than elsewhere in the Caribbean. There is an independence movement, whose more extremist members have been responsible for various bomb attacks and violent protests against high unemployment.

Both the main islands were discovered by Columbus on his second voyage in 1493, but no colonies were established by the Spanish because the islands were inhabited by the Caribs (who are now virtually extinct); it was not until 1635 that French settlers arrived.

Because of their wealth from sugar, the islands became a bone of contention between Britain and France; other French islands—Dominica, St. Lucia, Tobago—were lost by France in the Napoleonic wars. The important dates in the later history of the islands are 1848, when the slaves were freed under the influence of the French "Wilberforce", Victor Schoelcher, and 1946, when the islands ceased to be colonies and became Departments.

Climate The dry season, which is rather cooler, is December-May, with virtually no rain in February; the wet, warmer season is June-November. The average temperature is 26°C. Low season in the hotels is April 15-December 16.

One feature in common to the two main islands is the pre-Lenten Carnival, said to be more spontaneous and less touristy than most. There are also picturesque Ash Wednesday ceremonies, especially in Martinique, where the population dresses in black and white, and processions take place that combine the seriousness of the first day of the Christian Lent with the funeral of the Carnival King. Another common feature is the African dances—the *calinda, laghia, bel-air, haut-taille* and *gragé*—still performed in remote villages. The famous *béguine* is a more sophisticated dance from these islands.

The present-day economy of the main islands is based on sugar (from which a delicious, individual rum is distilled), bananas and pineapple. Tourism is very important.

Creole Cuisine is worth mentioning for its originality and interesting combination of French, Indian, and African traditions, seasoned with the exotic spices of the Antilles. Some typical dishes

FRENCH ANTILLES 1303

are: *calalou*, savoury soup made of local vegetables and herbs, served with *chiquetaille*, grilled cod, or with *feroce*, a mixture of avocado, sweet peppers, and manioc flour; *colombo*, an East Indian curry of seeds and beef, pork, kid, or fish, cooked with rice; *blaff*, a sort of *court-bouillon* made of *lambis* (conch), clams, or sea urchins, with onions, limes, and spices; *lambis* or *chatrous* (small octopus) stewed in tomatoes and onions and accompanied by red beans and rice; *accras*, an appetizer of African-style seafood fritters. The abundant seafood such as *langouste* (rock lobster) and *ouassous* (a crayfish almost as big as a lobster), as well as fresh-water *crabes* are most often served grilled or cold with mayonnaise; *tortue*, sea turtle, is eaten in curry, marinaded, or grilled; local fruits are particularly good.

Information on the French Antilles is contained in the *Guide de la France des Tropiques*, obtainable from France-Information-Loisirs DOM-TOM, 8 avenue de l'Opéra, 75001 Paris; or from the Commissariat à la Promotion des Départements et des Territoires d'Outre-Mer, 83, boulevard du Montparnasse, 75006 Paris; Tel.: 4325-80-40.

MARTINIQUE

Martinique (1,060 sq. km.) is an island 65 km. long and 31 km. wide situated at about 14° 40 N and 63° 30 W. To the W is the Caribbean and to the E, the Atlantic. To the S lies St. Lucia and to the N Dominica, with channels of about 40 km. between them and Martinique. The island is mountainous and volcanic; in the NW is the volcano Mont Pelée (1,384 metres), in the centre, Les Pitons du Carbet (368 metres at the highest point), and in the S the Vauclin and Diamant mountains. The population is about 400,000.

Martinique was discovered in 1493 by Christopher Columbus, but not visited and named until his fourth voyage in 1502, when he gave it the name of Martinica in honour of St. Martin. The natives called it Madinina, the island of flowers. Because of the hostility of the Indian tribes of Cibonney, Arawak and Carib, it was only in 1635 that the French, led by Chevalier Belain d'Esnambuc, were able to settle there. Apart from two brief periods, the Seven Years' War and the French Revolution, when the island was occupied by the British, Martinique has always remained French. Today, with its four-lane highways, it seems more like France than a Caribbean island.

The island's capital is **Fort-de-France** (population: 100,000) which lies on the north side of the largest bay. Originally called Fort Royal, it is a popular port of call for cruise ships and its streets are reminiscent of old New Orleans.

Among places of interest are Fort Saint-Louis, a military structure in Vauban style; La Savane square, a favourite promenade site, dominated by a marble statue of Napoleon's Empress Joséphine, a native of the island (her home, La Pagerie, is open to visitors, 15F entrance fee); Schoelcher library in typical late 19th-century style; the old part of town; Saint-Louis Cathedral, which was built in 1895; the Martinique museum at 9 rue de la Liberté, where can be found documents, crafts and old furniture of the Arawak and Carib period; the artisan centre near the Tourist Office (rue Ernest Deproge); the colourful market-places with their vast array of tropical fruits and spices; and the residential areas of Bellevue and Plateau Didier.

The Tourist Office suggests four main tours by car to see the island. These can equally well be combined to make two trips, which eliminates the necessity of returning to Fort-de-France each time.

1. The coastal road via Carbet to Saint-Pierre (24 km. N of Fort-de-France). Carbet is on a calm bay where Columbus paused in 1502 and the first French settlers landed in 1635. It was in this area that Gauguin lived and painted. Saint-Pierre, the first town founded by the French in 1635, was destroyed in 1902 by one of the worst volcanic disasters in history, the last eruption of Mont Pelée. Only one of its 30,000 inhabitants survived—a criminal who was safely imprisoned in a solitary vault deep beneath the ground. Once called the "little Paris of the West Indies", St.-Pierre had a splendid theatre which hosted the best operatic and dramatic companies on tour—now only its wide stone steps and a few vine-covered columns remain. You can explore the city's ruins, but there is very little to see. Also, visit the Musée Vulcanologique (open 0900 to 1200 and 1500 to 1700) for graphic documentation. There is an attractive beach (black sand) with bar at the southern end of town. Opposite the Shell station (the taxi pick-up for Fort-de-France) there is a café which serves excellent fish sandwiches and home-made fruit drinks. North of St.-Pierre is Le Precheur, once residence of Mme. de Maintenon, morganatic wife of King Louis XIV. Near the old city is the restored early 18th-century sugar plantation, now a hideaway resort hotel, *Plantation de Leyritz*. The main building is a manor-house full of antiques. Sleeping accommodation is in two other buildings which were once slaves' quarters. The hotel is part of the *Relais de la Martinique*

1304 FRENCH ANTILLES

chain (see *Hotels*). Return by the Trace road via Morne Rouge (where a guide can be hired for climbing Mont Pelée), then south through the lush rain forest. Bus, Morne Rouge to Mont Pelée, US$2. Turn-off for the trail to the summit is 2 km. outside Morne Rouge on the road to Ajoupa-Bouillon (a 2-hr. climb to the summit).

2. The second route cuts across the island to Trinité on the Atlantic coast and the picturesque Caravelle peninsula, dominating Galleon Bay and Treasure Bay. Good beaches at Tartane. See the ruins of Château du Buc and the Caravelle lighthouse.

3. To Trois-Ilets (35 km.), birthplace in 1763 of Joséphine Rose Tascher de la Pagerie, the Creole beauty who was to reign five years as Napoleon's Empress. Visit her house, La Pagerie, which was destroyed by a hurricane and partially restored, also the church where she was christened and a small museum with relics of the Napoleonic period. On Anse à l'Ane is the Courbaril campsite (which also has bungalows to let at reasonable prices). Anse-Mitan, nearby, has been developed as a tourist centre with a few hotels and small restaurants with tables along the beach—15 minutes by launch to Fort-de-France across the bay. Continue to Diamant and its beach (with a heavy undertow) facing "HMS Diamond Rock". This rock, jutting out of the sea just off the coast, was commissioned as a sloop of war by the Royal Navy in 1804, and held for 18 months against bombardments by the French coastal artillery. Reachable by boat. Continue west to the fishing village of Anses d'Arlets, from where there are also motor boats to the capital.

4. The fourth route suggested is to Vauclin, a colourful fishing village on the SE coast. The palm-fringed beach comes alive when the boats come in. See the church in Marin and the magnificent palm-backed beach at Sainte-Luce, also the charming village of Sainte-Anne and its coral beach lined with sea grapes. You can reach the Anse Macabout through the Macabout camping site. Nearby are the salt marshes and the Savane des Pétrifications, an eerie field in a dry, desert-like region, where the veins of a lava flow have been filled in with a crystalline substance which has given them the appearance of petrified wood.

Hotels Deluxe: *Bakoua*, Trois-Ilets, boat service to Fort-de-France (named after local fishermen's hats, and with a bar sheltered by a roof of the same shape), small beach, pool, animated weekly floor show, recommended, L, EP; *Méridien*, Pointe du Bout (Trois-Ilets), new, enormous complex, beach, pool, casino, L, EP; *Lido*, Schoelcher, traditional bungalows on lavishly landscaped hill overlooking dark sand beach and wharf, pool; *Martinique*, Schoelcher, actually a hotel school, but permitted to take guests when other hotels are full, 15 rooms only A, EP. *Latitude*, near Carbet, new, in lush green setting, Polynesian style, young crowd, pool, nightclub, L, AP; *Cap Est*, on Atlantic coast at Pointe de la Prairie (between Vauclin and François), tiny beach with shallow water, pool; *Auberge de L'Anse Mitan*, Trois-Ilets, typical run French inn, near the beach, private launch to Fort-de-France, A, MAP. Medium- to low-priced chain of hotels *Relais de la Martinique* offer an intimate, usually colonial atmosphere and Creole cuisine; *Plantation de Leyritz*, Basse-Pointe (see tour no. 1, above), A, CP; *Le Manoir de Beauregard*, Ste.-Anne, 1 km. from the beach, 18th century elegance, pool, A, CP; *La Vallée-Heureuse*, on the Ravine Vilaine just outside Fort-de-France, authentic colonial manor-house, Creole cuisine, pool; *L'Impératrice*, Fort-de-France, in city centre on La Savane, A, CP; *Le Bristol*, B, CP; *Victoria*, B, CP; and *Le Gommier* near centre of Fort-de-France, A-B, EP; *La Montemar*, Schoelcher, Creole cuisine, pool; *Les Brisants*, François, facing the Atlantic, Creole cuisine, B, CP. Other hotels in Fort-de-France: *Grillardin*, Left Bank atmosphere, friendly bar; *Malmaison*, La Savane, good, D, CP; *Lafayette*; B, EP; *L'Europe*; *Studio Laroc*; *Gallia*, on La Savane, recommended, with a good view of the harbour, the charge is higher if you pay in US$; *Bambou*, Trois-Ilets (Anse-Mitan beach), 10 rooms only, B, CP, A, MAP, pleasant outdoor dining on the beach, good, cheap meals and drinks; *Calalou*, Anse à l'Ane, A, MAP; *Chez André*, Trois-Ilets, C, CP, rooms a bit on the primitive side, but adequate; *Caridad Paradis*, Trois-Ilets; M. Claude Monlouis, Anse Mitan, Trois Ilets, rents apartments for 2-4 people at reasonable prices, book well in advance; *Diamant les Bains*, Diamant, B, CP, MAP; *Délices de la Mer*, Sainte-Luce, B, CP, A, MAP; *Le Vieux Chalet* and *Mont Pelée Hotel* at Morne-Rouge (the latter is not recommended); *Auberge de l'Atlantique* (C, EP other bases available) and *Les Alizés* (D, EP, B, AP) at Vauclin; *Tourist Hotel*, St.-Pierre (poor value); *Madras*, Tartane Beach, B, CP. (Almost no accommodation in St.-Pierre: stay at Morne Rouge for Mont Pelée, or Fort-de-France and commute); *Pension de Famille*, rue de Trissot 8, Fort-de-France, for young women only; *Typic Bellevue*, C, with bath; *Le Balisier*, Fort-de-France, noisy elevator; but good view over harbour from top floor, B-C, CP; *Hibiscus*, one block east of La Savane, cheap, recommended; *Club Méditerranée*, hotel-village also called *Les Boucaniers*, at Sainte-Anne, nice beaches (petrified forest nearby). Rates from US$680 a week p.p.: for further information, write Club Méditerranée, 516 Fifth Ave., New York, N.Y. 10036; or 5 South Molton Street, London W.1. In some hotels a 10% service charge and/or 5% government tax is added to the bill. AP—American Plan (room and full board); MAP—Modified American Plan (room, breakfast and dinner); CP—Continental Plan (room and breakfast); EP— European Plan (room only).

A fuller hotel list can be obtained from Office Départemental du Tourisme, B.P. 520, 97206 Fort-de-France Cédex, Martinique, and from French tourist offices at 178, Piccadilly, London W1V 0AL; 610, Fifth Avenue, New York, 10020; 372 Bay Street, Suite 610, Toronto; Berliner Allee 26, 4000 Düsseldorf; 93 via Veneto, Rome; 21 Av. de la Toison d'Or, 1050 Bruxelles; 2 rue Thalberg, CH 1201 Geneva. Hotels in Martinique are very expensive.

FRENCH ANTILLES

Camping There is a good campsite on the edge of St.-Luce, 30F for the first night, 25F thereafter. The nearest bank is in Pilote, 6 km. away and reachable by taxi, 12.50F. Or, take the ferry to Anse a l'Ane, Courbaril campsite (30F own tent, 47F rented tent).

Restaurants There are more restaurants than hotels, many are excellent, most are good. For current listing, check with the Tourist Office. Some traditional favourites; *Le Foyal*, behind La Savane in Fort-de-France, said to be best restaurant in the Caribbean, Maxim's tradition, elegant, intimate dining room, French and Creole cuisine, a favourite meeting spot for resident and visiting yachtsmen; *La Louisiane*, Didier, fashionable, elegant; *Chez Gérard*, rue Victor Sévère, tiny, friendly, French specialities; *L'Europe*, in hotel off La Savane, quiet, rustic atmosphere; *Ville Créole* (Anse Mitan), excellent French and Creole cooking. *Baalbeck*, blvd. de Gaulle, Lebanese specialities; at least 4 restaurants specialize in Vietnamese cuisine—one is the *Mandarin*, which is excellent; the *Bambou*, on Anse-Mitan beach at Trois-Ilets has budget-priced fixed menu, fine fish fare, outdoor dining in a gay ambience; *Aux Filets Bleus* offers lunches and dinners on the white sandy beach at Ste.-Anne; *La Dunette* is a small Creole inn and restaurant also at Ste.-Anne; *La Guinguette*, on the beach near St.-Pierre; *Diamant Plage*, Diamant beach; *Chez Sidonie*, Schoelcher. Another Creole restaurant is *L'Escalier*, on rue de Liberté; try the crab sauce and the octopus in red bean sauce. *Le Poisson d'Or*, *Le Matador* (both Trois-Ilets) and *L'Ecrevisse*, Anse-Mitan, all offer good quality Creole food. For cheap and cheerful Creole cuisine try *Octavie* in her yellow van parked on Place de la Savane, facing the bay.

Sports Snorkelling and scuba diving: instructors available at the *Méridien* and *Latitude* hotels, sailing, fishing, tennis, golf, horse riding. Yachts and other boats can be hired from the Marina de la Pointe-du-Bout; Ship Shop, 6 rue Joseph-Compère, F-de-F, Yachting Caraibe, Cité Mansarde, Robert; Mediawind-Shop, blvd. de la Marne; Carib Charter, Pte de Jaham, Schoelcher; Martinique Nauti Loisirs, Bakoua.

Shopping is pleasant in Martinique; many of the goods for sale are imported from France. There are also local handicrafts, including a doll souvenir dressed in the traditional Creole costume. There are wickerwork, jewellery, coral clusters, shells, leather goods, silk scarves etc. All French spirits can of course be purchased and the locally-produced rum is an excellent buy. Paris fashions are offered at continental prices in the many boutiques dotted about Fort-de-France. Purchases are exempt from tax when payment is made in foreign currency. Rue de la Liberté is good for shopping, and the colourful markets and handicrafts are to be found in shops mainly located on the rue Victor Hugo and near the Cathedral, in Fort-de-France. Small tourist market at La Savane. Remember 1200 to 1500 is siesta time, when most shops and banks are shut. Caisse Agricole is open until 1200 on Saturdays.

Useful Addresses *Tourist Office:* blvd. Alfassa and rue de la Liberté (near La Savane), open 0730 to 1200 and 1500 to 1730, Sat. from 0800 to 1200, Tel.: 71-79-60. Also at the airport. *US Consulate:* 10 rue Schoelcher, Tel.: 71-93-01. *British and Canadian Honorary Consulate:* Quartier Vieux Moulin, Didier (P.O. Box 465) 97205 Fort-de-France, Tel.: 71-25-44. *Office Départemental du Tourisme de la Martinique*, Boîte Postale 520, 97206, Fort-de-France. Tourist offices on Martinique are very helpful and friendly.

Transport on Martinique *Taxis* have official fixed prices, example: Lamentin Airport to Fort-de-France, 50F, to Trois-Ilets, 120F but drivers sometimes try to charge more. Buses no longer run between the airport and Fort-de-France. Colectivo 6.50F, but difficult to get. (It is easy to hitchhike.) For current list of prices, check the Tourist Board's monthly publication, *Points Chauds*. *Taxis collectives* (Peugeot station wagons) congregate in a parking lot near the Yacht Club and run to most parts of the island until about 2000. To St.-Pierre costs 12.50F; to St.-Luce 14F; to Ste.-Anne, near Les Boucaniers, 22F. There are also bus services to the main towns, which again leave from the parking lot on the quay. For *Bus Tours* of the island, check with Carib Tour, rue Ernest Deproge, Tel.: 71-25-56. For *Boat Tours:* Le Sider, Tel.: 71-70-28; Martinique Charter Services, Tel.: 71-80-80; Agence de Voyages Roger Albert, Tel.: 71-71-71; Agence de Voyages Marsan, Tel.: 71-19-21. *Self-drive hire cars* available at Lamentin Airport and in Fort-de-France; the main international agencies and several local firms. *Scooter-hire* from opposite the *Bakoua* hotel, and in the centre of Fort-de-France (check with Tourist Board), at Vespa Martinique, 3, rue Jules Monnerot, Terres Sainville (Tel.: 716003) 125 cc for 80F per day, 450F per week (700F insurance deposit and international driver's licence required). *Ferry boats* from Fort-de-France (Quai Desnambue) with Pointe du Bout, Anse Mitan and Anse à l'Ane. They leave every hour on the hour, 9F. The *Somatur*, plying between Fort-de-France and Pointe du Bout, costs 8.50F single, 13.50F return.

Entertainment Check with Tourist Board's monthly publication, *Points Chauds*, for current schedules. The Ballets Martiniquais, a local group of young people, perform Martinique's folk dances on cruise ships and in the major hotels. Cock fights, as well as mongoose vs. fer-de-lance snake fights, are held in specified arenas or *pitts* generally from December to May, accompanied by heavy betting. There are several night clubs, casinos, and cinemas, as well as equestrian and shooting clubs.

FRENCH ANTILLES

GUADELOUPE

Guadeloupe is surrounded by the small islands La Désirade, Marie Galante and Les Saintes, all of which can easily be visited from the main island, with each one offering something different. Including the two more distant islands of St.-Barthélémy and St.-Martin in the Leewards, the total area of the Department is 1,720 sq.km.

Guadeloupe (1,510 sq. km.) is rather less sophisticated than Martinique, and the forests and nature parks add to the feeling of timelessness. The island is really two small ones, separated by the narrow bridged strait of the Rivière Salée. To the west is mountainous egg-shaped Basse-Terre, which includes the administrative capital of the same name, with a population of 20,000. There can be found in the city some very pretty and authentic old buildings of the colonial period. Basse-Terre, with the volcano Grande Soufrière (1,484 metres) at its centre, has an area of 777 sq. km. and a total of 130,000 inhabitants. The commercial capital of Guadeloupe is Pointe-à-Pitre, with 60,000 inhabitants, situated in the flat half of the island, in Grande-Terre; it is a lively and picturesque centre with a beautiful natural harbour. Grande-Terre, triangular in shape and slightly smaller than Basse-Terre, has a total population of 160,000 inhabitants. The names of the two parts show a most un-Gallic disregard of logic as Basse-Terre is the higher and Grande-Terre is the smaller; it may be that they were named by sailors, who found the winds lower on the Basse-Terre and greater on the Grande-Terre side.

Christopher Columbus discovered Guadeloupe in 1493 and named it after the Virgin of Guadalupe, of Extremadura, Spain. The Caribs, who had inhabited the island, called it Karukera, meaning "island of beautiful waters". As in most of the Caribbean, the Spanish never settled, and Guadeloupe's history closely follows that of Martinique, beginning with French colonization in 1635. Other important dates are 1763, when Louis XV handed over Canada to Britain to secure his hold on these West Indian islands with the Treaty of Paris, and 1848, when the slaves were freed by Victor Schoelcher, now a local hero.

Guadeloupe is in some ways reminiscent of Normandy or Poitou, especially the farms, built in those regional styles. The island's Natural Park covers 30,000 hectares of forest land in the centre of Basse-Terre, which is by far the more scenic part. As the island is volcanic there are a number of related places to visit, including the fumaroles, the cauldrons and the sulphur fields of the Col de l'Echelle (Ladder Pass), the hot springs and waterfalls of the Carbet river, and the peaks of extinct volcanoes. One traveller has described the island as "idyllic— were it not for the noise of motorcycles".

Pointe-à-Pitre, at the S end of the Rivière Salée, is the chief port and commercial centre, whose early colonial buildings were largely destroyed by an earthquake in 1845. Pointe-à-Pitre has a lively and picturesque harbour with a colourful central market place. The tree-shaded Place de la Victoire was once the site of a guillotine, and the dock nearby is lined with inter-island schooners. Local handicrafts, particularly Madras cotton (from which the traditional costumes of the *doudous*, or local ladies, are made), are good buys, and French wines and perfumes are available at normal French domestic prices.

On Grande-Terre, the following are worth seeing: the ruins of the 18th-century fortress, Fort Fleur d'Epée, off the main road to Gosier; Gosier, the holiday centre of Guadeloupe, with its hotels, restaurants and night clubs; Sainte-Anne and its lovely beaches; and the rugged Pointe-de-Châteaux at the easternmost tip of the island. From here there is a good view of the flat island of Désirade. Also visit the eerie Beach of Skulls and Bones at Moule, which was once the main harbour of the island until it was destroyed in 1928 by a tidal wave (sea-quake). The beach is so named for the relics that have been exposed by the surging surf tearing away part of the cemetery in the rocks facing the sea. A precolumbian Arawak village, called Morel, has recently been uncovered on the beautiful sandy beaches N of Moule.

Basse-Terre, on the other wing of the island, is the administrative capital of Guadeloupe and the entire Department. It is a charming port town of narrow

FRENCH ANTILLES 1307

streets and well-laid-out squares with palm and tamarind trees, in a lovely setting between the sea and the great volcano La Soufrière. There is an interesting 17th-century cathedral, and nearby are the ruins of Fort St.-Charles. St.-Claude, a wealthy suburb and summer resort 8 km. into the hills, is surrounded by coffee trees and tropical gardens.

On Basse-Terre island one of the main sights is the volcano La Soufrière, reached through a primeval rain forest. A narrow road leads up from Basse Terre town to a car park from where the crater is a 300 metre climb. (The best clothing for the climb is the least; anoraks or coats worn against the dampness merely compound the problem but take a sweater; it can get quite chilly. Leave some spare clothes in the car.) From the top there is a spectacular view (if you are not enveloped in clouds, which is usually the case, but less likely to be so at mid-day and slightly after), above the lush jungle foliage and sulphurous fumes spurting over yellow and orange rock. Also visit the ancient Carib rock carvings near Trois Rivières. The most important of these is a drawing of the head of a Carib chief inside a cave where he is presumably buried; one can be led there for a few francs by one of the local boys. Nearby is a nature trail. Also see Sainte-Marie, where a statue commemorates the site of Columbus' landing in 1493, the calm clean beaches at Ferry and Grand-Anse and the rougher ones at Deshaies, as well as the Natural Park which one can cross from Pigeon by the Traversée road: an unspoiled tropical forest. Les Saintes can be reached from Trois Rivières. Matouba is an East Indian village in lovely surroundings with a good restaurant. On the SE side of Basse-Terre, along a forest path, are the Chutes de Carbet waterfalls. You can walk the Trace Victor Hugo, along the main ridge of Basse-Terre; it is a 29 km. hike.

Hotels Deluxe: *Auberge de la Vieille Tour*, Gosier, named after an 18th-century sugar tower incorporated into the main building, is on a bluff over the sea, beach, pool, tennis, L, CP; *Méridien*, St.-François, Air France's modern and confortable seaside complex, beach, pool, golf, tennis, flying school, dock, discothèque, and casino, L, EP; *Caraibe-Copatel*, Moule, 2 private beaches, pool, tennis, port, night club. At Gosier: *PLM Arawak* is of the Rothschilds' PLM group, beach, pool, L, CP; *Callinago* is slightly smaller, beach, pool, A, CP; also apartments at Callinago Village, A; *Le Montauban*, motel-style, 10 minutes from beach, pool; *Au Grand Corsaire*, a few cottages, private beach, good restaurant; *Seye Guest House*, on seafront, A, with breakfast and dinner. At Pointe-à-Pitre: *La Bougainvillée*, L, EP, CP, MAP; *Auberge Henri IV*, 83 rue Henri IV, central, C, EP, definitely not recommended; *Studiotel*; *Grand Hotel*; *Schoelcher*, rue Schoelcher, C, EP, not very clean; *Normandie*, Place de la Victoire, C, restaurant quite good; *Karukera*, rue Alsace-Lorraine, B, EP, not much better than *Auberge Henri IV*. On Bas du Fort Bay, *Fleur d'Epée-Novotel*, CP and *Frantel*, EP, A. At Saint-Claude: *Relais de la Grande Soufrière*, an elegant old plantation mansion, now a government-sponsored hotel school, A-B, EP. At Moule: *Les Alizés*, Canadian-owned, good horseshoe-shaped beach, pool, golf. At Ste.-Anne: *Auberge du Grand Large*, neither grand nor large, but friendly and with good restaurant on the beach, A, CP, MAP; *La Villa Créole*, cheaper but friendly and clean; and *Mini Beach*, also on the beach. At Vieux-Habitants: *Rocroy Hôtel*, bungalows on beach with good swimming, good food and in other ways delightful except for the occasional sounds of war from the absurdly-sited army range nearby, B, CP. In Basse-Terre: *Relaxe* EP (reasonable) and *Chez Charlery*, 52 rue Maurice Marie Claire, D, central, clean and cheap.

Other hotels: At Saint-François: *Hamak*, A, CP; *Trois Mâts*, B, CP, MAP; *Honoré's*, B, CP, MAP; *VVFG*, A, EP. At Gosier: *Salako*, A, CP; *Ecotel*, A, EP, CP, MAP; *Holiday Inn*, A, CP; *Callinago Village*, B, EP; *Les Flamboyants*; *Bungalows Village*, EP; *Serge's Guest House*, CP; *Auberge J.J.*, CP, MAP; *Canabis*, EP, CP. At Le Moule: *Le Réjeton*, B. At Sainte-Anne: *Relais du Moulin*, B, CP; *Motel Sainte-Anne*, MAP. La Marie-Gaillarde, *Marie-Gaillarde*, CP, MAP; *Basse-Terre*, EP. Check with Tourist Board for current price lists (they run an information desk at Raizet airport; they can also arrange for you to stay with local families for about US$12 a night). Club Méditerranée has two hotel-villages on the island (membership is required—see Martinique Hotels, page 1304): *La Caravelle* at Ste.-Anne is on a spectacular white sand beach, perhaps the best on Guadeloupe, surrounded by a 13-hectare preserve. Atmosphere strictly informal (topless beach), all sports equipment available, gourmet dining unlimited. Weekly rates are US$680-780 p.p. AP; bus from Pointe-à-Pitre. *Fort Royal* at Deshaies is a slightly run-down old luxurious hotel, more family-style than *La Caravelle* (which is mostly young and many singles), dramatically situated on a promontory between two beautiful but rather rough beaches. Similar prices to those of *La Caravelle*.

Camping A small but highly recommended campsite is Sable d'Or, near Deshaies, Basse-Terre. The charge is approximately US$2 per tent and per person. There are buses from Pointe-à-Pitre.

Restaurants Pointe-à-Pitre: *Oasis*; *Normandie*; *Relais des Antilles* (cheaper, but good Creole

1308 FRENCH ANTILLES

cooking); near the *Auberge Henri IV*, in a private house, good, cheap meals (ask Valentin at the *Auberge* for directions); Raizet airport: *Oiseau des Iles*; *Le Madras*. Gosier: *La Pergola* (*Hotel Au Grand Corsaire*); *Datcha*; *La Créole*; *Chez Rosette*; *Le Boukarou*; *Pavillon de Jade* (Vietnamese). Ste.-Anne: *Hotel au Grand Large* and *Chez Yvette* (budget-priced). Matouba: *Chez Paul* (Creole and East Indian cuisine). St.-François: *Madame Jerco* (good food in small creaking house).

Transport on Guadeloupe Taxis are rather expensive. There are modern air-conditioned Mercedes and Volvo buses, some equipped with video. Organized bus tours and boat excursions available. Check with Tourist Office and Petrelluzzi Travel Agency (American Express Agents), 2 rue Henri IV, Pointe-à-Pitre. The Tourist Office at Pointe-à-Pitre has excellent guidebooks with maps of various trails. Self-drive hire cars are available in Ponte-à-Pitre and Basse-Terre. Frequent buses between Pointe-à-Pitre and airport, 3.50F. Taxis, airport to Pointe-à-Pitre, US$5. Bus Pointe-à-Pitre to Basse-Terre, every 5 minutes, US$2.20 (a 65 km. journey, taking 2 hours. Taxi fare for the same trip is US$37). From there take a bus to St.-Claude, US$0.50 and then walk to the excellent Natural Park and climb Mt. Soufrière. Hot springs nearby.

Sailing Boats can be chartered for any length of time from Captain Lemaire, Carénage A, Route du Gosier, 97110 Pointe-à-Pitre. With a crew of 3 the cost works out at about US$50 p.p. per day, excluding food.

Food An unusual fruit, the *carambole*, can be bought in Pointe-à-Pitre.

The French Tourist Office addresses are: *London*: 178 Piccadilly, London W1V 0AL. Tel.: 01-493 3171. *New York*: 610 Fifth Avenue, New York, N.Y. 10020. Tel.: (212) 757-1125. *Paris*: 127 av. Champs-Elysées, 75008 Paris. Tel.: 225-12-80. *Guadeloupe*: 5, place de la Banque, 97181 Pointe-à-Pitre (Antilles Françaises). Tel.: 82-09-30.

OUTER ISLANDS OF GUADELOUPE

The outer islands of Guadeloupe are among the most beautiful and least visited of the West Indian islands; they can easily be reached by air or boat from Guadeloupe. One can still get on a trading schooner between the islands if patient.

At **Les Saintes** (a string of small islands: Terre-de-Haut, Terre-de-Bas and the Ilet-à-Cabrit are inhabited) the people are the greatest attraction, especially in Terre-de-Haut where they are descendants of Breton fisherfolk who have survived among themselves with little intermarriage with the dominant West Indian races. They even wear the same round hats that Breton fisherfolk used to wear, and fishing is still the main occupation on the islands. There are some excellent beaches including that of Pont Pierre (admission 1F) where camping is possible. Boats and diving equipment can be rented at *La Colline* hotel on Terre-de-Haut. On Terre-de-Haut is Fort Napoléon, which is being restored. There is a daily boat from Trois Rivières (Guadeloupe) to Terre-de-Haut (25F) and from Basse-Terre 4 times a week. *Hotels*: on Terre-de-Haut: *Bois Joli*, B, CP, MAP; *Kanoa*, B, EP; *Kanaoa*, B, CP; *La Saintoise*, B, CP; *La Colline*, bungalows. *Jeanne d'Arc*, CP, MAP. On Ile-à-Cabrit, *Hôtel du Fort Joséphine*.

Marie-Galante, a small round island of 153 sq. km., once an almost private rum-making empire, is simple and old-fashioned but surprisingly sophisticated when it comes to food and drink. Its beaches, so far almost completely untouched by the tourist flood, are superb. On the E coast the Plage de la Feuillère has fine sand beaches and is protected by the coral reef offshore. The Trou à Diable is a massive cave which runs deep into the earth. To visit it, it is advisable to have strong shoes, a torch with extra batteries, and a guide. The former plantation houses of Château Murat and Brûle are interesting. This island, which was named by Christopher Columbus after his own ship the *María Graciosa*, has three settlements. The largest is Grand-Bourg in the SW; Capesterre is in the SE and St.-Louis in the NW. There are no deluxe hotels on Marie-Galante but at Grand-Bourg there are the *Soledad*, B, EP, and *Le Quartier Latin*. *Le Belvédère* is near Capesterre (C, CP); in same area, *Chez Hajo*; *Le Salut* is at St.-Louis (C, EP). To get to the island there are regular flights (15 mins.) from Pointe-à-Pitre, which is only 43 km. away. There is also a ferry between Pointe-à-Pitre and Grand-Bourg (50F). On the island there are buses and taxis. Self-drive cars can be hired from M. Seytor, rue Beaurenom, Grand-Bourg.

La Désirade is an attractive but rather arid island with 1,600 inhabitants, who

FRENCH ANTILLES 1309

occupy themselves in fishing, sheep-rearing and cultivating cotton and maize. A road 10 km. long runs along the south coast to the E end of the island, where a giant cactus plantation can be seen. Also at the E end of the island is Pointe du Mornbin where there is an outstanding view of the coastline. There are excellent beaches. There are three boats weekly (2 hrs., 20F) from St.-François, Guadeloupe, to La Désirade, on which is found the *Hôtel La Guitourne*, C.

SAINT-MARTIN

St.-Martin, the largest of Guadeloupe's outer islands, is divided between France and the Netherlands. See Netherlands Antilles, page 1298, for general description and information.

Marigot, the capital of French St.-Martin, is a sleepy town between Simpson's Bay Lagoon and the sea. ("Marigot" is a French West Indian word meaning a spot from which rain water does not drain off, and forms marshy pools.) A modest waterfront marketplace offers local limes and vegetables, while mini-supermarkets abound in French delectables, as well as cheeses and wines. Boutiques offer French *prêt-à-porter* fashions and St. Barts batiks, and gift shops sell liqueurs, perfumes, and cosmetics at better duty-free prices than the Dutch side. A string of restaurants and small hotels line the beach along a narrow thread of land just outside Marigot.

Grand Case, 13 km. from the capital, is anything but grand: a quaint town between an old salt pond (which has been partially filled in to provide the airstrip, from which there are flights to St. Barts and Guadeloupe) and a long sandy and secluded beach. At the far NE end is another beach, Petite Plage, delightfully *petite* in a calm bay. On the Atlantic, Orient Bay is beautiful but rough; beware of its undertow. In Grand Case you can see fights between mongooses and snakes if you are so inclined.

Excursions From Marigot to Anguilla by ferry boat or with the *Hon-Me* ("paradise isle" in Vietnamese), a 49-foot ketch skippered by René Peyronnet, expert diver and chef (owner of *Restaurant Chez René*), who has crossed the Atlantic in it: US$40 includes day cruise and lobster-fish lunch with wine. Ferryboats go from Marigot to the Virgin Islands.

Hotels in French St. Martin *La Samanna*, rooms for A, without meals, in high season (2 and 3 bedroomed villas also available), one of the most exclusive resorts in the Caribbean. *Le Galion Beach Hotel et Club* offers a private beach on the northeast side of the island near Orient, A; it also has good water sport facilities; *Le Grand Saint-Martin*, with discothèque, A; *PLM St.-Tropez*, pool and discothèque, A, EP; *Le Pirate*, a favourite with island-hoppers, A, EP; *Yacht Club Résidence*, B; *Beauséjour*, in centre of Marigot, A, CP. At Grand Case: *Tackling's Beach Apartments*; *Hodge's Guest House*, A; *Goetz Guest House*, apartments about US$250-335 weekly; *Cagan's Guest House* and *Le Fish Spot* have a few reasonably-priced rooms; *Petite Plage*, housekeeping units on beach at US$280-420 a week. On a lonely point opposite Marigot is the multimillion dollar disaster, *La Belle Créole*, an eerie ghost of a hotel left in ruins when its developers went broke before its opening. Other hotels include the *Grand Case Beach Club*, EP; *Coralita Beach Hotel*, EP; *Club Orient* (naturist); *Hoa Mai*, CP; *Chez Martine*, EP.

Restaurants French cuisine in all hotel restaurants on the French side is quite good. Picturesque gourmet dining places on the seashore are the islanders' favourites: the *Mini-Club* with its bar and dining arbour and *Le Boucanier* for seafood specialities. Newest and very popular for its Créole specialities is *Chez Lolotte*, medium-priced with garden dining. Traditional French in centre of Marigot is *La Calanque*, and a new Vietnamese restaurant is *La Santal. Chez René* at the Lagoon Bridge promises really gourmet fare if given ample warning. *La Coupole* is French fare in 1930s ambience. *La Maison sur le Port*, *L'Aventure* and *Le Poisson d'Or* offer excellent seafood. *Le Radeau* is a floating bar and restaurant on the outskirts of Marigot with few but tasty French dishes. At Grand Case is *Fish Pot*, with only 8 tables overlooking the sea, exquisite sea food. Across the street is *Rosemary's* for Creole cooking. *Coralita* offers French/Creole fare. In the Tackling Building is the *New China Restaurant*.

SAINT-BARTHÉLÉMY

Saint-Barthélémy (St. Barts or St. Barth's), also in the Leewards, is 230 km. N of Guadeloupe, 240 km. E of the Virgin Islands, and 35 km. SE of St.-Martin. Its

1310 FRENCH ANTILLES

21 sq. km. are inhabited by a population of 2,500, mostly people of Breton, Norman, and Poitevin descent who live in quiet harmony with the small percentage of blacks. Thirty-two splendid white sandy beaches, most of which are protected by both cliff and reef, are surrounded by lush volcanic hillsides. The Norman dialect is still largely spoken while, as in the other non- British Leewards, most of the islanders also speak English. A few elderly women still wear traditional costumes (with their characteristic starched white bonnets called *kichnottes*); they cultivate sweet potato patches and weave palm fronds into hats and purses which they sell in the village of Corossol. The men traditionally smuggled rum among neighbouring islands and now import liqueurs and perfumes, raise cattle, and fish for lobsters offshore. Unspoiled as yet by mass tourism, the people are generally known for their courtesy and honesty. Although the Rockefellers, Fords, and Rothschilds own property on the island, there is little glitter or noise. In Gustavia, the capital, there are branches of several well-known French shops (such as Cartier). The small crowd of *habitués* is mostly young, chic, and French. The food, wine, and aromas are equally Gallic. Away from Gustavia, the fishing village Baie de Curazo is worth a visit. There is a good beach at Anse à Corossol, another fishing village.

History Named after Christopher Columbus' brother, St.-Barthélémy was first settled by French colonists from Dieppe in 1645. After a brief possession by the Order of the Knights of Malta, and ravaging by the Caribs, it was bought by the Compagnie des Iles and added to the French royal domain in 1672. In 1784, France ceded the island to Sweden in exchange for trading rights in the port of Göteborg. The harbour of Carénage was renamed Gustavia after the Swedish king, and became a free port, marking the beginning of the island's greatest prosperity. In 1801, St. Barts was attacked by the British, and in 1852 a fire severely damaged the capital, although the Swedish influence is still evidenced in the city hall and the trim stone houses which ring the harbour. The island was handed back to France after a referendum in 1878.

Hotels At St.-Jean beach (the best): *Eden Rock*, most picturesque, designed and owned by mayor of St. Barts, A, CP, good food; *Village St.-Jean*, modern bungalows, with kitchen facilities from A, CP; *Emeraude Plage*, similar, A, EP. At Lorient beach: *Autour du Rocher*, A, CP. At Flamands beach: *Hotel Baie des Flamands*, modern, near Anse Rockefeller, B, EP. *Les Castelets*, high in the hills, under new U.S. management, at A, CP. Least expensive: *La Presqu'Ile*, B, EP, MAP, with full board, and *Villas Prosper-Berry*, B, apartment for two with car included. Others: *PLM Jean Bart*, B; *Tropical*, A, EP; *Sereno Beach*, A, EP, *Filao Beach*, CP; *St. Barth Beach Hotel*, EP; *Grand Cul de Sac Beach Hotel*, EP; *Le P'tit Morne*, EP; *Auberge de la Petite Anse*, EP; *La Normandie*, EP. There are two car-hire companies at the airport, but their service leaves much to be desired. It is not easy to hire a car for only one day: ask your hotel to obtain a car if required.

Restaurants *Eden Rock*, good, terrace dining, average US$15 each, with wine. *Autour de Rocher*, good lobster salad lunch for US$10, indoors only. *Le Beach Club* (Village St.-Jean), reasonable lunches on the superb white sandy beach, water-sports equipment available here. *Lafayette*, again on a beach, good windsurfing, swimming pool for use of customers, recommended; *Taiwan Restaurant*, serving French food; *Club Estaminet* (Hotel Les Castelets), overpriced, in Alpine atmosphere. *La New Vieille France*, beachside with dancing at Corossol. In Gustavia: *L'Entrepont* for exquisite French cuisine; there is a good restaurant on the first floor of the *Yacht Club*, overlooking the harbour, offers few but well-prepared French dishes (also has a few rooms to let); *Auberge du Fort Oscar* specializes in Créole cooking, reserve first with Mme Jacque (Tel.: 208); *La Taverne* occupies an old warehouse and is open quite late; *La Cremaillère*, French cuisine. *Bar Le Select* is a central meeting spot and sort of general store, with a few tables in a small garden.

Transport to St.-Barts Scheduled flights from St.-Martin, Guadeloupe, and St. Thomas. Charters available locally. Day trips from Sint Maarten aboard *La Esperanza* (US$20 p.p.) and the *Maho* (twice weekly, US$35 p.p., including lunch). Full docking facilities are available at the Yacht Club in Gustavia, and anchor-place for yachts up to 10 ft. draft at St.-Jean Bay.

Information for Visitors

By Air Air France has direct flights from Paris to the international airports of Fort-de-France and Pointe-à-Pitre (about 8 hrs). Air Canada has direct flights from Montreal and Toronto. American and Eastern have flights from the USA. Inter-Caribbean connections on Air France, Eastern (Puerto Rico), Air Martinique (Dominica, Barbados, Grenada, Grenadines), St. Lucia, St Vincent, Trinidad, Antigua and the Dominican Republic), Liat.

By Sea The only company offering passenger transport is the Compagnie Générale Maritime, which has a twice-monthly service between Marseille and Fort-de-France. There are, however,

FRENCH ANTILLES 1311

numerous cruise lines departing from US and French ports, among which are the Italian Linea C and Siosa lines. Within the Caribbean, the *Delgrès*, a cargo ship with some facilities for passengers, sails regularly between Guadeloupe and St. Martin (150F), calling at St. Barthélémy. Every Tues. the *Dowes* cargo ship sails from Dominica to Guadeloupe, passengers are taken (EC$63) but there is only an awning on deck as shelter for the overnight trip. The *Independencia* connects Guadeloupe with Dominica (100F) several times a month.

Documents All travellers must be in possession of an outward ticket. Identity papers are required for US and Canadian citizens staying less than 21 days. French citizens need either their identity card or passport. A passport, but no visa, is needed by citizens of other EEC member-countries and most other nationalities. No vaccination is necessary.

Currency Exchange The banks are open from 0800 to 1200 and from 1430 to 1600, Mon. to Fri. There are money-changing offices in the big hotels and at airports. The French franc is the legal tender. There is no limit to travellers' cheques and letters of credit being imported, but a declaration of foreign banknotes in excess of 3,500 F must be made. 500 F in French banknotes may be exported and 3,500 F in foreign banknotes.

Tourists arriving in Guadeloupe would be advised to obtain a copy of a weekly booklet called *l Semaine de Loisirs* and those in Martinique, a booklet called *Choubouleoute*, both published by the Tourist Board. They give current information about entertainment, hotels, tours, prices etc. For commercial visitors the "Hints to Exporters" published by the UK Department of Trade has an interesting section on Martinique. The French Tourist Offices (addresses under Martinique and Guadeloupe) are most helpful.

Banks Royal Bank of Canada, Chase Manhattan Bank, Banque Nationale de Paris.

Many thanks to Dorothy Millgate for editorial work, and to Angela Allen (Swansea) and Paul Stearns (Derby), Pierre-Yves Atlan (Paris 18e), P.J. Spierenburg (Rotterdam), and Gustav-Adolf Yunge (Cologne), for valuable updating material.

NOTES

CLIMATIC TABLES

The following tables have been very kindly furnished by Mr. R. K. Headland. Each weather station is given with its altitude in metres (m.). Temperatures (Centigrade) are given as averages for each month; the first line is the maximum and the second the minimum. The third line is the average number of wet days encountered in each month.

MEXICO, CENTRAL AMERICA & CARIBBEAN

	Jan.	Feb.	Mar.	Apr.	May	June	July	Aug.	Sept.	Oct.	Nov.	Dec.
Acapulco, Mex. 3m.	29 21 0	31 21 0	31 21 0	31 22 0	32 23 2	32 24 9	32 24 7	32 24 7	31 24 12	31 23 6	31 22 1	31 21 0
Guatemala City 1490m.	23 11 2	25 12 2	27 14 2	28 14 5	29 16 8	27 16 20	26 16 17	26 16 16	26 16 17	24 15 13	23 14 6	22 13 2
Havana 49m.	26 18 6	27 18 4	28 19 4	29 21 4	30 22 7	31 23 10	31 24 9	32 24 10	31 24 11	29 23 11	27 21 7	26 19 6
Kingston 7m.	30 22 3	29 22 2	30 23 3	30 24 3	31 25 5	31 26 6	32 26 3	32 26 6	32 25 6	31 25 12	31 24 5	30 23 3
Managua, Nic. 46m.	30 23 0	30 24 0	30 26 0	32 28 0	32 27 6	31 26 12	31 26 11	31 25 12	31 26 15	31 26 16	30 24 4	30 24 1
Mérida, Mex. 22m.	28 17 4	29 17 2	32 19 1	33 21 2	34 22 5	33 23 10	33 23 11	33 23 12	32 23 13	31 23 7	29 19 3	28 18 3
Mexico City 2309m.	19 6 2	21 6 1	24 8 2	25 11 6	26 12 9	24 13 14	23 12 19	23 12 18	23 12 17	21 10 8	20 8 3	19 6 2
Monterrey, Mex. 538m.	20 9 3	22 11 3	24 14 3	29 17 4	31 20 4	33 22 4	32 22 4	33 22 3	30 21 8	27 18 5	22 13 4	18 10 4
Nassau 10m.	25 17 6	25 17 5	27 18 5	28 20 6	29 22 9	31 23 12	32 24 14	32 24 14	31 24 15	29 22 13	28 20 9	26 18 6
Panama City 36m.	31 21 4	31 21 2	32 22 1	32 23 6	31 23 15	30 23 16	30 23 15	31 23 15	30 23 15	30 22 16	29 22 18	30 23 12
Port-au-Prince 41m.	31 23 3	31 22 5	32 23 7	33 23 11	33 24 13	35 25 8	35 24 7	35 24 11	34 24 12	33 24 12	32 23 7	31 22 3
Port of Spain 12m.	30 20 11	32 21 8	31 21 2	32 21 8	31 23 9	31 23 19	31 23 23	31 23 17	32 23 16	31 23 13	31 22 17	30 21 16
San José, Costa Rica 1172m.	24 14 1	24 14 0	26 15 1	27 16 4	27 16 17	27 16 20	26 16 18	26 16 19	27 16 20	26 16 22	25 15 14	24 15 4
San Juan, PR 14m.	27 21 13	27 21 7	27 22 8	28 22 10	29 23 15	29 24 14	29 24 18	29 24 15	30 24 14	30 24 12	28 23 13	27 22 14
San Salvador 700m.	30 16 0	31 16 3	32 17 2	32 19 5	31 19 12	30 19 20	30 18 21	30 18 20	29 19 18	29 18 14	29 17 4	29 16 1
Santo Domingo 14m.	28 20 7	28 19 6	29 20 5	29 21 7	30 22 11	30 23 12	31 23 10	31 23 11	31 23 11	31 23 11	30 22 10	29 21 8
Tegucigalpa, Hond. 935m.	25 14 4	27 14 2	29 15 1	30 16 3	30 18 14	28 18 18	27 17 10	28 17 10	29 17 17	27 17 16	26 16 8	25 15 4
Willemstad 23m.	28 24 14	29 23 8	29 23 7	30 24 4	30 25 4	31 26 7	31 25 9	32 26 8	31 26 6	30 26 9	30 24 15	29 24 16

CLIMATIC TABLES (Cont.)

SOUTH AMERICA

	Jan.	Feb.	Mar.	Apr.	May	June	July	Aug.	Sept.	Oct.	Nov.	Dec.
Arica, Chile	26	26	25	23	21	19	19	18	19	21	22	24
29m.	18	18	17	16	14	14	12	13	13	14	16	17
	0	0	0	0	0	0	0	0	0	0	0	0
Asunción, Par.	34	34	33	28	25	22	24	25	27	29	31	33
64m.	22	22	21	18	14	13	14	14	16	17	19	21
	7	6	9	7	5	4	4	4	6	5	6	7
Bariloche, Arg.	21	21	18	14	10	7	6	8	10	11	16	18
825m.	8	8	6	4	2	1	0	0	1	3	5	6
	2	3	5	7	11	13	11	11	8	6	4	4
Barranquilla, Col.	31	31	32	33	34	33	33	33	32	32	32	30
12m.	22	22	23	24	25	25	25	25	25	24	24	23
	0	0	0	1	4	8	5	6	8	11	6	4
Belém, Braz.	31	30	30	31	31	32	32	32	32	32	32	32
24m.	23	23	23	23	23	23	22	22	22	22	22	22
	24	26	25	22	24	15	14	15	13	10	11	14
Belo Horizonte	27	27	27	27	25	24	24	25	27	27	27	26
857m.	18	18	17	16	12	10	10	12	14	16	17	18
	15	13	9	4	4	2	2	1	2	10	12	14
Bogotá	21	21	21	20	20	19	19	19	20	20	20	21
2560m.	7	7	9	10	10	9	8	8	8	9	8	7
	9	7	10	18	16	10	16	10	13	18	16	13
Brasilia	27	28	28	28	27	26	26	28	30	29	27	27
912m.	18	18	18	17	15	13	13	14	16	18	18	18
	19	16	15	9	3	1	0	2	4	11	15	20
Buenos Aires	30	29	26	22	18	15	15	16	18	21	25	29
25m.	18	17	15	12	9	6	6	6	8	11	13	16
	5	5	6	6	4	4	5	6	5	7	7	7
Caracas	26	26	28	28	28	27	26	27	28	27	27	26
1035m.	15	15	16	17	18	18	17	17	17	17	17	16
	4	3	2	4	8	13	13	11	11	11	8	6
Córdoba, Arg.	32	31	28	25	21	19	19	20	23	26	28	31
425m.	17	16	14	11	7	4	4	5	8	11	13	16
	8	9	9	6	4	2	2	1	3	7	9	10
Cuzco	20	21	21	22	21	21	21	21	22	22	23	22
3310m.	7	7	7	4	2	1	-1	1	4	6	6	7
	18	13	11	8	3	2	2	2	7	8	12	16
Guayaquil	31	31	32	31	31	29	28	29	30	29	30	31
6m.	22	22	23	23	22	21	20	20	20	21	21	22
	12	13	15	10	4	1	0	0	0	1	0	2
La Paz, Bol.	18	18	18	19	17	17	17	17	18	19	19	19
3632m.	6	6	6	5	3	2	1	2	3	5	6	6
	21	18	16	9	5	2	2	4	9	9	11	18
Lima	25	26	26	24	21	19	17	17	17	19	20	23
137m.	19	20	19	18	16	15	14	13	13	14	16	17
	1	0	0	0	1	1	1	2	1	0	0	0
Manaus	30	30	30	30	31	31	32	33	33	33	32	31
48m.	23	23	23	23	24	23	23	24	24	24	24	24
	20	18	21	20	18	12	12	5	7	4	12	16
Montevideo	28	28	26	22	18	15	14	15	17	20	23	26
22m.	17	16	15	12	9	6	6	6	8	9	12	15
	6	5	5	6	6	5	6	7	6	6	6	7
Porto Alegre, Braz.	31	30	29	25	22	20	20	21	22	24	27	29
10m.	20	20	19	16	13	11	10	11	13	15	17	19
	9	10	10	6	6	8	8	8	11	10	8	8
Punta Arenas, Chile	15	14	13	9	6	4	3	4	7	10	12	14
28m.	7	7	6	4	2	1	1	1	2	3	4	6
	6	5	7	9	6	8	6	5	5	5	5	8
Quito	21	21	20	21	21	21	21	22	22	21	21	21
2818m.	8	8	8	8	8	7	7	7	7	8	8	8
	9	11	11	15	10	9	3	3	8	13	13	7

SOUTH AMERICA (Cont.)

	Jan.	Feb.	Mar.	Apr.	May	June	July	Aug.	Sept.	Oct.	Nov.	Dec.
Recife, Braz.	30	30	30	30	29	28	27	27	28	29	30	30
56m.	24	25	24	23	23	22	21	21	22	23	24	24
	7	8	10	11	17	16	17	14	7	3	4	4
Rio de Janeiro	30	30	29	27	26	25	25	25	25	26	28	28
30m.	23	23	23	21	20	18	18	18	19	20	20	22
	13	11	9	9	6	5	5	4	5	11	10	12
Salvador (Bahia)	29	29	29	28	27	26	26	26	27	28	28	29
8m.	23	23	24	23	22	21	21	21	21	22	23	23
	6	9	17	19	22	23	18	15	10	8	9	11
Santa Cruz, Bol.	30	31	30	28	25	23	24	28	29	30	31	31
437m.	21	21	20	19	16	15	15	16	19	20	20	21
	14	10	12	9	11	8	5	4	5	7	8	11
Santiago de Chile	29	29	27	23	18	14	15	17	19	22	26	28
520m.	12	11	9	7	5	3	3	4	6	7	9	11
	0	0	1	1	5	6	6	5	3	3	1	0
São Paulo	28	28	27	25	23	22	21	23	25	25	25	26
792m.	18	18	17	15	13	11	10	11	13	14	15	16
	15	13	12	6	3	4	4	3	5	12	11	14

Sources:—H.M.S.O. Meteorological Reports
K.L.M. Climatic Data Publication

NOTES

STANDARD TIME ZONES

(Expressed as hours behind Greenwich Mean Time)

Argentina	3	Nicaragua	6
Falkland Islands	4	Costa Rica	6
Bolivia	4	Panama	5
Brazil	3*(2*1)	Cuba	5
Chile	4(3†)	Haiti	5
Colombia	5	Dominican Republic	4
Ecuador	5	Puerto Rico	4
Paraguay	4(3†)	Jamaica	5
Peru	5	Barbados	4
Uruguay	3	Trinidad & Tobago	4
Venezuela	4	Leeward Islands	4
Guyana	3¾	Windward Islands	4
Suriname	3½	Bahamas	5(4**)
Guyane	3	Turks & Caicos Islands	5
Mexico	6‡	Cayman Islands	5
Guatemala	6	Bermuda	4
Belize	6	Virgin Islands	4
El Salvador	6	Netherlands Antilles	4
Honduras	6	French Antilles	4

*Standard time, except for Fernando de Noronha (2); Amazonia W of the Jari and Xingu rivers and E of the Tabatinga-Porto Acre line, and the States of Mato Grosso and Mato Grosso do Sul (4); and Amazonia W of the Tabatinga-Porto Acre line (5).
†Summer time, October-March.
‡Standard time, except for Baja California Sur, Sonora, Sinaloa and Nayarit (7); and Baja California (8).
**Summer time, May-October.

WEIGHTS AND MEASURES

Metric

Weight:
1 kilogram (kg.) = 2,205 pounds
1 metric ton = 1.102 short tons
             = 0.984 long ton

Length:
1 millimetre (mm.) = 0.03937 inch
1 metre = 3.281 feet
1 kilometre (km.) = 0.621 mile

Area:
1 hectare = 2.471 acres
1 square km. (km²) = 0.386 sq. mile

Capacity:
1 litre = 0.220 Imperial gallon
       = 0.264 U.S. gallon

Volume:
1 cubic metre (m³) = 35.31 cubic feet
                   = 1.31 cubic yards

British and U.S.

1 pound (lb.) = 454 grams
1 short ton (2,000 lb.) = 0.907 metric ton
1 long ton (2,240 lb.) = 1.016 metric tons

1 inch = 25.417 millimetres
1 foot (ft.) = 0.305 metre
1 mile = 1.609 kilometres

1 acre = 0.405 hectare
1 square mile (sq. mile) = 2,590 km²

1 Imperial gallon = 4.546 litres
1 U.S. gallon = 3.785 litres
(5 Imperial gallons are approximately equal to 6 U.S. gallons)

1 cubic foot (cu. ft) = 0.028 m³
1 cubic yard (cu. yd.) = 0.765 m³

N.B. The *manzana*, used in Central America, is about 0.7 hectare (1.73 acres).

LATEST EXCHANGE AND INFLATION RATES

This information updates that given in the "Information for Visitors" sections of the country chapters.

	Exchange for tourists: Units per US dollar	Inflation: % increase in cost of living over last 12 months	
	End-May 1987	*Latest month*	*1987*
Argentina	1.61 (2.1)	April	103.0
Bolivia	2.10	April	19.0
Brazil	33.60 (36.3)	April	105.0
Chile	216.08 (226)	March	17.5
Columbia	237.84 (239)	February	19.8
Ecuador	178.50	March	29.5
Paraguay	798.00	December (86)	24.1
Peru	24.10	April	71.6
Uruguay	214.50	April	66.2
Venezuela	27.52	February	14.3
Mexico	1,257.00	April	128.7
Belize	2.00	December (86)	2.3
Costa Rica	61.30	January	17.7
El Salvador	5.00 (5.50)	February	26.5
Guatemala	2.50 (2.70)	December (86)	25.7
Honduras	2.00 (2.10)	September (86)	4.2
Nicaragua	70.00 (1,700)	December (86)	747.4
Panama	1.00	December (86)	1.9

Black ("parallel") market rates in brackets.

CALENDAR 1987

January
```
M  ..  5 12 19 26 ..
Tu ..  6 13 20 27 ..
W  ..  7 14 21 28 ..
Th  1  8 15 22 29 ..
F   2  9 16 23 30 ..
S   3 10 17 24 31 ..
S   4 11 18 25 .. ..
```

February
```
M  ..  2  9 16 23 ..
Tu ..  3 10 17 24 ..
W  ..  4 11 18 25 ..
Th ..  5 12 19 26 ..
F  ..  6 13 20 27 ..
S  ..  7 14 21 28 ..
S   1  8 15 22 .. ..
```

March
```
M  ..  2  9 16 23 30
Tu ..  3 10 17 24 31
W  ..  4 11 18 25 ..
Th ..  5 12 19 26 ..
F  ..  6 13 20 27 ..
S  ..  7 14 21 28 ..
S   1  8 15 22 29 ..
```

April
```
M  ..  6 13 20 27 ..
Tu ..  7 14 21 28 ..
W   1  8 15 22 29 ..
Th  2  9 16 23 30 ..
F   3 10 17 24 .. ..
S   4 11 18 25 .. ..
S   5 12 19 26 .. ..
```

May
```
M  ..  4 11 18 25 ..
Tu ..  5 12 19 26 ..
W  ..  6 13 20 27 ..
Th ..  7 14 21 28 ..
F   1  8 15 22 29 ..
S   2  9 16 23 30 ..
S   3 10 17 24 31 ..
```

June
```
M   1  8 15 22 29
Tu  2  9 16 23 30
W   3 10 17 24 ..
Th  4 11 18 25 ..
F   5 12 19 26 ..
S   6 13 20 27 ..
S   7 14 21 28 ..
```

July
```
M  ..  6 13 20 27 ..
Tu ..  7 14 21 28 ..
W   1  8 15 22 29 ..
Th  2  9 16 23 30 ..
F   3 10 17 24 31 ..
S   4 11 18 25 .. ..
S   5 12 19 26 .. ..
```

August
```
M  ..  3 10 17 24 31
Tu ..  4 11 18 25 ..
W  ..  5 12 19 26 ..
Tu ..  6 13 20 27 ..
F  ..  7 14 21 28 ..
S   1  8 15 22 29 ..
S   2  9 16 23 30 ..
```

September
```
M  ..  7 14 21 28 ..
T   1  8 15 22 29 ..
W   2  9 16 23 30 ..
Th  3 10 17 24 .. ..
F   4 11 18 25 .. ..
S   5 12 19 26 .. ..
S   6 13 20 27 .. ..
```

October
```
M  ..  5 12 19 26 ..
Tu ..  6 13 20 27 ..
W  ..  7 14 21 28 ..
Th  1  8 15 22 29 ..
F   2  9 16 23 30 ..
S   3 10 17 24 31 ..
S   4 11 18 25 .. ..
```

November
```
M  ..  2  9 16 23 30
Tu ..  3 10 17 24 ..
W  ..  4 11 18 25 ..
Th ..  5 12 19 26 ..
F  ..  6 13 20 27 ..
S  ..  7 14 21 28 ..
S   1  8 15 22 29 ..
```

December
```
M  ..  7 14 21 28 ..
Tu  1  8 15 22 29 ..
W   2  9 16 23 30 ..
Th  3 10 17 24 31 ..
F   4 11 18 25 .. ..
S   5 12 19 26 .. ..
S   6 13 20 27 .. ..
```

CALENDAR 1988 – Leap Year

January
M .. 4 11 18 25 ..
Tu .. 5 12 19 26 ..
W .. 6 13 20 27 ..
Th .. 7 14 21 28 ..
F 1 8 15 22 29 ..
S 2 9 16 23 30 ..
S 3 10 17 24 31 ..

February
M 1 8 15 22 29 ..
Tu 2 9 16 23 .. ..
W 3 10 17 24 .. ..
Th 4 11 18 25 .. ..
F 5 12 19 26 .. ..
S 6 13 20 27 .. ..
S 7 14 21 28 .. ..

March
M .. 7 14 21 28 ..
Tu 1 8 15 22 29 ..
W 2 9 16 23 30 ..
Th 3 10 17 24 31 ..
F 4 11 18 25 .. ..
S 5 12 19 26 .. ..
S 6 13 20 27 .. ..

April
M .. 4 11 18 25 ..
Tu .. 5 12 19 26 ..
W .. 6 13 20 27 ..
Th .. 7 14 21 28 ..
F 1 8 15 22 29 ..
S 2 9 16 23 30 ..
S 3 10 17 24 .. ..

May
M .. 2 9 16 23 30
Tu .. 3 10 17 24 31
W .. 4 11 18 25 ..
Th .. 5 12 19 26 ..
F .. 6 13 20 27 ..
S .. 7 14 21 28 ..
S 1 8 15 22 29 ..

June
M .. 6 13 20 27 ..
Tu .. 7 14 21 28 ..
W 1 8 15 22 29 ..
Th 2 9 16 23 30 ..
F 3 10 17 24 .. ..
S 4 11 18 25 .. ..
S 5 12 19 26 .. ..

July
M .. 4 11 18 25 ..
Tu .. 5 12 19 26 ..
W .. 6 13 20 27 ..
Th .. 7 14 21 28 ..
F 1 8 15 22 29 ..
S 2 9 16 23 30 ..
S 3 10 17 24 31 ..

August
M 1 8 15 22 29 ..
Tu 2 9 16 23 30 ..
W 3 10 17 24 31 ..
Tu 4 11 18 25 .. ..
F 5 12 19 26 .. ..
S 6 13 20 27 .. ..
S 7 14 21 28 .. ..

September
M .. 5 12 19 26 ..
T .. 6 13 20 27 ..
W .. 7 14 21 28 ..
Th 1 8 15 22 29 ..
F 2 9 16 23 30 ..
S 3 10 17 24 .. ..
S 4 11 18 25 .. ..

October
M .. 3 10 17 24 31
Tu .. 4 11 18 25 ..
W .. 5 12 19 26 ..
Th .. 6 13 20 27 ..
F .. 7 14 21 28 ..
S 1 8 15 22 29 ..
S 2 9 16 23 30 ..

November
M .. 7 14 21 28 ..
Tu 1 8 15 22 29 ..
W 2 9 16 23 30 ..
Th 3 10 17 24 .. ..
F 4 11 18 25 .. ..
S 5 12 19 26 .. ..
S 6 13 20 27 .. ..

December
M .. 5 12 19 26 ..
Tu .. 6 13 20 27 ..
W .. 7 14 21 28 ..
Th 1 8 15 22 29 ..
F 2 9 16 23 30 ..
S 3 10 17 24 31 ..
S 4 11 18 25 .. ..

CALENDAR 1989

January
M	..	2	9	16	23	30
Tu	..	3	10	17	24	31
W	..	4	11	18	25	..
Th	..	5	12	19	26	..
F	..	6	13	20	27	..
S	..	7	14	21	28	..
S	1	8	15	22	29	..

February
M	..	6	13	20	27	
Tu	..	7	14	21	28	
W	1	8	15	22	..	
Th	2	9	16	23	..	
F	3	10	17	24	..	
S	4	11	18	25	..	
S	5	12	19	26	..	

March
M	..	6	13	20	27	
Tu	..	7	14	21	28	
W	1	8	15	22	29	
Th	2	9	16	23	30	
F	3	10	17	24	31	
S	4	11	18	25	..	
S	5	12	19	26	..	

April
M	..	3	10	17	24
Tu	..	4	11	18	25
W	..	5	12	19	26
Th	..	6	13	20	27
F	..	7	14	21	28
S	1	8	15	22	29
S	2	9	16	23	30

May
M	1	8	15	22	29	
Tu	2	9	16	23	30	
W	3	10	17	24	31	
Th	4	11	18	25	..	
F	5	12	19	26	..	
S	6	13	20	27	..	
S	7	14	21	28	..	

June
M	..	5	12	19	26	
Tu	..	6	13	20	27	
W	..	7	14	21	28	
Th	1	8	15	22	29	
F	2	9	16	23	30	
S	3	10	17	24	..	
S	4	11	18	25	..	

July
M	..	3	10	17	24	31
Tu	..	4	11	18	25	..
W	..	5	12	19	26	..
Th	..	6	13	20	27	..
F	..	7	14	21	28	..
S	1	8	15	22	29	..
S	2	9	16	23	30	..

August
M	..	7	14	21	28	
Tu	1	8	15	22	29	
W	2	9	16	23	30	
Tu	3	10	17	24	31	
F	4	11	18	25	..	
S	5	12	19	26	..	
S	6	13	20	27	..	

September
M	..	4	11	18	25	
T	..	5	12	19	26	
W	..	6	13	20	27	
Th	..	7	14	21	28	
F	1	8	15	22	29	
S	2	9	16	23	30	
S	3	10	17	24	..	

October
M	..	2	9	16	23	30
Tu	..	3	10	17	24	31
W	..	4	11	18	25	..
Th	..	5	12	19	26	..
F	..	6	13	20	27	..
S	..	7	14	21	28	..
S	1	8	15	22	29	..

November
M	..	6	13	20	27	
Tu	..	7	14	21	28	
W	1	8	15	22	29	
Th	2	9	16	23	30	
F	3	10	17	24	..	
S	4	11	18	25	..	
S	5	12	19	26	..	

December
M	..	4	11	18	25	
Tu	..	5	12	19	26	
W	..	6	13	20	27	
Th	..	7	14	21	28	
F	1	8	15	22	29	
S	2	9	16	23	30	
S	3	10	17	24	31	

WANTED: MAPS

ARGENTINA – BRAZIL – MEXICO GUATEMALA – EL SALVADOR – THE CARIBBEAN ISLANDS

We would much appreciate receiving any surplus maps and diagrams, however rough, of towns and cities, walks, national parks and other interesting areas, to use as source material for the Handbook and other forthcoming titles.

The above regions are particularly needed but any maps of Latin America would be welcome.

The Editor
Trade & Travel Publications Ltd
5 Prince's Buildings
George Street
Bath BA1 2ED
England

INDEX TO TOWN AND REGIONAL MAPS

Argentina	Buenos Aires (Centre)	37
	North-West	60
	Andean Churches	78
	North-East	96
	Iguazú Falls	108
Bolivia	General	154
	La Paz (Centre)	158
Brazil	General	207
	Rio de Janeiro (Centre)	224
	Roads from Rio de Janeiro, São Paulo and Belo Horizonte	250
	São Paulo (Centre)	265
	Southern Brazil	280
	Salvador (Centre)	298
	Recife (Centre)	319
Chile	General	374
	Chilean Heartland	391
	Santiago (Centre)	395
	Easter Island	410
	South-Central	415
	The Lake District	421
Colombia	General	451
	Bogotá (Centre)	456
	Cartagena	468
	Central Colombia	479
	Upper Magdalena	518
Ecuador	General	536
	Quito (New City)	538
	Quito (Old City)	540
	Guayaquil	582
Paraguay	General	607
	Asunción	611
Peru	Lima (Centre)	635
	Lima to Callejón de Huaylas	661
	North	676
	South	693
	Cuzco (Centre)	713
	Cuzco Area	725
	Oroya to Pucallpa	747
Uruguay	General	767
	Montevideo	771
Venezuela	General	792
	Caracas (Centre)	796
The Guianas	General	864
Mexico	Mexico North	874
	Mexico City	911
	Mexico South	934
Central America	Guatemala	1011
	Belize	1059
	El Salvador	1073
	Honduras	1089
	Nicaragua	1117
	Costa Rica	1138
	Panama	1167
	Panama Canal	1171
Cuba	General	1194
	Havana	1197
Hispaniola	Haiti	1208
	Dominican Republic	1216
	Santo Domingo	1217

WILL YOU HELP US?

We do all we can to get our facts right in *The South American Handbook*. Each chapter is thoroughly revised each year, but Latin America and the Caribbean cover a vast area, and our eyes cannot be everywhere. A new highway or airport is built; a hotel, a restaurant, a cabaret dies; another, a good one is born; a building we describe is pulled down, a street renamed. Names and addresses of good hotels and restaurants for "budget-minded" travellers are always very welcome. We would especially like to receive maps and diagrams of towns and cities, walks, national parks and other interesting areas to use as source material for the Handbook and other forthcoming titles.

Your information may be far more up-to-date than ours. If your letter reaches us early enough in the year it will be used in the next edition, but write whenever you want to, for all your letters are used sooner or later.

Thank you very much indeed for your help.

Trade & Travel Publications Limited
5 Prince's Buildings, George Street,
Bath BA1 2ED. England

INDEX TO PLACES

Abaco 1273
Abancay 740
Acajutla 1082
Acapantzingo 945
Acapulco 948
Acarigua 817
Acatenango Volcano 1024
Acatepec 931
Acatlán 953
Acatzingo 942
Acayucán 939
Achacachi 170
Achao 434
Acobamba 741
Acolman 928
Acomayo 722
Actopán 873
Agua Azul 973
Agua Volcano 1024
Aguacatán 1044
Aguadulce 1181
Aguas Calientes (Peru) 729
Aguascalientes (Mex.) 885
Aguateca 1035
Aguaytía 748
Ahuachapán 1084
Ahuas 1112
Ajijic 901
Ajuda 310
Ajusco 926
Akumal 989
Alajuela 1153
Alamos 891
Alausí 565
Albina 855
Alcântara 331
Almolonga 1047
Alpuyeca 945
Alta Gracia 65
Altar 567
Altun Ha 1064
Amaichá del Valle 68
Amantaní 708
Amapala 1109
Amatenango del Valle 966
Amatitlán 1035
Ambalema 482
Ambato 568
Ambergris Caye 1063
Amecameca 929
Americana 277
Amozoc 933
Anaco 822
Anápolis 351
Ancón (Peru) 656
Ancón (Pan.) 1173
Ancud 433
Andacollo 389
Andahuaylas 740
Andalgalá 91
Andros 1273
Anegada 1286
Angastaco 74
Angel Falls 826
Angol 418

Angra dos Reis 245
Anguilla 1260
Antarctica (Chi.) 441
Antarctica (Arg.) 144
Antigua (Gua.) 1020
Antigua (WI) 1255
Antioquia 505
Antisana 588
Antofagasta 381
Antofagasta de la Sierra 91
Antonina 295
Aonara 862
Aparecida do Norte 279
Apartaderos 812
Apoera 855
Apuela 553
Ayquina 386
Aracaju 311
Aracataca 476
Araguaína 333
Araruama 241
Araxá 261
Arcoverde 323
Aregua 619
Arembepe 311
Arequipa 698
Argentina 31–151
Arica 377
Arima 1249
Armenia 509
Arriaga 960
Artigas 784
Aruba 1294
Asochinga 65
Asunción 609
Atacamés 562
Atibaia 279
Atlántida 777
Atlixco 953
Atotonilco 889
Auray 737
Avellaneda 52
Ayabaca 686
Ayacucho 739
Azángaro 705
Azogues 575
Azul 57

Bay Islands 1098
Baeza 588
Bahamas 1270–1274
Bahía Blanca 57
Bahía de Caráquez 560
Bahía de Los Angeles 994
Baja California 991
Balboa 1172
Balcarce 55
Ballestas Islands 691
Bambamarca 683
Bananal 352
Bananera 1031
Baños 570
Barahona 1223
Barbacena 249
Barbacoas 521

Barbados 1243–1246
Barbosa 497
Barbuda 1258
Barcelona 818
Barichara 498
Bariloche 114
Barinas 817
Barquisimeto 808
Barra da Tijuca 239
Barra de Navidad 902
Barra del Colorado 1151
Barra do Garças 352
Barranca 658
Barrancabermeja 480
Barrancas 826
Barranco 655
Barranquilla 465
Barro Colorado 1172
Bartica 842
Basaseachi 883
Basihuara 882
Basse-Terre (Guadeloupe) 1306
Basseterre (St. Kitts) 1259
Batopilas 882
Bauru 278
Becán 975
Beef Island 1286
Belém 334
Belén (Arg.) 90
Belén (Col.) 487
Belize 1057–1070
Belize City 1060
Bella Unión 784
Bello 506
Belmopan 1058
Belo Horizonte 251
Belterra 340
Benjamin Constant 346
Benque Viejo del Carmen 1066
Bequia 1269
Berlín 500
Bermuda 1280–1281
Bertioga 273
Bimini 1273
Biotopo del Quetzal 1026
Blanche Marie Falls 855
Bluefields 1131
Blumenau 290
Boa Vista 347
Boca Grande 520
Boca de Yuma 1224
Bocas del Toro 1184
Boconó 812
Bogotá 454
Bolivia 152–204
Bonaire 1296
Bonampak 973
Bonao 1220
Boquerón 1230
Boquete 1183
Boyuibe 187
Brasília 212
Brazil 205–371
Bridgetown 1243
British Virgin Islands 1285
Brownsberg 853
Brus Laguna 1112
Bucaramanga 498
Bucay 565

Buenaventura 513
Buenos Aires 36
Buga 510
Búzios 241

Caacupé 619
Cabanaconde 704
Cabo Blanco 688
Cabo Frio 241
Cabo San Lucas 996
Cabruta 823
Cacahuamilpa 945
Cacaxtla 930
Cáceres 357
Cacheuta 85
Cachi 74
Cachoeira 307
Cachoeira do Itapemirim 246
Caeté 253
Cafayate 73
Cahuita 1152
Caicara 823
Caicó 326
Caicos 1276
Caiobá 296
Cajabamba (Ecu.) 675
Cajabamba (Peru) 565
Cajamarca (Peru) 675
Cajamarca (Col.) 482
Cajamarquilla 656
Calafate 136
Calama 383
Calbuco 433
Calca 724
Caldas Novas 352
Caldera 387
Calderón 550
Caleta Olivia 133
Cali 510
California (Col.) 500
Calixtlahuaca 909
Callao 657
Callejón de Huaylas 668
Camagüey 1201
Camaná 696
Camargo 189
Camarones 131
Camboriú 290
Cambuquirá 260
Camiri 186
Campeche 975
Campina Grande 324
Campinas 277
Campo Grande 353
Campos 242
Campos do Jordão 279
Canaima 826
Cananéia 275
Cañar 577
Canchaque 686
Cancún 988
Candonga 64
Canela 284
Canelones 785
Cañete 417
Canoa Quebrada 328
Canouan 1269
Canta 743
Cantamarca 743

Cantel 1051
Cap Haitien 1210
Capiatá 618
Capilla del Monte 65
Caquetá 486
Caracaraí 348
Caracas 794
Caraguatatuba 274
Caranavi 175
Carás 660
Cárdenas (Cuba) 1201
Cárdenas (Mex.) 969
Carhuás 663
Carhué 58
Caripe 821
Carmelo 781
Carmen de Patagones 127
Carmen de Viboral 506
Carora 809
Carriacou 1269
Cartagena (Chi.) 406
Cartagena (Col.) 466
Cartago (Col.) 509
Cartago (Cr) 1148
Caruaru 323
Carúpano 819
Casas Grandes 880
Cascadas de Olaén 64
Casma 659
Cassino 286
Castries 1264
Castro 433
Cata 805
Catacaos 686
Catamarca 92
Catemaco 939
Caucasia 472
Caxambu 260
Caxias do Sul 285
Cayambe 550
Caye Caulker 1063
Cayma 703
Cayman Brac 1278
Cayman Islands 1277–1279
Cayo Largo 1201
Cedros 1095
Celaya 888
Celendín 678
Celestún 981
Cenotillo 985
Central America 1006–1009
Centú Cué 621
Cerro Colorado 65
Cerro Punta 1183
Cerro Verde 1082
Cerro de Pasco 743
Chachapoyas 679
Chaitén 435
Chala 695
Chalatenango 1085
Chalchuapa 1083
Chalma 909
Champaqui 65
Champerico 1052
Chamula 966
Chan Chan 673
Chañaral 387
Chanchamayo 742

Chancos 663
Changuinola 1184
Chapada dos Guimarães 358
Chapala 901
Chapingo 929
Charlestown 1259
Charlotte Amalie 1283
Chascomús 54
Chavín 666
Chepo 1184
Chetumal 974
Chiantla 1048
Chiapa de Corzo 963
Chicana 975
Chichén-Itzá 983
Chichicastenango 1041
Chichiriviche 807
Chiconcuac 929
Chihuahua 880
Chile 372–449
Chile Chico 437
Chilecito 89
Chilete 675
Chillán 413
Chiloé 433
Chilpancingo 947
Chimaltenango 1037
Chimborazo 569
Chimbote 659
Chinandega 1127
Chincheros 724
Chipaya 177
Chiquián 669
Chiquimula 1028
Chiquinquirá 493
Chirripó 1159
Chitré 1181
Chivacoa 809
Chivay 703
Choachí 464
Choele-Choel 123
Cholula 931
Choluteca 1109
Chomachi 883
Chonchi 434
Chongoyape 683
Chordeleg 577
Chorrillos 655
Chosica 734
Chota 683
Christiansted 1284
Chúa 172
Chucuíto 709
Chulucanas 686
Chulumani 174
Chuquicamata 384
Churubusco 926
Chuy 780
Ciénaga 476
Cienfuegos 1201
Ciudad Bolívar 822
Ciudad Camargo 883
Ciudad Constitución 994
Ciudad Guayana 824
Ciudad Hidalgo 908
Ciudad Juárez 880
Ciudad Neily 1161
Ciudad Obregón 891
Ciudad Presidente Stroessner 620

Ciudad Valles 873
Ciudad Victoria 872
Ciudad Vieja 1023
Ciudad del Carmen 975
Claromecó 57
Clisa 181
Clorinda 103
Coatepeque 1051
Coatzacoalcos 968
Cobá 991
Cobán 1026
Cobija 196
Coca 589
Cochabamba 177
Cochamó 432
Cochasqui 551
Cockburn Town 1276
Cockpit Country 1239
Cocobila 1112
Coconuco 516
Cocuy 497
Coina 674
Cojimíes 561
Cojutepeque 1079
Colima 902
Colombia 450–532
Colón (Arg.) 112
Colón (Pan.) 1169
Colonia 781
Colonia Sarmiento 132
Colonia Suiza 780
Colonia Tovar 804
Colonia Valdense 780
Comayagua 1107
Comacalco 970
Comalapa 1037
Comitán 966
Comodoro Rivadavia 131
Conceição da Barra 248
Concepción (Bol.) 193
Concepción (Chi.) 414
Concepción (Pan.) 1183
Concepción (Par.) 617
Concepción (Peru) 738
Concepción Chiquirichapa 1050
Concepción del Uruguay 112
Concón 406
Concordia 113
Congonhas do Campo 256
Constanza 1221
Constitución 413
Contadora 1173
Copacabana (Bol.) 171
Copacabana (Bra.) 237
Copahué Termas 123
Copán 1104
Copiapó 387
Coquimbo 389
Corcovado 238
Corcovado National Park 1160
Córdoba 61
Corinto 1127
Corn Islands 1132
Coro 807
Coroico 174
Coronel 416
Coronel Oviedo 619
Corozal 1065
Corrientes 101

Corriverton 842
Corumbá 354
Cosamaloapan 939
Cosquín 64
Costa Rica 1137–1165
Cotacachi 553
Cotopaxi 574
Cotzumalguapa 1036
Coveñas 472
Coyhaique 436
Coyoacán 927
Cozumel 989
Crateús 329
Crato 324
Creel 882
Cristalina 218
Cristóbal 1169
Cruz Azul 873
Cruz Chica 64
Cruz das Almas 308
Cruz del Eje 65
Cruzeiro do Sul 350
Cuautla 953
Cuba 1193–1205
Cucao 434
Cúcuta 500
Cuenca 575
Cuernavaca 943
Cuesta del Portezuelo 93
Cuetzalán 933
Cueva del Guácharo (Ven.) 821
Cueva de los Guácharos (Col.) 484
Cuiabá 357
Cuicocha 553
Cuicuilco 926
Cuilapan 959
Cuimón 411
Cuitzeo 907
Culiacán 892
Cumaná 819
Curaçao 1289
Curacautín 418
Curicó 412
Curitiba 292
Cusichaca 726
Cusipata 722
Cutervo 684
Cuzarare 882
Cuzco 710

Dainzu 958
Dalcahue 434
Dangriga 1067
Danlí 1110
David 1182
Desierto de los Leones 928
Diamantina 257
Dichato 416
Diriamba 1130
Dolores (Arg.) 54
Dolores (Uru.) 782
Dolores Hidalgo 889
Domingos Martins 248
Dominica 1261
Dominican Republic 1214–1226
Dos Pilas 1035
Duitama 496
Durango 883
Dzibilchaltun 981

East Caicos 1276
Easter Island 407
Ecuador 533–605
El Banco 480
El Bolsón 119
El Cajas 578
El Ceibal 1034
El Dorado (Ven.) 827
El Estor 1031
El Florido 1028
El Fuerte 892
El Hato del Volcán 1183
El Junquito 804
El Mirador 1035
El Naranjo (Arg.) 69
El Naranjo (Gua.) 1034
El Paraíso 1111
El Pauji 828
El Progreso 1097
El Salvador 1071–1087
El Tajín 876
El Tigre 822
El Tocuyo 809
El Triunfo 996
El Tule 958
El Valle 1181
El Vigía 811
El Zotz 1035
Eldorado (Arg.) 105
Eleuthera 1273
Embarcación 81
Embu 271
Empedrado 100
Encarnación 621
Engenheiro Passos 244
English Harbour 1256
Ensenada (Chi.) 429
Ensenada (Mex.) 993
Envigado 506
Epizana 181
Erandique 1107
Escuintla 1036
Esmeraldas 561
Espinal 482
Esquel 120
Esquías 1095
Esquipulas 1028
Estelí 1124
Etén 682
Exuma 1273

Facatativá 488
Falkland Islands 864–867
Falmouth 1240
Farellones 402
Fazenda Nova 323
Feira de Santana 307
Fernando de Noronha 323
Fiambalá 90
Filadelfia 624
Finca El Rey 69
Florencia 487
Flores 1031
Florianópolis 288
Florida 785
Floridablanca 499
Fontibón 488
Formosa 102
Fortaleza 326

Fort-de-France 1303
Fortín de las Flores 936
Foz do Iguaçu 109
Francisco Escárcega 973
Fray Bentos 782
Frederiksted 1284
Freeport 1272
French Antilles 1302–1311
Fresno 481
Frutillar 429
Fuego Volcano 1024
Fusagasugá 488

Gaiman 131
Galápagos Islands 594
Garanhuns 322
Garzón 484
George Town (Cayman Is.) 1277
Georgetown (Guy.) 839
Girardot 482
Girón 499
Gobernador Gregores 134
Goiânia 351
Goiás Velho 352
Golfito 1160
Gonaives 1210
Governador Valadares 259
Goya 100
Gracias 1106
Gramado 284
Granada (Col.) 490
Granada (Nic.) 1128
Grand Bahama Island 1272
Grand Case 1309
Grand Cayman 1277
Great Dog Island 1287
Great Thatch 1287
Grenada 1267
Grenadines 1269
Gruta de la Paz 555
Guachochi 882
Guacuí 242
Guadalajara 897
Guadeloupe 1306
Guaduas 488
Guajará Mirim 350
Gualaceo 577
Gualanday 482
Gualaquiza 594
Gualeguay 97
Gualeguaychú 112
Guaíra 276
Guaminí 58
Guamo 483
Guamote 565
Guana Island 1287
Guanabacoa 1200
Guanacaste 1156
Guanaja 1100
Guanajuato 886
Guanare 817
Guanay 175
Guano 567
Guanta 818
Guápiles 1151
Guaqui 171
Guaranda 569
Guarapari 246
Guaratuba 296

Guarujá 273
Guatavita Nueva 494
Guatemala 1010–1056
Guatemala City 1013
Guayaquil 580
Guayaramerín 195
Guaymas 891
Guelatao 959
Guerrero Negro 993
Guicán 497
Güiria 821
Guyana 837–848
Guyane 859–863

Haiti 1207–1213
Hamilton 1280
Hatillo 506
Havana 1195
Heredia 1152
Hermosillo 890
Hidalgo del Parral 883
Higüey 1224
Hispaniola 1206
Holbox 986
Holguín 1202
Honda 481
Honduras 1088–1115
Horcón 406
Huacachina 692
Huacarpay 722
Huacho 658
Huajuapan de León 958
Hualgayoc 684
Huallanca 660
Huamachuco 674
Huancabamba 686
Huancavelica 738
Huancayo 735
Huanchaco 673
Huánuco 744
Huánuco Viejo 745
Huaquillas 587
Huarás 664
Huarmey 659
Huaro 722
Huasco 388
Huatajata 172
Huaura 658
Huayna Potosí 170
Huaytará 691
Huehuetenango 1047
Huejotzingo 931
Huerta Grande 64
Huexotla 929
Huigra 565
Humahuaca 79
Humaitá 333

Ibagué 482
Ibarra 553
Ica 691
Igaraçu 322
Iguapé 275
Iguazú Falls 106
Ilave 708
Iles du Salut 861
Ilha da Maré 306
Ilha de São Sebastião 274
Ilha do Mel 296

Ilha Grande 245
Ilha Porchat 273
Ilhabela 274
Ilhéus 309
Illampu 170
Illapel 390
Ilo 697
Ilobasco 1079
Imbituba 288
Iñapari 733
Inca Trail 726
Ingapirca 578
Inzá 517
Ipiales 523
Iquique 380
Iquitos 750
Iraí 291
Irapuato 887
Isla de los Estados 143
Isla del Coco 1156
Isla Grande 1171
Isla Mujeres 986
Isla Victoria 114
Itá 621
Itabuna 309
Itacaré 309
Itacoatiara 345
Itacuruçá 245
Itaipú 620
Itajaí 290
Itamaracá 322
Itanhaém 275
Itaparica 306
Itatí 102
Itatiaia National Park 244
Itauguá 618
Itu 278
Itzán 1035
Ixcatlan 940
Iximché 1038
Ixmiquilpan 873
Ixtapa 951
Ixtapalapa 926
Ixtapan de la Sal 909
Ixtepec 960
Ixtlan del Río 896
Izalco 1082
Izamal 985
Izapa 961
Izcuchaca 736
Iztapa 1036
Izúcar de Matamoros 953

Jacmel 1211
Jacó 1156
Jaén 684
Jaguaribe 306
Jaji 815
Jalapa (Gua.) 1026
Jalapa (Mex.) 941
Jama 561
Jamaica 1235–1242
Janitzio 906
Jarabacoa 1221
Jauja 738
Jícaro Galán 1109
Jérémie 1212
Jibacoa 1201
Jicacal 939

Jilotepeque 1037
Jinotega 1124
Jinotepe 1130
Jipijapa 559
Joyabaj 1043
Joaçaba 291
João Pessoa 324
Jocotán 1028
Jocotepec 901
Jodensavanne 852
Joinville 291
Jost Van Dyke 1287
Juan Fernández Islands 407
Juazeiro 315
Juazeiro do Norte 324
Juchitán 960
Juiz de Fora 249
Jujuy 76
Juli 708
Juliaca 705
Jundiaí 277
Junín (Arg.) 81
Junín (Peru) 743
Junín de los Andes 123
Juticalpa 1111

Kabah 982
Kaieteur Fall 843
Kamarata 827
Kenscoff 1210
Kingston 1236
Kingstown 1266
Kirare 882
Klein Bonaire 1298
Kohunlich 975
Kourou 860
Kralendijk 1296
Kuelap 680

La Antigua 942
La Asunción 820
La Boquilla 472
La Ceiba 1097
La Ceja 506
La Congona 679
La Coronilla 779
La Cumbre 64
La Cumbrecita 66
La Democracia 1036
La Désirade 1308
La Dorada 480
La Esperanza (Ecu.) 554
La Esperanza (Hon.) 1106
La Falda 64
La Floresta 777
La Fría 811
La Grita 815
La Guaira 802
La Herradura 655
La Libertad (Ecu.) 558
La Libertad (El S.) 1078
La Lima 1102
La Merced 742
La Oroya 735
La Palma 1085
La Paloma 779
La Paz (Bol.) 157
La Paz (Entre Ríos) 100
La Paz (Hon.) 1108

La Paz (Mex.) 994
La Plata (Arg.) 53
La Plata (Ecu.) 516
La Punta 657
La Quiaca 79
La Rioja 91
La Romana 1224
La Serena 388
La Tinaja 940
La Tola 563
La Toma 82
La Tovara 895
La Unión (Col.) 509
La Unión (Peru) 745
La Unión/Cutuco 1080
La Vega 1220
La Victoria 509
Labadie 1211
Laberinto 733
Labná 983
Lago Agrio 589
Lagoa Santa 253
Lago de Tota 496
Lagoinha 274
Lagos de Moreno 885
Laguna 287
Laguna Colorada 188
Laguna de Alegría 1080
Laguna de Surucucho 578
Laguna La Cocha 521
Laguna Xelhá 990
Lagunas 746
Lagunas de Montebello 966
Lagunillas 403
Lajes 290
Lake Atitlán 1039
Lake Chapala 901
Lake Coatepeque 1083
Lake Güija 1084
Lake Ilopango 1077
Lake Nahuel Huapí 114
Lake Tequesquitengo 945
Lake Yojoa 1105
Lamas 682
Lambari 260
Lambayeque 684
Lambytieco 958
Lampa 705
Lanquín 1027
Laranjeiras 312
Las Cañas 1155
Las Cuevas 87
Las Grutas 127
Las Piedras 785
Las Tablas 1181
Latacunga 572
Lauca National Park 379
Lebu 417
Leeward Islands 1255–1260
Leguizamo 522
Leimebamba 679
Lençóis 308
León (Mex.) 886
León (Nic.) 1126
Lerma 910
Les Cayes 1212
Les Saintes 1308
Lethem 844
Leticia 490

Levanto 681
Líbano 481
Liberia 1158
Lican-Ray 422
Likin 1037
Lima 634
Limache 411
Limones 563
Linares 872
Linden 841
Linhares 248
Little Cayman 1278
Little Tobago 1250
Livingston 1030
Llaima 420
Llallagua 177
Llica 188
Llifén 426
Llolleo 406
Loja 579
Loltún 983
Loma Bonita 940
Loma Plata 624
Londres 90
Londrina 296
Loreto 994
Los Andes 411
Los Angeles 417
Los Chiles 1151
Los Chorros 1078
Los Cocos 65
Los Colorados 986
Los Encuentros 1041
Los Mochis 891
Los Reyes 904
Los Remedios 927
Los Roques 803
Los Santos 1181
Los Teques 804
Lota 417
Lubantum 1068
Lucea 1239
Luisiana 740
Luján 53
Luque 616

Macaé 241
Macapá 338
Macará 580
Macas 594
Maceió 312
Machachi 574
Machala 586
Machiques 811
Machu-Picchu 728
Macuro 821
Macuto 803
Magangué 480
Magdalena del Mar 655
Maicao 478
Maipo 406
Maiquetía 802
Malacatán 1050
Maldonado 778
Malinalco 909
Mamiña 381
Mana 862
Managua 1119
Manaus 341

Mandeville 1238
Mangaratiba 245
Manglaralto 559
Mango Creek 1068
Manhuaçu 259
Manhumirim 259
Manizales 506
Manta 559
Manu 722
Manuel Antonio 1156
Manzanillo 902
Mar del Plata 54
Mar Grande 306
Marabá 332
Maracay 805
Maracaibo 809
Maragogipe 308
Marajó 338
Marataizes 246
Marcahuasi 656
Marcala 1106
Marechal Deodoro 314
Margarita Island 820
Mariana 256
Marianao 1200
Marie-Galante 1308
Marigot 1309
Marina Cay 1286
Maringá 296
Mariquita 481
Mariscos 1031
Martín García 52
Martínez 52
Martinique 1303
Masachapa 1130
Masaya 1128
Mata de Limón 1155
Matagalpa 1124
Matamoros 871
Matanzas 1201
Matarani 696
Matehuala 877
Matinhos 296
Matucana 734
Maturín 821
Maullin 433
Mayagüez 1230
Mayapán 983
Mayreau 1269
Mazatenango 1051
Mazatlán 892
Medellín 502
Mehuin 426
Mejillones 383
Melaque 902
Melchor de Mencos 1033
Melgar 488
Melo 785
Mendoza 82
Mercaderes 519
Mercedes (Arg.) 81
Mercedes (Uru.) 782
Mérida (Arg.) 977
Mérida (Mex.) 813
Metapán 1084
Metepec 909
Mexicali 991
Mexico 867–1005
Mexico City 910

Middle Caicos 1270
Milagro 565
Milot 1211
Mina Clavero 65
Minas 784
Minas de Oro 1095
Minatitlán 968
Mira 555
Miraflores 655
Miramar 56
Miramar 95
Misahuallí 591
Misquitia 1111
Mitla 958
Mitú 490
Mixco Viejo 1025
Mocoa 522
Moengo 854
Molinos 74
Mollendo 696
Momostenango 1045
Momotombo 1125
Mompós 478
Monclova 876
Monday 620
Monte Albán 957
Monte Caseros 113
Monte Cristi (Dom. Rep.) 1222
Monte Hermoso 57
Monte Peruvia Lamud 681
Monte Santo 311
Monteagudo 186
Montecristi (Ecu.) 559
Montego Bay 1239
Montemorelos 872
Montería 473
Montero 193
Monterrey 871
Monteverde 1155
Montevideo 769
Montserrat 1260
Moquegua 696
Morales 1031
Morawhanna 842
Morelia 906
Morón 807
Morretes 295
Morro Branco 328
Morro de São Paulo 309
Mosqueiro 338
Mosquito Island 1287
Mossoró 326
Mount Orizaba 942
Mount Roraima 828
Moyobamba 681
Moyogalpa 1129
Mucuchíes 812
Muisné 561
Mulchén 418
Mulegé 994
Mustique 1269
Muzo 493

Nacaome 1109
Nagua 1223
Nahualá 1044
Nahuizalco 1083
Nakum 1035
Nandaime 1130

Naolinco 942
Nassau 1271
Natá 1181
Natal 325
Navajoa 891
Nazaré das Farinhas 307
Nazca 692
Nebaj 1044
Necochea 56
Negril 1238
Neiva 483
Nemocón 493
Netherlands Antilles 1289–1301
Neuquén 122
Nevis 1259
New Amsterdam 842
Nicoya 1157
Nicaragua 1116–1136
Nieuw Nickerie 854
Niterói 240
Nogales 890
Nohochtunich 1064
Norman Island 1286
Norogachi 882
North Caicos 1276
Nova Friburgo 243
Nova Jerusalém 323
Nova Lima 253
Nova Petrópolis 285
Nueva Ocotepeque 1104
Nueva Palmira 781
Nuevo Laredo 870

Oaxaca 954
Ocho Rios 1240
Ocongate 731
Ocós 1051
Ocosingo 971
Ocotal 1125
Ocú 1182
Ocumare de la Costa 805
Oeiras 330
Oiapoque 339
Oistins 1244
Ojinaga 881
Ojojona 1095
Olanchito 1100
Olinda 321
Olivos 52
Ollagüe 385
Ollantaitambo 725
Olocuilta 1081
Orán 80
Orange Walk 1064
Oranjestad 1294
Orizaba 935
Oropesa 722
Orosí 1149
Oruro 175
Osa Peninsula 1160
Osório 285
Osorno 426
Otatitlán 939
Otavalo 551
Otusco 674
Ouro Preto 254
Outeiro 337
Ovalle 389
Oxapampa 742

Oxcutzcab 983

Pacarijtambo 722
Pacasmayo 675
Pacaya 1025
Pachacámac 655
Pachuca 873
Paipa 495
Paita 687
Pajatén 674
Palenque 971
Palma Sola 807
Palmar Sur 1161
Palmira 510
Palín 1036
Pamplona 500
Panajachel 1039
Panama 1166–1192
Panama City 1174
Panamá Viejo 1179
Pañamarca 660
Panchimalco 1077
Pandi 488
Panguipulli 425
Pantanal 356
Pão de Açúcar 238
Papallacta 550
Papaloapan 940
Papantla 876
Paplaya 1112
Papudo 406
Paquetá Island 239
Paracas 690
Paracho 904
Paracuru 328
Paraguaná Peninsula 808
Paraguarí 621
Paraguay 606–629
Paraíso 970
Paramaribo 850
Paramonga 658
Paraná 98
Paranaguá 295
Parati 246
Paredón 961
Paricutín 904
Parika 842
Parinacota 379
Pariti 173
Parnaíba 329
Paso Canoas 1161
Paso de la Patria 102
Paso de los Libres 113
Paso de los Toros 785
Paso Río Mayo 132
Pasto 519
Pativilca 658
Patos 324
Patu 326
Pátzcuaro 905
Patzicía 1038
Patzún 1038
Paucartambo 722
Paulo Afonso 314
Paysandú 782
Pearl Islands 1173
Pedasí 1182
Pedernales (Ecu.) 561
Pedernales (Ven.) 822

Pedro Juan Caballero 618
Pelileo 570
Pelotas 286
Penedo 312
Penedo 244
Penonomé 1181
Pereira 508
Perito Moreno 133
Peru 630–765
Pespire 1109
Peter Island 1287
Pétionville 1210
Petit Martinique 1269
Petit St. Vincent 1269
Petrohué 429
Petrolina 315
Petrópolis 242
Peulla 429
Philipsburg 1298
Pica 381
Pichidangui 390
Pichucalco 970
Pico de Jaraguá 271
Pico Duarte 1221
Piedecuesta 500
Piedra Buena 135
Piedras Negras (Gua.) 1034
Piedras Negras (Mex.) 876
Pilar 618
Pimentel 682
Pinamar 54
Piñar del Río 1201
Pine Cay 1276
Pinotepa 951
Pirapora 258
Pirapora de Bom Jesus 278
Pirenópolis 352
Piriápolis 777
Piribebuy 619
Piripiri 330
Pisco 689
Pisté 984
Pitalito 484
Pitch Lake 1249
Piura 685
Placencia 1067
Planeta Rica 472
Playa Azul 950
Playa del Carmen 989
Playa del Coco 1157
Playa Dorada 1222
Playa Grande 1222
Playa Junquillal 1157
Playa Naranjo 1158
Playa San Rafael 779
Playa Tamarindo 1157
Playa Vicente 940
Playas 557
Plymouth 1261
Pochutla 953
Poços de Caldas 260
Pointe-à-Pitre 1306
Pomabamba 662
Pomaire 402
Pomata 708
Pomerode 291
Ponce 1230
Poneloya 1127
Ponta Grossa 296

Ponta Porã 354
Popayán 514
Popocatépetl 929
Poptún 1032
Porlamar 820
Port Antonio 1240
Port-au-Prince 1207
Port of Spain 1248
Port Royal 1238
Port Salut 1212
Portezuelo (Mex.) 873
Portezuelo (Uru.) 778
Portillo 402
Porto Alegre 281
Porto Seguro 310
Porto Velho 348
Portobelo 1170
Portoviejo 560
Porvenir 443
Posadas 103
Posorja 558
Potosí 181
Potrerillos (Arg.) 85
Potrerillos (Hon.) 1105
Poza Rica 875
Pozuzo 742
Prado 483
Prados 250
Praia do Francês 314
Prainha 328
Presidente Epitácio 276
Presidente Prudente 278
Progreso 981
Providencia 473
Providenciales 1276
Pucallpa 748
Pucón 422
Pucusana 689
Puebla 931
Pueblo Libre 655
Puente del Inca 87
Puerta de Talampaya 89
Puerto Acosta 173
Puerto Alvarado 938
Puerto Angel 952
Puerto Arista 961
Puerto Armuelles 1183
Puerto Asís 522
Puerto Ayacucho 824
Puerto Ayora 598
Puerto Aysén 436
Puerto Baquerizo Moreno 600
Puerto Barrios 1029
Puerto Bermúdez 743
Puerto Berrío 480
Puerto Bolívar 586
Puerto Boyacá 480
Puerto Cabello 806
Puerto Cabezas 1133
Puerto Carreño 489
Puerto Chacabuco 436
Puerto Colombia 466
Puerto Cortés 1096
Puerto Deseado 133
Puerto Escondido 951
Puerto Ibáñez 437
Puerto Iguazú 109
Puerto Juárez 986
Puerto La Cruz 818

Puerto Lempira 1111
Puerto Limón 1150
Puerto López (Col.) 489
Puerto López (Ecu.) 559
Puerto Madero 961
Puerto Madryn 128
Puerto Maldonado 731
Puerto Montt 430
Puerto Natales 441
Puerto Octay 427
Puerto Ordaz 824
Puerto Pirámides 129
Puerto Pizarro 689
Puerto Plata 1222
Puerto Quepos 1156
Puerto Rico 1227–1234
Puerto Rico (Col.) 487
Puerto Salgar 481
Puerto Suárez 194
Puerto Ubirique 742
Puerto Vallarta 896
Puerto Varas 428
Puerto Viejo 1152
Puerto Viejo de Sarapiquí 1152
Puerto Villarroel 194
Puerto Williams 443
Pujilí 572
Puno 705
Punta Arenas (Chi) 438
Punta Ballena 778
Punta Cana 1224
Punta Carnero 558
Punta del Este 778
Punta Gorda 1068
Punta Tombo 131
Puntarenas (CR) 1154
Punto Fijo 808
Puquío 694
Puracé 516
Puruchuco 656
Putumayo 521
Puya Raimondii 666
Puyo 590

Quebraya 173
Quelapa 1080
Quellón 435
Quequén 57
Querétaro 878
Quevedo 556
Quezaltenango 1046
Quibdó 506
Quíbor 809
Quiché 1042
Quillabamba 730
Quillacollo 180
Quillota 411
Quilmes 52
Quilotoa 573
Quilpue 411
Quincemil 731
Quinchamalí 413
Quintero 406
Quiriguá 1029
Quiroga 904
Quistacocha 750
Quito 537

Rabinal 1025

Ralún 430
Rama 1132
Rancagua 412
Raqchi 722
Ráquira 493
Rawson 130
Real de Catorce 877
Recife 315
Reconquista 100
Recuay 666
Redonda 1258
Registro 275
Resistencia 100
Retalhuleu 1051
Riberalta 196
Rincón 1230
Río Azul 1035
Río Blanco (Chi.) 411
Rio Branco (Bra.) 350
Río Branco (Uru.) 785
Río Claro 809
Río Cuarto 61
Rio das Ostras 241
Rio de Janeiro 218
Río Dulce 1031
Río Gallegos 135
Río Grande (Arg.) 142
Rio Grande (Bra.) 285
Río Lagartos 985
Río San Juan 1222
Río Turbio 136
Río Villegas 119
Riobamba 565
Riohacha 477
Rioja 681
Rionegro 505
Riosucio 508
Rivas 1130
Rivera 785
Road Town 1285
Roatán 1099
Rocafuerte 563
Rocha 779
Rodríguez Clara 940
Rondonópolis 359
Roque Sáenz Peña 94
Rosario (Arg.) 97
Rosario (Uru.) 781
Rosario de la Frontera 69
Roseau 1262
Runaway Bay 1240
Rurópolis 333

Saba 1300
Sabará 254
Sacapulas 1043
Sacsayhuamán 721
St.-Barthélémy 1309
St. Croix 1284
St. Eustatius 1300
St. George (Bermuda) 1280
St. George's (Grenada) 1267
St.-Georges de l'Oyapoc 862
St. John (Antigua) 1256
St. John's (USVI) 1283
St. Joseph 1249
St. Kitts 1258
St.-Laurent du Maroni 861
St. Lucia 1263
St.-Martin 1309
St. Thomas 1283
St. Vincent 1266
Sajama 177
Salamá 1025
Salasaca 569
Salaverry 670
Salcajá 1045
Salcedo 572
Saldaña 483
Salina Cruz 959
Salinas 558
Salinópolis 338
Salt Cay 1276
Salt Island 1286
Salta 69
Saltillo 876
Salto 783
Salto Grande 784
Salto de Tequendama 489
Salto del Laja 414
Salvador 297
Samachique 882
Samaná 1223
Sámara 1157
San Agustín 484
San Agustín del Valle Fértil 89
San Andrés 473
San Andrés de Pisimbalá 517
San Andrés Semetebaj 1041
San Andrés Tuxtla 938
San Angel 927
San Antón 945
San Antonio (Chi.) 406
San Antonio (Belize) 1068
San Antonio (Ven.) 816
San Antonio Aguas Calientes 1024
San Antonio de Areco 59
San Antonio de Ibarra 553
San Antonio de Oriente 1110
San Antonio de los Cobres 75
San Antonio Oeste 127
San Antonio Palopó 1041
San Bartolomé 734
San Bernardino 619
San Blas 894
San Blas Islands 1171
San Carlos (Arg.) 74
San Carlos (CR) 1153
San Carlos (Nic.) 1129
San Carlos (Pan.) 1181
San Carlos (Ven.) 817
San Cosme y Damián 621
San Cristóbal (DR) 1223
San Cristóbal (Ven.) 815
San Cristóbal de Las Casas 963
San Cristóbal Totonicapán 1045
San Cristóbal Verapaz 1026
San Felipe (Chi.) 411
San Felipe (Gua.) 1051
San Felipe (Mex.) 986
San Felipe (Mex.) 993
San Felipe (Ven.) 808
San Félix 824
San Fernando (Chi.) 412
San Fernando (TT) 1249
San Fernando de Apure 817
San Francisco 740
San Francisco El Alto 1045

San Gabriel 555
San Germán 1230
San Gil 497
San Ignacio (Belize) 1065
San Ignacio (Mex.) 993
San Ignacio Miní 105
San Isidro (Arg.) 52
San Isidro (Peru) 654
San Isidro de El General 1159
San Jacinto 472
San Jerónimo 738
San Jorge 1129
San José (Gua.) 1036
San José (CR) 1140
San José de Chiquitos 194
San José de Jachal 89
San José del Cabo 996
San José de la Montaña 1153
San José Purúa 908
San Juan (Arg.) 88
San Juan (PR) 1228
San Juan Bautista 621
San Juan Cosalá 901
San Juan de Los Morros 804
San Juan del Norte 1132
San Juan del Obispo 1023
San Juan del Río 879
San Juan del Sur 1131
San Juan de la Maguana 1224
San Juan Sacatepéquez 1025
San Juanito 882
San Julián 134
San Lorenzo (Arg.) 98
San Lorenzo (Ecu.) 563
San Lorenzo (Hon.) 1109
San Lorenzo (Par.) 618
San Lucas Sacatepéquez 1024
San Lucas Tolimán 1041
San Luis (Arg.) 81
San Luis (Hon.) 1103
San Luis (Mex.) 889
San Luis de la Paz 878
San Luis Potosí 878
San Marcos 1050
San Martín 1050
San Martín de los Andes 124
San Mateo Ixtatán 1049
San Miguel (Col.) 522
San Miguel (Uru.) 780
San Miguel de Allende 888
San Miguel Regla 875
San Pedro 1050
San Pedro Carchá 1027
San Pedro Colombia 1068
San Pedro de Atacama 385
San Pedro de Cajas 741
San Pedro de Macorís 1224
San Pedro La Laguna 1041
San Pedro Sacatepéquez 1024
San Pedro Sula 1101
San Quintín 993
San Rafael (Arg.) 82
San Rafael (Col.) 523
San Ramón (Peru) 742
San Ramón (CR) 1154
San Salvador 1072
San Sebastián 1079
San Vicente (Ecu.) 560
San Vicente (El S.) 1079

San Vito 1160
Sandoná 519
Sangay 594
Sangolquí 550
Santa Ana 1083
Santa Bárbara (Col.) 506
Santa Bárbara (Hon.) 1103
Santa Catalina Palopó 1041
Santa Clara 1181
Santa Clara 1201
Santa Clara de Choroní 805
Santa Cruz (Arg.) 134
Santa Cruz (Bol.) 190
Santa Cruz (CR) 1157
Santa Cruz (Mex.) 896
Santa Elena 1155
Santa Elena de Uairen 828
Santa Fe 99
Santa Leopoldina 248
Santa Lucía 1095
Santa María (Arg.) 69
Santa María (Peru) 689
Santa María de Dota 1159
Santa María de Jesús 1024
Santa María del Rosario 1201
Santa Marta 475
Santa Rosa (Arg.) 58
Santa Rosa (Peru) 682
Santa Rosa de Copán 1103
Santa Rosa de Lima 1080
Santa Rosalía 994
Santa Tecla 1077
Santa Teresa 238
Santa Teresa 248
Santana do Livramento 286
Santarém 339
Santiago (Chi.) 392
Santiago (Cuba) 1202
Santiago (Pan.) 1182
Santiago Atitlán 1040
Santiago de Chuco 674
Santiago de Los Caballeros 1221
Santiago del Estero 94
Santiago Tianpuistengo 909
Santiago Tuxtla 938
Santiago Volcano 1128
Santo Amaro da Purificação 307
Santo Ângelo 287
Santo Antônio de Pádua 242
Santo Domingo (Chi.) 407
Santo Domingo (DR) 1214
Santo Domingo (Uru.) 782
Santo Domingo de los Colorados 556
Santos 271
São Cristóvão 312
São Félix 307
São Francisco do Sul 291
São João del Rei 249
São Joaquim 290
São Lourenço 260
São Luís 330
São Miguel 287
São Paulo 262
São Pedro de Aldeia 241
São Sebastião 273
São Tomé das Letras 261
Saquarema 241
Saquisilí 573
Saraguro 579

Sarameriza 684
Sarchí 1154
Satipo 742
Saül 861
Sayaxché 1034
Sebol 1034
Sechín 659
Sechura 686
Sensuntepeque 1079
Serra Negra 278
Serro 258
Sete Cidades 330
Shell-Mera 590
Sibambe 565
Sibundoy 522
Sicuani 710
Sierra de la Ventana 58
Sierra Nevada de Mérida 811
Sierra Nevada del Cocuy 497
Sierras of Córdoba 63
Siguatepeque 1106
Sillustani 709
Silvia 515
Sincelejo 472
Sint Maarten 1298
Siquirres 1151
Sixaola 1152
Sobral 329
Socorro 497
Socosani 703
Sogamoso 496
Soledad 466
Solís 777
Sololá 1038
Sonsón 506
Sonsonate 1082
Sontecomapan 939
Sopó 464
Sorata 170
Sorocaba 278
Sosúa 1222
South Caicos 1276
Soyaltepec 940
Spanish Town 1238
Springlands 842
Stanley 864
Statia 1300
Stoelmanseiland 853
Súa 563
Sucre 184
Sucúa 592
Sullana 687
Sumpango 1037
Supe 658
Suriname 849–858

Tabatinga 346
Taboga Island 1173
Tacna 697
Tactic 1026
Tafí del Valle 68
Tairona 477
Talara 687
Talca 412
Talcahuano 416
Taltal 387
Tamazunchale 873
Tambo Colorado 691
Tambo de Mora 689

Tampico 872
Tandil 56
Tantamayo 744
Tapachula 960
Tapalpa 901
Taquile 708
Tarabuco 186
Tarapoto 682
Tarija 189
Tarma 741
Tastil 75
Taxco 946
Tazumal 1083
Teapa 970
Tecamachalco 935
Tecolutla 876
Tecomán 902
Tecpán 1038
Tecún Umán (Ayutla) 1051
Tefé 346
Tegucigalpa 1091
Tehuacán 935
Tehuantepec 959
Tekax 983
Tela 1096
Temascal 940
Temuco 419
Tena 592
Tenancingo 909
Tenango de Arista 909
Tenayuca 927
Tenejapa 966
Tenosique 981
Teófilo Otôni 259
Teotenango 909
Teotihuacán 928
Teotitlán del Valle 958
Tepeaca 933
Tepic 895
Tepozotlán 928
Tepoztlán 945
Tequesquiapán 880
Teresina 329
Teresópolis 242
Termas de Daymán 784
Termas de Jahuel 411
Termas de Puyehue 427
Termas de Reyes 77
Termas de Río Hondo 94
Termas de Socos 390
Termas del Arapey 784
Texcoco 929
Texmelucan 930
Teziutlán 942
Tiahuanaco 170
Ticul 983
Tierra Blanca 940
Tierra del Fuego (Arg.) 139
Tierra del Fuego (Chi.) 443
Tierradentro 517
Tigre 52
Tijuana 992
Tijuca National Park 239
Tikal 1033
Tilapa 1051
Tilcara 77
Timotes 812
Tingo 703
Tingo María 745

Tinharé 308
Tinogasta 90
Tinta 722
Tipitapa 1123
Tipón 722
Tiradentes 249
Tizimín 985
Tlacochahuaya 958
Tlacolula 958
Tlacotalpan 939
Tlalnepantla 927
Tlalpan 926
Tlalpujahua 908
Tlamacas 930
Tlaquepaque 899
Tlaxcala 930
Tlaxcalantzingo 931
Tobago 1250
Tocaima 489
Toconao 386
Tocopilla 381
Todos Los Santos 996
Todos Santos Cuchumatán 1049
Toluca 908
Tonalá 960
Tonantzintla 931
Tonchigüe 563
Tonina 971
Tonocatepeque 1079
Topolobampo 892
Toquepala 697
Torreón 883
Torres 284
Torres del Paine 442
Tortola 1285
Tortuguero 1151
Totness 854
Totonicapán 1044
Tovar 815
Tracunhaém 323
Tramandaí 284
Trancoso 310
Treinta y Tres 785
Trelew 130
Tres Arroyos 57
Tres Corações 261
Tres Lagoas 354
Tres Marias 258
Tres Valles 940
Tres Zapotes 938
Trevelin 121
Trinidad (Bol.) 195
Trinidad (Cuba) 1201
Trinidad (Par.) 622
Trinidad and Tobago 1247–1254
Triúnfo 323
Trujillo (Hon.) 1100
Trujillo (Peru) 670
Trujillo (Ven.) 812
Tubarão 288
Tucacas 807
Tucumán 66
Tucupita 825
Tula 929
Tulcán 555
Tulum 989
Tumaco 521
Tumbes 688
Tumeremo 827

Tungurahua 571
Tunja 494
Tupiza 188
Turbaco 472
Turbo 473
Turks and Caicos Islands 1275–1276
Turrialba 1149
Tutule 1108
Tuxpan 908
Tuxtepec 940
Tuxtla Gutiérrez 961
Tzintzuntzán 904

US Virgin Islands 1282
Uaxactún 1035
Ubajará 329
Ubatuba 275
Uberaba 261
Uberlândia 261
Ujarrás 1149
Union Island 1269
Unión Juárez 961
Urmiri 170
Uruapan 903
Urubamba; 724
Uruguaiana 286
Uruguay 766–790
Ushuaia 140
Uspallata 86
Usulután 1081
Utila 1098
Uyuni 187
Uxmal 982

Valdivia 423
Valença 308
Valencia 806
Valera 811
Valladolid 985
Valle de Angeles 1095
Valle de Bravo 908
Valle de la Luna (Ischigualasto) 89
Valle de las Leñas 86
Valle Hermoso 64
Valledupar 477
Vallenar 387
Valparaíso 403
Varadero 1201
Vedado 1200
Vélez 497
Venado Tuerto 61
Venecia 1153
Venezuela 791–835
Venustiano Carranza 966
Veracruz 936
Victoria 805
Vicuña 389
Viedma 127
Vila Velha 294
Vilcabamba 579
Vilcashuamán 740
Villa Carlos Paz 64
Villa de Leiva 495
Villa de María 65
Villa Dolores 65
Villa Florida 621
Villa General Belgrano 66
Villa Gesell 54
Villa Insurgentes 994

Villa Isla 940
Villa La Angostura 119
Villa María 61
Villa Mercedes 81
Villa Montes 186
Villa Obregón 927
Villa Serrano 186
Villa Traful 124
Villa Tunari 194
Villa Unión 89
Villahermosa 969
Villarrica (Chi.) 420
Villarrica (Par.) 619
Villavicencio 489
Villazón 188
Villeta (Col.) 488
Villeta (Par.) 616
Viña del Mar 405
Viñales 1201
Virgin Islands 1282–1288
Visconde de Mauá 244
Vistahermosa 490
Vitória 247
Vitória da Conquista 306
Volta Redonda 244

Wageningen 854
Washabo 855
Willcawain 666
Willemstad 1290
Windward Islands 1261–1269

X-Lapak 983
X-Puhil 975
Xavantina 352
Xcalak 975
Xcaret 989
Xochicalco 945
Xochimilco 926
Xunantunich 1066

Yacanto 65
Yacuiba 194
Yaguachi 565
Yaguarón 621

Yagul 958
Yaino 662
Yalape 681
Yanahuara 703
Yanhuitlán 958
Yare 803
Yarinacocha 749
Yarumal 505
Yavi 79
Yaviza 1185
Yaxchilán 973
Yaxhá 1035
Ybicuy 616
Yopal 497
Yukay 723
Yungay 662
Yunguyo 709
Yura 703
Yurimaguas 746
Yuriria 908
Yuscarán 1110

Zaachila 959
Zacapa 1027
Zacatecas 884
Zacatecoluca 1081
Zacatlán 875
Zacualpa 1043
Zacualpan 896
Zaculeu 1048
Zamora (Ecu.) 594
Zamora (Mex.) 903
Zapala 123
Zapallar 406
Zárate 97
Zempoala 942
Zepita 708
Zihuatanejo 950
Zimapán 873
Zinacantán 966
Zipaquirá 492
Zorritos 689
Zumbahua 573
Zunil 1051
Zunzal 1078
Zurite 724

INDEX TO ADVERTISERS

Page

AIRLINES
Air France, London	Endpaper 'd'
Iberia Airlines, London	Back Cover
Varig Brazilian Airlines, London	204
VIASA, London	Endpaper 'f'

BANKERS
Lloyds Bank PLC, London	Endpaper 'b'
Thomas Cook Travellers Cheques	Endpaper 'c'

BOOKS, GUIDES, ETC.
A. Burton Garbett, Morden, Surrey	Map Section
Bradt Publications, Chalfont St. Peter	669
Foster Cherrington, London	20
Traveller's Handbook	Endpaper 'e'

HOTELS AND RESTAURANTS
Hostal Barranco, Peru	643
Casa del Corregidor, Bolivia	161
Hotel El Casco, Argentina	115
Fort George Hotel, Belize	1056
Residencial Rosario, Bolivia	160
Hotel Las Dunas, Peru	Map Section
Hostal Residencial Torreblanca, Peru	645

LANGUAGE SCHOOLS
Academia de Espanol, Ecuador	546
Cuauhnahuac, Mexico	944
Experiencia, Mexico	945

PERUVIAN PRINTS AND DESIGNS
Silvania Prints, Peru	647

SAFETY MEASURES
Leg Pouch	28

TRANSPORT
Rosario Turibus, Bolivia	169
Colectur, Peru	706

TRAVEL SPECIALISTS
Coltur, Ecuador	598
Encounter Overland, London	268
Ecuador Travel, London	557
Exodus Expeditions, London	670
Galapagos Cruises, Ecuador	597
Holidays in Copacabana, Brazil	221
Journey Latin America, London	6
Ladatco Tours, Brazil	362
Melia Travel, London	Endpaper 'a'
Metropolitan Touring, Ecuador	593
Peruvian Andean Treks, Peru	719
Thomas Cook, Peterborough	Endpaper 'b'
Trailfinders, London	30
Turismo Balsa, Bolivia	171
Twickers World, Twickenham	Map Section
Vida Tours, Peru	726
Wilderness Expeditions, Peru	652

WHISKY
Johnnie Walker	4

THOMAS COOK TRAVELLERS CHEQUES EMERGENCY ASSISTANCE POINTS

Argentina

Buenos Aires	THOMAS COOK	25 de Mayo 140-8° piso	30-3988, 2790, 2730

Bolivia

Cochabamba	Banco del Estado	Calle Nataniel Aguirre, esq. Jordan No. 3860	4600
La Paz	Wagons-lits	Av. Mcal. Santa Cruz esq. Colón	358499, 372822
Oruro	Banco del Estado	Calle La Plata	50360
Santa Cruz	Banco del Estado	Plaza 24 de Septiembre	2-2171

Brazil

São Paulo	THOMAS COOK	Rua Haddock Lobo 337-2 Andar	259-3022
Aracaju	Banco do Brasil	Praça General Valadão 341	222-0234
Bagé	Banco do Brasil	Rua General Sampaio 99	2-2320
Belém	Banco do Brasil	Av. Presidente Vargas 248	223-5291
Belo Horizonte	Wagons-lits	Rua Pernambuco 1000, Lojas 35/6	224-2688
Blumenau	Banco do Brasil	Rua 15 de Novembro 1525	22-3144
Brasilia	Wagons-lits	Galeria Hotel Nacional 21/49	225-8084
Campina Grande	Banco do Brasil	Rua 7 de Setembro 52	321-3317
Campinas	Banco do Brasil	Rua Reg Feijo 914	31-5911
Corumbá	Banco do Brasil	Rua Treze de Junho 914	231-2713
Curitiba	Wagons-lits	Rue Marechal Deodoro 630, Loja 64	232-4344
Florianópolis	Banco do Brasil	Praça 15 de Novembro 20	22-7000
Fortaleza	Banco do Brasil	Rua Barão do Rio Branco 1515	226-7710
Foz do Iguaçu	Banco do Brasil	Av. Brasil 1365	72-3344
Ilhéus	Banco do Brasil	Rua Marquês de Paranaguá 112	231-1218
Itabuna	Banco do Brasil	Praça Olintho Leoni S/N	211-5321
Itajai	Banco do Brasil	Rua Felipe Schmitt 454	44-2602
João Pessoa	Banco do Brasil	Praça 1817 129	221-2203
Joinville	Banco do Brasil	Rua São Joaquim 128	22-2000
Maceió	Banco do Brasil	Rua Senador Mendonça 120	223-2489
Manaus	Wagons-lits	Av. Eduardo Ribeiro, 520 5/208	234-7553
Natal	Banco do Brasil	Av. Rio Branco 510	222-5411
Niterói	Banco do Brasil	Av. Amaral Peixoto 347	719-6006
Paranaguá	Banco do Brasil	Largo Cônego Alcidino 103	22-0958
Parnaiba	Banco do Brasil	Praça da Graça 340	322-1911
Passo Fundo	Banco do Brasil	Rua Bento Gonçalves 377	312-2566
Pelotas	Banco do Brasil	Rua Lobo da Costa 1315	22-7240
Porto Alegre	Wagons-lits	Rua Dos Andradas, 1273 S/1103/4	24-5044
Recife	Wagons-lits	Av. Conselheiro Aguiar, 3150-LJ I	326-4419
Rio de Janeiro	Wagons-lits	156 Av. Rio Branco, Salas 2506/7	262-3721
Rio Grande	Banco do Brasil	Rua Benjamin Constant 72	2-1001
Salvador	Wagons-lits	Rua Fonte Do Boi 216	248-4525
Santana do Livramento	Banco do Brasil	Rua dos Andradas 525	242-2488
Santos	Banco do Brasil	Rua 15 de Novembro 195	34-4496
São Francisco do Sul	Banco do Brasil	Rua Hercilio Luz 53	44-0375
São Luis	Banco do Brasil	Av. Gomes de Castro 46	222-0055
Teresina	Banco do Brasil	Rua Alvaro Mendes 1313	222-6611
Uruguaiana	Banco do Brasil	Rua Bento Martins 2609	412-2048
Vitória	Banco do Brasil	Praça Pio XII 30	223-4763

Chile

Concepción	Banco O'Higgins	Barros Araña 399	21110
Punta Areñas	Banco O'Higgins	Calle Roca No. 800	21344
Rancagua	Banco O'Higgins	Campos 350	22940
Santiago	Wagons-lits	Calle Agustinas 1058	698-2827/8
Valparaiso	Banco O'Higgins	Prat 882	52701

Colombia

Bogotá	Wagons-lits	Calle 85 No. 11-18	257-83-66
Cali	Banco Royal Colombiano	Carrera 3 No. 11-03	861105
Cartagena	Banco Royal Colombiano	Plaza del Ecuador	40-420
Medellin	Banco Royal Colombiano	Carrera 46 No. 49-19	421817

Ecuador

Quito	Ecuacambio	Av. de la Republica 192	445-885

Falkland Islands

Stanley	Falkland Islands Trading Company	Port Stanley	

French Guiana

Cayenne	Banque Française Commerciale	25 Rue François Arago	31-06-83

Guyana			
Georgetown	Royal Bank of Canada	38-39 Water Street	61691
Paraguay			
Asunción	Yguazú Casa de Cambios	Palma 547	90134
Ciudad Presidente Stroessner	Yguazú Casa de Cambios	Av. Monseñor Rodriguez E/7a y 8a	8121
Peru			
Cuzco	Wagons-lits	Calle San Agustin 327	221641
Lima	Wagons-lits	780 Calle Camaná, Oficina 508	287643
Surinam			
Paramaribo	De Surinaamsche Bank	Gravenstraat 26-28	71100
Uruguay			
Montevideo	Wagons-lits	Avenida Gral. Rondeau 1392	91-1426
Venezuela			
Caracas	THOMAS COOK	Edificio 'Cavendes', P1507 OFC706, Av. Francisco de Miranda, Los Palos Grandes, 1060	2-284-3866
Valencia	Wagons-lits	Edif. Hotel de Paris, local 7 Avenida Bolivar	213-965

CENTRAL AMERICA

Belize			
Belize	Belize Bank of Commerce and Industry	60 Market Square	02-3232
Costa Rica			
San José	Chase S.A.	50 M Sur Kiosko-Parque Morazán	21-6681
Guatemala			
Guatemala	Banco Nacional de la Vivienda	6A Avenue 1-22	31-4038
Honduras			
La Ceiba	Banco Atlántida	Av. San Isidro 1 Calle	42-2432
San Pedro Sula	Banco Atlántida	1 VP, 3 Av. 1 Calle	54-0107
Tegucigalpa	Banco Atlántida	5 Avenida No. 503	32-1742

Mexico

Telephone MasterCard New York 212 - 974 - 5696 (collect)

Mexico City	THOMAS COOK	Campos Eliseos No. 345-12 Floor, Col. Polanco	596-8430
Acapulco	Wagons-lits	Av. Costera Miguel Alemán 239	2-2864
Cancún	Wagons-lits	Hotel Camiño Real	3-0100
Chihuahua	Wagons-lits	1412 Avenida Independencia	15-7320
Ciudad Juárez	Wagons-lits	Ave. de Las Américas 168-7	3-5512/3
Cuernavaca	Wagons-lits	Melchor Ocampo, 1 Plaza Real	12-5950
Durango	Wagons-lits	409-B-Sur Calle Juárez	1-7204
Guadalajara	Wagons-lits	Avenida Vallarta 1447	25-8033/4
Guanajuato	Wagons-lits	Lobby, Hotel Real de Minas, Najayote No.17	2-1836
Hermosillo	Wagons-lits	86 Rosales, Local 1, Conjunto de Rosales y Morelia	2-2277
Ixtapa	Wagons-lits	Hotel Camino Real, Playa Vista, Hermosa	4-3188
León	Wagons-lits	Conjunto Estrella Local 5, Boulevard López Mateos 1303, Oriente	4-0918
Mazatlan	Wagons-lits	Angel Flores 806 Pte.	1-6294
Mérida	Wagons-lits	Plaza Colón 501-C, Local 108-D	554-11
Monterrey	Wagons-lits	Avenida Zaragoza 1000, Local C-1	42-7930
Morelia	Wagons-lits	Hotel Virrey de Mendoza, Portal Matamoros 16	2-7620
Puebla	Wagons-lits	43 Oriente No. 21, Local "L"-11	40-8743
Puerto Vallarta	Wagons-lits	Lobby Hotel Camino Real, Playa Las Estacas	2-0317
Querétaro	Wagons-lits	Centro Comercial, Plaza Niza, Poniente No. 2	4-3020
Saltillo	Wagons-lits	414 Guadalupe Victoria	2-0992
Toluca	Wagons-lits	Vicente Villada No. 125 Pte.C.	4-6895
Torreón	Wagons-lits	464 Avenida Morelos Poniente	2-4409
Tuxtla Gutiérrez	Wagons-lits	Lobby Hotel Flamboyant, Bd Dr. Belisario Dominguez 1081	2-9311
Veracruz	Wagons-lits	Hotel Prendes, 1076 Avenida 5 de Mayo	2-2257
Villahermosa	Wagons-lits	Gregorio Mendes y Pages Llergo, Centro Comercial Celorio	2-6268

Panama			
Panama	Banco General	Av. Cuba y Calle 34	25-0000

WEST INDIES

Telephone MasterCard New York 212-974-5696 (collect)

Antigua			
St. John's	Royal Bank of Canada	25-26 High Street, AT Market	4620325
Bahamas			
Nassau	Royal Bank of Canada	323 Bay Street	322-8700
Barbados			
Bridgetown	Royal Bank of Canada	Broad Street	65-200
Cayman Islands			
George Town	Royal Bank of Canada	Central	9-4600
Dominica			
Roseau	Royal Bank of Canada	Bayfront	2771
Dominican Republic			
La Romana	Banco del Comercio Dominicano	Calle Trinitaria 59 Esq. E. A. Miranda	556-2210
Puerto Plata	Banco del Comercio Dominicano	Calle Duarte, Esq. Padre Castellanos	586-2350
Santo Domingo	Banco del Comercio Dominicano	Ave. 27 de Febrero, Esq Winston Churchill	567-8871
Grenada			
St. George's	Grenada Bank of Commerce	Corner Cross & Halifax Streets	3521
Guadeloupe			
Pointe à Pitre	Société Générale de Banque aux Antilles	Rue Frébault 30	82-54-23
Haiti			
Port-au-Prince	Société Générale Hatienie de Banque	Rue Abraham Lincoln & Rue des Miracles 18	2-4800
Jamaica			
Kingston	Mutual Security Bank	37 Duke Street	922-6710
Mandeville	Mutual Security Bank	9 Manchester Square	962-2886
May Pen	Mutual Security Bank	52 Main Street	986-2592
Montego Bay	Mutual Security Bank	4 Sam Sharpe Square	952-3641
St. Elizabeth	Mutual Security Bank	High Street, Black River	965-2207
Martinique			
Fort-de-France	Crédit Martiniquais	Rue de la Liberté	71-1240
Montserrat			
Plymouth	Royal Bank of Canada	Parliament Street	2426
Netherlands Antilles			
Aruba	Caribbean Mercantile Bank	Nassaustraat 53, Oranjestad	3118
Bonaire	Maduro & Curiel's Bank	Kerkstraat/Breedestraat, Kraalendijk	8420
Curaçao	Maduro & Curiel's Bank	De Ruytersplein 2, Willemstad	11352
St. Maarten	Windward Islands Bank	Philipsburg	3485
Puerto Rico			
Hato Rey	Royal Bank of Canada	255 Ponce de León Avenue	753 2000
St. Kitts			
Basseterre	Royal Bank of Canada	Central	2389
St. Lucia			
Castries	St. Lucia Coop Bank	21 Bridge Street	2881
St. Vincent			
Kingstown	Caribbean Banking Corporation	No. 81 South River Road	61502
Trinidad & Tobago			
Port of Spain	National Commercial Bank	62 Independence Square	62-52893
San Fernando	National Commercial Bank	High & Penitence Streets	652-2757

In many Latin American countries there is a vigorous parallel (black) market for both travellers cheques and U.S. Dollar notes. (This may be with or without Government permission).

Rates are usually slightly better for notes but travellers cheques are obviously safer, which is especially important when theft is becoming more common.

You should shop around for rates since these may vary considerably. Hotel rates in particular tend to be poor.

Do not take currencies other than U.S. Dollar, if accepted at all the rate will be poor.

In some countries only specific bank branches may deal in foreign exchange and you may have difficulty obtaining local currency when far from capital cities.

AIR FRANCE TO LATIN AMERICA.
TWELVE WAYS
TO WING YOUR WAY IN STYLE.

AIR FRANCE

158 New Bond Street, London W1Y 0AY. Tel: 01-449 9511. Heathrow Airport: 01-759 2311
Manchester: 061-436 3800. Cargo Bookings: 01-897 2811. Prestel: 202423.

THE TRAVELLER'S HANDBOOK

EDITED BY MELISSA SHALES

New Edition - Completely Revised & Updated

New from Trade & Travel
The Completely Revised
5th Edition
864 pages
Paperback
ISBN 0 905802 04 7
£9.95

- designed to help plan any trip abroad
- everything the independent traveller needs to know
- 864 information packed pages
- 300 page Directory of useful names and addresses
- essential reference companion for foreign travel

"A gem of a guide. (Buy it to read in bed if you can't travel)."
OBSERVER

"Invaluable to the world-wide traveller."
VOGUE

"Justifiably billed as the indispensable guide to trouble-free travel".
GEOGRAPHICAL MAGAZINE

Available now from good bookshops, or from the publishers of The South American Handbook

Trade & Travel Publications Ltd.
5 Prince's Buildings, George Street,
Bath BA1 2ED. England.